Union List of Artist Names

James M. Bower
PROJECT MANAGER

Murtha Baca
SENIOR EDITOR

Volume 2

Published on behalf of
The Getty Art History Information Program

G. K. HALL & CO.
AN IMPRINT OF MACMILLAN PUBLISHING COMPANY
NEW YORK
1994

Published by G.K. Hall & Co., an imprint of Macmillan Publishing Company
866 Third Avenue, New York, NY 10022

Library of Congress Cataloging-in-Publication Data

Union list of artist names / project manager, James M. Bower ; senior editor, Murtha Baca. —
    New York : G.K. Hall, 1994–
       p. cm.
    "Published on behalf of the Getty Art History Information Program."
    Includes bibliographical references.
    Contents: v. 1. A–D. — v. 2. E–K. — v. 3. L–P. — v. 4. Q–Z.
    ISBN 0-8161-0725-4 (set)
       1. Artists—Registers. 2. Names, Personal (Cataloging) I. Bower, James M., 1958–.
II. Baca, Murtha. III. Getty Art History Information Program. IV. Title: ULAN.
LCCN: 9346739
L. C. CALL NO: N40.U54 1994
ID: DCLC9346739-B   CC: 9660   DCF: a
                                                    CIP

9 8 7 6 5 4 3 2 1

Printed in the United States of America
on acid-free paper

Designed by Jonathon Nix, Verso Design, Dalton, Massachusetts.
Illustration on facing page: Cosimo III's Hall of Artists' Self-Portraits, Uffizi Gallery. Pen-
and-ink drawing by Stefano Gaetano Neri, c. 1755. Photograph courtesy of Österreichische
Nationalbibliothek.

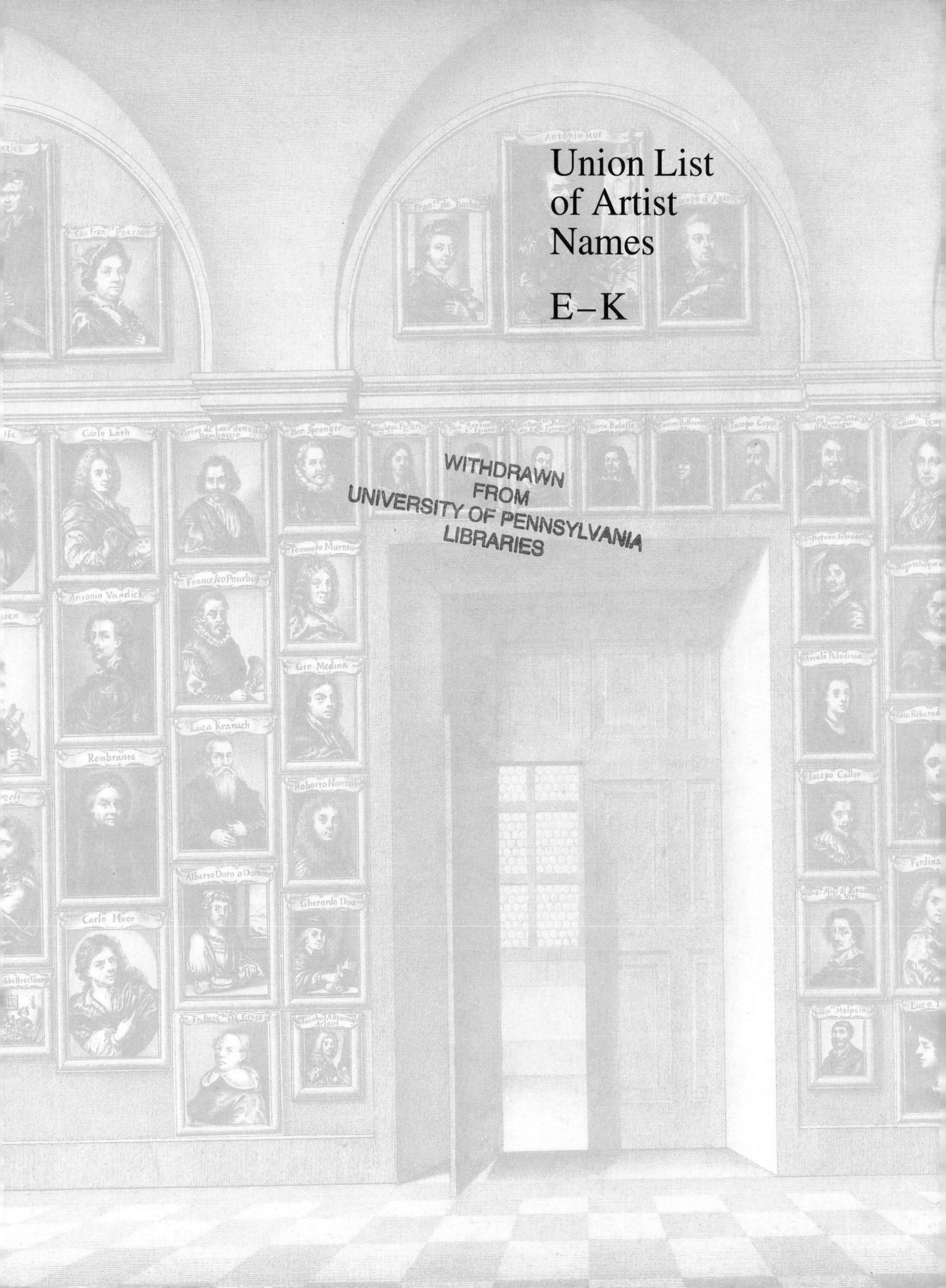

Union List
of Artist
Names

E–K

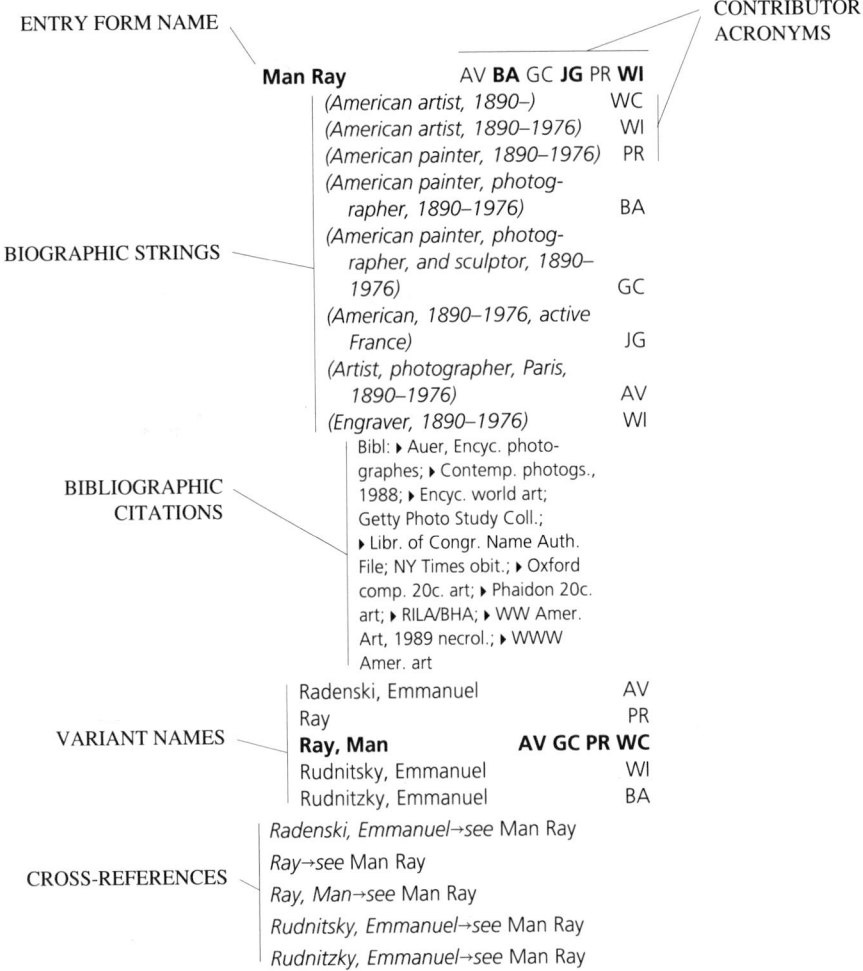

ENTRY FORM NAME

Man Ray   AV **BA** GC **JG** PR **WI**

CONTRIBUTOR
ACRONYMS

BIOGRAPHIC STRINGS

(American artist, 1890–) WC
(American artist, 1890–1976) WI
(American painter, 1890–1976) PR
*(American painter, photog-
rapher, 1890–1976)* BA
*(American painter, photog-
rapher, and sculptor, 1890–
1976)* GC
*(American, 1890–1976, active
France)* JG
*(Artist, photographer, Paris,
1890–1976)* AV
(Engraver, 1890–1976) WI

BIBLIOGRAPHIC
CITATIONS

Bibl: ▸ Auer, Encyc. photo-
graphes; ▸ Contemp. photogs.,
1988; ▸ Encyc. world art;
Getty Photo Study Coll.;
▸ Libr. of Congr. Name Auth.
File; NY Times obit.; ▸ Oxford
comp. 20c. art; ▸ Phaidon 20c.
art; ▸ RILA/BHA; ▸ WW Amer.
Art, 1989 necrol.; ▸ WWW
Amer. art

VARIANT NAMES

Radenski, Emmanuel AV
Ray PR
Ray, Man **AV GC PR WC**
Rudnitsky, Emmanuel WI
Rudnitzky, Emmanuel BA

CROSS-REFERENCES

Radenski, Emmanuel→*see* Man Ray
Ray→*see* Man Ray
Ray, Man→*see* Man Ray
Rudnitsky, Emmanuel→*see* Man Ray
Rudnitzky, Emmanuel→*see* Man Ray

AV Avery Index   **BA** Bibl Hist of Art   **CE** Census Antique Works   **FA** Fndn Docs of Arch   **GC** Getty Ctr Photo Study Coll

E'Spagnoletti → see Ribera, Jusepe de
(lo Spagnoletto)
E. A. Spilsbury → see Spilsbury, Edgar
Ashe
E. Aubrey Hunt → see Hunt, E. Aubrey
E. Charlton Fortune → see Fortune, E.
Charlton
E. Colyer → see Colyer, Edwaert
E. Conixloe → see Coninxloo, Gilles
van
E. Crayer → see Crayer, Gaspar de
E. Dayes → see Dayes, Edward
E. de Wit → see Witte, Emanuel de
E. de Witt → see Witte, Emanuel de
E. de Witte → see Witte, Emanuel de
E. Deveria → see Devéria, Eugène
François Marie Joseph
E. Dobson → see Dobson, William
E. Grace Mitchell Henry → see Henry,
Grace
E. H. → see Monogrammist E.H.
E. Heemskirk → see Heemskerck,
Egbert van (the elder)
E. Hemskerck → see Heemskerck,
Egbert van (the elder)
E. Hemskirk → see Heemskerck, Egbert
van (the elder)
E. Humskirk → see Heemskerck, Egbert
van (the elder)
E. Landt → see Landt, E. [Unidentified]
E. Le Seur → see Le Sueur, Eustache
E. Le Sueur → see Le Sueur, Eustache
E. Maxwell Albert → see Albert, E.
Maxwell
E. Mostard → see Mostaert, Gillis
E. Penny → see Penny, Edward
E. Quelinus → see Quellinus, Jan
Erasmus
E. Quellenus → see Quellinus, Jan
Erasmus
E. Quellines → see Quellinus, Jan
Erasmus
E. Quellinus → see Quellinus, Jan
Erasmus
E. Quilinus → see Quellinus, Jan
Erasmus
E. Quillinus → see Quellinus, Jan
Erasmus
E. Sarain → see Sirani, Elisabetta
E. Sarani → see Sirani, Elisabetta
E. Savani → see Sirani, Elisabetta
E. Serani → see Sirani, Elisabetta
E. Serini → see Sirani, Elisabetta
E. Sirani → see Sirani, Elisabetta
E. Terroux → see Terroux, Elisabeth
E. V. Broek → see Broeck, Elias van
den
E. van den Broeck → see Broeck, Elias
van den
E. Vanaerneer → see Neer, Eglon
Hendrik van der
E. Vande Velde → see Velde, Esaias I
van de
E. Vanderneer → see Neer, Eglon
Hendrik van der

E. Vandervelde → see Velde, Esaias I
van de
E. Vandevelde → see Velde, Esaias I
van de
E. Vandeveldt → see Velde, Esaias I
van de
E. Vaneck → see Vaneck, E.
[Unidentified]
E. Vonch → see Vonck, Elias
E. Wyatt Kimball → see Kimball, E.
Wyatt
E.A. Page → see Page, E.A.
E.A. Spilsbury → see Spilsbury, Edgar
Ashe
E.A.R.T.L.A.D.C.S., Madame
(French painter, critic, act.1785)   **BA**
Bibl: Cameron, WOMAN'S ART
JOURNAL, V/1 (spring-summer
1984) 8-11
E.C. Coates → see Coates, Edmund C.
E.G. (French, active ca. 1870)   **JG**
E.H. Vanderneer → see Neer, Eglon
Hendrik van der
E.J. → see J., E.
E.S. & Co   **JG**
E.V. der Neer → see Neer, Eglon
Hendrik van der
EA, Master → see Altdorfer, Erhard
Eadfrith, bishop of Lindisfarne
(English illuminator, act.698,
d.721)   **BA**
Bibl: Dict. Christian biog.; ▶Dict.
natl. biog.; Powick, HNDBK. OF
BRIT. CHRONOLOGY, 238
Eadie, Katherine M. (British artist,
op.1905-1932)   **WI**
Eadie, Robert (British artist, 1877-
1954)   **WI**
Eadie, William (British artist, op.
1871-1894)   **WI**
Eadmer of Canterbury (English, ca.
1055-1124)   **JG**
Eads, James Buchanan (American
engineer, inventor, 1820-1887)   **BA**
Bibl: Plowden, BRIDGE; ▶WWW
Amer.
Eadvius Basan → see Basan, Eadvius
Eadwine (English scribe, 12th c.)   **BA**
Bibl: ▶Thieme-Becker; Verfaillie-
Markey, D., SCRIPTORIUM,
XXXVII/2 (1983) 245-258
Eagar, W.   **WC WI**
(British artist, op.1831)   WC
(British artist, op.circa 1831-)   WI
Eagar, William H. (Irish painter in
CAN, 1796-1839)   **BA**
Bibl: Carter, Jrnl. of Canadian Art
Hist. VII, 2, 84 p.138-55; ▶Harper,
Ptg. Canada; ▶Witt checklist
Eagle Medalist (Italian medalist, act.
1490)   **BA**
Bibl: MON. & MEM. LXII (1979)
185-202; ▶Thieme-Becker
Eagle Painter   **GC JG**
(Etruscan vase-painter, 530-500)   GC
Bibl: Hemelrijk, Caeretan

Eagles → see Eagles, John
Eagles, Edmund (British artist, op.
1851-1877)   **WI**
Eagles, John   **PR WI**
(British artist, 1783-1855)   WI
(British artist, 1783/4-1855)   WC
(British painter, 1783-1855)   PR
Bibl: ▶RILA/BHA
Eagles   PR
Eagles, Rev. John   **WC**
John Eagles   PR
Eagles, Rev. John → see Eagles, John
Eakin, Garret (American architect)   **AV**
Bibl: Chicago architectural journal,
1985, v.5, p.97
Eakin, William (Canadian
photographer, filmmaker, b.1952)   **BA**
Bibl: Winnipeg (Man, CAN),
Winnipeg Art Gallery MY
FATHER'S GARDEN:
PHOTOGRAPHS BY WILLIAM
EAKIN
Eakins → see Eakins, Thomas
Eakins, Susan Macdowell   **BA WC WI**
(American artist, 1851-1938)   WC
(American artist, 1852-1938)   WI
(American painter, 1852-1938)   BA
Bibl: ▶Mallett's idx. artists
MacDowell, Susan Hannah, Miss   WI
Eakins, Thomas   **BA GC JG PR WC**
(American artist, 1844-1916)   WC WI
(American painter and sculptor,
1844-1916)   GC
(American painter, 1844-1916)   BA PR
(American, 1844-1916)   JG
Bibl: ▶Bénézit; ▶RILA/BHA;
▶Thieme-Becker
Eakins   PR
Eakins, Thomas Cowperthwait   **WI**
Thomas Eakins   PR
Eakins, Thomas Cowperthwait → see
Eakins, Thomas
Eakles → see Ekels, Jan (the younger)
Eames, Charles   **AV BA**
(American designer and
architect, 1907-1978)   AV
(American designer, architect,
1907-1978)   BA
Bibl: ▶Avery obit. idx.; Bangert,
Der Stil der 50er Jahre, p.144;
▶Contemp. archts.; Philadelphia
(PA, USA), Mus. of Art, Design
Since 1945 (1983), p.211; WW
Amer., 1976
Eames, J.   **WC WI**
(British artist, 18th cent.)   WC
(British artist, op.18th c.)   WI
Eames, Ray → see Eames, Ray Kaiser

Eames, Ray Kaiser BA
(American designer and artist, Los Angeles, Calif.; wife and partner of Charles Eames, 1916?-1988) AV
(American designer, 1912-1988) BA
Bibl: Architecture: the AIA journal, 1988 Oct., v.77, no.10, p.38; Contemp. designers, 1990; Kirkham, Furniture Hist. 26 (1990) p.132-141; ▶Libr. of Congr. Name Auth. File; ▶Macmillan encyc. archts.; Minneapolis (MN, USA), Walker Art Ctr., Nelson, Eames, Girard, Propst (1975-76); ▶MoMA libr. cat.; some sources give 1913 as b. date; WW Amer., 1976; ▶WWW Amer.

Eames, Ray AV
Eames, W.S. *(Engraver)* WI
Eanger Irving Couse→see Couse, Eanger Irving
Eankening, John Joseph→see Enneking, John Joseph
Eardley, Cynthia *(American sculptor, 20th c.)* BA
Bibl: Nadelman, C., in ART NEWS LXXXIII/1 (Jan 1984) 63
Eardley, Joan→see Eardley, Joan Kathleen Harding
Eardley, Joan Kathleen Harding BA WI
(British artist, 1921-1963) WC WI
(British painter, 1921-1963) BA
Bibl: ▶Bénézit; ▶Vollmer, Künst.-Lex. 20. Jhr.; ▶Who was who [GBR]
Eardley, Joan WC
Earl→see Earl, James
Earl→see Earl, Ralph
Earl Covis Kerkam→see Kerkam, Earl Cavis
Earl Horter→see Horter, Earl
Earl, Francis Charles *(British photographer, act.1860-1879)* BA
Bibl: Hallett, Hist. photo., XI (Apr.-Jun. 1987) pp.119-122
Earl, George *(British artist, op.1856-1883)* WC WI
Earl, Jack *(American sculptor, b.1934)* BA
Bibl: Hanover (NH, USA), Dartmouth College, Contemp. clay (1976)
Earl, James BA PR WI
(American artist, 1761-1796) WC WI
(American painter in GBR, 1761-1796) BA
(American painter, 1761-1796) PR
Bibl: ▶Artist biog. master idx.; ▶Fielding's Amer. ptrs., 1983; Stewart, Robert G., AMERICAN ART JOURNAL XX/4 (1988), p.34-58
Earl PR
Earle or Earl, James WC
James Earl PR

Earl, Maud WC WI
(British artist, 1848-1943) WI
(British artist, op.1884-1908) WC
Earl, Percy *(British artist, op.1907-1930)* WI
Earl, Phoebe, Miss→see Dighton, Phoebe
Earl, Ralph BA GC PR WI
(American artist, 1751-1801) WC WI
(American painter, 1751-1801) BA GC PR
Bibl: ▶Fielding's Amer. ptrs., 1983; ▶Groce, Artists Amer.; ▶RILA/BHA; ▶Young, Amer. artists
Earl PR
Earle or Earl, Ralph WC
Ralph Earl PR
Earl, Ralph E.W.→see Earl, Ralph Eleasen Whiteside
Earl, Ralph Eleasen Whiteside BA
(American artist, 1785-1838) WI
(American artist, 1788-1837) WC
(American painter, ca.1785-1838) BA
(American, 1788-1837) GC
Bibl: ▶Fielding's Amer. ptrs.; ▶Groce, Artists Amer.; ▶Witt checklist; ▶WWW Amer. art; ▶Young, Amer. artists
Earl, Ralph E.W. GC WC
Earl, Ralph Eleazer Whitesides WI
Earl, Ralph Eleazer Whitesides→see Earl, Ralph Eleasen Whiteside
Earl, Thomas *(British artist, op.1836-1885)* WC WI
Earl, William Robert *(British artist, op.1823-1867)* WC WI
Earle or Earl, James→see Earl, James
Earle or Earl, Ralph→see Earl, Ralph
Earle, Augustus BA WC WI
(British artist, 1793-1838) WI
(British artist, op.1806-1839) WC
(British painter, 1793-1838) BA
Bibl: ▶Bénézit; ▶Fisher, Watercolour ptrs.; ▶Mallalieu, Brit. watercolour artists; ▶Natl. union cat.; ▶Thieme-Becker
Earle, Charles *(British artist, 1832-1893)* WI
Earle, Eyvind WC WI
(American artist, 20th cent.) WC
(American artist, op.20th c.) WI
Earle, Lawrence C.→see Earle, Lawrence Carmichael
Earle, Lawrence Carmichael BA WI
(American artist, 1845-1921) WC WI
(American painter, 1845-1921) BA
Bibl: ▶Fielding's Amer. ptrs.
Earle, Lawrence C. WC
Earle, Maria Theresa *(British gardener, 1836-1925)* BA
Bibl: ▶Natl. union cat., pre-1956
Villiers, Maria Theresa BA
Earle, Paul Barnard *(Canadian artist, 1872-1930)* WC

Earle, Stephen C. *(American architect, 1839-1913)* BA
Bibl: Dall, C.; in WORCESTER ART MUS. JOURNAL VI (1982-83) 3; ▶Withey, Amer. archts.
Earles→see Earles, Chester
Earles, Chester *(British painter, act. 1842-1863)* PR
Bibl: ▶Thieme-Becker
Chester Earles PR
Earles PR
Earley, John Joseph *(American architectural sculptor, d.1945)* AV
Earlom, Richard BA WC WI
(British artist, 1743-1822) WC WI
(British printmaker, 1743-1822) BA
(Engraver, 1743-1822) WI
Bibl: ▶Dict. natl. biog.; ▶Thieme-Becker
Earlom, William *(British artist, 1772-1789)* WC WI
Early Olpai *(vase-painter, ca. 600-580 BC)* GC
Bibl: ▶Beazley, Attic bl.-fig. vase-ptrs.; Boardman, Attic Bl.-fig. Vases
Early, Kim *(British sculptor, b.1952)* BA
Bibl: Norwich (GBR), School of Art, Current Brit. sculp. (1979)
Earnshaw, Anthony *(British painter, printmaker, author, b.1924)* BA
Bibl: Arts Council GBR, A cold wind (1979)
Earnshaw, Harold *(British painter, act.1912-1926)* BA
Bibl: ▶Bénézit; ▶Johnson, Brit. artists
Earnshaw, Harold C., Mrs., (Mabel Lucie)→see Attwell, Mabel Lucie
Earnshaw, M. WC WI
(British artist, 19th cent.) WC
(British artist, op.19th c.) WI
Bibl: ▶Johnson, Brit. artists
Earp, Edwin *(British artist, op.1900-)* WI
Earp, G.→see Earp, George
Earp, George WI
(British artist, op.c.1834) WC
(British artist, op.circa 1834-) WI
Earp, G. WC
Earp, Henry→see Earp, Henry I
Earp, Henry I WI
(British artist, 1831-1914) WI
(British artist, op.1871-1884) WC
Earp, Henry WC
East, Alfred WI
(British artist, 1849-1913) WC WI
East, Sir Alfred WC
East, H.S. WC WI
(British artist, 19th cent.) WC
(British artist, op.1910-1918) WI
East, Lawrence *(American artist, op. 1931-1941)* WI
East, Roger *(American architect, San Francisco, Calif)* AV
Bibl: ▶AIA Pro File, 1987
East, Sir Alfred→see East, Alfred

Easterling, Keller *(American architect, New York City)* **AV**
Bibl: Metropolis, 1988 May, v.7, no.9, p.62

Easterly, Thomas M. *(American, 1809-1882, daguerreotypist)* **JG**

Eastlake, Caroline H. *(British artist, op.1868-1873)* **WC WI**
Bibl: ▶Wood, Victorian ptrs.

Eastlake, Charles Herbert **WC WI**
(British artist, 1885-1930) **WI**
(British artist, 19th cent.) **WC**
Bibl: ▶Waters, Brit. artists

Eastlake, Charles Lock **BA WI**
(British artist, 1793-1865) **WC WI**
(British painter, art historian, 1793-1865) **BA**
Bibl: ▶Natl. union cat.; ▶Thieme-Becker

Eastlake, Sir Charles Lock **WC**

Eastlake, Charles Locke *(British designer, author, 1836-1906)* **BA**
Bibl: ▶Avery Libr. cat.; ▶Fogg Mus. Libr. cat.; ▶Natl. union cat.; ▶Who was who [GBR]

Eastlake, Elizabeth, Lady → see Rigby, Elizabeth, Miss

Eastlake, Mrs. Mary A., (nee Bell) *(Canadian artist, 19th cent.)* **WC**

Eastlake, Sidney *(British artist, op. 20th c.)* **WI**

Eastlake, Sir Charles Lock → see Eastlake, Charles Lock

Eastley, J. **WC WI**
(British artist, op.c.1846) **WC**
(British artist, op.circa 1846-) **WI**

Eastley, Max *(British artist, b.1944)* **BA**
Bibl: Arts Council GBR, 6 Times (1976)

Eastley, S.R. **WC WI**
(British artist, op.19th c.) **WI**
(British(?) artist, 19th cent.) **WC**

Eastman → see Eastman, William Joseph

Eastman Johnson → see Johnson, Eastman

Eastman, Elizabeth *(Canadian painter, b.1905)* **BA**
Bibl: ▶Artists Canada; Kitchener (CAN), Kitchener-Waterloo Art Gallery, ELIZABETH EASTMAN (1982)

Eastman, Emily **WC WI**
(American artist, 1804-op.1900) **WI**
(American artist, 19th cent.) **WC**

Eastman, Emma *(American, b.ca. 1846)* **BA**
Bibl: Sutherland, Clarion (fall 1984) 55

Eastman, Frank S. → see Eastman, Frank Samuel

Eastman, Frank Samuel **WI**
(British artist, 1878-) **WC**
(British artist, 1878-op.1940) **WI**

Eastman, Frank S. **WC**

Eastman, George *(American, ca. 1844-ca.1891)* **BA**
Bibl: Sutherland, Clarion (fall 1984) 55

Eastman, George *(American inventor, businessman, 1854-1932)* **BA**
Bibl: ▶New Columbia encyc.; ▶WWW Amer.

Eastman, Jerome *(American interior designer)* **AV**
Bibl: Restaurant/hotel design international, 1988 May, v.10, no.5, p.56

Eastman, Lauren Chase *(American, 1844-1924)* **BA**
Bibl: ANTIQUES CXVIII (Nov 1980) 1048-1051

Eastman, Mary *(British artist, op. 1958-)* **WI**

Eastman, Maud *(British artist, op. 1902-1932)* **WI**
Mair, Maud, Miss **WI**

Eastman, Seth **BA GC JG WC WI**
(American artist, 1808-1875) **WC WI**
(American painter, 1808-1875) **BA GC**
(American, 1808-1875, daguerreotypist) **JG**
Bibl: ▶Fielding's Amer. ptrs.; ▶Mallett's idx. artists; ▶RILA/BHA; ▶Young, Amer. artists

Eastman, Tony *(British artist, b.1942)* **BA**
Bibl: Bristol (GBR), Arnolfini Gallery, Bristol sample (1979)

Eastman, William Joseph *(American painter, 1881-1950)* **PR**
Bibl: ▶WWW Amer. art
Eastman **PR**
William Joseph Eastman **PR**

Eastnor, Charles, Viscount → see Somers, Charles, 3rd Earl

Easton, Bob *(American architect, Santa Barbara, Calif)* **AV**
Bibl: House & garden, 1989 June, v.161, no.6, p.92

Easton, David Anthony *(American interior designer, New York City)* **AV**
Bibl: House & garden, 1989 Feb., v.161, no.2, p.165

Easton, Joseph → see Eaton, Joseph Oriel

Easton, Reginald *(British artist, 1807-1893)* **WC WI**

Eastwick-Field, Elizabeth *(British architect, 1919-)* **AV**

Eastwick-Field, John *(British architect, 1919-)* **AV**

Eastwood, Francis H. *(British artist, op.1875-1908)* **WI**

Eastwood, John S. *(1857-)* **AV**

Eastwood, Walter *(British artist, 1867-1943)* **WI**

Eatherton, Tom *(American artist, 20th c.)* **BA**
Bibl: JOURNAL... 32 (spring 1982) 57-61

Eaton → see Eaton, Charles Harry

Eaton → see Eaton, William Bradley

Eaton, B.M. Knight **WC WI**
(British artist, op.1914) **WC**
(British artist, op.1914-) **WI**

Eaton, Bertram *(British sculptor, b.1912)* **BA**
Bibl: Northampton (GBR), Central Museum and Art Gallery, RECENT SCULPTURE BY BERTRAM EATON (1975)

Eaton, C.C., Mrs., (Louise) → see Herreshoff, Louise C.

Eaton, Charles Harry **WI**
(American artist, 1850-1901) **WI**
(American painter, 1850-1901) **PR**
Bibl: ▶Thieme-Becker
Charles Henry Eaton **PR**
Eaton **PR**
Eaton, Charles Henry **PR**
Eaton, Henry **PR**

Eaton, Charles Henry → see Eaton, Charles Harry

Eaton, Charles Warren **BA WI**
(American artist, 1857-1937) **WI**
(American painter, 1857-1937) **BA**
Bibl: ▶Fielding's Amer. ptrs.; ▶WWW Amer.

Eaton, Elizabeth *(British interior designer)* **AV**
Bibl: The world of interiors, 1989 Oct., p.224

Eaton, Henry → see Eaton, Charles Harry

Eaton, Henry Barrington *(British architect, Romsey)* **AV**
Bibl: ▶RIBA members, 1987

Eaton, Janenne *(Australian painter, 20th c.)* **BA**
Bibl: ▶Intl. dir. exh. artists, 1982; McKenzie, Studio intl., CXCIX (Dec.-Feb. 1986-87) pp.22-39

Eaton, Jon Eric *(American photographer, b.1943)* **BA**
Bibl: Baltimore (MD, USA), Mus. Art, 5 Maryland photogs. (1980)

Eaton, Joseph Oriel **WC WI**
(American artist, 1829-1875) **WC WI**
(American, 1829-1875) **GC**
Bibl: ▶Encyc. world art
Easton, Joseph **GC**

Eaton, Maria *(British artist, op.1890-1937)* **WI**
Llewellyn, Ernest, Mrs.(Maria) **WI**

Eaton, Moses *(American stencil artist, 1796-1886)* **BA**
Bibl: ANTIQUES CVIII/4 (Oct 1975) 712-729

Eaton, Norman *(South African architect, 1902-1966)* **AV**
Bibl: ▶Contemp. archts.

Eaton, Robert *(British, 1819-1871, active Rome, Italy)* **JG**

Eaton, Valoy *(American artist, b.1938)* **WI**

Eaton, William B. → see Eaton, William Bradley

Eaton, William Bradley *(American painter, 1836-1896)*   **PR**
  Bibl: ▶WWW Amer. art
  Eaton   PR
  Eaton, William B.   PR
  William Bradley Eaton   PR
Eaton, Wyatt   **BA WC**
  (American painter, 1849-1896)   BA
  (Canadian artist, 1849-1896)   WC
  Bibl: ▶Fielding's Amer. ptrs.;
  ▶WWW Amer.
Eatwell, John *(British artist, b.1923)*   **WI**
Eaubonne, Louis Lucien d' *(French artist, 1834-1894)*   **WC**
Eaves, John   **WC WI**
  (British artist, 1929-)   WC
  (British artist, b.1929)   WI
Eayre, Thomas *(British artist, op. 18th c.)*   **WI**
Ebbesen, Torben *(Danish artist, b.1945)*   **BA**
  Bibl: København (DNK),
  Ordrupgaard, Kunst: Dag (1982);
  ▶Køie, Kunst.leks.
Ebel → see Ebel, Fritz
Ebel, Fritz   **PR WC**
  (German artist, 1835-1895)   WC
  (German painter, 1835-1895)   PR
  Bibl: ▶Thieme-Becker
  Ebel   PR
  Ebel, Fritz Carl Werner   PR
  Fritz Ebel   PR
Ebel, Fritz Carl Werner → see Ebel, Fritz
Ebel, Heinz *(German artist, 20th cent.)*   **WC**
Ebelmann, Hans Jakob *(German artist, op.c.1600)*   **WC**
Eben, Frederic Baron d' *(Swedish artist, op.1808)*   **WC**
Ebenezer Tull → see Tull, Ebenezer
Eberhard, Christian *(Austrian architect)*   **AV**
  Bibl: Planen Bauen Wohnen,
  1988, no.124, p.3
Eberhard, George Adam *(German artist, op.1656-1688)*   **WC**
Eberhard, Harold *(American designer, New York, NY)*   **AV**
  Bibl: Interior design, 1985 July,
  v.56, no.7, p.212
Eberhard, Konrad   **BA WC**
  (German artist, 1768-1859)   WC
  (German sculptor, 1768-1859)   BA
  Bibl: ▶Allgem. Deut. Biog.;
  ▶Thieme-Becker
Eberhard, Robert George *(Swiss artist, 1844-)*   **WC**
Eberhard, William T. *(American architect, Ohio)*   **AV**
  Bibl: ▶AIA Pro File, 1985
Eberhardt, Jacob *(German artist, 1820-1889)*   **WC**
Eberl, Frantisek Zdenek *(Czech artist, 1888-)*   **WC**
Eberle → see Eberle, Adolf

Eberle, Abastenia Saint Leger *(American sculptor, 1878-1942)*   **BA**
  Bibl: ▶Collins, Women artists
  Amer.; ▶Fielding's Amer. ptrs.
Eberle, Adam   **GC WC**
  (German artist, 1804-1832)   WC
  (German painter, 1804-1832)   GC
  Bibl: ▶Thieme-Becker
Eberle, Adolf   **PR WC**
  (German artist, 1843-1914)   WC
  (German painter, 1843-1914)   PR
  Bibl: ▶Thieme-Becker
  Adolf Eberle   PR
  Eberle   PR
  Eberle, Adolph   PR
Eberle, Adolph → see Eberle, Adolf
Eberle, Dietmar *(Austrian architect)*   **AV**
  Bibl: Deutsche Bauzeitung, 1988
  July, v.122, no.7, p.138
Eberle, Johann *(German artist, op.c. 1783-1788)*   **WC**
Eberle, Robert *(German artist, 1815-1862)*   **WC**
Eberlein, Gustav Heinrich *(German sculptor, painter, poet, 1847-1926)*   **BA**
  Bibl: Grimm, WERKVERZEICHNIS
  DES...PROF GUSTAV HEINRICH
  EBERLEIN (1983); ▶Natl. union
  cat., pre-1956; ▶Thieme-Becker;
  ▶Vollmer, Künst.-Lex. 20. Jhr.
Eberlein, Johann Friedrich   **BA GC**
  (German porcelain modeler, sculptor, 1696-1749)   BA
  (German porcelain modeller and sculptor, 1696-1749)   GC
  Bibl: ▶Neue deutsche Biog.;
  ▶RILA/BHA; ▶Thieme-Becker
Ebersbach, Hartwig *(German painter, b.1940)*   **BA**
  Bibl: Hamburg (DEU), Kunstverein,
  Zeitvergleich (1982)
Eberson, John   **AV BA**
  (American architect, 1875-1954)   AV
  (American architect, 1875?-1954)   BA
  Bibl: ▶Avery obit. idx.; NY Times
  obit., 7 Mar 1954, p.90
Eberson, Lucas Hermanus *(Dutch architect, 1822-1889)*   **BA**
  Bibl: Rosengerg, DE 19DE-EEUWSE
  KERKELIJKE BOUWKUNST IN NLD
  (1972) 96; Veenland-Heineman,
  LEIDS KUNSTHIST. JAARBOEK III
  (1984) 467-494
Ebert, Albert *(German painter, printmaker, 1906-1976)*   **BA**
  Bibl: Dresdener Kunstblatter, obit;
  ▶Fogg Mus. Libr. cat.; ▶Natl.
  union cat.
Ebert, Anton *(German artist, 1845-1896)*   **WC**
Ebert, Carl   **GC WC**
  (German artist, 1821-1885)   WC
  (German painter, 1821-1885)   GC
  Bibl: ▶Thieme-Becker

Ebert, Charles Henry *(American painter, illustrator, 1873-1959)*   **BA**
  Bibl: ▶Bénézit; ▶Fielding's Amer.
  ptrs.; New London (CT, USA),
  Lyman Allyn Museum, CHARLES
  EBERT (1979); ▶Vollmer,
  Künst.-Lex. 20. Jhr.; ▶Young,
  Amer. artists
Ebert, H. A. *(American, active Chicago early 20th century (Ebert Studios))*   **JG**
Ebert, Walter *(German architect)*   **AV**
  Bibl: Detail, 1980 Jan.-Feb., no.1,
  p.34
Eberth (Ebertts) *(German, active ca. 1920)*   **JG**
Eberts, Jean Henri *(French banker, printmaker, 18th c.)*   **BA**
  Bibl: ▶Dict. biog. fran.; Jahrb. der
  Staatl. Kunstsamml.
  Baden-Württemberg XV (1978)
  43-60
Eberwein, Anton *(Romanian sculptor, b.1936.)*   **BA**
  Bibl: ▶Barbosa, Art. romani
  contemp.
Eberz → see Eberz, Josef
Eberz, Josef   **GC PR WC**
  (German artist, 1880-1942)   WC
  (German painter, 1880-1942)   GC
  (German painter, b. 1880)   PR
  Bibl: ▶Thieme-Becker; ▶Witt
  checklist
  Eberz   PR
  Josef Eberz   PR
Ebetson → see Ibbetson, Julius Caesar
Ebhardt, Bodo *(German architect, 1965-)*   **AV**
  Bibl: ▶Thieme-Becker
Ebhardt, Bodo *(German architect, 1865-1945)*   **BA**
  Bibl: ▶Neue deutsche Biog.;
  ▶Thieme-Becker; ▶Vollmer,
  Künst.-Lex. 20. Jhr.
Ebihara, Eiji *(Japanese architect, 1945-)*   **AV**
  Bibl: GA houses, n.14, July 1983,
  p.227
Eble, Theo   **BA WC**
  (Swiss artist, 1899-)   WC
  (Swiss painter, printmaker, 1899-1974)   BA
  Bibl: ▶Lex. zeitgen. Schweiz.
  Künstler; ▶Vollmer, Künst.-Lex.
  20. Jhr.
Eburne, Emma Sophia, Miss → see Oliver, Emma Sophia
Eby, Kerr   **BA WI**
  (American artist, 1889-1946)   WI
  (American painter, printmaker, 1890-1946)   BA
  Bibl: Cold Spring Harbor (NY,
  USA), Harbor Gallery, HARBOR
  GALLERY PRESENTS (1979)
Ebyl, Franz *(German artist, 1806-1880)*   **WC**

Eccardt or Eckhardt, John Giles →*see*
Eccardt, John Giles
Eccardt, John Giles **WI**
 (British artist, op.1740-, d.1779) WI
 (British artist, op.1740-m.1779) WC
 Eccardt or Eckhardt, John Giles **WC**
 Eckhardt, John Giles WI
Eccheli, Maria Grazia *(Italian*
 architect) **AV**
  Bibl: Domus, 1988 July-Aug., no.
  696, p.10
Eccles, Jane *(Canadian artist,*
 b.1949) **BA**
  Bibl: Oshawa (Ont, CAN),
  McLaughlin Gallery, 14 artists
  from Durham (1979)
Eccleston, Harry Norman *(British*
 artist, b.1923) **WI**
Echalar, Juan de *(Spanish*
 woodworker, 17th c.) **BA**
  Bibl: Arch. esp. de arte, L/199
  (Jul-Sep 1977) 323-327
Echard or Eschard, Charles →*see*
Eschard, Charles
Echard, Charles →*see* Eschard,
Charles
Echard, G. *(French artist, op.1756)* **WC**
Echardt →*see* Eeckhout, Gerbrand van
den
Echarlinger *(German artist, 19th*
 cent.) **WC**
Echave →*see* Echave Rioja, Baltasar
de
Echave or Chaves the Elder,
 Balthasar *(Spanish artist, op.1603-*
 1630) **WC**
Echave Rioja →*see* Echave Rioja,
Baltasar de
Echave Rioja, Baltasar de *(Mexican*
 painter, 1632-1682) **BA PR**
  Bibl: Corpus Christi (TX, USA), Art
  Mus. So.Texas, Spain & new Spain
  (1979); ▶RILA/BHA;
  ▶Thieme-Becker
 Baltasar de Echave Rioja PR
 Echave PR
 Echave Rioja PR
 Echave, Balthasar PR
Echave, Balthasar →*see* Echave Rioja,
Baltasar de
Echena, Jose *(Spanish artist, 1845-p.*
 1883) **WC**
Echenique, Marcial *(Architect, lives*
 in Cambridge, England) **AV**
  Bibl: Toshi jutaku, 1983 July, no.
  189, p.58
Echevarria, Federico de *(Spanish*
 artist, 1916-) **WC**
Echevarria, Jesus *(Spanish sculptor,*
 20th c.) **BA**
  Bibl: Paris (FRA), Centre nat. G.
  Pompidou, JESUS ECHEVARRIA
  (1979)
Echevarria, Juan de *(Spanish artist,*
 1875-1931) **WC**

Echout →*see* Eeckhout, Gerbrand van
den
Echter, Michael *(German artist,*
 1812-1879) **WC**
Echtler, Adolf **BA WC**
 (German artist, 1843-1914) WC
 (German painter, 1843-1914) BA
  Bibl: ▶Thieme-Becker; ▶Vollmer,
  Künst.-Lex. 20. Jhr.
Ećimović, Dejan *(Yugoslavian*
 architect) **AV**
  Bibl: Architecture & urbanism,
  1986 Apr. no.4(187), p.15
Eck, Jeremiah *(American architect)* **AV**
Eck, van *[Unidentified]* *(Unknown*
 painter) **PR**
  Bibl: (February 21, 1815, lot 44,
  Coxe)
 Van Eck PR
 Vanneck PR
Eckardt, Aloys *(German artist, 1845-*
 1906) **WC**
Eckart, Christian *(Canadian painter,*
 b.1959) **BA**
  Bibl: Hart, ARTFORUM, XXVII
  (Sept 1988), 107-110; Leiber,
  ARTS, LXII (Mar 1988), 82-85;
  ▶WW Amer. Art
Eckbo, Garrett *(American architect,*
 1910-) **AV**
  Bibl: ▶Contemp. archts.
Eckel, van →*see* Hecke, Jan van den
(I)
Eckenbrecher, Karl Paul
 Themistocles von *(German artist,*
 1842-1921) **WC**
Eckener, Alexander *(German artist,*
 1870-1944) **WC**
Eckenfelder, Friedrich **GC WC**
 (Swiss artist, 1861-1938) WC
 (Swiss painter, 1861-1938) GC
  Bibl: ▶Thieme-Becker; ▶Witt
  checklist
Eckenhoff, Walter *(American*
 architect, Oakbrook, IL, 1950-) **AV**
  Bibl: ▶AIA Pro File, 1985
Ecker, Bogomir *(West German*
 sculptor, b.1950) **BA**
  Bibl: Guide exh. artists: N. Amer.
  ptrs.; ▶Intl. dir. exh. artists, 1983
Eckerle, Eberhard *(German sculptor,*
 b.1949) **BA**
  Bibl: Bremen (DEU), Kunsthalle,
  Natur-Landschaft-Kunst (1982)
Eckerman, Oscar A. *(American*
 architect, b.1873, d. after 1942) **BA**
  Bibl: JSAH XXXV/4 (Dec 1976)
  270
Eckersberg, C. W. →*see* Eckersberg,
Christoffer Wilhelm
Eckersberg, Christoffer Vilhelm →*see*
Eckersberg, Christoffer Wilhelm

Eckersberg, Christoffer Wilhelm **BA**
 (Danish artist, 1783-1853) WC
 (Danish painter, 1783-1853) AV BA
  Bibl: ▶Bénézit; ▶Libr. of Congr.
  Name Auth. File; ▶Thieme-Becker
Eckersberg, C. W. **AV**
Eckersberg, Christoffer Vilhelm **WC**
Eckersberg, Johan Fredrik **BA WC**
 (Norwegian artist, 1822-1870) WC
 (Norwegian painter, 1822-1870) BA
  Bibl: ▶Norsk Kunstner Leks.;
  ▶Thieme-Becker
Eckert, G.M. **JG**
 (German artist, 1828-1903) WC
 (German, active ca. 1870,
 Heidelberg) JG
Eckert, Georg Maria **WC**
Eckert, Georg Maria →*see* Eckert,
G.M.
Eckert, Heinrich Ambros *(German*
 artist, 1807-1840) **WC**
Eckert, Tom *(American craftsman,*
 b.1942) **BA**
  Bibl: Colorado Springs (CO, USA),
  Fine Arts Ctr., Woodworking in
  the Rockies (1982)
Eckert, Walter *(German artist,*
 1913) **WC**
Eckhardt, Carl Peter *(German artist,*
 1800-1850) **WC**
Eckhardt, Edris *(American sculptor,*
 b.1907) **BA**
  Bibl: ▶Archives Amer. Art Jrnl.,
  XI/1-4 (1971); ▶Vollmer,
  Künst.-Lex. 20. Jhr.
Eckhardt, Georg Ludwig **GC WC**
 (German artist, 1770-1794) WC
 (German, 1770-1794) GC
  Bibl: Getty Photo Study Coll.
  (Ptgs.); ▶Thieme-Becker; ▶Witt
  checklist
 Eckhardt, Louis GC
Eckhardt, H. W. *(West German*
 architect, Bielefeld) **AV**
  Bibl: Deutsche Bauzeitschrift,
  1986 Oct., v.34, no.10, p.1231
Eckhardt, Johannes Aegidius
 (German artist, 18th cent.) **WC**
Eckhardt, John Giles →*see* Eccardt,
John Giles
Eckhardt, Louis →*see* Eckhardt, Georg
Ludwig
Eckhardt, Rob *(Dutch interior*
 architect and designer) **AV**
  Bibl: The world of interiors, 1988
  Nov., p.116
Eckhart →*see* Eeckhout, Gerbrand van
den
Eckhaut →*see* Eeckhout, Gerbrand
van den
Eckhoote *[Unidentified]* *(Unknown*
 painter) **PR**
  Bibl: (September 15, 1802, lot 43,
  Langdon)
Eckhort →*see* Eeckhout, Gerbrand van
den

Eckhoudt→see Eeckhout, Gerbrand van den

Eckhouet→see Eeckhout, Gerbrand van den

Eckhout→see Eeckhout, Gerbrand van den

Eckhout, Albert→see Eeckhout, Albert van der

Eckhout, Albert van der→see Eeckhout, Albert van der

Eckl, Vilma *(Austrian painter, b.1892)* **BA**
  Bibl: ▶Bénézit; ▶MoMA libr. cat.; ▶Vollmer, Künst.-Lex. 20. Jhr.

Eckles→see Ekels, Jan (the younger)

Eckman, Jean **GC WC**
  (French artist, 1641-1677) WC
  (French painter, 1641-1677) GC
  Bibl: ▶Bénézit

Eckmann, Otto **BA WC**
  (German artist, 1865-1902) WC
  (German painter, 1865-1902) BA
  Bibl: ▶Bénézit; ▶Thieme-Becker

Eckout→see Eeckhout, Gerbrand van den

Eckrich, Jan *(American painter specializing in the restoration of mural painting and decoration, Milwaukee, Wisc, 1947-)* **AV**
  Bibl: Preservation news, 1988 Dec., v.28, no.12, p.18

Eckstein→see Eckstein, John II

Eckstein, František Řehoř Ignác **BA**
  (Czech painter, ca.1689-ca. 1736) BA
  (German artist, op.1700-1736) WC
  Bibl: ▶Bénézit; ▶Thieme-Becker

Eckstein, Franz Gregor Ignaz **WC**
  Egstein, Franz Gregor Ignaz BA
Eckstein, Franz Gregor Ignaz→see Eckstein, František Řehoř Ignác

Eckstein, Johann *(German painter, sculptor, printmaker in USA, ca. 1736-1817)* **BA**
  Bibl: ▶Groce, Artists Amer.

Eckstein, Johannes (John), I *(British artist, op.1762-1802)* **WC**
Eckstein, John→see Eckstein, John II

Eckstein, John II **WI**
  (British artist, op.1787-, d.1838) WI
  (German painter, act. 1787-1838) PR
  Bibl: ▶Thieme-Becker; ▶Waterhouse, Brit. 18c. ptrs.
  Eckstein PR

Eckstein, John **PR**
  John Eckstein PR

Eckstein, Sebastian *(in POL painter, ca.1711-after 1757)* **BA**
  Bibl: ▶Bénézit; Samsonowicz, BIULETIN HISTORII SZTUKI, XLVI/2-3 (1989), p. 271-292; ▶Thieme-Becker

Eckstorm, Christian *(American architect, Chicago, fl. early 1900's)* **AV**
  Bibl: Historic Illinois, 1989 June, v.12, no.1, p.9

Eckstut, Stanton *(American architect, New York, N.Y)* **AV**
  Bibl: ▶AIA Pro File, 1987-88

Eclair [Unidentified] *(Unknown painter)* **PR**
  Bibl: (July 23, 1803, lot 89, Farebrother)

Eco, Umberto *(Italian writer, architect, critic, 1932-)* **AV**
  Bibl: ▶Libr. of Congr. Name Auth. File, date added from note field

Ecobichon, Phillippa *(British photographer, printmaker, b.1949)* **BA**
  Bibl: Arts Council GBR, Aspects of landscape (1977)

Ecochard, Michel *(French architect, 1905-1985)* **AV**
  Bibl: ▶Contemp. archts.; Urbanisme, 1985 Dec.-1986 Jan., no.211, p.53

Econchatti, Nikkanochee, prince of→see Osceola Nickanochee

Economos, Michael **WC WI**
  (American artist, 1937-) WC
  (American artist, b.1937) WI

Economov, K. E. *(Architect, Greece)* **AV**
  Bibl: Design + art in Greece, 1982, v.13, p.92

Ecoot→see Eeckhout, Gerbrand van den

Ed. Vissinelli→see Vissinelli, Ed. [Unidentified]

Edbrooke, Frank E. *(American architect, active in Denver, Colo, 1840-1918)* **AV**
  Bibl: ▶Macmillan encyc. archts.

Edbrooke, W. J.→see Edbrooke, Willoughby J.

Edbrooke, Willoughby J. **FA**
  (1843-29.III.1896; Architect, United States of America) FA
  (American architect, 1843-1896) AV
  Bibl: ▶Lowry, Building natl. image; ▶Macmillan encyc. archts.

Edbrooke, W. J. **AV**

Eddelien, Mathias Heinrich Elias *(Danish painter, 1802-1852)* **BA**
  Bibl: ▶Thieme-Becker; ▶Weilbach, Kunst.leks.

Eddelink [Unidentified] *(Unknown painter)* **PR**
  Bibl: (June 18, 1803, lot 78, Christie's)

Eddington, William Clarke *(British artist, op.1860-1885)* **WC WI**
  Bibl: ▶Wood, Victorian ptrs.
  Clarke, William WI

Eddis→see Eddis, Eden Upton

Eddis, Eden→see Eddis, Eden Upton

Eddis, Eden Upton **GC PR WC WI**
  (British artist, 1812-1901) WC WI
  (British painter, 1812-1901) PR
  (British, 1812-1901) GC
  Bibl: ▶Thieme-Becker; ▶Witt checklist
  Eddis PR
  Eddis, Eden PR
  Eden Upton Eddis PR

Eddy, Don **BA WC WI**
  (American artist, 1944-) WC
  (American artist, b.1944) WI
  (American painter, b.1944) BA
  Bibl: ▶Babington Smith, Contemp. artists; ▶Intl. dir. exh. artists, 1982; ▶WW Amer. Art, 1989

Eddy, James *(Engraver, 1806-1888)* **WI**

Eddy, Oliver Tarbell **WC WI**
  (American artist, 1799-1868) WI
  (American artist, 19th cent.) WC

Ede, Basil **WC WI**
  (British artist, 20th cent.) WC
  (British artist, op.20th c.) WI

Ede, Bernard *(British landscape architect, Devon)* **AV**
  Bibl: Building, 1988 May 13, v.253, no.20, p.43

Ede, Frederick Charles Vipont *(Canadian artist, 1865-p.1909)* **WC**

Edeikins, Christine *(French architect)* **AV**
  Bibl: Architecture d'aujourd'hui, 1987 Dec. no.254,p.76

Edelbacher, Otmar *(Austrian architect)* **AV**
  Bibl: Bauforum, 1987, v.20, no. 119, p.52

Edelfelt→see Edelfelt, Albert Gustaf Aristides

Edelfelt, Albert Gustaf Aristides **BA PR WC**
  (Finnish artist, 1854-1905) WC
  (Finnish painter, 1854-1905) BA PR
  Bibl: ▶Bénézit; ▶RILA/BHA; ▶Thieme-Becker
  Albert Gustaf Aristides Edelfelt PR
  Edelfelt PR

Edelfelt, Carl Albert *(Finnish architect, act.1857-1862)* **BA**
  Bibl: Helsinki (FIN), Suomen Rakinnustaiteen Mus., Rautateiden Arkkitectuuri (1984); ▶Thieme-Becker

Edelinck, Gerard **BA GC WC**
  (Dutch engraver in FRA, 1640-1707) BA
  (Flemish artist, 1640-1707) WC
  (Flemish painter and draughtsman, 1640-1707) GC
  Bibl: ▶Bénézit; ▶Fogg Mus. Libr. cat.; ▶Thieme-Becker

Edelinck, Nicolas Etienne *(French artist, 1681-1767)* **WC**

Edell, Brad A. (American sculptor, b.1950)   **BA**
    Bibl: Syracuse (NY, USA), Syracuse Univ., Lowe Art Gallery, NY/8 (1980)

Edelman [**Unidentified**] (Unknown painter)   **PR**
    Bibl: (December 16, 1815, lots 18, 19 & 84, Christie's)

Edelmann   **PR**

Edelman, Gail Cohen (American printmaker, 20th c.)   **BA**
    Bibl: Brooklyn (NY, USA), Brooklyn Mus., Woman's Place (1982); DIEA 83

Edelman, Rita (American painter, b.1930.)   **BA**
    Bibl: ARTS MAG LV/2 (Oct 1980) 12; ▶WW Amer. Art, 1989

Edelmann→see Edelman [Unidentified]

Edelmann, Hanno (German artist, 1923-)   **WC**

Edelmann, Otto Robert (Canadian artist, 20th cent.)   **WC**

Edelmann, Yrjo (Finnish painter, printmaker, b.1941)   **BA**
    Bibl: ▶Babington Smith, Contemp. artists; ▶Intl. dir. exh. artists, 1982-1983

Edelschein, Henrietta (American ceramist, 20th c.)   **BA**
    Bibl: Philadelphia (PA, USA), Temple University, Samuel Paley Library, The Tyler show (1974)

Edelson, Mary Beth   **BA WI**
    (American artist, 20th c.)   BA
    (American artist, op.20th c.)   WI
    Bibl: ▶Intl. dir. exh. artists, 1982, 1983; Lucie Smith; ▶WW Amer. Art, 1984

Edelstein, Victor (British artist, op. 20th c.)   **WI**

Edema→see Edema, Gerard Van

Edema, Gerard Van   **GC PR WC**
    (Dutch artist, c.1652-c.1700)   WC
    (Dutch painter, ca.1652-ca. 1700)   PR
    (Dutch, ca.1652-ca.1700)   GC
    Bibl: ▶Thieme-Becker; ▶Witt checklist

Edema   PR
Gerard Edima   PR
Gerard Van Edema   PR

Eden Upton Eddis→see Eddis, Eden Upton

Eden, Bronson B. (American painter, sculptor, b.1949)   **BA**
    Bibl: ARTS MAGAZINE, LX/1 (Sept 1985) 12; ▶WW Amer. Art, 1986

Eden, Denis William (British artist, 1878-1949)   **WC WI**

Eden, Diane Burn (American interior designer, New York, NY)   **AV**
    Bibl: Architectural digest, 1986 Feb., v.43, no.2, p.86

Eden, Emily (British printmaker, author, 1797-1869)   **BA**
    Bibl: ▶Bénézit; ▶Thieme-Becker

Eden, John (American painter, 20th c.)   **BA**
    Bibl: JOURNAL S. CALIF. 27 (June-July 1980) 22-23

Eden, Marx (British artist, op.1934-)   **WI**

Eden, Sir William→see Eden, William, 7th Bt.

Eden, William, 7th Bt.   **WI**
    (British artist, 1849-1915)   WC WI

Eden, Sir William   **WC**

Edenborough, Edith, Miss→see Corbet, Edith

Edens or Eden, J. (Dutch artist, op. 1651)   **WC**

Edenshaw, Charles (Canadian artist, 1839-1924)   **BA**
    Bibl: VANGUARD XI/1 (Feb 1982) 20-25

Eder, Engelbert (Austrian architect, Vienna)   **AV**
    Bibl: ▶Verzeich. Öst. Ziviltech.

Eder, Susan (American photographer, b.1950)   **BA**
    Bibl: Pittsfield (MA, USA), Berkshire Museum, ASPECTS OF NEW NARRATIVE ART, 1984

Eder, Wolfram (European, contemporary)   **JG**

Ederd, Emma S. (Hungarian medalist, 20th c.)   **BA**
    Bibl: Pushkin

Ederer, Robert (Austrian painter, b.1920)   **BA**
    Bibl: Dortmund (DEU), Mus. Ostwald, Wiener Schule (1979)

Ederlein, Caspar→see Enderlein, Caspar

Edey, Moses Chamberlain   **AV FA**
    (1845-1919; Architect, Ottawa)   FA
    (Canadian architect, 1845-1918)   AV
    Bibl: ▶Hill, Archts. Canada, 1986

Edgar Alwin Payne→see Payne, Edgar Alwin

Edgar Ashe Spilsbury→see Spilsbury, Edgar Ashe

Edgar Parker→see Parker, Edgar

Edgar Spier Cameron→see Cameron, Edgar Spier

Edgar, James H.   **BA WC**
    (British artist, op.1857-1870)   WI
    (British artist, op.1860-1864)   WC
    (British painter, act.1857-1870)   BA
    Bibl: ▶Bénézit; Southport (GBR), Atkinson Art Gall., Victorian (1979); ▶Thieme-Becker; ▶Wood, Victorian ptrs.

Edgar, James R.   **WI**
Edgar, James R.→see Edgar, James H.

Edgar, Natalie (American painter, 20th c.)   **BA**
    Bibl: ARTS MAG. LV (Jan 1981) 7

Edgar, Robert (British architect)   **AV**
    Bibl: Journal of the Tiles & Architectural Ceramics Society, 1987, v.2, p.21

Edgard Farasyn→see Farasyn, Edgard

Edge→see Edy, John William

Edge [**Unidentified**] (Unknown painter)   **PR**
    Bibl: (July 7, 1810, lot 76, Christie's)

Edge, Douglas Benjamin (American sculptor, photographer, b.1942)   **BA**
    Bibl: Portland (OR, USA), Art Mus., West Coast now (1968); ▶WW Amer. Art, 1976

Edge, John (British artist, op.1827-1836)   **WI**

Edgerly, Josiah (American painter, 20th c.)   **BA**
    Bibl: Arts Mag. LI/8 (Apr 1977) 8; ▶Locus

Edgerton, Harold Eugene   **BA JG**
    (American electrical engineer, photographer, 1903-1990)   BA
    (American, 1903 -)   JG
    Bibl: BERKSHIRE EAGLE (5 Jan 1990) p.C8; ▶Contemp. photogs., 1988; ▶ICP encyc. photog.; WW Amer., 1989

Edie, Richard (American ceramist, b.1924)   **BA**
    Bibl: Brookings (SD, USA), S.D. Mem. Art center, RICHARD EDIE CERAMICS (1978)

Edie, Stuart Carson   **WC WI**
    (American artist, 1908-)   WC
    (American artist, b.1908)   WI

Edinburgh Painter (vase-painter, ca. 500-480 BC)   **GC**
    Bibl: ▶Beazley, Attic bl.-fig. vase-ptrs.; Boardman, Attic Bl.-fig. Vases

Edion, Henri (French artist, 1905-)   **WC**

Edis, Robert William   **BA**
    (British architect, 1838-1927)   AV
    (British architect, 1839-1927)   BA
    Bibl: ▶Arch. period. idx./RIBA; ▶Avery Libr. cat.; Country life, 1985 Nov.14, v.178, no.4604, p.1570; ▶Macmillan encyc. archts.; ▶Who was who [GBR]

Edis, Robert William, Sir   **AV**
Edis, Robert William, Sir→see Edis, Robert William

Edison, Thomas Alva (American inventor, 1847-1931)   **BA**
    Bibl: ▶New Columbia encyc.

Edith Cook→see Cook, Edith

Edith Corbet→see Corbet, Edith

Edito, Edson Jorge (Brazilian architect)   **AV**
    Bibl: Projeto, 1988 Apr., no.109, p.72

Editore, Baleri (Designer)   **AV**
    Bibl: Architecture intérieure crée, no.203, p.100

Edkins, John (British artist, 1931-1966)   **WC WI**

Edler, Anton (German, active
  Munich, Germany,
  daguerreotypist)   **JG**
Edlich, Stephen P.   **BA WI**
  (American artist, b.1944)   WI
  (American sculptor, painter,
  b.1944)   BA
  Bibl: ▶NY art yrbk.
Edlinger → see Edlinger, Josef Georg
  von
Edlinger or Etlinger, Joseph Georg
  von → see Edlinger, Josef Georg
  von
Edlinger, Johann Georg → see
  Edlinger, Josef Georg von
Edlinger, Josef Georg → see Edlinger,
  Josef Georg von
Edlinger, Josef Georg von   **BA GC PR**
  (German artist, 1741-1819)   WC
  (German painter, 1741-
  1819)   BA GC PR
  Bibl: ▶Bénézit; ▶Encyc. world art;
    ▶RILA/BHA; ▶Thieme-Becker
  Edlinger   PR
  **Edlinger or Etlinger, Joseph
    Georg von**   **WC**
  Edlinger, Johann Georg   PR
  Edlinger, Josef Georg   PR
  Etlinger, Josef Georg von   BA GC
  Ettlinger, Josef Georg von   BA GC
  Josef Georg Edlinger   PR
Edmisten, John   **AV**
Edmond Francois Aman-Jean → see
  Aman-Jean, Edmond François
Edmond Jean Pury → see Pury,
  Edmond Jean de
Edmond Jean, Baron de Pury → see
  Pury, Edmond Jean de
Edmond, Maggie (Australian
  architect)   **AV**
Edmond, Martin (Swedish artist,
  20th cent.)   **WC**
Edmonds, Francis William   **BA GC**
  (American artist, 1806-1863)   WC WI
  (American painter, 1806-
  1863)   BA GC
  Bibl: ▶Groce, Artists Amer.;
    ▶RILA/BHA; ▶WWW Amer.
Edmonds, John Francis W.   **WC**
Edmonds, John Francis William   **WI**
Edmonds, John Francis W. → see
  Edmonds, Francis William
Edmonds, John Francis William → see
  Edmonds, Francis William
Edmonds, Michael, Mrs. (British,
  20th c.)   **BA**
  Bibl: APOLLO CXIV/234 (Aug
    1981) 109-113
Edmonds, Nicholas Biddle
  (American sculptor, b.1937)   **BA**
  Bibl: ▶WW Amer. Art
Edmonds, R.M. (British artist, op.
  20th c.)   **WI**
Edmondson the Younger, E. → see
  Edmondson, Edward

Edmondson, Edward   **BA**
  (American artist, 1830-1884)   WI
  (American artist, 19th cent.)   WC
  (American painter, 1830-1884)   BA
  Bibl: ▶Groce, Artists Amer.; St.
    Louis (MO, USA), Art Mus., Ptg. in
    Midwest (1977)
Edmondson the Younger, E.   **WC**
Edmondson, Edward, Jr.   **WI**
Edmondson, Edward, Jr. → see
  Edmondson, Edward
Edmondson, James   **WC WI**
  (British artist, op.c.1810)   WC
  (British artist, op.circa 1810-)   WI
Edmondson, Leonard   **WC WI**
  (American artist, 1916-)   WC
  (American artist, b.1916)   WI
Edmondson, Simon (British painter,
  b.1955)   **BA**
  Bibl: ▶Intl. dir. exh. artists, 1982
Edmondson, William (American
  sculptor, ca.1870-1951)   **BA**
  Bibl: ▶Cederholm, Afro-Amer.
    artists; Nashville (TN, USA), Tenn.
    State Mus., William Edmondson
    (1981); ▶Vollmer, Künst.-Lex. 20.
    Jhr.
Edmonston, Samuel   **WC WI**
  (British artist, 1825-)   WC
  (British artist, 1825-op.1864)   WI
Edmonstone, Robert (British artist,
  1794-1834)   **WC WI**
Edmund Berninger → see Berninger,
  Edmund
Edmund Bristow → see Bristow,
  Edmund
Edmund Charles Tarbell → see Tarbell,
  Edmund Charles
Edmund Clarence Messer → see
  Messer, Edmund Clarence
Edmund Dorrell → see Dorrell,
  Edmund
Edmund Garvey → see Garvey,
  Edmund
Edmund Henry Osthaus → see
  Osthaus, Edmund Henry
Edmund Hodgson Smart → see Smart,
  Edmund Hodgson
Edmunds, David J. (Canadian
  architect, Calgary)   **AV**
  Bibl: ▶Canad. arch. dir., 1985
Edmunds, Keith McKay (British
  artist, op.1910-1922)   **WI**
Edoardo de Martino → see Martino,
  Edoardo de
Edouard Brandon → see Brandon,
  Edouard
Edouard de Beaumont → see
  Beaumont, Edouard de
Edouard Dufeu → see Dufeu, Edouard
Edouard Frere → see Frère, Pierre
  Edouard
Edouard Joseph Goerg → see Goerg,
  Edouard Joseph
Edouard Manet → see Manet, Edouard

Edouard Swebach → see Swebach,
  Edouard
Edouard Vuillard → see Vuillard,
  Edouard
Edouard-Leon Cortes → see Cortes,
  Edouard-Leon
Edouart, Augistin Amant Constant
  Fidele → see Edouart, Augustin
  Amant Constant Fidèle
**Edouart, Augustin Amant
  Constant Fidèle**   **BA**
  (French artist, 1789-1861)   WC
  (French silhouette artist, 1789-
  1861)   BA
  Bibl: ▶Bénézit; ▶Thieme-Becker
  **Edouart, Augistin Amant
    Constant Fidele**   **WC**
Edridge, Henry   **GC WC WI**
  (British artist, 1769-1821)   WC WI
  (British, 1769-1821)   GC
  Bibl: ▶Thieme-Becker; ▶Witt
    checklist
Edson, Aaron Allan   **BA**
  (British artist, op.1883-m.1888)   WC
  (Canadian painter, 1846-1888)   BA
  Bibl: ▶Artists Canada; ▶Bénézit;
    ▶Natl. Gall. Canada libr. cat.;
    ▶Thieme-Becker
Edson, Allan   **BA WC**
Edson, Allan → see Edson, Aaron Allan
Edstrand, Gert (Danish architect,
  20th c.)   **BA**
  Bibl: Koppel, Arkitektur, XXVII/1
    (Feb. 1983) p.5; Trap, Kongeriget
    DNK: personalregister
Eduard Bretschneider → see
  Bretschneider, Eduard
Eduard Charlemont → see Charlemont,
  Eduard
Eduard Dubois → see Dubois, Eduard
Eduard Jacobi → see Jacobi, Eduard
Eduard Julius Friedrich
  Bendemann → see Bendemann,
  Eduard Julius Friedrich
Eduard Merk → see Merk, Eduard
Eduard Post → see Post, Eduard
Eduard Robert Bary → see Bary,
  Eduard Robert
Eduard Seydel → see Seydel, Eduard
Eduard Strohling → see Ströhling,
  Eduard
Eduard von Gebhardt → see Gebhardt,
  Eduard von
Eduardo Javier Ramon Cano de la
  Pena → see Cano de la Peña,
  Eduardo Javier Ramón
Eduardo Tojetti → see Tojetti, Eduardo
Eduardo Zamacois y Zabala → see
  Zamacois y Zabala, Eduardo
Edugene, Pierre (Haitian artist,
  1941-)   **WC**
Edvard Munch → see Munch, Edvard
Edvards, Jes → see Edvars, Jes

Edvars, Jes (*Danish (?) architect*)   **AV**
    Bibl: Arkitektur DK, 1984 Oct.,
    v.28, no.6, p.226
    Edvards, Jes   AV
Edwaert Colyer→*see* Colyer, Edwaert
Edward Alcock→*see* Alcock, Edward
Edward B. Gay→*see* Gay, Edward B.
Edward Barnard Lintott→*see* Lintott,
    Edward Barnard
Edward Bird→*see* Bird, Edward
Edward Bruce→*see* Bruce, Edward
    Bright
Edward Burgess Butler→*see* Butler,
    Edward Burgess
Edward Burne-Jones→*see* Burne-
    Jones, Edward
Edward Calvert→*see* Calvert, Edward
Edward Charles Volkert→*see* Volkert,
    Edward Charles
Edward Clarke Cabot→*see* Cabot,
    Edward Clarke
Edward D. Boit→*see* Boit, Edward
    Darley
Edward Dayes→*see* Dayes, Edward
Edward Edwards→*see* Edwards,
    Edward
Edward Francis Burney→*see* Burney,
    Edward Francis
Edward Gabe→*see* Gabe, Edward
Edward H. Molyneux→*see* Molyneux,
    Edward H.
Edward Henry Potthast→*see*
    Potthast, Edward Henry
Edward Hill→*see* Hill, Edward
Edward Hopper→*see* Hopper,
    Edward
Edward L. Custer→*see* Custer,
    Edward L.
Edward Ladell→*see* Ladell, Edward
Edward Lamson Henry→*see* Henry,
    Edward Lamson
Edward Lear→*see* Lear, Edward
Edward Lutterell→*see* Lutterell,
    Edward
Edward Matthew Hale→*see* Hale,
    Edward Matthew
Edward Middleton Manigault→*see*
    Manigault, Edward Middleton
Edward Moran→*see* Moran, Edward
Edward Nash→*see* Nash, Edward
Edward Parker Hayden→*see* Hayden,
    Edward Parker
Edward Penfield→*see* Penfield,
    Edward
Edward Penny→*see* Penny, Edward
Edward Pritchett→*see* Pritchett,
    Edward
Edward Savage→*see* Savage, Edward
Edward Timothy Hurley→*see* Hurley,
    Edward Timothy
Edward Tojetti→*see* Tojetti, Eduardo
Edward VI (*British artist, 1537-*
    1553)   **WC WI**
Edward VII (*British artist, 1841-*
    1910)   **WC WI**

Edward William Cooke→*see* Cooke,
    Edward William
Edward Willis Redfield→*see* Redfield,
    Edward Willis
Edward, Albert S. (*British artist,*
    1852-1915)   **WI**
    Bibl: ▶Waters, Brit. artists
Edward, Alexander   **AV BA**
    (*Scottish architect, 1651-1708*)   AV
    (*Scottish architect, landscape,*
    architect, 1651-1708)   BA
    Bibl: ▶Colvin, Brit. archts.
Edward, Charles   **WC WI**
    (*British artist, op.1884*)   WC
    (*British artist, op.1884-*)   WI
Edward, Lindsay (*Australian painter,*
    b.1919)   **BA**
    Bibl: ▶Encyc. Australian art
Edwards (*American, active ca. 1860,*
    Atlanta (Edwards & Son))   **JG**
Edwards (*English upholsterer, 17th*
    c.)   **BA**
      Bibl: Mactaggart, COSTUME XIV
      (1980) 41-55
Edwards→*see* Edwards, Edward
Edwards Of Halifax→*see* Edwards of
    Halifax, William
Edwards of Halifax, William   **BA**
    (*British artist, 18th cent.*)   WC
    (*British artist, op.18th c.*)   WI
    (*British bookbinder, 1722-1808*)   BA
      Bibl: Baltimore (MD, USA), Mus.
      Art, Hist. bookbinding (1957),
      p.201; ▶Dict. natl. biog.; Harthan,
      BOOKBINDINGS, 1961, 16-17;
      Rees, E., NAT'L LIB. WALES J.,
      23/4 (wint 1984) 430-432
Edwards Of Halifax   **WC**
Edwards, (of Halifax)   **WI**
Edwards, (of Halifax)→*see* Edwards
    of Halifax, William
Edwards, Anthony (*British*
    architect)   **AV**
    Bibl: RIBA journal, 1985 Jan., v.92,
    no.1, p.17
Edwards, Arthur Sherwood (*British*
    artist, b.1887)   **WI**
Edwards, Barbara (*American artist,*
    1952-2052)   **WI**
Edwards, Benjamin A. (*American*
    cabinetmaker, 1773-1822)   **BA**
      Bibl: Keno, Antiques CXVII (May
      1980) 1100-1107
Edwards, C.A. (*British artist, op.*
    1792-1797)   **WI**
Edwards, Cyril W.→*see* Edwards,
    Cyril Walduck
Edwards, Cyril Walduck   **WI**
    (*British artist, 1902-*)   WC
    (*British artist, b.1902*)   WI
Edwards, Cyril W.   **WC**
Edwards, D.   **WC WI**
    (*British artist, 19th cent.*)   WC
    (*British artist, op.19th c.*)   WI
      Bibl: ▶Houfe, Brit. book illus.

Edwards, E.   **WI**
    (*British artist, 1766-1849*)   WI
    (*British artist, 19th cent.*)   WC
Edwards, The Rev.E.   **WC**
Edwards, Edward   **PR WC WI**
    (*British artist, 1738-1806*)   WC WI
    (*British painter, 1738-1806*)   PR
      Bibl: ▶Thieme-Becker;
      ▶Waterhouse, Brit. 18c. ptrs.
    Edward Edwards   PR
    Edwards   PR
Edwards, Edwin   **BA WC WI**
    (*British artist, 1823-1879*)   WC WI
    (*British painter, printmaker,*
    1823-1879)   BA
      Bibl: ▶Thieme-Becker; ▶Wood,
      Victorian ptrs.
Edwards, Emmet (*American painter,*
    b.1906)   **BA**
      Bibl: Arts Mag. CII/3 (Nov 1977),
      pp.105-107
Edwards, Ernest (*British*
    photographer, 19th c.)   **BA**
      Bibl: HIST OF PHOTOG. III (1979)
Edwards, Ethel (*American painter,*
    20th c.)   **BA**
      Bibl: ▶WW Amer. Art
Edwards, F.   **WC WI**
    (*British artist, 19th cent.*)   WC
    (*British artist, op.19th c.*)   WI
      Bibl: ▶Wood, Victorian ptrs.
Edwards, George   **BA WC WI**
    (*British artist, 1694-1773*)   WC WI
    (*English ornithologist, author,*
    illustrator, 1694-1773)   BA
      Bibl: ▶Dict. natl. biog.;
      ▶Thieme-Becker
Edwards, George Henry (*British*
    artist, op.1883-1910)   **WC WI**
Edwards, George Wharton   **WI**
    (*American artist, 1859-1950*)   WI
    (*Engraver, 1859-1950*)   WI
      Bibl: Who Was Who; ▶Who was
      who [GBR]
Edwards, Glen (*American artist,*
    1935-2035)   **WI**
Edwards, H. Sutherland→*see*
    Edwards, Henry Sutherland
Edwards, Harry C. (*American artist,*
    1868-1922)   **WC WI**
Edwards, Heide (*German painter,*
    b.1942)   **BA**
      Bibl: Bristol (GBR), Arnolfini
      Gallery, Bristol sample (1979)
Edwards, Henry Sutherland   **WI**
    (*British artist, b.1828*)   WI
    (*British artist, op.1867*)   WC
Edwards, H. Sutherland   **WC**
Edwards, James   **WC WI**
    (*British artist, 1820-1888*)   WI
    (*British artist, op.1868*)   WC
Edwards, Jay Dearborn (*American,*
    active 1860s)   **JG**
Edwards, Jeffery→*see* Edwards,
    Jeffrey

Eeckhoudt, Jean van den (*Belgian artist, 1875-1946*)   **WC**

Eeckhout → *see* Eeckhout, Gerbrand van den

Eeckhout, Albert van der   **BA GC**
   (*Dutch artist, op.1637-1664*)   WC
   (*Dutch painter and draughtsman, ca.1610-1666*)   GC
   (*Dutch painter, 1604-1666*)   BA
    Bibl: Dupare, ESSAYS IN NORTHERN EUR. ART..., 72; Rijksmuseum; ▶Thieme-Becker; ▶Witt checklist
   Eckhout, Albert   GC
   Eckhout, Albert van der   BA

Eeckholt or Eyckhout, Albert van der   **WC**
   Eyckhout, Albert van der   BA

Eeckhout, Anthonie van den
   (*Flemish artist, 1656-1695*)   **WC**

Eeckhout, Gerbrand Jansz. van den → *see* Eeckhout, Gerbrand van den

Eeckhout, Gerbrand van den   **BA GC JG PR**
   (*Dutch artist, 1621-1674*)   WC
   (*Dutch painter, 1621-1674*)   PR
   (*Dutch painter, printmaker, 1621-1674*)   BA
   (*Dutch, 1621-1674*)   GC JG
    Bibl: ▶Bénézit; ▶Grote Winkler Prins; ▶Nieuw NLD biog. woord., v.5, p.147; ▶RILA/BHA; ▶Thieme-Becker; ▶Wurzbach, NLD Künst.-Lex.
   Echardt   PR
   Echout   PR
   Eckhart   PR
   Eckhaut   PR
   Eckhort   PR
   Eckhoudt   PR
   Eckhouet   PR
   Eckhout   PR
   Eckout   PR
   Ecoot   PR
   Eeckhout   PR

Eeckhout, Gerbrand Jansz. van den   **WC**
   Eeckhout, Gerbrandt van den   PR
   Eekhoud   PR
   Eekhout   PR
   Eickhout   PR
   Escout   PR
   Eyckhout   PR
   G. Van Eckhout   PR
   G.V. Eckhout   PR
   Gerbrand van den Eeckhout   PR
   Gerbrant vander Eeckhout   PR
   V. den Eckhout   PR
   V. Eckhout   PR
   van den Eckhout   PR
   Van Eckhout   PR
   Van Eeckhoul   PR
   Van Eeckhout   PR
   Vanden Eckhout   PR
   Vander Eckhout   PR
   Vander Eeckhout   PR
   Vander Euckhout   PR
Eeckhout, Gerbrandt van den → *see* Eeckhout, Gerbrand van den
Eeckhout, Jacobus Josephus → *see* Eeckhout, Jakob Josef

Eeckhout, Jakob Josef   **GC PR**
   (*Belgian artist, 1793-1861*)   WC
   (*Belgian, 1793-1861*)   GC
   (*Dutch painter, 1793-1861*)   PR
    Bibl: ▶Thieme-Becker; ▶Witt checklist
   Eeckhoudt, Jacob Josef   PR

Eeckhout, Jacobus Josephus   **WC**
   Eeckhout, Jakob Joseph   PR
   Jakob Josef Eeckhout   PR
Eeckhout, Jakob Joseph → *see* Eeckhout, Jakob Josef

Eeckhout, Victor (*Belgian artist, 1821-1879*)   **WC**

Eegels [Unidentified] (*Unknown painter, act. 17th century*)   **PR**
    Bibl: Oilarts inventory, 1671

Eegre, Mathieu van → *see* Negre, Mathieu van

Eekhoud → *see* Eeckhout, Gerbrand van den

Eekhout → *see* Eeckhout, Gerbrand van den

Eekhout, Mick (*Industrial designer, Netherlands ?*)   **AV**
    Bibl: De Architect, 1986 June, v.17, no.6, p.78

Eekman, Nikolaas (*Belgian artist, 1889-*)   **WC**

Eeles, Bruce   **AV BA**
   (*Australian architect*)   AV
   (*Australian architect, 20th c.*)   BA
    Bibl: Architectural review, 1985 Dec., v.178, no.1066, p.54; ▶Avery period. idx., 6th suppl.

Eeles, Roger (*Australian architect*)   **AV**
    Bibl: Architecture Australia, 1985 May, v.74, no.3, p.41

Eelkema, Eelke Jelles   **GC WC**
   (*Dutch artist, 1788-1839*)   WC
   (*Dutch painter, 1788-1839*)   GC
    Bibl: ▶Thieme-Becker

Eemans, Marcel (Marc) (*Belgian artist, 1907-*)   **WC**

Eemon → *see* Eemont, Adriaen van

Eemont or Emont, Adriaen van → *see* Eemont, Adriaen van

Eemont, Adriaen van   **GC PR**
   (*Dutch artist, c.1627-1662*)   WC
   (*Dutch painter, c.1627-1662*)   GC
   (*Dutch painter, ca.1627-1662*)   PR
    Bibl: ▶Bénézit; ▶Thieme-Becker
   Adriaen van Eemont   PR
   Eemon   PR

Eemont or Emont, Adriaen van   **WC**
   Emont, Adriaen van   GC

Eenhooge, D. Van (*Belgian architect*)   **AV**
    Bibl: Monumentum en landscappe, 1984 May-June, v.3, no.2

Eenhoorn, Samuel van (*Dutch ceramist, 1655-1686/87*)   **BA**
    Bibl: ▶Boger, World pott. & porc.; Erkelens, NEDERLANDS KUNSTHIST. JAARBOEK XXXI (1980) 263-272; Fourest, DELFTWARE; ▶Grote Winkler Prins; ▶Honey, Euro. ceramic; ▶Mankowitz, Encyc. pott. & porc.; ▶Thieme-Becker

Eenzinger, Wolfgang (*Austrian architect*)   **AV**
    Bibl: Planen Bauen Wohnen, 1988, no.121, p.39

Eerelman, Otto   **GC WC**
   (*Dutch artist, 1839-1926*)   WC
   (*Dutch painter and draughtsman, 1839-1926*)   GC
    Bibl: ▶Bénézit

Eerenbeemt, Gérard Leonard van den *(Dutch painter, sculptor, b.1936)*   **BA**
     Bibl: ▶Scheen, Ned. beeldende kunst.

Eerenberch, Wilhelm van→see Ehrenberg, Wilhelm van

Eerikäinen, Petri *(Finnish architect, 20th century)*   **AV**
     Bibl: Byggekunst, 1986, v.68, no.7, p.F10

Eernis, J.G. *(Dutch painter)*   **GC**
     Bibl: Getty Photo Study Coll. (Douwes coll.)

Eertvelt→see Eertvelt, Andries van

Eertvelt or Artvelt, Andries van→see Eertvelt, Andries van

Eertvelt, Andries van   **BA GC PR**
   (Dutch painter, 1590-1652)   **PR**
   (Flemish artist, 1590-1652)   **WC**
   (Flemish painter, 1590-1652)   **BA GC**
     Bibl: ▶Encyc. world art; Gerson, Art & arch. Belgium; ▶RILA/BHA; ▶Thieme-Becker; ▶Witt checklist

Aertveldt   PR
Andries van Eertvelt   PR
Artvelt, Andries van   **BA GC**
Eertvelt   PR
Eertvelt or Artvelt, Andries van   **WC**
Ertvelt   PR

Eesteren, Cornelis van   **AV BA**
   (Dutch architect, city planner, b.1897)   **BA**
   (Dutch city planner, 1897-1988)   **AV**
     Bibl: ▶Avery Libr. cat.; ▶Avery period. idx.; ▶Encyc. world art; ▶Portoghesi, Diz. arch. e urbanistica; Stedebouw + volkhuisvesting, 1988 Apr., v.69, no.4, p.143; ▶Vollmer, Künst.-Lex. 20. Jhr.

Eewouts→see Eewouts, Claes [Unidentified]

Eewouts, Claes [Unidentified] *(Unknown painter, act. 17th century)*   **PR**
     Bibl: Bredius, Künstler-Inventare, pp.1868-1871; Claesz. inventory 1624

Claes Eewouts   PR
Eewouts   PR

Efanov, Vasilij Prokop'evič *(Russian painter, b.1900)*   **BA**
     Bibl: ▶Natl. union cat., pre-1956; Rome (ITA), Pal. Venezia, PITTURA RUSSE E SOVIETICA (1974)

Effel, Jean *(French artist, 20th cent.)*   **WC**

Effinger, Edwin *(W. German architect, Munich, 1939-)*   **AV**
     Bibl: Deutsche Bauzeitung, 1985 Oct., v.119, no.10, p.10

Effner, Joseph   **AV BA JG**
   (1687-1745)   **AV**
   (German architect, decorator, 1687-1745)   **BA**
   (German, 1687-1745)   **JG**
     Bibl: ▶Encyc. world art; ▶Met. Mus. Art libr. cat.; ▶Thieme-Becker

Efimov, Ivan *(Russian sculptor, illustrator, 1878-1959)*   **BA**
     Bibl: ▶Bénézit; ▶Fogg Mus. Libr. cat.

Yefimov, Ivan   BA

Efimova, Anna Maksimovna *(Russian ceramist, d.ca.1961)*   **BA**
     Bibl: DEK. ISKUSS. SSSR (May 1976) 42-45

Efrat, Benni *(Israeli artist, b.1936)*   **BA**
     Bibl: Wadsworth Atheneum, ANNUAL REPORT (1978) 17

Eg. Vanderneer→see Neer, Eglon Hendrik van der

Egan, Beresford *(British artist, author, actor, b.1905)*   **BA**
     Bibl: Portsmouth (GBR), City Museum and Art Gallery, BERESFORD EGAN (1979)

Egan, Felim *(Irish artist, b.1952)*   **BA**
     Bibl: London (GBR), Roundhouse Gallery, Irish art (1980)

Egan, George *(British artist, op.19th c.)*   **WI**

Egan, James J. *(American ecclesiastical architect, Chicago, Ill., noted for his Catholic church work; b. in Ireland, educated in England, moved to N.Y.C. as a youth. Estab. a practice in Chicago in 1871, 1839-1914)*   **AV**
     Bibl: ▶Withey, Amer. archts.

Egan, John J. *(American artist, 1810-1882)*   **WI**

Egan, Wilfred   **WC WI**
   (British artist, 20th cent.)   **WC**
   (British artist, op.20th c.)   **WI**
     Bibl: ▶Johnson, Brit. artists

Egan, William   **WC WI**
   (British artist, op.1850)   **WC**
   (British artist, op.1850-)   **WI**

Eganbyuri, Eli→see Iliazd

Egb, Hemskerck→see Heemskerck, Egbert van (the elder)

Egb. Hemskerck→see Heemskerck, Egbert van (the elder)

Egb. Hemskirk→see Heemskerck, Egbert van (the elder)

Egbert Heemskerck→see Heemskerck, Egbert van (the elder)

Egbert Heemskirk→see Heemskerck, Egbert van (the elder)

Egbert Hemskerck→see Heemskerck, Egbert van (the elder)

Egbert Hemskerk→see Heemskerck, Egbert van (the elder)

Egbert Hemskirk→see Heemskerck, Egbert van (the elder)

Egbert Hermskerck→see Heemskerck, Egbert van (the elder)

Egbert van der Poel→see Poel, Egbert van der

Egbert van Heemskerck (I)→see Heemskerck, Egbert van (the elder)

Egbert van Heemskerck (the younger)→see Heemskerck, Egbert van (the younger)

Egberts, Rik *(Dutch architect)*   **AV**
     Bibl: Architecture & urbanism, 1983 Dec., no.12(159), p.81

Egedius, Halfdan   **BA**
   (Norwegian artist, 1877-1899)   BA WC
     Bibl: NLK 1986; Oslo (NOR), Nasjonalgalleriet, Norsk malerkunst, p.82; ▶Thieme-Becker

Egedius, Halfdan Johnsen   **WC**

Egedius, Halfdan Johnsen→see Egedius, Halfdan

Egeler, Ernst *(1908-1978)*   **AV**

Egeler, Stefan *(German artist, 1894-1969)*   **WC**

Egell, Johann Paul   **BA GC**
   (German artist, 1691-1752)   **WC**
   (German sculptor and draughtsman, 1691-1752)   **GC**
   (German sculptor, 1691-1752)   AV BA
     Bibl: Anz. des Germ. Nationalmus. (1976) 151-158; ▶Neue deutsche Biog.; PANTHEON XLII/1 (Jan-Mar 1984) 12; ▶RILA/BHA; ▶Thieme-Becker

Egell, Paul   **AV GC WC**

Egell, Paul→see Egell, Johann Paul

Egenberger, Johannes Hinderikus *(Dutch artist, 1822-1897)*   **WC**

Egender, Karl *(Swiss architect)*   **AV**
     Bibl: Werk Bauen + Wohnen, 1989 July-Aug., no.7-8, p.56

Eger or Egger, Georg Adam *(German artist, 1727-1808)*   **WC**

Eger, John *(British architect, London)*   **AV**
     Bibl: ▶RIBA members, 1985

Eger, Selina *(British architect, London)*   **AV**
     Bibl: ▶RIBA members, 1985

Egeri, Carle von→see Aegeri, Carle von

Egermann, Friedrich *(German glass manufacturer, 1777-1864)*   **BA**
     Bibl: ▶Penguin dec. arts; ▶Thieme-Becker

Egersdorfer, Heinrich   **WC WI**
   (British artist, op.1909)   **WC**
   (British artist, op.1909-)   **WI**

Egerton Bush Coghill→see Coghill, Egerton Bush

Egerton Master *(French, active ca. 1405-1420)*   **JG**

Egerton Master→see Master of Egerton 1070

Egerton, 'Ariana' M.   **WC WI**
   (British artist, op.1777)   **WC**
   (British artist, op.1777-)   **WI**

Egerton, Daniel Thomas   WC WI
    (British artist, circa 1800-1842)   WI
    (British artist, op.1824-m.1842)   WC
Egerton, Francis, 1st Earl of
    Ellesmere *(British artist, op.circa*
    1850-)   WI
Egerton, M.   WC WI
    (British artist, op.1824-1827)   WI
    (British artist, op.c.1825)   WC
Egesandro → see Agesandros of
    Rhodes
Egg → see Egg, Augustus Leopold
Egg and Wave Group *(Apulian*
    vase-painters)   GC
    Bibl: Trendall, Attic red-fig. vases
    Apulia
Egg and Wave Painter *(Apulian*
    vase-painter)   GC
    Bibl: Trendall, Attic red-fig. vases
    Apulia
Egg, Augustus → see Egg, Augustus
    Leopold
Egg, Augustus Leopold   BA PR WC WI
    (British artist, 1816-1863)   WC WI
    (British painter, 1816-1863)   BA PR
    Bibl: ▶Bénézit; ▶Dict. natl. biog.;
    ▶RILA/BHA
    Autustus Leopold Egg   PR
    Egg   PR
    Egg, Augustus   PR
Egg, Durs *(Swiss gunsmith in GBR,*
    1745-1834)   BA
    Bibl: ▶Oxford dec. arts
Eggeling *(German architect, act.*
    1906)   BA
    Bibl: Pieske, DEU. KUNST UND
    DENK. XXXIII/1-2 (1975) 73-90
Eggeling, Helmuth Viking
    Fredrik → see Eggeling, Viking
Eggeling, Viking *(Swedish*
    filmmaker, painter, 1880-1925)   BA
    Bibl: ▶Encic. spettacolo; ▶Encyc.
    world art; ▶Phaidon 20c. art;
    ▶Seuphor, Abstract ptg.; ▶Svenskt
    konst.-lex.; ▶Vollmer, Künst.-Lex.
    20. Jhr.
    Eggeling, Helmuth Viking Fredrik   BA
Eggen, Nils Henrik *(Norwegian*
    architect, Trondheim, 1931-)   AV
    Bibl: Byggekunst: the Norwegian
    review of architecture, 1988,
    v.70, no.8, p.561
Eggenhofer, Nick   WC WI
    (American artist, 1897-op.1976)   WI
    (American artist, 20th cent.)   WC
Eggenschwiler, Franz   BA WC
    (Swiss artist, 20th cent.)   WC
    (Swiss sculptor, painter, b.1930)   BA
    Bibl: ▶Bénézit; ▶MoMA libr. cat.
Egger, Andreas *(Austrian architect)*   AV
    Bibl: Architektur + Wettbewerbe,
    1989 Mar., no.137, p.24
Egger, Jean *(Swiss artist, 1893-*
    1934)   WC

Egger-Lienz, Albin   BA GC WC
    (Austrian painter, 1868-1926)   BA GC
    (German artist, 1868-)   WC
    (German artist, 1868-1925)   WC
    Bibl: ▶Österr. biog. Lex. 1815-
    1950; ▶RILA/BHA;
    ▶Thieme-Becker; ▶Vollmer,
    Künst.-Lex. 20. Jhr.
    Lienz, Albin Egger   BA
Lienz, Egger   WC
Eggers, Bartholomeus *(Dutch*
    sculptor, ca.1630-1692)   BA
    Bibl: Leeuwenberg,
    Beeldhouwkunst Rijksmus.;
    ▶Thieme-Becker
Eggers, Otto R. *(4.VIII.1882-23.IV.*
    1964; Architect, United States of
    America)   FA
    Bibl: ▶Macmillan encyc. archts.,
    v.2, p.12 ff.; Natl. Archives
    object; NGA archives records
    Eggers, Otto Reinhold   FA
Eggers, Otto Reinhold → see Eggers,
    Otto R.
Eggert, Georg Peter Hermann   BA
    (1844-1914)   AV
    (German architect, 1844-1920)   BA
    Bibl: ▶Portoghesi, Diz. arch. e
    urbanistica; ▶Thieme-Becker
    Eggert, Herman   BA
Eggert, Hermann   AV BA
Eggert, Herman → see Eggert, Georg
    Peter Hermann
Eggert, Hermann → see Eggert, Georg
    Peter Hermann
Eggert, Sigmund *(German artist,*
    1839-1896)   WC
Egginton, Frank J. *(British artist,*
    b.1908)   WI
Egginton, Wycliffe *(British artist,*
    1875-1951)   WC WI
    Bibl: ▶Fisher, Watercolour ptrs.
Eggler, Fritz *(also Boissonnas &*
    Eggler)   JG
Eggleston, Benjamin Osro
    (American artist, 1867-1937)   WI
Eggleston, William   BA JG
    (American photographer,
    b.1939)   BA
    (American, 1939 -)   JG
    Bibl: ▶MoMA libr. cat.; ▶Parry,
    Photo idx.
Eggloffstein, von → see Egloffstein,
    F.W. von
Eggmann, Johann Melchior *(Swiss*
    painter, 1711-after 1751)   BA
    Bibl: ▶Jenny, Kunstführer Schweiz,
    v.1; MON. D'ART ET D'HISTOIRE
    DU CANTON DE FRIBOURG;
    Rorschacher Neujahrsblatt LXVIII
    (1978) 61
Eggstein, Hans *(Swiss architect,*
    Lucerne)   AV
    Bibl: ▶Schweiz. Ingen. u. Archit.,
    1984-1985
Egidio dall' Oglio → see Olio, Egidio
    dall'

Egidio dall'Oglio → see Olio, Egidio
    dall'
Egidio, Monsù [Unidentified]
    (Unknown painter)   PR
    Bibl: Maratti inventory, Rome,
    1711
    Monsù Egidio   PR
Egidius Mengelberg → see
    Mengelberg, Egidius
Egidius Sadeler (II) → see Sadeler,
    Egidius II
Egidius Van Tilborg → see Tilborgh,
    Gillis van
Eginton, Francis *(British glass*
    painter, 1737-1805)   BA
    Bibl: ▶Thieme-Becker
Eginton, John *(British artist, op.*
    1763-1800)   WC WI
Egl, Herbert *(West German painter,*
    b.1953)   BA
    Bibl: Stuttgart (DEU), Württemb.
    Kunstverein, Herbert Egla (1984)
Eglan, Maximilian T. → see Eglau,
    Maximilian T.
Eglau, Maximilian T. *(American*
    artist, 1825-circa 1900)   WI
    Eglan, Maximilian T.   WI
Eglen Vanderneer → see Neer, Eglon
    Hendrik van der
Egleton, W.H. *(Engraver, op.1833-*
    1862)   WI
Egley, William → see Egley, William E.
Egley, William E.   WI
    (British artist, 1798-1870)   WC WI
    (British, 1798-1870)   GC
    Bibl: ▶Thieme-Becker; ▶Witt
    checklist
Egley, William   GC WC
Egley, William Maw   WC WI
    (British artist, 1826-1916)   WI
    (British artist, op.1843-1898)   WC
Egli, Dorrit *(French interior designer,*
    Paris)   AV
    Bibl: Architectural digest, 1985
    Sept., v.42, no.9, p.202
Egli, Werner *(Swiss architect and*
    engineer)   AV
    Bibl: ▶Schweiz. Ingen. u. Archit.,
    1984-1985
Egli, Willi *(Swiss architect)*   AV
Eglington [Unidentified] *(Unknown*
    painter)   PR
    Bibl: (March 19, 1814, lot A7,
    Christie's)
Eglington, James T. *(British artist,*
    op.1835-1859)   WI
Eglinton, Samuel   WC WI
    (British artist, op.1830-1855)   WC
    (British artist, op.1830-1856)   WI
    Bibl: Paviere, Brit. sporting ptrs
Egloff, Anton *(Swiss sculptor,*
    b.1933)   BA
    Bibl: ▶Intl. dir. exh. artists, 1982;
    ▶Lex. zeitgen. Schweiz. Künstler

Egloff, Frank *(American artist, 20th c.)* **BA**
Bibl: Boston (MA, USA), ICA, Boston now (1982)

Egloffstein, F.W. von **BA**
(American printmaker, ca.1824-1898) **BA**
(American, active NY, U.S. 19th century) **JG**
Bibl: ART IN AMERICA LXIV (Jan-Feb 1976) 56; ▶Dawdy, Artists Amer. West; ▶Groce, Artists Amer.

Eggloffstein, von **JG**
Von Egloffstein, F.W. **BA**

Eglon Hendrik van der Neer→see Neer, Eglon Hendrik van der

Eglon V. der Neer→see Neer, Eglon Hendrik van der

Eglon V.D. Neer→see Neer, Eglon Hendrik van der

Eglon Van der Neer→see Neer, Eglon Hendrik van der

Eglon Vander Neer→see Neer, Eglon Hendrik van der

Eglon Vandermeer→see Neer, Eglon Hendrik van der

Eglon Vanderneer→see Neer, Eglon Hendrik van der

Egmont→see Egmont, Justus van

Egmont, Justus van **BA GC PR**
(Dutch artist, 1601-1674) **WC**
(Dutch painter, 1601-1674) **GC PR**
(Flemish painter, 1601-1674) **BA**
Bibl: ▶Bénézit; Getty Photo Study Coll.; ▶Thieme-Becker; ▶Witt checklist; ▶Wurzbach, NLD Künst.-Lex.

Egmont **PR**

Egmont, Justus van (Justus Verus ab Egmont) **WC**
Justus van Egmont **PR**
Justus Veerus ab Egmont **GC**

Egmont, Justus van (Justus Verus ab Egmont)→see Egmont, Justus van

Egmont, Theodore Juste d'
(Flemish artist, 1627-1672) **WC**

Egnazia Group *(Apulian vase-painters)* **GC**
Bibl: Trendall, Attic red-fig. vases Apulia

Egner, John *(American sculptor, b.1940)* **BA**
Bibl: New York (NY, USA), Guggenheim Mus., Young Amer. artists (1978)

Egner, Marie *(German artist, 1850-1940)* **WC**

Ego, Ernest **GC WC**
(French artist, 19th cent.) **WC**
(French painter, 19th century) **GC**
Bibl: ▶Bénézit

Egon Schiele→see Schiele, Egon

Egon, Nicholas **WC WI**
(British artist, 20th cent.) **WC**
(British artist, op.1953-) **WI**

Egornoff, Alexander Simionovitch *(Russian artist, 1858-1902)* **WC**

Egorov, Vladimir Evgen'evič *(Russian scenographer, b.1878)* **BA**
Bibl: ▶Encyc. world art; ▶Fogg Mus. Libr. cat.

Egorshina, N.A. *(Russian artist, 1926-)* **WC**

Egremont, Maud *(British artist, op. 1905-1915)* **WI**
Thorp, Burford, Mrs.(Maud) **WI**

Egry, József **BA WC**
(Hungarian artist, 1883-1951) **WC**
(Hungarian painter, 1883-1951) **BA**
Bibl: ▶Encyc. world art

Egstein, Franz Gregor Ignaz→see Eckstein, František Řehoř Ignác

Eguchi, Yasu *(Japanese painter, printmaker, b.1938.)* **BA**
Bibl: Guide exh. artists: N. Amer. ptrs.; ▶Intl. dir. exh. artists, 1983

Egusquiza, Rogelio *(Spanish artist, 1845-c.1920)* **WC**

Egville, James Herve d'→see D'Egville, James T. Herve

Egyed, Zoltan *(Architect, Austria?)* **AV**
Bibl: Bauforum, 1984, v.17, no. 105, p.77

Ehbisch, Johan Frederik *(Danish, 1668-1748)* **GC**
Bibl: ▶Thieme-Becker

Ehder, Johann Gottlieb *(German porcelain painter, 1717-1750)* **BA**
Bibl: ▶Thieme-Becker

Ehinger, Emanuel **GC WC**
(German artist, 17th cent.) **WC**
(German, 17th century) **GC**
Bibl: ▶Witt checklist

Ehinger, Gabriel **BA GC**
(German painter and printmaker, 1652-1736) **GC**
(German painter, printmaker, 1652-1736) **BA**
Bibl: ▶RILA/BHA; ▶Thieme-Becker

Ehlers, Carl *(German artist, 1854-)* **WC**

Ehlers, Karl *(German sculptor, printmaker, 1904-1973)* **BA**
Bibl: ▶Bénézit; Munster (DEU), Landesmus. fur Kunst und Kulturges., KARL EHLERS (1975)

Ehlers, Reinhold *(German architect, b.1934)* **BA**
Bibl: KUNSTWERK XXXII/2-3 (Apr-June 1979) 63-64

Ehlers, Reinhold *(1947-)* **AV**

Ehlers, Walter *(German architect, Munich)* **AV**
Bibl: Baumeister, 1986 Jan., v.83, no.1, p.42

Ehm, Josef **BA JG**
(Czech photographer, b.1909) **BA**
(Czech, 1909 -) **JG**
Bibl: HIST OF PHOTOGRAPHY III/3 (July 1979) 267

Ehmcke, Fritz Helmut *(German architect, printmaker, designer, 1878-1965)* **BA**
Bibl: ▶Brockhaus Enzyk.; Neuss (DEU), Clemens-Sels-Mus., F.H. Ehmcke et al. (1984); ▶Vollmer, Künst.-Lex. 20. Jhr.

Ehmsen, Heinrich **BA WC**
(German artist, 1886-1964) **WC**
(German painter, printmaker, 1886-1964) **BA**
Bibl: Berlin, Natl. Gall. cat.; ▶Vollmer, Künst.-Lex. 20. Jhr.

Ehn, Karl *(Austrian architect, act. 1925-1939)* **BA**
Bibl: Czeike, Wien Kunst & Kultur; Österr. Kunsttopographie XLIV

Ehninger, John Whetton **BA GC WI**
(American artist, 1827-1889) **WI**
(American painter, 1827-1889) **BA GC**
Bibl: ▶Fielding's Amer. ptrs.; ▶RILA/BHA; ▶Smith, Idx. Amer. artists; ▶Thieme-Becker

Ehnle, Adrianus Johannes **GC WC**
(Dutch artist, 1819-1863) **WC**
(Dutch painter and printmaker, 1819-1863) **GC**
Bibl: ▶Thieme-Becker

Ehrenberg→see Ehrenberg, Peter Schubert von

Ehrenberg→see Ehrenberg, Wilhelm van

Ehrenberg, Aerdenberg, Eerenberch, Hardenberg or Herdenberg, Wilhelm van (Wilhelm Schubert van Ehrenberg)→see Ehrenberg, Wilhelm van

Ehrenberg, Carl Ferdinand von *(German-born architect and painter, died in Switzerland, 1806-1841)* **AV**
Bibl: ▶Thieme-Becker

Ehrenberg, Felipe *(Mexican artist, publisher, author, 20th c.)* **BA**
Bibl: Gervor, AFTERIMAGE X/9 (Apr 1983) 12,16,17

Ehrenberg, Peter Schubert von *(Flemish painter, b. 1668)* **PR**
Bibl: ▶Thieme-Becker
Ehrenberg **PR**
Peter Schubert von Ehrenberg **PR**

Ehrenberg, Wilhelm Schubert van→see Ehrenberg, Wilhelm van

Ehrenberg, Wilhelm van **BA GC PR**
   (Flemish artist, 1630-c.1676) **WC**
   (Flemish painter, 1630-
     1676) **BA GC PR**
   (Flemish, 1630-ca. 1676) **JG**
   Bibl: ▶Bénézit; Getty Photo Study
     Coll. (Ptgs.); ▶RILA/BHA, 1986;
     ▶Thieme-Becker; ▶Witt checklist;
     ▶Wurzbach, NLD Künst.-Lex.
  Aerdenberg, Wilhelm van **BA**
  Eerenberch, Wilhelm van **BA**
  Ehrenberg **PR**
Ehrenberg, Aerdenberg,
  Eerenberch, Hardenberg or
  Herdenberg, Wilhelm van
  (Wilhelm Schubert van
  Ehrenberg) **WC**
Ehrenberg, Wilhelm Schubert
  van **JG**
  Ehrenberg, Wilhem van **PR**
  Ehrenberg, Willem van **GC**
  Erenberg **PR**
  Hardenberg, Wilhelm van **BA**
  Herdenberg, Wilhelm van **BA**
  marked Erenberg 1653 **PR**
  Schubert von Ehrenberg, Wilhelm
    van **BA**
  Van Erenburgh **PR**
  Wilhelm van Ehrenberg **PR**
Ehrenberg, Wilhem van → see
  Ehrenberg, Wilhelm van
Ehrenberg, Willem van → see
  Ehrenberg, Wilhelm van
Ehrenberger, Ludwig Lutz (German
  artist, op.c.1920) **WC**
Ehrenkrantz, Ezra (American
  architect, 1933-) **AV**
  Bibl: ▶Contemp. archts.
Ehrenstrahl, Anna Maria **BA**
  (Swedish artist, 1666-1729) **WC**
  (Swedish painter, 1666-1729) **BA**
  Bibl: ▶Svenskt konst.-lex.;
    ▶Thieme-Becker
  Klöcker, Anna Maria **BA**
Klocker, Anna Maria
  (Ehrenstrahl) **WC**
Ehrenstrahl, David Klöcker **BA**
  (German artist, 1629-1698) **WC**
  (German painter, 1629-1698) **GC**
  (Swedish painter, art historian,
    1628-1698) **BA**
  Bibl: ▶Encyc. world art; ▶Natl.
    union cat., pre-1956; ▶RILA/BHA;
    ▶Svenska konstnärer;
    ▶Thieme-Becker
  Klocker or Kloker, David
    (Ehrenstrahl) **WC**
  Klöcker, David **BA GC**
  Klöcker, David (Ehrenstrahl) **GC**
  Klöker, David **BA**
Ehrenström, Johan Albert (1762-
  1847) **AV**
Ehrensvaerd, Carl August → see
  Ehrensvärd, Carl August
Ehrensvard, Augustin → see
  Ehrensvärd, Augustin, greve

Ehrensvärd, Augustin, greve **BA**
  (Swedish artist, 1710-1772) **WC**
  (Swedish painter, printmaker,
    soldier, 1710-1772) **BA**
  Bibl: ▶Svenska konstnärer;
    ▶Svenskt konst.-lex.
Ehrensvard, Augustin **WC**
Ehrensvärd, Carl August **AV BA**
  (Swedish architect, aesthetician,
    1745-1800) **AV**
  (Swedish military commander,
    art historian, draftsman,
    1745-1800) **BA**
  Bibl: ▶Brockhaus Enzyk.; ▶Encyc.
    world art; ▶Macmillan encyc.
    archts.
Ehrensvaerd, Carl August **AV**
Ehrentraut, Julius (German artist,
  1841-1923) **WC**
Ehret, Georg Dionys → see Ehret,
  Georg Dionysius
Ehret, Georg Dionysius **BA**
  (German artist, 1710-1770) **WC**
  (German draughtsman, 1710-
    1770) **GC**
  (German painter, 1708-1770) **BA**
  Bibl: Calmann, EHRET, p.14;
    ▶Encyc. world art;
    ▶Thieme-Becker
Ehret, Georg Dionys **GC WC**
Ehrhardt, Adolf (Carl Ludwig
  Adolf) (German artist, 1813-1899) **WC**
Ehrhardt, Alfred (German, 1901-) **JG**
Ehrich, Bruno (German artist, 1861-) **WC**
Ehringer, J.W. (American artist, 19th
  cent.) **WC**
Ehrke, Eduard (German artist, 1837-
  p.1876) **WC**
Ehrler, Marianne (East German
  textile artist, 1939-1984) **BA**
  Bibl: Keisch, C., in BILDENDE
    KUNST 8 (1984) 346 (obit)
Ehrlich, Franz (German, active
  1920s, Bauhaus (also Franz Ehrlich
  & Heinz Loew)) **JG**
Ehrlich, Georg **BA WC WI**
  (Austrian sculptor, painter,
    printmaker, 1897-1966) **BA**
  (British artist, 1897-1966) **WC WI**
  Bibl: ▶Bénézit; ▶MoMA libr. cat.;
    ▶Vollmer, Künst.-Lex. 20. Jhr.
Ehrlich, Hugo (Yugoslav architect,
  1879-1936) **BA**
  Bibl: ▶Vollmer, Künst.-Lex. 20.
    Jhr., v.5
Ehrlich, R.A. (German artist, op.
  1828) **WC**
Ehrlich, Steven D. (American
  architect) **AV**
Ehrmann, François Emile **BA WC**
  (French artist, 1833-1910) **WC**
  (French painter, 1833-1910) **BA**
  Bibl: ▶Bénézit; ▶Thieme-Becker
Ehrmanns, C.B. (Austrian artist, op.
  1830) **WC**

Ehrmanns, Theodor von (German
  artist, 1846-) **WC**
Ehsan-Bryan, Noushin (Architect
  with Robert Bryan, New York, NY) **AV**
  Bibl: Architecture and planning,
    1984 Summer, p.30
Eibisch → see Eibisch, Eugeniusz
Eibisch, Eugene → see Eibisch,
  Eugeniusz
Eibisch, Eugeniusz **PR WC**
  (Polish artist, 1896-) **WC**
  (Polish painter, b. 1896) **PR**
  Bibl: ▶Witt checklist
  Eibisch **PR**
  Eibisch, Eugene **PR**
  Eugeniusz Eibisch **PR**
Eibl, Ludwig (German artist, 1842-
  1918) **WC**
Eibner → see Eibner, Friedrich
Eibner, Friedrich **GC PR WC**
  (German artist, 1825-1877) **WC**
  (German painter, 1825-1877) **GC PR**
  Bibl: ▶Thieme-Becker
  Eibner **PR**
  Friedrich Eibner **PR**
Eich, Johann Friedrich (German
  artist, 1748-1807) **WC**
Eichbaum, M.D. **WC WI**
  (British artist, op.1822) **WC**
  (British artist, op.1822-) **WI**
Eichbaum, Peter William (American
  glassmaker, act.1794-1797) **BA**
  Bibl: JOURNAL OF GLASS STUDIES
    XXI (1979) 102-114
Eichel the Younger, Emanuel
  (German artist, 1717-1782) **WC**
Eichel, Johann → see Santini Aichel,
  Johann
Eichenberg, Fritz (American
  illustrator, printmaker, b.1901) **BA**
  Bibl: ▶Archives Amer. Art Jrnl.,
    XI/1-4 (1971); BERKSHIRE EAGLE
    (2 Dec 1990) p.B6 (obit); ▶WW
    Amer. Art, 1976
Eichholtz, Jacob **BA WI**
  (American artist, 1776-1842) **WC WI**
  (American painter, 1776-1842) **BA**
  Bibl: ▶Fielding's Amer. ptrs.;
    ▶Groce, Artists Amer.
Eicholtz, Jacob **WC**
Eichhorn or Eichorn, Franz Joseph
  (German artist, c.1712-1785) **WC**
Eichhorn, Albert (German artist,
  1811-1851) **WC**
Eichinger, E. **GC WC**
  (German artist, 19th cent.) **WC**
  (German painter, 19th century) **GC**
  Bibl: ▶Witt checklist
Eichinger, Ernest (German artist,
  1929-) **WC**
Eichinger, Gregor-Gregor (Austrian
  architect, 1956-) **AV**
  Bibl: Ottagono, 1988 Mar., p.20
Eichler the Elder, Gottfried
  (German artist, 1677-1759) **WC**

Eichler the Younger, Johann
   Gottfried → see Eichler, Gottfried II
Eichler, Gottfried II   **BA GC**
   (German artist, 1715-1770)   WC
   (German draughtsman, 1715-
   1770)   GC
   (German painter, printmaker,
   1715-1770)   BA
      Bibl: ▶Bénézit; ▶Neue deutsche
      Biog.; ▶Thieme-Becker
   **Eichler the Younger, Johann
   Gottfried**   WC
   Eichler, Johann Gottfried II   GC
Eichler, Johann Conrad (Wollust)
   (German artist, 1688-1748)   WC
Eichler, Johann Gottfried II → see
   Eichler, Gottfried II
Eichler, Joseph (American
   developer, merchant builder)   AV
      Bibl: Arts + architecture, 1984,
      v.3, no.3, p.39
Eichler, Matthias Gottfried
   (German artist, 1748-p.1818)   WC
Eichler, Oldrich (Czech painter,
   b.1941)   BA
      Bibl: Jihlava (CSK), Oblastni Gal.
      Vysociny, OLDRICH EICHLER
      (1981)
Eichler, Reinhold Max (German
   artist, 1872-)   WC
Eichler, Wilhem (German artist, op.
   c.1830)   WC
Eicholtz, Jacob → see Eichholtz, Jacob
Eichstaedt, Rudolf (German artist,
   1857-1924)   WC
Eickelberg, Willem Hendrik   **GC WC**
   (Dutch artist, 1845-1920)   WC
   (Dutch painter, 1845-1920)   GC
      Bibl: ▶Wright, Ptgs. Dutch
      museums
Eickemeyer, Rudolf   **BA**
   (American photographer,
   author, illustrator, 1862-
   1932)   BA
   (American, 1862-1932)   JG
      Bibl: ▶Parry, Photo idx.; ▶WWW
      Amer.; ▶WWW Amer. art
Eickemeyer, Rudolph, Jr.   **JG**
Eickemeyer, Rudolph, Jr. → see
   Eickemeyer, Rudolf
Eickhoff, Gottfred   **BA**
   (Danish artist, 1902-)   WC
   (Danish sculptor, 1902-1982)   BA
      Bibl: Blue guide;
      ▶Nørregård-Nielsen, Dansk kunst
Eickhoff, Gottfried   WC
Eickhoff, Gottfried → see Eickhoff,
   Gottfred
Eickhout → see Eeckhout, Gerbrand
   van den
Eide, Palmer (American sculptor,
   designer, b.1906)   BA
      Bibl: ▶WW Amer. Art, 1976
Eidenbenz, Willi (Swiss, 1909-,
   active Basel, Switzerland 1930s
   (Eidenbenz Atelier))   JG

...eides   GC
      Bibl: ▶Beazley, Attic bl.-fig. vase-
      ptrs.
Eidlitz, Cyrus L. W. → see Eidlitz,
   Cyrus Lazelle Warner
Eidlitz, Cyrus Lazelle Warner   BA
   (American architect, 1853-
   1921)   AV BA
      Bibl: ▶Avery period. idx.; ▶Dict.
      Amer. biog.
Eidlitz, Cyrus L. W.   AV
Eidlitz, Leopold (American architect,
   1823-1908)   AV BA
      Bibl: ▶Dict. Amer. biog.;
      ▶Macmillan encyc. archts.;
      ▶Thieme-Becker; ▶Withey, Amer.
      archts.
Eiebakke, August (Norwegian
   artist, 1867-)   WC
Eiermann, Egon   **AV BA**
   (German architect, 1904-1970)   BA
   (West German architect, 1904-
   1970)   AV
      Bibl: ▶Brockhaus Enzyk.;
      ▶Contemp. archts.
Eiff, William von (German glass
   artist, 1890-1943)   BA
      Bibl: ▶Vollmer, Künst.-Lex. 20.
      Jhr.; WELTKUNST, LIV/10 (15 May
      1985) 1416-1419
Eiffe, Christian Wilhelm (German
   artist, 1826-1893)   WC
Eiffel, Alexandre Gustave (French
   engineer, 1832-1923)   AV BA
      Bibl: ▶Dict. biog. fran.; ▶Encyc.
      Britannica; ▶Encyc. world art;
      ▶Libr. of Congr. Name Auth. File;
      ▶New Columbia encyc.
Eiffel, Gustave   AV
Eiffel, Gustave → see Eiffel, Alexandre
   Gustave
Eiffler, Wolfgang H. (West German
   architect, Munich)   AV
      Bibl: Baumeister, 1987 Oct., v.84,
      no.10. p.46; Deutsche
      Bauzeitung, 1987 Dec., v.121,
      no.12, p.39
Eifler, John A. (American architect,
   Chicago, Ill)   AV
      Bibl: ▶AIA Pro File, 1987-88
Eige, Howard A.   **WC WI**
   (American artist, 20th cent.)   WC
   (American artist, op.20th c.)   WI
Eigenheer, Marianne (Swiss painter,
   b.1945)   BA
      Bibl: Bonn (DEU), Bonner
      Kunstverein, MARIANNE
      EIGENHEER, 1983; ▶Lex. zeitgen.
      Schweiz. Künstler; Munich (DEU),
      Galerie Tanit, MARIANNE
      EIGENHEER, 1983
Eigenmann, Urs Peter (Swiss
   architect, Gockhausen)   AV
      Bibl: ▶Schweiz. Ingen. u. Archit.,
      1984-1985

Eiger, Leonard (American
   photographer, 20th c.)   BA
      Bibl: Springfield (MA, USA), MFA,
      Platinum (1980)
Eight Bears → see Deming, Edwin
   Willard
Eigtved, Niels   BA
   (Danish architect, 1701-1754)   BA
   (Danish artist, 1701-1754)   WC
      Bibl: ▶Encyc. world art;
      ▶Thieme-Becker
Eigtved, Nikolai   AV
Eigtved, Nikolaj   WC
   Eigtwedt, Nikolaj   BA
Eigtved, Nikolai → see Eigtved, Niels
Eigtved, Nikolaj → see Eigtved, Niels
Eigtwedt, Nikolaj → see Eigtved, Niels
Eijk, Maria Johanna Louisa van
   (Dutch printmaker, b.1938)   BA
      Bibl: Paris (FRA), Inst. néerlandais,
      9 femmes constructivistes (1976);
      ▶Scheen, Ned. beeldende kunst.
   Eijk, Ria van   BA
   Eyk, Ria van   BA
Eijk, Ria van → see Eijk, Maria Johanna
   Louisa van
Eikelenberg or Eykelenberg,
   Symon → see Eikelenberg, Symon
Eikelenberg, Symon   GC
   (Dutch artist, 1663-1738)   WC
   (Dutch painter, 1663-1738)   GC
      Bibl: Getty Photo Study Coll.;
      ▶Thieme-Becker; ▶Witt checklist
   **Eikelenberg or Eykelenberg,
   Symon**   WC
Eikerman, Alma (American
   metalworker, jeweler, 20th c.)   BA
      Bibl: ▶Babington Smith, Contemp.
      artists; ▶WW Amer. Art, 1989
Eilat, Avraham (Israeli artist,
   b.1939)   BA
      Bibl: Haifa, Museum of Modern
      Art, AVRAHAM EILAT (1981)
Eilbracht, G. F. (Dutch printmaker,
   d.1854)   GC
      Bibl: ▶Bénézit
Eilshemius → see Eilshemius, Louis
   Michel
Eilshemius, Louis → see Eilshemius,
   Louis Michel
Eilshemius, Louis M. → see Eilshemius,
   Louis Michel
Eilshemius, Louis Michael → see
   Eilshemius, Louis Michel

Eilshemius, Louis Michel   BA PR WC WI
 (American artist, 1864-1941)   WC WI
 (American painter, 1864-1941)   PR
 (American painter, illustrator,
  1864-1941)   BA
  Bibl: ▶Bénézit; ▶RILA/BHA;
  ▶Vollmer, Künst.-Lex. 20. Jhr.;
  ▶WWW Amer.
 Eilshemius   PR
 Eilshemius, Louis   PR
 Eilshemius, Louis M.   PR
 Eilshemius, Louis Michael   PR
 Eilshemius, Louis N.   PR
 Eilshemius, Louis-Michel   PR
 Elshemius, Louis   WC
 Elshemius, Louis Michel   BA
 Louis Michel Eilshemius   PR
Eilshemius, Louis N. → see Eilshemius,
 Louis Michel
Eilshemius, Louis-Michel → see
 Eilshemius, Louis Michel
Eimart or Eimmart the Younger,
 Georg Christoph → see Eimmart,
 Georg Christoph II

Eimmart, Georg Christoph II   BA
 (German artist, 1638-1705)   WC
 (German painter, printmaker,
  1638-1705)   BA
  Bibl: ▶Bénézit; ▶Thieme-Becker

**Eimart or Eimmart the Younger,
Georg Christoph**   WC
Einbeck, Georg (German painter,
 photographer, 1870-1951)   BA
  Bibl: ▶Gernsheim, Hist. photog.;
  Image, XXVII/2 (Jun. 1984) pp.
  1-24; ▶Rosenblum, World hist.
  photog.; ▶Vollmer, Künst.-Lex. 20.
  Jhr.

Einberger, Andreas (Austrian
 painter, sculptor, 1878-1952)   BA
  Bibl: ▶Bénézit; ▶Vollmer,
  Künst.-Lex. 20. Jhr.

Einhorn, Helmut (New Zealand city
 planner, b. in Berlin, 1911-1988)   AV
  Bibl: Planning quarterly, 1988
  Sept., no.91, p.30

Einhorn, Steven L. (American
 architect)   AV
  Bibl: ▶AIA Pro File, 1983
Einsle → see Einsle, Anton

Einsle, Anton   BA PR WC
 (Austrian painter, 1801-1871)   BA PR
 (German artist, 1801-1871)   WC
  Bibl: ▶Busse, Maler u. Bildhauer
  19. Jahr.; ▶Österr. biog. Lex.
  1815-1950; ▶Thieme-Becker
 Anton Einsle   PR
 Einsle   PR

Einslie, S. (British artist, op.1785-
 1808)   WC WI

Einste, Joseph Bernhard (German
 painter, 1774-1829)   BA
  Bibl: ▶Bénézit; ▶Busse, Maler u.
  Bildhauer 19. Jahr.;
  ▶Thieme-Becker; WELTKUNST,
  LIV/20 (15 Oct 1984) 2900-2904

Einstein, William   WC WI
 (American artist, 1907-1972)   WI
 (American artist, 20th cent.)   WC

Einzig, Richard   AV BA
 (British architect, 1932-1980)   AV
 (British photographer, 1932-
  1980)   BA
  Bibl: ARCH REVIEW CLXVIII/9003
  (Sept 1980) 134, obit; RIBA
  Journal LXXXVII (10 Oct 1980) 12

Eirene (Greek painter, unknown)   GC
  Bibl: ▶Robertson, Greek art, p.712

Eiriz, Antonia (Cuban painter,
 b.1929)   BA
  Bibl: LaDuke, Woman's art jrnl.,
  V/2 (Fal.-Win. 1984-85) p.34

Eisch, Erwin (German glassmaker,
 b.1927)   BA
  Bibl: Cologne (DEU),
  Kunstgewerbemuseum, Glas von
  Jugendstil bis Heute (1981);
  ▶Encyc. glass; Frankfurt,
  MODERNEGLAS (1976)

Eischen, Ann (American interior
 designer, Houston, Tex)   AV
  Bibl: Southern accents, 1988 July-
  Aug., v.11, no.4, p.76

Eisel, Friedrich (German painter,
 b.1929)   BA
  Bibl: ▶Vollmer, Künst.-Lex. 20. Jhr.
 Eisel, Fritz   BA
Eisel, Fritz → see Eisel, Friedrich

Eisele, Johann (West German
 architect, Darmstadt)   AV
  Bibl: Bauwelt, 1989 May 19, v.80,
  no.20, p.932
Eisemann, Johann Anton → see
 Eismann, Johann Anton
Eisen → see Eisen, Charles Joseph
 Dominique

**Eisen, Charles Joseph
Dominique**   BA GC PR WC
 (French artist, 1720-1778)   WC
 (French painter, 1720-1778)   PR
 (French painter, printmaker,
  1720-1778)   BA
 (French, 1720-1778)   GC
  Bibl: ▶Bénézit; ▶Dict. biog. fran.;
  ▶RILA/BHA; ▶Thieme-Becker;
  ▶Witt checklist
 Charles Joseph Dominique Eisen   PR
 Eisen   PR

Eisen, François   BA GC PR WC
 (Flemish painter, ca.1695-aft.
  1778)   PR
 (Flemish painter, printmaker, ca.
  1695-after 1778)   BA
 (French artist, 1695-1778)   WC
 (French, 1695-1778)   GC
  Bibl: ▶Bénézit; ▶RILA/BHA;
  ▶Thieme-Becker; ▶Witt checklist;
  ▶Wurzbach, NLD Künst.-Lex.
 F. Eisen   PR
 Francois Eisen   PR

Eisenberg, baron d'   BA WC
 (French draftsman, author, 18th
  c.)   BA
 (German artist, 18th cent.)   WC
  Bibl: ▶Bénézit; ▶Thieme-Becker

Eisenberg, Marc (American sculptor,
 printmaker, b.1948)   BA
  Bibl: ▶NY art yrbk.

Eisenberg, Richard (American
 designer)   AV
  Bibl: Architectural lighting, 1988
  Mar., v.2, no.3, p.18

Eisenberger, Nikolaus Friedrich
 (German artist, 1707-1771)   WC

Eisendieck, Suzanne   BA GC WC
 (German painter, b.1908)   BA GC
 (Polish artist, 1908-)   WC
  Bibl: ▶Bénézit; ▶Vollmer,
  Künst.-Lex. 20. Jhr.

Eisendle, Helmut (Austrian
 architect, Linz)   AV
  Bibl: ▶Verzeich. Öst. Ziviltech.,
  1984

Eisenhauer, Collins (Canadian
 sculptor, b.1900)   BA
  Bibl: ARTSCANADA XXXVI (3 Oct-
  Nov 1979) 20

Eisenhower, Anne (American
 interior designer)   AV
  Bibl: Architectural digest, 1984
  Nov., v.41, no.11
Eisenhower, Dwight D. → see
 Eisenhower, Dwight David

Eisenhower, Dwight David   WI
 (American artist, 1890-1969)   WC WI
 Eisenhower, Dwight D.   WC

Eisenhut, Ferenc (Hungarian artist,
 1857-1903)   WC

Eisenköck, Hermann (Austrian
 architect, Salzburg, 1954-)   AV
  Bibl: Transparent, 1987, v.18,
  no.6/7, p.4

Eisenloeffel, Jan (Dutch silversmith,
 designer, 1876-1957)   BA
  Bibl: Bruckmann's Silber-Lex.;
  ▶Grote Winkler Prins; ▶Scheen,
  Ned. beeldende kunst.;
  ▶Thieme-Becker; ▶Winkler Prins
  van de kunst

Eisenlohr, Friedrich (German
 architect, 1805-1855)   BA
  Bibl: ▶Neue deutsche Biog.;
  ▶Thieme-Becker

Eisenman, Michael (American
 painter, 20th c.)   BA
  Bibl: Arts Mag. XLVII (Dec 1972)
  93
Eisenman, Peter → see Eisenman,
 Peter D.

Eisenman, Peter D.   BA
 (American architect and author,
  New York City, 1932-)   AV
 (American architect, b.1932)   BA
  Bibl: ▶AIA Pro File; ▶Contemp.
  archts.; ▶Libr. of Congr. Name
  Auth. File
 Eisenman, Peter   AV

Eisenmann, Georg *(German artist,*
18th cent.)   **WC**

Eisenmann, Germaine *(French*
artist, 1894-)   **WC**

Eisenmann, Michael *(Israeli painter,*
printmaker, b.1943)   **BA**
    Bibl: Cape Town (ZAF), S. African
    Natl. Gallery, Israeli art (1980)

Eisenmenger, August   **BA WC**
    (Austrian painter, 1830-1907)   BA
    (German artist, 1830-1907)   WC
    Bibl: ▶Bénézit; ▶Thieme-Becker

Eisenreich, Claudia *(E. German*
architect)   **AV**
    Bibl: Architektur der DDR, 1986
    Dec., v.35, no.12, p.751

Eisenschitz, Willy *(German artist,*
1889-)   **WC**

Eisenstadt, Eve *(American artist,*
20th c.)   **BA**
    Bibl: ▶Intl. dir. exh. artists, 1982

Eisenstaedt, Alfred *(American*
photographer, b.1898)   **BA**
    Bibl: ▶Auer, Encyc. photographes;
    ▶Contemp. photogs.; ▶Intl. dir.
    exh. artists, 1982; ▶Newhall,
    Photog.; ▶Parry, Photo idx.

Eisenstat, Ben   **WC WI**
    (American artist, 20th cent.)   WC
    (American artist, b.1915)   WI

Eisenstein, Bernice *(Canadian*
textile artist, b.1949)   **BA**
    Bibl: Stratford (Ont, CAN), Gallery
    Stratford, Natalie Novotny-Green
    (1981)

Eisentraut, Wolf R. *(East German*
architect, Berlin)   **AV**
    Bibl: Architektur der DDR, 1987
    Oct., v.36, no.10, p.22

Eisermann, Richard *(German artist,*
op.1878-1884)   **WC**

Eisl, Therese *(German artist, 20th*
cent.)   **WC**

Eisler, Georg   **BA WC**
    (Austrian painter, printmaker,
    b.1928)   BA
    (German artist, 1928-)   WC
    Bibl: ▶Bénézit; ▶Vollmer,
    Künst.-Lex. 20. Jhr.

Eisler, Johnny *(Architect,*
Czechoslovakia, 1946-)   **AV**
    Bibl: Architektur,
    Innenarchitektur, Technischer
    Ausbau, 1985 Jan.-Feb., v.93,
    no.1, p.10

Eisler, Otto   **AV**

Eisman-Semenowsky, Emile   **WC**
    (French artist, 19th cent.)   WC
    (Polish artist, op.c.1878)   WC
    Semenowsky, Eisman   **WC**
Eismann→see Eismann, Carlo
    (Brisighella)
Eismann→see Eismann, Johann Anton
Eismann or Leismann, Johann
Anton→see Eismann, Johann
    Anton

Eismann, Carlo (Brisighella)   **GC PR WC**
    (German painter, ca.1629-aft.
    1718)   PR
    (Italian antiquarian, late 17th
    cent)   AV
    (Italian artist, 1629(?)-p.1718)   WC
    (Italian, b. ca.1629-aft.1718)   GC
    Bibl: Getty Photo Study Coll.
    (Ptgs.); Notizie da Palazzo Albani,
    1987, v.16, no.1, p.102;
    ▶Thieme-Becker; ▶Witt checklist

Brisighella, Carlo   **AV**
    Brisighella, Carlo (Eismann)   GC
    Carlo Eismann (Brisighella)   PR
    Eismann   PR

Eismann, Johann Anton   **BA GC PR**
    (Austrian painter, 1604-1698)   GC
    (Austrian painter,
    1613/22-ca.1700)   BA
    (German artist, 1604-1698)   WC
    (German artist, op.1670)   WC
    (German painter, 1604-1698)   PR
    (German painter, act.1670)   GC
    Bibl: ▶Bénézit; Getty Photo Study
    Coll. (Ptgs.); ▶RILA/BHA; SAGGI E
    MEMORIE DI STORIA DELL'ARTE X
    (1976) 63-78; ▶Thieme-Becker;
    ▶Witt checklist

    Eisemann, Johann Anton   BA
    Eismann   PR

Eismann or Leismann, Johann
Anton   **WC**
    Giovanni Ant. Leisman   PR
    Giovanni Ismen   PR
    I. Vecchio   PR
    I. Veccio   PR
    Is. Vecchio   PR
    Isman Vacchio   PR
    Isman Vecchia   PR
    Isman Vecchio   PR
    Isman Veccio   PR

Isman, Johann   **GC WC**
    J. Veccio   PR
    Johann Anton Eismann   PR
    Js. Vecchio   PR
    Leismann, Johann Anton   BA GC
    Vecchio   PR

Eisner or Eissner, Joseph, II
    (German artist, 1788-1861)   **WC**

Eisner, Carole *(American painter,*
20th c.)   **BA**
    Bibl: Mass, J., in ARTS MAG LIX/2
    (Oct 1984) 12

Eisner, Dorothy *(American painter,*
collagist, b.1906)   **BA**
    Bibl: ▶WW Amer. Art

Eisner, Franz *(Austrian painter, 19th*
century)   **GC**
    Bibl: ▶Bénézit
Eisner, Jacob→see Elsner, Jakob
Eisselburg, Peter→see Isselburg,
    Peter

Eissler, Heinrich *(German architect)*   **AV**
    Bibl: Bauwelt, 1986 May 23, v.77,
    no.19-20, p.686

Eitel, Albert *(German architect,*
Stuttgart, 1866-1934)   **AV**

Eivind, Saxhaug *(Norwegian*
landscape architect, 1953-)   **AV**
    Bibl: Byggekunst 1988, v.70,
    no.5, p.364

Eizatt, Alexander *(Scottish*
woodcarver, act.1682-1706)   **BA**
    Bibl: COUNTRY LIFE CLXII/4180
    (11 Aug 1977) 372

Eizenberg, Julie *(American*
architect)   **AV**
    Bibl: GA houses, 1988 Oct.,
    no.24, p.146

Ejnar Hansen→see Hansen, Ejnar

Ejsmond, Franz *(Polish artist, 1859-)*   **WC**

Ejups, Gunars *(American architect)*   **AV**

Ek, Sandor *(Hungarian artist, 1902-)*   **WC**

Ekberg, Martin Axel *(Danish*
architect, 1882-1935)   **BA**

Ekeland, Arne *(Norwegian artist,*
20th cent.)   **WC**
Ekels→see Ekels, Jan (the elder)
Ekels→see Ekels, Jan (the younger)

Ekels, Jan (the elder)   **GC PR**
    (Dutch artist, 1724-1781)   WC
    (Dutch painter, 1724-1781)   GC PR
    Bibl: Getty Photo Study Coll.;
    Getty Photo Study Coll. (Ptgs.);
    ▶Thieme-Becker; ▶Witt checklist
    Ekels   PR

Ekels, Jan I   **GC**

Ekels, Jan, I   **WC**
    J. Eckels   PR
    Jan Ekels (the elder)   PR
    Van Ekels   PR

Ekels, Jan (the younger)   **GC PR**
    (Dutch artist, 1759-1793)   WC
    (Dutch painter and
    draughtsman, 1759-1793)   GC
    (Dutch painter, 1759-1793)   PR
    Bibl: ▶Thieme-Becker
    Eakles   PR
    Eckles   PR
    Ekels   PR

Ekels, Jan, II   **WC**
    Jan Ekels (the younger)   PR
Ekels, Jan I→see Ekels, Jan (the elder)
Ekels, Jan, I→see Ekels, Jan (the
    elder)
Ekels, Jan, II→see Ekels, Jan (the
    younger)

Ekhard, Godwin *(German artist,*
19th cent.)   **WC**

Ekhart, Heinz *(Austrian architect)*   **AV**
    Bibl: Architettura; cronache e
    storia, 1987 Oct.,v.33, no.10,
    p.726
Ekielski, Ladislaus→see Ekielski,
    Władysław

Ekielski, Władysław *(Polish*
architect, 1855-1927)   **BA**
    Bibl: ▶Słownik artystów polskich;
    ▶Thieme-Becker; ▶Wielka ilustr.
    encyk.
    Ekielski, Ladislaus   BA

Ekks, Redd (American ceramist, b.1937)   **BA**
    Bibl: Fullerton (CA, USA), CSU Art Gallery, Richard Shaw, Ed Blackburn (1976)

Ekludh, Claes (Swedish painter, b.1944)   **BA**
    Bibl: ▶Intl. dir. exh. artists, 1982; Mats, Flash art, 110 (Jan. 1983) pp.52-55

Eklund, Jarl (Finnish architect)   **AV**
    Bibl: Arkkitehti, 1985, no.2, p.63

Ekman, Kenneth (American architect)   **AV**

Ekman, Robert Wilhelm   **BA WC**
    (Finnish painter, 1808-1873)   BA
    (Scandinavian artist, 1808-1873)   WC
    Bibl: ▶Bénézit; ▶Busse, Maler u. Bildhauer 19. Jahr.; ▶Thieme-Becker

Ekphantos of Corinth (Greek painter, 7th c BC (3rd qtr))   **GC**
    Bibl: Getty Photo Study Coll.; ▶Robertson, Greek art, p.592

Ekster, Alexandra→see Exter, Alexandra

Ekstrom, Per (Swedish artist, 1844-1935)   **WC**

Ekvall, Hans (Swedish artist, 1918-)   **WC**

Ekvall, Knut (Scandinavian artist, 1843-1912)   **WC**

El Barbudo→see Vermeyen, Jan Cornelis

el cavallero Maxssimo→see Stanzione, Massimo

el divino Morales→see Morales, Luis de (el Divino)

el Dominico→see Greco, El (Domenico Theotocopuli)

el espanoletto→see Ribera, Jusepe de (lo Spagnoletto)

El Farouk, Omar (Egyptian architect and interior designer)   **AV**
    Bibl: Arts & the Islamic world, 1984 Summer, v.2, no.2, p.43
    Farouk, Omar el   AV

El Fattah, Ahmed Abd→see Abd El Fattah, Ahmed

el flamenco→see Fiammingo

El Greco→see Greco, El (Domenico Theotocopuli)

el griego→see Greco, El (Domenico Theotocopuli)

el Kafrawi, Kamal→see Kafrawi, Kamal el

El Lissitzky→see Lisickij, El'

El Mayo→see Vermeyen, Jan Cornelis

el mayorquin→see Mayorquin, el [Unidentified]

El Miniawy, A. (Algerian architect)   **AV**
    Bibl: Technique et architecture, 1982 Dec.-1983 Jan., no.34, p.88

El Miniawy, H. (Algerian architect)   **AV**
    Bibl: Technique et architecture, 1982 Dec.-1983 Jan., no.34, p.88

el mudo→see Fernández de Navarrete, Juan (el Mudo)

El Mulato→see Gómez, Sebastián (l)

el olandes→see Olandese [Unidentified]

el pequeño Ticiano→see Liaño, Teodoro Felipe de

el Racionero Cano→see Cano, Alonso

el Teatiño→see Seghers, Daniel

el Teattino→see Seghers, Daniel

el Tusino→see Tusino, el [Unidentified]

El'konin, Viktor Borisovič (Soviet artist, b.1910)   **BA**
    Bibl: Sokolov, Leonardo, XV/1 (Win. 1982) p.59

El-Wakil, Abdel Wahed→see El-Wakil, Abdelwahed

El-Wakil, Abdelwahed   **BA**
    (architect, b.1943)   BA
    (Egyptian architect, 1943-)   AV
    Bibl: Abel, Arch. Rev. CLXXX/1077 (Nov 1986), 52-60; Arts & the Islamic world, 1983/84 Winter, v.1, no.4, p.58; ▶Avery period. idx., 7th suppl.
    Al-Wakeel, Abdel Wahed   AV

El-Wakil, Abdel Wahed   **AV**
    Wakil, Abdel Wahed el   AV

El. Griego→see Greco, El (Domenico Theotocopuli)

Elam, Merrill (American architect, Atlanta, Ga)   **AV**
    Bibl: Assemblage, 1988 Oct., no.7, p.56

Eland, John Shenton (British artist, 1872-1933)   **WC WI**

Elander, Kristina (Swedish painter, b.1953)   **BA**
    Bibl: ▶Intl. dir. exh. artists, 1983, v.1; Mats, Flash art, 110 (Jan. 1983) pp.52-55

Elands, Cornelis→see Elandts, Cornelis

Elandt, Cornelis→see Elandts, Cornelis

Elandt, Elands or Elandts, Cornelis→see Elandts, Cornelis

Elandts, Cornelis   **GC**
    (Dutch artist, op.1663-1670)   WC
    (Dutch printmaker, act.1660-1666)   GC
    Bibl: ▶Bénézit; ▶Thieme-Becker
    Elands, Cornelis   GC
    Elandt, Cornelis   GC

Elandt, Elands or Elandts, Cornelis   **WC**

Elbertz, Joseph (German goldsmith, 1683-1774)   **BA**
    Bibl: Clasen, Wallraf-Richartz-Jahrb. XLIII (1982) 112; Scheffler, Goldschmiede Rheinland-Westfalens, v.2, p.862

Elbfas, Jacob Heinrich   **BA**
    (Swedish artist, op.1627-m. 1664)   WC
    (Swedish painter, ca.1600-1664)   BA
    Bibl: ▶Svenskt konst.-lex.; ▶Thieme-Becker; ▶Witt checklist

Elbfas, Jacob Hendrik   **WC**
Elbfas, Jacob Hendrik→see Elbfas, Jacob Heinrich

Elbo, Jose (Spanish artist, 1804-1844)   **WC**

Elborch, Jan van→see Elburcht, Jan van der

Elbows Out   **JG**

Elbows Out (The Painter of Louvre E 705) (vase-painter, ca. 550-530 BC)   **GC**
    Bibl: ▶Beazley, Attic bl.-fig. vase-ptrs.; Boardman, Attic Bl.-fig. Vases

Elbridge Ayer Burbank→see Burbank, E. A. (Elbridge Ayer)

Elbridge Wesley Webber→see Webber, Elbridge Wesley

Elburcht, Elborch, Elburg, Elsborch etc., Hans or Jan van der (Cleen Hansken)→see Elburcht, Jan van der

Elburcht, Jan van der   **BA GC**
    (early Netherlandish painter, act.1536-1553)   BA
    (Netherlandish painter, act. 1536-1553)   GC
    (Netherlands artist, op.1536-1553)   WC
    Bibl: ▶Bénézit; ▶Biog. Nat. Belgique; ▶Friedländer, Early Neth. ptg.; ▶RILA/BHA; ▶Thieme-Becker; ▶Wurzbach, NLD Künst.-Lex.
    Elborch, Jan van   BA

Elburcht, Elborch, Elburg, Elsborch etc., Hans or Jan van der (Cleen Hansken)   **WC**
    Elburg, Jan van   BA
    Elburg, Hans van der   GC
    Elsborch, Jan van   BA

Elburg, Jan G. (Dutch poet, printmaker, b.1919)   **BA**
    Bibl: ▶Grote Winkler Prins; JAN G. ELBURG: VROEGER KOMT LATER (1986)
    Elburg, Johannes Gommert   BA

Elburg, Jan van→see Elburcht, Jan van der

Elburg, Johannes Gommert→see Elburg, Jan G.

Elburgh, Hans van der→see Elburcht, Jan van der

Elcho, David Charteris (British, 1721-1787)   **BA**
    Bibl: BURLINGTON CXXII (Aug 1980) 564-567
    Charteris, David   BA

Eldem, Sedad Hakk *(Turkish
    architect, Istanbul, 1908-1988)*   **AV**
    Bibl: d. date from Mimar:
    architecture in development,
    1988 Dec., no.30, p.9; "Sedad
    Eldem, architect in Turkey,"
    Singapore: Mimar, 1988
Elder *(American, active Forest City,
    IA 1890s)*   **JG**
the elder Breughel → *see* Brueghel,
    Jan, the elder
the elder Brueghel → *see* Brueghel,
    Jan, the elder
*Elder Master of the Holy
    Kinship* → *see* Master of the Holy
    Kinship the elder
Elder Palma → *see* Palma, Jacopo il
    Vecchio
Elder Roberts → *see* Roberts, Thomas
Elder Teniers → *see* Teniers, David II
the elder Weenix → *see* Weenix, Jan
    Baptist
Elder, Andrew Taylor *(British artist,
    1908-1966)*   **WC WI**
Elder, John → *see* Elder, John Adams
Elder, John Adams   **WI**
    (American artist, 1833-1895)   WC WI
Elder, John   **WC**
Elderfield, John   **BA WC WI**
    *(British art historian, museum
    administrator, painter in USA,
    b.1943)*   BA
    (British artist, 1943-)   WC
    (British artist, b.1943)   WI
    Bibl: STUDIO INTERNATIONAL
    188/968 (July-Aug 1974),
    frontmatter; ▶WW Amer. Art,
    1984
Eldershaw, John Roy *(Australian
    painter, b.1896)*   **BA**
    Bibl: ▶Encyc. Australian art;
    ▶Johnson, Brit. artists; ▶Vollmer,
    Künst.-Lex. 20. Jhr.; ▶WW Art,
    1934
Eldin, Essam Safey → *see* Safey eldin,
    Essam
Eldred, Charles   **BA WC WI**
    (American artist, 1938-)   WC
    (American artist, b.1938)   WI
    (American sculptor, b.1938)   BA
    Bibl: Binghamton (NY, USA),
    Roberson Center, ELDRED...
    (1980)
Eldred, Dale   **AV BA**
    (American artist)   AV
    *(American sculptor, printmaker,
    b.1933.)*   BA
    Bibl: Coe, DALE ELDRED
    SCULPTURE... (1978); ▶Intl. dir.
    exh. artists, 1983; ▶MoMA libr.
    cat.; Utah architect, 1985 Fall,
    p.[10]
Eldredge, Stuart *(American painter,
    b.1902)*   **BA**
    Bibl: ▶WW Amer. Art
Eldridge, Charles Henry *(British
    artist, b.1869)*   **WI**

Eldridge, Martin   **WC WI**
    (British artist, 20th cent.)   WC
    (British artist, op.20th c.)   WI
Eldridge, Mildred E.   **BA WC WI**
    (British artist, 1909-)   WC
    (British artist, 1909-op.1970)   WI
    (British painter, b.1909)   BA
    Bibl: Guide exh. artists: N. Amer.
    ptrs.; ▶Intl. dir. exh. artists, 1982-
    1983; ▶Johnson, Brit. artists;
    ▶Waters, Brit. artists
Eleinko, Gary *(American artist, 20th
    c.)*   **BA**
    Bibl: Nawrocki, D.A., in NEW ART
    EXAMINER XI/9 (June 1984) 8
Elekfy, Jenő (Kirchner) *(Hungarian
    painter, printmaker, 1895-1968)*   **BA**
    Bibl: ▶Bénézit; Budapest (HUN),
    Mag. Menzeti Galeria, Elekfy Jeno
    (1978); ▶Vollmer, Künst.-Lex. 20.
    Jhr.
Elembrech, Theodoor → *see*
    Helmbreker, Dirk
Elen, Philip West *(British artist, op.
    1838-1872)*   **WC WI**
Elenus *(Spanish scribe, act. late
    11th, early 12th c.)*   **GC**
    Bibl: Janini, Catálogo manuscritos,
    pp.97-98, n.73
Eleőd, Akos *(Hungarian architect)*   **AV**
    Bibl: Magyar építőművészet,
    1988, v.79, no.2, p.36
Elers family *(Dutch ceramists in
    England, 17th-18th c.)*   **BA**
    Bibl: ▶Boger, World pott. & porc.;
    ▶Mankowitz, Encyc. pott. & porc.
Elers, David *(Dutch potter,
    silversmith, chemist in England,
    1656-1742)*   **BA**
    Bibl: ▶Mankowitz, Encyc. pott. &
    porc.; ▶Penguin dec. arts
Elers, John Philip *(Dutch potter,
    silversmith, chemist in England,
    1664-1738)*   **BA**
    Bibl: ▶Mankowitz, Encyc. pott. &
    porc.; ▶Penguin dec. arts
Eleszkievicz, Stanislaw *(Polish
    artist, 1900-1963)*   **WC**
Eleusinian Painter   **GC**
    Bibl: ▶Beazley, Attic red-fig. vase-
    ptrs.
Eleusis Painter *(vase-painter, ca.
    500-475 BC)*   **GC**
    Bibl: ▶Beazley, Attic red-fig. vase-
    ptrs.; Richter, Attic red-fig. vases
Eleutheriade, Micaela *(Romanian
    painter, b.1900)*   **BA**
    Bibl: ▶Bénézit; ▶Vollmer,
    Künst.-Lex. 20. Jhr.
Eley, Peter David *(British architect)*   **AV**
Elfeldar (Elfeldes, Alfeldes) Hanus
    (Czech artist, op.c.1511-1517)   **WC**
Elfers, Bernd *(West German interior
    designer, Bremen)*   **AV**
    Bibl: Architektur,
    Innenarchitektur, Technischer
    Ausbau, 1987 Sept., v.95, no.9,
    p.64

Elfert, Uwe *(West German painter,
    b.1944)*   **BA**
    Bibl: Berlin (DEU), Galerie
    Wewerka, 1979; exh.cat.
    Neuenkirchen, U.E., 1983
Elfever, Monsù [Unidentified]
    (French painter)   **PR**
    Bibl: Pamphilj inventory, Rome,
    1648
    Monsù Elfever francese   PR
Elfinger, Ant (Cajetan) *(German
    artist, 19th cent.)*   **WC**
Elford → *see* Elford, William, Bt.
Elford, Sir William → *see* Elford,
    William, Bt.
Elford, Victor *(British artist, op.
    1972-)*   **WI**
Elford, William → *see* Elford, William,
    Bt.
Elford, William, Bt.   **WI**
    (British artist, 1747-1837)   WC WI
    (British painter, 1747-1837)   PR
    Bibl: ▶Thieme-Becker
    Elford   PR
Elford, Sir William   **WC**
Elford, William   **PR**
    Elford, William, Sir   PR
    William Elford   PR
Elford, William, Sir → *see* Elford,
    William, Bt.
Elfrink, Theo *(Dutch painter,
    printmaker, b.1923)*   **BA**
    Bibl: Guide exh. artists: N. Amer.
    ptrs.; ▶Intl. dir. exh. artists, 1982;
    ▶Scheen, Ned. beeldende kunst.
Elgaard, Søren *(Danish painter,
    b.1951)*   **BA**
    Bibl: Hrymfaxe: Folkeligt
    kunsttidsskrift, XVI/3 (Sep. 1986)
    pp.1-47; ▶Nørregård-Nielsen,
    Dansk kunst
Elgart, Ruth C. *(American sculptor,
    20th c.)*   **BA**
    Bibl: Philadelphia (PA, USA),
    Temple University, Samuel Paley
    Library, The Tyler show (1974)
Elgood, George S. → *see* Elgood,
    George Samuel
Elgood, George Samuel   **WI**
    (British artist, 1851-1943)   WC WI
Elgood, George S.   **WC**
Elhafen, Ignaz *(German ivory carver,
    1685-1725)*   **BA**
    Bibl: Mezentseva, SOOBSCENJA,
    HERMITAGE XLII/42 (1977) 7-12;
    ▶Thieme-Becker
    Elhofer, Ignaz   BA
    Eulhofer, Ignaz   BA
    Helhafen, Ignaz   BA
    Oelhafen, Ignaz   BA
Elhanani, Aba *(Israeli architect)*   **AV**
    Bibl: Architettura; cronache e
    storia, 1981 Oct., v.27, no.
    10(312), p.[560]
Elhofer, Ignaz → *see* Elhafen, Ignaz

Eli, C.   **WC**
 (British artist, 19th cent.)   WC
 (German artist, 1800-1881)   WC
Eli, Christel (Johann Heinrich Christian)   **WC**
Eli, Christel (Johann Heinrich Christian)→see Eli, C.
Elia da Cortona *(Italian architect, ecclesiastic, d.1253)*   **BA**
 Bibl: ▶Portoghesi, Diz. arch. e urbanistica; ▶Thieme-Becker
Elia, Antonio Sant'→see Sant'Elia, Antonio
Eliadi, Emilios *(W. German interior designer, Munich)*   **AV**
 Bibl: Architektur, Innenarchitektur, Technischer Ausbau, 1986 Nov., v.94, no.11, p.34
Eliaerts, Jan Frans   **GC WC**
 (Belgian artist, 1761-1848)   WC
 (Belgian, 1761-1848)   GC
 Bibl: ▶Thieme-Becker; ▶Witt checklist
Eliakin, Daliah *(Brazilian architect)*   **AV**
 Bibl: Projeto, 1986 Mar., no.85, p.61
Elian, George P. *(American architect)*   **AV**
Elias *(Romanian monk, woodcarver, act.1730)*   **BA**
 Bibl: Burian, Tkadlcik, UMENI XXIII/3 (1975) 203-218
Elias Childe→see Childe, Elias
Elias Martin→see Martin, Elias
Elias or Elyas, Isaac→see Elias, Isaac
Elias van de Velde→see Velde, Esaias I van de
Elias van den Broeck→see Broeck, Elias van den
Elias van den Broek→see Broeck, Elias van den
Elias van Nijmegen→see Nijmegen, Elias van
Elias Vonck→see Vonck, Elias
Elias Vonk→see Vonck, Elias
Elias, Alfred *(British artist, op.1881-1911)*   **WI**
Elias, Annette   **WC WI**
 (British artist, op.1881-, d.1921)   WI
 (British artist, op.1881-m.1921)   WC
Elias, Brad *(Designer, New York, NY)*   **AV**
 Bibl: Interior design, 1985 Nov., v.56, no.11, p.185
Elias, Elie, Elyas or Elye, Matthieu→see Elias, Mathieu
Elias, Etienne *(Belgian painter, b.1936)*   **BA**
 Bibl: ▶Bénézit; ▶Dict. biog. artistes belges

Elias, Isaac   **BA GC PR**
 (Dutch artist, op.1620)   WC
 (Dutch painter, act. 1620)   PR
 (Dutch painter, act. ca.1620)   GC
 (Dutch painter, act.1620)   BA
 Bibl: Getty Photo Study Coll.; Rijksmuseum; ▶Thieme-Becker; ▶Witt checklist; ▶Wurzbach, NLD Künst.-Lex.
Elias or Elyas, Isaac   **WC**
 Elyas, Isack   GC PR
 Isaac Elias   PR
Elias, Ken *(British artist, b.1944)*   **BA**
 Bibl: Arts Council GBR, Welsh Comm., Ken Elias, Frances Woodley (1978)
Elias, Mathieu   **GC**
 (Flemish artist, 1658-1741)   WC
 (French painter, 1658-1741)   GC
 Bibl: ▶Bénézit
Elias, Elie, Elyas or Elye, Matthieu   **WC**
Elias, Nicolaes→see Pickenoy, Nicolaes Eliasz.
Elias, Sheila *(American painter, 20th c.)*   **BA**
 Bibl: Mission Viejo (CA, USA), Saddleback Art Gallery, Sheila Elias et al. (1981)
Elias, T.H. *(Dutch(?) artist, 18th cent.(?))*   **WC**
Eliasberg, Paul   **BA WC**
 (German artist, 1907-)   WC
 (German painter, printmaker, b.1907)   BA
 Bibl: ▶Vollmer, Künst.-Lex. 20. Jhr.; ▶Wer ist wer
Eliassen, Trond *(Norwegian architect, 20th century)*   **AV**
 Bibl: Byggekunst, 1986, v.68, no.7, p.385
Eliasz. Nicholas→see Pickenoy, Nicolaes Eliasz.
Eliasz. Nicholas (called Pickenoy)→see Pickenoy, Nicolaes Eliasz.
Eliasz. or Elias, Nicolaes (Nicolaes Eliasz. Pickenoy)→see Pickenoy, Nicolaes Eliasz.
Eliasz., Nicolaes→see Pickenoy, Nicolaes Eliasz.
Eliasz., Nicolaes (Nicolaes Eliasz. Pickenoy)→see Pickenoy, Nicolaes Eliasz.
Elie Lascaux→see Lascaux, Elie
Eliger→see Elliger, Ottmar II
Elihu Vedder→see Vedder, Elihu
Elinga, Pieter Janssens→see Janssens, Pieter
Elio Ciol→see Ciol, Elio
Eliot Candee Clark→see Clark, Eliot Candee

Eliot, Charles *(American landscape architect, Boston, Mass., partner of F.L. Olmsted, 1893-1897; son of Charles William Eliot, American educator, 1859-1897)*   **AV**
 Bibl: House & garden, 1987 Sept., v.159, no.9, p.56; ▶Macmillan encyc. archts.
Eliot, Charles William *(American city planner and landscape architect, 1899-)*   **AV**
Eliot, Nathaniel *(American woodworker)*   **AV**
 Bibl: Binney, Country Life, CLXXIX/4624 (3 Apr. 1986) p.861
Elisabeth Schultz→see Schultz, Elisabeth
Elisabeth Terroux→see Terroux, Elisabeth
Elisabeth Wright→see Wright, Elizabeth
Elisabetta Sirani→see Sirani, Elisabetta
Elisee Maclet→see Maclet, Elisée
Elisée, Jacques→see Reclus, Elisée
Eliseo Meifren y Roig→see Meifrén y Roig, Eliseo
Elisofon, Elin *(American artist, b.1952)*   **BA**
 Bibl: ▶Artweek idx.; San Francisco (CA, USA), SFMoMA, Desert project (1979)
Eliz. Serani→see Sirani, Elisabetta
Eliza Maskall→see Maskall, Eliza
Eliza Serani→see Sirani, Elisabetta
Elizabeth Anne Rigaud→see Rigaud, Elizabeth Anne
Elizabeth Engelhard→see Engelhard, Elizabeth
Elizabeth Jane Gardner Bouguereau→see Bouguereau, Elizabeth Jane Gardner
Elizabeth of France, Mme. *(French artist, 1764-1794)*   **WC**
Elizabeth Sirani→see Sirani, Elisabetta
Elizabeth Strong→see Strong, Elizabeth
Elizabeth Welles Perkins→see Perkins, Elizabeth Welles
Elizabeth Wentworth Roberts→see Roberts, Elizabeth Wentworth
Elizabeth, Lady Templetown *(British, designing for Wedgwood 1783-1787, d. 1823)*   **JG**
Elizabeth, Princess *(British artist, 1770-1840)*   **WC WI**
Elizabetha Serani→see Sirani, Elisabetta
Elizabetha Sirani→see Sirani, Elisabetta
Elizabethus Serani→see Sirani, Elisabetta

Elizondo, Alejandro (*Mexican architect, Mexico City*)   **AV**
    Bibl: Interiors, 1989 Sept., v.149, no.2, p.177

Elk, Gerard Pieter van (*Dutch artist, b.1941*)   **BA**
    Bibl: Basel (CHE), Kunsthalle, GER VAN ELK (1980); ▶DuMonts Künst.-Lex.; ▶Intl. dir. exh. artists, 1983

Elkan, Benno (*German sculptor, painter, author, 1877-1960*)   **BA**
    Bibl: Schubert. PANTHEON XLIII, 1985; ▶Vollmer, Künst.-Lex. 20. Jhr.

Elkan, David Levy (*German painter, printmaker, 1808-1865*)   **BA**
    Bibl: ▶Busse, Maler u. Bildhauer 19. Jahr.; ▶Thieme-Becker

Elkim, Maria   **WC WI**
    (*American artist, 20th cent.*)   WC
    (*American artist, op.20th c.*)   WI

Elkins, Frances Adler (*American interior designer, ca.1890-1953*)   **AV**
    Bibl: Connoisseur, Jan. 1984, v.214, n.863, p.[86]-93

Elkoury, Fouad (*Photographer, b. Lebanon, 1952?*)   **AV**
    Bibl: Architecture d'aujourd'hui, 1988 July, no.257, p.031; ▶Libr. of Congr. Name Auth. File

Elkus, Howard F. (*American architect, 1938-*)   **AV**

Ellacombe, Henry Nicholson (*1822-1915*)   **AV**

Ellaume, Jean-Charles (*French ébéniste, master 1754*)   **GC**
    Bibl: ▶Salverte, Ébénistes 18e s.

Elle → *see* Elle, Ferdinand

Elle, Edouard (*French artist, 1859-1911*)   **WC**

Elle, Elie or Helle, Ferdinand. → *see* Elle, Ferdinand

Elle, Elie or Helle, Louis ('Ferdinand fils') → *see* Elle, Louis

Elle, Elie, Helle or van Helle the Elder, Louis Ferdinand (Ferdinand le Vieux) → *see* Elle, Louis Ferdinand (the Elder)

Elle, Ferdinand   **PR**
    (*Flemish painter, ca.1585-1637*)   PR
    (*French artist, c.1585-m.1637/40*)   WC
    (*French, bef.1585-1637/40*)   GC
    Bibl: ▶Thieme-Becker; ▶Witt checklist
    Elle   PR

Elle, Elie or Helle, Ferdinand.   **WC**
Elle, Ferdinand I   **GC**
    Ferdinand Elle   PR

Elle, Ferdinand I → *see* Elle, Ferdinand

Elle, Louis   **GC**
    (*French artist, 1648-1717*)   WC
    (*French painter, 1648-1717*)   GC
    Bibl: ▶Thieme-Becker; ▶Witt checklist

Elle, Elie or Helle, Louis ('Ferdinand fils')   **WC**
    Elle, Louis ('Ferdinand fils')   GC
    Helle, Louis   GC

Elle, Louis ('Ferdinand fils') → *see* Elle, Louis

Elle, Louis Ferdinand (the Elder)   **GC**
    (*French artist, c.1612-1689*)   WC
    (*French, ca.1612-1689*)   GC
    Bibl: ▶Witt checklist

Elle, Elie, Helle or van Helle the Elder, Louis Ferdinand (Ferdinand le Vieux)   **WC**
    Ferdinand Le Vieux   GC
    Le Vieux, Ferdinand   GC
    Vieux, Ferdinand le   GC

Ellegaard Frederiksen, Erik (*Danish typographer, author, 20th c.*)   **BA**
    Bibl: KUNST ÅRSSKRIFT (1977-80); ▶Natl. union cat., 1973-1977
    Frederiksen, Erik Ellegaard   BA

Ellen Emmet Rand → *see* Rand, Ellen Emmet

Ellen Kendall Baker → *see* Baker, Ellen Kendall

Ellen Power → *see* Power, Ellen

Ellenborough, Edith, Miss → *see* Corbet, Edith

Ellender, Raphael   **WC WI**
    (*American artist, 1906-*)   WC
    (*American artist, b.1906*)   WI

Ellengast, Thomas → *see* Ölgast, Thomas

Ellenrieder, Maria (Anna Maria)
    (*German artist, 1791-1863*)   **WC**

Ellenshaw, Peter   **WC WI**
    (*American artist, 20th cent.*)   WC
    (*American artist, op.20th c.*)   WI

Ellenzweig, Harry   **AV**

Ellerbe, Thomas Farr (*American architect, Minneapolis, Minn, 1892-1987*)   **AV**
    Bibl: Architecture Minnesota, 1988 Mar.-Apr., v.14, no.2, p.21
    Ellerbe, Tom   AV

Ellerbe, Tom → *see* Ellerbe, Thomas Farr

Ellermann, Christoph (*German architect*)   **AV**
    Bibl: Arch plus, 1986 Mar., no.84, p.54

Ellermann, Karl (*German artist, 1887-1910*)   **WC**

Elleson, G.W. → *see* Ellison, G.W.

Ellett, Thomas Harlan (*American architect, 1880-1951*)   **AV**
    Bibl: ▶Avery obit. idx.

Ellice, Georgina, Miss → *see* Seymour, Georgina

Ellice, M.A. (*British artist, op.1906-*)   **WI**

Ellicombe, Charles (*British artist, 1783-1871*)   **WI**

Elliger, Antoni   **GC WC**
    (*Dutch artist, 1701-1781*)   WC
    (*Dutch painter, 1701-1781*)   GC
    Bibl: ▶Thieme-Becker

Elliger, Ottmar → *see* Elliger, Ottmar (the elder)

Elliger, Ottmar (I) → *see* Elliger, Ottmar (the elder)

Elliger, Ottmar (II) → *see* Elliger, Ottmar II

Elliger, Ottmar (the elder)   **GC PR**
    (*German artist, 1633-1679*)   WC
    (*German painter, 1633-1679*)   GC PR
    Bibl: Getty Photo Study Coll.; ▶Thieme-Becker; ▶Witt checklist
    Elliger, Ottmar   PR
    Elliger, Ottmar (I)   PR

Elliger, Ottmar I   **GC**
Elliger, Ottmar, I   **WC**
    Ottmar Elliger (the elder)   PR
    Ottoman Eliger   PR

Elliger, Ottmar (the younger) → *see* Elliger, Ottmar II

Elliger, Ottmar I → *see* Elliger, Ottmar (the elder)

Elliger, Ottmar II   **BA GC**
    (*German artist, 1666-1735*)   WC
    (*German painter and draughtsman, 1666-1735*)   GC
    (*German painter, 1666-1735*)   BA PR
    Bibl: ▶Thieme-Becker; ▶Witt checklist
    Eliger   PR
    Elliger, Ottmar (II)   PR

Elliger, Ottmar (the younger)   **GC PR**
Elliger, Ottmar, II   **WC**
    Ottmar Elliger (the younger)   PR

Elliger, Ottmar, I → *see* Elliger, Ottmar (the elder)

Elliger, Ottmar, II → *see* Elliger, Ottmar II

Elling, Herbert (*E. German architect, Bernau*)   **AV**

Elliot → *see* Elliott, William

Elliot Painter (*South Italian vase-painter, 330-275 BC*)   **GC**
    Bibl: McPhee & Trendall, Fish-Plates

Elliot, Archibald   **BA**
    (*Scottish architect, 1760-1823*)   AV BA
    Bibl: ▶Colvin, Brit. archts.; Edinburgh (GBR), Natl. Lib. Scotland, Scottish arch. (1978); ▶Thieme-Becker

Elliott, Archibald   **AV**

Elliot, Charles Loring → *see* Elliott, Charles Loring

Elliot, Daniel Girard (*American artist, op.1860-1877*)   **WC WI**

Elliot, George   **WC WI**
    (*British artist, op.1856*)   WC
    (*British artist, op.1856-*)   WI

Elliot, Harriet (*British artist, op.19th c.*)   **WI**

Elliot, Robert James *(British artist, 1790-1849)*   **WC WI**

Elliot, William P. *(fl. 1830s-1860s; Architect, District of Columbia)*   **FA**
Bibl: DC Catalog /Schwartz, 1974; ▶Macmillan encyc. archts., v.4, p.222 ff.; Natl. Archives object
Elliot, William Parker   **FA**
Elliot, William Parker →see Elliot, William P.

Elliott *(British, active 1860's-1890's (also Elliott & Fry))*   **JG**
Elliott →see Elliott, William
Elliott Daingerfield →see Daingerfield, Elliott

Elliott, Anne *(American sculptor, ceramist, b.1944.)*   **BA**
Bibl: Pittsburgh (PA, USA), Univ. of Pittsburgh, Sculp. by Women in the 80s (1985)
Elliott, Archibald →see Elliot, Archibald

Elliott, Charles Loring   **BA GC WC**
(American artist, 1812-1868)   WC WI
(American painter, 1812-1868) BA GC
Bibl: ▶Britannica encyc. Amer. art; ▶Fielding's Amer. ptrs.; ▶Groce, Artists Amer.; ▶RILA/BHA; ▶Thieme-Becker

Elliot, Charles Loring   **WI**

Elliott, David *(Canadian painter, sculptor, b.1953)*   **BA**
Bibl: ▶Idx. Ontario artists; Kingston (Ont, CAN), Queen's Univ., Agnes Etherington Art Centre, DAVID ELLIOTT (1979)

Elliott, Doug *(Builder, United States)*   **AV**
Bibl: Builder, 1985 Nov., v.8, no.11, p.55

Elliott, Glen *(American sculptor in CAN, b.1941)*   **BA**
Bibl: Stratford (Ont, CAN), Gallery/Stratford, KEN NUTT (1980)

Elliott, Henry *(American architect, 19th century, worked in Illinois)*   **AV**
Bibl: Historic Illinois, 1986 June, v.9, no.1, p.3

Elliott, John *(British artist, op.18th c.)*   **WI**

Elliott, Julian *(South African architect, 1928-)*   **AV**
Bibl: ▶Contemp. archts.

Elliott, Leo *(American architect, Tampa, FL)*   **AV**
Bibl: Historic preservation, 1985 Apr., v.37, no.2, p.11

Elliott, Owen Nelson *(American, 1886-1982)*   **BA**
Bibl: Clark Art Inst.; Iowa City (IA, USA), Univ. of Iowa, Mus. of Art, THE OWEN N. ELLIOTT COLLECTION... (1983)

Elliott, Peter   **AV BA**
(Australian architect)   AV
(Australian architect, 20th c.)   BA
Bibl: Architectural review, 1985 Dec., v.178, no.1066, p.94; ▶Avery period. idx., 6th suppl.

Elliott, Philip Clarkson   **WC WI**
(American artist, 1903)   WC
(American artist, b.1903)   WI
Elliott, Philip, Mrs., (Virginia) →see Cuthbert, Virginia

Elliott, Randall Lynn *(American architect, Oklahoma City, Okla)*   **AV**
Bibl: ▶AIA Pro File, 1985

Elliott, Rita *(American interior designer, Iowa)*   **AV**
Bibl: Iowa architect, 1984 July-Aug., v.31, no.4, p.28

Elliott, Robert Powell *(British artist, op.circa 1824-)*   **WI**

Elliott, Robinson *(British artist, 1814-1894)*   **WC WI**

Elliott, Ronnie Rose *(American artist, b.1916)*   **BA**
Bibl: ▶Cummings, Contemp. Amer. artists; ▶WW Amer. Art, 1976
Elliott, T. →see Elliott, Thomas

Elliott, Thomas   **WI**
(British artist, 18th cent.)   WC
(British artist, op.1793-1800)   WI
Elliott, T.   **WC**

Elliott, W., Lt. *(Engraver, op.1787-1792)*   **WI**

Elliott, William   **PR WI**
(British artist, op.1774-, d.1795)   WI
(British artist, op.1774-m.1792)   WC
(British painter, act. 1774, d. 1792)   PR
Bibl: ▶Thieme-Becker; ▶Waterhouse, Brit. 18c. ptrs.
Elliot   PR
Elliott   PR
Elliott, William (not Robert)   **WC**
L. Elliot   PR
Lieut. Elliot   PR
Elliott, William (not Robert) →see Elliott, William

Ellis, A.   **WC WI**
(American artist, op.1820-1830)   WC
(American artist, op.circa 1820-)   WI

Ellis, Alfred *(British, active London, England, U.K. 1890s-1920s)*   **JG**
Ellis, Bertram Clough →see Williams-Ellis, Bertram Clough

Ellis, C.Wynne *(British artist, op. 1880-, d.1915)*   **WI**

Ellis, Clifford & Rosemary *(British artist, b.1910)*   **WI**

Ellis, Dean *(Canadian sculptor, b.1948)*   **BA**
Bibl: ▶Artists Canada; Vancouver (BC, CAN), Art Gallery, Initial works (1977)

Ellis, Edmund L. *(Active Italy 20th century)*   **JG**

Ellis, Edwin *(British artist, 1841-1895)*   **WC WI**
Bibl: Hall, Nottinghamshire
Ellis, Fremond F. →see Ellis, Fremont F.

Ellis, Fremont F.   **BA**
(American artist, 1897-)   WC
(American artist, b.1897)   WI
(American painter, printmaker, b.1897)   BA
Bibl: ▶Bénézit; ▶Dawdy, Artists Amer. West; ▶Fielding's Amer. ptrs.

Ellis, Fremond F.   **WC WI**

Ellis, George B. *(Engraver, Philadelphia, PA., op.1821-1838)*   **WI**

Ellis, Gordon   **WC WI**
(British artist, 20th cent.)   WC
(British artist, op.20th c.)   WI

Ellis, Harvey   **AV BA WC WI**
(American architect, furniture designer, painter, 1852-1904)   AV
(American architect, painter, designer, 1852-1904)   BA
(American artist, 1852-1904)   WC WI
Bibl: ▶Avery obit. idx.; ▶Bénézit; ▶Thieme-Becker; ▶WWW Amer.

Ellis, Henry *(British hydrographer, public official, explorer, 1721-1806)*   **BA**
Bibl: ▶Dict. natl. biog.

Ellis, Jane *(British artist, b.1957)*   **WI**

Ellis, John *(American architect, New York City)*   **AV**
Bibl: ▶AIA Pro File, 1987-88

Ellis, Jonathan *(American sculptor, 20th c.)*   **BA**
Bibl: ARTS MAGAZINE, LVIII, 5 (Jan 1984) 137

Ellis, Joseph Francis   **WC WI**
(British artist, c.1783-1848)   WC
(British artist, circa 1783-1848)   WI

Ellis, Kenneth Lee *(American architectural student, Univ. of Ark., 1987-88)*   **AV**
Bibl: Association of Collegiate Schools of Architecture. News, 1988 Oct., v.18, no.2, p.14

Ellis, Lionel   **WC WI**
(British artist, 1903-)   WC
(British artist, b.1903)   WI

Ellis, Michael T. *(Unknown artist)*   **GC**
Bibl: Gernsheim, Corpus Photog. of Drawings, 1588

Ellis, Paul H.   **WC WI**
(British artist, 19th cent.)   WC
(British artist, op.1871-1900)   WI

Ellis, Peter   **BA**
(American architect)   AV
(British printmaker, sculptor, b.1950.)   BA
Bibl: Arts Council GBR, Welsh Comm., Some recent purchases (1979); Chicago architectural journal, 1989, no.7, p.198; ▶Intl. dir. exh. artists, 1982, 1983

Ellis, Peter G.   **AV**

Ellis, Peter G. → *see* Ellis, Peter
Ellis, Ray *(American artist, op.1988-)*   **WI**
Ellis, Ron *(American architect)*   **AV**
    Bibl: Arch. & urbanism, 4(223)
    (Apr.1989), p.111
Ellis, Thomas B. Harper *(British
    architect, 1911-1988)*   **AV**
    Bibl: Building design, 1988
    Mar.11, p.2
Ellis, Tristram J. → *see* Ellis, Tristram
    James
Ellis, Tristram James   **WI**
    (British artist, 1844-1922)   WI
    (British artist, 1844-p.1893)   WC
    Ellis, Tristram J.   **WC**
Ellis, William *(British artist, 1747-
    1810)*   **WC WI**
Ellis, William *(American architect,
    city planner and author, 1933-)*   **AV**
    Bibl: Oppositions, n.18 (Fall 1979)
    p.100
Ellis, William (Rev.) *(British, active
    Madagascar (now Malagasy
    Republic) 1873)*   **JG**
Ellis-Miller, Jonathan *(British
    architect, 1962-)*   **AV**
    Bibl: Ottagono, 1988 Dec., no.91,
    p.20
Elliscombe, Maj. Gen. → *see*
    Elliscombe, Major-Gen.
Elliscombe, Major-Gen.   **WI**
    (British artist, 18th cent.)   WC
    (British artist, op.18th c.)   WI
    Elliscombe, Maj. Gen.   **WC**
Ellison, G.W. *(Canadian
    photographer, act.1852-1879)*   **BA**
    Bibl: ▶Harper, Early ptrs. Canada;
    JOURNAL OF CAN. ART HIST. V/1
    (1980) 33-38; ▶Parry, Photo idx.
    Elleson, G.W.   BA
    Ellisson, G.W.   BA
Ellison, Nancy *(American artist,
    b.1936)*   **WI**
Ellisson, G.W. → *see* Ellison, G.W.
Ellmore → *see* Elmer, Stephen
Ellsley, Beverly *(American interior
    designer, Conn.(?))*   **AV**
    Bibl: House beautiful, 1987 Sept.,
    v.129, no.9, p.55
Ellsworth, Abigail Wolcott → *see*
    Wolcott, Abigail
Ellsworth, Clarence *(American
    artist, 1885-1961)*   **WC WI**
Ellsworth, James Sanford   **BA WC WI**
    (American artist, 1802-1874)   WC WI
    (American painter, 1802-1873?)   BA
    Bibl: ▶Encyc. world art; ▶Fielding's
    Amer. ptrs.; ▶Havlice, Idx. art.
    bio.; ▶Young, Amer. artists
Ellwood, Craig *(American architect,
    1922-)*   **AV**
    Bibl: ▶Contemp. archts.
Ellys, John   **WC WI**
    (British artist, 1700-1701-1757)   WI
    (British artist, 1700/1-1757)   WC
Elmer → *see* Elmer, Stephen

Elmer Forrest Hudson → *see* Hudson,
    Elmer Forrest
Elmer Wachtel → *see* Wachtel, Elmer
Elmer, Edwin R. → *see* Elmer, Edwin
    Romanzo
Elmer, Edwin Romanzo   **BA PR WI**
    (American artist, 1850-1920)   WC
    (American artist, 1850-1923)   WI
    (American painter, 1850-1923)   BA PR
    Bibl: ▶Bénézit; ▶Jakovsky, Peintres
    naïfs, p.209; ▶RILA/BHA
    Edwin Romanzo Elmer   PR
    Elmer, Edwin R.   **WC**
Elmer, Ivy (Betty Arundell) *(British
    painter, illustrator, 20th c.)*   **BA**
    Bibl: COSTUME, XIX (1985) 135-
    139
    Arundell, Betty   BA
Elmer, Stephen   **PR WC WI**
    (British artist, circa 1714-1796)   WI
    (British artist, op.1764-m.1796)   WC
    (British painter, ca.1714-1796)   PR
    Bibl: ▶Thieme-Becker;
    ▶Waterhouse, Brit. 18c. ptrs.
    Ellmore   PR
    Elmer   PR
    Elmor   PR
    Elmore   PR
    Mr. Elmer   PR
    Stephen Elmer   PR
Elmer, William   **WC WI**
    (British artist, 1762-op.1799)   WI
    (British artist, op.1772-1799)   WC
Elmes → *see* Elmes, William
Elmes, Harvey Lonsdale *(British
    architect, 1814-1847)*   **AV BA**
    Bibl: ▶Colvin, Brit. archts.;
    ▶Macmillan encyc. archts.
Elmes, William   **PR**
    (British artist, op.1797-1814)   WC
    (British painter, act. 1797-1814)   PR
    Bibl: ▶Bénézit; ▶Graves Royal
    Acad. contribs.; ▶Thieme-Becker
    Elmes   PR
    Elmes, William.   **WC**
    William Elmes   PR
Elmes, William. → *see* Elmes, William
Elmhirst, Dorothy Whitney
    (American, 1887-1968)   **BA**
    Bibl: Fricker, BEATRICE JONES
    FARRAND; ▶Who was who [GBR],
    v.7
Elmhirst, Leonard Knight *(British,
    1893-1974)*   **BA**
    Bibl: ▶Who was who [GBR], v.7
Elmiger, Franz *(Swiss painter, 1882-
    1934)*   **BA**
    Bibl: ▶Künst.-Lex. Schweiz 20.
    Jahrh.; ▶Schweiz. Künst.-Lex.,
    suppl.; ▶Vollmer, Künst.-Lex. 20.
    Jhr.
Elminger, Ignaz *(German artist,
    1843-1894)*   **WC**
Elmor → *see* Elmer, Stephen
Elmore → *see* Elmer, Stephen

Elmore, Alfred   **BA GC WC WI**
    (British artist, 1815-1881)   WC WI
    (British painter, 1815-1881)   BA
    (British, 1815-1881)   GC
    Bibl: ▶Johnson, Brit. artists;
    ▶Strickland, Irish artists;
    ▶Thieme-Becker; ▶Witt checklist
Elmore, Richard *(British artist, op.
    1852-1892)*   **WI**
Elms, Ray *(British architect)*   **AV**
    Bibl: Japan architect, 1988 Feb.,
    v.63, no.2(370), p.59
Elmslie, Essil R. *(British artist, 1880-
    1952)*   **WI**
    Rutherstone, C.L., Mrs.(Essil R.)   WI
Elmslie, George Grant *(American
    architect, 1871-1952)*   **AV BA**
    Bibl: ▶Avery obit. idx.; ▶Macmillan
    encyc. archts.
Elmslie, J.F.   **WC WI**
    (British artist, 19th cent.)   WC
    (British artist, op.19th c.)   WI
Elordi, Juan de *(Spanish altar
    sculptor, 16th cent)*   **AV**
    Bibl: Boletin del Museo e Instituto
    "Camón Aznar," 1987, no.28,
    p.145
Elouis, Henri (Jean Pierre Henri) → *see*
    Elouis, Jean Pierre Henri
Elouis, Jean Pierre Henri   **WI**
    (American artist, 1755-1840)   WI
    (French artist, 1755-1840)   WC
    Elouis, Henri (Jean Pierre Henri)   **WC**
Eloul, Kosso *(American sculptor,
    b.1920)*   **BA**
    Bibl: ▶Artists Canada; Hamilton
    (Ont, CAN), Art Gallery, KOSSO
    ELOUL (1980); ▶Havlice, Idx. art.
    bio.; ▶Idx. Ontario artists;
    ▶MoMA libr. cat.; ▶WW Amer.
    Art
    Kosso   BA
Elout, Franchoys *(Dutch painter,
    1608-1641)*   **GC**
    Bibl: Getty Photo Study Coll.;
    ▶Thieme-Becker; ▶Wright, Ptgs.
    Dutch museums
**Eloy, Mário (Mário Elói Jesus de
    Pereira)** *(Portuguese painter,
    printmaker, 1900-1951)*   **BA**
    Bibl: Tammock; ▶Tavares Chicó,
    Pint. portuguesa
Elozua, Raymon *(American sculptor,
    b.1947.)*   **BA**
    Bibl: Arts Mag. LIII/10 (June
    1979), p.23; ▶Babington Smith,
    Contemp. artists; Guide exh.
    artists: N. Amer. ptrs.
Elphick, Peter *(British architect,
    20th c.)*   **BA**
    Bibl: RIBA Journal LXXXVII/9 (Sept
    1980) 43-44
**Elphinstone, John, 11th Lord of
    Elphinstone** *(British artist, 1737-
    1794)*   **WI**

Elphinstone, Margaret Mercer,
Baroness Keith *(British artist, op.*
1825-, d.1867)   **WI**
Elpinikos Painter   **GC**
　　Bibl: ▶Beazley, Attic red-fig. vase-
　　ptrs.
Elrod, Biff *(American painter, 20th*
c.)   **BA**
　　Bibl: ARTS MAG LVI/10 (June
　　1982) 20
Elsaesser, Martin→see Elsässer,
Martin
Elsand, Jacob van *(Dutch, 18th*
century)   **GC**
　　Bibl: ▶Witt checklist
Elsasser, Friedrich August   **BA GC WC**
　　(German artist, 1810-1845)   **WC**
　　(German painter, 1810-1845)   **BA GC**
　　Bibl: ▶Bénézit; ▶Thieme-Becker
Elsässer, Hubert *(West German*
sculptor)   **AV**
　　Bibl: Das Münster, 1989, v.42,
　　no.3, p.189
Elsässer, Martin   **BA**
　　(German architect, 1884-
　　1957)   **AV BA**
　　Bibl: ▶Macmillan encyc. archts.;
　　▶Vollmer, Künst.-Lex. 20. Jhr.
Elsaesser, Martin   **AV**
Elsasser, Sigmund *(Austrian painter,*
act.1579, d.ca.1587)   **BA**
　　Bibl: ▶Bénézit; Scheicher, Jahrb. d.
　　Kunsthist. Samml. Wien, XLI
　　(1981) pp.119-153, 121-122;
　　▶Thieme-Becker
Elsborch, Jan van→see Elburcht, Jan
van der
Elscheid, Nikolaus *(German*
sculptor, 1835-1874)   **BA**
　　Bibl: Bloch, Jahrb. Preussisches
　　Kulturbesitz XXIV (1987), p. 251-
　　253; FESTSCHRIFT FUR OTTO
　　SIMSON p.504
Elschimier→see Elsheimer, Adam
Elsden, William *(British architect,*
military engineer, active in
Portugal in 1770's)   **AV**
　　Bibl: ▶Thieme-Becker
Else, Robert *(American painter,*
b.1918)   **BA**
　　Bibl: Sacramento (CA, USA), E.B.
　　Crocker Art Gallery, ROBERT
　　ELSE... (1977)
Elsen [Unidentified] *(Unknown*
painter)   **PR**
　　Bibl: Bruinenburg inventory, 1708,
　　Amsterdam
　　Van Elsen   PR
Elsen, Alfred *(Belgian artist, 1850-*
1914)   **WC**
Elsevier, Louys   **GC WC**
　　(Dutch artist, 1617/18-1675)   **WC**
　　(Dutch painter, 1617/18-1675)   **GC**
　　Bibl: Getty Photo Study Coll.;
　　▶Thieme-Becker; ▶Witt checklist
Elshameer→see Elsheimer, Adam
Elshamer→see Elsheimer, Adam

Elsheimar→see Elsheimer, Adam
Elsheimer→see Elsheimer, Adam
Elsheimer, Adam   **BA GC PR WC**
　　(German artist, 1578-1610)   **WC**
　　(German painter, 1578-1610)   **BA GC**
　　(German painter, ca.1578-1610)   **PR**
　　Bibl: ▶Bénézit; ▶RILA/BHA;
　　▶Thieme-Becker
　　A. Elsheimeer   PR
　　A. Elsheimer   PR
　　A. Elsheimer   PR
　　A. Elshimer   PR
　　Ad. Elsheimer   PR
　　Ad: Elsheimer   PR
　　Adam Elsheimer   PR
　　Adam Elshimer   PR
　　Adam Elzheimer   PR
　　Adam Eslchimr   PR
　　Adamo Elzheimer   PR
　　Adm. Elshiemer   PR
　　Elschimier   PR
　　Elshameer   PR
　　Elshamer   PR
　　Elsheimar   PR
　　Elsheimer   PR
　　Elsheiner   PR
　　Elsheinier   PR
　　Elshemar   PR
　　Elshemeer   PR
　　Elshemer   PR
　　Elshemier   PR
　　Elshermer   PR
　　Elshiemer   PR
　　Elshimar   PR
　　Elshimear   PR
　　Elshimer   PR
　　Elsmeer   PR
　　Eltheimer   PR
　　Elzheimer   PR
　　Eshiemer   PR
Elsheiner→see Elsheimer, Adam
Elsheinier→see Elsheimer, Adam
Elshemar→see Elsheimer, Adam
Elshemeer→see Elsheimer, Adam
Elshemer→see Elsheimer, Adam
Elshemier→see Elsheimer, Adam
Elshemius, Louis→see Eilshemius,
Louis Michel
Elshemus, Louis Michel→see
Eilshemius, Louis Michel
Elshermer→see Elsheimer, Adam
Elshiemer→see Elsheimer, Adam
Elshimar→see Elsheimer, Adam
Elshimear→see Elsheimer, Adam
Elshimer→see Elsheimer, Adam
Elshoecht, Carle *(French sculptor,*
1797-1856)   **BA**
　　Bibl: ▶Bénézit; Durey, REVUE DU
　　LOUVRE XXXIV/1 (1984) 15-21;
　　▶Lami, Sculp. fran. 19e s.; ▶Nouv.
　　biog. gén.; ▶Thieme-Becker
　　Elshoecht, Jean-Jacques-Marie-
　　Carle-Vital   BA
Elshoecht, Jean-Jacques-Marie-
Carle-Vital→see Elshoecht, Carle

Elsholtz, Ludwig   **GC WC**
　　(German artist, 1805-1850)   **WC**
　　(German painter, 1805-1850)   **GC**
　　Bibl: ▶Thieme-Becker
Elsken, Ed van der *(Dutch*
photographer, b.ca.1925)   **BA**
　　Bibl: Amsterdam (NLD), Stedelijk
　　Museum, EYE LOVE YOU (1977);
　　▶Image; ▶MoMA libr. cat.
Elsland, Jacob van *(Dutch artist,*
18th cent.)   **WC**
Elslandt→see Elslandt, Peeter
Elslandt, Peeter *(Flemish painter,*
act. 1595-1607)   **PR**
　　Bibl: ▶Thieme-Becker
　　Elslandt   PR
　　Peeter Elslandt   PR
Elsley, Arthur John   **WC WI**
　　(British artist, 1861-)   **WC**
　　(British artist, 1861-op.1927)   **WI**
Elsmeer→see Elsheimer, Adam
Elsner or Elszner, Jakob→see Elsner,
Jakob
Elsner, Jakob   **GC**
　　(German artist, op.1486-m.
　　1517)   **WC**
　　(German painter and
　　illuminator, ca.1460-1517)   **GC**
　　Bibl: ▶Bénézit; Germanisches
　　Nationalmuseum Cat.;
　　▶Thieme-Becker
　　Eisner, Jacob   GC
Elsner or Elszner, Jakob   **WC**
　　Elssner, Jacob   GC
　　Elzner, Jacob   GC
　　Ölszner, Jakob   GC
　　Ulszner, Jakob   GC
Elssner, Jacob→see Elsner, Jakob
Elst, Bartholomeus van der→see
Helst, Bartholomeus van der
Elst, F.J. van der *(Dutch(?)*
draughtsman, 17th century)   **GC**
　　Bibl: Sotheby's
Elst, Hieronymous van der *(Dutch*
artist, op.1595-1612)   **WC**
Elstrack or Elstrake, Renold→see
Elstrack, Renold
Elstrack, Renold   **WI**
　　(British artist, 1571-op.1625)   **WI**
　　(British artist, 1571-p.1625)   **WC**
Elstrack or Elstrake, Renold   **WC**
　　Elstrake, Renold   WI
Elstrake, Renold→see Elstrack,
Renold
Elsworth, John *(English clockmaker,*
17th c.)   **BA**
　　Bibl: Biavati, Boll. dei Mus. Civici
　　Genov., III/7-9 (Jan.-Dec. 1981),
　　pp. 5-68
Elten, D. van *(Dutch artist, op.1783)*   **WC**
Elten, Kruseman, van→see Kruseman
van Elten, Hendrik Dirk
Eltester, Christian *(German*
architect, 1671-1700)   **AV BA**
　　Bibl: ▶Allgem. Deut. Biog.;
　　▶Thieme-Becker

Eltheimer→*see* Elsheimer, Adam

Elton, Arthur *(British, 20th c.)*   **BA**
 Bibl: COUNTRY LIFE CLXV/4274
 (7 June 1979) 1861-1862

Elton, Carlos *(Chilean architect)*   **AV**
 Bibl: Projeto, 1985 Jan., no.71,
 p.38

Elton, Edmund Harry   **WC WI**
 (British artist, 1846-)   **WC**
 (British artist, b.1846)   **WI**

Elton, H. *(British artist, op.1868-)*   **WI**

Elton, Lynne *(British artist, 20th c.)*   **BA**
 Bibl: Arts Council GBR, Summer
 show 4 (1976)

Elton, Samuel Averill *(British artist,*
 1827-1886)   **WC WI**

Eltze, F.→*see* Eltze, Fritz

Eltze, Fritz   **WI**
 (British artist, 19th cent.)   **WC**
 (British artist, op.1864-, d.1870)   **WI**

Eltze, F.   **WC**

Eluard, Paul *(French artist, 20th*
 cent.)   **WC**

Elven→*see* Elven, Ivan

Elven, Ivan   **PR WC**
 (French artist, op.1871)   **WC**
 (French painter, act. 1871)   **PR**
 Bibl: ▶Witt checklist

Elven   PR
Ivan Elven   PR

Elvery, Beatrice→*see* Elvery, Beatrice
 Moss

Elvery, Beatrice Moss   **WI**
 (British artist, 1883-1970)   **WI**
 (British artist, 19th cent.)   **WC**
 Bibl: Irish Women Artists

Campbell, Gordon, Mrs., (Beatrice
 Moss)   WI

Elvery, Beatrice   **WC**
Glenavy, Beatrice Moss, Baroness   WI

Elvery, James   **WC WI**
 (British artist, op.1762)   **WC**
 (British artist, op.1762-)   **WI**

Elvira, Manuel de Diego *(Spanish*
 jeweler, 19th c.)   **BA**
 Bibl: REALES SITIOS XIX/71 (1982)
 37-44

Diego Elvira, Manuel de   BA

Elwell, Chip *(American printer,*
 publisher, 1940-1986)   **BA**
 Bibl: PRINT COLLECTOR'S
 NEWSLETTER, XVII/5 (Nov-Dec
 1986) p.169; ▶WW Amer. Art,
 1984

Elwell, D. Gerome *(American*
 painter, 1857-1912)   **PR**
 Bibl: ▶WWW Amer. art

D. Gerome Elwell   PR
Elwell, D. Jerome   PR

Elwell, D. Jerome→*see* Elwell, D.
 Gerome

Elwell, Francis Kenneth   **WC WI**
 (British artist, 1835-1940)   **WI**
 (British artist, 20th cent.)   **WC**

Elwell, Frederick W.→*see* Elwell,
 Frederick William

Elwell, Frederick William   **WI**
 (British artist, 1870-1958)   **WI**
 (British artist, 1870-p.1909)   **WC**

Elwell, Frederick W.   **WC**

Elwell, Mary Dawson *(British artist,*
 1874-1952)   **WI**

Bishop, Mary Dawson, Miss   WI

Elwell, R. Farrington→*see* Elwell,
 Robert Farrington

Elwell, Robert Farrington   **WI**
 (American artist, 1874-1962)   **WC WI**

Elwell, R. Farrington   **WC**

Elwes, Francis E. Carey   **WI**
 (British artist, 19th cent.)   **WC**
 (British artist, op.19th c.)   **WI**
 Bibl: ▶Wood, Victorian ptrs.

Elwes, Francis E. Cary   **WC**

Elwes, Francis E. Cary→*see* Elwes,
 Francis E. Carey

Elwes, Guy   **AV BA**
 (British architect, act.1931-
 1935)   **BA**
 (British interior designer)   **AV**
 Bibl: Architectural digest, 1984
 May, v.41, no.5, p.166; Pevsner,
 Lincolnshire, p. 233; Worsley, G.,
 COUNTRY LIFE, CLXXX/ 4650 (20
 Oct. 1986), p.1020-1023

Elwes, Helen *(British artist, op.*
 1958-)   **WI**

Elwes, Simon *(British artist, 1902-*
 1975)   **WC WI**

Elwick, Edward *(British*
 cabinetmaker, upholsterer, act.
 1748, d. after 1784)   **BA**
 Bibl: ▶Beard, Craftsmen; Jrnl.
 furniture hist., XII (1976) pp.
 34-50

Elwyn *(Australian (?))*   **GC**
 Bibl: Gernsheim, Corpus Photog.
 of Drawings, 1408

Elwyn, John *(British artist, b.1916)*   **WI**

Ely, Reginald *(English mason, act.*
 1438-1471)   **BA**
 Bibl: Harvey, Perpendicular style

Elyas, Isack→*see* Elias, Isaac

Elzer, Hendrik Jakob *(Dutch*
 draughtsman, 1808-1860)   **GC**
 Bibl: ▶Bénézit; Getty Photo Study
 Coll.

Elzheimer→*see* Elsheimer, Adam

Elzingre, Edouard *(Swiss artist, 20th*
 cent.)   **WC**

Elzner, Jacob→*see* Elsner, Jakob

Emanuel de Hoit→*see* Witte,
 Emanuel de

Emanuel de Wit→*see* Witte, Emanuel
 de

Emanuel de Witt→*see* Witte,
 Emanuel de

Emanuel de Witte→*see* Witte,
 Emanuel de

Emanuel Gottlieb Leutze→*see*
 Leutze, Emanuel Gottlieb

Emanuel Meurant→*see* Murant,
 Emanuel

Emanuel Murant→*see* Murant,
 Emanuel

Emanuel Nys→*see* Nys, Emanuel

Emanuel, Charles H.L. *(British,*
 active 1895-1928)   **JG**

Emanuel, Frank Lewis *(British*
 artist, 1865-1948)   **WC WI**

Emanuel, John *(British artist,*
 b.1930)   **WI**

Emanuel, K. *(Netherlands(?) artist,*
 17th/18th cent.)   **WC**

Emanuel, Peter *(German artist,*
 1799-1873)   **WC**

Emanuele Laggrazia→*see* Laggrazia,
 Emanuele [Unidentified]

Embde, August von der *(German*
 artist, 1780-1862)   **WC**

Emberton, Joseph   **AV BA**
 (1889-1956)   **AV**
 (British architect, 1889-1956)   **BA**
 Bibl: ▶Avery obit. idx.; ▶Macmillan
 encyc. archts.; ▶Who was who
 [GBR], v.5; ▶WW Arch.

Embriachi family *(Italian carvers,*
 15th c.)   **BA**
 Bibl: ▶Encic. italiana;
 ▶Thieme-Becker

Embring, Margaretha Christina
 (Swedish artist, 1756-1843)   **WC**

Embry, Norris   **BA WI**
 (American artist, 1921-1981)   **WI**
 (American painter, 1921-1981)   **BA**
 Bibl: NY Times obit., 20 Feb
 1981; ▶WW Amer. Art, 1973

Embury, Aymar *(American architect,*
 New York, NY)   **AV**
 Bibl: Metals in construction,
 1986, v.4, no.1, p.2

Embury, Aymar II *(American*
 architect, 1880-1966)   **BA**
 Bibl: ▶WWW Amer.

Emch, Peter *(Swiss painter, b.1945)*   **BA**
 Bibl: Guide exh. artists: N. Amer.
 ptrs.; ▶Intl. dir. exh. artists, 1982;
 ▶Lex. zeitgen. Schweiz. Künstler

Emck, Hans Jacob *(German*
 goldsmith, act.1591-1610)   **BA**
 Bibl: Scheffler, GOLDSCHMIEDE
 HESSENS, 559

Emden, H. *(German, active*
 Frankfurt, 1850's)   **JG**

Emele, Jakob *(German architect,*
 1707-1780)   **AV**
 Bibl: ▶Thieme-Becker

Emele, Wilhelm *(German artist,*
 1830-1905)   **WC**

Emenes, Jantje van [Unidentified]
 (Unknown painter)   **PR**
 Bibl: Wilmerdonx inventory (1686)

Jantje van Emenes   PR

Emeric, Honorine *(French artist,*
 1814-p.1880)   **WC**

Emerson, Edith *(American artist,*
 b.1888)   **WI**

Emerson, Larry *(American painter,*
b.1947)   **BA**
  Bibl: ▶Intl. dir. exh. artists; Regina
  (Sask, CAN), U.Sask. Gallery, A
  new generation (1982)
Emerson, P.H.   **WC WI**
  (American artist, 19th cent.)   WC
  (American artist, op.19th c.)   WI
Emerson, Peter Henry   **BA JG**
  (British photographer, physician,
  1856-1936)   BA
  (British, (b. Cuba), 1856-1936)   JG
  Bibl: Encyc. photography;
  ▶Gernsheim, Hist. photog.;
  ▶Newhall, Photog.
Emerson, William *(British architect,*
1843-1924)   **BA**
  Bibl: ▶Avery obit. idx.; ▶Bénézit;
  ▶Portoghesi, Diz. arch. e
  urbanistica; ▶Thieme-Becker
Emerson, William Ralph *(1833-*
1917)   **AV**
Emery, Charles E.   **WC WI**
  (British artist, 19th cent.)   WC
  (British artist, op.19th c.)   WI
Emery, John *(British artist, 1777-*
1822)   **WI**
Emery, Lin *(American sculptor, 20th*
c.)   **BA**
  Bibl: ▶WW Amer. Art, 1989
Emery, Matteo *(Swiss artist,*
b.1955)   **BA**
  Bibl: ▶Intl. dir. exh. artists, 1982,
  1983
Emery, Sergio *(Italian painter, 20th*
c.)   **BA**
  Bibl: ART INTERNATIONAL XXIV
  (Mar-Apr 1981) 58-62
Emery, Stephen *(American*
silversmith, 1749-1801)   **BA**
  Bibl: Antiques CXX/4 (Oct 1981)
  922-925; Kovel, Amer. silver
Emery, W.F.   **WC WI**
  (British artist, op.1870)   WC
  (British artist, op.1870-)   WI
Emeryk *(Hungarian carpenter, 14th*
c.)   **BA**
  Bibl: Sniezynskastolot, Acta Hist.
  Artium, XX/1-2 (1974) pp.13-36
Emes, John   **WC WI**
  (British artist, 1762-1810)   WI
  (British artist, op.1786-m.1810)   WC
Emes, Rebecca   **BA JG**
  (British silversmith, act.1808,
  d.1828)   BA
  Bibl: Country Life CLXI (20 Jan
  1977) 140; ▶Penguin dec. arts
Emes, William   **AV BA**
  (British landscape architect,
  '1729-1803)   AV
  (British landscape artist,
  1729/30-1803)   BA
  Bibl: Oxford comp. gardens;
  Pevsner, Derbyshire; Royal
  Commissions, CAMBRIDGESHIRE,
  v.1, p.217; Wilde, COUNTRY LIFE,
  CLXXXI (15 Oct. 1987), 152-156

Emeterius   **BA GC**
  (Spanish illuminator, act. ca.
  975)   GC
  (Spanish illuminator, act.970)   BA
  Bibl: Codex Gerundensis, v.1, pp.
  79-87; Domínguez Bordona, Span.
  illumination, v.1, p.15, pl.13;
  ▶Encic. univ. ilus.; SOCIEDAD
  ESPANOLA DE AMIGOS...CODICES
  MINIADOS ESPANOLES (1929),
  p.173
Emett, Rowland *(British artist,*
b.1906)   **WI**
  Bibl: ▶Johnson, Brit. artists
Emil Adam→*see* Adam, Emil
Emil Armin→*see* Armin, Emil
Emil Bisttram→*see* Bisttram, Emil
Emil Carlsen→*see* Carlsen, Emil
Emil Fuchs→*see* Fuchs, Emil
Emil Ganso→*see* Ganso, Emil
Emil Holm→*see* Holm, Emil
Emil Jacobs→*see* Jacobs, Emil
Emil Nolde→*see* Nolde, Emil
Emil Otto Grundmann→*see*
  Grundmann, Emil Otto
Emil Rode→*see* Rode, Emil
Emil Schwabe→*see* Schwabe, Emil
Emile Albert Gruppe→*see* Gruppe,
  Emile-Albert
Emile Auguste Carolus-Duran→*see*
  Carolus-Duran, Emile Auguste
Emile Bernard→*see* Bernard, Emile
Emile Blanche→*see* Blanche, Jacques-
  Emile
Emile Charles Lambinet→*see*
  Lambinet, Emile Charles
Emile Charles Wauters→*see* Wauters,
  Emile Charles
Emile Friant→*see* Friant, Emile
Emile Georges Weiss→*see* Weiss,
  Emile Georges
Emile Louis Vernier→*see* Vernier,
  Emile Louis
Emile Pierre Branchard→*see*
  Branchard, Emile Pierre
Emile Troncy→*see* Troncy, Emile
Emile van Marcke de Lummen→*see*
  Marcke de Lummen, Emile van
Emile Victor Cartier→*see* Cartier,
  Emile Victor
Emilie Charmy→*see* Charmy, Emilie
Emilio Pettoruti→*see* Pettoruti,
  Emilio
Emilio Sanchez Perrier→*see* Sánchez
  Perrier, Emilio
Emilio [Unidentified] *(Unknown*
painter)   **PR**
  Bibl: (July 15, 1809, lot 270,
  Phillips (Harry))
Emily Burling Waite→*see* Waite,
  Emily Burling
Emin, Evelyne *(French real estate*
developer)   **AV**
  Bibl: AMC, 1988 Oct., no.22,
  p.122

Emin, Patrick *(French real estate*
developer)   **AV**
  Bibl: AMC, 1988 Oct., no.22,
  p.122
Eminente, Grazia *(French*
photographer, 20th c.)   **BA**
  Bibl: Berlin (DEU), Akademie der
  Kunste, GRAZIA EMINENTE-
  EDOUARDO ARROYO... (1976)
Emk(?), J.M. van *(Dutch artist, 18th*
cent.)   **WC**
Emler, Bonaventura *(German artist,*
1831-1862)   **WC**
Emma Ciardi→*see* Ciardi, Emma
Emma McHenry Pond→*see* Pond,
  Emma McHenry
Emmanuel (Emmanuel Tzane)→*see*
  Zane, Emanuel
Emmanuel Decritz→*see* Decritz,
  Emmanuel
Emmanuele da Lampardo *(Italian*
artist, 16th cent.)   **WC**
Emmanuella de Matteis→*see*
  Matteis, Emmanuella de
Emmel, Andreas *(German*
goldsmith, 1759-after 1820)   **BA**
  Bibl: Heppe, WELTKUNST LII/18
  (15 Sept 1982) 2441-2443;
  Scheffler, Goldschmiede
  Rheinland-Westfalens, v.1, p.94
Emmelraet, Philip Augustyn I→*see*
  Immenraet, Philips Augustyn
Emmenegger, Hans   **BA WC**
  (Swiss artist, 1866-1940)   WC
  (Swiss painter, printmaker,
  1866-1940)   BA
  Bibl: ▶Bénézit; ▶Busse, Maler u.
  Bildhauer 19. Jahr.; ▶Schweiz.
  Künst.-Lex.; ▶Thieme-Becker
Emmerich, Charles-Louis *(French*
silversmith, master 1779)   **GC**
  Bibl: ▶Mabille, Orfèv. fran.
Emmerik, Govert van *(Dutch*
painter, 1808-1882)   **GC**
  Bibl: ▶Thieme-Becker
Emmerling, Mary Ellisor *(American*
interior designer)   **AV**
  Bibl: ▶Libr. of Congr. Name Auth.
  File
Emmerson, C.L., Col., Mrs., (Gladys
  Emma)→*see* Peto, Gladys Emma
Emmerson, Henry H.→*see* Emmerson,
  Henry Hetherington
Emmerson, Henry Hetherington **BA WI**
  (British artist, 1831-1895)   WI
  (British artist, op.1851-m.1895)   WC
  (British painter, 1831-1895)   BA
  Bibl: ▶Bénézit; ▶Johnson, Brit.
  artists; ▶Thieme-Becker
Emmerson, Henry H.   **WC**
Emmerson, Roger Frank *(British*
architect, Edinburgh)   **AV**
  Bibl: ▶RIBA members, 1987
Emmet→*see* Emmet, Lydia Field
Emmet family *(American artists,*
.19th-20th cs.)   **BA**
  Bibl: ▶Thieme-Becker

Emmet, Ellen G. → see Rand, Ellen Emmet

Emmet, Jane Erin → see De Glehn, Jane Erin

Emmet, Lydia Field   **BA PR WI**
  (American artist, 1866-)   **WC**
  (American artist, 1886-1952)   **WI**
  (American painter, 1866-1952)   **BA PR**
  Bibl: ▶Bénézit; ▶Collins, Women
    artists Amer.; ▶Fielding's Amer.
    ptrs.; ▶RILA/BHA;
    ▶Thieme-Becker; ▶Young, Amer.
    artists
  Emmet   **PR**
Emmet, Lydia. Field   **WC**
  Emmett, Lydia Field   **PR**
  Lydia Field Emmet   **PR**
Emmet, Lydia. Field → see Emmet,
  Lydia Field
Emmet, Rosina → see Sherwood,
  Rosina Emmet
Emmet, Rosina, Miss → see Sherwood,
  Rosina Emmet
Emmett, Lydia Field → see Emmet,
  Lydia Field

Emminger, Eberhard *(German
  artist, 1808-1885)*   **WC**
Emmons, Alexander H. → see
  Emmons, Alexander Hamilton
Emmons, Alexander Hamilton   **WI**
  (American artist, 1816-1879)   **WC WI**
Emmons, Alexander H.   **WC**
Emmons, Audrey *(American
  architect, San Francisco, CA)*   **AV**
  Bibl: ▶AIA Pro File, 1983
Emmons, Chansonetta Stanley
  *(American photographer, 1858-
  1937)*   **BA**
  Bibl: ▶Fogg Mus. Libr. cat.;
    ▶Macmillan photog. encyc.;
    ▶Parry, Photo idx.
Emmons, Donn *(American architect)* **AV**
Emmons, Frederick Earl *(American
  architect, partner in firm of Jones
  and Emmons, 1907-)*   **AV**
  Bibl: ▶Amer. archts. dir., 1970
Emmons, Nathaniel *(American
  artist, 1702-1740)*   **WC WI**
Emmons, Sylvia   **WC WI**
  (British artist, 1938-)   **WC**
  (British artist, b.1938)   **WI**
Emmons, Thomas *(American
  cabinetmaker, d.1825)*   **BA**
  Bibl: Antiques, CVII/5 (May 1975)
    pp.878-887; ▶Bjerkoe,
    Cabinetmkrs. Amer.
Emms, John *(British artist, 1843-
  1912)*   **WC WI**
  Bibl: ▶Mallalieu, Brit. watercolour
    artists
Emonds, P. *(French, active Paris mid-
  19th century)*   **JG**
Emons → see Emons, Jan
  [Unidentified]

Emons, Jan [Unidentified]
  *(Unknown painter, act. 17th
  century)*   **PR**
  Bibl: Schoonsteen inventory 1647
  Emons   **PR**
  Jan Emons   **PR**
Emont, Adriaen van → see Eemont,
  Adriaen van
Emory, Walter Leavitt *(American
  architect, Honolulu, 1868-1929)*   **AV**
  Bibl: ▶Withey, Amer. archts.
Emperaire, Achille   **BA WC**
  (French artist, 19th cent.)   **WC**
  (French painter, 1829-1898)   **BA**
  Bibl: ▶Bénézit
Emplmann, Franz *(Austrian
  goldsmith, act.1686, d.1707)*   **BA**
  Bibl: Simoniti, Zbornik za
    umetnostno zgodovino XVII
    (1981) 75-87
Empoli → see Jacopo da Empoli
  (Jacopo Chimenti)
Empoli, Jacopo da → see Jacopo da
  Empoli (Jacopo Chimenti)
Emporion Painter   **GC**
  Bibl: ▶Beazley, Attic bl.-fig. vase-
    ptrs.
Emrich de Podestá, Sylvio
  (Brazilian architect)   **AV**
  Bibl: Projeto, 1985 Mar., no.73,
    p.70
Ems, Rudolf von *(Austrian, ca.
  1200-1254)*   **JG**
Emslie, Alfred Edward   **WC WI**
  (British artist, 1848-1918)   **WI**
  (British artist, 1848-p.1897)   **WC**
Emslie, John Phillipps *(British
  painter, printmaker, 1839-1913)*   **BA**
  Bibl: ▶Fogg Mus. Libr. cat.;
    ▶Johnson, Brit. artists; ▶Mallalieu,
    Brit. watercolour artists; ▶Natl.
    union cat., pre-1956;
    ▶Thieme-Becker; V & A libr. cat.
Emslie, Rosalie *(British artist,
  b.1891)*   **WI**
Encarnacion, Mario Teruel
  (American artist, 20th c.)   **BA**
  Bibl: Leonhart, M.M., in NEW ART
    EXAMINER XI/2 (Nov 1983) 9
Encke, Erdmann *(German sculptor,
  1843-1896)*   **BA**
  Bibl: ▶Allgem. Deut. Biog.; ▶Busse,
    Maler u. Bildhauer 19. Jahr.;
    ▶Thieme-Becker
Encke, Fedor   **PR WC**
  (German artist, 1851-1926)   **WC**
  (German painter, 1851-1926)   **PR**
  Bibl: ▶Thieme-Becker; ▶Witt
    checklist
  Fedor Encke   **PR**
Enckell, Knut Magnus   **BA WC**
  (Finnish artist, 1870-1925)   **WC**
  (Finnish painter, 1870-1925)   **BA**
  Bibl: ▶Bénézit;
    TAIDEHISTORIALLISIA
    TUTKIMUKSIA III (1977) 115;
    ▶Thieme-Becker

End, Henry *(British-born designer
  based in Coral Gables, FL, 1915-)*   **AV**
  Bibl: Interior design, 1984 Jan.,
    v.55, no.1, p.182
Ende *(Spanish illuminator, act. ca.
  975)*   **GC**
  Bibl: Codex Gerundensis, v.1, pp.
    79-87; Getty Photo Study Coll.
    (Medieval)
  Nun Ende   **GC**
Ende *(Spanish illuminator, act.975)*   **BA**
  Bibl: ▶D'Ancona, Miniaturistes;
    Miner, Ptg. in Europe 800-1200
  Erde   **BA**
Ende, Edgar *(German artist, 1901-
  1965)*   **WC**
Ende, Felix von *(German¯painter,
  b.1856)*   **GC**
  Bibl: ▶Thieme-Becker
Ende, Hans am → see Am Ende, Hans
Ende, Hans an → see Am Ende, Hans
Ende, Hermann *(German architect,
  Berlin; partner of Wilhelm
  Bockmann, 1860-1895, 1829-1907)*   **AV**
  Bibl: ▶Thieme-Becker
**Ende, Johann or Hans Heinrich am
  (not Amende, Amendo or A.M.
  Ende)** *(German artist, 1645-1695)*   **WC**
Ende, Johanna Maria van den
  (Dutch painter, 1819-1853)   **GC**
  Bibl: ▶Scheen, Ned. beeldende
    kunst.
Endell, August   **BA**
  *(German architect and
    theoretical writer, 1871-1925)*   **AV**
  *(German architect, designer,
    author, 1871-1925)*   **BA**
  Bibl: ▶Avery Libr. cat.; ▶Busse,
    Maler u. Bildhauer 19. Jahr.;
    ▶Neue deutsche Biog.; ▶Vollmer,
    Künst.-Lex. 20. Jhr.; ▶WW Arch.
Endell, August.   **AV**
  Endell, Ernst Moritz August   **BA**
Endell, August. → see Endell, August
Endell, Ernst Moritz August → see
  Endell, August
*Enden, Ende or Eynde, Martinus, I
  van den* → see Enden, Martin I van
  den
Enden, Martin I van den   **BA**
  (Flemish artist, op.1630-1654)   **WC**
  *(Flemish print publisher,
    printmaker, act.1630-1654)*   **BA**
  Bibl: ▶Thieme-Becker; ▶Witt
    checklist; ▶Wurzbach, NLD
    Künst.-Lex.
**Enden, Ende or Eynde,
  Martinus, I van den**   **WC**
Ender → see Ender, Johann Nepomuk
Ender, Boris → see Ender, Boris
  Vladimirovič

Ender, Boris Vladimirovič   **BA**
(Russian artist, 20th cent.)   **WC**
(Russian painter, printmaker, 1893-1960)   **BA**
Bibl: ▶Bowlt, Russian avant-garde; Rome (ITA), Caliografia Nazionale BORIS ENDER (1977)

Ender, Boris   **WC**
Ender, Eduard   **BA WC**
(Austrian painter, 1822-1883)   **BA**
(German artist, 1822-1883)   **WC**
Bibl: ▶Busse, Maler u. Bildhauer 19. Jahr.; ▶Fuchs, Öst. Maler 19. Jahrh.; ▶Thieme-Becker

Ender, Johann → see Ender, Johann Nepomuk

Ender, Johann Nepomuk   **BA GC PR WC**
(Austrian painter, 1793-1854)   **BA GC PR**
(German artist, 1793-1854)   **WC**
Bibl: ▶Bénézit; ▶Busse, Maler u. Bildhauer 19. Jahr.; ▶Fuchs, Öst. Maler 19. Jahrh.; ▶RILA/BHA; ▶Thieme-Becker
Ender   **PR**
Ender, Johann   **PR**
Johann Nepomuk Ender   **PR**

Ender, Ksenija *(Russian painter, 1895-1955)*   **BA**
Bibl: ▶Petteys, Women artists; WOMEN ARTISTS NEWS,VII/4/(Jan-Feb 1982) 58

Ender, Rosa *(German artist, 1903-)*   **WC**
Ender, Thomas   **BA GC WC**
(Austrian painter and draughtsman, 1793-1875)   **GC**
(Austrian painter, printmaker, 1793-1875)   **BA**
(German artist, 1793-1875)   **WC**
Bibl: ▶Fuchs, Öst. Maler 19. Jahrh.; Getty Photo Study Coll.; Koschatzky, W.: THOMAS ENDER..., 1982; ▶Libr. of Congr. Name Auth. File; ▶Thieme-Becker; ▶Witt checklist

Enderle, Anton *(German artist, 18th cent.)*   **WC**
Enderle, Johann Baptist   **BA GC WC**
(German artist, 1725-1798)   **WC**
(German painter, 1725-1798)   **BA GC**
Bibl: ▶Neue deutsche Biog.; ▶RILA/BHA; ▶Thieme-Becker

Enderlein, Caspar *(Swiss pewterer in Germany, 1560-1633)*   **BA**
Bibl: ▶Thieme-Becker
Ederlein, Caspar   **BA**
Endterlein, Caspar   **BA**
Enterlin, Caspar   **BA**

Enders, Jean Joseph *(French artist, 1862-c.1930)*   **WC**
Endicott   **WC WI**
(American artist, op.1846)   **WC**
(American artist, op.1846-)   **WI**

Endlinger, Johann *(German artist, 1733-1789)*   **WC**
Endner, Gustav Georg *(German artist, 1754-1824)*   **WC**

Endo, Sei'ichi *(Japanese architect)*   **AV**
Endo, Takao *(Japanese architect, 1941-)*   **AV**
Bibl: Kenchiku bunka, 1987 Dec., v.42, no.494, p.64

Endogouroff, Jean (Jendoguroff) *(Russian artist, 1861-1898)*   **WC**
Endoios *(Greek sculptor, act. ca.530-500 BC)*   **GC**
Bibl: ▶Bowder, WWW Greek, p.102

Endre *(French artist, 20th cent.)*   **WC**
Endre, Béla *(Hungarian painter, potter, designer, 1874-1928)*   **BA**
Bibl: ▶Busse, Maler u. Bildhauer 19. Jahr.; ▶Uj magyar lexikon; ▶Vollmer, Künst.-Lex. 20. Jhr.

Endrikat, Klaus *(German printmaker, b.1939)*   **BA**
Bibl: ▶WW Arts DEU

Endsley, Fred Starr *(American photographer, b.1949)*   **BA**
Bibl: ▶WW Amer. Art

Endt, Walter Vom *(German artist, 1925-)*   **WC**
Endterlein, Caspar → see Enderlein, Caspar

Endura *(Spanish scribe, act.954)*   **GC**
Bibl: Millares, Manuscritos visigóticos, p.53, no.110

Enea Salmeggia → see Salmeggia, Enea (il Talpino)

Enerson, Larry *(American architect, 1909-1983)*   **AV**
Bibl: Dimensions, v.4, n.4, Oct. 1983, p.16

Enfantin, Barthelemy-Prosper   **AV GC**
(1796-1864)   **AV**
(French painter, 1796-1864)   **GC**
Bibl: ▶Bénézit

Eng, T. H. *(British architect)*   **AV**
Bibl: Architects' journal, 1989 Aug.23, v.190, no.8-9, p.24

Eng, William *(American architect, Champaign, Ill.; faculty member of the School of Architecture at the U. of Ill. Champaign-Urbana)*   **AV**
Bibl: ▶AIA Pro File, 1987-88

Engalière, Marius   **BA WC**
(French artist, 1824-1857)   **WC**
(French painter, 1824-1857)   **BA**
Bibl: ▶Busse, Maler u. Bildhauer 19. Jahr.; ▶Thieme-Becker

Engebrechtsz, Cornelis → see Engebrechtsz., Cornelis
Engebrechtsz. → see Engebrechtsz., Cornelis

Engebrechtsz., Cornelis   **BA GC PR**
(Dutch, ca. 1465-1527)   **JG**
(early Netherlandish painter, 1468-1533)   **BA**
(Netherlandish painter, 1468-1533)   **PR**
(Netherlands artist, 1468(?)-1533)   **WC**
(North Netherlandish painter, 1468-1533)   **GC**
Bibl: ▶Bénézit; ▶Encyc. world art; ▶RILA/BHA; ▶Thieme-Becker; ▶Wurzbach, NLD Künst.-Lex.
Corn. Enghelbrecht   **PR**
Cornelis Engebrechtsz.   **PR**
Cornelius Engelbrecht   **PR**
Engebrechtsz, Cornelis   **JG**
Engebrechtsz.   **PR**
Engebrechtsz., Engelbertsz., Engelbrechtsen or Engelbrechtsz., Cornelis   **WC**
Engelbertsz, Cornelis   **GC**
Engelbrecht   **PR**
Engelbrechtsen, Cornelis   **GC**
Engelbrechtsz, Cornelis   **PR**
Engelbrechtsz., Cornelis   **BA GC PR**
Enghelbrecht the Old   **GC**
Engebrechtsz., Engelbertsz., Engelbrechtsen or Engelbrechtsz., Cornelis → see Engebrechtsz., Cornelis

Engel, Adolf Karel Maximilian *(Belgian painter, 1801-1833)*   **GC**
Bibl: ▶Bénézit

Engel, Carl (Engel von der Rabenau) *(German artist, 1817-1870)*   **WC**
Engel, Carl Ludwig   **BA**
(German architect in FIN, 1778-1840)   **BA**
(German architect, Finland, 1778-1840)   **AV**
Bibl: ▶Bénézit; BHA/FIN; ▶Brockhaus Enzyk.; ▶Busse, Maler u. Bildhauer 19. Jahr.; Knaurs FINNLAND (1988), 206; ▶Macmillan encyc. archts.; ▶Neue deutsche Biog.; Reclams Kunst Finland, p.323; ▶Thieme-Becker
Engel, Carl Ludwig   **AV**
Engel, Johann Carl Ludwig   **AV BA**
Engel, Carl Ludwig → see Engel, Carl Ludwig

Engel, Dirk Tijse *(Dutch clockmaker, act.ca.1700)*   **BA**
Bibl: ANTIEK VIII/8 (Mar 1974) 627-640

Engel, Gerwin *(Swiss landscape architect, Zurich)*   **AV**
Bibl: Anthos, 1985, v.24, no.1, p.3

Engel, Hans *(German architect, Augsburg)*   **AV**
Bibl: Landscape architecture, 1985 Mar.-Apr., v.75, no.2, p.52

Engel, Jakob   AV BA
- (Court architect, Eichstätt, Germany, 1632-1714)   AV
- (Swiss architect, 1631-1714)   BA
  - Bibl: KDM KANTON BASEL-LANDSCHAFT, index; ▶Libr. of Congr. Name Auth. File; Popé, DOMKIRCHE IN ARLESHEIM, 1941, 11-16; Schmmid, ZEITSCHR. FÜR SCHWEIZ. KUNSTG. XLI/1 (1984) 39
- Angelini, Jacomo   AV
- Angelini, Jacopo   BA

Engel, Johann Carl Ludwig →see Engel, Carl Ludwig

Engel, Johann Friedrich (German artist, 1844-1921)   WC

Engel, Jules (American artist, op. 1966-)   WI

Engel, Otto Heinrich   BA WC
- (German artist, 1866-1949)   WC
- (German painter, printmaker, 1866-1949)   BA
  - Bibl: ▶Bénézit; ▶Busse, Maler u. Bildhauer 19. Jahr.; ▶Vollmer, Künst.-Lex. 20. Jhr.

Engel, Ramon (Spanish architect)   AV
- Bibl: Geometria, 1988, no.6, p.83

Engel, Robert (American, 20th c.)   BA
- Bibl: Santa Barbara (CA, USA), Mus. Art, Etchings of Rembrandt & His Followers (1978)

Engel, Tom (American painter, 20th c.)   BA
- Bibl: JOURNAL SO. CALIF 27 (Juen-July 1980) 23-24

Engel, Wolfgang (West German architect, Berlin)   AV
- Bibl: Techniques & architecture, 1989 June-July, no.384, p.136

Engelberg, Burkhard (German architect, ca.1450-1512)   BA
- Bibl: Kauffmann, Kunst des 16. Jahrhs. (Prop. Kunst. 8); ▶Neue deutsche Biog.; ▶Thieme-Becker
- Engelberger, Burkhard   BA

Engelberger, Burkhard →see Engelberg, Burkhard

Engelbert, S.   GC WC
- (Dutch artist, op.1751)   WC
- (Dutch draughtsman, act.1751)   GC
  - Bibl: ▶Witt checklist

Engelberts, Willem Jodocus Mattheus (Dutch draughtsman, 1809-1887)   GC
- Bibl: ▶Thieme-Becker

Engelbertsz, Cornelis →see Engebrechtsz., Cornelis

Engelbrecht →see Engebrechtsz., Cornelis

Engelbrecht, Martin   BA WC
- (German artist, 1684-1756)   WC
- (German printmaker, 1684-1756)   BA
  - Bibl: ▶Neue deutsche Biog.; ▶Thieme-Becker

Engelbrecht, Pieter (Dutch sculptor, carver)   AV
- Bibl: Country life, 1988 Oct.13, v.182, no.41, p.218

Engelbrechtsen, Cornelis →see Engebrechtsz., Cornelis

Engelbrechtsz, Cornelis →see Engebrechtsz., Cornelis

Engelbrechtsz., Cornelis →see Engebrechtsz., Cornelis

Engelen, Peter van   GC WC
- (Flemish artist, 1664-1711)   WC
- (Flemish painter, 1664-1711)   GC
  - Bibl: ▶Thieme-Becker

Engelen, Piet van (Belgian artist, 1863-1924)   WC

Engelhard →see Engelhard, Elizabeth

Engelhard, Elizabeth (American painter, 1893-aft.1945)   PR
- Bibl: ▶Petteys, Women artists
- Elizabeth Engelhard   PR
- Engelhard   PR

Engelhardt, Heinrich Adolph (Canadian landscape architect, 1830-1897)   AV
- Bibl: Society for the Study of Architecture in Canada. Bulletin, 1986 Sept., v.11, no.3, p.16

Engelhart, Catherine (Catherine Amyot) (Danish artist, 1845-)   WC

Engelhart, Josef   BA WC
- (Austrian painter, sculptor, printmaker, 1864-1941)   BA
- (German artist, 1864-1941)   WC
  - Bibl: ▶Bénézit; ▶Fuchs, Öst. Maler 19. Jahrh.; ▶Thieme-Becker; ▶Vollmer, Künst.-Lex. 20. Jhr.

Engelheart, Francis (British artist, 1775-1849)   WC WI

Engelman, Martin (French artist, 20th cent.)   WC

Engelman, Martin (Dutch painter, b.1924)   GC
- Bibl: ▶Bénézit

Engelmann, Gottfried   GC
- (German artist, 1788-1839)   WC
- (German, 1788-1839)   GC
  - Bibl: ▶Thieme-Becker; ▶Witt checklist

Engelmann, Gottfried or Godefroy   WC

Engelmann, Gottfried or Godefroy →see Engelmann, Gottfried

Engelmann, Paul (Austrian architect, Vienna)   AV
- Bibl: AMC, 1986 Oct., no.13, p.88

Engels, Bartholomeus (Dutch painter, act. ca.1656)   PR
- Bibl: ▶Thieme-Becker
- B. Engelz.   PR
- Bartholomeus Engels   PR

Engels, Friedrich (1820-1895)   AV
- Bibl: ▶Libr. of Congr. Name Auth. File

Engels, Jan Baptiste (Flemish, act. ca.1750)   GC
- Bibl: Getty Photo Study Coll.; ▶Thieme-Becker
- Engels, Joannes Baptista   GC

Engels, Joannes Baptista →see Engels, Jan Baptiste

Engels, L. (Netherlands artist, 17th cent.)   WC

Engels, Pieter   BA WC
- (Dutch artist, 1938)   WC
- (Dutch artist, b.1938)   BA
  - Bibl: ▶Bénézit; ▶MoMA libr. cat.; Rotterdam (NLD), Mus. Boymans-van Beuningen, PIETER ENGELS

Engelson, Carol (American painter, b.1944)   BA
- Bibl: ▶Intl. dir. exh. artists, 1982

Engelsz., Cornelis   BA GC
- (Dutch artist, 1575-c.1642/53)   WC
- (Dutch painter, 1575-ca.1650)   GC
- (Dutch painter, ca.1574/75-1650)   BA
  - Bibl: ▶Bénézit; Haarlem (NLD), Frans Halsmuseum, J.C. Verspronck (1979); ▶RILA/BHA; ▶Seyn, Écoles flam. et holl.; ▶Thieme-Becker; ▶Winkler Prins van de kunst; ▶Witt checklist; ▶Wurzbach, NLD Künst.-Lex.

Engelsz., Cornelis (Cornelis Engelsz. Verspronck)   WC
- Verspronck, Cornelis Engelsz.   GC

Engelsz., Cornelis (Cornelis Engelsz. Verspronck) →see Engelsz., Cornelis

Engelund, Svend (Danish painter, b.1908)   BA
- Bibl: ▶Nørregård-Nielsen, Dansk kunst

Engene Antoine Samuel Lavieille →see Lavieille, Eugène Antoine Samuel

Enger, Erling (Norwegian artist, 20th cent.)   WC

Engers, Lauzero (French artist, 20th cent.)   WC

Engert →see Engert, Erasmus

Engert, Erasmus   BA PR
- (Austrian painter, 1796-1871)   BA PR
- (German artist, 1796-1871)   WC
  - Bibl: ▶Bénézit; ▶Busse, Maler u. Bildhauer 19. Jahr.; ▶RILA/BHA; ▶Thieme-Becker
- Engert   PR

Engert, Erasmus Ritter von   WC
Engert, Erasmus, Ritter von   BA PR
- Erasmus Engert   PR
- Erasmus, Ritter von Engert   PR

Engert, Erasmus Ritter von →see Engert, Erasmus

Engert, Erasmus, Ritter von →see Engert, Erasmus

Engert, Ernst Moritz (German
  printmaker, b.1892) **BA**
    Bibl: Bonn (DEU), Reinisches
    Landesmuseum, ERNST MORITZ
    ENGERT (1977); ▶Vollmer,
    Künst.-Lex. 20. Jhr.

Engerth, Eduard von **WC**
  (German artist, 1818-1897) WC
  (German artist, 19th cent.) WC
  Eugerthe, Eduard von **WC**

Engesaeter, Erick (Norwegian in
  USA, act.1860-1870) **BA**
    Bibl: Minn. Inst. Arts Bull., LXIII
    (1976-1977), pp.63-73

Engh, Pål-Henry (Norwegian
  architect, Oslo) **AV**
    Bibl: Norske Ark. Lands. Årbok
    1987

Enghelbert (Flemish painter, 17th c.) **BA**
    Bibl: Díaz Padrón, Arch. esp. de
    arte, LV/220 (Oct-Dec 1982) 375-
    382

Enghelbrecht the Old→see
Engebrechtsz., Cornelis

Engkvist, Olle (Swedish architect) **AV**
    Bibl: Abitare, 1982 Nov., no.209,
    p.82

Engl, Joseph B. (German artist,
  1867-1907) **WC**

England, Jane (Australian
  photographer, b.1950) **BA**
    Bibl: Arts Council GBR, Summer
    Show 4 (1977)

England, Richard (Maltese architect,
  1937-) **AV**
    Bibl: ▶Contemp. archts.

England, William (British
  photographer, d.1896) **BA**
    Bibl: ▶MoMA libr. cat.; ▶Parry,
    Photo idx.; ▶Rosenblum, World
    hist. photog.

Englast, Thomas→see Ölgast,
Thomas

Engle, Horace (American
  mineralogist, photographer, 1861-
  1949) **BA**
    Bibl: Hist. of Photography I/1 (Jan
    1977) 17-30; ▶Rosenblum, World
    hist. photog.

Engle, Reed Lawrence (American
  landscape architect, Philadelphia,
  Penn) **AV**
    Bibl: Garden design, 1988
    Summer, v.7, no.2, p.38

Engledow, Susan (British artist,
  b.1947) **WI**

Englefield, Henry Charles (British
  artist, 1752-1822) **WI**

Engleheart, George (British artist,
  1752-1829) **WC WI**

Engleheart, Henry (British artist,
  1801-1885) **WC WI**

Engleheart, John Cox Dillman
  (British artist, 1783-1862) **WC WI**

Engleheart, Timothy Stansfeld→see
Engleheart, Timothy Stansfeld

Engleheart, Timothy Stansfield **WI**
  (British artist, 1803-1879) WC WI
  Engleheart, Timothy Stansfeld **WC**

Engleman, C.F. **WI**
  (American artist, op.1814-1831) WC
  (American artist, op.circa 1814-) WI

Engwiman, C.F. **WC**

Engler, Otto (German architect,
  1861-1940) **BA**
    Bibl: Grunsky, Otto Engler
    Geschafts... (1977);
    ▶Thieme-Becker

Englert, Rudolf (German painter,
  printmaker, b.1921) **BA**
    Bibl: Krefeld (DEU), Kaiser WIlhelm
    Museum, RUDOLF ENGLERT
    (1975)

Englerth, Emil (German artist,
  1882-) **WC**

English William→see William the
Englishman

English, Don (American, active
  Hollywood 1932 -) **JG**

English, Frank F. (American painter,
  b.1854) **BA**
    Bibl: ▶Fielding's Amer. ptrs.;
    ▶Mallett's idx. artists; ▶Young,
    Amer. artists

English, Frederick (British artist, op.
  1845-) **WI**

English, Grace (British artist, 1891-
  1956) **WI**

English, James Turner (British
  painter, printmaker, b.1916) **BA**
    Bibl: Bristol (GBR), Arnolfini
    Gallery, Bristol sample (1979)

English, Josias **WC WI**
  (British artist, c.1630-1718) WC
  (British artist, circa 1630-circa
  1718) WI

English, Michael **BA WI**
  (British artist, b.1941) WI
  (British painter, printmaker,
  b.1941) BA
    Bibl: ▶Intl. dir. exh. artists, 1982,
    1983

Englund, Lars (Swedish sculptor,
  b.1933) **BA**
    Bibl: ▶Intl. dir. exh. artists

Engman, Robert (American sculptor,
  b.1927) **BA**
    Bibl: ▶MoMA libr. cat.

Engonopoulos, Nicos (Greek artist,
  1910-) **WC**

Engqvist, Hans Henrik (Danish
  architect, b.1912) **BA**
    Bibl: ▶Weilbach, Kunst.leks.

Engramelle, R.P. (French artist, 18th
  cent.) **WC**

Engst, Georg (West German artist,
  1930-) **AV**
    Bibl: RLIN BKS file, CSUG

Engstrand, Bertil (Swedish
  architect, Stockholm, 1922-) **AV**
    Bibl: ▶Svenska Ark. Riks., 1984

Engstrom the Elder, Leander
  (Swedish artist, 1886-1927) **WC**

**Engstrom, Albert Laurentius
  Johannes** (Swedish artist, 1869-
  1940) **WC**

Engstrøm, Jytte Saabye (Danish
  architect, Hellerup, 1945-) **AV**
    Bibl: ▶Danske Arkitekters
    Landsforbund, 1984-85

Enguerrand Charonton→see Quarton,
Enguerrand

Enguídanos, Tomás López→see
López Enguídanos, Tomás

Engwiman, C.F.→see Engleman, C.F.

Enhuber, Carl→see Enhuber, Karl von

Enhuber, Karl von **GC**
  (German artist, 1811-1867) WC
  (German painter, 1811-1867) GC
    Bibl: ▶Thieme-Becker

Enhuber, Carl **WC**

Enid, Lorraine (Puerto Rican
  sculptor, b.1946) **BA**
    Bibl: Springfield (MA, USA), MFA,
    Clay from Puerto Rico (1980)

Enjolras, Christian (French
  architect) **AV**
    Bibl: AMC, 1988 Apr., no.20,
    p.90

Enjolras, Delphin (French artist,
  1857-) **WC**

Enneking→see Enneking, John Joseph

Enneking, John J.→see Enneking,
John Joseph

Enneking, John Joseph **BA PR WC WI**
  (American artist, 1841-1916) WC WI
  (American painter, 1841-1916) BA PR
    Bibl: ▶Fielding's Amer. ptrs.,
    1983; ▶RILA/BHA; ▶Young, Amer.
    artists
  Eankening, John Joseph PR
  Enneking PR
  Enneking, John J. PR
  John Joseph Enneking PR

Enness, Augustus William **WC WI**
  (British artist, 1876-) WC
  (British artist, 1876-1948) WI

Ennis, George Pearse (American
  artist, 1884-1936) **WC WI**

Ennis, Jacob **WC WI**
  (British artist, 1728-1770) WI
  (British artist, 1728-1771) WC

Ennis, T.J. (American, 1815-after
  1856, daguerreotypist) **JG**

Enns, Maureen (Canadian painter,
  sculptor, photography, 20th c.) **BA**
    Bibl: ▶Artists Canada; ▶Intl. dir.
    exh. artists, 1982, 1983

Eno, Brian (British composer,
  musician, artist in USA, b.1948) **BA**
    Bibl: WW Amer.

Enoch Seemann (the younger)→see
Seemann, Enoch II

Enoch Wood Perry→see Perry, Enoch
Wood

Enock, Arthur Henry *(British artist, op.1869-1912)* **WI**
Bibl: ▶Wood, Victorian ptrs.

Enomoto, Fumio *(Japanese designer)* **AV**
Bibl: Architecture intérieure créé, 1988 Oct.-Nov., no.226, p.112

Enos, Raoul *(American, 1944 -)* **JG**

Enri, Helene Berlewi *(French artist, 1873-)* **WC**

Enrico Coleman → see Coleman, Enrico

Enrico Cornelio Uroom → see Vroom, Hendrick Cornelisz.

Enrico Cornelio Uroom d'Atleme in Olanda, d. Enrico Spagnolo → see Vroom, Hendrick Cornelisz.

Enrico da Amsterdam *(Italian scribe, act. ca.1486)* **GC**
Bibl: Fava, Tesori, p.359

Enrico da Monreale (Erroneously called Monteregali) *(Italian artist, 15th cent.)* **WC**

Enrico di Tedice **GC**
(Italian artist, op.1254) **WC**
(Italian, act.1254) **GC**
Bibl: ▶Thieme-Becker; ▶Witt checklist

Tedice, Enrico di **WC**

Enrico fiamenco → see Hendricksz., Dirck, Teodoro d'Errico

Enrico Fiamengho → see Hendricksz., Dirck, Teodoro d'Errico

Enrico Fiamengo → see Hendricksz., Dirck, Teodoro d'Errico

Enrico Fiammingo → see Hendricksz., Dirck, Teodoro d'Errico

Enrico Oide' → see Oidè, Enrico [Unidentified]

Enrico Scifoni → see Scifoni, Enrico

Enrico Spagnolo → see Vroom, Hendrick Cornelisz.

Enrico, Giovanni d' → see D'Enrico, Giovanni

Enright, Walter Joseph *(American artist, b.1879)* **WI**

Enrigo Fiammingo → see Hendricksz., Dirck, Teodoro d'Errico

Enriques, Nicolas → see Enriquez, Nicolas

Enriquez, Nicolas **GC PR**
(Mexican artist, op.1738-m. 1780) **WC**
(Mexican painter, act. 1738-1770) **PR**
(Mexican, act.1738-1770) **GC**
Bibl: ▶Thieme-Becker; ▶Witt checklist

Enriques, Nicolas **WC**
Nicolas Enriquez **PR**

Enschedé, Christina Gérarda
(Dutch draughtsman, 1791-1873) **GC**
Bibl: ▶Thieme-Becker

Enschedé, Sandrina Christina Elisabeth E. *(Dutch draughtsman, 1794-1871)* **GC**
Bibl: ▶Bénézit; ▶Thieme-Becker
Troyen, Sandrina Christina Elisabeth van **GC**

Ensel *(French artist, 20th cent.)* **WC**

Enseñat Benlliure, L. *(Spanish architect)* **AV**
Bibl: Lotus international, 1989, no.59, p.38

Ensinck, Charles Victor → see Ensinck, Karel Victor

Ensinck, Karel Victor **GC**
(Dutch artist, 1846-1914) **WC**
(Dutch, 1846-1914) **GC**
Bibl: ▶Witt checklist
Ensinck, Charles Victor **GC**

Ensinck, Karel Victor (Charles Victor) **WC**
Ensinck, Karel Victor (Charles Victor) → see Ensinck, Karel Victor

Ensingen, Ulrich von *(German architect, ca.1350-1419)* **BA**
Bibl: ▶Portoghesi, Diz. arch. e urbanistica; ▶Thieme-Becker

Enslen, Carl Georg *(German artist, 1792-1866)* **WC**

Enslen, Johann Carl *(German artist, 1759-1848)* **WC**

Enslin Du Plessis → see Du Plessis, Enslin

Ensom, William *(Engraver, 1796-1832)* **WI**

Ensor → see Ensor, James

Ensor, James **BA GC JG PR WC**
(Belgian artist, 1860-1949) **WC**
(Belgian painter, 1860-1949) **PR**
(Belgian painter, printmaker, 1860-1949) **BA**
(Belgian, 1860-1949) **GC JG**
Bibl: ▶Bénézit; ▶Encyc. world art; ▶Kindlers Malerei Lex.; ▶RILA/BHA; ▶Thieme-Becker; ▶Witt checklist
Baron James Ensor **PR**
Ensor **PR**

Ensor, James, Baron **PR**
James Ensor **PR**
Ensor, James, Baron → see Ensor, James

Ensor, Mary *(British artist, op.1863-1897)* **WI**

Ensor, R. **WC WI**
(British artist, 20th cent.) **WC**
(British artist, op.20th c.) **WI**

Ensslen, Harald B. *(Canadian architect, Toronto)* **AV**
Bibl: Canadian architect, 1987 Aug., v.32, no.8, p.34

Enterlin, Caspar → see Enderlein, Caspar

Entwisle, William → see Entwistle, William

Entwistle, William **WI**
(British artist, 1943-) **WC**
(British artist, b.1943) **WI**

Entwisle, William **WC**

Enyeart, James Lyle *(American photographer, b.1943)* **BA**
Bibl: Lawrence (KS, USA), U. Kansas Mus. Art, Language of light (1974); ▶Macmillan photog. encyc.; ▶WW Amer. Art, 1986

Enzenhofer, Franz *(Austrian architect)* **AV**
Bibl: Detail, 1985 Jan.-Feb., v.25, no.1, p.29

Enzensberger, Entzensperger, Enzenberger or Enzensperger, Johann Baptist → see Enzensberger, Johann Baptist

Enzensberger, Johann Baptist **BA**
(German artist, 1733-1773) **WC**
(German painter, printmaker, 1732-1773) **BA**
Bibl: ▶Bénézit; Ohm und Reber, Festschrift fur P.W. Meister, p.155; ▶Thieme-Becker

Enzensberger, Entzensperger, Enzenberger or Enzensperger, Johann Baptist **WC**

Enzer, Joseph *(Scottish plasterer, 18th century)* **AV**
Bibl: Country life, 1986 Nov.20, v.180, no.4657, p.1621

Enzinger, Anton *(German artist, c.1683-1768)* **WC**

Enzinger, Hans *(Austrian artist, 1889-)* **WC**

Enzola, Gianfrancesco di Luca *(Italian goldsmith, medalist, act. 1456, d. after 1513)* **BA**
Bibl: ▶Forrer, Medallists; ▶Thieme-Becker

Eolli → see Joli, Antonio

Eondekoeter, Melchior de → see Hondecoeter, Melchior d'

Eosander, Johann Friedrich **BA**
(Danish architect, ca.1670-1729) **BA**
(Danish artist, c.1670-1729) **WC**
Bibl: ▶Portoghesi, Diz. arch. e urbanistica; ▶Thieme-Becker

Eosander, Johann Friedrich (Freiherr von Goethe) **WC**
Eosander, Johann Friedrich (Freiherr von Goethe) → see Eosander, Johann Friedrich

Eottes, Hans → see Ewouts, Hans

Ep'rem **JG**

Epeleios Painter **GC JG**
(vase-painter, ca. 530-500 BC) **GC**
Bibl: ▶Beazley, Attic red-fig. vase-ptrs.; Richter, Attic red-fig. vases

Ephedrismos Painter **JG**

Ephoros of Ephesos *(Greek painter, 4th c BC)* **GC**
Bibl: Getty Photo Study Coll.; ▶Robertson, Greek art, p.492

Ephraim *(Byzantine painter, 12th c.)* **BA**
Bibl: ▶Bénézit; ▶Thieme-Becker

Ephraim, Nathan Veitel Heine
*(German jeweler, banker, 1703-
1775)* **BA**
Bibl: Baedekers Berlin (1965) 270;
▶Neue deutsche Biog.

Epidromos Painter *(vase-painter, ca.
530-500 BC)* **GC**
Bibl: ▶Beazley, Attic red-fig. vase-
ptrs.; Richter, Attic red-fig. vases

Epigenes *(Greek potter, 450-420 BC)* **GC**
Bibl: ▶Beazley, Attic red-fig. vase-
ptrs., p.1247

Epignote Painter **GC**
Bibl: ▶Beazley, Attic bl.-fig. vase-
ptrs.

Epigonos *(Greek sculptor, 3rd c BC
(?))* **GC**
Bibl: Getty Photo Study Coll.;
▶Robertson, Greek art, p.533

Epiktetos → see Epiktetos II

Epiktetos II **BA**
(Greek vase painter, 6th c. B.C.) **BA**
(vase-painter, ca. 520-490 BC) **GC**
Bibl: ▶Beazley, Attic red-fig. vase-
ptrs.; Boardman, Athenian Red-
fig. Vases, Archaic Per.; ▶Encyc.
world art

Epiktetos **GC JG**
Epilykos Class **JG**
Epimedes Painter **GC**
Bibl: ▶Beazley, Attic red-fig. vase-
ptrs.

Epimenes *(Greek seal engraver, 5th
c BC (ca.500-480))* **GC**
Bibl: ▶Robertson, Greek art, p.148

Epimines **JG**

Epinat, Fleury *(French painter, 1764-
1830)* **GC**
Bibl: ▶Bénézit

Epinay, Prosper II, comte d'
*(French sculptor, caricaturist,
1836-1914)* **BA**
Bibl: ▶Artist biog. master idx.;
▶Bénézit; ▶Dict. biog. fran.;
▶Houfe, Brit. book illus.;
▶Thieme-Becker

Episcopio, Giustino *(Italian painter,
act.1527, d.1609)* **BA**
Bibl: ▶Bénézit; ▶Bolaffi; TCI
Marche; ▶Thieme-Becker; Urbino
(ITA), Gall. Naz. delle Marche
1631-1981 (1981)
Lavolini, Giustino **BA**
Salvolini, Giustino de' **BA**
Episcopius, Johannes → see Bisschop,
Jan de
Episcopo, Giuseppe → see Piscopo,
Giuseppe

Epitimos **GC JG**
Bibl: ▶Beazley, Attic bl.-fig. vase-
ptrs.

Epître Master → see Master of the
Epître d'Othéa

Epko **WC WI**
(American artist, 20th cent.) **WC**
(American artist, op.20th c.) **WI**

Epler *(American, active 1890s (also
Epler & Arnold))* **JG**
Epp → see Epp, Rudolf

Epp, Rudolf **GC PR WC**
(German artist, 1834-1910) **WC**
(German painter, 1834-1910) **GC PR**
Bibl: ▶Thieme-Becker
Epp **PR**
Epp, Rudolph **PR**
Rudolf Epp **PR**
Epp, Rudolph → see Epp, Rudolf

Eppele *(French artist, op.1970)* **WC**

Eppenstein, James F. *(American
architect)* **AV**

Epper, Ignaz *(Swiss printmaker,
painter, 1892-1969)* **BA**
Bibl: ▶Künst.-Lex. Schweiz 20.
Jahrh.; ▶Vollmer, Künst.-Lex. 20.
Jhr.; WERK 56/210 (Mar 1969)
obit

Epping, Franc *(American sculptor,
b.1910)* **GC**
Bibl: ▶Opitz, Amer. sculptors

Epple *(German artist, op.1823-1839)* **WC**

Eppler, Hermann *(Swiss architect,
Baden)* **AV**
Bibl: ▶Schweiz. Ingen. u. Archit.,
1984-1985

Eppler, Ruedi *(Architect, Swiss?)* **AV**
Bibl: Archithese 1985 Mar.4, v.15,
no.2, p.39

Epps, E. **WC WI**
(British artist, 1842-) **WC**
(British artist, b.1842) **WI**
Epps, Laura Teresa, Miss → see Alma-
Tadema, Laura Theresa Epps
Epps, Laura Theresa → see Alma-
Tadema, Laura Theresa Epps

Epstein *(Polish artist, 1892-1944)* **WC**

Epstein, David *(American real estate
developer, Boston, Mass)* **AV**
Bibl: Builder, 1988 July, v.11,
no.7, p.96

Epstein, Jacob **AV BA GC WI**
(British artist, 1880-1959) **WC WI**
(British sculptor, 1880-1959) **AV**
*(British sculptor, painter, 1880-
1959)* **BA**
(British, 1880-1959) **GC**
Bibl: Arts Council of GBR LEED'S
PAINTINGS... (1980); ▶Avery Libr.
cat.; ▶Phaidon 20c. art; ▶Vollmer,
Künst.-Lex. 20. Jhr.; ▶Who was
who [GBR], 1951-60; ▶Witt
checklist

Epstein, Sir Jacob **WC**

Epstein, Jehudo *(German artist,
1870-1946)* **WC**

Epstein, Mitch *(American
photographer, b.1952)* **BA**
Bibl: ▶WW Amer. Art, 1986
Epstein, Sir Jacob → see Epstein, Jacob

Er'zia, Stepan Dmitrievič *(Russian
sculptor, 1876-1959)* **BA**
Bibl: ▶Fogg Mus. Libr. cat.;
▶Vollmer, Künst.-Lex. 20. Jhr.
Ar'zia, Stepan Dmitrievič Nefedov **BA**
Nefedov Ar'zia, Stepan Dmitrievič **BA**
Er. Quelinus → see Quellinus, Jan
Erasmus

**Era, Giovanni Battista dell'
('Delara' or 'Dellara')** *(Italian
artist, 1765-1798)* **WC**
Erard de Bressuire → see Errard,
Charles II
Erard, Charles II → see Errard, Charles
II

Erard, Sébastien *(French musical
instrument maker, 1752-1831)* **BA**
Bibl: ▶Dict. biog. fran.; ▶Larousse
grande encyc.; ▶Nouv. biog. gén.
Erasme de Bie → see Bie, Erasme de
Erasmo da Zoagli → see Piaggio,
Teramo
Erasmus Engert → see Engert, Erasmus
Erasmus Quelinus → see Quellinus, Jan
Erasmus
Erasmus Quellinus → see Quellinus,
Jan Erasmus
Erasmus Quellinus (II) → see
Quellinus, Erasmus II
Erasmus Quellinus, jun. → see
Quellinus, Erasmus II
*Erasmus Quiellenius [the finest friend
and disciple of Rubens] → see*
Quellinus, Erasmus II
Erasmus Quilenus → see Quellinus, Jan
Erasmus
Erasmus Quillenus → see Quellinus,
Jan Erasmus
Erasmus Quillinus → see Quellinus, Jan
Erasmus
*Erasmus Quillinus, of the School of
Rubens → see* Quellinus, Jan
Erasmus

**Erasmus, Desiderius (Erasmus von
Rotterdam)** *(Netherlands artist,
1467-1536)* **WC**

Erasmus, Johann Georg *(German
artist, 1659-1710)* **WC**

Erasmus, Nel *(South African artist,
1928-)* **WC**
Erasmus, Ritter von Engert → see
Engert, Erasmus

Erassmy, Willes *(German architect,
Trier)* **AV**
Bibl: Deutsches Architektenblatt,
1985 Apr.1, v.17, no.4, p.428
Erastus Salisbury Field → see Field,
Erastus Salisbury

Erat, Bruno *(Finnish architect)* **AV**
Bibl: ▶Libr. of Congr. Name Auth.
File

Erba, Carlo *(Italian painter,
printmaker, 1884-1917)* **BA**
Bibl: ▶Comanducci, Diz.; ▶Vollmer,
Künst.-Lex. 20. Jhr.

Erba, Giorgio da (Italian architect, ca.1480-ca.1538)   **BA**
Bibl: ▶Bessone-Aurelj, Scult. & arch. ital.; ▶Portoghesi, Diz. arch. e urbanistica; ▶Thieme-Becker

Erba, Massimo (Italian architect)   **AV**
Bibl: Lotus international, 1986, no.48-49, p.61

Erbach Painter (vase-painter, ca. 400-366 BC)   **GC**
Bibl: ▶Beazley, Attic red-fig. vase-ptrs.; Richter, Attic red-fig. vases

Erbe, Gary Thomas (American painter, b.1944.)   **BA**
Bibl: ▶Intl. dir. exh. artists, 1983, v.1; ▶WW Amer. Art, 1986

Erbe, Julius (German artist, op.1866-1870)   **WC**

Erben, Josef (German sculptor, b.1936)   **BA**
Bibl: Berlin (DEU), Neuer Berliner Kunstverein, 8 from Berlin (1975); STUDIO 19 (Nov 1975) 250

Erben, Roman (Czech painter, b.1940)   **BA**
Bibl: ▶Bénézit; London (GBR), Camden Arts Ctr., Conroy Maddox (1979)

Erben, Tino (Austrian artist, 20th cent.)   **WC**

Erben, Ulrich   **BA WC**
(German artist, 1940-)   **WC**
(German painter, b.1940)   **BA**
Bibl: ▶Natl. union cat., 1975; ▶WW Arts DEU

Erber, Wolfram (German draftsman, b.1939)   **BA**
Bibl: Berlin (DEU), Neuer Berliner Kunstverein, 8 from Berlin (1975); STUDIO 19 (Nov. 1975) 250

Erbsloh→see Erbslöh, Adolf

Erbslöh, Adolf   **BA GC PR WC WI**
(American artist, 1881-1947)   **WC WI**
(German painter, 1881-1947)   **GC PR**
(German painter, printmaker, 1881-1947)   **BA**
Bibl: ▶Bénézit; ▶Phaidon 20c. art; ▶Thieme-Becker; ▶Vollmer, Künst.-Lex. 20. Jhr.; Yale UAG catalogue
Adolf Erbsloh   **PR**
Erbsloh   **PR**

Erceanu, Dan (Romanian artist, b.1943)   **BA**
Bibl: ARTA XXVIII/11 (1980) 16-17

Ercilla Abaitua, Roberto (Spanish architect)   **AV**
Bibl: ▶Guia secreta Hermandad, 1982-1983

Erck, J.M. van (Flemish(?) artist, 17th cent.)   **WC**

Ercolani, Gianpaolo (Italian architect, 1947-)   **AV**
Bibl: Controspazio, 1985 Jan.-June, v.16, no.1-2, p.86

Ercole da Ferrara→see Grandi, Ercole

Ercole de' Roberti→see Roberti, Ercole de'
Ercole Gennari→see Gennari, Ercole
Ercole Grandi→see Roberti, Ercole de'
Ercole Graziani (the younger)→see Graziani, Ercole II
Ercole Graziano→see Graziani, Ercole II
Ercole Procaccini→see Procaccini, Ercole II
Ercole Ruggieri, o Ercolino del Gessi→see Ruggieri, Ercole (Ercolino del Gessi)
Ercole Sarti→see Sarti, Ercole
Ercole Setti→see Setti, Ercole

Ercole, Giovanni Battista (Italian painter, architect, act.1788, d.1811)   **BA**
Bibl: ▶Thieme-Becker

Ercole, Paolo (Italian architect)   **AV**
Bibl: Ottagono, 1985 Sept., v.20, no.78, p.104

Ercoli, Alcide Carlo (Italian artist, op.1857-1866)   **WC**

Ercolino del Gessi→see Ruggieri, Ercole (Ercolino del Gessi)
Ercolo de' Roberti→see Roberti, Ercole de'
Erde→see Ende

Erdei, Andras (Hungarian architect)   **AV**
Bibl: Architecture and urbanism, 1984 Mar., no.3(162), p.81

Erdely, Francis de (American artist, 1904-1959)   **WC WI**

Erdély, Miklós (Hungarian architect or artist, 1928-1986)   **AV**
Bibl: Magyar építőművészet, 1988, v.79, no.1, p.28

Erdey, Dezső (Hungarian sculptor, 1902-1957)   **BA**
Bibl: ▶Fogg Mus. Libr. cat.; ▶Vollmer, Künst.-Lex. 20. Jhr.

Erdmann, Lothar (West German architect, Arolsen)   **AV**
Bibl: Architektur, Innenarchitektur, Technischer Ausbau, 1987 Nov., v.95, no.11, p.44

Erdmann, Moritz (Heinrich Edward Moritz) (German artist, 1845-1919)   **WC**

Erdmann, Otto (German artist, 1834-1905)   **WC**

Erdmannsdorff, Friedrich Wilhelm   **BA**
(Architect, Germany, 1736-1800)   **AV**
(German architect, 1736-1800)   **BA**
Bibl: ▶Libr. of Congr. Name Auth. File; ▶Neue deutsche Biog.; ▶Thieme-Becker

Erdmannsdorff, Friedrich Wilhelm von   **AV**
Von Erdmannsdorff, Friedrich Wilhelm   **AV**

Erdmannsdorff, Friedrich Wilhelm von→see Erdmannsdorff, Friedrich Wilhelm

Erdos, Paul (Rumanian artist, 1916-)   **WC**

Erdös, Stefan (German ceramist, 1906-1956)   **BA**
Bibl: KERAMOS 72 (May 1976) 55-56

Erdt, G. (Swiss architect, Zurich)   **AV**
Bibl: Schweizer Baumarkt, 1988 Sept.19, no.18, p.xiii

Erdt, Hans Rudi (German printmaker, 1883-ca.1918)   **BA**
Bibl: Barnicoat, Hist. posters; Hutchison, The poster; ▶MoMA libr. cat.; Strasbourg (FRA), Cabinet des estampes, BELLE EPOQUE (1981); ▶Thieme-Becker

Erdtelt, Alois   **BA**
(German artist, 1851-1911)   **WC**
(German painter, 1851-1911)   **BA**
Bibl: ▶Busse, Maler u. Bildhauer 19. Jahr.; ▶Thieme-Becker

Erdtuelt, Alois   **WC**
Erdtuelt, Alois→see Erdtelt, Alois

Eremita, or L'Ermite, Daniel (Flemish artist, 1584-1613)   **WC**

Erenberg→see Ehrenberg, Wilhelm van

Eretria Painter   **GC JG**
(vase-painter, ca. 450-420 BC)   **GC**
Bibl: ▶Beazley, Attic red-fig. vase-ptrs.; Richter, Attic red-fig. vases

Erfmann, Ferdinand George (Dutch painter, 1901-1968)   **BA**
Bibl: ▶Scheen, Ned. beeldende kunst.

Erfurth, Hugo   **BA JG**
(German photographer, 1874-1948)   **BA**
(German, 1874-1948)   **JG**
Bibl: ▶Gernsheim, Hist. photog.; ▶MoMA libr. cat.

Erger, Judith (American designer, New York, NY)   **AV**
Bibl: Interior design, 1983 May, v.54, no.5, p.193

Erginos (Greek potter, ca.420-390 BC)   **GC**
Bibl: ▶Beazley, Attic red-fig. vase-ptrs., p.1318; Richter, Attic red-fig. vases

Ergo, Engelbert   **BA GC WC**
(Flemish artist, op.c.1629/30-1652)   **WC**
(Flemish painter, act.1629-1652)   **BA GC**
Bibl: ▶Thieme-Becker; ▶Witt checklist

Ergoteles Son of Nearchos   **GC**
Bibl: ▶Beazley, Attic bl.-fig. vase-ptrs.

Ergotimos (potter, ca. 575-560 BC)   **GC**
Bibl: ▶Beazley, Attic bl.-fig. vase-ptrs.; Boardman, Attic Bl.-fig. Vases

---

Erhard GC
(German artist, 16th cent.) WC
(German painter, act. early 16th
century) GC
Bibl: Getty Photo Study Coll.
(Douwes coll.); ▶Thieme-Becker

Erhard von Augsburg GC **WC**

Erhard Altdorfer → see Altdorfer,
Erhard

Erhard Ludewig Winterstein → see
Winterstein, Erhard Ludewig

Erhard von Augsburg → see Erhard

Erhard, Johann Christoph BA GC WC
(German artist, 1795-1822) WC
(German draughtsman, 1795-
1822) GC
(German painter, printmaker,
1795-1822) BA
Bibl: ▶Busse, Maler u. Bildhauer
19. Jahr.; ▶Thieme-Becker; ▶Witt
checklist

Erhardt, Hans Martin (German
artist, 1935-) WC

Erhart, Gregor (German sculptor,
ca.1465-1540) **BA GC**
Bibl: ▶Encyc. world art; ▶Neue
deutsche Biog.; ▶RILA/BHA;
▶Thieme-Becker

Erhart, Michel (German sculptor, ca.
1440-after 1522) BA
Bibl: ▶Müller, Sculpture NLD DEU
FRA ESP, pp.115-116; ▶Neue
deutsche Biog.; ▶Thieme-Becker

Erhel, Jean-François (Architect) AV
Bibl: AA files, 1986 Autumn,
no.13, p.19

Erhlen, Jean-Jacques (French
silversmith, b.1700, master 1728) GC
Bibl: ▶Mabille, Orfèv. fran.

Erhlen, Johann Jacob GC

Erhlen, Johann Jacob → see Erhlen,
Jean-Jacques

Erič, Milan (Yugoslav painter,
printmaker, b.1956) BA
Bibl: ▶Intl. dir. exh. artists, 1981;
Medved, Flash art, 112 (May
1983) pp.52-55

Erich Buchholz → see Buchholz, Erich

Erich Heckel → see Heckel, Erich

Erich, August (German artist, op.
1620-1644) WC

Erichsen, Nelly → see Erichson, Nelly

Erichsen, Thorvald (Norwegian
artist, 1868-1939) WC

Erichsen, Vigilius GC WC
(Danish artist, 1722-1782) WC
(Danish, 1722-1782) GC
Bibl: ▶Thieme-Becker; ▶Witt
checklist

Erichson, Nelly WI
(British artist, op.1882-1893) WC
(British artist, op.1882-1917) WI

Erichsen, Nelly WC

Erickson, Arthur → see Erickson,
Arthur Charles

Erickson, Arthur Charles BA
(Canadian architect, 1924-) AV
(Canadian architect, b.1924) BA
Bibl: ▶Artists Canada; ▶Avery
period. idx.; ▶Contemp. archts.

Erickson, Arthur AV

Erickson, Bryce (Canadian painter,
20th c.) BA
Bibl: Erickson, LEONARDO XIX/3
(1986) 211-215

Erickson, C.O.A. WI
(American artist, 1893-1958) WC WI

Erickson, Carl O.A. WC

Erickson, Carl O.A. → see Erickson,
C.O.A.

Erickson, Delano D. (American
architect, Minneapolis) AV
Bibl: ▶AIA Pro File, 1987-88

Erickson, John (American artist,
b.1919) WI

Ericson, Anna Maria Gardell → see
Gardell-Ericson, Anna Maria

Ericson, Augustus William
(American photographer, 1848-
1927) BA
Bibl: Palmquist, FINE CALIF.
VIEWS, THE PHOTOS. OF A.W.
ERICSON (1975)

Ericson, David (American artist,
1869-1946) WI

Ericson, Johan Erik BA WC
(Swedish artist, 1849-1925) WC
(Swedish painter, 1849-1925) BA
Bibl: ▶Bénézit; ▶Svenska
konstnärer; ▶Svenskt konst.-lex.;
▶Thieme-Becker

Ericson, Nina (Swedish
photographer) AV
Bibl: Arkitektur: the Swedish
review of architecture, 1989 Jan.-
Feb., v.89, no.1, p.26

Ericson, Ronald (American architect,
Omaha, NE) AV
Bibl: ▶AIA Pro File, 1985

Ericsson, Erling (Swedish artist,
20th cent.) WC

Ericsson, John (Swedish engineer,
1803-1889) BA
Bibl: Columb. Gaz.; Knutsson,
KONSTHIST TIDSKRIFT
LV/1/(1986) 19-26; ▶Svenskt
konst.-lex.

Ericthonios Painter GC
Bibl: ▶Beazley, Attic red-fig. vase-
ptrs.

Eriksen, Dag (Norwegian architect) AV
Bibl: Byggekunst: the Norwegian
review of architecture, 1988
v.70, no.2, p.116

Eriksson, Liss (Swedish sculptor,
b.1919) BA
Bibl: Borgens Kulturguide Sverge,
14, 198; ▶Svenskt konst.-lex.;
WW Scand.

Erisalu, Enn (Canadian painter,
b.1943) BA
Bibl: Kangas, M., in VANGUARD
XII/1 (Feb 1983) 23

Erith, Raymond → see Erith, Raymond
Charles

Erith, Raymond Charles BA
(British architect, 1904-1973) AV BA
Bibl: ▶Avery obit. idx.; ▶Who's
Who [GBR], 1974; ▶WW Germany

Erith, Raymond AV

Erixson, Sven → see Erixson, Sven
Leonard (X-et)

Erixson, Sven Leonard (X-et) BA
(Swedish artist, 1899-) WC
(Swedish painter, printmaker,
designer, 1899-1970) BA
Bibl: ▶Bénézit; ▶Svenskt konst.-
lex.

Erixson, Sven WC
X-et BA

Erkelens, Abraham → see Erkelens,
Anthonie

Erkelens, Anthonie GC
(Dutch artist, op.1665(?)) WC
(Dutch draughtsman, act.1665) GC
Bibl: ▶Bénézit; ▶Thieme-Becker

Erkelens, Abraham GC

**Erkelens, Anthonie, (possibly
identified with Abraham
Erkeles)** WC

Erkelens, Anthonie, (possibly
identified with Abraham
Erkeles) → see Erkelens, Anthonie

Erlach, Johann Bernhard Fischer
von → see Fischer von Erlach,
Johann Bernhard

Erlandsen, Eric (Danish sculptor,
b.1934.) BA
Bibl: ▶Køie, Kunst.leks.

Erlanger, Rodolphe Francois d' → see
Erlanger, Rodolphe François d',
Baron

**Erlanger, Rodolphe François d',
Baron** AV
(French artist, 1872-1930/34) WC
(French artist, architect, b.1872) AV
Bibl: ▶Bénézit; ▶Thieme-Becker

Erlanger, Rodolphe Francois d' WC

Erlebacher, Martha Mayer
(American painter, printmaker,
b.1937) BA
Bibl: ▶Locus, 1977-78

Erler (Erler-Samaden), Erich
(German artist, 1870-) WC

Erler, Fritz GC WC
(German artist, 1868-1940) WC
(German painter, 1868-1940) GC
Bibl: ▶Thieme-Becker

Erlwein, Hans (German architect,
1872-) AV
Bibl: ▶Thieme-Becker

Ermakov, D. (Russian photographer,
act.1870-1914) BA
Bibl: HIST OF PHOTOG. II/1 (Jan
1978) 84

Erman→*see* Swanevelt, Herman van
Erman Swanevelt→*see* Swanevelt, Herman van
Erman, Erol *(West German engineer, Hannover)*   **AV**
  Bibl: Architektur, Innenarchitektur, Technischer Ausbau, 1989 Apr., v.97, no.4, p.30
Ermanno Gillis→*see* Gillis, Herman
Ermanno Stroiffi→*see* Stroiffi, Ermanno
Ermano Vandervert→*see* Swanevelt, Herman van
Ermels, Ermel or Ermelein, Georg Paul *(German artist, c.1666-p.1700)*   **WC**
Ermels, Johann Franciscus   **GC**
  (German artist, 1621-1693)   WC
  (German draughtsman, 1641-1693)   GC
  Bibl: Getty Photo Study Coll.; ▶Schweers, Gemälde deut. Museen; ▶Thieme-Becker; ▶Witt checklist
Ermels, Johann Franz   **WC**
Ermels, Johann Franz→*see* Ermels, Johann Franciscus
Ermenev, Ivan *(Russian artist, 1746-p.1789)*   **WC**
Ermilov, Vasilij Dmitrovič   **BA**
  (Russian artist, 1894-1968)   WC
  (Russian painter, sculptor, 1894-1967)   BA
  Bibl: John Bowlt corresp., Nov. 1976
Ermilov, Vassily   **WC**
Ermilov, Vassily→*see* Ermilov, Vasilij Dmitrovič
Ermini, Pietro *(Italian artist, op. 1799-1820)*   **WC**
Erminio, Carlo *(Italian architect)*   **AV**
  Bibl: L'industria delle costruzioni, 1989 June, v.23, no.212. p.34
Ermolaev, Boris Nicolaevich→*see* Ermolaev, Boris Nikolaevič
Ermolaev, Boris Nikolaevič   **BA**
  (Russian artist, 20th cent.)   WC
  (Russian printmaker, b.1903)   BA
  Bibl: ▶Fogg Mus. Libr. cat.; Paris (FRA), Grand Palais, L'ART RUSSE DES SCYTHES A NOS JOURS (1968)
Ermolaev, Boris Nicolaevich   **WC**
Erna, Johann Baptist de *(Czech architect, act.1643)*   **BA**
  Bibl: Jelínek, Česk. hrady; Plichta, Umění XXVIII, 2 (1980) 151-167
Ernest Fiene→*see* Fiene, Ernest
Ernest Harrison Barnes→*see* Barnes, Ernest Harrison
Ernest Joseph Laurent→*see* Laurent, Ernest Joseph
Ernest L. Ipsen→*see* Ipsen, Ernest Ludwig
Ernest Lawson→*see* Lawson, Ernest

Ernest Major→*see* Major, Ernest Lee
Ernest Parton→*see* Parton, Ernest
Ernest Procter→*see* Procter, Ernest
Ernest Wadsworth Longfellow→*see* Longfellow, Ernest Wadsworth
Ernest, E.   **WC WI**
  (British artist, 19th cent.)   WC
  (British artist, op.19th c.)   WI
Ernest, Ernest Pignon→*see* Pignon-Ernest, Ernest
Ernest, John   **BA WC WI**
  (American artist, 1922-)   WC
  (American artist, b.1922)   WI
  (American sculptor, b.1922)   BA
  Bibl: ▶Bénézit; ▶MoMA libr. cat.
Ernest, Sigismund von *(German, 18th c.)*   **BA**
  Bibl: KERAMOS 81-82 (July-Oct 1978) 11-12
Erneste E. Narjot→*see* Narjot, Erneste E.
Ernestine, Princess von Nassau-Hadamar *(German artist, -1668)*   **WC**
Ernestus, monk of Stavelot
  (Netherlandish scribe, act. late 11th century)   **GC**
  Bibl: Watson, British Library, p.321
Erneva, Monsù [Unidentified]
  (Unknown painter)   **PR**
  Bibl: Filomarino inventory, Naples, 1700: Labrot says "sconosciuto"
  Monsù Erneva   PR
  Monsù Et nevà   PR
  Monsu' Et neva'   PR
Erni, Hans   **BA GC WC**
  (Swiss artist, 1909-)   WC
  (Swiss painter, b.1909)   GC
  (Swiss painter, illustrator, printmaker, b.1909)   BA
  Bibl: ▶Bénézit; ▶Vollmer, Künst.-Lex. 20. Jhr.; WW Switz.
Erni, Vincenz *(Swiss architect)*   **AV**
  Bibl: Archithese, 1985 May, v.15, no.3, p.112
Erno, Vadas *(Hungarian, active ca. 1937)*   **JG**
Ernotte, Jacques *(Belgian illustrator, 1897-1964)*   **BA**
  Bibl: ▶Bénézit; Haskell, Word & Image III (Oct-Dec 1987), p. 248-258
Ernou, Pierre   **GC**
  (French artist, 1665-p.1739)   WC
  (French, 1664-aft.1739)   GC
  Bibl: ▶Thieme-Becker; ▶Witt checklist
Ernou, Pierre (Le Chevalier Ernou)   **WC**
Ernou, Pierre (Le Chevalier Ernou)→*see* Ernou, Pierre
Ernset Bucknall→*see* Bucknall, Ernest Pile
Ernst→*see* Ernst, Max
Ernst Adolf Meissner→*see* Meissner, Ernst Adolf

Ernst Kolbe→*see* Kolbe, Ernst
Ernst Ludwig Kirchner→*see* Kirchner, Ernst Ludwig
Ernst Stuiver→*see* Stuven, Ernst
Ernst Stuven→*see* Stuven, Ernst
Ernst, Alfred von *(Swiss artist, 1799-1850)*   **WC**
Ernst, Alphonsine Thuot *(American artist, 1873-1952)*   **WC WI**
Ernst, Helen *(German artist, 1904-1948)*   **BA**
  Bibl: Hübner, H., BILDENDE KUNST/II/(Nov.1987), 502-505
Ernst, Helge *(Danish painter, illustrator, b.1916)*   **BA**
  Bibl: ▶Nørregård-Nielsen, Dansk kunst; ▶Weilbach, Kunst.leks.
Ernst, Jimmy   **BA WC WI**
  (American artist, 1920-)   WC
  (American artist, 1920-1984)   WI
  (American painter, 1920-1984)   BA
  Bibl: Slivka, ARTS MAG. LXIII/10 (summer 1984) 4; ▶WW Amer. Art, 1976, 1984
Ernst, Johan Conrad→*see* Ernst, Johann Conrad
Ernst, Johann Conrad   **BA**
  (Danish architect, 1666-1750)   AV BA
  Bibl: ▶Thieme-Becker; ▶Weilbach, Kunst.leks.
Ernst, Johan Conrad   **AV**
Ernst, Karl Josef *(West German architect)*   **AV**
Ernst, Karl Mathias   **GC WC**
  (German artist, 1758-1830)   WC
  (German painter, 1758-1830)   GC
  Bibl: ▶Thieme-Becker
Ernst, Leopold *(1808-1862)*   **AV**
Ernst, Mark *(American architect, Chicago, Ill)*   **AV**
  Bibl: ARchitecture & urbanism, 1983 Sept., no.9(156), p.73
Ernst, Max   **BA GC PR WC WI**
  (German artist, 1891-)   WC
  (German artist, 1891-1976)   WI
  (German painter and sculptor, 1891-1976)   GC
  (German painter, 1891-1976)   PR
  (German painter, collagist, author, 1891-1976)   BA
  Bibl: ▶Bénézit; ▶Encyc. world art; ▶Marks, Dict. world artists; ▶New Columbia encyc.; ▶RILA/BHA
  Ernst   PR
  Max Ernst   PR
Ernst, Max, Mrs., (Dorothea)→*see* Tanning, Dorothea
Ernst, Philippe *(German educator, painter, 1862-1943)*   **BA**
  Bibl: Cologne (DEU), Kunstverein, Max Ernst in Köln (1980); Quinn, MAX ERNST
Ernst, Ralf *(West German architect)*   **AV**
  Bibl: Architektur + Wettbewerbe, 1984 June, no.118, p.80
Ernst, Rodolphe *(German artist, 1854-)*   **WC**

Ernt, Jimmy *(American painter,*
b.1920) **GC**
    Bibl: ▸RILA/BHA
Ernyei, Sandor *(Hungarian artist,*
20th cent.) **WC**
Eroli, Erulo **GC WC**
    (Italian artist, 1854-1916) WC
    (Italian painter, 1854-?) GC
    Bibl: ▸Thieme-Becker
    Eruli, Erulo GC
Eroli, Pierluigi *(Italian architect,*
1936-) **AV**
Eros and Hare Painter *(Campanian*
vase-painter) **GC**
    Bibl: ▸Trendall, Red-fig. vases
    Lucania
Eros, Bradley *(American artist, 20th*
c.) **BA**
    Bibl: Wooster, A.-S., in
    AFTERIMAGE XIII/4 (Nov 1985) 17
Erp, Theodoor Van *(Dutch army*
engineer) **AV**
    Bibl: Progressive architecture,
    1984 Nov., v.65, no.11, p.107
Erpikum, Leon *(Vuilleminot)*
    (French artist, 19th cent.) **WC**
Erra, Jyrki *(Finnish architect,*
Helsinki) **AV**
    Bibl: SAFA 87: Suomen Arkkit.
Errante, (Pellegrino Errante)
Giuseppe *(Italian artist, 1760-*
1821) **WC**
Errard, Charles I *(French, ca.1570-*
ca.1630) **GC**
    Bibl: ▸Thieme-Becker
Errard, Charles II **BA GC**
    (French artist, c.1606-1689) WC
    (French painter and
    draughtsman, 1606-1689) GC
    (French painter, printmaker,
    architect, 1606-1689) BA
    Bibl: ▸Bénézit; ▸Nouv. biog. gén.;
    ▸Thieme-Becker
    Erard de Bressuire GC
    Erard, Charles II **GC**
    Errard, Charles, II **WC**
Errard, Charles, II→see Errard,
    Charles II
Errard, Jean *(French engineer and*
festival designer, 1554-1623) **AV**
    Bibl: ▸Thieme-Becker
Errard, Léonard→see Hérard, Léonard
Errath, Jean-Pierre *(French*
architect) **AV**
    Bibl: Archives d'architecture
    moderne, 1987, no.35-36, p.50
Errera Painter *(Campanian vase-*
painter) **GC**
    Bibl: ▸Trendall, Red-fig. vases
    Lucania
Erri→see Erri, Agnolo degli
Erri→see Erri, Bartolomeo degli

Erri, Agnolo degli **GC PR WC**
    (Italian artist, op.1448-1482) WC
    (Italian painter, act. 1448-1482) PR
    (Italian, act.1448-1482) GC
    Bibl: ▸Fredericksen & Zeri, Census;
    ▸Thieme-Becker
    Agnolo degli Erri PR
    Erri PR
Erri, Bartolomeo degli **PR**
    (Italian artist, op.1460-1476) WC
    (Italian painter, act. 1460-1476) PR
    (Italian, act.1460-1476) GC
    Bibl: ▸Fredericksen & Zeri, Census;
    ▸Thieme-Becker; ▸Witt checklist
    Bartolomeo degli Erri PR
    Bartolommeo degli Erri PR
    Erri PR
    Erri, Bartolommeo degli **GC PR**
    Erri, Bartolomneo degli **WC**
Erri, Bartolommeo degli→see Erri,
    Bartolomeo degli
Erri, Bartolomneo degli→see Erri,
    Bartolomeo degli
Errico Fiamenco→see Hendricksz.,
    Dirck, Teodoro d'Errico
Errico Fiamengo→see Hendricksz.,
    Dirck, Teodoro d'Errico
Errico Fiammingo→see Hendricksz.,
    Dirck, Teodoro d'Errico
Erridetto [Unidentified] *(Unknown*
painter) **PR**
    Bibl: Doria inventory, Naples,
    1737
Errington, Elisabeth, Mrs. *(British*
artist, op.1843-1846) **WI**
Erro *(French artist, 20th cent.)* **WC**
Erró (Gudmundur Gudmundsson)
    (Icelandic painter in FRA, b.1932) **BA**
    Bibl: ▸ARTbibl. mod., 21/2,
    #07673; ▸Bénézit; ▸Gorenflo,
    Bild. Künstler; ▸Intl. dir. exh.
    artists, 1983; ▸MoMA libr. cat.;
    ▸WW France
    Ferro BA
    Gudmundsson, Gudmundur BA
    Gudmundur Gudmundsson BA
Erseghe, Alberto **AV**
Erskine Nicol→see Nicol, Erskine
Erskine, Colin **WC WI**
    (British artist, 18th cent.) WC
    (British artist, circa 1704-op.
    1743) WI
Erskine, Harold *(American sculptor,*
1879-1951) **GC**
    Bibl: Getty Photo Study Coll.;
    ▸Opitz, Amer. sculptors
    Erskine, Harold Perry GC
Erskine, Harold Perry→see Erskine,
    Harold
Erskine, John→see Mar, John Erskine,
    Earl of
Erskine, Peter *(American sculptor,*
b.1941) **BA**
    Bibl: ▸NY art yrbk.

Erskine, Ralph **AV BA**
    (British architect, city planner in
    SWE, b.1914) BA
    (Swedish architect, 1914-) AV
    Bibl: ▸Contemp. archts.; ▸Vollmer,
    Künst.-Lex. 20. Jhr.
Erskine, Vincent *(British artist, op.*
20th c.) **WI**
Erskine, W.C.C. **WC WI**
    (British artist, op.c.1879) WC
    (British artist, op.circa 1879-) WI
Ersoch, Gioacchino *(Italian*
architect, 1815-1902) **BA**
    Bibl: RICERCHE DI STORIA
    DELL'ARTE 3 (1976) 77
Erstet, Jean-Ulrich *(French ébéniste,*
master 1740, d.ca.1780) **GC**
    Bibl: ▸Salverte, Ébénistes 18e s.
    Herstel GC
Erté→see Erté (Romain de Tirtoff)
Erté (Romain de Tirtoff) **BA**
    (French artist) AV
    (French artist, 1892-) WC
    (French designer, sculptor,
    1892-1990) BA
    Bibl: ▸Bénézit; ERTE: SCULPTURE
    (1986); ▸Fogg Mus. Libr. cat.;
    ▸Libr. of Congr. Name Auth. File;
    NY Times obit., 22 Apr 1990;
    ▸NYPL Art & Arch. Div., Dict.
    catalog
    Erté **AV**
    Erte, Romain de Tirtoff **WC**
    Tirtoff, Romain de BA
Erte, Romain de Tirtoff→see Erté
    (Romain de Tirtoff)
Ertegun, Mica *(Rumanian-born*
interior designer, NYC) **AV**
    Bibl: House & garden, 1987 Mar.,
    v.159, no.3, p.100
Erthal, Philipp Christof von
    (German nobleman, architect, act.
    1700-1743) **BA**
    Bibl: Dehio: Rheinland-Pfälz
Ertinger *(German artist, 18th cent.)* **WC**
Ertinger, Franz **BA WC**
    (German artist, 1640-c.1710) WC
    (German printmaker in FRA,
    1640-ca.1710) BA
    Bibl: ▸Bénézit; ▸Thieme-Becker
Ertl, Roland *(Austrian architect,*
Linz) **AV**
    Bibl: ▸Verzeich. Öst. Ziviltech.,
    1984
Ertli, Jerzy *(Austrian builder in*
Russia, act.1672, d.1697) **BA**
    Bibl: Dreman, BIULETYN HISTORII
    SZTUKI XLII/2 (1980) 141-144
Ertvelt→see Eertvelt, Andries van
Ertz, Edward Frederick **WC WI**
    (American artist, 1862-) WC
    (American artist, 1862-1954) WI
Eruli, Erulo→see Eroli, Erulo
Ervi, Aarne *(Finnish architect, 1910-*
1977) **AV**
    Bibl: ▸Contemp. archts.

Erwin von Steinbach **BA**
  (German architect, act.ca.1277,
    d.1318) **BA**
  (German builder, d. 1318) **AV**
    Bibl: Liess, Wallraf-Richartz-
    Jahrbuch 46 (1985/86), p.75;
    ▶Macmillan encyc. archts.;
    ▶Thieme-Becker
  Steinbach, Erwin von **AV**
Erwitt, Elliott *(American*
  photographer, b.1928) **BA**
    Bibl: ▶Contemp. photogs.;
    ▶Naggar, Dict. photographes
Erwood, A. *(British artist, op.circa*
  1860-) **WI**
Erwull, I. *(German artist, 19th cent.)* **WC**
Erzagen, E. van *(Netherlands artist,*
  op.1736) **WC**
Es →see Es, Jacob Fopsen van
Es, Esch or Essen, Jacob Fopsen or
  Foppens van →see Es, Jacob
  Fopsen van
Es, Jacob Foppens van →see Es, Jacob
  Fopsen van
Es, Jacob Fopsen van **BA GC PR**
  (Flemish artist, op.1617-m.1666) **WC**
  (Flemish painter, ca.1596-
    1666) **BA PR**
  (Flemish, act.1617-d.1666) **GC**
    Bibl: ▶Bénézit; Getty Photo Study
    Coll. (Ptgs.); ▶RILA/BHA;
    ▶Thieme-Becker; ▶Witt checklist
  Es **PR**
  Es, Esch or Essen, Jacob Fopsen
    or Foppens van **WC**
  Es, Jacob Foppens van **PR**
  Es, Jacob van **PR**
  Esch, Jakob Foppeus van **BA**
  Essen, Jacob Fopsen **GC**
  Essen, Jakob Foppeus van **BA**
  Jacob Fopsen van Es **PR**
  Van Es **PR**
  Van Ess **PR**
Es, Jacob van →see Es, Jacob Fopsen
  van
Es, Niclaes van *(Flemish painter,*
  bef.1617-aft.1648) **GC**
    Bibl: ▶Bénézit
Esa. Vandervelde →see Velde, Esaias I
  van de
Esaias Boursse →see Boursse, Esaias
Esaias van de Velde →see Velde,
  Esaias I van de
Esaias van de Velde (I) →see Velde,
  Esaias I van de
Esaias van den Velden →see Velde,
  Esaias I van de
Esaias vande Velde →see Velde,
  Esaias I van de
Esaias Vandevelde →see Velde, Esaias
  I van de
Esaias Vandeveldt →see Velde, Esaias
  I van de
Esaias, Dēmētrōs *(Architect,*
  Greece) **AV**
    Bibl: Architektonika themata,
    1986, v.20, p.176

Esanatoglia Master **BA**
  (Italian artist, 14th cent.) **WC**
  (Italian painter, 14th c.) **BA**
    Bibl: BURLINGTON CXVI (Feb
    1974) 78
  Master of Esanatoglia **BA WC**
Esayas van de Velde →see Velde,
  Esaias I van de
Esbrard **GC WC**
  (French artist, op.1800-1830) **WC**
  (French painter, act.1800-1830) **GC**
    Bibl: ▶Thieme-Becker
Esbrat, Raymond Noel **GC WC**
  (French artist, 1809-1856) **WC**
  (French, 1809-1856) **GC**
    Bibl: ▶Witt checklist
Escalante →see Escalante, Juan
  Antonio de Frias y
Escalante, Juan Antonio →see
  Escalante, Juan Antonio de Frias y
Escalante, Juan Antonio de
  Frias y **BA GC PR WC**
  (Spanish artist, 1630-1670) **WC**
  (Spanish painter, 1633-1670) **BA PR**
  (Spanish, 1630-1670) **GC**
    Bibl: ▶Bénézit; ▶Kubler, Art &
    arch. ESP & PRT, p.426;
    ▶RILA/BHA; ▶Thieme-Becker;
    ▶Witt checklist
  Escalante **PR**
  Escalante, Juan Antonio **PR**
  Frias y Escalante, Juan Antonio de **BA**
  Juan Antonio de Frias y Escalante **PR**
  Juan de Escalante **PR**
  Juan de Esolante **PR**
Escalier, Marguerite *(French*
  painter, 19th century) **GC**
    Bibl: ▶Bénézit
Escallier, Eleonore-Caroline (Marie
  Caroline Eleonore) *(French artist,*
  1827-1888) **WC**
Escalón, Rafael *(Architect)* **AV**
    Bibl: Lotus international, 1989,
    no.61, p.102
Escamilla, Luis Tristan de →see
  Tristán de Escamilla, Luis
Esch, Jakob Foppeus van →see Es,
  Jacob Fopsen van
Esch, Mathilde *(German artist,*
  1820-p.1880) **WC**
Eschard, Charles **GC**
  (French artist, 1748-1810) **WC**
  (French painter, 1748-1810) **GC**
    Bibl: ▶Bénézit; ▶Thieme-Becker
  Echard or Eschard, Charles **WC**
  Echard, Charles **GC**
Escher, Fred *(American draftsman,*
  20th c.) **BA**
    Bibl: ARTS MAG LV (6 Feb 1982)
    25
Escher, Gielijn *(Dutch artist, 20th*
  cent.) **WC**
Escher, Hans *(German artist, 1918-)* **WC**
Escher, Hans Kaspar →see Escher,
  Johannes Caspar

Escher, Johannes Caspar *(Swiss*
  industrialist, architect, 1775-1859) **BA**
    Bibl: ▶Thieme-Becker
  Escher, Hans Kaspar **BA**
Escher, Maurits Cornelis **BA GC WC**
  (Dutch artist, 1898-) **WC**
  (Dutch printmaker, 1898-
    1972) **BA GC**
    Bibl: ▶Bénézit; Grosse Lex.
    Graphik; ▶Parry, Contemp. art;
    ▶Phaidon 20c. art; ▶Scheen, Ned.
    beeldende kunst.; ▶Vollmer,
    Künst.-Lex. 20. Jhr.
Escher, Rolf *(German printmaker,*
  b.1936) **BA**
    Bibl: ▶WW Arts DEU
Eschini, Angelo Maria d' *(Italian*
  painter, printmaker, d.1678) **BA**
    Bibl: ▶Bénézit; ▶Bryan, Ptrs. &
    engravers; ▶Thieme-Becker
  D'Eschini, Angelo Maria **BA**
  Meschini **BA**
Eschke, Hermann (Wilhelm
  Benjamin H.) *(German artist,*
  1823-1900) **WC**
Eschmann, Paul *(French architect, b.*
  in Nancy, 1902-) **AV**
    Bibl: Cahiers de la recherche
    architecturale, 1989, no.24-25,
    p.37
Eschoot, S. [Unidentified]
  (Unknown painter) **PR**
    Bibl: (November 2, 1803, lot 25,
    Langdon)
  S. Eschoot **PR**
Eschot →see Eschot, Jacques
Eschot, Jacques *(Flemish painter,*
  act. 1582-1610) **PR**
    Bibl: ▶Thieme-Becker
  Eschot **PR**
  Jacques Eschot **PR**
Eschout [Unidentified] *(Unknown*
  painter) **PR**
    Bibl: (December 14, 1803, lot 4,
    Edwards)
Eschwege, F.A. Elmar or Eilmar
  von *(German artist, 1856-)* **WC**
Escobar, Marisol →see Marisol
  (Marisol Escobar)
Escobar, Miriam *(Brazilian architect,*
  São Paulo) **AV**
    Bibl: Projecto, 1987 June, no.100,
    p.74
Escobar, Piergiorgio *(Italian*
  architect) **AV**
    Bibl: Abitare, 1986 Oct., no.248,
    p.194
Escobedo, Helen **AV BA**
  (Mexican sculptor) **AV**
  (Mexican sculptor, museum
    administrator, b.1936) **BA**
    Bibl: Architettura; cronache e
    storia, 1981 Apr., v.27, no.
    4(306), p.232; ▶Intl. dir. exh.
    artists, 1982; ▶MoMA libr. cat.;
    ▶WW Amer. Art, 1984
Escobedo, Jesus *(Mexican artist,*
  1917-) **WC**

Escombe, Jane *(British artist, op. 1869-1887)* — **WI**

Escot [Unidentified] *(Unknown painter)* — **PR**
Bibl: (March 17, 1810, lot 14, Christie's)

Escoudier *(Italian artist, 19th cent.)* — **WC**

Escout → see Eeckhout, Gerbrand van den

Escruche, Pierre *(French paintmaker, act.1555)* — **BA**
Bibl: Szilágyi, in RENAISSANCE STUDIES IN HONOR OF CRAIG HUGH SMYTH (1985) II 481

Escuyer, Pierre — **BA WC**
(Swiss artist, 1749-1834) — **WC**
(Swiss printmaker, 1749-1834) — **BA**
Bibl: ▶Bénézit; ▶Schweiz. Künst.-Lex.; ▶Thieme-Becker

Eselbrüggen, Johann *(Dutch painter, act.1793)* — **BA**
Bibl: ANTIEK VIII/9 (Apr 1974) 742

Esgueva, Manuel de *(Spanish goldsmith, act.1759)* — **BA**
Bibl: Arch. esp. de arte, LIII/209 (Jan-Mar 1980) 102-111

Eshault-Pelterie, Eugène-Emile *(French architect, 1842-)* — **AV**
Bibl: ▶Dict. biog. fran.
Pelterie, Eugène-Emile — **AV**

Esher, Barbra *(American photographer, b.1956)* — **BA**
Bibl: San Francisco (CA, USA), SFMoMA, Beyond color (1980)

Esherick, Joseph — **AV BA**
(American architect, 1914-) — **AV**
(American architect, b.1914) — **BA**
Bibl: ▶AIA Pro File, 1978; ▶Contemp. archts.; ▶Macmillan encyc. archts.; WW Amer., 1977

Eshet, Pinhas *(Israeli sculptor, b.1935)* — **BA**
Bibl: Haifa (ISR), Mus.of Mod. Art., PINHAS ESHET (1980)

Eshiemer → see Elsheimer, Adam

Esias van de Velde → see Velde, Esaias I van de

Esias Vandevelde → see Velde, Esaias I van de

Esijas van de Velde → see Velde, Esaias I van de

Eskelinen, Eero *(Finnish architect)* — **AV**
Bibl: Arkkitehti, 1985, v.82, no. 6-7, p.82

Eskell, Camille *(American painter, 20th c.)* — **BA**
Bibl: Bard, J., in ARTS MAG LIX/3 (Nov 1984) 12; ▶Intl. dir. exh. artists, 1983

Eskew, R. Allen *(American architect)* — **AV**

Eskilsson, Peter *(Swedish artist, 1820-1872)* — **WC**

Eskrich, Escricheus, Cruche, Couche, Cruzy, Vase or Du Vase, Pierre *(French artist, 1515/20-p.1590)* — **WC**

Eslaba, Pedro *(Spanish goldsmith, 16th c.)* — **BA**
Bibl: Goya, 153 (Nov.-Dec. 1979) pp.156-159

Esler, Annemarie *(Canadian ceramic sculptor, b.1937)* — **BA**
Bibl: ▶Artists Canada; ▶Natl. Gall. Canada libr. cat.; Oshawa (Ont, CAN), McLaughlin Gallery, 12 Canadian artists (1980)

Esler, John Kenneth *(Canadian printmaker, b.1933)* — **BA**
Bibl: ▶Artists Canada

Esmau *(French artist, 20th cent.)* — **WC**

Esmaysel → see Snyders, Frans

Esmenard, Ines d' *(French artist, op.1814-1851)* — **WC**

esnaira → see Snyders, Frans

esneide → see Snyders, Frans

esneyde → see Snyders, Frans

Esocoff, Philip A. *(American architect, Washington, D.C)* — **AV**
Bibl: ▶AIA Pro File, 1987-88

Espagnat → see Espagnat, Georges d'

Espagnat, Georges d' — **PR WC**
(French artist, 1870-1950) — **WC**
(French painter, 1870-1950) — **PR**
Bibl: ▶Thieme-Becker
d'Espagnat, Georges — **PR**
Espagnat — **PR**
Georges d'Espagnat — **PR**

Espagnat, Joseph d' *(French artist, 19th cent.)* — **WC**

Espagnolet → see Ribera, Jusepe de (lo Spagnoletto)

Espagnoletto → see Ribera, Jusepe de (lo Spagnoletto)

Espalargucs, Jose → see Despallargues, Pedro

Espalargucs, Pedro → see Despallargues, Pedro

Espalargues, Pedro → see Despallargues, Pedro

Espalter y Rull, Joaquin *(Spanish artist, 1809-1880)* — **WC**

españoletto → see Ribera, Jusepe de (lo Spagnoletto)

Esparbes, Jean d' *(French artist, 19th cent.)* — **WC**

Esper, Gaylord *(Haitian architect)* — **AV**
Bibl: Architecture d'aujourd'hui, 1989 Sept., no.264, p.70

Esper, Geneviève *(Haitian architect)* — **AV**
Bibl: Architecture d'aujourd'hui, 1989 Sept., no.264, p.70

Esper, Joseph → see Esperlin, Joseph

Espérandieu, Henri Jacques *(French architect, 1829-1874)* — **BA**
Bibl: ▶Dict. biog. fran.

Esperlin, Joseph — **GC WC**
(German artist, 1707-1775) — **WC**
(German painter and draughtsman, 1707-1775) — **GC**
Bibl: ▶Bénézit; Getty Photo Study Coll.; ▶Thieme-Becker; ▶Witt checklist
Esper, Joseph — **GC**
Esperling, Joseph — **GC**

Esperling, Joseph → see Esperlin, Joseph

Esperstedt, August Wilhelm *(German artist, 1814-p.1839)* — **WC**

Espin, John — **WC WI**
(British artist, 18th cent.) — **WC**
(British artist, op.18th c.) — **WI**

Espin, Thomas — **WC WI**
(British artist, 18th cent.) — **WC**
(British artist, circa 1768-1822) — **WI**

Espinal, Juan de — **BA WC**
(Spanish artist, -1783) — **WC**
(Spanish painter, 1714-1783) — **BA**
Bibl: ▶Ars Hispaniae, v.17, p.153; ▶Bénézit; ▶Ceán Bermúdez, Bellas artes ESP; ▶Encic. univ. ilus.; ▶Lafuente Ferrari, Pint. española; Sebastian, Goya 169-171 (July-Dec 1982) 29; ▶Thieme-Becker; ▶Witt checklist

Espinasse, François — **AV BA**
(French engineer, 1880-1925) — **BA**
(French engineer, architect, worked for Michelin Co., early 1900's) — **AV**
Bibl: Country life, 1987 Oct.8, v.181, no.41, p.113; Pearson, J., CONNOISSEUR, CXC/764 (Oct 1975) p.120-125

Espinasse, Raymond *(French artist, 1897-)* — **WC**

Espine, Isabeau de l' → see Aulan, Isabeau de l'Espine d'

Espinos, Benito — **GC WC**
(Spanish artist, 1748-1818) — **WC**
(Spanish, 1748-1818) — **GC**
Bibl: ▶Thieme-Becker; ▶Witt checklist

Espinosa → see Espinosa, Jerónimo Jacinto

Espinosa → see Espinosa, Jeronimo Rodriguez de

Espinosa → see Espinosa, Juan de

Espinosa Giménez, Pedro L. *(Spanish architect)* — **AV**
Bibl: Ianus, 1980, v.0, no.0, p.27

Espinosa or Espinossa, Joannes Baptista or Juan Bautista de *(Spanish artist, op.1616-1626)* — **WC**

Espinosa, Adelio *(Architect, Vienna)* — **AV**
Bibl: ▶Verzeich. Öst. Ziviltech.

Espinosa, Carlos *(Spanish, 18th century)* — **GC**
Bibl: ▶Thieme-Becker

Espinosa, Celestino *(Spanish silversmith, act.1805, d.1830)* — **BA**
Bibl: Martín, Reales sitios, XXI/79 (1984) pp.21-28

Espinosa, Eduardo *(Argentine artist, 20th cent.)*   **WC**

Espinosa, Jerónimo Jacinto   **BA GC PR WC**
   (Spanish artist, 1600-1680)   **WC**
   (Spanish painter, 1600-1680)   **BA GC PR**
      Bibl: ▶Aldana Fernández, Artistas valencianos; ▶Bénézit; ▶Thieme-Becker

   Espinosa   **PR**
   Jeronimo Jacinto Espinosa   **PR**

Espinosa, Jeronimo Rodriguez de *(Spanish painter, 1562-1638)*   **PR**
      Bibl: ▶Thieme-Becker

   Espinosa   **PR**
   Jeronimo Rodriguez de Espinosa   **PR**

Espinosa, Juan de *(Spanish painter, act. ca.1650)*   **PR**
      Bibl: ▶Thieme-Becker

   Espinosa   **PR**
   Juan de Espinosa   **PR**

Espinosa, Manuel *(Spanish artist, 20th cent.)*   **WC**

Espinosa, Susana *(Brazilian sculptor in PRT, 20th c.)*   **BA**
      Bibl: Springfield (MA, USA), MFA, Clay from Puerto Rico (1980)

Espinouze, Henri *(French artist, 1915-)*   **WC**

Espleghem, Frans Crabbe van→*see* Crabbe van Esplegem, Frans (The Crayfish Master)

Espley, Tom *(British artist, op.20th c.)*   **WI**

Esposito, Gaetano *(Italian artist, 1858-1911)*   **WC**

Esposito, Josefina *(Argentine architect, Buenos Aires)*   **AV**
      Bibl: AC: the fibrecement review XXX/1(iii) (Apr. 1985) p.73

Esposito, Piero *(Italian architect)*   **AV**
      Bibl: Abitare, 1984 Nov., no.229, p.52

Esposito, Richard *(American interior designer, New York City)*   **AV**
      Bibl: Interior design, 1988 Feb., v.59, no.3, p.292

Esquivel→*see* Esquivel, Antonio Maria

Esquivel, Antonio Maria   **BA PR WC**
   (Spanish artist, 1806-1857)   **WC**
   (Spanish painter, 1806-1857)   **BA PR**
      Bibl: ▶Busse, Maler u. Bildhauer 19. Jahr.; ▶Ossorio y Bernard, Artistas españoles 19s.; ▶RILA/BHA

   Antonio Maria Esquivel   **PR**
   Esquivel   **PR**

Esquivel, Miguel de *(Spanish painter, act.1609, d.1621)*   **BA**
      Bibl: ▶Bénézit; ▶Thieme-Becker; ▶Valdivieso, Pint. sevillana, act. 1609, d.1620

Esquivel, Vicente *(Spanish artist, 19th cent.)*   **WC**

Ess, Barbara *(American photographer, musician, performance artist, 20th c.)*   **BA**
      Bibl: Fisher, ARTFORUM XXIV (1985) 127; Gambrell, ART IN AMERICA LXXIII 1985) 158; Tatransky, ARTS LX (1985) 143

Ess, van [Unidentified] *(Unknown painter)*   **PR**
      Bibl: (December 20, 1811, lot 102, Christie's)

   Van Ess   **PR**

Essalat, Farrokh   **AV**

Essear, Béat-Antoine-François de Hennezel d'→*see* Hennezel d'Essert, Béat-Antoine-François de

Esselens→*see* Esselens, Jacob

Esselens, Jacob   **GC PR WC**
   (Dutch artist, 1626-1687)   **WC**
   (Dutch painter and draughtsman, 1626-1687)   **GC**
   (Dutch painter, 1626-1687)   **PR**
      Bibl: Getty Photo Study Coll.; ▶Thieme-Becker; ▶Witt checklist

   Esselens   **PR**
   Jacob Esselen   **PR**
   Jacob Esselens   **PR**
   Jacobus Esselens   **PR**

Esselin→*see* Asselyn, Jan

Essen Group   **GC**
      Bibl: ▶Beazley, Attic bl.-fig. vase-ptrs.

Essen or Esse, Cornelis van→*see* Essen, Cornelis van

Essen, Cornelis van   **GC PR**
   (Dutch artist, op.c.1700-1757)   **WC**
   (Dutch painter, act. 1700-1757)   **PR**
   (Dutch painter, act. ca.1700-1757)   **GC**
      Bibl: Getty Photo Study Coll.; ▶Thieme-Becker; ▶Witt checklist

   C. V. Essen   **PR**
   Cornelis van Essen   **PR**

Essen or Esse, Cornelis van   **WC**

Essen, Hans van   **BA WC**
   (Flemish artist, c.1587/9-p.1648)   **WC**
   (Flemish painter, ca.1589-after 1642)   **BA**
      Bibl: ▶Bénézit; ▶Thieme-Becker; ▶Wurzbach, NLD Künst.-Lex.

Essen, Jacob Fopsen→*see* Es, Jacob Fopsen van

Essen, Jakob Foppeus van→*see* Es, Jacob Fopsen van

Essen, Johannes Cornelis (Jan) van→*see* Essen, Johannes Cornelis van

Essen, Johannes Cornelis van   **GC**
   (Dutch artist, 1854-1936)   **WC**
   (Dutch painter and draughtsman, 1854-1936)   **GC**
      Bibl: ▶Wright, Ptgs. Dutch museums

Essen, Johannes Cornelis (Jan) van   **WC**

Essenwein, August Ottmar von   **BA**
   (German architect, 1831-1892)   **AV**
   (German architect, museum administrator, 1831-1892)   **BA**
      Bibl: ▶Libr. of Congr. Name Auth. File; ▶Neue deutsche Biog.; Restauro & città, 1988, v.3, no. 8-9, p.54 [dates]

Essenwein, August von   **AV**
Essenwein, August von→*see* Essenwein, August Ottmar von

Esser, Carl *(German sculptor, 1861-1929)*   **BA**
      Bibl: ▶Busse, Maler u. Bildhauer 19. Jahr.; ▶Vollmer, Künst.-Lex. 20. Jhr.; Weinstock, Aachner Kunstblatter XLIX (1980-1981), p. 220

Esser, Jerome   **WI**
   (British artist, 20th cent.)   **WC**
   (British artist, op.20th c.)   **WI**

Esser, Jerome E.   **WC**
Esser, Jerome E.→*see* Esser, Jerome

Esser, Johannes *(West German interior designer)*   **AV**
      Bibl: Architektur & Wohnen, 1988 Aug.-Sept., no.4, p.136

Esser, Max *(German sculptor, decorative artist, 1885-1943)*   **BA**
      Bibl: ▶Thieme-Becker; ▶Vollmer, Künst.-Lex. 20. Jhr.

Essers, Bernard *(Dutch draughtsman, 1893-1945)*   **GC**
      Bibl: ▶Vollmer, Künst.-Lex. 20. Jhr.

Essesteyn, Adrianus→*see* Ysselstein, Adrianus

Essex, Arthur Algernon Capell, 6th Earl of *(British artist, 1803-1892)*   **WI**

Essex, James   **AV BA**
   (1722-1784)   **AV**
   (British architect, 1722/23-1784)   **BA**
      Bibl: ▶Colvin, Brit. archts.; ▶Dict. natl. biog.; ▶Macmillan encyc. archts.; ▶Thieme-Becker

Essex, John *(English sculptor, 15th c.)*   **BA**
      Bibl: ▶Bénézit; ▶Thieme-Becker

Essex, Richard Hamilton *(British artist, 1802-1855)*   **WC WI**

Essex, Robert   **WC WI**
   (British artist, 18th cent.)   **WC**
   (British artist, op.18th c.)   **WI**

Essex, William   **PR WC WI**
   (British artist, 1784-1869)   **WC WI**
   (British painter, 1784-1869)   **PR**
      Bibl: ▶Thieme-Becker

   William Essex   **PR**

Esssier, Isabelle Emilie de→*see* Duval, Maria (Isabele Emilie de Tessier)

Estabrook, Reed *(American photographer, b.1944)*   **BA**
      Bibl: ▶Intl. dir. exh. artists, 1983; ▶Parry, Photo idx.; ▶WW Amer. Art

Estachon, Louis-Antoine *(French painter, 1819-1857)*   **GC**
      Bibl: ▶Bénézit

Estalban → see Albani, Francesco

Estall, William Charles (*British artist, 1857-1897*)   **WC WI**

Estapa, Domenech (*Spanish architect*)   **AV**
    Bibl: Process: architecture, 1985 Apr., no.57, p.94

Estcourt, Kathleen Beatrice (*British artist, 1909-op.1955*)   **WI**

Este, Baldassarre d'   **BA**
    (*Italian artist, op.1461-m.1504*)   WC
    (*Italian painter, 1432-1504*)   BA
    (*Italian painter, act. 1461, d. 1504*)   PR
    (*Italian, act.1461-d.1504*)   GC
    Bibl: Benati, Paragone, XXXIII/393 (1982) pp.3-26; Berenson, Cent. & N.Ital.; ▶Bolaffi; Campori, Artisti ital. e stranieri; ▶Diz. biog. ital.; ▶Shapley, Kress coll.; ▶Thieme-Becker; ▶Witt checklist

    Baldassare d'Este   GC PR
    Baldassare d'Este or Estense   **WC**
    Baldassare da Reggio   PR
    Baldassare Estense   GC **PR**
    Baldassarre Estense   PR
    Estense, Baldassare   PR

Esté, Florence   **BA WI**
    (*American artist, 1860-1926*)   WI
    (*American painter, printmaker, 1860-1926*)   BA
    Bibl: ▶Bénézit; ▶Fielding's Amer. ptrs., suppl.; ▶Thieme-Becker; ▶Vollmer, Künst.-Lex. 20. Jhr.

Esteban March → see March, Esteban

Esteban Marquez de Velasco → see Márquez de Velasco, Esteban

Esteban Noguera, Julio (*Spanish architect, Barcelona*)   **AV**
    Bibl: ▶Guia secreta Hermandad, 1982-1983

Estense, Baldassarre → see Este, Baldassarre d'

Esterer, Rudolf (*German architect, 20th c.*)   **BA**
    Bibl: KUNSTCHRONIK XXVII/4 (Apr 74) 110-112

Esterhuizen, Jac (*British artist, b.1949*)   **WI**

Esterl, Martin (*Architect*)   **AV**
    Bibl: DBZ, 1984 Oct., v.32, no.10, p.1343

Esterle, Max (*German artist, 1870-1947*)   **WC**

Estern, Neil (*American sculptor, b.1926*)   **BA**
    Bibl: ▶WW Amer. Art, 1978

Estes, Charles Edwin (*American architect, 1928-1982*)   **AV**
    Bibl: Texas architect, 1982 Sept.-Oct., v.32, no.5, p.75

Estes, Merion (*American painter, b.1938*)   **BA**
    Bibl: ▶Intl. dir. exh. artists, 1983; Oakland (CA, USA), Oakland Museum, ON AND OFF THE WALL (1983)

Estes, Richard   **BA GC WC WI**
    (*American artist, 1936-*)   WC
    (*American artist, b.1936*)   WI
    (*American painter, b.1932*)   BA
    (*American painter, b.1936*)   GC
    Bibl: ▶Babington Smith, Contemp. artists; ▶Contemp. artists; ▶Intl. dir. exh. artists, 1982-1983; ▶RILA/BHA; RLIN BKS file; ▶WW Amer. Art

Estevan Marquez → see Márquez de Velasco, Esteban

Esteve → see Esteve, Agustín

Esteve y Marques, Agustín → see Esteve, Agustín

Esteve y Vilella, Rafael   **BA GC**
    (*Spanish printmaker, 1772-1847*)   BA
    (*Spanish, 1772-1847*)   GC
    Bibl: ▶Bénézit; ▶Thieme-Becker
    Esteve, Rafael   BA

Esteve, Agustín   **BA GC PR WC**
    (*Spanish artist, 1753-p.1809*)   WC
    (*Spanish painter, 1753-ca.1820*)   BA PR
    (*Spanish, 1753-aft.1809*)   GC
    Bibl: Aren,LA PINTURA ESPANOLA (1971); ▶Bénézit; ▶Ceán Bermúdez, Bellas artes ESP; ▶Encic. univ. ilus.; ▶Ossorio y Bernard, Artistas españoles 19s.; ▶RILA/BHA; ▶Thieme-Becker; ▶Witt checklist

    Agustin Esteve   PR
    Esteve   PR
    Esteve y Marques, Agustín   BA
    Esteve, Augustin (y Marques)   PR
    Marques, Agustin Esteve y   PR

Esteve, Augustin (y Marques) → see Esteve, Agustín

Estève, José (*Architect, member of Association for the Development of an African Architecture and Urbanism (ADAUA)*)   **AV**
    Bibl: Architecture: the AIA journal, 1983 Aug., v.72, no.8, p.110

Estève, Maurice   **BA WC**
    (*French artist, 1904-*)   WC
    (*French painter, printmaker, b.1904*)   BA
    Bibl: ▶Bénézit; Guide exh. artists: N. Amer. ptrs.; ▶Intl. dir. exh. artists, 1982, v.1; ▶Vollmer, Künst.-Lex. 20. Jhr.

Esteve, Miguel (*Spanish artist, op. 1513-1520*)   **WC**

Esteve, Rafael → see Esteve y Vilella, Rafael

Esteves or Estevens, David (*Danish artist, op.1691-1703*)   **WC**

Esteves, Xavier   **AV BA**
    (*Portuguese architect*)   AV
    (*Portuguese engineer, act.1906*)   BA
    Bibl: Harris, Country Life, 179/4632 (29 May 1986) 1546

Estey, James (*American painter, b.1940*)   **BA**
    Bibl: Sacramento (CA, USA), Crocker Art Gallery, JAMES ESTEY (1981)

Esther Frances Alexander → see Alexander, Esther Frances

Esther Paris-Persennet → see Paris-Persennet, Esther

Estienne, Henry d' (*French artist, 1872-*)   **WC**

Estoppey, Pierre (*Swiss painter, printmaker, scenographer, b.1911*)   **BA**
    Bibl: ▶Künst.-Lex. Schweiz 20. Jahrh.; ▶Lex. zeitgen. Schweiz. Künstler

Estormes, Hernando → see Sturm, Fernando

Estrada, Adolfo (*Mexican artist, 1942-*)   **WC**

Estrada, Ernesto de (*Argentine architect, 1909-*)   **AV**
    Bibl: SCA: revista de la Sociedad Central de Arquitectos, 1985 Dec., no.135, p.44

Estrampes, Jean-Pierre (*French architect*)   **AV**
    Bibl: Techniques et architecture, 1986 Feb.-Mar., no.364, p.11

Estrin, Mary Lloyd (*American photographer, b.1944.*)   **BA**
    Bibl: Estrin,M.L.,To The Manor Born,1979; ▶Macmillan photog. encyc.

Estruch, Fernández y → see Fernández y Estruch

Etang, Henri de l' (*French artist, 1809-p.1844*)   **WC**

Etchells → see Etchells, Frederick

Etchells, Frederick   **BA PR WC WI**
    (*British artist, 1886-1973*)   WC WI
    (*British painter, 1886-1973*)   PR
    (*British painter, architect, 1886-1973*)   BA
    Bibl: ▶Phaidon 20c. art; ▶RILA/BHA; ▶Waters, Brit. artists
    Etchells   PR
    Frederick Etchells   PR

Etchells, Frederick (*1887-1953*)   **AV**

Etcheto, Jean François Marie (*Spanish sculptor, 1853-1889*)   **GC**
    Bibl: ▶Bénézit

Etcheverry, Hubert Denis (*French artist, 1867-p.1903*)   **WC**

Etex, Antoine   **BA GC**
    (*French artist, 1808-1888*)   WC
    (*French sculptor, architect, and painter, 1808-1888*)   GC
    (*French sculptor, painter, architect, 1808-1888*)   BA
    Bibl: ▶Bénézit; ▶RILA/BHA; ▶Thieme-Becker

    Etex, Antoine (Tony)   **WC**

Etex, Antoine (Tony) → see Etex, Antoine

Etex, Louis-Jules *(French painter, 1810-1889)* GC
Bibl: ▶Bénézit

Etgens, Jan Jiri or Johann Georg *(Czech artist, 1693-1757)* WC

Ethan Allen Greenwood→*see* Greenwood, Ethan Allen

Ethe, Solomon *(American painter, b.1924)* BA
Bibl: Arts Mag. LI (Jan 1977), p.51; ARTS MAGAZINE,v.52 (Dec. 1977),p.2; ▶NY art yrbk.

Ethel Sands→*see* Sands, Ethel
Ethel Walker→*see* Walker, Ethel
Ethelwyn Upton→*see* Upton, E.

Etheridge, William *(d.1776)* AV

Ethiop Painter GC
Bibl: ▶Beazley, Attic red-fig. vase-ptrs.

Ethofer, Theodor Josef *(German artist, 1849-p.1912)* WC

Etienne Allegrain→*see* Allegrain, Etienne
Etienne Aubry→*see* Aubry, Étienne
Etienne Barthelemy Garnier→*see* Garnier, Etienne Barthélemy
Etienne Jeaurat→*see* Jeaurat, Etienne
Etienne La Tour→*see* La Tour, Etienne
Etienne Parrocel→*see* Parrocel, Etienne (Le Romain)
Etienne Prosper Berne-Bellecour→*see* Berne-Bellecour, Etienne Prosper
Etienne Ret→*see* Ret, Étienne

Etienne, Francois-Paul *(French artist, 1874-)* WC

Etienne, Martin→*see* Etienne-Martin

Etienne-Martin *(French sculptor, b.1913)* BA
Bibl: ▶Vollmer, Künst.-Lex. 20. Jhr.; ▶WW France

Etienne, Martin BA

Etito *(Italian artist, 19th cent.)* WC

Etlinger, Josef Georg von→*see* Edlinger, Josef Georg von

Etna Group *(South Italian vase-painters, 4th century BC)* GC
Bibl: ▶Trendall, Red-fig. vases Lucania

Eto, Shinichi *(Japanese architect)* AV
Bibl: Bauforum, 1988, v.21, no. 127, p.9

Eton-Nika Painter *(Apulian vase-painter)* GC
Bibl: Trendall, Attic red-fig. vases Apulia

Etour→*see* Duchateau, Mme.

Etra, Bill *(American video artist, electronic designer, 20th c.)* BA
Bibl: Furlong, Afterimage (Sum. 1983) pp.37-38

Etra, Louise *(American video artist, 20th c.)* BA

Ettedgui, Joseph *(in GBR fashion designer, 20th c.)* BA
Bibl: Phone book

Joseph (Joseph Ettedgui) BA

Ettl, Georg *(West German painter, b.1940)* BA
Bibl: Krefeld (DEU),Kaiser Wilhelm Mus., GEORG ETTL (1983)

Ettlinger, Josef Georg von→*see* Edlinger, Josef Georg von

Ettner, Andreas Philipp *(German porcelain painter, act.1756-1787)* BA
Bibl: ▶Honey, Euro. ceramic; Keramos (Jan 1974) 11

Oettner, Andreas Philipp BA

Ettore Forti→*see* Forti, Ettore
Ettore Tito→*see* Tito, Ettore
Etty→*see* Etty, William

Etty, John *(English carpenter, architect, ca.1634-1707/08)* BA
Bibl: ▶Colvin, Brit. archts.

Etty, William AV BA GC PR WC WI
(British artist, 1787-1849) WC WI
(British painter, 1787-1849) BA PR
(British painter, York, England, 1787-1849) AV
(British, 1787-1849) GC
Bibl: ▶Encyc. world art; ▶RILA/BHA; ▶Thieme-Becker; ▶Witt checklist; York Georgian Society. Annual report, 1987, p.27

Etty PR
William Etty PR

Etty, William *(British carpenter, architect, ca.1675-1734)* AV
Bibl: ▶Colvin, Brit. archts.

Euaichme Painter *(vase-painter, ca. 475-450 BC)* GC
Bibl: ▶Beazley, Attic red-fig. vase-ptrs.; Richter, Attic red-fig. vases

Euainetos *(Greek coin designer, 5th/4th c BC)* GC
Bibl: ▶Brilliant, Anc. Greeks, p.242

Euaion Painter GC JG
(vase-painter, ca. 475-450 BC) GC
Bibl: ▶Beazley, Attic red-fig. vase-ptrs.; Richter, Attic red-fig. vases

Euanthes *(Greek painter, Hellenistic (3rd-1st c BC))* GC
Bibl: ▶Robertson, Greek art, p.589

Eucharides Painter GC JG
(vase-painter, ca. 500-475 BC) GC
Bibl: ▶Beazley, Attic red-fig. vase-ptrs.; Richter, Attic red-fig. vases

Eucheir of Corinth *(Greek clay-modeller, 7th c BC (3rd qtr))* GC
Bibl: Getty Photo Study Coll.; ▶Robertson, Greek art, p.592

Eucheir of Corinth (grandfather) *(Greek sculptor, 3rd c BC)* GC
Bibl: Getty Photo Study Coll. (Antiquities); ▶Robertson, Greek art, p.555

Eucheir of Corinth (grandson) *(Greek sculptor, 3rd c BC)* GC
Bibl: Getty Photo Study Coll. (Antiquities); ▶Robertson, Greek art, p.555

Eucheiros Son of Ergotimos *(potter, ca.560-540? BC)* GC
Bibl: ▶Beazley, Attic bl.-fig. vase-ptrs.; Boardman, Attic Bl.-fig. Vases

Euchel, Johann→*see* Santini Aichel, Johann

Eude, Jean Louis Adolphe *(French sculptor, 1818-1889)* GC
Bibl: ▶Bénézit

Eude, Nicolas→*see* Heude, Nicolas

Eudes de Guimard, Louise *(French artist, 1827-1904)* WC

Euenor of Ephesos *(Greek painter, 5th c BC (mid))* GC
Bibl: Getty Photo Study Coll.; ▶Robertson, Greek art, p.179

Euergides *(vase-painter and potter, ca. 515-500 BC)* GC
Bibl: ▶Beazley, Attic red-fig. vase-ptrs.; Boardman, Athenian Red-fig. Vases, Archaic Per.

Euergides Painter JG
Euergides Painter→*see* Euergides
Euertz, Jan→*see* Ewouts, Hans
eug.o caxes→*see* Caxés, Eugenio
Eugen Adam→*see* Adam, Eugen
Eugen Jettel→*see* Jettel, Eugen

Eugen Napoleon Nicolaus, prince BA
(Swedish artist, 1865-1947) WC
(Swedish painter, 1865-1947) GC PR
(Swedish painter, printmaker, 1865-1947) BA
Bibl: Heraldry of the Royal Families of Europe; ▶Libr. of Congr. Name Auth. File; ▶Svenskt konst-lex.; ▶Thieme-Becker; ▶Witt checklist

Duke of Narke PR

Eugen, Napoleon Nikolaus Prinz von WC

Eugen, Prince of Sweden GC PR

Eugene, Duke of Narke PR

Eugen Neuhaus→*see* Neuhaus, Eugen
Eugen Spiro→*see* Spiro, Eugen
Eugen, Napoleon Nikolaus Prinz von→*see* Eugen Napoleon Nicolaus, prince
Eugen, Prince of Sweden→*see* Eugen Napoleon Nicolaus, prince
Eugene Accard→*see* Accard, Eugène
Eugene Benoit Baudin→*see* Baudin, Eugène Benoît
Eugene Berman→*see* Berman, Eugene
Eugene Camerer→*see* Camerer, Eugene
Eugene Ciceri→*see* Cicéri, Eugène
Eugene Cyprien Boulet→*see* Boulet, Eugène Cyprien
Eugene Delacroix→*see* Delacroix, Eugène

Eugene Deshayes → see Deshayes,
     Eugène
Eugene Deveria → see Devéria, Eugène
     François Marie Joseph
Eugene E. Speicher → see Speicher,
     Eugene Edward
Eugene Emmanuel Lemercier → see
     Lemercier, Eugène Emmanuel
Eugene Faure → see Faure, Eugène
Eugene Fichel → see Fichel, Eugène
Eugene Francis Savage → see Savage,
     Eugene Francis
Eugene Fromentin → see Fromentin,
     Eugène
Eugene H. Pennell → see Pennell,
     Eugene H.
Eugene Higgins → see Higgins, Eugene
Eugene Lambert → see Lambert,
     Eugène
Eugene Louis Boudin → see Boudin,
     Eugène Louis
Eugene Louis Lami → see Lami,
     Eugène Louis
Eugene Paul Ullman → see Ullman,
     Eugene Paul
Eugene Verboeckhoven → see
     Verboeckhoven, Eugène
Eugene Zak → see Zak, Eugène
Eugene, Duke of Narke → see Eugen
     Napoleon Nicolaus, prince

Eugene, Frank   **BA JG**
     *(American photographer, 1865-
          1936)*   BA
     (German (b. USA), 1865-1936)   JG
     Bibl: ▶Gernsheim, Hist. photog.;
          ▶Image; Manchester (NH, USA),
          Currier Gallery, Stieglitz & photo-
          secession (1983); PA
     Smith, Frank Eugene   BA
Eugene. Carriere → see Carrière,
     Eugène
Eugenie Servieres → see Servières,
     Eugénie

Eugenikos, Manuel *(Byzantine
     painter, act.1384-1396)*   **BA**
     Bibl: Alpago-Novello, Art medieval
          Georgia, p. 100; Belting, CAHIERS
          ARCHEOL., 28 (1979) p.103-114;
          Lazarev, Pitt. bizantina;
          Lordkipanidze, L'ARE GEORGIANA
          DAL IX AL XIV s., 147-152;
          Lordkipanidze, L'ARE GEORGIANA
          DAL IX AL XIV s., p.147-152
Eugenio Caxes → see Caxés, Eugenio
Eugenio Lucas Villamil → see Lucas
     Villamil, Eugenio
Eugenio Lucas y Padilla → see Lucas y
     Padilla, Eugenio
Eugenio Zampighi → see Zampighi,
     Eugenio
Eugeniusz Eibisch → see Eibisch,
     Eugeniusz
Eugerthe, Eduard von → see Engerth,
     Eduard von

Eugrammos of Corinth *(Greek clay-
     modeller, 7th c BC (3rd qtr))*   **GC**
     Bibl: Getty Photo Study Coll.;
          ▶Robertson, Greek art, p.592
Eukleidas *(Greek die-sinker, 5th c
     BC)*   **GC**
     Bibl: ▶Robertson, Greek art, p.360
Eukleides of Athens *(Greek
     sculptor, Hellenistic (3rd-1st c BC))* **GC**
     Bibl: ▶Robertson, Greek art, p.555
Eulhofer, Ignaz → see Elhafen, Ignaz
Eumares *(Greek sculptor, 6th c BC
     (end))*   **GC**
     Bibl: ▶Robertson, Greek art, p.227
Eumaros of Athens *(Greek painter,
     6th c BC (end))*   **GC**
     Bibl: ▶Robertson, Greek art, p.227
Eumenides Painter *(Apulian vase-
     painter)*   **GC**
     Bibl: Trendall, Attic red-fig. vases
          Apulia
Euphemie Muraton → see Muraton,
     Euphémie
Euphiletos Painter *(vase-painter, ca.
     530-520 BC)*   **GC**
     Bibl: ▶Beazley, Attic bl.-fig. vase-
          ptrs.; Boardman, Attic Bl.-fig.
          Vases
Euphiletos?   **GC**
     Bibl: ▶Beazley, Attic bl.-fig. vase-
          ptrs.
Euphranor *(Greek sculptor, painter,
     375-335 B.C.)*   **BA**
     Bibl: ▶Bénézit; Schefold, Griechen
          u. ihre Nachbarn (Prop. Kunst. 1),
          p.223; ▶Thieme-Becker
Euphranor of Isthmia *(Greek
     sculptor, act. ca.360-330 BC)*   **GC**
     Bibl: ▶Bowder, WWW Greek,
          p.108
Euphronios   **BA GC JG**
     (Greek painter, act.ca.500 B.C.)   BA
     (vase-painter, ca. 520-505 BC)   GC
     Bibl: ▶Beazley, Attic red-fig. vase-
          ptrs.; Boardman, Athenian Red-
          fig. Vases, Archaic Per.; ▶Encyc.
          world art; ▶McGraw-Hill dict. art;
          ▶Thieme-Becker
Eupolemos of Argos *(Greek
     architect, 5th c (end)-4th c (beg)
     BC)*   **GC**
     Bibl: ▶Robertson, Greek art, p.396
Eupolis Painter *(vase-painter, ca.
     450-420 BC)*   **GC**
     Bibl: ▶Beazley, Attic red-fig. vase-
          ptrs.; Richter, Attic red-fig. vases
Eupompos of Sikyon *(Greek
     painter, 5th c (end)-4th c (beg)
     BC)*   **GC**
     Bibl: ▶Robertson, Greek art, p.484
Eurich, Richard Ernest → see Eurich,
     Richard Ernest

Eurich, Richard Ernst   **BA**
     (British artist, 1903-)   WC
     (British artist, b.1903)   WI
     (British painter, b.1903)   BA
     Bibl: ▶Dolman, Contemp. Brit.
          artists; ▶Johnson, Brit. artists
Eurich, Richard Ernest   **WC WI**
Europa Group *(Greek vase-painters,
     4th century BC)*   **GC**
     Bibl: McPhee & Trendall, Fish-
          Plates
Eusebi, Luis *(Spanish artist, op.1813-
     1830)*   **WC**
Eusebio da San Giorgio   **BA GC**
     *(Italian artist,
          1465/70-p.1539(?))*   WC
     *(Italian painter,
          1465/70-aft.1539)*   GC
     *(Italian painter, b.1465-1470, d.
          after 1540)*   BA
     Bibl: ▶Bénézit; ▶Bolaffi; Getty
          Photo Study Coll. (Ptgs.);
          ▶RILA/BHA; TCI Umbria;
          ▶Thieme-Becker
**Eusebio da San Giorgio
     (Eusepius Jacobi Cristofori;
     Eusepio Perugino)**   **WC**
Eusebio di Giacomo di Cristoforo   BA
Eusepio Perugino   GC
Eusepius Jacobi Cristofori   GC
*Eusebio da San Giorgio (Eusepius
     Jacobi Cristofori; Eusepio
     Perugino)* → see Eusebio da San
     Giorgio
*Eusebio di Giacomo di
     Cristoforo* → see Eusebio da San
     Giorgio
Eusebius, Johannes Alphen → see
     Alphen, Alf, Alfen or Alwen,
     Eusebius Johann
Eusepio Perugino → see Eusebio da
     San Giorgio
Eusepius Jacobi Cristofori → see
     Eusebio da San Giorgio
Eussenman, Georg *(German
     draughtsman, act.1715)*   **GC**
     Bibl: Christie's
Eustace, A.W. *(Australian artist,
     19th cent.)*   **WC**
Eustace, Samuel B.   **WC WI**
     (British artist, op.1819)   WC
     (British artist, op.1819-)   WI
Eustache Le Sueur → see Le Sueur,
     Eustache
Eustache, Charles François *(French
     painter, printmaker, 1820-1870)*   **BA**
     Bibl: ▶Bénézit; ▶Thieme-Becker
Euthychides of Sikyon *(Greek
     sculptor, act. ca.300 BC)*   **GC**
     Bibl: ▶Brilliant, Anc. Greeks, p.385
Euthykartides of Naxos *(Greek
     sculptor, 7th/6th c BC (ca.615-
     590))*   **GC**
     Bibl: Richter, Kouroi, p.53

Euthykrates of Sikyon *(Greek sculptor, 4th c (end)-3rd c (beg) BC)* **GC**
    Bibl: ▶Robertson, Greek art, p.478

Euthymides **GC JG**
    (vase-painter, ca. 530-500 BC) **GC**
    Bibl: ▶Beazley, Attic red-fig. vase-ptrs.; Richter, Attic red-fig. vases

Euw, Walter von *(Swiss architect)* **AV**
    Bibl: Abitare, 1982 July-Aug., no. 206, p.40

Euxeinidas *(Greek painter, 4th c BC (1st half))* **GC**
    Bibl: ▶Robertson, Greek art, p.484

Eva Almond Withrow→*see* Withrow, Eva Almond

Eva Gonzales→*see* Gonzalès, Eva

Eva Scott Fenyes→*see* Fenyes, Eva Scott

Evalde, Maurice-Bernard *(French ébéniste, master 1765)* **GC**
    Bibl: ▶Salverte, Ébénistes 18e s.
    Ewalde, Maurice-Bernard **GC**

Evalina **WC WI**
    (American artist, 20th cent.) **WC**
    (American artist, op.20th c.) **WI**

Evalo, Hans de→*see* De Vals, Hans

Evamy, Michael *(Canadian architect, 20th c.)* **BA**
    Bibl: White, Vanguard, XIII/4 (May 1984) p.26

Evance, Haunce→*see* Ewouts, Hans

Evangelista da Pian di Meleto→*see* Evangelista di Pian di Meleto

Evangelista de Predis→*see* Predis, Evangelista de

Evangelista di Pian di Meleto **BA GC WC**
    (Italian artist, c.1458-1549) **WC**
    (Italian painter, ca.1458-1549) **BA GC**
    Bibl: Berenson, Cent. & N.Ital.; ▶Bolaffi; ▶RILA/BHA, 1986; ▶Thieme-Becker; ▶Witt checklist
    Evangelista da Pian di Meleto **GC**

Evangelista Martinetti→*see* Martinetti, Evangelista [Unidentified]

Evangelisti, Filippo *(Italian artist, c.1684-1761)* **WC**

Evangulov, Sergej Pavlovič *(Russian sculptor, b.1893)* **BA**
    Bibl: ▶Fogg Mus. Libr. cat.; ▶Natl. union cat., 1956-1967

Evans, Allen *(1845-1925)* **AV**

Evans, Barry *(British painter, b.1923)* **BA**
    Bibl: Times 30 Sept 1978) 8

Evans, Bernard Walter **BA WC WI**
    (British artist, 1848-1922) **WC WI**
    (British painter, 1848-1922) **BA**
    Bibl: Evans, Hist. jewelry; ▶Johnson, Brit. artists; ▶Thieme-Becker

Evans, Bob *(British artist, b.1947)* **WI**

Evans, Charles *(18th cent. British carpenter/architect)* **AV**
    Bibl: ▶Colvin, Brit. archts.

Evans, Clifford *(American architect, 1889-1973)* **BA**
    Bibl: Prairie School Review, XII/1 (1975) pp.5-22

Evans, David *(British artist, b.1895)* **WI**
    Bibl: ▶Waters, Brit. artists

Evans, David Scott→*see* Evans, De Scott

Evans, De Scott **BA PR WI**
    (American artist, 1847-1898) **WI**
    (American painter, 1847-1898) **BA PR**
    Bibl: ▶Fielding's Amer. ptrs.; Indianapolis (IN, USA), Mus. Art, Mirages of memory (1976); ▶RILA/BHA
    De Scott Evans **PR**
    Evans, David Scott **BA**
    Evans, De Scott (S.S. David) **PR**

Evans, De Scott (S.S. David)→*see* Evans, De Scott

Evans, Dennis *(American sculptor, performance artist, b.1946)* **BA**
    Bibl: Artweek (Oct 23, 1976); New York (NY, USA), New Museum, OUTSIDE NY: SEATTLE (1983)
    Ubu Waugh **BA**

Evans, Dennis J. *(Canadian artist, 20th c.)* **BA**
    Bibl: Calgary (CAN), Glenbow-Albert Inst., BILL LAING, DENNIS EVANS...(1977)

Evans, Donald *(American artist, 1945-1977)* **BA**
    Bibl: ART IN AMERICA LXV/4 (July-Aug 1977) 15 (obit)

Evans, Donald F. *(American architect, Orlando)* **AV**
    Bibl: ▶AIA Pro File, 1987-89

Evans, Edmund **BA WI**
    (British artist, 1826-1905) **WI**
    (British printmaker, 1826-1905) **BA**
    Bibl: ▶Bénézit; ▶Thieme-Becker

Evans, Eldred **AV BA**
    (British architect, 1938-) **AV**
    (British architect, 20th c.) **BA**
    Bibl: ▶Avery period. idx.; Das Kunstwerk, n.3-4, Sept. 1983, p.92; Davies, ARCH REVIEW, CLXXVI/1049 (July 1984) 32-39

Evans, Etienne *(French porcelain painter, act.1752-1775, 1778-1806)* **GC**
    Bibl: ▶Brunet, Sèvres

Evans, Evan D. *(British, b. 1849, active U.S. until after 1902)* **JG**

Evans, F. Larry *(American architect, Ga)* **AV**
    Bibl: Restaurant and hotel design, 1988 Jan., v.10, no.1, p.50

Evans, Frederick H.→*see* Evans, Frederick Henry

Evans, Frederick Henry **BA JG**
    (British artist, 19th cent.) **WC**
    (British artist, op.19th c.) **WI**
    (British photographer, 1853-1943) **BA**
    (British, 1853-1943) **JG**
    Bibl: ▶Gernsheim, Hist. photog.; ▶Newhall, Photog.

Evans, Frederick H. **WC WI**

Evans, Frederick James McNamara **WC WI**
    (British artist, op.1886-1930) **WI**
    (British artist, op.1888-1911) **WC**

Evans, Garth **BA WC WI**
    (British artist, 20th cent.) **WC**
    (British artist, b.1934) **WI**
    (British sculptor, b.1934) **BA**
    Bibl: ▶Bénézit; ▶MoMA libr. cat.; ▶WW Art

Evans, George→*see* Evans, George II

Evans, George II **WI**
    (British artist, 1763-1819) **WC WI**

Evans, George **WC**

Evans, Gethin *(British artist, b.1954)* **WI**

Evans, Handel *(British artist, b.1932)* **WI**

Evans, Houghton *(British architect)* **AV**
    Bibl: Architects' journal, 1985 Apr.3, v.181, no.14, p.16

Evans, J. **BA WC**
    (American artist, 19th cent.) **WC**
    (American painter, act.1830-1850) **BA**
    Bibl: THREE NEW ENGLAND PAINTERS

Evans, James **AV GC**
    (American interior designer) **AV**
    (British) **GC**
    Bibl: Gernsheim, Corpus Photog. of Drawings, 1517; Southern accents, 1984 Sept.-Oct., v.7, no.5, p.106

Evans, James Guy *(American artist, op.circa 1840-)* **WI**

Evans, James I. *(American artist, op. 19th c.)* **WI**

Evans, Jeffrey **AV**

Evans, John I *(British artist, op.1813-1835)* **WI**

Evans, John II *(British artist, b.1951)* **WI**

Evans, John William *(Engraver, b.1855)* **WI**

Evans, Joyce Conway *(British designer, 20th c.)* **BA**
    Bibl: ARCHITECTURAL REVIEW CLX/955 (Sept 1976) 166

Evans, Kit **AV**

Evans, L. **WC WI**
    (British artist, 19th cent.) **WC**
    (British artist, op.19th c.) **WI**

Evans, Lesley→*see* Evans, Leslie

Evans, Leslie **WI**
    (British artist, 1945-) **WC**
    (British artist, b.1945) **WI**

Evans, Lesley **WC**

Evans, M.R. *(British artist, op.20th c.)* **WI**

Everbag, Frans→*see* Everbag,
Franciscus

Everbroeck, Frans van   **GC PR WC**
> *(Dutch painter, act. 1654-1672)*   PR
> *(Flemish artist, op.1654-1672)*   WC
> *(Flemish painter, act.1654-1672)*   GC
>> Bibl: ▶Thieme-Becker; ▶Witt
>> checklist

F.V. Ever Broeck   PR
Frans van Everbroeck   PR

Everdengen→*see* Everdingen, Allart
van
Everdengin→*see* Everdingen, Allart
van
Everding→*see* Everdingen, Allart van
Everdinge→*see* Everdingen, Allart
van
Everdingen→*see* Everdingen, Allart
van
Everdingen→*see* Everdingen, Caesar
Boetius van
Everdingen→*see* Everdingen, Jan van

Everdingen, Adriaen van   **GC**
> *(Dutch artist, 1832-1912)*   WC
> *(Dutch painter, 1832-1910)*   GC
>> Bibl: ▶Thieme-Becker

Everdingen, Adrianus van   **WC**
Everdingen, Adrianus van→*see*
Everdingen, Adriaen van
Everdingen, Allaert van→*see*
Everdingen, Allart van
*Everdingen, Allart or Aldert Pietersz.
van*→*see* Everdingen, Allart van

Everdingen, Allart van   **BA GC JG PR**
> *(Dutch artist, 1621-1675)*   WC
> *(Dutch painter and printmaker,*
> *1621-1675)*   GC
> *(Dutch painter, 1621-1675)*   PR
> *(Dutch painter, printmaker,*
> *1621-1675)*   BA
> *(Dutch, 1621-1675)*   JG
>> Bibl: ▶Bénézit; ▶RILA/BHA;
>> ▶Thieme-Becker

Albert van Everdingen   PR
Aldret Van Everdingen   PR
Allaert van Everdingen   PR
Allard van Everdingen   PR
Allart van Everdingen   PR
Allert van Everdingen   PR
Evendingen   PR
Everdengen   PR
Everdengin   PR
Everding   PR
Everdinge   PR
Everdingen   PR
Everdingen, Allaert van   PR

**Everdingen, Allart or Aldert
Pietersz. van**   **WC**
Everdingenn   PR
Everdingh   PR
Oude Everdingen   PR

Everdingen, Caesar Boetius van   **BA**
> *(Dutch artist,*
> *c.1616/17(?)-1678)*   WC
> *(Dutch painter and*
> *draughtsman, ca.1617-1678)*   GC
> *(Dutch painter, ca.1606-1678)*   BA
> *(Dutch painter, ca.1617-1678)*   PR
> *(Dutch, ca. 1617-1678)*   JG
>> Bibl: Getty Photo Study Coll.;
>> ▶RILA/BHA; ▶Thieme-Becker

Cesair of Everdingen   PR
Cesar Boetius van Everdingen   PR
Everdingen   PR

**Everdingen, Cesar Boetius
van**   **GC PR**
**Everdingen, Cesar Pietersz.
Cesar or Boetius van**   **WC**
Everdingen, Cesar van   **JG PR**
Everdingen, Cesar Van (?)   PR
Everdingen, Cesar Boetius van→*see*
Everdingen, Caesar Boetius van
*Everdingen, Cesar Pietersz. Cesar or
Boetius van*→*see* Everdingen,
Caesar Boetius van
Everdingen, Cesar van→*see*
Everdingen, Caesar Boetius van
Everdingen, Cesar Van (?)→*see*
Everdingen, Caesar Boetius van

Everdingen, Cornelis van *(Dutch
painter, b. 1646)*   **PR**
>> Bibl: ▶Thieme-Becker

Cornelis van Everdingen   PR

Everdingen, Jan van *(Dutch painter,
d. 1656)*   **PR**
>> Bibl: ▶Thieme-Becker

Everdingen   PR
Giovanni Van Everdigen   PR
Jan van Everdingen   PR

Everdingen, Pieter van   **GC PR**
> *(Dutch draughtsman, b. aft.*
> *1651-1739)*   GC
> *(Dutch painter, b. 1651)*   PR
>> Bibl: ▶Thieme-Becker

Pieter van Everdingen   PR

Everdingen, Tetar van   **GC WC**
> *(Dutch artist, 19th cent.)*   WC
> *(Dutch painter, 19th century)*   GC
>> Bibl: ▶Witt checklist

Everdingenn→*see* Everdingen, Allart
van
Everdingh→*see* Everdingen, Allart
van
Everen→*see* Van Everen, Jay
Everen, Jay van→*see* Van Everen, Jay
Everett Raymond Kinstler→*see*
Kinstler, Everett Raymond
Everett Shinn→*see* Shinn, Everett

Everett, Bruce   **BA WC WI**
> *(American artist, 1942-)*   WC
> *(American artist, b.1942)*   WI
> *(American painter, b.1942)*   BA
>> Bibl: Hartford (CT, USA),
>> Wadsworth Ath., NEW/PHOTO
>> REALISM (1974); Whitney

Everett, Edward *(American soldier,
painter, 1818-1903)*   **BA**
>> Bibl: Ahlborn, R.E., THE SAN
>> ANTONIO MISSIONS: EDWARD
>> EVERETT ... 1985; ▶Groce, Artists
>> Amer., p.216

Everett, John   **BA WC WI**
> *(British artist, 1876-1949)*   WI
> *(British artist, 20th cent.)*   WC
> *(British painter, 1876-1949)*   BA
>> Bibl: APOLLO (Mar 1974) 188

Everett, Roxanne *(American
photography, 20th c.)*   **BA**
>> Bibl: Archives Amer. Art Jrnl.,
>> XXIII/3 (1983) pp.34-37

Everett, Walter H. *(American artist,
op.20th c.)*   **WI**

Evergon *(Canadian photographer,
b.1946)*   **BA**
>> Bibl: ▶Artists Canada; ▶Idx.
>> Ontario artists; Paris (FRA), Centre
>> Culturel canadien, Evergon (1983)

Lunt, Albert   BA

Evergood, Philip   **BA**
> *(American artist, 1901-)*   WC
> *(American artist, 1901-1973)*   WI
> *(American painter, printmaker,*
> *1901-1973)*   BA
>> Bibl: ▶Bénézit; ▶Contemp. artists;
>> ▶Intl. dir. exh. artists, 1982;
>> ▶MoMA libr. cat.; ▶Oxford comp.
>> 20c. art; ▶Parry, Contemp. art;
>> ▶Vollmer, Künst.-Lex. 20. Jhr.;
>> ▶WW Amer. Art, 1970, 1976;
>> ▶WWW Amer.

Blashki, Howard Francis   WI
Dixon, Howard Francis   BA
Evergood, Philip Howard   **WC**
Evergood, Philip Howard Francis   **WI**
Evergood, Philip Howard→*see*
Evergood, Philip
*Evergood, Philip Howard
Francis*→*see* Evergood, Philip
Everhardus Koster→*see* Koster,
Everhardus

Everitt, Allen Edward *(British artist,
1824-1882)*   **WC WI**

Everitt, William *(British artist, 1809-
1879)*   **WI**

Evers, Albert J. *(American architect,
practiced in California in 1930s)*   **AV**
>> Bibl: Friends of Terra Cotta, 1982
>> Spring, p.3

Evers, Anton Clemens *(German
artist, 1802-1848)*   **WC**

Eversberg, Dirk *(West German
architect, Berlin)*   **AV**
>> Bibl: Architektur + Wettbewerbe,
>> 1986 Sept., no.127, p.53

Eversdijk, Willem→*see* Eversdyck,
Willem
Eversdyck or Eversdijck, Willem→*see*
Eversdyck, Willem

Eversdyck, Cornelis Willemsz.   GC WC
  (Dutch artist, op.1613-1635)   WC
  (Dutch painter, act.1613-d. bef.
    1644)   GC
    Bibl: ▶Thieme-Becker
Eversdyck, Willem   GC PR
  (Dutch artist, op.1633-m.1671)   WC
  (Dutch painter and
    draughtsman, act.1633-d.
    1671)   GC
  (Dutch painter, d. 1671)   PR
    Bibl: Getty Photo Study Coll.;
    ▶Thieme-Becker; ▶Witt checklist
  Eversdijk, Willem   PR
Eversdyck or Eversdijck, Willem   WC
  Willem Eversdyck   PR
Eversen → see Eversen, Adrianus
Eversen, Adrianus   GC PR WC
  (Dutch artist, 1818-1897)   WC
  (Dutch draughtsman and
    painter, 1818-1897)   GC
  (Dutch painter, 1818-1897)   PR
    Bibl: ▶Thieme-Becker
  Adrianus Eversen   PR
  Eversen   PR
Eversen, Jan H. → see Eversen,
  Johannes Hendrik
Eversen, Johannes Hendrik   GC
  (Dutch artist, 20th cent.)   WC
  (Dutch painter, b.1906)   GC
    Bibl: ▶Witt checklist
Eversen, Jan H.   WC
Evershed, Arthur *(British artist,*
  1836-1919)   WI
Eversley, Frederick John *(American*
  sculptor, b.1941)   BA
    Bibl: ▶WW Amer. Art, 1976
Eversley, H.Q. *(British artist, op.*
  1903-)   WI
Evert Bois → see Dubois, Eduard
Evert Marselus → see Marseus van
  Schrieck, Evert
Evert Marseus → see Marseus van
  Schrieck, Evert
Evert Marseus van Schrieck → see
  Marseus van Schrieck, Evert
Evert Olofs → see Olofs, Evert
  [Unidentified]
Evert Oudendyck → see Oudendyck,
  Evert
Evert Pieters → see Pieters, Evert
Everts, Wolfgang *(West German*
  architect, Stuttgart)   AV
    Bibl: Bauwelt, 1989 July 28, v.80,
    no.28-29, p.1318
Evertsen → see Everardi, Angiolo
  (Engelbertsz.)
Evertsz, → see Evertsz., Pieter
  [Unidentified]

Evertsz., Pieter [Unidentified]
  (Unknown painter, act. 17th
    century)   PR
    Bibl: Aelbertsz. inventory c.1640
  Evertsz,   PR
  Pieter Evertsz,   PR
  Pr. Evertsz.   PR
Everwin *(German illuminator, 12th*
  c.)   BA
    Bibl: Paris (FRA), Musée arts
    décoratifs, L'Art ancien en CSK;
    ▶Thieme-Becker
Eves, Reginald Grenville   BA WC WI
  (British artist, 1876-1941)   WC WI
  (British painter, 1876-1941)   BA
    Bibl: ▶Vollmer, Künst.-Lex. 20.
    Jhr.; ▶Who was who [GBR]
Evett, Kenneth   WC WI
  (American artist, 20th cent.)   WC
  (American artist, b.1913)   WI
Evison, David *(British sculptor,*
  b.1944)   BA
    Bibl: Arts Council GBR, Square
    Coll. cat. (1974)
Evitt, G.E. *(British artist, op.20th c.)*   WI
Evjen, Ellen *(American artist, 20th*
  c.)   BA
    Bibl: Arts Mag. 55/4 (1981)
    88-92
Evola, Giulio *(Italian painter, graphic*
  artist, b.1898)   BA
    Bibl: ▶Bénézit; ▶Bolaffi; London
    (GBR), Hayward Gallery, Dada &
    Surrealism (1978); ▶MoMA libr.
    cat.
  Evola, Julius   BA
Evola, Julius → see Evola, Giulio
Evrard, Adele *(Belgian artist, 1792-*
  1889)   WC
Evrard, Eurard, Everaerdt,
  Everard, Everards or Everardt,
  Perpete or Jacques *(Flemish*
  artist, 1662-1727)   WC
Evrard, Jean Marie *(French artist,*
  1776-1860)   WC
Evreinov, Dmitrij Ivanovič *(Russian*
  miniaturist, 1742-1814)   BA
    Bibl: SOOBSCENIJA, HERMITAGE
    XLIII (1978); ▶Thieme-Becker
  Jewreinoff, Dmitrij Iwanowitsch   BA
Ewald, Clara *(British artist, op.1911-*
  1930)   WI
Ewald, Ernst Deodat Paul
  Ferdinand *(German artist, 1836-*
  1904)   WC
Ewald, Reinhold *(German artist,*
  1890-)   WC
Ewalde, Maurice-Bernard → see
  Evalde, Maurice-Bernard
Ewart, Charles Joseph Frederick
  (British artist, 1816-1884)   WI
Ewart, David *(British artist, op.1919-*
  1955)   WC WI
    Bibl: ▶Waters, Brit. artists

Ewart, David   AV BA
  (Architect, active ca.1908)   AV
  (Canadian architect, act.1893)   BA
    Bibl: Canadian heritage, 1985
    Oct.-Nov., v.11, no.4, p.39;
    RACAR V/2 (1978-79) 113-115
Ewart, Elizabeth *(Canadian artist,*
  b.1949)   BA
    Bibl: Toronto (Ont, CAN), Art Gall.
    of Ont., Ewart (1981)
Ewart, John → see Ewart, John Albert
Ewart, John Albert   FA
  (20.IV.1872-21.IV.1964;
    Architect, Architectural
    draftsman, Ottawa)   FA
  (Canadian architect)   AV
    Bibl: Bulletin of the Society for
    the Study of Architecture in
    Canada, 1985 Dec., v.10, no.4,
    p.14; CAAD Finding Aid, J. Albert
    Ewart, 1963-752, 76703/13,
    77803/14; ▶Hill, Archts. Canada;
    Natl. Arch. of Canada, CAAD
    Finding Aid
Ewart, John   AV
Ewbank, John Wilson   WC WI
  (British artist, 1779-1847)   WI
  (British artist, c.1779-1847)   WC
Ewbank, T.John *(British artist, op.*
  1826-, d.1863)   WI
Ewen, Paterson *(Canadian painter,*
  sculptor, b.1925)   BA
    Bibl: ▶Babington Smith, Contemp.
    artists; Guide exh. artists: N.
    Amer. ptrs.; ▶Idx. Ontario artists;
    ▶Intl. dir. exh. artists, 1983; ▶WW
    Amer. Art, 1989
Ewing *(American, active WA, U.S.*
  ca. 1916 (also Harris & Ewing,
  Graphic Arts))   JG
Ewing, Charles Kermit *(American*
  painter, educator, 1910-1976)   BA
    Bibl: NY Times obit., 14 Sep
    1976; ▶WW Amer. Art, 1976
Ewing, Edgar Louis *(American*
  painter, b.1913)   BA
    Bibl: ▶Vollmer, Künst.-Lex. 20.
    Jhr.; ▶WW Amer. Art, 1976
Ewing, George Edwin *(British artist,*
  1828-1884)   WC WI
Ewing, Guilio *(British artist, 1828-*
  1884)   WI
Ewing, Lauren *(American artist,*
  b.1946)   BA
    Bibl: Art News, LXXX/5 (May
    1981) pp.74-94; ▶Babington
    Smith, Contemp. artists; ▶Intl. dir.
    exh. artists, 1982; New York (NY,
    USA), New Mus., Investigations,
    PROBE (1980)
Ewing, Louie H. *(American sculptor,*
  painter, printmaker, 20th c.)   BA
    Bibl: ARCHIVES OF A A JOURNAL,
    XXII/3 (1983) 39-40
Ewing, Margaret *(British artist, op.*
  1850-)   WI

Eworth, Eewouts, Eottes, Euerts,
    Ewottes, Ewoutsz, Evance or
    Huett, Hans Jan or Haunce →see
    Ewouts, Hans
Eworth, Hans →see Ewouts, Hans
Ewottes, John →see Ewouts, Hans
Ewouts →see Ewouts, Hans
Ewouts, Hans   **BA GC PR**
    (British artist, op.1540-1574)   WC
    (British artist, op.circa 1520-,
        d.1574)   WI
    (early Netherlandish painter in
        England, before 1525-after
        1578)   BA
    (Flemish painter in ENG, bef.
        1525-aft.1578)   GC
    (Netherlandish painter, bef.
        1525-aft.1578)   PR
    Bibl: ▶Encyc. world art; Getty
        Photo Study Coll. (Ptgs.); ▶Osten,
        Ptg. & sculp. DEU & NLD;
        ▶RILA/BHA; ▶Thieme-Becker;
        ▶Wilenski, Flem. ptrs.
    Eottes, Hans   BA
    Euertz, Jan   BA
    Evance, Haunce   BA
**Eworth, Eewouts, Eottes,
    Euerts, Ewottes, Ewoutsz,
    Evance or Huett, Hans Jan or
    Haunce**   **WC**
Eworth, Hans   BA GC PR WI
    Ewottes, John   BA
    Ewouts   PR
Ewoutsz., Hans   **GC**
    Hans Ewouts   PR
Ewoutsz., Hans →see Ewouts, Hans
Ewsum, Anna van (Dutch, 1640-
    1714)   **BA**
    Bibl: Formsma, W.J., DE
        OMMELANDER BORGEN EN
        STEENHUIZEN, 1973, 280; ▶Nieuw
        NLD biog. woord., v.1, p.840;
        Pathuis, A., GRONINGER
        GEDENKWAARDIGHEDEN, 1977,
        nos. 2712, 2713, 2719
Exall, Michael (British artist, b.1950)   WI
Exekias   **BA GC JG**
    (Greek pottery painter, 6th c.
        B.C.)   BA
    (vase-painter, ca. 545-530 BC)   GC
    Bibl: ▶Beazley, Attic bl.-fig. vase-
        ptrs.; Boardman, Attic Bl.-fig.
        Vases; ▶Encyc. world art; Oxford
        classical dict.; Praeger Enc. of
        Anc. Greek Civ.; ▶Thieme-Becker;
        WW Ancient World, p.105
Exeter Group (South Italian vase-
    painters, 4th century BC)   **GC**
    Bibl: ▶Trendall, Red-fig. vases
        Lucania
Exeter, Alexandra →see Exter,
    Alexandra
Exilious, John F. →see Exilious, John
    G.

Exilious, John G.   **WI**
    (American artist, op.1810-1814)   WC
    (American artist, op.circa 1810-
        circa 1814)   WI
    (Engraver, op.circa 1810-circa
        1814)   WI
Exilious, John F.   **WC**
Exner, Inger   **AV BA**
    (Danish architect, Århus, 1926-)   AV
    (Danish architect, b.1926)   BA
    Bibl: ▶Avery period. idx., 3rd
        suppl.; ▶Danske Arkitekters
        Landsforbund, 1984-85; Wistoft,
        Johannes Exner
Exner, Johan Julius (Danish artist,
    1825-1910)   **WC**
Exner, Johannes   **AV BA**
    (Danish architect, Århus, 1926-)   AV
    (Danish architect, b.1926)   BA
    Bibl: ▶Avery period. idx., 2nd
        suppl.; ▶Danske Arkitekters
        Landsforbund, 1984-85; Wistoft,
        Johannes Exner
Expert, Roger Henri (French
    architect, 1882-1955)   **BA**
    Bibl: ▶Avery obit. idx.; ▶Dict.
        biog. fran.
Export, Valie (Austrian artist,
    b.1942)   **BA**
    Bibl: Philadelphia (PA, USA), ICA,
        Video art (1975)
Exshaw, Charles   **BA WC WI**
    (British artist, circa 1710-1771)   WI
    (British artist, op.1747-m.1771)   WC
    (English painter, printmaker,
        d.1771)   BA
    Bibl: ▶Dict. natl. biog.;
        ▶Thieme-Becker
Exter →see Exter, Alexandra
Exter, Alexandra   **BA PR WC**
    (Russian artist, 20th cent.)   WC
    (Russian painter, 1884-1949)   PR
    (Russian painter, scenographer,
        1884-1949)   BA
    Bibl: ▶Bénézit; ▶Encyc. world art;
        ▶Met. Mus. Art libr. cat.;
        ▶RILA/BHA
    Alexandra Exter   PR
    Ekster, Alexandra   BA
    Exeter, Alexandra   PR
    Exter   PR
Exter, Julius (German artist, 1863-
    1930)   **WC**
Exworth, Ray (British sculptor,
    b.1930)   **BA**
    Bibl: London (GBR), Whitechapel
        Art Gallery, RAY EXWORTH...
        (1975)
Eybe, Carl Gottfried (German artist,
    1813-1893)   **WC**
Eyben, Bruno Ninaber van (Dutch
    designer, b.1950)   **BA**
    Bibl: Amsterdam (NLD), Stedelijk
        Museum, Atelier 14 (1977);
        ▶Avery period. idx., 9th suppl.;
        Dutch Art & Arch. Today, 8 (May
        1981) 26-31

Eybl or Eibl, Franz (German artist,
    1806-1880)   **WC**
Eyck →see Eyck, Jan van
Eyck →see Eyck, Kasper van
Eyck, Aldo van   **AV BA**
    (Dutch architect, 1918-)   AV
    (Dutch architect, b.1918)   BA
    Bibl: ▶Contemp. archts.;
        ▶Macmillan encyc. archts.
    van Eyck, Aldo   AV
Eyck, Barthélemy d'   **BA GC**
    (early Netherlandish painter,
        illuminator in FRA, act.1438,
        d.1476)   BA
    (French painter, act.1447-ca.
        1476)   GC
    Bibl: ▶Bénézit; Getty Photo Study
        Coll. (Medieval); Roques, LES
        APPORTS NEERLANDAIS DANS LA
        PEINT. DU SUD-EST DE LA
        FRANCE, 166-167; Sterling,
        Enguerrand Quarton, p.218, pp.
        173-183; ▶Thieme-Becker
    Barthélemy D'Eyck   GC
    Barthélemy de Clerc   BA GC
    Clerc, Barthélemy de   BA
Eyck, Charles Hubert   **BA**
    (Dutch painter, b.1897)   GC
    (Dutch painter, printmaker,
        b.1897)   BA
    Bibl: ▶Bénézit; ▶Scheen, Ned.
        beeldende kunst.; ▶Vollmer,
        Künst.-Lex. 20. Jhr.
Eyck, Charles Hubertus   **GC**
Eyck, Charles Hubertus →see Eyck,
    Charles Hubert
Eyck, Gaspard van →see Eyck, Kasper
    van
Eyck, Hannie van (Dutch architect)   **AV**
    Bibl: Architecture d'aujourd'hui,
        1984 Oct., no.235, p.18
    van Eyck, Hannie   AV
Eyck, Hubert van   **BA GC**
    (early Netherlandish painter,
        1366-1426)   BA
    (Netherlandish painter,
        ca.1366/70-1426)   GC
    (Netherlands artist,
        c.1366/70-1426)   WC
    Bibl: ▶Thieme-Becker; ▶Witt
        checklist
Eyck, Hubrecht or Hubert van   **WC**
Eyck, Hubrecht or Hubert van →see
    Eyck, Hubert van
Eyck, Jan Carel van (Flemish artist,
    1649-p.1685)   **WC**

Eyck, Jan van   **GC PR**
(Netherlandish painter, ca.1390-
1441)   GC PR
(Netherlands artist, op.1422-m.
1441)   WC
  Bibl: ▶RILA/BHA
A. V. Eyck   PR
Eyck   PR
Eyck, Jan, Jean or Johannes van   **WC**
J. V. Eycke   PR
J. Van Eyck   PR
J.V. Eyck   PR
Jan van Eyck   PR
Jan. Van Eyck   PR
Jean Van Eck   PR
Jean van Eick   PR
Jean van Eyk   PR
Jobnob. Eyck   PR
John van Eck   PR
John van Eyck   PR
John van Eycke   PR
Johnab. Eyck   PR
V. Eyck   PR
Van Eick   PR
Van Eyck   PR
Van Eycke   PR
Van. Eyck   PR
Eyck, Jan, Jean or Johannes van → see
Eyck, Jan van
**Eyck, Johannes Lodevicus Nicolaas
(Jan) van** (Dutch artist, 1927-)   **WC**
Eyck, Kasper van   **GC PR WC**
(Flemish artist, 1613-1673)   WC
(Flemish painter, 1613-1673)   GC PR
  Bibl: ▶Thieme-Becker
Eyck   PR
Eyck, Gaspard van   PR
Gaspar Van Eyck   PR
Gaspare delle Battaglie   PR
Gasparo delle Battaglie   PR
Gasper Van Eyck   PR
Kasper van Eyck   PR
Eyck, Margarethe van (early
Netherlandish, 1406-after 1456)   **BA**
  Bibl: Baldass, JAN VAN EYCK,
  p.282; ▶Biog. Nat. Belgique;
  Weale & Brockwell, THE VAN
  EYCKS AND THEIR ART, p.22
Eyck, Nicolaas van I   **GC**
(Flemish artist, 1617-1679)   WC
(Flemish painter and
  draughtsman, 1617-1679)   GC
  Bibl: ▶Thieme-Becker
Eyck, Nicolaas, I van   **WC**
Eyck, Nicolaas, I van → see Eyck,
Nicolaas van I
Eycke or Ecke, John (Netherlands(?)
artist, op.1618)   **WC**
Eycken, Charles van den (Belgian
artist, 1859-)   **WC**
Eycken, Felix van den (Dutch artist,
19th cent.)   **WC**
Eycken, Jan Baptist van (Belgian
artist, 1809-1853)   **WC**
Eyckens, Pieter → see Ykens, Pieter

Eyckhout → see Eeckhout, Gerbrand
van den
Eyckhout, Albert van der → see
Eeckhout, Albert van der
Eyden or Eyde, Jeremias van der
(Flemish artist, op.1658-m.1697)   **WC**
Eydt, P. Funck- → see Funck-Eydt, P.
Eye-Siren Group (vase-painters, ca.
530-510 BC)   **GC**
  Bibl: ▶Beazley, Attic bl.-fig. vase-
  ptrs.; Boardman, Attic Bl.-fig.
  Vases
Eyebrow Group (South Italian vase-
painters, 350-300 BC)   **GC**
  Bibl: McPhee & Trendall, Fish-
  Plates
Eyebrow Painter (South Italian vase-
painter, 350-300 BC)   **GC**
  Bibl: McPhee & Trendall, Fish-
  Plates
Eyes, Charles   **WC WI**
(British artist, c.1754-1803)   WC
(British artist, circa 1745-1803)   WI
Eyfells, Johann (American artist,
20th c.)   **BA**
  Bibl: Montgomery (AL, USA), Mus.
  of Fine Arts, MARATHON ART
  (1975)
Eyk or Yk, Abraham van der or
Abraham Vereyk → see Eyk,
Abraham van der
Eyk, Abraham van der   **GC**
(Dutch artist, op.1709-1725)   WC
(Dutch painter, act.1710-1725)   GC
  Bibl: Getty Photo Study Coll.;
  Getty Photo Study Coll. (Ptgs.);
  ▶Thieme-Becker; ▶Witt checklist
**Eyk or Yk, Abraham van der or
Abraham Vereyk**   **WC**
Vereyk, Abraham   GC
Yk, Abraham van der   GC
Eyk, Ria van → see Eijk, Maria Johanna
Louisa van
Eykes, John   **WC WI**
(British artist, 16th cent.)   WC
(British artist, op.17th c.)   WI
Eyles, John   **WC WI**
(British artist, 20th cent.)   WC
(British artist, op.20th c.)   WI
Eymar, Louis-Charles (French artist,
1882-1944)   **WC**
Eymer, Arnoldus Johannes   **GC WC**
(Dutch artist, 1803-1863)   WC
(Dutch draughtsman, 1803-
  1863)   GC
  Bibl: ▶Bénézit
Eymundsson, Sigfús (Icelandic
photographer, 1837-1911)   **BA**
  Bibl: Minneapolis (MN, USA),
  Walker Art Ctr., Frozen image
  (1982)
Eynard-Lullin, Jean-Gabriel (Swiss,
1775-1863, daguerreotypist (also
Eynard-Lullin & Rion))   **JG**

Eynde, Catharina van den (Flemish
tapestry maker, act.1605, d. after
1620)   **BA**
  Bibl: De Poorter, GENSTE
  BIJDRAGEN TOT DE KUNSTGESH.
  XXV (1979-1980) 208-221;
  Duverger, Gentse Bijdragen tot de
  Kunstgeschiedenis, XXVI (1981-
  1984) pp.161-193; ▶Encyc. world
  art; ▶Thieme-Becker; ▶Thomson,
  Tapestry, p.376
Eynde, Hubrecht van den (Flemish
sculptor, act.1620, d.1661)   **BA**
  Bibl: ▶Bénézit; ▶Thieme-Becker;
  ▶Wurzbach, NLD Künst.-Lex.
Eynden, Frans van (Dutch artist,
1694-1742)   **WC**
Eynden, Jacobus van   **GC**
(Dutch artist, 1733-1824)   WC
(Dutch draughtsman, 1733-
  1824)   GC
  Bibl: ▶Thieme-Becker
Eynden, Jacobus, II van   **WC**
Eynden, Jacobus, II van → see Eynden,
Jacobus van
Eyre, Edward   **WC WI**
(British artist, op.1771-1786)   WC
(British artist, op.1771-1792)   WI
Eyre, Elizabeth (British artist, op.
1890-)   **WI**
Eyre, Ivan → see Eyre, Ivan Kenneth
Eyre, Ivan Kenneth   **BA**
(Canadian artist, 20th cent.)   WC
(Canadian painter, b.1935)   BA
  Bibl: ▶Artists Canada; ▶MoMA
  libr. cat.; ▶WW Amer. Art
Eyre, Ivan   **WC**
Eyre, James (British artist, 1802-
1829)   **WI**
Eyre, John (English nobleman,
painter, 1680-1739)   **BA**
  Bibl: JOURNAL OF GARDEN HIST.,
  IV/4 (Oct-Dec 1984) 359-385
Eyre, John (Australian artist, op.
1806)   **WC**
Eyre, Wilson   **AV BA**
(American architect, 1858-1944)   BA
(American architect, in
  partnership with J. Gilbert
  McIlvaine, 1858-1944)   AV
  Bibl: ▶Withey, Amer. archts.;
  ▶Wodehouse, Amer. archts. WWI-
  pres.; ▶WWW Amer.
Eyres, Emily (British artist, op.circa
1892-)   **WI**
Eyries, J.B.B. (Swiss artist, op.c.
1800)   **WC**
Eysden, Robert van   **GC WC**
(Dutch artist, 1810-1890)   WC
(Dutch painter, 1810-1890)   GC
  Bibl: ▶Thieme-Becker
**Eysen, Eisen or Eyssen, Johann
Jacob** (German artist, op.1665-
1677)   **WC**

Eysen, Louis   **BA GC WC WI**
  (*British artist, 1843-1889*)   WI
  (*British artist, 1843-1899*)   WC
  (*German painter, 1843-1899*)   BA GC
    Bibl: ▶Bénézit; ▶Neue deutsche
    Biog.; ▶Thieme-Becker
Eysselinck, Gaston   **AV BA**
  (*Belgian architect, 1907-1953*)   AV
  (*Belgian architect, designer,
    1907-1953*)   BA
    Bibl: ▶Avery period. idx.; Ghent
    (BEL), Mus. voor Sierkunst,
    GASON EYSSELINCK (1978);
    Monumenten en landschappen,
    1986 Jan.-Feb., v.5, no.1, p.8
Eyssenhardt, Friedrich Albert
  (*German artist, 1801-1832*)   WC
Eyther, Joannes (*Yugoslav architect,
    active in Zagreb ca.1775-1810*)   AV
    Bibl: Peristil. v.22, 1979, p.111f.
Eytinge, Solomon (*American artist,
    1833-1905*)   WI
Eyton, Anthony →*see* Eyton, Anthony
    John Plowden
Eyton, Anthony John Plowden   **BA**
  (*British artist, b.1923*)   WI
  (*British painter, b.1923*)   BA
  (*Canadian artist, 20th cent.*)   WC
    Bibl: ▶Dolman, Contemp. Brit.
    artists; ▶Who's Who [GBR]; ▶WW
    Art, 1977
Eyton, Anthony   **WC WI**
Eyton-Jones, Philip (*British
    architect, Wales; director of
    architecture, planning and estates,
    Clwyd Co. Council Architects'
    Dept, Wales*)   AV
    Bibl: ▶Guide to RIBA practices,
    1987
**Ezdorf (not Etzdorf), Christian
    (Johann Christian Michael)**
  (*German artist, 1801-1851*)   WC
Ezekiel, Gottfried (*German artist,
    1744-1767*)   WC
Ezekiel, Moses Jacob (*American
    sculptor, 1844-1917*)   BA
    Bibl: ▶Opitz, Amer. sculptors
Ezpeleta, P. (*Spanish artist, op.
    1596*)   WC
Ezquerra, Jerónimo Antonio
  (*Spanish painter, b.1659/62, act.
    1730*)   BA
    Bibl: BOLETIN DEL MUSEO DEL
    PRADO, VI/18 (Sept.-Dec. 1985),
    p. 158-164 docs.; ▶Ceán
    Bermúdez, Bellas artes ESP;
    ▶Encic. univ. ilus.; ▶Kubler, Art &
    arch. ESP & PRT, p.284;
    ▶Thieme-Becker
Ezra Ames →*see* Ames, Ezra
F R Perrier →*see* Perrier, François (le
    Bourguignon)
F. Albano →*see* Albani, Francesco
F. Badens →*see* Badens, Francesco
F. Ball →*see* Bol, Ferdinand
F. Barocci →*see* Barocci, Federico
F. Baroccio →*see* Barocci, Federico

F. Barroccio →*see* Barocci, Federico
F. Barrocio →*see* Barocci, Federico
F. Bartolemeo →*see* Bartolomeo, Fra
F. Bartolomeo →*see* Bartolomeo, Fra
F. Bartolommeo →*see* Bartolomeo,
    Fra
F. Bassan →*see* Bassano, Francesco II
    (Francesco II da Ponte)
F. Bassano →*see* Bassano, Francesco II
    (Francesco II da Ponte)
F. Beloni →*see* Beloni, F.
    [Unidentified]
F. Bol →*see* Bol, Ferdinand
F. Bolanese →*see* Grimaldi, Giovanni
    Francesco
F. Boll →*see* Bol, Ferdinand
F. Bolognese →*see* Grimaldi, Giovanni
    Francesco
F. Bolonese →*see* Grimaldi, Giovanni
    Francesco
F. Bout →*see* Bout, Peeter
F. Brerewood →*see* Brerewood,
    Francis
F. Brina →*see* Brini, Francesco
F. Cagliari →*see* Veronese (Paolo
    Caliari)
F. Camillo →*see* Camilo, Francisco
F. Carre →*see* Carree, Franciscus
F. Castiglione →*see* Castiglione,
    Francesco
F. Collantes →*see* Collantes, Francisco
F. dan Legres →*see* Legres, F. dan
    [Unidentified]
F. de Cleyn →*see* Cleyn, Francis
F. de Mola →*see* Mola, Pier Francesco
F. Decker →*see* Decker, Frans
F. di Modena [Unidentified]
  (*Unknown painter*)   **PR**
    Bibl: (February 7, 1807, lot 38,
    Christie's)
F. Durand et Fils   **JG**
F. Eijkens →*see* Ijkens, Frans
F. Eisen →*see* Eisen, François
F. F. →*see* Fescourt, Félix
F. Ferg →*see* Ferg, Franz de Paula
F. Florio →*see* Floris, Frans, the elder
F. Floris →*see* Floris, Frans, the elder
F. Francia →*see* Francia, Francesco
    (Francesco Raibolini)
F. Furini →*see* Furini, Francesco
F. Furrini →*see* Furini, Francesco
F. Giovanni Gusman →*see* Guzmán,
    Juan
F. Hal →*see* Hals, Frans
F. Hall →*see* Hals, Frans
F. Halls →*see* Hals, Frans
F. Hals →*see* Hals, Frans
F. Hanfstängel (Munich) →*see*
    Hanfstaengl, Franz Seraph
F. Horemans →*see* Horemans, F.
    [Unidentified]
F. J. Mansirsch →*see* Manskirch, Franz
    Joseph
F. J. Manskirch →*see* Manskirch, Franz
    Joseph

F. J. Manskirsch →*see* Manskirch,
    Franz Joseph
F. Laura →*see* Lauri, Filippo
F. Laure →*see* Lauri, Filippo
F. Lauri →*see* Lauri, Filippo
F. Laurie →*see* Lauri, Filippo
F. Lawri →*see* Lauri, Filippo
F. le Moyne →*see* Le Moyne, François
F. Lindo →*see* Lindo, F.
F. Lisandroni →*see* Lisandroni, F.
F. Maes →*see* Maes, F. [Unidentified]
F. Mans →*see* Heeremans, Thomas
F. Mazzola →*see* Parmigianino
    (Francesco Mazzola)
F. Meiris →*see* Mieris, Frans I van
F. Miel →*see* Miel, Jan
F. Mieres →*see* Mieris, Frans I van
F. Mieris →*see* Mieris, Frans I van
F. Mieris, Jun. →*see* Mieris, Frans II
    van
F. Mieris, Sen. →*see* Mieris, Frans I
    van
F. Milè →*see* Millet, Jean François I
    (Francisque Millet)
F. Milee →*see* Millet, Jean François I
    (Francisque Millet)
F. Millé →*see* Millet, Jean François I
    (Francisque Millet)
F. Millee →*see* Millet, Jean François I
    (Francisque Millet)
F. Millet →*see* Millet, Jean François I
    (Francisque Millet)
F. Millie →*see* Millet, Jean François I
    (Francisque Millet)
F. Mola →*see* Mola, Pier Francesco
F. Molinaer →*see* Meulener, Pieter
F. Monaville →*see* Monnaville,
    François
F. Monti →*see* Monti, Francesco
    (Brescianino delle Battaglie)
F. Moucheron →*see* Moucheron,
    Frédéric de
F. Ochoa, of Seville →*see* Ochoa, F.,
    of Seville [Unidentified]
F. Oelenheinz →*see* Oelenhainz,
    Friedrich
F. P. Ferg →*see* Ferg, Franz de Paula
F. P. Verheyden →*see* Verheyden,
    Franck Pietersz.
F. Paul Ferg →*see* Ferg, Franz de Paula
F. Pourbus →*see* Pourbus, Frans, the
    younger
F. Reale →*see* Reale, F. [Unidentified]
F. Ricci →*see* Rizi, Francisco
F. Romanelli →*see* Romanelli,
    Giovanni Francesco
F. Sarani →*see* Sirani, Elisabetta
F. Snyders →*see* Snyders, Frans
F. Solimena →*see* Solimena, Francesco
F. Solimina →*see* Solimena, Francesco
F. Trevissani →*see* Trevisani,
    Francesco
F. Van Mieris →*see* Mieris, Frans I van
F. Van Stry →*see* Strij, Jacob van

F. van Vogelsang→see Vogelsang, F. van

F. Vanni→see Vanni, Francesco

F. Warburton→see Warburton, F.

F. Wheatley, Esq. R.A.→see Wheatley, Francis

F. Wheatley, R. A.→see Wheatley, Francis

F. Wolf→see Wolf, F.

F. Wooters→see Wouters, Frans

F. Wouters→see Wouters, Frans

F. Wych→see Wyck, Thomas

F. X. Fabre→see Fabre, François Xavier Pascal

F. Xavery→see Xavery, Frans

F. Zuccarelli→see Zuccarelli, Francesco

F. Zucchero→see Zuccari, Federico

F. Zuchero→see Zuccari, Federico

F., A. _(fl. 1930; draftsman (technical), Hamilton)_ **FA**
Bibl: CAAD Finding Aid, Ben Albert Dore 88957; Natl. Arch. of Canada, CAAD Finding Aid

F., J.A. _(fl. 1948; Architect, Ottawa)_ **FA**
Bibl: CAAD Finding Aid, J. Albert Ewart 76703/13; Natl. Arch. of Canada, CAAD Finding Aid

_F.B._→see Monogrammist F.B.

F.B. Group **GC**
Bibl: ▶Beazley, Attic red-fig. vase-ptrs.

F.F. Franck→see Franck, Franz Friedrich

F.I. Mannskirsch→see Manskirch, Franz Joseph

F.L. Neefs→see Neeffs, Lodewyck

F.M. Galetti→see Galletti, Filippo Maria

F.P. Ferg→see Ferg, Franz de Paula

F.V. Daellen→see Daellen, F.V.

F.V. Ever Broeck→see Everbroeck, Frans van

F.V. Hoeck→see Hoeck, F.V. [Unidentified]

_F.V.S._→see Schooten, Floris Gerritsz. van

F.W. Tamm→see Tamm, Franz Werner von

F: Bassan→see Bassano, Francesco II (Francesco II da Ponte)

F: Hals→see Hals, Frans

Faaborg, Finn _(Norwegian artist, 20th cent.)_ **WC**

Fabbi→see Fabbi, Fabio

Fabbi, Alberto _(Italian painter, b.1858)_ **GC**
Bibl: ▶Thieme-Becker

Fabbi, Fabbio→see Fabbi, Fabio

Fabbi, Fabio **GC PR**
(Italian painter, 1861-aft.1899) PR
(Italian painter, b.1861) GC
Bibl: ▶Thieme-Becker
Fabbi PR
Fabbi, Fabbio PR
Fabio Fabbi PR

Fabbri, Agenore **BA WC**
(Italian artist, 1911-) WC
(Italian sculptor, ceramist, b.1911) BA
Bibl: ▶Bénézit; ▶Vollmer, Künst.-Lex. 20. Jhr.

Fabbrica, Francesco _(Italian artist, op.c.1680)_ **WC**

Fabbrini or Fabrini, Giuseppe Antonio→see Fabbrini, Giuseppe Antonio

Fabbrini, Angiolo _(Italian artist, op. 1853)_ **WC**

Fabbrini, Giuseppe→see Fabbrini, Giuseppe Antonio

Fabbrini, Giuseppe Antonio **BA GC**
(Italian artist, 1740-p.1792) WC
(Italian painter, ca.1740-aft. 1793) GC
(Italian painter, ca.1740-after 1793) BA
Bibl: ▶Bénézit; ▶Bolaffi; Getty Photo Study Coll. (Ptgs.); ▶RILA/BHA; ▶Thieme-Becker; ▶Witt checklist

Fabbrini or Fabrini, Giuseppe Antonio **WC**
Fabbrini, Giuseppe GC
Fabrini, Giuseppe BA

Fabbris, G. _(Italian artist, op.1733)_ **WC**

Fabbrizio Boschi→see Boschi, Fabrizio

Fabbroni→see Fabbroni, Diacinto

Fabbroni, Cristoforo **GC WC**
(Italian artist, 18th cent.) WC
(Italian painter, act. mid.-18th century) GC
Bibl: ▶Thieme-Becker

Fabbroni, Diacinto _(Italian painter, b. 1712)_ **PR**
Bibl: Gabburri, Vite di Artisti, T.II, p. 762
Diacinto Fabbroni PR
Fabbroni PR

Fabbroni, Pier Giovanni [Unidentified] _(Unknown painter, act. 18th century)_ **PR**
Bibl: Riccardi inventory dated 1776
Pier Giovanni Fabbroni PR

Faber→see Faber, Traugott

Faber du Faur, Otto von **GC WC**
(German artist, 1828-1901) WC
(German, 1828-1901) GC
Bibl: ▶Thieme-Becker; ▶Witt checklist

Faber von Creuznach→see Faber von Creuznach, Conrad

Faber von Creuznach, Conrad **BA GC PR**
(German artist, c.1500-1552/3) WC
(German painter, ca.1500-ca. 1553) BA GC PR
Bibl: Bayerische Staatsgem. Samm.; Berlin Dahlem (1978); Getty Photo Study Coll. (Ptgs.); ▶Neue deutsche Biog.; ▶RILA/BHA; SOURCE IV/2-3 (winter-spring 1985) 68-71; ▶Thieme-Becker; ▶Witt checklist
Conrad Faber von Creuznach PR
Creuznach, Conrad von BA
Faber von Creuznach PR
Faber von Kreuzbach, Conrad BA
Faber von Kreuznach, Konrad GC
Faber, Conrad GC PR
Faber, Conrad (called Faber von Creuznach) GC
Faber, Conrad (Conrad von Creuznach) PR

Faber, Conrad (Conrad von Creuznach, Master of the Holzhausen Family) **WC**
Faber, Konrad GC
Master of the Holzhausen Family GC

Faber von Kreuzbach, Conrad→see Faber von Creuznach, Conrad

Faber von Kreuznach, Konrad→see Faber von Creuznach, Conrad

Faber, Conrad→see Faber von Creuznach, Conrad

Faber, Conrad (called Faber von Creuznach)→see Faber von Creuznach, Conrad

Faber, Conrad (Conrad von Creuznach)→see Faber von Creuznach, Conrad

Faber, Conrad (Conrad von Creuznach, Master of the Holzhausen Family)→see Faber von Creuznach, Conrad

Faber, Daniel _(German draughtsman, 18th century)_ **GC**
Bibl: ▶Thieme-Becker

Faber, du Faur, Christian Wilhelm _(German artist, 1780-1857)_ **WC**

Faber, Eusebius _(German painter, 1772-1852)_ **GC**
Bibl: ▶Thieme-Becker
Faber, Johann Theodor Eusebius GC

Faber, F. _(German(?) artist, op.1797)_ **WC**

Faber, Frederic Theodore _(Belgian artist, 1782-1844)_ **WC**

Faber, J. _(German artist, op.1763)_ **WC**

Faber, Jacob→see Faber, Jakob

Faber, Jakob **BA**
(Swiss artist, op.1516-1558) WC
(Swiss printmaker, act.1516-1550) BA
Bibl: ▶Bénézit; ▶Thieme-Becker

Faber, Jacob **WC**

Faber, Jean _(Flemish painter, d. 1674)_ **PR**
Jean Faber PR

Faber, Johann Friedrich *(German artist, 17th/18th cent.)* **WC**

Faber, Johann Joachim **GC WC**
   (German artist, 1778-1846) **WC**
   (German painter and draughtsman, 1778-1846) **GC**
     Bibl: ▶Thieme-Becker

Faber, Johann Theodor Eusebius → see Faber, Eusebius

Faber, John → see Faber, John II

Faber, John I **GC**
   (Dutch artist, c.1650/60-1721) **WC**
   (Dutch draughtsman, ca.1650/60-1721) **GC**
     Bibl: Getty Photo Study Coll.; ▶Witt checklist

Faber, John or Johan, I **WC**

Faber, John II **GC WI**
   (British artist, 1684-1756) **WC WI**
   (British, 1684-1756) **GC**
   (Engraver, circa 1695-1756) **WI**
     Bibl: Mackenzie; ▶Witt checklist

Faber, John **WI**

Faber, John, II **WC**

Faber, John or Johan, I → see Faber, John I

Faber, John, II → see Faber, John II

Faber, Karl Gottfried Traugott → see Faber, Traugott

Faber, Konrad → see Faber von Creuznach, Conrad

Faber, L.C. *(Engraver)* **WI**

Faber, Ludwig *(American artist, 1855-1913)* **WI**

Faber, Martin **BA GC**
   (German artist, 1587-1648) **WC**
   (German draughtsman, 1587-1648) **GC**
   (German painter, printmaker, architect, 1587-1648) **BA**
     Bibl: ▶Thieme-Becker

Faber, Martinus Hermanus **WC**

Faber, Martinus Hermanus → see Faber, Martin

Faber, Oscar *(English architect or engineer)* **AV**
     Bibl: Building, 1989 Jan.27, v.254, no.4, p.45

Faber, R. **WC WI**
   (British artist, 18th cent.) **WC**
   (British artist, op.18th c.) **WI**

Faber, Traugott **PR**
   (German artist, 1786-1863) **WC**
   (German painter, 1786-1863) **GC PR**
     Bibl: ▶Bénézit; ▶Thieme-Becker

Faber **PR**

Faber, Karl Gottfried Traugott **GC PR**

Faber, Traugott (Carl Gottfried Traugott) **WC**

Faber, Traugott (Karl Gottfried) **GC**

Traugott Faber **PR**

Faber, Traugott (Carl Gottfried Traugott) → see Faber, Traugott

Faber, Traugott (Karl Gottfried) → see Faber, Traugott

Faber, William *(German artist, 1901-)* **WC**

Fabergé, Karl Gustavovič *(Russian goldsmith, jeweler, 1846-1920)* **BA**
     Bibl: ▶Fogg Mus. Libr. cat.

Fabergé, Peter Carl **BA**

Fabergé, Peter Carl → see Fabergé, Karl Gustavovič

Fabert, Jacques **WC WI**
   (American artist, 20th cent.) **WC**
   (American artist, op.1967-) **WI**

Fabian, Gottfried *(German(?) artist, op.1959)* **WC**

Fabian, Victoria *(American restorationist, specializes in restoration of windows and in repainting historic buildings, Annapolis, Md)* **AV**
     Bibl: Preservation news, 1988 Aug., v.28, no.8, p.13

Fabiani, Max **AV BA**
   (Italian architect, city planner, 1865-1962) **AV**
   (Yugoslav architect, 1865-1962) **BA**
     Bibl: ▶Avery Libr. cat.; ▶Avery period. idx.; ▶Macmillan encyc. archts.; Parametro, 1983 Dec., no.122, p.2; ▶Thieme-Becker

Fabiano da Urbino, Frate *(Italian artist, op.1533)* **WC**

Fabigan, Hans *(Austrian artist, 1901-)* **WC**

Fabijanic, Nenad *(Yugoslav architect)* **AV**
     Bibl: Architectural record, 1988 Apr., v.183, no.1094, p.80

Fabio Berardi → see Berardi, Fabio

Fabio Fabbi → see Fabbi, Fabio

Fabisch, Joseph Hugues *(French sculptor, 1812-1886)* **BA**
     Bibl: ▶Bénézit; ▶Thieme-Becker

Fabius, Jan *(Dutch painter, 1820-1889)* **GC**
     Bibl: ▶Bénézit

Fabre → see Fabre, François Xavier Pascal

Fabre Painter **GC**
     Bibl: ▶Beazley, Attic red-fig. vase-ptrs.

Fabre, Francois → see Fabre, François Xavier Pascal

Fabre, Francois Xavier → see Fabre, François Xavier Pascal

Fabre, François Xavier Pascal **BA PR**
   (French artist, 1766-1837) **WC**
   (French painter, 1766-1837) **PR**
   (French painter, printmaker, collector, 1766-1837) **BA**
   (French, 1766-1837) **GC JG**
     Bibl: ▶Bénézit; ▶Dict. biog. fran.; ▶Havlice, Idx. art. bio.; ▶RILA/BHA; ▶Thieme-Becker; ▶Witt checklist

F. X. Fabre **PR**

Fabre **PR**

Fabre, Francois **PR**

Fabre, Francois Xavier **GC PR WC**

Fabre, Francois-Xavier **JG PR**

Francois Xavier Fabre **PR**

Francois Xavier Pascal Fabre **PR**

Fabre, Francois-Xavier → see Fabre, François Xavier Pascal

Fabre, Henri *(French artist, 19th/20th cent.)* **WC**

Fabre, J.H. **WC WI**
   (British artist, op.1797-) **WI**
   (British(?) artist, op.1797) **WC**

Fabre, Jean III *(French silversmith, 1676-ca.1729-1731, master 1709)* **GC**
     Bibl: ▶Mabille, Orfèv. fran.

Fabre, Louis Andre *(French artist, 1750-1814)* **WC**

Fabre, Louis Eugene *(French artist, 20th cent.)* **WC**

Fabre, Valentin *(French architect)* **AV**
     Bibl: ▶Annuaire archts. fran., 1978

Fabre, Xavier *(French architect, Paris)* **AV**
     Bibl: ▶Annuaire archts. fran., 1987

Fábregas de Sentmenat, Eulalia *(Spanish poet, sculptor, 20th c.)* **BA**
     Bibl: Tarin-Inglesiasin, REALES SITIOS XIX/73 (1982) 73-74

Sentmenat, Eulalia Fábregas de **BA**

Fabregas, Andres *(American architect)* **AV**

Fábregas, Salvador *(Spanish architect)* **AV**
     Bibl: Process: architecture, 1985 Apr., no.57, p.136

Fabregat, Joan *(Spanish architect, Barcelona)* **AV**
     Bibl: Architecture d'aujourd'hui, 1989 Apr., no.262, p.72

Fabregat, Joaquín *(Spanish printmaker, 1748-1807)* **BA**
     Bibl: ▶Encic. univ. ilus.; ▶Thieme-Becker

Fabres y Costa, Antonio Maria *(Spanish artist, 1854-)* **WC**

Fabri → see Fabri, Ralph

Fabri, A. *(Italian artist, op.1593)* **WC**

Fabri, Francisco Xavier *(Italian architect in PRT, d.1807)* **BA**
     Bibl: ▶Encyc. world art; ▶Kubler, Art & arch. ESP & PRT; ▶Portoghesi, Diz. arch. e urbanistica; ▶Thieme-Becker

Fabri, Ralph *(American painter,*
   1894-1975)   **PR**
   Bibl: ▶WWW Amer. art
   Fabri   PR
   Ralph Fabri   PR
Fabriano, Gentile da→see Gentile da
   Fabriano (Gentile di Niccolò di
   Giovanni Massi)
Fabricatore, Nicola *(Italian(?) artist,*
   op.1928)   **WC**
Fabrice→see Fabris, Pietro
Fabrice→see Fabritius, Carel
Fabricio Hastelo→see Castello,
   Fabrizio
Fabricius, Bernart→see Fabritius,
   Barent
Fabrini, Giuseppe→see Fabbrini,
   Giuseppe Antonio
Fabris→see Fabris, Pietro
Fabris Varion, Fiorina *(Italian*
   ceramist, act.1759-1781)   **BA**
   Bibl: Bertocchi, Carrobbio, XIV
   (1988) (docs); Lane, Ital.
   porcelain; Mottola, Porcellana
   Italia
Fabris, Antonio Zanotti→see Zanotti
   Fabris, Antonio
Fabris, Emilio de→see De Fabris,
   Emilio
Fabris, Giacomo→see Fabris, Jacopo
Fabris, Giampaolo *(Italian interior*
   designer)   **AV**
   Bibl: Domus, 1985 Dec., no.667,
   p.50
Fabris, Gino *(Italian artist, op.1768)* **WC**
Fabris, Jacob→see Fabris, Jacopo
Fabris, Jacopo   **BA**
   (Italian artist, 1689-1761)   WC
   (Italian painter, ca.1689-1761)   BA
   (Italian, ca.1689-1761)   GC
   Bibl: ▶Thieme-Becker; ▶Witt
   checklist
Fabris, Giacomo   **WC**
Fabris, Jacob   **GC**
Fabris, Michael   **BA**
   (Hungarian sculptor in ITA, ca.
   1644-1694)   BA
   (Hungarian sculptor, 1644-1684)   GC
   Bibl: Arte Veneta XXXIX (1985)
   87-100; Getty Photo Study Coll.
   (Sculp.); TCI Venezia
   Fabris, Michele   GC
   Ongaro Michele   BA
   Ongaro, Michele   GC
   Ungaro Michele   BA
Ungaro, Michele   **GC**
Fabris, Michele→see Fabris, Michael
Fabris, Pietro   **BA GC PR WC**
   (Italian artist, op.1768-1778)   WC
   (Italian painter, act. 1768-1778)   PR
   (Italian painter, act.1768-1778) BA GC
   Bibl: ▶Bolaffi; ▶RILA/BHA;
   ▶Thieme-Becker
   Fabrice   PR
   Fabris   PR
   Pietro Fabris   PR

Fabris, Placido   **GC WC**
   (Italian artist, 1802-1859)   WC
   (Italian, 1802-1859)   GC
   Bibl: ▶Thieme-Becker; ▶Witt
   checklist
Fabritio Chiari→see Chiari, Fabrizio
Fabritio S.ta fede→see Santafede,
   Fabrizio
Fabritio Santa Fede→see Santafede,
   Fabrizio
fabritio Santafede→see Santafede,
   Fabrizio
Fabritiq, 1664→see Fabritius, Barent
Fabritius→see Fabritius, Barent
Fabritius→see Fabritius, Carel
Fabritius or Fabricius Barent or
   Bernard Pietersz. →see Fabritius,
   Barent
Fabritius or Fabricius, Carel or
   Carolus Pietersz. →see Fabritius,
   Carel
Fabritius or Fabricius, Johannes
Pietersz. *(Dutch artist, 1636-p.*
   1693)   **WC**
Fabritius, Barend→see Fabritius,
   Barent
Fabritius, Barent   **BA GC PR**
   (Dutch artist, 1624-1673)   WC
   (Dutch painter and
   draughtsman, 1624-1673)   GC
   (Dutch painter, 1624-1673)   BA PR
   Bibl: ▶Bénézit; ▶Bernt, Neth. ptrs.
   17c.; Brown, CAREL FABRITIUS,
   p.15; ▶Encyc. world art; Getty
   Photo Study Coll.; ▶Grote Winkler
   Prins; ▶Nieuw NLD biog. woord.;
   ▶Rosenberg, Dutch art & arch.;
   ▶Thieme-Becker; ▶Witt checklist;
   ▶Wurzbach, NLD Künst.-Lex.
   B. Fabritius   PR
   Barent Fabritius   PR
   Fabricius, Bernart   GC
   Fabritiq, 1664   PR
   Fabritius   PR
Fabritius or Fabricius Barent or
Bernard Pietersz.   **WC**
   Fabritius, Barend   PR
Fabritius, Carel   **BA GC PR**
   (Dutch artist, 1622-1654)   WC
   (Dutch painter and
   draughtsman, 1622-1654)   GC
   (Dutch painter, 1622-1654)   BA
   (Dutch painter, 1624-1654)   PR
   Bibl: ▶Bénézit; Brown, CAREL
   FABRITIUS, p.15; Getty Photo
   Study Coll.; ▶Grote Winkler Prins;
   ▶Nieuw NLD biog. woord., v.8,
   p.526; ▶RILA/BHA;
   ▶Thieme-Becker; ▶Wurzbach, NLD
   Künst.-Lex.
   Carel Fabritius   PR
   Fabrice   PR
   Fabritius   PR
Fabritius or Fabricius, Carel or
Carolus Pietersz.   **WC**

Fabritius, Carl Ferdinand   **GC WC**
   (Austrian draughtsman, 1637-
   1673)   GC
   (German artist, 1637-1673)   WC
   Bibl: ▶Bénézit; Getty Photo Study
   Coll.; ▶Thieme-Becker
Fabritius, Chilian *(German artist, op.*
   1612-m.1633)   **WC**
Fabritius, Jean *(Dutch painter, 17th*
   century)   **GC**
   Bibl: ▶Bénézit
Fabrizi, F. or S. *(Italian artist, op.*
   1881)   **WC**
Fabrizi, Fabrizio *(Italian painter, act.*
   1470-1522)   **BA**
   Bibl: ▶Bolaffi; TCI Marche;
   ▶Thieme-Becker
Fabrizio Boschi→see Boschi, Fabrizio
Fabrizio Castello→see Castello,
   Fabrizio
Fabrizio Chiari→see Chiari, Fabrizio
Fabrizio Santafede→see Santafede,
   Fabrizio
Fabro, Luciano *(Italian artist,*
   b.1936)   **BA**
   Bibl: ▶Bénézit
Fabry, Emile   **BA**
   (Belgian artist, 1865-1966)   WC
   (Belgian painter, 1865-1966)   BA
   Bibl: ▶Bénézit; ▶Thieme-Becker
Fabry, Emile Barthelemy   **WC**
Fabry, Emile Barthelemy→see Fabry,
   Emile
Fabullus→see Famulus
Facchetti or Fachetto, Pietro→see
   Facchetti, Pietro
Facchetti, Gianfranco *(Italian*
   architect)   **AV**
   Bibl: Ottagono, 1984 Sept.,
   no.74, p.98
Facchetti, Pietro   **BA GC**
   (Italian artist, 1535-1619)   WC
   (Italian painter, printmaker,
   1535/39-1619)   BA
   (Italian, 1535-1619)   GC
   Bibl: ▶Bolaffi; ▶Thieme-Becker;
   ▶Witt checklist
Facchetti or Fachetto, Pietro   **WC**
   Fachetto, Pietro   BA
Facchinetti, Giuseppe *(Italian*
   painter, d.1777)   **BA**
   Bibl: ▶Bolaffi; ▶Nouv. biog. gén.;
   ▶Thieme-Becker
Faccini or Facini, Pietro→see Faccini,
   Pietro

Faccini, Pietro   BA GC PR
   (*Italian artist, 1562-1602*)   WC
   (*Italian painter and printmaker,*
     ca.1562-1602)   GC
   (*Italian painter, ca.1562-1602*)   PR
   (*Italian painter, printmaker, ca.*
     1562-1602)   BA
     Bibl: ▶Bolaffi; Boll. d'arte LXIV
     (Apr-June 1979) 103-105;
     ▶RILA/BHA; ▶Thieme-Becker
  Faccini or Facini, Pietro   WC
  Facini   PR
  Pietro Faccini   PR
  Pietro Faccini da Bologna   PR
  Pietro Faccino   PR
  Pietro Faccino Bolognese   PR
  Pietro Faccino da Bologna   PR
  Pietro Facini   PR
Faccino [Unidentified] (*Unknown*
   painter)   PR
     Bibl: Aldobrandini inventory,
     Frascati, 1603, possibly Pietro /
     Bartolommeo / Girolamo Faccini?
Faccioli, Girolamo (*Italian*
   metalworker, act.1560, d.1573)   BA
     Bibl: ▶Forrer, Medallists;
     ▶Thieme-Becker; Tuttle, ITALIAN
     MEDALS (1987) 230
  Facinoli, Girolamo   BA
  Fagiuoli, Girolamo   BA
Faccioli, Raffaello (*Italian artist,*
   1846-)   WC
Facciotto, Bernardino (*16th century*
   Italian architect)   AV
Faceni [Unidentified] (*Unknown*
   painter)   PR
     Bibl: (March 17, 1808, lot 124,
     Squibb)
Facey, Martin (*American painter,*
   20th c.)   BA
     Bibl: ARTS MAG LV/2 (Oct
     19890) 9
Facheris, Agostino   GC
   (*Italian artist, 1500-p.1552*)   WC
   (*Italian painter, ca.1500-aft.*
     1552)   GC
     Bibl: ▶Bolaffi; ▶Thieme-Becker;
     ▶Witt checklist
  Agostino Facheris da Caversegno   GC
  Facheris, Agostino (da
   Caversegno)   WC
  Facheris, Agostino (da
   Caversegno)→see Facheris,
   Agostino
  Fachetto, Pietro→see Facchetti,
   Pietro
Facht von Andernach, Jacob
   (*German architect, 16th c.*)   BA
     Bibl: Wiener Jahrb. für
     Kunstgesch. XXVII (1974) 66, n.5
  Feucht, Jacob   BA
  Keull, Jacob   BA
  Kevl, Jacob   BA
  Voygh von Andernach, Jacob   BA
  Facini→see Faccini, Pietro

Facini, Antonio (*Italian*
   draughtsman)   GC
     Bibl: ▶Contemp. photogs.;
     Gernsheim, Corpus Photog. of
     Drawings
Facinoli, Girolamo→see Faccioli,
  Girolamo
Facio, E. C.   AV
Facius→see Facius, Friedrich Wilhelm
Facius, Friedrich Wilhelm   BA
   (*Engraver, op.1802-*)   WI
   (*German medalist, gem*
     engraver, 1764-1843)   BA
     Bibl: ▶Forrer, Medallists;
     ▶Thieme-Becker
  Facius   WI
Facius, Lepidus (*Italian printer,*
   publisher, act.1591-1626)   BA
     Bibl: Werner, Ripa's Iconologia
Fackere, Jef van de (*Belgian artist,*
   1879-1946)   WC
Facteur Cheval→see Cheval, Joseph
  Ferdinand (Facteur Cheval)
Facundus (*Spanish scribe, act.1047*)   GC
     Bibl: Williams, Early Span. mss.
     illum., p.13
Faczynski, Jerzy (*Polish artist, 20th*
   cent.)   WC
Faden, W.   WC WI
   (*American artist, op.1776*)   WC
   (*American artist, op.1776-*)   WI
Fadino→see Aleni, Tommaso (il
  Fadino)
Fadrusz, János (*Hungarian sculptor,*
   1858-1903)   BA
     Bibl: ▶Encyc. world art;
     ▶Thieme-Becker
Faed→see Faed, John
Faed family (*British painters, 19th*
   c.)   BA
     Bibl: ▶Fisher, Watercolour ptrs.;
     ▶Wood, Victorian ptrs.
Faed, James→see Faed, James II
Faed, James II   WI
   (*British artist, 1857-1920*)   WC WI
  Faed, James   WC
Faed, John   BA GC PR WC WI
   (*British artist, 1820-1902*)   WC WI
   (*British painter, 1820-1902*)   BA PR
   (*British, 1820-1902*)   GC
     Bibl: RB; ▶RILA/BHA;
     ▶Thieme-Becker; ▶Witt checklist
  Faed   PR
  John Faed   PR
Faed, Susan (*British artist, op.1866-*
   1868)   WI
Faed, Thomas   BA GC PR WC WI
   (*British artist, 1826-1900*)   WC WI
   (*British painter, 1826-1900*)   BA PR
   (*British, 1826-1900*)   GC
     Bibl: ▶RILA/BHA; ▶Thieme-Becker;
     ▶Witt checklist
  Thomas Faed   PR
Faed, William C. (*British artist, op.*
   1880-1897)   WI

Faeli (*Italian draughtsman*)   GC
     Bibl: ▶Contemp. photogs.;
     Gernsheim, Corpus Photog. of
     Drawings
Faen, Guillaem de→see Fal, Guillaem
  de
Faenza, Marco da→see Marchetti,
  Marco (Marco da Faenza)
Faes→see Faes, Peter
Faes, Peter   GC PR WC
   (*Dutch painter, 1750-1814*)   PR
   (*Flemish artist, 1750-1814*)   WC
   (*Flemish, 1750-1814*)   GC
     Bibl: ▶Thieme-Becker; ▶Witt
     checklist
  D. Faes   PR
  De Faes   PR
  Faes   PR
  Faes, Pieter   PR
  Peter Faes   PR
Faes, Pieter→see Faes, Peter
Faes, van der→see Falens, Carel van
Faesch, Johann Ludwig
  Wernhard→see Fäsch, Johann
  Ludwig Wernhard
Faesi-Gessner, Johann Konrad→see
  Gessner, Johann Conrad
Faesy, A. Robert (*American*
   architect, Wilton, CT)   AV
     Bibl: ▶AIA Pro File, 1987-88
Faeta, Francesco (*Italian*
   photographer, 20th c.)   BA
     Bibl: Rome (ITA), Gall. Naz. d'Arte
     Moderno, Imago mortis (1980)
Fafard, Joseph Yvon (*Canadian*
   sculptor, b.1942)   BA
     Bibl: ▶Artists Canada; ▶WW
     Amer. Art, 1978, 1982
Faffeo, Cristiano (*Italian painter,*
   15th-16th cs.)   BA
     Bibl: Alparone, ARTE CRISTIANA
     LXXII/703 (July-Aug 1984) 232-
     237; ▶Bolaffi
Faffeo, Cristoforo (*Italian painter,*
   15th-16th cs.)   BA
     Bibl: ▶Bolaffi; TCI Campania
Fafournoux, C. (*French, active ca.*
   1915)   JG
Fagan, A. [Unidentified] (*Unknown*
   painter)   PR
     Bibl: (April 10, 1813, lot 41,
     Christie's)
  A. Fagan   PR
Fagan, Betty Maud Christian   WC WI
   (*British artist, -1932*)   WC
   (*British artist, d.1932*)   WI
  Smith, Betty Maud Christian, Miss   WI
Fagan, Robert   PR WC WI
   (*British artist, c.1745-1816*)   WC
   (*British artist, circa 1745-1816*)   WI
   (*British painter, 1761-1816*)   PR
     Bibl: ▶Thieme-Becker;
     ▶Waterhouse, Brit. 18c. ptrs.
  Fagen   PR
  Fegan   PR
  Robert Fagan   PR

Fagen → see Fagan, Robert

Fagen, B. (British artist, op.19th c.) **WI**

Fagerholt, Nils **AV BA**
(Danish architect) AV
(Danish architect, 20th c.) BA
Bibl: ▶Avery period. idx., 3rd
suppl.; Meedam, Living
Architecture 1 (1983) 128

Fagerkvist, Thor (Swedish artist,
1884-1960) **WC**

Faverkvist, Thor **WC**

Fagerlin, Ferdinand Julius (Swedish
artist, 1825-1907) **WC**

Fages, Arthur R. (French artist,
1902-) **WC**

**Faget, Athalie Josephine Melanie
du** (French artist, 1811-p.1844) **WC**

Faget, Mignon (American designer,
20th c.) **BA**
Bibl: ARTS QUARTERLY III (Apr-
June 1981) 16, 36-37

Faggioli, Giovanni (Italian architect) **AV**
Bibl: Ville giardini, 1985 Mar., no.
194, p.14

Faghih, Nasrine (Iranian architect,
working in France) **AV**
Bibl: Maison francais, 1989 July-
Aug., no.428, p.80

Fagin, Steve (American artist, 20th
c.) **BA**
Bibl: ▶Art Index, v.35; Tamblyn,
Afterimage XV (summer 1987),
22-24

Fagioli, Massimo (Italian architect,
Monte San Savino) **AV**
Bibl: Abitare, 1988 Nov., no.269,
p.215

Fagioni → see Fagioni, B.A.

Fagioni, B.A. (American painter, act.
1876) **PR**
Bibl: ▶Hughes, Artists California
B.A. Fagioni PR
Fagioni PR

Fagiuoli, Girolamo → see Faccioli,
Girolamo

Faglia, Michele (Italian architect) **AV**
Bibl: Ville giardini, 1988 Jan.-Feb.,
no.223, p.24

Faglia, Vittorio (Italian architect) **AV**
Bibl: ▶Libr. of Congr. Name Auth.
File

Fagnani → see Fagnani, Giuseppe

Fagnani, Giuseppe **GC PR WC**
(Italian artist, 1819-1873) WC
(Italian painter, 1819-1873) PR
(Italian, 1819-1873) GC
Bibl: ▶Thieme-Becker; ▶Witt
checklist
Fagnani PR
Giuseppe Fagnani PR

Fagnola, Ferdinand (Italian
architect) **AV**
Bibl: Domus, 1984 Mar., no.648,
p.48

Fagnoni, Pier Guido (Italian
architect) **AV**
Bibl: Ottagono, 1984 Sept.,
no.74, p.18

Fagnoni, Pietro (Italian architect) **AV**
Bibl: Abitare, 1984 Apr., no.223,
p.34

Faguelin, Jean (French artist, 16th
cent.) **WC**

Fagundes, Ary (Brazilian artist, 20th
cent.) **WC**

Fahey, Aelfred (British artist, op.
1902-1909) **WI**

Fahey, Edward Henry (British artist,
1844-1907) **WC WI**

Fahey, James (British artist, 1804-
1885) **WC WI**

Fahey, Michael G. (American
architect) **AV**
Bibl: Architecture, the AIA
journal, 1986 Oct., v.75, no.10,
p.21

Fahlcrantz, Carl Johan (Swedish
artist, 1774-1861) **WC**

Fahlen, Charles (American sculptor,
b.1939) **BA**
Bibl: ▶Intl. dir. exh. artists, 1982-
1983; Whitney

Fahlman, Esse (Swedish architect,
Sundsvall) **AV**
Bibl: ▶Svenska Ark. Riks., 1987

Fahlsten, Lars (Swedish architect.
Stockholm) **AV**
Bibl: ▶Svenska Ark. Riks., 1984

Fahlström, Oyvind **BA WC**
(Scandinavian artist, 1928-) WC
(Swedish painter in USA, 1928-
1976) BA
Bibl: ▶Bénézit; ▶Svenskt konst.-
lex.; ▶WW Amer. Art, 1976, 1986

Fahnestock → see Fahnestock, Wallace
Weir

Fahnestock, Henry Reigert
(American artist, 1830-1909) **WI**

Fahnestock, Wallace Weir
(American painter, 1877-aft.1929) **PR**
Bibl: ▶WWW Amer. art
Fahnestock PR
Wallace Weir Fahnestock PR

Fahr, Barry (American artist, b.1949) **BA**
Bibl: Pasadena (CA, USA), Cal
Tech, Baxter Art Gall., Barry Fahr
(1981)

Fahr, Ekkehard (W. German
architect, Munich) **AV**
Bibl: Architektur,
Innenarchitektur, Technischer
Ausbau, 1986 Oct., v.94, no.10,
p.56

Fahrbach, Carl Ludwig **BA**
(German artist, 1835-1902) WC
(German painter, printmaker,
1835-1902) BA
Bibl: Bergisch Gladbach (DEU)
Stadtische Galerie, 27 Apr-2 June
1985; Karlsruhe, Kunsthalle;
▶Thieme-Becker

Fahrbach, Carl Ludwug **WC**
Fahrbach, Carl Ludwug → see
Fahrbach, Carl Ludwig

Fahrenheit, Daniel Gabriel (German
physicist, instrument maker, 1686-
1736) **BA**
Bibl: ▶Brockhaus Enzyk.; ▶Encyc.
Britannica

Fahrenkrog, Ludwig (German artist,
1867-1952) **WC**

Fahrenschon, František Kašpar
(Czech painter, 1726-1796) **BA**
Bibl: ▶Bénézit; ▶Thieme-Becker;
UMENI XXV/2 (1977) 169-183

Fahringer, Carl (German artist,
1874-) **WC**

Fahrlander, Franz (German artist,
1793-p.1850) **WC**

Fahrner, Kurt (Swiss painter, 1932-
1977) **BA**
Bibl: Schubarth, DER FAHRNER-
PROZESS (1983) (RILA/CHE)

Faichtmair, Johann Michael II → see
Feichtmayr, Johann Michael II

Faichtmair, Joseph Anton → see
Feichtmayer, Joseph Anton

Faidherbe, Lukas → see Fayd'herbe,
Lucas

Failde Gago, Antonio (Spanish
sculptor, b.1907) **BA**
Bibl: ▶Campoy, Español contemp.;
Trabazo, PIEDRO, BARRO, BRONCE
EN TRES ESCULTORES GALLEGOS
(1978)

Faille, Charles della (early
Netherlandish, b.1545) **BA**
Bibl: BULL. D'INST PATR.
(1971-72) 82

Faille, Monique della (French artist,
op.1914) **WC**

Faine, Duran (Spanish artist, 20th
cent.) **WC**

Faini, Fausto (Italian painter,
b.1955) **BA**
Bibl: Testori, Fausto Faini..., 1985

Fainsilber, Adrien **AV BA**
(French architect) AV
(French architect, 20th c.) BA
Bibl: Architects' journal, 1985
Apr.17, v.181, no.16, p.20;
▶Avery period. idx., suppl. 4,6,7

Fairbairn (British artist, 18th cent.) **WC**

Fairbairn, Hilda (British artist, op.
1893-, d.circa 1917) **WI**
Bibl: ▶Houfe, Brit. book illus.

Fairbairn, Sue (British artist, op.20th
c.) **WI**

Fairbairn, William   **AV BA**
    (British engineer, 1789-1874)   BA
    (British engineer, millwright,
      1789-1874)   AV
      Bibl: Country life, 1986 Mar.20,
      v.179, no.4622, p.714; ▶Dict.
      natl. biog.; ▶Macmillan encyc.
      archts.
Fairbanks Painter (Etruscan vase-
    painter)   **GC**
      Bibl: ▶Szilagyi, Etruszko-korinthosi
Fairbanks, Avard→see Fairbanks,
    Avard Tennyson
Fairbanks, Avard Tennyson
    (American sculptor, b.1897)   **GC**
      Bibl: Getty Photo Study Coll.;
      ▶Opitz, Amer. sculptors
    Fairbanks, Avard   GC
Fairburn (British artist, op.18th c.) **WI**
Fairburn→see Fairburn, John
Fairburn→see Freebairn, Robert
Fairburn, John   **WI**
    (British artist, 19th cent.)   WC
    (British artist, op.19th c.)   WI
    Fairburn   **WC**
Fairchild, Anson P. (American
    cabinetmaker, act.1790-1816)   **BA**
      Bibl: Keno, Antiques CXVII (May
      1980) 1100-1107
Fairchild, Cameron Douglas
    (American architect, active in
      Houston, TX, 1902-1985)   **AV**
      Bibl: ▶Amer. archts. dir.; Texas
      architect, 1985 Sept.-Oct., v.35,
      no.5, p.32
Fairchild, Charlotte (Active NY, U.S.
    ca. 1920-ca. 1940)   **JG**
Fairchild, Hurlstone (American
    painter, 1893-1966)   **PR**
      Bibl: ▶WWW Amer. art
    Hurlstone Fairchild   PR
Fairchild, Louis   **WC WI**
    (American artist, 1800-op.1855)   WI
    (American artist, 1800-p.1840)   WC
Fairchild, Lucia→see Fuller, Lucia
    Fairchild
Fairchild, Mary, Miss→see Low, Mary
    Fairchild MacMonnies
Fairclough, Wilfred   **BA WC WI**
    (British artist, 1907-)   WC
    (British artist, b.1907)   WI
    (British painter, printmaker,
      b.1907)   BA
      Bibl: ▶Intl. dir. exh. artists, 1983;
      ▶Waters, Brit. artists; ▶Who's
      Who [GBR], 1977; ▶WW Art,
      1974, 1982
Faire, Leandro de→see Ferro,
    Leandro
Fairfax-Lucy, Edmund   **WC WI**
    (British artist, 20th cent.)   WC
    (British artist, op.20th c.)   WI
Fairfax-Muckley, Louis→see Muckley,
    Louis Fairfax
Fairfeldt→see Fairfield, Charles
Fairfield→see Fairfield, Charles

Fairfield, A.N.   **WC WI**
    (British artist, 19th cent.)   WC
    (British artist, op.19th c.)   WI
Fairfield, Charles   **PR WC WI**
    (British artist, 1759-1761-1804)   WI
    (British artist, 1759/61-1804)   WC
    (British painter, ca.1760-1804)   PR
      Bibl: ▶Thieme-Becker;
      ▶Waterhouse, Brit. 18c. ptrs.
    Charles Fairfield   PR
    Fairfeldt   PR
    Fairfield   PR
    Farefeldt   PR
    Fayerfield   PR
Fairgrieve, James (British artist, op.
    20th c.)   **WI**
Fairhaven, Henry Rogers
    Broughton (British, 1900-1973) **BA**
      Bibl: Debrett's
    Broughton, Henry Rogers   BA
Fairholme, Georgina (American
    interior designer)   **AV**
      Bibl: House beautiful, 1987 Feb.,
      v.130, no.2, p.76
Fairholt, Frederick William (British
    artist, 1814-1866)   **WC WI**
Fairlam, Eleanor, Miss→see Brown,
    Eleanor
Fairland, Thomas   **WC WI**
    (British artist, c.1804-1852)   WC
    (British artist, circa 1804-1852)   WI
Fairless, Thomas Kerr   **WC WI**
    (British artist, 1825-1853)   WI
    (British artist, c.1825-1853)   WC
Fairley, Barker (Canadian educator,
    author, painter, b.1887)   **BA**
      Bibl: ▶Artists Canada; Kingston
      (Ont,CAN), Queen's Univ., A.
      Etherington Arts Centre, BARKER
      FAIRLEY (1980); ▶Natl. Gall.
      Canada libr. cat.
Fairley, Graham   **AV**
Fairlie Harmar→see Harmar, Fairlie
Fairlie Harmar, Viscountess
    Harberton→see Harmar, Fairlie
Fairman, Frances C. (British artist,
    1836-1923)   **WI**
      Bibl: ▶Wood, Victorian ptrs.
    Fairman, Frances L., Miss   WI
Fairman, Frances L., Miss→see
    Fairman, Frances C.
Fairman, James (American artist,
    1826-1904)   **WI**
Fairn, Leslie (Canadian architect,
    Nova Scotia, 1875-1971)   **AV**
      Bibl: Society for the Study of
      Architecture in Canada. Bulletin,
      1989 Mar., v.14, no.1, p.15
Fairs, Tom (British artist, op.1985-) **WI**
Fairweather, George (British
    architect, 1906-1986)   **AV**
      Bibl: Building design, 1986 July
      18, no.796, p.8

Fairweather, Ian   **BA WC**
    (Australian artist, 20th cent.)   WC
    (Australian painter, b.1891)   BA
      Bibl: ▶Bénézit; ▶Encyc. Australian
      art
Faisant, Daniel (French architect)   **AV**
      Bibl: Architecture d'aujourd'hui,
      1985 Feb., no.237, p.XIX
Faistauer→see Faistauer, Anton
Faistauer, Anton   **BA PR WC**
    (Austrian painter, 1887-1930)   BA PR
    (German artist, 1887-1930)   WC
      Bibl: ▶Bénézit; ▶Brockhaus Enzyk.;
      ▶Österr. biog. Lex. 1815-1950;
      ▶RILA/BHA; ▶Vollmer, Künst.-Lex.
      20. Jhr.
    Anton Faistauer   PR
    Faistauer   PR
Faistenberger→see Faistenberger,
    Anton
Faistenberger (not Feistenberger),
    Andreas, II (German artist, 1647-
      1736)   **WC**
Faistenberger, Anton   **GC PR**
    (Austrian, 1663-1708)   GC
    (German artist, 1663-1708)   WC
    (German painter, 1663-1708)   PR
      Bibl: ▶Thieme-Becker; ▶Witt
      checklist
    Anton Faistenberger   PR
    Faistenberger   PR
Faistenberger, Anton, I   **WC**
    Feistenberger   PR
Faistenberger, Anton, I→see
    Faistenberger, Anton
Faistenberger, Anton, II (German
    artist, 1678-1722)   **WC**
Faistenberger, Faistenperger or
    Feistenberger, Simon Benedikt
    (German artist, 1695-1759)   **WC**
Faistenberger, Ignaz (German
    artist, 1662-1728)   **WC**
Faistenberger, Joseph (German
    artist, 1675-1724)   **WC**
Faistenberger, Wilhelm (Austrian
    painter, 1623-ca.1690)   **BA**
      Bibl: ▶Bénézit; ▶Thieme-Becker
    Feistenberger, Wilhelm   BA
Fait, Joe (American designer and
    builder, Arizona)   **AV**
      Bibl: Earthbuilder, 1984, no.43,
      p.5
Faithful Christopher Pack→see Pack,
    Faithful Christopher
Faithfull, Leila   **WC WI**
    (British artist, 20th cent.)   WC
    (British artist, b.1898)   WI
    Reynolds, Leila, Miss   WI
Faithorne the Elder, William→see
    Faithorne, William
Faithorne, William (English
    printmaker, 1656-ca.1701)   **BA**
      Bibl: ▶Dict. natl. biog.; Hind, Hist.
      engraving & etching; ▶Nagler,
      Neues Künst.-Lex.; ▶Redgrave,
      Engl. school; ▶Thieme-Becker

Falconetti, Gian Maria **BA** GC **PR**
    (Architect, painter,
      draughtsman, 1468-1535) CE
    (Italian artist, c.1486-a.1540) WC
    (Italian painter and architect,
      ca.1468-1535) GC
    (Italian painter, architect, ca.
      1468-1535) BA
    (Italian painter, ca.1468-1535) PR
    Bibl: ▶Bolaffi; ▶Encic. italiana;
    ▶RILA/BHA, 1986;
    ▶Thieme-Becker; ▶Witt checklist
    Falconetti PR
    Falconetti, Giovanni Maria PR
    Falconetto, Gian Maria CE PR
Falconetto, Giovanni Mari **WC**
Falconetto, Giovanni
    Maria BA **CE GC PR**
    Gian Maria Falconetti PR
    Iohannes Maria Falconetus CE
Falconetti, Giovanni Maria→see
    Falconetti, Gian Maria
Falconetto, Gian Maria→see
    Falconetti, Gian Maria
Falconetto, Giovanni Mari→see
    Falconetti, Gian Maria
Falconetto, Giovanni Maria→see
    Falconetti, Gian Maria
Falconi, Bernardo di Nello di
    Giovanni **BA**
    (Italian artist, 14th cent.) WC
    (Italian painter, 14th c.) BA
    (Italian, late 14th century) GC
    Bibl: ▶Bolaffi; ▶Thieme-Becker;
    ▶Witt checklist
    Bernardo di Nello di Giovanni
    Falconi BA **GC WC**
Falconi, Giovanni *(Italian*
    illuminator, act. ca.1432-1437) **GC**
    Bibl: ▶Thieme-Becker
Falconi, Giovanni Battista *(Italian*
    architect in POL, act.1625-1660) **BA**
    Bibl: ▶Slownik artystów polskich;
    ▶Thieme-Becker; ▶Wielka ilustr.
    encyk.
Falconi, Silvio *(Italian artist, op.c.*
    1514) **WC**
Falconieri, Paolo Francesco *(Italian,*
    1626-1696) **BA**
    Bibl: Howard, BURLINGTOON
    MAGAZINE, 130/1023 (Jun
    1988), 457-459; Storia dell'arte
    38-40 (Jan-Dec 1980) 335-338
Falconnet, Judith Marie Agnes de
    Palezieux *(British, d.1856)* **BA**
    Bibl: Blue guide: Rome, p.172;
    Fehl, ARS AURO PRIOR, STUDIA
    IOANNI BIAŁOSTOCKI (1981),
    647, n.2; Istituto di studi romani,
    S. Andrea delle Fratte, fold-out
Falcrantz [Unidentified] *(Unknown*
    painter) **PR**
    Bibl: (May 17, 1806, lots 4,5,7,8,
    11,12, Christie's)

Falda, Giovanni Battista **AV BA GC WC**
    (Italian architectural engraver,
      1648?-1678) AV
    (Italian artist, op.1655-m.1678) WC
    (Italian printmaker,
      1640/43-1678) BA GC
    Bibl: Assunto, VILLE E GIARDINI
    (1980); ▶Bénézit; ▶Bolaffi; ▶Encic.
    italiana; ▶Encyc. world art; ▶Illus.
    Bartsch, v.21, pp.138-146; ▶Libr.
    of Congr. Name Auth. File;
    ▶RILA/BHA; Strut; TCI Roma e
    dintorni; ▶Thieme-Becker
Faldi, Arturo *(Italian artist, 1856-*
    1911) **WC**
Faldoni, Giovanni Antonio **GC WC**
    (Italian artist, 1690-1770) WC
    (Italian, 1690-1770) GC
    Bibl: ▶Thieme-Becker; ▶Witt
    checklist
Falen, Johannes *(Netherlands artist,*
    op.1672) **WC**
Falens→see Falens, Carel van
Falens or Valens, Carel van→see
    Falens, Carel van
Falens, Carel van **GC PR**
    (Flemish artist, 1683-1733) WC
    (Flemish painter, 1683-1733) PR
    (Flemish, 1683-1733) GC
    Bibl: (December 18, 1811, lot 22,
    Shaw); Getty Photo Study Coll.
    (Ptgs.); ▶Thieme-Becker; ▶Witt
    checklist
    Carel van Falens PR
    Faes, van der PR
    Falens PR
    Falens or Valens, Carel van **WC**
    V. Falens PR
    Valens, Carel van GC
    Van Faelens PR
    Van Falen PR
    Van Falens PR
    Van. Falens PR
    Vanderfaes PR
Falens, J. van *(Netherlands artist,*
    17th/18th cent.) **WC**
Falero, Luis Riccardo *(Spanish*
    artist, 1851-1896) **WC**
Falguière, Alexandre→see Falguière,
    Jean Alexandre Joseph
Falguière, Jean Alexandre
    Joseph **BA GC WC**
    (French artist, 1831-1900) WC
    (French sculptor, 1831-1900) BA GC
    Bibl: ▶Bénézit; ▶Fogg Mus. Libr.
    cat.; ▶RILA/BHA; ▶Thieme-Becker
    Falguière, Alexandre BA
Fali, Giuseppe *(Italian painter, ca.*
    1697-1772) **BA**
    Bibl: ▶Bolaffi; ▶Thieme-Becker
Falileev, Vadim *(Russian printmaker,*
    b.1879) **BA**
    Bibl: ▶Fogg Mus. Libr. cat.; ▶Met.
    Mus. Art libr. cat.

Faliscan Barbarano Group
    (Etruscan, Faliscan vase-painters) **GC**
    Bibl: Del Chiaro, Caere
Falize, Alexis *(French goldsmith,*
    1811-1898) **BA**
    Bibl: ▶Dict. biog. fran.; ▶Penguin
    dec. arts; ▶Thieme-Becker
Falize, Jean **AV**
Falize, Lucien *(French goldsmith,*
    jeweler, 1842-1897) **BA**
Falk *(Active Sydney, Australia,*
    1890's) **JG**
Falk, G. Devoto *(Italian, 20th c.)* **BA**
    Bibl: Mallory, METROPOLITAN
    MUS. JOURNAL IX (1974) 187-202
Falk, Gathie *(Canadian artist,*
    b.1928) **BA**
    Bibl: ▶Artists Canada; ▶Intl. dir.
    exh. artists, 1982, 1983
Falk, Hans **BA WC**
    (Swiss artist, 1918-) WC
    (Swiss painter, printmaker,
      b.1918) BA
    Bibl: ▶MoMA libr. cat.; ▶Vollmer,
    Künst.-Lex. 20. Jhr.
Falk, Jeremias→see Falck, Jeremias
Falk, Robert Rafailovič **BA**
    (Russian artist, 1886-p.1931) WC
    (Russian painter, 1886-1958) BA
    Bibl: ▶Bénézit; ▶Vollmer,
    Künst.-Lex. 20. Jhr.
Falk, Robert Rafailowitsh **WC**
Falk, Robert Rafailowitsh→see Falk,
    Robert Rafailovič
Falkeisen, Sebastian *(Swiss artist,*
    1719-1788) **WC**
Falken, Herbert *(German painter,*
    b.1932) **BA**
    Bibl: ▶WW Arts DEU
Falkenberg, Richard *(German artist,*
    1875-) **WC**
Falkenbury, Stephen D. **AV**
Falkener, Erhart *(German sculptor,*
    act.1496-1510) **BA**
    Bibl: Dehio: Hessen; Dehio:
    Rheinland-Pfälz; Dölling, in KUNST
    UND KULTUR AM MITTELRHEIN
    (1982) 290-297; Schäfke, Der
    Rhein; ▶Thieme-Becker
    Falckener, Erhart BA
Falkenstein, Claire **BA WC WI**
    (American artist, 1908-) WC
    (American artist, b.1908) WI
    (American sculptor, b.1908) BA
    Bibl: ▶MoMA libr. cat.; ▶Parry,
    Contemp. art; ▶WW Amer. Art,
    1978, 1980
    McCarthy, C. Lindley, Mrs., (Claire) WI
Falkner, Avery *(American painter,*
    20th c.) **BA**
    Bibl: Malibu (CA, USA),
    Pepperdine U., Sue Dirksen et al.
    (1979)
Falkner, Harold *(British architect,*
    1875-1963) **BA**
    Bibl: ▶Avery obit. idx.; Pevsner,
    Surrey; ▶Wodehouse, Brit. archts.

Falkner, Rubert *(Austrian architect, 20th c.)* **BA**
Bibl: ▶Avery period. idx., v.2, 6th suppl.

Falkner, Rupert *(Austrian architect, Vienna)* **AV**
Bibl: ▶Verzeich. Öst. Ziviltech.

Falkowska, Barbara *(Polish weaver, 20th c.)* **BA**
Bibl: Warsaw (POL), Centrlne Biuro Wystaw Artystycznych, BARBARA FALKOWSKA TAPESTRIES (1979)

Falla, Gordon *(Finnish architect)* **AV**
Bibl: Arkkitehti, 1986, no.2-3, p.64

Fallah, Christina *(Interior designer, London)* **AV**
Bibl: Interiors, 1988 Sept., v.148, no.2, p.50

Fallani, Bernardo **AV BA**
(Florentine 18th cent. architect) AV
(Italian architect, act.1775-1792) BA
Bibl: Mignani Galli, Labyrinthos I/1-2 (1982) 165-202; ▶Portoghesi, Diz. arch. e urbanistica; Santi et al., Comp. della SS. Annunziata a Firenze; TCI Firenze; ▶Thieme-Becker

Fallaro, Foller or Follador(?), Jacopo *(Italian artist, 16th cent.)* **WC**

Fallender of Fallenter, Franz *(Swiss artist, op.1577-m.1612)* **WC**

Faller, Dieter *(German architect, Stuttgart, 1936-)* **AV**
Bibl: Deutsche Bauzeitung, 1985 Aug., v.119, no.8, p.94

Faller, Felix *(German artist, 1835-1887)* **WC**

Faller, Marion *(American photographer, b.1941)* **BA**
Bibl: ▶WW Amer. Art

Faller, Matthias *(Swiss sculptor, act. 1764-1767)* **BA**
Bibl: ▶Jenny, Kunstführer Schweiz, v.1, p.629; Kasper, ZAK XL/3 (1983) 209; Kunstdenkmäler Thurgau, v.1, pp.230, 248

Faller, Peter **AV BA**
(German architect, b.1931) BA
(West German architect, 1931-) AV
Bibl: Kunstwerk XXXII/2-3 (Apr-June 1979) 54-55

Falletti, Anna *(Italian architect, Milan)* **AV**
Bibl: Area, 1989 Jan.-Feb., v.9, no.44, p.48

Fallon, Mark *(Irish goldsmith, act. 1730-ca.1742)* **BA**
Bibl: Bennet, IR. GEORGIAN SILVER, 207; Gordon, IRISH GEORGIAN SOC. XXV (1982) 19-24; Jackson, Engl. goldsmiths, p.705

Fallon, Sarah W.M. *(British artist, op.1880-1895)* **WI**

Fallot **GC JG**
(French porcelain gilder, act. 1773-1790) GC
(French, active at Sevres 1773-1790) JG
Bibl: ▶Brunet, Sèvres; Dauterman, Wrightsman coll.: Porc.
Falot GC

Fallours, Samuel *(Dutch painter, printmaker, 18th c.)* **BA**
Bibl: ▶Bénézit; Landwehr, Buchillus. 18. Jahrh., p.200; ▶Thieme-Becker

Fallow Deer Painter, Tyrrhenian Group **JG**

Fally, Erich *(Austrian architect, Salzburg)* **AV**
Bibl: ▶Verzeich. Öst. Ziviltech.

Falmouth Painter *(vase-painter, ca. 585-570 BC)* **GC**
Bibl: ▶Beazley, Attic bl.-fig. vase-ptrs.; Boardman, Attic Bl.-fig. Vases, (Komast Group)

Faloci, Pierre Louis→see Faloci, Pierre-Louis

Faloci, Pierre-Louis **BA**
(French architect) AV
(French architect, 20th c.) BA
Bibl: Architecture intérieure CREE, 1984, no.200, p.130; ▶Avery period. idx., 1986; Faloci, MONUMENTS HISTORIQUES DE LA FRANCE, CLIV (Oct 1987), 58-59

Faloci, Pierre Louis **AV**
Falot→see Fallot

Falot or Fallot, J. *(French artist, op. 1764-1825)* **WC**

Falter, John Philip *(American artist, b.1910)* **WI**
Bibl: ▶Fielding's Amer. ptrs.

Falturini→see Perino del Vaga (Pietro Buonaccorsi)

Faltz, Raymond *(Swedish medalist, wax modeler, painter in Germany, 1658-1703)* **BA**
Bibl: ▶Forrer, Medallists; ▶Neue deutsche Biog.; ▶Pyke, Wax modellers; ▶Svenskt konst.-lex.; ▶Thieme-Becker
Falz, Raimund BA

Falz, Raimund→see Faltz, Raymond
Falzagalloni da Ferrara, Stefano (Stefano da Ferrara)→see Falzagalloni, Stefano

Falzagalloni, Stefano **PR**
(Italian artist, -1500) WC
(Italian painter, d. 1500) PR
Bibl: ▶Thieme-Becker

Falzagalloni da Ferrara, Stefano (Stefano da Ferrara) **WC**
Stefano Falzagalloni PR

Falzoni, Giordino *(Italian artist, 20th cent.)* **WC**

Fama, Joe *(American architect, Troy, N.Y)* **AV**
Bibl: Architecture, the AIA journal, 1984 Jan., v.73, no.1, p.80

Famechon, Jacques *(French silversmith, b. ca.1733, master 1770)* **GC**
Bibl: ▶Mabille, Orfèv. fran.

Famechon, Pierre-Antoine *(French silversmith, master 1785)* **GC**
Bibl: ▶Nocq, Poinçon de Paris

Famery, Jacques *(French designer, 20th c.)* **BA**
Bibl: Zadova, DEK. ISKUSSTVO 1 (Jan 1974) 41-45

Famin, Auguste Pierre Sainte Marie *(French architect, 1776-1859)* **BA**
Bibl: ▶Dict. biog. fran.; ▶Macmillan encyc. archts.; ▶Natl. union cat., pre-1956

Famin, Charles *(French, active 1860s-1870s)* **JG**

Famulus **BA CE**
(Painter, artist, ante 69-post 63) CE
(Roman painter, act.64-68 A.D.) BA
Bibl: J.J. Politt, THE ART OF ROME, c.753 B.C.-337 A.D. sOURCES AND DOCUMENTS, Englewood Cliffs, NJ, 1966, 143 and 146; Kraus, Römische Weltreich (Prop. Kunst. 2), 64, 209; Pliny the Elder, Nat. hist., XXXV, 120; Strong, Roman art, pp.60-70
Amulius CE

Fabullus **CE**

Fancelli, Chiarissimo *(Italian sculptor, d.1632)* **GC**
Bibl: TCI Firenze

Fancelli, Cosimo *(Italian sculptor, 1620-1688)* **BA**
Bibl: ▶Bénézit; ▶Bessone-Aurelj, Scult. & arch. ital.; ▶Encic. italiana; ▶Encyc. world art; ▶Thieme-Becker

Fancelli, G. *(Italian artist, 16th cent.)* **WC**

Fancelli, Giacomo Antonio *(Italian sculptor, stucco artist, 1619-1671)* **BA**
Bibl: ▶Encyc. world art; ▶Thieme-Becker

Fancelli, Giovanni *(Italian sculptor, doca.1568, d.1586)* **GC**
Bibl: TCI Firenze

Fancelli, Luca *(Italian sculptor, architect, engineer, 1430-1495)* **BA**
Bibl: ▶Thieme-Becker

Fancelli, Petronio (Italian, 1734-
1800) **GC**
   Bibl: ▶Thieme-Becker
Fancelli, Pietro **BA WC**
   (Italian artist, 1764-1850) WC
   (Italian painter, 1764-1850) BA
    Bibl: ▶Bolaffi; ▶Thieme-Becker
Fancher, Louis → see Fancher, Luis
Fancher, Luis **WI**
   (American artist, 1884-) WC
   (American artist, 1884-1944) WI
   Fancher, Louis **WC**
Fane, E. **WC WI**
   (British artist, 18th cent.) WC
   (British artist, op.18th c.) WI
Fane, Lawrence (American sculptor,
b.1933) **BA**
    Bibl: Lincoln (MA, USA),
    DeCordova and Dana Mus, NEW
    WORK BY OLD FRIENDS (1987);
    ▶Locus, 1977-78; ▶MoMA libr.
    cat.
Fanelli, Francesco **BA GC**
   (Italian sculptor in England, act.
   1608-1665) BA
   (Italian sculptor, act.1608-1665) GC
    Bibl: ▶Grant, Brit. sculptors;
    ▶RILA/BHA; ▶Thieme-Becker;
    Whinney, Sculp. GBR 1530-1830
   Fanelli, Francis BA
Fanelli, Francis → see Fanelli,
   Francesco
Faneuil, Benjamin (American, 18th
c.) **BA**
    Bibl: ▶Dict. Amer. biog.
Fanfani, Enrico (Italian artist, op.
1847-1861) **WC**
Fangel, H.G. → see Fangel, Henry Guy
Fangel, Henry Guy **WI**
   (British artist, op.19th c.) WI
   (British(?) artist, 19th cent.) WC
   Fangel, H.G. **WC**
Fanger, Walter (German, 20th c.) **BA**
    Bibl: WAFFEN- UND KOST. XXII.
    (1980) 65-70
Fangor, Wojciech (Polish artist,
1922-) **WC**
Fanneck [Unidentified] (Unknown
painter) **PR**
    Bibl: (April 12, 1810, lot 40,
    Winstanley)
Fannen, J. **WC WI**
   (British artist, 20th cent.) WC
   (British artist, op.1887-1892) WI
Fanner, Alice Maud **WI**
   (British artist, 1844-1907) WC
   (British artist, 1865-1930) WI
   **Fanner, Alice Maud (Alice Maud
   Taite)** **WC**
   Taite, Alice Maud, Mrs. WI
Fanner, Alice Maud (Alice Maud
   Taite) → see Fanner, Alice Maud
Fano, Dorothea Natalie Sophia Da,
   Mrs. → see Landau, Dorothea
   Natalie Sophia
Fanquires → see Fouquières, Jacques

Fantacchiotti, Cesare (Italian
sculptor, 1844-1922) **GC**
    Bibl: ▶Bénézit
Fantacchiotti, Odoardo (Italian
sculptor, 1809-1877) **GC**
    Bibl: TCI Firenze
Fantaguzzi, Giuseppe (Italian
painter, 1771-1837) **BA**
    Bibl: ▶Bénézit; ▶Bolaffi; Modena
    (ITA), Palazzo dei Musei, CENTO
    DISEGNI DI GIUSEPPE FANTAGUZZI
    (1976); ▶Thieme-Becker
Fantastici, Agostino **AV BA**
   (Italian architect, cabinetmaker,
   1782-1845) BA
   (Sienese architect, son of
   Bernardino Fantastici, chief
   architect of the city of Siena,
   1782-1845) AV
    Bibl: ▶Encic. italiana, v.31, 712e;
    Furniture history, v.20, p.[45]-46;
    TCI Toscana
Fantetti, Cesare (Italian printmaker,
act.1675) **BA**
    Bibl: ▶Bénézit; ▶Bolaffi; ▶Encic.
    italiana; ▶Thieme-Becker
Fanti, Corrado (Italian
photographer, b.1947) **BA**
    Bibl: Pieve di Cento (ITA), Pinac.
    Civica, L'Occhi Pubblico 1984
    p.95
Fanti, Ercole Antonio Gaetano → see
   Fanti, Gaetano
Fanti, Gaetano (Italian painter in
AUT, 1687-1759) **BA**
    Bibl: ▶Bolaffi; ▶Thieme-Becker
   Fanti, Ercole Antonio Gaetano BA
   Fanti, Giovanni Gaetano BA
Fanti, Giovanni Gaetano → see Fanti,
   Gaetano
Fantin, Paolo (Italian architect) **AV**
    Bibl: Ville giardini, 1984 Oct., no.
    190, p.15
Fantin-Latour → see Fantin-Latour,
   Henri
Fantin-Latour family (French
painters, 19th c.) **BA**
    Bibl: ▶Dict. biog. fran.;
    ▶Thieme-Becker
Fantin-Latour, (Ignace) Henri
   (Jean-Theodore) → see Fantin-
   Latour, Henri

Fantin-Latour, Henri **BA GC PR**
   (French artist, 1836-1904) WC
   (French painter, 1836-1904) PR
   (French painter, printmaker,
   1836-1904) BA
   (French, 1836-1904) GC
    Bibl: ▶Bénézit; Montreal (CAN),
    Mus. of Fine Arts, 19TH C. SMALL
    PAINTINGS (1980); ▶RILA/BHA;
    ▶Thieme-Becker
   Fantin-Latour PR
   Fantin-Latour, (Ignace) Henri (Jean-
   Theodore) PR
   Fantin-Latour, Ignace Henri PR
   **Fantin-Latour, Ignace Henri Jean
   Theodore** **PR WC**
   Fantin-Latour, Ignace-Henri Jean
   Theodore PR
   Fantin-Latour, Ignace-Henri-Jean-
   Theodore PR
   Henri Fantin-Latour PR
Fantin-Latour, Ignace Henri → see
   Fantin-Latour, Henri
Fantin-Latour, Ignace Henri Jean
   Theodore → see Fantin-Latour,
   Henri
Fantin-Latour, Ignace-Henri Jean
   Theodore → see Fantin-Latour,
   Henri
Fantin-Latour,
   Ignace-Henri-Jean-Theodore → see
   Fantin-Latour, Henri
Fantin-Latour, Victoria Dubourg → see
   Dubourg, Victoria
Fantin-Latour, Victoria, (nee
   Dubourg) → see Dubourg, Victoria
Fantini, Guglielmetto (Italian
painter, d.1465) **BA**
    Bibl: Di Macco, ARTE DEL
    QUATTROCENTO (1988)
Fantini, Italo (Italian craftsman,
Milan, specializes in laying
Venetian mosaic floors with
traditional techniques) **AV**
    Bibl: Abitare, 1987, suppl. 251
Fantini, Luigi (Italian photographer,
1895-1928) **BA**
    Bibl: Bologna (ITA), S. Giorgio in
    Poggiale, church, PAESAGGISMO E
    PAESE (1983)
Fantini, Marco (Italian craftsman,
Milan, specializes in laying
Venetian mosaic floors with
traditional techniques) **AV**
    Bibl: Abitare, 1987, suppl. 251
Fanto, Leonhard (German artist,
1874-) **WC**
Fanton, Anthoine → see Fantuzzi,
   Antonio
Fantone, Francesco **GC**
   (Italian artist, op.1530) WC
   (Italian, act.1530) GC
    Bibl: Getty Photo Study Coll.
    (Ptgs.); ▶Thieme-Becker; tyb
Fantoni da Norcia, Francesco **WC**
   Fatone, Francesco GC

Fantoni da Norcia, Francesco → see
Fantone, Francesco

Fantoni family (Italian sculptors,
woodcarvers, 15th-18th cs.) **BA**
Bibl: ▶Bénézit; ▶Encic. italiana;
▶Thieme-Becker

Fantoni, Andrea (Italian
woodcarver, sculptor,
cabinetmaker, architect, 1659-
1734) **BA**
Bibl: ▶Thieme-Becker

Fantoni, Donato Andrea (Italian
sculptor, 1746-1817) **BA**
Bibl: ▶Bénézit; ▶Thieme-Becker

Fantoni, Giacomo (Italian sculptor,
1504-1540) **GC**
Bibl: Getty Photo Study Coll.
(Sculp.); TCI Venezia, 1969

Fantoni. Iacopo **GC**

Fantoni, Marco (Italian architect) **AV**
Bibl: Ottagono, 1984 Sept.,
no.74, p.98

Fantoni. Iacopo → see Fantoni,
Giacomo

Fantuzzi di Bologna, Rodolfo → see
Fantuzzi, Rodolfo

Fantuzzi, Antonio **BA CE GC WC**
(Italian artist, c.1510-p.1550) **WC**
(Italian painter, ca.1510-d. aft.
1550) **GC**
(Italian painter, printmaker, ca.
1510-ca.1550) **BA**
(Painter, engraver, c.1510-post
1549/ante 1600) **CE**
Bibl: ▶Bénézit; ▶Bolaffi; ▶Diz.
biog. ital.; ▶Encic. italiana;
▶Nagler, Neues Künst.-Lex.;
▶Thieme-Becker; ▶Witt checklist

Anthoine Fanton **CE**
Antonio da Trento **GC**
Antonio Fantuzzi **CE**
Fanton, Anthoine **CE**

Fantuzzi, Eliano (Italian artist,
1909-) **WC**

Fantuzzi, Rodolfo **BA**
(Italian artist, 1779-1832) **WC**
(Italian painter, 1781-1832) **BA**
(Italian, 1779-1832) **GC**
Bibl: ▶Bolaffi; Bologna (ITA), S.
Giorgio in Poggiale, OMMAGGIO
A BOLOGNA (1980), 108F;
▶Comanducci, Diz.; ▶Witt
checklist

Fantuzzi di Bologna, Rodolfo **GC WC**

Fanzago, Cosimo **AV BA GC**
(1591-1678) **AV**
(Italian architect, sculptor, 1591-
1678) **BA**
(Italian sculptor and architect,
1591-1678) **GC**
Bibl: ▶Bénézit; ▶Encic. italiana;
Naples (ITA), Museo
Capodimonte, Civiltà del 600 a
Napoli (1984); ▶Portoghesi, Diz.
arch. e urbanistica;
TCI Napoli e dintorni;
▶Thieme-Becker

Fanzeres, Evany (Brazilian painter,
sculptor, b.1940) **BA**
Bibl: ▶Bénézit

Fanzoni, Ferrau → see Fenzoni, Ferraù
Fapresto → see Giordano, Luca

Fara, Vitezslav (Czech architect,
1946-) **AV**
Bibl: Deutsche Bauzeitung, 1981
Oct., v.115, no.10, p.138

Faragó, János (Hungarian architect,
trained and practices in Geneva) **AV**
Bibl: ▶Schweiz. Ingen. u. Archit.,
1984-1985

Farasyn, Edgard **PR WC**
(Belgian artist, 1858-1938) **WC**
(Belgian painter, 1858-1938) **PR**
Bibl: ▶Thieme-Becker; Walker Art
Gal catalogue

Edgard Farasyn **PR**

Farasyn, L. (Belgian painter, 1822-
1889) **PR**
Bibl: ▶Thieme-Becker

L. Farasyn **PR**

Farb, Adrienne (American painter,
20th c.) **BA**
Bibl: ARTS MAG LV (June 1981)
11

Farb, Nathan (American
photographer, b.ca.1941) **BA**
Bibl: ▶Art Index, v.36; Yau, ART
NEWS, LXXXVII (Apr 1988), p.
85-86

Farber, Damon (American landscape
architect, Minneapolis, Minn) **AV**
Bibl: Architecture Minnesota,
1989 July-Aug., v.15, no.4, p.15

Farber, Dennis (American painter,
photographer, b.1946.) **BA**
Bibl: Guide exh. artists: N. Amer.
ptrs.; Jrnl. of So. Calif. 27 (June-
July 1980) 25-26; ▶WW Amer.
Art, 1989

Farber, Manny (American painter,
critic, b.1917) **BA**
Bibl: ▶Havlice, Idx. art. bio.; ▶Intl.
dir. exh. artists, 1983; ▶MoMA
libr. cat.

Farcus, Joseph **AV**

Fardella di Calvello (Italian painter,
act.1684) **BA**
Bibl: ▶Thieme-Becker; Ugo
Procacci festchrift, pp.554-566

Fardella, Giuseppe **BA**
Fardella, Giuseppe → see Fardella di
Calvello

Fardelli, Francesco Neri (Italian
sculptor, act.1379) **BA**
Bibl: Kreytenberg, MITTEILUNGEN
XXIV/3 (1980) 379

Fardon, George Robinson (British) **JG**
Farefeldt → see Fairfield, Charles
Farelli → see Farelli, Giacomo
Farelli, Fardella or Farella
Giacomo → see Farelli, Giacomo
Farelli, Farella or Fardella,
Giacomo → see Farelli, Giacomo

Farelli, Giacomo **BA GC PR**
(Italian artist, 1624-1706) **WC**
(Italian painter, 1624-1706) **BA GC PR**
Bibl: ▶Bolaffi; ▶RILA/BHA;
▶Thieme-Becker

Cavalier Farelli **PR**
Cavalier Farello **PR**
Cavalier Giacomo Farella **PR**
Cavaliere Farelli **PR**
Cavalliero Farelli **PR**
Farelli **PR**

**Farelli, Fardella or Farella
Giacomo** **WC**

**Farelli, Farella or Fardella,
Giacomo** **WC**

Farello **PR**
Fariello **PR**
Giacomo Farelli **PR**
Farello → see Farelli, Giacomo

Faresin, Ilario (Italian architect,
Vicenza) **AV**
Bibl: Architettura, cronache e
storia, 1987 Apr., v.33, no.4,
p.258

Faresin, Silvano (Italian architect,
Vicenza) **AV**
Bibl: Architettura, cronache e
storia, 1987 Apr., v.33, no.4,
p.258

Farey, Cyril **WC WI**
(British artist, op.1922) **WC**
(British artist, op.1922-) **WI**
Bibl: ▶Houfe, Brit. book illus.

Farfan [Unidentified] (Unknown
painter) **PR**

Farfan, Juan (Spanish painter, act.
1489) **PR**
Bibl: ▶Thieme-Becker

Juan Farfan **PR**

Farge, Henri (French artist, 1884-) **WC**
Farge, John La → see La Farge, John

Farge, P. (French artist, 20th cent.) **WC**
Fargue → see Fargue, Maria la
Fargue → see Fargue, Paulus
Constantijn la

Fargue, Jacob Elias la **BA**
(Dutch artist, 1738-1771) **WC**
(Dutch painter, 1735-after 1776) **BA**
(Dutch, 1738-aft.1771) **GC**
Bibl: ▶Thieme-Becker; ▶Witt
checklist

La Fargue, Jacob Elias **GC WC**
Fargue, Karel la → see La Fargue, Karel

Fargue, Maria la **GC PR**
(Dutch artist, 1743-1813) **WC**
(Dutch painter and
draughtsman, 1743-1813) **GC**
(Dutch painter, 1732-1782) **PR**
Bibl: ▶Bénézit; Ringling Museum
catalogue; ▶Thieme-Becker

Fargue **PR**
La Fargue, Maria **GC PR**

La Fargue, Maria Margaretha **WC**
Maria la Fargue **PR**

Fargue, Paulus Constantijn la **BA PR**
  (Dutch artist, 1729-1782)   WC
  (Dutch painter and
    draughtsman, ca.1732-1782)   GC
  (Dutch painter, 1724-1782)   PR
  (Dutch painter, printmaker,
    1729-1782)   BA
    Bibl: ▶Bénézit; Getty Photo Study
    Coll.; ▶RILA/BHA; ▶Scheen, Ned.
    beeldende kunst.; Silleris, DOOR
    HOLLAND MET DE TREKSCHENIT;
    ▶Thieme-Becker; ▶Winkler Prins
    van de kunst; ▶Witt checklist;
    ▶Wurzbach, NLD Künst.-Lex.
  C. F. la Fargue, 1777   PR
  Fargue   PR
Fargue, Paulus Constantin la   GC
  La Fargue   PR
La Fargue, Paulus Constantijn PR WC
  P. C. la Fargue   PR
  P. G. Fargue   PR
  Paulus Constantijn la Fargue   PR
Fargue, Paulus Constantin la→see
  Fargue, Paulus Constantijn la
Faricy, Richard T.   AV
Fariello→see Farelli, Giacomo
Fariello, MaryAnn *(American*
  ceramist, sculptor, 20th c.)   BA
    Bibl: Craig, R.M., in
    SOUTHEASTERN COLLEGE ART
    CONF. REVIEW X/4 (spring 1984)
    201
Farina, Achille *(Italian artist, 1804-*
  1879)   WC
Farina, Baldassare *(Italian, 17th*
  century)   GC
    Bibl: ▶Thieme-Becker
Farina, Ernesto *(Italian artist, 20th*
  cent.)   WC
Farina, Paolo *(Italian architect,*
  1949-)   AV
Farina, Pietro Francesco *(Italian*
  artist, op.1695)   WC
Farinati→see Farinati, Paolo
Farinati, Orazio   BA
  (Italian artist, 1559-p.1616)   WC
  (Italian painter, printmaker,
    1559-after 1616)   BA
  (Italian, 1559-aft.1616)   GC
    Bibl: ▶Thieme-Becker; ▶Witt
    checklist
Farinato, Orazio   GC WC

Farinati, Paolo   BA GC PR
  (Italian artist, 1524-p.1606)   WC
  (Italian painter, 1524-1606)   PR
  (Italian painter, printmaker, and
    architect, 1524-1606)   GC
  (Italian painter, printmaker,
    architect, 1524-1606)   BA
    Bibl: ▶Artist biog. master idx.;
    ▶Bolaffi; ▶Encic. italiana;
    ▶RILA/BHA; ▶Thieme-Becker;
    ▶Witt checklist
  Farinati   PR
  Farinato   PR
Farinato, Paolo   PR WC
  Farinatti   PR
  P. Faranatti   PR
  P. Farinati   PR
  P. Farinati   PR
  Paolo Farinati   PR
  Paolo Farinato   PR
  Paulus Fernatus   PR
Farinato→see Farinati, Paolo
Farinato, Battista→see Zelotti,
  Giovanni Battista
Farinati, Orazio→see Farinati, Orazio
Farinati, Paolo→see Farinati, Paolo
Farinatti→see Farinati, Paolo
Farinatti, Giambattista→see Zelotti,
  Giovanni Battista
Farington→see Farington, Joseph
Farington, George *(British artist,*
  1752-1788)   WC WI
Farington, Joseph   BA GC PR WC WI
  (British artist, 1747-1821)   WC WI
  (British painter, 1747-1821)   BA PR
  (British, 1747-1821)   GC
    Bibl: ▶Dict. natl. biog.;
    ▶RILA/BHA; ▶Thieme-Becker;
    ▶Witt checklist
  Farington   PR
  Farringdon   PR
  Farrington   PR
  Joseph Farington   PR
  T. Farrington, R. A.   PR
Farini, Antonio *(Italian architect,*
  1710-1794)   BA
    Bibl: Bandini & Pirazzoli, ANTONIO
    FARINI (1981); Ricci, Guida di
    Ravenna
Farino→see Furini, Francesco
Faris, Charles *(American silversmith,*
  1764-1800)   BA
    Bibl: Antiques, CXI/2 (Feb. 1977)
    pp.378-385; ▶Penguin dec. arts;
    Pleasants, Silversmiths 1715-1830
Faris, William I *(American*
  clockmaker, silversmith, painter,
  1728-1804)   BA
    Bibl: Antiques, CXI/2 (Feb. 1977)
    pp.378-385; ▶Penguin dec. arts;
    Pleasants, Silversmiths 1715-1830
Farissol, Abraham *(Hebrew*
  illuminator, ca.1451-ca.1525)   BA
    Bibl: Encyc. Judaica

Farjat, Benoît *(French printmaker,*
  1646-ca.1720)   BA
    Bibl: ANTICHITĀ VIVA, XXV/5-6
    (Sept-Dec 1986) 45-50; ▶Bénézit;
    ▶Dict. biog. fran.; ▶Thieme-Becker
Farkas→see Farkas, István
Farkas, André→see François, André
Farkas, Etienne→see Farkas, István
Farkas, István   PR WC
  (Hungarian artist, 1887-1947)   WC
  (Hungarian painter, 1887-1947)   PR
    Bibl: ▶Witt checklist
  Farkas   PR
  Farkas, Etienne   PR
  Istvan Farkas   PR
Farkas, Tamás F. *(Hungarian artist,*
  20th c.)   BA
    Bibl: Farkas & Erdi in LEONARDO
    XVIII/3 (1985) 179
Farkasdy, Zoltán *(Hungarian*
  architect)   AV
    Bibl: Magyar építőművészet,
    1987, v.78, no.4-5., p.7
Farkasvölgyi, István *(Brazilian*
  architect)   AV
    Bibl: Projeto, 1985 Sept., no.79,
    p.104
Farleigh, F.W.C. *(British artist, op.*
  circa 1920-circa 1930)   WI
Farleigh, John   BA WC
  (British artist, 1900-)   WC
  (British artist, 1900-1965)   WI
  (British painter, illustrator,
    printmaker, 1900-1965)   BA
    Bibl: ▶Johnson, Brit. artists;
    ▶Vollmer, Künst.-Lex. 20. Jhr.;
    ▶Who was who [GBR]
Farleigh, John Frederick William
  Charles   WI
Farleigh, John Frederick William
  Charles→see Farleigh, John
Farma, Charles *(Nigerian sculptor in*
  GBR, b.1958)   BA
    Bibl: London (GBR), Camden Arts
    Ctr., Sculp. in garden (1982)
Farmantou→see Fromantiou, Hendrik
  de
Farmatou→see Fromantiou, Hendrik
  de
Farmer, Alexander, Mrs. *(British*
  artist, op.1855-1867)   WC WI
Farmer, Corrall *(British artist, op.*
  1893-1929)   WI
Farmer, Edward Herbert *(New*
  South Wales, Australia government
  architect, 1909-)   AV
Farmer, Emily   WC WI
  (British artist, c.1826-1905)   WC
  (British artist, circa 1826-1905) WI
Farmer, Josephus *(American artist,*
  b.1894)   BA
    Bibl: Milwaukee (WI, USA), Univ.
    of Wisc., Art Hist. Gallery, THE
    GIFT OF JOSEPHUS FARMER (1982)
Farmer, Paul W.   AV
    Bibl: ▶Libr. of Congr. Name Auth.
    File

AV Avery Index   **BA** Bibl Hist of Art   **CE** Census Antique Works   **FA** Fndn Docs of Arch   **GC** Getty Ctr Photo Study Coll

Farmer, Peter *(British artist, op.20th c.)*   **WI**

Farmer, Walter *(British artist, 1887-1947)*   **WI**

Farnam, Henry *(American silversmith, 1773-1833?)*   **BA**
  Bibl: Avery, Early Amer. silver; Buhler, Amer. silver; ▶Thieme-Becker

Farnborough, Amelia Long, Lady → see Long, Amelia

Farnborough, Charles Long, Lord → see Long, Charles

Farndon, Walter *(American artist, 1876-1964)*   **WI**

Farnelli, G. *(Italian artist, 19th cent.)* **WC**

Farnerius, Abraham → see Furnerius, Abraham

Farnham, Mrs. Paulding → see Farnham, Sally James

Farnham, Sally → see Farnham, Sally James

Farnham, Sally James *(American sculptor, b.1898)*   **GC**
  Bibl: Getty Photo Study Coll.; ▶Opitz, Amer. sculptors
  Farnham, Mrs. Paulding   GC
  Farnham, Sally   GC

Farnsworth, Emma Justine *(American, active 1890s, 1900s)*   **JG**

Farnsworth, Jerry *(American painter, b. 1895)*   **PR**
  Bibl: ▶WWW Amer. art
  Jerry Farnsworth   PR

Farnsworth, Louise Richard *(American artist, 1878-1969)*   **WI**

Farny, François Henry → see Farny, Henry François

Farny, Henry F. → see Farny, Henry François

Farny, Henry François   **BA WI**
  (American artist, 1847-1916) WC WI
  (American painter, printmaker, 1847-1916)   BA
  Bibl: ▶Bénézit; ▶Fielding's Amer. ptrs.; ▶WWW Amer.; ▶Young, Amer. artists
  Farny, François Henry   BA
  Farny, Henry F.   **WC**

Farochon, Jean Baptiste Eugene *(French artist, 1812-1871)*   **WC**

Farolfi, Marco *(Italian architect)*   **AV**
  Bibl: L'Arca, 1989 July-Aug., no.29, p.75

Farouk, Omar el → see El Farouk, Omar

Farquarson, A. *(British artist, op. 19th c.)*   **WI**

Farquarson, Robert C. *(British artist, op.20th c.)*   **WI**

Farquhar, Robert D. *(American architect)*   **AV**
  Bibl: Architectural digest, 1985 Nov., v.42, no.11, p.184

Farquharson, David   **GC WC WI**
  (British artist, 1839-1907)   WC WI
  (Scottish draughtsman, 1839-1907)   GC
  Bibl: ▶Thieme-Becker

Farquharson, David   **BA VO**
  (American architect, act.1854-1868)   BA
  (Architect, born Scotland, active in San Francisco and Sacramento, Calif. (1827-1914))   VO
  Bibl: Ehrich, Photo guide to UC Berkeley, p.22; Jrnl. Soc. Arch. Historians; ▶Macmillan encyc. archts., v.2, p.46

Farquharson, Joseph   **BA GC WC WI**
  (British artist, 1846-1935)   WC WI
  (British painter, 1846-1935)   BA
  (British, 1846-1935)   GC
  Bibl: ▶Thieme-Becker; ▶Vollmer, Künst.-Lex. 20. Jhr.; ▶Waters, Brit. artists; ▶Who was who [GBR]; ▶Witt checklist

Farr, Charles Griffin *(American painter, 1908-1984)*   **BA**
  Bibl: Laguna Beach (CA, USA), Mus. Art, West Coast realism (1983); Oakland (CA, USA), Oakland Mus. CHARLES GRIFFIN FARR (1984)

Farran, Kalil *(Brazilian architect)*   **AV**
  Bibl: Projeto, 1987 Dec.-1988 Jan., no.106, p.126

Farran, Richard M. → see Betjeman, John, Sir

Farran, Thomas   **WC WI**
  (British artist, 19th cent.)   WC
  (British artist, op.19th c.)   WI

Farrand, Beatrix → see Farrand, Beatrix Jones

Farrand, Beatrix Jones   **BA**
  (American landscape architect, 1872-1959)   AV BA
  Bibl: Capitol Losses, p.70; ▶Libr. of Congr. Name Auth. File; ▶Natl. union cat., pre-1956; ▶Who was who [GBR]

  Farrand, Beatrix   **AV**

Farrela [Unidentified] *(Unknown painter)*   **PR**
  Bibl: (March 2, 1809, Dublin)

Farrell, Anthony   **BA WI**
  (British artist, b.1945)   WI
  (British painter, printmaker, b.1945)   BA
  Bibl: ▶Intl. dir. exh. artists, 1983

Farrell, Bill *(American sculptor, 20th c.)*   **BA**
  Bibl: Ceramics monthly, XXVIII (1980)

Farrell, Edward Cornelius *(British silversmith, ca.1775-1854)*   **BA**
  Bibl: Connoisseur, CXC/763 (Sept 1975) 26-41

Farrell, Michael   **BA WI**
  (British artist, 1940-)   WC
  (British artist, b.1940)   WI
  (Irish painter, printmaker, b.1940)   BA
  Bibl: Belfast (GBR), Ulster Mus., Irish directions (1975), p.15

Farrell, Micheal   **WC**
Farrell, Micheal → see Farrell, Michael

Farrell, Terry   **AV BA**
  (British architect, b.1938)   BA
  (British architect. Since 1965 partner in Terry Farrell Partnership (formerly Farrell Grimshaw Partnership), 1938-)   AV
  Bibl: ▶Avery period. idx., 7th suppl.; Transactions 3, v.2, n.1, p.97

Farren, Robert *(British artist, 1832-op.1891)*   **WI**

Farrer → see Farrer, Thomas Charles

Farrer, Henry   **WC WI**
  (British artist, op.1826)   WC
  (British artist, op.1826-)   WI
  Bibl: ▶Engen, Victorian engravers

Farrer, Julia *(British artist, b.1950)*   **WI**

Farrer, Nicholas *(British artist, 1750-1805)*   **WC WI**

Farrer, Thomas C. → see Farrer, Thomas Charles

Farrer, Thomas Charles   **PR WI**
  (British artist, 1839-1891)   WC WI
  (British painter, 1839-1891)   PR
  Bibl: ▶Engen, Victorian engravers; ▶Thieme-Becker
  Farrer   PR
  Farrer, Thomas C.   **PR WC**
  Thomas C. Farrer   PR

Farreras, Francisco   **BA WC**
  (Spanish artist, 1927-)   WC
  (Spanish painter, b.1927)   BA
  Bibl: ▶Bénézit; ▶Campoy, Español contemp.

Farret, Coenraad or Coenraet *(Dutch artist, op.1712-1727)*   **WC**

Farri, Stanislao *(Italian photographer, 20th c.)*   **BA**
  Bibl: Reggio Emilia (ITA), Sala Comunale delle Esposizioni, STANISLAS FARNI (1976)

Farriello, Gioseppe → see Farriello, Giuseppe [Unidentified]

Farriello, Giuseppe [Unidentified] *(Italian painter, act. 17th century)*   **PR**
  Bibl: Persico inventory, Naples, 1698; ▶Thieme-Becker, has Giuseppe Fardella 17c.; says he may be identical to Giacomo Farelli
  Farriello, Gioseppe   PR
  Gioseppe Farriello   PR
  Giuseppe Farriello   PR

Farrier, Robert *(British artist, 1796-1879)*   **WC WI**

Farringdon → see Farington, Joseph

Farrington → *see* Farington, Joseph

Farrington, Florence A., Mrs. → *see* Claxton, Florence A.

Farsetti, Daniele *(Italian, 18th c.)*   **BA**
Bibl: Boll. Musei Veneziani XXVII/1-4 (1983-84), p. 58-59; Brusatin:VENEZIA NEL SETTECENTO (1980), p.79

Farsetti, Maffeo *(Italian, act.1704)*   **BA**
Bibl: ARTE VENETA XXXII (1978) 359-361

Farthing, John *(British artist, op. 1885-)*   **WI**

Farthing, Stephen *(British artist, b.1950)*   **WI**

Faruffini, Federico   **BA GC WC**
(Italian artist, 1831-1869)   **WC**
(Italian painter and printmaker, 1831-1869)   **GC**
(Italian painter, printmaker, 1831-1869)   **BA**
Bibl: ▶Bénézit; ▶RILA/BHA; ▶Thieme-Becker

Farulli, Fernando *(Italian painter, printmaker, scenographer, b.1923)*   **BA**
Bibl: ▶Comanducci, Diz.; ▶Havlice, Idx. art. bio.; Prato (ITA), Galleria Comunale di Palazzo Pretorio, FERNANDO FARULLI (1976)

Farwick, Hermann J. *(German architect, Emsdetten)*   **AV**
Bibl: Detail, 1982 Mar.-Apr., no.2, p.146

Fasanella, Ralph *(American painter, b.1914)*   **BA**
Bibl: ▶MoMA libr. cat.

Fasano → *see* Fasano, Tommaso

Fasano, Michelangelo *(Italian artist, 1750-1775)*   **WC**

Fasano, Tommaso *(Italian painter, d. ca.1716)*   **PR**
Bibl: ▶Thieme-Becker
Fasano   **PR**
Tomaso Fasano   **PR**
Tommaso Fasano   **PR**

Fasce, Gianfranco *(Italian artist, 1927-)*   **WC**

Fäsch, Johann Ludwig Wernhard   **BA**
(Swiss artist, 1738-1778)   **WC**
(Swiss painter, ca.1738-1778)   **BA**

Faesch, Johann Ludwig Wernhard   **WC**

Faskel, Bernd *(West German architect, Berlin)*   **AV**
Bibl: Abitare, 1984 July-Aug., no. 226

Fasolo or Fasuolo, Giovanni Antonio → *see* Fasolo, Giovanni Antonio

Fasolo or Fazolo, Bernardino → *see* Fasolo, Bernardino

Fasolo or Fazolo, Lorenzo (Lorenzo da Pavia) → *see* Fasolo, Lorenzo

Fasolo, Antonio → *see* Fasolo, Giovanni Antonio

Fasolo, Bernardino   **BA GC**
(Italian artist, 1489-p.1526)   **WC**
(Italian painter, 1489-1526/27)   **BA GC**
Bibl: ▶Bolaffi; ▶RILA/BHA, 1986; ▶Thieme-Becker
de' Fasoli, Bernardino   **BA**

Fasolo or Fazolo, Bernardino   **WC**
Fazolo, Bernardino   **BA**

Fasolo, Furio *(Italian architect, author, b.1897)*   **BA**
Bibl: ▶Avery Libr. cat.; ▶Avery period. idx.; ▶Portoghesi, Diz. arch. e urbanistica

Fasolo, Giovanni Antonio   **AV BA GC PR**
(Italian artist, c.1530-1572)   **WC**
(Italian painter, 1530-1572)   **BA GC PR**
(Italian painter, b. Vincenza)   **AV**
Bibl: ▶Bolaffi; ▶Encyc. world art; ▶Freedberg, Ptg. Italy; ▶RILA/BHA, 1986; ▶Thieme-Becker

Fasolo or Fasuolo, Giovanni Antonio   **WC**
Fasolo, Antonio   **BA**
Fassolo, Giovanni Antonio   **BA**
Fasuolo, Giovanni Antonio   **BA**
Giovanni Antonio Fasolo   **PR**

Fasolo, Lorenzo   **BA**
(Italian artist, op.1494-m.1516/8)   **WC**
(Italian painter, 1463-1516/18)   **BA**
Bibl: ▶Bolaffi; ▶Thieme-Becker; ▶Witt checklist

Fasolo or Fazolo, Lorenzo (Lorenzo da Pavia)   **WC**
Fazolo, Lorenzo   **BA**
Lorenzo da Pavia   **BA**

Fasolo, Vincenzo *(Italian architect, author, engineer, b.1885)*   **BA**
Bibl: ▶Avery period. idx.; ▶Chi è?; ▶Natl. union cat.; ▶Portoghesi, Diz. arch. e urbanistica

Fassauer, Johann Adam *(German painter, act.1754-d.1787?)*   **GC**
Bibl: Getty Photo Study Coll.; ▶Thieme-Becker

Fassbender, Josef   **BA**
(German artist, 1903-)   **WC**
(West German painter, 1903-1974)   **BA**
Bibl: KUNSTWERK, 27 (MAR 1974), 81 (obit); ▶Vollmer, Künst.-Lex. 20. Jhr.; ▶Witt checklist

Fassbender, Joseph   **WC**
Fassbender, Joseph → *see* Fassbender, Josef

Fässer, Roland *(Swiss architect)*   **AV**
Bibl: Archithese, 1988 Jan.-Feb., v.18, no.1, p.56

Fasset, Kaffe *(British artist, op.20th c.)*   **WI**

Fassett, Cornelia A. → *see* Fassett, Cornelia Adele Strong

Fassett, Cornelia Adele Strong   **WI**
(American artist, 1831-1898)   **WC WI**

Fassett, Cornelia A.   **WC**
Strong, Cornelia Adele, Miss   **WI**

Fassett, Francis Henry *(American architect, Portland, Me, d. 1908?)*   **AV**
Bibl: ▶Withey, Amer. archts., p.204

Fassett, Samuel Montague *(Canadian, b. 1824-1825, active Chicago, IL, U.S.)*   **JG**

Fassianos, Alecos *(Spanish artist, 20th cent.)*   **WC**

Fassin → *see* Fassin, Nicolas Henri Joseph (Chevalier de)

Fassin, Nicolas Henri Joseph (Chevalier de)   **PR**
(Belgian painter, 1728-1811)   **PR**
(Flemish artist, 1728-1811)   **WC**
Bibl: ▶Thieme-Becker
Fassin   **PR**

Fassin, Nicolas Henri Joseph de (Chevalier de Fassin)   **WC**
[le Chevalier...] Fassin   **PR**
Nicolas Henri Joseph (Chevalier de) Fassin   **PR**

Fassin, Nicolas Henri Joseph de (Chevalier de Fassin) → *see* Fassin, Nicolas Henri Joseph (Chevalier de)

Fassler-Kamstra, Mira *(South African architect, 1938-)*   **AV**
Bibl: UIA international architect, 1985, no.8, inside back cover

Fassolo, Giovanni Antonio → *see* Fasolo, Giovanni Antonio

Fasstallis, Giovanni Baptista → *see* Austalis de Sala, Giovanni Baptista

Fasting, Lars *(Norwegian architect)*   **AV**
Bibl: Byggekunst, 1984, v.66, no.7, p.380

Fastolf Master   **BA GC**
(French illuminator, act. ca. 1425)   **GC**
(French, active Paris before ca. 1420, active Rouen from ca. 1420, active England ca. 1440-1450)   **JG**
(illuminator, 15th c.)   **BA**
Bibl: Getty Photo Study Coll. (Medieval); Sotheby's; Sotheby's London, June 25, 1985, Lot 97; Speculum, (Apr. 1979) p.366

Master of Sir John Fastolf   **GC JG**

Fasulo, Filippo *(Italian engineer, act. 1754)*   **BA**
Bibl: Strazzullo, Napoli nobilissima, XXII, XXIII, XXIV (May-Aug. 1983) pp.145-146

Fasuolo, Giovanni Antonio → *see* Fasolo, Giovanni Antonio

Fat Duck Painter *(Apulian vase-painter)*   **GC**
Bibl: Trendall, Attic red-fig. vases Apulia

Fat-Runner Group   **GC**
Bibl: ▶Beazley, Attic bl.-fig. vase-ptrs.

Fath, Jacques *(French couturier, ca. 1911-1954)* **BA**
    Bibl: Denver (CO, USA), Art Mus., 25 yrs. couturiers (1975); NY Times obit.

Fath, Rene Maurice *(French artist, 1850-1922)* **WC**

Father Baptiest → *see* Monnoyer, Jean-Baptiste I

Fathy, Hassan *(Egyptian architect, 1899-)* **AV**
    Bibl: ▶Contemp. archts.

Fatio, Edmond *(Swiss architect, collector, 1871-1959)* **BA**
    Bibl: ▶Avery Libr. cat.; Geneva (CHE), Musee d'Art et d'Histoire, DESSINS ANCIENS D'ARCH. (1979)

Fatio, Emile **AV BA**
    (French architect) AV
    (Swiss architect, 20th c.) BA
    Bibl: ▶Avery period. idx., 1987; Country life, 1987 Jan.22, v.181, no.4, p.66

Fatio, Maurice *(American architect, Palm Beach, Fla, 1897-1943)* **AV**
    Bibl: ▶Macmillan encyc. archts.

Fatius de Castoldis → *see* Presbiter Fatius de Castoldis

Fatone, Francesco → *see* Fantone, Francesco

Fatou *(French weapons maker, act. 1796-1805)* **BA**
    Bibl: Beckert, Dresdener Kunstblatter XXX/1 (1986) 22

Fatouros, Dimitri → *see* Fatouros, Dimitris

Fatouros, Dimitris **AV**
    (Greek archtect) AV
    (Greek artist, 1928-) WC

Fatouros, Dimitri **WC**

Fatqua [**Unidentified**] *(Unknown painter)* **PR**
    Bibl: (June 1812, lots 396 & 397, European Museum)

Fatteruso, Nicola [**Unidentified**] *(Unknown painter, act. 17th century)* **PR**
    Bibl: Cuomo inventory dated 1687

    Fattorusso, Nicola PR
    Nicola Fattoruso PR
    Nicola Fattorusso PR

Fattore → *see* Penni, Giovanni Francesco (il Fattore)

Fattori, Giovanni **BA GC WC**
    (Italian artist, 1825-1908) WC
    (Italian painter, 1825-1908) GC
    (Italian painter, printmaker, 1825-1908) BA
    Bibl: ▶Comanducci, Diz.; ▶Thieme-Becker; ▶Witt checklist

Fattorusso, Nicola → *see* Fatteruso, Nicola [Unidentified]

Fau, Fernand *(French artist, 19th cent.)* **WC**

Faubert, Pierre *(French painter, d.1681)* **GC**
    Bibl: ▶Thieme-Becker

Fauché Gudin → *see* Gudin, Herminie (Madame Fauchier)

Faucher, Paul *(Canadian architect, Quebec)* **AV**
    Bibl: ▶Canad. arch. dir., 1985

Fauchier, Laurent **BA WC**
    (French artist, 1643-1672) WC
    (French painter, printmaker, 1643-1672) BA
    Bibl: ▶Bénézit; ▶Thieme-Becker

Fauck, Francois *(French artist, 19th cent.)* **WC**

Faucon, Bernard *(French conceptual artist, photographer, b.1950)* **BA**
    Bibl: ▶Auer, Encyc. photographes; ▶Babington Smith, Contemp. artists; ▶Contemp. photogs.; ▶Intl. dir. exh. artists, 1983

Fauconnet, François *(French architect and designer)* **AV**
    Bibl: Architecture d'aujourd'hui, 1988 Sept., no.258, p.98

Fauconnier, Nicolas *(French silversmith, master 1785)* **GC**
    Bibl: ▶Nocq, Poinçon de Paris

Faudel *(French architect, act.1629)* **BA**
    Bibl: Congrès archéologique de France 135e (1977, Champagne)

Faudie, Fred *(American painter, photographer, b.1941)* **BA**
    Bibl: ▶WW Amer. Art

Faudran, Jean Baptiste de *(French artist, 1620-1694)* **WC**

Faudran, Jean-Baptiste de *(French painter, 1611-1669)* **BA**
    Bibl: ▶Bénézit; ▶Marseille (FRA), Musée B.-A., Peinture Provence 17e s. (1978); ▶Thieme-Becker

Fauerbach, Michael *(American painter, 20th c.)* **BA**
    Bibl: AMERICAN ART REVIEW IX/6 (Nov 1978) 80-83

Fauerholdt, Viggo *(Danish artist, 1832-1883)* **WC**

Faueur [**Unidentified**] *(Unknown painter)* **PR**
    Bibl: Delahaye inventory dated 1753
    Faueur[?] PR

Faueur[?] → *see* Faueur [Unidentified]

Faugeron, Adolphe *(German artist, 1866-)* **WC**

Faugigny *(French artist, op.1797)* **WC**

Faulkner, Amanda **BA WI**
    (British artist, b.1953) WI
    (British painter, b.1953) BA
    Bibl: Januszczak, W., in STUDIO INT'L: CXCVII/1007 (1984) 12; ▶RILA/BHA, [phone call to artist's gallery (Angela Flowers Gallery, London)]

Faulkner, Benjamin Rawlinson *(British artist, 1787-1849)* **WC WI**

Faulkner, C. → *see* Faulkner, Charles

Faulkner, Charles **WI**
    (British artist, op.1874) WC
    (British artist, op.1874-) WI

Faulkner, C. **WC**

Faulkner, Frank **BA WI**
    (American painter, b.1946) BA
    (British artist, op.1977-1981) WI
    Bibl: ▶Locus; ▶WW Amer. Art, 1989

Faulkner, George *(British artist, op. 19th c.)* **WI**

Faulkner, John **PR WC WI**
    (British artist, circa 1830-op. 1887) WI
    (British artist, op.1852-1887) WC
    (Irish painter, act. 1852-1887) PR
    Bibl: ▶Thieme-Becker
    John Faulkner PR

Faulkner, Joshua Wilson **WC WI**
    (British artist, 1780-op.circa 1820) WI
    (British artist, 1780-p.1820) WC

Faulkner, Patricia **WC WI**
    (British artist, 1946-) WC
    (British artist, b.1946) WI

Faulkner, Winthrop W. **AV**

Faull, Emma *(British artist, b.1956)* **WI**

Faulque, Louis *(French painter, 19th century)* **GC**
    Bibl: ▶Bénézit

Faulte, Michel *(French artist, op. 1619-1638)* **WC**

Fauquet, Maria Luisa [**Unidentified**] *(Unknown painter, act. 18th century)* **PR**
    Bibl: Riccardi inventory dated 1776
    Maria Luisa Fauquet PR

Fauquez family *(French ceramists, 18th c.)* **BA**
    Bibl: ▶Honey, Euro. ceramic; ▶Thieme-Becker

Fauquier → *see* Fouquières, Jacques

Fauquier, W. **WC WI**
    (British artist, 18th cent.) WC
    (British artist, op.18th c.) WI

Fauquiers → *see* Fouquières, Jacques

Faure → *see* Faure, Eugène

Faure Walker, James **BA**
    (British artist, op.1974-1984) WI
    (British painter, critic, b.1948) BA
    Bibl: Bristol (GBR), Arnolfini Gallery, Style in the 70s (1979)

Walker, James Faure **WI**

Faure, Amedee (Victor Amedee) *(French artist, 1801-1878)* **WC**

Faure, Elisa *(French artist, 19th cent.)* **WC**

Faure, Eugène **GC PR WC**
    (French artist, 1822-1879) WC
    (French painter, 1822-1879) PR
    (French, 1822-1879) GC
    Bibl: ▶Thieme-Becker; ▶Witt checklist
    Eugene Faure PR
    Faure PR

Faure, Geneviève (*Interior
decorator, New York City*) **AV**
Bibl: House & garden, 1989 May,
v.161, no.5, p.171

Faure, Jean **GC WC**
(*French artist, op.c.1820-1840*) **WC**
(*French, act.1820-1840*) **GC**
Bibl: ▶Thieme-Becker; ▶Witt
checklist

Faure, L. (*French artist, op.1770*) **WC**

Faure, Leon (*French artist, 1819-
1887*) **WC**

Faure-Beaulieu, Emile (*French artist,
op.1864*) **WC**

Faurer, Louis **BA JG**
(*American photographer,
b.1916*) **BA**
(*American, 1916 -*) **JG**
Bibl: ▶WW Amer. Art

Fausett, Dean→see Fausett, William
Dean

Fausett, William Dean (*American
painter, printmaker, b.1913*) **BA**
Bibl: ▶Vollmer, Künst.-Lex. 20.
Jhr.; ▶WW Amer. Art, 1976
Fausett, Dean **BA**

Faust, Carl (*German artist, 1874-
1935*) **WC**

Faust, Heinrich (*German artist,
1843-1891*) **WC**

Faust, Robert L. (*American
architect*) **AV**

Faust, Sara (*American landscape
architect*) **AV**

Faustina the younger (*ca.125-176*) **BA**
Bibl: ▶Columbia encyc.; ▶New
Columbia encyc.; ▶Petit Robert 2

Faustini, Modesto **BA WC**
(*Italian artist, 1839-1891*) **WC**
(*Italian painter, 1839-1891*) **BA**
Bibl: ▶Bolaffi; ▶Thieme-Becker

Faustner, Luitpold (*German artist,
1845-1925*) **WC**

Fausto Pirandello→see Pirandello,
Fausto

Fausto, Pirandello→see Pirandello,
Fausto

Fausto, Vettor (*Italian naval
architect, ca.1490-ca.1540*) **BA**
Bibl: Avery, Ital. Ren. encyc.

Faustus Painter (*South Italian vase-
painter, 350-300 BC*) **GC**
Bibl: McPhee & Trendall, Fish-
Plates

Fauteux, André Lucien (*Canadian
sculptor, b.1946*) **BA**
Bibl: ▶Artists Canada; Sackville
(CAN), Mount Allison Univ.,
Owens Art Gallery, ANDRE
FAUTEUX (1976)

Fauteux, Roger (*Canadian
draftsman, 20th c.*) **BA**
Bibl: Montreal (Que, CAN), Mus.
d'art contemp., Dessins &
surréalisme (1979)

Fauteux-Masse, Henriette
(*Canadian artist, 20th cent.*) **WC**

Fautier, Jean→see Fautrier, Jean

Fautrier, Jean **BA WC**
(*French artist, 1898-*) **WC**
(*French painter, sculptor,
printmaker, 1898-1964*) **BA**
(*French sculptor, painter, and
printmaker, 1898-1964*) **GC**
Bibl: ▶Bénézit; ▶RILA/BHA;
▶Vollmer, Künst.-Lex. 20. Jhr.

Fautier, Jean **GC**

Fauveau, Félicie de (*French
sculptor, 1799-1886*) **BA**
Bibl: ▶Bellier, Artistes fran.;
▶Busse, Maler u. Bildhauer 19.
Jahr.; ▶Dict. biog. fran.; ▶Mackay,
Western sculp. bronze;
▶Thieme-Becker

Fauvel (*French artist, op.1789*) **WC**

Fauvel Painter **GC**
Bibl: ▶Beazley, Attic red-fig. vase-
ptrs.

Fauvelet→see Fauvelet, Jean Baptiste

Fauvelet, Jean Baptiste **GC PR WC**
(*French artist, 1819-1883*) **WC**
(*French painter, 1819-1883*) **PR**
(*French, 1819-1883*) **GC**
Bibl: ▶Thieme-Becker; ▶Witt
checklist
Fauvelet **PR**
Jean Baptiste Fauvelet **PR**

Faux, Gilbert-Maurice (*French
architect, Asnieres*) **AV**
Bibl: ▶Annuaire archts. fran.,
1987

Faux-Froidure, Eugenie Juliette
(*French artist, 1886-*) **WC**

Fava, Gian Giacomo de→see Macrino
d'Alba

Fava, Giangiacomo→see Macrino
d'Alba

Favanne, Henri Antoine de **BA WC**
(*French artist, 1668-1752*) **WC**
(*French painter, 1668-1752*) **BA GC**
Bibl: ▶Bénézit; ▶Dict. biog. fran.;
▶Thieme-Becker

Favanne, Henri-Antoine **GC**
Favanne, Henri-Antoine→see
Favanne, Henri Antoine de

Favanne, Jacques de (*French artist,
1716-1770*) **WC**

Favaretto, Paolo (*Interior designer,
New York City(?)*) **AV**
Bibl: Interiors, 1987 July, v.146,
no.12, p.64

Favaro, James B. (*American
architect*) **AV**

**Favart, Maurice Genevieve (nee
Bellot)** (*French artist, op.1780-
1808*) **WC**

Favelle, R. (*British artist, op.1865-*) **WI**

Faven, Yrjo Antti (*Scandinavian
artist, 1882-1948*) **WC**

Faverkvist, Thor→see Fagerkvist,
Thor

Favermann, Mark (*American artist,
20th c.*) **BA**
Bibl: Norton (MA, USA), Wheaton
Coll., Allusive illusions (1979)

Favero, Luciano (*Italian architect or
interior designer*) **AV**
Bibl: Ottagono, 1988 June, no.89,
p.98

Faverot, Joseph (*French artist,
1862-*) **WC**

Faverzani, Graziella (*Italian
architect*) **AV**
Bibl: Ottagono, 1984 Sept.,
no.74, p.106

Favier, Antoine (*French silversmith,
act.1510-1532*) **BA**
Bibl: Mons. Hist. de la France 2
(1977) 33-47

Favier, Philippe (*French painter,
b.1957*) **BA**
Bibl: ▶Intl. dir. exh. artists, 1983

Favole, Paolo (*Italian architect*) **AV**
Bibl: Arca, 1987 Oct., no.10, p.62

Favorskij, Vladimir Andreevič **BA**
(*Russian artist, 1886-*) **WC**
(*Russian artist, 1886-1964*) **BA**
Bibl: ▶Fogg Mus. Libr. cat.; ▶Great
Soviet encyc.

Favorsky, Vladimir Andreyevich **WC**
Favorsky, Vladimir Andreyevich→see
Favorskij, Vladimir Andreevič

Favory, Andre (*French artist, 1889-
1937*) **WC**

Favray (not Fauray), Antoine de→see
Favray, Antoine de

Favray, Antoine→see Favray, Antoine
de

Favray, Antoine de **BA GC PR**
(*French artist, 1706-1791/2*) **WC**
(*French painter, 1706-ca.1791*) **BA PR**
(*French, 1706-1791*) **GC**
Bibl: ▶Bellier, Artistes fran.;
▶RILA/BHA; ▶Thieme-Becker;
▶Witt checklist
Antoine de Favray **PR**

Favray (not Fauray), Antoine de **WC**
Favray, Antoine **PR**

Favre, Alexandre (*French architect*) **AV**
Bibl: Garden design, 1985
Autumn, v.4, no.3, p.70

Favre, Jacques (*French silversmith,
master 1774*) **GC**
Bibl: ▶Nocq, Poinçon de Paris

Favre, Jacques (*Swiss architect,
1921-1973*) **BA**
Bibl: Lausanne (CHE), Ecole Poly.
Fed., JACQUES FAVRE (1981)

Favre, Pierrette (Bedie) (*French
artist, 1827-p.1864*) **WC**

Favresse, Marc (*French painter,
sculptor, printmaker, b.1938*) **BA**
Bibl: ▶Bénézit; Saint Quentin
(FRA), Musee Antonio-Lecuyer,
MARC FAVRESSE (1979)

Favretti, Rudy *(American landscape architect)*   **AV**
  Bibl: Historic preservation, 1984, v.36, no.5
Favretto → see Favretto, Giacomo
Favretto, Giacomo   **GC PR WC**
  (Italian artist, 1849-1887)   WC
  (Italian painter, 1849-1887)   PR
  (Italian, 1849-1887)   GC
  Bibl: ▶Thieme-Becker; ▶Witt checklist
  Favretto   PR
  Giacomo Favretto   PR
Favrin, Louis *(French artist, op.1789-1813)*   **WC**
Favro, Murray *(Canadian artist, b.1940)*   **BA**
  Bibl: ▶Artists Canada; ▶Idx. Ontario artists; ▶WW Amer. Art
Faw *(Engraver)*   **WI**
Fawcett, Benjamin *(British artist, 1808-1893)*   **WI**
Fawcett, William Milner *(British architect, 1832-1908)*   **BA**
  Bibl: ▶Avery obit. idx.; ▶Who was who [GBR]
Fawizah bte Haji Kamal *(Malaysian architect)*   **AV**
  Bibl: Pertubuhan Akitek Malaysia, 1984 membership list
  Kamal, Fawizah bte Haji   AV
Fawkes, L.G. → see Fawkes, Lionel Grimston
Fawkes, Lionel Grimston   **WI**
  (British artist, 1849-1931)   WI
  (British artist, op.1895)   WC
  Fawkes, L.G.   **WC**
Faworski → see Faworski, Józef
Faworski, Józef   **BA**
  (Polish artist, 18th cent.)   WC
  (Polish painter, act.1790-1805)   BA
  Bibl: ▶Slownik artystów polskich; ▶Thieme-Becker
  Faworski   **WC**
Fawr, Llywelwyn *(Welsh architect, 1190-1240)*   **BA**
  Bibl: ARCHAEOLOGICAL JOURNAL CXXXII (1975) 237-243
Faxon, Richard *(French artist, op.c. 1865-1870)*   **WC**
Fay, Augustus   **WC WI**
  (American artist, circa 1824-op. 1860)   WI
  (American artist, op.1854-)   WC
  (Engraver, circa 1824-op.1860)   WI
Fay, Joe *(American painter, printmaker, b.1950)*   **BA**
  Bibl: ▶WW Amer. Art, 1978
Fay, Joseph   **GC WC**
  (German artist, 1813-1875)   WC
  (German painter, 1813-1875)   GC
  Bibl: ▶Bénézit; ▶Thieme-Becker
  Fey, Joseph   GC
Fayd'herbe, Luc → see Fayd'herbe, Lucas

Fayd'herbe, Lucas   **BA**
  (Flemish architect and sculptor, 1617-1697)   GC
  (Flemish sculptor, architect, 1617-1697)   BA
  Bibl: ▶Bénézit; ▶Biog. Nat. Belgique; ▶Encyc. world art; ▶Grote Winkler Prins; ▶RILA/BHA; ▶Thieme-Becker
  Faidherbe, Lukas   BA
  Fayd'herbe, Luc   **GC**
  Fiderbe, Luc   BA
Fayd'herbe, Marie *(Flemish sculptor, 1587-1643)*   **BA**
  Bibl: ▶Bénézit; Coekelberghs, S. Jean Baptiste au Béguinage à Bruxelles; ▶Thieme-Becker
Fayerfield → see Fairfield, Charles
Fayermann, Anne Charlotte, Miss → see Bartholomew, Anne Charlotte
Fayet, Carlos Maximiliano *(Brazilian architect, 20th c.)*   **BA**
  Bibl: Muller, Munster, XXVII (1974) pp.295-302
Fayet, Gustave *(French artist, 1865-1925)*   **WC**
Fayet, Suzy Brücker *(Brazilian architect, 20th c.)*   **BA**
  Bibl: Muller, Munster, XXVII (1974) pp.295-302
  Brücker, Suzy   BA
Fayn, Etienne   **AV BA**
  (Belgian architect and engraver, 1712-1790)   AV
  (Flemish architect, printmaker, 1712-1790)   BA
  Bibl: ▶Avery period. idx.; ▶Bénézit; ▶Thieme-Becker
Fayos Molet, Ricard *(Spanish architect)*   **AV**
  Bibl: Arquitectura, LXV/250 (Sept. -Oct. 1984)
Fayram, John   **WC WI**
  (British artist, op.1713-1743)   WI
  (British artist, op.1727-1743)   WC
Fayre, Leandro de la → see Ferro, Leandro
Fayrer, Fanny Jane, Miss → see Maltese, Fanny Jane
Fazekas, Magdolna *(Hungarian artist, 1933-)*   **WC**
Fazolo, Bernardino → see Fasolo, Bernardino
Fazolo, Lorenzo → see Fasolo, Lorenzo
Fazzi, Arnaldo *(Italian sculptor, 1855-1944)*   **GC**
  Bibl: TCI Toscana
Fazzini, Pericle   **BA WC**
  (Italian artist, 1913-)   WC
  (Italian sculptor, b.1913)   BA
  Bibl: ▶Bénézit; ▶Bolaffi 20c.; ▶Vollmer, Künst.-Lex. 20. Jhr.
Fazzino, Massimo *(Italian architect)*   **AV**
  Bibl: Abitare, 1988 June, no.265, p.208

Fearey, Mike *(British photographer, b.1950)*   **BA**
  Bibl: Bristol (GBR), Arnolfini Gallery, Houses & homes (1983)
Fearing, William Kelly *(American painter, b.1918)*   **BA**
  Bibl: ▶WW Amer. Art, 1984
Fearnley, Neill *(American artist, b.1949)*   **BA**
  Bibl: Lincoln (MA, USA), DeCordova & Dana Mus., 3 Boston ptrs. (1983)
Fearnley, Thomas   **GC WC**
  (Norwegian artist, 1802-1842)   WC
  (Norwegian, 1802-1842)   GC
  Bibl: ▶Thieme-Becker; ▶Witt checklist
Fearnside, Viola *(American, 20th c.)*   **BA**
  Bibl: Kinkead, MASTER DRAWINGS XX/3 (autumn 1982) 257-258
Fearnside, W. → see Fearnside, William
Fearnside, William   **WI**
  (British artist, op.1791-1801)   WC WI
  Fearnside, W.   **WC**
Fearon → see Fearon, Hilda
Fearon, Ann, Miss → see Walke, Ann Fearon
Fearon, Hilda   **PR WC WI**
  (British artist, 1878-1917)   WI
  (British artist, 20th cent.)   WC
  (British painter, d. 1917)   PR
  Bibl: Minneapolis catalogue; ▶Witt checklist
  Fearon   PR
  Hilda Fearon   PR
Feary → see Feary, John
Feary, John   **PR WC WI**
  (British artist, 1745-1750-1788)   WI
  (British artist, 1745/50-1788)   WC
  (British painter, 1745/50-1788)   PR
  Bibl: ▶Thieme-Becker
  Feary   PR
  John Feary   PR
Featherston, Grant *(Australian furniture designer)*   **AV**
  Bibl: Transition, 1988 winter, no.25, p.88
Featherston, William *(Canadian painter, b.1927)*   **BA**
  Bibl: ▶Artists Canada; ▶Bénézit; ▶Canad. artists exh., 1972-1974
Febvre, Edouard *(French artist, 20th cent.)*   **WC**
Fechelm, Carl Traugott → see Fechhelm, Carl Traugott
Fechhelm, Carl Traugott   **GC WC**
  (German artist, 1748(?)-1819)   WC
  (German painter, 1748-1819)   GC
  Bibl: ▶Bénézit; ▶Thieme-Becker
  Fechelm, Carl Traugott   GC
Fechin → see Fechin, Nicolai Ivanovich
Fechin, Nicolai → see Fechin, Nicolai Ivanovich

Fechin, Nicolai Ivanovich BA PR
 (American artist, 1881-1955) WI
 (Russian painter, 1881-1955) PR
 (Russian sculptor, painter in
   USA, 1881-1955) BA
   Bibl: ▶Bénézit; ▶Fogg Mus. Libr.
   cat.; ▶Havlice, Idx. art. bio.;
   ▶RILA/BHA; ▶Vollmer, Künst.-Lex.
   20. Jhr.
 Fechin PR
 Fechin, Nicolai PR
 Fechin, Nikolai PR
 Fechin, Nikolai Ivanovich WI
 Feshin, Nikolai Ivanovich BA
 Fešin, Nikolai Ivanovič BA
 Nicolai Ivanovich Fechin PR
 Fechin, Nikolai→see Fechin, Nicolai
   Ivanovich
 Fechin, Nikolai Ivanovich→see
   Fechin, Nicolai Ivanovich
Fechner, Eduard Clemens *(German*
   artist, 1799-1861) WC
Fechner, Hans *(German artist, 1860-*
   1931) WC
Fechter IV, Johann Ulrich *(Swiss*
   artist, 1742-1796) WC
Feckert, Gustav Heinrich Gottlob
   (German artist, 1820-1899) WC
Feddema, Anne Hendrik Berend
   (Dutch painter, b.1961) BA
   Bibl: Leeuwarden, Fries Museum,
   Pim Lenos & Anne Feddema
   (1986)
 Fedden, A. Romilly→see Fedden,
   Arthur Romilly
Fedden, Arthur Romilly WI
 (British artist, 1875-) WC
 (British artist, 1875-1939) WI
 Fedden, A. Romilly WC
Fedden, Mary WC WI
 (British artist, 1915-) WC
 (British artist, b.1915) WI
 Trevelyan, Julian Otto, Mrs., (Mary) WI
Fedder, Otto *(German artist, 1873-*
   1919) WC
 Feddersen the Younger, Hans
   Peter→see Feddersen, Hans Peter
   II
Feddersen, Hans Peter II BA
 (German artist, 1848-1941) WC
 (German painter, 1848-1941) BA
   Bibl: ▶Brockhaus Enzyk.;
   ▶Thieme-Becker; ▶Vollmer,
   Künst.-Lex. 20. Jhr.
 Feddersen the Younger, Hans
   Peter WC
 Feddes, Petrus (Pieter van
   Harlingen)→see Feddes, Pieter van
   (Pieter van Harlingen)
 Feddes, Petrus or Pieter (Pieter van
   Harlingen)→see Feddes, Pieter van
   (Pieter van Harlingen)

Feddes, Pieter van (Pieter van
   Harlingen) BA
 (Dutch artist, 1586-1634(?)) WC
 (Dutch painter and
   draughtsman, 1586-1634) GC
 (Dutch painter, printmaker,
   1586-ca.1634) BA
   Bibl: ▶Bénézit; Getty Photo Study
   Coll.; ▶Seyn, Écoles flam. et holl.;
   ▶Thieme-Becker; ▶Witt checklist;
   ▶Wurzbach, NLD Künst.-Lex.
Feddes, Petrus (Pieter van
   Harlingen) GC
Feddes, Petrus or Pieter (Pieter
   van Harlingen) WC
 Harlingen, Pieter van BA
 Pieter van Harlingen GC
 Fede Galizia→see Galizia, Fede
Fedele da Urbino *(Italian ceramist,*
   16th c.) BA
   Bibl: Douglas, Tuscany Majolica,
   pp.9-10; ▶Encic. italiana, v.41,
   p.718; Luccarelli, Faenza LXIX/3-4
   (1983) 197-201
Fedele di San Biagio, Padre *(Italian*
   artist, 18th cent.) WC
Fedele [Unidentified] *(Unknown*
   painter) PR
   Bibl: Salernitano inventory,
   Naples, 1648
Fedele, Antonio *(Italian architect)* AV
   Bibl: Ville giardini, 1989 Sept., no.
   240, p.12
 Fedeli, Francesco→see Maggiotto,
   Francesco
Fedeli, Matteo de' *(Italian painter,*
   act.1481, d.1505) BA
   Bibl: ▶Bolaffi; ▶Thieme-Becker
Fedeli, Stefano de' BA GC
 (Italian painter, act.1472-1481) BA
 (Italian, act.1472-1481) GC
   Bibl: ▶Bolaffi; ▶Thieme-Becker;
   Welch, BURLINGTON, CXXVII/986
   (May 1985) 296; ▶Witt checklist
Feder, Adolphe *(French artist,*
   1886-) WC
Feder, Gottfried *(German city*
   planner, 1883-1941) AV
   Bibl: Alte Stadt, 1986, v.13, no.3,
   p.192
Federici, Gaetano *(American*
   sculptor, 1880-1964) BA
   Bibl: Paterson (NJ, USA), Passaic
   Cty Hist. Soc., GAETANO FEDERICI
   (1980)
 Federico Barocci→see Barocci,
   Federico
 Federico Barocci da Urbino→see
   Barocci, Federico
 Federico Baroccio da Urbino→see
   Barocci, Federico
 Federico Baroci→see Barocci,
   Federico
 Federico Barozi→see Barocci,
   Federico
 Federico Barroccio→see Barocci,
   Federico

 federico Barrozio→see Barocci,
   Federico
 Federico Bencovich→see Bencovich,
   Federico (Dalmatino)
 Federico Bianchi→see Bianchi,
   Federico
 Federico Cervelli→see Cervelli,
   Federico
 Federico çucar→see Zuccari, Federico
 Federico de Madrazo y Kuntz→see
   Madrazo y Kuntz, Federico de
 Federico Franch→see Franck, Franz
   Friedrich
 Federico Joni→see Joni, Icilio
   Federico
 Federico Mazzotta→see Mazzotta,
   Federico
 Federico Varrozio→see Barocci,
   Federico
 Federico Zuccari→see Zuccari,
   Federico
 Federico Zuccaro→see Zuccari,
   Federico
 Federico Zuccheri→see Zuccari,
   Federico
 Federico Zucharo→see Zuccari,
   Federico
 Federighetto→see Bencovich,
   Federico (Dalmatino)
 Federighi dei Tolomei, Antonio→see
   Federighi, Antonio
Federighi, Antonio BA CE GC
 (Draughtsman, architect,
   sculptor, 1420-1490) CE
 (Italian architect, sculptor, and
   designer, ca.1423-1490) GC
 (Italian artist, c.1420-1490) WC
 (Italian sculptor, architect, ca.
   1423-1490) BA
   Bibl: ▶Encic. italiana; ▶Encyc.
   world art; ▶RILA/BHA; ▶Seymour,
   Sculp. Italy; Siena (ITA), Pal.
   Pubb., Jacopo della Quercia
   (1975); ▶Thieme-Becker
 Antonio di Federigo GC
 Antonio Federighi CE GC
 Antonio Federighi dei Tolomei BA CE GC
 Antonio Federighi or di
   Federigo dei Tolomei WC
 Di Federigo, Antonio CE
 Federighi dei Tolomei, Antonio CE
 Federighi, Antonio dei Tolomei GC
 Federighi, Antonio dei Tolomei→see
   Federighi, Antonio
 Federigo Andreotti→see Andreotti,
   Federigo
 Federigo Barocci d'Urbino→see
   Barocci, Federico
 Federigo Baroccio→see Barocci,
   Federico
 Federigo Baroccj→see Barocci,
   Federico
 Federigo Barroccio→see Barocci,
   Federico

Federigo Bianchi → see Bianchi, Federico

Federigo Nerly → see Nerly, Friedrich

Federigo Zuccaro, Cavaliere → see Zuccari, Federico

Federigo Zuccheri → see Zuccari, Federico

Federle, Helmut M. *(Swiss painter, b.1944)*   **BA**
Bibl: Basel, HELMUT M. FEDERLE; ▶Bénézit

Federley, Birger *(Finnish architect, fl. early 20th cent)*   **AV**
Bibl: Arkkitehti, 1987, v.84, no. 4-5, p.81

Federlin, Hans Balthasar *(Swiss artist, op.1571)*   **WC**

Fedi, Antonio *(Italian painter, 1771-1843)*   **BA**
Bibl: ▶Bolaffi; ▶Thieme-Becker

Fedi, Pio   **BA GC WC**
(Italian artist, 1816-1892)   **WC**
(Italian sculptor, 1816-1892)   **BA GC**
Bibl: ▶Bénézit; ▶Encic. univ. ilus.; ▶Mackay, Western sculp. bronze; ▶RILA/BHA, 1986; ▶Thieme-Becker; Vigezzi, Scult. ital., p.119

Fedi, Rolando *(Italian architect)*   **AV**
Bibl: Architettura; cronache e storia, 1988 Nov., v.34, no.11, p.806

Fedier, Franz *(Swiss artist, 1920-)*   **WC**

Fedin, Konstantin Aleksandrovič *(Russian painter, b.1892)*   **BA**
Bibl: ▶Bowlt, Russian avant-garde

Fedini, Giovanni → see Fedini, Giovanni di Domenico di Lorenzo

Fedini, Giovanni di Domenico di Lorenzo   **BA**
(Italian artist, op.1565-1582)   **WC**
(Italian painter, act.1565-1599)   **BA**
Bibl: ▶Bolaffi; ▶Thieme-Becker

Fedini, Giovanni   **WC**

Fedor Encke → see Encke, Fedor

Fedorov, Ivan *(Russian printer, metalworker, ca.1510-1583)*   **BA**
Bibl: ▶Great Soviet encyc., v.27, p.131 (sv. Fedorov, I., Russian printer)

Moskvitin, Ivan Fedorov   **BA**

Fedorova, M. *(Russian architect)*   **AV**
Bibl: Process: architecture, 1985 Jan., no.54, p.153

Fedorovitch, Sophie   **BA**
(British painter, 1903-1953)   **BA**
(Russian artist, -1953)   **WC**
Bibl: ▶Bénézit; ▶Johnson, Brit. artists; ▶London Times obit.; Southport (GBR), Atkinson Art Gall., Seven & Five Society (1979); ▶Vollmer, Künst.-Lex. 20. Jhr.

Fedorowitsch, Sophia   **WC**

Fedorovskij, Fedor Fedorovič   **BA**
(Russian artist, 1883-1955)   **WC**
(Russian scenographer, 1883-1955)   **BA**
Bibl: ▶Encyc. world art; ▶Fogg Mus. Libr. cat.

Fedorovsky, Feodor   **WC**

Fedorovsky, Feodor → see Fedorovskij, Fedor Fedorovič

Fedorowitsch, Sophia → see Fedorovitch, Sophie

Fedoseeva, G. *(Russian architect)*   **AV**
Bibl: Process: architecture, 1985 Jan., no.54, p.153

Fedotoff, Pauwel Andreievitch → see Fedotov, Pavel Andreevič

Fedotov, Pavel Andreevič   **BA**
(Russian artist, 1815-1852)   **WC**
(Russian painter, poet, 1815-1852)   **BA**
Bibl: ▶Encyc. world art; ▶Thieme-Becker

Fedotoff, Pauwel Andreievitch   **WC**

fedricho borosio → see Barocci, Federico

Feduchi Benlliure, Javier *(Spanish architect)*   **AV**
Bibl: Arquitectura, 1988 Mar.-June, v.69, no.271-272, p.74

Feduchi Canosa, Pedro *(Spanish architect)*   **AV**
Bibl: Arquitectura, 1988 Mar.-June, v.69, no.271-272, p.74; Arquitectura, 1988 Nov.-1989 Feb., v.70, no.275, p.16

Feeley, Paul   **BA WC**
(American artist, 1910-)   **WC**
(American artist, 1910-1966)   **WI**
(American painter, sculptor, 1910-1966)   **BA**
Bibl: ▶Britannica encyc. Amer. art; ▶Cummings, Contemp. Amer. artists, 1971; ▶Phaidon 20c. art

Feeley, Paul Terence   **WI**

Feeley, Paul Terence → see Feeley, Paul

Feeney, Lawrence *(American printmaker, b.1937)*   **BA**
Bibl: Davenport (IA, USA), Munic. Art Gall., Family album (1975)

Feeny, Peter *(British architect)*   **AV**
Bibl: ▶RIBA members, 1983

Feer, Anna van der (Anneke) *(Dutch artist, 1902-)*   **WC**

Feer, Leandro de → see Ferro, Leandro

Feetag, R. *(German artist, 19th cent.)*   **WC**

Feferbaum, Jorge *(Argentine architect, Buenos Aires)*   **AV**
Bibl: Progressive architecture, 1983 June, v.64, no.6, p.85

Feff, Catherine *(French artist, Paris)*   **AV**
Bibl: Architectural record, 1988 Nov., p.51

Fegan → see Fagan, Robert

Fegatelli, Mauro *(Italian architect or engineer)*   **AV**
Bibl: L'industria delle costruzioni, 1988 June, v.22, no.200, p.49

Fegiz, Carlo *(Italian architect)*   **AV**
Bibl: Architettura: Cronache e storia, 1984 July, v.30, no.7, p.512

Feguide *(French artist, 20th cent.)*   **WC**

Fehily, James A. *(Irish landscape architect, Dublin)*   **AV**
Bibl: Landscape architecture, 1985 Nov.-Dec., v.75, no.6, p.80

Fehling, Carl Heinrich Jacob *(German draughtsman, 1683-1753)*   **GC**
Bibl: ▶Bénézit

Fehling, Heinrich Christoph   **GC**
(German artist, 1654-1725)   **WC**
(German, 1654-1725)   **GC**
Bibl: ▶Thieme-Becker; ▶Witt checklist

Fehling, Heinrich Christoph (not Christian)   **WC**

Fehling, Heinrich Christoph (not Christian) → see Fehling, Heinrich Christoph

Fehling, Hermann   **AV BA**
(1909-)   **AV**
(German architect, b.1909)   **BA**
Bibl: ▶Avery period. idx., 6th suppl.; ▶Contemp. archts.

Fehmel, Klaus *(German architect, Fellbach, 1942-)*   **AV**
Bibl: Deutsche Bauzeitung, 1985 Nov., v.119, no.11, p.126

Fehn, Sverre   **AV BA**
(Norwegian architect, 1924-)   **AV**
(Norwegian architect, b.1924)   **BA**
Bibl: ▶Contemp. archts.; ▶Libr. of Congr. Name Auth. File

Fehr   **WC WI**
(British artist, op.1793)   **WC**
(British artist, op.1793-)   **WI**

Fehr, Carl Friedrich Bartholomaeus *(Swiss artist, op.1834-1841)*   **WC**

Fehr, Konrad *(German artist, 1854-1933)*   **WC**

Fehr, Peter, *(German artist, 1681-1740)*   **WC**

Fehr, Siegfried *(German architect)*   **AV**
Bibl: Bauwelt, 1985 Oct.4, v.76, no.37, p.1514

Fehrenbach, E. *(Active London, England, U.K., daguerreotypist)*   **JG**

Fehrenbach, Gerson *(West German sculptor, b.1932)*   **BA**
Bibl: ▶Bénézit; ▶WW Arts DEU

Fehrer, Oscar *(American painter, b.1872)*   **BA**
Bibl: Fehrer, Drawing, IV/2 (Jul.-Aug. 1982) pp.25-28; ▶Fielding's Amer. ptrs.; ▶Vollmer, Künst.-Lex. 20. Jhr.; ▶Young, Amer. artists

Fehringer, Franz *(Austrian architect)*   **AV**
Bibl: Planen Bauen Wohnen, 1986, no.115, p.35

Fehrle, Jakob Wilhelm *(German
 sculptor, painter, 1884-1974)* **BA**
  Bibl: ▶Bénézit; Schwabisch Gmund
  (DEU), Stadtisches Museum, JWF:
  JAKOB WILHELM FEHRLE... (1974);
  ▶Thieme-Becker; ▶Who's Who
  [GBR]
 Fehrle, Wilhelm **BA**
Fehrle, Wilhelm → see Fehrle, Jakob
 Wilhelm
Fehrmann, Jakob *(German artist,
 1760-1837)* **WC**
Fei, Alessandro → see Fei, Alessandro
 (Alessandro del Barbiere)
**Fei, Alessandro (Alessandro del
 Barbiere)** **BA**
  (Italian artist, 1543-1592) **WC**
  (Italian painter, 1543-1592) **BA**
  (Italian, 1543-1592) **GC**
  Bibl: ▶Bénézit; ▶Bolaffi; ▶Encyc.
  world art; ▶Thieme-Becker; ▶Witt
  checklist
 Alessandro del Barbiere **BA**
 Barbiere, Alessandro del **BA**
Fei, Alessandro **GC**
**Fei, Alessandro (di Vincenzio)
 del Barbiere** **WC**
*Fei, Alessandro (di Vincenzio) del
 Barbiere → see* Fei, Alessandro
 (Alessandro del Barbiere)
Fei, Paolo di Giovanni → see Paolo di
 Giovanni Fei
*Fei, Paolo di Giovanni
 (Frederici) → see* Paolo di Giovanni
 Fei
Feibusch, Hans → see Feisbuch, Hans
Feichtmayer, Joseph Anton **BA**
  (German artist, 1696-1770) **WC**
  *(German draughtsman, 1696-
  1770)* **GC**
  *(German sculptor, stucco artist,
  printmaker, 1696-1770)* **BA**
  Bibl: ▶Bénézit; ▶Encyc. world art;
  Getty Photo Study Coll.; ▶Met.
  Mus. Art libr. cat.; ▶Neue
  deutsche Biog.; ▶Schweiz.
  Künst.-Lex.; ▶Thieme-Becker;
  ▶Witt checklist
 Faichtmair, Joseph Anton **BA**
Feichtmayr, Joseph **GC**
Feichtmayr, Joseph Anton **WC**
 Feuchtmair, Joseph **GC**
 Feuchtmayer, Joseph **GC**
 Feuchtmayer, Joseph Anton **BA**
*Feichtmayr, Faichtmair, Feichtmayer,
 Feichtmeier, Feuchtmair or
 Feuchtmayer, Franz Xaver, I → see*
 Feichtmayr, Franz Xavier I

Feichtmayr, Franz Xavier I **BA**
  (German artist, 1705-1764) **WC**
  *(German stucco artist, sculptor,
  printmaker, 1705-1763)* **BA**
  Bibl: ▶Neue deutsche Biog.;
  ▶Thieme-Becker; ▶Witt checklist
**Feichtmayr, Faichtmair,
 Feichtmayer, Feichtmeier,
 Feuchtmair or Feuchtmayer,
 Franz Xaver, I** **WC**
Feichtmayr, Johan Michael, I
  (German artist, c.1666-1713) **WC**
Feichtmayr, Johann Michael → see
 Feichtmayr, Johann Michael II
Feichtmayr, Johann Michael II **BA**
  *(German sculptor, stucco artist,
  1709?-1772)* **BA**
  *(German stucco-worker, 1709 or
  1710-1772)* **AV**
  Bibl: ▶Avery Libr. cat.; ▶Bénézit;
  ▶Encyc. world art; ▶Neue
  deutsche Biog.; ▶Thieme-Becker;
  ▶Witt checklist
 Faichtmair, Johann Michael II **BA**
Feichtmayr, Johann Michael **AV**
 Feuchtmayer, Johann Michael II **BA**
Feichtmayr, Joseph → see
 Feichtmayer, Joseph Anton
Feichtmayr, Joseph Anton → see
 Feichtmayer, Joseph Anton
Feid, Joseph *(German artist, 1806-
 1870)* **WC**
Feidt, Daniel *(American architect,
 Minneapolis, Minn)* **AV**
  Bibl: ▶AIA Pro File, 1987-88
Feiffer, Jules *(American cartoonist,
 playwright, filmmaker, b.1929)* **BA**
  Bibl: WW Amer., 1976; ▶WW
  Amer. Art, 1976
Feigel, Carl *(German artist, 19th
 cent.)* **WC**
Feigenbaum, Harriet **AV BA**
  *(American environmental artist,
  1939-)* **AV**
  (American sculptor, b.1939) **BA**
  Bibl: Heresies, 1987, v.6, no.
  2(22). p.46; ▶NY art yrbk.; ▶WW
  Amer. Art, 1976
 Chamberlain, Harriet **BA**
Feiger, Thomas *(Austrian architect,
 Vienna)* **AV**
  Bibl: ▶Verzeich. Öst. Ziviltech.,
  1984
Feigin, Marsha *(American
 printmaker, b.1946)* **BA**
  Bibl: St. Louis (MO, USA), U.
  Missouri, Amer. women
  printmakers (1975)
Feijt → see Fyt, Jan
Feilberg, Ludvig *(Danish
 philosopher, engineer, 1849-1912)* **BA**
  Bibl: ▶Natl. union cat., pre-1956;
  Trap, Kongeriget DNK:
  personalregister, v.22, p.901

Feilchenfeldt, Walter II *(Swiss,
 b.1944)* **BA**
  Bibl: 26 Jahre Feilchenfeldt in
  Zurich
Feild, E. Maurice **WI**
  (British artist, 20th cent.) **WC**
  (British artist, op.1982-) **WI**
 Feild, Maurice **WI**
Field, Maurice **WC**
Feild, Maurice → see Feild, E. Maurice
Feildel, Coralie *(French(?) interior
 designer)* **AV**
  Bibl: Maison française, 1988 Jan.-
  Feb., no.413, p.98
Feilden, Bernard *(British architect,
 1919-)* **AV**
  Bibl: ▶Contemp. archts.
Feiler, Jo Alison *(American, 1951 -)* **JG**
Feiler, Paul **WC WI**
  (British artist, 1918-) **WC**
  (British artist, b.1918) **WI**
Feiller, R. *(German artist, 18th cent.)* **WC**
Feillet, Helene *(French artist, op.c.
 1836-1848)* **WC**
Feilner, Simon *(German ceramist,
 modeler, act.1747, d.1798)* **BA**
  Bibl: ▶Boger, World pott. & porc.;
  ▶Honey, Euro. ceramic; ▶Penguin
  dec. arts; ▶Thieme-Becker
 Feylner, Simon **BA**
Feilt, Gaspard *(French ébéniste, act.
 ca.1715, master ca.1736, d. 1763)* **GC**
  Bibl: ▶Salverte, Ébénistes 18e s.
Fein, Randy *(American sculptor,
 potter, Camden, Maine)* **AV**
  Bibl: Landmarks observer, 1987
  July-Sept., v.14, no.3, p.12
Feinberg, David Jay *(American
 architect, Miami, Fla)* **AV**
  Bibl: ▶AIA Pro File, 1987-88
Feinberg, Elen *(American painter,
 20th c.)* **BA**
  Bibl: ▶Intl. dir. exh. artists, 1983
Feinberg, Jean E. *(American painter,
 20th c.)* **BA**
  Bibl: ▶Art Index, Apr. 1981, p.99;
  Artforum 19 Sept 1980 p.20
Feininger → see Feininger, Lyonel
Feininger, Andreas **BA**
  (American (b. France), 1906 -) **JG**
  *(American photographer,
  b.1906)* **BA**
  Bibl: ▶MoMA libr. cat.; ▶Parry,
  Photo idx.
**Feininger, Andreas Bernhard
 Lyonel** **JG**
*Feininger, Andreas Bernhard
 Lyonel → see* Feininger, Andreas
Feininger, Lyonel **BA GC PR WC WI**
  (American artist, 1871-1956) **WC WI**
  (American painter, 1871-1956) **BA PR**
  (American, 1871-1956) **GC**
  Bibl: ▶Phaidon 20c. art;
  ▶RILA/BHA; ▶Witt checklist;
  ▶WWW Amer. art
 Feininger **PR**
 Lyonel Feininger **PR**

Feininger, T. Lux **BA**
   (American (b. Germany), 1910 -) JG
   (American painter, author,
    b.1910) **BA**
    Bibl: ▶MoMA librr. cat.; ▶Vollmer,
    Künst.-Lex. 20. Jhr.; ▶WW Amer.
    Art
Feininger, T. Lux (Theodore
   Lukas) JG
Feininger, T. Lux (Theodore
   Lukas)→see Feininger, T. Lux
Feint, Adrian **WC WI**
   (British artist, 1894-) WC
   (British artist, b.1894) WI
Feintuch, Robert *(American painter,*
   20th c.) **BA**
    Bibl: ▶Art Index, v.37; Pardee,
    Arts Mag. LXI/3 (Nov 1986) p.64
Feisbuch, Hans **WI**
   (British artist, 1898-) WC
   (British artist, b.1898) WI
Feibusch, Hans **WC**
Feislachen, F. *(W. German architect,*
   Dortmund) **AV**
    Bibl: Detail, 1986 Sept.-Oct., v.26,
    no.5
Feist, Dieter *(West German*
   architect, Schloss Holte-
   Stukenbrock) **AV**
    Bibl: Architektur,
    Innenarchitektur, Technischer
    Ausbau, 1986 Oct., v.94, no.10,
    p.50
Feist, Harold Elmer *(American*
   painter, graphic artist in CAN,
   b.1945) **BA**
    Bibl: ▶Artists Canada; Sackville
    (NB,CAN), Owens Art Gallery, Mt.
    Allison Univ., FIVE ARTISTS
Feist, Werner David *(German,*
   1909-, Bauhaus) **JG**
Feistenberger→see Faistenberger,
   Anton
Feistenberger, Wilhelm→see
   Faistenberger, Wilhelm
Feit, Jürgen **AV BA**
   (German architect, b.1928) BA
   (West German architect, 1928-) AV
    Bibl: KUNSTWERK XXXII/2-3 (Apr-
    June 1979) 16-17
Feitama, Sybrand→see Feitama,
   Sybrand II
Feitama, Sybrand II **BA**
   (Dutch artist, 1694-1758) WC
   (Dutch poet, draftsman,
   collector, 1694-1758) **BA**
    Bibl: ▶Aa, Biog. woordenboek
    NLD, v.6, pp.55-57; Bross, Oud
    Holland 98/1 (1984) 20-22;
    ▶Nieuw NLD biog. woord., v.1,
    p.849; ▶Witt checklist
Feitama, Sybrand **WC**
Feitelson→see Feitelson, Lorser
Feitelson, Helen Lundeberg→see
   Lundeberg, Helen

Feitelson, Lorser **BA PR WI**
   (American artist, 1898-1978) WI
   (American painter, 1898-1978) BA PR
    Bibl: ART GALLERY (July 1978)
    p.100, obit.; ▶RILA/BHA; ▶WW
    Amer. Art
   Feitelson PR
   Lorser Feitelson PR
Feitelson, Lorser, Mrs., (Helen
   Lundeberg)→see Lundeberg, Helen
Feito, Luis *(Spanish artist, 1929-)* **WC**
Fejér, Csaba *(Hungarian painter,*
   20th c.) **BA**
    Bibl: Hatvan (HUN), Muvelodesi
    Kozpont Galeriaja, Hat festo
    (1975)
Feke→see Feke, Robert
Feke, Robert *(American painter,*
   1707-1752) **BA PR**
    Bibl: ▶Dict. Amer. biog.; ▶Encyc.
    world art; ▶RILA/BHA;
    ▶Thieme-Becker; Worcester Art
    Mus. Jrnl. II (1978-79) 3-11
   Feke PR
   Robert Feke PR
Feke, Robert **GC WC WI**
   (American artist, 1724-1769) WC WI
   (American, 1724-1769) GC
    Bibl: ▶Groce, Artists Amer.;
    ▶Thieme-Becker; ▶Witt checklist
Fekete, Iosif *(Hungarian painter,*
   sculptor in ROM, b.1903) **BA**
    Bibl: ▶Barbosa, Art. romani
    contemp.; MUVESZETTORTENETI
    ERTESITO XXVII/1 (1978) 111-113
Fekner, John A. *(American painter,*
   b.1950) **BA**
    Bibl: Oberlin (OH, USA), Oberlin
    Coll., Allen Mem. Art Mus., Art &
    social change (1983)
Felaert, Dirk Jacobsz.→see Vellert,
   Dirk
Felber, Herbert *(Swiss architect,*
   Lucerne) **AV**
    Bibl: Schweizer Baumarkt, 1989
    Apr.17, no.7, p.l
Felber, Robert *(Austrian*
   architectural student, 1957-) **AV**
    Bibl: Kenchiku bunka, 1984 Dec.,
    v.39, p.458, p.84
Felbermeyer, Johannes *(German*
   photographer, d.1987) **GC**
    Bibl: Getty Photo Study Coll.
Felbinger, Bartol *(Croatian*
   architect, 1785-1871) **AV**
    Bibl: ▶Libr. of Congr. Name Auth.
    File
Felcey, Trevor *(British artist,*
   b.1945) **WI**
Feldbauer, Max **BA WC**
   (German artist, 1869-1948) WC
   (German painter, printmaker,
   1869-1948) BA
    Bibl: ▶Bénézit; ▶Busse, Maler u.
    Bildhauer 19. Jahr.;
    ▶Thieme-Becker; ▶Vollmer,
    Künst.-Lex. 20. Jhr.

Felder, Hans, der Ältere *(German*
   architect, late 15th cent) **AV**
    Bibl: ▶Thieme-Becker
Felder, van der [Unidentified]
   (Unknown painter) **PR**
    Bibl: (July 22, 1813, lot 49,
    Brydone)
   Vander Felder PR
Felder, Wolfgang *(West German*
   architect, Cologne) **AV**
    Bibl: ▶Bund Deut. Arch. Hdbch.,
    1987
Felderman, Stanley *(American*
   designer, Los Angeles, CA) **AV**
    Bibl: Design directory '84
Feldhutter→see Feldhütter, Ferdinand
Feldhütter, Ferdinand **PR WC**
   (German artist, 1842-1898) WC
   (German painter, 1842-1898) PR
    Bibl: ▶Thieme-Becker
   Feldhutter PR
   Ferdinand Feldhutter PR
Feldman, Bella Tabak *(American*
   sculptor, 20th c.) **BA**
    Bibl: ▶WW Amer. Art, 1984
Feldman, Carel Albert *(Dutch*
   painter, b.1894) **GC**
    Bibl: ▶Vollmer, Künst.-Lex. 20. Jhr.
Feldman, Howard A. *(American,*
   20th c.) **BA**
    Bibl: Antiques CVIII/4 (Oct 1975)
    764
Feldman, Hyman Isaac *(American*
   architect, 1897-1981) **BA**
    Bibl: ▶Avery period. idx.; NY
    Times obit., 27 Jan 1981
Feldman, Murray *(American*
   designer, Calif, 1923-1987) **AV**
    Bibl: L.A. architect, 1987 Sept.,
    p.11
Feldman, Pauline *(American interior*
   designer, New York) **AV**
    Bibl: House beautiful, 1986 Feb.,
    v.128, no.2, p.56
Feldman, Simone *(American interior*
   designer) **AV**
    Bibl: House beautiful, 1989 June,
    v.131, no.6, p.39
Feldman, Walter Sidney *(American*
   painter, b.1925) **BA**
    Bibl: ▶MoMA librr. cat.; ▶WW
    Amer. Art, 1976
Feldmann, Elisabeth *(West German*
   architect, Aachen) **AV**
    Bibl: Bauwelt, 1987 May 29, v.78,
    no.21, p.730
Feldmann, Hans Peter *(West*
   German artist, b.1941.) **BA**
    Bibl: ▶Babington Smith, Contemp.
    artists; ▶Intl. dir. exh. artists,
    1983
Feldmann, Louis *(German artist,*
   1856-1938) **WC**

Feldmann, Otto *(German painter, act.1911-1914)*   BA
  Bibl: Hannover (DEU), Kestner-Gesellschaft, August Macke (1979)
Feldmann, Wilhelm *(German artist, 1859-1932)*   WC
Feldsien, Werner *(German architect, Kaltenkirchen)*   AV
  Bibl: Detail, 1980 May-June, no.3, p.364
Feldstein, Mark *(American photographer, 20th c.)*   BA
  Bibl: ▶Intl. dir. exh. artists, 1983
Felgentreff, Paul *(German artist, 1854-1933)*   WC
Felguerez, Manuel *(Mexican painter, b.1928)*   BA
  Bibl: AFI; ▶Havlice, Idx. art. bio.
Félibien, André, sieur des Avaux et de Javersy *(French architect, author, 1619-1695)*   BA
  Bibl: ▶Avery Libr. cat.; ▶Dict. biog. fran.; ▶Lance, Dict. archts. fran.; ▶Larousse grande encyc.
Felice Bernabe → see Bernabe, Felice [Unidentified]
Felice Brusasorci → see Brusasorci, Felice
Felice Carena → see Carena, Felice
Felice Casorati → see Casorati, Felice
Felice de Matteis → see Matteis, Felice de
Felice de' Fiori → see Biggi, Felice Fortunato
Felice Ficherelli → see Ficherelli, Felice (Felice Riposo)
Felice Riccio → see Brusasorci, Felice
Felice Riposo → see Ficherelli, Felice (Felice Riposo)
Felice Torelli → see Torelli, Felice
Felice Truglia → see Truglia, Felice [Unidentified]
Felice, Giuseppe *(Italian painter, 1656-1734)*   BA
  Bibl: LE ARTI IN SICILIA NEL SETTECENTO, ACCASCINA FESTSCHR., p. 553; TCI Sicilia
Felici, Matteo *(Italian illuminator, act. late 15th century)*   GC
  Bibl: Daneu Lattanzi, Bibliofilia, LXXV (1973) pp.1-43
Feliciano da Foligno (Mutis) *(Italian artist, a.1490-p.1518)*   WC
Feliciano, Felice *(Scribe, 1433-1478/79)*   CE
  Felicianus Antiquarius Veronensis   CE
  Felix Antiquarius   CE
  Felicianus Antiquarius Veronensis → see Feliciano, Felice
Feliciati, Lorenzo *(Italian artist, 1732-1799)*   WC
Felicie Howell → see Howell, Felicie Waldo

Feline, Edward *(British silversmith, act. from 1720)*   GC
  Bibl: ▶Grimwade, London goldsmiths, 1982
Felipe Champaña → see Champaigne, Philippe de
Felipe [Unidentified] *(Unknown painter)*   PR
  Bibl: 1621 Montoya de Càrdenas inventory
felippo → see Filippo Napoletano
Felippo dell'Angeli → see Filippo Napoletano
Felippo Giannetti → see Giannetti, Filippo
Felippo Ginnetti → see Giannetti, Filippo
Felippo Nap.no → see Filippo Napoletano
felippo napolitano → see Filippo Napoletano
Felippo Romano → see Gagliardi, Filippo
Felippo Tranghino → see Franchino, Filippo [Unidentified]
Felisker [Unidentified] *(Unknown painter)*   PR
  Bibl: (February 18, 1807, lot 121, Langdon)
Feliú, Ventura *(Spanish cabinetmaker, designer, act.1910)*   BA
  Bibl: Fernández-Miranda, REALES SITIOS, XXI/79 (1984) 4-7
Felix *(American painter, 20th c.)*   BA
  Bibl: ARTFORUM XXV/1 (Sept 1986) 92-93
Felix *(Roman gem engraver, 1st c. A.D.)*   BA
  Bibl: Enciclopedia dell'Arte Antica; ▶Thieme-Becker
Felix Antiquarius → see Feliciano, Felice
Felix Boisselier → see Boisselier, Felix
Felix Edouard Vallotton → see Vallotton, Félix Edouard
Felix Elie Tobeen → see Tobeen, Felix Elie
Felix Francois Georges Philibert Ziem → see Ziem, Félix François Georges Philibert
Felix Maria Diog → see Diog, Felix Maria
Felix Meyer → see Meyer, Felix
Felix Muller → see Felixmüller, Conrad (Felix Müller)
Felix Pissarro → see Pissarro, Félix
Felix Saturnin Brissot de Warville → see Brissot de Warville, Felix Saturnin
Felix, Eugen *(German artist, 1837-1906)*   WC
Félix, Laurent *(French ébéniste, master 1755, act. to ca.1785)*   GC
  Bibl: ▶Salverte, Ébénistes 18e s.
Felix, Leon Pierre *(French artist, 1869-1940)*   WC

Felix, Nicholas *(British artist, 1804-1876)*   WC WI
Felixmuller → see Felixmüller, Conrad (Felix Müller)
Felixmuller, Conrad → see Felixmüller, Conrad (Felix Müller)
Felixmüller, Conrad (Felix Müller)   BA PR
  (German artist, 1897-)   WC
  (German painter, 1897-1977)   GC PR
  (German painter, printmaker, 1897-1977)   BA
  Bibl: Dresden (DDR), Gemaldegalerie Neue Meister, CONRAD FELIXMULLER (1977); Getty Photo Study Coll.; Phaidon; ▶RILA/BHA; ▶Thieme-Becker; ▶Vollmer, Künst.-Lex. 20. Jhr.; ▶Wer ist wer; ▶WW Arts DEU
  Conrad Felixmuller   PR
  Felix Muller   PR
  Felixmuller   PR
  Felixmuller, Conrad   GC PR WC
  Müller, Felix   BA PR
  Müller, Felix Conrad   GC
Felixmüller, Titus F. *(West German architect, b.1920)*   BA
  Bibl: Kinkel,WELTKUNST,LV/10/(May, 1985),p.1442; ▶WW Arts DEU
Fell, Ella May *(American, 20th c.)*   BA
  Bibl: Vancouver (BC, USA), Art Gallery, THE FELL COLLECTION (1979)
Fell, Herbert Granville *(British artist, 1872-1951)*   WC WI
Fell, J.C.   WC WI
  (British artist, op.1844)   WC
  (British artist, op.1844-)   WI
Fell, Sheila → see Fell, Sheila Mary
Fell, Sheila Mary   BA
  (British artist, 1931-)   WC
  (British artist, b.1931)   WI
  (British painter, 1931-1979)   BA
  Bibl: Royal Soc. of Arts Jrnl. CXXVIII/5284 (Mar 1980) 237; ▶Who's Who [GBR], 1980; ▶WW Art, 1977
Fell, Sheila   WC WI
Feller, Frank *(Swiss artist, 1848-1908)*   WC
Fellig, Arthur H. → see Weegee (Arthur H. Fellig)
Fellini, Federico *(Italian filmmaker, b.1920)*   BA
  Bibl: ▶Chi è?; Hannover (DE), Wilhelm Busch Mus., Fellini:... (1984); Intl. who's who
Fellner or Felner, Coloman (Pater Colomanus or Kolomanus) *(German artist, 1750-1818)*   WC
Fellner, Ferdinand   AV BA
  (Austrian architect, 1847-1916)   BA
  (Austrian architect, Vienna, 1847-1916)   AV
  Bibl: ▶Macmillan encyc. archts.; ▶Österr. biog. Lex. 1815-1950; ▶Thieme-Becker

Fellner, Ferdinand → *see* Fellner,
Ferdinand August Michael

**Fellner, Ferdinand August
Michael**   **BA WC**
 (*German artist, 1799-1859*)   WC
 (*German printmaker, painter,
 1799-1859*)   BA
 (*German, 1799-1859*)   GC
 Bibl: ▶Bénézit; ▶Thieme-Becker;
 ▶Witt checklist

Fellner, Ferdinand   **GC**

Fellner, Ferdinand III (*Austrian
architect, b.1872, act.1904*)   **BA**
 Bibl: Lehne, Öster. Zeit. für Kunst
 u. Denk. 35/1-2 (1981) 49-50;
 Osterreichisches
 Kunsttopographie, Wien III, IV, V
 1980

Fellowes, James   **WC WI**
 (*British artist, op.1710-1745*)   WC
 (*British artist, op.1710-1751*)   WI

Fellowes, W.M.   **WC WI**
 (*British artist, op.1827*)   WC
 (*British artist, op.1827-*)   WI

Fellowes, William (*British surveyor,
architect*)   **AV**
 Bibl: Country life, 1987 Nov.12,
 v.181, no.46, p.192

Fellows, Alice (*American painter,
sclptor, b.1935*)   **BA**
 Bibl: ▶Intl. dir. exh. artists, 1983;
 Washington, DC (USA), Hirshhorn
 Mus., Directions (1986), p.49

Fellows, William Dorset (*British
artist, op.1807-1878*)   **WC WI**
 Bibl: Paviere, Brit. sporting ptrs

Felon, Joseph (*French artist, 1818-
1896*)   **WC**

Felpacher   **PR**
 (*Dutch artist, op.1639*)   WC
 (*Dutch painter, act. 1639*)   PR
 Bibl: ▶Thieme-Becker

Felpacher or Felpacker, J.   **WC**
 J. Felpacker   PR

Felpacher or Felpacker, J. → *see*
Felpacher

Fels, Jan Jacob   **GC WC**
 (*Dutch artist, 1816-1883*)   WC
 (*Dutch painter, 1816-1883*)   GC
 Bibl: ▶Thieme-Becker

Felsen, Dirk van (*Netherlands artist,
op.1650*)   **WC**

Felsenhardt, Cristina (*Chilean
architect*)   **AV**
 Bibl: ARQ, 1986 May, no.11, p.12

Felter, Susan (*American
photographer, b.1945*)   **BA**
 Bibl: ▶Intl. dir. exh. artists, 1983;
 London (GBR), ICA, New Amer.
 colour photog.

Feltman, Hendrik (*German painter,
draughtsman, and printmaker, ca.
1610-aft.1670*)   **GC**
 Bibl: ▶Schweers, Gemälde deut.
 Museen

Felton family (*English metalworkers,
17th-18th cs.*)   **BA**
 Bibl: Hall & Homer,
 MONTGOMERYSHIRE
 COLLECTIONS, LXXI (1983) 42-47

Felton Group   **JG**

Felton Painter (*Apulian vase-painter*)   **GC**
 Bibl: Trendall, Attic red-fig. vases
 Apulia

Felton, Jan (*Australian architect*)   **AV**
 Bibl: Architectural review, 1988
 Oct., v.184, no.1100, p.94

Felton, Mehitable Berry (*b.1837,
act.1864*)   **BA**
 Bibl: DRESS VI (1980) 83-88

**Feltrini, Andrea di Giovanni di
Lorenzo**   **CE**
 (*Italian artist, c.1490-c.1554*)   WC
 (*Painter, 1477-1548*)   CE
 Andrea del Fornajo   CE
 Andrea di Cosimo   CE
 Andrea di Cosimo (Feltrini)   **WC**

Felts, Don (*American architect, New
Mexico (AIA member)*)   **AV**
 Bibl: New Mexico architecture,
 1986 July-Aug., v.27, no.4, p.15

Feltus, Alan Evan (*American
painter, b.1943.*)   **BA**
 Bibl: ARTS MAG LI/8 (Apr 1977)
 20; ▶WW Amer. Art, 1989

Felu, Charles Francois (*Belgian
artist, 1830-1900*)   **WC**

Felvideki, Andras (*Hungarian artist,
20th cent.*)   **WC**

Femenella, Art (*American stained
glass conservator, New York City*)   **AV**
 Bibl: Preservation news, 1988
 Apr., v.28, no.4, p.7

Fémes-Beck, Vilmos (*Hungarian
sculptor, 1885-1918*)   **BA**
 Bibl: ▶Vollmer, Künst.-Lex. 20. Jhr.

Femminck, H.C. (*German artist, op.
1842*)   **WC**

Fen, Hsiao-lin (*Canadian architect*)   **AV**
 Bibl: Arts of Asia, 1988 Jan.-Feb.,
 v.18, no.1, p.103

Fenbaum(?), Ivan (*Russian artist,
20th cent.*)   **WC**

Fend, Peter (*American artist, 20th
c.*)   **BA**
 Bibl: Pasadena (CA, USA), Cal
 Tech, Baxter Art Gall., Poetry of
 Systems (1978)

Fenderich, Charles   **BA WI**
 (*American artist, 1805-1887*)   WI
 (*American printmaker, painter,
 act.1830-1870*)   BA
 Bibl: ▶Groce, Artists Amer.;
 ▶Thieme-Becker

Fendi, Peter (*German artist, 1796-
1842*)   **WC**

Fendrick, Charles (*American artist,
c.1841-*)   **WC**

Fendt, Tobias (*German artist, op.
1566-m.1576*)   **WC**

Fenesi, Paolo (*Italian artist, 18th
cent.*)   **WC**

Fenger, Ludvig (*Danish architect*)   **AV**
 Bibl: Arkitektur DK, 1986 Nov.,
 v.30, no.6-7, p.245

Fenley, Karen (*American sculptor,
b.1945*)   **BA**
 Bibl: Sacramento (CA, USA),
 Crocker Art Mus., KAREN
 FENLEY..., 1984

Fenn, Alice S.Manville (*British
artist, op.1883-1885*)   **WI**

Fenn, George (*British artist, 1810-
1871*)   **WI**

Fenn, Harry   **BA WC WI**
 (*American painter, illustrator,
 1838/45-1911*)   BA
 (*British artist, 1845-1911*)   WC WI
 Bibl: ▶Amer. art annual, 1911;
 ▶Bénézit; ▶Fielding's Amer. ptrs.;
 ▶Samuels, Artists Amer. West;
 ▶Thieme-Becker; ▶WWW Amer.

Fenn, Otto (*European, active
1940's*)   **JG**

Fenn, William Wilthieu (*British
artist, circa 1827-1906*)   **WI**

Fennell → *see* Fennell, John Greville
Fennell, John → *see* Fennell, John
Greville

Fennell, John Greville   **BA PR WC WI**
 (*British artist, 1807-1885*)   WC WI
 (*British painter, 1807-1885*)   PR
 (*British painter, printmaker,
 1807-1885*)   BA
 Bibl: ▶Bénézit; ▶RILA/BHA
 Fennell   PR
 Fennell, John   PR
 John Greville Fennell   PR

Fennell, Patricia (*American painter,
b.1952*)   **BA**
 Bibl: Milwaukee (WI, USA), Art
 Mus., Emerging imagists (1983)

Fennema, G.D. (*Dutch artist, op.
1650*)   **WC**

Fennemore, James   **BA JG**
 (*American photographer, act.
 1872-1877*)   BA
 (*American, 1849-1941*)   JG
 Bibl: ▶Current, Photog. & Old
 West, 91-92; HIST OF PHOTOG,
 VIII/1 (Jan-Mar 1984) 65-66;
 Photog. in America; Taft, Photo.
 & Amer. scene, p.290

**Fennitzer, Fenitzer or Venitzer,
Georg** (*German artist, op.1697-
1700*)   **WC**

Fenoglio, Pietro (*Italian architect,
d.1927*)   **AV**
 Bibl: Architettura; cronache e
 storia, 1979 May, v.25, no.
 5(283), p.262

Fenosa, Apeles (*Spanish sculptor,
b.1899*)   **BA**
 Bibl: ▶Bénézit; ▶Campoy, Español
 contemp.; ▶MoMA libr. cat.;
 ▶Phaidon 20c. art; ▶Vollmer,
 Künst.-Lex. 20. Jhr.

Fenouil or Fenouilh, Jean Cesar
(*French artist, op.1738-1746*)   **WC**

Fenouil or Fenouilh, P. (Paul?)
(French artist, op.1738-1746) **WC**
Fenoulet, W. *(British artist, op.1836-1839)* **WC WI**
Fensonius → *see* Finson, Louis
Fenster, Fred *(American metalsmith, b.1934)* **BA**
  Bibl: St. Petersburg (FL, USA), MFA, Contemp. silversmiths (1979)
Fenton, Alan *(American painter, b.1927)* **BA**
  Bibl: ▶Cummings, Contemp. Amer. artists; ▶WW Amer. Art, 1976
Fenton, John **WC WI**
  (British artist, 18th cent.) WC
  (British artist, op.18th c.) WI
Fenton, Joseph *(American architect)* **AV**
  Bibl: Architecture and urbanism, 1986 Aug., no.81(191), p.63
Fenton, Michael **WC WI**
  (American artist, 20th cent.) WC
  (American artist, op.20th c.) WI
Fenton, Roger **AV BA JG**
  (British architectural photographer, 1819-1869) AV
  (British photographer, 1819-1869) BA
  (British, 1819-1869) JG
  Bibl: ▶Gernsheim, Hist. photog.; ▶Libr. of Congr. Name Auth. File; ▶Newhall, Photog.
Fenwick, Alice *(British, 19th c.)* **BA**
  Bibl: Parris, BURLINGTON (Apr 1983) 220
  Ashby, Alice BA
Fenwick, C.G. **WC WI**
  (British artist, 19th cent.) WC
  (British artist, op.19th c.) WI
Fenwick, Mark J. *(Architect)* **AV**
  Bibl: Arquitectura, 1988 July-Aug., v.69, no.273, p.48
Fenwick, Thomas **WC WI**
  (British artist, -1850) WC
  (British artist, op.1750-, d.1850) WI
Fenyes → *see* Fenyes, Eva Scott
Fenyes, Adolf *(Hungarian artist, 1867-1945)* **WC**
Fényes, Adolf *(Hungarian painter, 1867-1945)* **GC**
  Bibl: ▶Bénézit; Getty Photo Study Coll.
  Feynes, Adolf GC
Fenyes, Eva Scott *(American painter, 1846-1930)* **PR**
  Bibl: ▶Hughes, Artists California
  Eva Scott Fenyes PR
  Fenyes PR
Fenzi, Warren S. *(American craftsman, b.1947)* **BA**
  Bibl: Colorado Springs (CO, USA), Fine Arts Ctr., Woodworking in the Rockies (1982)
Fenzoni, Faenzoni or Fanzoni, Ferrau (Ferrau da Faenza) → *see* Fenzoni, Ferraù

Fenzoni, Ferraù **GC PR**
  (Italian artist, 1562-1645) WC
  (Italian painter, 1562-1645) PR
  (Italian, 1562-1645) GC
  Bibl: ▶Thieme-Becker; ▶Witt checklist
  Fanzoni, Ferrau GC
Fenzoni, Faenzoni or Fanzoni, Ferrau (Ferrau da Faenza) **WC**
  Ferraù da Faenza GC PR
  Ferrau Fenzoni PR
Feo, Charles de *(American artist, op.19th-20th c.)* **WI**
Feodor Feodorowitsch Buchholz → *see* Buchholz, Feodor Feodorowitsch
Feofilaktov, Nikolaj Petrovič *(Russian painter, 1878-1941)* **BA**
  Bibl: ▶Bowlt, Russian avant-garde
Feoli Painter *(Etruscan vase-painter)* **GC**
  Bibl: ▶Szilagyi, Etruszko-korinthosi
Feoli, Carlo [Unidentified]
  (Unknown painter) **PR**
  Bibl: Cardenas inventory dated 1699
  Carlo Feoli PR
  Carlo Fuoli PR
Feoli, Francesco [Unidentified]
  (Unknown painter) **PR**
  Bibl: Carlo de Cardenas inventory, 1699
  Francesco Feoli PR
Fer. Bol → *see* Bol, Ferdinand
Fera, Bernardino *(Italian painter, d. 1714)* **PR**
  Bibl: ▶Thieme-Becker
  Bernardino Fera PR
  Giovanni Bernardino Fera PR
Ferabech, Giovanni *(German sculptor in ITA, act.1393-1405)* **BA**
  Bibl: ▶Bessone-Aurelj, Scult. & arch. ital.; TCI Emilia-Romagna; ▶Thieme-Becker
  Ferrabech, Giovanni BA
Feragutti Visconti, Adolfo **BA**
  (Italian artist, 20th cent.) WC
  (Italian painter, 1850-1924) BA
  Bibl: Cesura, ADOLFO FERAGUTTI VISCONTI PITTURE: PURA, 1850-MILANO, 1924 (Milan, 1982); ▶Comanducci, Diz.; ▶Thieme-Becker
  Visconti, Adolfo Feragutti BA
Visconti, Adolfo Ferragiti **WC**
Feraiuoli, Menzio → *see* Ferraiuoli, Nunzio (Afflitti)
Ferat, Serge **BA WC**
  (Russian artist, 1881-1958) WC
  (Russian painter, printmaker in FRA, 1881-1958) BA
  Bibl: ▶Bénézit; ▶Dict. biog. fran.; ▶Havlice, Idx. art. bio.; ▶Thieme-Becker; ▶Witt checklist
  Jastrebzoff, Serge BA
Féraud, Albert *(French sculptor, b.1921)* **BA**
  Bibl: ▶Bénézit

Ferber, Herbert *(American sculptor, painter, b.1906)* **BA**
  Bibl: ARTNEWS (Oct 1991) p.29; ▶Cummings, Contemp. Amer. artists; ▶WW Amer. Art, 1976
Ferd. Bol → *see* Bol, Ferdinand
Ferdenandes, J. → *see* Ferdinand, Pieter
Ferdinand → *see* Bury, Ferdinand
Ferdinand Bol → *see* Bol, Ferdinand
Ferdinand Boll → *see* Bol, Ferdinand
Ferdinand de Navarette → *see* Fernández de Navarrete, Juan (el Mudo)
Ferdinand Elle → *see* Elle, Ferdinand
Ferdinand Feldhutter → *see* Feldhütter, Ferdinand
Ferdinand Hauptner → *see* Hauptner, Ferdinand
Ferdinand Heilbuth → *see* Heilbuth, Ferdinand
Ferdinand Hodler → *see* Hodler, Ferdinand
Ferdinand Humbert → *see* Humbert, Ferdinand
Ferdinand Jean Monchablon → *see* Monchablon, Ferdinand Jean
Ferdinand Kobell → *see* Kobell, Ferdinand
Ferdinand Le Vieux → *see* Elle, Louis Ferdinand (the Elder)
Ferdinand Leon Victor Roybet → *see* Roybet, Ferdinand Léon Victor
Ferdinand Minor → *see* Minor, Ferdinand
Ferdinand Philippe, Duke of Orleans *(French artist, 1810-1842)* **WC**
Ferdinand Schauss → *see* Schauss, Ferdinand
Ferdinand Voet → *see* Voet, Jakob-Ferdinand
Ferdinand, Pieter **GC**
  (Dutch artist, 17th cent.) WC
  (Dutch painter, 1631-aft.1664) GC
  Bibl: ▶Thieme-Becker
Ferdenandes, J. **GC WC**
Ferdinando → *see* Voet, Jakob-Ferdinand
Ferdinando Campani → *see* Campani, Ferdinando Maria
Ferdinando Fuga → *see* Fuga, Ferdinando
Ferdinando Galli Bibiena → *see* Bibiena, Ferdinando Galli
Ferdinando Gregori → *see* Gregori, Ferdinando
Ferdinando Maria Campani → *see* Campani, Ferdinando Maria
Ferdinando Messini → *see* Messini, Ferdinando [Unidentified]
Ferdinando Ruggeri → *see* Ruggeri, Ferdinando
Ferdinando Sassone → *see* Sassone, Ferdinando [Unidentified]

Ferdinando Voet → *see* Voet, Jakob-Ferdinand

Ferdinandus Bol → *see* Bol, Ferdinand

Ferdinandus Boll → *see* Bol, Ferdinand

Ferdinandus, J. [Unidentified]

  (Unknown painter)   **PR**

    Bibl: P. de la Court inventory, Amsterdam, 1707; ▶Thieme-Becker, cf. under ''Ferdinandus, Philips''

  J. Ferdinand   PR.

Ferdinard Boll → *see* Bol, Ferdinand

Ferenczy, Béni   **BA WC**

  (Hungarian artist, 1890-)   WC

  (Hungarian sculptor, medalist, 1890-1967)   BA

    Bibl: ▶Bénézit; ▶Encyc. world art; ▶Vollmer, Künst.-Lex. 20. Jhr.

Ferenczy, Br. Hatvany *(Hungarian artist, 20th cent.)*   **WC**

Ferenczy, István *(Hungarian sculptor, 1792-1856)*   **BA**

    Bibl: ▶Bénézit; ▶Thieme-Becker

Ferenczy, Júlia *(Hungarian painter, printmaker, b.1909)*   **BA**

    Bibl: MUVESZETTORTENETI ERTENITO XXIV/1 (1975) 71

Ferenczy, Károly   **BA WC**

  (Hungarian artist, 1862-1917)   WC

  (Hungarian painter, 1862-1917)   BA

    Bibl: ▶Fogg Mus. Libr. cat.; ▶Thieme-Becker; ▶Vollmer, Künst.-Lex. 20. Jhr.

  Freund, Karl   BA

Ferenczy, Károlyné → *see* Fialka, Olga

Ferenczy, Noémi *(Hungarian textile artist, 1890-1957)*   **BA**

    Bibl: Budapest (HUN), Magyar Nemz.Gal., NOEMI FERENCZY (1979); ▶Encyc. world art; ▶Vollmer, Künst.-Lex. 20. Jhr.

Ferenczy, Valér *(Hungarian painter, printmaker, b.1885)*   **BA**

    Bibl: ▶Bénézit; ▶Vollmer, Künst.-Lex. 20. Jhr.

Fereol Bonnemaison → *see* Bonnemaison, Féréol de

Feresino [Unidentified] *(Unknown painter)*   **PR**

    Bibl: Doria inventory, Naples, 1690

Feret, Baptiste *(French painter, act. 1677)*   **PR**

    Bibl: ▶Bénézit; ▶Thieme-Becker, sv. Feret, Jean-Baptiste

  Baptiste Feret   PR

  Monsieur Batista Ferretti   PR

Feret, Jean Baptiste   **GC**

  (French artist, 1664/5-1739)   WC

  (French painter, 1665-1739)   GC

    Bibl: ▶Bénézit

Feret, Jean-Baptiste   **WC**

Feret, Jean-Baptiste → *see* Feret, Jean Baptiste

Ferg → *see* Ferg, Franz de Paula

Ferg, Franz de Paula   **BA GC PR**

  (Austrian painter, 1689-1740)   PR

  (Austrian painter, printmaker, 1689-1740)   BA

  (Austrian, 1689-1740)   GC

  (German artist, 1689-1740)   WC

    Bibl: ALTE UND MODERNE KUNST, XXX/201-202 (1985), p. 17-19; ▶Neue deutsche Biog.; ▶Thieme-Becker; ▶Waterhouse, Brit. 18c. ptrs.; ▶Witt checklist

  F. Ferg   PR

  F. P. Ferg   PR

  F. Paul Ferg   PR

  F.P. Ferg   PR

  Ferg   PR

Ferg, Franz de Paula (Franz Josef or Paul)   **WC**

  Fergue   PR

  Ferz   PR

  Francis Paul Ferg   PR

  Franz de Paula Ferg   PR

  Furge   PR

  P. Ferg   PR

  Paul Ferg   PR

Ferg, Franz de Paula (Franz Josef or Paul) → *see* Ferg, Franz de Paula

Ferg. V. der Pool → *see* Poel, Egbert van der

Fergeson → *see* Ferguson, William Gowe

Ferghetto → *see* Bencovich, Federico (Dalmatino)

Fergola, Salvatore   **GC WC**

  (Italian artist, 1799-p.1877)   WC

  (Italian, 1799-aft.1877)   GC

    Bibl: ▶Thieme-Becker; ▶Witt checklist

Fergue → *see* Ferg, Franz de Paula

Ferguson → *see* Ferguson, William Gowe

Ferguson, Amos *(Bahamian painter, b.1920)*   **BA**

    Bibl: ▶Art Index; Hartford (CT, USA), Wadsworth Ath. PAINT BY MR‡AMOS...1985

Ferguson, C. J. *(British architect, active at Naworth Castle in 1880's)*   **AV**

    Bibl: Country life, 1987 Feb.26, v.181, no.8, p.91

Ferguson, Catherine *(American sculptor, 20th c.)*   **BA**

    Bibl: ▶Babington Smith, Contemp. artists; Omaha (Neb, USA), Joslyn Art Mus., CATHERINE FERGUSON (1981)

Ferguson, Frank W. *(1861-1926)*   **AV**

Ferguson, George Robin Paget *(British architect, Bristol, England; founder of Acanthus)*   **AV**

    Bibl: Traditional homes, 1988 Sept., v.4, no.12, p.88

Ferguson, Gerald *(Canadian artist, b.1937)*   **BA**

    Bibl: ▶Natl. Gall. Canada libr. cat.

Ferguson, Henri A. → *see* Ferguson, Henry A.

Ferguson, Henry A.   **WI**

  (American artist, 1842-1911)   WI

  (American painter, 1842-1911)   GC

    Bibl: ▶Bénézit

Ferguson, Henri A.   **GC**

Ferguson, James → *see* Ferguson, James I

Ferguson, James → *see* Ferguson, James II

Ferguson, James I   **WI**

  (British artist, 1710-1776)   WC WI

  (British, 1710-1776)   GC

    Bibl: ▶Witt checklist

Ferguson, James   **GC WC**

Ferguson, James II   **WI**

  (British artist, op.1817-1858)   WC WI

Ferguson, James   **WC**

Ferguson, John Knox   **WC WI**

  (British artist, op.1886)   WC

  (British artist, op.1886-)   WI

Ferguson, Kathleen Elizabeth *(American sculptor, b.1931)*   **BA**

    Bibl: ▶WW Amer. Art, 1978

Ferguson, Roy Young   **WC WI**

  (British artist, 1907-)   WC

  (British artist, b.1907)   WI

Ferguson, William Gowe   **GC PR WC WI**

  (British artist, 1632-1633-circa 1695)   WI

  (British artist, 1632/3-p.1695)   WC

  (British painter, ca.1632-aft. 1695)   PR

  (British, ca.1632-aft.1695)   GC

    Bibl: ▶Thieme-Becker; ▶Witt checklist

  Fergeson   PR

  Ferguson   PR

  Fergusson   PR

  Furgeson   PR

  Vergeson   PR

  William Gowe Ferguson   PR

Ferguson, William J. → *see* Ferguson, William James

Ferguson, William James   **WI**

  (British artist, op.1849-1886)   WC WI

Ferguson, William J.   **WC**

Fergusson → *see* Ferguson, William Gowe

Fergusson, John Duncan   **BA GC WC WI**

  (British artist, 1874-1961)   WC WI

  (British painter, 1874-1961)   BA

  (Scottish sculptor and painter, 1874-1961)   GC

    Bibl: ▶Bénézit; ▶RILA/BHA; ▶Vollmer, Künst.-Lex. 20. Jhr.; ▶Waters, Brit. artists

Ferino, Benedetto → *see* Ferrini, Benedetto

Feriti, Claudio [Unidentified] *(Unknown painter)*   **PR**

    Bibl: Botteri inventory, Milan, 1697

  Claudio Feriti   PR

Ferjantz, Birgit (*West German architecture student, Karlsruhe*)   **AV**
Bibl: Architektur + Wettbewerbe, 1987 Sept., no.131, p.91

Ferkai, András (*Hungarian architect, Budapest, 1953-*)   **AV**
Bibl: Magyar építőművészet, 1987, v.78, no.6, p.33

Ferlenga, Alberto (*Architect*)   **AV**
Bibl: De Architect, 1988 Oct., v.19, no.10, p.94

Ferlita, Nelson (*American interior designer, New York City*)   **AV**
Bibl: NYC phone bk., 1987

Ferlito, Francesco   **AV**

Ferloni, Pietro (*Italian tapestry maker, act.1717, d.1770*)   **BA**
Bibl: Olszewski, Apollo, CXVI/246 (Aug. 1982) pp.103-111; ▶Thieme-Becker; ▶Thomson, Tapestry, p.468

Ferlov-Mancoba, Sonja (*Danish sculptor, b.1911*)   **BA**
Bibl: ▶Bénézit
Mancoba, Sonja Ferlov   BA

Fermo da Caravaggio →see Ghisoni, Fermo di Stefano (Fermo da Caravaggio)

Fermout (Fremout), Gilliam (*Dutch painter, act. 17th century*)   **PR**
Bibl: ▶Thieme-Becker
Fermout (Fremout), Gilliam or Willem Jansz.   PR
Straccio de Volute   PR
Stratio de Valuto   PR
Fermout (Fremout), Gilliam or Willem Jansz. →see Fermout (Fremout), Gilliam

Fern, Dan (*British artist, op.20th c.*)   **WI**
Fern, Dan (*British illustrator, 20th c.*)   **BA**
Bibl: Arts Council GBR, Welsh Comm., Images to order (1979)

Fernancez, Alexo →see Fernández, Alejo

Fernand Leger →see Léger, Fernand

Fernand Lungren →see Lungren, Fernand Harvey

Fernand Sabatte →see Sabatté, Fernand

Fernand-Trochain, Jean (*French artist, 1879-*)   **WC**

Fernandes, César da Silva (*Brazilian architect*)   **AV**
Bibl: Projeto, 1988 Mar., no.108, p.94

Fernandes, Garcia (*Portuguese artist, op.1514-1551*)   **WC**

Fernandes, Glícia (*Brazilian architect*)   **AV**
Bibl: Projeto, 1988 May, no.110, p.98

Fernandes, João Manuel (*Brazilian architect, São Paulo*)   **AV**
Bibl: Projeto, 1989 July, no.123, p.89

Fernandes, Mateus, the elder (*Portuguese architect, act.ca.1490-1515*)   **BA**
Bibl: ▶Encic. univ. ilus.; ▶Portoghesi, Diz. arch. e urbanistica; Smith, Art Portugal; ▶Thieme-Becker

Fernandes, Michael (*Canadian artist, b.1944*)   **BA**
Bibl: ▶Artists Canada

Fernandes, Vasco →see Fernandes, Vasco (Grão Vasco)

Fernandes, Vasco (Grão Vasco)   **BA**
(*Portuguese artist, -1541/3*)   WC
(*Portuguese painter, ca.1475-1542/3*)   BA
Bibl: ▶Kubler, Art & arch. ESP & PRT; ▶Pamplona, Pint. escult. PRT; ▶Thieme-Becker; ▶Witt checklist

Fernandes, Vasco   **WC**
Grão Vasco   BA

Fernández Alba, Angel (*Spanish architect, 1943-*)   **AV**
Bibl: Arquitectura, 1984 May-June, v.65, no.248

Fernández Alba, Antonio (*Spanish architect, 1927-*)   **AV**
Alba, Antonio Fernández   AV

Fernandez Balbuena, Gustavo (*Spanish architect and city planner, 1888-1931*)   **AV**
Bibl: Urbanismo, 1989 Jan., no.6, p.84

Fernández Caballero, Jerónimo (*Spanish sculptor, b. 1668*)   **AV**
Bibl: Arch. esp. de arte, LXI/243 (Jul-Sep 1988) 257

Fernández Cruzado, Joaquín Manuel   **BA**
(*Spanish artist, 1791-1856*)   WC
(*Spanish painter, 1781-1856*)   BA
Bibl: ▶Bénézit; ▶Lafuente Ferrari, Pint. española; ▶Ossorio y Bernard, Artistas españoles 19s.; ▶Thieme-Becker

Cruzado, J.Fernandez   **WC**
Cruzado, Joaquín Manuel Fernández   BA

Fernandez da Guadalupe, Pedro (*Spanish artist, op.1506-1539*)   **WC**

Fernández de la Vega, Luis (*Spanish sculptor, 1601-1675*)   **BA**
Bibl: ▶Encic. univ. ilus.; Oviedo, exhb. 1983, LUIS FÉRNANDEZ DE LA VEGA (1601-1676); ▶Thieme-Becker
Vega, Luis Fernández de la   BA
Fernandez de Navarette →see Fernández de Navarrete, Juan (el Mudo)
Fernandez de Navarette →see Fernández de Navarrete, Juan (el Mudo)

Fernández de Navarrete, Juan (el Mudo)   **BA PR WC**
(*Spanish artist, 1526-1579*)   WC
(*Spanish painter, 1526-1579*)   PR
(*Spanish painter, ca.1526-1579*)   BA
Bibl: ▶Ceán Bermúdez, Bellas artes ESP; ▶Encyc. world art; ▶RILA/BHA; ▶Thieme-Becker
el mudo   PR
Ferdinand de Navarette   PR
Fernandez de Navarette   PR
Fernandez de Navarette   PR
Fernández Navarrete   PR
Fernández Navarrete, Juan   BA
Hernando Del Mudo   PR
Juan (El Mudo) Fernandez de Navarrete   PR
Mudo   BA PR
Navarette   PR
Navarette, Juan Fernandez de   **WC**
Navarrete, Juan   PR
Navarrete, Juan Fernández de   BA

Fernandez de Peñaranda, Jose Maria Toro (*Spanish architect*)   **AV**
Bibl: El croquis, 1987 Nov., v.6, no.31, p.55

Fernandez family (*Spanish ceramists, 16th-17th cs.*)   **BA**
Bibl: Gonzalez Muñoz, Arch. esp. de arte, LIII/211 (1980) 345-366

Fernández Larrañaga, Teodoro (*Chilean architect*)   **AV**
Bibl: ARQ, 1986 May, no.11, p.12
Fernandez Navarrete →see Fernández de Navarrete, Juan (el Mudo)
Fernández Navarrete, Juan →see Fernández de Navarrete, Juan (el Mudo)

Fernández y Estruch (*Spanish medalist, 19th c.*)   **BA**
Bibl: ▶Forrer, Medallists; Pardo, GOYA CLXXII (1983) 210
Estruch, Fernández y   BA

Fernández, Agustin (*American painter, b.1928*)   **BA**
Bibl: ▶MoMA libr. cat.; ▶Vollmer, Künst.-Lex. 20. Jhr.

Fernández, Alberto (*Spanish printmaker, act.1595-1611*)   **BA**
Bibl: Moreno Garrido, Grabado en Granada, p.51

Fernández, Alejo   **BA PR**
(*Spanish artist, c.1470-p.1543*)   WC
(*Spanish painter, ca.1470-1543*)   BA PR
(*Spanish, ca.1470-1543*)   GC
Bibl: ▶Ceán Bermúdez, Bellas artes ESP; ▶Encic. univ. ilus.; Padrón Mérida, Arch. esp. de arte, LVII/227 (Jul-Sep 1984) 324; ▶Thieme-Becker; ▶Witt checklist
Alexo Fernandez   PR
Fernancez, Alexo   PR
Fernández, Alexo   **GC PR**
Fernández, Alexo or Alejo   **WC**
Hernández, Alejo   BA

Fernández, Alexo → *see* Fernández, Alejo

Fernandez, Alexo or Alejo → *see* Fernández, Alejo

Fernandez, Amalio *(Spanish artist, 19th/20th cent.)*   **WC**

Fernandez, Antonio Arias → *see* Arias Fernandez, Antonio

Fernandez, Armand → *see* Arman (Armand Fernandez)

Fernández, Carlos Puente → *see* Puente Fernández, Carlos

Fernández, Christian *(Chilean architect)*   **AV**
   Bibl: Projeto, 1985 Jan., no.71, p.42

Fernandez, Domingo *(Spanish artist, 1862-)*   **WC**

Fernández, Francisco *(Spanish sculptor, act.1535)*   **BA**
   Bibl: Estella, Arch. esp. de arte, LIV/215 (Jul-Sep 1981) 273-296

Fernandez, Frank *(American architect, N. J)*   **AV**
   Bibl: Architecture New Jersey, 1988, v.24, no.3, p.24

Fernández, Gregorio *(Spanish sculptor, ca.1576-1636)*   **BA**
   Bibl: ▶Ceán Bermúdez, Bellas artes ESP; ▶Encic. univ. ilus.; ▶Kubler, Art & arch. ESP & PRT; ▶Thieme-Becker
   Hernández, Gregorio   BA

Fernández, José *(Colombian architect)*   **AV**
   Bibl: Proa, 1988 July, no.373, p.40

Fernández, José Lopez → *see* López Fernández, José

Fernández, José Luis *(Spanish sculptor, b.1948)*   **BA**
   Bibl: Marin Medina, JOSE LUIS FERNANDEZ...

Fernández, Juan (el Labrador)
(Spanish painter, d. after 1636)   **BA**
   Bibl: ▶Bénézit; ▶Ceán Bermúdez, Bellas artes ESP; De Moura Sobral, COLL. ARTES 55 (Dec 1982) 5-11; ▶Encic. univ. ilus.; ▶Encyc. world art; Harris, Arch. esp. de arte, XLVII/186 (Apr-Jun 1974) 162-164; ▶Lafuente Ferrari, Pint. española; ▶Ossorio y Bernard, Artistas españoles 19s.; Paviere, v.1; ▶Thieme-Becker; Torres Martin, LA NATURAL MUERTA (1971); Valdovieso, Arch. esp. de arte, XLV/179 (Jul-Sep 1972) 323-324
   Labrador, Juan   BA

Fernandez, Louis   **BA**
   (French painter, b.1900)   BA
   (Spanish artist, 1900-)   WC
   Bibl: ▶Bénézit; ▶Vollmer, Künst.-Lex. 20. Jhr.

Fernandez, Luis   **WC**

Fernandez, Luis *(Spanish artist, op. 1543-1579)*   **WC**

Fernández, Luis   **BA WC**
   (Spanish artist, 1596-1654)   WC
   (Spanish painter, 1596-1654)   BA
   Bibl: ▶Ceán Bermúdez, Bellas artes ESP; ▶Kubler, Art & arch. ESP & PRT; ▶Thieme-Becker

Fernandez, Luis → *see* Fernandez, Louis

Fernandez, Margarita *(Puerto Rican artist, 20th c.)*   **BA**
   Bibl: La Duke, Women Artists News X/1 (fall 1984) 10

Fernández, Pedro *(Spanish painter in ITA, act.1499-1519)*   **BA**
   Bibl: PROSPETTIVA, 42 (July 1985) 58-61, 62-64; ▶Thieme-Becker
   Pietro Spano   BA
   Spano, Pietro   BA

Fernandez, Rendell *(American interior designer, NYC)*   **AV**
   Bibl: Architectural digest, 1987 Feb., v.44, no.2, p.96

Fernandez, Waldo *(American interior designer, Calif)*   **AV**
   Bibl: Architectural digest, 1987 Oct., v.44, no.10, p.128

Fernandi → *see* Fernandi, Francesco (Imperiali)

Fernandi, Francesco → *see* Fernandi, Francesco (Imperiali)

Fernandi, Francesco (Imperiali)   **BA GC PR**
   (Italian artist, op.1723-1737)   WC
   (Italian painter, 1679-1740)   BA GC PR
   Bibl: ▶Bolaffi; Clark, BURLINGTON CVI (1964) 226-233; Getty Photo Study Coll.; ▶RILA/BHA, 1986; ▶Thieme-Becker; Waterhouse, in Arte lombarda III/1 (1958), pp. 101-106; ▶Wittkower, Art & arch. Italy
   Fernandi   PR

Fernandi, Francesco   **GC**
   Ferrando, Francesco   BA
   Francesco Fernandi   PR
   Francesco Fernandi (Imperiali)   PR
   Imperiale   PR
   Imperiali   BA PR
   Imperiali, Fernandi   GC
   Imperiali, Francesco   GC

Imperiali, Francesco (also Fernandi or Ferrando)   **WC**

Fernando de Bruselas → *see* Bruselas, Arnau de

Fernando del Rincón del Figueroa → *see* Rincón del Figueroa, Fernando del

Fernando Fique, Luis *(Colombian architect)*   **AV**
   Bibl: Proa, 1986 Sept., no.354, p.48

Fernando Gallego → *see* Gallego, Fernando

Fernau, Helga *(E. German architect)*   **AV**
   Bibl: Architektur der DDR, 1986 Dec., v.35, no.12, p.730

Fernau, Richard *(American architect, Berkeley, Calif)*   **AV**
   Bibl: Progressive architecture, 1981 Apr., v.62, no.4, p.138

Fernehten, Matheus *(German)*   **GC**
   Bibl: Gernsheim, Corpus Photog. of Drawings, 1429

Ferneley → *see* Ferneley, John E.

Ferneley the Younger, John → *see* Ferneley, John II

Ferneley, Claude → *see* Ferneley, Claude Lorraine

Ferneley, Claude Lorraine   **WI**
   (British artist, 1822-1891)   WI
   (British artist, op.1851-1868)   WC

Ferneley, Claude   **WC**

Ferneley, John → *see* Ferneley, John E.

Ferneley, John E.   **GC PR WC WI**
   (British artist, 1781-1860)   WI
   (British artist, 1782-1860)   WC
   (British painter, 1781-1860)   PR
   (British, 1782-1860)   GC
   Bibl: ▶Thieme-Becker; ▶Witt checklist
   Ferneley   PR
   Ferneley, John   PR
   Ferneley, John E., Sr.   PR
   Fernely   PR
   John E. Ferneley   PR

Ferneley, John E., Sr. → *see* Ferneley, John E.

Ferneley, John II   **WI**
   (British artist, 1815-1862)   WC WI
   Bibl: Mitchell

Ferneley the Younger, John   **WC**

Ferneley, Margaret   **WC WI**
   (British artist, op.1851)   WC
   (British artist, op.1851-)   WI

Ferneley, Mary *(British artist, op. 1842-)*   **WI**

Ferneley, Sarah   **WC WI**
   (British artist, 1812-1893)   WI
   (British artist, op.1836)   WC
   Bibl: Mitchell; Paviere, Brit. sporting ptrs

Fernely → *see* Ferneley, John E.

Fernex, Jean Baptiste → *see* Defernex, Jean Baptiste

Fernex, Jean Baptiste de → *see* Defernex, Jean Baptiste

Fernhout, Edgar   **BA GC**
   (Dutch artist, 1912-)   WC
   (Dutch painter, 1912-1976)   BA
   (Dutch painter, b.1912)   GC
   Bibl: ▶Bénézit; ▶Contemp. artists; ▶Havlice, Idx. art. bio.; Holland (MI, USA), Hope College, De Pree Art Center & Gallery, DUTCH ART AND MODERN LIFE (1982); ▶MoMA libr. cat.; ▶Vollmer, Künst.-Lex. 20. Jhr.

Fernhout, Edgar Richard Johannes   **WC**

Fernhout, Edgar Richard Johannes → *see* Fernhout, Edgar

Ferniani family (*Italian ceramists,*
17th-19th cs.)   **BA**
  Bibl: ▶Honey, Euro. ceramic;
  ▶Thieme-Becker
Fernier, Jean-Jacques (*1931-*)   **AV**
Fernique, Albert   **BA JG**
  (*French photographer, engineer,*
  19th c.)   **BA**
  (*French, died 1898*)   **JG**
  Bibl: PORTFOLIO III (July-Aug
  1981) 46-49
Fernkorn, Anton Dominik   **BA**
  (*German sculptor, 1813-1878*)   **BA GC**
  Bibl: ▶Bénézit; Krause, DIE
  PLASTIK DER WIENER
  RINGSTRASSE (1980); ▶RILA/BHA;
  ▶Thieme-Becker
  Fernkorn, Anton Dominik Ritter
  von   **GC**
  Fernkorn, Anton von   GC
  Von Fernkorn, Anton Ritter   GC
Fernkorn, Anton Dominik Ritter
  von → *see* Fernkorn, Anton Dominik
Fernkorn, Anton von → *see* Fernkorn,
  Anton Dominik
Fernley, Clifford (*British architect*) **AV**
  Bibl: ▶RIBA members, 1984
Fernow, Carl Ludwig (*German*
  artist, 1763-1808)   **WC**
Fero, Leandro de → *see* Ferro, Leandro
Ferogio, Fortune (*Francois Fortune*
  Antoine) (*French artist, 1805-*
  1888)   **WC**
Feron, Eloi Firmin   **GC WC**
  (*French artist, 1802-1876*)   **WC**
  (*French, 1802-1876*)   **GC**
  Bibl: ▶Thieme-Becker; ▶Witt
  checklist
Feron, Paul (*French artist, 20th*
  cent.)   **WC**
Feroni, Francesco   **AV**
Feroni, Paolo (*Italian artist, 1807-*
  1864)   **WC**
Ferrabech, Giovanni → *see* Ferabech,
  Giovanni
Ferrabosco → *see* Forabosco, Girolamo
Ferrabosco, Girolamo → *see*
  Forabosco, Girolamo
Ferracina, Bartolomeo (*Italian*
  watchmaker, blacksmith, 1692-
  1777)   **BA**
  Bibl: ANTICHITÀ VIVA, XXIII, 6
  (Nov-Dec 1984) 16-24; ▶Baillie,
  Watch- & clockmkrs.; ▶Encic.
  italiana; ▶Libr. of Congr. Name
  Auth. File; TCI Veneto
Ferradini, Francesco (*Italian stucco*
  artist, act.1687-1695)   **GC**
  Bibl: TCI Abruzzo-Molise
Ferragamo, Anthony E. (*American*
  architect, East Sandwich, Mass)   **AV**
  Bibl: ▶AIA Pro File, 1987-88

Ferraiuoli, Nunzio (*Afflitti*)   **BA PR**
  (*Italian artist, 1660/1-1735*)   **WC**
  (*Italian painter, 1661-1735*)   **BA PR**
  Bibl: ▶Bénézit; ▶Bolaffi;
  ▶RILA/BHA; ▶Thieme-Becker
  Afflitti   BA
  Feraiuoli, Menzio   BA
Ferrajuoli, Nunzio   **WC**
  Ferrauoli   PR
  Firajouli   PR
  N. Ferrajuoli   PR
  Nunzio Ferraiuoli (Afflitti)   PR
  Nuzio Firajouli   PR
Ferrajuoli, Nunzio → *see* Ferraiuoli,
  Nunzio (Afflitti)
Ferramola, Floriano   **BA GC**
  (*Italian artist, 1480-1528*)   **WC**
  (*Italian painter, 1480-1528*)   **BA GC**
  Bibl: ▶Bolaffi; ▶RILA/BHA, 1986;
  ▶Thieme-Becker
  Ferramola, Floriano or
  Fioravante   **WC**
Ferramola, Floriano or
  Fioravante → *see* Ferramola,
  Floriano
Ferran, Anne (*Australian*
  photographer, 20th c.)   **BA**
  Bibl: Moore, C., in AFTERIMAGE
  XIV/2 (Sept 1986) 5
Ferrand, Jacques Philippe (*French*
  artist, 1653-1732)   **WC**
Ferrand, Louis (*French painter,*
  b.1905)   **BA**
  Bibl: ▶Bénézit; ▶MoMA libr. cat.;
  Nantes (FRA), Musee des Beaux-
  Arts, HOMMAGE A LOUIS
  FERRAUD (1976)
Ferrand, Marylène (*French*
  architect, Paris)   **AV**
  Bibl: Landscape architecture,
  1989 Jan., v.79, no.1, p.25
Ferrand, Patrick (*French architect,*
  Lille)   **AV**
  Bibl: Le Moniteur architecture
  AMC, 1989, no.2, p.48
Ferrandini, Robert (*American artist,*
  20th c.)   **BA**
  Bibl: Boston (MA, USA), ICA,
  Boston now (1982)
Ferrando de Almedina → *see* Yañez de
  la Almedina, Fernando
Ferrando, Francesco → *see* Fernandi,
  Francesco (Imperiali)
Ferrandus, Thomas (*Italian printer,*
  author, ecclesiastic, ca.1441-ca.
  1510)   **BA**
  Bibl: Febvre, Coming of the bk.;
  M. Murtri THE BOOK p.279;
  ▶Natl. union cat., pre-1956;
  Rhodes. BULL OF THE J. RYLANDS
  UNIV. LIB OF MAN. LXVII, 1
  autumn '84 p.544-559

Ferrant Vázquez, Angel (*Spanish*
  sculptor, 1891-1961)   **BA**
  Bibl: ▶Campoy, Español contemp.;
  ▶Encic. univ. ilus., suppl. 1961-62;
  GOYA CLXXV-VI (1983) 56;
  Madrid (ESP), Palacio de Cristal
  del Retiro, ANGEL FERRANT
  (1983); ▶Vollmer, Künst.-Lex. 20.
  Jhr.
Ferrant y Fischermans, Alejandro
  (*Spanish painter, 1843-1917*)   **BA**
  Bibl: ▶Bénézit; ▶Encic. univ. ilus.;
  ▶Ossorio y Bernard, Artistas
  españoles 19s.; REALES SITIOS
  XIX/71 (1982) 49-56;
  ▶Thieme-Becker
  Ferrant, Alejandro   BA
  Fischermans, Alejandro Ferrant y   BA
Ferrant y Llamas (y Llausas) → *see*
  Ferrant y Llausas, Luis
Ferrant y Llamas, Fernando → *see*
  Ferrant y Llausas, Fernando
Ferrant y Llamas, Luis → *see* Ferrant y
  Llausas, Luis
Ferrant y Llausas, Fernando
  (*Spanish painter, 1810-1856*)   **BA**
  Bibl: ▶Bénézit; ▶Ossorio y Bernard,
  Artistas españoles 19s.;
  ▶Thieme-Becker
  Ferrant y Llamas, Fernando   BA
  Ferrant, Fernando   BA
  Llausas, Fernando Ferrant y   BA
Ferrant y Llausas, Luis   **BA**
  (*Spanish artist, 1806-1868*)   **WC**
  (*Spanish painter, 1806-1868*)   **BA**
  Bibl: ▶Bénézit; ▶Ossorio y Bernard,
  Artistas españoles 19s.;
  ▶Thieme-Becker
  Ferrant y Llamas (y Llausas)   **WC**
  Ferrant y Llamas, Luis   BA
  Ferrant, Luis   BA
  Llausas, Luis Ferrant y   BA
Ferrant, Alejandro → *see* Ferrant y
  Fischermans, Alejandro
Ferrant, Fernando → *see* Ferrant y
  Llausas, Fernando
Ferrant, Luis → *see* Ferrant y Llausas,
  Luis
Ferrante Amendola → *see* Amendola,
  Ferrante
Ferrante, Francesco (*Italian artist,*
  op.1672)   **WC**
Ferrante, Paolo (*Italian architect*) **AV**
  Bibl: Abitare, 1983 May, no.214,
  p.90
Ferrara, Giovanni Battista (*Italian*
  sculptor, 17th-18th cs.)   **BA**
  Bibl: Antichità viva (Jul.-Aug.
  1980) pp.24-29
Ferrara, Guido (*Italian architect*) **AV**
  Bibl: Ville giardini, 1985 May, no.
  196, p.48

Ferrara, Jackie   **AV BA**
  (American sculptor)   AV
  (American sculptor, b.1929)   BA
    Bibl: Philadelphia (PA, USA), U
    Penn, ICA, CONNECTIONS (1983);
    Process: architecture, 1989 May,
    no.82, p.128
Ferrari→see Ferrari, Defendente
Ferrari→see Ferrari, Gaudenzio
Ferrari→see Ferrari, Giovanni Andrea
  de
Ferrari→see Ferrari, Luca (Luca da
  Reggio)
Ferrari→see Ferraro, Orazio
Ferrari Hardoy, Jorge *(Argentine
  architect, 1914-)*   **AV**
    Bibl: Encic. arte en America
*Ferrari or de Ferrari,
  Defendente→see* Ferrari,
  Defendente
*Ferrari or Deferrari, Giovanni
  Andrea→see* Ferrari, Giovanni
  Andrea de
Ferrari, Agostini *(Italian artist,
  b.1938)*   **BA**
    Bibl: Milan (ITA), Rotonda Besana,
    Agostini Ferrari et al. (1975)
Ferrari, Alessandro *(Italian
  architect)*   **AV**
    Bibl: Abitare, 1985 Oct., no.238,
    p.46
Ferrari, Ambrogio *(Italian engineer,
  act.1490-1500)*   **BA**
    Bibl: ARTE LOMBARDA 62 (1982)
    93-140
Ferrari, Andrea *(Italian illuminator,
  act. late 16th century)*   **GC**
    Bibl: Sotheby's London.
    06/25/85, Lot 33
  Ferrari, Andreas   GC
Ferrari, Andreas→see Ferrari, Andrea
Ferrari, Antoni *(Italian(?) architect,
  active in Poland, 18th cent)*   **AV**
    Bibl: Rocznik historii sztuki, 1988,
    v.17, p.301
  Ferrarich, Antoniego   AV
Ferrari, Antonio Felice *(Italian
  painter, 1667-1720)*   **BA**
    Bibl: ▶Bolaffi; ▶Thieme-Becker
Ferrari, Bernardo *(Italian artist, op.
  1626-1649)*   **WC**
Ferrari, Bianco *(Italian painter, act.
  1479, d.ca.1489)*   **BA**
    Bibl: Itinerari, V (1988)
**Ferrari, Cesare (Cesare Augusto
  Ferrarese)** *(Italian artist, 17th
  cent.)*   **WC**
Ferrari, Claudio *(Chilean architect)*   **AV**
    Bibl: ARQ, 1986 May, no.11, p.12

Ferrari, Defendente   **BA GC JG PR**
  (Italian artist, c.1490-p.1535)   WC
  (Italian painter, act. 1510-1535)   PR
  (Italian painter, act.1510-1535)   BA
  (Italian, ca.1490-aft.1535)   GC
  *(Italian, Piedmontese, active
  1511-1535)*   JG
    Bibl: ▶Bolaffi; ▶Encyc. world art;
    Mallè, SPANZOTTI, DEFENDENTE
    (1971); ▶RILA/BHA;
    ▶Thieme-Becker; ▶Witt checklist
  Defendente de Ferrari   BA
  Defendente Ferrari   PR
  Ferrari   PR
**Ferrari or de Ferrari,
  Defendente**   **WC**
Ferrari, Domenico   **GC WC**
  (Italian artist, 16th cent.)   WC
  (Italian painter, 16th century)   GC
    Bibl: ▶Witt checklist
Ferrari, Donnino *(Italian architect,
  1739-1817)*   **BA**
    Bibl: AUREA PARMA LXIV (Aug
    1980) 173-180; ▶Thieme-Becker
Ferrari, Ettore *(Italian sculptor,
  1848-1929)*   **BA GC**
    Bibl: ▶Bénézit; ▶Encic. italiana;
    ▶RILA/BHA; ▶Thieme-Becker
Ferrari, Eusebio   **BA WC**
  (Italian artist, a.1470-a.1533)   WC
  *(Italian painter, before 1470-
  before 1533)*   BA
    Bibl: ▶Bolaffi; Malle, L., in
    INCONTRI CON GAUDENZIO, p.
    189-194; ▶Thieme-Becker; ▶Witt
    checklist
Ferrari, Federico   **BA**
  (Italian artist, op.1768-1781)   WC
  (Italian painter, 18th c.)   BA
    Bibl: ▶Bolaffi; Coppa, ARTE
    CRISTIANA 77/731 (Mar-Apr
    1989) 121-130; TCI Milano;
    ▶Thieme-Becker; ▶Witt checklist
Ferrari, Federigo   **WC**
Ferrari, Federigo→see Ferrari,
  Federico
Ferrari, Francesco   **GC WC**
  (Italian artist, 1634-1708)   WC
  (Italian, 1634-1708)   GC
    Bibl: ▶Thieme-Becker; ▶Witt
    checklist
Ferrari, Francesco   **BA GC**
  *(Italian architect, painter, act.
  1703-1744)*   BA
  (Italian, act.1721-1744)   GC
    Bibl: ▶Bénézit; ▶Bolaffi; Spetia, in
    Notizie da Palazzo Albani XVI, 2
    (1987), p. 122; ▶Thieme-Becker
Ferrari, Francesco Bernardino   **AV BA**
  (Italian architect, 1744-1821)   BA
  (Milanese architect, 1744-1821)   AV
    Bibl: Arte lombarda 55-57 (1980),
    pp.273, 344-345
Ferrari, Francesco de'→see Bianchi
  Ferrari, Francesco de'

Ferrari, Francesco di Bianco *(Italian
  painter, 1457/60-1510)*   **BA**
    Bibl: ▶Bénézit; Berenson, NORTH
    ITALIAN PAINTERS OF THE
    RENAISSANCE (1927); ▶Bolaffi;
    ▶Encic. italiana; ▶Encic. univ. ilus.;
    Itinerari, V (1988);
    ▶Thieme-Becker
Ferrari, Gaudenzio   **BA GC PR**
  (Italian artist, 1470/80-1546)   WC
  *(Italian painter and sculptor, ca.
  1470-1546)*   GC
  (Italian painter, d. 1546)   PR
  *(Italian painter, sculptor,
  1475/80-1546)*   BA
    Bibl: ▶Bolaffi; ▶Freedberg, Ptg.
    Italy; ▶RILA/BHA; TCI Piemonte;
    ▶Thieme-Becker; Turin (ITA),
    Accademia Albertina, GAUDENZIO
    FERRARI E LA SUA SCUOLA (1982)
  Ferrari   PR
**Ferrari, Gaudenzio (Gaudenzio
  de Vincio)**   **WC**
  Ferrari, Gaudinzio   PR
  Gaudenzio da Vincio   GC
  Gaudenzio Ferrari   PR
  Godiancure   PR
*Ferrari, Gaudenzio (Gaudenzio de
  Vincio)→see* Ferrari, Gaudenzio
Ferrari, Gaudinzio→see Ferrari,
  Gaudenzio
**Ferrari, Giacomo (Giuseppe
  Giacomo)** *(Italian artist, 1747-
  1807)*   **WC**
Ferrari, Giovanni *(Italian artist, op.
  1585)*   **WC**
Ferrari, Giovanni Andrea d'→see
  Ferrari, Giovanni Andrea de
Ferrari, Giovanni Andrea de   **BA PR**
  (Italian artist, 1598-1669)   WC
  (Italian painter, 1598-1669)   BA GC PR
    Bibl: ▶Bénézit; ▶Bolaffi; ▶Encic.
    italiana; ▶Encyc. world art;
    ▶Fredericksen & Zeri, Census;
    ▶RILA/BHA, 1986; TCI Liguria,
    p.476; ▶Thieme-Becker
  and.a de ferrari   PR
  Deferrari, Giovanni Andrea   BA
  Ferrari   PR
**Ferrari or Deferrari, Giovanni
  Andrea**   **WC**
  Ferrari, Giovanni Andrea d'   PR
Ferrari, Giovanni Andrea de'   **GC PR**
  G. A. Ferrari   PR
  Gio: Andrea   PR
  Giovanni andrea   PR
  Giovanni Andrea d' Ferrari   PR
  Giovanni Andrea de Ferrari   PR
  Giovanni Andrea de' Ferrari   PR
  Giovanni Andrea Ferrari   PR
Ferrari, Giovanni Andrea de'→see
  Ferrari, Giovanni Andrea de
Ferrari, Girolamo *(Italian artist,
  16th cent.)*   **WC**
Ferrari, Giuseppe *(Italian artist,
  1921-)*   **WC**

Ferrari, Giuseppe *(Italian stucco*
artist, act.1769-1781)   **BA**
 Bibl: Chiappini di Sorio, Not. Pal.
 Albani, XI/1-2 (1982), p.101
Ferrari, Giuseppe *(Italian*
cabinetmaker in USA, b.1848, act.
1880)   **BA**
 Bibl: Jarvan, B.B., PHILADELPHIA
 MUS OF ART BULLETIN, LXXX,
 343-344 (summer-fall 1984)
 24-26; ▶Thieme-Becker
Ferrari, Gregorio de'   **BA GC WC**
 (Italian artist, 1644-1726)   **WC**
 (Italian painter, 1644-1726)   **BA GC**
 Bibl: ▶RILA/BHA, 1986;
 ▶Thieme-Becker; ▶Wittkower, Art
 & arch. Italy
 Deferrari, Gregorio   BA
 Gergorio de Ferrari   BA
Ferrari, Lorenzo de'   **BA FA GC**
 (1680-20.VIII.1744; Artist,
 Painter, Italia)   **FA**
 (Italian artist, 1680-1744)   **WC**
 (Italian painter, 1680-1744)   **BA GC**
 Bibl: ▶Bolaffi; Getty Photo Study
 Coll. (Ptgs.); NGA (Uffizi) objects;
 ▶RILA/BHA, 1986, Subject, 1988;
 ▶Thieme-Becker, v.11, p.457 ff.
 Abate de Ferrari, l'   BA
 Abate de'Ferrari, Lorenzo l'   FA
 Abate Ferrari   GC
 de'Ferrari, Lorenzo   FA
 Defarrari, Lorenzo   FA
 Deferrari, Lorenzo   BA
 Ferrari, Lorenzo de' (L'Abate
 de' Ferrari)   **WC**
Ferrari, Lorenzo de' (L'Abate de'
 Ferrari) → *see* Ferrari, Lorenzo de'
Ferrari, Luca → *see* Ferrari, Luca (Luca
 da Reggio)
Ferrari, Luca (Luca da
Reggio)   **BA GC PR WC**
 (Italian artist, 1605-1654)   **WC WI**
 (Italian painter, 1605-1654) **BA GC PR**
 Bibl: ▶Bolaffi; ▶RILA/BHA, 1986;
 ▶Thieme-Becker
 Ferrari   PR
 Ferrari, Luca   **GC PR**
 Ferrari, Luca, da Reggio   **WI**
 L. da Reggio   PR
 Luca da Reggio   BA GC PR WI
 Luca Ferrari   PR
 Reggio, Luca da   BA
Ferrari, Luca, da Reggio → *see* Ferrari,
 Luca (Luca da Reggio)
Ferrari, Marino *(Italian architect,*
1948-)   **AV**
 Bibl: Frames, porte & finestre,
 1988 Jan.-Mar., no.18, p.64
Ferrari, Orazio de' → *see* Ferraro,
 Orazio
Ferrari, Pietro *(Italian painter, act.*
1683-1685)   **BA**
 Bibl: Le Stampe e la diffusione
 delle immagini ... (CIHA 24,
 Bologna 1979), pp.62-65

Ferrari, Pietro Melchiorre   **BA GC WC**
 (Italian artist, 1735-1787)   **WC**
 (Italian painter, 1735-1787)   **BA GC**
 Bibl: ▶Bolaffi; ▶RILA/BHA, 1986;
 ▶Thieme-Becker
Ferrari, Pompeo   **AV BA**
 (Italian architect in POL, ca.
 1660-1736)   **BA**
 (Italian(?) architect, active in
 Poland, 18th cent)   **AV**
 Bibl: ▶Hempel, Baroque central
 Euro.; ▶Thieme-Becker; ▶Wielka
 ilustr. encyk.
 Ferrarich, Pompea   AV
Ferrari, Renzo *(Italian painter,*
b.1939)   **BA**
 Bibl: ▶Intl. dir. exh. artists, 1983;
 ▶Lex. zeitgen. Schweiz. Künstler
Ferrari, Vincenzo   **WC**
 (Italian artist, op.1780-1793)   **WC**
 (Italian artist, op.1790-1793)   **WC**
 Ferreri, Vincenzo   **WC**
Ferrarich, Antoniego → *see* Ferrari,
 Antoni
Ferrarich, Pompea → *see* Ferrari,
 Pompeo
Ferrarini, Pier Giuseppe *(Italian*
artist, 1846-p.1882)   **WC**
Ferrario, Carlo   **GC WC**
 (Italian artist, 1833-1907)   **WC**
 (Italian, 1833-1907)   **GC**
 Bibl: ▶Thieme-Becker; ▶Witt
 checklist
Ferrario, Luigi *(Italian architect,*
Milan)   **AV**
 Bibl: Abitare, 1988 Oct., no.268,
 p.242
Ferrario, Roberto *(Italian architect)*   **AV**
 Bibl: Abitare, 1989 Oct., no.278,
 p.188
Ferraris → *see* Ferraris, Artur
Ferraris, Arthur von → *see* Ferraris,
 Artur
Ferraris, Artur   **PR**
 (Hungarian artist, 1856-)   **WC**
 (Hungarian painter, 1856-aft.
 1908)   **PR**
 Bibl: ▶Thieme-Becker
 Artur Ferraris   PR
 Ferraris   PR
 Ferraris, Arthur von   **PR WC**
Ferraro, Antonino *(Italian painter,*
sculptor, stucco artist, 16th c.)   **BA**
 Bibl: ▶Bolaffi; ▶Thieme-Becker
Ferraro, Giuseppe *(Italian engineer,*
act.1782)   **BA**
 Bibl: Strazzullo, Napoli
 nobilissima, XXII, XXIII, XXIV
 (May-Aug. 1983) pp.145-146
Ferraro, Giuseppe *(Italian sculptor,*
act.1607-1623)   **BA**
 Bibl: ▶Bénézit; ▶Thieme-Becker

Ferraro, Orazio   **BA**
 (Italian artist, 1605-1657)   **WC**
 (Italian painter, 1605-1657)   **GC PR**
 (Italian painter, stucco artist,
 16th-17th cs.)   **BA**
 Bibl: ▶Bolaffi; ▶Thieme-Becker;
 ▶Witt checklist
 Ferrari   PR
 Ferrari, Orazio de'   **GC PR WC**
 Orazio de' Ferrari   PR
Ferraro, Tommaso *(Italian painter,*
stucco artist, act.1589)   **BA**
 Bibl: ▶Bolaffi; ▶Thieme-Becker
Ferrat, Charles Hippolyte Marcellin
 (French sculptor, 1830-1882)   **BA**
 Bibl: ▶Bénézit; ▶Camard, Ptrs. &
 sculps. provençaux; ▶Lami, Sculp.
 fran. 19e s.; ▶Thieme-Becker
 Ferrat, Hippolyte Marcellin   BA
Ferrat, Dominique *(French painter,*
b.1954)   **BA**
 Bibl: ▶Intl. dir. exh. artists, 1982
Ferrat, Hippolyte → *see* Ferrat, Jean
 Joseph Hippolyte Romain
Ferrat, Hippolyte Marcellin → *see*
 Ferrat, Charles Hippolyte Marcellin
Ferrat, Jean Joseph Hippolyte
 Romain *(French sculptor, 1822-*
 1882)   **BA**
 Bibl: ▶Bénézit; ▶Camard, Ptrs. &
 sculps. provençaux; ▶Lami, Sculp.
 fran. 19e s.; ▶Thieme-Becker
 Ferrat, Hippolyte   BA
Ferrata, Ercole *(Italian sculptor,*
1610-1686)   **BA GC**
 Bibl: ▶Bessone-Aurelj, Scult. &
 arch. ital.; ▶Encyc. world art;
 ▶RILA/BHA; ▶Thieme-Becker
Ferrater, Carles *(Spanish architect)*   **AV**
 Bibl: Quaderns d'arquitectura i
 urbanisme, 1981 Jan.-Feb., no.
 144, p.40
Ferratini, Gaetano *(Italian artist,*
1697-1765)   **WC**
Ferraù da Faenza → *see* Fenzoni,
 Ferraù
Ferrau Fenzoni → *see* Fenzoni, Ferraù
Ferrauoli → *see* Ferraiuoli, Nunzio
 (Afflitti)
Ferraz, Marcelo *(Brazilian architect,*
Sao Paulo)   **AV**
 Bibl: Abitare, 1983 Dec., no.220,
 p.64
Ferraz, Mário Sérgio *(Brazilian*
architect)   **AV**
 Bibl: Projeto, 1986 Feb., no.84,
 p.73
Ferrazana, Pietro *(Italian artist,*
19th cent.)   **WC**
Ferrazzi, Ferruccio   **BA PR WC**
 (Italian artist, 1891-)   **WC**
 (Italian painter, 1891-1978)   **BA PR**
 Bibl: ▶Bénézit; ▶Bolaffi 20c.;
 ▶Comanducci, Diz.; ▶RILA/BHA
 Ferruccio Ferrazzi   PR
Ferrazzi, Luigi *(Italian artist, op.*
1887)   **WC**

Ferre →*see* Ferré, Georges E.

Ferre, Georges →*see* Ferré, Georges E.

Ferré, Georges E.   **PR**
  (French artist, op.1886)   WC
  (French painter, act. 1885-1890)   PR
    Bibl: ▶Thieme-Becker

Ferre   PR

Ferre, Georges   PR **WC**

Georges E. Ferre   PR

Ferré, Gianfranco   **AV BA**
  (Italian architect, interior designer)   AV
  (Italian fashion designer, 20th c.)   BA
    Bibl: Architectural digest, 1985 Jan., v.41, no.1; Contemp. designers, 1984; Time (9 May 1983) p.74-77

Ferré, Jean-Pierre *(French architect)*   **AV**
    Bibl: Architecture d'aujourd'hui, 1983 Dec., no.230, p.liv

Ferreira, Flávio *(Brazilian architect)*   **AV**
    Bibl: Projeto, 1988 Feb., no.107, p.110

Ferreira, Paulo *(Portuguese painter, printmaker, designer in FRA, b.1911)*   **BA**
    Bibl: ▶Tavares Chicó, Pint. portuguesa; ▶Vollmer, Künst.-Lex. 20. Jhr.; ▶WW France; ▶WW Graphic Art

Rodrigues-Ferreira, Paulo   BA

Ferreiro, Esteban *(Spanish sculptor)*   **AV**
    Bibl: Country life, v.177, no.4580, p.1502

Ferrell, Sarah Coleman *(American landscape gardener, ca.1817-1903)*   **BA**
    Bibl: Jrnl. of Garden Hist. II/4 (Oct-Dec 1982) 343-360

Ferren, John   **BA WC WI**
  (American artist, 1905-)   WC
  (American artist, 1905-1970)   WI
  (American painter, sculptor, 1905-1970)   BA
    Bibl: ▶Seuphor, Abstract ptg.; ▶WWW Amer.; ▶Young, Amer. artists

Ferrer →*see* Ferrer, Jaime

Ferrer Bassa (Ferrarius Bassa or de Baco) →*see* Bassa, Ferrer

Ferrer y Miro, Juan *(Spanish artist, 1850-)*   **WC**

Ferrer, Albert *(Spanish publisher, artist, b.ca.1950)*   **BA**
    Bibl: Graves, Connoisseur CCXIV/865 (Mar 1984) 122

Ferrer, Bassa →*see* Bassa, Ferrer

Ferrer, Jaime   **GC PR**
  (Spanish artist, 15th cent.)   WC
  (Spanish painter, act. 1436)   PR
  (Spanish, act.1457)   GC
    Bibl: ▶RILA/BHA; ▶Thieme-Becker; ▶Witt checklist

Ferrer   PR

Ferrer, Jaime II   PR

Jaime Ferrer   PR

Master of the Paheria Altarpiece (identified with Ferrer, Jaime, II)   **WC**

Master of Verdu (identified with Ferrer, Jaime, II)   **WC**

Ferrer, Jaime II →*see* Ferrer, Jaime

Ferrer, Jaime, I and II *(Spanish artist, op.1457)*   **WC**

Ferrer, Javier Carvajal →*see* Carvajal Ferrer, Javier

Ferrer, Rafael *(American painter, sculptor, b.1933)*   **BA**
    Bibl: ▶WW Amer. Art, 1980

Ferrer, Ramón *(Spanish scribe, act. late 14th, early 15th c.)*   **GC**
    Bibl: Domínguez Bordona, Mss., v.1, no.52

Ferrer, Tomás *(Spanish painter, act. 1753)*   **BA**
    Bibl: ▶Thieme-Becker

Ferrer, Vincentius *(Spanish artist, op.1372)*   **WC**

Ferrera, Raúl   **AV**

Ferrère family *(French sculptors, 17th-18th cs.)*   **BA**
    Bibl: ▶Bénézit; ▶Dict. biog. fran.; ▶Thieme-Becker

Ferreri, Andrea *(Italian sculptor, 1673-1744)*   **BA**
    Bibl: ▶Bessone-Aurelj, Scult. & arch. ital.; TCI Emilia-Romagna (1957), p.710; ▶Thieme-Becker

Ferreri, Giuseppe *(Italian sculptor, b.1702, act.1745)*   **BA**
    Bibl: Baruffaldi, Vite pitt. e scult. ferraresi; ▶Bessone-Aurelj, Scult. & arch. ital.; ▶Thieme-Becker

Ferreri, Vincenzo →*see* Ferrari, Vincenzo

Ferreris or Freres, Dirck or Theodorus *(Dutch artist, 1639-1693)*   **WC**

Ferreris, Heindrick *(Dutch artist, op. 1617-1625)*   **WC**

Ferrero, Harvey *(American architect, Ferndale, MI, 1934-)*   **AV**
    Bibl: Architecture and urbanism, no.174, p.124; Building design & construction, 1985 Sept., v.26, no.9, p.129

Ferrers, Benjamin   **WC WI**
  (British artist, op.1695-, d.1732)   WI
  (British artist, op.1697-m.1732)   WC

Ferrers, Rebecca Dulcibella   **WC WI**
  (British artist, 19th cent.)   WC
  (British artist, op.19th c.)   WI

Ferretti →*see* Ferretti, Giovanni Domenico

Ferretti da Imola, Giovanni Domenico →*see* Ferretti, Giovanni Domenico

Ferretti, Giovanni →*see* Ferretti, Giovanni Domenico

Ferretti, Giovanni Domenico **BA GC PR**
  (Italian artist, 1692-a.1769)   WC
  (Italian painter, 1692-1768)   BA PR
  (Italian painter, 1692-ca.1766/69)   GC
    Bibl: ▶Bénézit; ▶Bolaffi; ▶RILA/BHA; ▶Thieme-Becker; ▶Witt checklist

Ferretti   PR

Ferretti da Imola, Giovanni Domenico   **GC WC**

Ferretti, Giovanni   PR

Giovanni Domenico Ferretti   PR

Giovanni Ferretti   PR

Ferretti, Massimo *(Italian architect)*   **AV**
    Bibl: L'Industria delle costruzioni, 1989 Mar., v.23, no.209, p.18

Ferretti, Paolo *(Italian artist, 1866-)*   **WC**

Ferretti, Stefania Foschi →*see* Foschi Ferretti, Stefania

Ferrey, Benjamin   **BA WC WI**
  (1810-1880)   AV
  (British archiect, 1810-1880)   BA
  (British artist, 1810-1880)   WC WI
    Bibl: ▶Dict. natl. biog.

Ferry, Benjamin   **AV**

Ferrez, Marc *(Brazilian, 1843-1923)*   **JG**

Ferri →*see* Ferri, Ciro

Ferri di Bologna, Domenico *(Italian artist, 1829-1896)*   **WC**

Ferri, Antonio   **BA**
  (Florentine architect, d.1716)   AV
  (Italian architect, d.1716)   BA
  (Italian artist, 1651-1716)   WC
    Bibl: ▶Portoghesi, Diz. arch. e urbanistica; ▶Thieme-Becker; Zangheri, L., ANTICHITA VIVA, 11/6 (1972) 45-56 [BHA/ITA]

Ferri, Antonio Maria   **AV WC**

Ferri, Antonio Maria →*see* Ferri, Antonio

Ferri, Augusto *(Italian artist, 1829-)*   **WC**

Ferri, Ciro   **BA FA GC PR WC**
  (1634-13.IX.1689; Artist,
    Painter, Italia)   **FA**
  (Italian artist, 1634-1689)   **WC**
  (Italian painter, 1634-1689)   **PR**
  (Italian painter, sculptor, 1634-
    1689)   **BA**
  (Italian, 1634-1689)   **GC**
  Bibl: ▶Bénézit; ▶Bolaffi; ▶Encyc.
    world art; NGA (Uffizi) objects;
    ▶RILA/BHA, Subject, 1988;
    ▶Thieme-Becker, v.11, p.479 ff.;
    ▶Witt checklist
    C. Ferri   PR
    Ciro   PR
    Ciro Feri   PR
    Ciro Ferri   PR
    Ciro Ferri Scolare di Pietro da
      Cortona   PR
    Ciro Ferro   PR
    Cirofer   FA
    Ciroferri   PR
    Ciroferro   PR
    Cirofiori   PR
    Cirro Ferri   PR
    Ferri   PR
    Le Cyre   FA
Ferri, Domenico *(Italian artist, 1808-*
1865)   **WC**
Ferri, Domenico   **AV BA**
  (Italian architect, scenographer,
    decorator, 1797-1869)   **BA**
  (Italian decorator and scenic
    designer, fl. 1853)   **AV**
  Bibl: Colle, Antichità viva XXVII
    (Jan.-Feb. 1988), p. 50;
    ▶Portoghesi, Diz. arch. e
    urbanistica; ▶Thieme-Becker
Ferri, Gesualdo →see Ferri, Gesualdo
  Francesco
Ferri, Gesualdo Francesco   **PR WC**
  (Italian artist, 1728-c.1788)   **WC**
  (Italian painter, 1728-1788)   **PR**
  Bibl: ▶Thieme-Becker
    Ferri, Gesualdo   PR
    Gesualdo Ferri   PR
    Gesualdo Francesco Ferri   PR
Ferri, Giovanni (Giovanni Senese)
  (Italian painter, act. ca. 1620)   **PR**
  Bibl: Colonna inventory, Rome,
    1648; Salerno, La natura morta
    italiana, pp. XXI, 405
    Gio: Sanese   PR
    Gio: Sannese   PR
    Gio: Senese   PR
    Gio: Senesio   PR
    Giovanni Senese   PR
Ferri, Roger C.   **AV BA**
  (American architect, 1948-)   **AV**
  (American architect, ca.1949-
    1991)   **BA**
  Bibl: ARCH. REVIEW CLXVIII/9005
    (Nov 1980) 268-277; ▶Avery
    period. idx.; NY Times obit., 24
    Nov 1991, p.50; Space design,
    1982 Aug., no.215, p.132

Ferriday, Aileen *(British*
photographer, 20th c.)   **BA**
  Bibl: Arts Council GBR, 3
    perspectives photography (1979)
Ferrier, A. →see Ferrier, Jacques
  Alexandre
Ferrier, Alexandre →see Ferrier,
  Jacques Alexandre
Ferrier, Arthur *(British artist, op.*
20th c.)   **WI**
Ferrier, C. →see Ferrier, C.M.
Ferrier, C.M.   **GC**
  (French photographer, act.
    1850s-1860s)   **GC**
  (French, 1811-1889 (also Ferrier;
    Ferrier & Soulier; Ferrier)   **JG**
  Bibl: Getty Photo Study Coll.;
    ▶Idx. Amer. photog. colls.
    Ferrier, C.   GC
Ferrier, Claude-Marie   **JG**
Ferrier, Claude-Marie →see Ferrier,
  C.M.
Ferrier, Gabriel   **GC**
  (French artist, 1847-1914)   **WC**
  (French painter, 1847-1914)   **GC**
  Bibl: ▶Thieme-Becker
Ferrier, Gabriel Joseph Marie
Augustin   **WC**
Ferrier, Gabriel Joseph Marie
  Augustin →see Ferrier, Gabriel
Ferrier, George Stratton *(British*
artist, 1852-1912)   **WI**
Ferrier, Jacques Alexandre   **JG VO**
  (French photographer, 1831-
    1912)   **VO**
  (French photographer, act.
    1860s-1890s)   **GC**
  (French, 1811-1912 (also Ferrier;
    Ferrier & Soulier))   **JG**
  Bibl: Getty Photo Study Coll.;
    ▶Idx. Amer. photog. colls.; ▶Libr.
    of Congr. Name Auth. File,
    NAFR9242725; Vues
    stéréoscopiques de Ferrier et
    Soulier (1992), p. 8
    Ferrier, A.   GC
Ferrier, Alexandre   **GC**
Ferrier, James *(British artist, op.*
1873-1883)   **WI**
Ferrier, Leonard Jozef *(Flemish*
silversmith, 1726-ca.1801)   **BA**
  Bibl: Ren, Antiek XXII/10 (May
    1988), p.541-545
Ferrier, Marcel *(Swiss architect,*
b.1951)   **BA**
  Bibl: ▶RILA/BHA; Röllin, Unsere
    Kunstdenkmäler XXXV, 4 (1984)
Ferriere, Francois *(Swiss artist,*
1752-1839)   **WC**
Ferrieres, Martin   **WC**
  (French artist, 1893-)   **WC**
  (French artist, 20th cent.)   **WC**
Martin-Ferrieres, Jac   **WC**
Ferrieres, Martin *(French artist, op.*
1700)   **WC**

Ferrieri, Anna Castelli *(Italian*
architect, 1918-)   **AV**
Ferrini, Benedetto   **AV BA**
  (Italian architect and engineer,
    d.1479)   **AV**
  (Italian architect, d.1479)   **BA**
  Bibl: ▶Portoghesi, Diz. arch. e
    urbanistica; ▶Thieme-Becker
    Ferino, Benedetto   BA
Ferrini, Rino *(Italian architect,*
Milan)   **AV**
  Bibl: Abitare, 1987 May, no.254,
    p.164
Ferrior, John *(British architect, act.*
1754)   **BA**
  Bibl: Slade, PROCEEDINGS OF SOC.
    OF ANTIQUARIES IN SCOTLAND
    CX (1978-80) 432-474
Ferris, Hugh →see Ferriss, Hugh
Ferris, Jean Leon Gerome   **BA**
  (American artist, 1863-1930)   **WI**
  (American painter, 1863-1930)   **BA**
  Bibl: ▶Fielding's Amer. ptrs.;
    ▶WWW Amer.
Ferris, Jean Leon Jerome   **WI**
Ferris, Jean Leon Jerome →see Ferris,
  Jean Leon Gerome
Ferris, Robert *(American painter,*
b.1944)   **BA**
  Bibl: Montclair (NJ, USA), Art
    Museum, ROBERT FERRIS
Ferris, Roger P. *(American architect,*
Southport, Conn)   **AV**
  Bibl: ▶AIA Pro File, 1987-88
Ferris, Stephen James   **WC WI**
  (American artist, 1835-1915)   **WI**
  (American artist, 1835-p.1881)   **WC**
  (Engraver, 1835-1915)   **WI**
Ferriss, Hugh   **AV BA**
  (American architect, 1889-
    1962)   **AV BA**
  (American artist, 1889-1962)   **WI**
  Bibl: ▶Avery obit. idx.; ▶Libr. of
    Congr. Name Auth. File; ▶WWW
    Amer.
Ferris, Hugh   **WI**
Ferro →see Erró (Gudmundur
  Gudmundsson)
Ferro Caaveiro, Lucas Antonio
  (Spanish architect, ca.1700-1770)   **BA**
  Bibl: ▶Encic. univ. ilus.;
    ▶Portoghesi, Diz. arch. e
    urbanistica; ▶Thieme-Becker
Ferro Caaveiro, Miguel *(Spanish*
architect, ca.1740-1804)   **BA**
  Bibl: ▶Encic. univ. ilus.; España
    entre el Mediterraneo y el
    Atlántico (1973), v.3, p.445;
    ▶Portoghesi, Diz. arch. e
    urbanistica; ▶Thieme-Becker

Ferro, Francesco *(Unknown painter,*
d. aft. 1618)   **PR**
   Bibl: Delfino, 'Documenti inediti
      per alcuni pittori napoletani del
      '600...' in Ricerche sul '600
      napoletano, p.100
   Fran.co Ferro   PR
   Francesco Ferro   PR
Ferro, Gregorio   **BA WC**
   (Spanish artist, 1742-1812)   WC
   (Spanish painter, 1742-1812)   BA
   Bibl: ▶Bénézit; Prado: Cat.
      pinturas, p.219; ▶Thieme-Becker
Ferro, John *(American artist,*
b.1942)   **BA**
   Bibl: Ithaca (NY, USA), Cornell,
      Johnson Museum of Art, NEW
      YORK STATE ARTISTS SERIES
      (1977); ▶Natl. Faculty Dir., 1979
Ferro, Leandro *(Italian glass worker,*
act.1668-1711)   **BA**
   Bibl: Antiek, XVIII/10 (May 1984)
      pp.516-523; Gasparetto, Vetro di
      Murano, pp.54-55; Hudig, Glas,
      pp.82-84
   Faire, Leandro de   BA
   Fayre, Leandro de la   BA
   Feer, Leandro de   BA
   Fero, Leandro de   BA
Ferro, Maximilian L. *(American*
architect)   **AV**
Ferro, Sérgio *(Brazilian architect)* **AV**
   Bibl: Projeto, 1986 Apr., no.86,
      p.68
Ferroggio, Francesco Benedetto
   (18th century Italian architect) **AV**
Ferroli, Amadeo *(Italian, 1901-1971)* **JG**
Ferron, Marcelle   **BA WC**
   (Canadian artist, 1924-)   WC
   (Canadian painter, glass artist,
b.1929)   BA
   Bibl: ▶Artists Canada; Montreal
      (Que, CAN), Musee d'Art
      contemp., LA REVOLUTION
      (1980); ▶WW Amer. Art
Ferroni, Egisto   **GC WC**
   (Italian artist, 1835-1912)   WC
   (Italian painter, 1835-1912)   GC
   Bibl: ▶Thieme-Becker
Ferroni, Gianfranco *(Italian artist,*
1927-)   **WC**
Ferroni, Joseph *(Spanish artist, act.*
1803)   **BA**
   Bibl: Arch. esp. de arte,
      XLVIII/189 (Jan-Mar 1975) 139-
      142
Ferroni, Violante   **PR WC**
   (Italian artist, 1720-)   WC
   (Italian painter, b. 1720)   PR
   Bibl: ▶Thieme-Becker
   Violante Ferroni   PR
Ferrucci da Fiesole, Francesco di
Simone →see Ferrucci, Francesco di
Simone
Ferrucci or Ferruzzi, Andrea di Piero
(Andrea da Fiesole) →see Ferrucci,
Andrea

Ferrucci, Andrea   **GC**
   (Italian artist, 1465-1526)   WC
   (Italian sculptor, 1465-1526) GC
   Bibl: TCI Firenze
Ferrucci or Ferruzzi, Andrea di
Piero (Andrea da Fiesole)   **WC**
Ferrucci, Francesco di Giovanni →see
   Ferrucci, Francesco di Giovanni
   (Francesco del Tadda)
Ferrucci, Francesco di Giovanni
(Francesco del Tadda)   **BA**
   (Italian sculptor, 1497-1585) GC
   (Italian sculptor, 1497-1586) BA
   Bibl: ▶Bénézit; Di Castro Moscati,
      Apollo CXXVI/308 (Oct 1987)
      248; ▶Encic. italiana; TCI Firenze;
      ▶Thieme-Becker
   del Tadda, Francesco   BA
Ferrucci, Francesco di Giovanni **GC**
   Francesco del Tadda   GC
   Tadda, Francesco del   BA
Ferrucci, Francesco di Simone **BA GC**
   (Italian artist, 1437-1493)   WC
   (Italian sculptor, 1437-1493) BA GC
   Bibl: ▶Encyc. world art;
      ▶RILA/BHA; ▶Thieme-Becker
Ferrucci da Fiesole, Francesco di
Simone   **WC**
   Francesco di Simone da Fiesole   BA
Ferrucci, Nicodemo (Niccolo) di
Michelangelo →see Ferrucci,
Nicodemo di Michelangelo
Ferrucci, Nicodemo di
Michelangelo   **GC**
   (Italian artist, 1574-1650)   WC
   (Italian, 1574-1650)   GC
   Bibl: ▶Thieme-Becker; ▶Witt
      checklist
Ferrucci, Nicodemo (Niccolo) di
Michelangelo   **WC**
Ferrucci, Pompeo di Giovanni
Battista *(Italian, ca.1566-1637)* **GC**
   Bibl: ▶Thieme-Becker
Ferrucci, Romolo di Francesco
   (Italian sculptor, d.1621)   **GC**
   Bibl: TCI Firenze
   Romolo del Tadda   GC
Ferrucci, Simone *(Italian sculptor,*
1402-1469)   **GC**
   Bibl: TCI Firenze
Ferruccio Ferrazzi →see Ferrazzi,
Ferruccio
Ferry, Benjamin →see Ferrey,
Benjamin
Ferry, François *(French military*
engineer, act.1680-1686)   **BA**
   Bibl: ▶Bauchal, Archtes. fran.;
      Faucherre, MON. HIST. DE LA
      FRANCE 147 (Oct-Nov 1986)
      12m15; Hautecoeur, v.2, pt.1, pp.
      501-502
Ferry, Jean-Georges *(French*
painter, 1851-1926)   **GC**
   Bibl: ▶Bénézit

Ferry, Jules Jean   **BA**
   (French artist, 1844-)   WC
   (French painter, b.1844)   BA
Ferry, Jules-Jean   **WC**
Ferry, Jules-Jean →see Ferry, Jules
Jean
Ferryman, Cornelia, Miss →see
Brockman, Cornelia
Ferstel, E. *(German artist, 19th*
cent.)   **WC**
Ferstel, Heinrich Freiherr von →see
Ferstel, Heinrich, Freiherr von
Ferstel, Heinrich, Freiherr von **AV BA**
   (Austrian architect, 1828-1883) AV BA
   (German artist, 1828-1883)   WC
   Bibl: ▶Avery Libr. cat.; ▶Encyc.
      world art; ▶Thieme-Becker
Ferstel, Heinrich Freiherr von **WC**
Ferstel, Max, Freiherr von
   (Austrian architect, 1859-1936) **BA**
   Bibl: ▶Österr. biog. Lex. 1815-
      1950; ▶Portoghesi, Diz. arch. e
      urbanistica; ▶Thieme-Becker
Ferster, Hans *(German architect in*
SWE, d.1653)   **BA**
   Bibl: KONSTHIST. TIDSKRIFT
      XLVI/3 (1977) 126; Konsthist.
      Tidskrift, XLV/1-2 (1976) pp.
      39-51; ▶Svenska konstnärer;
      ▶Thieme-Becker
   Förster, Hans   BA
   Freester, Hans   BA
Ferstler, Heinrich *(German artist,*
1800-)   **WC**
Fertbauer →see Fertbauer, Leopold
Fertbauer, Leopold   **PR WC**
   (Austrian painter, 1802-1875) PR
   (German artist, 1802-1875)   WC
   Bibl: ▶Thieme-Becker
   Fertbauer   PR
   Leopold Fertbauer   PR
Fertel, Martin-Dominique *(French*
printer, 1684-1752)   **BA**
   Bibl: ▶Dict. biog. fran.; ▶Natl.
      union cat., pre-1956
Ferville, L. *(French artist, op.1825)* **WC**
Fery, John   **BA WI**
   (American artist, 1859-1934)   WI
   (American painter, 1859-1934) BA
   Bibl: St. Paul (MN, USA), Minn.
      Mus. of Art, Iron Horse West
      (Jan-Jul 1976)
Ferz →see Ferg, Franz de Paula
Fesch, C.A. *(British artist, op.1885-)* **WI**
Fescourt, Félix *(French*
photographer, act. ca.1860-1880) **GC**
   Bibl: ▶Idx. Amer. photog. colls.
   F. F.   GC
Fesel, Christoph *(German artist,*
1737-1805)   **WC**
Fesel, Gerd   **AV BA**
   (German architect, b.1924)   BA
   (West German architect, 1924-
1984)   AV
   Bibl: KUNSTWERK XXXII/2-3 (Apr-
      June) 1979 56

Feselein, Melchior→see Feselen,
  Melchior
Feselen→see Feselen, Melchior
Feselen or Feselein, Melchior→see
  Feselen, Melchior
Feselen, Melchior   **GC PR**
  (German artist, op.1521-m.
    1538)   **WC**
  (German painter and
    draughtsman, ca.1495-1538)   **GC**
  (German painter, d. 1538)   **PR**
    Bibl: Munich, Alte Pinakothek,
    (1983); ▶Thieme-Becker; ▶Witt
    checklist
  Feselein, Melchior   **GC**
  Feselen   **PR**
Feselen or Feselein, Melchior   **WC**
  Melchior Feselen   **PR**
Fesenmaier, Bartholomäus→see
  Fesenmayer, Bartholomäus
Fesenmaier, Helene   **BA**
  (American artist, op.20th c.)   **WI**
  (American sculptor, b.1937)   **BA**
    Bibl: Norwich (GBR), Univ. of E.
    Anglia, Sainsbury Center, Four
    Amer. Sculptors (1981)
  Fesenmailer, Helen   **WI**
Fesenmailer, Helen→see Fesenmaier,
  Helene
Fesenmair, Bartholomäus→see
  Fesenmayer, Bartholomäus
Fesenmair, Hans Christoph II
  (German goldsmith, 1587-1664)   **BA**
    Bibl: Eckerbom, KONSTHIST.
    TIDSKRIFT LII/1 (1983) 15-22;
    ▶Neue deutsche Biog.; ▶Seling,
    Augsburger Goldschmiede, v.3,
    p.452; ▶Thieme-Becker
  Fesenmayr, Hans Christoph   BA
  Veslmair, Hans Christoph   BA
Fesenmayer, Bartholomäus
  (German draughtsman, act.1572-d.
    1597)   **GC**
    Bibl: ▶Thieme-Becker
  Fesenmaier, Bartholomäus   GC
  Fesenmair, Bartholomäus   GC
  Veslmair, Bartholomäus   GC
Fesenmayr, Hans Christoph→see
  Fesenmair, Hans Christoph II
Feshbach, Oriole Farb (American
  painter, b.1931)   **BA**
    Bibl: Amherst (MA, USA), U Mass.
    Art Gallery, 11 Alumni (1983)
Feshin, Nikolai Ivanovich→see Fechin,
  Nicolai Ivanovich
Fešin, Nikolai Ivanovič→see Fechin,
  Nicolai Ivanovich
Fessard, Etienne   **BA WC**
  (French artist, 1714-1777)   **WC**
  (French engraver, 1714-1777)   **BA**
    Bibl: ▶Bénézit; Clark Art Inst.
    Photo & Slide Dept.; ▶Encyc.
    world art; ▶Thieme-Becker
Fessler, Robert A. (American
  architect, Toledo, OH, 1958-)   **AV**
    Bibl: ▶AIA Pro File, 1987-88

Fessy, Georges (French
  photographer, b.1937)   **BA**
    Bibl: Arc-et-Senans (FRA), Salines
    Royales, Itinérance (1985), p.31
**Festa, Matilde Piacentini (or
  Bianca)** (Italian artist, op.1830)   **WC**
Festa, Tano (Italian painter, b.1938) **BA**
    Bibl: ▶Bolaffi 20c.; ▶Comanducci,
    Diz.; ▶Havlice, Idx. art. bio.
Feszl, Frigyes (Hungarian architect,
  1821-1884)   **AV**
    Bibl: ▶Thieme-Becker
Feszt, Ladislau (Romanian painter,
  printmaker, b.1930)   **BA**
    Bibl: ▶Vollmer, Künst.-Lex. 20. Jhr.
Feszti, Árpád→see Feszty, Árpád
Feszty, Árpád (Hungarian painter,
  author, 1856-1914)   **BA**
    Bibl: ▶Bénézit; ▶Thieme-Becker
  Feszti, Árpád   BA
Fet→see Fyt, Jan
Fetherolf, James (American painter,
  20th c.)   **BA**
    Bibl: Shreveport (LA, USA), Norton
    Art Gallery, America the beautiful
    (1975)
Fetherstonhaugh, Harold Lea
  (Canadian architect, 1887-1971)   **AV**
    Bibl: Journal of the Society for
    the Study of Architecturte in
    Canada, 1987 Mar., v.12, no.1,
    p.16
Fethi, Ihsan (Iraqi architect)   **AV**
    Bibl: Process: architecture, 1985
    May, no.58, p.151
Feti→see Fetti, Domenico
Feti or Fetti, Domenico→see Fetti,
  Domenico
Feti, Camillo (Italian artist, 17th
  cent.)   **WC**
Feti, Domenico→see Fetti, Domenico
Fette→see Fetti, Domenico
Fetti→see Fetti, Domenico
Fetti Genovese→see Fetti, Domenico

Fetti, Domenico   **BA GC PR**
  (Italian artist, 1589-1624)   **WI**
  (Italian artist, c.1589-1624)   **WC**
  (Italian painter, ca.1589-1624)   **BA PR**
  (Italian, ca.1589-1624)   **GC**
    Bibl: ▶Bénézit; ▶Bolaffi; ▶Encyc.
    world art; ▶Oxford comp. art;
    ▶RILA/BHA; ▶Thieme-Becker;
    ▶Witt checklist
  D Feti   PR
  D Fetti   PR
  D. Feti   PR
  D. Fette   PR
  D. Fetti   PR
  D. Fitti   PR
  Dé Feté   PR
  De Feti   PR
  De Fetti   PR
  Dom : Feti   PR
  Dom Fetti   PR
  Dom. Feti   PR
  Dom. Fetti   PR
  Dom: Fetti   PR
  Domenico Feti   PR
  Domenico Fetti   PR
  Domenico Fetti Genovese   PR
  Domin. Feti   PR
  Domini Fetti   PR
  Dominico Feti   PR
  Dominico Fetti   PR
  Dominico Fetto   PR
  Dominifitti   PR
  Dominique Feti   PR
  Feti   PR
  Feti or Fetti, Domenico   **WC**
  Feti, Domenico   **BA PR WI**
  Fette   PR
  Fetti   PR
  Fetti Genovese   PR
Fetti, Francesco [Unidentified]
  (Italian painter, act. bef.1648)   **PR**
    Bibl: Salernitano inventory,
    Naples, 1648
  Franc.o Fetti   PR
  Francesco Fetti   PR
Fetti, Giovanni di Francesco
  (Italian sculptor, architect, act.
    1355-1386)   **BA**
    Bibl: ▶Bessone-Aurelj, Scult. &
    arch. ital.; MITTEILUNGEN DES
    KUNSTHIST. INST IN FLORENZ
    XX/2 (1976) 127-158;
    ▶Thieme-Becker
Fetti, Mariano (Italian artist, 17th
  cent.)   **WC**
Fetting, Rainer (West German
  painter, filmmaker, b.1949)   **BA**
    Bibl: Flash art, 101 (Jan.-Feb.
    1981) pp.27-31; London (GBR),
    Royal Academy of Arts, A NEW
    SPIRIT IN PAINTING (1981)
Fetz, Hans-Peter (German architect,
  20th c.)   **BA**
    Bibl: Fetz, Jahrb. für Architektur
    (1985-86) 198

Fetzer, Eberhard *(German interior architect)*   **AV**
   Bibl: Architektur, Innenarchitektur, Technischer Ausbau, 1985 Mar., v.93, no.2, p.78

Fetzer, J. *(Swiss, active 1870s-1880s)*   **JG**

Fetzer, John *(American architect, 1882-1965)*   **BA**
   Bibl: ▶Avery obit. idx.; Prairie School Review, XII/1 (1975) pp. 5-22; ▶Withey, Amer. archts.

Feuchère, Jean-Jacques   **BA WC**
   (French artist, 1807-1852)   WC
   (French sculptor, printmaker, 1807-1852)   BA
   Bibl: ▶Bénézit; ▶Dict. biog. fran.; ▶Thieme-Becker

Feuchere, L. F. *(French, b. ca. 1750, d. 1828)*   **JG**

Feucht, Jacob → see Facht von Andernach, Jacob

Feuchtmair, Joseph → see Feichtmayer, Joseph Anton

Feuchtmayer, Johann Michael II → see Feichtmayr, Johann Michael II

Feuchtmayer, Joseph → see Feichtmayer, Joseph Anton

Feuchtmayer, Joseph Anton → see Feichtmayer, Joseph Anton

Feudel, Arthur *(American artist, b.1857)*   **WI**

Feuerbach → see Feuerbach, Anselm Friedrich

Feuerbach, Anselm → see Feuerbach, Anselm Friedrich

Feuerbach, Anselm Friedrich   **BA PR**
   (German artist, 1829-1880)   WC
   (German painter, 1829-1880)   BA PR
   (German, 1829-1880)   GC
   Bibl: ▶Brockhaus Enzyk.; ▶Encyc. world art; ▶Natl. union cat., pre-1956; ▶RILA/BHA; ▶Thieme-Becker
   Anselm Friedrich Feuerbach   PR
   Feuerbach   PR

Feuerbach, Anselm   **GC PR WC**

Feuerlein, Johann Peter *(German artist, 1668-1728)*   **WC**

Feuerman, Carole Jeane *(American sculptor, 20th c.)*   **BA**
   Bibl: Huntington (NY, USA), Heckscher Mus., 4 II: Shifting focus (1981)

Feuermüller, Carl → see Müller, Moritz Karl Friedrich

Feuerstein, Bedřich   **AV BA**
   (Czech architect and artist, 1892-1936)   AV
   (Czech architect, scenographer, 1892-1936)   BA
   Bibl: ▶Encic. spettacolo; ▶Encyc. world art; Umění, 1987, no.2, p.104

Feuerstein, Günther *(Austrian architect)*   **AV**
   Bibl: Transparent, 1984, v.15, no. 5-6, p.38

Feuerstein, J. *(Swiss, active ca. 1900)*   **JG**

Feuerstein, Martin   **GC WC**
   (French painter, 1856-1931)   GC
   (German artist, 1856-1931)   WC
   Bibl: ▶Bénézit

Feugas, Jean Pierre *(French architect, Paris, 1944-)*   **AV**

Feuillée, Louis *(French painter, 1660-1732)*   **BA**
   Bibl: ▶Marseille (FRA), Musée B.-A., Peinture Provence 17e s. (1978)

Feuillee, Rev. Pere L. *(French artist, 18th cent.)*   **WC**

Feuillois *(French menuisier, act. ca. 1776)*   **GC**
   Bibl: Feulner, Pantheon, v.9, no.4 (September 1929): 410

Feure, Georges de → see Feure, Georges de (George van Sluijters)

Feure, Georges de (George van Sluijters)   **BA**
   (Dutch painter in FRA, 1868-1943)   BA
   (French artist, 1868-)   WC
   Bibl: GBA LXXXII (Oct 1974) 231

Feure, Georges de   **WC**
   Sluijters, George van   BA

Feurer, René *(Swiss painter, architect, b.1940)*   **BA**
   Bibl: ▶Lex. zeitgen. Schweiz. Künstler

Feurstein, Joseph *(French ébéniste, 1733-1809, master 1767)*   **GC**
   Bibl: ▶Salverte, Ébénistes 18e s.

Feuser, Gerhard *(West German architect, Munich)*   **AV**
   Bibl: ▶Bund Deut. Arch. Hdbch., 1987

Fevre *(French artist, op.1765)*   **WC**

Fèvre, Marguerite De Gas *(French, 1842-1895)*   **BA**
   Bibl: Cabanne, Degas (1958); Fevre, Mon oncle Degas (1949); YALE UNIV. ART GALL. BULLETIN XXXVII (1978) 10-13
   Degas, Marguerite   BA

Février, Pierre *(French architect)*   **AV**
   Bibl: Connaissance des arts, 1984 Sept., no.391, p.71

Few, Elsie *(British artist, b.1909)*   **WI**
   Rogers, Claude Maurice, Mrs., (Elsie)   WI

Fey, Joseph → see Fay, Joseph

Feyen, Jacques Eugene   **GC WC**
   (French artist, 1815-1908)   WC
   (French painter, 1815-1908)   GC
   Bibl: ▶Thieme-Becker

Feyen-Perrin, François Nicolas Auguste   **GC WC**
   (French artist, 1826-1888)   WC
   (French painter, 1826-1888)   GC
   Bibl: ▶Thieme-Becker

Feyer, Cornelia *(West German landscape architect, Landshut)*   **AV**
   Bibl: Deutsches Architektenblatt, 1988 May, v.20, no.5, p.681

Feyerabend, Franz *(Swiss artist, 1755-1800)*   **WC**

Feyerabend, Johann Rudolf *(Swiss artist, 1779-1814)*   **WC**

Feylner, Simon → see Feilner, Simon

Feynes, Adolf → see Fényes, Adolf

Feys, Jan *(Belgian architect)*   **AV**
   Bibl: Monumenten en landschappen, 1986 May-June, v.5, no.3, p.8

Feytaud, Sophia *(French painter, 19th century)*   **GC**
   Bibl: ▶Bénézit

Ffaringdon, R. → see Ffarington, R.

Ffarington, R.   **WI**
   (British artist, 18th cent.)   WC
   (British artist, op.late 18th c.)   WI

Ffaringdon, R.   **WC**

Ffarington, Susan Maria *(British artist, 1808-1894)*   **WI**

Fi, József *(Hungarian craftsman, b.1908)*   **BA**
   Bibl: Kecskemeti, KERAMIK-FREUNDE-DER SCHWEIZ 98 (Sept 1983) 16

Fiacco or Flacco, Orlando → see Flacco, Orlando

Fiacco, Orlando → see Flacco, Orlando

Fiala, Jaromír *(Czech sculptor, 20th c.)*   **BA**
   Bibl: LEONARDO XII (summer 1979) 183-186

Fiala, R. *(Italian artist, 20th cent.)*   **WC**

Fiala, Ronald J. *(Architect, American)*   **AV**
   Bibl: GA houses, 1983 Mar., 13, p.168

Fialetti, Odoardo   **BA GC WC**
   (Italian artist, 1573-1638)   WC
   (Italian painter and printmaker, 1573-1638)   GC
   (Italian painter, printmaker, 1573-1638)   BA
   Bibl: ▶Bénézit; ▶Bolaffi; ▶RILA/BHA, 1986; ▶Thieme-Becker

Fialho, J.A. Judice *(Portuguese, 20th c.)*   **BA**
   Bibl: BELAS ARTES 31 (1977) 59-64

Fiali, Carl *(German(?) artist, 18th cent.)*   **WC**

Fialka, Olga *(Czech painter in HUN, 1848-1930)*   **BA**
   Bibl: Champlin, Cycl. ptrs.; ▶Havlice, Idx. art. bio.; Maguar Nemzeti Gal. Evkonyve, II, 1974
   Ferenczy, Károlyné   BA

Fiamberti, Tommaso   **BA GC**
   (Italian sculptor, d.1524/25)   BA
   (Italian sculptor,
    d.ca.1524/1525)   GC
    Bibl: ▶Bénézit; ▶Encyc. world art;
    ▶RILA/BHA; ▶Seymour, Sculp.
    Italy; TCI Firenze; ▶Thieme-Becker
   Flamberti, Tommaso   BA GC
   Framberti, Tommaso   BA
Fiamenco → see Fiammingo
fiamenghi → see Fiammingo
Fiamenghino → see Fiammingo
Fiamengho → see Fiammingo
fiamengo → see Fiammingo
Fiamengo, Iacobus *(Italian*
   cabinetmaker, act.1594-1602)   **BA**
    Bibl: Jervis, S., in V & A ALBUM IV
    (1985) 48-56
fiamingo → see Fiammingo
Fiamingo, Luigi *(Flemish painter,*
   act. ca.1533-ca.1560)   **GC**
    Bibl: Langedijk, Medici portraits,
    p.386
Fiammengo → see Fiammingo
Fiammeri or Fammieri,
   Giambattista → see Fiammeri,
   Giovanni Battista
Fiammeri, Giovanni Battista   **BA**
   (Italian artist, p.1530-1606)   WC
   (Italian painter, sculptor, after
    1530-1606)   BA
    Bibl: ▶Bolaffi; ▶Thieme-Becker;
    ▶Witt checklist
   Fiammeri or Fammieri,
    Giambattista   **WC**
Fiammingo *(Unknown painter)*   **PR**
   el flamenco   PR
   Fiamenco   PR
   fiamenghi   PR
   Fiamenghino   PR
   Fiamengho   PR
   fiamengo   PR
   fiamingo   PR
   Fiammengo   PR
   Flamengo   PR
Fiammingo (François
   Duquesnoy) → see Duquesnoy,
   François (il Fiammingo)
Fiammingo, Arrigo → see Broeck,
   Hendrick van den
Fiammingo, Enrico *(Italian artist,*
   op.c.1650)   **WC**
Fiammingo, Paolo → see Paolo
   Fiammingo
fiasella → see Fiasella, Domenico

Fiasella, Domenico   **BA GC PR**
   (Italian artist, 1589-1669)   WC
   (Italian painter, 1589-1669)   BA GC PR
    Bibl: ▶Bénézit; ▶Bolaffi;
    ▶RILA/BHA, 1986;
    ▶Thieme-Becker; Whitfield, Ptg.
    Naples 1606-1705; ▶Witt
    checklist
   Dom.o Fiasella   PR
   Domenico Fiasella   PR
   Domenico Fiaselle   PR
   fiasella   PR
Fiasella, Domenico (il
   Sarzana)   **GC WC**
   fiosella   PR
   Sarazana   BA
   Sarsana   PR
   Sarzana   PR
   Sarzano   PR
Fiasella, Domenico (il Sarzana) → see
   Fiasella, Domenico
Ficara, Franz *(Italian artist, 1926-)*   **WC**
Ficarelli, Felice → see Ficherelli, Felice
   (Felice Riposo)
Fichard, C. *(Dutch artist, 17th cent.)*   **WC**
Fichard, Johannes → see Fichard,
   Johannes C.
Fichard, Johannes C. *(Scribe,*
   traveller, 1512-1581)   **CE**
   Fichard, Johannes   CE
   Fichardus, Joannes   CE
Fichardus, Joannes → see Fichard,
   Johannes C.
Fichel → see Fichel, Eugène
Fichel, Eugène   **GC PR**
   (French artist, 1826-1895)   WC
   (French painter, 1826-1895)   PR
   (FRench, 1826-1895)   GC
    Bibl: ▶Thieme-Becker; ▶Witt
    checklist
   Eugene Fichel   PR
   Fichel   PR
Fichel, Eugene (Benjamin)   **WC**
Fichel, Eugene (Benjamin) → see
   Fichel, Eugène
Ficherelli or Ficarelli, Felice (Il
   Riposo) → see Ficherelli, Felice
   (Felice Riposo)
Ficherelli, Felice → see Ficherelli, Felice
   (Felice Riposo)
Ficherelli, Felice (Felice Riposo)   **BA PR**
   (Italian artist, 1605-1660)   WC
   (Italian painter, 1605-1669?)   BA
   (Italian painter, 1692-1768)   PR
    Bibl: ▶Bolaffi; CONNOISSEUR
    CC/805 (Mar 1979) 170; Gregori,
    Pitt. e scult. del 600 e 700;
    ▶RILA/BHA; ▶Thieme-Becker
   Felice Ficherelli   PR
   Felice Riposo   BA PR
   Ficarelli, Felice   BA
   Ficherelli or Ficarelli, Felice (Il
    Riposo)   **WC**
   Ficherelli, Felice   PR
   Roposo, Felice   BA

Fichet, Alexandre Lucien *(French*
   painter, 20th century)   **GC**
    Bibl: ▶Bénézit
Fichi, Ercole *(1595-1665)*   **AV**
Fichot, Charles *(French painter,*
   1817-1903)   **GC**
    Bibl: ▶Thieme-Becker
   Fichot, Michel Charles   GC
Fichot, Michel Charles → see Fichot,
   Charles
Fichtenberger, Bartholomaeus
   (German artist, op.1561-m.1592)   **WC**
Fichter, Robert *(American*
   photographer, b.1939)   **BA**
    Bibl: ▶Image; Los Angeles (CA,
    USA), UCLA Wight Gallery, Amer.
    photos (1976)
Fichtler, Jürgen *(East German*
   architect, professor at
   Bauakademie der DDR)   **AV**
    Bibl: Architektur der DDR, 1987
    Aug., v.36, no.8, p.46
Fichtner, J. *(German artist, 19th*
   cent.)   **WC**
Fick, David *(American painter, 20th*
   c.)   **BA**
    Bibl: Arts Mag. LVI/7 (Mar 1982),
    p.21; ▶Intl. dir. exh. artists, 1983
Fick, Gottfried *(Austrian architect,*
   Vienna)   **AV**
    Bibl: ▶Verzeich. Öst. Ziviltech.,
    1984
Fick, Roderich *(German architect,*
   1886-1955)   **BA**
    Bibl: ▶Neue deutsche Biog.;
    ▶Vollmer, Künst.-Lex. 20. Jhr.
Ficke, Fuk or Fyk, Nicolaes → see
   Ficke, Nicolaes
Ficke, Nicolaes   **GC PR**
   (Dutch artist, op.1642-m.c.1702) WC
   (Dutch painter, act. 1642-bef.
    1702, d. by 1702)   PR
   (Dutch painter, act.1642-d. ca.
    1702)   GC
    Bibl: Getty Photo Study Coll.;
    Getty Photo Study Coll. (Ptgs.);
    ▶Thieme-Becker; ▶Witt checklist
   Ficke, Fuk or Fyk, Nicolaes   **WC**
   Fuk, Nicolaes   GC
   Fyk, Nicolaes   GC
   Nicolaes Ficke   PR
Ficquet or Fiquet, Etienne *(French*
   artist, 1719-1794)   **WC**
Fictor → see Victors, Jan
Fida Ali, Habib *(Pakistani architect,*
   1936-)   **AV**
    Bibl: Mimar, 1982 Oct-Dec., no.6,
    p.7
Fidani → see Fidani, Orazio

Fidani, Orazio GC PR WC
  (Italian artist, c.1610-p.1656) WC
  (Italian painter, ca.1610-aft. 1656) PR
  (Italian, ca.1610-1656) GC
    Bibl: ▶Thieme-Becker; ▶Witt checklist
  Fidani PR
  Orazio Fidani PR
Fidanza → see Fidanza, Giuseppe
Fidanza, Francesco BA GC JG PR
  (Italian painter, 1747-1819) BA GC PR
  (Italian, active 1900-1910, Varese, Como) JG
    Bibl: ▶Bolaffi; ▶RILA/BHA, 1986; ▶Thieme-Becker
  Francesco Fidanza PR
Fidanza, Giuseppe *(Italian painter, 1750-1820)* PR
    Bibl: ▶Thieme-Becker
  Fidanza PR
  Giuseppi Fidanza PR
Fidanza, Gregorio GC WC
  (Italian artist, 1759-1823) WC
  (Italian painter, 1759-1823) GC
    Bibl: ▶Thieme-Becker
Fidanza, Prospero *(Italian painter, act. ca.1663)* PR
    Bibl: Andrea Sacchi, Ann Sutherland Harris, 1977, pp. 115 sqq.
  Prospero Fidanza PR
Fidanza, Raffaele *(Italian artist, 1797-1846)* WC
Fidelia Bridges → see Bridges, Fidelia
Fidelis *(Italian scribe, act.1502)* GC
    Bibl: Sotheby's London, July 3, 1984, lot 67
Fidelle, Marc *(French architect)* AV
    Bibl: AMC, 1987 Oct., no.17, p.44
Fiderbe, Luc → see Fayd'herbe, Lucas
Fidler, Anton *(German artist, op. 1828-1850)* WC
Fidler, Frank WC WI
  (British artist, 1910-) WC
  (British artist, b.1910) WI
Fidler, Harry WC WI
  (British artist, -1935) WC
  (British artist, op.1891-, d.1935) WI
Fidler, Laura WI
  (British artist, 20th cent.) WC
  (British artist, op.20th c.) WI
Fidler, Nora WC
Fidler, Nora → see Fidler, Laura
Fidman, Vladimir *(Russian architect, 20th c.)* BA
    Bibl: Dek. Iskusstvo SSSR, 246 (May 1978) p.32
Fidolini, Marco *(Italian painter, b.1945)* BA
    Bibl: Gallarate (ITA), Galleria Civica d'Arte moderna, FIDOLINI..., 1986 (RILA, ITA)
Fidus (Hugo Hoppener) *(German artist, 1868-1948)* WC

Fiebiger, Julius (Gottlieb Moritz Julius) *(German artist, 1813-1883)* WC
Fiechter, Arnold *(Swiss artist, 1879-1943)* WC
Fiedler, Bernhard *(Austrian artist, 1816-1904)* WC
Fiedler, Carl Christian *(German artist, 1789-1851)* WC
Fiedler, Günther *(West German architect, Heiligenhaus)* AV
    Bibl: ▶Bund Deut. Arch. Hdbch., 1987
Fiedler, Joachim *(German artist, 20th cent.)* WC
Fiedler, Johan-Christian *(German ébéniste, act.1750-1800, master 1786)* GC
    Bibl: ▶Salverte, Ébénistes 18e s.
Fiedler, Johann Christian GC WC
  (German artist, 1697-1765) WC
  (German painter, 1697-1765) GC
    Bibl: ▶Thieme-Becker
Fiedler, Wolfgang *(German architect, Stuttgart, 1930-)* AV
    Bibl: Deutsche Bauzeitung, 1985 Apr., v.119, no.4, p.128
Fiedorow, Michail *(Russian artist, 20th cent.)* WC
Fiedotow, Aleksandr *(Russian artist, 20th cent.)* WC
Fieffe, Jean-Jacques *(French, d. 1770)* JG
Fieger of Vienna [Unidentified] *(Unknown painter)* PR
    Bibl: (June 25, 1808, lot 83, Christie's)
Fiekierz, Szykier *(Polish artist, 19th cent.)* WC
Field, Dorothie → see Field, Dorothie S.
Field, Dorothie S. WI
  (British artist, 20th cent.) WC
  (British artist, op.1937-1939) WI
Field, Dorothie WC
Field, Duggie → see Fields, Duggie
Field, Erastus Salisbury BA PR WC WI
  (American artist, 1805-1900) WC WI
  (American painter, 1805-1900) BA PR
    Bibl: ▶Bénézit; Garbisch, 101 MASTERPIECES OF AM. PRIM. PRINTMAKING; ▶Groce, Artists Amer.; ▶RILA/BHA; ▶Young, Amer. artists
  Erastus Salisbury Field PR
Field, Freke *(British artist, op.1884-1894)* WI
Field, G.C. WC WI
  (British artist, op.1911-) WI
  (British(?) artist, op.1911) WC
Field, Hamilton Easter BA WC WI
  (American artist, 1873-1922) WC WI
  (American painter, printmaker, 1873-1922) BA
    Bibl: ▶Fielding's Amer. ptrs.; ▶Vollmer, Künst.-Lex. 20. Jhr.

Field, I. WC WI
  (British artist, op.1815) WC
  (British artist, op.1815-) WI
Field, John → see Field, John M.
Field, John L. *(American architect)* AV
Field, John M. WI
  (British artist, 1771-1841) WC WI
Field, John WC
Field, Maurice → see Feild, E. Maurice
Field, Robert BA WC WI
  (British artist, op.1810-m.1819) WC
  (British engraver, circa 1769-1819) WI
  (Canadian painter, ca.1769-1819) BA
    Bibl: ▶Harper, Early ptrs. Canada; ▶Thieme-Becker
  Fish, R. BA
Field, Robert (R. Fish) *(Canadian artist, b.1948)* BA
    Bibl: Vancouver (BC, CAN), Art Gallery, R.FISH (1978)
Field, Walter *(British artist, 1837-1901)* WC WI
Field, William *(British artist, 1848-1885)* WI
Field, William Scott *(American architect in the Office of the Architect of the Capitol, Austin, Tex)* AV
    Bibl: ▶AIA Pro File, 1987-88
Fielding → see Fielding, Nathan Theodore
Fielding family *(British painters, 19th c.)* BA
    Bibl: ▶Dict. natl. biog.
Fielding, Anthony Vandyke Copley BA WC WI
  (British artist, 1787-1855) WC WI
  (British painter, 1787-1855) BA
  (British, 1787-1855) GC
    Bibl: ▶Havlice, Idx. art. bio.; ▶Thieme-Becker
Fielding, Copley GC
Fielding, Basil WC WI
  (British artist, 1907-) WC
  (British artist, b.1907) WI
Fielding, Brian BA WC WI
  (British artist, 1933-) WC
  (British artist, b.1933) WI
  (British painter, b.1933) BA
    Bibl: ▶Dolman, Contemp. Brit. artists
Fielding, Copley → see Fielding, Anthony Vandyke Copley
Fielding, Felix Ferdinand Frederick Raffael *(British artist, circa 1874-1853)* WI
Fielding, Mary Anne *(British painter, act. 1821-1835)* PR
    Bibl: ▶Thieme-Becker
  Mary Anne Fielding PR
  Miss Walton PR

Fielding, Nathan Theodore   **PR WC WI**
   (British artist, 1747-circa 1814)   WI
   (British artist, op.1775-1818)   WC
   (British painter, 1747-ca.1814)   PR
    Bibl: ▶Mallalieu, Brit. watercolour
     artists; ▶Thieme-Becker
  Fielding   PR
  Nathan Theodore Fielding   PR
Fielding, Newton Smith →see
  Fielding, Newton Smith Limbird
Fielding, Newton Smith Limbird   **WI**
   (British artist, 1799-1856)   WC WI
    Bibl: ▶Engen, Victorian engravers
Fielding, Newton Smith   **WC**
Fielding, Thales →see Fielding, Thales
  Henry Augustus
Fielding, Thales Henry Augustus   **WI**
   (British artist, 1793-1837)   WC WI
Fielding, Thales   **WC**
Fielding, Theodore Henry
  Adolphus *(British artist, 1781-*
  1851)   **WC WI**
    Bibl: ▶Engen, Victorian engravers
Fielding, Thomas H. *(British artist,*
  op.19th c.)   WI
Fields, Darrell *(American*
  architecture student, Harvard,
  1988)   **AV**
    Bibl: Harvard Grad. Sch. of Design
     news, 1988 Spring, v.16, no.4,
     p.1
Fields, Duggie   **BA**
   (British artist, op.20th c.)   WI
   (British painter, 20th c.)   BA
    Bibl: CONNOISSEUR CCVIII/836
     (Oct 1981) 138-141; ▶Intl. dir.
     exh. artists, 1982
Field, Duggie   **WI**
Fiene →see Fiene, Ernest
Fiene, Ernest   **PR WC WI**
   (American artist, 1894-)   WC
   (American artist, 1894-1965)   WI
   (American painter, 1894-1966)   PR
    Bibl: Falk, Turner; ▶WWW Amer.
     art
  Ernest Fiene   PR
  Fiene   PR
Fiene, Paul *(American sculptor, exh.*
  1934)   **GC**
    Bibl: ▶Opitz, Amer. sculptors
Fienga Painter *(South Italian vase-*
  painter, 4th century BC)   **GC**
    Bibl: ▶Trendall, Red-fig. vases
     Lucania
Fier, Bruce *(American artist, 20th c.)*   **BA**
    Bibl: JOURNAL OF THE L.A. INST.
     OF CONT. ART 7 (Aug-Sept 1975)
     40-41
Fieravanti, Aristotele →see Fioravanti,
  Aristotele
Fieravino →see Fieravino, Francesco

Fieravino, Francesco   **GC PR**
   (Italian artist, op.1650-1680)   WC
   (Italian painter, act. 1650-1680)   PR
   (Italian, act. ca.1650-1680)   GC
    Bibl: (September, 1813, lot 66,
     Anderson); ▶Thieme-Becker; ▶Witt
     checklist
  Fieravino   PR
Fieravino, Francesco (Il Maltese
  or Le Maltais)   **WC**
  Francesco Fieravino   PR
  Il Maltese   GC PR
  Maltese   PR
  Mattessey   PR
Fieravino, Francesco (Il Maltese or Le
  Maltais) →see Fieravino, Francesco
Fierfort, Vincent *(French architect,*
  Epernay)   **AV**
    Bibl: Architectes architecture,
     1988 July-Aug., no.189, p.17
Fierlants, Edmond *(Belgian*
  photographer, 1819-1869)   **BA**
    Bibl: Antiek, IX/8 (Mar. 1975) pp.
     786-797; BN 31 suppl 3
Fierlants, Nicolaas Marten   **BA WC**
   (Dutch artist, c.1622-1694)   WC
   (Flemish painter, ca.1622-1694)   BA
    Bibl: ▶Bénézit; ▶Thieme-Becker
Fierros, Dionisio *(Spanish artist,*
  c.1830-a.1899)   **WC**
Fieschi, Giannetto *(Italian artist,*
  1921-)   **WC**
Fiesel, Christopher →see Füssl,
  Christopher
Fiesole Illuminator   **JG**
Fiesole, Giovanni da →see Angelico,
  Fra
Fiesole, Mino da →see Mino da
  Fiesole
Fiesole, Silvio da →see Cosini, Silvio
Fiess, Géo *(French interior designer)*   **AV**
    Bibl: Architecture intérieure créé,
     1985 Aug.-Sept., no.207, p.103
Fiessinger, Franz Gabriel *(German*
  printmaker, 1752-1807)   **BA**
    Bibl: ▶Bénézit; Jahrb. der Staatl.
     Kunstsamml. Baden-Württemberg
     XXII (1985) 90; ▶Thieme-Becker
Fiesso, Sigismondo da →see
  Sigismondo da Fiesso
Fieve, Cárlos Luis de Ribera y →see
  Ribera y Fieve, Cárlos Luis de
Fievre, Yolande *(French artist, 20th*
  cent.)   **WC**
Fife, Ivy G. *(New Zealander painter,*
  1905-1976)   **BA**
    Bibl: Christchurch (NZL), Robt.
     McDougall Art Gallery, IVY FIFE
     (1977)
Fife, Phyllis *(American artist,*
  b.1948)   **BA**
    Bibl: Regina (Sask, CAN), U.Sask.
     Gallery, A new generation (1982)
Fifield, William *(British painter,*
  1777-1857)   **BA**
    Bibl: ▶Honey, Euro. ceramic;
     ▶Thieme-Becker

Figanieres, Henry de *(French artist,*
  20th cent.)   **WC**
Figari, Andrea *(Italian artist, 20th*
  cent.)   **WC**
Figari, Filippo *(Italian artist, 1885-)*   **WC**
Figari, Pedro *(South and Central*
  American artist, 1861-1938)   **WC**
Figini, Luigi   **AV BA**
   (Italian architect, 1903-1984)   AV
   (Italian architect, b.1903)   BA
    Bibl: ▶Contemp. archts.;
     ▶Portoghesi, Diz. arch. e
     urbanistica
Figino, Ambrogio
  Giovanni   **BA GC WC WI**
   (Italian artist, 1548-1608)   WC WI
   (Italian painter, 1548-1608)   BA GC
    Bibl: ▶Bénézit; ▶Bolaffi;
     ▶RILA/BHA, 1986;
     ▶Thieme-Becker
Figino, Gerolamo →see Figino,
  Girolamo
Figino, Girolamo *(Italian painter,*
  act. 2nd half 16th cent.)   **PR**
    Bibl: ▶RILA/BHA; ▶Thieme-Becker
  Girolamo Figino   PR
Figino, Girolamo *(Italian painter,*
  16th c.)   **BA**
    Bibl: ▶Thieme-Becker
Figino, Girolamo *(Draughtsman,*
  painter, ante 1600-post 1550)   **CE**
  Figino, Gerolamo   CE
Figlia di Mr. Luigi [Unidentified]
  (Unknown painter)   **PR**
    Bibl: Corsini inventory, Rome,
     1750
figlia di Paolo de Matteis →see
  Matteis, Emmanuella de
figlia di Paolo de Matteis →see
  Matteis, Felice de
Figlia di Paolo de Matteis →see
  Matteis, Mariangela de
figlio di Brucoli →see Brueghel,
  Abraham (Ryngraaf)
figlio di Giovanni Benedetto
  Castiglione →see Castiglione,
  Francesco
figlio di Recco →see Recco, Giuseppe
figlio di Riviano →see Codazzi,
  Niccolò
figlio di Scipione Compagno →see
  Compagno, Scipione (son of)
  [Unidentified]
figlio di Viviano →see Codazzi,
  Niccolò
figliolo del Tintoretto →see
  Tintoretto, Domenico (Domenico
  Robusti)
Figonetto →see Granello, Niccolò
  (Figonetto)
Figoretto, Francesco [Unidentified]
  (Unknown painter)   **PR**
    Bibl: Pignatelli inventory, Naples,
     1723, (originally read as
     "Tigoretto" and changed after
     Delfino correction)
  Francesco Figoretto   PR

Figueiredo, Christovaeo de
 (Portuguese artist, op.1518-1540) **WC**
Figuera, Juan *(Spanish artist, op.c.
 1455-1456)* **WC**
Figueroa, Leonardo de *(Spanish
 architect, ca.1650-1730)* **BA**
  Bibl: ▶Encyc. world art; ▶Kubler,
  Art & arch. ESP & PRT;
  ▶Thieme-Becker
Figueroa, Miguel de *(Spanish
 architect, act.ca.1692-1731)* **BA**
  Bibl: ▶Portoghesi, Diz. arch. e
  urbanistica; ▶Thieme-Becker
Figuière, François *(French painter,
 b.1828, act.1847)* **BA**
  Bibl: Hardouin-Fugier, Bull. Soc.
  Hist. Art Fran. (1981) pp.240-245,
  n.34
Figurelli, Giuilio *(Italian architect)* **AV**
  Bibl: Architecture d'aujourd'hui,
  1984 Oct., no.235, p.50
Figurino→see Tonducci, Giulio (il
 Figurino)
Fijałkowski, Stanisław *(Polish
 printmaker, b.1922)* **BA**
  Bibl: Cincinnati (OH, USA), Art
  Mus., Eastern Euro. printmkrs.
  (1975)
Fijt, Joannes→see Fyt, Jan
Fikentscher, Jenny *(German painter,
 printmaker, 1869-1959)* **BA**
  Bibl: ▶Bénézit; Karlsruhe (DEU),
  Staat. Kunsthalle, Grotzinger
  Malerkolonie (1975);
  ▶Thieme-Becker
 Nottebohin, Jenny **BA**
Fikentscher, Otto *(German painter,
 printmaker, sculptor, 1862-1945)* **BA**
  Bibl: ▶Bénézit; Karlsruhe (DEU),
  Staat. Kunsthalle, Grotzinger
  Malerkolonie (1975);
  ▶Thieme-Becker; ▶Vollmer,
  Künst.-Lex. 20. Jhr.
Filarete→see Filarete (Antonio
 Averlino)
Filarete (Antonio Averlino) **BA**
 (15th century) **AV**
 *(Italian architect, sculptor, ca.
 1400-1469)* **BA**
 (Italian, ca.1400-ca.1469) **GC**
 *(Sculptor, architect,
 draughtsman, c.1400-c.1469)* **CE**
  Bibl: ▶Diz. biog. ital.; ▶Forrer,
  Medallists; ▶Thieme-Becker
 Averlino, Antonio **BA**
 Averlino, Antonio, detto Filarete **CE**
 Filarete **CE**
 **Filarete, Antonio Averlino,
  known as** **AV**
 **Filarete, Antonio di Pietro
  Averlino** **GC**
*Filarete, Antonio Averlino, known
 as→see* Filarete (Antonio Averlino)
*Filarete, Antonio di Pietro
 Averlino→see* Filarete (Antonio
 Averlino)

Filarski, Dirk Herman Willem **GC WC**
 (Dutch artist, 1885-1964) **WC**
 *(Dutch painter and
 draughtsman, 1885-1964)* **GC**
  Bibl: ▶Thieme-Becker
Filassier, Michel-Étienne *(French
 silversmith, master 1745)* **GC**
  Bibl: ▶Nocq, Poinçon de Paris
Filatčev, Oleg *(Russian painter,
 b.1937)* **BA**
  Bibl: John Bowlt corresp.
Filbert, Sadie→see Adams, Beatrice
Filcer, Luis *(Dutch artist, b.1927)* **BA**
  Bibl: ▶MoMA libr. cat.;
  Woesterburg, LUIS FILCER (1979)
Fildes, Denis→see Fildes, Quinton
Fildes, Fanny *(British artist, op.
 1875-, d.circa 1927)* **WI**
 Woods, Fanny, Miss **WI**
Fildes, Luke **BA**
 (British artist, 1843-1927) **WI**
 (British artist, 1844-1927) **WC**
 (British painter, 1844-1927) **BA**
 (British, 1844-1927) **GC**
  Bibl: ▶Dict. natl. biog., 1922-1930
  suppl.; ▶Thieme-Becker; ▶Witt
  checklist
 Fildes, Samuel Luke **WI**
 Fildes, Sir Samuel Luke **GC WC**
Fildes, Quinton **WI**
 (British artist, 1889-) **WC**
 (British artist, b.1889) **WI**
 Fildes, Denis **WC**
Fildes, Samuel Luke→see Fildes, Luke
Fildes, Sir Samuel Luke→see Fildes,
 Luke
Filguéiras Lima, João *(Brazilian
 architect, 1932-)* **AV**
  Bibl: ▶Contemp. archts.
Filho, Augusto Alves *(Brazilian
 architect)* **AV**
  Bibl: Projeto, 1987 Oct., no.104,
  p.140
Filho, José Daher *(Brazilian
 architect)* **AV**
  Bibl: Projeto, 1987 Sept., no.103,
  p.128
Filho, Lourenço Diegues *(Brazilian
 architect, Rio de Janeiro)* **AV**
  Bibl: Projeto, 1988 Mar., no.108,
  p.82
Filho, Ney Pompeo *(Brazilian
 architect)* **AV**
  Bibl: Projeto, 1985 May, no.75,
  p.74
Filhol, Alain *(French architect)* **AV**
  Bibl: Architecture intérieure créé,
  1985 June-July, no.206, p.86
Filiasi *(Italian artist, op.1749)* **WC**
Filiger, Charles **BA WC**
 (French artist, 1863-1928) **WC**
 *(French painter, printmaker,
 musician, 1863-1928)* **BA**
  Bibl: ▶Bénézit; ▶Havlice, Idx. art.
  bio.; ▶Vollmer, Künst.-Lex. 20.
  Jhr.
 Filliger, Charles **BA**

Filinov, Pavel Nikolaevič→see
 Filonov, Pavel Nikolaevič
Filipart, Jean Jacques→see Flipart,
 Jean Jacques
Filipe, Ricardo da Cruz→see Cruz-
 Filipe, Ricardo da
Filipkiewicz, Stephan *(Polish artist,
 1879-)* **WC**
filipo de ligorno→see Filippo
 Napoletano
Filipo Lauri→see Lauri, Filippo
Filipov, I.F. *(Russian artist, 20th
 cent.)* **WC**
Filipovic, Franio *(Yugoslav artist,
 1930-)* **WC**
Filippelli, Cafiero *(Italian painter,
 1889-1973)* **BA**
  Bibl: ▶Comanducci, Diz.; Donzelle,
  CAFIERO FILIPPELLI (1982);
  ▶Vollmer, Künst.-Lex. 20. Jhr.
Filippi, Camillo **BA PR WC**
 (Italian artist, 1500-1574) **WC**
 (Italian artist, ca.1500-1574) **BA PR**
  Bibl: ▶Bolaffi; ▶RILA/BHA; TCI
  Emilia-Romagna; ▶Thieme-Becker
 Camillo Filippi **PR**
Filippi, Cesare *(Italian painter, 1536-
 1602)* **PR**
  Bibl: ▶Thieme-Becker
 Cesare Filippi **PR**
Filippi, Fernando de *(Italian artist,
 filmmaker, b.1940)* **BA**
  Bibl: ▶Bénézit; ▶MoMA libr. cat.;
  Vancouver (BC, CAN), Art Gallery,
  Mannerism (1982)
 De Filippi, Fernando **BA**
Filippi, Giovanni Maria *(Italian
 sculptor, architect, 16th-17th cs.)* **BA**
  Bibl: ▶Bénézit; ▶Encic. italiana;
  ▶Portoghesi, Diz. arch. e
  urbanistica; ▶Thieme-Becker
Filippi, Sebastiano (Bastianino) **BA PR**
 (Italian artist, 1532-1602) **WC**
 *(Italian mural painter, Ferrara,
 1532-1602)* **AV**
 (Italian painter, 1532-1602) **BA PR**
 (Italian painter, ca. 1532-1602) **GC**
  Bibl: ▶Bolaffi; ▶Diz. biog. ital.;
  Mezzetti & Mattaliano, idx.
  Baruffaldi's ''Vite pitt. ferraresi'',
  v.3, p.19; ▶RILA/BHA;
  ▶Thieme-Becker
 Bastianino **AV BA PR**
 Bastianino, Sebastiano (Filippi) **WC**
 **Filippi, Sebastiano (called
  Bastianino)** **GC**
 **Filippi, Sebastiano, called
  Bastianino** **AV**
 Sebastiano Filippi **PR**
 Sebastiano Filippi (Bastianino) **PR**
*Filippi, Sebastiano (called
 Bastianino)→see* Filippi,
 Sebastiano (Bastianino)
*Filippi, Sebastiano, called
 Bastianino→see* Filippi, Sebastiano
 (Bastianino)

Filippini, Felice *(Italian artist, 20th cent.)*   **WC**

Filippini, Francesco *(Italian artist, 1853-1895)*   **WC**

Filippino Fiorentino→see Lippi, Filippino

Filippino Lippi→see Lippi, Filippino

Filippo *(Italian architect and stonemason, act. 1210-1231)*   **GC**
  Bibl: ▶Thieme-Becker
  Maestro Filippo   GC
  Master Filippo   GC

Filippo *(Italian sculptor, act.1162)*   **BA**
  Bibl: Arte e cult. artistica a Lucca, 21-33; ▶Bessone-Aurelj, Scult. & arch. ital.; TCI Toscana, p.245

Filippo Abbiati→see Abbiati, Filippo

Filippo Agricola→see Agricola, Filippo

Filippo Andreola→see Andreola, Filippo

Filippo Andreoli→see Andreola, Filippo

Filippo Bellini→see Bellini, Filippo

Filippo Carcano→see Carcano, Filippo

Filippo Ceppaluni→see Ceppaluni, Filippo

Filippo d'Angeli→see Filippo Napoletano

Filippo da Carona *(Italian sculptor, act.1509)*   **BA**
  Bibl: Pulin, C., EARLY RENAISSANCE SCULPTURE, PH.D. 1984, Univ. of TX at Austin; ▶Thieme-Becker
  Carona, Filippo da   BA

Filippo da Venezia *(Italian sculptor, act.1332-1334)*   **BA**
  Bibl: ▶Bénézit; ▶Thieme-Becker
  Filippo de'Santi da Venezia   BA
  Santi, Filippo de'   BA

Filippo da Verona   **BA WC**
  (Italian artist, op.1509-1515)   WC
  (Italian painter, act.1509-1514)   BA
  Bibl: ▶Bolaffi; ▶Thieme-Becker; ▶Witt checklist

Filippo dalle prospettive→see Gagliardi, Filippo

Filippo de gli Angioli→see Filippo Napoletano

Filippo de Pisis→see De Pisis, Filippo (Luigi Tibertelli)

Filippo de Veris→see Veris, Filippolo de'

Filippo de'Santi da Venezia→see Filippo da Venezia

Filippo degl'Angeli→see Filippo Napoletano

Filippo degl'Angioli→see Filippo Napoletano

Filippo degli Angeli→see Filippo Napoletano

Filippo del Lauro→see Lauri, Filippo

Filippo dell'Angeli→see Filippo Napoletano

Filippo delle Prospettive→see Gagliardi, Filippo

Filippo di Giovanni *(Italian master mason, act.1419, d. before 1456)*   **BA**
  Bibl: Battisti, Brunelleschi; ▶Thieme-Becker
  Giovanni, Filippo di   BA
  Pippo di Giovanni   BA

Filippo di Lauro→see Lauri, Filippo

Filippo di Liagno→see Filippo Napoletano

filippo di liviano→see Filippo Napoletano

Filippo di Matteo Torelli→see Torelli, Filippo di Matteo

Filippo di Memmo→see Lippo Memmi

Filippo di Rosa→see Roos, Philipp Peter

Filippo Falciatore→see Falciatore, Filippo

Filippo Franghino→see Franchino, Filippo [Unidentified]

Filippo Furini→see Furini, Filippo

Filippo Gagliardi→see Gagliardi, Filippo

Filippo Gagliardo→see Gagliardi, Filippo

Filippo Gherardi→see Gherardi, Filippo (Sancasciani)

Filippo Giannetti→see Giannetti, Filippo

Filippo Indoni→see Indoni, Filippo

Filippo Latini→see Latini, Filippo

Filippo Laura→see Lauri, Filippo

Filippo Lauri→see Lauri, Filippo

Filippo Lauro→see Lauri, Filippo

Filippo lavoro→see Lauri, Filippo

Filippo Leni→see Filippo Napoletano

Filippo Lippi→see Lippi, Filippo

Filippo Lucatelli→see Lucatelli, Filippo [Unidentified]

Filippo Lucci→see Lucci, Filippo [Unidentified]

Filippo Maria Burci Steccuti→see Steccuti, Filippo Maria Burci [Unidentified]

Filippo Maria Galletti→see Galletti, Filippo Maria

Filippo Maurili Genovese→see Maurili, Filippo [Unidentified]

Filippo Mazzola→see Mazzola, Filippo

Filippo Naldini→see Naldini, Filippo

Filippo Napoletano   **BA PR VO**
  (Italian artist, c.1600-c.1640)   WC
  (Italian painter, ca. 1587-ca. 1629)   VO
  (Italian painter, ca.1587-aft. 1629)   PR
  (Italian painter, ca.1600-ca. 1640)   GC
  (Italian painter, printmaker, ca. 1587-after 1629)   BA
  Bibl: ▶Bolaffi; ▶Bryan, Ptrs. & engravers; ▶Diz. biog. ital., III, p. 196 (often erroneously confused with the Spanish painter Felipe Liaño, 'el pequeño Tiziano'); ▶Libr. of Congr. Name Auth. File, NAFR9130690; Pilkington's dict. of ptrs.; ▶RILA/BHA; Rome, Villa Farnesina, Incisori napoletani (1981); ▶Thieme-Becker

Angeli, Filippo d'   **BA GC**
Angeli, Filippo de Liano d' (Il Napoletano)   **WC**
  felippo   PR
  Felippo dell'Angeli   PR
  Felippo Nap.no   PR
  felippo napolitano   PR
  filipo de ligorno   PR
  Filippo d'Angeli   BA PR
  Filippo de gli Angioli   PR
  Filippo degl'Angeli   PR
  Filippo degl'Angioli   PR
  Filippo degli Angeli   PR
  Filippo dell'Angeli   PR
  Filippo di Liagno   BA
  filippo di liviano   PR
  Filippo Leni   PR

Filippo Napoletano (Filippo d'Angeli)   **PR**
  Filippo Napolitano   PR
  Filippo napulitano   PR
  Il Napolitano   PR
  Leni   PR
  Liagno, Filippo di   BA
  Liagno, Teodoro Filippo de   BA
  Napoletano, Filippo   BA
  Ph. Napolitain   PR
  Ph.e Napolitano   PR
  Philippe Napolitain   PR
  Philippo Neapolitano   PR

Filippo Napoletano (Filippo d'Angeli)→see Filippo Napoletano

Filippo Napolitano→see Filippo Napoletano

Filippo napulitano→see Filippo Napoletano

Filippo Romano→see Gagliardi, Filippo

Filippo Roos→see Roos, Philipp Peter

Filippo Tarchiani→see Tarchiani, Filippo

Filippo Villari→see Villari, Filippo [Unidentified]

Filippo Vitale→see Vitale, Filippo

Filiputti, G. *(Italian architect)* **AV**
Bibl: Lotus ionternational, 1987, no.54, p.114

Filjanskaja, Vera Grigorevna
(Russian ceramist, b.ca.1900) **BA**
Bibl: Dek Iskusstvo (Jan 1976) 42-43

Fill, Charles W. *(American architect)* **AV**
Bibl: Chicago architectural journal, 1989,no.7, p.106

Filla, Emil **BA WC**
(Czech artist, 1882-1953) WC
(Czech painter, sculptor, 1882-1953) BA
Bibl: ▶Bénézit; ▶Fogg Mus. Libr. cat.; ▶Vollmer, Künst.-Lex. 20. Jhr.

Fillebrown, F.E. *(Engraver, op.1850-)* **WI**

Filler, Robert *(American interior designer, San Francisco, Calif)* **AV**
Bibl: Interior design, 1987 Aug., v.58, no.10, p.220

Fillet Group *(South Italian vase-painters, 4th century BC)* **GC**
Bibl: ▶Trendall, Red-fig. vases Lucania

Fillet Painter *(Campanian vase-painter)* **GC**
Bibl: ▶Trendall, Red-fig. vases Lucania

Filleul, Anne Rosalie de (nee Bocquet) *(French artist, 1752-1794)* **WC**

Fillia, Luigi Colombo **GC WC**
(Italian artist, 1904-) WC
(Italian draughtsman, 1904-1936) GC
Bibl: ▶Bénézit
Colombo, Luigi GC

Fillian, John **WC WI**
(British artist, op.1658-, d.circa 1680) WI
(British artist, op.1658-1680) WC

Filliger, Charles→see Filiger, Charles
Filliou→see Filliou, Robert

Filliou, Robert **BA**
(French artist, 20th cent.) WC
(French artist, b.1926) BA
Bibl: ▶Art Index, v.39; ▶Bénézit; ▶Gorenflo, Bild. Künstler; ▶Intl. dir. exh. artists; ▶Natl. union cat., 1956

Filliou **WC**

Fillipo Laura→see Lauri, Filippo
Fillippo Laura→see Lauri, Filippo

Fillon *(French, active late 19th century (also Fillon & Heuse))* **JG**

Fillon, Arthur *(French artist, 1900-)* **WC**

Fillpot, Bob G. *(Architect, Houston, TX)* **AV**
Bibl: ▶AIA Pro File, 1983

Filmer, F. *(Engraver)* **WI**

Filmer, H. *(Engraver)* **WI**

Filmus, Anatol→see Filmus, Tully

Filmus, Michael *(American painter, b.1943)* **BA**
Bibl: Pittsfield (MA, USA), Berkshire Mus., Filmus (1980)

Filmus, Stephen *(American painter, b.1948)* **BA**
Bibl: Pittsfield (MA, USA), Berkshire Mus., Filmus (1980)

Filmus, Tully *(American painter, b.1908)* **BA**
Bibl: ▶MoMA libr. cat.; ▶WW Amer. Art
Filmus, Anatol BA

Filocamo, Antonio *(Italian painter, 1699-1743)* **PR**
Bibl: ▶Thieme-Becker
Antonio Filocamo PR
Domenico Antonio Filocamo PR

Filocamo, Paolo *(Italian painter, act. 18th century)* **PR**
Bibl: ▶Thieme-Becker
D. Paolo Filocamo PR
Paolo Filocamo PR

Filonio [Unidentified] *(Unknown painter)* **PR**
Bibl: Filomarino inventory dated 1634

Filonov, Pavel→see Filonov, Pavel Nikolaevič

Filonov, Pavel Nikolaevič **BA**
(Russian artist, op.1912) WC
(Russian painter, theorist, 1883-1941) BA
Bibl: Misler & Bowlt; ▶Oxford comp. 20c. art; ▶Phaidon 20c. art; ▶Witt checklist
Filinov, Pavel Nikolaevič BA

Filonov, Pavel **WC**

Filosa, Giovanni Battista *(Italian artist, 1850-1935)* **WC**

Filosof, Alber *(Finnish architect)* **AV**

Filottrano Painter **GC**
Bibl: ▶Beazley, Attic red-fig. vase-ptrs.

Filson, Ron→see Filson, Ronald

Filson, Ronald *(American architect)* **AV**
Filson, Ron AV

Filugelli, Filippo *(Italian woodcarver, b.1477, act.1542)* **BA**
Bibl: Morselli, ANTICHITA VIVA XXI/1 (1982) 46

Filüts [Unidentified] *(Unknown painter)* **PR**
Bibl: Closterman inventory, Amsterdam, 1711

filz dud. Sr. Cornu→see Cornu, Nicolas

Fima, Efraim *(Israeli painter, b.1916)* **BA**
Bibl: ▶Bénézit; Cape Town (ZAF), S. African Natl. Gallery, Israeli art (1980); ▶MoMA libr. cat.
Roeytenberg, Ephraïm BA

Finart, (David) Noel Dieudonne→see Finart, David Noël Dieudonné

Finart, David Noël Dieudonné **GC**
(French artist, 1797-1852) WC
(French painter, 1797-1852) GC
Bibl: ▶Bénézit

Finart, (David) Noel Dieudonne **WC**

Finch *(American, active 1880s (Finch Studio))* **JG**

Finch, Alfred William **BA**
(Belgian artist, 1854-1930) WC
(Belgian ceramist, printmaker, painter in FIN, 1854-1930) BA
Bibl: ▶Bénézit; ▶Boger, World pott. & porc.; ▶Encyc. world art; ▶Penguin dec. arts; ▶Thieme-Becker; ▶Vollmer, Künst.-Lex. 20. Jhr.

Finch, Alfred William (Willy) **WC**
Finch, Alfred William (Willy)→see Finch, Alfred William

Finch, Barbara *(American sculptor, 20th c.)* **BA**
Bibl: Swimeley

Finch, Daniel **WI**
(British artist, 1789-1868) WC WI

Finch, The Hon. Daniel **WC**

Finch, E.E. *(American artist, op.1833-1850)* **WI**

Finch, Elizabeth **WC WI**
(British artist, 19th cent.) WC
(British artist, op.1853-) WI

Finch, Francis Oliver **BA GC WC WI**
(British artist, 1802-1862) WC WI
(British painter, 1802-1862) BA
(British, 1802-1862) GC
Bibl: ▶Dict. natl. biog.; ▶Thieme-Becker; ▶Witt checklist; ▶Wood, Victorian ptrs.

Finch, George *(British architect, Lewes)* **AV**
Bibl: ▶RIBA members, 1984

Finch, James H. **AV**

Finch, Keith **WC WI**
(American artist, 1920-) WC
(American artist, 1920-2020) WI

Finch, Ray *(British ceramist, b.1914)* **BA**
Bibl: Ceramics monthly, XXVIII/3 (Mar. 1980) pp.61-65

Finch, The Hon. Daniel→see Finch, Daniel

Fincher, John H. *(American painter, b.1941)* **BA**
Bibl: ▶WW Amer. Art, 1981

Finck, Giuseppe *(Austrian ceramist in ITA, 1735/36-1789)* **BA**
Bibl: Bertocchi, Carrobbio, XIV (1988) (docs), pp.37-46

Finck, Johann Lorenz→see Fink, Johann Lorenz
Finck, Lorenz→see Fink, Johann Lorenz

Finck, Thiébaud *(French wigmaker, photographer, 1798-1890)* **BA**
Bibl: Morand, CAHIERS ALSACIENS D'ARCHAEOLOGIE, D'ART, ET D'HISTOIRE, XXX (1987), p. 225-242

Fincke, Caspar *(Danish ironsmith, ca.1584-1655)* **BA**
Bibl: ▶Thieme-Becker; ▶Weilbach, Kunst.leks.

Find, Ludwig Frederik *(Danish artist, 1869-1945)* **WC**

Finlay, H. *(Australian artist, 19th cent.)*   **WC**

Finlay, Hugh *(American cabinetmaker, 19th c.)*   **BA**
  Bibl: Baltimore (MD, USA), Mus. Art, Baltimore furniture (1947); Elder, Baltimore furniture

Finlay, Ian Hamilton   **AV BA WI**
  (British artist, b.1925)   **WI**
  (British poet, artist, b.1925)   **BA**
  (Scottish artist, garden designer, 1925-)   **AV**
  Bibl: Archives of Amer. art jrnl. XIV/4 (1974); CONNAISSANCE DES ARTS 342 (Aug 1980) 38-47; Contemp. poets of Eng. language; ▶Libr. of Congr. Name Auth. File

Finlay, John *(American cabinetmaker, 19th c.)*   **BA**
  Bibl: Baltimore (MD, USA), Mus. Art, Baltimore furniture (1947); Elder, Baltimore furniture

Finlayson, A.S. *(British artist, op. 1940-)*   **WI**

Finlayson, John *(British artist, 1730-1776)*   **WC WI**

Finlayson, Walter Allen *(American artist, 1919-op.1990)*   **WI**

Finn, Alfred Charles *(American architect, 1883-1964)*   **AV**
  Bibl: Alfred C. Finn: builder of Houston

Finn, Christopher J. *(Canadian artist, b.1950)*   **BA**
  Bibl: ▶Artists Canada; Paris (FRA), Ctr culturel canadien, The grand western Canadian screen shop (1977)

Finn, David *(American photographer, b.1921)*   **BA**
  Bibl: ▶WW Amer. Art, 1984

Finn, David *(American painter, 20th c.)*   **BA**
  Bibl: ART MAG, LIX/1 (Sept 1984) 15

Finn, David Thurman *(American artist, b.1952)*   **BA**
  Bibl: Köcher. KUNSTFORUM INT'L 67, 11, nov '83, p.177-181

Finn, Herbert J. → *see* Finn, Herbert John

Finn, Herbert John   **WI**
  (British artist, 1860)   **WC**
  (British artist, 1861-1942)   **WI**

Finn, Herbert J.   **WC**

Finn, Paul *(British artist, b.1957)*   **WI**

Finn-Kelcey, Rose *(British artist, 20th c.)*   **BA**
  Bibl: ▶Art Index, Nov. 1979-Oct. 1980; Tickner, OXFORD ART JOURNAL III/1 (Apr 1980) 58-72

Kelcey, Rose Finn   **BA**

Finnberg, Gustaf Wilhelm   **BA**
  (Finnish artist, 1784-1833)   **WC**
  (Finnish painter, printmaker, 1784-1833)   **BA**
  Bibl: ▶Svenskt konst.-lex.; ▶Thieme-Becker

Finnberg, Gustav Wilhelm   **WC**
Finnberg, Gustav Wilhelm → *see* Finnberg, Gustaf Wilhelm

Finne, Gunnar *(Finnish sculptor, 1886-1952)*   **BA**
  Bibl: ATENEUMIN TAIDEMUSEO XX (1975-76) 2-9;38-41; ▶Vollmer, Künst.-Lex. 20. Jhr.

Finnegan, Sharyn Marie *(American painter, art administrator, b.1946)*   **BA**
  Bibl: ▶WW Amer. Art, 1980

Finnemore, Joseph *(British artist, 1860-1939)*   **WI**

Finney, Harry *(American artist, op. 1875-1925)*   **WI**

Finney, Samuel *(British artist, 1718-1719-1798)*   **WI**
  Bibl: ▶Fisher, Watercolour ptrs.

Finnie, John *(British artist, 1829-1907)*   **WC WI**

Finnis, Valerie *(British artist, op.20th c.)*   **WI**

Finnur Jonsson → *see* Jonsson, Finnur

Finoglia → *see* Finoglia, Paolo

Finoglia, Paolo   **BA GC PR**
  (Italian artist, op.1620-m.1656)   **WC**
  (Italian painter, 1590-1645)   **BA GC**
  (Italian painter, ca.1590-1645)   **PR**
  Bibl: ▶Bolaffi; ▶RILA/BHA, 1986; ▶Thieme-Becker; Whitfield, Ptg. Naples 1606-1705, p. 157; ▶Witt checklist

Finoglia   **PR**

Finoglia, Paolo Domenico   **GC PR WC**
Paolo Domenico Finoglia   **PR**
Paolo Finocchio   **PR**
Paolo Finoglia   **PR**
Paolo finoglio   **PR**
Paulo Finoglia   **PR**
Finoglia, Paolo Domenico → *see* Finoglia, Paolo

Finot, Alfred *(French sculptor, 1876-1947)*   **BA**
  Bibl: ▶Bénézit

Finschi, Luzi *(Swiss architect)*   **AV**
  Bibl: ▶Schweiz. Ingen. u. Archit., 1984-1985

Finsler, Hans   **BA JG**
  (Swiss photographer, 1891-1972)   **BA**
  (Swiss, 1891-1972)   **JG**
  Bibl: ▶Auer, Encyc. photographes; ▶Contemp. photogs., 1988; NEW ART EXAMINER, 9-6 (Mar 1982) p.1,7

Finson → *see* Finson, Louis

Finson or Finsonius, David → *see* Finson, David

Finson, David   **GC**
  (Dutch artist, c.1597-p.1625)   **WC**
  (Dutch painter, c.1597-aft.1625)   **GC**
  Bibl: ▶Thieme-Becker

Finson or Finsonius, David   **WC**
Finsonius, David   **GC**

Finson, Finsonius or Vinson, Ludovicus or Louis → *see* Finson, Louis

Finson, Louis   **BA PR**
  (Flemish artist, a.1580-1617)   **WC**
  (Flemish painter, ca.1580-1617)   **BA PR**
  (Flemish, ca.1580-1617)   **GC**
  Bibl: ▶Encyc. world art; ▶Grote Winkler Prins; ▶RILA/BHA; ▶Seyn, Écoles flam. et holl.; Spear, Caravaggio, p.93; ▶Thieme-Becker; ▶Witt checklist; ▶Wurzbach, NLD Künst.-Lex.

Fensonius   **PR**
Finson   **PR**

Finson, Finsonius or Vinson, Ludovicus or Louis   **WC**

Finson, Ludovicus   **GC PR**
Finsonius, Ludovicus   **BA PR**
Finzone   **PR**
Fynson, Louis   **BA**
L. Finsonio   **PR**
Ludovicus Finson   **PR**
Luigi Finzone   **PR**
Tenzonius   **PR**
Vinson, Louis   **BA**

Finson, Ludovicus → *see* Finson, Louis

Finson, Pieter *(Dutch painter, act. 1632)*   **GC**
  Bibl: ▶Thieme-Becker

Finsonius, David → *see* Finson, David
Finsonius, Ludovicus → *see* Finson, Louis

Finster, Howard *(American clergyman, artist, b.1916)*   **BA**
  Bibl: New York (NY, USA), New Museum, REV. HOWARD FINSTER (1982)

Finsterer, Alfred *(German painter, printmaker, b.1908)*   **BA**
  Bibl: ▶MoMA libr. cat.; ▶Vollmer, Künst.-Lex. 20. Jhr.; ▶WW Arts DEU

Finsterlin, Hermann   **AV BA**
  (1887-1973)   **AV**
  (German painter, architect, poet, 1887-1973)   **BA**
  Bibl: ▶Brockhaus Enzyk.; Kunstwerk, XXVI (Nov. 1973), p.79 (obit)

Finsterwalder, Ulrich *(West German engineer, Karlsruhe)*   **AV**
  Bibl: Deutsche Bauzeitung, 1989 Apr., v.123, no.4, p.94

Finta, József *(Hungarian architect, 1935-)*   **AV**
  Bibl: ▶Contemp. archts.

Finzi, Sylvia *(British artist, b.1948)*   **WI**

Finzone → *see* Finson, Louis

Fio, Zvjezdana (*Yugoslav painter, b.1954*)   **BA**
Bibl: ▶Intl. dir. exh. artists, 1983, v.1

Fiocchi, Alexandre (*French artist, 1803-p.1858*)   **WC**

Fiocchi, Lídia (*Brazilian architect*)   **AV**
Bibl: Projeto, 1987 July, no.101, p.92

Fiocchi, Massimo (*Brazilian architect*)   **AV**
Bibl: Projeto, 1987 July, no.101, p.92

Fiol, Victorio del (*Argentine architect*)   **AV**
Bibl: Summa, 1985 Oct., no.218, p.46

Fior, Robin   **WC WI**
(*British artist, 20th cent.*)   WC
(*British artist, op.1970-*)   WI

Fioravanti   **PR**
(*Italian artist, op.1620-1660*)   WC
(*Italian painter, act. 1620-1660*)   PR
Bibl: ▶Thieme-Becker

Fioravanti (Fieravanti)   **WC**
Fioravantj   PR
Fioraventi   PR
Fioravanti (Fieravanti) → see Fioravanti

Fioravanti family (*Italian architects, 15th c.*)   **BA**
Bibl: ▶Portoghesi, Diz. arch. e urbanistica

Fioravanti, Aristotele (*Italian architect, engineer, medalist, ca.1415-1485/86*)   **BA**
Bibl: ▶Avery Libr. cat.; ▶Bessone-Aurelj, Scult. & arch. ital.; ▶Encic. italiana; ▶Encyc. world art; ▶Thieme-Becker
Aristotile da Bologna   BA
Bologna, Aristotile da   BA
Fieravanti, Aristotele   BA

Fioravanti, Cosimo [**Unidentified**]
(*Unknown painter, act. 18th century*)   **PR**
Bibl: Riccardi inventory dated 1776
Cosimo Fioravanti   PR
Fioravantj → see Fioravanti
Fioraventi → see Fioravanti

Fiore Furlan dei Liberi da Premariacco (*Italian, b. ca. 1340-1350*)   **JG**
Fiore, Cesare de' → see Fiori, Cesare

Fiore, Francesco del (*Italian painter, d. 1405-1415*)   **PR**
Bibl: ▶Thieme-Becker
Francesco del Fiore   PR

Fiore, Nicola   **BA WC**
(*Italian artist, op.1775*)   WC
(*Italian engineer, act.1787*)   BA
Bibl: Strazzullo, Napoli nobilissima, XXII, XXIII, XXIV (May-Aug. 1983) pp.145-146

Fiorentino [**Unidentified**] (*Italian painter*)   **PR**
Bibl: Doria inventory, Naples, 1690

Fiorentino, Arnolfo → see Arnolfo di Cambio

Fiorentino, Mario (*Italian architect, 1918-*)   **AV**

Fiorentino, Pier Francesco → see Pier Francesco Fiorentino

Fiorentino, Pseudo Pier Francesco → see Pseudo Pier Francesco Fiorentino

Fiorenza, Carlo [**Unidentified**] (*Unknown painter*)   **PR**
Bibl: (June 1810, lot 203 and November 1810, lot 203, European Museum)
Carlo Fiorenza   PR

Fiorenzo di Lorenzo   **BA GC PR WC**
(*Italian artist, c.1445-a.1525*)   WC
(*Italian painter, ca.1445-ca.1525*)   BA GC PR
Bibl: ▶Bénézit; ▶Bolaffi; ▶RILA/BHA; ▶Thieme-Becker

Fiorenzoli, Giuliano (*Architect, 1943-*)   **AV**
Bibl: Space design, 1982 Aug., no.215, p.132

Fiorese, Giorgio (*Italian architect, 1942-*)   **AV**
Bibl: Architettura: Cronache e storia, 1985 Jan., v.31, no.1(351), p.16

Fioretti, Carles Vergen (*Spanish artist, 19th cent.*)   **WC**

Fiori da Urbino → see Barocci, Federico

Fiori, Cesare   **BA GC WC**
(*Italian artist, 1636-1702*)   WC
(*Italian painter, architect, and printmaker, ca.1636-1702*)   GC
(*Italian painter, architect, printmaker, ca.1636-1702*)   BA
Bibl: ▶Bolaffi; Getty Photo Study Coll. (Ptgs.); ▶RILA/BHA; ▶Thieme-Becker
Fiore, Cesare de'   GC

Fiori, Leonardo (*Italian architect, 1926-*)   **AV**

Fiori, Paolo   **AV**
Fiorillo → see Fiorillo, L.

Fiorillo, Francesco or Domenico (*Italian artist, op.1521*)   **WC**

Fiorillo, L.   **GC**
Bibl: Getty Photo Study Coll.; ▶Idx. Amer. photog. colls.
Fiorillo   GC

Fiorini, Gabriele (*Italian sculptor, act.1571-1605*)   **BA**
Bibl: ▶Bénézit; ▶Bessone-Aurelj, Scult. & arch. ital.; Rubenstein, PALAZZO MAGNANI; TCI Emilia-Romagna; ▶Thieme-Becker

Fiorini, Giovanni Battista   **GC**
(*Italian artist, c.1540-c.1600*)   WC
(*Italian painter, ca.1540-ca.1600*)   GC
Bibl: ▶Thieme-Becker

Fiorino or Fiorini, Giovanni Battista, II   **WC**

Fiorini, Guido (*Italian engineer and architect*)   **AV**
Bibl: Casabella, 1988 Sept., v.52, no.549, p.42

Fiorini, Pietro (*Italian architect, 1539-1629*)   **BA**
Bibl: ▶Portoghesi, Diz. arch. e urbanistica; Ricci/Zucchini, Bologna; TCI Emilia-Romagna, p.742; ▶Thieme-Becker

Fiorino or Fiorini, Giovanni Battista, II → see Fiorini, Giovanni Battista

Fiorino, Jeremias David Alexander (*German artist, 1797-1847*)   **WC**

Fioriti, Bernardo (*Italian sculptor, 17th century*)   **GC**
Bibl: TCI Roma e dintorni

Fioroni, Luigi (*Italian artist, 1795-1864*)   **WC**

fiosella → see Fiasella, Domenico

Fiozzi, Aldo (*Italian artist, op.1921*)   **WC**

Fiquet, Hortense (*French, ca.1850-after 1906*)   **BA**
Bibl: Dorival, CEZANNE; Kendall, CEZANNE..., p.318; Rewald, CEZANNE
Cézanne, Madame   BA

Firabet (of Rapperswil) (*Swiss artist, op.1465-80*)   **WC**

Firajouli → see Ferraiuoli, Nunzio (Afflitti)

Firebrace, William (*British architect*)   **AV**
Bibl: AA files, 1984 Jan., no.5, p.75

Firens or Fierens, Pierre (*Flemish artist, op.1597-m.c.1636/9*)   **WC**

Firens, Pierre (*French artist, 1637-c.1673*)   **WC**

Firenze, Biagio d'Antonio da → see Biagio d'Antonio da Firenze

Firfires, Nicholas S.   **WC WI**
(*American artist, 20th cent.*)   WC
(*American artist, b.1917*)   WI

Firle, Walter   **GC**
(*German artist, 1859-1929*)   WC
(*German painter, 1859-1929*)   GC
Bibl: ▶Bénézit

Firle, Walther   **WC**
Firle, Walther → see Firle, Walter

Firmian, Nicolas von → see Nicolas von Firmian

Firmin, Claude (*French artist, 1864-*)   **WC**

Firmin, Eric Henry (*British architect, London*)   **AV**
Bibl: ▶RIBA members, 1984

Firmin-Gerard, Marie Francois → see Girard, Marie-François-Firmin

Firmin-Girard → see Girard, Marie-François-Firmin

Firmstone, Christopher John Eldon
  (English architect, Charlbury)   **AV**
    Bibl: ▶RIBA members, 1987

Firsov, Ivan   **BA**
  (Russian artist, op.1747-1756)   **WC**
  (Russian painter, 18th c.)   **BA**
    Bibl: ▶Bénézit; ▶Thieme-Becker

Firssoff, Iwan   **WC**

Firssoff, Iwan → see Firsov, Ivan

First Master of Bible Historiale of
  Jean de Berry   **JG**

First Master of Sant'Eugenio
  (Italian illuminator, act ca.1340)   **GC**
    Bibl: Siena (ITA), Pal. Pubb.,
    Gotico a Siena (1982)

Firth, Robert *(American architect)*   **AV**

Firth-Smith, John *(Australian*
  painter, b.1943.)   **BA**
    Bibl: Artscribe, 23 (June 1980)
    22-29; ▶Encyc. Australian art

Firthaler, Barthlmä *(Austrian*
  architect, act.1500-1518)   **BA**
    Bibl: Acta Historiae Artium
    XXIII/1-2 (1977) 21-56;
    ▶Thieme-Becker

Fisael [Unidentified] *(Unknown*
  painter)   **PR**
    Bibl: Bianco inventory, Naples,
    1693

Fisberg, Luiz *(Brazilian architect)*   **AV**
    Bibl: Projeto, 1987 Sept., no.103,
    p.119

Fisch vom Stein, Hans Ulrich I   **GC**
  (Swiss artist, 1583-1647)   **WC**
  (Swiss, 1583-1647)   **GC**
    Bibl: ▶Witt checklist

Fisch vom Stein, Hans Ulrich, I
  or H. von Fisch the Elder   **WC**

Fisch vom Stein, Hans Ulrich, I or H.
von Fisch the Elder → see Fisch vom
Stein, Hans Ulrich I

Fisch, Hans Ulrich II   **BA GC**
  (Swiss painter, 1613-1686)   **BA**
  (Swiss, ca.1613-1686)   **GC**
    Bibl: ▶Bénézit; ▶Thieme-Becker

Fischbach, Johann *(German artist,*
  1797-1871)   **WC**

Fischel, Hartwig *(Austrian architect,*
  furniture designer, art historian,
  1861-1938)   **BA**
    Bibl: Lewis, BURLINGTON
    CCXXV/969 (May 1983) 297-289;
    ▶Natl. union cat.; ▶Thieme-Becker

Fischer → see Fischer, Vinzenz

Fischer von Erlach, Johann
Bernard → see Fischer von Erlach,
Johann Bernhard

Fischer von Erlach, Johann
  Bernhard   **AV BA**
  (Austrian architect, 1656-1723)   **AV BA**
  (German artist, 1656-1723)   **WC**
    Bibl: ▶Macmillan encyc. archts.;
    ▶Thieme-Becker

  Erlach, Johann Bernhard Fischer
  von   **AV BA**

Fischer von Erlach, Johann
  Bernard   **WC**

Fischer von Erlach, Johann
  Emanuel → see Fischer von Erlach,
  Joseph Emanuel

Fischer von Erlach, Joseph
  Emanuel   **BA WC**
  (Austrian architect, 1693-1742)   **BA**
  (Austrian architect, Vienna,
  1693-1742)   **AV**
  (German artist, 1693-1742)   **WC**
    Bibl: ▶Neue deutsche Biog.;
    ▶Portoghesi, Diz. arch. e
    urbanistica; ▶Thieme-Becker

Fischer von Erlach, Johann
  Emanuel   **AV**

Fischer, Adam *(Danish sculptor,*
  1888-1968)   **BA**
    Bibl: ▶Bénézit; ▶Vollmer,
    Künst.-Lex. 20. Jhr.; ▶Weilbach,
    Kunst.leks.

Fischer, Adolf *(Austrian painter,*
  1856-1908)   **GC**
    Bibl: ▶Bénézit

Fischer, Adolf (Fischer-Gurig) Carl
  Franz Adolf *(German artist, 1860-*
  1918)   **WC**

Fischer, Alfred Friedrich Kurt
  (Cuno) *(German painter,*
  printmaker, 1914-1973)   **BA**
    Bibl: ▶MoMA libr. cat.;
    Nuremberg (DEU), Germansiches
    Nationalmus., DOKUMENTE ZU
    LEBEN UND WERK... (1978);
    ▶Vollmer, Künst.-Lex. 20. Jhr.

Fischer, Andreas *(German farmer,*
  woodcarver, act.ca.1930)   **BA**
    Bibl: PANTHEON XXXIII/2 (1975)
    145

Fischer, Anton Otto   **BA WI**
  (American artist, 1882-1962)   **WI**
  (German painter in USA,
  b.1882)   **BA**
    Bibl: ▶Bénézit; ▶Vollmer,
    Künst.-Lex. 20. Jhr.

Fischer, Arno *(East German*
  photographer, b.1927)   **BA**
    Bibl: BILDENDE KUNST 4 (1984)
    160

Fischer, Benno Joachim Theodor
  (German artist, 1828-1865)   **WC**

Fischer, Carl von → see Fischer,
  Heinrich Karl Joseph von

Fischer, Clemens *(German painter,*
  b.1918)   **BA**
    Bibl: ▶WW Arts DEU

Fischer, Ellen *(Danish painter, 1889-*
  1966)   **BA**
    Bibl: ▶Bénézit; København (DNK),
    Statens Mus. Kunst,
    København/Paris (1982);
    ▶Weilbach, Kunst.leks.

Fischer, Erhard *(Architect, Munich*
  since 1965)   **AV**
    Bibl: AC, 1984 Oct, v.29, no.
    2(110), p.77; ▶Arch. period.
    idx./RIBA, 1983

Fischer, Ernst (Georg Ernst)
  (German artist, 1815-1874)   **WC**

Fischer, Eva *(Yugoslav artist, 20th*
  cent.)   **WC**

Fischer, Friedrich *(Austrian*
  architect, Vienna)   **AV**
    Bibl: ▶Verzeich. Öst. Ziviltech.,
    1984

Fischer, Friedrich Theodor *(German*
  architect, 1803-1868)   **BA**
    Bibl: ▶Avery obit. idx.;
    ▶Thieme-Becker

Fischer, Fritz *(East German painter,*
  printmaker, 1911-1968)   **BA**
    Bibl: FRITZ FISCHER:
    WERKKATALOG DER
    ILLUSTRIERTEN BUCHER, 1935-
    1984 (RILA, DEU); ▶Vollmer,
    Künst.-Lex. 20. Jhr.

Fischer, Gerd *(W. German architect,*
  Michelau and Munich)   **AV**
    Bibl: Baumeister, 1986 Dec., v.83,
    no.12, p.60

Fischer, Günther *(West German*
  architect, Berlin)   **AV**
    Bibl: ▶Bund Deut. Arch. Hdbch.,
    1987

Fischer, Hanna → see Nagel, Hanna

Fischer, Hans *(Swiss artist, 1909-*
  1958)   **WC**

Fischer, Heinrich Karl Joseph von   **BA**
  (German architect, 1782-1820)   **BA**
  (German artist, 1782-1820)   **WC**
  (German sculptor, 1782-1820)   **AV**
    Bibl: Ars bavarica, 1988, v.49-50,
    p.93; ▶Macmillan encyc. archts.;
    ▶Neue deutsche Biog.

  Fischer, Carl von   **BA**

Fischer, Karl von   **AV WC**

Fischer, Hervé *(French artist,*
  b.1941)   **BA**
    Bibl: ▶Bénézit; ▶Contemp. artists

Fischer, Horst *(W. German architect,*
  Munich, 1935-)   **AV**
    Bibl: Deutsche Bauzeitung, 1985
    Oct., v.119, no.10, p.10

Fischer, Isaac   **GC**
  (German artist, 1677-1705)   **WC**
  (German painter and
  draughtsman, bef.1677-1705)   **GC**
    Bibl: ▶Bénézit

Fisches the Younger, Isaac F.   **WC**
  Fisches, Isaac II   **GC**

Fischer, Jacob Adolph *(German*
  artist, 1755-p.1799)   **WC**

Fischer, Jamie *(American architect,*
  Chicago)   **AV**
    Bibl: Inland architect, 1982 July-
    Aug., v.26, no.4, p.16

Fischer, Johann Christian
  Richard → see Fischer, Richard

Fischer, Johann Christian Richard
  (Richard) → see Fischer, Richard

Fischer, Johann Georg *(German*
  architect, 1673-1747)   **BA**
    Bibl: ▶Neue deutsche Biog.;
    ▶Portoghesi, Diz. arch. e
    urbanistica; ▶Thieme-Becker

Fischer, Johann Georg	GC
(German artist, 1580-1643)	WC
(German artist, c.1570/80-1643)	WC
(German painter and sculptor, 1580-1643)	GC
Bibl: ▶Schweers, Gemälde deut. Museen; ▶Thieme-Becker	
Fischer, Johannes or Hans Vischer or Fischer, Johann	WC
Georg	WC
Fischer, Johann Michael	AV BA
(ca.1691-1766)	AV
(German architect, 1692-1766)	BA
Bibl: ▶Encyc. world art; ▶Neue deutsche Biog.; ▶Thieme-Becker	
Fischer, Johannes (German artist, 1888-1955)	WC
Fischer, Johannes August (Danish artist, 1854-1921)	WC
Fischer, Johannes or Hans → see Fischer, Johann Georg	
Fischer, Josef	BA
(Austrian painter, printmaker, 1769-1822)	BA
(German artist, 1769-1822)	WC
Bibl: ▶Fuchs, Öst. Maler 19. Jahrh.; Rosza, MITTEILUNGEN DER SOTERR. GALERIE XVI/XVII (1982-83) 148-169; ▶Thieme-Becker	
Fischer, Joseph	WC
Fischer, Josef Anton (German painter, 1814-1859)	BA
Bibl: ▶Busse, Maler u. Bildhauer 19. Jahr.; ▶Thieme-Becker	
Fischer, Joseph → see Fischer, Josef	
Fischer, Joseph Anton (German artist, c.1700-1750)	WC
Fischer, Karl von → see Fischer, Heinrich Karl Joseph von	
Fischer, Leo L. (American architect, South Orange, N.J)	AV
Bibl: ▶AIA Pro File, 1985	
Fischer, Leopold (German artist, 1814-1864)	WC
Fischer, Lili (German painter, performance artist, b.1947)	BA
Bibl: ▶Intl. dir. exh. artists, 1982	
Fischer, Lothar (German sculptor, b.1933)	BA
Bibl: ▶DuMonts Künst.-Lex.	
Fischer, Louis (German artist, 1784-1845)	WC
Fischer, Ludwig Hans (German artist, 1848-1915)	WC
Fischer, Manfred (Swiss interior architect [not same as Manfred F.])	AV
Bibl: Architektur, Innenarchitektur, Technischer Ausbau, 1986 Mar., v.94, no.3, p.44	
Fischer, Paul (Johann Georg Paul)	
(German artist, 1786-1875)	WC
Fischer, Paul Gustaf → see Fischer, Paul Gustav	

Fischer, Paul Gustav	BA
(Danish painter, 1860-1934)	BA
(Scandinavian artist, 1860-1934)	WC
Bibl: ▶Nørregård-Nielsen, Dansk kunst; ▶Weilbach, Kunst.leks.; ▶Witt checklist	
Fischer, Paul Gustaf	WC
Fischer, Raymond (French architect, 1898-1988)	AV
Bibl: Casabella, 1988 Nov., v.52, no.551, p.30	
Fischer, Ricarda (German painter, b.1958)	BA
Bibl: ▶Art Index, v.34; Schweinebraden, KUNSTWERK, XXXVIII(SEPT 1985), 48-49	
Fischer, Richard	GC
(German artist, 1826-p.1872)	WC
(German painter, 1826-d. aft. 1872)	GC
Bibl: ▶Bénézit; ▶Thieme-Becker	
Fischer, Johann Christian Richard	GC
Fischer, Johann Christian Richard (Richard)	WC
Fischer, Ron M. (American sculptor, b.1947)	BA
Bibl: ARTS MAG LIV (June 1980); ▶WW Amer. Art, 1982	
Fischer, Theodor	AV BA
(1862-1938)	AV
(German architect, 1862-1938)	BA
Bibl: ▶Brockhaus Enzyk.; ▶Thieme-Becker; ▶Vollmer, Künst.-Lex. 20. Jhr.	
Fischer, Tora → see Garde, Tora	
Fischer, Vinzenz	GC PR WC
(German artist, 1729-1810)	WC
(German painter, 1729-1810)	PR
(German, 1729-1810)	GC
Bibl: ▶Thieme-Becker; ▶Witt checklist	
Fischer	PR
V. Fischer	PR
Vinzenz Fischer	PR
Fischer, Werner (West German architect, Ehingen, 1947-)	AV
Bibl: Deutsche Bauzeitung, 1988 Feb., v.122, no.2, p.146	
Fischer-Klemm, Ursula (German artist, 20th c.)	BA
Bibl: Baden (DEU), Gal. Trudelhaus, Aus der Ittenschule (1984)	
Klemm, Ursula	BA
Fischermans, Alejandro Ferrant y → see Ferrant y Fischermans, Alejandro	
Fischerová-Rösslerová, Gertruda	
(Czech photographer, 1894-1976)	BA
Bibl: HIST OF PHOTOGRAPHY III/3 (July 1979) 265	
Fisches the Elder, Isaac (Jesaias Isaics) → see Fisches, Isaac I	
Fisches the Younger, Isaac F. → see Fischer, Isaac	

Fisches, Isaac I	BA
(German artist, 1638-1706)	WC
(German painter, 1638-1706)	BA
Bibl: Adriani, Malerei ... 17. Jhrh. (1977); Augsburg (DEU), St.Kunst., DEUTSCHE BAROCKGAL. (1970); ▶Bénézit; Forniz, Noncello 52 (1981) 5-34; ▶Nagler, Neues Künst.-Lex.; ▶Thieme-Becker	
Fisches the Elder, Isaac (Jesaias Isaics)	WC
Fisches, Isaac, the elder	BA
Fisches, Isaac II → see Fischer, Isaac	
Fisches, Isaac, the elder → see Fisches, Isaac I	
Fischetti, Fedele	BA GC WC
(Italian artist, 1734-1789)	WC
(Italian painter, 1734-1789)	BA GC
Bibl: ▶Bolaffi; ▶RILA/BHA, 1986	
Fischetti, John (American cartoonist, 1916-1980)	BA
Bibl: NY Times obit., 21 Nov 1980; ▶WW Amer. Art, 1976	
Fischhof, George (German artist, 1859-)	WC
Fischinger, Oskar (German filmmaker, painter in USA, 1900-1967)	BA
Bibl: Long Beach (CA, USA), Mus. of Art, Milton Wichner Coll. (1981); ▶MoMA libr. cat.; ▶Oxford comp. film	
Fischl, Eric	BA WI
(American artist, b.1948)	WI
(American painter, b.1948)	BA
Bibl: ▶Intl. dir. exh. artists, 1982-1983; Vancouver (BC, CAN), Art Gallery, 17 Canadian artists (1976)	
Fischli, Hans	AV BA WC
(Swiss architect, 1909-)	AV
(Swiss artist, 1909-)	WC
(Swiss painter, sculptor, architect, printmaker, b.1909)	BA
Bibl: Archithese, 1985 Sept.-Oct., v.15, no.5, p.40; ▶Lex. zeitgen. Schweiz. Künstler; ▶Vollmer, Künst.-Lex. 20. Jhr.	
Fischli, Peter (Swiss artist, b.1952)	BA
Bibl: ▶Intl. dir. exh. artists, 1982-1983	
Fisco, Claude Joseph Antoine (Belgian architect, 1736-1825)	AV
Bibl: Monumenten en landschappen, 1986 Jan.-Feb., v.5, no.1, p.36	
Fisen, Englebert (Flemish artist, 1655-1733)	WC
Fišer, František (Czech art historian, painter, restorer, 20th c.)	BA
Bibl: Uměni, XXV/4 (1977) pp. 340-350	

Fish, Anne Harriet   **WI**
   (British artist, 20th cent.)   WC
   (British artist, op.circa 1919-,
    d.1964)   WI
  Fish, Anne Harriet (Anne
   Sefton)   **WC**
   Sefton, Walter, Mrs., (Anne
    Harriet)   WI
 Fish, Anne Harriet (Anne
   Sefton)→see Fish, Anne Harriet
Fish, Janet   **BA WI**
   (American artist, b.1938)   WI
   (American painter, b.1938)   BA
    Bibl: ▶Art Index, Jul. 1985; ▶WW
    Amer. Art, 1989
Fish, Margery *(British gardener,*
   author, 1892-1969)   **AV**
    Bibl: Country life, 1985 Feb.7,
    v.177, no.4564, p.314; ▶Libr. of
    Congr. Name Auth. File
Fish, Peter *(British cabinetmaker,*
   act.1748-1788)   **BA**
    Bibl: FURNITURE HISTORY XIV
    (1978) 65-67
Fish, R. →see Field, Robert
Fish, Seena *(American painter, 20th*
   c.)   **BA**
    Bibl: Brooklyn (NY, USA), Brooklyn
    Mus., Woman's Place (1982);
    ▶Intl. dir. exh. artists, 1983
Fisher →see Fisher, Jonathon
Fisher, A. Robert *(American*
   architect, 1930-)   **AV**
Fisher, Alfred Hugh *(British artist,*
   1867-1945)   **WC WI**
Fisher, Alice →see Fisher, Alice R.
Fisher, Alice R. *(American painter, b.*
   1882)   **PR**
    Bibl: ▶Petteys, Women artists
   Alice R. Fisher   PR
   Fisher, Alice   PR
Fisher, Alvan →see Fisher, Alvan T.
Fisher, Alvan T.   **BA PR WI**
   (American artist, 1792-1863)   WC WI
   (American painter, 1792-1863)   BA PR
   (American painter, engraver,
    Boston, Mass., worked in
    France, 1792-1863)   AV
    Bibl: ▶Fielding's Amer. ptrs.;
    ▶Groce, Artists Amer.;
    ▶RILA/BHA; source: Antiques,
    1988 July, v.134, no.1, p.152;
    ▶Young, Amer. artists
   Alvan T. Fisher   PR
Fisher, Alvan   **AV PR WC**
Fisher, Amy E. *(British artist, op.*
   1866-1890)   **WC WI**
Fisher, Brian *(Canadian artist, 20th*
   cent.)   **WC**
Fisher, Carole Gorney *(American*
   painter, sculptor, 20th c.)   **BA**
    Bibl: ▶WW Amer. Art, 1989
Fisher, Charles *(British artist, op.*
   1881-1890)   **WI**
Fisher, Chris Hugh *(British artist,*
   op.20th c.)   **WI**

Fisher, E.J. *(British artist, op.1836-*
   1853)   **WI**
Fisher, Edward *(British artist, 1722-*
   1785)   **WC WI**
    Bibl: Mackenzie
Fisher, Elizabeth Campbell, Miss→see
   Clay, Elizabeth Campbell Fisher
Fisher, F.   **WC WI**
   (British artist, 18th cent.)   WC
   (British artist, op.18th c.)   WI
Fisher, Frederick *(American*
   architect, active in California,
   1949-)   **AV**
    Bibl: Space design, 1982 Aug.,
    no.215, p.4
Fisher, Gareth *(British sculptor,*
   b.1951)   **BA**
    Bibl: Glasgow (GBR), Third Eye
    Centre, Built in Scotland (1983)
Fisher, George *(British bookbinder,*
   designer, 1879-1970)   **BA**
    Bibl: Rees, NATIONAL LIBRARY OF
    WALES JOURNAL, XXVII (Summer
    1987), p.121-22
Fisher, George Bulteel   **BA WI**
   (British artist, 1764-1834)   WC WI
   (British artist, 1764-after 1796)   BA
    Bibl: APOLLO (May 1976) 412;
    ▶Bénézit; ▶Fisher, Watercolour
    ptrs.; ▶Groce, Artists Amer.;
    ▶Harper, Ptg. Canada;
    ▶Thieme-Becker
  Fisher, Sir George Bulteel   **WC**
Fisher, Harrison   **BA WC WI**
   (American artist, 1875-1934)   WC WI
   (American illustrator, painter,
    1875-1934)   BA
    Bibl: ▶Fielding's Amer. ptrs.;
    ▶Vollmer, Künst.-Lex. 20. Jhr.;
    ▶WWW Amer.; ▶Young, Amer.
    artists
Fisher, Horace   **WC WI**
   (British artist, op.1882-1903)   WI
   (British artist, op.1882-m.1893)   WC
Fisher, Howard T. *(American*
   architect)   **AV**
Fisher, J.   **WC WI**
   (American artist, op.1858-)   WI
   (British artist, 19th cent.)   WC
Fisher, J.H. Vignoles →see Fisher,
   Vignoles
Fisher, J.P. *(British artist, op.19th c.)*   **WI**
Fisher, James →see Fisher, James II
Fisher, James I *(British artist, op.*
   circa 1750-)   **WI**
Fisher, James II   **WI**
   (British artist, 1818-1896)   WC WI
  Fisher, James   **WC**
Fisher, Jan *(British artist, op.1985-)*   **WI**
Fisher, Janet *(British artist, 1867-*
   1926)   **WI**
Fisher, Joel A. *(American artist,*
   b.1947)   **BA**
    Bibl: ▶Bénézit; ▶Intl. dir. exh.
    artists, 1983; ▶MoMA libr. cat.;
    ▶WW Amer. Art

Fisher, John →see Fisher, John, bishop
   of Salisbury
Fisher, John S. *(American architect,*
   Los Angeles, CA)   **AV**
    Bibl: ▶AIA Pro File, 1985
Fisher, John, bishop of Salisbury   **BA**
   (British artist, 1748-1825)   WI
   (British painter, 1748-1825)   BA
    Bibl: Beckett, JOHN CONSTABLE
    AND THE FISHERS, p.2; ▶Mallalieu,
    Brit. watercolour artists
  Fisher, John   **WI**
Fisher, Jonathan *(American painter,*
   printmaker, 1768-1847)   **BA**
    Bibl: ▶Groce, Artists Amer.;
    ▶WWW Amer.
Fisher, Jonathan →see Fisher,
   Jonathon
Fisher, Jonathon   **WI**
   (British artist, op.1763-, d.1809)   WI
   (Irish painter, act. 1763, d.
    1809)   PR
    Bibl: ▶Fisher, Watercolour ptrs.;
    ▶Thieme-Becker
   Fisher   PR
Fisher, Jonathan   **PR**
   I. Fisher   PR
   Jonathan Fisher   PR
Fisher, Joseph *(British painter, 1796-*
   1890)   **PR**
    Bibl: Ashmolean Museum
    catalogue
   Joseph Fisher   PR
Fisher, Joseph H. Vignoles →see
   Fisher, Vignoles
Fisher, Joshua Brewster *(British*
   artist, 1859-op.1918)   **WI**
Fisher, K.A. *(Russian, active*
   Moscow, early 20th century)   **JG**
Fisher, Mabel *(British painter, 20th*
   c.)   **BA**
    Bibl: Jankowicz, Leonardo XX/1
    (1987), p. 39-45
Fisher, Margaret *(American painter,*
   20th c.)   **BA**
    Bibl: Chicago (IL, USA), Art Inst.,
    MARG. FISHER (1975)
Fisher, Mark   **PR WI**
   (British artist, 1841-1923)   WI
   (British painter, 1841-1923)   PR
    Bibl: ▶Thieme-Becker; ▶Witt
    checklist
   Fisher, William Mark   PR
   Mark Fisher   PR
Fisher, Millicent Margaret, Miss →see
   Prout, Millicent Margaret Fisher
Fisher, Moricz *(Hungarian porcelain*
   manufacturer, act.1838, d.1880)   **BA**
    Bibl: ▶Penguin dec. arts
Fisher, Percy Harland *(British artist,*
   1867-op.1930)   **WI**
Fisher, Robert   **WC WI**
   (British artist, op.1655)   WC
   (British artist, op.1655-)   WI

Fisher, Robert Norman (*American sculptor, b.1939*)   **BA**
  Bibl: Fisher & Masters. LEONARDO XVIII, 3 1985 p.133; ▶WW Amer. Art

Fisher, Rowland (*British artist, 1885-1969*)   **WI**

Fisher, Samuel Melton (*British artist, 1859-1939*)   **WI**

Fisher, Sandra   **BA WI**
  (*American painter in GBR, b.1947*)   BA
  (*British artist, op.1981-*)   WI
  Bibl: ▶Intl. dir. exh. artists, 1982; Washington, DC (USA), Hirshhorn Mus., Representation abroad (1985), p.209

Fisher, Sir George Bulteel → see Fisher, George Bulteel

Fisher, Stefani Melton (*British artist, 1861-1939*)   **WC WI**
  Bibl: ▶Waters, Brit. artists

Fisher, Theodore (*American painter, 1789-1819*)   **PR**
  Bibl: ▶Young, Amer. artists
  Theodore Fisher   PR

Fisher, Thomas   **BA WC WI**
  (*British artist, 1782-1836*)   WC WI
  (*British painter, printmaker, antiquary, 1782-1836*)   BA
  Bibl: ▶Bénézit; ▶Dict. natl. biog.; ▶Fisher, Watercolour ptrs.; ▶Mallalieu, Brit. watercolour artists; Sotheby & Co., London June 12, 1980; ▶Thieme-Becker

Fisher, Vernon (*American artist, b.1943*)   **BA**
  Bibl: ▶WW Amer. Art, 1978

Fisher, Vignoles   **WC WI**
  (*British artist, 19th cent.*)   WC
  (*British artist, op.1920's-*)   WI
  (*British painter, 1864-1945*)   PR
  Bibl: Ashmolean Museum catalogue; ▶Bénézit; ▶Johnson, Brit. artists
  Fisher, J.H. Vignoles   PR
  Fisher, Joseph H. Vignoles   **PR**
  Joseph H. Vignoles Fisher   PR

Fisher, William (*American artist, op. 1672-1682*)   **WI**

Fisher, William → see Fisher, William, (GBR.)

Fisher, William Mark → see Fisher, Mark

Fisher, William, (GBR.)   **WI**
  (*British artist, 1817-1895*)   WC WI
  Fisher, William   **WC**

Fisherman, Hercules (*British painter, sculptor, performance artist, 20th c.*)   **BA**
  Bibl: ▶Intl. dir. exh. artists, 1983

Fishlock, Michael Tom (*British architect, London*)   **AV**
  Bibl: ▶RIBA members, 1984

Fishman, Louise   **BA WI**
  (*American artist, op.1981-*)   WI
  (*American painter, b.1939*)   BA
  Bibl: ARTS MAG LIV/3 (Nov 1979) 105-107; ▶Intl. dir. exh. artists, 1982-1983; Yonkers (NY, USA), Hudson River Mus., 6 ptrs. (1983)

Fishman, Richard (*American sculptor, b.1941*)   **BA**
  Bibl: ▶MoMA libr. cat.; ▶Natl. Faculty Dir.

Fisk, Anita (*American artist, 20th c.*)   **BA**
  Bibl: Honolulu (HI, USA), Acad. Arts, Matter-Memory (1981)

Fisk, William Henry (*British artist, 1827-1884*)   **WC WI**

Fiske Boyd → see Boyd, Fiske

Fiske, George   **BA JG**
  (*American photographer, 1835-1918*)   BA
  (*American, 1835-1918, active Yosemite, CA, U.S. (also Watkins)*)   JG
  Bibl: Sacramento (CA, USA), Crocker, LARGE SPACES (1980); Tuscon (AZ, USA), Univ of Ariz., Center for Creative Photog. GEORGE FISKE (1980)

Fiske, Gertrude   **BA PR WI**
  (*American artist, 1878-1961*)   WI
  (*American painter, 1878-1961*)   BA PR
  Bibl: Columbia (SC, USA), Museum of Art, GERTRUDE FISKE (1975); ▶Mallett's idx. artists; ▶RILA/BHA; ▶WW Amer. Art, 1959, 1966
  Gertrude Fiske   PR

Fiske, J. Warren   **WC WI**
  (*American artist, 19th cent.*)   WC
  (*American artist, op.19th c.*)   WI

Fisker, Kay → see Fisker, Kay Otto

Fisker, Kay Otto   **BA**
  (*Danish architect, 1893-1965*)   AV BA
  Bibl: ▶Contemp. archts.; ▶Encyc. world art; ▶WW Arch.
  Fisker, Kay   **AV**

Fiskin, Judy (*American photographer, b.1945*)   **BA**
  Bibl: ▶WW Amer. Art, 1986

Fissette, Leopold (*German artist, 1814-*)   **WC**

Fiszer, Stanislas   **AV BA**
  (*French architect, 20th c.*)   BA
  (*French architect, Paris; born in Warsaw, 1935-*)   AV
  Bibl: Architectural review, 1982 Apr., v.171, no.1022, p.48; Devillers, MONUMENTS HISTORIQUES DE LA FRANCE, CLIV(DEC.1987), 13-19

Fiszman, Gilles (*Belgian artist, 20th cent.*)   **WC**

fit → see Fyt, Jan

Fitch, Beriah, Capt. → see Fitch, Simon, Captain

Fitch, Beriah, Captain → see Fitch, Simon, Captain

Fitch, Captain → see Fitch, Simon, Captain

Fitch, George Hopper (*American, 20th c.*)   **BA**
  Bibl: New Haven (CT, USA), Yale Univ., Art Gallery, AMERICAN WATERCOLORS FROM THE COLLECTION... (1980)

Fitch, Marc (*British, 20th c.*)   **BA**
  Bibl: TRIBUTE TO AN ANTIQUARY (1976)

Fitch, Simon, Captain   **VO**
  (*American artist, op.1795-1805*)   WI
  (*American artist, op.1800*)   WC
  (*American painter, 1758-1835*)   VO
  Bibl: ▶Ebert, Amer. folk ptrs., p.208; ▶Groce, Artists Amer., p. 229; ▶Libr. of Congr. Name Auth. File, NAFR9224064
  Fitch, Beriah, Capt.   **WI**
  Fitch, Beriah, Captain   VO
  Fitch, Captain   **WC**

Fitch, Steve (*American, 1949-*)   **JG**

Fitch, Steve (*American photographer, b.1949*)   **BA**
  Bibl: ▶WW Amer. Art, 1989

Fitch, Walter H. (*British artist, op. 1835-1874*)   **WI**

Fitchen, Dorothy (*British artist, op. 1910-1922*)   **WI**

Fitches, William (*Canadian artist, b.1945*)   **BA**
  Bibl: Oshawa (Ont, CAN), McLaughlin Gallery, Christmas: another dimension (1980)

Fite, Harvey (*American sculptor, 1903-1976*)   **BA**
  Bibl: ART NEWS 76 (Oct 1977) 23-24, obit; ▶MoMA libr. cat.; ▶WW Amer. Art, 1976

Fitger → see Fitger, Arthur

Fitger, Arthur (*German painter, 1840-1909*)   **PR**
  Bibl: ▶Thieme-Becker
  Arthur Fitger   PR
  Fitger   PR
  Fitger, Arthur Heinrich Wilhelm   PR

Fitger, Arthur Heinrich Wilhelm → see Fitger, Arthur

Fitler, William Crothers (*American artist, 1857-1900*)   **WI**

Fitler, William Crothers, Mrs., (Claude Raguet) → see Hirst, Claude Raguet

Fitting, Louise (*American interior designer*)   **AV**
  Bibl: Architectural digest, 1985 Sept., v.42, no.9, p.184

Fittler, James (*British artist, 1758-1835*)   **WC WI**

Fitton, Hedley   AV BA WC WI
(British architectural etcher)   AV
(British artist, 1857-1929)   WI
(British artist, 1859-1929)   WC
(British printmaker, 1859-1929)   BA
    Bibl: ▶Johnson, Brit. artists; Print
    collector, v.1-2/no.55-56 (1982),
    p.2; ▶Vollmer, Künst.-Lex. 20.
    Jhr.; ▶Waters, Brit. artists; ▶Who
    was who [GBR]

Fitton, James   BA WC WI
(British artist, 1899-)   WC
(British artist, b.1899)   WI
(British painter, b.1899)   BA
    Bibl: ▶Dolman, Contemp. Brit.
    artists

Fitton, Margaret (British artist, op.
1930-1940)   WI
Cook, Margaret, Miss   WI

Fitton, Peter (English, act.1631-
1655)   BA
    Bibl: JWCI XXXVIII (1975) 339
Biddulph, Peter   BA

Fitz Hugh Lane → see Lane, Fitz Hugh

Fitz, William (British artist, op.1880-
1891)   WI

Fitzcook, Mary (British artist, 1824-
op.1898)   WI

Fitzenreiter, Wilfried (German
sculptor, b.1932)   BA
    Bibl: ▶Intl. dir. exh. artists, 1982

**FitzGeorge-Balfour, Robert
George Victor** (British, b.1913)   BA
    Bibl: ▶Who's Who [GBR]

FitzGerald, Barry (British architect,
Ipswich)   AV
    Bibl: Architects' journal, 1989
    Mar.22, v.189, no.12, p.15

Fitzgerald, Edward (British artist,
1809-1883)   WC WI

Fitzgerald, Florence   WC WI
(British artist, op.1887-, d.1927)   WI
(British artist,
op.1887/1893-m.1927)   WC
Bishop, Walter Follen, Mrs.,
(Florence)   WI

Fitzgerald, Frederick R. (British
artist, op.1897-1938)   WI

Fitzgerald, Gerald, Lord   WI
(British artist, 1821-1886)   WC WI
Fitzgerald, Lord Gerald   WC

Fitzgerald, Harrington (American
painter, 1847-1930)   PR
    Bibl: ▶WWW Amer. art
Harrington Fitzgerald   PR

Fitzgerald, Hazlewood B. (British
artist, op.circa 1925-)   WI

*Fitzgerald, James → see Fitzgerald,
James Edward*

Fitzgerald, James Edward   BA
(American painter, 1894-1971)   PR
(American painter, 1899-1971)   BA
    Bibl: ▶Bénézit; Rockland,
    Farnsworth Library and Art Nus.,
    JAMES FITZGERALD (1984); Univ
    of Arizona MA catalogue; ▶WWW
    Amer. art

Fitzgerald, James   PR
James Fitzgerald   PR
Fitzgerald, John Anster   WC WI
(British artist, 1832-1906)   WI
(British artist, 1832-p.1906)   WC
    Bibl: ▶Johnson, Brit. artists

Fitzgerald, Kit (American video
artist, b.1953)   BA
    Bibl: ARTWEEK X (28 July 1979)
    14; ▶Intl. dir. exh. artists, 1982

FitzGerald, Lionel Lemoine   BA WC
(Canadian artist, 1890-1956)   WC
(Canadian painter, printmaker,
1890-1956)   BA
    Bibl: ▶Artists Canada;
    ▶MacDonald, Can. artists

*Fitzgerald, Lord Gerald → see
Fitzgerald, Gerald, Lord*

*Fitzgerald, M. → see Fitzgerald,
Michael*

Fitzgerald, Mary (Irish painter,
b.1956)   BA
    Bibl: Belfast (GBR), ARts Council
    Gallery, FOUR ARTISTS FROM
    IRELAND, 1985 (RILA, GBR)

Fitzgerald, Michael   WI
(British artist, op.1875-1885)   WC WI
    Bibl: ▶Houfe, Brit. book illus.

Fitzgerald, M.   WC
FitzGerald, Robert   BA
(British, 1716-1781)   BA
(Irish nobleman and amateur
gardener, 1716-1781)   AV
    Bibl: Jrnl. garden hist., VI/4 (Oct.-
    Dec. 1986) pp.321-329

**Fitzgerald, Robert, Knight of
Kerry**   AV
*Fitzgerald, Robert, Knight of
Kerry → see FitzGerald, Robert*

Fitzgerald, Thornthwaite
(Engraver)   WI

Fitzgerald, V. (British artist, op.20th
c.)   WI

Fitzgerald, Zelda Sayre (American
dancer, painter, author, 1900-
1948)   BA
    Bibl: ▶Dict. Amer. biog.

Fitzgibbon, James W. (American
architect, 1915-1985)   AV
    Bibl: Fine homebuilding, 1986
    June-July, no.33, p.24

Fitzgibbons, J. Frank (American
architect, Los Angeles, Calif)   AV
    Bibl: ▶AIA Pro File, 1987-88

Fitzhardinge, Michael (Australian
architect)   AV
    Bibl: The Architect, W.A., 1988
    summer, v.29, no.4, p.13

Fitzi, Johann Ulrich (Swiss artist,
1798-p.1850)   WC
*Fitzmaurice, Capt. E. → see
Fitzmaurice, E.*
Fitzmaurice, E.   WI
(British artist, op.1833)   WC
(British artist, 1833-)   WI
Fitzmaurice, Capt. E.   WC

Fitzpatrick (American sculptor, 20th
century)   GC
    Bibl: Juley coll., NMAA

Fitzpatrick, Arthur (British artist,
op.1862-1868)   WI

Fitzpatrick, Charles (American
sailor, carpenter, d.ca.1932)   BA
    Bibl: ARCHIVES OF AMERICAN
    ART, XXIV/3 (1984) 2-16

Fitzpatrick, Daniel Robert
(American artist, 1891-1969)   WI

Fitzpatrick, Kirby Ward (American
architect)   AV

Fitzpatrick, Louise (American
painter, d.1933)   BA
    Bibl: ARCHIVES OF AMERICAN
    ART, XXIV/3 (1984) 2-16;
    ▶Petteys, Women artists; ▶WWW
    Amer. art

Fitzralph, Richard (D. 1360)   JG
FitzRobert, Geoffrey (Irish, act.
1192, d.1211)   BA
    Bibl: Barry, T.B., et al in PROC. OF
    THE ROYAL IRISH ACAD. LXXXIV
    (1984) 161

**FitzRoy Newdegate, Francis
Humphrey Maurice** (British,
b.1921)   BA
    Bibl: BURLINGTON CXIX (Apr
    1977) 272; Kelly's Handbook;
    ▶Who's Who [GBR]
Newdegate, Francis Humphrey
Maurice F.   BA
*Fitzroy, Caroline Blanche Elizabeth,
Miss → see Lindsay, Blanche*

Fitzroy, Cyril D. (British artist, op.
1885-1895)   WI

Fitzroy, Robert (British artist, op.
19th c.)   WI

Fitzsimmons Hall, E. (Australian (?))   GC
    Bibl: Gernsheim, Corpus Photog.
    of Drawings, 1417

Fitzsimmons, Joan (American
photographer, 20th c.)   BA
    Bibl: Amherst (MA, USA), U Mass.
    Art Gallery, Criticism of
    photography (1978)

Fitzwilliam, Anne (English, 14th c.)   BA
    Bibl: ▶Burke's dormant & extinct;
    ▶Dict. natl. biog.; Le Strange, Brit.
    brasses, p.100; Lewis's; Murrays
    Northants, p.84

Fiumani, Katherine (French
architect, Paris)   AV
    Bibl: Techniques et architecture,
    1984 Dec., no.357, p.111

Fiume, Salvatore (Italian painter,
b.1915)   BA
    Bibl: ▶Bolaffi

Fiumi, Napoleone G. *(Italian artist, 1898-)*   **WC**

Fiumicelli or Fumicelli, Lodovico →see Fiumicelli, Ludovico

Fiumicelli, Ludovico   **BA**
(Italian artist, op.1527-1570)   **WC**
(Italian painter, act.1527-1570)   **BA**
Bibl: ▶Bénézit; ▶Bolaffi;
▶Thieme-Becker; ▶Witt checklist

Fiumicelli or Fumicelli, Lodovico   **WC**
Fumicelli, Lodovico   **BA**

Fiuza, Ione *(Brazilian architect)*   **AV**
Bibl: Projeto, 1988 May, no.110,
p.93

Fiuza, Luiz *(Brazilian architect)*   **AV**
Bibl: Projeto, 1988 May, no.110,
p.93

Five Linked by the Handle-Floral
(vase-painter, ca. 500-475 BC)   **GC**
Bibl: ▶Beazley, Attic bl.-fig. vase-
ptrs.; Boardman, Attic Bl.-fig.
Vases

Fivet, Daniel [Unidentified]
(Unknown painter)   **PR**
Bibl: 1682 Benning inventory
Daniel Fivet   **PR**

Fivian, Bendicht *(Swiss painter, b.1940)*   **BA**
Bibl: ▶Lex. zeitgen. Schweiz.
Künstler; Olten, Kunstmuseum,
BENDICHT FIVIAN (1985)

Fix-Masseau, Pierre Félix *(French sculptor, b.1869)*   **BA**
Bibl: ▶Art Index, 1929-1932, v.1,
p.534

Fixon, Claude Pierre *(French artist, 18th cent.)*   **WC**

Fixon, E. *(Active Paris, France, daguerreotypist)*   **JG**

Fixon, Louis Pierre   **BA WC**
(French artist, 1748-1792)   **WC**
(French sculptor, painter, ca. 1748-1792)   **BA**
Bibl: ▶Dict. biog. fran.;
▶Thieme-Becker

Fizeau, Armand-Hippolyte-Louis →see Fizeau, Hippolyte Louis

Fizeau, Hippolyte Louis   **BA**
(French photographer, 1819-1896)   **BA**
(French, 1819-1896, daguerreotypist)   **JG**
Bibl: ▶Gernsheim, Hist. photog.;
▶Newhall, Photog.

Fizeau, Armand-Hippolyte-Louis   **JG**

Fizelle, Rah   **GC WC**
(Australian artist, 1891-1964)   **WC**
(British, 1891-1964)   **GC**
Bibl: ▶Witt checklist

Fjaestad, Gustav Edolf *(Swedish artist, 1868-)*   **WC**

Fjell, Kai *(Norwegian artist, 20th cent.)*   **WC**

Fjellboe, Paul *(American artist, 1873-1948)*   **WI**

Fjuk, Ignar *(Estonian architect, 20th century)*   **AV**
Bibl: Crit, 1983 Fall, no.13, p.53

Flacco or Fiacco, Orlando →see Flacco, Orlando

Flacco, Orlando   **BA GC**
(Italian artist, c.1530-c.1590)   **WC**
(Italian artist, c.1530-p.1591)   **WC**
(Italian painter, b. ca.1530; act. to ca.1590)   **GC**
(Italian painter, ca.1530-ca. 1592)   **BA**
Bibl: ▶Bolaffi; ▶Encic. italiana;
SIEVENHUNER FESTSCHRIFT, 138;
▶Thieme-Becker

Fiacco or Flacco, Orlando   **WC**
Fiacco, Orlando   **BA GC**

Flacco or Fiacco, Orlando   **WC**

Flaccus, Peter *(American painter, 20th c.)*   **BA**
Bibl: ARTS MAG LIV/1 (Sept
1979) 2; Guide exh. artists: N.
Amer. ptrs.

Flach, Hannes Maria   **BA JG**
(German photographer, 1901-1936)   **BA**
(German, 1901-, active Cologne, Germany)   **JG**
Bibl: BULLETIN DER MUSEEN DER
STADT KOLN (1983) 47; Cologne
(DEU), Museum Ludwig,HANNES
MARIA FLACH (1983)

Flach, Thomas *(British artist, op. 1736-)*   **WI**

Flacheron, Jean-Francois-Charles-Andre *(French, 1813-1883)*   **JG**

Flack, Audrey →see Flack, Audrey L.

Flack, Audrey L.   **BA**
(American artist, 1931-)   **WC**
(American artist, b.1931)   **WI**
(American painter, b.1931)   **BA**
Bibl: ▶WW Amer. Art

Flack, Audrey   **WC WI**

Flagellan [Unidentified] *(Unknown painter)*   **PR**
Bibl: (June 13, 1812, lot 2,
Phillips)

Flagg, Ernest *(American architect, 1857-1947)*   **AV BA**
Bibl: ▶Macmillan encyc. archts.;
▶Withey, Amer. archts.; ▶WWW
Amer.

Flagg, George Whiting   **BA WI**
(American artist, 1816-1897)   **WI**
(American painter, 1816-1897)   **BA**
Bibl: ▶Fielding's Amer. ptrs.;
▶Thieme-Becker

Flagg, James Montgomery   **BA WC WI**
(American artist, 1877-)   **WC**
(American artist, 1877-1960)   **WI**
(American illustrator, painter, author, 1877-1960)   **BA**
Bibl: ▶MoMA libr. cat.; ▶WWW
Amer.

Flagg, Jared Bradley *(American artist, 1820-1899)*   **WC WI**

Flaherty, Robert Joseph *(American, 1884-1951)*   **JG**

Flamand *(French menuisier, act. ca. 1760)*   **GC**
Bibl: Sotheby's London, April
22-24, 1982, lot 449

Flamberti, Tommaso →see Fiamberti, Tommaso

Flamen or Flamand the Elder, Anselme →see Flamen, Anselme

Flamen, Albert   **BA GC**
(Dutch painter, printmaker, b.ca. 1620, act.1669)   **BA**
(Flemish artist, op.1648-1669)   **WC**
(Flemish, act.1648-1669)   **GC**
Bibl: ▶Thieme-Becker; ▶Wurzbach,
NLD Künst.-Lex.

Flamen, Flaman or Flamand, Albert   **WC**

Flamen, Anselme   **BA JG**
(French artist, 1647-1717)   **WC**
(French sculptor, 1647-1717)   **BA**
(French, 1647-1717)   **GC JG**
Bibl: ▶Bénézit; ▶Dict. biog. fran.;
▶Larousse grande encyc.;
▶Thieme-Becker

Flamen or Flamand the Elder, Anselme   **WC**

Flamen, Anselme I   **GC**

Flamen, Anselme I →see Flamen, Anselme

Flamen, Flaman or Flamand, Albert →see Flamen, Albert

Flameng →see Flameng, François

Flameng, François   **GC PR WC**
(French artist, 1856-1923)   **WC**
(French painter, 1856-1923)   **GC PR**
Bibl: ▶Bénézit; ▶Thieme-Becker

Flameng   **PR**
Francois Flameng   **PR**

Flameng, Léopold   **BA WC**
(Belgian artist, 1831-1911)   **WC**
(French printmaker, painter, 1831-1911)   **BA**
Bibl: ▶Bénézit; ▶Thieme-Becker

Flameng, Marie Auguste *(French artist, 1843-1893)*   **WC**

Flamengo →see Fiammingo

Flaminio Allegrini →see Allegrini, Flaminio

Flaminio Tori →see Torri, Flaminio

Flaminio Torre →see Torri, Flaminio

Flaminio Torri →see Torri, Flaminio

Flamm, Albert   **GC WC**
(German artist, 1823-1906)   **WC**
(German painter, 1823-1906)   **GC**
Bibl: ▶Bénézit

Flanagan, Barry   **BA WI**
(British artist, b.1941)   **WI**
(British sculptor, painter, conceptual artist, b.1941)   **BA**
Bibl: ▶Babington Smith, Contemp.
artists; ▶Bénézit; ▶Contemp.
artists; ▶Intl. dir. exh. artists,
1983; ▶MoMA libr. cat.

Flanagan, John F. *(American sculptor, 1865-1952)*   **BA GC**
Bibl: ▸Bénézit; ▸Fielding's Amer. ptrs.; ▸Havlice, Idx. art. bio.; ▸RILA/BHA; ▸Schwab, Life & death; ▸WW Amer. Art, 1940-1941, 1953 obit.; ▸WWW Amer.; ▸Young, Amer. artists

Flanagan, Patrick *(Irish "student of architecture," 19th cent)*   **AV**
Bibl: The world of interiors, 1988 Feb., p.118

Flanders, Dennis   **BA WC WI**
(British artist, 20th cent.)   WC
(British artist, b.1915)   WI
(British painter, b.1915)   BA
Bibl: ▸Waters, Brit. artists

Flanders, French *(British artist, op. 1856-1866)*   **WI**

Flandes, Cobos de *(Spanish sculptor, act.1554, d.ca.1581)*   **BA**
Bibl: ▸Ars Hispaniae, p.199; Parrado del Olmo, Escult. seguid. Berruguete, 341-362

Flandes, Juan de → see Juan de Flandes

Flandes, Pedro de *(Spanish sculptor, ca.1498-ca.1566)*   **BA**
Bibl: ▸Ars Hispaniae, v.13, p.199; ▸Ceán Bermúdez, Bellas artes ESP; Parrado del Olmo, Escult. seguid. Berruguete, 193-194; ▸Thieme-Becker

Flandin, Eugene   **AV GC WC**
(French painter, 1809-1876)   GC
(French writer, archaeologist(?), 1809-1876)   AV
(Italian artist, 1809-1876)   WC
Bibl: ▸Libr. of Congr. Name Auth. File; ▸Thieme-Becker

Flandrin → see Flandrin, Jean-Paul

Flandrin family *(French painters, 19th-20th cs.)*   **BA**

Flandrin, Auguste Réné → see Flandrin, Réné-Auguste

Flandrin, Hippolyte → see Flandrin, Hippolyte-Jean

Flandrin, Hippolyte Jean → see Flandrin, Hippolyte-Jean

Flandrin, Hippolyte-Jean   **AV BA GC PR**
(French artist, 1809-1864)   WC
(French painter, 1809-1864)   BA GC PR
(French painter, muralist, 1808-1864)   AV
Bibl: ▸Bénézit; ▸Dict. biog. fran.; ▸Encyc. world art; ▸RILA/BHA; ▸Thieme-Becker; ▸Witt checklist
Flandrin, Hippolyte   GC
Flandrin, Hippolyte Jean   PR

Flandrin, Jean Hippolyte   **WC**
Hippolyte-Jean Flandrin   PR

Flandrin, Jean Hippolyte → see Flandrin, Hippolyte-Jean

Flandrin, Jean Paul → see Flandrin, Jean-Paul

Flandrin, Jean-Paul   **BA**
(French artist, 1811-1902)   WC
(French painter, 1811-1902)   BA GC PR
Bibl: ▸Bénézit; ▸Dict. biog. fran.; ▸Thieme-Becker; ▸Witt checklist
Flandrin   PR
Flandrin, Jean Paul   GC

Flandrin, Paul   **GC PR**

Flandrin, Paul (Jean Paul)   **WC**
Paul Flandrin   PR

Flandrin, Jules Leon   **GC WC**
(French artist, 1871-1947)   WC
(French painter, 1871-1947)   GC
Bibl: ▸Bénézit

Flandrin, Paul → see Flandrin, Jean-Paul

Flandrin, Paul (Jean Paul) → see Flandrin, Jean-Paul

Flandrin, Paul Hippolyte *(French painter, 1856-1921)*   **GC**
Bibl: ▸Thieme-Becker

Flandrin, René-Auguste   **BA**
(French artist, 1804-1843)   WC
(French painter, 1804-1843)   GC
(French painter, printmaker, 1804-1843)   BA
Bibl: ▸Bénézit; ▸Dict. biog. fran.; ▸Thieme-Becker; ▸Witt checklist

Flandrin, Auguste Réné   **GC WC**

Flannagan, John B. → see Flannagan, John Bernard

Flannagan, John Bernard   **BA WI**
(American artist, 1895-1942)   WI
(American artist, 1898-1942)   WC
(American sculptor, 1895-1942)   BA
Bibl: ▸Bénézit; ▸Cummings, Contemp. Amer. artists, 1971; ▸Havlice, Idx. art. bio.; ▸MoMA libr. cat.; ▸Vollmer, Künst.-Lex. 20. Jhr.; ▸WW Amer. Art, 1941

Flannagan, John B.   **WC**

Flannery → see Flannery, Vaughn

Flannery, Vaughn *(American painter, 1898-1955)*   **BA PR**
Bibl: ▸RILA/BHA; ▸Vollmer, Künst.-Lex. 20. Jhr.; ▸WWW Amer., v.3
Flannery   PR
Vaughn Flannery   PR

Flansburgh, Earl R. *(American architect)*   **AV**
Bibl: ▸AIA Pro File, 1985

Flashar, Max *(German artist, 1855-1915)*   **WC**

Flasschoen, Gustave *(Belgian artist, 1868-)*   **WC**

Flat-Head Painter *(Apulian vase-painter)*   **GC**
Bibl: Trendall, Attic red-fig. vases Apulia

Flatfish Painter *(South Italian vase-painter, 350-300 BC)*   **GC**
Bibl: McPhee & Trendall, Fish-Plates

Flatman, Thomas   **BA WC WI**
(British artist, 1635-1688)   WI
(British artist, 1637-1688)   WC
(English poet, miniaturist, 1637-1688)   BA
Bibl: ▸Bénézit; Encyc. Americana; ▸Thieme-Becker

Flatt, David Gary *(American cabinetmaker, b.1952)*   **BA**
Bibl: Milwaukee (WI, USA), Art Museum, OUT OF THE WOODS (1980)

Flattely, Alastair F. *(British artist, b.1922)*   **WI**

Flatters, Richard *(German artist, 1822-1876)*   **WC**

Flattner, Peter → see Flötner, Peter

Flatz, Gebhard *(German artist, 1800-1881)*   **WC**

Flatz, Wolfgang *(German artist, 20th c.)*   **BA**
Bibl: Munich (DEU), Stadt. gal. im Lenbachhaus, Kunstf. Max., FLATZ MORGENROT & DAMMERYN (1981)

Flaugé, José → see Flaugier, Josée

Flaugier, Josée *(French painter in ESP, 1775-1813)*   **BA**
Bibl: Bassegoda Novell, Reales Sitios XXI, 81 1984, p.45-64; ▸Encic. univ. ilus.; ▸Ossorio y Bernard, Artistas españoles 19s.; ▸Rafols, Artistas Cataluña; ▸Thieme-Becker
Flaugé, José   BA
Flaugier, Josep Bernat   BA
Flaugier, Joseph Bernard   BA

Flaugier, Josep Bernat → see Flaugier, Josée

Flaugier, Joseph Bernard → see Flaugier, Josée

Flavelle, William   **WC WI**
(British artist, c.1786-p.1813)   WC
(British artist, circa 1786-op. 1813)   WI

Flavet, Claude *(French artist, 1940-)*   **WC**

Flaviens, C. Chusseau *(French photographer, act.ca.1900-ca. 1914)*   **BA**
Bibl: IMAGE XXI/1 (Mar 1978) 1-31

Flavin, Dan   **AV BA WC WI**
(American artist, 1933-)   AV WC
(American artist, author, b.1933)   BA
(American artist, b.1933)   WI
Bibl: ▸Contemp. artists; ▸WW Amer. Art, 1984

Flavin, John *(British artist, op.20th c.)*   **WI**

Flávio-Shiró *(Brazilian painter, b.1928)*   **BA**
Bibl: ▸Bénézit; Laude, Colóquio: Artes 59 (Dec 1983)
Shiró, Flávio   BA

Flawiizky, Konstantin Dmitrejewitsch (Russian artist, 1830-1866) **WC**

Flaxman, Ann (British, d.1820) **BA**
Bibl: ▶Dict. natl. biog.; Irwin, JOHN FLAXMAN

Flaxman, John **BA GC WC WI**
(British artist, 1755-1826) WC WI
(British sculptor, 1755-1826) GC
(British sculptor, designer, 1755-1826) BA
Bibl: ▶Bénézit; ▶Dict. natl. biog.; ▶RILA/BHA; ▶Thieme-Becker

Flaxman, Mary Ann (British artist, 1768-1833) **WC WI**

Flay, William H.G. (fl. 1920; draftsman (technical), Ottawa) **FA**
Bibl: CAAD Finding Aid, Ben Albert Dore 88957; Natl. Arch. of Canada, CAAD Finding Aid

Flecha, Giuseppe→see Frecha, José

Flechy, Pierre (French ébéniste, 1715-1769, master 1756) **GC**
Bibl: ▶Salverte, Ébénistes 18e s.

Fleck→see Fleck, Joseph A.

Fleck, Joseph→see Fleck, Joseph A.

Fleck, Joseph A. **WC WI**
(American artist, 1892-) WC
(American artist, b.1892) WI
(American painter, b. 1893) PR
Bibl: ▶WWW Amer. art

Fleck PR

Fleck, Joseph PR

Fleck, Joseph Amadeus **PR**

Joseph Amadeus Fleck PR

Fleck, Joseph Amadeus→see Fleck, Joseph A.

Fleck, Ralph (German painter, b.1951) **BA**
Bibl: Kunstwerk, XXXIII/6 (1980) pp.3-38

Fleckenstein, Charles (American architect) **AV**

Fleckenstein, Louis (American, 1866-1943) **JG**

Fleckseder, Erwin (Austrian architect, Vienna) **AV**
Bibl: Der Aufbau, 1987 July, v.42, no.6, p.294

Fleer, Fritz (German sculptor, b.1921) **BA**
Bibl: ▶Vollmer, Künst.-Lex. 20. Jhr.; ▶WW Arts DEU

Fleet, George (Architect, Harare, Zimbabwe) **AV**
Bibl: Yearbook - The Institute of Architects of Zimbabwe, 1984

Fleetwood-Hesketh, Peter (British architectural writer and illustrator) **AV**
Bibl: Thirties Society Journal no.1, p.13

Fleetwood-Walker, Bernard (British artist, 1893-1965) **WC WI**

Flegel→see Flegel, Georg

Flegel, Georg **BA GC PR WC**
(Czech painter in Germany, 1566-1638) BA
(Czechoslovakian painter, 1566-1638) PR
(German artist, 1563-1638) WC
(German painter and draughtsman, 1566-1638) GC
Bibl: ▶Encyk. českého výtv. umění; Munich, Alte Pinakothek, (1983); ▶RILA/BHA; ▶Thieme-Becker

Flegel PR

Georg Flegel PR

Fleig-Harbauer, Gisela (West German landscape architect, Emmendingen) **AV**
Bibl: Baumeister, 1986 Aug., v.83, no.8, p.59

Fleischer, Alain (French filmmaker, photographer, b. 1944) **BA**
Bibl: ▶Art Index, v.38; ▶ARTbibl. mod., 21/1; ▶Auer, Encyc. photographes; CAHIERS DU MUSÉE NATL. D'ART MODERNE, 12 (1983) 178-181

Fleischer, Hieronymus (German, d.1559) **BA**
Bibl: Wallraf-Richartz-Jahrb. XXXIX (1977)

Fleischer, Joseph L. (American architect) **AV**
Bibl: ▶AIA Pro File, 1985

Fleischer, Karin (German artist, b.1943) **BA**
Bibl: Arts Council GBR, Summer show 3 (1977)

Fleischer, Karl Christoph Wilhelm (German architect, engineer, 1727-1787) **BA**
Bibl: ▶Portoghesi, Diz. arch. e urbanistica; ▶Thieme-Becker

Fleischer, Lutz (East German painter, b.1956) **BA**
Bibl: Berlin (DEU), Nationalgalerie, Expressivität Heute (1985)

Fleischer, Max **GC WC WI**
(American artist, 1861-1930) WI
(American artist, 20th cent.) WC
(German draughtsman, b.1861) GC
Bibl: ▶Thieme-Becker

Fleischer, Max (Czech architect in AUT, 1841-1905) **BA**
Bibl: ▶Avery Librr. cat.; ▶Thieme-Becker

Fleischer, Richard (American artist) **AV**
Bibl: Architecture: the AIA journal, 1986 Feb., v.75, no.2, p.39

Fleischman, Lloyd **AV**

Fleischman, Richard J. (American architect, Cleveland Heights, Ohio) **AV**
Bibl: ▶AIA Pro File, 1984

Fleischmann→see Fleischmann, Adolf Richard

Fleischmann, Adolf Richard **PR WC**
(German artist, 1892-) WC
(German painter, b. 1892) PR
Bibl: ▶Witt checklist

Adolf Richard Fleischmann PR

Fleischmann PR

Fleischmann, Adolph PR

Fleischmann, Adolph→see Fleischmann, Adolf Richard

Fleischmann, Carl (German artist, 1853-) **WC**

Fleischmann, Frank (West German architect, Munich) **AV**
Bibl: Deutsches Architektenblatt, 1989 Jan.1, v.21, no.1, p.45

Fleischmann, Friedrich (German artist, 1791-1834) **WC**

Fleischmann, Karel (Czech physician, author, artist, 1897-1944) **BA**
Bibl: Umeni XXIV/1 (1976) 85

Fleischner, Richard **AV BA**
(American environmental artist) AV
(American sculptor, b.1944) BA
Bibl: Arts Mag. LI/8 (Apr 1977) 118; Landscape architecture, 1985 July-Aug., v.75, no.4, p.78; ▶NY art yrbk.

Fleishman, Maurice H. **AV**

Flejsar, Josef (Czech artist, 1922-) **WC**

Flemal→see Flemal, Bertholet (I)

Flemal, Bertholet (I) **PR**
(Flemish artist, 1614-1675) WC
(Flemish painter, 1614-1675) PR
(Flemish, 1614-1675) GC
Bibl: ▶Thieme-Becker; ▶Witt checklist

Bartolet Flamael PR

Bertholet Flemal (I) PR

Flemal PR

Flemal, Bertholet I **GC**

Flemal, Flemael or Flemalle, Bertholet **WC**

Hammeil PR

Flemal, Bertholet I→see Flemal, Bertholet (I)

Flemal, Flemael or Flemalle, Bertholet→see Flemal, Bertholet (I)

Flémalle, Master of→see Campin, Robert

Fleming, Eden→see Box, Eden (Eden Fleming)

Fleming, Edward S. (American architect, Washington, D.C) **AV**
Bibl: Fine homebuilding, 1988 June-July, no.47, p.79

Fleming, Fr. v. (German(?) artist, op.1726) **WC**

Fleming, Jane→see Harrington, Jane

Fleming, John→see Fleming, John B.

Fleming, John B. **WI**
(British artist, 1792-1845) WC WI

Fleming, John **WC**

Fleming, Mary (British artist, op. 20th c.) **WI**

Fleming, Patricia (*American painter, 20th c.*) **BA**
Bibl: Haaren, Arts mag., LVII/5 (Jan. 1983) p.6

Fleming, Thomas (*Engraver*) **WI**

Fleming, Thomas (*American interior designer, New York City*) **AV**
Bibl: Architectural digest, 1984 Apr, v.41, no.4, p.148

Fleming-Williams, C.P. (*British artist, op.1899-1925*) **WI**
Bibl: ▶Houfe, Brit. book illus.

Flemming, Hertz (*1936-*) **AV**

Flemwell, George → see Flemwell, George Jackson

Flemwell, George Jackson **WI**
(*British artist, 1865-1928*) **WI**
(*British artist, 19th cent.*) **WC**

Flemwell, George **WC**

Flensburg, Nicolaus Andree von
(*German artist, 16th cent.*) **WC**

Fleps, Peter (*American sculptor, b.1955*) **BA**
Bibl: Washington, DC (USA), Hirshhorn Mus., Directions (1986), p.50

Fleri, Joseph → see Fleri, Joseph C.

Fleri, Joseph C. (*American sculptor, 1889-1965*) **GC**
Bibl: Getty Photo Study Coll.;
▶Opitz, Amer. sculptors

Fleri, Joseph **GC**

Flers, Camille **GC WC**
(*French artist, 1802-1868*) **WC**
(*French, 1802-1868*) **GC**
Bibl: ▶Bénézit; ▶Witt checklist

Flesch-Brunningen, Ludmilla von (Luma) (*German artist, 1856-p. 1915*) **WC**

Flessiers, Balthasar **GC WC**
(*Flemish artist, op.c.1575-m.c.1619/27*) **WC**
(*Flemish painter, act.1575-d. bef.1626*) **GC**
Bibl: Getty Photo Study Coll.;
▶Thieme-Becker

Flessiers, Benjamin (*Flemish artist, op.1629-1666*) **WC**

Flessiers, Willem (*Dutch artist, op.c. 1627*) **WC**

Fletcher [Unidentified] (*Unknown painter*) **PR**
Bibl: (November 26, 1814, lot 96, Christie's)

Fletcher, Aaron Dean **BA WI**
(*American artist, 1817-1902*) **WI**
(*American painter, 1817-1902*) **BA**
Bibl: ANTIQUES CXV/1 (Jan 1979) 184-193; ▶Groce, Artists Amer.;
▶Young, Amer. artists

Fletcher, Alex (*American painter, 1866-1952*) **BA PR**
Bibl: CARNEGIE MAG. LIV/3 (Mar 1980) 11; ▶RILA/BHA
Alex Fletcher **PR**

Fletcher, Alison (*American interior designer*) **AV**
Bibl: Metropolitan home, 1989 May, v.21, no.5, p.190

Fletcher, Blandford → see Fletcher, William Teulon Blandford

Fletcher, Edward Henry Eugene
(*British artist, op.20th c.*) **WI**

Fletcher, Edwin **WC WI**
(*British artist, 19th cent.*) **WC**
(*British artist, op.1910-*) **WI**

Fletcher, G.H.Benton (*British artist, d.1944*) **WI**

Fletcher, Hanslip **WC WI**
(*British artist, 1874-*) **WC**
(*British artist, 1874-1955*) **WI**

Fletcher, Henry (*British artist, b.1901*) **WI**

Fletcher, John Henry (*British artist, op.circa 1884-*) **WI**

Fletcher, Leone W. (*American artist, 1932-2032*) **WI**

Fletcher, Margaret, Miss → see Leadbitter, Margaret Fletcher

Fletcher, Norman C. (*American architect, 1917-*) **AV**

Fletcher, Patricia (*French interior designer*) **AV**
Bibl: Maison française, 1988 Jan.-Feb., no.413, p.98

Fletcher, Thomas **WC WI**
(*British artist, op.1789*) **WC**
(*British artist, op.1789-*) **WI**

Fletcher, Thomas (*American silversmith, 1787-1866*) **BA**
Bibl: ANTIQUES CXV (Jan 1979) 180-183

Fletcher, U.R (*British artist, op.circa 1925-*) **WI**

Fletcher, William **WC WI**
(*British artist, op.1644*) **WC**
(*British artist, op.1644-*) **WI**

Fletcher, William Teulon Blandford **WI**
(*British artist, 1858-1936*) **WI**
(*British artist, 1866-1936*) **WC**
(*British painter, 1866-1936*) **PR**
Bibl: ▶Witt checklist
Blandford Fletcher **PR**

Fletcher, Blandford **PR WC**

Fletner, Peter → see Flötner, Peter

Flettrich, Leonard T. (*American painter, 1916-1970*) **BA**
Bibl: New Orleans (LA, USA), Museum of Art, LEONARD T. FLITTRICH (1974)

Fleuren, W. L. H. M. (*Dutch architect*) **AV**
Bibl: Gemeentewerken, 1986 Feb., v.15, no.2, p.34

Fleuret (*French artist, op.1820-1850*) **WC**

Fleury (*French architect, act.1680-1685*) **BA**
Bibl: Laurent, Mons. Hist. Fran., 145 (Jun.-Jul. 1986), p.20;
▶Portoghesi, Diz. arch. e urbanistica

Fleury Chenu → see Chenu, Augustin Pierre Bienvenu

Fleury, Adrien (*French ébéniste, 1721-d. bef.1775*) **GC**
Bibl: ▶Salverte, Ébénistes 18e s.

Fleury, Albert-François (*French artist, muralist, worked in the U.S, 1848-*) **AV**

Fleury, Antoine Claude (*French artist, op.1795-1822*) **WC**

Fleury, Ch. Rohault de → see Rohault de Fleury, Charles

Fleury, Fanny, Mme. (*French artist, 1848-p.1888*) **WC**

Fleury, François Antoine Léon **BA GC WC**
(*French artist, 1804-1858*) **WC**
(*French painter, 1804-1858*) **BA GC**
Bibl: ▶Bellier, Artistes fran.;
▶Bénézit; ▶Dict. biog. fran.;
▶Thieme-Becker

Fleury, H. **WC WI**
(*British artist, 19th cent.*) **WC**
(*British artist, op.1885-1890*) **WI**

Fleury, J.V. de (*French artist, op. 1847-1868*) **WC**

Fleury, Joseph Nicolas Robert → see Robert-Fleury, Joseph Nicolas

Fleury, Lucien (*French artist, 20th cent.*) **WC**

Fleuss, Henry → see Fleuss, Henry J.

Fleuss, Henry J. **WI**
(*British artist, 1847-1874*) **WC**
(*British artist, op.1847-1874*) **WI**

Fleuss, Henry **WC**

Flexner, Roland (*French painter, b.1944*) **BA**
Bibl: Arts Council GBR, French art (1979)

Fliccius, Garlicke → see Flicke, Gerlach

Flick, Auguste Emile (*French artist, 19th cent.*) **WC**

Flick, Robbert (*Canadian photographer in USA, b.1939*) **BA**
Bibl: Afterimage VIII/5 (Dec 1980) 10-11; ▶MoMA libr. cat.; ▶Natl. Gall. Canada libr. cat.; ▶Parry, Photo idx.; ▶WW Amer. Art

Flicke or Fliccius, Gerlach or Garlicke → see Flicke, Gerlach

Flicke, Gerlach **GC WI**
(*British artist, op.1545-, d.1558*) **WI**
(*British artist, op.1547-1558*) **WC**
(*British, act.1547-1558*) **GC**
Bibl: ▶Thieme-Becker; ▶Witt checklist

Fliccius, Garlicke **WI**

Flicke or Fliccius, Gerlach or Garlicke **WC**

Flieger, Rainer (*German artist, 20th cent.*) **WC**

Flierl, Peter (*German architect*) **AV**
Bibl: Architektur der DDR, 1985 July, v.34, no.7, p.405

Fliess, Henry *(1956?-1975?;*
Architect, Toronto)   **FA**
    Bibl: CAAD Finding Aid, J. Austin
    Floyd, 82303/27 Proj. 67011,
    69031; Natl. Arch. of Canada,
    CAAD Finding Aid; Toronto City
    Directories

Flight, Claude   **BA WC WI**
    (British artist, 1881-)   WC
    (British artist, 1881-1955)   WI
    (British painter, printmaker,
      sculptor, 1881-1955)   BA
    Bibl: ▶Johnson, Brit. artists;
    ▶Peppin, Bk. illus. 20c.; ▶Waters,
    Brit. artists; ▶Who was who
    [GBR], 1957-60

Flinck → see Flinck, Govert
Flinck, Govaert → see Flinck, Govert

Flinck, Govert   **BA GC PR**
    (Dutch artist, 1615-1660)   WC
    (Dutch painter and
      draughtsman, 1615-1660)   GC
    (Dutch painter, 1615-1660)   BA PR
    (Dutch, 1616-1660)   JG
    Bibl: Getty Photo Study Coll.;
    ▶Grote Winkler Prins; ▶Nieuw NLD
    biog. woord.; ▶RILA/BHA;
    ▶Thieme-Becker

    Flinck   PR

Flinck, Govaert   **JG PR**
Flinck, Govert Teunisz. or
    Anthonisz.   **WC**
    Flink   PR
    G. Flinch   PR
    G. Flinck   PR
    G. Flink   PR
    Govaert Flinck   PR
    Govaert Flink   PR
    Goverd Flink   PR
    Govert Flinck   PR
    Govert Flink   PR

Flinck, Govert Teunisz. or
Anthonisz. → see Flinck, Govert

Flinck, Ingitta Claedr. Thoveling
    (Dutch, act.1645, d.1651)   BA
    Bibl: ISRAEL MUSEUM JOURNAL, II
    (spring 1983) 58-61; ▶Nieuw NLD
    biog. woord.

Flinck, Nicolaes Anthoni *(Dutch*
    artist, 1646-1723)   **WC**

Flindt, Flint, Flynt, Flynth or Vlindt
    the Younger, Paul *(German*
    artist, op.1592-1618)   **WC**

Flink → see Flinck, Govert

Flinsch, Alexander *(German artist,*
    1834-1912)   **WC**

Flint, Andreas *(Danish artist, c.1768-*
    1824)   **WC**

Flint, Anthony Ray *(British engineer,*
    1924-)   **AV**
    Bibl: Building design, 1989 June,
    suppl., p.5

Flint, Francis M.R. → see Flint, Francis
Murrau Russell

Flint, Francis Murrau Russell   **WI**
    (British artist, 1915-)   WC
    (British artist, b.1915)   WI

Flint, Francis M.R.   **WC**

Flint, R. Purves → see Flint, Robert
Purves

Flint, Robert Purves   **WI**
    (British artist, 1883-)   WC
    (British artist, 1883-1947)   WI

Flint, R. Purves   **WC**

Flint, Sir William Russell → see Flint,
William Russell

Flint, William Russell   **BA GC WI**
    (British artist, 1880-1969)   WC WI
    (British painter, 1880-1969)   BA
    (British, 1880-1969)   GC
    Bibl: George Goldner; ▶Harris,
    Scottish ptrs.; ▶Waters, Brit.
    artists; ▶Witt checklist

Flint, Sir William Russell   **WC**

Flintoe, Johan   **BA WC**
    (Norwegian artist, 1786-1870)   WC
    (Norwegian painter, 1786-1870)   BA
    Bibl: ▶Bénézit; Naess, Arne
    Walentin; Wielbach

Flipart → see Flipart, Charles Joseph

Flipart, Charles Joseph   **BA GC PR WC**
    (French artist, 1721-1797)   WC
    (French painter, 1721-1797)   PR
    (French painter, printmaker,
      1721-1797)   BA
    (French, 1721-1797)   GC
    Bibl: ▶Bénézit; Getty Photo Study
    Coll. (Ptgs.); ▶RILA/BHA;
    ▶Thieme-Becker; ▶Witt checklist

    Charles Joseph Flipart   PR
    Flipart   PR
    Flipart, Charles-Joseph   PR
    Flipart, Giuseppe   BA
    Flipart, Joseph   GC

Flipart, Charles-Joseph → see Flipart,
Charles Joseph
Flipart, Giuseppe → see Flipart,
Charles Joseph

Flipart, Jean Jacques   **BA WC**
    (French artist, 1719-1782)   WC
    (French artist, 18th cent.)   WC
    (French painter, 1719-1782)   GC
    (French printmaker, printmaker,
      1719-1782)   BA
    Bibl: ▶Bénézit; ▶Dict. biog. fran.;
    ▶Thieme-Becker; ▶Witt checklist

Filipart, Jean Jacques   **WC**
Flipart, Jean-Jacques   **GC**

Flipart, Jean-Jacques → see Flipart,
Jean Jacques
Flipart, Joseph → see Flipart, Charles
Joseph

Flir, Erich *(Austrian architect,*
    Salzburg)   **AV**
    Bibl: Bauforum, 1987, v.20, no.
    123, p.68

Flisak, Jerzy *(Polish artist, 20th*
    cent.)   **WC**

Flitcroft, Henry   **AV BA**
    (1697-1769)   AV
    (English architect, 1697-1769)   BA
    Bibl: ▶Colvin, Brit. archts.; ▶Dict.
    natl. biog.

Flobert, Antonio Federico *(Italian*
    military engineer, act.1756)   **BA**
    Bibl: ▶RILA/BHA

Floch → see Floch, Joseph
Floch, Josef → see Floch, Joseph

Floch, Joseph   **BA PR**
    (American painter, 1895-1977) BA PR
    (German artist, 1894-)   WC
    Bibl: ▶Bénézit; ▶Cummings,
    Contemp. Amer. artists; ▶Fogg
    Mus. Libr. cat.; ▶Locus;
    ▶RILA/BHA; ▶Vollmer, Künst.-Lex.
    20. Jhr.; ▶WW Amer. Art, 1976

    Floch   PR

Floch, Josef   **WC**
    Joseph Floch   PR

Flockhart, William *(British architect,*
    1814-1913)   **AV**
    Bibl: ▶Gray, Edwardian arch.

Flockton, Frederick S. *(British artist,*
    op.1854-1879)   **WI**

Flocon, Albert → see Flocon, Albert
(Mentzel)

Flocon, Albert (Mentzel)   **BA**
    (French artist, 1909-)   WC
    (French printmaker, b.1909)   BA
    Bibl: ▶Bénézit

Flocon, Albert   **WC**

Floding, Per Gustaf   **BA**
    (Swedish artist, 1731-1791)   WC
    (Swedish printmaker, 1731-
      1791)   BA
    Bibl: ▶Svenskt konst.-lex.;
    ▶Thieme-Becker

Floding, Per Gustav   **WC**

Floding, Per Gustav → see Floding, Per
Gustaf
Flodner, Peter → see Flötner, Peter

Floeter, Kent *(American sculptor,*
    b.1937.)   **BA**
    Bibl: ▶Intl. dir. exh. artists, 1982;
    ▶Locus; ▶WW Amer. Art, 1989

Flöge, Emilie *(Austrian fashion*
    designer, 1874-1952)   **BA**
    Bibl: Nebehay, GUSTAV KLIMT;
    Novotny & Dobai, Gustav Klimt;
    Powell, APOLLO CXVI/ 246 (Aug
    1982) 112-114

Floience, P.   **WC WI**
    (British artist, 19th cent.)   WC
    (British artist, op.19th c.)   WI

Floirat, Marie *(French artist, 1900-)* **WC**

Flood, Edward C. *(American*
    painter, sculptor, b.1944)   **BA**
    Bibl: ▶Intl. dir. exh. artists, 1983

Flood, Paul *(American artist, 20th*
    c.)   **BA**
    Bibl: Arts Mag., Arts review,
    Wash DC, 3 Nov 1982

Flood, Rex *(British artist, op.20th c.)* **WI**

Floor, Marcia (*American sculptor, b.1947.*)   **BA**
   Bibl: Honolulu (HI, USA), Acad. Arts, Matter-Memory (1981); ▶Intl. dir. exh. artists, 1982

Floors, Dolf (*Dutch architect*)   **AV**
   Bibl: De Architect, 1985 Sept., v.16, no.9, p.58

Floquet → see Floquet, Lucas (I)

Floquet, Flocket or Flocquet, Lucas, I → see Floquet, Lucas (I)

Floquet, Flocket or Flocquet, Simon (*Flemish artist, op.c.1634/5*)   **WC**

Floquet, Lucas (I)   **PR**
   (*Flemish artist, 1578-1635*)   WC
   (*Flemish painter, 1578-1635*)   PR
   Bibl: ▶Thieme-Becker
   Floquet   PR

Floquet, Flocket or Flocquet, Lucas, I   **WC**
   Lucas Flockett   PR
   Lucas Floquet (I)   PR

Flor, Ede (*Hungarian painter, printmaker in NLD, b.1925*)   **BA**
   Bibl: Paris (FRA), Inst. néerlandais, L'Atelier de Piet Clement (1976); ▶Scheen, Ned. beeldende kunst.
   Flor, Eduard   BA

Flor, Eduard → see Flor, Ede

Flor, Ferdinand   **BA WC**
   (*German artist, 1793-1881*)   WC
   (*German painter, 1793-1881*)   BA
   Bibl: ▶Bénézit; ▶Thieme-Becker

Flora MacLean Reeder → see Reeder, Flora MacLean

Flora, Paul (*Austrian printmaker, b.1922*)   **BA**
   Bibl: ▶Vollmer, Künst.-Lex. 20. Jhr.; ▶WW Austria

Florakis, Mathèos (*Greek painter, printmaker in DEU, b.1935*)   **BA**
   Bibl: ▶WW Arts DEU

Florance, Colden   **AV**

Floreani, Francesco (*Italian artist, op.1534-m.1593*)   **WC**

Floren, Lars (Lasse) (*Swedish artist, 1899-*)   **WC**

Florena, Mario (*Italian architect*)   **AV**
   Bibl: Ville giardini, 1985 July-Aug., no.198, p.14

Florence Caeretan Painter (*Etruscan vase-painter*)   **GC**
   Bibl: Del Chiaro, Caere

Florence Painter   **GC**
   Bibl: ▶Beazley, Attic red-fig. vase-ptrs.

Florence, Henry Louis (*British artist, 1844-1916*)   **WC WI**

Florence, Hercules (*French photographer, inventor in BRA, 1804-1879*)   **BA**
   Bibl: ARTFORUM XIV/6 (Feb 1976) 57-59

Florence, Mary (nee Sargant) → see Florence, Mary Sargant

Florence, Mary Sargant   **WI**
   (*British artist, 1857-*)   WC
   (*British artist, 1857-1954*)   WI
   Florence, Mary (nee Sargant)   **WC**
   Sargant, Mary, Miss   WI

Florencio (*Spanish scribe, 920-978*)   **BA**
   Bibl: ▶Encic. univ. ilus.

Florensa, Adolfo (*Spanish architect, 1889-1969*)   **AV**
   Bibl: AA files, 1987 Spring, no.14, p.65

Florent Willems → see Willems, Florent

Florentino (*Italian architect*)   **AV**
   Bibl: Conservation news, 1985 Nov., no.28, p.29

Florentinus → see Fontius, Bartolomeus

Florentius (*Spanish scribe, 10th century*)   **GC**
   Bibl: Williams, Early Span. mss. illum., pp.55-56

Florenzuoli → see Pier Francesco da Viterbo

Florer, Ignaz → see Flurer, Ignaz Franz Joseph

Flores → see Floris, Frans, the elder

flores → see Foro, Francesco [Unidentified]

Flores, Aurélio Martinez (*Brasilian architect*)   **AV**
   Bibl: Projeto, 1987 June (suppl.), no.100, p.4

Flores, Daniel (*Salvadoran poet, painter, 20th c.*)   **BA**
   Bibl: ARTS MAG LVIII/5 (Jan 1984) 80

Flores, Gilbert (*American architect*)   **AV**
   Bibl: Architectural digest, 1985 Oct., v.42, no.10, p.124

Flores, Javier (*Venezuelan artist, op. c.1774*)   **WC**

Flores, Pedro (*Spanish artist, 20th cent.*)   **WC**

Flores, Ricardo (*French artist, 1878-1918*)   **WC**

Florescu, Vlad (*Romanian painter, b.1923.*)   **BA**
   Bibl: ARTS XXI/7 (July 1974) 22-25; ▶Barbosa, Art. romani contemp.

Florett (*German(?) artist, 19th cent.*)   **WC**

Florez, Francisco (*Spanish painter, act.1546-1594*)   **BA**
   Bibl: Relações artisticas entre PRT e ESP (1987), pp.9-64

Florian (*Engraver*)   **WI**
Florian → see Florian, Walter

Florian, Maximilian (*German artist, 1901-*)   **WC**

Florian, Olga Winsinger (*German artist, 1844-1926*)   **WC**
   Wisinger-Florian, Olga   **WC**

Florian, Paul (*American architect, Chicago*)   **AV**
   Bibl: Chicago architectural journal, 1989, v.7, p.78

Florian, Walter (*American painter, 1878-1909*)   **PR**
   Bibl: ▶WWW Amer. art
   Florian   PR
   Walter Florian   PR

Floriani, Sergio (*Italian artist, b.1948*)   **BA**
   Bibl: Rome (ITA), Ist. It.-Lat. Amer., Narcissus (1982)

Floriano da Brescia (*Italian artist, 16th cent.*)   **WC**

Florigerio, Sebastiano   **BA GC WC WI**
   (*Italian artist, c.1500-p.1543*)   WC
   (*Italian artist, circa 1500-op. 1543*)   WI
   (*Italian painter, ca.1500-1543*)   BA GC
   Bibl: ▶Bolaffi; ▶RILA/BHA, 1986; ▶Thieme-Becker

Florimi, Matteo (*Italian, act.1580-1603*)   **GC**
   Bibl: ▶Thieme-Becker

Florin, Gudrun Müsse (*West German artist, 1935-*)   **AV**
   Bibl: Das Münster, 1989, v.42, no.2, p.102

Florindo, Alonso Ruiz (*Spanish artist, 17th cent.(?)*)   **WC**

Florine Stettheimer → see Stettheimer, Florine

Floris → see Floris, Frans, the elder

Floris de Vriendt, Cornelis, II → see Floris, Cornelis II

Floris de Vriendt, Frans → see Floris, Frans, the elder

Floris de Vriendt, Frans, I → see Floris, Frans, the elder

Floris de Vriendt, Jacob, I → see Floris, Jacob (the Elder)

Floris de Vrient, Frans → see Floris, Frans, the elder

Floris Gerritsz. van Schooten → see Schooten, Floris Gerritsz. van

Floris, Cornelis (the Younger) → see Floris, Cornelis II

Floris, Cornelis de Vriendt, called → see Floris, Cornelis II

Floris, Cornelis II   **BA**
   (*Dutch architect and designer, 1514-1575*)   AV
   (*early Netherlandish sculptor, architect, 1514-1575*)   BA
   (*Flanders draughtsman, 1514-1575*)   GC
   (*Netherlands artist, 1514-1575*)   WC
   Bibl: ▶Encyc. world art; ▶Nagler, Neues Künst.-Lex.; ▶Thieme-Becker

Floris de Vriendt, Cornelis, II   **WC**
Floris, Cornelis (the Younger)   **GC**
Floris, Cornelis de Vriendt, called   **AV**

Floris, Cornelis III *(early Netherlandish painter, sculptor, 1551-1615)* — BA
    Bibl: ▶Bénézit; ▶Thieme-Becker; ▶Wurzbach, NLD Künst.-Lex.
    Vriendt, Cornelis III de — BA
Floris, Frans → see Floris, Frans, the elder
Floris, Frans (I) → see Floris, Frans, the elder
Floris, Frans (the Elder) → see Floris, Frans, the elder
Floris, Frans I → see Floris, Frans, the elder
Floris, Frans, the elder — BA
    (early Netherlandish painter, printmaker, ca.1519-1570) — BA
    (Flanders painter and draughtsman, ca.1519-ca. 1570) — GC
    (Netherlandish painter, 1516-1570) — PR
    (Netherlands artist, c.1518-1570) — WC
    (Painter, etcher, woodcutter, artist, 1519/20-1570) — CE
    Bibl: ▶Bénézit; ▶Friedländer, Early Neth. ptg., v.13, pp.34+; Getty Photo Study Coll.; ▶RILA/BHA; ▶Thieme-Becker; ▶Witt checklist
    de Vriendt, Frans — CE
    F. Florio — PR
    F. Floris — PR
    Flores — PR
    Floris — PR
    Floris de Vriendt, Frans — BA
    Floris de Vriendt, Frans, I — WC
    Floris de Vrient, Frans — BA
    Floris, Frans — CE PR
    Floris, Frans (I) — PR
    Floris, Frans (the Elder) — GC
    Floris, Frans I — BA
    Fran. Flores — PR
    Francis Floris — PR
    Francisco Flores — PR
    Franck Flore — PR
    Frank Floris — PR
    Frans de Vrient — BA
    Frans Floris — PR
    Frans Floris (I) — PR
    Frans Florisz — PR
    Frans Florisz. — PR
    Frans Florus — PR
    Fransje Floris — PR
    Fras: Floris — PR
    Vriendt, Frans de — BA
    Vrient, Frans de — BA
Floris, Jacob (the Elder) — GC
    (Flanders painter and stained glass designer, 1524-1581) — GC
    (Netherlands artist, 1524-1581) — WC
    Bibl: ▶Bénézit; ▶Thieme-Becker; ▶Witt checklist
    Floris de Vriendt, Jacob, I — WC
    Floris, Jacob de Vrendt — GC

Floris, Jacob de Vrendt → see Floris, Jacob (the Elder)
Floris, Jan Baptista *(early Netherlandish painter, b.1549/50)* — BA
    Bibl: ▶Bénézit; Hafnia-Copenhagen Papers 8 (1981) 51-71; ▶Thieme-Becker; ▶Wurzbach, NLD Künst.-Lex.
    Vriendt, Jan Baptista de — BA
Floris, Johan *(early Netherlandish architect, sculptor in DNK, act. 1576-1581)* — BA
    Bibl: Hanne Honnens de Lichtenberg, in HAFNIA 8 (1981), 51-58
Florquin, Louis *(French artist, 20th cent.)* — WC
Florsheim, Lillian — BA
    (American artist, 20th cent.) — WC
    (American artist, op.1966-) — WI
    (American sculptor, 20th c.) — BA
    Bibl: ▶Bénézit; Krantz, NEW ART EXAMINER X/8 (May 1983) 12,33; ▶MoMA libr. cat.
Florsheim, Lillian H. — WC WI
Florsheim, Lillian H. → see Florsheim, Lillian
Florsheim, Richard Aberle *(American painter, printmaker, 1916-1979)* — BA
    Bibl: ART GALLERY (Jan 1980) obit; ▶MoMA libr. cat.; ▶WW Amer. Art, 1980 necrol.
Flotner or Flettner, Peter → see Flötner, Peter
Flötner, Peter — BA GC
    (German artist, c.1485-1546) — WC
    (German draughtsman, ca.1485-1546) — GC
    (German sculptor, woodcarver, goldsmith, ca.1485-1546) — BA
    Bibl: ▶Bénézit; ▶Encyc. world art; Getty Photo Study Coll.; ▶Thieme-Becker; ▶Witt checklist
    Flattner, Peter — BA GC
    Fletner, Peter — BA
    Flodner, Peter — GC
    Flotner or Flettner, Peter — WC
Floud, Mathilda *(British artist, op. 19th c.)* — WI
Flouest, Joseph Marie *(French artist, 1747-1833)* — WC
Flouquet, Pierre *(Belgian artist, 1900-)* — WC
Flower, Bernard *(English glazier, act.ca.1496, d.1517)* — BA
    Bibl: ▶Bénézit; Blue guide: Oxford & Camb.; ▶Penguin dec. arts; ▶Thieme-Becker; Woodforde, Engl. stained glass
Flower, Cedric — GC WC
    (Australian artist, 1920-) — WC
    (British, b.1920) — GC
    Bibl: ▶Witt checklist
Flower, Clement — WC WI
    (British artist, 19th cent.) — WC
    (British artist, op.1899-1917) — WI

Flower, E.M. *(British artist, op.19th c.)* — WI
Flower, Frederick William *(British businessman, photographer, 1815-1889)* — BA
    Bibl: COLOQUIO ARTES 46 (Sept 1980) 38-45
Flower, John — WC WI
    (British artist, 1793-1861) — WI
    (British artist, 1795-1861) — WC
Flower, Marmaduke C.William — WI
    (British artist, op.1873-, d.1910) — WI
Flowers, Elisha Beauregard — AV
    (American architect) — AV
Flowers, J. — WC WI
    (British artist, 19th cent.) — WC
    (British artist, op.19th c.) — WI
Flowers, Peter *(British artist, b.1955)* — WI
Floyd, Chad — AV BA
    (American architect) — AV
    (American architect, 20th c.) — BA
    Bibl: Architecture: the AIA journal, 1986 Jan., v.75, no.1, p.89; ▶Avery period. idx., 4th suppl., 6th suppl.; NEW CRITERION, IV/3 (Nov 1985) 45-52
Floyd, Christina *(British artist, b.1949)* — WI
Floyd, Donald H. *(British artist, op. circa 1907-)* — WI
Floyd, J. Austin *(18.IV.1910-1981; Landscape architect, Toronto)* — FA
    Bibl: CAAD Finding Aids; Natl. Arch. of Canada, CAAD Finding Aid
Floyd, James *(British artist, op.circa 1936-)* — WI
Floyd, W. *(Engraver, op.1845-)* — WI
fluele Breugel → see Brueghel, Jan, the elder
Fluerer, Ignaz → see Flurer, Ignaz Franz Joseph
Flugelman, Bert *(Australian sculptor, b.1923)* — BA
    Bibl: ▶Encyc. Australian art
Fluggen, Gisbert *(German artist, 1811-1859)* — WC
Fluggen, Josef *(German artist, 1842-1906)* — WC
Flughs [Unidentified] *(Unknown painter)* — PR
    Bibl: (May 29, 1804, lot 18, Farebrother)
Fluid Group *(Etruscan, Faliscan vase-painters)* — GC
    Bibl: Beazley, Etruscan vase-ptrs.
Flulk, A. *(German artist, 20th cent.)* — WC
Flurer, Flor, Florer or Fluerer, Ignaz (Franz Ignaz Joseph) → see Flurer, Ignaz Franz Joseph

Flurer, Ignaz Franz Joseph   **BA**
  (Austrian painter, act.1729,
    d.1742)   **BA**
  (German artist, op.1729-m.
    1742)   **WC**
    Bibl: ▶Bénézit; Dehio, Steiermark;
    ▶Thieme-Becker; ▶Witt checklist
  Florer, Ignaz   **BA**
  Fluerer, Ignaz   **BA**
Flurer, Flor, Florer or Fluerer,
  Ignaz (Franz Ignaz Joseph)   **WC**
Flurschütz, Gero *(German painter,*
  printmaker, b.1935)   **BA**
    Bibl: ▶WW Arts DEU
fluwele Breugel→*see* Brueghel, Jan,
  the elder
fluwelen Breugel→*see* Brueghel, Jan,
  the elder
Fly, Camillus S. *(American*
  photographer, 1849-1901)   **BA**
    Bibl: ▶Current, Photog. & Old
    West
Flying Bird Painter *(Etruscan vase-*
  painter)   **GC**
    Bibl: ▶Szilagyi, Etruszko-korinthosi
Flying-Angel Painter   **GC**
    Bibl: ▶Beazley, Attic red-fig. vase-
    ptrs.
Flynn, Anne *(British artist, op.20th*
  c.)   **WI**
Flynte, William *(English mason, 16th*
  c.)   **BA**
    Bibl: White, ARCHITECTURAL
    REVIEW CLXXI/1024 (June 1982)
    52-58
  Gatton, William of   **BA**
  William of Gatton   **BA**
Foard, James F. *(British, active*
  Liverpool, England, U.K. ca. 1853)   **JG**
Focardi, Ruggero *(Italian painter,*
  1864-1934)   **GC**
    Bibl: ▶Thieme-Becker
Fochi, Ferdinando   **GC WC**
  (Italian artist, 18th cent.)   **WC**
  (Italian painter, act.1702)   **GC**
    Bibl: ▶Thieme-Becker
Focht, Bernhard *(German architect)*   **AV**
    Bibl: Deutsche Bauzeitschrift,
    1985 Feb., v.33, no.2, p.182
Fock, Hermanus   **GC WC**
  (Dutch artist, 1766-1822)   **WC**
  (Dutch draughtsman, 1766-
    1822)   **GC**
    Bibl: Getty Photo Study Coll.;
    ▶Witt checklist
Focke, Carl *(German artist, op.1803-*
  1810)   **WC**
Fockeer→*see* Fouquières, Jacques
Fockens, Elisabeth Geertruida→*see*
  Wassenbergh, Elisabet Geertruda
Foclise, H. *(German artist, 1757-*
  1821)   **WC**
Focosi, Alessandro   **GC WC**
  (Italian artist, 1836-1869)   **WC**
  (Italian painter, 1836-1869)   **GC**
    Bibl: ▶Thieme-Becker

Focosi, Roberto *(Italian artist, 18th*
  cent.)   **WC**
Focus, Georges   **GC**
  (French artist, 1641-1708)   **WC**
  (French painter, 1641-1708)   **GC**
    Bibl: ▶Thieme-Becker
Focus, Georges (Faucas)   **WC**
Focus, Georges (Faucas)→*see* Focus,
  Georges
Fodchuk, Roman   **AV**
Fodon, A.J. *(Netherlands artist,*
  op.1665/85)   **WC**
Foelix, Heinrich *(German artist,*
  1757-1821)   **WC**
Foentes, Giorgio→*see* Fuentes,
  Giorgio
Foerster, Emil *(American artist,*
  1822-1906)   **WC WI**
Foerster, Heinrich von *(German*
  artist, 1832-1889)   **WC**
Foerster, Karin *(West German*
  architect-interior designer,
  Stuttgart)   **AV**
    Bibl: Architektur & Wohnen, 1989
    Mar.-Apr., no.2, p.81
Foerster, Karl *(German gardener,*
  1874-1970)   **AV**
    Bibl: Landscape architecture,
    1985 Nov.-Dec., v.75, no.6, p.82;
    ▶Libr. of Congr. Name Auth. File
Foerster, Peter *(German artist,*
  1887-1948)   **WC**
Fogarty, Anne *(American*
  couturiere, b.1919)   **BA**
    Bibl: WW Amer., 1976
Fogarty, Thomas   **BA WI**
  (American artist, 1873-1938)   **WI**
  (American illustrator, 1873-
    1938)   **BA**
    Bibl: ▶Fielding's Amer. ptrs.;
    ▶Vollmer, Künst.-Lex. 20. Jhr.;
    ▶WWW Amer.; ▶Young, Amer.
    artists
Fogas, Peter *(Hungarian artist, 20th*
  cent.)   **WC**
Fogel, Seymour   **BA WC WI**
  (American artist, 1911-)   **WC**
  (American artist, b.1911)   **WI**
  (American painter, sculptor,
    b.1911)   **BA**
    Bibl: ▶Vollmer, Künst.-Lex. 20.
    Jhr.; ▶WW Amer. Art, 1976
Fogelberg, Bengt Erland *(Swedish*
  sculptor, 1786-1854)   **BA**
    Bibl: ▶Thieme-Becker
Fogerty, Brian *(American lighting*
  designer)   **AV**
    Bibl: Architectural lighting, 1989
    June, v.3, no.6, p.40
Fogg Group *(Apulian vase-painters)*   **GC**
    Bibl: Trendall, Attic red-fig. vases
    Apulia
Foggia Group *(Apulian vase-*
  painters)   **GC**
    Bibl: Trendall, Attic red-fig. vases
    Apulia

Foggia, Michele *(Italian artist, op.*
  1832)   **WC**
Foggie, David   **WC WI**
  (British artist, 1878-)   **WC**
  (British artist, 1878-1948)   **WI**
Foggini, Domenico *(Italian medalist,*
  16th c.)   **BA**
    Bibl: Avery, FIRENZE E TOSCANA
    DEI MEDICI (1983) 885-897
Foggini, Giovanni
  Battista   **AV BA GC JG WC**
  (1652-1725)   **AV**
  (Italian architect and sculptor,
    1652-1725)   **GC**
  (Italian architect, sculptor, 1652-
    1725)   **BA**
  (Italian artist, 1652-1725)   **WC**
  (Italian, 1652-1725)   **JG**
    Bibl: ▶Encyc. world art;
    ▶RILA/BHA, 1986;
    ▶Thieme-Becker
Foggini, Vincenzo *(Italian sculptor,*
  act.1725-1755)   **BA**
    Bibl: ▶Bénézit; ▶Bessone-Aurelj,
    Scult. & arch. ital.; Lankheit,
    Floren. Barockplastik;
    ▶Thieme-Becker
Foggo, K. Peter *(British architect,*
  London)   **AV**
    Bibl: ▶Guide to RIBA practices,
    1987
Fogli, Marco *(Italian architect and*
  exhibition designer)   **AV**
    Bibl: Domus, 1988 July-Aug., no.
    696, p.4
Fogolino, Marcello   **BA CE GC WC**
  (Italian artist, c.1470-a.1550)   **WC**
  (Italian painter and printmaker,
    act.1519-1548)   **GC**
  (Italian painter, printmaker, act.
    1519-1548)   **BA**
  (Painter, engraver, post
    1482/ante 1489-post 1547)   **CE**
    Bibl: ▶Bolaffi; ▶RILA/BHA, 1986;
    ▶Thieme-Becker; ▶Witt checklist
Fogt, Mimi *(French painter, b.1921)*   **BA**
    Bibl: Wohl, BURLINGTON
    CXIX/896 (Nov 1977) 763-772
Fohn, Emanuel *(German painter,*
  1881-1966)   **GC**
    Bibl: ▶Schweers, Gemälde deut.
    Museen
Fohn, Max *(Architect)*   **AV**
    Bibl: Planen bauen wohnen, no.
    106, p.11
Fohn, Sofie *(German artist, 1899-)*   **WC**
Fohr, Carl Philipp   **BA GC WC**
  (German artist, 1795-1818)   **WC**
  (German painter, 1795-1818)   **BA**
  (German, 1795-1818)   **GC**
    Bibl: ▶Bénézit; ▶RILA/BHA;
    ▶Thieme-Becker
Fohr, Daniel *(German artist, 1801-*
  1862)   **WC**
Foied Painter *(Etruscan, Faliscan*
  vase-painter)   **GC**
    Bibl: Beazley, Etruscan vase-ptrs.

Foin, Jean *(French architect)* **AV**
    Bibl: AMC, 1988 Apr., no.20,
    p.90
Foisse, Francois *(French, 18th*
    century) **GC**
    Bibl: ▶Thieme-Becker
Foix, Louis de *(French architect,*
    engineer, ca.1530-after 1606) **BA**
    Bibl: ▶Bauchal, Archtes. fran.;
    ▶Dict. biog. fran.; ▶Nouv. biog.
    gén.; ▶Portoghesi, Diz. arch. e
    urbanistica; ▶Thieme-Becker
Fokke, Jan **GC WC**
    (Dutch artist, c.1745-1812) **WC**
    (Dutch draughtsman, 1745-
    1812) **GC**
    Bibl: ▶Thieme-Becker
Fokke, Simon **GC WC**
    (Dutch artist, 1712-1784) **WC**
    (Dutch draughtsman and
    printmaker, 1712-1784) **GC**
    Bibl: ▶Thieme-Becker
Fokko Tadama→see Tadama, Fokko
Folberg, Neil H. *(American, 1950 -)* **JG**
Folchard **BA**
    (Frankish scribe and illuminator,
    act. ca.875-900) **GC**
    (scribe, act.864-872) **BA**
    Bibl: Eggenberger, RIFORME
    RELIGIOSA E ARTI NELL'EPOCA
    CAROLINGIA 99-107;
    ▶Thieme-Becker
Folchart **GC**
Folchart→see Folchard
Folchetti da Sanginesio, Stefano→see
    Folchetti, Stefano
Folchetti, Stefano **GC PR**
    (Italian artist, op.1492-1513) **WC**
    (Italian painter, act. 1492-1513) **PR**
    (Italian painter, act.1492-1513) **GC**
    Bibl: Getty Photo Study Coll.;
    ▶Thieme-Becker; ▶Witt checklist
Folchetti da Sanginesio, Stefano **WC**
Folchetti, Stefano (da S. Ginesio) GC
Folchetti, Stefano, da San Genesio PR
Stefano Folchetti PR
Folchetti, Stefano (da S.
    Ginesio)→see Folchetti, Stefano
Folchetti, Stefano, da San
    Genesio→see Folchetti, Stefano
Folchi, Clemente *(Italian engineer,*
    1780-1868) **BA**
    Bibl: Blue guide: Rome, p.366;
    Boll. dei musei com. di Roma
    XXIII/1-4 (1976) 53; ▶Encic.
    italiana, v.33, p.946
Foldes, Peter **WC WI**
    (British artist, 1924-) **WC**
    (British artist, b.1924) **WI**
Foldsone, Anne, Miss→see Mee,
    Anne
Foldsone, John **WC WI**
    (British artist, op.1769-, d.1784) **WI**
    (British artist, op.1769-m.c.
    1784) **WC**

Foler or Foller, Antonio→see Foler,
    Antonio
Foler, Antonio **GC**
    (Italian artist, 1528-1616) **WC**
    (Italian, 1528-1616) **GC**
    Bibl: ▶Witt checklist
Foler or Foller, Antonio **WC**
Foley, Henry *(British artist, op.19th*
    c.) **WI**
Foley, Joan Tuckerman *(American*
    photographer, 20th c.) **BA**
    Bibl: Amherst (MA, USA), U Mass.
    Art Gallery, Criticism of
    photography (1978)
Foley, Kyoko Asano *(American*
    painter, b.1933) **BA**
    Bibl: JOURNAL OF S. CALIF. 27
    (June-July 1980) 28; ▶WW Amer.
    Art
Foley, Lois *(American painter, 20th*
    c.) **BA**
    Bibl: ▶Intl. dir. exh. artists, 1982
Foley, Margaret F. *(American*
    sculptor, 1827-1877) **BA**
    Bibl: Arts Mag. LVI/5 (Jan 1982)
    88-95; ▶Fielding's Amer. ptrs.;
    ▶Groce, Artists Amer.; ▶Young,
    Amer. artists
Foley, Richard **AV**
Folguera Grassi, Joaquim *(Spanish*
    architect) **AV**
    Bibl: old Avery Index
Folguera, Francesc *(Spanish*
    architect, 1891-1960) **AV**
    Bibl: AA files, 1987 Spring, no.14,
    p.65
Folin, Nicolas-Alexandre *(French,*
    master 1784) **JG**
Folingsby, George Frederick
    (Australian painter, illustrator,
    1830-1891) **BA**
    Bibl: ▶Bénézit; ▶Encyc. Australian
    art; ▶Thieme-Becker
Folinsbee, John Fulton *(American*
    artist, 1892-1972) **WI**
Folinus, Jeffrey J. *(American*
    architect, Atlanta, Ga. (Profile
    1987-1988)) **AV**
Foliot, François *(French menuisier,*
    master 1749, d. 1761) **GC**
    Bibl: Getty Photo Study Coll. (Dec.
    arts); ▶Salverte, Ébénistes 18e s.
Foliot, François I GC
Foliot, François le jeune GC
Foliot, François I→see Foliot,
    François
Foliot, François II→see Foliot,
    François-Toussaint
Foliot, François le jeune→see Foliot,
    François
Foliot, François-Toussaint *(French*
    menuisier, b.1748, master 1773) **GC**
    Bibl: ▶Salverte, Ébénistes 18e s.;
    Verlet, MeublesFr (1982)
Foliot, François II GC
Foliot, Toussaint-François GC

Foliot, Nicolas-Quinibert **GC JG**
    (French menuisier, 1706-1776) GC
    (French, 1706-1776) JG
    Bibl: ▶Salverte, Ébénistes 18e s.
Foliot, Toussaint *(French*
    woodcarver, act.1732-1778) **GC**
    Bibl: ▶Vial, Artistes décorateurs
Foliot, Toussiant-François→see Foliot,
    François-Toussaint
Folkard, Julia B.→see Folkard, Julia
    Bracewell
Folkard, Julia Bracewell **WI**
    (British artist, 1849-1933) WI
    (British artist, op.1872-1902) WC
Folkard, Julia B. **WC**
Folkard, R.W. *(British artist, op.*
    1831-1844) **WI**
Folkema, Jacob *(Dutch printmaker,*
    1692-1767) **GC**
    Bibl: ▶Bénézit
Folkema, Jacob *(Dutch artist, 1692-*
    1767) **WC**
Folkestad, Bernhard Dorotheus
    (Norwegian artist, 1879-1933) **WC**
Folkvord, Malfrid Takle *(Norwegian*
    landscape architect) **AV**
    Bibl: Byggekunst, 1986, v.68,
    no.1, p.43
Follenweider, Rudolf *(Swiss artist,*
    1774-1847) **WC**
Follet, J. *(English architect, early*
    20th c., resident in Argentina) **AV**
    Bibl: Restauro, no.73-74, p.222
Follett, J.R., Mrs., (Cathleen
    Sabine)→see Mann, Cathleen
    Sabine
Follett, Jean *(American artist,*
    b.1917) **WI**
Folli, Sebastiano **BA WC**
    (Italian artist, 1568-1621) WC
    (Italian painter, architect, 1568-
    1621) BA
    Bibl: ▶Bolaffi; ▶Thieme-Becker
Follina, Toni *(Italian architect)* **AV**
Follini, Carlo *(Italian artist, 1848-)* **WC**
Follmer, Jack *(American florist and*
    floral designer, New York City) **AV**
    Bibl: House beautiful, 1988 Dec.,
    v.130, no.12, p.52
Follot, Paul *(French designer, 1877-*
    1941) **BA**
    Bibl: ▶Bénézit; ▶Penguin dec. arts;
    ▶Thieme-Becker
Followers of Douris: Unascribed **GC**
    Bibl: ▶Beazley, Attic red-fig. vase-
    ptrs.
Following of the Seireniske
    Painter **GC**
    Bibl: ▶Beazley, Attic red-fig. vase-
    ptrs.
Folmar, Wilson *(American fashion*
    designer, 1911-1975) **BA**
    Bibl: Montgomery (AL, USA),
    Museum of Fine Arts, AMERICAN
    FASHION DESIGNS BY (1978)

Folon, Jean Michel   **BA WC**
(*Belgian painter, printmaker,*
  b.1934)   BA
(*French artist, 1934-*)   WC
  Bibl: ARTNEWS LXXXI/4 (Apr
  1982) 126-130; ▶Bénézit; ▶MoMA
  libr. cat.
Folonis, Michael W. (*American
  architect*)   **AV**
Folsom, Elizabeth A.   **WI**
  (*American artist, 1812-1899*) WC WI
  Folsom, Levi, Mrs., (Clara A.)   WI
**Folsom, Mrs. Elizabeth A.
  (Clara)**   **WC**
  Freeman, Elizabeth, A., Miss   WI
Folsom, Fred III (*American painter,
  20th c.*)   **BA**
  Bibl: ART INTERNATIONAL
  XXIV/55-6 (Jan-Feb 1981) 204-
  208; ART INTERNATIONAL
  XXXVI/5 (Nov-Dec 1983) 61
Folsom, Levi, Mrs., (Clara A.)→see
  Folsom, Elizabeth A.
Folsom, Miss (*American sculptor,
  20th century*)   **GC**
  Bibl: Juley coll., NMAA
*Folsom, Mrs. Elizabeth A.
  (Clara)→see* Folsom, Elizabeth A.
Foltyn (*French artist, 19th cent.*)   **WC**
Foltýn, František (*Czech painter,
  b.1892*)   **BA**
  Bibl: Hlusicka, UMENI XXIII/3
  (1975) 193-203
Foltyn, Hugo (*Czechoslovak
  architect*)   **AV**
  Bibl: AMC, 1985 Mar., no.7, p.52
Foltz, Philipp von (*German artist,
  1805-1877*)   **WC**
Folwell, Elizabeth (*American
  needleworker, 1770-1824*)   **BA**
  Bibl: ANTIQUES CXIX (Feb 1981)
  420-423
Folwell, Samuel   **BA WC WI**
  (*American artist, 1765-1813*) WC WI
  (*American painter, printmaker,
  1764-1813*)   BA
  Bibl: ▶Dict. Amer. biog.;
  ▶Thieme-Becker; WINTERTHUR
  PORTFOLIO XIV/1 (spring 1979)
  41; ▶WWW Amer.
Fomin, Ivan Aleksandrovič (*Russian
  architect, ca.1872-1936*)   **BA**
  Bibl: ▶Encyc. world art; ▶Vollmer,
  Künst.-Lex. 20. Jhr.
Fomison, Tony (*New Zealander
  painter, 20th c.*)   **BA**
  Bibl: Cartwright, Art New Zealand
  LII (Spr 1989), 66-69; ▶Intl. dir.
  exh. artists, 1982
Fonatsch, Franz (*Austrian architect*) **AV**
  Bibl: Domus, 1984 Oct., no.654,
  p.52
Fonatti, Franco (*Architect*)   **AV**
  Bibl: Bauforum, 1985, v.18, no.
  109, p.13
Fonceca, S. (*British artist, op.1846-*) **WI**

Fondati, Agostino→see Fondulo,
  Agostino
Fondi, Ottaviano (*Italian, d.ca.1555*) **BA**
  Bibl: Riedl, DAS FONDI-GRABMAL
  IN S. AGOSTINO (1979), p.30
Fonduli, Agostino→see Fondulo,
  Agostino
Fondulis, Agostino de'→see Fondulo,
  Agostino
**Fondulli, Fondulio, Fondulo or
  Fundulli, Giovanni Paolo** (*Italian
  artist, op.1574-1592*)   **WC**
Fondulo, Agostino   **BA VO**
  (*Italian architect and sculptor,
  doca.1483-1516*)   GC
  (*Italian architect, sculptor, act.
  1483-1517*)   BA
  (*Italian sculptor, decorator, and
  architect, fl. 1483-1517*)   VO
  Bibl: Bandirali, Arte lombarda,
  III/1 (1958) pp.29-44;
  ▶Bessone-Aurelj, Scult. & arch.
  ital.; Bistoletti Bandera, S. "Il
  gruppo del 'sepolcro' di Agostino
  de' Fondulis," in Il sacello di San
  Satiro ... (Milano, 1990), pp.
  49-57; ▶Encyc. world art; Getty
  Photo Study Coll. (Sculp.);
  ▶Heydenreich, Arch. Italy; ▶Libr.
  of Congr. Name Auth. File,
  NAFR9216183; TCI Lombardia,
  idx.; TCI Milano e laghi;
  ▶Thieme-Becker; W. Terni de
  Gregory, "Non 'de Fondutis,'" in
  Archivio storico lombardo LXXV-
  LXXVI (1948-49), pp. 238-240
De Fondutis, Agostino   **BA GC**
  De' Fondulis, Agostino   VO
  Fondati, Agostino   VO
  Fonduli, Agostino   BA
  Fondulis, Agostino de'   VO
Fonduti, Agostino de   **BA**
  Fondutis, Agostino de   GC
Fonduti, Agostino de→see Fondulo,
  Agostino
Fondutis, Agostino de→see Fondulo,
  Agostino
Fong, Flora (*Cuban painter, b.1941*) **BA**
  Bibl: LaDuke, Woman's art jrnl.,
  V/2 (Fal.-Win. 1984-85) p.34
Fong, Lia (*Oriental artist, op.1899*) **WC**
Fong, Steven (*Canadian(?) architect,
  Toronto*)   **AV**
  Bibl: Progressive architecture,
  1987 Jan., v.68, no.1, p.94
Fongario, Bernardino→see Fungai,
  Bernardino
Fonhave, Hinrich→see Funhof,
  Hinrich
Fonnart (*French artist, op.1807*)   **WC**
Fonner, F. (*German artist, 18th
  cent.*)   **WC**

Fonnesbech-Sandberg, Elna
  (*Danish painter, collector, b.1892*) **BA**
  Bibl: Andreasen, E.: ELNA
  FONNESBECH-SANDBERG..., 1985;
  Dansk biog. leks.
  Sandberg, Elna Fonnesbach   BA
Fonseca, António Manuel da **BA WC**
  (*Portuguese artist, 1796-1890*)   WC
  (*Portuguese painter, sculptor,
  1796-1890*)   BA
  Bibl: ▶Bénézit; ▶Encic. univ. ilus.;
  ▶Tavares Chicó, Pint. portuguesa;
  ▶Thieme-Becker
Fonseca, Gonzalo (*Uruguayan
  sculptor, b.1922*)   **BA**
  Bibl: ARTS MAG. 45/3 (Dec-Jan
  1971) 53; Henry, ART
  INTERNATIONAL XV/2 (1971) 79;
  Mennin, ARTS MAG. LXI/2 (Oct
  1986) 112; ▶MoMA libr. cat.
Fonseca, Harry (*American painter,
  b.1946*)   **BA**
  Bibl: ▶Intl. dir. exh. artists; Regina
  (Sask, CAN), U.Sask. Gallery, A
  new generation (1982)
Fonseca, José da (*Portuguese
  sculptor, 1884-1956*)   **BA**
  Bibl: ▶Tannock, Port. 20c. artists
Font Arellano, Antonio (*Spanish
  architect, Barcelona*)   **AV**
  Bibl: ▶Guia secreta Hermandad,
  1982-1983
Font y Gamà, José (*Spanish
  architect, 1859-1922*)   **BA**
  Bibl: ▶Encic. univ. ilus.;
  ▶Macmillan encyc. archts.
Fonta, Henri La (*French architect,
  Paris*)   **AV**
  Bibl: Architecture intérieure cree,
  1986 Apr.-May, no.211, p.150
Fontaine, Antoine (*act.1781*)   **BA**
  Bibl: Honour, APOLLO CIV/176
  (Oct 1976) 290-297
Fontaine, Charles-Joseph (*French
  silversmith, master 1765*)   **GC**
  Bibl: ▶Nocq, Poinçon de Paris
Fontaine, Edme Adolphe (*French
  painter, 1814-1883*)   **GC**
  Bibl: ▶Bénézit
Fontaine, Gabriel (*Swiss artist,
  1696-1767*)   **WC**
Fontaine, Jacques   **GC JG**
  (*French porcelain painter, act.
  1752-1775*)   GC
  (*French, active 1752-1775 and
  1778-1807*)   JG
  Bibl: ▶Brunet, Sèvres
*Fontaine, Jacques Francois
  Joseph→see* Swebach, Jacques
  François Joseph
Fontaine, Louis de (*French artist,
  op.1723-1757*)   **WC**

Fontaine, Pierre François
Léonard   **AV BA GC WC**
    (French architect, 1762-1853)   AV
    (French architect, printmaker,
       1762-1853)   BA
    (French artist, 1762-1853)   WC
    (French, 1762-1853)   GC
    Bibl: ▶Bénézit; ▶Petit Robert 2;
      ▶Portoghesi, Diz. arch. e
      urbanistica; ▶Thieme-Becker;
      ▶Witt checklist

Fontaine, Thomas Sherwood, la
    (British artist, b.1915)   **WI**

Fontaine, Victor (Belgian painter,
    1837-1884)   **GC**
    Bibl: ▶Bénézit

Fontaines, Andre des (French artist,
    1869-)   **WC**

Fontallard, Jean Francois Gerard
    (French artist, 1777-1858)   **WC**

Fontana→see Fontana, Lavinia
Fontana→see Fontana, Prospero
Fontana da Melide, Giovanni→see
    Fontana, Giovanni

Fontana di Cento, Riccardo (Italian
    artist, 1840-1915)   **WC**

Fontana family (Italian ceramists,
    16th-17th cs.)   **BA**
    Bibl: ▶Honey, Euro. ceramic;
      ▶Penguin dec. arts
    Pellipario family   BA

Fontana Hidalgo, Maria José   **AV**
    (Spanish architect)   AV
    (Spanish artist, 19th cent.) WC
    Bibl: Process: architecture, 1985
      Apr., no.57, p.13
    Hidalgo, Maria   WC
    Hidalgo, Maria José Fontana   AV
Fontana l'Abate, Carlo→see Fontana,
    Carlo Stefano

Fontana, Alberto (Italian artist, op.
    1518-m.1558)   **WC**

Fontana, Andrea (di) (Italian artist,
    op.c.1516)   **WC**

Fontana, Annibale   **BA GC**
    (Italian sculptor, medalist, and
      gem carver, 1540-1587)   GC
    (Italian sculptor, medalist, gem
      carver, 1540-1587)   BA
    Bibl: ▶Bénézit; ▶Encic. italiana;
      ▶Encyc. world art; ▶RILA/BHA,
      1986; ▶Thieme-Becker

Fontana, Baldasar (Italian sculptor,
    stucco artist, architect in POL,
    1661-1733)   **BA**
    Bibl: ▶Encyc. world art; ▶Hempel,
      Baroque central Euro.; Karpowicz,
      BALDASAR FONTANA, 1661-1733.
      ..(1990); ▶Slownik artystów
      polskich; ▶Thieme-Becker
    Fontana, Baldassare   BA
Fontana, Baldassare→see Fontana,
    Baldasar

Fontana, Bill (American conceptual
    artist, sculptor, b.1947)   **BA**
    Bibl: Fontana DAIDALOS
      17/15/Sept '85; ▶WW Amer. Art

Fontana, Camillo (Italian ceramist,
    act.1549-1589)   **BA**
    Bibl: ▶Honey, Euro. ceramic;
      ▶Thieme-Becker

Fontana, Carlo   **AV BA CE FA GC PR**
    (1634-5.II.1714; Architect,
      Engineer, Roma)   FA
    (Architect, engineer, 1634-1714) CE
    (Italian architect, 1634-1714) AV BA
    (Italian painter, 1634-1714)   PR
    (Italian sculptor and architect,
      1634-1714)   GC
    Bibl: ▶Macmillan encyc. archts.;
      ▶Portoghesi, Diz. arch. e
      urbanistica; ▶RILA/BHA, Subject,
      1988; ▶Thieme-Becker, v.12,
      p.170 ff.
    Carlo Fontana   FA PR
    Cavalier Fontana   PR
    Signor Cavaliere Carlo Fontana PR

Fontana, Carlo Stefano   **FA**
    (fl. 1700-1719; Late Baroque
      Classical Architect, Popes
      Architect, Roma)   FA
    (Italian artist, op.c.1700-1711) WC
    Bibl: NGA (Acc. San Luca) objects;
      ▶Thieme-Becker, v.12, p.174 ff.
    Fontana l'Abate, Carlo   FA

Fontana, Carlo Stefano
(l'Abbate)   **WC**
Fontana, Carlo Stefano
    (l'Abbate)→see Fontana, Carlo
    Stefano

Fontana, Corsin (Swiss artist, 1944-) **WC**

Fontana, Domenico   **AV BA CE FA GC**
    (1543-1607; Architect, Painter,
      Sculptor, Roma)   FA
    (Architect, 1543-1607)   CE
    (Italian architect, 1543-1607) AV BA
    (Italian painter and sculptor,
      1543-1607)   GC
    Bibl: ▶Macmillan encyc. archts.;
      Nash, Dictionary, 1961.;
      ▶Portoghesi, Diz. arch. e
      urbanistica; ▶RILA/BHA; ULAN
      1988, (CENSUS)
    Domenico Fontana   FA

Fontana, Flaminio (Italian ceramist,
    act.1571-1591)   **BA**
    Bibl: ▶Honey, Euro. ceramic;
      ▶Thieme-Becker

Fontana, Francesco (Italian
    architect, 1668-1708)   **BA GC**
    Bibl: Di Goia, Antologia di B-A
      21-22 (1984) 65-69; ▶Macmillan
      encyc. archts.; ▶Portoghesi, Diz.
      arch. e urbanistica; ▶RILA/BHA,
      1986; TCI Roma e dintorni;
      ▶Thieme-Becker

Fontana, Franco (Italian
    photographer, painter, b.1933)   **BA**
    Bibl: ▶Auer, Encyc. photographes;
      ▶Intl. dir. exh. artists, 1982-1983

Fontana, Gerardo (Italian artist,
    16th cent.)   **WC**

Fontana, Giacomo (16th cenuty
    Italian architect and engineer,
    active in Ancona)   **AV**
    Bibl: Storia architettura, 1982 Jan.
      -June, v.5, no.1, p.25
Fontana, Giacomo→see Fontana,
    Jakub

Fontana, Giovanni (Italian artist,
    op.1731)   **WC**

Fontana, Giovanni (Italian engineer,
    theorist, ca.1393-ca.1455)   **BA**
    Bibl: Battisti, E., Le Macchine
      Cifrate di Giovanni Fontana,
      1984; ▶Encic. italiana, index

Fontana, Giovanni   **BA GC**
    (Italian architect, 1540-1614) GC
    (Italian architect, engineer,
      1540-1614)   BA
    Bibl: ▶Macmillan encyc. archts.;
      TCI Lazio, (var.); ▶Thieme-Becker

Fontana da Melide, Giovanni   **GC**
Fontana, Giovanni
Battista   **BA GC PR WC**
    (Italian artist, c.1524-1587)   WC
    (Italian painter and printmaker,
      ca.1524-1587)   GC
    (Italian painter, ca.1524-1587) PR
    (Italian painter, printmaker, ca.
      1524-1587)   BA
    Bibl: ▶Bénézit; ▶Encyc. world art;
      ▶RILA/BHA, 1986;
      ▶Thieme-Becker
    Giovanni Battista Fontana   PR
    Juan Baptista Fontano   PR

Fontana, Girolamo   **AV BA WC**
    (Italian architect, act.1690-
      1714)   BA
    (Italian artist, op.1690-1714) WC
    (Roman architect, son of
      Giovanni Battista Fontana and
      nephew of Carlo Fontana,
      d.1701)   AV
    Bibl: Commentari v.28, p.273;
      ▶Portoghesi, Diz. arch. e
      urbanistica; ▶Thieme-Becker

Fontana, Giulio Cesare (Italian
    architect, act.1593-1627)   **BA**
    Bibl: ▶Encyc. world art;
      ▶Macmillan encyc. archts.; Pane,
      Arch. barocca Napoli, pp.50-53;
      ▶Portoghesi, Diz. arch. e
      urbanistica; ▶Thieme-Becker
    Fontana, Sebastiano Giulio Cesare BA

Fontana, Ivan (Swiss architect,
    Bellinzona)   **AV**
    Bibl: Ville giardini, 1987 Sept., no.
      219, p.30

Fontana, Jakub (Polish architect,
    1710-1773)   **BA**
    Bibl: ▶Hempel, Baroque central
      Euro., pp.307-308; ▶Łozínski,
      Arch. Poland, p.252; Slaski,
      Barocco fra ITA e POL, p.134;
      ▶Wielka ilustr. encyk.
    Fontana, Giacomo   BA

Fontana, Lavinia   BA GC PR
  (Italian artist, 1552-1614)   WC
  (Italian painter, 1552-1614)   BA PR
  (Italian, 1552-1614)   GC
  Bibl: Getty Photo Study Coll.
    (Ptgs.); ▶RILA/BHA;
    ▶Thieme-Becker; ▶Witt checklist
  Fontana   PR
Fontana, Lavinia (Zappi)   WC
  L. Fontana   PR
  Lavigna Fontana   PR
  Lavinia Fontana   PR
  Livia Fontana   PR
  Zappi, Lavinia   GC
Fontana, Lavinia (Zappi) → see
  Fontana, Lavinia
Fontana, Lucio   AV BA GC PR WC
  (Italian artist, 1899-1968)   WC
  (Italian painter and sculptor,
    1899-1968)   GC
  (Italian painter, 1899-1968)   PR
  (Italian painter, sculptor, 1899-
    1968)   BA
  (Italian sculptor, 1899-1968)   AV
  Bibl: ▶Bénézit; ▶Comanducci, Diz.;
    ▶Libr. of Congr. Name Auth. File;
    ▶MoMA libr. cat.; ▶RILA/BHA,
    1986; ▶Vollmer, Künst.-Lex. 20.
    Jhr.
  Lucio Fontana   PR
Fontana, Luigi   GC WC
  (Italian artist, 1827-1908)   WC
  (Italian painter, 1827-1908)   GC
  Bibl: ▶Thieme-Becker
Fontana, Luigi *(Italian architect,*
  1812-1877)   AV BA
  Bibl: TCI Milano e laghi;
    ▶Thieme-Becker
Fontana, Orazio   BA JG
  (Italian ceramist, act.1540-1571)   BA
  (Italian, b. Casteldurante 1510,
    active in Urbino, d. 1571)   JG
  Bibl: ▶Bénézit; ▶Thieme-Becker
Fontana, Paolo Antonio *(Italian*
  architect in POL, act.1735-1756)   BA
  Bibl: Bildhdbch. Kunst. Pol.; Łoza;
    ▶Łozínski, Arch. Poland; POLISH
    ART STUDIES, V (1984) 21-22
Fontana, Pietro *(Italian architect,*
  1934-)   AV
  Bibl: Die Kunst, v.96, no.8, 1984,
    p.569
Fontana, Prospero   AV BA GC PR WC
  (Italian artist, 1512-1597)   WC
  (Italian painter, 1512-1597)   BA GC PR
  (Italian painter, Bologna, 1512-
    1597)   AV
  Bibl: ▶Bolaffi; ▶RILA/BHA, 1986;
    ▶Thieme-Becker
  Fontana   PR
  Prospero Fontana   PR
  Prospero Fontana Bolognese   PR
Fontana, Roberto   GC WC
  (Italian artist, 1844-1907)   WC
  (Italian painter, 1844-1907)   GC
  Bibl: ▶Thieme-Becker

Fontana, Sebastiano Giulio
  Cesare → see Fontana, Giulio
  Cesare
Fontanals, Manuel *(Spanish*
  illustrator, 1895-1972)   BA
  Bibl: Reyero Hermosilla, Goya,
    178 (Jan.-Feb. 1984) pp.215-217
Fontanarosa, Lucien *(French artist,*
  1912-)   WC
Fontanesi, Antonio   BA GC WC
  (Italian artist, 1818-1882)   WC
  (Italian painter, 1818-1882)   BA GC
  Bibl: ▶RILA/BHA, 1986;
    ▶Thieme-Becker
Fontanesi, Francesco → see Fontanesi,
  Francesco Salvator
Fontanesi, Francesco Salvator   GC
  (Italian artist, 1751-1795)   WC
  (Italian, 1751-1795)   GC
  Bibl: Getty Photo Study Coll.
    (Ptgs.); ▶Thieme-Becker; ▶Witt
    checklist
  Fontanesi, Francesco   GC WC
Fontayne, Charles H. *(American,*
  1814-1858, active Cincinnati, OH,
  U.S. 1848-1853)   JG
Fontayne, Rene *(French artist, 20th*
  cent.)   WC
Fontbuoni, Anastasio → see
  Fontebuoni, Anastasio
Fonte, Giovanni Battista della → see
  Della Fonte, Giovanni Battista
Fontebasso → see Fontebasso,
  Francesco
Fontebasso, Francesco   BA GC PR
  (Italian artist, 1709-1768/9)   WC
  (Italian painter and printmaker,
    1709-1769)   GC
  (Italian painter, 1709-1769)   PR
  (Italian painter, printmaker,
    1707-1769)   BA
  Bibl: Magrini, M., FRANCESCO
    FONTEBASSO, 1707-1769 (1988);
    ▶RILA/BHA; ▶Thieme-Becker
  Fontebasso   PR
Fontebasso, Francesco Salvator   WC
  Francesco Fontebasso   PR
Fontebasso, Francesco Salvator → see
  Fontebasso, Francesco
Fonteboni, Tommaso
  [Unidentified] *(Unknown painter,*
  act. 18th century)   PR
  Bibl: Riccardi inventory dated
    1776
  Tommaso Fonteboni   PR
Fontebuoni, Anastasio   BA GC WC
  (Italian artist, c.1580-1626)   WC
  (Italian painter, ca.1580-1626)   BA GC
  Bibl: ▶Bénézit; ▶Bolaffi;
    ▶RILA/BHA; ▶Thieme-Becker
  Fontbuoni, Anastasio   GC
Fontenay de Saint-Afrique *(French*
  artist, 20th cent.)   WC

Fontenay, Christophe François Le
  Prudhomme, comte de *(French*
  ceramics manufacturer, act.1712)   BA
  Bibl: PAYS LORRAIN LX/3 (1979)
    159-160
Fontenay, Eugène *(French artist,*
  1824-)   WC
Fontenay, Henry Francois *(French*
  artist, 1657-p.1704)   WC
Fontenay, Jean-Baptiste Belin de → see
  Belin, Jean Baptiste II (Blin de
  Fontenay)
Fontenay, Louis Henri de *(Dutch*
  artist, 1800-)   WC
Fontené, Robert   BA WC
  (French artist, 1892-)   WC
  (French painter, b.1892)   BA
  Bibl: ▶Bénézit; Pontoise (FRA),
    Musee de Pontoise, ROBERT
    FONTENE (1977); ▶Vollmer,
    Künst.-Lex. 20. Jhr.
Fonteny, C.D. *(Dutch artist, 18th*
  cent.)   WC
Fontes, E. *(French, active 1870s)*   JG
Fonteyn, Adriaen Lucasz.   GC PR WC
  (Dutch painter, d. 1661)   PR
  (Flemish artist, op.1626-m.1661)   WC
  (Flemish, act.1626-d.1661)   GC
  Bibl: ▶Thieme-Becker; ▶Witt
    checklist
  A. Fontijn   PR
  Adriaen Lucasz. Fonteyn   PR
Fonteyn, Jan Anthonisz. *(Dutch*
  painter, 17th century)   GC
  Bibl: ▶Bénézit
Fonteyn, Pieter → see Fontyn, Pieter
Fonti, Bartolomeo → see Fontius,
  Bartolomeus
Fontio, Bartholomeo → see Fontius,
  Bartolomeus
Fontius, Barthius → see Fontius,
  Bartolomeus
Fontius, Bartholomaeus → see Fontius,
  Bartolomeus
Fontius, Bartolomeus *(Humanist,*
  draughtsman, poet, orator, 1445-
  1513)   CE
  Della Fonte, Bartholomeo   CE
  Della Fonte, Bartolomeo   CE
  Florentinus   CE
  Fonti, Bartolomeo   CE
  Fontio, Bartholomeo   CE
  Fontius, Barthius   CE
  Fontius, Bartholomaeus   CE
  Fontius, Benuandinus   CE
  Fontus, Bartolomeus   CE
  Fonzio, Bartholomeo   CE
  Fonzio, Bartolomeo   CE
Fontius, Benuandinus → see Fontius,
  Bartolomeus
Fonton, Marcel → see Fontón, Marcelo

Fontón, Marcelo   BA
   (Architect, pupil of Luigi
    Vanvitelli, 1722-1797)   AV
   (Spanish architect in FRA, act.
    1751-1780)   BA
    Bibl: Apollo, CXXI/279 (May
    1985) pp.321-327; Arch. esp. de
    arte, LVIII/231 (Jul-Sep 1985)
    230-238; ▶Diz. artisti ital. in
    Spagna
  Fonton, Marcel   AV
Fontrouge, François *(French*
  silversmith, 18th century)   GC
    Bibl: ▶Mabille, Orfèv. fran.
Fontserè i Mestres, Josep *(Spanish*
  architect, 1829-1897)   AV
    Bibl: Ianus, 1980, v.0, no.0, p.27
Fontus, Bartolomeus→see Fontius,
  Bartolomeus
Fontyn, Pieter   GC WC
   (Dutch artist, 1773-1839)   WC
   (Dutch painter, 1773-1839)   GC
    Bibl: Getty Photo Study Coll.;
    Getty Photo Study Coll. (Ptgs.);
    ▶Witt checklist
  Fonteyn, Pieter   GC
Fonvizin, Artur Vladimirovič
  (Russian painter, b.1882)   BA
    Bibl: ▶Fogg Mus. Libr. cat.;
    ▶Vollmer, Künst.-Lex. 20. Jhr.
Fońyi, Géza (Friml) *(Hungarian*
  painter, b.1899)   BA
    Bibl: Budapest (HUN), Mag.
    Nemzeti Galeria, FONYI GEZI
    (1979); ▶Vollmer, Künst.-Lex. 20.
    Jhr.
Fonzio, Bartholomeo→see Fontius,
  Bartolomeus
Fonzio, Bartolomeo→see Fontius,
  Bartolomeus
Fonzio, Niccolò *(Italian scribe, act.*
  ca.1480-1485)   GC
    Bibl: Sotheby's London, June 27,
    1982, Lot 5b
Foo Fat, Dulcie *(Canadian painter,*
  20th c.)   BA
    Bibl: ARTSCANADA XXXV/4 (Dec
    78-Jan 79) 60-61
Foornvliet→see Toorenvliet, Jacob
Foot, D.D.   WC WI
   (American artist, op.1815-1835)   WI
   (American artist, op.c.1820-
    1830)   WC
  Foot, F. *(British artist, op.1857-*
   1874)   WC WI
Foote, Jonathan L. *(American*
  architect, Livingston, Mont)   AV
    Bibl: ▶AIA Pro File, 1985
Foote, Mary Anna Hallock   WI
   (American artist, 1847-1938)   WI
   (American artist, 20th cent.)   WC
  Foote, Mary Hallock   WC
    Hallock, Mary Anna, Miss   WI
Foote, Mary Hallock→see Foote,
  Mary Anna Hallock
Foote, Steven M.   AV

Foote, Will Howe   BA
   (American artist, 1874-1965)   WI
   (American painter, 1874-1965)   BA
    Bibl: ▶Fielding's Amer. ptrs.;
    Gibson, Artists of early Michigan;
    ▶WWW Amer.
  Foote, William Howe   WI
Foote, William Howe→see Foote,
  Will Howe
Foottet, Frederick Francis   WC WI
   (British artist, 1850-1935)   WI
   (British artist, op.1873-1901)   WC
Foppa→see Foppa, Vincenzo
Foppa, Cristoforo→see Caradosso
  (Cristoforo Foppa)
Foppa, Vincenzo   BA GC PR WC
   (Italian artist, 1427/30-1515/16)   WC
   (Italian painter, ca.1427-ca.
    1515)   BA GC PR
    Bibl: ▶Bolaffi; ▶RILA/BHA;
    ▶Thieme-Becker; ▶Witt checklist
  Foppa   PR
  Foppa, Vincenzo da Brescia   PR
  Vincenzo Foppa   PR
Foppa, Vincenzo da Brescia→see
  Foppa, Vincenzo
Forabosco→see Forabosco, Girolamo
Forabosco (Ferrabosco)
  Girolamo→see Forabosco,
  Girolamo
Forabosco, Gerolamo→see
  Forabosco, Girolamo
Forabosco, Girolamo   BA GC PR WI
   (Italian artist, c.1605-1679)   WC
   (Italian artist, circa 1605-1697)   WI
   (Italian painter, ca.1605-1679)   BA PR
   (Italian, 1631-aft.1675)   GC
    Bibl: ▶Bolaffi; Getty Photo Study
    Coll. (Ptgs.); TCI Venezia, 1969;
    ▶Thieme-Becker; ▶Witt checklist
  Ferrabosco   PR
  Ferrabosco, Girolamo   BA GC WI
  Forabosco   PR
  Forabosco (Ferrabosco)
   Girolamo   WC
  Forabosco, Gerolamo   PR
  Girolamo Forabosco   PR
Forain→see Forain, Jean Louis
Forain, Jean→see Forain, Jean Louis
Forain, Jean Louis   BA GC PR WC
   (French artist, 1852-1931)   WC
   (French painter, 1852-1931)   PR
   (French painter, printmaker,
    1852-1931)   BA
   (French, 1852-1931)   GC
    Bibl: ▶Bénézit; ▶Encyc. world art;
    ▶RILA/BHA; ▶Thieme-Becker
  Forain   PR
  Forain, Jean   PR
  Forain, Jean-Louis   PR
  Jean Louis Forain   PR
Forain, Jean-Louis→see Forain, Jean
  Louis

Forakis, Peter *(American architect,*
  sculptor, b.1927)   BA
    Bibl: ▶MoMA libr. cat.; ▶WW
    Amer. Art, 1976
Forasassi, Daniela *(Italian architect)*   AV
    Bibl: Parametro, 1985 July, no.
    138, p.50
Forasassi, Paolo *(Italian architect)*   AV
    Bibl: Parametro, 1985 July, no.
    138, p.50
Forattini, Giorgio *(Italian*
  caricaturist, b.1931)   BA
    Bibl: Amsterdam (NLD),
    Nieuwekerk, Europa quo vadis?
    (1984)
Forbát, Alfred *(Hungarian architect,*
  city planner, 1897-1972)   BA
    Bibl: Rome (ITA), Pal. Barberini, Gli
    otto egli attivisiti (1980)
Forberg, Charles *(Architect)*   AV
    Bibl: ▶Avery period. idx.
Forbes   WC WI
   (British artist, 19th cent.)   WC
   (British artist, op.19th c.)   WI
Forbes→see Forbes, James G.
Forbes→see Forbes, Kenneth K.
Forbes→see Forbes, Stanhope
  Alexander
Forbes family *(American*
  silversmiths, 18th-19th cs.)   BA
    Bibl: NY state silversmiths;
    Phillips, Collectors' encyc. of
    antiques
Forbes, A. →see Forbes, Alexander
Forbes, Alexander   WI
   (British artist, -1839)   WC
   (British artist, 1802-1839)   WI
  Forbes, A.   WC
Forbes, Andrew Alexander
  (American photographer, 1862-
  1921)   BA
    Bibl: ▶Current, Photog. & Old
    West
Forbes, Anne *(British artist, 1745-*
  1834)   WC WI
Forbes, Charles S. *(American*
  painter, b.1860, act.1913)   BA
    Bibl: ▶Bénézit; ▶Thieme-Becker
Forbes, Edward   WC WI
   (British artist, 19th cent.)   WC
   (British artist, op.19th c.)   WI
Forbes, Edwin   GC WI
   (American artist, 1839-1895)   WI
   (American draughtsman, 1839-
    1895)   GC
    Bibl: ▶Bénézit
Forbes, Elizabeth→see Forbes,
  Elizabeth Adela Stanhope

Forbes, Elizabeth Adela Stanhope **BA**
  (British artist, 1859-1912) **WC WI**
  (British painter, 1859-1912) **BA**
   Bibl: ▶Johnson, Brit. artists;
   ▶Waters, Brit. artists
  Armstrong, Elizabeth Adela, Miss **WI**
Forbes, Elizabeth **WI**
Forbes, Elizabeth Adela, (nee
  Armstrong) (Mrs. Eliz.
  Stanhope Forbes) **WC**
  Stanhope Forbes, Elizabeth **BA**
Forbes, Elizabeth Adela, (nee
  Armstrong) (Mrs. Eliz. Stanhope
  Forbes) → see Forbes, Elizabeth
  Adela Stanhope
Forbes, Ernest **WC WI**
  (British artist, 20th cent.) **WC**
  (British artist, op.circa 1905-,
  d.1962) **WI**
Forbes, Heather *(New Zealander*
  photographer, b.1948) **BA**
   Bibl: Arts Council GBR, Summer
   Show 4 (1977)
Forbes, Ian *(British architect)* **AV**
   Bibl: Country life, 1987 July 23,
   v.181, no.30, p.107
Forbes, J. → see Forbes, J. I
Forbes, J. I **WI**
  (British artist, 17th cent.) **WC**
  (British artist, op.17th c.) **WI**
  Forbes, J. **WC**
Forbes, J. II *(British artist, op.early*
  19th c.) **WI**
Forbes, James G. **PR WI**
  (British artist, 1800-op.1859) **WI**
  (British painter, 1800-aft.1870) **PR**
   Bibl: ▶Thieme-Becker
  Forbes **PR**
  James G. Forbes **PR**
Forbes, Kenneth K. **PR WC**
  (Canadian artist, 1892-) **WC**
  (Canadian painter, b. 1892) **PR**
   Bibl: ▶Witt checklist
  Forbes **PR**
  Kenneth K. Forbes **PR**
Forbes, Maud C.Stanhope *(British*
  artist, op.circa 1903-) **WI**
Forbes, Nigel Ivan *(British, b.1918)* **BA**
   Bibl: ▶Who's Who [GBR], 1980
Forbes, Peter *(American architect,*
  1942-) **AV**
   Bibl: Architecture & urbanism,
   1989 Mar., no.3(222), p.110
Forbes, Stanhope → see Forbes,
  Stanhope Alexander
Forbes, Stanhope
  Alexander **BA PR WC WI**
  (British artist, 1857-1947) **WC WI**
  (British painter, 1857-1947) **BA PR**
   Bibl: ▶RILA/BHA; ▶Wood,
   Victorian ptrs.
  Forbes **PR**
  Forbes, Stanhope **PR**
  Stanhope Alexander Forbes **PR**
Forbes, Vivian *(British artist, 1891-*
  1937) **WC WI**

Forbes, William G. *(American*
  silversmith, 1752-1840) **BA**
   Bibl: Kovel, Amer. silver
Forbes-Robertson → see Forbes-
  Robertson, Johnstone
Forbes-Robertson, Eric → see Forbes-
  Robertson, Eric J.
Forbes-Robertson, Eric J. **WI**
  (British artist, 1865-1935) **WC WI**
  Forbes-Robertson, Eric **WC**
Forbes-Robertson, Johnston → see
  Forbes-Robertson, Johnstone
Forbes-Robertson, Johnstone **WI**
  (British artist, 1853-) **WC**
  (British artist, 1853-1937) **WI**
  (British painter, 1853-1937) **PR**
   Bibl: Nat Gal of Ireland catalogue;
   ▶Thieme-Becker
  Forbes-Robertson **PR**
  Forbes-Robertson, Johnston **PR**
  Forbes-Robertson, Sir
   Johnstone **WC**
  Johnston Forbes-Robertson **PR**
Forbes-Robertson, Sir Johnstone → see
  Forbes-Robertson, Johnstone
Forbin, Comte de *(French painter,*
  b. ca.1721) **GC**
   Bibl: ▶Bénézit
Forbin, Louis Nicolas Philippe
  Auguste, comte de **BA WC**
  (French artist, 1777-1841) **WC**
  (French painter, 1777-1841) **GC**
  (French painter, archaeologist,
  museum administrator, 1777-
  1841) **BA**
   Bibl: ▶Bénézit; ▶Dict. biog. fran.;
   ▶Larousse grande encyc.;
   ▶Thieme-Becker
  Forbin, Louis-Nicolas-Philippe-
  Auguste **GC**
Forbin,
  Louis-Nicolas-Philippe-Auguste → see
  Forbin, Louis Nicolas Philippe
  Auguste, comte de
Forbin-Janson, N. de *(French artist,*
  19th cent.) **WC**
Forcella, Giacomo [Unidentified]
  (Italian painter) **PR**
   Bibl: Gagliano inventory, Naples,
   1699
  Giacomo Forcella **PR**
Forcellini, Simone *(Italian artist, op.*
  1686-1691) **WC**
Forchert, Johann *(German artist,*
  18th cent) **AV**
   Bibl: Abitare, 1988 Dec., no.270,
   p.98
Ford Madox Brown → see Brown, Ford
  Madox
Ford, Charles **WC WI**
  (British artist, op.1801-1870) **WI**
  (British artist, op.1830-1856) **WC**
Ford, Edward Onslow *(British*
  sculptor, 1852-1901) **BA**
   Bibl: ▶Bénézit; ▶Thieme-Becker

Ford, Emily *(British artist, 1851-*
  1930) **WI**
Ford, F.Clare *(British artist, op.1853-*
  1865) **WI**
Ford, F.J. *(British artist, op.1845-*
  1853) **WC WI**
Ford, Gordon Onslow *(British artist,*
  op.1913-1942) **WI**
Ford, Harriet *(British artist, op.1822-*
  1825) **WC WI**
Ford, Henry Chapman *(American*
  painter, printmaker, 1828-1894) **BA**
   Bibl: ▶Groce, Artists Amer.;
   ▶Moure, Art So. Calif.; ▶Young,
   Amer. artists
Ford, Henry Justice *(British artist,*
  1860-1941) **WC WI**
Ford, Hugh Hubbard *(British*
  architect, 1906-1980) **AV**
Ford, J.A. **WC WI**
  (British artist, op.1911) **WC**
  (British artist, op.1911-) **WI**
Ford, James **BA**
  (American sculptor, 20th c.) **BA**
  (American, active San Francisco
  and Sacramento, CA, U.S.
  1854-) **JG**
   Bibl: NY Times obit., 17 Apr
   1992; Wortz, Arts Mag. XVII/9
   (May 1983) 142
Ford, James M. **JG**
Ford, James M. → see Ford, James
Ford, Jo *(British artist, op.20th c.)* **WI**
Ford, Kenneth *(British sculptor,*
  20th c.) **BA**
   Bibl: ▶Intl. dir. exh. artists, 1982-
   1983; Stonyer, LEONARDO XIX/1
   (1986) 35-38
Ford, Lauren *(American painter,*
  1891-1973) **PR**
   Bibl: ▶WWW Amer. art
  Lauren Ford **PR**
Ford, Marianne, Lady *(British artist,*
  op.19th c.) **WI**
Ford, Michael *(British artist, b.1920)* **WI**
Ford, O'Neil *(American architect,*
  1905-1982) **AV**
   Bibl: AIA journal, v.71, n.11, Sept.
   1982, p.11; ▶Contemp. archts.
Ford, Piers *(British architect)* **AV**
   Bibl: Architects' journal, 1981
   Sept.16, v.174, no.37, p.541
Ford, Richard *(British artist, 1796-*
  1858) **WC WI**
Ford, Robert *(British artist, op.20th*
  c.) **WI**
Ford, Rudolph Onslow **WC WI**
  (British artist, circa 1880-op.
  1914) **WI**
  (British artist, op.1880-1914) **WC**
Ford, William **WC WI**
  (British artist, op.1848-, d.1880) **WI**
  (British artist, op.1848-m.1880) **WC**
Ford, William Bishop *(British artist,*
  op.1847-1892) **WC WI**

Ford, Wolfram Onslow   WC WI
  (British artist, 1880-)   WC
  (British artist, b.1880)   WI
Fordanes [Unidentified] *(Unknown
  painter)*   PR
    Bibl: (May 22, 1813, lot 31,
    White)
Forde, Samuel *(British artist, 1805-
  1828)*   WC WI
Förderer, Walter M.   AV BA
  (Architect, 1928-)   AV
  *(West German architect,
  b.1928)*   BA
    Bibl: ▶Avery period. idx., 1st
    suppl.; Pohl, Daidalos 9 (Sept
    1983) 40; ▶WW Arts DEU
Fordet, Comtesse de *(French artist,
  19th cent.)*   WC
Fordham, Max *(British architect)*   AV
    Bibl: Architects' journal, 1989
    Aug.16, v.190, no.7, p.25
Fore, George *(American
  architectural conservator and paint
  analyst, Raleigh, N.C)*   AV
    Bibl: Historic preservation, 1988
    Jan.-Feb., v.40, no.1, p.68
Fore, Philippe *(French artist, 1917-)* WC
Foreau, Louis Henri *(French artist,
  1866-1940)*   WC
Forel, Alexis *(Swiss printmaker,
  author, 1852-1922)*   BA
    Bibl: ▶Bénézit; ▶Künst.-Lex.
    Schweiz 20. Jahrh.; ▶Natl. union
    cat., pre-1956; ▶Schweiz.
    Künst.-Lex.; ▶Thieme-Becker
Forel, Emmeline *(Swiss painter,
  1860-1957)*   BA
    Bibl: ▶Bénézit; ▶Künst.-Lex.
    Schweiz 20. Jahrh.; ▶Petteys,
    Women artists; ▶Schweiz.
    Künst.-Lex.; ▶Thieme-Becker
Foreman, Margaret *(British artist,
  op.1981-)*   WI
Foreman, Richard *(American artist,
  20th c.)*   BA
    Bibl: ▶Art Index, v.48, no.1; v.49,
    no.1
*Forenberg, Alexander van→see
  Fornenbergh, Alexandre van*
Forero, Laureano *(Colombian
  architect)*   AV
    Bibl: Proa, 1987 Aug., no.364, p.7
Fores, S.W. *(British artist, op.1785-
  1825)*   WI
Forest *(French, active 19th century
  (also Gouchenheim & Forest))*   JG
Forest, Fred *(French artist, b.1933)*   BA
    Bibl: ▶Bénézit; COLOQUIO (Mar
    180) 50-55
Forest, Jean Baptiste   GC WC
  (French artist, 1635-1712)   WC
  (French painter, 1635-1712)   GC
    Bibl: ▶Thieme-Becker
*Forest, Roy de→see De Forest, Roy
  Dean*
*Forest, Roy Dean de→see De Forest,
  Roy Dean*

Forest, Thomas *(British architect, fl.
  15th cent)*   AV
    Bibl: Country life, 1989 Jan.19,
    v.183, no.3, p.68
Foresti, Maffeo *(Italian painter, act.
  1756)*   BA
    Bibl: Rossi, ARTE VENETA XXXVII
    (1983) 237, 241
Forestier   JG
Forestier, Adolphe *(French, 1801-
  1885)*   GC
    Bibl: ▶Thieme-Becker
Forestier, Amedee   WC WI
  (British artist, -1930)   WC
  (British artist, 1854-1930)   WI
    Bibl: ▶Peppin, Bk. illus. 20c.
Forestier, Henri Joseph de   GC WC
  (French artist, 1787-1872)   WC
  (French painter, 1787-1872)   GC
    Bibl: ▶Thieme-Becker
Forestier, Henri-Claude *(Swiss
  artist, 1875-1922)*   WC
Forestier, Henry-Claudius *(Swiss
  illustrator, printmaker, 1875-1922)*   BA
    Bibl: ▶Bénézit; Giroud, GENAVA,
    XXXV(1987),155-184; KUNSTER-
    LEXIKON; ▶Thieme-Becker
*Forestier, Jacques le→see Le
  Forestier, Jacques*
Forestier, Marie Anne Julie *(French
  artist, 1789-)*   WC
Forestier, Marius *(French artist,
  19th cent.)*   WC
Forestier, Pierre-Auguste *(French
  bronzier, 1755-1835)*   GC
    Bibl: ▶Penguin dec. arts
Förg, Günther *(West German artist,
  b.1952)*   BA
    Bibl: Munich (DEU), Kunstraum
    Munchen, GUNTHER FORG (1984)
Forge, Andrew Murray   BA WI
  (British artist, b.1923)   WI
  *(British painter, author in USA,
  b.1923)*   BA
    Bibl: WW Amer., 1974; ▶WW
    Amer. Art, 1989
Forge, F. de *(French artist, 18th
  cent.)*   WC
Forgeot *(French artist, op.1711)*   WC
Forges Davanzati, Lorenzo *(Italian
  architect, Milan)*   AV
    Bibl: Architettura: Cronache e
    storia, 1984 July, v.30, no.7,
    p.560
Forgioli, Attilio *(Italian painter,
  b.1933)*   BA
    Bibl: ▶Bolaffi 20c.
Forin, John *(Canadian architect,
  19th c.)*   BA
    Bibl: Jrnl. Canadian art hist.,
    III/1-2 (1976) pp.83-94
Forini→see Furini, Francesco
Forino→see Furini, Francesco
Forino, Vincenzo *(Italian architect)*   AV
    Bibl: Architettura; cronache e
    storia, 1979 Jan., v.25, no.1(279),
    p.52

Forissier, Roger *(French artist, 19th
  cent.)*   WC
Forlati, Ferdinando *(Italian
  architect, 1882-1975)*   BA
    Bibl: ▶Chi è?, 1961; Öster. Zeit.
    für Kunst u. Denk. 29/3-4 (1975)
    164-167, obit
Forli→see Forlì, Giovan Vincenzo
Forlì Painter *(Apulian vase-painter)*   GC
    Bibl: Trendall, Attic red-fig. vases
    Apulia
Forlì, Giovan Vincenzo   BA PR
  (Italian painter, act. 1592-1639)   PR
  (Italian painter, act.1592-1639)   BA
    Bibl: ▶Bolaffi; Marini, Pittori a
    Napoli, p. 86; Previtali,
    Cinquecento a Napoli;
    ▶Thieme-Becker

  D'Onofrio, Giovan Vincenzo   BA
  Forli   PR
  Giovan Vincenzo Forli   PR
  Vincenzo Forli   PR

*Forlì, Melozzo da→see Melozzo da
  Forlì*
Formal Group *(Etruscan vase-
  painters)*   GC
    Bibl: Beazley, Etruscan vase-ptrs.
Forman, Steven *(American
  architect, NYC, 1954-)*   AV
    Bibl: ▶AIA Pro File, 1987-88;
    Domus, 1987 Feb., no.680
Formánek, Petr *(Czech medalist,
  20th c.)*   BA
    Bibl: Vytvarna Kultura V/3 (1981)
    48-49
*Forment or Formente, Damian→see
  Forment, Damián*
Forment, Damián   BA
  (Spanish artist, c.1480-c.1542)   WC
  (Spanish sculptor, 1480-1541)   BA
    Bibl: ▶Ars Hispaniae, v.13; ▶Encic.
    univ. ilus.; ▶Encyc. world art;
    ▶Kubler, Art & arch. ESP & PRT;
    ▶Thieme-Becker
Forment or Formente, Damian   WC
Formenti, Tommaso (Formentino)
  (Italian artist, op.1720-1729)   WC
Formentin, Mlle. *(French artist, 18th
  cent.)*   WC
Formentone, Tommaso *(Italian
  architect, 1440-1491/92)*   BA
    Bibl: Belluschi, GUIDA DI BRESCIA
    (1920's), p.90; ▶Bessone-Aurelj,
    Scult. & arch. ital.; Frati, Brescia
    (1989), p. 69, 102; Hemsoll, ARTE
    LOMBARDA, LXXXVI/LXXXVII
    (1988), p. 172; ▶Thieme-Becker;
    Zamboni, MEMORIE...DI BRESCIA
    (1728)
Formichi, Carlo *(Italian architect)*   AV
    Bibl: Domus, 1985 Oct., no.665,
    p.32
Formicola, John Joseph *(American
  painter, b.1941)*   BA
    Bibl: ARTS MAG LV (Sept 1980) 6;
    ▶WW Amer. Art, 1989
*Formis Befani, Achille→see Formis,
  Achille*

Formis, Achille   **BA GC**
  (Italian artist, 1832-1906)   WC
  (Italian painter, 1832-1906)   BA GC
    Bibl: ▶Bolaffi; ▶Thieme-Becker;
    ▶Witt checklist
  Formis Befani, Achille   GC
Formis-Befani, Achille   **WC**
Formis-Befani, Achille → see Formis,
  Achille
Formois [Unidentified] (Unknown
  painter)   **PR**
    Bibl: Le Hon inventory, dated
    1868 (item 12)
Formosa, Romualdo (Italian artist,
  op.1755)   **WC**
Fornaino di Frediano di Baronio
  (Italian goldsmith, act.1331-1372)   **BA**
    Bibl: Capitanio, REVISTA D'ARTE,
    XL(1988)
Fornara, Carlo   **GC WC**
  (Italian artist, 1871-)   WC
  (Italian painter, 1871-1968)   GC
    Bibl: ▶Bénézit
**Fornaretto Mantovano (Giovan
  Francesco Biceso)** (Italian
  painter, stucco artist, 16th c.)   **BA**
    Bibl: Quaderni Pal. Te, IV/6 (Jan-
    June 1987) 65-70; TCI Lombardia
  Biceso, Giovan Francesco   BA
Fornari, duc de (French architect,
  act.1704-1711)   **BA**
    Bibl: Strandberg, R.:GAZETTE DES
    BEAUX ARTS, 99 (Apr 1982),
    p.137
  Fornaro, duc de   BA
Fornari, E. (Italian artist, 19th cent.) **WC**
Fornaro, duc de → see Fornari, duc de
Fornaroli, Antonio (Italian architect) **AV**
    Bibl: Rassegna, 1985 Dec., v.7,
    no.24, p.54
Fornasetti, Piero   **AV BA**
  (Italian designer, 1913-)   AV
  (Italian designer, b.1913)   BA
    Bibl: Bossaglia, APOLLO, 131/336
    (Feb 1990) p.92-95;
    ▶Comanducci, Diz.; Milan
    phonebook; Studio dict. design &
    dec.; Wasserman, JOURNAL OF
    DEC AND PROP ARTS III (Winter
    1987), p.108-119
Fornenbergh, Alexandre van
  (Flemish painter, author, act.1621,
  d. after 1663)   **BA**
    Bibl: ▶Bénézit; BN;
    ▶Thieme-Becker; ▶Wurzbach, NLD
    Künst.-Lex.
  Forenberg, Alexander van   BA
**Fornenburgh, Jan Baptist
  van**   **BA GC WC**
  (Dutch artist, op.1621-1649)   WC
  (Dutch painter and
    draughtsman, act.1608-1656)   GC
  (Dutch painter, act.1608-1656)   BA
    Bibl: Bol, Goede Onbekenden;
    Getty Photo Study Coll.; Paviere;
    ▶RILA/BHA; ▶Witt checklist
Forner, Master Robin (French artist,
  15th cent.)   **WC**

Forner, Pedro (Argentine architect) **AV**
    Bibl: Architecture d'aujourd'hui,
    1986 Feb., no.243, p.XLVIII
Forner, Raquel (Argentine artist,
  1902-)   **WC**
Fornerod, Rodolphe (Swiss artist,
  1877-p.1913)   **WC**
Forni, Girolamo   **GC PR WC**
  (Italian artist, 16th cent.)   WC
  (Italian painter, act. 2nd half
    16th cent.)   PR
  (Italian painter, act. 2nd half
    16th century)   GC
    Bibl: ▶Bolaffi; ▶Thieme-Becker
  Girolamo Forni   PR
**Forniè, Giovanni Battista
  [Unidentified]** (Unknown painter)   **PR**
    Bibl: Colonna inventory, Rome,
    1714
  Gio: Ba Forniè Fiammengo   PR
  Gio: Ba Fornie' Fiammengo   PR
Forno, Marcantonio del (Italian
  painter, act.1574)   **BA**
    Bibl: ANTICHITA VIVA XV/3 (May-
    June 1976) 14-22
Foro Group (Etruscan, Faliscan vase-
  painters)   **GC**
    Bibl: Beazley, Etruscan vase-ptrs.
Foro, Francesco [Unidentified]
  (Unknown painter)   **PR**
    Bibl: Doria inventory, Naples, 17th
    c.
  flores   PR
  Francescho Frorez   PR
  Francesco Foro   PR
Forrer Painter (Apulian vase-painter) **GC**
    Bibl: Trendall, Attic red-fig. vases
    Apulia
Forrest, A.S. → see Forrest, Archibald
  Stevenson
Forrest, Archibald Stevenson   **WI**
  (British artist, 1869-1963)   WI
  (British artist, op.1897-1905)   WC
Forrest, A.S.   **WC**
Forrest, Brian (American
  photographer, b.1951)   **BA**
    Bibl: Los Angeles (CA, USA), Calif.
    State Univ., Fine Arts Gall., Brian
    Forrest (1979)
Forrest, Charles   **WC WI**
  (British artist, op.1765-1776)   WC
  (British artist, op.circa 1748-)   WI
Forrest, Douglas (Scottish architect) **AV**
    Bibl: Country life, 1985 Dec.19,
    v.178, no.4609, p.1972
Forrest, Erik   **WC WI**
  (British artist, 20th cent.)   WC
  (British artist, op.20th c.)   WI
Forrest, H. (British artist, op.1879) **WC**
Forrest, Ian B. → see Forrest, John B.
Forrest, John B. (Engraver, 1814-
  1870)   **WI**
  Forrest, Ian B.   **WI**
Forrest, John Haughton (British
  artist, 1825-1924)   **WI**

Forrest, Robert (American interior
  designer)   **AV**
Forrest, Thomas Theodosius
  (British artist, 1728-1784)   **WC WI**
Forrest, W.S. → see Forrest, William
Forrest, William   **BA**
  (British artist, op.1840-1866)   WI
  (British artist, op.1851)   WC
  (British printmaker, 1805-1889)   BA
    Bibl: Hunnisett, Brit. steel
    engravers; Mackenzie;
    ▶Thieme-Becker
  Forrest, W.S.   **WC**
  Forrest, William S.   **WI**
Forrest, William S. → see Forrest,
  William
Forrestall, Thomas DeVany
  (Canadian artist, b.1936)   **BA**
    Bibl: ▶Creative Canada;
    ▶MacDonald, Can. artists; ▶WW
    Amer. Art, 1976
Forrester, Alfred Henry,
  (Crowquill) → see Crowquill, Alfred
Forrester, Charles II   **WI**
  (British artist, op.1828-1876)   WC WI
  Forster the Younger, Charles   **WC**
Forrester, Denzil (British artist, op.
  20th c.)   **WI**
Forrester, J.J. → see Forrester, Joseph
  James, baron de
Forrester, James   **WC WI**
  (British artist, 1729-1775)   WC
  (British artist, 1730-1775)   WI
Forrester, Jay Wright (American
  engineer, educator, b.1918)   **BA**
    Bibl: WW Amer.
Forrester, John   **WC WI**
  (British artist, 1922-)   WC
  (British artist, b.1922)   WI
Forrester, Joseph James → see
  Forrester, Joseph James, baron de
Forrester, Joseph James, baron de **BA**
  (British artist, 1809-1861)   WI
  (British artist, op.1834)   WC
  (British merchant, author,
    photographer in PRT, 1809-
    1861)   BA
    Bibl: ▶Dict. natl. biog.; ▶Mallalieu,
    Brit. watercolour artists
  Forrester, J.J.   **WC**
  Forrester, Joseph James   **WI**
Forrester, Patricia Tobacco
  (American painter, printmaker,
  b.1940)   **BA**
    Bibl: ▶Art Index, v.31; Guide exh.
    artists: N. Amer. ptrs.; ▶Intl. dir.
    exh. artists, 1982-1983;
    University Park (PA, USA), Penn.
    State Univ., Palmer Mus.of Art,
    REALIST WATERCOLORS (1990)
    [exhibition]; ▶WW Amer. Art,
    1989-1990
Forsberg the Elder, Nils (Swedish
  artist, 1842-1934)   **WC**
Forsberg, Nils (Swedish artist,
  1870-)   **WC**

Forsby, Ola *(Swedish architect,*
Göteborg)   **AV**
    Bibl: Arkitektur: the Swedish
    review of architecture, 1987 July-
    Aug., v.87, no.6, p.36
Forser, Bengt *(Swedish architect)*   **AV**
    Bibl: ▶Svenska Ark. Riks., 1985
Forseth, Einar *(Swedish artist,*
1892-)   **WC**
Forsgren, John *(American glass*
painter)   **AV**
    Bibl: Glass studio, 1985, no.45,
    p.4
Forshall, Francis S.Hyde *(British*
artist, op.1893-1899)   **WI**
Forsman, Chuck *(American painter,*
b.1944)   **BA**
    Bibl: Guide exh. artists: N. Amer.
    ptrs.; ▶WW Amer. Art
Forsman, Erkki *(Finnish architect,*
Helsinki)   **AV**
    Bibl: Arkkitehti, 1987, v.84, no.6,
    p.70
Forss, George *(American*
photographer, b.ca.1941)   **BA**
    Bibl: Wilson, J., in ART NEWS,
    LXXXIII/7 (Sept 1984) 66
Forssell, Victor *(Swedish artist,*
1846-1931)   **WC**
Forsslund, Jonas *(Swedish artist,*
1754-1809)   **WC**
Forst, Johann Hubert Anton
(German artist, 1756-p.1815)   **WC**
Forster the Younger, Charles → see
Forrester, Charles II
Förster, Christian Friedrich Ludwig
von   **BA**
    (1797-1863)   **AV**
    (German architect, author in
    AUT, 1797-1863)   **BA**
    Bibl: ▶Brockhaus Enzyk.;
    ▶Thieme-Becker
    Förster, Ludwig von   **AV BA**
Forster, Cornelia *(Swiss painter,*
sculptor, b.1906)   **BA**
    Bibl: Curonici, Cornelis Forster
    (1984); ▶Künst.-Lex. Schweiz 20.
    Jahr.; ▶Lex. zeitgen. Schweiz.
    Künstler
Forster, Ernst *(German artist, 1800-*
1885)   **WC**
Forster, F.L.M. → see Forster, Francis
L.M.
Forster, Francis L.M.   **WI**
    (British artist, 19th cent.)   **WC**
    (British artist, op.1891-1900)   **WI**
    Forster, F.L.M.   **WC**
Forster, Frank Joseph *(American*
architect, New York, 1886-1948)   **AV**
    Bibl: ▶Withey, Amer. archts.
Forster, G. → see Forster, George,
(USA)
Forster, George → see Forster,
George, (GBR)

Forster, George, (GBR)   **WI**
    (British artist, op.1816-1842)   **WC WI**
    Forster, George   **WC**
Forster, George, (USA)   **WI**
    (American artist, op.1860-1880)   WI
    (American artist, op.1866)   WC
    Forster, G.   **WC**
Forster, Günter *(West German*
architect, Munich)   **AV**
    Bibl: Detail, 1987 July-Aug., v.27,
    no.4, p.365
Förster, Hans *(German painter,*
printmaker, 1885-1966)   **BA**
    Bibl: Altonaer Mus. in Hamburg,
    Jahrb. 16-17 (1978-79) 59-74;
    ▶Bénézit; ▶Thieme-Becker
Forster, Hans *(Swiss painter,*
b.1917)   **BA**
    Bibl: ▶Künst.-Lex. Schweiz 20.
    Jahrh.; ▶Lex. zeitgen. Schweiz.
    Künstler
Förster, Hans → see Ferster, Hans
Forster, Hendrik *(Australian*
silversmith, 20th c.)   **BA**
    Bibl: ▶Intl. dir. exh. artists, 1983,
    v.2; O'Callaghan, Art Bulletin of
    Victoria, 24 (1983) pp.67-71
Forster, J.G.A.   **WC WI**
    (British artist, op.1774)   WC
    (British artist, op.1774-)   WI
Förster, Jens *(West German*
architect(?))   **AV**
    Bibl: Deutsche Bauzeitschrift,
    1989 June, v.37, no.6, p.728
Forster, Joseph Wilson *(British*
artist, op.1889-1916)   **WI**
Förster, Ludwig von → see Förster,
Christian Friedrich Ludwig von
Forster, Noel   **BA WC WI**
    (British artist, 20th cent.)   WC
    (British artist, b.1932)   WI
    (British painter, b.1932)   BA
    Bibl: Bristol (GBR), Arnolfini
    Gallery, Style in the 70s (1979);
    ▶Dolman, Contemp. Brit. artists;
    ▶MoMA libr. cat.
Forster, Robert Edward *(British*
artist, op.circa 1838-)   **WI**
Forster, Thomas   **GC WC WI**
    (British artist, circa 1677-op.
    1713)   WI
    (British artist, op.1695-1712)   WC
    (British, ca.1677-aft.1712)   GC
    Bibl: ▶Brit. Mus. cat.; ▶Witt
    checklist
Förster, Wieland *(German sculptor,*
painter, b.1930)   **BA**
    Bibl: Keisch, WIELAND FORSTER
    (1977); ▶Vollmer, Künst.-Lex. 20.
    Jhr.
Forsterling, Otto *(German artist,*
1843-1904)   **WC**
Forstl, Michael *(American architect,*
Chappaqua, NY)   **AV**
    Bibl: ▶AIA Pro File, 1985

Forstner, Leopold   **BA WC**
    (Austrian mosaicist, sculptor,
    painter, 1878-1936)   BA
    (German artist, 1878-1936)   WC
    Bibl: ▶Bénézit; ▶Fuchs, Öst. Maler
    19. Jahrh.; ▶Österr. biog. Lex.
    1815-1950; ▶Vollmer, Künst.-Lex.
    20. Jhr.
Forsyth, Alan *(British architect)*   **AV**
Forsyth, Gordon Mitchell   **BA WC WI**
    (British artist, 1879-)   WC
    (British artist, 1879-1952)   WI
    (British painter, ceramist,
    designer, 1879-1952)   BA
    Bibl: ▶Fisher, Watercolour ptrs.;
    ▶Johnson, Brit. artists; ▶Waters,
    Brit. artists
Forsyth, Mina *(Canadian painter,*
b.1920)   **BA**
    Bibl: ▶Artists Canada; ▶Intl. dir.
    exh. artists, 1982; Yorkton (Sask,
    CAN), Dean Cultural Centre, Mina
    Forsyth (1985), p.18
Forsyth, Moira *(British ceramist,*
stained glass artist, b.1905)   **BA**
    Bibl: ▶Johnson, Brit. artists; WW
    Amer., 1977
Forsyth, William J. *(American*
painter, 1854-1935)   **BA**
    Bibl: ▶Fielding's Amer. ptrs.;
    Hoosier Group (1985) 155;
    ▶WWW Amer., v.1; ▶WWW
    Amer. art
Forsythe, Victor Clyde *(American*
artist, 1885-1962)   **WI**
Fort → see Fort, Théodore
Fort, Jean Antoine Simeon   **GC WC**
    (French artist, 1793-1861)   WC
    (French painter, 1793-1861)   GC
    Bibl: Getty Photo Study Coll.;
    ▶Witt checklist
    Fort, Simeon   GC
Fort, Simeon → see Fort, Jean Antoine
Simeon
Fort, Théodore   **PR WC**
    (French artist, 19th cent.)   WC
    (French painter, act. 1842)   PR
    Fort   PR
    Theodore Fort   PR
Fort-Brescia, Bernardo *(American*
architect, 1951-)   **AV**
Forte Neto, Luiz *(1935-)*   **AV**
Forte, Gaetano *(Italian artist, 1790-*
1871)   **WC**
Forte, Giacomo → see Forti, Giacomo

Forte, Luca   **BA GC JG PR WC**
   (*Italian artist, op.1640-1670*)   WC
   (*Italian painter,
      1600/15-bef.1670, act. 1640-
      1670*)   PR
   (*Italian painter, act. ca.1625-
      1670*)   GC
   (*Italian painter, act.ca.1625-
      1670*)   BA
   (*Italian, Neapolitan, active ca.
      1625-1655*)   JG
     Bibl: ▶Bolaffi; ▶RILA/BHA, 1986;
     ▶Thieme-Becker; ▶Witt checklist
   Forti, Luca   PR
   Luca Forte   PR
Forte, Miguel (*Brazilian architect*)   AV
     Bibl: Projeto, 1986 Mar., no.85,
     p.72
Fortenagel, Lucas → see Furtenagel,
   Lukas
Fortes, Cláudio (*Brazilian architect*)   AV
     Bibl: Projeto, 1985 Jan., no.71,
     p.73
Fortes, Vitor (*Portuguese artist,
   1943-*)   WC
Fortescue, Henrietta Anne   WI
   (*British artist, c.1765-1841*)   WC
   (*British artist, circa 1765-1841*)   WI
   Acland, Thomas Dyke, 9th Bt.,
     Lady, (Henrietta Anne)   WI
   Fortescue, Hon. Henrietta, Anne   WC
Fortescue, Hon. Henrietta, Anne → see
   Fortescue, Henrietta Anne
Fortescue, William B. → see Fortescue,
   William Banks
Fortescue, William Banks   BA
   (*British artist, circa 1855-1924*)   WI
   (*British artist, op.1880-m.1924*)   WC
   (*British painter, ca.1855-1924*)   BA
     Bibl: ▶Johnson, Brit. artists;
     Newlyn (GBR), Art Gallery, Artists
     of Newlyn (1979); ▶Waters, Brit.
     artists
   Fortescue, William B.   WC WI
*Fortescue-Brickdale, Eleanor,
   Miss → see* Brickdale, Eleanor
   Fortescue
Forth, Nathaniel Parker, Mrs.
   (*British, 18th c.*)   BA
     Bibl: APOLLO, CXXIII/292 (June
     1986) 386-389
Forthun, Louise (*Australian artist*)   AV
     Bibl: Transition, 1987 summer,
     no.22-23, p.90
Forti → see Forti, Ettore
Forti or Forte, Giacomo → see Forti,
   Giacomo
Forti, Edoardo → see Forti, Edwardo
Forti, Edwardo   GC WC
   (*Italian artist, 19th cent.*)   WC
   (*Italian, 19th century*)   GC
     Bibl: Getty Photo Study Coll.
     (Ptgs.); ▶Witt checklist
   Forti, Edoardo   GC

Forti, Ettore   **JG PR WC**
   (*Italian artist, op.c.1892-1935*)   WC
   (*Italian painter, act. 1893-1897*)   PR
   (*Italian, active end 19th century-
     early 20th century*)   JG
     Bibl: ▶Thieme-Becker
   Ettore Forti   PR
   Forti   PR
Forti, Giacomo   **GC**
   (*Italian artist, op.1483-1485(?)*)   WC
   (*Italian, act.1483-1485(?)*)   GC
     Bibl: Getty Photo Study Coll.
     (Ptgs.); ▶Witt checklist
   Forte, Giacomo   GC
Forti or Forte, Giacomo   **WC**
Forti, Luca → see Forte, Luca
Fortier, Alexandre   **JG**
Fortier, Bruno (*Italian architect,
   20th c.*)   BA
     Bibl: ▶Avery period. idx.; Culot,
     Mons. Hist. France, 133 (Jun.-Jul.
     1984) pp.97-101; Ricerche di
     storia dell'arte 7 (1978-79) p.38
Fortier, Francois Alphonse (*French,
   1825-1882*)   JG
Fortin, André (*Canadian architect*)   AV
     Bibl: Section a, 1985 Jan., v.2, no.
     5-6, p.12
Fortin, Augustin Félix   BA
   (*French artist, 1763-1832*)   WC
   (*French sculptor, painter,
     printmaker, 1763-1832*)   BA
     Bibl: ▶Bénézit; ▶Thieme-Becker
   Fortin, Augustin-Felix   WC
Fortin, Augustin-Felix → see Fortin,
   Augustin Félix
Fortin, Charles (*French painter,
   1815-1865*)   GC
     Bibl: ▶Bénézit
Fortin, Jean Patrick (*French
   architect*)   AV
Fortin, Jeanne Besnard (*French
   artist, 19th cent.*)   WC
Fortin, Joseph Ernest (*Canadian
   architect, 1875 or 6-1945*)   AV
     Bibl: Society for the Study of
     Architecture in Canada. Bulletin,
     1986 Dec., v.11, no.4, p.10
Fortin, L. (*French ébéniste, act. ca.
   1750*)   GC
     Bibl: Getty Photo Study Coll. (Dec.
     arts); Theunissen, Meubles
Fortin, Marc Aurèle   BA
   (*Canadian artist, 1888-*)   WC
   (*Canadian painter, 1888-1970*)   BA
     Bibl: ▶Artists Canada; ▶Bénézit;
     ▶MacDonald, Can. artists;
     ▶MoMA libr. cat.
   Fortin, Marc-Aurele   WC
Fortin, Marc-Aurele → see Fortin, Marc
   Aurèle

Fortini, Giovacchino   **BA GC**
   (*Italian sculptor, architect, and
     medalist, 1671-1736*)   GC
   (*Italian sculptor, architect,
     medalist, 1671-1736*)   BA
     Bibl: ▶Bénézit; ▶Forrer, Medallists;
     Nava Cellini, Scult. del'700,
     p.255; ▶RILA/BHA; TCI Firenze,
     p.476; ▶Thieme-Becker
Fortling, Jacob   BA
   (*Danish architect, 1711-1761*)   AV
   (*Danish architect, sculptor,
     ceramist, 1711-1761*)   BA
     Bibl: ▶Thieme-Becker; ▶Weilbach,
     Kunst.leks.
   Fortling, Jakob   AV
Fortling, Jakob → see Fortling, Jacob
Fortnagel, Lanx → see Furtenagel,
   Lukas
Fortner, Georg   **BA WC**
   (*German artist, 1814-1879*)   WC
   (*German painter, 1814-1879*)   BA
     Bibl: ▶Busse, Maler u. Bildhauer
     19. Jahr.; ▶Thieme-Becker
Fortner, Ludwig (*Bohemian
   silversmith, 1797-1872*)   BA
     Bibl: ▶Thieme-Becker
Fortsch, Hans (*German artist, 1859-*)   WC
Fortsch, Hans (*German artist, 1924-*)   WC
Fortt, Frederick W. (*British artist,
   op.1848-1861*)   WI
Fortuna, Gianfrancesco (*16th
   century Paduan architect, author
   of manuscript treatise on
   architecture*)   AV
     Bibl: Padua, Museo Civico,
     Bollettino, v.67, p.42-58
Fortuna, Pietro (*Italian painter,
   b.1950*)   BA
     Bibl: Acireale (ITA), Palazzo di
     Città, Incursioni oltre le linee
     (1982)
Fortunata Guadagni → see Guadagni,
   Fortunata [Unidentified]
Fortunati da Gubbio, Agostino → see
   Fortunati, Agostino
Fortunati, Agostino (*Draughtsman,
   ante 1583-post 1583*)   CE
   Fortunati da Gubbio, Agostino   CE
Fortunato (*Italian painter, b.1500-
   1510, d. after 1550*)   BA
     Bibl: ▶Bolaffi; Cleri, Not. Pal.
     Albani, XIV/1 (1985) pp.44-49;
     ▶Thieme-Becker
   Ridolfi, Fortunato   BA
Fortunato Arriola → see Arriola,
   Fortunato
Fortune → see Fortune, E. Charlton
*Fortune Joseph Seraphin
   Layraud → see* Layraud, Fortuné
   Joseph Séraphin
Fortune Medalist (*Italian medalist,
   act.1495*)   BA
     Bibl: ▶Forrer, Medallists
Fortune, Charlton → see Fortune, E.
   Charlton

Fortune, E. Charlton *(American painter, 1885-1969)* **PR**
 Bibl: De Young Mus. cat.; ▶WWW Amer. art
 E. Charlton Fortune PR
 Fortune PR
 Fortune, Charlton PR
Fortuny→see Fortuny y Carbó, Mariano José María Bernardo
Fortuny y Carbó→see Fortuny y Carbó, Mariano José María Bernardo
Fortuny y Carbo, Mariano→see Fortuny y Carbó, Mariano José María Bernardo
Fortuny y Carbó, Mariano José María Bernardo **BA GC PR WC**
 (Spanish artist, 1838-1874) WC
 (Spanish painter, 1838-1874) BA PR
 (Spanish, 1838-1874) GC
 Bibl: ▶Bénézit; ▶Encic. univ. ilus.; ▶Natl. union cat., pre-1956; ▶Ossorio y Bernard, Artistas españoles 19s.; ▶RILA/BHA; ▶Thieme-Becker; ▶Witt checklist
 Carbó, Mariano Fortuny y BA
 Fortuny PR
 Fortuny y Carbó PR
 Fortuny y Carbo, Mariano PR
 Fortuny y Marsal, Mariano BA
 Fortuny, Mariano PR
 Mariano Jose Maria Bernardo Fortuny y Carbo PR
 Marsal, Mariano Fortuny y BA
Fortuny y Madrazo, Mariano
 (Spanish painter, couturier, scenographer, photographer in ITA, 1871-1949) **BA**
 Bibl: ▶Bénézit; ▶Encic. spettacolo; ▶Encic. univ. ilus.; Lorenzetti, Venice & its Lagoon; ▶Thieme-Becker; Venezia (ITA), Mus. di Pal. Fortuny, Immagini e materiali del Laboratorio Fortuny (1978)
Fortuny y Marsal, Mariano→see Fortuny y Carbó, Mariano José María Bernardo
Fortuny, Cecilia de Madrazo
 (Spanish, d.1933) **BA**
 Bibl: Cecchi, GIOVANNI BOLDINI, 68, 285; Venezia (ITA), Mus. di Pal. Fortuny, Immagini e materiali del Laboratorio Fortuny (1978), p.37
 Madrazo, Cecilia de BA
Fortuny, Lucia *(French artist, 20th cent.)* **WC**
Fortuny, Mariano→see Fortuny y Carbó, Mariano José María Bernardo
Fortur, Arthur John *(British artist, op.circa 1860-)* **WI**
Fortuzzi, Fabio *(Italian architect)* **AV**
 Bibl: Architettura; cronache e storia, 1988 Nov., v.34, no.11, p.806

Forzetta da Treviso, Oliviero→see Forzetta, Oliviero
Forzetta, Oliviero *(Scribe, post 1250/ante 1335-post 1335/ante 1400)* **CE**
 Da Treviso, Oliviero Forzetta CE
 Forzetta da Treviso, Oliviero CE
 Oliviero Forzetta CE
 Oliviero Forzetta da Treviso CE
Forzoni, Giovanna Gastona→see Forzoni-Accolti, Giovanna Gastona
Forzoni-Accolti, Giovanna Gastona
 (Italian painter, act. 18th century) **PR**
 Bibl: ▶Thieme-Becker
 Forzoni, Giovanna Gastona PR
 Giov. Gastona Forzoni-Accolti PR
 Giovanna Gastona Forzoni PR
 Giovanna Gastona Forzoni-Accolti PR
Fos, Urbano *(Spanish painter, act. 1648-1650)* **BA**
 Bibl: Kowal, Francisco Ribalta, p.191
Fosburgh, James Whitney **BA WC WI**
 (American artist, 1910-) WC
 (American artist, 1910-1978) WI
 (American painter, collector, author, 1910-1978) BA
 Bibl: NY Times obit., 25 Apr 1978, p.40; ▶WW Amer. Art, 1976
Foscari, Antonio **AV BA**
 (Italian architect, architectural historian, 20th c.) BA
 (Italian architect, Venice. Teaches at Istituto universitario di architettura di Venezia, 1938-) AV
 Bibl: Clark Art Inst. Libr.; Kaufmann, E., in H.-R. Hitchcock Festsch. 1982, 31; ▶Libr. of Congr. Name Auth. File
Foschi→see Foschi, Francesco
Foschi Ferretti, Stefania *(Italian architect)* **AV**
 Bibl: Architettura; cronache e storia, 1981 June, v.27, no. 6(308), p.373
 Ferretti, Stefania Foschi AV
Foschi, Francesco **GC PR**
 (Italian artist, op.c.1750) WC
 (Italian painter, act. ca.1750) PR
 (Italian, act. ca.1750) GC
 Bibl: ▶Thieme-Becker; ▶Witt checklist
 Foschi PR
Foschi, Francesco (not Ferdinando) **WC**
 Fosky PR
 Francesco Foschi PR
Foschi, Francesco (not Ferdinando)→see Foschi, Francesco

Foschi, Pier Francesco **BA GC WC**
 (Italian artist, 1502-1567) WC
 (Italian painter, 1502-1567) BA GC
 Bibl: ▶Bolaffi; ▶Freedberg, Ptg. Italy; Getty Photo Study Coll. (Ptgs.); ▶RILA/BHA, 1986; ▶Thieme-Becker
 Toschi, Pier Francesco GC
Foschi, Sigismondo **GC WC**
 (Italian artist, op.1520-1532) WC
 (Italian, act.1520-d.1532) GC
 Bibl: ▶Thieme-Becker; ▶Witt checklist
Foschini→see Foschini, Michele
Foschini, Antonio **AV BA**
 (Italian architect, 1741-1813) BA
 (Italian architect, worked in Ferrara, 1741-1813) AV
 Bibl: ▶Portoghesi, Diz. arch. e urbanistica; ▶Thieme-Becker
Foschini, Michele **GC PR**
 (Italian painter, 1711-1770) PR
 (Italian, 1711-1770) GC
 Bibl: ▶Thieme-Becker
 Foschini PR
 Michele Foschini PR
Fosdick, Cheryl *(American architect, Minn)* **AV**
 Bibl: Architecture Minnesota, 1989 Nov.-Dec., v.15, no.6, p.27
Fosdick, James William *(American artist, 1858-1937)* **WI**
Fosino [Unidentified] *(Unknown painter)* **PR**
 Bibl: Colonna inventory, Rome, 1714
Fosky→see Foschi, Francesco
Foss, John *(British architect, 1745-1827)* **AV BA**
 Bibl: ▶Colvin, Brit. archts.
Foss, Ole *(1937-)* **AV**
Fossano, Ambrogio da→see Ambrogio da Fossano (il Bergognone)
Fossati family *(Italian architects, sculptors, 18th c.)* **BA**
 Bibl: ▶Bénézit; ▶Bolaffi; ▶Comanducci, Diz.; ▶Thieme-Becker
Fossati, Andrea *(Italian painter, b.1844 - d. aft. 1900)* **GC**
 Bibl: ▶Thieme-Becker
Fossati, Davide Antonio **BA GC**
 (Italian artist, 1708-1780) WC
 (Italian draughtsman, 1708-1780) GC
 (Swiss painter, printmaker, 1708-ca.1780) BA
 Bibl: ▶Artist biog. master idx.; ▶Bénézit; ▶Havlice, Idx. art. bio.; ▶Nagler, Neues Künst.-Lex.; ▶Schweiz. Künst.-Lex.; ▶Thieme-Becker
Fossati, Davide-Antonio **WC**
Fossati, Davide-Antonio→see Fossati, Davide Antonio

Fossati, Domenico   GC WC
   (Italian artist, 1743-1784)   WC
   (Italian, 1743-1784)   GC
   Bibl: ▶Thieme-Becker; ▶Witt
     checklist
Fossati, Gaspare *(Swiss artist, 1809-*
   1883)   WC
Fossati, Giorgio   AV BA
   (Swiss architect and theorist,
    active in northern Italy, 1706-
    1778)   AV
   (Swiss architect, printmaker,
    1705-1785)   BA
   Bibl: Arte lombarda, 55-57 (1980)
    346-364; ▶Avery Libr. cat.;
    ▶Portoghesi, Diz. arch. e
    urbanistica; ▶Thieme-Becker
Fosse, Coessin de la→*see* Coessin de
   la Fosse, Charles Alexandre
Fosse, Désiré *(French sculptor,*
   d.1913)   GC
   Bibl: ▶Thieme-Becker
Fosse, Jena-Charles De la→*see*
   Delafosse, Jean Charles
Fosse, Louis Remy de la→*see* La
   Fosse, Louis Remy de
Fossi, Fra Domenico de' *(Italian*
   artist, 1479-p.1547)   WC
Fossland, Geir *(Norwegian architect,*
   1954-)   AV
   Bibl: Byggekunst: the Norwegian
    review of architecture, 1988,
    v.70, no.5, p.350
Fossland, Geir *(Norwegian*
   architect)   AV
   Bibl: Byggekunst: the Norwegian
    review of architecture, 1988
    v.70, no.2, p.116
Fossland, Kari *(Norwegian architect,*
   1957-)   AV
   Bibl: Byggekunst: the Norwegian
    review of architecture, 1988,
    v.70, no.5, p.346
Foster, Alan   WC WI
   (American artist, 1892-)   WC
   (American artist, b.1892)   WI
Foster, Anne-Marie *(British artist,*
   b.1955)   WI
Foster, Arthur Joseph *(British*
   artist, op.circa 1874-)   WI
Foster, Barbara Lynn *(American*
   printmaker, painter, b.1947)   BA
   Bibl: ▶WW Amer. Art, 1976
Foster, Ben   PR WC WI
   (American artist, 1852-1926) WC WI
   (American painter, 1852-1926)   PR
   Bibl: ▶WWW Amer. art
   Ben Foster   PR
Foster, Birket→*see* Foster, Myles
   Birket
Foster, Charles   WI
   (American artist, 1850-1931) WC WI
   Foster, Charles A.   WC
Foster, Charles A.→*see* Foster,
   Charles

Foster, Charles Andrew *(American*
   painter, 1817-1886)   PR
   Bibl: ▶Young, Amer. artists
   Charles Andrew Foster   PR
Foster, David *(British artist, b.1936)* WI
Foster, Deryck   WC WI
   (British artist, 20th cent.)   WC
   (British artist, b.1924)   WI
Foster, Diana *(American collagist,*
   20th c.)   BA
   Bibl: ▶Intl. dir. exh. artists, 1982;
    New art examiner, VIII/2 (Nov.
    1980)
Foster, Edward Ward *(British artist,*
   1761-1864)   WC WI
Foster, Elizabeth, Lady *(British*
   artist, 1760-1824)   WI
Foster, George Washington *(Black*
   American architect, Park Ridge,
   N.J, 1866-1923)   AV
   Bibl: House beautiful, 1988 Jan.,
    v.130, no.1, p.23
Foster, Gilbert (William G.)→*see*
   Foster, William Gilbert
Foster, Graham *(British artist,*
   b.1950)   WI
Foster, Herbert Wilson *(British*
   artist, op.1870-1899)   WC WI
   Bibl: Morris &Morris(Birm.)
Foster, J.R. *(American, active Civil*
   War)   JG
Foster, John *(British sculptor,*
   b.1951)   BA
   Bibl: Norwich (GBR), School of
    Art, Current Brit. sculp. (1979)
Foster, John→*see* Foster, John, (GBR)
Foster, John→*see* Foster, John, (USA)
Foster, John, (GBR)   WI
   (British artist, c.1787-1846)   WC
   (British artist, circa 1787-1846) WI
   Foster, John   WC
Foster, John, (USA)   WI
   (American artist, 1648-1681)   WC
   (American artist, engraver,
    1648-1681)   WI
   (Engraver, 1648-1681)   WI
   Bibl: ▶Groce, Artists Amer.
   Foster, John   WC WI
Foster, Jonathan S. *(American*
   architect, New York City)   AV
   Bibl: ▶AIA Pro File, 1987-88
Foster, Michael *(British architect*
   and president of the Architectural
   Association, London)   AV
   Bibl: Building, 1989 Sept.29,
    v.254, no.39, p.28
Foster, Myles Birket   BA WC WI
   (British artist, 1825-1899)   WC WI
   (British painter, printmaker,
    1825-1899)   BA
   (British, 1825-1899)   GC
   Bibl: ▶Thieme-Becker
   Foster, Birket   GC
Foster, Norman→*see* Foster, Norman
   Robert

Foster, Norman Robert   BA
   (British architect and author. In
    practice with Richard Rogers
    as Team 4, London, 1963-67
    and then with his wife
    Wendy as Foster Associates,
    London, 1967-, 1935-)   AV
   (British architect, b.1935)   BA
   Bibl: ▶Avery period. idx.;
    ▶Contemp. archts.; ▶Who's Who
    [GBR]
   Foster, Norman   AV
Foster, Paul *(British artist, op.1845-)* WI
Foster, Peter Le Neve *(British*
   lawyer, photographer, 1809-1879) BA
   Bibl: ▶Dict. natl. biog.
Foster, Philip *(Australian artist, 20th*
   cent.)   WC
Foster, Richard   AV
Foster, Richard *(British artist, op.*
   20th c.)   WI
Foster, Thomas *(British artist, 1798-*
   1826)   WC WI
Foster, Tim *(British architect)*   AV
   Bibl: Architects' journal, 1985
    Apr.3, v.181, no.14, p.16
Foster, Tim *(British artist, b.1951)* WI
Foster, Walter H.W. *(British artist,*
   op.1861-1888)   WI
Foster, Wendy *(British architect)*   AV
Foster, William *(British artist, op.*
   1772-, d.1812)   WI
Foster, William Dewey *(American*
   architect, New York City, fl.
   1930's)   AV
   Bibl: Metropolis, 1989 Mar., v.8,
    no.7, p.88
Foster, William Fred *(American*
   artist, 1883-1953)   WI
Foster, William Gilbert *(British*
   artist, 1855-1906)   WC WI
   Foster, Gilbert (William G.)   WC
Foster, William Harnden *(American*
   artist, circa 1886-1941)   WI
Fothergill, Charles *(British artist,*
   op.1850-1883)   WC WI
Fothergill, George Algernon
   (British artist, 1868-1945)   WI
Fothergill, John *(English*
   metalworker, ca.1700-1782)   BA
   Bibl: ▶Dict. natl. biog.
Fothergill, Waston *(British architect,*
   1841-1928)   BA
   Bibl: Pevsner, Nottinghamshire, p.
    36
   Watson, Fothergill   BA
Fotheringham, Michael *(American*
   landscape architect)   AV
   Bibl: Landscape architecture,
    1989 June, v.79, no.5, p.16
Foto-Ars *(Active ca. 1920)*   JG
Fotr *(Viking sculptor, act.1040-1060)* BA
   Bibl: Crocker, FOTR RISTI: A
    RUNOGRAPHER'S STYLE (1982)
    (diss.)

Fouace, Guillaume Romain *(French artist, 1827-1895)*   **WC**

Foubert, Emile Louis *(French artist, -1910/11)*   **WC**

Foucart, Joseph *(Belgian architect in United States, 1848-after 1906)*   **AV**
Bibl: Blueprints, 1984 Fall, v.3, no.1, p.11

Fouceel, Jan *(Flemish artist, op.c. 1670)*   **WC**

Fouche or Foucher, Nicolas *(French artist, 1653-1733)*   **WC**

Fouchier, Bartram de   **GC WC**
(Dutch artist, 1609-1673)   **WC**
(Dutch painter, 1609-1673)   **GC**
Bibl: ▶Thieme-Becker

Fouchier, Bernard *(French architect, 15th c.)*   **BA**
Bibl: BULLETIN MONUMENTAL CXXXVIII/3 (1980) 293-345

Foucou, Jean Joseph *(French sculptor, 1739-1815/1816)*   **GC**
Bibl: ▶Thieme-Becker

Foucquier→see Fouquières, Jacques

Foudras *(French artist, 19th cent.)*   **WC**

Fougeras-Lavergnolle, Arnaud *(French architect)*   **AV**
Bibl: Architecture d'aujourd'hui, 1988 Apr., no.256, p.74

Fougerel, F. *(French artist, op.1791)*   **WC**

Fougeron, André   **BA WC**
(French artist, 1912-)   **WC**
(French painter, printmaker, b.1913)   **BA**
Bibl: ▶Bénézit; ▶Larousse grande encyc.

Fougeron, J. *(Engraver, op.1761-)*   **WI**

Fougstedt, Arvid *(Swedish artist, 1888-1949)*   **WC**

Fouilhoux, Jacques André *(American architect, 1879-1945)*   **AV**
Bibl: ▶Macmillan encyc. archts.

Foujioka→see Foujioka, Noboru

Foujioka, Noboru *(American painter, act. 20th century)*   **PR**
Foujioka   PR
Noboru Foujioka   PR

Foujita→see Foujita, Tsugouharu

Foujita, Léonard→see Foujita, Tsugouharu

Foujita, Tsugouharu   **BA PR**
(French artist, 1886-)   **WC**
(French painter, 1886-1968)   **PR**
(French painter, printmaker, 1886-1968)   **BA**
(Japanese painter in FRA, 1886-1968)   **GC**
Bibl: ▶Bénézit; ▶RILA/BHA; Selz, FOUJITA (1981); ▶Vollmer, Künst.-Lex. 20. Jhr.
Foujita   PR
Foujita, Léonard   BA

Foujita, Tsugouharu Léonard   **WC**
Fujita, Tsugouharu   BA

Tsugouhari, Foujita   **GC**
Tsugouharu Foujita   PR

Foujita, Tsugouharu Leonard→see Foujita, Tsugouharu

Foulger, Howson Rutherford *(British artist, op.circa 1890-)*   **WI**

Foulkes, Llyn   **BA WC WI**
(American artist, 1934-op.1965)   WI
(American artist, 20th cent.)   WC
(American painter, b.1934)   BA
Bibl: Clark Art Inst. Photo & Slide Dept.; ▶WW Amer. Art, 1976

Foullet, Antoine *(French, 1710-1775, master 1749)*   **JG**

Foullet, Pierre-Antoine *(French ébéniste, master 1765, act. to ca. 1780)*   **GC**
Bibl: ▶Salverte, Ébénistes 18e s.

Foullon or Foulon, Lucile, (nee Vachot) *(French artist, c.1775-1865)*   **WC**

Foulon or Foullon, Benjamin→see Foulon, Benjamin

Foulon, Benjamin   **GC**
(French artist, c.1550-c.1612)   WC
(French painter, ca.1550-ca. 1612)   GC
Bibl: ▶Thieme-Becker

Foulon or Foullon, Benjamin   **WC**

Foulque Nerra *(French nobleman, architect, 987-1040)*   **BA**
Bibl: ▶Columbia encyc.; Deyres, BULL. MON. CXXXII/1 (1974) 7-28
Fulk Nerra   BA
Nerra, Foulque   BA

Foulquier, Jean Antoine Valentin→see Foulquier, Valentin

Foulquier, Jean-Antoine-Valentin→see Foulquier, Valentin

Foulquier, Valentin   **GC**
(French artist, 1822-1896)   WC
(French, 1822-1896)   GC
Bibl: Getty Photo Study Coll. (Ptgs.); ▶Thieme-Becker; ▶Witt checklist
Foulquier, Jean Antoine Valentin   GC

Foulquier, Jean-Antoine-Valentin   **WC**

Foulston, John   **AV WC WI**
(1772-1842)   AV
(British artist, 1772-1842)   WC WI

Foundling Group *(Campanian vase-painters)*   **GC**
Bibl: ▶Trendall, Red-fig. vases Lucania

Foundry Painter   **GC JG**
(vase-painter, ca. 500-475 BC)   GC
Bibl: ▶Beazley, Attic red-fig. vase-ptrs.; Richter, Attic red-fig. vases

Fountain, Cherryl *(British artist, op. 20th c.)*   **WI**

Fountain, William *(British silversmith, act. from 1791)*   **GC**
Bibl: ▶Grimwade, London goldsmiths, 1982

Fountaine, F.   **WC WI**
(British artist, op.1908)   WC
(British artist, op.1908-)   WI

Fouque, Jean Marius (not Jean Marie Baptiste) *(French artist, 1822-)*   **WC**

Fouqueire→see Fouquières, Jacques

Fouqueirs→see Fouquières, Jacques

Fouquet family *(French jewelers, 19th-20th cs.)*   **BA**
Bibl: ▶Newman, Jewelry; RLIN BKS file; Vever, Bijoutérie fran.

Fouquet or Foucquet, Jean→see Fouquet, Jean

Fouquet, Alphonse *(French jeweler, 1828-1911)*   **BA**
Bibl: ▶Newman, Jewelry; Vever, Bijoutérie fran., v.3, p.365 ff.

Fouquet, Francois   **GC**
(French artist, 15th cent.)   WC
(French, 15th century)   GC
Bibl: ▶Witt checklist

Fouquet, Francois (Maitre Francois?) et Louis   **WC**

Fouquet, Francois (Maitre Francois?) et Louis→see Fouquet, Francois

Fouquet, Georges *(French jeweler, 1862-1957)*   **BA**
Bibl: ▶Newman, Jewelry; Vever, Bijoutérie fran., v.3, p.623 ff.

Fouquet, Jacques   **GC WC**
(Flemish painter, 17th century)   GC
(French artist, op.1685-1704)   WC
Bibl: ▶Bénézit

Fouquet, Jean   **AV BA GC JG**
(French artist, c.1420-1477/81)   WC
(French painter and illuminator, ca.1418-1480?)   GC
(French painter, ca.1420-ca. 1480)   AV
(French painter, illuminator, ca. 1420-ca.1480)   BA
(French, ca. 1420-1481)   JG
Bibl: ▶Bénézit; ▶Dict. biog. fran.; ▶Libr. of Congr. Name Auth. File; ▶RILA/BHA; ▶Thieme-Becker

Fouquet or Foucquet, Jean   **WC**

Fouquet, Jean *(French artist, op. 1781-1798)*   **WC**

Fouquet, Jean *(French jeweler, b.1899)*   **BA**
Bibl: ▶Newman, Jewelry

Fouquet, Louis Vincent *(French artist, 1803-1869)*   **WC**

Fouquier→see Fouquières, Jacques

Fouquier, Focquier, Fouquiere or Fouquieres, Jacques→see Fouquières, Jacques

Fouquier, Jacques→see Fouquières, Jacques

Fouquiere→see Fouquières, Jacques

Fouquieres→see Fouquières, Jacques

Fouquières, Jacques **BA PR**
(Flemish artist, c.1580/90-1659) WC
(Flemish painter in FRA, ca.1580-
1659) BA
(Flemish painter, 1580/90-1659) PR
(Flemish, 1580/90-1659) GC
Bibl: ▶Bénézit; ▶RILA/BHA;
▶Thieme-Becker; ▶Witt checklist
Fanquires PR
Fauquier PR
Fauquiers PR
Fockeer PR
Foucquier PR
Fouqueire PR
Fouqueirs PR
Fouquier PR
Fouquier, Focquier, Fouquiere
or Fouquieres, Jacques **WC**
Fouquier, Jacques **GC PR**
Fouquiere PR
Fouquieres PR
Fouquiers PR
Fouquires PR
J. Fouquieres PR
Jacques Fouquieres PR
Fouquiers→see Fouquières, Jacques
Fouquires→see Fouquières, Jacques
Fourau or Foureau, Hugues (French
artist, 1803-1873) **WC**
Fouraut, Marie (Mother Saint
Croix) (American nun,
photographer, 1854-1940) **BA**
Bibl: Freeman, ARTS QUARTERLY
IV/4 (Oct-Dec 1982) 30-33; New
Orleans (LA, USA), Mus. of Art,
THE PHOTOGRAPHS OF MOTHER
ST. CROIX
Mother Saint Croix BA
Fourcade, Anne (French architect) **AV**
Bibl: Architectes architecture,
1987 May, no.177, p.28
Fourcade, Vincent (American
interior designer) **AV**
Bibl: House & garden, 1985 June,
v.157, no.6, p.102
Fourdinois, Alexandre Georges
(French cabinetmaker, 1799-1871) **BA**
Bibl: ANTIQUES CX/2 (Aug 1976)
336-343; Ledoux-Lebard, LES
EBENISTES PARISIENS, p.180
Fourdinois, Henri Auguste (French
cabinetmaker, 1830-after 1894) **BA**
Bibl: ANTIQUES CX/2 (Aug 1976)
336-343; ▶Bénézit; Ledoux-
Lebard, LES EBENISTES PARISIENS,
181; ▶Thieme-Becker
Fourdrinier, Pierre **BA WI**
(Engraver, op.1720-1760) WI
(French printmaker in GBR,
d.1758) BA
Bibl: Connoisseur CCVI/828 (Feb
1981) 158-161; ▶Dict. natl. biog.
Foureau, Louis (French ébéniste,
master 1755, act. to ca.1785) **GC**
Bibl: ▶Salverte, Ébénistes 18e s.
Fourie, Albert Auguste (French
artist, 1854-) **WC**

Fourier, Charles (1772-1837) **AV**
Bibl: ▶Libr. of Congr. Name Auth.
File
Fourment, Susanne (Flemish, 1599-
1628) **BA**
Bibl: Evers, Rubens u. zein Werk;
Vlieghe, RINGLING MUSEUM OF
ART JOURNAL (1983) 107-108
Lunden, Susanne BA
Fourmois, Théodore **BA WC**
(Belgian artist, 1814-1871) WC
(French painter, printmaker,
1814-1871) BA
Bibl: ▶Bénézit; ▶Busse, Maler u.
Bildhauer 19. Jahr.;
▶Thieme-Becker
Fourneau, Charles-Antoine de
(Flemish, 1658-1729) **BA**
Bibl: Delmarcel, Ringling Mus. Art
Jrnl. (1983), p.197, n.11
Cruyckenbourg, Charles-Antoine
de Fourneau de BA
Fournier→see Fournier, Louis
Edouard
Fournier, Alain (French architect) **AV**
Bibl: Architecture d'aujourd'hui,
1988 Dec., no.260, p.096
Fournier, Alexandre de (French
artist, 1831-) **WC**
Fournier, Alexis Jean **BA**
(American artist, 1865-1948) WI
(American painter, 1865-1948) BA
Bibl: ▶Vollmer, Künst.-Lex. 20.
Jhr.; ▶WWW Amer. art
Fournier, Alexis-Jean **WI**
Fournier, Alexis-Jean→see Fournier,
Alexis Jean
Fournier, Charles (French artist,
1803-1854) **WC**
Fournier, Fortune→see Fournier,
Fortune (Jean Baptiste Fortune)
Fournier, Fortune (Jean Baptiste
Fortune) **GC WC**
(French artist, 1798-1864) WC
(French, 1798-1864) GC
Bibl: ▶Thieme-Becker; ▶Witt
checklist
Fournier, Fortune GC
Fournier, Gabriel (French painter,
1605-after 1666) **BA**
Bibl: ▶Dict. biog. fran.; Roudie, P.,
BULL. DE LA SOC. DE l'HIST. De
L'ART FRAN. (1983) 57-66;
▶Thieme-Becker
Fournier, Gabriel Francisque→see
Gabriel-Fournier
Fournier, Jean (French artist, c.1700-
1765) **WC**
Fournier, Jean Simon (French artist,
op.1791-1799) **WC**

Fournier, Louis Edouard **GC PR**
(French artist, 1857-) WC
(French painter, 1857-aft.1903) PR
(French painter, b.1857) GC
Bibl: ▶Thieme-Becker
Fournier PR
Fournier, Louis Edouard Paul **WC**
Louis Edouard Fournier PR
Fournier, Louis Edouard Paul→see
Fournier, Louis Edouard
Fournier, Marcel (French artist,
1869-1917) **WC**
Fournier, Mary (British artist, op.
18th c.) **WI**
Fournier, Paul (Canadian painter,
printmaker, b.1939) **BA**
Bibl: ▶Artists Canada
Fournier, R. [Unidentified]
(Unknown painter) **PR**
Bibl: (May 23, 1801, lot 12, Coxe,
Burrel & Foster)
R. Fournier PR
Fournier, Sheila (British ceramist,
b.1930) **BA**
Bibl: Intl. ceramics 1972
Fourquier, Alain (French architect) **AV**
Bibl: Architecture intèrieure créé,
1985 June-July, no.206, p.86
Fourquier, Joanna (French
architect) **AV**
Bibl: Architecture intèrieure créé,
1985 June-July, no.206, p.86
Fourtina, Annie (French artist, 20th
cent.) **WC**
Fous, Jear (French artist, 1901-) **WC**
Fousek, Frank Daniel (American
artist, b.1913) **WI**
Fouson, Pieter Jozef (Flemish
silversmith, 1713-1799) **BA**
Bibl: De Ren, Antiek, XIX/3 (Oct.
1984) pp.121-122, pp.121-122;
Hernmarck, Euro. silversmith
Foweraker, A. Moulton (British
artist, 1873-1942) **WI**
Fowke, Francis **AV BA**
(British architect, 1823-1865) AV
(British engineer, architect,
1823-1865) BA
Bibl: ▶Dict. natl. biog.;
▶Macmillan encyc. archts.
Fowke, Margaret→see Walsh,
Margaret Benn
Fowler, Charles **AV BA**
(1791-1867) AV
(British architect, 1792-1867) BA
Bibl: ▶Colvin, Brit. archts.;
▶Thieme-Becker
Fowler, Charles B. (fl.1914;
Architect, Vancouver) **FA**
Bibl: CAAD Finding Aid, RG 11M
77803/39; Natl. Arch. of Canada,
CAAD Finding Aid
Fowler, Daniel (Canadian painter,
1810-1894) **BA**
Bibl: ▶Harper, Ptg. Canada;
Hubbard, 300 yrs. of Canadian
art; ▶Thieme-Becker

Fowler, Francis   **AV BA**
    (19th century British architect)   AV
    (British architect, act.1875)   BA
      Bibl: ▶Avery period. idx.;
      COUNTRY LIFE CLXX (12 Nov)
      1700-1703

Fowler, Frank   **PR WI**
    (American artist, 1852-1910)   WI
    (American painter, 1852-1910)   PR
      Bibl: ▶WWW Amer. art
    Frank Fowler   PR

Fowler, Graham *(English interior
    designer, London)*   **AV**
      Bibl: The World of interiors, 1988
      Apr., p.130

Fowler, Henry Day *(British artist,
    op.1855-)*   **WI**

Fowler, John → see Fowler, John
    Beresford

Fowler, John Beresford   **BA**
    *(British decorator, restorer,
    1906-1977)*   BA
    *(English interior designer, 1906-
    1977)*   AV
      Bibl: Kelly's Handbook; ▶Libr. of
      Congr. Name Auth. File, d. date
      from 670 field; Times issue 29,
      Oct. 1977, p.16

    Fowler, John   **AV**
Fowler, John, Sir *(1817-1898)*   **AV**
Fowler, Laurence Hall *(American
    architect, 1876-1971)*   **BA**
      Bibl: ▶WWW Amer., v.5

Fowler, Mary Lemon, Miss → see
    Waller, Mary Lemon

Fowler, O. S. *(American
    phrenologist, author, and designer,
    1809-1887)*   **AV**
      Bibl: ▶Libr. of Congr. Name Auth.
      File

Fowler, O.K.   **WC WI**
    (American artist, op.1838)   WC
    (American artist, op.1838-)   WI

Fowler, Paul *(British artist, op.
    1977-)*   **WI**

Fowler, Robert   **WC WI**
    (British artist, 1853-1854-1926)   WI
    (British artist, 1853/4-1926)   WC

Fowler, Trevor Thomas   **WC WI**
    (British artist, c.1800)   WC
    *(British artist, circa 1800-op.
    1844)*   WI

Fowler, Walter *(British artist, op.
    1887-1902)*   **WC WI**

Fowler, William *(British artist, 1761-
    1826)*   **WI**

Fowler, William II   **WI**
    (British artist, op.1825-1867)   WC WI
    Fowler, William, II   **WC**

Fowler, William III   **WI**
    (British artist, 1796-c.1880)   WC
    (British artist, 1796-circa 1880)   WI
    Fowler, William, III   **WC**

Fowler, William, II → see Fowler,
    William II

Fowler, William, III → see Fowler,
    William III

Fowles, Arthur Wellington   **WC WI**
    (British artist, c.1815-1883)   WC
    (British artist, circa 1815-1883)   WI

Fowles, Joseph *(Australian artist,
    op.19th c.)*   **WI**

Fowlkes, Isabel *(American interior
    designer)*   **AV**
      Bibl: House beautiful, 1988 July,
      v.130, no.7, p.35

Fownes [Unidentified] *(Unknown
    painter)*   **PR**
      Bibl: (June 23, 1813, lot 82,
      Hermon)

Fox *(British, active London, England,
    U.K. 1860s (also Maull & Fox))*   **JG**

Fox family *(British silversmiths, 18th-
    20th cs.)*   **BA**
      Bibl: Mallalieu, COUNTRY LIFE,
      CLXXXII/50 (15 Dec 88), p.74-75

Fox, Alfred *(British landscape
    designer, 19th cent)*   **AV**
      Bibl: Ville giardini, 1989 Feb., no.
      234, p.56

Fox, Augustus Henry Lane → see Pitt-
    Rivers, Augustus Henry Lane-Fox

Fox, Barry M. *(American interior
    designer)*   **AV**
      Bibl: Southern accents, 1988
      Sept.-Oct., v.11, no.5, p.176

Fox, Bridell → see Bridell-Fox, Eliza
    Florence

Fox, Charles   **JG**

Fox, Charles E. *(American architect,
    1870-1926)*   **AV**
      Bibl: ▶Withey, Amer. archts.

Fox, Charles I   **WI**
    (British artist, 1749-1809)   WC WI
    Fox, Charles, I   **WC**

Fox, Charles II   **WI**
    (British artist, 1794-1849)   WC WI
    Fox, Charles, II   **WC**

Fox, Charles James   **WC WI**
    (British artist, c.1860-)   WC
    (British artist, op.1883-1904)   WI

Fox, Charles, I → see Fox, Charles I
Fox, Charles, II → see Fox, Charles II

Fox, Connie *(American painter, 20th
    c.)*   **BA**
      Bibl: Slivka, R., in ARTS MAG
      LIX/9 (MAy 1985) 22

Fox, Dan R. *(American architect,
    Minneapolis, Minn)*   **AV**
      Bibl: ▶AIA Pro File, 1987-88

Fox, Edward   **WC WI**
    (British artist, 1791-op.1854)   WI
    (British artist, op.1813-1854)   WC

Fox, Emanuel Phillips   **BA**
    (Australian artist, 1865-1915)   WC
    (Australian painter, 1865-1915)   BA
    (British artist, 1865-1915)   WI
      Bibl: ▶Johnson, Brit. artists
    Fox, Emmanuel Philips   **WC WI**

*Fox, Emanuel Phillips, Mrs.,
    (Ethel) → see* Carrick, Ethel

Fox, Emmanuel Philips → see Fox,
    Emanuel Phillips

Fox, Ernest R. *(British artist, circa
    1860-op.1919)*   **WI**
      Bibl: Morris & Morris(Birm.)

Fox, G.M.   **WC WI**
    (British artist, op.1852)   WC
    (British artist, op.1852-)   WI

Fox, George   **WC WI**
    (British artist, 1851-op.1889)   WI
    (British artist, op.1870-1900)   WC

Fox, George *(British Victorian
    interior designer)*   **AV**

Fox, George E. *(British architect,
    act.1866)*   **BA**
      Bibl: ▶Avery period. idx.;
      CONNOISSEUR CCVIII (Oct 1981)
      97-100; Johnson, NATL TRUST BK
      OF CASTLES (1978); ▶Wodehouse,
      Brit. archts.

Fox, Henry Charles *(British artist,
    1860-op.1922)*   **WI**

Fox, James Henry *(London-born
    19th century Australian architect)*   **AV**
      Bibl: House & garden, 1984 Feb.,
      v.157, no.2, p.100

Fox, Jim *(American architect,
    Highlands, N.C)*   **AV**
      Bibl: Fine homebuilding, 1988
      June-July, no.47, p.84

Fox, John *(British artist, op.1830-
    1846)*   **WC WI**

Fox, John Shirley *(British artist,
    circa 1860-op.1902)*   **WI**

Fox, Kathleen   **WC WI**
    (British artist, 1880-1963)   WI
    (British artist, 19th cent.)   WC

Fox, Milton S.   **BA WI**
    (American artist, 1904-1971)   WI
    *(American painter, printmaker,
    editor, 1904-1971)*   BA
      Bibl: ART STUDIES FOR AN
      EDITOR, 25 ESSAYS IN MEMORY
      OF MILTON S. FOX; ▶WW Amer.
      Art, 1970

Fox, R. → see Fox, Robert

Fox, Revel *(South African architect;
    worked in Zimbabwe for 3 years,
    in Stockholm in Anders Tengbom's
    office, opened practice in Cape
    Town in 1953, 1924-)*   **AV**
      Bibl: ▶Contemp. archts.

Fox, Robert   **WI**
    (British artist, 1810-op.1883)   WI
    (British artist, 19th cent.)   WC
    Fox, R.   **WC**

Fox, Sir William *(New Zealand
    artist, 1812-1893)*   **WC**

Fox, Terry Alan *(American artist,
    b.1943)*   **BA**
      Bibl: ▶Artweek idx.; ▶Intl. dir. exh.
      artists, 1983; ▶WW Amer. Art,
      1976

Fox, William *(American movie theater owner/builder, New York, N.Y, 1879-1952)* **AV**
Bibl: ▶Libr. of Congr. Name Auth. File; Marquee, v.19, no.4, p.1 (death date)

Fox, William Edward **WC WI**
(British artist, 1872-) WC
(British artist, b.1872) WI

Fox-Pitt, Douglas→see Pitt, Douglas Fox

Fox-Pitt-Rivers, Augustus Henry Lane→see Pitt-Rivers, Augustus Henry Lane-Fox

Foxcroft, Lesley **BA WI**
(British artist, b.1949) BA
(British artist, op.20th c.) WI
Bibl: Eindhoven (NLD), Stedelijk van Abbemuseum, Christa Dichgans, Lili Dujourie (1985)

Foxley, Anne *(American interior designer, New York City)* **AV**
Bibl: NYC phone bk., 1988-89

Foy, James *(American interior designer, Fort Worth, TX)* **AV**
Bibl: Interior design, 1984 June, v.55, no.6, p.189
Foy, Tonny AV

Foy, Katherine **WC WI**
(British artist, op.1879) WC
(British artist, op.1879-) WI

Foy, Tonny→see Foy, James

Foy, William **WC WI**
(British artist, 1791-1861) WI
(British artist, 1791-p.1861) WC

Foyatier, Denis *(French sculptor, 1793-1863)* **GC**
Bibl: ▶Thieme-Becker

FP Class **GC**
Bibl: Paralipomena

Fr. Apollodoro→see Apollodoro, Francesco (il Porcia)

Fr. Apollodoro, detto di Porcia→see Apollodoro, Francesco (il Porcia)

Fr. Bartolomeo→see Bartolomeo, Fra

Fr. Bolognese→see Grimaldi, Giovanni Francesco

Fr. Candido→see Candido, Francesco Saverio

Fr. de Solis→see Solis, Francisco de

Fr. Fracanzani→see Fracanzano, Francesco

Fr. Furini→see Furini, Francesco

Fr. Hale→see Hals, Frans

Fr. Mieris→see Mieris, Frans I van

Fr. Millé→see Millet, Jean François I (Francisque Millet)

Fr. Mola→see Mola, Pier Francesco

Fr. Mueda→see Mueda, Fr. [Unidentified]

Fr. Pourbus→see Pourbus, Frans, the younger

Fr. Vanni→see Vanni, Francesco

Fr: Bolognese→see Grimaldi, Giovanni Francesco

[Fr: Candido]→see Candido, Francesco Saverio

Fr: Guardi→see Guardi, Francesco

Fr: Mieris→see Mieris, Frans I van

Fr: Vecelli→see Vecellio, Francesco

Fra Angelico→see Angelico, Fra

Fra Antonio→see Lorenzini, Giovanni Antonio

Fra Bartolomeo→see Bartolomeo, Fra

Fra Bartolomeo da s. Marco→see Bartolomeo, Fra

Fra Bartolomeo da S. Marco Maestro di Raffaello→see Bartolomeo, Fra

Fra Bartolomeo Davellano→see Davellano, Bartolomeo, Fra [Unidentified]

Fra Bartolomeo de S. Marco Domenicano→see Bartolomeo, Fra

Fra Bartolomeo della Minerva→see Bartolomeo, Fra

Fra Bartolommeo→see Bartolomeo, Fra

Fra Bartolommeo della Porta→see Bartolomeo, Fra

Fra Bartolommeo di S. Marco→see Bartolomeo, Fra

fra bastiano del piombo→see Sebastiano del Piombo (Sebastiano Luciani)

Fra Bonfantino→see Bonfantinus Antiquior de Bonona, Frater

Fra Carnevale→see Carnevale, Fra (Bartolomeo di Giovanni Corradini)

Fra Damiano Zambelli→see Zambelli, Damiano

Fra Diamante→see Diamante di Feo

Fra Domenico de'Servitori→see Servitori, Domingo Maria, Fra

Fra Domingo Maria Servitori→see Servitori, Domingo Maria, Fra

Fra Evangelista da Reggio *(Italian scribe, act. ca.1477)* **GC**
Bibl: Salmi, Pitt. a Ferrara, p.43

Fra Filippo→see Lippi, Filippo

Fra Filippo del Carmine→see Lippi, Filippo

Fra Galgario→see Ghislandi, Vittore Giuseppe

Fra Giacomo Filippo da Milano *(Italian scribe, act.1490)* **GC**
Bibl: Fava, Tesori, p.368

Fra Giovanni Angelico da Fiesole→see Angelico, Fra

Fra Giovanni da Siena *(Italian scribe, act. ca.1464)* **GC**
Bibl: Alessi, Osservanza Siena, pp. 240-242

Fra Giovanni da Verona→see Giocondo, Fra (Giovanni da Verona)

Fra Giovanni di Guido Barbiere *(Italian scribe, act.1451-1454)* **GC**
Bibl: Chiarelli, Mus. San Marco, p.61
Barbiere, Giovanni di Guido GC
Giovanni di Guido Barbiere GC

Fra Iacopo del Tonghio→see Giacomo del Tonghio

Fra Innocenzo da Palermo→see Innocenzo da Palermo (Fra)

Fra Lorenzo da Castro→see Lorenzo da Castro, Fra

Fra Marino Angeli da Santa Vittoria→see Angeli, Marino

Fra Niccodemo da Livorno→see Niccodemo da Livorno, Fra [Unidentified]

Fra Paolino→see Paolino da Pistoia

Fra Sebastiano del Piombo→see Sebastiano del Piombo (Sebastiano Luciani)

Fra Semplice→see Semplice da Verona, Fra

Frà Semplice Cappuccino→see Semplice da Verona, Fra

Fra Semplice da Verona→see Semplice da Verona, Fra

Fra Servita→see Servitori, Domingo Maria, Fra

Fra Vicentius a Fundis **JG**

Fra Vittore Ghislandi→see Ghislandi, Vittore Giuseppe

fra' Bastian del Piombo→see Sebastiano del Piombo (Sebastiano Luciani)

fra' Bastiano del Piombo→see Sebastiano del Piombo (Sebastiano Luciani)

Fra. Bartolomeo→see Bartolomeo, Fra

Fra. Bartolomeo Baccio→see Bartolomeo, Fra

Fra. Bartolomeo da St. Marco→see Bartolomeo, Fra

Fra. Bartolomeo di San Marco→see Bartolomeo, Fra

Fra. Bartolommeo di San Marco→see Bartolomeo, Fra

Fra. Bartolomo→see Bartolomeo, Fra

Fra. Bartooneo→see Bartolomeo, Fra

Fra. Mieris→see Mieris, Frans I van

Fra. Mile→see Millet, Jean François I (Francisque Millet)

Fra: Bartolomeo Baccio→see Bartolomeo, Fra

Fracanzani or Fracanzano, Cesare→see Fracanzano, Cesare

Fracanzani, Cesare→see Fracanzano, Cesare

Fracanzani, Francesco (il Ciccio)→see Fracanzano, Francesco

Fracanzani, Michelangelo→see Fracanzano, Michelangelo

Fracanzano→see Fracanzano, Francesco

Fracanzano, Cesare   **PR**
   (Italian artist, c.1600-a.1653)   WC
   (Italian painter, ca.1605-1651,
     act. ca.1622)   PR
   (Italian, ca.1600-bef.1653)   GC
    Bibl: ▶Fredericksen & Zeri, Census;
    ▶Thieme-Becker; Whitfield, Ptg.
    Naples 1606-1705, with birth &
    death dates; ▶Witt checklist
   Cesare Cacansano   PR
   Cesare Fracanzani   PR
   Cesare Fracanzano   PR
   Cesare Fraganzano   PR
   Cesare Fragazzano   PR
   Cesare Fragozzano   PR
   Cesare Frecanzano   PR
   Cesare Freganzone   PR
   Cesaro Fracanzano   PR
Fracanzani or Fracanzano,
   Cesare   **WC**
Fracanzani, Cesare   **GC PR**
   Fraganzano   PR
   Fraganzano il vecchio   PR
   Fragazzano   PR
   Fragonzano   PR
Fracanzano, Francesco   **BA** GC **PR**
   (Italian artist, c.1612-1656(?))   WC
   (Italian painter, 1612-1656)   BA GC PR
    Bibl: ▶Bolaffi; ▶Fredericksen &
    Zeri, Census; ▶RILA/BHA, 1986;
    ▶Thieme-Becker; ▶Witt checklist
   Ciccio Fracanzano   PR
   Cicco Fraganzano   PR
   Fr. Fracanzani   PR
Fracanzani, Francesco (il Ciccio)   **GC**
   Fracanzano   PR
Fracanzano, Francesco (Il Ciccio)   **WC**
   Francanzano, Francesco   PR
   Francesco Fracanzano   PR
   Francesco Fraganzano   PR
Fracanzano, Francesco (Il
   Ciccio) → *see Fracanzano,*
   Francesco
Fracanzano, Michelangelo   **PR**
   (Italian artist, p.1644-c.1685)   WC
   (Italian painter, b. 1644)   PR
    Bibl: ▶Thieme-Becker
Fracanzani, Michelangelo   **WC**
   Michel Angelo Fraganzano   PR
   Michelangelo Fracanzano   PR
Fracassini or Fracassi, Cesari → *see*
   Fracassini, Cesari
Fracassini, Cesari   **GC**
   (Italian artist, 1838-1868)   WC
   (Italian, 1838-1868)   GC
    Bibl: ▶Witt checklist
Fracassini or Fracassi, Cesari   **WC**
Fraccaroli, Innocenzo *(Italian*
   sculptor, 1805-1882)   **GC**
    Bibl: TCI Lombardia
Fraciocome, Pietro → *see Fragiacomo,*
   Pietro
Frączek, Franciszek *(Polish painter,*
   act.1929-1936)   **BA**
    Bibl: Biuletyn Historii Sztuki, 3
    (1974) p.303ff.

Frączkiewicz, Anton *(Polish*
   sculptor, act.1726-1765)   **BA**
    Bibl: ▶Thieme-Becker
Fradan, Cyril *(British artist, op.*
   1966-)   **WI**
Fradelle, Henri Joseph *(French*
   artist, 1778-1865)   **WC**
Fradi[nand] Bol → *see Bol, Ferdinand*
Fraenckel, Liepmann *(German*
   artist, 1772-1857)   **WC**
Fraeuly, Charles *(French artist, op.*
   1936)   **WC**
Fragantoni, Ingrid *(American*
   designer, Newport Beach, Calif)   **AV**
    Bibl: Interior design, 1987 Aug.,
    v.58, no.10, p.198
Fraganzano → *see Fracanzano, Cesare*
Fraganzano il vecchio → *see*
   Fracanzano, Cesare
Fragazzano → *see Fracanzano, Cesare*
Fragelli, Marcello *(Brazilian*
   architect, 1928-)   **AV**
Fragiacomo → *see Fragiacomo, Pietro*
Fragiacomo, Pietro   **BA GC PR WC**
   (Italian artist, 1856-1922)   WC
   (Italian painter, 1856-1922)   BA GC PR
    Bibl: ARTE IN FRIULI, VIII, 1985,
    199-202, ▶Bolaffi; PTGSPROC; TCI
    Friuli-Venezia-Giulia;
    ▶Thieme-Becker; ▶Witt checklist
   Fraciocome, Pietro   GC
   Fragiacomo   PR
   Pietro Fragiacomo   PR
Fragner, Jaroslav *(Czech architect,*
   1898-1967)   **AV**
    Bibl: ▶Macmillan encyc. archts.
Fragonard → *see Fragonard, Jean*
   Honoré
Fragonard (Honorè) → *see Fragonard,*
   Jean Honoré
Fragonard family *(French artists,*
   18th-19th cs.)   **BA**
    Bibl: ▶Bénézit; ▶Thieme-Becker
Fragonard, Alexandre Evariste → *see*
   Fragonard, Alexandre-Evariste
Fragonard, Alexandre-Evariste   **BA**
   (French artist, 1780-1850)   WC
   (French painter, 1780-1850)   PR
   (French painter, sculptor,
    printmaker, 1780-1850)   BA
   (French, 1780-1850)   GC
    Bibl: ▶Bénézit; ▶Dict. biog. fran.;
    ▶Thieme-Becker; ▶Witt checklist
   Alexandre Evariste Fragonard   PR
Fragonard, Alexandre
   Evariste   **GC PR WC**
Fragonard, Etienne Theophile
   Evariste → *see Fragonard, Theophile*
   Evariste Hippolyte Etienne
Fragonard, Honoré → *see Fragonard,*
   Jean Honoré

Fragonard, Jean Honoré   **BA GC PR WC**
   (French artist, 1732-1806)   WC
   (French painter, 1732-1806)   BA GC PR
   (French, 1732-1806)   JG
    Bibl: ▶Bénézit; Getty Photo Study
    Coll. (Ptgs.); ▶RILA/BHA;
    ▶Thieme-Becker
   Fragonard   PR
   Fragonard (Honorè)   PR
   Fragonard, Honoré   GC
   Fragonard, Jean-Honore   **JG PR**
   Frangnoard   PR
   Frangonard   PR
   Frangouard   PR
   Frogonard   PR
   Jean Honore Fragonard   PR
Fragonard, Jean-Honore → *see*
   Fragonard, Jean Honoré
Fragonard, Mme. Marie-Anne
   (French, 1745-1823)   **GC**
    Bibl: Getty Photo Study Coll.
    (Ptgs.); ▶Thieme-Becker
   Gerard, Marie Anne   GC
Fragonard, Theophile Evariste
   Hippolyte Etienne   **GC**
   (French artist, 1806-1876)   WC
   (French painter, 1806-1876)   GC
    Bibl: ▶Bénézit
Fragonard, Etienne Theophile
   Evariste   **WC**
Fragonzano → *see Fracanzano, Cesare*
Fragoso, João Diniz *(Portuguese*
   sculptor, b.1913)   **BA**
    Bibl: ▶Bénézit; ▶Tannock, Port.
    20c. artists
Frai, Felicita *(Italian artist, 20th*
   cent.)   **WC**
Fraichot, Pierre Antoine *(French*
   artist, 1690-c.1763)   **WC**
Fraile *(French artist, 20th cent.)*   **WC**
Frailey, Stephen A. *(American*
   photographer, critic, b.1957)   **BA**
    Bibl: Pincus-Witten, Arts mag.,
    LVIII/3 (Nov. 1983) p.96; ▶WW
    Amer. Art, 1989
Frain, R.   **WC WI**
   (British artist, 19th cent.)   WC
   (British artist, op.1869-)   WI
Fraisinger, Caspar   **GC WC**
   (German artist, op.1581-1599)   WC
   (German, act.1581-1599)   GC
    Bibl: ▶Thieme-Becker; ▶Witt
    checklist
Fraisse, Jean Antoine *(French artist,*
   op.1733-1740)   **WC**
Fraker, Harrison *(American architect*
   and architectural school head)   **AV**
    Bibl: Architecture Minnesota,
    1984 Sept.-Oct., v.10, no.5, p.42
Fraker, William A. *(American, active*
   1930's)   **JG**
Framberti, Tommaso → *see Fiamberti,*
   Tommaso
Frampton, Christabel A., Lady → *see*
   Cockerell, Christabel A.

Frampton, Edward Reginald
(British artist, 1873-1923)   **WC WI**
Frampton, George James   **BA WI**
(British artist, 1860-1928)   WC WI
(British sculptor, 1860-1928)   BA
　　Bibl: ▶Bénézit; ▶Thieme-Becker;
　　▶Who was who [GBR], 1916-28
Frampton, Sir George James   **WC**
Frampton, George, Lady → see
　Cockerell, Christabel A.
Frampton, Hollis *(American*
　filmmaker, 1936-1984)   **BA**
　　Bibl: AFTERIMAGE XI/10 (May
　　1984) 2, obit; ▶WW Amer. Art
Frampton, Kenneth   **AV BA**
　(American architect, critic, 20th
　c.)   BA
　(British architect and
　architectural historian,
　Professor of Architecture,
　Columbia Univ, 1930-)   AV
　　Bibl: Transactions 3, v.2, n.1,
　　1982-83, p.[15]; ▶Wodehouse,
　　Amer. archts. WWI-pres.
Frampton, Meredith   **BA WC WI**
　(British artist, 1894-)   WC
　(British artist, b.1894)   WI
　(British painter, b.1894)   BA
　　Bibl: ▶Johnson, Brit. artists;
　　▶Vollmer, Künst.-Lex. 20. Jhr.;
　　▶Waters, Brit. artists; ▶Who's
　　Who [GBR], 1978
Frampton, Sir George James → see
　Frampton, George James
Fran Mille → see Millet, Jean François I
　(Francisque Millet)
Fran. Bartolomeo → see Bartolomeo,
　Fra
Fran. Bolognese → see Grimaldi,
　Giovanni Francesco
Fran. Flores → see Floris, Frans, the
　elder
Fran. Mieres → see Mieris, Frans I van
Fran. Mille → see Millet, Jean François
　I (Francisque Millet)
Fran. Mola → see Mola, Pier Francesco
Fran. Post → see Post, Frans Jansz.
Fran. Snyders → see Snyders, Frans
Fran.co Albano → see Albani,
　Francesco
Fran.co Bassano → see Bassano,
　Francesco II (Francesco II da Ponte)
Fran.co Bassi → see Bassi, Francesco
　Maria
Fran.co Bassi Veronese → see Bassi,
　Francesco Maria
Fran.co Ferro → see Ferro, Francesco
fran.co fiammengo → see Francesco
　Fiammingo (Monsù Francesco)
　[Unidentified]
Fran.co Giovane → see Francesco
　Giovane [Unidentified]
Fran.co la Questa → see Cuosta,
　Francesco della
Fran.co Mola → see Mola, Pier
　Francesco

Fran.co Pavesi → see Pavesi, Francesco
Fran.co Rosa → see Rosa, Francesco
　de (Pacecco de Rosa)
Fran.co Solimena → see Solimena,
　Francesco
fran.co Yznaire → see Snyders, Frans
Fran:co Mola → see Mola, Pier
　Francesco
Fran:co Passano → see Bassano,
　Francesco II (Francesco II da Ponte)
Franc → see Francken, Frans II
Franc Halls → see Hals, Frans
Franc Hals → see Hals, Frans
Franc Walls → see Hals, Frans
Franc, François *(French ébéniste,*
　1722-1799, master 1756)   **GC**
　　Bibl: ▶Salverte, Ébénistes 18e s.
Franc, Stanislav *(Czech architect,*
　1928-)   **AV**
　　Bibl: Architektura ČSR, 1988,
　　v.47, no.4, p.76
Franc. Halls → see Hals, Frans
Franc. Mille → see Millet, Jean
　François I (Francisque Millet)
Franc.co Albano → see Albani,
　Francesco
Franc.o Cario → see Curia, Francesco
Franc.o Fetti → see Fetti, Francesco
　[Unidentified]
Franc.o Manzini → see Manzini,
　Francesco
Franc.o Petrarca → see Petrarca,
　Francesco [Unidentified]
Franc.o Roppoli → see Ruoppolo,
　Francesco
Franc.o S. Fede → see Santafede,
　Fabrizio
Franc.o Salviati → see Salviati,
　Francesco (Francesco de' Rossi)
Franca → see Franca, Manuel Joachim
　de
Franca, de → see Franca, Manuel
　Joachim de
Franca, Manuel Joachim de   **PR WC WI**
　(American artist, 1808-1865)   WC WI
　(American painter, 1808-1865)   PR
　　Bibl: ▶Groce, Artists Amer.; ▶Witt
　　checklist; ▶Young, Amer. artists
　　Franca   PR
　　Franca, de   PR
　　Manuel Joachim de Franca   PR
Francais → see Français, Louis
Francais, François Louis → see
　Français, Louis
Français, Louis   **PR**
　(French artist, 1814-1897)   WC
　(French painter, 1814-1897)   GC PR
　　Bibl: ▶Bénézit; ▶Thieme-Becker
　　Francais   PR
Francais, François Louis   **GC PR WC**
　　Louis Francais   PR
Francaise Mole → see Mola, Pier
　Francesco
Francanzano, Francesco → see
　Fracanzano, Francesco

Francareccio, Francesco *(Italian,*
　18th c.)   **BA**
　　Bibl: Spinosa, Arte figurative a
　　Napoli
Francart or Francquart, Jacques, II
　(Flemish artist, 1582/3-1651)   **WC**
Francart, Franckaert, Francquaert or
　Francquart, Jacques, I → see
　Francart, Jacques (the Elder)
Francart, Francois   **JG**
　(French artist, c.1622-1672)   WC
　(French, 1622-1672)   JG
Francart, Francois, I   **WC**
Francart, Francois, I → see Francart,
　Francois
Francart, Jacques (the Elder)   **GC**
　(Flanders painter, 1550-1601)   GC
　(Netherlands artist, op.1571-m.
　1601)   WC
　　Bibl: ▶Thieme-Becker
Francart, Franckaert,
　Francquaert or Francquart,
　Jacques, I   **WC**
Francavilla, Pietro → see Francqueville,
　Pierre de
Francavilla, Pietro → see Franqueville,
　Pierre
France, Charles *(British artist, op.*
　1881-1892)   **WI**
France, John Mark *(British artist,*
　op.20th c.)   **WI**
Francelli, Luca *(Italian architect)*   **AV**
　　Bibl: Abitare, 1983 May, no.214,
　　p.12
Frances → see Francés, Nicolás
Frances Parmigianino → see
　Parmigianino (Francesco Mazzola)
Frances, Esteban *(Spanish artist,*
　20th cent.)   **WC**
Francés, Juan   **AV BA**
　(Spanish builder, mason)   AV
　(Spanish mason, act.1537, d.ca.
　1550)   BA
　　Bibl: Arch. esp. de arte, LIX/235
　　(Jul-Sep 1986) 96; Estella Marcos,
　　Arch. esp. de arte, LIX/233 (Jan-
　　Mar 1986) 96-106
Francés, Juana   **BA WC**
　(Spanish artist, 20th cent.)   WC
　(Spanish painter, b.1926)   BA
　　Bibl: ▶Bénézit; ▶Campoy, Español
　　contemp.
Francés, Nicolás   **BA PR WC**
　(Spanish artist, op.1480)   WC
　(Spanish painter, act. 1425-
　1468)   PR
　(Spanish painter, act.1425-1468)   BA
　(Spanish painter, ca.1400-1460)   GC
　　Bibl: ▶Ars Hispaniae, v.9; Blanch,
　　GOTISCHE KUNST IN SPANIEN;
　　Blue guide: Spain; ▶RILA/BHA;
　　▶Thieme-Becker
　　Frances   PR
　　Nicolas Frances   PR
Nicolas, Francés   **GC**

Francesc Comes→see Comes,
Francesc
Francesc'Antonio Pisacane→see
Pisacano, Francesco Antonio
Francesc'Antonio Pisacano→see
Pisacano, Francesco Antonio
Francesca Mola→see Mola, Pier
Francesco
Francesca Stradetti→see Stradetti,
Francesca [Unidentified]
Franceschi→see Franceschi,
Francesco de'

Franceschi, Domenico dei (Italian,
act. ca.1560-1565)   **GC**
   Bibl: ▶Thieme-Becker

Franceschi, Edgar (American
painter, sculptor, 20th c.)   **BA**
   Bibl: ▶Intl. dir. exh. artists, 1983

Franceschi, Emilio (Italian sculptor,
1839-1890)   **GC**
   Bibl: TCI Napoli e dintorni

Franceschi, Francesco de'   **WC WI**
   (Italian artist, op.1445-1456)   WC WI
   (Italian painter, act. 1445-1456)   PR
   (Italian, act.1445-1456)   GC
      Bibl: ▶Thieme-Becker; ▶Witt
      checklist
   Franceschi   PR

Franceschi, Francesco dei   **GC PR**
   Francesco de'Franceschi   PR
   Francesco dei Franceschi   PR
   Francesco dei Francheschi   PR
Franceschi, Francesco dei→see
Franceschi, Francesco de'

Franceschi, Jules (French sculptor,
1825-1893)   **GC**
   Bibl: ▶Thieme-Becker

Franceschi, Mariano de (Italian
artist, 1849-1896)   **WC**
Franceschiello→see Mura, Francesco
.de
Franceschiello Muro→see Mura,
Francesco de
Franceschini→see Franceschini,
Baldassare (Il Volterrano)
Franceschini→see Franceschini, Marc
Antonio
Franceschini di Bologna→see
Franceschini, Marc Antonio
Franceschini, Baldassare→see
Franceschini, Baldassare (Il
Volterrano)

**Franceschini, Baldassare (Il
Volterrano)**   **BA GC PR**
   (Italian artist, 1611-1689)   WC
   (Italian painter from Volterra,
      15th cent)   AV
   (Italian painter, 1611-1689) BA GC PR
   (Italian, 1611-1689)   JG
      Bibl: ▶Bolaffi; Critica d'arte, 1988
      Oct..-Dec., v.53, no.18, p.70;
      ▶Encyc. world art; ▶RILA/BHA
   Baldassar Franceschini detto il
      Volterrano   PR
   Baldassar Volterrano   PR
   Baldassare Franceschini   PR
   Baldassare Franchescini   PR
   Baldassare Franchescini, called
      Volterrano   PR
   Bardassar Franceschini detto il
      Volterrano   PR
   Franceschini   PR
   Franceschini, Baldassare   GC PR

**Franceschini, Baldassarre (Il
Volterrano)**   **WC**
   Franchechini   PR
   Francheschino   PR
   Franchescini   PR
   Franzesino   PR
   Il Volterrano   GC PR
Volterrano   **AV JG PR**
Franceschini, Baldassarre (Il
Volterrano)→see Franceschini,
Baldassare (Il Volterrano)

Franceschini, Carlo (Italian artist,
17th cent.)   **WC**

Franceschini, Marc Antonio **BA PR WC**
   (Italian architect, 1648-1729)   AV
   (Italian artist, 1648-1729)   WC
   (Italian painter, 1648-1729)   BA PR
   (Italian, 1648-1729)   GC
      Bibl: ▶Bolaffi; NOTE:
      "Franceschino da Bologna" can
      be Franceschino CARRACCI (rec.
      6461); TCI Abruzzo-Molise;
      ▶Thieme-Becker; ▶Witt checklist
   Franceschini   PR
   Franceschini di Bologna   PR
   Franceschini, Marcantonio   GC PR
**Franceschini, Marco
Antonio**   **AV GC PR**
   Franceschino di Bologna   PR
   Marc'Antonio Franceschini   PR
   Marco Antonio Franceschini   PR
Franceschini, Marcantonio→see
Franceschini, Marc Antonio
Franceschini, Marco Antonio→see
Franceschini, Marc Antonio

Franceschini, Mattia (Italian artist,
op.c.1745)   **WC**

Franceschinis, Giampietro (Italian
architect)   **AV**
   Bibl: GAS houses, 1988 Aug.,
      no.23, p.174
Franceschino di Bologna→see
Franceschini, Marc Antonio
Francescho Frorez→see Foro,
Francesco [Unidentified]

Francesco (Ciccio) della Torre→see
Torre, Francesco (Ciccio) della
Francesco Albani→see Albani,
Francesco
Francesco Albani Bolognese→see
Albani, Francesco
Francesco Albano→see Albani,
Francesco
Francesco Allegrini→see Allegrini,
Francesco
Francesco Andrea di Anguilla→see
Anguilla, Francesco Andrea di
Francesco Antonio Aldobello→see
Altobello, Francesco Antonio
Francesco Antonio Altobello→see
Altobello, Francesco Antonio
Francesco Antonio Pisacano→see
Pisacano, Francesco Antonio
Francesco Antonozzi→see Antonozzi,
Francesco
Francesco Apollodoro→see
Apollodoro, Francesco (il Porcia)
Francesco Apraiti→see Apratti,
Francesco
Francesco Apratti→see Apratti,
Francesco
Francesco Badens→see Badens,
Francesco
Francesco Barberi d.o il
Guercino→see Guercino (Giovanni
Francesco Barbieri)
Francesco Bartolozzi→see Bartolozzi,
Francesco
Francesco Basile→see Basile,
Francesco
Francesco Bassano→see Bassano,
Francesco II (Francesco II da Ponte)
Francesco Bassano (II)→see Bassano,
Francesco II (Francesco II da Ponte)
Francesco Battaglioli→see Battaglioli,
Francesco
Francesco Beccaruzzi→see
Beccaruzzi, Francesco
Francesco Benaglio→see Benaglio,
Francesco
Francesco Bissolo→see Bissolo,
Francesco
Francesco Bolognese→see Grimaldi,
Giovanni Francesco
Francesco Bolonese→see Grimaldi,
Giovanni Francesco
Francesco Bonsignori→see
Bonsignori, Francesco
Francesco Boschi→see Boschi,
Francesco
Francesco Botti→see Botti, Francesco
Francesco Botticini→see Botticini,
Francesco
Francesco Brini→see Brini, Francesco
Francesco Brizio→see Brizio,
Francesco
Francesco Capella→see Capella,
Francesco (Daggiù)
Francesco Caracci→see Carracci,
Francesco

Francesco dai Libri → *see* Libri,
Francesco dai, the elder

Francesco de Bais Imolese   **GC WC**
   (Italian artist, 16th cent.)   WC
   (Italian painter, 16th century)   GC
     Bibl: ▶Witt checklist

Francesco de la Questa → *see* Cuosta,
Francesco della

Francesco de Maria → *see* Maria,
Francesco di

Francesco de Marini [Unidentified]
   (Unknown painter)   **PR**
     Bibl: Ronca inventory, Naples,
     1686

Francesco de Minzocchi da Forlì → *see*
Menzocchi, Francesco (Vecchio di
San Bernardo)

Francesco de Mura → *see* Mura,
Francesco de

Francesco de Muro → *see* Mura,
Francesco de

Francesco de Nepe' → *see* Neve, Frans
de (Bloosaerken)

Francesco de Rosa → *see* Rosa,
Francesco de (Pacecco de Rosa)

Francesco de Veris *(Italian artist,*
op.1400-1420)   **WC**

Francesco de' Bianchi Ferrari → *see*
Bianchi Ferrari, Francesco de'

Francesco de' Bianchi-Ferrari → *see*
Bianchi Ferrari, Francesco de'

Francesco de' Rossi → *see* Salviati,
Francesco (Francesco de' Rossi)

Francesco de'Franceschi → *see*
Franceschi, Francesco de'

Francesco de'Rossi → *see* Salviati,
Francesco (Francesco de' Rossi)

Francesco dei Franceschi → *see*
Franceschi, Francesco de'

Francesco dei Francheschi → *see*
Franceschi, Francesco de'

Francesco del Borgo   **AV BA**
   (Italian architect)   AV
   (Italian architect, ca.1425-1468)   BA
     Bibl: ▶Art Index, lists death date
     as bef.1467; Frommel, Römisches
     Jahrb. XXI (1984) 131;
     ▶Macmillan encyc. archts., lists
     death date as 1468

   Borgo, Francesco del   **AV**
   Del Borgo, Francesco   AV

Francesco del Cairo → *see* Cairo,
Francesco del

Francesco del Cossa → *see* Cossa,
Francesco del

Francesco del Fiore → *see* Fiore,
Francesco del

Francesco Del Nome Spagnolo → *see*
Nomé, François Didier de

Francesco del Pò → *see* Pò, Francesco
Carlo Giovanni Battista del

Francesco del Po' → *see* Pò, Francesco
Carlo Giovanni Battista del

Francesco del Tadda → *see* Ferrucci,
Francesco di Giovanni (Francesco
del Tadda)

Francesco dela Cuesta → *see* Cuosta,
Francesco della

Francesco dell' Orioli *(Italian artist,*
15th cent.)   **WC**

Francesco dell'Orcagna *(Italian, act.*
Pistoia 1347)   **GC**
     Bibl: Getty Photo Study Coll.
     (Ptgs.); Zeri, Dipinti toscani ...
     Cini (1984)
   Orcagna, Francesco   GC

Francesco della Cuesta → *see* Cuosta,
Francesco della

Francesco della Cuosta → *see* Cuosta,
Francesco della

Francesco della Torre → *see* Torre,
Francesco (Ciccio) della

Francesco Desiderio (Francois Didier
Nome) → *see* Nomé, François Didier
de

Francesco di Antonio → *see* Francesco
di Antonio di Bartolomeo

Francesco di Antonio da
Viterbo → *see* Francesco d'Antonio
(Balletta)

Francesco di Antonio di
Bartolomeo   **BA GC PR**
   (Italian artist, 1394-op.1433)   WI
   (Italian artist, op.1409(?)-1429)   WC
   (Italian painter, act. 1393-1433)   PR
   (Italian painter, act.1393-
     1433)   BA GC
     Bibl: Berenson; ▶Bolaffi; Getty
     Photo Study Coll. (Ptgs.); MEISS
     FESTSCHRIFT (1977) 48-53;
     ▶RILA/BHA
   Banchi, Francesco d'Antonio   GC
   Francesco d'Antonio   PR

Francesco d'Antonio di
Bartolomeo (Banchi,
Francesco Fiorentino)   **WC**
   Francesco di Antonio   PR
   Francesco Fiorentino   GC

Francesco, di Antonio di
Bartolomeo   **WI**

Francesco di Bartolomeo Alfei → *see*
Alfei, Francesco di Bartolomeo

Francesco di Bosio Zaganelli → *see*
Zaganelli, Francesco di Bosio
(Francesco da Cotignola)

Francesco di Castello *(Italian*
illuminator, ca.1447-after 1502)   **BA**
     Bibl: Dykmans, Scriptorium
     XXXVII/2/1983, p.226

Francesco di Cecco → *see* Ghissi,
Francescuccio (Francesco di Cecco)

Francesco di Cristofano → *see*
Franciabigio (Francesco di
Cristofano)

Francesco di Cristofano
(Franciabigio) → *see* Franciabigio
(Francesco di Cristofano)

Francesco di Cristofano Bigi → *see*
Franciabigio (Francesco di
Cristofano)

Francesco di Duccio → *see* Francesco
di Guccio di Bindo

Francesco di Gentile → *see* Francesco
di Gentile da Fabriano

Francesco di Gentile da
Fabriano   **BA GC PR WC**
   (Italian artist, op.c.1460-1500)   WC
   (Italian painter, 15th c.)   BA
   (Italian painter, act. 2nd half
     15th cent.)   PR
   (Italian, act.ca.1460-1500)   GC
     Bibl: ▶Bolaffi; ▶Encyc. world art;
     ▶Fredericksen & Zeri, Census;
     ▶Thieme-Becker; ▶Witt checklist

Francesco di Gentile   **GC**
   Gentile da Fabriano, Francesco di   PR

Francesco di Giacomo Tacconi → *see*
Tacconi, Francesco di Giacomo

Francesco di Giorgio → *see* Francesco
di Giorgio Martini

Francesco di Giorgio
Martini   **BA CE FA GC PR WC**
   (23.IX.1439 - early 1502;
     Architect, Artist, Painter,
     Marche, Napoli, Siena,
     Toscana)   FA
   (Italian architect, sculptor,
     painter, theorist, 1439-1501)   BA
   (Italian artist, 1439-1502)   WC
   (Italian painter, 1439-1501)   PR
   (Italian painter, architect,
     sculptor, and illuminator,
     1439-1501)   GC
   (Italian sculptor and architect,
     1439-1502)   AV
   (Italian, Sienese, 1439-1502)   JG
   (Painter, sculptor, architect,
     draughtsman, writer, 1439-
     1501)   CE
     Bibl: ▶Fredericksen & Zeri, Census;
     Getty Photo Study Coll.
     (Medieval); ▶Libr. of Congr. Name
     Auth. File; ▶Macmillan encyc.
     archts., v.2, pp.108-111; NGA
     (Uffizi) objects; ▶Portoghesi, Diz.
     arch. e urbanistica; ▶RILA/BHA,
     Subject, 1988; ▶Thieme-Becker,
     v.12, p.303 ff.
   di Giorgio Martini, Francesco   AV FA
   di Giorgio, Francesco   FA
   Di Giorgio, Francesco Maurizio   AV

Francesco di Giorgio   **AV FA GC JG PR**
   Francesco Maurizio di Giorgio di
     Martino Pollaiuolo   CE
   Francesco Maurizo di Giorgio di
     Martini Pollaiuolo   FA
   Giorgio Martini, Francesco di   AV
   Giorgio, Francesco di   AV

Martini, Francesco di
Giorgio   **AV BA CE FA**

Francesco di Giovannetto *(Italian*
artist, 15th cent.)   **WC**

Francesco di Giovanni (Italian
artist, op.1491)   **WC**
Francesco di Giovanni (Italian
goldsmith, act.1465-1480)   **BA**
Bibl: Antichità viva XIX (May-Jun.
1980) pp.47-53; ▶Bunt,
Goldsmiths Italy; ▶Thieme-Becker
Francesco di Giovanni di Guccio
(Italian cabinetmaker, wood
inlayer, b.1393/97, d.1440-47)   **BA**
Bibl: Haines, Sacrestia di Firenze,
pp.52-55; ▶Thieme-Becker
Francesco di Guccio di Bindo
(Italian illuminator, 1414-1480/84)   **GC**
Bibl: ▶Levi d'Ancona, Miniatura a
Firenze, pp.120-121
Francesco di Duccio   GC
Francesco di Guido di Virio (Italian
sculptor and architect, d.ca.1532)   **GC**
Bibl: TCI Umbria
Francesco di Ladi [**Unidentified**]
(Unknown painter)   **PR**
Bibl: (March 15, 1805, lot 51,
Christie's)
Francesco di Lorenzo (Italian artist,
15th cent.)   **WC**
Francesco di Luca (Italian artist,
16th cent.)   **WC**
**Francesco di Marco (Checco di
Marchisse)** (Italian stonecarver,
ca.1382-after 1430)   **BA**
Bibl: Frosinini, RIVISTA D'ARTE
XXXIX (1987), 435-441
Checco di Marchisse   BA
Marchisse, Checco di   BA
Marco, Francesco di   BA
Francesco di Marco India
Torbido → see Torbido, Francesco
(il Moro)
Francesco di Maria → see Maria,
Francesco di
Francesco di Marra → see Marra,
Francesco la
Francesco di Matteo (Italian
sculptor, b.ca.1530)   **BA**
Bibl: NORTH CAROLINA MUSEUM
OF ART XII/4 (1976) 37
Francesco di Michele (Italian
painter, act.1385)   **BA**
Bibl: Bellosi, Paragone,
XXXVI/419-423 (Jan.-Mar. 1985)
pp.57-63; ▶Bolaffi;
▶Thieme-Becker; ▶Witt checklist
Francesco Fiorentino   BA
Francesco di Muro → see Mura,
Francesco de
Francesco di Neri (Sellaio) (Italian
sculptor, act.1354-1383)   **BA**
Bibl: Cavallucci, S. Maria del Fiore,
pp.134-135; Grote, DAS
SOMBAUAMT IN FLORENZ; Paatz,
Kirchen von Florenz;
▶Thieme-Becker
Sellaio, Francesco   BA
Francesco di niccolò → see Francesco
Niccolai

Francesco di Piedimonte
[**Unidentified**] (Italian painter)   **PR**
Bibl: Gagliano inventory, Naples,
1699
Francesco di Pietro d'Assisi (Italian
sculptor, act.1345-1362)   **BA**
Bibl: ▶Bénézit; ▶Diz. biog. ital.;
TCI Toscana; ▶Thieme-Becker
**Francesco di Pietro del Fusari da
Faenza** (Italian artist, op.1448-m.
1453)   **WC**
Francesco di Rinaldo (Italian
architect, act.1339-1344)   **GC**
Bibl: ▶Thieme-Becker
Francesco di Rosa → see Rosa,
Francesco de (Pacecco de Rosa)
**Francesco di Segna di
Bonaventura** (Italian artist, op.
1399)   **WC**
**Francesco di Ser Nardo da
Barberino**   **GC**
(Italian artist, 14th cent.)   WC
(Italian scribe, 14th century)   GC
Bibl: Brieger, Divine comedy, v.1,
pp.240-322; Scuricini Greco,
Miniature Riccardiane, p.176
Barberino, Francesco da   **WC**
Francesco di Ser Nardo da
Barberino in Val di Pesa   GC
Francesco di Ser Nardo da Barberino
in Val di Pesa → see Francesco di
Ser Nardo da Barberino
Francesco di Simone da Fiesole → see
Ferrucci, Francesco di Simone
Francesco di Stefano → see Pesellino,
Francesco (Francesco di Stefano)
Francesco di Tiziano → see Vecellio,
Francesco
Francesco di Ubertini → see Bachiacca
(Francesco Ubertini)
Francesco di Valdambrino   **BA GC**
(Italian sculptor and goldsmith,
act.1401/02-1435)   GC
(Italian sculptor, goldsmith, act.
1401-1435)   BA
Bibl: Bagnoli, A., SCULTURA
DIPINTA (1987), p.133; Del Bravo,
SCULTURA SENESE; Getty Photo
Study Coll. (Sculp.); Krautheimer
Festschrift; Pope-Hennessey;
▶RILA/BHA; ▶Thieme-Becker
Valdambrino, Francesco di   BA GC
Francesco di Vannuccio   **BA GC PR WC**
(Italian artist, op.1361-1388)   WC
(Italian painter, act. 1361-1388)   PR
(Italian painter, act.1361-1388) BA GC
Bibl: ▶Bolaffi; ▶Encyc. world art;
▶RILA/BHA; ▶Thieme-Becker
Vannuccio, Francesco   PR
Francesco di Zolofra → see Guarino,
Francesco
Francesco Feoli → see Feoli, Francesco
[Unidentified]
Francesco Fernandi → see Fernandi,
Francesco (Imperiali)

Francesco Fernandi (Imperiali) → see
Fernandi, Francesco (Imperiali)
Francesco Ferro → see Ferro,
Francesco
Francesco Fetti → see Fetti, Francesco
[Unidentified]
Francesco Fiammengo → see
Francesco Fiammingo (Monsù
Francesco) [Unidentified]
**Francesco Fiammingo (Monsù
Francesco)** [**Unidentified**]
(Unknown painter)   **PR**
Bibl: Colonna inventory, Rome,
1714, Duquesnoy somtimes called
"Francesco Fiammengo"--this
needs further checking
fran.co fiammengo   PR
Francesco Fiammengo   PR
Monsù franc.o   PR
Francesco Fidanza → see Fidanza,
Francesco
Francesco Fieravino → see Fieravino,
Francesco
Francesco Figoretto → see Figoretto,
Francesco [Unidentified]
Francesco Fiorentino (Italian
architect, sculptor in POL, act.
1502-1505)   **BA**
Bibl: ARTE LOMBARDA 44-45
(1976) 217-224; ▶Łozínski, Arch.
Poland, p.116
Francesco Fiorentino → see Francesco
di Antonio di Bartolomeo
Francesco Fiorentino → see Francesco
di Michele
Francesco Fontebasso → see
Fontebasso, Francesco
Francesco Foro → see Foro, Francesco
[Unidentified]
Francesco Foschi → see Foschi,
Francesco
Francesco Fracanzano → see
Fracanzano, Francesco
Francesco Fraganzano → see
Fracanzano, Francesco
Francesco Franchi fiammingo → see
Francken, Frans II
Francesco Francia → see Francia,
Francesco (Francesco Raibolini)
Francesco Furini → see Furini,
Francesco
Francesco Galli Bibiena → see Bibiena,
Francesco Galli
Francesco Gessi → see Gessi, Giovan
Francesco
Francesco Giovane [**Unidentified**]
(Unknown painter)   **PR**
Bibl: Colonna inventory, Rome,
1679
Fran.co Giovane   PR
Francesco Giuseppe Casanova → see
Casanova, Francesco Giuseppe
Francesco Granacci → see Granacci,
Francesco

Francesco Graziani→*see* Graziani, Francesco

Francesco Grigiotti→*see* Grigiotti, Francesco

Francesco Grimaldi→*see* Grimaldi, Francesco

Francesco Grimaldi called Il Bolognese→*see* Grimaldi, Giovanni Francesco

Francesco Grimaldi, called Il Bolognese→*see* Grimaldi, Giovanni Francesco

Francesco Guardi→*see* Guardi, Francesco

Francesco Guarini→*see* Guarino, Francesco

Francesco Half→*see* Hals, Frans

Francesco Ignazio Bavarese→*see* Oefele, Franz Ignaz

Francesco La Cuesta→*see* Cuosta, Francesco della

Francesco la Cuosta→*see* Cuosta, Francesco della

Francesco la Marra→*see* Marra, Francesco la

Francesco la Questa→*see* Cuosta, Francesco della

Francesco Laurana→*see* Laurana, Francesco

Francesco Leisdes→*see* Leisdes, Francesco [Unidentified]

Francesco Levo→*see* Levo, Francesco [Unidentified]

Francesco Londonio→*see* Londonio, Francesco

Francesco Lorenzi→*see* Lorenzi, Francesco

Francesco M.a→*see* Maria, Francesco di

Francesco Maffei→*see* Maffei, Francesco

Francesco Mancini→*see* Mancini, Francesco

Francesco Mancini di S. Angelo in Vado→*see* Mancini, Francesco

Francesco Manzini→*see* Manzini, Francesco

Francesco Manzino→*see* Manzini, Francesco

Francesco Marchissi→*see* Marchissi, Francesco [Unidentified]

Francesco Maria→*see* Maria, Francesco di

Francesco Maria Bassi→*see* Bassi, Francesco Maria

Francesco Maria Rondani→*see* Rondani, Francesco Maria

Francesco Massola→*see* Parmigianino (Francesco Mazzola)

Francesco Maurizio di Giorgio di Martino Pollaiuolo→*see* Francesco di Giorgio Martini

Francesco Maurizo di Giorgio di Martini Pollaiuolo→*see* Francesco di Giorgio Martini

Francesco Mazzola→*see* Parmigianino (Francesco Mazzola)

Francesco Mazzuoli detto il Parmigianino→*see* Parmigianino (Francesco Mazzola)

Francesco Mazzuoli, detto il Parmigianino→*see* Parmigianino (Francesco Mazzola)

Francesco Melzi→*see* Melzi, Francesco

Francesco Menzocchi→*see* Menzocchi, Francesco (Vecchio di San Bernardo)

Francesco Merano→*see* Merano, Francesco (Il Paggio)

Francesco Mile→*see* Millet, Jean François I (Francisque Millet)

Francesco Millé→*see* Millet, Jean François I (Francisque Millet)

Francesco Mille, Called, Francisque→*see* Millet, Jean François I (Francisque Millet)

Francesco Mingucci di Giovan Francesco→*see* Mengucci, Giovanni Francesco

Francesco Mola→*see* Mola, Pier Francesco

Francesco Mola di Lugano→*see* Mola, Pier Francesco

Francesco Montelatici→*see* Cecco Bravo (Francesco Montelatici)

Francesco Montelatici, detto Cecco Bravo→*see* Cecco Bravo (Francesco Montelatici)

Francesco Montemezzano→*see* Montemezzano, Francesco

Francesco Monti→*see* Monti, Francesco (Bolognese)

Francesco Monti (Brescianino delle Battaglie)→*see* Monti, Francesco (Brescianino delle Battaglie)

Francesco Montlatici→*see* Cecco Bravo (Francesco Montelatici)

Francesco Morandini→*see* Morandini, Francesco (il Poppi)

Francesco Morone→*see* Morone, Francesco

Francesco Muro→*see* Mura, Francesco de

Francesco Napoletano→*see* Galli, Francesco

Francesco Naselli→*see* Naselli, Francesco

Francesco Neri→*see* Francesco da Volterra

Francesco Niccolai *(Italian goldsmith, act.1361-1371)* **BA**
    Bibl: Gai, Altare argenteo di Pistoia; Rossi, Oreficeria ital., p.17; ▶Thieme-Becker

Francesco di niccolò **BA**

Francesco Nome→*see* Nomé, François Didier de

Francesco Orizonte→*see* Bloemen, Jan Frans van (Orizonte)

Francesco Padovanino *(Italian artist, 1561-1617)* **WC**

Francesco Padremio→*see* Padremio, Francesco [Unidentified]

Francesco Pamfilo→*see* Panfili, Francesco

Francesco Panfili→*see* Panfili, Francesco

Francesco Panfilo→*see* Panfili, Francesco

Francesco Paolo Michetti→*see* Michetti, Francesco Paolo

Francesco Paresi→*see* Parise, Francesco

Francesco Parise→*see* Parise, Francesco

Francesco Parisi→*see* Parise, Francesco

Francesco Parmesano→*see* Parmigianino (Francesco Mazzola)

Francesco Parmigianino→*see* Parmigianino (Francesco Mazzola)

Francesco Parmigiano→*see* Parmigianino (Francesco Mazzola)

Francesco Parone→*see* Parone, Francesco

Francesco Pascucci→*see* Pascucci, Francesco

Francesco Pavesi→*see* Pavesi, Francesco

Francesco Penni il Fattore→*see* Penni, Giovanni Francesco (il Fattore)

Francesco Peres → *see* Peres, Francesco [Unidentified]

Francesco Pereyas → *see* Pereyas, Francesco [Unidentified]

Francesco Peselli → *see* Pesellino, Francesco (Francesco di Stefano)

Francesco Petrarca → *see* Petrarca, Francesco [Unidentified]

Francesco Polazzo → *see* Polazzo, Francesco

Francesco Porbus il giovane → *see* Pourbus, Frans, the younger

Francesco Primaticcio → *see* Primaticcio, Francesco

Francesco Questa → *see* Cuosta, Francesco della

Francesco Raibolini → *see* Francia, Francesco (Francesco Raibolini)

Francesco Rivet → *see* Rivet, Francesco

Francesco Rizzi da Santacroce → *see* Francesco Rizzi da Santacroce (Francesco di Bernardo)

Francesco Rizzi da Santacroce (Francesco di Bernardo) **PR**
  (Italian artist, a.1490-p.1548) WC
  (Italian painter, act. 1508-1545) PR
  (Italian, act.1492-d.1508) GC
    Bibl: ▶Fredericksen & Zeri, Census; ▶Witt checklist; Zeri, Walters Ital. ptgs.
  Francesco Rizzi da Santacroce GC PR
  Francesco Rizzo da Santacroce PR
  Santa Croce, Francesco II GC

Santa Croce, Francesco, II, di Bernardo de' Vecchi or de' Galizzi (Francesco Rizzo da Santa Croce) **WC**

Santacroce, Francesco Rizzo da **GC**

Francesco Rizzo da Santacroce → *see* Francesco Rizzi da Santacroce (Francesco di Bernardo)

Francesco Romanelli → *see* Romanelli, Giovanni Francesco

Francesco Roppoli → *see* Ruoppolo, Francesco

Francesco Rubino → *see* Rubino, Francesco [Unidentified]

Francesco Ruoppolo → *see* Ruoppolo, Francesco

Francesco Ruschi → *see* Ruschi, Francesco

Francesco Rustici → *see* Rustici, Francesco

Francesco Salviati → *see* Salviati, Francesco (Francesco de' Rossi)

Francesco Santa Fede → *see* Santafede, Francesco

Francesco Santafede → *see* Santafede, Francesco

Francesco Saraceni → *see* Saraceni, Francesco

Francesco Saracino → *see* Saraceni, Francesco

Francesco Saverio Candido → *see* Candido, Francesco Saverio

Francesco Scardua → *see* Scardua, Francesco

Francesco Sebastiano del Piombo → *see* Sebastiano del Piombo (Sebastiano Luciani)

Francesco Siciliano → *see* Ciccio Siciliano [Unidentified]

Francesco Silvestro → *see* Silvestro, Francesco [Unidentified]

Francesco Simonini → *see* Simonini, Francesco

Francesco Soderini → *see* Soderini, Francesco

Francesco Solimani → *see* Solimena, Francesco

Francesco Solimena → *see* Solimena, Francesco

Francesco Solimene → *see* Solimena, Francesco

Francesco Solimeni → *see* Solimena, Francesco

Francesco Solimeno → *see* Solimena, Francesco

Francesco Squarcione → *see* Squarcione, Francesco

Francesco Tifernate → *see* Francesco da Città di Castello (Francesco Tifernate)

Francesco Traini → *see* Traini, Francesco

Francesco Trevisani → *see* Trevisani, Francesco

Francesco Trevisano → *see* Trevisani, Francesco

Francesco Trivisani → *see* Trevisani, Francesco

Francesco Ubertini → *see* Bachiacca (Francesco Ubertini)

Francesco [Unidentified] *(Unknown painter)* **PR**
    Bibl: Francone inventory, Naples, 1718

Francesco Utam → *see* Tamm, Franz Werner von

Francesco Vamblomen detto Orizonte → *see* Bloemen, Jan Frans van (Orizonte)

Francesco Van Bloemen → *see* Bloemen, Jan Frans van (Orizonte)

Francesco Vanni → *see* Vanni, Francesco

Francesco Vanni da Siena → *see* Vanni, Francesco

Francesco Vecellio → *see* Vecellio, Francesco

Francesco Veneiro → *see* Veniero, Francesco [Unidentified]

Francesco Veneto *(Italian artist, op. 1561)* **WC**

Francesco Veniero → *see* Veniero, Francesco [Unidentified]

Francesco Zaganelli (da Cotignola) → *see* Zaganelli, Francesco di Bosio (Francesco da Cotignola)

Francesco Zaganelli da Cotignola → *see* Zaganelli, Francesco di Bosio (Francesco da Cotignola)

Francesco Zoppolo → *see* Ruoppolo, Francesco

Francesco Zuccarelli → *see* Zuccarelli, Francesco

Francesco Zuccherelli → *see* Zuccarelli, Francesco

Francesco Zugno → *see* Zugno, Francesco

Francesco, de *(Italian artist, 19th cent.)* **WC**

Francesco, di Antonio di Bartolomeo → *see* Francesco di Antonio di Bartolomeo

Francesco, Domenico *(Italian painter, 16th c.)* **BA**
    Bibl: SOOBSIENIJA, HERMITAGE XL (1975) 8-10

Francesco, maestro → *see* Master Francesco

Francesco, Padre [Unidentified]
  (Unknown painter) **PR**
    Bibl: Poliastri inventory, Naples, 1741
  Padre Francesco PR

Francesco, S. [Unidentified]
  (Unknown painter) **PR**
    Bibl: Capecelatro inventory, Naples, 1661
  S. Francesco PR

Francesconi, Anselmo → *see* Anselmo

Francescuccio da Fabriano → *see* Ghissi, Francescuccio (Francesco di Cecco)

Francescuccio Ghissi → *see* Ghissi, Francescuccio (Francesco di Cecco)

Francese, Franco **BA WC**
  (Italian artist, 1920-) WC
  (Italian painter, b.1920) BA
    Bibl: ▶Bénézit; ▶Fogg Mus. Libr. cat.

Francesi, Alessandro *(Italian painter, act.1710)* **GC**
    Bibl: ▶Thieme-Becker

Francesque → *see* Millet, Jean François I (Francisque Millet)

Franch [Unidentified] *(Unknown painter)* **PR**
    Bibl: Riccardi inventory, Florence, n.d., In the same inventory there is a "Bonfranch"

Franchechini → *see* Franceschini, Baldassare (Il Volterrano)

Franchère, Joseph Charles *(Canadian painter, 1866-1921)* **BA**
    Bibl: ▶Artists Canada; ▶Natl. Gall. Canada libr. cat., suppl.

Francheschino → *see* Franceschini, Baldassare (Il Volterrano)

Franchescini → *see* Franceschini,
Baldassare (Il Volterrano)

Francheville, Pierre de → *see*
Francqueville, Pierre de

Franchi → *see* Franchi, Antonio
(Lucchese)

Franchi, Alesandro → *see* Franchi,
Alessandro

Franchi, Alessandro   **BA GC**
   (Italian artist, 1828-1914)   WC
   (Italian painter and copyist,
   1828-1914)   GC
   (Italian painter, 1838-1914)   BA
     Bibl: ▶Comanducci, Diz.;
     ▶Thieme-Becker; ▶Witt checklist

Franchi, Alesandro   **WC**

Franchi, Antonio → *see* Franchi,
Antonio (Lucchese)

Franchi, Antonio
   (Lucchese)   **BA GC PR WC**
   (Italian artist, 1634-1709)   WC
   (Italian painter, 1634-1709) BA GC PR
     Bibl: ▶Bénézit; ▶Bolaffi; ▶Encyc.
     world art; ▶RILA/BHA, 1986;
     ▶Thieme-Becker
   Antonio Franchi   PR
   Franchi   PR

Franchi, Antonio   **GC**
   Lucchese   BA PR

Franchi, Francesco *(Italian sculptor,*
   act.1712-1728)   **BA**
     Bibl: Paliaga, PARAGONE,
     XXXIX/465 (Nov. 1988), p. 48-58

Franchi, Giuseppe *(Italian sculptor,*
   1731-1806)   **BA**
     Bibl: ▶Bénézit; ▶Thieme-Becker

Franchi, Isidoro *(Italian sculptor,*
   d.1719)   **BA**
     Bibl: Viscone, Antichita viva,
     XXVII/2 (Apr.-Jun. 1988) pp.22-31

Franchi, Lorenzo *(Italian painter,*
   1565-1632)   **BA**
     Bibl: ▶Bénézit; ▶Bolaffi; Reggio
     Emilia (ITA), Palazzo del Capitano
     del Popolo, NOSTRA DI LORENZO
     FRANCHI; ▶Thieme-Becker
   Franco, Lorenzo   BA

Franchi, Luigi *(Italian engineer, 19th*
   cent)   **AV**
     Bibl: Abitare, 1988 June, no.265,
     p.214

Franchi, Roberto *(Italian, 20th c.)*   **BA**

Franchi, Rossello di
   Jacopo   **BA GC PR WC WI**
   (Italian artist, c.1377-1456)   WC
   (Italian artist, circa 1377-1456)   WI
   (Italian painter, 1377-1456)   PR
   (Italian painter, ca.1376-1456)   BA
   (Italian, ca.1377-1456)   GC
     Bibl: ▶Bénézit; Peters, ROSSELLO
     DI JACOPO FRANCHI; TCI Firenze;
     ▶Thieme-Becker
   Rossello di Jacopo Franchi   GC PR

Franchine, Alexander → *see* Francini,
Alexandre

Franchini di Messina → *see* Franchino,
Filippo [Unidentified]

Franchini family → *see* Lafranchini
family

Franchini, Giorgio *(Italian architect)*   **AV**
     Bibl: Lotus international, 1986,
     no.48-49, p.51

Franchini, Giuliano *(Italian*
   architect)   **AV**
     Bibl: Area, 1984 Nov.-Dec., v.4,
     no.19, p.38

Franchini, Niccolo *(Italian artist,*
   1704-1783)   **WC**

Franchini, Paul → *see* Lafranchini,
Paolo

Franchini, Philip → *see* Lafranchini,
Filippo

Franchini, Pietro Natale → *see*
Lafranchini, Pietro-Natale

Franchino di Messina → *see* Franchino,
Filippo [Unidentified]

Franchino, Filippo [Unidentified]
   (Italian painter)   **PR**
     Bibl: Pignatelli inventory, Naples,
     1723
   Felippo Tranghino   PR
   Filippo Franghino   PR
   Franchini di Messina   PR
   Franchino di Messina   PR

Franchisco Mola → *see* Mola, Pier
Francesco

Franchoijs, Peeter → *see* Franchoys,
Peeter

Franchois Francken → *see* Francken,
Frans II

Franchoys → *see* Franchoys, Peeter

Franchoys, Franchois or Franchoijs,
Peeter → *see* Franchoys, Peeter

Franchoys, Franchois, Franchoijs or
Francois Lucas, II → *see* Franchoys,
Lucas (the Younger)

Franchoys, Lucas (II) → *see* Franchoys,
Lucas (the Younger)

Franchoys, Lucas (the Younger) **GC PR**
   (Flemish artist, 1616-1681)   WC
   (Flemish painter, 1616-1681)   PR
   (Flemish, 1616-1681)   GC
     Bibl: ▶Thieme-Becker; ▶Witt
     checklist

Franchoys, Franchois, Franchoijs
   or Francois Lucas, II   **WC**
   Franchoys, Lucas (II)   PR
   Lucas Franchoys (the younger)   PR

Franchoys, Paul → *see* Paolo
Fiammingo

Franchoys, Peeter   **GC PR**
   (Flemish artist, 1606-1654)   WC
   (Flemish painter, 1606-1654)   PR
   (Flemish, 1606-1654)   GC
     Bibl: ▶Thieme-Becker; ▶Witt
     checklist
   Franchoijs, Peeter   PR
   Franchoys   PR

Franchoys, Franchois or
   Franchoijs, Peeter   **WC**
   Peeter, Franchoys   PR

Franci [Unidentified] *(Unknown*
   painter)   **PR**
     Bibl: Bargagli inventory, Siena,
     1740

Franci, Li [Unidentified] *(Unknown*
   painter)   **PR**
     Bibl: Carafa inventories, Naples,
     1648 and 1649: some confusion
     about how many artists are
     referred to by the article "delli";
     Labrot suggests either delli Franci
     or li Franci for the full name.
   Delli Franci   PR
   delli Franzi   PR
   li Franci   PR
   li Franzi   PR

Francia → *see* Francia, Francesco
(Francesco Raibolini)

Francia bolognese → *see* Francia,
Francesco (Francesco Raibolini)

Francia Gasparrini, Elda *(Italian,*
   20th c.)   **BA**
     Bibl: Broccoli, RIVISTA DI ARCH.
     CRIST. LV (1979) 183-199

Francia vecchio → *see* Francia,
Francesco (Francesco Raibolini)

Francia vecchio bolognese → *see*
Francia, Francesco (Francesco
Raibolini)

Francia, Alexandre *(French artist,*
   1815/2-c.1884)   **WC**

Francia, Aniello *(Italian architect,*
   18th century)   **GC**
     Bibl: TCI Abruzzo-Molise

Francia, Domenico   **BA WC**
   (Italian artist, 1702-1758)   WC
   (Italian painter, 1702-1758)   BA
     Bibl: ▶Bolaffi; ▶Thieme-Becker
   Domenico Francia   BA

Francia, Francesco → *see* Francia,
Francesco (Francesco Raibolini)

**Francia, Francesco (Francesco
    Raibolini)**   **BA GC PR**
(Italian artist, c.1450-1517)   WC
(Italian goldsmith, medalist, and
    painter, ca.1450-1517)   GC
(Italian goldsmith, medalist,
    painter, ca.1450-after 1526)   BA
(Italian painter, ca.1450-1517)   PR
    Bibl: ▶Bolaffi; Dempsey, STUDIES
    IN THE HIST. OF ART 17 (1986)
    65, col.1-2, 70, n.58; ▶Forrer,
    Medallists; ▶RILA/BHA;
    ▶Thieme-Becker, (var)
F. Francia   PR
Francesco Francia   PR
Francesco Raibolini   PR
Francia   PR
Francia bolognese   PR
Francia vecchio   PR
Francia vecchio bolognese   PR
Francia, Francesco   GC PR
**Francia, Francesco di Marco di
    Giacomo Raibolini, II**   **WC**
François Francia   PR
frangi   PR
Frangia   PR
Frangia Vecchio   PR
Franza   PR
Raibolini, Francesco   BA PR
Raibolini, Francesco di Marco   PR
Raibolini, Francesco di Marco di
    Giacomo   GC
*Francia, Francesco di Marco di
    Giacomo Raibolini, II→see Francia,
    Francesco (Francesco Raibolini)*
**Francia, François Louis
    Thomas**   **BA GC WC**
(French artist, 1772-1839)   WC
(French painter in GBR, 1772-
    1839)   BA
(French, 1772-1839)   GC
    Bibl: ▶Bellier, Artistes fran.;
    ▶Bénézit; ▶Dict. natl. biog.;
    ▶Fisher, Watercolour ptrs.;
    ▶Mallalieu, Brit. watercolour
    artists; ▶Redgrave, Engl. school;
    ▶Thieme-Becker; ▶Witt checklist
Francia, Louis   BA

Francia, Giacomo   **BA** CE **GC PR WC WI**
(Engraver, goldsmith,
    draughtsman, post 1450/ante
    1486-1557)   CE
(Italian artist, 1486-1557)   WI
(Italian artist, c.1486-1557)   WC
(Italian painter, bef.1486-1557)   PR
(Italian painter, ca.1486-1557)   GC
(Italian painter, goldsmith,
    printmaker, ca.1486-1557)   BA
    Bibl: ▶Bénézit; ▶Bessone-Aurelj,
    Scult. & arch. ital.; ▶Bolaffi;
    Boschetto, in Panazza, GIOVANNI
    GERALOMO SAVOLDO, p. 29-37;
    Faietti, Bologna e l'umanesimo,
    p.361; Getty Photo Study Coll.
    (Douwes coll.); Getty Photo Study
    Coll. (Ptgs.); Hind, Hist. engraving
    & etching; TCI Emilia-Romagna,
    artist idx.; ▶Thieme-Becker; ▶Witt
    checklist
Francia, Giacomo (Giacomo
    Raibolini)   GC
Francia, Jacopo   **CE**
Giacomo Francia   CE PR
Giacomo Franco   PR
Jacopo Francia   CE
Raibolini, Giacomo   GC
*Francia, Giacomo (Giacomo
    Raibolini)→see Francia, Giacomo*
Francia, Giulio   **GC PR WC**
(Italian artist, 1487-1540)   WC
(Italian painter, 1487-1540)   GC PR
    Bibl: ▶Thieme-Becker
Giulio Francia   PR
*Francia, Jacopo→see Francia,
    Giacomo*
*Francia, Louis→see Francia, François
    Louis Thomas*
*Francia, Peter de→see de Francia,
    Peter*
*Franciabigi→see Franciabigio
    (Francesco di Cristofano)*
*Franciabigio→see Franciabigio
    (Francesco di Cristofano)*
**Franciabigio (Francesco di
    Cristofano)**   **BA GC PR WC**
(Italian artist, 1482/3-1525)   WC
(Italian painter, 1482/3-1525)   GC
(Italian painter, 1482/83-1525)   BA PR
(Painter, post 1481/ante 1484-
    1525)   CE
    Bibl: ▶Bénézit; ▶Bolaffi; ▶Encyc.
    world art; ▶RILA/BHA;
    ▶Thieme-Becker
Bigi, Francesco   BA
Cristofano, Francesco di   BA
Cristofano, Francesco di
    (Franciabigio)   PR
Francesco di Cristofano   CE GC PR
Francesco di Cristofano
    (Franciabigio)   PR
Francesco di Cristofano Bigi   BA
Franciabigi   PR
Franciabigio   **CE** GC **PR**

Francillon, René *(Swiss painter,
    printmaker, 1876-1973)*   **BA**
    Bibl: ▶Künst.-Lex. Schweiz 20.
    Jahrh.; ▶Lex. zeitgen. Schweiz.
    Künstler
Francin, Guillaume *(French sculptor,
    1741-1830)*   **GC**
    Bibl: ▶Thieme-Becker
*Francine, Thomas→see Francini,
    Thomas*
*Francini family→see Lafranchini
    family*
Francini, Alexandre   **GC**
(Italian artist, op.1598-m.1648)   WC
(Italian, act.1598-d.1648)   GC
    Bibl: Getty Photo Study Coll.
    (Ptgs.); ▶Thieme-Becker; ▶Witt
    checklist
Franchine, Alexander   GC
**Francini, Franchine or Francyne,
    Alexander**   **WC**
*Francini, Franchine or Francyne,
    Alexander→see Francini,
    Alexander*
*Francini, Girolamo→see Franzini,
    Girolamo*
Francini, Thomas   **BA**
(Italian architect, worked at
    French court, 1571-1651)   AV
(Italian engineer, architect in
    FRA, 1571-1651)   BA
    Bibl: Bull. Soc. Hist. Art. Fran.,
    (1980) p.71, C; Mousset, LES
    FRANCINE, p.3; ▶Thieme-Becker,
    sv. Francini, Thomas, 1571-1651
Francine, Thomas   BA
Francini, Tommaso   **AV**
Francini, Tommaso de   BA
Tommaso de Francini   BA
*Francini, Tommaso→see Francini,
    Thomas*
*Francini, Tommaso de→see Francini,
    Thomas*
**Francione, Francesco di Giorgio di
    Matteo** *(Italian sculptor and
    architect, 1428-1495)*   **GC**
    Bibl: TCI Firenze
Francione, Pietro (Pietro Hispano)
(Spanish painter in ITA, act.1510-
    1512)   **BA**
    Bibl: ▶Bolaffi; ▶Thieme-Becker
Frangione, Pietro   BA
Pietro Hispano   BA
Francioni, Bernabeo *(Italian painter)*   **PR**
    Bibl: Bershad, Antologia di B-A
    25-26 (1985) p.65, n.3
Bernabeo Francioni   PR
*Franciosino→see Cordier, Nicolas (il
    Franciosino)*
*Francis Albano→see Albani,
    Francesco*
*Francis Alexander→see Alexander,
    Francis*
Francis Ball→see Bol, Ferdinand
Francis Barlow→see Barlow, Francis

Francisco Mazzuoli, called
Parmegiano→see Parmigianino
(Francesco Mazzola)
Francisco Meneses Osorio→see
Meneses Osorio, Francisco
Francisco Mile→see Millet, Jean
François I (Francisque Millet)
Francisco Mille→see Millet, Jean
François I (Francisque Millet)
Francisco Miralles→see Miralles,
Francisco
Francisco Mola→see Mola, Pier
Francesco
Francisco Molu→see Mola, Pier
Francesco
Francisco Pacheco→see Pacheco,
Francisco
Francisco Parmegiano→see
Parmigianino (Francesco Mazzola)
Francisco Ribalta→see Ribalta,
Francisco
Francisco Rizi→see Rizi, Francisco
Francisco Simonini→see Simonini,
Francesco
Francisco Vanni→see Vanni,
Francesco
Francisco Vicelli→see Vecellio,
Francesco

Francisco, John Bond (American
artist, 1863-1931)   **WI**
Francisco, Richard (American
painter, b.1942)   **BA**
    Bibl: ARTFORUM (Oct 1974) 76;
    ARTS MAG. LIV/1 (Sept 1979) 9
Franciscus (Hungarian painter in
POL, act.ca.1450)   **BA**
    Bibl: BIULETYN HISTORII SZTUKI
    XXXVII/2 (1975) 114-134
Franciscus Carree→see Carree,
Franciscus
Franciscus Francks, the elder→see
Francken, Frans I
Franciscus Francks, the Younger→see
Francken, Frans II
Franciscus Leonardus Johannes→see
Moormans, Frans
Franciscus Weert→see Weert,
Franciscus
Francisque→see Millet, Jean François
I (Francisque Millet)
Francisque Mille→see Millet, Jean
François I (Francisque Millet)
Francisque Millet→see Millet, Jean
François I (Francisque Millet)
Francisquito or Francesquitto
(Spanish artist, 18th cent.)   **WC**
Franciszek Streitt→see Streitt,
Franciszek
Franck→see Franck, Franz Friedrich
Franck Flore→see Floris, Frans, the
elder
Franck Halls→see Hals, Frans
Franck Hals→see Hals, Frans
Franck Pietersz. Verheyden→see
Verheyden, Franck Pietersz.

Franck von Bubendorf→see Franck,
Hans
Franck von Bubendorf, Hans→see
Franck, Hans
Franck, Albert (Canadian artist,
20th cent.)   **WC**
Franck, Christoffel Frederik   **GC WC**
    (Dutch artist, 1758-1818)   WC
    (Dutch painter, 1758-1816)   GC
    Bibl: ▶Bénézit
Franck, Fance (American ceramist,
b.1931)   **BA**
    Bibl: Keramos, 114 (Oct 1986) 45
Franck, Florence Gertrude Vale
(Canadian painter, b.1909)   **BA**
    Bibl: ▶Artists Canada; ▶Idx.
    Ontario artists
    Vale, Florence Gertrude   BA
Franck, Frans (the Elder)→see
Francken, Frans I
Franck, Frans I→see Francken, Frans I
Franck, Frans III→see Francken, Frans
III
Franck, Franz→see Franck, Franz
Friedrich
Franck, Franz Friedrich   **GC PR**
    (German artist, 1627-1687)   WC
    (German painter, 1627-1687)   PR
    (German, 1627-1687)   GC
    Bibl: Getty Photo Study Coll.
    (Ptgs.); ▶Thieme-Becker; ▶Witt
    checklist
    F.F. Franck   PR
    Federico Franch   PR
    Franck   PR
Franck, Franz   **GC WC**
    Franz Friedrich Franck   PR
Franck, Gabriel   **GC**
    (Flemish artist, op.1605-m.1639)   WC
    (Flemish painter, act.1605-d.
    1639)   GC
    Bibl: ▶Thieme-Becker
**Francken, Franck, Franckx,
Franken or Vranken, Gabriel**   **WC**
    Francken, Gabriel   GC
Franck, Georg Christian (German
gem carver, 1736-1780)   **BA**
    Bibl: Netzer, Niederdeutsche
    Beiträge, XXII (1983) p.142
**Franck, Gobinet de Villecholle,
Francois-Marie-Louis-Alexandre**
(French, 1816-1906)   **JG**
Franck, Hans   **BA GC WC**
    (German artist, op.1485-m.a.
    1522)   WC
    (Swiss artist, op.1505-m.a.1522)   WC
    (Swiss draughtsman, act.1505-
    1522)   GC
    (Swiss painter, act.1505-1522)   BA
    Bibl: ▶RILA/BHA; ▶Schweiz.
    Künst.-Lex.; SOURCE II/2 (winter
    1983) 16; ▶Thieme-Becker; ▶Witt
    checklist
    Franck von Bubendorf   BA
Franck von Bubendorf, Hans   **WC**
    Frank, Hans   BA

Franck, Hans→see Lützelburger, Hans
Franck, Hans Ulrich   **BA GC**
    (German artist, 1603-1680)   WC
    (German draughtsman, 1603-
    1680)   GC
    (German painter, printmaker,
    1603-1680)   BA
    Bibl: ▶Bénézit; ▶Bryan, Ptrs. &
    engravers; Getty Photo Study
    Coll.; ▶Hollstein, German;
    ▶Thieme-Becker; ▶Witt checklist
**Franck, Hans Ulrich
(Monogrammist H.V.F.
1647?)**   **WC**
Frank, Hans Ulrich   **GC**
    Monogrammist H V F 1647?   GC
Franck, Hans Ulrich (Monogrammist
H.V.F. 1647?)→see Franck, Hans
Ulrich
Franck, Heinz (Austrian architect) **AV**
Franck, Hieronymus I→see Francken,
Hieronymus I
Franck, Hieronymus II→see Francken,
Hieronymus II
Franck, Jan (Flemish artist,
16th/17th cent.)   **WC**
Franck, Johan Willem (Dutch
painter, ca.1720-1761)   **GC PR**
    Bibl: ▶Thieme-Becker
    J.W. Frank   PR
    Johan Willem Franck   PR
Franck, Johann Leonhard (German
gem carver, 1708-1782)   **BA**
    Bibl: Netzer, Niederdeutsche
    Beiträge, XXII (1983) p.142
Franck, Johannes (German
printmaker, d.ca.1687)   **BA**
    Bibl: ▶Bénézit; ▶Hollstein, German,
    v.8, p.180; Lettere e altri
    documenti
Franck, Kaj (Finnish craftsman,
b.1911)   **BA**
    Bibl: Sunderland (GBR), Arts Ctr.,
    Suomen Lasi--Finnish glass (1979)
Franck, Maximilian (German artist,
c.1780-1830)   **WC**
Franck, Michel (French designer)   **AV**
    Bibl: Interiors, 1986 Nov., v.146,
    no.4, p.138
Franck, Pauwels→see Paolo
Fiammingo
Franck, Pauwels (Paul Franchoys or
Paolo Fiammingo or dei
Franceschi)→see Paolo Fiammingo
Franck, Philipp   **BA WC**
    (German artist, 1860-1944)   WC
    (German painter, printmaker,
    1860-1944)   BA
    Bibl: ▶Bénézit; ▶Thieme-Becker;
    ▶Vollmer, Künst.-Lex. 20. Jhr.
Franck, Philipp (German artist,
c.1780-1837)   **WC**
Franck, Simon→see Aschaffenburg,
Simon von

Francke, Bernhard   **GC**
   (German artist, op.1693-m.
    1729)   WC
   (German painter, d.1729)   GC
    Bibl: ▶Thieme-Becker
Francke, Christoph Bernard   **WC**
   Francke, Christoph Bernhard   GC
Francke, Christoph Bernard → see
   Francke, Bernhard
Francke, Christoph Bernhard → see
   Francke, Bernhard
Francke, Master → see Master Francke
Francke, Paul *(German architect,*
   1538-1615)   **AV**
    Bibl: ▶Macmillan encyc. archts.
Francken → see Francken, Frans II
Francken → see Francken, Hieronymus
   I
Francken or Franck, Ambrosius,
   I → see Francken, Ambrosius I
Francken or Franck, Ambrosius, II
   (Flemish artist, op.1616-m.1632)   **WC**
Francken or Franck, Frans, I → see
   Francken, Frans I
Francken or Franck, Frans, II → see
   Francken, Frans II
Francken or Franck, Frans, III → see
   Francken, Frans III
Francken or Franck, Hieronymus,
   I → see Francken, Hieronymus I
Francken or Franck, Hieronymus,
   II → see Francken, Hieronymus II
Francken or Franck, Maximilaen
   (Flemish artist, -1651)   **WC**
Francken or Franck, Thomas
   (Flemish artist, op.1601-1626)   **WC**
Francken, Ambrosius (the Elder) → see
   Francken, Ambrosius I
Francken, Ambrosius I   **BA** GC
   (early Netherlandish painter,
    1544-1618)   BA
   (Flanders painter, 1544-1618)   GC
   (Flemish artist, 1544-1618)   WC
    Bibl: Getty Photo Study Coll.;
     Harting, Studien z.
     Kabinettbildmalerei des Frans
     Franckens, II (1983), p.9;
     ▶RILA/BHA; ▶Thieme-Becker
Francken or Franck, Ambrosius,
   I   **WC**
Francken, Ambrosius (the Elder)   **GC**
Francken, Constantinus *(Flemish*
   painter, 1661-1717)   **GC**
    Bibl: ▶Bénézit
Francken, Franck, Franckx, Franken or
   Vranken, Gabriel → see Franck,
   Gabriel
Francken, Frans → see Francken, Frans
   II
Francken, Frans (I) → see Francken,
   Frans I
Francken, Frans (II) → see Francken,
   Frans II
Francken, Frans (III) → see Francken,
   Frans III

Francken, Frans (the elder) → see
   Francken, Frans I
Francken, Frans (the younger) → see
   Francken, Frans II
Francken, Frans I   **BA**
   (early Netherlandish painter,
    1542-1616)   BA
   (Flanders painter and
    draughtsman, 1542-1616)   GC
   (Flemish artist, 1542-1616)   WC
   (Flemish painter, 1542-1616)   PR
    Bibl: Getty Photo Study Coll.;
     Harting, Studien z.
     Kabinettbildmalerei des Frans
     Franckens, II (1983), p.9;
     ▶Thieme-Becker; ▶Witt checklist;
     ▶Wurzbach, NLD Künst.-Lex.
   Franciscus Francks, the elder   PR
   Franck, Frans (the Elder)   GC
   Franck, Frans I   BA
Francken or Franck, Frans, I   **WC**
Francken, Frans (I)   **PR**
Francken, Frans (the elder)   **GC** PR
   Frans Francken (I)   PR
Francken, Frans II   **BA GC WI**
   (Flemish artist, 1581-1642)   WC WI
   (Flemish painter, 1581-1642)   BA PR
   (Flemish, 1581-1642)   GC JG
    Bibl: ▶Encyc. world art; Harting,
     Studien z. Kabinettbildmalerei des
     Frans Franckens, II (1983), p.9;
     ▶RILA/BHA; ▶Thieme-Becker
   de jonge Franck   PR
   Franc   PR
   Francesco Franchi fiammingo   PR
   Franchois Francken   PR
   Francis Franck Jun. called Young
    Francks   PR
   Franciscus Francks, the Younger   PR
   Francken   PR
Francken or Franck, Frans, II   **WC**
Francken, Frans   **JG**
Francken, Frans (II)   **PR**
   Francken, Frans (the younger)   PR
   Francken, Frans, II   PR
   Franken, Frans II   PR
   Frans Francken (II)   PR
   marked Young Francks   PR
   petit Franc   PR
   Young Franks   PR

Francken, Frans III   **BA GC**
   (Flemish artist, 1607-1667)   WC
   (Flemish painter, 1607-1667)   BA PR
   (Flemish, 1607-1667)   GC
    Bibl: ▶Bénézit; Gerson, Art & arch.
     Belgium, p.181, n.32; Harting,
     Studien z. Kabinettbildmalerei des
     Frans Franckens, II (1983), p.9;
     ▶RILA/BHA; ▶Thieme-Becker;
     ▶Witt checklist; ▶Wurzbach, NLD
     Künst.-Lex.
   Franck, Frans III   BA
Francken or Franck, Frans, III   **WC**
Francken, Frans (III)   **PR**
   Francken, Frans, III   PR
   Frank   PR
   Frans Francken (III)   PR
Francken, Frans, II → see Francken,
   Frans II
Francken, Frans, III → see Francken,
   Frans III
Francken, Gabriel → see Franck,
   Gabriel
Francken, Hans *(Flemish, 1581-*
   1624)   **GC**
    Bibl: ▶Bénézit
Francken, Hieronymus (I) → see
   Francken, Hieronymus I
Francken, Hieronymus (the
   Elder) → see Francken, Hieronymus
   I
Francken, Hieronymus I   **BA**
   (early Netherlandish painter,
    1540-1610)   BA
   (Flanders painter, 1540-1610)   GC
   (Flemish painter, 1540-1610)   PR
   (Netherlands artist, 1540-1610)   WC
    Bibl: ▶Bénézit; ▶Encyc. world art;
     Harting, Studien z.
     Kabinettbildmalerei des Frans
     Franckens, II (1983), p.9;
     ▶RILA/BHA; ▶Thieme-Becker
   Franck, Hieronymus I   BA
   Francken   PR
Francken or Franck,
   Hieronymus, I   **WC**
Francken, Hieronymus (I)   **PR**
Francken, Hieronymus (the
   Elder)   **GC**
   Francken, Jerome (I)   PR
   Frank   PR
   H. Franck   PR
   Hieronymus Francken (I)   PR
Francken, Hieronymus II   **BA GC**
   (Flemish artist, 1578-1623)   WC
   (Flemish painter, 1578-1623)   BA
   (Flemish, 1578-1623)   GC
    Bibl: Harting, Studien z.
     Kabinettbildmalerei des Frans
     Franckens, II (1983), p.9;
     ▶Thieme-Becker; ▶Wurzbach, NLD
     Künst.-Lex.
   Franck, Hieronymus II   BA
Francken or Franck,
   Hieronymus, II   **WC**

Francken, Hieronymus III *(Flemish painter, b.1611)* GC
  Bibl: ▶Thieme-Becker
Francken, Jan Baptist *(Flemish painter, 1599-1653)* PR
  Jan Baptist Francken PR
  John Baptiste Franck PR
Francken, Jerome (I) → see Francken, Hieronymus I
Francken, P.H. *(Flemish artist, op. 1655)* WC
Francken, Ruth *(Czech artist, 20th cent.)* WC
Franckenberger the Elder, Hans → see Franckenberger, Hans (the Elder)
Franckenberger the Younger, Tobias *(German artist, c.1600-m.p. 1660)* WC
Franckenberger, Hans (the Elder) GC
  (German artist, op.c.1530) WC
  (German painter, act.1530) GC
  Bibl: ▶Thieme-Becker
Franckenberger the Elder, Hans WC
Francks, C. *(Netherlands artist, op. 1610)* WC
Franco → see Franco, Battista
Franco Bolognese BA
  (Italian artist, op.1312-1313) WC
  (Italian illuminator, 14th c.) BA
  Bibl: ▶Bolaffi; ▶Bradley, Miniaturists; ▶Thieme-Becker
  Bologna, Franco da BA
Franco Bolognese (possibly Franco di Bonavita) WC
Franco Bolognese (possibly Franco di Bonavita) → see Franco Bolognese
Franco de Liege → see Defrance, Léonard
Franco de Russi → see Russi, Francesco di Giovanni de' (Franco Ferrarese)
Franco Ferrarese → see Russi, Francesco di Giovanni de' (Franco Ferrarese)
Franco L, Eduardo *(Colombian architect)* AV
  Bibl: ▶Proa, 1986 July, no.352, p.28
Franco Salamanca, Germàn *(Colombian architect, historic preservationist, prof. of architecture)* AV
  Bibl: ▶Escala, 1988, v.20, no.139, p.4
Franco Ysneire → see Snyders, Frans
Franco, Alfonso (Argentero) *(Italian artist, 1466-1523)* WC

Franco, Battista BA CE GC PR
  (Italian artist, 1498-1561) WC
  (Italian painter, 1498-1561) PR
  (Italian painter, printmaker, 1498?-1561) BA
  (Italian, 1498-1561) GC
  (Painter, draughtsman, engraver, 1498-1561) CE
  Bibl: ▶Bolaffi; ▶Encyc. world art; ▶RILA/BHA; ▶Thieme-Becker; ▶Witt checklist
  Bap. Franco PR
  Bapt. Franco PR
  Baptiste Franc PR
  Battista di Franchi BA GC
  Battista Franco PR
  Battista Franco Veneziano PR
  Battta Franco PR
  Franco PR
  Franco, Giovanni Battista BA
  Franco, Giovanni Battista (Il Semolei) GC
Franco, Giovanni Battista (Il Semolei) (Battista di Franchi) WC
  Il Semolei CE
  Semolei BA
Franco, Cesare *(Italian architect, sculptor, act.1575-1599)* BA
  Bibl: ▶Bessone-Aurelj, Scult. & arch. ital.; ▶Thieme-Becker
Franco, Francisco *(Portuguese sculptor, 1885-1955)* BA
  Bibl: ▶Pamplona, Pint. escult. PRT; ▶Tannock, Port. 20c. artists; ▶Vollmer, Künst.-Lex. 20. Jhr.
  Sousa, Francisco Franco de BA
Franco, Francisco *(Spanish sculptor, d. 1694)* AV
  Bibl: ▶Thieme-Becker
Franco, Giacomo *(Italian painter, 1818-1895)* GC
  Bibl: ▶Thieme-Becker
Franco, Giacomo BA GC WC
  (Italian artist, 1550-1620) WC
  (Italian printmaker, 1550-1620) GC
  (Italian printmaker, publisher, 1550-1620) BA
  Bibl: ▶Bolaffi; ▶RILA/BHA, 1986; ▶Thieme-Becker
Franco, Giovanni Battista → see Franco, Battista
Franco, Giovanni Battista (Il Semolei) → see Franco, Battista
Franco, Giovanni Battista (Il Semolei) (Battista di Franchi) → see Franco, Battista
Franco, Giuseppe *(Italian artist, c.1550-1628)* WC
Franco, Lorenzo → see Franchi, Lorenzo
Franco, Salvatore *(Italian sculptor, act.1720-1793)* BA
  Bibl: ▶Bénézit; ▶Bessone-Aurelj, Scult. & arch. ital.; ▶Thieme-Becker

Francoi, Hans Antoni *(Netherlands artist, op.1591)* WC
Françoijs Eyckens → see Ijkens, Frans
François → see François, Alexandre
François Albane → see Albani, Francesco
François Alfred Delobbe → see Delobbe, François Alfred
François Andre Vincent → see Vincent, François André
François Auguste Biard → see Biard, François-Auguste
François Bassan → see Bassano, Francesco II (Francesco II da Ponte)
François Batens → see Badens, Francesco
François Boucher → see Boucher, François
François Cachoud → see Cachoud, François
François Clouet → see Clouet, François
François de Nome → see Nomé, François Didier de
François de Troy → see Troy, Francois de
François Decker → see Decker, Frans
François du Moulin → see Du Moulin, François
François Eduard Picot → see Picot, François Eduard
François Eisen → see Eisen, François
François Emile Barraud → see Barraud, François Emile
François Flameng → see Flameng, François
François Francia → see Francia, Francesco (Francesco Raibolini)
François Girardon → see Girardon, François
François Guardi → see Guardi, Francesco
François Guillaume Menageot → see Ménageot, François Guillaume
François Henri Mulard → see Mulard, François Henri
François Herrera (le jeune) → see Herrera, Francisco II
François Hubert Drouais → see Drouais, François Hubert
François Jacques Boileau → see Boileau, François Jacques
François Joseph Dupressoir → see Dupressoir, François Joseph
François Joseph Navez → see Navez, François Joseph
François Knibbergen → see Knibbergen, Francois
François Knipbergen → see Knibbergen, Francois
François Lamoriniere → see Lamorinière, François
François Le Moyne → see Le Moyne, François
François Marius Granet → see Granet, François Marius

François Mazzuoli→see Parmigianino (Francesco Mazzola)

François Mieris→see Mieris, Frans I van

François Miris→see Mieris, Frans I van

François Monnaville→see Monnaville, François

François or Franceschi, Marie Catherine, (nee Fredou) *(French artist, c.1712-1773)* **WC**

François or Francoys, Simon→see François, Simon

Francois Perrier→see Perrier, François (le Bourguignon)

Francois Pourbus→see Pourbus, Frans, the younger

Francois Quesnel (I)→see Quesnel, François (I)

Francois Snijders→see Snyders, Frans

Francois Snyders→see Snyders, Frans

Francois Spierre→see Spierre, François

François Verdier→see Verdier, François

Francois Vernay→see Vernay, François

Francois Vivares→see Vivarès, François

Francois Xavier Fabre→see Fabre, François Xavier Pascal

Francois Xavier Pascal Fabre→see Fabre, François Xavier Pascal

Francois, Alexander→see François, Alexandre

François, Alexandre *(Flemish painter, 1824-1912)* **PR**
Bibl: ▶Thieme-Becker
Alexandre Francois PR
Francois PR
Francois, Alexander PR

François, André **BA WC**
(French artist, 1915-) WC
(French artist, b.1915) BA
Bibl: ▶MoMA libr. cat.; ▶Vollmer, Künst.-Lex. 20. Jhr.; ▶WW France
Farkas, André BA

Francois, Ange *(French, 1800-aft. 1869)* **GC**
Bibl: ▶Thieme-Becker

François, Bonvin→see Bonvin, François

Francois, Charles Emile *(French artist, 1821-)* **WC**

François, Christian *(French architect)* **AV**
Bibl: Architectes architecture, 1987 May, no.177, p.20

François, Claude→see Luc, Frère (Claude François)

Francois, Claude (Frere Luc)→see Luc, Frère (Claude François)

Francois, F.L. *(French artist, 19th cent.)* **WC**

Francois, Gustave (Gustave Francois Barraud) *(Swiss artist, 1883-1968)* **WC**

François, Guy **BA GC**
(French artist, c.1578-1650) WC
(French painter, 1578-1650) GC
(French painter, ca.1578-ca. 1650) BA
Bibl: ▶Bénézit; ▶Larousse grande encyc.; ▶Thieme-Becker

Francois, Guy or Guide ('Le Grand Francois') **WC**

Francois, Guy or Guide ('Le Grand Francois')→see François, Guy

Francois, Henri J. **GC**
(French artist, op.1785-1806) WC
(French, act.1785-1806) GC
Bibl: ▶Thieme-Becker; ▶Witt checklist

Francois, Henri-J. **WC**

Francois, Henri-J.→see Francois, Henri J.

Francois, Jean→see Francois, Jean II

Francois, Jean Charles *(French artist, 1717-1769)* **WC**

Francois, Jean II **GC**
(French artist, -1684) WC
(French, d.1684) GC
Bibl: ▶Bénézit

Francois, Jean **WC**

Francois, Joseph **GC**
(Belgian artist, 1759-1851) WC
(Belgian, 1759-1851) GC
Bibl: ▶Thieme-Becker; ▶Witt checklist

Francois, Pierre Joseph Celestin **WC**

François, Lucien *(1894?-)* **AV**

Francois, Pierre Joseph Celestin→see Francois, Joseph

Francois, Simon **GC**
(French artist, 1606-1671) WC
(French, 1606-1671) GC
Bibl: Getty Photo Study Coll. (Ptgs.); ▶Witt checklist

Francois or Francoys, Simon **WC**
Francoys, Simon GC
le Petit Francois GC

Tours, Simon Francois or Francoys de **WC**

François-Codou, P. *(French architect)* **AV**
Bibl: Architecture intérieure créé, 1985 Mar.-Apr., no.204, p.97

François-Robert, J. *(French architect, Paris)* **AV**
Bibl: Architecture intérieure créé, 1988 Oct.-Nov., no.226, p.172; ▶Libr. of Congr. Name Auth. File
Robert, J.-François AV

Francois-Xavier Vispre→see Vispré, François-Xavier

Francolin, Johann von **JG**

Francolin, Robert *(French artist, 20th cent.)* **WC**

Francolini, F. *(Italian artist, 19th cent.)* **WC**

Francolini, Ferdinando *(Italian painter, 19th c.)* **BA**
Bibl: De Palma, Mitteil. des Kunsthist. Inst. Florenz XXXII/ 1-2 (1988), p.294-322; ▶Witt checklist

Francoys Dancx→see Dancx, Francoys (Schildpad)

Francoys, Simon→see Francois, Simon

Francqueville, Pierre de **BA GC**
(early Netherlandish sculptor, architect, painter in FRA, 1548-1615) BA
(Netherlandish architect, painter, and sculptor, 1548-1615) GC
Bibl: ▶Bénézit; COMMENTARI XXVI/3-4 (July-Dec 1975) 333-344; ▶Encyc. world art; Getty Photo Study Coll.; ▶Nouv. biog. gén.; R. de Francqueville, monograph; ▶RILA/BHA; ▶Thieme-Becker
Francavilla, Pietro GC
Francheville, Pierre de GC
Pierre de Francheville GC
Pierre de Francqueville GC

Francucci, Innocenzo→see Francucci, Innocenzo (Innocenzo da Imola)

Francucci, Innocenzo (Innocenzo da Imola) **BA**
(Italian artist, 1490/4-1547/50) WC
(Italian artist, circa 1494-circa 1550) WI
(Italian painter, ca.1490-ca. 1550) BA PR
(Italian, 1485-1550) JG
(Italian, 1490/94-1547/50) GC
Bibl: ▶Bénézit; ▶Bolaffi; ▶Encyc. world art; ▶Fredericksen & Zeri, Census; Getty Photo Study Coll. (Ptgs.); ▶RILA/BHA; ▶Thieme-Becker; ▶Witt checklist
Francucci, Innocenzo GC PR
Francucci, Innocenzo di Pietro WI
Imola, Innocenzo da GC
Innoc.o da Imola PR
Innocent d'Imola PR
Innocent Francucci PR
Innocenza da Imola PR

Innocenzo da Imola **BA GC JG PR WI**
Innocenzo da Imola (Francucci) **WC**
Innocenzo da Imola (Innocenzo Francucci) **PR**
Innocenzo Francucci PR
Innocenzo Francucci da Imola PR
Innoco da Imola PR

Francucci, Innocenzo di Pietro→see Francucci, Innocenzo (Innocenzo da Imola)

Frandsen, Sophus *(Danish architect, b.1927)* **BA**
Bibl: Arkitekten, LXXXV/3 (1983) pp.45-50; ▶Libr. of Congr. Name Auth. File

Frangella, Roberto *(Argentine architect)* **AV**
    Bibl: Proa, 1985 Apr., no.340, p.28

frangi → *see* Francia, Francesco (Francesco Raibolini)

Frangia → *see* Francia, Francesco (Francesco Raibolini)

Frangia Vecchio → *see* Francia, Francesco (Francesco Raibolini)

Frangiamore, Salvatore *(British artist, op.1897-)* **WI**

Frangione, Pietro → *see* Francione, Pietro (Pietro Hispano)

Frangipane → *see* Frangipane, Niccolò

Frangipane, Niccolò   **BA GC PR WC**
    (Italian artist, op.1563-1597)   **WC**
    (Italian painter, 1555-1600)   **BA GC**
    (Italian painter, act. 1563-1597)   **PR**
    Bibl: ▶Bénézit; ▶Bolaffi; ▶RILA/BHA, 1986; SAGGI E MEMORIE DI STORIA DELL'ARTE VIII; ▶Thieme-Becker
    Frangipane   **PR**
    Frangipani   **PR**
    Niccolo Frangipane   **PR**

Frangipani → *see* Frangipane, Niccolò

Frangipanni, F. *(Italian artist, 18th cent.)* **WC**

Frangipanni, Francesco *(Italian painter, 17th c.)* **BA**
    Bibl: Mravik MUVESZETTORTENETI ERTESITO XXXI/4 (1982) 241-246; Pallucchini, Pitt. venez. '600, 291; ▶Witt checklist

Frangnoard → *see* Fragonard, Jean Honoré

Frangonard → *see* Fragonard, Jean Honoré

Frangouard → *see* Fragonard, Jean Honoré

Frank → *see* Francken, Frans III

Frank → *see* Francken, Hieronymus I

Frank Alfred Bicknell → *see* Bicknell, Frank Alfred

Frank Brangwyn → *see* Brangwyn, Frank

Frank Cairo → *see* Cairo, Francesco del

Frank Duveneck → *see* Duveneck, Frank

Frank Floris → *see* Floris, Frans, the elder

Frank Fowler → *see* Fowler, Frank

Frank Hall → *see* Hals, Frans

Frank Halls → *see* Hals, Frans

Frank Hals → *see* Hals, Frans

Frank Henry Shapleigh → *see* Shapleigh, Frank Henry

Frank Holl → *see* Holl, Frank

Frank M. Boggs → *see* Boggs, Frank Myers

Frank M. Pebbles → *see* Pebbles, Frank M.

Frank Morgan O'Brien → *see* O'Brien, Frank Morgan

Frank Mura → *see* Mura, Frank

Frank O. Salisbury → *see* Salisbury, Frank Owen

Frank Reynolds → *see* Reynolds, Frank

Frank Stone → *see* Stone, Frank

Frank V. Dudley → *see* Dudley, Frank V.

Frank Weston Benson → *see* Benson, Frank Weston

Frank, Alfred *(German painter, printmaker, 1884-1945)* **BA**
    Bibl: ▶Vollmer, Künst.-Lex. 20. Jhr.

Frank, Audrey *(American painter, 20th c.)* **BA**
    Bibl: Brooklyn (NY, USA), Brooklyn Mus., Woman's Place (1982); ▶Intl. dir. exh. artists, 1983

Frank, Barbara *(American artist, 20th c.)* **BA**
    Bibl: Washington, DC (USA), Womens Arts Center, Founders (1980)

Frank, Dale   **BA WI**
    (American artist, op.1987-)   **WI**
    (Australian painter, collagist, b.1959)   **BA**
    Bibl: ▶Intl. dir. exh. artists, 1983; New York (NY, USA), Guggenheim Mus., Australian visions (1984)

Frank, Edvard *(German painter, printmaker, 1909-1971)* **BA**
    Bibl: Rump, KUNSTNACHRICHTEN XVII/1 (Jan 1981) 13-18; ▶Vollmer, Künst.-Lex. 20. Jhr.

Frank, Ellen   **BA WI**
    (American artist, 20th c.)   **BA**
    (British artist, op.1899-1912)   **WI**
    Bibl: ▶Artist biog. master idx.; Lindenberger, ARTS MAG, LXI/5 (Jan 1987) 108

Frank, Fernando *(Brazilian architect)* **AV**
    Bibl: Architecture d'aujourd'hui, 1987 June,no.251,p.50

Frank, Francke or Franke, Johann (Johann Andreas Joseph) *(German artist, 1756-1804)* **WC**

Frank, Friedrich *(German artist, 1900-)* **WC**

Frank, Hans → *see* Franck, Hans

Frank, Hans Ulrich → *see* Franck, Hans Ulrich

Frank, Hartmut *(West German architect and architectural historian, Hamburg, 1942-)* **AV**
    Bibl: ▶Libr. of Congr. Name Auth. File; Werk Bauen + Wohnen, 1989 Mar., no.3, p.11 [date]

Frank, Heinz *(Austrian artist, 1939-)* **AV**
    Bibl: Institute for Architecture and Urban Studies. Catalogue, n.13, 1980, p.82

Frank, Jan *(American artist, 20th c.)* **BA**
    Bibl: Rubenstein, Arts Mag. LXI/5 (Jan 1987) 94-95

Frank, Jay *(American architect, Dallas, TX)* **AV**
    Bibl: ▶AIA Pro File, 1985

Frank, Josef   **AV BA**
    (Austrian architect and designer, 1885-1967)   **AV**
    (Austrian architect, author, 1885-1967)   **BA**
    Bibl: Clark Art Inst.; ▶MoMA libr. cat.; ▶Vollmer, Künst.-Lex. 20. Jhr.

Frank, Klaus *(German architect, Stuttgart, 1940-)* **AV**
    Bibl: Deutsche Bauzeitung, 1985 June, v.119, no.6, p.136

Frank, Larry *(American, 20th c.)* **BA**
    Bibl: Roswell (NM, USA), Museum, Larry Frank Coll. (1975-76)

Frank, Lucien *(Belgian artist, 1857-1920)* **WC**

Frank, Mary   **BA WI**
    (American artist, b.1933)   **WI**
    (American sculptor, b.1933)   **BA**
    Bibl: ▶MoMA libr. cat.; ▶WW Amer. Art, 1976

Frank, Raoul *(German artist, 1867-1939)* **WC**

Frank, Robert → *see* Frank, Robert Louis

Frank, Robert Louis   **BA**
    (American (b. Switzerland), 1924)   **JG**
    (American photographer, b.1924)   **BA**
    Bibl: ▶Newhall, Photog.; ▶Szarkowski, Photog's eye

Frank, Robert   **JG**

Frank, Roger *(American photographer, painter, b.ca.1957)* **BA**
    Bibl: HISTORIC PRES. XXXII (May-June 1980)

Frank, Sepp *(Architect, Austria)* **AV**
    Bibl: Planen bauen wohnen, 1984, no.107, p.5

Frank, Thomas *(American painter, b.1949)* **BA**
    Bibl: ▶Intl. dir. exh. artists

Frank, William Arnee   **WC WI**
    (British artist, op.1889)   **WC**
    (British artist, op.1889-)   **WI**

Frank-Krauss, Robert *(German artist, 1893-1950)* **WC**

Frank?, Heinrich *(German artist, 1805-1890)* **WC**

Franke family *(Austrian leather goods makers, bookbinders, 19th-20th cs.)* **BA**
    Bibl: WELTKUNST I (Nov 1980) 3081-3083

Franke, Albert Joseph *(German artist, 1860-1924)* **WC**

Franke, Heinrich (Johann Heinrich Christian *(German artist, 1738-1792)* **WC**

Franke, Julius *(Austrian leather goods maker, 1831-1917)* **BA**
    Bibl: WELTKUNST L (1980) 710-715

Franke, Klaus *(East German engineer)*   **AV**
 Bibl: Architektur der DDR, 1989 June, v.38, no.6, p.13

Franke, Rainer *(German architect)*   **AV**
 Bibl: Bauwelt, 1986 May 23, v.77, no.19-20, p.721

Frankeberger, Robert R. *(American architect, Phoenix, Ariz)*   **AV**
 Bibl: ▶AIA Pro File, 1987-88

Frankel *(American, active 1920's)*   **JG**

Frankel, Neil P. *(American architect, Chicago, IL)*   **AV**
 Bibl: Chicago architectural journal, 1989, no.7, po.168

Franken, Bruno *(German architect)*   **AV**
 Bibl: Die Kunst, 1986 June, v.96, no.6, p.469

Franken, Chris *(Dutch architect, Eindhoven)*   **AV**
 Bibl: Open house international, 1984, v.9, no.4, p.55

Franken, Frans II → see Francken, Frans II

Franken, Marianne *(Dutch artist, 1884-1945)*   **WC**

Franken, Paul von *(German artist, 1818-1884)*   **WC**

Franken, Petrus Johannes Cornelis *(Dutch painter, 1866-1911)*   **GC**
 Bibl: ▶Bénézit

Frankenburg *(Hungarian(?) artist, 16th cent.)*   **WC**

Frankenburger, Johann *(German artist, 1807-1874)*   **WC**

Frankenstein, Godfrey N. *(American painter, 1820-1873)*   **BA**
 Bibl: ▶Groce, Artists Amer.; ▶WWW Amer.

Frankenstein, John Peter   **BA WI**
 (American artist, 1816-1817-1881)   **WI**
 (American painter, sculptor, 1816/17-1881)   **BA**
 Bibl: ▶Bénézit; ▶Fielding's Amer. ptrs.; ▶Groce, Artists Amer.; ▶Thieme-Becker; ▶WWW Amer.

Frankenstein, von *(Active Vienna, Austria ca. 1900)*   **JG**

Frankenstein, Wolfgang   **BA WC**
 (German artist, 1918-)   **WC**
 (German painter, printmaker, b.1918)   **BA**
 Bibl: ▶Vollmer, Künst.-Lex. 20. Jhr.

Frankenthaler, Helen   **AV BA GC WC WI**
 (American artist, 1928-)   **AV WC**
 (American artist, b.1928)   **WI**
 (American painter, b.1928)   **BA GC**
 Bibl: ▶Contemp. artists; ▶Libr. of Congr. Name Auth. File; ▶RILA/BHA; ▶WW Amer. Art, 1989; ▶WW Art, 1988
 Motherwell, Robert Burns, Mrs., (Helen)   **WI**

Frankfort, Eduard *(Dutch painter, 1864-1920)*   **GC**
 Bibl: ▶Thieme-Becker

Frankhalls → see Hals, Frans

Frankie, A.F. *(French(?) artist, 19th cent.)*   **WC**

Frankl, Gerhard   **WI**
 (German artist, 1901-)   **WC**
 (German artist, 1901-1965)   **WI**

Frankl, Gerhardt   **WC**

Frankl, Gerhardt → see Frankl, Gerhard

Frankl, Volfango   **BA**
 (Italian architect, 1907-)   **AV**
 (Italian architect, 20th c.)   **BA**
 Bibl: Arquitectura, 1988 Mar.-June, v.69, no.271-272, p.124; Terni (ITA), Pal. Mazzancolli, THE ARCH. OF RIDOLFI AND FRANKL (1979)

Frankl, Wolfgang   **AV**

Frankl, Wolfgang → see Frankl, Volfango

Frankland, Robert II *(British artist, b.1938)*   **WI**

Frankland, Robert Russell, 7th Bt. → see Frankland, Robert, baronet

Frankland, Robert, baronet   **BA**
 (British artist, 1784-1849)   **WC WI**
 (British painter, 1784-1849)   **BA**
 Bibl: COMPLETE BARONETGE, III 144, v.3, p.144; Wilton, A., Turner Studies IV, 2 p.60; ▶Witt checklist

Frankland, Robert Russell, 7th Bt.   **WI**

Frankland, Sir Robert   **WC**
 Frankland-Russell, Robert   **BA**

Frankland, Sir Robert → see Frankland, Robert, baronet

Frankland-Russell, Robert → see Frankland, Robert, baronet

Franklin Chenault Watkins → see Watkins, Franklin

Franklin De Haven → see Haven, Franklin de

Franklin Jay Lewis → see Lewis, Franklin Jay

Franklin, Beatrice M. *(Irish painter, d.1895)*   **BA**
 Bibl: Dublin (IRL), Nat. Gallery, THE EARLY CELTIC REVIVAL (1980)
 Samuel, Beatrice M. Franklin, viscountess   **BA**

Franklin, Deborah Read *(American, 1738-1815)*   **BA**
 Bibl: ANTIQUES CVIII/2 (Aug 1975) 114-122; ▶Dict. Amer. biog.

Franklin, George *(British artist, op. 1825-1847)*   **WC WI**

Franklin, Gilbert A. *(American sculptor, b.1919)*   **BA**
 Bibl: ▶WW Amer. Art, 1989

Franklin, Jenny-Ann *(British artist, b.1949)*   **WI**

Franklin, John   **WC WI**
 (British artist, c.1800-p.1868)   **WC**
 (British artist, circa 1800-op. circa 1868)   **WI**

Franklin, Mary   **WC WI**
 (British artist, op.1823)   **WC**
 (British artist, op.1823-)   **WI**

Franklin, Maud *(British, 1857-ca. 1941)*   **BA**
 Bibl: MacDonald, M.F., in STUDIES IN THE HIST OF ART, 19 (1987) 13-26

Franklin, Stanley Arthur   **WC WI**
 (British artist, 20th cent.)   **WC**
 (British artist, op.20th c.)   **WI**

Franklyn, Lesley *(British artist, op. 1965-)*   **WI**

Franko, Nancy *(Cuban painter, b.1951)*   **BA**
 Bibl: LaDuke, Woman's art jrnl., V/2 (Fal.-Win. 1984-85) p.34

Franks Hals → see Hals, Frans

Frano Albani → see Albani, Francesco

Frano Vanni → see Vanni, Francesco

Franque, François   **AV BA WC**
 (French architect, 1710-1786)   **BA**
 (French architect, 1710-ca.1792)   **AV**
 (French artist, 1710-1786)   **WC**
 Bibl: ▶Lance, Dict. archts. fran.; ▶Macmillan encyc. archts.; ▶Thieme-Becker

Franque, Jean Pierre → see Franque, Pierre

Franque, Jean-Baptiste *(1683-1758)*   **AV**

Franque, Joseph   **BA GC WC**
 (French artist, 1774-1833)   **WC**
 (French painter, 1774-1833)   **BA**
 (French, 1774-1833)   **GC**
 Bibl: ▶Bénézit; ▶Dict. biog. fran.; ▶Thieme-Becker; ▶Witt checklist

Franque, Lucile *(French painter, author, 1780-1802)*   **BA**
 Bibl: ▶Bénézit; ▶Thieme-Becker

Franque, Pierre   **BA**
 (French artist, 1774-1860)   **WC**
 (French painter, 1774-1860)   **BA**
 (French, 1774-1860)   **GC**
 Bibl: ▶Bénézit; ▶Larousse grande encyc.; ▶Thieme-Becker; ▶Witt checklist

Franque, Jean Pierre   **BA GC WC**

Franquelin → see Franquelin, Jean Augustin

Franquelin, Jean Augustin   **GC PR WC**
 (French artist, 1798-1839)   **WC**
 (French painter, 1798-1839)   **GC PR**
 Bibl: ▶Thieme-Becker; ▶Witt checklist
 Franquelin   **PR**
 Jean Augustin Franquelin   **PR**

Franquet, L. *(Belgian artist, 19th cent.)*   **WC**

Franqueville, Pierre *(French painter, act. in Italy, d. ca. 1553)*   **AV**
 Bibl: ▶Thieme-Becker
 Francavilla, Pietro   **AV**

Frans Daems→see Daems, Frans
Frans Dames→see Daems, Frans
Frans de Hulst→see Hulst, Franz de
Frans de Momper→see Momper,
  Frans de
Frans de Neve→see Neve, Frans de
  (Bloosaerken)
Frans de Vrient→see Floris, Frans, the
  elder
Frans Decker→see Decker, Frans
Frans Dekker→see Decker, Frans
Frans family *(Italian potters in Low
  Countries, 16th c.)*   **BA**
  Bibl: Dumortier, Faenza,
  LXXIII/4-5 (1987) pp.161-172
Frans Floris→see Floris, Frans, the
  elder
Frans Floris (I)→see Floris, Frans, the
  elder
Frans Florisz→see Floris, Frans, the
  elder
Frans Florisz.→see Floris, Frans, the
  elder
Frans Florus→see Floris, Frans, the
  elder
Frans Francken (I)→see Francken,
  Frans I
Frans Francken (II)→see Francken,
  Frans II
Frans Francken (III)→see Francken,
  Frans III
Frans Hals→see Hals, Frans
Frans Hals (I)→see Hals, Frans
Frans Heremans→see Heeremans,
  Thomas
Frans Ijkens→see Ijkens, Frans
Frans Jansz. Post→see Post, Frans
  Jansz.
Frans Masereel→see Masereel, Frans
Frans Moormans→see Moormans,
  Frans
Frans Pieter Ter Meulen→see Ter
  Meulen, Frans Pieter
Frans Post→see Post, Frans Jansz.
Frans Pourbus (the Elder)→see
  Pourbus, Frans, the elder
Frans Pourbus (the Younger)→see
  Pourbus, Frans, the younger
Frans Rijckhals→see Rijckhals, Frans
Frans Snyders→see Snyders, Frans
Frans van Cuyck→see Cuyck, Frans
  van
Frans van Doornik→see Doornik,
  Frans van
Frans van Everbroeck→see
  Everbroeck, Frans van
Frans van Mieris (the Elder)→see
  Mieris, Frans I van
Frans van Mieris (the younger)→see
  Mieris, Frans II van
Frans van Oosten→see Oosten, Frans
  van
Frans Wouters→see Wouters, Frans
Frans Xaver Hendrik Verbeeck→see
  Verbeeck, Frans Xaver Hendrik

Frans Xavery→see Xavery, Frans
Frans, Nicolaus *(Netherlands artist,
  1539-)*   **WC**
Franse, Cornelis (Kees) *(Dutch
  artist, 1924-)*   **WC**
Franse, P. *(Netherlands artist, 17th
  cent.)*   **WC**
Fransie van den Heuvel→see Heuvel,
  Fransie van den [Unidentified]
Fransie vanden Heuvel→see Heuvel,
  Fransie van den [Unidentified]
Fransioli, Thomas Adrian *(American
  artist, b.1906)*   **WI**
Fransje Floris→see Floris, Frans, the
  elder
Franta, Aleksander *(Polish
  architect, 1925-)*   **AV**
  Bibl: ▶Contemp. archts.
Frantisek Kupka→see Kupka,
  František
Frantz, Alison *(American
  photographer and author)*   **GC**
  Bibl: Getty Photo Study Coll.;
  ▶Libr. of Congr. Name Auth. File
Frantz, Johann Martin *(German
  porcelain painter, act.1717-1756)*   **BA**
  Bibl: ▶Thieme-Becker
Frantzke, H. R. *(West German
  architect, Karlsruhe)*   **AV**
  Bibl: Deutsches Architektenblatt,
  1989 June 1, p.915
Franz→see Franz, Carl Joseph
Franz Anton Maulbertsch→see
  Maulbertsch, Franz Anton
Franz Christoph Janneck→see
  Janneck, Franz Christoph
Franz Cleyn→see Cleyn, Francis
Franz de Hulst→see Hulst, Franz de
Franz de Paula Ferg→see Ferg, Franz
  de Paula
Franz Dietrich→see Dietrich, Franz
Franz Edmund Weirotter→see
  Weirotter, Franz Edmund
Franz Friedrich Franck→see Franck,
  Franz Friedrich
Franz Ignaz Oefele→see Oefele,
  Franz Ignaz
Franz Joseph Manskirch→see
  Manskirch, Franz Joseph
Franz Kels→see Kels, Franz
Franz Linder→see Linder, Franz
Franz Marc→see Marc, Franz
Franz Maria Ingenmey→see
  Ingenmey, Franz Maria
Franz Rederer→see Rederer, Franz
Franz Seraph von Lenbach→see
  Lenbach, Franz Seraph von
Franz Theodor Aerni→see Aerni,
  Franz Theodor
Franz von Defregger→see Defregger,
  Franz Jacob von
Franz von Rohden→see Rohden,
  Franz von
Franz von Stuck→see Stuck, Franz
  von

Franz Werner von Tamm→see Tamm,
  Franz Werner von
Franz Wilhelm Seiwert→see Seiwert,
  Franz Wilhelm
Franz Xaver Petter→see Petter, Franz
  Xaver
Franz Xaver Winterhalter→see
  Winterhalter, Franz Xaver
Franz Xavier Karl Palko→see Palko,
  Franz Xavier Karl
Franz, A. *(German artist, 19th cent.)* **WC**
Franz, Carl Joseph   **PR WC**
  (German artist, 1829-1875)   **WC**
  (German painter, 1829-1875)   **PR**
  Bibl: ▶Thieme-Becker
  Carl Joseph Franz   **PR**
  Franz   **PR**
Franz, Ettore Roesler→see Roesler
  Franz, Ettore
Franz, Johann Michael *(German
  artist, op.1760-1768)*   **WC**
Franz, Klaus   **AV BA**
  (German architect, b.1923)   **BA**
  (West German architect, 1923-)   **AV**
  Bibl: ▶WW Arts DEU
Franz-Dreber, Heinrich→see Dreber,
  Heinrich
Franza→see Francia, Francesco
  (Francesco Raibolini)
Franzel [Unidentified] *(Unknown
  painter)*   **PR**
  Bibl: Anonymous inventory,
  Florence, 1750
Franzen, A.W. *(fl. 1959;
  Architectural draftsman, United
  States of America)*   **FA**
  Bibl: drawing inscription; Natl.
  Archives object
Franzen, August   **PR WI**
  (American artist, 1863-1938)   **WI**
  (American painter, 1863-1938)   **PR**
  Bibl: ▶WWW Amer. art
  August Franzen   **PR**
  Franzen, August Reinhold   **PR**
Franzen, August Reinhold→see
  Franzen, August
Franzen, John Erik *(Swedish painter,
  b.1942)*   **BA**
  Bibl: ▶Intl. dir. exh. artists, 1983
Franzen, Karl *(West German
  architect, fl. ca. 1900)*   **AV**
  Bibl: Deutsche Bauzeitschrift,
  1989 June, v.37, no.6, p.733
Franzen, Ulrich→see Franzen, Ulrich
  Joseph
Franzen, Ulrich Joseph   **BA**
  (American architect, 1921-)   **AV**
  (American architect, b.1921)   **BA**
  Bibl: ▶Avery period. idx.;
  ▶Contemp. archts.; Wolf,
  EVOLVING CITY, p.10
Franzen, Ulrich   **AV**
Franzesino→see Franceschini,
  Baldassare (Il Volterrano)

Franzheim, Elizabeth *(American painter, collagist, b.1923)*   **BA**
Bibl: Arnault, CIMAISE 38/210(Janv.Fev.Mars 1991), p.65; ▶Babington Smith, Contemp. artists; ▶Intl. dir. exh. artists, 1982

Franzheim, Kenneth *(American architect, Houston, Tex, 1891?-1959)*   **AV**
Bibl: ▶Avery obit. idx.

Franzi, Gino *(Italian architect)*   **AV**
Bibl: Domus, 1988 Apr., no.693, p.72

Franzini, Girolamo *(Woodcutter, author, ante 1571-post 1589)*   **CE**
Franzini, Hieronymus   CE
Girolamo Franzini   CE

Franzini, Girolamo *(Italian printmaker, act.1588)*   **BA**
Bibl: Howe, Gaz. des B.-A. CVI (Dec 1985) 196; ▶Natl. union cat., pre-1956
Francini, Girolamo   BA
Franzini, Hieronymus → see Franzini, Girolamo

Franzoia, Ferruccio *(Italian architect)*   **AV**
Bibl: Area, 1984 Nov.-Dec., v.4, no.19, p.26

Franzoni, A.G. *(Italian artist, 20th cent.)*   **WC**

Franzoni, Filippo *(Swiss painter, 1857-1911)*   **BA**
Bibl: ▶Bénézit; ▶Bolaffi; ▶Comanducci, Diz.; ▶Künst.-Lex. Schweiz 20. Jahrh.; ▶Schweiz. Künst.-Lex.; ▶Thieme-Becker

Franzoni, Francesco Antonio *(Sculptor, 1734-1818)*   **CE**

Franzoni, Roberto *(Italian painter, 1882-1960)*   **BA**
Bibl: Bologna (ITA), Galleria comunale d'arte moderna, IL LIBERTY A BOLOGNA (1977); ▶Comanducci, Diz.
Franzosino → see Gare, Domenico

Frappa, Jose   **GC WC**
(French painter, 1854-1904)   GC
(German artist, 1854-1904)   WC
Bibl: ▶Thieme-Becker

Fraprie, Frank *(American photographer, 20th c.)*   **BA**
Bibl: New Mex. Studies Fine Arts, II (1977) pp.13-19
Fraro, Francesco → see Bianchi Ferrari, Francesco de'

Frary, Michael   **WC WI**
(American artist, 1918-)   WC
(American artist, b.1918)   WI
Fras. Furini → see Furini, Francesco
Fras. Meiris → see Mieris, Frans I van
Fras: Floris → see Floris, Frans, the elder

Frasa, Carlo *(Italian artist, op.1711)*   **WC**

Frasca, Robert J. *(American architect)*   **AV**

Frascheri, Giuseppe   **GC WC**
(Italian artist, 1809-1886)   WC
(Italian painter, 1809-1886)   GC
Bibl: ▶Thieme-Becker

Frascino, Lívio *(Brazilian architect)*   **AV**
Bibl: Projeto, 1986 Apr., no.86, p.47
Frascino, Tito Lívio   AV
Frascino, Tito Lívio → see Frascino, Lívio

Frasconi, Antonio   **BA WC**
(American illustrator, painter, b.1919)   BA
(South American artist, 1919-)   WC
Bibl: ▶Archives Amer. Art Jrnl., XI/1-4 (1971); ▶WW Amer. Art, 1976
Fraser → see Fraser, William

Fraser family *(British painters, 19th c.)*   **BA**
Bibl: ▶Harris, Scottish ptrs.; ▶Thieme-Becker
Fraser, Alexander → see Fraser, Alexander III
Fraser, Alexander (the elder) → see Fraser, Alexander I
Fraser, Alexander (the Younger) → see Fraser, Alexander II

Fraser, Alexander I   **WI**
(British artist, 1786-1865)   WC WI
(British painter, 1786-1865)   PR
Bibl: ▶Thieme-Becker
A. Frazer   PR
Alexander Fraser (the elder)   PR
Fraser, Alexander (the elder)   **PR**
Fraser, Alexander, I   **WC**
Fraser, Alexander II   **WI**
(British artist, 1827-1828-1899)   WI
(British artist, 1827/8-1899)   WC
(Scottish painter, 1828-1899)   GC
Bibl: ▶Bénézit
Fraser, Alexander (the Younger)   **GC**
Fraser, Alexander, II   **WC**
Fraser, Alexander III   **WI**
(British artist, 20th cent.)   WC
(British artist, op.20th c.)   WI
Fraser, Alexander   **WC**
Fraser, Alexander, I → see Fraser, Alexander I
Fraser, Alexander, II → see Fraser, Alexander II

Fraser, Arthur Anderson, (of Huntingdonshire) *(British artist, 1861-1904)*   **WI**

Fraser, Carol Lucille Hoorn *(Canadian painter, b.1930)*   **BA**
Bibl: ▶Artists Canada; ▶Natl. Gall. Canada libr. cat.

Fraser, Charles   **BA WC WI**
(American artist, 1782-1860)   WC WI
(American painter, 1782-1860)   BA
Bibl: ▶Bénézit; ▶Fielding's Amer. ptrs.; ▶Groce, Artists Amer.; ▶Thieme-Becker; ▶WWW Amer.

Fraser, Charles Mackenzie *(British, d.1871)*   **BA**
Bibl: ▶Dict. natl. biog.; Slade, PROCEEDINGS OF SOC. OF ANTIQUARIES OF SCOTLAND CIX (1977-78) 233-301

Fraser, Claud Lovat   **BA WC WI**
(British artist, 1890-1921)   WC WI
(British designer, illustrator, printmaker, 1890-1921)   BA
Bibl: ▶Dict. natl. biog.; ▶Johnson, Brit. artists; ▶Vollmer, Künst.-Lex. 20. Jhr.; ▶Waters, Brit. artists

Fraser, Donald Hamilton   **BA WC WI**
(British artist, 1929-)   WC
(British artist, b.1929)   WI
(British painter, b.1929)   BA
Bibl: ▶Dolman, Contemp. Brit. artists; ▶MoMA libr. cat.; ▶WW Art, 1977

Fraser, Elyza *(British, 1736-1814)*   **BA**
Bibl: Slade, PROCEEDINGS OF SOC. OF ANTIQUARIES OF SCOTLAND CIX (1977-78) 233-301

Fraser, Eric George *(British painter, designer, b.1902)*   **BA**
Bibl: ▶Vollmer, Künst.-Lex. 20. Jhr.; ▶WW Art
Fraser, Francis Arthur → see Fraser, Francis Arthur Anderson, (of Huntingdonshire)

Fraser, Francis Arthur Anderson, (of Huntingdonshire)   **WI**
(British artist, 1846-1924)   WI
(British artist, op.1867-1883)   WC
Fraser, Francis Arthur   **WC**

Fraser, George Gordon, (of Huntingdonshire) *(British artist, 1859-1895)*   **WI**

Fraser, Hamilton *(British artist, op. 1966-)*   **WI**

Fraser, Ian   **AV WC WI**
(British architect, London)   AV
(British artist, 1933-)   WC
(British artist, b.1933)   WI
Bibl: ▶Libr. of Congr. Name Auth. File
Fraser, J.A. → see Fraser, John Arthur

Fraser, James   **AV BA**
(1793-1863)   AV
(Irish landscape architect, 1793-1863)   BA
Bibl: Bowe, NATIONAL TRUST STUDIES 7-16; Malins, IRISH GARDENS.& DEMESNES FROM 1830; ▶Natl. union cat., pre-1956

Fraser, James Baillie   **BA WC WI**
(British artist, 1783-1856)   WC WI
(British merchant, artist, 1783-1856)   BA
Bibl: ▶Dict. natl. biog.; ▶Encyc. Britannica

Fraser, James Earle BA GC
  (American medalist and
    sculptor, 1876-1953) GC
  (American sculptor, medalist,
    1876-1953) BA
    Bibl: ▶Encyc. world art;
    ▶RILA/BHA; ▶Vollmer, Künst.-Lex.
    20. Jhr.
Fraser, John WC WI
  (British artist, 1858-1927) WI
  (British artist, 1858-p.1914) WC
Fraser, John Arthur BA
  (Canadian artist, 20th cent.) WC
  (Canadian painter, 1838-1898) BA
    Bibl: ▶Bénézit; ▶Encyc. world art;
    ▶Harper, Ptg. Canada;
    ▶MacDonald, Can. artists

Fraser, J.A. WC
Fraser, Justina WC WI
  (British artist, op.1822) WC
  (British artist, op.1822-) WI
Fraser, Oliver *(American artist,*
  1808-1864) WC WI
  Frazer, Oliver WI

Fraser, Robert Winchester, (of
  Huntingdonshire) *(British artist,*
  1848-1906) WI
Fraser, Simon Barron *(British*
  architect, London) AV
    Bibl: ▶RIBA members, 1983
Fraser, Thomas WC WI
  (British artist, -1851) WC
  (British artist, op.1851-) WI
Fraser, Vivian AV BA
  (Australian architect) AV
  (Australian architect, 20th c.) BA
    Bibl: Architectural review, 1985
    Dec., v.178, no.1066, p.58;
    ▶Avery period. idx., 6th suppl.
Fraser, William PR WC WI
  (British artist, 19th cent.) WC
  (British artist, op.1808-) WI
  (British painter, act. 1806-1811) PR
    Bibl: ▶Thieme-Becker
  Fraser PR
  Frazer PR
  W. Fraser PR
  William Fraser PR
Fraser, William Lewis *(American*
  artist, 1841-1905) WI
Fraser-Brunner, A. *(British artist,*
  op.20th c.) WI
Fraser-Gardener, William →see
  Garden, W.F.
Frasnedi, Alfonso *(Italian artist,*
  1934-) WC
Frassanito, John R. *(American*
  designer, San Antonio, TX) AV
    Bibl: Design directory '84
Frassine, Heinz AV
Frassinelli, G. *(Italian architect)* AV
    Bibl: Lotus international, 1983,
    no.40, p.4

Frassinelli, Gian Piero BA
  (Italian architect) AV
  (Italian architect, 20th c.) BA
    Bibl: ▶Avery period. idx.; Pettena,
    Superstudio 1966-1982 (1982);
    Walker
Frassinelli, Piero AV
Frassinelli, Piero →see Frassinelli, Gian
  Piero
Frate →see Bartolomeo, Fra
Frate da Deruta *(Italian pottery*
  painter, 16th c.) BA
    Bibl: Fiocco, Faenza, LXX/5-6
    (1984) pp.403-416; ▶Honey, Euro.
    ceramic; ▶Thieme-Becker
Frate Eustachio →see Tommaso di
  Baldassare (Frate Eustachio)
Frate Felice Della Sambuca →see
  Viscosi, Gioachino (Felice da
  Sambuca)
Frate Fiammingo Benedettino →see
  Frate Fiammingo [Unidentified]
Frate Fiammingo [Unidentified]
  (Unknown painter) PR
    Bibl: Corsini inventory, Rome,
    1750
  Frate Fiammingo Benedettino PR
Frate Niccholas *(Italian scribe, act.*
  ca.1350) GC
    Bibl: ▶Levi d'Ancona, Miniatura a
    Firenze; P. D'Ancona, Miniatura
    fiorentina (1914), v.2, p.1701
Frate, Domenico (di Sante) del →see
  Del Frate, Domenico
Frate, Domenico del →see Del Frate,
  Domenico
Frateili, Mariella *(Italian architect,*
  Milan) AV
    Bibl: Abitare, 1983 Oct., no.218,
    p.14
Fratellina →see Fratellini, Giovanna
Fratellini, Giovanna PR
  (Italian artist, 1666-1731) WC
  (Italian painter, 1666-1731) PR
    Bibl: ▶Thieme-Becker
  Fratellina PR
Fratellini, Giovanna, (nee
  Marmocchini Cortesi) WC
  Giovanna Fratellini PR
  Marmocchini Cortesi PR
Fratellini, Giovanna, (nee
  Marmocchini Cortesi) →see
  Fratellini, Giovanna
Fratellini, Lorenzo *(Italian artist,*
  1691/3-1729) WC
fratello del Guercin da cento →see
  Barbieri, Paolo Antonio
Frater Amadeus *(Italian scribe, act.*
  late 14th, early 15th c) GC
    Bibl: Meiss, Visconti Hours
Frater Francisinus *(Italian scribe,*
  act.1300) GC
    Bibl: Venice, Miniature Italiane
    Cini, p.13

Frater Guilielmus *(Italian scribe, act.*
  1421) GC
    Bibl: Chiarelli, Mus. San Marco,
    p.64; Getty Photo Study Coll.
    (Medieval)
  Guilielmus, Frater GC
Frater Iohannes Aurifex de
  Venetiis *(Italian scribe, act.1425)* GC
    Bibl: Mazzatinti, Inventari, v.3,
    p.165
  Johannes Aurifex de Venetiis GC
Frater Iohannes Magno de
  Veneciis *(Italian scribe, act.1445)* GC
    Bibl: Getty Photo Study Coll.
    (Medieval); Mazzatinti, Inventari,
    v.3, p.167
  Johannes Magno de Veneciis GC
F[rater] L[udovicus] Neeffs →see
  Neeffs, Lodewyck
Frater Romanus →see Romanus,
  Frater
Frater, William *(Australian artist,*
  1890-) WC
Frati [Unidentified] *(Unknown*
  painter) PR
    Bibl: Riccardi inventory, Florence,
    1752
Frati, Leonardo *(Italian painter, d.*
  1808-1813) PR
    Bibl: ▶Thieme-Becker
  Leonardo Frati PR
Fratin, Christophe BA GC
  (French sculptor,
    ca.1800/02-1864) BA
  (French sculptor,
    ca.1800/1802-1864) GC
    Bibl: ▶Bénézit; ▶Lami, Sculp. fran.
    19e s.; ▶RILA/BHA;
    ▶Thieme-Becker
Fratino, Giovanni →see Fratino,
  Giovanni (Giovanni de' Mio)
Fratino, Giovanni (de Mio or
  Visentin) →see Fratino, Giovanni
  (Giovanni de' Mio)

Fratino, Giovanni (Giovanni de' Mio)   **BA** GC **PR**
- (Italian artist, op.1538-1560)   WC
- (Italian painter and mosaicist, act.1537-1563, d.ca.1570)   GC
- (Italian painter, act. 1537-1563, d. ca.1570)   PR
- (Italian painter, mosaicist, act. 1537, d.ca.1570)   BA
  - Bibl: ▶Bolaffi; ▶RILA/BHA, 1986; ▶Thieme-Becker; Vicenza (ITA), Temp. di S. Corona, Palladio e la maniera (1980)
- De' Mio, Giovanni   BA
- De'Mio, Giovanni   BA
- Demio, Giovanni   GC PR
- **Fratino, Giovanni**   **GC** PR
- **Fratino, Giovanni (de Mio or Visentin)**   **WC**
- Giovanni de' Mio   BA PR
- Giovanni de'Mio   BA
- Giovanni Fratino   PR
- Indemio, Giovanni   BA
- Mio, Giovanni de'   BA GC
- Visentin   GC

Fratrel → see Fratrel, Joseph (I)
Fratrel the Elder, Joseph → see Fratrel, Joseph (I)
Fratrel, Joseph (I)   **PR**
- (French artist, 1730-1783)   WC
- (French painter, 1730-1783)   PR
  - Bibl: ▶Thieme-Becker
- Fratrel   PR
Fratrel the Elder, Joseph   **WC**
- Joseph Fratel (I)   PR
Fratta, Domenico → see Fratta, Domenico Maria
Fratta, Domenico Maria   **BA GC WC**
- (Italian artist, 1696-1763)   WC
- (Italian painter, 1696-1763)   BA
- (Italian, 1696-1763)   GC
  - Bibl: ▶Bolaffi; Getty Photo Study Coll. (Ptgs.); ▶Thieme-Becker; ▶Witt checklist
- Fratta, Domenico   GC
Fratte Group *(South Italian vase-painters, 4th century BC)*   **GC**
- Bibl: ▶Trendall, Red-fig. vases Lucania
Fratte Painter *(Campanian vase-painter)*   **GC**
- Bibl: ▶Trendall, Red-fig. vases Lucania
Frattini Magnusson, Emanuela → see Magnusson, Emanuela
Frattini, Gianfranco *(Italian architect)*   **AV**
- Bibl: Ottagono, 1985 Dec., v.20, no.79, p.86
Frattini, Vittore *(Italian painter, b.1937)*   **BA**
- Bibl: Bellini, VOTTORE FRATTINI (1988)

Frau, Luigi [Unidentified] *(Unknown painter, act. 18th century)*   **PR**
- Bibl: Riccardi inventory dated 1776
- Luigi Frau   PR
Frau. Mola → see Mola, Pier Francesco
Frauen, Asmus *(Dutch sculptor, 1709-1799)*   **BA**
- Bibl: Gelder, van, H.E., KUNSTGESCHIEDENIS... NEDERLANDEN (1946), p.654; Jensma, Preekstoel in onze lieve vrouwekerk; KUNSTREISBOEK VOOR NEDERLAND (1977), p.430; ▶Thieme-Becker
Frauenfeld, Eduard *(Austrian architect, fl. 1903)*   **AV**
- Bibl: Planen Bauen Wohnen, 1988, no.123, p.21
Frauenpreis, Matthäus, the elder *(German armorer, ca.1505-1549)*   **BA**
- Bibl: Becher, Jahrb. Kunsthist. Sammlung. Wien, XL (1980) p.28; ▶Neue deutsche Biog.; ▶Thieme-Becker
Frauenpreis, Matthäus, the younger *(German armorer, ca. 1530-1575)*   **BA**
- Bibl: Becher, Jahrb. Kunsthist. Sammlung. Wien, XL (1980) p.28; ▶Neue deutsche Biog.; ▶Thieme-Becker
Fraunhofer, Rosemarie *(German architect, Munich)*   **AV**
- Bibl: Detail, 1981 Jan.-Feb., no.1, p.54
Fraustadt, Friedrich August *(German artist, 1821-1880)*   **WC**
Fray Miguel de Herrera → see Herrera, Fray Miguel de
Fray, James   **JG**
Fraye, André   **BA WC**
- (French artist, 1887-1963)   WC
- (French painter, illustrator, 1888-1963)   BA
  - Bibl: ▶Bénézit; ▶Dict. biog. fran.; ▶Vollmer, Künst.-Lex. 20. Jhr.
Fraysse *(French printmaker, 18th c.)*   **BA**
- Bibl: REVUE DU lOUVRE, XXXIII, 5-6 (1983) 398-399
Frazee, John *(American sculptor, 1790-1852)*   **BA**
- Bibl: ▶Thieme-Becker; ▶WWW Amer.
Frazer → see Fraser, William
Frazer, Hugh *(British artist, op.1813-1861)*   **WI**
Frazer, James *(American photographer, painter, b.1949)*   **BA**
- Bibl: ▶WW Amer. Art
Frazer, Jim *(American, 1949 -)*   **JG**
Frazer, Mabel Pearl *(American artist, 1887-1981)*   **WI**
Frazer, Oliver → see Fraser, Oliver
Frazer, Sally *(American artist, op. 20th c.)*   **WI**

Frazer, William Miller *(British artist, 1864-1961)*   **WC WI**
Frazer, William, Capt. *(American artist, op.1795-1805-1905)*   **WI**
Frazetta, Frank *(American illustrator, 20th c.)*   **BA**
- Bibl: Kresge Art Ctr. Bull., IX/2 (Dec. 1975) pp.16-20
Frazier, Charles *(American artist, b.1930)*   **BA**
- Bibl: ART NEWS 76 (May 1977) 106; ARTS MAG 50 (Mar 1976) 25; ▶MoMA libr. cat.
Frazier, John Robinson *(American artist, 1889-1966)*   **WC WI**
Frazier, Kenneth   **BA WI**
- (American artist, 1867-1949)   WI
- (American painter, 1867-1949)   BA
  - Bibl: ▶Bénézit; ▶Fielding's Amer. ptrs.; ▶Smith, Idx. Amer. artists; ▶WWW Amer.; ▶Young, Amer. artists
Frazier, Thelma Winter *(American ceramist, 1903-1977)*   **BA**
- Bibl: ▶Clark, Ceramics US; Syracuse (NY, USA), Everson Mus., Diversions of Keramos (1983)
- Winter, Thelma Frazier   BA
fra' Sebastiano del Piompo → see Sebastiano del Piombo (Sebastiano Luciani)
Fra' Semplice Cappuccino → see Semplice da Verona, Fra
Freake, Elizabeth Clarke *(English in America, 1642-1713)*   **BA**
- Bibl: AMERICAN ART FROM THE WORCESTER ART MUSEUM; Dresser, Worcester Art Mus. Bull., XXIX/5 (1964); Strickler, WORCESTER ART MUS. JOURNAL V (1981-82) 55, n.7
Freake, Mary *(English in America, 1674-1752)*   **BA**
- Bibl: Dresser, Worcester Art Mus. Bull., XXIX/5 (1964); Strickler, WORCESTER ART MUSEUM JOURNAL V (1981-82) 49
- Wolcott, Josiah, Mrs.   BA
Freame, Margaret Penn *(American, 1704-1751)*   **BA**
- Bibl: Fleischer, Amer. art jrnl., XIX/3 (1987) pp.4-18
Frebairn → see Freebairn, Robert
Freccia, Giuseppe → see Frecha, José
Frecha, José *(Italian sculptor, cabinetmaker in ESP, act.1575, d.1591)*   **BA**
- Bibl: ▶Ceán Bermúdez, Bellas artes ESP; ▶Diz. artisti ital. in Spagna; Estal, Reales Sitios XXII, 84, p.56; ▶Thieme-Becker
- Flecha, Giuseppe   BA
- Freccia, Giuseppe   BA
- Giuseppe di Luciano Fraccia   BA
Frecher, Daniel *(Polish artist, op. 1664)*   **WC**

Fréchon, Emile *(French photographer, act.1900)*   **BA**
Bibl: ▶Art Index, v.36; Jeffrey, COUNTRY LIFE/ CLXXXI / (18 June 1987), pp 172-173

Frechou, Charles *(French artist, op. 1841-1887)*   **WC**

Freckelton, Sondra *(American painter, b.1936.)*   **BA**
Bibl: Guide exh. artists: N. Amer. ptrs.; ▶WW Amer. Art, 1986

Frecketter, Hubernis [Unidentified] *(Unknown painter)*   **PR**
Bibl: (1813, lot 29, Andrews)
Hubernis Frecketter   **PR**

Freckleton, Harry *(British artist, op. circa 1949-)*   **WI**

Frecknall, Graham *(British architect)*   **AV**
Bibl: Building, 1984 June 22, p.41

Fred Baroccio → see Barocci, Federico
Fred Grayson Sayre → see Sayre, Fred Grayson
Fred W. Wright → see Wright, Fred W.
Fred Zucchero → see Zuccari, Federico
Fred. Baroccio → see Barocci, Federico
Fred. Barrocio → see Barocci, Federico

Freddi, Eva *(Italian architect)*   **AV**
Bibl: Abitare, 1984 Nov., no.229, p.56

Freddie (Frederick Wilhelm Christian Carlsen)   **BA**
(Danish artist, 1909-)   **WC**
(Danish painter, printmaker, b.1909)   **BA**
Bibl: ▶Vollmer, Künst.-Lex. 20. Jhr.; ▶Weilbach, Kunst.leks.
Carlsen, Frederick Wilhelm Christian   **BA**
Carlsen, Frederik Wilhelm Christian   **WC**

Fredeau, Ambroise   **GC WC**
(French artist, 1589-1673)   **WC**
(French painter, 1589-1673)   **GC**
Bibl: ▶Bénézit

Fredeau, Mathieu *(Flemish artist, op.1629-1634)*   **WC**

Fredenburgh, Harold *(American architect. Partner, I. M. Pei & Partners)*   **AV**
Bibl: GA document, no.12, p.91

Fredendall, Bruce *(American builder and house restorer, Solebury, Penn)*   **AV**
Bibl: Colonial homes, 1989 Oct., v.15, no.5, p.69

Fredenthal, David   **BA WC WI**
(American artist, 1914-)   **WC**
(American artist, 1914-1958)   **WI**
(American painter, illustrator, 1914-1958)   **BA**
Bibl: ▶Vollmer, Künst.-Lex. 20. Jhr.; ▶WW Amer. Art, 1958, 1959; ▶WWW Amer. art, p.214

Freder → see Freder, Frederick C.
Freder, Frederick → see Freder, Frederick C.

Freder, Frederick C. *(American painter, 1895-1954)*   **PR**
Bibl: ▶WWW Amer. art
Freder   **PR**
Freder, Frederick   **PR**
Frederick C. Freder   **PR**

Frederic Baroche → see Barocci, Federico
Frederic Baroci → see Barocci, Federico
Frederic Bazille → see Bazille, Frédéric
Frederic Charles Knight → see Knight, Frederic Charles
Frederic de Moucheron → see Moucheron, Frédéric de
Frederic Dubois → see Dubois, Frédéric
Frederic Edwin Church → see Church, Frederic Edwin
Frederic Kerseboom → see Kerseboom, Frederic
Frederic Leighton → see Leighton, Frederic, baron
Frederic Leighton, Lord Leighton → see Leighton, Frederic, baron
Frederic Moucheron → see Moucheron, Frédéric de
Frederic Remington → see Remington, Frederic
Frederic Schopin → see Schopin, Frédéric
Frederic Thomas Somerby → see Somerby, Frederic Thomas

Frederic [Unidentified] *(Unknown painter)*   **PR**
Bibl: (June 7, 1806, lot 19, Christie's)

Frederic Zuccheri → see Zuccari, Federico

Frédéric, Léon   **BA GC**
(Belgian artist, 1856-1940)   **WC**
(Belgian painter, 1856-1940)   **BA GC**
Bibl: ▶Bénézit; ▶Busse, Maler u. Bildhauer 19. Jahr.; ▶Thieme-Becker

Frederic, Leon Henri Marie   **WC**
Frederic, Leon Henri Marie → see Frédéric, Léon
Frederick Andrew Bosley → see Bosley, Frederick Andrew
Frederick Arthur Bridgman → see Bridgman, Frederick Arthur
Frederick Ballard Williams → see Williams, Frederick Ballard
Frederick Baroccio → see Barocci, Federico
Frederick C. Freder → see Freder, Frederick C.
Frederick Carl Frieseke → see Frieseke, Frederick Carl
Frederick Clay Bartlett → see Bartlett, Frederic Clay
Frederick de Moucheron → see Moucheron, Frédéric de

Frederick Dickinson Williams → see Williams, Frederick Dickinson
Frederick E. Cohen → see Cohen, Frederick Elmore
Frederick Ellwood Wallace → see Wallace, Frederick Ellwood
Frederick Etchells → see Etchells, Frederick
Frederick Goodall → see Goodall, Frederick
Frederick James Porter → see Porter, Frederick James
Frederick Judd Waugh → see Waugh, Frederick Judd
Frederick Morgan → see Morgan, Frederick
Frederick Papsdorf → see Papsdorf, Frederick
Frederick Porter Vinton → see Vinton, Frederick Porter
Frederick Richard Lee → see Lee, Frederick Richard
Frederick Sandys → see Sandys, Frederick
Frederick Stuart Church → see Church, Frederick Stuart
Frederick W. Watts → see Watts, Frederick Waters
Frederick Yeates Hurlstone → see Hurlstone, Frederick Yeates

Frederick, Anthony E. *(American architect, Houston, TX)*   **AV**
Bibl: ▶AIA Pro File, 1985

Frederick, Douglas Brent *(Designer)*   **AV**
Bibl: Parametro, 1988 July-Aug., v.19, no.167, p.32

Frederick, Empress of Germany *(German artist, 1840-1901)*   **WC**

Frederick, Helen *(American artist, 20th c.)*   **BA**
Bibl: Houston (TX, USA), UH Blaffer Gallery, New American paperworks (1982)

Frederick, William *(British artist, op. circa 1825-circa 1840)*   **WI**

Fredericke *(Spanish artist, op.1833)*   **WC**

Fredericks, Alfred *(American artist, op.1853-1881)*   **WI**

Frederico Zucchero → see Zuccari, Federico
Frederik Hendrik Kaemmerer → see Kaemmerer, Frederik Hendrik
Frederik Jacobus van Rossum du Chattel → see Chattel, Frederik Jacobus van Rossum du
Frederik Marianus Kruseman → see Kruseman, Frederik Marianus
Frederik van Steenlandt → see Steenlandt, Frederik van
Frederik Vroom → see Vroom, Frederik
Frederiksen, Erik Ellegaard → see Ellegaard Frederiksen; Erik
Frederix → see Frederix, Gillis [Unidentified]

Frederix, Gillis [Unidentified]
(Unknown painter, act. 17th century)   **PR**
Bibl: Schoonsteen inventory 1647
Frederix   PR
Gillis Frederix   PR
Fredi, Bartolo di → see Bartolo di Fredi
Frediani, Vincenzo di Antonio
(Italian painter, act.1481-1505)   **BA**
Bibl: RICERCHE DI STORIA
DELL'ARTE, 26 (1985) 4-17
Fredoli, Berengarius *(Active 1305-1323)*   **JG**
Fredou, Jean Martial → see Frédou, Jean-Martial
Frédou, Jean-Martial   **BA**
(French artist, 1711-1795)   WC
(French painter, 1710-1795)   BA
(French, 1711-1795)   GC
Bibl: ▶Bénézit; ▶Dict. biog. fran.;
▶Thieme-Becker; ▶Witt checklist
Fredou, Jean Martial   **GC WC**
Fredricks, Charles De Forest   **BA JG**
(American photographer, b.1823, act.1880)   **BA**
Bibl: HIST. OF PHOTOG., VIII/1
(Jan-Mar 1984) 43-46; ▶Parry, Photo idx.
Fredsberg, Olof *(Swedish artist, 1728-1795)* **WC**
Fredusser → see Verdussen, Jan Peeter
Free, Abigail *(American interior designer)*   **AV**
Bibl: Architectural digest, 1989
June, v.46, no.6, p.182
Freebain → see Freebairn, Robert
Freebaine → see Freebairn, Robert
Freebairn → see Freebairn, Robert
Freebairn, Robert   **PR WC WI**
(British artist, 1764-1808)   WI
(British artist, 1765-1808)   WC
(British painter, 1764-1808)   PR
Bibl: ▶Thieme-Becker;
▶Waterhouse, Brit. 18c. ptrs.
Fairburn   PR
Frebairn   PR
Freebain   PR
Freebaine   PR
Freebairn   PR
Freebairne   PR
Freebrain   PR
Robert Freebairn   PR
Freebairne → see Freebairn, Robert
Freeborn, Victor   **WC WI**
(British artist, 20th cent.)   WC
(British artist, op.20th c.)   WI
Freebrain → see Freebairn, Robert
Freed, David *(American printmaker, photographer, b.1936)*   **BA**
Bibl: ▶WW Amer. Art, 1976
Freed, Douglass *(American painter, b.1944)*   **BA**
Bibl: ARTS MAG LIV/8 (Apr 1980) 20

Freed, Hermine *(American artist, author, b.1940)*   **BA**
Bibl: ▶WW Amer. Art, 1976
Freed, James Ingo   **AV BA**
(American architect, 1930-)   AV
(American architect, b.1930)   BA
Bibl: ▶Amer. archts. dir., 1970;
▶Avery period. idx.; WW Amer.
Freed, William *(American painter, b.1902)*   **BA**
Bibl: Kuchta, PROVINCETOWN
PAINTERS (1977); Provincetown
(RI, USA), Art Museum, FREED IN
RETROSPECT (1981); ▶WW Amer.
Art
Freedman, Barnett   **BA WC WI**
(British artist, 1901-1958)   WC WI
(British painter, printmaker, 1901-1958)   BA
Bibl: ▶Johnson, Brit. artists;
▶Vollmer, Künst.-Lex. 20. Jhr.;
▶Waters, Brit. artists
Freedman, Deborah S. *(American painter, b.1947)*   **BA**
Bibl: Miller: Lives & works
Freedman, Jill *(American photographer, b.1939)*   **BA**
Bibl: Du, XXXVII/439 (Sep. 1977)
pp.30-83; ▶MoMA libr. cat.
Freedman, Maurice   **WC WI**
(American artist, 1904-)   WC
(American artist, b.1904)   WI
Freeman   **WC WI**
(British artist, op.1853)   WC
(British artist, op.1853-)   WI
Freeman → see Freeman, William R.
Freeman of Cambridge → see Freeman, (of Cambridge)
Freeman, (of Cambridge)   **WI**
(British artist, 18th cent.)   WC
(British artist, op.18th c.)   WI
Freeman of Cambridge   **WC**
Freeman, Dan *(American painter, 20th c.)*   **BA**
Bibl: ARTS MAG LV (June 1981)
16; Guide exh. artists: N. Amer.
ptrs.; ▶MoMA libr. cat.; ▶WW
Amer. Art, 1980
Freeman, Elizabeth, A., Miss → see Folsom, Elizabeth A.
Freeman, Emma Belle *(American photographer, 1880-1928)*   **BA**
Bibl: Palmquist, WITH NATURE'S
CHILDREN: EMMA FREEMAN
(1976)
Freeman, Geoffrey *(American architect)*   **AV**
Freeman, George   **BA WC WI**
(American artist, 1789-1868)   WI
(American painter, 1789-1868)   BA
(British artist, op.1828-1833)   WC
Bibl: ▶Fielding's Amer. ptrs.;
▶Groce, Artists Amer.; ▶Havlice,
Idx. art. bio.; ▶Thieme-Becker;
▶Young, Amer. artists

Freeman, James *(British photographer, act.ca.1850)*   **BA**
Bibl: Photographic jrnl CXIX/4
(Jul-Aug 1979) pp.196-197
Freeman, James   **WC WI**
(American artist, 20th cent.)   WC
(American artist, op.20th c.)   WI
Freeman, James Edward   **BA WC WI**
(American artist, 1808-1884)   WI
(American artist, 1808-1884/5)   WC
(American painter, 1808-1884)   BA
Bibl: ▶Fielding's Amer. ptrs.;
▶Kubler, Art & arch. ESP & PRT
Freeman, John   **AV BA**
(British amateur architect, ca. 1684-1752)   AV
(English architect, ca.1689-1752)   BA
Bibl: ▶Colvin, Brit. archts.
Freeman, John   **WC WI**
(British artist, op.1670-1720)   WC
(British artist, op.circa 1660-)   WI
Freeman, Kathryn *(American painter, b.1956.)*   **BA**
Bibl: Guide exh. artists: N. Amer.
ptrs.; Koslow, ARTS MAG LVII/9
(May 1983) 17; ▶WW Amer. Art,
1989
Freeman, Michael *(American architect, Santa Fe, N.M)*   **AV**
Bibl: Architecture, the AIA
journal, 1989 Oct., v.78, no.10,
p.85
Freeman, Milton H. *(American engineer)*   **AV**
Bibl: Lotus international, 1988,
no.56, p.87
Freeman, Paul *(American sculptor, painter, ca.1929-1980)*   **BA**
Bibl: NY Times obit., 12 Aug
1980
Freeman, Ralph *(British artist, op. 20th c.)*   **WI**
Freeman, Roland L. *(American photographer, b.1936)*   **BA**
Bibl: ▶Intl. dir. exh. artists, 1983
Freeman, S. Pearl *(American architect)*   **AV**
Bibl: Progressive architecture,
1980 Feb., v.61, no.2, p.82
Freeman, Samuel *(Engraver, 1773-1857)*   **WI**
Freeman, Tina *(American photographer, art administrator, 20th c.)*   **BA**
Bibl: WOMEN ARTISTS NEWS VI/1
(May 1980) 5
Freeman, William Henry *(British artist, op.1840-1844)*   **WI**
Freeman, William Philip Barnes
(British artist, 1813-1897)   **WC WI**
Freeman, William R. *(American painter, ca.1820-ca.1906)*   **PR**
Bibl: ▶WWW Amer. art
Freeman   PR
William R. Freeman   PR

Freeman-Smith, Ralph *(British interior decorator, d.1940)*   **BA**
  Bibl: Gilbert, FURNITURE AT TEMPLE NEWSAM HOUSE AND LOTHERTON HALL, v. 2, p.375; Wells-Cole, LEEDS ARTS CALENDAR, CI (1987), p. 24-30

Freer, Frederick Warren *(American artist, 1849-1908)*   **WI**

Freer, H. Branston   **WI**
  (British artist, op.1870-1900)   WC WI

  Freer, H.B.   **WC**
Freer, H.B. → see Freer, H. Branston

Freer, Mary *(British artist, op.1985-)*   **WI**
Freer, Mary Ellen, Mrs → see Edwards, Mary Ellen

Freer, Roy *(British artist, op.20th c.)*   **WI**
Freese → see Freese, N.
Freese, Daniel → see Frese, Daniel

Freese, N.   **WC WI**
  (American artist, op.1794-1814)   WI
  (American artist, op.1798)   WC
  (British painter, act. 1794-1814)   PR
  Bibl: ▶Graves Royal Acad. contribs.; ▶Thieme-Becker; ▶Waterhouse, Brit. 18c. ptrs.

  Freese   PR
  Freese, Nathaniel   **PR**
  Friese   PR
  Nathaniel Freese   PR
Freese, Nathaniel → see Freese, N.
Freester, Hans → see Ferster, Hans
Freeth, Herbert Andrew → see Freeth, Hubert Andrew

Freeth, Hubert Andrew   **WI**
  (British artist, 1912-)   WC
  (British artist, b.1912)   WI
  Freeth, Herbert Andrew   **WC**

Freeth, Peter *(British artist, op.20th c.)*   **WI**

Freeth, W.   **WC WI**
  (British artist, 18th cent.)   WC
  (British artist, op.18th c.)   WI

Freeto, David Harmon *(Architect)*   **AV**
  Bibl: Interiors, 1984 Oct., v.144, no.3, p.96

Freezor, George Augustus *(British artist, op.1861-1879)*   **WI**

Fregevize, Fraigevise or Fregevise, Frederic *(Swiss artist, 1770-1849)*   **WC**

Fregna, Roberto *(Italian architect)*   **AV**

Fregoli, Matteo *(Italian artist, 16th cent.)*   **WC**

Freher, Paul *(German artist, op. 1688)*   **WC**

Frei, C. *(Swiss architect, Zurich)*   **AV**
  Bibl: Architektur + Wettbewerbe, 1986 Dec., no.128, p.37
Frei, Ignatz Alois → see Frey, Ignatz Alois

Frei, Peter *(Swiss architect, Suhr)*   **AV**
  Bibl: ▶Schweiz. Ingen. u. Archit., 1984-1985

Frei, Robert *(Swiss architect, Geneva)*   **AV**
  Bibl: ▶Schweiz. Ingen. u. Archit., 1984-1985

Frei, Roland *(Swiss architect)*   **AV**
  Bibl: ▶Schweiz. Ingen. u. Archit., 1984-1985

Frei, Sisto *(German sculptor in ITA, act.1500-1515)*   **BA**
  Bibl: Bortolotti, G., ARTE VENETA, XLA (1987), p.176-185

Frei, Urs *(Swiss artist in AUT, b.1958)*   **BA**
  Bibl: ▶Art Index, v.36; Schenker, Flash art, CXXVIV (1987)

Freiberg, Jens *(French architect)*   **AV**
  Bibl: Architecture d'aujourd'hui, 1984 Sept., no.234, p.56

Freiberg, Maria von *(German artist, 18th cent.)*   **WC**

Freidhoff, Johann Joseph *(German printmaker, 1768-1818)*   **GC**
  Bibl: ▶Thieme-Becker
Freier, Werner Barth → see Barth, Werner

Freifeld, Eric *(Canadian artist, 20th cent.)*   **WC**

Freijmuth, Alphons *(Dutch painter, printmaker, b.1940)*   **BA**
  Bibl: Amsterdam (NLD), Stedelijk Museum, ALPHOS FREIJMUTH (1977)

Freilicher, Jane   **BA WC WI**
  (American artist, 1924-)   WC
  (American artist, b.1924)   WI
  (American painter, printmaker, b.1924)   BA
  Bibl: ▶WW Amer. Art, 1989

Freiman, Lillian   **BA WC**
  (Canadian artist, 1908-)   WC
  (Canadian painter, b.1908)   BA
  Bibl: ▶Bénézit; ▶MacDonald, Can. artists; ▶Vollmer, Künst.-Lex. 20. Jhr.

Freising, Gerhard *(German architect, Trier)*   **AV**
  Bibl: Deutsches Architektenblatt, 1985 Apr.1, v.17, no.4, p.428

Freisinger, Lienhart *(German, act. 1498-99)*   **GC**
  Bibl: ▶Thieme-Becker

Freitag, Fritz *(German painter, b.1915)*   **BA**
  Bibl: Schulze, FRITZ FREITAG (1983); ▶Vollmer, Künst.-Lex. 20. Jhr.

Freitag, Johann Isaak *(Austrian sculptor, 1682-1734)*   **BA**
  Bibl: ▶Bénézit; ▶Thieme-Becker; ZEITSCH. FUR SCHW. ARCHAEOLOGIE U. KUNSTGES. XXXII/1 (1975) 78

  Freytag, Johann   BA

Freitas, Ivan *(Brazilian painter, sculptor, b.1932)*   **BA**
  Bibl: ▶Pontual, Artes plásticas Brasil; Toronto (Ont, CAN), Art Gal. of Ont., 10 Brazilian artists (1975)

Freitas, Lima de *(Portuguese artist, 20th cent.)*   **WC**

Freixas, Vivo *(Spanish artist, 20th cent.)*   **WC**

Freixes, Dani *(Spanish architect, Barcelona)*   **AV**
  Bibl: El croquis, 1988 Aug.-Sept., v.7, no.35, p.78
Frelaut → see Frélaut, Jean

Frélaut, Jacques *(Swiss printer, 20th c.)*   **BA**
  Bibl: Geneva (CHE), Mus. d'art et d'hist., MARC CHAGALL (1980)

Frélaut, Jean   **BA PR WC**
  (French artist, 1879-1954)   WC
  (French painter, 1879-1954)   PR
  (French painter, printmaker, 1879-1954)   BA
  Bibl: ▶Bénézit; ▶RILA/BHA; ▶Vollmer, Künst.-Lex. 20. Jhr.

  Frelaut   PR
  Jean Frelaut   PR

Freling, B. *(French architect)*   **AV**
  Bibl: Techniques et architecture, 1984 June-July, no.354, p.62

Frelinghuysen, S.   **WI**
  (American artist, 1912-)   WC
  (American artist, b.1912)   WI

Frelinghuysen, Suzy   **WC**
Frelinghuysen, Suzy → see Frelinghuysen, S.

Fremantle, Chloe *(British artist, op. 20th c.)*   **WI**

Frémery, Etienne *(French silversmith, master beg. 18th century)*   **GC**
  Bibl: ▶Mabille, Orfèv. fran.

Fremez, Jose Gomez Fresquet *(South American artist, 20th cent.)*   **WC**

Frémiet, Emmanuel   **BA GC WC**
  (French artist, 1824-1910)   WC
  (French sculptor, 1824-1910)   BA GC
  Bibl: ▶Bénézit; ▶Fogg Mus. Libr. cat.; ▶RILA/BHA; ▶Thieme-Becker

Frémin, René   **BA GC WC**
  (French artist, 1672-1744)   WC
  (French sculptor, 1672-1744)   BA GC
  Bibl: ▶Bénézit; ▶RILA/BHA; ▶Thieme-Becker
Fréminel, Martin → see Fréminet, Martin

Freminet, Louis de   **GC WC**
  (French artist, -c.1651)   WC
  (French, d. ca.1651)   GC
  Bibl: ▶Witt checklist

Fréminet, Martin   **AV BA GC PR WC**
    (French architect, 1567-1619) AV
    (French artist, 1567-1619) WC
    (French painter, 1567-1619) PR
    (French painter, printmaker,
    1567-1619) BA
    (French, 1567-1619) GC
      Bibl: ▶Bénézit; ▶Dict. biog. fran.;
      ▶Thieme-Becker; ▶Witt checklist
    Fréminel, Martin BA
    Fremynet PR
    Martin Freminet PR
Fremund, Richard *(Czech artist,*
    1928-) **WC**
Frémy, Edouard Pierre *(French*
    sculptor, 1829-1888) **GC**
      Bibl: ▶Thieme-Becker
Fremy, Jacques Noel Marie *(French*
    artist, 1782-1867)* **WC**
Fremynet → see Fréminet, Martin
French Monogrammist LAM → see
    Monogrammist L.A.M.
French, Albert E. **AV**
French, Annie **WC WI**
    (British artist, 1872-1965) WI
    (British artist, op.c.1900-1915) WC
    Rhead, George Wooliscroft, Mrs.
    (Annie) WI
French, Daniel Chester *(American*
    sculptor, 1850-1931) **AV BA GC**
      Bibl: ▶Fielding's Amer. ptrs.; ▶Libr.
      of Congr. Name Auth. File;
      ▶RILA/BHA
French, Dick *(British artist, b.1942)* **WI**
French, Frank **WC WI**
    (American artist, 1850-1933) WC WI
    (Engraver, 1850-1933) WI
French, Jared *(American painter,*
    sculptor, b.1905) **BA**
      Bibl: ▶WW Amer. Art, 1978
French, John *(British photographer,*
    1907-1966) **BA**
      Bibl: ▶Hall-Duncan, Fashion
      photog., p.226; ▶London Times
      obit.
French, Jotham A. *(American, 1834-*
    1898) **JG**
French, Leonard *(Australian artist,*
    1928-) **WC**
French, Margaret **BA VO**
    (American photographer, act|
    1937-ca.1950) VO
    (American, 20th c.) BA
      Bibl: Arts Mag. LIII/4 (Dec 1978),
      118-119
    Hoening, Margaret VO
French, Nathanael → see French,
    Nathaniel
French, Nathaniel **WI**
    (British artist, op.1747) WC
    (British artist, op.1747-) WI
French, Nathanael **WC**
French, Percy *(British artist, 1854-*
    1920) **WI**
French, Richard *(British artist, op.*
    18th c.) **WI**

French, Stephen *(British designer)* **AV**
      Bibl: Architects' journal, 1989
      May 10, v.189, no.19, p.82
French, William *(American*
    landscape architect, 19th cent) **AV**
      Bibl: 1987 Sept.-Oct., v.77, no.5,
      p.88
French, William **WC WI**
    (British artist, c.1815-1898) WC
    (British artist, circa 1815-1898) WI
Frénet, Jean Baptiste *(French*
    painter, sculptor, printmaker,
    1814-1889) **BA**
      Bibl: ▶Bénézit; ▶Thieme-Becker
Frenkel, J. *(Active Hamburg,*
    Germany 1882) **JG**
Frenkel, S. *(Active Hamburg,*
    Germany 1882) **JG**
Frenkel, Vera *(Canadian artist,*
    b.1938) **BA**
      Bibl: ▶Art Index, Jan. 1978;
      ▶Artists Canada; Vancouver (BC,
      USA), Art Gallery, LIES & TRUTHS
      (1978)
Frenken, Antonius Wilhelmus
    Maria → see Frenken, Ton
Frenken, Jaak → see Frenken, Jacques
    Antoon Charles
Frenken, Jacques Antoon Charles
    (Dutch painter, sculptor, b.1929) **BA**
      Bibl: ▶Bénézit; ▶Scheen, Ned.
      beeldende kunst.
    Frenken, Jaak BA
Frenken, Ton *(Dutch painter,*
    printmaker, b.1930) **BA**
      Bibl: Nijmegen (NLD), Nijmegen
      Mus. Commanderie van S. Jun.,
      TON FRENKEN..., 1986; ▶Scheen,
      Ned. beeldende kunst.
    Frenken, Antonius Wilhelmus
    Maria BA
Frenkiel, Stanislaw *(Polish artist,*
    1918-) **WC**
Frennesson, Britt *(British artist, op.*
    20th c.) **WI**
Frentiu, Sever *(Rumanian artist,*
    20th cent.) **WC**
Frenzel, Christa *(East German*
    architect, Berlin) **AV**
      Bibl: Architektur der DDR, 1985
      Apr., v.34, no.4, p.236
Frenzel, Friedrich August *(German,*
    1814-1898?) **GC**
      Bibl: ▶Thieme-Becker
Frenzel, Oskar *(German artist, 1855-*
    1915) **WC**
Frenzeny, Paul **WC WI**
    (American artist, 1840-1902) WI
    (American artist, op.c.1898) WC
Frequin, A. *(Dutch photographer)* **GC**
      Bibl: Getty Photo Study Coll.;
      ▶Libr. of Congr. Name Auth. File
    A. Frequin (The Hague) GC
Frere → see Frère, Charles Théodore
Frere → see Frère, Pierre Edouard
Frere Andre → see Andre, Jean

Frère, Charles Théodore **BA PR WC**
    (French artist, 1814-1888) WC
    (French painter, 1814-1888) BA PR
    (French, 1814-1888) GC
      Bibl: ▶Bénézit; ▶Encyc. world art;
      Getty Photo Study Coll. (Ptgs.);
      ▶Thieme-Becker; ▶Witt checklist
    Frere PR
    Frere, Charles-Theodore GC
Frère, Théodore **BA GC PR**
    Theodore Frere PR
Frere, Charles-Theodore → see Frère,
    Charles Théodore
Frere, E.J. *(British artist, op.circa*
    1860-circa 1870) **WI**
Frère, Edouard → see Frère, Pierre
    Edouard
Frere, P. Joseph *(Swedish(?) artist,*
    op.1789) **WC**
Frère, Pierre Edouard **BA GC PR WC**
    (French artist, 1819-1886) WC
    (French painter, 1819-1886) BA PR
    (French, 1819-1886) GC
      Bibl: ▶Havlice, Idx. art. bio.;
      ▶Thieme-Becker; ▶Witt checklist
    Edouard Frere PR
    Frere PR
Frère, Edouard **PR**
    Frere, Pierre-Edouard PR
Frere, Pierre-Edouard → see Frère,
    Pierre Edouard
Frère, Théodore → see Frère, Charles
    Théodore
Freret, William A. → see Freret,
    William Alfred
Freret, William Alfred **BA**
    (1833-after 1887; Architect,
    United States of America) FA
    (American architect, 1833-1911) BA
      Bibl: ▶Avery period. idx.; ▶Lowry,
      Building natl. image; ▶Withey,
      Amer. archts.; Wodehouse, S.E.
      COLLEGE ART CONFERENCE REV.,
      XI (1987), p. 135-143
Freret, William A. **FA**
Frerichs, William Charles Anthony **BA**
    (American artist, 1829-1905) WC WI
    (American painter, 1829-1905) BA
      Bibl: ▶Fielding's Amer. ptrs.;
      ▶Groce, Artists Amer.
Frerichs, William Charles
Antony **WC WI**
Frerichs, William Charles
    Antony → see Frerichs, William
    Charles Anthony
Freron [Unidentified] *(Unknown*
    painter) **PR**
      Bibl: (April 25, 1804, lot 44,
      Langdon)
Freschel, Daniel → see Fröschl, Daniel
Freschi, Bruno *(Canadian architect,*
    Vancouver) **AV**
      Bibl: ▶Canad. arch. dir., 1985

Frese, Daniel *(German painter, cartographer, 1540-1611)*   **BA**
    Bibl: ▶Neue deutsche Biog.; ▶Thieme-Becker; ▶Witt checklist
Freese, Daniel   BA
Friese Dietmarsiensis   BA
Friesze, Daniel   BA
Freset, Georges Eugene *(French artist, 1894-)*   **WC**
Freshfield [Unidentified] *(Unknown painter)*   **PR**
    Bibl: (July 4, 1815, lots 137[a] or 137[b], Christie's)
Freshwater, Sally *(British artist, b.1958)*   **WI**
Fresnaye→see La Fresnaye, Roger de
Fresnaye, de la Roger→see La Fresnaye, Roger de
Fresnaye, Roger de la→see La Fresnaye, Roger de
Fresnes [Unidentified] *(Unknown painter)*   **PR**
    Bibl: (Bonne de Brassac de Buisse inventory dated 1794)
Fresnoy, Charles Alphonse du→see Du Fresnoy, Charles Alphonse
Frets, Barbara *(American painter, 20th c.)*   **BA**
    Bibl: Omaha (NE, USA), Joslyn AM, Regionalism (1979)
Fretton, Tony *(British interior designer)*   **AV**
    Bibl: Blueprint (London), 1989 May, no.57, p.50
Freud, Lucian   **BA WI**
    (British artist, 1922-)   WC
    (British artist, b.1922)   WI
    (British painter, b.1922)   BA
    Bibl: ▶Bénézit; ▶Phaidon 20c. art
Freud, Lucien   **WC**
Freud, Lucien→see Freud, Lucian
Freudeberg or Freudenberger, Sigmund→see Freudenberger, Sigmund
Freudemann, Victor *(German artist, 1857-c.1919)*   **WC**
Freudenberg, Ernst *(Dutch businessman, printmaker, 1901-1960)*   **BA**
    Bibl: LOS ANGELES INST. OF CONT. ART JOURNAL 12 (Oct-Nov 1976) 17
Freudenberg, Jacobus *(Dutch painter, 1818-1873)*   **GC**
    Bibl: ▶Scheen, Ned. beeldende kunst.
Freudenberger, Sigmund   **GC**
    (Swiss artist, 1745-1801)   WC
    (Swiss, 1745-1801)   GC
    Bibl: ▶Thieme-Becker
Freudeberg or Freudenberger, Sigmund   **WC**

Freudenreich, Gabriel de *(Swiss architect, Geneva)*   **AV**
    Bibl: ▶Schweiz. Ingen. u. Archit., 1984-1985
De Freudenreich, Gabriel   AV
Freudenreich, Marek *(Polish artist, 20th cent.)*   **WC**
Freudenthal, Dan *(German painter, b.1945)*   **BA**
    Bibl: ▶Art Index; Neeske, KUNSTWERK, XXXVIII(SEP 1985), 50-51
Freudweiler, Heinrich   **BA WC**
    (Swiss artist, 1755-1795)   WC
    (Swiss painter, printmaker, 1755-1795)   BA
    Bibl: ▶Thieme-Becker
Freund, B. *(German)*   **GC**
    Bibl: Gernsheim, Corpus Photog. of Drawings, 1735
Freund, Bernhard   **AV BA**
    (1939-)   AV
    (German architect, b.1939)   BA
    Bibl: KUNSTWERK XXXII/2-3 (Apr-June 1979) 107-108
Freund, Christoph (Johann Christoph) *(German artist, op.c. 1720-1750)*   **WC**
Freund, Georg Christian *(Danish sculptor, 1821-1900)*   **BA**
    Bibl: ▶Thieme-Becker; ▶Weilbach, Kunst.leks.
Freund, Gisèle *(German photographer, b.1912)*   **BA**
    Bibl: CONNAISSANCE DES ARTS 293 (July 1976) 54; ▶MoMA libr. cat.
Freund, Harry Louis *(American painter, illustrator, b.1905)*   **BA**
    Bibl: ▶WW Amer. Art, 1976
Freund, Hermann Ernst *(Danish sculptor, 1786-1840)*   **BA**
    Bibl: ▶Thieme-Becker; ▶Weilbach, Kunst.leks.
Freund, Karl→see Ferenczy, Károly
Freundlich, Otto   **BA GC WC**
    (German artist, 1878-1943)   WC
    (German painter, 1878-1943)   GC
    (German painter, sculptor, 1878-1943)   BA
    Bibl: ▶Bénézit; ▶Encyc. world art
Freundova, Zdena *(Architect, Czechoslovakia, 1931-)*   **AV**
    Bibl: Architektur, Innenarchitektur, Technischer Ausbau, 1985 Jan.-Feb., v.93, no.1, p.10
Frevisani→see Trevisani, Francesco
Frew, Alexander, Mrs., (Bessie)→see MacNicol, Bessie
Frey Carlos→see Carlos, Frey
Frey or Freij, Anna de *(Dutch artist, c.1775-1808)*   **WC**
Frey the Elder, Johan Jacob (Giacomo) *(Swiss artist, 1681-1752)*   **WC**

Frey, Albert *(American architect, 1904?-)*   **AV**
    Bibl: Progressive architecture, 1987 Jan., v.68, no.1, p.31
Frey, Anna de *(Dutch painter, d.1808)*   **GC**
    Bibl: ▶Thieme-Becker
Frey, Gilbert *(Swiss architect)*   **AV**
    Bibl: Archithese, 1985 May, v.15, no.3, p.118
Frey, Hans *(German artist, -1523)*   **WC**
Frey, Ignatz Alois *(German painter, 1752/54-1835)*   **GC**
    Bibl: ▶Thieme-Becker
Frei, Ignatz Alois   GC
Frey, Johann Jakob   **GC WC**
    (Swiss artist, 1813-1865)   WC
    (Swiss, 1813-1865)   GC
    Bibl: ▶Witt checklist
Frey, Johann Wilhelm *(German artist, 1830-)*   **WC**
Frey, Johannes Pieter de *(Dutch painter and printmaker, 1770-1834)*   **GC**
    Bibl: ▶Scheen, Ned. beeldende kunst.
Frey, Konrad *(Austrian architect, Graz)*   **AV**
    Bibl: Architectural review, 1988 Dec., p.84
Frey, Viola *(American sculptor, painter, b.1933)*   **BA**
    Bibl: ▶WW Amer. Art
Frey, Werner *(Swiss architect, Zurich)*   **AV**
    Bibl: ▶Schweiz. Ingen. u. Archit., 1984-1985
Frey, Wilhelm *(German artist, 1826-1911)*   **WC**
Frey, Wilhelm *(German artist, c.1816-1841)*   **WC**
Frey-Moock, Adolf *(German artist, 20th cent.)*   **WC**
Frey-Surbek, Marguerite *(Swiss artist, 1886-)*   **WC**
Freyberg, Conrad *(German artist, 1842-)*   **WC**
Freyberg, Electrina von *(German artist, 1797-1847)*   **WC**
Freyberger, Johann *(German artist, 1571-1631)*   **WC**
Freyburg, Frank P.→see Freyburg, Frank Proschwitzry
Freyburg, Frank Proschwitzry   **WI**
    (British artist, 1862-op.1903)   WI
    (British artist, op.c. 1896)   WC
Freyburg, Frank P.   **WC**
Freyder, Michael *(French silversmith, master 1606)*   **GC**
    Bibl: ▶Mabille, Orfèv. fran.
Freyer, Achim *(East German scenographer, painter in DEU, b.1934)*   **BA**
    Bibl: Freyer, A., in DAIDALOS 14 (15 Dec 1984) 104

Freyhoff, Eduard (German artist,
c.1810-1842/4)   **WC**
Freyhold, Carl von (German artist,
1878-1944)   **WC**
Freymark, Dieter (West German
architect)   **AV**
Freymund, Jörg   **AV BA**
 (German sculptor, act.1633)   BA
 (Swiss sculptor, Lausanne, 17th
 cent)   AV
   Bibl: Fontannaz, UNSERE
   KUNSTDENKMALER, XXXVIII/4
   (1987), p. 533-539; Unsere
   Kunstdenkmäler, 1987, v.38,
   no.4, p.533
Freyse, Albert (German artist, op.
1643-m.1652)   **WC**
Freyssinet, Eugène   **AV BA**
 (French architect, 1879-1962)   AV
 (French engineer, 1879-1962)   BA
   Bibl: ▶Contemp. archts.; ▶Dict.
   biog. fran.; ▶Macmillan encyc.
   archts.; ▶Portoghesi, Diz. arch. e
   urbanistica
Freystein, Johanna Marianne
 (German, 1760-1807)   **GC**
   Bibl: ▶Thieme-Becker
Freytag, Johann → see Freitag, Johann
Isaak
Freytag, Johann Konrad, I (Swiss
artist, 1770-1837)   **WC**
Freytag, Otto   **GC WC**
 (German artist, 20th cent.)   WC
 (German draughtsman, b.1888)   GC
   Bibl: Getty Photo Study Coll.;
   ▶Schweers, Gemälde deut.
   Museen; ▶Witt checklist
Freytag-Loringhoaven, Elsa von,
baroness (German artist, poet,
model in USA, 1874-1927)   **BA**
   Bibl: DADA/SURREALISM, 14
   (1985) 81-101; ▶Petteys, Women
   artists
Freytom, Frederik van → see Frytom,
Frederik van
Frezza, Giovanni Girolamo (Italian
artist, 1659-p.1741)   **WC**
Friant → see Friant, Emile
Friant, Emile   **BA GC PR WC**
 (French artist, 1863-1932)   WC
 (French painter and engraver,
 1863-1932)   GC
 (French painter, 1863-1932)   PR
 (French painter, printmaker,
 sculptor, 1863-1932)   BA
   Bibl: ▶Bénézit; ▶Larousse grande
   encyc.; ▶Thieme-Becker; ▶Vollmer,
   Künst.-Lex. 20. Jhr.
 Emile Friant   PR
 Friant   PR
Friar Andrés de León → see León, Friar
Andrés de
Friar Julian de la Fuente del Saz → see
Fuente del Saz, Friar Julian de la

Frias y Escalante, Juan Antonio
de → see Escalante, Juan Antonio
de Frias y
Friberg, Arnold   **WC WI**
 (American artist, 19th cent.)   WC
 (American artist, b.1913)   WI
Friboulet, Jef (French artist, 20th
cent.)   **WC**
Frich, Joachim Christian
Geelmuyden Gyldenkrantz
 (Norwegian artist, 1810-1858)   **WC**
Frick, A.H. (American, active
Hudson, Wisconsin ca. 1890)   **JG**
Frick, Johann Friedrich (German
printmaker, 1774-1850)   **BA GC**
   Bibl: ▶Bénézit; ▶Busse, Maler u.
   Bildhauer 19. Jahr.; Kilarski, ZEIT.
   D. DEUT. VEREINS F.
   KUNSTWISSEN. XXXV/1-4 (1981)
   95-120; ▶Thieme-Becker
Frick, Oliver, Mrs., (Winifred Marie
Louise) → see Austen, Winifred
Marie Louise
Frick, Peter (American cabinetmaker,
1743-1822)   **BA**
   Bibl: Antiques CVII/5 (May 1975),
   969
Fricke, August (German artist,
1875-)   **WC**
Fricx, Bernard (Flemish artist, 1754-
1814)   **WC**
Fridel, Christof   **GC**
 (German artist, op.1600)   WC
 (German draughtsman, act. ca.
 1600)   GC
   Bibl: ▶Thieme-Becker; ▶Witt
   checklist
Friedel, Christof   **GC WC**
Fridell, Axel   **BA WC**
 (Swedish artist, 1894-1935)   WC
 (Swedish painter, printmaker,
 1894-1935)   BA
   Bibl: ▶Svenskt konst.-lex.;
   ▶Vollmer, Künst.-Lex. 20. Jhr.
 Fridell, John Axel   BA
Fridell, John Axel → see Fridell, Axel
Fridfinnsson, Hreinn (Icelandic
photographer, painter, sculptor,
b.1943)   **BA**
   Bibl: ▶Intl. dir. arts; New York
   (NY, USA), Guggenheim Mus.,
   Sleeping beauty (1982)
Fridlander, Ernest David
Emmanuel (British painter, 1870-
1960)   **BA**
   Bibl: London, Leighton House Art
   Gallery and Museum, A
   retrospective exhibition of the
   work of Ernest David ...(1962)
Fridrich or Friedrich, Jacob
Andreas → see Fridrich, Jacob
Andreas I

Fridrich, Jacob Andreas I   **GC**
 (German artist, 1684-1751)   WC
 (German draughtsman, 1684-
 1751)   GC
   Bibl: ▶Thieme-Becker
Fridrich or Friedrich, Jacob
Andreas   **WC**
 Friedrich, Jacob Andreas I   GC
Fridsberg, O. (Swedish artist, 19th
cent.)   **WC**
Frie, Peter (British artist, op.1986-) **WI**
Friebe, Wolfgang (German
architect)   **AV**
   Bibl: Deutsche Bauzeitschrift,
   1985 May, v.33, no.5, p.566
Friebert, Joseph (American painter,
b.1908)   **BA**
   Bibl: Milwaukee (WI, USA), Univ.
   of Wisc., Fine Arts Gallery,
   GEORGE GOUNDI...JOSEPH
   FRIEBERT... (1977); ▶Natl. Faculty
   Dir.
Fried, Elaine Maria Catherine,
Miss → see de Kooning, Elaine
Fried, Heinrich Jakob (German
artist, 1802-1870)   **WC**
Fried, Howard Lee (American
sculptor, b.1946)   **BA**
   Bibl: ▶WW Amer. Art, 1976
Fried, Nancy (American artist,
b.1945)   **BA**
   Bibl: Claremont (CA, USA),
   Galleries of the Claremont
   Colleges, Contemp. triptychs
   (1982)
Fried, Pal (Hungarian artist, 1893-) **WC**
Friedberg, Alan B. (American real
estate developer, New York City)   **AV**
   Bibl: Better buildings, 1989 Oct.,
   v.8, no.10, p.28
Friedberg, M. Paul (American
landscape architect, 1931-)   **AV**
   Bibl: ▶Contemp. archts.
 Friedberg, Paul   AV
Friedberg, Paul → see Friedberg, M.
Paul
Friedberg, Richard (American
sculptor, b.1943)   **BA**
   Bibl: ARTS MAG. LIII/8 (Apr 1972)
   2; New Haven (CT, USA), Yale Art
   Gallery, 20 artists (1981)
Friedeberg, Pedro (American
painter, sculptor, b.1937)   **BA**
   Bibl: ▶MoMA libr. cat.; ▶WW
   Amer. Art
Friedeberg, Peter (German
architect, Mainz)   **AV**
   Bibl: Deutsche Bauzeitschrift,
   1984 Aug., v.32, p.1003
Friedel, Christof → see Fridel, Christof
Friedensohn, Elias   **BA WC WI**
 (American artist, 1924-)   WC
 (American artist, b.1924)   WI
 (American painter, sculptor,
 b.1924)   BA
   Bibl: ▶WW Amer. Art

Friedenson, Arthur A.   **WC WI**
   (British artist, 1872-)   WC
   (British artist, 1872-1955)   WI
Friedensreich Hundertwassser → see
   Hundertwasser, Friedensreich
   (Friedrich Stowasser)
Friedkli, Markus *(Swiss architect,*
   Schaffhausen and Zurich)   **AV**
   Bibl: Schweizer Baumarkt, 1989
   May 12, no.8, p.l
Friedlaender → see Friedlaender,
   Johnny
Friedlaender, Alfred *(Austrian*
   artist, 1860-)   **WC**
Friedlaender, Bilgé *(American*
   painter, 20th c.)   **BA**
   Bibl: ▶Collins, Women artists
   Amer.; ▶Havlice, ldx. art. bio.;
   Houston (TX, USA), UH Blaffer
   Gallery, New American
   paperworks (1982); ▶NY art yrbk.
Friedlaender, Johnny   **BA**
   (French artist, 1912-)   WC
   (German artist, 1912-)   WC
   (German printmaker in FRA,
   b.1912)   BA
   Bibl: ▶Bénézit; ▶Phaidon 20c. art
Friedlaender   **WC**
Friedlander, Johnny   **WC**
Friedlaender, Stephen *(American*
   architect, Cambridge, Mass)   **AV**
   Bibl: ▶AIA Pro File, 1987-88
Friedland, Jeffrey   **WC WI**
   (American artist, 20th cent.)   WC
   (American artist, b.1942)   WI
Friedlander, August Maurice
   (American artist, 1856-1897)   **WI**
Friedlander, Camilla → see Friedländer,
   Camilla von Malheim
Friedländer, Camilla von Malheim   **GC**
   (Austrian painter, b.1856)   GC
   (German artist, 1856-)   WC
   Bibl: ▶Bénézit
Friedlander, Camilla   **WC**
Friedlander, Dan *(American*
   architect)   **AV**
Friedlander, Friedrich, Ritter von
   Malheim *(German artist, 1825-*
   1901)   **WC**
Friedlander, Hedwig *(Austrian*
   artist, 1863-)   **WC**
Friedlander, Johnny → see
   Friedlaender, Johnny
Friedlander, Lee *(American artist,*
   b.1890)   **WI**
Friedlander, Lee Norman *(American*
   photographer, b.1934)   **BA**
   Bibl: Beaton, Magic image; ▶Natl.
   union cat., 1968-1972; ▶Parry,
   Photo idx.; Thornton, Master of
   the camera

Friedlander, Leo *(American*
   sculptor, 1890-1966)   **BA GC**
   Bibl: ▶Bénézit; ▶Cummings,
   Contemp. Amer. artists, 1971;
   ▶MoMA libr. cat.; NY Times obit.;
   ▶RILA/BHA; ▶Smith, Idx. Amer.
   artists; ▶Vollmer, Künst.-Lex. 20.
   Jhr.
Friedländer, Marguerite → see
   Wildenhain, Marguerite
Friedlander, Max *(German artist,*
   1867-1958)   **WC**
Friedley, Duer *(American artist, op.*
   20th c.)   **WI**
Friedman, Arnold → see Friedman,
   Arnold Aaron
Friedman, Arnold Aaron   **BA PR WI**
   (American artist, 1879-1946)   WI
   (American painter, 1874-1946)   PR
   (American painter, printmaker,
   1874-1946)   BA
   Bibl: ARTS MAG LIV/10 (June
   1980) 6; ▶MoMA libr. cat.; NY
   Times obit., 30 Dec 1946, p.22:2;
   ▶RILA/BHA; ▶Schwab, Life &
   death; ▶Vollmer, Künst.-Lex. 20.
   Jhr.; ▶WW Amer. Art, 1947
   Arnold Aaron Friedman   PR
   Friedman, Arnold   PR
Friedman, Arthur   **WC WI**
   (British artist, op.c.1912-1940)   WC
   (British artist, op.circa 1912-)   WI
Friedman, Barbara *(American*
   painter, 20th c.)   **BA**
   Bibl: Cohrs, T., in ARTS MAG
   LX/10 (June 1986) 106; ▶Intl. dir.
   exh. artists, 1983
Friedman, Benno *(American*
   photographer, b.1945)   **BA**
   Bibl: ▶WW Amer. Art, 1989
Friedman, Dan   **AV BA**
   (American graphic designer,
   b.1945)   BA
   (American graphic designer,
   interior designer)   AV
   Bibl: Art News, LXXX/2 (Feb.
   1981) pp.80-86; Progressive
   architecture, 1982 Sept., v.63,
   no.9
Friedman, Howard A. *(American*
   architect)   **AV**
Friedman, James G. *(American*
   photographer, b.1950)   **BA**
   Bibl: ▶Gernsheim, Hist. photog.;
   Photog. in America
Friedman, Jonathan *(Professor,*
   University of Kentucky; principal
   of Amatuzzo Roccanova and
   Friedman)   **AV**
   Bibl: Design action, 1(2), 1982,
   p.10
Friedman, Ken *(American sculptor,*
   art historian, 20th c.)   **BA**
   Bibl: telephonic communication
   from Hood Museum; ▶WW Amer.
   Art

Friedman, Martin *(American*
   painter, 1896-1980)   **BA PR**
   Bibl: ▶MoMA libr. cat.; NY Times
   obit., 16 Sep 1980; ▶RILA/BHA;
   ▶Vollmer, Künst.-Lex. 20. Jhr.
   Martin Friedman   PR
Friedman, Roberta *(American artist,*
   20th c.)   **BA**
   Bibl: Afterimage, XV/2 (Sep.
   1987) pp.10-11; ▶Art Index, Nov.
   1987-Dec. 1988
Friedman, Rodney F. *(American*
   architect, 1935-)   **AV**
Friedman, Stanley *(American*
   interior designer)   **AV**
   Bibl: Maison Française, 1985 Feb.,
   no.384, p.132
Friedman, Warner *(American*
   painter, b.1934)   **BA**
   Bibl: Pittsfield (MA, USA), 1981
   INVITATIONAL
Friedman, Yona *(French architect,*
   1923-)   **AV**
   Bibl: ▶Contemp. archts.
Friedmann *(French artist, 20th*
   cent.)   **WC**
Friedmann, John *(American urban*
   planner, author and prof. at UCLA)   **AV**
   Bibl: ▶Libr. of Congr. Name Auth.
   File
Friedmann, Robert *(West German*
   architect, 1888-1940)   **AV**
   Bibl: Bauwelt, 1988 Mar. 11,
   v.79, no.11, p.402
Friedmann, Walter *(West German*
   architect, Mannheim; practices
   with Hans Richter)   **AV**
   Bibl: ▶Bund Deut. Arch. Hdbch.,
   1987
Friedrich → see Friedrich, Adolf
Friedrich August von Kaulbach → see
   Kaulbach, Friedrich August von
Friedrich Eibner → see Eibner, Friedrich
Friedrich Heimerdinger → see
   Heimerdinger, Friedrich
Friedrich Horner → see Horner,
   Friedrich
Friedrich III, Kaiser, (Victoria
   Adelaide Mary Louise) → see
   Victoria, Princess, (Empress
   Frederick of Germany)
Friedrich Johan Gottlieb Lieder → see
   Lieder, Friedrich Johan Gottlieb
Friedrich Kraus → see Kraus, Friedrich
Friedrich Moritz Wendler → see
   Wendler, Friedrich Moritz
Friedrich Nerly → see Nerly, Friedrich
Friedrich Oelenhainz → see
   Oelenhainz, Friedrich
Friedrich Pacher → see Pacher,
   Friedrich
Friedrich Peter Hiddeman → see
   Hiddeman, Friedrich Peter
Friedrich Pondel → see Pondel,
   Friedrich

Friedrich Rehberg→see Rehberg,
    Frederick
Friedrich Rosenberg→see Rosenberg,
    Friedrich
Friedrich Roth→see Roth, Friedrich
Friedrich Voltz→see Voltz, Friedrich
Friedrich von Aschaffenburg
    (German artist, op.1448-1462)   **WC**
Friedrich
    Vordemberge-Gildewart→see
    Vordemberge-Gildewart, Friedrich
Friedrich Walther→see Walther,
    Friedrich
Friedrich Wilhelm Heine→see Heine,
    Friedrich Wilhelm
Friedrich Wilhelm Heinrich
    Martersteig→see Martersteig,
    Friedrich Wilhelm Heinrich
Friedrich Wilhelm IV *(German artist,*
    1795-1861)   **WC**
Friedrich Wolf→see Wolf, Friedrich
Friedrich, Adolf   **PR WC**
    (German artist, 1824-1889)   WC
    (German painter, 1824-1889)   PR
        Bibl: ▶Thieme-Becker
    Adolf Friedrich   PR
    Friedrich   PR
    Friedrich, Gustave Adolf   PR
Friedrich, August *(German*
    draughtsman, 1789-1843)   **GC**
        Bibl: ▶Bénézit; ▶Thieme-Becker
    Friedrich, Johann Heinrich August   GC
Friedrich, Caroline Friederike   **BA WC**
    (German artist, 1749-1815)   WC
    (German painter, 1749-1815)   BA
        Bibl: ▶Bénézit; ▶Nagler, Neues
        Künst.-Lex.; ▶Thieme-Becker;
        ▶Witt checklist
Friedrich, Caspar David   **AV BA GC WC**
    (1774-1840)   AV
    (German artist, 1774-1840)   WC
    (German painter, 1774-1840)   BA
    (German, 1774-1840)   GC
        Bibl: ▶Bénézit; ▶Thieme-Becker
Friedrich, Gustave Adolf→see
    Friedrich, Adolf
Friedrich, Harald *(German artist,*
    1858-)   **WC**
Friedrich, Jacob   **GC**
    (German artist, 1746-1813)   WC
    (German painter, 1746-1813)   GC
        Bibl: ▶Thieme-Becker
Friedrich, Jacob (Johann
    Christian Jacob)   **WC**
    Friedrich, Johann Christian Jacob   GC
Friedrich, Jacob (Johann Christian
    Jacob)→see Friedrich, Jacob
Friedrich, Jacob Andreas I→see
    Friedrich, Jacob Andreas I
Friedrich, Johann Christian
    Jacob→see Friedrich, Jacob
Friedrich, Johann Heinrich
    August→see Friedrich, August

Friedrich, Lothar *(German architect,*
    Dusseldorf)   **AV**
        Bibl: Detail, 1980 July-Aug., no.3,
        p.516
Friedrich, Otto *(German artist,*
    1862-1937)   **WC**
Friedrich, Otto Bernhard *(German*
    furniture manufacturer, 1838-ca.
    1913)   **BA**
        Bibl: Arnold, Jahrb. der Staatl.
        Kunstsamml. Dresden XV (1983)
        129
Friedrich, Peter *(German artist,*
    -1616)   **WC**
Friend, Donald   **GC WC**
    (Australian artist, 1914-)   WC
    (British, b.1914)   GC
        Bibl: ▶Witt checklist
Friend, Ian *(British artist, b.1951)*   **WI**
Friend, Washington F.   **BA WC WI**
    (American artist, circa 1820-
    1886)   WI
    (American artist, op.c.1870)   WC
    (British painter, ca.1820-1886)   BA
        Bibl: ▶Bénézit; ▶Harper, Ptg.
        Canada
Frienz, Eduard de *(French(?) artist,*
    19th cent.)   **WC**
Frier, Walter   **WC WI**
    (British artist, c.1721)   WC
    (British artist, op.1715-1731)   WI
Fries, Adriaen de→see Vries, Adriaen
    de
Fries, Anna Susanna *(Swiss artist,*
    1827-1901)   **WC**
Fries, Anton *(German artist,*
    1764/8-1834)   **WC**
Fries, Bernhard *(German artist,*
    1820-1879)   **WC**
Fries, Ernst   **BA GC WC**
    (German artist, 1801-1833)   WC
    (German painter and
    printmaker, 1801-1833)   GC
    (German painter, printmaker,
    1801-1833)   BA
        Bibl: Bott, Elisabeth, dissertation,
        1978; ▶RILA/BHA;
        ▶Thieme-Becker
Fries, Félix *(French architect, 1800-*
    1859)   **BA**
        Bibl: Levine, 19c. French arch.;
        ▶Thieme-Becker
Fries, Hans   **GC WC**
    (Swiss artist, c.1465-1520)   WC
    (Swiss painter and
    draughtsman, ca.1465-ca.
    1520)   GC
        Bibl: ▶Thieme-Becker
Fries, Willy *(Swiss artist, 1881-)*   **WC**
Friesach, Konrad von→see Konrad
    von Friesach
Friese→see Freese, N.
Friese Dietmarsiensis→see Frese,
    Daniel
Friese, Richard *(German artist,*
    1854-1918)   **WC**

Frieseke→see Frieseke, Frederick Carl
Frieseke, Frederick C. →see Frieseke,
    Frederick Carl
Frieseke, Frederick
    Carl   **BA GC PR WC WI**
    (American artist, 1874-1939)   WC WI
    (American painter, 1874-1939)   BA PR
    (American, 1874-1939)   GC
        Bibl: ▶Bénézit; ▶RILA/BHA;
        ▶Thieme-Becker; ▶Witt checklist
    Frederick Carl Frieseke   PR
    Frieseke   PR
    Frieseke, Frederick C.   PR
Frieselhem (Freislhien), P. *(German*
    artist, 18th cent.)   **WC**
Friesz→see Friesz, Othon
Friesz, Achille Emile Othon→see
    Friesz, Othon
Friesz, Emile Othon→see Friesz,
    Othon
Friesz, Othon   **BA GC PR**
    (French artist, 1879-)   WC
    (French artist, 1879-1949)   WI
    (French painter and engraver,
    1879-1949)   GC
    (French painter, 1879-1949)   BA PR
        Bibl: ▶Bénézit; Getty Photo Study
        Coll.; ▶MoMA libr. cat.; ▶Phaidon
        20c. art; ▶RILA/BHA; ▶Vollmer,
        Künst.-Lex. 20. Jhr.
    Friesz   PR
Friesz, Achille Emile Othon   **BA GC**
Friesz, Emile Othon   **GC PR WC WI**
    Othon Friesz   PR
Friesze, Daniel→see Frese, Daniel
Frietsch, Joseph   **AV BA**
    (Bohemian landscape gardener,
    1774-1867)   BA
    (Bohemian landscape gardener,
    worked in Italy)   AV
        Bibl: Zangheri, Antichità viva
        XXIII/3 (May-June 1984) pp.28,
        32,42
    Fritsch, Giuseppe   BA
Frigerio, Eduardo *(Architect)*   **AV**
        Bibl: Interior design, 1983 Aug.,
        v.54, no.8, p.178
Frigerio, Ezio *(Italian scenographer)*   **AV**
        Bibl: Domus, 1988 July-Aug., no.
        696, p.74
Frigerio, Ismael *(Chilean artist in*
    USA, b.1955)   **BA**
        Bibl: New York (NY, USA), New
        Mus., Art & Ideology (1984)
Frigimelica, Francesco, Francesco,
    the elder *(Italian painter, ca.1570-*
    after 1646)   **BA**
        Bibl: Belluno (ITA), Palazzo
        Crepadova, Arte del'600 (1981);
        ▶Bénézit; ▶Bolaffi; ▶Thieme-Becker
Frigimelica, Girolamo *(Italian*
    architect, 1653-1732)   **AV**
        Bibl: ▶Thieme-Becker
Frignano Group *(South Italian vase-*
    painters, 4th century BC)   **GC**
        Bibl: ▶Trendall, Red-fig. vases
        Lucania

Frignano Painter *(Campanian vase-painter)*   GC
  Bibl: ▶Trendall, Red-fig. vases Lucania

Friis, Erna Sonne *(Danish landscape architect and/or author)*   AV
  Bibl: Landskab, 1988 May, v.69, no.3, p.44

Friis, Hans Gabriel *(Danish artist, 1839-1892)*   WC

Friis, Knud *(Danish architect, 1926-)*   AV

Frijns, Bert *(Dutch glass artist, b.1953)*   BA
  Bibl: Broos, K, BEELDEN IN GLAS. GLASS SCULPTURE (1986); ▶Intl. dir. exh. artists, 1982

Frillie, Felix Nicolas *(French artist, 1821-1863)*   WC

Friman, Kimmo *(Finnish architect(?))*   AV
  Bibl: Arkkitehti, 1988, v.85, no.1, p.74

Frimkess, Michael *(American ceramist, b.1937.)*   BA
  Bibl: Craft Horizon, Oct 1977; ▶Intl. dir. exh. artists, 1982; Los Angeles (CA, USA), LAICA, Foundations in Clay (1977)

Frimlargst, P.A. *(Danish artist, op. 1667)*   WC

Frink, Elisabeth   BA
  (British artist, 1930-)   WC
  (British artist, b.1930)   WI
  (British sculptor, b.1930)   BA
  Bibl: ▶Bénézit; ▶MoMA libr. cat.; ▶Vollmer, Künst.-Lex. 20. Jhr.; ▶Who's Who [GBR], 1927

Frink, Elizabeth   WC WI
Frink, Elizabeth→see Frink, Elisabeth

Fripp, Alfred Downing   BA WC WI
  (British artist, 1822-1895)   WC WI
  (British painter, 1822-1895)   BA
  Bibl: ▶Bénézit

Fripp, Charles Edwin *(British artist, 1854-1906)*   WC WI

Fripp, George Arthur   BA WC WI
  (British artist, 1813-1896)   WC WI
  (British painter, 1813-1896)   BA
  Bibl: ▶Johnson, Brit. artists; ▶Thieme-Becker

Fripp, Innes *(British artist, 1867-op. 1904)*   WI

Fripp, J.H.   WC WI
  (British artist, 19th cent.)   WC
  (British artist, op.19th c.)   WI

Fripp, Paul *(British artist, b.1890)*   WI

Fripp, S.C. *(British artist, 18th c.)*   BA
  Bibl: ▶Busse, Maler u. Bildhauer 19. Jahr.; Smith, Medieval mons.

Fripp, Susan Beatrice, Mrs.→see Lock, Beatrice Fripp

Friquet de Vauroze, Jacques Antoine   GC
  (French artist, 1638-1716)   WC
  (French, 1648-1716)   GC
  Bibl: ▶Bénézit

Friquet, Jacques ('de Vauroze')   WC

Friquet, Jacques ('de Vauroze')→see Friquet de Vauroze, Jacques Antoine
Fris→see Fris, Pieter
Fris or Frits, Pieter→see Fris, Pieter
Fris, Jan→see Fris, Jan (Johannes)
Fris, Jan (Johannes)   PR
  (Dutch artist, 1627/8-1672)   WC
  (Dutch painter, 1627/28-1672)   GC PR
  Bibl: Getty Photo Study Coll.; ▶Thieme-Becker; ▶Witt checklist

Fris, Jan   GC PR
Fris, Jan or Johannes   WC
  J. Fris   PR
  Jan Fris   PR
Fris, Jan or Johannes→see Fris, Jan (Johannes)

Fris, Pieter   GC PR
  (Dutch artist, 1627/8-a.1708)   WC
  (Dutch painter, 1627/28-1708)   GC PR
  Bibl: Brul inventory 1653; Getty Photo Study Coll.; Getty Photo Study Coll. (Ptgs.); ▶Thieme-Becker; ▶Witt checklist
  Fris   PR

Fris or Frits, Pieter   WC
  Frits, Pieter   GC
  Pieter Fris   PR

Frisbee, Peter E. *(American architect)*   AV
  Bibl: Chicago architectural journal, 1985, v.5, p.158

Friscara, Oreste *(French architect)*   AV
  Bibl: Architecture d'aujourd'hui, 1987 Oct., no.253, p.77

Frisch, Johan Didrik *(Norwegian artist, 1835-1867)*   WC

Frisch, Johann Christoph   GC WC
  (German artist, 1738-1815)   WC
  (German, 1738-1815)   GC
  Bibl: ▶Thieme-Becker; ▶Witt checklist

Frisch, Victor *(American sculptor (b. Austria), b.1876)*   GC
  Bibl: ▶Opitz, Amer. sculptors

Frische, Heinrich Ludwig *(German artist, 1831-1901)*   WC

Frischknecht, Paul *(Australian architect)*   AV
  Bibl: Architecture Australia, 1986 May, v.75, no.3, p.56

Frischman, Ralph *(American architect, San Francisco, Calif)*   AV
  Bibl: Interior design, 1986 Sept., v.57, no.9, p.224

Friscia, Albert *(American painter, sculptor in ITA, 20th c.)*   BA
  Bibl: Friscia, LEONARDO, XXI (1988), 145-149; ▶WW Amer. Art, 1989

Frisia, Elio *(Italian architect)*   AV
Frisius or Vriesius, Simon Wynhoutsz or Weynouts (Simon Wynhoutsz. de Vries)→see Vries, Simon Wynhoutsz.
Frisius, Simon Wynhoutsz.→see Vries, Simon Wynhoutsz.

Frisius, Theodorus→see Vries, Dirck de
Friso, Alvise dal→see Benfatto, Luigi (Alvise dal Friso)
Frisoni [Unidentified] *(Unknown painter)*   PR
  Bibl: Corsini inventory, Rome, 1750

Frisoni, Donato Giuseppe   AV BA
  (Italian architect, stuccator, active in Germany, 1683-1735)   AV
  (Italian architect, stucco artist, 1683-1735)   BA
  Bibl: Dehio, I, 290; ▶Macmillan encyc. archts.; ▶Thieme-Becker

Frisse, Courtney *(American photographer, b.1953)*   BA
  Bibl: Syracuse (NY, USA), Everson Mus., New works in clay (1981)

Frissell, Toni   BA WC
  (American artist, 20th cent.)   WC
  (American photographer, b.1907)   BA
  Bibl: Beaton, Magic image; ▶Hall-Duncan, Fashion photog.; ▶MoMA libr. cat.; ▶Parry, Photo idx.
  Bacon, Antoinette Montgomery Frissell   BA

Frister, Carl (Johann Carl) *(German artist, 1742-1783)*   WC

Fristom, Claus Edward *(New Zealand artist, -1942)*   WC

Friston, Adrian de   WC WI
  (British artist, 1900-)   WC
  (British artist, b.1900)   WI

Friston, David Henry *(British artist, op.circa 1853-circa 1869)*   WI
Frith→see Frith, William Powell
Frith, Clifford   WC WI
  (British artist, 20th cent.)   WC
  (British artist, op.20th c.)   WI

Frith, F.   WC WI
  (American artist, op.1776-1786)   WI
  (American artist, op.1781)   WC

Frith, Francis   AV BA JG
  (British photographer, 1822-1898)   BA GC
  (British, 1822-1898)   JG
  (English photographer, 1822-1898)   AV
  Bibl: ▶Eastman House database; ▶Gernsheim, Hist. photog.; ▶Idx. Amer. photog. colls.; ▶Libr. of Congr. Name Auth. File; ▶Newhall, Photog.

Francis Frith   GC
Frith, Frederick *(British artist, op. 19th c.)*   WI

Frith, William Powell   **BA GC PR WC WI**
(British artist, 1819-1909)   **WC WI**
(British painter, 1819-1909)   **BA PR**
(British, 1819-1909)   **GC**
Bibl: ▶Encyc. world art;
▶RILA/BHA; ▶Thieme-Becker;
▶Who was who [GBR]; ▶Witt
checklist
Frith   **PR**
William Powell Frith   **PR**
Frith, William Silver (British
sculptor, 1849-1924)   **BA**
Bibl: ▶Grant, Brit. sculptors;
▶Johnson, Brit. artists;
▶Thieme-Becker; ▶Vollmer,
Künst.-Lex. 20. Jhr.; ▶Waters, Brit.
artists
Frits Thaulow → see Thaulow, Fritz
Frits, Pieter → see Fris, Pieter
Fritsch (French porcelain painter,
act.1763-1764)   **GC**
Bibl: ▶Brunet, Sèvres
Fritsch, Dieter (West German
architect)   **AV**
Bibl: Architektur + Wettbewerbe,
1984 Sept., no.119
Fritsch, Elizabeth (British ceramist,
b.1940.)   **BA**
Bibl: Guide exh. artists: N. Amer.
ptrs.; ▶Intl. dir. exh. artists, 1983;
Leeds Art Calendar
Fritsch, Ellen (West German
architect, Trautheim/Darmstadt)   **AV**
Bibl: Architektur,
Innenarchitektur, Technischer
Ausbau, 1987 Oct., v.95, no.10,
p.44
Fritsch, Ernst   **BA WC**
(German artist, 1892-)   **WC**
(German painter, 1892-1962)   **BA**
Bibl: ▶Bénézit; ▶MoMA libr. cat.;
▶Vollmer, Künst.-Lex. 20. Jhr.
Fritsch, F.J.   **WC WI**
(American artist, op.1843-)   **WI**
(American artist, op.1843/4)   **WC**
Fritsch, Franz (West German interior
designer, Baden-Baden)   **AV**
Bibl: Architektur,
Innenarchitektur, Technisicher
Ausbau, 1987 Nov., v.95, no.11,
p.58
Fritsch, Giuseppe → see Frietsch,
Joseph
Fritsch, Heinrich (West German
architect, Trautheim/Darmstadt)   **AV**
Bibl: Architektur,
Innenarchitektur, Technischer
Ausbau, 1987 Oct., v.95, no.10,
p.44
Fritsch, Lutz (West German sculptor,
b.1955)   **BA**
Bibl: ▶Intl. dir. exh. artists, 1983;
Karlsruhe (DEU), Badischer
Kunstverein, Ars Viva 84/85
(1984)
Fritsch, Melchior (German artist,
1826-1889)   **WC**
Fritsch, Reinhard (1935-)   **AV**

Fritsch, Rüdiger (German architect,
Munich)   **AV**
Bibl: 1984 Aug., v.34, p.1016
**Fritsche or Fritzsche, George
Christian** (German artist, op.1681-
1709)   **WC**
Fritsche, Hans (East German
engineer?, 1929-)   **AV**
Bibl: Architektur der DDR, 1989
June, v.38, no.6, p.5
Fritz Ebel → see Ebel, Fritz
Fritz Glarner → see Glarner, Fritz
Fritz Karl Hermann von Uhde → see
Uhde, Fritz Karl Hermann von
Fritz Pfeiffer → see Pfeiffer, Fritz
Fritz Steinmetz-Noris → see Steinmetz-
Noris, Fritz
Fritz Stuckenberg → see Stuckenberg,
Fritz
Fritz Wucherer → see Wucherer, Fritz
Fritz, August (German artist, 1843-
p.1878)   **WC**
Fritz, Johann Friedrich (German
painter, printmaker, 1798-1870)   **BA**
Bibl: Deutsche Künstlerkolonien u.
Künstlerorte; ▶Thieme-Becker
Fritz, Nicolas (West German
architect, Darmstadt)   **AV**
Bibl: Bauwelt, 1989 May 19, v.80,
no.20, p.932
Fritzel, Wilhelm (German artist,
1870-1943)   **WC**
Fritzius, Harry (American painter,
b.ca.1933)   **BA**
Bibl: Art News LXXX (May 1981)
74-94
Fritzsch or Fritsch, Christian
Friedrich → see Fritzsch, Christian
Friedrich
Fritzsch, Christian (German
printmaker, 1695-1769)   **BA**
Bibl: ▶Thieme-Becker;
Williamstown (MA, USA), Clark
Art Inst., Dürer through other
eyes (1975)
Fritzsch, Christian Friedrich   **GC**
(German artist, 1719-a.1774)   **WC**
(German printmaker, ca.1719-d.
bef.1774)   **GC**
Bibl: ▶Bénézit
**Fritzsch or Fritsch, Christian
Friedrich**   **WC**
Fritzsch, Claudius Ditlev (Danish
artist, 1763-1841)   **WC**
Frize, Bernard (French painter,
b.1949)   **BA**
Bibl: ▶Intl. dir. exh. artists;
Lausanne (CHE), Musée Cantonal
B.-A., Rite, rock, rêve (1984);
Paris (FRA), Ctr Pompidou, Murs
(1981-82)
Frizzell, Dick (New Zealander
painter, b.1943)   **BA**
Bibl: Auckland (NZL), City Art
Gallery, New image (1983)
Frobenius, Hermann (German artist,
1871-c.1954)   **WC**

Frobisher, Lucy Marguerite (British
artist, op.1915-1940)   **WI**
Fröde, Wolfgang (German painter,
b.1952)   **BA**
Bibl: Aachen (DEU), Neue Gal.-
Samm. Ludwig, Wolfgang Frode
(1977)
Froehlich, Arthur (Architect, United
States, 1909-1985)   **AV**
Bibl: ▶Amer. archts. dir., 3rd ed.,
1970
Froehlich, J.W. (German, 20th c.)   **BA**
Bibl: Monchengladbach (DEU),
Stadt. Mus. Abteiburg
Monchengladbach, PALERMO
(1983)
Froehlich-Müller, Lilly (German
artist, 20th c.)   **BA**
Bibl: Baden (DEU), Gal.
Trudelhaus, Aus der Ittenschule
(1984)
Müller, Lilly   **BA**
Froelicher, Joseph Antoine (Swiss
architect, 1790-1866)   **BA**
Bibl: BULL. DE LA SOC. DE L'HIST.
DE L'ART FRANCAIS (1976) 381;
ZEITSCH. FUR SCHWEIZ. ARCH.
XXXIII (1976) 211
Froelix, H. (German artist, op.1721) **WC**
Froer, Veit (German artist, 1828-c.
1900)   **WC**
Froeschl, Daniel → see Fröschl, Daniel
Frogonard → see Fragonard, Jean
Honoré
Frohawk, Fredrick William (British
artist, 1861-1942)   **WI**
Fröhli family (Swiss cabinetmakers,
woodcarvers, 17th-18th cs.)   **BA**
Bibl: Fruh, Zeits. Schweiz. Arch. u.
Kunst, XXXVIII/1 (1981) pp.59-79;
Kunstdenkmäler Thurgau, v.2,
p.411
Fröhli, Chrysotimus I (Swiss
cabinetmaker, woodcarver,
b.1652, act.1704)   **BA**
Bibl: Fruh, Zeits. Schweiz. Arch. u.
Kunst, XXXVIII/1 (1981) pp.59-79;
▶Jenny, Kunstführer Schweiz, v.1,
pp.619-630; Kunstdenkmäler
Thurgau, v.1, pp.228, 256-260
Frohlich, Betty (Bogner) (German
artist, 1798-1878)   **WC**
Fröhlich, Elfi (West German
photographer, b.1951)   **BA**
Bibl: Munich (DEU), Kunstverein,
Neuer Realismus (1983)
Fröhlich, L.Ch. (in CSK architect,
act.1835-1855)   **BA**
Bibl: Zatloukal, Umění, XXVIII/4
(1980) pp.359-364

Frohman, Philip Hubert   **AV BA**
  (American architect, 1887-)   AV
  (American architect, 1887-1972)   BA
    Bibl: ▶Amer. archts. dir., 1970;
    ▶Avery obit. idx., 1980; ▶Avery
    period. idx.; ▶Withey, Amer.
    archts.; WPA GUIDE TO
    WASHINGTON, D.C. (1942), pp.
    398, 403

Frohner, Adolf   **BA WC**
  (Austrian painter, printmaker,
    sculptor, b.1934)   BA
  (German artist, 1934-)   WC
    Bibl: ▶Bénézit; ▶WW Arts DEU

Frohnwieser, H. (Architect, Austria)   **AV**
    Bibl: Techniques et architecture,
    1979 Nov., no.327, p.102

Froidevauz, Denis (French architect,
   Nevers)   **AV**
    Bibl: ▶Annuaire archts. fran.,
    1987

Froimon, Johann Clemens→see
  Froimont, Jean Clément

Froimont, Jean Clément (French
   architect in Germany, act.1717-
   1731)   **BA**
    Bibl: Colombier, L'ARCH. FRAN.
    EN ALLEMAGNE... 18E. S.; Dehio:
    Baden-Württemberg; ▶Portoghesi,
    Diz. arch. e urbanistica; Reclams,
    II; Schneider, Jahrb. der Staatl.
    Kunstsamm. in
    Baden-Württemberg XVII (1980)
    111-124; ▶Thieme-Becker; Walter,
    BAUWERKE D. KURFURSTENZEIT,
    18 ·
  Froimon, Johann Clemens   BA

Froisart (Flemish(?) artist, 18th
   cent.)   **WC**

Froissart, Jean (French, b.
   Valenciennes ca. 1337, d. ca.
   1405)   **JG**

Froissart, Louis-Antoine (French,
   1815-1860)   **JG**

Frojd, David Fripp (American
   interior designer)   **AV**
    Bibl: Architectural digest, 1984
    May, v.41, no.5, p.145

Frolen, Stune (Swedish architect)   **AV**
    Bibl: Architects' journal, 1989
    Sept.6, v.190, no.10, p.45

Frölich, Anton→see Frölich, Franz
  Anton

Frölich, Franz Anton (German
   sculptor, painter, 1770-1841)   **BA**
    Bibl: ▶Busse, Maler u. Bildhauer
    19. Jahr.; Loffler, WELTKUNST
    LII/19 (1 Oct 1982) 2642-2644;
    ▶Thieme-Becker
  Frölich, Anton   BA

Frølich, Kare (Norwegian architect)   **AV**
    Bibl: Architectural review, 1988
    May, v.183, no.1095, p.55

Frolich, Lorens (Danish artist, 1820-
   1908)   **WC**

**Frolich, Lucas (Laux Frelich)
  (Monogrammist L.F.)** (Danish
   artist, op.1490-1511)   **WC**

Frølich, Torburg Zimmer
  (Norwegian landscape architect,
   Bergen)   **AV**
    Bibl: Landskab, 1987 Sept., v.68,
    no.5, p.81
  Zimmer, Torburg   AV

Frölicher, Johann Wolfgang
  (German sculptor, 1652-1700)   **BA**
    Bibl: Dehio: Rheinland-Pfälz;
    Roning, F.J., in IMAGINATION
    UND IMAGO (1983) 273-280;
    ▶Thieme-Becker

Frölicher, Otto   **BA WC**
  (Swiss artist, 1840-1890)   WC
  (Swiss painter, 1840-1890)   BA
    Bibl: ▶Schweiz. Künst.-Lex.;
    ▶Thieme-Becker

Frolov, V.A. (Russian artist, 20th
   cent.)   **WC**

from Metzu→see Metsu, Gabriel
from Raphael→see Raffaello Sanzio
from Rembrandt→see Rembrandt
  Harmensz. van Rijn
From the School of Rubens→see
  Rubens, Peter Paul

Fromageau, Jean-Baptiste (French
   ébéniste, ca.1726, master 1755,
   act. to ca.1777)   **GC**
    Bibl: ▶Salverte, Ébénistes 18e s.

Froman, Ann (American sculptor,
   b.1942)   **GC**
    Bibl: ▶Opitz, Amer. sculptors

Fromanger, Gérard (French painter,
   sculptor, b.1939)   **BA**
    Bibl: ▶Bénézit; XXe Siecle,
    XXXI/42 (June 1974) 178

Fromantiou→see Fromantiou,
  Hendrik de
Fromantiou, Hendrik→see
  Fromantiou, Hendrik de

Fromantiou, Hendrik de   **GC PR WC**
  (Dutch artist,
    1633/4-1694/1700)   WC
  (Dutch painter, 1633/34-1694)   GC
  (Dutch painter,
    1633/34-1694/1700)   PR
    Bibl: ▶Bénézit; ▶Thieme-Becker
  Farmantou   PR
  Farmatou   PR
  Fromantiou   PR
  Fromantiou, Hendrik   PR
  Fromentiou   PR
  Hendrik de Fromantiou   PR

Fromboluti, Sideo (American
   painter, b.1920)   **BA**
    Bibl: ▶MoMA libr. cat.; ▶NY art
    yrbk.; ▶WW Amer. Art, 1976

Frömder, Wolfgang (East German
   architect)   **AV**
    Bibl: Architektur der DDR, 1989
    Aug., v.38, no.8, p.32

Frömel, Gerda (Czech sculptor in
   IRL, b.1931)   **BA**
    Bibl: Belfast (GBR), Ulster Mus.,
    Irish directions (1975), p.17

Froment→see Froment, Nicolas

Froment, Eugene (French painter,
   1844-1900)   **GC**
    Bibl: ▶Thieme-Becker

Froment, Nicholas→see Froment,
  Nicolas

Froment, Nicolas   **BA GC PR WC**
  (French artist, op.1450-1490)   WC
  (French painter,
    ca.1435-1483/84)   BA GC PR
    Bibl: Art Bull. LVIII/3 (Sept 1976),
    350; ▶Bénézit; ▶Encyc. world art;
    Grayson, Documentary hist.
    (diss.); ▶RILA/BHA;
    ▶Thieme-Becker
  Froment   PR
  Froment, Nicholas   PR
  Nicolas Froment   PR

Froment, Nicolas, the younger
  (French painter, 1467-1522)   **BA**
    Bibl: Grayson, Documentary hist.
    (diss.)

Froment-Meurice, Emile (French
   goldsmith, jeweler, 1837-1913)   **BA**
    Bibl: Gere, Jewellery; ▶Newman,
    Jewelry; ▶Thieme-Becker

Froment-Meurice, François Désiré
  (French goldsmith, jeweler, 1802-
   1855)   **BA**
    Bibl: Gere, Jewellery; ▶Newman,
    Jewelry; ▶Thieme-Becker

Fromentin→see Fromentin, Eugène

Fromentin, Eugène   **BA PR**
  (French artist, 1820-1876)   WC
  (French painter, 1820-1876)   PR
  (French painter, art historian,
    1820-1876)   BA
  (French, 1820-1876)   GC
    Bibl: ▶Bénézit; ▶RILA/BHA;
    ▶Thieme-Becker; ▶Witt checklist
  Eugene Fromentin   PR
  Fromentin   PR

**Fromentin-Dupeux, Eugene
  Samuel Auguste**   **GC WC**

Fromentin-Dupeux, Eugene Samuel
  Auguste→see Fromentin, Eugène
Fromentiou→see Fromantiou,
  Hendrik de

Fromiller, Josef Ferdinand   **BA GC WC**
  (Austrian draughtsman, 1693-
   1760)   GC
  (Austrian painter, printmaker,
    1693-1760)   BA
  (German artist, 1693-1760)   WC
    Bibl: ▶Bénézit; ▶Encyc. world art;
    Getty Photo Study Coll.;
    ▶RILA/BHA; ▶Thieme-Becker;
    ▶Witt checklist

Fromkes→see Fromkes, Maurice

Fromkes, Maurice (American
   painter, 1872-1931)   **PR**
    Bibl: ▶WWW Amer. art
  Fromkes   PR
  Maurice Fromkes   PR

Fromm, Dorit (American architect)   **AV**
    Bibl: Places, 1984 Summer, v.1,
    no.4, p.81

Fromm, Günther *(West German architect, Berlin)*   **AV**
  Bibl: ▶Bund Deut. Arch. Hdbch., 1987
Frommel, Carl Ludwig   **BA GC WC**
  (German artist, 1789-1863)   **WC**
  (German painter, draughtsman, and printmaker, 1789-1863)   **GC**
  (German painter, printmaker, 1789-1863)   **BA**
  Bibl: ▶Bénézit; ▶RILA/BHA; ▶Thieme-Becker
Frommer, Wilhelm   **GC WC**
  (German artist, op.1638-1653)   **WC**
  (German, act.1638-1653)   **GC**
  Bibl: ▶Thieme-Becker; ▶Witt checklist
Fromouth, Charles Henry   **WI**
  (American artist, 1861-)   **WC**
  (American artist, 1861-1937)   **WI**
  Fromuth, Charles Henry   **WC**
  Fromuth, Charles Henry →see Fromouth, Charles Henry
Fronius, Hans *(Austrian painter, printmaker, illustrator, b.1903)*   **BA**
  Bibl: ▶Bénézit; ▶Vollmer, Künst.-Lex. 20. Jhr.; ▶WW Austria
Frontado, Guillermo *(Venezuelan architect)*   **AV**
  Bibl: Spazio e societa, 1987 July-Sept., v.10, no.37, p.116
Frontal Rooster Circle *(Etruscan vase-painter)*   **GC**
  Bibl: ▶Szilagyi, Etruszko-korinthosi
Frontal Satyr Caeretan Painter *(Etruscan vase-painter)*   **GC**
  Bibl: Del Chiaro, Caere
Frontier, Jean Charles   **GC WC**
  (French artist, 1701-1763)   **WC**
  (French, 1701-1763)   **GC**
  Bibl: ▶Thieme-Becker
Frood, Hester   **WI**
  (British artist, 1882-)   **WC**
  (British artist, 1882-1971)   **WI**
  Frood, Hester (Gwynne-Evans)   **WC**
  Gwynne-Evans, Frank, Mrs., (Hester)   **WI**
  Frood, Hester (Gwynne-Evans) →see Frood, Hester
Froschel, Hanns *(German artist, op. 1620)*   **WC**
Fröscher, K. *(West German architect, Detmold)*   **AV**
  Bibl: Deutsches Architektenblatt, 1987 Oct., v.18, no.10, p.1196
Froschl →see Fröschl, Daniel
Froschl, Carl *(German artist, 1848-)*   **WC**

Fröschl, Daniel   **GC PR**
  (Czechoslovakian painter, bef. 1572-1613)   **PR**
  (German artist, a.1570-1613)   **WC**
  (German painter, bef.1572-1613)   **GC**
  Bibl: Getty Photo Study Coll.; Getty Photo Study Coll. (Ptgs.); ▶Thieme-Becker; ▶Witt checklist
  Daniel Froschl   **PR**
  Freschel, Daniel   **GC**
  Froeschl, Daniel   **PR**
  Froschl   **PR**
Froschl, Freschel, Froschlein or Frossley, Daniel   **WC**
  Fröschlein, Daniel   **GC**
  Frossley, Daniel   **GC**
  Froschl, Freschel, Froschlein or Frossley, Daniel →see Fröschl, Daniel
  Fröschlein, Daniel →see Fröschl, Daniel
Frosini [Unidentified] *(Unknown painter)*   **PR**
  Bibl: Salvi inventory, Florence, 1792
Frosino, Luca   **GC WC**
  (Italian artist, 15th cent.)   **WC**
  (Italian painter, 15th century)   **GC**
  Bibl: Getty Ctr: I Tatti database; ▶Witt checklist
  Luca di Frosinone   **GC**
Frosne, Jean *(French artist, c.1623-p.1676)*   **WC**
Frossard, Claude *(French artist, 20th cent.)*   **WC**
Frossard, L. *(French artist, 19th cent.)*   **WC**
Frossard, Maryvonne *(French architect)*   **AV**
  Bibl: Architecture & urbanism, 1986 Oct., no.10, p.54
Frossley, Daniel →see Fröschl, Daniel
Frost →see Frost, J.
Frost →see Frost, John
Frost family *(American artists, 19th-20th cs.)*   **BA**
  Bibl: Montclair (NJ, USA), Montclair Art Museum, THE WORLD OF A.B. FROST: HIS FAMILY AND THEIR CIRCLE
Frost, Andy *(British sculptor, 20th c.)*   **BA**
  Bibl: ▶ARTbibl. mod., v.15 (1984), 1
Frost, Anthony *(British artist, b.1951)*   **WI**
Frost, Arthur Burdett →see Frost, Arthur Burdett I

Frost, Arthur Burdett I   **BA**
  (American artist, 1851-1928)   **WC WI**
  (American illustrator, author, 1851-1928)   **BA**
  (American, 1851-1921)   **GC**
  Bibl: Earle, Costume in Amer.; ▶Encyc. world art; ▶Fielding's Amer. ptrs.; ▶Smith, Idx. Amer. artists; ▶Witt checklist; ▶WWW Amer.
Frost, Arthur Burdett   **GC WC WI**
Frost, Arthur Burdett II   **BA**
  (American artist, 1887-1917)   **WI**
  (American painter, 1887-1917)   **BA**
  Bibl: Baigell, Dict. Amer. art; ▶Phaidon 20c. art
Frost, Arthur Burdett, Jr.   **WI**
Frost, Arthur Burdett, Jr. →see Frost, Arthur Burdett II
Frost, Brian *(British architect)*   **AV**
  Bibl: ▶Avery period. idx.
Frost, Charles Sumner *(American architect. Partner in firm of Cobb & Frost, Chicago (1882-1898). Later practiced with Alfred H. Granger in firm of Frost & Granger, Chicago (1898-1910), 1856-1931)*   **AV**
  Bibl: ▶Withey, Amer. archts.
Frost, Flemming *(Danish architect, Copenhagen)*   **AV**
  Bibl: ▶Danske Arkitekters Landsforbund, 1984-85
Frost, George   **GC WC WI**
  (British artist, c.1754-1821)   **WC**
  (British artist, circa 1754-1821)   **WI**
  (British, ca.1754-1821)   **GC**
  Bibl: ▶Mallalieu, Brit. watercolour artists; ▶Thieme-Becker; ▶Witt checklist
Frost, George Albert   **WC WI**
  (American artist, 1843-)   **WC**
  (American artist, 1843-circa 1900)   **WI**
Frost, H. *(British artist, op.1857-)*   **WI**
Frost, J.   **WI**
  (British artist, 18th cent.)   **WC**
  (British artist, op.18th c.)   **WI**
  Frost   **WC**
Frost, J.O.J. →see Frost, John Orne Johnson
Frost, James *(British artist, op.1766-1783)*   **WC WI**
Frost, John *(British painter, act. 1758-1785)*   **PR**
  Bibl: ▶Waterhouse, Brit. 18c. ptrs.
  Frost   **PR**
  John Frost   **PR**
Frost, John Orne Johnson   **BA WI**
  (American artist, 1852-1928)   **WC WI**
  (American painter, 1852-1928)   **BA**
  Bibl: New York (NY, USA), Whitney Mus., Amer. folk ptrs. (1980)
  Frost, J.O.J.   **WC**

Frost, Susan Pringle *(American preservationist, Charleston, S.C, 1873-1960)* **AV**
Bibl: Historic preservation, v.39, no.1, p.33
Frost, Terence Ernest Manitou → see Frost, Terry
Frost, Terry **BA WC WI**
(British artist, 1917-) WC
(British artist, b.1915) WI
(British painter, b.1915) BA
Bibl: ▶Bénézit; ▶MoMA libr. cat.; ▶Vollmer, Künst.-Lex. 20. Jhr.; ▶Waters, Brit. artists; ▶WW Art, 1974
Frost, Terence Ernest Manitou BA
Frost, William Edward **BA PR WC WI**
(British artist, 1810-1877) WC WI
(British painter, 1810-1877) BA PR
Bibl: ▶Bénézit; ▶Dict. natl. biog.; ▶RILA/BHA; ▶Thieme-Becker
William Edward Frost PR
Froste, Sebastien *(French, 1790-1856)-* **GC**
Bibl: ▶Thieme-Becker
Frosterus, Sigurd **AV BA**
(Finnish architect, 1876-1956) AV
(Finnish architect, critic, 1876-1956) BA
Bibl: Arkkitehti, 1988, v.85, no.6, p.60; ▶Avery obit. idx.; ▶Natl. union cat., pre-1956
Frothingham → see Frothingham, James
Frothingham, Benjamin *(American cabinetmaker, 1734-1809)* **BA**
Bibl: Boston Furn. 18th ce.; Complete encyc. antiques
Frothingham, James **PR WC WI**
(American artist, 1786-1864) WC WI
(American painter, 1786-1864) PR
Bibl: ▶Fielding's Amer. ptrs., 1983
Frothingham PR
James Frothingham PR
Froud, Jonathan *(British sculptor, b.1958)* **BA**
Bibl: Cambridge (GBR), Cambridge Univ., Kettle's Yard, Ptgs. & sculps. (1983)
Froude, Rev. Robert Hurrell → see Froude, Robert Hurrell
Froude, Robert Hurrell **WI**
(British artist, 1779-1859) WI
(British artist, 18th cent.) WC
Bibl: ▶Fisher, Watercolour ptrs.
Froude, Rev. Robert Hurrell **WC**
Frowein, Dieter *(German architect, Berlin, 1938-)* **AV**
Bibl: Archithese, 1984 Nov.-Dec., v.14, no.6, p.60
Froy, Martin **BA WC WI**
(British artist, 1926-) WC
(British artist, b.1926) WI
(British painter, b.1926) BA
Bibl: ▶MoMA libr. cat.; ▶WW Art
Frs. Mola → see Mola, Pier Francesco

Fruchter, Louis *(American sculptor, 20th c.)* **BA**
Bibl: ARTS MAG. XILX/5 (Jan 1975) 60-61
Frudakis, Evangelos → see Frudakis, Evangelos William
Frudakis, Evangelos William *(American sculptor, b.1921)* **GC**
Bibl: Getty Photo Study Coll.; ▶Opitz, Amer. sculptors
Frudakis, Evangelos GC
Frueauf → see Frueauf, Rueland, the elder
Frueauf, Rueland → see Frueauf, Rueland, the elder
Frueauf, Rueland (the elder) → see Frueauf, Rueland, the elder
Frueauf, Rueland (the Younger) → see Frueauf, Rueland, the younger
Frueauf, Rueland I → see Frueauf, Rueland, the elder
Frueauf, Rueland, I → see Frueauf, Rueland, the elder
Frueauf, Rueland, II → see Frueauf, Rueland, the younger
Frueauf, Rueland, the elder **BA**
(Austrian painter, 1440-1507) GC
(Austrian painter, ca.1440-1507) BA PR
(German artist, 1440/50-1507) WC
Bibl: ▶Bénézit; ▶RILA/BHA; ▶Thieme-Becker
Frueauf PR
Frueauf, Rueland PR
Frueauf, Rueland (the elder) **GC PR**
Frueauf, Rueland I GC
Frueauf, Rueland, I **WC**
Fruehauf, Rueland, the Elder PR
Rueland Frueauf PR
Rueland Frueauf (the elder) PR
Frueauf, Rueland, the younger **BA**
(Austrian painter, act.1498, d. after 1545) BA
(German artist, op.1498-1545) WC
(German painter, ca.1470-1546) GC
Bibl: ▶Bénézit; ▶Thieme-Becker
Frueauf, Rueland (the Younger) **GC**
Frueauf, Rueland, II **WC**
Frueh, Alfred J. *(American painter, printmaker, 1880-1968)* **BA**
Bibl: ▶Fielding's Amer. ptrs.; NY Times obit.; ▶Vollmer, Künst.-Lex. 20. Jhr.
Fruehauf, Rueland, the Elder → see Frueauf, Rueland, the elder
Frugale [Unidentified] *(Unknown painter)* **PR**
Bibl: (May 22, 1813, lot 51, White)
Fruhbeck, Franz *(German(?) artist, op.1795-1830)* **WC**
Fruhtrunk, Gunter *(German artist, 1923-)* **WC**
Fruhwirth or Fruwirth, Carl *(German artist, 1810-1878)* **WC**
Fruit, Paul → see Fruit, Pol

Fruit, Pol **GC JG**
(Netherlandish illuminator, act. ca.1470-72) GC
Bibl: ▶Euw, Ludwig mss., v.3, pp. 250-256
Fruit, Paul GC
Fruitiers, Philip → see Fruytiers, Philip
Frulli, Giovanni Battista *(Italian draughtsman, d.1826)* **GC**
Bibl: ▶Thieme-Becker
Frullini, Luigi *(Italian sculptor, 1839-1897)* **BA**
Bibl: ▶Thieme-Becker
Frumi, Lotte *(Italian artist, 20th cent.)* **WC**
Frutet, Frans or Francesco *(Netherlands artist, op.1548)* **WC**
Frutiers → see Fruytiers, Philip
Frutius [Unidentified] *(Unknown painter)* **PR**
Bibl: (January 17, 1803, lot 43, Christie's)
Frutom, Frederik van → see Frytom, Frederik van
Frutos Espinosa, Alberto de *(Student at the Escuela de Arquitectura de Madrid, 1987)* **AV**
Bibl: El croquis, 1987 Oct., v.5, no.30, p.99
Fruttiers [Unidentified] *(Unknown painter)* **PR**
Bibl: (January 15, 1803, lot 77, Christie's)
Fruytiers → see Fruytiers, Philip
Fruytiers or Fruitiers, Philip → see Fruytiers, Philip
Fruytiers, Philip **BA GC JG PR**
(Flemish artist, 1610-1666) WC
(Flemish painter, 1610-1666) BA PR
(Flemish, 1610-1666) GC JG
Bibl: Getty Photo Study Coll. (Ptgs.); ▶Thieme-Becker; ▶Witt checklist; ▶Wurzbach, NLD Künst.-Lex.
Fruitiers, Philip BA GC
Frutiers PR
Fruytiers PR
Fruytiers or Fruitiers, Philip **WC**
P. Fruytiers PR
Philip Fruytiers PR
Fry → see Fry, Georgia Timken
Fry → see Fry, John Hemming
Fry, Anthony **WC WI**
(British artist, 1927-) WC
(British artist, b.1927) WI
Fry, C. Arthur **WC WI**
(British artist, 20th cent.) WC
(British artist, op.20th c.) WI
Fry, Clement Edward *(British, active 1863 (also Elliott & Fry))* **JG**
Fry, E. Maxwell, (Edwin Maxwell) → see Fry, Edwin Maxwell

Fry, Edwin Maxwell   **BA FA**
   (born 1899; Architect, United
     Kingdom)   *FA*
   (British architect, 1899-1987)   *AV*
   (British architect, painter, 1899-
     1987)   *BA*
   (British artist, op.20th c.)   *WI*
     Bibl: Building design, 1987
     Sept.11, no.852, p.2 [death date];
     ▶Contemp. archts.; Dannatt, T.,
     ARCHITECT: RIBA, XCIV/10 (Oct
     1987) p.56-57; Le Corbusier,
     Sketchbooks, v.3; ▶Libr. of Congr.
     Name Auth. File; ▶Who's Who
     [GBR], 1978; ▶WW Arch.
   Fry, E. Maxwell, (Edwin Maxwell)   AV
Fry, Maxwell   **AV FA WI**
Fry, Georgia Timken *(American*
   painter, 1864-1921)   **PR**
     Bibl: ▶WWW Amer. art
   Fry   PR
   Georgia Timken Fry   PR
Fry, Helen   **WC WI**
   (British artist, -1937)   *WC*
   (British artist, d.1937)   *WI*
Fry, Henry Lindley *(American*
   decorator and wood-carver,
   d.1895)   *AV*
     Bibl: Nineteenth century, 1982,
     v.8, no.3-4, p.173
Fry, John Hemming *(American*
   painter, 1861-1946)   **PR**
     Bibl: ▶WWW Amer. art
   Fry   PR
   John Hemming Fry   PR
Fry, Lewis George *(British artist,*
   1860-1933)   **WI**
Fry, Malcolm   **WC WI**
   (British artist, 1909-)   *WC*
   (British artist, b.1909)   *WI*
Fry, Margery   **WC WI**
   (British artist, 20th cent.)   *WC*
   (British artist, op.20th c.)   *WI*
Fry, Marta *(American landscape*
   architect)   **AV**
     Bibl: Landscape architecture,
     1989 Mar., v.79, no.2, p.16
Fry, Maxwell → see Fry, Edwin
   Maxwell
Fry, Roger → see Fry, Roger Eliot
Fry, Roger Eliot   **BA PR WI**
   (British artist, 1866-1934)   *WC WI*
   (British critic, painter, 1866-
     1934)   *BA*
   (British painter, 1866-1934)   *PR*
     Bibl: ▶Encyc. world art; ▶Houfe,
     Brit. book illus.; ▶McGraw-Hill
     dict. art; ▶RILA/BHA
   Fry, Roger   PR **WC**
   Roger Eliot Fry   PR
Fry, S.   **WC WI**
   (British artist, op.1783)   *WC*
   (British artist, op.1783-)   *WI*
Fry, Sherry Edmundson *(American*
   sculptor, 1879-1966)   **GC**
     Bibl: ▶Opitz, Amer. sculptors

Fry, Todd *(American landscape*
   architect, La Jolla, Calif)   **AV**
     Bibl: Garden design, 1988
     Autumn, v.7, no.3, p.34
Fry, W.T. *(Engraver)*   **WI**
Fry, William Henry *(American*
   decorator and wood-carver,
   d.1929)   **AV**
     Bibl: Nineteenth century, 1982,
     v.8, no.3-4, p.173
Fryberg *(German artist, 18th cent.)* **WC**
Frycz, Karol *(Polish painter, b.1877)* **BA**
     Bibl: ▶Thieme-Becker; ▶Vollmer,
     Künst.-Lex. 20. Jhr., v.1; ▶Wielka
     ilustr. encyk.
Frye, Louis Tudor *(American*
   designer, San Diego, Calif)   **AV**
     Bibl: Interior design, 1987 Jan.,
     v.58, no.1, p.260
Frye, Thamas (not Theodore) → see
   Frye, Thomas
Frye, Thomas   **BA PR WI**
   (British artist, 1710-1762)   *WC WI*
   (Irish painter, 1710-1762)   *BA PR*
     Bibl: ▶Bénézit; ▶RILA/BHA;
     ▶Thieme-Becker
   Frye, Thamas (not Theodore)   **WC**
   Thomas Frye   PR
Fryer, Edward H. *(British artist, op.*
   1819-1843)   **WC WI**
Fryer, Elmer *(American, active Los*
   Angeles, CA, U.S. ca. 1900)   **JG**
Fryer, Finley *(American artist,*
   b.1952)   **BA**
     Bibl: New York (NY, USA), New
     Museum, exh., 30 June-15 Sept
     1979
Fryer, G → see Fryer, George G.
Fryer, George G.   **WI**
   (British artist, 19th cent.)   *WC*
   (British artist, op.1870-)   *WI*
   Fryer, G   **WC**
Fryer, Katherine May *(British artist,*
   b.1910)   **WI**
Fryer, William   **WC WI**
   (British artist, 19th cent.)   *WC*
   (British artist, op.circa 1850-)   *WI*
Fryman, John G.   **AV**
Frymeier, Jacob → see Frymire, Jacob
Frymire, Jacob *(American painter,*
   1765/74-1822)   **BA**
     Bibl: ▶Groce, Artists Amer.;
     Washington, DC (USA), Corcoran
     Gallery, Charles Peale Polk (1981)
   Frymeier, Jacob   BA
Frys, Adriaen de → see Vries, Adriaen
   de
Frytom, Frederick van → see Frytom,
   Frederik van

Frytom, Frederik van   **GC**
   (Dutch artist, op.1658-1600)   *WC*
   (Dutch draughtsman, act.
     1658-d. aft.1690)   *GC*
     Bibl: ▶Bénézit; ▶Thieme-Becker
   Freytom, Frederik van   GC
   Frutom, Frederik van   GC
   Frytom, Frederick van   **WC**
Frytom, Joanna van *(Dutch artist,*
   17th cent.)   **WC**
Fucci, Lorenzo di Mariano → see
   Lorenzo di Mariano Fucci (il
   Marrina)
Fuchs, Bohuslau   **BA**
   (Czech architect, 1895-1972)   *BA*
   (Czechoslovak architect, 1895-
     1972)   *AV*
     Bibl: ▶Contemp. archts.; ▶Encyk.
     českého výtv. uměni; ▶Vollmer,
     Künst.-Lex. 20. Jhr.
Fuchs, Bohuslav   **AV**
Fuchs, Bohuslav → see Fuchs, Bohuslau
Fuchs, Emil   **BA PR WC**
   (American painter, sculptor,
     medalist, 1866-1929)   *BA*
   (Austrian painter, 1866-1929)   *PR*
   (German artist, 1866-1929)   *WC*
     Bibl: ▶Bénézit; ▶Fielding's Amer.
     ptrs.; ▶Smith, Idx. Amer. artists;
     ▶Thieme-Becker; ▶Vollmer,
     Künst.-Lex. 20. Jhr.; ▶WWW
     Amer. art; ▶Young, Amer. artists
   Emil Fuchs   PR
Fuchs, Ernst   **BA WC**
   (Austrian painter, printmaker,
     designer, b.1930)   *BA*
   (German artist, 1930-)   *WC*
     Bibl: ▶Bénézit; ▶Vollmer,
     Künst.-Lex. 20. Jhr.
Fuchs, Felix Cajetan Christoph
   (Swiss artist, 1749-1814)   **WC**
Fuchs, Feodor   **WC WI**
   (American artist, 19th cent.)   *WC*
   (American artist, op.1856-1876)   *WI*
Fuchs, Georg Mathias *(German*
   artist, 1719-1797)   **WC**
Fuchs, Inken *(West German*
   architecture student,
   Fachhochschule Coburg)   **AV**
     Bibl: Architektur,
     Innenarchitektur, Technischer
     Ausbau, 1987 Nov., v.95, no.11,
     p.48
Fuchs, Jack   **WC WI**
   (American artist, 20th cent.)   *WC*
   (American artist, op.20th c.)   *WI*
Fuchs, Jacques *(Swiss painter,*
   sculptor, 1922-1980)   **BA**
     Bibl: ▶Künst.-Lex. Schweiz 20.
     Jahrh.; Lausanne (CHE), Musee
     historique de l'Ancien Eveche,
     HOMMAGE A JACQUES FUCHS
     (1983); ▶Lex. zeitgen. Schweiz.
     Künstler

Fuchs, Johann (German organ
builder, ca.1670-1738) **BA**
Bibl: Dehio: Oberbayern, p.128;
Lampl, Jahrb. Bayer.
Denkmalpflege XXXIV (1980) 333-
353; Lieb, BAROCK KIRCHEN, 141
Fux, Johann **BA**
Fuchs, Joseph (German artist, 1810-
1880) **WC**
Fuchs, Kamil (Architect, son of
architect Bohuslav Fuchs, 1895-
1972) **AV**
Bibl: Architecture, the AIA
journal, 1986 Nov., v.75, no.11,
p.13
Fuchs, Peter (German sculptor,
1829-1898) **AV BA**
Bibl: ▶Bénézit; ▶Thieme-Becker
Fuchs, Waldemar (German, active
Italy 1890s) **JG**
Fucigna, Andrea **AV BA**
(Italian sculptor) **AV**
(Italian sculptor, act.1697-1701) **BA**
Bibl: Hager, Commentari XXIX
(Jan.-Dec. 1978) 201-216; Hager,
Commentari XXVIII (1977) 285;
Haus, PETERS-PLATZ IM ROM
(PhD. diss. Frieburg, 1976) 114
Fucina, Andrea **BA**
Fusina, Andrea **BA**
Fucina, Andrea → see Fucigna, Andrea
Fuechsel → see Fuechsel, Hermann
Fuechsel, Herman → see Fuechsel,
Hermann
Fuechsel, Hermann **PR WC WI**
(American artist, 1833-1915) **WC WI**
(American painter, 1833-1915) **PR**
Bibl: ▶WWW Amer. art
Fuechsel **PR**
Fuechsel, Herman **PR**
Herman Fuechsel **PR**
Füeg, Franz (Swiss architect) **AV**
Fuente del Saz, Friar Julian de la
(Spanish illuminator, act. ca.1568-
1589) **GC**
Bibl: Domínguez Bordona, Span.
illumination, v.2, p.157; Getty
Photo Study Coll.
Friar Julian de la Fuente del Saz **GC**
Fuente, Juan Leandro de la
(Spanish painter, 1600-1654) **BA**
Bibl: ▶Ceán Bermúdez, Bellas artes
ESP; ▶Encic. univ. ilus.;
▶Thieme-Becker
Fuente, Jullian de la → see Lafuente,
Julio
Fuente, Larry (American artist, 20th
c.) **BA**
Bibl: ARTS MAG LVII/1 (Sept 82)
18
Fuente, Luis de la (Spanish
architect) **AV**
Bibl: Arquitectura, LXV/250 (Sept.
-Oct. 1984), p.21

Fuentes, Giorgio (Italian
scenographer, 1756-1821) **BA**
Bibl: ▶Bolaffi; ▶Encic. spettacolo;
▶Thieme-Becker
Foentes, Giorgio **BA**
Fuerst, Shirley Miller (American
sculptor, painter, b.1928) **BA**
Bibl: ▶WW Amer. Art, 1978
Fuertes, Louis Agassiz **BA**
(American artist, 1874-1927) **WC WI**
(American painter, naturalist,
1874-1927) **BA**
Bibl: ▶Fielding's Amer. ptrs.;
Norelli, Amer. wildlife ptg.;
▶WWW Amer.; ▶Young, Amer.
artists
Fuertes, Louis Agassize **WC WI**
Fuertes, Louis Agassize → see Fuertes,
Louis Agassiz
Fueter, E (German artist, 18th cent.) **WC**
Fuga, Ferdinando **AV BA FA**
(1699-1781; Architect, Firenze,
Napoli, Roma) **FA**
(Italian architect, 1699-1781) **AV BA**
Bibl: ▶Macmillan encyc. archts.;
▶Thieme-Becker, v.12, p.576 ff.
Ferdinando Fuga **FA**
Fugate-Wilcox, Terry **AV BA**
(American sculptor, b.1944) **BA**
(Artist, New York City, 1944-) **AV**
Bibl: Art news, 1987 Dec., v.86,
no.10, p.30; ▶WW Amer. Art,
1976
Wilcox, Terry Fugate **BA**
Fugazza, Gian Pietro (Italian
cabinetmaker, act.1497) **BA**
Bibl: ▶Bessone-Aurelj, Scult. &
arch. ital.; Ippolito, ARTE
LOMBARDA, LXXXVI-LXXXVII
(1988), p. 141
Fuge, James **WC WI**
(British artist, op.1830-, d.1838) **WI**
(British artist, op.1830-m.1838) **WC**
Fugel, Gebhard **BA**
(German painter, 1863-1939) **BA GC**
Bibl: ▶Bénézit; ▶Brockhaus Enzyk.;
▶RILA/BHA; ▶Thieme-Becker;
▶Vollmer, Künst.-Lex. 20. Jhr.
Fugel, Gebhardt **GC**
Fugel, Gebhardt → see Fugel, Gebhard
**Fugelschaug, Fiigenschoug or
Fügenschaug, Elias** (Norwegian
artist, op.1635-1652) **WC**
Fuger → see Füger, Heinrich
Fuger, Friedrich Heinrich → see Füger,
Heinrich
Füger, Heinrich **BA GC PR**
(German artist, 1751-1818) **WC**
(German painter, 1751-1818) **BA PR**
(German, 1751-1818) **GC**
Bibl: ▶Encyc. world art;
▶RILA/BHA; ▶Thieme-Becker;
▶Witt checklist
Fuger **PR**
Fuger, Friedrich Heinrich **WC**
Heinrich Füger **PR**

Fugère, Henry (French sculptor,
b.1872) **BA**
Bibl: ▶Bénézit; Catley, Art deco
Fugl, Jan (Danish architect, Aarhus,
1952-) **AV**
Bibl: ▶Danske Arkitekters
Landsforbund, 1984-85
Fuglsang, Hans (German painter,
printmaker, 1889-1917) **BA**
Bibl: ▶MoMA libr. cat.; ▶Vollmer,
Künst.-Lex. 20. Jhr.
Fuglu, Jan Herman (Norwegian
architect, 1956-) **AV**
Bibl: Byggekunst: the Norwegian
review of architecture, 1988,
v.70, no.5, p.352
Fugman, Robert (American
architect) **AV**
Bibl: Chicago architectural journal,
1989, no.7, p.136
Fugo, Will (American architect,
Cleveland, Ohio) **AV**
Bibl: Inland architect, 1987 May-
June, v.31, no.3, p.46
Fuher, W. (German artist, op.1843) **WC**
Fuhr → see Fuhr, Xavier
Fuhr, Xaver → see Fuhr, Xavier
Fuhr, Xavier **PR WC**
(German artist, 1898-) **WC**
(German draughtsman, 1898-
1973) **GC**
(German painter, b. 1898) **PR**
Bibl: ▶Bénézit; Getty Photo Study
Coll.; ▶Schweers, Gemälde deut.
Museen; ▶Witt checklist
Fuhr **PR**
Fuhr, Xaver **GC**
Xavier Fuhr **PR**
Führich, Josef Ritter von → see
Führich, Josef von
Führich, Josef von **BA GC**
(Austrian painter, printmaker,
1800-1876) **BA**
(German artist, 1800-1876) **WC**
(German draughtsman, 1800-
1876) **GC**
Bibl: Getty Photo Study Coll.;
▶Österr. biog. Lex. 1815-1950;
▶Thieme-Becker; ▶Witt checklist
Führich, Josef Ritter von **GC**
Fuhrich, Joseph Ritter von **WC**
Fürich, Josef von **GC**
Fuhrich, Joseph Ritter von → see
Führich, Josef von
Fuhriman, Jerry (American artist,
b.1942) **WI**
Fuhrimann, Hans Ulrich (Swiss
architect, Ennetbaden) **AV**
Bibl: ▶Schweiz. Ingen. u. Archit.,
1984-1985

Fuhrlohg, Christopher *(Swedish cabinetmaker in GBR, b.ca.1737, d. after 1787)*   **BA**
    Bibl: BURLINGTON CXI/800 (Nov 1969) 648; BURLINGTON CXIV/835 (Oct 1972) 704; ▸Penguin dec. arts
Fürloh, Christopher   BA
Fuhrman, Paul → see Fuhrmann, Paul
Fuhrmann, C.G. *(German artist, op. 1842-1850)*   **WC**
Fuhrmann, Ernst *(German, 1886-1956)*   **JG**
Fuhrmann, Paul   **BA**
    (German painter, printmaker, 1893-1952)   BA
    (Interior designer)   AV
    Bibl: Interiors, 1988 Sept., v.148, no.2, p.50; ▸Vollmer, Künst.-Lex. 20. Jhr.
    Fuhrman, Paul   **AV**
Fuijck, Maerten van der *(Dutch artist, op.1660-1683)*   **WC**
Fujie, Kazuko *(Japanese furniture designer)*   **AV**
    Bibl: Space design, 1989 Nov., no. 302, p.5
Fujii, Hiromi *(Japanese architect, 1935-)*   **AV**
    Bibl: ▸Contemp. archts.; GA houses, n.14, July 1983, p.68
Fujii, Koji *(Japanese architect)*   **AV**
    Bibl: Toshi jutaku: 1985 Nov., no. 217, p.9
Fujiki, Tadayoshi *(Japanese architect, 1933-)*   **AV**
    Bibl: Kenchiku bunka, 1987 Dec., v.42,no.494, p.250
Fujimoto, Masaya *(Japanese architect, 1937-)*   **AV**
    Bibl: Kenchiku bunka, 1987 Dec., v.42, no.494, p.254
Fujishima, Takeji *(Japanese, 1867-1943)*   **GC**
    Bibl: ▸Vollmer, Künst.-Lex. 20. Jhr.
Fujita, Junya *(Japanese architect)*   **AV**
    Bibl: Space design, 1985 Dec., no. 255, p.5
Fujita, Kenji *(American sculptor, 20th c.)*   **BA**
    Bibl: Rubinstein, ARTS, LXII (Sept 1987), p.26
Fujita, Koichi *(Japanese architect, 1940-)*   **AV**
    Bibl: Kenchiku bunka, 1987 Dec., v.42, no.494, p.252
Fujita, Tsugouharu → see Foujita, Tsugouharu
Fujita, Yoshishige *(Japanese landscape architect, 1938-)*   **AV**
    Bibl: Process: architecture, 1985 June, no.59, p.143
Fujiwara, David K. *(Canadian architect, Toronto, Ont)*   **AV**
    Bibl: ▸Canad. arch. dir., 1987
Fuk, Nicolaes → see Ficke, Nicolaes

Fukao, Seiichi *(Japanese architect)*   **AV**
    Bibl: Kenchiku bunka, 1988 July, v.43, no.501, p.55
Fukaya, Kenji *(Japanese architect)*   **AV**
    Bibl: Toshi jutaku, 1983 May, no. 187, p.25
Fukerider, Herbert *(Architect, Nuremberg)*   **AV**
    Bibl: Baumeister, 1985 Feb., v.82, no.2, p. 37
Fuksas, Massimiliano *(Italian architect, 1944-)*   **AV**
    Bibl: Controspazio, XVI/1-2 (Jan.-Jun. 1985) p.108
Fukuzawa, Kenji *(Japanese architect, 1941-)*   **AV**
    Bibl: Japan architect, 1985 June, v.60, no.6(338), p.20
Fulcher, Raf *(British sculptor, b.1948)*   **BA**
    Bibl: Arts Council GBR, Summer show 3 (1977)
Fulchram, Jean Harriet → see Harriet, Fulchran Jean
Fulco di Verdura *(Italian designer, 1898-1978)*   **BA**
    Bibl: Letson, CONNOISSEUR CCXIII/853 (Mar 1983) 52-53; 62
Santostefano della Cerda, Fulco, duca di Verdura   BA
Verdura, Fulco Santostefano della Cerda, duca di   BA
Fulda, Albert *(German artist, op. 1820-1854)*   **WC**
Fulde, Edward B. *(American artist, op.1896-1912)*   **WC WI**
Fulk Nerra → see Foulque Nerra
Fulla, Ludovít   **BA WC**
    (Czech artist, 1909-)   WC
    (Czech painter, printmaker, b.1902)   BA
    Bibl: ▸Bénézit; ▸Fogg Mus. Libr. cat.; ▸Vollmer, Künst.-Lex. 20. Jhr.
Fullaondo Errazu, Daniel *(Spanish Architect)*   **AV**
    Bibl: Architecture d'aujourd'hui, no.236, p.58
Fullard, George   **BA WI**
    (British artist, 1925-1973)   WI
    (British sculptor, 1923-1973)   BA
    Bibl: ▸Bénézit; ▸Parry, Contemp. art; ▸Waters, Brit. artists; ▸Who was who [GBR]
Fuller → see Fuller, Isaac
Fuller, Albert W. *(American architect, Albany, 1854-1934)*   **AV**
    Bibl: ▸Withey, Amer. archts., p.225
Fuller, Arthur P. *(British artist, op. circa 1926-)*   **WI**
Fuller, Buckminster → see Fuller, Richard Buckminster
Fuller, Charles A. *(fl. 1846; Architectural draftsman, Louisville)*   **FA**
    Bibl: drawing inscription; Natl. Archives object

Fuller, Edmund G. *(British artist, op. 1888-1930)*   **WI**
Fuller, Ella *(American photographer, 1872-1968)*   **BA**
    Bibl: HIST. OF PHOTOGRAPHY III/4 (Oct 1979) 310
Fuller, Emily *(American painter, sculptor, b.1941)*   **BA**
    Bibl: ▸WW Amer. Art, 1978
Kingston, Emily Fuller   BA
Fuller, Florence Ada *(British artist, op.1897-1904)*   **WI**
Fuller, George   **BA GC PR WI**
    (American artist, 1822-1884)   WC WI
    (American painter, 1822-1884)   BA GC PR
    Bibl: ▸Fielding's Amer. ptrs.; ▸RILA/BHA; ▸Thieme-Becker; ▸Witt checklist
Fuller, George F.   **GC WC**
George Fuller   PR
Fuller, George F. → see Fuller, George
Fuller, Henry Brown   **WC WI**
    (American artist, 1867-)   WC
    (American artist, 1867-1934)   WI
Fuller, Isaac   **BA GC PR WC WI**
    (British artist, 1606-1672)   WC WI
    (British painter, 1606-1672)   PR
    (British, 1606-1672)   GC
    (English painter, printmaker, 1606-1672)   BA
    Bibl: ▸Bénézit; ▸Brit. Mus. cat.; ▸Dict. natl. biog.; ▸RILA/BHA; ▸Thieme-Becker; ▸Witt checklist
Fuller   PR
Isaac Fuller   PR
Fuller, John Charles *(American art historian, photographer, b.1937)*   **BA**
    Bibl: The Camera Viewed, Writings of 20th Cent. Photography; ▸WW Amer. Art
Fuller, Leland F. *(American architect)*   **AV**
Fuller, Leonard John *(British artist, 1891-1973)*   **WI**
Fuller, Lucia Fairchild *(American painter, 1872-1924)*   **BA**
    Bibl: ARCHIVES OF AMERICAN ART, XXVI/4 (1986) 2-16; ▸Petteys, Women artists; ▸WWW Amer. art
Fairchild, Lucia   BA
Fuller, Martin   **WC WI**
    (British artist, 1943-)   WC
    (British artist, b.1943)   WI
Fuller, Moss *(British artist, op.1978-)*   **WI**
Fuller, R. Buckminster → see Fuller, Richard Buckminster

Fuller, Richard Buckminster   AV **BA**
   (American architect, 1895-1983)   BA
   (American architect, designer
      and author, 1895-1983)   AV
      Bibl: ▶Libr. of Congr. Name Auth.
        File; ▶MoMA libr. cat.; NY Times
        obit., 3 Jul 1983, p.1
   Fuller, Buckminster   BA
   Fuller, R. Buckminster   AV
Fuller, Samuel   **WC WI**
   (American artist, 19th cent.)   WC
   (American artist, op.19th c.)   WI
Fuller, Thomas   **AV BA FA**
   (1823-1898; Architect,
      Government architect,
      draftsman (technical),
      Albany, Antigua, England,
      Ottawa, Toronto)   FA
   (Canadian architect, 19th c.)   BA
   (English architect, moved to
      Ottawa in 1857, 1822-1898)   AV
      Bibl: Arthur, Toronto; ▶Hill,
        Archs. Canada; Jrnl. Canadian art
        hist., III/1-2 (1976) pp.83-94;
        ▶Macmillan encyc. archts.
Fuller, Thomas William (1865-1951;
   Architect, Ottawa)   FA
      Bibl: CAAD Finding Aid, RG 11M
        77803/39; ▶Hill, Archts. Canada,
        1986; Ottawa City Directories
Fullerton, Arnie W. (Canadian
   architect, Edmonton)   AV
      Bibl: ▶Canad. arch. dir., 1985
Fullerton, Leonard (British artist,
   1909-1968)   BA
      Bibl: Council for Museums and
        Galleries in Scotland, PAINTINGS
        AND DRAWINGS BY L.F. (1973-75)
Fulleylove, John   **BA WC WI**
   (British architect, illustrator,
      painter, 1845-1908)   BA
   (British artist, 1845-1908)   WC WI
      Bibl: ▶Johnson, Brit. artists;
        ▶Mallalieu, Brit. watercolour
        artists; ▶Thieme-Becker
Fullmaurer, Heinrich (Swiss artist,
   op.1536-1543)   WC
Fullwood, Albert Henry   **WC WI**
   (British artist, 1863-)   WC
   (British artist, 1863-1930)   WI
      Bibl: ▶Johnson, Brit. artists
Fullwood, John   **WC WI**
   (British artist, 1854-1931)   WI
   (British artist, op.1881-1915)   WC
Fulmer, O. Kline (American
   architect, Princeton, N.J)   AV
      Bibl: ▶AIA Pro File, 1985
Fulmer, Thomas (American
   architect, Princeton, N.J)   AV
      Bibl: ▶AIA Pro File, 1985
Fulton, David (British artist, 1848-
   1930)   WI
Fulton, Don Hendry (Australian
   architect, 1925-)   AV
      Bibl: ▶Contemp. archts.
Fulton, Frederick (British artist, op.
   1889-)   WI

Fulton, Hamish   **BA WC WI**
   (British artist, 20th cent.)   WC
   (British artist, b.1946)   BA WI
      Bibl: Arts Council GBR, Beyond
        ptg & sculp. (1974); ▶MoMA libr.
        cat.
Fulton, Jack (American
   photographer, b.1939)   BA
      Bibl: San Francisco (CA, USA),
        Mus. of Modern Art, JACK
        FULTON'S PUNS...(1979)
Fulton, Robert   **BA GC WC WI**
   (American artist, 1765-1815)   WC WI
   (American engineer, painter,
      1765-1815)   BA
   (American, 1765-1815)   GC
      Bibl: ▶Columbia encyc.;
        ▶Thieme-Becker; ▶Witt checklist;
        ▶WWW Amer. hist.
Fulton, Samuel (British artist, 1855-
   1941)   WI
Fuluto, Piero   GC
      Bibl: ▶Bolaffi; ▶Witt checklist
   Fulutti or Fulutto, Pietro   GC
Fulutti or Fulutto, Pietro (Italian
   artist, op.1512-1519)   WC
Fulutti or Fulutto, Pietro → see Fuluto,
   Piero
Fumagalli, Gerolamo (Italian artist,
   16th cent.)   WC
Fumeron, Rene (French artist, 20th
   cent.)   WC
Fumez (French porcelain painter, act.
   1777-1804)   GC
      Bibl: ▶Brunet, Sèvres
Fumiani → see Fumiani, Giovanni
   Antonio
Fumiani, Giovanni
   Antonio   **BA GC PR WC**
   (Italian artist, 1643-1710)   WC
   (Italian painter, 1643-1710)   GC PR
   (Italian painter, 1650-1710)   BA
      Bibl: ▶Bolaffi; ▶RILA/BHA; TCI
        Venezia; ▶Thieme-Becker
   Fumiani   PR
   Giovanni Antonio Fumiani   PR
Fumicelli, Lodovico → see Fiumicelli,
   Ludovico
Fumo, Gaetano (Italian goldsmith,
   act.1737-1759)   BA
      Bibl: ▶Thieme-Becker
Fumo, Nicolò (Italian sculptor,
   d.1725)   BA
      Bibl: ▶Bessone-Aurelj, Scult. &
        arch. ital.; CB; TCI Napoli e
        dintorni, p.631; ▶Thieme-Becker
Funakoshi, Tohru (Japanese
   architect, 1931-)   AV
      Bibl: Kenchiku bunka, 1987 Dec.,
        v.42, no.494, p.256
Funaro, Gabriella (Italian architect)   AV
      Bibl: L'Industria delle costruzioni,
        1988 Mar., v.22, no.197, p.44
Funaro, Giuseppe (Italian painter,
   act.1762-1763)   BA
      Bibl: ▶Bénézit; Rizzo, NAPOLI
        NOB. XX/1-2 (1981) 33;
        ▶Thieme-Becker

Funck or Vonck, Cornelis (Dutch
   artist, op.1693-1712)   WC
Funck, Theodor (German painter,
   1867-1919)   GC
      Bibl: ▶Thieme-Becker
Funck, Valerian (German artist, op.
   1754-1770)   WC
Funck-Eydt, P.   AV
   Eydt, P. Funck-   AV
Fundarò, Anna Maria (Italian
   architect, 1936-)   AV
      Bibl: Architecture & urbanism,
        1987 Oct., no.10(205), p.48
Fung, Ming (American architect,
   Santa Monica, Calif)   AV
      Bibl: Bauwelt, 1989 Apr.28, v.80,
        no.16-17, p.770
Fungai → see Fungai, Bernardino
Fungai, Bernardino   **BA GC JG PR**
   (Italian artist, c.1460-1516)   WC
   (Italian painter, 1460-1516)   BA GC PR
   (Italian, Sienese, 1460-1516)   JG
      Bibl: ▶Bolaffi; Getty Photo Study
        Coll. (Ptgs.); ▶RILA/BHA, 1986;
        ▶Thieme-Becker
   Bernardino da Fongaia   BA
   Bernardino Fungai   PR
   Fongario, Bernardino   BA GC
   Fungai   PR
   Fungai, Fongario or Fungari,
      Bernardino   **WC**
   Fungari, Bernardino   BA
Fungai, Fongario or Fungari,
   Bernardino → see Fungai,
   Bernardino
Fungari, Bernardino → see Fungai,
   Bernardino
Funghoff, Hinrich → see Funhof,
   Hinrich
Funhof, Fonhave, Funghoff or
   Vonhoff (not Van Hof)
   Heinrich → see Funhof, Hinrich
Funhof, Hinrich   **GC**
   (German artist,
      op.1475-m.1484/5)   WC
   (German painter, d. ca.1485)   GC
      Bibl: ▶Thieme-Becker
   Fonhave, Hinrich   GC
   Funghoff, Hinrich   GC
   Funhof, Fonhave, Funghoff or
      Vonhoff (not Van Hof)
      Heinrich   **WC**
   Vonhoff, Hinrich   GC
Funi, Achille   **AV BA WC**
   (Italian artist, 1890-)   WC
   (Italian painter, muralist,
      Ferrara, 1890-)   AV
   (Italian painter, printmaker,
      1890-1972)   BA
      Bibl: ▶Comanducci, Diz.; Ferrara
        (ITA), Pal. dei Diamanti, Achille
        Funi (1976); ▶MoMA libr. cat.;
        ▶Vollmer, Künst.-Lex. 20. Jhr.

Funk, Hans (the Elder)   GC
   (Swiss artist, c.1470-1539)   WC
   (Swiss painter, 1470-1539)   GC
     Bibl: ▶Bénézit
Funk, Hans, I   WC
Funk, Hans, I→see Funk, Hans (the
   Elder)
Funk, Hans, II (Swiss artist, op.1523-
   m.1562)   WC
Funk, Heinrich   GC WC
   (German artist, 1807-1877)   WC
   (German painter, 1807-1877)   GC
     Bibl: ▶Thieme-Becker
Funk, Marc (Swiss architect,
   Ennetbaden)   AV
     Bibl: ▶Schweiz. Ingen. u. Archit.,
     1984-1985
Funkat, Walter   BA JG
   (German artist, art
     administrator, b.1906)   BA
   (German, 1906-, Bauhaus)   JG
     Bibl: ▶Natl. union cat., 1968-1972
Funke, Jaromír   BA JG
   (Czech photographer, 1896-
     1945)   BA
   (Czech, 1896-1945)   JG
     Bibl: Hist. of Photography III/3
     (July 1979) 259
Funke, Wilfried (West German
   architect, Detmold)   AV
     Bibl: Deutsches Architektenblatt,
     1988 Mar., v.20, no.3, p.513
Funnel Group (Etruscan vase-
   painters, 350-300 BC)   GC
     Bibl: Beazley, Etruscan vase-ptrs.;
     Del Chiaro, Funnel Group
Funnell, Suzanne (Canadian painter,
   b.1954)   BA
     Bibl: ▶Intl. dir. exh. artists, 1983;
     Winnipeg, Art Gallery, SUZANNE
     FUNNELL (1982)
Funo, Shūji (Japanese architect(?)
   and writer, 1949-)   AV
     Bibl: RLIN BKS file, MIUO87-B4208
Fuontebuoni, Anastasia (Italian
   artist, 17th cent.)   WC
Furbeck, Allen (painter, 20th c.)   BA
     Bibl: Bell, Flash art, 112 (May
     1983) pp.40-46
Furck, Sebastian (German artist,
   c.1600-1655)   WC
Furet, Catherine (French architect)   AV
     Bibl: Architecture intérieure créé,
     1988 June-July, no.224, p.56
Furge→see Ferg, Franz de Paula
Furgeson→see Ferguson, William
   Gowe
Fürich, Josef von→see Führich, Josef
   von
Furini→see Furini, Filippo
Furini→see Furini, Francesco
Furini, Filippo (Italian painter, act.
   1572-1614)   PR
     Bibl: ▶Thieme-Becker
   Filippo Furini   PR
   Furini   PR

Furini, Francesco   BA GC PR VO WC
   (Italian artist, 1600/4-1646)   WC
   (Italian painter and poet, 1603-
     1646)   VO
   (Italian painter, ca.1600-1646) GC PR
   (Italian painter, poet, 1604-
     1646)   BA
     Bibl: ▶Bénézit; ▶Bolaffi; Corti, G.
     'Contributi alla vita e alle opere di
     Francesco Furini,' in Antichità viva
     X/2 (1971), pp. 14-23; ▶Libr. of
     Congr. Name Auth. File,
     NAFR9128777; ▶RILA/BHA, 1986;
     ▶Thieme-Becker; Toesca, E.
     Francesco Furini (1950), p. 7
   F. Furini   PR
   F. Furrini   PR
   Farino   PR
   Forini   PR
   Forino   PR
   Fr. Furini   PR
   Francesco Furini   PR
   Fras. Furini   PR
   Furini   PR
   Furino   PR
Furino→see Furini, Francesco
Furlani Pedoja, Anna (Italian
   landscape architect)   AV
     Bibl: Ville giardini, 1989 June, no.
     238, p.58
Fürloh, Christopher→see Fuhrlohg,
   Christopher
Furlong→see Furlong, Charles
   Wellington
Fúrlong Cárdiff, Guillermo
   (Argentine architect, 1889-1974)   AV
     Bibl: dates: Summa, 1985 Aug.,
     no.215-216, p.26; ▶Libr. of
     Congr. Name Auth. File
Furlong, Charles W. →see Furlong,
   Charles Wellington
Furlong, Charles Wellington   PR WI
   (American artist, b.1874)   WI
   (American painter, 1874-aft.
     1962)   PR
     Bibl: ▶WWW Amer. art
   Charles Wellington Furlong   PR
   Furlong   PR
   Furlong, Charles W.   PR
Furlong, Thomas (American painter,
   illustrator, act.1921, d.1952)   BA
     Bibl: ▶Amer. art annual, 1933;
     ▶Bénézit; Glens Falls (NY, USA),
     Hyde Coll., Artists of Lake George
     (1976), pp.39-41; ▶Havlice, Idx.
     art. bio.; ▶Mallett's idx. artists;
     ▶WW Amer. Art, 1947; ▶Young,
     Amer. artists
Furlong, Weber→see Furlong,
   Wilhelmina Weber
Furlong, Wilhelmina Weber
   (American painter, 1878-1962)   BA
     Bibl: Glens Falls (NY, USA), Hyde
     Coll., Artists of Lake George
     (1976), pp.39-41
   Furlong, Weber   BA

Furlotti, Nicola [Unidentified]
   (Unknown painter)   PR
     Bibl: Furlotti, Nicola [Unidentified]
   Nicola Furletti   PR
   Nicola Furlotti   PR
Furnass, John Mason→see Furness,
   John Mason
Furne Fils (French, active Paris,
   France 1858-1861 (also Furne Fils
   & H. Tournier)   JG
Furnerius or Farnerius, Abraham→see
   Furnerius, Abraham
Furnerius, Abraham   BA GC
   (Dutch artist, c.1628-p.1648)   WC
   (Dutch painter and
     draughtsman, 1628-1654)   GC
   (Dutch painter, 1628-1654)   BA
     Bibl: Getty Photo Study Coll.;
     Getty Photo Study Coll. (Ptgs.);
     Gilfay, in ESSAYS IN NORTHERN
     EUR. ART... (1983) 97-101;
     ▶RILA/BHA, Rosenberg, Dutch
     art & arch.; ▶Thieme-Becker;
     ▶Witt checklist; ▶Wurzbach, NLD
     Künst.-Lex.
   Farnerius, Abraham   BA GC
Furnerius or Farnerius, Abraham WC
Furness, Frank   AV BA
   (American architect, 1839-1912)   AV
   (American architect, designer,
     1839-1912)   BA
     Bibl: ▶Britannica encyc. Amer. art;
     ▶Macmillan encyc. archts.
Furness, John Mason   WI
   (American artist, 1763-1804)   WC WI
   Furnass, John Mason   WC WI
Furness, Sydney Charles (British
   architect with the firm Cambridge
   Design, London)   AV
     Bibl: ▶RIBA members, 1987
Furniss, Harry   BA WC WI
   (British artist, 1855-1941)   WC WI
   (British caricaturist, illustrator,
     1854-1925)   BA
     Bibl: ▶Bénézit; ▶Houfe, Brit. book
     illus.; ▶Johnson, Brit. artists;
     ▶Met. Mus. Art libr. cat.;
     ▶Thieme-Becker
Furnival, John   WC WI
   (British artist, 20th cent.)   WC
   (British artist, op.20th c.)   WI
Furnstahl, Stephen (American
   architect, Brooklyn)   AV
     Bibl: Progressive architecture,
     1985 Feb., v.66, no.2, p.33
Furon, Aime Joseph (French, 1687-
   1729)   GC
     Bibl: ▶Thieme-Becker
Furrer, Walter (Swiss architect,
   1870-1949)   BA
     Bibl: ▶Avery obit. idx.; Winterthur
     (CHE), Kunstmus., Rittmeyer &
     Furrer (1986)
Furse→see Furse, Charles Wellington
Furse, Charles→see Furse, Charles
   Wellington

Furse, Charles Wellington PR WC WI
  (British artist, 1868-1904) WC WI
  (British painter, 1868-1904) PR
    Bibl: ▶Thieme-Becker
  Charles Wellington Furse PR
  Furse PR
  Furse, Charles PR
Furse, Roger WC WI
  (British artist, 20th cent.) WC
  (British artist, op.20th c.) WI
Furse, W.H. *(British artist, op.1830-1850)* WC WI
Furse, W.J.C. *(British artist, op. 1850's-)* WI
Fursman, Frederick Frary *(American painter, 1874-1943)* BA
    Bibl: ▶Bénézit; ▶Fielding's Amer. ptrs.; St. Louis (MO, USA), Art Mus., Ptg. in Midwest (1977); ▶Vollmer, Künst.-Lex. 20. Jhr.
Furst, Anton *(American production designer)* AV
    Bibl: Progrressive architecture, 1989 Sept., v.70, no.9, p.21
Furst, Josef *(German artist, op. 1798)* WC
Fürst, Moritz *(Hungarian medalist in USA, 1782-after 1841)* BA
    Bibl: ▶Groce, Artists Amer.; ▶Thieme-Becker; ▶WWW Amer.
Furst, Paul *(German artist, c.1605-1666)* WC
Fürst, Rosina Helena *(German textile artist, act.1676)* BA
    Bibl: Wilckens, KUNST U. ANTIQ 5 (Sept-Oct 1982) 58
Fürstchen, Georg Friedrich *(German architect, 1848-1884)* BA
    Bibl: DEUT. KUNST UND DENKMALPFLEGE XXXIII/1-2 (1975) 29-37
Furstenberg, Theodor Caspar, Baron von *(German artist, op. 1624-m.1675)* WC
Furtenagel or Fortenagel, Lucas or Laux → see Furtenagel, Lukas
Furtenagel, Laux → see Furtenagel, Lukas
Furtenagel, Lucas → see Furtenagel, Lukas
Furtenagel, Lukas BA
  (German artist, 1505-p.1546) WC
  (German painter, 1505-ca. 1546) BA GC
    Bibl: Pelican Hist. of Art; ▶RILA/BHA; ▶Thieme-Becker
  Fortenagel, Lucas BA
  Fortnagel, Lanx GC
Furtenagel or Fortenagel, Lucas or Laux WC
Furtenagel, Laux GC
  Furtenagel, Lucas GC
Furtenbach, Josef, the elder → see Furttenbach, Josef, the elder

Furter, Hans *(Swiss architect)* AV
    Bibl: Archithese 1985 Mar.4, v.15, no.2, p.39
Fürtler, Anton *(Austrian architect, Modling)* AV
    Bibl: ▶Verzeich. Öst. Ziviltech.
Furtmayr, Berthold BA GC
  (German illuminator, act.1470-1501) GC
  (German illuminator, ca.1435/40-after 1501) BA
    Bibl: ▶Allgem. Deut. Biog.; ▶Bénézit; Regensburg (DEU), Museen der Stadt Regensburg, REGENSBURGER BUCHMALEREI: VON FRUHKAROLINGSCHER ZEIT BIS ZUM AUSGANG DES MITTELALTERS (1987); ▶RILA/BHA; ▶Thieme-Becker
  Furtmeyr, Berthold BA
Furtmeyr, Berthold → see Furtmayr, Berthold
Furtrer, Ruprecht *(German painter, act.1455, d.1477)* BA
    Bibl: Liedke, ARS BAVARICA XLIII-XLIV (1986) 35-62
Furttenbach or Furttembach the Elder, Josef → see Furttenbach, Josef, the elder
Furttenbach, Josef, the elder BA
  (1591-1667) AV
  (German architect, 1591-1667) BA
  (German artist, 1591-1667) WC
    Bibl: ▶Portoghesi, Diz. arch. e urbanistica; ▶Thieme-Becker
  Furtenbach, Josef, the elder BA
Furttenbach or Furttembach the Elder, Josef WC
Fürttenbach, Joseph AV
Fürttenbach, Joseph → see Furttenbach, Josef, the elder
Furuya, Nobuaki *(Japanese architect, 1955-)* AV
    Bibl: Japan architect, 1988 Nov.-Dec., v.63, no.11-12, p.52
Fuscillo Painter *(Campanian vase-painter)* GC
    Bibl: ▶Trendall, Red-fig. vases Lucania
Fusco Girard, Luigi AV
    Bibl: ▶Libr. of Congr. Name Auth. File
  Girard, Luigi Fusco AV
Fuseli → see Fuseli, Henry
Fuseli R.A. → see Fuseli, Henry
Fuseli, Henri → see Fuseli, Henry

Fuseli, Henry BA GC JG PR
  (British artist, 1741-1825) WI
  (Swiss artist, 1741-1825) WC
  (Swiss painter in GBR, 1741-1825) BA
  (Swiss painter, 1741-1825) GC PR
  (Swiss, 1741-1825) JG
    Bibl: ▶Bénézit; Getty Photo Study Coll. (Ptgs.); ▶RILA/BHA; ▶Thieme-Becker
  Fuseli PR
  Fuseli R.A. PR
  Fuseli, Henri PR
  Fuseli, Jean-Henri PR
Fuseli, Johann Heinrich PR WI
  Fuseli, John Henry PR
  Fuseli, R. A. PR
  Fuseli, R.A. PR
  Fuselli PR
Fussli, Fuseli, Fusslin or Fussly the Younger, Henry or Johann Heinrich WC
  Füssli, Heinrich GC
  Füssli, Johann Heinrich BA
  Fuzeli PR
  Fuzelli PR
  H. Fuseli PR
  H. Fuseli, Esq.R.A. PR
  Henry Fuseli PR
Fuseli, Jean-Henri → see Fuseli, Henry
Fuseli, Johann Heinrich → see Fuseli, Henry
Fuseli, John Henry → see Fuseli, Henry
Fuseli, R. A. → see Fuseli, Henry
Fuseli, R.A. → see Fuseli, Henry
Fuseli, Sophia Rawlins *(18th-19th cs.)* BA
    Bibl: ▶Dict. natl. biog.; Pantheon Oct-Dec 1974, 379-381
Fuselli → see Fuseli, Henry
Fuses, Josep *(Spanish architect)* AV
    Bibl: El croquis, 1986 Apr., v.5, no.24, p.44
Fusi, Francesco *(Italian painter, act. 1748)* BA
    Bibl: ▶Bolaffi; ▶Thieme-Becker
Fusiano [Unidentified] *(Unknown painter)* PR
    Bibl: Spinelli inventory, Naples, 1655
Fusina, Andrea *(Italian sculptor, doca.1495, d.1526)* GC
    Bibl: TCI Milano e laghi
Fusina, Andrea → see Fucigna, Andrea
Fussel, Alexander *(British artist, op. 1838-1881)* WC WI
Fussell, Charles Lewis WC WI
  (American artist, 1840-1909) WC WI
  (American painter, b.1840) GC
    Bibl: ▶Bénézit
Fussell, Charles Louis GC
Fussell, Charles Louis → see Fussell, Charles Lewis
Fussell, Joseph WC WI
  (British artist, 1818-1912) WI
  (British artist, op.1821-1845) WC

Fussell, Michael	**WC WI**	
(British artist, 1927-)	WC	
(British artist, b.1927)	WI	
Fussell, Solomon (American cabinetmaker, 1704?-1762)	**BA**	
Bibl: WINTERTHUR PORT. XV (1980) 41-64		
Füssl, Christopher (Hungarian medalist, act.1536, d.1561)	**BA**	
Bibl: ▶Forrer, Medallists; MEDAL, 10 (winter 1986), p. 3-10; ▶Thieme-Becker		
Fiesel, Christopher	BA	
Fussli the Elder, Johann (Hans) Caspar → see Füssli, Johann Kaspar I		
Fussli, Friedrich Salomon (Swiss artist, 1802-1847)	**WC**	
Fussli, Fuseli, Fusslin or Fussly the Younger, Henry or Johann Heinrich → see Fuseli, Henry		
Füssli, Heinrich (Swiss painter, dealer in FRA, 1751-1829)	**BA**	
Bibl: ▶Bénézit; ▶Schweiz. Künst.-Lex.; ▶Thieme-Becker; Weinglass, Blake quarterly, XXI/4 (Spr. 1988) pp.144-146		
Füssli, Heinrich → see Fuseli, Henry		
Fussli, Heinrich, I (Swiss artist, 1720-1802)	**WC**	
Fussli, Heinrich, II (Swiss artist, 1755-1829)	**WC**	
Füssli, Johann Heinrich → see Fuseli, Henry		
Füssli, Johann Kaspar I	**BA**	
(Swiss art historian, painter, 1706-1782)	BA	
(Swiss artist, 1706-1782)	WC	
Bibl: ▶Allgem. Deut. Biog.; ▶Brockhaus Enzyk.; ▶Nagler, Neues Künst.-Lex.; ▶Neue deutsche Biog.; ▶Thieme-Becker		
Fussli the Elder, Johann (Hans) Caspar	**WC**	
Füssli, Johann Melchior	**BA**	
(Swiss artist, 1677-1736)	WC	
(Swiss printmaker, 1677-1736)	BA	
Bibl: ▶Schweiz. Künst.-Lex.; ▶Thieme-Becker		
Füssli, Melchior	BA	
Fussli, Melchior (Johann Melchior)	**WC**	
Füssli, Johann Rudolph	**BA**	
(Swiss artist, 1737-1806)	WC	
(Swiss painter, printmaker, art historian, 1737-1806)	BA	
Bibl: Singer, Allgem. Bildniskat., v.1; ▶Thieme-Becker		
Fussli, Rudolf, III Johann Rudolf)	**WC**	
Fussli, Mathias, I (Swiss artist, 1598-1665)	**WC**	
Fussli, Mathias, III (Swiss artist, 1671-1739)	**WC**	
Füssli, Melchior → see Füssli, Johann Melchior		

Fussli, Melchior (Johann Melchior) → see Füssli, Johann Melchior		
Füssli, Rudolf Heinrich (Swiss painter, 1791-1828)	**GC**	
Bibl: ▶Bénézit		
Fussli, Rudolf, I (Johann Rudolf) (Swiss artist, 1680-1761)	**WC**	
Fussli, Rudolf, II (Johann or Hans Rudolf) (Swiss artist, 1709-1793)	**WC**	
Fussli, Rudolf, III Johann Rudolf) → see Füssli, Johann Rudolph		
Fussli, Wilhelm Heinrich (Swiss artist, 1830-1916)	**WC**	
Fussmann, Klaus (West German painter, b.1938)	**BA**	
Bibl: Berlin (DEU), Staatlich Mus., Nationalgal. KLAUS FUSSMANN (1971); Washington, DC (USA), Hirshhorn Mus., Representation abroad (1985)		
Fusterz, Petre (Romanian, active Bucharest 1930s)	**JG**	
Fusto, F. (Italian artist, 17th cent.)	**WC**	
Futagawa, Yukio (Japanese author and architectural photographer, 1932-)	**AV**	
Bibl: ▶Libr. of Congr. Name Auth. File		
Futerer, Fuetrer, Furtrer, Futrer etc., Ulrich (German artist, op.1460-m.1496/1500)	**WC**	
Futterer, Josef (German artist, 1871-1930)	**WC**	
Futterman, E. L. (American architect)	**AV**	
Bibl: Architectural digest, 1984 Dec, v.41, no.12		
Futterman, Marc (American city planner, Calif)	**AV**	
Bibl: L.A. architect, 1989 June, p.5		
Futura 2000 (American artist, 20th c.)	**BA**	
Bibl: ▶Art Index, v.54, no.1; Nadelman, Artnews, LXXXI/8 (Oct. 1982) p.76		
Fux, Franz (German artist, 1745-p. 1787)	**WC**	
Fux, Johann → see Fuchs, Johann		
Fux, Johann Adam (German artist, op.1750-1753)	**WC**	
Fuzeli → see Fuseli, Henry		
Fuzelli → see Fuseli, Henry		
FVB Group (Campanian vase-painters)	**GC**	
Bibl: ▶Trendall, Red-fig. vases Lucania		
FVS → see Schooten, Floris Gerritsz. van		
Fye, Christine (British artist, op. 1982-)	**WI**	
Fyfe, William Baxter → see Fyfe, William Baxter Collier		

Fyfe, William Baxter Collier	**WI**	
(British artist, 1836-1882)	WC WI	
Fyfe, William Baxter	**WC**	
Fyk, Nicolaes → see Ficke, Nicolaes		
Fynson, Louis → see Finson, Louis		
Fyol, Conrad → see Fyol, Konrad		
Fyol, Konrad	**GC**	
(German artist, op.1448-m.1499/1500)	WC	
(German painter, d.1499/1500)	GC	
Bibl: ▶Thieme-Becker		
Fyol, Conrad	**WC**	
Fyre, S.H. (British artist, op.1867-1870)	**WI**	
Fyt → see Fyt, Jan		
Fyt or Fijt, Joannes or Jan → see Fyt, Jan		
Fyt, Jan	**BA GC PR**	
(Flemish artist, 1611-1661)	WC	
(Flemish painter, 1611-1661)	BA PR	
(Flemish, 1611-1661)	GC	
Bibl: Getty Photo Study Coll. (Ptgs.); ▶RILA/BHA; ▶Thieme-Becker; ▶Wurzbach, NLD Künst.-Lex.		
Feijt	PR	
Fet	PR	
Fijt, Joannes	GC	
fit	PR	
Fyt	PR	
Fyt or Fijt, Joannes or Jan	**WC**	
Fyt, Joannes	PR	
Fyte	PR	
Fyth	PR	
Fytt	PR	
I. Fyt	PR	
J. Fyt	PR	
J. Fytt	PR	
Jan Fyt	PR	
Jan Fytt	PR	
John Fytt	PR	
Ju.o feitto	PR	
Juan esfelt	PR	
Juan Fit	PR	
Fyt, Joannes → see Fyt, Jan		
Fyte → see Fyt, Jan		
Fyth → see Fyt, Jan		
Fytt → see Fyt, Jan		
G Dow → see Dou, Gerrit		
G Hamilton → see Hamilton, Gavin		
G Morland → see Morland, George		
G Myer → see Myer, G. [Unidentified]		
G Poussin → see Dughet, Gaspard (Gaspard Poussin)		
G Smith of Chichester → see Smith, George		
G, Morland → see Morland, George		
G. A. Ferrari → see Ferrari, Giovanni Andrea de		
G. A. Laurentini → see Laurentini, Giovanni (Arrigoni)		
G. Amicona → see Amigoni, Jacopo		
G. Angel → see Angel, G. [Unidentified]		
G. Arnald → see Arnald, George		

G. Arnald, Esq. A.R.A. →see Arnald, George

G. Arnold →see Arnald, George

G. Arnold, A.R.A. →see Arnald, George

G. B. Basini →see Bassi, Giambattista

G. B. Buccolo →see Brueghel, Jan Baptist

G. B. Caracciolo →see Caracciolo, Giovanni Battista (Battistello)

G. Baptt. Weeninghs →see Weenix, Jan Baptist

G. Bassan →see Bassano, Jacopo (Jacopo da Ponte)

G. Bassani →see Bassano, Jacopo (Jacopo da Ponte)

G. Bassano →see Bassano, Jacopo (Jacopo da Ponte)

G. Bassau →see Bassano, Jacopo (Jacopo da Ponte)

G. Bega →see Bega, Cornelis Pietersz.

G. Bellini →see Bellini, Giovanni

G. Bellino →see Bellini, Giovanni

G. Bemmel →see Bemmel, Johann Georg von

G. Benedetto Castiglioni →see Castiglione, Giovanni Benedetto (il Grechetto)

G. Berkheide →see Berckheyde, Gerrit Adriaensz.

G. Berkheyde →see Berckheyde, Gerrit Adriaensz.

G. Berkheyden →see Berckheyde, Gerrit Adriaensz.

G. Bosch →see Bosch, Gerrit van den

G. Botler →see Boteler, Gasper [Unidentified]

G. Brandi →see Brandi, Giacinto

G. Cagnacci →see Cagnacci, Guido

G. Camillio →see Camillio, G. [Unidentified]

G. Carpione →see Carpioni, Giulio I

G. Carracci →see Bonzi, Pietro Paolo (Gobbo dei Carracci)

G. Castiglione →see Castiglione, Giacomo [Unidentified]

G. Cesare da Sesto →see Cesare da Sesto

G. Chiari →see Chiari, Giuseppe Bartolomeo

G. Coionet →see Congnet, Gillis (I)

G. Coques →see Coques, Gonzales

G. Cortesi, called (Bourguignon) →see Courtois, Jacques (le Bourguignon)

G. Cortesi, overo il Borgognone →see Courtois, Jacques (le Bourguignon)

G. Covona →see Congnet, Gillis (I)

G. Crayer →see Crayer, Gaspar de

G. Croyer →see Crayer, Gaspar de

G. D. Witte →see Witte, Gaspar de

G. Da Bellino →see Bellini, Giovanni

G. da Carpi →see Girolamo da Carpi

G. da St. Giovanni →see Giovanni da San Giovanni (Giovanni Mannozzi)

G. Dathan →see Dathan, G. [Unidentified]

G. Daw →see Dou, Gerrit

G. de Bellini →see Bellini, Giovanni

G. De Crayer →see Crayer, Gaspar de

G. De Crayers →see Crayer, Gaspar de

G. de Heusch →see Heusch, Willem de

G. de la Notte →see Honthorst, Gerrit van

G. de la Rive →see La Rive, Pierre Louis de

G. de Lairesse →see Lairesse, Gerard de

G. De. Vrise 1664 →see Vrise, G. de [Unidentified]

G. del Notta →see Honthorst, Gerrit van

G. del Sole →see Sole, Giovan Gioseffo dal

G. Della Notte →see Honthorst, Gerrit van

G. della Notti →see Honthorst, Gerrit van

G. Desmarcsa →see Desmarcsa, G. [Unidentified]

G. di Bellini →see Bellini, Giovanni

G. di Bellino →see Bellini, Giovanni

G. di Vicenza [Unidentified]
(Unknown painter)　　　　　　**PR**
　　Bibl: (February 29, 1812, lot 130, Christie's)

G. Donck →see Donck, G.

G. Dou →see Dou, Gerrit

G. Douun →see Dou, Gerrit

G. Douw →see Dou, Gerrit

G. Dow →see Dou, Gerrit

G. Dow, 1671 →see Dou, Gerrit

G. Dowe →see Dou, Gerrit

G. Du Hamel →see Du Hamel, G.

G. Duhamel →see Du Hamel, G.

G. F. Grimaldi →see Grimaldi, Giovanni Francesco

G. Flinch →see Flinck, Govert

G. Flinck →see Flinck, Govert

G. Flink →see Flinck, Govert

G. Genga →see Genga, Girolamo

G. Ghilsolfi →see Ghisolfi, Giovanni

G. Ghisolfi →see Ghisolfi, Giovanni

G. Goeldorf →see Geldorp Gortzius

G. Guillon le Thiere →see Lethiere, Guillaume

G. Hamilton →see Hamilton, Gavin

G. Hamilton →see Hamilton, Johann Georg de

G. Head →see Head, Guy

G. Hoet →see Hoet, Gerard I

G. Hondekoeter →see Hondecoeter, Gysbert Gillisz. de

G. Hontherst →see Honthorst, Gerrit van

G. Honthorst →see Honthorst, Gerrit van

G. Honthurst →see Honthorst, Gerrit van

G. Hoor →see Hoet, Gerard I

G. Houet →see Hoet, Gerard I

G. James →see James, George, (GBR.)

G. Jansens →see Johnson, Cornelius I

G. Jordaens →see Jordaens, Jacob

G. Kalf →see Kalf, Willem

G. Kneller →see Kneller, Godfrey, baronet

G. L. Romanino →see Romanino (Girolamo di Romano)

G. L. Romano →see Giulio Romano (Giulio Pippi)

G. la Hire →see La Hyre, Laurent de

G. la Ris →see Lairesse, Gerard de

G. Lairaisse →see Lairesse, Gerard de

G. Lairess →see Lairesse, Gerard de

G. Lairesse →see Lairesse, Gerard de

G. Lambert →see Lambert, George

G. Laraiss →see Lairesse, Gerard de

G. Laraisse →see Lairesse, Gerard de

G. Laresse →see Lairesse, Gerard de

G. Larisse →see Lairesse, Gerard de

G. Larresse →see Lairesse, Gerard de

G. Lopez →see Lopez, Gasparo

G. Lunden →see Lundens, Gerrit

G. Lundens →see Lundens, Gerrit

G. Lunder →see Lundens, Gerrit

G. Lunders →see Lundens, Gerrit

G. Mazzola →see Bedoli, Girolamo Mazzola

G. Metsu →see Metsu, Gabriel

G. Metsue →see Metsu, Gabriel

G. Metz →see Metsu, Gabriel

G. Metzu →see Metsu, Gabriel

G. Mieris →see Mieris, Willem van

G. Moreland →see Morland, George

G. Morland →see Morland, George

G. Morland, 1793 →see Morland, George

G. Morlhnd →see Morland, George

G. Mortand →see Morland, George

G. Mostert →see Mostaert, Gillis

G. Mutiano →see Muziano, Girolamo

G. Netcher →see Netscher, Caspar

G. Netscher →see Netscher, Caspar

G. Notti →see Honthorst, Gerrit van

G. Occhiale →see Wittel, Gaspar van

G. Occhiali →see Wittel, Gaspar van

G. Occhialli →see Wittel, Gaspar van

G. Ocehiali →see Wittel, Gaspar van

G. Ochialle →see Wittel, Gaspar van

G. Ochialli →see Wittel, Gaspar van

G. Oechialli →see Wittel, Gaspar van

G. Palma →see Palma Giovane (Jacopo Negretti)

G. Paulyni →see Paulyni, G. [Unidentified]

G. Peeters →see Peeters, G. [Unidentified]

G. Pens →see Pencz, Georg

G. Peters →see Peeters, Gillis (I)

G. Petrie →see Petrie, George

G. *Philips* → see Philips, G.
[Unidentified]
G. *Piscopo* → see Piscopo, Giuseppe
G. *Pousin* → see Dughet, Gaspard
(Gaspard Poussin)
G. *Poussi* → see Dughet, Gaspard
(Gaspard Poussin)
G. *Poussin* → see Dughet, Gaspard
(Gaspard Poussin)
G. *Poussiu* → see Dughet, Gaspard
(Gaspard Poussin)
G. *Raco* → see Recco, Giuseppe
G. *Ralph* → see Ralph, George Keith
G. *Reni* → see Reni, Guido
G. *Romanino* → see Romanino
(Girolamo di Romano)
G. *Romano* → see Giulio Romano
(Giulio Pippi)
G. *Santacroze* → see Santacroce,
Girolamo da
G. *Schalken* → see Schalcken, Godfried
G. *Segars* → see Seghers, Gerard
G. *Seger* → see Seghers, Gerard
G. *Segers* → see Seghers, Gerard
G. *Sergers* → see Seghers, Gerard
G. *Siciolante da Sermoneta* → see
Siciolante, Girolamo (Girolamo da
Sermoneta)
G. *Simonelli* → see Simonelli, Giuseppe
G. *Smith* → see Smith, George
G. *Smitz* → see Smits, Casparus
G. *Smitzs* → see Smits, Casparus
G. *Stijls* → see Stijls, Gerard
[Unidentified]
G. *Stuart* → see Stuart, Gilbert
G. *Stubbs* → see Stubbs, George
G. *Terbourg* → see Terborch, Gerard II
G. *Terburg* → see Terborch, Gerard II
G. *Terburgh* → see Terborch, Gerard II
G. *Tilborg* → see Tilborgh, Gillis van
G. *Tilburg* → see Tilborgh, Gillis van
G. *Turner* → see Turner, George I
G. *V. Netcher* → see Netscher, Caspar
G. *van Aalst* → see Aelst, Willem van
G. *van Aelst* → see Aelst, Willem van
G. *Van B.* → see Monogrammist G.
van B.
G. *Van Eckhout* → see Eeckhout,
Gerbrand van den
G. *van Herp* → see Herp, Willem I van
G. *Vasari* → see Vasari, Giorgio
G. *Vongk* → see Vonck, Jan
G.B. *Califano* → see Califano, Giovanni
G.B. *Caracciolo* → see Caracciolo,
Giovanni Battista (Battistello)
G.B. *Viola* → see Viola, Giovanni
Battista
G.C. *Groth* → see Grooth, Georg
Cristoph
G.D *(French, active ca. 1880)*   JG
G.F. *Grimaldi detto Il Bolognese* → see
Grimaldi, Giovanni Francesco
G.F. *Penni* → see Penni, Giovanni
Francesco (il Fattore)

G.F. *Romanel* → see Romanelli,
Giovanni Francesco
G.H *(Active Belgium 1890s)*   JG
G.H. → see Monogrammist G.H.
G.K. → see Monogrammist G.K.
G.K.F. → see Monogrammist G.K.F.
G.M. *Crespi* → see Crespi, Giuseppe
Maria (lo Spagnuolo)
G.N. *Poussin* → see Dughet, Gaspard
(Gaspard Poussin)
G.P. *Rugendas* → see Rugendas, Georg
Philipp (I)
G.S. → see Sommer, Giorgio
G.T. *Serres* → see Serres, John Thomas
G.T. *Stubbs* → see Stubbs, George
Townley
G.V. *Bentem* → see Bentem, G. van
[Unidentified]
G.V. *Eckhout* → see Eeckhout,
Gerbrand van den
G: *Dow* → see Dou, Gerrit
Gaal → see Gael, Barend
Gaal, *Adriaen II* → see Gael, Adriaen II
Gaal, *Barend* → see Gael, Barend
Gaal, Pieter   GC WC
(Dutch painter, 1770-1819)   GC
(German artist, 1770-1819)   WC
Bibl: ▶Thieme-Becker
Gaap, Johann Adolf   BA GC
(German goldsmith in ITA,
1667-1724)   BA
(German, b.1664/69)   GC
Bibl: ▶Bulgari, Argentieri d'Italia,
v.1, p.477; ▶Forrer, Medallists;
▶Seling, Augsburger
Goldschmiede, v.3, p.282, no.
1895; ▶Thieme-Becker
Gaarder, LeRoy *(American
architect)*   AV
Gaast, Koenraadvan der *(Dutch
railway architect)*   AV
Bibl: Forum voor architectuur en
daarmee verbonden kunsten,
1984-1985, v.29, no.4, p.152
Gabai, Samuele *(Italian painter,
b.1949)*   BA
Bibl: Testori, GABAI, ... (1986)
Gabain, *Ethel* → see Gabain, Ethel
Leontine
Gabain, Ethel Leontine   WI
(British artist, 1883-1950)   WC WI
Copley, John, Mrs., (Ethel
Leontine)   WI
Gabain, Ethel   WC
Gabao → see Goubau, Antoon
Gabay, Dianna *(American painter,
20th c.)*   BA
Bibl: Staten Island (NY, USA), Inst
of Arts & Sciences, Study of a
Community
Gabbaria Mistrangelo, Pasquale
(Italian architect)   AV
Bibl: Architettura; cronache e
storia, 1979 Nov., v.25, no.
11(289), p.626

Gabbert, John *(American interior
designer, Lake Minnetonka, Minn)*   AV
Bibl: Architecture Minnesota,
1988 Mar.-Apr., v.15, no.5, p.13
Gabbert, Martha *(American real
estate developer, Lake
Minnetonka, Minn)*   AV
Bibl: Architecture Minnesota,
1988 Mar.-Apr., v.15, no.5, p.13
Gabbi *(Italian artist, 18th cent.)*   WC
Gabbiana → see Gabbiani, Anton
Domenico
Gabbiani → see Gabbiani, Anton
Domenico
Gabbiani, Anton Domenico   BA GC PR
(Italian artist, 1652-1726)   WC
(Italian painter, 1652-1726)   BA GC PR
Bibl: ▶Bénézit; Getty Photo Study
Coll. (Ptgs.); ▶RILA/BHA, 1986;
▶Thieme-Becker
Anton Domenico Gabbiani   PR
Gabbiana   PR
Gabbiani   PR
Gabbiani, Antonio Domenico   GC WC
Gibbiani   PR
Gabbiani, *Antonio Domenico* → see
Gabbiani, Anton Domenico
Gabe → see Gabe, Edward
Gabe, Edward   PR
(French artist, 1814-1865)   WC
(French painter, 1814-1865)   GC PR
Bibl: ▶Bénézit; ▶Thieme-Becker
Edward Gabe   PR
Gabe   PR
Gabe, Nicolas Edward   GC WC
Gabe, *Nicolas Edward* → see Gabe,
Edward
Gaberel, Rudolf *(Swiss architect,
Davos, 1882-1963)*   AV
Bibl: Archithese, 1986 Nov.-Dec.,
v.16, no.6, p.33
Gabetti, Giovanni *(Italian real
estate developer, Turin, 1927-)*   AV
Bibl: Architects' journal, 1989 July
26, v.190, no.4, p.15
Gabetti, Roberto *(Italian architect,
Turin, 1925-)*   AV
Bibl: Arkkitehti, 1987, v.84, no.3,
p.52
Gabilán Tomé, Simón   AV BA
(Spanish architect, painter,
sculptor, 1708-1781)   BA
(Spanish architect, sculptor and
painter, 1708-ca.1781)   AV
Bibl: Arch. esp. de arte (1949)
258-260; ▶Ceán Bermúdez, Bellas
artes ESP; ▶Encic. univ. ilus.;
Rodriguez Guttierrez de Ceballos,
Arch. esp. de arte, LIV/213 (Jan.-
Mar. 1981) 29-60;
▶Thieme-Becker; ▶Viñaza,
Adiciones Ceán-Berm.
Gavilán Tomé, Simón   BA
Gavilán, Simón Tomé y   AV
Tomé Gavilán, Simóm   BA
Tomé y Gavilán, Simón   AV

Gabino, Amadeo   **BA WC**
  (Spanish artist, 20th cent.)   WC
  (Spanish sculptor, b.1922)   BA
    Bibl: ▶Campoy, Español contemp.;
    Jahrb. der Hamburger
    Kunstsammlungen XIX (1974)
    123-128

Gabl, Alois *(German artist, 1845-*
  1893)   WC

Gabler, Ambrosius *(German artist,*
  1762-1834)   WC

Gabler, Josef *(German organ*
  builder, 1700-1771)   BA
    Bibl: ▶Allgem. Deut. Biog.; ▶Neue
    deutsche Biog.

Gablik, Suzi *(American painter,*
  author, b.1934)   BA
    Bibl: ▶WW Amer. Art, 1984

Gabo, Miriam Israels *(American,*
  20th c.)   BA
    Bibl: Clark Art Inst.; GABO (1957),
    eds. Read and Martin, p.186

Gabo, Naum   **BA GC WC**
  (Russian artist, 1890-1977) WC
  (Russian sculptor, designer in
  USA, 1890-1977)   BA
  (Russian-American sculptor,
  1890-1977)   GC
    Bibl: ▶Bénézit; ▶Encyc. world art;
    ▶Met. Mus. Art libr. cat.; ▶Natl.
    union cat., 1956-1967; NY Times
    obit., 24 Aug 1977, p.34;
    ▶RILA/BHA; ▶Vollmer, Künst.-Lex.
    20. Jhr.
  Pevsner, Naum Neemia   BA

Gábor, Marianne *(Hungarian*
  painter, b.1917)   **BA**
    Bibl: ▶Bénézit; ▶Vollmer,
    Künst.-Lex. 20. Jhr.
  Ronay, Marianne Gábor   BA

Gaboriaud, Josue *(French artist,*
  20th cent.)   WC

Gaboury, Etienne J.   **AV BA**
  (Canadian architect, 1930-) AV
  (Canadian architect, 20th c.) BA
    Bibl: ▶Arch. period. idx./RIBA,
    X/2 (1982); ▶Avery period. idx.;
    Building with words..., 1981,
    p.52; NBC

Gabrelli, Gaspare→see Gabrielli,
  Gaspare

Gabriel *(French artist, 18th cent.)* WC
Gabriel Blanchet→see Blanchet, Louis
  Gabriel
Gabriel Cornelius Ritter von
  Max→see Max, Gabriel Cornelius
  Ritter von
Gabriel de la Corte→see Corte,
  Gabriel de la
Gabriel de Leone→see Leeuw, Govert
  van der
Gabriel de Lyon→see Leeuw, Govert
  van der
Gabriel de terraças→see Terrasa,
  Gabriel
Gabriel de Terrazas→see Terrasa,
  Gabriel

Gabriel delacortte→see Corte,
  Gabriel de la
Gabriel family *(French architects,*
  17th-18th cs.)   **BA**
    Bibl: ▶Portoghesi, Diz. arch. e
    urbanistica; ▶Thieme-Becker
Gabriel Francois Doyen→see Doyen,
  Gabriel François
Gabriel Jacques de Saint-Aubin→see
  Saint-Aubin, Gabriel Jacques de
Gabriel Lemonnier→see Lemonnier,
  Anicet Charles Gabriel
Gabriel Metsu→see Metsu, Gabriel
Gabriel Metzu→see Metzu, Gabriel
Gabriel Perelle→see Perelle, Gabriel
Gabriel terraza→see Terrasa, Gabriel
Gabriel terrazas→see Terrasa, Gabriel
Gabriel von Hackl→see Hackl, Gabriel
  von
Gabriel, Ange Jacques→see Gabriel,
  Jacques Ange
Gabriel, Christopher *(British*
  manufacturer, 1746-1809)   **BA**
    Bibl: Goodman, FURNITURE
    HISTORY XVII (1981) 23-41
Gabriel, Claus *(German sculptor,*
  d.1654)   **BA**
    Bibl: Behling, H., in
    KUNSTPLITTER...(1984) 88-99;
    ▶Bénézit; ▶Thieme-Becker
Gabriel, G. L.→see Gabriel, G.L.
Gabriel, G.L.   **BA**
  (German painter, b.1958)   BA
  (West German painter, Berlin,
  1958-)   AV
    Bibl: ▶Babington Smith, Contemp.
    artists; ▶Intl. dir. exh. artists;
    ▶Libr. of Congr. Name Auth. File
Gabriel, G. L.   **AV**
Gabriel, Georges François Marie
  (French painter, b.1775)   GC
    Bibl: ▶Thieme-Becker
Gabriel, Jacques→see Gabriel,
  Jacques V
Gabriel, Jacques Ange   **AV BA GC WC**
  (1698-1782)   AV
  (French architect, 1698-1782) BA
  (French artist, 1698-1782)   WC
  (French, 1698-1782)   GC
    Bibl: ▶Bénézit; ▶Encyc. world art;
    ▶Lance, Dict. archts. fran.; ▶Lex.
    Kunst; ▶Nouv. biog. gén.;
    Pevsner, Dict. of arch.;
    ▶Thieme-Becker; ▶Witt checklist
  Gabriel, Ange Jacques   AV BA
Gabriel, Jacques Jules→see Gabriel,
  Jacques V
Gabriel, Jacques V   **BA**
  (1667-1742)   AV
  (French architect, 1667-1742) BA
    Bibl: ▶Dict. biog. fran.;
    ▶Macmillan encyc. archts.;
    ▶Portoghesi, Diz. arch. e
    urbanistica; ▶Thieme-Becker
Gabriel, Jacques   **AV**
  Gabriel, Jacques Jules   BA

Gabriel, Jacques-Jules *(French*
  architect, Paris, 1678-1753) AV
    Bibl: ▶Libr. of Congr. Name Auth.
    File
Gabriel, Jean *(1669-1718)*   GC
    Bibl: ▶Thieme-Becker
Gabriel, Julio *(American architect)* AV
Gabriel, Justin (Joseph Marie
  Justin) *(French artist, 1838-)* WC
Gabriel, Michal *(Czech architect)* AV
    Bibl: Architektura ČSR, 1988,
    v.47, no.3, p.62
Gabriel, Paul Joseph
  Constantin   **BA GC WC**
  (Dutch artist, 1828-1903)   WC
  (Dutch draughtsman and
  painter, 1828-1903)   GC
  (Dutch painter, 1828-1903)   BA
    Bibl: ▶Bénézit; ▶Busse, Maler u.
    Bildhauer 19. Jahr.; ▶Scheen, Ned.
    beeldende kunst., suppl.;
    ▶Thieme-Becker; ▶Wurzbach, NLD
    Künst.-Lex.
Gabriel, Richard   **WC WI**
  (British artist, 1924-)   WC
  (British artist, b.1924)   WI
Gabriel, Romano *(American*
  gardener, ca.1887-1977)   BA
    Bibl: ART NEWS LXXVIII/4 (Apr
    1979) 96; Wampler, ALL THEIR
    OWN, p.94
Gabriel-Fournier   **GC**
  (French artist, 1893-)   WC
  (French painter, b.1893)   GC
    Bibl: ▶Bénézit
Fournier, Gabriel Francisque   **WC**
Gabriele Bella→see Bella, Gabriele
Gabriele Cagliari→see Caliari,
  Gabriele
Gabriele Caliari→see Caliari, Gabriele
Gabriele Capellini→see Capellini,
  Gabriele
Gabriele Cappellini→see Capellini,
  Gabriele
Gabriele da Como→see Gabriele di
  Battista
Gabriele di Battista *(Italian*
  sculptor, act.1475, d.1505)   BA
    Bibl: Di Marzo, I Gagini, v.1, p.49;
    Kruft, DOMENICO GAGINI; TCI
    Sicilia (1968); ▶Thieme-Becker
  Gabriele da Como   BA
Gabriele Munter→see Münter,
  Gabriele
Gabriele Ricciardelli→see Riccardelli,
  Gabriele
Gabrieli, Antonio *(Italian painter,*
  ca.1694-1789)   BA
    Bibl: ▶Bolaffi; ▶Thieme-Becker;
    Vizzutti, Arte Veneta XL (1986)
    200-203
Gabrieli, Gabriel *(Austrian architect,*
  1671-1747)   AV
Gabrieljan, Nona *(Russian ceramist,*
  20th c.)   BA
    Bibl: DEK. ISKUSS. SSSR (Aug
    1976) 11-12

Gabrielli→see Gabrielli, Gaspare
Gabrielli da Viterbo, Francesco dei (Francischo Ghabriellis) *(Italian artist, op.1426-1427)*   **WC**
Gabrielli or Gabriello, Onofrio→see Gabrielli, Onofrio
Gabrielli, Antonio *(Italian, b. ca. 1625)*   **GC**
　　Bibl: ▶Thieme-Becker
Gabrielli, Gaspar→see Gabrielli, Gaspare
Gabrielli, Gaspare　　**BA GC PR WC**
　　(Italian artist, op.1805-m.1828)   WC
　　(Italian painter and printmaker, d.1828)   GC
　　(Italian painter, d. 1828)   PR
　　(Italian painter, printmaker, d.1828)   BA
　　Bibl: ▶Bénézit; ▶Bolaffi; ▶RILA/BHA, 1986; ▶Thieme-Becker
　　Gabrelli, Gaspare   BA
　　Gabrielli   PR
　　Gabrielli, Gaspar   PR
　　Gaspare Gabrielli   PR
Gabrielli, Onofrio   **GC**
　　(Italian artist, 1616-1705/6)   WC
　　(Italian, 1616-1705/06)   GC
　　Bibl: ▶Thieme-Becker; ▶Witt checklist
　　Gabrielli or Gabriello, Onofrio   **WC**
Gabrielsen, Eilert *(Norwegian architect)*   **AV**
　　Bibl: Byggekunst: the Norwegian review of architecture, 1988, v.70, no.4, p.262
Gabrielson, Walter *(American painter, sculptor, b.1935.)*   **BA**
　　Bibl: ▶Art Index, v.23; ARTFORUM (June 1972); Guide exh. artists: N. Amer. ptrs.; ▶Intl. dir. exh. artists, 1983; ▶WW Amer. Art, 1989
Gabriner, Ralph   **GC**
　　Bibl: ▶Idx. Amer. photog. colls.
Gabrini, Pietro *(Italian artist, 1856-1926)*   **WC**
Gabritschevsky, Eugene *(Russian artist, 20th cent.)*   **WC**
Gabron, Guilliam   **GC**
　　(Flemish artist, 1619-1678)   WC
　　(Flemish, 1619-1678)   GC
　　Bibl: ▶Thieme-Becker; ▶Witt checklist
　　Gabron, Guilliam or Willem   **WC**
Gabron, Guilliam or Willem→see Gabron, Guilliam
Gachet, Paul Ferdinand   **BA**
　　(French artist, 1828-1909)   WC
　　(French physician, artist, collector, 1828-1909)   BA
　　Bibl: ▶Dict. biog. fran.
　　Ryssel, Paul Van (Docteur Gachet)   **WC**

Gaci, Ludovico de *(Italian illuminator, scribe, act.1498)*   **BA**
　　Bibl: ▶Bolaffi; ▶D'Ancona, Miniaturistes; Daneu Lattanzi, Studi in onore di Roberto Salvini, pp.335-345; ▶Thieme-Becker
　　De Gazis, Ludovico   BA
　　Gadiis, Ludovico de   BA
　　Gazi, Ludovico de   BA
Gacs, Gyorgy Z. *(Hungarian sculptor, b.1914)*   **BA**
　　Bibl: Budapest (HUN), Magyar Nemzeti Gal., HOMMAGE A GYORGY Z. GACS (1974)
Gacsi, Mihaly *(Hungarian artist, 1926-)*   **WC**
Gactano→see Pulzone, Scipione (il Gaetano)
Gacy, John Wayne *(American, 20th c.)*   **BA**
　　Bibl: New Art Examiner XIII/3 (Nov 1985) 26-27
Gadaev, Lazar' *(Russian sculptor, 20th c.)*   **BA**
　　Bibl: Soviet sculp. 1977
Gadanyi, Jeno *(Hungarian artist, 1896-1960)*   **WC**
Gadbois→see Gadbois, L.
Gadbois, L.   **GC**
　　(French artist, op.1791-m.c. 1826)   WC
　　(French painter, d.1826)   GC
　　Bibl: ▶Bénézit
　　Gadbois   **WC**
Gaddi→see Gaddi, Agnolo
Gaddi→see Gaddi, Taddeo
Gaddi family *(Italian artists, 13th-16th cs.)*   **BA**
　　Bibl: ▶Bénézit; ▶Encic. italiana; ▶Thieme-Becker
Gaddi, Agnolo　　**BA GC PR WI**
　　(Italian artist, c.1350-1396)   WC
　　(Italian artist, circa 1350-1396)   WI
　　(Italian painter, ca.1350-1396)   GC
　　(Italian painter, d. 1396)   PR
　　(Italian painter, d.1396)   BA
　　Bibl: ▶Bolaffi; ▶Encyc. world art; ▶RILA/BHA, 1986; ▶Thieme-Becker; ▶Witt checklist
　　Agnolo Gaddi   PR
　　Gaddi   PR
　　Gaddi, Agnolo de Taddeo   PR
　　Gaddi, Agnolo di Taddeo   GC PR
　　Gaddi, Angelo or Agnolo di Taddeo   **WC**
Gaddi, Agnolo de Taddeo→see Gaddi, Agnolo
Gaddi, Agnolo di Taddeo→see Gaddi, Agnolo
Gaddi, Angelo or Agnolo di Taddeo→see Gaddi, Agnolo
Gaddi, Gaddo→see Gaddi, Gaddo di Zanobi

Gaddi, Gaddo di Zanobi　　**BA GC WC**
　　(Italian artist, op.c.1308-1330)   WC
　　(Italian painter and mosaicist, ca.1260-ca.1333)   GC
　　(Italian painter, mosaicist, ca. 1260-1333?)   BA
　　Bibl: ▶Bénézit; ▶Bolaffi; Ladis, TADDEO; ▶Thieme-Becker
　　Gaddi, Gaddo   GC
Gaddi, Giovanni di Taddeo *(Italian artist, op.1369-m.1383)*   **WC**
Gaddi, Taddeo　　**BA GC PR**
　　(Italian artist, circa 1300-1366)   WI
　　(Italian artist, op.1334-m.1366)   WC
　　(Italian painter, ca.1300-1366)   BA GC PR
　　Bibl: ▶Bénézit; ▶Bolaffi; ▶Fremantle, Florentine Gothic; Ladis; ▶RILA/BHA; ▶Thieme-Becker
　　Gaddi   PR
　　Gaddi, Taddeo di Gaddo   **WC WI**
　　Taddeo Gaddi   PR
Gaddi, Taddeo di Gaddo→see Gaddi, Taddeo
Gaddiana Master→see Gaddiani Master
Gaddiani Master *(Italian illuminator, act. late 13th century)*   **GC**
　　Bibl: Garrison, Ital. ptg. IV, p.88; Getty Photo Study Coll.
　　Gaddiana Master   GC
　　Master of Gaddiani   GC
　　Master of Gadiana   GC
Gadegaard, Paul *(Danish painter, b.1920)*   **BA**
　　Bibl: ▶Vollmer, Künst.-Lex. 20. Jhr.
Gadiis, Ludovico de→see Gaci, Ludovico de
Gado Romano [Unidentified] *(Unknown painter)*   **PR**
　　Bibl: (February 21, 1809, lot 90, Dawson (Thomas))
Gádor, Istvan *(Hungarian ceramist, b.1891)*   **BA**
　　Bibl: Faenza, LXVI/1-6 (1980) pp. 367-370; ▶Vollmer, Künst.-Lex. 20. Jhr.
Gadsby, Eric　　**WC WI**
　　(British artist, 1943-)   WC
　　(British artist, b.1943)   WI
Gadsby, William Hippon *(British artist, 1844-1924)*   **WI**
Gael→see Gael, Barend
Gael, Adriaen II   **GC**
　　(Dutch artist, c.1618/24-1665)   WC
　　(Dutch painter, 1618/24-1665)   GC
　　Bibl: ▶Bénézit; ▶Thieme-Becker
　　Gaal, Adriaen II   GC
　　Gael, Adriaen, II   **WC**
Gael, Adriaen, II→see Gael, Adriaen II

Gael, Barend   GC PR WC
  (Dutch artist, op.1658-1681)   WC
  (Dutch painter and
    draughtsman, ca.1620-1687
    or 1703)   GC
  (Dutch painter, ca.1635-1681)   PR
    Bibl: ▶Bénézit; Getty Photo Study
    Coll.; ▶Thieme-Becker; ▶Witt
    checklist
    B. Gaal   PR
    B. Gael   PR
    B. Gale   PR
    Barend Gael   PR
    Barent Gaal   PR
    Barent Gael   PR
    Barent Gaell   PR
    Barent Gale   PR
    Baron Soal   PR
    Berent Gaal   PR
    Gaal   PR
    Gaal, Barend   GC
    Gael   PR
    Gael, Barent   PR
  Gael, Barent→see Gael, Barend
Gael, Cornelis Adriaensz, I (Dutch
    artist, c.1589/90-p.1672)   WC
Gael, Cornelis Adriaensz, II (Dutch
    artist, c.1618/24-c.1654/60)   WC
  Gaelen→see Gaelen, Alexander van
  Gaelen or Gaalen, Alexander
    van→see Gaelen, Alexander van
Gaelen, Alexander van   PR
  (Dutch artist, 1670-1728)   WC
  (Dutch painter, 1670-1728)   PR
    Bibl: ▶Thieme-Becker
    Alexander van Gaelen   PR
    Gaelen   PR
  **Gaelen or Gaalen, Alexander
    van**   WC
    Van Gaelen   PR
Gaenssler, Michael (West German
    architect)   AV
    Bibl: Baumeister, 1989 Apr., v.86,
    no.4, p.28
Gaep, Thomas de (Dutch painter,
    17th century)   GC
    Bibl: ▶Thieme-Becker
Gaertner de la Pena, Jose (Spanish
    artist, c.1860-)   WC
Gaertner, Carl   WI
  (American artist, 1898-1952)   WC WI
Gaertner, Carl Frederick   WC
  Gaertner, Carl Frederick→see
    Gaertner, Carl
  Gaertner, Christoph→see Gertner,
    Christoph
  Gaertner, Eduard→see Gärtner,
    Johann Philipp Eduard
  Gaertner, Georg II→see Gärtner,
    Georg II
Gaertner, Johann Jacob (German
    painter, 1697-1750)   GC
    Bibl: ▶Bénézit
    Gärtner, Johann Jacob   GC
  Gaertner, Peter→see Gertner, Peter

Gaesbeeck, Adriaen van (Dutch
    artist, 1621/2-1650)   WC
Gaesbeeck, Adriaen van (Dutch
    painter, 1621/22-1650)   GC
    Bibl: ▶Bénézit
  Gaeta, Francesco→see Gaetano,
    Francesco
  Gaetan→see Pulzone, Scipione (il
    Gaetano)
  Gaetani→see Pulzone, Scipione (il
    Gaetano)
Gaetani, Benedetto di Oddone
  (Italian, d.1312)   BA
    Bibl: Wollesen, Fresken von S.
    Piero a Grado bei Pisa p.147
  Gaetano Brandi→see Brandi, Gaetano
  Gaetano Brando→see Brandi,
    Gaetano
  Gaetano Criscuolo→see Criscuolo,
    Gaetano
  Gaetano Cusano→see Cusati,
    Gaetano
  Gaetano Cusati→see Cusati, Gaetano
  Gaetano de Rosa→see Roos, Cajetan
  Gaetano Gandolfi→see Gandolfi,
    Gaetano
  Gaetano Lapis→see Lapis, Gaetano
  Gaetano Lapis di Cagli→see Lapis,
    Gaetano
  Gaetano Marsich→see Marsich,
    Gaetano [Unidentified]
  Gaetano Martorelli→see Martoriello,
    Gaetano
  Gaetano Martoriello→see
    Martoriello, Gaetano
  Gaetano Marturelli→see Martoriello,
    Gaetano
  Gaetano Neri→see Neri, Gaetano
  Gaetano Piattoli→see Piattoli,
    Gaetano
  Gaetano Recco→see Recco, Gaetano
  Gaetano Romanelli→see Romanelli,
    Gaetano
Gaetano, Alvise (Italian mosaicist,
    d.1631)   BA GC
    Bibl: ▶Bolaffi; ▶Thieme-Becker
    Gaetano, Luigi   GC
Gaetano, Francesco   BA
  (Italian artist, 17th cent.)   WC
  (Italian draughtsman, act.1664)   GC
  (Italian painter, act.1665-1687)   BA
    Bibl: ▶Bénézit; ▶Bolaffi; Ruotolo,
    Ricerche sul '600 Napoletano
    (1988); ▶Thieme-Becker
  Gaeta, Francesco   GC WC
  Gaetano, Luigi→see Gaetano, Alvise
  Gaetino→see Pulzone, Scipione (il
    Gaetano)
Gaffuri, Giorgio di Cristofano
  (Italian gem carver, act.1576,
    d.1591)   BA
    Bibl: Fock, Arti del principato
    mediceo, pp.319-320; Fock,
    Jahrb. der Kunstsamml. in Wien
    LXX (1974) 95; ▶Thieme-Becker

Gäfgen, Wolfgang (West German
    painter, printmaker, b.1936)   BA
    Bibl: Guide exh. artists: N. Amer.
    ptrs.; ▶Intl. dir. exh. artists, 1982-
    1983
Gág, Wanda (American printmaker,
    painter, illustrator, 1893-1946)   BA
    Bibl: ▶Vollmer, Künst.-Lex. 20.
    Jhr.; ▶WW Amer. Art, 1940,
    1947; ▶WWW Amer.
  Gagarin, Gregori Grigorievltch,
    Prince→see Gagarin, Grigorij
    Grigor'evič, prince
**Gagarin, Grigorij Grigor'evič,
    prince**   BA
  (Russian artist, 1810-1893)   WC
  (Russian painter, 1810-1893)   BA
    Bibl: ▶Bénézit; ▶Thieme-Becker
  **Gagarin, Gregori Grigorievltch,
    Prince**   WC
Gage, Elizabeth (British jeweler,
    20th c.)   BA
    Bibl: Watts, Connoisseur
    CCXIV/872 (Oct 1984) 122
Gage, Stephen (British architect)   AV
    Bibl: AA files, 1986 Autumn,
    no.13, p.46
Gage, Thomas, Bt. (British artist,
    circa 1780-1820)   WI
Gageiro, Eduardo (Portuguese
    photographer, b.1935)   BA
    Bibl: Gageiro, MULHER (1976)
Gagen, Robert Ford (British artist,
    1847-1926)   WC WI
Gageos   GC
    Bibl: ▶Beazley, Attic bl.-fig. vase-
    ptrs.
Gagern, Jurgen, freiherr von (West
    German architect)   AV
Gagerri [Unidentified] (Unknown
    painter)   PR
Gagès, René (French architect,
    Lyon)   AV
    Bibl: ▶Annuaire archts. fran.,
    1987
Gaggini family (Italian sculptors,
    15th-19th cs.)   BA
    Bibl: ▶Bénézit; ▶Thieme-Becker,
    v.13, p.52; chart
    Gagini family   BA
Gaggini, Antonello   BA GC
  (Italian artist, 1478-1536)   WC
  (Italian sculptor, 1478-1536)   BA GC
    Bibl: ▶Bénézit; ▶Bessone-Aurelj,
    Scult. & arch. ital.; ▶RILA/BHA;
    ▶Thieme-Becker
  Gagini or Gaggini, Antonello   WC
    Gagini, Antonello   GC
Gaggini, Antonio (Italian
    draughtsman, act. ca.1504-ca.
    1532)   GC
    Bibl: ▶Thieme-Becker; ▶Witt
    checklist

Gaggini, Domenico (*Italian sculptor, d.1492*)   **BA**
Bibl: ▶Bénézit; ▶Bessone-Aurelj, Scult. & arch. ital.; ▶Thieme-Becker

Gaggini, Elia (*Italian sculptor, d. before 1511*)   **BA**
Bibl: ▶Encyc. world art; Kruft; ▶Seymour, Sculp. Italy; ▶Thieme-Becker

Gaggini, Fazio (*Italian sculptor, ca. 1520-1567*)   **BA**
Bibl: ▶Bénézit; ▶Thieme-Becker

Gaggini, Giovanni II (*Italian sculptor, ca.1470-1517*)   **BA**
Bibl: ▶Bénézit; ▶Bessone-Aurelj, Scult. & arch. ital.; ▶Thieme-Becker

Gaggini, Pace (*Italian sculptor, act. 1493-1522*)   **BA**
Bibl: ▶Bessone-Aurelj, Scult. & arch. ital.; ▶Diz. artisti ital. in Spagna; Kruft; ▶Thieme-Becker

Gaggini, Vincenzo (*Italian sculptor, ca.1527-1595*)   **BA**
Bibl: ▶Bénézit; ▶Thieme-Becker

Gaggiotti-Richards, Emma (*Italian artist, 1825-1912*)   **WC**

Gagini family →see Gaggini family

Gagini or Gaggini, Antonello →see Gaggini, Antonello

Gagini, Antonello →see Gaggini, Antonello

Gagliardi →see Gagliardi, Filippo

Gagliardi, Bernardino (*Italian artist, 1609-1660*)   **WC**

Gagliardi, Filippo   **BA GC PR WC**
(*Italian architect, painter, d.1659*)   BA
(*Italian artist, op.1640-m.1659*)   WC
(*Italian painter, d. 1659*)   PR
(*Italian painter, d.1659, act. 1643-1659*)   GC
Bibl: ▶Portoghesi, Diz. arch. e urbanistica; ▶Thieme-Becker

Felippo Romano   PR
Filippo dalle prospettive   PR
Filippo delle Prospettive   PR
Filippo Gagliardi   PR
Filippo Gagliardo   PR
Filippo Romano   PR
Gagliardi   PR
Gagliardo, Filippo   PR

Gagliardi, Giovanni (*Italian painter, act. 1865-1898*)   **GC**
Bibl: ▶Thieme-Becker

Gagliardi, Pietro   **GC WC**
(*Italian artist, 1809-1890*)   WC
(*Italian painter, 1809-1890*)   GC
Bibl: ▶Thieme-Becker

Gagliardi, Rosario   **AV BA**
(*Italian architect, b.1685-1690, d.ca.1762*)   BA
(*Sicilian architect, b. 1698?*)   AV
Bibl: Blunt, Sicilian baroque; Lockwood Adler, Konsthist. Tidskrift, LV/3 (1986), p. 128; ▶Macmillan encyc. archts.; Tobriner, Genesis of Noto... (1982)

Gagliardini, Julien Gustave (*French artist, 1846-1927*)   **WC**

Gagliardo, Filippo →see Gagliardi, Filippo

Gagnaire, Aline (*French artist, 20th cent.*)   **WC**

Gagneraux cadet →see Gagneraux, Baptiste (Gagneraux cadet)

Gagneraux, Baptiste →see Gagneraux, Baptiste (Gagneraux cadet)

Gagneraux, Baptiste (Gagneraux cadet)   **BA**
(*French painter, 1765-1846*)   GC
(*French painter, printmaker, 1765-1846*)   BA
Bibl: ▶Bénézit; ▶Thieme-Becker

Gagneraux cadet   BA
Gagneraux, Baptiste   GC

Gagneraux, Bénigne   **BA GC**
(*French artist, 1756-1795*)   WC
(*French painter, printmaker, 1756-1795*)   BA
(*French, 1756-1795*)   GC
Bibl: ▶Bénézit; ▶Thieme-Becker; ▶Witt checklist

Gagneraux, Benigne (not Benjamin or Benedetto)   **WC**

Gagneraux, Benigne (not Benjamin or Benedetto) →see Gagneraux, Bénigne

Gagnery, Jean Auguste   **GC WC**
(*French artist, 1778-p.1845*)   WC
(*French painter, b.1778*)   GC
Bibl: ▶Thieme-Becker

Gagneux (*French artist, op.-1733*)   **WC**

Gagneux, Marie-Christine (*French architect, 1947-*)   **AV**
Bibl: Das Kunstwerk, n.3-4, Sept. 1983, p.59

Gagnon, Charles   **BA WC**
(*Canadian artist, 1934-*)   WC
(*Canadian painter, photographer, b.1934*)   BA
Bibl: ▶Artists Canada; ▶MacDonald, Can. artists; Sackville (NB, CAN), Mt. Allison Univ. Owens Gall., 5 photographers

Gagnon, Clarence A.   **BA WC**
(*Canadian artist, 1881-1942*)   WC
(*Canadian painter, printmaker, 1881-1942*)   BA
Bibl: ▶Dict. Amer. biog.; En. Can.; ▶Encyc. world art; ▶Thieme-Becker; ▶Vollmer, Künst.-Lex. 20. Jhr.

Gagnon, Claude (*Canadian architect, Montreal, Quebec*)   **AV**
Bibl: ▶Canad. arch. dir., 1985

Gago, Ignacio (*Chilean architect*)   **AV**
Bibl: ARQ, 1986 May, no.11, p.21

Gahan, Gordon →see Gahan, Gordon W.

Gahan, Gordon W. (*American photographer*)   **GC**
Bibl: ▶Idx. Amer. photog. colls.; ▶Libr. of Congr. Name Auth. File

Gahan, Gordon   GC

Gahler, Ernst (*East German architect, Rostock*)   **AV**
Bibl: Architektur der DDR, 1988 June, v.37, no.6, p.9

Gahn, Wolter Barclay (*Swedish architect, Stockholm, 1890-1985*)   **AV**
Bibl: Arkitektur; the Swedish review of architecture, 1985 Nov., v.85, no.9, p.43; ▶Svenska Ark. Riks., 1984

Gahrlieb von der Muhlen, Gustaf Casimir (*German artist, 1630-1717*)   **WC**

Gai, Antonio (*Italian sculptor, 1686-1769*)   **BA GC**
Bibl: ▶RILA/BHA; TCI Roma e dintorni; TCI Veneto; ▶Thieme-Becker

Gai, Francesco (*Italian, 17th century*)   **GC**
Bibl: ▶Thieme-Becker

Gai, Giovanni Maria (*Italian sculptor, 18th c.*)   **BA**
Bibl: ▶Bénézit; ▶Bessone-Aurelj, Scult. & arch. ital.; RIV. DELL'IST. NAZ. DI ARCH E ST. DELL'ARCH. 3, p.192; ▶Thieme-Becker

Gaiani, Carlo (*Italian artist, 1929-*)   **WC**

Gaibano, Giovanni (de Gaibana) →see Giovanni da Gaibana

Gaidano, Paolo (*Italian artist, 1861-1917*)   **WC**

Gaidon, Antonio (*Italian architect, sculptor and engineer, 1738-1829*)   **AV**

Gaig, G.M.M.   **WC WI**
(*British artist, 1638-op.1659*)   WI
(*British(?) artist, 1638-p.1659*)   WC

Gail, Joseph (*German artist, op. 1796-p.1818*)   **WC**

Gail, Wilhelm (*German artist, 1804-1890*)   **WC**

Gaildrau, Jules (*French painter, 1816-1898*)   **GC**
Bibl: ▶Bénézit

Gailhofer family (*German tinsmiths, 17th-20th cs.*)   **BA**
Bibl: ARS BAVARICA, 31-32 (1983) 67-76

Gailhoustet, Renée (*French architect, Paris*)   **AV**
Bibl: ▶Annuaire archts. fran., 1978

Gaillard, André *(Swiss architect,
Geneva)*   **AV**
 Bibl: ▶Schweiz. Ingen. u. Archit.,
 1984-1985
Gaillard, Antoine *(French menuisier,
master 1781, act. to ca.1815)*   **GC**
 Bibl: ▶Salverte, Ébénistes 18e s.;
 ▶Vial, Artistes décorateurs
 Gaillardi, Antoine   GC
Gaillard, Claude Ferdinand → see
 Gaillard, Claude-Ferdinand
Gaillard, Claude-Ferdinand   **GC**
 (French artist, 1834-1887)   WC
 (German painter, 1834-1887)   GC
 Bibl: ▶Bénézit; ▶Thieme-Becker
 Gaillard, Claude Ferdinand   **WC**
Gaillard, Eugène *(French designer,
1862-1933)*   **BA**
 Bibl: ▶Larousse grande encyc.;
 ▶Penguin dec. arts
Gaillard, Francois *(Flemish artist,
op.1634-m.1664)*   **WC**
Gaillard, Jean *(French architect, act.
1631-1640)*   **BA**
 Bibl: Fregnac, Merveilles des
 châteaux, IV, p.178; Jestaz, B., in
 Congrès archéologique de France
 138 (1980), p. 200
Gaillard, Maryvonne *(French
architect)*   **AV**
 Bibl: Architecture & urbanism,
 1986 Oct., no.10, p.54
Gaillard, Paul *(French, before 1835-
1890)*   **JG**
Gaillard, René   **BA GC**
 *(French printmaker, ca.1719-
 1790)*   BA
 (French, d.1790)   GC
 Bibl: ▶Bellier, Artistes fran.; Getty
 Photo Study Coll. (Ptgs.);
 ▶Thieme-Becker
 Gaillard, Robert   GC
Gaillard, Robert → see Gaillard, René
Gaillardi, Antoine → see Gaillard,
 Antoine
Gailliard, Jean Jacques *(Belgian
painter, 1890-1976)*   **BA**
 Bibl: ▶Bénézit; BULLETIN DE LA
 CLASSE DES BEAUX-ARTS LXII/4-9
 (1980) 61-73; ▶Natl. union cat.,
 1968-1972; ▶Vollmer, Künst.-Lex.
 20. Jhr.
Gailliard, Pierre *(French artist, 20th
cent.)*   **WC**
Gaillot, Bernard *(French painter,
printmaker, 1780-1847)*   **BA**
 Bibl: ▶Dict. biog. fran.;
 ▶Thieme-Becker
Gain, Jacob (the Elder) → see Gheyn,
 Jacob I de
Gainborough → see Gainsborough,
 Thomas

Gaines, Charles *(American
printmaker, sculptor, 20th c.)*   **BA**
 Bibl: ▶Art Index, 1980; ▶Intl. dir.
 exh. artists, 1983; Print
 collector's newsletter X (July
 1979), p. 93
Gainey, Ryan *(American gardener,
Decatur, Ga)*   **AV**
 Bibl: House beautiful, 1988 Nov.,
 v.130, no.11, p.104
Gainsboro → see Gainsborough,
 Thomas
Gainsboro Dupont → see Dupont,
 Gainsborough
Gainsboro' → see Gainsborough,
 Thomas
[Gainsborough] → see Gainsborough,
 Thomas
Gainsborough Dupont → see Dupont,
 Gainsborough
Gainsborough, &c. → see
 Gainsborough, Thomas
**Gainsborough,
 Thomas**   **BA GC JG PR WC WI**
 (British artist, 1727-1788)   WC WI
 (British painter, 1727-1788) BA GC PR
 (English, 1727-1788)   JG
 Bibl: ▶Bénézit; ▶RILA/BHA;
 ▶Thieme-Becker; ▶Waterhouse,
 Brit. 18c. ptrs.
 Gainborough   PR
 Gainsboro   PR
 Gainsboro'   PR
 [Gainsborough]   PR
 Gainsborough, &c.   PR
 Gainsbro   PR
 Gainsbro'   PR
 T. Gainsborough   PR
 T. Gainsbro   PR
 Thomas Gainsborough   PR
Gainsbro → see Gainsborough,
 Thomas
Gainsbro' → see Gainsborough,
 Thomas
Gainsford, F.G. *(British artist, op.
1805-1822)*   **WC WI**
Gainza, Carlos Alberto *(Argentine
architect)*   **AV**
 Bibl: Summa, 1986 Mar., no.223,
 p.48
Gais, Christoph M. *(West German
painter, b.1951.)*   **BA**
 Bibl: ▶Intl. dir. exh. artists, 1983;
 Munich (DEU), Kunstverein, Neue
 Tendenzen der Zeichnung (1981)
Gaismayer, J. *(West German
architect, Düsseldorf)*   **AV**
 Bibl: Deutsche Bauzeitschrift,
 1987 Sept., v.35, no.9, p.1079
Gaisne, Claude   **AV**
Gaiso, Giovanni del → see Del Gaizo,
 Giovanni
Gaisser, Jakob Emanuel *(German
artist, 1825-1899)*   **WC**

Gaisser, Max   **GC WC**
 (German artist, 1857-1922)   WC
 (German painter, 1857-1922)   GC
 Bibl: ▶Thieme-Becker
Gaitán, Pedro *(Spanish sculptor, act.
1700)*   **BA**
 Bibl: ▶Bénézit; ▶Thieme-Becker
Gaither, James Orme *(American
silversmith, b.1792, act.1817)*   **BA**
 Bibl: JOURNAL OF EARLY SOUTH.
 DEC. ARTS, XI/1 (MAy 1985) 1-13
Gaither, John *(American silversmith,
1784/88-1819)*   **BA**
 Bibl: S. EARLY S. DEC. ARTS IX/.1
 (May 1983) 35
Gaitis, Yannis *(Greek artist, 1923-)* **WC**
Gaius Julius Caesar Octavianus → see
 Augustus, Emperor of Rome
Gaizo, Giovanni del → see Del Gaizo,
 Giovanni
Gaj, Jacek *(Polish printmaker,
b.1938)*   **BA**
 Bibl: Paris (FRA), Grand Palais,
 L'art polonais romantique (1977)
Gajda, Wiktor *(Polish sculptor,
b.1938)*   **BA**
 Bibl: Paris (FRA), Mus. d'art mod
 de la ville, Sculptures polonaises
 (1980)
Gajewski, Henryk *(Polish artist,
b.1948)*   **BA**
 Bibl: Hoffberg, JOURNAL: A
 CONTEMP. ART MAGAZINE 35
 (1982-83) 54-58; ▶Intl. dir. exh.
 artists, 1982
Gal (Gerard Alsteens) *(Belgian
cartoonist, printmaker, b.1940)*   **BA**
 Bibl: ▶Dict. biog. artistes belges;
 ▶Intl. dir. exh. artists, 1983
 Alsteens, Gerard   BA
Gal'berg, I.I. *(Russian architect, 19th
c.)*   **BA**
 Bibl: DEKORATIVNOE ISKUSSTVO
 11 (1974) 46-47
Gal'berg, Samuil Ivanovič *(Russian
sculptor, 1787-1839)*   **BA**
 Bibl: Akademie Nauk SSSR,
 Russische Kunst, v.8, pt.1
 Halberg, Samuel   BA
 Hallberg, Samuel Friedrich
 Ivanovich   BA
Gal, Menchu *(Spanish artist, 20th
cent.)*   **WC**
Gal, Serge *(French, 1950 -)*   **JG**
Gál, Vera *(Hungarian tapestry
maker, b.1942)*   **BA**
 Bibl: Budapest (HUN), Magyar
 Nemzeti Gal., EXPOSITION DE
 VERA GAL (1974)
Galait, Louis → see Gallait, Louis
Galaktionov, Stepan Filippovič
 *(Russian painter, printmaker, 1778-
 1854)*   **BA**
 Bibl: ▶Thieme-Becker; Wulff,
 Neurissische Kunst

Galán y González Carvajal, Julio
(*Spanish architect, 20th c.*)   **BA**
 Bibl: Anguiano, MISCELANEA DE
  ARTE 254-258
Galán, Julio   BA
Galán, Julio → see Galán y González
 Carvajal, Julio
Galanda, Mikulas (*Czech artist,
1895-1938*)   **WC**
Galani-Papala, E. (*Architect, Greece*)   **AV**
 Bibl: Themata chorov + technon,
  1984, v.15, p.155
Galanini, Baldassare → see Aloisi
 Galanini, Baldassare (Galanino)
Galanini, Baldassare Aloisi → see Aloisi
 Galanini, Baldassare (Galanino)
Galanino → see Aloisi Galanini,
 Baldassare (Galanino)
Galanis → see Galanis, Demetrios
Galanis, Demetrios   **PR WC**
 (*French artist, 1882-1966*)   WC
 (*French painter, 1880/2-1966*)   GC
 (*Greek painter, 1880-1966*)   PR
 Bibl: ▸Bénézit; ▸Thieme-Becker;
  ▸Witt checklist
Demetrios Galanis   PR
Demetrius, Galanis   **GC**
Galanis   PR
Galanos, James (*American
couturier, b.1922*)   **BA**
 Bibl: ▸Columbia encyc.
Galanos, Markellos (*Greek
architect, Athens*)   **AV**
 Bibl: American School of Classical
  Studies at Athens. Newsletter,
  1989 spring, no.23, p.1
Galante, Francesco (*Italian artist,
1884-*)   **WC**
Galantini, Ippolito (*Italian artist,
1627-1706*)   **WC**
Galantino, Mauro (*Italian architect,
Milan*)   **AV**
 Bibl: Domus, 1988 Oct., no.698,
  p.46
Galanyk, Edward Andrew
(*Canadian architect, Toronto*)   **AV**
 Bibl: ▸Canad. arch. dir., 1985,
  p.52
Galard, Gustave → see Galard,
 Gustave, comte de
Galard, Gustave Comte de → see
 Galard, Gustave, comte de
Galard, Gustave, comte de   **BA**
 (*French artist, c.1777-1840*)   WC
 (*French painter, 1777-1840*)   GC
 (*French painter, 1779-1841*)   BA
 Bibl: ▸Bénézit; ▸Thieme-Becker
Galard, Gustave   **WC**
Galard, Gustave Comte de   **GC**
Galardi, Alberto (*Italian architect,
1930-*)   **AV**
Galas, Diamanda (*American singer,
20th c.*)   **BA**
 Bibl: Frank, Flash art, 125 (Dec.
  1985-Jan. 1986) p.73

Galasso di Matteo Piva   GC **PR**
 (*Italian artist, op.c.1450*)   WC
 (*Italian painter, act. 2nd half
  15th cent.*)   PR
 (*Italian, d.1573*)   GC
 Bibl: ▸Thieme-Becker
Alghisi, Galasso   **GC**
**Galasso di Matteo Piva
(Galasso, Galassi or Alghisi)**   **WC**
Galasso Galassi   PR
*Galasso di Matteo Piva (Galasso,
 Galassi or Alghisi) → see* Galasso di
 Matteo Piva
Galasso Galassi → see Galasso di
 Matteo Piva
Galberio, Giuseppe (*Italian painter,
16th c.*)   **BA**
 Bibl: ARTE LOMBARDA 51 (1979)
  29-38
Galbrund, Alphonse Louis   **GC WC**
 (*French artist, 1810-1885*)   WC
 (*French painter, 1810-1885*)   GC
 Bibl: ▸Bénézit
Galdi, Vicenzo (*Italian, active ca.
1890-ca. 1910*)   **JG**
Gale, Benjamin   **WC WI**
 (*British artist, 1741-1832*)   WI
 (*British artist, op.c.1775-1830*)   WC
Gale, Denise (*American painter,
b.1950*)   **BA**
 Bibl: ▸Artweek idx.; JOURNAL OF
  THE LOS ANGELES INST. OF CONT.
  ART 19 (June-July 1978) 25
Gale, Jonathan → see Gale, Simon
 Jonathan
Gale, Joseph (Col.) (*British, d.
1906*)   **JG**
Gale, Martin (*Irish painter, 20th c.*)   **BA**
 Bibl: ▸Babington Smith, Contemp.
  artists; London (GBR),
  Roundhouse Gallery, Irish art
  (1980)
Gale, Simon Jonathan (*English
architect, London*)   **AV**
 Bibl: ▸RIBA members, 1986
Gale, Jonathan   AV
Gale, William (*British artist, op.
1747-1757*)   **WI**
Gale, William (*British artist, 1823-
1909*)   **WC**
Galea → see Galea, Luigi Maria
Galea, L. → see Galea, Luigi Maria
Galea, Luigi → see Galea, Luigi Maria
Galea, Luigi Maria   **WI**
 (*British artist, 1847-1917*)   WI
 (*British artist, op.1894*)   WC
 (*British painter, act. 1894*)   PR
 Bibl: Columbus M of A catalogue;
  ▸Witt checklist
Galea   PR
Galea, L.   **WC**
Galea, Luigi   **PR**
Luigi Galea   PR

Galeani, Orfeo (*Italian engineer and
soldier in the service of Farnese
dukes and Charles III of Lorraine
(16th century)*)   **AV**
 Bibl: Quaderni. Istituto di storia
  dell'arch., 1977-78, p.57
Galeazzi, Conte Enrico (*fl. mid-20th
century; Architect, Italia*)   **FA**
 Bibl: ▸Blunt, Baroque Rome
Galeazzo Campi → see Campi,
 Galeazzo
Galen, G.D. (*Dutch artist, op.1779*)   **WC**
Galen, Nicolaes van   **GC WC**
 (*Dutch artist, c.1620-p.1683*)   WC
 (*Dutch painter, ca.1620-aft.
  1683*)   GC
 Bibl: Getty Photo Study Coll.;
  ▸Thieme-Becker; ▸Witt checklist
Galen, Thyman van (*Dutch artist,
1590-p.1632*)   **WC**
Galeotti, Anna [Unidentified]
(*Unknown painter, act. 18th
century*)   **PR**
 Bibl: Riccardi inventory dated
  1776
Anna Galeotti   PR
Galeotti, Giuseppe (*Italian artist,
1708-1778*)   **WC**
Galeotti, Pietro Paolo (*Italian
goldsmith, medalist, ca.1520-1584*)   **BA**
 Bibl: ▸Encic. italiana; ▸Forrer,
  Medallists; Hill, Portrait medals;
  ▸Thieme-Becker
Galeotto, Pietro Paolo   BA
Pier Paolo Romano   BA
Romano, Pier Paolo   BA
Galeotti, Sebastiano   **BA**
 (*Italian artist, c.1676-1746*)   WC
 (*Italian painter, 1676-1746*)   BA
 Bibl: ▸Bénézit; ▸Bolaffi;
  ▸Thieme-Becker
Galeotti, Sebastiano (Bastiano)   **WC**
Galeotti, Sebastiano (Bastiano) → see
 Galeotti, Sebastiano
Galeotto, Pietro Paolo → see Galeotti,
 Pietro Paolo
Galerne, Prosper (*French painter,
b.1836*)   **GC**
 Bibl: ▸Thieme-Becker
Galeron, Albert (*French architect,
19th century*)   **AV**
 Bibl: Archives d'architecture
  moderne, 1986, no.32, p.76
Gales Painter (*vase-painter, ca. 530-
500 BC*)   **GC**
 Bibl: ▸Beazley, Attic red-fig. vase-
  ptrs.; Richter, Attic red-fig. vases
Galestruzzi → see Galestruzzi,
 Giovanni Battista

Galestruzzi, Giovanni Battista BA GC PR WC
  (Italian artist, 1615/8-p.1669) WC
  (Italian painter and printmaker, 1618-aft.1661) GC
  (Italian painter, 1619-1661) PR
  (Italian painter, printmaker, 1618-after 1661) BA
  Bibl: ▶Bolaffi; Giglioli, INCISORI TOSCANI DEL SEICENTO (1942); ▶RILA/BHA, 1986; ▶Thieme-Becker
  Galestruzzi PR
  Giovanni Battista Galestruzzi PR
Galetti → see Galletti, Filippo Maria
Galey, Gaston Pierre *(French artist, 1880-)* WC
Galeyev, Bulat M. *(Russian physicist, artist, 20th c.)* BA
  Bibl: Galeyev, LEONARDO, XXI/4 (1988), p. 386-396
Galfetti, Aurelio AV BA
  (Swiss architect, b.1936) BA
  (Swiss architect, Lugano, 1936-) AV
  Bibl: ▶Avery period. idx.; Ianus, 1980, v.0, no.0, p.99; ▶RILA/BHA; UNSERE KDM, XXXV, 4 (1984) 471-477
Galgano di Giovanni → see Gano da Siena
Galgano di Minuccio *(Italian painter, d.1387)* GC
  Bibl: ▶Thieme-Becker
Galgario, Fra → see Ghislandi, Vittore Giuseppe
Galgiani, Phillip *(American photographer, b.1951)* BA
  Bibl: Santa Barbara (CA, USA), UCSB Art Mus., Invented images (1980)
Galí, Beth *(Spanish architect and author, 1950-)* AV
  Bibl: Garten und Landschaft, 1986 Apr., v.96, no.4, p.49
Galí, Jordi *(Spanish architect, Barcelona)* AV
  Bibl: El croquis, 1988 Aug.-Sept., v.7, no.35, p.82
Galiani, Rossano *(Italian artist, 19th cent.)* WC
Galiano, Alvaro Alcala *(Spanish artist, 19th cent.)* WC
Galibert, Pierre *(French artist, op. 1870-1876)* WC
Galice, Louis *(French artist, 19th cent.)* WC
Galiegue, Marcel *(French artist, 20th cent.)* WC
Galien-Laloue or Gallien-Laloue, Eugene WC
  (French artist, 1854-) WC
  (French artist, 1854-1941) WC
  Laloue, Galien Eugene WC

Galilei, Alessandro AV BA GC
  (Italian architect, 1691-1736) AV BA
  (Italian, 1691-1736) GC
  Bibl: ▶Encyc. world art; ▶Portoghesi, Diz. arch. e urbanistica; ▶Thieme-Becker
Galimard, Auguste → see Galimard, Nicolas-Auguste
Galimard, Auguste (Nicolas Auguste) → see Galimard, Nicolas-Auguste
Galimard, Nicolas-Auguste BA GC
  (French artist, 1813-1880) WC
  (French painter, 1813-1880) GC
  (French painter, printmaker, author, 1813-1880) BA
  Bibl: ▶Bellier, Artistes fran.; ▶Bénézit; Getty Photo Study Coll.; ▶Thieme-Becker
  Galimard, Auguste GC
  Galimard, Auguste (Nicolas Auguste) WC
Galimberti, D. *(Swiss architect)* AV
  Bibl: Ville giardini, 1988 May, no. 224, p.18
Galimberti, Francesco GC WC
  (Italian artist, 1755-1803) WC
  (Italian, 1755-1803) GC
  Bibl: ▶Thieme-Becker; ▶Witt checklist
Galimberti, Giuseppe *(Italian architect)* AV
  Bibl: Ville giardini, 1989 June, no. 238, p.20
Galimberti, Sándor *(Hungarian painter, 1883-1915)* BA
  Bibl: ▶Bénézit; ▶Vollmer, Künst.-Lex. 20. Jhr.
Galimberti, Valeria *(Hungarian painter, 1885-1915)* BA
  Bibl: ▶Bénézit; ▶Thieme-Becker; ▶Vollmer, Künst.-Lex. 20. Jhr.
  Dénes, Valeria BA
Galindo, Juan *(Colombian architect)* AV
  Bibl: Proa, 1985 Sept., no.345, p.22
Galindo, Victoriano P. *(Spanish artist, 20th cent.)* WC
Galinin, Igor *(Russian painter in USA, b.ca.1940)* BA
  Bibl: ART NEWS (Dec 1974) 45
Galion, Christian *(French interior designer)* AV
  Bibl: Maison Française, 1984 Nov., no.382, p. 91
Galitzine, Andrew *(British artist, op. 1983-)* WI
Galizia or Gallizi, Fede → see Galizia, Fede

Galizia, Fede BA GC PR
  (Italian artist, 1578(?)-1630(?)) WC
  (Italian painter, 1578-ca. 1630) BA GC PR
  Bibl: ▶Bolaffi; Getty Photo Study Coll. (Ptgs.); ▶RILA/BHA; ▶Thieme-Becker
  Fede Galizia PR
  Galizia or Gallizi, Fede WC
  Gallizi, Fede GC
Galizzi, Giovanni GC WC
  (Italian artist, op.1543) WC
  (Italian painter, act.1543-1565) GC
  Bibl: ▶Thieme-Becker
Galkin, G. *(Russian artist, 20th c.)* BA
  Bibl: ISKUSSTVO XXXVIII/4 (1985) 3
Galkus, Juozas *(Russian artist, 20th cent.)* WC
Gall → see Gall, Joseph
Gall, Francois *(French artist, 1912-1945)* WC
Gall, Joseph PR WC
  (French artist, 1807-1886) WC
  (French painter, 1807-1886) PR
  Bibl: ▶Thieme-Becker
  Gall PR
  Joseph Gall PR
Gall, Sally *(American photographer, b.1956)* BA
  Bibl: ▶Babington Smith, Contemp. artists; ▶Intl. dir. exh. artists
Gallagher, Barrett *(American photographer, 20th c.)* BA
  Bibl: ▶Intl. dir. exh. artists, 1982; ▶MoMA libr. cat.
Gallagher, Brendan *(Irish architect, Dublin)* AV
  Bibl: Irish architect, 1988 Feb. Mar., no.65, p.22
Gallagher, Cynthia *(American painter, 20th c.)* BA
  Bibl: ▶Intl. dir. exh. artists, 1983
Gallagher, Michael *(American painter, b.1945)* BA
  Bibl: Springfield (MA, USA), MFA, Abstract illusionism (1978)
Gallagher, Winifred *(American painter, 20th c.)* BA
  Bibl: ARTS MAG LV (Feb 1981) 8
Gallaher, Mabel L. *(British artist, op.1909-1940)* WI
Gallait, Louis BA WC
  (Belgian artist, 1810-1887) WC
  (Belgian painter and draughtsman, 1810-1887) GC
  (Belgian painter, printmaker, 1810-1887) BA
  Bibl: ▶Bénézit; ▶RILA/BHA; ▶Thieme-Becker
  Galait, Louis GC
Galland, Pierre Victor GC WC
  (French painter, 1822-1892) GC
  (Swiss artist, 1822-1892) WC
  Bibl: ▶Bénézit

Gallarati, Mario (Italian architect)   **AV**
Bibl: Anfione zeto, 1988, v.1, no.0, p.204

Gallard, Didier (French architect)   **AV**
Bibl: Architecture d'aujourd'hui, 1989 Oct., no.265, p.134

Gallard, Michel de (French artist, 1921-)   **WC**

Gallard-Lepinay, Emmanuel (French artist, 1842-1885)   **WC**

Gallardo, Francisco (Spanish painter, act.1764)   **BA**
Bibl: GOYA, 1983 (Nov-Dec 1984) 154

Gallardo, Luis (Spanish artist, 19th cent.)   **WC**

Gallasini, Andrea (Italian architect, stucco artist in Germany, act.1710-1759)   **BA**
Bibl: ▶Thieme-Becker; ZEITSCH. DES DEUT. VEREINS FUR KUNSTWISSENSCHAFT XXX/1-4 (1976) 26-43

Gallatin → see Gallatin, Albert Eugene

Gallatin Class (Greek, 450-400 BC)   **GC**
Bibl: McPhee & Trendall, Fish-Plates

Gallatin Neck-Amphora   **GC**
Bibl: Paralipomena

Gallatin Painter (vase-painter, ca. 500-475 BC)   **GC**
Bibl: ▶Beazley, Attic red-fig. vase-ptrs.; Richter, Attic red-fig. vases

Gallatin, A.E. (American artist, 20th cent.)   **WC**

Gallatin, Albert Eugene   **BA PR WI**
(American artist, 1882-1952)   WI
(American painter, 1882-1952)   PR
(American painter, art historian, 1882-1952)   BA
Bibl: ▶RILA/BHA; Trenton (NJ, USA), State Mus., Beyond the plane (1983); ▶Witt checklist; ▶WW Amer. Art, 1984 necrol.; ▶WWW Amer.
Albert Eugene Gallatin   PR
Gallatin   PR

Gallaway (American artist, op.20th c.)   **WI**

Gallaway, Alexander (British artist, op.1794-1812)   **WI**

Gallay, Jacques (French architect, 1708-1755)   **BA**
Bibl: Ludmann, Cahiers Alsaciens XXIX (1986) 115

Galle → see Galle, Hieronymus (I)

Galle family (French bronze gilders, 18th-19th cs.)   **BA**
Bibl: ▶Thieme-Becker

Galle, A. (Active Paris, France, daguerreotypist)   **JG**

Galle, Andr'e   **GC**
(French bronzier, 1761-1833)   GC
(French, active ca. 1785-1825)   JG
Bibl: ▶Thieme-Becker

Galle, Andre   **JG**
Galle, Andre → see Galle, Andr'e

Galle, Cornelis I   **BA GC**
(Flemish artist, 1576-1650)   WC
(Flemish printmaker, 1576-1650)   BA
(Flemish, 1576-1650)   GC
Bibl: ▶Bénézit; ▶Encyc. world art; ▶Thieme-Becker; ▶Witt checklist; ▶Wurzbach, NLD Künst.-Lex.

Galle, Cornelis, I   **WC**
Galle, Cornelis, I → see Galle, Cornelis I

Galle, Cornelis, II (Flemish artist, 1615-1678)   **WC**

Gallé, Emile (French designer, craftsman, 1846-1904)   **BA**
Bibl: ▶Encyc. world art; ▶Oxford dec. arts; Studio dict. design & dec.; ▶Thieme-Becker

Galle, Hieronymus (I)   **PR**
(Flemish artist, 1625-p.1679)   WC
(Flemish painter, 1625-aft.1679)   PR
(Flemish, 1625-aft.1679)   GC
Bibl: ▶Thieme-Becker; ▶Witt checklist

Galle   PR

Galle, Hieronymus I   **GC**
Galle, Hieronymus, I   **WC**
Hier. Galle   PR
Hieronymus Galle (I)   PR
Galle, Hieronymus I → see Galle, Hieronymus (I)
Galle, Hieronymus, I → see Galle, Hieronymus (I)
Galle, Joan or Joannes → see Galle, Joannes

Galle, Joannes   **BA**
(Flemish artist, 1600-1676)   WC
(Flemish printmaker, print publisher, 1600-1676)   BA
Bibl: ▶Bénézit; ▶Seyn, Écoles flam. et holl.; ▶Wurzbach, NLD Künst.-Lex.

Galle, Joan or Joannes   **WC**

Galle, Philip   **BA GC**
(early Netherlandish printmaker, 1537-1612)   BA
(Engraver, 1537-1612)   CE
(Netherlandish printmaker, 1537-1612)   GC
(Netherlands artist, 1537-1612)   WC
Bibl: Getty Photo Study Coll.; Hollstein; ▶RILA/BHA; ▶Thieme-Becker

Galle, Philipp   **CE WC**
Philip Galle   GC
Galle, Philipp → see Galle, Philip

Galle, Theodoor   **BA**
(Flemish artist, c.1571-1633)   WC
(Flemish printmaker, 1571-1633)   BA
Bibl: ▶Hollstein, Dutch & Flemish; ▶Wurzbach, NLD Künst.-Lex.

Galle, Theodor   **WC**
Galle, Theodor → see Galle, Theodoor

Galle, Tibor (Hungarian artist, 1896-1944)   **WC**

Gallé-Reinemer, Charles (French glass manufacturer, ceramist, act. 1844)   **BA**
Bibl: Arts in Virginia XX (fall 1979) 30-37; ▶Thieme-Becker

Gallecus, Fernandus → see Gallego, Fernando

Gallee, Elias (German artist, 17th cent.)   **WC**

Gallego → see Gallego, Fernando

Gallego, Fernando   **BA JG PR**
(Spanish (Castile), ca. 1440/45-ca. 1507)   JG
(Spanish artist, c.1440-p.1507)   WC
(Spanish painter, 1440/45-ca.1507)   BA
(Spanish painter, act. 1466-1506)   PR
(Spanish, ca.1440-aft.1507)   GC
Bibl: ▶Bénézit; ▶Ceán Bermúdez, Bellas artes ESP; ▶Encyc. world art; ▶Lafuente Ferrari, Pint. española, p.576; ▶O'Neil, Spanish ptrs.; ▶Post, Spanish ptg., v.9; Quinn, Fernando Gallego, pp. 10-13; ▶RILA/BHA; ▶Thieme-Becker; ▶Witt checklist; Young, Pantheon, XXIX/2 (Apr.-Jun. 1981) pp.129-132
Fernando Gallego   PR
Gallecus, Fernandus   BA
Gallego   PR

Gallegos, Fernando   **GC PR**
Gallegos, Fernando (Fernandus Galecus)   **WC**

Gallego, Francisco   **BA**
(Spanish artist, op.1500)   WC
(Spanish painter, act.ca.1500)   BA
(Spanish, act. ca.1500)   GC
Bibl: ▶Bénézit; ▶Encyc. world art; ▶Lafuente Ferrari, Pint. española, p.576; ▶Post, Spanish ptg., v.9; Quinn, Fernando Gallego, pp. 16-17; ▶Thieme-Becker; ▶Witt checklist

Gallegos, Francisco   **GC WC**

Gallego, Manuel (Spanish architect)   **AV**
Bibl: Process: architecture, 1985 Apr., no.57, p.128

Gallegos y Arnosa, Jose   **GC WC**
(Spanish artist, 1859-1917)   WC
(Spanish, 1859-1917)   GC
Bibl: ▶Witt checklist

Gallegos, Fernando → see Gallego, Fernando
Gallegos, Fernando (Fernandus Galecus) → see Gallego, Fernando
Gallegos, Francisco → see Gallego, Francisco
Gallèn-Kallela, Akseli → see Gallén-Kallela, Akseli Valdemar

Gallén-Kallela, Akseli Valdemar **BA WC**
  (Finnish architect and graphic
    artist, 1865-1931) AV
  (Finnish painter, printmaker,
    1865-1931) BA
  (Swedish artist, 1865-1931) WC
    Bibl: ▶Bénézit; ▶Macmillan encyc.
    archts.; ▶Thieme-Becker
  Gallén-Kallela, Akseli AV
Gallenstein, Kuntz *(German artist,*
  19th cent.) WC
Galler, Michael T. *(West German*
  architect) AV
    Bibl: Arch plus, no.86, p.56
Galleri, Charles *(French artist, op.*
  1601-1602) WC
Galles, Juan *(Spanish artist, op.c.*
  1850) WC
Gallet, Louis Jacques *(Swiss*
  sculptor, painter, 1873-1955) BA
    Bibl: ▶Künst.-Lex. Schweiz 20.
    Jahrh.; ▶Vollmer, Künst.-Lex. 20.
    Jhr.
Galletti→see Galletti, Filippo Maria
Galletti, Filippo Maria **BA PR WC**
  (Italian artist, 1636-1714) WC
  (Italian painter, 1636-1714) BA PR
    Bibl: ▶Bolaffi; ▶Thieme-Becker
  F.M. Galetti PR
  Filippo Maria Galletti PR
  Galetti PR
  Galletti PR
Gallhof, Wilhelm *(German artist,*
  1878-1918) WC
Galli *(German painter, 20th c.)* BA
    Bibl: ▶Art Index, v.35; Guide exh.
    artists: N. Amer. ptrs.; Ohff,
    Kunstwerk, XXXVIII (Sep 1985)
    pp.56-69
Galli Bibiena family→see Bibiena
  family
Galli da Bibiena family→see Bibiena
  family
Galli da Bibiena, Antonio→see
  Bibiena, Antonio Galli
Galli da Bibiena, Ferdinando→see
  Bibiena, Ferdinando Galli
Galli da Bibiena, Francesco→see
  Bibiena, Francesco Galli
Galli da Bibiena, Giuseppe→see
  Bibiena, Giuseppe Galli
Galli, Alfredo *(Italian artist, 20th*
  cent.) WC
Galli, Angelo *(Italian painter, act.ca.*
  1600-ca.1650) BA
    Bibl: ▶Bénézit; ▶Bolaffi; TCI
    Milano; ▶Thieme-Becker
  Gallo, Angelo BA
Galli, Federica *(Italian printmaker,*
  b.1932) BA
    Bibl: ▶Bolaffi 20c.

Galli, Francesco VO
  (Italian artist, op.c.1500) WC
  (Italian painter, act.1500) BA
  (Italian painter, d. 1501) PR VO
  (Italian, act. ca.1500) GC
    Bibl: ▶Bolaffi; ▶Libr. of Congr.
    Name Auth. File, NAFR9230635;
    Shell, J. & G. Sironi, Raccolta
    Vinciana XXIII (1989), pp. 155-
    166; ▶Thieme-Becker; ▶Witt
    checklist
  Francesco Napoletano **BA GC VO WC**
  Galli, Francesco (Francesco
    Napoletano) PR
  Napoletano PR
  Napoletano, Francesco BA PR VO
  Napolitano, Francesco PR
  Galli, Francesco (Francesco
  Napoletano)→see Galli, Francesco
Galli, Giacomo **BA PR**
  (Italian painter, act.ca.1605-
    1623) BA
  (Italian painter, ca.1605-1623) PR
    Bibl: ▶Bolaffi; Mariscola,
    PROSPETTIVA, 16 (Jan 1979),
    45-52; Paragone XXXVII/435
    (May 1986) pp.20-28;
    PARAGONE, XXXVII/435 (May
    1986) 20-28
  Gallo, Giacomo BA
  Giacomo Galli PR
Galli, Gino *(Italian artist, 1893-)* WC
Galli, Giovanni *(Italian artist, op.*
  1547-1568) WC
Galli, Giovanni Antonio→see Galli,
  Giovanni Antonio (lo Spadarino)
Galli, Giovanni Antonio (lo
  Spadarino) BA
  (Italian artist, op.1615-1650) WC
  (Italian painter, act.1615-1650) GC
  (Italian painter, b.1585, d.1651-
    1653) BA
    Bibl: ▶Bénézit; ▶Bolaffi; Paragone
    XXXVII/435 (May 1986) pp.20-28;
    PROSPETTIVA 16 (Jan 1979)
    45-52; ▶Thieme-Becker; ▶Witt
    checklist
  Galli, Giovanni Antonio GC
  Gallo (or Galli), Giovanni
    Antonio (lo Spadarino or
    Spadaro) WC
  Gallo, Giovanni Antonio BA GC
  Spadarino BA GC
  Spadaro BA GC
Galli, Guido *(Sculptor, 1873-1956)* CE
    Bibl: Galli 1923-1924, pp. 473-
    474
Galli, Luigi **GC WC**
  (Italian artist, 1820-1906) WC
  (Italian painter, 1820-1906) GC
    Bibl: ▶Thieme-Becker

Galli, Pietro **AV BA GC**
  (Italian architect) AV
  (Italian sculptor, 1804-1877) BA GC
    Bibl: ▶Bénézit; ▶RILA/BHA;
    ▶Thieme-Becker; Ville giardini,
    1988 May, no.226, p.30
Galli, Q. *(German artist, 18th cent.)* WC
Galli, Riccardo *(Italian artist, 1839-*
  m.p.1890) WC
Gallia, Hermine *(Austrian, d.1936)* BA
    Bibl: Coradeschi , KLIMT , p.102;
    Melbourne (AUS), Natl. Gall. of
    Victoria, Vienna 1913 (1984)
Galliani, Omar *(Italian painter,*
  b.1954) BA
    Bibl: ▶Art Index, vs.27, 29, 36;
    ▶Babington Smith, Contemp.
    artists
Galliard, Henry *(English tailor, act.*
  1588-1593) BA
    Bibl: Stern, Costume, XV (1981)
    pp.13-23
  Gallyard, Henry BA
Galliari family *(Italian painters,*
  scenographers, architects, 18th-
  19th cs.) BA
    Bibl: ▶Bénézit; ▶Thieme-Becker
Galliari, Bernardino **BA GC WC**
  (Italian artist, 1707-1794) WC
  (Italian scenographer, painter,
    1707-1794) BA
  (Italian, 1707-1794) GC
    Bibl: ▶Bolaffi; ▶Encic. spettacolo;
    ▶Thieme-Becker; ▶Witt checklist
Galliari, Fabrizio **BA GC WC**
  (Italian artist, 1709-1790) WC
  (Italian scenographer, 1709-
    1790) BA GC
    Bibl: ▶Bolaffi; ▶RILA/BHA, 1986
Galliari, Gaspare **BA GC**
  (Italian artist, c.1760-1818) WC
  (Italian scenographer, architect,
    1761-1823) BA
  (Italian, ca.1760-1818) GC
    Bibl: ▶Bolaffi; ▶Encic. spettacolo;
    ▶Thieme-Becker; ▶Witt checklist
Galliari, Gasparo WC
Galliari, Gasparo→see Galliari,
  Gaspare
Galliari, Giovanni Antonio **BA GC WC**
  (Italian artist, 1718-1783) WC
  (Italian painter, scenographer,
    1714-1783) BA
  (Italian, 1718-1783) GC
    Bibl: ▶Bolaffi; ▶Encic. italiana;
    ▶Encic. spettacolo;
    ▶Thieme-Becker; ▶Witt checklist
Gallibert, Geneviève **WC WI**
  (French artist, 1888-) WC
  (French artist, b.1888) WI
Gallicus, Johannes→see Wale, Johan
  (Johannes Gallicus)
Gallie, P. **GC WC**
  (French artist, 18th cent.) WC
  (French, 18th century) GC
    Bibl: ▶Witt checklist

Gallie, Tommie J. (*Canadian sculptor, printmaker, b.1946*) **BA**
Bibl: ▶Artists Canada

Gallien, Pierre-Antoine **BA WC**
(*French artist, op.c.1919*) WC
(*French painter, printmaker, 1896-1963*) BA
Bibl: ▶Bénézit; ▶Dict. biog. fran.

Gallien, Simon **GC JG**
(*French silversmith, d.1757, master 1714*) GC
(*French, master 1714, d. 1757*) JG
Bibl: ▶Nocq, Poinçon de Paris

Gallier, James (*American architect, New Orleans, La.; son of James Gallier, Sr. (1798-1868), 1827-1868*) **AV**
Bibl: ▶Withey, Amer. archts.

Gallier, James (*Architect, native of Ireland, came to New York, 1832, then set set up practice in New Orleans; father of James Gallier, Jr. (1827-1868), 1798-1868*) **AV**
Bibl: ▶Withey, Amer. archts.

Galligné, Pierre-Antoine (*French ébéniste, master 1767, d. ca.1782*) **GC**
Bibl: ▶Salverte, Ébénistes 18e s.

Gallimard, Claude Olivier (*French artist, 1718/19-1774*) **WC**

Gallin, Saara **AV**
(*American artist*) AV
(*Stained glass artist, NYC*) AV
Bibl: Stained glass, 1984 Fall, v.79, no.3, p.225; Stained glass, 1986 Winter, v.81, no.4, p.294

Gatlin, Saara **AV**

Gallina, Lodovico **BA GC WC**
(*Italian artist, 1752-1787*) WC
(*Italian painter, 1752-1787*) BA GC
Bibl: ▶Bolaffi; ▶Thieme-Becker; ▶Witt checklist

Gallina, Remy Canta → *see* Cantagallina, Remigio

Gallinari, Giacomo (*Italian, act. ca. 1676-1685*) **GC**
Bibl: ▶Thieme-Becker

Gallione, M. (*Italian architect*) **AV**
Bibl: Domus, 1984 July-Aug., no. 652, p.58

Galliori, Giulio (*Italian architect, 1715-1795*) **BA**
Bibl: TCI Milano; ▶Thieme-Becker

Gallis → *see* Gallis, Pieter

Gallis, Pieter **GC PR WC**
(*Dutch artist, 1633-1697*) WC
(*Dutch painter, 1633-1697*) GC PR
Bibl: Getty Photo Study Coll.; ▶Thieme-Becker; ▶Witt checklist
Gallis PR
Pieter Gallis PR

Gallissá y Soqué, Antonio Maria (*Spanish architect, 1861-1903*) **BA**
Bibl: ▶Encic. univ. ilus.; ▶Macmillan encyc. archts.

Gallizi, Fede → *see* Galizia, Fede

Gallizio, Pinot (*Italian artist, 1902-*) **WC**

Gallizzioli, Vettoria → *see* Gallizzioli, Vettoria [Unidentified]

Gallizzioli, Vettoria [Unidentified]
(*Unknown painter*) **PR**
Bibl: Riccardi inventory dated 1776
Gallizzioli, Vettoria PR
Vettoria Gallizzioli PR

Gallo (or Galli), Giovanni Antonio (lo Spadarino or Spadaro) → *see* Galli, Giovanni Antonio (lo Spadarino)

Gallo, Angelo → *see* Galli, Angelo

Gallo, Doreen (*American artist, New York City*) **AV**
Bibl: AIT, 1989 Jan.-Feb., v.97, no.1, p.32

Gallo, Francesco (*Italian architect*) **AV**
Bibl: Abitare, 1989 Mar., no.272, p.172

Gallo, Francesco (*Italian sculptor, act.ca.1807*) **BA**
Bibl: ▶Bénézit; ▶Bessone-Aurelj, Scult. & arch. ital.; Catello, Napoli Nobilissima XIX/3-4 (May-Aug 1980) 117-126; Strazzullo, LE MANIFATTURE D'ARTE DI CARLO DI BORBONE; ▶Thieme-Becker

Gallo, Frank (*American sculptor, b.1933*) **BA GC**
Bibl: ▶RILA/BHA; ▶WW Amer. Art, 1989

Gallo, Giacomo → *see* Galli, Giacomo

Gallo, Giovanni (*Italian, 16th century*) **GC**
Bibl: ▶Thieme-Becker

Gallo, Giovanni Antonio → *see* Galli, Giovanni Antonio (lo Spadarino)

Gallo, Girolamo (*Italian artist, 17th cent.(?)*) **WC**

Gallo, Giuseppe (*Italian painter, b.1954*) **BA**
Bibl: ▶Art Index, v.32; Verzotti, FLASH ART, CXXXVI (1987)

Gallo, Maria (*Nicaraguan painter, b.1951*) **BA**
Bibl: La Duke, WOMEN ARTISTS NEWS VIII (1982-83) 23-24

Gallo, Oscar (*Italian sculptor, b.1909*) **BA GC**
Bibl: ▶Chi è?; Del Bravo, ANTICHITA VIVA XX/4 (July-Aug 1981) 32-46; ▶RILA/BHA; ▶Vollmer, Künst.-Lex. 20. Jhr.

Gallo, Paolo (*Italian, active Milan, Italy late 19th century*) **JG**

Galloche → *see* Galloche, Louis

Galloche, Louis **BA GC PR WC**
(*French artist, 1670-1761*) WC
(*French painter, 1670-1761*) BA PR
(*French, 1670-1761*) GC
Bibl: ▶Bénézit; ▶RILA/BHA; ▶Thieme-Becker; ▶Witt checklist
Galloche PR
Louis Galloche PR

Gallon, Robert **WC WI**
(*British artist, 1845-1925*) WI
(*British artist, op.1868-1905*) WC

Gallon, Robert Samuel Ennis (*British artist, op.1830-1868*) **WI**

Gallonios Group (*Etruscan vase-painters*) **GC**
Bibl: Beazley, Etruscan vase-ptrs.

Gallori, Emilio (*Italian sculptor, 1846-1924*) **GC**
Bibl: TCI Roma e dintorni

Galloway, A. (*British artist, 19th cent.*) **WC**

Galloway, J. (*British artist, op.1866-*) **WI**

Galloway, Kit (*American artist, 20th c.*) **BA**
Bibl: ARTWEEK XI/44 (27 Dec 1980) 5

Gallucci, Pietro → *see* Galluzzi, Pietro

Galluzzi, Pietro (*Italian painter, 17th c.*) **BA**
Bibl: ▶Bolaffi; ▶Thieme-Becker
Gallucci, Pietro BA

Gallwitz, Peter (*West German architect, Oberursel, 1938-*) **AV**
Bibl: Deutsche Bauzeitung, 1986 May, v.120, no.5, p.172

Gallyard, Henry → *see* Galliard, Henry

Galmiche, Jean-François (*French architect*) **AV**

Galofre y Gimenez, Baldemiro (*Spanish artist, 1849-1902*) **WC**

Galotto [Unidentified] (*Unknown painter*) **PR**
Bibl: Pignatelli inventory, Naples, 1723

Galserandus (*Spanish scribe, act. early 15th century*) **GC**
Bibl: Sotheby's London, June 25, 1985, Lot 37

Galston, Beth (*American sculptor, 20th c.*) **BA**
Bibl: Galston, LEONARDO XV/4 (autumn 1982) 291

Galsworthy, Frank (*British artist, 1863-op.1936*) **WI**

Galsworthy, Gordon C. **WC WI**
(*British artist, 20th cent.*) WC
(*British artist, op.1890-1925*) WI

Galsworthy, Olive → *see* Galsworthy, Olive Edis

Galsworthy, Olive Edis **BA**
(*British artist, 19th cent.*) WC
(*British artist, op.1887-*) WI
(*British photographer, 1876-1955*) BA
Bibl: London (GBR), Natl. Port. Gall., People in Camera 1839-1914 (1979)

Galsworthy, Olive **WC WI**

Galt → *see* Galt, Charles Franklin

Galt, Charles Franklin (*American painter, 1884-aft.1926*) **PR**
Bibl: ▶WWW Amer. art
Charles Franklin Galt PR
Galt PR

Galt, John (*British artist, op.1917-*) **WI**

Galtier-Boissiere, Jean   **BA GC**
    (French draftsman, author,
    1891-1966)   **BA**
    (French draughtsman, 1891-
    1966)   **GC**
    Bibl: ▶Bénézit; ▶Dict. biog. fran.;
    ▶Larousse grande encyc.;
    ▶Vollmer, Künst.-Lex. 20. Jhr.

Galtier-Boissiere, Louise *(French*
    artist, 19th cent.)   **WC**

Galton, Ada Mary   **WC WI**
    (British artist, 19th cent.)   **WC**
    (British artist, op.1899-1928)   **WI**

Galton, Douglas Strutt *(British*
    engineer, 1822-1899)   **BA**
    Bibl: ▶Dict. natl. biog.

Galton, Francis *(British eugenist,*
    photographer, 1822-1911)   **BA**
    Bibl: ▶Dict. natl. biog.; OXFORD
    ART JOURNAL, XII/2 (1984) 3-16

Galton, H.   **WC WI**
    (British artist, 19th cent.)   **WC**
    (British artist, op.19th c.)   **WI**

Galvan y Candela, Jose Maria
    (Spanish artist, 1864-)   **WC**

Galvan, Jesus Guerrer *(Mexican*
    artist, 1912-)   **WC**

Galvez→see Gálvez, Juan

Gálvez, Isidro *(Spanish aritst, 18th*
    c.)   **BA**
    Bibl: Arch. esp. de arte, LVIII/230
    (Apr-Jun 1985) 157-162

Gálvez, Juan   **PR WC**
    (Spanish artist, 1774-1847)   **WC**
    (Spanish painter, 1774-1847)   **PR**
    Bibl: ▶Thieme-Becker
    Galvez   **PR**
    Juan Galvez   **PR**

Galway, R.E. *(British artist, op.19th*
    c.)   **WI**

Gama, Amelia *(Brazilian architect)*   **AV**
    Bibl: Architecture d'aujourd'hui,
    1987 june,no.251,p.56

Gamar, A. *(Italian artist, 19th cent.)* **WC**

Gamard, Michel *(French architect)*   **AV**
    Bibl: AMC, 1988 Apr., no.20,
    p.90

Gamba, Crescenzo→see Gamba,
    Crescenzo della

Gamba, Crescenzo della   **BA**
    (Italian painter, act.1766-1779)   **BA**
    (Italian, act. ca.1759-1779)   **GC**
    Bibl: ▶Bolaffi; ▶Thieme-Becker

Gamba, Crescenzo   **GC**

Gamba, Enrico *(Italian painter,*
    1831-1883)   **GC**
    Bibl: ▶Thieme-Becker

Gambacciani, Francesco *(Italian*
    artist, 1701-p.1771)   **WC**

Gambacciani, Giuseppe
    [Unidentified] *(Unknown painter,*
    act. 18th century)   **PR**
    Bibl: Riccardi inventory dated
    1776
    Giuseppe Gambacciani   **PR**

Gambacciani, Piero *(Italian*
    architect)   **AV**
    Bibl: Casabella, 1980 June, v.44,
    no.459, p.16

Gambado, Geoffrey →see Bunbury,
    Henry William

Gambara, Antonio *(Italian sculptor,*
    ca.1416-ca.1462)   **BA**
    Bibl: Malignaggi, Arte in Sicilia
    1302-1458 (1986) 150;
    Malignaggi, ARTE IN SICILIA 1302-
    1458 (1986), p.147; Meli, ARTE
    MEDIEVALE, 4/1 (1990), 151-173;
    TCI Sicilia (1968), p.135;
    ▶Thieme-Becker

Gambara, Lattanzio   **BA GC JG WC**
    (Italian artist, c.1530-1573/4)   **WC**
    (Italian painter, ca.1530-1574)   **BA GC**
    (Italian, ca. 1530-1574)   **JG**
    Bibl: ▶Bolaffi; ▶Encic. italiana;
    ▶Encyc. world art; ▶RILA/BHA,
    1986; ▶Thieme-Becker

Gambarato, Gambarotto or
    Gamberati, Girolamo →see
    Gambarato, Girolamo

Gambarato, Girolamo   **GC**
    (Italian artist, op.1591-m.1628)   **WC**
    (Italian, act.1591-d.1628)   **GC**
    Bibl: Getty Photo Study Coll.
    (Ptgs.); ▶Witt checklist

Gambarato, Gambarotto or
    Gamberati, Girolamo   **WC**
    Gamberati, Girolamo   **GC**

Gambard, Henri Augustin   **BA**
    (French painter, 1819-1882)   **BA**
    (French, b.1819; act. 1845-1869)   **GC**
    Bibl: ▶Bénézit; BULL. OF THE
    DETROIT INST OF ART LXVII
    (1979) 72-81; ▶Thieme-Becker

Gambard, Henri-Augustin   **GC**

Gambard, Henri-Augustin →see
    Gambard, Henri Augustin

Gambardella, Spiridione   **PR WC WI**
    (British artist, op.1842-1868)   **WC WI**
    (British painter, act. 1842-1868)   **PR**
    Bibl: ▶Witt checklist
    Spiridione Gambardella   **PR**

Gambardi *(Italian artist, 19th cent.)* **WC**

Gambarini →see Gambarini, Giuseppe

Gambarini, Giuseppe   **BA GC PR WC**
    (Italian artist, 1680-1725)   **WC**
    (Italian painter, 1680-1725)   **BA**
    (Italian painter, 1680-1775)   **PR**
    (Italian, 1680-1725)   **GC**
    Bibl: ▶Bolaffi; ▶Thieme-Becker;
    ▶Witt checklist
    Gambarini   **PR**
    Giuseppe Gambarini   **PR**

Gambaro, E. James *(American*
    architect, N.Y., N.Y, 1902-1983)   **AV**
    Bibl: the AIA journal, 1984 Mar.,
    v.73, no.3, p.97

Gambaruccio or Gamberucci,
    Cosimo →see Gamberucci, Cosimo

Gambel   **WC WI**
    (British artist, op.1773)   **WC**
    (British artist, op.1773-)   **WI**

Gambello, Antonio di Marco
    (Italian architect, sculptor, d.ca.
    1481)   **BA**
    Bibl: ▶Portoghesi, Diz. arch. e
    urbanistica; ▶Thieme-Becker

Gambello, Vettore →see Gambello,
    Vittore

Gambello, Vittore   **BA CE GC**
    (Italian sculptor and medalist,
    ca.1460-1537)   **GC**
    (Italian sculptor, medalist, ca.
    1460-1537)   **BA**
    (Sculptor, medallist, c.1460-
    1537)   **CE**
    Bibl: ▶Diz. biog. ital.; ▶Forrer,
    Medallists; ▶RILA/BHA;
    ▶Thieme-Becker
    Cambello, Vettore   **CE**
    Camelio   **CE**
    Camelio, Vettore   **CE**
    Camelio, Vittore   **BA**
    Camelius, Victorius   **CE**
    Camelus, Victorius   **CE**
    Gambello, Vettore   **CE**

Gamberati, Girolamo →see
    Gambarato, Girolamo

Gamberelli, Antonio →see Rossellino,
    Antonio

Gamberelli, Antonio di Matteo →see
    Rossellino, Antonio

Gamberelli, Bernardo →see Rossellino,
    Bernardo

Gamberini, Giovacchino   **GC WC**
    (Italian artist, 1859-)   **WC**
    (Italian, b.1859)   **GC**
    Bibl: ▶Thieme-Becker; ▶Witt
    checklist

Gamberini, Italo   **AV BA**
    (Italian architect)   **AV**
    (Italian architect, b.1907)   **BA**
    Bibl: Art e dossier, no.26, p.10;
    ▶Avery period. idx., 3rd suppl.;
    PRATO: STORIA E ARTE XXVIII/70
    (June 1987) 16-19; Santini, P.C.,
    CRITICA D'ARTE, LIII/18 (Oct-Dec
    1988) p.54-59

Gambert de Loche, Jeanne *(French*
    interior designer, Paris)   **AV**
    Bibl: Maison Française, 1985 July-
    Aug., no.389, p.108

Gamberucci, Cosimo   **BA GC**
    (Italian artist, op.1598-1619)   **WC**
    (Italian painter, ca.1560-1621)   **BA GC**
    Bibl: ▶Bolaffi; MITTEILUNGEN DES
    KUNSTHIST. INST. IN FLORENZ
    XVIII/3 (1974) 383-392;
    ▶RILA/BHA, 1986;
    ▶Thieme-Becker

Gambaruccio or Gamberucci,
    Cosimo   **WC**

Gamberucci, Marco *(Italian*
    goldsmith, 1630-1697)   **BA**
    Bibl: Dittmann, in THIEM
    FESTSCHRIFT, p.19

Gambini, Silvio *(Italian architect, b.1877)*   **BA**
    Bibl: Bossaglia, SITUAZIONE DEGLI STUDI SUL LIBERTY, 237

Gambino, Giuseppe *(Italian artist, 1928-)*   **WC**

Gambiño, José *(Spanish sculptor, architect, ca.1722-1775)*   **AV BA**
    Bibl: ▶Ceán Bermúdez, Bellas artes ESP, v.2; ▶Encic. univ. ilus.; Jackson-Stops, G., COUNTRY LIFE CLXXVII/4579/23 May 1985; ▶Thieme-Becker

Gambirasio, Giuseppe *(Italian architect, Ferrara)*   **AV**
    Bibl: Parametro, 1987 Aug.-Sept., v.16, no.159, p.44

Gamble → see Gamble, John Marshall

Gamble, Erik *(Canadian painter, b.1950)*   **BA**
    Bibl: ▶Idx. Ontario artists

Gamble, John M. → see Gamble, John Marshall

Gamble, John Marshall   **PR WI**
    (American artist, b.1863)   WI
    (American painter, 1863-1915)   PR
    Bibl: ▶WWW Amer. art
    Gamble   PR
    Gamble, John M.   PR
    John Marshall Gamble   PR

Gamble, Roy → see Gamble, Roy C.

Gamble, Roy C. *(American painter, 1887-1964)*   **PR**
    Bibl: ▶WWW Amer. art
    Gamble, Roy   PR
    Roy C. Gamble   PR

Gamborino, Miguel *(Spanish printmaker, 1760-ca.1828)*   **BA**
    Bibl: ▶Bénézit; ▶Thieme-Becker; ▶Viñaza, Adiciones Ceán-Berm.

Gambs or Gams, Benedickt *(Swiss artist, op.1745-1751)*   **WC**

Gambs, Heinrich *(German cabinetmaker, 1765-1831)*   **BA**
    Bibl: Cheneviere, ESTAMPILLE. L'OBJET D'ART, 236(1990), 52-67; ▶Thieme-Becker

Gamelin, Jacques   **GC WC**
    (French artist, 1738-1803)   WC
    (French, 1738-1803)   GC
    Bibl: ▶Witt checklist

Gamerith, Walter *(Austrian painter, photographer, 1903-1949)*   **BA**
    Bibl: ▶Österr. biog. Lex. 1815-1950

Gamichon, Jean-Baptiste *(French ébéniste, act.1790-1805)*   **GC**
    Bibl: ▶Salverte, Ébénistes 18e s.

Gamiczer, Christoph → see Jamnitzer, Christoph

Gámiz, Pedro López de → see López de Gámiz, Pedro

Gamm, A. *(Engraver)*   **WI**

Gammarano, Bianca *(Brazilian architect)*   **AV**
    Bibl: Projeto, 1986 Feb., no.84, p.73

Gammon, James *(British artist, op. 1660-1670)*   **WC WI**

Gammon, Reginald *(British artist, b.1894)*   **WI**

Gammon, Reginald Adolphus *(American painter, b.1921)*   **BA**
    Bibl: ▶WW Amer. Art

Gammucci, Caterina *(Italian, d.1517)*   **BA**
    Bibl: ANTICHITA VIVA XIX (July-Aug 1980) 43-46

Gamondi, Gianni *(Italian architect)*   **AV**
    Bibl: Ville Giardini, 1989 Feb., no. 234, p.14

Gampenrieder, Karl *(German artist, 1860-)*   **WC**

Gamper, Gustav Adolf *(Swiss artist, 1873-)*   **WC**

Gampert, Otto *(Swiss artist, 1842-1924)*   **WC**

Gamrekeli, Iraklij Il'ič *(Russian scenographer, 1894-1943)*   **BA**
    Bibl: ▶WWW USSR

Gamucci, Bernardo *(Italian, 16th c.)*   **BA**
    Bibl: Bury,BURLINGTON MAG,CXXIX/1011(JUNE) 1987),p. 388; ▶Natl. union cat.

Gan, Aleksej Mihajlovič *(Russian designer, critic, 1893-1942)*   **BA**
    Bibl: ▶Bowlt, Russian avant-garde

Gan, Tat'jana Konstantinovna *(Russian sculptor, b.1931)*   **BA**
    Bibl: Hudozniki Narodov SSSR, v.2

Ganassoni, Giacomo *(Italian artist, 18th cent.)*   **WC**

Gancedo, Teresa *(Spanish artist, b.1937)*   **BA**
    Bibl: New York (NY, USA), Guggenheim Mus., New images from Spain (1980)

Gand, Juste de → see Joos van Gent (Joos van Wassenhove)

Gandaglia, Luca *(Italian artist, 18th cent.)*   **WC**

Gandar, A.A. *(French artist, op. 1799)*   **WC**

Gandara, Antonio de la   **GC WC**
    (French artist, 1862-1917)   WC
    (Italian painter, 1862-1917)   GC
    Bibl: ▶Bénézit; ▶Thieme-Becker
    La Gandara, Antonio de   GC

Gandat *(French artist, op.1779-m. 1797)*   **WC**

Gandelsonas, Mario   **AV BA**
    (American architect and author, 1938-)   AV
    (Argentine architect, b.1938)   BA
    Bibl: Art in Amer., LXIX/6 (Sum. 1981) pp.114-123; ▶Avery period. idx.

Gander, Ambrosius *(Tyrolean painter, act.1448-1479)*   **BA**
    Bibl: ▶Bolaffi

Gander, Ralph H. *(Swiss microscopist, artist, 20th c.)*   **BA**
    Bibl: Gander, LEONARDO XIII/3 (summer 1980) 211-212

Gandi, Bonaventura   **BA GC**
    (Italian painter, ca.1668-1734)   BA
    (Italian, act.1680-1732)   GC
    Bibl: ▶Bolaffi; ▶Thieme-Becker

Gandia, Juan de (Juan Fernandez de Gandia) *(Spanish artist, op. 1659)*   **WC**

Gandini del Grano → see Gandini, Giorgio

Gandini del Grano, Giorgio → see Gandini, Giorgio

Gandini or Gandino, Antonio → see Gandini, Antonio

Gandini, Alessandro *(Italian, 2nd half of 16th c.)*   **GC**
    Bibl: ▶Thieme-Becker

Gandini, Antonio   **BA**
    (Italian artist, op.1602-m.1630)   WC
    (Italian painter, 1565-1630)   BA
    Bibl: ▶Bolaffi; ▶Thieme-Becker

Gandini or Gandino, Antonio   **WC**
    Gandino, Antonio   BA

Gandini, Francesco *(Italian artist, 1723-p.1778)*   **WC**

Gandini, Franco *(Italian architect, Alessandria)*   **AV**
    Bibl: Architettura; cronache e storia, 1989 Aug., v.35, no.7-8, p.496

Gandini, Giorgio   **GC**
    (Italian artist, 1489-1538)   WC
    (Italian painter, 1489-1538)   GC
    Bibl: ▶Thieme-Becker
    Gandini del Grano   GC

Gandini del Grano, Giorgio   **WC**

Gandini, Saverio *(Italian, ca.1729-1796)*   **GC**
    Bibl: ▶Thieme-Becker

Gandini, Sergio *(Italian designer)*   **AV**
    Bibl: Domus, 1985 Sept., no.664, p.62

Gandino, Antonio → see Gandini, Antonio

Gandino, Christoforo da *(Renaissance engineer)*   **AV**
    Bibl: Burlington Mag., Nov. 1980, p.763

Gandolfi → see Gandolfi, Ubaldo

Gandolfi family *(Italian painters, stucco artists, 18th c.)*   **BA**
    Bibl: ▶Bénézit; ▶Thieme-Becker

Gandolfi, Francesco   **GC WC**
    (Italian artist, 1824-1873)   WC
    (Italian painter, 1824-1873)   GC
    Bibl: ▶Thieme-Becker

Gandolfi, Gaetano   **BA GC PR WC**
    (Italian artist, 1734-1802)   WC
    (Italian painter and printmaker, 1734-1802)   GC
    (Italian painter, 1734-1802)   PR
    (Italian painter, printmaker, 1734-1802)   BA
    Bibl: ▶Bolaffi; ▶RILA/BHA; ▶Thieme-Becker
    Gaetano Gandolfi   PR

Gandolfi, José Maria (*Brazilian architect*)   **AV**
    Bibl: Projeto, 1985 Dec., no.82, p.80

Gandolfi, Mauro   **BA GC WC**
  (*Italian artist, 1764-1834*)   **WC**
  (*Italian painter, printmaker, 1764-1834*)   **BA**
  (*Italian, 1764-1834*)   **GC**
    Bibl: ▶Bolaffi; ▶Thieme-Becker; ▶Witt checklist

Gandolfi, Paola (*Italian painter, b.1949*)   **BA**
    Bibl: Washington, DC (USA), Hirshhorn Mus., New romanticism (1985), p.112

Gandolfi, Roberto (*Brazilian architect*)   **AV**
    Bibl: Projeto, 1985 Dec., no.82, p.80

Gandolfi, Tommaso (*Italian sculptor, 17th c.*)   **BA**
    Bibl: Baruffaldi, Vite pitt. e scult. ferraresi; ▶Bessone-Aurelj, Scult. & arch. ital.; TCI Emilia-Romagna; ▶Thieme-Becker

Gandolfi, Ubaldo   **BA GC PR WC**
  (*Italian artist, 1728-1781*)   **WC**
  (*Italian painter, 1728-1781*)   **PR**
  (*Italian painter, printmaker, sculptor, 1728-1781*)   **BA**
  (*Italian sculptor, painter, and printmaker, 1728-1781*)   **GC**
    Bibl: ▶Bolaffi; ▶Encyc. world art; ▶Fredericksen & Zeri, Census; ▶RILA/BHA; ▶Thieme-Becker
  Gandolfi   **PR**
  Ubaldo Gandolfi   **PR**

Gandolfi, Vittorio (*Italian architect, 1919-*)   **AV**

Gandolfino d'Asti   **BA GC**
  (*Italian artist, op.1493-1510*)   **WC**
  (*Italian painter, act.1493-1510*)   **BA**
  (*Italian, act. ca.1493-1510*)   **GC**
    Bibl: ▶Bolaffi; ▶Thieme-Becker; ▶Witt checklist
  Asti, Gandolfino d'   **BA**
  Gandolfino da Roreto   **BA**

Gandolfino di Boreto or de Roretis d'Asti   **WC**
  Roreto, Gandolfino da   **BA**
Gandolfino da Roreto →see Gandolfino d'Asti
Gandolfino di Boreto or de Roretis d'Asti →see Gandolfino d'Asti

Gandon, James   **AV BA WC WI**
  (*1743-1823*)   **AV**
  (*British architect, 1743-1823*)   **BA**
  (*British artist, 1742-1823*)   **WC WI**
    Bibl: ▶Macmillan encyc. archts.; ▶Mallalieu, Brit. watercolour artists; ▶Thieme-Becker

Gandon, Pierre (*French artist, 1899-*)   **WC**

Gandy, Herbert   **WC WI**
  (*British artist, 19th cent.*)   **WC**
  (*British artist, op.1879-, d.circa 1920*)   **WI**

Gandy, James (*British artist, 1619-1689*)   **WC WI**

Gandy, John Peter →see Deering, John Peter, (Gandy)
Gandy, John Peter, afterwards J. P. Deering →see Deering, John Peter, (Gandy)

Gandy, Joseph Michael   **AV BA GC WC WI**
  (*1771-1843*)   **AV**
  (*British architect, painter, 1771-1843*)   **BA**
  (*British artist, 1771-1843*)   **WC WI**
  (*British, 1771-1843*)   **GC**
    Bibl: ▶Dict. natl. biog.; ▶Fisher, Watercolour ptrs.; ▶Mallalieu, Brit. watercolour artists; ▶Thieme-Becker; ▶Witt checklist

Gandy, Michael (*1778-1862*)   **AV**

Gandy, Thomas (*British artist, op. 1848-1859*)   **WC WI**

Gandy, William   **WC WI**
  (*British artist, c.1660-1729*)   **WC**
  (*British artist, op.1655-1729*)   **WI**

Ganf, Natal'ja Jul'evna (*Russian designer, b.1926*)   **BA**
    Bibl: Hudozniki Narodov SSSR, v.2

Gangelen, H. van (*Dutch, 20th c.*)   **BA**
    Bibl: ANTIEK XIV (1980)

Gangl, Alojz (*Yugoslav sculptor, 1859-1935*)   **BA**
    Bibl: ▶Busse, Maler u. Bildhauer 19. Jahr.; Hootz, JUGOSLAVIEN, v. I(1981),p.385; ▶Vollmer, Künst.-Lex. 20. Jhr., suppl.

Gangnet, Pierre (*French architect, 1943-*)   **AV**
    Bibl: Das Kunstwerk, n.3-4, Sept. 1983, p.58

Gangneux, Marie-Christine (*French architect*)   **AV**
    Bibl: Architecture d'aujourd'hui, 1981 Sept., no.216, p.65

Ganière, Jean (*French painter, d.1666*)   **GC**
    Bibl: ▶Thieme-Becker

Ganju, Ashish (*Indian architect*)   **AV**
    Bibl: Architectural review, 1987 Aug., v.181, no.1086, p.48

Ganju, Ioan (*Rumanian artist, 1942-*)   **WC**

Ganne, Yves (*French artist, 1931-*)   **WC**

Gannett, Brainard Joy (*American architect*)   **AV**

Gannon, Patrick (*Irish architect, Dublin*)   **AV**
    Bibl: Plan: architecture + interior design in Ireland, 1989 Feb., v.20, no.2, p.50

Gano da Siena (*Italian sculptor, act. ca.1303, d.ca.1318*)   **BA**
    Bibl: Bardotti Biasion, PROSPETTIVA 37 (1984), 5-18; ▶Portoghesi, Diz. arch. e urbanistica; TCI Toscana; ▶Thieme-Becker; ▶White, Art & arch. Italy
  Galgano di Giovanni   **BA**
  Gano di Fazio   **BA**
Gano di Fazio →see Gano da Siena

Gano, Peter (*American architect and engineer, Calif*)   **AV**
    Bibl: Historic preservation, 1984 Apr., v.36, no.2, p.10

Gans, Frederick C. (*American architect, 1911?-1976*)   **BA**
    Bibl: NY Times obit., 7 Apr 1976, p.36

Gans, Tojvo (*Russian designer, 20th c.*)   **BA**
    Bibl: DEKORATIVNOE ISKUSSTVO SSSR 207 (Feb 1975) 38

Gansevoort Limner (*American, 1730-1845*)   **GC**
    Bibl: Getty Photo Study Coll.; ▶Witt checklist
  Limner, Gansevoort   **GC**
Ganso →see Ganso, Emil

Ganso, Emil   **BA PR WC WI**
  (*American artist, 1895-1941*)   **WC**
  (*American artist, 1895-1945*)   **WI**
  (*American painter, 1895-1941*)   **PR**
  (*American painter, printmaker, 1895-1941*)   **BA**
    Bibl: ▶Avery obit. idx.; ▶Bénézit; ▶Havlice, Idx. art. bio.; ▶RILA/BHA; ▶Vollmer, Künst.-Lex. 20. Jhr.
  Emil Ganso   **PR**
  Ganso   **PR**

Gansöder, Steffan (*German printmaker, act.1533, d.1582/83*)   **BA**
    Bibl: ▶Hollstein, German; ▶Thieme-Becker; Timann, Anz. des Germ. Nationalmus. (1987) 195-204

Gant, James Y. (*British artist, op. 1827-1841*)   **WI**

Gantar, Bert (*Austrian architect*)   **AV**
    Bibl: Architecture, the AIA journal, 1983 Aug., v.72, no.8, p.94

Gantenbein, Werner (*Swiss architect, Zurich*)   **AV**
    Bibl: ▶Schweiz. Ingen. u. Archit., 1984-1985

Ganter, Bernard (*French artist, 1928-*)   **WC**

Ganter, Dionys (*German artist, 1800-1864*)   **WC**

Ganter, Nikolaus (*German artist, 19th cent.*)   **WC**

Ganter, W. (*German artist, op.c. 1800*)   **WC**

Gantt, Harvey B. *(American architect and city planner, mayor of Charlotte, N.C., 1984, 1943-)*   **AV**
    Bibl: ▶AIA Pro File, 1987-88; Architecture, the AIA journal, 1984 Feb., v.73, no.2, p.30 [date]

Gantz, John *(British artist, 1772-1853)*   **WI**

Gantz, Justinian   **WC WI**
    (British artist, 1802-1862)   WI
    (British artist, op.1850)   WC

Gantz, William *(American architect, St. Louis, MO, 1941-)*   **AV**
    Bibl: Inland architect, 1985 Nov.-Dec., v.29, no.6, p.36

Ganymede Painter *(Apulian vase-painter)*   **GC**
    Bibl: Trendall, Attic red-fig. vases Apulia

Ganz, Edwin   **GC WC**
    (Swiss artist, 1871-)   WC
    (Swiss painter, b.1871)   GC
    Bibl: ▶Bénézit

Ganz, Henry F.W. *(British artist, op. 1883-1907)*   **WI**

Ganz, Joachim   **AV BA**
    (German architect, b.1942)   BA
    (West German archtect, 1942-)   AV
    Bibl: KUNSTWERK XXXII/2-3 (Apr-June 1979) 58

Ganža, Aleksandr *(Ukranian sculptor, potter, 20th c.)*   **BA**
    Bibl: DEKORATIVNOE ISKUSSTVO (May 1974) 43-44

Ganzel, Bill *(American photographer, 20th c.)*   **BA**
    Bibl: Glowen, Artweek XIV/16 (23 Par 1983) 15; Seattle (WA, USA), Univ. of Washington, Henry Art Gallery, RADICAL, RATIONAL (1983)

Ganzinotto, G.P. *(Italian artist, 17th cent.(?))*   **WC**

Gaponenko, Taras Gur'evič *(Russian painter, b.1906)*   **BA**
    Bibl: ▶Vollmer, Künst.-Lex. 20. Jhr.; Vronskaya, Biog. dict. USSR

Gappnigg, Valentin *(Austrian painter, act.1697-1728)*   **BA**
    Bibl: ▶Bénézit; ▶Thieme-Becker

Gaputyte, Elena   **WC WI**
    (British artist, 1927-)   WC
    (British artist, b.1927)   WI

Gar. Marrat →see Maratti, Carlo

Garabedian, Charles *(American painter, sculptor, b.1923)*   **BA**
    Bibl: ▶MoMA libr. cat.; ▶NY art yrbk.

Garafalo →see Garofalo, Benvenuto Tisi da

Garafaol →see Garofalo, Benvenuto Tisi da

Garanjoud, Claude *(French artist, 1926-)*   **WC**

Garat, Francis *(French artist, op.c. 1898)*   **WC**

Garatti, Vittorio *(Italian architect, Milan)*   **AV**
    Bibl: Interior design, 1987 May, v.58, no.7, p.258

Garau, Giorgio *(Italian architect)*   **AV**
    Bibl: Parametro, 1985 Apr.-May, no.135-136, p.48

Garaud, G.B. *(French artist, op.c. 1750-1778)*   **WC**

Garavaggi →see Caravaggio, Michelangelo Merisi da

Garay, Helene de *(Venezuelan architect)*   **AV**

Garay, Miguel   **AV BA**
    (Spanish architect, 1936-)   AV
    (Spanish architect, 20th c.)   BA
    Bibl: Das Kunstwerk, n.3-4, Sept. 1983, p.15; MONUMENTS HIST. DE LA FRANCE 108 (1980) 71-787

Garbas, Marco *(Italian artist, 18th cent.)*   **WC**

Garbe, Richard *(British sculptor, 1876-1957)*   **BA**
    Bibl: ▶Johnson, Brit. artists; ▶Thieme-Becker; ▶Waters, Brit. artists

Garbe-Roeder, Emy →see Roeder, Emy

Garbell, Alexandre *(French artist, 1903-)*   **WC**

Garber, Daniel   **BA PR WC WI**
    (American artist, 1880-)   WC
    (American artist, 1880-1958)   WI
    (American painter, 1880-1958)   BA PR
    Bibl: ▶Fielding's Amer. ptrs.; ▶RILA/BHA; ▶WWW Amer. art; ▶Young, Amer. artists
    Daniel Garber   PR

Garbett, Edward Lacy *(British architect, designer, act.1850)*   **BA**
    Bibl: ▶Avery period. idx.; ▶Natl. union cat., pre-1956

Garbett, Gordon   **WC WI**
    (British artist, 19th cent.)   WC
    (British artist, op.19th c.)   WI

Garbett, Keith *(British architect)*   **AV**
    Bibl: Area, 1985 Mar.-Apr., v.5, no.21, p.26

Garbi →see Garbi, Anton Maria

Garbi, Anton Maria *(Italian painter, 1718-1797)*   **PR**
    Bibl: ▶Thieme-Becker
    Anton Maria Garbi   PR
    Garbi   PR

Garbi, Domenico   **BA WC**
    (Italian artist, op.1797-1812)   WC
    (Italian painter, act.1797-1812)   BA
    Bibl: ▶Bolaffi; ▶Thieme-Becker; ▶Witt checklist

Garbiani, G.B. *(Italian artist, 17th cent.)*   **WC**

Garbieri →see Guercino (Giovanni Francesco Barbieri)

Garbieri, Lorenzo   **GC WC**
    (Italian artist, 1580-1654)   WC
    (Italian, 1580-1654)   GC
    Bibl: ▶Thieme-Becker; ▶Witt checklist

Garbini, Ludovicus →see Cruse, Ludovicus

Garbizza, Angela   **GC**
    (French artist, op.c.1810)   WC
    (French, act.ca.1810)   GC
    Bibl: ▶Witt checklist

Garbizza, Angelo   **WC**

Garbizza, Angelo →see Garbizza, Angela

Garbo, Raffaellino del →see Raffaellino del Garbo

Garbrand, Caleb J. →see Garbrand, Caleb John

Garbrand, Caleb John   **WI**
    (British artist, 1748-1794)   WI
    (British artist, op.1775-1789)   WC

Garbrand, Caleb J.   **WC**

Garbutt, John *(British artist, op. 1981-)*   **WI**

Garcement, Alfred *(British artist, op.1868-1903)*   **WC**

Garcés, Jordi *(Spanish architect, 1945-)*   **AV**
    Bibl: ▶Contemp. archts.

Garcet, Robert *(Belgian artist, 20th c.)*   **BA**
    Bibl: Lennep, KUNSTFORUM INT. 51 (July 1982) 37

Garci Aguirre, Pedro *(Spanish architect, printmaker, 1752-1809)*   **BA**
    Bibl: Arch. esp. de arte, XLIX/193 (Jan-Mar 1976) 41-57; ▶Encyc. world art

García Barrena, Carmelo   **BA**
    (Spanish artist, 20th cent.)   WC
    (Spanish painter, b.1926)   BA
    Bibl: ▶Campoy, Español contemp.; Campoy, LA PINTURA DE GARCIA BARRENA

Barrena, Carmelo García   **WC**

García Bryce, José *(Peruvian architect, 1928-)*   **AV**
    Bibl: Projeto, 1987 Oct., no.104, p.126

Bryce, José García   **AV**

García Chicano, José *(Spanish painter, act.ca.1838, d.1858)*   **BA**
    Bibl: Banda y Vargas, GOYA 169-171 (July-Dec 1982) 52-58; ▶Bénézit; ▶Ossorio y Bernard, Artistas españoles 19s.; ▶Thieme-Becker

Chicano, José García   **BA**

Garcia de Benabarre →see García de Benabarre, Pedro

García de Benabarre,
Pedro　　　　　　　**BA GC PR WC**
- *(Spanish artist, op.1455-1456)*　WC
- *(Spanish painter, act. 1455)*　PR
- *(Spanish painter, act.1455)*　BA
- *(Spanish, act.1455-56)*　GC
  Bibl: ▶Bénézit; Gardner Mus. cat.;
  Post, CAT. SCH. OF LATE MIDDLE
  AGES , p.265; ▶Rafols, Artistas
  Cataluña; ▶RILA/BHA; ▶Witt
  checklist
- Benabarre, Pedro García de　BA PR
- Garcia de Benabarre　PR
- Garcia, Pedro de Benabarre　GC
- Pedro Garcia de Benabarre　PR

García de Cubillas *(Spanish
architect, 16th c.)*　　　　**BA**
  Bibl: Arch. esp. de arte, LI/201
  (Jan-Mar 1978) 29-51
- Cubillas, García de　BA

García de Dueñas, Alonso *(Spanish
mason, act.1653)*　　　　**BA**
  Bibl: Barrio Moya, GOYA 164-165
  (Sept-Dec 1981) 91
- Dueñas, Alonso García de　BA

*Garcia de Miranda → see García de
Miranda, Juan*

García de Miranda, Juan　**BA PR WC**
- *(Spanish artist, 1677-1749)*　WC
- *(Spanish painter, 1677-1749)*　BA PR
  Bibl: ▶Ceán Bermúdez, Bellas artes
  ESP; ▶RILA/BHA; ▶Thieme-Becker
- Garcia de Miranda　PR
- Juan Garcia de Miranda　PR
- Miranda, Juan García de　BA
- Miranda, Juan Garcia de la　PR

Garcia de Paredes, José Maria
(Spanish architect, 1924-)　　**AV**

García de Sahagún *(Spanish
goldsmith, act.1602-1607)*　　**BA**
  Bibl: Arch. esp. de arte, LI/202
  (Apr-Jun 1978) 170-174

**Garcia del Diestro, Jerónimo
Junquerra** *(Spanish architect)*　**AV**
  Bibl: Bauwelt, 1988 Feb.19, v.79,
  no.7-8, p.298

*Garcia el Hidalgo, Jose → see García
Hidalgo, José*

Garcia Faria, Pedro *(Spanish
architect, 1858-1927)*　　**AV**

García Gil, Luis *(Student at the
Escuela de Arquitectura de
Madrid, 1987))*　　**AV**
  Bibl: El croquis, 1987 Oct., v.5,
  no.30, p.107

García Hidalgo, José　　**BA**
- *(Spanish artist, c.1650-1717)*　WC
- *(Spanish painter, 1646-1717)*　BA
- *(Spanish, ca.1650-1717)*　GC
  Bibl: ▶Ceán Bermúdez, Bellas artes
  ESP; ▶Encic. univ. ilus.; ▶O'Neil,
  Spanish ptrs.; Piedra, Arch. esp.
  de arte, LXIII/250 (Apr-Jun 1990)
  325-326; ▶Thieme-Becker; ▶Witt
  checklist
- **Garcia el Hidalgo, Jose**　　**GC WC**

García Joya, Mario *(Cuban
photographer, b.1938?)*　　**BA**
  Bibl: ▶Art Index, v.54, no.2
- Joya, Mario García　BA
- Mayito　BA

*Garcia La Fuente, M. Clara → see
Garcia Lafuente, Clara*

Garcia Lafuente, Clara *(Italian
architect, 1955-)*　　**AV**
  Bibl: Controspazio, 1985 Jan.-
  June, v.16, no.1-2, p.8; Domus,
  1988 Nov., no.699, p.14
- Garcia La Fuente, M. Clara　AV

Garcia Melgarejo, Diego *(Spanish
artist, -1724)*　　**WC**

Garcia Mercadal, Fernando *(20th
century Spanish architect)*　**AV**
- Mercadal, Fernando García　AV

García Nuñez, Julián *(Argentine
architect, 1875-1944)*　　**BA**
  Bibl: CONNOISSEUR 189/759,
  p.56

García Pedrosa, Ignacio *(Spanish
architect)*　　**AV**
  Bibl: Arquitectura, LXV/250 (Sept.
  -Oct. 1984), p.21

Garcia Rodero, Cristina
(photographer, b.1949)　　**GC**
  Bibl: Getty Photo Study Coll.
- Rodero, Cristina Garcia　GC

*Garcia y Barcia, Manuel → see García
y García, Manuel*

García y García, Manuel　　**BA**
- *(Spanish artist, op.1858-1877)*　WC
- *(Spanish painter, 1836-1898)*　BA
  Bibl: ▶Encic. univ. ilus.; ▶Ossorio y
  Bernard, Artistas españoles 19s.;
  ▶Thieme-Becker
- **Garcia y Barcia, Manuel**　　**WC**

Garcia y Garcia, Rafael **(Garcia
Hispaleto)** *(Spanish artist, 1833-
1854)*　　**WC**

*Garcia y Ramos → see García y
Ramos, José*

García y Ramos, José　　**PR WC**
- *(Spanish artist, 1852-1912)*　WC
- *(Spanish painter, 1852-1912)*　PR
  Bibl: ▶Thieme-Becker
- Garcia y Ramos　PR
- Jose Garcia y Ramos　PR

Garcia y Reynoso, Antonio
(Spanish artist, c.1623-1677)　**WC**

Garcia y Rodriguez, Manuel
(Spanish artist, 1863-)　　**WC**

Garcia y Salmeron, Cristobal　**WC**
- *(Spanish artist, c.1603-1660)*　WC
- *(Spanish artist, c.1603-1666)*　WC
- **Salmeron, Cristobal Garcia y**　**WC**

Garcia, Angel *(Venezuelan architect)*　**AV**
  Bibl: Spazio e societa, 1987 July-
  Sept., v.10, no.37, p.116

Garcia, Fernandez *(Spanish artist,
op.1519-1540)*　　**WC**

García, Gerónimo *(Spanish painter,
sculptor, 17th c.)*　　**BA**
  Bibl: ▶Ceán Bermúdez, Bellas artes
  ESP; ▶Encic. univ. ilus.;
  ▶Thieme-Becker

García, Hector *(Mexican
photographer, 20th c.)*　　**BA**
  Bibl: Berlin (DEU), SMPK,
  Nationalgalerie, WAND, BILD,
  MEXICO (1982)

Garcia, Jacques *(French interior
designer)*　　**AV**
  Bibl: Maison Française, 1985 Apr.,
  no.386, p.116

*Garcia, Joaquin Torres → see
Torres-García, Joaquín*

García, José *(Colombian architect)*　**AV**
  Bibl: Proa, 1985 Sept., no.345,
  p.44

Garcia, Juan *(American architect)*　**AV**
  Bibl: Pratt jrnl. of architecture,
  1985 Fall, v.1, p.41

Garcia, Luis Ignacio de Homa
(Spanish artist, 20th cent.)　**WC**

García, Miguel *(Spanish painter,
sculptor, 17th c.)*　　**BA**
  Bibl: ▶Ceán Bermúdez, Bellas artes
  ESP; ▶Encic. univ. ilus.

*Garcia, Pedro de Benabarre → see
García de Benabarre, Pedro*

Garcia, Rupert *(American artist,
b.1941)*　　**BA**
  Bibl: ▶Artweek idx.; San Francisco
  (CA, USA), MOMA, Rupert Garcia
  (1978)

García, Simón *(Spanish architect,
b.ca.1651, act.1681)*　　**BA**
  Bibl: Hispanic Soc., Libr. cat.;
  ▶Natl. union cat., pre-1956;
  Sanabria, JSAH XLI/4 (Dec 1982)
  282

Garcia, Stephanus *(illuminator, 11th
c.)*　　**BA**
  Bibl: Avril, ACTAS DEL SIMPOSIO
  PARA EL ESTUDIO DE LOS
  CODICES DEL COMENTARIO AL
  APOCALIPSIS DE BEATO..., Madrid
  (1976) II, 261-271; Domínguez
  Bordona, Codices miniados esp.;
  Domínguez Bordona, Span.
  illumination; Schapiro,
  ROMANESQUE..., p.311
- Garsia, Stephan　BA

García, Tomás *(Argentine architect)*　**AV**
  Bibl: Ianus, 1980, v.0, no.0, p.121

Garciandía, Flavio *(Cuban artist,
20th c.)*　　**BA**
  Bibl: Lippard, Art in Amer.,
  LXXIV/4 (Apr. 1986) p.27

Garcias, Jean-Claude *(French
architect and author, 1940-)*　**AV**
  Bibl: Intl. archt., 1 (1983) p.[61]

Garcin, Gilles   **BA GC WC**
   (French artist, op.1690-1700)   WC
   (French painter, 1647-1702)   BA
   (French painter, ca.1700)   GC
     Bibl: ▶Bénézit; ▶Marseille (FRA),
     Musée B.-A., Peinture Provence
     17e s. (1978); ▶Thieme-Becker
   Garcin, Louis   BA
Garcin, Laure (French artist, 1896-)   **WC**
Garcin, Louis→see Garcin, Gilles
Gard, De   **WC WI**
   (British artist, 17th cent.)   WC
   (British artist, op.17th c.)   WI
Gardanne, Paméla de→see Brame,
   Paméla
Garde→see Guardi, Francesco
Garde, Tora (Danish, 20th c.)   **BA**
     Bibl: ▶København (DNK), Statens
     Mus. Kunst, København/Paris
     (1982)
   Fischer, Tora   BA
Gardell-Ericson, Anna Maria
   (Swedish painter, 1853-1939)   **BA**
     Bibl: ▶Bénézit; ▶Svenska
     konstnärer; ▶Svenskt konst.-lex.;
     ▶Thieme-Becker
   Ericson, Anna Maria Gardell   BA
Gardella, Ignazio (Italian architect,
   1905-)   **AV**
     Bibl: ▶Contemp. archts.
Gardelle the Younger, Robert→see
   Gardelle, Robert II
Gardelle, Elie(?) (Swiss artist, 1688-
   1748)   **WC**
Gardelle, Robert II   **GC**
   (Swiss artist, 1682-1766)   WC
   (Swiss, 1682-1766)   GC
     Bibl: ▶Thieme-Becker; ▶Witt
     checklist
   Gardelle the Younger, Robert   **WC**
Gardelle, Theodore (Swiss artist,
   1722-1761)   **WC**
Garden, Hugh Mackie Gordon
   (Canadian architect, 1873-1961)   **AV**
     Bibl: ▶Macmillan encyc. archts.
Garden, Phillips   **JG**
Garden, Simon (British artist, op.
   1985-)   **WI**
Garden, W.F. (British artist, 1856-
   1921)   **WI**
     Bibl: ▶Fisher, Watercolour ptrs.
   Fraser-Gardener, William   WI
Gardener, Jon (English gardener,
   14th c.)   **BA**
     Bibl: ▶Encyc. Britannica, v.7,
     p.902; Garden History XIII/2
     (autumn 1985) 83; ▶Natl. union
     cat., pre-1956
Gardener, Rev. William→see
   Gardener, William
Gardener, William   **WI**
   (British artist, 18th cent.)   WC
   (British artist, op.18th c.)   WI
   Gardener, Rev. William   **WC**
Gardi→see Guardi, Francesco

Gardie, Mrs. (British artist, op.1824-
   1837)   **WC WI**
Gardier, Fernand (French assistant
   to Le Corbusier)   **AV**
     Bibl: Archithese, 1987 Sept.-Oct.,
     v.17, no.5, p.32
Gardier, Raoul de   **PR**
   (French artist, 1871-1952)   WC
   (French painter, 1871-1952)   PR
     Bibl: Detroit Inst of Arts
     catalogue; ▶Thieme-Becker
Gardier, Raoul du   **PR WC**
   Raoul de Gardier   PR
Gardier, Raoul du→see Gardier,
   Raoul de
Gardijn, Karel du→see Dujardin, Karel
Gardiner, Alfred Clive   **WI**
   (British artist, 1891-1960)   WI
   (British artist, 1891-1970)   AV
   (British artist, 20th cent.)   WC
   (British painter, 1891-1960)   PR
     Bibl: Ashmolean Museum
     catalogue; RLIN BKS file, NYCX86-
     B62542; ▶Witt checklist
   Clive Gardiner   PR
Gardiner, Clive   **AV PR WC**
Gardiner, Alfred Clive, Mrs.,
   (Lilian)→see Lancaster, Lilian
   Gardiner
Gardiner, Clive→see Gardiner, Alfred
   Clive
Gardiner, Eliza→see Gardiner, Eliza,
   (GBR)
Gardiner, Eliza Draper (American
   artist, 1871-1955)   **WI**
Gardiner, Eliza, (GBR)   **WI**
   (British artist, op.1802)   WC
   (British artist, op.1802-)   WI
   Gardiner, Eliza   **WC**
Gardiner, Gerald (British artist,
   b.1902)   **WI**
Gardiner, Jeremy (British artist, op.
   1981-)   **WI**
Gardiner, Margaret (British, 20th
   c.)   **BA**
     Bibl: Arts Council of GBR, THE
     PIER GALLERY COLLECTION
     (1978)
Gardiner, Mary   **WI**
   (British artist, op.1759)   WC
   (British artist, op.1759-1783)   WI
   Gardiner, Miss   **WC**
Gardiner, Miss→see Gardiner, Mary
Gardiner, Sidney (American
   silversmith, d.1827)   **BA**
     Bibl: Fales, Early Amer. silver,
     p.72; Hood, Amer. silver, p.197
Gardiner, Stanley (British architect,
   ca.1906-1975)   **BA**
     Bibl: ▶RILA/BHA, LXXXII/11-12
     (Nov.-Dec. 1975) 4
Gardiner, Stanley→see Gardiner,
   Stanley Horace

Gardiner, Stanley Horace   **VO WI**
   (British artist, 1888-1952)   WI
   (British painter, 1888-1952)   VO
     Bibl: ▶Johnson, Brit. artists, p.
     192; ▶Libr. of Congr. Name Auth.
     File, NAFR938401; ▶Waters, Brit.
     artists
Gardiner, Stanley   **WI**
Gardiner, William Nelson (British
   artist, 1766-1814)   **WC WI**
Gardis→see Guardi, Francesco
Gardner→see Gardner, Daniel
Gardner, Alexander   **BA JG**
   (American (b. Scotland, UK),
   1821-1882)   JG
   (American photographer, 1821-
   1882)   BA
     Bibl: ▶Gernsheim, Hist. photog.;
     ▶Newhall, Photog.
Gardner, Daniel   **BA GC PR WC WI**
   (British artist, 1750-1805)   WC WI
   (British painter, 1750-1805)   BA PR
   (British, 1750-1805)   GC
     Bibl: ▶Bénézit; ▶RILA/BHA;
     ▶Thieme-Becker; ▶Witt checklist
   Daniel Gardner   PR
   Gardner   PR
Gardner, Derek George
   Montague   **WC WI**
   (British artist, 1914-)   WC
   (British artist, b.1914)   WI
Gardner, Edwin Alexander (1902-
   1986; Architect, Government
   architect, Ottawa)   **FA**
     Bibl: CAAD Finding Aid RG 11M
     79003/36 Item 22; Dube; ▶Hill,
     Archts. Canada, 1986; The
     Ottawa Citizen 24.XII.1986
Gardner, Elizabeth→see Bouguereau,
   Elizabeth Jane Gardner
Gardner, Elizabeth Jane   **WI**
   (American artist, 1851-1922)   WC WI
   Bouguereau, Adolphe William,
   Mrs., (Elizabeth Jane Gardner)   WI
   Gardner, Elizabeth Jane
   (Elizabeth Jane Bouguereau)   **WC**
Gardner, Elizabeth Jane (Elizabeth
   Jane Bouguereau)→see Gardner,
   Elizabeth Jane
Gardner, F. (American artist, op.
   20th c.)   **WI**
Gardner, G.B.→see Gardner, George
   B.
Gardner, George B.   **WI**
   (American artist, 1835-1904)   WI
   (American artist, 19th cent.)   WC
   Gardner, G.B.   **WC**
Gardner, George W. (American
   photographer, b.1940)   **BA**
     Bibl: Pittsfield (MA, USA),
     Gerkshire Mus. GEORGE W.
     GARDNER (1983)

Gardner, Ian   **BA WI**
  (*British artist, b.1944*)   **WI**
  (*British painter, b.1944*)   **BA**
    Bibl: Bradford (GBR), City Art
    Gallery, Aislabie's gardens (1981)
Gardner, James (*British designer,
  b.1907*)   **BA**
    Bibl: Gardner, J., ROYAL SOCIETY
    OF ARTS JOURNAL, CXXXIII/5344
    (Mar 1985) 257-266
Gardner, Joan A. (*American
  printmaker, b.1933*)   **BA**
    Bibl: Guide exh. artists: N. Amer.
    ptrs.; ▶Intl. dir. exh. artists, 1982;
    ▶WW Amer. Art
Gardner, John (*British artist, op.
  20th c.*)   **WI**
Gardner, Linda (*American painter,
  20th c.*)   **BA**
    Bibl: Breslow, Arts mag., LVII/1
    (Sep. 1982) p.13
Gardner, Robert (*American
  anthropologist, photographer,
  filmmaker, author, b.1925*)   **BA**
    Bibl: ▶Natl. union cat.
Gardner, W. Biscambe → see Gardner,
  William Biscombe
Gardner, Walter (*American, active
  1880s Gloucester, Massachusetts*)   **JG**
Gardner, William Biscombe   **WI**
  (*British artist, 1847-1919*)   **WC WI**
  Gardner, W. Biscambe   **WC**
Gardner-Soper, James Hamlin
  (*American artist, b.1877*)   **WI**
Gardnor → see Gardnor, John
Gardnor, John   **PR WI**
  (*British artist, 1729-1808*)   **WC WI**
  (*British painter, 1729-1808*)   **PR**
    Bibl: ▶Thieme-Becker;
    ▶Waterhouse, Brit. 18c. ptrs.
    Gardnor   **PR**
  Gardnor, Rev. John   **WC**
    John Gardnor   **PR**
Gardnor, Rev. John → see Gardnor,
  John
Gardy-Artigas, Joan (*Spanish
  ceramist, sculptor, b.1938*)   **BA**
    Bibl: Dallas (TX, USA), So. Meth.
    Univ. Meadows Mus. & Sculp. Ct.
    JOAN GARDY-ARTIGAS 1984;
    Pierre Matisse Gallery, MIRO,
    ARTIGAS..., 1985
    Artigas, Joan Gardy   **BA**
Gare, Domenico (*French sculptor in
  ITA, act.1520*)   **BA**
    Bibl: REVUE DE L'ART 36 (1977)
    7-26; ▶Thieme-Becker
    Franzosino   **BA**
    Garello, Domenico   **BA**
    Ghare, Domenico   **BA**
Gareis, Franz   **GC WC**
  (*German artist, 1775-1803*)   **WC**
  (*German draughtsman, 1775-
    1803*)   **GC**
    Bibl: Getty Photo Study Coll.;
    ▶Thieme-Becker; ▶Witt checklist
    Gareis, Johann Franz Peter Paul   **GC**

Gareis, Johann Franz Peter Paul → see
  Gareis, Franz
Garel, Leo (*American painter,
  b.1917*)   **BA**
    Bibl: ▶WW Amer. Art, 1976
Garel, Patrick (*French interior
  designer, Paris*)   **AV**
    Bibl: Restaurant and hotel design,
    1986 Nov., v.8, no.9, p.76
Garella, Antonio (*Italian sculptor,
  1864-1919*)   **GC**
    Bibl: TCI Toscana
**Garelli or Garello, Tommaso
  d'Alberto (Masacodo)** (*Italian
  artist, op.1452-1495*)   **WC**
Garelli, David di Tommaso (*Italian
  illuminator, act. ca.1487*)   **GC**
    Bibl: Bellosi, S. Petronio Bologna,
    v.1, p.15
Garelli, Henri (*French designer*)   **AV**
    Bibl: Maison française, 1987 Apr.,
    no.405, p.74
Garello, Domenico → see Gare,
  Domenico
*Garemyn or Gaeremyn, Jan
  Anton → see* Garemyn, Jan Anton
Garemyn, Jan Anton   **GC**
  (*Flemish artist, 1712-1799*)   **WC**
  (*Flemish, 1712-1799*)   **GC**
    Bibl: ▶Thieme-Becker; ▶Witt
    checklist
  **Garemyn or Gaeremyn, Jan
  Anton**   **WC**
Garet, Jedd   **BA WI**
  (*American artist, b.1955*)   **WI**
  (*American painter, b.1955*)   **BA**
    Bibl: ARTS MAG LV (June 1981)
    158-160; Santa Barbara (CA,
    USA), UCSB Art Mus., Figuration
    (1982)
Garets, Odette des (*French artist,
  1891-*)   **WC**
Garf, Salomon   **GC WC**
  (*Dutch artist, 1879-1943*)   **WC**
  (*Dutch painter, 1879-1943*)   **GC**
    Bibl: Getty Photo Study Coll.;
    ▶Witt checklist
Garfield, Abram (*American
  architect, son of President James
  Garfield, 1872?-1958*)   **AV**
    Bibl: ▶Avery obit. idx.
Gargallo, Pablo   **BA**
  (*Spanish sculptor, 1881-1934*) **BA GC**
    Bibl: ▶Bénézit; ▶Havlice, Idx. art.
    bio.; ▶McGraw-Hill dict. art;
    ▶Met. Mus. Art libr. cat.;
    ▶Phaidon 20c. art; ▶RILA/BHA
  Gargello, Pablo   **GC**
Gargello, Pablo → see Gargallo, Pablo
Garginli, Domenico → see Gargiulo,
  Domenico (Micco Spadaro)
Gargiolli, Giovanni (*Italian engineer,
  photographer, 1838-1913*)   **BA**
    Bibl: Martinelli Coco, XENIA, 12
    (1986), p. 103-104

Gargiolli, Giovanni (*Italian architect,
  d.1608*)   **BA**
    Bibl: ▶Portoghesi, Diz. arch. e
    urbanistica; ▶Thieme-Becker
*Gargiuli, Domenico (Micco
  Spadaro) → see* Gargiulo, Domenico
  (Micco Spadaro)
Gargiulo, Domenico → see Gargiulo,
  Domenico (Micco Spadaro)
**Gargiulo, Domenico (Micco
  Spadaro)**   **BA GC PR**
  (*Italian artist, 1612-a.1679*)   **WC**
  (*Italian painter, 1612-1675*) **BA GC PR**
    Bibl: ▶Bolaffi; ▶Encyc. world art;
    Getty Photo Study Coll. (Ptgs.);
    Musei d'Italia, Meraviglie d'Italia,
    4: BARI PINACOTECA
    PROVINCIALE (1972) picture #130
    on p.44; ▶RILA/BHA;
    ▶Thieme-Becker

    Dom.o Gargiulo alias Spataro   **PR**
    Domenico Gargiulo   **PR**
    Domenico Micco detto lo Spataro **PR**
    Domenico Spadaro   **PR**
    Domenico Sparano   **PR**
    Domenico Spataro   **PR**
    Dominico Spadaro   **PR**
    Garginli, Domenico   **GC**
  **Gargiuli, Domenico (Micco
  Spadaro)**   **WC**
  Gargiulo, Domenico   **GC PR**
    Miccho Spataro   **PR**
    Micco Spadaro   **GC PR**
    Micco spatare   **PR**
    Micco Spataro   **PR**
    Mico Spadaro   **PR**
    Nicco Spadaro   **PR**
    Nico Spadaro   **PR**
    Spadaro   **PR**
    Spadaro, Micco   **BA**
    Spataro   **PR**
Gari, A. (*German artist, 18th cent.*) **WC**
**Garibaldi or Garibaldo, Marc
  Antonio** (*Flemish artist, 1620-
  1678*)   **WC**
Garibaldi, Joseph (*French artist,
  1863*)   **WC**
Garibbo, Luigi (*Italian artist, 1784-
  1869*)   **WC**
Gariboldi, Giancarlo (*Italian
  architect*)   **AV**
    Bibl: Abitare, 1985 Sept., no.237,
    p.42
Garinei, Giuseppe (*Italian artist, op.
  1887*)   **WC**
Gariot, Paul Cesaire (*French
  painter, b.1811*)   **GC**
    Bibl: n
Garipuy, Jules (*French artist, 1817-
  1893*)   **WC**
Garland, Charles Trevor (*British
  artist, op.1874-1901*)   **WI**

Garland, David *(British ceramist, painter, b.1941)* **BA**
  Bibl: ▶Art Index, Nov. 1987-Oct. 1988; Geddes-Brown, L., COUNTRY LIFE/ CLXXXI/ 14/ 2/ (April 1987), 91; ▶Intl. dir. exh. artists, 1983

Garland, Henry **WC WI**
  (British artist, op.1854-1890) WC
  (British artist, op.1854-1892) WI

Garland, Margaret Lester *(British artist, op.1926-1964)* **WI**
  Bibl: ▶Wood, Victorian ptrs.
  Garland, Margaret Vallis Mary Lester   WI

Garland, Margaret Vallis Mary Lester→see Garland, Margaret Lester

Garland, Valentine Thomas **WC WI**
  (British artist, op.1867-, d.1914) WI
  (British artist, op.1867-1893) WC

Garland, William *(British artist, op. 1853-, d.1882)* **WI**

Garle(?) *(German(?) artist, 18th cent.)* **WC**

Garling, Henry *(British architect, 1789-1870)* **AV**
  Bibl: ▶Colvin, Brit. archts.

Garlington, Susie *(American interior designer)* **AV**
  Bibl: Southern accents, 1986 Jan.-Feb., v.9, no.1, p.112

Garman, Ed *(American painter, author, b.1914)* **BA**
  Bibl: Albuquerque (NM, USA), Museum, Transcendental ptg group (1982); ▶WW Amer. Art, 1982

Garms, Coenraad Matthias *(Dutch painter, 1863-1944)* **GC**
  Bibl: ▶Wright, Ptgs. Dutch museums

Garnache, Jehançon *(French master mason, act.1485, d.ca.1529)* **BA**
  Bibl: GESTA XIX (1980) 37-49; ▶Lance, Dict. archts. fran.; ▶Thieme-Becker

Garnell, Jean-Louis *(French photographer)* **AV**
  Bibl: RLIN BKS file, NYCG84-b58910

Garnelo y Alda, Jose Ramon *(Spanish artist, 1867-)* **WC**

Garner, Edith Mary **WI**
  (British artist, 1881-) WC
  (British artist, b.1881) WI
  Garner, Edith Mary (Edith Mary Lee-Hankey) **WC**
  Hankey, William Lee, Mrs., (Edith Mary)   WI
  Lee-Hankey, William Lee, Mrs., (Edith Mary)   WI
Garner, Edith Mary (Edith Mary Lee-Hankey)→see Garner, Edith Mary

Garner, Frederick *(British artist, op. 1900-)* **WI**

Garner, Gretchen *(American photographer, 20th c.)* **BA**
  Bibl: ARTNEWS LXXIX/5 (May 1980) 78

Garner, Thomas *(Engraver)* **WI**

Garner, Thomas **AV BA**
  (1839-1906) AV
  (British architect, 1839-1906) BA
  Bibl: ▶Portoghesi, Diz. arch. e urbanistica; ▶Thieme-Becker

Garneray→see Garneray, Ambroise-Louis

Garneray, Ambroise Louis→see Garneray, Ambroise-Louis

Garneray, Ambroise-Louis **BA**
  (French artist, 1783-1857) WC
  (French painter, 1783-1857) GC PR
  (French painter, printmaker, author, 1783-1857) BA
  Bibl: ▶Bellier, Artistes fran.; ▶Dict. biog. fran.; Getty Photo Study Coll. (Ptgs.); ▶Thieme-Becker; ▶Witt checklist
  Garneray   PR
  Garneray, Ambroise Louis   GC

Garneray, Louis **GC PR**
Garneray, Louis (Ambroise Louis) **WC**
  Garnerey   PR
  Garnerey, Ambroise-Louis   BA
  Garnerey, Louis   GC
  L. Garnerey   PR
  Louis Garnerey   PR

Garneray, Auguste Simon→see Garnerey, Auguste Simon

Garneray, Jean Francois→see Garnerey, Francois Jean

Garneray, Louis→see Garneray, Ambroise-Louis

Garnerey, Louis (Ambroise Louis)→see Garneray, Ambroise-Louis

Garnerey→see Garneray, Ambroise-Louis

Garnerey (not Garneray), Francois Jean→see Garnerey, Francois Jean

Garnerey, Ambroise-Louis→see Garneray, Ambroise-Louis

Garnerey, Auguste Simon **GC WC**
  (French artist, 1785-1824) WC
  (French, 1785-1824) GC
  Bibl: ▶Bénézit; ▶Witt checklist
  Garnerey, Auguste Simon   GC

Garnerey, Francois Jean **GC**
  (French artist, 1755-1837) WC
  (French, 1755-1837) GC
  Bibl: Getty Photo Study Coll. (Ptgs.); ▶Witt checklist
  Garnerey, Jean Francois   GC

Garnerey (not Garneray), Francois Jean **WC**

Garnerey, Hippolyte Jean Baptiste *(French artist, 1787-1858)* **WC**

Garnerey, Louis→see Garneray, Ambroise-Louis

Garnet, Eldon *(Canadian poet, filmmaker, photographer, 20th c.)* **BA**
  Bibl: Dault, Vanguard, XI/7 (Sep. 1982) pp.18-20

Garnett, Angelica *(British artist, b.1918)* **WI**

Garnett, Charles Claude *(British artist, op.1920-1930)* **WI**

Garnett, Patrick *(British architect, London)* **AV**
  Bibl: ▶RIBA members, 1987

Garnett, Ruth *(British artist, op. 1893-1919)* **WI**

Garnett, William A. **BA JG**
  (American photographer, b.1916) BA
  (American, 1916 -) JG
  Bibl: ▶Newhall, Photog.; ▶Szarkowski, Photog's eye

Garney, William **WC WI**
  (British artist, op.1772) WC
  (British artist, op.1772-) WI

Garnier→see Garnier, Etienne Barthélemy

Garnier→see Garnier, Michel

Garnier, Antoine *(French artist, 1611-1694)* **WC**

Garnier, Charles *(French architect, 1825-1898)* **AV BA**
  Bibl: ▶Avery Libr. cat.; ▶Encyc. world art; ▶Havlice, Idx. art. bio.; ▶Macmillan encyc. archts.; ▶Met. Mus. Art libr. cat.; Penguin dict. arch.
  Garnier, Jean Louis Charles   AV BA

Garnier, Claude *(French artist, 20th cent.)* **WC**

Garnier, Etienne Barthélemy **BA GC PR WC**
  (French artist, 1759-1849) WC
  (French painter, 1759-1849) BA GC PR
  Bibl: ▶Bellier, Artistes fran.; ▶Bénézit; ▶RILA/BHA; ▶Thieme-Becker
  Etienne Barthelemy Garnier   PR
  Garnier   PR

Garnier, François *(French painter, d.1672)* **GC**
  Bibl: ▶Bénézit

Garnier, Francois *(French artist, 1590-1658)* **WC**

Garnier, Friederich Ernst von→see Garnier, Friedrich Ernst von

Garnier, Friedrich Ernst von **BA**
  (German architect, designer, b.1935) BA
  (West German psychologist?, expert on effects of color in architecture) AV
  Bibl: Architektur, Innenarchitektur, Technischer Ausbau, 1988 Oct., p.32; ▶WW Arts DEU

Garnier, Friederich Ernst von **AV**

Garnier, Geoffroy *(French artist, 20th cent.)* **WC**

Garnier, Jean   GC WC
    (French artist, 1632-1705)   WC
    (French painter, 1632-1705)   GC
       Bibl: ▶Bénézit

Garnier, Jean Baptiste *(French*
    artist, -1759)   WC
Garnier, Jean Louis Charles → see
    Garnier, Charles
Garnier, Jules Arsene → see Garnier,
    Jules-Arsène
Garnier, Jules-Arsène   BA
    (French artist, 1847-1889)   WC
    (French painter, 1847-1889)   BA
       Bibl: ▶Dict. biog. fran.;
        ▶Thieme-Becker, v.13, p.207;
        ▶Witt checklist
    Garnier, Jules Arsene   WC
Garnier, Louis   BA GC
    (French sculptor, 1639-1728)   BA
    (French sculptor, ca.1639-1728)   GC
       Bibl: ▶Bénézit; ▶Lami, Sculp. fran.
        19e s.; ▶Thieme-Becker
Garnier, Michel   GC PR WC
    (French artist, op.1793-1814)   WC
    (French painter, act. 1793-1814)   PR
    (French, act.1793-1814)   GC
       Bibl: ▶Bénézit; ▶Thieme-Becker
    Garnier   PR
    Michel Garnier   PR
Garnier, Pierre   BA GC JG
    (French cabinetmaker, act.1742-
    1789)   BA
    (French ébéniste, 1720-ca.1800,
    master 1742)   GC
    (French, 1726-1800, master
    1742)   JG
       Bibl: ▶Salverte, Ébénistes 18e s.;
        ▶Thieme-Becker; Watson, Wallace
        Coll.
Garnier, Tony *(French architect,*
    1869-1948)   AV BA
       Bibl: ▶Avery obit. idx.; ▶Contemp.
        archts.; ▶Encyc. world art
Garof, Francesco → see Garovo,
    Francesco
Garof, Leone → see Garovo, Leone
Garofali → see Garofalo, Benvenuto
    Tisi da
Garofalini or Garofolini,
    Giacinto → see Garofalini, Giacinto
Garofalini, Giacinto   GC
    (Italian artist, 1661-1723)   WC
    (Italian painter, 1661-1723)   GC
       Bibl: ▶Thieme-Becker
    Garofalini or Garofolini,
    Giacinto   WC
    Garofolini, Giacinto   GC
Garofallo → see Garofalo, Benvenuto
    Tisi da
Garofalo → see Garofalo, Benvenuto
    Tisi da
Garofalo (Benvenuto Tisi) → see
    Garofalo, Benvenuto Tisi da
Garofalo Benvenuto → see Garofalo,
    Benvenuto Tisi da

Garofalo, Benvenuto Tisi
da   BA GC PR WI
    (Italian artist, 1481-1559)   WC WI
    (Italian painter, 1481-1559)   BA PR
    (Italian, 1481-1559)   GC
       Bibl: ▶Bolaffi; ▶RILA/BHA, 1986;
        ▶Thieme-Becker; ▶Witt checklist
    B. Da Garofolo   PR
    B. Garafalo   PR
    B. Garaffalo   PR
    B. Garofaldo   PR
    B. Garofalo   PR
    B. Garofolo   PR
    Ben. Garofallo   PR
    Benev. Garofalo   PR
    Benvento Garofolo   PR
    Benvenuti Garofalo   PR
    Benvenuto   PR
    Benvenuto da Garafano   PR
    Benvenuto da Garofalo   PR
    Benvenuto da Garofano   PR
    Benvenuto del Garofalo   PR
    Benvenuto di Garofano   PR
    Benvenuto Garofali   PR
    Benvenuto Garofalo   PR
    Benvenuto Garofano   PR
    Benvenuto Garofoli   PR
    Benvenuto Garofolo   PR
    Benvenuto Garofolo Ferrarese
      Discepolo di Raffaello   PR
    Benvenuto Tisi   PR
    Benvenuto Tisi da Garofalo   BA PR
    Garafalo   PR
    Garafaol   PR
    Garofali   PR
    Garofallo   PR
    Garofalo   PR
    Garofalo (Benvenuto Tisi)   PR
    Garofalo Benvenuto   PR
    Garofalo, Benvenuto Tisio da   WC
    Garofano   PR
    Garoffalo   PR
    Garofoli   PR
    Garofolo   PR
    Garrofolo   PR
    Gorafalo   PR
    Gurafalo   PR
    Il Garofalo   PR
    Tisi   PR
    Tisi, Benvenuto   BA PR
Garofalo, Benvenuto Tisio da → see
    Garofalo, Benvenuto Tisi da
Garofalo, Carlo *(Italian painter, act.*
    17th century)   PR
       Bibl: ▶Thieme-Becker
    Abbate Carlo Garofalo   PR
    Carlo Garofalo   PR
Garofano → see Garofalo, Benvenuto
    Tisi da
Garoffalo → see Garofalo, Benvenuto
    Tisi da
Garofoli → see Garofalo, Benvenuto
    Tisi da
Garofolini, Giacinto → see Garofalini,
    Giacinto

Garofolo → see Garofalo, Benvenuto
    Tisi da
Garoli or Garola, Pier Francesco → see
    Garoli, Pietro Francesco
Garoli, Pietro Francesco   GC
    (Italian artist, 1638-1716)   WC
    (Italian, 1638-1716)   GC
       Bibl: ▶Thieme-Becker; ▶Witt
        checklist
    Garoli or Garola, Pier Francesco   WC
Garouste, Elizabeth *(French*
    designer)   AV
       Bibl: Space design, 1985 Feb., no.
        245, p.52
Garouste, Gérard *(French painter,*
    b.1946)   BA
       Bibl: ▶Bénézit; ▶Intl. dir. exh.
        artists, 1983
Garovaglio Painter *(Etruscan vase-*
    painter)   GC
       Bibl: ▶Szilagyi, Etruszko-korinthosi
Garovo, Francesco *(Italian architect*
    in Moravia, d.1589)   BA
       Bibl: Krčálová, Umění, XXXIII/5
        (1985) p.424; ▶Portoghesi, Diz.
        arch. e urbanistica;
        ▶Thieme-Becker; Umělecké
        Památky CSK, I, 239-241
    Garof, Francesco   BA
    Garuo, Francesco   BA
Garovo, Leone *(Italian architect in*
    Moravia, 16th c.)   BA
       Bibl: Krčálová, Umění, XXXIII/5
        (1985) p.424
    Garof, Leone   BA
    Garuo, Leone   BA
Garper Pausin → see Dughet, Gaspard
    (Gaspard Poussin)
Garrad, Charles *(British sculptor,*
    b.1952)   BA
       Bibl: Arts Council GBR, 6 Times
        (1976)
Garrard → see Garrard, George
Garrard, George   BA GC PR WC WI
    (British artist, 1760-1826)   WC WI
    (British painter, 1760-1826)   PR
    (British painter, sculptor, 1760-
    1826)   BA
    (British sculptor and painter,
    1760-1826)   GC
       Bibl: ▶Redgrave, Engl. school;
        ▶RILA/BHA; ▶Thieme-Becker
    Garrard   PR
    George Garrard   PR
    Mr. G. Garrard, A.R.A.   PR
Garrard, Marcus II → see Geeraerts,
    Marcus, the younger
Garrard, Peter *(British artist, op.*
    1978-1985)   WI
Garrard, Robert → see Garrard, Robert
    I

Garrard, Robert I   **BA GC**
 (British silversmith, 1758-1818)   BA
 (British silversmith, b.1758, act.
    from 1792)   GC
    Bibl: ▶Grimwade, London
    goldsmiths, 1982; Los Angeles
    (CA, USA), LACMA, Monumental
    silver (1977); ▶Penguin dec. arts
Garrard, Robert   JG
Garrard, Rose *(British artist, 20th c.)* BA
    Bibl: Arts Council GBR, Lives
    (1979)
Garrard, Sandra *(American painter,*
    1952-1984)   BA
    Bibl: Olsen, V.L., in ARTS
    QUARTERLY VII/4 (Oct-Dec 1985)
    26
Garrat, Arthur Paine   WI
    (British artist, 1873-op.1908)   WI
    (British artist, op.1899-1908)   WC
    Bibl: ▶Waters, Brit. artists
Garratt, Arthur P.   WC
Garratt, Arthur P.→see Garrat, Arthur
    Paine
Garratt, Robert *(American artist,*
    op.1987-)   WI
Garraud, Leon *(French artist, 1877-)* WC
Garreau, Alphonse *(French painter,*
    1792-d. aft. 1831)   GC
    Bibl: ▶Thieme-Becker
Garret, H. *(British artist, op.18th c.)* WI
Garret, Marcus→see Geeraerts,
    Marcus, the elder
Garret, Marcus I→see Geeraerts,
    Marcus, the elder
Garret, Marcus II→see Geeraerts,
    Marcus, the younger
Garretson, Della *(American painter,*
    1860-1940)   PR
    Bibl: Detroit Inst of Arts
    catalogue; ▶Thieme-Becker
    Della Garretson   PR
Garrett *(American, active 1860s-*
    1870s)   JG
Garrett, Albert Charles *(British*
    painter, printmaker, author,
    b.1915)   BA
    Bibl: ▶WW Art, 1974
Garrett, Alice Warder *(American,*
    1877-1952)   BA
    Bibl: ▶WWW Amer.
Garrett, Dana *(American painter,*
    20th c.)   BA
    Bibl: ARTS MAG LVI/8 (Apr 1982)
    120
Garrett, Daniel   **AV BA**
    (British architect, act.ca.1721-
    1754)   BA
    (British architect, d.1753)   AV
    Bibl: ▶Avery period. idx.; ▶Colvin,
    Brit. archts.
Garrett, Edmund Henry   WI
    (American artist, 1853-1929)   WI
    (Engraver, 1853-1929)   WI
Garrett, H. *(British artist, op.1650)* WC

Garrett, Priscilla Longshore
    (American painter, b.1907)   BA
    Bibl: Ahrens, K., in WOMAN's
    ART JRL. VI/1 (spring-summer
    1985) 12; ▶Collins, Women artists
    Amer.
Garrett, Stephen George
    (American architect, art
    administrator, author, b.1922)   BA
    Bibl: WW Amer., 1978
Garretti, Paolo *(Italian architect)* AV
    Bibl: Abitare, 1985 Sept., no.237,
    p.18
Garrez, Pierre Joseph→see Garrez,
    Rene Joseph
Garrez, Rene Joseph   GC
    (French artist, 1802-1852)   WC
    (French painter, 1802-1852)   GC
    Bibl: ▶Bénézit
Garrez, Pierre Joseph   WC
Garri, Giorgio *(Italian artist, -c.1731)* WC
Garrick, Robert *(British artist, op.*
    19th c.)   WI
Garrido→see Garrido, Leandro
    Ramón
Garrido, Eduardo Leon *(Spanish*
    artist, 1856-)   WC
Garrido, Juan Bautista *(Spanish*
    sculptor, architect, act.1585,
    d.1644)   BA
    Bibl: Mazon de la Toree,
    Miscelanea de Arte 137-139
Garrido, Leandro Ram6n→see
    Garrido, Leandro Ramón
Garrido, Leandro Ramón   PR
    (French artist, 1868-1909)   WC
    (Spanish painter, 1868-1901)   PR
    Bibl: ▶Thieme-Becker
    Garrido   PR
Garrido, Leandro Ram6n   WC
    Leandro Ramon Garrido   PR
Garrido, Pedro *(Spanish silversmith,*
    17th-18th cs.)   BA
    Bibl: Arch. esp. de arte, LII/206
    (Apr-Jun 1979) 145-168
Garriga, Umberto Pena *(South*
    American artist, 20th cent.)   WC
Garriot *(French artist, 18th cent.)* WC
Garrison, Benjamin   **WC WI**
    (British artist, op.-1757)   WC
    (British artist, op.1757-)   WI
Garrison, Eve   **WC WI**
    (American artist, 20th cent.)   WC
    (American artist, op.20th cent.)   WI
Garrison, J. S. *(American architect*
    and builder, act. in Georgia,
    1960s)   AV
    Bibl: Southern accent, 1985 May-
    June, v.8, no.3, p.[77]
Garrison, James G. *(American*
    architect, 1953-)   AV
    Bibl: ▶AIA Pro File, 1987-88
Garrison, T.   **WC WI**
    (British artist, op.1713)   WC
    (British artist, op.1713-)   WI

Garro, Andrés *(Spanish silversmith,*
    act.1651)   BA
    Bibl: Arch. esp. de arte, LII/206
    (Apr-Jun 1979) 145-168
Garro, Jorge *(Peruvian architect,*
    Lima)   AV
    Bibl: Proa, 1988 Mar., no.369,
    p.51
Garrofolo→see Garofalo, Benvenuto
    Tisi da
Garroni, Nicoletta *(Italian architect)* AV
    Bibl: Architettura; cronache e
    storia, 1981 Dec., v.27, no.
    12(314), p.728
Garsea *(Spanish scribe, act.976)*   GC
    Bibl: Antolin, Códices latinos, v.1,
    pp.368-404
Garsia, Stephan→see Garcia,
    Stephanus
Garside, Helen   **WC WI**
    (British artist, 1893-)   WC
    (British artist, b.1893)   WI
Garstenauer, Gerhard *(Austrian*
    architect, Salzburg, 1925-)   AV
    Bibl: Transparent, 1987, v.18,
    no.6/7, p.21
Garstin→see Garstin, Norman
Garstin, Alethea   **BA WC**
    (British artist, 1894-op.1970)   WI
    (British artist, op.1910-1970)   WC
    (British painter, 1894-1978)   BA
    Bibl: ▶Johnson, Brit. artists; Saint
    Ives (GBR), Penwith Gall., Norman
    & Alethea Garstin (1978); Wters;
    ▶WW Art, 1977
Garstin, Althea   WI
Garstin, Althea→see Garstin, Alethea
Garstin, Norman   **BA PR WC WI**
    (British artist, 1855-1926)   WC WI
    (British painter, 1847-1926)   BA PR
    Bibl: ▶Bénézit; ▶Johnson, Brit.
    artists; ▶RILA/BHA; Saint Ives
    (GBR), Penwith Gall., Norman &
    Alethea Garstin (1978); ▶Vollmer,
    Künst.-Lex. 20. Jhr.; ▶Waters, Brit.
    artists
    Garstin   PR
    Norman Garstin   PR
Garten, Richard *(German goldsmith,*
    20th c.)   BA
    Bibl: KUNST UL ANTIQUITATEN 2
    (Mar-Apr 1982) 55
Garthwaite, W.   **WC WI**
    (British artist, 19th cent.)   WC
    (British artist, op.1850-1852)   WI
Gartner→see Gärtner, Johann Philipp
    Eduard
Gärtner, Andreas *(German*
    architect, 1744-1826)   BA
    Bibl: ▶Portoghesi, Diz. arch. e
    urbanistica
Gärtner, Eduard→see Gärtner,
    Johann Philipp Eduard
Gartner, Eduard (Johann Philipp
    Eduard)→see Gärtner, Johann
    Philipp Eduard

Gartner, Friedrich (German artist, 1824-1905)   **WC**

Gärtner, Friedrich von   **AV BA**
(1792-1847)   AV
(German architect, 1792-1847)   BA
Bibl: ▶Brockhaus Enzyk.; Hederer, F. VON GARTNER; ▶Thieme-Becker

Gartner, Fritz (Czech artist, 1882-1958)   **WC**

Gärtner, Georg II   **BA**
(German painter, d.1654)   BA GC
Bibl: ▶Bénézit; ▶Thieme-Becker

Gaertner, Georg II   **GC**
Gertner, Georg II   GC

Gartner, Heinrich (German artist, 1828-1909)   **WC**

Gartner, Jacob (in CSK architect, act.1897)   **BA**
Bibl: Zatloukal, Umění, XXVIII/4 (1980) pp.359-364

Gärtner, Johann Jacob → see Gaertner, Johann Jacob

Gärtner, Johann Philipp Eduard   **BA PR**
(German artist, 1801-1877)   WC
(German painter, 1801-1877)   PR
(German painter, architect, printmaker, 1801-1877)   BA
(German, 1801-1877)   GC
Bibl: ▶Brockhaus Enzyk.; ▶Encyc. world art; ▶Neue deutsche Biog.; ▶RILA/BHA; ▶Thieme-Becker; ▶Witt checklist

Gaertner, Eduard   BA PR
Gartner   PR

Gärtner, Eduard   **BA GC**

Gartner, Eduard (Johann Philipp Eduard)   **WC**
Johann Philipp Eduard Gartner   PR

Garuo, Francesco → see Garovo, Francesco

Garuo, Leone → see Garovo, Leone

Garusambo, Domenico (Italian architect, act.1676-1683)   **BA**
Bibl: Magni, Paragone XXXIV/401-403 (July-Sept 1983) 143

Garutti, Alberto (Italian painter, b.1948)   **BA**
Bibl: Acireale (ITA), Palazzo di Città, Incursioni oltre le linee (1982)

Garvan, Mabel Brady (American, 20th c.)   **BA**
Bibl: American silver in Yale U. Gallery; Clark Art Inst.

Garvey → see Garvey, Edmund

Garvey, Edmund   **PR WC WI**
(British artist, op.1767-, d.1813)   WI
(British artist, op.1767-m.1813)   WC
(British painter, act. 1767, d. 1813)   PR
Bibl: ▶Thieme-Becker; ▶Waterhouse, Brit. 18c. ptrs.

Edmund Garvey   PR
Garvey   PR

Garvie, Thomas Bowman   **BA WC WI**
(British artist, 1859-1934)   WC WI
(British painter, 1859-1944)   BA
Bibl: ▶Bénézit; Natl. Trust, Principal oil ptgs.; ▶Thieme-Becker

Garwood, Tirzah (British printmaker, painter, 1908-1951)   **BA**
Bibl: ▶Art Index, Jan. 1929-Sep. 1932; Constable, THE ENGLAND OF ERIC RAVILIOUS (1982); Geddes-Brown, COUNTRY LIFE/ CLXXXI (26 May 1987), pp 180-181; ▶Johnson, Brit. artists; THE STUDIO, 99 (1930), p.171

Garwood-Jones, Trevor P.
(Canadian architect)   **AV**

Garza, Mary Jessie (American photographer, b.1950)   **BA**
Bibl: San Antonio (TX, USA), Mus. of Art, Mary Jessie Garza (1983)

Garzarelli, Matjaž (Yugoslavian architect, Ljubljana)   **AV**
Bibl: Bauwelt, 1989 Jan.27, v.80, no.5, p.156

Garzarolli, Matiaž (Austrian architect)   **AV**
Bibl: Abitare, 1989 Jan.-Feb., p.154

Garzi → see Garzi, Luigi

Garzi, Luigi   **BA GC JG PR WC**
(Italian artist, 1638-1721)   WC
(Italian painter, 1638-1721)   BA GC PR
(Italian, Roman, 1638-1721)   JG
Bibl: ▶Bolaffi; ▶RILA/BHA, 1986; ▶Thieme-Becker

Garzi   PR
L. Garzi   PR
Lud. Garzi   PR
Luigi Garzi   PR

Garzia, Giuseppe (Italian artist, op. 1922)   **WC**

Garzio, Angelo C. (American ceramist, b.1922.)   **BA**
Bibl: Ceramics Monthly XXIX/1 (Jan 1981) 29-33; ▶Natl. Faculty Dir.; ▶WW Amer. Art, 1989

Garzón (Spanish photographer)   **GC**
Bibl: ▶Idx. Amer. photog. colls.

Garzoni, Giovanna   **BA GC PR WC**
(Italian artist, 1600-1670)   WC
(Italian painter, 1600-1670)   BA GC PR
Bibl: ▶Bénézit; ▶Bolaffi; ▶Encic. italiana; ▶RILA/BHA, 1986; ▶Thieme-Becker

Giovana Garzoni   PR
Giovanna Garzoni   PR

Garzotti family (Italian masons, 17th-18th cs.)   **BA**
Bibl: Vio, Arte veneta, XL (1986) pp.225-229

Garzotti, Baldassare (Italian stonecarver, 1659-1716)   **BA**
Bibl: Puppi, L. in Interpretazioni veneziane (1984), pp. 389-391

Gas, Estelle Musson de (American, 1843-1909)   **BA**
Bibl: ▶Dict. biog. fran.; New Orleans Museum of Art, HANDBOOK OF THE COLLECTION; Rewald, DEGAS AND HIS FAMILY IN NEW ORLEANS

De Gas, Estelle   BA
Degas, Estelle   BA
Musson, Estelle   BA

Gas. Poussin → see Dughet, Gaspard (Gaspard Poussin)

Gasc, Anna Rosina de → see Lisiewska, Anna Rosina

Gâscă, Eugen (Romanian painter, b.1908)   **BA**
Bibl: ARTA XXVIII/4-5 (Apr-May 1980) 15-17; ARTA, XXXVI/7 (1989), 26

Gascar → see Gascard, Henri
Gascar, Henri → see Gascard, Henri
Gascard → see Gascard, Henri

Gascard, Henri   **BA PR**
(French artist, 1634/5-1701)   WC
(French painter, 1634/5-1701)   PR
(French painter, 1635-1701)   BA
(French, 1634/35-1701)   GC
Bibl: ▶Bénézit; ▶Larousse grande encyc.; ▶RILA/BHA; ▶Thieme-Becker; ▶Witt checklist

Gascar   PR

Gascar, Henri   **BA GC WC**
Gascard   PR
Henri Gascard   PR

Gasco, Joan (Spanish artist, op. 1502-1529)   **WC**

Gasco, Pere or Pedro (Spanish artist, op.1522-1546)   **WC**

Gascoigne, Beatrix (English, act. 1403)   **BA**
Bibl: ▶Dict. natl. biog.

Gascoyne, George (British artist, 1862-1933)   **WI**

Gascoyne, George, Mrs., (Ethel Slade) → see King, Ethel Slade

Gash, Walter Bonner (British artist, 1869-1928)   **WI**

Gasilewskij, Nikolay, I (Russian artist, 20th cent.)   **WC**

Gasiorowski, Gérard (French painter, b.1930)   **BA**
Bibl: ▶Intl. dir. exh. artists, 1983

Gaskell, George Arthur (British artist, op.1871-1900)   **WI**

Gaskell, George Percival → see Gaskell, Percival

Gaskell, Percival (British artist, 1868-1934)   **WC WI**
Bibl: ▶Waters, Brit. artists

Gaskell, George Percival   WI

Gaskin, Arthur Joseph   **BA WC WI**
  (British artist, 1862-1928)   WC WI
  (British painter, illustrator,
    craftsman, 1862-1928)   BA
    Bibl: Gere, Jewellery; ▶Houfe, Brit.
    book illus.; ▶Waters, Brit. artists;
    ▶WW Art, 1929
Gaskin, Georgina Evelyn *(British*
  illustrator, craftsman, 1866-1934)   **BA**
    Bibl: Gere, Jewellery; ▶Houfe, Brit.
    book illus.; ▶WW Art, 1929
  Cave France, Georgina Evelyn   BA
Gasner, Johann Nikolaus   **GC WC**
  (German artist, 18th cent.)   WC
  (German painter, 18th century)   GC
    Bibl: Sotheby's; ▶Witt checklist
  Gasper, Johann Nikolaus   GC
Gasnier [Unidentified] *(Unknown*
  painter)   **PR**
    Bibl: (June 24, 1815, lot 72,
    Robins)
Gasolphi→*see* Ghisolfi, Giovanni
Gasp. Netscher→*see* Netscher,
  Caspar
Gasp. Poussin→*see* Dughet, Gaspard
  (Gaspard Poussin)
Gaspar→*see* Dughet, Gaspard
  (Gaspard Poussin)
Gaspar Dagli Occhiali→*see* Wittel,
  Gaspar van
Gaspar de Crayer→*see* Crayer,
  Gaspar de
Gaspar de Witte→*see* Witte, Gaspar
  de
Gaspar Jacob van Opstal (II)→*see*
  Opstal, Gaspar Jacob II van
Gaspar Lopez→*see* Lopez, Gasparo
Gaspar Nescher→*see* Netscher,
  Caspar
Gaspar Peeter de Verbruggen→*see*
  Verbruggen, Gaspar Peeter II de
Gaspar Pousin→*see* Dughet, Gaspard
  (Gaspard Poussin)
Gaspar Poussijn→*see* Dughet,
  Gaspard (Gaspard Poussin)
Gaspar Poussin→*see* Dughet,
  Gaspard (Gaspard Poussin)
Gaspar Poussin, or Dughet→*see*
  Dughet, Gaspard (Gaspard Poussin)
Gaspar Pousssin→*see* Dughet,
  Gaspard (Gaspard Poussin)
Gaspar Pusin→*see* Dughet, Gaspard
  (Gaspard Poussin)
Gaspar Schmidtz→*see* Smits,
  Casparus
Gaspar Smitz→*see* Smits, Casparus
Gaspar Van Eyck→*see* Eyck, Kasper
  van
Gaspar van Wittel→*see* Wittel,
  Gaspar van
Gaspard Dughet→*see* Dughet,
  Gaspard (Gaspard Poussin)
Gaspard Netscher→*see* Netscher,
  Caspar

Gaspard Poussin→*see* Dughet,
  Gaspard (Gaspard Poussin)
Gaspard, Leon   **BA PR WC**
  (American artist, 1882-1964)   WI
  (American painter, 1882-1964)   BA
  (Russian artist, 1882-)   WC
  (Russian painter, 1882-1964)   PR
    Bibl: ART NEWS (Feb 1968) 12;
    ▶RILA/BHA; ▶WW Amer. Art,
    1940-1941; ▶Young, Amer. artists
Gaspard, Leon Schulman   **WI**
  Leon Gaspard   PR
Gaspard, Leon Schulman→*see*
  Gaspard, Leon
[Gaspare]→*see* Wittel, Gaspar van
Gaspare Cusino→*see* Dughet,
  Gaspard (Gaspard Poussin)
Gaspare da Como *(Italian sculptor,*
  16th century)   **GC**
    Bibl: TCI Umbria
Gaspare da Corte→*see* Ruina,
  Gaspare
Gaspare da Imola→*see* Sacchi,
  Gaspare (Gaspare da Imola)
Gaspare da Pesaro *(Italian artist,*
  op.1421-m.a.1462)   **WC**
Gaspare degl'Occhiali→*see* Wittel,
  Gaspar van
Gaspare degli Occhiali→*see* Wittel,
  Gaspar van
Gaspare dei Fiori→*see* Lopez,
  Gasparo
Gaspare dell'Occhiali→*see* Wittel,
  Gaspar van
Gaspare dell'Ochiali→*see* Wittel,
  Gaspar van
Gaspare delle Battaglie→*see* Eyck,
  Kasper van
Gaspare di Jacopo da Foligno
  (Italian sculptor, 1st half 15th
  century)   **GC**
    Bibl: TCI Umbria
Gaspare Diziani→*see* Diziani,
  Gaspare
Gaspare ferrarese→*see* Venturini,
  Gaspare
Gaspare Gabrielli→*see* Gabrielli,
  Gaspare
Gaspare Giovanni Traversi→*see*
  Traversi, Gaspare Giovanni
Gaspare Negro→*see* Negro, Gaspare
Gaspare or Guaspare d'Agostino
  (Italian artist, op.1451-1455)   **WC**
Gaspare Posini→*see* Dughet, Gaspard
  (Gaspard Poussin)
Gaspare Posino→*see* Dughet,
  Gaspard (Gaspard Poussin)
Gaspare Pusini→*see* Dughet, Gaspard
  (Gaspard Poussin)
Gaspare Pusino→*see* Dughet,
  Gaspard (Gaspard Poussin)
Gaspare Pussino→*see* Dughet,
  Gaspard (Gaspard Poussin)
Gaspare Serenari→*see* Serenario,
  Gaspare

Gaspare Traversi→*see* Traversi,
  Gaspare Giovanni
Gaspare Vannutelli→*see* Wittel,
  Gaspar van
Gaspare Vannutelli detto
  degl'Occhiali→*see* Wittel, Gaspar
  van
Gaspare Vannutelli detto
  dell'Occhiali→*see* Wittel, Gaspar
  van
Gaspare Vanvitelli→*see* Wittel,
  Gaspar van
Gaspare Vanvitelli detto
  degl'Occhiali→*see* Wittel, Gaspar
  van
Gaspare Venturini→*see* Venturini,
  Gaspare
Gaspari or Caspari, Giovanni
  Paolo→*see* Gaspari, Giovanni
  Paolo
Gaspari or Caspari, Pietro→*see*
  Gaspari, Pietro
Gaspari, Antonio   **AV BA**
  (ca.1670-ca.1730)   AV
  (Italian architect, painter, ca.
    1660-after 1738)   BA
    Bibl: Bassi, SAGGI E MEMORIE III
    (1963) 99-103; ▶Macmillan encyc.
    archts.; ▶Portoghesi, Diz. arch. e
    urbanistica; ▶Thieme-Becker
  Caspari, Antonio   BA
Gaspari, Antonio *(Italian artist,*
  1793-p.1823)   **WC**
Gaspari, Carlo *(Italian painter, d.ca.*
  1800)   **BA**
    Bibl: ▶Bolaffi; ▶Thieme-Becker
Gaspari, Giovanni Paolo   **GC**
  (Italian artist, 1714-1775)   WC
  (Italian, 1714-1775)   GC
    Bibl: Getty Photo Study Coll.
    (Ptgs.); ▶Thieme-Becker; ▶Witt
    checklist
  Caspari, Giovanni Paolo   GC
Gaspari or Caspari, Giovanni
  Paolo   **WC**
Gaspari, Pietro   **GC**
  (Italian artist, c.1720-c.1785)   WC
  (Italian, ca.1720-ca.1785)   GC
    Bibl: Getty Photo Study Coll.
    (Ptgs.); ▶Witt checklist
  Caspari, Pietro   GC
Gaspari or Caspari, Pietro   **WC**
Gasparini, Antonio *(Italian*   **BA**
  embroiderer in ESP, act.1775-1803)
    Bibl: Arch. esp. de arte,
    XLVII/185 (Jan-Mar 1974) 81-82;
    Gudiol, Goya
Gasparini, Ercole *(1771-1829)*   **AV**
Gasparini, Gasparo *(Italian artist,*
  op.1570)   **WC**
Gasparini, Graziano *(Venezuelan*
  architect)   **AV**
    Bibl: Armitano arte, 1983 Apr.,
    no.3, p.97

Gasparini, Luigi *(Italian painter, b.1779)* **GC**
  Bibl: ▶Thieme-Becker

Gasparini, Matías *(Italian embroiderer in ESP, 18th c.)* **BA**
  Bibl: Arch. esp. de arte, XLVII/187 (Jul-Sep 1974) 281-282

Gasparini, Matteo *(Italian ceramist, cabinetmaker, decorator, act.1760-1774)* **BA**
  Bibl: Antologia di B-A II/5 (Mar 1978) 73; ▶Diz. artisti ital. in Spagna; ▶Thieme-Becker

Gasperini, Matteo **BA**

Gasparino Lopes→see Lopez, Gasparo

Gasparino Lopez→see Lopez, Gasparo

Gasparino [Unidentified] *(Unknown painter)* **PR**
  Bibl: Della Quadra inventory, Naples, 18th c.

Gasparo dagli Occhiali→see Wittel, Gaspar van

Gasparo degl'Occhiali→see Wittel, Gaspar van

Gasparo degli Occhiali→see Wittel, Gaspar van

Gasparo dell'Occhiali→see Wittel, Gaspar van

Gasparo delle Battaglie→see Eyck, Kasper van

Gasparo Diziani→see Diziani, Gaspare

Gasparo Duchet detto Pussino→see Dughet, Gaspard (Gaspard Poussin)

Gasparo Ferrarese→see Venturini, Gaspare

Gasparo Lopes→see Lopez, Gasparo

Gasparo Lopez→see Lopez, Gasparo

[Gasparo] Loppes→see Lopez, Gasparo

Gasparo Posino→see Dughet, Gaspard (Gaspard Poussin)

Gasparo Possini→see Dughet, Gaspard (Gaspard Poussin)

Gasparo Poussin→see Dughet, Gaspard (Gaspard Poussin)

Gasparo Pusino→see Dughet, Gaspard (Gaspard Poussin)

Gasparo Pussini→see Dughet, Gaspard (Gaspard Poussin)

Gasparo Pussino→see Dughet, Gaspard (Gaspard Poussin)

Gasparo Romano da Padova *(Italian illuminator, act.1477)* **GC**
  Bibl: Getty Photo Study Coll. (Medieval); Salmi, Pitt. a Ferrara, p.49

Romano da Padova, Gasparo **GC**

Gasparo Soversi→see Traversi, Gaspare Giovanni

Gasparo Veronensis *(Italian artist, op.1550)* **WC**

Gasparoli *(Italian artist, op.c.1830)* **WC**

Gasparrino Lopes→see Lopez, Gasparo

Gasparro Lopes→see Lopez, Gasparo

Gasparro Lopez→see Lopez, Gasparo

Gaspearo Pussino→see Dughet, Gaspard (Gaspard Poussin)

Gasper Boteler→see Boteler, Gasper [Unidentified]

Gasper Pousin→see Dughet, Gaspard (Gaspard Poussin)

Gasper Poussin→see Dughet, Gaspard (Gaspard Poussin)

Gasper Smitzs→see Smits, Casparus

Gasper Van Eyck→see Eyck, Kasper van

Gasper Van Lanan→see Lanen, Jasper van [Unidentified]

Gasper, Johann Nikolaus→see Gasner, Johann Nikolaus

Gasperini, Gian Carlo *(Brazilian architect, São Paulo, 1926-)* **AV**
  Bibl: Projeto, 1988 May, no.110, p.74

Gasperini, Matteo→see Gasparini, Matteo

Gaspero degl'Occhiali→see Wittel, Gaspar van

Gaspero degli occhiali→see Wittel, Gaspar van

Gaspero Duchet detto Pussino→see Dughet, Gaspard (Gaspard Poussin)

Gaspero Duchet, detto Pussino→see Dughet, Gaspard (Gaspard Poussin)

Gaspero Ducket detto Pussino→see Dughet, Gaspard (Gaspard Poussin)

Gaspero Posini→see Dughet, Gaspard (Gaspard Poussin)

Gaspero Pussini→see Dughet, Gaspard (Gaspard Poussin)

Gaspero Pussino→see Dughet, Gaspard (Gaspard Poussin)

Gaspero Serenari di Palermo→see Serenario, Gaspare

Gaspero Serenari Palermitano→see Serenario, Gaspare

Gaspero Vallitelli→see Wittel, Gaspar van

Gaspero Vamvitelli detto degli Occhiali→see Wittel, Gaspar van

Gaspero Vanvitelli detto degli Occhiali→see Wittel, Gaspar van

Gaspero Vanvitelli, detto degli Occhiali→see Wittel, Gaspar van

Gaspero Wanvitelli→see Wittel, Gaspar van

Gaspers, Jan Baptist→see Jaspers, Jan Baptist

Gass, Thomas *(Designer, NYC)* **AV**
  Bibl: Interior design, LV/9 (Sep. 1984) p.224

Gasse, Stefano *(Italian architect, 1778-1840)* **BA**
  Bibl: ▶Portoghesi, Diz. arch. e urbanistica; TCI Napoli e dintorni; ▶Thieme-Becker

Gassebner, Hans *(German artist, 1902-1966)* **WC**

Gassel→see Gassel, Lucas

Gassel, Lucas **GC PR WC**
  (Netherlandish painter, act. 1538-1568) **GC**
  (Netherlandish painter, ca.1500-1570) **PR**
  (Netherlands artist, op.1538-1568) **WC**
  Bibl: Getty Photo Study Coll. (Duits coll.); ▶Thieme-Becker; ▶Witt checklist

Gassel **PR**
Helmond, Lucas van **GC**
Lucas Gassel **PR**

Gasselin, Francois *(French artist, c.1683-1703)* **WC**

Gasselin, Noel (?) *(French artist, op. 1703)* **WC**

Gasser, Anton **GC WC**
  (German artist, op.1610-1615) **WC**
  (German draughtsman, act. 1610-1615) **GC**
  Bibl: ▶Thieme-Becker

Gasser, Bruno *(Swiss painter, b.1947)* **BA**
  Bibl: Gasser, MEI-MAI (1982); ▶Lex. zeitgen. Schweiz. Künstler

Gasser, Hans **BA GC WC**
  (Austrian painter, sculptor, 1817-1868) **BA**
  (Austrian sculptor and painter, 1817-1868) **GC**
  (German artist, 1817-1868) **WC**
  Bibl: ▶Bénézit; ▶Fuchs, Öst. Maler 19. Jahrh.; ▶RILA/BHA; ▶Thieme-Becker

Gasser, Leonardo *(Italian artist, 1831-)* **WC**

Gasser, Peter *(Swiss photographer, b.1947)* **BA**
  Bibl: IMAGES: THE PHOTOGRAPHS OF PETER GASSER, 1984 (RILA, CHE)

Gassies→see Gassies, Arnaldo

Gassies, Arnaldo **PR**
  (Spanish artist, op.1434-m.c. 1456) **WC**
  (Spanish painter, act. 1434-1456, d. 1456) **PR**
  Bibl: ▶Witt checklist

Arnaldo Gassies **PR**
Gassies **PR**

Gassies, Arnaldo (Master of Elne) **WC**

Gassies, Arnaldo (Master of Elne)→see Gassies, Arnaldo

Gassies, Jean Bruno **GC WC**
  (French artist, 1786-1832) **WC**
  (French painter, 1786-1823) **GC**
  Bibl: ▶Bénézit

Gassisi, Joan *(American painter, 20th c.)* **BA**
  Bibl: ARTS MAG LVI/10 (June 1982) 16

Gässler, Fridolin (W. German
architect, Sigmaringen) **AV**
Bibl: Architektur + Wettbewerbe,
1986 Dec., no.128, p.44

Gassmann, Gerd (West German
architect, Karlsruhe) **AV**
Bibl: ▶Bund Deut. Arch. Hdbch.,
1987

Gassner, Beat (Swiss architect,
Thun) **AV**
Bibl: ▶Schweiz. Ingen. u. Archit.,
1988-1989

Gassó, José María (Argentine
architect) **AV**
Bibl: Summa, 1985 Oct., no.218,
p.63

Gasson, Barry → see Gasson, Gorgon
Barry

Gasson, Gorgon Barry **BA**
(British architect) **AV**
(British architect, b.ca.1942) **BA**
Bibl: ▶Art Index, v.23; ▶Avery
period. idx., 2nd suppl.;
Connaissance des arts, 1984
Sept., no.391, p.76; McEwen, J.,
Art in AMerica, LXXII/2 (Feb.
1984) 30

Gasson, Barry **AV BA**

Gastaidi, Andrea → see Gastaldi,
Andrea

Gastaldi, Andrea **GC**
(Italian artist, 1826-1889) **WC**
(Italian painter, 1826-1889) **GC**
Bibl: ▶Thieme-Becker

Gastaidi, Andrea **WC**

Gastaud, Pierre (French artist, 20th
cent.) **WC**

Gaste, Georges Constant (French
artist, 1869-1910) **WC**

Gaste, Pierre (French artist, b.1938) **BA**
Bibl: ▶Bénézit; Tanlay (FRA),
Château de Tanlay, Matisse:
dessins (1985)

Gasteiger, Anna Sophie (German
painter, 1877-1954) **BA**
Bibl: Munich (DEU), Verwaltung
Staatl. Schlösser, Mathias u. Anna
Gasteiger (1985); ▶Thieme-Becker;
▶Vollmer, Künst.-Lex. 20. Jhr.

Gasteiger, Mathias (German
sculptor, 1871-1934) **BA**
Bibl: Munich (DEU), Verwaltung
Staatl. Schlösser, Mathias u. Anna
Gasteiger (1985); ▶Thieme-Becker;
▶Vollmer, Künst.-Lex. 20. Jhr.

Gasti, (?) (Italian(?) artist, op.1861) **WC**

Gastineau, Henry **BA WC**
(British artist, 1791-1876) **WC WI**
(British painter, ca.1791-1876) **BA**
Bibl: Country Life CLX (14 Oct
1976) 1044; ▶Dict. natl. biog.;
▶Fisher, Watercolour ptrs.;
▶Thieme-Becker; ▶Wood,
Victorian ptrs.; ▶Yale Brit. artists
list

Gastineau, Henry G. **WI**

Gastineau, Henry G. → see Gastineau,
Henry

Gastineau, Maria G. (British artist,
op.1855-, d.1890) **WI**

Gastini, Marco (Italian painter,
b.1938) **BA**
Bibl: ▶Bénézit; ▶Contemp. artists;
▶MoMA libr. cat.

Gaston (French, 1331-1391) **JG**

Gaston (French, active 1870s (also
Gaston et Mathieu)) **JG**

Gaston de Latouche → see Latouche,
Gaston de

Gaston Duchamp → see Villon,
Jacques (Gaston Duchamp)

Gat, Eliahu (Israeli painter, b.1919) **BA**
Bibl: Haifa (ISR), Mus. of Mod.
Art, ELIAHU GAT (1979)

Gata, Gabor (Hungarian medalist,
20th c.) **BA**
Bibl: Pushkin

Gatch, Lee **BA GC WC WI**
(American artist, 1902-) **WC**
(American artist, 1902-1968) **WI**
(American painter, 1902-1968) **BA GC**
Bibl: ▶Cummings, Contemp.
Amer. artists; ▶Havlice, Idx. art.
bio.; NY Times obit.; ▶RILA/BHA;
Saint Louis Art Museum Bull. XI/4
(July-Aug 1975) 67-69

Gate, Carl Oskar Simon (Swedish
glass designer, painter, sculptor,
1883-1945) **BA**
Bibl: ▶Arwas, Glass, p.171;
▶Penguin dec. arts; ▶Svenskt
konst.-lex.

Gate, Simon **BA**

Gate, Simon → see Gate, Carl Oskar
Simon

Gatellier, Boulard de (French, 18th
c.) **BA**
Bibl: METROPOLITAN MUSEUM
JOURNAL XII (1977) 107-130

Gately, David K. (American
architect, Tiburon, Calif) **AV**
Bibl: ▶AIA Pro File, 1987-88

Gates, Henry L. **WC WI**
(British artist, 20th cent.) **WC**
(British artist, op.1943-) **WI**

Gates, Jeff (American, 1949 -) **JG**

Gatewood, Charles (American
photographer, b.1942) **BA**
Bibl: ▶Contemp. photogs.; ▶Parry,
Photo idx.

Gatewood, Maud → see Gatewood,
Maud Florance

Gatewood, Maud Florance **WI**
(American artist, 20th cent.) **WC**
(American artist, b.1934) **WI**

Gatewood, Maud **WC**

Gathe, Asbjorn (Architect) **AV**
Bibl: Canadian architect, 1985
June, v.30, no.6, p.20

Gatier, Pierre Louis **BA**
(French artist, 1878-) **WC**
(French painter, printmaker,
1878-1944) **BA**
Bibl: ▶Bénézit; ▶Vollmer,
Künst.-Lex. 20. Jhr.

Gatier, Pierre-Louis **WC**

Gatier, Pierre-Louis → see Gatier,
Pierre Louis

Gatine, Georges Jacques (French
artist, 1773-1831) **WC**

Gatje, Robert F. (American
architect) **AV**

Gätke, Heinrich (German painter,
1814-1897) **BA**
Bibl: ▶Neue deutsche Biog.

Gatley, E.A., Miss (British artist, op.
20th c.) **WI**

Gatlin, Saara → see Gallin, Saara

Gaton, Juan (Spanish artist, op.
1518) **WC**

Gatschet or Gachet, Niklaus (Swiss
artist, 1736-1817) **WC**

Gatta, Bartolomeo della → see Della
Gatta, Bartolomeo (Pier d'Antonio
Dei)

Gatta, Domenico [Unidentified]
(Italian painter) **PR**
Bibl: Montecorvino inventory,
Naples, 1698; Diaz Pimienta
inventory, Naples, 1684;
Dom:co Gatta **PR**
Domenico Gatta **PR**
Domenico Gatto **PR**

Gatta, Saverio or Xavier della → see
Gatta, Saviero della

Gatta, Saviero della **GC**
(Italian artist, op.1777-1811) **WC**
(Italian, act.1777-1811) **GC**
Bibl: ▶Witt checklist

Gatta, Saverio or Xavier della **WC**

Gattapone (Italian architect, act.
1345-1374) **GC**
Bibl: Bigotti, Narni, 43, p.362; TCI
Umbria; ▶Thieme-Becker
Gattaponi **GC**
Matteo di Giovanello **GC**
Matteo di Giovanello di Maffeo **GC**
Matteo Gattapone **GC**

Gattaponi → see Gattapone

Gatteaux, Edouard → see Gatteaux,
Jacques-Edouard

Gatteaux, Jacques Edouard → see
Gatteaux, Jacques-Edouard

Gatteaux, Jacques-Edouard **BA**
(French sculptor and medalist,
1788-1881) **GC**
(French sculptor, medalist,
1788-1881) **BA**
Bibl: ▶Bénézit; ▶Dict. biog. fran.;
▶Forrer, Medallists; ▶RILA/BHA;
▶Thieme-Becker
Gatteaux, Edouard **GC**

Gatteaux, Jacques Edouard **GC**

Gatteri, Giuseppe Lorenzo (Italian
artist, 1829-1884) **WC**

Gatti→see Gatti, Bernardino (il
   Sojaro)

Gatti de Sanctis, Diambra *(Italian*
   architect, Naples(?))   **AV**
    Bibl: Architectural review, 1988
     Nov., v.184, no.1101, p.68

Gatti, Alberto *(Italian architect,*
   Naples(?))   **AV**
    Bibl: Architectural review, 1988
     Nov., v.184, no.1101, p.68

Gatti, Annibale   **BA GC WC**
   (Italian artist, 1828-1909)   WC
   (Italian painter, 1827-1909)   BA
   (Italian painter, 1828-1909)   GC
    Bibl: ▶Bolaffi; ▶Thieme-Becker;
     ▶Witt checklist; Zappie,
     LABYRINTHOS II/3-4 (1983) 70-90

Gatti, Bernardino→see Gatti,
   Bernardino (il Sojaro)

Gatti, Bernardino (il Sojaro)   **BA GC PR**
   (Italian artist, c.1495-1575)   WC
   (Italian painter, ca.1495-1575)   BA PR
   (Italian, ca. 1495-1575)   JG
   (Italian, ca.1495-1575)   GC
    Bibl: ▶Bénézit; ▶Bolaffi;
     ▶RILA/BHA, 1986;
     ▶Thieme-Becker
   Bernardino Gatti   PR
   Gatti   PR
   Gatti, Bernardino   **GC JG** PR
   Gatti, Bernardino or Bernardo
    (Il Sojaro)   **WC**
   Il Sojaro   GC PR
   Sojaro (Bernardino Gatti)   BA
Gatti, Bernardino or Bernardo (Il
   Sojaro)→see Gatti, Bernardino (il
   Sojaro)

Gatti, Camillo *(Italian ceramist,*
   d.1567)   **BA**
    Bibl: ▶Honey, Euro. ceramic;
     ▶Thieme-Becker

Gatti, Gervasio (il Sojaro)   **BA WC**
   (Italian artist, 1549-1631)   WC
   (Italian painter, 1549-1631)   BA
    Bibl: ▶Bolaffi; ▶Thieme-Becker
   Sojaro (Gervasio Gatti)   BA

Gatti, Girolamo *(Italian artist, 1662-*
   1726)   **WC**

Gatti, Ilaria *(Italian architect)*   **AV**
    Bibl: Controspazio, 1985 Jan.-
     June, v.16, no.1-2, p.77

Gatti, L. *(Italian artist, 19th cent.)*   **WC**

Gatti, Oliviero   **BA GC**
   (Italian painter, printmaker,
    b.1579, act.1626)   BA
   (Italian, act.1626)   GC
    Bibl: ▶Bolaffi; ▶Thieme-Becker

Gatti, Saturnino   **BA**
   (Italian artist, 1463-c.1521)   WC
   (Italian painter, 1463-1521)   PR
   (Italian painter, sculptor, 1463-
    1521)   BA
   (Italian sculptor and painter,
    1463-1521)   GC
    Bibl: ▶Bénézit; ▶Bolaffi;
     ▶Fredericksen & Zeri, Census;
     ▶Thieme-Becker

Gatti, Saturnino de   **GC**
Gatti, Saturnino de'   **PR WC**
   Saturnino de' Gatti   PR
   Saturnino de'Gatti   PR
Gatti, Saturnino de→see Gatti,
   Saturnino
Gatti, Saturnino de'→see Gatti,
   Saturnino

Gattiker, Herman *(Swiss artist,*
   1865-1951)   **WC**
Gatton, William of→see Flynte,
   William

Gau, François Chrétien   **BA**
   (French architect, 1790-1853)   BA
   (German artist, 1790-1853)   WC
    Bibl: ▶Portoghesi, Diz. arch. e
     urbanistica; Rassart-Debergh,
     Ann. de l'inst. de Philologie et
     d'hist. orientales, 25 (1981) 79-
     113

Gau, Franz Christian   BA **WC**
Gau, Franz Christian→see Gau,
   François Chrétien

Gaubert, Pierre   **BA**
   (French artist, 1662-1744)   WC
   (French painter, 1662-1744)   PR
   (French painter, ca.1659-ca.
    1744)   BA
   (French, 1662-1744)   GC
    Bibl: ▶Bellier, Artistes fran.;
     ▶Bénézit; ▶Thieme-Becker; ▶Witt
     checklist
   Gobert   PR
   Gobert, Pierre   **BA GC PR WC**
   Pierre Gobert   PR

Gaucher de Reims *(French master*
   builder, act.1252-1258)   **BA**
    Bibl: Bull. Monumental,
     CXXXVII/1 (1979) p.7; ▶Encyc.
     world art; ▶Thieme-Becker

Gaucher, Alain *(French architect,*
   Paris)   **AV**
    Bibl: ▶Annuaire archts. fran.,
     1978

Gaucher, Charles Etienne or
   Stephan *(French artist, 1741-*
   1802)   **WC**

Gaucher, Yves   **BA WC**
   (Canadian artist, 1934-)   WC
   (Canadian printmaker, painter,
    b.1934)   BA
    Bibl: ▶Artists Canada; ▶Bénézit;
     ▶MacDonald, Can. artists;
     ▶MoMA libr. cat.; Toronto (Ont,
     CAN), Art Gallery of Ont, YVES
     GAUCHER... 91979)

Gaucherel, Lion *(French artist, 1816-*
   1886)   **WC**

Gauci, A.M. *(British artist, op.1848-*
   1868)   **WI**

Gauci, M.   **WC WI**
   (British artist, op.1810-1846)   WI
   (British artist, op.c.1810-1846)   WC

Gauci, Paul *(British artist, op.1834-*
   1866)   **WC WI**

Gauci, William   **WC WI**
   (British artist, op.1825-1840)   WC
   (British artist, op.1825-1854)   WI

Gaud, Lion *(Swiss artist, 1844-1908)*   **WC**
Gauda→see Guardi, Francesco

Gaudar De La Verdine, Auguste
   Alphonse *(French painter, 1780-*
   1804)   **GC**
    Bibl: ▶Thieme-Becker

Gaudens, Augustus Saint-→see Saint-
   Gaudens, Augustus

Gaudenzi, Marco *(Italian architect)*   **AV**
    Bibl: L'Arca, 1989 July-Aug.,
     no.29, p.83

Gaudenzio da Vincio→see Ferrari,
   Gaudenzio

Gaudenzio Ferrari→see Ferrari,
   Gaudenzio

Gaudernack, Gustav *(Norwegian*
   artist, 1865-1914)   **BA**
    Bibl: Oslo (NOR),
     Kunstindustrimuseet, GUSTAV
     GAUDERNACK (1979)

Gaudez, Adrien Etienne *(French*
   sculptor, 1845-1902)   **GC**
    Bibl: ▶Thieme-Becker

Gaudí i Cornet, Antoni→see Gaudí y
   Cornet, Antonio

Gaudí y Cornet, Antonio *(Spanish*
   architect, 1852-1926)   **AV BA**
    Bibl: ▶Contemp. archts.; ▶Encic.
     univ. ilus.; ▶Encyc. world art;
     ▶Libr. of Congr. Name Auth. File;
     ▶Natl. union cat.; ▶Thieme-Becker
   Cornet, Antonio Gaudí y   AV
   Gaudí i Cornet, Antoni   AV
   Gaudí, Antoni   **AV**
   Gaudí, Antonio   AV
Gaudí, Antoni→see Gaudí y Cornet,
   Antonio
Gaudí, Antonio→see Gaudí y Cornet,
   Antonio

Gaudier-Brzeska→see Gaudier-
   Brzeska, Henri

Gaudier-Brzeska, Henri   **BA PR**
   (British artist, 1891-1915)   WC WI
   (British, 1891-1915)   GC
   (French painter, 1891-1915)   PR
   (French sculptor, 1891-1915)   BA
    Bibl: ▶Mackay, Western sculp.
     bronze; ▶Maillard, Sculpt. mod.;
     ▶RILA/BHA; ▶Witt checklist
   Gaudier-Brzeska   PR
   Gaudier-Brzeska, Henry   **GC WC WI**
   Henri Gaudier-Brzeska   PR
Gaudier-Brzeska, Henry→see Gaudier-
   Brzeska, Henri

Gaudin, Henri   **AV BA**
  (French architect, 1933-)   AV
  (French architect, b.1933)   BA
    Bibl: ▶Avery period. idx., 1988
    suppl.; International architect,
    issue 1, 1983, p.[1]; Loyer, Mons.
    Hist. Fran., CLX (1988-89) pp.
    73-80
Gaudin, Jean Daniel (Swiss, 1780-
  1856)   **BA**
    Bibl: REVUE HISTORIQUE
    VANDOISE, XCI (1983) 93-118
Gaudio, Cavalier del [Unidentified]
  (Unknown painter)   **PR**
    Bibl: Coppola inventory, Naples,
    1724
  Cavalier del Gaudio   PR
Gaudion, Andre (French artist, op.
  1612-1634)   **WC**
Gaudioso, Pietro (Italian artist, op.
  1674-1682)   **WC**
Gaudnek, Walter (American painter,
  sculptor, b.1931)   **BA**
    Bibl: Montgomery (AL, USA),
    Museum of Fine Arts, WALTER
    GAUDNEK RETROSPECTIVE
Gaudreau, Antoine-Robert→see
  Gaudreaus, Antoine-Robert
Gaudreaus family (French
  cabinetmakers, 18th c.)   **BA**
    Bibl: Antologia di B-A 27-28
    (1985) 73-97; ▶Dict. biog. fran.;
    ▶Salverte, Ébénistes 18e s.
Gaudreaus, Antoine-Robert   **BA**
  (French cabinetmaker, ca.1682-
  1746)   BA
  (French ébéniste, ca.1680-1751)   GC
    Bibl: Antologia di B-A 27-28
    (1985) 73-97; ▶Dict. biog. fran.;
    ▶Penguin dec. arts; ▶Salverte,
    Ébénistes 18e s.; ▶Thieme-Becker;
    Watson, Wallace Coll.
Gaudreau, Antoine-Robert   **GC**
  Gaudreaux, Antoine-Robert   GC
Gaudreaus, François-Antoine
  (French cabinetmaker, act.1739,
  d.1753)   BA
    Bibl: Antologia di B-A 27-28
    (1985) 75, 81; ▶Dict. biog. fran.;
    ▶Salverte, Ébénistes 18e s.;
    ▶Thieme-Becker
Gaudreaux, Antoine-Robert→see
  Gaudreaus, Antoine-Robert
Gaudron, Antoine (Master 1675,
  jure 1699, died ca. 1707)   **JG**
Gaudron, Auburtin (French
  ébéniste, act. ca.1670-ca.1713)   **GC**
    Bibl: ▶Salverte, Ébénistes 18e s.
Gaudy, Thomas   **WC WI**
  (British artist, op.1849)   WC
  (British artist, op.1849-)   WI

Gauermann, Friedrich   **BA GC WC**
  (Austrian draughtsman, 1807-
  1862)   GC
  (Austrian painter, 1807-1862)   BA
  (German artist, 1807-1862)   WC
    Bibl: ▶Bénézit; ▶Bryan, Ptrs. &
    engravers; ▶Fuchs, Öst. Maler 19.
    Jahrh.; ▶RILA/BHA;
    ▶Thieme-Becker
Gauermann, Jacob→see Gauermann,
  Jakob
Gauermann, Jakob   **BA**
  (Austrian painter, printmaker,
  1773-1843)   BA
  (German artist, 1773-1843)   WC
    Bibl: ▶Fuchs, Öst. Maler 19.
    Jahrh.; Nagel, Schwabische Maler;
    ▶Österr. biog. Lex. 1815-1950;
    ▶Thieme-Becker; ▶Witt checklist
Gauermann, Jacob   **WC**
Gauffier→see Gauffier, Louis
Gauffier, Cath. (French artist, 19th
  cent.)   **WC**
Gauffier, Louis   **BA GC PR WC**
  (French artist, 1761-1801)   WC
  (French painter, 1761-1801)   BA PR
  (French, 1761-1801)   GC
    Bibl: ▶Bellier, Artistes fran.;
    ▶Bénézit; ▶Dict. biog. fran.;
    ▶RILA/BHA; ▶Thieme-Becker;
    ▶Witt checklist
  Gauffier   PR
  Louis Gauffier   PR
Gauffier, MMe Pauline   **GC**
  (French artist, -1801)   WC
  (French painter, d.1801)   GC
    Bibl: ▶Thieme-Becker
Gauffier, Pauline   **WC**
Gauffier, Pauline→see Gauffier, MMe
  Pauline
Gaugain, Philip A.   **WC WI**
  (British artist, op.1783-1847)   WI
  (British artist, op.1808-1842)   WC
Gaugain, Thomas (French artist,
  1748-1812)   **WC**
Gaugengigl→see Gaugengigl, Ignaz
  Marcel
Gaugengigl, Ignaz Marcel   **PR WC**
  (German artist, 1855-1932)   WC
  (German painter, 1855-1932)   PR
    Bibl: ▶Thieme-Becker
  Gaugengigl   PR
  Ignaz Marcel Gaugengigl   PR
Gaugin, Paul→see Gauguin, Paul
Gauguin→see Gauguin, Paul
Gauguin, (Eugene-Henri) Paul→see
  Gauguin, Paul

Gauguin, Paul   **BA GC JG PR WC WI**
  (French artist, 1848-1903)   WC WI
  (French painter, 1848-1903)   PR
  (French painter, printmaker,
    1848-1903)   BA
  (French painter, printmaker, and
    sculptor, 1848-1903)   GC
  (French, 1848-1903)   JG
    Bibl: ▶Bénézit; ▶RILA/BHA;
    ▶Thieme-Becker
  Gaugin, Paul   PR
  Gauguin   PR
  Gauguin, (Eugene-Henri) Paul   PR
  Paul Gauguin   PR
Gauguin, Paul Rene (Danish artist,
  1911-)   **WC**
Gauguin, Pola (Paul) Rollon (Danish
  artist, 1883-)   **WC**
Gaul (German artist, 20th cent.)   **WC**
Gaul→see Gaul, Gilbert
Gaul [Unidentified] (Unknown
  painter)   **PR**
    Bibl: (September 9, 1801, lot 11b,
    Edwards)
Gaul, August   **BA WC**
  (German artist, 1869-1921)   WC
  (German sculptor, 1869-1921)   BA
Gaul, Franz (German artist, 1837-
  1906)   **WC**
Gaul, Gilbert   **BA PR**
  (American artist, 1855-1919)   WC WI
  (American painter, 1855-1919)   BA PR
    Bibl: ▶Bénézit; ▶Dict. Amer. biog.;
    ▶Fielding's Amer. ptrs.;
    ▶RILA/BHA; Smith;
    ▶Thieme-Becker; ▶Vollmer,
    Künst.-Lex. 20. Jhr.; ▶Who was
    who [GBR]; ▶Young, Amer. artists
  Gaul   PR
Gaul, Gilbert William   **BA WC WI**
  Gaul, William Gilbert   BA
  Gilbert Gaul   PR
Gaul, Gilbert William→see Gaul,
  Gilbert
Gaul, Gustav (German artist, 1836-
  1888)   **WC**
Gaul, Robert (American interior
  designer, New York City)   **AV**
    Bibl: NYC phone bk., 1987
Gaul, William Gilbert→see Gaul,
  Gilbert
Gaul, Winfred   **BA**
  (German artist, 1928-)   WC
  (German painter, b.1928)   BA
    Bibl: ▶Bénézit; ▶WW Arts DEU
Gaul, Winifred   **WC**
Gaul, Winifred→see Gaul, Winfred
Gauld, David   **WC WI**
  (British artist, 1866-)   WC
  (British artist, 1866-1936)   WI
    Bibl: ▶Wood, Victorian ptrs.
Gauld, John Richardson   **WC WI**
  (British artist, op.1913-, d.1962)   WI
  (British artist, op.1913-1960)   WC

Gaulle, Edme (French painter, 1762-
1841) **GC**
  Bibl: ▶Bénézit
Gaulli → see Gaulli, Giovanni Battista
(Baciccio)
Gaulli, Giovanni Battista → see Gaulli,
Giovanni Battista (Baciccio)
**Gaulli, Giovanni Battista
(Baciccio)** **BA** GC **PR**
    (Italian artist, 1639-1709) WC
    (Italian painter, 1639-1709) BA GC PR
    (Italian, Genoese, 1639-1709) JG
    Bibl: ▶Bolaffi; ▶Diz. biog. ital.;
    ▶Encyc. world art; ▶RILA/BHA,
    1986; ▶Thieme-Becker
    Abbaciccio PR
    bacchio PR
    Bacciccia PR
    Bacciccio BA GC
    Baccici PR
    Bacicci PR
    Bacciccia GC PR
  **Baciccia, Giovanni Battista (Il
    Gaulli)** **WC**
    Baciccio BA PR
    Bacici PR
    Bacicio PR
    Baptiste Gauli PR
    Batista Bacici PR
    Gaulli PR
  Gaulli, Giovanni Battista **GC JG** PR
    Gio: Batta Gauli detto il Baciccio PR
    Gio: Battista Gauli detto il Baciccio PR
    Gio: Battista Gauli, detto Baciccio PR
    Giovanni Battista Gaulli PR
*Gault de Saint Germain, Mme. E.
de* → see Rajecka, Anna
Gault de Saint-Germain → see Rajecka,
Anna
**Gault de Saint-Germain, Pierre
  Marie** (French artist, 1754-1842) **WC**
Gaultier, Germain (French architect,
  sculptor, 1571-after 1635) **BA**
    Bibl: ▶Bénézit; ▶Thieme-Becker
    Gautier, Germain BA
Gaultier, Jacques (French (Paris),
  active first half of the 18th c.) **JG**
Gaultier, Léonard **BA GC WC**
    (French artist, 1561-c.1641) WC
    (French painter, 1561-1641) GC
    (French painter, printmaker,
    illustrator, 1561?-1630/41) BA
    Bibl: ▶Bénézit; ▶Fogg Mus. Libr.
    cat.; ▶Havlice, Idx. art. bio.; ▶Natl.
    union cat., pre-1956;
    ▶Thieme-Becker
Gaultier, P. (French artist, 19th
  cent.) **WC**
Gaultier, Pierre Jacques (French
  artist, op.1740) **WC**
Gauneray, J.F. (French artist, 18th
  cent.) **WC**

Gaunt, William **BA WC WI**
    (British artist, 1874-) WC
    (British artist, b.1900) WI
    (British author, painter, b.1900) BA
    Bibl: ▶Who's Who [GBR], 1975
Gaupmann, Rudolf (German artist,
  1815-1877) **WC**
Gaupp, Gustav Adolf (German
  painter, 1844-1918) **BA**
    Bibl: ▶Bénézit; ▶Busse, Maler u.
    Bildhauer 19. Jahr.;
    ▶Thieme-Becker; ▶Vollmer,
    Künst.-Lex. 20. Jhr.
Gaurion (potter, ca. 420-390 BC) **GC**
    Bibl: ▶Beazley, Attic red-fig. vase-
    ptrs.; Richter, Attic red-fig. vases
Gauron, Nicolas François (French
  porcelain modeler, b.ca.1736, act.
  1773) **BA**
    Bibl: Clifford, T., ROCOCO IN
    ENGLAND (1986) p.161-174;
    ▶Danckert, Euro. Porzellans;
    ▶Honey, Euro. ceramic;
    ▶Thieme-Becker
Gause, Wilhelm (German artist,
  1853-1916) **WC**
Gausling, Georg Michael (West
  German glass artist, with studio in
  Pécs, Hungary) **AV**
    Bibl: Művészet, 1987 Aug., v.28,
    no.8, p.44
Gausson, Leo (French artist, 1860-) **WC**
Gaut, Justinien (French painter,
  1817-1880) **BA**
    Bibl: ▶Baille, Petits maîtres;
    ▶Bénézit
Gautherot, Claude (French, 1729-
  1802) **GC**
    Bibl: ▶Thieme-Becker
Gautherot, Pierre (French artist,
  1769-1825) **WC**
Gauthey, Emiland Marie **AV BA**
    (French architect and engineer,
    1732-1806) AV
    (French architect, engineer,
    1732-1806) BA
    Bibl: ▶Avery Libr. cat.; ▶Dict.
    biog. fran.; ▶Thieme-Becker
Gauthier, Camille (French
  cabinetmaker, 1870-1963) **BA**
    Bibl: Munich (DEU), Stadtmus.,
    Nancy 1900 (1980)
Gauthier, Dominique (French
  painter, b.1953) **BA**
    Bibl: Arts Council GBR, French art
    (1979); Bordeaux (FRA), Centre
    d'arts plastiques, DOM. GAUTHIER
    91979); Lausanne (CHE), Musée
    Cantonal B.-A., Rite, rock, rêve
    (1984)
Gauthier, Eric (Canadian architect,
  Montreal) **AV**
    Bibl: ▶Canad. arch. dir., 1987

Gauthier, Léon-Ambroise (French
  painter, 1822-1901) **BA**
    Bibl: ▶Bellier, Artistes fran.;
    ▶Bénézit; ▶Thieme-Becker; Wilson
    Bareau, J., Burlington Mag
    CXXVI/981 (Dec 1984) 756
Gauthier, Martin Pierre **BA GC**
    (French architect and sculptor,
    1790-1855) GC
    (French architect, 1790-1855) BA
    Bibl: ▶Lance, Dict. archts. fran.;
    ▶RILA/BHA; ▶Thieme-Becker
Gauthier, Oscar (French artist,
  1921-) **WC**
Gautié, Arnaud (French silversmith,
  1647-1723, master 1675) **GC**
    Bibl: ▶Mabille, Orfèv. fran.
Gautier D'Agoty, Arnauld Eloi **BA**
    (French artist, 1741-a.1780) WC
    (French printmaker,
    1741-1780/83) BA
    Bibl: ▶Bénézit; ▶Thieme-Becker
    Dagoty, Arnauld Eloi Gautier BA
  **Gautier Dagoty, or D'Agoty,
    Arnaud Eloi** **WC**
Gautier D'Agoty, Edouard **BA**
    (French artist, 1744-1783/4) WC
    (French printmaker, 1744-1784) BA
    (French, 1744-1783/4) GC
    Bibl: ▶Bénézit; ▶Dict. biog. fran.;
    ▶Thieme-Becker; ▶Witt checklist
    D'Agoty, Edouard GC
    Dagoty, Edouard Gautier BA
  **Gautier Dagoty or d'Agoty,
    Edouard** **WC**
  Gautier Dagoty, Edouard **GC**
Gautier D'Agoty, Jacques Fabien **BA**
    (French artist, 1710-1781) WC
    (French painter, printmaker,
    1710-1781) BA
    (French, 1710-1781) GC
    Bibl: ▶Bénézit; ▶Encyc. world art;
    ▶Thieme-Becker
  **Gautier Dagoty or d'Agoty,
    Jacques** **WC**
  Gautier Dagoty, Jacques Fabien **GC**
*Gautier Dagoty or d'Agoty,
  Edouard* → see Gautier D'Agoty,
  Edouard
*Gautier Dagoty or d'Agoty,
  Jacques* → see Gautier D'Agoty,
  Jacques Fabien
**Gautier Dagoty or d'Agoty, Jean
  Baptiste Andre (Gautier Fils)**
    (French artist, 1740-1786) **WC**
Gautier Dagoty, Edouard → see
  Gautier D'Agoty, Edouard
Gautier Dagoty, Jacques Fabien → see
  Gautier D'Agoty, Jacques Fabien
*Gautier Dagoty, or D'Agoty, Arnaud
  Eloi* → see Gautier D'Agoty, Arnauld
  Eloi

Gautier Lebaube atelier *(French illuminator, act. ca.1240)*   **GC**
  Bibl: ▶Branner, Ms. ptg. Paris, p.72; Getty Photo Study Coll. (Medieval)
  Gautier Lebaube shop   GC
  Gautier Lebaube workshop   GC
  Lebaube, Gautier   GC
Gautier Lebaube shop → see Gautier Lebaube atelier
Gautier Lebaube workshop → see Gautier Lebaube atelier
Gautier, Amand Desire → see Gautier, Armand-Désiré
Gautier, Armand-Désiré   **GC**
  (French artist, 1825-1894)   WC
  (French painter, 1825-1894)   GC
  Bibl: ▶Bénézit
Gautier, Amand Desire   **WC**
Gautier, Germain → see Gaultier, Germain
Gautier, J.   **AV**
Gautier, Louis François Léon
  (French painter, sculptor, 1855-1947)   **BA**
  Bibl: ▶Bénézit; ▶Camard, Ptrs. & sculps. provençaux
Gautier, Lucien Marcelin *(French printmaker, 1850-1925)*   **BA**
  Bibl: ▶Baille, Petits maîtres; ▶Bénézit; ▶Busse, Maler u. Bildhauer 19. Jahr.; ▶Camard, Ptrs. & sculps. provençaux; ▶Thieme-Becker
Gautier, Rodolphe (Jean Rodolphe)   **GC WC**
  (Swiss artist, 1764-1820(?))   WC
  (Swiss, 1764-1820?)   GC
  Bibl: ▶Witt checklist
Gautier, Saint-Elme *(French, b.1849)*   **GC**
  Bibl: ▶Thieme-Becker
Gautier, Theophile *(French artist, 1811-1873)*   **WC**
Gautier-Dagoty, Fabien *(French artist, 1747-p.1781)*   **WC**
Gautier-Dagoty, Louis (Honore Louis) *(French artist, 1746-p.1787)*   **WC**
Gautier-Dagoty, Pierre Edouard *(French artist, 1775-1871)*   **WC**
Gautiez, Pierre *(French artist, 20th cent.)*   **WC**
Gauvain, Mansuy *(French sculptor, act.1506/7, d.before 1551)*   **BA**
  Bibl: ▶Bénézit; ▶Thieme-Becker
Gauvin, Alain *(French painter, 20th c.)*   **BA**
  Bibl: Grout, Flash art, 130 (Oct.-Nov. 1986) pp.98-100
Gauvreau, Claude *(Canadian draftsman, 1925-1971)*   **BA**
  Bibl: ▶Artists Canada; Montreal (Que, CAN), Mus. d'art contemp., Dessins & surréalisme (1979)

Gauvreau, Pierre *(Canadian architect, 19th c.)*   **BA**
  Bibl: Jrnl. Canadian art hist., III/1-2 (1976) pp.83-94
Gauvreau, Pierre *(Canadian painter, printmaker, b.1922)*   **BA**
  Bibl: ▶Artists Canada; ▶Bénézit
Gauw, Gerrit Adriaensz. *(Dutch, act.1604-d.1638)*   **GC**
  Bibl: ▶Thieme-Becker
Gavard, C. *(French artist, op.1833/4)*   **WC**
Gavard, Charles *(French engineer, inventor, 1794-1871)*   **BA**
  Bibl: ▶Bénézit; ▶Dict. biog. fran.; ▶Natl. union cat., pre-1956
Gavarni, Chevalier Hippolyte Guillaume Sulpice → see Gavarni, Paul (Hippolyte-Guillaume-Sulpice Chevalier)
Gavarni, Paul → see Gavarni, Paul (Hippolyte-Guillaume-Sulpice Chevalier)
Gavarni, Paul (Hippolyte-Guillaume-Sulpice Chevalier)   **BA**
  (French artist, 1804-1866)   WC
  (French printmaker, illustrator, painter, 1804-1866)   BA
  (French, 1804-1866)   GC
  Bibl: ▶Bénézit; ▶Dict. biog. fran.; ▶Thieme-Becker
Gavarni, Chevalier Hippolyte Guillaume Sulpice   **WC**
Gavarni, Paul   **GC**
Gavarni, Pierre *(French painter, b.1846)*   **GC**
  Bibl: ▶Bénézit
Gavarotti, Giovanni Battista *(Italian painter, act. ca.1663)*   **PR**
  Bibl: Pirovano, Natura morta in Italia, 1989, I, p. 382; Salerno, Natura morta, p.406; ▶Thieme-Becker
  Chiavarotti   PR
  Giovanni Battista Gavarotti   PR
Gavasetti or Gavassette, Camillo → see Gavasetti, Camillo
Gavasetti, Camillo   **BA GC**
  (Italian artist, op.1625-m.1628)   WC
  (Italian painter, act.1624/25, d.ca.1630)   BA
  (Italian painter, d.1628)   GC
  Bibl: ▶Bénézit; ▶Bolaffi; BULLETIN VAN HET RIJKSMUSUEM XXIV/4(1976); ▶Thieme-Becker; ▶Witt checklist
Gavasetti or Gavassette, Camillo   **WC**
  Gavassete, Camillo   GC
  Gavassetti, Camillo   BA
Gavasio or Gavazzi, Giovanni Giacomo → see Gavazzi, Giovanni di Giacomo
Gavassete, Camillo → see Gavasetti, Camillo
Gavassetti, Camillo → see Gavasetti, Camillo

Gavaudan, Francesco *(Italian architect, act.1859)*   **BA**
  Bibl: Dell'Aja,IL PANTHEON DEI BORBONI IN S.CHIARA DI NAPOLI(1987)p.28
Gavazzi → see Gavazzi, Giovanni di Giacomo
Gavazzi, Agostino *(Italian, act. 1527)*   **GC**
  Bibl: ▶Thieme-Becker; ▶Witt checklist
Gavazzi, Elizabeth *(Italian architect)*   **AV**
  Bibl: Ottagono, 1988 June, no.89, p.110
Gavazzi, Giacomo *(Italian painter, 15th c.)*   **BA**
  Bibl: ▶Bolaffi; Zampetti, Pitt. bergamaschi, v.3
Gavazzi, Giovanni di Giacomo   **BA GC PR**
  (Italian artist, op.1512)   WC
  (Italian painter, d. 1512)   PR
  (Italian painter, d.1512)   BA GC
  Bibl: ▶Bolaffi; ▶Fredericksen & Zeri, Census; ▶RILA/BHA, 1986; ▶Thieme-Becker; Zampetti, Pitt. bergamaschi, v.3
Gavasio or Gavazzi, Giovanni Giacomo   **WC**
  Gavazzi   PR
Gavazzi, Giovanni Giacomo   **GC**
  Giovanni di Giacomo Gavazzi   PR
Gavazzi, Giovanni Giacomo → see Gavazzi, Giovanni di Giacomo
Gavelin, Margareta, (nee Capsius) *(Finnish artist, op.1725-1751)*   **WC**
Gavenchak, Theodora *(American artist, 20th c.)*   **BA**
  Bibl: ▶Art Index, v.30; ART MAGAZINE, LVI/9(MAY 1982), 17
Gavencky, Frank J. *(American artist, 1888-1968)*   **WC WI**
Gavet, Emile *(French architect, 1830-1904)*   **BA**
  Bibl: Boston, MFA, J-F MILLET(1984); Lepoitterin, J-F MILET(1984); Tomson, J-F MILLET AND THE BARBIZON SCHOOL, 93
Gavilán Tomé, Simón → see Gabilán Tomé, Simón
Gavilán, Simón Tomé y → see Gabilán Tomé, Simón
Gavin Hamilton → see Hamilton, Gavin
Gavin, Robert *(British artist, 1827-1883)*   **WC WI**
Gavrilenko, P.N. *(Russian painter, 20th c.)*   **BA**
  Bibl: Drobov, Zivopis Sovetskoj Belorussij
Gaw → see Gaw, William A.
Gaw, William A.   **PR WC WI**
  (American artist, 1895-)   WC
  (American artist, b.1891)   WI
  (American painter, 1891-1973)   PR
  Bibl: ▶Hughes, Artists California
  Gaw   PR
  William A. Gaw   PR

Gawdy or Gawdie, Sir John →see
Gawdy, John
Gawdy, John　　　　　　　**WI**
　(British artist, 1639-1699/1709)　WC
　(British artist, 1639-1708-1709)　WI
　　Gawdy or Gawdie, Sir John　**WC**
Gawell, Oscar *(German artist, 1888-*
　1955)　　　　　　　　　**WC**
Gawen Hamilton →see Hamilton,
　Gawen
Gawinski, Antoni *(Polish artist,*
　1876-)　　　　　　　　**WC**
Gawlak, Annie *(American painter,*
　b.1943)　　　　　　　　**BA**
　　Bibl: New art examiner, VIII (May
　　1981) pp.12-15
Gay →see Gay, Edward B.
Gay →see Gay, Walter
Gay or Ge, Nikolai Nikolajevitch
　(Nicolas Gue') →see Ge, Nikolaj
　Nikolaevič
Gay, Arthur *(American*
　photographer, 1895-1981)　　**BA**
　　Bibl: Milwaukee (WI, USA), Art
　　Mus., Photos collections
Gay, Bernard　　　　　**WC WI**
　(British artist, 20th cent.)　WC
　(British artist, op.20th c.)　WI
Gay, C.H. *(American, active New*
　London, CT, U.S. 1850-1851,
　daguerreotypist)　　　　　**JG**
Gay, Duncan *(American painter,*
　1865-1949)　　　　　　　**BA**
　　Bibl: Archives Amer. Art Jrnl.,
　　XXIII/3 (1983) pp.34-37
Gay, Edward →see Gay, Edward B.
Gay, Edward B.　**BA GC PR WC WI**
　(American artist, 1837-1928)　WC WI
　(American painter, 1837-1928)　BA PR
　(American, 1837-1928)　　GC
　　Bibl: ▶Groce, Artists Amer.;
　　▶Havlice, Idx. art. bio.; ▶Mallett's
　　idx. artists; ▶RILA/BHA; ▶Witt
　　checklist
　　Edward B. Gay　　　　　PR
　　Gay　　　　　　　　　PR
　　Gay, Edward　　　　　PR
Gay, George Howell　　　**BA WI**
　(American artist, 1858-1931)　WI
　(American painter, 1858-1931)　BA
　　Bibl: ▶Amer. art annual, 20;
　　▶Fielding's Amer. ptrs.; ▶Young,
　　Amer. artists
Gay, Jacques *(French menuisier,*
　master 1779, act. to ca.1799)　**GC**
　　Bibl: ▶Salverte, Ébénistes 18e s.
Gay, John *(American, active 19th*
　century)　　　　　　　**JG**
Gay, N. *(French artist, op.1780)*　**WC**
Gay, P. or B. *(German(?) artist, op.*
　1792)　　　　　　　　**WC**
Gay, Roland *(Swiss architect)*　**AV**
　　Bibl: ▶Schweiz. Ingen. u. Archit.,
　　1984-1985

Gay, Walter　　　**BA PR WC WI**
　(American artist, 1856-1937)　WC WI
　(American painter, 1856-1937)　BA PR
　　Bibl: Dayton (OH, USA), Amer.
　　expatriate ptrs. (1976); ▶Fielding's
　　Amer. ptrs.; ▶RILA/BHA;
　　▶Vollmer, Künst.-Lex. 20. Jhr.;
　　▶WWW Amer., 1897
　　Gay　　　　　　　　　PR
　　Walter Gay　　　　　　PR
Gay, Wicksworth Allen →see Gay,
　Winckworth Allan
Gay, Winckworth Allan　　**BA PR**
　(American artist, 1821-1910)　WI
　(American painter, 1821-1910)　BA PR
　　Bibl: ▶Fielding's Amer. ptrs.;
　　▶RILA/BHA; ▶Thieme-Becker;
　　▶Young, Amer. artists
　　Gay, Wicksworth Allen　　PR
　Gay, Winkworth Allan　　**WI**
　　Winckworth Allan Gay　　PR
Gay, Winkworth Allan →see Gay,
　Winckworth Allan
Gayart, Jean *(French architect, 18th*
　cent)　　　　　　　　**AV**
　　Bibl: Architektur der DDR, 1988
　　June, v.37, no.6, p.23
Gaye, Juliet de *(British artist, op.*
　20th c.)　　　　　　　**WI**
Gayette, Peter van　　　　**BA**
　(Architect, d.1747)　　AV
　(French architect in Germany,
　d.1747)　　　　　　　BA
　　Bibl: Dehio BERLIN/POTSDAM;
　　▶Portoghesi, Diz. arch. e
　　urbanistica; ▶Thieme-Becker
　　Gayette, Peter von　　**AV**
Gayette, Peter von →see Gayette,
　Peter van
Gayford, T.　　　　　**WC WI**
　(British artist, 18th cent.)　WC
　(British artist, op.18th c.)　WI
Gayle, Margot *(American*
　preservationist, head of Friends of
　Cast Iron Architecture, New York
　City)　　　　　　　　**AV**
　　Bibl: Historic preservation, 1988
　　July-Aug., v.40, no.4, p.18
Gaylor →see Gaylor, Samuel Wood
Gaylor, Samuel Wood *(American*
　painter, b. 1883)　　　　**PR**
　　Bibl: ▶WWW Amer. art
　　Gaylor　　　　　　　PR
　　Samuel Wood Gaylor　　PR
Gaylord, William *(American interior*
　designer)　　　　　　　**AV**
　　Bibl: Architectural digest, 1985
　　Apr., v.41, no.4, p.198
Gayman, Brian *(American sculptor,*
　20th c.)　　　　　　　**BA**
　　Bibl: Grove, N., in ARTS MAG
　　Lx/6 (Feb 1986) 104
Gaynor, Alan *(American architect,*
　NYC)　　　　　　　　**AV**
　　Bibl: ▶AIA Pro File, 1987-88

Gáyor, Tibor *(Hungarian painter,*
　b.1929)　　　　　　　　**BA**
　　Bibl: ▶Bénézit; Bonn (DEU), Stadt.
　　Kunstmus., Neue ungarische
　　Konstruktivisten (1975)
Gayot-Du Buisson, Jean Baptiste →see
　Dubuisson, Jean Baptiste Gayot
Gays, Howard　　　　　**WC WI**
　(British artist, 19th cent.)　WC
　(British artist, op.1886-)　WI
Gaytán family *(Spanish ceramists,*
　16th-17th cs.)　　　　　**BA**
　　Bibl: Gonzalez Muñoz, Arch. esp.
　　de arte, LIII/211 (1980) 345-366
Gayton family *(Spanish ceramists,*
　16th-17th cs.)　　　　　**BA**
　　Bibl: Gonzalez Muñoz, Arch. esp.
　　de arte, LIII/211 (1980) 345-366
Gayton, Anna M. *(British artist, op.*
　1874-1910)　　　　　　**WI**
Gaywood, Richard *(British artist,*
　op.1650-1680)　　　　**WC WI**
　　Bibl: ▶Fisher, Watercolour ptrs.
Gazard, Francois Valentin *(French*
　artist, -1817)　　　　　**WC**
Gaze, Harold　　　　　**WC WI**
　(British artist, 20th cent.)　WC
　(British artist, op.20th c.)　WI
Gazeau, Philippe *(French architect)*　**AV**
　　Bibl: Techniques et architecture,
　　1985 Dec.-1986 Jan., no.363,
　　p.104
Gazera, Carlo Antonio *(Italian*
　scenographer, act.1757)　　**BA**
　　Bibl: ARTE LOMBARDA, 41(1974),
　　83-91
Gaži, Dragan　　　　　**BA WC**
　(Yugoslav artist, 1930-)　WC
　(Yugoslav painter, b.1930)　BA
　　Bibl: ▶Bénézit
Gazi, Ludovico de →see Gaci,
　Ludovico de
Gazon, Luc *(Belgian draftsman,*
　b.1957)　　　　　　　　**BA**
　　Bibl: Duchese, AER & FACT,
　　1(1982), 74
Gažovič, Vladimir　　　　**BA WC**
　(Czech artist, 1939-)　WC
　(Czech printmaker, painter,
　b.1939)　　　　　　　BA
　　Bibl: Cincinnati (OH, USA), Art
　　Mus., Eastern Euro. printmkrs.
　　(1975); Guide exh. artists: Euro.
　　ptrs.
Gazzard, Donald *(Australian*
　architect, 1929-)　　　　**AV**
Gazzetta *(Italian artist, op.1795)*　**WC**
Ge, Nikolaj Nikolaevič　　　**BA**
　(Russian artist, 1831-1894)　WC
　(Russian painter, 1831-1894)　GC
　(Russian painter, sculptor, 1831-
　1894)　　　　　　　　BA
　　Bibl: ▶Bénézit; ▶Encyc. world art;
　　▶Fogg Mus. Libr. cat.; ▶RILA/BHA
　　Gay or Ge, Nikolai Nikolajevitch
　　　(Nicolas Gue')　　　**WC**
　　Ge, Nikolaj Nikolaevitch　**GC**

Ge, Nikolaj Nikolaevitch→see Ge, Nikolaj Nikolaevič

Gealst, S. (Netherlands(?) artist, op. 1697)   **WC**

Gear, A.Handel (British artist, op. 1877-1894)   **WI**

Gear, John W.   **WC WI**
   (British artist, 1806-1866)   WI
   (British artist, op.1821-m.1866)   WC

Gear, Mabel (British artist, b.1900)   **WI**
   Bibl: ▶Waters, Brit. artists
   Symes, Ivor J.J., Mrs.(Mabel)   WI

Gear, William   **BA WC WI**
   (British artist, 1915-)   WC
   (British artist, b.1915)   WI
   (British painter, b.1915)   BA
   Bibl: ▶Bénézit; ▶WW Art

Geare, H.L., Mrs., (Marjorie Violet)→see Watherston, Marjorie Violet

Geare, Reginald (American architect, Washington, D.C)   **AV**
   Bibl: Historic preservation, 1987 Sept.-Oct., v.39, no.5, p.74

Gearo (American, active NY, U.S. 1910-1920s)   **JG**

Geary [Unidentified] (Unknown painter)   **PR**
   Bibl: (January 17, 1803, lot 22, Christie's)

Geary, Stephen   **AV BA**
   (British architect, entrepreneur, 1797-1854)   BA
   (English architect, civil engineer, inventor and specialist in cemetery design, ca. 1797-1854)   AV
   Bibl: ▶Colvin, Brit. archts.; ▶Macmillan encyc. archts.

Gebaud, Y. (French artist, op.1828)   **WC**

Gebauer, Arno (East German architect, Weimar)   **AV**
   Bibl: Architectur der DDR, 1989 Apr., v.38, no.4, p.14

Gebauer, Christian David (German artist, 1777-1831)   **WC**

Gebauer, Joachim (West German architect, 20th cent)   **AV**
   Bibl: Das Münster, 1989, v.42, no.2, p.138

Gebauer, Paul Erngt (German artist, 1782-1865)   **WC**

Gebel, Matthes (German sculptor, medalist, ca.1500-1574)   **BA**
   Bibl: ▶Forrer, Medallists; ▶Neue deutsche Biog.; ▶Thieme-Becker

Gebelein, George Christian (American silversmith, 1878-1945)   **BA**
   Bibl: Fredyma, Boston Silversmiths; ▶WWW Amer., 1943

Gebert, Hansik (West German painter, sculptor, photographer, b.1947)   **BA**
   Bibl: ▶Babington Smith, Contemp. artists; ▶Intl. dir. exh. artists, 1983

Gebhard, Albert (Finnish artist, 1869-)   **WC**

Gebhard, Andreas (German artist, 1704-1774)   **WC**

Gebhard, Johann (German artist, 1676-1756)   **WC**

Gebhard, Otto→see Gebhardt, Otto

Gebhard, Rainer (German architect)   **AV**
   Bibl: Bauwelt, 1986 May 23, v.77, no.19-20, p.721

Gebhardt→see Gebhardt, Eduard von

Gebhardt, Carl (German artist, 1860-1917)   **WC**

Gebhardt, Eduard (Carl Franz Eduard von)→see Gebhardt, Eduard von

Gebhardt, Eduard von   **BA GC PR**
   (German artist, 1838-1925)   WC
   (German painter, 1838-1925)   BA GC PR
   Bibl: ▶Bénézit; Reclams Künstlerlex.; ▶RILA/BHA; ▶Thieme-Becker
   Eduard von Gebhardt   PR
   Gebhardt   PR

Gebhardt, Eduard (Carl Franz Eduard von)   **WC**
   Gebhardt, Karl Franz Edouard von   PR
   Gebhardt, Karl Franz Eduard von   GC

Gebhardt, Ignaz Heinrich (German painter, 1869-1946)   **BA**
   Bibl: ▶Busse, Maler u. Bildhauer 19. Jahr.; Ludwig, Münchener Maler; ▶Vollmer, Künst.-Lex. 20. Jhr.
   Gebhardt, Karl Franz Edouard von→see Gebhardt, Eduard von
   Gebhardt, Karl Franz Eduard von→see Gebhardt, Eduard von

Gebhardt, Ludwig (German artist, 1830-1908)   **WC**

Gebhardt, Otto   **GC**
   (German artist, 1700-1773)   WC
   (German painter, ca.1700-1773)   GC
   Bibl: ▶Thieme-Becker

Gebhard, Otto   **WC**

Gebhardt, Wolfgang Magnus (German artist, op.1730-1750)   **WC**

Gebler, Friedrich Otto   **GC**
   (German artist, 1838-1917)   WC
   (German painter, 1838-1917)   GC
   Bibl: ▶Thieme-Becker

Gebler, Otto (Friedrich Otto)   **WC**
Gebler, Otto (Friedrich Otto)→see Gebler, Friedrich Otto

Gebouw→see Goubau, Antoon

Geccelli, Johannes   **BA WC**
   (German artist, op.1959)   WC
   (German painter, b.1925)   BA
   Bibl: ▶Bénézit; ▶WW Arts DEU

Gechter, Jean François Théodore→see Gechter, Théodore

Gechter, Théodore (French sculptor, 1796-1844)   **GC**
   Bibl: Getty Photo Study Coll. (Sculp.); ▶Thieme-Becker
   Gechter, Jean François Théodore   GC

Gechtoff, Sonia   **BA WC WI**
   (American artist, 1926-)   WC
   (American artist, b.1926)   WI
   (American painter, b.1926)   BA
   Bibl: ▶MoMA libr. cat.; ▶WW Amer. Art, 1976

Geckels, Lothar (German architect)   **AV**
   Bibl: Architektur, Innenarchitektur, technischer Ausbau, 1984 Mar., v.92, no.2, p.54

Geddes→see Geddes, Andrew

Geddes, Andrew   **BA GC PR WC WI**
   (British artist, 1783-1844)   WC WI
   (British painter, 1783-1844)   PR
   (British painter, printmaker, 1783-1844)   BA
   (British, 1783-1844)   GC
   Bibl: ▶Dict. natl. biog.; ▶RILA/BHA; ▶Thieme-Becker; ▶Witt checklist
   Andrew Geddes   PR
   Geddes   PR

Geddes, Fiona (British artist, b.1949)   **BA**
   Bibl: Arts Council GBR, Scot. Comm., Small tapestries (1976)

Geddes, Margaret Sarah, Miss→see Carpenter, Margaret Sarah

Geddes, Norman Bel   **AV BA**
   (American architect, 1893-1958)   AV
   (American designer, 1893-1958)   BA
   Bibl: ▶Libr. of Congr. Name Auth. File; ▶MoMA libr. cat.; NY Times obit.; ▶WW Amer. Art
   Bel Geddes, Norman   AV

Geddes, Patrick   **BA WC WI**
   (British artist, op.1895/6)   WC
   (British artist, op.1985-)   WI
   (British biologist, town planner, 1854-1932)   BA
   (Scottish city planner, 1854-1932)   AV
   Bibl: ▶Who was who [GBR], 1929-40

Geddes, Patrick, Sir   **AV**
Geddes, Patrick, Sir→see Geddes, Patrick

Geddes, Peter (American architect)   **AV**

Geddes, Robert (American architect, 1923-)   **AV**
   Bibl: ▶Contemp. archts.

Geddes, Wilhelmina→see Geddes, Wilhelmina Margaret

Geddes, Wilhelmina Margaret   **BA**
   (Irish glass painter, illustrator, decorative artist, 1887-1955)   BA
   (Irish stained glass artist, 1887-1955)   AV
   Bibl: Bowe, Jrnl. of Dec. & Propaganda Arts 8 (Spring 1988), 58-79; Irish arts review, 1987 Autumn, v.4, no.3, p.53; ▶Johnson, Brit. artists

Geddes, Wilhelmina   **AV**

Geddes, William WC WI
　(British artist, op.1850-) WI
　(British artist, op.c.1850) WC
Gedeler or Goedeler, Elias *(German artist, 1620-1693)* **WC**
Gedlek, Ludwig *(Polish artist, 1847-)* **WC**
Gee, David **BA WI**
　(British artist, 1793-1872) WI
　(British painter, printmaker, 1793-1872) BA
　Bibl: Coventry(GBR), Herbert Art Gallery and Museum, DAVID GEE, 1978; ▶Wood, Victorian ptrs.
Gee, John *(British turner, cabinetmaker, act.1799-ca.1824)* **BA**
　Bibl: ▶Heal, London furniture mkrs., (1979); Jarvis, FURNITURE HISTORY, XV(2979), 69; Wills, Engl. furniture
Gee, Joseph **WC WI**
　(British artist, 19th cent.) WC
　(British artist, op.1915-) WI
Gee, Peter *(Designer)* **AV**
　Bibl: Metropolis, 1983 July-Aug., v.3, no.1, p.10
Gee, Yun *(American painter, 1906-1963)* **BA**
　Bibl: ▶Bénézit; Storrs(CONN,USA), U.of Conn., William Benton Museum of Art, THE PAINT-INGS OF YUN GEE, 1979; ▶Vollmer, Künst.-Lex. 20. Jhr.
Geefs, Isabelle Marie Francoise (Fanny), (nee Corr) *(Belgian artist, 1807-1883)* **WC**
Geefs, Joseph Germain *(Belgian sculptor, 1808-1885)* **BA**
　Bibl: ▶Bénézit; ▶Thieme-Becker; ▶Wurzbach, NLD Künst.-Lex.
Geel → see Geel, Jacob Jacobsz. van
Geel, Daniel van *(Dutch artist, op. 1635-1660)* **WC**
Geel, Jacob Jacobsz. van **BA GC PR WC**
　(Dutch artist, c.1585-p.1638) WC
　(Dutch painter and draughtsman, ca.1585-aft.1638) GC
　(Dutch painter, ca.1585-aft.1638) PR
　(Dutch painter, ca.1585-after 1638) BA
　Bibl: Getty Photo Study Coll.; ▶RILA/BHA; ▶Thieme-Becker; ▶Witt checklist; ▶Wurzbach, NLD Künst.-Lex.
　Geel PR
　Geel, Jacob van PR
　J.V. Geel PR
　Jacob Jacobsz. van Geel PR
Geel, Jacob van → see Geel, Jacob Jacobsz. van

Geel, Joost van **BA GC PR WC**
　(Dutch artist, 1631-1698) WC
　(Dutch painter, 1631-1698) BA GC PR
　Bibl: ▶Bénézit; Getty Photo Study Coll.; ▶Nieuw NLD biog. woord.; ▶RILA/BHA; ▶Thieme-Becker; ▶Witt checklist; ▶Wurzbach, NLD Künst.-Lex.
　Joost van Geel PR
Geelen, Christiaan, I van *(Dutch artist, 1755-1824)* **WC**
Geelen, Christiaan, II van *(Dutch artist, 1794-1826)* **WC**
Geenvaars [Unidentified] *(Unknown painter)* **PR**
　Bibl: 1712 Hiel inventory
　Geevaars PR
Geer, Maximilian von **BA WC**
　(German artist, 1680-1768) WC
　(German miniaturist, 1680-1768) BA
　Bibl: ▶Thieme-Becker
Geeraardts → see Zyl, Gerard Pietersz. van
Geeraerts → see Geeraerts, Marcus, the younger
Geeraerts, Jasper → see Gerardi, Jasper
Geeraerts, Marcus (the elder) → see Geeraerts, Marcus, the elder
Geeraerts, Marcus (the younger) → see Geeraerts, Marcus, the younger
Geeraerts, Marcus, the elder **BA**
　(British artist, 1516-1521-op. 1604) WI
　(British artist, 1516/21-a.1604) WC
　(early Nethrlandish painter, printmaker, ca.1520-before 1604) BA
　(Flanders printmaker, ca.1530-ca.1590) GC
　(Flanders printmaker, painter, and draughtsman, 1516/21-bef.1604) GC
　(Netherlandish painter, ca.1520-bef.1640) PR
　Bibl: ▶Bénézit; ▶Biog. Nat. Belgique; ▶Dict. natl. biog.; ▶Encyc. world art; Getty Photo Study Coll. (Ptgs.); ▶RILA/BHA; ▶Thieme-Becker; ▶Witt checklist
　Garret, Marcus GC
　Garret, Marcus I WI
Geeraerts, Marcus (the elder) **GC PR**
　Geerards, Marcus (the Elder) GC
　Gerard, Marcus (the Elder) GC
　Gerard, Marcus I WI
Gerards, Marcus (the Elder) **GC**
Gheeraerts, Garret, Geeraerts or Gerard the Elder, Marcus **WC**
　Gheeraerts, Marcus (the Elder) GC PR
Gheeraerts, Marcus I **WI**
　Marcus Geeraerts (the elder) PR

Geeraerts, Marcus, the younger **BA**
　(British artist, 1561-1635) WC WI
　(British painter, 1561-1635) PR
　(Flemish painter, 1561-1635) BA GC
　Bibl: ▶Encyc. world art; ▶RILA/BHA; ▶Thieme-Becker; ▶Witt checklist
　Garrard, Marcus II WI
　Garret, Marcus II WI
　Geeraerts PR
Geeraerts, Marcus (the younger) **GC PR**
　Gerard, Marcus II WI
　Gerards PR
　Gheeraerts PR
Gheeraerts, Garrard, Garret, Geeraerts or Gerard the Younger, Marcus **WC**
　Gheeraerts, Marc (the Younger) PR
　Gheeraerts, Marcus PR
　Gheeraerts, Marcus (the Younger) GC PR
Gheeraerts, Marcus II **WI**
　Gheeraerts, Marcus, the Younger PR
　Marcus Geeraerts (the younger) PR
Geeraerts, Marten Jozef **BA GC WC**
　(Flemish artist, 1707-1791) WC
　(Flemish painter, 1707-1791) BA
　(Flemish, 1707-1791) GC
　Bibl: ▶RILA/BHA; ▶Seyn, Écoles flam. et holl.; ▶Thieme-Becker; ▶Witt checklist; ▶Wurzbach, NLD Künst.-Lex.
Geerards, Marcus (the Elder) → see Geeraerts, Marcus, the elder
Geering, Robert J. *(American architect, 1935-)* **AV**
Geerlings, Gerald Kenneth *(American printmaker, architect, b.1897)* **BA**
　Bibl: ▶WW Amer. Art, 1984
Geerlof, Johan *(Flemish painter, 17th c.)* **BA**
　Bibl: Vlieghe, REVUE DU LOUVRE ET DES MUSÉE DE FRANCE, XXXVIII/1 (1988), 37-38
Geertgen tot Sint Jans **BA GC PR**
　(early Netherlandish painter, ca. 1465-ca.1495) BA
　(Netherlandish painter, ca.1465-ca.1495) PR
　(Netherlands artist, c.1455/65-c.1485/95) WC
　(North Netherlandish painter, ca.1465-ca.1495) GC
　Bibl: ▶Encyc. world art; Getty Photo Study Coll.; ▶RILA/BHA; ▶Thieme-Becker; ▶Witt checklist; ▶Wurzbach, NLD Künst.-Lex.
Geertgen tot Sint Jans (Gerard or Gerrit van Haarlem) **WC**
　Gerard van Haarlem GC
　Gerrit van Haarlem GC
　Sint Jans PR
　Sint Jans, Geertgen tot PR

Geertgen tot Sint Jans (Gerard or Gerrit van Haarlem) → *see* Geertgen tot Sint Jans

Geertgen, Pseudo → *see* Master of the Figdor Deposition

Geertruij Pranger → *see* Pranger, Geertruij [Unidentified]

Geertruijd Pieters → *see* Pietersz., Gertrude

Geertsen, Ib (*Danish painter, b.1919*)   **BA**
    Bibl: ▶Vollmer, Künst.-Lex. 20. Jhr.; ▶Weilbach, Kunst.leks.

Geertz, Julius (*German artist, 1837-1902*)   **WC**

Geesink, Johan Louis (Joop) (*Dutch artist, 1913-*)   **WC**

Geest, Arie van (*Dutch artist, b.1948*)   **BA**
    Bibl: Hague, The, Haags Gemeentemuseum, Arie van Geest...(1986)

Geest, Chris van (*Dutch painter, b.1942*)   **GC**
    Bibl: Getty Photo Study Coll. (Douwes coll.)

Geest, Julius or Juliaen Franciscus de (*Dutch artist, op.1657-m.1699*)   **WC**

Geest, Uwe (*Architect, worked in Barcelona, Spain*)   **AV**
    Bibl: Architecture mouvement et continuité 1984 Dec., no.6, p.84

Geest, Wybrand Simonsz. de → *see* Geest, Wybrand Simonsz. de, the elder

Geest, Wybrand Simonsz. de, the elder   **BA**
    (*Dutch artist, 1592-p.1667*)   **WC**
    (*Dutch painter and draughtsman, 1592-aft.1667*)   **GC**
    (*Dutch painter, ca.1592-ca.1661*)   **BA**
    Bibl: ▶Bénézit; Getty Photo Study Coll.; Leeuwarden, WYBRAND DE GEEST(1982); ▶Thieme-Becker; ▶Witt checklist; ▶Wurzbach, NLD Künst.-Lex.

Geest, Wybrand Simonsz. de   **GC WC**

Geets → *see* Geets, Willem

Geets, Willem   **PR WC**
    (*Belgian artist, 1838-1919*)   **WC**
    (*Belgian painter, 1838-1919*)   **PR**
    Bibl: ▶Thieme-Becker; ▶Witt checklist

Geets   **PR**

Willem Geets   **PR**

Geevaars → *see* Geenvaars [Unidentified]

Geffcken, Walter   **GC WC**
    (*German artist, 1872-1950*)   **WC**
    (*German painter, 1872-1950*)   **GC**
    Bibl: ▶Thieme-Becker

Geffels, Frans   **BA GC**
    (*Flemish painter, act.1635-1699*)   **GC**
    (*Flemish painter, printmaker, architect, act.1680*)   **BA**
    Bibl: ▶Bénézit; ▶Encyc. world art; ▶Thieme-Becker

Gefflis, Frans   **GC**

Geuffels, Frans   **GC**

Gielfis, Frans   **GC**

Geffert, Alfred, Jr. (*fl. 1937; Landscape architect, District of Columbia, United States of America*)   **FA**
    Bibl: Natl. Archives object (inscription); Natl. Archives object file

Gefflis, Frans → *see* Geffels, Frans

Geffroy, Edmond Aimé Florentin   **GC WC**
    (*French artist, 1804-1895*)   **WC**
    (*French painter, 1804-1895*)   **GC**
    Bibl: ▶Bénézit

Gegenbauer, A. von (*German artist, 1800-1876*)   **WC**

Gegerfelt, Vilhelm (*Swedish artist, 1844-1920*)   **WC**

Gehbe, Eduard (*German artist, 1845-*)   **WC**

Gehlhausen, Guy (*American architect, Schaumburg, Ill*)   **AV**
    Bibl: Inland architect, 1989 Nov.-Dec., v.33, no.6, p.40

Gehr, Ferdinand (*Swiss artist, 1896-*)   **WC**

Gehrig, Thomas (*West German interior architect*)   **AV**
    Bibl: Interiors, 1987 June, v.146, no.11, p.54

Gehrmann, Johann Michael (*German artist, -1770*)   **WC**

Gehrts, Carl (*German artist, 1853-1898*)   **WC**

Gehrts, Johannes   **GC WC**
    (*German artist, 1855-p.1884*)   **WC**
    (*German painter, 1855-aft.1898*)   **GC**
    Bibl: ▶Thieme-Becker

Gehry, Frank O. → *see* Gehry, Frank Owen

Gehry, Frank Owen   **BA**
    (*American architect, 1929-*)   **AV**
    (*American architect, b.1929*)   **BA**
    Bibl: ▶AIA Pro File; ▶Contemp. archts.

Gehry, Frank O.   **AV**

Gehse, Karl F. (*German architect, Bochum*)   **AV**
    Bibl: Detail, 1981 Nov.-Dec., no.6, p.795

Gehtmann, Anton (*Prussian architect, 19th cent*)   **AV**
    Bibl: The world of interiors, 1987 Nov., p.176

Geibel, Casimir   **GC WC**
    (*German artist, 1839-1896*)   **WC**
    (*German painter, 1839-1896*)   **GC**
    Bibl: ▶Bénézit

Geier, Ingeborg (*West German architect, Stuttgart*)   **AV**
    Bibl: Detail, 1987 Nov.-Dec., v.27, no.6, p.629

Geier, Rudolf (*West German architect, Stuttgart*)   **AV**
    Bibl: ▶Bund Deut. Arch. Hdbch., 1987

Geigenberger, Otto   **GC WC**
    (*German artist, 1881-1946*)   **WC**
    (*German painter, 1881-1946*)   **GC**
    Bibl: ▶Thieme-Becker

Geiger, Benno (*Swiss ceramist, b.1903*)   **BA**
    Bibl: Schnyder, VIER BERNER KERAMIKER (1985)

Geiger, Carl Joseph (*German artist, 1822-1905*)   **WC**

Geiger, Conrad (*German artist, 1751-1808*)   **WC**

Geiger, David H. (*American engineer, New York*)   **AV**
    Bibl: Architectural record, 1988 Sept., v.176, no.10, p.128

Geiger, Karl-Georg (*West German architect, Frankfurt*)   **AV**
    Bibl: ▶Bund Deut. Arch. Hdbch., 1985

Geiger, Margarete (*German artist, 1783-1809*)   **WC**

Geiger, Markus (*Swiss painter in AUT, b.1958*)   **BA**
    Bibl: ▶Art Index, v.36; Schenker, Flash art, CXXVIV (1987)

Geiger, Nicolaus (*German sculptor, painter, 1849-1897*)   **BA**
    Bibl: ▶Bénézit; ▶Thieme-Becker

Geiger, Peter Johann Nepomuk (*German artist, 1805-1880*)   **WC**

Geiger, Philip Neil (*American painter, b.1956*)   **BA**
    Bibl: ARTS MAG, LX/7 (Mar 1986) 106; ▶WW Amer. Art, 1986

Geiger, R. → *see* Geiger, Robert

Geiger, Ray W. (*American architect*)   **AV**
    Bibl: ▶AIA Pro File, 1983

Geiger, Robert   **WI**
    (*British artist, 20th cent.*)   **WC**
    (*British artist, op.1961-*)   **WI**

Geiger, R.   **WC**

Geiger, Rupprecht   **BA WC**
    (*German artist, 1908-*)   **WC**
    (*German painter, printmaker, b.1908*)   **BA**
    Bibl: ▶Bénézit; ▶MoMA libr. cat.; ▶Vollmer, Künst.-Lex. 20. Jhr.; ▶WW Germany

Geiger, Willi (*German artist, 1878-*)   **WC**

Geigerfeld, Hans Georg (*in Slovenia painter, act.1641*)   **BA**
    Bibl: Lipoglavšek, Zbornik za umetnostno zgodovino, pp.115-116

Geijp, Adriaan Marinus → *see* Geyp, Adriaan Marinus

Geikie, Walter   BA WC WI
  (British artist, 1795-1837)   WC WI
  (British painter, printmaker,
    1795-1837)   BA
  Bibl: ▶Bénézit; ▶Thieme-Becker

Geipel, Finn *(West German*
  architect, 1958 or 9-)   AV
  Bibl: Architecture d'aujourd'hui,
    1989 Feb., no.261, p.58

Geirnaert, Hendrik-Lucianus
  (Belgian architect, Ghent, 1860-
    1928)   AV
  Bibl: Gentse bijdragen tot de
    kunstgeschiedenis en
    oudheidkunde, 1988, v.27, p.88

Geirnaert, Jozef   GC
  (Belgian artist, 1791-1859)   WC
  (Belgian painter, 1791-1859)   GC
  Bibl: ▶Thieme-Becker

Geirnaert, Jozef Lodevyk   WC
Geirnaert, Jozef Lodevyk→see
  Geirnaert, Jozef

Geis, William III *(American artist,*
  b.1940)   BA
  Bibl: Artforum 12 (Sep 1973) 22;
    Portland (OR, USA), Art Mus.,
    West Coast now (1968)

Geisendörfer, Manfred *(West*
  German architect, Würzburg)   AV
  Bibl: ▶Bund Deut. Arch. Hdbch.,
    1987

Geiser, Frank *(Swiss architect, Bern)*   AV
  Bibl: ▶Schweiz. Ingen. u. Archit.,
    1984-1985

Geiser, Leonhard *(German porcelain*
  painter, 1776-1830)   BA
  Bibl: ▶Bénézit; Glaser,
    WELTKUNST/ LVII/20/15 (Oct.
    1987), p.2892-2894;
    ▶Thieme-Becker

Geisler, Johan Tobias *(Swedish*
  artist, musician, author, 1683-
    1729)   BA
  Bibl: KUNST IN HESSEN, XXII
    (1982) 71-75; ▶Svenskt konst.-lex.

Geisler, Siegfried *(West German*
  architect, Ettlingen)   AV
  Bibl: Deutsche Bauzeitung, 1988
    Feb., v.122, no.2, p.40

Geisler, Tim *(American architect)*   AV
  Bibl: Architecture Minnesota,
    1982 Oct.-Nov., v.8, no.5, p.40

Geisler-Hansson, Manfred *(West*
  German architect, Hamburg)   AV
  Bibl: Architektur,
    Innenarchitektur, Technischer
    Ausbau, 1988 Sept., v.96, no.9,
    p.100

Geismar, Hans von *(German artist,*
  op.1499)   WC

Geismar, Thomas *(American*
  architect)   AV

Geiss, Johann Conrad *(German*
  ironsmith, goldsmith, 1771-1846)   BA
  Bibl: Arenhovel, Weltkunst LII/22
    (15 Nov 1982) pp.3292-3295;
    ▶Neue deutsche Biog.

Geisselbrun, Jeremias *(German*
  sculptor, 1594/96-1659/64)   BA
  Bibl: ▶Thieme-Becker; Zeitschrift,
    Verein für Kunstwissenschaft
    XXXII/1-4 (1978), 168-173

Geissler, Christian Gottfried
  Heinrich *(German artist, 1770-*
    1844)   WC

Geissler, Christian Gottlieb
  (German artist, 1729-1814)   WC

Geissler, J.G. *(German artist, op.c.*
  1780-1800)   WC

Geissler, Johann Martin Friedrich
  (German draughtsman, 1778-1853)   GC
  Bibl: ▶Bénézit

Geissler, Rudolf Carl Gottfried
  (German artist, 1834-1906)   WC

Geissler, Wilhelm *(German artist,*
  1848-1928)   WC

Geissler, Wilhelm *(German*
  printmaker, b.1895)   BA
  Bibl: Stadtisches Gustav-Lubcke
    Museum. AUSSTELLUNG WILHEIM
    GEISSLER. EXH. 1975

Geist, August Christian→see Geiste,
  August Christian

Geist, Sidney *(American sculptor,*
  author, b.1914)   BA
  Bibl: ▶Natl. union cat.; ▶WW
    Amer. Art

Geiste, August Christian   BA
  (German artist, 1835-1868)   WC
  (German painter, graphic artist,
    1835-1868)   BA
  Bibl: ▶Bénézit; ▶Thieme-Becker

Geist, August Christian   WC

Geit, Geil or Gell(?), F. van
  (Netherlands(?) artist, 19th
    cent.(?))   WC

Gela Group *(Sicilian vase-painters)*   GC
  Bibl: ▶Trendall, Red-fig. vases
    Lucania

Gela Painter   GC JG
  (vase-painter, ca. 500-450 B.C.)   GC
  Bibl: ▶Beazley, Attic bl.-fig. vase-
    ptrs.; Boardman, Attic Bl.-fig.
    Vases

Gelardin, Robert *(American*
  architect, 1940-)   AV
  Bibl: Process: architecture, n.7,
    1978, p.213

Gelasio di Niccolò   PR
  (Italian artist, op.1242)   WC
  (Italian painter, act. ca.1242)   PR
  Bibl: ▶Thieme-Becker

  Gelasio di Niccolo ('della
    Masnada di S. Giorgio')   WC
  Gelasio di Nicolo   PR
  Gelasio di Nicolo della Masnada di
    S. Giorgio   PR
Gelasio di Niccolo ('della Masnada di
  S. Giorgio')→see Gelasio di
  Niccolò
Gelasio di Nicolo→see Gelasio di
  Niccolò

Gelasio di Nicolo della Masnada di S.
  Giorgio→see Gelasio di Niccolò

Gelati, Lorenzo *(Italian painter,*
  1824-1893)   GC
  Bibl: ▶Thieme-Becker

Gelbe, Eduard *(German artist, 19th*
  cent.)   WC

Gelber, Martin B. *(American*
  architect)   AV

Gelberg, Murry *(American designer,*
  New York, NY)   AV
  Bibl: Interior design, 1986 Mar.,
    v.57, no.3, p.216

Geld, Hendrik van der *(Dutch*
  sculptor, 1838-1914)   BA
  Bibl: ▶Scheen, Ned. beeldende
    kunst.

Geldart, Joseph *(British artist, 1808-*
  1882)   WC WI

Gelde Macker→see Geldemacker
  [Unidentified]

Geldemacker [Unidentified]
  (Unknown painter)   PR
  Bibl: (May 1, 1802, lot 25,
    Christie's)
  Gelde Macker   PR

Gelden, George Van *(Architect,*
  Katonah NY)   AV
  Bibl: Interior design 1985 May,
    v.56, no.5, p.296

Gelder→see Gelder, Aert de

Gelder, Aert de   BA GC JG PR
  (Dutch artist, 1645-1727)   WC
  (Dutch painter and
    draughtsman, 1645-1727)   GC
  (Dutch painter, 1645-1727)   BA PR
  (Dutch, 1645-1727)   JG
  Bibl: ▶Bénézit; ▶Grote Winkler
    Prins; ▶RILA/BHA, 1986;
    ▶Thieme-Becker; ▶Wurzbach, NLD
    Künst.-Lex.

  A. De Gelder   PR
  Aert de Gelder   PR
  Arant de Gelder   PR
  De Gelder   PR
  De Gilder   PR
  Gelder   PR
  Gelder, Arent or Aert de   WC
  Petrus van Gelder   PR
  Van Gelder   PR
Gelder, Arent or Aert de→see
  Gelder, Aert de

Gelder, Dirk van *(Dutch painter,*
  printmaker, b.1907)   BA
  Bibl: ▶Scheen, Ned. beeldende
    kunst.; ▶Vollmer, Künst.-Lex. 20.
    Jhr.

Gelder, J. van *(Belgian(?) artist,*
  19th cent.)   WC

Gelder, L.D. van *(Dutch designer,*
  19th c.)   BA
  Bibl: Greenwald, A.M., JOURNAL
    OF JEWISH ART X (1984) 87-101;
    Meestertekens NLD goud- en
    zilversmeden, v.1, #7502

Gelder, Lucia Mathilde van
   (German painter, 1865-1899)   **PR**
     Bibl: ▶Thieme-Becker
   Gelder, Lucia Mathilde von   PR
   Lucia Mathilde van Gelder   PR
Gelder, Lucia Mathilde von → see
   Gelder, Lucia Mathilde van
Gelder, Nicolaes (Claes) van → see
   Gelder, Nicolaes van
Gelder, Nicolaes van   **GC PR**
   (Dutch artist, c.1625 or
     c.1635-1675/7)   **WC**
   (Dutch painter, 1636-1675/77)   PR
   (Dutch painter, ca.1625
     or1635-1675/77)   GC
     Bibl: ▶Bénézit; ▶Thieme-Becker
   Gelder, Nicolaes (Claes) van   **WC**
   Nicolaes van Gelder   PR
   Van Gelder   PR
Gelderman, G.J. *(Dutch artist, op.*
   1828)   **WC**
Geldorp → see Geldorp Gortzius
Geldorp → see Geldorp, Melchior
Geldorp Gortzius   **PR**
   (Flemish artist, 1553-c.1616)   WC
   (Flemish painter, 1553-ca.1616)   PR
   (Flemish, 1553-ca.1616)   GC
     Bibl: Getty Photo Study Coll.
     (Ptgs.); ▶Thieme-Becker; ▶Witt
     checklist
   de Oude Geldorp   PR
   G. Goeldorf   PR
   Geldorp   PR
   Geldorp or Gualdorp, Gortzius   **WC**
   Geldorp, Gortzius   **GC PR**
   Gortzius Geldorp   PR
   Gualdorp, Gorzius   GC
Geldorp or Gualdorp, Gortzius → see
   Geldorp Gortzius
Geldorp, Georg or Jorge *(Flemish*
   artist, op.1610-1653)   **WC**
Geldorp, Gortzius → see Geldorp
   Gortzius
Geldorp, Melchior   **GC PR WC**
   (Flemish painter, 17th century)   GC
   (German artist, op.1615-1637)   WC
   (German painter, act. 1615-
     1637)   PR
     Bibl: ▶Bénézit; ▶Thieme-Becker
   Geldorp   PR
   Melchior Geldorp   PR
Geldorp, Niclas [Unidentified]
   (Unknown painter)   **PR**
     Bibl: (May 14 & ff, 1804, lots
     289, 799, 815, Truchsessian
     Gallery)
   Gueldorf   PR
   N. Goeldorf   PR
   Niclas Geldorp   PR
Geldton, Toussaint → see Gelton,
   Toussaint
Gelduinus, Bernardus *(French*
   sculptor, 11th c.)   **BA**
     Bibl: CAHIERS DE SAINT-MICHEL
     DE CUXA, IX(JUNE 1978)

Gelée, Antoine François *(French*
   printmaker, 1796-1860)   **BA**
     Bibl: ▶Bénézit; ▶Dict. biog. fran.;
     ▶Thieme-Becker
Gelee, Claude → see Claude Lorrain
Geleng, Otto *(German artist, 19th*
   cent.)   **WC**
Gelernter, Mark *(British architect,*
   20th c.)   **BA**
     Bibl: Gelernter, ARCH. REV.,
     CLXXXI, 1083 (May 1987),
     p.86-88
Gelez, Edme *(French goldsmith,*
   b.1784, act.1838)   **BA**
     Bibl: Macé de Lépinay,F.REVUE DU
     LOUVRE...XXXVI/4-5(1986) 311
Gelfman, Marilynn *(American artist,*
   20th c.)   **BA**
     Bibl: McConathy, D., in ARTS
     MAG LIX/4 (Dec 1984) 108
Gelger, J. *(German artist, 19th cent.)*   **WC**
Gelhay, Edouard *(French artist,*
   1856-)   **WC**
Gelibert, Jules Bertrand *(French*
   artist, 1834-1916)   **WC**
Gelick, Michael *(American architect,*
   1940-)   **AV**
     Bibl: ▶AIA Pro File, 1985
Gelinet, Marcel *(French artist, op.*
   1927-1931)   **WC**
Gelissen, Maximilien Lambert
   (Belgian painter, 1786-1867)   **GC**
     Bibl: ▶Bénézit
Geliton, T. *(French artist, 17th cent.)*   **WC**
Gelius, Aegidius *(Netherlands artist,*
   op.1616)   **WC**
Gelle, Claude (le Lorrain) → see
   Claude Lorrain
Gelle, Johann   **GC WC**
   (German artist, c.1580-1625)   WC
   (German printmaker, 1580/89-d.
     bef.1625)   GC
     Bibl: ▶Thieme-Becker
Gellée, Claude → see Claude Lorrain
Geller → see Geller, Todros
Geller, Abraham W. *(American*
   architect, New York City)   **AV**
     Bibl: ▶AIA Pro File, 1987-88
Geller, Johann Nepomuk *(German*
   artist, 1860-1954)   **WC**
Geller, Todros *(American painter,*
   1889-1949)   **PR**
     Bibl: ▶WWW Amer. art
   Geller   PR
   Todros Geller   PR
Geller, W. *(Engraver)*   **WI**
Geller, William Overend *(British,*
   act. ca.1834-1853)   **GC**
     Bibl: ▶Thieme-Becker
Gellerstedt, Albert Theodor
   (Swedish painter, architect,
   printmaker, 1836-1914)   **BA**
     Bibl: ▶Busse, Maler u. Bildhauer
     19. Jahr.; ▶Portoghesi, Diz. arch. e
     urbanistica; ▶Svenskt konst.-lex.;
     ▶Thieme-Becker

Gellert Painter *(South Italian vase-*
   painter, 350-300 BC)   **GC**
     Bibl: McPhee & Trendall, Fish-
     Plates
Gellert, Thomas *(Austrian architect)*   **AV**
     Bibl: Bauforum, 1989, v.22, no.
     131, p.64
Gellez, Antoine-Joseph *(French*
   silversmith, master 1749)   **GC**
     Bibl: ▶Mabille, Orfèv. fran.
Gellhorn, Alfred *(German architect,*
   b.1885)   **BA**
     Bibl: ▶Vollmer, Künst.-Lex. 20. Jhr.
Gelli → see Gelli, Odoardo
Gelli, Edoardo → see Gelli, Odoardo
Gelli, Odoardo   **PR WC**
   (Italian artist, 1852-1933)   WC
   (Italian painter, 1852-1916)   PR
     Bibl: ▶Thieme-Becker
   Gelli   PR
   Gelli, Edoardo   PR
   Odoardo Gelli   PR
Gellig, Jakob → see Gillig, Jakob
Gellinek, Jost *(West German*
   architect, Aachen)   **AV**
     Bibl: Bauwelt, 1987 May 29, v.78,
     no.21, p.730
Gellner, Edda *(Austrian architect,*
   Graz)   **AV**
     Bibl: ▶Verzeich. Öst. Ziviltech.
Geltner, Danita *(American sculptor,*
   20th c.)   **BA**
     Bibl: Cameron, D., in ARTS MAG
     LIX/9 (May 1985) 74
Gelton → see Gelton, Toussaint
Gelton, Geldton or Geltton, Toussaint
   or Tousseijn → see Gelton,
   Toussaint
Gelton, Toussaint   **GC PR**
   (Dutch artist, c.1630-1680)   WC
   (Dutch painter, ca.1630-1680)   GC PR
     Bibl: Getty Photo Study Coll.;
     Getty Photo Study Coll. (Ptgs.);
     ▶Thieme-Becker; ▶Witt checklist
   Geldton, Toussaint   GC
   Gelton   PR
   Gelton, Geldton or Geltton,
     Toussaint or Tousseijn   **WC**
   Toussaint Gelton   PR
Geltrudi, Daniele   **AV**
Geluwe, Johan van *(Belgian*
   printmaker, b.1929)   **BA**
     Bibl: Antwerp (BEL),
     INTERNATIONAL CULTURAL
     CENTRUM, MUSEUM OF
     MUSEUMS: JOHAN VAN GELUWE,
     1981; ▶Intl. dir. exh. artists, 1982
Gemberling, Stephen *(American*
   trompe l'oeil painter, New York
   City)   **AV**
     Bibl: House & garden, 1987 Dec.,
     v.159, no.12, p.40
Gemell or Gemelli, H. → see Gemell,
   H.

Gemell, H. WI
 (British artist, 18th cent.) WC
 (British artist, op.1723-) WI
 Gemell or Gemelli, H. WC
Gemeniani→see Gimignani, Giacinto
Gemignani→see Gimignani, Giacinto
Gemin, Luciano *(Italian architect)* AV
 Bibl: Ottagono, 1987 June, v.22,
  no.85, p.56
Gemini, Gustavo *(Argentine
 architect)* AV
 Bibl: Summa, 1985 Oct., no.218,
  p.31
Geminiani, Giacinto→see Gimignani,
 Giacinto
Geminiano Cozzi→see Cozzi,
 Geminiano Francesco Antonio
Geminus, Thomas BA WC
 *(early Netherlandish printmaker,
  printer, physician, act.1524-
  1570)* BA
 *(Netherlands artist, c.1500-c.
  1570)* WC
 Bibl: ▶Bénézit; ▶Dict. natl. biog.;
  ▶Natl. union cat., pre-1956;
  ▶Thieme-Becker
Gemito, Vincenzo BA GC JG WC
 (Italian artist, 1852-1929) WC
 (Italian sculptor, 1852-1929) BA GC
 (Italian, 1852-1929) JG
 Bibl: ▶Bénézit; ▶Comanducci, Diz.;
  ▶Encyc. world art; ▶RILA/BHA;
  ▶Thieme-Becker
Gemmani, Davide *(Italian architect)* AV
 Bibl: L'Arca, 1989 June, no.28,
  p.58
Gemmill, Thomas *(Scottish armorer,
 18th c.)* BA
 Bibl: Scottish Weapons &
  Fortifications, 1100-1800, pp.
  399-402
Gemperle (Gemperlinus), Tobias
 (German artist, c.1550-1601/2) WC
Gempt, Bernard te GC WC
 (Dutch artist, 1826-1879) WC
 (Dutch painter, 1826-1879) GC
 Bibl: ▶Thieme-Becker
Gemünder, George *(American
 violin maker, 1816-1899)* BA
 Bibl: ▶Dict. Amer. biog.
Gen-Paul, (Eugene Paul) *(French
 artist, 1895-)* WC
Genaille, Felix-François *(French
 painter, 1826-1883)* GC
 Bibl: ▶Thieme-Becker
Genari→see Gennari, Benedetto II
Genaro→see Gennari, Benedetto II
Genasci, Donald B. *(American
 architect, Eugene, OR)* AV
 Bibl: Progressive architecture,
  1985 Jan., v.66, no.1, p.136
Genberg, Anton *(Swedish artist,
 1862-1939)* WC
Gence, Gabriel→see Gence, Robert
 Gabriel
Gence, Robert→see Gence, Robert
 Gabriel

Gence, Robert Gabriel GC
 (French artist, op.1713) WC
 (French painter, 1713-1719) GC
 Bibl: Getty Photo Study Coll.;
  ▶Thieme-Becker
 Gence, Gabriel GC
Gence, Robert WC
Gendall, John BA WC WI
 (British artist, 1790-1865) WC WI
 *(British painter, printmaker,
  1789-1865)* BA
 Bibl: ▶Fisher, Watercolour ptrs.;
  ▶Mallalieu, Brit. watercolour
  artists; ▶Wood, Victorian ptrs.
Gendreau, Gerald *(American
 architect, New York City)* AV
 Bibl: Architecture & urbanism,
  1989 Apr., no.4, p.128
Gendron, Ernest *(Canadian painter,
 b.ca.1912)* BA
 Bibl: ▶Artists Canada;
  ▶MacDonald, Can. artists;
  Montreal (QUE, CAN), Museum of
  Fine Arts, QUEBEC, TV AND
  COMPANY: THE PAINTINGS OF
  ERNEST GENDRON, 1976
Gendron, Ernest Augustin GC WC
 (French artist, 1817-1881) WC
 (French painter, 1817-1881) GC
 Bibl: ▶Bénézit
Gendron, Pierre *(Canadian artist,
 1934-)* WC
Gendt, Adolf Leonard van *(Dutch
 architect, Amsterdam, 1835-1901)* AV
 Bibl: ▶Macmillan encyc. archts.;
  ▶Thieme-Becker
Geneleos *(Greek sculptor, act. 1st
 half 6th c BC)* GC
 Bibl: ▶Brilliant, Anc. Greeks, p.80;
  ▶Robertson, Greek art, p.76
Genelli or Genelly, Janus→see
 Genelli, Janus
Genelli, Bonaventura BA GC
 (German artist, 1798-1868) WC
 (German painter, 1798-1868) BA GC
 Bibl: ▶Artist biog. master idx.;
  ▶Encyc. world art; ▶RILA/BHA;
  ▶Thieme-Becker; ▶Witt checklist
**Genelli, Bonaventura (Giovanni
 Bonaventura)** WC
*Genelli, Bonaventura (Giovanni
 Bonaventura)→see* Genelli,
 Bonaventura
Genelli, Camillo→see Genelli, Camilo
Genelli, Camilo BA
 (German artist, 1840-1867) WC
 (German painter, 1840-1867) BA
 Bibl: ▶Thieme-Becker; ▶Witt
  checklist
Genelli, Camillo WC
Genelli, Friedrich *(Danish
 printmaker, 1765-1793)* BA
 Bibl: ▶Bénézit; ▶Thieme-Becker

Genelli, Hans Christian *(Danish
 architect, scholar, 1763-1823)* BA
 Bibl: ▶Dict. natl. biog.; ▶Encyc.
  world art; ▶Portoghesi, Diz. arch.
  e urbanistica; ▶Thieme-Becker
Genelli, Janus BA
 (Danish artist, 1761-1813) WC
 (Danish painter, 1761-1813) BA
 Bibl: ▶Bénézit; ▶Thieme-Becker
Genelli or Genelly, Janus WC
**Gener or Jener, Gerado, Gerardo,
 Gerau or Guerau** *(Spanish artist,
 1369-p.1407)* WC
General Lambert→see Lambert, John
 (I)
Generalić, Ivan BA WC
 (Yugoslav artist, 1914-) WC
 (Yugoslav painter, b.1914) BA
 Bibl: ▶Natl. union cat., 1976;
  ▶Phaidon 20c. art
Generalic, Josip *(Yugoslav artist,
 20th cent.)* WC
Generalic, Milan *(Yugoslav artist,
 1938-)* WC
Genere→see Gennari, Benedetto II
Generès, Louis *(French sculptor,
 act.1671, d.1710)* BA
 Bibl: ▶Bénézit; Cortade, MONUM.
  HISTORIQUES DE LA FRANCE,
  127(JUNE-JUL 1983), 35-41;
  ▶Thieme-Becker
Genero dl Guercino→see Gennari,
 Ercole
Genesini, Cristoforo→see Cristoforo
 da Lendinara
Genesini, Lorenzo→see Lorenzo da
 Lendinara
Genesis Master *(French glass
 painter, 13th c.)* BA
 Bibl: GESTA, XIII/1(1974), 27-38
Genest, Jean-Baptiste-Etienne
 (French, active 1752-1788) JG
Genet, Alexandre *(French artist, op.
 1838)* WC
Geneva Group *(Campanian vase-
 painters)* GC
 Bibl: Beazley, Etruscan vase-ptrs.;
  ▶Trendall, Red-fig. vases Lucania
Geneva Painter *(vase-painter, ca.
 475-450 BC)* GC
 Bibl: ▶Beazley, Attic red-fig. vase-
  ptrs.; Richter, Attic red-fig. vases
Geneve Rixford Sargeant→see
 Sargeant, Geneve Rixford
Geneverino [Unidentified]
 (Unknown painter) PR
 Bibl: Colonna inventory, Rome,
  1763
**Genevois, Genovese or Lomellini,
 Manuel** *(Italian artist, op.1509-
 1557)* WC
Genga→see Genga, Girolamo
Genga, Bartolomeo *(Italian painter,
 architect, 1516-1558)* BA
 Bibl: ▶Portoghesi, Diz. arch. e
  urbanistica; ▶Thieme-Becker

Genga, Girolamo   **BA GC PR WC**
  (Italian artist, c.1476-1551)   WC
  (Italian painter, ca.1476-1551)   PR
  (Italian painter, sculptor, and
    architect, ca.1476-1551)   GC
  (Italian painter, sculptor,
    architect, ca.1476-1551)   BA
  Bibl: ▶Bolaffi; ▶Encyc. world art;
    ▶Fredericksen & Zeri, Census;
    ▶RILA/BHA, 1986;
    ▶Thieme-Becker
  G. Genga   PR
  Genga   PR
  Girolamo Genga   PR
Genga, Simone (Italian architect, ca.
  1530-ca.1595)   **BA**
  Bibl: ▶Portoghesi, Diz. arch. e
    urbanistica; ▶Thieme-Becker
Genge, Charles   **WC WI**
  (British artist, 20th cent.)   WC
  (British artist, op.1895-1929)   WI
Gengembre, Joseph Zephyris
  (French painter, 19th century)   **GC**
  Bibl: ▶Bénézit
Gengembre, Sophie, Miss→see
  Anderson, Sophie
Gengenbach, Joseph→see Canabas
Genheimer, Dieter (German
  architect)   **AV**
  Bibl: Deutsche Bauzeitung, 1986
    Aug., v.120, no.8, p.34
Genia (French artist, 20th cent.)   **WC**
Genicot, Robert (French artist,
  1890-)   **WC**
Genik, Christopher (American
  architect, Houston, TX)   **AV**
  Bibl: Progressive architecture,
    1985 Jan., v.66, no.1, p.118
Genillion, Jean Baptiste
  François   **GC WC**
  (French artist, 1750-1829)   WC
  (French painter, 1750-1829)   GC
  Bibl: ▶Bénézit
Genin→see Genin, Robert
Genin, Lucien (French artist, 1894-
  1958)   **WC**
Genin, Robert   **PR WC**
  (Russian artist, 1884-)   WC
  (Russian painter, 1884-aft.1916)   PR
  Bibl: ▶Thieme-Becker
  Genin   PR
  Robert Genin   PR
Geniol→see Géniole, Alfred André
Géniole→see Géniole, Alfred André
Géniole, Alfred André   **PR WC**
  (French artist, 1813-1861)   WC
  (French painter, 1813-1861)   PR
  Bibl: ▶Bénézit; ▶Thieme-Becker
  Alfred Andre Geniole   PR
  Geniol   PR
  Géniole   PR
Genis, Fred (Dutch printer, b.1934)   **BA**
  Bibl: Melbourne (AUS), National
    Gallery of Victoria, THE ARTIST
    AND THE PRINTER..., 1982
Genis, Renee (French artist, 1922-)   **WC**

Genisson→see Génisson, Jules Victor
Génisson, Jules Victor   **GC PR WC**
  (Belgian artist, 1805-1860)   WC
  (Belgian painter, 1805-1860)   GC PR
  Bibl: ▶Thieme-Becker
  Genisson   PR
  Genisson, Victor   PR
  Jules Victor Genisson   PR
Genisson, Victor→see Génisson, Jules
  Victor
Genkinger, Friez (German artist,
  1934-)   **WC**
Genn, Nancy Thompson (American
  artist, 20th c.)   **BA**
  Bibl: ART NEWS(OCT 1975); Los
    Angeles (CA, USA), LAICA, Nancy
    Glenn, John Okulick, et al. (1976)
Gennari→see Gennari, Benedetto II
Gennari→see Gennari, Cesare
Gennari the Elder, Benedetto→see
  Gennari, Benedetto (I)
Gennari the Younger, Benedetto→see
  Gennari, Benedetto II
Gennari, Benedetto (I)   **PR**
  (Italian artist, op.1585-m.1610)   WC
  (Italian painter, d. 1610)   PR
  (Italian, act.1585-d.1610)   GC
  Bibl: ▶Thieme-Becker; ▶Witt
    checklist
  Benedetto Gennari (I)   PR
  Benedetto Gennari Seniore   PR
  Gennari the Elder, Benedetto   **WC**
  Gennari, Benedetto I   **GC**
Gennari, Benedetto (II)→see Gennari,
  Benedetto II
Gennari, Benedetto (the
  Younger)→see Gennari, Benedetto
  II
Gennari, Benedetto I→see Gennari,
  Benedetto (I)
Gennari, Benedetto II   **BA GC**
  (Italian artist, 1633-1715)   WC
  (Italian painter, 1633-1715)   BA GC PR
  (Italian, Bolognese, 1633-1715)   JG
  Bibl: ▶Bolaffi; ▶RILA/BHA, 1986;
    ▶Thieme-Becker; ▶Witt checklist
  Benedetto Gennari (II)   PR
  Benedetto Gennari Juniore   PR
  Benedict Gennari   PR
  Beneditto Genaro   PR
  Genari   PR
  Genaro   PR
  Genere   PR
  Gennari   PR
  Gennari the Younger,
    Benedetto   **WC**
  Gennari, Benedetto (II)   **PR**
  Gennari, Benedetto (the Younger) PR
  Gennari, Benedettos   **JG**
  Gennaro   PR
  nipote del Guercino   PR
  uno dei decij nipote del Guercino PR
  uno delli due nipoti del Guercino PR
Gennari, Benedettos→see Gennari,
  Benedetto II

Gennari, Carlo   **BA WC**
  (Italian artist, 1712-1790)   WC
  (Italian lawyer, painter, 1712-
    1790)   BA
  Bibl: Bagni, IL GUERCINO E IL SUO
    FALSARIO (1985);
    ▶Thieme-Becker; ▶Witt checklist
Gennari, Cesare   **BA GC PR WC WI**
  (Italian artist, 1637-1688)   WC WI
  (Italian painter, 1637-1688)   BA PR
  (Italian, 1637-1688)   GC
  Bibl: ▶Bolaffi; Clerici Bagozzi
    PARAGONE 419-423, Jan-May '85
    p.243; ▶Thieme-Becker; ▶Witt
    checklist
  Cesare Gennari   PR
  Gennari   PR
  nipote del Guercino   PR
  uno dei decij nipote del Guercino PR
  uno delli due nipoti del Guercino PR
Gennari, Domenico (Italian artist,
  18th cent.)   **WC**
Gennari, Ercole (Italian painter,
  1597-1658)   **PR**
  Bibl: ▶Thieme-Becker, (The variant
    "Genero dl Guercino" may NOT
    refer to Ercole G., Guercino's
    brother-in-law [not son-in-law].)
  Ercole Gennari   PR
  Genero dl Guercino   PR
  Gennaro   PR
Gennari, Massimo   **AV**
Gennaro→see Gennari, Benedetto II
Gennaro→see Gennari, Ercole
Gennaro de Mura→see Mura,
  Gennaro de
Gennaro Greco→see Greco, Gennaro
Gennaro Landi→see Landi, Gennaro
Gennaro Muro→see Mura, Gennaro
  de
Gennaro, Antonio Maria de (Italian
  medalist, 1679-1744)   **BA**
  Bibl: ▶Forrer, Medallists;
    ▶Thieme-Becker
Gennay, Franciscus   **GC JG**
  (Italian scribe, act. early 15th
    century)   GC
  Bibl: ▶Euw, Ludwig mss., v.4, pp.
    305-313
Génod, Michel Philibert   **BA GC WC**
  (French artist, 1796-1862)   WC
  (French painter, 1795-1862)   GC
  (French painter, printmaker,
    1796-1862)   BA
  Bibl: ▶Bénézit; ▶Thieme-Becker
Genoels→see Genoels, Abraham
  (Archimedes)

**Genoels, Abraham
(Archimedes) **BA PR WC**
(Flemish artist, 1640-1723) WC
(Flemish painter, 1640-1723) PR
*(Flemish painter, printmaker,
1640-1723)* BA
(Flemish, 1640-1723) GC
Bibl: ▶Bénézit; HOLLSTEIN;
▶RILA/BHA; ▶Thieme-Becker
Abraham Genoels PR
Genoels PR
Genoels, Abraham II GC
Genouls PR
*Genoels, Abraham II→see Genoels,
Abraham (Archimedes)*
Genoese→see Strozzi, Bernardo
Genoir [Unidentified] *(Unknown
painter)* PR
Bibl: 1706 De Letter inventory
Genoud, Nanette *(Swiss artist,
1907-)* WC
*Genouls→see Genoels, Abraham
(Archimedes)*
Genoves, Juan *(Spanish artist,
1930-)* WC
Genovese→see Strozzi, Bernardo
Genovese, Federico *(Italian
architect, 1934-)* AV
Genovese, Gaetano *(Italian
architect, 1795-ca.1860)* BA
Bibl: ▶Portoghesi, Diz. arch. e
urbanistica; ▶Thieme-Becker
Genser→see Gessner, Johann Conrad
Gensler, Gunther *(German artist,
1803-1884)* WC
Gensler, Jacob→see Gensler, Jakob
Gensler, Jakob GC
(German artist, 1808-1845) WC
*(German draughtsman, 1808-
1845)* GC
Bibl: ▶Thieme-Becker
Gensler, Jacob WC
Gensler, M. Arthur *(American
architect)* AV
Bibl: ▶AIA Pro File, 1985
Gensler, Martin *(German artist,
1811-1881)* WC
Gent, G.W. *(British artist, op.1804-
1822)* WC WI
*Gent, Joos van→see Joos van Gent
(Joos van Wassenhove)*
Genter, Heinrich *(German artist,
1854-)* WC
Genth→see Genth, Lillian
Genth, Lillian *(American painter,
1876-1953)* PR
Bibl: Detroit Inst of Arts
catalogue; ▶WWW Amer. art
Genth PR
Genth, Lillian Matilda PR
Lillian Genth PR
*Genth, Lillian Matilda→see Genth,
Lillian*

Genthe, Arnold **BA JG**
*(American (b. Germany), 1869-
1942)* JG
*(American photographer, 1869-
1942)* BA
Bibl: ▶Gernsheim, Hist. photog.,
(1868-1942); ▶MoMA libr. cat.;
▶Newhall, Photog.
Gentil, François *(French gardener,
author, act.1704)* BA
Bibl: ▶Larousse grande encyc.;
▶Natl. union cat., pre-1956;
▶Nouv. biog. gén.
*Gentile→see Gentile, Luigi (Louis
Cousin)*
Gentile Bellini→see Bellini, Gentile
*Gentile Bellini Pittore Antico
Veneziano→see Bellini, Gentile*
*Gentile da Fabriano→see Gentile da
Fabriano (Gentile di Niccolò di
Giovanni Massi)*
**Gentile da Fabriano (Gentile di
Niccolò di Giovanni Massi)** **BA PR**
(Italian artist, 1360/70-1427) WC
*(Italian painter, ca.1370-
1427)* BA GC PR
(Italian, ca. 1370-1427) JG
Bibl: ▶Bolaffi; ▶Fredericksen &
Zeri, Census; ▶RILA/BHA;
▶Thieme-Becker; ▶Witt checklist
Fabriano, Gentile da GC
Gentile da Fabriano GC JG PR
**Gentile da Fabriano (Gentile di
Niccolò di Giovanni Mossi)** GC
Gentile di Niccolo di Giovanni
Massi GC
**Gentile di Niccolo di Giovanni
Massi (Gentile da Fabriano or
Gentilino)** WC
Gentile di Noccolo di Giovanni
Massi PR
*Gentile da Fabriano (Gentile di
Niccolò di Giovanni Mossi)→see
Gentile da Fabriano (Gentile di
Niccolò di Giovanni Massi)*
*Gentile da Fabriano, Francesco
di→see Francesco di Gentile da
Fabriano*
Gentile da Sulmona *(Italian artist,
13th cent.)* WC
*Gentile di Niccolo di Giovanni
Massi→see Gentile da Fabriano
(Gentile di Niccolò di Giovanni
Massi)*
*Gentile di Niccolo di Giovanni Massi
(Gentile da Fabriano or
Gentilino)→see Gentile da
Fabriano (Gentile di Niccolò di
Giovanni Massi)*
*Gentile di Noccolo di Giovanni
Massi→see Gentile da Fabriano
(Gentile di Niccolò di Giovanni
Massi)*

Gentile, Charles *(Canadian painter,
1835-1893)* BA
Bibl: Mattisin, Hist. of Photog.
XL/4 (Oct-Dec 1987), 261-263
*Gentile, Luigi→see Gentile, Luigi
(Louis Cousin)*
*Gentile, Luigi (Louis Cousin or Luigi
Primo; Gentiel)→see Gentile, Luigi
(Louis Cousin)*
Gentile, Luigi (Louis Cousin) **BA PR**
(Flemish artist, 1606-1667) WC
*(Flemish painter,
1604/06-1667)* BA PR
(Flemish painter, 1606-1667) GC
Bibl: ▶Bénézit; Getty Photo Study
Coll.; ▶Thieme-Becker;
WURLBACHH
Cousin, Louis GC
Gentile PR
Gentile, Luigi GC
**Gentile, Luigi (Louis Cousin or
Luigi Primo; Gentiel)** WC
Luigi Gentile PR
Primo, Luigi GC
Gentile, Michele, the elder *(Italian,
d.1595)* BA
Bibl: Testini, NAPOLI
NOBILISSIMA, XXV/3-4(MAY-AUG
1986)p.101-106
*Gentileschi→see Gentileschi,
Artemisia*
Gentileschi→see Gentileschi, Orazio
Gentileschi, Artemisia **BA GC PR**
(Italian artist, 1597-p.1651) WC
(Italian painter, 1593-aft.1651) GC
*(Italian painter, 1593-after
1651)* BA
(Italian painter, 1597-aft.1651) PR
Bibl: ▶Bolaffi; ▶Encyc. world art;
▶RILA/BHA, 1986;
▶Thieme-Becker
Artemesia Gentileschi PR
Artemiggia PR
Artemiscia Gentoleschi PR
Artemiscia PR
Artemisia Gentilesca PR
Artemisia Gentileschi PR
Artemitia Gentilesca PR
Artemizia Gentilesca PR
Artimisia PR
Gentileschi PR
**Gentileschi, Artemisia Lami
(Schiattesi?)** WC
Lomi, Artemisia BA
*Gentileschi, Artemisia Lami
(Schiattesi?)→see Gentileschi,
Artemisia*
Gentileschi, Francesco *(Italian
artist, 1599-p.1665)* WC

Gentileschi, Orazio   **BA GC JG PR WI**
   (Italian artist, 1562-1647)   WC WI
   (Italian painter, 1563-1639)   BA GC PR
   (Italian, Roman, 1563-1639)   JG
   Bibl: ▶Bolaffi; ▶Encyc. world art;
     ▶RILA/BHA, 1986;
     ▶Thieme-Becker
   Gentileschi   PR
Gentileschi, Orazio Lami   **WC**
   Geutileschi   PR
   Horace Gentileschi   PR
   Oratio Gentileschi   PR
   Orazio Gentileschi   PR
Gentileschi, Orazio Lami → see
   Gentileschi, Orazio
Gentili family *(Italian ceramists,*
   17th-19th cs.)   **BA**
   Bibl: ▶Honey, Euro. ceramic;
     ▶Thieme-Becker
Gentili or Gentile, Antonio (Antonio
   da Faenza) → see Gentili, Antonio
   (Antonio da Faenza)
Gentili Tedeschi, Eugenio *(Italian*
   architect, Milan)   **AV**
   Bibl: Architettura, cronache e
     storia, 1989 Jan., v.35, no.1(399),
     p.6
   Tedeschi, Eugenio Gentili   AV
Gentili, Antonio (Antonio da
   Faenza)   **BA**
   (Italian artist, c.1519-1609)   WC
   (Italian goldsmith, 1519-1609)   BA
   Bibl: ▶Bulgari, Argentieri d'Italia,
     v.1, p.509; ▶Thieme-Becker
Gentili or Gentile, Antonio
   (Antonio da Faenza)   **WC**
Gentili, Giorgio *(Italian architect,*
   Milan)   **AV**
   Bibl: Ottagono, 1987 Mar.,v.22,
     no.84, p.98
Gentili, L. *(Italian architect)*   **AV**
   Bibl: Lotus international, 1983,
     no.39, p.78
Gentili, Pietro *(Italian goldsmith,*
   1563-1626)   **BA**
   Bibl: ▶Bulgari, Argentieri d'Italia,
     v.1, p.510; Storia arte, 48 (May-
     Aug. 1983) pp.117-125
Gentili, Tommaso [Unidentified]
   (Unknown painter, act. 18th
   century)   **PR**
   Bibl: Riccardi inventory dated
     1776
   Tommaso Gentili   PR
Gentilini, Franco   **AV BA WC**
   (Italian archtiect(?), Rome, fl.
   1930's)   AV
   (Italian artist, 1909-)   WC
   (Italian painter, 1909-1981)   BA
   Bibl: Parametro, 1988 July-Aug.,
     v.19, no.167, p.80
Gentillâtre, Jacques *(French*
   architect, 1578-after 1610)
     BA
   Bibl: London, RIBA, Library.
     CATALOGUE OF DRAWINGS, v.6,
     p.11; Pays Lorrain LIX/2 (1978),
     65-955

Gentille, Thomas *(American jeweler,*
   b.1936)   **BA**
   Bibl: ▶Intl. dir. exh. artists, 1983;
     Lisbon (PRT), Fund. Gulbenkian,
     Thomas Gentille, 1983
Gentils, Vic → see Gentils, Victor A.
Gentils, Victor A.   **BA**
   (Belgian sculptor, b.1919)   BA
   (British artist, b.1919)   WI
   Bibl: ▶Phaidon 20c. art
Gentils, Vic   **WI**
Gentilucci, Sergio *(Italian architect)*   **AV**
   Bibl: L'Arca, 1989 July-Aug.,
     no.29, p.75
Gentimer Fiammingo, Monsù
   [Unidentified] *(Unknown painter)*   **PR**
   Bibl: Colonna inventory, Rome,
     1714
   Monsù Gentimer Fiammengo   PR
Gentleman, David   **BA WC WI**
   (British artist, 1930-)   WC
   (British artist, b.1930)   WI
   (British painter, printmaker,
   b.1930)   BA
   Bibl: ▶Babington Smith, Contemp.
     artists; ▶Intl. dir. exh. artists,
     1983
Gentner, Alois *(German musical*
   instrument maker, 1825-1900)   **BA**
   Bibl: Layer, Jahrb. Hist. Vereins
     Dillingen, LXXXVI (1984), p.172
Gentot, Blaise *(French metal*
   engraver, b.1658, act.1700)   **BA**
   Bibl: ▶Bénézit; ▶Thieme-Becker
Gentry, Herbert *(Swedish artist, op.*
   1959-1961)   **WC**
Genty, Denis *(French ébéniste,*
   master 1754, d. 1770)   **GC**
   Bibl: ▶Salverte, Ébénistes 18e s.
Gentz → see Gentz, Wilhelm
Gentz, Heinrich   **AV BA WC**
   (1766-1811)   AV
   (German architect, 1766-1811)   BA
   (German artist, 1766-1811)   WC
   Bibl: Klingenburg, K.-H., in
     BILDENDE KUNST 5 (1983) 229;
     ▶Macmillan encyc. archts.
Gentz, Ismael (Wolfgang
   Christian) *(German artist, 1862-*
   1914)   **WC**
Gentz, Wilhelm   **GC PR**
   (German artist, 1822-1890)   WC
   (German painter, 1822-1890)   PR
   (German, 1822-1890)   GC
   Bibl: ▶Thieme-Becker; ▶Witt
     checklist
   Gentz   PR
Gentz, Wilhelm Carl   **WC**
   Gentz, Wilhelm Karl   PR
   Wilhelm Gentz   PR
Gentz, Wilhelm Carl → see Gentz,
   Wilhelm
Gentz, Wilhelm Karl → see Gentz,
   Wilhelm
Genu, Marie-Joseph-Gabriel
   (French silversmith, master 1788)   **GC**
   Bibl: ▶Nocq, Poinçon de Paris

Genucchi, Giovanni *(Italian*
   sculptor, 1904-1979)   **BA**
   Bibl: Castiglioni, GIOVANNI
     GENUCCHI:BELLINZONA,
     1984:bANCE DELLA STATA DEL
     CANTONS, 1904-1979;
     ▶Künst.-Lex. Schweiz 20. Jahrh.
Genucilia Group *(Etruscan vase-*
   painters, 330-290 BC)   **GC**
   Bibl: Beazley, Etruscan vase-ptrs.;
     Del Chiaro, Caere
Genuino, Vespasiano *(Italian*
   sculptor, 1552-ca.1637)   **BA**
   Bibl: TCI Puglia; ▶Thieme-Becker;
     Vaccari, ITMERARI:CONTRIBUTI
     ALLA STORICA DELL'ARTE...,I, 99-
     103
Genuys, Charles Louis *(French*
   architect, painter, craftsman,
   b.1852)   **BA**
   Bibl: ▶Bénézit; ▶Thieme-Becker
Genzken, Isa *(German sculptor,*
   photographer, b.1948)   **BA**
   Bibl: Krefeld (DEU), Mus. Haus
     Lange, Isa Genzken (1979)
Genzmer → see Genzmer, Berthold
Genzmer, Berthold   **PR WC**
   (German artist, 1858-1927)   WC
   (German painter, 1858-aft.1899)   PR
   Bibl: ▶Thieme-Becker
   Berthold Genzmer   PR
   Genzmer   PR
Geo. Dom. Porta → see Porta,
   Giovanni Domenico
Geo. Morland → see Morland, George
Geoffrey, Eqbal M.J.I. → see Geoffrey,
   Iqbal M.J.I.
Geoffrey, Iqbal M.J.I.   **WI**
   (British artist, 1939-)   WC
   (British artist, b.1939)   WI
Geoffrey, Eqbal M.J.I.   **WC**
Geoffroi, Harry *(British artist, op.*
   1884-1892)   **WI**
Geoffroy de Meaux *(French,*
   flourished ca. 1310)   **JG**
Geoffroy, Henry Jules Jean   **GC**
   (French artist, 1853-1924)   WC
   (French painter, 1853-1924)   GC
   Bibl: ▶Bénézit
Geoffroy, Jean Jules Henri   **WC**
Geoffroy, Jean Jules Henri → see
   Geoffroy, Henry Jules Jean
Geoffroy-Dechaume, Adolphe
   Victor *(French sculptor,*
   goldsmith, 1816-1892)   **BA**
   Bibl: ▶Bénézit; ▶Lami, Sculp. fran.
     18e s.; Paris (FRA), Grand Palais,
     Viollet-le-Duc (1980), 406;
     ▶Thieme-Becker
Georg Anton Rasmussen → see
   Rasmussen, Georg Anton
Georg Cristoph Grooth → see Grooth,
   Georg Cristoph
Georg Decker → see Decker, Georg
Georg Flegel → see Flegel, Georg
Georg Friedrich Adolph Schoner → see
   Schoner, Georg Friedrich Adolph

Georg Hoefnagel→see Hoefnagel, Joris

Georg Jacob Johann Os→see Os, Georg Jakob Johann

Georg Muche→see Muche, Georg

Georg Oeder→see Oeder, Georg

Georg or George, Johann Wilhelm or Jean Guillaume→see Georg, Johann Wilhelm

Georg Pencz→see Pencz, Georg

Georg Philipp Rugendas (I)→see Rugendas, Georg Philipp (I)

Georg Tappert→see Tappert, Georg

Georg von Hoesslin→see Hoesslin, Georg von

Georg Weikert→see Weikert, Georg

Georg, Johann Wilhelm **WI**
   (British artist, 1728-1791) **WC WI**
   Georg or George, Johann Wilhelm or Jean Guillaume **WC**

Georg, Victor *(American, active Chicago, IL, U.S. ca. 1915)* **JG**

Georgalides, Stephane P (Le Grec)
   (Greek artist, 20th cent.) **WC**

George A. Boyle→see Boyle, George A.

George A. Grainger→see Grainger, George A.

George Albert Thompson→see Thompson, George Albert

George Alexander Picken→see Picken, George Alexander

George Armfield→see Armfield, George, (Smith)

George Arnald→see Arnald, George

George Augustus Wallis→see Wallis, George Augustus

George Barret (I)→see Barret, George I

George Barret (II)→see Barret, George II

George Beare→see Beare, George

George Benjamin Luks→see Luks, George Benjamin

George Bernard Butler→see Butler, George Bernard

George Biddle→see Biddle, George

George Caleb Bingham→see Bingham, George Caleb

George Carter→see Carter, George

George Catlin→see Catlin, George

George Chambers (I)→see Chambers, George I

George Chinnery→see Chinnery, George

George Clausen→see Clausen, George

George Cochran Lambdin→see Lambdin, George Cochran

George Constant→see Constant, George

George Copeland Ault→see Ault, George Copeland

George Cuitt (the elder)→see Cuitt, George I

George Cuitt (the younger)→see Cuitt, George II

George Curtin Stanson→see Stanson, George Curtin

George de Forest Brush→see Brush, George de Forest

George de Marees→see Marees, George de

George Elgar Hicks→see Hicks, George Elgar

George F. Carline→see Carline, George F.

George Francis Joseph→see Joseph, George Francis

George Frederic Watts→see Watts, George Frederick

George Fuller→see Fuller, George

George Garrard→see Garrard, George

George Glen Newell→see Newell, George Glen

George Goodwin Kilburne→see Kilburne, George Goodwin

George Gower→see Gower, George

George Grosz→see Grosz, George

George Hayter→see Hayter, George

George Heming Mason→see Mason, George Heming

George Hendrik Breitner→see Breitner, George Hendrik

George Henry Boughton→see Boughton, George Henry

George Henry Durrie→see Durrie, George Henry

George Henry Harlow→see Harlow, George Henry

George Henry Melcher→see Melcher, George Henry

George Hirst Bogert→see Bogert, George Hirst

George Howland Beaumont→see Beaumont, George Howland

George Huddesford→see Huddesford, George

George III **WI**
   (British artist, 1738-1820) **WC WI**
   George III, King **WC**

George III, King→see George III

George Inness→see Inness, George

George J. Robertson→see Robertson, George J.

George James→see James, George, (GBR.)

George James Howard→see Carlisle, George James Howard, earl of

George James Howard, Earl of Carlisle→see Carlisle, George James Howard, earl of

George Jamesone→see Jamesone, George

George Jones→see Jones, George

George Kars→see Kars, George

George Keith Ralph→see Ralph, George Keith

George Knapton→see Knapton, George

George L. Clough→see Clough, George L.

George Lambert→see Lambert, George

George Lance→see Lance, George

George Loring Brown→see Brown, George Loring

George Lothian Hall→see Hall, George Lothian

George Louis Roose→see Roose, George Louis

George M. Hathaway→see Hathaway, George M.

George Mayer-Marton→see Marten, George Mayer

George Morland→see Morland, George

George Mullins→see Mullins, George

George Oberteuffer→see Oberteuffer, George

George Overbury Hart→see Hart, George Overbury

George Percy Jacomb-Hood→see Jacomb-Hood, George Percy

George Peter Alexander Healey→see Healy, George Peter Alexander

George Petrie→see Petrie, George

George Richmond→see Richmond, George

George Robertson→see Robertson, George

George Romney→see Romney, George

George Ropes→see Ropes, George

George Roth→see Roth, George II

George Sayer→see Sayer, George

George Simon Harcourt→see Harcourt, George Simon, 2nd Earl

George Simon, Earl Harcourt→see Harcourt, George Simon, 2nd Earl

George Smith (of Chichester)→see Smith, George

George Southward→see Southward, George

George Stubbs→see Stubbs, George

George Townley Stubbs→see Stubbs, George Townley

George Turner→see Turner, George I

George Vicat Cole→see Cole, George Vicat

George Vincent→see Vincent, George

George W. Horlor→see Horlor, George W.

George W. White→see White, George W.

George Washington Tyler→see Tyler, George Washington

George Watson→see Watson, George

George Watson James, Jr.→see James, George Watson, Jr.

George Webster → see Webster, George

George Wesley Bellows → see Bellows, George Wesley

George William Dinckel → see Dinckel, George William

George Willison → see Willison, George

George, Adrian WC WI
(*British artist, 20th cent.*) WC
(*British artist, op.1973-1986*) WI

George, Dan (*20th c.*) BA
Bibl: George, LEONARDO, XIX/2(1986), 117-121

George, Eric WC WI
(*British artist, 1881-*) WC
(*British artist, b.1881*) WI

George, Ernest BA WI
(*British architect, 1839-1922*) AV BA
(*British artist, 1839-1922*) WC WI
Bibl: ▶Bénézit; ▶Thieme-Becker; ▶Who was who [GBR], 1916-28; ▶Wodehouse, Brit. archts.

George, Ernest, Sir AV
George, Sir Ernest WC

George, Ernest, Sir → see George, Ernest

George, Esther, Miss → see Johnson, Ernest & Esther Borough

George, Herbert (*American sculptor, b.1940*) BA
Bibl: ▶MoMA libr. cat.; ▶NY art yrbk.

George, J. (*British artist, op.1821-1838*) WC WI

George, Jean Philippe GC WC
(*French artist, 1818-1888*) WC
(*French painter, 1818-1888*) GC
Bibl: ▶Witt checklist

George, John (*British artist, op. 1763-1771*) WC WI

George, Patrick BA WC WI
(*British artist, 1923-*) WC
(*British artist, b.1923*) WI
(*British painter, b.1923*) BA
Bibl: Serpentine Gallery, London, PATRICK GEORGE. 1980

George, Philip (*American interior designer, NYC*) AV
Bibl: NYC phone bk., 1986-87

George, Sir Ernest → see George, Ernest

George, T. → see George, T. I

George, T. I WI
(*British artist, op.1819-1838*) WC WI
Bibl: Rees

George, T. WC

George, T. II (*British artist, op.20th c.*) WI

George, Thomas BA WC WI
(*American artist, 1918-*) WC
(*American artist, b.1918*) WI
(*American painter, printmaker, b.1918*) BA
Bibl: ▶MoMA libr. cat.; ▶NY art yrbk.; ▶WW Amer. Art, 1976

George, W. Herbert (*fl.1927; Architect, Ottawa*) FA
Bibl: CAAD Finding Aid, J. Albert Ewart 77803/14; ▶Hill, Archts. Canada, 1986; Ottawa City Directories

George, W.Pettit (*British artist, op. 1847-1854*) WI

George, William (*American artist, b.1926*) WI

Georgelas, Thomas G. (*American architect, McLean, VA*) AV
Bibl: ▶AIA Pro File, 1983

Georgeon → see Giorgione (Giorgio da Castelfranco)

Georgeonia → see Giorgione (Giorgio da Castelfranco)

Georges (*French, (dates unknown, active second half of the 18th century)*) JG

Georges (*French artist, op.1798*) WC

Georges Braque → see Braque, Georges

Georges d'Espagnat → see Espagnat, Georges d'

Georges du Mesnil de La Tour → see La Tour, Georges de

Georges Dufrenoy → see Dufrenoy, Georges Léon

Georges E. Ferre → see Ferré, Georges E.

Georges Emile Capon → see Capon, Georges Emile

Georges Giorgion → see Giorgione (Giorgio da Castelfranco)

Georges Jean Marie Haquette → see Haquette, Georges Jean Marie

Georges Jeannin → see Jeannin, Georges

Georges Jeanniot → see Jeanniot, Georges

Georges Lacombe → see Lacombe, Georges

Georges Lemmen → see Lemmen, Georges

Georges Michel → see Michel, Georges

Georges Papazoff → see Papazoff, Georges

Georges Pierre Seurat → see Seurat, Georges Pierre

Georges Ribemont-Dessaignes → see Ribemont-Dessaignes, Georges

Georges Rouault → see Rouault, Georges

Georges Rouget → see Rouget, Georges

Georges Vasari → see Vasari, Giorgio

Georges, Claude BA WC
(*French artist, 1929-*) WC
(*French painter, b.1929*) BA
Bibl: ▶Bénézit; ▶Vollmer, Künst.-Lex. 20. Jhr.

Georges, Emile (Geo-Weiss) → see Weiss, Emile Georges

Georges, Paul BA WC WI
(*American artist, 20th cent.*) WC
(*American artist, b.1923*) WI
(*American painter, b.1923*) BA
Bibl: ▶Havlice, Idx. art. bio.; ▶WW Amer. Art, 1976

Georgesco, Christopher (*American sculptor, b.1950*) BA
Bibl: ART NEWS, 76(MAY 1977), 106; La Jolla (CA, USA), Mus. of Contemp. Art, Four Californians (1977)

Georgescu, Ion (*Romanian sculptor, 1857-1899*) BA
Bibl: ▶Bénézit; ▶Encyc. world art; ▶Thieme-Becker

Georgescu, Sergiu (*Rumanian artist, 20th cent.*) WC

Georgi, Friedrich Traugott (*German artist, 1783-1838*) WC

Georgi, Giovanni BA WC
(*Italian artist, op.1617-1656*) WC
(*Italian printmaker, act.1617-1663*) BA
Bibl: ▶Bolaffi; ▶Thieme-Becker; ▶Witt checklist

Georgi, Otto (Friedrich Otto) (*German artist, 1819-1874*) WC

Georgi, Walter (*German artist, 1871-1924*) WC

Georgia O'Keeffe → see O'Keeffe, Georgia

Georgia Timken Fry → see Fry, Georgia Timken

Georgiadis, Nicholas BA WC WI
(*British artist, 1925-*) WC
(*British artist, b.1925*) WI
(*Greek designer in GBR, 20th c.*) BA
Bibl: Arts Council GBR, Welsh Comm., Nicholas Georgiadis: Designs for Theatre

Georgidis, N. (*Greek architect*) AV
Bibl: Architektonika themata — Architecture in Greece, 1988, v.22, p.166

Georgii, Nils (*Swedish medalist, 1717-1790*) BA
Bibl: ▶Svenskt konst.-lex.; ▶Thieme-Becker

Georgini → see Giorgione (Giorgio da Castelfranco)

Georgione → see Giorgione (Giorgio da Castelfranco)

Georgioni → see Giorgione (Giorgio da Castelfranco)

Georgios or Georgius (*Greek artist, op.1454*) WC

Georgius (*Polish artist, op.1517*) WC

Georgone → see Giorgione (Giorgio da Castelfranco)

Georgoni → see Giorgione (Giorgio da Castelfranco)

Georgsen, Georg (*Danish landscape architect, 1893-1976*) AV
Bibl: Landskab, 1984 Sept., v.65, no.6, p.127; Landskab, 1987 Nov., v.68, no.7, p.135

Geppert, Eugeniusz Stanisław
(Polish painter, b.1890) **BA**
    Bibl: ▶Vollmer, Künst.-Lex. 20. Jhr.
Ger. de la Notte → *see* Honthorst,
    Gerrit van
Ger. Del Notti → *see* Honthorst, Gerrit
    van
Ger. Douw → *see* Dou, Gerrit
Ger. Dow → *see* Dou, Gerrit
Ger. Laeresse → *see* Lairesse, Gerard
    de
Ger. Lairesse → *see* Lairesse, Gerard
    de
Ger.mo Colomes → *see* Colomes,
    Jerome
Ger: Lairesse → *see* Lairesse, Gerard
    de
Gera → *see* Jacopo di Michele, Il Gera
Gera, Jacopo di Michele, Il → *see*
    Jacopo di Michele, Il Gera
Geraardts → *see* Zyl, Gerard Pietersz.
    van
Geraci, Paolo *(Italian painter, 17th*
c.) **BA**
    Bibl: Spadaro, ULTIMO
    CARAVAGGIO E LA CULTURA ...
    (1987) 289-292
Geraedts, Wijnandus Aloisius
(Wijnand) *(Dutch artist, 1883-*
1958) **WC**
Gerald Festus Kelly → *see* Kelly, Gerald
    Festus
Gerald Leake → *see* Leake, Gerald
Gerald Leslie Brockhurst → *see*
    Brockhurst, Gerald Leslie
Gerald Murphy → *see* Murphy, Gerald
Gerard → *see* Gérard, François Pascal
    Simon, baron
Gerard → *see* Gérard, Marguerite
Gerard → *see* Zyl, Gerard Pietersz. van
Gerard (Mad.) → *see* Gérard,
    Marguerite
Gerard Berkheyden → *see* Berckheyde,
    Gerrit Adriaensz.
Gerard Chowne → *see* Chowne,
    Gerard
Gerard d'Orleans *(French artist, op.*
c.1359) **WC**
Gerard David → *see* David, Gerard
Gerard de la Notte → *see* Honthorst,
    Gerrit van
Gerard de Lairesse → *see* Lairesse,
    Gerard de
Gerard de Larisse → *see* Lairesse,
    Gerard de
Gerard de Lauresse → *see* Lairesse,
    Gerard de
Gerard Dou → *see* Dou, Gerrit
Gerard Douw → *see* Dou, Gerrit
Gerard Dow → *see* Dou, Gerrit
Gerard Edima → *see* Edema, Gerard
    Van
Gerard Ernest Albert Schneider → *see*
    Schneider, Gérard Ernest Albert
Gerard Hoet → *see* Hoet, Gerard I

Gerard Hoet (I) → *see* Hoet, Gerard I
Gerard Honthorst → *see* Honthorst,
    Gerrit van
Gerard Honthurst → *see* Honthorst,
    Gerrit van
Gerard Hontorst → *see* Honthorst,
    Gerrit van
Gerard Houckgeest → *see* Houckgeest,
    Gerard
Gerard Huet → *see* Hoet, Gerard I
Gerard Lairesse → *see* Lairesse, Gerard
    de
Gerard Lanscroon → *see* Lanscroon,
    Gerard
Gerard Laresse → *see* Lairesse, Gerard
    de
Gerard Lundens → *see* Lundens, Gerrit
Gerard M. Barry → *see* Barry, Gerard
    M.
Gerard Melder → *see* Melder, Gerard
Gerard Peeters → *see* Peeters, Gerard
Gerard Peters → *see* Peeters, Gerard
Gerard Pietersz. van Zyl → *see* Zyl,
    Gerard Pietersz. van
Gerard Sanders → *see* Sanders, Gerard
Gerard Schoof (the Elder) → *see*
    Schoof, Gerard (the elder)
Gerard Seghers → *see* Seghers, Gerard
Gerard Seyers → *see* Seghers, Gerard
Gerard Soest → *see* Soest, Gerard
Gerard Stijls → *see* Stijls, Gerard
    [Unidentified]
Gerard ter Burg → *see* Terborch,
    Gerard II
Gerard Terberg → *see* Terborch,
    Gerard II
Gerard Terborch (II) → *see* Terborch,
    Gerard II
Gérard Terburg → *see* Terborch,
    Gerard II
Gerard Terburgh → *see* Terborch,
    Gerard II
Gerard [Unidentified] *(Unknown*
painter) **PR**
    Bibl: (July 18, 1814, lot 187,
    Owston)
Gerard van der Puyl → *see* Puyl,
    Gerard van der
Gerard Van Edema → *see* Edema,
    Gerard Van
Gerard van Haarlem → *see* Geertgen
    tot Sint Jans
Gerard van Kuijl → *see* Kuijl, Gerard
    van
Gerard van Spaendonck → *see*
    Spaendonck, Gerard van
Gerard van Zijl → *see* Zyl, Gerard
    Pietersz. van
Gerard Wigmana → *see* Wigmana,
    Gerard
Gerard, Baron → *see* Gérard, François
    Pascal Simon, baron
Gerard, Baron Francis → *see* Gérard,
    François Pascal Simon, baron

Gérard, Claude Charles **GC WC**
(French artist, 1757-1826) **WC**
(French porcelain painter, act.
1771-1825) **GC**
    Bibl: ▶Brunet, Sèvres
Gerard, E. → *see* Gerard, Ebenezer
Gerard, Ebenezer **WI**
(British artist, circa 1790-1826) **WI**
(British artist, op.1815) **WC**
  Gerard, E. **WC**
Gerard, Francis, Baron → *see* Gérard,
    François Pascal Simon, baron
Gerard, Francois → *see* Gérard,
    François Pascal Simon, baron
Gérard, François Pascal Simon,
baron **BA PR WC**
(French artist, 1770-1837) **WC**
(French painter, 1770-1837) **BA PR**
(French, 1770-1837) **GC**
    Bibl: ▶Encyc. world art; George
    Goldner; ▶RILA/BHA;
    ▶Thieme-Becker
  Baron Francois Pascal Simon
    Gerard **PR**
  Gerard **PR**
  Gerard, Baron **PR**
  Gerard, Baron Francis **PR**
  Gerard, Francis, Baron **PR**
  Gerard, Francois **GC PR**
  Gerard, Francois, Baron **PR**
Gerard, Francois, Baron → *see* Gérard,
    François Pascal Simon, baron
Gerard, Gaston (Louis Gaston)
(French artist, 1859-) **WC**
Gerard, Ippolito *(French, act.1808)* **BA**
    Bibl: Bershad, Antologia di B-A
    II/6 (May 1978) 162-167
Gerard, Jean Ignace Isidore → *see*
    Grandville (Jean Ignace Isidore
    Gérard)
Gerard, Jean Ignace Isidore
    ('Grandville') → *see* Grandville (Jean
    Ignace Isidore Gérard)
Gerard, John *(British artist, 1545-*
1612) **WC**
Gerard, Joseph *(Belgian artist, 1821-*
1895) **WC**
Gérard, Judith *(French painter,*
b.1881) **BA**
    Bibl: Danielsson, GAUGUIN IN THE
    SOUTH SEAS, 149; Jirat-
    Wasintynski, VINCENT VAN
    GOGH'S SELF PORTRAIT...,17, 18,
    21; Monneret, Impressionisme,
    v.1, p.240
Gerard, Lucien *(French artist, 19th*
cent.) **WC**
Gerard, Marcus (the Elder) → *see*
    Geeraerts, Marcus, the elder
Gerard, Marcus I → *see* Geeraerts,
    Marcus, the elder
Gerard, Marcus II → *see* Geeraerts,
    Marcus, the younger

Gérard, Marguerite   **BA GC PR WC**
    (French artist, 1761-1837)   WC
    (French painter, 1761-1837)   BA PR
    (French, 1761-1837)   GC
    Bibl: ▶Bénézit; ▶Nagler, Neues
    Künst.-Lex.; ▶RILA/BHA;
    ▶Thieme-Becker
    Gerard   PR
    Gerard (Mad.)   PR
    Gerards   PR
    Gerardt   PR
    Mad. Gerard   PR
    Mad.elle Gérard   PR
    Marguerite Gerard   PR
Gerard, Marie Anne → see Fragonard,
    Mme. Marie-Anne
Gérard, Michel *(French painter,*
    printmaker, sculptor, b.1938)   **BA**
    Bibl: ART MAGAZINE,
    LVI/10(JUNE 1982), 20; Dadoun,
    ART PRESS, 146 (Apr 1990),
    44-46; Guide exh. artists: Sculp.
Gerard, Theodore   **GC WC**
    (Belgian artist, 1829-1895)   WC
    (Belgian, 1829-1895)   GC
    Bibl: ▶Witt checklist
Gerardi → see Gerardi, Jasper
Gerardi, Geerardi or Geeraerts,
    Jasper → see Gerardi, Jasper
Gerardi, Jasper   **BA GC PR**
    (Dutch painter, act.1634, d.
    before 1654)   BA
    (Flemish artist, op.1634-m.a.
    1655)   WC
    (Flemish painter, act. 1634/35,
    d. 1654)   PR
    (Flemish, act.1634-d.bef 1655)   GC
    Bibl: Getty Photo Study Coll.
    (Ptgs.); ▶Thieme-Becker; ▶Witt
    checklist; ▶Wurzbach, NLD
    Künst.-Lex.
    Geeraerts, Jasper   GC
    Gerardi   PR
Gerardi, Geerardi or Geeraerts,
    Jasper   **WC**
    Gerardi, Jasper (Geeraerts)   PR
    Jasper Gerardi   PR
Gerardi, Jasper (Geeraerts) → see
    Gerardi, Jasper
Gerardin, Auguste *(French, b.1849)*   GC
    Bibl: ▶Thieme-Becker
Gerardin, Desire Delplace *(French*
    artist, 20th cent.)   WC
Gérardin, René → see Girardin, René
    Louis, marquis de
Gerardo delle notti → see Honthorst,
    Gerrit van
Gerardo fiamengo → see Honthorst,
    Gerrit van
Gérardo Lairets → see Lairesse, Gerard
    de
Gerards → see Geeraerts, Marcus, the
    younger
Gerards → see Gérard, Marguerite
Gerards → see Zyl, Gerard Pietersz.
    van

Gerards [Unidentified] *(Unknown*
    painter)   **PR**
    Bibl: (1802 Edinburgh sale, lot 60)
Gerards, Marcus (the Elder) → see
    Geeraerts, Marcus, the elder
Gerardt → see Gérard, Marguerite
Geras Painter   **GC JG**
    (vase-painter, ca. 500-475 BC)   GC
    Bibl: ▶Beazley, Attic red-fig. vase-
    ptrs.; Richter, Attic red-fig. vases
Gerasch, August *(German artist,*
    1892-)   **WC**
Gerasimov, A. *(Russian artist,*
    1885-)   **WC**
Gerasimov, Aleksandr Mikhailovič
    (Russian painter, 1881-1963)   **BA**
    Bibl: ▶Brockhaus Enzyk.; ▶Natl.
    union cat., pre-1956; ▶WWW
    USSR
Gerasimov, Sergei Vasilyevich → see
    Gerasimov, Sergej Vasil'evič
Gerasimov, Sergej Vasil'evič   **BA**
    (Russian artist, 1885-)   WC
    (Russian painter, b.1885)   BA
    Bibl: ▶Bénézit; ▶Fogg Mus. Libr.
    cat.; ▶Vollmer, Künst.-Lex. 20. Jhr.
    Gerasimov, Sergei Vasilyevich   **WC**
    Guerassimov, Sergei Vasilevich   BA
Gerbarg, Darcy *(American painter,*
    printmaker, b.1949)   **BA**
    Bibl: Syracuse (NY, USA), Everson
    Mus., New works in clay (1981)
Gerbaud, Abel *(French artist, 1888-)*   **WC**
Gerbault, Henry *(French artist,*
    1863-)   **WC**
Gerbel, Anton *(German artist, op.*
    1480-1510)   **WC**
Gerber, Alan *(American architect)*   **AV**
Gerber, Eckhard *(West German*
    architect, Dortmund)   **AV**
    Bibl: ▶Bund Deut. Arch. Hdbch.,
    1987
Gerber, Gaylen   **BA WI**
    (American artist, op.1987-)   WI
    (American painter, 20th c.)   BA
    Bibl: ▶Art Index, Jan. 1989;
    Hixson, K., ARTS MAGAZINE/ LXIII
    / 2 / (Oct. 1988), 88
Gerber, Hans *(Swiss sculptor, 1910-*
    1978)   **BA**
    Bibl: ▶Künst.-Lex. Schweiz 20.
    Jahrh.; Walter, HANS GERBER:DER
    MENSCH UND SEIN WERK...(1982)
Gerber, Michel *(French architect)*   **AV**
    Bibl: Techniques et architecture,
    1984 June-July, no.354, p.76
Gerber, Theo   **BA WC**
    (Swiss artist, 1928-)   WC
    (Swiss painter, sculptor, b.1928)   BA
    Bibl: ▶Bénézit; ▶Künst.-Lex.
    Schweiz 20. Jahrh.; ▶MoMA libr.
    cat.
Gerbes, H. *(German artist, op.1866)*   **WC**
Gerbier → see Gerbier d'Ouvilly,
    Balthazar

Gerbier d'Ouvilly, Balthazar   **BA GC WC**
    (Dutch artist, c.1591/3-1667)   WC
    (Dutch painter, 1592-1667)   PR
    (Dutch painter, 1593-1667)   GC
    (Flemish painter, architect,
    author, diplomat in England,
    ca.1592-1667)   BA
    Bibl: ▶Bénézit; BN; ▶Dict. natl.
    biog.; ▶RILA/BHA;
    ▶Thieme-Becker; ▶Wurzbach, NLD
    Künst.-Lex.
    Balthazar Gerbier   PR
    Gerbier   PR
    Gerbier, Balthazar   **GC PR**
Gerbier, Balthazar → see Gerbier
    d'Ouvilly, Balthazar
Gerbig, Alexander *(German painter,*
    printmaker, 1878-1948)   **BA**
    Bibl: ▶Busse, Maler u. Bildhauer
    19. Jahr.; Knop, W., BILDENDE
    KUNST/9/(Sept.1987), 406-408;
    Knop, W., in DRESDENER
    KUNSTBLÄTTER XXIX/6 (1985)
    176; ▶Vollmer, Künst.-Lex. 20.
    Jhr.
Gerbrand van den Eeckhout → see
    Eeckhout, Gerbrand van den
Gerbrands, Roelof *(Dutch painter,*
    1891-1954)   **GC**
    Bibl: ▶Vollmer, Künst.-Lex. 20. Jhr.
Gerbrandt [Unidentified] *(Unknown*
    painter)   **PR**
    Bibl: (Thursday, Feb. 5, 1801, lot
    65, Christie's)
Gerbrant vander Eeckhout → see
    Eeckhout, Gerbrand van den
Gerbu, Gabriel *(French silversmith,*
    master 1782)   **GC**
    Bibl: ▶Nocq, Poinçon de Paris
Gerchman, Rubens *(Brazilian*
    painter, b.1942)   **BA**
    Bibl: ▶Pontual, Artes plásticas
    Brasil; Toronto (Ont, CAN), Art
    Gal. of Ont., 10 Brazilian artists
    (1975)
Gercken, Diderik *(Danish, d. ca.*
    1748)   **GC**
    Bibl: ▶Thieme-Becker
Gerdes, Eduard *(Dutch painter,*
    1887-1945)   **GC**
    Bibl: ▶Vollmer, Künst.-Lex. 20. Jhr.
Gerdes, Ingeborg *(American*
    photographer, b.1938)   **BA**
    Bibl: ▶Artweek idx.; San Francisco
    (CA, USA), SFMoMA, Jerry
    Burchard (1979)
Gerdes, Ludger *(West German*
    artist, b.1954)   **BA**
    Bibl: ▶Intl. dir. exh. artists, 1983
Gere, Charles March   **WC WI**
    (British artist, 1869-1934)   WC
    (British artist, 1869-1957)   WI
    Bibl: ▶Peppin, Bk. illus. 20c.
Gere, Margaret   **WC WI**
    (British artist, 1878-)   WC
    (British artist, 1878-1965)   WI

Geremia Cristoforo → *see* Cristoforo di Geremia

Gérente, Henri *(French glass painter, 1814-1849)* **BA**
  Bibl: ▶Bénézit; Brisac, REVUE DE L'ART, 47(1980), 72-75; ▶Thieme-Becker

Gererd Lairesse → *see* Lairesse, Gerard de

Gerg, Blasius *(German designer)* **AV**
  Bibl: Detail, 1984 Nov.-Dec., v.24, no.6, p.645

Gergely, Sándor *(Hungarian sculptor, printmaker, 1888-1932)* **BA**
  Bibl: Rome (ITA), Pal. Barberini, Gli otto egli attivisiti (1980)

Gergen, Peter *(West German architect)* **AV**

Gergorio de Ferrari → *see* Ferrari, Gregorio de'

Gergs, Herbert *(West German architect, Stuttgart)* **AV**
  Bibl: Deutsche Bauzeitung, 1988 Mar., v.122, no.3, p.54

Gergs, Siegfried *(German architect, 20th c.)* **BA**
  Bibl: ▶Arch. period. idx./RIBA, XV/1 (1987); Gergs, "Block 234 an der Lützowstrasse, südliches Tier ...", Jahrb. für Architektur 1985-86, p.192-197

Gerhaert, Niclaus *(early Netherlandish? sculptor in Germany, act.1462, d.1473)* **BA**
  Bibl: ▶Encyc. world art, index; Ohnmacht, KRUZIFIX DES NICLAUS GERHAERT VON LEYDEN, 1973, 2; ▶Thieme-Becker

Gerhard Douw → *see* Dou, Gerrit
Gerhard Dow → *see* Dou, Gerrit
Gerhard Lairesse → *see* Lairesse, Gerard de
Gerhard or Gerard, Johann Friedrich → *see* Gerhard, Johann Friedrich

Gerhard, Hubert **BA GC**
  (early Netherlandish sculptor, 1540/50-1620) **BA**
  (North Netherlandish draughtsman and sculptor, 1540/60-1620) **GC**
  Bibl: ▶RILA/BHA; ▶Thieme-Becker; ▶Wurzbach, NLD Künst.-Lex.

Gerhard, Johann Friedrich **GC**
  (German artist, c.1695-1748) **WC**
  (German painter, ca.1695-1748) **GC**
  Bibl: ▶Bénézit

Gerhard or Gerard, Johann Friedrich **WC**

Gerhardi, Ida *(German artist, 1867-1927)* **WC**

Gerhardinger Constantin → *see* Gerhardinger, Constantin

Gerhardinger, Constantin **GC**
  (German artist, 1888-) **WC**
  (German painter, 1888-1970) **GC**
  Bibl: ▶Schweers, Gemälde deut. Museen

Gerhardinger Constantin **WC**

Gerhardt, Eduard *(German artist, 1813-1888)* **WC**

Gerhardt, Karl *(American sculptor, 1853-1940)* **BA**
  Bibl: ▶Fielding's Amer. ptrs.; NEWARK MUSEUM QUARTERLY, XXV/1(WINTER 1975), 1-31; ▶Young, Amer. artists

Gerhart, Nikolaus *(German sculptor, b.1944)* **BA**
  Bibl: Kunstwerk, XXXIII/6 (1980) pp.3-38

Gericaule, Jean Louis Andre Theodore → *see* Géricault, Jean Louis André Théodore

Gericault → *see* Géricault, Jean Louis André Théodore

Gericault, Jean Louis Andre → *see* Géricault, Jean Louis André Théodore

Géricault, Jean Louis André Théodore **BA GC PR WC**
  (French artist, 1791-1824) **WC**
  (French painter and sculptor, 1791-1824) **GC**
  (French painter, 1791-1824) **BA PR**
  (French, 1791-1824) **JG**
  Bibl: ▶Bénézit; ▶Libr. of Congr. Name Auth. File; ▶Petit Robert 2; ▶RILA/BHA; ▶Witt checklist

  Gericaule, Jean Louis Andre Theodore **PR**
  Gericault **PR**
  Gericault, Jean Louis Andre **PR**
  Gericault, Jean Louis Theodore **PR**

Gericault, Theodore **GC JG PR**
  Jean Louis Andre Theodore Gericault **PR**

Gericault, Jean Louis Theodore → *see* Géricault, Jean Louis André Théodore

Gericault, Theodore → *see* Géricault, Jean Louis André Théodore

Gericke, Samuel Theodor **BA WC**
  (German artist, 1665-1730) **WC**
  (German painter, 1665-1729) **BA**
  Bibl: ▶Neue deutsche Biog.; ▶Thieme-Becker; ▶Witt checklist

Gérin, Claude Humbert *(French porcelian chemist, act.1747)* **BA**
  Bibl: D'Albis, A., FAENZA, LXX/5-6 (1984) 479-493; ▶Honey, Euro. ceramic

Gerin-La Joie, Guy **BA**
  (Canadian architect) **AV**
  (Canadian architect, b.1928) **BA**
  Bibl: Section a, 1984 Aug., suppl., p.12; ▶WW Amer. Art

Gérin-Lajoie, Guy **AV**

Gérin-Lajoie, Guy → *see* Gerin-La Joie, Guy

Gerini → *see* Gerini, Niccolò di Pietro

Gerini, Carlo, Marchese [Unidentified] *(Unknown painter, act. 18th century)* **PR**
  Bibl: Riccardi inventory dated 1776
  Marchese Carlo Gerini **PR**
  Sig.r Marchese Carlo Gerini **PR**

Gerini, Lorenzo → *see* Lorenzo di Niccolò di Martino

Gerini, Lorenzo de Niccolo → *see* Lorenzo di Niccolò di Martino

Gerini, Lorenzo di Niccolò → *see* Lorenzo di Niccolò di Martino

Gerini, Niccolo → *see* Gerini, Niccolò di Pietro

Gerini, Niccolò di Pietro **BA GC PR WC**
  (Italian artist, op.1368-m.1415) **WC**
  (Italian painter, act. 1368-1415) **PR**
  (Italian painter, act.1368-1415) **BA GC**
  Bibl: APOLLO, CVIII/202(DEC 1978), 374; ▶Bolaffi; ▶Encyc. world art; ▶RILA/BHA; ▶Thieme-Becker

  Gerini **PR**
  Gerini, Niccolo **PR**
  Niccolo di Pietro Gerini **PR**

Gerino d'Antonio Gerini → *see* Gerino da Pistoia (Gerino d'Antonio Gerini)

Gerino da Pistoia → *see* Gerino da Pistoia (Gerino d'Antonio Gerini)

Gerino da Pistoia (Gerino d'Antonio Gerini) **BA GC PR**
  (Italian artist, 1480-op.1529) **WI**
  (Italian artist, 1480-p.1529) **WC**
  (Italian painter, 1480-act.1529) **GC**
  (Italian painter, b. 1480, act. 1529) **PR**
  (Italian painter, b.1480, act. 1529) **BA**
  Bibl: ▶Bénézit; ▶Bolaffi; ▶RILA/BHA, 1986; ▶Thieme-Becker; ▶Witt checklist

  Gerino d'Antonio Gerini **GC WI**

Gerino da Pistoia **GC PR WI**

Gerino da Pistoja (Gerino d'Antonio Gerini) **WC**

Gerino da Pistoja (Gerino d'Antonio Gerini) → *see* Gerino da Pistoia (Gerino d'Antonio Gerini)

Gerischer, Angela Oedekoven → *see* Oedekoven-Gerischer, Angela

Gerischer, Wolf *(West German architect, Düsseldorf)* **AV**
  Bibl: Architektur, Innenarchitektur, Technischer Ausbau, 1989 June, v.97, no.6, p.100

Gerkan, Meinhard von *(West German architect, 1935-)* **AV**
  Bibl: ▶Libr. of Congr. Name Auth. File
  Von Gerkan, Meinhard **AV**

Gerke Henkes → *see* Henkes, Gerke

Gerlach, Erich (*German painter, b.1909*) **BA**
    Bibl: Ebert. FORSCHUNGEN und Berichte XXIII, 1983 p.154; ▶Vollmer, Künst.-Lex. 20. Jhr.

Gerlachus (*German glass painter, 12th-13th cs.*) **BA**
    Bibl: ▶Encyc. world art; ▶Thieme-Becker

Gerleman, Bruce (*American real estate developer, Des Moines, Iowa; specializes in converting historic properties to commercial use*) **AV**
    Bibl: Iowa architect, 1987 Sept.-Oct., v.35, no.4, p.16

Gerli, Agostino **BA WC**
    (*Italian architect, act.1759-1784*) **BA**
    (*Italian artist, op.1759-1787*) **WC**
    Bibl: ▶Portoghesi, Diz. arch. e urbanistica; ▶Thieme-Becker

Gerli, Eugenio (*Italian architect, 1923-*) **AV**

Gerling, Johann Kasper (*German artist, 18th cent.*) **WC**

Germain family (*French silversmiths, 17th-18th cs.*) **BA**
    Bibl: ▶Penguin dec. arts; ▶Thieme-Becker

Germain, Alphonse (Thil) (*French artist, 19th cent.*) **WC**

Germain, François-Thomas **BA GC JG**
    (*French silversmith, 1726-1791*) **BA GC**
    (*French, 1726-1791, master 1748*) **JG**
    Bibl: ▶Mabille, Orfèv. fran.; ▶Penguin dec. arts; ▶Thieme-Becker

Germain, Louise (*French painter, 1874-1939*) **BA**
    Bibl: ▶Baille, Petits maîtres; ▶Bénézit

Germain, Louise Denise (*French bookbinder, 1870-1963*) **BA**
    Bibl: Paris (FRA), Bibl. Nationale, Joseph Šimá (1979)

Germain, Nicolas II (*French potter in HUN, act.1744, d.1787*) **BA**
    Bibl: ▶Bruckmann's Fayence-Lex.; ▶Honey, Euro. ceramic; Langer,WELTKUNST,LVI/2/ (15,Jan.1986) 138-139

Germain, Pierre I (*French, ca.1644-1684*) **GC**
    Bibl: ▶Thieme-Becker

Germain, Pierre II **GC**
    (*French artist, 1716-1783*) **WC**
    (*French, 1716-1783*) **GC**
    Bibl: ▶Thieme-Becker; ▶Witt checklist

Germain, Pierre, II (Le Romain) **WC**
Germain, Pierre, II (Le Romain) → *see* Germain, Pierre II

Germain, Thomas **GC JG WC**
    (*French artist, 1673-1748*) **WC**
    (*French, 1673-1748*) **GC**
    (*French, 1673-1748, master 1720, orfevre du Roi 1723*) **JG**
    Bibl: ▶Thieme-Becker; ▶Witt checklist

German y Llorente → *see* Germán y Llorente, Bernardo

Germán y Llorente, Bernardo **PR WC**
    (*Spanish artist, 1680/1-1759*) **WC**
    (*Spanish painter, 1680/81-1759*) **PR**
    Bibl: ▶Thieme-Becker

    Bernardo German y Llorente **PR**
    German y Llorente **PR**
    Germano Lhorente **PR**

Germanaz, Christian (*French architect*) **AV**
    Bibl: Techniques et architecture, 1989 Aug.-Sept., no.385, p.142

Germanello, Angelo (*Writer, scribe, ante 1515-post 1525*) **CE**

Germani [**Unidentified**] (*Unknown painter*) **PR**
    Bibl: (August 3, 1811, lot 103, Jones)

Germani, Roberto (*Argentine architect*) **AV**
    Bibl: Ianus, 1980, v.0, no.0, p.121

Germann, Charles (Franz Carl Andreas) (*Swiss artist, 1755-1830*) **WC**

Germann, Thomas (*Swiss architect*) **AV**
    Bibl: Lotus international, 1986, no.48-49, p.95

Germann-Jahn, Charlotte Annemarie (*Swiss sculptor, b.1921*) **BA**
    Bibl: ▶Künst.-Lex. Schweiz 20. Jahrh.; ▶Lex. zeitgen. Schweiz. Künstler

Germano Lhorente → *see* Germán y Llorente, Bernardo

Germela, Raimund (*German artist, 1868-*) **WC**

Germisoni, Filippo **BA WC**
    (*Italian artist, op.1682-m.1743*) **WC**
    (*Italian painter, d.1743*) **BA**
    Bibl: ▶Bénézit; ▶Bolaffi; ▶Thieme-Becker

Germon, Washington L. (*American, 1823-1878, active Philadelphia, PA, U.S. 1847-afterly; Malta 1860, active Washington, D.C., U.S. 1857-1861, daguerreotypist.*) **JG**

Gernandt, Siegfried (*West German architect, Fachhochschule, Darmstadt*) **AV**
    Bibl: Architektur, Innenarchitektur, Technischer Ausbau, 1989 Apr., v.97, no.4, p.56; Architektur, Innenarchitektur, Technisicher Ausbau, 1987 Nov., v.95, no.11, p.54

Gernes, Poul (*Danish artist, b.1925*) **BA**
    Bibl: Lyngby(DNK), Sophienholm, POUL GERNES..., 1980

Gernez, Paul Elie (*French artist, 1888-1948*) **WC**

Gerngross, Heidulf (*Austrian architect, 1939-*) **AV**
    Bibl: Das Kunstwerk, n.3-4, Sept. 1983, p.50

    Gerngrosz, Heidulf **AV**
Gerngrosz, Heidulf → *see* Gerngross, Heidulf

Gernreich, Rudi (*American couturier, b.1922*) **BA**
    Bibl: ▶Columbia encyc.

Gerő, László (*Hungarian architect or architectural historian, 1909-*) **AV**
    Bibl: ▶Libr. of Congr. Name Auth. File

Geroff **WC WI**
    (*British artist, op.18th c.*) **WI**
    (*British(?) artist, 18th cent.*) **WC**

Gerofi, Robert (*Belgian architect*) **AV**
    Bibl: Architectural digest, 1988 Jan., v.45, no.1, p.104

Gerola, Stefano (*Italian sculptor, 15th-16th cs.*) **BA**
    Bibl: San Benedetto(ITA), Museum Civico Pol., SECOLI DI POLIONE, 1981

Gerolamo Arena → *see* Arena, Giovanni Geronimo d'

Gerolamo Bassano → *see* Bassano, Gerolamo (Gerolamo da Ponte)

Gerolamo da Ponte → *see* Bassano, Gerolamo (Gerolamo da Ponte)

Gerolamo da Santa Croce → *see* Santacroce, Girolamo da

Gerolamo da Santacroce → *see* Santacroce, Girolamo da

Gerolamo da Treviso (the younger) → *see* Girolamo da Treviso the younger (Girolamo Pennacchi)

Gerolamo da Vicenza → *see* Girolamo Vicentino

Gerolamo dai Libri → *see* Girolamo dai Libri

Gerolamo della Pacchia → *see* Pacchia, Girolamo del

Gerolamo di Giovanni da Camerino → *see* Girolamo Da Camerino

Gerolamo di Matteo da Gualdo (*Italian artist, 15th cent.*) **WC**

Gerolamo Giovenone → *see* Giovenone, Gerolamo

Gerolamo Panza → *see* Panza, Girolamo

Gerolamo [**Unidentified**] (*Unknown painter*) **PR**
    Bibl: (December 16, lot 39, Coxe; December 17, lot 9, Coxe)

Geroldi, Alberto (*Italian architect*) **AV**

Geroldus, cleric of Amiens (French
  scribe, act.1218)   GC
    Bibl: ▶Branner, Ms. ptg. Paris,
    p.210
Gerome→see Gérôme, Jean Léon
Gerome, Jean→see Gérôme, Jean
  Léon
Gérôme, Jean Léon   BA GC PR WC
    (French artist, 1824-1904)   WC
    (French painter and sculptor,
    1824-1904)   GC
    (French painter, 1824-1904)   PR
    (French painter, sculptor, 1824-
    1904)   BA
    (French, 1824-1904)   JG
    Bibl: ▶Encyc. world art; Getty
    Photo Study Coll. (Sculp.);
    ▶RILA/BHA
  Gerome   PR
  Gerome, Jean   GC PR
  Gerome, Jean-Leon   JG PR
  Jean Leon Gerome   PR
Gerome, Jean-Leon→see Gérôme,
  Jean Léon
Geron Group   GC
    Bibl: Paralipomena
Geron, Mathias→see Gerung,
  Matthias
Gerondelis, Ann Schoelles
    (American architect, Atlanta, GA) AV
    Bibl: Faith & form, 1986 Spring,
    v.19, p.32
Geronimo Cenatiempo→see
  Cenatiempo, Geronimo
Geronimo Colomes→see Colomes,
  Jerome
Geronimo Colones→see Colomes,
  Jerome
Geronimo d'Arena→see Arena,
  Giovanni Geronimo d'
Geronimo de Bobadilla→see
  Bobadilla, Geronimo de
Geronimo Massaro→see Massaro,
  Girolamo
Geronimo Mutiano→see Muziano,
  Girolamo
Geronimo Riccardo→see Riccardo,
  Geronimo [Unidentified]
Geronimo Solari→see Solari,
  Girolamo
Geronimo Timessa→see Timessa,
  Geronimo [Unidentified]
Geronzi, Lele (Italian architect)   AV
    Bibl: Architecture & urbanism,
    1988 June, no.6(213), p.97
Gerosa Lusena, Adaranca (Italian
  architect, Milan)   AV
    Bibl: Abitare, 1987 May, no.254,
    p.186
Gerosa, Franco (Italian architect)   AV
    Bibl: Abitare, 1984 Nov., no.229,
    p.70
Gerowitz, Judy→see Chicago, Judy
Gerrard Douw→see Dou, Gerrit
Gerrard Dow→see Dou, Gerrit
Gerrard Hoed→see Hoet, Gerard I

Gerrard Melder→see Melder, Gerard
Gerrard, Roy (British artist, op.1981-
  1983)   WI
Gerresheim, Bert (German sculptor,
  printmaker, b.1935)   BA
    Bibl: ▶WW Arts DEU
Gerrid Stijls→see Stijls, Gerard
  [Unidentified]
Gerrish, Benjamin (American
  gunsmith, ca.1686-1750)   BA
    Bibl: ANTIQUES, CXII(AUG 1977),
    282-4
Gerrit Adriaensz, Berckheyde→see
  Berckheyde, Gerrit Adriaensz.
Gerrit Albertus Beneker→see
  Beneker, Gerrit Albertus
Gerrit Andriaensz. de Heer→see
  Heer, Gerrit Adriaensz. de
Gerrit Battem→see Battem, Gerrit
  van
Gerrit Berckheijde→see Berckheyde,
  Gerrit Adriaensz.
Gerrit Bergheiden→see Berckheyde,
  Gerrit Adriaensz.
Gerrit Berkheide→see Berckheyde,
  Gerrit Adriaensz.
Gerrit Blycker→see Bleker, Gerrit
  Claesz
Gerrit Claesz Bleker→see Bleker,
  Gerrit Claesz
Gerrit Cornelisz.→see Cornelisz.,
  Gerrit
Gerrit de Heer→see Heer, Gerrit
  Adriaensz. de
Gerrit de Wet→see Wet, Gerrit de
Gerrit Douw→see Dou, Gerrit
Gerrit Douwen→see Dou, Gerrit
Gerrit Heer→see Heer, Gerrit
  Adriaensz. de
Gerrit Hees→see Hees, Gerrit van
Gerrit Hoet→see Hoet, Gerard I
Gerrit Hondius→see Hondius, Gerrit
Gerrit Larisse→see Lairesse, Gerard
  de
Gerrit Lundens→see Lundens, Gerrit
Gerrit Pietersz.→see Sweelinck,
  Gerrit Pietersz.
Gerrit Pietersz. Sweelinck→see
  Sweelinck, Gerrit Pietersz.
Gerrit Pompe→see Pompe, Gerrit
Gerrit Rademaker→see Rademaker,
  Gerrit
Gerrit Uylenburgh→see Uylenburgh,
  Gerrit
Gerrit van Battem→see Battem,
  Gerrit van
Gerrit van den Bosch→see Bosch,
  Gerrit van den
Gerrit van Haarlem→see Geertgen
  tot Sint Jans
Gerrit van Heda→see Heda, Gerrit
  Willemsz.
Gerrit van Hees→see Hees, Gerrit
  van

Gerrit van Honthorst→see Honthorst,
  Gerrit van
Gerrit van Linde→see Lundens, Gerrit
Gerrit van Velsen→see Velsen, Gerrit
  van [Unidentified]
Gerrit van Vucht→see Vucht, Gerrit
  van
Gerrit Willemsz. Heda→see Heda,
  Gerrit Willemsz.
Gerrit Willemsz. Horst→see Horst,
  Gerritt Willemsz.
Gerrit Zegelaar→see Zegelaar, Gerrit
Gerritsz, Hessel   BA
    (Dutch artist, 1581-1632)   WC
    (Dutch draughtsman, 1581-
    1632)   GC
    (Dutch printmaker, publisher,
    1581-1632)   BA
    Bibl: Getty Photo Study Coll.;
    HOLLSTEIN; ▶Natl. union cat., pre-
    1956; ▶Thieme-Becker; ▶Witt
    checklist
  Gerritsz., Gerrits or Gerryts,
    Hessel   WC
  Gerritsz., Hessel   GC
Gerritsz., Gerrits or Gerryts,
  Hessel→see Gerritsz, Hessel
Gerritsz., Hessel→see Gerritsz, Hessel
Gerritsz., Joost (Dutch brass
  founder, 1598-1652)   BA
    Bibl: OUD HOLLAND, XCIII, 1979
Gerritt Willemsz. Horst→see Horst,
  Gerritt Willemsz.
Gerritz, Hendrikus Antonius (Dutch
  printmaker, b.1940)   BA
    Bibl: Paris (FRA), Inst. néerlandais,
    L'Atelier de Piet Clement (1976);
    ▶Scheen, Ned. beeldende kunst.
Gerritz., Claes   GC
    (Netherlandish painter, act. ca.
    1560)   GC
    (Netherlands artist, op.c.1560) WC
    Bibl: ▶Witt checklist
  Gerritz., Claes or Claus   WC
Gerritz., Claes or Claus→see Gerritz.,
  Claes
Gerry, Samuel Lancaster   BA WC WI
    (American artist, 1813-1891)   WC WI
    (American painter, 1813-1891)   BA
    Bibl: ▶Groce, Artists Amer.
Gerschel Freres (French, active
  Strasbourg, 1860s)   JG
Gershoy, Eugenie (American
  sculptor and painter (b. Russia),
  b.1901)   GC
    Bibl: ▶Opitz, Amer. sculptors
Gershuni, Moshe (Israeli sculptor,
  painter, printmaker, b.1936)   BA
    Bibl: Apter-Gabriel, Israel Mus.
    Jrnl. IV (1985) 67; ▶ARTbibl.
    mod., 19/1; ▶Gorenflo, Bild.
    Künstler; ▶Intl. dir. exh. artists,
    1983
Gerson, Jean (French, b. in the
  vicinity of Rethel in the Ardennes
  1363)   JG

Gerson, Lotte *(German, 1905 -)*   **JG**
Gerson, Wojciech (Adalbert) → see
Gerson, Wojciech Henryk Wilhelm
Gerson, Wojciech Henryk Wilhelm   **BA**
(Polish artist, 1831-1901)   WC
(Polish painter, illustrator,
printmaker, 1831-1901)   BA
Bibl: ▶Slownik artystów polskich;
▶Thieme-Becker
Gerson, Wojciech (Adalbert)   **WC**
Gerssen, Peter J. *(Dutch architect,*
Rotterdam)   **AV**
Bibl: ▶Federatie O jrbk., 1984
Gerst, Johann Karl Jakob *(German*
painter, 1792-1854)   **GC**
Bibl: ▶Thieme-Becker
Gerstel, Wilhelm *(German sculptor,*
1879-1963)   **BA**
Bibl: ▶Bénézit; ▶Fogg Mus. Libr.
cat.; ▶Vollmer, Künst.-Lex. 20. Jhr.
Gerster, Franz *(illustrator in CHE,*
16th c.)   **BA**
Bibl: Basel (CHE), Universitätsbib.,
Oberrheinische Buchillustration 2:
Basler Buchillustration 1500-1545
Gerstl, Hermina   **WC WI**
(British artist, 20th cent.)   WC
(British artist, op.20th c.)   WI
Gerstl, Richard   **BA WC**
(Austrian painter, 1883-1908)   BA
(German artist, 1883-1908)   WC
Bibl: ▶Österr. biog. Lex. 1815-
1950; ▶Vollmer, Künst.-Lex. 20.
Jhr.; ▶Witt checklist
Gerstmaier or Gerstmayer, Joseph
(German artist, 1801-1870)   **WC**
Gerstmyer, William *(Architect)*   **AV**
Bibl: Inland architect, 1984 Nov.-
Dec., v.28, no.6, p.50
Gerstner, Karl *(Swiss painter,*
printmaker, b.1930)   **BA**
Bibl: ▶Künst.-Lex. Schweiz 20.
Jahrh.; ▶Lex. zeitgen. Schweiz.
Künstler; ▶Parry, Contemp. art
Gerth, Helmut *(East German*
architect)   **AV**
Bibl: Architektur der DDR, 1988
Mar., v.37, no.3, p.25)6
Gerthener, Madern *(German*
architect, 1360-1430/31)   **BA**
Bibl: ▶Nagler, Neues Künst.-Lex.;
▶Neue deutsche Biog.;
▶Thieme-Becker
Gertler → see Gertler, Mark
Gertler, Mark   **BA GC PR WC WI**
(British artist, 1892-1939)   WC WI
(British painter, 1892-1939)   BA PR
(British, 1892-1939)   GC
Bibl: ▶Bénézit; ▶RILA/BHA;
▶Vollmer, Künst.-Lex. 20. Jhr.;
▶Who was who [GBR], v.3; ▶Witt
checklist
Gertler   PR
Mark Gertler   PR
Gertner or Gaertner, Peter
(Monogrammist P.G.) → see
Gertner, Peter

Gertner, Christoph   **BA**
(German artist, op.1604-1621)   WC
(German draughtsman, act.
1604-1621)   GC
(German painter, ca.1575-after
1623)   BA
Bibl: Dehio, BREMEN/NIEDER;
Niederdeutsche Beiträge XXIII
(1984) 117-138; ▶Thieme-Becker;
▶Witt checklist
Gaertner, Christoph   **GC**
Gerttner or Gaernter, Christoff   **WC**
Gerttner, Christoph   GC
Gertner, Georg II → see Gärtner,
Georg II
Gertner, Johan Vilhelm *(Danish*
artist, 1818-1871)   **WC**
Gertner, Lazarus *(German painter,*
act.1510)   **BA**
Bibl: BIULETYN HISTORII SZTUKI,
XXXVII/4(1975), 305-11
Gertner, Peter   **PR**
(German artist, op.1524-1537)   WC
(German painter and
draughtsman, act.1524-1537)   GC
(German painter, act. 1524-
1537)   PR
Bibl: ▶Witt checklist
Gaertner, Peter   GC PR
Gertner or Gaertner, Peter
(Monogrammist P.G.)   **WC**
Gertner, Peter (Monogrammist
P G)   **GC**
Peter Gertner   PR
Gertner, Peter (Monogrammist P
G) → see Gertner, Peter
Gertrude Fiske → see Fiske, Gertrude
Gertrude Partington → see Partington,
Gertrude
Gertrude Pietersz. → see Pietersz.,
Gertrude
Gertsch, Franz   **BA WC**
(Swiss artist, 1930-)   WC
(Swiss painter, b.1930)   BA
Bibl: Berlin (DEU), Akad. der
Künste, Franz Gertsch (1975);
▶DuMonts Künst.-Lex.
Gerttner or Gaernter, Christoff → see
Gertner, Christoph
Gerttner, Christoph → see Gertner,
Christoph
Gertz, Rennveig *(Norwegian interior*
designer)   **AV**
Bibl: Byggekunst: the Norwegian
review of architecture, 1989,
v.71, no.1, p.24
Gerum, P. *(German architect)*   **AV**
Bibl: Architektur,
Innenarchitektur, Technischer
Ausbau, 1984 Jan-Feb., v.92,
no.1, p.36
Gerung → see Gerung, Matthias
Gerung or Geron, Mathias or
Mathis → see Gerung, Matthias
Gerung, Mathis → see Gerung,
Matthias

Gerung, Matthias   **BA PR**
(German artist, c.1500-1568/70)   WC
(German painter, 1500-1568/70)   PR
(German painter, printmaker,
tapestry designer, ca.1500-ca.
1568)   BA
(German, ca.1500-1568/70)   GC
Bibl: ▶Allgem. Deut. Biog.; Getty
Photo Study Coll. (Ptgs.); ▶Libr. of
Congr. Name Auth. File;
▶Thieme-Becker; ▶Witt checklist
Geron, Mathias   GC
Gerung   PR
Gerung or Geron, Mathias or
Mathis   **WC**
Gerung, Mathis   **GC**
Matthias Gerung   PR
Géruzet, family *(Belgian*
photographers, 19th c.)   **BA**
Geruzzi, S. *(Italian artist, 19th cent.)*   **WC**
Gervais, Charles → see Jervas, Charles
Gervais, Elie   **WC WI**
(British artist, op.1758)   WC
(British artist, op.1758-)   WI
Gervais, Leo *(Canadian sculptor,*
b.1917)   **BA**
Bibl: ▶Artists Canada;
▶MacDonald, Can. artists; Paris
(FRA), Ctr culturel canadien,
Métiers d'art/3 (1979)
Gervais, Paul Jean Louis *(French*
artist, 1859-1934(?))   **WC**
Gervais, Raymond *(Canadian artist,*
b.1946)   **BA**
Bibl: Paris, Centre Cultural
Canadian, TENDANCES
ACTUELLES, 1977
Gerverot, Victor Louis *(French*
ceramist, arcanist, 1747-1829)   **BA**
Bibl: ▶Honey, Euro. ceramic; Ohm
und Reber, Festschrift fur P.W.
Meister, pp. 240-245;
▶Thieme-Becker
Gervex, Henri   **GC WC**
(French artist, 1852-1929)   WC
(French painter, 1852-1929)   GC
Bibl: ▶Bénézit
Gerwen, Reymer van → see Gherwen,
Reynier van
Gerz, Jochen *(West German artist in*
FRA, b.1940)   **BA**
Bibl: ▶Bénézit; ▶DuMonts
Künst.-Lex.; ▶MoMA libr. cat.
Gerzso, Gunther *(Mexican painter,*
b.1915)   **BA**
Bibl: AFI; Catlin, Art Lat. Amer.,
p.174
Gesellius, Herman *(Finnish*
architect, 1874-1916)   **AV BA**
Bibl: ▶Macmillan encyc. archts.,
p.188; ▶Thieme-Becker
Geselschap, Eduard *(Dutch artist,*
1814-1878)   **WC**
Geselschap, Friedrich   **GC WC**
(German artist, 1835-1898)   WC
(German painter, 1835-1898)   GC
Bibl: ▶Thieme-Becker

Gesemann, Heinrich (German artist, 1886-)   **WC**

Gesina Terborch→see Terborch, Gesina

Gésinus (Visser), Bob   **GC**
  (Dutch artist, 1898-)   WC
  (Dutch painter, b.1898)   GC
    Bibl: ▶Vollmer, Künst.-Lex. 20. Jhr.

Gesinus, Bob (Johannes Gesinus Visser)   **WC**

Gesinus, Bob (Johannes Gesinus Visser)→see Gésinus (Visser), Bob

Gesio, Giovanni Battista (Italian philosopher, cosmographer, military engineer in ESP, act.1565-1580)   **BA**
    Bibl: ▶Encic. univ. ilus.; Relações artisticas entre PRT e ESP (1987), pp.147-183

Geske, Allan (Canadian printmaker, b.1945)   **BA**
    Bibl: Winnipeg (Man, CAN), Art Gallery, Artists' proof (1981)

Gesler, Alejandrina Anselma de (Spanish artist, 1831-)   **WC**

Geslin, Jean Charles (French painter, 1814-1885)   **GC**
    Bibl: ▶Bénézit

Geslin, P. (French artist, 19th cent.)   **WC**

Gesmar, C. (French artist, op.c. 1925)   **WC**

Gesner→see Gessner, Johann Conrad
Gesner→see Gessner, Salomon

Gesner, Abelard (South American artist, 1922-)   **WC**

Gesner, Conrad (Swiss artist, op.c. 1730)   **WC**

Gesol. →see Ghisolfi, Giovanni
Gessi→see Gessi, Giovan Francesco
Gessi, Francesco→see Gessi, Giovan Francesco

Gessi, Giovan Francesco   **BA GC PR**
  (Italian artist, 1588-1649)   WC
  (Italian painter, 1588-1649)   BA GC PR
    Bibl: ▶Bolaffi; ▶RILA/BHA, 1986; ▶Thieme-Becker, (as Francesco Gessi)
    Francesco Gessi   PR
    Gessi   PR

Gessi, Francesco   **GC WC**
    Gesso   PR
    Giovan Francesco Gessi   PR

Gessi, Giovanni Battista →see Ruggieri, Giovanni Battista
Gessner→see Gessner, Johann Conrad
Gessner→see Gessner, Salomon
Gessner, Conrad (Johann Conrad)→see Gessner, Johann Conrad

Gessner, Hans Heinrich (Swiss, d.1622)   **GC**
    Bibl: ▶Thieme-Becker

Gessner, Hubert (Austrian architect, b.1871)   **BA**
    Bibl: ▶Thieme-Becker

Gessner, Johann Conrad   **BA PR**
  (Swiss artist, 1764-1826)   WC
  (Swiss artist, 1796-1870)   WC
  (Swiss painter, 1764-1826)   PR
  (Swiss painter, printmaker, 1764-1826)   BA
    Bibl: ▶RILA/BHA; ▶Schweiz. Künst.-Lex.; ▶Thieme-Becker

Faesi-Gessner, Johann Konrad   **WC**
    Genser   PR
    Gesner   PR
    Gessner   PR

Gessner, Conrad (Johann Conrad)   **WC**
    Johann Conrad Gessner   PR

Gessner, Richard (German artist, 1894-)   **WC**

Gessner, Robert S. (Swiss painter, sculptor, printmaker, b.1903)   **BA**
    Bibl: ▶Lex. zeitgen. Schweiz. Künstler; ▶Vollmer, Künst.-Lex. 20. Jhr.

Gessner, Salomon   **BA GC PR WC**
  (Swiss artist, 1730-1788)   WC
  (Swiss painter and printmaker, 1730-1788)   GC
  (Swiss painter, 1730-1788)   PR
  (Swiss poet, painter, printmaker, 1730-1788)   BA
    Bibl: ▶Neue deutsche Biog.; ▶RILA/BHA; ▶Schweiz. Künst.-Lex.; ▶Thieme-Becker; ▶Witt checklist
    Gesner   PR
    Gessner   PR
    Ghessner   PR
    Salomon Gessner   PR
    Sol. Gesner, Jun   PR

Gesso→see Gessi, Giovan Francesco

Gestel, A. van (Dutch artist, 17th cent.)   **WC**

Gestel, Leendert (Leo)→see Gestel, Leo

Gestel, Leo   **BA GC**
  (Dutch artist, 1881-1941)   WC
  (Dutch painter and draughtsman, 1881-1941)   GC
  (Dutch painter, printmaker, 1881-1941)   BA
    Bibl: ▶Bénézit; ▶Scheen, Ned. beeldende kunst.; ▶Vollmer, Künst.-Lex. 20. Jhr.

Gestel, Leendert (Leo)   **WC**

Gesuado, Vincenzo (Italian glass painter, 17th c.)   **BA**
    Bibl: Gonzales-Palacios, Hist. furniture, v.7, p.11; Naples (ITA), Museo Capodimonte, Civiltà del 600 a Napoli (1984), p.423

Gesualdo Ferri→see Ferri, Gesualdo Francesco
Gesualdo Francesco Ferri→see Ferri, Gesualdo Francesco
Gesuita→see Courtois, Jacques (le Bourguignon)
Gesuita→see Seghers, Daniel

Getchell, Edith Loring Peirce   **BA WI**
  (American artist, 1855-1940)   WI
  (American printmaker, 1855-1940)   BA
    Bibl: ▶Fielding's Amer. ptrs.; Fitchburg (MA, USA), Art Mus., Eleanor Norcross (1980); ▶Vollmer, Künst.-Lex. 20. Jhr.

Gethin, Percy Francis (British artist, 1874-1916)   **WC WI**
    Bibl: ▶Mallalieu, Brit. watercolour artists

Gette, Paul Armand (French sculptor, b.1927)   **BA**
    Bibl: ▶Bénézit; ▶MoMA libr. cat.

Getto di Jacopo   **GC WC**
  (Italian artist, op.1391)   WC
  (Italian painter, act.1391)   GC
    Bibl: ▶Thieme-Becker

Getty, George F. II, Mrs. (American, 20th c.)   **BA**

Getz, Ilse   **BA**
  (American artist, 20th cent.)   WC
  (American artist, b.1917)   WI
  (American painter, artist, b.1917)   BA
    Bibl: ▶Vollmer, Künst.-Lex. 20. Jhr.; ▶WW Amer. Art, 1978

Getz, Ilse Bechhold   **WI**
Getz, Ilse Bechold   **WC**
Getz, Ilse Bechhold→see Getz, Ilse
Getz, Ilse Bechold→see Getz, Ilse

Geubels family (Flemish tapestry makers, 16th-17th cs.)   **BA**
    Bibl: ▶Thieme-Becker; ▶Thomson, Tapestry

Geubels, Jacques I (Flemish tapestry maker, act.1580-1605)   **BA**
    Bibl: DePoorter, GENTSE BIJDAGTOT KUNST, XXV(1979-80), 208-224; ▶Encyc. world art; ▶Thieme-Becker; ▶Thomson, Tapestry, pp.376-377

Geubels, Jacques II (Flemish tapestry maker, act.1626, d. before 1633)   **BA**
    Bibl: Duverger, ARTES TEXTILES, VII (1971) 89; Duverger, Gentse Bijdragen tot de Kunstgeschiedenis, XXVI (1981-1984) pp.161-193; ▶Thieme-Becker

Geuens, J. (French artist, 20th cent.)   **WC**

Geuer, Jan W. (Canadian artist, b.1917)   **BA**
    Bibl: ▶Artists Canada; ▶Idx. Ontario artists; ▶MacDonald, Can. artists; Rotterdam (NLD), Mus. Boymans-van Beuningen, Juan Geuer (1985)

Geuffels, Frans→see Geffels, Frans
Geurcino→see Guercino (Giovanni Francesco Barbieri)

Geurts, Jerry W. (American architect)   **AV**

Geurts, Joris *(Dutch painter,*
b.1958)   **BA**
    Bibl: Rotterdam (NLD), Mus.
    Boymans-van Beuningen, Veertien
    Kunstenaars (1983)

Geusendam, Gerrit Jacobus *(Dutch*
artist, 1771-p.1815)   **WC**

Geuslain, Geslin, Geuslin or
Gueslin, Charles *(French artist,*
1685-1865)   **WC**

Geutileschi→see Gentileschi, Orazio

Gevers, P. *(Belgian architect,*
Kasterlee)   **AV**
    Bibl: Monumenten en
    landschappen, 1989 Sept.-Oct.,
    v.8, no.5, p.7

Geyelin, Sherry *(American interior*
designer, Washington, D.C)   **AV**
    Bibl: Architectural digest, 1988
    July, v.45, no.7, p.138

Geyer, Elias *(German artist, op.*
1572-m.1634)   **WC**

Geyer, Georg *(German artist, 1823-*
1912)   **WC**

Geyer, George *(American ceramist,*
20th c.)   **BA**
    Bibl: ▶Art Index, Apr. 1976;
    Smith, LAICA Jrnl., 8 (Nov.-Dec.
    1975) pp.38-49

Geyer, Johann *(German artist, 1807-*
1875)   **WC**

Geyer, Ludwig Heinrich Christiani
(German artist, 1779-1821)   **WC**

Geyer, Otto *(German sculptor,*
1843-1914)   **BA**
    Bibl: ▶Bénézit

Geyer, Otto M. *(German artist,*
1955-)   **WC**

Geyling, Carl *(German artist, 1814-*
1880)   **WC**

Geyling, Remigius *(German artist,*
1878)   **WC**

Geyp, Adriaan Marinus *(Dutch*
painter, 1855-1926)   **GC**
    Bibl: ▶Scheen, Ned. beeldende
    kunst.

    Geijp, Adriaan Marinus   **GC**

Geyra, Don *(American painter,*
b.1953)   **BA**
    Bibl: Hamilton (NY, USA), Colgate
    Univ., 3 Artists (1979)

Geyst, P.J. *(Netherlands artist, op.*
1764)   **WC**

Geyter, Xaveer de *(Dutch architect)*   **AV**
    Bibl: GA document, 1989 Apr.,
    no.23, p.85

Gezelius, Jan *(Swedish architect,*
Stockholm, 1923-)   **AV**
    Bibl: ▶Svenska Ark. Riks., 1984

Gfall, Johann *(German artist, 1725-*
p.1800)   **WC**

Ghachet, Bernard *(Swiss architect)*   **AV**
    Bibl: Parametro, 1985 Nov., no.
    141, p.54

Ghare, Domenico→see Gare,
Domenico

Ghedini, Giuseppe Antonio   **PR WC**
(Italian artist, 1707-1791)   WC
(Italian painter, 1707-1791)   PR
    Bibl: ▶Thieme-Becker
    Giuseppe Antonio Ghedini   PR
    Giuseppe Ghedini   PR

Gheduzzi di Crespellano, Ugo
(Italian artist, 1853-1925)   **WC**

Gheeraerts→see Geeraerts, Marcus,
the younger

Gheeraerts, Garrard, Garret,
Geeraerts or Gerard the Younger,
Marcus→see Geeraerts, Marcus,
the younger

Gheeraerts, Garret, Geeraerts or
Gerard the Elder, Marcus→see
Geeraerts, Marcus, the elder

Gheeraerts, Marc (the Younger)→see
Geeraerts, Marcus, the younger

Gheeraerts, Marcus→see Geeraerts,
Marcus, the younger

Gheeraerts, Marcus (the Elder)→see
Geeraerts, Marcus, the elder

Gheeraerts, Marcus (the
Younger)→see Geeraerts, Marcus,
the younger

Gheeraerts, Marcus I→see Geeraerts,
Marcus, the elder

Gheeraerts, Marcus II→see
Geeraerts, Marcus, the younger

Gheeraerts, Marcus, the
Younger→see Geeraerts, Marcus,
the younger

Gheest, Francois de *(Netherlands*
artist, 17th cent.)   **WC**

Ghelli, Francesco *(Italian artist,*
1637-1703)   **WC**

Ghémar family *(Belgian*
photographers, 19th c.)   **BA**
    Bibl: ▶Thieme-Becker

Ghémar, Louis Joseph *(Belgian*
printmaker, photographer, 1820-
1873)   **BA**
    Bibl: ▶Thieme-Becker

Ghendt, Emmanuel Jean
Nepomucene de *(Flemish artist,*
1738-1815)   **WC**

Ghent, Justus of→see Joos van Gent
(Joos van Wassenhove)

Ghent, Peter *(British artist, 1875-*
1911)   **WI**
    Bibl: ▶Wood, Victorian ptrs.

Gheorghe, Alexandra *(Romanian*
ceramist, sculptor, 20th c.)   **BA**
    Bibl: Arta, XXVIII/10-11 (1981)

Gheorghe, Mihai *(Rumanian artist,*
20th cent.)   **WC**

Gheorghiu, Ion *(Romanian painter,*
b.1929)   **BA**
    Bibl: ARTA, XXVI(AUG 1979),
    38-40; ▶Barbosa, Art. romani
    contemp.; ▶Bénézit

Ghequier, Alexis de *(French artist,*
1817-1869)   **WC**

Gherard Dow→see Dou, Gerrit

Gherard Honthorst→see Honthorst,
Gerrit van

Gherard, Eugene de→see Guérard,
Eugène von

Gherardi→see Gherardi, Filippo
(Sancasciani)

Gherardi, Antonio   **AV BA GC PR**
(Italian architect and painter,
Rome, 1644-1702)   AV
(Italian artist, 1644-1702)   WC
(Italian painter, 1644-1702)   PR
(Italian painter, printmaker, and
architect, 1644-1702)   GC
(Italian painter, printmaker,
architect, 1644-1702)   BA
    Bibl: ▶Bénézit; ▶Bolaffi; Getty
    Photo Study Coll. (Ptgs.);
    ▶Macmillan encyc. archts.; Pelican
    Hist. of Art; ▶RILA/BHA, 1986;
    ▶Thieme-Becker; ▶Witt checklist

    Ant:o Gherardi   PR
    Antonio Gherardi   PR
Gherardi, Antonio (Reatino)   **GC WC**
    N. N. Gherardi   PR
    Reatino   GC PR

Gherardi, Antonio (Reatino)→see
Gherardi, Antonio

Gherardi, Cristofano→see Gherardi,
Cristofano (Doceno)

Gherardi, Cristofano (Cristofano dal
Borgo or Doceno)→see Gherardi,
Cristofano (Doceno)

Gherardi, Cristofano (Doceno)   **BA GC**
(Italian artist, 1508-1556)   WC
(Italian painter, 1508-1556)   BA GC
    Bibl: Getty Photo Study Coll.
    (Ptgs.); ▶RILA/BHA, 1986;
    ▶Thieme-Becker; ▶Witt checklist

Gherardi, Cristofano   **GC**
Gherardi, Cristofano (Cristofano
dal Borgo or Doceno)   **WC**

Gherardi, Filippo→see Gherardi,
Filippo (Sancasciani)

Gherardi, Filippo
(Sancasciani)   **BA GC PR WC**
(Italian artist, 1643-1704)   WC
(Italian painter, 1643-1704) BA GC PR
    Bibl: ▶Bolaffi; ▶Encyc. world art;
    Getty Photo Study Coll. (Ptgs.);
    ▶RILA/BHA; ▶Thieme-Becker

    Filippo Gherardi   PR
    Gherardi   PR
    Gherardi, Filippo   PR
    Lucchesini   PR
    Lucchesini [Gherardi]   PR
    Sancasciani   GC PR
Gherardi, Giuseppe   **BA WC**
(Italian artist, op.1850)   WC
(Italian painter, 1788/90-1884)   BA
    Bibl: ANTICHITA VIVA, XV(JAN-FEB
    1976), 40-47; ▶Thieme-Becker

Gherardini, Alessandro   **BA GC PR WC**
   (Italian artist, 1655-1723)   WC
   (Italian painter, 1655-1723) BA GC PR
   Bibl: ▶Encyc. world art;
   ▶RILA/BHA, 1986;
   ▶Thieme-Becker
   Alessandro Gherardini   PR
Gherardini, Giovanni Battista
   (Italian painter, act. c.1700)   **GC**
   Bibl: ▶Thieme-Becker
Gherardini, Melchior → see Gherardini,
   Melchiorre
Gherardini, Melchiorre   **BA GC PR WC**
   (Italian artist, -1675)   WC
   (Italian painter and printmaker,
   1607-1675)   GC
   (Italian painter, 1607-1675)   PR
   (Italian painter, printmaker,
   1607-1675)   BA
   Bibl: ▶Bolaffi; Getty Photo Study
   Coll.; PARAGONE, XXIX/345(NOV
   1978), 87; ▶RILA/BHA, 1986;
   ▶Thieme-Becker
   Gherardini, Melchior   GC
   Gilardino Vecchio   PR
   Melchiorre Gherardini   PR
Gherardini, Stefano *(Italian painter,*
   1696-1756)   **GC**
   Bibl: ▶Thieme-Becker
Gherardini, Tommaso   **BA GC PR WC**
   (Italian artist, 1715-1797)   WC
   (Italian painter, 1715-1797) BA GC PR
   Bibl: ▶Bolaffi; Pellegrini, Paragone
   XXXIII (1982), 387, 86;
   ▶RILA/BHA, 1986;
   ▶Thieme-Becker
   Tommaso Gherardini   PR
Gherardo Borgognone, Michelozzo di
   Bartolommeo di → see Michelozzo
   di Bartolommeo
Gherardo del Fora → see Gherardo di
   Giovanni del Fora
Gherardo del Fora (Gherardo di
   Giovanni Master of the Triumph of
   Chastity) → see Gherardo di
   Giovanni del Fora
Gherardo della Notte → see
   Honthorst, Gerrit van
Gherardo delle Notti → see Honthorst,
   Gerrit van
Gherardo di Giovanni → see Gherardo
   di Giovanni del Fora
Gherardo di Giovanni (di
   Miniato) → see Gherardo di
   Giovanni del Fora

Gherardo di Giovanni del Fora   **BA** GC
   (Italian artist, 1444/5-1497)   WC
   (Italian artist, 15th cent.)   WC
   (Italian artist, circa 1432-op.
   1497)   WI
   (Italian painter, 1444/45-1497)   PR
   (Italian painter, illuminator,
   printmaker, and mosaicist, ca.
   1445-1497)   GC
   (Italian painter, printmaker,
   mosaicist, ca.1445-1497)   BA
   Bibl: ▶Bolaffi; ▶Encyc. world art;
   ▶Fredericksen & Zeri, Census;
   Getty Photo Study Coll. (Ptgs.);
   ▶RILA/BHA, 1986;
   ▶Thieme-Becker; ▶Witt checklist
Gherardo del Fora   **GC PR**
Gherardo del Fora (Gherardo di
Giovanni Master of the
Triumph of Chastity)   **WC**
Gherardo di Giovanni   GC **WI**
   Gherardo di Giovanni (di Miniato)   PR
   Gherardo di Giovanni di Miniato   GC
Master of the Triumph of
Chastity   GC **WC** WI
Gherardo di Giovanni di
   Miniato → see Gherardo di
   Giovanni del Fora
Gherardo di Jacopo → see Starnina,
   Gherardo
Gherardo Fiamengo → see Honthorst,
   Gerrit van
Gherardo Fiammingo → see Honthorst,
   Gerrit van
Gherardo Segers → see Seghers,
   Gerard
Gherardo Segers detto delle
   Notti → see Seghers, Gerard
Gherardo Segers, detto delle
   Notti → see Seghers, Gerard
Gherardo Starnina → see Starnina,
   Gherardo
Gherarducci, Silvestro de' → see
   Silvestro dei Gherarducci
Gherarducci, Silvestro dei → see
   Silvestro dei Gherarducci
Gherasim, Marin *(Romanian artist,*
   b.1937)   **BA**
   Bibl: ARTA 78, XXV, 1978
Gherasim, Paul *(Romanian painter,*
   20th c.)   **BA**
   Bibl: STUDII SI CERCETARI DE
   ISTORIA ARTEI, XXII(1975), 139-
   148
Gherban, Alexandre *(Romanian*
   artist, b.1943)   **BA**
   Bibl: ▶Art Index, v.39; ▶Intl. dir.
   exh. artists, 1983
Gheri, Cosimo *(Italian painter, act.*
   1600)   **BA**
   Bibl: ▶Bolaffi; Paragone
   XXXVII/437 (July 1986), p.25-34;
   Santi et al., Comp. della SS.
   Annunziata a Firenze;
   ▶Thieme-Becker

Gheri, Goro *(Italian, act.1518-1519)*   **BA**
   Bibl: ▶Encic. italiana; Sherr,
   BURLINGTON, CXXV, 958(JAN
   1983), 31-32
Gheringh, Anton Günther   **BA GC**
   (Flemish artist, op.1662-m.1668)   WC
   (Flemish painter, d.1668)   BA
   (Flemish, act.1662-d.1668)   GC
   (German artist, op.1641-m.
   1668)   WC
   Bibl: ▶Bénézit; ▶RILA/BHA;
   ▶Thieme-Becker
   Gheringh, Anton Gunther (also,
   erroneously, Jan)   **WC**
   Gunther van Geringh, Antonius   **WC**
Gheringh, Anton Gunther (also,
   erroneously, Jan) → see Gheringh,
   Anton Günther
Gherra, G. *(Swiss architect)*   **AV**
   Bibl: Ville giardini, 1988 May, no.
   224, p.18
Gherwen or Gerwen, Reynier
   van → see Gherwen, Reynier van
Gherwen, Reynier van   **BA GC**
   (Dutch artist, op.1652-m.c.1661)   WC
   (Dutch painter, act.1640-ca.
   1660)   BA
   (Dutch painter, act.1640-d. ca.
   1660)   GC
   Bibl: ▶Bernt, Neth. ptrs. 17c., v.4,
   no.98; Getty Photo Study Coll.;
   Getty Photo Study Coll. (Ptgs.);
   ▶RILA/BHA; ▶Thieme-Becker;
   ▶Witt checklist
   Gerwen, Reymer van   GC
   Gherwen or Gerwen, Reynier
   van   **WC**
Ghesolfi → see Ghisolfi, Giovanni
Ghessner → see Gessner, Salomon
Gheție, Alexandrina *(Romanian*
   draftsman, b.1935)   **BA**
   Bibl: ARTA, XXVIII(6 JUNE 1980),
   24
Ghetti, Antonio *(Italian sculptor,*
   act.1645-1689)   **GC**
   Bibl: TCI Napoli e dintorni
Ghetti, Bartolomeo   **AV BA**
   (Italian marble worker, sculptor,
   act. 1645-1689)   AV
   (Italian marble worker, sculptor,
   act.1645-1689)   BA
   Bibl: ▶Bénézit; ▶Bessone-Aurelj,
   Scult. & arch. ital.; ▶RILA/BHA;
   ▶Thieme-Becker
Ghetti, Pietro   **AV**
Ghetti, Pietro *(Italian marble*
   worker, sculptor, act.1645-1689)   **BA**
   Bibl: ▶Bénézit; ▶Bessone-Aurelj,
   Scult. & arch. ital.;
   ▶Thieme-Becker
Gheyn → see Gheyn, Jacob III de
Gheyn family *(Dutch painters,*
   printmakers, 16th-17th cs.)   **BA**
   Bibl: ▶Thieme-Becker; ▶Wurzbach,
   NLD Künst.-Lex.
Gheyn or Geyn, Guilliam or Willem
de *(Dutch artist, 1610-p.1650)*   **WC**

Gheyn or Geyn, Jacob, III de→see
    Gheyn, Jacob III de
Gheyn or Geyn, Jacques or Jacob, II
    de→see Gheyn, Jacob II de
Gheyn, Gain, Geyn etc., Jacob, I
    Jansz. de→see Gheyn, Jacob I de
Gheyn, Jacob de (II)→see Gheyn,
    Jacob II de
Gheyn, Jacob de (III)→see Gheyn,
    Jacob III de
Gheyn, Jacob de (the Elder)→see
    Gheyn, Jacob I de
Gheyn, Jacob de, III→see Gheyn,
    Jacob III de
Gheyn, Jacob I de   **BA**
    (early Netherlandish painter,
        glass painter, printmaker, ca.
        1537-1581)   BA
    (Netherlands artist, c.1532-
        1582)   WC
    (North Netherlandish painter,
        printmaker, glass painter, and
        draughtsman, ca.1537-1581)   GC
        Bibl: ▶Bénézit; Getty Photo Study
        Coll. (Ptgs.); ▶RILA/BHA;
        ▶Thieme-Becker; ▶Witt checklist;
        ▶Wurzbach, NLD Künst.-Lex.
    Gain, Jacob (the Elder)   GC
Gheyn, Gain, Geyn etc., Jacob, I
    Jansz. de   **WC**
Gheyn, Jacob de (the Elder)   **GC**
Gheyn, Jacob II de   **BA GC**
    (Dutch painter, 1565-1629)   PR
    (Dutch painter, draughtsman,
        and printmaker, 1565-1629)   GC
    (Dutch painter, printmaker,
        1565-1629)   BA
    (Dutch, 1565-1629)   JG
    (Flemish artist, 1565-1629)   WC
        Bibl: ▶Encyc. world art;
        ▶RILA/BHA; ▶Thieme-Becker;
        ▶Witt checklist
    de Gheyn, Jacques   **JG**
    Gheyn or Geyn, Jacques or
        Jacob, II de   **WC**
    Gheyn, Jacob de (II)   **PR**
    Gheyn, Jacques de   PR
    Gheyn, Jacques de (the Elder)   PR
    Gheyn, Jacques II de   GC
    Jacob de Gheyn (II)   PR

Gheyn, Jacob III de   **BA GC**
    (Dutch artist, c.1596-1641)   WC
    (Dutch painter, 1596-1641)   PR
    (Dutch painter, draughtsman,
        and printmaker, ca.1596-
        1641)   GC
    (Dutch printmaker, painter, ca.
        1596-1641)   BA
        Bibl: Regteren Altena, JACQUES
        DE GHEYN,I, 164; ▶RILA/BHA;
        ▶Thieme-Becker; ▶Witt checklist;
        ▶Wurzbach, NLD Künst.-Lex.
    De Gheyn   PR
    Gheyn   PR
    Gheyn or Geyn, Jacob, III de   **WC**
    Gheyn, Jacob de (III)   **PR**
    Gheyn, Jacob de, III   PR
    Jacob de Gheyn (III)   PR
Gheyn, Jacques de→see Gheyn,
    Jacob II de
Gheyn, Jacques de (the Elder)→see
    Gheyn, Jacob II de
Gheyn, Jacques II de→see Gheyn,
    Jacob II de
Gheyn, Jan Baptist de (Dutch)   **GC**
        Bibl: Getty Photo Study Coll.
Ghez, Gilles (French painter, b.1945)   **BA**
        Bibl: ▶Bénézit; London (GBR),
        Camden Arts Ctr., Conroy
        Maddox (1979)
Ghezzi, Domenico di Bartolo→see
    Domenico di Bartolo
Ghezzi, Giuseppe   **BA GC PR WC**
    (Italian artist, 1634-1721)   WC
    (Italian painter and printmaker,
        1634-1721)   GC
    (Italian painter, 1634-1721)   PR
    (Italian painter, printmaker,
        1634-1721)   BA
        Bibl: ▶Bolaffi; ▶RILA/BHA, 1986;
        ▶Thieme-Becker; Waterhouse,
        Roman baroque ptg.
    Giuseppe Ghezzi   PR
Ghezzi, Pier Leone   **BA GC PR WC**
    (Italian artist, 1674-1755)   WC
    (Italian painter, 1674-1755)   BA GC PR
        Bibl: ▶Encyc. world art;
        ▶RILA/BHA; ▶Thieme-Becker
    Cavalier Ghezzi   PR
    Cavaliere Pietro Leone Ghezzi   PR
    Cave. Ghezzi   PR
    Ghezzi, Pier Leono   PR
    P. Ghezzi   PR
    Pier Leone Ghezzi   PR
    Pietro Leone Ghezzi   PR
    Pietro Leoni Ghezzi   PR
Ghezzi, Pier Leono→see Ghezzi, Pier
    Leone
Ghiai, Heydar (Iranian architect,
    1922-)   **AV**
Ghianda, Pierluigi (Italian cabinet-
    and furniture-maker, Milan)   **AV**
        Bibl: Abitare, 1987, suppl. 251

Ghiare, Michele [Unidentified]
    (Unknown painter, act. 18th
        century)   **PR**
        Bibl: Riccardi inventory dated
        1776
    Michele Ghiare   PR
Ghiaţă, Dumitru   **BA WC**
    (Romanian painter, 1888-1972)   BA
    (Rumanian artist, 1888-)   WC
        Bibl: ▶Barbosa, Art. romani
        contemp.; ▶Bénézit
Ghiausche, Acchille→see Giansche,
    Achille
Ghiberti, Buonaccorso (Italian
    architect, engineer, 1451-1516)   **BA**
        Bibl: ▶Portoghesi, Diz. arch. e
        urbanistica; ▶Thieme-Becker
Ghiberti, Lorenzo   **AV BA CE GC WC**
    (1378-1455)   AV
    (Italian artist, 1378-1455)   WC
    (Italian sculptor, ca.1381-1455)   GC
    (Italian sculptor, theorist, ca.
        1381-1455)   BA
    (Sculptor, architect, painter,
        goldsmith, writer, 1378-1455)   CE
        Bibl: ▶Encyc. world art;
        ▶RILA/BHA; ▶Thieme-Becker
    Lorenzo Ghiberti   CE
Ghiberti, Vittorio   **BA GC**
    (Italian goldsmith, sculptor, ca.
        1418-1496)   BA
    (Italian sculptor, ca.1418-1496)   GC
        Bibl: ▶Bessone-Aurelj, Scult. &
        arch. ital.; ▶RILA/BHA;
        ▶Thieme-Becker
Ghidiglia Quintavalle, Augusta→see
    Quintavalle, Augusta Ghidiglia
Ghidoni, Domenico (Italian
    sculptor, ca.1860-1920/1921)   **GC**
        Bibl: ▶Busse, Maler u. Bildhauer
        19. Jahr.; TCI Lombardia
Ghieteels, Jan (early Netherlandish
    tapestry artist, b.ca.1488, act.
    1554)   **BA**
        Bibl: Gobel, Lowlands Tapestries,
        p.64; Hulst, Tapisséries
        flamandes, p.156
Ghifolzi→see Ghisolfi, Giovanni
Ghiglia→see Ghiglia, Oscar
Ghiglia, Oscar   **BA GC PR WC**
    (Italian artist, 1876-)   WC
    (Italian painter, 1876-1945)   BA GC PR
        Bibl: ▶Bénézit; ▶Bolaffi;
        ▶RILA/BHA; ▶Thieme-Becker;
        ▶Vollmer, Künst.-Lex. 20. Jhr.
    Ghiglia   PR
    Ghiglia, Oskar   PR
    Oscar Ghiglia   PR
Ghiglia, Oskar→see Ghiglia, Oscar
Ghiglion-Green, Maurice (French
    artist, 1913-)   **WC**
Ghika, Nicolas   **BA**
    (Greek artist, 1906-)   WC
    (Greek painter, b.1906)   BA
        Bibl: ▶Bénézit
    Ghika, Nikolaos Alexander
        Hadjikyriacos   **WC**

Ghika, Nikolaos Alexander
   Hadjikyriacos→see Ghika, Nicolas
Ghika-Budeşti, Nicolae (Romanian
   architect, 1869-1943)   BA
      Bibl: ▶Fogg Mus. Librr. cat.; ▶Met.
      Mus. Art libr. cat.

Ghilain (Austrian? painter, act.1901)   BA
      Bibl: Kunstjahrb. Stadt Linz (1979)
      pp.39-48

Ghilchick, David   BA
   (British artist, 1892-)   WC
   (British artist, b.1892)   WI
   (British painter, illustrator,
      b.1892)   BA
      Bibl: ▶Johnson, Brit. artists;
      ▶Waters, Brit. artists

   Ghilchik, David   WC
   Ghilchik, David L.   WI
Ghilchik, David→see Ghilchick, David
Ghilchik, David L. →see Ghilchick,
   David
Ghilsolfi→see Ghisolfi, Giovanni
Ghilsolphi→see Ghisolfi, Giovanni
Ghin, J. (French artist, 20th cent.)   WC
Ghinelli, Vicenzo (Italian architect)   AV
      Bibl: Architectural review, 1983
      June, v.173, no.1036, p.66
Ghinghi, Francesco (Italian gem
   carver, 1689-1762)   BA
      Bibl: Antologia di B-A I/3 (Sept
      1977) 271-281; ▶Thieme-Becker
Ghini, Antonio→see Ghini, Antonio
   di Paolo
Ghini, Antonio di Paolo (Italian
   sculptor and painter, d.1482)   GC
      Bibl: Getty Photo Study Coll.
      (Sculp.); TCI Toscana
   Ghini, Antonio   GC
Ghino d'Antonio di Ghino (Italian
   painter, act.1524-1552)   BA
      Bibl: ▶Bolaffi; Corti, in
      PARAGONE, XXXVII/439 (Sept.
      1986), p. 57-60; TCI Toscana;
      ▶Thieme-Becker
Ghio di Pantaleo, Pietro Giovanni
   (Italian painter, act.1610)   BA
      Bibl: Lopez Torrijos, Arch. esp. de
      arte, LI/202 (Apr-Jun 1978) 184-
      186
Ghirardelli→see Ghirardelli, Alida
Ghirardelli, Alida (American painter,
   1881-1909)   PR
      Bibl: De Young Mus. cat.; ▶WWW
      Amer. art
   Alida Ghirardelli   PR
   Ghirardelli   PR
Ghirardo→see Honthorst, Gerrit van
Ghirardo fialdengo→see Honthorst,
   Gerrit van
Ghirardo fiamengo→see Honthorst,
   Gerrit van
Ghirardoni, Giovanni Andrea
   (Italian painter, d. ca.1628)   PR
      Bibl: ▶Thieme-Becker
   Gio. Andrea Ghirardoni   PR
   Giovanni Andrea Ghirardoni   PR

Ghirlandai→see Ghirlandaio,
   Domenico (Domenico Bigordi)
Ghirlandaio→see Ghirlandaio,
   Benedetto
Ghirlandaio→see Ghirlandaio,
   Domenico (Domenico Bigordi)
Ghirlandaio→see Ghirlandaio, Ridolfo
   (Ridolfo di Domenico Bigordi)
Ghirlandaio (Domenico Bigordi)→see
   Ghirlandaio, Domenico (Domenico
   Bigordi)
Ghirlandaio, Benedetto   GC PR WC
   (Italian artist, 1458-1497)   WC
   (Italian painter, 1458-1497)   PR
   (Italian, 1458-1497)   GC
      Bibl: ▶Thieme-Becker; ▶Witt
      checklist
   Benedetto Ghirlandaio   PR
   Ghirlandaio   PR
Ghirlandaio, Davide→see
   Ghirlandaio, Davide (Davide
   Bigordi)
**Ghirlandaio, Davide (Davide
   Bigordi)**   BA GC PR
   (Italian artist, 1452-1525)   WC
   (Italian painter and mosaicist,
      1452-1525)   GC
   (Italian painter, 1452-1525)   PR
   (Italian painter, mosaicist, 1452-
      1525)   BA
      Bibl: ▶Bolaffi; ▶Encyc. world art;
      ▶RILA/BHA, 1986;
      ▶Thieme-Becker
   Davide Bigordi   PR
   Davide Ghirlandaio   PR
Ghirlandaio, Davide   GC PR WC
   Ghirlandajo, Davide   PR
Ghirlandaio, Domenico→see
   Ghirlandaio, Domenico (Domenico
   Bigordi)
Ghirlandaio, Domenico (Bigordi),
   II→see Ghirlandaio, Domenico
   (Domenico Bigordi)
**Ghirlandaio, Domenico (Domenico
   Bigordi)**   BA GC PR
   (Italian artist, 1449-1494)   WC
   (Italian painter, 1449-1494)   BA GC PR
      Bibl: ▶Bolaffi; Getty Photo Study
      Coll. (Ptgs.); Hutzel; ▶RILA/BHA;
      ▶Thieme-Becker
   Bigordi, Domenico   GC
   Domenico Ghirlandaio   PR
   Domenico Ghirlandaio (Domenico
      Bigordi)   PR
   Domenico Ghirlandajo   PR
   Domenico Ghirlandajo Maestro di
      Michelangelo   PR
   Ghirlandai   PR
   Ghirlandaio   PR
   Ghirlandaio (Domenico Bigordi)   GC
   Ghirlandaio, Domenico   GC PR
**Ghirlandaio, Domenico
   (Bigordi), II**   WC

Ghirlandaio, Ridolfo→see
   Ghirlandaio, Ridolfo (Ridolfo di
   Domenico Bigordi)
Ghirlandaio, Ridolfo (Bigordi), II→see
   Ghirlandaio, Ridolfo (Ridolfo di
   Domenico Bigordi)
**Ghirlandaio, Ridolfo (Ridolfo di
   Domenico Bigordi)**   BA GC PR
   (Italian artist, 1483-1561)   WC
   (Italian painter, 1483-1561) BA GC PR
      Bibl: ▶Bolaffi; ▶Encyc. world art;
      Getty Photo Study Coll. (Ptgs.);
      ▶RILA/BHA; ▶Thieme-Becker
   Bigordi, Ridolfo di Domenico   GC
   Ghirlandaio   PR
   Ghirlandaio, Ridolfo   GC PR
Ghirlandaio, Ridolfo (Bigordi), II WC
   Ridolfo del Crilandaio   PR
   Ridolfo di Domenico Bigordi
      Ghirlandaio   PR
   Ridolfo Ghirlandaio   PR
   Ridolfo Grillandajo   PR
   Ridolpho Grilandajo   PR
Ghirlandajo, Davide→see
   Ghirlandaio, Davide (Davide
   Bigordi)
Ghirri, Luigi (Italian photographer,
   b.1943)   BA
      Bibl: Parma(ITA), Universita,
      Centro studi...,GHIRRI, 1979
Ghisdplu→see Ghisolfi, Giovanni
Ghisholfi→see Ghisolfi, Giovanni
Ghisi, Adamo→see Scultori, Adamo
   (Mantovano)
Ghisi, Diana→see Scultori, Diana
   (Mantovana)
Ghisi, Francescuccio→see Ghissi,
   Francescuccio (Francesco di Cecco)
Ghisi, Giorgio   BA CE GC
   (Engraver, c.1520-1582)   CE
   (Italian artist, 1520-1582)   WC
   (Italian printmaker, 1520-1582)   BA
   (Italian, 1520-1582)   GC
      Bibl: ▶Bolaffi; ▶Thieme-Becker;
      ▶Witt checklist
Ghisi, Giorgio (Mantuano)   WC
   Mantuano, Giorgio   CE
Ghisi, Giorgio (Mantuano)→see
   Ghisi, Giorgio
Ghisi, Giovanni Battista
   Mantovano→see Scultori, Giovanni
   Battista (Mantovano)
Ghisi, Teodoro   BA GC
   (Italian artist, 1536-1601)   WC
   (Italian painter, 1536-1601)   BA GC
      Bibl: ▶Bénézit; ▶Bolaffi;
      ▶RILA/BHA, 1986; TCI Lombardia;
      ▶Thieme-Becker
Ghisi, Teodoro (Mantovano)   WC
Ghisi, Teodoro (Mantovano)→see
   Ghisi, Teodoro
Ghisilieri, Filippo Carlo, marchese
   (Italian majolica manufacturer,
   d.1759)   BA
      Bibl: Bertocchi, Faenza LXVIII
      (1982), 255-7

Ghislandi → see Ghislandi, Vittore
  Giuseppe
Ghislandi, Fra Vittore → see Ghislandi,
  Vittore Giuseppe
Ghislandi, Fra Vittore (Fra Paolotto or
  Fra Galgario) → see Ghislandi,
  Vittore Giuseppe
Ghislandi, Fra Vittorio → see Ghislandi,
  Vittore Giuseppe
Ghislandi, Giuseppe → see Ghislandi,
  Vittore Giuseppe
Ghislandi, Giuseppe, called Fra
  Vittore di Galgario → see Ghislandi,
  Vittore Giuseppe
Ghislandi, Vittore → see Ghislandi,
  Vittore Giuseppe

Ghislandi, Vittore Giuseppe   **BA**
  (Italian artist, 1655-1743)   WC
  (Italian painter, 1655-1743)   BA PR
  (Italian, 1655-1743)   GC
    Bibl: ▶Bolaffi; ▶Fredericksen &
    Zeri, Census; Getty Photo Study
    Coll. (Ptgs.); ▶Thieme-Becker;
    ▶Witt checklist
  Fra Galgario   PR
  Fra Vittore Ghislandi   PR
  Galgario, Fra   GC
  Ghislandi   PR
Ghislandi, Fra Vittore   **GC PR**
**Ghislandi, Fra Vittore (Fra
  Paolotto or Fra Galgario)**   **WC**
  Ghislandi, Fra Vittorio   PR
  Ghislandi, Giuseppe   PR
  Ghislandi, Giuseppe, called Fra
    Vittore di Galgario   PR
  Ghislandi, Vittore   PR
  Paolotto, Fra   GC
  Paulotto il Frate   PR
Ghisolfe → see Ghisolfi, Giovanni
Ghisolfi → see Ghisolfi, Giovanni
Ghisolfi (not Grisolfi), Giovanni → see
  Ghisolfi, Giovanni

Ghisolfi, Giovanni   **BA GC PR**
  (Italian artist, c.1623-1683)   WC
  (Italian painter, ca.1623-1683)   BA PR
  (Italian, ca.1623-1683)   GC
    Bibl: ▶Bolaffi; ▶Thieme-Becker;
    ▶Witt checklist
  Crisolfi   PR
  G. Ghilsolfi   PR
  G. Ghisolfi   PR
  Gasolphi   PR
  Gesol.   PR
  Ghesolfi   PR
  Ghifolzi   PR
  Ghilsolfi   PR
  Ghilsolphi   PR
  Ghisdplu   PR
  Ghisholfi   PR
  Ghisolfe   PR
  Ghisolfi   PR
Ghisolfi (not Grisolfi), Giovanni   **WC**
  Ghisolfo   PR
  Ghisolph   PR
  Ghisolphi   PR
  Ghisolpi   PR
  Ghisolzi   PR
  Ghisophi   PR
  Ghsiolfi   PR
  Gio. Grisolfi milanese   PR
  Gio: Ghisolfi   PR
  Giovanni Ghisolfi   PR
  Giovanni Ghisolfo   PR
  Gisolfi   PR
  Gisolphi   PR
  Gizolphi   PR
  Gosolphi   PR
  Grisolfi   PR
  Guisolfi   PR
Ghisolfo → see Ghisolfi, Giovanni
Ghisolph → see Ghisolfi, Giovanni
Ghisolphi → see Ghisolfi, Giovanni
Ghisolpi → see Ghisolfi, Giovanni
Ghisolzi → see Ghisolfi, Giovanni
Ghisoni or Guisoni, Fermo di Stefano
  (Fermo da Carravaggio) → see
  Ghisoni, Fermo di Stefano (Fermo
  da Caravaggio)
Ghisoni, Fermo → see Ghisoni, Fermo
  di Stefano (Fermo da Caravaggio)
**Ghisoni, Fermo di Stefano (Fermo
  da Caravaggio)**   **BA**
  (Italian artist, c.1505-1575)   WC
  (Italian painter, ca.1505-1575)   BA
  (Italian, ca.1505-1575)   GC
    Bibl: ▶Bolaffi; ▶Thieme-Becker;
    ▶Witt checklist
  Fermo da Caravaggio   GC
**Ghisoni or Guisoni, Fermo di
  Stefano (Fermo da
  Carravaggio)**   **WC**
Ghisoni, Fermo   **GC**
  Guisoni, Fermo di Stefano   GC
Ghisophi → see Ghisolfi, Giovanni
Ghissi → see Ghissi, Francescuccio
  (Francesco di Cecco)

Ghissi, Francescuccio → see Ghissi,
  Francescuccio (Francesco di Cecco)
**Ghissi, Francescuccio (Francesco
  di Cecco)**   **BA GC PR**
  (Italian artist, op.1359-1374)   WC
  (Italian painter, act. 1359-1374)   PR
  (Italian painter, act.1359-1374)   BA GC
    Bibl: ▶Encyc. world art;
    ▶McGraw-Hill dict. art;
    ▶RILA/BHA, 1986;
    ▶Thieme-Becker
  Francesco di Cecco   PR
  Francescuccio da Fabriano   GC
  Francescuccio Ghissi   PR
  Ghisi, Francescuccio   PR
  Ghissi   PR
Ghissi, Francescuccio   **GC PR**
**Ghissi, Francescuccio or
  Francesco (Francescuccio da
  Fabriano)**   **WC**
Ghissi, Francescuccio or Francesco
  (Francescuccio da Fabriano) → see
  Ghissi, Francescuccio (Francesco di
  Cecco)
Ghitti, Pompeo   **BA GC WC**
  (Italian artist, 1631-1703)   WC
  (Italian painter, printmaker,
    1631-1703)   BA
  (Italian, 1631-1703)   GC
    Bibl: ▶Bénézit; ▶Bolaffi;
    ▶Thieme-Becker; ▶Witt checklist
Ghittoni, Francesco (Italian painter,
  1855-1928)   **BA**
    Bibl: ▶Bolaffi; ▶Thieme-Becker
Ghiulamila, Alexander (French
  architect, Paris)   **AV**
    Bibl: Abitare, 1987 Apr., no.253,
    p.262
Ghizzardi, Bernardino (Italian artist,
  c.1730-1770)   **WC**
Ghobert, Bernard (Belgian artist,
  20th cent.)   **WC**
Ghsiolfi → see Ghisolfi, Giovanni
Ghysis, Nicolas (Greek artist, 1842-
  1906)   **WC**
GI → see Monogrammist G.I.
Giabonetto Nobile → see Nobile,
  Giabonetto [Unidentified]
Giacciuoli (Italian painter, act.
  1730/50)   **PR**
    Bibl: ▶Thieme-Becker
  Giacciuoli Scolare d'Orizonte   PR
  Giacciuoli Scolare di Orizonte   PR
Giacciuoli Scolare d'Orizonte → see
  Giacciuoli
Giacciuoli Scolare di Orizonte → see
  Giacciuoli
Giaccoms Bassan → see Bassano,
  Jacopo (Jacopo da Ponte)
Giacento, J.-B. de (French architect,
  Bordeaux)   **AV**
    Bibl: ▶Annuaire archts. fran.
Giachi, E. (Italian artist, 19th cent.) **WC**
**Giachinetti Gonzalez, Giovanni
  (Borgognone dalle Teste)**
  (Spanish artist, c.1630-1696)   **WC**

Giachosa, Fernando *(German artist, op.1836-1849)* **WC**
Giacinto (Brandi) →*see* Brandi, Domenico (Micco)
Giacinto Brandi →*see* Brandi, Giacinto
Giacinto Brandj →*see* Brandi, Giacinto
Giacinto Calandrucci →*see* Calandrucci, Giacinto
Giacinto Camassei →*see* Camassei, Giacinto
Giacinto de Popoli →*see* Populi, Giacinto de
Giacinto de Populi →*see* Populi, Giacinto de
Giacinto del Popolo →*see* Populi, Giacinto de
Giacinto del Populo →*see* Populi, Giacinto de
Giacinto Diana →*see* Diano, Giacinto
Giacinto Gimignani →*see* Gimignani, Giacinto
Giacinto Gimignano →*see* Gimignani, Giacinto
Giacinto Giminiani →*see* Gimignani, Giacinto
Giacinto lo Calabrese →*see* Giacinto lo Calavrese [Unidentified]
Giacinto lo Calavrese [Unidentified] *(Italian painter)* **PR**
    Bibl: inventory of Francesco Cavallino, dated 1677/05/29
    Giacinto lo Calabrese   **PR**
Giacobbe [Unidentified] *(Unknown painter, act. 17th century)* **PR**
    Bibl: Neapolitan inventories (D'Amore 1656, De Costanzo 1692, Marciano 1702, De Palma 1716, Pignatelli 1723) and Rome (Pamphilj, 1648). [Labrot thinks he is Flemish]
    Giacobe   **PR**
    Giacobo   **PR**
    Giacobo fiammengo   **PR**
Giacobe →*see* Giacobbe [Unidentified]
Giacobo →*see* Giacobbe [Unidentified]
Giacobo fiammengo →*see* Giacobbe [Unidentified]
Giacoboni, Giorgio **PR WC**
    (Italian artist, op.1739-m.c. 1777)   **WC**
    (Italian painter, act. 1739, d. 1777)   **PR**
    Bibl: ▶Thieme-Becker
    Giorgio Giacobini   **PR**
    Giorgio Giacoboni   **PR**
    Giorgio Jacoboni scolare di Gio: Paolo Pannini   **PR**
    Giorgio Tacoboni   **PR**
Giacoma, Antonio della *(Italian painter, act.1787-1796)* **BA**
    Bibl: Akademie Nauk SSSR, Russische Kunst, v.6
Giacome Migliori →*see* Migliori, Giacome [Unidentified]

Giacomelli, Hector *(French artist, 1822-1904)* **WC**
Giacomelli, Mario **BA JG**
    (Italian painter, poet, photographer, b.1925)   **BA**
    (Italian, 1925 -)   **JG**
    Bibl: Brunswick (ME, USA), Bowdoin Coll., New landscape (1978); ▶Image
Giacometti family *(Swiss artists, 19th-20th cs.)* **BA**
    Bibl: PHAIDON
Giacometti, Alberto **BA GC WC**
    (Swiss artist, 1901-1966)   **WC**
    (Swiss painter, sculptor, and printmaker, 1901-1966)   **GC**
    (Swiss painter, sculptor, printmaker, 1901-1966)   **BA**
    Bibl: ▶RILA/BHA; ▶Vollmer, Künst.-Lex. 20. Jhr.; WBG
Giacometti, Augusto **BA WC**
    (Swiss artist, 1877-1947)   **WC**
    (Swiss painter, 1877-1947)   **BA**
    Bibl: ▶Encyc. world art; PHAIDON
Giacometti, Diego *(Swiss sculptor, furniture designer, 1902-1985)* **BA**
    Bibl: Lord, Giacometti; Marchesseau, DIEGO GIACOMETTI
Giacometti, Giovanni **BA WC**
    (Swiss artist, 1868-1933)   **WC**
    (Swiss painter, 1868-1933)   **BA**
    Bibl: PHAIDON; ▶Schweiz. Künst.-Lex.; ▶Vollmer, Künst.-Lex. 20. Jhr.
Giacomo →*see* Po, Giacomo del
Giacomo (or Jacopo) da Campli →*see* Giacomo da Campli
Giacomo Antonio Ceruti →*see* Ceruti, Giacomo Antonio (Pitocchetto)
Giacomo Bambini →*see* Bambini, Giacomo
Giacomo Barozzi →*see* Vignola (Giacomo Barozzi)
Giacomo Barozzi da Vignuola →*see* Vignola (Giacomo Barozzi)
Giacomo Bassan →*see* Bassano, Jacopo (Jacopo da Ponte)
Giacomo Bassani →*see* Bassano, Jacopo (Jacopo da Ponte)
Giacomo Bassano →*see* Bassano, Jacopo (Jacopo da Ponte)
Giacomo Berger →*see* Berger, Giacomo
Giacomo Bertoja →*see* Bertoja, Giacomo (Giacomo Zanguidi)
Giacomo Borgognone →*see* Courtois, Jacques (le Bourguignon)
Giacomo Brandi →*see* Brandi, Giacinto
Giacomo Cavedone →*see* Cavedone, Giacomo
Giacomo Ceruti →*see* Ceruti, Giacomo Antonio (Pitocchetto)
Giacomo Cortese →*see* Courtois, Jacques (le Bourguignon)

Giacomo Cortese detto il Borgognone →*see* Courtois, Jacques (le Bourguignon)
Giacomo Cortesi, called Borgognone →*see* Courtois, Jacques (le Bourguignon)
Giacomo d'Alemanii →*see* Griesinger, Jakob
Giacomo da Bassano →*see* Bassano, Jacopo (Jacopo da Ponte)
Giacomo da Campli **GC WC**
    (Italian artist, op.1461-1479)   **WC**
    (Italian painter, act.1461-d. aft. 1490)   **GC**
    Bibl: TCI Abruzzo-Molise
Giacomo (or Jacopo) da Campli **WC**
Jacopo da Campli **WC**
Giacomo da Castello →*see* Kerckhoven, Jacob van der
Giacomo da Pontolmo →*see* Pontormo (Jacopo Carrucci)
Giacomo da Pontorno →*see* Pontormo (Jacopo Carrucci)
Giacomo da Recanati →*see* Giacomo di Nicola da Recanati
Giacomo da Vicenza *(Italian painter, act.1504)* **BA**
    Bibl: Barbieri, Pittori di Vicenza
Giacomo de Castro →*see* Castro, Giacomo di
Giacomo del Duca →*see* Del Duca, Giacomo
Giacomo del Pisano **GC PR**
    (Italian artist, 15th cent.)   **WC**
    (Italian painter, 15th century)   **GC**
    (Italian painter, act. 2nd half 15th cent.)   **PR**
    Bibl: ▶Fredericksen & Zeri, Census; Getty Photo Study Coll. (Ptgs.); ▶Thieme-Becker; ▶Witt checklist
Jacomo del Pisano **WC**
Pisano, Giacomo del   **GC PR**
Pisano, Jacopo del **GC**
Pisano, Jacopo or Giacomo del **WC**
Giacomo del Po →*see* Po, Giacomo del
Giacomo del Po' →*see* Po, Giacomo del
Giacomo del Ponte da Bassano →*see* Bassano, Jacopo (Jacopo da Ponte)
Giacomo del Ponte da Bassano Stato Veneto →*see* Bassano, Jacopo (Jacopo da Ponte)
Giacomo del Po' →*see* Po, Giacomo del
Giacomo del Tonghio *(Italian sculptor, metalworker(?), and enameler(?), d.1390)* **GC**
    Bibl: Getty Photo Study Coll. (Medieval); ▶Thieme-Becker
    Fra Iacopo del Tonghio   **GC**
    Jacopo del Tonghi   **GC**
    Jacopo del Tonghio   **GC**
    Tonghio, Giacomo del   **GC**

Giacomo della Porta→*see* Della
Porta, Giacomo
Giacomo di Benedetto *(Italian
sculptor, act.1490-1525)*   **BA**
   Bibl: Di Marzo, I Gagini, v.1, p.49;
   ▶Thieme-Becker
Giacomo di Castro→*see* Castro,
Giacomo di
Giacomo di Giovanni *(Italian
painter, act. 1st half 16th c.)*   **GC**
   Bibl: TCI Umbria
Giacomo di Martino *(Italian mason,
act.1543-1553)*   **BA**
   Bibl: Battilotti, ARTICHITA VIVA,
   XX/1(1981)
*Giacomo di Mino di Neri del
Pellicciaio*→*see* Jacopo di Mino del
Pellicciaio
**Giacomo di Nicola da
Recanati**   **BA GC WC**
   (Italian artist, ca.1390-ca.1466)   WC
   (Italian painter, ca.1390-1466?)   GC
   *(Italian painter, ca.1390-ca.
   1466)*   BA
   Bibl: ▶Bolaffi; Donnini, NOT. DA
   PALAZZO ALBANI, 18/2 (1989)
   p.5-14; TCI Marche; ▶Witt
   checklist
   Giacomo da Recanati   GC
   Recanati, Giacomo da   GC
Giacomo di Pontormo→*see* Pontormo
(Jacopo Carrucci)
Giacomo Farelli→*see* Farelli, Giacomo
Giacomo Favretto→*see* Favretto,
Giacomo
Giacomo Fiammingo *(German ivory
carver in ITA, act.1594-1596)*   **BA**
   Bibl: Antologia di B-A II/6 (May
   1975-76); PANTHEON,
   XXXVII/2(APR-JUN 1979, 141;
   ▶Thieme-Becker
Giacomo Forcella→*see* Forcella,
Giacomo [Unidentified]
Giacomo Francesco Cipper→*see*
Cipper, Giacomo Francesco
(Todeschini)
Giacomo Francia→*see* Francia,
Giacomo
Giacomo Franco→*see* Francia,
Giacomo
Giacomo Galli→*see* Galli, Giacomo
Giacomo Giacquetto→*see*
Giacquetto, Giacomo
[Unidentified]
Giacomo Guardi→*see* Guardi,
Giacomo
Giacomo Ligozzi→*see* Ligozzi,
Jacopo
Giacomo Manecchia→*see*
Mannecchia, Giacomo
Giacomo Mannecchia→*see*
Mannecchia, Giacomo
Giacomo Nani→*see* Nani, Giacomo
Giacomo Pacchiarotti→*see*
Pacchiarotti, Giacomo

Giacomo Parolini→*see* Parolini,
Giacomo
Giacomo Recco→*see* Recco,
Giacomo
Giacomo Robusti→*see* Tintoretto,
Jacopo (Jacopo Robusti)
*Giacomo Robusti detto il
Tintoretto*→*see* Tintoretto, Jacopo
(Jacopo Robusti)
*Giacomo Robusti di Venezia detto il
Tintoretto*→*see* Tintoretto, Jacopo
(Jacopo Robusti)
*Giacomo Robusti, detto il
Tintoretto*→*see* Tintoretto, Jacopo
(Jacopo Robusti)
Giacomo Romano [Unidentified]
(Italian painter)   **PR**
   Bibl: Poliastri inventory, Naples,
   1741
Giacomo Rosa→*see* Russo, Jacopo
Giacomo Russo→*see* Russo, Jacopo
Giacomo Sementi→*see* Sementi,
Giovanni Giacomo
Giacomo Tintoret→*see* Tintoretto,
Jacopo (Jacopo Robusti)
Giacomo Tintoretto→*see* Tintoretto,
Jacopo (Jacopo Robusti)
Giacomo Todesco→*see* Cipper,
Giacomo Francesco (Todeschini)
Giacomo Zanguidi→*see* Bertoja,
Giacomo (Giacomo Zanguidi)
Giacomo Zanguidi Bertoja→*see*
Bertoja, Giacomo (Giacomo
Zanguidi)
Giacomo Zoboli→*see* Zoboli,
Giacomo
Giacomotti, Felix Henri   **GC WC**
   (French artist, 1828-1909)   WC
   (French painter, 1828-1909)   GC
   Bibl: ▶Thieme-Becker
Giacoms Bassan→*see* Bassano,
Jacopo (Jacopo da Ponte)
**Giacquetto, Giacomo
[Unidentified]** *(Italian painter)*   **PR**
   Bibl: Cella inventory, Naples,
   1680; Diaz Pimienta inventory,
   Naples, 1684, (as ''Giaquinto
   Capuano)
   Giacomo Giacquetto   PR
   Giaquinto Capuano   PR
Gialdi, Giorgio *(Italian sculptor,
architect in CSK, 1586-1623)*   **BA**
   Bibl: ▶Bénézit; Krčálová, Umění,
   XXIII/2 (1975) pp.127-141;
   ▶Thieme-Becker
Giamb.tta Ruoppoli→*see* Ruoppolo,
Giovanni Battista
Giambattista Bassano→*see* Bassano,
Giambattista (Giambattista da
Ponte)
Giambattista Bassi→*see* Bassi,
Giambattista
Giambattista da Ponte→*see* Bassano,
Giambattista (Giambattista da
Ponte)

Giambattista Dossi→*see* Dossi,
Battista
Giambattista Lanzetti→*see* Langetti,
Giovanni Battista
Giambattistiello Caracciolo→*see*
Caracciolo, Giovanni Battista
(Battistello)
Giambattistiello Caracciuolo→*see*
Caracciolo, Giovanni Battista
(Battistello)
Giambelli, Pietro *(Italian)*   **GC**
   Bibl: Gernsheim, Corpus Photog.
   of Drawings, 1345
Giambert, Francesco→*see* Sangallo,
Francesco da (il Margotta)
Giamberti, Antonio→*see* Sangallo,
Antonio da, the elder (Antonio
Giamberti)
Giamberti, Giuliano→*see* Sangallo,
Giuliano da
Giamberti, Marco del Buono→*see*
Marco del Buono Giamberti
Giambologna→*see* Giambologna
(Jean Boulogne)
Giambologna (Jean Boulogne)   **BA**
   *(1529-13.VIII.1608; Architect,
   Mannerist Sculptor, Bologna,
   Firenze, Roma)*   FA
   *(Flemish (Italian School), 1529-
   1608)*   JG
   *(Flemish sculptor in ITA, 1529-
   1608)*   BA
   (Italian artist, 1529-1608)   WI
   (Italian artist, c.1524-1608)   WC
   *(Italian sculptor (b. in
   Netherlands), 1529-1608)*   GC
   *(Sculptor, goldsmith, 1529-
   1608)*   CE
   Bibl: Avery & Radcliffe,
   GIAMBOLOGNA... (1978);
   ▶Bénézit; Dhanens, JEAN
   BOULOGNE; ▶Diz. biog. ital.;
   ▶Encyc. world art; Getty Photo
   Study Coll. (Sculp.); Oxford Dict.
   art, pp.199-200; ▶RILA/BHA,
   Subject, 1988; TCI Firenze;
   ▶Thieme-Becker
   Bologna, Giovanni   CE FA **GC**
   Bologna, Giovanni da   **WC WI**
   Bologne, Jean   FA
   Bologne, Jean de   FA
   Boulogne, de Jean   CE
   Giambologna   CE FA GC **JG** WI
   Jean Boulogne   FA
   Jean de Bologne   FA GC
Giambono→*see* Giambono, Michele

Giambono, Michele   **BA GC JG PR**
  (Italian artist, op.1420-1460)   WC
  (Italian painter and mosaicist,
    act.1420-1462)   GC
  (Italian painter, act. 1420-1462)   PR
  (Italian painter, mosaicist, act.
    1420-1462)   BA
  (Italian, documented 1420-
    1462)   JG
    Bibl: ▶Bolaffi; ▶RILA/BHA;
    ▶Thieme-Becker
  Bono, Michele di Taddeo   GC
Bono, Michele di Taddeo
  (Giambono or Zambone)   **WC**
  Giambono   PR
  Michele Giambono   PR
Giammelardino→see Azzolino
  (Giovanni Bernardino Ragano)
Giampetrino→see Giampietrino
Giampetrino Master→see
  Giampietrino
Giampetrino, Giovanni Pedrini→see
  Giampietrino
Giampiccoli, Giuliano *(Italian*
  printmaker, printer, 1703-1759)   **BA**
    Bibl: ▶Bolaffi; ▶Thieme-Becker
Giampietrino   **BA CE GC PR**
  (Draughtsman, post 1440/ante
    1530-post 1540-ante 1575)   CE
  (Italian artist, op.1510-1540)   WI
  (Italian artist, op.c.1520-1540)   WC
  (Italian painter, act. 1520-1540)   PR
  (Italian painter, act. ca.1520-
    1540)   GC
  (Italian painter, act.1520-1540)   BA
    Bibl: ▶Bolaffi; Brown, Seymour
    festschrift, pp.167-186; ▶Encyc.
    world art; ▶Fredericksen & Zeri,
    Census; Getty Photo Study Coll.
    (Ptgs.); ▶RILA/BHA;
    ▶Thieme-Becker; ▶Witt checklist
  Giampetrino   **BA PR WI**
  Giampetrino Master   PR
  Giampetrino, Giovanni Pedrini   PR
  Gianpietrino   WI
  Gianpietrino (Giovanni Pietro
    Rizzo Pedrini)   **WC**
  Pedrini, Giovanni   **CE GC**
  Pietro Rizzo Milanese   CE
  Rizzi, Giampietro   **CE**
  Rizzo, Giampietro   CE
Gian Benedetto Castiglione→see
  Castiglione, Giovanni Benedetto (il
  Grechetto)
Gian Bernardo Siciliano→see
  Azzolino (Giovanni Bernardino
  Ragano)
Gian Francesco Bembo→see Bembo,
  Gian Francesco
Gian Francesco da Tolmezzo→see
  Gianfrancesco da Tolmezzo
  (Giovanni Francesco dal Zotto)
Gian Francesco de' Maineri→see
  Maineri, Gian Francesco de

Gian Giacombo de' Caprotti→see
  Salaj (Gian Giacomo de' Caprotti)
Gian Giacomo de Alladio→see
  Macrino d'Alba
Gian Giacomo de' Caprotti→see Salaj
  (Gian Giacomo de' Caprotti)
Gian Gioseffo del Sole→see Sole,
  Giovan Gioseffo dal
Gian Giuseppe dl Sole→see Sole,
  Giovan Gioseffo dal
Gian Lorenzo Bernini→see Bernini,
  Gian Lorenzo
Gian Maria Falconetti→see
  Falconetti, Gian Maria
Gian Paolo di Pace→see Pace, Gian
  Paolo
Gianakos, Cristos *(American*
  sculptor, b.1934)   **BA**
    Bibl: ▶Intl. dir. exh. artists; ▶WW
    Amer. Art
Gianakos, Steven *(American*
  painter, printmaker, b.1938)   **BA**
    Bibl: ARTFORUM, 15(NOV 1976),
    73; New York (NY, USA), Solomon
    Guggenheim Museum, NINE
    ARTISTS: THEADORON AWARDS,
    1977
Gianbattista da Venezia *(Italian*   **BA**
  architect in Poland, act.1540-1570)
    Bibl: BIULETYN HIST. SZTUKI, XLV,
    1 (1983) 25-48; ▶Łozínski, Arch.
    Poland, pp.51, 187, 199
Gianbattista Zelotti→see Zelotti,
  Giovanni Battista
Gianbettino Cignaroli→see Cignaroli,
  Giambettino
Giancarli or Zancarli, Polifilo→see
  Giancarli, Polifilo
Giancarli, Polifilo   **GC**
  (Italian artist, op.1628-1636)   WC
  (Italian, act.1628-1636)   GC
    Bibl: ▶Witt checklist
  Giancarli or Zancarli, Polifilo   **WC**
  Zancarli, Polifilo   GC
Gianetti, Gino *(Italian sculptor,*
  b.1951)   **BA**
    Bibl: Michel, P., in BILDENDE
    KUNST 12 (1984) 546
Gianfrancesco da Tolmezzo
  (Giovanni Francesco dal Zotto)   **BA**
  (Italian artist, c.1450-p.1510)   WC
  (Italian painter, ca.1450-1510)   BA
  (Italian painter, ca.1450-aft.
    1510)   GC
    Bibl: ▶Bolaffi; TCI Friuli-Venezia-
    Giulia; ▶Thieme-Becker; ▶Witt
    checklist
  Gian Francesco da Tolmezzo   GC
  Giovanni Francesco da
    Tolmezzo   **GC WC**
  Tolmezzo, Gianfrancesco da   BA
  Zotto, Giovanni Francesco dal   **BA GC**
  Zotto, Giovanni Francesco dal
    (da Tolmezzo)   **WC**
Gianfresco da Rimini→see Giovanni
  Francesco da Rimini

Giangiacomo Fava de Alladio→see
  Macrino d'Alba
Giangiacomo, Tertulliano *(Italian*
  artist, 19th cent.)   **WC**
Giani di Portogallo, Luigi→see Giani,
  Luigi
Giani or Gianni, Felice→see Giani,
  Felice
Giani, Davide *(Italian architect and*
  missionary lay-brother in India,
  1908-)   **AV**
    Bibl: Arte cristiana, n.678
Giani, Felice   **AV BA GC**
  (1760?-1823)   AV
  (Italian artist, 1757/60-1823)   WC
  (Italian painter and illustrator,
    1758-1823)   GC
  (Italian painter, illustrator, 1758-
    1823)   BA
    Bibl: ▶Bolaffi; ▶Encyc. world art;
    ▶RILA/BHA, 1986; TCI Emilia-
    Romagna, p.722; ▶Thieme-Becker
  Giani or Gianni, Felice   **WC**
Giani, Giovanni *(Italian painter,*
  b.1866; act.1884-1913)   **GC**
    Bibl: ▶Thieme-Becker
Giani, Luigi   **GC**
  (Italian artist, op.1452)   WC
  (Italian painter, act.1472)   GC
    Bibl: ▶Thieme-Becker
  Giani di Portogallo, Luigi   **GC WC**
Giani, Vincenzo *(Italian sculptor,*
  1831-aft.1883)   **GC**
    Bibl: TCI Liguria
Gianlisi, Antonia *(Italian artist, 18th*
  cent.)   **WC**
Gianlorenzo Bernini→see Bernini,
  Gian Lorenzo
Giannattasio, Giovanni *(Italian*
  architect)   **AV**
    Bibl: Domus, 1986 Feb., no.669,
    p.18
Giannattasio, Ugo *(Italian artist,*
  1888-)   **WC**
Giannelli [Unidentified] *(Unknown*
  painter)   **PR**
    Bibl: Riccardi inventory, Florence,
    1715, Another Riccardi inventory
    cites a self-portrait done in 1772
    by "Prete Ambrogio Giannelli"
    but because of the difference in
    date we have assumed these are
    two different artists.
Giannelli, Ambrogio, Prete
  [Unidentified] *(Unknown painter,*
  act. 18th century)   **PR**
    Bibl: Riccardi inventory dated
    1776, has his self-portrait;
    another Riccardi inventory dated
    1715 lists a still life with flowers
    and birds by "Giannelli", but
    because of the difference in
    dates we assume that these are
    two different artists
  Prete Ambrogio Giannelli   PR
Giannetti→see Giannetti, Filippo

Giannetti, Filippo *(Italian painter,*
ca.1640-1702)   **PR**
   Bibl: ▶Thieme-Becker
   Felippo Giannetti   PR
   Felippo Ginnetti   PR
   Filippo Giannetti   PR
   Giannetti   PR
   Giannettini   PR
   Ginetti   PR
   Ginnetti   PR
Giannetti, Raffaele   **GC WC**
   (Italian artist, 1832-1916)   WC
   (Italian painter, 1832-1916)   GC
   Bibl: ▶Thieme-Becker
Giannettini → see Giannetti, Filippo
Gianni, Giambattista *(stucco artist,*
act.1687-1695)   **GC**
   Bibl: TCI Abruzzo-Molise
Gianni, Giancinto *(Italian artist,*
19th cent.)   **WC**
Gianni, Giovanni Battista *(Italian*
architect, act.1741)   **GC**
   Bibl: TCI Abruzzo-Molise
Gianni, Giuseppe *(Swiss artist,*
1829-1885)   **WC**
Giannicola di Paolo → see Giannicola
di Paolo (Smicca)
Giannicola di Paolo (Smicca)   **BA PR**
   (Italian artist, c.1460-1544)   WC
   (italian painter, ca.1460-1544) BA PR
   (Italian, ca.1460-1544)   GC
   Bibl: ▶Encyc. world art;
    ▶Fredericksen & Zeri, Census;
    ▶McGraw-Hill dict. art;
    ▶Thieme-Becker; ▶Witt checklist
   Giannicola di Paolo   GC PR
   Manni   PR
   Manni, Giannicola di Paolo GC PR WC
   Smicca   PR
Giannini family *(Italian stationers,*
bookbinders, publishers, 19th-20th
cs.)   **BA**
   Bibl: Ercoli, I GIANNINI (1986)
Giannino Lanfranchi → see Lanfranco,
Giovanni
Giannizzero → see Hofman, Pieter
(Giannizzero)
Giannizzero d'Anversa → see Hofman,
Pieter (Giannizzero)
Giannone → see Giannone, Onofrio
Giannone, Onofrio   **BA PR**
   (Italian painter, b. 1698, act.
   1732)   PR
   (Italian painter, b.1698, act.
   1732)   BA
   Bibl: ▶Bolaffi; BURLINGTON,
    CXX/901(APR 1978), 207;
    ▶Thieme-Becker
   Cavalier Giannone   PR
   Cavalier' Giannone   PR
   Giannone   PR
   Onofrio Giannone   PR
Gianol, A. *(Danish(?) artist, 19th*
cent.(?))   **WC**

Gianola, Ivano   **AV BA**
   (Swiss architect, 1944-)   AV
   (Swiss architect, b.1944)   BA
   Bibl: Botta, M. in Daidalos 13 (15
    Sept. 1984); Das Kunstwerk,
    n.3-4, Sept. 1983, p.42
Gianoli → see Gianoli, Pietro
Francesco
Gianoli, Louis *(Swiss artist, 1868-)* **WC**
Gianoli, Pietro → see Gianoli, Pietro
Francesco
Gianoli, Pietro Francesco   **PR WC**
   (Italian artist, op.1679-1690)   WC
   (Italian painter, d. 1690)   PR
   Bibl: ▶Thieme-Becker
   Gianoli   PR
   Gianoli, Pietro   PR
   Pietro Francesco Gianoli   PR
Gianpaolo Pannini → see Pannini,
Giovanni Paolo
Gianpietrino → see Giampietrino
Gianpietrino (Giovanni Pietro Rizzo
Pedrini) → see Giampietrino
Gianquinto, Alberto *(Italian painter,*
b.1929)   **BA**
   Bibl: ▶Bénézit; ▶Comanducci, Diz.
Giansche, Achille *(Draughtsman,*
ante 1510-post 1540)   **CE**
   Ghiausche, Acchille   CE
Giansimoni, Nicola   **AV BA**
   (Italian architect, act.1772,
   d.1800)   BA
   (Italian architect, born in
   Velletri, died in Rome,
   d.1800)   AV
   Bibl: Musei ferraresi, v.9-10;
    ▶Portoghesi, Diz. arch. e
    urbanistica; ▶Thieme-Becker, sv.
    Giansimoni, Niccolà
Giaquinto → see Giaquinto, Corrado
Giaquinto Capuano → see Giacquetto,
Giacomo [Unidentified]
Giaquinto, Corrado   **AV BA GC PR WC**
   (Italian artist, 1699-c.1765)   WC
   (Italian painter, 1699-1765)   AV
   (Italian painter, 1699-ca.1765)   PR
   (Italian painter, 1703-1765)   BA GC
   Bibl: ▶Bénézit, lists b.1690;
    ▶Bolaffi; ▶RILA/BHA, 1986;
    ▶Thieme-Becker; ▶Witt checklist
   Cavaliere Corrado   PR
   Chevalier Currado   PR
   Corrado Giaquinto   PR
   Giaquinto   PR
Giardelli, Arthur *(British artist,*
b.1911)   **WI**
Giardini, Giovanni   **GC WC**
   (Italian artist, 1646-1722)   WC
   (Italian, 1646-1722)   GC
   Bibl: ▶Thieme-Becker; ▶Witt
    checklist
Giardini, Lorenzo *(Italian architect*
in FRA, d. before 1724)   **BA**
   Bibl: ▶Portoghesi, Diz. arch. e
    urbanistica; ▶Thieme-Becker

Giardoni, José *(Spanish silversmith,*
act.1768, d.1804)   **BA**
   Bibl: Marton, REALES SITIOS, XXII,
    85, p.41-42
Giarghio → see Giarghio[?] [Illegible]
Giarghio[?] [Illegible] *(Unknown*
painter)   **PR**
   Bibl: Giuliano inventory, Naples
    (1702)
   Giarghio   PR
   Giayhio   PR
Giarola or Gerola, Antonio (Il
Cavaliere Coppa) → see Giarola,
Antonio (Cavalier Coppa)
Giarola, Antonio → see Giarola,
Antonio (Cavalier Coppa)
Giarola, Antonio (Cavalier
Coppa)   **BA GC**
   (Italian artist, c.1595-1665)   WC
   (Italian painter, ca.1595-1665) BA GC
   Bibl: ▶Bénézit; ▶Bolaffi; Getty
    Photo Study Coll. (Douwes coll.);
    ▶RILA/BHA, 1986;
    ▶Thieme-Becker
Giarola or Gerola, Antonio (Il
Cavaliere Coppa)   **WC**
   Giarola, Antonio   GC
Giarre, Pietro *(French painter, act.*
18th century)   **PR**
   Bibl: ▶Thieme-Becker
   Pietro Giarre   PR
Giarrizzo, Carmelo *(Italian artist,*
1850-1917)   **WC**
Giauffret, Maurice *(French*
architect)   **AV**
   Bibl: Connaissance des arts, 1984
    Sept., no.391, p.71
Giaverg [Unidentified] *(Unknown*
painter)   **PR**
   Bibl: Fesch inventory 1841, lot
    455
Giayhio → see Giarghio[?] [Illegible]
Gibb → see Gibb, Henry Phelan
Gibb, Alexander, Sir *(British*
architect)   **AV**
Gibb, H. Phelan → see Gibb, Henry
Phelan
Gibb, Harry Phelan → see Gibb, Henry
Phelan
Gibb, Henry Phelan   **WC WI**
   (British artist, 1870-1948)   WC WI
   (British painter, 1870-1948)   PR
   Bibl: ▶Johnson, Brit. artists
   Gibb   PR
   Gibb, H. Phelan   PR
   Gibb, Harry Phelan   **PR**
   Harry Phelan Gibb   PR
Gibb, J.   **WC WI**
   (British artist, 19th cent.)   WC
   (British artist, op.19th c.)   WI
Gibb, John *(British artist, op.1871-)* **WI**
Gibb, Levi Taylor → see Gibb, Lewis
Taylor
Gibb, Lewis Taylor   **WI**
   (British artist, 20th cent.)   WC
   (British artist, op.1918-1939)   WI
Gibb, Levi Taylor   **WC**

AV Avery Index   **BA** Bibl Hist of Art   **CE** Census Antique Works   **FA** Fndn Docs of Arch   **GC** Getty Ctr Photo Study Coll

Gibb, P.J. (*British artist, op.20th c.*) **WI**
Gibb, Robert → see Gibb, Robert I
Gibb, Robert → see Gibb, Robert II
Gibb, Robert I **WI**
  (*British artist, 1801-1837*) WC WI
  (*British painter, 1801-1837*) PR
    Bibl: ▶Witt checklist
  Gibb, Robert **PR WC**
  Robert Gibb PR
Gibb, Robert II **WI**
  (*British artist, 1845-1932*) WC WI
  Gibb, Robert **WC**
Gibb, T. or J. **WC WI**
  (*British artist, op.1820*) WC
  (*British artist, op.1820-*) WI
Gibbens, Abiah (*Dutch artist, op. 1629-1635*) **WC**
Gibbens, Abiah (*Dutch painter, act. 1629-1635*) **GC**
    Bibl: Getty Photo Study Coll. (Douwes coll.); ▶Witt checklist
  Gibbens, Abraham GC
Gibbens, Abraham → see Gibbens, Abiah
Gibberd, Eric **WC WI**
  (*British artist, 20th cent.*) WC
  (*British artist, op.20th c.*) WI
Gibberd, Frederick **BA**
  (*British architect, 1908-1984*) AV BA
    Bibl: ▶Arch. period. idx./RIBA, v.12, 1984; ▶Contemp. archts.; Heritage outlook, 1984, v.4, no.5, p.102; ▶Who's Who [GBR], 1980; ▶Wodehouse, Brit. archts.
  Gibberd, Frederick, Sir **AV**
Gibberd, Frederick, Sir → see Gibberd, Frederick
Gibberd, Vernon **AV BA**
  (*British architect*) AV
  (*British architect, 20th*) BA
    Bibl: ▶Avery period. idx., suppl. 7 & 9; House & garden, 1986 June, v.158, no.6, p.142; ▶RILA/BHA, [phone call to Gibberd's firm]
Gibbiani → see Gabbiani, Anton Domenico
Gibbings, Robert → see Gibbings, Robert John
Gibbings, Robert John **BA WI**
  (*British artist, 1889-1958*) WC WI
  (*British printmaker, illustrator, author, 1889-1958*) BA
    Bibl: ▶Johnson, Brit. artists; ▶Waters, Brit. artists; ▶Who was who [GBR], 1951-60
  Gibbings, Robert **WC**
Gibbins, Olaf (*West German architect, Hamburg*) **AV**
    Bibl: ▶Bund Deut. Arch. Hdbch., 1987
Gibbon, James M.C. (*British artist, op.1905-*) **WI**
Gibbons, Arthur (*American sculptor, b.1947*) **BA**
    Bibl: ▶NY art yrbk.

Gibbons, Carole (*British artist, b.1935*) **WI**
Gibbons, Edmund (*Bermudian landscape architect*) **AV**
    Bibl: Architectural digest, 1985 Mar., v.41, no.3, p.198
Gibbons, F. **WC WI**
  (*British artist, 19th cent.*) WC
  (*British artist, op.1880-1884*) WI
Gibbons, Grinling **AV BA GC**
  (*British, 1648-1721*) GC
  (*English sculptor, woodcarver, 1648-1721*) BA
  (*English woodcarver, sculptor, 1648-1721*) AV
    Bibl: ▶Brit. Mus. cat.; ▶Dict. natl. biog.; ▶Encyc. world art; ▶Grant, Brit. sculptors; ▶Thieme-Becker
Gibbons, J. Harold (*British architect*) **AV**
Gibbons, John (*British sculptor, b.1949*) **BA**
    Bibl: Bristol (GBR), Arnolfini Gallery, Style in the 70s (1979)
Gibbons, William (*British artist, op. 1880-1890*) **WI**
Gibbs, Alexander (*British mosaicist and stained glass artist, act. ca. 1868-1882*) **GC**
    Bibl: Pevsner, Oxfordshire, p. 229
Gibbs, Denyse (*Australian printmaker, b.1950*) **BA**
    Bibl: London, Commonwealth Institute, DENYSE GIBBS:PRINTS AND DRAWINGS, 1977
Gibbs, Donald H. (*American architect, Long Beach, Calif*) **AV**
    Bibl: ▶AIA Pro File, 1987-88
Gibbs, Evelyn **WI**
  (*British artist, 1905-*) WC
  (*British artist, 1905-op.1939*) WI
  Gibbs, Evelyn (Evelyn) **WC**
Gibbs, Evelyn (Evelyn) → see Gibbs, Evelyn
Gibbs, George (*American artist, 1870-1942*) **WI**
Gibbs, Henry **WC WI**
  (*British artist, op.1865-1907*) WC WI
  (*English landowner and gardener, d. 1907*) AV
    Bibl: Garden history, 1986 Autumn, v.14, no.2, p.173
  Gibbs, Henry Hucks **AV**
Gibbs, Henry (*American artist, op. 1670*) **WC**
Gibbs, Henry Hucks → see Gibbs, Henry
Gibbs, Horatio **WC WI**
  (*British artist, 18th cent.*) WC
  (*British artist, op.18th c.*) WI
Gibbs, J.B. **WC WI**
  (*British artist, 19th cent.*) WC
  (*British artist, op.19th c.*) WI

Gibbs, James **AV BA GC**
  (*British architect, 1682-1754*) AV
  (*British, 1682-1754*) GC
  (*English architect, 1682-1754*) BA
    Bibl: ▶Colvin, Brit. archts.; ▶Dict. natl. biog.; ▶Encyc. world art; ▶Thieme-Becker
Gibbs, James (*British artist, op. 1819-1835*) **WI**
    Bibl: ▶Mallalieu, Brit. watercolour artists
Gibbs, James Walter (*British artist, 1854-1906*) **WI**
Gibbs, Jonathon (*British artist, b.1953*) **WI**
Gibbs, Mary (*British artist, op.1860-1878*) **WI**
Gibbs, Mary Ann (*American artist, op.1825-1835*) **WI**
Gibbs, Percy William **WC WI**
  (*British artist, op.1894-1925*) WI
  (*British artist, op.c. 1895-1925*) WC
Gibbs, Philip (*Australian architect, 1940-*) **AV**
Gibbs, Snow **WC WI**
  (*British artist, 1882-*) WC
  (*British artist, 1882-circa 1970*) WI
Gibbs, Thomas Binney (*British artist, b.1870*) **WI**
Gibbs, Vicary **AV BA**
  (*British lawyer, gardener, 1853-1932*) BA
  (*English landowner, gardener, and author on gardening, d. 1932*) AV
    Bibl: ▶Dict. natl. biog.; Garden history, 1986 Autumn, v.14, no.2, p.173
Gibbs, William Woodruff (*American painter, 1821-1902*) **BA**
    Bibl: East Lansing (MI, USA), MSU, Kresge Gallery, Early Michigan ptgs. (1977); Gibson
Gibelin, Esprit (*French painter, 1852-1909*) **BA**
    Bibl: ▶Baille, Petits maîtres
Gibelin, Esprit Antoine **BA GC WC**
  (*French artist, 1739-1813*) WC
  (*French painter, printmaker, author, 1739-1813*) BA
  (*French, 1739-1813*) GC
    Bibl: ▶Bénézit; ▶Thieme-Becker; ▶Witt checklist
Gibello, Cleto (*Italian artist, 1896-*) **WC**
Giberne, George de (*British artist, 1797-1875*) **WC WI**
Gibert, Antoine Placide (*French painter, 1806-1875*) **GC**
    Bibl: ▶Thieme-Becker
Gibert, Jean Amedee (*French painter, b.1869*) **GC**
    Bibl: ▶Thieme-Becker
Gibert, Joseph Marc (*French painter, 1806-1884*) **BA**
    Bibl: ▶Baille, Petits maîtres; ▶Bénézit

Gibil Gabib Group (*Sicilian vase-painters*)   **GC**
    Bibl: ▶Trendall, Red-fig. vases Lucania

Gibney, Arthur (*Irish architect, Dublin*)   **AV**
    Bibl: Building, 1989 Mar.17, v.254, no.11, p.16

Gibon, Jacques Alphonse (*Belgian potter, act.1808-1810*)   **BA**
    Bibl: Antiek XIII/7 (Feb 1978), 486-487

Gibs, J.   **WC WI**
    (*British artist, op.1823-*)   **WI**
    (*British artist, op.1832*)   **WC**

Gibson (*American, active Chicago ca. 1900*)   **JG**

Gibson→see Gibson, Richard (Dwarf Gibson)

Gibson family (*British photographers, 19th-20th cs.*)   **BA**

Gibson, A. J. (*American architect, Missoula, Mont., fl. early 1900's*)   **AV**
    Bibl: Historic preservation, 1988 Sept.-Oct., v.40, no.5, p.52

Gibson, Alec (*American architect*)   **AV**

Gibson, Alexander (*British photographer, b.1857*)   **BA**
    Bibl: London (GBR), Natl. Maritime Mus., Photos West Country shipwrecks (1984)

Gibson, Charles (*Canadian architect, Toronto*)   **AV**
    Bibl: Section a, 1985 May, v.3, no.2, p.15

Gibson, Charles Dana   **BA WC WI**
    (*American artist, 1867-1944*)   **WC WI**
    (*American illustrator, 1867-1944*)   **BA**
    Bibl: ▶Encyc. world art; ▶WWW Amer., v.2

Gibson, Colin (*British artist, b.1948*)   **WI**

Gibson, D.   **WC WI**
    (*British artist, op.1655-1660*)   **WI**
    (*British artist, op.c.1655-1660*)   **WC**
    Bibl: ▶Foskett, Brit. miniature ptrs.

Gibson, David (*British artist, op. 1790-1796*)   **WC WI**

Gibson, David Cooke (*British artist, 1827-1856*)   **WI**

Gibson, Edward (*British artist, 1668-1701*)   **WC WI**

Gibson, Emily Grassick (*Landscape designer; b. in Dublin, Ireland, emigrated to Australia in 1911, 1887-1974*)   **AV**
    Bibl: Transition, 1988 Winter, no.25, p.61

Gibson, F. (*British artist, op.1786-1834*)   **WC WI**

Gibson, Herbert (*British photographer, 19th c.*)   **BA**
    Bibl: London (GBR), Natl. Maritime Mus., Photos West Country shipwrecks (1984)

Gibson, James Brown (*British artist, b.1880*)   **WI**

Gibson, Jean   **BA WI**
    (*British artist, op.1981-1983*)   **WI**
    (*British painter, sculptor, b.1935*)   **BA**
    Bibl: Cardiff (GBR), ORiel, BREAKING THE SURFACE..., 1985 (RILA, GBR); ▶Intl. dir. exh. artists, 1982, 1983

Gibson, Jesse (*British architect, ca. 1748-1828*)   **BA**
    Bibl: ▶Colvin, Brit. archts.

Gibson, John   **BA WC WI**
    (*British artist, 1790-1866*)   **WC WI**
    (*British sculptor, 1790-1866*)   **BA**
    Bibl: ▶Dict. natl. biog.; ▶Havlice, Idx. art. bio.; ▶Thieme-Becker

Gibson, John   **AV BA**
    (*British architect*)   **AV**
    (*British architect, 1817-1892*)   **BA**
    Bibl: Country life, 1985 Feb.6, v.179, no.4616, p.302; Dixon, Victorian arch., p.258; ▶Thieme-Becker

Gibson, John (*British market gardener, act.1691*)   **BA**
    Bibl: Malins, ENG. LANDSCAPING, 15

Gibson, Joseph Vincent   **WC WI**
    (*British artist, op.1857-1888*)   **WC**
    (*British artist, op.1861-1893*)   **WI**
    Bibl: ▶Mallalieu, Brit. watercolour artists

Gibson, Lloyd (*British sculptor, b.1945*)   **BA**
    Bibl: Sunderland(GRB), Arts Centre, LLOYD GIBSON, 1977

Gibson, Lorraine (*British artist, op. 1980-*)   **WI**

Gibson, Patrick   **WI**
    (*British artist, 1782-1829*)   **WC WI**

Gibson, Patrick or Peter   **WC**

Gibson, Patrick or Peter→see Gibson, Patrick

Gibson, Peter (*English restorer, York*)   **AV**
    Bibl: Stained glass, 1982 Fall, v.77, no.3, p.252

Gibson, Ralph (*American photographer, b.1939*)   **BA**
    Bibl: ▶Image; Los Angeles (CA, USA), UCLA Wight Gallery, Amer. photos (1976); ▶MoMA libr. cat.

Gibson, Richard→see Gibson, Richard (Dwarf Gibson)

Gibson, Richard (Dwarf Gibson)   **BA PR**
    (*British artist, 1615-1690*)   **WC WI**
    (*British painter, 1605-1690*)   **PR**
    (*British, 1615-1690*)   **GC**
    (*English miniaturist, 1615-1690*)   **BA**
    Bibl: ▶Bénézit; ▶Brit. Mus. cat.; ▶Redgrave, Engl. school; ▶RILA/BHA; ▶Thieme-Becker; ▶Witt checklist

Dwarf Gibson   **PR**
Gibson   **PR**

Gibson, Richard   **GC PR WC**
Gibson, Richard, (The Dwarf)   **WI**
Gibson, the Dwarf   **PR**
Rich. Gibson   **PR**
Richard Gibson   **PR**

Gibson, Richard, (The Dwarf)→see Gibson, Richard (Dwarf Gibson)

Gibson, Robert W. (*American architect, active in New York, 1854-1927*)   **AV**
    Bibl: ▶Withey, Amer. archts.

Gibson, Robin (*Australian architect, 1930-*)   **AV**
    Bibl: ▶Contemp. archts.

Gibson, Susan Penelope, Miss→see Rosse, Susan Penelope

Gibson, the Dwarf→see Gibson, Richard (Dwarf Gibson)

Gibson, Thomas   **GC WC WI**
    (*British artist, c.1680-1751*)   **WC**
    (*British artist, circa 1680-1751*)   **WI**
    (*British, ca.1680-1751*)   **GC**
    Bibl: ▶Witt checklist

Gibson, Thomas Kent Hamilton (*Canadian painter, photographer, b.1930*)   **BA**
    Bibl: ▶Artists Canada; ▶MacDonald, Can. artists; Sackville (NB, CAN), Mt. Allison Univ. Owens Gall., 5 photographers

Gibson, W. Hamilton   **WC WI**
    (*American artist, 20th cent.*)   **WC**
    (*American artist, op.1900-1928*)   **WI**

Gibson, William   **WC WI**
    (*British artist, c.1644-1702*)   **WC**
    (*British artist, circa 1644-1702*)   **WI**
    Bibl: ▶Waterhouse, Brit. 18c. ptrs.

Gibson, William Alfred (*British artist, 1866-1931*)   **WC WI**

Gibson, William J. (*Scottish architect and businessman, 1870-*)   **AV**
    Bibl: Charles Rennie Mackintosh Society. Newsletter, 1989 Summer, no.51, p.6

Gid, Raymond (*French artist, 1905-*)   **WC**

Gidal, Tim (*German photographer, b.1909*)   **BA**
    Bibl: ▶Auer, Encyc. photographes; ▶Contemp. photogs.; ▶Idx. Amer. photog. colls.; Jerusalem, Israel Museum, IN THE THIRTIES: PHOTOGRAPHS BY TIM GIDAL (1975); ▶Parry, Photo idx.

Giddens, David *(American landscape architect, Fla)*   **AV**
   Bibl: Ville giardini, 1987 Sept., no. 219, p.54

Giddings, Edward *(American architect, lives at Cabo San Lucas, Mexico)*   **AV**
   Bibl: House beautiful, 1988 Oct., v.130, no.10, p.98

Giddings, Pat → see Giddings, Patricia

Giddings, Patricia   **VO**
   (American interior designer)   **VO**
   (American interior designer, lives at Cabo San Lucas, Mexico)   **AV**
   Bibl: House beautiful, 1988 Oct., v.130, no.10, p.98; L.A. Times, Aug 11 '93, A-14

   Giddings, Pat   **AV**
   Hall, Paige   **VO**

Gide, Theophile (Francois Theophile Etienne) *(French artist, 1822-1890)*   **WC**

Gideon Jacques Denny → see Denny, Gideon Jacques

Giebe, Hubertus *(East German painter, printmaker, b.1953)*   **BA**
   Bibl: Berlin (DEU), Nationalgalerie, Expressivität Heute (1985); Schumann, Bindende Kunst, 7 (1983) pp.324-326

Giebel, Selma *(German painter, printmaker, b.1883)*   **BA**
   Bibl: ▶Vollmer, Künst.-Lex. 20. Jhr.

Giebicz, Matouš *(Czech sculptor, 17th c.)*   **BA**
   Bibl: Plichta, Umění XXVIII, 2 (1980) 151-167

Giefer, Alois *(W. German architect)*   **AV**
   Bibl: Arcus, 1983, no.4, p.168

Giegengack, Richard *(American architect)*   **AV**
   Bibl: Architecture: the AIA journal, 1985 Nov., v.74, no.11, p.64

Giegerich, Jill *(American artist, b.1952)*   **BA**
   Bibl: Santa Barbara (CA, USA), UCSB Art Mus., Contemp. drawings (1981)

Gielder, Gerrit op *(Dutch artist, op. 1620)*   **WC**

Gielfis, Frans → see Geffels, Frans

Gielniak, Józef *(Polish printmaker, 1932-1972)*   **BA**
   Bibl: PRINT REVIEW, 3(1974), 68-77

Giencke, Volker *(Austrian architect, 1947-)*   **AV**
   Bibl: Kenchiku bunka, 1984 Dec., v.39, no.458, p.76

Gierowski, Stefan *(Polish painter, b.1925)*   **BA**
   Bibl: ▶Bénézit; ▶MoMA libr. cat.; ▶Phaidon 20c. art

Giers, Walter *(German artist, 1937-)*   **WC**

Giersbach, Marilyn *(American painter, b.1940)*   **BA**

Giersing, Harald   **BA WC**
   (Danish artist, 1881-1927)   **WC**
   (Danish painter, 1881-1927)   **BA**
   Bibl: ▶Thieme-Becker; ▶Weilbach, Kunst.leks.

Gierymski, Aleksandr   **BA GC**
   (Polish artist, 1849-1901)   **WC**
   (Polish painter, 1850-1901)   **BA GC**
   Bibl: ▶RILA/BHA; ▶Thieme-Becker; ▶Witt checklist

   Gierymski, Alexander   **WC**
Gierymski, Alexander → see Gierymski, Aleksandr

Gierymski, Maksymilian   **BA**
   (Polish artist, 1846-1874)   **WC**
   (Polish painter, 1846-1874)   **BA**
   Bibl: ▶Thieme-Becker; ▶Witt checklist

   Gierymski, Maximilian, (Maks)   **WC**
Gierymski, Maximilian, (Maks) → see Gierymski, Maksymilian

Gies → see Gies, Joseph W.

Gies, Joseph W.   **PR WI**
   (American artist, 1860-1935)   **WI**
   (American painter, 1859-1935)   **PR**
   Bibl: Detroit Inst of Arts catalogue; ▶WWW Amer. art
   Gies   **PR**
   Joseph W. Gies   **PR**

Gies, Ludwig *(German sculptor, medalist, 1887-1966)*   **BA**
   Bibl: ▶Bénézit; ▶Brockhaus Enzyk.; ▶Vollmer, Künst.-Lex. 20. Jhr.; ▶Wer ist wer, 1967-1968

Giesbrecht, Milly *(Canadian artist, b.1945)*   **BA**
   Bibl: Winnipeg (Man, CAN), Winnipeg Art Gallery, MILLY GIESBRECHT..., 1985, p.8

Giese, Gottlieb Christian Johannes *(German artist, 1787-1838)*   **WC**

Gieselmann, Reinhard *(Austrian architect, Vienna)*   **AV**
   Bibl: ▶Verzeich. Öst. Ziviltech., 1984

Gieseman, David *(French interior designer)*   **AV**
   Bibl: ▶AIA Pro File, 1985

Giessen, G. van   **GC WC**
   (Dutch artist, 18th cent.)   **WC**
   (Dutch printmaker, 18th century)   **GC**
   Bibl: ▶Witt checklist

Giesser, Pierre Alain *(Swiss artist, b.1955)*   **BA**
   Bibl: Lausanne (CHE), Musée Cantonal B.-A., Jeunes vaudois (1983)

Giessmann, Friedrich *(German artist, 1810-1847)*   **WC**

Giesuita → see Courtois, Jacques (le Bourguignon)

Giesuita Borgognone → see Courtois, Jacques (le Bourguignon)

Giesuita Olandese → see Seghers, Daniel

Giesuppino → see Cesari, Giuseppe (Cavalier d'Arpino)

Gietl, Josua von   **GC WC**
   (German artist, 1847-1922)   **WC**
   (German painter, 1847-1922)   **GC**
   Bibl: ▶Thieme-Becker

Giezen, Krijn *(Dutch painter, b.1939)*   **BA**
   Bibl: ▶Bénézit; ▶Scheen, Ned. beeldende kunst.

Giffart, Gifart or Giffard, Pierre *(French artist, c.1637-1723)*   **WC**

Giffin, Don *(American painter, 20th c.)*   **BA**
   Bibl: JOURNAL OF THE L.A. INSTITUTE OF CONTEMPORARY ART, 8(AUG-SEP 1975), 32-34

Giffone, Luigi *(Italian architect, Milan, has practiced in London)*   **AV**
   Bibl: Abitare, 1987 Nov., no.259, p.214

Gifford → see Gifford, Sanford Robinson

Gifford Reynolds Beal → see Beal, Gifford Reynolds

Gifford, Charles Alling *(American architect, practiced in New York City, 1861-1937)*   **AV**
   Bibl: ▶Withey, Amer. archts.

Gifford, Charles Henry *(American artist, 1839-1904)*   **WI**

Gifford, E.A.   **WC WI**
   (British artist, op.1843-1858)   **WI**
   (British artist, op.1843-58)   **WC**

Gifford, George   **WC WI**
   (British artist, op.c.1635-1640)   **WC**
   (British artist, op.circa 1635-)   **WI**

Gifford, John   **WC WI**
   (British artist, 19th cent.)   **WC**
   (British artist, op.19th c.)   **WI**

Gifford, Robert Swain   **BA WC WI**
   (American artist, 1840-1905)   **WC WI**
   (American painter, 1840-1905)   **BA**
   Bibl: ▶Fielding's Amer. ptrs.

Gifford, Sanford → see Gifford, Sanford Robinson

Gifford, Sanford Robinson   **BA GC PR WC WI**
   (American artist, 1823-1880)   **WC WI**
   (American painter, 1823-1880)   **BA PR**
   (American, 1823-1880)   **GC**
   Bibl: ▶Dict. Amer. biog.; ▶RILA/BHA; ▶Witt checklist
   Gifford   **PR**
   Gifford, Sanford   **PR**
   Sanford Robinson Gifford   **PR**

Gigante, Achille   **BA GC WC**
(Italian artist, 1828-1846)   WC
(Italian painter and printmaker,
    1823-1846)   GC
(Italian painter, printmaker,
    1823-1846)   BA
Bibl: ▶Comanducci, Diz.;
    ▶RILA/BHA, 1986;
    ▶Thieme-Becker

Gigante, Ercole   **GC WC**
(Italian artist, 1815-1860)   WC
(Italian, 1815-1860)   GC
Bibl: ▶Bolaffi; ▶Witt checklist

Gigante, Gaetano (Italian artist, op.
    1811-1822)   **WC**

Gigante, Giacinto   **BA GC**
(Italian artist, 1806-1876)   WC
(Italian painter and printmaker,
    1806-1876)   GC
(Italian painter, printmaker,
    1806-1876)   BA
Bibl: ▶Bénézit; ▶Encyc. world art;
    ▶RILA/BHA, 1986;
    ▶Thieme-Becker

Giganti, Giacinto   **WC**

Gigante, José (Portuguese architect,
    1952-)   **AV**
Bibl: AMC, 1985 Mar., no.7, p.15

Gigantes, Eleni (Greek(?) architect)   **AV**
Bibl: Architectural design, 1988,
    v.58, no.7-8, p.54

Giganti, Andrea   **AV BA**
(18th century Sicilian architect)   AV
(Italian architect, 1731-1787)   BA
Bibl: Antichità viva, v.20, n.2,
    p.27; Blue guide: Sicily; Blunt,
    Sicilian baroque; ▶Encyc. world
    art; ▶Wittkower, Art & arch. Italy

Giganti, Giacinto → see Gigante,
    Giacinto

Giger, H.R. (Swiss painter,
    filmmaker, b.1940)   **BA**
Bibl: ▶Lex. zeitgen. Schweiz.
    Künstler

Giger, Hansruedi (Swiss artist,
    1940-)   **WC**

Gigl family (German stucco artists,
    18th c.)   **BA**
Bibl: ▶Schweiz. Künst.-Lex.;
    ▶Thieme-Becker

Gigl, Hans Georg (German stucco
    artist, act.1738, d.1765)   **BA**
Bibl: ▶Thieme-Becker

Gigl, Matthias II (German stucco
    artist, act.1761)   **BA**
Bibl: Knoepfli, DIVERSARUM
    ARTIUM STUDIA, 1982, 217-18;
    ▶Thieme-Becker

Gigli, Andrea (Bolzoni) (Italian
    artist, 16th cent.)   **WC**

Gigli, Guido (Italian architect)   **AV**
Bibl: L'Arca, 1988 June, no.17,
    p.71

Giglio Pisano (Italian goldsmith, act.
    1342-1353)   **BA**
Bibl: Gai, Altare argenteo di
    Pistoia; ▶Honour, Gold- &
    silversmiths, p.45; Rossi,
    Oreficeria ital., p.17;
    ▶Thieme-Becker

Gigliotti, Vittorio   **AV**
Gigniani → see Cignani, Carlo

Gignous, Eugenio   **BA GC WC**
(Italian artist, 1850-1906)   WC
(Italian painter, 1850-1906)   BA GC
Bibl: ▶Bolaffi; ▶Thieme-Becker

Gignoux → see Gignoux, Régis
    François

Gignoux, Alain   **AV**
Bibl: Techniques et architecture,
    1984 June-July, no.354, p.109

Gignoux, Pierre (Swiss artist,
    c.1646-1716)   **WC**

Gignoux, Régis François   **BA PR WC WI**
(American artist, 1816-1882)   WC WI
(French painter in USA, 1816-
    1882)   BA
(French painter, 1816-1882)   PR
Bibl: ▶Fielding's Amer. ptrs.;
    ▶RILA/BHA; ▶Thieme-Becker

Gignoux   PR
Regis Francois Gignoux   PR

Gigola, Giovanni Battista   **BA WC**
(Italian artist, 1769-1841)   WC
(Italian painter, 1769-1841)   BA
Bibl: ▶Comanducci, Diz.;
    ▶Thieme-Becker

Cigola, Giovanna Battista   **WC**
Gigoli, Lodovico → see Cigoli
    (Ludovico Cardi)

Gigoux, Jean Francois   **GC WC**
(French artist, 1806-1894)   WC
(French, 1806-1894)   GC
Bibl: ▶Witt checklist

Giguère, Roland (Canadian
    printmaker, painter, poet, b.1929)   **BA**
Bibl: ▶Artists Canada; ▶Bénézit

Gihon, Clarence Montfort
(American artist, 1871-1929)   **WC WI**
Gijsaerts, Gualterus → see Gysaerts,
    Wouter
Gijsbert Sibilla → see Sibilla, Gijsbert
Gijsbrechts, Cornelis Norbertus → see
    Gysbrechts, Cornelis Norbertus

Gijselingh, Daniel [Unidentified]
(Unknown painter)   **PR**
Daniel Gijselingh   PR

Gijsen, Jo (Dutch sculptor, b.1943)   **BA**
Bibl: Boyens, De Druppel Holt de
    Steen Uit, p.166; ▶Intl. dir. exh.
    artists, 1982, 1983

Gikow, Ruth   **WC WI**
(American artist, 1914-)   WC
(American artist, 1915-op.1960)   WI
Bibl: ▶Who was who [GBR]

Gil Borsoi, Marco Antônio
(Brazilian architect)   **AV**
Bibl: Projeto, 1985 Sept., no.79,
    p.100

Gil de Biedma, Gabriel Allende
(Spanish architect)   **AV**
Bibl: Bauwelt, 1988 Feb.19, v.79,
    no.7-8, p.284

Gil de Camillo, Rubens (Brazilian
    architect)   **AV**
Bibl: Projeto, 1985 Mar., no.73,
    p.76

Gil de Hontañón, Juan   **AV BA**
(before 1480-1531)   AV
(Spanish architect, ca.1480-
    1531)   BA
Bibl: ▶Kubler, Art & arch. ESP &
    PRT; ▶Portoghesi, Diz. arch. e
    urbanistica; ▶Thieme-Becker

Gil de Hontañón, Rodrigo   **AV BA**
(Spanish architect, ca. 1500-
    1577)   AV
(Spanish architect, ca.1500-
    1577)   BA
Bibl: ▶Portoghesi, Diz. arch. e
    urbanistica; Proa, 1985 Apr., no.
    340, p.16

Hontañón, Rodrigo Gil de   AV
Gil Master → see Master of the Gil
    Picture
Gil, Geronimo Antonio → see Gil,
    Jerónimo Antonio

Gil, Jerónimo Antonio   **BA**
(Spanish artist, 1732-1798)   WC
(Spanish printmaker, medalist,
    1732-1798)   BA
Bibl: ▶Encic. univ. ilus.; ▶Forrer,
    Medallists, suppl.; ▶Thieme-Becker

Gil, Geronimo Antonio   **WC**
Gil, Jose (Spanish artist, 1759-1828)   **WC**
Gil, José M. (Spanish architect)   **AV**
Bibl: Process: architecture, 1985
    Apr., no.57, p.85

Gil, Josep Maria   AV
Gil, Josep Maria → see Gil, José M.

Gil, Moshe (Israeli architect)   **AV**
Gil, Vicente (Portuguese painter,
    act.1491, d.1518)   **BA**
Bibl: Dias, Coimbra no
    Renascimento, pp.102-103;
    ▶Pamplona, Pint. escult. PRT;
    ▶Thieme-Becker

Gilabertus   **BA GC**
(French sculptor, 12th c.)   BA
(French sculptor, act. ca.1120-
    1140)   GC
Bibl: ▶Lami, Sculp. fran. 19e s.;
    ▶Thieme-Becker; Toulouse, Musée
    des Augustins, Les Sculptures
    romanes

Gilabertus of Toulouse   GC
Gilabertus of Toulouse → see
    Gilabertus

Gilardi family (Swiss artists,
    conservators, 19th-20th cs.)   **BA**
Bibl: Mendrisio (CHE), Mus. Arte, I
    Gilardi (1986)

Gilardi, Alessandro (Swiss artist,
    conservator, b.1932)   **BA**
Bibl: Mendrisio (CHE), Mus. Arte, I
    Gilardi (1986)

Gilardi, Domenico *(Swiss architect
in Russia, 1785-1845)*   **BA**
    Bibl: Belecskaja, DOMENICO
    GILARDI, 1984, 39; ▶Great Soviet
    encyc.; ▶Portoghesi, Diz. arch. e
    urbanistica; ▶Schweiz.
    Künst.-Lex., suppl.;
    ▶Thieme-Becker

Gilardi, Emilio *(Swiss printmaker,
b.1938)*   **BA**
    Bibl: Mendrisio (CHE), Mus. Arte, I
    Gilardi (1986)

Gilardi, Italo *(Swiss painter,
printmaker, b.1928)*   **BA**
    Bibl: Mendrisio (CHE), Mus. Arte, I
    Gilardi (1986)

Gilardi, Mario *(Swiss painter,
conservator, 1904-1970)*   **BA**
    Bibl: Mendrisio (CHE), Mus. Arte, I
    Gilardi (1986)

Gilardi, Mauro *(Swiss architect,
conservator, b.1945)*   **BA**
    Bibl: Mendrisio (CHE), Mus. Arte, I
    Gilardi (1986)

Gilardi, Pasquale *(Swiss sculptor,
author, 1885-1934)*   **BA**
    Bibl: ▶Künst.-Lex. Schweiz 20.
    Jahrh.; Mendrisio (CHE), Mus.
    Arte, I Gilardi (1986)

Gilardi, Pier Celestino *(Italian artist,
op.1888)*   **WC**

Gilardi, Piero *(Swiss painter,
sculptor, b.1942)*   **BA**
    Bibl: Mendrisio (CHE), Mus. Arte, I
    Gilardi (1986)

Gilardi, Pietro *(Swiss painter, 1875-
1970)*   **BA**
    Bibl: Mendrisio (CHE), Mus. Arte, I
    Gilardi (1986)

Gilardi, Pietro   **BA WC**
    (Italian artist, 1679-1730)   WC
    (Italian painter, 1679-1730)   BA
    Bibl: ▶Bénézit; ▶Bolaffi;
    ▶Thieme-Becker

Gilardi, Silvano *(Swiss painter,
conservator, b.1933)*   **BA**
    Bibl: Mendrisio (CHE), Mus. Arte, I
    Gilardi (1986)

Gilardi, Silvio *(Swiss painter,
conservator, 1873-1943)*   **BA**
    Bibl: Mendrisio (CHE), Mus. Arte, I
    Gilardi (1986)

Gilardino Vecchio→see Gherardini,
    Melchiorre

Gilardoni, Pietro *(Italian architect,
1763-1839)*   **AV BA**
    Bibl: ▶Portoghesi, Diz. arch. e
    urbanistica; ▶Thieme-Becker

Gilarte, Mateo   **BA WC**
    (Spanish artist, c.1620-p.1680)   WC
    *(Spanish painter, ca.1620-ca.
    1680)*   BA
    Bibl: ▶Thieme-Becker

Gilbert→see Gilbert, Arthur
Gilbert→see Gilbert, Arthur Hill

Gilbert & George *(British artist,
b.1942)*   **WI**

Gilbert Gaul→see Gaul, Gilbert

Gilbert Spencer→see Spencer, Gilbert
Gilbert Stuart→see Stuart, Gilbert
Gilbert Stuart Newton→see Newton,
    Gilbert Stuart
Gilbert Tucker Margeson→see
    Margeson, Gilbert Tucker

Gilbert, Achille Isidore *(French
artist, 1828-1899)*   **WC**

Gilbert, Albert→see Gilbert, Albert
    Thomas Jarvis

Gilbert, Albert Thomas Jarvis   **WI**
    (British artist, 18th cent.(?))   WC
    (British artist, d.1927)   WI

Gilbert, Albert   **WC**

Gilbert, Alfred   **AV BA WI**
    (1854-1934)   AV
    (British artist, 1854-1934)   WC WI
    (British sculptor, 1854-1934)   BA
    Bibl: ▶Bénézit; ▶Dict. natl. biog.;
    ▶Thieme-Becker; ▶Vollmer,
    Künst.-Lex. 20. Jhr.

Gilbert, Sir Alfred   **WC**

Gilbert, André-Louis *(French
ébéniste, 1746-1809, master 1774)*   **GC**
    Bibl: ▶Salverte, Ébénistes 18e s.

Gilbert, Arthur   **BA**
    (British artist, 1819-1895)   WC WI
    (British painter, 1819-1895)   BA
    Bibl: Reynolds, Williams family of
    ptrs.; ▶Thieme-Becker
    Gilbert   WI

Williams, Arthur (Gilbert)   **WC**
Williams, Arthur, (Gilbert)   **WI**

Gilbert, Arthur Hill *(American
painter, b. 1894)*   **PR**
    Bibl: ▶WWW Amer. art
    Arthur Hill Gilbert   PR
    Gilbert   PR

Gilbert, Auguste *(French artist,
1822-)*   **WC**

Gilbert, Bradford Lee *(American
architect, 1853-1911)*   **AV**
    Bibl: ▶Macmillan encyc. archts.

Gilbert, Camille *(French artist, 17th
cent.)*   **WC**

Gilbert, Cass   **AV BA FA**
    *(1859-1934; Architect, United
    States of America)*   FA
    *(American architect, 1859-
    1934)*   AV BA
    Bibl: Guide Arch.Wash DC/Cox,
    1974; ▶Hitchcock, Arch. 19 &
    20cs, p.250; ▶Withey, Amer.
    archts.; ▶WWW Amer., 1897

Gilbert, Charles Allan   **WC WI**
    (American artist, 1873-)   WC
    (American artist, 1873-1925)   WI

Gilbert, Charles Pierrepont H.
    (American architect, 1861-1952)   **AV**

Gilbert, Dave *(British artist, b.1928)*   **WI**

Gilbert, Emile Jacques *(French
architect, 1793-1874)*   **BA**
    Bibl: ▶Portoghesi, Diz. arch. e
    urbanistica; ▶Thieme-Becker

Gilbert, Horace W. →see Gilbert,
    Horace Walter

Gilbert, Horace Walter   **WI**
    (British artist, 1855-op.1885)   WI
    (British artist, op.1873-1885)   WC

Gilbert, Horace W.   **WC**

Gilbert, J. *(British artist, op.1867-)*   **WI**

Gilbert, J.M. *(British artist, op.1825-
1855)*   **WC WI**

Gilbert, Jim *(British artist, b.1933)*   **WI**

Gilbert, John   **BA GC WI**
    (British artist, 1817-1897)   WC WI
    *(British painter, illustrator, 1817-
    1897)*   BA
    (British, 1817-1897)   GC
    Bibl: ▶Bénézit; ▶Johnson, Brit.
    artists; ▶Thieme-Becker; ▶Who
    was who [GBR], 1897; ▶Witt
    checklist

Gilbert, Sir John   **WC**

Gilbert, John Graham   **WI**
    (British artist, 1794-1866)   WC WI
    Graham, John   WI

Graham-Gilbert, John   **WC**

Gilbert, Joseph Francis   **GC WC WI**
    (British artist, 1792-1855)   WC WI
    (British, 1792-1855)   GC
    Bibl: Chichester Artists;
    ▶Thieme-Becker; ▶Witt checklist

Gilbert, Josiah *(British artist, 1814-
1892)*   **WC WI**

Gilbert, Kate Elizabeth *(British
artist, 1843-op.1888)*   **WI**
    Hughes, Kate Elizabeth, Mrs.   WI

Gilbert, Norman   **WC WI**
    (British artist, 20th cent.)   WC
    (British artist, op.1965-)   WI

Gilbert, Pierre Julien *(French artist,
1783-1860)*   **WC**

Gilbert, Pierre-Vincent *(French
artist, 1801-1883)*   **WC**

Gilbert, Ralph *(American printmaker,
b.1948)*   **BA**
    Bibl: ▶Intl. dir. exh. artists, 1983;
    Long Beach (CA, USA), Mus. Art,
    2: New & unique (1982)

Gilbert, Rene Joseph *(French artist,
1858-1914)*   **WC**

Gilbert, Sarah *(English upholsterer,
act.1734)*   **BA**
    Bibl: JOURNAL OF THE COSTUME
    SOCIETY, 11(1977), 56-72

Gilbert, Sir Alfred→see Gilbert,
    Alfred
Gilbert, Sir John→see Gilbert, John

Gilbert, Stephen   **BA WI**
    (British artist, 1910-op.1948)   WI
    *(British painter, sculptor,
    b.1910)*   BA
    Bibl: Lambert, Cobra, pp.253-257;
    ▶WW Art

Gilbert, Stephen Hamilton
    (Australian architect)   **AV**

Gilbert, Thomas *(English architect,
18th c.)*   **BA**
    Bibl: COUNTRY LIFE,
    CLX/4124(JUL 1976), 146-48

Gilbert, Van H. *(American architect, Albuquerque, NM)* **AV**
  Bibl: ▶AIA Pro File, 1985
Gilbert, Victor Gabriel **BA PR WC**
  (French artist, 1847-1935) WC
  (French painter, 1847-1935) BA PR
  Bibl: ▶Bénézit; Cleveland(OH,USA), Museum of Art, THE REALIST TRADITION...,(1980); ▶RILA/BHA; ▶Thieme-Becker
  Victor Gabriel Gilbert PR
Gilbert, W.J. *(British artist, op.1835-1851)* **WI**
Gilbert, William S. → see Gilbert, William Schwenk, (Bab)
Gilbert, William Schwenk, (Bab) **WI**
  (British artist, 1836-1911) WC WI
Gilbert, William S. **WC**
Gilbert-Rolfe, Jeremy *(British painter, critic, b.1945)* **BA**
  Bibl: Arts Mag. LI/8 (Apr 1977) p.19; Gilbert-Rolfe, IMMANENCE AND CONTRADICTION...(1985); ▶Intl. dir. exh. artists, 1982; ▶NY art yrbk.; ▶WW Amer. Art, 1991
Gilbody, Samuel *(British ceramist, act.1754-1761)* **BA**
  Bibl: ▶Honey, Euro. ceramic; ▶Thieme-Becker; Watney, Engl. ceramics circle trans., X/4-5 (1980) pp.346-368
Gilbreath, Ford *(American photographer, b.1951)* **BA**
  Bibl: Pullman (WA, USA), Washington St. Univ. Mus. Art, A partial view (1979)
Gilbreth, Bruce G. *(British architect, London)* **AV**
  Bibl: ▶RIBA members, 1983
Gilchrist, Herbert Harlakenden
  (British painter, act.1876-1914) **BA**
  Bibl: ▶Johnson, Brit. artists; Nahum, Monograms; ▶Thieme-Becker
Gilchrist, Mrs → see Gilchrist, Mrs.
Gilchrist, Mrs. **WI**
  (British artist, op.1774-) WI
  (British artist, op.1774-5) WC
Gilchrist, Mrs **WC**
Gilchrist, Philip Thomson *(British artist, 1865-1956)* **WI**
Gilchrist, William Wallace
  (American artist, 1879-1926) **WI**
Gilder, Henry *(British artist, op. 1773-1778)* **WC WI**
Gildewart, Vordemberge → see Vordemberge-Gildewart, Friedrich
Gile, Selden Connor *(American painter, 1877-1947)* **BA**
  Bibl: ▶Dawdy, Artists Amer. West
Gilemans, A. *(Netherlands artist, op. 1615)* **WC**
Giles de Winter → see Winter, Gillis de
Giles Neyts → see Neyts, Gillis
Giles or Gyles, Henry → see Gyles, Henry

Giles, ('Giles') *(British artist, op.20th c.)* **WI**
Giles, Alfred **AV BA**
  (American architect, 1853-1920) AV
  (British architect in USA, 1853-1920) BA
  Bibl: ▶Avery period. idx.; JOURNAL FOR SOC.OF ARCH.HIST. (MAY 1974), 175; Texas Homes of the 19th c.
Giles, Geoffrey Douglas *(British artist, 1857-1941)* **WC WI**
  Bibl: ▶Waters, Brit. artists
Giles, Henry → see Gyles, Henry
Giles, Howard → see Giles, Howard Everett
Giles, Howard Everett **WI**
  (American artist, 1876-) WC
  (American artist, 1876-1955) WI
  (American painter, 1876-1955) PR
  Bibl: ▶WWW Amer. art
Giles, Howard **PR WC**
  Howard Giles PR
Giles, James *(British porcelain painter, 1718-1780)* **BA**
  Bibl: ▶Boger, World pott. & porc.; Coke, In Search of James Giles (1983); ▶Mankowitz, Encyc. pott. & porc.
Giles, James William *(British artist, 1801-1870)* **WC WI**
Giles, John West **WC WI**
  (British artist, op.1830-1865) WI
  (British artist, op.1834) WC
Giles, William, Mrs., (Ada Mathilda) → see Shrimpton, Ada M.
Gilfillan, John Alexander **WC WI**
  (British artist, 1793-1864) WI
  (British artist, op.1830-1840) WC
Gilfillan, Tom *(British artist, op. 1953-)* **WI**
Gilfoy, J. *(British artist, op.1830-1835)* **WC WI**
Gilgenast, Gerhard *(West German engineer and ship designer)* **AV**
  Bibl: House & garden, 1989 Aug., v.161, no.7, p.122
Gilhooly, David James *(American sculptor, b.1943)* **BA**
  Bibl: AFI; ▶WW Amer. Art, 1976
Gili, Katherine *(British sculptor, b.1948)* **BA**
  Bibl: Arts Council GBR, Condition of sculp. (1975), p.26; London (GBR), Marble Hill House, Sculp. in landscape (1975)
Gili, Raymond *(1940-)* **AV**
Gilibert *(French artist, 19th cent.)* **WC**
Giliberto, Tony *(American painter, b.1942)* **BA**
  Bibl: NEW ART EXAMINER, VII/1(OCT 1979), 4-5

Gilio di Pietro **GC**
  (Italian artist, op.1258) WC
  (Italian, act.1258) GC
  Bibl: Getty Photo Study Coll. (Ptgs.); ▶Witt checklist
Gilio di Pietro (Pseudo Maestro Gilio) **WC**
  Pseudo Maestro Gilio GC
Gilio di Pietro (Pseudo Maestro Gilio) → see Gilio di Pietro
Gilioli, Emile **BA WC**
  (French artist, 1911-) WC
  (French sculptor, painter, tapestry designer, b.1911) BA
  Bibl: ▶Bénézit; Cape Town (ZAF), S. African Natl. Gallery, Contemp. French tapestries (1976); ▶MoMA libr. cat.
Gilke, Alexander **AV**
Gilkey, Gordon Waverly *(American printmaker, art administrator, b.1912)* **BA**
Gilks, William *(British architect, act. 1696, d.1727)* **BA**
  Bibl: ▶Colvin, Brit. archts.; Pevsner, Derbyshire, p. 120
Gill → see Gill, Charles
Gill, Alison Margaret → see Smithson, Alison
Gill, André → see Gill, André (Louis Alexandre Gosset de Guines)
Gill, André (Louis Alexandre Gosset de Guines) **BA**
  (French artist, 1840-1885) WC
  (French painter, 1840-1885) GC
  (French painter, printmaker, 1840-1885) BA
  Bibl: ▶Bénézit; ▶Thieme-Becker
Gill, André **GC**
Gosset de Guines, Louis Alexandre (Andre Gill) **WC**
Gill, Arthur Eric Rowton → see Gill, Eric
Gill, Basil *(British artist, op.20th c.)* **WI**
Gill, Bob **WC WI**
  (British artist, 20th cent.) WC
  (British artist, op.20th c.) WI
Gill, C.R. **WC WI**
  (British artist, 19th cent.) WC
  (British artist, op.circa 1800-) WI
Gill, Charles *(Canadian painter, 1871-1918)* **BA**
  Bibl: ▶Artists Canada; ▶Natl. Gall. Canada libr. cat., suppl.
Gill, Charles *(British artist, op.1749-1819)* **WC**
Gill, Charles *(British painter, act. 1769, d. ca.1828)* **PR**
  Bibl: ▶Thieme-Becker; ▶Waterhouse, Brit. 18c. ptrs.
  Charles Gill PR
  Gill PR
Gill, Colin → see Gill, Colin Unwin

Gill, Colin Unwin PR WC WI
   (British artist, 1892-1940) WC WI
   (British painter, 1892-1940) PR
     Bibl: ▶Witt checklist
   Colin Unwin Gill PR
   Gill, Colin PR
Gill, DeLancey W. *(American painter, photographer, illustrator, 1859-1940)* BA
     Bibl: Glenn, HISTORY OF PHOTOGRAPHY, 1(1983), 7-22; McMahan, WASHINGTON, DC ARTISTS BORN BEFORE 1900
Gill, Edmund Marriner GC WC WI
   (British artist, 1820-1894) WC WI
   (British, 1820-1894) GC
     Bibl: ▶Fisher, Watercolour ptrs.; ▶Witt checklist
Gill, Edmund Ward GC WC WI
   (British artist, op.1843-1868) WC
   (British artist, op.1843-1872) WI
   (British, act.1843-1868) GC
     Bibl: ▶Thieme-Becker; ▶Witt checklist
Gill, Edward WC WI
   (British artist, 19th cent.) WC
   (British artist, op.1860-1886) WI
Gill, Edwin WC WI
   (British artist, op.1809-1810) WC
   (British artist, op.1810-, d.1868) WI
Gill, Eric AV BA GC WI
   (British artist, 1882-1940) WC WI
   (British stone carver, engraver, typographer, author; apprenticed as an architect before becoming an artist, 1882-1940) AV
   (British stonecarver, printmaker, author, 1882-1940) BA
   (British, 1882-1940) GC
     Bibl: ▶Encyc. world art; ▶Libr. of Congr. Name Auth. File; Speaight. THE LIFE OF ERIC GILL; ▶Thieme-Becker; ▶Waters, Brit. artists; ▶Who was who [GBR], 1929-40; ▶Witt checklist
   Gill, Arthur Eric Rowton AV
   Gill, Eric (Arthur Eric Rovton Peter Joseph) WC
   Gill, Eric (Arthur Eric Rovton Peter Joseph)→see Gill, Eric
Gill, Grattan *(American architect)* AV
Gill, Irving J. BA
   (American architect, 1870-1936) AV BA
     Bibl: ▶Macmillan encyc. archts.; ▶Withey, Amer. archts.
   Gill, Irving John AV
   Gill, Irving John→see Gill, Irving J.
Gill, James WC WI
   (American artist, 20th cent.) WC
   (American artist, op.1965-) WI
Gill, Leslie *(American architect, New York City, 1957-)* AV
     Bibl: Ottagono, 1987 Sept., v.22, no.86, p.26

Gill, Leslie *(American photographer, 1908-1958)* BA
     Bibl: New Orleans(LA,USA), Museum of Art, LESLIE GILL(1983)
Gill, Madge *(British draftsman, 1882-1961)* BA
     Bibl: ▶MoMA libr. cat.; Thevoz, ART BRUT, p.148-50
Gill, Nigel *(British sculptor, b.1954)* BA
     Bibl: London (GBR), Serpentine Gallery, Problems of picturing (1984), p.12
Gill, Robert *(British army officer, photographer in IND, 1804-1879)* BA
     Bibl: ▶Gernsheim, Hist. photog., p.288; Thomas, Hist. of Photog. VII (1983), pp.323-27
Gill, Rosalie Lorraine *(American artist, 1867-1898)* WI
   Chalon, Rosalie Lorraine, Comtesse de WI
Gill, Samuel Thomas *(Australian artist, 1818-1880)* WC
Gill, Spencer *(American architect, Portland, Oreg)* AV
     Bibl: Urban design international, 1985 Winter, v.5,no.2, p.34
Gill, William WC WI
   (British artist, 1826-1869) WC
   (British artist, op.1826-1869) WI
     Bibl: Morris & Morris
Gill, Winifred *(British artist, 1891-1976)* WI
Gillaboz, de *(German artist, op. 1796-1800)* WC
Gillam, Bernard *(American cartoonist, 1856-1896)* BA
     Bibl: Berkeley (CA, USA), UCB Art Mus., Amer. presidency political cartoons (1976); ▶Dict. Amer. biog.; ▶Fielding's Amer. ptrs.; ▶Mallett's idx. artists
Gillam, James *(American architect)* AV
Gillam, Victor *(British artist, op.19th c.)* WI
Gillar, Jan *(Czechoslovak architect, 1904-1967)* AV
     Bibl: Czech functionalism 1918-1938 (1987)
Gillard, Alan *(British architect, Kendal)* AV
     Bibl: Architects' journal, 1989 May 24, v.189, no.21, p.34
Gillard, William WC WI
   (British artist, c.1812-p.1876) WC
   (British artist, circa 1812-op. 1876) WI
     Bibl: Paviere, Brit. sporting ptrs
Gillberg, Jacob *(Swedish printmaker, 1724-1793)* BA
     Bibl: ▶Svenskt konst.-lex.; ▶Thieme-Becker
Gillberg, Jakob Axel *(Swedish artist, 1769-1845)* WC
Gilbert, I. *(American artist, op.1833-1844)* WI
Gille→see Gille, Christian Friedrich

Gille, Christian Friedrich GC PR WC
   (German artist, 1805-1899) WC
   (German painter, 1805-1899) PR
   (German, 1805-1899) GC
     Bibl: ▶Thieme-Becker; ▶Witt checklist
   Christian Friedrich Gille PR
   Gille PR
Gille, Sighard *(East German painter, printmaker, b.1941)* BA
     Bibl: Hamburg (DEU), Kunstverein, Zeitvergleich (1982); Schumann, Bindende Kunst, 7 (1983) pp.324-326
Gillemans, Jan Paulwel, I or Joan Paulo→see Gillemans, Jan Pauwel I
Gillemans, Jan Paulwel, II→see Gillemans, Jan Pauwel II
Gillemans, Jan Pauwel I GC
   (Flemish artist, 1618-1675) WC
   (Flemish, 1618-1675) GC
     Bibl: ▶Witt checklist
   Gillemans, Jan Paulwel, I or Joan Paulo WC
Gillemans, Jan Pauwel II GC
   (Flemish artist, 1651-1704) WC
   (Flemish, 1651-1704) GC
     Bibl: ▶Witt checklist
   Gillemans, Jan Paulwel, II WC
Gilles Backereel→see Backereel, Gillis
Gilles Hallet→see Hallet, Gilles
Gilles Hondekoeter→see Hondecoeter, Gysbert Gillisz. de
Gilles, Barthel *(German painter, 1891-1977)* BA
     Bibl: Oellers, A.C., in AACHENER KUNSTBLÄTTER LII (1984) 9; ▶Vollmer, Künst.-Lex. 20. Jhr.
Gilles, Jean Francois→see Colson, Jean François
Gilles, Jean Francois (Colson)→see Colson, Jean François
Gilles, Joseph (Provençal) *(French painter, 1679-1749)* BA
     Bibl: ▶Bénézit; ▶Thieme-Becker
Gilles, Joseph Jean *(Haitian painter, 20th c.)* BA
     Bibl: Pau-Llosa, Art intl XXVIII/1 (Jan-Mar 1984) pp.28-29
Gilles, Werner BA GC PR WC
   (German artist, 1894-1961) WC
   (German painter and printmaker, 1894-1961) GC
   (German painter, 1894-1961) PR
   (German painter, printmaker, 1894-1961) BA
     Bibl: ▶Bénézit; ▶RILA/BHA; ▶Vollmer, Künst.-Lex. 20. Jhr.
   Werner Gilles PR
Gillespie, Dorothy Merle *(American painter, sculptor, b.1920)* BA
     Bibl: ▶Collins, Women artists Amer.; ▶WW Amer. Art, 1976, 1980, 1982, 1984
Gillespie, Gregory→see Gillespie, Gregory Joseph

Gillespie, Gregory Joseph   **BA WI**
  (American artist, 1936-)   WC
  (American artist, b.1936)   WI
  (American painter, b.1936)   BA
  Bibl: ART NEWS, LXXVI/3(MAR
   1977), 79; ▶WW Amer. Art, 1976
Gillespie, Gregory   WC
Gillespie, James *(Canadian glass*
  painter, b.1945)   BA
  Bibl: Stratford (ONT, CAN),
   Gallery/Stratford, Portfolio 80
   (1980)
Gillespie, James→see Graham, James
  Gillespie
Gillespie, John Gaff   **AV BA**
  (British architect, 1870-1926)   BA
  (Scottish architect working in
  Glasgow)   AV
  Bibl: Architectural history, 1985,
   v.28, p.198; Service, Edwardian
   arch., p.236
Gillet, Edward Frank *(British artist,*
  1874-1927)   WI
  Bibl: ▶Waters, Brit. artists
Gillet, François→see Gillet, Nicolas
  François
Gillet, Guillaume *(French architect,*
  1912-1987)   AV
  Bibl: Architecture d'aujourd'hui,
   1988 Feb., no.255, p.016
Gillet, Jacques   **AV BA**
  (Belgian architect, 1931-)   AV
  (Belgian architect, 20th c.)   BA
  Bibl: Architecture and urbanism,
   no.174, p.88; ▶Bénézit; Luigi,
   Revue de l'art LXXVI (1987), pp.
   91-93
Gillet, Jean-Baptiste *(French*
  silversmith, ca.1719-1786, master
  1734)   GC
  Bibl: ▶Mabille, Orfèv. fran.
Gillet, Nicolas François *(French*
  sculptor, 1709-1791)   **BA GC**
  Bibl: ▶Bénézit; Getty Photo Study
   Coll. (Sculp.); ▶Lami, Sculp. fran.
   18e s.; ▶Thieme-Becker
  Gillet, François   GC
Gillet, Numa Francois *(French artist,*
  1868-)   WC
Gillet, Pierre *(French silversmith,*
  act. ca.1753-1788)   GC
  Bibl: ▶Mabille, Orfèv. fran.
Gillet, Roger Edgard *(French artist,*
  1924-)   WC
Gillett, M. Louise *(British artist, op.*
  1922-1939)   WI
Gillett, Rosemary *(American interior*
  designer, Florida)   AV
  Bibl: Interior design, 1983 Jan.,
   v.54, no.1, p.173
Gillette, Frank *(American artist,*
  b.1941)   BA
  Bibl: Artforum (Jan 1975) 68;
   Philadelphia (PA, USA), ICA, Video
   art (1975)

Gillette, Leon N. *(American*
  architect, 1878-1945)   AV
  Bibl: ▶Withey, Amer. archts.
Gillette, Richard *(American*
  decorative painter)   AV
  Bibl: Wilsonline Name Authority
Gillette, Stewart *(American*
  architect, New York, 19th century)   AV
  Bibl: House & garden, 1986 Sept.,
   v.158, no.9, p.194
Gillette, W. Dean *(American*
  painter, dealer, 20th c.)   BA
  Bibl: ▶WW Amer. Art, 1976
Gilli *(Italian artist, 20th cent.)*   WC
Gilli, Alberto Maso   **GC WC**
  (Italian artist, 1840-1894)   WC
  (Italian painter, 1840-1894)   GC
  Bibl: ▶Thieme-Becker
Gilliam, Sam   **BA WC WI**
  (American artist, 20th cent.)   WC
  (American artist, b.1933)   WI
  (American painter, b.1933)   BA
  Bibl: ▶Cederholm, Afro-Amer.
   artists; ▶WW Amer. Art, 1976
Gillier, Pierre *(French menuisier,*
  master 1749, act. to 1773)   GC
  Bibl: ▶Salverte, Ébénistes 18e s.
Gillies, Margaret   **BA WC WI**
  (British artist, 1803-1887)   WC WI
  (British painter, 1803-1887)   BA
  Bibl: ▶Dict. natl. biog.; ▶Foskett,
   Brit. miniature ptrs.; ▶Johnson,
   Brit. artists
Gillies, Mary Ann *(American artist,*
  d.1984)   BA
  Bibl: Feminist art jrnl., V/2 (Sum.
   1976) pp.36-37; WOMEN ARTISTS
   NEWS(1984)
Gillies, William George   **BA WC WI**
  (British artist, 1898-1973)   WC WI
  (British painter, .1898-1973)   BA
  Bibl: ▶Waters, Brit. artists
Gillig→see Gillig, Jakob
Gillig or Gellig, Jakob→see Gillig,
  Jakob
Gillig, Jacob→see Gillig, Jakob
Gillig, Jakob   **BA GC PR**
  (Dutch artist, c.1636-1701)   WC
  (Dutch painter and
  draughtsman, ca.1636-1701)   GC
  (Dutch painter, ca.1636-1701)   BA PR
  Bibl: ▶Bénézit; ▶Bryan, Ptrs. &
   engravers; Getty Photo Study
   Coll.; Getty Photo Study Coll.
   (Ptgs.); ▶Havlice, Idx. art. bio.;
   ▶RILA/BHA; ▶Witt checklist
  Gellig, Jakob   GC
  Gillig   PR
  Gillig or Gellig, Jakob   WC
  Gillig, Jacob   PR
  Jakob Gillig   PR
Gilliland, Hector *(Australian artist,*
  1912-)   WC
Gillingwater, Denis Claude
  (American sculptor, b.1946)   BA
  Bibl: ▶WW Amer. Art

Gillio Comoglio, Adriana *(Italian*
  architect, 1946-)   AV
  Bibl: Controspazio, 1985 Jan.-
   June, v.16, no.1-2, p.18
Gillion-Crowet, Anne Marie
  (Belgian, 20th c.)   BA
Gillis Backereel→see Backereel, Gillis
Gillis Claesz. d' Hondecoeter→see
  Hondecoeter, Gillis Claesz. d'
Gillis Congnet (I)→see Congnet,
  Gillis (I)
Gillis de Hondekoutere→see
  Hondecoeter, Gysbert Gillisz. de
Gillis de Winter→see Winter, Gillis
  de
Gillis Frederix→see Frederix, Gillis
  [Unidentified]
Gillis Hondecoeter→see
  Hondecoeter, Gillis Claesz. d'
Gillis Hondekoeter→see
  Hondecoeter, Gysbert Gillisz. de
Gillis Mostaert→see Mostaert, Gillis
Gillis Neyts→see Neyts, Gillis
Gillis Peeters (I)→see Peeters, Gillis
  (I)
Gillis Rombouts→see Rombouts,
  Gillis
Gillis van Coninxloo→see Coninxloo,
  Gilles van
Gillis van Tilborgh→see Tilborgh,
  Gillis van
Gillis, Ermanno→see Gillis, Herman
Gillis, Herman *(Dutch painter, b.*
  1733)   PR
  Bibl: ▶Thieme-Becker
  Ermanno Gillis   PR
  Gillis, Ermanno   PR
  Herman Gillis   PR
Gillis, J. *(Flemish(?) artist, 18th/19th*
  cent.)   WC
Gillis, Nicolaes   **BA GC PR WC**
  (Dutch artist, op.1601-1632)   WC
  (Dutch painter, act. 1601-1632)   PR
  (Dutch painter, act.1601-1632)   GC
  (Flemish painter, act.1601-1632)   BA
  Bibl: ▶Encyc. world art;
   ▶RILA/BHA; Stockholm(SWE),
   Universitat, COLLEGE OF
   PAINTINGS(1978), 112;
   ▶Thieme-Becker
  Claes Gillis   PR
  Nicolaes Gillis   PR
Gillman, Tricia *(British painter,*
  b.1951)   BA
  Bibl: ▶Intl. dir. exh. artists, 1983;
   Sunderland(GBR), Arts
   Centre(TRICIA GILLMAN...(1982)
Gillon, Didier   AV
Gillot, Alain *(1927-)*   AV
Gillot, Claude   **BA GC JG WC**
  (French artist, 1673-1722)   WC
  (French painter, printmaker,
  1673-1722)   BA
  (French, 1673-1722)   GC JG
  Bibl: ▶Encyc. world art;
   ▶Thieme-Becker; ▶Witt checklist

Gillot, Eugene Louis *(French artist, 1867-1925)* **WC**
Gillot, Firmin *(French printmaker, 1820-1872)* **BA**
   Bibl: ▶Bénézit; ▶Larousse grande encyc.
Gillot, Thomas *(British artist, 1886-1913)* **WI**
Gillott, Joseph *(British manufacturer, collector, 1799-1872)* **BA**
   Bibl: ▶Dict. natl. biog.; ▶Natl. union cat., pre-1956
Gillray, James **BA GC WC WI**
   (British artist, 1757-1815) **WC WI**
   (British caricaturist, 1757-1815) **BA**
   (British, 1757-1815) **GC**
   Bibl: ▶Dict. natl. biog.; ▶Thieme-Becker; ▶Witt checklist
Gilly, David *(Architect, Germany, 1748-1808)* **AV**
   Bibl: ▶Libr. of Congr. Name Auth. File; ▶Thieme-Becker
Gilly, Friedrich→see Gilly, Friedrich David
Gilly, Friedrich David **BA GC**
   (1772-1800) **AV**
   (German architect, 1772-1800) **BA GC**
   Bibl: ▶Allgem. Deut. Biog.; ▶Avery Libr. cat.; ▶Macmillan encyc. archts.; ▶RILA/BHA; ▶Thieme-Becker
Gilly, Friedrich **AV GC**
Gilman→see Gilman, Harold
Gilman, Arthur Delevan **AV BA**
   (American architect, 1821-1882) **BA**
   (American architect, practiced in Boston, 1821-1908) **AV**
   Bibl: ▶Avery Libr. cat.; ▶Macmillan encyc. archts.; ▶WWW Amer.
Gilman, Hap *(American architect, Los Angeles, Calif)* **AV**
   Bibl: House beautiful, 1987 Feb., v.130, no.2, p.49
Gilman, Harold **BA PR**
   (British artist, 1876-1919) **WC WI**
   (British painter, 1876-1919) **BA PR**
   (British, 1876-1919) **GC**
   Bibl: ▶Bénézit; ▶RILA/BHA; ▶Vollmer, Künst.-Lex. 20. Jhr.; ▶Waters, Brit. artists; ▶Witt checklist; ▶Yale Brit. artists list
Gilman **PR**
Gilman, Harold J.W. **GC WC**
Gilman, Harold John Wilde **WI**
Harold Gilman **PR**
Gilman, Harold J.W.→see Gilman, Harold
Gilman, Harold John Wilde→see Gilman, Harold
Gilman, Rosemary *(American interior designer)* **AV**
   Bibl: House & garden, 1987 Sept., v.159, no.9, p.180
Gilmor the Younger, Robert→see Gilmor, Robert, Jr.

Gilmor, Robert, Jr. **WI**
   (American artist, op.1800) **WC**
   (American artist, op.1800-1837) **WI**
Gilmor the Younger, Robert **WC**
Gilmore, Gerard G. *(American architect)* **AV**
Gilmore, William H. *(American architect, Midland, Mich)* **AV**
   Bibl: ▶AIA Pro File, 1987-88
Gilot, Françoise **BA**
   (French artist, 1922-) **WC**
   (French painter, b.1921) **BA**
   Bibl: ▶Bénézit; ▶MoMA libr. cat.; ▶Vollmer, Künst.-Lex. 20. Jhr.; ▶WW France
Gilot, Francoise (Francoise Picasso) **WC**
Gilot, Francoise (Francoise Picasso)→see Gilot, Françoise
Gilpin→see Gilpin, Sawrey
Gilpin, John Bernard *(British artist, 1701-1776)* **WC WI**
Gilpin, Laura **BA JG**
   (American photographer, 1891-1979) **BA**
   (American, 1891-1979) **JG**
   Bibl: BOSTON HERALD AMERICAN(SUN,DEC 4 1979); St. Louis (MO, USA), Univ. of Missouri, Gallery 210, Aspects of Amer. Photog. (1976)
Gilpin, Rev. William→see Gilpin, William, Rev.
Gilpin, Sawrey **GC PR WC WI**
   (British artist, 1733-1807) **WC WI**
   (British painter, 1733-1807) **PR**
   (British, 1733-1807) **GC**
   Bibl: ▶Thieme-Becker; ▶Waterhouse, Brit. 18c. ptrs.; ▶Witt checklist
   Gilpin **PR**
   S. Gilpin **PR**
   S. Gilpin R.A. **PR**
   S. Gilpin, Esq. **PR**
   Sawrey Gilpin **PR**
Gilpin, William→see Gilpin, William, Rev.
Gilpin, William Sawrey **AV BA WC WI**
   (British artist, 1762-1843) **WC WI**
   (British landscape architect, 1762-1843) **AV**
   (British painter, landscape gardener, 1762-1843) **BA**
   Bibl: ▶Dict. natl. biog.; ▶Encyc. world art; ▶Hadfield, Brit. gardeners
Gilpin, William, Rev. **WI**
   (British artist, 1724-1804) **WC WI**
   (British, 1724-1804) **GC**
   Bibl: ▶Thieme-Becker; ▶Witt checklist
Gilpin, Rev. William **WC**
Gilpin, William **GC**
Gilroy *(British artist, 20th cent.)* **WC**
Gilroy, John→see Gilroy, John T. Young

Gilroy, John T. Young **BA PR**
   (British artist, 1898-op.1963) **WI**
   (British painter, b. 1898) **PR**
   (British painter, b.1898) **BA**
   Bibl: ▶Johnson, Brit. artists; ▶RILA/BHA; ▶Waters, Brit. artists
Gilroy, John **PR**
Gilroy, John Thomas Young **WI**
John T. Young Gilroy **PR**
Gilroy, John Thomas Young→see Gilroy, John T. Young
Gilroy, John William *(British artist, 1898-op.1921)* **WI**
   Bibl: ▶Wood, Victorian ptrs.
Gilson, Jake *(American sculptor, ceramist, b.1946)* **BA**
   Bibl: Los Angeles(CA,USA), MSMC, Art Gallery. JAKE GIBSON...(1979)
Gilson, Warren *(American inventor, manufacturer, 20th c.)* **BA**
   Bibl: Milwaukee(WI,USA), Art Museum. AMERICAN AND EUROPEAN SILVER...(1982)
Gilsoul, Benoit *(Glass designer, Bronx, NY; educated in Belgium)* **AV**
   Bibl: Stained glass, 1985 Fall, v.80, no.3, p.249
Gilsoul, Victor Olivier **BA GC WC**
   (Belgian artist, 1867-1939) **WC**
   (Belgian painter, 1867-1939) **BA**
   (Belgian painter, 1867-aft.1900) **GC**
   Bibl: ▶Berko, Belgian ptrs.; ▶Thieme-Becker; ▶Witt checklist
Giltinger, Gumpolt (the Elder)→see Giltlinger, Gumpolt I
Giltlinger, Gueltineer, Gultlineer or Gutlineer, Gumpolt→see Giltlinger, Gumpolt I
Giltlinger, Gumpolt (the Elder)→see Giltlinger, Gumpolt I
Giltlinger, Gumpolt I **BA**
   (German artist, op.1481-m.1522) **WC**
   (German painter, 1455-1522) **BA GC**
   Bibl: ▶Bénézit; ▶Kindlers Malerei Lex.; ▶Neue deutsche Biog.; ▶Thieme-Becker
Giltlinger, Gumpolt (the Elder) **GC**
Giltlinger, Gueltineer, Gultlineer or Gutlineer, Gumpolt **WC**
Giltlinger, Gumpolt (the Elder) **GC**
Gültlinger, Gumpolt (the Elder) **GC**
Gimachi, Carlo *(fl. 1722; Architect, Roma, Sovereign State of Malta)* **FA**
   Bibl: ▶Blunt, Baroque Rome
Gimber, Stephen Henry *(Engraver, op.circa 1806-, d.1862)* **WI**
Gimbere, Joseph Napoleon→see Gimbrede, Joseph Napoleon
Gimbert, René *(French architect)* **AV**
   Bibl: Architecture d'aujourd'hui, 1983 Sept., no.228, p.72
Gimblett, Maxwell *(American painter, b.1935)* **BA**
   Bibl: ▶NY art yrbk.

Gimbrede, Joseph Napoleon   **WI**
  (American artist, 1820-op.1860)   WI
  (Engraver, 1820-op.1860)   WI
  Gimbere, Joseph Napoleon   WI
Gimbrede, Thomas *(American*
  artist, 1781-1832)   **WC WI**
Giménez Lacal, José Felipe
  (Spanish architect, Granada, 1884-
  1937)   **AV**
    Bibl: Ianus, 1980, v.0, no.0, p.59
Giménez, Carlos *(Spanish*
  printmaker, b.1941)   **BA**
    Bibl: Revilla, Coloquio: Artes 58
    (Sept 1983) 52
Gimenez, Edgardo Miguel
  (Argentine artist, 20th cent.)   **WC**
Gimenez, Raymond *(French*
  architect)   **AV**
    Bibl: AMC, 1988 Oct., no.22,
    p.109
Gimignani→see Gimignani, Giacinto
Gimignani, Gemignani or Geminiani,
  Giacinto→see Gimignani, Giacinto
Gimignani, Giacinto   **BA GC PR**
  (Italian artist, 1611-1681)   WC
  (Italian painter and printmaker,
  1606-1681)   GC
  (Italian painter, 1611-1681)   PR
  (Italian painter, printmaker,
  1606-1681)   BA
    Bibl: ▶Bolaffi; Getty Photo Study
    Coll. (Ptgs.); Revue du Louvre,
    XXVIII/5 (1978) pp.343-358;
    ▶RILA/BHA, 1986;
    ▶Thieme-Becker; ▶Witt checklist
  Gemeniani   PR
  Gemignani   PR
  Geminiani, Giacinto   GC
  Giacinto Gimignani   PR
  Giacinto Gimignano   PR
  Giacinto Giminiani   PR
  Gimignani   PR
  Gimignani, Gemignani or
  Geminiani, Giacinto   **WC**
Gimignani, Lodovico   **BA GC WC**
  (Italian artist, 1643-1697)   WC
  (Italian painter, 1643-1697)   BA GC
    Bibl: ▶Bénézit; ▶Bolaffi;
    ▶RILA/BHA; ▶Thieme-Becker
Gimmer, Adam *(German painter,*
  d.1596/98)   **GC**
    Bibl: ▶Thieme-Becker
Gimmi, Wilhelm   **BA WC**
  (Swiss artist, 1886-)   WC
  (Swiss painter, printmaker,
  1886-1965)   BA
    Bibl: ▶Art Index, v.15; ▶Bénézit;
    ▶Künst.-Lex. Schweiz 20. Jahrh.;
    ▶MoMA libr. cat.; ▶Vollmer,
    Künst.-Lex. 20. Jhr.
Gimond, Marcel *(French artist,*
  1894-)   **WC**
Gimonet, Christian *(1935-)*   **AV**
Gimson, Ernest→see Gimson, Ernest
  William

Gimson, Ernest William   **BA**
  (1864-1919)   AV
  (British architect, designer,
  1864-1919)   BA
    Bibl: London (GBR), V & A Mus.,
    Victorian church art (1971-1972),
    p.156
  Gimson, Ernest   **AV**
Ginain, Louis Eugene *(French artist,*
  1818-1886)   **WC**
Ginandes, Carol *(American*
  photographer, b.1947)   **BA**
    Bibl: FEMINIST ART JOURNAL,
    v.5(FALL 1976), 42; OCLC
Gindriez, Charles *(French artist,*
  19th cent.)   **WC**
Gindroz, Raymond L. *(American*
  architect)   **AV**
Gindter, Samuel *(Bohemian painter,*
  act.1680)   **BA**
    Bibl: Štěpánek, Arch. esp. de arte,
    LVII/227 (Jul-Sep 1984) 321-324;
    ▶Thieme-Becker; Umělecké
    Památky ČSK, II, 78, sv Koči
Ginelli, Anatol *(West German*
  architect, b.1927)   **BA**
    Bibl: ▶Avery period. idx.; ▶WW
    Arts DEU
Giner, Francisco *(Spanish artist,*
  15th cent.)   **WC**
Giner, Tomás   **BA WC**
  (Spanish artist, 15th cent.)   WC
  (Spanish painter, act.1466-1468)   BA
    Bibl: ▶Ars Hispaniae, v.9; Post,
    ARAGONESE SCHOLL...LATE
    MIDDLE AGES; Tesoros artisticos
    de España
Giner, Vicente *(Spanish artist, op.*
  1676-1677)   **WC**
Ginés de Aguirre, Andrés   **BA**
  (Spanish artist, 1731-c.1785)   WC
  (Spanish painter, act.1755)   BA
    Bibl: ▶Ars Hispaniae, v.17
  Aguirre, Gines Andres de   **WC**
Ginesi, Edna   **WC WI**
  (British artist, 1902-)   WC
  (British artist, b.1902)   WI
  Coxon, Raymond James, Mrs.
  (Edna)   WI
Ginetti→see Giannetti, Filippo
Ginevra Cantofoli→see Cantofoli,
  Ginevra
Ginevri, Arnaldo *(Italian engineer,*
  act.1897-1902)   **BA**
    Bibl: ▶Natl. union cat., pre-1956;
    Rotondi, in Misc. di Studi in
    Memoria di Anna Saitta Revignas
    (1988)
Gingelen, Jacques van *(Belgian*
  artist, 1801-)   **WC**
Gingell, John *(British artist, b.1935)* **BA**
    Bibl: Cardiff (GBR), Oriel, Garden
    of Pleasures (1983)
Gingell, Vernon R. *(American*
  architect)   **AV**
Ginger, Phyllis→see Ginger, Phyllis
  Ethel

Ginger, Phyllis Ethel   **WI**
  (British artist, 20th cent.)   WC
  (British artist, b.1907)   WI
  Durbin, Leslie, Mrs., (Phyllis Ethel) WI
  Ginger, Phyllis   **WC**
Gingles, Diane *(American interior*
  designer)   **AV**
    Bibl: Interiors, 1986 Dec., v.146,
    no.5, p.180
Gingold, Madelynn *(American*
  artist, 20th c.)   **BA**
    Bibl: ARTS MAGAZINE, LVII(4 DEC
    1982), 32-33
Ginn, Michael *(English architect,*
  London)   **AV**
    Bibl: ▶RIBA members, 1987
Ginna, Arnaldo (Arnaldo Corradini
  Ginanni) *(Italian painter, b.1890)* **BA**
    Bibl: ▶Bénézit; ▶Bolaffi
Ginnasi, Caterina *(Italian artist,*
  c.1590-1660)   **WC**
Ginner→see Ginner, Charles
Ginner, Charles   **BA PR**
  (British artist, 1878-1952)   WC WI
  (British painter, 1878-1952)   BA PR
    Bibl: ▶RILA/BHA; ▶Vollmer,
    Künst.-Lex. 20. Jhr.; ▶Waters, Brit.
    artists; ▶Who was who [GBR],
    1951
  Charles Ginner   PR
  Ginner   PR
  Ginner, Charles Isaac   **WC WI**
Ginner, Charles Isaac→see Ginner,
  Charles
Ginnett, Louis *(British artist, 1875-*
  1946)   **WC WI**
Ginnetti→see Giannetti, Filippo
Ginnever, Charles *(American*
  sculptor, b.1931)   **BA**
    Bibl: ▶WW Amer. Art, 1976
Ginns, Malcolm *(British builder,*
  Essex)   **AV**
    Bibl: Period homes, 1987 July,
    p.30
Gino Micheli *(Italian sculptor, act.*
  1341)   **BA**
    Bibl: ANTICHITA VIVA,
    XVIII/3(MAY-JUNE 1979), 31-37
Gino Severini→see Severini, Gino
Ginori family *(Italian porcelain*
  manufacturers, 18th-19th cs.)   **BA**
    Bibl: Apollo, CV/179 (Jan. 1977)
    p.34; ▶Encic. italiana; TCI Firenze
Ginori, Carlo Lorenzo, marchese
  (Italian porcelain manufacturer,
  1702-1757)   **BA**
    Bibl: ▶Encic. italiana; ▶Penguin
    dec. arts, 1989
Ginori, Lorenzo II *(Italian porcelain*
  manufacturer, 1823-1878)   **BA**
    Bibl: Faenza, LXV/6 (1979), 399-
    405
Ginosa Painter *(Apulian vase-*
  painter)   **GC**
    Bibl: Trendall, Attic red-fig. vases
    Apulia
Ginoulhiac, Francesco   **AV**

Ginovszky or Ginowski, Josef
(Hungarian artist, 1800-1857) **WC**
Gins, Madeline *(American artist,*
20th c.) **BA**
Bibl: Tracks III/3 (Fall 1977), 109
Ginsborg, Michael **BA WI**
(British artist, b.1943) **WI**
(British painter, b.1943) **BA**
Bibl: ▶Babington Smith, Contemp.
artists
Ginsburg, Randy *(American interior*
designer, New York, NY) **AV**
Bibl: Interior design, 1985 Oct.,
v.56, no.10, p.246
Ginter, Ignaz → see Günther, Ignaz
Ginther, Ignaz → see Günther, Ignaz
Ginther, Joachim *(Austrian*
architect) **AV**
Bibl: Bauforum, 1987, v.20, no.
124, p.26
Gintner, Anton **WC WI**
(American artist, 1941-) **WC**
(American artist, 1941-op.1971) **WI**
Gintrac, Jean Louis *(French artist,*
1808-) **WC**
Ginzburg, Carlos *(Argentine artist in*
FRA, b.1946) **BA**
Bibl: ▶Babington Smith, Contemp.
artists; Ginzburg, LEONARDO
XIX/4 (1986) 289-291; ▶Intl. dir.
exh. artists, 1982
Ginzburg, Moisě Iﾍkovlevich → see
Ginzburg, Moisej Jakovlevič
Ginzburg, Moisej Jakovlevič **BA**
(Russian architect, 1892-1946) **AV BA**
Bibl: ▶Avery Libr. cat.; ▶Great
Soviet encyc.
Ginzburg, Moisě Iﾍkovlevich **AV**
Ginzel, Andrew *(American artist,*
b.1954) **BA**
Bibl: Cameron, Arts mag., LXI
(Sep. 1986) pp.40-46; ▶WW
Amer. Art, 1989-1990
Ginzel, Roland *(American painter,*
printmaker, b.1921) **BA**
Bibl: ▶Who was who [GBR], 1976
Gio Batta detto Castiglione → see
Castiglione, Giovanni Benedetto (il
Grechetto)
Gio Batta Pace → see Pace, Giovanni
Battista
Gio Battista Weeninx → see Weenix,
Jan Baptist
Gio Bellini → see Bellini, Giovanni
Gio Bellino → see Bellini, Giovanni
Gio da Belino → see Bellini, Giovanni
Gio de Belino → see Bellini, Giovanni
Gio del Soli → see Sole, Giovan
Gioseffo dal
Gio Domo Cerrini Perugino → see
Cerrini, Giovanni Domenico
(Cavalier Perugino)
Gio Domo Perugino → see Cerrini,
Giovanni Domenico (Cavalier
Perugino)
Gio Miele → see Miel, Jan

Gio-Batta Viola → see Viola, Giovanni
Battista
Gio. And. Donducci called
Mastelletta → see Donducci,
Giovanni Andrea (Mastelletta)
Gio. Andrea Ghirardoni → see
Ghirardoni, Giovanni Andrea
Gio. Angelo Vicino → see Vicino,
Giovanni Angelo
Gio. Ant. d'Amato → see Amato,
Giovanni Antonio d'
Gio. B. Caracciolo → see Caracciolo,
Giovanni Battista (Battistello)
Gio. B.a Caracciolo → see Caracciolo,
Giovanni Battista (Battistello)
Gio. Ba. Boncore → see Bonocore,
Giovanni Battista
Gio. Baptista Weenincx → see Weenix,
Jan Baptist
Gio. Bassano → see Bassano, Jacopo
(Jacopo da Ponte)
Gio. Batt. Naldini → see Naldini,
Giovanni Battista
Gio. Batta Busirri → see Busiri,
Giovanni Battista
Gio. Batta Carlone → see Carlone,
Giovanni Battista
Gio. Batta Castello → see Castello,
Giovanni Battista (Genovese)
Gio. Batta Castello → see Castello,
Giovanni Battista (il Bergamasco)
Gio. Batta Poggi → see Paggi,
Giovanni Battista
Gio. Batta Viola → see Viola, Giovanni
Battista
Gio. Battista Benvenuti detto
l'Ortolano → see Ortolano
(Giovanni Battista Benvenuti)
Gio. Battista Caracciolo → see
Caracciolo, Giovanni Battista
(Battistello)
Gio. Battista dalla Torre → see Torre,
Giovanni Battista dalla
Gio. Battista Piazzetta → see
Piazzetta, Giovanni Battista
Gio. Battista Tiepolo → see Tiepolo,
Giovanni Battista
Gio. Battistello Caracciolo il
buono → see Caracciolo, Giovanni
Battista (Battistello)
Gio. Bellini → see Bellini, Giovanni
Gio. Bellino → see Bellini, Giovanni
Gio. Benedetto Castiglione
sopranominato il Greghetto → see
Castiglione, Giovanni Benedetto (il
Grechetto)
Gio. Benedetto Castiglioni → see
Castiglione, Giovanni Benedetto (il
Grechetto)
Gio. Bernardo → see Azzolino
(Giovanni Bernardino Ragano)
Gio. Bettino Cignaroli → see Cignaroli,
Giambettino
Gio. Breughel → see Brueghel, Jan, the
elder

Gio. del Borgo → see Vecchi, Giovanni
de' (Giovanni del Borgo)
Gio. Donati → see Donati, Gio.
[Unidentified]
Gio. Fiamengo → see Giovanni
Fiammingo [Unidentified]
Gio. Fran.co Grimaldi → see Grimaldi,
Giovanni Francesco
Gio. Francesco Barbieri → see
Guercino (Giovanni Francesco
Barbieri)
Gio. Francesco Bolognese → see
Grimaldi, Giovanni Francesco
Gio. Francesco Bolognesi → see
Grimaldi, Giovanni Francesco
Gio. Francesco Braccioli → see
Braccioli, Giovanni Francesco
Gio. Francesco della Nunziatella → see
Giovanni Francesco della
Nunziatella [Unidentified]
Gio. Francesco Grimaldi → see
Grimaldi, Giovanni Francesco
Gio. Francesco Penni detto il
Fattore → see Penni, Giovanni
Francesco (il Fattore)
Gio. Francesco Surchi detto
Dielai → see Surchi, Giovanni
Francesco
Gio. Franco Bolognese → see Grimaldi,
Giovanni Francesco
Gio. Gioseffo del Sole → see Sole,
Giovan Gioseffo dal
Gio. Giuseppe → see Sole, Giovan
Gioseffo dal
Gio. Giuseppe d. Sole → see Sole,
Giovan Gioseffo dal
Gio. Giuseppe del Sole → see Sole,
Giovan Gioseffo dal
Gio. Giuseppe dl Sole → see Sole,
Giovan Gioseffo dal
Gio. Grisolfi milanese → see Ghisolfi,
Giovanni
Gio. Miel → see Miel, Jan
Gio. Miele → see Miel, Jan
Gio. Paolo Graccini → see Grazzini,
Giovanni Paolo
Gio. Paolo Pannini → see Pannini,
Giovanni Paolo
Gio. Vincenzo Barbalonga → see
Barbalonga, Giovanni Vincenzo
[Unidentified]
Gio. Ziter figlio di M. Leandro → see
Reder, Giovanni
Gio: Andrea → see Ferrari, Giovanni
Andrea de
Gio: Angelo Milone → see Milone,
Giovanni Angelo [Unidentified]
Gio: Ant. d'Amato → see Amato,
Giovanni Antonio d'
Gio: Antonio d'Amato → see Amato,
Giovanni Antonio d'
Gio: B.ttanello → see Caracciolo,
Giovanni Battista (Battistello)

Gio: Ba Forniè Fiammengo→see
Forniè, Giovanni Battista
[Unidentified]

Gio: Ba Fornie' Fiammengo→see
Forniè, Giovanni Battista
[Unidentified]

Gio: Bacco Recco→see Recco,
Giovanni Battista

Gio: Baglioni→see Baglione, Giovanni

Gio: Balducci→see Balducci, Giovanni
(Cosci)

Gio: Balduccio→see Balducci,
Giovanni (Cosci)

Gio: Bapta Caracciolo→see
Caracciolo, Giovanni Battista
(Battistello)

Gio: Batistielo→see Caracciolo,
Giovanni Battista (Battistello)

Gio: Batta Binasco→see Benaschi,
Giovanni Battista

Gio: Batta Boella→see Boel, Jan
Baptiste

Gio: Batta Boncore→see Bonocore,
Giovanni Battista

Gio: Batta Caracci→see Caracciolo,
Giovanni Battista (Battistello)

Gio: Batta Caracciolo→see
Caracciolo, Giovanni Battista
(Battistello)

Gio: Batta Caracciuoli→see
Caracciolo, Giovanni Battista
(Battistello)

*Gio: Batta Gauli detto il
Baciccio*→see Gaulli, Giovanni
Battista (Baciccio)

Gio: Batta Paggi→see Paggi,
Giovanni Battista

Gio: Batta Roppoli→see Ruoppolo,
Giovanni Battista

Gio: Battista Busirri→see Busiri,
Giovanni Battista

*Gio: Battista Gauli detto il
Baciccio*→see Gaulli, Giovanni
Battista (Baciccio)

*Gio: Battista Gauli, detto
Baciccio*→see Gaulli, Giovanni
Battista (Baciccio)

Gio: Battista il Veneziano→see
Giovanni Battista il Veneziano
[Unidentified]

Gio: Battista Veneziano→see
Giovanni Battista il Veneziano
[Unidentified]

Gio: Battistanello→see Caracciolo,
Giovanni Battista (Battistello)

Gio: Battistello Caracciolo→see
Caracciolo, Giovanni Battista
(Battistello)

Gio: Battistiello Caraccioli→see
Caracciolo, Giovanni Battista
(Battistello)

Gio: Belardino Siciliano→see
Azzolino (Giovanni Bernardino
Ragano)

Gio: Bellin→see Bellini, Giovanni

Gio: Bellini→see Bellini, Giovanni

Gio: Bellinj→see Bellini, Giovanni

Gio: Bellino→see Bellini, Giovanni

Gio: Bened.o Castiglioni→see
Castiglione, Giovanni Benedetto (il
Grechetto)

Gio: Benedetto Castiglione→see
Castiglione, Giovanni Benedetto (il
Grechetto)

Gio: ber.do→see Azzolino (Giovanni
Bernardino Ragano)

Gio: Ber.no Siciliano→see Azzolino
(Giovanni Bernardino Ragano)

Gio: Berardino→see Azzolino
(Giovanni Bernardino Ragano)

Gio: Berardino Siciliano→see
Rodriguez, Bernardino

Gio: Bernardino→see Azzolino
(Giovanni Bernardino Ragano)

Gio: Bernardino Siciliano→see
Azzolino (Giovanni Bernardino
Ragano)

Gio: Bernardo→see Azzolino
(Giovanni Bernardino Ragano)

Gio: Bernardo Lama→see Lama,
Giovan Bernardo

Gio: Dom:co Perugino→see Cerrini,
Giovanni Domenico (Cavalier
Perugino)

Gio: Do'→see Dò, Giovanni

*Gio: Do' allievo dello
Spagnoletto*→see Dò, Giovanni

Gio: Fiamenco→see Giovanni
Fiammingo [Unidentified]

Gio: Fiamengo→see Giovanni
Fiammingo [Unidentified]

Gio: Fiamingo→see Giovanni
Fiammingo [Unidentified]

Gio: Fran.co Bolognese→see
Grimaldi, Giovanni Francesco

Gio: Fran:co Bola→see Bola, Giovanni
Francesco [Unidentified]

Gio: Fran:co Bolognese→see
Grimaldi, Giovanni Francesco

*Gio: Francesco Barbieri detto il
Guercino*→see Guercino (Giovanni
Francesco Barbieri)

*Gio: Francesco Barbieri detto il
Guercino da Cento*→see Guercino
(Giovanni Francesco Barbieri)

Gio: Francesco Bola→see Bola,
Giovanni Francesco [Unidentified]

*Gio: Francesco Grimaldi
Bolognese*→see Grimaldi, Giovanni
Francesco

*Gio: Francesco Grimaldi detto il
Bolognese*→see Grimaldi, Giovanni
Francesco

Gio: Francesco Mola→see Mola, Pier
Francesco

Gio: Francesco Mola di Lugano→see
Mola, Pier Francesco

*Gio: Francesco Romanelli
Viterbese*→see Romanelli,
Giovanni Francesco

Gio: Franco Bolognese→see Grimaldi,
Giovanni Francesco

Gio: Ghisolfi→see Ghisolfi, Giovanni

Gio: Giuseppe dal Sole→see Sole,
Giovan Gioseffo dal

Gio: Giuseppe del Sole→see Sole,
Giovan Gioseffo dal

Gio: Lanfranco→see Lanfranco,
Giovanni

Gio: Lanfranco Parmigiano→see
Lanfranco, Giovanni

Gio: Maria della Torre→see Torre,
Giovanni della (Giovanniello del
Beinaschi)

Gio: Maria Morandi→see Morandi,
Giovanni Maria

Gio: Miele→see Miel, Jan

Gio: Pace→see Pace, Giuseppe

Gio: Paolo Milchiori→see Melchiori,
Giovanni Paolo

Gio: Paolo Vannini→see Vannini,
Giovanni Paolo

Gio: Pavolo Schor→see Schor,
Johann Paul (Giovanni Paolo
Tedesco)

Gio: Pettorali→see Pettorali,
Giovanni [Unidentified]

Gio: Sanese→see Ferri, Giovanni
(Giovanni Senese)

Gio: Sannese→see Ferri, Giovanni
(Giovanni Senese)

Gio: Senese→see Ferri, Giovanni
(Giovanni Senese)

Gio: Senesio→see Ferri, Giovanni
(Giovanni Senese)

Gio: Seric→see Seric, Giovanni
[Unidentified]

Gio: Stanchi→see Stanchi, Giovanni

Gio: Tabacco→see Tabacco, Giovanni
[Unidentified]

*Gio: Tabacco di nazione
olandese*→see Tabacco, Giovanni
[Unidentified]

Gio: Torelli→see Torelli, Gio.
[Unidentified]

Gio: Vandaneinden→see Heyden, Jan
van der

Gio:Batt. Caracciolo→see Caracciolo,
Giovanni Battista (Battistello)

Gio:Batta Benasco→see Benaschi,
Giovanni Battista

Gio:Battistello Caraccio→see
Caracciolo, Giovanni Battista
(Battistello)

Gio:Battistello Caracciolo→see
Caracciolo, Giovanni Battista
(Battistello)

Gio:Battistiello Caracciolo→see
Caracciolo, Giovanni Battista
(Battistello)

Gio:mo de Arena→see Arena,
Giovanni Geronimo d'

Gioacchino Assereto→see Assereto,
Gioacchino

Gioacchino Giuseppe Serangeli→see
    Serangeli, Gioacchino Giuseppe
Gioacchino Martorana→see
    Martorana, Gioacchino
Gioacchino Martorani→see
    Martorana, Gioacchino
Gioachino Assereto→see Assereto,
    Gioacchino
Gioan Antonio d'Amato→see Amato,
    Giovanni Antonio d'
Gioan Fiamengo→see Giovanni
    Fiammingo [Unidentified]

Gioanetti, Vittorio Amedeo *(Italian
    porcelain manufacturer, chemist,
    1729-1815)*   **BA**
        Bibl: ▶Boger, World pott. & porc.;
        ▶Encic. italiana, v.9, 771c;
        ▶Honey, Euro. ceramic;
        ▶Mankowitz, Encyc. pott. & porc.
Gioanne Fiamengo→see Giovanni
    Fiammingo [Unidentified]
Gioannen Fiamengo→see Giovanni
    Fiammingo [Unidentified]
Gioanni Rosa→see Roos, Jan (I)
Giobbe, Nicola *(Italian contractor,
    1705-1748)*   **BA**
        Bibl: Brunel, PIRANESE ET LES
        FRANCAIS, 77-146
Giobbi, Edward→see Giobbi, Edward
    Giochino
Giobbi, Edward Giochino   **WI**
    (American artist, 20th cent.)   WC
    (American artist, b.1926)   WI
Giobbi, Edward   **WC**
Giocchi, Ulisse *(Italian painter, ca.
    1570-1631)*   **BA**
        Bibl: ▶Bolaffi; ▶Diz. biog. ital.;
        PRATO STORIA E ARTE, XXVIII/70
        (June 1987), p. 4-15;
        ▶Thieme-Becker
Giocomin, P. *(Italian architect)*   **AV**
        Bibl: Lotus international, 1983,
        no.38, p.90
**Giocondo, Fra (Giovanni da
    Verona)**   **BA**
    *(Architect, writer, draughtsman,
        engineer, translator, c.1433-
        1515)*   CE
    *(Italian architect, engineer,
        humanist, ca.1433-1515)*   BA
    (Italian artist, c.1457-1525)   WC
    *(Italian sculptor and architect,
        ca.1457-1525)*   GC
        Bibl: ▶Encic. italiana; ▶Encyc.
        world art; ▶New Columbia encyc.;
        ▶Portoghesi, Diz. arch. e
        urbanistica; TCI Lombardia
    Fra Giovanni da Verona   GC
Giocondo, Fra Giovanni   **CE**
Giovanni da Verona   CE **GC**
Giovanni da Verona, Fra   **WC**
Giocondo, Fra Giovanni→see
    Giocondo, Fra (Giovanni da
    Verona)

Gioffredo, Mario   **AV BA**
    (1718-1785)   AV
    (Italian architect, 1718-1785)   BA
        Bibl: ▶Thieme-Becker;
        ▶Wittkower, Art & arch. Italy
Giogone→see Giorgione (Giorgio da
    Castelfranco)
Gioia del Colle Painter *(Apulian
    vase-painter)*   **GC**
        Bibl: Trendall, Attic red-fig. vases
        Apulia
Gioja, Belisario *(Italian artist, 1829-
    1906)*   **WC**
Gioja, Edoardo *(Italian artist, 1862-
    1936)*   **WC**
Giol Draper, Pere *(Spanish
    architect)*   **AV**
        Bibl: Arquitectura, LXV/250 (Sept.
        -Oct. 1984)
Giolfino→see Giolfino, Niccolò, the
    younger
Giolfino, Niccolò→see Giolfino,
    Niccolò, the younger
Giolfino, Niccolò (the Younger)→see
    Giolfino, Niccolò, the younger
Giolfino, Niccolò, the younger   **BA**
    (Italian artist, 1476/7-1555)   WC
    (Italian painter, 1476-1555)   BA GC PR
        Bibl: ▶Bolaffi; ▶Fredericksen &
        Zeri, Census; ▶RILA/BHA, 1986;
        ▶Thieme-Becker
    Giolfino   PR
Giolfino, Niccolò   **PR WC**
**Giolfino, Niccolò (the
    Younger)**   **GC PR**
    Niccolo Giolfino   PR
    Niccolò Giolfino (the Younger)   PR
Gioli, Antonio→see Joli, Antonio
Gioli, Francesco   **GC WC**
    (Italian artist, 1846-1922)   WC
    (Italian painter, 1846-1922)   GC
        Bibl: ▶Thieme-Becker
Giolli, Raffaello *(Italian architect)*   **AV**
        Bibl: Casabella, 1985 Dec., v.49,
        no.519, p.30
Giona Ebreo [Unidentified]
    (Unknown painter)   **PR**
        Bibl: Riccardi inventory, Florence,
        1715
Gionima, Antonio   **BA GC WC**
    (Italian artist, 1697-1732)   WC
    (Italian painter, 1697-1732)   BA
    (Italian, 1697-1732)   GC
        Bibl: ▶Bolaffi; ▶Thieme-Becker;
        ▶Witt checklist
Giordanello→see Giordano, Luca
Giordani→see Giordano, Luca
Giordani, Pietro *(Italian artist, 14th
    cent.)*   **WC**
Giordanico, Pietro *(Italian artist, op.
    1493)*   **WC**
Giordaniello→see Giordano, Luca
Giordano→see Giordano, Luca
Giordano d'Olanda→see Jordaens,
    Jacob

Giordano giovane→see Giordano,
    Luca
Giordano, Antonio *(Italian painter,
    1597-1681)*   **PR**
        Bibl: ▶Thieme-Becker
    Antonio Giordano   PR
    Padre di Luca Giordano   PR
Giordano, Baron *(Italian railway
    engineer, architect)*   **AV**
        Bibl: Area, 1982 Oct.-Nov., v.2,
        no.7, p.48
Giordano, Biagio *(Italian goldsmith,
    act.1774-1790)*   **BA**
        Bibl: Antol. di B-A II/5 (Mar 1978)
        49-51
Giordano, Joe *(American painter,
    20th c.)*   **BA**
        Bibl: ARTS MAG LX/8 (Apr 1986)
        107; ▶WW Amer. Art, 1986

Giordano, Luca   BA GC JG PR
  (Italian artist, 1632-1705)   WC
  (Italian painter, 1632-1705)   GC PR
  (Italian painter, printmaker,
    1632-1705)   BA
  (Italian, Neapolitan, 1634-1705)   JG
  Bibl: ▶Bolaffi; ▶Encic. italiana;
    Ferrari & Scavizzi:LUCA
    GIORDANO, I, p. 231 + 242;
    ▶RILA/BHA, 1986;
    ▶Thieme-Becker; ▶Witt checklist;
    ▶Wittkower, Art & arch. Italy,
    p.305
  Fapresto   PR
  Giordanello   PR
  Giordani   PR
  Giordaniello   PR
  Giordano   PR
  Giordano giovane   PR
Giordano, Luca Fapresto   WC
  Jardaeno   PR
  Jiardano   PR
  Jiordano   PR
  Jordan   PR
  Jordano   PR
  L'Giordano   PR
  L. Giodano   PR
  L. Giondano   PR
  L. Giordana   PR
  L. Giordani   PR
  L. Giordano   PR
  L. Giordino   PR
  L. Gordano   PR
  L. Guardano   PR
  L. Jordanes   PR
  L. Jordano   PR
  L. Jordans   PR
  L: Giordano   PR
  Luc Jordani   PR
  Luc Jordans   PR
  Luc. Giordano   PR
  Luc. Jordano   PR
  Luc. Jordans   PR
  Luca fa Presto   PR
  Luca Giardano   PR
  Luca Giardino   PR
  Luca Giordani   PR
  Luca Giordano   PR
  Luca Giordano, called Luca fa
    Presto   PR
  Luca Giordano, Called, Luca fa
    Presto   PR
  Luca Jordano   PR
  Lucas Jordan   PR
  Lucca fa Presto   PR
  Lucca Giedano   PR
  Lucca Giedanoo   PR
  Lucca Giordano   PR
  Lucca Jordano   PR
  Lucco Giordano   PR
  Lucia Jordana   PR
  Luco Giordano   PR
  Luco Jordano   PR
  S. Giordano   PR
  Zordano   PR

Giordano, Luca Fapresto →see
  Giordano, Luca
Giordano, Stefano   BA PR WC
  (Italian artist, op.1540)   WC
  (Italian painter, act. ca.1541)   PR
  (Italian painter, act.ca.1541)   BA
  Bibl: ▶Bénézit; Blue guide: Sicily;
    Maucen, Boll. d'arte X/1916,
    144-146; TCI Sicilia;
    ▶Thieme-Becker; ▶Witt checklist
  S. Giordano   PR
  Stefano Giordano   PR
Giorgetta, F. *(Italian architect)*   AV
  Bibl: Domus, 1985 Oct., no.665,
    p.62
Giorgetti, Antonio   FA GC
  (died before 22.VIII.1670;
    Architect, Roma)   FA
  (Italian sculptor, d.1670)   GC
  Bibl: ▶RILA/BHA, Subject, 1988;
    TCI Roma e dintorni;
    ▶Thieme-Becker, v.14, p.80 ff.
Giorgetti, Ercole *(Italian artist,*
    1814-1860)   WC
Giorgetti, Giacomo *(Italian painter,*
    1603-1679)   GC
  Bibl: ▶Thieme-Becker
Giorgi →see Giorgi, Antonio Ruggero
Giorgi da Piacenza, Giuseppe
    (Italian artist, op.1823-1842)   WC
Giorgi, Antonio de' *(Italian artist,*
    1720-1793)   WC
Giorgi, Antonio Ruggero   BA
  (Italian artist, 20th cent.)   WC
  (Italian painter, printmaker,
    b.1887)   BA
  Bibl: ▶Comanducci, Diz.
Giorgi   WC
Giorgi, Giovanni   GC
  (Italian artist, c.1684-1717)   WC
  (Italian painter, ca.1684-1717)   GC
  Bibl: ▶Thieme-Becker
  Giorgi, Giovanni de'   GC
Giorgi, Giovanni de' (Torellino)   WC
  Torellino   GC
Giorgi, Giovanni de' →see Giorgi,
  Giovanni
Giorgi, Giovanni de' (Torellino) →see
  Giorgi, Giovanni
Giorgi, Vita *(American printmaker,*
    painter, 20th c.)   BA
  Bibl: ▶NY art yrbk.; ▶WW Amer.
    Art, 1978
Giorgini, Simone *(Italian sculptor,*
    act.1697)   BA
  Bibl: ▶Bénézit; ▶Thieme-Becker
Giorgini, Vittorio *(Italian architect,*
    1926-)   AV
Giorgino →see Vasari, Giorgio
Giorgino di Rezzo →see Vasari,
  Giorgio
Giorgio →see Giorgione (Giorgio da
  Castelfranco)
Giorgio Barbarelli, Called, Giorgione
  di Castel Franco →see Giorgione
  (Giorgio da Castelfranco)

Giorgio d'Alemagna   BA GC PR
  (Italian illuminator, act.1441-
    1479)   BA
  (Italian illuminator, d.1479)   GC
  (Italian painter, act. 1441-1479)   PR
  Bibl: ▶Bénézit; ▶Bolaffi;
    ▶D'Ancona, Miniaturistes;
    ▶RILA/BHA
  Alemagna, Giorgio d'   PR
  Tedesco, Zorzo   GC
Giorgio da Castelfranco →see
  Giorgione (Giorgio da
  Castelfranco)
Giorgio da Gubbio →see Andreoli,
  Giorgio
Giorgio da Sebenico →see Giorgio da
  Sebenico (Giorgio Orsini)
Giorgio da Sebenico (Giorgio
  Dalmatico) →see Giorgio da
  Sebenico (Giorgio Orsini)
Giorgio da Sebenico (Giorgio
  Orsini)   BA GC
  (Italian architect, sculptor, act.
    1440, d.1475)   BA
  (Italian sculptor and architect,
    act.ca.1440-d.1475)   GC
  (Italian(?) artist, op.1441-m.
    1475)   WC
  Bibl: ▶Bessone-Aurelj, Scult. &
    arch. ital.; ▶Encic. italiana;
    ▶Encyc. world art; Getty Photo
    Study Coll. (Sculp.); ▶RILA/BHA;
    ▶Seymour, Scult. Italy, p.265
  Giorgio da Sebenico   GC
Giorgio da Sebenico (Giorgio
  Dalmatico)   WC
  Giorgio Orsini   GC
  Orsini, Giorgio   GC
Giorgio Dalmatico →see Schiavone,
  Giorgio di Tomaso
Giorgio de Chirico →see Chirico,
  Giorgio de
Giorgio di Andrea di Bartolo
  (Italian painter, act.1389-1412)   BA
  Bibl: ARTE CRISTIANA LXXIV/712
    (Jan-Feb, 1986) 15-28; ▶Bolaffi;
    ▶Diz. biog. ital.; ▶Thieme-Becker
Giorgio di Tomaso Schiavone →see
  Schiavone, Giorgio di Tomaso
Giorgio Fiorentino →see Marchesi,
  Giorgio, called Giorgio Fiorentino
Giorgio Giacobini →see Giacoboni,
  Giorgio
Giorgio Giacoboni →see Giacoboni,
  Giorgio
Giorgio Jacoboni scolare di Gio:
  Paolo Pannini →see Giacoboni,
  Giorgio
Giorgio Martini, Francesco di →see
  Francesco di Giorgio Martini
Giorgio Morandi →see Morandi,
  Giorgio
Giorgio Orsini →see Giorgio da
  Sebenico (Giorgio Orsini)
Giorgio Schiavone →see Schiavone,
  Giorgio di Tomaso

Giorgio Sommer (Naples) → see
Sommer, Giorgio
Giorgio Tacoboni → see Giacoboni,
Giorgio
Giorgio Vaccari → see Vasari, Giorgio
Giorgio Vasaio → see Vasari, Giorgio
Giorgio Vasari → see Vasari, Giorgio
Giorgio Vasaro → see Vasari, Giorgio
Giorgio Vasarri → see Vasari, Giorgio
Giorgio Vassalii → see Vasari, Giorgio
Giorgio Vassari → see Vasari, Giorgio
Giorgio Vassaro → see Vasari, Giorgio

**Giorgio Veneziano (Master
Giorgio, called "Greco")** (Italian,
act.1534)   **GC**
> Bibl: Malaguzzi-Valeri, Pinac. di
> Brera (1908)

Giorgio, Ettore di (Italian artist,
1890-)   **WC**

Giorgio, Francesco di → see Francesco
di Giorgio Martini

Giorgioli, Francesco Antonio
*(Swiss painter, printmaker, ca.
1655-1725)*   **BA**
> Bibl: ▶Bénézit; ▶Encyc. world art;
> ▶Thieme-Becker

Giorgion → see Giorgione (Giorgio da
Castelfranco)
Giorgion di Castelfranco → see
Giorgione (Giorgio da
Castelfranco)
Giorgione → see Giorgione (Giorgio da
Castelfranco)

**Giorgione (Giorgio da
Castelfranco)**   **BA GC PR**
  (Italian artist, 1477-1510)   **WI**
  (Italian artist, 1477/8-1510)   **WC**
  *(Italian painter,
   1477/78-1510)*   **BA GC PR**
> Bibl: ▶Bolaffi; Pignatti,
> GIORGIONE; ▶RILA/BHA;
> ▶Thieme-Becker

Cavalier Georgione	PR
Georgeon	PR
Georgeonia	PR
Georges Giorgion	PR
Georgini	PR
Georgione	PR
Georgioni	PR
Georgone	PR
Georgoni	PR
Giogone	PR
Giorgio	PR
Giorgio Barbarelli, Called,
Giorgione di Castel Franco	PR
Giorgio da Castelfranco	PR
Giorgion	PR
Giorgion di Castelfranco	PR
Giorgione	GC PR
Giorgione da Castelfranco	PR
Giorgione del Castel-franco	PR
Giorgione di Castel Franco	PR
Giorgione di Castelfranco	PR

Giorgione, Giorgio Barbarelli   **WC WI**

Giorgioni	PR
Giorgioni di Castelfranco	PR
Giorgone	PR
Giorgoni	PR
Gorgione	PR
Gorgione del Castel-franco	PR
Gorgioni	PR
Gorgone	PR
Jorge del Castel Franco	PR
Jorjion de Castelfranco	PR

Giorgione d'Arezzo → see Vasari,
Giorgio
Giorgione da Castelfranco → see
Giorgione (Giorgio da
Castelfranco)
Giorgione del Castel-franco → see
Giorgione (Giorgio da
Castelfranco)
Giorgione di Castel Franco → see
Giorgione (Giorgio da
Castelfranco)
Giorgione di Castelfranco → see
Giorgione (Giorgio da
Castelfranco)
Giorgione, Giorgio Barbarelli → see
Giorgione (Giorgio da
Castelfranco)
Giorgioni → see Giorgione (Giorgio da
Castelfranco)
Giorgioni di Castelfranco → see
Giorgione (Giorgio da
Castelfranco)
Giorgitta → see Giorgitto
[Unidentified]

Giorgitto [Unidentified] *(Unknown
painter)*   **PR**
> Bibl: Tuttavilla inventory, Naples,
> 1679 & 1681
  Giorgitta   PR

Giorgo Dalmatico → see Schiavone,
Giorgio di Tomaso
Giorgone → see Giorgione (Giorgio da
Castelfranco)
Giorgoni → see Giorgione (Giorgio da
Castelfranco)

Giorla, J. G. *(Architect)*   **AV**
> Bibl: Lotus international, 1984,
> no.43, p.88

Giorla, Jean-Gerard *(Swiss
architect)*   **AV**
> Bibl: ▶Schweiz. Ingen. u. Archit.,
> 1984-1985

Gios. d'Arpino → see Cesari, Giuseppe
(Cavalier d'Arpino)
Gios. Recco → see Recco, Giuseppe
Gios. Riviera → see Ribera, Jusepe de
(lo Spagnoletto)
Gios.e Castellano → see Castellano,
Giuseppe
Gios.e d'Arpino → see Cesari,
Giuseppe (Cavalier d'Arpino)
Gios.e di Ribera → see Ribera, Jusepe
de (lo Spagnoletto)
Gios.e Pasquino → see Pasquino,
Giuseppe [Unidentified]
Gios.e Piscopo → see Piscopo,
Giuseppe
Gios.e Pollio → see Pollio, Giuseppe
[Unidentified]
Gios.e Recco → see Recco, Giuseppe
Gios.e Scarpato → see Scarpato,
Giuseppe [Unidentified]
Gioseffe Cesari d'Arpino → see Cesari,
Giuseppe (Cavalier d'Arpino)
Gioseffe Salviati → see Porta,
Giuseppe (Giuseppe Salviati)
Gioseppe → see Giuseppe
[Unidentified]
Gioseppe → see Iovine, Giuseppe
Gioseppe Castellano → see Castellano,
Giuseppe
Gioseppe Cesari d'Arpino → see
Cesari, Giuseppe (Cavalier
d'Arpino)
Gioseppe Coppolo → see Coppolo,
Giuseppe [Unidentified]
Gioseppe d'Amato → see Amato,
Giuseppe d'
Gioseppe d'Arpino → see Cesari,
Giuseppe (Cavalier d'Arpino)
Gioseppe de Arpino → see Cesari,
Giuseppe (Cavalier d'Arpino)
Gioseppe de Quedo → see Quedo,
Giuseppe de [Unidentified]
Gioseppe de Reviera → see Ribera,
Jusepe de (lo Spagnoletto)
Gioseppe de Ribera → see Ribera,
Jusepe de (lo Spagnoletto)

Gioseppe de Rivera→see Ribera,
Jusepe de (lo Spagnoletto)
Gioseppe de Riviera→see Ribera,
Jusepe de (lo Spagnoletto)
Gioseppe di Revera→see Ribera,
Jusepe de (lo Spagnoletto)
Gioseppe di Ribera→see Ribera,
Jusepe de (lo Spagnoletto)
Gioseppe di Rivera→see Ribera,
Jusepe de (lo Spagnoletto)
Gioseppe di Riviera→see Ribera,
Jusepe de (lo Spagnoletto)
Gioseppe Farriello→see Farriello,
Giuseppe [Unidentified]
Gioseppe Napoletano→see Piscopo,
Giuseppe
Gioseppe Napolitano→see Piscopo,
Giuseppe
Gioseppe Piscopo→see Piscopo,
Giuseppe
Gioseppe Pollio→see Pollio, Giuseppe
[Unidentified]
Gioseppe Recco→see Recco,
Giuseppe
Gioseppe Revera→see Ribera, Jusepe
de (lo Spagnoletto)
Gioseppe Reviera→see Ribera, Jusepe
de (lo Spagnoletto)
Gioseppe rivera→see Ribera, Jusepe
de (lo Spagnoletto)
*Gioseppe Rivera, detto il
Spagnolo*→see Ribera, Jusepe de
(lo Spagnoletto)
Gioseppe Riviera→see Ribera, Jusepe
de (lo Spagnoletto)
Gioseppe Rivieras→see Ribera,
Jusepe de (lo Spagnoletto)
Gioseppe Salviati→see Porta,
Giuseppe (Giuseppe Salviati)
Gioseppe Scarpato→see Scarpato,
Giuseppe [Unidentified]
Gioseppe Simonelli→see Simonelli,
Giuseppe
Gioseppe Trombatore→see
Trombatore, Giuseppe
Gioseppino→see Cesari, Giuseppe
(Cavalier d'Arpino)
Gioseppino d'Arpino→see Cesari,
Giuseppe (Cavalier d'Arpino)
Giotti→see Giotto di Bondone
Giottino→see Giottino, Giotto di
Maestro Stefano
Giottino→see Tommaso di Stefano
*Giottino (Giotto di Maestro
Stefano)*→see Giottino, Giotto di
Maestro Stefano
Giottino di Maestro Stefano→see
Giottino, Giotto di Maestro
Stefano

**Giottino, Giotto di Maestro
Stefano**   **WC WI**
    (Italian artist, op.1368)   WC
    (Italian artist, op.1368-)   WI
    *(Italian painter, act. 14th
    century)*   PR
    (Italian, ca.1320/30-aft. 1369)   GC
    Bibl: Smart, Dawn of Ital. Ptg.,
    p.84; ▶Thieme-Becker; Uffizi Gen
    Cat; ▶Witt checklist
Giottino   GC PR
**Giottino (Giotto di Maestro
Stefano)**   **GC PR**
    Giottino di Maestro Stefano   GC
Giottino, Maso di Banco→see Maso
di Banco
Giotto→see Giotto di Bondone
Giotto di Bondone   **BA GC PR WC**
    (Italian artist, 1267-1337)   WI
    (Italian artist, 1276-1337)   WC
    *(Italian painter and architect,
    ca.1266-1337)*   GC
    (Italian painter, 1276-1337)   PR
    *(Italian painter, architect, ca.
    1266-1337)*   BA
    Bibl: Getty Photo Study Coll.
    (Ptgs.); ▶RILA/BHA;
    ▶Thieme-Becker
Giotti   PR
Giotto   GC PR
Giotto, Ambrogio di Bondone   **WI**
Giotto, Ambrogio di Bondone→see
Giotto di Bondone
Giouanni Bellini→see Bellini, Giovanni
Giouanni Bellino→see Bellini,
Giovanni
Giov Frano Romanelli→see Romanelli,
Giovanni Francesco
Giov. Antonio Iovino→see Iovino,
Giovanni Antonio [Unidentified]
Giov. Battista di Conegla→see Cima
da Conegliano, Giovanni Battista
Giov. Battista il veneziano→see
Giovanni Battista il Veneziano
[Unidentified]
Giov. Battistiello Caracciolo→see
Caracciolo, Giovanni Battista
(Battistello)
Giov. Battistino→see Caracciolo,
Giovanni Battista (Battistello)
Giov. Bellini→see Bellini, Giovanni
Giov. Benedetto Castiglione→see
Castiglione, Giovanni Benedetto (il
Grechetto)
Giov. Bernardo→see Azzolino
(Giovanni Bernardino Ragano)
Giov. da Bellino→see Bellini,
Giovanni
Giov. di Bellini→see Bellini, Giovanni
Giov. Francesco Grimaldi→see
Grimaldi, Giovanni Francesco
Giov. Gastona Forzoni-Accolti→see
Forzoni-Accolti, Giovanna Gastona
Giov. Maldura→see Maldura,
Giovanni

Giovan Andrea da Caldarola→see
Magistris, Giovanni Andrea de
Giovan Batista Cimaroli→see
Cimaroli, Giovanni Battista
Giovan Battista Ambra→see Ambra,
Giovan Battista [Unidentified]
Giovan Battista Benini→see Benini,
Giovan Battista [Unidentified]
Giovan Battista Cipriani→see
Cipriani, Giovanni Battista
Giovan Battista Hassunt→see
Hassunt, Giovan Battista
[Unidentified]
Giovan Battista Naldini→see Naldini,
Giovanni Battista
Giovan Battista Scarlatti→see
Scarlatti, Giovan Battista
[Unidentified]
Giovan Battista Vannetti→see
Vannetti, Giovan Battista
[Unidentified]
Giovan battistiello Caracciolo→see
Caracciolo, Giovanni Battista
(Battistello)
Giovan Bernardo Lama→see Lama,
Giovan Bernardo
Giovan Breughel→see Brueghel, Jan,
the elder
Giovan Domenico Picchianti→see
Picchianti, Giovanni Domenico
Giovan Filippo Criscuolo→see
Criscuolo, Giovan Filippo
*Giovan Francesco Barbieri detto il
Guercino da Cento*→see Guercino
(Giovanni Francesco Barbieri)
Giovan Francesco Gessi→see Gessi,
Giovan Francesco
Giovan Francesco Rigaud→see
Rigaud, John Francis
Giovan Francesco Romanelli→see
Romanelli, Giovanni Francesco
Giovan Gioseffo dal Sole→see Sole,
Giovan Gioseffo dal
Giovan Giuseppe del Sole→see Sole,
Giovan Gioseffo dal
Giovan Giuseppe Romei→see Romei,
Giuseppe
Giovan Iacopo [Unidentified]
    (Unknown painter)   PR
    Bibl: Mamiani della Rovere
    inventory, Urbino, 1624; possibly
    SALAJ (GIAN GIACOMO
    DE'CAPROTTI)?
Giovan Leonardo→see Giovanni
Leonardo [Unidentified]
Giovan Maria Morandi→see Morandi,
Giovanni Maria
Giovan Paolo Graccini→see Grazzini,
Giovanni Paolo
Giovan Paolo Pannini→see Pannini,
Giovanni Paolo
Giovan Pietro Birago→see Birago,
Giovan Pietro
Giovan Vincenzo Forli→see Forlì,
Giovan Vincenzo

Giovana Garzoni→*see* Garzoni, Giovanna

Giovanbattista Ruoppolo→*see* Ruoppolo, Giovanni Battista

Giovanbattistiello Caracciuolo→*see* Caracciolo, Giovanni Battista (Battistello)

Giovanetti da Viterbo→*see* Matteo di Giovanetto

Giovanetti, Mario *(Italian sculptor, b.1932)*   **BA**
Bibl: Pieve di Cento (ITA), Pinacoteca Civica, GIOVANETTI..., 1983 p.22 (RILA, ITA)

Giovanfrancesco di Mariotto *(Italian illuminator, 1477-1526/34)*   **GC**
Bibl: ▶Levi d'Ancona, Miniatura a Firenze, pp.139-142

Giovani Bellini→*see* Bellini, Giovanni

Giovani Viani→*see* Viani, Giovanni Maria

Giovanino Fiamingo→*see* Giovanni Fiammingo [Unidentified]

Giovanna Fratellini→*see* Fratellini, Giovanna

Giovanna Garzoni→*see* Garzoni, Giovanna

Giovanna Gastona Forzoni→*see* Forzoni-Accolti, Giovanna Gastona

Giovanna Gastona Forzoni-Accolti→*see* Forzoni-Accolti, Giovanna Gastona

Giovanne Bernardo→*see* Azzolino (Giovanni Bernardino Ragano)

Giovannelli, Benedetto *(Italian architect, 1601-1676)*   **BA**
Bibl: ▶Encic. italiana; ▶Portoghesi, Diz. arch. e urbanistica; TCI Toscana, p.771; ▶Thieme-Becker

Giovannello d'Italia (Itala) *(Italian artist, op.1504-1531)*   **WC**

Giovannetti, Matteo→*see* Matteo Giovannetti

Giovanni (di Barcellona?) *(Italian artist, 15th cent.)*   **WC**

Giovanni (di Giorgio) da Padova *(Italian artist, op.1367-1397)*   **WC**

Giovanni (or Zuanne) da Brescia (Zuane da Asola)→*see* Giovanni da Brescia

Giovanni (Zuanne) da Brescia→*see* Giovanni da Brescia

Giovanni Adamo Verlin→*see* Verlin, Giovanni Adamo

Giovanni Agostino Cassana→*see* Cassana, Giovanni Agostino (Abate Cassana)

Giovanni Agostino da Lodi   **BA GC**
(Italian artist, op.c.1500)   **WC**
(Italian painter, act. ca.1500)   **GC**
(Italian painter, act. early 16th cent.)   **PR**
(Italian painter, act.1500-ca. 1520)   **BA**
Bibl: Berenson, Cent. & N.Ital.; ▶Bolaffi; ▶Diz. biog. ital.; ▶Encic. italiana; ▶Fredericksen & Zeri, Census; Getty Photo Study Coll. (Ptgs.); Moro, PARAGONE, 40/473 (July 1989) p.23-61; ▶Thieme-Becker; ▶Witt checklist

Agostino da Lodi   **BA GC**
Boccaccino   **PR**
Boccaccino (pseudo)   **PR**
Boccaccino, Pseudo   **BA**

Boccaccino, Pseudo (Giovanni Agostino da Lodi)   **WC**

Master known as the Pseudo-Boccaccino   **PR**

Pseudo Boccaccino   **GC**

Pseudo-Boccaccino   **BA PR**

Giovanni Ambrogio de Predis→*see* Predis, Giovanni Ambrogio de

Giovanni andrea→*see* Ferrari, Giovanni Andrea de

Giovanni Andrea Coppola→*see* Coppola, Giovanni Andrea

Giovanni Andrea d' Ferrari→*see* Ferrari, Giovanni Andrea de

Giovanni Andrea de Ferrari→*see* Ferrari, Giovanni Andrea de

Giovanni Andrea de' Ferrari→*see* Ferrari, Giovanni Andrea de

Giovanni Andrea Donducci→*see* Donducci, Giovanni Andrea (Mastelletta)

Giovanni Andrea Ferrari→*see* Ferrari, Giovanni Andrea de

Giovanni Andrea Ghirardoni→*see* Ghirardoni, Giovanni Andrea

Giovanni Andrea Sirani→*see* Sirani, Giovanni Andrea

Giovanni Angelo di Antonio da Camerino→*see* Angelo da Camerino

Giovanni Angelo di Antonio da Camerino→*see* Carnevale, Fra (Bartolomeo di Giovanni Corradini)

Giovanni Angelo Milone→*see* Milone, Giovanni Angelo [Unidentified]

Giovanni Angelo Vicino→*see* Vicino, Giovanni Angelo

Giovanni Ant. Leisman→*see* Eismann, Johann Anton

Giovanni Antionio da Pordenone→*see* Pordenone (Giovanni Antonio de Sacchis)

Giovanni Antonio Bazzi→*see* Sodoma (Giovanni Antonio Bazzi)

Giovanni Antonio Boltraffio→*see* Boltraffio, Giovanni Antonio

Giovanni Antonio Crecolini→*see* Grecolini, Giovanni Antonio

Giovanni Antonio d'Amato→*see* Amato, Giovanni Antonio d'

Giovanni Antonio da Brescia   **BA CE GC WC**
(Engraver, printmaker, post 1440/ante 1485-post 1507/ante 1585)   **CE**
(Italian artist, 16th cent.)   **WC**
(Italian artist, op.c.1500-1520)   **WC**
(Italian printmaker, act.1490-ca. 1520)   **BA**
(Italian, act. ca.1500-1520)   **GC**
Bibl: ▶Bolaffi; Getty Photo Study Coll. (Ptgs.); ▶Thieme-Becker; ▶Witt checklist

Antonio da Brescia, Giovanni   **WC**
Brescia, Giovanni Antonio da   **CE GC**
Da Brescia, Giovanni Antonio   **CE**
Ioan Brixia   **CE**

Giovanni Antonio da Lucoli *(Italian painter, sculptor, b.ca.1491, act. 1537)*   **BA**
Bibl: ▶Bolaffi; Croceffi, NOTIZIE DA PALAZZO ALBANI, XIV, 1 (1985); ▶Thieme-Becker

Giovanni Antonio da Mesco *(Italian artist, op.1450)*   **WC**

Giovanni Antonio da Milano *(Italian sculptor, act.1492)*   **BA**
Bibl: Barbieri, Scultori a Vicenza; TCI Veneto; ▶Thieme-Becker

Giovanni Antonio da Parma *(Italian artist, 15th cent.)*   **WC**

Giovanni Antonio da Pesaro→*see* Giovanni Antonio di Gaspare da Pesaro

Giovanni Antonio da Pordenone→*see* Pordenone (Giovanni Antonio de Sacchis)

Giovanni Antonio da Spinola *(Italian scribe, 15th century)*   **GC**
Bibl: Getty Photo Study Coll. (Medieval); Rome (ITA), Pal. di Venezia, Miniatura (1953), p.554

Spinola, Giovanni Antonio da   **GC**

Giovanni Antonio de Sacchis→*see* Pordenone (Giovanni Antonio de Sacchis)

Giovanni Antonio di Francesco Sogliani→*see* Sogliani, Giovanni Antonio di Francesco

Giovanni Antonio di Gaspare da Pesaro   **BA GC PR WC**
(Italian artist, op.1462-1511)   **WC**
(Italian painter, act. 1462-1511)   **PR**
(Italian painter, act.1462-1511)   **BA GC**
Bibl: ▶Bolaffi; PARAGONE, XXVII/317-319(JULY-SEPT 1976), 59-62; ▶RILA/BHA, 1986; TCI Emilia-Romagna, p.723

Giovanni Antonio da Pesaro   **GC PR**

Giovanni Antonio Fasolo→*see* Fasolo, Giovanni Antonio

Giovanni Antonio Fumiani→see
Fumiani, Giovanni Antonio
Giovanni Antonio Guardi→see
Guardi, Giovanni Antonio
Giovanni Antonio Lelli→see Lelli
(Lellio), Giovanni Antonio
Giovanni Antonio Licinio da
Pordenone→see Pordenone
(Giovanni Antonio de Sacchis)
Giovanni Antonio Licinio, called
Pordenone→see Pordenone
(Giovanni Antonio de Sacchis)
Giovanni Antonio Morandi→see
Morandi, Giovanni Antonio
Giovanni Antonio Paracca→see
Paracca, Giovanni Antonio
Giovanni Antonio Pellegrini→see
Pellegrini, Giovanni Antonio
Giovanni Badile→see Badile, Giovanni
Giovanni Baglione→see Baglione,
Giovanni
Giovanni Baglioni→see Baglione,
Giovanni
Giovanni Balducci→see Balducci,
Giovanni (Cosci)
Giovanni Balduccio→see Balducci,
Giovanni (Cosci)
Giovanni Baptista Salvi, Called,
Sassaferrato→see Sassoferrato
(Giovanni Battista Salvi)
Giovanni Baptista Viola→see Viola,
Giovanni Battista
Giovanni Baronzio→see Baronzio,
Giovanni
Giovanni Battista Balducci→see
Balducci, Giovanni (Cosci)
Giovanni Battista Beinaschi→see
Benaschi, Giovanni Battista
Giovanni Battista benacco→see
Benaschi, Giovanni Battista
Giovanni Battista Benaso→see
Benaschi, Giovanni Battista
Giovanni Battista Benazzo→see
Benaschi, Giovanni Battista
Giovanni Battista Bernasca→see
Benaschi, Giovanni Battista
Giovanni Battista Bertucci→see
Bertucci, Giovanni Battista, the
elder
Giovanni Battista Boncori→see
Bonocore, Giovanni Battista
Giovanni Battista Braceli→see
Bracelli, Giovanni Battista
Giovanni Battista Bracelli→see
Bracelli, Giovanni Battista
Giovanni Battista Bue'→see Buè,
Giovanni Battista [Unidentified]
Giovanni Battista Busiri→see Busiri,
Giovanni Battista
Giovanni Battista Caccini→see
Caccini, Giovanni Battista
Giovanni Battista Canevari→see
Canevari, Giovanni Battista
Giovanni Battista Capanna→see
Capanna, Giovanni Battista

Giovanni Battista Caraccio→see
Caracciolo, Giovanni Battista
(Battistello)
Giovanni Battista Caracciolo→see
Caracciolo, Giovanni Battista
(Battistello)
Giovanni Battista Carlone→see
Carlone, Giovanni Battista
Giovanni Battista Castello→see
Castello, Giovanni Battista
(Genovese)
Giovanni Battista Castello→see
Castello, Giovanni Battista (il
Bergamasco)
Giovanni Battista Cavazza→see
Cavazza, Giovanni Battista
Giovanni Battista Cima→see Cima da
Conegliano, Giovanni Battista
Giovanni Battista Cima da
Conegliano→see Cima da
Conegliano, Giovanni Battista
Giovanni Battista Cimaroli→see
Cimaroli, Giovanni Battista
Giovanni Battista Cipriani→see
Cipriani, Giovanni Battista
Giovanni Battista Costa→see Costa,
Giovanni Battista
Giovanni Battista Crescenzi→see
Crescenzi, Giovanni Battista
Giovanni Battista Crespi→see Crespi,
Giovanni Battista (Cerano)
Giovanni Battista Crespi detto il
Cerano→see Crespi, Giovanni
Battista (Cerano)
Giovanni Battista Crosato→see
Crosato, Giovanni Battista
Giovanni Battista da Citta di
Castello→see Battista da Città di
Castello
Giovanni Battista da Cortona *(fl.*
1525-1540; Architect, Umbria) **FA**
Bibl: TCI Umbria
Cortona, Giovanni Battista da FA
da Cortona, Giovanni Battista FA
Giovanni Battista da Faenza→see
Bertucci, Giovanni Battista, the
elder
Giovanni Battista da Lugano→see
Discepoli, Giovanni Battista (Zoppo
da Lugano)
Giovanni Battista da Milano
(Italian artist, op.1495) **WC**
Giovanni Battista da Sangallo→see
Sangallo, Giovanni Battista da
(Gobbo)
Giovanni Battista da Udine→see
Martini, Giovanni (Giovanni da
Udine)
Giovanni Battista da Vicenza **GC WC**
(Italian artist, 14th cent.) WC
(Italian, 14th century) GC
Bibl: ▶Witt checklist
Giovanni Battista dalla Torre→see
Torre, Giovanni Battista dalla

Giovanni Battista del Cavalletto→see
Cavalletto, Giovanni Battista de
Giovanni Battista del Porto *(Italian*
artist, op.c.1503) **WC**
Giovanni Battista del Sole→see Sole,
Giovanni Battista del
Giovanni Battista della Porta→see
Della Porta, Giovanni Battista
Giovanni Battista di Bernardino
Bonsignori→see Bonsignori,
Giovanni Battista di Bernardino
Giovanni Battista di Jacopo di
Guasparre→see Rosso Fiorentino
(Giovanni Battista di Jacopo)
Giovanni Battista di Jacoppo→see
Rosso Fiorentino (Giovanni Battista
di Jacopo)
Giovanni Battista Discepoli→see
Discepoli, Giovanni Battista (Zoppo
da Lugano)
Giovanni Battista Fontana→see
Fontana, Giovanni Battista
Giovanni Battista Galestruzzi→see
Galestruzzi, Giovanni Battista
Giovanni Battista Gaulli→see Gaulli,
Giovanni Battista (Baciccio)
Giovanni Battista Gavarotti→see
Gavarotti, Giovanni Battista
Giovanni Battista il Veneziano
[Unidentified] *(Unknown painter,*
act. 18th century) **PR**
Bibl: Inventory of Filippo Pisacane,
1702; possibly Giovanni Battista
LANGETTI.
Gio: Battista il Veneziano PR
Gio: Battista Veneziano PR
Giov. Battista il veneziano PR
Giovanni Battista Innocenzo
Colombo→see Colombo, Giovanni
Battista Innocenzo
Giovanni Battista Lama→see Lama,
Giovanni Battista
Giovanni Battista Langetti→see
Langetti, Giovanni Battista
Giovanni Battista Lenardi→see
Lenardi, Giovanni Battista
Giovanni Battista Lusieri→see Lusieri,
Giovanni Battista
Giovanni Battista Maganza (I)→see
Maganza, Giovanni Battista I
Giovanni Battista Moroni→see
Moroni, Giovanni Battista
Giovanni Battista Muti→see Muti,
Giovanni Battista
Giovanni Battista Naldini→see
Naldini, Giovanni Battista
Giovanni Battista of Faenza→see
Bertucci, Giovanni Battista, the
elder
Giovanni Battista Paggi→see Paggi,
Giovanni Battista
Giovanni Battista Palumba→see
Palumba, Giovanni Battista
Giovanni Battista Passaro→see
Passeri, Giovanni Battista

Giovanni Battista Passeri → *see*
Passeri, Giovanni Battista
Giovanni Battista Passero → *see*
Passeri, Giovanni Battista
Giovanni Battista Piazzetta → *see*
Piazzetta, Giovanni Battista
Giovanni Battista Piranesi → *see*
Piranesi, Giovanni Battista
*Giovanni Battista Pittoni (the
younger)* → *see* Pittoni, Giovanni
Battista, the younger
Giovanni Battista Procaccini → *see*
Procaccini, Giovanni Battista
[Unidentified]
Giovanni Battista Recco → *see* Recco,
Giovanni Battista
Giovanni Battista Reppoli → *see*
Ruoppolo, Giovanni Battista
Giovanni Battista Ruoppoli → *see*
Ruoppolo, Giovanni Battista
Giovanni Battista Ruoppolo → *see*
Ruoppolo, Giovanni Battista
Giovanni Battista Salvi → *see*
Sassoferrato (Giovanni Battista
Salvi)
*Giovanni Battista Salvi da
Sassoferrato* → *see* Sassoferrato
(Giovanni Battista Salvi)
Giovanni Battista Spinelli → *see*
Spinelli, Giovanni Battista
Giovanni Battista Stomo → *see* Stomo,
Giovanni Battista [Unidentified]
Giovanni Battista Tiepolo → *see*
Tiepolo, Giovanni Battista
Giovanni Battista Troccoli → *see*
Troccoli, Giovanni Battista
*Giovanni Battista Trotti
(Malosso)* → *see* Trotti, Giovanni
Battista (Malosso)
Giovanni Battista Vanni → *see* Vanni,
Giovanni Battista
Giovanni Battista Viola → *see* Viola,
Giovanni Battista
Giovanni Battista Volpato → *see*
Volpato, Giovanni Battista
Giovanni Battista Zelotti → *see* Zelotti,
Giovanni Battista
Giovanni battistello → *see* Caracciolo,
Giovanni Battista (Battistello)
Giovanni Battistello Caracciolo → *see*
Caracciolo, Giovanni Battista
(Battistello)
Giovanni Battistiello Caracciolo → *see*
Caracciolo, Giovanni Battista
(Battistello)
Giovanni Battistino Caracciolo → *see*
Caracciolo, Giovanni Battista
(Battistello)
Giovanni Belardino Siciliano → *see*
Azzolino (Giovanni Bernardino
Ragano)
Giovanni Bellini → *see* Bellini, Giovanni
Giovanni Bellino → *see* Bellini,
Giovanni

Giovanni Bellino, or Bellini → *see*
Bellini, Giovanni
Giovanni Benedetto Castiglione → *see*
Castiglione, Giovanni Benedetto (il
Grechetto)
*Giovanni Benedetto Castiglione,
Called, Grechetto* → *see*
Castiglione, Giovanni Benedetto (il
Grechetto)
Giovanni Benedetto Castiglioni → *see*
Castiglione, Giovanni Benedetto (il
Grechetto)
Giovanni Berardino → *see* Azzolino
(Giovanni Bernardino Ragano)
Giovanni Berardino Seciliano → *see*
Azzolino (Giovanni Bernardino
Ragano)
Giovanni Berardino Siciliano → *see*
Azzolino (Giovanni Bernardino
Ragano)
Giovanni bernardino → *see* Azzolino
(Giovanni Bernardino Ragano)
Giovanni Bernardino Fera → *see* Fera,
Bernardino
Giovanni bernardino napoletano → *see*
Azzolino (Giovanni Bernardino
Ragano)
Giovanni Bernardino Ragano → *see*
Azzolino (Giovanni Bernardino
Ragano)
Giovanni Bernardino Siciliano → *see*
Azzolino (Giovanni Bernardino
Ragano)
Giovanni Bernardo → *see* Azzolino
(Giovanni Bernardino Ragano)
Giovanni Bernardo Azzolini → *see*
Azzolino (Giovanni Bernardino
Ragano)
Giovanni Bernardo Carboni → *see*
Carboni, Giovanni Bernardo
Giovanni Bilivert → *see* Bilivert,
Giovanni
Giovanni Biliverti → *see* Bilivert,
Giovanni
Giovanni Boccati → *see* Boccati,
Giovanni di Piermatteo da
Camerino
Giovanni Boldini → *see* Boldini,
Giovanni
Giovanni Bonati → *see* Bonatti,
Giovanni (Il Ferraresino)
Giovanni Bonatti → *see* Bonatti,
Giovanni (Il Ferraresino)
Giovanni Bonatti (Il Ferraresino) → *see*
Bonatti, Giovanni (Il Ferraresino)
Giovanni Bonsi → *see* Bonsi, Giovanni
Giovanni Bontalenti → *see* Bontalenti,
Giovanni [Unidentified]
Giovanni Boulanger → *see* Boulanger,
Jean
Giovanni Breughel → *see* Brueghel,
Jan, the elder
Giovanni Briglia → *see* Briglia,
Giovanni Francesco

Giovanni Buonconsiglio → *see*
Buonconsiglio, Giovanni (il
Marescalco)
Giovanni Busi → *see* Cariani, Giovanni
(Giovanni de'Busi)
Giovanni Busi (Cariani) → *see* Cariani,
Giovanni (Giovanni de'Busi)
Giovanni Califano → *see* Califano,
Giovanni
Giovanni Camillo Sagrestani → *see*
Sagrestani, Giovanni Camillo
Giovanni Cariani → *see* Cariani,
Giovanni (Giovanni de'Busi)
Giovanni Caroto → *see* Caroto,
Giovanni

Giovanni Cieco [Unidentified]
*(Unknown painter, act. 17th
century)* **PR**
Bibl: inventory of Giulio Cesare
Caiafa, dated 1676/05/07
Giovanni Coli → *see* Coli, Giovanni
Giovanni Contarini → *see* Contarini,
Giovanni
Giovanni Costa → *see* Costa, Giovanni
(Nino)
Giovanni Currado → *see* Currado,
Giovanni [Unidentified]

Giovanni d'Agostino *(Italian
sculptor, architect, ca.1310-after
1347)* **BA**
Bibl: ▶Portoghesi, Diz. arch. e
urbanistica; TCI Toscana;
▶Thieme-Becker
Giovanni d'Alamagna → *see* Giovanni
d'Alemagna

Giovanni d'Alemagna **BA GC PR**
*(German artist, op.1440-m.
1450)* **WC**
(German painter in ITA, d.1450) **BA**
(German painter, d. 1450) **PR**
*(Italian painter, act.1441-d.
1450)* **GC**
Bibl: ▶Bolaffi; ▶RILA/BHA; TCI
Veneto; ▶Thieme-Becker;
▶Vollmer, Künst.-Lex. 20. Jhr.;
▶Witt checklist
Alamagna, Giovanni de **GC**
D'Alemagna, Giovanni **PR**
Giovanni d'Alamagna **GC**
Giovanni da Murano **GC**

**Giovanni de Alamagna (Johanes
Alamanus, Zuane or Giovanni
da Murano)** **WC**
Giovanni d'Alessio d'Antonio → *see*
Nanni Unghero (Giovanni d'Alessio
d'Antonio)

Giovanni d'Ambrogio **BA CE**
(Italian sculptor, act.1366-1418) **BA**
*(Sculptor, post 1318/ante 1366-
post 1418/ante 1466)* **CE**
Bibl: ▶Bessone-Aurelj, Scult. &
arch. ital.; ▶Seymour, Sculp. Italy;
▶Thieme-Becker
D'Ambrogio, Giovanni **CE**

Giovanni d'Antonio Varnucci→see Varnucci, Giovanni d'Antonio di Luca di Jacopo

Giovanni d'Apparecchiato da   **BA**
  Lucca *(Italian painter, act.ca.1302)*
  Bibl: Waldenburg, Miniatura ital., pp.207-221

Giovanni d'Asciano   **GC PR WC**
  (Italian artist, op.1372)   **WC**
  (Italian painter, act. 14th century)   **PR**
  (Italian painter, act.1372-1381)   **GC**
  Bibl: TCI Toscana; ▶Thieme-Becker
  Asciano, Giovanni d'   **PR**
  Giovanni da Asciano   **GC**

Giovanni d'Enrico→see D'Enrico, Giovanni

Giovanni da Asciano→see Giovanni d'Asciano

Giovanni da Asola→see Giovanni da Brescia

Giovanni da Bellino→see Bellini, Giovanni

Giovanni da Biolo *(Italian artist, op. 1433)*   **WC**

Giovanni da Bologna   **BA GC PR WC**
  (Italian artist, op.1377-1389)   **WC**
  (Italian painter, act. ca.1389)   **GC PR**
  (Italian painter, act.ca.1389)   **BA**
  Bibl: ▶Bolaffi; ▶RILA/BHA, 1986; ▶Thieme-Becker; ▶Witt checklist

Giovanni da Brescia   **BA GC PR**
  (Italian artist, op.1512-m.1531)   **WC**
  (Italian painter, act. 1512, d. 1531)   **PR**
  (Italian painter, act.1512, d.1531)   **BA**
  (Italian painter, act.1512-d. 1531)   **GC**
  Bibl: Berenson, Venetian; ▶Bolaffi; ▶RILA/BHA, 1986; ▶Thieme-Becker
  Asola, Giovanni da   **PR**
  Giovanni (or Zuanne) da Brescia (Zuane da Asola)   **WC**
  Giovanni (Zuanne) da Brescia   **GC**
  Giovanni da Asola   **GC PR**
  Zuane da Isola   **GC**

Giovanni da Brunico→see Da Brunico, Giovanni

Giovanni da Calcar→see Calcar, Jan Stephan van

Giovanni da Ciclonio da Eggi *(Italian artist, 14th cent.(?))*   **WC**

Giovanni da Como→see Giovanni da Milano

Giovanni da Cremona→see Da Cremona, Giovanni

Giovanni da Fiesole→see Angelico, Fra

Giovanni da Firenze *(Italian sculptor, act.1343-1345)*   **BA**
  Bibl: TCI Napoli e dintorni; ▶Thieme-Becker; ▶White, Art & arch. Italy

Giovanni da Firenze, Fra (Pietro Carettai) *(Italian artist, 1572-1619/20)*   **WC**

Giovanni da Gaeta   **BA GC WC**
  (Italian artist, op.1456)   **WC**
  (Italian painter, act.1448-1472)   **BA GC**
  Bibl: ▶Bolaffi; Gaeta (ITA), Palazzo de Vio, Arte a Gaeta (1976), p.36; ▶RILA/BHA, 1986; ▶Witt checklist

Giovanni da Gaibana   **GC**
  (Italian artist, op.1253)   **WC**
  (Italian scribe, act.1259)   **GC**
  Bibl: Bellinati, Epistolario Gaibana
  Gaibano, Giovanni (de Gaibana)   **WC**

Giovanni da Imola *(Italian sculptor and designer, doca. Siena 1419-1423)*   **GC**
  Bibl: Aronow, Siena; Carli, Duomo di Siena
  Giovanni di Francesco da Imola   **GC**

Giovanni da Magno *(Italian sculptor, 1438-1478)*   **BA**
  Bibl: ▶Bessone-Aurelj, Scult. & arch. ital.; Eisenberg, BURLINGTON, (MAR 1981), 134-148

Giovanni da Mel→see Rossi, Giovanni (Giovanni da Mel)

Giovanni da Milano *(Italian engineer, d.1451)*   **GC**
  Bibl: Arrigoni, Castello Sforzesco, p.12

Giovanni da Milano   **BA GC PR**
  (Italian artist, op.c.1350-1370)   **WC**
  (Italian painter, act. 1346-1369)   **PR**
  (Italian painter, act. ca.1350-1370)   **GC**
  (Italian painter, act.1346-1369)   **BA**
  Bibl: ▶Bénézit; ▶Bolaffi; ▶Fredericksen & Zeri, Census; ▶Thieme-Becker; ▶Witt checklist
  Giovanni da Como   **GC**
  Giovanni da Milano (Giovanni di Jacopo di Guido da Kaverzaio or Giovanni da Como)   **WC**

Giovanni da Milano (Giovanni di Jacopo di Guido da Kaverzaio or Giovanni da Como)→see Giovanni da Milano

Giovanni da Modena   **BA GC**
  (Italian artist, op.1420-1451)   **WC**
  (Italian painter, act.1420-1451)   **BA**
  (Italian, act.1420-1451)   **GC**
  Bibl: ▶Witt checklist
  Giovanni di Modena (Giovanni di Pietro Faloppi)   **WC**
  Giovanni di Pietro Faloppi   **GC**

Giovanni da Monte *(Italian painter, act.1557)*   **BA**
  Bibl: Prijatelj, Ars auro prior: Studia Ioanni Białostocki Sexagenario Dicata (1981) pp. 257-259

Giovanni da Monte Cremasco *(Italian artist, op.1580)*   **WC**

Giovanni da Monte Rubiano *(Italian artist, op.1506)*   **WC**

Giovanni da Montecassino *(Italian illuminator, act.1278-1282)*   **BA**
  Bibl: ▶Bolaffi; Daneu Lattanzi, in MISCELLANEA DI STUDI IN MEMORIA DI ANNA SAITA REVIGNAS (1988) (RILA-ITA)

Giovanni da Montorfano→see Montorfano, Giovanni Donato

Giovanni da Murano→see Giovanni d'Alemagna

Giovanni da Napoli *(Italian, act. 1431-d.ca.1450)*   **GC**
  Bibl: ▶Thieme-Becker; ▶Witt checklist

Giovanni da Nola→see Marigliano, Giovanni (Giovanni da Nola)

Giovanni da Oriolo   **PR**
  (Italian artist, op.1443-m.1473/4)   **WC**
  (Italian painter, d. 1473/74)   **PR**
  Bibl: ▶Thieme-Becker
  Giovanni da Oriolo (Giovanni di Giuliano Savoretti ? Giovanni Marcio or Giovanni di Faenza?)   **WC**

Giovanni da Oriolo (Giovanni di Giuliano Savoretti ? Giovanni Marcio or Giovanni di Faenza?)→see Giovanni da Oriolo

Giovanni da Padova   **BA**
  (15th century Florentine architect (do not confuse with 14th cent. painter of same name))   **AV**
  (Italian engineer, 15th c.)   **BA**
  Bibl: Rodella, CIVILTÀ MANTOVANA 6, 1985, p.11
  Giovanni da Padua   **AV**
  Padua, Giovanni da   **AV**

Giovanni da Padua→see Giovanni da Padova

Giovanni da Pedemuro *(Italian sculptor, architect, act.1495-1550)*   **BA**
  Bibl: Puppi, Palladio, p.6; TCI Veneto

Giovanni da Pisa   **BA**
  (Italian artist, op.1358-1423)   **WC**
  (Italian painter, act. 1358-1360)   **PR**
  (Italian painter, act.1401-1421)   **BA**
  (Italian, act.1358-1423)   **GC**
  Bibl: ▶Bolaffi; ▶Fredericksen & Zeri, Census; ▶Thieme-Becker; ▶Witt checklist

Giovanni di Niccola da Pisa   **GC WC**
Giovanni di Niccolo da Pisa   **PR**
  Giovanni di Nicola da Pisa   **PR**

Giovanni da Rimini   **GC WC**
  (Italian artist, op.1439-c.1463)   **WC**
  (Italian, act.1439-ca.1463)   **GC**
  Bibl: ▶Witt checklist

Giovanni da Rimini *(Italian painter, act.1292-1336)*   **BA**
  Bibl: TCI Marche, p.682

Giovanni da Rimini (Giovanni
  Baronzio) → see Baronzio, Giovanni
Giovanni da Rovezzano → see
  Giovanni di Francesco da
  Rovezzano
Giovanni da S. Giovanni → see
  Giovanni da San Giovanni
  (Giovanni Mannozzi)
Giovanni da San Giovanni → see
  Giovanni da San Giovanni
  (Giovanni Mannozzi)
**Giovanni da San Giovanni
  (Giovanni Mannozzi)**   **BA PR**
  (Italian artist, 1592-1636)   WC
  (Italian painter, 1592-1636)   BA PR
  (Italian, 1592-1636)   GC
  Bibl: ▶Bolaffi; ▶Encyc. world art;
    George Goldner; ▶RILA/BHA;
    ▶Thieme-Becker; ▶Witt checklist
  G. da St. Giovanni   PR
  Giovanni da S. Giovanni   PR
  Giovanni da San Giovanni   **GC PR**
  Giovanni da St Giovanni   PR
  Giovanni di S: Giovanni   PR
  Giovanni Mannozzi   PR
  Mannozzi   PR
  Mannozzi, Giovanni   GC PR
  **Mannozzi, Manozzi or Mannozi,
    Giovanni (Giovanni da San
    Giovanni)**   **WC**
  San Giovanni, Giovanni da   GC
Giovanni da Santo Pietro (Italian
  artist, 17th cent.)   **WC**
Giovanni da Siena (Neri) (Italian
  artist, op.1426-1462)   **WC**
Giovanni da St Giovanni → see
  Giovanni da San Giovanni
  (Giovanni Mannozzi)
Giovanni da Sulmona (Italian
  painter and woodcarver, act.1440)   **GC**
  Bibl: ▶Thieme-Becker
Giovanni da Tolentino (Italian, act.
  1490)   **BA**
  Bibl: Jrnl. Warburg & Courtauld
    Insts. XLIII (1980), 246-256
Giovanni da Trau → see Giovanni
  Dalmata
Giovanni da Udine → see Giovanni da
  Udine (Giovanni di Francesco
  Ricamador)
Giovanni da Udine → see Martini,
  Giovanni (Giovanni da Udine)

**Giovanni da Udine (Giovanni di
  Francesco Ricamador)**   **BA**
  (Italian artist, 1487/94-1564)   WC
  (Italian decorator and
    stuccatore, 1487-1564)   AV
  (Italian painter, architect, and
    sculptor, 1487-1564)   GC
  (Italian painter, architect,
    sculptor, stucco artist, 1487-
    1564)   BA
  (Painter, draughtsman,
    stuccatore, plasterworker,
    architect, 1487-1564)   CE
  Bibl: ▶Bénézit; ▶Bessone-Aurelj,
    Scult. & arch. ital.; ▶Bolaffi; Clark
    Art Inst. Libr.; Dacos, N., Giovanni
    da Udine; ▶Encic. italiana;
    ▶Thieme-Becker
  Da Udine, Giovanni   **CE**
  Giovanni da Udine   GC
  **Giovanni da Udine or
    Recamatori (Nanni)**   **WC**
  Giovanni dei Recamatori   GC
  Giovanni, Recamador   GC
  Nanni, Giovanni   CE GC
  Ricamatore, Giovanni   CE
  Udine, Giovanni da   **AV GC**
Giovanni da Udine or Recamatori
  (Nanni) → see Giovanni da Udine
  (Giovanni di Francesco Ricamador)
Giovanni da Varese (Italian artist,
  17th cent.)   **WC**
Giovanni da Verona → see Giocondo,
  Fra (Giovanni da Verona)
Giovanni da Verona, Fra → see
  Giocondo, Fra (Giovanni da
  Verona)
Giovanni dal Ponte → see Giovanni dal
  Ponte (Giovanni di Marco)
**Giovanni dal Ponte (Giovanni di
  Marco)**   **BA PR**
  (Italian artist, 1385-1437(?))   WC
  (Italian painter, 1385-ca.1437)   BA PR
  (Italian, 1385-1437(?))   GC
  Bibl: Art Bull. idx. 2, 1949-1973;
    ▶Bolaffi; ▶Fredericksen & Zeri,
    Census; Getty Photo Study Coll.
    (Ptgs.); ▶Thieme-Becker; ▶Witt
    checklist
  Giovanni dal Ponte   **GC PR**
  **Giovanni dal Ponte or da San
    Stefano (Giovanni di Marco)**   **WC**
  Giovanni del Ponte   PR
  Giovanni di Marco   PR
  Ponte, Giovanni dal   GC PR
Giovanni dal Ponte or da San Stefano
  (Giovanni di Marco) → see Giovanni
  dal Ponte (Giovanni di Marco)

Giovanni Dalmata   **BA GC**
  (Italian sculptor and architect,
    ca.1440-ca.1509)   GC
  (Italian sculptor, architect, ca.
    1440-ca.1509)   BA
  (Sculptor, 1440-post 1509)   CE
  Bibl: ▶Bessone-Aurelj, Scult. &
    arch. ital.; ▶Encyc. world art;
    ▶Portoghesi, Diz. arch. e
    urbanistica; ▶RILA/BHA;
    ▶Thieme-Becker
  Da Trau, Giovanni   CE
  Dalmata, Giovanni   **CE**
  De Tragusia, Johannes Duknowich   CE
  Giovanni da Trau   CE
  Johannes Duknowich de Tragusia   CE
Giovanni de Alamagna (Johanes
  Alamanus, Zuane or Giovanni da
  Murano) → see Giovanni
  d'Alemagna
Giovanni de Cramariis → see
  Cramariis, Giovanni de
Giovanni de Luteri (Lutero) or de
  Costantino → see Dossi, Dosso
  (Giovanni de Lutero)
Giovanni de Lutero → see Dossi,
  Dosso (Giovanni de Lutero)
**Giovanni de Savi (Johannes de
  Sapientibus)** (Swiss painter in
  ITA, act.1475-1478)   **BA**
  Bibl: Welch, Arte Lomb., 70-71
    (1984) 156-158
Giovanni de' Mio → see Fratino,
  Giovanni (Giovanni de' Mio)
Giovanni de' Rettori (Italian
  sculptor, act.1474-1492)   **GC**
  Bibl: TCI Abruzzo-Molise, p.109;
    ▶Thieme-Becker
  Giovanni de' Rettorii   GC
Giovanni de' Rettorii → see Giovanni
  de' Rettori
Giovanni de' Vajenti Speranza → see
  Speranza, Giovanni de' Vajenti
Giovanni de' Vecchi → see Vecchi,
  Giovanni de' (Giovanni del Borgo)
Giovanni de'Mio → see Fratino,
  Giovanni (Giovanni de' Mio)
Giovanni de'Vecchij → see Vecchi,
  Giovanni de' (Giovanni del Borgo)
Giovanni degli Eremitani (Italian
  architect, engineer, act.1289-1318)   **BA**
  Bibl: Bettini-Puppi, La Chiesa degli
    Eremitani; ▶Encic. italiana; TCI
    Veneto; ▶Thieme-Becker
Giovanni dei Recamatori → see
  Giovanni da Udine (Giovanni di
  Francesco Ricamador)

Giovanni del Biondo   **BA GC PR**
> *(Italian artist, op.1356-1392)*   WC
> *(Italian painter, act. 1356, d. 1398)*   PR
> *(Italian painter, act.1356, d.1399)*   BA
> *(Italian, act.1356-1392)*   GC
> Bibl: ▶Bolaffi; George Goldner; Offner, Flor. ptg.; ▶RILA/BHA; ▶Thieme-Becker; ▶Witt checklist
> Biondo, Giovanni del   PR

Giovanni del Biondo (dei Landini ?) dal Casentino   **WC**
Giovanni del Biondo (dei Landini ?) dal Casentino → see Giovanni del Biondo
Giovanni del Borgo → see Vecchi, Giovanni de' (Giovanni del Borgo)
Giovanni del Pio → see Bonatti, Giovanni (Il Ferraresino)
Giovanni del Ponte → see Giovanni dal Ponte (Giovanni di Marco)
Giovanni del Sega → see Del Sega, Giovanni
Giovanni dell'Opera → see Bandini, Giovanni (Giovanni dell'Opera)
Giovanni dell'Opera del Duomo → see Bandini, Giovanni (Giovanni dell'Opera)
Giovanni della Robbia → see Della Robbia, Giovanni

Giovanni di Andrea di Domenico
> *(Italian artist, 1455-p.1488)*   **WC**

Giovanni di Angelo di Balduccio   **GC WC**
> *(Italian artist, c.1370-1452)*   WC
> *(Italian painter, ca.1370-1452)*   GC
> Bibl: ▶Bénézit; ▶Thieme-Becker
Giovanni di Baccio Bigio → see Nanni di Baccio Bigio

Giovanni di Balduccio *(Italian sculptor, act.ca.1315-1349)*   **BA**
> Bibl: ▶Bénézit; ▶Encic. italiana; ▶Encyc. world art; Pope-Hennessy, Ital. Gothic sculp., pp.25-26; ▶Thieme-Becker

Giovanni di Bartolomeo *(Italian sculptor, 15th c.)*   **BA**
> Bibl: ▶Bessone-Aurelj, Scult. & arch. ital.

Giovanni di Bartolomeo Cristiani   **BA**
> *(Italian artist, op.1366-1396/8)*   WC
> *(Italian artist, op.1366-1398)*   WC
> *(Italian painter, act. 1366-1398, d. ca.1400)*   PR
> *(Italian painter, act.1347, d.ca. 1400)*   BA
> *(Italian, act.1366-1396/8)*   GC
> Bibl: Getty Photo Study Coll. (Ptgs.); ▶RILA/BHA; ▶Witt checklist
> Cristiani   PR

Cristiani, Giovanni di Bartolomeo   **GC PR**
Cristiani, Giovanni di Bartolommeo da Pistoia   **WC**
Giovanni di Bartolommeo Cristiani   **GC PR WC**
Giovanni di Bartolommeo Cristiani → see Giovanni di Bartolomeo Cristiani
Giovanni di Bellini → see Bellini, Giovanni

Giovanni di Benedetto   **GC WC**
> *(Italian artist, op.1352-1361/78)*   WC
> *(Italian painter and scribe(?), act.1352-1361/78)*   GC
> Bibl: ▶Witt checklist
> Giovanni di Benedetto da Como   GC
Giovanni di Benedetto Cianfanini → see Cianfanini, Giovanni di Benedetto
Giovanni di Benedetto da Como → see Giovanni di Benedetto
Giovanni di Bindino da Travale → see Giovanni di Bindino di Cialli

Giovanni di Bindino di Cialli   **BA**
> *(Italian artist, op.1392-m.1417)*   WC
> *(Italian painter, d.1417)*   BA
> *(Italian, act.1392-d.1417)*   GC
> Bibl: ▶Bolaffi; ▶Thieme-Becker; ▶Witt checklist

Giovanni di Bindino da Travale   **GC WC**
Giovanni di Bonino *(Italian glass painter, mosaicist, 14th c.)*   **BA**
> Bibl: ▶Bolaffi; ▶Fremantle, Florentine Gothic; ▶Thieme-Becker
Giovanni di Brucolo → see Brueghel, Jan, the elder
Giovanni di Brunico → see Da Brunico, Giovanni

Giovanni di Cecco *(Italian architect, sculptor, and designer, act.1357-1397)*   **GC**
> Bibl: Brandi, Palazzo Pubblico, 57; ▶Thieme-Becker

Giovanni di Consalvo   **BA GC**
> *(Portuguese artist, op.1436-1439)*   WC
> *(Portuguese painter in ITA, 15th c.)*   BA
> *(Portuguese, act.1436-1439)*   GC
> Bibl: Arte in Friuli VIII, 1984, 39-51; ▶Bolaffi; TCI Firenze; ▶Witt checklist

Giovanni di Consalvo (or Jean de Portugal)   **WC**
> Jean de Portugal   GC
> Juan de Portugal   GC
Giovanni di Consalvo (or Jean de Portugal) → see Giovanni di Consalvo

Giovanni di Corraduccio   **BA GC WC**
> *(Italian artist, op.1413-1422)*   WC
> *(Italian painter, act.1404-1437)*   BA GC
> Bibl: ▶Bénézit; ▶Bolaffi; ▶RILA/BHA, 1986; Scarpellini, GIOVANNI DI CORRADUUCIO(OCLC); ▶Thieme-Becker; ▶Witt checklist; Zeri, Diari di lavoro 2, p.22

Giovanni di Cosma *(Italian mosaicist, act.ca.1296-ca.1303)*   **BA**
> Bibl: ▶Bolaffi; ▶Thieme-Becker

Giovanni di Cristoforo *(Italian goldsmith, act.1871)*   **BA**
> Bibl: Öster. Zeit. für Kunst u. Denk. 28/1-2 (1974), 1-4

Giovanni di Domenico *(Italian ecclesiastic, glass painter, act. 1503)*   **BA**
> Bibl: STUDIES IN THE HISTORY OF ART, VII(1975), 81-89

Giovanni di Domenico da Gaiole
> *(Italian architect, 1403-1479)*   **BA**
> Bibl: Paatz, Kirchen von Florenz, v.6; ▶Portoghesi, Diz. arch. e urbanistica; ▶Thieme-Becker

Giovanni di Filippo da Fiesole
> *(Italian cabinetmaker, decorative artist, act.1470-1474)*   **BA**
> Bibl: ▶Bénézit; ▶Thieme-Becker
Giovanni di Filippo del Campo → see Ducamps, Jean

Giovanni di Francesco   **GC JG**
> *(Italian, act.1446-d.1459)*   GC
> *(Italian, Florentine, 1412-ca. 1462)*   JG
> Bibl: ▶Witt checklist
Giovanni di Francesco → see Giovanni di Francesco da Rovezzano
Giovanni di Francesco (Cervelliera) → see Giovanni di Francesco da Rovezzano

Giovanni di Francesco (il Cicchia)
> *(Italian woodcarver, act.1390)*   **BA**
> Bibl: ANTICHITA VIVA, XVII/1(JAN/FEB 1978), 25-39; Lusini, Duomo di Siena, pp.272-273

Giovanni di Francesco d'Arezzo
> *(Italian sculptor, act.1369-1375)*   **BA**
> Bibl: ▶Bénézit; ▶Thieme-Becker

Giovanni di Francesco da Imola→*see* Giovanni da Imola

Giovanni di Francesco da Rovezzano   **BA PR**
  (Italian painter, 15th c.)   BA
  (Italian painter, act. 15th century)   PR
    Bibl: ▶Bolaffi; ▶RILA/BHA
  Giovanni da Rovezzano   PR
  Giovanni di Francesco   PR
  Giovanni di Francesco (Cervelliera)   PR

Giovanni di Francesco del Cervelliera   **BA**
  (Italian artist, op.1446-m.1459)   WC
  (Italian painter, act.1446, d.1459)   BA
    Bibl: ▶Bolaffi; Firenze (ITA), Casa Buonarroti, PITTURA DI LUCE (Aug 1990); ▶Thieme-Becker

Giovanni di Francesco del Cervelliera (Master of the Carrand Triptych or Giovanni Rovezzano)   **WC**
  Master of the Carrand Triptych   BA

Giovanni di Francesco del Cervelliera (Master of the Carrand Triptych or Giovanni Rovezzano)→*see* Giovanni di Francesco del Cervelliera

Giovanni di Francesco Toscani→*see* Toscani, Giovanni di Francesco

Giovanni di Francia→*see* Charlier, Giovanni (Giovanni di Francia)

Giovanni di Francia (Giovanni Charlier)→*see* Charlier, Giovanni (Giovanni di Francia)

Giovanni di Francis *(Italian artist, op.1429-1432)*   **WC**

Giovanni di Francis→*see* Charlier, Giovanni (Giovanni di Francia)

Giovanni di Gherardo da Prato
  (Italian architect, scholar, ca.1367-1442/46)   **BA**
    Bibl: ▶Encic. italiana; ▶Portoghesi, Diz. arch. e urbanistica; ▶Thieme-Becker

Giovanni di Giacomo Gavazzi→*see* Gavazzi, Giovanni di Giacomo

Giovanni di Giuliano Boccardi→*see* Boccardi, Giovanni (Boccardino Vecchio)

Giovanni di Guido Barbiere→*see* Fra Giovanni di Guido Barbiere

Giovanni di Guitone→*see* Giovanni di Guittone

Giovanni di Guittone *(Italian marbleworker, act.1210-1220)*   **GC**
    Bibl: Getty Photo Study Coll. (Medieval); Lehmann-Brockhaus, Abruzzen u. Molise; Moretti, Abruzzo, pp.329-331
  Giovanni di Guitone   GC
  Guittone, Giovanni di   GC
  Maestro Giovanni di Guido   GC
  Master Giovanni di Guido   GC

Giovanni di Lorenzo *(Italian painter, 16th c.)*   **BA**
    Bibl: Moran, GALLONERO, IV/1(JAN-FEB 1981), 31-33

Giovanni di Marco→*see* Giovanni dal Ponte (Giovanni di Marco)

Giovanni di Martino da Fiesole   **BA GC**
  (Italian sculptor, 15th c.)   BA
  (Italian sculptor, 15th century)   GC
    Bibl: ▶Bénézit; ▶Bessone-Aurelj, Scult. & arch. ital.; ▶RILA/BHA; ▶Thieme-Becker

Giovanni di Modena (Giovanni di Pietro Faloppi)→*see* Giovanni da Modena

Giovanni di Nanni da Udine *(Italian painter, act.1517)*   **BA**
    Bibl: Tempestini, Scritti ... in onore di Roberto Salvini, 385-89

Giovanni di Niccola da Pisa→*see* Giovanni da Pisa

Giovanni di Nicola da Pisa→*see* Giovanni da Pisa

Giovanni di Niccolo Mansueti→*see* Mansueti, Giovanni di Niccolò

Giovanni di Nicola *(Italian mosaicist, act. ca.1286)*   **GC**
    Bibl: Aurigemma, Circeo, p.58

Giovanni di Nicola da Pisa→*see* Giovanni da Pisa

Giovanni di Paolo   **GC JG PR VO**
  (Italian artist, 1403-1483)   WC
  (Italian painter and illuminator, 1403(?)-1482)   GC
  (Italian painter, 1403(?)-1482)   PR
  (Italian painter, illuminator, 1403?-1482)   BA
  (Italian painter, illuminator, ca. 1403-ca. 1482)   VO
  (Italian, ca. 1403-1482)   JG
    Bibl: ▶Bolaffi; ▶Encic. italiana; ▶Fredericksen & Zeri, Census; Getty Photo Study Coll. (Medieval); ▶Libr. of Congr. Name Auth. File, NAFL8642313; ▶RILA/BHA; ▶Thieme-Becker; Wormhoudt, K., Manuscript illuminations by Giovanni di Paolo (1984)

Giovanni di Paolo di Grazia   **BA GC PR WC**
  Paolo, Giovanni di   PR

Giovanni di Paolo da Venezia→*see* Giovanni di Paolo Veneziano

Giovanni di Paolo di Grazia→*see* Giovanni di Paolo

Giovanni di Paolo Veneziano   **BA**
  (Italian artist, op.1345-1358)   WC
  (Italian painter, act. 1333-1358)   PR
  (Italian painter, act.1345-1358)   BA
  (Italian, act.1345-1358)   GC
    Bibl: ▶Bolaffi; ▶Fredericksen & Zeri, Census; ▶Thieme-Becker; ▶Witt checklist

Giovanni di Paolo da Venezia   **GC WC**
Giovanni Veneziano   **PR**
  Veneziano   PR

Giovanni di Piamonte   **BA**
  (Italian artist, op.1456)   WC
  (Italian painter, act.1456)   GC
  (Italian painter, act.1456-1472)   BA
    Bibl: Bellosi, PROSPETTIVA, 50 (July, 1987), p. 15-35; ▶Bolaffi; ▶Thieme-Becker; ▶Witt checklist

Giovanni di Piamonte (not Piemontese)   **WC**
Giovanni Piemontese   **GC**

Giovanni di Piamonte (not Piemontese)→*see* Giovanni di Piamonte

Giovanni di Pieriacopo→*see* Giovanni di Pieriacopo da San Severino

Giovanni di Pieriacopo da San Severino *(Italian sculptor, doca. 1481-1525)*   **GC**
    Bibl: TCI Umbria
  Giovanni di Pieriacopo   GC

Giovanni di Piermatteo→*see* Boccati, Giovanni di Piermatteo da Camerino

Giovanni di Piermatteo da Camerino Boccati→*see* Boccati, Giovanni di Piermatteo da Camerino

Giovanni di Pietro   **BA JG**
  (Italian painter, act.1432-1479)   BA
  (Italian, Sienese, active 1432-before 1479)   JG
    Bibl: Cleveland (OH, USA), Mus. Art, Euro. ptgs. bef. 1500 (1974), p.73; ▶Thieme-Becker

Giovanni di Pietro→*see* Giovanni di Pietro (Lo Spagna)

Giovanni di Pietro (Lo Spagna)   **BA PR**
  (Italian artist, c.1450-1528)   WC
  (Italian painter, ca.1450-1528)   BA PR
  (Italian, ca.1450-1528)   GC
    Bibl: ▶Bénézit; ▶Bolaffi; ▶Encyc. world art; ▶Fredericksen & Zeri, Census; ▶RILA/BHA; ▶Thieme-Becker

  Giovanni di Pietro   GC PR
  Lo Spagna   **GC PR**
  Lo Spagna, Giovanni di Pietro   PR
  Spagna   PR
  Spagna (Giovanni di Pietro)   PR
  Spagna, Giovanni Lo   PR
  Spagna, Lo   PR
  Spagna, Lo (Giovanni di Pietro)   **WC**

Giovanni di Pietro (Master of the Olive Annunciation) *(Italian painter, ca.1432-bef.1479)*   **GC**
    Bibl: Cleveland (OH, USA), Mus. Art, Euro. ptgs. bef. 1500 (1974), p.73; ▶Thieme-Becker
  Master of the Olive Annunciation   GC
  Nanni di Pietro   GC

Giovanni di Pietro da Napoli   **GC PR WC**
  (Italian artist, op.1402-1405)   WC
  (Italian painter, act. 14th century)   PR
  (Italian, act.1402-1405)   GC
    Bibl: ▶Thieme-Becker; ▶Witt checklist

Giovanni di Pietro da Pisa *(Italian painter, 15th c.)*   **BA**
  Bibl: ▶Bolaffi; STUDI DI STORIA DELLE ARTI, II(1978/79), 97-103; ▶Thieme-Becker

Giovanni di Pietro di Francia→see Charlier, Giovanni (Giovanni di Francia)

Giovanni di Pietro Faloppi→see Giovanni da Modena

Giovanni di Rigino *(Italian sculptor, act.1331-1392)*   **BA**
  Bibl: Critica d'arte, XLII/151-153 (Jan.-Jun. 1977) pp.39-54; TCI Veneto, artist idx.; ▶Thieme-Becker

Giovanni di Riguzzo *(Italian sculptor, act.1384-1394)*   **BA**
  Bibl: ▶Bessone-Aurelj, Scult. & arch. ital.; Grandi, Della Quercia e S. Pietro, pp.177-215; ▶Thieme-Becker

Giovanni di S: Giovanni→see Giovanni da San Giovanni (Giovanni Mannozzi)

Giovanni di Santuccio *(Italian architect, act. ca.1458)*   **GC**
  Bibl: Anderson; TCI Umbria; Todi, Città, p.291
  Giovanni di Santuccio da Fiorenzola di Spoleto   GC
  Giovanni di Santuccio da Spoleto   GC

Giovanni di Santuccio da Fiorenzola di Spoleto→see Giovanni di Santuccio

Giovanni di Santuccio da Spoleto→see Giovanni di Santuccio

Giovanni di ser Giovanni→see Guidi, Giovanni di ser Giovanni (lo Scheggia)

Giovanni di ser Giovanni Guidi→see Guidi, Giovanni di ser Giovanni (lo Scheggia)

Giovanni di Simone   **BA**
  (Italian architect)   AV
  (Italian architect, act.1260-1286)   BA
  Bibl: ▶Bessone-Aurelj, Scult. & arch. ital.; Cristiani Testi, M.L., in CRITICA D'ARTE LII/13 (Apr-June 1987) 26; Critica d'arte, 1986 Apr.-June, 4th ser., v.51, no.9, p.57; TCI Toscana
  Simone, Giovanni di   **AV**

Giovanni di Stefano   **BA GC**
  (Italian artist, c.1446-a.1506)   WC
  (Italian sculptor and bronze founder, b ca.1446-d.bef. 1506)   GC
  (Italian sculptor, ca.1446-before 1506)   BA
  Bibl: ▶Bénézit; ▶RILA/BHA; ▶Seymour, Sculp. Italy; ▶Thieme-Becker

Giovanni di Stefano da Siena   **GC WC**

Giovanni di Stefano da Siena→see Giovanni di Stefano

Giovanni di Turino *(Italian sculptor and metalworker, ca.1385-1455)*   **GC**
  Bibl: TCI Toscana

Giovanni di Ugolino da Milano   **GC WC**
  (Italian artist, op.1436)   WC
  (Italian, act.1436)   GC
  Bibl: ▶Witt checklist

Giovanni di Zanello *(Italian artist, 14th cent.)*   **WC**

Giovanni Dò→see Dò, Giovanni

Giovanni Domenico Campiglia→see Campiglia, Giovanni Domenico

Giovanni Domenico Capellino→see Cappellino, Giovanni Domenico

Giovanni Domenico Cappellino→see Cappellino, Giovanni Domenico

Giovanni Domenico Cerrini→see Cerrini, Giovanni Domenico (Cavalier Perugino)

Giovanni Domenico Desiderii→see Desiderii, Giovanni Domenico

Giovanni Domenico Ferretti→see Ferretti, Giovanni Domenico

Giovanni Domenico Piastrini→see Piastrini, Giovanni Domenico

Giovanni Domenico Picchianti→see Picchianti, Giovanni Domenico

Giovanni Domenico Porta→see Porta, Giovanni Domenico

Giovanni Domenico Tiepolo→see Tiepolo, Giovanni Domenico

giovanni dominico capelino→see Cappellino, Giovanni Domenico

Giovanni Elia Morghen→see Morghen, Giovanni Elia

Giovanni Enrico ovvero Angericch→see Schönfeld, Johann Heinrich

Giovanni Fei, Paolo di→see Paolo di Giovanni Fei

Giovanni Ferretti→see Ferretti, Giovanni Domenico

Giovanni Fiamengo→see Giovanni Fiammingo [Unidentified]

Giovanni Fiamengo/Fiamingo/Flamingo→see Giovanni Fiammingo [Unidentified]

Giovanni Fiammingo [Unidentified]
  (Unknown painter)   **PR**
  Bibl: Arici inv. dated 1744; Cuomo inventory dated 1687; Doria inventory dated 1690 and 1693; possibly JEAN BAPTISTE BOEL? [Labrot thinks he is Giovanni Van Houbraken]
  Gio. Fiamengo   PR
  Gio: Fiamenco   PR
  Gio: Fiamengo   PR
  Gio: Fiamingo   PR
  Gioan Fiamengo   PR
  Gioanne Fiamengo   PR
  Gioannen Fiamengo   PR
  Giovanino Fiamingo   PR
  Giovanni Fiamengo   PR
  Giovanni Fiamengo/Fiamingo/Flamingo   PR
  Giovanni Flamingo   PR
  Monsù Gio: Fiamengo   PR
  Monsu Giovani   PR
  Monsù Giovanni   PR
  Monsù Giovanni il Fiamenco   PR

Giovanni Flamingo→see Giovanni Fiammingo [Unidentified]

Giovanni Francesco Barbieri→see Guercino (Giovanni Francesco Barbieri)

Giovanni Francesco Bezzi→see Bezzi, Giovanni Francesco (il Nosadella)

Giovanni Francesco Bola→see Bola, Giovanni Francesco [Unidentified]

Giovanni Francesco Bolognese→see Grimaldi, Giovanni Francesco

Giovanni Francesco Braccioli→see Braccioli, Giovanni Francesco

Giovanni Francesco Briglia→see Briglia, Giovanni Francesco

Giovanni Francesco Caroto→see Caroto, Giovanni Francesco

Giovanni Francesco Cassana→see Cassana, Giovanni Francesco

Giovanni Francesco da Rimini   **GC PR WC**
  (Italian artist, op.1459-1470)   WC
  (Italian painter, act. 1441, d. ca. 1470)   PR
  (Italian, act.1459-d.1470)   GC
  Bibl: ▶Fredericksen & Zeri, Census; ▶Thieme-Becker; ▶Witt checklist
  Gianfresco da Rimini   PR

Giovanni Francesco da Sangallo→see Sangallo, Giovanni Francesco da

Giovanni Francesco da Tolmezzo→see Gianfrancesco da Tolmezzo (Giovanni Francesco dal Zotto)

Giovanni Francesco della Nunziatella [Unidentified]
  (Unknown painter)   **PR**
  Bibl: Inventory of Giovanni Battista Borghese, principe di Rossano from 1693/04/07
  Gio. Francesco della Nunziatella   PR
  Nunziatella   PR

Giovanni Francesco Grimaldi → *see* Grimaldi, Giovanni Francesco

Giovanni Francesco Penni → *see* Penni, Giovanni Francesco (il Fattore)

Giovanni Francesco Romanelli → *see* Romanelli, Giovanni Francesco

Giovanni Francesco Surchi → *see* Surchi, Giovanni Francesco

Giovanni Fratino → *see* Fratino, Giovanni (Giovanni de' Mio)

Giovanni Ghisolfi → *see* Ghisolfi, Giovanni

Giovanni Ghisolfo → *see* Ghisolfi, Giovanni

Giovanni Girolamo Savoldo → *see* Savoldo, Giovanni Girolamo

Giovanni Grasso da Carpi   **JG**

Giovanni Guidi → *see* Guidi, Giovanni di ser Giovanni (lo Scheggia)

Giovanni Hoc → *see* Hoc, Giovanni [Unidentified]

Giovanni Holben → *see* Holbein, Hans, the younger

Giovanni Holbeno → *see* Holbein, Hans, the younger

Giovanni Holbense → *see* Holbein, Hans, the younger

Giovanni Ismen → *see* Eismann, Johann Anton

Giovanni Jacopo (Gianiacopo) da Castrocaro (Mattoncini, Master of the Gottineen Crucifixion)
(Italian artist, op.1525-m.1581)   **WC**

Giovanni Lanfranco → *see* Lanfranco, Giovanni

Giovanni Lanfranco, Cavaliere → *see* Lanfranco, Giovanni

Giovanni Laurentini → *see* Laurentini, Giovanni (Arrigoni)

Giovanni Le Duc → *see* Ducq, Johan le

Giovanni Leonardo [Unidentified]
(Unknown painter)   **PR**
    Bibl: Orsini inventory, Naples, 1704, possibly Giovan Leonardo Pinto?
    Giovan Leonardo   PR

Giovanni Lorenzo Bernini → *see* Bernini, Gian Lorenzo

Giovanni Lupicini → *see* Lupicini, Giovanni Battista

Giovanni Maldura → *see* Maldura, Giovanni

Giovanni Malerg → *see* Maler, Hans

Giovanni Malerg Tedesco → *see* Maler, Hans

Giovanni Mannozzi → *see* Giovanni da San Giovanni (Giovanni Mannozzi)

Giovanni Maria Butteri → *see* Butteri, Giovanni Maria

Giovanni Maria da Brescia   **BA WC**
(Italian artist, op.1500-1512)   WC
(Italian painter, printmaker, 16th c.)   BA
(Italian, act.1500-1512)   GC
    Bibl: ▶Bénézit; ▶Bolaffi; ▶Thieme-Becker; ▶Witt checklist

Giovanni Maria da Brescia (Trevisano)   **GC**
Giovanni Maria da Brescia (Trevisano) → *see* Giovanni Maria da Brescia

Giovanni Maria da Treviso (Trevisano) *(Italian artist, op. 1506-1513)*   **WC**

Giovanni Maria dalle Piane → *see* Piane, Giovanni Maria dalle

Giovanni Maria de Torre → *see* Torre, Giovanni della (Giovanniello del Beinaschi)

Giovanni Maria Morandi → *see* Morandi, Giovanni Maria

Giovanni Maria Padovano → *see* Mosca, Giovanni Maria

Giovanni Maria Scupola → *see* Scupola, Giovanni Maria

Giovanni Maria Tamburini → *see* Tamburini, Giovanni Maria

Giovanni Maria Viani → *see* Viani, Giovanni Maria

Giovanni Maria Zaffoni (called "Calderari") → *see* Calderari, Giovanni Maria (Zaffoni)

Giovanni Martinelli → *see* Martinelli, Giovanni (19th c.)

Giovanni Martini → *see* Martini, Giovanni (Giovanni da Udine)

Giovanni Martini da Udine → *see* Martini, Giovanni (Giovanni da Udine)

Giovanni Martino Spanzotti → *see* Spanzotti, Giovanni Martino

Giovanni Masoni → *see* Masoni, Giovanni [Unidentified]

Giovanni Matteo di Corado d'Alemagna → *see* Teutonico, Giovanni Matteo

Giovanni Mazone → *see* Mazone, Giovanni

Giovanni Meel → *see* Miel, Jan

Giovanni Mell → *see* Miel, Jan

Giovanni Mellino → *see* Mellino, Giovanni [Unidentified]

Giovanni Michele Graneri → *see* Graneri, Giovanni Michele

Giovanni Michele Granieri → *see* Granieri, Giovanni Michele

Giovanni Miele → *see* Miel, Jan

Giovanni Miele Scolare di Pussino → *see* Miel, Jan

Giovanni Monti → *see* Monti, Giovanni

Giovanni Morandi → *see* Morandi, Giovanni Antonio

Giovanni Morandi → *see* Morandi, Giovanni Maria

Giovanni Morghen → *see* Morghen, Giovanni Elia

Giovanni Niccola Rombaux → *see* Rombaux, Giovanni Niccola [Unidentified]

Giovanni Niccolo Servandoni → *see* Servandoni, Giovanni Niccolò

Giovanni Nicolo Servandoni → *see* Servandoni, Giovanni Niccolò

Giovanni Odazzi → *see* Odazzi, Giovanni

Giovanni Olandese [Unidentified]
(Unknown painter)   **PR**
    Bibl: Pamphilj inventory, Rome, 1648

Giovanni Paolo Castelli, detto Spadino → *see* Spadino, Giovanni Paolo (Giovanni Paolo Castelli)

Giovanni Paolo dal Borgo *(Italian artist, op.1542-1561)*   **WC**

Giovanni Paolo de' Agostini → *see* Agostini, Giovanni Paolo de'

Giovanni Paolo di Agostino → *see* Agostini, Giovanni Paolo de'

Giovanni Paolo Graccini → *see* Grazzini, Giovanni Paolo

Giovanni Paolo Lomazzo → *see* Lomazzo, Giovanni Paolo

Giovanni Paolo Melchiori → *see* Melchiori, Giovanni Paolo

Giovanni Paolo Panini → *see* Pannini, Giovanni Paolo

Giovanni Paolo Pannini → *see* Pannini, Giovanni Paolo

Giovanni Paolo Pasta → *see* Pasta, Giovanni Paolo

Giovanni Paolo Pisani → *see* Pisani, Giovanni Paolo

Giovanni Paolo Spadino → *see* Spadino, Giovanni Paolo (Giovanni Paolo Castelli)

Giovanni Paolo Tedesco → *see* Schor, Johann Paul (Giovanni Paolo Tedesco)

Giovanni Paolo Vannini → *see* Vannini, Giovanni Paolo

Giovanni Parcellis → *see* Porcellis, Jan

Giovanni Petitot → *see* Petitot, Jean

Giovanni Pettorali → *see* Pettorali, Giovanni [Unidentified]

Giovanni Piemontese → *see* Giovanni di Piamonte

Giovanni Piero da Gemona *(Italian artist, op.1401)*   **WC**

Giovanni Piero del Tuccio *(Italian architect, act.1438-1445)*   **BA**
    Bibl: Battisti, Brunelleschi

Giovanni Pietro da Cemmo *(Italian painter, act.1474-1504)*   **BA GC**
    Bibl: ▶Bolaffi; Pirovano, Pittura in Lombardia (1973), p. 83, fig. 93; ▶RILA/BHA, 1986; ▶Thieme-Becker

Giovanni Pietro da San Vito *(Italian artist, op.1485-1529)*   **WC**

Giovanni Pisano→*see* Pisano, Giovanni

Giovanni Pudina→*see* Pudina, Giovanni [Unidentified]

Giovanni Raggi→*see* Raggi, Giovanni

Giovanni Reder→*see* Reder, Giovanni

Giovanni Reider→*see* Reder, Giovanni

Giovanni Ricca→*see* Ricca, Giovanni

Giovanni Riccio→*see* Ricca, Giovanni

Giovanni Romagnoli→*see* Romagnoli, Giovanni

Giovanni Rosa→*see* Roos, Jan (I)

Giovanni Rossi→*see* Roos, Jan (I)

Giovanni Rosso→*see* Roos, Jan (I)

Giovanni Rossos→*see* Rossos, Giovanni

Giovanni Santi→*see* Santi, Giovanni

Giovanni Segala→*see* Segala, Giovanni

Giovanni Segalla→*see* Segala, Giovanni

Giovanni Segantini→*see* Segantini, Giovanni

Giovanni Senese→*see* Ferri, Giovanni (Giovanni Senese)

Giovanni Seric→*see* Seric, Giovanni [Unidentified]

Giovanni Stanchi→*see* Stanchi, Giovanni

Giovanni Stanghi→*see* Stanchi, Giovanni

Giovanni Stefano→*see* Maja, Giovanni Stefano

Giovanni Stefano Maja→*see* Maja, Giovanni Stefano

Giovanni Stefano Montalti→*see* Danedi, Stefano (Stefano Montalto)

Giovanni Stefano Montalto→*see* Danedi, Stefano (Stefano Montalto)

Giovanni Stradano→*see* Straet, Jan van der (Giovanni Stradano)

Giovanni Tabacco→*see* Tabacco, Giovanni [Unidentified]

Giovanni Tabbacco→*see* Tabacco, Giovanni [Unidentified]

Giovanni Tedeschi *(Italian artist, -1752)*   **WC**

Giovanni Tognolli→*see* Tognolli, Giovanni

Giovanni Van Everdigen→*see* Everdingen, Jan van

Giovanni Vanberghen→*see* Berghen, Giovanni van [Unidentified]

Giovanni Vandaneinden→*see* Heyden, Jan van der

Giovanni Vannanen→*see* Vannanen, Giovanni [Unidentified]

Giovanni Varardino Siciliano→*see* Azzolino (Giovanni Bernardino Ragano)

Giovanni Varricco→*see* Schönfeld, Johann Heinrich

Giovanni Veneziano→*see* Giovanni di Paolo Veneziano

Giovanni Verkruis→*see* Verkruis, Giovanni [Unidentified]

giovanni vildens→*see* Wildens, Jan

Giovanni Vincenzo Barbalonga→*see* Barbalonga, Giovanni Vincenzo [Unidentified]

Giovanni Weenix Olandese→*see* Weenix, Jan Baptist

Giovanni Wildens→*see* Wildens, Jan

Giovanni, Filippo di→*see* Filippo di Giovanni

Giovanni, Luigi di *(Italian artist, 1856-)*   **WC**

Giovanni, Matteo di→*see* Matteo di Giovanni di Bartolo

Giovanni, Piero di (Lorenzo Monaco)→*see* Lorenzo Monaco

Giovanni, Recamador→*see* Giovanni da Udine (Giovanni di Francesco Ricamador)

Giovannini *(Italian artist, act.1611)*   **BA**
Bibl: BIULETYN HISTORII SZTUKI, XXXVIII/19(1976), 23

Giovannini, Giacomo Maria   **BA GC**
(Italian painter and printmaker, 1667-1716)   **GC**
(Italian painter, printmaker, 1667-1717)   **BA**
Bibl: ▶Bénézit; ▶Bolaffi; ▶RILA/BHA, 1986; ▶Thieme-Becker

Giovannini, Joseph *(American architect; architectural critic for the New York Times, formerly wrote for the Los Angeles Herald Examiner)*   **AV**
Bibl: Architecture: the AIA jour., v.73, no.12, p.84

Giovannini, Massimo *(Italian architect, 1945-)*   **AV**
Bibl: Controspazio, 1985 Jan.-June, v.16, no.1-2, p.101

Giovannini, Vincenzio [**Unidentified**] *(Unknown painter, act. 18th century)*   **PR**
Bibl: Riccardi inventory dated 1776

Vincenzio Giovannini   **PR**

Giovannino (Zannino) di Pietro da Venezia→*see* Giovannino di Pietro da Venezia

Giovannino dei Grassi→*see* Grassi, Giovannino de'

Giovannino di Pietro da Venezia   **GC**
(Italian artist, op.1407)   **WC**
(Italian, act.1407)   **GC**
Bibl: ▶Witt checklist

Giovannino (Zannino) di Pietro da Venezia   **WC**

Zannino di Pietro da Venezia   **GC**

Zannino Pietro Venezia   **GC**

Giovannino of Genoa *(Italian scribe, 14th c.)*   **BA**
Bibl: Waldenburg, Miniatura ital., 489-499

Giovannio Scledio→*see* Scledio, Giovannio

Giovannoli, Alo(isio) *(Italian artist, c.1550-1618)*   **WC**

Giovannoni, Gustavo   **AV BA**
(Italian arch. conservator, 1873-1947)   **AV**
(Italian architect, author, 1873-1947)   **BA**
Bibl: ▶Natl. union cat., pre-1956; ▶Portoghesi, Diz. arch. e urbanistica; RLIN BKS file

Giovara, V. *(Italian, active 1920s)*   **JG**

Giovarrich→*see* Schönfeld, Johann Heinrich

Giovenale da Orvieto *(Italian painter, mosaicist, act.1425-1441)*   **BA**
Bibl: ▶Bolaffi; ▶Thieme-Becker

Giovenale, Giovanni Battista *(Italian architect, 1849-1934)*   **BA**
Bibl: ▶Avery obit. idx.; ▶Portoghesi, Diz. arch. e urbanistica; ▶Thieme-Becker

Giovene→*see* Vittoria, Giovanni [Unidentified]

Giovenone→*see* Giovenone, Gerolamo

Giovenone the Elder, Girolamo→*see* Giovenone, Gerolamo

Giovenone the Younger, Giuseppe *(Italian artist, 1524-a.1609)*   **WC**

Giovenone, Gerolamo   **BA GC PR**
(Italian artist, c.1490-1555)   **WC**
(Italian painter, 1486/87-1555)   **BA GC**
(Italian painter, 1486/87-1555, act. 1513)   **PR**
Bibl: ▶Bolaffi; ▶Fredericksen & Zeri, Census; ▶RILA/BHA, 1986; ▶Thieme-Becker; ▶Witt checklist

Gerolamo Giovenone   **PR**

Giovenone   **PR**

Giovenone the Elder, Girolamo   **WC**

Giovenone, Girolamo   **PR**

Giovenone, Girolamo I   **GC**

Girolamo Giovenone   **PR**

Giovenone, Giovanni Battista *(Italian artist, op.1548-79)*   **WC**

Giovenone, Girolamo→*see* Giovenone, Gerolamo

Giovenone, Girolamo I→*see* Giovenone, Gerolamo

Giovenone, Raffaelo *(Italian artist, op.1572-1604)*   **WC**

Gipkyn, John   **WC WI**
(British artist, op.1616)   **WC**
(British artist, op.1616-)   **WI**

Gips, Wilhelmine (Wilhelmine Carbin) *(Dutch artist, 1897-)*   **WC**

Gipstein, Yaacov→*see* Agam, Yaacov

Giradet, Abraham→*see* Girardet, Abraham

Giradet, Carl→*see* Girardet, Karl

Giradet, Edouard Henri→see
Girardet, Edouard Henri
Giradon→see Girardon, François
Giral, Jean Antoine *(French*
architect, ca.1720-1787)   **BA**
  Bibl: ▶Dict. biog. fran.; Kalnein,
  18c. France; ▶Larousse grande
  encyc.; ▶Macmillan encyc. archts.;
  ▶Thieme-Becker
Giraldi or Ziraldi di Guglielmo (del
Magro)→see Giraldi, Guglielmo
Giraldi, Domenico *(Italian architect,*
act.1819-1850)   **BA**
  Bibl: Fanelli, Firenze arch., p.390;
  Paatz, Kirchen von Florenz, v.4,
  p.345; Zangheri, Filippo
  Brunelleschi, II, p. 680
Giraldi, Guglielmo   **GC JG**
  (Italian artist, 15th cent.)   **WC**
  (Italian artist, op.1445-m.c.
  1480)   **WC**
  (Italian illuminator, act.1470-
  1480)   **GC**
  (Italian, active 1445-1489)   **JG**
  Bibl: Salmi, Pitt. a Ferrara, p.11
  Giraldi or Ziraldi di Guglielmo
  (del Magro)   **WC**
  Girardi, Guglielmo   **WC**
Giraldo, José L. *(Colombian*
architect)   **AV**
  Bibl: Escala, 1988, v.20, no.139,
  p.42
Giralte *(early Netherlandish sculptor*
in ESP, act.1560-1569)   **BA**
Giralte, Francisco *(Spanish sculptor,*
ca.1510-1576)   **BA**
  Bibl: ▶Bénézit; ▶Ceán Bermúdez,
  Bellas artes ESP; Parrado del
  Olmo, Escult. seguid. Berruguete,
  p.109; Portela Sandoval, Escult.
  sig. 16 en Palencia, p.250-252;
  ▶Thieme-Becker
Giran, Max Leon *(French artist,*
1867-1927)   **WC**
Girand *(French artist, 19th cent.)*   **WC**
Girard *(French porcelain painter and*
porcelain gilder, act.1772-1817)   **GC**
  Bibl: ▶Brunet, Sèvres
Girard, Albert *(French painter, 1839-*
1920)   **GC**
  Bibl: ▶Thieme-Becker
Girard, Alexander Hayden
(American designer, architect,
b.1907)   **BA**
Girard, Christian *(French architect)*   **AV**
  Bibl: AMC, 1988 June, no.21,
  p.92
Girard, Claude *(Canadian artist,*
1938-)   **WC**
Girard, Daniel *(French painter,*
illustrator, b.1890)   **BA**
  Bibl: ▶Bénézit

Girard, Dominique   **AV BA**
(French landscape architect,
d.1738)   **BA**
(Landscape architect, d.1738)   **AV**
  Bibl: ▶Hempel, Baroque central
  Euro.; Lieb: München;
  ▶Portoghesi, Diz. arch. e
  urbanistica; ▶Thieme-Becker
Girard, Edith *(French architect, wife*
of Olivier Girard, 1949-)   **AV**
  Bibl: Das Kunstwerk, n.3-4, Sept.
  1983, p.60; Intl. archt., 1 (1983)
  p.[61]
Girard, Ernest J.A.   **GC WC**
(French artist, 1813-1898)   **WC**
(French, 1813-1898)   **GC**
  Bibl: ▶Witt checklist
Girard, Firmin→see Girard,
Marie-François-Firmin
Girard, Jacques *(French interior*
designer)   **AV**
  Bibl: Maison Française, 1985
  June, no.388, p.108
Girard, Luigi Fusco→see Fusco
Girard, Luigi
Girard, Marie-Francois-Fermin→see
Girard, Marie-François-Firmin
Girard, Marie-François-Firmin   **VO**
(French artist, 1828-1921)   **WC**
(French painter, 1838-1921)   **VO**
(French, 1838-1921)   **GC**
  Bibl: ▶Bénézit, v. 5, p. 34; Getty
  Photo Study Coll. (Ptgs.);
  ▶Thieme-Becker
  Firmin-Gerard, Marie Francois   **WC**
  Firmin-Girard   **VO**
  Girard, Firmin   **GC**
  Girard, Marie-Francois-Fermin   **GC**
Girard, Olivier *(French architect,*
1947-)   **AV**
  Bibl: Intl. archt., 1 (1983) p.[61]
Girard, Pedro→see Girard, Pere
Girard, Pere   **GC PR**
(Spanish painter, act. 1479)   **PR**
(Spanish, act.1479-1490)   **GC**
  Bibl: Getty Photo Study Coll.
  (Ptgs.); ▶Thieme-Becker; ▶Witt
  checklist
  Girard, Pedro   **GC PR**
  Pere Girard   **PR**
Girard, Romain   **GC WC**
(French artist, c.1751-)   **WC**
(French, act. ca.1751)   **GC**
  Bibl: ▶Thieme-Becker
Girard, Sylvie *(Canadian architect,*
Montreal)   **AV**
  Bibl: ▶Canad. arch. dir., 1987
Girardel, E. *(French artist, 19th*
cent.)   **WC**
Girardet family *(Swiss printmakers,*
publishers, printers, 18th-19th cs.)   **BA**
  Bibl: ▶Bénézit; ▶Schweiz.
  Künst.-Lex.; ▶Thieme-Becker

Girardet, Abraham   **GC**
(Swiss artist, 1764-1823)   **WC**
(Swiss painter, 1764-1823)   **GC**
  Bibl: ▶Bénézit
  Giradet, Abraham   **WC**
Girardet, Charles Samuel *(Swiss*
painter, 1780-1863)   **GC**
  Bibl: ▶Bénézit
Girardet, Edouard Henri   **GC**
(Swiss artist, 1819-1880)   **WC**
(Swiss painter, 1819-1880)   **GC**
  Bibl: ▶Bénézit
  Giradet, Edouard Henri   **GC WC**
Girardet, Eugene *(French artist,*
1853-1907)   **WC**
Girardet, F. *(French)*   **GC**
  Bibl: Gernsheim, Corpus Photog.
  of Drawings, 1386
Girardet, Jean   **GC WC**
(French artist, 1709-1778)   **WC**
(French, 1709-1778)   **GC**
  Bibl: ▶Witt checklist
Girardet, Jules   **GC WC**
(French artist, 1856)   **WC**
(French painter, b.1856)   **GC**
  Bibl: ▶Bénézit
Girardet, Karl   **GC**
(Swiss artist, 1813-1871)   **WC**
(Swiss painter, 1813-1871)   **GC**
  Bibl: ▶Bénézit
  Giradet, Carl   **WC**
Girardet, Leon *(French artist, 1857-*
1895)   **WC**
Girardet, Leopold Henri *(Swiss*
artist, 1848-)   **WC**
Girardet, Michel *(Swiss architect)*   **AV**
  Bibl: L'Arca, 1989 Sept., no.
  30(suppl.), p.100
Girardi, Guglielmo→see Giraldi,
Guglielmo
Girardin, Alexandre Francois
Louis, Comte de *(French artist,*
1777-p.1836)   **WC**
Girardin, E. *(French artist, 19th*
cent.)   **WC**
Girardin, Laurent *(French glass*
painter, act.1440, d.1478)   **BA**
  Bibl: ▶Bénézit; ▶Thieme-Becker
Girardin, René Louis, marquis de
(French landscape architect, 1735-
1808)   **AV BA**
  Bibl: ▶Libr. of Congr. Name Auth.
  File; ▶New Columbia encyc.;
  Oxford comp. Fr. lit.
  Gérardin, René   **AV**
Girardon→see Girardon, François
Girardon, François   **BA GC JG PR WC**
(French artist, 1628-1715)   **WC**
(French painter, 1628-1715)   **PR**
(French sculptor, 1628-1715)   **BA GC**
(French, 1628-1715)   **JG**
  Bibl: ▶Bénézit; ▶Dict. biog. fran.;
  ▶RILA/BHA; ▶Thieme-Becker
  Francois Girardon   **PR**
  Giradon   **PR**
  Girardon   **PR**

Girardon, Gustave *(French artist, 1821-1888)* **WC**
Girardot, Ernest Gustave **WC WI**
   (British artist, op.1855-1904) WI
   (British artist, op.1860-1893) WC
Girardot, Louis Auguste **GC WC**
   (French artist, 1858-1933) WC
   (French painter, 1856-1933) GC
   Bibl: ▶Bénézit
Giraud, Charles (Sebastian Charles)→see Giraud, Sébastien Charles
Giraud, Emile *(French painter, 1825-1892)* **GC**
   Bibl: ▶Thieme-Becker
Giraud, Emile *(French painter, pharmacist, 1850-1918)* **BA**
   Bibl: ▶Baille, Petits maîtres; ▶Camard, Ptrs. & sculps. provençaux
Giraud, Etienne *(French printmaker, act.1767-1771)* **BA**
Giraud, Eugène→see Giraud, Pierre François Eugène
Giraud, Eugene (Pierre Francois Eugene)→see Giraud, Pierre François Eugène
Giraud, Georges *(French artist, 1882-)* **WC**
Giraud, Jean Baptiste→see Giraud, Jean-Baptiste
Giraud, Jean-Baptiste **BA**
   (French artist, 1752-1830) WC
   (French sculptor, collector, 1752-1830) BA
   Bibl: ▶Dict. biog. fran.; ▶Thieme-Becker; ▶Witt checklist
Giraud, Jean Baptiste **WC**
Giraud, Pierre François Eugène **BA**
   (French artist, 1806-1881) WC
   (French painter, 1806-1881) GC
   (French painter, printmaker, 1806-1881) BA
   Bibl: ▶Bénézit; ▶Busse, Maler u. Bildhauer 19. Jahr.; ▶Thieme-Becker
Giraud, Eugène **GC**
Giraud, Eugene (Pierre Francois Eugene) **WC**
Giraud, Sébastien Charles **BA GC**
   (French artist, 1819-1892) WC
   (French painter, 1819-1892) BA GC
   Bibl: ▶Bénézit; ▶Busse, Maler u. Bildhauer 19. Jahr.; ▶Thieme-Becker
Giraud, Charles (Sebastian Charles) **WC**
Giraud, Victor Julien *(French painter, 1840-1871)* **GC**
   Bibl: ▶Thieme-Becker
Giraudeau, Jean-Baptiste *(French silversmith, d.1764, master 1715)* **GC**
   Bibl: ▶Mabille, Orfèv. fran.
Girault, Charles→see Girault, Charles Louis

Girault, Charles Louis **BA**
   (1851-1932) AV
   (French architect, 1851-1932) BA
   Bibl: ▶Thieme-Becker; ▶WW Arch.
Girault, Charles **AV**
Girbau, Lluís Domenech→see Domènech Girbau, Luis
Girbino, Domenico *(Italian sculptor, 20th c.)* **BA**
   Bibl: Privitera, S., ARTE CRISTIANA, LXXII/703 (July-Aug 1984) p.255-258
Girgenti→see Girgenti, Paolino
Girgenti, Paolino *(Italian painter, act. 1st half 19th cent.)* **PR**
   Bibl: ▶Thieme-Becker
   Girgenti PR
   Paolino Girgenti PR
Girier, Cyr Jean Aimé (Saint-Cyr) *(French painter, 1837-1912)* **BA**
   Bibl: ▶Bénézit; ▶Thieme-Becker
Girieud, Pierre→see Girieud, Pierre Paul
Girieud, Pierre Paul **BA WC**
   (French artist, 1875-1940) WC
   (French painter, 1875-1940) BA GC
   Bibl: ▶Bénézit; ▶Thieme-Becker; ▶Vollmer, Künst.-Lex. 20. Jhr.
Girieud, Pierre **GC**
Girin, David-Eugene *(French artist, 1848-1917)* **WC**
Giriodi, Sisto *(Italian architect)* **AV**
   Bibl: Controspazio, 1985 Jan.-June, v.16, no.1-2, p.21
Girke, Raimund *(West German painter, b.1930)* **BA**
   Bibl: ▶Vollmer, Künst.-Lex. 20. Jhr.; ▶WW Arts DEU
Girling, Edmund *(British artist, 1796-1871)* **WC WI**
Girling, Oliver *(Canadian artist, 20th c.)* **BA**
   Bibl: Dault, G.M., in VANGUARD XI/4 (May 1982) 13
Girling, Richard *(British artist, 1799-1863)* **WC WI**
Girling, Sheila *(British painter, 20th c.)* **BA**
   Bibl: Syracuse (NY, USA), Everson Mus., New works in clay (1981)
Giró, Ramon *(Spanish architect, Barcelona)* **AV**
   Bibl: Quaderns d'arquitectura i urbanisme, 1984 Jan.-Mar., no. 160, p.102
Girod *(French artist, 19th cent.)* **WC**
Girod, Patrice *(Dutch architect, Amsterdam)* **AV**
   Bibl: Architecture d'aujourd'hui, 1988 July, no.257, p.72
Girodet→see Girodet-Trioson, Anne-Louis
Girodet de Roucy Trioson, Anne Louis→see Girodet-Trioson, Anne-Louis

Girodet de Roucy-Trioson, Anne-Louis→see Girodet-Trioson, Anne-Louis
Girodet de Roucy-Trioson, Anne-Louise→see Girodet-Trioson, Anne-Louis
Girodet de Roussy, Anne-Louis→see Girodet-Trioson, Anne-Louis
Girodet, Anne Louis de Roucy Trioson→see Girodet-Trioson, Anne-Louis
Girodet, Anne-Louis→see Girodet-Trioson, Anne-Louis
Girodet, Anne-Louis de Roucy-Trioson→see Girodet-Trioson, Anne-Louis
Girodet-Trioson→see Girodet-Trioson, Anne-Louis
Girodet-Trioson, Anne Louis→see Girodet-Trioson, Anne-Louis
Girodet-Trioson, Anne Louis (Anne Louis Girodet de Roussy)→see Girodet-Trioson, Anne-Louis
Girodet-Trioson, Anne Louis de Roussy→see Girodet-Trioson, Anne-Louis
Girodet-Trioson, Anne-Louis **BA GC PR**
   (French artist, 1767-1824) WC
   (French painter, 1767-1824) PR
   (French painter, printmaker, 1767-1824) BA
   (French, 1767-1824) GC JG
   Bibl: ▶RILA/BHA; ▶Thieme-Becker; ▶Witt checklist
   Anne Louis Girodet-Trioson PR
   Girodet PR
   Girodet de Roucy Trioson, Anne Louis PR
Girodet de Roucy-Trioson, Anne-Louis **JG**
   Girodet de Roucy-Trioson, Anne-Louise PR
   Girodet de Roussy, Anne-Louis BA
   Girodet, Anne Louis de Roucy Trioson PR
   Girodet, Anne-Louis BA
   Girodet, Anne-Louis de Roucy-Trioson BA
   Girodet-Trioson PR
   Girodet-Trioson, Anne Louis PR
Girodet-Trioson, Anne Louis (Anne Louis Girodet de Roussy) **PR**
Girodet-Trioson, Anne Louis de Roussy **WC**
Girodon, Gabriel Charles *(French painter, sculptor, b.1884)* **BA**
   Bibl: ▶Bénézit; ▶Vollmer, Künst.-Lex. 20. Jhr.
Girolama da Carpi→see Girolamo da Carpi
Girolami Pennacchi→see Girolamo da Treviso the elder (Girolamo Pennacchi)

Girolami, Filippo di Zanobi de'
(Italian, act.1475-1500)   **BA**
Bibl: Callmann, Art Bull., LXVI/3
(Sep. 1984) pp.493-495;
Lightbown, Botticelli, v.1, p.145;
v.2, p.106

Girolami, Zanobi di Filippo de'
(Italain, act.1500)   **BA**
Bibl: Callmann, Art Bull., LXVI/3
(Sep. 1984) pp.493-495
Girolamo Bedoli-Mazzola→see
Bedoli, Girolamo Mazzola
Girolamo Bonini→see Bonini,
Girolamo
Girolamo Carpi→see Girolamo da
Carpi
Girolamo Chignoli→see Chignoli,
Girolamo
Girolamo Comes→see Colomes,
Jerome
Girolamo d'Arena→see Arena,
Giovanni Geronimo d'
Girolamo da Brescia *(Italian artist,*
op.1501-1519)   **WC**
Girolamo Da Camerino   **WI**
(Italian artist, op.1450-1473)   WC WI
(Italian painter, 1450-1473)   PR
(Italian, act.1450-1473)   GC
Bibl: ▶Fredericksen & Zeri, Census;
▶Thieme-Becker; ▶Witt checklist

Gerolamo di Giovanni da
Camerino   **WC**
Girolamo di Giovanni da
Camerino   **GC PR WC**
Girolamo da Carpi   **BA JG PR**
(Draughtsman, painter, 1501-
1556)   CE
(Italian artist, 1501-1556)   WC
(Italian painter, 1501-1556)   GC PR
(Italian pàinter, architect, 1501-
1556)   BA
(Italian, Emilian, ca. 1501-1556)   JG
Bibl: ▶RILA/BHA; ▶Thieme-Becker
Carpi   PR
Carpi, Girolamo da   **GC PR**
Da Carpi, Girolamo   **CE**
De Livizzani, Girolamo   CE
G. da Carpi   PR
Girolama da Carpi   PR
Girolamo Carpi   PR
Girolamo da Carpi, Grassi,
de'Livizzani or Sellari   **WC**
Girolamo Sellari da Carpi   PR
Gironimo da Carpi   PR
Sellari, Girolamo   CE
Girolamo da Carpi, Grassi,
de'Livizzani or Sellari→see
Girolamo da Carpi
Girolamo da Cotignola→see
Marchesi, Girolamo (Girolamo da
Cotignola)

Girolamo da Cremona   **BA GC PR WC**
(Italian artist, 1467-1475)   WC
(Italian painter and illuminator,
act.1467-1475)   GC
(Italian painter, act. 1467-1475)   PR
(Italian painter, illuminator, act.
1467-1475)   BA
Bibl: ▶RILA/BHA, 1986
Cremona, Girolamo da   PR
Girolamo da Ferrara→see Lombardo,
Girolamo (Girolamo Solari)
Girolamo da Ponte→see Bassano,
Gerolamo (Gerolamo da Ponte)
Girolamo da Santa Croce→see
Santacroce, Girolamo da
Girolamo da Santacroce→see
Santacroce, Girolamo da
Girolamo da Sermoneta→see
Siciolante, Girolamo (Girolamo da
Sermoneta)
Girolamo da Trento *(Italian artist,*
op.1492-1502)   **WC**
Girolamo da Treviri→see Girolamo
da Treviso the elder (Girolamo
Pennacchi)
Girolamo da Treviso→see Girolamo
da Treviso the elder (Girolamo
Pennacchi)
Girolamo da Treviso→see Girolamo
da Treviso the younger (Girolamo
Pennacchi)
Girolamo da Treviso (the elder)→see
Girolamo da Treviso the elder
(Girolamo Pennacchi)
Girolamo da Treviso (the
younger)→see Girolamo da
Treviso the younger (Girolamo
Pennacchi)
Girolamo da Treviso the Elder→see
Girolamo da Treviso the elder
(Girolamo Pennacchi)
Girolamo da Treviso the elder
(Girolamo Pennacchi)   **BA**
(Italian artist, c.1450-1496(?))   WC
(Italian painter, b.1450-1455,
d.1496/97)   BA
(Italian painter, c.1450-1496)   GC
(Italian painter,
ca.1450/55-1496/97)   PR
Bibl: ▶Bolaffi; ▶Fredericksen &
Zeri, Census; Getty Photo Study
Coll. (Ptgs.); ▶McGraw-Hill dict.
art; ▶RILA/BHA; ▶Thieme-Becker;
▶Witt checklist
Girolami Pennacchi   PR
Girolamo da Treviri   PR
Girolamo da Treviso   PR
Girolamo da Treviso (the
elder)   **GC PR**
Girolamo da Treviso the Elder   **WC**
Pennacchi   PR
Pennacchi, Gerolamo (the Elder)   GC
Pennacchi, Girolamo   PR
Pennachi, Girolamo da Treviso
(the Elder)   **GC**
Treviso, Girolamo da   PR

Girolamo da Treviso the younger
(Girolamo Pennacchi)   **BA**
(Italian artist, 1497(?)-1544)   WC
(Italian painter and sculptor,
1497-1544)   GC
(Italian painter, 1497-1544)   PR
(Italian painter, 16th cent)   AV
(Italian painter, sculptor,
architect, 1497-1544)   BA
Bibl: ▶Bénézit; ▶Bolaffi;
▶Fredericksen & Zeri, Census;
Getty Photo Study Coll. (Ptgs.);
Getty Photo Study Coll. (Sculp.);
Paragone arte, 1987 No9v., no.
453, p.37; ▶RILA/BHA;
▶Thieme-Becker; ▶Witt checklist
Gerolamo da Treviso (the younger)   PR
Girolamo da Treviso   GC
Girolamo da Treviso (the
younger)   **PR**
Girolamo Pennacchi (the younger)   PR
Pennacchi (?), Gerolamo di Pier
Maria (?) (Gerolamo da
Treviso II)   **WC**
Pennacchi, Gerolamo (the
Younger)   GC
Pennacchi, Girolamo (the younger)   PR
Pennachi, Girolamo da Treviso   **GC**
Treviso, Gerolamo da   **AV**
Girolamo da Udine→see Girolamo di
Bernardino da Udine
Girolamo da Vicenza→see Girolamo
Vicentino
Girolamo da Vicenza (Girolamo di
Stefano d'Alemagna)→see
Girolamo Vicentino
Girolamo da Vicenzo→see Girolamo
Vicentino
Girolamo dai Libri   **GC PR**
(Italian artist, 1474-1555)   WC
(Italian illuminator, 1474-1555)   GC
(Italian painter, 1474?-1555)   PR
Bibl: ▶Fredericksen & Zeri, Census;
▶Thieme-Becker; ▶Witt checklist
Gerolamo dai Libri   PR
Girolamo dai Libri (Veccia)   GC
Girolamo dai Libri (Veccio)   **WC**
Girolamo dai Libri (Veccia)→see
Girolamo dai Libri
Girolamo dai Libri (Veccio)→see
Girolamo dai Libri
Girolamo dal Santo→see Tessari,
Girolamo (Girolamo dal Santo)
Girolamo dei Maggi   **GC WC**
(Italian artist, op.c.1500)   WC
(Italian, op.c.1500)   GC
Bibl: ▶Witt checklist
Girolamo del Pacchia→see Pacchia,
Girolamo del
Girolamo della Pacchia→see Pacchia,
Girolamo del
Girolamo Dente→see Dente,
Girolamo (Girolamo di Tiziano)

Girolamo di Benvenuto   BA GC **JG PR**
  (*Italian artist, 1470-1524*)   WC
  (*Italian painter, 1470-1524*) BA GC PR
  (*Italian, Sienese, 1470-1524*)   JG
  Bibl: ▶Bolaffi; Fredericksen.
  BENVENUTO DI GIOVANNI,
  GIROLAMO DI BENVENUTO...,
  ▶RILA/BHA; ▶Witt checklist
Girolamo di Benvenuto del
  Guasta   GC WC
  Girolamo di Benvenuto di Giovanni
    del Guasta   PR
  Girolamo di Benvenuto del
    Guasta→see Girolamo di
    Benvenuto
  Girolamo di Benvenuto di Giovanni
    del Guasta→see Girolamo di
    Benvenuto
Girolamo di Bernardino da
  Udine   BA GC PR WC
  (*Italian artist, op.1506-m.1512*)   WC
  (*Italian painter, act. 1506, d.*
    1512)   PR
  (*Italian painter, act.1506,*
    d.1512)   BA
  (*Italian painter, act.1506-d.*
    1512)   GC
  Bibl: Berenson, Venetian; ▶Bolaffi;
  ▶RILA/BHA, 1986;
  ▶Thieme-Becker; ▶Witt checklist
  Girolamo da Udine   PR
Girolamo di Giovanni da
  Camerino→see Girolamo Da
  Camerino
Girolamo di Santa Croce→see
  Santacroce, Girolamo da
Girolamo di Tiziano→see Dente,
  Girolamo (Girolamo di Tiziano)
Girolamo Donnini→see Donnini,
  Girolamo
Girolamo Figino→see Figino,
  Girolamo
Girolamo Forabosco→see Forabosco,
  Girolamo
Girolamo Forni→see Forni, Girolamo
Girolamo Francesco Maria
  Mazzola→see Parmigianino
  (Francesco Mazzola)
Girolamo Franzini→see Franzini,
  Girolamo
Girolamo Genga→see Genga,
  Girolamo
Girolamo Giovenone→see
  Giovenone, Gerolamo
Girolamo Marchesi→see Marchesi,
  Girolamo (Girolamo da Cotignola)
Girolamo Marchesi da
  Cotignola→see Marchesi,
  Girolamo (Girolamo da Cotignola)
Girolamo Massaro→see Massaro,
  Girolamo
Girolamo Mazzola Bedoli→see
  Bedoli, Girolamo Mazzola
Girolamo Mazzuola→see Bedoli,
  Girolamo Mazzola

Girolamo Mocetto→see Mocetto,
  Girolamo
Girolamo Mutiani→see Muziano,
  Girolamo
Girolamo Mutiano→see Muziano,
  Girolamo
Girolamo Muziano→see Muziano,
  Girolamo
Girolamo Padovano→see Tessari,
  Girolamo (Girolamo dal Santo)
Girolamo Panza→see Panza,
  Girolamo
Girolamo Pennacchi (the
  younger)→see Girolamo da
  Treviso the younger (Girolamo
  Pennacchi)
Girolamo Pesci→see Pesci, Girolamo
Girolamo Piola→see Piola, Paolo
  Gerolamo
Girolamo Rivera→see Ribera, Jusepe
  de (lo Spagnoletto)
Girolamo Sellari da Carpi→see
  Girolamo da Carpi
Girolamo Siciolante→see Siciolante,
  Girolamo (Girolamo da Sermoneta)
Girolamo Sordo→see Tessari,
  Girolamo (Girolamo dal Santo)
Girolamo Sordo, del Santo di Padova
  or Padovano→see Tessari,
  Girolamo (Girolamo dal Santo)
Girolamo Troppa→see Troppa,
  Girolamo
Girolamo Vicentino   BA GC PR
  (*Italian artist, op.c.1500*)   WC
  (*Italian painter and sculptor,*
    act.1481-ca.1510)   GC
  (*Italian painter, act. 1481-ca.*
    1510)   PR
  (*Italian painter, act.1481-ca.*
    1510)   BA
  Bibl: Barbieri, Pittori di Vicenza;
  ▶Bénézit; ▶Bolaffi; Borenius, Ptrs.
  Vicenza; Getty Photo Study Coll.
  (Sculp.); ITATTI2, 2; ▶RILA/BHA,
  1986; TCI Abruzzo-Molise;
  ▶Thieme-Becker
  Gerolamo da Vicenza   PR
Girolamo da Vicenza   GC PR
  Girolamo da Vicenza (Girolamo di
    Stefano d'Alemagna)   GC
Girolamo da Vicenzo   WC
  Vicentino   PR
  Vicentino, Girolamo   GC PR
Giron, Charles   BA GC WC
  (*Swiss artist, 1850-1914*)   WC
  (*Swiss painter, 1850-1914*) BA GC
  Bibl: ▶Bénézit
Gironcoli, Bruno (*Austrian sculptor,*
  painter, b.1936)   BA
  Bibl: ▶Bénézit; Munich (BRD),
  Städtische Galerie im
  LEnbachhaus, BRUNO GIRONCOLI,
  1977
Gironde, Victor de (*French artist,*
  1788-1866)   WC
Gironella (*Italian artist, op.1962*)   WC

Gironimo da Carpi→see Girolamo da
  Carpi
Girot, Antoine Marie (*French artist,*
  1809-1885)   WC
Girouard, Tina (*American artist,*
  b.1946)   BA
  Bibl: ART NEWS, vol. 74, Nov
  1975, p.121; New Orleans (LA,
  USA), Museum of Art, FIVE FROM
  LOUISIANA, 1977
Giroud, Michel (*French organ*
  builder, 20th c.)   BA
  Bibl: Michel, MON. HIST. DE LA
  FRANCE 146 (Sept 1986) 18-23
Giroust, Jean Antoine Theodore
  (*French artist, 1753-1817*)   WC
  Giroust, Marie Suzanne→see Roslin,
    Suzanne
Giroust, R. (*French artist, op.1897*)   WC
Giroux [Unidentified] (*Unknown*
  painter)   PR
  Bibl: (June 16, 1806, lot 305,
  Phillips)
Giroux, André   BA GC JG PR WC
  (*French artist, 1801-1879*)   WC
  (*French painter, 1801-1879*) BA GC PR
  (*French, 1801-1879*)   JG
  Bibl: ▶Bénézit; Miquel, Paysage
  fran. 19e s., v.1, p.176;
  ▶RILA/BHA; ▶Thieme-Becker
  Andre Giroux   PR
Giroux, Charles (*American artist,*
  b.1861)   WI
Giroux, Ernest (*French painter,*
  b.1851)   GC
  Bibl: ▶Bénézit
Giroux, Raphaël (*Canadian*
  architect, act.1855)   BA
  Bibl: Journal of Can Art Hist, I, 1
  '74 p.8
Girsberger, Werner (*West German*
  architectural firm, Kempton)   AV
  Bibl: Deutsches Architektenblatt,
  1988 Mar., v.20, no.3, p.513
Girscher, Bernhard Moritz (*German*
  artist, 1822-1870)   WC
Girtin→see Girtin, Thomas
Girtin, James (*British painter, ca.*
  1780-aft.1820)   PR
  Bibl: ▶Thieme-Becker
  J. Girtin   PR
  James Girtin   PR
Girtin, Thomas   BA GC PR WC WI
  (*British artist, 1775-1802*)   WC WI
  (*British painter, 1775-1802*)   PR
  (*British painter, printmaker,*
    1775-1802)   BA
  (*British, 1775-1802*)   GC
  Bibl: ▶Encyc. world art;
  ▶RILA/BHA; ▶Thieme-Becker;
  ▶Witt checklist
  Girtin   PR
  Girton   PR
  Thomas Girtin   PR
  Girton→see Girtin, Thomas

Gisbern, Horace (American architect, New York) **AV**
Bibl: Harvard architecture review, 1982, v.2, p.51

Gisbert, Antonio (Spanish artist, 1835-p.1899) **WC**

Giscard, Joseph (French artisan of architectural terracotta, Toulouse) **AV**
Bibl: Archives d'architecture moderne, 1989, no.39, p.96

Gischia, Léon **BA WC**
(French artist, 1903) **WC**
(French painter, scenographer, b.1903) **BA**
Bibl: ▶Artist biog. master idx.; ▶Bénézit; ▶McGraw-Hill dict. art; ▶Oxford comp. 20c. art; ▶Thieme-Becker

Giseken, Georgi (Russian artist, 20th cent.) **WC**

Gisel, Ernst (Swiss architect, Zurich) **AV**
Bibl: Detail, 1984 Nov.-Dec., v.24, no.6, p.641

Gisela, Josef (Reznicek) (German artist, 1851-1899) **WC**

Giselaer, Nicolaes de→see Gyselaer, Nicolaes de

Giselbrecht, Ernst (Austrian architect, 1951-) **AV**
Bibl: Ottagono, 1988 Mar., p.20

Gislander, William (Scandinavian artist, 1890-1937) **WC**

Gislebertus (French sculptor, 12th cent.) **AV**
Bibl: RLIN BKS file, CSUG12458422

Gisleni or Ghiseni, Giambattista.→see Gisleni, Giovanni Battista

Gisleni, Giovanni Battista **BA**
(Italian architect, sculptor, 1600-1672) **BA**
(Italian artist, 1600-1672) **WC**
Bibl: ▶Portoghesi, Diz. arch. e urbanistica; ▶Thieme-Becker

Gisleni or Ghiseni, Giambattista. **WC**

Gisler, Edouard (Belgian artist, op. 1836-1851) **WC**

Gismondi, Jean (French interior designer) **AV**
Bibl: Connaissance des arts, 1988 Nov., no.441, p.92

Gismondi, Paolo (Paolo Perugino) (Italian artist, 1612-c.1685) **WC**

Gismondo Betti→see Betti, Sigismondo

Gisolfi→see Ghisolfi, Giovanni

Gisolfi, Onofrio Antonio (Italian engineer, act.1620, d.1656) **BA**
Bibl: Storia dell'arte 26 (Jan-Apr 1976) 61-72; TCI; ▶Thieme-Becker

Gisolphi→see Ghisolfi, Giovanni

Gisors, Guy de (1762-1835) **AV**

Gispen, Willem Hendrik (Dutch architect, designer, painter, b.1890) **BA**
Bibl: Amsterdam, Stedelijk Mus., GISPENLAMPEN 1916-1949 (1980); Koch, A., INDUSTRIELL ONTWERPER W.H. GISPEN, 1890-1981 (Ph.d. diss); ▶Natl. union cat., pre-1956; ▶Scheen, Ned. beeldende kunst.

Gissey, Germain (French sculptor, 1594-1640) **BA**
Bibl: ▶Bénézit; ▶Lami, Sculp. fran. 19e s.; ▶Thieme-Becker

Gissey, Gesse, Gessey or Jesse, Henry→see Gissey, Henry

Gissey, Henry **BA**
(French artist, 1621-1673) **WC**
(French costume designer, 1621-1673) **BA**
Bibl: ▶Bénézit; ▶Dict. biog. fran.; ▶Encic. spettacolo; La Gorce, J. de, Revue de l'Art 66 (1984) 40; ▶Thieme-Becker

Gissey, Gesse, Gessey or Jesse, Henry **WC**

Gissinger, Robert (Swiss landscape architect) **AV**
Bibl: Schweizer Baumarkt, 1989 Jan.5, no.1, p.II

Gisske, Ehrhardt (East German architect, 1924-) **AV**
Bibl: Architektur der DDR, 1989 Mar., p.41 (birth date); ▶Libr. of Congr. Name Auth. File

Gissler, Gary (American painter, 20th c.) **BA**
Bibl: Douglas, New art examiner, XI/9 (Jun. 1984) p.12

Gisson (American artist, op.circa 1970-) **WI**

Giszinger, J. (Hungarian artist, op.c. 1880) **WC**

Gitlin, Michael (American sculptor, b.1943) **BA**
Bibl: Arts Mag. LI (Jan 1977), p.18; ▶Intl. dir. exh. artists, 1982; ▶Locus; ▶WW Amer. Art, 1989

Gitschmann the Elder, Hans (Hans von Ropstein or Raperstein) (German artist, op.1515-m.1564) **WC**

Gittard, Alexandre Charles Joseph (French artist, 1832-1904) **WC**

Gittard, Daniel (French architect, 1625-1686) **AV**
Bibl: RLIN BKS file, NYCG84-B30820

Gitz-Johansen, Aage Rudolf Hans (Danish painter, printmaker, 1897-1972) **BA**
Bibl: ▶Vollmer, Künst.-Lex. 20. Jhr.; ▶Weilbach, Kunst.leks.

Giuda→see Carolis, Lorenzo di Maestro Giovanni de (Giuda)

Giudice, Carlo Giovanni Francesco **AV BA**
(1747-1774) **AV**
(Italian architect in NLD, 1746-1819) **BA**
Bibl: ▶Encyc. world art; KUNSTREISBOEK; Molen-den Outer, NEDERLANDS KUNSTHIST. JAABK., XXXI (1980) 423-438; ▶Portoghesi, Diz. arch. e urbanistica; ▶Rosenberg, Dutch art & arch., p.251; ▶Thieme-Becker

Giudice, Niccolò del (1660-1729) **AV**

Giudici, Carlo Maria (Italian artist, 1723-1804) **BA**
Bibl: ▶Thieme-Becker

Giudici, Luigi del (Italian artist, op. 1777-1811) **WC**

Giudici, Rinaldo (Italian artist, op. 1886-) **WC**

Giudo Cagnaci→see Cagnacci, Guido

Giudo Reni→see Reni, Guido

Giuffre, Antonino **GC**
(Italian artist, 15th cent.) **WC**
(Italian, 15th century) **GC**
Bibl: ▶Witt checklist

Antonello da lu Re **GC**

Giuffre, Juffre or Jufre, Antonino or Antonio (Antonello de lu Re) **WC**

Juffre, Antonio **GC**

Giuffre, Juffre or Jufre, Antonino or Antonio (Antonello de lu Re)→see Giuffre, Antonino

Giuffrida, Paul (British artist, b.1956) **BA**
Bibl: Arts Council GBR, Welsh Comm., Coming out (1979)

Giugno, Francesco (Italian painter, 1574-after 1651) **BA**
Bibl: ▶Bolaffi

Giulia Lama→see Lama, Giulia

Giulianelli, Sandro (Italian architect) **AV**
Bibl: Domus, 1985 May, no.661, p.12

Giuliani, Giovanni **BA WC**
(Italian artist, 1663-1744) **WC**
(Italian sculptor in AUT, 1663-1744) **BA**
Bibl: ▶Bénézit; ▶Hempel, Baroque central Euro.; ▶Thieme-Becker

Giuliani, Paola (Italian architect) **AV**
Bibl: Lotus international, 1986, no.48-49, p.61

Giuliani, R. (Italian architect) **AV**
Bibl: Lotus international, 1983, no.38, p.90

Giuliano Bugiardini→see Bugiardini, Giuliano

Giuliano d'Arrighi→see Pesello, Giuliano (Giuliano d'Arrighi)

Giuliano da Fano→see Presciutti, Giuliano

Giuliano da Firenze, Fra (Italian, d.1487) **GC**
Bibl: ▶Thieme-Becker

Giuliano da Maiano →*see* Giuliano da
Maiano (Giuliano di Leonardo di
Antonio)

**Giuliano da Maiano (Giuliano di
Leonardo di Antonio)**   **BA** GC

   *(Italian architect and sculptor,
1432-1490)*   GC

   (Italian architect, 1432-1490)   AV

   *(Italian architect, sculptor,
wood inlayer, 1432-1490)*   BA

   (Italian artist, 1432-1490)   WC

   Bibl: ▶Encyc. world art;
   ▶Macmillan encyc. archts.;
   ▶Portoghesi, Diz. arch. e
   urbanistica; ▶RILA/BHA;
   ▶Thieme-Becker

Giuliano da Maiano   GC

**Giuliano da Maiano, Giuliano di
Leonardo (Nardo) d'Antonio**   WC

Maiano, Giuliano da   AV

*Giuliano da Maiano, Giuliano di
Leonardo (Nardo) d'Antonio* →*see*
Giuliano da Maiano (Giuliano di
Leonardo di Antonio)

Giuliano da Rimini   **BA GC PR WC**

   (Italian artist, op.1307-m.1346)   WC

   *(Italian painter, act. 1370, d.
bef.1345)*   PR

   *(Italian painter, act.1307, d.
before 1345)*   BA

   (Italian, act.1307-d.1346)   GC

   Bibl: Bellinati, Padova, p. 222,
   p.222; Bettini-Puppi, La Chiesa
   degli Eremitani; ▶Bolaffi; ▶Encyc.
   world art; ▶RILA/BHA;
   ▶Thieme-Becker; ▶Witt checklist

Giuliano da Sangallo →*see* Sangallo,
Giuliano da

Giuliano di Biagio *(Italian sculptor
and designer, act.1482)*   GC

   Bibl: ▶Thieme-Becker

Giuliano di Bugiardini →*see*
Bugiardini, Giuliano

**Giuliano di Giovanni da
Poggibonsi** *(Italian sculptor, act.
1407-1424)*   **BA GC**

   Bibl: Pelican Hist. of Art;
   ▶RILA/BHA; ▶Thieme-Becker

Giuliano di Simone →*see* Giuliano di
Simone da Lucca

Giuliano di Simone da Lucca   **BA** GC **PR**

   (Italian artist, op.c.1389)   WC

   (Italian painter, 14th c.)   BA

   *(Italian painter, act. 14th
century)*   PR

   (Italian painter, act. ca.1389)   GC

   Bibl: ▶Bénézit; ▶Bolaffi; Offner,
   Flor. ptg.; ▶RILA/BHA, 1986;
   ▶Thieme-Becker; ▶Witt checklist

Giuliano di Simone   GC **PR WC**

Giuliano di Tomaso di Guccio

   (Italian scribe, act.1425)   **BA**

   Bibl: Parrouchi, in SCRITTI IN
   ONORE DI OTTARIO MORISANI,
   167-169

Giuliano family *(Italian jewelers,
19th c.)*   **BA**

   Bibl: ▶Newman, Jewelry

Giuliano Finelli →*see* Finelli, Giuliano

Giuliano Finello →*see* Finelli, Giuliano

Giuliano Giamberti →*see* Sangallo,
Giuliano da

Giuliano Traballesi →*see* Traballesi,
Giuliano

Giuliano, Bartolommeo   **GC WC**

   (Italian artist, 1825-1909)   WC

   (Italian painter, 1825-1909)   GC

   Bibl: ▶Thieme-Becker

Giuliano, Carlo *(Italian jeweler in
GBR, 1831-1895)*   **BA**

   Bibl: Gere, Jewellery

Giuliano, Fra *(Italian artist, op.1487)*   **WC**

Giulianotti, Filippo *(Italian sculptor,
1852-1903)*   **GC**

   Bibl: ▶RILA/BHA

Giuliari, Giorgio *(Italian architect)*   **AV**

   Bibl: Abitare, 1989 Mar., no.272,
   p.172

Giulio →*see* Giulio Romano (Giulio
Pippi)

Giulio Avellino →*see* Avellino, Giulio

Giulio Benso →*see* Benso, Giulio

Giulio Bruni →*see* Bruni, Giulio

Giulio Bruno →*see* Bruni, Giulio

Giulio Campi →*see* Campi, Giulio

Giulio Carpioni →*see* Carpioni, Giulio
I

Giulio Carpioni (I) →*see* Carpioni,
Giulio I

Giulio Ces.e Procaccino →*see*
Procaccini, Giulio Cesare

Giulio Cesare →*see* Procaccini, Giulio
Cesare

Giulio Cesare Amidano →*see*
Amidano, Giulio Cesare

Giulio Cesare Precacchino →*see*
Procaccini, Giulio Cesare

Giulio Cesare Procaccini →*see*
Procaccini, Giulio Cesare

Giulio Cesare Procaccino →*see*
Procaccini, Giulio Cesare

Giulio Cesare Procacino →*see*
Procaccini, Giulio Cesare

Giulio Cesare proccacino →*see*
Procaccini, Giulio Cesare

Giulio Cesare Semino →*see* Semino,
Giulio Cesare

Giulio Cromer →*see* Cromer, Giulio

Giulio da Urbino *(Italian porcelain
painter, painter, act.1533-1569)*   **BA**

   Bibl: ▶Bénézit; ▶Bolaffi; ▶Honey,
   Euro. ceramic; Rasmussen, Jahrb.
   der Hamburger Kunst. XXV, 1980,
   81-96; ▶Thieme-Becker

Giulio del'Ocha →*see* Giulio dell'Oca

Giulio dell'Oca *(Italian painter, act.
17th century)*   **PR**

   Bibl: Prota-Giurleo, Pitt.
   Napoletani del '600

Giulio del'Ocha   PR

Giulio dell'Ocha   PR

Giulio dell'Ocha →*see* Giulio dell'Oca

Giulio di Antonio Bonasone →*see*
Bonasone, Giulio

Giulio di Pietro de' Gianuzzi →*see*
Giulio Romano (Giulio Pippi)

Giulio di Pietro de'Gianuzzi →*see*
Giulio Romano (Giulio Pippi)

Giulio Francia →*see* Francia, Giulio

Giulio Pierino da Amelia *(Italian
artist, op.1543-1581)*   **WC**

Giulio Pignatta →*see* Pignatta, Giulio

Giulio Pippi →*see* Giulio Romano
(Giulio Pippi)

*Giulio Pippi detto Giulio
Romano* →*see* Giulio Romano
(Giulio Pippi)

*Giulio Pippi, Called, Giulio
Romano* →*see* Giulio Romano
(Giulio Pippi)

Giulio Pomano →*see* Giulio Romano
(Giulio Pippi)

Giulio Rom. →*see* Giulio Romano
(Giulio Pippi)

Giulio Rom.o →*see* Giulio Romano
(Giulio Pippi)

Giulio Romano →*see* Giulio Romano
(Giulio Pippi)

*Giulio Romano (Giulio Pippi or di
Pietro de Gianuzzi)* →*see* Giulio
Romano (Giulio Pippi)

Giulio Romano (Giulio Pippi)   BA PR
  (1499 ?-1546; Artist, Painter,
    Mantova, Roma)   FA
  (1499-1546)   AV
  (Architect, painter,
    draughtsman, 1499-1546)   CE
  (Italian artist, 1499-1546)   WC
  (Italian painter and architect,
    1499-1546)   GC
  (Italian painter, 1499-1546)   PR
  (Italian painter, architect,
    1492/99-1546)   BA
  (Italian, ca. 1499-1546)   JG
  Bibl: ▶Bolaffi; ▶Encic. italiana;
    ▶Encyc. world art; ▶Libr. of
    Congr. Name Auth. File;
    ▶Macmillan encyc. archts.; ▶Petit
    Robert 2; ▶Portoghesi, Diz. arch.
    e urbanistica; ▶RILA/BHA;
    ▶Thieme-Becker; ▶Witt checklist
  G. L. Romano   PR
  G. Romano   PR
  Giulio   AV PR
  Giulio di Pietro de' Gianuzzi   CE
  Giulio di Pietro de'Gianuzzi   GC
  Giulio Pippi   GC PR
  Giulio Pippi detto Giulio Romano   PR
  Giulio Pippi, Called, Giulio Romano   PR
  Giulio Pomano   PR
  Giulio Rom.   PR
  Giulio Rom.o   PR
Giulio Romano   FA GC JG PR
Giulio Romano (Giulio Pippi or
    di Pietro de Gianuzzi)   WC
  Giulio Romano, Giulio Pippi   AV
  Giulio Romo   PR
  J. Romano   PR
  Juilo Romano   PR
  Jul. Romano   PR
  Jules Romain   PR
  Julia Romana   PR
  Julia Romano   PR
  Julio Romano   PR
  Julles Romain   PR
  Jullio Romano   PR
  Marco Giulio Romano   PR
  Pippi, Giulio   AV CE FA GC
  Romain   PR
  Romano   PR
Romano, Giulio   AV CE FA GC PR
Giulio Romano, Giulio Pippi→see
  Giulio Romano (Giulio Pippi)
Giulio Romo→see Giulio Romano
  (Giulio Pippi)
Giunni, Piero *(Italian artist, 1912-)*   WC
Giunta di Tugio *(Italian, b.*
  Bacchereto)   JG
Giunta Pisano→see Giunta Pisano
  (Giunta Capitini)

Giunta Pisano (Giunta Capitini)   BA
  (Italian artist,
    op.c.1202-m.1255/67)   WC
  (Italian painter, act.1202, d.ca.
    1257)   BA
  (Italian, act.ca.1202-d.1255/67)   GC
  Bibl: ▶Bénézit; ▶Bolaffi; TCI
    Umbria; ▶Thieme-Becker; ▶Witt
    checklist
Giunta Pisano   GC
Giunta, Pisano   WC
Giunta, Pisano→see Giunta Pisano
  (Giunta Capitini)
Giunti family *(Italian printers, 15th-*
  16th c.)   BA
  Bibl: ▶Encic. italiana
Giunti, Domenico *(Italian architect,*
  painter, 1505-1560)   BA
  Bibl: ▶Avery period. idx.; ▶Bénézit;
    ▶Bolaffi; ▶Encic. italiana; ▶Encyc.
    world art; ▶Heydenreich, Arch.
    Italy; ▶Portoghesi, Diz. arch. e
    urbanistica; TCI Milano e laghi;
    ▶Thieme-Becker
Giuntini, Gilles Jean *(American*
  sculptor, b.1946)   BA
  Bibl: Purchase (NY, USA), SUNY,
    Area codes (1983)
Giuntotardi, Filippo   BA WC
  (Italian artist, 1768-1831)   WC
  (Italian painter, printmaker,
    sculptor, 1768-1831)   BA
  Bibl: ▶Bolaffi; ▶Thieme-Becker;
    ▶Witt checklist
Giura Longo, Tommaso→see Giura-
  Longo, Tommaso
Giura-Longo, Tommaso   BA
  (Italian architect, 20th c.)   BA
  (Italian architect, city planner)   AV
  Bibl: ARCHITECTURAL REVIEW
    CLXIV/977 (July 1978) p.56;
    ▶Avery period. idx.; Parametro,
    1984 Jan.-Mar., no.123-124, p.8
Giura Longo, Tommaso   AV
Giurgola, Romaldo   AV BA
  (American architect, 1920-)   AV
  (American architect, b.1920)   BA
  Bibl: ▶AIA Pro File; ▶Contemp.
    archts.; Williamstown (MA, USA),
    Williams Coll. Mus. of Art, Three
    architects... (1976)
Gius. C. d'Arpino→see Cesari,
  Giuseppe (Cavalier d'Arpino)
Gius. Chiari→see Chiari, Giuseppe
  Bartolomeo
Gius. Recco→see Recco, Giuseppe
Gius.e d'Arpino→see Cesari,
  Giuseppe (Cavalier d'Arpino)
Gius.e de Guida→see Giuseppe di
  Guido [Unidentified]
Gius.e di Rivera→see Ribera, Jusepe
  de (lo Spagnoletto)
Gius.e Passeri→see Passeri, Giuseppe
Gius.e Piscopo→see Piscopo,
  Giuseppe
Gius.e Recco→see Recco, Giuseppe

Gius.e Riviera→see Ribera, Jusepe de
  (lo Spagnoletto)
Gius.e Riviero→see Ribera, Jusepe de
  (lo Spagnoletto)
Gius:e Napolitano→see Piscopo,
  Giuseppe
Giuseffi, Girolamo *(American*
  designer, 20th c.)   BA
  Bibl: Indianapolis (IN, USA), Mus.
    Art, A rustle of silk (1979)
Giusepe di Riviera→see Ribera,
  Jusepe de (lo Spagnoletto)
Giuseppe Alpina→see Alpina,
  Giuseppe [Unidentified]
Giuseppe Angeli→see Angeli,
  Giuseppe
Giuseppe Antonio Ghedini→see
  Ghedini, Giuseppe Antonio
Giuseppe Arcimboldi→see
  Arcimboldi, Giuseppe
Giuseppe Avanzi→see Avanzi,
  Giuseppe
Giuseppe Baronti→see Baronti,
  Giuseppe [Unidentified]
Giuseppe Bartolomeo Chiari→see
  Chiari, Giuseppe Bartolomeo
Giuseppe Bazzani→see Bazzani,
  Giuseppe
Giuseppe Bernardino Bison→see
  Bison, Giuseppe Bernardino
Giuseppe Bonaiuti→see Bonaiuti,
  Giuseppe [Unidentified]
Giuseppe Bonati→see Bonatti,
  Giovanni (Il Ferraresino)
Giuseppe Bonito→see Bonito,
  Giuseppe
Giuseppe Bottani→see Bottani,
  Giuseppe
Giuseppe Buoccolo→see Brueghel,
  Jan, the elder
Giuseppe Cadenasso→see
  Cadenasso, Giuseppe
Giuseppe Cades→see Cades,
  Giuseppe
Giuseppe Calabrese [Unidentified]
  (Italian painter)   PR
  Bibl: Montecorvino inventory,
    Naples, 1698
Giuseppe Caletti→see Caletti,
  Giuseppe (il Cremonese)
Giuseppe Caletti (Il Cremonese)→see
  Caletti, Giuseppe (il Cremonese)
Giuseppe Carminno→see Carminno,
  Giuseppe [Unidentified]
Giuseppe Carmino→see Carminno,
  Giuseppe [Unidentified]
Giuseppe Casini→see Casini,
  Giuseppe [Unidentified]
Giuseppe Castellano→see Castellano,
  Giuseppe
Giuseppe Cesari→see Cesari,
  Giuseppe (Cavalier d'Arpino)
Giuseppe Chiari→see Chiari,
  Giuseppe Bartolomeo

Giuseppe Colzi de'Cavalcanti→see
Colzi, Giuseppe

Giuseppe Coppolo→see Coppolo,
Giuseppe [Unidentified]

Giuseppe Corentil→see Corentil,
Giuseppe [Unidentified]

Giuseppe Crespi, detto lo
Spagnoletto→see Crespi, Giuseppe
Maria (lo Spagnuolo)

Giuseppe d'Amato→see Amato,
Giuseppe d'

Giuseppe d'Arpino→see Cesari,
Giuseppe (Cavalier d'Arpino)

Giuseppe de Gobbis→see Gobbis,
Giuseppe de

Giuseppe de Guida→see Giuseppe di
Guido [Unidentified]

Giuseppe de Nittis→see Nittis,
Giuseppe de

Giuseppe de Quedo→see Quedo,
Giuseppe de [Unidentified]

Giuseppe de Ribera→see Ribera,
Jusepe de (lo Spagnoletto)

Giuseppe de Rivera→see Ribera,
Jusepe de (lo Spagnoletto)

Giuseppe del Moro→see Moro,
Giuseppe del

Giuseppe del Sole→see Sole, Giovan
Gioseffo dal

Giuseppe della Porta Salviati→see
Porta, Giuseppe (Giuseppe Salviati)

Giuseppe di Arpino→see Cesari,
Giuseppe (Cavalier d'Arpino)

Giuseppe di Guido→see Giuseppe di
Guido [Unidentified]

Giuseppe di Guido [Unidentified]
*(Unknown painter, act. 17th
century)*   **PR**
    Bibl: inventory of Carlo de
    Cardenas, dated 1699/12/23;
    inventory of Francesco Cavallino,
    dated 1677/05/29
    Gius.e de Guida   PR
    Giuseppe de Guida   PR
    Giuseppe di Guido   PR

Giuseppe di Luciano Fraccia→see
Frecha, José

Giuseppe di Ribera detto lo
Spagnoletto→see Ribera, Jusepe de
(lo Spagnoletto)

Giuseppe di Rivera→see Ribera,
Jusepe de (lo Spagnoletto)

Giuseppe di Rivero→see Ribera,
Jusepe de (lo Spagnoletto)

Giuseppe di Riviera→see Ribera,
Jusepe de (lo Spagnoletto)

Giuseppe di Riviero→see Ribera,
Jusepe de (lo Spagnoletto)

Giuseppe Dromatoro→see
Trombatore, Giuseppe

Giuseppe Episcopo→see Piscopo,
Giuseppe

Giuseppe Fagnani→see Fagnani,
Giuseppe

Giuseppe Farriello→see Farriello,
Giuseppe [Unidentified]

Giuseppe fiammengo→see Giuseppe
Fiammingo [Unidentified]

Giuseppe Fiammingo
[Unidentified] *(Unknown painter)* **PR**
    Bibl: Colonna inventory, Rome,
    1714
    Giuseppe fiammengo   PR

Giuseppe Filippo Liberati Marchi→see
Marchi, Giuseppe Filippo Liberati

Giuseppe Gambacciani→see
Gambacciani, Giuseppe
[Unidentified]

Giuseppe Gambarini→see Gambarini,
Giuseppe

Giuseppe Ghedini→see Ghedini,
Giuseppe Antonio

Giuseppe Ghezzi→see Ghezzi,
Giuseppe

Giuseppe Gricci→see Gricci,
Giuseppe

Giuseppe Grifoni→see Grisoni,
Giuseppe

Giuseppe Grisoni→see Grisoni,
Giuseppe

Giuseppe Grisson→see Grisoni,
Giuseppe

Giuseppe Iovine→see Iovine,
Giuseppe

Giuseppe Libera detto lo
Spagnoletto→see Ribera, Jusepe
de (lo Spagnoletto)

Giuseppe Macpherson→see
MacPherson, Joseph, James or
Giuseppe

Giuseppe Mafferson→see
MacPherson, Joseph, James or
Giuseppe

Giuseppe Magni→see Magni,
Giuseppe

Giuseppe Manfriani→see Manfriani,
Giuseppe [Unidentified]

Giuseppe Maria Crespi→see Crespi,
Giuseppe Maria (lo Spagnuolo)

Giuseppe Maria Crespi detto lo
Spagnolo→see Crespi, Giuseppe
Maria (lo Spagnuolo)

Giuseppe Marulli→see Marullo,
Giuseppe

Giuseppe Marullo→see Marullo,
Giuseppe

Giuseppe Mazzuoli (Il
Bastarolo)→see Mazzuoli,
Giuseppe (Bastarolo)

Giuseppe Mazzuoli detto il
Bastarolo→see Mazzuoli, Giuseppe
(Bastarolo)

Giuseppe Menabuoni→see
Menabuoni, Giuseppe

Giuseppe Montper→see Momper,
Joos de, the younger

Giuseppe Morullo→see Marullo,
Giuseppe

Giuseppe Napolitano→see Piscopo,
Giuseppe

Giuseppe Nobili→see Nobili,
Giuseppe [Unidentified]

Giuseppe Nogari→see Nogari,
Giuseppe

Giuseppe Nuvolone→see Nuvolone,
Giuseppe

Giuseppe Pace→see Pace, Giuseppe

Giuseppe Palizzi→see Palizzi,
Giuseppe

Giuseppe Panfilo→see Nuvolone,
Giuseppe

Giuseppe Parenti→see Parenti,
Giuseppe [Unidentified]

Giuseppe Pasquino→see Pasquino,
Giuseppe [Unidentified]

Giuseppe Passeri→see Passeri,
Giuseppe

Giuseppe Pennasilico→see
Pennasilico, Giuseppe

Giuseppe Perri→see Perri, Giuseppe
[Unidentified]

Giuseppe Piattoli→see Piattoli,
Giuseppe

Giuseppe Piscopo→see Piscopo,
Giuseppe

Giuseppe Pollio→see Pollio, Giuseppe
[Unidentified]

Giuseppe Porta→see Porta, Giuseppe
(Giuseppe Salviati)

Giuseppe Raggio→see Raggio,
Giuseppe

Giuseppe Recco→see Recco,
Giuseppe

Giuseppe Revera→see Ribera, Jusepe
de (lo Spagnoletto)

Giuseppe Ribera→see Ribera, Jusepe
de (lo Spagnoletto)

Giuseppe Ribera detto lo
Spagnoletto→see Ribera, Jusepe
de (lo Spagnoletto)

Giuseppe Ribera, detto lo
Spagnoletto→see Ribera, Jusepe
de (lo Spagnoletto)

Giuseppe Rivela→see Ribera, Jusepe
de (lo Spagnoletto)

Giuseppe Rivera→see Ribera, Jusepe
de (lo Spagnoletto)

Giuseppe Romei→see Romei,
Giuseppe

Giuseppe Roppoli→see Ruoppolo,
Giuseppe

Giuseppe Roppolo→see Ruoppolo,
Giuseppe

Giuseppe Ruoppoli→see Ruoppolo,
Giuseppe

Giuseppe Ruoppolo→see Ruoppolo,
Giuseppe

Giuseppe Sacconi→see Sacconi,
Giuseppe

Giuseppe Salviati→see Porta,
Giuseppe (Giuseppe Salviati)

Giuseppe Scampato→see Scarpato,
Giuseppe [Unidentified]

Giuseppe Scarpato→see Scarpato, Giuseppe [Unidentified]

Giuseppe Scono→see Scono, Giuseppe [Unidentified]

Giuseppe Simonelli→see Simonelli, Giuseppe

Giuseppe Tassone→see Tassoni, Giuseppe

Giuseppe Tassoni→see Tassoni, Giuseppe

Giuseppe Tomassi→see Tommasi, Giuseppe

Giuseppe Tommasi→see Tommasi, Giuseppe

Giuseppe Tommasi Scolare di Carlo Cignani→see Tommasi, Giuseppe

Giuseppe Trombatore→see Trombatore, Giuseppe

Giuseppe [Unidentified] *(Unknown painter)* **PR**
Bibl: April 10, 1813, lot 9, Christie's; Doria inventory, Naples, 17th c.
Gioseppe **PR**

Giuseppe Vermiglio→see Vermiglio, Giuseppe

Giuseppe Vernet→see Vernet, Joseph

Giuseppe Verrazzani→see Verrazzani, Giuseppe [Unidentified]

Giuseppe Vincenzino→see Vincenzino, Giuseppe

Giuseppe Zais→see Zais, Giuseppe

Giuseppe Zocchi→see Zocchi, Giuseppe

Giuseppe Zola→see Zola, Giuseppe

Giuseppi Fidanza→see Fidanza, Giuseppe

Giuseppina [Unidentified] *(Unknown painter)* **PR**
Bibl: anonymous inventory, Florence, 17th c.

Giuseppini→see Cesari, Giuseppe (Cavalier d'Arpino)

Giuseppini, Filippo *(Italian artist, 1815-1862)* **WC**

Giuseppino→see Cesari, Giuseppe (Cavalier d'Arpino)

Giuseppino d'Arpino→see Cesari, Giuseppe (Cavalier d'Arpino)

Giuseppo Ribera→see Ribera, Jusepe de (lo Spagnoletto)

Giussani, Roberto *(Italian architect)* **AV**
Bibl: Domus, 1986 July-Aug., no. 674, p.4

Giust'→see Suttermans, Justus

Giusti→see Suttermans, Justus

Giusti da Pistoja, Gregorio *(Italian artist, 1732-p.1756)* **WC**

Giusti, Alessandro *(Italian sculptor in PRT, 1715-1799)* **BA**
Bibl: ▶Bénézit; ▶Thieme-Becker

Giusti, Antonio *(Italian painter, 1624-1705)* **PR**
Bibl: ▶Thieme-Becker
Ant. Giusti **PR**
Antonio Giusti **PR**

Giusti, Giovan Francesco *(Abbot and architect in Lucca, whose only known activity was in connection with the restoration of Lucca Cathedral and project in Segromigno)* **AV**
Bibl: Prospettiva n.19, 1979, p.52-53

Giusti, Guglielmo *(Italian artist, 1824-p.1916)* **WC**

Giusti, T. *(Italian artist, 19th cent.)* **WC**

Giusti, Tommaso **AV BA**
(Italian architect, painter in Germany, 1644-1729) **BA**
(Venetian architect, worked in Hanover, Germany, ca.1644-1729) **AV**
Bibl: ▶Thieme-Becker

Giusti, Ugo *(Italian architect, 1880-1926)* **AV**
Bibl: Architecture and urbanism, 1984 Dec., no.12(171), p.11; L'Arca, 1989 Jan., no.23, p.10

Giustiniani family *(Italian ceramists, 18th-19th cs.)* **BA**
Bibl: Conti, Maiolica, pp.179, 181; ▶Honey, Euro. ceramic; ▶Mankowitz, Encyc. pott. & porc.; Napoli (ITA), Mus. Ceramica, Maoilica del '700 (1980); ▶Thieme-Becker

Giustiniani, Michelangelo *(Italian engineer, act.1761-1788)* **BA**
Bibl: Fiengo Gioffredo e Vanvitelli nei palazzi dei Casacalenda; Fiengo, Preti della Missione (1990); Reclams, NEAPEL, 279; TCI Napoli e dintorni, p.258

Giustiniano→see Justinian, I, Emperor of the East

Giustiniano d'Arpino→see Cesari, Giuseppe (Cavalier d'Arpino)

Giustiniano, Ignazio *(Italian tile maker, act.1729)* **BA**
Bibl: Napoli nobilissima, XVII/6 (Nov.-Dec. 1978) pp.206-231

Giustiniano, Matteo *(Italian tile maker, act.1724)* **BA**
Bibl: Napoli nobilissima, XVII/6 (Nov.-Dec. 1978) pp.206-231

Giustino di Gherardino da Forlì *(Italian illuminator, act.1365)* **GC**
Bibl: Rome (ITA), Pal. di Venezia, Miniatura (1953), p.247

Giusto→see Suttermans, Justus

Giusto d'Andrea di Giusto **GC**
(Italian artist, 1440-1496) **WC**
(Italian painter, 1440-1496) **GC**
Bibl: ▶Thieme-Becker

Giusto, d'Andrea di Giusto **WC**

Giusto da Firenze *(Italian goldsmith, act.1457)* **BA**
Bibl: ▶Bessone-Aurelj, Scult. & arch. ital.; Mancini, CORTONA (1909), p.61-63; TCI Toscana, p.438; ▶Thieme-Becker

Giusto da Guanto→see Joos van Gent (Joos van Wassenhove)

Giusto de' Menabuci→see Menabuoi, Giusto di Giovanni de'

Giusto de' Menabuoi→see Menabuoi, Giusto di Giovanni de'

Giusto de'Menabuoi→see Menabuoi, Giusto di Giovanni de'

Giusto di Andrea di Giusto→see Andrea di Giusto

Giusto di Francesco da Settignano *(Italian sculptor, act.1427)* **BA**
Bibl: Parronchi, FILIPPO BRUNELLESCHI, I, 239-255

Giusto di Francesco del Castello dell' Incisa *(Italian cabinetmaker, decorative artist, act.1470-1474)* **BA**
Bibl: ▶Bénézit; ▶Thieme-Becker

Giusto di Giovanni de'Menabuoi→see Menabuoi, Giusto di Giovanni de'

Giusto di Menabuoi→see Menabuoi, Giusto di Giovanni de'

Giusto family→see Juste family

Giusto Fiamengo→see Suttermans, Justus

Giusto fiammengo→see Suttermans, Justus

Giusto Guanto→see Joos van Gent (Joos van Wassenhove)

Giusto Praisler→see Preissler, Johann Justin

Giusto Subtermans→see Suttermans, Justus

Giusto Sutterman→see Suttermans, Justus

Giusto, d'Andrea di Giusto→see Giusto d'Andrea di Giusto

Giusto, Felice (Giuseppe Giusti) *(Italian artist, 1872-)* **WC**

Giusto, Giovanni di→see Juste, Jean I

Giustoni Menescardi→see Menescardi, Giustino

Giutti, G. *(Italian artist, 19th cent.)* **WC**

Givenchy, Hubert de **AV BA**
(French couturier, b.1927) **BA**
(French designer) **AV**
Bibl: House beautiful, 1988 July, v.130, no.7, p.35; ▶New Columbia encyc.

Gizolphi→see Ghisolfi, Giovanni

Gizycki, Paweł *(Painter and architect, Poland, d.1762)* **AV**
Bibl: ▶Thieme-Becker

Gjerding, Per *(Danish architect, Lyngby, 1926-1989)* **AV**
Bibl: Arkitekten, 1989 Mar.28, v.91, no.6, p.144 [dates]; ▶Danske Arkitekters Landsforbund, 1988-89

Glab, Charles (*American architect, Dubuque, IA*)   **AV**
    Bibl: Iowa architect, 1986 Sept-Oct., v.34, no.5, p.18
Glabbeeck → see Glabbeeck, Gysbert van
Glabbeeck, Gladbeek or Gladbek, Jan van → see Glabbeeck, Jan van
Glabbeeck, Gysbert van (*Dutch painter, act. 1630-1648*)   **PR**
    Bibl: ▶Thieme-Becker
    Glabbeeck   PR
    Gladbeeck   PR
    Gladtbeeck   PR
    Gysbert van Glabbeeck   PR
Glabbeeck, Jan van   **BA GC**
    (*Dutch artist, op.1653-m.c.1686*) WC
    (*Dutch painter, act.1630, d.1687?*)   BA
    (*Dutch painter, d. bef.1634-1686*)   GC
    Bibl: ▶Bénézit; ▶Thieme-Becker; ▶Wurzbach, NLD Künst.-Lex.
Glabbeeck, Gladbeek or Gladbek, Jan van   **WC**
    Gladbek, Jan van   GC
Glabman, Thom (*American painter, 20th c.*)   **BA**
    Bibl: ▶Art Index; Arts Mag. LVII (2 Oct 1982), 24-25
Glackens → see Glackens, William James
Glackens, Louis (*American illustrator, 20th c.*)   **BA**
    Bibl: Wilmington (Del, USA), Delaware Art Mus., City life..., 1980
Glackens, William → see Glackens, William James
Glackens, William J. → see Glackens, William James
Glackens, William James   **BA GC PR WC WI**
    (*American artist, 1870-1938*) WC WI
    (*American painter, 1870-1938*) BA PR
    (*American, 1870-1938*)   GC
    Bibl: ▶Cummings, Contemp. Amer. artists; ▶Fielding's Amer. ptrs., suppl.; ▶RILA/BHA; ▶Witt checklist
    Glackens   PR
    Glackens, William   PR
    Glackens, William J.   PR
    William James Glackens   PR
Gladbeeck → see Glabbeeck, Gysbert van
Gladbek, Jan van → see Glabbeeck, Jan van
Gladstone, Gerald (*Canadian sculptor, b.1929*)   **BA**
    Bibl: ▶Artists Canada; ▶Intl. dir. arts
Gladstone, Thomas (*British artist, 1803-1832*)   **WC WI**
Gladtbeeck → see Glabbeeck, Gysbert van

Gladwell, Rodney   **WC WI**
    (*British artist, 20th cent.*)   WC
    (*British artist, b.1934*)   WI
Gladysz, Christopher (*German artist, 19th cent.*)   **WC**
Glaeser, Gotthelf Lebrecht (*German artist, 1784-1851*)   **WC**
Glain, Léon   **BA**
    (*French artist, op.1749-1778*)   WC
    (*French painter, miniaturist, act. 1752-1778*)   BA
    (*French, act.1749-1778*)   GC
    Bibl: ▶Bénézit; Schidlof, Miniature in Europe; ▶Thieme-Becker; ▶Witt checklist
Glain, Leon or Pascal(?)   **GC**
Glain, Lion or Pascal(?)   **WC**
Glain, Leon or Pascal(?) → see Glain, Léon
Glain, Lion or Pascal(?) → see Glain, Léon
Glaister, Christopher G. (*British city planner, has worked in New York City since 1970's*)   **AV**
    Bibl: ▶AIA Pro File, 1987-88
Glaize, Auguste Barthélemy   **BA GC WC**
    (*French artist, 1807-1893*)   WC
    (*French painter, 1807-1893*)   GC
    (*French painter, lithographer, 1807-1893*)   BA
    Bibl: ▶Bellier, Artistes fran.; ▶Bénézit; ▶Busse, Maler u. Bildhauer 19. Jahr.; ▶Havlice, Idx. art. bio.; ▶Thieme-Becker
Glaize, Léon   **PR**
    (*French artist, 1842-1932*)   WC
    (*French painter, 1842-1932*) GC PR
    Bibl: ▶Bénézit; NY Met catalogue; ▶Thieme-Becker
Glaize, Leon (Pierre Paul Lion)   **WC**
    Glaize, Pierre Paul Leon   PR
Glaize, Pierre Paul-Léon   **GC**
    Leon Glaize   PR
Glaize, Leon (Pierre Paul Lion) → see Glaize, Léon
Glaize, Pierre Paul Leon → see Glaize, Léon
Glaize, Pierre Paul-Léon → see Glaize, Léon
Glanber → see Glauber, Johannes (Polidoro)
Glankoff, Sam (*American painter, printmaker, 1894-1982*)   **BA**
    Bibl: Goldman, ARTNEWS, LXXXI, 7 (Sept 1982) 70-71; ▶Intl. dir. exh. artists, 1982; New Brunswick, Rutgers U., June v.2. art mus, SAM GLANKOFF (1894-1982) (1984); UC Santa Barbara cat. sheets
Glantschnigg, Ulrich (*German artist, 1661-1722*)   **WC**
Glantzman, Judith (*American painter, 20th c.*)   **BA**
    Bibl: Haaren, P.E., in ARTS MAG LVII/5 (Jan 1983

Glanville, Roy (*British artist, op. 1950-1959*)   **WI**
Glardon, Charles Louis Francois (Glardon-Leubel) (*Swiss artist, 1825-1887*)   **WC**
Glarner → see Glarner, Fritz
Glarner, Fritz   **BA PR WC**
    (*American artist, 1899-*)   WC
    (*American painter, 1899-1972*) BA PR
    Bibl: ▶Art Index, v.21; Clark; ▶Cummings, Contemp. Amer. artists; ▶Havlice, Idx. art. bio.; ▶Phaidon 20c. art; ▶RILA/BHA; ▶Seuphor, Abstract ptg.; ▶WW Amer. Art, 1973; ▶WWW Amer., v.5
    Fritz Glarner   PR
    Glarner   PR
Glasco, Joseph → see Glasco, Joseph M.
Glasco, Joseph M.   **BA**
    (*American artist, 1925-*)   WC
    (*American artist, b.1925*)   WI
    (*American painter, sculptor, b.1925*)   BA
    Bibl: ▶MoMA libr. cat.; ▶WW Amer. Art, 1978
Glasco, Joseph   **WC WI**
Glaser, Anthony (*Swiss artist, 1490-1551*)   **WC**
Glaser, Hans Wolff (*German artist, op.c.1560*)   **WC**
Glaser, Milton   **AV BA**
    (*American designer, NYC, 1929-*)   AV
    (*American printmaker, illustrator, b.1929*)   BA
    Bibl: ▶Libr. of Congr. Name Auth. File; ▶WW Amer. Art, 1976
Glaser, Peter (*Austrian architect*)   **AV**
    Bibl: Bauforum, 1988, v.21, no. 126, p.49
Glaser-Hinder, April (*Australian sculptor, painter, 20th c.*)   **BA**
    Bibl: Art International XXI/4 July-Aug 1977, p.35
Glasgow, Alexander (*British artist, op.1859-1884*)   **WC WI**
Glasgow, Edwin (*British artist, 1874-1955*)   **WC WI**
Glasgow, Robert   **WC WI**
    (*British artist, op.c.1828*)   WC
    (*British artist, op.circa 1828-*)   WI
Glasier, John (*English glass painter, act.1472-ca.1500*)   **BA**
    Bibl: Marks, Crown in glory, (07) p.37
    Browne, John   BA
Gläsker, Horst (*German artist, 20th c.*)   **BA**
    Bibl: Aachen (DEU), Neue Gal. Samm. Ludwig, New Fauves (1980)
Glasmeier, Ernst Otto (*West German architect, Gelsenkirchen*)   **AV**
    Bibl: Deutsches Architektenblatt, 1988 Nov.1, v.20, no.11, p.1563

Glass, Alan *(Canadian painter, printmaker, b.1932)* **BA**
Bibl: ▶Artists Canada; Montreal (Que, CAN), Mus. d'art contemp., Dessins & surréalisme (1979)

Glass, Hans *(American architect, San Francisco, Calif)* **AV**
Bibl: Design solutions, 1987 Fall, v.7, no.3, p.22

Glass, Ingo *(West German sculptor, b.1941)* **BA**
Bibl: Regensburg (DEU), Ostdeutsche Gal. Regensburg, Ingo Glass, 1985-86

Glass, James William *(American artist, 1825-1857)* **WC WI**

Glass, John Hamilton **WC WI**
(British artist, 1820-1885) WI
(British artist, op.c.1920) WC

Glass, Peter *(Australian landscape architect)* **AV**
Bibl: Landscape Australia, 1985 Winter, v.7, no.2, p.128

Glass, Rhoda **WC WI**
(British artist, 20th cent.) WC
(British artist, op.20th c.) WI

Glass, William Mervyn *(British artist, 1885-1965)* **WC WI**

Glässer, Alexander *(German printmaker, act.1738-1743)* **BA**
Bibl: ▶Bénézit; Jahrb. Staat. Kunst. Dresden, XIII (1981) pp.101-105; ▶Thieme-Becker

Glasser, David E. *(American architect, Milwaukee, Wisc)* **AV**
Bibl: Kenchiku bunka, 1989 Feb., v.44, no.508, p.95

Glassie, Henry H. *(American lawyer and preservationist, 1914-)* **AV**
Bibl: Preservation news, 1987 Sept., v.27, no.9, p.11

Glasson, Lancelot Myles **WC WI**
(British artist, 1894-) WC
(British artist, b.1894) WI

Glatz, Oszkár **BA WC**
(Hungarian artist, 1872-) WC
(Hungarian painter, printmaker, 1872-1958) BA
Bibl: ▶Bénézit; Revai Nagy Lex.; ▶Thieme-Becker; ▶Uj magyar lexikon; ▶Vollmer, Künst.-Lex. 20. Jhr.

Glatz, Theodor *(Austrian painter, 1818-1871)* **BA**
Bibl: ▶Bénézit; ▶Thieme-Becker

Glaube→see Glauber, Johannes (Polidoro)

Glauber→see Glauber, Johannes (Polidoro)

Glauber, Diana *(Dutch painter, 1650-ca.1721)* **PR**
Bibl: ▶Thieme-Becker
Diana Glauber PR
juffrouw Globers PR

Glauber, Gheorghe *(Rumanian artist, 1921-)* **WC**

Glauber, Hans *(German painter, sociologist, b.1933)* **BA**
Bibl: Lyon (FRA), Mus. des B.-A., Artistes francofortois contemp. (1975); ▶WW Arts DEU

Glauber, Johannes→see Glauber, Johannes (Polidoro)

Glauber, Johannes (Polidoro) **BA GC PR**
(Dutch artist, 1646-c.1726) WC
(Dutch painter and draughtsman, 1646-ca.1726) GC
(Dutch painter, 1646-ca.1726) PR
(Dutch painter, printmaker, 1646-ca.1726) BA
Bibl: ▶Bernt, Neth. ptrs. 17c.; Getty Photo Study Coll.; ▶Nieuw NLD biog. woord.; ▶RILA/BHA; ▶Thieme-Becker
Clauber PR
Glanber PR
Glaube PR
Glauber PR
Glauber, Johannes PR

Glauber, Johannes or Jan (Polidoro or Polidoor) **WC**
Glaubert PR
Glober PR
Glouber PR
J. Glauber PR
Johannes Glauber PR

Glauber, Johannes Gottlieb *(German artist, c.1656-1703)* **WC**

Glauber, Johannes or Jan (Polidoro or Polidoor)→see Glauber, Johannes (Polidoro)

Glaubert→see Glauber, Johannes (Polidoro)

Glaubitz, Jan Krzysztof *(Polish architect, act.1732-1765)* **BA**
Bibl: Drema, Biuletyn Hist. Sztuki XLII/1 (1980) 63-75; Kowalczyk, Polish Art Studies 8 (1984) 20; Pałubicki, in BIULETYN HISTORII SZTUKI XLII, 1 (1980) 76

Glaude d'Loraine→see Claude Lorrain
Glaudo Lorineses→see Claude Lorrain

Glaukion of Corinth *(Greek painter, Hellenistic (3rd-1st c BC))* **GC**
Bibl: ▶Robertson, Greek art, p.584

Glaukos *(Greek sculptor, 6th c BC)* **GC**
Bibl: Avery, New Century classical hbk., p. 499

Glaukytes **GC**
Bibl: ▶Beazley, Attic bl.-fig. vase-ptrs.

Glazbrook, Howard *(American architect, Dallas, Tex)* **AV**
Bibl: Texas architect, 1987 Sept.-Oct., v.37, no.5, p.14

Glazebrook, Hugh de Twenebrokes **WC WI**
(British artist, 1870-1935) WC
(British artist, 1870-1937) WI

Glazier or Glisier, P. *(French artist, op.c.1754)* **WC**

Glazier, Louise M. **WC WI**
(British artist, 20th cent.) WC
(British artist, op.1899-1912) WI

Glazunov, Il'ja **BA**
(Russian artist, 1921-) WC
(Russian painter, b.1930) BA
Bibl: ▶Fogg Mus. Libr. cat.; NYTimes (31 Aug 1977) p.31; NYTimes 31 Aug 1977, p.31

Glazunov, Ilya **WC**
Glazunov, Ilya→see Glazunov, Il'ja

Gleadah, Joseph *(British artist, op. 19th c.)* **WI**

Gleason, Duncan→see Gleason, Joe Duncan

Gleason, Herbert Wendell *(American, 1855-1937)* **JG**

Gleason, Joe Duncan **PR WI**
(American artist, 1881-1959) WI
(American painter, 1881-1959) PR
Bibl: ▶WWW Amer. art
Gleason, Duncan PR
Joe Duncan Gleason PR

Gleb-Krakotchwil, Maria *(Polish artist, 20th cent.)* **WC**

Gleber, Conrad *(American artist, b.1949)* **BA**
Bibl: Santa Barbara (CA, USA), UCSB Art Mus., Dark/light..., 1980

Glebova, Arina *(Russian ceramist, painter, 20th c.)* **BA**
Bibl: Dek Isss SSSR Aug 1976, p.6-8

Gleckman, William B. *(American architect, New York City)* **AV**
Bibl: NYC phone bk., 1987

Gledhill, Blaine→see Larson, Blaine

Gledhill, Carolyn Even *(American, d. 1935 (also Carolyn & Edwin Gledhill))* **JG**

Gledhill, William Edwin *(American, d. 1976 (also Carolyn & Edwin Gledhill))* **JG**

Gledstanes, Elsie *(British artist, 1891-op.1940)* **WI**

Gleeson, James *(American painter, 20th c.)* **BA**
Bibl: ▶MoMA libr. cat.

Gleeson, James *(Australian artist, 1915)* **WC**

Gleeson, Joseph Michael *(American artist, b.1861)* **WI**

Gleghorn, Thomas **GC WC**
(Australian artist, 1925-) WC
(British, b.1925) GC
Bibl: ▶Witt checklist

Glehn, Jane de→see De Glehn, Jane Erin

Glehn, Jane Erin de→see De Glehn, Jane Erin

Glehn, Oswald von **WC WI**
(British artist, 1858-) WC
(British artist, 1858-op.1908) WI

Glehn, Wilfred Gabriel de→see De Glehn, Wilfred Gabriel

Glehn, Wilfred Gabriel von →see De Glehn, Wilfred Gabriel

Gleichen, Feodora Georgina Maud
(British sculptor, 1861-1922)   **BA**
    Bibl: ▶Bénézit; ▶Dict. natl. biog.;
    ▶Grant, Brit. sculptors;
    ▶Thieme-Becker

Gleichen-Russworm, Heinrich Ludwig, Freiherr von →see Gleichen-Russwurm, Heinrich Ludwig, Freiherr von Gleichen-Russwurm

Gleichen-Russwurm, Heinrich Ludwig, Freiherr von Gleichen-Russwurm   **BA**
    (German artist, 1836-1901)   **WC**
    (German painter, printmaker, 1836-1901)   **BA**
    Bibl: ▶Brockhaus Enzyk.;
    ▶Thieme-Becker; ▶Witt checklist

Gleichen-Russworm, Heinrich Ludwig, Freiherr von   **WC**

Gleichmann, Otto   **BA WC**
    (German artist, 1887-)   **WC**
    (German painter, graphic artist, 1887-1963)   **BA**
    Bibl: Hamann; ▶Phaidon 20c. art;
    ▶Vollmer, Künst.-Lex. 20. Jhr.

Gleim, Eduard *(German painter, 1812-1899)*   **BA**
    Bibl: ▶Bénézit; ▶Thieme-Becker

Gleizes →see Gleizes, Albert

Gleizes, Albert   **BA GC PR WC**
    (French artist, 1881-1953)   **WC**
    (French painter, 1881-1953)   **PR**
    (French painter, author, 1881-1953)   **BA**
    (French, 1881-1953)   **GC**
    Bibl: ▶Bénézit; ▶Encyc. world art;
    ▶Fogg Mus. Libr. cat.;
    ▶McGraw-Hill dict. art; ▶Oxford
    comp. art; ▶RILA/BHA; ▶Vollmer,
    Künst.-Lex. 20. Jhr.; ▶Witt
    checklist
    Albert Gleizes   **PR**
    Gleizes   **PR**
    Gleizes, Albert Leon   **PR**
Gleizes, Albert Leon →see Gleizes, Albert

Gleizes, Philippe *(French artist, -a. 1801)*   **WC**

Glembrandt, Per *(Swedish architect)*   **AV**
    Bibl: Arkitektur: the Swedish
    review of architecture, 1988 Apr.,
    v.88, no.3, p.6

Glen, Graham   **WC WI**
    (British artist, 20th cent.)   **WC**
    (British artist, op.1897-1925)   **WI**

Glen, Robert *(American sculptor)*   **AV**
    Bibl: Architecture: the AIA
    journal, 1985 Dec., v.74, no.12,
    p.61

Glenavy, Beatrice Moss, Baroness →see Elvery, Beatrice Moss

Glendening, Alfred Augustus I   **WI**
    (British artist, op.1861-, d.1903)   **WI**
    (British artist, op.1861-1903)   **WC**

Glendenning or Glendinning the Younger, Alfred   **WC**

Glendening, Alfred Augustus II
    (British artist, 1861-1907)   **WI**

Glendening, Ronald *(British artist, b.1926)*   **WI**

Glendenning or Glendinning the Younger, Alfred →see Glendening, Alfred Augustus I

Glenk, G. *(German artist, 18th cent.)*   **WC**

Glennie, Arthur *(British artist, 1803-1890)*   **WC WI**

Glennie, Ian *(American architect)*   **AV**
    Bibl: Cite, 1986 Summer, p.8

Glennie, John David *(British artist, 1796-1874)*   **WC WI**

Glessner, John Jacob *(American manufacturer, 1843-1936)*   **BA**
    Bibl: ▶WWW Amer.

Glette, Erich *(German painter, 1896-1980)*   **BA**
    Bibl: Munich (BRD),
    Residensmuseum, Der Mahler Emil
    Glette..., 1982; Roh; ▶Vollmer,
    Künst.-Lex. 20. Jhr.

Glew, Edward Lees *(British artist, 1817-1870)*   **WI**

Gleyre →see Gleyre, Charles

Gleyre, Charles   **BA GC PR**
    (Swiss artist, 1806-1874)   **WC**
    (Swiss painter in FRA, 1806-1874)   **BA**
    (Swiss painter, 1806-1874)   **GC PR**
    Bibl: ▶Bénézit; ▶Brockhaus Enzyk.;
    ▶Encyc. world art; Getty Photo
    Study Coll. (Ptgs.); ▶Larousse
    grande encyc.; Novotny, Ptg. &
    sculp. Europe 1780-1880;
    ▶RILA/BHA; ▶Schweiz.
    Künst.-Lex.; ▶Thieme-Becker
    Charles Gleyre   **PR**
    Gleyre   **PR**

Gleyre, Charles (Mare Charles Gabriel)   **WC**
    Gleyre, Marc Gabriel Charles   **PR**
    Gleyre, Marc-Gabriel-Charles   **GC**
Gleyre, Charles (Mare Charles Gabriel) →see Gleyre, Charles
Gleyre, Marc Gabriel Charles →see Gleyre, Charles
Gleyre, Marc-Gabriel-Charles →see Gleyre, Charles

Glicenstein, Enoch (Henryk)
    (Russian artist, 1870-1942)   **WC**

Glick, Rani *(American sculptor, b.1956)*   **BA**
    Bibl: Framingham (MA, USA),
    Danforth Mus., Abstract art New
    Engl. (1983)

Glick, Richard *(American interior designer, New York and Boston)*   **AV**
    Bibl: Restaurant and hotel design,
    1986 Sept., v.8, no.7, p.52

Glick, Robert *(Interior designer, planner)*   **AV**
    Bibl: Interior design, 1985 Feb.,
    v.56, no.2, p.198

Glickher, Johann Georg →see Glyckher, Johann Georg

Glickman, Michael *(British architect, London)*   **AV**
    Bibl: ▶RIBA members, 1983

Glicone →see Glykon

Gliddon, Anne   **WC WI**
    (British artist, op.1840-)   **WI**
    (British artist, op.c.1840)   **WC**

Gliemann →see Gliemann, Albert

Gliemann, Albert *(German painter, 1822-1871)*   **PR**
    Bibl: ▶Thieme-Becker
    Albert Gliemann   **PR**
    Gliemann   **PR**
    Gliemann, Philipp Albert   **PR**
Gliemann, Philipp Albert →see Gliemann, Albert

Glier, Mike *(American painter, b.1953)*   **BA**
    Bibl: ▶Intl. dir. exh. artists; Oberlin
    (OH, USA), Oberlin Coll., Allen
    Mem. Art Mus., Art & social
    change (1983)

Gliha, Oton *(Yugoslav artist, 1914-)*   **WC**

Glimes →see Glimes, Pierre de
Glimes, P. de →see Glimes, Pierre de

Glimes, Pierre de   **WI**
    (British artist, op.c.1780-1793)   **WC**
    (British artist, op.circa 1780-)   **WI**
    (British, act. ca.1780-1793)   **GC**
    (Flemish painter, act. 1750-1800)   **PR**
    Bibl: ▶Thieme-Becker; ▶Witt
    checklist
    Glimes   **PR**

Glimes, P. de   **GC PR WC**
    P. de Glimes   **PR**

Glimette *(French, active 19th century)*   **JG**

Glindoni, Henry Gillard *(British artist, 1852-1913)*   **WC WI**

Glink, Franz Xaver *(German artist, 1795-1873)*   **WC**

Glintenkamp, Hendrick   **WI**
    (American artist, -1946)   **WC**
    (American artist, 1887-1946)   **WI**

Glintenkamp, Hendrik   **WC**
Glintenkamp, Hendrik →see Glintenkamp, Hendrick

Glintenramp, Hendrik *(American painter, 1887-1946)*   **BA**
    Bibl: ▶MoMA libr. cat.; ▶WWW
    Amer., v.2

Glinz, Theo *(Swiss artist, 1890-)*   **WC**

Glinzer, Karl *(German artist, 1802-1878)*   **WC**

Gliri, Nicola *(Italian artist, op.1658-1680)*   **WC**

Glisenti, Achille　　　GC WC
　(Italian artist, 1906-)　　WC
　(Italian painter, d.1906)　GC
　Bibl: ▶Thieme-Becker
Glitsch, Val *(American architect)*　AV
Gliwa, Stanislas *(Polish artist, act.*
　1929-1936)　　BA
　Bibl: Biuletyn Historii Sztuki, 3
　(1974) p.303ff.
Gloag, Isobel Lilian *(British artist,*
　1865-1917)　　WC WI
Glober → see Glauber, Johannes
　(Polidoro)
Glockendon family *(German*
　illuminators, 15th-16th cs.)　BA
　Bibl: ▶Encyc. world art;
　▶Thieme-Becker
Glockendon the Elder, Georg or
　Jorg → see Glockendon, Georg (the
　Elder)
Glockendon the Elder, Nicolaus → see
　Glockendon, Nikolaus
Glockendon, Albrecht (the
　Younger)　　　　GC
　(German artist, op.1547-1568)　WC
　(German painter, act.1547-1568)　GC
　Bibl: ▶Witt checklist
Glockendon, Glockenthon,
　Glockenton etc., the
　Younger, Albrecht　　WC
Glockendon, Albrecht, the elder
　(German printmaker, 15th c.)　BA
　Bibl: ▶Shestack, 15c. engravings,
　nos. 121-122; ▶Strutt, Dict.
　engravers; ▶Thieme-Becker
Glockendon, Georg (the Elder)　GC
　(German artist, op.1484-m.
　1514)　　　WC
　(German draughtsman, d.1514)　GC
　Bibl: ▶Bénézit; ▶Thieme-Becker
Glockendon the Elder, Georg or
　Jorg　　　　WC
　Glockenthon, Georg (the Elder)　GC
　Glogkenthon, Jorg (the Elder)　GC
Glockendon, Glockenthon,
　Glockenton etc., the Younger,
　Albrecht → see Glockendon,
　Albrecht (the Younger)
Glockendon, Nikolaus　　BA GC
　(German artist, op.c.1514-m.
　1534)　　　WC
　(German illuminator, d.1534)　BA GC
　Bibl: ▶Bradley, Miniaturists;
　▶D'Ancona, Miniaturistes;
　▶RILA/BHA; ▶Thieme-Becker
Glockendon the Elder, Nicolaus　WC
Glockenthon, Georg (the Elder) → see
　Glockendon, Georg (the Elder)
Glocker or Glockler, Johann
　(German artist, op.1637-1646)　WC
Glöckner, Emil *(German painter,*
　b.1868)　　　BA
　Bibl: ▶Bénézit; ▶Thieme-Becker

Glöckner, Hermann *(German*
　painter, sculptor, b.1889)　　BA
　Bibl: Dresden (DDR),
　Kupferstichkabinett.GLOCKNER:...
　(1989); Frommhold BILDENDE
　KUNST 1, 1984, p.28-30;
　▶Gorenflo, Bild. Künstler; Guide
　exh. artists: Sculp.; ▶Intl. dir. exh.
　artists, 1983; ▶Vollmer,
　Künst.-Lex. 20. Jhr.
Gloeckler, Raymond *(American*
　painter, printmaker, b.1928)　　BA
　Bibl: Milwaukee (Wis, USA), Art
　Center, Raymond Gloeckler...,
　1980
Gloeden, Wilhelm von　　BA
　(German photographer in ITA,
　1856-1931)　　BA
　(German, 1856-1916)　　JG
　Bibl: OCLC; ▶Parry, Photo idx.;
　PRINT COLLECTOR'S NEWSLETTER,
　IX/6 (J-F 1979), p.198-201
Gloeden, Wilhelm von (Baron)　JG
Gloeden, Wilhelm von (Baron) → see
　Gloeden, Wilhelm von
Gloersen, Jacob *(Norwegian artist,*
　1852-1912)　　WC
Glogkenthon, Jorg (the Elder) → see
　Glockendon, Georg (the Elder)
Glogowsky, Georg *(Czech artist,*
　1777-1838)　　WC
Glogstein, J.W. *(Danish artist, op.c.*
　1835)　　　WC
Glombiza *(East German printmaker,*
　20th c.)　　　BA
　Bibl: Dresden (DEU), Galerie Kunst
　der Zeit, Glas (1985)
Gloriefloren, Lambert *(German(?)*
　artist, op.c.1762)　　WC
Gloss, Isaak Jakob → see Clauce, Isaak
　Jakob
Gloss, Ludwig　　　BA WC
　(Austrian sculptor, painter,
　1851-1903)　　BA
　(German artist, 1851-1903)　WC
　Bibl: ▶Bénézit; ▶Fuchs, Öst. Maler
　19. Jahrh.; ▶Thieme-Becker
Glossner, M. *(German, active*
　Munich, Germany 1880s)　　JG
Glötzle, Ludwig *(German painter,*
　illustrator, 1847-1929)　　BA
　Bibl: ▶Bénézit; ▶Thieme-Becker;
　▶Vollmer, Künst.-Lex. 20. Jhr.
Glouber → see Glauber, Johannes
　(Polidoro)
Gloutchenko, N.P. *(Russian artist,*
　20th cent.)　　WC
Glover → see Glover, John
Glover, George → see Glover, George I
Glover, George I　　　WI
　(British artist, 1618-op.1653)　WI
　(British artist, op.1625-1653)　WC
Glover, George　　　WC
Glover, George II *(British artist, op.*
　19th c.)　　　WI

Glover, John　　BA GC PR WC WI
　(British artist, 1767-1849)　WC WI
　(British painter, 1767-1849)　BA PR
　(British, 1767-1849)　　GC
　Bibl: ▶Dict. natl. biog.;
　▶Thieme-Becker; ▶Witt checklist
　Glover　　　　PR
　John Glover　　　PR
Glover, William　　GC WC WI
　(British artist, op.1808-1839)　WC WI
　(British, act.1808-1839)　GC
　Bibl: ▶Johnson, Brit. artists;
　▶Thieme-Becker; ▶Witt checklist
Glowacki, Jan Nepomucen *(Polish*
　artist, 1802-1847)　　WC
Gluck *(British painter, 1895-1978)*　BA
　Bibl: APOLLO, v.97, May 1973,
　p.515; BURLINGTON v.115, June
　1973, p.411; ▶Johnson, Brit.
　artists; Times (14 Jan 1978) p.16
Glück, Harry *(Austrian architect,*
　Vienna)　　　AV
　Bibl: ▶Verzeich. Öst. Ziviltech.
Glück, Heidi *(American painter,*
　b.1944)　　　BA
　Bibl: ARTFORUM, XVI, Apr 1978,
　p.62-3; ARTS, LII, Mar 1978,
　p.92-2; New York (NY, USA),
　Guggenheim Mus., 19 artists
　(1981)
Gluck, Louis T.E. → see Gluck, Louis
　Théodore Eugène
Gluck, Louis Théodore Eugène　BA
　(French painter, 1820-1898)　BA
　(German artist, 1820-1898)　WC
　Bibl: ▶Bellier, Artistes fran.;
　▶Bénézit; ▶Busse, Maler u.
　Bildhauer 19. Jahr.;
　▶Thieme-Becker
Gluck, Louis T.E.　　WC
Gluck, M.　　　WC WI
　(British artist, 1895-)　　WC
　(British artist, b.1895)　　WI
Gluck, Peter L. *(American architect)*　AV
　Bibl: ▶AIA Pro File, 1983
Gluck, Walter *(American artist in*
　NLD, b.1929)　　BA
　Bibl: Amsterdam (NLD), Stedelijk
　Mus., Who Needs the Pacific
　Ocean (1977)
Glückher, Johann Georg → see
　Glyckher, Johann Georg
Glücklich, Simon　　BA WC
　(Australian painter, 1863-1943)　BA
　(German artist, 1863-1943)　WC
　Bibl: ▶Bénézit; Hamburg (DEU),
　Kunsthalle, Meister des 19 Jahrh.
　(1969); ▶Thieme-Becker
Gluckman, Richard *(American*
　architect)　　　AV
　Bibl: Abitare, 1985 May, no.234,
　p.70
Gluckmann → see Gluckmann, Grigory

Gluckmann, Grigory   **BA PR WC**
(Russian artist, 1898-)   WC
(Russian painter in USA, 1898-
1973)   BA
(Russian painter, 1898-1973)   PR
Bibl: ▶Met. Mus. Art libr. cat.;
▶MoMA libr. cat.; Univ of Arizona
MA catalogue; ▶WWW Amer. art
Gluckmann   PR
Grigory Gluckmann   PR
Glueckman, Joan (American artist,
20th c.)   **BA**
Bibl: Feminist art jrnl., V/2 (Sum.
1976) pp.36-37; NYC phone bk.
Gluhov, V.A. (Russian artist, 20th c.)   **BA**
Bibl: Moscow (RUS), Assc. Comm.
Graphic Artists, 2nd exh. (1979)
Glume, Friedrich Christian (German
sculptor, 1714-1752)   **BA**
Bibl: ▶Bénézit; ▶Thieme-Becker
Glume, Johann Gottlieb   **GC WC**
(German artist, 1711-1778)   WC
(German draughtsman and
printmaker, 1711-1778)   GC
Bibl: ▶Bénézit
Glunder→see Lundens, Gerrit
Gluth, John (American architect,
partner in firm with Rob. W.
Quigley)   **AV**
Bibl: ▶AIA Pro File, 1980
Glyckher, Johann Georg   **GC**
(German artist, op.1691-1697)   WC
(German draughtsman, act.
1691-1697)   GC
Bibl: Getty Photo Study Coll.;
▶Thieme-Becker; ▶Witt checklist
Glickher, Johann Georg   GC
Glückher, Johann Georg   **GC WC**
Glycon→see Glykon
Glykon (Sculptor, post 100/ante 200-
post 220/ante 270)   **CE**
Glicone   CE
Glycon   CE
Glykon of Athens (Roman copyist,
2nd c AD)   **GC**
Bibl: ▶Brilliant, Anc. Greeks,
p.270; Havelock, Hellenistic Art
Glymes, Jan III van (Flemish, act.ca.
1500)   **BA**
Bibl: Kunstreisbk
Glyn Warren Philpot→see Philpot,
Glyn Warren
Glyn, Susan (British sculptor, painter
in FRA, 20th c.)   **BA**
Bibl: Glyn, Susan, LEONARDO,
"The development of my
sculpture..., XIII, 4 autumn 1980
265
Glynn, John (British artist, op.1891-
1940)   **WI**
Gmelin, Georg (Johann Georg)
(German artist, 1810-1854)   **WC**

Gmelin, Wilhelm Friedrich   **BA WC**
(German artist, 1760-1820)   WC
(German printmaker, 1760-
1820)   BA
Bibl: ▶Encyc. world art; ▶Neue
deutsche Biog.; ▶Thieme-Becker
Gmür, Silvia (Swiss architect, Basel)   **AV**
Bibl: ▶Schweiz. Ingen. u. Archit.,
1984-1985
Gnaccarini, Otello (Italian painter,
b.1957)   **BA**
Bibl: Macerata (I), Pinacoteca
Comunale GNACCARINI..., 1982
Gnaiger, Roland (Austrian architect,
1951-)   **AV**
Bibl: Ottagono, 1988 Mar., p.20
Gnaios (Greek gem engraver, act.
2nd half 1st c BC)   **GC**
Bibl: Treasure Houses of Britain,
p.287
Gnamuš, Gustav (Yugoslav painter,
b.1941)   **BA**
Bibl: Ljubljana (Yu), Mala galerija,
GUSTAV Gnamuš, 1977
Gnass, Peter (German sculptor,
painter in CAN, b.1936)   **BA**
Bibl: ▶Artists Canada; ▶Bénézit;
Guide exh. artists: N. Amer. ptrs.
Gnecchi-Ruscone, Aldo (Italian
architect)   **AV**
Bibl: Area, 1986 Nov.-Dec., v.6,
no.31, p.11
Gnecchi-Ruscone, Marco (Italian
architect)   **AV**
Bibl: Area, 1986 Nov.-Dec., v.6,
no.31, p.11
Gnehm, Peter (German artist, 1712-
1799)   **WC**
**Gnocchi, Giovanni Pietro
(Gnocheus)** (Italian artist, op.
1579-1603)   **WC**
Gnoli, Domenico   **BA WC**
(Italian artist, 1933-)   WC
(Italian painter in USA, 1933-
1970)   BA
Bibl: ▶Bolaffi; ▶Phaidon 20c. art;
▶Vollmer, Künst.-Lex. 20. Jhr.
Gnosis (Greek mosaicist, 4th c BC
(late))   **GC**
Bibl: ▶Brilliant, Anc. Greeks, p.250
Gnudtzmann, Johannes Emil (1837-
1922)   **AV**
Goad, Derek (British architect)   **AV**
Goalen, Martin John (British
architect, London)   **AV**
Bibl: ▶RIBA members, 1987
Goateed Siren Painter   **JG**
Gobaerts, Hendrick→see Govaerts,
Hendrick
Gobaut, Gaspard   **BA GC WC**
(French artist, 1814-1882)   WC
(French painter, 1814-1882)   BA GC
Bibl: ▶Bénézit; ▶Thieme-Becker
Gobban→see Goubau, Antoon
Gobbau'→see Goubau, Antoon
Gobbis→see Gobbis, Giuseppe de

Gobbis, Giuseppe→see Gobbis,
Giuseppe de
Gobbis, Giuseppe de   **BA GC PR**
(Italian artist, op.1772-1783)   WC
(Italian painter, ca.1730-
1787)   BA GC PR
Bibl: Arte veneta, XXXII (1978)
pp.366-370; ▶Bolaffi; ▶RILA/BHA,
1986; ▶Thieme-Becker; ▶Witt
checklist
Giuseppe de Gobbis   PR
Gobbis   PR
Gobbis, Giuseppe   **GC PR WC**
Gobbo→see Bonzi, Pietro Paolo
(Gobbo dei Carracci)
Gobbo→see Solari, Cristoforo
Gobbo Caracci→see Bonzi, Pietro
Paolo (Gobbo dei Carracci)
Gobbo Carache→see Bonzi, Pietro
Paolo (Gobbo dei Carracci)
Gobbo Caracic→see Bonzi, Pietro
Paolo (Gobbo dei Carracci)
Gobbo Carracci→see Bonzi, Pietro
Paolo (Gobbo dei Carracci)
Gobbo Carree→see Bonzi, Pietro
Paolo (Gobbo dei Carracci)
Gobbo de Caracci→see Bonzi, Pietro
Paolo (Gobbo dei Carracci)
Gobbo de Caraggi→see Bonzi, Pietro
Paolo (Gobbo dei Carracci)
Gobbo de Carracci→see Bonzi, Pietro
Paolo (Gobbo dei Carracci)
Gobbo dei Caracci→see Bonzi, Pietro
Paolo (Gobbo dei Carracci)
Gobbo del Caraggi→see Bonzi, Pietro
Paolo (Gobbo dei Carracci)
Gobbo del Carracci→see Bonzi,
Pietro Paolo (Gobbo dei Carracci)
Gobbo delli Caracci→see Bonzi,
Pietro Paolo (Gobbo dei Carracci)
Gobbo delli frutti→see Bonzi, Pietro
Paolo (Gobbo dei Carracci)
Gobbo detto Carraci→see Bonzi,
Pietro Paolo (Gobbo dei Carracci)
Gobbo di Caracci→see Bonzi, Pietro
Paolo (Gobbo dei Carracci)
Gobbo di Caraggi→see Bonzi, Pietro
Paolo (Gobbo dei Carracci)
Gobbo di Carani→see Bonzi, Pietro
Paolo (Gobbo dei Carracci)
Gobbo di Roma→see Bonzi, Pietro
Paolo (Gobbo dei Carracci)
Gobbo dj Caracci→see Bonzi, Pietro
Paolo (Gobbo dei Carracci)
Gobbo, Giovanni Battista il→see
Sangallo, Giovanni Battista da
(Gobbo)
Gobbo, Il→see Sangallo, Giovanni
Battista da (Gobbo)
Gobel Johann Emanuel→see Göbel,
Johann Emanuel
Gobel, Angilbert Wunibald→see
Göbel, Angilbert Wuniblad

Göbel, Angilbert Wuniblad   **BA**
   (German artist, 1821-1882)   WC
   (German printmaker, painter,
     1821-1882)   BA
     Bibl: ▶Bénézit; ▶Thieme-Becker
Gobel, Angilbert Wunibald   **WC**
Goebel, Angilbert Wunibald   **WC**
Göbel, Bernd *(German sculptor,*
   b.1942)   **BA**
     Bibl: Arta, 28/4-5 (Apr-May 1980)
     58-76
Göbel, Johann Emanuel   **GC**
   (German artist, 1720-1759)   WC
   (German draughtsman, 1720-
     1759)   GC
     Bibl: ▶Thieme-Becker
Gobel Johann Emanuel   **WC**
Göbel, Jürgen *(Finnish(?) architect)*   **AV**
     Bibl: Architektur + Wettbewerbe,
     1986 Sept., no.127, p.12
Göbell, Gerrit Hendrik *(Dutch*
   draughtsman, 1786-1833)   **GC**
     Bibl: ▶Thieme-Becker
Gobellinus, Johannes *(Italian scribe,*
   act.1459)   **GC**
     Bibl: Paris, 10 siècles, no.142
Gober, Robert *(American sculptor,*
   b.1954)   **BA**
     Bibl: Cooke, ARTSCRIBE
     INTERNATIONAL, 65 (Sept-Oct
     1987), p.55-59; Decter, ARTS, LX
     (Dec 1985), p.124; Heartney, ART
     PRESS, 146 (Apr 1990), 36-39; NY
     ART NOW: SAACHI COLLECTION,
     (1987)
Gobert→see Gaubert, Pierre
Gobert, Alfred Thompson *(French*
   painter, ceramist, 1822-1895)   **BA**
     Bibl: ▶Thieme-Becker
Gobert, Henri Toussaint *(French*
   artist, op.1831-1881)   **WC**
Gobert, Paul de *(Belgian painter,*
   b.1945)   **BA**
     Bibl: ▶Dict. biog. artistes belges;
     Loze, P., in KUNSTFORUM INT'L
     57 (Jan 1983) 135
Gobert, Philippe de *(Belgian artist,*
   b.1952)   **BA**
     Bibl: Artnews LXXXI 4 Apr '82
     144-7
Gobert, Pierre→see Gaubert, Pierre
Gobert, Thomas *(French architect,*
   ca.1630-1703)   **BA**
     Bibl: ▶Bauchal, Archtes. fran.;
     Congrès archéologique de France
     135e (1977, Champagne);
     Laurent, Mons. Hist. Fran., 145
     (Jun.-Jul. 1986), p.24;
     ▶Thieme-Becker
Gobiet, Armand *(French, 20th c.)*   **BA**
Gobillard, Paule *(French painter,*
   1867-1946)   **BA**
     Bibl: ▶Bénézit; Fourreau. Berthe
     morisot; Juynball; ▶Thieme-Becker
Gobin, Daniel *(American designer,*
   Columbus, IN)   **AV**
     Bibl: Earth shelter living, 1985
     Jan.-Feb., no.37, p.15

Gobin, Michel   **GC WC**
   (French artist, op.1681)   WC
   (French, act.1681)   GC
     Bibl: ▶Witt checklist
Gobius, Hendrik Anthony Frederik
   Agathus *(Dutch artist, 1815-1899)*   **WC**
Gobl, Friedrich *(Austrian architect,*
   Krems)   **AV**
     Bibl: ▶Verzeich. Öst. Ziviltech.,
     1984
Göbl-Wahl, Camilla *(Australian*
   painter, b.1871)   **BA**
     Bibl: ▶Bénézit; ▶Fuchs, Öst. Maler
     19. Jahrh.; ▶Thieme-Becker;
     ▶Vollmer, Künst.-Lex. 20. Jhr.
Goblain, Antoine Louis   **GC WC**
   (French artist, 1779-p.1838)   WC
   (French, 1779-aft.1838)   GC
     Bibl: ▶Witt checklist
Goble, Anthony *(British artist, 20th*
   c.)   **BA**
     Bibl: Arts Council GBR, Welsh
     Comm., Some recent purchases
     (1979)
Goble, Robert *(Irish silversmith)*   **BA**
     Bibl: Antiques, CXX/4 (Oct. 1981)
     pp.915-921
Goble, Steven *(Dutch artist, 1749-*
   1799)   **WC**
Goble, Warwick *(British artist, op.*
   circa 1893-, d.1943)   **WI**
Gobo del Caracci→see Bonzi, Pietro
   Paolo (Gobbo dei Carracci)
Gobo, Georges   **WC WI**
   (American artist, 1876-)   WC
   (American artist, b.1876)   WI
Gobrecht, Christian *(Engraver,*
   1785-1844)   **WI**
Gočár, Josef   **AV BA**
   (Czech architect, 1880-1945)   BA
   (Czechoslovak architect, 1880-
     1945)   AV
     Bibl: Czech functionalism 1918-
     1938 (1987); ▶Portoghesi, Diz.
     arch. e urbanistica; ▶Vollmer,
     Künst.-Lex. 20. Jhr., v.1
Godaert Kamper→see Kamper,
   Godaert
Godano, Lia *(Italian sculptor,*
   b.1927)   **BA**
     Bibl: Coloquio Arte, June 1981
Godard, Octave   **AV BA**
   (French landscape architect)   AV
   (French landscape architect,
     20th c.)   BA
     Bibl: ▶Avery period. idx., 1987;
     Country life, 1987 Jan.22, v.181,
     no.4, p.66
Godart, André *(1933-)*   **AV**
Godart, Thomas *(British artist, op.*
   circa 1852-)   **WI**
Goday, Josep *(Spanish architect,*
   1882-1936)   **AV**
     Bibl: AA files, 1987 Spring, no.14,
     p.63
Godbarge, Henri *(architect)*   **BA**

Godbold, Samuel Barry→see
   Godbold, Samuel Berry
Godbold, Samuel Berry   **WI**
   (British artist, op.1842-1875)   WI
   (British artist, op.c.1842-1875)   WC
Godbold, Samuel Barry   **WC**
Godby, James *(British artist, op.*
   1790-1820)   **WC WI**
Godchain *(French artist, 19th cent.)*   **WC**
Goddard family *(American*
   cabinetmakers, 18th-19th cs.)   **BA**
     Bibl: ▶Honour, Cabinet mkrs.
Goddard, Beatrice Romaine,
   Miss→see Brooks, Romaine
Goddard, Charles *(British artist, op.*
   1853-)   **WI**
Goddard, Eliza *(British artist, op.*
   1884-1897)   **WI**
Goddard, Emerson *(American,*
   1817-1893, active 1860s,
   daguerreotypist)   **JG**
Goddard, George Bouverie   **BA WI**
   (British artist, 1832-1886)   WI
   (British painter, 1832-1886)   BA
     Bibl: ▶Bénézit; ▶Dict. natl. biog.;
     ▶Johnson, Brit. artists;
     ▶Thieme-Becker
Goddard, J.→see Goddard, John
Goddard, John   **WI**
   (British artist, op.1811-1842)   WC WI
Goddard, J.   **WC**
Goddard, John *(American*
   cabinetmaker, 1723/24-1785)   **BA**
     Bibl: Complete encyc. antiques;
     ▶Honour, Gold- & silversmiths;
     Nagel, Amer. furniture
Goddard, Louis Charles *(British*
   artist, op.1901-1921)   **WI**
Goddard, Thomas *(British artist, op.*
   1779-1788)   **WI**
Goddé, Jules *(French painter,*
   illustrator, 1812-1876)   **BA**
     Bibl: ▶Bénézit; ▶Thieme-Becker
Godding, Emil Hendrik Karel
   Passchaal *(German artist, 1841-*
   1898)   **WC**
Godeau, André   **AV BA**
   (17th century French landscape
     architect, probably related to
     Siméon Godeau)   AV
   (French landscape architect, act.
     ca.1671)   BA
     Bibl: Aikema, Arte veneta, XXXIV
     (1980) pp.127-137
Godeau, Siméon   **AV BA**
   (French landscape architect,
     b.1632, act.1696)   BA
   (Garden designer, 17th century)   AV
     Bibl: Jrnl. of Garden Hist. V/4
     (Oct.-Dec. 1985) 322;
     ▶Thieme-Becker

Godefroid de Huy   **BA GC**
 *(early Netherlandish goldsmith,
 enamelist, act.1146-ca.1174)*   BA
 *(Flemish goldsmith and
 silversmith, act. ca.1145)*   GC
 Bibl: ▶Bénézit; ▶Encyc. world art;
 Helbig: L'ART MOSAN, p.38-44;
 ▶Honour, Gold- & silversmiths;
 Lasko, Ars sacra; ▶Thieme-Becker;
 V & A libr. cat.
Godefroid, Marie Eleonore→see
 Godefroy, Marie Eléonore
Godefroy   **GC WC**
 (French artist, op.1482)   WC
 (French painter, 15th century)   GC
 Bibl: ▶Bénézit
Godefroy le Batave→see Godofredus
 Batavus
*Godefroy or Godefroid, Maria
 Eleanore→see* Godefroy, Marie
 Eléonore
Godefroy or Godefroij, Jan *(Dutch
 artist, 1882-1958)*   **WC**
Godefroy, Abraham Nikolaas
 (Dutch architect, 1822-1899)   **BA**
 Bibl: ▶Nieuw NLD biog. woord.,
 v.9
**Godefroy, Adrien Pierre Francois
 (Godefroy jeune)** *(French artist,
 1777-1805)*   **WC**
Godefroy, C. *(French painter, 19th
 century)*   **GC**
 Bibl: ▶Bénézit
Godefroy, E. *(French artist, op.
 1856)*   **WC**
Godefroy, François   **BA WC**
 (French artist, 1743-1819)   WC
 (French engraver, 1743-1819)   BA
 Bibl: ▶Bénézit; ▶Thieme-Becker
**Godefroy, Francois Ferdinand
 Joseph** *(French artist, 1729-1788)*   **WC**
Godefroy, H.C. *(French, active
 1870s)*   **JG**
Godefroy, Jean   **GC**
 (French artist, 1771-1839)   WC
 (French, 1771-1839)   GC
 Bibl: ▶Thieme-Becker; ▶Witt
 checklist
Godefroy, Jean or John   **WC**
Godefroy, Jean François *(French
 painter, 18th century)*   **GC**
 Bibl: ▶Bénézit
Godefroy, Jean or John→see
 Godefroy, Jean
Godefroy, Maria Eleanore→see
 Godefroy, Marie Eléonore

Godefroy, Marie Eléonore   **BA**
 (French artist, 1778-1849)   WC
 (French painter, 1778-1849)   BA
 (French, 1778-1849)   GC
 Bibl: ▶Bellier, Artistes fran.;
 ▶Bénézit; ▶Dict. biog. fran.; Getty
 Photo Study Coll. (Ptgs.);
 ▶Petteys, Women artists;
 ▶Thieme-Becker; ▶Witt checklist
 Godefroid, Marie Eleonore   GC
**Godefroy or Godefroid, Maria
 Eleanore**   **WC**
Godefroy, Maria Eleanore   **GC**
Godefroy, Maximilian   **AV BA**
 (fl.1806-1824)   AV
 *(French architect in USA, act.
 1806-1824)*   BA
Godefroy, P.L. de Larive→see La
 Rive, Pierre Louis de
Goderanus, monk of Stavelot
 *(Netherlandish scribe, act. late
 11th century)*   **GC**
 Bibl: Watson, British Library,
 p.321
Goderis→see Goderis, Hans
Goderis, Hans   **GC PR WC**
 (Dutch artist, op.1622-1638)   WC
 *(Dutch painter, act. 1625/38, d.
 1643)*   PR
 *(Dutch painter, act.1622-d. bef.
 1643)*   GC
 Bibl: Gaillard inventory 1639;
 Getty Photo Study Coll.;
 ▶Thieme-Becker; ▶Witt checklist
 Goderis   PR
 Goderus   PR
 Hans Goderis   PR
Goderus→see Goderis, Hans
Godet *(French, active 1860s-1870s)*   **JG**
Godet, Christine *(French architect)*   **AV**
 Bibl: AMC, 1987 Oct., no.17,
 p.43
Godet, Julius   **WC WI**
 (British artist, op.1844-1884)   WC
 (British artist, op.1844-1894)   WI
Godewyk, Margaret van→see
 Godewyk, Margaretha van
Godewyk, Margaretha van   **BA GC**
 (Dutch artist, 1627-1677)   WC
 (Dutch painter, 1627-1677)   BA GC
 Bibl: Houbraken, Groote
 Schouburgh der nederlantsche
 Kunstschilders ... 1753, deel 1;
 ▶Thieme-Becker; ▶Wurzbach, NLD
 Künst.-Lex.
Godewyk, Margaret van   **WC**
Godfrey Kneller→see Kneller,
 Godfrey, baronet
Godfrey Schalcken→see Schalcken,
 Godfried
Godfrey Skalken→see Schalcken,
 Godfried
Godfrey, Betsy *(Builder and interior
 designer, Florida)*   **AV**
 Bibl: Builder, 1985 Aug., v.8,
 no.8, p.93

Godfrey, Eliza *(British silversmith,
 act. from 1741)*   **GC**
 Bibl: ▶Grimwade, London
 goldsmiths, 1982
 Godfrey, Elizabeth   GC
Godfrey, Elizabeth→see Godfrey,
 Eliza
Godfrey, Jane *(American artist,
 b.1948)*   **WI**
Godfrey, Richard Bernard   **WI**
 (British artist, 1728-op.1794)   WI
 (British artist, 1728-p.1794)   WC
**Godfrey, Richard Bernard (not
 Rene)**   **WC**
*Godfrey, Richard Bernard (not
 Rene)→see* Godfrey, Richard
 Bernard
Godfrey, Robert *(American painter,
 20th c.)*   **BA**
 Bibl: Arts Mag. LIV/7 (Mar 1980),
 p.12
Godfrey, Walter Hindes   **AV BA**
 *(British architect, author, 1881-
 1961)*   BA
 (English architect, 1881-1961)   AV
 Bibl: ▶Avery obit. idx.;
 ▶RILA/BHA, cum. idx 1-5; ▶Who
 was who [GBR], 1961
Godfridus→see Gofridus
Godfried Schalken→see Schalcken,
 Godfried
Godhaux *(French artist, 19th cent.)*   **WC**
Godiancure→see Ferrari, Gaudenzio
Godie, Lee *(American painter, 20th
 c.)*   **BA**
 Bibl: Bonesteel, Art in Amer.,
 LXXIII/2 (Feb. 1985) pp.128-134
Godin, Charles *(French porcelain
 répareur, act.1770-1816)*   **GC**
 Bibl: ▶Brunet, Sèvres
Godin, Edme-François *(French
 silversmith, d.1760, master 1747)*   **GC**
 Bibl: ▶Nocq, Poinçon de Paris
Godin, Raymonde *(Canadian
 painter, b.1930)*   **BA**
 Bibl: ▶Artists Canada; ▶Natl. Gall.
 Canada libr. cat.
Göding, Andreas   **GC**
 (German artist, 1570-1625)   WC
 *(German draughtsman, ca.1570-
 ca.1625)*   GC
 Bibl: ▶Thieme-Becker
Goeding, Andreas   **WC**
 Götting, Andreas   GC
*Goding, Goddeck, Goddigen, Gotting
 etc., the Elder, Heinrich→see*
 Göding, Heinrich, the elder
Göding, Heinrich (the Elder)→see
 Göding, Heinrich, the elder

Göding, Heinrich, the elder — BA WC
(German artist, 1531-1606) WC
(German painter, printmaker, 1531-1606) BA
(German, 1531-1606) GC
Bibl: ▶Allgem. Deut. Biog.; ▶Bénézit; ▶Thieme-Becker; ▶Witt checklist

Goding, Goddeck, Goddigen, Gotting etc., the Elder, Heinrich WC
Göding, Heinrich (the Elder) GC
Godinho de Almeida, Maria Manuel *(Portuguese architect)* AV
Bibl: Domus, 1984 Nov., no.655, p.14

Godio, Paolo *(Italian architect, 1949-)* AV
Bibl: Controspazio, 1985 Jan.-June, v.16, no.1-2, p.38

Godivier, Jean-Louis *(French architect)* AV
Bibl: Techniques et architecture, 1988 Dec.-1989 Jan., no.381, p.34

Gödl-Brandhuber, Lilli *(Australian painter, graphic artist, sculptor, b.1875)* BA
Bibl: ▶Bénézit; ▶Thieme-Becker; ▶Vollmer, Künst.-Lex. 20. Jhr.

Godla, Joseph *(American craftsman, b.1955)* BA
Bibl: Colorado Springs (CO, USA), Fine Arts Ctr., Woodworking in the Rockies (1982)

Godlevsky, Ivan Ivanovich *(Russian artist, 20th cent.)* WC

Godley, Frederick A. *(American architect, d.1961)* AV

Godó, Ramon *(Spanish architect, Barcelona)* AV
Bibl: Quaderns d'arquitectura i urbanisme, 1984 Jan.-Mar., no. 160, p.102

Godofredus Batavus BA GC
(early Netherlandish illuminator in FRA, act.1516-1526) BA
(Netherlandish illuminator, act. 1516-1526) GC
Bibl: ▶Bénézit; ▶Bradley, Miniaturists; ▶D'Ancona, Miniaturistes; Getty Photo Study Coll. (Medieval); Kren, Ren. ptg. in mss., index; Orth, Fr. ms. illum.; ▶RILA/BHA; ▶Thieme-Becker

Batavus, Godofredus GC
Godefroy le Batave GC
Godon, François Louis *(French clockmaker, act.1787-1790)* BA
Bibl: ▶Baillie, Watch- & clockmkrs.; ▶Britten, Old clocks

Godor *(French artist, 20th cent.)* WC
Godou [Unidentified] *(Unknown painter)* PR
Bibl: (August 3, 1814, lot 16, Ballantyne)

Godward→see Godward, John William
Godward, John William BA GC JG PR WC WI
(British artist, 1861-1922) WI
(British artist, op.1887-1905) WC
(British painter, 1861-1922) BA PR
(British, act.1887-1905) GC
(English, 1861-1922) JG
Bibl: ▶Bénézit; ▶Johnson, Brit. artists; ▶Thieme-Becker; ▶Waters, Brit. artists; ▶Witt checklist; ▶Wood, Victorian ptrs.

Godward PR
John William Godward PR
Godwin, Edward William AV BA
(1833-1886) AV
(British architect, designer, 1833-1886) BA
Bibl: ▶Dict. natl. biog.; ▶Encyc. world art; ▶Hitchcock, Arch. 19 & 20cs; ▶Macmillan encyc. archts.; ▶Thieme-Becker

Godwin, Fay *(British photographer, b.1931)* BA
Bibl: Arts Council GBR, Welsh Comm., Fay Godwin, Arthur Williamson (1977); COUNTRY LIFE, V.158, Nov 1975, p.1456

Godwin, George AV BA
(British architect, antiquary, 1815-1888) BA
(English architect, archaeologist and journalist, ed. of The Builder; son of George Godwin, Sr. (1789-1863), 1813-1888) AV
Bibl: ▶Colvin, Brit. archts.; ▶Dict. natl. biog.; ▶Macmillan encyc. archts.

Godwin, Henry *(British tile manufacturer, 1828-1910)* AV
Bibl: Journal of the Tiles of Architectural Ceramics Society, 1982, v.1, p.8

Godwin, James WC WI
(British artist, op.1846-, d.1876) WI
(British artist, op.1846-m.1876) WC

Godwin, Judith Whitney *(American painter, designer, 20th c.)* BA
Bibl: ▶WW Amer. Art, 1980

Godwin, Margery *(British artist, b.1910)* WI
Godwin, Mary *(British artist, 1887-1960)* WC WI
Godwin, William AV BA
(British brick and tile maker, 1813-1883) AV
(British tile manufacturer, 1813-1883) BA
Bibl: Austwick, THE DECORATED TILE, 75; Barnard, VICT CERAMIC TILES, 37, 160; Greene, IND. ARCH REV, V, 3 (autumn 1981) 241; Journal of the Tiles of Architectural Ceramics Society, 1982, v.1, p.8

Godwin-Austin, Henry Haversham *(British artist, op.1903-1907)* WI
Godyn or Goddyn, Abraham→see Godyn, Abraham
Godyn or Goddyn, Pieter Matthias *(Flemish artist, 1752-1811)* WC
Godyn, Abraham BA
(Dutch artist, op.c.1680-1723) WC
(Flemish painter, act.ca.1679-ca. 1724) BA
Bibl: ▶Bénézit; ▶Biog. Nat. Belgique; ▶Thieme-Becker

Godyn or Goddyn, Abraham WC
Godyn, Izaak *(Flemish painter, act. 1688-1712)* BA
Bibl: ▶Bénézit; ▶Thieme-Becker

Goebel, Angilbert Wunibald→see Göbel, Angilbert Wuniblad
Goebel, Carl *(German artist, 1824-1899)* WC
Goebel, Carl Peter *(German artist, 1791-1823)* WC
Goebel, Carol *(American sculptor, 20th c.)* BA
Bibl: ARTS MAG, LIX (Mar 1985), p.68; Marter, ARTS MAG, LXII (Oct 1987), p.96

Goebel, Otto Julius *(German painter, 1865-1903)* BA
Bibl: ▶Bénézit; ▶Thieme-Becker

Goebel, Renate *(German sculptor, b.1934)* BA
Bibl: Baden-Baden (BRD), Staatliche Kunsthalle. Besucher der Kunsthalle: Renate Goebel, Bildwerke und zeichnungen, 1976; ▶Bénézit; ▶MoMA libr. cat.

Goebeler, Elise *(German painter, 1847-1913)* BA
Bibl: ▶Bénézit; ▶Thieme-Becker

Goebertus, Billy *(Colombian architect, Bogotá)* AV
Bibl: Proa, 1988 Feb., no.368, p.14

Goebertus, Willem AV
Goebertus, Willem→see Goebertus, Billy
Goecke, Irma *(German textile designer, 1885-1976)* BA
Bibl: Anz. des Germ. Nationalmus. (1977); ▶WW Arts DEU

Goedaert or Godaard Johannes→see Goedaert, Johannes

Goedaert, Johannes   **BA GC**
(Dutch artist, c.1620-1668)   WC
(Dutch naturalist, painter, 1617-
1668)   BA
(Dutch painter, 1620-1668)   PR
(Dutch painter, ca.1620-1668)   GC
Bibl: Gaillard inventory 1639;
Getty Photo Study Coll.;
Landwehr, Buchillus. 18. Jahrh.,
pp.190-191; ▶Thieme-Becker;
▶Witt checklist; ▶Wurzbach, NLD
Künst.-Lex.

Goedaert or Godaard Johannes   WC
Goedart   PR
Goedart, Johannes   **PR**
Hans Goederen   PR
Johannes Goedart   PR
Goedart→see Goedaert, Johannes
Goedart, Johannes→see Goedaert,
Johannes

Goede, Jules de (Dutch artist,
1937-)   WC

Goede, Kees de (Dutch sculptor,
painter, b.1954)   BA
Bibl: Imanse, de Nederlandse
Identiteit in de Schilderkunst na
1945, p.243; ▶Intl. dir. exh.
artists, 1982

Goede, Paul (Dutch artist, 20th c.) BA
Bibl: Eindhoven(NLD),Stedel.Van
Abbemus.,PAUL
GOEDE,1988(RILA/NLD)

Goede, Piet (Dutch sculptor,
b.1918)   BA
Bibl: Amsterdam (NLD), Mus.
Fodor, Uitdrukkingen van... (1978)

Goedeljee, Jan (Dutch
photographer, 1824-1905)   BA
Bibl: Antiek, IX/8 (Mar. 1975) pp.
786-797
Goedhart, Jan C. A. →see Goedhart,
Jan Catharinus Adriaan

Goedhart, Jan Catharinus Adriaan
(Dutch painter, 1893-1975)   GC
Bibl: from postcard; ▶Vollmer,
Künst.-Lex. 20. Jhr.
Goedhart, Jan C. A.   GC

Goedike, Shirl (American painter,
b.1923)   BA
Bibl: ▶WW Amer. Art, 1978
Goeding, Andreas→see Göding,
Andreas

Goedschalksz., Jacobus Kops   **GC WC**
(Dutch artist, 1736-1773)   WC
(Dutch draughtsman, 1736-
1773)   GC
Bibl: ▶Witt checklist
Kops, Jacobus   GC

Goedvriend, Theo (Dutch painter,
b.1879)   GC
Bibl: ▶Bénézit

Goehle, Gerhard (Swedish architect,
Goteborg, 1932-)   AV
Bibl: ▶Svenska Ark. Riks., 1987

Goehner, Hans Werner (German
architect, 1943-)   AV
Bibl: Das Kunstwerk, n.3-4, Sept.
1983, p.123

Goeje, Pieter de   **GC WC**
(Dutch artist, 1779-1859)   WC
(Dutch draughtsman, 1789-
1859)   GC
Bibl: ▶Thieme-Becker

Goeller, Charles Louis (American
artist, 1901-1955)   WI
Goemare, Goeimare or Goeymare,
Joos→see Goemare, Joos

Goemare, Joos   GC
(Flemish artist, c.1575-1618)   WC
(North Netherlandish painter,
1575-1610)   GC
Bibl: ▶Thieme-Becker

**Goemare, Goeimare or
Goeymare, Joos**   WC
Goenberger, S. (Dutch artist, 19th
cent.)   WC

Goeneutte, Norbert   **BA GC WC**
(French artist, 1854-1894)   WC
(French painter, 1854-1894)   GC
(French painter, printmaker,
1854-1894)   BA
Bibl: Baltimore (Md, USA),
Museum of Art. The George A.
Lucas collection: selected prints,
1976; ▶Bénézit; ▶Thieme-Becker

Goepfert, Hermann (German
painter, sculptor, b.1929)   BA
Bibl: ▶Bénézit; Lyon (FRA), Mus.
des B.-A., Artistes francofortois
contemp. (1975); ▶MoMA libr.
cat.; ▶WW Arts DEU

Goeree, Jan   **BA GC WC**
(Dutch artist, 1670-1731)   WC
(Dutch draughtsman and
printmaker, 1670-1731)   GC
(Dutch printmaker, painter,
author, 1670-1731)   BA
Bibl: Getty Photo Study Coll.;
▶Nieuw NLD biog. woord.;
▶Thieme-Becker; ▶Witt checklist
Goerg→see Goerg, Edouard Joseph

Goerg, Cbristian (German artist,
19th cent.)   WC
Goerg, Edouard→see Goerg, Edouard
Joseph

Goerg, Edouard Joseph   **PR**
(French artist, 1893-)   WC
(French painter, 1893-1969)   PR
Bibl: ▶Bénézit; ▶Witt checklist
Edouard Joseph Goerg   PR
Goerg   PR
Goerg, Edouard   PR
Goerg, Edward   **PR WC**
Goerg, Edward→see Goerg, Edouard
Joseph

Goergen, Anton (German architect,
Cologne)   AV
Bibl: Faith & form, 1985 Spring,
v.18, p.17

Goergens, Gert (W. German
architect, Munich)   AV
Bibl: Baumeister, 1986 Dec., v.83,
no.12, p.24

Goeritz, Mathias   **AV BA WC**
(French artist, 1915-)   WC
(German architect, painter and
sculptor, 1915-)   AV
(German sculptor, author,
architect in MEX, b.1915)   BA
Bibl: ▶Bénézit; ▶Contemp. archts.;
▶Havlice, Idx. art. bio.; ▶MoMA
libr. cat.; ▶Vollmer, Künst.-Lex.
20. Jhr.

Goertschacher, Urban   **BA**
(Australian painter, 16th c.)   BA
(German artist, op.1508)   WC
(German painter, act. 1508)   PR
(German, act. ca.1508)   GC
Bibl: Baldass, Öst. Tafelmal. d.
Spätgotik; ▶Bénézit; Pächt. Österr.
Tafelmal. d. Gotik; ULAN 1988,
(Witt, Prov.Idx., PHOA); ▶Witt
checklist
Gortschacher   PR
**Gortschacher (not
Dortschacher) Urban**   **WC**
Görtschacher, Urban   **GC PR**
Urban Gortschacher   PR

Goertz, Augustus (American
painter, b.1948)   BA
Bibl: Art News, Nov '74, p.92

Goertz, Jürgen (West German
sculptor, b.1939)   BA
Bibl: Kunstwerk, XXX/2 (Apr.
1977) pp.3-33; ▶WW Arts DEU
Goes→see Goes, Hugo van der

Goes, Hugo van der   **BA GC PR WC**
(early Netherlandish painter, ca.
1440-1482)   BA
(Flanders painter, ca.1440-1482)   GC
(Netherlandish painter, ca.1440-
1482)   PR
(Netherlands artist, op.1467-m.
1482)   WC
Bibl: ▶Encyc. world art;
▶RILA/BHA; ▶Thieme-Becker;
▶Wurzbach, NLD Künst.-Lex.
Goes   PR
Hugo van der Goes   PR

Goeschl, Roland (Austrian sculptor,
Vienna, 1932-)   AV
Bibl: Transparent, 1988, v.19, no.
9-10, p.20

Goetghebuer, Pierre Jacques
(Belgian printmaker, architect,
1788-1866)   BA
Bibl: ▶Biog. Nat. Belgique;
▶Thieme-Becker

Goethals, Eugene Raymond
(French artist, 1804-1864)   WC

Goethe, Johann Wolfgang
von AV GC WC
(1749-1832) AV
(German artist, 1749-1832) WC
(German author and
draughtsman, 1749-1832) GC
Bibl: ▶Thieme-Becker
Goethem, Jan van *(Dutch painter,*
20th c.) BA
Bibl: Amsterdam. Museum Fodor.
exh. cat. 1973
Goetkindt, Antoine *(Flemish*
printmaker, print publisher in FRA,
act.1598, d.1644) BA
Bibl: ▶Bénézit; ▶Biog. Nat.
Belgique; ▶Thieme-Becker;
▶Wurzbach, NLD Künst.-Lex.
Goetkint, Goetkind or Goetkindt,
Peter, I→see Goetkint, Peter (the
Elder)
Goetkint, Peter (the Elder) GC
(Netherlandish painter, act.
1555-d.1583) GC
(Netherlands artist, op.1555-m.
1583) WC
Bibl: ▶Thieme-Becker
Goetkint, Goetkind or
Goetkindt, Peter, I WC
Goets, A. *(Dutch(?) artist, op.1767)* WC
Goettelmann, Paul A. *(5.V.1907-16.*
IX.1976; Architectural draftsman,
District of Columbia) FA
Bibl: drawing inscription; Natl.
Archives object
Goettingen Painter GC
Bibl: ▶Beazley, Attic red-fig. vase-
ptrs.
Goettsch, James C. *(American*
architect, Chicago, Ill, 1941-) AV
Bibl: ▶AIA Pro File, 1983; New
Chicago architecture, 1981,
p.134
Goetz, Gottfried Bernhard→see Götz,
Gottfried Bernhard
Goetz, Henri→see Goetz, Henri
Bernard
Goetz, Henri Bernard BA
(French artist, 1909-) WC
(French painter, b.1909) BA
Bibl: ▶Bénézit; ▶Vollmer,
Künst.-Lex. 20. Jhr.; ▶Young,
Amer. artists
Goetz, Henri WC
Goetz, Martin *(German interior*
architect) AV
Bibl: Architektur,
Innenarchitektur, Technischer
Ausbau, 1986 Mar., v.94, no.3,
p.46
Goetz, Mary Anna *(American artist,*
b.1947) WI
Goetz, Peter *(Canadian artist, 20th*
cent.) WC
Goetze, Leopold *(Engraver)* WI

Goetze, Otto *(German painter,*
graphic artist, 1868-1931) BA
Bibl: ▶Bénézit; ▶Thieme-Becker;
▶Vollmer, Künst.-Lex. 20. Jhr.
Goetze, Sigismund Christian
Hubert *(British artist, 1866-*
1939) WC WI
Goetzeberger, E. *(German painter,*
18th century(?)) GC
Bibl: Getty Photo Study Coll.
(Douwes coll.)
Goetzee, M. J. *(Dutch(?)*
draughtsman, 18th century) GC
Bibl: from postcard
Goeverts→see Govaerts, Abraham
Goey, Marijke de *(Dutch artist,*
b.1947) BA
Bibl: BEELDEN AAN DE LINGE:...,
Utrecht: Reflex, 1984, 25; Breda
(NLD), De Beyerd, Marijke de
Goey... Utrecht: Reflex, 1984
Goez, Josef Franz Freiherr von→see
Goez, Joseph Franz Freiherr von
Goez, Joseph Franz Freiherr von GC
(German artist, 1754-1815) WC
(German, 1754-1815) GC
Bibl: ▶Thieme-Becker; ▶Witt
checklist
Goez, Josef Franz Freiherr von WC
Goff, Bruce→see Goff, Bruce Alonzo
Goff, Bruce Alonzo BA
(American architect, 1904-
1982) AV BA
Bibl: AIA journal, Sept. 1982,
p.16; ▶Avery Libr. cat.;
▶Contemp. archts.; ▶Macmillan
encyc. archts.; Milwaukee (WI,
USA), Art Ctr., Amer. arch.
(1977); ▶MoMA libr. cat.; ▶WW
Arch.
Goff, Bruce AV
Goff, David *(American architect*
student) AV
Bibl: Historic preservation, 1985
Apr., v.37, no.2, p.8
Goff, Fred E.J. *(British artist, 1855-*
1931) WC WI
Goff, Lloyd Lozes *(American*
painter, illustrator, b.1919) BA
Bibl: ▶WW Amer. Art, 1976
Goff, Robert Charles *(British artist,*
1837-1922) WC WI
Goffredo→see Wals, Goffredo
Goffredo Wals→see Wals, Goffredo
Gofridus *(French scribe)* GC
Godfridus GC
Gog, Gregor *(German artist, 20th*
c.) BA
Bibl: Bildende kunst 7 1980
321-23
Gogdano→see Bogdany, Jakob
Gogel, Daniel AV BA
(West German architect, 1927-) AV
(West German architect,
b.1927) BA
Bibl: ▶Contemp. archts.

Göger, Franz *(West German*
architect, Dittelbrunn, 1945-) AV
Bibl: ▶Bund Deut. Arch. Hdbch.,
1987; Deutsche Bauzeitung, 1986
June, v.120, no.6, p.164
Gogh→see Gogh, Vincent van
Gogh, Elisabeth Huberta van→see Du
Quesne-van Gogh, Elisabeth
Huberta
Gogh, Peter van *(Dutch artist of*
fantastic architecture) AV
Bibl: Architettura; cronache e
storia, 1979 June, v.25, no.
6(284), p.362
van Gogh, Peter AV
Gogh, Vincent van BA GC JG PR WC WI
(Dutch artist, 1853-1890) WC
(Dutch painter, 1853-1890) BA PR
(Dutch painter, draughtsman,
and printmaker, 1853-1890) GC
(Dutch, 1853-1890) JG
(Netherlands artist, 1853-1890) WI
Bibl: ▶Bénézit; Blue guide:
Yugoslavia, p.402; ▶Encyc. world
art; Getty Photo Study Coll.;
▶RILA/BHA; ▶Thieme-Becker
Gogh PR
Gogh, Vincent Willem van PR
Vincent van Gogh PR
Gogh, Vincent Willem van→see
Gogh, Vincent van
Gogh-Bonger, Johanna Gesina
(Dutch, 1862-1925) BA
Bibl: ▶Natl. union cat., 1973-
1977, v.42, p.243; WW Neth.
Gogh-Carbentus, Anna Cornelia
van *(Dutch, 1819-1906)* BA
Bibl: Hanson, PASS.
PILGRIM(1955),; Leymarie, Van
Gogh
Gogin, Charles *(British artist, 1844-*
1931) WC WI
Gogly, Pierre-François→see Goguelye,
Pierre-François
Goguelye, Pierre-François *(French*
silversmith, master 1768) GC
Bibl: ▶Nocq, Poinçon de Paris
Gogly, Pierre-François GC
Goguen, Jean BA WC
(Canadian artist, 1928-) WC
(Canadian painter, b.1927) BA
Bibl: ▶Artists Canada; ▶Bénézit;
Montreal (Que, CAN), Mus. d'art
contemp., Dix ans (1979)
Gohl, Johann Christian Samuel
(German artist, 1743-1825) WC
Gohl, Theodor *(Swiss architect,*
1844-1914) BA
Bibl: ▶Thieme-Becker
Gohler, Hermann *(German artist,*
op.1890) WC
Gohlke, Frank *(American*
photographer, b.1942) BA
Bibl: Kalamazoo (MI, USA), Inst.
Art, Young Amer. photogs.
(1975)

Goicoechea, Juana Galarza de
(Spanish, act.1775-1805)   **BA**
  Bibl: Beruete, GOYA AS PORTRAIT
  PTR; BOLETÍN D. MUS. D. PRADO,
  I (Jan-Apr 1980) 12-16; Stokes
  GOYA
Goien, Jan Josephsz. van→see
Goyen, Jan Josephsz. van
Goines, David Lance *(American*
printmaker, b.1945)   **BA**
  Bibl: D.L. GOINES POSTERBOOK,
  1978; ▶Natl. union cat., 1974; UC
  Santa Barbara cat. sheets
Goings, Ralph→see Goings, Ralph
Ladell
Goings, Ralph Ladell   **BA GC WI**
  (American artist, 1928-)   WC
  (American artist, b.1928)   WI
  (American painter, b.1928)   BA GC
  Bibl: ▶RILA/BHA; ▶WW Amer. Art
Goings, Ralph   **WC**
Gois, Etienne Pierre Adrien   **GC WC**
  (French artist, 1731-1823)   WC
  (French sculptor, 1731-1823)   GC
  Bibl: ▶Thieme-Becker
Goita, Fernando Chueca→see Chueca
Goita, Fernando
Goitia, Francisco *(Mexican artist,*
1884-)   **WC**
Goitia, Pedro de *(Spanish sculptor,*
act.1534-1542)   **BA**
  Bibl: Estella, Arch. esp. de arte,
  LVIII/229 (Jan-Mar 1985) 58-65
Gojowczyk, Hubertus *(German*
artist, poet, b.1943)   **BA**
  Bibl: ▶Bénézit; Krefeld (BRD),
  Kaiser Wilhelm Museum,
  HUBERTUS GOJOWCZYK 1975;
  ▶WW Arts DEU
Göknil, Ulya→see Vogt-Göknil, Ulya
Gola, Ádám *(Hungarian*
photographer, act.1840s)   **BA**
  Bibl: HISTORY OF PHOTOGRAPHY
  II/1 (Jan 1978), p.53
Gola, Emilio *(Italian artist,*
1851/2-1923)   **WC**
Golan, Ruth *(Israeli architect,*
practices in West Berlin, 1944-)   **AV**
  Bibl: Deutsche Bauzeitung, 1986
  Nov., v.120, no.11, p.25
Golanda, Nella *(Sculptor, Greece)*   **AV**
  Bibl: Themata chorov + technon,
  1984, v.15, p.162
Gołaski, Karol *(Polish architect,*
20th c.)   **BA**
  Bibl: Szcześniewska-Ochnio,
  ROCZNIK MUSEUM NARODOWE
  W WARSZAWIE XXVI (1982) 7-88
Golcius→see Goltzius, Hendrik
Gold Scroll Master→see Gold Scrolls
Group
Gold Scrolls Group *(Flemish*
illuminators, act. ca.1415-1450)   **GC**
  Bibl: Brussels, Miniature Flamande
  (1959), p.17; Getty Photo Study
  Coll. (Medieval); Marrow, Dutch
  illus. mss.
  Gold Scroll Master   GC
  Master of the Gold Scroll   GC

Gold, Charles Emilius   **WC WI**
  (British artist, op.1806-, d.1842)   WI
  (British artist, op.1806-m.1842)   WC
Gold, Mike *(British architect)*   **AV**
  Bibl: Architectural design, 1984,
  v.54, no.3-4, p.66
Gold, Sharon Cecile *(American*
painter, b.1949)   **BA**
  Bibl: ▶WW Amer. Art, 1978
Golda, János *(Hungarian architect,*
Miskolc)   **AV**
  Bibl: Architecture: the AIA
  journal, 1989 Sept., v.78, no.9,
  p.68
Goldapp, Wolfram   **AV BA**
  (German architect, b.1950)   BA
  (West German architect, 1950-)   AV
  Bibl: Kunstwerk, XXXII/2-3 (Apr.-
  Jun. 1979) p.59
Goldar, John *(British artist, 1729-*
1795)   **WC WI**
Goldbach, Helmut *(West German*
architect)   **AV**
  Bibl: Detail, 1987 Nov.-Dec., v.27,
  no.6, p.621
Goldbacher, Sandra *(British artist,*
b.1960)   **WI**
Goldbacker, J. *(German artist, 19th*
cent.)   **WC**
Goldbeck, Eugene Omar *(American*
photographer, b.1892)   **BA**
  Bibl: ▶Artist biog. master idx.;
  Davenport, Unpretentious post;
  ▶Idx. Amer. photog. colls.
Goldbeck, Walter Dean *(American*
artist, 1882-1925)   **WI**
Goldberg, B.J. *(American artist,*
20th c.)   **BA**
  Bibl: Journal of the L.A. Institute
  of Contemporary Art, 7 (Aug-Sept
  1975), 38
Goldberg, Bertrand   **AV BA**
  (American architect, 1913-)   AV
  (American architect, b.1913)   BA
  Bibl: ▶Contemp. archts.; WW
  Amer., 1980
Goldberg, Carl *(Designer)*   **AV**
  Bibl: Interior design, LV/9 (Sep.
  1984) p.225
Goldberg, Elias   **BA WC WI**
  (American artist, op.1964-)   WI
  (American painter, b.1886)   BA
  (American(?) artist, 20th cent.)   WC
  Bibl: ▶Archives Amer. Art Jrnl.,
  XI/1-4 (1971)
Goldberg, Eric *(Canadian artist,*
1890-)   **WC**
Goldberg, Glenn *(American artist,*
op.1986-)   **WI**
Goldberg, Gustav Adolf *(German*
painter, 1848-1911)   **BA**
  Bibl: ▶Bénézit; ▶Thieme-Becker
Goldberg, Jim *(American*
photographer, b.1953)   **BA**
  Bibl: UC Santa Barbara cat. sheets

Goldberg, Joseph *(American*
painter, b.1947)   **BA**
  Bibl: ▶Intl. dir. exh. artists, 1983;
  Kangas, M., in VANGUARD XII/1
  (Feb 1983) 23
Goldberg, Michael   **AV BA WC WI**
  (American architect, New York,
NY)   AV
  (American artist, 1924-)   WC
  (American artist, b.1924)   WI
  (American painter, b.1924)   BA
  Bibl: ▶Archives Amer. Art Jrnl.,
  XI/1-4 (1971); Interior design,
  1984 Apr., v.55, no.4, p.180;
  ▶WW Amer. Art
Goldberg, Steven M. *(American*
architect, 1941-)   **AV**
  Bibl: Process: architecture, n.2,
  1977, p.40
Goldberg, Theo *(Canadian artist,*
b.1921)   **BA**
  Bibl: Goldberg, Leonardo XIX/1
  (1986) p.11-17; ▶Intl. dir. exh.
  artists, 1983
Golden, Daniel (Daan) van→see
Golden, Daniel van
Golden, Daniel van   **BA**
  (Dutch artist, 1936-)   WC
  (Dutch painter, photographer,
b.1936)   BA
  Bibl: Rotterdam (NLD), Mus.
  Boymans-van Beuningen, DAAN
  VAN GOLDEN, 1982; ▶Scheen,
  Ned. beeldende kunst.
Golden, Daniel (Daan) van   **WC**
Golden, Grace L. *(British artist,*
b.1904)   **WI**
Golden, Jack *(American architect &*
painter, 1928-)   **AV**
  Bibl: A + U, no.174, p.100
Golden, Judith *(American*
photographer, b.1934)   **BA**
  Bibl: Los Angeles (CA, USA),
  UCLA, 18 faculty artists (1975),
  p.14
Golden, Robert *(British*
photographer, b.1945)   **BA**
  Bibl: Arts Council GBR, 3
  perspectives photography (1979)
Golden, William O. *(American artist,*
b.1874)   **WI**
Goldenson, Leonard H. *(American*
painter, 20th c.)   **BA**
  Bibl: Palm Springs (Calif, USA),
  Desert Museum, LEONARD H.
  GOLDENSON, 1978
Golder, C.H.   **WC WI**
  (American artist, 19th cent.)   WC
  (American artist, op.1878-)   WI
Golderman, Mark *(American*
photographer, 20th c.)   **BA**
  Bibl: Arts Magazine LIII 3 (Nov
  1978) 2
Goldes, David *(American*
photographer, 20th c.)   **BA**
  Bibl: Roth, N., in AFTERIMAGE
  XIII/3 (Oct 1985) 5

Goldfarb, Shirley *(American painter in FRA, 20th c.)* **BA**
Bibl: Art News Annual 1966, p.144-45

Goldfinger, Ernö **AV BA**
(British architect, b.1902) **BA**
(British architect, born in Hungary, immigrated to Switzerland, studied architecture at the Ecole des Beaux-arts 1920-1934; moved to London in 1934, 1902-1987) **AV**
Bibl: ▶Arch. period. idx./RIBA; ▶Art Index, v.37 (obits); Building design, 1987 Nov.20, no.862, p.10; ▶Contemp. archts.; ▶Who's Who [GBR], 1983; ▶Wodehouse, Brit. archts.

Goldfinger, Myron *(American architect, 1933-)* **AV**
Bibl: Process: architecture, n.7, 1978, p.208

Goldhammer, Albert *(American architect, 1890-1956)* **AV**
Bibl: Sites, 1989, no.21-22, p.41

Goldicutt, John *(British artist, 1793-1842)* **WC WI**

Goldie, Charles Frederick *(New Zealand artist, op.1903)* **WC**

Goldin, Leon *(American painter, b.1923)* **BA**
Bibl: ▶WW Amer. Art

Goldin, Nan *(American photographer, b.1953)* **BA**
Bibl: Cincinnati (OH, USA), Taft Museum, Presentation (1983)

Golding, John **BA WC WI**
(British artist, 1929-) **WC**
(British artist, b.1929) **WI**
(British author, painter, b.1929) **BA**
Bibl: Edinburgh (GB), Natl. Gallery of Modern Art, JOHN GOLDING, 1977; lectures at the Courtauld & at Royal College of Arts; ▶MoMA libr. cat.

Golding, Stuart *(American restoration architect, Clearwater, Fla)* **AV**
Bibl: Colonial homes, 1988 Aug., v.14, no.4, p.22

Goldingham *(British army officer, painter, act.ca.1875)* **BA**
Bibl: Aijazuddin, Sikh portraits..., 1979

Goldman, György *(Hungarian sculptor, 1904-1944)* **BA**
Bibl: Budapest (HUN), Magyar Nemz. Gal., Goldman György (1980); ▶Vollmer, Künst.-Lex. 20. Jhr.

Goldman, Harvey *(American ceramist, b.1951)* **BA**
Bibl: Amherst (MA, USA), U Mass. Art Gallery, 11 Alumni (1983)

Goldman, James P. *(American architect)* **AV**

Goldman, John *(American architect)* **AV**
Bibl: Architecture California, 1986 May-June, v.8, no.3, p.25

Goldman, Ronald E. *(American architect, Malibu, CA)* **AV**
Bibl: ▶AIA Pro File, 1983

Goldman, Saul *(American interior designer, New York, NY)* **AV**
Bibl: Interior design, 1983 Apr., v.54, no.4, p.174

Goldner, Daniel Louis **AV**

Goldring, Elizabeth *(American environmental artist, b.1945)* **BA**
Bibl: ▶WW Amer. Art, 1989-1990

Goldring, Nancy Deborah *(American printmaker, photographer, b.1945)* **BA**
Bibl: SITES, The Photographer's Hand (1980-82); ▶WW Amer. Art, 1980

Goldschmid → see Goldschmid, Hans

Goldschmid, Hans **PR WC**
(German artist, op.1521-1535) **WC**
(German painter, act. 1517-1534) **PR**
Bibl: ▶Thieme-Becker
Goldschmid **PR**
Hans Goldschmid **PR**

Goldschmidt, David *(Swiss artist, 20th cent.)* **WC**

Goldschmidt, Edmond *(French photographer, 1863-1934)* **BA**
Bibl: Glowen in ARTWEEK XII/38 (14 Nov 1987), p.11; Godeau in PORTFOLIO III (Jan-Feb 1981), p.44; Vancouver (BC, CND), Art Gallery. LOUIS AMÉDÉE MANTÉ..., 1981

Goldschmidt, Hilde *(German painter, printmaker, b.1897)* **BA**
Bibl: Innsbruck (A), Tiroler Landesmuseum Ferdinandeum, HILDE GOLDSCHMIDT, 1977; ▶Vollmer, Künst.-Lex. 20. Jhr.

Goldsleger, Cheryl *(American painter, b.1951)* **BA**
Bibl: ▶WW Amer. Art

Goldsmith → see Arnold, Harriet

Goldsmith, Bill *(American artist and ceramic designer)* **AV**
Bibl: House beautiful, 1988 June, v.130, no.6, p.72

Goldsmith, Derek *(British artist, b.1951)* **BA**
Bibl: London, Whitechapel Art Gallery, Derek Goldsmith: OUR HOUSE IN STILL AND ANIMATED PICTURES, 1976

Goldsmith, J. **WC WI**
(British artist, op.1815) **WC**
(British artist, op.1815-) **WI**

Goldsmith, Jonathan → see Goldsmith, Jonothan

Goldsmith, Jonathan **BA**
(American architect, 1783-1847) **BA**
(American master builder, 1783-1847) **AV**
Bibl: ▶Who was who [GBR]; ▶Withey, Amer. archts.

Goldsmith, Jonathan **AV**

Goldsmith, Lloyd *(American artist, 20th c.)* **BA**
Bibl: Arts Mag. LVI/8 (Apr 1982) p.19-20

Goldsmith, Myron *(American architect, 1918-)* **AV**
Bibl: ▶Contemp. archts.

Goldsmith, Nicholas *(Designer)* **AV**
Bibl: Interiors, 1986 Mar., v.145, no.8, p.139

Goldsmith, Walter H. *(British artist, op.1880-1898)* **WI**

Goldstein, Alfredo *(Argentine painter, b.1921)* **BA**
Bibl: ▶MoMA libr. cat.

Goldstein, Barbara → see Goodstein, Barbara

Goldstein, Daniel Joshua *(American printmaker, sculptor, b.1950)* **BA**
Bibl: Brooklyn (NY, USA), Brooklyn Mus., Daniel Joshua Goldstein: Wood Block Prints & Paper 1974-1982 (1983); ▶WW Amer. Art

Goldstein, Eliot W. *(American architect, N.J)* **AV**
Bibl: ▶AIA Pro File, 1987-88

Goldstein, Frederik *(British artist, op.1986-)* **WI**

Goldstein, Harriet *(British artist, op. 19th c.)* **WI**

Goldstein, Jack **BA WI**
(American artist, b.1945) **BA**
(British artist, op.20th c.) **WI**
Bibl: ▶WW Amer. Art, 1991-92

Goldstein, Johann Theodor **GC WC**
(German painter, 1798-1871) **GC**
(Polish artist, 1798-p.1871) **WC**
Bibl: ▶Thieme-Becker

Goldstein, Lipa *(1950-)* **AV**

Goldstein, Milton *(American artist, b.1914)* **BA**
Bibl: ▶Natl. Faculty Dir., 1978; Pierson, Arts in US; ▶WW Amer. Art, 1976

Goldstein, Nathan *(American painter, author, b.1927)* **BA**
Bibl: ▶WW Amer. Art, 1978

Goldstein, Serge *(1947-)* **AV**

Goldstein, Zvi *(Israeli artist, b.1947)* **BA**
Bibl: ▶Art Index, v.36; ▶ARTbibl. mod., 1982, v.13/2, p.176; ▶Intl. dir. arts, 1989; Jaar, ART IN AMERICA, 77 (1989), p.132

Goldstine, Irvin *(American architect)* **AV**
Bibl: Abitare, 1984 Dec., new ser., v.83, no.230, p.42

Goldston, Bill *(American printer, 20th c.)* **BA**
Bibl: Amer. Fed. Arts, The painter & the printer

Goldstone, Harmon H. *(American preservationist, New York, N.Y, 1911-)* **AV**
    Bibl: ▶Libr. of Congr. Name Auth. File

Goldstraw, G. A. **AV**

Goldthwaite→see Goldthwaite, Anne

Goldthwaite, Anne **BA PR WC WI**
    (American artist, 1869-1944) WI
    (American artist, 1875-1944) WC
    (American painter, 1869-1944) PR
    (American painter, printmaker, 1869-1944) BA
    Bibl: ▶Art Index, v.6; ▶Bénézit;
    ▶Collins, Women artists Amer.;
    ▶Havlice, Idx. art. bio.; ▶MoMA
    libr. cat.; Montgomery, Museum
    of Fine Art, Anne Goldthwaite
    1869-1944; ▶RILA/BHA; ▶Vollmer,
    Künst.-Lex. 20. Jhr.
        Anne Goldthwaite PR
        Goldthwaite PR
        Goldwaithe, Anne PR

Goldwaithe, Anne→see Goldthwaite, Anne

Goldwasser, Penny *(Interior designer)* **AV**
    Bibl: Southern accents, 1985 Mar.
    -Apr., v.8, no.2, p.56

Goldworthy, Andy *(British photographer, b.1956)* **BA**
    Bibl: ▶Babington Smith, Contemp.
    artists

Goldyne, Joseph *(American printmaker, b.1942)* **BA**

Gole, Jacob **BA GC WC**
    (Dutch artist, c.1660-c.1737) WC
    (Dutch draughtsman, ca.1660-ca.1737) GC
    (Dutch printmaker, 1660-1737) BA
    Bibl: ▶Aa, Biog. woordenboek
    NLD; ▶Bénézit; Getty Photo Study
    Coll.; ▶Thieme-Becker; ▶Witt
    checklist

Gole, Pierre **BA GC**
    (Dutch cabinetmaker in FRA, act.1653, d.1684) BA
    (French ébéniste, d.1684) GC
    (French, active 1670-1690) JG
    Bibl: ▶Thieme-Becker

Golle, Pierre **GC JG**

Goleta Group *(Apulian vase-painters)* **GC**
    Bibl: Trendall, Attic red-fig. vases
    Apulia

Golfe [Unidentified] *(Unknown painter)* **PR**
    Bibl: (February 18, 1809, lot 5,
    Christie's)

Golfinopoulos, Peter *(American painter, b.1928)* **BA**

Golia (Eugenio Colmo) *(Italian ceramist, caricaturist, 1885-1967)* **BA**
    Bibl: Faenza (ITA), Mus. Internaz.
    delle Ceramiche. Golia..., 1981

Golicyn, Illarion Vladimirovič *(Soviet printmaker, b.1928)* **BA**
    Bibl: ▶Bénézit; ▶Fogg Mus. Libr.
    cat.; ISO

Golike, William Alexandrowitsch *(Russian artist, op.1819-m.1848)* **WC**

Golikov, Ivan Ivanovič *(Russian painter, scenographer, illustrator, 1886/87-1937)* **BA**
    Bibl: ▶Vollmer, Künst.-Lex. 20.
    Jhr.; ▶WWW USSR

Golikova, Nina Anatol'evna *(Russian designer, 20th c.)* **BA**
    Bibl: Dek. Iskusstvo SSSR, 262
    (Sep. 1979) pp.12-17

Goll van Franckenstein, Johann **GC**
    (Dutch artist, op.1722-m.1785) WC
    (Dutch draughtsman, 1722-1785) GC
    Bibl: ▶Witt checklist

Goll van Frankenstein or Franckerstein, Johann, I. **WC**

Goll van Frankenstein or Franckerstein, Johann, I.→see Goll van Franckenstein, Johann

Göll, Oskar→see Döll, Oskar

Golle, Pierre→see Gole, Pierre

Goller, Bruno **BA WC**
    (German artist, 1901-) WC
    (German painter, b.1901) BA
    Bibl: ▶Vollmer, Künst.-Lex. 20.
    Jhr.; ▶WW Arts DEU

Goller, Christian *(German painter, b.ca.1943)* **BA**
    Bibl: NY Times 18 Nov 1977 p.A2

Gollifel, Sue *(British artist, op.20th c.)* **WI**

Golling, Leonard *(German draughtsman, 1604-1667)* **GC**
    Bibl: ▶Bénézit

Gollings, Edward **WC WI**
    (American artist, op.1916) WC
    (American artist, op.1916-) WI

Gollings, Elling William **BA**
    (American artist, 1878-1932) WI
    (American artist, 20th cent.) WC
    (American painter, 1878-1932) BA
    Bibl: ▶Dawdy, Artists Amer. West

Gollings, William **WC WI**

Gollings, William→see Gollings, Elling William

Gollini, Alberto *(Italian architect, b.1942)* **BA**
    Bibl: Rome (ITA), Ist. naz. arch.,
    Alberto Gollini (1979)

Gollins, Frank *(British architect)* **AV**

Gollut, Christophe *(Swiss interior designer, based in London)* **AV**
    Bibl: The world of interiors, 1988
    Oct., p.226

Gollwitzer, Gerda *(West German landscape architect, writer, 1907-)* **AV**
    Bibl: ▶Libr. of Congr. Name Auth.
    File

Gollwitzer, Hans *(West German architect(?), Deggendorf)* **AV**
    Bibl: Deutsches Architektenblatt,
    1988 May, v.20, no.5, p.681

Golonos Group **GC**
    Bibl: ▶Beazley, Attic bl.-fig. vase-ptrs.

Golosov, Il'ja Aleksandrovič **BA FA**
    (1883-1945; Russian Architect, Moscow) FA
    (Russian architect, 1883-1945) BA
    Bibl: ▶Macmillan encyc. archts.,
    v.2, p.226; ▶RILA/BHA, Subject,
    1988; ▶WWW USSR
        Golosov, Ilya FA

Golosov, Ilya→see Golosov, Il'ja Aleksandrovič

Golosov, Pantelemon *(1882-1945; Russian Architect, Moscow)* **FA**
    Bibl: ▶Macmillan encyc. archts.

Golovanov, L.F. *(Russian artist, 20th c.)* **BA**
    Bibl: Iskusstvo XXXVIII/5 (1975)
    28-30; ▶Vollmer, Künst.-Lex. 20.
    Jhr.

Golovin, Aleksandr Jakovlevič **BA**
    (Russian artist, 1863-1930) WC
    (Russian scenographer, painter, 1863-1930) BA
    Bibl: ▶Bénézit; ▶Encic. spettacolo;
    ▶Fogg Mus. Libr. cat.;
    ▶Thieme-Becker

Golovin, Alexander Yakovlevitch **WC**

Golovin, Alexander Yakovlevitch→see Golovin, Aleksandr Jakovlevič

Golovin, Willard *(American, 20th c.)* **BA**
    Bibl: Ugo Procacci festchrift, v.1,
    pp.137-139

Golovine, Countess *(Russian artist, 18th cent.)* **WC**

Golpaia, Bernardo della→see Della Volpaia, Bernardo

Golpazo, Bernardo dello→see Della Volpaia, Bernardo

Golsius→see Goltzius, Hendrik
Goltino→see Goltzius, Hendrik
Goltius→see Goltzius, Hendrik
Goltius, Hendrik→see Goltzius, Hendrik
Goltsius→see Goltzius, Hendrik

Goltyr Painter **GC**
    Bibl: ▶Beazley, Attic bl.-fig. vase-ptrs.

Goltz, Alexander Demetrius **BA WC**
    (Australian painter, 1857-1944) BA
    (German artist, 1857-1944) WC
    Bibl: ▶Fuchs, Öst. Maler 19.
    Jahrh.; ▶Thieme-Becker; ▶Vollmer,
    Künst.-Lex. 20. Jhr.

Goltz, Hendrick→see Goltzius, Hendrik

Goltz, Hendrick→see Goltzius, Hendrik
Goltzius→see Goltzius, Hendrik
Goltzius→see Goltzius, Hubertus
Goltzius→see Goltzius, Scipio
Goltzius, Hendrick→see Goltzius, Hendrik

Goltzius, Hendrik   **BA GC** PR
     (Dutch artist, 1558-1617)   WC
     (Dutch painter, 1558-1617)   PR
     (Dutch painter, printmaker,
      1558-1617)   BA
     (Dutch, 1558-1617)   JG
     (North Netherlandish painter,
      draughtsman, and printmaker,
      1558-1617)   GC
     (Painter, draughtsman, engraver,
      1558-1617)   CE
      Bibl: ▶Encyc. world art; Hollstein;
      ▶RILA/BHA; ▶Thieme-Becker
   Golcius   PR
   Golsius   PR
   Goltino   PR
   Goltius   PR
   Goltius, Hendrik   GC
   Goltsius   PR
   Goltz, Hendrick   CE
   Goltz, Hendrick   GC
   Goltzius   PR
Goltzius, Hendrick   **CE GC JG PR WC**
   Goltzius, Henrik   CE
   Golzious   PR
   Golzius   PR
   Golzius, Hendrick   CE
   Golzius, Hendrik   GC PR
   Gousius   PR
   H. Goltzius   PR
   Hendrick Goltius   PR
   Hendrick Goltzius   PR
   Hendrik Goltsius   PR
   Hendrik Goltzius   PR
   Henri Goltz   PR
   Henry Goltzius   PR
   Goltzius, Henrik → see Goltzius,
     Hendrik
   Goltzius, Hubert → see Goltzius,
     Hubertus
   Goltzius, Hubert, Hubertus or
     Hubrecht Goltz → see Goltzius,
     Hubertus
Goltzius, Hubertus   **BA**
     (early Netherlandish painter,
      printmaker, numismatist,
      1525-1583)   BA
     (Flemish painter, 1526-1583)   PR
     (Netherlands artist, 1526-1583)   WC
      Bibl: Cat. Bruges, Stedelijke
      Musea, HUBERTUS GOLTZIUS EN
      BRUGGE, 1583-1983, 1983;
      ▶Hollstein, Dutch & Flemish, v.8,
      p.139; ▶Thieme-Becker
   Goltzius   PR
Goltzius, Hubert   **PR**
Goltzius, Hubert, Hubertus or
   Hubrecht Goltz   **WC**
   Golzius   PR
   Hubert Goltzius   PR
Goltzius, Hugo *(Netherlandish*
   draughtsman, 16th century)   GC
     Bibl: Getty Photo Study Coll.
     (Duits coll.)

Goltzius, Jacob (the Elder) → see
   Goltzius, Jacob I
Goltzius, Jacob I   **BA**
     (Netherlandish engraver, ca.
      1535-1609)   BA
     (North Netherlandish painter
      and draughtsman, ca.1535-
      1609)   GC
      Bibl: ▶Bénézit; Getty Photo Study
      Coll.; ▶Hollstein, Dutch & Flemish;
      ▶Thieme-Becker; ▶Wurzbach, NLD
      Künst.-Lex.
Goltzius, Jacob (the Elder)   **GC**
Goltzius, Scipio *(Flemish painter,*
   act. 16th century)   **PR**
   Goltzius   PR
   Scipio Goltzius   PR
Goltzsche, Dieter Herbert *(German*
   printmaker, b.1934)   **BA**
     Bibl: Berlin (DDR), Staatliche
     Museum, Kupfer..., DIETER
     GOTTZSCHE 1982; ▶Intl. dir. exh.
     artists, 1983
Golub, Leon Albert   **BA WC WI**
     (American artist, 1922-)   WC
     (American artist, b.1922)   WI
     (American painter, b.1922)   BA
      Bibl: ▶WW Amer. Art
Golubkina, Anna Semenovna
   (Russian sculptor, 1864-1927)   **BA**
      Bibl: ▶Encyc. world art; ▶Fogg
      Mus. Libr. cat.
Golubov, Maurice *(American*
   painter, b.1905)   **BA**
      Bibl: ▶Locus, 1977-78; ▶NY art
      yrbk.
Goluchow Painter *(vase-painter, ca.*
   530-500 BC)   **GC**
      Bibl: ▶Beazley, Attic red-fig. vase-
      ptrs.; Richter, Attic red-fig. vases
Golvol Group   **GC JG**
      Bibl: ▶Beazley, Attic bl.-fig. vase-
      ptrs.
Golyscheff, Jefim *(Russian painter,*
   graphic artist, b.1897)   **BA**
      Bibl: ▶Met. Mus. Art libr. cat.;
      ▶MoMA libr. cat.
Golyšev, Ivan Aleksandrovič
   (Russian printmaker, 1838-1896)   **BA**
      Bibl: ▶Fogg Mus. Libr. cat.
   Golzious → see Goltzius, Hendrik
   Golzius → see Goltzius, Hendrik
   Golzius → see Goltzius, Hubertus
   Golzius, Hendrick → see Goltzius,
     Hendrik
   Golzius, Hendrik → see Goltzius,
     Hendrik
Golzl, Andre   **WC WI**
     (American artist, op.1763)   WC
     (American artist, op.1763-)   WI
Goma, Francesco *(Italian artist, op.*
   1797)   **WC**
Goma, Xavier *(Spanish architect)*   **AV**
     Bibl: Architecture d'aujourd'hui,
     1985 June, no.239, p.LVI
Gomar y Gomar, Antonio *(Spanish*
   artist, 1853-1911)   **WC**

Gomar, Francisco *(Spanish sculptor,*
   act.1443-ca.1493)   **BA**
      Bibl: ▶Ars Hispaniae, v.8, p.282;
      ▶Ceán Bermúdez, Bellas artes ESP;
      ▶Encic. univ. ilus.; Janke, Metr
      Mus Journal, XVIII (1983) 65-83;
      ▶Thieme-Becker
Gombar, Richard *(American artist,*
   20th c.)   **BA**
      Bibl: Hempstead (NY, USA),
      Hofstra Univ., Lowe Gall.,
      Abstract ptg...1981
Gombert, Thomas François Joseph
   (Flemish architect, 1725-1801)   **BA**
      Bibl: ▶Portoghesi, Diz. arch. e
      urbanistica; ▶Thieme-Becker
Gomery *(French artist, 20th cent.)*   **WC**
Gomery, Emeric *(French painter,*
   1902-1969)   **BA**
      Bibl: ▶Bénézit; Budapest, Magyar
      Nemzeti Gáleria, TISZTELETADÁS
      GÖMÖR..., 1980; ▶MoMA libr.
      cat.
Gomes, Augusto de Oliveira
   (Portuguese painter, 1910-1976)   **BA**
      Bibl: Belas Artes 30 (1976) 45;
      ▶Tavares Chicó, Pint. portuguesa
Gomes, Dordio → see Dórdio Gomes,
   Simão César
Gomes, Fernando *(Portuguese*
   artist, 16th cent.)   **WC**
Gomes, Oton *(Brazilian architect)*   **AV**
      Bibl: Architecture d'aujourd'hui,
      1987 June, no.251,p.50
Gomez → see Gómez, Sebastián (I)
Gómez Cotán, Juan *(Spanish*
   painter, act.1608-1626)   **BA**
      Bibl: Arch. esp. de arte, LI/204
      (Oct-Dec 1978) 409-426
Gomez da Silva, Enrique
   (Architect)   **AV**
      Bibl: Lotus international, 1989,
      no.61, p.102
Gómez de los Elgueros, Andrés → see
   Helgueros, Andrés de los
Gómez de Mora, Juan   **AV BA WC**
     (Spanish architect, 1586-1648)   BA
     (Spanish architect, ca.1580-
      1648)   AV
     (Spanish artist, c.1580-1648)   WC
      Bibl: ▶Encic. univ. ilus.; ▶Encyc.
      world art; ▶Kubler, Art & arch.
      ESP & PRT
   Mora, Juan Gómez de   AV
Gomez de Valencia, Felipe *(Spanish*
   artist, c.1634-1694)   **WC**
Gómez Sánchez, Ramón *(Spanish*
   architect)   **AV**
      Bibl: Arquitectura, 1988 July-Aug.,
      v.69, no.273, p.10
Gomez the Elder, Sebastian → see
   Gómez, Sebastián (I)
Gómez y Cros, Antonio *(Spanish*
   painter, 1809-1863)   **BA**
      Bibl: ▶Bénézit; ▶Encic. univ. ilus.;
      Goya, v.167-168, Mar-June 1982;
      ▶Ossorio y Bernard, Artistas
      españoles 19s.; ▶Thieme-Becker

Gomez y Gil, Guillermo (*Spanish artist, 19th cent.*) **WC**

Gomez y Pastor, Jacinto (*Spanish painter, 1746-1812*) **BA**
Bibl: ▶Thieme-Becker; ▶Viñaza, Adiciones Ceán-Berm.

Gomez, Bernard (*French photographer, b.1944*) **BA**
Bibl: Amsterdam (NLD), Stedelijk Museum, Foto-sequenties (1977)

Gomez, Didier (*French interior designer*) **AV**
Bibl: Maison Française, 1985 Apr., no.386, p.110

Gómez, Juan **BA WC**
(*Spanish artist, op.1555-m.1597*) **WC**
(*Spanish painter, d.1597*) **BA**
Bibl: ▶Ceán Bermúdez, Bellas artes ESP; ▶Encic. univ. ilus.; ▶Thieme-Becker

Gomez, Mariette Himes (*American interior designer*) **AV**
Bibl: House beautiful, 1985 Jan., p.13

Gómez, Martín, the elder (*Spanish painter, act.1550-1600*) **BA**
Bibl: ▶Bénézit; Bermejo Díez, LA CATEDRAL DE CUENCA, 1977; ▶Ceán Bermúdez, Bellas artes ESP; ▶Thieme-Becker

Gómez, Patricia (*Colombian architect, Medellín*) **AV**
Bibl: Proa, 1987 Nov., no.366, p.10

Gómez, Pedro (*Colombian architect*) **AV**
Bibl: Proa, 1985 Aug., no.344, p.17

Gomez, Richard Vincente Jose (*Canadian sculptor, b.1942*) **BA**
Bibl: ▶Artists Canada; Artscanada XXXIV (May-June '77) p.56; Regina Univ. of Saskatchewan, Norman Mackenzie Art Gallery, RIC GOMEZ, 1977

Gómez, Sebastián (I) **PR**
(*Spanish artist, 1646-c.1682*) **WC**
(*Spanish painter, ca.1646-1682*) **PR**
Bibl: ▶Thieme-Becker
El Mulato **PR**
Gomez **PR**
Gomez the Elder, Sebastian **WC**
Mulato **PR**
Sebastian Gomez (I) **PR**

Gomez, T. (*Spanish artist, 17th cent.*) **WC**

Gomez-Estern, Luis Fernando (*Spanish architect*) **AV**
Bibl: El croquis, 1987 Nov., v.6, no.31, p.55

Gomez-Pimienta, Bernardo (*Mexican architect*) **AV**
Bibl: Interiors, 1989 Sept., v.149, no.2, p.178

Gomi, Kenji (*Japanese artist, Tokyo, 1956-*) **AV**
Bibl: Process: architecture, 1988 Aug., no.74, p.157

Gomien, Paul (*French artist, 1799-1846*) **WC**

Gomis, André (*1926-*) **AV**

Gomis, Joaquim (*Spanish photographer, b.1902*) **BA**
Bibl: London, Riverside Studios, HOMAGE TO MIRÓ (1983); ▶MoMA libr. cat.

Gomm, Richard (*British cabinetmaker, ca.1729-1794*) **BA**
Bibl: BURLINGTON MAG., CXXII (June 1980), 395-400

Gomm, William (*British cabinetmaker, ca.1698-1780*) **BA**
Bibl: ▶Beard, Engl. furniture; NATIONAL TRUST BOOK OF ENGLISH FURNITURE

Gomont, Maurice Augustin (*French painter, 1839-1909*) **BA**
Bibl: ▶Bellier, Artistes fran.; ▶Bénézit; ▶Busse, Maler u. Bildhauer 19. Jahr.; ▶Thieme-Becker

Gompertz, M. (*British artist, op. 1833-1835*) **WC WI**

Gonçalves, Enrico Manuel de Melo (*Portuguese painter, b.1932*) **BA**
Bibl: ▶Tannock, Port. 20c. artists; ▶Tavares Chicó, Pint. portuguesa

Goncalves, Luis (*Portuguese artist, 1936-*) **WC**

Gonçalves, Nuno **BA GC WC**
(*Portuguese artist, op.1450-1471*) **WC**
(*Portuguese painter, act.1450-1471*) **BA**
(*Portuguese, act.1450-1471*) **GC**
Bibl: ▶Encyc. world art; Figueiredo; ▶Pamplona, Pint. escult. PRT; Smith, Art Portugal; ▶Thieme-Becker; ▶Witt checklist

Gončarov, Andrej Dmitrievič (*Russian painter, printmaker, scenographer, author, 1903-1979*) **BA**
Bibl: Dek. iskusstvo 262 (Sept 79), p.46; ▶Vollmer, Künst.-Lex. 20. Jhr.

Gončarova, Natalija Sergeevna **BA**
(*Russian artist, 1881-*) **WC**
(*Russian painter, sculptor, designer, 1881-1962*) **BA**
(*Russian, b.1881*) **GC**
Bibl: Art news LXXV Mar 1976, p.52; ▶ARTbibl. mod., ind. 1-3, vs. 19-21; ▶Bénézit; ▶Castagno, Eur. Sigs.; ▶Gorenflo, Bild. Künstler; Leonardo, spring 79, p.137-143; Moskva-Parizh 1900-1930; ▶Witt checklist
Goncharova, Natalija Sergeevna **BA**
Gontcharova, Nathalie **GC WC**
Goncharova, Natalija Sergeevna → see Gončarova, Natalija Sergeevna

Goncourt, Jules de **GC**
(*French artist, 1830-1870*) **WC**
(*French painter, 1830-1870*) **GC**
Bibl: ▶Bénézit

Goncourt, Jules Huot de **WC**
Goncourt, Jules Huot de → see Goncourt, Jules de

Gondelach, Johann Heinrich II (*German glass engraver, act.1716-1750*) **BA**
Bibl: Dreier, F.A., BURLINGTON MAGAZINE, CXXIX/1010 (May 1987), p.309-313

Gondoin or Gondouin, Jacques → see Gondoin, Jacques

Gondoin, Jacques **AV BA GC**
(*1737-1818*) **AV**
(*French architect, 1737-1818*) **BA**
(*French artist, 1737-1818*) **WC**
(*French, 1737-1818*) **GC**
Bibl: ▶Dict. biog. fran.; Getty Photo Study Coll. (Ptgs.); ▶Macmillan encyc. archts.; ▶Thieme-Becker; ▶Witt checklist

Gondoin or Gondouin, Jacques **WC**
Gondouin, Jacques **GC**
Gondolach, Matthäus → see Gundelach, Matthäus

Gondor, Bertalan (*Hungarian artist, 1908-1945*) **WC**

Gondouin, Emmanuel (*French artist, 1883-1934*) **WC**
Gondouin, Jacques → see Gondoin, Jacques

Gonella [Unidentified] (*Unknown painter*) **PR**
Bibl: Doria inventory, Naples, 1690

Gonfreville-Dumon, Brigitte (*French architect, Bordeaux*) **AV**
Bibl: Dialogues d'architecture, 1984, no.2, p.68

Góngora, Leonel (*Colombian painter, b.1932*) **BA**
Bibl: ▶Havlice, Idx. art. bio.

Gongora, Mario (*Chilean architect, teacher*) **AV**
Bibl: ARQ, 1986 May, no.11, p.39

Gonin, Francesco **GC WC**
(*Italian artist, 1808-1889*) **WC**
(*Italian painter, 1808-1889*) **GC**
Bibl: ▶Thieme-Becker

Gonne, Christian Friedrich **BA**
(*German artist, 1813-1906*) **WC**
(*German painter, 1813-1906*) **BA**
Bibl: ▶Bénézit; ▶Thieme-Becker

Gonne, Friedrich (Christian Friedrich) **WC**
Gonne, Friedrich (Christian Friedrich) → see Gonne, Christian Friedrich
Gonnelli, Giovanni Francesco → see Cieco da Gambassi

Gonord, Francois (*French artist, 1756-1819/25*) **WC**
Gonsales → see Coques, Gonzales

Gooch, Thomas   PR WI
   (British artist, 1750-1802)   WI
   (British artist, op.1777-1802)   WC
   (British painter, 1750-1802)   PR
    Bibl: ▶Waterhouse, Brit. 18c. ptrs.
   Gooch   PR
Gooch, T.   WC
   Mr. Gooch   PR
   T. Gooch   PR
   Thomas Gooch   PR
Good, Frank Mason *(British, active*
   London, England, U.K. and Near
   East ca. 1860-1890)   JG
Good, Thomas →see Good, Thomas
   Sword
Good, Thomas Sword   PR WC WI
   (British artist, 1789-1872)   WC WI
   (British painter, 1789-1872)   PR
    Bibl: ▶Thieme-Becker
   Good, Thomas   PR
   Thomas Sword Good   PR
Goodall →see Goodall, Frederick
Goodall, Edward Alfred →see
   Goodall, Edward Alfred, (Angelo)
Goodall, Edward Alfred, (Angelo)   WI
   (British artist, 1819-1908)   WC WI
    Bibl: ▶Mallalieu, Brit. watercolour
    artists
   Goodall, Edward Alfred   WC
Goodall, Frederick   BA PR WC WI
   (British artist, 1822-1904)   WC WI
   (British painter, 1822-1904)   BA PR
    Bibl: DBN; ▶Johnson, Brit. artists;
    ▶RILA/BHA
   Frederick Goodall   PR
   Goodall   PR
Goodall, Frederick Trevelyan
   (British artist, 1848-1871)   WC WI
Goodall, George *(British artist, op.*
   1926-)   WI
Goodall, Herbert   WC WI
   (British artist, op.1890-, d.1907)   WI
   (British artist, op.1890-m.1907)   WC
    Bibl: ▶Fisher, Watercolour ptrs.
Goodall, J. Edward   WC WI
   (British artist, 19th cent.)   WC
   (British artist, op.1890-1911)   WI
Goodall, J.F. *(British photographer,*
   19th c.)   BA
    Bibl: Art Jrnl., XLI/1 (Spr. 1981)
    pp.26-32
Goodall, John *(British artist, b.1940)*   WI
Goodall, John Strickland   WC WI
   (British artist, 1908-)   WC
   (British artist, b.1908)   WI
Goodall, R. Graham   AV
Goodall, Thomas F.   WC WI
   (British artist, 1856-1857-1944)   WI
   (British artist, 1856/7-1944)   WC
Goodall, Walter *(British artist, 1830-*
   1889)   WC WI
Goodall, William   WC WI
   (American artist, 20th cent.)   WC
   (American artist, op.1900-1972)   WI

Goodden, Robert Yorke *(British*
   architect, designer, b.1909)   BA
    Bibl: Roy. Soc. of Arts Journal,
    v.130, n.5306, Jan '82 p.74p-84;
    ▶Who's Who [GBR], 1982
Goodden, Ted *(Canadian glass*
   painter, b.1947)   BA
    Bibl: Stratford (ONT, CAN),
    Gallery/Stratford, Portfolio 80
    (1980)
Goode, J. →see Goode, John
Goode, Joe   BA WC WI
   (American sculptor, painter,
   b.1937)   BA
   (British artist, 20th cent.)   WC
   (British artist, op.1966-)   WI
    Bibl: ART NEWS. JAn 1975 p.62;
    ARTFORUM. June 1974, p.36;
    ▶MoMA libr. cat.; Russell, POP
    ART REDIFINED. NY 1969; ▶WW
    Amer. Art, 1973, 1976
Goode, John   WI
   (British artist, op.1810-1865)   WI
   (British artist, op.1815-1860)   WC
   Goode, J.   WC
Goode, Louise, Miss →see Jopling,
   Louise
Goode, Mervyn *(British artist, op.*
   20th c.)   WI
Goodell, Ira C. *(American painter,*
   ca.1810-after 1860)   BA
    Bibl: ▶Groce, Artists Amer.
Gooden, James Chisholm   WC WI
   (British artist, 1892-1955)   WI
   (British artist, op.1835-1865)   WC
    Bibl: ▶Wilson, Brit. marine ptrs.
Gooden, Stephen Frederick *(British*
   artist, 1892-1955)   WC WI
Goodenow, George *(American*
   photographer, b.1942)   BA
    Bibl: San Antonio (TX, USA),
    Witte Mem. Mus., 4 Texans
    (1978)
Gooderson, Thomas Youngerman   WI
   (British artist, op.1846-1860)   WC WI
    Bibl: ▶Wood, Victorian ptrs.
Gooderson, Thomas Youngman   WC
Gooderson, Thomas Youngman →see
   Gooderson, Thomas Youngerman
Goodes, Edward Ashton *(American*
   artist, 1832-1910)   WI
Goodey, Brian *(British architect)*   AV
    Bibl: Projeto, 1986 Mar., no.85,
    p.90
Goodhall, H.   WC WI
   (British artist, op.1780-)   WI
   (British artist, op.c.1780)   WC
Goodhall, Thomas F. *(British*
   photographer, act.1885)   BA
    Bibl: ▶Parry, Photo idx.
Goodhart Ducciesque Master →see
   Goodhart Master

Goodhart Master   BA
   (Italian artist, op.c.1300)   WC
   (Italian painter, act. 1300-1325)   PR
   (Italian painter, act.1310-1325)   BA
   (Italian, act. 1st quarter 14th c)   GC
    Bibl: ▶Fredericksen & Zeri, Census;
    ▶Shapley, Kress coll.; Stubblebine,
    Duccio, v.6, p.106; ▶Witt
    checklist
   Goodhart Ducciesque Master   GC PR
Master known as the Goodhart
   Ducciesque Master   PR
Master of Goodhart (Goodhart
   Master)   WC
   Master of Goodhart Madonna   PR
Master of the Goodhart
   Madonna   GC PR
Goodhart-Rendel, Harry Stuart   AV BA
   (1887-1959)   AV
   (British architect, 1887-1959)   BA
    Bibl: ▶Macmillan encyc. archts.;
    ▶Vollmer, Künst.-Lex. 20. Jhr.
Goodhue, Bertram →see Goodhue,
   Bertram Grosvenor
Goodhue, Bertram Grosvenor   AV BA
   (American architect, 1869-
   1924)   AV BA
   (American artist, 1869-1924)   WI
    Bibl: ▶Dict. Amer. biog.;
    ▶Macmillan encyc. archts.;
    ▶Vollmer, Künst.-Lex. 20. Jhr.
   Goodhue, Bertram   WI
Goodison, Benjamin *(English*
   cabinetmaker, ca.1700-1767)   BA
    Bibl: Burlington CXIX/892 (July
    1977) p.483; ▶Oxford dec. arts;
    ▶Penguin dec. arts
Goodlife, Kent P. *(American artist,*
   b.1946)   WI
Goodman [Unidentified] *(Unknown*
   painter)   PR
    Bibl: (February 1, 1812, lots 66,
    94, 95, & 102, Robins)
Goodman, Brenda Joyce *(American*
   painter, b.1943)   BA
    Bibl: ▶WW Amer. Art, 1978
Goodman, James John *(Designer,*
   New York, NY)   AV
    Bibl: Interior design, 1984 Apr.,
    v.56, no.4, p.174
Goodman, Janis *(American artist,*
   20th c.)   BA
    Bibl: Wash, D.C., Womens Arts
    Center, The founders, 1980
Goodman, Jeremiah *(American*
   interior designer, New York City)   AV
    Bibl: NYC phone bk., 1987
Goodman, Ken *(American painter,*
   b.1950)   BA
    Bibl: Art in Amer., LXVIII/8 (Oct.
    1980) pp.113-117; Cambridge
    (MA, USA), MIT, Hayden Gallery,
    Body language (1981)
Goodman, Lori Ellen *(American*
   artist, 20th c.)   BA
    Bibl: Arts Mag., "Arts reviews", 3
    Nov 1982

Goodman, Maude WC WI
    (British artist, op.1860-, d.1938) WI
    (British artist, op.1874-m.1938) WC
    Scanes, Maude, Mrs. WI
Goodman, Michael (American,
    contemporary) JG
Goodman, Robert Gwelo (South
    African artist, 1871-1939) WC
Goodman, Ronald D. (Architect,
    Great Neck, NY) AV
    Bibl: ▶AIA Pro File, 1983
Goodman, Sidney BA WC WI
    (American artist, 1936-) WC
    (American artist, b.1936) WI
    (American painter, printmaker,
    b.1936) BA
    Bibl: ▶Havlice, Idx. art. bio.; ▶WW
    Amer. Art, 1976
Goodman, Thomas Edward
    (Architect, Jackson, MS) AV
    Bibl: ▶AIA Pro File, 1983
Goodman, Tom (American
    photographer, b.1948) BA
    Bibl: ▶MoMA libr. cat.; San
    Antonio (TX, USA), Witte Mem.
    Mus., 4 Texans (1978)
Goodman, Walter (20th c.) BA
Goodman, Walter WC WI
    (British artist, 1838-) WC
    (British artist, 1838-op.1890) WI
Goodnough, Robert WC WI
    (American artist, 19th cent.) WC
    (American artist, op.circa 1889-) WI
Goodnough, Robert →see
    Goodnough, Robert Arthur
Goodnough, Robert Arthur BA WI
    (American artist, 1917-) WC
    (American artist, b.1917) WI
    (American painter, b.1917) BA
    Bibl: ▶Bénézit; ▶Contemp. artists;
    ▶Intl. dir. exh. artists; ▶MoMA
    libr. cat.; ▶NY art yrbk.; ▶Parry,
    Contemp. art; ▶Vollmer,
    Künst.-Lex. 20. Jhr.; ▶WW Amer.
    Art
    Goodnough, Robert WC
Goodovitch, Israel M. AV
Goodrich, Ansel (American
    cabinetmaker, d.1803) BA
    Bibl: Keno, Antiques CXVII (May
    1980) 1100-1107
Goodrich, Jerome (British artist, op.
    1829-1859) WC WI
Goodrich, Thomas White (British
    artist, op. 1853-1856) WI
Goodrich, W.R.E. (British artist, op.
    1912-) WI
Goodrich, William (American
    architect, act.1802) BA
    Bibl: ▶Withey, Amer. archts.
Goodridge, Eliza (American artist,
    1798-1882) WC WI

**Goodridge, Henry
    Edmund** AV BA WC WI
    (British architect, 1797-1864) BA
    (British architect, 1797-1864)) AV
    (British artist, op.1835) WC
    (British artist, op.1835-) WI
    Bibl: ▶Colvin, Brit. archts.
Goodridge, James (British artist,
    1766-1849) WI
Goodridge, Sarah BA WC WI
    (American artist, 1788-1853) WC WI
    (American miniaturist, 1788-
    1853) BA
    Bibl: ▶Fielding's Amer. ptrs.;
    ▶Groce, Artists Amer.;
    Washington, DC (USA), Natl.
    Gallery, Portrait Miniatures
    (1976-77)
Goodstein, Barbara BA
    (American architectural
    journalist) AV
    (American sculptor, b.1945) BA
    Bibl: ▶Intl. dir. exh. artists, 1983;
    Perl, J., in NEW CRITERION IV/4
    (Sept 1985) 60;
    Goldstein, Barbara AV
Goodstein, Edward H. (American
    painter, ca.1932-1981) BA
    Bibl: NY Times 8 Dec 1981
Goodwin, A.C. →see Goodwin,
    Arthur Clifton
Goodwin, Albert BA WC WI
    (British artist, 1845-1932) WC WI
    (British painter, 1845-1932) BA
    Bibl: ▶Bénézit; ▶Wood, Victorian
    ptrs.
Goodwin, Arthur Clifton BA PR WC WI
    (American artist, 1866-1929) WC
    (American artist, 1866-1933) WI
    (American painter, 1864-1929) PR
    (American painter, illustrator,
    1864-1929) BA
    Bibl: ▶Fielding's Amer. ptrs.;
    ▶RILA/BHA; ▶Vollmer, Künst.-Lex.
    20. Jhr.; ▶WWW Amer., 1897;
    ▶Young, Amer. artists
    Arthur Clifton Goodwin PR
    Goodwin, A.C. PR
Goodwin, Betty Roodish (Canadian
    artist, b.1923) BA
    Bibl: ▶Artists Canada;
    ▶MacDonald, Can. artists;
    Vancouver (BC, CAN), Art Gallery,
    17 Canadian artists (1976)
Goodwin, Edward (British artist,
    op.1802-1816) WC WI
    Bibl: ▶Mallalieu, Brit. watercolour
    artists
Goodwin, Edwin Weyburn WC WI
    (American artist, 1800-1845) WI
    (American artist, 1800-m.1845) WC
Goodwin, Edytha M., Miss (British
    artist, 1882-op.1912) WI
    Longstaff, Ralph, Mrs.(Edytha) WI
Goodwin, Francis (British architect,
    1784-1835) BA
    Bibl: ▶Colvin, Brit. archts.; ▶Dict.
    natl. biog.; ▶Thieme-Becker

Goodwin, Gary (British artist,
    b.1956) WI
Goodwin, Guy (American painter,
    b.1940) BA
    Bibl: ▶WW Amer. Art, 1986
Goodwin, Harry WC WI
    (British artist, -1925) WC
    (British artist, op.1868-, d.1925) WI
    Bibl: ▶Wood, Victorian ptrs.
Goodwin, Henry B. (Swedish
    photographer, 1878-1931) BA
    Bibl: Minneapolis (MN, USA),
    Walker Art Ctr., Frozen image
    (1982)
Goodwin, Mary (British interior
    designer and conservator for the
    National Trust) AV
    Bibl: The world of interiors, 1987
    May, p.100
Goodwin, Nancy AV
Goodwin, Philip L. →see Goodwin,
    Philip Lippincott
Goodwin, Philip Lippincott BA
    (American architect, 1885-
    1958) AV BA
    Bibl: ▶Avery obit. idx.; Hunt,
    Amer. arch.; ▶Macmillan encyc.
    archts.
Goodwin, Philip L. AV
Goodwin, Philip R. BA
    (American artist, 1882-1935) WI
    (American painter, illustrator,
    1882-1935) BA
    Bibl: ▶Fielding's Amer. ptrs.;
    ▶Vollmer, Künst.-Lex. 20. Jhr.
Goodwin, Philip Russell WI
Goodwin, Philip Russell →see
    Goodwin, Philip R.
Goodwin, Richard La Barre BA
    (American artist, 1840-1910) WC WI
    (American painter, 1840-1910) BA
    Bibl: Smith; ▶Young, Amer. artists
Goodwin, Richard Labarre WC WI
Goodwin, Richard Labarre →see
    Goodwin, Richard La Barre
Goodwin, Sydney P. (British artist,
    1867-1944) WI
Goodwin, W.Kate Malleson (British
    artist, op.1873-1893) WI
    Malleson, W.Kate, Miss WI
Goodwine, S. (British artist, op.
    1748-) WI
Goodwyn, John (English, 16th c.) BA
    Bibl: TRANS OF THE MOM. BRASS
    SOC. XII/2 (1976) 155-158
Goody, Joan E. (American architect) AV
    Bibl: ▶AIA Pro File, 1983
Goody, Marvin E. (1929-1980) AV
Goodyear, John L. (American
    painter, sculptor, b.1930) BA
    Bibl: Trenton (NJ, USA), State
    Mus., Beyond the plane (1983);
    ▶WW Amer. Art, 1984
Gooij →see Goyen, Jan Josephsz. van
Gool →see Gool, Jan van

Gool, Jan van   **BA GC PR WC**
  (*Dutch artist, 1685(?)-1763/5)*   WC
  (*Dutch painter and*
    draughtsman, 1685?-1763/5)   GC
  (*Dutch painter, 1685?-1763/65)*   PR
  (*Dutch painter, critic, 1685-*
    1763)   BA
    Bibl: Getty Photo Study Coll.;
    ▶Scheen, Ned. beeldende kunst.;
    ▶Thieme-Becker; ▶Witt checklist
  Gool   PR
  J.V. Goal   PR
  J.V. Goal   PR
  Jan van Gool   PR
  V. Gool   PR
  Van Gol   PR
  Van Gool   PR
  Van Zool   PR
Goolrick, Robert Cooke (*American*
  artist, 20th c.)   BA
    Bibl: UC Santa Barbara cat. sheets
Goor, G. van → *see* Goor, Gerrit van
Goor, Gerrit van   BA
  (*Dutch artist, c.1694(?))*   WC
  (*Dutch painter, act.1674-1694)*   BA
    Bibl: ▶Art Index, v.36; ▶Kraam,
    Holl. en Vlaamsche kunst., v.2,
    p.590; ▶Thieme-Becker; van Gool,
    v.I (1750), p.375; Van Thiel, Ptgs
    Rijksmus., p.714; Wansink, OUD
    HOLLAND, CI/3 (1987), 218-221;
    ▶Wurzbach, NLD Künst.-Lex.
  Goor, G. van   WC
Goor, Martien van (*Dutch architect,*
  Amsterdam)   AV
    Bibl: ▶Federatie O jrbk., 1984
Goor, Simon van [**Unidentified**]
  (*Unknown painter)*   PR
    Bibl: (May 14 & ff, 1804, lot 519,
    Truchsessian Gallery)
  S. van Goor   PR
Goor, Steven Jansz. van   GC PR WC
  (*Dutch artist, c.1606-c.1657/63)*   WC
  (*Dutch painter,*
    ca.1608-1657/63)   GC
  (*Dutch painter,*
    ca.1608-ca.1657/63)   PR
    Bibl: ▶Thieme-Becker
  Steven Jansz. van Goor   PR
  Steven van Ghoor   PR
  Steven van Goor   PR
  Van Goar   PR
  Van Goor   PR
Goos, Berend (*German artist, 1815-*
  1885)   WC
Goosen, Jan van (*Dutch artist,*
  op.1667/8)   WC
Goossens, Josse (*German artist,*
  1876-1929)   WC
Goossens, Miek (*Belgian architect)*   AV
    Bibl: Monumenten en
    landschappen, 1986 May-June,
    v.5, no.3, p.8
Gootfried, A. (*British artist, op.*
  1870-)   WI

Goovaerts, Hendrick → *see* Govaerts,
  Hendrick
Gopal-Chowdhury, Paul   WC WI
  (*British artist, 1949-)*   WC
  (*British artist, b.1949)*   WI
Göpfert, Heiner (*German architect)*   AV
    Bibl: Kunst und Kirche, 1984,
    no.2, p.125
Goppel, Thomas (*West German*
  State Sec., Bavarian State Ministry
  for Science and Art)   AV
    Bibl: Deutsche Bauzeitschrift,
    1989 May, v.37, no.5, p.5564
Gor, Pierre (*French bell founder, act.*
  ca.1752-ca.1768)   BA
    Bibl: Albinus, RYTTERSTATUEN
    AMALIENBORG...(1982);
    ▶Thieme-Becker
Gorafalo → *see* Garofalo, Benvenuto
  Tisi da
Gorbitz, Johan (*Norwegian artist,*
  1782-1853)   WC
Gorchov, Ron   BA WI
  (*American artist, b.1930)*   WI
  (*American painter, b.1930)*   BA
    Bibl: ▶WW Amer. Art, 1976
Gorczyn, Jan Alexander (*Polish*
  artist, op.1645-1704)   WC
Gordigiani, Edoardo   GC
  (*Italian artist, 1866-)*   WC
  (*Italian painter, b.1867)*   GC
    Bibl: ▶Thieme-Becker
Gordigiani, Eduardo   WC
Gordigiani, Eduardo → *see* Gordigiani,
  Edoardo
Gordigiani, Michele   BA GC WC
  (*Italian artist, 1830-1909)*   WC
  (*Italian painter, 1830-1909)*   BA
  (*Italian, 1830-1909)*   GC
    Bibl: ▶Bénézit; ▶Thieme-Becker
Gordillo, Luis (*Spanish painter,*
  b.1934)   BA
    Bibl: ▶Campoy, Español contemp.;
    ▶Intl. dir. exh. artists
Gordin, Sidney (*American sculptor,*
  painter, printmaker, b.1918)   BA
    Bibl: Artforum III May 1965, p.39;
    ▶MoMA libr. cat.; Portland (OR,
    USA), Art Mus., West Coast now
    (1968); ▶Vollmer, Künst.-Lex. 20.
    Jhr.
Gordon Coutts → *see* Coutts, Gordon
Gordon, Alexander John (*British*
  architect)   AV
Gordon, Arthur   WC WI
  (*British artist, 19th cent.)*   WC
  (*British artist, op.19th c.)*   WI
Gordon, Bonnie (*American artist,*
  b.1941)   BA
    Bibl: New York (NY, USA), New
    Mus.,
    Deconstruction/reconstruction
    (1980)
Gordon, Catherine Susan, Lady → *see*
  Chesham, Lady
Gordon, Col.& Mrs. (*British artist,*
  op.1849-1892)   WI

Gordon, Eleanor, Miss → *see* Boyle,
  Eleanor Vere
Gordon, Eugene (*American*
  photographer, b.1923)   GC
    Bibl: ▶Libr. of Congr. Name Auth.
    File
Gordon, George (*Unknown artist)*   GC
    Bibl: Gernsheim, Corpus Photog.
    of Drawings, 1591
Gordon, Hilda May   BA WI
  (*British artist, 1874-1972)*   WI
  (*British painter, 1874-1972)*   BA
    Bibl: ▶Artist biog. master idx.;
    ▶Johnson, Brit. artists; ▶Petteys,
    Women artists; ▶Waters, Brit.
    artists
Gordon, Jack L. (*American*
  architect)   AV
Gordon, James   WI
  (*British artist, op.c.1646)*   WC
  (*British artist, op.circa 1646-)*   WI
Gordon, Rev. James   WC
Gordon, James Riely   AV BA
  (*American architect, 1863-1937)*   BA
  (*American architect, active in*
    Texas, 1863-1937)   AV
    Bibl: ▶Withey, Amer. archts.
Gordon, Jeff (*American architectural*
  student)   AV
    Bibl: Architecture: the AIA
    journal, 1985 May, v.74, no.5,
    p.56
Gordon, John S. (*American sculptor,*
  b.1946)   BA
    Bibl: ARTS MAGAZINE, v.51, Mar
    1977, p.17; ▶WW Amer. Art,
    1976
Gordon, John Sloan (*Canadian*
  artist, 1868-1940)   WC
Gordon, John Watson   BA GC PR WI
  (*British artist, 1788-1864)*   WC WI
  (*British painter, 1788-1864)*   BA PR
  (*Scottish painter, 1788-1864)*   GC
    Bibl: ▶Bénézit; ▶Dict. natl. biog.;
    Getty Photo Study Coll.; ▶Harris,
    Scottish ptrs.; ▶RILA/BHA;
    ▶Thieme-Becker; ▶Witt checklist
  Gordon, John Watson, Sir   PR
  Gordon, Sir John Watson   GC WC
  John Watson Gordon   PR
  Watson Gordon, Sir John   GC
  Watson, John II   WI
Gordon, John Watson, Sir → *see*
  Gordon, John Watson
Gordon, Julia Isabella Levina
  (*British artist, 1772-1867)*   WI
    Bibl: ▶Mallalieu, Brit. watercolour
    artists
  Bennet, Julia Isabella Levina, Miss   WI
Gordon, Lee (*American artist,*
  b.1957)   BA
    Bibl: New York (NY, USA), New
    Mus., Extended sensibilities
    (1982)
Gordon, Max (*British architect,*
  London)   AV
    Bibl: ▶RIBA members, 1983

Gordon, Mel *(British artist, b.1943)* **WI**
Gordon, N. L. *(American, active
     Chicago ca. 1900)*   **JG**
Gordon, Neil *(British artist, b.1958)* **WI**
Gordon, Pat S. *(American painter,
     20th c.)*   **BA**
     Bibl: Tulsa (OK, USA), Philbrook
        Art Center, P.S. GORDON (1985);
        Tulsa (OK, USA), Philbrook Art
        Center. WORKS ON PAPER; PAT S.
        GORDON WATERCOLORS, 1977
Gordon, Peter   **WC WI**
     (American artist, op.1730-1740)   **WI**
     (American artist, op.c.1735)   **WC**
Gordon, Rev. James → *see* Gordon,
     James
Gordon, Richard   **BA JG**
     *(American photographer,
        b.1945)*   **BA**
     (American, contemporary)   **JG**
     Bibl: Afterimage VI/9 (Apr 79),
        p.18
Gordon, Robert Jacob *(Dutch
     soldier, explorer, draftsman, 1743-
     1795)*   **BA**
     Bibl: ▶Natl. union cat., pre-1956;
        Rookmaaker, Bull. v. het Rijks,
        XXIX/3 (1981) pp.123-135
Gordon, Robert James   **WC WI**
     (British artist, 19th cent.)   **WC**
     (British artist, op.1871-1894)   **WI**
Gordon, Sir John Watson → *see*
     Gordon, John Watson
Gordon, T.J.L.   **WC WI**
     (British artist, op.1807)   **WC**
     (British artist, op.1807-)   **WI**
Gordot, Claude Marie   **GC WC**
     (French artist, op.1774)   **WC**
     (French, act. ca.1774)   **GC**
     Bibl: ▶Thieme-Becker; ▶Witt
        checklist
Gordy, Robert P. *(American painter,
     b.1933)*   **BA**
     Bibl: ▶WW Amer. Art, 1976
Gore → *see* Gore, Spencer Frederick
Gore, Allan *(British architect, 20th
     c.)*   **BA**
     Bibl: Gaillemin, Mons. hist.
        France, 108 (1980) pp.68-70
Gore, Charles   **BA GC WC WI**
     (British artist, 1729-1807)   **WC WI**
     (British painter, 1729-1807)   **BA GC**
     Bibl: ▶Bénézit; ▶Mallalieu, Brit.
        watercolour artists; ▶RILA/BHA
Gore, Frederick → *see* Gore, Frederick
     John Pym
Gore, Frederick John Pym   **BA WI**
     (British artist, 1913-)   **WC**
     (British artist, b.1913)   **WI**
     (British painter, b.1913)   **BA**
     Bibl: Kelly's Handbook; ▶Who's
        Who [GBR], 1977
Gore, Frederick   **WC**

**Gore, Spencer
     Frederick**   **BA GC PR WC WI**
     (British artist, 1878-1914)   **WC WI**
     (British painter, 1878-1914)   **BA PR**
     (British, 1878-1914)   **GC**
     Bibl: ▶Bénézit; ▶RILA/BHA;
        ▶Vollmer, Künst.-Lex. 20. Jhr.;
        ▶Waters, Brit. artists; ▶Who was
        who [GBR], 1897; ▶Witt checklist;
        ▶Yale Brit. artists list
     Gore   **PR**
     Spencer Frederick Gore   **PR**
Gore, William Crampton *(British
     artist, 1877-1946)*   **WI**
     Bibl: ▶Waters, Brit. artists
     Gore, William Crampton Crawford **WI**
*Gore, William Crampton
     Crawford* → *see* Gore, William
     Crampton
Gore, William Henry   **WC WI**
     (British artist, 1880-1916)   **WI**
     (British artist, 19th cent.)   **WC**
Gore-Booth, Colum *(British artist,
     op.1937-1955)*   **WI**
Gorecki or Goretzky, Tadeusz von
     (Polish artist, 1825-1868)   **WC**
Goreleigh, Rex *(American painter,
     printmaker, b.1902)*   **BA**
     Bibl: ▶Cederholm, Afro-Amer.
        artists; ▶WW Amer. Art, 1976
Gorelick, Shirley *(American painter,
     printmaker, b.1924)*   **BA**
     Bibl: ▶WW Amer. Art, 1978
Gorella, Arwed D. *(German painter,
     b.1937)*   **BA**
     Bibl: Lübeck (DEU), Overbeck-
        Gesellschaft, 3 Berliner Realisten
        (1975); ▶Natl. union cat., 1968-
        1972
Gorey, Edward St. John *(American
     illustrator, author, b.1925)*   **BA**
     Bibl: ▶Natl. union cat., 1975;
        ▶New Columbia encyc.
Gorge, Paul *(Belgian artist, 19th
     cent.)*   **WC**
Gorgiard, Laurence *(French
     architect)*   **AV**
     Bibl: Le moniteur architecture
        AMC, 1989 Oct., no.5, p.12
Gorgias *(Greek sculptor, 5th c BC
     (early))*   **GC**
     Bibl: Getty Photo Study Coll.;
        ▶Robertson, Greek art, p.104
Gorgione → *see* Giorgione (Giorgio da
     Castelfranco)
Gorgione del Castel-franco → *see*
     Giorgione (Giorgio da
     Castelfranco)
Gorgioni → *see* Giorgione (Giorgio da
     Castelfranco)
Gorgon Painter   **GC JG**
     (vase-painter, ca. 600-580 BC)   **GC**
     Bibl: ▶Beazley, Attic bl.-fig. vase-
        ptrs.; Boardman, Attic Bl.-fig.
        Vases
Gorgone → *see* Giorgione (Giorgio da
     Castelfranco)

Gorgoni, Gianfranco *(Italian
     photographer, b.1941)*   **BA**
     Bibl: ▶Artweek idx.; ▶MoMA libr.
        cat.; San Francisco (CA, USA),
        MOMA, Art of the 70's: Photos
        by... (1978)
Gorgu, Claude *(French menuisier,
     master 1770, act. to ca.1790)*   **GC**
     Bibl: ▶Salverte, Ébénistes 18e s.
Gorguet, August François Marie   **BA**
     (French artist, 1862-1927)   **WC**
     (French painter, 1862-1927)   **BA GC**
     Bibl: ▶Bénézit; ▶Met. Mus. Art
        libr. cat.; ▶Vollmer, Künst.-Lex.
        20. Jhr.
Gorguet, Auguste Francois   **GC WC**
Gorguet, Auguste Francois → *see*
     Gorguet, August François Marie
Gorham, John *(d.1801)*   **AV**
Gori, Alessandro   **GC WC**
     (Italian artist, 17th cent.)   **WC**
     (Italian, 17th century)   **GC**
     Bibl: ▶Witt checklist
Gori, Angiolo   **BA WC**
     (Italian artist, op.1658)   **WC**
     (Italian painter, d.1678)   **BA**
     Bibl: ▶Bolaffi; Nesi, ANTICHITA
        VIVA, XXVII/2 (Apr-June 1988), p.
        10-21; ▶Thieme-Becker; ▶Witt
        checklist
Gori, Giuseppe *(Italian architect,
     1906-)*   **AV**
Gori, Lamberto Cristiano *(Italian
     artist, 1730-1801)*   **WC**
Gori, Ottavio *(Italian artist, 18th
     cent.)*   **WC**
Gori, Rosalba *(Italian artist, 18th
     cent.(?))*   **WC**
Gorin, Jean *(French painter,
     b.1899)*   **BA**
     Bibl: ▶Bénézit; ▶Encyc. world art
Gorin, Jean-Albert *(French artist,
     20th cent.)*   **WC**
Gorin, Rosalind E. *(American real
     estate developer, president of H.N.
     Gorin Associates, Boston, Mass)* **AV**
     Bibl: Boston Preservation Alliance
        letter, 1989 Jan., v.10, no.1, p.5
Gorin, Stanislas *(French painter,
     19th century)*   **GC**
     Bibl: ▶Bénézit
Goris, Gérard *(Flemish woodcarver,
     act.1438-1441)*   **BA**
     Bibl: ▶Bénézit; ▶Thieme-Becker
Gorjaev, Vitalij Nikolaevič *(Russian
     printmaker, b.1910)*   **BA**
     Bibl: ▶Fogg Mus. Libr. cat.;
        Voronov, VITALIJ GORIAEV, 1979
Gorjup, Tomaž *(Yugoslav painter,
     b.1950)*   **BA**
     Bibl: TOMAZ GORJUP(1979),
        Ljubljana, Mala Galerija
Gorka, Gèza *(Hungarian ceramist,
     b.1894)*   **BA**
     Bibl: Faenza, LXVI/1-6 (1980) pp.
        367-370; ▶Vollmer, Künst.-Lex.
        20. Jhr.

Gorka, Wiktor (Polish artist, 20th
cent.)   WC
*Gorky, Arshile→see Gorky, Arshile
(Vosdanig Manoog Adoian)*
**Gorky, Arshile (Vosdanig Manoog
Adoian)**   BA GC
   (American artist, 1904-1948)   WC WI
   (American painter, 1904-1948)   BA GC
     Bibl: ▶Bénézit; ▶Cummings,
     Contemp. Amer. artists, 1971;
     ▶Encyc. world art; ▶Fogg Mus.
     Libr. cat.; Getty Photo Study Coll.;
     ▶RILA/BHA
   Adoian, Vosdanig Manoog   WI
   Gorky, Arshile   GC WC WI
Gorlier, Bruno (French silversmith,
1725-1804, master 1750)   GC
     Bibl: ▶Mabille, Orfèv. fran.
*Gorman, Richard→see Gorman,
Richard C.*
Gorman, Richard C.   WI
   (American artist, 20th cent.)   WC
   (American artist, op.1963-)   WI
   Gorman, Richard   WC
Gorman, Rudolf Carl (American
painter, dealer, b.1933)   BA
     Bibl: OCLC; WW Amer., 1978;
     ▶WW Amer. Art, 1978, 1982
*Gormley, Anthony→see Gormley,
Antony*
Gormley, Antony   BA
   (British artist, b.1950)   WI
   (British sculptor, b.1950)   BA
     Bibl: Archer, STUDIO
     INTERNATIONAL,
     CXCVI/1004(1984), 44; ▶Intl. dir.
     exh. artists, 1983
   Gormley, Anthony   WI
Gormy, Anthony (American artist,
20th c.)   BA
     Bibl: Arts Mag., LV/9 (May 1981)
     pp.88-92
Gorn, Edward (Soviet photographer,
b.ca.1933)   BA
     Bibl: Jacoby, S., CONNOISSEUR,
     CCXIV/870 (Aug. 1984) 71
Gornell, Robert (American architect) AV
     Bibl: Marquee, 1987 Fourth
     quarter, v.19, no.4, p.20
Gorni, Giuseppe   BA
   (Italian artist, 1894-)   WC
   *(Italian sculptor, painter,
   printmaker, 1894-1975)*   BA
     Bibl: ▶Bolaffi; ▶Comanducci, Diz.;
     Suzzara(ITA), Galleria civica...,
     GUISEPPE GORNI(1979); ▶Vollmer,
     Künst.-Lex. 20. Jhr.
   Gorni, Giuseppe di Nuvolato   WC
*Gorni, Giuseppe di Nuvolato→see
Gorni, Giuseppe*
Gornik, April (American painter,
b.1953)   BA
     Bibl: ▶Intl. dir. exh. artists, 1983;
     ▶WW Amer. Art
Gorny, Alan (American architect)   AV
     Bibl: Design solutions, 1984
     Summer, v.4, no.2, p.23

Górny, Anthony-Petr (American
printmaker, b.1950)   BA
     Bibl: ART NEWS LXXXV/8 (Oxt
     1986); ▶Intl. dir. exh. artists,
     1982; New York (NY, USA),
     Guggenheim Mus., New horizons
     (1985)
Goro di Gregorio (Italian sculptor,
act.ca.1324-1333)   BA
     Bibl: ▶Encyc. world art;
     ▶Thieme-Becker; ▶White, Art &
     arch. Italy, p.287
Goro di ser Neroccio (Italian
goldsmith and sculptor, 1387-
doca.1456)   GC
     Bibl: ▶Bénézit; Getty Photo Study
     Coll.; ▶Thieme-Becker
   Neroccio, Goro di ser   GC
Gorowski, Mieczyslaw (Polish
artist, 20th cent.)   WC
Gorp, Henri Nicolas van   GC WC
   (French artist, op.1793-1819)   WC
   (French, act.1793-1819)   GC
     Bibl: ▶Thieme-Becker; ▶Witt
     checklist
Gorra, Giulio (Italian artist, 1832-
1884)   WC
Görres, Heinrich (West German
architect)   AV
     Bibl: ▶Bund Deut. Arch. Hdbch.,
     1987
Gorrie, John (American physician,
inventor, 1803-1855)   BA
     Bibl: ▶Webster's Bio. Dict.
Gorski, Gilbert (American architect) AV
     Bibl: Chicago architectural journal,
     1989, no.7, p.170
Gorski, Joel (Brazilian architect)   AV
     Bibl: Projeto, 1987 sept., no.103,
     p.69
Gorski, Maria Cecília Barbieri
(Brazilian architect)   AV
     Bibl: Projeto, 1988 Mar., no.108,
     p.110
Gorski, Michel Todel (Brazilian
architect, São Paulo)   AV
     Bibl: Projeto, 1987 July, no.101,
     p.96
Gorsline, Douglas Warner
(American painter, printmaker,
illustrator, author, b.1913)   BA
     Bibl: Minneapolis (MN, USA), U.
     Minn. Gallery, American Scene
     (1976); ▶WW Amer. Art, 1976
Gorson→see Gorson, Aaron Henry
*Gorson, A.H.→see Gorson, Aaron
Henry*
*Gorson, Aaron→see Gorson, Aaron
Henry*
*Gorson, Aaron Harry→see Gorson,
Aaron Henry*

Gorson, Aaron Henry   WC WI
   (American artist, 1872-1933)   WC WI
   (American painter, 1872-1933)   PR
     Bibl: ▶WWW Amer. art
   Aaron Harry Gorson   PR
   Gorson   PR
   Gorson, A.H.   PR
   Gorson, Aaron   PR
   Gorson, Aaron Harry   PR
Gorst, Thom (British architect,
London)   AV
     Bibl: Architects' journal, 1989
     Oct.18, v.190, no.16, p.26
Görstner, Alfred (East German
architect)   AV
     Bibl: Architektur der DDR, 1986
     aug., v.35, no.8, p.476
Gort (Dutch(?) artist, op.1661)   WC
Gort (Dutch painter, act.1661)   GC
     Bibl: ▶Bénézit
Gortano, Jacob (Austrian goldsmith,
jeweler, 19th c.)   BA
     Bibl: Simoniti, Zbornik za
     umetnostno zgodovino XIV-XV
     (1978-1979) 199-209
*Gortazar, Fernando Gonzalez→see
Gonzalez Gortazar, Fernando*
Gorter→see Gorter, Arnold Marc
Gorter, Arnold Marc   BA GC PR WC
   (Dutch artist, 1866-1933)   WC
   (Dutch painter, 1866-1933)   BA GC PR
     Bibl: ▶Bénézit; ▶Scheen, Ned.
     beeldende kunst.;
     ▶Thieme-Becker; ▶Witt checklist
   Arnold Marc Gorter   PR
   Gorter   PR
Gorter, Paul (Dutch painter, b.1952) BA
     Bibl: Leeuwarden (NLD), Fries
     Museum, Paul Gorter: Schilderijen
     1981-1985 (1986)
Gorton, Assheton (British artist,
b.1930)   WI
*Gortschacher→see Goertschacher,
Urban*
*Gortschacher (not Dortschacher)
Urban→see Goertschacher, Urban*
*Görtschacher, Urban→see
Goertschacher, Urban*
*Gortzius Geldorp→see Geldorp
Gortzius*
Görz, Mathias von (Austrian
painter, ca.1670-1731)   BA
     Bibl: ▶Bénézit; ▶Thieme-Becker
Gos, Albert (Swiss artist, 1852-)   WC
Gosar, Marko (Yugoslav painter,
b.1953)   BA
     Bibl: Ljubljana(YUG), Modernema
     Galerij, Likoma..., 10
     MLADIH(1982)
Gosc (British artist, op.1617-)   WI
Gösch, Paul (German architect and
painter, 1885-1940)   AV
Goscimski, Wladislaw (Polish artist,
1904-)   WC
Gose, Francisco Xavier (Spanish
artist, 1876-1915)   WC

Goser, Simon *(Swiss artist, op.1772-1814)* **WC**

Gosewitz, Ludwig *(German draftsman, b.1936)* **BA**
 Bibl: ▶Bénézit; Berlin (DEU), Neuer Berliner Kunstverein, 8 from Berlin (1975), p.250; ▶WW Arts DEU

Goshow, F. Eric *(American architect)* **AV**
 Bibl: ▶AIA Pro File, 1985

Gosling, C.H. *(British artist, op.1886-)* **WI**

Gosling, William W. *(British artist, 1824-1883)* **WC WI**

Gosnell, Stephen *(American painter, b.1961)* **BA**
 Bibl: Norman (OK, USA), U of OK Mus. Art, Visions 83 (1983)

Gosolphi→see Ghisolfi, Giovanni

Goss, William Henry *(British potter, 1833-1906)* **BA**
 Bibl: ▶Boger, World pott. & porc.; ▶Mankowitz, Encyc. pott. & porc.

Gossaert→see Gossaert, Jan

Gossaert, Jan   **BA CE GC JG PR** WI
 (early Netherlandish painter, ca. 1472-ca.1533)   **BA**
 (Flanders painter, ca.1472-ca. 1533)   **GC**
 (Flemish, ca. 1478-1532)   **JG**
 (Netherlandish painter, ca.1478-1533/6)   **PR**
 (Netherlands artist, circa 1478-1533)   **WI**
 (Netherlands artist, op.1503-m. 1532)   **WC**
 (Painter, draughtsman, c.1478-post 1532/ante 1537)   **CE**
 Bibl: ▶Friedländer, Early Neth. ptg.; Getty Photo Study Coll. (Ptgs.); ▶RILA/BHA; ▶Thieme-Becker

Gossaert   PR
Gossaert, Jan (Mabuse)   PR
Gossaert, Jan called Mabuse   PR
Gossart, Jan   CE PR
Gossart, Jan (Mabuse)   PR
Gossart, Jan van   WI
J. dd Mabeuse   PR
J. de Mabeuge   PR
J. De Mabeuse   PR
J. de Mabuge   PR
J. de Mabuse   PR
J. de Mabuze   PR
J. de Maubege   PR
J. de Maubeuge   PR
J. De Maubeuse   PR
J. de Maubuse   PR
J. de Maugeuge   PR
J. Mabuse   PR
J. Maubeuge   PR
J. of Maubeuge   PR
J.D. Mabuge   PR
Jan de Mabeuge   PR
Jan de Mabuse   PR
Jan Gossaert   PR
Jean de Mabeuse   PR
Jean de Maubeuge   PR
Jean of Maubeuge   PR
John de Mabeuse   PR
John de Mabuse   PR
Mabeuge   PR
Mabuge   PR
Mabuse   CE GC PR **WI**
Mabuse or Mauberge, Jennyn or Jan Gossaert or Gossart van (Joannes Malbodius)   **WC**
Maubauge   PR
Mauberge, Jennyn   WI
Maubeuge   PR
Maubeuse   PR
Gossaert, Jan (Mabuse)→see Gossaert, Jan
Gossaert, Jan called Mabuse→see Gossaert, Jan

Gossage, John R. *(American photographer, b.1946)* **BA**
 Bibl: Baltimore (MD, USA), Baltimore Mus., JOHN R. GOSSAGE (1975)

Gossart or Gosser, Jean or Jen *(Netherlands artist, op.1428-1430)* **WC**

Gossart, Jan→see Gossaert, Jan

Gossart, Jan (Mabuse)→see Gossaert, Jan

Gossart, Jan van→see Gossaert, Jan

Gosse→see Gosse, Laura Sylvia

Gosse, H. *(French artist, op.1831)* **WC**

Gosse, Laura Sylvia   **BA PR WC WI**
 (British artist, 1881-1968)   **WC WI**
 (British painter, 1881-1968)   **PR**
 (British painter, printmaker, 1881-1968)   **BA**
 Bibl: ▶Houfe, Brit. book illus.; ▶RILA/BHA; ▶Waters, Brit. artists; ▶Who's Who [GBR], 1961

Gosse   PR
Gosse, Sylvia   PR
Laura Sylvia Gosse   PR

Gosse, Nicolas Louis Francois   **GC WC**
 (French artist, 1787-1878)   **WC**
 (French, 1787-1878)   **GC**
 Bibl: ▶Thieme-Becker; ▶Witt checklist

Gosse, Philip Henry *(British artist, 1810-1888)* **WI**

Gosse, Sylvia→see Gosse, Laura Sylvia

Gosse, Thomas *(British artist, 1765-1844)* **WC WI**
 Bibl: ▶Houfe, Brit. book illus.

Gosse, W. *(British artist, op.1814-1839)* **WC WI**
 Bibl: ▶Foskett, Brit. miniature ptrs.

Gossee, B. *(French artist, op.1779)* **WC**

Gosselin, Albert (Ferdinand Jules Albert) *(French artist, 1862-)* **WC**

Gosselin, Louis *(Canadian ceramist, 20th c.)* **BA**
 Bibl: ▶Artists Canada; Saint-Paul-de-Vence(FRA), Foundation Maeght. LOUIS GOSSELIN(1975)

Gossens *(Flemish(?) artist, 18th cent.)* **WC**

Gosset de Guines, Louis Alexandre (Andre Gill)→see Gill, André (Louis Alexandre Gosset de Guines)

Gosset, Isaac *(British artist, 1713-1799)* **WC WI**

Gossin, Gerard→see Goswin, Gerard

Gostl, Johana Baptist *(German artist, 1813-1895)* **WC**

Gostoli, Francesco *(Italian architect)* **AV**
 Bibl: Domus, 1988 Sept., no.697, p.6

Gostomski, Zbigniew *(Polish painter, sculptor, b.1932)* **BA**
Bibl: ▶Bénézit; Buffalo (NY, USA), Albright-Knox, 17 contemp. artists Poland (1976); ▶Phaidon 20c. art

Gosvami, Gopal Krishna *(Indian photographer, act.1887)* **BA**
Bibl: HISTORY OF PHOTOG., IX/3 (July-Sept 1985) 247-250

Goswin van der Weyden → see Weyden, Goswin van der

Goswin, Gerard **GC**
(Flemish artist, 1616-1691) WC
(Flemish, 1616-1691) GC
Bibl: Getty Photo Study Coll. (Ptgs.); ▶Witt checklist
Gossin, Gerard GC

Goswin, Gossin or Gosuin, Gerard **WC**
Goswin, Gossin or Gosuin, Gerard → see Goswin, Gerard

Gotch, Bernard Cecil **WC WI**
(British artist, 1876-) WC
(British artist, b.1876) WI

Gotch, Thomas Cooper **BA WC WI**
(British artist, 1854-1931) WC WI
(British painter, printmaker, 1854-1931) BA
Bibl: ▶Vollmer, Künst.-Lex. 20. Jhr.; ▶Waters, Brit. artists; ▶Who was who [GBR], 1929

Goth, Moricz *(Hungarian artist, 1873-)* **WC**

Gotha Cup **GC**
Bibl: ▶Beazley, Attic red-fig. vase-ptrs.

Gothard, Barbara *(American artist, 20th c.)* **BA**
Bibl: Chavis, 10 Michigan Afro-Amer. artists

Gothard, Eugen von *(Hungarian astronomer, photographer, 1857-1909)* **BA**
Bibl: HISTORY OF PHOTOGRAPHY, II/1(JAN 1978), 53; ▶Österr. biog. Lex. 1815-1950

Gothart-Nithart, Mathis → see Grünewald, Matthias

Göthe, Gustav *(Swedish sculptor, 1779-1838)* **BA**
Bibl: ▶Encyc. world art; ▶Natl. union cat., 1975; ▶Thieme-Becker

Gothe, H. *(German artist, 19th cent.)* **WC**

Gothein, Werner *(German artist, 1890-)* **WC**

Gothereau *(French(?) artist, 19th cent.(?))* **WC**

Gotlib → see Gotlib, Henryk

Gotlib, Henryk **BA PR WC**
(Polish artist, 1892-1966) WC
(Polish painter, 1890-1966) BA PR
Bibl: ▶Bénézit; ▶Contemp. artists; ▶MoMA libr. cat.; ▶RILA/BHA
Gotlib PR
Henryk Gotlib PR

Gotlieb, Al *(American artist, 20th c.)* **BA**
Bibl: Kuhn ARTS MAG LIX/1 Sept '84

Gotman, Miles Edmund → see Cotman, Miles Edmund

Goto, John *(British photographer, b.1949)* **BA**
Bibl: Arts Council GBR, Summer Show 4 (1977)

Goto, Joseph **WC WI**
(American artist, 1926-) WC
(American artist, b.1920) WI

Goto, Mariko *(Japanese architect, 1948-)* **AV**
Bibl: Kenchiku bunka, 1987 Dec., v.42,no.494, p.116

Gotsch, Friedrich Karl **BA GC**
(German painter, 1900-1984) GC
(German painter, printmaker, 1900-1984) BA
Bibl: Albstadt (DEU), Stadt. Galerie, FRIEDRICH KARL GOTSCH (1985); ▶MoMA libr. cat.; PHAIDON; ▶Schweers, Gemälde deut. Museen; ▶Vollmer, Künst.-Lex. 20. Jhr.; ▶WW Germany

Götsch, Joseph *(Austrian sculptor in Germany, 1728-1793)* **BA**
Bibl: ▶Thieme-Becker; Unger, Joseph Gotsch: ein bayerischer Bildhauer des Rokokos aus Tirol (1972), 10

Gott, Joseph *(British sculptor, 1785-1860)* **BA**
Bibl: ▶Bénézit; ▶Thieme-Becker

Gottardo Piazzoni → see Piazzoni, Gottardo

Gottfried Pulian → see Pulian, Gottfried

Gottfried, A. *(British artist, op. 1870)* **WC**

Gottfried, Hermann *(German painter, 20th cent)* **AV**
Bibl: Colonia romanica, 1988, v.3, p.148

Gottfried, Michael *(American interior designer, New York)* **AV**
Bibl: Architectural digest, 1985 Aug., v.42, no.8, p.132

Gottfrois, Roland *(French architect, Paris)* **AV**
Bibl: Architektur + Wettbewerbe, 1989 Mar., no.137, p.52

Gottgetreu, Rudolf Wilhelm *(German artist, 1821-p.1877)* **WC**

Gotthardt Kuehl → see Kuehl, Gotthardt Johann

Gotti, Arcangelo *(Italian, act.1733)* **BA**
Bibl: Haines, Memorie domenicane, XII (1981) pp.269-286

Götti, Oskar *(Architect, Switzerland)* **AV**

Gotti, Vincenzio → see Gotti, Vincenzo

Gotti, Vincenzo *(Italian painter, act. 18th century)* **PR**
Bibl: ▶Bolaffi
Gotti, Vincenzio PR
Vincenzio Gotti PR
Vincenzo Gotti PR

Götting, Andreas → see Göding, Andreas

Gottlandt, Peter *(German, act.1548/49-1572)* **GC**
Bibl: ▶Thieme-Becker

Gottlieb or Gotlieb, Leopold *(Polish artist, 1883-1933)* **WC**

Gottlieb, Adolph **BA GC WC WI**
(American artist, 1903-) WC
(American artist, 1903-1974) WI
(American painter, 1903-1974) BA GC
Bibl: ▶RILA/BHA; Syracuse(NY, USA), Everson Museum of Art, PROVINCETOWN PAINTERS(1977)

Gottlieb, Harry **BA PR**
(American painter, b. 1895) PR
(American painter, printmaker, b.1895) BA
Bibl: ▶Bénézit; ▶MoMA libr. cat.; ▶RILA/BHA; RLIN BKS file
Harry Gottlieb PR

Gottlieb, Maurycy **BA**
(Polish artist, 1856-1879) WC
(Polish painter, 1856-1879) BA
Bibl: ▶Slownik artystów polskich; ▶Thieme-Becker

Gottlieb, Moritz **WC**
Gottlieb, Moritz → see Gottlieb, Maurycy

Gottlob, Fernand Louis *(French artist, 1873-)* **WC**

Gottlob, Kaj *(Danish architect)* **AV**
Bibl: Landskab, 1984 Sept., v.65, no.6, p.130

Gottloeber, Christine *(West German painter, b.1958)* **BA**
Bibl: Ingolstadt (DEU), Kulturpalast, Christian Bauer (1984)

Gottman, Lorens *(Swedish artist, 1708-1779)* **WC**

Gottmann, Ernst, the elder *(German photographer, b.1874)* **BA**
Bibl: Heidelberg (DEU), Kunstverein, Beruf: Photo. Heidelberg (1980) 2 exhs.

Gottmann, Ernst, the younger *(German photographer, 20th c.)* **BA**
Bibl: Heidelberg (DEU), Kunstverein, Beruf: Photo. Heidelberg (1980) 2 exhs.

Gotto, Frederick *(British architect)* **AV**
Bibl: Country life, 1989 Feb.23, v.183, no.8, p.110

Gottschalk, Albert **BA WC**
(Danish artist, 1866-1906) WC
(Danish painter, 1866-1906) BA
Bibl: ▶Bénézit; ▶Thieme-Becker; ▶Weilbach, Kunst.leks.

Gottschalk, Joachim *(Danish artist, op.1667)* **WC**

Gottschalk-Walter, Ulla *(East German painter, printmaker, b.1955)*   **BA**
> Bibl: Frankfurt am der Oder, Galerie junge kunst, ULLA GOTTSCHALK-WALTER (1985)

Gottscho, Samuel *(American, 1875-1971)*   **JG**

Gottsmann, Werner *(German artist, 20th cent.)*   **WC**

Gottwald, Laura *(American interior designer, New York City)*   **AV**
> Bibl: NYC phone bk., 1988-89

Götz, Axel *(German artist, b.1952)* **BA**
> Bibl: London (GBR), Goethe Inst., Young German artists (1982)

Gotz, Claude des → see Desgots, Claude

Gotz, Franz Augustin *(German artist, 1752-1827)*   **WC**

Götz, Gottfried Bernhard   **BA**
(German artist, 1708-1774)   **WC**
(German painter, printmaker, 1708-1774)   **BA**
(German, 1708-1774)   **GC**
> Bibl: ▶Encyc. world art; ▶Neue deutsche Biog.; ▶Thieme-Becker; ▶Witt checklist

Goetz, Gottfried Bernhard   **GC WC**

Götz, Joseph Matthias *(German sculptor, architect, 1696-1760)*   **BA**
> Bibl: Dehio: Niederösterreich; ▶Neue deutsche Biog.; ▶Thieme-Becker

Götz, Karl Otto   **BA GC WC**
(German artist, 1914-)   **WC**
(German painter, b.1914)   **GC**
(West German painter, b.1914)   **BA**
> Bibl: ▶Bénézit; ▶Vollmer, Künst.-Lex. 20. Jhr.; ▶Wer ist wer

Götz, Lother *(West German architect, 1925-)*   **AV**
> Bibl: Deutsche Bauzeitung, 1985 Feb., v.119, no.2, p.96

Götz, Peter *(Swiss architect, Schaffhausen)*   **AV**
> Bibl: ▶Schweiz. Ingen. u. Archit., 1984-1985

Gotz, Pierre des → see Desgots, Pierre

Götz, Sebastian *(German, 17th century)*   **GC**
> Bibl: ▶Thieme-Becker

Gotz, Theodor von *(German artist, 1826-1892)*   **WC**

Götze, Inge *(East German textile artist, 20th c.)*   **BA**
> Bibl: BILDENDE KUNST 8 (1984) 342

Götzebach, Dieter *(1937-)*   **AV**

Götzen, Heinrich *(West German architect, Düsseldorf)*   **AV**
> Bibl: Deutsche Bauzeitschrift, 1987 Sept., v.35, no.9, p.1092

Götzen, Reiner *(West German architect, Düsseldorf)*   **AV**
> Bibl: Deutsche Bauzeitschrift, 1987 Sept., v.35, no.9, p.1092

Gotzenberger, Jacob → see Götzenberger, Jakob

Götzenberger, Jakob   **BA**
(German artist, 1800-1866)   **WC**
(German painter, 1800-1866)   **BA**
> Bibl: ▶Allgem. Deut. Biog.; ▶Bénézit; ▶Bryan, Ptrs. & engravers; ▶Busse, Maler u. Bildhauer 19. Jahr.; ▶Thieme-Becker

Gotzenberger, Jacob   **WC**

Gotzinger, Hans *(German artist, 1867-)*   **WC**

Gotzkowsky, Johann Ernst *(German porcelain manufacturer, 1710-1775)*   **BA**
> Bibl: Baer, VON GOTZKOWSKY ZUR KPM, (1986) (RILA/DEU); ▶Penguin dec. arts, p. 80; RLIN BKS file

Gotzloff, Carl Wilhelm   **GC WC**
(German artist, 1799-1866)   **WC**
(German, 1799-1866)   **GC**
> Bibl: ▶Witt checklist

Gouarchin → see Guercino (Giovanni Francesco Barbieri)

Gouaspre → see Dughet, Gaspard (Gaspard Poussin)

Goubau, Antoine → see Goubau, Antoon

Goubau, Antoni I → see Goubau, Antoon

Goubau, Antoni or Antoon → see Goubau, Antoon

Goubau, Antoon   **BA PR**
(Flemish artist, 1616-1698)   **WC**
(Flemish painter, ca.1616-1698) **BA PR**
(Flemish, 1616-1698)   **GC**
> Bibl: ▶Bénézit; ▶RILA/BHA; ▶Thieme-Becker; ▶Witt checklist; ▶Wurzbach, NLD Künst.-Lex.

Antoon Goubau   PR
Anttonio Guo   PR
Gabao   PR
Gebouw   PR
Gobban   PR
Gobbau'   PR
Goubau, Antoine   PR

Goubau, Antoni I   **GC PR**
Goubau, Antoni or Antoon   **WC**
Monsu Gobau   PR

Goubau, Frans *(Flemish artist, 1622-1678)*   **WC**

Goubau, Laureys   **GC WC**
(Flemish artist, op.1651-1670)   **WC**
(Flemish painter, act.1651-1670)   **GC**
> Bibl: ▶Thieme-Becker

Goubaud, Innocent Louis   **GC WC**
(French artist, c.1780-1847)   **WC**
(French, ca.1780-1847)   **GC**
> Bibl: ▶Witt checklist

Goubie → see Goubie, Jean Richard

Goubie, Jean Richard   **PR WC**
(French artist, 1842-1899)   **WC**
(French painter, 1842-1899)   **PR**
> Bibl: ▶Thieme-Becker

Goubie   PR
Jean Richard Goubie   PR

Goubier, E. *(French, active late 19th century)*   **JG**

Gouchenheim *(French, active 19th century (also Gouchenheim & Forest))*   **JG**

Gouda, Cornelis van *(North Netherlandish painter, 1510-1550)*   **GC**
> Bibl: Getty Photo Study Coll.; ▶Thieme-Becker

Cornelis van Gouda   GC

Goudge, Edward *(English plasterer, act.1684-1688)*   **BA**
> Bibl: ▶Colvin, Brit. archts.; Jackson-Stops, COUNTRY LIFE CLXXX/4644 (21 Aug 1986) 588; NATIONAL TRUST STUDIES, 1979, 20-27; Pevsner, Northants, p. 326

Goudiachvili → see Gudiašvili, Lado
Goudiachvili, Lado → see Gudiašvili, Lado

Goudie, Alexander *(British artist, op.1970-)*   **WI**

Goudoin, Jacques *(French cabinetmaker, act.1779)*   **BA**
> Bibl: Apollo, CXI/216 (Feb. 1980) pp.127-134

Goudreaux or Gaudreau, Pierre Louis *(French artist, 1694-1731)*   **WC**

Goudstikker, Sophie *(Dutch photographer in Germany, 1865-1924)*   **BA**
> Bibl: Munich, Münchner Stadtmuseum, Fotomuseum, HOF-ATELIER...(1985)

Goudt, Hendrick → see Goudt, Hendrik

Goudt, Hendrik   **BA**
(Dutch artist, 1585-1630)   **WC**
(Dutch draughtsman, 1585-1630)   **GC**
(Dutch printmaker, ca.1582-1648)   **BA**
> Bibl: Getty Photo Study Coll.; ▶Grote Winkler Prins; ▶Hollstein, Dutch & Flemish, v.8; Stampfle, in ESSAYS IN NORTHERN EUROP. ART...(1983); ▶Thieme-Becker; ▶Witt checklist; ▶Wurzbach, NLD Künst.-Lex.

Goudt, Hendrick   **GC WC**

Gouel, Gilles *(French silversmith, d.1743, master 1694)*   **GC**
> Bibl: ▶Mabille, Orfèv. fran.

Gouel, Gilles-Claude *(French silversmith, d.1769, master 1727)*   **GC**
> Bibl: ▶Nocq, Poinçon de Paris

Gouers, Daniel *(Dutch goldsmith in FRA, act.1717-1740)*   **BA**
> Bibl: REVUE DU LOUVRE, XXXIX(1979); ▶Thieme-Becker

Gouezou, Joseph Rene (French artist, 1821-1880) **WC**
Gouge, E. → see Gouge, Edward
Gouge, Edward **WI**
    (British artist, op.1690-1735) WI
    (British artist, op.1719-1742) WC
    Gouge, E. **WC**
Gougeon, Diane (Canadian artist, 20th c.) **BA**
    Bibl: Vanguard (Dec. 1981-Jan. 1982) pp.25-29
Gough, Alexander Dick (1804-1871) **AV**
Gough, Hugh Roumieu (British architect, 1843-1904) **AV BA**
    Bibl: Clarke, Parish Churches of London, p.286; Country life, 1986 Dec.4, v.180, no.4659, p.1758; ▶Dict. natl. biog.
Gough, J.H. (British artist, op.1884-1886) **WI**
Gough, Piers (English architect) **AV**
    Bibl: World of interiors, 1987 Jan., p.117
Gough, Richard (1735-1809) **AV**
Gough, Thomas (British artist, b.1858) **WI**
Gouillet, Jules (French artist, 1826-p.1882) **WC**
Gouiot, J. (French artist, 19th cent.) **WC**
Goujon, Jean **AV BA GC WC**
    (French architect, 16th century) AV
    (French architect, printmaker, and sculptor, act.1540, d.ca. 1568) GC
    (French artist, op.1526-1564/8) WC
    (French sculptor, architect, printmaker, act.1540, d.ca. 1568) BA
    Bibl: Blunt, Art & arch. FRA; ▶Encyc. world art; ▶Larousse grande encyc.; ▶Libr. of Congr. Name Auth. File; ▶Macmillan encyc. archts., [gives dates as ca.1510-ca.1568]; ▶RILA/BHA; ▶Thieme-Becker
Gouk, Alan (British painter, b.1939) **BA**
    Bibl: Arts Council GBR, Scot. Comm., 4 abstract artists (1977); STUDIO, 187(JUNE 1974), 292-5
Goula, Richard (American artist, geologist, gardener) **AV**
    Bibl: Southern accents, 1988 May-June, v.11, no.3, p.176
Goulandris Master **GC JG**
    (Aegean (Cycladic) sculptor, 28th/25th c BC) GC
    Bibl: Getty Photo Study Coll.
Goulandris, Niki (Greek patron, painter, public official, 20th c.) **BA**
    Bibl: Spours, J., CONNOISSEUR, CCXIV/865 (Mar 1984) 47
Gould, Alec Carruthers **WC WI**
    (British artist, 1870-) WC
    (British artist, 1870-1948) WI

Gould, Chester (American cartoonist, b.1900) **BA**
    Bibl: WW Amer., 1980-81
Gould, David (British artist, op.1885-1930) **WI**
Gould, Elizabeth **WC WI**
    (British artist, 1804-1841) WI
    (British artist, 19th cent.) WC
    Coxon, Elizabeth, Miss WI
Gould, Francis Carruthers (British artist, 1844-1925) **WC WI**
Gould, John **BA WC WI**
    (British artist, 1804-1881) WC WI
    (British painter, ornithologist, 1804-1881) BA
    Bibl: ▶Dict. natl. biog.
Gould, Katherine (American sculptor, 20th c.) **BA**
    Bibl: Gould, LEONARDO, XIV/1(WINTER 1981), 1
Gould, Michael → see Ayrton, Michael
Gould, Thomas James (American architect, 1849-) **AV**
Gould, Thomas Ridgeway (American sculptor, 1818-1881) **BA**
    Bibl: ▶Thieme-Becker; ▶WWW Amer.
Gould, Walter → see Gould, Walter G.
Gould, Walter G. **BA**
    (American artist, 1829-1893) WI
    (American painter, 1829-1893) BA
    Bibl: ▶Bénézit; ▶Fielding's Amer. ptrs.; ▶Thieme-Becker; Washington, DC (USA), Smith. Inst., Natl. Port. Gall., Abroad in America (1976)
Gould, Walter **WI**
Gould, William Buelow (Australian artist, 1801-1852) **WC**
Goulding, Frederick **WI**
    (British artist, 1842-1909) WI
    (Engraver, London, GTL, 1842-1909) WI
Goulding, Frederik **WI**
Goulding, Frederik → see Goulding, Frederick
Goulding, Tim (Irish painter, b.1945) **BA**
    Bibl: Belfast (GBR), Ulster Mus., Irish directions (1975), p.19
Gouldsmith → see Arnold, Harriet
Gouldsmith, Harriet, Miss → see Arnold, Harriet
Goulesque, Jean-Luc (French (?) architect) **AV**
    Bibl: Architecture d'aujourd'hui, 1985 June, no.239, p.50
Goulet, Lorrie (American sculptor, b.1925) **BA**
    Bibl: ▶WW Amer. Art, 1976
Goulet, Michel (Canadian sculptor, b.1944) **BA**
    Bibl: Montreal (Ont, CAN), Musée d'art contemp., MICHEL GOULET (1980)
Goulet, Patrice (French architect) **AV**
    Bibl: ▶Libr. of Congr. Name Auth. File

Goulet, Rose-Marie (Canadian architect) **AV**
    Bibl: Section a, 1985 Jan, v.2, no. 5-6, p.16
Goulinat, Jean Gabriel (French artist, 1883-) **WC**
Goullin or Goulin, Francis (French artist, 18th cent.) **WC**
Goun → see Goun, Karl Theodor Fiodorovitch
Goun, Karl Theodor Fiodorovitch **PR**
    (Russian artist, 1830-1877) WC
    (Russian painter, 1830-1877) PR
    Goun PR
    Goune, Theodore PR
    Huhn, Carl Theodor Fjodorawitsch **WC**
    Karl Theodor Fiodorovitch Goun PR
Gounaro (French artist, 20th cent.) **WC**
Goundie, George (American sculptor, b.1913) **BA**
    Bibl: Milwaukee(WI, USA), Univ. of WI, Fine Arts Galleries, GEORGE GOUNDIE, SCULPTURE-JOSEPH FRIE...(1977); ▶Natl. Faculty Dir.; UC Santa Barbara cat. sheets
Goune, Theodore → see Goun, Karl Theodor Fiodorovitch
Gounod, Francois Louis (French artist, 1758-1823) **WC**
Goupil (French photographer, act. ca.1855) **GC**
    Bibl: ▶Idx. Amer. photog. colls.
    Goupil & Cie GC
Goupil → see Goupil, Jules Adolphe
Goupil & Cie → see Goupil
Goupil, Jules Adolphe **GC PR WC**
    (French artist, 1839-1883) WC
    (French painter, 1839-1883) PR
    (French, 1839-1883) GC
    Bibl: ▶Thieme-Becker; ▶Witt checklist
    Goupil PR
    Jules Adolphe Goupil PR
Goupil, Leon Lucien **GC WC**
    (French artist, 1834-1890) WC
    (French, 1834-1890) GC
    Bibl: ▶Witt checklist
Goupil-Fesquet, Frederic (French artist, op.c.1839-1842) **WC**
Goupy → see Goupy, Joseph
Goupy, Joseph **BA PR WC WI**
    (British artist, 1680(?)-1768(?)) WC
    (British artist, 1680-1768) WI
    (British painter, ca.1680-1763) PR
    (English printmaker, painter, ca. 1680-1763) BA
    Bibl: ▶Bryan, Ptrs. & engravers; ▶Dict. natl. biog.; ▶Mallalieu, Brit. watercolour artists; ▶RILA/BHA; ▶Waterhouse, Brit. 18c. ptrs.
    Goupy PR
    Gupey PR
    Joseph Goupy PR

Goupy, Louis or Lewis *(French artist, 1700-1747)*   **WC**

Goupy, Thomas *(British artist, op. 18th c.)*   **WI**

Gouranopoulos, George *(Greek artist, 20th cent.)*   **WC**

Gouraud, François *(French photographer, act.1840)*   **BA**
Bibl: ▶Natl. union cat.; Newhall, Daguerreotype in Amer., p.32; Rudisill, Mirror image, pp.58-69

Gourdain, Michel→see Gourdin, Michel

Gourdaine, Jean Pierre Norblin de la→see Norblin, Jean Pierre (de la Gourdaine)

Gourdal, Diane *(American interior designer, Los Angeles)*   **AV**
Bibl: Interior design, LVI/5 (May 1985) p.254

Gourdault, Pierre *(French artist, 1880-1915)*   **WC**

Gourdel, Pierre   **GC**
(French artist, op.1555-1588)   WC
(French painter, 16th century)   GC
Bibl: ▶Bénézit

Gourdelle or Gourdel, Pierre (Goudet)   **WC**

Gourdelle or Gourdel, Pierre (Goudet)→see Gourdel, Pierre

Gourdin le Jeune→see Gourdin, Michel

Gourdin, Jean *(French menuisier, act.1737-1763)*   **GC**
Bibl: ▶Salverte, Ébénistes 18e s.; Theunissen, Meubles
Gourdin, Jean le Père   GC

Gourdin, Jean le Père→see Gourdin, Jean

Gourdin, Jean-Baptiste *(French menuisier, master 1748, act. to 1776)*   **GC**
Bibl: ▶Salverte, Ébénistes 18e s.

Gourdin, Michel *(French menuisier, master 1752, act. to ca.1782)*   **GC**
Bibl: ▶Salverte, Ébénistes 18e s.; ▶Vial, Artistes décorateurs
Gourdain, Michel   GC
Gourdin le Jeune   GC

Gourdon, R. *(French artist, 19th cent.)*   **WC**

Goureau, Charles *(French artist, 1797-p.1834)*   **WC**

Gourevitch, Jacqueline *(American painter, b.1933)*   **BA**
Bibl: Hartford, Wadsworth Atheneum, JACQUELINE GOUREVITCH; ▶WW Amer. Art, 1976

Gourfain, Peter *(American sculptor, 20th c.)*   **BA**
Bibl: Art in Amer. LXXVII (May/June 1979), 128-131

Gourgaud, General *(French artist, op.1818)*   **WC**

Gourjon-Bouis, Amedee→see Gourjon-Bours, Amédée

Gourjon-Bours→see Gourjon-Bours, Amédée

Gourjon-Bours, Amédée *(French painter, act. 1907)*   **PR**
Amedee Gourjon-Bours   PR
Gourjon-Bouis, Amedee   PR
Gourjon-Bours   PR

Gourley, Ronald *(American architect)*   **AV**
Bibl: ▶Contemp. archts.

Gourlier, Charles Pierre *(French architect, 1786-1857)*   **AV**
Bibl: ▶Thieme-Becker

Gourmont the Younger, Jean de *(French artist, op.1565-1585)*   **WC**

Gourmont, Jean de   **GC WC**
(French artist, c.1483-p.1557)   WC
(French painter, 16th century)   GC
Bibl: ▶Bénézit

Gourmont, Remy de *(French artist, op.1895)*   **WC**

Goursat, Georges (sem)→see Sem (Georges Goursat)

Gousius→see Goltzius, Hendrik

Goussier→see Goussier, Louis-Jacques

Goussier, Louis-Jacques   **BA**
(French artist, 18th cent.)   WC
(French illustrator, 1722-1799)   BA
Bibl: ▶Dict. biog. fran.; Pinault, M., REVUE DE L'ART 66 (1984) 19-20; ▶Witt checklist

Goussier   **WC**

Gout, Jean Francois *(German artist, c.1748-1812)*   **WC**

Goutes, K. *(Architect, Greece)*   **AV**
Bibl: Architektonika themata, 1986, v.20, p.174

Gouthière, Pierre→see Gouthière, Pierre Joseph Désiré

Gouthière, Pierre Joseph Désiré   **BA GC**
(French artist, 1732-1813/14)   WC
(French bronze worker, gilder, designer, 1732-1813/14)   BA
(French sculptor, bronzier, gilder, and designer, 1732-1813/1814)   GC
(French, 1732-1813/1814, master 1758)   JG
Bibl: ▶Bénézit; ▶Encyc. world art; ▶Penguin dec. arts; ▶RILA/BHA; ▶Thieme-Becker

Gouthière, Pierre   **GC JG WC**

Gouthro, Steve *(Canadian printmaker, b.1951)*   **BA**
Bibl: Winnipeg (Man, CAN), Art Gallery, Artists' proof (1981)

Gouveia, André de→see André de Gouveia

Gouwi, Jacob Peter→see Gowy, Jacob Peter

Gouy, de *(French artist, 18th cent.)*   **WC**

Gouy, M.A.   **WC WI**
(American artist, 20th cent.)   WC
(American artist, op.20th c.)   WI

Gouzien, J.-D. *(French architect, 20th c.)*   **BA**
Bibl: ▶Avery period. idx.; Paris phone book, 1988

Govaert Flinck→see Flinck, Govert

Govaert Flink→see Flinck, Govert

Govaerts→see Govaerts, Abraham

Govaerts or Goovaerts, Hendrick→see Govaerts, Hendrick

Govaerts, Abraham   **BA GC PR**
(Flemish artist, 1589-1626)   WC
(Flemish painter, 1589-1626)   PR
(Flemish painter, ca.1589-1626)   BA
(Flemish, 1589-1626)   GC
Bibl: ▶Bénézit; ▶RILA/BHA; ▶Thieme-Becker
Abraham Govaerts   PR
Goeverts   PR
Govaerts   PR

Govaerts, Goevaerts, Gouvaert or Goyvaert, Abraham   **WC**

Govaerts, Goevaerts, Gouvaert or Goyvaert, Abraham→see Govaerts, Abraham

Govaerts, Hendrick   **GC**
(Flemish artist, 1669-1720)   WC
(Flemish, 1669-1720)   GC
Bibl: Getty Photo Study Coll. (Ptgs.); ▶Witt checklist
Gobaerts, Hendrick   GC
Goovaerts, Hendrick   GC

Govaerts or Goovaerts, Hendrick   **WC**

Govaerts, Jan Baptiste   **GC WC**
(Flemish artist, op.1713-m.1746)   WC
(Flemish, act.1713-d.1746)   GC
Bibl: ▶Witt checklist

Govaerts, Jean *(Belgian artist, 1898-)*   **WC**

Govan, Mary Maitland *(British artist, op.1884-1925)*   **WI**

Goverd Flink→see Flinck, Govert

Governatori, Aroldo *(Italian painter, b.1937)*   **BA**
Bibl: Saint Omer(FRA), Musee Sandelin, AROLO GOVERNATORI(1976)

Govert Dircksz. Camphuysen→see Camphuysen, Govert Dircksz.

Govert Flinck→see Flinck, Govert

Govert Flink→see Flinck, Govert

Govert Jans Mijnheer→see Jansz., Govert

Govert Jansz.→see Jansz., Govert

Govert van der Leeuw→see Leeuw, Govert van der

Govert van der Meye→see Meye, Govert van der [Unidentified]

Govertsen, Jan→see Govertsz. van der Aar, Jan

Govertsz. van der Aar, Jan (*Dutch merchant and patron, 1544/45-1612*) **BA**
Bibl: Nichols, L.W., NEDERLANDS KUNSTHISTOR. JAARBOEK 38 (1987), 24-255; Reznicek, in ESSAYS IN NORTHERN EUR. ART... (1983) 212
Govertsen, Jan   BA

Govertsz., Goversz. or Goverts, Dirck (*Dutch artist, c.1580-c.1645/54*) **WC**

Govett, William Romaine   **WC WI**
(*British artist, op.1828-1837*)   WC
(*British artist, op.1828-1846*)   WI

Gow, Andrew Carrick (*British artist, 1848-1920*)   **WC WI**

Gow, Charles   **WC WI**
(*British artist, 19th cent.*)   WC
(*British artist, op.1844-1872*)   WI

Gow, James   **WC WI**
(*British artist, -1886*)   WC
(*British artist, op.1852-, d.1886*)   WI

Gow, Mary L.   **WI**
(*British artist, 1851-1929*)   WI
(*British artist, 19th cent.*)   WC

Gow, Mary L. (Mrs. Sydney Prior Hall)   **WC**
Hall, Sydney Prior, Mrs., (Mary L.)   WI
Gow, Mary L. (Mrs. Sydney Prior Hall)→see Gow, Mary L.

Gowa, H. Henry (*German scenographer, painter, b.1902*)   **BA**
Bibl: ▶WW Arts DEU

Gowan, James (*British architect, 1923-*)   **AV**
Bibl: ▶Contemp. archts.
Gower→see Gower, George

Gower, George   **GC PR WC WI**
(*British artist, circa 1540-1596*)   WI
(*British artist, op.1579-c.1596*)   WC
(*British painter, 1540-1596*)   PR
(*British, act.1579-ca.1596*)   GC
Bibl: Indianapolis M of A catalogue; ▶Thieme-Becker; ▶Witt checklist
George Gower   PR
Gower   PR
Gower, Henry de→see Gower, Henry, bishop of St. David's

Gower, Henry, bishop of St. David's   **BA**
(*English architect, ca.1278-1347*)   BA
(*Welsh bishop and architect, 1278?-1347*)   AV
Bibl: Blue guide: Wales, pp.353-358; ▶Dict. natl. biog., Gower, Henry, d. 1347; Williams, Archaeologia Cambrensis, CXXX (1981)
Gower, Henry de   **AV**

Gower, Ronald Charles Sutherland   **BA**
(*British sculptor, 1845-1916*)   AV BA
Bibl: ▶Grant, Brit. sculptors; ▶Libr. of Congr. Name Auth. File; ▶Natl. union cat.; ▶Thieme-Becker

Gower, Ronald Sutherland, Lord   **AV**
Gower, Ronald Sutherland, Lord→see Gower, Ronald Charles Sutherland

Gower, T.   **WC WI**
(*British artist, op.1790*)   WC
(*British artist, op.1790-*)   WI

Gowers, David   **WC WI**
(*British artist, op.1799-1808*)   WI
(*British artist, op.1801-1808*)   WC

Gowin, Emmet (*American photographer, b.1941*)   **BA**
Bibl: Boston (MA, USA), MFA, Private Realities (1974)

Gowing, Lawrence   **BA**
(*British artist, 1918-*)   WC
(*British artist, b.1918*)   WI
(*British painter, b.1918*)   BA
Bibl: ▶Dolman, Contemp. Brit. artists; NY Times obit., 7 Feb 1991

Gowing, Lawrence Burnett   **WC WI**
Gowing, Lawrence Burnett→see Gowing, Lawrence
Gowy, Gouwi or Gowi, Jacob Peter→see Gowy, Jacob Peter

Gowy, Jacob Peter   **GC**
(*Flemish artist, op.1632-1661(?)*)   WC
(*Flemish, act.1632-1661(?)*)   GC
Bibl: Getty Photo Study Coll. (Ptgs.); ▶Witt checklist
Gouwi, Jacob Peter   GC

Gowy, Gouwi or Gowi, Jacob Peter   **WC**

Goya→see Goya y Lucientes, Francisco José de
Goya y Lucientes→see Goya y Lucientes, Francisco José de
Goya y Lucientes, Francisco→see Goya y Lucientes, Francisco José de
Goya y Lucientes, Francisco de→see Goya y Lucientes, Francisco José de

Goya y Lucientes, Francisco José de   **AV BA GC JG PR WC**
(*Spanish artist, 1746-1828*)   WC WI
(*Spanish painter and printmaker, 1746-1828*)   GC
(*Spanish painter, 1746-1828*)   AV PR
(*Spanish painter, printmaker, 1746-1828*)   BA
(*Spanish, 1746-1828*)   JG
Bibl: ▶Encic. univ. ilus.; ▶Encyc. world art; George Goldner; ▶Kindlers Malerei Lex.; ▶Libr. of Congr. Name Auth. File; ▶Ossorio y Bernard, Artistas españoles 19s.; ▶Petit Larousse; ▶RILA/BHA; ▶Thieme-Becker
De Goya, Francisco   AV
Francisco Jose de Goya y Lucientes   PR
Goya   PR
Goya y Lucientes   PR
Goya y Lucientes, Francisco   PR
Goya y Lucientes, Francisco de   PR
Goya, Francisco   **AV GC**
Goya, Francisco de   PR
Goya, Francisco Jose de   PR
Goya, Francisco Jose y Lucientes de   **WI**
Goya, Francisco→see Goya y Lucientes, Francisco José de
Goya, Francisco de→see Goya y Lucientes, Francisco José de

Goya, Francisco Javier de (*Spanish, b.1784, act.1828*)   **BA**
Bibl: Camón Aznar, Goya, v.1, p.70; v.4, p.227; García de la Rasilla, Goya: nueves visiones (1987) pp.133-153; Gassier, Goya, 1983
Goya, Francisco Jose de→see Goya y Lucientes, Francisco José de
Goya, Francisco Jose y Lucientes de→see Goya y Lucientes, Francisco José de

Goyder, Alice Kirkby (*British artist, 1875-op.1903*)   **WI**
Goyen→see Goyen, Jan Josephsz. van

Goyen, Jan Josephsz. van **BA GC PR WC**
    (Dutch artist, 1596-1656) WC
    (Dutch painter, 1596-1656) PR
    (Dutch painter, draughtsman,
      and printmaker, 1596-1656) GC
    (Dutch painter, printmaker,
      1596-1656) BA
    (Dutch, 1596-1656) JG
      Bibl: ▶Aa, Biog. woordenboek
      NLD; George Goldner;
      ▶RILA/BHA; ▶Thieme-Becker;
      ▶Wurzbach, NLD Künst.-Lex.
    Goien, Jan Josephsz. van GC
    Gooij PR
    Goyen PR
    Goyen, Jan Josephszoon van PR
Goyen, Jan van GC JG PR
    J.v. Goijen PR
    Jan Gooijen PR
    Jan Josephsz. van Goyen PR
    Jan van Goien PR
    Jan van Goijen PR
    Jan van Gojen PR
    Jan van Goyen PR
    John Van Goyen PR
    V ngoyen PR
    V. Goyen PR
    Van Gayen PR
    Van Goen PR
    Van Gogen PR
    Van Goien PR
    Van Goijen PR
    Van Goin PR
    Van Gojen PR
    van Gooijen PR
    Van Gooyen PR
    Van Gouen PR
    Van Gowan PR
    Van Goyen PR
    Van. Goyen PR
    Vangloolen PR
    Vangoen PR
    Vangogen PR
    Vangoin PR
    Vangoing PR
    Vangoupen PR
    Vangoyen PR
    Vangoyer PR
    Vangoyou PR
    Vaugoyen PR
Goyen, Jan Josephszoon van→see
    Goyen, Jan Josephsz. van
Goyen, Jan van→see Goyen, Jan
    Josephsz. van
Goyet, Eugene *(French painter,*
    1798-1857) GC
      Bibl: ▶Bénézit
Goyrand, Antoine-Gabriel *(French*
    artist, 1754-1826) WC
Goyrand, Claude *(French*
    printmaker, ca.1620-ca.1662) BA
      Bibl: ▶Bénézit; ▶Bryan, Ptrs. &
      engravers; ▶Encyc. world art;
      ▶Thieme-Becker

Gozian, Leon Duval *(French artist,*
    1853-) WC
Gozzard→see Gozzard, J.W.
Gozzard, J.W. WI
    (British artist, 19th cent.) WC
    (British artist, op.19th c.) WI
Gozzard WC
Gozzi, Alberto *(Italian architect)* AV
      Bibl: Abitare, 1989 Mar., no.272,
      p.212
Gozzi, Elsie McNeill Lee, contessa
    (American textile manufacturer in
    ITA, 20th c.) BA
      Bibl: Nadelson, CONNOISSEUR, CC
      XIII, 856(JUNE 1983), 78-81
Gozzi, Luigi *(Yugoslav, 1457-1538)* BA
      Bibl: Ancona, Pinacoteca
      Comunale Podesti, TIZIANO, LA
      PALA GOZZI...(23 Apr-30 Oct
      1988), p.34, 100; Crowe &
      Cavalcaselle, Titian, pp.233, 235;
      Lafenestre, TITIEN (1886); MEISS
      FESTSCHRIFT(1977), 83-87;
      Pallucchini, TIZIANO (1969), p.53;
      Wethey, Titian, I, p. 110
Gozzi, Marco BA WC
    (Italian artist, 1759-1839) WC
    (Italian painter, 1759-1839) BA
      Bibl: ▶Bolaffi; ▶Thieme-Becker;
      ▶Witt checklist
Gozzi, Maria Maddalena *(Italian*
    painter, 1718-1782) PR
      Bibl: ▶Thieme-Becker
    Baldacci, Maria Maddalena PR
    Baldacci-Gozzi, Maria Maddalena PR
    Maria Maddalena Baldacci PR
    Maria Maddalena Baldacci-Gozzi PR
    Maria Maddalena Gozzi PR
Gozzi, P. *(Italian architect)* AV
      Bibl: Ville giardini, 1985 June, no.
      197, p.24
Gozzi, Romano *(Italian architect)* AV
      Bibl: Ville giardini, 1989 Mar., no.
      235, p.28
Gozzini, Giuseppe *(Italian artist, op.*
    1824-1870) WC
Gozzini, Vincenzo *(Italian artist,*
    19th cent.) WC
Gozzo, Bruno *(Italian artist, 20th*
    cent.) WC
Gozzoli, Alessio *(Italian painter,*
    1473-1528) BA
      Bibl: ANTICHITA VIVA, XIX(MAY-
      JUNE 1980); Padoa Rizzo,
      Antichità viva 19/3 (May-June
      1980) p.14-19; Padoa Rizzo, ARTE
      E COMMITTENZA A PISTOIA ALLA
      FINE DEL XV SECOLO.... (1989)

Gozzoli, Benozzo BA GC PR
    (Italian artist, 1420-1497) WC
    (Italian painter, 1420-1497) BA GC PR
      Bibl: ▶Diz. biog. ital.;
      ▶Fredericksen & Zeri, Census;
      Getty Photo Study Coll. (Ptgs.);
      ▶RILA/BHA; ▶Thieme-Becker;
      ▶Witt checklist
    Benozzo PR
    Benozzo di Lese PR
    Benozzo di Lese di Sandro GC PR
    Benozzo Gozzoli GC PR
    Benozzo Gozzoli (Benozzi di
      Lese di Sandro) WC
    Gozzoli, Benozzo di Lese PR
Gozzoli, Benozzo di Lese→see
    Gozzoli, Benozzo
Gr. de Cayer→see Crayer, Gaspar de
Gra, Guilio *(Italian architect)* AV
      Bibl: Interior design, 1987 Oct.,
      v.58, no.13, p.316
Graadt van Roggen, Johannes
    Mattheus *(Dutch painter, b.1867)* GC
      Bibl: ▶Thieme-Becker
Graaf→see Graf, Johann
Graaf, Erik de *(Dutch(?) designer,*
    20th c.) BA
      Bibl: Leeds Art Calendar, 87
      (1980) pp.21-30
Graaf, Hans PR
    (Austrian painter, 1680-1734) PR
    (German artist, 1680-1734) WC
      Bibl: ▶Bénézit
    Graf or Fraaf, Hans WC
    Hans Graaf PR
Graaf, Heinz AV BA
    (German architect, b.1910) BA
    (West German architect, 1910-
    1980) AV
      Bibl: KUNSTWERK,
      XXXII/2-3(APR-JUNE 1979), 60-62
Graaf, Josua de→see Grave, Josua de
Graaf, Kees *(Dutch artist, 20th*
    cent.) WC
Graaf, Timotheus de→see Graef,
    Timotheus de
Graafland, Robert Archibalt *(Dutch*
    painter, 1870-1940) GC
      Bibl: ▶Bénézit
Graag, Julie *(Dutch printmaker,*
    1877-1924) GC
      Bibl: ▶Vollmer, Künst.-Lex. 20. Jhr.
Graan→see Gran, Daniel
Graat→see Graat, Barent
Graat or Graet, Barend→see Graat,
    Barent
Graat, Barend→see Graat, Barent

Graat, Barent **BA PR**
(Dutch artist, 1628-1709) WC
(Dutch painter and
draughtsman, 1628-1709) GC
(Dutch painter, 1628-1709) BA PR
Bibl: Getty Photo Study Coll.;
▶RILA/BHA; ▶Thieme-Becker;
▶Witt checklist; ▶Wurzbach, NLD
Künst.-Lex.
B. Graat PR
B. Graat, 1668 PR
B. Graetz PR
B. Graict PR
Barend Graat PR
Barent Graat PR
Barent Graet PR
Barent Gratz PR
Graat PR
Graat or Graet, Barend **WC**
Graat, Barend **GC**
Graedt PR
Graet PR
Graatsma, William (Dutch architect,
b.1925) **BA**
Bibl: Maastricht (NLD),
Bonnefantenmus., Gerrit Rietveld
(1978)
Graauw or Grauw, Hendrick (de)
(Dutch artist, c.1627-1693) **WC**
Grab, Bertha von (Czech artist,
1846-) **WC**
Grab, Udo-Falk (West German
architect, Münstertal) **AV**
Bibl: Arch Plus, 1987 Nov., no.92,
p.77
Grabach→see Grabach, John R.
Grabach, John R. **BA PR WI**
(American artist, 1886-1981) WI
(American painter, 1886-1981) BA PR
Bibl: ▶Bénézit; ▶RILA/BHA;
Washington, D.C.,Smithsonian,
Nat'l Coll. of Fine Arts:JOHN
R.GRABACH,(1980); ▶WW Amer.
Art; ▶Young, Amer. artists
Grabach PR
John R. Grabach PR
Grabar, Igor' Ėmmanuilovič **BA**
(Russian artist, 1872-) WC
(Russian artist, art historian,
restorer, 1871-1960) BA
Bibl: ▶Great Soviet encyc.;
McGraw-Hill encyc. Russia &
USSR; ▶Natl. union cat.; ▶NYPL
Art & Arch. Div., Dict. catalog
Grabar, Jigor Emmanuilovitsch **WC**
Grabar, Jigor Emmanuilovitsch→see
Grabar, Igor' Ėmmanuilovič
Grabenberger, Johann Bernard
(German artist, 1637-1710) **WC**
Grabenberger, Michael Cristoph
(German artist, op.1674-m.1684) **WC**
Graber, Ted (American interior
designer) **AV**
Bibl: Architectural digest, 1983
May, v.40, no.5

Grabill, John C.H. (American
photographer, act.ca.1887-1891) **BA**
Bibl: ▶Current, Photog. & Old
West
Grabmullerova, Eva (Czech artist,
20th cent.) **WC**
Grabone, Arnold (French artist,
20th cent.) **WC**
Grabowski, Andrzej (Polish artist,
1938-1969) **WC**
Grabowski, Henry (American
architect, Chicago, Ill) **AV**
Bibl: ARchitecture & urbanism,
1983 Sept., no.9(156), p.73
Grabowski, Tadeusz (Polish artist,
20th cent.) **WC**
Graby, John (Irish architect, Dublin) **AV**
Bibl: Royal Institute of Architects
of Ireland. Directory
Grace Clements→see Clements,
Grace
Grace Henry→see Henry, Grace
Grace, Alfred Fitzwalter (British
artist, 1844-1903) **WC WI**
Grace, Frances Lily (British artist,
op.1876-1909) **WI**
Grace, Louise N. (American painter,
1876-1954) **PR**
Bibl: Univ of Arizona MA
catalogue; ▶WWW Amer. art
Louise N. Grace PR
Grace, Oliver (Irish architect, act.
1797) **BA**
Bibl: Eiffe IRISH GEORGIAN SOC
XXVII '84 p. 1-37 (RILA, GBR)
Grace, W. **WC WI**
(British artist, 19th cent.) WC
(British artist, op.19th c.) WI
Gracht, Cornelis van der (Dutch,
act.1635) **BA**
Bibl: Kunstmuseets Arsskrift, LXII
(1975) pp.30-37
Gracht, Jacob van der **GC WC**
(Dutch artist, 1593-1652) WC
(Dutch painter, 1593-1652) GC
Bibl: ▶Bénézit
Gracia Soria, Francisco de (Spanish
architect) **AV**
Bibl: Bauwelt, 1988 Feb.19, v.79,
no.7-8, p.294
Gracie, Vernon (City planner) **AV**
Bibl: Spazio e societa, 1982 Dec.,
v.5, no.20, p.108
Grad, Bernard J. (American
architect) **AV**
Grad, Dora (Israeli architect) **AV**
Grad, Howard (American architect) **AV**
Grada, Raffaele de→see De Grada,
Raffaele
Gradidge, Roderick **AV BA**
(British architect) AV
(British architect, 20th c.) BA
Bibl: Aslet, Country Life CLXXIV,
4500-01 (17-24 Nov 1983) 1430-
1433, 1502-1505; ▶Libr. of
Congr. Name Auth. File;
▶Wodehouse, Brit. archts.

Grado, Arcangelo de (Italian artist,
18th cent.) **WC**
Graeb→see Graeb, Carl Georg Anton
Graeb, Carl Georg
Anton **AV BA GC PR WC**
(German artist, 1816-1884) WC
(German painter and
printmaker, 1816-1884) GC
(German painter, 1816-1884) AV PR
(German painter, printmaker,
1816-1884) BA
Bibl: ▶Bénézit; Berlin, Natl. Gall.
cat.; ▶RILA/BHA; ▶Thieme-Becker
Carl, Georg Anton Graeb PR
Graeb PR
Graeb, Paul **GC WC**
(German artist, 1842-1892) WC
(German painter, 1842-1892) GC
Bibl: ▶Bénézit
Graeber, David C. (American
architect, Austin, TX) **AV**
Bibl: ▶AIA Pro File, 1983
Graedt→see Graat, Barent
Graef, Graaf or Graaff, Timotheus
de→see Graef, Timotheus de
Graef, Gustav (German artist, 1821-
1895) **WC**
Graef, Manfred (West German
artist, b.1928) **BA**
Bibl: ▶Babington Smith, Contemp.
artists; Graef, LEONARDO XIX/4
(1986) 293-296
Graef, Oscar (German artist, 1861-
1912) **WC**
Graef, Timotheus de **GC**
(Dutch artist, op.1682-1718) WC
(Dutch, act.1682-1718) GC
Bibl: ▶Thieme-Becker; ▶Witt
checklist
Graaf, Timotheus de GC
**Graef, Graaf or Graaff,
Timotheus de** **WC**
Graefel, Albert (British artist, 1807-
1887) **WI**
Bibl: ▶Wood, Victorian ptrs.
Graefer, John Andrew (British
gardener, act.1787-1799) **BA**
Bibl: Chigiotti, Antologia di B-A
V/19-20 (1981) 193-198; ▶Encic.
italiana; ▶Natl. union cat., pre-
1956; TCI Campania
Graeff→see Gryef, Adriaen de
Graeff, Cornelis de (Dutch, 1650-
1678) **BA**
Bibl: Dudok van Heel, in Essays in
No. Europ. Art (1983) 71
Graeff, Robert (American industrial
designer, architecture professor at
Vir. Polytechnic Institute and State
Univ) **AV**
Bibl: Progressive architecture,
1989 May, v.70, no.5, p.117
Graeff, Werner (German artist,
1901-) **WC**

Grael, Johann Friedrich *(German architect, 1708-1740)* **AV**
  Bibl: ▶Thieme-Becker
Graeme, Colin **WC WI**
  (British artist, 1858-1910) **WI**
  (British artist, 19th cent.) **WC**
Graeme, James **WC WI**
  (British artist, op.1820) **WC**
  (British artist, op.1820-) **WI**
Graenicher, Samuel *(German artist, 1758-1813)* **WC**
Graenie [?]→see Graenie [Unidentified]
Graenie [Unidentified] *(Unknown painter)* **PR**
  Bibl: 1682 Zeeman inventory
  Graenie [?] **PR**
Graesböck→see Craesbeeck, Joos van
Graesboeck→see Craesbeeck, Joos van
Graesdorp→see Grasdorp, Jan Gerrit
Graeser, Camille→see Graeser, Camille Louis
Graeser, Camille Louis **BA**
  (Swiss artist, 1892-) **WC**
  (Swiss artist, interior designer, b.1892) **BA**
  Bibl: ▶Havlice, Idx. art. bio.; ▶Künst.-Lex. Schweiz 20. Jahrh.; ▶Vollmer, Künst.-Lex. 20. Jhr.
Graeser, Camille **WC**
Graet→see Graat, Barent
Graether, Frederick C. *(fl. 1891; Architectural draftsman, United States of America)* **FA**
  Bibl: ▶Lowry, Building natl. image; Natl. Archives object
Graetz, Gidon *(Italian sculptor, b.1929)* **BA**
  Bibl: ▶Art Index, 1973; Munich (BRD), Kunstverein München, GIDON GRAETZ, 1977
Graetz, René *(German sculptor, painter, b.1908)* **BA**
  Bibl: Berlin(DDR), Staatliche Museen, Kupperstichkabinett und Sammlungen derZeichnungen, RENE GRAETZ...(1978); ▶Vollmer, Künst.-Lex. 20. Jhr.
Graevenitz, Gerhard van→see Graevenitz, Gerhard von
Graevenitz, Gerhard von **BA**
  (Dutch artist, 20th cent.) **WC**
  (West German sculptor, 1934-1983) **BA**
  Bibl: ▶Bénézit; ▶MoMA libr. cat.; Otterlo (NLD), Rijksmus. Kroller-Muller, GERHARD VON GRAVENITZ (1984); ▶Wer ist wer, 1978; Winter, P., KUNSTWERK, XXXVI/5 (Nov 1983) p.85-86
Graevenitz, Gerhard van **WC**
Graf→see Graf, Johann
Graf or Fraaf, Hans→see Graaf, Hans
Graf or Graff the Elder, Urs→see Graf, Urs, the elder

Graf, Caecilie *(German painter, b.1868)* **GC**
  Bibl: ▶Thieme-Becker
  Bader-Pfaff, Caecilie **GC**
  Graf-Pfaff, Caecilie **GC**
Graf, F. *(Dutch(?) artist, op.1733)* **WC**
Graf, Gerd *(Swiss architect)* **AV**
  Bibl: Abitare, 1984 Mar., no.222, p.10
Graf, Gottfried *(German painter, printmaker, author, 1881-1938)* **BA**
  Bibl: ▶Natl. union cat., pre-1956; ▶Vollmer, Künst.-Lex. 20. Jhr.; Wirth, KUNSTWERK, XXXIV/6(1981), 74-75
Graf, Graaf, Graef or Graff, Johann or Hans→see Graf, Johann
Graf, Johann **PR**
  (German artist, 1653-1710) **WC**
  (German painter, 1653-1710) **PR**
  Bibl: ▶Thieme-Becker
  Graaf **PR**
  Graf **PR**
Graf, Graaf, Graef or Graff, Johann or Hans **WC**
  Hans Graf **PR**
  Johann Graf **PR**
Graf, Oscar **GC WC**
  (German artist, 1870-1957) **WC**
  (German painter, 1870-1957) **GC**
  Bibl: ▶Thieme-Becker
Graf, Sieglinde *(West German architect)* **AV**
  Bibl: Bauwelt, 1988 Jan.29, v.79, no.5, p.202
Graf, Urs (the Elder)→see Graf, Urs, the elder
Graf, Urs (the Younger) *(Swiss painter, 1512-ca.1560)* **GC**
  Bibl: ▶Thieme-Becker
Graf, Urs, the elder **BA**
  (Swiss artist, c.1485-1527) **WC**
  (Swiss painter, printmaker, and goldsmith, ca.1485-1527/29) **GC**
  (Swiss painter, printmaker, goldsmith, ca.1485-1527/29) **BA**
  Bibl: ▶Bénézit; ▶Encyc. world art; ▶RILA/BHA; ▶Schweiz. Künst.-Lex.; ▶Thieme-Becker
Graf or Graff the Elder, Urs **WC**
Graf, Urs (the Elder) **GC**
Graf-Pfaff, Caecilie→see Graf, Caecilie
Grafait, P. *(French artist, op.1695-1700)* **WC**
Graff→see Graff, Anton

Graff, Anton **BA GC PR WC**
  (Swiss artist, 1736-1813) **WC**
  (Swiss painter and printmaker, 1736-1813) **GC**
  (Swiss painter, 1736-1813) **PR**
  (Swiss painter, printmaker in Germany, 1736-1813) **BA**
  Bibl: ▶RILA/BHA; ▶Schweiz. Künst.-Lex.; ▶Thieme-Becker
  Anton Graff **PR**
  Graff **PR**
Graff, Carl Anton **GC WC**
  (German artist, 1774-1832) **WC**
  (German, 1774-1832) **GC**
  Bibl: ▶Thieme-Becker
Graff, Dorothea Maria Henrietta→see Gsell, Dorothea Maria Henrietta
Graff, Graf or Grav, Johann Andreas→see Graff, Johann Andreas
Graff, Graf or Grav, Michael *(German artist, op.c.1520-m.1550)* **WC**
Graff, Harald *(West German architect, Stade)* **AV**
  Bibl: ▶Bund Deut. Arch. Hdbch., 1987
Graff, Johann Andreas **GC**
  (German artist, 1637-1701) **WC**
  (German, 1637-1701) **GC**
  Bibl: ▶Witt checklist
Graff, Graf or Grav, Johann Andreas **WC**
Graff, Jummy *(South African architect)* **AV**
  Bibl: Architect & builder, 1985 Aug., p.30
Graff, Leslie Frederick *(Canadian painter, b.1936)* **BA**
  Bibl: ▶MacDonald, Can. artists
Graff, Maria Sibylla→see Merian, Maria Sibylla
Graff, Philipp *(German photographer, 19th c.)* **BA**
  Bibl: Eder, Hist. photography; ▶Kempe, Daguerreotypie DEU
Graffin, David *(French artist, b.1938)* **BA**
  Bibl: Amsterdam (NLD), Stedelijk Mus., Daniel Graffin (1977)
Graffione *(Giovanni di Michele Scheggini)* **BA**
  (Italian artist, 1455-1527) **WC**
  (Italian painter, 1455-ca.1527) **BA**
  (Italian, 1455-1527) **GC**
  Bibl: ▶Bénézit; ▶Bolaffi; ▶Thieme-Becker
Graffione, Giovanni **GC**
Graffione, Giovanni di Michele Scheggini da Larciano **WC**
Graffione, Giovanni→see Graffione (Giovanni di Michele Scheggini)
Graffione, Giovanni di Michele Scheggini da Larciano→see Graffione (Giovanni di Michele Scheggini)

Graffman, Carl Samuel *(Swedish artist, 1802-1842)* **WC**
Grafi, Carlo *(Italian architect, 1925-)* **AV**
Grafle, Albert *(German artist, 1807-1889)* **WC**
Grafly, Charles *(American sculptor, 1862-1929)* **BA**
  Bibl: ▶Bénézit; NBD; ▶Vollmer, Künst.-Lex. 20. Jhr.; ▶Who was who [GBR]
Grafstrom→see Grafström, Jonas Olof
Grafström, Jonas Olof *(Swedish painter, 1855-1933)* **BA PR**
  Bibl: ▶RILA/BHA; ▶Svenska konstnärer; ▶Vollmer, Künst.-Lex. 20. Jhr.
  Grafstrom **PR**
  Grafstrom, Olof **PR**
  Olof Jonas Grafstrom **PR**
Grafstrom, Olof→see Grafström, Jonas Olof
Gragera y Herboso, José *(Spanish sculptor, 1818-1897)* **BA**
  Bibl: ▶Encic. univ. ilus.; Goya, CLXI/2 (1981) pp.350-353; ▶Ossorio y Bernard, Artistas españoles 19s.; ▶Thieme-Becker
Gragg, Samuel *(American cabinetmaker, 1772-ca.1855)* **BA**
  Bibl: ST.LOUIS ART MUSEUM BULL.,XV(SUMMER 1980), 2-48
Graglia, Andrea *(Italian artist, op. 1777-1792)* **WC**
Graham *(Engraver)* **WI**
Graham→see Graham, John
Graham the Younger, John→see Graham, John
Graham, Alexander **WC WI**
  (British artist, 1858-op.1893) **WI**
  (British artist, 1858-p.1893) **WC**
Graham, Brett *(New Zealander sculptor, 20th c.)* **BA**
  Bibl: Dunn, Art New Zealand LII (spr.1989), 52-53
Graham, Bruce *(American architect, born in Bogota, Colombia, joined SOM in 1951, since 1960 partner in SOM, 1925-)* **AV**
  Bibl: ▶Contemp. archts.
Graham, C. *(British artist, op.1839-1850)* **WC WI**
Graham, Charles *(American painter, illustrator, 1852-1911)* **BA**
  Bibl: ▶Dawdy, Artists Amer. West; ▶Groce, Artists Amer.; ▶Samuels, Artists Amer. West
Graham, Chauncey G. *(fl. 1892; Draftsman, United States of America)* **FA**
  Bibl: ▶Lowry, Building natl. image; Natl. Archives object
Graham, Dan **WC WI**
  (British artist, 20th cent.) **WC**
  (British artist, op.20th c.) **WI**
Graham, Dan→see Graham, Daniel H.

Graham, Daniel H. **BA**
  (American artist, b.1942) **BA**
  (American sculptor, 1942-) **AV**
  Bibl: ▶Libr. of Congr. Name Auth. File; NGB; Philadelphia (PA, USA), ICA, Video art (1975); ▶WW Amer. Art, 1976
Graham, Dan **AV**
Graham, David *(New Zealand artist, 1928-)* **WC**
Graham, Edith *(British artist, op. 1880-1920)* **WI**
Graham, Ernest Robert *(1868-1936)* **AV**
Graham, Fergus *(British artist, op. 1928-1937)* **WI**
Graham, Florence E. *(British artist, op.1861-1891)* **WI**
Graham, George→see Graham, George I
Graham, George→see Graham, George II
Graham, George I **WI**
  (British artist, op.1786-1813) **WC**
  (British artist, op.1788-1813) **WI**
  (Engraver, op.1788-1813) **WI**
Graham, George **WC WI**
Graham, George II **WI**
  (British artist, 1881-1949) **WC WI**
  Bibl: ▶Wilson, Brit. marine ptrs.
Graham, George **WC**
Graham, H.B. **WC WI**
  (British artist, 20th cent.) **WC**
  (British artist, op.20th c.) **WI**
Graham, J. *(American interior designer, Mississippi)* **AV**
  Bibl: Southern accents, 1986 Mar.-Apr., v.9, no.2, p.70
Graham, James Gillespie **AV BA**
  (Scottish architect, 1776-1855) **AV**
  (Scottish architect, ca.1777-1855) **BA**
  Bibl: ▶Colvin, Brit. archts.; ▶Dict. natl. biog.; ▶Thieme-Becker
  Gillespie, James **AV**
Graham, James Lillie *(Canadian artist, 1890-1965)* **WC**
Graham, John *(American artist, 1890-)* **WC**
Graham, John **BA PR**
  (British artist, 1754-1817) **WC WI**
  (British painter, 1754-1817) **BA**
  (British painter, 1755-1817) **PR**
  Bibl: ▶Bénézit; ▶Dict. natl. biog.; ▶RILA/BHA
  Graham **PR**
Graham the Younger, John **WC**
Graham, John II **WI**
  Graham, R. A. **PR**
  John Graham **PR**
Graham, John→see Gilbert, John Graham
Graham, John→see Graham, John II

Graham, John D. **BA PR WC WI**
  (American artist, 1881-1961) **WC WI**
  (American painter, 1881-1961) **BA PR**
  Bibl: Arts Mag LIX/9 (May 1985), p.95; Clark Art Inst. Libr.; ▶Cummings, Contemp. Amer. artists; ▶Fielding's Amer. ptrs.; ▶Oxford comp. 20c. art; ▶RILA/BHA; ▶WW Amer. Art, necrol.; ▶WWW Amer. art; ▶Young, Amer. artists
  Dabrowski, Ivan **BA**
  Dombrovsky, Ivan Gratianovich **BA**
Graham, John D. (Ivan Dabrowski) **PR**
  Ivan Dabrowski **PR**
  John D. Graham **PR**
  Servus, Ioannes Magnus **BA**
Graham, John D. (Ivan Dabrowski)→see Graham, John D.
Graham, John II **BA**
  (American architect, 1908-) **AV**
  (American architect, 20th c.) **BA**
  Bibl: ▶AIA Pro File; ▶Avery period. idx.; Clausen, JSAH, XLII/2 (May 1984) 144
Graham, John **AV**
Graham, John II→see Graham, John
Graham, Kay M. *(Canadian painter, b.1913)* **BA**
  Bibl: ▶Artists Canada; ▶WW Amer. Art, 1976
Graham, Maria→see Callcott, Maria
Graham, Maria, Mrs.→see Callcott, Maria
Graham, Montague William, Lord *(British artist, 1807-1878)* **WI**
  Bibl: ▶Mallalieu, Brit. watercolour artists
Graham, Paul *(British photographer, b.1956)* **BA**
  Bibl: ▶Intl. dir. exh. artists
Graham, Peter **BA WC WI**
  (British artist, 1836-1921) **WC WI**
  (British painter, 1836-1921) **BA**
  Bibl: Paviere, Landscape; ▶Vollmer, Künst.-Lex. 20. Jhr.; ▶Waters, Brit. artists; ▶Who was who [GBR], 1916
Graham, R. A.→see Graham, John
Graham, Rigby *(British author, illustrator, b.1931)* **BA**
  Bibl: ▶Natl. union cat., 1973-1977; V & A libr. cat.
Graham, Robert *(American sculptor, b.1938)* **BA**
  Bibl: Oakland (CA, USA), Mus. of Art, A sense of scale (1977)
Graham, Robert *(British artist, op. 20th c.)* **WI**
Graham, Robert *(British, act.1840-1870)* **BA**
  Bibl: HISTORY OF PHOTOG., VIII/3 (July-Sept 1984) 231-235

Graham, Robert Alexander
(American painter, 1873-1946) **PR**
  Bibl: ▶WWW Amer. art
Robert Alexander Graham PR
Graham, Robert E. *(British artist,*
op.1857-1873) **WI**
Graham, Roy Eugene *(American*
architect) **AV**
  Bibl: Historic preservation, 1986
  Sept.-Oct., v.38, no.5, p.32
Graham, Thomas Alex
Fergusson→see Graham, Thomas
Alexander Fergusson
Graham, Thomas Alexander→see
Graham, Thomas Alexander
Fergusson
Graham, Thomas Alexander
Ferguson→see Graham, Thomas
Alexander Fergusson
Graham, Thomas Alexander
Fergusson **WI**
  (British artist, 1840-1906) WC WI
  (British painter, 1840-1906) PR
  Bibl: ▶Thieme-Becker
Graham, Thomas Alex
Fergusson **WC**
Graham, Thomas Alexander PR
Graham, Thomas Alexander
Ferguson **PR**
Thomas Alexander Ferguson
  Graham PR
Graham, Wilhelmina Barns→see
  Barns-Graham, Wilhelmina
Graham, William *(American artist,*
1841-1910) **WC WI**
Graham-Gilbert, John→see Gilbert,
  John Graham
Grahl, August *(German artist, 1791-*
1868) **WC**
Grahn, Hjalmar *(Swedish artist,*
1882-1949) **WC**
Graillon, Pierre Adrien **GC WC**
  (French artist, 1807/9-1872) WC
  (French painter, 1809-1872) GC
  Bibl: ▶Bénézit
Grailly, Victor de **BA PR WC**
  (French artist, 1804-1889) WC
  (French painter, 1804-1889) BA PR
  Bibl: ▶Bénézit; ▶RILA/BHA;
  ▶Thieme-Becker
Victor de Grailly PR
Graimberg, Carl, Graf von (Charles
de) *(German artist, 1774-1865)* **WC**
Graindorge, Thomas→see Jourdain,
  Frantz
Graine, Colin *(British artist, op.*
1906) **WC**
Graine, de la [Unidentified]
  (Unknown painter) **PR**
  Bibl: (1802, April 2, lot 18,
  Christie's)
Grainger→see Grainger, George A.

Grainger, George A. *(British*
painter, act. 1782-1836) **PR**
  Bibl: ▶Thieme-Becker
George A. Grainger PR
Grainger PR
Granger PR
Grainger, Ian **BA WI**
  (British artist, b.1942) WI
  (British printmaker, b.1942) BA
  Bibl: ▶Babington Smith, Contemp.
  artists; Cardiff (GBR), Oriel, The
  final proof (1981)
Grainger, James *(British artist, op.*
20th c.) **WI**
Grainger, Rowan *(British artist,*
b.1936) **WI**
Grale, Conrad *(German printmaker,*
woodcutter, act.1614, d.1630) **BA**
  Bibl: ▶Bénézit; ▶Hollstein, German;
  ▶Thieme-Becker
Gralleni, H. **WC WI**
  (British artist, op.1845-) WI
  (British(?) artist, op.c.1845) WC
Gram, Lennart *(Swedish artist,*
1910-) **WC**
Gramaglia, Maggiorino *(Italian, b.*
1895) **JG**
Gramatica→see Gramatica,
  Antiveduto
Gramatica, Anteveduto→see
  Gramatica, Antiveduto
Gramatica, Antiveduto **BA PR**
  (Italian artist, 1571-1626) WC
  (Italian painter, 1571-1626) BA GC PR
  Bibl: ▶Bénézit; ▶Bolaffi; ▶Encyc.
  world art; ▶RILA/BHA;
  ▶Thieme-Becker; ▶Witt checklist;
  ▶Wittkower, Art & arch. Italy
Antiveduto PR
Antiveduto Gramatica PR
Gramatica PR
Gramatica, Anteveduto GC
Grammatica, Anteveduto **GC**
Grammatica, Antiveduto **WC**
Gramatica, Imperiale *(Italian*
painter, 1599-1634) **BA**
  Bibl: ▶Bolaffi; ▶Thieme-Becker
Gramatky, Hardie *(American*
author, illustrator, 1907-1979) **BA**
  Bibl: NY Times obit., 1 May 1979;
  ▶WW Amer. Art, 1978
Gramatté, Walter **BA WC**
  (German artist, 1897-1929) WC
  (German painter, printmaker,
1897-1929) BA
  Bibl: ▶Bénézit; ▶Vollmer,
  Künst.-Lex. 20. Jhr.
Gramatzki, Eve *(French artist, 20th*
cent.) **WC**
Gramiccia→see Gramiccia, Lorenzo

Gramiccia, Lorenzo **BA GC PR WC**
  (Italian artist, 1702-1795) WC
  (Italian painter, 1702-1795) BA PR
  (Italian, 1702-1795) GC
  Bibl: ▶Bolaffi; ▶Thieme-Becker;
  ▶Witt checklist
Gramiccia PR
Lorenzo Gramiccia PR
Grammatica, Anteveduto→see
  Gramatica, Antiveduto
Grammatica, Antiveduto→see
  Gramatica, Antiveduto
Grammenopoulos, Anthony
(American architect) **AV**
Grammont *(French artist, 19th*
cent.) **WC**
Grammorseo→see Grammorseo,
  Pietro
Grammorseo, Pietro **BA GC PR WC**
  (Italian artist, op.1523-1533) WC
  (Italian painter, act. 1523-1533) PR
  (Italian painter, act.1523, d.
before 1531) BA
  (Italian, act.1523-1533) GC
  Bibl: ▶Bénézit; ▶Bolaffi; Romano,
  CASALESI DEL CINQUECENTO
  (1970) 36; ▶Thieme-Becker; ▶Witt
  checklist
Grammorseo PR
Pietro Grammorseo PR
Gramont(?) *(French(?) artist, 18th*
cent.) **WC**
Gran→see Gran, Daniel
Gran Re, Achille *(Italian painter, act.*
1602-1606) **BA**
  Bibl: Chappell, Prospettiva, 25
  (Apr. 1981) pp.59-64
Gran, Daniel **BA GC PR WC**
  (Austrian painter and
draughtsman, 1694?-1757) GC
  (Austrian painter, 1694-1757) BA
  (German artist, 1694-1757) WC
  (German painter, 1694-1757) PR
  Bibl: ▶Encyc. world art; Getty
  Photo Study Coll.; ▶RILA/BHA;
  ▶Thieme-Becker
D. Graan PR
Daniel Gran PR
Graan PR
Gran PR
Granacci→see Granacci, Francesco
Granacci, Francesco **BA GC PR WC**
  (Italian artist, 1477-1543) WC
  (Italian painter, 1469-1543) PR
  (Italian painter, 1477-1543) BA GC
  Bibl: ▶Bolaffi; ▶Encyc. world art;
  ▶Fredericksen & Zeri, Census,
  (who have used earlier birth
  date); ▶RILA/BHA, 1986;
  ▶Thieme-Becker
Francesco Granacci PR
Granacci PR
Granacci, Francesco d'Andrea di
  Marco PR
Granacci, Francesco d'Andrea di
Marco→see Granacci, Francesco

Granacci, Pseudo →see Master
  Known as the Pseudo Granacci
Granát, Aleš (Czech architect)   **AV**
  Bibl: Architektura ČSR, 1988,
  v.47, no.3, p.58
Granberg, Gunnar (Norwegian
  architect)   **AV**
  Bibl: Byggekunst: the Norwegian
  review of architecture, 1988,
  v.70, no.7, p.522
Granche, Pierre (Canadian sculptor,
  b.1948)   **BA**
  Bibl: Paris (FRA), Ctr culturel
  canadien, Annick Doideau (1981)
Grancini, Amos (Italian artist, op.
  1809)   **WC**
Grand'Homme, Paul V (French
  artist, 19th cent.)   **WC**
Grand, France (French interior
  designer)   **AV**
  Bibl: Maison Française, 1985 May,
  no.387, p.130
Grand, Olivier de →see Olivier de
  Gand
Grand, Toni (French sculptor,
  b.1935)   **BA**
  Bibl: Sainte Etienne, Musee d'Art
  et d'Industrie.TONI GRAND;
  BERNARD PAGES; STUDIO
  188(DEC 1974), 5
Grandadam, Hervé (French
  architect, Grenoble)   **AV**
  Bibl: ▶Annuaire archts. fran.,
  1978
Grandart, Monsieur [Unidentified]
  (Unknown painter)   **PR**
  Bibl: Colonna inventory, Rome,
  1763
  Monsieur Grandart   **PR**
Grande →see Roberti, Ercole de'
Grande, Antonio del →see Del
  Grande, Antonio
Grande, Salvatore (Italian architect)   **AV**
  Bibl: Ottagono, 1984 June, no.73,
  p.88
Grandee, Joe   **WC WI**
  (American artist, 20th cent.)   **WC**
  (American artist, op.1962-)   **WI**
Grandgerard, Lucien Henri →see
  Grandgérard, Lucien-Henri
Grandgérard, Lucien-Henri   **BA**
  (French artist, 1880)   **WC**
  (French painter, printmaker,
  1880-1970)   **BA**
  Bibl: ▶Bénézit; ▶Dict. biog. fran.;
  ▶Vollmer, Künst.-Lex. 20. Jhr.;
  ▶Witt checklist
  Grandgerard, Lucien Henri   **WC**
Grandhomme (French architect,
  18th cent)   **AV**
  Bibl: Architectural digest, 1989
  Jan., v.46, no.1, p.148
Grandhomme, Jacques (the
  Younger) →see Granthomme,
  Jacques (the Younger)
Grandi (Italian artist, op.1782)   **WC**

Grandi, Ercole   **BA**
  (Italian artist, c.1463-a.1525)   **WC**
  (Italian painter, architect, ca.
  1463-ca.1531)   **BA**
  (Italian, ca.1463-d. bef.1525)   **GC**
  Bibl: ▶Bessone-Aurelj, Scult. &
  arch. ital.; ▶Thieme-Becker; ▶Witt
  checklist
  Ercole da Ferrara   **GC**
Grandi, Ercole de Giulio Cesare
  (Ercole da Ferrara)   **WC**
Grandi, Ercole di Giulio Cesare   **GC**
Grandi, Ercole →see Roberti, Ercole
  de'
Grandi, Ercole de Giulio Cesare
  (Ercole da Ferrara) →see Grandi,
  Ercole
Grandi, Ercole di Giulio Cesare →see
  Grandi, Ercole
Grandi, Francesco (Italian artist,
  1831-1891)   **WC**
Grandi, Gianmatteo (Italian
  sculptor, act.1523)   **BA**
  Bibl: Bellinati, Padova, p. 212
Grandi, Giovanni Battista de'
  (Italian painter, 1643-1718)   **BA**
  Bibl: Arte lombarda, 42/43
  (1975) pp.211-212; ▶Bolaffi;
  ▶Thieme-Becker
Grandi, Girolamo   **GC WC**
  (Italian artist, op.c.1530-48)   **WC**
  (Italian, act. ca.1530-1548)   **GC**
  Bibl: ▶Witt checklist
Grandi, Girolamo de' (Italian
  painter, 1653-1718)   **BA**
  Bibl: Arte lombarda, 42/43
  (1975) pp.211-212; ▶Bolaffi;
  ▶Thieme-Becker
Grandi, Giuseppe (Italian sculptor,
  1843-1894)   **BA GC**
  Bibl: ▶RILA/BHA; ▶Thieme-Becker
Grandi, Mario Dario (Argentine
  painter, 1918-1971)   **BA**
  Bibl: Buenos Aires (ARG), Mus.
  Nac. de Bellas Artes, Mario Dario
  Grandi (1977)
Grandin, Jacques Louis Michel
  (French artist, 1780-p.1814)   **WC**
Grandio, Constantino (Spanish
  artist, 1924-)   **WC**
Grandjean de Montigny, Auguste
  Henri Victor (French architect in
  BRA, 1776-1850)   **BA**
  Bibl: ▶Hitchcock, Arch. 19 & 20cs;
  ▶Macmillan encyc. archts.;
  ▶Portoghesi, Diz. arch. e
  urbanistica
Grandjean, Edmond Georges
  (French artist, 1844-1908)   **WC**
Grandjean, Jean   **BA GC WC**
  (Dutch artist, 1755-1781)   **WC**
  (Dutch draughtsman, 1755-
  1781)   **GC**
  (Dutch painter, 1752-1781)   **BA**
  Bibl: ▶Aa, Biog. woordenboek
  NLD; Getty Photo Study Coll.;
  ▶Thieme-Becker; ▶Witt checklist

Grandjean, Lee (British artist,
  b.1949)   **BA**
  Bibl: Kingston-upon-Hull (GBR),
  Ferens Art Gallery, Drawing in
  action (1978)
Grandjean, Phillipe (Architect)   **AV**
  Bibl: ▶Libr. of Congr. Name Auth.
  File
Grandjouan, Jules (French
  printmaker, 1875-1968)   **BA**
Grandma Moses →see Moses, Anna
  Mary Robertson
Grandmaison, Nickola de
  (Canadian painter, b.1892)   **BA**
  Bibl: ▶Havlice, Idx. art. bio.;
  ▶MacDonald, Can. artists; ▶WW
  Amer. Art, 1970
Grandon, Charles (French artist,
  c.1691-1762)   **WC**
Grandpierre-Deverzy, Adrienne
  Marie Louise (French painter,
  b.1798, act.1822-1855)   **BA**
  Bibl: ▶Bénézit; ▶Thieme-Becker
Grandsire, Pierre Eugène   **GC WC**
  (French artist, 1825-1905)   **WC**
  (French painter, 1825-1905)   **GC**
  Bibl: ▶Bénézit
Grandville (Jean Ignace Isidore
  Gérard)   **BA**
  (French artist, 1803-1847)   **WC**
  (French illustrator, cartoonist,
  printmaker, 1803-1847)   **BA**
  (French, 1803-1847)   **GC**
  Bibl: ▶Bénézit; ▶Encyc. world art;
  Getty Photo Study Coll. (Ptgs.);
  ▶Larousse grande encyc.; ▶Witt
  checklist
  Gerard, Jean Ignace Isidore   **GC**
  Gerard, Jean Ignace Isidore
  ('Grandville')   **WC**
  Grandville, J.I.   **GC**
Grandville, J.I. →see Grandville (Jean
  Ignace Isidore Gérard)
Grane, W.D. (American, 20th c.)   **BA**
Granell, E.F. →see Granell, Eugenio
  Fernández
Granell, Eugenio Fernández   **BA**
  (French artist, 20th cent.)   **WC**
  (Spanish painter, b.1912)   **BA**
  Bibl: Arean, Cuadernos
  hispanoaméricanos (Nov.-Dec.
  1989) pp.17-28; ▶Bénézit; ▶Blas,
  Pintores españoles contemp.;
  Guide exh. artists: Sculp.; ▶MoMA
  libr. cat.
  Granell, E.F.   **WC**
Granello or Granelo, Niccola →see
  Granello, Niccolò (Figonetto)
Granello, Niccola (Figonetto) →see
  Granello, Niccolò (Figonetto)

Granello, Niccolò (Figonetto) BA
   (Italian artist, op.1567-m.1593) WC
   (Italian painter, act. 1562, d.
     1593) PR
   (Italian painter, sculptor in ESP,
     act.1562, d.1593) BA
     Bibl: ▶Bolaffi; ▶Diz. artisti ital. in
     Spagna; ▶RILA/BHA;
     ▶Thieme-Becker
   Figonetto PR
Granello or Granelo, Niccola WC
Granello, Niccola (Figonetto) PR
   Niccola Granello (Figonetto) PR
Granelo, Francisco (Spanish painter,
   act.1610, d.1629) BA
     Bibl: ▶Ceán Bermúdez, Bellas artes
     ESP; ▶Thieme-Becker
Graner y Arrufi, Luis (Spanish artist,
   1867-1927) WC
Graner y Vinuelas, Antonio
   (Spanish artist, 19th cent.) WC
Graner, Ernst (German artist, 1865-) WC
Graneri, Giovanni Michele → see
   Granieri, Giovanni Michele
Graneri, Giovanni Michele(?) → see
   Granieri, Giovanni Michele
Granet → see Granet, François Marius
Granet, François Marius BA GC PR WC
   (French artist, 1775-1849) WC
   (French painter, 1775-1849) BA PR
   (French, 1775-1849) GC
     Bibl: ▶Bénézit; ▶Encyc. world art;
     ▶RILA/BHA; ▶Thieme-Becker;
     ▶Witt checklist
   Francois Marius Granet PR
   Granet PR
   Granet, Francois-Marius PR
   Grenet PR
Granet, Francois-Marius → see Granet,
   François Marius
Grange, Jacques AV BA
   (French interior designer) AV
     Bibl: Architectural digest, 1985
     Apr., v.41, no.4, p.86
Grange, Kenneth Henry (British
   designer, b.1929) BA
     Bibl: ▶Who's Who [GBR]
Grange, Robert (French(?) artist,
   18th cent.) WC
Granger → see Grainger, George A.
Granger, Alfred Hoyt (American
   architect. In partnership with
   Charles S. Frost, Frost & Granger,
   Chicago (1898-1910), 1867-1939) AV
     Bibl: ▶Withey, Amer. archts.
Granger, David → see Des Granges,
   David
Granger, Jean Pierre GC WC
   (French artist, 1779-1840) WC
   (French painter, 1779-1840) GC
     Bibl: ▶Bénézit
Granger, Mme (French artist, 19th
   cent.) WC
Granger, Richard (British architect,
   1797-1861) AV
     Bibl: ▶Colvin, Brit. archts.

Granges, David des → see Des
   Granges, David
Granholm, Bruno F. (Finnish
   architect, 19th-20th cs.) BA
     Bibl: Helsinki (FIN), Suomen
     Rakinnustaiteen Mus.,
     Rautateiden Arkkitectuuri (1984)
**Granicher, Samuel (Johann
   Samuel)** (Swiss artist, 1758-1813) WC
Granie, Joseph (French artist, 1866-
   1915) WC
Granier, Jean Marie (French
   printmaker, b.1922) BA
     Bibl: NOUVELLES DE L'ESTAMPE,
     54(NOV-DEC 1980), 20-23
Granier, Pierre (French sculptor,
   1635-1715) BA
     Bibl: ▶Dict. biog. fran.;
     ▶Thieme-Becker
Granieri → see Granieri, Giovanni
   Michele
Granieri, Giovanni Michele PR
   (Italian artist, op.c.1730-m.a.
     1778) WC
   (Italian painter, act. ca.1742-ca.
     1789) PR
   (Italian, act.ca.1730-bef.1778) GC
     Bibl: ▶Fredericksen & Zeri, Census;
     ▶Witt checklist
   Giovanni Michele Graneri PR
   Giovanni Michele Granieri PR
Graneri, Giovanni Michele GC PR
Graneri, Giovanni Michele(?) WC
   Granieri PR
Graninger, Leopold (German artist,
   19th cent.) WC
Granit, Michael (Architect) AV
     Bibl: Places, 1984, v.1, no.3, p.4
Grano, Antonino Nino → see Grano,
   Antonio
Grano, Antonio BA
   (Italian artist, op.1680-m.1718) WC
   (Italian painter, printmaker, act.
     1683, d.1718) BA
     Bibl: ▶Bolaffi; Garstang, Antologia
     di B-A 23-24 (1984) 40;
     ▶Thieme-Becker
Grano, Antonino Nino WC
Granpré Molière, Marinus Jan BA
   (Dutch architect, 1883-) AV
   (Dutch architect, theorist, 1883-
     1972) BA
     Bibl: ▶Avery period. idx.; ▶Grote
     Winkler Prins
Granpré Molière, Marius Jan AV
Granpré Molière, Marius Jan → see
   Granpré Molière, Marinus Jan
Grant → see Grant, Duncan
Grant → see Grant, J. Jeffery
Grant DeVolson Wood → see Wood,
   Grant
Grant Wood → see Wood, Grant
Grant, A. → see Grant, A. I
Grant, A. → see Grant, A. II

Grant, A. I WI
   (British artist, op.1786-1789) WC WI
Grant, A. WC
Grant, A. II WI
   (British artist, op.1852) WC
   (British artist, op.1852-) WI
Grant, A. WC
Grant, Alexander (British, act.1770) BA
     Bibl: BULLETIN OF THE ART
     INSTITUTE OF CHICAGO,
     LXXII(JAN-FEB 1978), 8
Grant, Alice (British artist, op.1879-
   1904) WI
Grant, Alistair WC WI
   (British artist, 1925-) WC
   (British artist, b.1925) WI
Grant, Baron WC WI
   (British artist, 19th cent.) WC
   (British artist, op.19th c.) WI
Grant, C.J. WC WI
   (British artist, op.1832) WC
   (British artist, op.1832-) WI
     Bibl: ▶Houfe, Brit. book illus.
Grant, Carlton (British artist, op.
   1883-1899) WI
     Bibl: Paviere, Landscape
Grant, Clement Rollins (American
   artist, 1849-1893) WC WI
Grant, Donald (British artist, op.
   1989-) WI
Grant, Dorothy Marion (English
   stained glass artis, London, 1912-
   1988) AV
     Bibl: Transactions of the Ancient
     Monuments Society, 1989, v.33,
     p.209
Grant, Duncan BA PR WC WI
   (1885-) AV
   (British artist, 1885-) WC
   (British artist, 1885-1978) WI
   (British painter, 1885-1978) BA PR
     Bibl: ▶Johnson, Brit. artists;
     N.ADAMS(MA, USA),
     TRANSCRIPT(MAY 11 1978);
     ▶RILA/BHA
   Duncan Grant PR
   Grant PR
Grant, Duncan James Corrows AV PR
Grant, Duncan James Corrows → see
   Grant, Duncan
Grant, Francis PR WI
   (British artist, 1803-1878) WC WI
   (British painter, 1803-1878) PR
     Bibl: ▶Thieme-Becker
   Francis Grant PR
Grant, Sir Francis WC
Grant, Frederick M. (American
   artist, b.1886) WI
Grant, George (American sculptor,
   20th c.) BA
     Bibl: ▶Art Index, v.25; Arts Mag.
     LII/2 (Feb 1978), 12
Grant, Gordon WC WI
   (American artist, 1875-) WC
   (American artist, 1875-1962) WI

Grant, Ian MacDonald WC WI
(British artist, 1904-) WC
(British artist, b.1904) WI
Grant, Ian, Mrs.(Margaret) → see
Gunuchian, Margaret, Miss
Grant, J. Jeffery WI
(American artist, 1883-1960) WI
(American painter, 1883-1960) PR
Bibl: ▶WWW Amer. art
Grant PR
Grant, J. Jeffrey PR
J. Jeffrey Grant PR
Grant, J. Jeffrey → see Grant, J.
Jeffery
Grant, James A. (British artist,
b.1887) WI
Grant, James M. (City Planning
Director, Des Moines, Iowa) AV
Bibl: Iowa architect, 1987 Sept-
Oct., v.35, no.4, p.22
Grant, Joe (American artist, b.ca.
1950) BA
Bibl: Los Angeles (CA, USA),
LAICA, Architectural sculp. (1980)
Grant, John WC WI
(British artist, -1873) WC
(British artist, d.1873) WI
Grant, Keith BA WC WI
(British artist, 20th cent.) WC
(British artist, b.1930) WI
(British painter, sculptor,
b.1930) BA
Bibl: ▶Bénézit
Grant, Margaret Ross → see Hislop,
Margaret Ross
Grant, Margo (American interior
designer) AV
Bibl: Interior design, 1987 Dec.,
v.58, no.15, p.152
Grant, Martin H. (Canadian
photographer, act.1855-1857) BA
Bibl: Jrnl. Canadian art hist., IV/1
(Spr. 1977) pp.25-45
Grant, Norah (British artist, op.
1911-) WI
Grant, Robertson (British architect,
d.1975) BA
Bibl: RIBA Jrnl., LXXXII/11-12
(Nov.-Dec. 1975) p.4
Grant, Sir Francis → see Grant, Francis
Grant, Thomas (British artist, op.
1819-1849) WC WI
Grant, William BA WI
(British artist, op.1752-) WI
(Scottish, act.1781-1782) BA
Bibl: McLanathan, Gilbert Stuart,
pp.45-46
Grant, William James (British artist,
1829-1866) WC WI
Granthomme, Jacques → see
Granthomme, Jacques (the
Younger)

**Granthomme, Jacques (the
Younger)** GC
(French artist, op.1574-1613) WC
(German draughtsman, c.1560-c.
1613) GC
Bibl: ▶Bénézit; ▶Thieme-Becker
Grandhomme, Jacques (the
Younger) GC
Granthomme, Jacques WC
Granucci, Bartolommeo (Italian
artist, 18th cent.) WC
Granveaud, Pierre (1939-) AV
Granville Perkins → see Perkins,
Granville
Granville Redmond → see Redmond,
Granville
Granville, John (British, 1779-1800) BA
Bibl: Bull. Detroit Inst. Arts, LVII/1
(1979) pp.41-45
Granville, Mary → see Delany, Mary
Granville
Granville, Walter L.B. (British
architect, ca.1819-1874) BA
Bibl: ROYAL SOCIETY OF ARTS
JOURNAL, CXXIX, 5298(MAY
1981), 357-79
Granzow, Wladislaw (Polish artist,
1872-) WC
Grão Vasco → see Fernandes, Vasco
(Grão Vasco)
Grape-Vine Group (Apulian vase-
painters) GC
Bibl: Trendall, Attic red-fig. vases
Apulia
Grapiglia, Giovanni Girolamo
(Italian architect, doca.1572-1621) GC
Bibl: TCI Venezia, 1969
Grapinelli, Flaminio (Italian artist,
-c.1750) WC
Grapp, Wendling → see Dietterlin,
Wendel
Grappe-Roy, C. (French artist, op.
1922) WC
Gras, Amedée (French painter,
b.1805) GC
Bibl: ▶Bénézit
Gras, Caspar BA GC
(German metalworker and
sculptor, 1584-1674) GC
(German sculptor, metalworker
in AUT, 1584-1674) BA
(German, 1590-1674) JG
Bibl: ▶Brockhaus Enzyk.; ▶Encyc.
world art; ▶Neue deutsche Biog.;
▶RILA/BHA
Gras, Kaspar JG
Gras, Kaspar → see Gras, Caspar
Gras, Willem GC WC
(Dutch artist, 17th cent.) WC
(Dutch painter, 17th century) GC
Bibl: Getty Photo Study Coll.;
▶Thieme-Becker; ▶Witt checklist
Grasberger, Helmut (Austrian
architect) AV
Bibl: Planen Bauen Wohnen,
1986, no.115, p.35

Grasdorp → see Grasdorp, Jan Gerrit
Grasdorp, Jan Gerrit GC PR WC
(Dutch artist, 1651-1693) WC
(Dutch painter and
draughtsman, 1651-1693) GC
(Dutch painter, 1651-1693) PR
Bibl: Getty Photo Study Coll.;
▶Thieme-Becker; ▶Witt checklist
Graesdorp PR
Grasdorp PR
Jan Gerrit Grasdorp PR
Grasdorp, Willem GC WC
(Dutch artist, 1678-1723) WC
(Dutch painter, 1678-1723) GC
Bibl: ▶Thieme-Becker
Grasel (German artist, 20th cent.) WC
Gräsel, Friedrich (German sculptor,
b.1927) BA
Bibl: Jahrb. Hamburger
Kunstsamm. XX (1975) p.131-137
Grashey-Straub, Irmingard
(German draughtsman, 19th
century(?)) GC
Bibl: Getty Photo Study Coll.
(Douwes coll.)
Grashorn, Burkhard AV BA
(German architect, b.1940) BA
(West German architect, 1940-) AV
Bibl: Grashorn, B., in DAIDALOS
10 (DEc 1983) 104
Grashow, James AV BA
(American artist, 20th c.) BA
(American sculptor, printmaker,
1942-) AV
Bibl: ARTS MAGAZINE,
LVI/10(JUNE 1982), 12; ▶WW
Amer. Art
**Grasmair, Grasmayer, Grasmayr or
Graszmayer, Johann Georg
Dominikus** (German artist, 1691-
1751) WC
Grasmere Group (Etruscan vase-
painters) GC
Bibl: ▶Szilagyi, Etruszko-korinthosi
Grass, Adolf (Joseph Adolf)
(German artist, 19th cent.) WC
Grass, Carl Gotthard (German
artist, 1767-1814) WC
Grass, Günter (German author,
printmaker, b.1927) BA
Bibl: ▶New Columbia encyc.;
▶Wer ist wer
Grass-Mick, Augustin (French artist,
19th cent.) WC
Grassel, Franz (German artist, 1861-
c.1921) WC
Grasser, Erasmus (German sculptor,
architect, ca.1450-after 1526) BA
Bibl: ▶Bénézit; ▶Thieme-Becker
Grasset, Adèle (French painter, 19th
century) GC
Bibl: ▶Bénézit
Grasset, Auguste (French artist,
1829-p.1884) WC

Grasset, Eugène Samuel   **BA WC**
  (*French painter, printmaker,*
    architect, 1841-1917)   BA
  (*Swiss artist, 1841-1917*)   WC
  (*Swiss painter, 1841-1917*)   GC
  Bibl: ▶Bénézit; ▶Dict. biog. fran.;
    ▶Encyc. world art; ▶Schweiz.
    Künst.-Lex.; ▶Thieme-Becker

Grasset, Samuel   **GC**
Grasset, Samuel→see Grasset,
  Eugène Samuel

Grasshopper Group (*South Italian*
  vase-painters, 350-300 BC)   **GC**
  Bibl: McPhee & Trendall, Fish-
    Plates

Grasshopper Painter (*South Italian*
  vase-painter, 350-300 BC)   **GC**
  Bibl: McPhee & Trendall, Fish-
    Plates
Grassi→see Grassi, Nicola
Grassi or Grassy, Joseph→see Grassi,
  Josef

Grassi Painter (*South Italian vase-*
  painter, 360-330 BC)   **GC**
  Bibl: McPhee & Trendall, Fish-
    Plates

Grassi, Anton (*Austrian porcelain*
  modeler, 1755-1807)   **BA**
  Bibl: ▶Boger, World pott. & porc.;
    ▶Penguin dec. arts

Grassi, Bartolomeo (*Italian artist,*
  16th cent.)   **WC**

Grassi, Giorgio   **AV BA**
  (*Italian architect, 1935-*)   AV
  (*Italian architect, b.1935*)   BA
  Bibl: ▶Avery period. idx., suppl.
    4,6; ▶Libr. of Congr. Name Auth.
    File
Grassi, Giovanni→see Grassi,
  Giovannino de'

Grassi, Giovanni Battista (*Italian*
  painter, act.1716-1755)   **BA**
  Bibl: ▶Bolaffi

Grassi, Giovanni Battista di
  Raffaello (*Italian artist, op.1545-*
  m.1578)   **WC**
Grassi, Giovannino de→see Grassi,
  Giovannino de'

Grassi, Giovannino de'   **BA WC**
  (*Italian architect, sculptor,*
    illuminator, painter, act.1389-
    1410)   BA
  (*Italian artist, op.1389-m.1398*)   WC
  (*Italian illuminator, d.1398*)   GC
  Bibl: ▶Bolaffi;
    ▶D'Ancona, Miniaturistes, p.99;
    Gatti Perer, M.L., ARTE
    LOMBARDA, 84-85 (1988) p.5-32;
    ▶Portoghesi, Diz. arch. e
    urbanistica; ▶RILA/BHA;
    ▶Thieme-Becker; ▶Witt checklist
  Giovannino dei Grassi   GC
Grassi, Giovanni   **AV**
Grassi, Giovannino de   **GC**
Grassi, Giuseppe→see Grassi, Josef

Grassi, Guy (*American architect,*
  Boston, Mass)   **AV**
  Bibl: Builder, 1988 July, v.11,
    no.7, p.96

Grassi, Josef   **BA GC**
  (*Austrian painter, ca.1757-1838*)   BA
  (*German artist, c.1758-1838*)   WC
  (*Italian painter, 18-19c*)   GC
  Bibl: ▶Fuchs, Öst. Maler 19.
    Jahrh.; Ryszliewicz,
    MITTEILUNGEN DER
    OSTERREICHISCHEN GALERCE, XVI-
    XVII(1982-83), 121-147;
    ▶Thieme-Becker

Grassi or Grassy, Joseph   **WC**
  Grassi, Giuseppe   GC

Grassi, Luciano (*Italian architect*)   **AV**
  Bibl: Domus, 1985 Apr., no.660,
    p.54

Grassi, Marta (*Italian architect*)   **AV**
  Bibl: Ville giardini, 1987 Dec., no.
    222 suppl., p.38

Grassi, Nicola   **BA GC PR**
  (*Italian artist, a.1682-c.1750*)   WC
  (*Italian painter, 1682-1748*)   BA GC
  (*Italian painter, 1682-ca.1750*)   PR
  Bibl: ▶RILA/BHA, 1986;
    ▶Thieme-Becker
  Grassi   PR
Grassi, Nicola (Giannicola)   **WC**
  N. Grassi   PR
  Nicola Grassi   PR
Grassi, Nicola (Giannicola)→see
  Grassi, Nicola

Grassi, Orazio   **BA GC**
  (*Italian architect, 1583-1654*)   GC
  (*Italian ecclesiastic, architect,*
    mathematician, 1583-1654)   BA
  Bibl: ▶Bessone-Aurelj, Scult. &
    arch. ital.; ▶Portoghesi, Diz. arch.
    e urbanistica; ▶RILA/BHA, 1986;
    ▶Thieme-Becker

Grassi, Salomone de' (*Italian*
  illuminator, act.1399-1400)   **BA**
  Bibl: ▶Bénézit; ▶Bolaffi;
    ▶Thieme-Becker

Grassia, Francesco   **BA GC**
  (*Italian sculptor, 17th century*)   GC
  (*Italian sculptor, act.1640-1687*)   BA
  Bibl: Chappell, SE COLLEGE ART
    CONF. REVIEW, X/3 (1983) 130;
    TCI Roma e dintorni
Grassin→see Grassin, Alexandre-
  Marie
Grassin, A.→see Grassin, Alexandre-
  Marie

Grassin, Alexandre-Marie (*French*
  painter, b. 1883, act. 1912)   **PR**
  Bibl: ▶Bénézit; Indianapolis M of
    A catalogue
  Alexandre-Marie Grassin   PR
  Grassin   PR
  Grassin, A.   PR
Grassman, Marcelo (*Brazilian artist,*
  1925-)   **WC**

Grassmann, Ulrich (*Austrian*
  architect)   **AV**
  Bibl: Deutsche Bauzeitung, 1988
    July, v.122, no.7, p.138

Grasso, Filippo D. (*Italian artist, op.*
  1644)   **WC**

Grasso, Francesco di Giannino
  (Francesco da Pavia) (*Italian*
  artist, op.1490-1502)   **WC**

Grasso, Luciano (*Italian architect*)   **AV**
  Bibl: Abitare, 1987 Oct., no.258,
    p.242

Grassy, Percy (*British artist, op.*
  1913-)   **WI**

Gratama, Gerrit David (*Dutch*
  artist, 1874-1965)   **WC**

Gratama, Jan (*Dutch architect,*
  1877-1947)   **AV**
  Bibl: Assemblage, 1987 July, no.3,
    p.122

Grati, Alessandro (*Italian artist,*
  18th/19th cent.)   **WC**

Grati, Antonio (*Italian*)   **GC**
  Bibl: Gernsheim, Corpus Photog.
    of Drawings, 1451

Grati, Giovanni Battista   **BA WC**
  (*Italian artist, 1681-1758*)   WC
  (*Italian painter, 1681-1758*)   BA
  Bibl: ▶Bolaffi; ▶Thieme-Becker
Gratia, Leonardo→see Grazia,
  Leonardo

Gratian (*Italian, d. by 1159*)   **JG**
Gratiese→see Gratise, Sebastian
Gratise→see Gratise, Sebastian

Gratise, Sebastian   **PR WC**
  (*German artist, op.1785-1795*)   WC
  (*German painter, act. 1785-*
    1795)   PR
  Bibl: ▶Thieme-Becker
  Gratiese   PR
  Gratise   PR
  Sebastian Gratise   PR

Graton, Milton (*American restorer*
  and builder of covered bridges, ca.
  1090-)   **AV**
  Bibl: Historic preservation, v.38,
    no.4, p.20

Grattan, George (*British artist,*
  1787-1819)   **WC WI**

Grattan, William (*British artist, circa*
  1792-op.1821)   **WI**

Gratz, Carl Mayr   **WC**
  (*German artist, 1850-1929*)   WC
  (*German artist, 20th cent.*)   WC
  Mayr-Graetz, Carl   **WC**

Grau Santos, Julián (*Spanish*
  painter, b.1937)   **BA**
  Bibl: ▶Blas, Pintores españoles
    contemp.; ▶Campoy, Español
    contemp.

Grau y Andreu, Francisco (*Spanish*
  artist, 1772-1834)   **WC**

Grau, Gustave Adolphe (*French*
  artist, 1873-1919)   **WC**

Grau, Otto *(German painter,
printmaker, b.1913)* **BA**
    Bibl: ▶Vollmer, Künst.-Lex. 20.
    Jhr.; ▶WW Arts DEU
Grau, Peter *(German painter,
printmaker, b.1928)* **BA**
    Bibl: ▶Vollmer, Künst.-Lex. 20.
    Jhr.; ▶WW Arts DEU
Grau, Xavier *(Spanish painter,
b.1951)* **BA**
    Bibl: ▶ARTbibl. mod., 16/1;
    Madrid (ESP), Mus.esp.de arte
    contemporaneo, VIII DE LOS 16
    (1988) BHA/FRA; Moure, Flash
    Art 111 (Mar. 1983) pp.48-51
Grau-Garriga, Josep *(Spanish
painter, tapestry artist, b.1929)* **BA**
    Bibl: ▶Art diary int'l., 1990; ▶Art
    Index, v.38; ▶ARTbibl. mod., 16,
    #5850; ▶Bénézit; ▶Campoy,
    Español contemp.; Clark Art Inst.
    Libr.; ▶Contemp. artists; ▶Intl. dir.
    arts; ▶Intl. dir. exh. artists
Grau-Sala, Emilio *(French artist,
1911-)* **WC**
Graubner, Gotthard **BA JG WC**
    (German artist, 1930-) WC
    (German, 1930-) JG
    (West German painter, b.1930) BA
    Bibl: Hamburg, Gotthard Braubner
    (1976); ▶WW Arts DEU; ▶WW
    Germany
Grauer, Sherry *(Canadian painter,
sculptor, b.1939)* **BA**
    Bibl: ▶Artists Canada; Ottawa
    (Ont, CAN), Natl. Gall., Some
    Canadian women artists (1975),
    pp.42-52
Grauerholz, Angela *(Canadian
photographer, b.1952)* **BA**
    Bibl: Kingston (Ont, CAN),
    Queen's U. Etherington Art Ctr.,
    April, Davey, Grauerholz (1985)
Grault [Unidentified] *(Unknown
painter)* **PR**
    Bibl: Le Marois inventory dated
    1870
Graumann, Julius *(German artist,
1878-)* **WC**
Graupe-Pillard, Grace *(American
painter, b.1941)* **BA**
    Bibl: ▶WW Amer. Art
Grausman, Philip **BA WC WI**
    (American artist, 20th cent.) WC
    (American artist, b.1931) WI
    (American sculptor, b.1935) BA
    Bibl: ▶WW Amer. Art, 1978
Grauss, Gerardus Hendrik (Geert)
(Dutch artist, 1882-1929) **WC**
Grauwels, J. *(Flemish artist, op.
1798)* **WC**
Graval, Jehan de *(French goldsmith,
act.1493-1553)* **BA**
    Bibl: Hérold, Michel, L'orfèvrerie
    aménoise au XVI siècle: RENEDE
    l'ART 67 (1985) 78;
    ▶Thieme-Becker

Gravanbroeck, Orazio →*see*
    Grevenbroeck, Orazio
Gravant, François *(French ceramist,
act.1738, d.1765)* **BA**
    Bibl: ▶Honey, Euro. ceramic;
    ▶Mankowitz, Encyc. pott. & porc.
Gravatt, W. →*see* Gravatt, William
Gravatt, William **WI**
    (British artist, 18th cent.) WC
    (British artist, d.circa 1852) WI
    Bibl: ▶Fisher, Watercolour ptrs.
    Gravatt, W. **WC**
Grave or Graaf, Josua de →*see* Grave,
    Josua de
Grave, Charles **WC WI**
    (British artist, 1886-) WC
    (British artist, b.1886) WI
Grave, Jan Evert *(Dutch artist,
1759-1805)* **WC**
Grave, Josua de **GC**
    (Dutch artist, op.1660-m.c.1712) WC
    *(Dutch painter and
    draughtsman, d.1712)* GC
    Bibl: ▶Getty Photo Study Coll.;
    ▶Thieme-Becker; ▶Witt checklist
    Graaf, Josua de GC
Grave or Graaf, Josua de **WC**
Gravelot, Hubert Francois →*see*
    Gravelot, Hubert François
    Bourguignon
*Gravelot, Hubert Francois
(Bourguignon)* →*see* Gravelot,
    Hubert François Bourguignon
**Gravelot, Hubert François
Bourguignon** **BA**
    (French artist, 1699-1773) WC
    *(French painter, printmaker,
    1699-1773)* BA
    (French, 1699-1773) GC
    Bibl: ▶Encyc. world art; ▶Larousse
    grande encyc.; ▶New Columbia
    encyc.; ▶Thieme-Becker; ▶Witt
    checklist
    Gravelot, Hubert Francois **GC**
    **Gravelot, Hubert Francois
    (Bourguignon)** **WC**
Gravenor, James *(English
woodcarver, act.1760-1770)* **BA**
    Bibl: CONNOISSEUR,
    CXCVIII/797(JULY 1978), 188;
    ▶Gunnis, Brit. sculp.
Graves, Abbott Fuller **BA GC PR WI**
    (American artist, 1859-1936) WI
    *(American painter, 1859-
    1936)* BA GC PR
    Bibl: ▶Fielding's Amer. ptrs.;
    ▶RILA/BHA; ▶WW Amer. Art,
    1987
    Abbott Fuller Graves PR
Graves, Frederick Percy *(British
artist, 1837-1903)* **WC WI**
    Bibl: ▶Mallalieu, Brit. watercolour
    artists
Graves, George Palmer *(American
architect)* **AV**

Graves, Henry Richard, Hon. **WI**
    (British artist, 1818-1882) WI
    (British artist, op.1846-1881) WC
    Graves, the Hon. Henry Richard **WC**
Graves, Michael **AV BA**
    (American architect, b.1934) BA
    *(American architect, Princeton,
    N.J, 1934-)* AV
    Bibl: ▶Contemp. archts.; ▶MoMA
    libr. cat.; Oxford UP, 5 archts.
Graves, Morris **BA GC WC WI**
    (American artist, 1910-) WC
    (American artist, b.1910) WI
    (American painter, b.1910) BA GC
    Bibl: ▶Bénézit; ▶Who was who
    [GBR]; ▶WW Amer. Art
Graves, Nancy →*see* Graves, Nancy
    Stevenson
Graves, Nancy Stevenson **BA WI**
    (American artist, 20th cent.) WC
    (American artist, b.1940) WI
    *(American painter, sculptor,
    b.1940)* BA
    Bibl: ▶WW Amer. Art
    Graves, Nancy **WC**
Graves, P. de **WC WI**
    (British artist, 17th cent.) WC
    (British artist, op.17th c.) WI
Graves, Robert *(British artist, 1798-
1873)* **WC WI**
Graves, the Hon. Henry Richard →*see*
    Graves, Henry Richard, Hon.
**Gravesande, Arent Adriaansz.
van 's** *(Dutch architect, b.1600,
act.1649)* **BA**
    Bibl: ▶Portoghesi, Diz. arch. e
    urbanistica; ▶Thieme-Becker;
    ▶Wurzbach, NLD Künst.-Lex.
Gravett, Dale P. *(American city
planner, Philadelphic, Penn.;
Director of Planning &
Development for Philadelphia,
1988-)* **AV**
    Bibl: Journal of housing, 1988
    July-Aug., v.45, no.4, p.197
Gravier, Nicole *(French painter,
photographer, b.1949)* **BA**
    Bibl: Vancouver (BC, CAN), Art
    Gallery, Mannerism (1982)
Gravière, Francis *(French architect,
Saintes)* **AV**
    Bibl: ▶Annuaire archts. fran.,
    1978
Gravina Painter **GC JG**
    (Apulian vase-painter) GC
    Bibl: Trendall, Attic red-fig. vases
    Apulia
Gray →*see* Gray, Percy
Gray, B.C. *(American, active early
20th century, Colorado)* **JG**
Gray, Cedric **WC WI**
    (British artist, 19th cent.) WC
    (British artist, op.1880-) WI

Gray, Cleve   BA WI
  (American artist, b.1918)   WI
  (American painter, sculptor,
    b.1918)   BA
  Bibl: ▶MoMA libr. cat.; ▶WW
    Amer. Art, 1976
Gray, Clive (British architectural
  student)   AV
  Bibl: Architects' journal, 1986
    Oct.22, v.184, no.43, p.26
Gray, David (British architect, 1928-)   AV
  Bibl: ▶Contemp. archts.
Gray, Don   WC WI
  (American artist, 20th cent.)   WC
  (American artist, op.20th c.)   WI
Gray, Douglas Stannus (British
  artist, 1890-1959)   WC WI
Gray, Eileen   AV BA
  (Irish architect, designer, 1879-
    1976)   BA
  (Irish-born architect and
    designer, lived in Paris from
    1907-1976, 1879-1976)   AV
  Bibl: ▶Avery Libr. cat.; ▶Dict. natl.
    biog., 1971-80; Garner,
    Connoisseur CLXXXIII (May 1973)
    2-11; Johnson, EILEEN GRAY,
    MOMA, 1979; ▶Libr. of Congr.
    Name Auth. File; ▶Penguin dec.
    arts; ▶Petteys, Women artists;
    ▶Phaidon dec. arts
Gray, Felix de (French artist, 1889-)   WC
Gray, Fiona (British designer)   AV
  Bibl: Country life, 1988 Mar.24,
    v.182, no.12, p.128
Gray, George (British artist, op.
  1880-1909)   WI
  Bibl: ▶Waters, Brit. artists
Gray, H.G. (British artist, 19th cent.)   WC
Gray, Henry (British artist, op.1849-
  1897)   WC WI
Gray, Henry Peters (American
  artist, 1819-1877)   WI
Gray, J. M. (American architect,
  Boston, Mass., fl. 1930's)   AV
  Bibl: Boston Preservation Alliance
    letter, 1988 Aug., v.9, no.7, p.1
Gray, J.C. (British artist, op.20th c.)   WI
Gray, John   BA
  (British artist, b.1942)   WI
  (British painter, b.1942)   BA
  Bibl: Arts Council GBR, Summer
    show 4 (1976)
  Gray, John II   WI
Gray, John → see Gray, John I
Gray, John I   WI
  (British artist, op.1906-)   WI
  (British artist, op.c.1906)   WC
  Gray, John   WC
Gray, John II → see Gray, John
Gray, Joseph (British artist, 1890-
  1962)   WI
Gray, Kate   WC WI
  (British artist, 19th cent.)   WC
  (British artist, op.1870-1897)   WI

Gray, Ken (British artist, 20th c.)   BA
  Bibl: Colchester(GBR), Minories,
    KEN GRAY ELECTRO
    SCULPTURE(1978)
Gray, M.Etheldreda (British artist,
  op.1910-)   WI
Gray, Nicolas Henry de (French
  artist, 19th cent.)   WC
Gray, Norah Nielsen (British artist,
  d.1931)   WI
Gray, Paul (American architect,
  1935-)   AV
  Bibl: Process: architecture, n.7,
    1978, p.209
Gray, Paul Mary (British artist,
  1842-1866)   WC WI
Gray, Percy (American painter,
  1869-1952)   PR
  Bibl: ▶WWW Amer. art
  Gray   PR
  Percy Gray   PR
Gray, Ray (American interior
  designer)   AV
  Bibl: Architectural digest, 1986
    May, v.43, no.5, p.155
Gray, Ronald (British artist, 1868-
  1951)   WC WI
Gray, Sharon R. (American artist,
  b.1947)   WI
Gray, Spalding (American artist,
  author, b.1941)   BA
  Bibl: Battock + Nickas, ART OF
    PERFORMANCE, (1984), p. 122;
    Judson, Carnegie mag., LVIII (Sep.-
    Oct. 1986) pp.16-26; RLIN BKS
    file
Graybill (American, active ca. 1860-
  1870)   JG
Grayson, Clifford Prevost   WC WI
  (American artist, 1857-1951)   WI
  (American artist, 1857/9-)   WC
Grayson, William (British artist, op.
  1894-1940)   WI
Graz Group (Campanian vase-
  painters)   GC
  Bibl: ▶Trendall, Red-fig. vases
    Lucania
Graz Painter (Apulian vase-painter)   GC
  Bibl: Trendall, Attic red-fig. vases
    Apulia
Grazebrook, Ellen Lucy (British
  artist, op.1887-1908)   WI
Grazi, Giulio Cesare (Italian artist,
  op.1583-1589)   WC
Grazi, L. (Italian artist, 19th cent.)   WC

Grazia, Leonardo   GC PR WI
  (Italian artist, 1497-op.1548)   WI
  (Italian artist, c.1502-p.1548)   WC
  (Italian painter, b. 1505)   GC
  (Italian painter, b. ca.1502)   PR
  Bibl: ▶Bolaffi; Briganti, La pittura
    in Italia, II (1986);
    ▶Thieme-Becker; ▶Witt checklist
  Gratia, Leonardo   GC WI
  Grazia, Leonardo (Pistoia)   PR
  **Grazia. or Gratia, Leonardo
    (Leonardo da Pistoia)**   WC
  Grazzi, Leonardo   GC
  Leonardo da Pistoia   GC PR
  Leonardo di Pistoia   WI
  Leonardo Grazia   PR
  Pistala   PR
  Pistoia   PR
  Pistoio   PR
Grazia, Leonardo (Pistoia) → see
  Grazia, Leonardo
Grazia. or Gratia, Leonardo
  (Leonardo da Pistoia) → see Grazia,
  Leonardo
Graziani → see Graziani, Ercole II
Graziani → see Graziani, Pietro
Graziani II, Ercole → see Graziani,
  Ercole II
Graziani the Younger, Ercole → see
  Graziani, Ercole II
Graziani, Ciccio and/or Pietro
  (Italian artist, 17th cent.)   WC
Graziani, Ercole → see Graziani, Ercole
  II
Graziani, Ercole (il Giovane) → see
  Graziani, Ercole II
Graziani, Ercole (the younger) → see
  Graziani, Ercole II
Graziani, Ercole II   BA
  (Italian artist, 1688-1765)   WC
  (Italian painter, 1688-1765)   BA PR
  (Italian, 1688-1765)   GC
  Bibl: ▶Bolaffi; ▶Thieme-Becker;
    ▶Witt checklist
  Ercole Graziani (the younger)   PR
  Ercole Graziano   PR
  Graziani   PR
  Graziani II, Ercole   PR
  Graziani the Younger, Ercole   WC
  Graziani, Ercole   PR
  Graziani, Ercole (il Giovane)   GC
  Graziani, Ercole (the younger)   PR
Graziani, Francesco (Italian painter,
  act. 17th century)   PR
  Bibl: ▶Fredericksen & Zeri, Census
  Francesco Graziani   PR
Graziani, Giuseppe (Italian painter,
  1699-after 1760)   BA
  Bibl: ▶Bolaffi; ▶Rigon, Pitt.
    vicentini '700; ▶Thieme-Becker

Graziani, Pietro   **GC PR**
   (Italian painter, act. 18th
     century)   PR
   (Italian, 18th century)   GC
     Bibl: ▶Bénézit; ▶Thieme-Becker
   Graziani   PR
   Graziano   PR
   Petruccio napolitano   PR
   Pietro Gratiani   PR
   Pietro Gratiano   PR
   Pietro Graziani   PR
   Pietro Graziano   PR
   Pietro Napolitano   PR
Graziani, Sante   **BA WC WI**
   (American artist, 1920-)   WC
   (American artist, b.1920)   WI
   (American painter, b.1920)   BA
     Bibl: UC Santa Barbara cat.
     sheets; WW Amer., 1976; ▶WW
     Amer. Art, 1976
Graziano →see Graziani, Pietro
Grazioli, Francesco *(Italian*
   architect, sculptor, d.1536)   **BA**
     Bibl: ▶Bénézit; ▶Thieme-Becker
Grazioli, Walmar *(Italian artist, 20th*
   cent.)   **WC**
Graziosi, Giuseppe *(Italian sculptor,*
   painter, printmaker, 1879-1942) **BA**
     Bibl: ▶Bénézit; ▶Comanducci, Diz.;
     ▶Thieme-Becker; ▶Vollmer,
     Künst.-Lex. 20. Jhr.
Grazzi, Leonardo →see Grazia,
   Leonardo
Grazzini, Gaetano *(Italian sculptor,*
   1786-1858)   **GC**
     Bibl: TCI Firenze
Grazzini, Giovanni Paolo *(Italian*
   painter, ca. 1560-1632)   **PR**
     Bibl: Aldobrandini inventory,
     Frascati, 1603; ▶Thieme-Becker
   Gio. Paolo Graccini   PR
   Giovan Paolo Graccini   PR
   Giovanni Paolo Graccini   PR
Greacen, Edmund William   **BA WC WI**
   (American artist, 1877-1949)   WC WI
   (American painter, 1877-1949)   BA
     Bibl: ▶Havlice, Idx. art. bio.;
     ▶Schwab, Life & death; ▶Vollmer,
     Künst.-Lex. 20. Jhr.; ▶WWW
     Amer., 1943-1950
Grease, Jack →see Gresse, John
   Alexander
Greason →see Greason, William
Greason, William *(American painter,*
   1884-1945)   **PR**
     Bibl: Detroit Inst of Arts
     catalogue; ▶WWW Amer. art
   Greason   PR
   William Greason   PR
Great Neck Painter *(Etruscan vase-*
   painter)   **GC**
     Bibl: ▶Szilagyi, Etruszko-korinthosi

Greatbach, William *(British*
   ceramist, 1735-1813)   **BA**
     Bibl: CONNOISSEUR CXC/764 (Oct
     1975) 108 ff.; ▶Honey, Euro.
     ceramic; ▶Mankowitz, Encyc.
     pott. & porc.; ▶Penguin dec. arts,
     1989
Greatorex, Eliza Pratt →see Greatorix,
   Eliza Pratt
Greatorix, Eliza Pratt   **BA**
   (American artist, 1820-1897)   WI
   (American painter, printmaker,
     1820-1897)   BA
     Bibl: ▶Bénézit; ▶Met. Mus. Art
     libr. cat.; ▶Natl. union cat., pre-
     1956; ▶Thieme-Becker
   Greatorex, Eliza Pratt   **WI**
Greaves →see Greaves, Walter
Greaves, Derrick   **BA WC WI**
   (British artist, 1927-)   WC
   (British artist, b.1927)   WI
   (British painter, b.1927)   BA
     Bibl: ▶Bénézit; ▶Dolman,
     Contemp. Brit. artists; ▶MoMA
     libr. cat.
Greaves, Harry Siddon *(Architect,*
   South Africa)   **AV**
     Bibl: Architect & builder, 1985
     Nov., p.2
Greaves, Henry *(British artist, 1850-*
   1900)   **WC WI**
Greaves, Leonard *(British artist,*
   1918-1949)   **WI**
Greaves, Walter   **BA GC PR WC WI**
   (British artist, 1846-1930)   WC WI
   (British painter, 1846-1930)   BA PR
   (British, 1846-1930)   GC
     Bibl: ▶Dict. natl. biog.;
     ▶RILA/BHA; ▶Waters, Brit. artists;
     ▶Witt checklist
   Greaves   PR
   Walter Greaves   PR
Greaves, William   **WC WI**
   (British artist, op.1885-1910)   WC
   (British artist, op.1885-1922)   WI
Greaves-Lord, Sally *(British*
   architect, 20th c.)   **BA**
     Bibl: Farrelly, E.M., in
     ARCHITECTURAL REVIEW,
     CLXXIX/1072 (June 1986), p. 89
Greb *(Russian artist, op.1832)*   **WC**
Grebber →see Grebber, Anthony
   Claesz.
Grebber →see Grebber, Pieter Fransz.
   de
Grebber, Adriaen Claesz. de   **BA WC**
   (Dutch artist, 1576-1661(?))   WC
   (Dutch goldsmith, silversmith,
     medalist, 1576-1661)   BA
     Bibl: Frederiks, Dutch silver, v.4,
     pp.12-13; ▶Thieme-Becker;
     ▶Wurzbach, NLD Künst.-Lex.

Grebber, Anthony Claesz.   **GC PR**
   (Dutch painter, 1622-1683)   PR
   (Dutch painter, 1622-d. aft.
     1683)   GC
     Bibl: ▶Thieme-Becker
   Anthony Claesz. Grebber   PR
   [Anton] Grebber   PR
   Grebber   PR
Grebber, Frans Pietersz. de *(Dutch*
   artist, 1573-1649)   **WC**
Grebber, Maria *(Dutch artist, op.*
   1628-1631)   **WC**
Grebber, Pieter de →see Grebber,
   Pieter Fransz. de
Grebber, Pieter Fransz, de →see
   Grebber, Pieter Fransz. de
Grebber, Pieter Fransz.
   de   **BA GC PR WC**
   (Dutch artist, c.1600-c.1652/3)   WC
   (Dutch artist, circa 1600-circa
     1653)   WI
   (Dutch painter and draughts-
     man, ca.1600-ca.1652)   GC
   (Dutch painter,
     ca.1600-1652/53)   PR
   (Dutch painter, printmaker,
     ca.1600-1652/53)   BA
   (Dutch, ca. 1600-ca. 1653)   JG
     Bibl: Getty Photo Study Coll.;
     ▶Thieme-Becker; Washington,
     D.C., National Gallery, GODS,
     SAINTS AND HEROS...,(1980-
     1981); ▶Wurzbach, NLD
     Künst.-Lex.
   Grebber   PR
   Grebber, Pieter de   **JG PR**
   Grebber, Pieter Fransz, de   **WI**
   Pedro Grebber   PR
   Pieter Fransz. de Grebber   PR
Grebe, Fritz   **GC WC**
   (German artist, 1850-)   WC
   (German painter, b.1850)   GC
     Bibl: ▶Bénézit
Grebe, Johan Georg *(Dutch*
   silversmith, 1803-1862)   **BA**
     Bibl: Cat. Great Exh. 1851, p.290;
     Voorts tot Voorst, NLD Kunsthist.
     Jaarb.., XXXI (1980) pp.476-492
Greber family *(French sculptors,*
   stucco artists, ceramists,
   architects, 19th-20th cs.)   **BA**
     Bibl: ▶Larousse grande encyc.;
     ▶Thieme-Becker
Greber, Henri Léon *(French*
   sculptor, b.1854)   **GC**
     Bibl: ▶Thieme-Becker
Greber, Jacques   **AV FA**
   (1882-ca.1950; Architect,
     Ottawa)   FA
   (French architect, city planner) AV
     Bibl: CAAD Finding Aids; The
     Canadian Architect, Odds and
     Ends, pg. 6, vol. 5, no. 5, May
     1960; ▶Hill, Archts. Canada; Natl.
     Arch. of Canada, CAAD Finding
     Aid; Urban design international,
     1983 Winter, v.4, no.2, p.25

Greca, Felice della→*see* Della Greca, Felice

Greca, Vincenzo della→*see* Della Greca, Vincenzo

Greche, Domenicho dalle *(Italian artist, op.1543-1549)*   **WC**

Grechetto (Giovanni Benedetto Castiglione)→*see* Castiglione, Giovanni Benedetto (il Grechetto)

Grechetto, Alessandro Cesati→*see* Cesati, Alessandro

Grecho→*see* Greco, Gennaro

Grecian Williams→*see* Williams, Hugh William (Grecian Williams)

Greco→*see* Greco, El (Domenico Theotocopuli)

Greco→*see* Greco, Gennaro

Greco (Alessandro Cesati)→*see* Cesati, Alessandro

Greco or Griego, Nicolas (El Greco Segoviano) *(Spanish artist, 16th cent.)*   **WC**

Greco [Unidentified] *(Unknown painter)*   **PR**

Greco, Domenico Theotokopuli El→*see* Greco, El (Domenico Theotocopuli)

Greco, El→*see* Greco, El (Domenico Theotocopuli)

Greco, El (Domenico Theotocopuli)   **BA PR**
   (d.1614)   AV
   (Greek painter in ESP, 1541-1614)   BA
   (Greek painter, 1541-1614)   PR
   (Greek/Spanish, 1541-1614)   JG
   (Spanish artist, 1541-1614)   WC
   (Spanish painter, 1541-1614)   GC
   Bibl: ▶Encic. univ. ilus.; ▶Encyc. world art; Getty Photo Study Coll. (Ptgs.); ▶Petit Robert 2; ▶RILA/BHA; ▶Thieme-Becker; TY
   Domenico Theotocopouli   GC
   Domenico Theotocopouli   PR
   Domingo Greco   PR
   Dominico Greco   PR
   el Dominico   PR
   El Greco   AV GC PR
   el griego   PR
   El. Griego   PR
   Greco   JG PR
Greco, Domenico Theotokopuli El   WC
   Greco, El   GC PR
   Theotocopoulos, Domenikos   PR
   Theotocopoulos, Domenikos (El Greco)   PR
   Theotocopuli, Domenico (El Greco)   PR
Theotocopuli, Dominico, called El Greco   AV
   Theotokopoulos, Domenicos   PR

Greco, Emilio   **BA GC WC**
   (Italian artist, 1913-)   WC
   (Italian sculptor, b.1913)   BA GC
   Bibl: ▶Comanducci, Diz.; ▶RILA/BHA

Greco, Gennaro   **PR**
   (Italian artist, 1663-1714)   WC
   (Italian painter, 1663-1714)   GC PR
   Bibl: Getty Photo Study Coll. (Ptgs.); ▶Thieme-Becker; ▶Witt checklist
   Gennaro Greco   PR
   Grecho   PR
   Greco   PR
Greco, Gennaro ('Mascacotta')   **WC**
Greco, Gennaro (Mascacotta)   **GC**
   Il Mascacotta   GC
   Mascacotta   PR
Greco, Gennaro ('Mascacotta')→*see* Greco, Gennaro
Greco, Gennaro (Mascacotta)→*see* Greco, Gennaro
Greco, George Manuel Theotokopuli→*see* Theotocopuli, Jorge Manuel

Greco, Michele (Michele Lucchese) *(Italian painter, printmaker, publisher, b.ca.1529)*   **BA**
   Bibl: ▶Bénézit; ▶Bolaffi; ▶Thieme-Becker

Greco, Vettor (Vittore)   **WC**
   (Greek artist, op.1522)   WC
   (Greek artist, op.1522-1539)   WC
   Vittore Greco   WC
Grecolini, Giovanni Antonio   **BA**
   (Italian artist, 1675-c.1736)   WC
   (Italian painter, 1675-1736)   BA PR
   Bibl: ▶Bolaffi; ▶Diz. biog. ital.; ▶Thieme-Becker; ▶Witt checklist
   Antonio Crecolini   PR
Crecolini, Cricolini or Gregolini, Giovanni Antonio   **WC**
Crecolini, Giovanni Antonio   **PR**
   Giovanni Antonio Crecolini   PR
Gree→*see* Gree, Pieter Jan Balthazar de
Gree, Pieter Jan Balthazar de *(Dutch painter, 1751-1789)*   **PR**
   Bibl: ▶Thieme-Becker
   De Grea'   PR
   De Gree   PR
   De Gree, Peter   PR
   Gree   PR
   Pieter Jan Balthazar de Gree   PR
Greef→*see* Gryef, Adriaen de
Greef, Jean or Jan de, or Jean Degreef→*see* Degreef, Jean Baptiste
Greeley, Mellen Clark *(American architect, 1880-1981)*   **AV**
   Bibl: "AIA Journal" Dec. 1981, p.87
Greely, Ann *(American interior designer)*   **AV**
   Bibl: Architectural digest, 1985 Nov., v.42, no.11, p.142

Green→*see* Green, William
Green, Alan   **BA WC WI**
   (British artist, 20th cent.)   WC
   (British artist, b.1932)   WI
   (British painter, b.1932)   BA
   Bibl: ▶Dolman, Contemp. Brit. artists
Green, Alexander *(British artist, op. 19th c.)*   **WI**
Green, Alfred H. *(British artist, op. 1844-1862)*   **WC WI**
Green, Amos   **BA WC WI**
   (British artist, 1735-1807)   WC WI
   (British painter, 1735-1807)   BA
   Bibl: ▶Dict. natl. biog.; ▶Thieme-Becker
Green, Anthony   **BA WC WI**
   (British artist, 20th cent.)   WC
   (British artist, b.1939)   WI
   (British painter, b.1939)   BA
   Bibl: ▶Bénézit; ▶MoMA libr. cat.
Green, Art *(American painter, b.1941)*   **BA**
   Bibl: ARTS MAGAZINE, LI/9(MAY 1977), 16; ▶WW Amer. Art, 1976
Green, Benjamin   **WC WI**
   (British artist, c.1736-1800)   WC
   (British artist, circa 1736-1800)   WI
   (Engraver, London, GTL., circa 1736-1800)   WI
Green, Benjamin Richard *(British artist, 1808-1876)*   **WC WI**
   Bibl: Hall
Green, C.E.L.→*see* Green, Charles Edwin Lewis
Green, Cedric *(British architect)*   **AV**
   Bibl: RIBA journal, 1985 Oct., v.92, no.10, p.25
Green, Charles   **BA WC**
   (British artist, 1840-1898)   WC WI
   (British illustrator, 1840-1898)   BA
   Bibl: ▶Johnson, Brit. artists
   Green, Charles I   **WI**
Green, Charles→*see* Green, Charles II
Green, Charles Edwin Lewis *(American painter, 1844-1915)*   **BA PR**
   Bibl: ▶Bénézit; ▶RILA/BHA; Salem(MA,USA), Essex Inst., CHARLES EDWIN LEWIS GREEN... (1980)
   Charles Edwin Lewis Green   PR
   Green, C.E.L.   PR
Green, Charles I→*see* Green, Charles
Green, Charles II   **WI**
   (British artist, 20th cent.)   WC
   (British artist, op.20th c.)   WI
Green, Charles   **WC**
Green, David Gould *(British artist, 1854-1918)*   **WC WI**
   Bibl: ▶Fisher, Watercolour ptrs.
Green, Denise G. *(American painter, b.1946)*   **BA**
   Bibl: ▶WW Amer. Art, 1978

Green, Derek (*Irish architect, asst. principal architect Dublin Office of Public Works*) **AV**
    Bibl: Plan: architecture + interior design in Ireland, 1989 Feb., v.20, no.2, p.50

Green, Donald E. (*British artist, op. 1968-*) **WI**

Green, Dora (*British artist, op.1900-1926*) **WI**

Green, Edward B. (*American architect, 1855-1950*) **AV**
    Bibl: Preservation League of New York State. Newsletter, 1984 Nov.-Dec., v.10, no.6, p.2

Green, Edward Frederick **WI**
    (*British artist, c.1767-1850*) **WC**
    (*British artist, circa 1767-1851*) **WI**

Green, F. **WC**

Green, Elizabeth Shippen **BA WC WI**
    (*American painter, illustrator, 1871-1954*) **BA**
    (*British artist, 20th cent.*) **WC**
    (*British artist, op.20th c.*) **WI**
    Bibl: ▶Amer. art annual; ▶Collins, Women artists Amer.; ▶Fielding's Amer. ptrs.; Wilmington(DE,USA), Delaware Art Museum.THE STUDIES AT COOPEN(1976)

Green, F. → see Green, Edward Frederick

Green, George D. (*American painter, b.1943*) **BA**
    Bibl: ▶WW Amer. Art, 1978, 1984

Green, George Pycock Everett **WC WI**
    (*British artist, op.1840-, d.1893*) **WI**
    (*British artist, op.1841-1873*) **WC**

Green, George Thurman (*American sculptor, painter, b.1942*) **BA**
    Bibl: Fort Worth (TX, USA), Art Museum, Great Amer. rodeo (1976); ▶WW Amer. Art, 1976

Green, Gregory (*American artist, op.1987-*) **WI**

Green, Guy (*British ceramist, act. 1756-1799*) **BA**
    Bibl: ▶Honey, Euro. ceramic; ▶Mankowitz, Encyc. pott. & porc.

Green, Harold → see Green, Harold Abbott

Green, Harold Abbott (*American painter, b. 1883*) **PR**
    Bibl: ▶WWW Amer. art
    Green, Harold **PR**
    Harold Abbott Green **PR**

Green, Harriet **WC WI**
    (*British artist, 1751-op.1807*) **WI**
    (*British artist, 1751-p.1807*) **WC**
    Lister, Harriet, Miss **WI**

Green, Henry (*American cabinetmaker, 1844-1931*) **BA**
    Bibl: ANTIQUES, CV/5, p.115

Green, Henry Towneley (*British artist, 1836-1899*) **WC WI**

Green, Herbert J. (*British architect*) **AV**
    Bibl: Japan architect, 1989 Aug.10, v.183, no.32, p.66

Green, J. (*Engraver, op.1725-*) **WI**

Green, J. F. (*Irish architect, Dublin*) **AV**
    Bibl: Irish architect, 1988 Feb.-Mar., p.49

Green, James **GC PR WC WI**
    (*British artist, 1771-1834*) **WC WI**
    (*British painter, 1771-1834*) **GC PR**
    Bibl: ▶Thieme-Becker; ▶Witt checklist
    James Green **PR**

Green, Jasha **BA WI**
    (*American artist, b.1923*) **WI**
    (*American painter, sculptor, b.1923*) **BA**
    Bibl: ▶NY art yrbk.

Green, John → see Green, John Hippisley

Green, John Hippisley **WI**
    (*British artist, c.1729-c.1757*) **WC**
    (*British artist, circa 1729-circa 1757*) **WI**

Green, John **WC**

Green, Jonathan (*American photographer, art historian, 20th c.*) **BA**
    Bibl: CAMERA WORKS: A CRITICAL ANTHOLOGY; ▶MoMA libr. cat.

Green, Joshua **WC WI**
    (*British artist, 19th cent.*) **WC**
    (*British artist, op.1852-1868*) **WI**
    Bibl: ▶Mallalieu, Brit. watercolour artists

Green, Josiah (*British artist, op. 1862-1868*) **WI**

Green, Kenneth **WC WI**
    (*British artist, 1916-*) **WC**
    (*British artist, b.1916*) **WI**

Green, Leonard (*British photographer, b.1883*) **BA**
    Bibl: DeVille, LENARE:THE HEART OF SOCIETY PHOTOG.(1981); RLIN BKS file

Green, Lionel (*American, active Cambodia 1920's*) **JG**

Green, Madeline (*French artist, -1947*) **WC**

Green, Margaret (*British artist, op. 20th c.*) **WI**

Green, Mary **WI**
    (*British artist, 1776-1846*) **WC WI**
    Byrne, Mary, Miss **WI**

Green, Mary, (nee Byrne) **WC**

Green, Mary (*American textile designer, 1788-1817*) **BA**
    Bibl: Ring, Worcester Art Mus. Jrnl., V (1981-1982) pp.21-25

Green, Mary, (nee Byrne) → see Green, Mary

Green, Nathaniel Everett (*British artist, op.1833-, d.1899*) **WI**

Green, Peter **WC WI**
    (*British artist, 20th cent.*) **WC**
    (*British artist, b.1934*) **WI**

Green, Roland (*British artist, 1896-1972*) **WI**

Green, Stan (*British architectural designer, Cold Ash*) **AV**
    Bibl: Building design, 1989 Aug., suppl., p.46

Green, T. **WC WI**
    (*British artist, op.1747*) **WC**
    (*British artist, op.1747-*) **WI**

Green, Tom (*American sculptor, b.1942*) **BA**
    Bibl: ▶WW Amer. Art

Green, Tony (*American artist, b.1954*) **WI**

Green, Valentine **BA WC WI**
    (*British artist, 1739-1813*) **WC WI**
    (*British printmaker, 1739-1813*) **BA**
    (*Engraver, 1739-1813*) **WI**
    Bibl: ▶Bénézit; ▶Redgrave, Engl. school; ▶Thieme-Becker

Green, W. (*British artist, op.1765*) **WC**

Green, William (*Canadian, act.1827*) **BA**
    Bibl: Levenson, JOURNAL OF CANADIAN ART HISTORY, VII/1(1983)

Green, William **BA PR WC WI**
    (*British artist, 1760-1823*) **WC WI**
    (*British painter, 1761-1823*) **PR**
    (*British painter, printmaker, 1760-1823*) **BA**
    Bibl: ▶Dict. natl. biog.; ▶Fielding's Amer. ptrs.; ▶Mallalieu, Brit. watercolour artists; ▶Thieme-Becker; ▶Waterhouse, Brit. 18c. ptrs.; ▶Witt checklist
    Green **PR**
    William Green **PR**

Green, William Curtis **AV BA**
    (*British architect, 1875-1960*) **AV**
    (*British architect, draftsman, 1875-1960*) **BA**
    Bibl: ▶Avery Libr. cat.; ▶Macmillan encyc. archts.; ▶Who was who [GBR], 1951-60

Greenamyer, George Mossman (*American sculptor, b.1939*) **BA**
    Bibl: ▶WW Amer. Art, 1978

Greenaway, Kate **BA GC WC WI**
    (*British artist, 1846-1901*) **WC WI**
    (*British illustrator, painter, 1846-1901*) **BA**
    (*British, 1846-1901*) **GC**
    Bibl: ▶Encyc. world art; ▶Fogg Mus. Libr. cat.; ▶Met. Mus. Art libr. cat.; ▶Thieme-Becker; ▶Witt checklist

Greenbank, Arthur **WC WI**
    (*British artist, op.1880-1899*) **WI**
    (*British artist, op.1888-1899*) **WC**

Greenbaum → see Greenbaum, Joseph

Greenbaum, Joseph (*American painter, b. 1864*) **PR**
    Bibl: ▶Dawdy, Artists Amer. West
    Greenbaum **PR**
    Joseph Greenbaum **PR**

Greenbaum, Marty (*American painter, sculptor, b.1934*) **BA**
    Bibl: ▶WW Amer. Art

Greenbaum, Steffi (American
sculptor, painter, 20th c.) BA
Bibl: Philadelphia (PA, USA),
Temple University, Samuel Paley
Library, The Tyler show (1974)
Greenberg, Allan AV BA
(American architect, b.1938) BA
(American architect, New
Haven, CT) AV
Bibl: Design solutions, 1985 Fall,
v.5, no.3, p.15; New York (NY,
USA), MoMA, Bldgs. for Best
Products (1980); Northampton
(MA, USA), Smith Coll. Art Mus.,
New classicism (1981)
Greenberg, Stephen AV
Greenblat, Rodney Alan (American
artist, b.1960) BA
Bibl: Glaser, D., in ARTS MAG
LVIII/3 (Nov 1983) 126; New York
(NY, USA), Whitney Mus., Biennial
(1985)
Greenburg, Richard BA
(British artist, op.1622-c.1670) WC
(British artist, op.1622-circa
1670) WI
(English painter, d.ca.1670) BA
Bibl: ▶Dict. natl. biog.; Jrnl. of
Warburg & Courtauld Inst. (1952),
253; ▶Thieme-Becker;
▶Waterhouse, Brit. 18c. ptrs.
Greenbury, Richard WI
**Greenbury, Richard (not
Robert)** WC
Greenbury, Richard → see Greenburg,
Richard
Greenbury, Richard (not Robert) → see
Greenburg, Richard
Greene, Balcomb BA WC WI
(American artist, 1904-) WC
(American artist, b.1904) WI
(American painter, b.1904) BA
Bibl: Hale, THE ART OF BALCOMB
GREENE; NY TIMES (13 Nov 1990);
▶WW Amer. Art, 1976
Greene, Charles Sumner (American
architect, 1868-1957) AV BA
Bibl: ▶Britannica encyc. Amer. art;
▶Contemp. archts.
Greene, Daniel (American painter,
20th c.) BA
Bibl: Findsen, Arts Mag. LX/2
(Oct 1985) 121
Greene, Douglas Lowell (American
designer) AV
Bibl: Design solutions, 1985 Fall,
v.5, no.3, p.38
Greene, Gertrude (American
painter, sculptor, 1904-1956) BA
Bibl: ▶WW Amer. Art, 1956,
1959, 1984
Greene, Henry Mather (American
architect, 1870-1954) AV BA
Bibl: ▶Avery Libr. cat.; ▶Britannica
encyc. Amer. art; ▶Contemp.
archts.
Greene, Herb → see Greene, Herbert

Greene, Herbert BA
(American architect, 1929-) AV
(American architect, painter,
b.1929) BA
Bibl: ▶Avery period. idx.;
▶Contemp. archts.; ▶Natl. Faculty
Dir., 1977
Greene, Herb AV
Greene, Isabelle (American
landscape designer, Calif) AV
Bibl: House & garden, 1987 July,
v.159, no.7, p.90
Greene, John B. BA
(American photographer, 1832-
1856) BA
(American, 1832-1856, active
Egypt and Algeria) JG
Bibl: Alinder, Discovery &
recognition
Greene, John Beasly JG
Greene, John Beasly → see Greene,
John B.
Greene, Stephen BA WC WI
(American artist, 1917-) WC
(American artist, b.1918) WI
(American painter, b.1918) BA
Bibl: ▶Who was who [GBR]; ▶WW
Amer. Art
Greene, Walter L. WC WI
(American artist, 19th/20th
cent.) WC
(American artist, op.1898-1901) WI
Greene-Mercier, Marie Zoe
(American sculptor, b.1911) BA
Bibl: ▶WW Amer. Art, 1978
Greenfield-Sanders, Timothy
(American photographer, b.1952) BA
Bibl: ▶WW Amer. Art, 1986
Greengrass, Sarah (British painter,
b.1951) BA
Bibl: ARTSCRIBE, 22(APR 1980),
49-51
Greenhalgh, Derek (British artist,
op.1985-) WI
Greenhalgh, Thomas (British artist,
op.1884-) WI
Greenham, Peter BA
(British artist, 1909-) WC
(British artist, b.1909) WI
(British painter, b.1909) BA
Bibl: ▶Intl. dir. exh. artists, 1982-
1983
Greenham, Peter George WC WI
Greenham, Peter George → see
Greenham, Peter
Greenham, Robert Duckworth
(British artist, 1906-1980) WI
Bibl: ▶Waters, Brit. artists
Greenhead, B., Miss → see Greenly, B.,
Miss
Greenhill → see Greenhill, John

Greenhill, John GC PR WC WI
(British artist, 1649-1676) WC WI
(British painter, 1649-1676) PR
(British, 1640/45-1676) GC
Bibl: ▶Brit. Mus. cat.;
▶Thieme-Becker; ▶Witt checklist
Greenhill PR
John Greenhill PR
Greening, Robert (British landscape
architect, 18th c.) BA
Bibl: COUNTRY LIFE, CLXVI(SEPT
1979), 658-661; 758-762; Hussey,
Engl. houses, v.1: Early Georgian
Greenland, B., Miss → see Greenly, B.,
Miss
Greenlaw, Alexander (British
amateur photographer; English
officer in the Indian army, fl.
1856) AV
Bibl: Archaeology, 1989 Sept.-
Oct., v.42, no.5, p.40
Greenleaf, Benjamin (American
painter, 1769-1821) BA
Bibl: ▶Groce, Artists Amer.; Kern,
Clarion (spr-sum 1985), 40-47
Greenleaf, Jacob I. (American artist,
op.20th c.) WI
Greenleaf, Kenneth Lee (American
sculptor, b.1945) BA
Bibl: ▶NY art yrbk.; ▶WW Amer.
Art
Greenlees, Georgina Mossman
(British artist, op.1874-1880) WI
Greenlees, James (British artist, op.
1860-1883) WI
Greenlees, Robert M. (British artist,
1820-1894) WC WI
Bibl: ▶Mallalieu, Brit. watercolour
artists
Greenley, B., Miss → see Greenly, B.,
Miss
Greenly, B., Miss WI
(British artist, op.1795-1801) WC WI
Greenhead, B., Miss WI
Greenland, B., Miss WI
Greenley, B., Miss WI
Greenly, Miss B. WC
Greenly, Miss B. → see Greenly, B.,
Miss
Greenman, Frances Cranmer
(American painter, b.1890) BA
Bibl: ▶Bénézit; Minneapolis(MN,
USA), Univ.Gallery, THREE
WOMEN ARTISTS(1980); ▶Vollmer,
Künst.-Lex. 20. Jhr.
Greenough, Horatio BA WI
(American artist, 1805-1852) WI
(American sculptor, 1805-1852) BA
Bibl: ▶McGraw-Hill dict. art
Greenough, John (American artist,
1801-1852) WI
Greenough, Richard Saltonstall
(American sculptor, 1819-1904) BA
Bibl: ▶Fielding's Amer. ptrs.;
▶Groce, Artists Amer.; ▶Young,
Amer. artists

Greensmith, John *(British artist, op. 1976-)* WI

Greenspan, David A. *(Architect)* AV
Bibl: Inland architect, 1984 Nov.-Dec., v.28, no.6, p.50

Greenup, Joseph *(British artist, op. 1913-, d.1946)* WI

Greenwald, Caroline *(American artist, 20th c.)* BA
Bibl: ▶Intl. dir. exh. artists, 1983; Print collector's newsletter X/3 (July-Aug. 1979), pp. 77-79

Greenway, Francis Howard *(British architect, active in Australia, 1777-1837)* AV
Bibl: ▶Colvin, Brit. archts.

Greenway, Joseph *(British sculptor, act.ca.1760)* BA
Bibl: LEEDS ART CALENDAR, 75, p.29-32

Greenwell, A. *(British artist, op. 1819-)* WI

Greenwold, Mark *(20th c.)* BA
Bibl: Johnson, ARTS MAGAZINE, LX/5(JAN 1987), 70-72; ▶Natl. Faculty Dir.

Greenwood→see Greenwood, Ethan Allen

Greenwood, C.J. WC WI
(British artist, 19th cent.) WC
(British artist, op.19th c.) WI

Greenwood, Ernest BA WC WI
(British artist, 1913-) WC
(British artist, b.1913) WI
(British painter, b.1913) BA
Bibl: ▶Waters, Brit. artists

Greenwood, Ethan Allen PR WC WI
(American artist, 1779-1856) WC WI
(American painter, 1779-1856) PR
Bibl: ▶Fielding's Amer. ptrs.
Ethan Allen Greenwood PR
Greenwood PR

Greenwood, Frans *(Dutch glass engraver, 1680-1763)* BA
Bibl: Smit, WELKUNST, LII/19(1 OCT 1982), 2620-24; ▶Thieme-Becker; ▶Wurzbach, NLD Künst.-Lex.

Greenwood, George Parker *(British artist, op.1884-1904)* WI

Greenwood, John BA GC WC WI
(American artist, 1727-1792) WC WI
(American painter, printmaker, 1727-1792) BA
(American, 1727-1792) GC
Bibl: ▶Groce, Artists Amer.; ▶Thieme-Becker; ▶Witt checklist

Greenwood, Joseph H. *(American painter, 1857-1927)* PR
Bibl: ▶WWW Amer. art
Joseph H. Greenwood PR

Greenwood, Marion *(American painter, 1909-1970)* BA
Bibl: ▶MoMA libr. cat.; ▶WWW Amer., 1976

Greenwood, Orlando WC WI
(British artist, b.1892) WI
(British artist, op.1920) WC

Greenwood, Sydney *(British architect)* AV
Bibl: old Avery Index

Greenwood, Thomas *(British, d.1797)* GC
Bibl: ▶Thieme-Becker

Greer, A.D. *(American artist, op. 20th c.)* WI

Greer, Blanche *(British artist, b.1883)* WI

Greer, John Sydney *(Canadian sculptor, b.1944)* BA
Bibl: ▶Artists Canada; ▶WW Amer. Art

Greer, Lulu WC WI
(British artist, 20th cent.) WC
(British artist, op.20th c.) WI

Greeve, S.→see Greeve, Stephanus

Greeve, Stephanus *(Dutch painter, ca.1760-d. aft.1815)* GC
Bibl: ▶Bénézit; ▶Thieme-Becker
Greeve, S. GC

Greeven, Bendrik *(Dutch artist, 1787-1854)* WC

Gref, Franz Heinrich *(German painter, printmaker, 1872-1957)* BA
Bibl: ▶Thieme-Becker; ▶Vollmer, Künst.-Lex. 20. Jhr.

Grefe, Konrad *(German artist, 1823-1907)* WC

Greff, Hieronymus *(German painter, printmaker, ca.1460-after 1507)* BA
Bibl: ▶Bénézit; Nürnberg (DEU), Stadtgesch. Mus., Wirkung u. Nachleben Durers (1976); ▶Thieme-Becker

Greffier→see Griffier, Jan I
Greffs→see Gryef, Adriaen de

Grefice, Victoria WC WI
(British artist, 20th cent.) WC
(British artist, op.20th c.) WI

Greg, Rada *(Canadian painter, b.1941)* BA
Bibl: Kingston (Ont, CAN), Queen's U. Etherington Art Ctr., Contemp. primitives (1982)

Gregersen, Emil *(Danish painter, b.1921)* BA
Bibl: Aarhus (DNK), Kunstbygning, Emil Gregersen (1981)

Gregg, Alfred Holden *(1868-1945; Architect, Toronto)* FA
Bibl: Arthur, Toronto

Gregg, Glenn H. AV

Gregg, William Rufus *(1851-1930; Architect, Toronto)* FA
Bibl: Arthur, Toronto

Gregga, Bruce *(American interior designer, Chicago)* AV
Bibl: Architectural digest, 1985 May, v.42, no.5, p.184

Gregga, John *(American interior designer, Chicago)* AV
Bibl: Architectural digest, 1984 Oct., v.41, no.10, p.102

Greghetto→see Castiglione, Giovanni Benedetto (il Grechetto)
Greghetto da Leone→see Leeuw, Govert van der

Gregoire, Aleandre *(Haitian artist, 1922-)* WC

Gregoire, Gaspard GC WC
(French artist, 1751-1846) WC
(French, 1751-1846) GC
Bibl: ▶Witt checklist

Gregoire, Paul GC WC
(French artist, op.1781-1823) WC
(French, act.1781-1823) GC
Bibl: ▶Witt checklist

Gregoor, Pieter Martinus GC WC
(Dutch artist, 1784-1846) WC
(Dutch draughtsman, 1786-1846) GC
Bibl: ▶Bénézit

Gregor von Bochmann→see Bochmann, Gregor von

Gregor, Harold BA WC WI
(American artist, 1929-) WC
(American artist, b.1929) WI
(American painter, b.1929) BA
Bibl: West Palm Beach (FL, USA), Norton Gallery, Imagist realism (1974-1975)

Gregor, Helen Frances *(Canadian textile artist, b.1921)* BA
Bibl: ▶Artists Canada; Paris, Centre cultural Canadien. HELEN FRANCES GREGOR(1977)

Gregoratos, K. *(Greek architect)* AV
Bibl: Architektonika Themata — Architecture in Greece, 1989, no.23, p.185

Gregori→see Gregori, Carlo
Gregori→see Gregori, Ferdinando
Gregori, Antonio (di Taddeo?)→see Gregori, Antonio di Taddeo

Gregori, Antonio di Taddeo BA
(Italian artist, 1583-1646) WC
(Italian painter, 1583-1646) BA
Bibl: ▶Bénézit; ▶Bolaffi; ▶Thieme-Becker; ▶Witt checklist

Gregori, Antonio (di Taddeo?) WC

Gregori, Bruno *(Italian architect, Milan)* AV
Bibl: AIT, 1989 Jan.-Feb., v.97, no.1, p.26

Gregori, Carlo PR WC
(Italian artist, 1719-1759) WC
(Italian painter, 1719-1759) PR
Bibl: ▶Thieme-Becker
Carlo Gregori PR
Gregori PR

Gregori, Ferdinando PR WC
(Italian artist, 1743-1804) WC
(Italian painter, 1743-1804) PR
Bibl: ▶Thieme-Becker
Ferdinando Gregori PR
Gregori PR

Gregori, Girolamo *(Italian painter,*
ca.1692-1773) **BA**
  Bibl: ▶Thieme-Becker
Gregori, Luigi *(Italian painter, art*
historian, 1819-1896) **BA**
  Bibl: ▶Bénézit; ▶Bolaffi;
  Indianapolis (IN, USA), Mus. Art,
  Mirages of memory (1976);
  ▶Thieme-Becker
Gregori, Massimo *(Italian architect)* **AV**
  Bibl: Ville giardini, 1985 Nov., no.
  201, p.24
Gregori, Nello *(British architect,*
London) **AV**
  Bibl: Architects' journal, 1989
  Mar.29, v.189, no.13, p.46
Gregorietti, Salvatore *(Italian*
architect, Milan) **AV**
  Bibl: Abitare, 1987 May, no.254,
  p.206
Gregoriev *(Russian artist, 20th*
cent.) **WC**
Gregorini, Antonio **[Unidentified]**
(Unknown painter) **PR**
  Bibl: Sacripante inventory, Rome,
  1743; ▶Thieme-Becker, lists as
  variant for Giovanni Antonio
  Crecolini (1675-1736), church ptr.
  Rome; dates do not correlate
  with Sacripante inventory ptg.
  done with B. Torreggiani (d.1675)
  Antonio Gregorini   PR
Gregorini, Domenico *(Italian*
architect, ca.1700-1777) **AV BA**
  Bibl: ▶Bessone-Aurelj, Scult. &
  arch. ital.; ▶Encic. italiana;
  ▶Encyc. world art; Paragone arte,
  1988 Jan., v.39, no.7, p.62;
  ▶Thieme-Becker, gives dates as
  ca.1700-1770; ▶Wittkower, Art &
  arch. Italy, p.248
Gregorio D'Arezzo **GC PR WC**
  (Italian (Aretine), documented
  1315-ca. 1340) JG
  (Italian artist, op.1315) WC
  (Italian painter, act. 1315) PR
  (Italian, act. ca.1315) GC
  Bibl: ▶Witt checklist
  Arezzo, Gregorio   **JG**
Gregorio di Cecco da Lucca→see
  Gregorio di Cecco di Luca
Gregorio di Cecco di Luca **BA GC WC**
  (Italian artist, op.1389-1423) WC
  (Italian painter, act.1389-1423) BA GC
  Bibl: ▶Bénézit; ▶Bolaffi; Boston
  MFA catalogue; ▶RILA/BHA,
  1986; ▶Thieme-Becker
  Gregorio di Cecco da Lucca   GC
Gregorio di Lorenzo *(Italian*
sculptor, doca.1461-1473) **GC**
  Bibl: TCI Firenze
Gregorio Guglielmi→see Guglielmi,
  Gregorio
Gregorio Lazzarini→see Lazzarini,
  Gregorio

Gregorio López Martín, Eduardo
(Spanish sculptor, 1903-1974) **BA**
  Bibl: ▶Ars Hispaniae, v.22, p.324;
  ▶Campoy, Español contemp.;
  Perez Reyes, Arch. esp. de arte,
  LV/217 (Jan-Mar 1982) 50-53
Gregorio Pagani→see Pagani,
  Gregorio
Gregorio, Giuseppe de→see De
  Gregorio, Giuseppe
Gregorio, Marco di *(Italian artist,*
1829-1876) **WC**
Gregorio, N.H. de *(Italian artist, op.*
1875) **WC**
Gregorius de Coninck→see Coninck,
  Gregorius de
Gregorius, Albert Jakob Frans
(Belgian artist, 1774-1853) **WC**
Gregorovius, Michael Carl *(German*
artist, op.1814-1834) **WC**
Gregory *(Italian, ca. 540-604)* **JG**
Gregory, Charles→see Gregory,
  Charles I
Gregory, Charles→see Gregory,
  Charles II
Gregory, Charles I **WI**
  (British artist, 1850-1920) WC WI
  Bibl: ▶Johnson, Brit. artists
Gregory, Charles **WC**
Gregory, Charles II **WI**
  (British artist, op.1838-1854) WC WI
Gregory, Charles **WC**
Gregory, Edward John *(British*
artist, 1850-1909) **WC WI**
Gregory, Eliot *(American artist,*
1854-1915) **WI**
Gregory, George **WC WI**
  (British artist, 1849-1938) WI
  (British artist, 19th cent.) WC
Gregory, John *(American sculptor,*
1879-1958) **BA GC**
  Bibl: ▶RILA/BHA; ▶Vollmer,
  Künst.-Lex. 20. Jhr.; ▶WWW
  Amer., 1951
Gregory, Josef *(German artist,*
1774-1810) **WC**
Gregory, Jules *(American architect,*
Princeton, NJ, 1921-1985) **AV**
  Bibl: dates from Progressive
  architecture, 1985 June, v.66,
  no.6, p.28; ▶Libr. of Congr. Name
  Auth. File
Gregory, Mary Alice *(American*
glass painter, 1856-1908) **BA**
  Bibl: Barlow, Glass industry, v.4;
  ▶Encyc. glass
Gregory, Robert *(British artist, op.*
1912-1915) **WI**
Gregory, Waylande Desantis
(American sculptor, designer,
1905-1971) **BA**
  Bibl: ▶Clark, Ceramics US, pp.293-
  294; Syracuse (NY, USA), Everson
  Mus., Diversions of Keramos
  (1983); ▶WW Amer. Art, 1982

Gregotti, Vittorio **AV BA**
(Italian architect, b.1927) BA
(Italian architect, partner in firm
  of Gregotti Associati, editor
  of journals Casabella and
  Rassegna, 1927-) AV
  Bibl: ▶Arch. period. idx./RIBA;
  ▶Avery Libr. cat.; ▶Contemp.
  archts.
Grégr, Vladimír *(Czech architect)* **AV**
  Bibl: Architectural review, 1988
  Mar., v.183, no.1093, p.72
Gregson, Henry *(British artist, op.*
1870-1900) **WI**
Gregson, Judith *(British artist,*
b.1959) **WI**
Gregson, Sally *(Canadian painter,*
b.1939) **BA**
  Bibl: ▶Natl. Gall. Canada libr. cat.
Greiffenhagen→see Greiffenhagen,
  Maurice William
Greiffenhagen, Maurice→see
  Greiffenhagen, Maurice William
Greiffenhagen, Maurice William **WI**
  (British artist, 1862-1931) WC WI
  (British painter, 1862-1931) PR
  Bibl: Carnegie Inst AM catalogue;
  ▶Thieme-Becker
  Greiffenhagen   PR
Greiffenhagen, Maurice **PR WC**
  Maurice Greiffenhagen   PR
Greifswald Painter **GC**
  Bibl: ▶Beazley, Attic red-fig. vase-
  ptrs.
Greig, E. **WC WI**
  (British artist, 19th cent.) WC
  (British artist, op.19th c.) WI
Greig, James *(British artist, 1861-*
1941) **WI**
  Bibl: ▶Houfe, Brit. book illus.
Greig, John **WC WI**
  (British artist, op.1803-1853) WI
  (British artist, op.1803-1853(?)) WC
Greig, John Russell *(British artist,*
1870-op.1939) **WI**
Greig, Rita *(British artist, op.20th c.)* **WI**
Greig, S.H. *(British artist, op.1860-)* **WI**
Greil, Alois **BA WC**
  (Austrian painter, 1841-1902) BA
  (German artist, 1841-1902) WC
  Bibl: ▶Österr. biog. Lex. 1815-
  1950; ▶Thieme-Becker
Greil, Philipp Jakob *(German artist,*
1729-1787) **WC**
Greim, Michal *(Polish printer,*
photographer in Russia, 1827-
1890) **BA**
  Bibl: Hist. photography, I/1 (Jan.
  1977) pp.39-62
Greiman, April *(Designer, Los*
Angeles, 1948-) **AV**
  Bibl: ▶Art Index
Grein, Caspar Arnold *(German*
artist, 1764-1835) **WC**

Greiner, Annie *(French painter, printmaker, b.1953)* **BA**
  Bibl: Strasbourg (FRA), Mus. d'Art moderne, ANNIE GREINER..., 1986

Greiner, Dick *(Dutch architect, father of Onno, 1891-1964)* **AV**
  Bibl: Assemblage, 1987 July, no.3, p.142

Greiner, H. *(German artist, op.1840-1860)* **WC**

Greiner, Onno **AV BA**
  (Dutch architect, Amsterdam) AV
  (Dutch architect, b.1924) BA
  Bibl: ▶Federatie O jrbk., 1984; M. van der MArck, ONNO GREINER: ARCHITECT, Amsterdam, 1985 (RILA, NLD)

Greiner, Otto **GC WC**
  (German artist, 1869-1916) WC
  (German painter and draughtsman, 1869-1916) GC
  Bibl: ▶Thieme-Becker

Greippel, Johann Franz (not Johann Georg) *(German artist, 1720-1798)* **WC**

Greis, Otto *(West German painter, b.1913)* **BA**
  Bibl: ▶Bénézit; ▶MoMA libr. cat.; ▶Vollmer, Künst.-Lex. 20. Jhr.

Greisch, Marcel *(Belgian architect, 20th c.)* **BA**
  Bibl: Luigi, Revue de l'art LXXVI (1987), pp. 91-93

Greissing, Joseph *(German architect, 1664-1721)* **AV**
  Bibl: ▶Thieme-Becker

Greither, Elias → see Greuter, Elias I
Greither, Elias II → see Greuter, Elias II
Greitherer, Elias → see Greuter, Elias I
Greitherer, Elias II → see Greuter, Elias II

Greive, Johan Conrad **GC WC**
  (Dutch artist, 1837-1891) WC
  (Dutch painter and draughtsman, 1837-1891) GC
  Bibl: ▶Thieme-Becker

Grekou, Titsa *(Greek artist, b.1951)* **BA**
  Bibl: Antwerp (BEL), Intl. Cult. Centrum, Beeldend Verbeelden (1982)

Grekov, Aleksej Fedorovič *(Russian photographer, ca.1800-ca.1855)* **BA**
  Bibl: Hist. photography, I/4 (Oct. 1977) pp.327-347

Grekov, Mitrofan Borisovič *(Russian painter, 1882-1934)* **BA**
  Bibl: ▶Bénézit; ▶Encyc. world art; ▶Vollmer, Künst.-Lex. 20. Jhr.; WW USSR

Grela, Juan *(Spanish artist, 1914-)* **WC**

Grellet, Alexandre Athanese *(French artist, 19th cent.)* **WC**

Grellin, W. **WC WI**
  (British artist, 19th cent.) WC
  (British artist, op.19th c.) WI

Grelot, Guillaume Joseph *(French painter, b. ca.1630)* **GC**
  Bibl: ▶Bénézit

Gremaux → see Grimou, Alexis

Gremillion, Charles Paxton *(American interior designer)* **AV**
  Bibl: Architectural digest, 1986 May, v.43, no.5, p.109

Gremion *(French painter, 18th century)* **GC**
  Bibl: ▶Bénézit

Grémont jeune, Etienne-Jean *(French porcelain painter, act. 1769-1775, 1778-1781)* **GC**
  Bibl: ▶Brunet, Sèvres

Gren → see Gren, Nils

Gren, Nils *(American painter, act. 1939)* **PR**
  Bibl: ▶WWW Amer. art
  Gren PR
  Nils Gren PR

Gren, van [Unidentified] *(Unknown painter)* **PR**
  Bibl: (August 3, 1811, lot 76, Jones)
  Van Gren PR

Grenander, Alfred *(German architect, Berlin, e. 20th cent)* **AV**
  Bibl: Detail, 1989 Mar.-Apr., v.29, no.2, p.105

Grendel, A. **GC**
  (Dutch artist, op.1781) WC
  (Dutch painter, act.1781) GC
  Bibl: ▶Witt checklist

Grendels A. **WC**
Grendels A. → see Grendel, A.
Grenet → see Granet, François Marius

Grenfell-Baines, George, Sir *(British architect)* **AV**

Grenier de Saint Martin, Henry *(French artist, op.1857-66)* **WC**

Grenier de Saint-Martin, Francois *(French artist, 1793-1867)* **WC**

Grenier family *(early Netherlandish tapestry makers, 15th-16th cs.)* **BA**
  Bibl: ▶Encyc. world art; ▶Thieme-Becker; Wauters, Tapisséries bruxelloises, p.17

Grenier, Jean *(early Netherlandish tapestry maker, act.1497-1513)* **BA**
  Bibl: New York (NY, USA), Masterpieces of Tapestry, p.56; ▶Thieme-Becker

Grenier, Pasquier *(early Netherlandish tapestry maker, act. 1459, d.1493)* **BA**
  Bibl: ▶Encyc. world art; ▶Met. Mus. Art libr. cat.; ▶Thieme-Becker

Grenoble, Mathieu Jacquet de → see Jacquet, Mathieu

Grenon, Nathalie *(Architect, Rome and New York City)* **AV**
  Bibl: Progressive architecture, 1988 Feb., v.69, no.2, p.76

Grenot, Bernard **AV**

Grenzbach, Ted *(American architect)* **AV**
  Bibl: House & garden, 1985 Oct., v.157, no.10, p.148

Greppi, Giovanni Battista *(Italian artist, c.1600-1647)* **WC**

Grès, Alix *(French fashion designer, b.1899)* **BA**
  Bibl: Denver (CO, USA), Art Mus., 25 yrs. couturiers (1975); ▶Hall-Duncan, Fashion photog.

Gres, Gerard du *(French(?) artist, 18th cent.)* **WC**

Grésely, Gaspard **BA GC**
  (French artist, 1712-1756) WC
  (French painter, 1712-1756) BA
  (French, 1712-1756) GC
  Bibl: ▶Bénézit; ▶Dict. biog. fran.; ▶Thieme-Becker; ▶Witt checklist

Gresely, Greseli or Gresly Gaspard (not Gabriel) **WC**
Gresely, Greseli or Gresly Gaspard (not Gabriel) → see Grésely, Gaspard

Gresely, Nicolas *(French artist, c.1715-p.1777)* **WC**

Gresham, James A. *(American architect)* **AV**

Gresham, John Fuller *(American interior designer)* **AV**
  Bibl: Southern accents, 1987 Jan.-Feb., v.10, no.1, p.110

Gresleri, Giuliano *(Italian architect)* **AV**
  Bibl: Parametro, 1987 May, no. 156, p.43

Gresleri, Glauco *(Italian architect, 1930-)* **AV**

Gresley, Harold *(British artist, 1892-1967)* **WI**
  Bibl: ▶Mallalieu, Brit. watercolour artists

Gresley, James Stephen *(British artist, 1829-1908)* **WI**
  Bibl: ▶Mallalieu, Brit. watercolour artists

Gresnigt, Adelbert *(Dutch architect, artist, ecclesiastic, 1877-1965)* **BA**
  Bibl: New Cath. encyc., 9:910a, 911 (illus.); ▶Scheen, Ned. beeldende kunst.; ▶Thieme-Becker

Gresse → see Gresse, John Alexander

Gresse, John Alexander **PR WI**
  (British artist, 1741-1794) WC WI
  (British painter, ca.1740-1794) PR
  Bibl: ▶Thieme-Becker
  Grease, Jack WI
  Gresse PR

Gresse, John Alexander (Jack Grease or Greese) **WC**
  John Alexander Gresse PR

Gresse, John Alexander (Jack Grease or Greese) → see Gresse, John Alexander

Gresset, Philippe *(1947-)* **AV**

Gressler, Eduardo M. (*Brazilian architect*) **AV**
  Bibl: Projecto, 1987 June, no.100, p.91
Gresswell, Nicola (*British artist, op. 1985-*) **WI**
Gresty **WC WI**
  (*British artist, op.1854*) **WC**
  (*British artist, op.1854-*) **WI**
Gresty, Hugh (*British artist, 1899-1958*) **WI**
Gresty, Kenneth H. (*British artist, b.1928*) **WI**
Gresy, Prosper → see Grésy, Prosper Joseph
Grésy, Prosper Joseph **BA**
  (*French artist, 1804-1874*) **WC**
  (*French painter, 1804-1874*) **BA**
  Bibl: ▶Bellier, Artistes fran.; ▶Dict. biog. fran.; ▶Encyc. world art; ▶Thieme-Becker
Gresy, Prosper **WC**
Grethe, Carlos **GC WC**
  (*German artist, 1864-1913*) **WC**
  (*German painter, 1864-1913*) **GC**
  Bibl: ▶Thieme-Becker
Gretsch, Hermann (*German designer, ceramist, 1895-1950*) **BA**
  Bibl: Jahrb. der Staatl. Kunstsamml. Baden-Württemberg XII (1975) 213-224; ▶Vollmer, Künst.-Lex. 20. Jhr.
Greuell, Arthur (*Belgian artist, 1891-1966*) **WC**
Greulich, Lothar (*German architect, Darmstadt, 1940-*) **AV**
  Bibl: Deutsche Bauzeitung, 1985 Sept., v.119, no.9, p.25
Greune, Karl Heinrich (*German painter, printmaker, b.1933*) **BA**
  Bibl: Bremen (BRD), Kunsthalle, KARL HEINRICH GREUNE: PAINTINGS, DRAWINGS, PRINTS; Guide exh. artists: N. Amer. ptrs.
Greuse → see Greuze, Jean Baptiste
Greuter or Greuther, Matthaus → see Greuter, Matthäus
Greuter, Elias I **GC**
  (*German artist, op.1591-m. 1646*) **WC**
  (*German painter, act.1591, d.1646*) **GC**
  Bibl: ▶Thieme-Becker
  Greither, Elias **GC**
  Greitherer, Elias **GC**
Greuter, Greither, Kreitter or Kreuter, Elias, I **WC**
  Kreitter, Elias **GC**
  Kreuter, Elias **GC**

Greuter, Elias II **GC**
  (*German artist, c.1595-1641/2*) **WC**
  (*German painter, ca.1595-1641/2*) **GC**
  Bibl: ▶Thieme-Becker
  Greither, Elias II **GC**
  Greitherer, Elias II **GC**
Greuter, Greither, Greitherer, Kreitter or Kreuter, Elias, II **WC**
  Kreitter, Elias II **GC**
  Kreuter, Elias II **GC**
Greuter, Greither, Greitherer, Kreitter or Kreuter, Elias, II → see Greuter, Elias II
Greuter, Greither, Greitherer, Kreitter or Kreuter, Johann or Hans (*German artist, op.1607-m. 1641*) **WC**
Greuter, Greither, Kreitter or Kreuter, Elias, I → see Greuter, Elias I
Greuter, Johann Friedrich (*German printmaker in ITA, 1590/93-1662*) **BA**
  Bibl: ▶Hollstein, German; ▶Thieme-Becker
Greuter, Lorenzo (*Italian artist, 1620-1668*) **WC**
Greuter, Matthäus **BA**
  (*German artist, c.1564/6-1638*) **WC**
  (*German printmaker in ITA, 1564/66-1638*) **BA**
  Bibl: ▶Bryan, Ptrs. & engravers; ▶Hollstein, German, v.12, p.107; ▶Nagler, Neues Künst.-Lex.; ▶Strutt, Dict. engravers; ▶Thieme-Becker
Greuter or Greuther, Matthaus **WC**
Greux, Amedee Paul (*French artist, 1836/8-1919*) **WC**
Greuze → see Greuze, Jean Baptiste
Greuze, Anne Genevieve (*French artist, 1762-1842*) **WC**
Greuze, Jean Baptiste **BA PR**
  (*French artist, 1725-1805*) **WC**
  (*French painter, 1725-1805*) **BA PR**
  (*French, 1725-1805*) **GC JG**
  Bibl: ▶Bénézit; ▶RILA/BHA; ▶Thieme-Becker
  Creuse **PR**
  Creuze **PR**
  Cruise **PR**
  De Gruse **PR**
  Greuse **PR**
  Greuze **PR**
Greuze, Jean-Baptiste **GC JG PR WC**
  Grouse **PR**
  Gruce **PR**
  Gruze **PR**
  Jean Baptiste Greuze **PR**
  Jean-Baptiste Greuze **PR**
Greuze, Jean-Baptiste → see Greuze, Jean Baptiste
Greve, Guillaume Ernest (*French artist, op.1612-m.1639*) **WC**
Greve, Hedwig (*German artist, 1850-*) **WC**

Greve, Hennyq (*Dutch architect, Boskop*) **AV**
  Bibl: De Architect, 1989 June, v.20, no.6, p.101
Greve, W. (*Dutch architect*) **AV**
  Bibl: Assemblage, 1987 July, no.3, p.122
Grevedon, Henri **GC**
  (*French artist, 1776-1860*) **WC**
  (*French, 1776-1860*) **GC**
  Bibl: Getty Photo Study Coll. (Ptgs.); ▶Thieme-Becker; ▶Witt checklist
Grevedon, Henri or Pierre Louis **WC**
  Grevedon, Pierre-Louis **GC**
Grevedon, Henri or Pierre Louis → see Grevedon, Henri
Grevedon, Pierre-Louis → see Grevedon, Henri
Grevenbroeck, Alessandro **GC WC**
  (*Dutch painter, act.1717-1720*) **GC**
  (*Italian artist, op.1717-1724*) **WC**
  Bibl: Getty Photo Study Coll.; ▶Thieme-Becker
Grevenbroeck, Charles Leopold van **GC**
  (*Dutch artist, op.1731-1799*) **WC**
  (*Dutch painter, act.1731-1799*) **GC**
  Bibl: Getty Photo Study Coll.; ▶Witt checklist
Grevenbroeck, Charles-Leopold van **WC**
Grevenbroeck, Charles-Leopold van → see Grevenbroeck, Charles Leopold van
Grevenbroeck, Jan II **BA**
  (*Dutch painter in ITA, 1731-1807*) **BA**
  (*Italian artist, 1731-1807*) **WC**
  Bibl: ▶Thieme-Becker; ▶Witt checklist
Grevenbroeck, Jan, II **WC**
Grevenbroeck, Jan, II → see Grevenbroeck, Jan II
Grevenbroeck, Martinus van **WC**
  (*Dutch artist, 1646-p.1670*) **WC**
Grevenbroeck, Orazio **GC**
  (*Dutch artist, 1678(?)-*) **WC**
  (*Dutch painter, ca.1678-*) **GC**
  Bibl: Getty Photo Study Coll.; Getty Photo Study Coll. (Ptgs.); ▶Thieme-Becker; ▶Witt checklist
  Gravanbroeck, Orazio **GC**
Grevenbroeck, Orazlo **WC**
Grevenbroeck, Orazlo → see Grevenbroeck, Orazio
Grevenich, Nicolas (*French ébéniste, master 1768*) **GC**
  Bibl: ▶Salverte, Ébénistes 18e s.
Greville, Charles (*British, 1695-1769*) **BA**
  Bibl: Harris, Jrnl. garden history, I/2 (Apr.-Jun. 1981) pp.167-178

Greville, Louisa Augusta   WI
   (British artist, 1743-op.1770)   WI
   (British artist, op.1757-1770)   WC
   Grevilte, Lady Louisa Augusta   WC
Grevilte, Lady Louisa Augusta→see
  Greville, Louisa Augusta
Grévin, Alfred   BA GC WC
   (French artist, 1827-1892)   WC
   (French illustrator, 1827-1892)   BA
   (French painter, 1827-1892)   GC
   Bibl: ▶Bénézit; ▶Thieme-Becker
Grewe family *(German ceramists,*
  18th-19th cs.)   BA
   Bibl: Ducret, Furstenberger
   Porzellan I
Grewenig, Leo *(German painter,*
  printmaker, b.1898)   BA
   Bibl: ▶Vollmer, Künst.-Lex. 20.
   Jhr.; ▶WW Arts DEU
Grey or Caey, J. de→see Grey, J. de
Grey, Alfred *(British artist, op.1869-,*
  d.1926)   WI
Grey, Edith F. *(British artist, op.*
  1889-1913)   WI
Grey, Elmer *(American architect,*
  1871-1962)   BA
   Bibl: ▶Avery period. idx.; GUIDE
   TO ARCH. OF LA; Pasadena (CA,
   USA), Baxter Art Gallery, Cal.
   Tech. 1910-1950 (1983);
   ▶Wodehouse, Amer. archts. WWI-
   pres.; ▶WWW Amer., v.4
Grey, Gregor *(British artist, op.1880-*
  1911)   WI
Grey, J. de   WI
   (British artist, op.1720(?))   WC
   (British artist, op.1720-)   WI
   Grey or Caey, J. de   WC
Grey, Jane *(English, 1537-1554)*   BA
   Bibl: ▶Dict. natl. biog.
Grey, Johnny *(British furniture*
  designer, 1951-)   AV
   Bibl: Traditional homes, 1988
   Dec., v.5, no.3, p.47
Grey, Lady *(British artist, op.18th c.)* WI
Grey, Roger de→see de Grey, Roger
Grey, Thomas Philip de, earl
  (British architect, 1781-1859)   BA
   Bibl: ▶Colvin, Brit. archts.; ▶Dict.
   natl. biog.
Grezna, C.   WC WI
   (British artist, op.1785)   WC
   (British artist, op.1785-)   WI
Griar, L.H. *(German(?) artist, op.*
  1767)   WC
Gribble, Bernard Finegan   WC WI
   (British artist, 1872-)   WC
   (British artist, 1872-1962)   WI
   Bibl: ▶Wilson, Brit. marine ptrs.

Gribble, Herbert   BA
   (British architect, 1847-1894)   BA
   (British artist, op.1874-1882)   WC WI
   (English architect, 1847-1894)   AV
   Bibl: ▶Arch. period. idx./RIBA;
   Robinson APOLLO CXXI/277, Mar
   1985 p.182-83; ▶Thieme-Becker,
   [cited as Herbert G., father of
   Bernard Finegan]; Ware, Brit.
   architects
Gribble, Herbert A.   AV
Gribble, Herbert Augustine
  Keate   WC WI
Gribble, Herbert A. →see Gribble,
  Herbert
Gribble, Herbert Augustine
  Keate→see Gribble, Herbert
Gribble, Kenneth *(British artist,*
  b.1925)   WI
Gribble, Vivien *(British artist,*
  d.1932)   WI
   Jones, Douglas, Mrs., (Vivien)   WI
Gribbon, Charles Edward *(British*
  artist, op.1925-1935)   WI
Gribbroek, Robert *(American*
  painter, 1907-1970)   BA
   Bibl: Albuquerque (NM, USA),
   Museum, Transcendental ptg
   group (1982)
Gribelin the Younger, Simon→see
  Gribelin, Simon II
Gribelin, Simon II   BA
   (English printmaker, 1661-1733)   BA
   (French artist, 1661-1733)   WC
   Bibl: ▶Thieme-Becker
  Gribelin the Younger, Simon   WC
Gribl, Jörg *(German architect,*
  Munich)   AV
   Bibl: Detail, 1985 May, v.25,
   no.3, p.267
Gricci, Giuseppe   BA PR
   (Italian painter, act. 18th
   century)   PR
   (Italian painter, act.1757-1788)   BA
   Bibl: ▶Bolaffi; TCI Toscana;
   ▶Thieme-Becker
   Giuseppe Gŕicci   PR
Gricci, Giuseppe *(Italian sculptor,*
  modeler, act.1744, d.1770)   BA
   Bibl: ▶Bénézit; ▶Boger, World
   pott. & porc.; ▶Honey, Euro.
   ceramic; Lane, Ital. porcelain, pp.
   51-55; ▶Thieme-Becker
   Gricci, José   BA
   Grici, Giuseppe   BA
Gricci, José→see Gricci, Giuseppe
Grici, Giuseppe→see Gricci, Giuseppe
Gricjuk, Nikolaj Dem'janovič
  (Soviet painter, 1922-1976)   BA
   Bibl: Manin, V.: Nikolai Grizjuk...,
   1984
   Grizjuk, Nikolai   BA
Gridaine, Maurice *(Belgian*
  architect, Brussels, fl. 1930's)   AV
   Bibl: Monumenten en
   landschappen, 1988 Sept-Oct.,
   v.7, no.5, p.48

Gridasov, O. *(Russian architect)*   AV
   Bibl: Process: architecture, 1985
   Jan., no.54, p.153
Gridnley, David *(British architect)*   AV
   Bibl: Building design, 1989 Mar.3,
   no.926, p.24
Grido→see Reni, Guido
Grieb, Ludwig *(German artist,*
  1884-)   WC
Griebel, Fritz *(German artist, 1877-)* WC
Griebel, Otto   BA WC
   (German artist, 1895)   WC
   (German painter, b.1895)   BA
   Bibl: ▶ARTbibl. mod., 20/2; Berlin,
   Natl. Gall. cat.; ▶Gorenflo, Bild.
   Künstler; ▶Kindlers Malerei Lex.;
   ▶Vollmer, Künst.-Lex. 20. Jhr.
Grieco, Gennaro *(Italian painter,*
  18th c.)   BA
   Bibl: Borrelli, NAPOLI
   NABOLISSIMA XVIII/6 (Nov-Dec
   1979) 201-229
Grieder, Walter *(Swiss artist, 1914-)* WC
Grief→see Gryef, Adriaen de
Griefen, John   BA WC WI
   (American artist, 20th cent.)   WC
   (American artist, b.1942)   WI
   (American painter, b.1942)   BA
   Bibl: Guide exh. artists: N. Amer.
   ptrs.; ▶NY art yrbk.; ▶WW Amer.
   Art, 1986
Grieff→see Gryef, Adriaen de
Grieffier→see Griffier, Jan I
Grieger, Walter Scott *(American*
  sculptor, b.1946)   BA
   Bibl: ▶WW Amer. Art, 1976
Griemer, Jacob→see Grimmer, Jacob
Grien, Hans Baldung→see Baldung,
  Hans (Hans Baldung Grien)
Grieninger, Johann Georg *(German*
  porcelain manufacturer, 1716-
  1798)   BA
   Bibl: DRESDENER KUNSTBLÄTTER,
   XXVI, 5 (1982) 150-153; ▶Neue
   deutsche Biog., v.6, p.690
Grient, Cornelis de   GC WC
   (Dutch artist, 1691-1783)   WC
   (Dutch draughtsman, 1691-
   1783)   GC
   Bibl: Getty Photo Study Coll.;
   ▶Witt checklist
Griep→see Gryef, Adriaen de
Griepenkerl, Christian *(German*
  artist, 1839-1916)   WC
Grier, Edmund Wyly, Sir *(British*
  artist, 1862-1957-1958)   WI
Grier, Louis *(British artist, 1864-*
  1920)   WI
   Bibl: ▶Waters, Brit. artists
   Grier, Louis Monro   WI
Grier, Louis Monro→see Grier, Louis
Grierson, Charles MacIvor *(British*
  artist, 1864-1939)   WI
   Bibl: ▶Fisher, Watercolour ptrs.
Grierson, William   AV

Griesedieck, Ellen *(American painter, 20th c.)*   **BA**
  Bibl: ARTS MAGAZINE, LX/1 (Sept 1985) 7
Griesemer, Paul *(American architect)*   **AV**
  Bibl: Oz, 1985, v.7, p.66
Grieshaber, H.A.P. → see Grieshaber, HAP
Grieshaber, HAP   **BA**
  (German artist, 1909-)   **WC**
  (West German painter, printmaker, 1909-1981)   **BA**
  Bibl: ▶Vollmer, Künst.-Lex. 20. Jhr.; ▶Witt checklist; ▶WW Arts DEU
  Grieshaber, H.A.P.   **WC**
Grieshaber, Karl *(American landscape architect)*   **AV**
  Bibl: House & garden, 1987 June, v.159, no.6, p.142
Griesinger, Jakob *(German painter, 1407-1491)*   **PR**
  Bibl: ▶Thieme-Becker
  Giacomo d'Alemanii   PR
  Jacques Almand   PR
  Jakob Griesinger   PR
Grieve family *(British scenographers, 19th c.)*   **BA**
  Bibl: ▶Fisher, Watercolour ptrs.; ▶Mallalieu, Brit. watercolour artists
Grieve, Alec *(British artist, op.1891-, d.1933)*   **WI**
Grieve, Bob *(Australian draughtsman, 1924-)*   **GC**
  Bibl: ▶Encyc. Australian art
  Grieve, Robert   GC
  Grieve, Robert Henderson   GC
  Grieve, Robert → see Grieve, Bob
  Grieve, Robert Henderson → see Grieve, Bob
Grieve, Thomas *(British artist, 1799-1882)*   **WC WI**
Grieve, Walter Graham   **WI**
  (British artist, -1937)   **WC**
  (British artist, op.1837-, d.1937)   **WI**
  Grieve, Walter Grahan   **WC**
  Grieve, Walter Grahan → see Grieve, Walter Graham
Grieve, William *(British artist, 1800-1844)*   **WC WI**
Grieves, James R. *(American architect, Baltimore, Md)*   **AV**
  Bibl: ▶AIA Pro File, 1987-88
Griff → see Gryef, Adriaen de
Griff. → see Gryef, Adriaen de
Griffa, Giorgio *(Italian painter, b.1936)*   **BA**
  Bibl: ▶Bénézit; ▶Bolaffi
Griffe → see Gryef, Adriaen de
Griffear → see Griffier, Jan I
Griffen → see Griffen, William Davenport
Griffen, Davenport → see Griffen, William Davenport

Griffen, Hayden *(British stage set designer)*   **AV**
  Bibl: Architects' journal, 1988 Mar.16, v.187, no.11, p.74
Griffen, William Davenport *(American painter, b. 1894)*   **PR**
  Bibl: ▶WWW Amer. art
  Griffen   PR
  Griffen, Davenport   PR
  William Davenport Griffen   PR
Griffere → see Griffier, Jan I
Griffier → see Griffier, Jan I
Griffier → see Griffier, Robert
Griffier, A.R. *(Netherlands(?) artist, 18th cent.(?))*   **WC**
Griffier, Jan (I) → see Griffier, Jan I
Griffier, Jan (the elder) → see Griffier, Jan I
Griffier, Jan I   **BA GC**
  (Dutch artist, c.1652/6-1718)   **WC**
  (Dutch painter and draughtsman, ca.1652/56-1718)   **GC**
  (Dutch painter in GBR, ca.1645-1718)   **BA**
  (Dutch painter, ca.1652/56-1718)   **PR**
  Bibl: ▶Bernt, Neth. ptrs. 17c.; ▶Dict. natl. biog.; Getty Photo Study Coll.; ▶RILA/BHA; ▶Thieme-Becker; ▶Witt checklist; ▶Wurzbach, NLD Künst.-Lex.
  Greffier   PR
  Grieffier   PR
  Griffear   PR
  Griffere   PR
  Griffier   PR
  Griffier, Jan (I)   **PR**
  Griffier, Jan (the elder)   PR
  Griffier, Jan, I   **WC**
  Griffin   PR
  Grifir   PR
  I. Griffier   PR
  J. Greffier   PR
  J. Griffier   PR
  Jan Griffier (I)   PR
  O Griffier   PR
  O. Griffier   PR
  Old Gray Freres   PR
  Old Greffier   PR
  Old Griffier   PR
  P. Greffier   PR
Griffier, Jan II   **BA GC**
  (Dutch artist, -c.1750(?))   **WC**
  (Dutch painter in GBR, ca.1690-1750)   **BA**
  (Dutch painter, 1688-ca.1760)   **GC**
  Bibl: Getty Photo Study Coll.; Grant, Old Engl. landscape ptrs., v.1; ▶RILA/BHA; ▶Thieme-Becker; ▶Witt checklist
  Griffier, Jan, II   **WC**
Griffier, Jan, I → see Griffier, Jan I
Griffier, Jan, II → see Griffier, Jan II

Griffier, Robert   **BA GC PR WC**
  (Dutch artist, 1688-c.1760)   **WC**
  (Dutch painter in GBR, 1688-ca.1760)   **BA**
  (Dutch painter, 1688-1760)   **GC PR**
  Bibl: Getty Photo Study Coll.; GRant DBLP; ▶RILA/BHA; ▶Thieme-Becker; ▶Witt checklist
  Griffier   PR
  Robert Griffier   PR
  Young Greffier   PR
  Young Griffier   PR
Griffin → see Griffier, Jan I
Griffin, Brian *(British photographer, b.1948)*   **BA**
  Bibl: Arts Council GBR, 3 perspectives photography (1979)
Griffin, G. Gerry *(American sculptor, 20th c.)*   **BA**
  Bibl: Syracuse (NY, USA), Syracuse Univ., Lowe Art Gallery, NY/8 (1980)
Griffin, James *(British sculptor, b.1950)*   **BA**
  Bibl: London (GBR), Marble Hill House, Sculp. in landscape (1975)
Griffin, Marion Lucy   **BA**
  (1871-1962; Architect, Draftsman, Australia, Chicago)   **FA**
  (American architect, 1871-1962)   **BA**
  (American architect, wife of Walter Burley Griffin (1876-1937), 1871-1962)   **AV**
  Bibl: ▶Macmillan encyc. archts.; ULAN 1988, (Avery); ▶Wodehouse, Amer. archts. WWI-pres.
  Griffin, Marion Mahony   **AV FA**
  Mahony Griffin, Marion   FA
  Mahony, Marion   AV
Griffin, Marion Mahony → see Griffin, Marion Lucy
Griffin, Phil *(British artist, op.1982-)*   **WI**
Griffin, Robert *(English architect)*   **AV**
  Bibl: Building design, 1985 Aug.15, no.800. p.6
Griffin, Walter   **BA PR WC WI**
  (American artist, 1861-1935)   **WI**
  (American artist, 1861-1953)   **WC**
  (American painter, 1861-1935)   **BA PR**
  Bibl: ▶Bénézit; Boston (MA, USA), Vose Galleries, WALTER GRIFFIN, AMERICAN IMPRESSIONIST; ▶Vollmer, Künst.-Lex. 20. Jhr.; ▶WWW Amer. art
  Walter Griffin   PR
Griffin, Walter Burley *(American architect, 1876-1937)*   **AV BA**
  Bibl: Amer. Fed. of Arts, 200 Yrs. of Amer. Architectural Drawings (1977-78); ▶Avery Libr. cat.; ▶Libr. of Congr. Name Auth. File; ▶Natl. union cat., 1970; ▶Natl. union cat., pre-1956
Griffin, William *(British artist, 1742-op.1841)*   **WI**

Griffin-Bird Painter *(vase-painter, ca. 575-555 BC)* **GC**
    Bibl: ▶Beazley, Attic bl.-fig. vase-ptrs.; Boardman, Attic Bl.-fig. Vases

Griffini, Enrico A. *(Italian architect)* **AV**

Griffins, S.S. Bouton **WI**
    (American artist, op.1885) **WC**
    (American artist, op.1885-) **WI**

    Griffins, S.S.Boulton **WC**

Griffins, S.S.Boulton → see Griffins, S.S. Bouton

Griffith, Hugh *(British artist, b.1916)* **WI**

Griffith, Lauren *(American landscape architect, Tex)* **AV**
    Bibl: Texas architect, 1989 Nov.-Dec., v.39, no.6, p.15

Griffith, Moses **BA WC WI**
    (British artist, 1749-1819) **WC**
    (British artist, 1769-1819) **WI**
    (British illustrator, printmaker, 1749-1819) **BA**
    Bibl: ▶Dict. natl. biog.; ▶Fisher, Watercolour ptrs.; ▶Redgrave, Engl. school; ▶Thieme-Becker

Griffith, Roberta **WI**
    (American artist, 1937-) **WC**
    (American artist, b.1937) **WI**

    Griffith, Roberta Jean **WC**

Griffith, Roberta Jean → see Griffith, Roberta

Griffith, William A. → see Griffith, William Alexander

Griffith, William Alexander
    (American painter, 1866-1940) **PR**
    Bibl: ▶Hughes, Artists California
    Griffith, William A. **PR**
    William Alexander Griffith **PR**

Griffiths → see Griffiths, John I

Griffiths, Andrew *(British photographer, b.1949)* **BA**
    Bibl: Bradford (GBR), City Art Gallery, Aislabie's gardens (1981)

Griffiths, C.J. **WC WI**
    (British artist, op.1820) **WC**
    (British artist, op.1820-) **WI**

Griffiths, Colin *(Australian architect, 1936-)* **AV**

Griffiths, John → see Griffiths, John I
Griffiths, John → see Griffiths, John II

Griffiths, John I **WI**
    (British artist, 18th cent.) **WC**
    (British artist, op.1764-1774) **WI**
    (British painter, act. 1764-1774) **PR**
    Bibl: ▶Thieme-Becker; ▶Waterhouse, Brit. 18c. ptrs.
    Griffiths **PR**

    Griffiths, John **PR WC**
    John Griffiths **PR**

Griffiths, John II **WI**
    (British artist, 1837-1918) **WC WI**
    Bibl: ▶Waters, Brit. artists

    Griffiths, John **WC**

Griffiths, Julia *(British artist, 20th c.)* **BA**
    Bibl: the artist in wOMEN ARTISTS NEWS VII/6 (summer 1982) 19

Griffoni or Grifoni, Girolamo
    (Italian artist, op.1620) **WC**

Griffoni, C. M. **GC**
    (Italian artist, op.1776) **WC**
    (Italian painter, act. 2nd half 18th century) **GC**
    Bibl: ▶Thieme-Becker

    Griffoni, C.M. **WC**

Griffoni, C.M. → see Griffoni, C. M.

Griffoni, Floriano di Floriano
    (Italian, act.1457-1483) **BA**
    Bibl: Torella, Musei Ferraresi: Boll. annuale XV (1985-87) pp.43-60

Griffoni, Fulvio *(Italian artist, op. 1604-1650)* **WC**

Griffoni, Giovanni Maria **BA WC**
    (Italian artist, op.c.1800) **WC**
    (Italian painter, act.1770-1798) **BA**
    Bibl: Antologia di B-A II/5 (Mar 1978) 69; ▶Bolaffi; ▶Thieme-Becker

Griffoul, E. *(German artist, 19th cent.)* **WC**

Grifir → see Griffier, Jan I

Grifone, Marisa *(Italian architect)* **AV**

Griggs Master → see Toscani, Giovanni di Francesco

Griggs, Frank *(British artist, op. 1933-)* **WI**

Griggs, Frederick Landseer Maur **BA WC WI**
    (British artist, 1876-1938) **WC WI**
    (British printmaker, 1876-1938) **BA**
    Bibl: ▶Vollmer, Künst.-Lex. 20. Jhr.; ▶Waters, Brit. artists; ▶Who was who [GBR], 1929-40

Griggs, Noel *(British photographer, 20th c.)* **BA**
    Bibl: Oxford (GBR), MoMA, Mod. British photog. (1980)

Grighi, Antonio *(Italian architect, act.1676-1683)* **BA**
    Bibl: Magni, Paragone XXXIV/401-403 (July-Sept 1983) 143

Grigi, Giovanni Giacomo de'
    (Italian architect, sculptor, act.ca. 1550, d.1572) **BA**
    Bibl: Bassi, Palazzi di Venezia; ▶Bénézit; ▶Bessone-Aurelj, Scult. & arch. ital.; Blue guide: Venice; ▶Encic. italiana; ▶Portoghesi, Diz. arch. e urbanistica; TCI Venezia; ▶Thieme-Becker

Grigi, Guglielmo de' **BA**
    (Italian architect, sculptor, act. 1515, d.1550) **BA**
    (Italian sculptor and architect, act.fr.1515, d.ca.1550) **GC**
    Bibl: ▶Encic. italiana; Howard, ARCHITECTURAL HISTORY OF VENICE, 129; Lorenzetti, Venice & its Lagoon; McAndres, VENETIAN ARCHITECTURE OF THE EARLY RENAISSANCE; Paoletti, 123; ▶Portoghesi, Diz. arch. e urbanistica; TCI Venezia, 1969; ▶Thieme-Becker

    Bergamasco, Guglielmo **GC**
    Dei Grigi, Guglielmo **GC**

Grigiotti, Francesco **PR WC**
    (Italian artist, op.1604-1635) **WC**
    (Italian painter, act. 1604-1635) **PR**
    Bibl: ▶Thieme-Becker

    Francesco Grigiotti **PR**
    Grisotti **PR**

Griglik, Peter R. *(American interior designer)* **AV**
    Bibl: Architectural digest, 1989 Dec., p.208

Grignani, Dimitri *(Italian architect)* **AV**
    Bibl: Abitare, 1986 Nov., no.249, p.188

Grignani, Franco *(Italian printmaker, painter, b.1908)* **BA**
    Bibl: ▶Bénézit; ▶Bolaffi; Reggio Emilia (ITA), Sala comunale...., FRANCO GRIGNANI (1979)

Grignion (not Grignon) the elder, Charles → see Grignion, Charles I
Grignion the Younger, Charles → see Grignion, Charles II
Grignion, C. → see Grignion, Charles II
Grignion, Charles → see Grignion, Charles I

Grignion, Charles I **WI**
    (British artist, 1717-1810) **WC WI**
    (Engraver, 1717-1810) **WI**

    Grignion (not Grignon) the elder, Charles **WC**
    Grignion, Charles **WI**

Grignion, Charles II **WI**
    (British artist, 1754-1804) **WC WI**
    (British painter, 1754-1804) **GC**
    Bibl: ▶Thieme-Becker

    Grignion the Younger, Charles **WC**
    Grignion, C. **GC**

Grignoli, Sergio *(Swiss architect)* **AV**
    Bibl: Abitare, 1983 Oct., no.218, p.62

Grigny, Alexandre Charles **BA**
    (French architect, 1815-1867) **BA**
    (Swiss architect, 1815-1867) **AV**
    Bibl: ▶Schweiz. Künst.-Lex.; ▶Thieme-Becker

    Grigny, Alexandre-Charles **AV**

Grigny, Alexandre-Charles → see Grigny, Alexandre Charles

Grigoletti, Michelangelo   **BA GC WC**
  (Italian artist, 1801-1870)   WC
  (Italian painter, 1801-1870)   BA GC
    Bibl: ▶Thieme-Becker
Grigor'ev → see Grigor'ev, Boris
  Dmitrievič
Grigor'ev, Boris Dmitrievič   **BA**
  (Russian artist, 1886-1939)   BA WC
  (Russian painter, 1886-1939)   PR
    Bibl: ▶Bénézit; ▶Fogg Mus. Libr.
    cat.; ▶Great Soviet encyc.;
    ▶RILA/BHA; ▶Vollmer, Künst.-Lex.
    20. Jhr.
  Boris Dmitrievich Grigor'ev   PR
  Grigor'ev   PR
Grigor'ev, Boris Dmitrievich   **PR**
  Grigoriev, Boris   PR
Grigorjeff, Boris   **WC**
  Grigoryev, Boris Dmitryevich   PR
Grigor'ev, Boris Dmitrievich → see
  Grigor'ev, Boris Dmitrievič
Grigor'ev, Sergej *(Russian designer,*
  19th c.)   BA
    Bibl: SOOBSCENIJA HERMITAGE
    LXVI (1982) 28-31
Grigor'janc, Karapet *(Russian artist,*
  1870-1938)   BA
    Bibl: ▶Bowlt, Russian avant-garde
Grigore, Ion *(Rumanian artist, 20th*
  cent.)   WC
Grigore, Vasile *(Rumanian artist,*
  1935-)   WC
Grigore, Zincovschi *(Rumanian*
  artist, 20th cent.)   WC
Grigorescu, Lucien *(Rumanian artist,*
  1894-)   WC
Grigorescu, Nicolae   **BA**
  (Romanian painter, 1838-1907)   BA
  (Rumanian artist, 1838-1907)   WC
    Bibl: ▶Encyc. world art; ▶Havlice,
    Idx. art. bio.; ▶Kindlers Malerei
    Lex.
Grigorescu, Nicolae Jon   **WC**
Grigorescu, Nicolae Jon → see
  Grigorescu, Nicolae
Grigorescu, Octav *(Romanian*
  painter, printmaker, b.1933)   BA
    Bibl: ARTA (Oct 1974) 9-10;
    ▶Barbosa, Art. romani contemp.
Grigoriadis, Mary *(American*
  painter, b.1942)   BA
    Bibl: ▶WW Amer. Art, 1978
Grigoriev, Boris → see Grigor'ev, Boris
  Dmitrievič
Grigorjeff, Boris → see Grigor'ev, Boris
  Dmitrievič
Grigory Gluckmann → see Gluckmann,
  Grigory
Grigoryants, G. *(Russian architect)*   **AV**
    Bibl: Process: architecture, 1985
    Jan., no.54, p.153
Grigoryev, Boris Dmitryevich → see
  Grigor'ev, Boris Dmitrievič
Grigsby, John *(British artist, op.*
  1893-)   WI

Grijn, Erik Adriaan van der *(Dutch*
  painter in IRL, b.1941)   **BA**
    Bibl: Belfast (GBR), Ulster Mus.,
    Irish directions (1975)
Grijó, João *(Brazilian sculptor,*
  painter, 20th c.)   **BA**
    Bibl: Costa, Colóquio: Artes 68
    (Mar 1986), p. 22-25; Doctors,
    COLOQUIO: ARTES, 68 (Mar
    1986), p. 26-29
Grijst → see Gryef, Adriaen de
Grill, K. *(German, active Bauhaus*
  1920's)   **JG**
Grillo, Esther Angela *(American*
  sculptor, printmaker, b.1954)   **BA**
    Bibl: ▶Intl. dir. exh. artists, 1983,
    v.2; ▶WW Amer. Art, 1986
Grillo, John   **BA WC WI**
  (American artist, 1917-)   WC
  (American artist, b.1917)   WI
  (American painter, b.1917)   BA
    Bibl: ▶Archives Amer. Art Jrnl.,
    XI/1-4 (1971); ▶WW Amer. Art,
    1976
Grimaldi → see Grimaldi, Giovanni
  Francesco
Grimaldi, Alessandro *(Italian*
  painter, 1630-1663)   **GC**
    Bibl: ▶Thieme-Becker
Grimaldi, Francesco   **BA CE GC**
  (Architect, c.1545-1630)   CE
  (Italian architect, 1560-aft.1626)   GC
  (Italian ecclesiastic, architect,
    founder, 1560-after 1626)   BA
    Bibl: ▶Bessone-Aurelj, Scult. &
    arch. ital.; ▶RILA/BHA, 1986; TCI
    Napoli e dintorni, artist idx.;
    ▶Thieme-Becker
  Francesco Grimaldi   CE
Grimaldi, Giacomo   **BA**
  (Italian artist, c.1560-1623)   WC
  (Italian ecclesiastic, archivist,
    archaeologist, draftsman, ca.
    1560-1623)   BA
  (Italian painter, ca.1560-1623)   GC
    Bibl: ▶Bolaffi; ▶Thieme-Becker
Grimaldi, Jacopo   **GC WC**

Grimaldi, Giovanni Francesco   **BA GC PR**
  (Italian artist, 1606-1680)   WC
  (Italian painter, 1606-1680)   GC PR
  (Italian painter, printmaker,
    architect, 1606-1680)   BA
    Bibl: ▶Bénézit; ▶Bolaffi;
    ▶RILA/BHA, 1986;
    ▶Thieme-Becker
  after F. Bolonese   PR
  Boglognese   PR
  Bolanese   PR
  Bolaniese   PR
  Bolognese   PR
  Bolonese   PR
  F. Bolanese   PR
  F. Bolognese   PR
  F. Bolonese   PR
  Fr. Bolognese   PR
  Fr: Bolognese   PR
  Fran. Bolognese   PR
  Francesco Bolognese   PR
  Francesco Bolonese   PR
  Francesco Grimaldi called Il
    Bolognese   PR
  Francesco Grimaldi, called Il
    Bolognese   PR
  Francis Bolognese   PR
  Francis Grimaldi   PR
  Francisco Bolognese   PR
  G. F. Grimaldi   PR
  G.F. Grimaldi detto Il Bolognese   PR
  Gio. Fran.co Grimaldi   PR
  Gio. Francesco Bolognese   PR
  Gio. Francesco Bolognesi   PR
  Gio. Francesco Grimaldi   PR
  Gio. Franco Bolognese   PR
  Gio: Fran.co Bolognese   PR
  Gio: Fran:co Bolognese   PR
  Gio: Francesco Grimaldi Bolognese   PR
  Gio: Francesco Grimaldi detto il
    Bolognese   PR
  Gio: Franco Bolognese   PR
  Giov. Francesco Grimaldi   PR
  Giovanni Francesco Bolognese   PR
  Giovanni Francesco Grimaldi   PR
  Grimaldi   PR
Grimaldi, Giovanni Francesco (Il
  Bolognese)   **WC**
  Il Bolognese   PR
Grimaldi, Giovanni Francesco (Il
  Bolognese) → see Grimaldi,
  Giovanni Francesco
Grimaldi, Jacopo → see Grimaldi,
  Giacomo
Grimaldi, Lazzaro   **GC WC**
  (Italian artist, op.1496-1504)   WC
  (Italian painter, act.1496)   GC
    Bibl: ▶Thieme-Becker
Grimaldi, Ron *(American designer,*
  Long Island, N.Y)   **AV**
    Bibl: House beautiful, 1987 Aug.,
    v.129, no.8, p.76
Grimaldi, William *(British artist,*
  1751-1830)   **WC WI**

Grimaldo, Alberto [Unidentified]
(Unknown painter)   **PR**
    Bibl: Colonna inventory, Rome,
    1714
    Alberto Grimaldo   **PR**
Grimani da Stroncone, Gregorio → see
    Grimani, Gregorio
Grimani, Gasparo   **AV BA**
    (18th cent. Italian architect,
        publisher of A Topographical
        and Historical Description of
        Ancient and Modern Rome
        (Bath, 1783))   **AV**
    (Italian educator, architect, act.
        1776-1783)   **BA**
    Bibl: Durand, Revue de l'art 58-59
    (1982-83) 142
Grimani, Giovanni *(Italian*
    nobleman, probable designer of
    parts of his family palace, 1501-
    1593)   **AV**
    Bibl: Apollo, v.113, n.230,
    p.218ff.
Grimani, Gregorio *(Italian stucco*
    artist, act.1635-1637)   **GC**
    Bibl: TCI Lazio
    Grimani da Stroncone, Gregorio   **GC**
Grimani, Zanetta *(Italian, b.ca.*
    1450)   **BA**
    Bibl: Festsch. Otto von Simson,
    pp. 197-208
Grimaux, Louis *(French painter,*
    1811-1879)   **GC**
    Bibl: ▶Bénézit
Grimbach, Joseph *(German*
    woodcarver, 1718-1789)   **BA**
    Bibl: Dehio: Baden-Württemberg,
    p.464; Fruh, Zeits. Schweiz. Arch.
    u. Kunst, XXXVIII/1 (1981) pp.
    59-79
Grimbaldson, Walter   **WC WI**
    (British artist, op.1711-1738)   **WI**
    (British artist, op.1738)   **WC**
Grimbrede, Thomas *(American?*
    printmaker, act.ca.1800-1809)   **BA**
    Bibl: Cunningham, THE IMAGE OF
    THOMAS JEFFERSON (1981)
Grimelund, Johannes Martin
    (Norwegian artist, 1842-1917)   **WC**
Grimer → see Grimmer, Abel
Grimer, Jacob → see Grimmer, Jacob
Grimes, Frances *(American sculptor,*
    1869-1963)   **BA GC**
    Bibl: NY Times obit.; ▶Opitz,
    Amer. sculptors; ▶Thieme-Becker;
    ▶Who was who [GBR], v.4; ▶WW
    Amer. Art, necrol.; ▶WWW Amer.
    art
Grimes, John *(American artist, 1804-*
    1837)   **WC WI**
Grimes, Margaret *(American*
    painter, 20th c.)   **BA**
    Bibl: ARTS MAG LV/3 (Nov 1980)
    13
Grimes, W.M. *(American, active*
    Hollywood 1930s)   **JG**

Grimiale, Simon *(Italian sculptor,*
    act.ca.1753)   **BA**
    Bibl: Baranyai, ARS HUNGARICA
    VIII/1 (1980) 149-154
Grimleby, David *(British artist,*
    b.1949)   **WI**
Grimley, J.H. *(Engraver)*   **WI**
Grimm, Arthur *(German artist,*
    1883-1948)   **WC**
Grimm, Franz Anton   **AV BA**
    (Austrian architect, ca.1710-
        1784)   **AV**
    (Czech architect, ca.1710-1784)   **BA**
    Bibl: ▶Portoghesi, Diz. arch. e
    urbanistica; ▶Thieme-Becker
Grimm, Hieronymus → see Grimm,
    Samuel Hieronymus
Grimm, Hugo *(German artist, 1866-*
    1944)   **WC**
Grimm, Johann Karl *(Swiss, 1630-*
    1701)   **BA**
    Bibl: UNSERE KUNSTDENK.
    XXXIII/7 (1982) 74-81
Grimm, Ludwig Emil   **BA GC WC**
    (German artist, 1790-1863)   **WC**
    (German painter and
        draughtsman, 1790-1863)   **GC**
    (German painter, author, 1790-
        1863)   **BA**
    Bibl: ▶Bénézit; ▶Natl. union cat.;
    ▶Thieme-Becker
Grimm, Max von *(German artist,*
    op.1783-1797)   **WC**
Grimm, P.H. *(German artist, 19th*
    cent.)   **WC**
Grimm, Samuel Hieronymus   **BA GC WC**
    (Swiss artist, 1733-1794)   **WC**
    (Swiss painter, 1733-1794)   **BA**
    (Swiss, 1733-1794)   **GC**
    Bibl: ▶Bénézit; Getty Photo Study
    Coll. (Ptgs.); ▶Redgrave, Engl.
    school; ▶Schweiz. Künst.-Lex.;
    ▶Thieme-Becker; ▶Witt checklist
    Grimm, Hieronymus   **GC**
Grimm, Simon *(German*
    draughtsman, act.1654-1669)   **GC**
    Bibl: ▶Thieme-Becker
Grimm, Stanley   **WC WI**
    (British artist, 1891-)   **WC**
    (British artist, 1891-1966)   **WI**
Grimm, Wilhelm (Willem) *(German*
    artist, 1904-)   **WC**
Grimmaer, Jacob → see Grimmer,
    Jacob
Grimmer → see Grimmer, Abel
Grimmer → see Grimmer, Jacob
Grimmer (not Griemer) Adam   **WC**
    (German artist, op.1562-m.1596/8)
Grimmer or Grimer, Hans or
    Johannes → see Grimmer, Hans

Grimmer, Abel   **BA GC PR**
    (Flemish painter, architect, ca.
        1570-ca.1619)   **BA**
    (Flemish painter, ca.1570-bef.
        1619)   **PR**
    (Flemish, ca.1570-d. bef.1619)   **GC**
    (Netherlands artist, op.1592-
        1614)   **WC**
    Bibl: ▶Bénézit; ▶Grote Winkler
    Prins; Orth, Fr. ms. illum.;
    ▶Thieme-Becker; ▶Witt checklist;
    ▶Wurzbach, NLD Künst.-Lex.
    Abel Grimmer   **PR**
    Grimer   **PR**
    Grimmer   **PR**
Grimmer, Grimer or Grimmaert,
    Abel   **WC**
Grimmer, Griemer, Grimer or
    Grimmaer, Jacob → see Grimmer,
    Jacob
Grimmer, Grimer or Grimmaert,
    Abel → see Grimmer, Abel
Grimmer, Hans   **GC**
    (German artist, op.1560)   **WC**
    (German painter, act.1560)   **GC**
    Bibl: ▶Thieme-Becker
Grimmer or Grimer, Hans or
    Johannes   **WC**
    Grimmer, Johannes   **GC**
Grimmer, Jacob   **BA GC PR**
    (early Netherlandish painter, ca.
        1525-1590)   **BA**
    (Flanders painter, ca.1525-1590)   **GC**
    (Netherlandish painter, ca.1525-
        1590)   **PR**
    (Netherlands artist, c.1525-
        1590)   **WC**
    Bibl: Getty Photo Study Coll.;
    ▶RILA/BHA; ▶Thieme-Becker;
    ▶Witt checklist; ▶Wurzbach, NLD
    Künst.-Lex.
    Griemer, Jacob   **GC**
    Grimer, Jacob   **GC**
    Grimmaer, Jacob   **GC**
    Grimmer   **PR**
Grimmer, Griemer, Grimer or
    Grimmaer, Jacob   **WC**
    I. Grimmer   **PR**
    Jacob Grimmer   **PR**
    Jacob Grimmer, 1587   **PR**
Grimmer, Johannes → see Grimmer,
    Hans
Grimmer, Mineko *(American*
    sculptor, 20th c.)   **BA**
    Bibl: Guide exh. artists: N. Amer.
    ptrs.; MacNaughton, ARTS, LXII
    (Nov 1987), p.54; ▶WW Amer.
    Art, 1989-1990
Grimmond, William   **WC WI**
    (British artist, 1884-)   **WC**
    (British artist, b.1884)   **WI**
Grimoldi, Alberto *(Architect)*   **AV**
    Bibl: Techniques et architecture,
    1985 Aug.-Sept., no.361, p.167
Grimou → see Grimou, Alexis

Grimou or Grimoult, Alexis (not Jean
or Nicolas Grimoud or
Grimoux) → see Grimou, Alexis

Grimou, Alexis   **BA GC PR**
(French artist, 1678-1733)   WC
(French painter, 1678-1733)   PR
(French, 1678-1733)   GC
(Swiss painter in FRA, 1678-
1733)   BA
Bibl: ▶Nouv. biog. gén.;
▶RILA/BHA; ▶Thieme-Becker;
▶Witt checklist
Alexis Grimou   PR
Gremaux   PR
Grimou   PR
**Grimou or Grimoult, Alexis (not
Jean or Nicolas Grimoud or
Grimoux)**   **WC**
Grimou, Jean-Alexis   PR
Grimoux   PR
Grimoux, Alexis   PR
[Jean] Grimoux   PR
Grimou, Jean-Alexis → see Grimou,
Alexis
Grimoux → see Grimou, Alexis
Grimoux, Alexis → see Grimou, Alexis
Grimsdale, Sarah (British painter,
sculptor, b.1956)   BA
Bibl: Nottingham (GBR), Univ. of
Nottingham, Art Gallery, SARAH
GRINSDALE..., 1984 (RILA, GBR)
Grimshaw → see Grimshaw, John
Atkinson
Grimshaw, Arthur E. (British artist,
1868-1913)   **WC WI**
Grimshaw, Atkinson → see Grimshaw,
John Atkinson
Grimshaw, Elaine (British artist, op.
1897-)   **WI**
Grimshaw, John Atkinson   **BA PR WI**
(British artist, 1836-1893)   WC WI
(British painter, 1836-1893)   BA PR
(British, 1836-1893)   GC
Bibl: ▶Mallalieu, Brit. watercolour
artists; ▶RILA/BHA;
▶Thieme-Becker; ▶Witt checklist;
▶Wood, Victorian ptrs.
Grimshaw   PR
Grimshaw, Atkinson   **GC PR WC**
John Atkinson Grimshaw   PR
Grimshaw, Louis → see Grimshaw,
Louis H.
Grimshaw, Louis H.   **WI**
(British artist, 1870-1944)   WC WI
Bibl: ▶Wood, Victorian ptrs.
Grimshaw, Louis   **WC**
Grimshaw, Nicholas Thomas
(British architect)   **AV**
Grimshaw, Reginald (British artist,
1910-op.1983)   **WI**
Grimshaw, Thomas   **WC WI**
(British artist, op.1844)   WC
(British artist, op.1844-)   WI
Grimshaw, W.H. Murphy (British
artist, op.1886-1907)   **WC WI**

Grimson, Samuel Grimson, Mrs.,
(Malvina Cornell) → see Hoffman,
Malvina
Grimstead, Richard L.   **AV**
Grimston, Katherine, Lady → see
Clarendon, Lady
Grimstone, Edward (British artist,
op.1837-1879)   **WI**
Grimwood, Alan (British sculptor,
b.1949)   **BA**
Bibl: Walsall (GBR), E.M. Flint
Gallery, INNER WORLDS (1982)
Grimwood, Brian (British illustrator,
20th c.)   **BA**
Bibl: Arts Council GBR, Welsh
Comm., Images to order (1979)
Grinage, Theron E. (American
architect)   **AV**
Grinberg, Jacques (Belgian artist,
20th cent.)   **WC**
Grinberg, Jaime (Argentinian
architect)   **AV**
Bibl: Open house international,
1984, v.9, no.4, p.51
Grindlay, Robert Melville   **WC WI**
(British artist, 1786-1877)   WI
(British artist, op.1828)   WC
Grindley, David (British architect,
20th c.)   **BA**
Bibl: ▶Arch. period. idx./RIBA,
XVII/1 (Jan-Mar 1989); Pearce,
Journal of Inst. Brit. Arch. XCIV/3
(Mar. 1987), pp. 43-43
Grinnell, Peter (American merchant,
craftsman, 1764-1836)   **BA**
Bibl: ANTIQUES CXVII/1 (Jan
1980) 212-219
Grinnell, William Taylor (American
merchant, craftsman, 1788-1835)   **BA**
Bibl: ANTIQUES CXVII/1 (Jan
1980) 212-219; ▶Natl. union cat.,
pre-1956
Grino, Sylvia (French architect)   **AV**
Bibl: Maison française, 1989
Mar., no.424, p.100
Grinstein, Elyse (American architect,
Los Angeles, CA)   **AV**
Bibl: ▶AIA Pro File, 1985
Grintzner (German artist, 19th cent.)   **WC**
Gripenberg, Sebastian (Finnish
architect)   **AV**
Bibl: Arkkitehti, 1985, no.2, p.48
Grippi (American sculptor, 20th
century)   **GC**
Bibl: Juley coll., NMAA
Grippi, Salvatore William (American
painter, printmaker, b.1921)   **BA**
Bibl: ▶Vollmer, Künst.-Lex. 20.
Jhr.; ▶WW Amer. Art, 1978
Grips, Carel Jozeph (Belgian artist,
1825-1920)   **WC**
Gris → see Gris, Juan
Gris, Jean-Noël (French architect)   **AV**
Bibl: Techniques et architecture,
1984 Aug.-Sept., no.355, p. 120

Gris, Juan   **BA GC PR VO WC**
(Spanish artist, 1887-1927)   WC
(Spanish painter, 1887-1927)   BA PR
(Spanish, 1887-1927)   GC
Bibl: ▶Encyc. world art; Gaya
Nuño, Juan Gris (1974), p. 25;
▶Lex. Kunst; ▶Libr. of Congr.
Name Auth. File, NAFL79139620;
▶RILA/BHA; ▶Witt checklist
González Pérez, José Victoriano
Carmelo Carlos   VO
González, José Victoriano   VO
Gris   PR
Juan Gris   PR
**Grisebach, Hans Otto Friedrich
Julius** (German architect,
bibliophile, 1848-1904)   **BA**
Bibl: ▶Neue deutsche Biog.
Grisée, Louis-Joseph (French
porcelain painter, 19th century)   **GC**
Bibl: ▶Thieme-Becker
Griselli, Italo → see Griselli, Italo
Orlando
Griselli, Italo Orlando   **BA**
(Italian sculptor, 1880-1958)   BA GC
Bibl: ▶Comanducci, Diz.;
▶RILA/BHA; TCI Firenze; ▶Vollmer,
Künst.-Lex. 20. Jhr.
Griselli, Italo   **GC**
Griset, Ernest Henry   **BA GC WC WI**
(British artist, 1844-1907)   WC WI
(French painter, 1844-1907)   GC
(French printmaker, illustrator in
GBR, 1844-1907)   BA
Bibl: ▶Bénézit; ▶Busse, Maler u.
Bildhauer 19. Jahr.;
▶Thieme-Becker
Grisolfi → see Ghisolfi, Giovanni
Grison → see Grison, Adolphe
Grison, Adolphe   **PR WC**
(French artist, 1845-)   WC
(French artist, 1845-1914)   WC
(French painter, 1845-1914)   PR
Bibl: ▶Thieme-Becker
Adolphe Grison   PR
Grison   PR
Grison, Francois Adolphe   PR
Grison, Francois-Adolphe   **WC**
Grison, Francois Adolphe → see
Grison, Adolphe
Grison, Francois-Adolphe → see
Grison, Adolphe
Grisoni → see Grisoni, Giuseppe
Grisoni or Grifoni, Giuseppe (Pierre
Joseph Grison) → see Grisoni,
Giuseppe

Grisoni, Giuseppe   PR
  (Italian artist, 1699-1769)   WC
  (Italian painter, 1699-1769)   PR
    Bibl: ▶Thieme-Becker
  Giuseppe Grifoni   PR
  Giuseppe Grisoni   PR
  Giuseppe Grisson   PR
  Grisoni   PR
Grisoni or Grifoni, Giuseppe
  (Pierre Joseph Grison)   WC
  Mons Grizon   PR
Grisotti → *see* Grigiotti, Francesco
Grispi → *see* Crespi, Giuseppe Maria
  (lo Spagnuolo)
Grisson, Giovanni Maria *(Italian*
  artist, 18th cent.)   WC
Griswold, Harlan H. *(American*
  preservationist, Conn)   AV
    Bibl: Connecticut preservation:
    news, 1989 Jan.-Feb., v.12, no.1,
    p.1
Griswold, Roger *(American*
  architect)   AV
    Bibl: Abitare, 1984 June, no.225,
    p.20
Grita, Salvatore *(Italian sculptor,*
  d.1912)   GC
    Bibl: ▶Bénézit
Gritchenko → *see* Gritchenko, Alexis
Gritchenko, Alexis   PR WC
  (Russian artist, 20th cent.)   WC
  (Russian painter, 1883-1977)   PR
    Bibl: Univ of Arizona MA
    catalogue; ▶Witt checklist
  Alexis Gritchenko   PR
  Gritchenko   PR
Gritsay or Grizai, Aleksey
  Mikhaylovich *(Russian artist,*
  1914-)   WC
Gritten → *see* Gritten, Henry C.
Gritten, Henry → *see* Gritten, Henry C.
Gritten, Henry C.   BA
  (Australian painter, 1818-1873)   BA
  (British artist, op.1835-1848)   WC WI
  (British painter, act. 1835-1848)   PR
    Bibl: ▶Bénézit; ▶Encyc. Australian
    art; ▶Thieme-Becker
  Gritten   PR
Gritten, Henry   PR WC WI
  Henry Gritten   PR
Gritzner, Gunter *(German artist,*
  20th cent.)   WC
Gritzner, Johann *(Austrian*
  architect)   AV
    Bibl: 9H, 1985, no.7, p.40
Grivaz, Eugene *(Swiss artist, 1852-*
  1915)   WC
Griveau, Lucien *(French artist, 1858-*
  1923)   WC
Grivolas, Pierre *(French artist, 1823-*
  1906)   WC

Grixopolus *(Italian painter, 13th c.)*   BA
    Bibl: Fiaccadori, in FELIX
    RAVENNA, CXXXI-CXXXII/1-2
    (1986), p. 33-37; Pittura in Italia,
    Duegento & Trecento, v.2, p.584;
    TCI Lombardia, p.534
Griyantara, P. T. *(Indonesian*
  architect)   AV
    Bibl: Architectural review, 1989
    Nov., v.186, no.113, p.109
Griziotti, Laura *(Italian architect)*   AV
    Bibl: Abitare, 1983 Apr., no.213,
    p.32
Grizjuk, Nikolai → *see* Gricjuk, Nikolaj
  Dem'janovič
Grob, Konrad *(Swiss artist, 1828-*
  1904)   WC
Grobe, German *(German painter,*
  1857-1938)   BA
    Bibl: ▶Bénézit; ▶Schweers,
    Gemälde deut. Museen;
    ▶Thieme-Becker
Grobet, Lourdes *(Mexican painter,*
  photographer, conceptual artist,
  b.1940)   BA
    Bibl: Goldman, Woman's art jrnl.
    III/2 (Fal.-Win. 1982-1983) pp.1-7
Grobéty, Claude *(French painter,*
  printmaker, b.1940)   BA
    Bibl: ▶MoMA libr. cat.; Pontoise
    (FRA), Mus. de Pontoise, Claude
    Grobety (1982)
Grobon, Eugene Anthelme *(French*
  painter, 1820-1878)   GC
    Bibl: ▶Bénézit
Grobon, Jean Michel   BA GC
  (French artist, 1770-1853)   WC
  (French painter and engraver,
  1770-1853)   GC
  (French painter, printmaker,
  1770-1853)   BA
    Bibl: ▶Busse, Maler u. Bildhauer
    19. Jahr.; ▶Thieme-Becker; ▶Witt
    checklist
Grobon, Michel   GC
Grobon, Michel (Jean Michel)   WC
Grobon, Michel → *see* Grobon, Jean
  Michel
Grobon, Michel (Jean Michel) → *see*
  Grobon, Jean Michel
Groborne, Robert *(French painter,*
  b.1939)   BA
    Bibl: ▶Art Index, v.36; ▶ARTbibl.
    mod., 13/2, 13/2, 21/2; ▶Intl.
    dir. arts, 1989
Grocholski, Stanislaw Tadeusz
  (Polish painter, 1858-1932)   BA
    Bibl: ▶Bénézit; ▶Slownik artystów
    polskich
Grochowiak, Thomas *(German*
  painter, museum administrator,
  b.1914)   BA
    Bibl: ▶Artist biog. master idx.;
    Hahne, WELTKUNST, LVII/20 (15
    Oct. 1987), p.2895-2896;
    ▶Phaidon 20c. art; ▶Vollmer,
    Künst.-Lex. 20. Jhr.; ▶WW Arts
    DEU

Grodecki, Wlodzimierz *(Polish*
  artist, 20th cent.)   WC
Groder, Edward Thomas *(American*
  architect, New York, NY)   AV
    Bibl: ▶AIA Pro File, 1983
Groeber, Hermann *(German artist,*
  1865-1935)   WC
Groeger, Friedrich Carl → *see* Gröger,
  Friedrich Carl
Groell, Carl *(Polish artist, 1770-*
  1857)   WC
Groell, Theophil *(American painter,*
  b.1932)   BA
    Bibl: St. Petersburg, Museum of
    Fine Arts, FIGURE AS FORM
    (1975-76); ▶WW Amer. Art, 1976
Groen, A. van der *(Dutch artist, op.*
  1774-m.c.1788)   WC
Groenedael, Cornelis *(Belgian*
  artist, 1785-1834)   WC
Groenestein, Jan → *see* Groenestein,
  Johannes Maria
Groenestein, Johannes Maria
  (Dutch painter, b.1919)   GC
    Bibl: ▶Scheen, Ned. beeldende
    kunst.
  Groenestein, Jan   GC
Groenewegen, Adrianus
  Johannes   GC WC
  (Dutch artist, 1874-1963)   WC
  (Dutch painter and
  draughtsman, 1874-1963)   GC
    Bibl: ▶Bénézit
Groenewegen, Gerrit   GC WC
  (Dutch artist, 1754-1826)   WC
  (Dutch draughtsman, 1754-
  1826)   GC
    Bibl: Getty Photo Study Coll.;
    ▶Thieme-Becker; ▶Witt checklist
Groenewegen, Pieter Anthonisz.
  van   GC WC
  (Dutch artist, op.1623-1657)   WC
  (Dutch painter, act.1623-1657)   GC
    Bibl: Getty Photo Study Coll.;
    Rijksmuseum; ▶Thieme-Becker;
    ▶Witt checklist
Groenia, Petrus *(Dutch artist, 1767-*
  1844)   WC
Groenning, Gerard P.   GC
  (Flanders draughtsman, 16th
  century (second half))   GC
  (Netherlands artist, op.1573)   WC
    Bibl: ▶Thieme-Becker
Groenning, Groennig or
  Groningus, Gerard P. van
  (Gerard Paludanus van
  Groningen?)   WC
Groenning, Groennig or Groningus,
  Gerard P. van (Gerard Paludanus
  van Groningen?) → *see* Groenning,
  Gerard P.
Groer, Ferdinand *(German artist,*
  op.c.1830)   WC
Groesbeck, Carl T. *(Architect)*   AV
    Bibl: Inland architect, 1984 Nov.-
    Dec., v.28, no.6, p.50

Groethuysen, Herbert (Architect, Munich)   **AV**
    Bibl: Bauwelt, 1984, v.75, no.34, p.1398

Grofe family (Silesian bellfounders, metalworkers, 15th-16th cs.)   **BA**
    Bibl: Anz. des Germ. Nationalmus. (1976) 47-55; ▶Thieme-Becker

Grogan, Nathaniel   **BA WC**
    (British artist, c.1740-1807)   WC
    (British artist, circa 1740-1807)   WI
    (Irish painter, ca.1740-1807)   BA
    Bibl: Crookshank, Ptrs. Ireland; ▶Dict. natl. biog.; ▶Redgrave, Engl. school; ▶Strickland, Irish artists; ▶Thieme-Becker

Grogan, Nathaniel I   **WI**
Grogan, Nathaniel I → see Grogan, Nathaniel

Grogan, Nathaniel II (British artist, op.1809-)   **WI**

Groger, Ferdinand (German artist, 18th cent.)   **WC**

Gröger, Friedrich Carl   **BA WC**
    (German artist, 1766-1838)   WC
    (German draughtsman, 1766-1838)   GC
    (German painter, graphic artist, 1766-1838)   BA
    Bibl: ▶Bénézit; Berlin, Natl. Gall. cat.; ▶Thieme-Becker

Groeger, Friedrich Carl   **GC**
Grögler, Wilhelm   **GC WC**
    (German artist, 1839-1897)   WC
    (German painter, 1839-1897)   GC
    Bibl: ▶Thieme-Becker

Grognard, Alexis (French artist, 1752-1840)   **WC**

Groh, Carol (American designer)   **AV**
    Bibl: Interior design, LV/10 (Oct. 1984) p.195

Gróh, István (Hungarian painter, decorator, b.1867)   **BA**
    Bibl: ▶Bénézit; ▶Met. Mus. Art libr. cat.; ▶Thieme-Becker

Groh, Maria (Austrian architect)   **AV**
    Bibl: Transparent, 1985, v.16, no. 5-6, p.sonderseiten 1

Groh, Werner (German architect)   **AV**
Grohain, Pierre Joseph (French artist, 1780-1872)   **WC**

Grohar, Ivan (Yugoslav artist, 1867-1911)   **WC**

Grohmann, Peer (West German architect)   **AV**
    Bibl: Bauwelt, 1989 Aug.18, v.80, no.32, p.1478

Groin, Jost van (Dutch artist, 17th cent.)   **WC**

Grois, Josef (German artist, op. 1830-c.1850)   **WC**

Grolig → see Grolig, Curt Victor Clemens

Grolig, Curt Victor Clemens (French painter, 1805-1863)   **PR**
    Bibl: ▶Thieme-Becker
    Curt Victor Clemens Grolig   PR
    Grolig   PR

Groll → see Groll, Albert Lorey
Groll, Albert → see Groll, Albert Lorey

Groll, Albert Lorey   **PR WC WI**
    (American artist, 1866-1952)   WC
    (American artist, 1868-1952)   WI
    (American painter, 1866-1952)   PR
    Bibl: ▶Who was who [GBR]; ▶WWW Amer. art
    Albert Lorey Groll   PR
    Groll   PR
    Groll, Albert   PR

Groll, Henriette (French artist, 20th cent.)   **WC**

Groll, Theodor (American artist, 1857-1913)   **WC WI**

Grolleron → see Grolleron, Paul Louis Narcisse
Grolleron, P. → see Grolleron, Paul Louis Narcisse

Grolleron, Paul Louis Narcisse   **PR WC**
    (French artist, 1848-1901)   WC
    (French painter, 1848-1901)   PR
    (French, active 19th century)   JG
    Bibl: ▶Thieme-Becker
    Grolleron   PR

Grolleron, P.   **JG**
    Grolleron, Paul Narcisse   PR
    Paul Louis Narcisse Grolleron   PR
Grolleron, Paul Narcisse → see Grolleron, Paul Louis Narcisse

Grollier, Marquise de, (nee de Fuligny Damas) (French artist, 1742-1828)   **WC**

Gromaire → see Gromaire, Marcel

Gromaire, Marcel   **BA PR WC**
    (French artist, 1892-)   WC
    (French painter, 1892-1971)   PR
    (French painter, printmaker, 1892-1971)   BA
    Bibl: ▶Bénézit; ▶RILA/BHA; ▶Vollmer, Künst.-Lex. 20. Jhr.
    Gromaire   PR
    Marcel Gromaire   PR

Gromort, Georges (French architect)   **AV**

Gromyko, Viktor (Russian painter, 20th c.)   **BA**
    Bibl: ISKUSSTVO, XXXVIII/12(1975), 28; ISKUSSTVO, XXXVIII/4(1975), 31-33; Prom. persons USSR

Grondona, Tom (American architect, active in San Diego, CA)   **AV**
    Bibl: GA houses, 1984 July, no.16, p.7

Grone, Ferdinand E. (British artist, circa 1845-1920)   **WI**

Grone, Johann Baptist   **GC WC**
    (German artist, 1682-1748)   WC
    (German draughtsman, 1682-1748)   GC
    Bibl: ▶Thieme-Becker
    Groni, Johann Baptist   GC

Gronen, Bruno (German artist, 20th cent.)   **WC**

Groner, Anton (German artist, 1823-1889)   **WC**

Groni, Johann Baptist → see Grone, Johann Baptist
Groningen, Jan Swart van → see Swart van Groningen, Jan
Gröninger, Gerdt → see Gröninger, Gerhard

Gröninger, Gerhard (German sculptor, 1582-1652)   **GC**
    Bibl: Getty Photo Study Coll. (Sculp.); ▶Thieme-Becker
    Gröninger, Gerdt   GC
    Gruniger, Gerdt   GC
    Gruniger, Gerhard   GC
    Gruninger, Gerdt   GC
    Gruninger, Gerhard   GC
    Grunninger, Gerdt   GC
    Grunninger, Gerhard   GC

Gröninger, Heinrich (German sculptor, 1589-1631)   **GC**
    Bibl: Getty Photo Study Coll. (Sculp.); ▶Thieme-Becker
    Gruniger, Heinrich   GC
    Gruninger, Heinrich   GC
    Grunninger, Heinrich   GC

Gröninger, Johann Wilhelm (German sculptor, 1675/1677-aft.1732)   **GC**
    Bibl: Getty Photo Study Coll. (Sculp.); ▶Thieme-Becker
    Gruniger, Johann Wilhelm   GC
    Gruninger, Johann Wilhelm   GC
    Grunninger, Johann Wilhelm   GC

Gronland → see Grönland, Theude

Grönland, Theude   **BA GC PR WC**
    (German painter, 1817-1876)   BA PR
    (Swedish artist, 1817-1876)   WC
    (Swedish, 1817-1876)   GC
    Bibl: ▶Bénézit; ▶RILA/BHA; ▶Thieme-Becker; ▶Witt checklist
    Gronland   PR
    Theude Gronland   PR

Gronninger, J.H. (German artist, op. 1771)   **WC**

Gronon (French artist, 19th cent.)   **WC**

Gronsveld, Groensveld or Gronsvelt, Johannes (Dutch artist, c.1660-1728)   **WC**

Gronvold, Bert Borchgrewink (Norwegian artist, 1859-p.1894)   **WC**

Gronvold, Hendrik (British artist, 1858-1940)   **WC WI**
    Bibl: ▶Waters, Brit. artists

Groom, Jon   **BA WI**
  (British artist, b.1953)   WI
  (British painter, b.1953)   BA
    Bibl: ▶Babington Smith, Contemp.
    artists; ▶Intl. dir. exh. artists
Groombridge, William   **WC WI**
  (British artist, 1748-1811)   WI
  (British artist, op.1770-1796)   WC
Groome, William Henry Charles
  (British artist, op.1881-1914)   **WI**
Grooms, Charles Roger→see Grooms,
  Red
Grooms, Mimi Gross *(American*
  artist, 20th c.)   **BA**
    Bibl: Fort Worth (TX, USA), Art
    Museum, Great Amer. rodeo
    (1976); ▶NY art yrbk.
Grooms, Red   **BA WC WI**
  (American artist, 1937-)   WC
  (American artist, b.1937)   WI
  (American painter, sculptor,
  b.1937)   BA
    Bibl: ▶Intl. dir. exh. artists; ▶WW
    Amer. Art, 1976
  Grooms, Charles Roger   WI
Groosman, E. F. *(Dutch architect,*
  Rotterdam)   **AV**
    Bibl: ▶Federatie O jrbk., 1984,
    p.290
Groot, Adelaide Milton de→see de
  Groot, Adelaide Milton
Groot, David *(Dutch artist, b.1949)*   **BA**
    Bibl: Amsterdam (NLD), Stedelijk
    Museum, Ansuya Blom (1978)
Groot, Els de *(Dutch sculptor,*
  printmaker, b.1940)   **BA**
    Bibl: ▶Bénézit; Paris (FRA), Inst.
    néerlandais, 9 femmes
    constructivistes (1976)
Groot, Gerardus de *(Dutch painter,*
  b.1878)   **GC**
    Bibl: ▶Vollmer, Künst.-Lex. 20. Jhr.
Groot, Johannes de   **GC**
  (Dutch artist, 1650(?)-1726)   WC
  (Dutch painter and
  draughtsman, 1650-1726)   GC
    Bibl: Getty Photo Study Coll.;
    ▶Thieme-Becker; ▶Witt checklist
Groot, Johannes or Jan de   **WC**
Groot, Johannes or Jan de→see
  Groot, Johannes de
Groot, Johannes Willem Simon de
  (Dutch artist, 1877-1956)   **WC**
Groot, Mieke *(Dutch glass worker,*
  b.1949)   **BA**
    Bibl: Amsterdam (NLD), Stedelijk
    Museum, Atelier 16 (1980)
Groot, Pieter de   **GC WC**
  (Dutch artist, 1742-)   WC
  (Dutch painter, b.1742)   GC
    Bibl: Getty Photo Study Coll.;
    ▶Thieme-Becker; ▶Witt checklist
Groot, Willem de *(Dutch painter,*
  b.1734)   **GC**
    Bibl: ▶Bénézit
Groote, A. de *(Dutch artist, 19th*
  cent.)   **WC**

Groote, Otto von *(German artist,*
  1883-)   **WC**
Grooteclaes, Hubert *(German,*
  1927-)   **JG**
Grooth, Georg Christoph→see
  Grooth, Georg Cristoph
Grooth, Georg Cristoph   **PR**
  (German artist, 1716-1749)   WC
  (German painter, 1716-1749)   GC PR
    Bibl: ▶Thieme-Becker
  G.C. Groth   PR
  Georg Cristoph Groth   PR
  Grooth, Georg Christoph   **GC PR**
  Grooth, George Christof   **WC**
Grooth, George Christof→see
  Grooth, Georg Cristoph
Grooth, Jacob *(German painter, act.*
  late 18th cent.)   **PR**
    Bibl: ▶Thieme-Becker
  Jacob Grooth   PR
Grooth, Johann Friedrich *(German*
  artist, 1717-1801)   **WC**
Grooth, Johann Nikolaus   **GC PR WC**
  (German artist, 1721/3-1797)   WC
  (German painter, 1721/23-1797)   PR
  (German painter, 1723?-1797)   GC
    Bibl: ▶Thieme-Becker
  Johann Nikolaus Grooth   PR
Grootvelt, Jan Hendrick van   **GC**
  (Dutch artist, 1808-1855)   WC
  (Dutch painter, 1808-1855)   GC
    Bibl: ▶Thieme-Becker
  Grootvelt, Jan Hendrik van   **WC**
Grootvelt, Jan Hendrick van→see
  Grootvelt, Jan Hendrick van
Grootz., F. *(Netherlands artist, 17th*
  cent.)   **WC**
Groover, Jan *(American*
  photographer, b.1943)   **BA**
    Bibl: ▶Intl. dir. exh. artists, 1983
Gropeanu, Nicolae *(Rumanian artist,*
  1864-1936)   **WC**
Gropius, Carl Wilhelm *(German*
  artist, 1793-1870)   **WC**
Gropius, Martin→see Gropius, Martin
  Philipp
Gropius, Martin Philipp   **BA**
  (German architect, 1824-
  1880)   AV BA
    Bibl: ▶Macmillan encyc. archts.;
    ▶Portoghesi, Diz. arch. e
    urbanistica; ▶Thieme-Becker
  Gropius, Martin   **AV**
Gropius, Walter→see Gropius, Walter
  Adolf
Gropius, Walter Adolf   **BA**
  (American architect, 1883-
  1969)   AV BA
    Bibl: ▶Contemp. archts.; ▶Libr. of
    Congr. Name Auth. File;
    ▶Macmillan encyc. archts.; ▶New
    Columbia encyc.; ▶WWW Amer.
  Gropius, Walter   **AV**
Gropp or Grapp, Balthasar *(Swiss*
  artist, op.1549)   **WC**

Groppelli family *(Italian sculptors,*
  17th-18th cs.)   **BA**
    Bibl: ▶Bessone-Aurelj, Scult. &
    arch. ital.; ▶Thieme-Becker; Vio,
    Arte veneta, XXXVII (1983) pp.
    223-227
Groppelli, Giovanni Battista I
  (Italian sculptor, ca.1640-1714)   **BA**
    Bibl: Vio, Arte veneta, XXXVII
    (1983) pp.223-227
Groppelli, Marino   **BA**
  (Italian architect, doca.1700-
  1715)   GC
  (Italian sculptor, architect, ca.
  1664-1723)   BA
    Bibl: ARTE VENETA, XXIV(1970),
    238; ▶Bessone-Aurelj, Scult. &
    arch. ital.; Guide Bleu, YUG, 243;
    TCI Venezia; TCI Venezia, 1969;
    ▶Thieme-Becker
  Groppelli, Marino (the Younger)   **GC**
Groppelli, Marino (the
  Younger)→see Groppelli, Marino
Gropper→see Gropper, William
Gropper, William   **BA GC PR WC WI**
  (American artist, 1897-)   WC
  (American artist, 1897-1977)   WI
  (American painter, 1897-1977)   GC PR
  (American painter, printmaker,
  1897-1977)   BA
    Bibl: ▶Cummings, Contemp.
    Amer. artists; ▶Fielding's Amer.
    ptrs.; NY Times obit.; ▶RILA/BHA;
    ▶WW Amer. Art
  Gropper   PR
  William Gropper   PR
Groppi, A. *(Italian artist, 18th cent.)*   **WC**
Groppino, Domenico *(Italian*
  architect, act.1584-1594)   **BA**
    Bibl: Mantese, PALLADIO,
    XIX(1977), 85-105
Groppoli, Francesco *(Italian artist,*
  17th cent.)   **WC**
Gros→see Gros, Antoine Jean, baron
Gros, Antoine Jean→see Gros,
  Antoine Jean, baron
Gros, Antoine Jean, baron   **BA PR**
  (French artist, 1771-1835)   WC
  (French painter, 1771-1835)   BA PR
  (French, 1771-1835)   GC JG
    Bibl: George Goldner; ▶RILA/BHA;
    ▶Thieme-Becker
  Baron Antoine Jean Gros   PR
  Baron Gros   PR
  Gros   PR
  Gros, Antoine Jean   **GC WC**
  Gros, Antoine-Jean, Baron   **JG PR**
  Gros, Jean-Antoine, Baron   PR
  Monsieur Gros   PR
  Monssieur Gros   PR
  Moussieur Gros   PR
Gros, Antoine-Jean, Baron→see Gros,
  Antoine Jean, baron
Gros, Henri *(French artist, 19th*   •
  cent.)   **WC**

Gros, Jean Baptiste Louis (Baron)
*(French, 1793-1870, active France,
Greece, and Switzerland)*   JG
Gros, Jean-Antoine *(French artist,
1725-p.1786)*   WC
*Gros, Jean-Antoine, Baron → see Gros,
Antoine Jean, baron*
Gros, Lucien Alphonse *(French,
1845-1913)*   GC
    Bibl: ▶Thieme-Becker
Grosch, Christian Henrik *(1801-
1865)*   AV
Groschwitz, Gustave von
(American printmaker, 20th c.)   BA
    Bibl: Greengard, Jrnl. dec. &
    propaganda arts I (Sept 1986)
*Grosclaude, Louis Aime → see
Grosclaude, Louis-Aimé*
Grosclaude, Louis-Aimé   BA
(Swiss artist, 1784-1869)   WC
(Swiss painter, 1784-1869)   BA
    Bibl: ▶Schweiz. Künst.-Lex.;
    ▶Thieme-Becker; ▶Witt checklist
Grosclaude, Louis Aime   WC
Grosdebeler, Thierry *(French
architect)*   AV
    Bibl: Maison française, 1989
    Mar., no.424, p.100
*Grose or Grosse, Francis → see Grose,
Francis*
Grose, Daniel Charles *(American
artist, op.1860-)*   WI
Grose, Francis   WI
(British artist, 1731-1791)   WI
(British artist, c.1731-1791)   WC
Grose or Grosse, Francis   WC
**Grosjean, Henry (Marie Gustave
Henry)** *(French artist, 1866-)*   WC
Grosjean, Robert *(French architect)*   AV
    Bibl: ▶Engen, Victorian engravers;
    Techniques et architecture, 1985
    Dec.-1986 Jan., no.363, p.48
Grosman, Johann *(Czech artist, op.
1707-1730)*   WC
Grosperrin, Claude *(French artist,
1936-)*   WC
*Grospietsch or Grosspietsch,
Florian → see Grospietsch, Florian*
Grospietsch, Florian   GC
(German artist, 1789-p.1830)   WC
*(German printmaker, 1789-
1830)*   GC
    Bibl: ▶Bénézit
**Grospietsch or Grosspietsch,
Florian**   WC
Gross, Anthony   BA GC WC WI
(British artist, 1905-)   WC
(British artist, 1905-1984)   WI
*(British painter, printmaker,
1905-1984)*   BA
(British, b.1905)   GC
    Bibl: Ackroyd, ART MONTHLY, 82
    (DEC-JAN 1984-85), 31; ▶Bénézit;
    ▶MoMA libr. cat.; ▶Witt checklist
Gross, Arnold *(Hungarian artist,
1929-)*   WC

Gross, Chaim   BA GC WC WI
(American artist, 1904-)   WC
(American artist, b.1904)   WI
*(American sculptor (b. Austria),
b.1904)*   GC
(American sculptor, b.1904)   BA
    Bibl: ▶Intl. dir. exh. artists, 1983;
    NY Times obit., 7 May 1991;
    ▶RILA/BHA
Gross, František *(Czech painter,
printmaker, b.1909)*   BA
    Bibl: ▶Vollmer, Künst.-Lex. 20. Jhr.
Gross, Fritz M. *(German artist,
1895-1969)*   WC
Gross, Hans *(German painter,
printmaker, b.1893)*   BA
    Bibl: ▶Vollmer, Künst.-Lex. 20. Jhr.
Gross, Heinrich *(German
draughtsman, 16th century)*   GC
    Bibl: ▶Thieme-Becker
Gross, Howard *(American
photographer, 20th c.)*   BA
    Bibl: Powell, ARTS MAGAZINE,
    LVII/10(JUNE 1983), 20
Gross, Jacques *(Swiss architect,
Jouxtens)*   AV
    Bibl: ▶Schweiz. Ingen. u. Archit.,
    1984-1985
Gross, James *(American painter,
20th c.)*   BA
    Bibl: Morgan, R.C., in ARTS MAG
    LIX/5 (Jan 1985) 20
Gross, Julie *(American architect)*   AV
    Bibl: Architecture: the AIA
    journal, 1985 Oct., v.74, no.10,
    p.18
Gross, Leopold *(German artist, op.
1830-1845)*   WC
Gross, Michael *(Israeli painter,
sculptor, b.1920)*   BA
    Bibl: ▶Art Index, 1975, 1988;
    ▶Intl. dir. exh. artists, 1989-1990;
    Worcester(MA, USA), Worester
    Art Museum. 3 ISRAELI
    ARTISTS(1975)
Gross, Nora *(Swiss painter,
ceramist, 1871-1928)*   BA
    Bibl: Ball, GENAVA, XXXVI (1988),
    p. 117-135; ▶Bénézit; ▶Künst.-Lex.
    Schweiz 20. Jahrh.; ▶Petteys,
    Women artists; ▶Schweiz.
    Künst.-Lex.
Gross, P.A. *(French artist, 19th
cent.)*   WC
Gross, Patricio *(Chilean architect)*   AV
    Bibl: ARQ, 1986 May, no.11, p.12
Gross, Peter Alfred *(American
painter, 1849-1914)*   BA
    Bibl: ▶Smith, Idx. Amer. artists;
    ▶Young, Amer. artists
Gross, Rainer *(German painter in
USA, b.1951)*   BA
    Bibl: ▶Art Index, v.50, 1984;
    Hanover, kestner Gesells-chaft,
    MOMENT BILD; ▶Intl. dir. exh.
    artists, 1983; Lausanne(CHE),
    Musee cantonal des Beaux-Arts
    Lausanne. RAINER GROSS

Grossbach, Peter *(German sculptor,
printmaker, b.1934)*   BA
    Bibl: ▶WW Arts DEU
Grossberg, Carl   BA WC
(German artist, 1894-1940)   WC
*(German painter, printmaker,
1894-1940)*   BA
    Bibl: ▶Bénézit; ▶Vollmer,
    Künst.-Lex. 20. Jhr.
Grossberg, Jake *(American sculptor,
b.1932)*   BA
    Bibl: ▶Art Index, v.36; ▶Intl. dir.
    exh. artists, 1983; ▶WW Amer.
    Art, 1989
*Grossberg, Yitzroch Loiza → see
Rivers, Larry*
Grosse, Theodor *(German artist,
1829-1891)*   WC
Grossen, Francoise *(Swiss textile
artist in USA, b.1943)*   BA
    Bibl: ▶Intl. dir. exh. artists, 1982;
    Portland (OR, USA), Reed Coll. Art
    Gall., Francoise Grossen (1978);
    ▶WW Amer. Art
Grossenheider, Richard Philip
(American artist, 1911-1975)   WI
Grosser, Hubertus *(West German
architect, Neuss)*   AV
    Bibl: ▶Bund Deut. Arch. Hdbch.,
    1987
Grosser, Maurice Richard
(American painter, b.1903)   BA
    Bibl: ▶Havlice, Idx. art. bio.;
    ▶Locus, 1977-78; ▶Natl. union
    cat., 1968-1972
Grosseteste, Robert *(English, ca.
1168-1253)*   JG
Grossi Bianchi, Luciano *(Italian
engineer)*   AV
    Bibl: Abitare, 1987 June, no.255,
    p.206
Grossi, Bartolino de   GC
(Italian artist, op.1425-m.1464)   WC
(Italian painter, d.1464)   GC
    Bibl: ▶Thieme-Becker
**Grossi, Bartolino or
Bartolommeo de'**   WC
Grossi, Bartolommeo   GC
*Grossi, Bartolino or Bartolommeo
de' → see Grossi, Bartolino de*
*Grossi, Bartolommeo → see Grossi,
Bartolino de*
Grossi, Giovanni Battista *(Italian
sculptor, act.1760)*   BA
    Bibl: ▶Bénézit; ▶Thieme-Becker
Grossi, Giuseppe *(Italian architect,
1944-)*   AV
    Bibl: ▶Contemp. archts.
Grossi, W. *(Unknown artist)*   GC
    Bibl: Gernsheim, Corpus Photog.
    of Drawings, 1561
Grossman, Barbara *(American
painter, 20th c.)*   BA
    Bibl: ▶Intl. dir. exh. artists, 1982
Grossman, Irving *(Canadian
architect, 1926-)*   AV
    Bibl: ▶Contemp. archts.

Grossman, Joseph (German
architect, act.1770-1784) BA
Bibl: Mithay,
MUVESZETTORTENETI ERTESITO,
XXVIII/2(1979), 131-150

Grossman, Julio (Argentine
architect, Buenos Aires) AV
Bibl: Progressive architecture,
1989 Apr., v.70, no.4, p.22

Grossman, Leo (Brazilian architect) AV
Bibl: Projecto, 1985 Apr., no.74,
p.84

Grossman, Luis (Argentine architect,
Buenos Aires) AV
Bibl: Progressive architecture,
1989 Apr., v.70, no.4, p.22

Grossman, Nancy (American
painter, sculptor, b.1940) BA
Bibl: ▶Collins, Women artists
Amer.

Grossman, Robert (American
cartoonist, b.1940) BA
Bibl: Berkeley (CA, USA), UCB Art
Mus., Amer. presidency political
cartoons (1976)

Grossman, Sid (American
photographer, 1915-1955) BA
Bibl: Ottawa(ONT, CAN), Nat'l
Gallery of Canada.
PHOTOGRAPHIC CROSSROADS
IN1978; ▶Parry, Photo idx.

Grossmann, Rudolf GC WC
(German artist, 1882-1941) WC
(German, 1882-1941) GC
Bibl: ▶Witt checklist

Grossmann, Thomas (West German
architect) AV
Bibl: Bauwelt, 1988 Mar. 11,
v.79, no.11, p.404

Grossmann-Hensel, Gert (West
German architect, Heiligenhaus) AV
Bibl: ▶Bund Deut. Arch. Hdbch.,
1987

Grossmith, Weedon (British artist,
1854-1919) WC WI
Bibl: ▶Wood, Victorian ptrs.

Grosso, Frank S. (American
architect, Rochester, NY) AV
Bibl: ▶AIA Pro File, 1985

Grosso, Giacomo (Italian artist,
1860-1938) WC

Grosso, James del (American artist,
b.1941) WI
Del Grosso, James WI

Grosso, Luigi BA WC
(Italian artist, 20th c.) BA
(Italian artist, 20th cent.) WC
Bibl: Di Genova, GENERAZIONE
ANNI DIECI, 1983; ▶Intl. dir. exh.
artists, 1989-1990

Grosso, Mariella (Italian architect,
Milan) AV
Bibl: Abitare, 1983 Nov., no.219,
p.68

Grosso, Niccolo (Caparra) (Italian
artist, op.c.1500) WC

Grostein, Marcia (American painter,
20th c.) BA
Bibl: Bradley, ARTS MAGAZINE,
LVII/9(MAY 1983), 10

Grosvenor, Caroline (British artist,
op.1889-, d.1940) WI
Norman, Caroline H. WI
Stewart-Wortley, Caroline, Miss WI

Grosvenor, Robert (American
sculptor, b.1937) BA
Bibl: ▶Babington Smith, Contemp.
artists; ▶Intl. dir. exh. artists,
1982; ▶Parry, Contemp. art; ▶WW
Amer. Art, 1982

Grosz → see Grosz, George

Grosz, August J. (German artist,
1847-1917) WC

Grosz, Georg (German
draughtsman, act.1727) GC
Bibl: Christie's photo

Grosz, George BA GC PR WC
(German artist, 1893-1959) WC
(German painter, 1893-1959) PR
(German painter, printmaker,
1893-1959) BA
(German, 1893-1959) GC
Bibl: ▶Bénézit; ▶Neue deutsche
Biog.; ▶New Columbia encyc.;
▶RILA/BHA; ▶Vollmer, Künst.-Lex.
20. Jhr.; ▶Witt checklist; ▶WW
Amer. Art, 1956; ▶WWW Amer.,
v.3
George Grosz PR
Grosz PR

Groten, Henrik 's (Netherlandish
painter, act.1631-1638) GC
Bibl: Gorissen, Conspectus Cliviae
(1964)

Grotenfelt, Georg (Finnish
architect) AV
Bibl: Arkkitehti, 1986, no.2-3,
p.32

Groth Jensen, Jens Peter (Danish
painter, printmaker, b.1918) BA
Bibl: ▶Vollmer, Künst.-Lex. 20.
Jhr.; ▶Weilbach, Kunst.leks.

Groth, Berent (American architect,
Albuquerque, NM) AV
Bibl: ▶AIA Pro File, 1987-88

Groth, Jan (Norwegian tapestry
maker, b.1938) BA
Bibl: ▶Art Index, v.25, 1976-1977;
ARTS MAGAZINE, LIII/5(JAN
1979); ▶Bénézit; ▶MoMA libr. cat.

Groth, John (British artist, op.20th
c.) WI

Grottger, Artur BA WC
(Polish artist, 1837-1867) WC
(Polish painter, draftsman, 1837-
1867) BA
Bibl: ▶Bénézit; ▶Busse, Maler u.
Bildhauer 19. Jahr.; ▶Slownik
artystów polskich;
▶Thieme-Becker

Grötzebach, Dietmar AV BA
(German architect, 1937-1985) AV
(German architect, b.1937) BA
Bibl: Bauwelt, 1985 Apr.5, v.76,
no.13, p.498; ▶WW Germany,
1974

Grouard, Charles (French painter,
sculptor, act.1651) BA
Bibl: ▶Thieme-Becker

Groueff, Lillian (American interior
designer, Southhamptom, N.Y) AV
Bibl: Architectural digest, 1988
June, v.45, no.6, p.128

Groult, Nicole (French fashion
designer, 1887-1967) BA
Bibl: Lynam, Couture; Paris (FRA),
Musée de la mode et du
Costume, PAUL POIRET ET NICOLE
GROULT..., 1986

Groumelec, Loïc le → see Le
Groumelec, Loïc

Grounds, Roy, Sir (Australian
architect, 1905-1981) AV
Bibl: ▶Tanner, Archts. Australia

Group JG

Group E (vase-painters, ca. 550-530
BC) GC
Bibl: ▶Beazley, Attic bl.-fig. vase-
ptrs.; Boardman, Attic Bl.-fig.
Vases

Group G GC
Bibl: ▶Beazley, Attic red-fig. vase-
ptrs.

Group London B 265 GC
Bibl: Paralipomena

Group of Acropolis 1441 (vase-
painters, ca. 575-555 BC) GC
Bibl: ▶Beazley, Attic bl.-fig. vase-
ptrs.; Boardman, Attic Bl.-fig.
Vases

Group of Acropolis 410 GC
Bibl: ▶Beazley, Attic red-fig. vase-
ptrs.

Group of Acropolis 787 GC
Bibl: ▶Beazley, Attic red-fig. vase-
ptrs.

Group of Acropolis 96 GC
Bibl: ▶Beazley, Attic red-fig. vase-
ptrs.

Group of Adria B 300 GC
Bibl: ▶Beazley, Attic red-fig. vase-
ptrs.

Group of Agora P 1073 GC
Bibl: ▶Beazley, Attic red-fig. vase-
ptrs.

Group of Agora P 18953 GC
Bibl: ▶Beazley, Attic red-fig. vase-
ptrs.

Group of Agora P 24327 GC
Bibl: Paralipomena

Group of Agora P 24340 GC
Bibl: Paralipomena

Group of Agora P 24366 GC
Bibl: Paralipomena

Group of Agora P 24377 GC
Bibl: Paralipomena

Group of Agora P 24381 GC
Bibl: Paralipomena

Group of Agora P 24402   GC
    Bibl: Paralipomena
Group of Agora P 24486   GC
    Bibl: Paralipomena
Group of Agora P 5562   GC
    Bibl: ▶Beazley, Attic red-fig. vase-
    ptrs.
Group of Agora P 7891   GC
    Bibl: Paralipomena
Group of Athens 10452   GC
    Bibl: ▶Beazley, Attic red-fig. vase-
    ptrs.
Group of Athens 12144   GC
    Bibl: ▶Beazley, Attic red-fig. vase-
    ptrs.
Group of Athens 14645   GC
    Bibl: ▶Beazley, Attic bl.-fig. vase-
    ptrs.
Group of Athens 15260   GC
    Bibl: ▶Beazley, Attic red-fig. vase-
    ptrs.
Group of Athens 1686   GC
    Bibl: Paralipomena
Group of Athens 1810   GC
    Bibl: ▶Beazley, Attic red-fig. vase-
    ptrs.
Group of Athens 1834   GC
    Bibl: ▶Beazley, Attic red-fig. vase-
    ptrs.
Group of Athens 1887   GC
    Bibl: ▶Beazley, Attic red-fig. vase-
    ptrs.
Group of Athens 2001   GC
    Bibl: ▶Beazley, Attic red-fig. vase-
    ptrs.
Group of Athens 2025   GC
    Bibl: ▶Beazley, Attic red-fig. vase-
    ptrs.
Group of B.M. F 196 *(Campanian
vase-painters)*   GC
    Bibl: ▶Trendall, Red-fig. vases
    Lucania
Group of B.M. F 308 *(Apulian vase-
painters)*   GC
    Bibl: Trendall, Attic red-fig. vases
    Apulia
Group of B.M. F 500 *(South Italian
vase-painters, 4th century BC)*   GC
    Bibl: ▶Trendall, Red-fig. vases
    Lucania
Group of Bari 3720 *(Apulian vase-
painters)*   GC
    Bibl: Trendall, Attic red-fig. vases
    Apulia
Group of Bari 5924 *(Apulian vase-
painters)*   GC
    Bibl: Trendall, Attic red-fig. vases
    Apulia
Group of Berkeley 8.3376   GC
    Bibl: Paralipomena
Group of Berkeley 8/61 *(Apulian
vase-painters)*   GC
    Bibl: Trendall, Attic red-fig. vases
    Apulia
Group of Berlin 1803   GC
    Bibl: ▶Beazley, Attic bl.-fig. vase-
    ptrs.

Group of Berlin 2092   GC
    Bibl: ▶Beazley, Attic bl.-fig. vase-
    ptrs.
Group of Berlin 2095   GC
    Bibl: ▶Beazley, Attic bl.-fig. vase-
    ptrs.
Group of Berlin 2406   GC
    Bibl: ▶Beazley, Attic red-fig. vase-
    ptrs.
Group of Berlin 2415   GC
    Bibl: ▶Beazley, Attic red-fig. vase-
    ptrs.
Group of Berlin 2459   GC
    Bibl: ▶Beazley, Attic red-fig. vase-
    ptrs.
Group of Berlin 4039 *(Etruscan
vase-painters)*   GC
    Bibl: Beazley, Etruscan vase-ptrs.
Group of Berlin 4077 *(Etruscan,
Faliscan vase-painters)*   GC
    Bibl: Beazley, Etruscan vase-ptrs.
Group of Bologna 16 *(vase-
painters, ca. 530-510 BC)*   GC
    Bibl: ▶Beazley, Attic bl.-fig. vase-
    ptrs.; Boardman, Attic Bl.-fig.
    Vases
Group of Bologna 33 *(vase-
painters, ca. 530-510 BC)*   GC
    Bibl: ▶Beazley, Attic bl.-fig. vase-
    ptrs.; Boardman, Attic Bl.-fig.
    Vases
Group of Bologna 440   GC
    Bibl: ▶Beazley, Attic red-fig. vase-
    ptrs.
Group of Bologna 53   GC
    Bibl: Paralipomena
Group of Bologna 572 *(Apulian
vase-painters)*   GC
    Bibl: Trendall, Attic red-fig. vases
    Apulia
**Group of Bologna 585/Trieste S
403** *(Apulian vase-painters)*   GC
    Bibl: Trendall, Attic red-fig. vases
    Apulia
Group of Bologna PU 289   GC
    Bibl: ▶Beazley, Attic red-fig. vase-
    ptrs.
Group of Bonn 602   GC
    Bibl: Paralipomena
Group of Bonn 73A   GC
    Bibl: ▶Beazley, Attic red-fig. vase-
    ptrs.
Group of Bonn 94   GC
    Bibl: ▶Beazley, Attic red-fig. vase-
    ptrs.
Group of Boston 10.190 *(vase-
painters)*   GC
    Bibl: ▶Beazley, Attic red-fig. vase-
    ptrs.
Group of Brussels A 1311 *(vase-
painters, ca. 500-480 BC)*   GC
    Bibl: ▶Beazley, Attic bl.-fig. vase-
    ptrs.; Boardman, Attic Bl.-fig.
    Vases

Group of Brussels A 137 *(South
Italian vase-painters, 4th century
BC)*   GC
    Bibl: ▶Trendall, Red-fig. vases
    Lucania
Group of Brussels A 156   GC
    Bibl: ▶Beazley, Attic red-fig. vase-
    ptrs.
Group of Brussels A 3096   GC
    Bibl: ▶Beazley, Attic red-fig. vase-
    ptrs.
Group of Brussels R 243 *(vase-
painters, ca. 525-500 BC)*   GC
    Bibl: ▶Beazley, Attic bl.-fig. vase-
    ptrs.; Boardman, Attic Bl.-fig.
    Vases
Group of Brussels R 304 *(South
Italian vase-painters, 4th century
BC)*   GC
    Bibl: ▶Trendall, Red-fig. vases
    Lucania
Group of Brussels R 309   GC
    Bibl: ▶Beazley, Attic bl.-fig. vase-
    ptrs.
Group of Brussels R 312 *(vase-
painters, ca. 500-475 BC)*   GC
    Bibl: ▶Beazley, Attic bl.-fig. vase-
    ptrs.; Boardman, Attic Bl.-fig.
    Vases
Group of Brussels R 380   GC
    Bibl: ▶Beazley, Attic red-fig. vase-
    ptrs.
Group of Bryn Mawr P 123
(Campanian vase-painters)   GC
    Bibl: ▶Trendall, Red-fig. vases
    Lucania
Group of Cambridge 62   GC
    Bibl: Paralipomena
Group of Cambridge 73   GC
    Bibl: ▶Beazley, Attic red-fig. vase-
    ptrs.
Group of Carlsruhe 237   GC
    Bibl: ▶Beazley, Attic red-fig. vase-
    ptrs.
Group of Carlsruhe 280   GC
    Bibl: ▶Beazley, Attic red-fig. vase-
    ptrs.
Group of Catania 4292 *(South
Italian vase-painters, 4th century
BC)*   GC
    Bibl: ▶Trendall, Red-fig. vases
    Lucania
Group of Catania 737 *(South
Italian vase-painters, 4th century
BC)*   GC
    Bibl: ▶Trendall, Red-fig. vases
    Lucania
Group of Chur K 55 *(South Italian
vase-painters, 4th century BC)*   GC
    Bibl: McPhee & Trendall, Fish-
    Plates
Group of Class W   GC
    Bibl: ▶Beazley, Attic red-fig. vase-
    ptrs.
Group of Cleveland 16.1061   GC
    Bibl: Paralipomena

Group of Como C 62 (*Apulian vase-painters*)   GC
Bibl: Trendall, Attic red-fig. vases Apulia

Group of Como C 63 (*Apulian vase-painters*)   GC
Bibl: Trendall, Attic red-fig. vases Apulia

Group of Compiégne 985   GC
Bibl: ▶Beazley, Attic bl.-fig. vase-ptrs.

Group of Compiégne 988 (*vase-painters, ca. 530-510 BC*)   GC
Bibl: ▶Beazley, Attic bl.-fig. vase-ptrs.; Boardman, Attic Bl.-fig. Vases

Group of Copenhagen 114   GC
Bibl: ▶Beazley, Attic bl.-fig. vase-ptrs.

Group of Copenhagen 335 (*Apulian vase-painters*)   GC
Bibl: Trendall, Attic red-fig. vases Apulia

Group of Copenhagen 4223 (*Greek vase-painters*)   GC
Bibl: Trendall, Attic red-fig. vases Apulia, v.2, pp.462-470

Group of Copenhagen 453 (*Etruscan vase-painters*)   GC
Bibl: Beazley, Etruscan vase-ptrs.

Group of Copenhagen 505 (*Etruscan vase-painters*)   GC
Bibl: Beazley, Etruscan vase-ptrs.

Group of Copenhagen 509 (*Etruscan vase-painters*)   GC
Bibl: Beazley, Etruscan vase-ptrs.

Group of Copenhagen 6442   GC
Bibl: ▶Beazley, Attic red-fig. vase-ptrs.

Group of Copenhagen 99   GC
Bibl: ▶Beazley, Attic bl.-fig. vase-ptrs.

Group of Copenhagen ABc 1059 (*Etruscan vase-painters*)   GC
Bibl: Beazley, Etruscan vase-ptrs.

Group of Copenhagen inv. 3817 (*Etruscan vase-painters*)   GC
Bibl: Beazley, Etruscan vase-ptrs.

Group of Faina 75 (*vase-painters, ca. 525-500 BC*)   GC
Bibl: ▶Beazley, Attic bl.-fig. vase-ptrs.; Boardman, Attic Bl.-fig. Vases

Group of Ferrara T. 132   GC
Bibl: ▶Beazley, Attic red-fig. vase-ptrs.

Group of Ferrara T. 376 B   GC
Bibl: ▶Beazley, Attic red-fig. vase-ptrs.

Group of Ferrara T. 459 B   GC
Bibl: ▶Beazley, Attic red-fig. vase-ptrs.

Group of Ferrara T. 800   GC
Bibl: Paralipomena

Group of Ferrara T. 981   GC
Bibl: ▶Beazley, Attic red-fig. vase-ptrs.

Group of Ferrara T585 (*Etruscan vase-painters*)   GC
Bibl: Beazley, Etruscan vase-ptrs.

Group of Ferrara T785 (*Etruscan vase-painters*)   GC
Bibl: Beazley, Etruscan vase-ptrs.

Group of Florence 3983   GC
Bibl: Paralipomena

Group of Geneva MF142 (*Etruscan vase-painters, 4th century BC*)   GC
Bibl: Pianu, Ceramiche etrusche

Group of Harvard 2685   GC
Bibl: ▶Beazley, Attic red-fig. vase-ptrs.

Group of Harvard 3066 (*Etruscan vase-painters*)   GC
Bibl: Beazley, Etruscan vase-ptrs.

Group of "Hoplite-Leaving-Home" (*vase-painters, ca. 525-500 BC*)   GC
Bibl: ▶Beazley, Attic bl.-fig. vase-ptrs.; Boardman, Attic Bl.-fig. Vases

Group of Karlsruhe 66/140 (*South Italian vase-painters, 350-300 BC*)   GC
Bibl: McPhee & Trendall, Fish-Plates

Group of Lecce 660 (*Apulian vase-painters*)   GC
Bibl: Trendall, Attic red-fig. vases Apulia

Group of Lecce 686 (*Apulian vase-painters*)   GC
Bibl: Trendall, Attic red-fig. vases Apulia

Group of Lecce 727 (*Apulian vase-painters*)   GC
Bibl: Trendall, Attic red-fig. vases Apulia

Group of Lecce 847 (*Apulian vase-painters*)   GC
Bibl: Trendall, Attic red-fig. vases Apulia

Group of Lecce 875 (*Apulian vase-painters*)   GC
Bibl: Trendall, Attic red-fig. vases Apulia

Group of Leningrad 1469   GC
Bibl: ▶Beazley, Attic bl.-fig. vase-ptrs.

Group of Leningrad 2023   GC
Bibl: ▶Beazley, Attic red-fig. vase-ptrs.

Group of Leyden 192 (*Etruscan vase-painters, later 4th century*)   GC
Bibl: Beazley, Etruscan vase-ptrs.

Group of Leyden 1957   GC
Bibl: ▶Beazley, Attic red-fig. vase-ptrs.

Group of London 460   GC
Bibl: ▶Beazley, Attic bl.-fig. vase-ptrs.

Group of London B 145   GC
Bibl: ▶Beazley, Attic bl.-fig. vase-ptrs.

Group of London B 174   GC
Bibl: ▶Beazley, Attic bl.-fig. vase-ptrs.

Group of London B 25   GC
Bibl: ▶Beazley, Attic bl.-fig. vase-ptrs.

Group of London B 250   GC
Bibl: ▶Beazley, Attic bl.-fig. vase-ptrs.

Group of London B 338 (*vase-painters, ca. 520-500 BC*)   GC
Bibl: ▶Beazley, Attic bl.-fig. vase-ptrs.; Boardman, Attic Bl.-fig. Vases, (Leagros Group)

Group of London B 339   GC
Bibl: ▶Beazley, Attic bl.-fig. vase-ptrs.

Group of London B 632   GC
Bibl: ▶Beazley, Attic bl.-fig. vase-ptrs.

Group of London D 65   GC
Bibl: ▶Beazley, Attic red-fig. vase-ptrs.

Group of London E 2 (*vase-painters, ca. 520-500 BC*)   GC
Bibl: ▶Beazley, Attic bl.-fig. vase-ptrs.; Boardman, Attic Bl.-fig. Vases, (Leagros Group)

Group of London E 230   GC
Bibl: ▶Beazley, Attic red-fig. vase-ptrs.

Group of London E 245   GC
Bibl: ▶Beazley, Attic red-fig. vase-ptrs.

Group of London E 311   GC
Bibl: ▶Beazley, Attic red-fig. vase-ptrs.

Group of London E 33   GC
Bibl: ▶Beazley, Attic red-fig. vase-ptrs.

Group of London E 445   GC
Bibl: ▶Beazley, Attic red-fig. vase-ptrs.

Group of London E 614   GC
Bibl: ▶Beazley, Attic red-fig. vase-ptrs.

Group of London E 631   GC
Bibl: ▶Beazley, Attic red-fig. vase-ptrs.

Group of London E 777   GC
Bibl: ▶Beazley, Attic red-fig. vase-ptrs.

Group of Louvre C 11000   GC
Bibl: ▶Beazley, Attic red-fig. vase-ptrs.

Group of Louvre CA 3205 (*Apulian vase-painters*)   GC
Bibl: Trendall, Attic red-fig. vases Apulia

Group of Louvre CA 928   GC
Bibl: ▶Beazley, Attic red-fig. vase-ptrs.

Group of Louvre F 110   GC
Bibl: ▶Beazley, Attic bl.-fig. vase-ptrs.

Group of Louvre F 125   GC
Bibl: ▶Beazley, Attic red-fig. vase-ptrs.

Group of Louvre F 137   GC
Bibl: ▶Beazley, Attic bl.-fig. vase-ptrs.

Group of Louvre F 166   GC
Bibl: ▶Beazley, Attic bl.-fig. vase-ptrs.

Group of Louvre F 314 (vase-painters, ca. 520-500 BC)   GC
Bibl: ▶Beazley, Attic bl.-fig. vase-ptrs.; Boardman, Attic Bl.-fig. Vases, (Leagros Group)

Group of Louvre F 81   GC
Bibl: ▶Beazley, Attic bl.-fig. vase-ptrs.

Group of Louvre G 99   GC
Bibl: ▶Beazley, Attic red-fig. vase-ptrs.

Group of Louvre K 366 (South Italian vase-painters, 4th century BC)   GC
Bibl: ▶Trendall, Red-fig. vases Lucania

Group of Madrid 11099   GC
Bibl: ▶Beazley, Attic red-fig. vase-ptrs.

Group of Madrid 11111   GC
Bibl: ▶Beazley, Attic red-fig. vase-ptrs.

Group of Montauban 11   GC
Bibl: ▶Beazley, Attic red-fig. vase-ptrs.

Group of Moscow 4332   GC
Bibl: ▶Beazley, Attic red-fig. vase-ptrs.

Group of Munich   JG

Group of Munich 1501   GC
Bibl: ▶Beazley, Attic bl.-fig. vase-ptrs.

Group of Munich 1938   GC
Bibl: ▶Beazley, Attic bl.-fig. vase-ptrs.

Group of Munich 2388   GC
Bibl: ▶Beazley, Attic red-fig. vase-ptrs.

Group of Munich 2562   GC
Bibl: ▶Beazley, Attic red-fig. vase-ptrs.

Group of Munich 872 (Etruscan vase-painters)   GC
Bibl: Beazley, Etruscan vase-ptrs.

Group of Munich 878 (Etruscan vase-painters)   GC
Bibl: Beazley, Etruscan vase-ptrs.

Group of Munich 883 (Etruscan vase-painters)   GC
Bibl: Beazley, Etruscan vase-ptrs.

Group of Munich 886 (Etruscan vase-painters)   GC
Bibl: Beazley, Etruscan vase-ptrs.

Group of Munich 891 (Etruscan vase-painters)   GC
Bibl: Beazley, Etruscan vase-ptrs.

Group of Munich 912 (Etruscan vase-painters)   GC
Bibl: Beazley, Etruscan vase-ptrs.

Group of Munich 980 (Etruscan vase-painters)   GC
Bibl: Beazley, Etruscan vase-ptrs.

Group of Mytilene 590   GC
Bibl: ▶Beazley, Attic red-fig. vase-ptrs.

Group of Naples 128100 (South Italian vase-painters, 4th century BC)   GC
Bibl: ▶Trendall, Red-fig. vases Lucania

Group of Naples 2246   GC
Bibl: ▶Beazley, Attic red-fig. vase-ptrs.

Group of Naples 2473   GC
Bibl: Paralipomena

Group of Naples 3067   GC
Bibl: ▶Beazley, Attic red-fig. vase-ptrs.

Group of Naples 3169   GC
Bibl: ▶Beazley, Attic red-fig. vase-ptrs.

Group of Naples 3208   GC
Bibl: ▶Beazley, Attic red-fig. vase-ptrs.

Group of Naples 3227 (Campanian vase-painters)   GC
Bibl: ▶Trendall, Red-fig. vases Lucania

Group of Naples 3231   GC JG
(Apulian red-figure painter)   JG
(Apulian vase-painters)   GC
Bibl: Trendall, Attic red-fig. vases Apulia

Group of Naples 3235   GC
Bibl: ▶Beazley, Attic red-fig. vase-ptrs.

Group of Naples 735 (South Italian vase-painters, 4th century BC)   GC
Bibl: ▶Trendall, Red-fig. vases Lucania

Group of Naples Stg. 252   GC
Bibl: ▶Beazley, Attic red-fig. vase-ptrs.

Group of New York 17.120.240 (Apulian vase-painters)   GC
Bibl: Trendall, Attic red-fig. vases Apulia

Group of New York GR 517 (Etruscan vase-painters)   GC
Bibl: Beazley, Etruscan vase-ptrs.

Group of North Slope AP 942 (vase-painters, ca. 565-555 BC)   GC
Bibl: ▶Beazley, Attic bl.-fig. vase-ptrs.; Boardman, Attic Bl.-fig. Vases

Group of Olynthos 5.141   GC
Bibl: ▶Beazley, Attic red-fig. vase-ptrs.

Group of Orvieto 28 (Etruscan, Faliscan vase-painters)   GC
Bibl: Beazley, Etruscan vase-ptrs.

Group of Oxford 1940.74   GC
Bibl: Paralipomena

Group of Oxford 1945.73 (Campanian vase-painters)   GC
Bibl: ▶Trendall, Red-fig. vases Lucania

Group of Oxford 216   GC
Bibl: ▶Beazley, Attic bl.-fig. vase-ptrs.

Group of Oxford 412 (Etruscan vase-painters)   GC
Bibl: Beazley, Etruscan vase-ptrs.

Group of Oxford 570 (Etruscan, Faliscan vase-painters)   GC
Bibl: Beazley, Etruscan vase-ptrs.

Group of Oxford G 269 (Apulian vase-painters)   GC
Bibl: Trendall, Attic red-fig. vases Apulia

Group of Oxford V 460 (Campanian vase-painters)   GC
Bibl: ▶Trendall, Red-fig. vases Lucania

Group of Palermo 16   GC
Bibl: ▶Beazley, Attic red-fig. vase-ptrs.

Group of Philadelphia 2272   GC
Bibl: ▶Beazley, Attic red-fig. vase-ptrs.

Group of Pnyx 37   GC
Bibl: ▶Beazley, Attic red-fig. vase-ptrs.

Group of Polygnotos   GC
Bibl: ▶Beazley, Attic red-fig. vase-ptrs.

Group of Reading 51.7.13 (Apulian vase-painters)   GC
Bibl: Trendall, Attic red-fig. vases Apulia

Group of Rhodes 11941   GC
Bibl: Paralipomena

Group of Rhodes 11966   GC
Bibl: ▶Beazley, Attic red-fig. vase-ptrs.

Group of Rhodes 12264   GC
Bibl: ▶Beazley, Attic bl.-fig. vase-ptrs.

Group of Rhodes 13485   GC
Bibl: ▶Beazley, Attic bl.-fig. vase-ptrs.

Group of Rhodes 6474 (vase-painters, ca. 565-555 BC)   GC
Bibl: ▶Beazley, Attic bl.-fig. vase-ptrs.; Boardman, Attic Bl.-fig. Vases

Group of Rodin 152   GC
Bibl: ▶Beazley, Attic bl.-fig. vase-ptrs.

Group of Ruvo 1401 (Apulian vase-painters)   GC
Bibl: Trendall, Attic red-fig. vases Apulia

Group of Ruvo 423 (Apulian vase-painters)   GC
Bibl: Trendall, Attic red-fig. vases Apulia

Group of Ruvo 730 (Apulian vase-painters)   GC
Bibl: Trendall, Attic red-fig. vases Apulia

Group of Ruvo 892 (Apulian vase-painters)   GC
Bibl: Trendall, Attic red-fig. vases Apulia

Group of Salonica 510   GC
Bibl: ▶Beazley, Attic red-fig. vase-ptrs.

Group of Salonica 93   GC
Bibl: ▶Beazley, Attic red-fig. vase-ptrs.

Group of Syracuse 51288 *(Sicilian vase-painters)*   GC
Bibl: ▶Trendall, Red-fig. vases Lucania

Group of Taranto 7013 *(Apulian vase-painters)*   GC
Bibl: Trendall, Attic red-fig. vases Apulia

Group of Taranto 9243 *(Apulian vase-painters)*   GC
Bibl: Trendall, Attic red-fig. vases Apulia

Group of the Arming Lekythoi *(vase-painters, ca. 575-500 BC)*   GC
Bibl: ▶Beazley, Attic bl.-fig. vase-ptrs.; Boardman, Attic Bl.-fig. Vases

Group of the Athena-Head Pyxides   GC
Bibl: ▶Beazley, Attic red-fig. vase-ptrs.

Group of the Belly Amphorae *(South Italian vase-painters)*   GC
Bibl: Rumpf, Chalkidische Vasen

Group of the Boeotian Dancers *(vase-painters, ca. 585-500 BC)*   GC
Bibl: ▶Beazley, Attic bl.-fig. vase-ptrs.; Boardman, Attic Bl.-fig. Vases, (Komast Group)

Group of the Bonn Amphorae *(South Italian vase-painters)*   GC
Bibl: Rumpf, Chalkidische Vasen

Group of the Bonn Askos   GC
Bibl: ▶Beazley, Attic red-fig. vase-ptrs.

Group of the Cambridge Askos   GC
Bibl: ▶Beazley, Attic red-fig. vase-ptrs.

Group of the Cambridge Hydria *(South Italian vase-painters)*   GC
Bibl: Rumpf, Chalkidische Vasen

Group of the Camiros Palmettes   GC
Bibl: ▶Beazley, Attic bl.-fig. vase-ptrs.

Group of the Cracow Alabastron   GC
Bibl: ▶Beazley, Attic red-fig. vase-ptrs.

Group of the Cracow Peleus   GC
Bibl: Paralipomena

Group of the Dot-Wreath Plates *(Etruscan vase-painters)*   GC
Bibl: Beazley, Etruscan vase-ptrs.

Group of the Dresden Amphora *(Apulian vase-painters)*   GC
Bibl: Trendall, Attic red-fig. vases Apulia

Group of the Dresden Lekanis *(vase-painters, ca. 590-570 BC)*   GC
Bibl: ▶Beazley, Attic bl.-fig. vase-ptrs.; Boardman, Attic Bl.-fig. Vases

Group of the Dublin Situlae *(Apulian vase-painters)*   GC
Bibl: Trendall, Attic red-fig. vases Apulia

Group of the Floral Nolans   GC JG
Bibl: ▶Beazley, Attic red-fig. vase-ptrs.

Group of the Hamburg Askos *(Apulian vase-painters)*   GC
Bibl: Trendall, Attic red-fig. vases Apulia

Group of the Hawk-Jugs   GC
Bibl: ▶Beazley, Attic red-fig. vase-ptrs.

Group of the Huge Lekythoi   GC
Bibl: ▶Beazley, Attic red-fig. vase-ptrs.

Group of the Inscribed Amphorae *(South Italian vase-painters)*   GC
Bibl: Rumpf, Chalkidische Vasen

Group of the Leipzig Amphora *(South Italian vase-painters)*   GC
Bibl: Rumpf, Chalkidische Vasen

Group of the Leyden Kyathos *(Etruscan vase-painters)*   GC
Bibl: Beazley, Etruscan vase-ptrs.

Group of the Louvre Deer-askos *(Etruscan vase-painters)*   GC
Bibl: Beazley, Etruscan vase-ptrs.

Group of the Naples Psykter-Amphora *(vase-painters, ca. 545-530 BC)*   GC
Bibl: ▶Beazley, Attic bl.-fig. vase-ptrs.; Boardman, Attic Bl.-fig. Vases

Group of the Nego Alabastra   GC
Bibl: ▶Beazley, Attic red-fig. vase-ptrs.

Group of the Orvieto Hydria *(South Italian vase-painters)*   GC
Bibl: Rumpf, Chalkidische Vasen

Group of the Oxford Boar-Head *(Apulian vase-painters)*   GC
Bibl: Trendall, Attic red-fig. vases Apulia

Group of the Oxford Lid   GC
Bibl: ▶Beazley, Attic bl.-fig. vase-ptrs.

Group of the Paidikos Alabastra *(vase-painters, ca. 520-500 BC)*   GC
Bibl: ▶Beazley, Attic red-fig. vase-ptrs.; Boardman, Athenian Red-fig. Vases, Archaic Per.

Group of the Perseus Dance   GC
Bibl: ▶Beazley, Attic red-fig. vase-ptrs.

Group of the Rodin Lekanis   GC
Bibl: ▶Beazley, Attic red-fig. vase-ptrs.

Group of the Sotheby Amphorae and Louvre K 74 *(Apulian vase-painters)*   GC
Bibl: Trendall, Attic red-fig. vases Apulia

Group of the Spina Bulls *(Etruscan vase-painters)*   GC
Bibl: Beazley, Etruscan vase-ptrs.

Group of the Spouted Hydriai *(Etruscan vase-painters)*   GC
Bibl: Beazley, Etruscan vase-ptrs.

Group of the St. Louis Pelike *(Apulian vase-painters)*   GC
Bibl: Trendall, Attic red-fig. vases Apulia

Group of the Tarquinia Belly Amphora *(South Italian vase-painters)*   GC
Bibl: Rumpf, Chalkidische Vasen

Group of the Temple Hydria *(Apulian vase-painters)*   GC
Bibl: Trendall, Attic red-fig. vases Apulia

Group of the Thorvaldsen Mastoids   GC
Bibl: ▶Beazley, Attic bl.-fig. vase-ptrs.

Group of the Trieste Askoi (S 444-5) *(Apulian vase-painters)*   GC
Bibl: Trendall, Attic red-fig. vases Apulia

Group of the Vienna Amphora *(South Italian vase-painters)*   GC
Bibl: Rumpf, Chalkidische Vasen

Group of the Vienna Lekanis   GC
Bibl: ▶Beazley, Attic red-fig. vase-ptrs.

Group of the Vine Phialai *(Etruscan vase-painters)*   GC
Bibl: Beazley, Etruscan vase-ptrs.

Group of the White Horses   JG

Group of the Yale Pelike *(Apulian vase-painters)*   GC
Bibl: Trendall, Attic red-fig. vases Apulia

Group of Thebes R. 102   GC
Bibl: ▶Beazley, Attic bl.-fig. vase-ptrs.

Group of Thorvaldsen 119   GC
Bibl: ▶Beazley, Attic red-fig. vase-ptrs.

Group of Todi 515 *(Etruscan vase-painters)*   GC
Bibl: Beazley, Etruscan vase-ptrs.

Group of Toronto 289   GC
Bibl: ▶Beazley, Attic bl.-fig. vase-ptrs.

Group of Toronto 305 *(vase-painters, ca. 530-510 BC)*   GC
Bibl: ▶Beazley, Attic bl.-fig. vase-ptrs.; Boardman, Attic Bl.-fig. Vases

Group of Toronto 387 *(South Italian vase-painters, 4th century BC)*   GC
Bibl: ▶Trendall, Red-fig. vases Lucania

Group of Toronto 495 *(Etruscan vase-painters)*   GC
Bibl: Beazley, Etruscan vase-ptrs.

Group of Toronto 564 *(Etruscan vase-painters)*   GC
Bibl: Beazley, Etruscan vase-ptrs.

Group of Toronto 573 *(Etruscan vase-painters)*   GC
Bibl: Beazley, Etruscan vase-ptrs.

Group of Trieste S 427 *(Apulian vase-painters)*   GC
Bibl: Trendall, Attic red-fig. vases Apulia

Group of Tübingen D 41   GC
Bibl: ▶Beazley, Attic bl.-fig. vase-ptrs.

Group of Vatican 127 (*Etruscan potter*)   GC
Bibl: ▶Szilagyi, Etruszko-korinthosi

Group of Vatican 246 (*Etruscan vase-painters*)   GC
Bibl: Beazley, Etruscan vase-ptrs.

Group of Vatican 347   GC
Bibl: ▶Beazley, Attic bl.-fig. vase-ptrs.

Group of Vatican 424 (*vase-painters, ca. 520-500 BC*)   GC
Bibl: ▶Beazley, Attic bl.-fig. vase-ptrs.; Boardman, Attic Bl.-fig. Vases, (Leagros Group)

Group of Vatican 480 (*Attic black-figure painter*)   JG

Group of Vatican G. 23   GC
Bibl: ▶Beazley, Attic bl.-fig. vase-ptrs.

Group of Vatican G. 30 (*vase-painters, ca. 500-475 BC*)   GC
Bibl: ▶Beazley, Attic bl.-fig. vase-ptrs.; Boardman, Attic Bl.-fig. Vases

Group of Vatican G. 48   GC
Bibl: ▶Beazley, Attic bl.-fig. vase-ptrs.

Group of Vatican G. 52   GC
Bibl: ▶Beazley, Attic bl.-fig. vase-ptrs.

Group of Vatican G. 57   GC
Bibl: ▶Beazley, Attic bl.-fig. vase-ptrs.

Group of Vatican G. 58 (*vase-painters, ca. 510-500 BC*)   GC
Bibl: ▶Beazley, Attic bl.-fig. vase-ptrs.; Boardman, Attic Bl.-fig. Vases

Group of Vatican G. 66   GC
Bibl: ▶Beazley, Attic bl.-fig. vase-ptrs.

Group of Vatican G.61   GC
Bibl: Paralipomena

Group of Vatican G113 (*Etruscan vase-painters*)   GC
Bibl: Beazley, Etruscan vase-ptrs.

Group of Vatican G116 (*Etruscan vase-painters*)   GC
Bibl: Beazley, Etruscan vase-ptrs.

Group of Vatican G119 (*Etruscan vase-painters*)   GC
Bibl: Beazley, Etruscan vase-ptrs.

Group of Vatican U 46-47 (*Campanian vase-painters*)   GC
Bibl: ▶Trendall, Red-fig. vases Lucania

Group of Vatican V 21 (*Apulian vase-painters*)   GC
Bibl: Trendall, Attic red-fig. vases Apulia

Group of Vatican V 5 (*Apulian vase-painters*)   GC
Bibl: Trendall, Attic red-fig. vases Apulia

Group of Vatican W 4 (*Apulian vase-painters*)   GC
Bibl: Trendall, Attic red-fig. vases Apulia

Group of Vatican X 5   GC
Bibl: ▶Beazley, Attic red-fig. vase-ptrs.

Group of Vatican Y 14 (*Apulian vase-painters*)   GC
Bibl: Trendall, Attic red-fig. vases Apulia

Group of Vatican Z 16 (*Apulian vase-painters*)   GC
Bibl: Trendall, Attic red-fig. vases Apulia

Group of Vienna 1025   GC
Bibl: ▶Beazley, Attic red-fig. vase-ptrs.

Group of Vienna 1104   GC
Bibl: ▶Beazley, Attic red-fig. vase-ptrs.

Group of Vienna 116 (*vase-painters, ca. 400-366 BC*)   GC
Bibl: ▶Beazley, Attic red-fig. vase-ptrs.; Richter, Attic red-fig. vases

Group of Vienna 4013 (*Apulian vase-painters*)   GC
Bibl: Trendall, Attic red-fig. vases Apulia

Group of Vienna 888   GC
Bibl: ▶Beazley, Attic red-fig. vase-ptrs.

Group of Vienna 943   GC
Bibl: ▶Beazley, Attic red-fig. vase-ptrs.

Group of Vienna O. 565 (*Etruscan vase-painters*)   GC
Bibl: Beazley, Etruscan vase-ptrs.

Group of Villa Giulia 1607 (*Etruscan, Faliscan vase-painters*)   GC
Bibl: Beazley, Etruscan vase-ptrs.

Group of Villa Giulia 1664 (*Etruscan, Faliscan vase-painters*)   GC
Bibl: Beazley, Etruscan vase-ptrs.

Group of Villa Giulia 2303 (*Etruscan vase-painters*)   GC
Bibl: Beazley, Etruscan vase-ptrs.

Group of Villa Giulia 3559   GC
Bibl: ▶Beazley, Attic bl.-fig. vase-ptrs.

Group of Villa Giulia 3597 (*Etruscan, Faliscan vase-painters*)   GC
Bibl: Beazley, Etruscan vase-ptrs.

Group of Walters 48.42 (*vase-painters, ca. 520-500 BC*)   GC
Bibl: ▶Beazley, Attic bl.-fig. vase-ptrs.; Boardman, Attic Bl.-fig. Vases

Group of Warsaw 147188 (*Campanian vase-painters*)   GC
Bibl: ▶Trendall, Red-fig. vases Lucania

Group of Washington 136389   GC
Bibl: ▶Beazley, Attic red-fig. vase-ptrs.

Group of Würzburg 179 (*vase-painters, ca. 530-510 BC*)   GC
Bibl: ▶Beazley, Attic bl.-fig. vase-ptrs.; Boardman, Attic Bl.-fig. Vases

Group of Würzburg 199 (*vase-painters, ca. 530-510 BC*)   GC
Bibl: ▶Beazley, Attic bl.-fig. vase-ptrs.; Boardman, Attic Bl.-fig. Vases

Group of Würzburg 210 (*vase-painters, ca. 520-500 BC*)   GC
Bibl: ▶Beazley, Attic bl.-fig. vase-ptrs.; Boardman, Attic Bl.-fig. Vases, (Leagros Group)

Group of Würzburg 221   GC JG
(*Attic black-figure painter*)   JG
(*vase-painters, ca. 480-450 BC*)   GC
Bibl: ▶Beazley, Attic bl.-fig. vase-ptrs.

Group of Würzburg 461   GC
Bibl: ▶Beazley, Attic bl.-fig. vase-ptrs.

Group of Würzburg 577   GC
Bibl: ▶Beazley, Attic red-fig. vase-ptrs.

Group of Würzburg G 230   GC
Bibl: Paralipomena

Group of Zurich 2659 (*Apulian vase-painters*)   GC
Bibl: Trendall, Attic red-fig. vases Apulia

Group R   GC
Bibl: ▶Beazley, Attic red-fig. vase-ptrs.

Group Recalling the Painter of London E 342 or the Ethiop Painter   GC
Bibl: Beazley Addenda

Group YZ   GC
Bibl: ▶Beazley, Attic red-fig. vase-ptrs.

Grouse→see Greuze, Jean Baptiste

Grout→see Grout, John H.

Grout, John H. (*American painter, act. 1833*)   PR
Bibl: ▶Young, Amer. artists
Grout   PR
John H. Grout   PR

Groux, Charles Corneille Auguste de   BA WC
(*Belgian artist, 1825-1870*)   WC
(*Belgian painter, printmaker, 1825-1870*)   BA
Bibl: ▶Bénézit; ▶Thieme-Becker

Groux, Charles de (*French artist, 18th cent.*)   WC

Groux, Henri de   BA
(*Belgian artist, 1867-1930*)   WC
(*Belgian draughtsman, 1867-1930*)   GC
(*Belgian painter, sculptor, printmaker, 1867-1930*)   BA
Bibl: ▶Bénézit; ▶Thieme-Becker

Groux, Henry Jules Charles Corneille de   GC WC

Groux, Henry Jules Charles Corneille de→see Groux, Henri de

Grove, J. (*British artist, op.1789-1805*)   WC WI

Grove, Nordahl (*Danish artist, 1822-1885*)   WC

Grover, Kit (American painter, 20th c.) **BA**
Bibl: O'Beil, H., in ARTS MAG LIX/10 (summer 1985) 20

Grover, Oliver Dennett **WC WI**
(American artist, 1861-) WC
(American artist, 1861-1927) WI

Grover, Satish (Indian architect) **AV**
Bibl: Mimar, 1981 Oct.-Dec., no.2, p.21

Grover, William **AV**

Groves, Alan Joseph (English architect) **AV**
Bibl: ▶RIBA members, 1984

Groves, Robert E. (British artist, op. 1887-, d.circa 1944) **WI**

Growald, Martin C. (Principal of Growald Associates, Fort Worth, TX) **AV**
Bibl: ▶AIA Pro File, 1983

Groz, Walther (German, 20th c.) **BA**

Groze, Jan de la (early Netherlandish tapestry designer, act.1575-1583) **BA**
Bibl: Festsch. S. Müller-Christensen

Grozer, Joseph **WC WI**
(British artist, circa 1755-op. 1799) WI
(British artist, op.1784-1797) WC

Gru or Grue, Giuseppe le (Italian artist, c.1715-1775(?)) **WC**

Gruau, René (French printmaker, b.1910) **BA**
Bibl: Bure, GRUAU (1989); ▶Castagno, Artists illustrators; ▶WW France, 1990; ▶WW Graphic Art, v.2

Grub, Horst (West German architect, Zweibrücken) **AV**
Bibl: Deutsches Architektenblatt, 1988 Mar., v.20, no.3, p.341

Grubacs, Carlo **GC WC**
(German painter, act. ca.1840-1870) GC
(Italian artist, op.c.1840-1870) WC
Bibl: ▶Bénézit

Grubacs, Giovanni (Italian artist, -1919) **WC**

Grube, Georg Ernst (German artist, op.1694-1701) **WC**

Grube, Joachim C. (West German architect) **AV**
Bibl: Architektur + Wettbewerbe, 1987 Sept., no.131, p.13

Grubenmann, Johannes (Swiss engineer, b.1707, act.1758) **BA**
Bibl: ▶Schweiz. Künst.-Lex.; ▶Thieme-Becker

Grubenmann, Ulrich **AV BA**
(Swiss architect and engineer, 1709-1783) AV
(Swiss architect, 1709-1783) BA
Bibl: ▶Portoghesi, Diz. arch. e urbanistica; ▶Schweiz. Künst.-Lex., suppl.; ▶Thieme-Becker; Widmer, Fünf Schweizer Brückenbauer (1985)

Gruber or Grueber, Johann Friedrich (German artist, op.1662-m.1681) **WC**

Gruber, Aaronel de Roy (American sculptor, painter, 20th c.) **BA**
Bibl: Arts Mag. LI (Jan 1977), p.69; ▶MoMA libr. cat.; ▶WW Amer. Art, 1976

Gruber, Augustin (Czech porcelain painter, b.1773, act.1820) **BA**
Bibl: Nejdl, Umění, XXX/4 (1982) pp.370-371

Gruber, Francis **BA GC WC**
(French artist, 1912-1948) WC
(French painter, 1912-1948) BA GC
Bibl: ▶Bénézit; ▶Vollmer, Künst.-Lex. 20. Jhr.

Gruber, Franz Xaver **GC WC**
(Austrian painter, 1801-1862) GC
(German artist, 1801-1862) WC
Bibl: ▶Bénézit

Gruber, Harald (German painter, b.1950) **BA**
Bibl: Kunstwerk, XXXIII/6 (1980) pp.3-38

Gruber, Hetum (West German artist, b.1937) **BA**
Bibl: ▶DuMonts Künst.-Lex.

Gruber, Jacques (French painter, designer, craftsman, 1870-1936) **BA**
Bibl: Champigneule, L'Art Nouveau; Chicago(IL,USA), ART NOUVEAU, BELGIUM, FRANCE(1976); ▶Thieme-Becker; ▶Vollmer, Künst.-Lex. 20. Jhr.; Waddell, ART NOUVEAU STYLE

Gruber, Jan Pavel (Czech porcelain painter, d.1816) **BA**
Bibl: Nejdl, Umění, XXX/4 (1982) pp.370-371

Gruber, Karl (German city planner and writer, 1885-1966) **AV**
Bibl: Bauwelt, 1984 Dec.28, v.75, no.48, p.418; ▶Libr. of Congr. Name Auth. File

Gruber, Leopold (Czech porcelain painter, d.1826) **BA**
Bibl: Nejdl, Umění, XXX/4 (1982) pp.370-371

Gruber, T. (French architect) **AV**
Bibl: Techniques et architecture, 1986 Oct.-Nov., v.368, p.17

Gruber, Terry de Ray (American, contemporary) **JG**

Gruber, Ziva S. (Design consultant, New York) **AV**
Bibl: Interior design, LV/9 (Sep. 1984) p.225

Grubhofer, Tony (German artist, 1854-1935) **WC**

Grubicy de Dragon, Vittore **BA WC**
(Italian artist, 1851-1920) WC
(Italian painter, critic, 1851-1920) BA
Bibl: ▶Bolaffi; ▶Encic. italiana; ▶Thieme-Becker; ▶Witt checklist

Grubin, D.B. (German artist, 20th cent.) **WC**

Gruce→see Greuze, Jean Baptiste

Gruchot, Heinz (West German painter, b.1918) **BA**
Bibl: Guide exh. artists: N. Amer. ptrs.; ▶Intl. dir. exh. artists, 1983; ▶WW Arts DEU

Gruden, France (Yugoslav painter, b.1952) **BA**
Bibl: ▶Intl. dir. exh. artists, 1981

Grudmann (German artist, 19th cent.) **WC**

Grue family (Italian ceramists, 16th-18th cs.) **BA**
Bibl: ▶Honey, Euro. ceramic; ▶Thieme-Becker

Grue, Carlo Antonio (Italian pottery painter, 1655-1723) **BA**
Bibl: ▶Bénézit; ▶Bolaffi; ▶Penguin dec. arts; ▶Thieme-Becker

Grue, Francesco Antonio I di Giovanni (Italian artist, 1594-c. 1680) **WC**

Grue, Francesco Antonio II Saverio (Italian porcelain painter, printmaker, 1686-1746) **BA**

Grue, Francesco Saverio **BA**
(Italian painter, 1720-1755) BA
(Italian, 1731-1799) JG
Bibl: ▶Bénézit; ▶Honey, Euro. ceramic; ▶Thieme-Becker

Grue, Francesco Saverio II Maria **JG**
Grue, Francesco Saverio II Maria→see Grue, Francesco Saverio

Grue, Giovanni II (Italian ceramist, 1698-1752) **BA**
Bibl: Uggeri, Itinerari contributi alla storia dell'arte..., I, 157-162

Grueby, William H. (American potter, 1867-1925) **BA**
Bibl: ▶Boger, World pott. & porc.; ▶Penguin dec. arts

Gruelle, Richard B. →see Gruelle, Richard Buckner

Gruelle, Richard Buckner **BA WC**
(American artist, 1851-1914) WC WI
(American painter, 1851-1914) BA
Bibl: ▶Fielding's Amer. ptrs.; Indianapolis, John Herron Art Inst. (cat 1942); ▶Natl. union cat., pre-1956; ▶WWW Amer. art

Gruelle, Richard B. **WI**

Gruembroech, Gruenbroeck or Gruenbroek, Johann (German(?) artist, op.1757) **WC**

Gruembroech, Johann   **GC PR**
  (German painter, act. ca.1680)   PR
  (German, act. ca.1680)   GC
    Bibl: Safarik spells the name:
    GREVENBROECK; ▶Thieme-Becker;
    ▶Witt checklist
  Johann Gruembroech   PR
  Monsu' Solfarolo   PR
  Solfaroli   PR
Gruen, Victor (American architect,
  1903-1980)   **AV**
    Bibl: ▶Libr. of Congr. Name Auth.
    File
Gruffydd, Pegi (British artist, op.
  1985-)   **WI**
Gruft, Andrew (Canadian architect) **AV**
    Bibl: Section a, v.2, no.1, p.24
Gruger, Frederic Rodrigo   **BA**
  (American artist, 1871-1953)   WI
  (American illustrator, 1871-
    1953)   BA
    Bibl: ▶Fielding's Amer. ptrs.; NYT
    Obit 1858-1968; WWEA, V;
    ▶Young, Amer. artists
  Gruger, Frederick Rodrigo   **WI**
Gruger, Frederick Rodrigo → see
  Gruger, Frederic Rodrigo
Gruijter or Gruyter, Willem → see
  Gruyter Jr., Willem
Grumbach, Antoine   **AV BA**
  (French architect, b.1942)   BA
  (French archtect, 1942-)   AV
    Bibl: ▶Avery period. idx.; Culot,
    Mons. Hist. France, 133 (Jun.-Jul.
    1984) pp.97-101
Grumeaux (French(?) artist, 19th
  cent.)   **WC**
Grummer, Hansjurgen (German
  artist, 20th cent.)   **WC**
Grün, Ingo (German planner,
  Ratingen)   **AV**
    Bibl: Detail, 1982 Nov.-Dec., no.6,
    p.662
Grün, Jules Alexandre   **BA WC**
  (French artist, 1869-)   WC
  (French painter, printmaker,
    illustrator, 1868-1934)   BA
    Bibl: ▶Busse, Maler u. Bildhauer
    19. Jahr.; ▶MoMA libr. cat.; ▶Petit
    Larousse; ▶Thieme-Becker; ▶Witt
    checklist
Grün, Mathis → see Grünewald,
  Matthias
Grun, Maurice (French painter,
  b.1869)   **GC**
    Bibl: ▶Bénézit
Grunbaum (Netherlands(?) artist,
  18th cent.)   **WC**
Grunbaum, Laurent (German artist,
  c.1760-p.1830)   **WC**
Grünberger, Arno (Austrian
  architect, Vienna)   **AV**
    Bibl: Bauwelt, 1989 Jan.20, v.80,
    no.4, p.134
Grünberger, Friedrich Florian
  (Austrian architect, Vienna)   **AV**
    Bibl: ▶Verzeich. Öst. Ziviltech.

Grünberger, Robert (Danish
  architect, 1944-)   **AV**
    Bibl: Das Kunstwerk, n.3-4, Sept.
    1983, p.100
Grund → see Grund, Norbert Joseph
  Carl
Grund, Detlef (East German
  architect, Rostock)   **AV**
    Bibl: Architektur der DDR, 1987
    Dec., v.36, no.12, p.18
Grund, I. (East German architect,
  Berlin)   **AV**
    Bibl: Architektur der DDR, 1989
    Jan., v.38, no.1, p.18
Grund, Johann   **GC WC**
  (Austrian draughtsman, 1808-
    1887)   GC
  (German artist, 1808-1887)   WC
    Bibl: ▶Bénézit; Getty Photo Study
    Coll.; ▶Thieme-Becker
Grund, Johann Gottfried (German
  sculptor in DNK, 1733-1796)   **BA**
    Bibl: ▶Thieme-Becker; ▶Weilbach,
    Kunst.leks.
Grund, Johann Jacob Norbert
  (German painter, 1755-1812)   **GC**
    Bibl: ▶Thieme-Becker
**Grund, Norbert Joseph
  Carl**   **BA GC PR WC**
  (Bohemian painter, 1717-1767)   BA
  (Czech painter, 1717-1767)   GC
  (German artist, 1717-1767)   WC
  (German painter, 1717-1767)   PR
    Bibl: Getty Photo Study Coll.;
    ▶Neue deutsche Biog.;
    ▶Thieme-Becker; ▶Witt checklist
  Grund   PR
  N. Grund   PR
  Norbert Joseph Carl Grund   PR
Grunder, Mariann (Swiss sculptor,
  b.1926)   **BA**
    Bibl: ▶Intl. dir. exh. artists, 1982;
    ▶Künst.-Lex. Schweiz 20. Jahrh.;
    ▶Lex. zeitgen. Schweiz. Künstler
Grundig, Hans   **BA WC**
  (German artist, 1901-1958)   WC
  (German painter, printmaker,
    1901-1958)   BA
    Bibl: ▶Kindlers Malerei Lex.;
    ▶Vollmer, Künst.-Lex. 20. Jhr.
Grundig-Langer, Lea   **BA WC**
  (German artist, 1906-)   WC
  (German painter, printmaker,
    b.1906)   BA
    Bibl: ▶Bénézit; ▶Fogg Mus. Libr.
    cat.; ▶Kindlers Malerei Lex.;
    ▶Vollmer, Künst.-Lex. 20. Jhr.
Grundmann → see Grundmann, Emil
  Otto
Grundmann, Basilius   **GC WC**
  (German artist, 1726-1798)   WC
  (German, 1726-1798)   GC
    Bibl: ▶Thieme-Becker; ▶Witt
    checklist

Grundmann, Emil Otto (German
  painter, 1844-1890)   **PR**
    Bibl: ▶Thieme-Becker
  Emil Otto Grundmann   PR
  Grundmann   PR
Grundmann, Friedhelm (German
  architect, Hamburg)   **AV**
    Bibl: BDA Mitglieder 1960
Grundy, Cuthbert Cartwright, Sir
  (British artist, 1846-1946)   **WI**
    Bibl: Paviere, Landscape
Grundy, Robert Hindmarsh (British
  artist, 1816-1865)   **WC WI**
Grune, Johann Samuel Benedictus
  (German artist, c.1782-1848)   **WC**
Grune, Mathis (German painter,
  d.1532)   **BA**
    Bibl: ▶Neue deutsche Biog.;
    PANTHEON, XXXV/3(JULY-SEPT
    1977), 188-197; ▶Thieme-Becker
Grunenwaid, Jakob (German artist,
  1822-1896)   **WC**
Gruner, Elioth   **GC WC**
  (Australian artist, 1882-1939)   WC
  (British, 1882-1939)   GC
    Bibl: ▶Witt checklist
Grüner, Ludwig → see Gruner,
  Wilhelm Heinrich Ludwig
Gruner, Vincenz Raimund (Czech
  artist, 1771-1832)   **WC**
**Gruner, Wilhelm Heinrich
  Ludwig**   **BA WC**
  (German artist, 1801-1882)   WC
  (German designer/author, 1801-
    1882)   AV
  (German printmaker, 1801-
    1882)   BA
    Bibl: Country life, 1986 Dec.4,
    v.180, no.4659, p.1762; ▶Engen,
    Victorian engravers;
    ▶Thieme-Becker
  Grüner, Ludwig   **AV**
Grünewald → see Grünewald,
  Matthias
Grunewald, Isaac (Swedish artist,
  1889-1946)   **WC**
Grunewald, Mathis → see Grünewald,
  Matthias

Grünewald, Matthias   BA GC PR
  (German artist, 1470/80-c.1530) WC
  (German painter and
    draughtsman, 1475/80-1528) GC
  (German painter, ca.1480-1528) BA PR
    Bibl: ▶Encyc. world art; Lucking,
    MATHIS, NACHFORSCHUNGER
    UKER GRUNEWALD(1983);
    Munich, Alte Pinakothek, (1983);
    ▶Neue deutsche Biog.; Pevsner,
    MATTHIAS GRUNEWALD;
    ▶RILA/BHA; ▶Thieme-Becker;
    ▶Witt checklist
  Gothart-Nithart, Mathis   BA
  Grün, Mathis   BA
  Grünewald   PR
  Grunewald, Mathis   PR
Grunewald, Matthias, Mathis,
  Matthaeus or Mathes
  (Neithardt, Nithardt or
  Gothardt) (Monogrammist
  M.G.N. or M.N.)   WC
  Mathis of Aschaffenburg   BA
  Matthias Grunewald   PR
  Neithardt, Mathis Gothardt   BA
  Nithart, Mathis Gothart   BA
  Grunewald, Matthias, Mathis,
  Matthaeus or Mathes (Neithardt,
  Nithardt or Gothardt)
  (Monogrammist M.G.N. or
  M.N.)→see Grünewald, Matthias
  Grünewald, Pseudo→see
  Aschaffenburg, Simon von
Grünfeld, Thomas *(German*
  sculptor, b.1955)   BA
    Bibl: ▶Art Index, v.36; Beyer, Flash
    art, 133 (Apr. 1987) p.97
Grunier, de [Unidentified]
  (Unknown painter)   PR
    Bibl: (June 27, 1807, lot 39, Coxe
    (Peter))
  De Grunier   PR
  Gruniger, Gerdt→see Gröninger,
  Gerhard
  Gruniger, Gerhard→see Gröninger,
  Gerhard
  Gruniger, Heinrich→see Gröninger,
  Heinrich
  Gruniger, Johann Wilhelm→see
  Gröninger, Johann Wilhelm
  Gruninger, Gerdt→see Gröninger,
  Gerhard
  Gruninger, Gerhard→see Gröninger,
  Gerhard
  Gruninger, Heinrich→see Gröninger,
  Heinrich
  Gruninger, Johann Wilhelm→see
  Gröninger, Johann Wilhelm
Grunler, Ehregott (Heinrich
  Ehregott) *(German artist, 1797-*
  1881)   WC
  Grunninger, Gerdt→see Gröninger,
  Gerhard
  Grunninger, Gerhard→see Gröninger,
  Gerhard

  Grunninger, Heinrich→see Gröninger,
  Heinrich
  Grunninger, Johann Wilhelm→see
  Gröninger, Johann Wilhelm
Grunsfeld, Ernest Alton, Jr.
  (American architect, worked
  mostly in Illinois; do not confuse
  with Ernest Alton Grunsfeld III,
  1897-)   AV
    Bibl: Historic Illinois, 1986 June,
    v.9, no.1, p.12
Grunt, Jaroslav *(Czechoslovak*
  architect)   AV
    Bibl: AMC, 1985 Mar., no.7, p.52
  Grunwaid, Bela Ivanyi→see
  Iványi-Grünwald, Béla
Grunwald, Carl *(German artist,*
  1907-)   WC
  Gruoppoli→see Ruoppolo, Giovanni
  Battista
  Grupello, Gabriel→see Grupello,
  Gabriel de
Grupello, Gabriel de   BA
  (Flemish artist, 1644-1730) WC
  (Flemish sculptor, 1644-1730) BA GC
    Bibl: ▶Bénézit; ▶Brockhaus Enzyk.;
    ▶Grote Winkler Prins; ▶RILA/BHA;
    ▶Thieme-Becker; ▶Wurzbach, NLD
    Künst.-Lex.
Grupello, Gabriel   GC WC
  Gruppe→see Gruppe, Charles Paul
Gruppe, Charles Paul   BA PR WC WI
  (American artist, 1860-1940) WC WI
  (American painter, 1860-1940) BA PR
    Bibl: ▶RILA/BHA
  Charles Paul Gruppe   PR
  Gruppe   PR
  Gruppe, Emile A.→see Gruppe, Emile-
  Albert
  Gruppe, Emile Albert→see Gruppe,
  Emile-Albert
Gruppe, Emile-Albert   WI
  (American artist, 1896-1978) WI
  (American painter, b. 1896) PR
    Bibl: ▶WWW Amer. art
  Emile Albert Gruppe   PR
  Gruppe, Emile A.   PR
Gruppe, Emile Albert   PR
  Gruppe, Karl→see Gruppe, Karl
  Heinrich
Gruppe, Karl Heinrich *(American*
  sculptor, 1893-1982)   GC
    Bibl: Getty Photo Study Coll.;
    ▶Opitz, Amer. sculptors
  Gruppe, Karl   GC
Gruppo *(Italian artist, 20th cent.)* WC
Grus, Josef *(Czech architect, 20th*
  c.)   BA
    Bibl: Svácha, Umêní, XXVIII/4
    (1980) pp.368-379
Grusdin, Artemij Michailovltsch
  (Russian artist, 1825-1891)   WC
Gruson, François *(French architect,*
  Paris)   AV
    Bibl: Architecture d'aujourd'hui,
    1988 Oct., no.259, p.084

Gruson, Johann David *(German*
  artist, 1780-1848)   WC
Grusovin, Maria Teresa *(Italian*
  architect)   AV
    Bibl: Parametro, 1985 Apr.-May,
    no.135-136, p.74
Gruss, Agneta *(Swedish-American*
  interior designer)   AV
    Bibl: House beautiful, 1988 July,
    v.130, no.7, p.35
Gruss, Julius Theodor *(Czech artist,*
  1825-1865)   WC
Gruss, Walter *(Austrian architect)*   AV
    Bibl: 9H, 1985, no.7, p.40
Gruszczyński, Włodzimierz *(Polish*
  architect and professor, Cracow,
  Poland, 1906-1973)   AV
    Bibl: Polska Akademia Nauk.
    Komisja Urbanistyki i
    Architektury. Teka, 1984, v.18,
    p.170
Grut, L. *(French architect)*   AV
    Bibl: AMC, 1988 Feb., no.10, p.2
Grutter, Pierre *(French architect)*   AV
    Bibl: Architect & builder, 1985
    July, p.30
Gruttner, Erhard *(German artist,*
  20th cent.)   WC
Grüttner, Rudolf   BA WC
  (German artist, 20th cent.) WC
  (German printmaker, b.1933) BA
    Bibl: Gassner, KUTTER UND KUNST
    IN DER DDR SEIT(1970), p.229
Grützke, Johannes *(German painter,*
  b.1937)   BA
    Bibl: Jahrb. Hamburger
    Kunstsamm., XIX (1974) pp.117-
    122
  Grutzner, Eduard→see Grützner,
  Eduard von
Grützner, Eduard von   BA GC
  (German artist, 1846-1925) WC
  (German painter, 1846-1925) BA GC
    Bibl: ▶Bénézit; ▶Vollmer,
    Künst.-Lex. 20. Jhr.
Grutzner, Eduard   WC
Gruyère, Théodore Charles *(French*
  sculptor, 1814-1885)   BA
    Bibl: ▶Bénézit; ▶Thieme-Becker
Gruygutis, Barbara *(American*
  sculptor, ceramist, b.1946)   BA
    Bibl: Guide exh. artists: N. Amer.
    ptrs.; ▶WW Amer. Art
Gruyter Jr., Willem   GC
  (Dutch artist, 1817-1880) WC
  (Dutch painter, 1817-1880) GC
    Bibl: ▶Bénézit
Gruijter or Gruyter, Willem   WC
Gruyter, E. de   GC WC
  (Dutch artist, 17th cent.) WC
  (Dutch, 17th century) GC
    Bibl: ▶Thieme-Becker; ▶Witt
    checklist

Gruyter, Jacob de GC WC
(Dutch artist, op.1655-m.1681) WC
(Dutch painter, act. ca.1655-d.
1681) GC
Bibl: ▶Thieme-Becker
Gruyter, Jacob Willem (Dutch
painter, 1856-1908) GC
Bibl: ▶Scheen, Ned. beeldende
kunst.
Gruze → see Greuze, Jean Baptiste
Gruzen, Barnett Sumner (American
architect, 1903-1974) AV
Bibl: ▶Contemp. archts.
Gruzen, Jordan L. AV
Gryef → see Gryef, Adriaen de
Gryef, Adriaen de GC PR
(Flemish artist, op.1687-m.
1715) WC
(Flemish painter, act. 1687, d.
1715) PR
(Flemish, act.1687-d.1715) GC
Bibl: ▶Thieme-Becker; ▶Witt
checklist
A. Griff PR
A. Gryef PR
Adriaan Grijs PR
Adriaen de Gryef PR
Graeff PR
Greef PR
Greffs PR
Grief PR
Grieff PR
Griep PR
Griff PR
Griff. PR
Griffe PR
Grijst PR
Gryef PR
**Gryef, Grief(f), Grif, Gryeff or
Gryf(f), Adriaen de** WC
Gryeff PR
Gryffe PR
R. Gryef PR
Gryef, Grief(f), Grif, Gryeff or
Gryf(f), Adriaen de → see Gryef,
Adriaen de
Gryeff → see Gryef, Adriaen de
Gryffe → see Gryef, Adriaen de
Grygar, Milan (Czech artist, 20th
cent.) WC
Gryglewski, Alexander (Polish
artist, 1833-1879) WC
Grylls, Vaughan (British
photographer, b.1943) BA
Bibl: ▶Intl. dir. exh. artists; ▶Parry,
Photo idx.
Grym, Jacob (German sculptor in
Lithuania, b.1709) BA
Bibl: Biuletyn Historii Sztuki,
XXXVI/2 (1974) pp.158-168
Grymbault, Paoul (French artist,
15th cent.) WC
Gryphe, Sébastien (French printer,
1493-1556) BA
Bibl: ▶Larousse grande encyc.;
▶Larousse, Grand dict. 19e s.

Grzimek, Waldemar (German
sculptor, b.1918) BA
Bibl: ▶Fogg Mus. Libr. cat.; ▶Wer
ist wer
Grzybcwski, Ryszard Kuba (Polish
artist, 20th cent.) WC
Gsell, Dorothea Maria Henrietta GC
(German artist, 1678-1743) WC
(German painter, 1678-1743) GC
Bibl: ▶Bénézit; ▶Thieme-Becker
Graff, Dorothea Maria Henrietta GC
**Gsell, Gesell, Ksell, Xell, etc.
Dorothea Maria Henrietta,
(nee Graff)** WC
Gsell, Gesell, Ksell, Xell, etc.
Dorothea Maria Henrietta, (nee
Graff) → see Gsell, Dorothea Maria
Henrietta
**Gsell, Gesell, Ksell, Xell, etc.
Georg** (Swiss artist, 1673-1740) WC
Gsell, Johann Julius Kaspar
(Swiss glass painter, designer,
1814-1904) BA
Bibl: ▶Bénézit; ▶Schweiz.
Künst.-Lex.; ▶Thieme-Becker
Gsöllpointner, Helmut (Austrian
sculptor, 20th c.) BA
Bibl: Maar, Kunstjahrb. Stadt Linz,
(1984) p.102
Gstrein, Alois (Swiss architect,
1869-1945) AV
Bibl: Unsere Kunstdenkmäler,
1989, no.1, p.3
Gsur, Karl Friedrich (German artist,
1871-) WC
Guacci, Antonio AV BA
(Italian architect) AV
(Italian architect, 20th c.) BA
Bibl: ▶Avery period. idx.;
Parametro, 1985 Apr.-May, no.
135-136, p.56; Walcher,
TRIESTE:EDIZIONI 'ITALO
SVEVO'(1977)
Guaccimanni, Vittorio (Italian artist,
1859-1938) WC
Guada → see Guardi, Francesco
Guadagni, Fortunata [Unidentified]
(Unknown painter, act. 18th
century) PR
Bibl: Riccardi inventory dated
1776
Fortunata Guadagni PR
Guadagni, Violante [Unidentified]
(Unknown painter, act. 18th
century) PR
Bibl: Riccardi inventory dated
1776
Violante Guadagni PR
Guadagnino → see Zoan Andrea
Guadal → see Quadal, Martin
Ferdinand
Guadalupe, Pedro de (Spanish
sculptor, ca.1470-before 1531) BA
Bibl: ▶Ceán Bermúdez, Bellas artes
ESP; ▶Thieme-Becker
Guadel → see Quadal, Martin
Ferdinand

Guadet, Julien AV BA
(French architect and
theoretician, 1834-1908) AV
(French architect, 1834-1908) BA
Bibl: ▶Avery Libr. cat.; ▶Macmillan
encyc. archts.; ▶Thieme-Becker
Guagnini, Marchese → see Scapitta,
Giacomo Bernardino
Guaita, Maria Luigia (Italian
printmaker, 20th c.) BA
Bibl: IL BISONTE (1987)
Guaitoli, Alfio (Italian architect) AV
Bibl: Domus, 1985 Mar., no.659,
p.20
Gual, Adrian (Spanish artist, 19th
cent.) WC
Guala or Gualla, Pier Francesco → see
Guala, Pier Francesco
Guala, Pier Francesco BA GC
(Italian artist, 1698-1760) WC
(Italian painter, 1698-1757) BA GC
Bibl: ▶Bolaffi; Martinotti, P.F.
GUALA; ▶RILA/BHA, 1986;
▶Thieme-Becker; ▶Wittkower, Art
& arch. Italy, p.400
Guala or Gualla, Pier Francesco WC
Gualla, Pietro GC
Gualdi, Antonio WC WI
(American artist, op.1847) WC
(American artist, op.1847-) WI
Gualdi, Pietro BA WC
(Italian artist, 1716-) WC
(Italian painter, b.1716) BA
Bibl: ▶Bénézit; ▶Bolaffi;
▶Thieme-Becker
Gualdini, Angelo (Sculptor, post
1500/ante 1580-post 1600/ante
1690) CE
Angelo Gualdini CE
Gualdo, Bernardo Girolamo da → see
Bernardo Girolamo da Gualdo
Gualdorp, Gorzius → see Geldorp
Gortzius
Gualla, Pietro → see Guala, Pier
Francesco
Gualterio, Giovanni Antonio
(Italian ivory carver, act.1599) BA
Bibl: ▶Bénézit; ▶Thieme-Becker
Gualterius de Alemagna (German
sculptor, act.1393-1432) GC
Bibl: Lehmann-Brockhaus,
Abruzzen u. Molise; TCI Abruzzo-
Molise; ▶Thieme-Becker
Gualtiero Alemanno GC
Gualtiero d'Alemagna GC
Gualtiero di Alemagna GC
Walter di Monaco GC
Gualterotti or Gualdarotti,
Raffaello → see Gualterotti,
Raffaello

Gualterotti, Raffaello   **PR**
   (Italian artist, op.1580-c.1600)   WC
   (Italian painter, 1544-1638)   PR
     Bibl: ▶Fredericksen & Zeri, Census;
     ▶Thieme-Becker

Gualterotti or Gualdarotti,
   Raffaello   **WC**
   Raffaello Gualterotti   PR

Gualther Hermenius Rivius→see
   Rivius, Gualther Hermenius

Gualtieri di Giovanni→see Gualtieri di
   Giovanni da Pisa

Gualtieri di Giovanni da Pisa   **BA GC PR**
   (Italian artist, op.1389-1445)   WC
   (Italian painter, act. 1400-1445)   PR
   (Italian painter, act.1400-1445)   BA
   (Italian painter, doca.1389-aft.
    1445)   GC
     Bibl: ▶Bénézit; ▶Bolaffi; ▶Encyc.
     world art; ▶RILA/BHA, 1986;
     ▶Thieme-Becker; Torriti, Siena 12-
     15c

Gualtieri di Giovanni   **GC PR**
Gualtieri or Gualtiero di
   Giovanni da Pisa or
   Dellunigiana   **WC**
Gualtieri Gualtiero   **BA**
   (Italian artist, op.1539-a.1560)   WC
   (Italian painter, ca.1500-before
    1560)   BA
     Bibl: ▶Bolaffi; TCI Veneto; Vicenza
     (ITA), Temp. di S. Corona, Palladio
     e la maniera (1980)

Gualtieri or Gualtiero,
   Girolamo(?)   **WC**

Gualtieri or Gualtiero di Giovanni da
   Pisa or Dellunigiana→see Gualtieri
   di Giovanni da Pisa
Gualtieri or Gualtiero,
   Girolamo(?)→see Gualtieri
   Gualtiero
Gualtiero Alemanno→see Gualterius
   de Alemagna
Gualtiero d'Alemagna→see
   Gualterius de Alemagna
Gualtiero di Alemagna→see
   Gualterius de Alemagna
Guarana→see Guarana, Jacopo

Guarana, Jacopo   **BA GC PR WC**
   (Italian artist, 1720-1808)   WC
   (Italian painter, 1720-1808) BA GC PR
     Bibl: ▶Bolaffi; ▶Encic. italiana;
     Pelican Hist. of Art; ▶RILA/BHA,
     1986; ▶Thieme-Becker
   Guarana   PR
   Jacopo Guarana   PR

Guarana, Vicenzo *(Italian painter,*
   ca.1753-1815)   **GC**
     Bibl: ▶Thieme-Becker

Guarchi del Zenato→see Guercino
   (Giovanni Francesco Barbieri)
Guarchin del zintto→see Guercino
   (Giovanni Francesco Barbieri)
Guarchino→see Guercino (Giovanni
   Francesco Barbieri)

Guard, Mark *(British architect,*
   London)   **AV**
     Bibl: ▶RIBA members, 1986

Guardabassi, Giacomo *(Italian*
   artist, 19th cent.)   **WC**

Guardabassi, Guerrino *(Italian*
   artist, 1841-)   **WC**

Guardassoni, Alessandro *(Italian*
   artist, 1819-1888)   **WC**

Guarde→see Guardi, Francesco
Guardet→see Guardi, Francesco
Guardi→see Guardi, Francesco
Guardi→see Guardi, Giacomo
Guardi→see Guardi, Giovanni
   Antonio

Guardi family *(Italian painters, 18th*
   c.)   **BA**
     Bibl: ▶Bolaffi; ▶Encic. italiana;
     ▶Thieme-Becker

Guardi, Andrea di Francesco
   (Italian sculptor, act.1451-1470) **BA GC**
     Bibl: ▶Bessone-Aurelj, Scult. &
     arch. ital.; Middeldorf, Revue de
     l'art, 36 (1977) pp.7-26;
     ▶RILA/BHA; ▶Thieme-Becker

Guardi, Antonio→see Guardi,
   Giovanni Antonio

Guardi, Francesco   **BA GC PR WC WI**
   (Italian artist, 1712-1793)   WC WI
   (Italian painter, 1712-1793) BA GC PR
     Bibl: ▶RILA/BHA; ▶Thieme-Becker
   Fr: Guardi   PR
   Francesco Guardi   PR
   François Guardi   PR
   Garde   PR
   Gardi   PR
   Gardis   PR
   Gauda   PR
   Guada   PR
   Guarde   PR
   Guardet   PR
   Guardi   PR

Guardi, Giacomo   **BA GC PR WC**
   (Italian artist, 1764-1835)   WC
   (Italian painter, 1764-1835) BA PR
   (Italian, 1764-1835)   GC
     Bibl: ▶Encyc. world art;
     ▶RILA/BHA; ▶Thieme-Becker;
     ▶Witt checklist
   Giacomo Guardi   PR
   Guardi   PR

Guardi, Gian Antonio→see Guardi,
   Giovanni Antonio

Guardi, Giovanni Antonio **BA GC PR WC**
   (Italian artist, 1698-1760)   WC
   (Italian painter, 1699-1760) BA PR
   (Italian, 1698-1760)   GC
     Bibl: ▶Fredericksen & Zeri, Census;
     ▶RILA/BHA; ▶Thieme-Becker;
     ▶Witt checklist; ▶Wittkower, Art
     & arch. Italy
   Giovanni Antonio Guardi   PR
   Guardi   PR
   Guardi, Antonio   PR
   Guardi, Gian Antonio   PR

Guardi, Niccolò   **GC WC**
   (Italian artist, 1715-1785)   WC
   (Italian painter, 1715-1785)   GC
     Bibl: ▶Thieme-Becker

Guardia, Gabriel *(Spanish artist, op.*
   1501)   **WC**

Guardiola, Oriol Bohigas→see
   Bohigas, Oriol

Guarienti, Carlo   **BA WC**
   (Italian artist, 1923-)   WC
   (Italian painter, b.1923)   BA
     Bibl: ▶Comanducci, Diz.

Guarienti, Pase *(Italian, 16th c.)*   **BA**
     Bibl: Hornig, Cavazzola

Guariento   **BA GC PR WC**
   (Italian (Paduan School), active
    1338-died by 1370)   JG
   (Italian artist, op.1338-, d.1378) WI
   (Italian artist,
    op.1338-m.1368/70)   WC
   (Italian painter, ca.1310-ca.
    1370)   BA GC PR
     Bibl: ▶Fogg Mus. Libr. cat.; Getty
     Photo Study Coll. (Douwes coll.);
     ▶RILA/BHA; ▶Thieme-Becker;
     ▶Witt checklist
   Guariento d'Arpo   PR

Guariento di Arpo   **GC JG PR**
Guariento, Ridolfo   **GC WI**

Guariento d'Arpo→see Guariento
Guariento di Arpo→see Guariento
Guariento, Ridolfo→see Guariento

Guarine [Unidentified] *(Unknown*
   painter)   **PR**
     Bibl: Blanchard inventory, dated
     1638 (item 4)

Guarini or Guarino, Francesco→see
   Guarino, Francesco
Guarini, Francesco→see Guarino,
   Francesco

Guarini, Guarino   **AV BA FA**
   (1624-1683)   AV
   (1624-1683; Architect, Nice,
    Paris, Piemonte)   FA
   (Italian architect, 1624-1683)   BA
     Bibl: ▶RILA/BHA, Subject, 1988;
     ▶Thieme-Becker

Guariniello, Biagio *(Italian*
   goldsmith, 18th c.)   **BA**
     Bibl: Catello, Napoli Nobilissima,
     XX/3-4 (1981) pp.129-134

Guarino family *(Italian painters,*
   17th c.)   **BA**
     Bibl: ▶Bolaffi; ▶Encyc. world art;
     Spinosa, Pitt. napoletana; TCI
     Napoli e dintorni

Guarino, Domenico *(Italian, 1683-*
   1750)   **GC**
     Bibl: ▶Thieme-Becker

Guarino, Francesco   **BA** GC
  (Italian artist, 1611-1654)   WC
  (Italian painter, 1611-1654) BA GC PR
    Bibl: ▶Bolaffi; ▶RILA/BHA;
    Spinosa, Pitt. napoletana; TCI
    Napoli e dintorni; ▶Thieme-Becker
  Francesco di Zolofra   PR
  Francesco Guarini   PR
  Guarini or Guarino, Francesco   **WC**
  Guarini, Francesco   BA **GC** PR
  Zoppo Solofre   PR
Guarino, Luigi *(Italian artist, 1853-)* **WC**
Guarinoni, Giovanni Battista   **BA**
  (Italian artist, op.1576-1580)   WC
  (Italian painter, act.1576)   GC
  *(Italian painter, ca.1548-after
    1580)*   BA
    Bibl: ▶Bolaffi; ▶Thieme-Becker;
    Zampetti, Pitt. bergamaschi, p.85
Guerinoni, Giovanni Battista **GC WC**
Guarnacci Painter *(Etruscan vase-
  painter)*   **GC**
    Bibl: ▶Szilagyi, Etruszko-korinthosi
Guarnieri, Aurora [Unidentified]
  *(Unknown painter, act. 18th
    century)*   **PR**
    Bibl: Riccardi inventory dated
    1776
  Aurora Guarnieri   PR
Guarnieri, Giuseppe *(Italian, b. late* **JG**
  19th century, active 1930's, Turin)
Guarnieri, Luciano   **BA WC**
  (Italian artist, 1930-)   WC
  (Italian painter, b.1930)   BA
    Bibl: ▶Comanducci, Diz.; ▶MoMA
    libr. cat.
Guas, Juan   **BA WC**
  *(Spanish architect, sculptor,
    d.1496)*   BA
  *(Spanish artist, op.1459-m.a.
    1497)*   WC
    Bibl: ▶Bénézit; ▶Encic. univ. ilus.;
    ▶Encyc. world art; Pevsner;
    ▶Thieme-Becker
Guasco, Charles Fortune *(French
  artist, 1826-1869)*   **WC**
Guascone, Nicolò *(Italian sculptor,
  doca. 1546)*   **GC**
    Bibl: TCI Firenze
Guasparini, Giuseppe *(Italian
  painter, act.1669)*   **BA**
    Bibl: Bruschetti, LE LUNETTE DEL
    CONVENTO DI
    SAUT'AGOSTINO(1983)
Guaspre, Le → see Dughet, Gaspard
  (Gaspard Poussin)
Guastalla, Pierre *(French artist,
  1891-)*   **WC**
Guastavino, Rafael *(Catalonian
  architect who moved to New York
  City in 1881; famous for the
  fireproof tile vaulting system he
  developed and patented, 1842-
  1908)*   **AV**
    Bibl: Brownstoner, 1988 Summer,
    p.4; RLIN BKS file, NYCG87-
    B27879

Guayazamin *(South American artist,
  20th cent.)*   **WC**
Guazza, Carlo Antonio *(Italian
  painter, act.1711)*   **BA**
    Bibl: Bisogni, in Craig Hugh Smyth
    festchrift, v.2, pp.39-43
Guazzalotti, Andrea *(Italian
  medalist, printmaker, ca.1435-ca.
  1495)*   **BA**
    Bibl: ▶Bessone-Aurelj, Scult. &
    arch. ital.; ▶Encic. italiana; Pelican
    Hist. of Art; ▶Thieme-Becker
Guazzi, Anselmo *(Italian painter,
  act.1527-1549)*   **BA**
    Bibl: ▶Bolaffi; Piva, P., QUADERNI
    PALAZZO Te, I/2 (Jan-June 1985)
    p. 9; ▶Thieme-Becker
Guazzoni, Edoardo *(Italian
  architect)*   **AV**
Gubai(?) *(Italian artist, 19th cent.)*   **WC**
Gubbins Browne, Victor *(Architect,
  Chile)*   **AV**
    Bibl: AC: the fibrecement review
    1985 Apr, v.30, no.1(iii), p.74
  Gubbins, Victor   AV
Gubbins, Victor → see Gubbins
  Browne, Victor
Gubelmann, James *(American
  architect, N.J)*   **AV**
    Bibl: Architectural digest, 1986
    Nov., v.43, no.11, p.198
Gubern, Silvia *(Spanish interior
  designer)*   **AV**
    Bibl: Architectural record, 1983
    Sept.l, v.171, no.10, p.129
Gubernatis, Giovanni Battista de
  (Italian artist, 1774-1837)   **WC**
Guberti, Silvia *(Italian artist,
  b.1944)*   **BA**
    Bibl: Modena (ITA), Galleria
    Civica, Forma senza forma (1982)
Gubig *(German(?) artist, 19th cent.)*   **WC**
Gubin, V.I. *(Russian painter, 20th c.)*   **BA**
    Bibl: Iskusstvo, 6 (1979) pp.39-44
Gubitz, Friedrich Wilhelm   **BA GC**
  *(German printmaker, 1786-
    1870)*   GC
  *(German printmaker, journalist,
    publisher, theater critic, 1786-
    1870)*   BA
    Bibl: ▶Bénézit; ▶Neue deutsche
    Biog.; ▶Thieme-Becker
Gubler, Max   **BA WC**
  (Swiss artist, 1898-1958)   WC
  (Swiss painter, 1898-1973)   BA
    Bibl: ▶Bénézit; ▶Künst.-Lex.
    Schweiz 20. Jahrh.; ▶Lex. zeitgen.
    Schweiz. Künstler; Olten(CHE),
    KUnstmus.,
    SAMMLUNGSKATALOG(1983);
    ▶Witt checklist
Gubler, Thomas Ernst *(Swiss
  sculptor, painter, 1895-1958)*   **BA**
    Bibl: ▶Künst.-Lex. Schweiz 20.
    Jahrh.; ▶Vollmer, Künst.-Lex. 20.
    Jhr.

Gubsch, Dietmar *(East German
  painter, printmaker, b.1941)*   **BA**
    Bibl: Dresden (DDR), Galerie Kunst
    der Zeit, DIETMAR GUBSCH, 1985
Gucci, Santi (Santi della Cammilla)
  *(Italian sculptor, architect in POL,
  ca.1535-1600)*   **BA**
    Bibl: ▶Bénézit; ▶Encyc. world art;
    N.C. Mus. of Art Bull. XIII/4
    (1976), p.1-70; ▶Portoghesi, Diz.
    arch. e urbanistica; Slownik
    Artystow Polskich PAN, v.II (BHA-
    Paris); ▶Thieme-Becker
Guccio di Mannaia   **BA GC**
  *(Italian goldsmith, act.1292-
    1298)*   GC
  *(Italian goldsmith, enamelist,
    act.1292-1318)*   BA
    Bibl: Prospettiva 17 (Apr 1979),
    47-58; ▶Thieme-Becker
Guccione, Piero   **BA WC**
  (Italian artist, 1935-)   WC
  (Italian painter, b.1935)   BA
    Bibl: ▶Bénézit; ▶Comanducci, Diz.
Guchez, Henri *(Architect, Belgium)*   **AV**
    Bibl: Bauwelt, 1985 Nov. 8, v.76,
    no.41-42, p.1651
Gucht, Benjamin van der   **GC WC WI**
  (British artist, op.1767-, d.1794)   WI
  (British artist, op.1767-m.1794)   WC
  (British, d.1794)   GC
    Bibl: ▶Thieme-Becker; ▶Witt
    checklist
Gucht, Gerard van der *(British
  artist, 1696-1776)*   **WC WI**
Gucht, John van der *(British artist,
  1697-1776)*   **WC WI**
Gucht, Maximiliaan van der *(Dutch
  tapestry weaver, act.1637-1689)*   **BA**
    Bibl: Nijmegen (NLD), Mus.
    Commanderie van S.Jan, Stadhuis
    van Nijmegen (1982);
    ▶Thieme-Becker; ▶Thomson,
    Tapestry
Gucht, Michiel van der *(British
  artist, 1660-1725)*   **WC WI**
Guckh, Gordian *(German artist, op.
  1513-m.a.1545)*   **WC**
Gudaitis, Antanas *(Russian painter,
  b.1904)*   **BA**
    Bibl: ▶Fogg Mus. Libr. cat.
Gudbrod, Rolf   **BA**
  (German archtiect, b.1910)   BA
  (West German architect, 1910-)   AV
    Bibl: ▶Contemp. archts.;
    ▶Macmillan encyc. archts.
Gutbrod, Rolf   **AV**
Gude, Hans Fredrik   **BA WC**
  (Norwegian artist, 1825-1903)   WC
  (Norwegian painter, 1825-1903)   BA
    Bibl: ▶Bénézit; ▶Busse, Maler u.
    Bildhauer 19. Jahr.;
    ▶Thieme-Becker

Gudgell, Henry *(American craftsman, ca.1826-1895)*   **BA**
  Bibl: New York (NY, USA), Met. Mus., 19c. Afro-American art (1976); Parry, Image of Indian and Black Man in American art:1826-1895

Gudgeon, Ralston *(British artist, op. 1932-1950)*   **WI**

Gudiašvili, Lado   **BA**
  (Russian painter, b. 1896)   PR
  (Russian painter, b.1896)   BA
  Bibl: ▶Encyc. world art; Kagan, GUDIASHVILI(1984)
  Goudiachvili   PR

Goudiachvili, Lado   **PR**
  Lado Goudiachvili   PR

Gudin → see Gudin, Herminie (Madame Fauchier)

Gudin, Herminie → see Gudin, Herminie (Madame Fauchier)

Gudin, Herminie (Herminie Fauchier) → see Gudin, Herminie (Madame Fauchier)

Gudin, Herminie (Madame Fauchier)   **PR**
  (French artist, 19th cent.)   WC
  (French painter, act. 1849-1853)   PR
  Bibl: ▶Bénézit; ▶Thieme-Becker
  Fauché Gudin   PR
  Gudin   PR
  Gudin, Herminie   PR

Gudin, Herminie (Herminie Fauchier)   **WC**
  H. Gudin   PR
  Herminie Gudin   PR

Gudin, Jacques *(French, 1706-1744, master 1726)*   **JG**

Gudin, Jacques Gérôme   **BA WC**
  (French artist, 1769-1784)   WC
  (French clockmaker, act.1768-1784)   BA
  Bibl: ▶Thieme-Becker

Gudin, Theodore → see Gudin, Théodore, baron

Gudin, Theodore (Jean Antoine Theodore) → see Gudin, Théodore, baron

Gudin, Théodore, baron   **BA**
  (French artist, 1802-1880)   WC
  (French painter, printmaker, 1802-1880)   BA
  (French, 1802-1880)   GC
  Bibl: ▶Bénézit; ▶Thieme-Becker; ▶Witt checklist

Gudin, Theodore   **GC**

Gudin, Theodore (Jean Antoine Theodore)   **WC**

Gudmand-Høyer, Jan *(Danish (?) architect)*   **AV**
  Bibl: Arkitektur DK, 1984 Oct., v.28, no.6, p.210

Gudmonas, Jonas *(Russian artist, 20th cent.)*   **WC**

Gudmundsson, Gudmundur → see Erró (Gudmundur Gudmundsson)

Gudmundsson, Sigurdur   **AV BA**
  (Icelandic artist in NLD, b.1942)   BA
  (Icelandic artist in the Netherlands, 1942-)   AV
  Bibl: DUTCH ART & ARCH.TODAY, 4(NOV 1978), 8-13; ▶RILA/BHA

Gudmundur Gudmundsson → see Erró (Gudmundur Gudmundsson)

Gudmundur Jónsson   **BA**
  (Icelandic architect)   AV
  (Icelandic scribe, act.1665)   BA
  Bibl: Byggekunst: the Norwegian review of architecture, 1985, v.67, no.4, p.180

Jonsson, Gudmundur   **AV**

Gudnason, Svavar *(Scandinavian artist, 1909-)*   **WC**

Gududio   **JG**

Gue → see Gué, Julien Michel

Gué, Julien Michel   **GC PR WC**
  (French artist, 1789-1843)   WC
  (French painter, 1789-1843)   GC PR
  Bibl: ▶Bénézit; ▶Thieme-Becker
  Gue   PR
  Julien Michel Gue   PR

Guebels, François *(early Netherlandish tapestry maker, act. 1545-1577)*   **BA**
  Bibl: Hunter, Tapestry; ▶Thieme-Becker; ▶Thomson, Tapestry

Guébels, Monique *(South African painter, b.1921)*   **BA**
  Bibl: Brussels (BEL), Nouvelle subjectivité (1979)

Guedes, Amancio → see Guedes, Amâncio d'Alpoim Miranda (Pancho)

Guedes, Amancio d'Alpoim Miranda → see Guedes, Amâncio d'Alpoim Miranda (Pancho)

Guedes, Amâncio d'Alpoim Miranda (Pancho)   **BA**
  (Portugese architect, painter and sculptor; practices and teaches in Witwatersrand, South Africa, 1925-)   AV
  (Portuguese sculptor, 20th c.)   BA
  Bibl: ▶Libr. of Congr. Name Auth. File; Tavares, Colóquio: Artes 32 (Apr 1977), 14-23
  Alpoim Miranda Guedes, Amancio d'   AV
  D'Alpoim Miranda Guedes, Amancio   AV

Guedes, Amancio   **AV**
  Guedes, Amancio d'Alpoim Miranda   AV
  Guedes, Pancho   AV
  Miranda Guedes, Amancio d'Alpoim   AV

Guedes, Joaquim *(Brazilian architect, 1932-)*   **AV**
  Bibl: ▶Contemp. archts.

Guedes, Pancho → see Guedes, Amâncio d'Alpoim Miranda (Pancho)

Gueldorf → see Geldorp, Niclas [Unidentified]

Gueldry, Ferdinand Joseph   **GC**
  (French artist, 1858-)   WC
  (French painter, b.1859)   GC
  Bibl: ▶Bénézit

Gueldry, Joseph Ferdinand   **WC**

Gueldry, Joseph Ferdinand → see Gueldry, Ferdinand Joseph

Guell, Lluis *(Spanish designer/artist)*   **AV**
  Bibl: Interior design, 1987 Apr., v.58, no.6, p.270

Guemeres, Pedro de *(Spanish illuminator, act.1472)*   **BA**
  Bibl: Silva Maroto, Miscelánea de arte, pp.54-56

Gueniot, Arthur *(French artist, 1866-1951)*   **WC**

Guenzburger, Ernest   **AV**

Guerard, Bernhard, von *(German artist, op.1793-m.1836)*   **WC**

Guerard, Charles-Francois-Eugene → see Guérard, Eugène Charles François

Guerard, Eugen von → see Guérard, Eugène von

Guerard, Eugene → see Guérard, Eugène Charles François

Guérard, Eugène Charles François   **BA WC**
  (French artist, 1821-1866)   WC
  (French painter, printmaker, 1821-1866)   BA
  (French, 1821-1866)   GC
  Bibl: ▶Dict. biog. fran.; Getty Photo Study Coll. (Ptgs.); ▶Thieme-Becker; ▶Witt checklist
  Guerard, Charles-Francois-Eugene   GC

Guerard, Eugene   **GC**

Guérard, Eugène von   **BA**
  (Austrian painter and draughsman, 1811-1901)   GC
  (Austrian painter in AUS, 1811-1901)   BA
  Bibl: ▶Bénézit; ▶Encyc. Australian art; ▶Thieme-Becker
  Gherard, Eugene de   GC

Guerard, Eugen von   **GC**

Guerard, H. *(Engraver)*   **WI**

Guerard, Henri (Charles Henri) → see Guérard, Henri Charles

Guérard, Henri Charles   **BA**
  (French artist, 1846-1897)   WC
  (French painter, printmaker, 1846-1897)   BA
  Bibl: ▶Bénézit; ▶Thieme-Becker

Guerard, Henri (Charles Henri)   **WC**

Guerard, Nicolas *(French artist, op. 1680-m.1719)*   **WC**

Guerassimov, Sergei Vasilevich → see Gerasimov, Sergej Vasil'evič

Guerau, Antonio *(Spanish artist, op. 1411-1439)*   **WC**

Guerceni → *see* Guercino (Giovanni Francesco Barbieri)

Guerchin → *see* Guercino (Giovanni Francesco Barbieri)

Guerchino → *see* Guercino (Giovanni Francesco Barbieri)

Guercin → *see* Guercino (Giovanni Francesco Barbieri)

Guercin da Cento → *see* Guercino (Giovanni Francesco Barbieri)

Guercin da Cento pittor → *see* Guercino (Giovanni Francesco Barbieri)

Guercin del Cento → *see* Guercino (Giovanni Francesco Barbieri)

Guercin di Cento → *see* Guercino (Giovanni Francesco Barbieri)

Guercine → *see* Guercino (Giovanni Francesco Barbieri)

Guercini → *see* Guercino (Giovanni Francesco Barbieri)

Guercino → *see* Guercino (Giovanni Francesco Barbieri)

Guercino (Giovanni Francesco Barbieri)   **BA GC PR**
(Italian artist, 1591-1666)   WC
(Italian painter, 1591-1666)   BA GC PR
(Italian, Bolognese, 1591-1666)   JG
  Bibl: ▶Bénézit; ▶Bolaffi; Getty Photo Study Coll. (Ptgs.); ▶RILA/BHA; ▶Thieme-Becker

After Guercino   PR
Barbieri   PR
Barbieri, Francesco (Il Guercino)   PR
Barbieri, Giovanni Francesco   GC PR
Corchino   PR
Francesco Barberi d.o il Guercino   PR
Garbieri   PR
Geurcino   PR
Gio. Francesco Barbieri   PR
Gio: Francesco Barbieri detto il Guercino   PR
Gio: Francesco Barbieri detto il Guercino da Cento   PR
Giovan Francesco Barbieri detto il Guercino da Cento   PR
Giovanni Francesco Barbieri   PR
Gouarchin   PR
Guarchi del Zenato   PR
Guarchin del zintto   PR
Guarchino   PR
Guerceni   PR
Guerchin   PR
Guerchino   PR
Guercin   PR
Guercin da Cento   PR
Guercin da Cento pittor   PR
Guercin del Cento   PR
Guercin di Cento   PR
Guercine   PR
Guercini   PR
Guercino   GC **JG** PR
Guercino d'acento   PR
Guercino da Cento   PR
Guercino, Giovanni Francesco Barbieri   **WC**
Guerino   PR
Guiercino   PR
Guirchino   PR
Guircino   PR
Gurchino   PR
Gursin del Cinto   PR
Gvarcino   PR
Huerchino   PR
Il Guercino   PR
Il Guercino (Giovanni Francesco Barbieri)   PR
Jean François Barbieri   PR
John Francis Barbieri, called Guercino   PR
Le Guerchin   PR
Quercino   PR
Guercino d'acento → *see* Guercino (Giovanni Francesco Barbieri)
Guercino da Cento → *see* Guercino (Giovanni Francesco Barbieri)

Guercino, Giovanni Francesco Barbieri → *see* Guercino (Giovanni Francesco Barbieri)

Guerfurt → *see* Querfurt, August

Guerhard *(French artist, op.1786-1829(?))*   **WC**

Guerin → *see* Guérin, Pierre Narcisse, baron

Guerin, A.M. *(French artist, 1913)*   **WC**

Guerin, Charles → *see* Guérin, Charles François Prosper

Guérin, Charles François Prosper   **GC PR WC**
(French artist, 1875-1939)   WC
(French painter, 1875-1939)   GC PR
  Bibl: ▶Bénézit; San Francisco F.A. Museums; ▶Thieme-Becker

Charles Francois Prosper Guerin   PR
Guerin, Charles   PR
Guerin, Christophe   **GC WC**
(French artist, 1758-1831)   WC
(French painter, 1758-1831)   GC
  Bibl: ▶Bénézit

Guérin, Eloi *(French silversmith, ca. 1714-1765, master 1727)*   **GC**
  Bibl: ▶Mabille, Orfèv. fran.

Guerin, Ernest-Pierre *(French artist, 19th/20th cent.)*   **WC**

Guerin, Francois   **GC WC**
(French artist, op.1751-1791)   WC
(French, d.1791)   GC
  Bibl: ▶Thieme-Becker; ▶Witt checklist

Guérin, Gilles   **BA GC**
(French sculptor, ca.1606-1678)   BA
(French sculptor, d.1678)   GC
  Bibl: ▶Bénézit; ▶Encyc. world art; ▶Thieme-Becker

Guerin, Gustave *(French artist, op. 1810)*   **WC**

Guerin, Jean *(French artist, 1734-1787)*   **WC**

Guerin, Jean *(French painter, d. ca. 1670)*   **GC**
  Bibl: ▶Thieme-Becker

Guerin, Jean Urbain   **GC WC**
(French artist, 1760-1836)   WC
(French painter, 1760-1836)   GC
  Bibl: ▶Thieme-Becker; ▶Witt checklist

Guérin, Jean-Louis *(French menuisier, master 1778, act. to ca. 1789)*   **GC**
  Bibl: ▶Salverte, Ébénistes 18e s.

Guerin, Jules *(French artist, op.c. 1845)*   **WC**

Guerin, Jules   BA FA PR WC WI
 (18.XI.1866-1946; Architectural
 draftsman, United States of
 America)   FA
 (American artist, 1866-1946)   WC WI
 (American painter, 1866-1946)   PR
 (American painter, illustrator,
 1866-1946)   BA
 Bibl: ▶Bénézit, v.5, p.271;
 ▶Fielding's Amer. ptrs.; ▶Havlice,
 Idx. art. bio.; ▶Lowry, Building
 natl. image; NY Times obit.;
 ▶RILA/BHA; ▶Thieme-Becker;
 ▶Vollmer, Künst.-Lex. 20. Jhr.
 Jules Guerin   PR
Guerin, Louis   GC WC
 (French artist, op.1751)   WC
 (French, act.1751)   GC
 Bibl: ▶Thieme-Becker; ▶Witt
 checklist
Guerin, Nicolas *(French painter, ca.*
 1645-1714)   GC
 Bibl: ▶Bénézit
Guerin, Paulin → see Guérin, Paulin
 Jean Baptiste
Guerin, Paulin (Jean Baptiste
 Paulin) → see Guérin, Paulin Jean
 Baptiste
Guérin, Paulin Jean Baptiste   BA
 (French artist, 1783-1855)   WC
 (French painter, 1783-1855)   BA
 (French, 1783-1855)   GC
 Bibl: ▶Bénézit; ▶Thieme-Becker;
 ▶Witt checklist
 Guerin, Paulin   GC
 Guerin, Paulin (Jean Baptiste
 Paulin)   WC
Guérin, Pierre *(French architect)*   AV
 Bibl: AMC, 1988 Feb., no.19, p.21
Guerin, Pierre Narcisse → see Guérin,
 Pierre Narcisse, baron
Guérin, Pierre Narcisse,
 baron   BA PR WC
 (French artist, 1774-1833)   WC
 (French painter, 1774-1833)   PR
 (French painter, printmaker,
 1774-1833)   BA
 (French, 1774-1833)   GC
 Bibl: ▶Bénézit; ▶Encyc. world art;
 ▶RILA/BHA; ▶Thieme-Becker;
 ▶Witt checklist
 Baron Pierre Narcisse Guerin   PR
 Guerin   PR
 Guerin, Pierre Narcisse   GC PR
 Guerin, Pierre-Narcisse   PR
Guerin, Pierre-Narcisse → see Guérin,
 Pierre Narcisse, baron
Guerin, Thomas Francois *(French*
 artist, 1767-1829)   WC
Guérineau, René *(French*
 printmaker, dealer, print publisher,
 act.1664)   BA
 Bibl: ▶Thieme-Becker
Guerino → see Guercino (Giovanni
 Francesco Barbieri)

Guerinoni, Giovanni Battista → see
 Guarinoni, Giovanni Battista
Guérinot, Antoine-Gaëtan *(French*
 architect, 1830-1891)   AV
 Bibl: ▶Thieme-Becker
Guérinot, Pierre *(French silversmith,*
 master 1734)   GC
 Bibl: Helft, Provinces (1985);
 ▶Mabille, Orfèv. fran.
Guerins → see Quirins [Unidentified]
Gueritte, T.J. *(French engineer,*
 19th-20th cs.)   BA
 Bibl: Cusack, Arch. history, XXVIII
 (1985) p.198, n.3
Guermacheff, Michel Markinovitch
 (Russian artist, 1867-)   WC
Guerne *(French artist, 1748-)*   WC
Guernerey *(French artist, op.1830)*   WC
Guernier, Charles Joseph du
 (French artist, 1820-1881)   WC
Guernier, Louis I du *(French artist,*
 1614-1659)   WC
Guernier, Louis, II du → see Du
 Guernier the Younger, Louis
Guerniero, Giovanni Francesco
 (Italian architect, sculptor, ca.
 1665-1745)   BA
 Bibl: ▶Avery period. idx.;
 ▶Bessone-Aurelj, Scult. & arch.
 ital.; ▶Thieme-Becker
Gueroult de Pau, J. *(French painter,*
 18th century)   GC
 Bibl: ▶Bénézit
Guerra, Achille *(Italian painter,*
 1832-1903)   PR
 Achille Guerra   PR
Guerra, Antoine (the younger)
 (French painter, 1666-1711)   GC
 Bibl: ▶Bénézit
Guerra, Camillo   BA GC WC
 (Italian artist, p.1797-1852)   WC
 (Italian painter, 1797-1852)   GC
 (Italian painter, 1797-1874)   BA
 Bibl: ▶Bolaffi; ▶Encic. italiana;
 ▶Thieme-Becker; ULAN 1988,
 (RILA)
Guerra, Enrique *(Argentine*
 architect)   AV
 Bibl: Summa, 1985 Jan.-Feb., no.
 208-209, p.90
Guerra, Giovanni   AV BA GC WC
 (Italian artist, 1544-1608)   AV
 (Italian artist, c.1540-1618)   WC
 (Italian painter, printmaker, and
 architect, 1544-1618)   GC
 (Italian painter, printmaker,
 architect, 1544-1618)   BA
 Bibl: ▶Bolaffi; ▶Libr. of Congr.
 Name Auth. File, (dates do not
 agree with Thieme-Becker);
 Modena, Pal. de Musei, Libri
 d'immagini (1978); ▶RILA/BHA,
 1986; ▶Thieme-Becker,
 [dates=c.1540-1618]; ▶Witt
 checklist
Guerra, Giuseppe, I *(Italian artist,*
 op.1740-m.1761)   WC

Guerra, Glenn *(American*
 woodworker, Barrington, Ill)   AV
 Bibl: Fine homebuilding, 1989
 Oct.-Nov., no.56, p.74
Guerrazzi, Temistocle *(Italian*
 sculptor, 1806-1884)   GC
 Bibl: TCI Firenze
Guerrera, Maria *(Italian architect)*   AV
 Bibl: L'Arca, 1989 July-Aug.,
 no.29, p.75
Guerrero y Torres, Francisco
 Antonio *(ca.1725-ca.1793)*   AV
Guerrero, Emilio *(Mexican*
 architect)   AV
Guerrero, José   BA WC WI
 (American artist, 1914-)   WC
 (American artist, b.1913)   WI
 (Spanish painter, graphic artist
 in USA, b.1914)   BA
 Bibl: ▶Campoy, Español contemp.;
 ▶Havlice, Idx. art. bio.; NY Times
 obit., 5 Jan 1992; ▶Seuphor,
 Abstract ptg.; ▶Vollmer,
 Künst.-Lex. 20. Jhr.; ▶WW Amer.
 Art, 1976
Guerrero, Pedro → see Guerrero,
 Pedro E.
Guerrero, Pedro E.   BA
 (American architectural
 photographer)   AV
 (American photographer, 20th
 c.)   BA
 Bibl: Architecture, the AIA
 journal, 1984 Mar., v.73, no.3,
 p.129; ▶MoMA libr. cat.; New
 York (NY, USA), Whitney Mus.,
 Louise Nevelson (1980)
 Guerrero, Pedro   AV
Guerrero, Raul *(American artist,*
 20th c.)   BA
 Bibl: LAICA JOURNAL(OCT-NOV
 1977), 31
Guerreschi, Giuseppe *(Italian artist,*
 1929-)   WC
Guerri or Guerra, Dionisio → see
 Guerri, Dionisio
Guerri, Danilo *(Italian architect)*   AV
 Bibl: Spazio e società, 1989 Apr.-
 June, v.12, no.46, p.64
Guerri, Dionisio   GC
 (Italian artist, 1598-1640)   WC
 (Italian, 1598-1640)   GC
 Bibl: ▶Thieme-Becker; ▶Witt
 checklist
 Guerri or Guerra, Dionisio   WC
Guerri, Giovan Battista *(Italian*
 intarsia artist, act.1669)   BA
 Bibl: Modena (ITA), Museo Civico,
 Opere restaurate
Guerrier, Francis *(French architect)*   AV
 Bibl: Architecture & urbanism,
 1986 Oct., no.10, p.54
Guerrier, Raymond *(French artist,*
 1920-)   WC

Guerrieri, Giovanni Francesco **BA GC**
  (Italian artist, 1589-c.1655/9)   **WC**
  (Italian painter and printmaker,
    1589-1655/59)   **GC**
  (Italian painter, printmaker,
    1589-1657)   **BA**
    Bibl: ▶Bolaffi; Emiliani, GIOVAN
    FRANCESCO GUERRIERI (exhib.cat)
    (1988), p.53 docs.; ▶RILA/BHA,
    1986; ▶Thieme-Becker
Guerrieri, Guerini or Guerreri,
    Giovanni Francesco   **WC**
Guerrieri, Guerini or Guerreri,
  Giovanni Francesco → see Guerrieri,
  Giovanni Francesco
Guerriero, Alessandro (Italian
  designer, Milan, co-founder of
  Studio Alchimia)   **AV**
    Bibl: ▶Architektur & Wohnen, 1989
    Jan.-Feb., no.1, p.26
Guerrini, Lorenzo (Italian artist,
  1914-)   **WC**
Guerrini, Mino (Italian painter,
  b.1927)   **BA**
    Bibl: ▶Bénézit; ▶Seuphor, Abstract
    ptg.; ▶Vollmer, Künst.-Lex. 20.
    Jhr.
Guerrini, Olindo (Italian poet,
  photographer, 1845-1916)   **BA**
    Bibl: CARROBIO, XII (1986) 5-9;
    ▶Encic. italiana
Guerst, J. (Dutch architect, The
  Hague)   **AV**
    Bibl: ▶De Architect, 1988 Oct.,
    v.19, no.10, p.73
Guerue, Tony (American artist, op.
  1935-)   **WI**
Guery, Armand (French artist, 1850-
  1912)   **WC**
Guesdon, René (French architect)   **AV**
    Bibl: ▶Annuaire archts. fran.,
    1978
Guesoan (French artist, 19th cent.)   **WC**
Guest → see Guest, Thomas Douglas
Guest, Barbara (American artist, op.
  20th c.)   **WI**
Guest, Thamas Douglas → see Guest,
  Thomas Douglas
Guest, Thomas → see Guest, Thomas
  Douglas
Guest, Thomas Douglas   **PR WI**
  (British artist, 1781-op.1839)   **WI**
  (British artist, 1781-p.1839)   **WC**
  (British painter, 1781-aft.1839)   **PR**
  (British silversmith, act. from
    1805)   **GC**
    Bibl: ▶Bénézit; ▶Grimwade,
    London goldsmiths, 1982;
    ▶Thieme-Becker
  Douglas Guest   **PR**
  Guest   **PR**
Guest, Thamas Douglas   **WC**
Guest, Thomas   **GC**
  Thomas Douglas Guest   **PR**

Guet, Charlemagne Oscar   **GC WC**
  (French artist, 1801-1871)   **WC**
  (French, 1801-1871)   **GC**
    Bibl: ▶Thieme-Becker; ▶Witt
    checklist
Guet, Jean Baptiste (French artist,
  op.1682/3)   **WC**
Guetin, Victor Oscar (French
  painter, b.1873)   **GC**
    Bibl: ▶Bénézit
Guetzlaff, Tim (American designer,
  New York)   **AV**
    Bibl: Metropolitan home, 1989
    May, v.21, no.5, p.154
Guevara, Alvaro   **BA WC**
  (Chilean painter, 1894-1951)   **BA**
  (South and Central American
    artist, 1894-1951)   **WC**
    Bibl: ▶Art Index, Nov. 1950-Oct.
    1953; CONNOISSEUR,
    189/762(AUG'75), 276
Guevara, Juan 'Nino' de → see Niño
  de Guevara, Juan
Guevara, Melchor de (Spanish
  artist, op.c.1660-1690)   **WC**
Guevara, Meraud Guinness (British
  painter, b.1904)   **BA**
    Bibl: ▶Bénézit
Guévrékian, Gabriel (French
  architect, landscape architect, act.
  1923-1928)   **BA**
    Bibl: ▶Avery Libr. cat.; ▶Avery
    period. idx.; Imbert, D., JOURNAL
    OF THE SOCIETY OF
    ARCHITECTURAL HISTORIANS,
    49/4 (Dec 1990) 449-450;
    ▶Oudin, Dict. architectes
Guffens, Egide Godfried
  (Godfried) (Belgian artist, 1823-
  1901)   **WC**
Gugel, Carl Adolf (German artist,
  1820-1885)   **WC**
Gugelot, Hans (Dutch designer,
  architect in DEU, 1920-1965)   **BA**
    Bibl: Blaser, W.: Element, System,
    Möbel..., 1984; RLIN: dates
Gugg, Hugo (German artist, 1878-)   **WC**
Guggenberger, Thomas (German
  artist, 1866-)   **WC**
Guggenblicher, Johann Meinrad
  (Austrian sculptor, 1649-1723)   **GC**
    Bibl: ▶Thieme-Becker
Guggenheimer, Peter (American
  architect)   **AV**
    Bibl: Arch. & urbanism, 4(223)
    (Apr.1989), p.111
Guggenheimer, Richard Henry
  (American painter, author, 1906-
  1977)   **BA**
    Bibl: NYTIMES, 14 March 1977,
    p.32; ▶WW Amer. Art, 1976
Guglielmelli, Arcangelo (Italian
  architect, painter, sculptor, 17th
  c.)   **BA**
    Bibl: Amirante, Architettura
    napoletana... (1990); ▶Bolaffi;
    ▶Thieme-Becker

Guglielmelli, Marcello (Italian
  architect, 18th c.)   **BA**
    Bibl: Amirante, Napoli
    Nobilissima, XVIII/3 (May-June
    1979), 88-104; ▶Thieme-Becker
Guglielmetti, Camillo (Italian
  architect, act.1860)   **BA**
    Bibl: ANTICHITA VIVA,
    V.XVI(MAY-JUNE 1977), 27
Guglielmi Group   **GC**
    Bibl: ▶Beazley, Attic bl.-fig. vase-
    ptrs.
Guglielmi Painter   **GC**
    Bibl: ▶Beazley, Attic red-fig. vase-
    ptrs.
Guglielmi, Gregorio   **BA GC PR WC**
  (Italian artist, 1714-1773)   **WC**
  (Italian painter, 1714-1773)   **BA GC PR**
    Bibl: ▶Bolaffi; ▶RILA/BHA, 1986;
    ▶Thieme-Becker
  Gregorio Guglielmi   **PR**
Guglielmi, Guillaume (Italian
  painter, b.1832, act.1854)   **BA**
    Bibl: GENAVA, XXVII(1979), 231-
    241
Guglielmi, Luigi (Italian sculptor,
  1834-1907)   **BA**
    Bibl: ▶Bénézit; ▶Thieme-Becker
Guglielmi, O. Louis → see Guglielmi,
  Osvaldo Louis
Guglielmi, Osvaldo Louis   **BA WI**
  (American artist, 1906-)   **WC**
  (American artist, 1906-1956)   **WI**
  (American painter, 1906-1956)   **BA**
    Bibl: ▶Cummings, Contemp.
    Amer. artists, 1971; ▶Schwab,
    Life & death; ▶Young, Amer.
    artists
Guglielmi, O. Louis   **WC**
Guglielmino, Luigi (Italian artist,
  19th cent.)   **WC**
Guglielmo (Italian painter, act.1138)   **BA**
    Bibl: ▶Bolaffi; TCI Liguria
Guglielmo (Italian sculptor, act.
  1162)   **BA**
    Bibl: Art Bull. idx.; Pope-Hennessy,
    Ital. Gothic sculp.; TCI,
    SARDEGNA; ▶Thieme-Becker
Guglielmo Baur → see Baur, Johann
  Wilhelm
Guglielmo Baver → see Baur, Johann
  Wilhelm
Guglielmo Borgognone → see
  Courtois, Guillaume
Guglielmo Borgognoni → see Courtois,
  Guillaume
Guglielmo Caccia → see Caccia,
  Guglielmo (Moncalvo)
Guglielmo da Forli   **GC**
  (Italian artist, 14th cent.)   **WC**
  (Italian, 14th Century)   **GC**
    Bibl: ▶Thieme-Becker; ▶Witt
    checklist
Guglielmo da Forli (degli
  Organi)   **WC**
Guglielmo da Forli (degli
  Organi) → see Guglielmo da Forli

Guglielmo da Modena → see
Wiligelmo da Modena
Guglielmo da Venezia *(Italian, act.
1353-1358)* **GC**
  Bibl: ▶Thieme-Becker
Guglielmo della Porta → see Della
Porta, Guglielmo
Guglielmo di Guido di Perruccino
*(Italian painter, act. early 15th
century)* **GC**
  Bibl: Archi, Pinac. di Faenza
  (1957)
Guglielmo di Pietro de Marcillat → see
Marcillat, Guillaume de
Guglielmo Fiamengo → see Guglielmo,
Monsù [Unidentified]
Guglielmo Fiammingo → see Tetrode,
Willem Danielsz. van
Guglielmo Tedesco → see Tetrode,
Willem Danielsz. van
Guglielmo Terranova → see Nieulandt,
Willem II van (Guglielmo
Terranova)
Guglielmo Todescho → see Baur,
Johann Wilhelm
Guglielmo Veneziano *(Italian artist,
op.1382)* **WC**
Guglielmo von Alst → see Aelst,
Willem van
Guglielmo, Fra *(Italian sculptor,
architect, ca.1235-1312)* **BA**
  Bibl: ▶Bessone-Aurelj, Scult. &
  arch. ital.; Bruni, FRA GUGLIELMO
  DA PISA, p.27; ▶Thieme-Becker
*Guglielmo, Lorenzo di Ludovico
di* → see Lorenzetto (Lorenzo di
Ludovico di Guglielmo Lotti)
Guglielmo, Monsù [Unidentified]
(Unknown painter) **PR**
  Bibl: Pignatelli inventory, Naples,
  1723
  Guglielmo Fiamengo **PR**
  Guglielmo, Monsu' **PR**
  gugliermo fiamengo **PR**
  Monsù Guglielmo fiammengo **PR**
  Monsu' Guglielmo **PR**
  nonsù Guglielmo **PR**
Guglielmo, Monsu' → see Guglielmo,
Monsù [Unidentified]
gugliermo fiamengo → see Guglielmo,
Monsù [Unidentified]
Gugliotta, José *(Brazilian architect)* **AV**
  Bibl: Projeto, 1986 Apr., no.86,
  p.43
Guhl, Willy *(Swiss designer, b.1915)* **BA**
  Bibl: ▶Künst.-Lex. Schweiz 20.
  Jahrh.; RLIN BKS file; Zürich,
  kunstgewerbe mus. der Stadt,
  WILLY GUHL (1985)
Guhr, Jerzy **BA**
Guhr, Richard *(German artist, 1873-)* **WC**
Gui, J. Romano *(Spanish artist, 17th
cent.)* **WC**
Guiard, Adélaïde Labille → see Labille-
Guiard, Adélaïde

Guiard, Laurent *(French sculptor,
1723-1788)* **BA**
  Bibl: ▶Bénézit; ▶Dict. biog. fran.;
  ▶Thieme-Becker
*Guiard, Mme. Adelaide Labille (Mme.
Vincent)* → see Labille-Guiard,
Adélaïde
*Guiard, Mme. Adelaide Labille (Mme.
Vincent) nee Labille des
Vertus* → see Labille-Guiard,
Adélaïde
Guiaud, Jacques **GC WC**
  (French artist, 1811-1876) **WC**
  (French painter, 1811-1876) **GC**
  Bibl: ▶Bénézit
Guibal, Barthélemy *(French
sculptor, 1699-1757)* **BA**
  Bibl: ▶Thieme-Becker
Guibal, Nicolas **BA GC WC**
  (French artist, 1725-1784) **WC**
  (French painter, 1725-1784) **BA**
  (French, 1725-1784) **GC**
  Bibl: ▶Bénézit; ▶Thieme-Becker;
  ▶Witt checklist
Guibert, Danielle *(French architect)* **AV**
  Bibl: AMC, 1988 Oct., no.22,
  p.138
Guibert, Francois *(French artist,
18th cent.)* **WC**
Guichard, Benoit Joseph → see
Guichard, Joseph Benoît
Guichard, Didier *(French architect,
b.1936)* **BA**
  Bibl: ▶WW France, 1988
Guichard, E. *(French, active 19th
century)* **JG**
Guichard, H. Th. *(French artist, 19th
cent.)* **WC**
Guichard, Joseph Benoît **BA**
  (French artist, 1806-1880) **WC**
  (French painter, 1806-1880) **BA**
  Bibl: ▶Bellier, Artistes fran.;
  ▶Bénézit; ▶Thieme-Becker
Guichard, Benoit Joseph **WC**
Guichard, Joseph-Nicolas *(French
sculptor and woodcarver, act. ca.
1765-ca.1786)* **GC**
  Bibl: ▶Vial, Artistes décorateurs
Guid → see Reni, Guido
Guida da Siena → see Guido da Siena
Guida, Harold *(American architect,
1941-)* **AV**
  Bibl: Process: architecture, n.2,
  1977, p.40
**Guidabombarda, Giovanni
Battista** **AV BA**
  *(17th century Italian architect,
  worked in Milan)* **AV**
  *(Italian architect, act.1627-
  1643)* **BA**
  Bibl: Baroni, Documenti a Milano;
  ▶Thieme-Becker
Guidaccio → see Guidaccio da Imola
(Antonio Checchi)

**Guidaccio da Imola (Antonio
Checchi)** **BA**
  (Italian artist, op.1470) **WC**
  (Italian painter, act. 1470) **PR**
  (Italian painter, act.1463-1481) **BA**
  (Italian, act.1470) **GC**
  Bibl: ▶Bolaffi; Tambini,
  PARAGONE XXXVIII (Sept 1987)
  48-67; TCI Emilia-Romagna, pp.
  520, 746; ▶Thieme-Becker
  Antonio Checchi **BA**
  Antonio da Imola **GC PR WC**
  Guidaccio **PR**
Guiddo Reni → see Reni, Guido
Guide → see Reni, Guido
Guide-line Class *(potters, ca. 500-
475 BC)* **GC**
  Bibl: ▶Beazley, Attic bl.-fig. vase-
  ptrs.; Boardman, Attic Bl.-fig.
  Vases
**Guide-Line Class (Class of Vatican
G.47)** **GC**
  Bibl: ▶Beazley, Attic bl.-fig. vase-
  ptrs.; Paralipomena
Guiderone → see Reni, Guido
Guidetti, Antonio *(Italian architect,
engineer, act.1680-1730)* **BA**
  Bibl: Rizzo, NAPOLI NOB.,
  XXI/3-4(MAY-AUG 1982), 113;
  TCI Napoli e dintorni;
  ▶Thieme-Becker
Guidetti, Guidetto *(Italian architect,
act.1561-1564)* **BA**
  Bibl: ▶Portoghesi, Diz. arch. e
  urbanistica; ▶Thieme-Becker
Guidi → see Guidi, Giovanni di ser
Giovanni (lo Scheggia)
Guidi family *(Italian painters, 15th-
17th cs.)* **BA**
  Bibl: Procacci, Rivista d'arte, IV/1
  (1984) pp.235-268
Guidi the Elder, Giovanni → see Guidi,
Giovanni di ser Giovanni (lo
Scheggia)
Guidi, Antonio Francesco *(Italian
painter, ca.1441-1476)* **BA**
  Bibl: ▶Bolaffi; Procacci, Rivista
  d'arte, IV/1 (1984) pp.235-268;
  ▶Thieme-Becker
Guidi, Baccio *(Italian painter,
d.1616)* **BA**
  Bibl: Procacci, Rivista d'arte, IV/1
  (1984) pp.235-268
Guidi, Domenico **BA GC WC**
  (Italian artist, 1625-1701) **WC**
  (Italian sculptor, 1625-1701) **BA GC**
  Bibl: ▶Bénézit; ▶RILA/BHA;
  ▶Thieme-Becker
Guidi, Giorgio *(Italian architect, fl.
1930's)* **AV**
  Bibl: Journal of architectural
  education, 1989 spring,m v.42,
  no.3, p.38
Guidi, Giovanni → see Guidi, Giovanni
di ser Giovanni (lo Scheggia)

Guidi, Giovanni (the Elder) →see
Guidi, Giovanni di ser Giovanni (lo
Scheggia)

Guidi, Giovanni Citosibio (Italian
painter, printmaker, act.1628-
1635)   **BA**
  Bibl: ▶Bénézit; ▶Bolaffi; ▶Illus.
  Bartsch, v.21; ▶Thieme-Becker

Guidi, Giovanni de ser Giovanni (Lo
Scheggia) →see Guidi, Giovanni di
ser Giovanni (lo Scheggia)

Guidi, Giovanni di ser Giovanni →see
Guidi, Giovanni di ser Giovanni (lo
Scheggia)

**Guidi, Giovanni di ser Giovanni
(lo Scheggia)**   **BA PR**
  (Italian artist, 1407-1480/90)   WC
  (Italian artist, 1407-1480/98)   WC
  (Italian artist, 15th cent.)   WC
  (Italian painter, 1406-1486)   BA PR
  (Italian, act. ca.1430-1460)   GC
  (Italian, act.1435-1460(?))   GC
  (Italian, b.1406-1480/98)   GC
  (Italian, Florentine, 1407-ca.
   1480/98)   JG
  Bibl: Arte nell'Aretino (1974);
  ▶Bolaffi; ▶Fremantle, Florentine
  Gothic; ▶Thieme-Becker; ▶Witt
  checklist

Giovanni di ser Giovanni   GC
Giovanni di ser Giovanni Guidi   PR
Giovanni Guidi   PR
Guidi   PR

Guidi the Elder, Giovanni   **WC**
Guidi, Giovanni   **JG PR**
Guidi, Giovanni (the Elder)   **GC**
Guidi, Giovanni de ser Giovanni
  (Lo Scheggia)   PR
Guidi, Giovanni di ser Giovanni   PR
Lo Scheggia   PR
Master of Fucecchio   **GC PR WC**
Master of the Adimari
  Cassone   **GC WC**
Master of the Fucecchio Altarpiece   PR
Scheggia, Giovanni di Ser
  Giovanni (Guidi)   **WC**

Guidi, Giovanni, the younger (lo
  Scheggia) (Italian painter, ca.
  1472-1546)   **BA**
  Bibl: ▶Bolaffi; Procacci, Rivista
  d'arte, IV/1 (1984) pp.235-268;
  ▶Thieme-Becker

Guidi, Giuseppe (Italian artist, 1884-
  1931)   **WC**
Guidi, Guido (Italian photographer,
  b.1941)   **BA**
  Bibl: Naples (ITA), Museo
  Capodimonte, Napoli '82 (1982)
Guidi, Guido (Italian artist, op.1867-
  c.1911)   **WC**
Guidi, Mauro (Italian architect,
  1761-1829)   **BA**
  Bibl: Faenza(ITA), Pal.Milzetti,
  L'ETA NEOCLASSICA...(1979)

Guidi, Michelangelo (Italian painter,
  d. by 1670)   **PR**
  Bibl: His inventory, dated
  1670/10/18, where he is
  described as a painter
Michelangelo Guidi   PR
Guidi, Nedda (Italian sculptor,
  ceramist, b.1927)   **BA**
  Bibl: ▶Intl. dir. arts; LAZIO
Guidi, Paolo Antonio (Italian
  painter, 1675-1704)   **GC**
  Bibl: ▶Thieme-Becker
Guidi, Pietro   **GC WC**
  (Italian artist, op.1490-1530)   WC
  (Italian, act.1490-1530)   GC
  Bibl: ▶Thieme-Becker; ▶Witt
  checklist
Guidi, Raffaello (Italian artist,
  c.1540-p.1614)   **WC**
Guidi, Tommaso (Italian painter,
  d.1567)   **BA**
  Bibl: Procacci, Rivista d'arte, IV/1
  (1984) pp.235-268
Guidi, Tommaso →see Masaccio
  (Tommaso di ser Giovanni di Mone
  Guidi)
Guidi, Virgilio   **BA GC WC**
  (Italian artist, 1892-)   WC
  (Italian painter, b.1892)   BA GC
  Bibl: ▶Bénézit; ▶Comanducci, Diz.;
  ▶RILA/BHA, 1986; ▶Vollmer,
  Künst.-Lex. 20. Jhr.
Guidino →see Abbatini, Guido Ubaldo
Guido (Italian scribe, act. ca.1200) **GC**
  Bibl: ▶Branner, Ms. ptg. Paris,
  p.201
Guido →see Reni, Guido
Guido Abbatini →see Abbatini, Guido
  Ubaldo
Guido Arena →see Arena, Guido
  [Unidentified]
Guido Bollonees →see Reni, Guido
Guido bolognes →see Reni, Guido
Guido Bolognese →see Reni, Guido
Guido Caganacci →see Cagnacci,
  Guido
Guido Cagnacci →see Cagnacci,
  Guido
Guido Cagnacci Celebre discepolo di
  Guido Reno →see Cagnacci, Guido
Guido Cagnaci →see Cagnacci, Guido
Guido Cagnasi →see Cagnacci, Guido
Guido Canlassi →see Cagnacci, Guido
Guido Cugnacci →see Cagnacci,
  Guido
Guido da Bologna (Italian artist,
  14th cent.)   **WC**

Guido da Siena   **BA GC PR WC WI**
  (Italian artist, op.1221(?))   WC
  (Italian artist, op.1250-1300)   WI
  (Italian painter, 13th c.)   BA
  (Italian painter, act. 13th
   century)   PR
  (Italian, act. 2nd half 13th c.)   GC
  Bibl: ▶Bolaffi; Clark Art Inst. Libr.;
  Clark Art Inst. Photo & Slide
  Dept.; ▶RILA/BHA; Stubblebine,
  Guido da Siena; ▶Thieme-Becker;
  Torriti, Siena 12-15c; ▶Witt
  checklist
Guida da Siena   PR
Siena, Guido da   PR
Guido de Reny →see Reni, Guido
guido de Reyna →see Reni, Guido
Guido di Cino or Cinatti →see
  Cinatti, Guido
Guido di Graziano (Italian, doca.
  Siena 1278-1302)   **GC**
  Bibl: ▶Thieme-Becker
Guido di Palmerucci →see Guido di
  Palmeruccio
Guido di Palmeruccio   **BA**
  (Italian artist, c.1280-p.1345)   WC
  (Italian painter, b.ca.1280, act.
   1315-1349)   BA
  (Italian, ca.1280-aft.1345)   GC
  Bibl: ▶Bolaffi; ▶Thieme-Becker;
  ▶Witt checklist
Guido di Palmerucci   **GC WC**
Palmerucci, Guido de   GC
Guido di Prato (Italian sculptor and
  architect, act.1211)   **GC**
  Bibl: Marchini, Prato, p.24
Guido di Savino (Italian potter in
  Low Countries, act.1508, d.1541)   **BA**
  Bibl: BURLINGTON XVI (Dec 1972)
  288; Dumortier, Faenza,
  LXXIII/4-5 (1987) pp.161-172;
  ▶Thieme-Becker
Guido Redi →see Reni, Guido
Guido Ren →see Reni, Guido
Guido Rena →see Reni, Guido
Guido René →see Reni, Guido
Guido Reni →see Reni, Guido
Guido Renni →see Reni, Guido
Guido Reno →see Reni, Guido
Guido Reno Bolognese →see Reni,
  Guido
Guido Reyna →see Reni, Guido
Guido Rhene →see Reni, Guido
Guido Rheni →see Reni, Guido
Guido Rueni →see Reni, Guido
Guido Ubaldo Abbatini →see
  Abbatini, Guido Ubaldo
Guido, &c. →see Reni, Guido
Guido, Angel Francisco (Argentine
  architect, 1896-1960)   **AV**
  Bibl: Encic. arte en America
Guido, Francesco (Italian architect) **AV**
  Bibl: L'industria delle costruzioni,
  1988 May, v.22, no.199, p.3

Guido, Marcello *(Italian architect,*
Calabria) **AV**
> Bibl: Architettura; cronache e
> storia, 1989 Feb., v.35, no.2(400),
> p.86

Guidobaldo Abbatini →see Abbatini,
Guido Ubaldo

Guidobon, Bartolommeo →see
Guidobono, Bartolomeo

Guidobono, Bartolomeo **BA GC PR**
> *(Italian artist, 1657-1709)* **WC**
> *(Italian painter, 1654-1709)* BA GC PR
> Bibl: ▶Bolaffi; ▶Encic. italiana;
> ▶Encyc. world art; ▶RILA/BHA,
> 1986; ▶Thieme-Becker

> Bartolomeo Guidobono **PR**
> Guidobon, Bartolommeo **PR**
> Guidobono, Bartolommeo **PR**

Guidobono, Bartolommeo ('Il
Prete Savonese') **WC**

Guidobono, Bartolommeo →see
Guidobono, Bartolomeo

Guidobono, Bartolommeo ('Il Prete
Savonese') →see Guidobono,
Bartolomeo

Guidobono, Domenico *(Italian*
artist, 1670-1746) **WC**

Guidoccio di Giovanni
Cozzarelli →see Cozzarelli,
Guidoccio di Giovanni

Guidon, Jacques *(Swiss artist,*
1931-) **WC**

Guidop →see Reni, Guido
Guidoraine →see Reni, Guido
guidoreni →see Reni, Guido
Guidoreno →see Reni, Guido

Guidorici, Bonaventura
[Unidentified] *(Italian painter)* **PR**
> Bibl: Nepita inventory, Naples,
> 1705

> Bonaventura Guidorici **PR**

Guidotti, Dario *(Italian sculptor,*
doca.1892-1900) **GC**
> Bibl: TCI Firenze; ▶Thieme-Becker

Guidotti, Paolo →see Guidotti, Paolo
(Cavaliere Borghese)

Guidotti, Paolo (Cavaliere
Borghese) **BA**
> *(Italian painter, 1560-1629)* **PR**
> *(Italian painter, ca.1560-1629)* **BA**
> Bibl: ▶Bolaffi; ▶Thieme-Becker

> Cavaliere Borghese **PR**
> **Guidotti, Paolo** **PR**
> Paolo Borghese **PR**
> Paolo Guidotti **PR**

Guiducci, Roberto *(Italian architect)* **AV**
> Bibl: Architecture & urbanism,
> 1987 Nov., no.11, p.105

Guiduccio Palmerucci →see
Palmerucci, Giuduccio

Guiercino →see Guercino (Giovanni
Francesco Barbieri)

Guiette, Rene *(Belgian artist, 1893-)* **WC**

Guignard, Alberto da Veiga
(Brazilian artist, 1893/6-) **WC**

Guignard, Gaston (Alexandre
Gaston) *(French artist, 1848-1922)* **WC**

Guignard, Pierre-François →see
Quéniard, Pierre-François

Guignebert, Jean-Claude (Vincent)
(French artist, 1921-) **WC**

Guignet →see Guignet, Jean Adrien

Guignet, Adrien →see Guignet, Jean
Adrien

Guignet, Jean Adrien **BA PR**
> *(French artist, 1816-1854)* **WC**
> *(French painter, 1816-1854)* **BA PR**
> *(French, 1816-1854)* **GC**
> Bibl: ▶Bellier, Artistes fran.;
> ▶Bénézit; ▶Nouv. biog. gén.;
> ▶RILA/BHA; ▶Thieme-Becker

> Guignet **PR**

Guignet, Adrien **WC**

Guignet, Jean Adrien (the
younger) **GC**

> Jean Adrien Guignet **PR**

Guignet, Jean Adrien (the
younger) →see Guignet, Jean
Adrien

Guigon, Charles Louis *(Swiss*
painter, 1807-1882) **GC**
> Bibl: ▶Bénézit

Guigou →see Guigou, Paul Camille

Guigou, Paul →see Guigou, Paul
Camille

Guigou, Paul Camille **BA GC PR WC**
> *(French artist, 1834-1871)* **WC**
> *(French painter, 1834-1871)* **BA PR**
> *(French, 1834-1871)* **GC**
> Bibl: ▶Bénézit; ▶RILA/BHA;
> ▶Thieme-Becker; ▶Witt checklist

> Guigou **PR**
> Guigou, Paul **PR**
> Paul Camille Guigou **PR**

Guiguet, Francois Joseph *(French*
artist, 1860-) **WC**

Guilbert, Albert Désiré **BA**
> *(French architect, 1866-)* **AV**
> *(French architect, b.1866)* **BA**
> Bibl: ▶Avery period. idx.; Du
> Molin, LES EGLISES DE FRANCE...
> (1956); ▶Natl. union cat., pre-
> 1956; ▶Thieme-Becker

Guilbert, Albert-Désiré **AV**

Guilbert, Albert-Désiré →see Guilbert,
Albert Désiré

Guilbert, Narcisse *(French artist,*
1878-1942) **WC**

Guilding, Lansdown **WI**
> *(British artist, 1798-1831)* WC WI

Guilding, The Rev. Lansdown **WC**

Guilding, The Rev. Lansdown →see
Guilding, Lansdown

Guilgelmus *(Italian scribe, act. late*
14th century) **GC**
> Bibl: Sotheby's London, June 25,
> 1985, Lot 60

Guilielmus, Frater →see Frater
Guilielmus

Guill(elmus) *(French scribe, act.*
1266) **GC**
> Bibl: Ducrat-Granderye, Miracles,
> pp.36-41; Getty Photo Study Coll.
> (Medieval)

Guillelmus **GC**

Guillain, Simon →see Guillain, Simon I

Guillain, Simon (the Elder) →see
Guillain, Simon I

Guillain, Simon I **BA GC**
> *(French artist, c.1581-1658)* **WC**
> *(French sculptor, ca.1581-*
> *1658)* **BA GC**
> Bibl: Getty Photo Study Coll.
> (Sculp.); ▶Lami, Sculp. fran. 19e
> s.; ▶Thieme-Becker

Guillain, Simon **WC**
> Guillain, Simon (the Elder) **GC**

Guillain, Simon II *(French painter,*
b.1618) **GC**
> Bibl: ▶Thieme-Becker

Guillam Dubois →see Dubois, Guillam

Guillaume Courtois →see Courtois,
Guillaume

Guillaume de Marcillat →see
Marcillat, Guillaume de

Guillaume de Sens **BA**
> *(French architect of the Gothic*
> *choir at Canterbury Cathedral*
> *from 1174 to 1179)* **AV**
> *(French architect, act.1174,*
> *d.1180)* **BA GC**
> Bibl: ▶Bauchal, Archtes. fran.;
> ▶Encyc. world art; ▶Harvey, Engl.
> med. archts.; ▶Macmillan encyc.
> archts.; ▶RILA/BHA;
> ▶Thieme-Becker

William of Sens **AV BA GC**

Guillaume de Vienne →see Willelmus
Martini

Guillaume de Volpiano, S. *(abbot,*
architect, 962-1031) **BA**
> Bibl: Book of saints; ▶Portoghesi,
> Diz. arch. e urbanistica; Reau,
> ICONOGRAPHIE DE L'ART
> CHRETIEN; ▶Thieme-Becker

> William of Dijon, S. **BA**

Guillaume Du Choul →see Duchoul,
Guillaume

Guillaume Duchoul →see Duchoul,
Guillaume

Guillaume Lepaulle →see Lépaulle,
François Gabriel Guillaume

Guillaume Lethière →see Lethiere,
Guillaume

Guillaume Miéris →see Mieris, Willem
van

Guillaume Scrots →see Scrots,
Guillaume

Guillaume Seignac →see Seignac,
Guillaume

Guillaume, Albert **PR WC**
> *(French artist, 1873-1942)* **WC**
> *(French painter, 1873-1942)* **PR**
> Bibl: ▶Thieme-Becker

> Albert Guillaume **PR**
> Guillaume, Albert P. **PR**

Guillaume, Albert P. → see Guillaume,
Albert

Guillaume, Edmond Jean Baptiste
(French architect, 1826-1894) **BA**
Bibl: ▶Avery obit. idx.; ▶Larousse
grande encyc.; ▶Portoghesi, Diz.
arch. e urbanistica;
▶Thieme-Becker

Guillaume, Eugène **BA GC**
(French painter, 1822-1905) GC
(French sculptor, 1822-1905) BA
Bibl: ▶Dict. biog. fran.; ▶Lami,
Sculp. fran. 19e s.; Shedd, BEAUX-
ARTS CXII/1 (1988) p.51-60;
▶Thieme-Becker

Guillaume, Louis Mathieu Didier
(French artist, op.1837-1852) **WC**

Guillaume, Toussaint-Claude
*(French silversmith, master ca.
1745)* **GC**
Bibl: ▶Mabille, Orfèv. fran.

Guillaumet, Gustave → see Guillaumet,
Gustave Achille

Guillaumet, Gustave Achille **PR WC**
(French artist, 1840-1887) WC
(French painter, 1840-1887) GC PR
Bibl: ▶Bénézit; ▶Thieme-Becker

Guillaumet, Gustave **GC PR**
Gustave Achille Guillaumet PR
Guillaumet, Jean Baptiste
Antoine → see Guillemet, Jean
Baptiste Antoine

Guillaumin → see Guillaumin, Armand

Guillaumin, Armand **BA GC PR**
(French artist, 1841-1927) WC
(French painter, 1841-1927) BA PR
(French, 1841-1927) GC
Bibl: ▶Artist biog. master idx.;
▶Bénézit; Getty Photo Study Coll.
(Ptgs.); ▶Thieme-Becker; ULAN
1988; ▶Witt checklist
Armand Guillaumin PR
Guillaumin PR
Guillaumin, Jean Baptiste
Armand GC PR

**Guillaumin, Jean-Baptiste
Armand** **WC**
Guillaumin, Jean-Baptiste-Armand PR
Guillaumin, Jean Baptiste
Armand → see Guillaumin, Armand
Guillaumin, Jean-Baptiste
Armand → see Guillaumin, Armand
Guillaumin,
Jean-Baptiste-Armand → see
Guillaumin, Armand

Guillaumot, Bernard *(French
architect, Vitry sur Seine)* **AV**
Bibl: ▶Annuaire archts. fran.,
1987

Guillaumot, Charles-Axel
*(Architect, born in Stockholm,
active in France, 1730-1807)* **AV**
Bibl: ▶Thieme-Becker
Guillelmo van Aalst → see Aelst,
Willem van

Guillelmo van Aelst → see Aelst,
Willem van

Guillelmus *(Italian artist, op.1138)* **WC**
Guillelmus → see Guill(elmus)

Guillelmus dictus miler Parisiensis
(French scribe, act.1244) **GC**
Bibl: ▶Branner, Ms. ptg. Paris,
p.213; Getty Photo Study Coll.
(Medieval)
Parisiensis, Guillelmus dictus miler GC

Guillemard, Pierre Michel *(French
artist, op.c.1705)* **WC**

Guillemer, Ernest *(French artist,
1839-)* **WC**
Guillemet → see Guillemet, Jean
Baptiste Antoine
Guillemet, Antoine → see Guillemet,
Jean Baptiste Antoine
Guillemet, Antoine (Jean Baptiste
Antoine) → see Guillemet, Jean
Baptiste Antoine

**Guillemet, Jean Baptiste
Antoine** **BA GC PR**
(French artist, 1843-1918) WC
(French painter, 1843-1918) BA GC PR
Bibl: ▶Bellier, Artistes fran.;
▶Bénézit; ▶Busse, Maler u.
Bildhauer 19. Jahr.; ▶RILA/BHA,
1987; ▶Thieme-Becker; ▶Witt
checklist
Guillaumet, Jean Baptiste Antoine GC
Guillemet PR
Guillemet, Antoine GC

**Guillemet, Antoine (Jean
Baptiste Antoine)** **WC**

**Guillemet, Jean-Baptiste-
Antoine** **GC**
Jean Baptiste Antoine Guillemet PR
Guillemet, Jean-Baptiste-Antoine → see
Guillemet, Jean Baptiste Antoine

Guillemin, Alexandre Marie *(French
artist, 1817-1880)* **WC**

Guillemin, Robert *(American artist,
20th c.)* **BA**
Bibl: Framingham (MA, USA),
Danforth Mus., Homage (1981)

Guilleminet, Claude *(French artist,
1821-)* **WC**

Guillemot, Alexandre Charles **GC WC**
(French artist, 1786-1831) WC
(French, 1786-1831) GC
Bibl: ▶Thieme-Becker; ▶Witt
checklist

Guillen, Asilia *(South and Central
American artist, 1887-)* **WC**

Guillén, Diego *(Spanish sculptor,
act.1521-1548)* **BA**
Bibl: ▶Bénézit; ▶Ceán Bermúdez,
Bellas artes ESP; ▶Thieme-Becker

Guillermo, Juan *(Spanish artist,
1916-)* **WC**

Guillerot **BA WC**
(French artist, op.c.1672-1680) WC
*(French painter, ca.1620-ca.
1670)* BA
Bibl: ▶Bénézit; ▶Thieme-Becker

Guillet-Galland, Zacharie *(French
architect, entrepreneur, 1761-
1821)* **BA**
Guilliam Nieulandt → see Nieulandt,
Willem II van (Guglielmo
Terranova)

**Guillibaud or Guillebaud, Jean
Francois** *(Swiss artist, 1718-1799)* **WC**

Guillibaud, Barthemy *(Swiss artist,
1697-a.1742)* **WC**

Guillier, Emile Antoine **GC WC**
(French artist, 19th cent.) WC
(French painter, 19th century) GC
Bibl: ▶Bénézit

Guilliot, Charles *(French painter,
1695-1762)* **GC**
Bibl: ▶Thieme-Becker

Guillobel, Joaquim Candido
(Brazilian architect, act.1847) **BA**
Bibl: L'OEIL 275(JUNE 1978),
32-37

Guillod, Thomas Walker *(British
artist, op.1839-1860)* **WI**

Guillon, Adolphe Irenée **GC WC**
(French artist, 1829-1896) WC
(French painter, 1829-1896) GC
Bibl: ▶Thieme-Becker

Guillon, Charles Nicolas *(French
artist, 18th cent.)* **WC**

Guillon, Eugene Antoine **GC WC**
(French artist, 1834-p.1914) WC
(French, 1834-aft.1914) GC
Bibl: ▶Witt checklist

Guillon, Maurice *(French artist,
1924-)* **WC**

Guillonnet, Octave Denis Victor
(French artist, 1872-) **WC**

Guillot, Bernard *(contemporary,
active NY, U.S.)* **JG**

Guillot, Laure Albin *(French, 18††-
1962, active Paris, France 1930s)* **JG**

Guilloteau, Jean-François *(French
architect)* **AV**
Bibl: Architectes architecture,
1987 Oct., no.181, p.21

Guillou, Alfred *(French artist, 1844-
1926)* **WC**

Guilt, Roger *(French artist, 19th
cent.)* **WC**

Guimarães, José de *(Portuguese
painter, b.1939)* **BA**
Bibl: STAFF OF COLOQUIO ARTES

**Guimaraes-Gutma, Antonio
Ferreira de Oliveira** *(Portuguese
artist, 20th cent.)* **WC**
Guimard → see Guimard, Adeline
Guimard, A.O. → see Guimard,
Adeline

Guimard, Adeline   PR **WC WI**
  *(American artist, 1872-circa
   1960)*   WI
  (American artist, 1875-)   WC
  *(American painter, 1872-ca.
   1960)*   PR
   Bibl: ▶Petteys, Women artists
  Adeline Oppenheim Guimard   PR
  Guimard   PR
  Guimard, A.O.   PR
Guimard, Adeline Oppenheim   **PR**
  Oppenheim, Adeline, Miss   WI
*Guimard, Adeline Oppenheim→see
  Guimard, Adeline*
Guimard, Barnabe *(French artist,
  op.1765-m.1792)*   **WC**
Guimard, Hector   **AV BA**
  *(French architect, sculptor,
   1867-1942)*   BA
  *(French Art Nouveau architect
   and designer, 1867-1942)*   AV
   Bibl: ▶Bénézit; Munster (DEU),
   Landesmus. fur Kunst und
   Kulturges., HECTOR GUIMARD
   (1975)
Guimera *(Spanish artist, 15th cent.)*   **WC**
Guimond, Pierre *(Canadian artist,
  b.1946)*   **BA**
   Bibl: Paris(FRA), Centre Cultural
   Canadian. PIERRE
   GUIMOND:PHOTOMONTAGES
**Guinaccia, Deodato (Deodato
  Napoletano)** *(Italian painter,
  b.1510/15)*   **BA**
   Bibl: ▶Bolaffi; ▶Encyc. world art
Guinan, Robert   **BA WI**
  (American artist, b.1934)   WI
  (American painter, b.1934)   BA
   Bibl: ▶Bénézit; Brussels (BEL),
   Nouvelle subjectivité (1979)
*Guinard→see Guinard, Robert Raoul
  André*
Guinard, Robert Raoul André
  (French painter, b. 1896)   **PR**
  Guinard   PR
  Robert Raoul Andre Guinard   PR
Guindaleri, Pietro *(Italian
  illuminator, d.1506)*   **GC**
   Bibl: ▶Thieme-Becker
Guindon, Richard Gordon
  (American cartoonist, b.1935)   **BA**
   Bibl: WW Amer., 1984-85
Guindrand, Antoine *(French artist,
  1801-1843)*   **WC**
Guines atelier *(French illuminators,
  act. ca.1230-1250)*   **GC**
   Bibl: ▶Branner, Ms. ptg. Paris,
   p.69; Getty Photo Study Coll.
   (Medieval)
  Guines shop   GC
  Guines workshop   GC
Guines shop→see Guines atelier
Guines workshop→see Guines atelier
Guinet, Claude *(French artist,
  op.1496-m.1512/13)*   **WC**

Guingot, Louis *(French artist, 1864-
  1948)*   **BA**
   Bibl: PAYS LORRAIN, LXI(1980),
   173-174
Guinier, Henri Jules *(French artist,
  1867-1927)*   **WC**
Guiniforte da Vicomercate *(Italian
  calligrapher, illuminator, 15th c.)*   **BA**
   Bibl: ▶Bolaffi; ▶Thieme-Becker
*Guinigi Master→see Master of the
  Lathrop Tondo*
Guinness, Elizabeth Sarah, Miss
  (British artist, op.1873-1900)   **WI**
Guinness, Lindy *(British artist, op.
  1975-1980)*   **WI**
Guinness, May *(British artist, 1863-
  1955)*   **WI**
Guino, Michel *(French sculptor,
  printmaker, b.1926)*   **BA**
   Bibl: ▶Bénézit; Knaurs Lex. mod.
   Plastik; ▶Maillard, Sculpt. mod.
Guinovart, Jose *(Spanish artist,
  1927-)*   **WC**
Guinut, Serge *(French architect, La
  Rochelle)*   **AV**
   Bibl: ▶Annuaire archts. fran.,
   1978
*Guinzberg, Frederick Victor→see
  Guinzburg, Frederick Victor*
Guinzburg, Frederick Victor   **BA**
  *(American sculptor and painter,
   1897-1978)*   GC
  *(American sculptor, painter,
   1897-1978)*   BA
   Bibl: ▶Bénézit; NY Times obit., 27
   Dec 1978, B-7; ▶RILA/BHA;
   ▶Vollmer, Künst.-Lex. 20. Jhr.
Guinzberg, Frederick Victor   **GC**
Guiot, Hector *(French artist, 1825-
  1903)*   **WC**
Guipon, Leon *(French artist, 1872-
  1910)*   **WC**
Guiramand→see Guiramand, Paul
Guiramand, Jean I *(French painter,
  sculptor, d.1557)*   **BA**
   Bibl: ▶Bénézit; ▶Thieme-Becker
Guiramand, Paul   **BA**
  (French artist, 20th cent.)   WC
  (French artist, b.1926)   BA
   Bibl: ▶Fogg Mus. Libr. cat.; ▶Natl.
   union cat.; ▶WW France, 1975
Guiramand   **WC**
**Guirand (de Scevola), Lucien-
  Victor** *(French artist, 1871-1950)*   **WC**
*Guirchino→see Guercino (Giovanni
  Francesco Barbieri)*
*Guircino→see Guercino (Giovanni
  Francesco Barbieri)*
Guirey, Sylvia *(British artist, b.1931)*   **WI**
Guiritti, Bernardino *(Italian
  architect, sculptor, act.1506,
  d.1511)*   **BA**
Guise   **WC WI**
  (British artist, op.18th c.)   WI
  (British(?) artist, 18th cent.)   WC

*Guise Master→see Master of the
  Guise Hours*
Guise, Constantin *(Swiss artist,
  1811-1858)*   **WC**
*Guiseppe Chiari→see Chiari,
  Giuseppe Bartolomeo*
*Guiseppe D'Arpino→see Cesari,
  Giuseppe (Cavalier d'Arpino)*
*Guiseppe Porta called Salivati→see
  Salviati, Francesco (Francesco de'
  Rossi)*
*Guiseppi Cesari→see Cesari,
  Giuseppe (Cavalier d'Arpino)*
Guisolfi→see Ghisolfi, Giovanni
*Guisoni, Fermo di Stefano→see
  Ghisoni, Fermo di Stefano (Fermo
  da Caravaggio)*
*Guisto, Andrea di→see Andrea da
  Firenze*
*Guisuppe Chiari→see Chiari,
  Giuseppe Bartolomeo*
Guiter, Hermann Hendrik de I
  (Unknown artist)   **GC**
   Bibl: Gernsheim, Corpus Photog.
   of Drawings, 1528;
   ▶Thieme-Becker
Guitet, James   **BA WC**
  (French artist, 1925-)   WC
  (French painter, b.1925)   BA
   Bibl: ▶Bénézit; ▶Witt checklist
Guitonio   **AV BA**
  (Italian sculptor, 11th c.)   BA
  *(Italian sculptor, Montemonaco,
   fl. 1039-1050)*   AV
   Bibl: Sensi, Riv. Ist. Naz. d'Arch.,
   VI-VII (1983-84) pp.221-236
Guitry, Sacha *(French artist, 20th
  cent.)*   **WC**
Guitti, Francesco *(Italian
  scenographer, architect, engineer,
  1605-1645)*   **BA**
   Bibl: ▶Encic. spettacolo;
   ▶Portoghesi, Diz. arch. e
   urbanistica; ▶Thieme-Becker
Guitton, E. *(Dutch(?) artist, op.
  1882)*   **WC**
*Guittone, Andrea di→see Master
  Andrea of Rome*
*Guittone, Giovanni di→see Giovanni
  di Guittone*
Guizzardi, Giuseppe *(Italian painter,
  1779-1861)*   **BA**
   Bibl: ▶Bénézit; ▶Havlice, Idx. art.
   bio.
Guizzelmi, Michele di Francesco
  (Italian painter, act.1512)   **BA**
   Bibl: Antichità viva XXV/4 (July-
   Aug. 1986) 18-32; Morselli, S.
   Maria delle carceri
Gujral, Satish *(Indian architect,
  1925-)*   **AV**
   Bibl: Architects' journal, 1985
   Mar.20, v.181, no.12, p.38

Gulácsy, Lajos   **BA**
  (Hungarian artist, 1882-1932)   WC
  (Hungarian painter, 1882-1932)   BA
   Bibl: Ars Hungarica V/1 (1977),
   1-43; ▶Vollmer, Künst.-Lex. 20.
   Jhr.

Gulacsy, Lajos Kalman   **WC**
Gulacsy, Lajos Kalman→see Gulácsy,
  Lajos

Gulagi(?), I.(?) *(Italian artist, 18th*
  cent.)   **WC**

Gulbransson, O.→see Gulbransson,
  Olaf

Gulbransson, Olaf   **BA GC**
  (Norwegian painter, printmaker,
   1873-1958)   BA
  (Scandinavian artist, 1873-1958)   WC
  (Scandinavian, 1873-1958)   GC
   Bibl: ▶Bénézit; ▶Thieme-Becker;
   ▶Witt checklist

Gulbransson, O.   **WC**

Guldager or Gullager, Christian→see
  Gullager, Christian

Guldenmund, Guldenmundt or
  Guldenmundt, Hans→see
  Guldenmund, Hans

Guldenmund, Hans   **BA GC**
  (German artist, op.c.1490-m.
   1560)   WC
  (German illuminator,
   printmaker, act.1490-1560)   BA
  (German printmaker, act. ca.
   1490-d.1560)   GC
   Bibl: ▶Bénézit; Getty Photo Study
   Coll.; ▶RILA/BHA;
   ▶Thieme-Becker; ▶Witt checklist

Guldenmund, Guldenmundt or
  Guldenmundt, Hans   **WC**

Güldenpfennig, Hans Alex *(German*
  architect, 1875-1945)   **AV BA**
   Bibl: ▶Avery period. idx., 7th
   suppl.; Kölner Domblatt, 1986,
   v.51, p.285

Guldenwagen→see Guldewagen, Jan
  Jacobsz.

Guldewagen→see Guldewagen, Jan
  Jacobsz.

Guldewagen, Jan Jacobsz. *(Dutch*
  painter, act. 1624/30)   **PR**
   Bibl: Gaillard inventory 1639;
   ▶Thieme-Becker
  Guldenwagen   PR
  Guldewagen   PR
  Jan Guldenwagen   PR
  Jan Jacobsz. Guldewagen   PR

Guldi, Heinrich *(Swiss artist, 1606-p.*
  1650)   **WC**

Guldsmed, Hans *(Danish goldsmith,*
  d.1632)   **BA**
   Bibl: MIV: Museerne I Viborg Amt,
   XIII (1985) pp.126-129

Gülgönen, Ahmet *(Turkish*
  architect, 1940-)   **AV**
   Bibl: Mimar, 1982 July-Sept., no.5,
   p.62

Gulich   **WC WI**
  (British artist, op.1760-)   WI
  (British(?) artist, op.1760)   WC

Gulich, John Percival *(British artist,*
  1864-1898)   **WC WI**
   Bibl: ▶Engen, Victorian engravers

Gulino *(Italian artist, 20th cent.)*   **WC**

Gullager or Guldager, Christian→see
  Gullager, Christian

Gullager, Christian   **BA WI**
  (American artist, 1759-1826)   WI
  (American artist, 1762-1826)   WC
  (Danish painter in USA, 1759-
   1826)   BA
   Bibl: ART IN AMERICA, 51(JULY
   1949), 105; ▶Bénézit; ▶Fielding's
   Amer. ptrs., suppl., p.1759;
   ▶Groce, Artists Amer.;
   ▶Thieme-Becker; Washington (DC,
   USA), Smithsonian, Nat'l. Port.
   Gall., Christian Gullager: Port. Ptr.
   to Federal America

Guldager or Gullager, Christian   **WC**
Gullager or Guldager, Christian   **WC**

Gullelmo van Aalst→see Aelst,
  Willem van

Gullesson, Håkan *(Swedish sculptor,*
  act.1520-1570)   **BA**
   Bibl: ▶Bénézit; ▶Svenska
   konstnärer; ▶Thieme-Becker

Gulliband, J.F.   **WC WI**
  (British artist, op.1758)   WC
  (British artist, op.1758-)   WI

Gullichsen, Kristian *(Finnish*
  architect, 1932-)   **AV**
   Bibl: Process: architecture, n.37,
   1983, p.100

Gully, John *(British artist, 1819-*
  1888)   **WC WI**

Gulsrud, Mark Eric *(American artist,*
  Gig Harbor, Wash)   **AV**
   Bibl: Stained glass, 1982-83
   winter, v.77, no.4, p.374

Gültlinger, Gumpolt (the Elder)→see
  Giltlinger, Gumpolt I

Gulyás, Gyula   **BA WC**
  (Hungarian artist, 20th cent.)   WC
  (Hungarian sculptor, 20th c.)   BA
   Bibl: ▶Art Index, v.22; Asztalos,
   Studio Intl. 187/964 (Mar 1974),
   105-111

Gumery, Adolphe Ernest *(French*
  artist, 1861-)   **WC**

Gumery, Charles Alphonse Achille
  (French sculptor, 1827-1871)   **GC**
   Bibl: ▶Thieme-Becker

Gumley, Elizabeth *(English*
  cabinetmaker, glass manufacturer,
  act.1694-1729)   **BA**
   Bibl: ▶Heal, London furniture
   mkrs.

Gumley, John *(English*
  cabinetmaker, glass manufacturer,
  act.1694-1729)   **BA**
   Bibl: Gloag, Engl. furniture; ▶Heal,
   London furniture mkrs.; ▶Penguin
   dec. arts

Gummelt, Sam *(American painter,*
  b.1944)   **BA**
   Bibl: ▶Art Index, v.22; Fort
   Worth(TX, USA), Art Museum.
   FOCUS:SAM GAMMELT(1979);
   ▶WW Amer. Art, 1989-1990

Gummer, Don *(American sculptor,*
  b.1946)   **BA**
   Bibl: ▶Art Index, v.28; ▶WW
   Amer. Art, 1989-1990

Gummer, William H. *(Architect,*
  New Zealand)   **AV**
   Bibl: New Zealand architect,
   1985, no.3, p.53

Gumowski, Jan *(Polish artist, 1883-)*   **WC**

Gumpp family *(Austrian architects,*
  engineers, printmakers, painters,
  16th-18th cs.)   **BA**
   Bibl: ▶Encyc. world art;
   ▶Portoghesi, Diz. arch. e
   urbanistica; ▶Thieme-Becker

Gumpp, Gumb or Gump the Elder,
  Johann Baptist *(German artist,*
  1651-1728)   **WC**

Gumpp, Johann Anton   **BA WC**
  (German artist, 1654-1719)   WC
  (German painter, 1654-1719)   BA
   Bibl: ▶Thieme-Becker

Gumpp, Rainer *(West German*
  architect)   **AV**
   Bibl: Detail, 1989 Aug.-Sept.,
   v.29, no.4, p.356

Gunawan, J. H. *(Indonesian*
  architect)   **AV**
   Bibl: Arca, 1987 Mar., no.4, p.51

Gunckel, Friedrich Ludwig *(German*
  architect in NLD, act.1767-1793)   **BA**
   Bibl: ▶Rosenberg, Dutch art &
   arch., p.250; ▶Thieme-Becker

Gund, Graham   **AV BA**
  (American architect, 1922-)   AV
  (American architect, 20th c.)   BA
   Bibl: ▶AIA Pro File, 1985

Gundelach, Gondelach or Gondolach,
  Matthäus→see Gundelach,
  Matthäus

Gundelach, Matthäus   **GC**
  (German artist, c.1566-1653)   WC
  (German painter, ca.1566-1653)   GC
   Bibl: ▶Thieme-Becker; ▶Witt
   checklist
  Gondolach, Matthäus   GC

Gundelach, Gondelach or
  Gondolach, Matthaus   **WC**

Gundelfinger, Gyula *(Hungarian*
  painter, 1833-1894)   **BA**
   Bibl: Szinyei Merse,
   MUVESZETTAORTENETI ERTESITO,
   XXXIV/1-2 (1985), p. 32-47

Gundelfinger, John *(American*
  painter, b.1937)   **BA**
   Bibl: ▶NY art yrbk.

Günder, Ignaz→see Günther, Ignaz

Gundersen, Gunnar S. *(Norwegian*
  artist, 20th cent.)   **WC**

Gunderson, Bruce (*American artist, b.1948)*   BA
Bibl: New York(NY, USA), New Museum. IN APICTORIAL FRAME... (30 JUNE-15 SEPT 1979

Gunderson, Karen (*American painter, 20th c.)*   BA
Bibl: Campbell, L., in ARTS MAG LVIII/7 (Mar 1984) 20

Gundophinus (*French scribe, act. 754)*   GC
Bibl: Autun, Bibliothèque Municipale

Gündter, Ignaz →see Günther, Ignaz

Gunetzrhainer, Johann (*German artist, 1692-1763)*   WC

Gunge, Morten (*Danish architect, Copenhagen)*   AV
Bibl: ▶Danske Arkitekters Landsforbund, 1984-85

Gunija, Georgij (*Russian scenographer, 20th c.)*   BA
Bibl: Kovalenko, Dek. Iskusstvo SSSR 259 (June 1979), 26-29

Gunkleman, Thomas R. (*American interior designer)*   AV
Bibl: Architecture Minnesota, 1986 Jan.-Feb., v.12, no.1, p.44

Gunn, Herbert James   WI
(*British artist, 1893-1964)*   WC WI
Gunn, Sir Herbert James   WC
Gunn, Sir Herbert James →see Gunn, Herbert James

Gunnarshaug, Johannes
(*Norwegian architect, Trondheim)*   AV
Bibl: Baumeister, 1987 Aug., v.84, no.8, p.61

Gunnell, James (*British artist, op. 1985-)*   WI

Gunneweg, Hermanus Petrus Antonius (*Dutch painter and draughtsman, 1846-1904)*   GC
Bibl: ▶Scheen, Ned. beeldende kunst.

Gunnill, Edward F.   AV
Gunnis, Louis (*American artist, op. 1887-1897)*   WI
Gunnløgsson, Halldor   AV BA
(*Danish architect, 20th c.)*   BA
(*Danish architect, Copenhagen, 1918-1985)*   AV
Bibl: Arkitekten, 1985 June 18, v.87, no.12, p.256; ▶Avery period. idx., 2nd suppl.; ▶Danske Arkitekters Landsforbund, 1984-85; Skriver, Arkitektur DNK, XXVII (1 Feb. 1983) p.21; Trap, Kongeriget DNK: personalregister

Gunot, Serge (*French architect, Martinique)*   AV
Bibl: Urbanisme, 1985 Dec.-1986 Jan., no.211, p.109

Günschel, Günter (*German architect(?))*   AV
Bibl: Daidalos, 1988 Sept.15, no.29, p.96

Gunschmann, Carl (*German artist, 1895-)*   WC
Gunson, John (*British artist, op. 1800-)*   WI
Gunst, Pieter Stevens van (*Dutch artist, 1659-c.1724)*   WC
Gunston, G.W. (*British artist, op. 1823-1833)*   WC WI
Gunsul, Brooks R. W. (*American architect)*   AV
Gunten, Roger von (*Swiss painter in MEX, b.1933)*   BA
Bibl: ▶Art Index, v.23; GOYA, 119(MAR 1974), 315

Guntenaar, Ben (*Dutch sculptor, medalist, b.1922)*   BA
Bibl: ▶Scheen, Ned. beeldende kunst.

Günter, Anna (*Polish painter in USA, b.1933)*   BA
Bibl: Irvine (CA, USA), UCI Art Gallery, Female fantasies (1977); ▶MoMA libr. cat.

Gunter, Marcus (*Swedish printmaker, designer, ca.1660-1739)*   BA
Bibl: MASTER DRAWINGS, XV/3(AUTUMN 1977), 269-278

Gunter, Virginia (*American artist, 20th c.)*   BA
Bibl: ▶Art Index, v.29; Norton (MA, USA), Wheaton Coll., Allusive illusions (1979)

Gunther van Geringh, Antonius →see Gheringh, Anton Günther

Günther, Axel M. (*German ceramist, b.1956)*   BA
Bibl: Philippi, KERAMOS 107 (1985) 15-59

Gunther, Christian August
(*German artist, 1759-1824)*   WC
Günther, Franz Ignaz →see Günther, Ignaz
Gunther, Gindter, Ginter or Gundter, Matthaus →see Günther, Matthäus
Gunther, Ginter, Ginther, Gunder or Gundter, Ignaz (Franz Ignaz) →see Günther, Ignaz

Gunther, Harri (*West German landscape architect)*   AV
Bibl: Garten und Landschaft, 1989, v.99, no.9, p.13

Günther, Hertha (*German painter, b.1934)*   BA
Bibl: Wenzkat, HERTHA GUNTHER(1983)

Günther, Ignaz   BA GC
(*German artist, 1725-1775)*   WC
(*German sculptor, 1725-1775)*   BA GC
Bibl: ▶Encyc. world art; Getty Photo Study Coll. (Sculp.); ▶Thieme-Becker
Ginter, Ignaz   GC
Ginther, Ignaz   GC
Günder, Ignaz   GC
Gündter, Ignaz   GC
Günther, Franz Ignaz   GC
Gunther, Ginter, Ginther, Gunder or Gundter, Ignaz (Franz Ignaz)   WC
Gunther, Manfred (*German artist, 20th cent.)*   WC
Günther, Matthäus   BA PR
(*German artist, 1705-1788)*   WC
(*German painter, 1705-1788)*   BA PR
(*German, 1705-1788)*   GC
Bibl: ▶Bénézit; ▶RILA/BHA; ▶Thieme-Becker; ▶Witt checklist
Gunther, Gindter, Ginter or Gundter, Matthaus   WC
Günther, Matthüs   GC
Matthaus Gunther   PR
Günther, Matthüs →see Günther, Matthäus
Guntz, Thaddaeus →see Kuntze, Tadeusz

Gunuchian, Margaret, Miss (*British artist, b.1927)*   WI
Grant, Ian, Mrs.(Margaret)   WI
Guol (*French artist, op.c.1795)*   WC
Gupey →see Goupy, Joseph
Guptill, Arthur Leighton (*American author, architect, 1891-1956)*   BA
Bibl: ▶WWW Amer., v.3
Gurafalo →see Garofalo, Benvenuto Tisi da
Gurbrand (*German artist, op.1778)*   WC
Gurchino →see Guercino (Giovanni Francesco Barbieri)
Gurdiani [Unidentified] (*Unknown painter)*   PR
Bibl: (February 3, 1804, lot 192, Phillips)
Guregian, Sally A.   AV
Bibl: ▶Libr. of Congr. Name Auth. File
Gürel, Seda (*Architect, Turkey, 1925-)*   AV
Bibl: Deutsche Bauzeitung, 1986 June, v.120, no.6, p.47
Gurk, Eduard   BA WC
(*Austrian painter, printmaker, 1801-1841)*   BA
(*German artist, 1801-1841)*   WC
Bibl: ▶Bénézit; ▶Fuchs, Öst. Maler 19. Jahrh.; ▶Thieme-Becker; ▶Witt checklist
Gurland, Gerald (*American architect, 1935-)*   AV
Bibl: ▶Amer. archts. dir., 1970
Gurlitt, Heinrich Louis Theodor →see Gurlitt, Louis

Gurlitt, Louis   GC
   (German artist, 1812-1897)   WC
   (German painter, 1812-1897)   GC
   Bibl: ▶Bénézit; ▶Thieme-Becker
Gurlitt, Heinrich Louis Theodor   GC
Gurlitt, Louis (Heinrich Louis Theodor)   WC
Gurlitt, Ludwig Heinrich Theordo   GC
Gurlitt, Louis (Heinrich Louis Theodor) → see Gurlitt, Louis
Gurlitt, Ludwig Heinrich Theordo → see Gurlitt, Louis
Gurney, J.   WC WI
   (British artist, 19th cent.)   WC
   (British artist, op.19th c.)   WI
Gurney, Jeremiah, (Gurney & Son)
   (American, 1812-after 1886, daguerreotypist)   JG
Gurney, L. → see Gurney, L., Miss
Gurney, L., Miss   WI
   (British artist, 20th cent.)   WC
   (British artist, op.19th c.)   WI
Gurney, L.   WC
Gurney, Priscilla   WC WI
   (British artist, 20th cent.)   WC
   (British artist, op.19th c.)   WI
Gurney, Richenda   WC WI
   (British artist, 20th cent.)   WC
   (British artist, op.19th c.)   WI
Guro, Elena Genrihovna (Eleonora Genrihovna Notenberg) *(Russian poet, painter, 1877-1913)*   BA
   Bibl: ▶Bowlt, Russian avant-garde
Gurrentz, Susan *(American painter, 20th c.)*   BA
   Bibl: Gurrentz, Women Artists News VIII/3 (Spr 1983), 19
Gurschner, Herbert *(German artist, 1901-)*   WC
Gursin del Cinto → see Guercino (Giovanni Francesco Barbieri)
Gurskas, Albertas *(Russian artist, 20th cent.)*   WC
Gürtler, Andrej *(Architect, act. in Poland)*   AV
   Bibl: Casabella, 1989 Oct., v.53, no.561, p.38
Gürtler, Ivan *(Architect, act. in Poland)*   AV
   Bibl: Casabella, 1989 Oct., v.53, no.561, p.38
Gus Mager → see Mager, Gus
Guscelli, Girolamo *(Italian mathematician, theorist, architect, 1538-1604)*   BA
   Bibl: ▶Portoghesi, Diz. arch. e urbanistica; ▶Thieme-Becker
Gusevich, Miriam *(Architect, born Cuba, 1953-)*   AV
   Bibl: Inland architect, 1985 Nov.-Dec., v.29, no.6, p.46
Gush, William *(British artist, op. 1833-1874)*   WC WI
Gusman, Adolphe *(Engraver, 1821-1905)*   WI
Gusmand, Adolphe   WI

Gusman, Pierre *(French artist, 1862-)*   WC
Gusmand, Adolphe → see Gusman, Adolphe
Gusmin *(German sculptor, goldsmith, ca.1340-after 1381)*   BA
   Bibl: ▶Bénézit; Firenze (ITA), Città da Vita, Ghiberti e la sua... (1979); Krautheimer, LORENZO GHIBERTI; ▶Thieme-Becker
Gusquin → see Joosken van Utrecht
Gussmann, Otto *(German artist, 1869-1926)*   WC
Gussow → see Gussow, Karl
Gussow, Alan *(American painter, sculptor, b.1931)*   BA
   Bibl: ▶WW Amer. Art, 1976, 1984
Gussow, Carl → see Gussow, Karl
Gussow, Karl   GC PR
   (German artist, 1843-1907)   WC
   (German painter, 1843-1907)   GC PR
   Bibl: ▶Thieme-Becker
Gussow   PR
Gussow, Carl   PR WC
Karl Gussow   PR
Gustav Adolf Schmidt → see Schmidt, Gustav Adolf
Gustav Hesselius (the elder) → see Hesselius, Gustavus
Gustav III, King of Sweden
   (Swedish artist, 18th cent.)   WC
Gustav Jacob Canton → see Canton, Gustav Jacob
Gustave Achille Guillaumet → see Guillaumet, Gustave Achille
Gustave Adolph Wiegand → see Wiegand, Gustav Adolph
Gustave Caillebotte → see Caillebotte, Gustave
Gustave Courbet → see Courbet, Gustave
Gustave Courtois → see Courtois, Gustave Claude Etienne
Gustave Dore → see Doré, Gustave
Gustave Jean Jacquet → see Jacquet, Gustave Jean
Gustave Klimt → see Klimt, Gustav
Gustave Leonard de Jonghe → see Jonghe, Gustave Léonard de
Gustave Loiseau → see Loiseau, Gustave
Gustave Madelain → see Madelain, Gustave
Gustave Moreau → see Moreau, Gustave
Gustave Ricard → see Ricard, Gustave
Gustavs, Erland *(Canadian architect)*   AV
Gustavsson, Roland *(Danish landscape architect and/or author)*   AV
   Bibl: Landskab, 1988 May, v.69, no.3, p.62

Gustawa, Jørgen Flemming *(Danish painter, b.1951)*   BA
   Bibl: Mumgaard, HRYMFAXE:FOLKELIGT, XVII (Dec 1987)
Guston, Philip   BA GC WC WI
   (American artist, 1913-)   WC
   (American artist, 1913-1980)   WI
   (American painter, 1913-1980)   BA GC
   Bibl: NY TIMES, 10 JUNE 1980; ▶RILA/BHA; ▶Vollmer, Künst.-Lex. 20. Jhr.; ▶WW Amer. Art, 1976
Guta *(French nun, scribe, act.1154)*   BA
   Bibl: Hotz, Hdbch. Künstdenk. Elsass u. Lothringen; ▶Thieme-Becker
Gutagaza, Gyula Nemeth *(Hungarian artist, 1880-)*   WC
Gutbrod, Rolf → see Gudbrod, Rolf
Gutch, John Wheeley Gough *(British, 1806-1862)*   JG
Gutekunst, Frederick *(American, 1831-1917, active Philadelphia, PA, U.S.)*   JG
Gutenberg, Johann *(German printer, ca.1397-1468)*   BA
   Bibl: ▶Brockhaus Enzyk.; ▶Neue deutsche Biog.
Guterbock, Leopold *(German artist, c.1820-1881)*   WC
Gutersloh, Albert Paris → see Gütersloh, Paris von
Gütersloh, Paris von   BA
   (Austrian painter, sculptor, designer, author, 1887-1973)   BA
   (German artist, op.1956)   WC
   Bibl: ▶Bénézit; ▶MoMA libr. cat.; ▶Natl. union cat., pre-1956; ▶Thieme-Becker
Gütersloh, Albert Paris   WC
Gutersohn, Peter *(Swiss architect)*   AV
   Bibl: ▶Schweiz. Ingen. u. Archit., 1984-1985
Gutfreund, Otto   BA WC
   (Czech artist, 1889-1927)   WC
   (Czech artist, 19th cent.)   WC
   (Czech sculptor, 1889-1927)   BA
   Bibl: ▶Bénézit; ▶Encyc. world art; ▶Vollmer, Künst.-Lex. 20. Jhr.
Guttfreund, Otto   WC
Guth, Hella *(German artist, 1912-)*   WC
Guther, Max *(West German architect, 1909-)*   AV
   Bibl: Deutsches Architektenblatt, 1989 Apr.1, v.21, no.4, p.104
Gutherz, Carl *(American artist, 1844-1907)*   WC WI
Guthfeldt(?) or Guyfeldt (?), O.(?) *(Netherlands(?) artist, op.1655)*   WC
Güthlein, Georg *(West German architect, Erlangen)*   AV
   Bibl: ▶Bund Deut. Arch. Hdbch., 1987
Guthrie, Derek *(British artist, op. 20th c.)*   WI

Guthrie, J. Gordon *(Scottish stained glass designer, U.S, 1874-1961)*   **AV**
Bibl: Stained glass, 1982-83 Winter, v.77, no.4, p.356

Guthrie, James   **BA WI**
(British artist, 1859-1930)   **WC WI**
(British painter, 1859-1930)   **BA**
Bibl: ▶Harris, Scottish ptrs.; ▶Who was who [GBR]

Guthrie, Sir James   **WC**

Guthrie, Robin   **BA**
(British artist, 1902-1971)   **WC WI**
(British painter, 1902-1971)   **BA**
Bibl: ▶London Times obit., 1971-1975; ▶Vollmer, Künst.-Lex. 20. Jhr.

Guthrie, Robin Craig   **WC WI**

Guthrie, Robin Craig→see Guthrie, Robin

Guthrie, Sir James→see Guthrie, James

Gutiérrez de la Vega, José   **BA WC**
(Spanish artist, 1815-1865)   **WC**
(Spanish painter, 1791-1865)   **BA**
Bibl: ▶Encic. univ. ilus.; Pardo Canalis, GOYA, 169-171(JULY-DEC 1982), 153; ▶Thieme-Becker; ▶Witt checklist

Gutiérrez de San Martín, Pedro Luis→see Afanador, Pedro Luis

Gutiérrez Lega, Jaime *(Colombian designer, architect)*   **AV**
Bibl: Proa, 1986 Nov., no.356, p.12

Gutierrez Solana→see Gutiérrez Solana, José

Gutiérrez Solana, José   **BA PR**
(Spanish artist, 1886-1945)   **WC**
(Spanish painter, 1886-1945)   **PR**
(Spanish painter, author, 1886-1945)   **BA**
Bibl: ▶Bénézit; ▶Campoy, Español contemp.; ▶Encic. univ. ilus.; ▶RILA/BHA; ▶Vollmer, Künst.-Lex. 20. Jhr.

Gutierrez Solana   **PR**
Jose Gutierrez Solana   **PR**
Solana, Jose Gutierrez   **PR WC**

Gutiérrez Soto, Luis *(Spanish architect)*   **AV**
Bibl: Abitare, 1986 July-Aug., no. 246, p. 160

Gutiérrez, Alberto Díaz→see Díaz Gutierrez, Alberto

Gutiérrez, Ana Rosa *(Cuban painter, printmaker, b.1925)*   **BA**
Bibl: La Duke WOMEN ARTISTS NEWS 1046/IX (2) winter 1983-84, p.19-20

Gutiérrez, Dione *(Colombian architect)*   **AV**
Bibl: Proa, 1985 Sept., no.345, p.56

Gutiérrez, Domingo *(Venezuelan artist, 1709-1793)*   **BA**
Bibl: Duarte, DOMINGO GUTIERREZ:EL MAESTRO...(1977)

Gutierrez, Ernesto *(Spanish artist, 19th cent.)*   **WC**

Gutiérrez, Esteban *(17th century Spanish architect, associated with Cathedral of Oaxaca)*   **AV**
Bibl: Arch. esp. de arte, LII/207 (Jul-Sep 1979) 313

Gutiérrez, Francisco *(Spanish painter, act.1642-1657)*   **BA**
Bibl: Agulló Cobo, Pintores madrileños sig. 16 y 17 (1978); Berute y Moret, THE SCHOOL OF MADRID; ▶Ceán Bermúdez, Bellas artes ESP, v.2, p.245; ▶Thieme-Becker

Gutiérrez, Juan Manuel *(Colombian architect)*   **AV**
Bibl: Proa, 1988 June, no.372, p.17

Gutierrez, Juan Simón   **PR WC**
(Spanish artist, 1644-1718)   **WC**
(Spanish painter, 1644-1718)   **PR**
Bibl: ▶Thieme-Becker

Juan Simon Gutierrez   **PR**

Gutierrez, Marlene Zander
(American artist, 20th c.)   **BA**
Bibl: Nelson, Leonardo XIX/3 (1986) 223-229

Gutiérrez, Rafael *(Colombian architect)*   **AV**
Bibl: Proa, 1986 July, no.352, p.20

Gutiérrez-Ambrossi Robles, Miguel
(Spanish architect)   **AV**
Bibl: Arquitectura, 1988 Mar.-June, v.69, no.271-272, p.18

Gutierriez-Blanchard, María→see Blanchard, María

Gutjahr, Silvana *(West German interior designer, Munich)*   **AV**
Bibl: Architektur, Innenarchitektur, Technischer Ausbau, 1989 June, v.97, no.6, p.64

Gutkin, Peter *(American sculptor, b.1944)*   **BA**
Bibl: ▶WW Amer. Art, 1989-1990

Gutkind, Erwin Anton *(German architect, Berlin, 1920s)*   **AV**
Bibl: Casabella, 1982 July-Aug., v.46, no.482, p.38

Gutman, N. *(German artist, 19th cent.)*   **WC**

Gutman, Nahum *(Israeli illustrator, author, painter, 1898-1980)*   **BA**
Bibl: Encyc. Judaica; ▶Intl. dir. exh. artists, 1983, v.1; ▶Natl. union cat., 1978; Zalmona, ISREALI MUSEUM JOURNAL, II(SP.83), 23-34

Gutman, Robert *(American architect, Princeton, N.J)*   **AV**
Bibl: ▶Libr. of Congr. Name Auth. File

Gutman, Willi *(Swiss sculptor, b.1927)*   **BA**
Bibl: ▶Künst.-Lex. Schweiz 20. Jahrh.

Gutmann, Franz *(West German sculptor, 1928-)*   **AV**
Bibl: ▶Libr. of Congr. Name Auth. File

Gutmann, John *(American painter, photographer, b.1905)*   **BA**
Bibl: Toronto(CAN), Art Gallery of Ontario, GUTMANN(1985); ▶WW Amer. Art, 1984

Gütner, Franz *(German architect, Munich)*   **AV**
Bibl: Architektur, Innenarchitektur, Technischer Ausbau, 1985 Mar., v.93, no.2, p.58

Guton, Raja *(Danish artist, 19th cent.)*   **WC**

Gutrecht, Matthaus, I *(Swiss artist, c.1450-1505)*   **WC**

Gutrecht, Matthaus, II *(Swiss artist, op.1506-1524)*   **WC**

Gutruf, Gerhard *(German artist, 20th cent.)*   **WC**

Gutschow, Arvid *(German, b. 1880)*   **JG**

Guttchen, Daniel *(Architect, Switzerland)*   **AV**
Bibl: DBZ, 1985 Jan., v.33, no.1, p.29

Guttenberg *(German)*   **GC**
Bibl: Gernsheim, Corpus Photog. of Drawings, 1777

Guttenberg or Guttenberger, Carl Gottlieb or Gottfried→see Guttenberg, Carl

Guttenberg, Carl   **GC**
(German artist, 1743-1790)   **WC**
(German, 1743-1790)   **GC**
Bibl: ▶Thieme-Becker; ▶Witt checklist

Guttenberg or Guttenberger, Carl Gottlieb or Gottfried   **WC**

Guttenbrunn, J.A. *(German artist, 18th cent.)*   **WC**

Guttenbrunn, Ludwig   **GC**
(Austrian painter, ca.1750-1819)   **GC**
(German artist, op.1770-1813)   **WC**
Bibl: Getty Photo Study Coll.; ▶Schweers, Gemälde deut. Museen; ▶Thieme-Becker

Guttenbrunn, Ludwig (not Lorenz)   **WC**

Guttenbrunn, Ludwig (not Lorenz)→see Guttenbrunn, Ludwig

Guttere, Alfredo *(Italian artist, 19th cent.)*   **WC**

Guttfreund, Otto→see Gutfreund, Otto

Gutti, Rosina Mantovani *(Italian artist, 20th cent.)*   **WC**

Guttilla, Carolyn *(American interior designer)*   **AV**
Bibl: House & garden, 1984 Sept., v.156, no.9, p.198

Guttmann, E. *(German, active ca. 1920)*   **JG**

Guttmann, Martin *(American photographer, 20th c.)* **BA**
Bibl: Welchman, FLASH ART 130 (Oct-Nov 1986) 70-71

Guttmann, Rudolf *(Austrian engineer, Graz)* **AV**
Bibl: ▶Verzeich. Öst. Ziviltech.

Gutton, Henri *(French architect, 1874-1963)* **BA**
Bibl: ▶Macmillan encyc. archts.; Mons. Hist. Fran., 141 (Oct.-Nov. 1985) p.44

Gutton, Henri B. *(French architect, engineer, 1851-1933)* **BA**
Bibl: ▶Macmillan encyc. archts.; Mons. Hist. Fran., 141 (Oct.-Nov. 1985) p.44

Guttoso, Renate → *see* Guttuso, Renato

Guttuso, Renato **BA GC WC**
(Italian artist, 1912-) WC
(Italian painter, author, 1912-1987) BA
(Italian painter, b.1912) GC
Bibl: Biog. idx., v.15, p.316; ▶Comanducci, Diz.; Getty Photo Study Coll.; ▶RILA/BHA, 1986; ▶Vollmer, Künst.-Lex. 20. Jhr.
Guttoso, Renate GC

Guttwein, Johann Georg *(German printmaker, painter, act.1698, d.1718)* **BA**
Bibl: ▶Bénézit; HOLLSTEIN; ▶Thieme-Becker

Gutzeit, Ernst *(scenographer, 20th c.)* **BA**
Bibl: Bauer, Wagner

Gutzeit, Fred *(American painter, b.1940)* **BA**
Bibl: ART MAGAZINE, LI/8(APR 1977), 16; ▶NY art yrbk.

Gutzon Borglum → *see* Borglum, Gutzon

Gutzwiller, Sebastian *(German artist, 1800-1872)* **WC**

Guvan, Aydin *(French architect)* **AV**
Bibl: Architettura: Cronache e storia, 1984 July, v.30, no.7, p.522

Guvina, Andrea → *see* Buvina, Andrea

Guy Carleton Wiggins → *see* Wiggins, Guy Carleton

[Guy Head] → *see* Head, Guy

Guy Pene Du Bois → *see* Du Bois, Guy Pène

Guy, Francis *(British artist, 1760-1820)* **WC WI**

Guy, Head → *see* Head, Guy

Guy, Hippolyte **GC**
(French artist, 1868-) WC
(French painter, b.1868) GC
Bibl: ▶Thieme-Becker

Guy, Hippolyte (Maurice Hippolyte) **WC**
Guy, Maurice-Hippolyte GC
Guy, Hippolyte (Maurice Hippolyte) → *see* Guy, Hippolyte

Guy, J.B. Louis *(French artist, 1824-1888)* **WC**

Guy, James M. *(American painter, 1910-1983)* **BA**
Bibl: ▶WW Amer. Art, 1984

Guy, John *(American architect, Wharton, Tex)* **AV**
Bibl: Victorian homes, 1989 summer, v.8, no.3, p.17

Guy, Maurice-Hippolyte → *see* Guy, Hippolyte

Guy, Seymour Joseph **BA GC PR WC WI**
(American artist, 1824-1910) WC WI
(American painter, 1824-1910) BA GC PR
Bibl: ▶Dict. Amer. biog.; ▶Fielding's Amer. ptrs.; ▶RILA/BHA; ▶Thieme-Becker; ▶Young, Amer. artists
Seymour Joseph Guy PR

Guy, Willy *(British photographer, b.1940)* **BA**
Bibl: Bristol (GBR), Arnolfini Gallery, Bristol sample (1979); ▶MoMA libr. cat.

Guyard *(French artist, op.1774-1778)* **WC**

Guyer, Esther *(Swiss architect)* **AV**
Bibl: ▶Schweiz. Ingen. u. Archit., 1984-1985

Guyer, Lux **AV BA**
(Swiss architect, 1894-1955) BA
(Swiss architect, interior designer, 1894-1955) AV
Bibl: ▶Vollmer, Künst.-Lex. 20. Jhr.; Zürich, ETH, DIE ARCHITEKTIN LUX GUYER, 1894-1955 (1983)

Guyer, Rudolf *(Swiss architect)* **AV**
Bibl: ▶Schweiz. Ingen. u. Archit., 1984-1985

Guyhead → *see* Head, Guy

Guyomard *(French artist, 20th cent.)* **WC**

Guyon, Jean Louis *(French, ca.1672-1736)* **GC**
Bibl: ▶Thieme-Becker

Guyon, Maximilienne (Goepp) *(French artist, 1868-1903)* **WC**

Guyot, Adelin *(Belgian painter, b.1950)* **BA**
Bibl: Minguet, ART AND FACT, 1(1982), 79

Guyot, Antoine Patrice (the Younger) → *see* Guyot, Antoine Patrice II

Guyot, Antoine Patrice II *(French painter, 1777-1845)* **GC**
Bibl: ▶Thieme-Becker
Guyot, Antoine Patrice (the Younger) GC

Guyot, Charles (Géo-Charles) *(French painter, poet, 1892-1963)* **BA**
Bibl: ▶Bénézit; ▶Natl. union cat.

Guyot, Fred N. *(American painter, b.1937)* **BA**
Bibl: ▶Art Index, v.22; ART NEWS, 72(SEPT 1973), 82

Guyot, Laurent **BA WC**
(French artist, op.1600-1664) WC
(French painter, tapestry designer, d.1610) BA
Bibl: ▶Bénézit; ▶Encyc. world art; ▶Thieme-Becker

Guyot, Laurent **PR WC**
(French artist, 1756-p.1806) WC
(French painter, b. 1756, act. 1793-1806) PR
Bibl: ▶Thieme-Becker
Laurent Guot PR
Laurent Guyot PR

Guyot, Louise *(French artist, op. 1841-1845)* **WC**

Guyot, R. *(French artist, op.1827)* **WC**

Guyot, Rémy *(French silversmith, master 1717)* **GC**
Bibl: ▶Mabille, Orfèv. fran.

Guys, Constantin **BA GC**
(French artist, 1805-1892) WC
(French painter, illustrator, 1802-1892) BA
(French, 1805-1892) GC
Bibl: ▶Bénézit; ▶Encyc. world art; ▶Thieme-Becker

Guys, Constantin (Ernest Adolphe Hyacinthe Constantin) **WC**
Guys, Constantin (Ernest Adolphe Hyacinthe Constantin) → *see* Guys, Constantin

Guz, Vladimir Vasil'evič *(Russian woodcarver, 20th c.)* **BA**
Bibl: DEKORATIVNOE ISKUSSTVO SSSR, 259(JUNE 1979), 30

Guzelimian, Vahé *(American photographer, 20th c.)* **BA**
Bibl: ▶Intl. dir. exh. artists, 1983

Guzman → *see* Guzmán, Juan

Guzmán, Alicia de *(Thai architect, Bangkok)* **AV**
Bibl: Abitare, 1988 June, no.265, p.156

Guzmán, Juan *(Spanish painter, 1611-1680)* **PR**
Bibl: ▶Thieme-Becker
F. Giovanni Gusman PR
Guzman PR
Juan Guzman PR

Guznan, Rodriguez de → *see* Rodríguez de Guzman, Manuel

Guzzardi, Giuseppe *(Italian painter, d.1914)* **GC**
Bibl: ▶Thieme-Becker

Guzzardi, Leonardo *(Italian artist, op.1799)* **WC**

Guzzi, Beppe *(Italian artist, 1902-)* **WC**

Guzzone, Sebastiano **GC WC**
(Italian artist, 1856-1890) WC
(Italian painter, 1856-1890) GC
Bibl: ▶Thieme-Becker

Gvarcino → *see* Guercino (Giovanni Francesco Barbieri)

Gvardjančič, Herman *(Yugoslav painter, b.1943)* **BA**
Bibl: Ljubljana(YUG), Mala Galerija. HERMAN GVARDJANIC(1981)

Gwathmey, Charles **AV BA**
(American architect, 1938-) AV
(American architect, b.1938) BA
Bibl: ▶AIA Pro File; ▶Contemp. archts.; Turner, Judith Turner Photographs Five Architects (1980)

Gwathmey, Robert **BA WC WI**
(American artist, 1903-) WC
(American artist, b.1903) WI
(American painter, b.1903) BA
Bibl: ▶Art Index, July 1990; ▶ARTbibl. mod., 20/2, #08645; ▶Marks, Dict. world artists; ▶Oxford comp. 20c. art; ▶Phaidon 20c. art; St. Mary's City (MD, USA), St. Mary's College Of Maryland. ROBERT GWATHMEY(1976); WW Amer., 1976

Gwatkin, Joshua Reynolds *(British artist, op.1832-1851)* **WI**

Gwennap, Thomas *(British artist, op.1821-1828)* **WC WI**

Gwerk, Edmund *(Czech artist, 1895-)* **WC**

Gwiazda, M. *(German architect, Munich)* **AV**
Bibl: Deutsche Bauzeitschrift, 1988, no.1, p.41

Gwillim, Elizabeth *(British painter, naturalist, 1763-1807)* **BA**
Bibl: Oshawa(ONT, CAN), McLaughlin Gallery. ELIZABETH GWILLIM...(1980)

Gwim, Gwin, Gvinn or Gvyn, James → see Gwim, James

Gwim, James **WI**
(British artist, 1700-1769) WI
(British artist, p.1700-1769) WC
Bibl: ▶Houfe, Brit. book illus.

Gwim, Gwin, Gvinn or Gvyn, James **WC**

Gwyn, Woody *(American painter, 20th c.)* **BA**
Bibl: ▶Art Index, v.28; ARTS MAGAZINE, LV(SEPT 1980), 15; Guide exh. artists: N. Amer. ptrs.

Gwynn, John **BA WI**
(British architect, d.1786) BA
(British artist, op.1755-, d.1786) WI
Bibl: ▶Dict. natl. biog.

Gwynn, W. → see Gwynn, William

Gwynn, William **WI**
(British artist, op.1807-1817) WC WI

Gwynn, W. **WC**

Gwynne, Patrick *(British architect, 1913-)* **AV**
Bibl: ▶Contemp. archts.

Gwynne-Evans, Frank, Mrs., (Hester) → see Frood, Hester

Gwynne-Jones, Allan **BA WC WI**
(British artist, 1892-) WC
(British artist, b.1892) WI
(British painter, printmaker, 1892-1982) BA
Bibl: ▶Art Index, v.31; ▶Johnson, Brit. artists; WW Amer., 1982

Gwynne-Jones, Emilie **WC WI**
(British artist, 20th cent.) WC
(British artist, op.20th c.) WI

Gwynne-Jones, Rosemary Allan, Mrs. → see Allan, Rosemary

Gyarfas, Jeno (Eugen) *(Hungarian artist, 1857-1925)* **WC**

Gyarmathy, M. **WC**
(French artist, 20th cent.) WC
(Hungarian artist, 20th cent.) WC

Gyrmathy **WC**

Gyarmathy, Tihamér **BA VO**
(Hungarian painter, act. Paris, b. 1915) VO
(Hungarian painter, b.1915) BA
Bibl: Aszalos, Gyarmathy Tihamér (1979); ▶Bénézit; ▶Németh, Mod. ungarische Kunst

Gyenes, Gitta *(Hungarian painter, 1888-1960)* **BA**
Bibl: ▶Bénézit; Budapest(HUN), Mag.Nemzeti Galeria. GYENES GITTA 1888-1960(1978); ▶Vollmer, Künst.-Lex. 20. Jhr.

Gyfford, Edward *(British artist, 1772-1834)* **WC WI**

Gyffoths *(Dutch(?) artist, 18th cent.)* **WC**

Gygax, Hugo *(Swiss architect)* **AV**
Bibl: ▶Schweiz. Ingen. u. Archit., 1984-1985

Gyles, Althea *(Irish artist, book designer, act.1890s)* **BA**
Bibl: ▶Natl. union cat.

Gyles, Henry **BA GC**
(British artist, c.1640-1709) WC
(British artist, circa 1640-1709) WI
(British, 1645-1709) GC
(English glass painter, 1645-1709) BA
Bibl: Brighton, "Henry Gyles", YORK HISTORIAN IV(1984); ▶Brit. Mus. cat.; ▶Dict. natl. biog.; ▶Thieme-Becker; ▶Witt checklist

Giles or Gyles, Henry **WC**

Giles, Henry **WI**

Gyllenpalm, Kim *(Swedish architect, Stockholm)* **AV**
Bibl: ▶Svenska Ark. Riks., 1984

Gyongyi, Yvonne *(Hungarian artist, 20th cent.)* **WC**

Gyorgel or Giergl, Alajos or Alois *(Hungarian artist, 1821-1863)* **WC**

György of Kolozsvár → see Kolozsvári, György

Györgyi, Dénes *(Hungarian architect(?), 1886-1961)* **AV**
Bibl: Magyar építőművészet, 1987, v.78, no.4-5, p.39

Gyozo, Szilas *(Hungarian artist, 20th cent.)* **WC**

Gyp (Sybille-Gabrielle-Marie Antoinette de Riquetti-Mirabeau, Comtesse de Martel de Janville) *(French artist, 1850-1932)* **WC**

Gyraldus *(French scribe, act. late 11th century)* **GC**
Bibl: Paris, Mss. 7-12e s., p.192

Gyrmathy → see Gyarmathy, M.

Gysaerts or Gijseerts, Gualterus → see Gysaerts, Wouter

Gysaerts, F.G. → see Gysaerts, Wouter

Gysaerts, Wouter **GC**
(Flemish artist, 1649-p.1674) WC
(Flemish, 1649-aft.1674) GC
Bibl: Getty Photo Study Coll. (Ptgs.); ▶Thieme-Becker

Gijsaerts, Gualterus **GC**

Gysaerts or Gijseerts, Gualterus **WC**

Gysaerts, F.G. **GC**

Gysbert Gillisz. de Hondecoeter → see Hondecoeter, Gysbert Gillisz. de

Gysbert van Glabbeeck → see Glabbeeck, Gysbert van

Gysbrecht Hondekoeter → see Hondecoeter, Gysbert Gillisz. de

Gysbrecht Leytens → see Leytens, Gysbrecht

Gysbrechts → see Gysbrechts, Cornelis Norbertus

Gysbrechts, Cornelis Norbertus **BA GC PR WC**
(Flemish artist, op.1659-1672) WC
(Flemish painter, act. 1659-1672) PR
(Flemish painter, act.1659-1672) BA
(Flemish, act.1659-1672) GC
Bibl: ▶Thieme-Becker; ▶Witt checklist

Cornelis Norbertus Gysbrechts **PR**

Gijsbrechts, Cornelis Norbertus **PR**

Gysbrechts **PR**

Gysbrechts, Franciscus **GC WC**
(Dutch artist, op.1674) WC
(Dutch painter, act.1674) GC
Bibl: ▶Thieme-Becker

Gyseiaer or Giselaer, Nicolaes de → see Gyselaer, Nicolaes de

Gyselaer → see Gyselaer, Nicolaes de

Gyselaer or Giselaer, Philip *(Flemish artist, op.1634/5)* **WC**

Gyselaer, Nicolaes de   **GC PR**
  (Dutch artist, op.1616-1654)   WC
  (Dutch painter, 1590/95-1654)   PR
  (Dutch painter,
    1590/95-aft.1654)   GC
    Bibl: ▶Bénézit; Getty Photo Study
    Coll.; Getty Photo Study Coll.
    (Ptgs.); ▶Thieme-Becker; ▶Witt
    checklist
  D. Giselaer   PR
  Giselaer, Nicolaes de   GC PR
Gyseiaer or Giselaer, Nicolaes
    de   **WC**
  Gyselaer   PR
  Nicolaes de Gyselaer   PR
Gyselinck, Jos   **GC**
  (Belgian artist, 19th cent.)   WC
  (Belgian painter, act.1851)   GC
    Bibl: ▶Bénézit
Gyselinckx, Joseph   **WC**
  Gyselinckx, Joseph → *see* Gyselinck,
    Jos
  Gysels → *see* Gysels, Peeter
  Gysels, Geysels, Gheysels, Gijsels,
    Gyssels, Gysens etc. Peeter → *see*
    Gysels, Peeter
Gysels, Peeter   **GC PR**
  (Flemish artist, 1621-1690/1)   WC
  (Flemish painter, 1621-1690/1)   PR
  (Flemish, 1621-1690/91)   GC
    Bibl: ▶Thieme-Becker
  Gysels   PR
Gysels, Geysels, Gheysels,
    Gijsels, Gyssels, Gysens etc.
    Peeter   **WC**
  Gysels, Pieter   PR
  Gysson   PR
  P. Gysons   PR
  Peeter Gysels   PR
  Pieter Gheese   PR
  Pietro Gheys   PR
  Gysels, Pieter → *see* Gysels, Peeter
Gysin, Brion *(American painter,*
    author, b.1916)   **BA**
    Bibl: ▶Art Index, Nov. 1983-Oct.
    1984, Nov. 1983-Oct. 1984; Jan.
    1991; ▶ARTbibl. mod., 9,10,18;
    ▶Natl. union cat.; Perrot,
    ARTENSION, 10 (1989) p.34-35;
    ▶WW Amer. Art, 1984, 1989
Gysis, Nicolaos   **BA**
  (Greek artist, 1842-1901)   WC
  (Greek painter in Germany,
    1842-1901)   BA
    Bibl: Papastamos, D., in Thiasos
    Tōn Mousōn (1984) 217-221;
    ▶Thieme-Becker; ▶Witt checklist
Gysis, Nikolaus   **WC**
  Gysis, Nikolaus → *see* Gysis, Nicolaos
Gyssler, Felix *(Swiss artist, 20th*
    cent.)   **WC**
  Gysson → *see* Gysels, Peeter
  Gyula Benczur → *see* Benczúr, Gyula

Gyurkovits, Ferenc *(Hungarian*
    painter, 1876-1968)   **BA**
    Bibl: MUVESZETTORTENETI
    ERTESITE, XXV/4(1976), 352-355;
    ▶Vollmer, Künst.-Lex. 20. Jhr.
  H de C → *see* Monogrammist H. de C.
  H Howard, R.A. → *see* Howard, Henry
  H V Limborch → *see* Limborch,
    Hendrik van
  H, Swanefeld → *see* Swanevelt,
    Herman van
  H. Aldegraef → *see* Aldegrever,
    Heinrich
  H. Aldegraf → *see* Aldegrever,
    Heinrich
  H. Aldegraff → *see* Aldegrever,
    Heinrich
  H. Aldegraft → *see* Aldegrever,
    Heinrich
  H. Antonis → *see* Anthonissen,
    Hendrick van
  H. B. 1552 → *see* Monogrammist H.B.
  H. B. Chalon → *see* Chalon, Henry
    Bernard
  H. B. Thier → *see* Thier, Bernhard
    Heinrich
  H. Berckheyde → *see* Berckheyde, Job
    Adriaensz.
  H. Berkheide → *see* Berckheyde, Job
    Adriaensz.
  H. Berkheyde → *see* Berckheyde, Job
    Adriaensz.
  H. Blomaert → *see* Bloemaert,
    Hendrick
  H. Bolch → *see* Bolch, H. [Unidentified]
  H. Boulangier → *see* Bollongier, Hans
  H. Breughel → *see* Brueghel, Jan, the
    elder
  H. Brooke → *see* Brooke, Henry
  H. Brosamer → *see* Brosamer, Hans
  H. Brosimer → *see* Brosamer, Hans
  H. Brughel → *see* Brueghel, Pieter, the
    younger
  H. Carracci → *see* Carracci, Annibale
  H. Carre → *see* Carree, Hendrik
  H. de C. → *see* Monogrammist H. de
    C.
  H. F. Breughel → *see* Brueghel, Pieter,
    the younger
  H. F. Brueghels → *see* Brueghel, Pieter,
    the younger
  H. Franck → *see* Francken, Hieronymus
    I
  H. Fuseli → *see* Fuseli, Henry
  H. Fuseli, Esq.R.A. → *see* Fuseli, Henry
  H. Gobbo Caracci → *see* Bonzi, Pietro
    Paolo (Gobbo dei Carracci)
  H. Gobo Caracci → *see* Bonzi, Pietro
    Paolo (Gobbo dei Carracci)
  H. Goltzius → *see* Goltzius, Hendrik
  H. Gudin → *see* Gudin, Herminie
    (Madame Fauchier)
  H. Holbein → *see* Holbein, Hans, the
    younger

  H. Holbien → *see* Holbein, Hans, the
    younger
  H. Hondius → *see* Hondius, Abraham
  H. Howard → *see* Howard, Henry
  H. Howard R.A. → *see* Howard, Henry
  H. Howard, A.R.A. → *see* Howard,
    Henry
  H. Howard, R.A. → *see* Howard, Henry
  H. Hulley → *see* Hulley, H.
  H. Hulsman → *see* Hulsman, Johann
  H. Kuibbers → *see* Cuyper, Hendrick
  H. Ledyard Towle → *see* Towle, H.
    Ledyard
  H. Lemens → *see* Lemens, H.
    [Unidentified]
  H. Lofthouse → *see* Lofthouse, H.
    [Unidentified]
  H. Mans → *see* Heeremans, Thomas
  H. Meyer, &c. → *see* Meijer, Hendrik
    de
  H. Moore → *see* Moore, H.
    [Unidentified]
  H. Morland → *see* Morland, Henry
    Robert
  H. Muller → *see* Muller, Hermann
    [Unidentified]
  H. Pagna → *see* La Pegna, Hyacinth de
  H. Paulyn → *see* Paulyn, Horatius
  H. Potuyl → *see* Potuyl, Henrik
  H. Ravestein → *see* Ravesteyn, Hubert
    van
  H. Rigaud → *see* Rigaud, Hyacinthe
  H. Roos → *see* Roos, Johann Heinrich
  H. Sachleven → *see* Saftleven, Herman
  H. Sachtleven → *see* Saftleven,
    Herman
  H. Sagtleben → *see* Saftleven, Herman
  H. Sagtleven → *see* Saftleven, Herman
  H. Satchleven → *see* Saftleven,
    Herman
  H. Schoenfelder → *see* Schönfeld,
    Johann Heinrich
  H. Schweickhardt → *see* Schweickardt,
    Heinrich Wilhelm
  H. Schwickhardt → *see* Schweickardt,
    Heinrich Wilhelm
  H. Serin → *see* Serin, Harmen
  H. Singleton → *see* Singleton, Henry
  H. Snellinck → *see* Snellinck, Jan I
  H. Stoccade → *see* Helt Stockade,
    Nicolaes van
  H. Stoffee → *see* Stoffe, Jan Jacobsz.
    van der
  H. Swanefeld → *see* Swanevelt,
    Herman van
  H. Swaneveldt → *see* Swanevelt,
    Herman van
  H. Swinburne, Esq. → *see* Swinburne,
    Henry
  H. Tresham → *see* Tresham, Henry
  H. Tresham R.A. → *see* Tresham, Henry
  H. Tresham, R. A. → *see* Tresham,
    Henry
  H. V. E. → *see* Monogrammist H.V.E.

H. van Buren Magonigle→*see* Magonigle, H. van Buren

H. van de Velde→*see* Velde, Adriaen van de

H. Van Ravestyn→*see* Ravesteyn, Hubert van

H. van Vliet→*see* Vliet, Hendrik Cornelisz. van

H. Vander Botcht→*see* Borcht, Hendrik van der (the elder)

H. Vandermyn→*see* Myn, Herman van der

H. Vanhoven→*see* Hoven, H. van [Unidentified]

H. Veccelli→*see* Vecellio, Orazio

H. Vecelli→*see* Vecellio, Orazio

H. Verelst→*see* Verelst, Herman

H. Verschuring→*see* Verschuring, Hendrik

H. W. Schweickhardt→*see* Schweickardt, Heinrich Wilhelm

H. Wild→*see* Wild, H. [Unidentified]

H. Williams→*see* Williams, H.

H. Wootton→*see* Wootton, John

H. Zachtleven→*see* Saftleven, Herman

H., Caterina van→*see* Hemessen, Katharina van

H.A. and Suckling-Salting Group   JG

H.A. Hellwegen→*see* Hellwegen, H.A.

"H.A." Painter *(Apulian vase-painter)*   GC
Bibl: Trendall, Attic red-fig. vases Apulia

H.B. →*see* Doyle, John (HB)

H.B. →*see* Monogrammist H.B.

H.B. Chalon→*see* Chalon, Henry Bernard

H.D. →*see* Monogrammist H.D.

H.D. 1667→*see* Monogrammist H.D.

H.F. Raspe→*see* Raspe, H.F. [Unidentified]

H.P. Painter   GC
Bibl: ▶Beazley, Attic red-fig. vase-ptrs.

H.V.D. Burg→*see* Burch, Hendrick van der

Ha os de Valdes→*see* Ha os de Valdès [Unidentified]

Ha os de Valdès [Unidentified]
(Unknown painter)   PR
Bibl: Soult inventory, dated 1852 (item B4)
Ha os de Valdes   PR

Haach, Ludwig *(German artist, 1813-1842)*   WC

Haacke, Hans Christoph *(German artist in USA, b.1936)*   BA
Bibl: ▶Contemp. artists; ▶Intl. dir. exh. artists, 1983; ▶WW Amer. Art, 1976, 1984

Haacke, Harald *(German sculptor, b.1924)*   BA
Bibl: ▶Vollmer, Künst.-Lex. 20. Jhr.; ▶WW Arts DEU

Haag Funnel Group Painter
(Etruscan vase-painters, 350-300 BC)   GC
Bibl: Del Chiaro, Funnel Group

Häag, Axel Herman→*see* Hägg, Axel Herman

Haag, Carl   BA GC WC
(German artist, 1820-1915)   WC
(German draughtsman, 1820-1915)   GC
(German painter in GBR, 1820-1915)   BA
Bibl: ▶Bénézit; ▶Johnson, Brit. artists; ▶Thieme-Becker

Haag, Charles Oscar *(Swedish sculptor in USA, 1867-1933)*   BA
Bibl: ▶Svenska konstnärer; ▶Vollmer, Künst.-Lex. 20. Jhr.; ▶Young, Amer. artists

Haag, Cornelius Pieter *(German painter, 18th century)*   GC
Bibl: Getty Photo Study Coll. (Duits coll.)

Haag, Edgar *(American landscape architect)*   AV
Bibl: Process: architecture, 1985 Aug., no.61, p.62

Haag, Hans *(German artist, 1841-)*   WC

Haag, Horst *(West German architect, Stuttgart)*   AV
Bibl: Architektur + Wettbewerbe, 1986 Sept., no.127, p.64

Haag, Peter [Unidentified]
(Unknown painter)   PR
Bibl: (1805, lot 39)
Peter Haag   PR

Haag, Richard *(American landscape architect, Seattle, Wash)*   AV
Bibl: Landscape architecture, 1986 Sept.-Oct., v.76, no.5, p.54

Haag, Tethart Philip Christian   BA WC
(Dutch painter, printmaker, 1737-1812)   BA
(German artist, 1737-1812)   WC
Bibl: ▶Thieme-Becker; ▶Wurzbach, NLD Künst.-Lex.

Haag, Wilhelm *(West German architect, Stuttgart)*   AV
Bibl: Deutsches Architektenblatt, 1987 Oct., v.19, no.10, p.1161

Haaga, Edouard *(German artist, op. 1888-1897)*   WC

Haage, Franciscus   BA GC
(Dutch artist, op.1686)   WC
(Dutch painter, act.1686)   BA GC
Bibl: ▶Bénézit; ▶Thieme-Becker; ▶Wurzbach, NLD Künst.-Lex.

Haagen or Haage, Franciscus   WC
Haagen, Franciscus   GC
Hagen, Franciscus   GC

Haagen or Haage, Franciscus→*see* Haage, Franciscus

Haagen, Franciscus→*see* Haage, Franciscus

Haagen, Joris van der→*see* Hagen, Joris van der

Haagmans, Fons *(Dutch painter, b.1948)*   BA
Bibl: Maastricht (NLD), Bonnefantenmus., Kunst/Limburg: Een Keuze (1984).; Maastricht (NLD), Bonnefantenmus., Toon Teeken, Fons Haagmans (1986)

Haak, Christie van der *(Dutch artist, b.1950)*   BA
Bibl: Eindhoven (NLD), Stedelijk van Abbemuseum, LA CAUSE DE NOTRE JOIE: CHRISTIE VAN DER HAAK, 1985; Welter, METROPOLIS M V/6 (Nov-Dec 1984), 6-9 (RILA, NLD)

Haak, Lex *(Dutch architect and professor, Delft)*   AV
Bibl: De Architect, 1988 Nov., v.19, no.11 suppl., p.66

Haake   WC WI
(British artist, 16th cent.)   WC
(British artist, op.16th c.)   WI

Haakman, Cornelia Maria→*see* Warnsinck, Cornelia Maria

Haaland, Knut Magne *(Norwegian architect, 1955-)*   AV
Bibl: Byggekunst: the Norwegian review of architecture, 1988, v.70, no.5, p.326

Haaland, Per Oscar *(Norwegian architect, 1953-)*   AV
Bibl: Byggekunst: the Norwegian review of architecture, 1988, v.70, no.5, p.354

Haan→*see* Haan, Meyer Isaac de

Haan or Haen, Dirk de *(Dutch artist, 1832-1886)*   WC

Haan, Franciscus Antonius de *(Dutch artist, 1823-1873)*   WC

Haan, Jacob Glaudianna de *(Dutch painter, 1824-1901)*   GC
Bibl: ▶Scheen, Ned. beeldende kunst.

Haan, Jurjen de *(Dutch painter, b.1936)*   BA
Bibl: Norwich (GBR), Castle Mus., Watercolours from The Hague (1978); ▶Scheen, Ned. beeldende kunst.

Haan, Meijer Isaac de→*see* Haan, Meyer Isaac de

Haan, Meyer Isaac de   BA GC PR
(Dutch artist, 1852-1895)   WC
(Dutch painter, 1852-1895)   BA GC PR
Bibl: ▶Bénézit; ▶Busse, Maler u. Bildhauer 19. Jahr.; ▶RILA/BHA; ▶Thieme-Becker; ▶Wurzbach, NLD Künst.-Lex.
Haan   PR

Haan, Meijer Isaac de   WC
Meyer de Haan, Jacob Isaac   GC
Meyer Isaac de Haan   PR

Haan, Willem Jacob de *(Dutch artist, 1913-1967)*   BA
Bibl: Amsterdam (NLD), Stedelijk Mus., Ex cat. 1976; ▶Scheen, Ned. beeldende kunst.

Haanebrink, Willem Albertus→see
Hannebrink, Willem Albertus

Haanen, Adriana Johanna   GC WC
 (Dutch artist, 1814-1895)   WC
 (Dutch painter, 1814-1895)   GC
  Bibl: ▶Bénézit

Haanen, Casparis (Dutch artist,
 1778-1849)   WC

Haanen, Cecil van   GC WC
 (Dutch artist, 1844-)   WC
 (Dutch painter, 1844-aft.1873)   GC
  Bibl: ▶Bénézit

Haanen, Elisabeth Alida   GC WC
 (Dutch artist, 1809-1845)   WC
 (Dutch painter, 1809-1845)   GC
  Bibl: ▶Thieme-Becker
 Kiers, Elisabeth Alida   GC

Haanen, Georg Gillis   GC
 (Dutch artist, 1807-1879/81)   WC
 (Dutch painter, 1807-1879)   GC
  Bibl: ▶Thieme-Becker

Haanen, George Gillis   WC
Haanen, George Gillis→see Haanen,
 Georg Gillis

Haanen, Remigius Adrianus (Remi)   GC
 (Dutch artist, 1812-1894)   WC
 (Dutch painter, 1812-1894)   GC
  Bibl: ▶Thieme-Becker

**Haanen, Remigius Adrianus
 (Remy or Remi van Haanen)**   WC
Haanen, Remigius Adrianus (Remy or
 Remi van Haanen)→see Haanen,
 Remigius Adrianus (Remi)
Haansberg→see Haensbergen, Johan
 van
Haansbergen→see Haensbergen,
 Johan van
Haansbergen, Johannes van→see
 Haensbergen, Johan van

Haaren, Dirk Johannes van (Dutch
 painter, 1878-1953)   GC
  Bibl: ▶Vollmer, Künst.-Lex. 20. Jhr.
Haarlem, Cornelis van→see
 Cornelisz. van Haarlem, Cornelis
Haarlem, Jan Mandyn van→see
 Mandyn, Jan

Haars, Peter (Norwegian artist, 20th
 cent.)   WC

Haas (American, active NY and SC,
 U.S. 1846-1867 (also Haas &
 Peale))   JG
Haas→see Haas, Maurits Frederik
 Hendrik de

Haas, Adrianus Johannes de
 (Dutch painter, printmaker, 1920-
 1972)   BA
  Bibl: ▶Grote Winkler Prins;
  ▶Scheen, Ned. beeldende kunst.

Haas, Alois (Austrian architect,
 1805-1879)   BA
  Bibl: ▶Österr. biog. Lex. 1815-
  1950

Haas, Andréa   AV

Haas, Bruno (Austrian architect,
 Graz)   AV
  Bibl: ▶Verzeich. Öst. Ziviltech.

Haas, Carl (Austrian goldsmith, act.
 1860s)   BA
  Bibl: Simoniti, Zbornik za
  umetnostno zgodovino XVII
  (1981) 75-87

Haas, Daniel (Architectural
 photographer)   AV
  Bibl: Proa, [1984], no.332, p.10

Haas, Ernst (American
 photographer, b.1921)   BA
  Bibl: ▶Auer, Encyc. photographes;
  ▶Contemp. photogs.; ▶Gernsheim,
  Hist. photog.; ▶Parry, Photo idx.

Haas, Franz Sebastian (German
 artist, op.1730-1737)   WC

Haas, Fritz (Austrian architect, fl.
 1920's-1940's)   AV
  Bibl: Magyar építőművészet,
  1987, v.78, no.4-5., p.18

Haas, Georg (Johann Jakob Georg)
 (Danish artist, 1756-1817)   WC

Haas, Hendrik de (Dutch
 bookbinder, publisher, author,
 1732-1809)   BA
  Bibl: J. Storm van Leeuwen, in
  QUAERENDO X (1980), 237-249

Haas, Jan de (Dutch painter,
 b.1943)   GC
  Bibl: ▶Scheen, Ned. beeldende
  kunst.

Haas, Jean (German(?) artist, 18th
 cent.)   WC

Haas, Johannes (American
 cabinetmaker, 1814-1856)   BA
  Bibl: Lewisburg (PA, USA),
  Bucknell U, Center Gallery,
  DECORATED FURNITURE... (1987),
  p.75ff

**Haas, Johannes Hubertus
 Leonardus de**   BA GC WC
 (Dutch artist, 1832-1908)   WC
 (Dutch painter and
  draughtsman, 1832-1908)   GC
 (Dutch painter, 1832-1908)   BA
  Bibl: Getty Photo Study Coll.;
  ▶Thieme-Becker; ▶Witt checklist

Haas, Jürg (Swiss architect)   AV
  Bibl: ▶Schweiz. Ingen. u. Archit.,
  1984-1985
Haas, M.F.H. de→see Haas, Maurits
 Frederik Hendrik de
Haas, Maurits Frederik de→see Haas,
 Maurits Frederik Hendrik de

**Haas, Maurits Frederik Hendrik
 de**   BA PR WC
 (Dutch artist, 1832-1895)   WC
 (Dutch painter, 1832-1895)   BA PR
  Bibl: ▶Bénézit; ▶Scheen, Ned.
  beeldende kunst.;
  ▶Thieme-Becker; ▶Wurzbach, NLD
  Künst.-Lex.
 Haas   PR
 Haas, M.F.H. de   PR
 Haas, Maurits Frederik de   PR
 Maurits Frederik Hendrik de Haas   PR

Haas, Meno (Johann Meno)
 (German artist, 1752-1833)   WC

Haas, P. (Austrian architect)   AV
  Bibl: Planen Bauen Wohnen,
  1989, no.127, p.34

Haas, P.   WC WI
 (American artist, op.1835-1845)   WI
 (American artist, op.c.1840)   WC
 (Engraver, Washington, DC., op.
  1835-1845)   WI

Haas, Peter (West German architect,
 Stuttgart)   AV
  Bibl: Detail, 1982 July-Aug., no.4,
  p.397

Haas, Peter (Christian Peter Jonas)
 (German artist, 1754-p.1804)   WC

Haas, Philip (American
 photographer, act.1839-1857)   BA
  Bibl: ▶Image; METROPOLITAN
  MUSEUM JOURNAL XII (1977),
  p.151

Haas, Plinio (Swiss architect, Arbon)   AV
  Bibl: Deutsche Bauzeitschrift,
  1986 Oct., v.34, no.10, p.1251
Haas, Richard→see Haas, Richard
 John

Haas, Richard John   BA
 (American painter, printmaker,
  b.1936)   BA
 (American trompe l'oeil painter,
  1936-)   AV
  Bibl: ▶Cummings, Contemp.
  Amer. artists; ▶Libr. of Congr.
  Name Auth. File; ▶WW Amer. Art,
  1976

Haas, Richard   AV

Haas, Rudolf (Austrian sculptor,
 b.1937)   BA
  Bibl: Acatos, Kohler & Kyrias:
  RUDOLF HAAS..., 1984
Haas, William Frederik de→see
 Haas, William Frederik de

Haas, William Frederik de   WI
 (American artist, 1830-1880)   WC WI

Haas, William Frederik de   WC

Haas, Wynand de (Dutch artist, op.
 1698-1700)   WC

Haasbroek, Geraerd   GC WC
 (Dutch artist, op.1775)   WC
 (Dutch draughtsman, 18th
  century)   GC
  Bibl: ▶Bénézit

Haase, Karl (German artist, -c.1877)   WC

Haase, Ove (Danish painter, b.1894)   BA
  Bibl: Haase: Tilbageblik

Haase-Jastrow, Kurt   BA WC
 (German artist, 1885-1958)   WC
 (German painter, 1885-1958)   BA
  Bibl: ▶Bénézit; ▶Thieme-Becker;
  ▶Vollmer, Künst.-Lex. 20. Jhr.

Haasen, D. (German architect,
 Dusseldorf)   AV
  Bibl: Deutsche Bauzeitschrift,
  1985 June, v.33, no.6, p.759

Haasen, Raymond (French print
 publisher, painter, printmaker,
 1911-1983)   BA
  Bibl: Nouvelle de l'estampe 68
  (Mar-Apr 1983) 15-19

Haass, Terry BA WC
   (Dutch artist, 1923-) WC
   (German artist, 20th c.) BA
     Bibl: Bochum (BRD), Mus., TERRY
     HAASS, 1978
Haastert, Isaac van → see Haastert,
   Isaak van
Haastert, Isaak van BA
   (Dutch artist, 1753-1834) WC
   (Dutch draughtsman, 1753-
     1834) GC
   (Dutch painter, printmaker,
     poet, 1753-1834) BA
     Bibl: ▶Thieme-Becker; ▶Witt
     checklist; ▶Wurzbach, NLD
     Künst.-Lex.
   Haastert, Isaac van GC WC
Haastrup, Lars (Danish architect) AV
     Bibl: Arkitektur DK, 1988 v.32,
     no.4, p.152
Haasz., Jacobus (Netherlands(?)
   artist, op.1655) WC
Haaxman, Pieter (Dutch painter,
   1854-1937) GC
     Bibl: ▶Bénézit
Habbima → see Hobbema, Meindert
Habel, van der [Unidentified]
   (Unknown painter) PR
     Bibl: (July 10, 1813, lot 15,
     Squibb)
   Vanderhabel PR
Habenicht, Carl Gotthelf (German
   porcelain modeller, 1800-1849) BA
     Bibl: Jedding, Meissener Porz.,
     p.148
Habenschaden, Sebastian (German
   artist, 1813-1868) WC
Haber, Ira Joel (American sculptor,
   b.1947) BA
     Bibl: New Brunswick (NJ, USA),
     Rutgers U., Response to the
     environment (1975); ▶WW Amer.
     Art, 1976
Haberer, Godfrid AV BA
   (German architect, Cologne,
     1941-) AV
   (West German architect,
     b.1941) BA
     Bibl: ▶Avery period. idx., 4th
     suppl.; Deutsche Bauzeitung,
     1985 June, v.119, no.6, p.136
Haberes, Matthäus Eustachius
   (German sculptor, 1753-1824) BA
     Bibl: ▶Bénézit; Mainzer Zeitschrift
     LXIX (1974) p.190-196;
     ▶Thieme-Becker
Haberjahn, Gabriel Eduard (Swiss
   artist, 1890-1956) WC
Haberle → see Haberle, John

Haberle, John BA GC PR WC WI
   (American artist, 1856-1933) WI
   (American artist, 20th cent.) WC
   (American painter, 1856-1933) BA PR
   (American, 20th century) GC
     Bibl: ▶Britannica encyc. Amer. art;
     ▶Encyc. world art; ▶RILA/BHA;
     ▶Vollmer, Künst.-Lex. 20. Jhr.;
     ▶Witt checklist
   Haberle PR
   John Haberle PR
Habermann, Franz Edler von
   (Czech artist, 1788-) WC
Habermann, Franz Xaver BA GC
   (German artist, 1721-1796) WC
   (German designer, sculptor,
     1721-1796) BA
   (German draughtsman, 1721-
     1796) GC
     Bibl: ▶Bénézit; ▶Penguin dec. arts;
     ▶Thieme-Becker
Habermann, Franz Xavier WC
Habermann, Franz Xavier → see
   Habermann, Franz Xaver
Habermann, Hugo van → see
   Habermann, Hugo von
Habermann, Hugo von BA GC PR WC
   (German artist, 1849-1929) WC
   (German painter, 1849-
     1929) BA GC PR
     Bibl: ▶Bénézit; NY Met catalogue;
     ▶RILA/BHA; ▶Thieme-Becker;
     ▶Vollmer, Künst.-Lex. 20. Jhr.
   Habermann, Hugo von PR
Habermann, Hugo, Freiherr von PR
   Hugo von Habermann PR
   Hugo, Freiherr von Habermann PR
Habermann, Hugo, Freiherr von → see
   Habermann, Hugo von
Habermehl, Erasmus (Bohemian
   instrument maker, act.1576,
     d.1606) BA
     Bibl: ▶Encyc. world art; Jahrb. der
     Hamburger Kunstsammlungen XXI
     1976, 55-92; ▶Thieme-Becker
Habermehl, Josua (Bohemian
   goldsmith, instrument maker, 16th
     c.) BA
     Bibl: ▶Thieme-Becker
Haberschrack, Nicolas → see
   Haberschrek, Nikolaus
Haberschrek, Nikolaus GC
   (Polish artist, op.1454-1481) WC
   (Polish painter, act.1454-d.1516) GC
     Bibl: ▶Thieme-Becker
Haberschrack, Nicolas WC
Habert, Francois GC WC
   (French artist, op.c.1645) WC
   (French, act. ca.1645) GC
     Bibl: ▶Witt checklist
Habert, Nicolas (French artist,
   c.1650-p.1715) WC
Habich, Edward (German, 19th c.) BA
     Bibl: ▶Natl. union cat.

Habich, Ludwig (German sculptor,
   1872-1948) BA
     Bibl: ▶Bénézit; ▶Neue deutsche
     Biog.; ▶Thieme-Becker; ▶Vollmer,
     Künst.-Lex. 20. Jhr.; Weyrauch,
     KUNST IN HESSEN U.A.
     MITTELRHEIN, XX (1980) 85-105
Habilius, Johannes (German(?)
   artist, 17th cent.(?)) WC
Habl, Willi Paul Rudolf (German
   artist, 1888-) WC
Hablig, Beatrice (American painter,
   20th c.) BA
     Bibl: Art News, LXXX/5 (May
     1981) pp.74-94
Hablik, Wenzel AV BA
   (Czech painter, printmaker,
     decorative artist in Germany,
     1881-1934) BA
   (German painter, etcher, and
     designer, 1881-1934) AV
     Bibl: Feuss, A., NORDELBINGEN, LI
     (1982) 131-150; ▶Thieme-Becker;
     ▶Vollmer, Künst.-Lex. 20. Jhr.
Hablot Knight Browne → see Browne,
   Hablot Knight
Habraken, Nicolaas John (Dutch
   architect, theorist and teacher,
     1928-) AV
     Bibl: Architecture, the AIA
     journal, 1986 Oct., v.75, no. 10,
     p.90; ▶Contemp. archts.
Habuka, Takao (Japanese architect,
   1945-) AV
     Bibl: Kenchiku bunka, 1987 Dec.,
     v.42, no.494, p.228
Haburg, Johann Peter (German
   painter, act.1737) BA
     Bibl: ▶Bénézit; Singer, Allgem.
     Bildniskat.; ▶Thieme-Becker
Haccou → see Haccou, Johannes
   Cornelis
Haccou, Johannes Cornelis GC PR WC
   (Dutch artist, 1798-1839) WC
   (Dutch painter, 1798-1839) GC PR
     Bibl: ▶Thieme-Becker
   Haccou PR
   Johannes Cornelis Haccou PR
Hache Bibi → see Hache,
   Christophe-André
Hache l'aîné → see Hache,
   Jean-François
Hache, Christophe-André (French
   ébéniste, 1748-1831) GC
     Bibl: ▶Salverte, Ébénistes 18e s.;
     ▶Vial, Artistes décorateurs
   Hache Bibi GC
   Hache-Lagrange GC
Hache, Jean-François (French
   ébéniste, 1730-1801) GC
     Bibl: ▶Salverte, Ébénistes 18e s.;
     ▶Vial, Artistes décorateurs
   Hache l'aîné GC
Hache, Pierre (French ébéniste,
   1703-1776) GC
     Bibl: ▶Salverte, Ébénistes 18e s.

Hache-Lagrange → see Hache, Christophe-André

Hachenberg, Heinrich P. *(West German architect)*   AV

Hachman, Albert *(German brass founder, act.1520-1565)*   BA
> Bibl: Dorgolo, Niederrhein. Jrbch. VIII (1965) pp.158-166; ▶Thieme-Becker

Hachman, Wilhelm *(German brass founder, ca.1560-1615)*   BA
> Bibl: Dorgolo, Niederrhein. Jrbch. VIII (1965) pp.158-166; ▶Thieme-Becker; Werd, G., ANTIEK, XXII/ 9/ (April 1988), p.474-481

Hachtmann-Pütz, Birgit *(West German architect, Hamburg)*   AV
> Bibl: Bauwelt, 1987 Mar.6, v.78, no.10, p.322

Hachulle, Ulrich *(German artist, 20th c.)*   BA
> Bibl: Altenburg (DEU), Staat. Lindenau-Mus., Etching & engraving (1979)

Hacin, Janez *(Swiss architect, Geneva)*   AV
> Bibl: ▶Schweiz. Ingen. u. Archit., 1984-1985

Hack, Howard Edwin *(American painter, b.1932)*   BA
> Bibl: ▶WW Amer. Art

Hack, Johann G. *(Austrian architect, Vienna)*   AV
> Bibl: Der Aufbau, 1987 July, v.42, no.6, p.293

Hack, Wilhelm *(German, 20th c.)*   BA

Hackaert → see Hackaert, Jan

Hackaert → see Hackert, Jacob Philipp

Hackaert → see Hackert, Johann Gottlieb

Hackaert of Naples → see Hackert, Jacob Philipp

Hackaert or Hackert, Jan or Joan → see Hackaert, Jan

Hackaert, Jacob Philip → see Hackaert, Jan

Hackaert, Jan   BA GC PR
   (Dutch artist, c.1629-c.1685)   WC
   (Dutch painter and draughtsman, 1629-ca.1700)   GC
   (Dutch painter, 1629-ca.1700)   PR
   (Dutch painter, printmaker, 1629-ca.1700)   BA
> Bibl: ▶Bénézit; ▶RILA/BHA; ▶Thieme-Becker
   Hackaert   PR

Hackaert or Hackert, Jan or Joan   WC
   Hackaert, Jacob Philip   GC
   Hackaert, Jan Janss   PR
   Hackaert, Johannes   PR
   Hacker   PR
   Hackert   PR
   Hackert, Joan   GC
   Hakkert, Jan   GC
   I. Hackaart   PR
   J. Hackert   PR
   Jan Hackaert   PR
   Jan Hacker   PR
   Jan Hackert   PR
   Jan. Hackert   PR
   Jean Hackert   PR

Hackaert, Jan Janss → see Hackaert, Jan

Hackaert, Johannes → see Hackaert, Jan

Hackelsberger, Christoph *(West German architect, Munich)*   AV
> Bibl: ▶Bund Deut. Arch. Hdbch., 1987

Hackenberg, Gregory J. *(American architectural student, Tulane Univ., 1987-88)*   AV
> Bibl: Assoc. of Collegiate Schools of Architecture. News, 1988 Oct., v.18, no.2, p.13

Hacker → see Hackaert, Jan

Hacker, Arthur   BA WC WI
   (British artist, 1858-1919)   WC WI
   (British painter, 1858-1919)   BA
> Bibl: ▶Wood, Victorian ptrs.

Hacker, David *(German (Prussian), active 1770-1820)*   JG

Hacker, Dieter *(German painter, b.1942)*   BA
> Bibl: Munich (BRD) Städtische Galerie im LEhbachhaus; Die Kunst muss...

Hacker, F. *(American, active Providence, RI, U.S. 1870s)*   JG

Hacker, Horst *(German artist, 1842-1906)*   WC

Hacker, L. *(Swedish(?) artist, 18th cent.(?))*   WC

Hacker, Thomas *(American architect, Eugene, Ore)*   AV
> Bibl: Center: a journal for architecture in America, 1987, v.3, p.116

Hackert → see Hackaert, Jan

Hackert → see Hackert, Jacob Philipp

Hackert → see Hackert, Johann Gottlieb

Hackert d'Italie → see Hackert, Jacob Philipp

Hackert, Carl Ludwig   GC WC
   (German artist, 1740-1796)   WC
   (German painter, 1740-1796)   GC
> Bibl: ▶Thieme-Becker

Hackert, Georg Abraham *(German painter, 1755-1805)*   GC
> Bibl: ▶Bénézit

Hackert, Jacob Philipp   BA GC PR WC
   (German artist, 1737-1807)   WC
   (German landscape painter, 1737-1807)   AV
   (German painter and draughtsman, 1737-1807)   GC
   (German painter in ITA, 1737-1807)   BA
   (German painter, 1737-1807)   PR
> Bibl: ▶Bénézit; ▶Encic. italiana; Getty Photo Study Coll.; ▶Libr. of Congr. Name Auth. File; ▶Natl. union cat., pre-1956; ▶RILA/BHA; ▶Thieme-Becker

   Hackaert   PR
   Hackaert of Naples   PR
   Hackert   PR
   Hackert d'Italie   GC
   Hackert, Jakob Philipp   AV
   Hackert, Johann Philipp   GC
   Hackert, Philipp   AV
   Hackhaert   PR
   P. Hackart   PR
   Peter Hackert   PR
   Phil. Hackaert   PR
   Philip Hackert   PR
   Philipp Jacob Hackert   PR

Hackert, Jakob Philipp → see Hackert, Jacob Philipp

Hackert, Jbhann Gottlieb → see Hackert, Johann Gottlieb

Hackert, Joan → see Hackaert, Jan

Hackert, Johann Gottlieb   GC PR
   (German artist, 1744-1773)   WC
   (German painter, 1744-1773)   GC PR
> Bibl: ▶Bénézit; ▶Thieme-Becker
   Hackaert   PR
   Hackert   PR

Hackert, Jbhann Gottlieb   WC
   Johann Gottlieb Hackert   PR

Hackert, Johann Philipp → see Hackert, Jacob Philipp

Hackert, Philipp → see Hackert, Jacob Philipp

Hackett, Bill *(British goldsmith, 20th c.)*   BA
> Bibl: Becker, V., in CONNOISSEUR CCXIII/851 (Jan 1983) 45

Hackett, Brian *(British landscape architect and writer)*   AV
> Bibl: ▶Libr. of Congr. Name Auth. File

Hackhaert → see Hackert, Jacob Philipp

Hackhl, Joseph (German potter, act.
1749-1768) **BA**
Bibl: ▶Bénézit; ▶Honey, Euro.
ceramic; ▶Thieme-Becker
Hackhofer, Johann Cyriak (Austrian
artist, 1675-1731) **WC**
Hacking, Nicholas (British artist,
b.1947) **WI**
Hackl → see Hackl, Gabriel von
Hackl, Donald J. **AV**
Hackl, Gabriel von **GC PR WC**
(German artist, 1843-) **WC**
(German painter and
draughtsman, 1843-1926) **GC**
(German painter, 1843-aft.1919) **PR**
Bibl: ▶Thieme-Becker
Gabriel von Hackl **PR**
Hackl **PR**
Hackman, Vida (American
printmaker, b.1935) **BA**
Bibl: Long Beach (CA, USA), CSU,
Black dolphin prints (1978)
Hackney, Alfred **WC WI**
(British artist, 1926-) **WC**
(British artist, b.1926) **WI**
Hackney, Arthur **WC WI**
(British artist, 1925-) **WC**
(British artist, b.1925) **WI**
Hackney, Mary (British artist, op.
1983-) **WI**
Hackney, Roderick Peter (British
architect, developer, RIBA
President, 1987-, 1942-) **AV**
Bibl: ▶RIBA members, 1983
Hackwood, William **JG**
Hacq, François (French architect) **AV**
Bibl: Ville giardini, 1984 Nov., no.
191, p.8
Hacq, Martine (French architect) **AV**
Bibl: Ville giardini, 1984 Nov., no.
191, p.8
Hacquin, Jean Louis (French painter,
restorer, d.1783) **BA**
Bibl: Mâle, FLORENCE ET LA
FRANCE (1979) 237-249;
▶Thieme-Becker
Hadamard, Auguste (French artist,
1823-1886) **WC**
Haddad, Farid (Lebanese painter,
20th c.) **BA**
Bibl: Arts Mag. LIII/10 (June
1979), p.14
Haddelsey, Vincent → see Haddesley,
Vincent
Haddesley, Vincent **WI**
(British artist, 1929-) **WC**
(British artist, b.1929) **WI**
Haddelsey, Vincent **WC**
Haddoca, A. **WC WI**
(American artist, op.c.1830) **WC**
(American artist, op.circa 1830-) **WI**
Haddon, Arthur Trevor **WI**
(British artist, 1864-1941) **WC WI**
Haddon, Trevor **WC**
Haddon, David W. (British artist,
op.1884-1911) **WI**

Haddon, Joyce (British artist, op.
1983-) **WI**
Haddon, Julia (British artist, b.1960) **WI**
Haddon, Trevor → see Haddon, Arthur
Trevor
Haddrell, John Trevor (British artist,
b.1945) **WI**
Haden, Francis Seymour **BA GC WI**
(British artist, 1818-1910) **WC WI**
(British printmaker, 1818-1910) **BA**
(British, 1818-1910) **GC**
Bibl: ▶Dict. natl. biog.; ▶Encyc.
world art; Getty Photo Study Coll.
(Ptgs.); ▶Thieme-Becker; ▶Who
was who [GBR]
Haden, Seymour **GC**
Seymour-Haden, Sir Francis **WC**
Haden, Seymour → see Haden, Francis
Seymour
Hadfield, Charles **AV BA**
(British architect, 1840-1916) **AV**
(British architect, 1841-1916) **BA**
Bibl: ▶Avery obit. idx.
Hadfield, George **AV FA**
(ca.1767-5.II.1826; Architect,
District of Columbia) **FA**
(d.1826) **AV**
Bibl: Nat'l Register of Hist. Places,
1972; National Register, 1972
Hadfield, Maria Cecilia Louisa
Catherine, Miss → see Cosway,
Maria Hadfield
Hadfield, Maria Louisa Catherine
Cecilia → see Cosway, Maria
Hadfield
Hadfield, Matthew Ellison **AV BA**
(1812-1885) **AV**
(British architect, 1812-1885) **BA**
Bibl: ▶Dict. natl. biog.;
▶Thieme-Becker
Hadid, Zaha **AV BA**
(British architect, 1950-) **AV**
(West German architect,
b.1950) **BA**
Bibl: AA FILES (Summer 1987), p.
83; ▶Avery period. idx., 1988
suppl.; GA document, 1985 Sept.,
no.13, p.77; Schroth, Daidalos
XXII (Dec 1986), p. 98-103
Hädler, Emil (West German
architect, Darmstadt, 1952-) **AV**
Bibl: Deutsche Bauzeitung, 1988
July, v.122, no.7, p.138
Hadley, Albert (American interior
designer, New York City) **AV**
Bibl: Interior design, 1986 Dec.,
v.57, no.12, p.156
Hadol, Paul (French painter, 1835-
1875) **GC**
Bibl: ▶Bénézit

Hadrian **CE GC**
(76-138 AD) **AV**
(Architect, emperor, 76-138) **CE**
(Roman architect, 76-138 AD) **GC**
Bibl: Boëthius, Etr. Rom. arch.,
p.264; ▶Libr. of Congr. Name
Auth. File
Adrian **AV**
Aelius Hadrianus, Publius **CE**
Hadrian, Emperor of Rome **AV**
Publius Aelius Hadrianus **CE**
Hadrian, Emperor of Rome → see
Hadrian
Hadzi, Dimitri (American sculptor,
printmaker, b.1921) **BA**
Bibl: ART NEWS, V. LXXVII, n.6,
Sept 1978, p.78; ▶Bénézit; ▶WW
Amer. Art, 1978
Hadziewicz, Rafał (Polish painter,
printmaker, 1803-1886) **BA**
Bibl: ▶Bénézit; ▶Thieme-Becker;
▶Wielka ilustr. encyk.
Hadzimichalis, N. (Architect,
Greece) **AV**
Bibl: Design + art in Greece,
1982, v.13, p.118
Hadzimichalis-Schwartz, H.
(Architect, Greece) **AV**
Bibl: Design + art in Greece,
1982, v.13, p.118
Haeberlin Group (Campanian vase-
painters) **GC**
Bibl: ▶Trendall, Red-fig. vases
Lucania
Haeberlin, Carl von (German artist,
1832-1911) **WC**
Haecht, Tobias van → see Verhaecht,
Tobias
Haecht, Tobias van, or Tobias
Verhaagt, Verhaecht or,
Verhaeght → see Verhaecht, Tobias
Haecht, Willem II van **BA GC**
(Flemish artist, 1593-1637) **WC**
(Flemish painter, printmaker,
1593-1637) **BA**
(Flemish, 1593-1637) **GC**
Bibl: ▶RILA/BHA; ▶Thieme-Becker;
▶Wurzbach, NLD Künst.-Lex.
Haecht, Willem, II van **WC**
Haecht, Willem van (the Elder)
(Netherlandish painter, 16th
century) **GC**
Bibl: Getty Photo Study Coll.;
▶Thieme-Becker
Haecht, Willem, II van → see Haecht,
Willem II van
Haecken → see Haecken, Alexander
van
Haecken, Alexander van **PR WC**
(Flemish artist, 1701(?)-c.1758) **WC**
(Flemish painter, 1701-1758) **PR**
Bibl: ▶Thieme-Becker
Alexander van Haecken **PR**
Haecken **PR**
Haecker, George W. (American
architect) **AV**

Haedt, J.H.W. *(Dutch painter, 17th century)*   GC
Bibl: Getty Photo Study Coll. (Duits coll.)

Haefeli, Georges-Jacques *(Swiss architect, La Chaux-de-Fonds)*   AV
Bibl: ▶Schweiz. Ingen. u. Archit., 1988-1989

Haefeli, Markus *(Swiss architect, Klingnau)*   AV
Bibl: ▶Schweiz. Ingen. u. Archit., 1984-1985

Haefeli, Max *(Swiss architect, fl. ca. 1900; father of Max Ernst Haefeli?)*   AV
Bibl: Archithese, 1988 Mar.-Par., v.19, no.2, p.50

Haefeli, Max Ernst *(Swiss architect, Zurich, 1901-1976)*   AV
Bibl: ▶Macmillan encyc. archts.
Häfeli, Max Ernst   AV

Haefliger, Leopold *(Swiss painter, sculptor, b.1929)*   BA
Bibl: ▶Künst.-Lex. Schweiz 20. Jahrh.; ▶Lex. zeitgen. Schweiz. Künstler

Haeften, Nicolas van → see Haften, Nicolas van

Hael, María *(Argentine architect)*   AV
Bibl: Summa, 1985 Jan.-Feb., no. 208-209, p.90

Haelszel, Johann Baptist   GC
(German artist, 1710/12-1777)   WC
(German painter, 1712-1777)   GC
Bibl: ▶Thieme-Becker
Hälszel, Johann Baptist   GC
Halszel, Johann Baptist (von?)   WC

Haelweg, Albert → see Haelwegh, Albert

Haelwegh, Adriaen   GC WC
(Dutch artist, c.1637-c.1696)   WC
(Dutch printmaker, b.1637)   GC
Bibl: ▶Bénézit

Haelwegh, Albert   GC WC
(Danish artist, c.1600-1673)   WC
(Dutch printmaker, ca.1610-d. aft.1677)   GC
Bibl: ▶Bénézit
Haelweg, Albert   GC

Haen or Haan, David de   WC
(Dutch artist, 17th cent.)   WC
(Flemish artist, op.1619-m.1622)   WC

Haen or Haan, German *(Dutch artist, op.1667-1682)*   WC

Haen or Haan, Joseph Charles de *(Dutch artist, 1777-1836)*   WC

Haen, Abraham I de *(Dutch, 17th century)*   GC
Bibl: ▶Thieme-Becker

Haen, Abraham II de   GC WC
(Dutch artist, 1707-1748)   WC
(Dutch painter and draughtsman, 1707-1748)   GC
Bibl: ▶Thieme-Becker

Haen, Anthony de *(Dutch artist, 1640-c.1675)*   WC

Haen, G. de → see Haen, Gerrit de
Haen, Gerrit de *(Dutch painter, act. 1667-1682)*   GC
Bibl: Rijksmuseum; ▶Thieme-Becker
Haen, G. de   GC
Haen, Pieter de *(Dutch painter, act. 1630-1638)*   GC
Bibl: ▶Thieme-Becker

Haenen, F. de *(French artist, 19th cent.)*   WC

Haensbergen → see Haensbergen, Johan van
Haensbergen or Haansbergen, Johan or Jan van → see Haensbergen, Johan van

Haensbergen, Johan van   GC PR
(Dutch artist, 1642-1705)   WC
(Dutch painter, 1642-1705)   GC PR
Bibl: Getty Photo Study Coll.; ▶Thieme-Becker; ▶Witt checklist
Haansberg   PR
Haansbergen   PR
Haansbergen, Johannes van   PR
Haensbergen   PR
Haensbergen or Haansbergen, Johan or Jan van   WC
Hansbergen   PR
Hensberch   PR
Hensbergen   PR
Johan van Haensbergen   PR
Van Haansbergen   PR

Haer, C.V. *(Netherlandish)*   GC
Bibl: Gernsheim, Corpus Photog. of Drawings, 1529

Haerdtl, Oswald *(Austrian architect, designer, 1899-1959)*   BA
Bibl: ▶Avery Libr. cat.; ▶Vollmer, Künst.-Lex. 20. Jhr.

Haerer, Carol *(American painter, b.1933)*   BA
Bibl: ▶WW Amer. Art, 1980

Haering, Johann Georg → see Hering, Hans

Haert, Hendrik Anna Victoria van der *(Belgian artist, 1790-1846)*   WC

Haertl, Wilfried *(Austrian architect, Vienna)*   AV
Bibl: ▶Verzeich. Öst. Ziviltech.

Haes, Carlos de *(Belgian, 1829-1898)*   GC
Bibl: ▶Thieme-Becker

Haes, Johannes de *(Dutch painter, act. 1661-1667)*   PR
Bibl: ▶Thieme-Becker
de Haes   PR
Johannes de Haes   PR

Haese, D. de (Possibly identified with Haan) *(Dutch artist, op. 1700)*   WC

Haese, Günter *(German sculptor, painter, b.1924)*   BA
Bibl: ▶Fogg Mus. Libr. cat.; Junge Kunstler

Haese, Reinhoud d' *(Belgian sculptor, b.1928)*   BA
Bibl: Brussels (BEL), Mus roy des b-a de Bel, Mus mod, REINHOUD (1973); Brussels. Musées royaux des beaux-arts de Belgique. Musée moderne. Reinhoud, exh. cat. 1973

Haese, Roel d' *(Belgian sculptor, b.1921)*   BA
Bibl: ▶Bénézit; ▶Vollmer, Künst.-Lex. 20. Jhr.

Haeseker, Alexandra *(Canadian painter, b.1945)*   BA
Bibl: ?AC?; ?NGC?; Oshawa (Ont, CAN), McLaughlin Gallery, 12 Canadian artists (1980)

Haesele, Emmy *(German artist, 1894-)*   WC

Haeselich, Johann Marcus *(German artist, 1807-1856)*   WC

Haeskel *(Dutch artist, op.1647)*   WC

Haesler, Otto   AV BA
(German architect, b.1880)   BA
(West German architect, 1880-1962)   AV
Bibl: ▶Art Index, 1961-1963; ▶Avery period. idx., 9th suppl.; Bauwelt, v.71, n.24, July 11, 1980, p.1130-131; ▶Portoghesi, Diz. arch. e urbanistica; ▶Vollmer, Künst.-Lex. 20. Jhr.

Haeslich, Johann Georg *(German artist, 1806-1894)*   WC

Haestar or Haaster, Leendert Maertensz. van → see Haestar, Leendert van

Haestar, Leendert van   GC
(Dutch artist, op.1639-m.1675)   WC
(Dutch painter, act.1639-d. 1675)   GC
Bibl: ▶Thieme-Becker

Haestar or Haaster, Leendert Maertensz. van   WC

Häfele, Melchior → see Hefele, Melchior
Häfeli, Max Ernst → see Haefeli, Max Ernst

Hafen, John *(American artist, 1856-1910)*   WI

Haffe, E. *(German artist, 19th cent.)*   WC

Haffenecker, Tomáš *(Czech architect, act.1713, d.1731)*   BA
Bibl: Baedeker's TSCH, 33; Horyna, UMENI, XXIX, 5 (1981) 437-447; ▶Portoghesi, Diz. arch. e urbanistica; ▶Thieme-Becker

Haffengiesser, Heinrich *(Swiss bell founder, 15th c.)*   BA
Bibl: Zeit. Schw. Arch. u. Kunst., XXXIII/2 (1976) pp.112-118

Haffenrichter, Hans *(German painter, sculptor, designer, 1897-1981)*   BA
Bibl: ▶Bénézit; ▶Vollmer, Künst.-Lex. 20. Jhr.; Wangler, Schüler des Bauhauses, p.20

Haffield, Cooper **WC WI**
  (British artist, -1821) WC
  (British artist, op.1721-, d.1821) WI
Haffmanns, Paul (Dutch architect) **AV**
  Bibl: De Architect, 1985 Mar.,
  v.16, no.3, p.64
Haffner (American sculptor, 20th
  century) **GC**
  Bibl: Juley coll., NMAA
**Haffner, Affner or Aufner, Anton
  Maria** (Italian artist, 1654-1732) **WC**
*Haffner, Affner or Aufner, Enrico (Il
  Tenente)*→see Haffner, Enrico
Haffner, Enrico **GC**
  (Italian artist, 1640-1702) WC
  (Italian, 1640-1702) GC
  Bibl: ▶Thieme-Becker; ▶Witt
  checklist
**Haffner, Affner or Aufner,
  Enrico (Il Tenente)** **WC**
Hafftka, Michael **BA WI**
  (American artist, op.1987-) WI
  (American painter, b.1953) BA
  Bibl: Pittsburg (PA, USA),
  Carnegie-Mellon Univ., Hewlett
  Gallery. MICHAEL HAFFTKA'S
  PAINTINGS 1983-1984 (1984)
Hafif, Marcia (American painter,
  photographer, b.1929) **BA**
  Bibl: ▶MoMA libr. cat.; UC Santa
  Barbara cat. sheets; ▶WW Amer.
  Art
Hafkenscheid, Michiel **BA**
Hafner, Bernhard (Austrian
  architect, Graz) **AV**
  Bibl: ▶Verzeich. Öst. Ziviltech.
Hafner, Charles (American artist,
  1888-op.1953) **WI**
Hafner, Dorothy (American
  ceramist, b.1952) **BA**
  Bibl: Providence (RI, USA), RISD,
  Clay (1981)
Hafner, Jonas (German painter,
  sculptor, b.1940) **BA**
  Bibl: ▶WW Arts DEU
Hafstrom, Axel Gillis (Swedish
  artist, 1841-1909) **WC**
Håfström, Jan **BA WC**
  (Scandinavian artist, 20th cent.) WC
  (Swedish painter, b.1937) BA
  Bibl: ▶Art Index, Nov. 1972-Oct.
  1973; ▶Svenska konstnärer; UC
  Santa Barbara cat. sheets; Vem ar
  det 1989
Haften→see Haften, Nicolas van
*Haften or Haeften, Nicolas van
  (Nicolas Walraven van
  Haften)*→see Haften, Nicolas van

Haften, Nicolas van **GC PR**
  (Dutch artist, c.1663-1715) WC
  (Dutch painter, 1663-1715) PR
  (Dutch painter, draughtsman,
  and printmaker, ca.1663-
  1715) GC
  Bibl: Getty Photo Study Coll.;
  ▶Thieme-Becker; ▶Witt checklist
  Haeften, Nicolas van GC PR
  Haften PR
**Haften or Haeften, Nicolas van
  (Nicolas Walraven van
  Haften)** **WC**
  Nicolas van Haften PR
Hag de Dillingen, Lenhart **GC WC**
  (German artist, 17th cent.) WC
  (German draughtsman, 17th
  century) GC
  Bibl: ▶Witt checklist
Hagaman, J. (American artist, op.
  19th c.) **WI**
Hagan, Harri F. (Finnish(?) architect) **AV**
  Bibl: Arkkitehtuurikilpailuja, 1989,
  no.3, p.2
Hagan, Victoria (American interior
  decorator, New York City) **AV**
  Bibl: House & garden, 1989 May,
  v.161, no.5, p.188
Hagarth, William (British artist, op.
  circa 1810-) **WI**
Hagarty, James (British artist, op.
  1767-1782) **WC WI**
Hagarty, Mary S. (British artist, op.
  1885-1919) **WI**
  Bibl: ▶Waters, Brit. artists
Hagarty, Parker (British artist, 1859-
  1934) **WI**
Hagasawa, Hsuko (Architect, Japan,
  1941-) **AV**
  Bibl: De architect, 1984 July-Aug.,
  v.15, no.7-8
Hagbore, Otto (British artist, op.
  circa 1887-) **WI**
  Bibl: ▶Johnson, Brit. artists
**Hagborg, August (Vilhelm
  Nikolaus August)** (Swedish artist,
  1852-1921) **WC**
Hage, Christian (German architect,
  Berlin) **AV**
  Bibl: Bauwelt, 1985 July 5, no.25,
  p.1028
Hage, Hendrick→see Hage, Hendrik
  Anton
Hage, Hendrik Anton (Dutch
  painter, 1879-1961) **PR**
  Bibl: ▶Scheen, Ned. beeldende
  kunst.
  Hage, Hendrick PR
  Hendrik Anton Hage PR
Hagedorn, Alfried (German painter,
  b.1940) **BA**
  Bibl: ▶WW Arts DEU
Hagedorn, Christian Ludwig von
  (German artist, 1712-1780) **WC**
Hagedorn, Herman Conrad
  (German artist, op.1828-1838) **WC**

Hagedorn, Karl (British artist, 1889-
  1969) **WI**
  Bibl: ▶Waters, Brit. artists
**Hagelgans, Michael Cristoph
  Emanuel** (German artist, 1725-
  1766) **WC**
*Hagelstein, Jakob Ernst
  Thomann*→see Thomann von
  Hagelstein, Jakob Ernst
Hagemann, Carl (German architect,
  1843-1916) **BA**
  Bibl: ▶Neue deutsche Biog.
Hagemann, Eva (German painter,
  b.1908) **BA**
  Bibl: EVA HAGEMANN:
  STATIONEN E WERKES, 1978;
  ▶Vollmer, Künst.-Lex. 20. Jhr.
Hagemann, Godefroy de (German
  artist, op.1861-m.1877) **WC**
Hagemann, Oskar H. (German
  painter, b.1888) **BA**
  Bibl: ▶Bénézit; Karlsruhe,
  Kunsthalle; ▶Thieme-Becker;
  ▶Vollmer, Künst.-Lex. 20. Jhr.
Hagemeister, Karl **BA GC WC**
  (German artist, 1848-1933) WC
  (German painter, 1848-1933) BA GC
  Bibl: ▶Bénézit; ▶Neue deutsche
  Biog.; ▶Thieme-Becker; ▶Vollmer,
  Künst.-Lex. 20. Jhr.
Hagemeyer, Georg-Maria (West
  German architecture student, FHT,
  Stuttgart) **AV**
  Bibl: Architektur,
  Innenarchitektur, Technischer
  Ausbau, 1987 Dec., v.95, no.12,
  p.62
Hagemeyer, Johan **BA JG**
  (American (b. Netherlands),
  1884-1962) JG
  (American photographer, 1884-
  1962) BA
  Bibl: ▶Parry, Photo idx.; Travis,
  Photog. rediscovered
Hagen→see Hagen, Joris van der
Hagen→see Hagen, Willem van der
**Hagen or Haagen, Jacob Jorisz.
  van der, or Jacob Verhagen**
  (Dutch artist, 1657-1715) **WC**
*Hagen or Haagen, Joris Abrahamsz.
  van der or Joris Verhaegen or
  Verhagen*→see Hagen, Joris van
  der
*Hagen or Haagen, Joris Cornelisz.
  van der*→see Hagen, J.C. van der
*Hagen or Hagens, Christian (also
  erroneousiy, Christoph)*→see
  Hagen, Christian
Hagen, Christian **GC**
  (Dutch artist, op.1663-1688) WC
  (Dutch draughtsman, act.1663-
  1688) GC
  Bibl: ▶Thieme-Becker
**Hagen or Hagens, Christian
  (also erroneousiy, Christoph)** **WC**
  Hagens, Christian GC

Hagen, Dingeman van der   **GC WC**
  (Flemish artist,
   c.1610/20-a.1682)   **WC**
  (Flemish, ca.1610/20-d bef.
   1682)   **GC**
    Bibl: ▶Witt checklist
Hagen, Franciscus→see Haage,
  Franciscus
Hagen, Franz *(German painter, act.*
  1686)   **GC**
    Bibl: ▶Thieme-Becker
Hagen, J. *(British artist, op.1710-*
  1746)   **WC**
Hagen, J. *(Dutch artist, 1703-p.*
  1791)   **WC**
Hagen, J.C. van der   **GC PR**
  (Dutch artist, 1676-c.1745)   **WC**
  (Dutch painter, 1676?-1745)   **GC**
  (Dutch painter, act. 18th
   century)   **PR**
    Bibl: R. Preston; ▶Thieme-Becker
Hagen or Haagen, Joris
  Cornelisz. van der   **WC**
  J.C. van der Hagen   **PR**
  Vander Hagen   **PR**
  Vanderhagen   **PR**
Hagen, Jacobus van der   **GC PR**
  (Dutch painter, act. 1666-1673)   **PR**
  (Dutch painter, act.1666-1680)   **GC**
    Bibl: ▶Thieme-Becker
  Jacobus van der Hagen   **PR**
  Van Hagen   **PR**
  Verhagen, Jacobus van der   **GC**
Hagen, Johann van der *(British*
  artist, 1675-circa 1745)   **WI**
Hagen, Joris van der   **BA GC PR**
  (Dutch artist, c.1615-1669)   **WC**
  (Dutch painter and
   draughtsman, ca.1615-1669)   **GC**
  (Dutch painter, act.1615-1669)   **BA PR**
    Bibl: ▶Bénézit; ▶RILA/BHA;
    ▶Thieme-Becker; ▶Wurzbach, NLD
    Künst.-Lex.
  Haagen, Joris van der   **GC PR**
  Hagen   **PR**
Hagen or Haagen, Joris
  Abrahamsz. van der or Joris
  Verhaegen or Verhagen   **WC**
  John Van Hagen   **PR**
  Joris van der Hagen   **PR**
  mark'd Vanderhagen   **PR**
  V. Hagen   **PR**
  van der Hagen   **PR**
  Van Hagen   **PR**
  Van Hager   **PR**
  Vanderhagen   **PR**
  Vanhagen   **PR**
  Verhaege, Joris   **GC**
  Verhaegen, Joris   **GC**
  Verhagen   **PR**
  Verhagen, Joris   **GC**

Hagen, Ludwig von   **GC**
  (German artist, 1819-1898)   **WC**
  (German painter, 1819-1898)   **GC**
    Bibl: Getty Photo Study Coll.
    (Douwes coll.)
Hagn, Ludwig von   **WC**
Hagn, Ole *(Danish architect)*   **AV**
    Bibl: Arkitektur DK, 1989, v.33,
    no.3, p.124
Hagen, Theodor Joseph   **GC WC**
  (German artist, 1842-1919)   **WC**
  (German painter, 1842-1919)   **GC**
    Bibl: ▶Thieme-Becker
Hagen, van [Unidentified]
  (Unknown painter)   **PR**
    Bibl: December 18, 1813, lots 34
    & 39, Christie's; December 9,
    1814, lot 5, Christie's; July 9,
    1814, lot 13, Christie's; May 27,
    1814, lot 97, Christie's
  Van Hagen   **PR**
  Vander Hagen   **PR**
Hagen, Willem van der   **GC PR WC**
  (Dutch artist, 17th/18th cent.)   **WC**
  (Dutch painter, 17th -18th
   centuries)   **GC**
  (Dutch painter, act. 18th
   century)   **PR**
    Bibl: ▶Bénézit; Croft-Murray, Dec.
    ptg. England, v.1, p.255; Getty
    Photo Study Coll.; R. Preston;
    ▶Thieme-Becker; ▶Waterhouse,
    Brit. 18c. ptrs.; ▶Witt checklist
  Hagen   **PR**
  Vander Hagen   **PR**
  Vanderhagen   **PR**
  W. Vanderhagen   **PR**
  Willem van der Hagen   **PR**
Hagenah, Charles *(American*
  architect)   **AV**
    Bibl: Arch. & urbanism, 3(222)
    (Mar.1989) p.82
Hagenau, Niclaus von→see
  Hagenauer, Nikolaus
Hagenauer, Carl *(Austrian metal*
  engraver, 1872-1928)   **BA**
    Bibl: Beger, WELTKUNST LVI/21
    (1 Nov 1986) 3366
Hagenauer, Friedrich *(German*
  woodcarver, medalist, act.1520-
  1545)   **BA**
    Bibl: ▶Bénézit; ▶Forrer, Medallists;
    Kobler, Jahrb. Zentralinst.
    Kunstgeschichte, I (1985) p.409
Hagenauer, Johann Baptist
  (German artist, 1732-1810)   **WC**
Hagenauer, Nikolaus *(German*
  sculptor, b.ca.1455, d.1526-1528)   **BA**
    Bibl: ▶Bénézit; ▶Encyc. world art;
    Müller, Sculpture NLD DEU FRA
    ESP, pp.170-171; ▶Neue deutsche
    Biog.; ▶Thieme-Becker
  Hagenau, Niclaus von   **BA**
  Hagenover, Nikolaus   **BA**
  Nikolaus von Hagenau   **BA**

Hagenbach, Caspar, the elder   **BA**
  (Swiss artist, op.1534-1553)   **WC**
  (Swiss painter, ca.1500-before
   1579)   **BA**
    Bibl: Früh, UNSERE KUNSTDENKM.,
    XXXVII/1 (1986) 33; ▶Schweiz.
    Künst.-Lex., suppl.;
    ▶Thieme-Becker; ▶Witt checklist
Hagenbuch the Elder, Caspar   **WC**
Hagenbuch the Elder, Caspar→see
  Hagenbach, Caspar, the elder
Hagenbuch, Caspar, the younger
  (Swiss painter, ca.1525-1579)   **BA**
    Bibl: ▶Schweiz. Künst.-Lex.,
    suppl.; ▶Thieme-Becker
Hagenover, Nikolaus→see
  Hagenauer, Nikolaus
Hagens, Christian→see Hagen,
  Christian
Hagens, Erik *(Danish painter,*
  printmaker, b.1940)   **BA**
    Bibl: Hauch
    FASCINATION/INSPIRATION.....(1985);
    ▶Nørregård-Nielsen, Dansk kunst
Hager, Gary *(American interior*
  designer, NYC)   **AV**
    Bibl: House & garden, 1988 Apr.,
    v.160, no.4, p.94
Hagerman, Thomas *(American*
  architect)   **AV**
    Bibl: Architectural digest, 1985
    July, v.42, no.7, p.48
Hagerup→see Hagerup, Nels
Hagerup, Nels *(American painter,*
  1864-1922)   **PR**
    Bibl: ▶Dawdy, Artists Amer. West
  Hagerup   **PR**
  Nels Hagerup   **PR**
Hagesander→see Agesandros of
  Rhodes
Hagesander Rhodus→see Agesandros
  of Rhodes
Hagesandros→see Agesandros of
  Rhodes
Hägg, Axel Herman   **BA WC**
  (German architectural
   illustrator, England, 1835-
   1921)   **AV**
  (Swedish architect, printmaker
   in GBR, 1835-1921)   **BA**
  (Swedish artist, 1835-1921)   **WC**
  (Swedish draughtsman, 1835-
   1921)   **GC**
    Bibl: ▶Bénézit; RLIN BKS file;
    ▶Svenskt konst.-lex.;
    ▶Thieme-Becker; ▶Waters, Brit.
    artists
  Häag, Axel Herman   **AV**
  Haig, Axel Herman   **GC**
Hägg, Göran *(Swedish sculptor,*
  b.1949)   **BA**
    Bibl: ▶Intl. dir. exh. artists, 1982;
    Paris (FRA), Ctr Pompidou,
    Sextant (1981)
Hagg, Jakob *(Swedish artist, 1839-*
  1931)   **WC**

AV Avery Index   **BA** Bibl Hist of Art   **CE** Census Antique Works   **FA** Fndn Docs of Arch   **GC** Getty Ctr Photo Study Coll

Haggar, Reginald George (*British painter, author, b.1905*)　**BA**
Bibl: ▶Johnson, Brit. artists; ▶Natl. union cat., pre-1956; RSA, 137 (Mar 1989) 250; ▶Waters, Brit. artists; ▶WW Art

Haggard, Kenneth　**AV**

Haggerty, Gerard (*American artist, op.20th c.*)　**WI**

Haggerty, William (*Canadian photographer, 1874-1934*)　**BA**
Bibl: Toronto (Ont, CAN), Art Gallery of Ont. WILLIAM NOTMAN: THE STAMP OF A STUDIO

Haghe, C. →see Haghe, Charles

Haghe, Charles　**BA WI**
　(*Belgian painter, printmaker in GBR, 1810-1888*)　**BA**
　(*British artist, op.1848*)　**WC**
　(*British artist, op.1848-, d.1888*)　**WI**
　Bibl: ▶Bénézit; ▶Berko, Belgian ptrs.; ▶Dict. biog. artistes belges

Haghe, C.　**WC**

Haghe, Louis　**BA GC WC WI**
　(*Belgian draughtsman, 1806-1885*)　**GC**
　(*British artist, 1806-1885*)　**WC WI**
　(*British painter, printmaker, 1806-1885*)　**BA**
　Bibl: ▶Bénézit; ▶Mallett's idx. artists

Hagimichalis, Niko (*Greek architect, Rhodes*)　**AV**
Bibl: House & garden, 1988 Feb., v.160, no.2, p.82

Hagin, Nancy (*American painter, 20th c.*)　**BA**
Bibl: Arts Mag. LII/5 (Jan 1978), p.4; ▶Locus

Hagino, Kiichiro (*Japanese architect*)　**AV**
Bibl: Japan architect, 1989 Jan., v.64, no.1(381), p.61

Hagiopetrites, Theodore (*Byzantine scribe, act.ca.1277-ca.1308*)　**BA**
Bibl: Nelson, R.S., in (07) INTERNATIONALER BYZANTINISTEN II. 4, p.79

Hagius (*Netherlands artist, op.1657*)　**WC**

Hagiwara, Takeshi (*Japanese architect*)　**AV**
Bibl: Space design, 1985 Dec., no. 255, p.5

Hagman, A. (*Engraver*)　**WI**

Hagman, Donald G. (*American city planner and author, 1932-1982*)　**AV**
Bibl: Journal of American Planning Assoc. v.48, n.4 1982, p.496

Hagmann, John S. (*American architect*)　**AV**

Hagmüller, Roland (*Austrian architect, 1941-*)　**AV**
Bibl: Das Kunstwerk, n.3-4, Sept. 1983, p.51

Hagn, J. (*Austrian? painter, act. 1910*)　**BA**
Bibl: Kunstjahrb. Stadt Linz (1979) pp.39-48

Hagn, Ludwig von →see Hagen, Ludwig von

Hagnauer, Eugen →see Hagnauer, Eugene

Hagnauer, Eugene　**GC**
　(*French painter, ca.1820*)　**GC**
　(*German artist, op.c.1820-1848*)　**WC**
　Bibl: ▶Thieme-Becker

Hagnauer, Eugen　**WC**

Hagreen, Henry Browne (*British artist, 1831-1912*)　**WC WI**

Hagstette, Guy (*American architect, Houston, TX*)　**AV**
Bibl: Texas architect, 1986 July-Aug., v.36, no.4, p.60

Hague →see Hague, Maurice Stewart

Hague, J. Anderson →see Hague, Joshua Anderson

Hague, J. Edward Homerville　**WC WI**
　(*British artist, op.1884-1917*)　**WI**
　(*British artist, op.1885-1917*)　**WC**

Hague, Joshua Anderson　**WI**
　(*British artist, 1850-1916*)　**WC WI**

Hague, J. Anderson　**WC**

Hague, Maurice Stewart (*American painter, 1862-1943*)　**PR**
Bibl: ▶WWW Amer. art
　Hague　PR
　Maurice Stewart Hague　PR

Hague, Raoul (*American sculptor, b.1905*)　**BA**
Bibl: ▶Phaidon 20c. art; ▶Vollmer, Künst.-Lex. 20. Jhr.; ▶WW Amer. Art, 1976

Haguenot, Haincelin de →see Haincelin de Hagenau

Hahn (*German artist, op.c.1820*)　**WC**

Hahn →see Hahn, Karl Wilhelm

Hahn or Han, Hermann →see Hahn, Hermann

Hahn, Albert (*German artist, b.1910*)　**BA**
Bibl: ▶Libr. of Congr. Name Auth. File; ▶Natl. union cat., 1973-1977

Hahn, Andrea (*American painter, 20th c.*)　**BA**
Bibl: ARTS MAG. LV (Sept 1980) 10

Hahn, Arthur W. (*American draftsman, 20th c.*)　**BA**
Bibl: UC Santa Barbara cat. sheets

Hahn, Betty (*American photographer, b.1940*)　**BA**
Bibl: ▶Natl. Faculty Dir.; St. Louis (MO, USA), Univ. of Missouri, Gallery 210, Aspects of Amer. Photog. (1976)

Hahn, Friedemann (*German painter, b.1949*)　**BA**
Bibl: Stuttgart (DEU), Württemb. Kunstverein, 16 Künstler (1978)

Hahn, Friedrich (*Swiss architect, 19th c.*)　**BA**
Bibl: Mathus, UNSERE KUNSTDENKMALER XXXVII (1986)

Hahn, Friedrich (Jacob Friedrich) (*German artist, c.1805-1870(?)*)　**WC**

Hahn, Georg (*German artist, 1741-1889*)　**WC**

Hahn, Gerhard (*German architect, 1948-*)　**AV**
Bibl: Deutsche Bauzeitung, 1986 June, v.120, no.6, p.55

Hahn, Gustav Adolph (*German artist, 1819-1872*)　**WC**

Hahn, Hermann　**GC**
　(*German artist, c.1570-1628*)　**WC**
　(*German draughtsman, ca.1570-1628*)　**GC**
　Bibl: ▶Thieme-Becker

Hahn or Han, Hermann　**WC**
　Han, Hermann　GC

Hahn, Hermann (*German sculptor, medalist, 1868-1942*)　**BA**
Bibl: ▶Bénézit; ▶Neue deutsche Biog.; ▶Thieme-Becker

Hahn, Joseph (*German artist, 1839-1906*)　**WC**

Hahn, Karl (*American artist, 19th cent.*)　**WC**

Hahn, Karl Karlovich (*Russian jeweler, 19th c.*)　**BA**
Bibl: Solodkoff, Russian gold & silver

Hahn, Karl Wilhelm　**BA PR WC WI**
　(*American artist, 1829-1887*)　**WI**
　(*German artist, 1829-1887*)　**WC**
　(*German painter in USA, 1829-1887*)　**BA**
　(*German painter, 1829-1887*)　**PR**
　Bibl: ▶Bénézit; Oakland, Oakland Museum, WILLIAM HAHN (1975); ▶RILA/BHA; ▶Thieme-Becker
　Hahn　PR

Hahn, William　**PR WI**
　Karl Wilhelm Hahn　PR

Hahn, Lothar (*East German architect, Karl-Marx-Stadt, 1930-1988*)　**AV**
Bibl: Architectur der DDR, 1989 May, v.38, no.5, p.39

Hahn, Otto (*Polish painter, printmaker, b.1904*)　**BA**

Hahn, Samuel (*Austrian, act.1885*)　**BA**
Bibl: Asenbaum, OTTO WAGNER, 300 Villa für Samuel Ritter von Hahn...1885; Vyoral-Tschapka, Öster. Zeit. für Kunst u. Denk. 38/1-2 (1984) 43-56

Hahn, Siegbert (*German painter, b.1937*)　**BA**
Bibl: Solingen (BRD), Deutsches Klingenmuseum, Siegbert Hahn (1978)

Hahn, Ulrich (*West German architect, Aachen*)　**AV**
Bibl: Baumeister, 1988 June, v.85, no.6, p.22

Hahn, William *(American artist,*
1840(?)-1890(?))   **WC**

Hahn, William → see Hahn, Karl
Wilhelm

Hähnel, Ernst Julius   **BA WC**

(*German artist, 1811-1891*)   WC

(*German sculptor, 1811-1891*)   BA

Bibl: ▶Bénézit; ▶Thieme-Becker

Hahnisch, Anton *(German artist,*
1817-1897)   **WC**

Hahnloser-Buhler, Hedy *(Swiss*
artist, 19th cent.)   **WC**

Hahs, Erwin *(German painter,*
printmaker, 1887-1970)   **BA**

Bibl: Schulze, FORSCHUNGEN UND
BERICHTE, STAATLICHE MUSEEN
ZU BERLIN (XXIII, 1983)

Haickenburg → see Huchtenburgh, Jan
van

Haid or Hayd, Johann Jakob

(*German artist, 1704-1767*)   **WC**

Haid or Hayd, Johann Philipp → see
Haid, Johann Philipp

Haid, C. *(German artist, op.1722)*   **WC**

Haid, David *(American architect,*
Chicago, IL, 1928-)   **AV**

Bibl: ▶Amer. archts. dir., 3rd ed.,
1970

Haid, Johann Elias *(German artist,*
1739-1809)   **WC**

Haid, Johann Gottfried   **GC**

(*German artist, 1710-1776*)   WC

(*German draughtsman, 1710-*
1776)   GC

Bibl: ▶Thieme-Becker

Haid, John Gottfried   **WC**

Haid, Johann Philipp   **GC**

(*German artist, 1730-c.1806*)   WC

(*German draughtsman, 1730-*
1806)   GC

Bibl: ▶Thieme-Becker

Haid or Hayd, Johann Philipp   **WC**

Haid, John Gottfried → see Haid,
Johann Gottfried

Haider, Andreas *(Swiss artist, op.*
1530-1532)   **WC**

Haider, Gulzar *(Pakistan born*
architect and engineer, living in
Ottawa, Canada)   **AV**

Bibl: Arts & the Islamic world,
1985 Autumn, v.3, no.3, p.48

Haider, Karl   **GC WC**

(*German artist, 1846-1912*)   WC

(*German painter, 1846-1912*)   GC

Bibl: ▶Thieme-Becker

Haider, M. *(Engraver)*   **WI**

Haidt, John Valentin → see Haidt, John
Valentine

Haidt, John Valentine   **BA**

(*American painter, 1700-1780*)   BA

(*German artist, 1700-1780*)   WC

Bibl: ▶Fielding's Amer. ptrs.;
▶Witt checklist; ▶WWW Amer.
hist.

Haidt, John Valentin   **WC**

Haier or Hayer, Joseph *(German*
artist, 1816-1891)   **WC**

Haifa Group *(Apulian vase-painters)*   **GC**

Bibl: Trendall, Attic red-fig. vases
Apulia, p.568

Haifa Painter   **GC JG**

(*Apulian vase-painter*)   GC

Bibl: Trendall, Attic red-fig. vases
Apulia

Haig, Adrianne *(British artist,*
b.1929)   **WI**

Haig, Axel Herman → see Hägg, Axel
Herman

Haig, Earl *(British artist, 1861-*
1928)   **WC WI**

Haig, George Alexander Eugene
Douglas, earl of *(British painter,*
b.1918)   **BA**

Bibl: ▶Vollmer, Künst.-Lex. 20.
Jhr.; ▶Waters, Brit. artists; ▶Who's
Who [GBR], 1978

Haig, Richard *(Landscape architect)*   **AV**

Bibl: Garten und Landschaft, 1985
Aug., v.95, no.8, p.37

Haig, Thomas *(Scottish*
cabinetmaker, upholsterer, act.
1770-1796)   **BA**

Bibl: ▶Edwards, Engl. furniture

Haigh, Alfred G. *(British artist,*
1870-1963)   **WI**

Haigh, Paul *(American architect)*   **AV**

Haight, Charles Coolidge *(American*
architect, 1841-1917)   **AV BA**

Bibl: ▶Macmillan encyc. archts.;
▶Withey, Amer. archts.

Haight, Charles T. *(American*
interior decorator, ca.1904-1980)   **BA**

Bibl: Art Gallery, May 1980

Haigis, Ulrich *(Architect,*
Korntal-Münchingen)   **AV**

Bibl: Deutsche Bauzeitschrift,
v.32, 1984, p.1147

Hail, Anthony *(American interior*
designer)   **AV**

Bibl: Architectural digest, 1985
Mar., v.41, no.3, p.162

Haile, Sam → see Haile, Samuel

Haile, Samuel   **BA**

(*British artist, 1909-1948*)   WI

(*British painter, ceramist, 1909-*
1948)   BA

(*British(?) artist, 20th cent.*)   WC

Bibl: ▶Johnson, Brit. artists; Leeds
Art Calendar, 87 (1980) pp.21-30;
London (GBR), Hayward Gallery,
Dada & Surrealism (1978); Tate
Gallery collections

Haile, Sam   **WC WI**

Hailer or Hailler, Daniel *(German*
artist, op.1604-a.1630)   **WC**

Haileybury Painter *(Campanian*
vase-painter)   **GC**

Bibl: ▶Trendall, Red-fig. vases
Lucania

Hailman → see Hailman, Johanna
K.Woodwell

Hailman, Johana K.W. → see Hailman,
Johanna K.Woodwell

Hailman, Johanna K. Woodwell → see
Hailman, Johanna K.Woodwell

Hailman, Johanna K.Woodwell   **WI**

(*American artist, 1871-*)   WC

(*American artist, b.1871*)   WI

(*American painter, 1871-1958*)   PR

Bibl: ▶WWW Amer. art

Hailman   PR

Hailman, Johanna K.W.   PR

Hailman, Johanna K.
Woodwell   **PR WC**

Hailman, Johanna Knowles
Woodwell   PR

Johanna K. Woodwell Hailman   PR

Woodwell, Johanna Knowles, Miss   WI

Hailman, Johanna Knowles
Woodwell → see Hailman, Johanna
K.Woodwell

Hailstone, Bernard *(British artist,*
b.1910)   **WI**

Haiman → see Hayman, Francis

Haimon Group   **GC JG**

(*Attic vase-painters*)   GC

Bibl: ▶Beazley, Attic bl.-fig. vase-
ptrs., pp.538-583

Haimon Painter *(vase-painter, ca.*
460-435 BC)   **GC**

Bibl: ▶Beazley, Attic bl.-fig. vase-
ptrs.; Boardman, Attic Bl.-fig.
Vases

Hainard, Robert   **BA WC**

(*Swiss artist, 1906-*)   WC

(*Swiss painter, printmaker,*
sculptor, author, b.1906)   BA

Bibl: ▶Künst.-Lex. Schweiz 20.
Jahrh.; ▶Lex. zeitgen. Schweiz.
Künstler

Hainault or Henault *(French artist,*
op.1752-1789)   **WC**

Haincelin de Hagenau   **BA GC**

(*French artist, op.1403-1448*)   WC

(*French illuminator, act. ca.*
1403-1448)   GC

(*French illuminator, act.1403-*
1448)   BA

Bibl: Getty Photo Study Coll.
(Medieval); ▶RILA/BHA

Haguenot, Haincelin de   GC

Haincelin de Haguenot or
Hagueneau (Hanslein von
Hagenau or Jean Haincelin or
Haimelin)   **WC**

Haincelin de Haguenot or Hagueneau
(Hanslein von Hagenau or Jean
Haincelin or Haimelin) → see
Haincelin de Hagenau

Haindl, Friedrich C. *(German*
architect, Munich)   **AV**

Bibl: BDA Mitglieder 1960;
Deutsche Bauzeitschrift, 1985
Mar., v.33, no.3, p.299

Haindl, Friedrich F. *(German architect, Munich)* **AV**
   Bibl: BDA Mitglieder 1960; Deutsche Bauzeitschrift, 1985 Mar., v.33, no.3, p.299
Haine → see Heins, D.
Haine → see Heins, John Theodore
Haines, Elizabeth *(English embroiderer, act.ca.1720)* **BA**
   Bibl: CONNOISSEUR CC/808 (June 1979) p.86; Kendric ENG NEEDLEWORK
Haines, Ephraim *(American cabinetmaker, act.1770-1826)* **BA**
   Bibl: Schwarz, Girard coll.
Haines, Eugene S.M. *(American, active Albany, NY, U.S. ca. 1865-1882)* **JG**
Haines, Jeffrey B. *(American interior designer, Far Hills, NJ)* **AV**
   Bibl: Colonial homes, 1989 June, v.15, no.3, p.42
Haines, Lett **BA WI**
   (British artist, 20th c.) **BA**
   (British artist, op.circa 1970-1971-) **WI**
   Bibl: Colchester (GBR), Minories, 24 Essex & Suffolk artists (1979)
Haines, Richard **WC WI**
   (American artist, 1906-) **WC**
   (American artist, 1906-op.1956) **WI**
Haines, William *(British artist, 1778-1848)* **WC WI**
Haines, William *(American interior designer)* **AV**
   Bibl: Architectural digest, 1984 Dec., v.41, no.12
Haines, William Henry **WI**
   (British artist, 1812-1884) **WC WI**
   Haines, William Henry (William Henry) **WC**
Haines, William Henry (William Henry) → see Haines, William Henry
Hains, Adam *(American cabinetmaker, 1768-after 1815)* **BA**
   Bibl: ANTIQUES, CXVIII (May 1980) 1112-1116
Hains, Raymond **BA WC**
   (French artist, 20th cent.) **WC**
   (French painter, photographer, b.1929) **BA**
   Bibl: ▶Art Index; ▶Bénézit; Sainte Etienne (FRA), Musée d'Art et d'Industrie, Beautés Volées, p.19
Haintzmann, Michael **JG**
Hainz, Georg → see Hinz, Georg
Hainz, Heintz, Hinz or Hintzsch, Georg (Johann Georg) → see Hinz, Georg
Hainz, Johann Georg → see Hinz, Georg
Hainz, Josef → see Heintz, Joseph, the elder
Hainzelmann or Heinzelmann, Johann *(German artist, 1641-1693/1700)* **WC**

Hair, Thomas H. **WC WI**
   (British artist, 1810-1882) **WI**
   (British artist, op.1838-1849) **WC**
Haire, Susan *(British artist, b.1952)* **WI**
Haisch, Gerhard *(Architect, Munich)* **AV**
   Bibl: Detail, 1981 Mar.-Apr., no.2, p.173
Haisne, Abbe de *(French artist, op. c.1785-1786)* **WC**
Haite, George Charles **WC WI**
   (British artist, 1855-1924) **WI**
   (British artist, 1855-c.1919) **WC**
Haizlip, Selden P. *(American architect, New Orleans, La)* **AV**
   Bibl: ▶AIA Pro File, 1987-88; phone call to office 3/30/88
Haizmann, Richard *(German painter, sculptor, designer, 1895-1963)* **BA**
   Bibl: ▶MoMA librr. cat.; Schleswig (DEU), Schleswig-Holst. Landesmuseum, Cesar Klein; ▶Vollmer, Künst.-Lex. 20. Jhr.
Hajdu, Étienne *(French sculptor, b.1907)* **BA**
   Bibl: ▶Bénézit; ▶Fogg Mus. Libr. cat.
Hajek, Katja *(West German painter, 20th c.)* **BA**
   Bibl: Kerber, B., in ART INT'l XXVII/2 (Apr-June 1984) 47
Hajek, Otto Herbert **AV BA**
   (West German sculptor, printmaker, b.1927) **BA**
   (West German sculptor, Stuttgart, 1927-) **AV**
   Bibl: ▶DuMonts Künst.-Lex.; ▶Libr. of Congr. Name Auth. File; Stuttgart (BRD), Staatsgalerie. OH HAJEK, 1979; ▶Wer ist wer; ▶WW Arts DEU
Hajema, Freerk *(Dutch artist, op. 1717-1746)* **WC**
Hajo, Rose (Hans-Joachim) *(German, 1910 -)* **JG**
Hajzig, Bernhard → see Heisig, Bernhard
Hak, Miroslav *(Czech, 1911-1977)* **JG**
Hakatch, Petrus van [Unidentified]
   (Unknown painter) **PR**
   Bibl: (May 16, 1809, lot 87, Robins)
   Petrus Van Hakatch **PR**
Haken Group *(Campanian vase-painters)* **GC**
   Bibl: ▶Trendall, Red-fig. vases Lucania
Haken Painter *(South Italian vase-painter, 4th century BC)* **GC**
   Bibl: ▶Trendall, Red-fig. vases Lucania
Hakenjos, Hermann I *(German ceramist, painter, 1879-1961)* **BA**
   Bibl: Schuly, DIE FAYENCE-MANUFAKTUR KANDERN (1985)
Hakewill or Hakewell, John *(British artist, 1742-1791)* **WC**

Hakewill, Henry *(English architect, 1771-1830)* **AV**
   Bibl: ▶Colvin, Brit. archts.
Hakewill, James **BA WC WI**
   (British architect, 1778-1843) **BA**
   (British artist, 1778-1843) **WC WI**
   Bibl: ▶Colvin, Brit. archts.; ▶Dict. natl. biog.; ▶Thieme-Becker
Hakim, Besim S. *(Tunisian(?) architect, educated at Harvard, professor at Technical University of Nova Scotia, Halifax)* **AV**
   Bibl: ▶Libr. of Congr. Name Auth. File
Hakkert, Jan → see Hackaert, Jan
Häkli, Seppo *(Finnish architect)* **AV**
   Bibl: Arkkitehti, 1989, v.86, no.3, p.18
Hal, Jacob van **GC WC**
   (Flemish artist, 1672-1750) **WC**
   (Flemish painter, 1672-1750) **GC**
   Bibl: ▶Thieme-Becker
Hal, M. van *(Dutch painter, 17th century)* **GC**
   Bibl: Getty Photo Study Coll. (Duits coll.)
Halaby, Samia A. *(American painter, b.1936)* **BA**
   Bibl: Guide exh. artists: N. Amer. ptrs.; ▶WW Amer. Art, 1989-1990
Haladay, Edward P. *(American architect)* **AV**
Halápy, János **BA WC**
   (Hungarian artist, 1893-1961) **WC**
   (Hungarian painter, printmaker, 1893-1960) **BA**
   Bibl: ▶Vollmer, Künst.-Lex. 20. Jhr.
Halard, Michelle *(French fabric designer, Paris)* **AV**
   Bibl: House & garden, 1987 Dec., v.159, no.12, p.126
Halard, Yves *(French fabric designer, Paris)* **AV**
   Bibl: House & garden, 1987 Dec., v.159, no.12, p.126
Halasiewicz *(Polish artist, 19th cent.)* **WC**
Halász, Gyula → see Brassaï (Gyula Halász)
Halauska, Ludwig *(German artist, 1827-1882)* **WC**
Halbax, Michael Wenzel **GC WC**
   (Austrian draughtsman, 1661-1711) **GC**
   (German artist, 1661-1711) **WC**
   Bibl: ▶Thieme-Becker
Halbeeck or Haelbeck, Jan van *(Flemish(?) artist, op.1600-1618)* **WC**
Halberg, Samuel → see Gal'berg, Samuil Ivanovič
Halberg-Krauss, Fritz *(German artist, 1874-1951)* **WC**
Halberstadt, Ernst **WC WI**
   (American artist, 20th cent.) **WC**
   (American artist, op.20th c.) **WI**

Halbou, Louis Michel   **BA GC**
    (French artist, 1730-1809)   WC
    (French printmaker, 1730-ca.
      1809)   BA
    (French, 1730-1809)   GC
      Bibl: ▶Bellier, Artistes fran.;
      ▶Bénézit; ▶Thieme-Becker; ▶Witt
      checklist
Halbou, Louis Michel (not Jean
    Louis)   **WC**
Halbou, Louis Michel (not Jean
    Louis) → see Halbou, Louis Michel
Halbower, Kathy *(American painter,*
    20th c.)   **BA**
      Bibl: JRL SO CALIF 27/June-July
      '80, p.29-30
Halbritter, Kurt *(German illustrator,*
    caricaturist, b.1924)   **BA**
Hald, Niels Tove Edward *(Swedish*
    glass designer, painter, printmaker,
    1883-1980)   **BA**
      Bibl: ▶Arwas, Glass, p.171; Jrl of
      Dec Arts Soc V (1981) 5-11;
      ▶Penguin dec. arts; ▶Svenskt
      konst.-lex.
Hald, Smitz(?) *(Danish(?) artist, 19th*
    cent.(?))   **WC**
Haldenby, Eric William *(1893-1971;*
    Architect, Ottawa, Toronto)   **FA**
      Bibl: Dube, Parliament bldgs.;
      ▶Hill, Archts. Canada, 1986
Haldenwang, Christian *(German*
    printmaker, 1770-1831)   **BA**
Haldenwang, Friedrich *(Swiss*
    artist, -1820)   **WC**
Haldenwanger, Henri *(German*
    artist, op.1766-1770)   **WC**
Hale *(Active New York, NY, U.S.*
    (also Meade & Hale,
    daguerreotypist))   **JG**
Hale, Edward → see Hale, Edward
    Matthew
Hale, Edward Matthew   **PR WC WI**
    (British artist, 1852-)   WC
    (British artist, 1852-1924)   WI
    (British painter, 1852-1924)   PR
      Bibl: Nat Gal of Ireland catalogue;
      ▶Thieme-Becker
    Edward Matthew Hale   PR
    Hale, Edward   PR
Hale, Ellen Day   **BA WI**
    (American artist, 1855-1940)   WI
    (American painter, 1855-1940)   BA
      Bibl: Smith; York, Richard, Gallery
      exh cat. 1981; ▶Young, Amer.
      artists
Hale, Frank L. *(American, active*
    Hartford, CT, U.S. 1880s)   **JG**
Hale, John Howard *(British artist,*
    1863-1955)   **WI**
Hale, Kathleen   **WC WI**
    (British artist, 20th cent.)   WC
    (British artist, b.1898)   WI
      Bibl: ▶Waters, Brit. artists
    McClean, Kathleen, Mrs.   WI

Hale, Lilian Westcott   **BA WI**
    (American artist, 1880-1963)   WI
    (American artist, 1881-)   WC
    (American painter, 1881-1963)   BA
      Bibl: ▶Bénézit; ▶Vollmer,
      Künst.-Lex. 20. Jhr.; ▶WW Amer.
      Art, 1959; ▶WWW Amer.
Hale, Lillian (nee Westcott)   **WC**
Hale, Lillian (nee Westcott) → see
    Hale, Lilian Westcott
Hale, Luther Holman *(American,*
    1821-1885, active Boston, MA,
    U.S. 1846-1864,)   **JG**
Hale, Philip Leslie   **BA**
    (American artist, 1865-1931)   WC WI
    (American painter, 1865-1931)   BA
      Bibl: ▶Fielding's Amer. ptrs., &
      Add.; ▶Young, Amer. artists
Hale, Phillip L.   **WC**
Hale, Phillip Leslie   **WI**
Hale, Phillip L. → see Hale, Philip Leslie
Hale, Phillip Leslie → see Hale, Philip
    Leslie
Hale, Robert Beverly *(American*
    painter, art administrator, b.1901)   **BA**
      Bibl: ▶Archives Amer. Art Jrnl.,
      XI/1-4 (1971); ▶WW Amer. Art,
      1976
Hale, Walter *(American artist, 1869-*
    1917)   **WC WI**
Hale, William Matthew   **WC WI**
    (British artist, 1837-1929)   WI
    (British artist, 1852-1924)   WC
      Bibl: ▶Witt checklist
Hale, Willis *(American architect)*   **AV**
Halem, Henry *(American glass artist,*
    ceramist, b.1938)   **BA**
      Bibl: Akron (OH, USA), Akron Art
      Mus., Akron collaboration (1982);
      ▶Intl. dir. exh. artists, 1983
Halemans, Thomas → see Halleman,
    Thomas
Halen, Arnoud or Arend van
    (Aquila) → see Halen, Arnoud van
    (Aquila)
Halen, Arnoud van (Aquila)   **BA GC**
    (Dutch artist, op.1679-m.1732)   WC
    (Dutch draughtsman and
      printmaker, act.1679-d.1732)   GC
    (Dutch painter, poet, 1673-
      1732)   BA
      Bibl: ▶Bénézit; Bulletin van het
      Rijksmuseum XXVI/1 (1978)
      11-26; Getty Photo Study Coll.;
      ▶Thieme-Becker; ▶Witt checklist
Halen, Arnoud or Arend van
    (Aquila)   **WC**
Halen, Francisco de Paula van
    (Spanish artist, -1887)   **WC**

Halen, Peter van   **GC PR WC**
    (Flemish artist, 1612-1687)   WC
    (Flemish painter, 1612-1687)   PR
    (Flemish, 1612-1687)   GC
      Bibl: ▶Thieme-Becker; ▶Witt
      checklist
    P. Halen   PR
    Peter van Halen   PR
Hales, John → see Hayls, John
Haley, Henry James   **WC WI**
    (British artist, 1874-op.1919)   WI
    (British artist, op.1901-1919)   WC
Haley, John   **WC WI**
    (American artist, 20th cent.)   WC
    (American artist, b.1905)   WI
Haley, Katherine H. *(American, 20th*
    c.)   **BA**
      Bibl: Oklahoma City (OK, USA),
      Natl. Cowboy Hall of Fame,
      Edward Borein (1979)
Haley, Marj *(American interior*
    designer, Iowa)   **AV**
      Bibl: Iowa architect, 1986 Mar.-
      Apr., v.34, no.2, p.44
Haley, Nade *(American sculptor,*
    20th c.)   **BA**
      Bibl: ▶Art Index, v.36; Nadelman,
      ARTS MAGAZINE, LXII/9 (May
      1988), p. 94
Halfmann, Jasper   **AV BA**
    (West German architect, 20th
      c.)   BA
    (West German architect, Berlin,
      1941-)   AV
      Bibl: Architektur + Wettbewerbe,
      1988 Mar., no.133, p.96; the
      artist in KUNSTFORUM INT'L 60
      (Apr 1983) 136; ▶Avery period.
      idx., 6th suppl.; Cook, AA FILES 9
      (summer 1985) 65
Halfnight, Richard William   **WC WI**
    (British artist, 1855-1925)   WI
    (British artist, op.1878-1892)   WC
Halford, Henry   **WI**
    (British artist, 1766-1844)   WC WI
Halford, Sir Henry   **WC**
Halford, Mary, Miss → see Davis,
    Mary
Halford, Sir Henry → see Halford,
    Henry
Halfpenny or Alpenny, Joseph
    Samuel → see Halfpenny, Joseph
    Samuel
Halfpenny, Joseph → see Halfpenny,
    Joseph S.
Halfpenny, Joseph S.   **WC WI**
    (British artist, 1748-1811)   WC WI
    (British painter, 1748-1811)   GC
      Bibl: ▶Bénézit
Halfpenny, Joseph   **GC**
Halfpenny, Joseph Samuel   **WI**
    (British artist, 1787-1858)   WC WI
    Alpenny, Joseph Samuel   WI
    Halfpenny or Alpenny, Joseph
      Samuel   **WC**

Hall, Mark (*American Architect, Los Angeles, CA*)   **AV**
Bibl: ▶AIA Pro File, 1983
Hall, Michael David (*American sculptor, b.1941*)   **BA**
Bibl: ▶WW Amer. Art, 1976
Hall, Nigel   **BA WC WI**
(*British artist, 1943-op.1968*)   WI
(*British artist, 20th cent.*)   WC
(*British sculptor, b.1943*)   BA
Bibl: Arts Council GBR, Square Coll. cat. (1974); Arts Council of GB
Hall, Oliver   **PR WC WI**
(*British artist, 1869-1957*)   WC WI
(*British painter, 1869-1957*)   PR
Bibl: ▶Thieme-Becker
Oliver Hall   PR
Hall, Paige→see Giddings, Patricia
Hall, Patrick   **WC WI**
(*British artist, 1906-*)   WC
(*British artist, b.1906*)   WI
Hall, Peder Adolf→see Hall, Peter Adolf
Hall, Peter (*British city planner, London; Chairman (1988-), Economic and Social Science Research Council, Gt. Britain*)   **AV**
Bibl: Architects' journal, 1988 Jan.13, v.187, no.2, p.17
Hall, Peter Adolf   **BA GC**
(*Swedish artist, 1739-1793*)   WC
(*Swedish painter in FRA, 1739-1793*)   BA
(*Swedish painter, draughtsman, 1739-1793*)   GC
Bibl: ▶Encyc. world art; ▶Svenskt konst.-lex.; ▶Thieme-Becker; ▶Witt checklist
Hall, Peder Adolf   GC WC
Hall, Ralph (*British potter, act.1805-1849*)   **BA**
Bibl: ▶Mankowitz, Encyc. pott. & porc.
Hall, Richard (*American painter, 20th c.*)   **BA**
Bibl: ▶Intl. dir. exh. artists, 1983
Hall, Rosemary (*British artist, op. 20th c.*)   **WI**
Hall, Susan (*American painter, b.1943*)   **BA**
Bibl: Art News, nov. 1974, p.93; exh cat
Hall, Sydney→see Hall, Sydney Prior
Hall, Sydney Prior   **PR WC WI**
(*British artist, 1842-1922*)   WI
(*British artist, 1842-p.1920*)   WC
(*British painter, 1842-1922*)   PR
Bibl: Nat Gal of Ireland catalogue; ▶Thieme-Becker
Hall, Sydney   PR
Sydney Prior Hall   PR
Hall, Sydney Prior, Mrs., (Mary L.)→see Gow, Mary L.
Hall, T. (*Engraver, op.early 19th c.*)   **WI**

Hall, Thomas P.   **WC WI**
(*British artist, op.1827-1886*)   WI
(*British artist, op.1837-1867*)   WC
Hall, van [Unidentified] (*Unknown painter*)   **PR**
Bibl: (April 13, 1813, lot 85, Johnson)
Vanhall   PR
Hall, Warren (*American sculptor, b.1939*)   **BA**
Bibl: exh cat
Hall, William   **WC WI**
(*British artist, op.1859-, d.circa 1885*)   WI
(*British artist, op.1859-1885*)   WC
Hallaert, Denis van (*Dutch painter in AUT, act.1571/72*)   **BA**
Bibl: Jahrb. der Kunsthist. Samml. in Wien LXXI 1975; ▶Thieme-Becker
Hallam, Lisa (*British artist, op.1901-1921*)   **WI**
Bibl: ▶Foskett, Brit. miniature ptrs.
Hallart, Jean (*French artist, 1616-1685*)   **WC**
Hallas, Harold W. (*British artist, op. circa 1928-*)   **WI**
Hallatz, Emil (*German artist, 1837-1888*)   **WC**
Hallbeck, Carl Svante (*Swedish artist, 1826-1897*)   **WC**
Hallberg, Lawrence (*American architect, 1844-1915*)   **AV**
Bibl: ▶Withey, Amer. archts.
Hallberg, Samuel Friedrich Ivanovich→see Gal'berg, Samuil Ivanovič
Hallblad, Erik (*Swedish painter, restorer, 1720-1814*)   **BA**
Bibl: ▶Bénézit; ▶Svenskt konst.-lex.; ▶Thieme-Becker
Hallbrock, Jo   **WC WI**
(*British artist, op.circa 1620-*)   WI
(*C*)   WC
Halle→see Hallé, Noël
Halle, C. A. von (*West German architect, Berlin*)   **AV**
Bibl: Architektur + Wettbewerbe, 1988 Dec., no.136, p.81
Halle, Charles Edward (*British artist, 1846-1914*)   **WC WI**
Bibl: ▶Waters, Brit. artists
Halle, Claude Guy→see Hallé, Claude-Guy
Hallé, Claude-Guy   **BA**
(*French artist, 1652-1736*)   WC
(*French painter, printmaker, 1652-1736*)   BA
(*French, 1652-1736*)   GC
Bibl: ▶Bénézit; ▶Thieme-Becker; ▶Witt checklist
Halle, Claude Guy   **GC WC**
Halle, Daniel   **GC WC**
(*French artist, 1614-1675*)   WC
(*French, 1614-1675*)   GC
Bibl: ▶Witt checklist

Hallé, Elinor Jessie Marie (*British sculptor, medalist, b.1856, act. 1908*)   **BA**
Bibl: Attwood, MEDAL, 6 (spring 1985) 16-22; ▶Forrer, Medallists; ▶Johnson, Brit. artists; Macray; ▶Thieme-Becker
Hallé, Kiuston (*French dancer, photographer, b.1952*)   **BA**
Bibl: Paris (FRA), Musée Rodin, Rodin: 5 photographes (1985), p.66
Halle, Ludwig→see Halle, Samuel Baruch
Hallé, Noël   **BA GC WC**
(*French artist, 1711-1781*)   WC
(*French painter, 1711-1781*)   PR
(*French painter, printmaker, 1711-1781*)   BA
(*French, 1711-1781*)   GC
Bibl: ▶RILA/BHA; ▶Thieme-Becker; ▶Witt checklist
Halle   PR
Hallé, Noïl   **PR**
Noel Halle   PR
Hallé, Noïl→see Hallé, Noël
Halle, Samuel Baruch   **BA**
(*French painter, printmaker, 1824-1889*)   BA
(*German artist, 1824-1889*)   WC
Bibl: ▶Bénézit; ▶Thieme-Becker
Halle, Ludwig   **WC**
Halle, William   **WC WI**
(*British artist, 20th cent.*)   WC
(*British artist, op.20th c.*)   WI
Halledine, G.H. (*British artist, op. 20th c.*)   **WI**
Hallek, Enno (*Swedish painter, b.1931*)   **BA**
Bibl: ▶Svenska konstnärer
Halleman, Haleman or Halemans, Thomas→see Halleman, Thomas
Halleman, Thomas   **GC**
(*Dutch artist, 1665-p.1690*)   WC
(*Dutch, 1665-aft.1690*)   GC
Bibl: Getty Photo Study Coll. (Ptgs.); ▶Witt checklist
Halemans, Thomas   GC
Halleman, Haleman or Halemans, Thomas   **WC**
Hallen, Ernest (*American photographer, 1875-1947*)   **BA**
Bibl: Art Journal XXXVI/2 (winter 76/76) 123-125
Hallen, Hans Heyerdahl (*South African architect, Durban, 1957-, 1930-*)   **AV**
Bibl: ▶Contemp. archts.; UIA international architect, 1985, no.8, inside front & back covers
Haller von Hallerstein, Carl→see Haller von Hallerstein, Johann Carl Christoph Wilhelm Joachim

Haller von Hallerstein, Christoph GC
  (German artist, 1771-1839) WC
  (German, 1771-1839) GC
    Bibl: George Goldner;
    ▶Thieme-Becker; ▶Witt checklist
**Haller, Christoph Jakob Wilhelm
  Carl Joachim, (Freiherr von
  Hallerstein)** WC
**Haller von Hallerstein, Johann Carl
  Christoph Wilhelm Joachim** BA
  (German architect, 1774-1817) AV
  *(German architect,
    archaeologist, 1774-1817)* BA
  (German artist, 1774-1817) WC
  (German, 1774-1817) GC
    Bibl: ▶Brockhaus Enzyk.; ▶Libr. of
    Congr. Name Auth. File;
    ▶Macmillan encyc. archts.; ▶Neue
    deutsche Biog.; ▶Portoghesi, Diz.
    arch. e urbanistica;
    ▶Thieme-Becker; ▶Witt checklist
Haller von Hallerstein, Carl GC
**Haller von Hallerstein, Karl,
  Freiherr** AV
**Haller, Johann Carl Christoph
  Joachim, (Freiherr von
  Hallerstein)** WC
*Haller von Hallerstein, Karl,
  Freiherr →see Haller von
  Hallerstein, Johann Carl Christoph
  Wilhelm Joachim*
Haller, Andre or Andra *(German
  artist, op.1509-1522)* WC
*Haller, Christoph Jakob Wilhelm Carl
  Joachim, (Freiherr von
  Hallerstein) →see Haller von
  Hallerstein, Christoph*
Haller, Fritz P. *(Swiss architect,
  Zurich)* AV
    Bibl: ▶Schweiz. Ingen. u. Archit.,
    1984-1985
Haller, George *(American, 20th c.)* BA
Haller, Hans Peter *(engineer, 20th
  c.)* BA
    Bibl: Piano DAIDALOS/17 (15
    Sept) 1985 p.84-87
Haller, Hermann BA WC
  (Swiss artist, 1880-) WC
  (Swiss sculptor, 1880-1950) BA
    Bibl: ▶Künst.-Lex. Schweiz 20.
    Jahrh.; ▶Vollmer, Künst.-Lex. 20.
    Jhr.
*Haller, Johann Carl Christoph
  Joachim, (Freiherr von
  Hallerstein) →see Haller von
  Hallerstein, Johann Carl Christoph
  Wilhelm Joachim*
Haller, Joseph *(German artist, 1737-
  1773)* WC
Haller, Jost *(German painter, act.
  1453, d. before 1485)* BA
    Bibl: Sterling, Wiener Jahrb. XXXIII
    (1980) p.109
Haller, Philipp *(German artist, 1698-
  1772)* WC

Hallermann, Klaus *(German
  architect, b.1930)* BA
    Bibl: KUNSTWERK XXXII/2-3 (Apr-
    June) 1979 74-76
Hallet, Gilles *(Flemish painter, 1620-
  1694)* PR
    Bibl: ▶Thieme-Becker
  Gilles Hallet PR
  Monsu' Egidio fiammengo PR
*Hallet, Hendricks A. →see Hallett,
  Hendricks A.*
Hallett →see Hallett, Hendricks A.
Hallett, Hendricks A. *(American
  painter, 1847-1921)* PR
    Bibl: ▶WWW Amer. art
  Hallet, Hendricks A. PR
  Hallett PR
  Hendricks A. Hallett PR
*Hallett, William →see Hallett, William
  I*
Hallett, William I BA
  (1707-1781) AV
  *(British cabinetmaker, 1707-
    1781)* BA
    Bibl: Beard, Studies hist. furniture,
    p.220 (1707-1781); ▶Heal,
    London furniture mkrs., (active
    1732, died 1781)
Hallett, William AV
Hallett, William II *(British
  cabinetmaker, 1730-1767)* BA
    Bibl: Beard, Studies hist. furniture,
    p.223
Hallewell, Ben *(British artist, op.
  1865-1869)* WC WI
Halley, Peter *(American artist,
  b.1953)* WI
Hallez, Germain-Joseph *(Belgian
  artist, 1769-1840)* WC
Halliday, Alan *(British artist, b.1952)* WI
Halliday, Charlotte WC WI
  (British artist, 20th cent.) WC
  (British artist, op.20th c.) WI
Halliday, Edward Irvine BA WC WI
  (British artist, 1902-) WC
  (British artist, b.1902) WI
  (British painter, b.1902) BA
    Bibl: ▶Johnson, Brit. artists;
    ▶Vollmer, Künst.-Lex. 20. Jhr.;
    ▶Who's Who [GBR], 1976
Halliday, Frank Ernest *(British artist,
  op.20th c.)* WI
Halliday, Iain *(Australian interior
  designer)* AV
    Bibl: Interiors, 1989 Sept., v.149,
    no.2, p.179
Halliday, Irene WC WI
  (British artist, 1932-) WC
  (British artist, b.1932) WI
*Halliday, Michael Frederick or
  Michael Henry →see Halliday,
  Michael Fredrick (or Michael
  Henry)*

**Halliday, Michael Fredrick (or
  Michael Henry)** WI
  (British artist, 1822-1869) WC WI
    Bibl: ▶Houfe, Brit. book illus.
**Halliday, Michael Frederick or
  Michael Henry** WC
Halliday, Trevor BA WC WI
  (British artist, 1939-) WC
  (British artist, b.1939) WI
  (British painter, b.1939) BA
    Bibl: Nottingham (GBR), Univ. Art
    Gallery, Maurice Cockrill (1980)
Hallien [Unidentified] *(Unknown
  painter)* PR
    Bibl: (January 17, 1803, lot 7,
    Christie's)
Hallman, Gary *(American
  photographer, b.1940)* BA
    Bibl: Baltimore (MD, USA), exhib.
    cat. 1975
Hallock, Absolom B. *(American
  architect, engineer, surveyor,
  1826-1892)* AV
    Bibl: Portland friends of cast-iron
    architecture newsletter, 1981,
    no.18
*Hallock, Mary Anna, Miss →see
  Foote, Mary Anna Hallock*
Hallock, Ruth Mary *(American
  artist, 1876-1945)* WI
Halloran, O. WC WI
  (British artist, 19th cent.) WC
  (British artist, op.19th c.) WI
Halloran, Sue *(American,
  contemporary)* JG
Hallot, William *(British
  cabinetmaker, act.1769)* BA
    Bibl: Beard, Studies hist. furniture,
    pp.221, 224
Hallowell, George Hawley
  (American artist, 1872-1926) WI
Halls →see Hals, Frans
Halls, John James WC WI
  (British artist, 1776-1834) WI
  (British artist, op.1791-1834) WC
Hallstrom, Eric *(Swedish artist,
  1893-1946)* WC
Hallstrom, Gunnar August
  (Swedish artist, 1875-1943) WC
Hallward, Reginald F. *(British artist,
  1858-1948)* WI
Halm, Felix GC WC
  (German artist, 1758-1810) WC
  *(German draughtsman, 1758-
    1810)* GC
    Bibl: ▶Thieme-Becker
Halm, M. →see Halm, Matthäus
Halm, Matthäus GC
  (German artist, op.1766) WC
  *(German draughtsman, 18th
    century)* GC
    Bibl: ▶Thieme-Becker
Halm, M. WC

Hals, Nicolaes　　　　　GC PR
　(Dutch artist, 1628-1686)　WC
　(Dutch painter, 1628-1668)　PR
　(Dutch painter, 1628-1686)　GC
　　Bibl: Getty Photo Study Coll.;
　　Getty Photo Study Coll. (Ptgs.);
　　▶Thieme-Becker; ▶Witt checklist
　Hals　　　　　　　　　　PR
　Hals, Claes　　　　　　GC PR
Hals, Nicolaes (Claes)　　WC
　Nicolaes Hals　　　　　PR
Hals, Nicolaes (Claes) → see Hals,
　Nicolaes
Hals, Reynier → see Hals, Reynier
　Fransz.
Hals, Reynier Fransz.　　VO
　(Dutch artist, 1627(?)-1671)　WC
　(Dutch painter, 1627-1671)　GC
　(Dutch painter, 1627-1672)　VO
　　Bibl: ▶Libr. of Congr. Name Auth.
　　File, NAFR9137833;
　　▶Thieme-Becker
Hals, Reynier　　　　　GC WC
Hals, Thierry → see Hals, Dirck
Hals, Willem　　　　　GC WC
　(Dutch painter, 17th century)　GC
　(Netherlands artist, 17th cent.)　WC
　　Bibl: ▶Thieme-Becker
Halsband, Frances (American
　architect, New York, NY, 1943-)　AV
　　Bibl: ▶AIA Pro File, 1985
Halse, Anders (Danish architect)　AV
Halsey, Louise McCallum (American
　weaver, b.1949)　　　　BA
　　Bibl: Greenville (SC, USA), County
　　Mus. Art, 5 South Carolina artists
　　(1975)
Halskov, Lasse (Danish architect,
　Naerum, 1937-)　　　　AV
　　Bibl: Arkitekten, 1988 June 28,
　　v.90, no.12, p.337, [dates];
　　▶Danske Arkitekters
　　Landsforbund, 1984-85
Halsman, Philippe　　　BA JG
　(American (b. Latvia, Russia,
　now USSR), 1906-1979)　JG
　(American photographer,
　author, 1906-1979)　　BA
　　Bibl: ▶Newhall, Photog.; NYT, 26
　　(June 1979); WW Amer., 1976-77
Halst, Frans → see Hals, Frans
Halstead, Samuel (British artist, op.
　circa 1893-)　　　　　WI
Halstijn → see Holsteijn, Cornelis
Halswelle → see Halswelle, Keeley
Halswelle, Keeley　　PR WC WI
　(British artist, 1832-1891)　WC WI
　(British painter, 1832-1891)　PR
　　Bibl: ▶Thieme-Becker
　Halswelle　　　　　　　PR
　Keeley Halswelle　　　PR
Hälszel, Johann Baptist → see Haelszel,
　Johann Baptist
Halszel, Johann Baptist (von?) → see
　Haelszel, Johann Baptist

Haltiner, Hans Jakob (Swiss
　architect, 1728-1805)　　BA
　　Bibl: ▶Jenny, Kunstführer Schweiz;
　　▶Schweiz. Künst.-Lex.;
　　▶Thieme-Becker
Haltmayr, Veit (German 18th cent.
　architect, active in Ingolstadt)　AV
　　Bibl: Ars Bavarica. v.3, 1975, p.82
Halton, H. Russell (Canadian
　architect)　　　　　　AV
　　Bibl: Society for the Study of
　　Architecture in Canada. Bulletin,
　　1984 Oct., v.9, no.3, p.4
Haly, Robert → see Healy, Robert
Ham, J. van　　　　　GC WC
　(Dutch artist, 17th cent.)　WC
　(Dutch painter, 17th century)　GC
　　Bibl: ▶Witt checklist
Ham, Marie (American interior
　decorator)　　　　　　AV
　　Bibl: Colonial homes, 1985 Jan.-
　　Feb., v.11, no.1, p.109
Ham, Roderick (British architect)　AV
Hamacher, Willy (German artist,
　1865-1909)　　　　　WC
Hamada, Shoji (Japanese potter,
　1894-1978)　　　　　BA
　　Bibl: ▶Boger, World pott. & porc.;
　　Intl. who's who, 1977, 1978-79
Hamada, Tetsuzo (Japanese
　architect, 1945-)　　　AV
　　Bibl: Kenchiku bunka, 1987 Dec.,
　　v.42, no.494, p.230
Hamaguchi, Yozo　　　BA WC
　(Japanese printmaker, b.1909)　BA
　(Westernized Oriental artist,
　1909-)　　　　　　　WC
　　Bibl: ▶Bénézit; ▶Libr. of Congr.
　　Name Auth. File; ▶Witt checklist
Hamaici, Samir (Tunisian architect,
　Tunis)　　　　　　　　AV
　　Bibl: Ordre architectes Tunisie,
　　1984
Haman, Oleg (Czech city planner)　AV
　　Bibl: Architektura ČSR, 1988,
　　v.47, no.2, p.10
Hamayon, C. (French architect)　AV
　　Bibl: Techniques et architecture,
　　1981 Dec., no.339, p.118
Hambach, Johann Michael　GC WC
　(German artist, op.1672-1675)　WC
　(German painter, act.1672-1686)　GC
　　Bibl: Getty Photo Study Coll.;
　　▶Schweers, Gemälde deut.
　　Museen; ▶Thieme-Becker; ▶Witt
　　checklist
Hambidge, Jay　　　　BA WC WI
　(American art historian, artist,
　1867-1924)　　　　　BA
　(American artist, 1867-1924)　WI
　(American artist, 1867-p.1900)　WC
　　Bibl: ▶Dict. Amer. biog.; LC card;
　　▶Who was who [GBR]
Hamble, J.R. (Engraver, London,
　GTL., op.1775-1825)　　WI

Hamblen, Sturtevant J.　　BA
　(American artist, op.1837-1856)　WI
　(American painter, act.1837-
　1856)　　　　　　　　BA
　　Bibl: ▶Groce, Artists Amer.;
　　▶Young, Amer. artists
Hamblin, Sturtevant J.　　WI
Hambleton, Richard A. (Canadian
　artist, 20th c.)　　　　BA
　　Bibl: ▶Intl. dir. exh. artists, 1982,
　　1983
Hambleton, Toni (Mexican sculptor
　in PRI, b.1934)　　　　BA
　　Bibl: ▶Bénézit; Springfield (MA,
　　USA), MFA, Clay from Puerto Rico
　　(1980)
Hamblett → see Hamblett, Theora
Hamblett, Theora　　BA PR WC WI
　(American artist, 1895-)　WC
　(American artist, 1895-1977)　WI
　(American painter, 1895-1977)　BA PR
　　Bibl: NY Times obit., 7 Mar 1977,
　　28; ▶Petteys, Women artists;
　　▶RILA/BHA; ▶WW Amer. Art,
　　necrol.
　Hamblett　　　　　　　PR
　Theora Hamblett　　　PR
Hamblin, Sturtevant J. → see Hamblen,
　Sturtevant J.
Hambling, Maggi　　　BA
　(British artist, 1943-)　WC
　(British artist, b.1945)　WI
　(British painter, b.1945)　BA
　　Bibl: ▶Dolman, Contemp. Brit.
　　artists
Hambling, Maggie　　　WC WI
Hambling, Maggie → see Hambling,
　Maggi
Hambly, Arthur → see Hambly, Arthur
　Creed
Hambly, Arthur Creed　　WI
　(Australian (?))　　　GC
　(British artist, b.1900)　WI
　　Bibl: Gernsheim, Corpus Photog.
　　of Drawings, 1418; ▶Johnson,
　　Brit. artists
Hambly, Arthur　　　GC
Hambourg, Andre (French artist,
　1909-)　　　　　　　WC
Hambrecht, Edward C. (American
　architect)　　　　　　AV
Hambro, Nathalie (British interior
　designer)　　　　　　AV
　　Bibl: The world of interiors, 1989
　　Oct., p.224
Hambüchen, Georg (German
　painter, 1901-1972)　　BA
　　Bibl: Kocks, D., WELTKUNT,
　　LIII/18 (15 Sept 1983) 2368;
　　▶Vollmer, Künst.-Lex. 20. Jhr.
Hambüchen, Wilhelm　　BA WC
　(German artist, 1869-)　WC
　(German painter, graphic artist,
　1869-1939)　　　　　BA
　　Bibl: ▶Bénézit; Berlin, Natl. Gall.
　　cat.; ▶Thieme-Becker

Hambuck, Carl (American painter, act.1874, d.1879)   **BA**
> Bibl: Wright, R.L., Clarion (winter 1983-84) 46

Hamburg Painter (Lucanian vase-painter)   **GC**
> Bibl: ▶Trendall, Red-fig. vases Lucania

Hamburger, Bernard (French architect, 1940-1982)   **AV**
> Bibl: Architecture d'aujourd'hui, 1982 Apr., no.220, p.VII

Hamburger, Johann Conrad
> (German artist, 1809-a.1870)   **WC**

Hamdi, Osman Bey → see Hamdy Bey, Osmân

Hamdy Bey → see Hamdy Bey, Osmân

Hamdy Bey, Osmân (Turkish painter, 1842-1910)   **PR**
> Bibl: ▶Thieme-Becker

Hamdi, Osman Bey   PR
Hamdy Bey   PR
Osman Hamdy Bey   PR

Hameel or Hamel, Alart du → see Hameel, Alart du

Hameel, Alart du   **BA GC**
> (early Netherlandish architect, sculptor, printmaker, 1449-1509)   BA
> (Netherlands artist, c.1449-c.1509)   WC
> (North Netherlandish printmaker, 1449-ca.1509)   GC
> Bibl: Getty Photo Study Coll.; ▶Portoghesi, Diz. arch. e urbanistica; ▶Thieme-Becker; ▶Wurzbach, NLD Künst.-Lex.

Du Hameel, Alart   GC

Hameel or Hamel, Alart du   **WC**

Hamel, Jack (Dutch painter, 1890-1951)   **GC**
> Bibl: ▶Vollmer, Künst.-Lex. 20. Jhr.

Hamel, Julius (German artist, 1834-1907)   **WC**

Hamel, Théophile   **BA WC**
> (Canadian artist, op.1846)   WC
> (Canadian painter, 1817-1870)   BA
> Bibl: ▶Artists Canada; ▶Natl. Gall. Canada libr. cat., suppl.

Hamel, Willem   **GC WC**
> (Dutch artist, 1860-1924)   WC
> (Dutch painter, 1860-1924)   GC
> Bibl: ▶Thieme-Becker

Hamen y Leon → see Hamen y León, Juan van der

Hamen y León, Juan van der   **BA GC PR WC**
> (Spanish artist, 1596-a.1632)   WC
> (Spanish painter, 1596-1631)   BA PR
> (Spanish, 1596-bef.1632)   GC
> Bibl: Jordan, Span. Still Life in the Golden Age (1985); ▶RILA/BHA; ▶Thieme-Becker; ▶Witt checklist; ▶Wurzbach, NLD Künst.-Lex.

Balderamen   PR
Hamen y Leon   PR
Juan van der Hamen y León   PR
Leon, Juan van der Hamen y   GC
Valderamen   PR
Valderan   PR
valderramen   PR
Van Derhamen Y Leon, Juan de   PR

Hamen, Jan van der (Flemish painter in ESP, act.ca.1595)   **BA**
> Bibl: ▶Encyc. world art; ▶Kubler, Art & arch. ESP & PRT; ▶Thieme-Becker

Hamer, Christopher (British artist, b.1953)   **BA**
> Bibl: Birmingham (GBR), Ikon Gall., Colored constructions (1982)

Hämer, Hardt-Waltherr (West German architect, 20th c.)   **BA**
> Bibl: ▶Wer ist wer, 1986-1987

Hamer, Leo I. M. (Dutch architect, 's-Gravenhage)   **AV**
> Bibl: ▶Federatie O jrbk., 1984

Hamer, Rawthmal   **WC WI**
> (American artist, op.1859-1861)   WC
> (American artist, op.20th c.)   WI

Hamer, Robert (British artist, op. 20th c.)   **WI**

Hamer, Stefan   **BA GC**
> (German printmaker, act.1534-1554)   BA
> (German woodcutter and publisher, act.1534-1554)   GC
> Bibl: ▶Bénézit; ▶RILA/BHA; ▶Thieme-Becker

Hamerani family (Italian medalists, metal engravers, 17th-19th cs.)   **BA**
> Bibl: ▶Encyc. world art; ▶Thieme-Becker

Ameriani family   BA

Hamerani, Caterina (Italian gem engraver, act.1670-1674)   **BA**
> Bibl: ▶Bulgari, Argentieri d'Italia, v.2, p.8; Chadour, Wallraf-Richartz-Jahrb. XLIII (1982) 133-193

Hamerani, Giovanni (Italian, 1763-1846)   **GC**
> Bibl: ▶Thieme-Becker

Hamerani, Giovanni Martino (Italian, 1646-1705)   **GC**
> Bibl: ▶Thieme-Becker

Hamerano, Juan (Spanish medalist, 17th c.)   **BA**
> Bibl: GOYA//143 Mar-Apr 1978 p.278-279

Hamerton, Philip Gilbert (British artist, critic, 1834-1894)   **BA**

Hamerton, Robert Jacob   **WC WI**
> (British artist, op.1830-1891)   WI
> (British artist, op.1831-1858)   WC

Hames, William (Australian architect, Perth)   **AV**
> Bibl: The architect, W.A., 1989, v.29, no.2, p.18

Hamesse, Paul   **AV BA**
> (Belgian architect, 1877-1956)   BA
> (Belgian architect, Brussels, 1877-)   AV
> Bibl: Brussels (BEL), École supérieur, Brussels 1900 (1972); ▶Thieme-Becker

Hamill, Tim J. (American painter, printmaker, b.1942)   **BA**
> Bibl: ▶WW Amer. Art

Hamilton → see Hamilton, Gavin
Hamilton → see Hamilton, Gawen
Hamilton → see Hamilton, Johann Georg de
Hamilton → see Hamilton, William
Hamilton Achille Wolf → see Wolf, Hamilton Achille
Hamilton Gibbs Wilde → see Wilde, Hamilton Gibbs

Hamilton Painter (Apulian vase-painter)   **GC**
> Bibl: Trendall, Attic red-fig. vases Apulia

Hamilton, Anne, Lady   **WI**
> (British artist, 1766-1846)   WC WI

Hamilton, Lady Anne   **WC**

Hamilton, Anton Ignaz (German artist, 1696-1770)   **WC**

Hamilton, C.   **WC WI**
> (British artist, op.1831-1867)   WC
> (British artist, op.19th c.)   WI

Hamilton, C.C.   **WC WI**
> (British artist, op.1810)   WC
> (British artist, op.1810-)   WI

Hamilton, Charles   **AV BA**
> (British landscape architect, 1704-1786)   AV
> (English landscape gardener, 1704-1786)   BA
> Bibl: ▶Hadfield, Brit. gardeners, pp.141-142

Hamilton, Charles (British artist, op. 1831-1867)   **WI**

Hamilton, Cuthbert   **BA WC WI**
> (British artist, 1884-1959)   WI
> (British artist, 1885-1959)   WC
> (British painter, 1884-1959)   BA
> Bibl: CONNOISSEUR. CXC: 764, Oct 1975, p.98; London. Hayward. VORTICISM & ITS ALLIES. 1974; Tate Gallery collections; ▶Waters, Brit. artists

Hamilton, David (Scottish architect, 1768-1843)   **BA**
> Bibl: Boase, Engl. art; ▶Dict. natl. biog.; Fletcher's arch., p.986; ▶Thieme-Becker

---

Hamilton, Edward Wilbur Dean BA WI
(*American artist, 1864-1943*) WI
(*American painter, 1864-1943*) BA PR
Bibl: Boston (MA, USA), Mus. of
Fine Arts, The Bostonians...,
1986; Canton AI catalogue;
▶Fielding's Amer. ptrs., 1983;
NYT; ▶Thieme-Becker; ▶Vollmer,
Künst.-Lex. 20. Jhr., v.6; ▶WWW
Amer., v.2; ▶WWW Amer. art;
▶Young, Amer. artists
Hamilton, Wilber Dean PR
Hamilton, Wilbur Dean PR
Wilbur Dean Hamilton PR
Hamilton, Emma (*British, ca.1765-
1815*) BA
Bibl: Connoisseur, CXCI, (Feb
1976) p.116; ▶Dict. natl. biog.;
GAZ. D. B-A, XCIV (Dec 1979)
219-226; ▶New Columbia encyc.
Hart, Emma BA
Hamilton, Eugene L. (*American
painter, sculptor, b.1947*) BA
Bibl: Des Moines (Ia, USA), Art
Center, RECENT WORKS BY
EUGENE L. HAMILTON, 1978
Hamilton, Eva Henrietta (*British
artist, 1880-1959*) WI
Bibl: Irish Women Artists
Hamilton, Frances (*American artist,
20th c.*) BA
Bibl: Boston (MA, USA), ICA,
Boston now (1982)
Hamilton, Franz de GC WC
(*Flemish artist, op.1661-1695*) WC
(*Flemish, act.1661-1695*) GC
Bibl: ▶Thieme-Becker; ▶Witt
checklist
Hamilton, Gavin BA GC PR WC WI
(*British artist, 1723-1798*) WC WI
(*British painter, 1723-1798*) PR
(*British painter, antiquary, 1723-
1798*) BA
(*British, 1723-1798*) GC
Bibl: ▶Bénézit; ▶Dict. natl. biog.;
▶RILA/BHA; ▶Thieme-Becker
G Hamilton PR
G. Hamilton PR
Gavin Hamilton PR
Hamilton PR
Hamilton, Gavin (*Scottish painter
act. in Rome, 1723-1798*) AV
Bibl: ▶Libr. of Congr. Name Auth.
File; ▶RILA/BHA; ▶Thieme-Becker
Hamilton, Gawen PR WC WI
(*British artist, c.1697-1737*) WC
(*British artist, circa 1697-1737*) WI
(*British painter, 1697-1737*) PR
Bibl: ▶Thieme-Becker
Gawen Hamilton PR
Hamilton PR
Hamilton, Gustavus WC WI
(*British artist, c.1739-1775*) WC
(*British artist, circa 1739-1775*) WI
Hamilton, Hamilton (*American
artist, 1847-1928*) WI

**Hamilton, Hugh
Douglas** BA GC PR WC WI
(*British artist, 1739-1808*) WC WI
(*Irish painter and draughtsman,
c.1739-1808*) GC
(*Irish painter, ca.1739-1808*) BA PR
Bibl: ▶Dict. natl. biog.; ▶Redgrave,
Engl. school; ▶RILA/BHA;
▶Strickland, Irish artists;
▶Thieme-Becker
Hugh Douglas Hamilton PR
Hamilton, Ian (*British architect*) AV
Bibl: Glazed expressions/Tiles &
Architectural Ceramics Society,
1986 Summer, no.12, p.1
Hamilton, Jacob or James de→*see*
Hamilton, Jacob, (or James de)
Hamilton, Jacob, (or James de) WI
(*British artist, c.1640-1720*) WC
(*British artist, circa 1640-1720*) WI
Hamilton, Jacob or James de WC
Hamilton, James (*American potter,
19th c.*) BA
Bibl: Ceramics monthly, XXVIII
(Sep. 1980) pp.30-36
Hamilton, James BA WC
(*American painter, 1819-1878*) BA
(*British artist, 1819-1878*) WC WI
Bibl: ▶Archibald, Sea ptrs.;
Binghamton (NY, USA), SUNY,
19c. ptrs. Delaware Valley (1983);
▶Strickland, Irish artists;
▶Thieme-Becker; ▶Witt checklist;
▶WWW Amer. hist.
Hamilton, James I WI
Hamilton, James I→*see* Hamilton,
James
Hamilton, James II (*British artist,
1855-1894*) WI
Hamilton, James Whitelaw (*British
artist, 1860-1932*) WC WI
Hamilton, Johann (*German artist, -c.
1750*) WC
Hamilton, Johann Georg de GC PR WC
(*Austrian painter, 1672-1737*) PR
(*Flemish artist, 1672-1737*) WC
(*Flemish painter, 1672-1737*) GC
Bibl: ▶Bénézit; ▶Thieme-Becker
G. Hamilton PR
Hamilton PR
Johann Georg de Hamilton PR
Hamilton, John Bruce→*see* Hamilton,
Juan B.
Hamilton, John McLure (*American
artist, 1853-1936*) WC WI
Hamilton, Juan B. (*American potter,
sculptor, b.1945*) BA
Bibl: ART NEWS, LXXVI (Dec
1977), p.37; Decker, ART NEWS,
LXXXVI (Apr 1987), p.120-127;
NYT, Nov 17, 1977,p.C2; NYT,
Nov 20, 1978, p.B10; ▶WW
Amer. Art, 1989-1990
Hamilton, John Bruce BA

Hamilton, Karl Wilhelm de GC PR
(*Flemish artist, 1668-1754*) WC
(*Flemish painter, 1668-1754*) PR
(*Flemish, 1668-1754*) GC
Bibl: ▶Thieme-Becker; ▶Witt
checklist
**Hamilton, Karl Wilhelm or
Charles William de** WC
Hamilton, Karl Willem de PR
Karl Wilhelm de Hamilton PR
*Hamilton, Karl Wilhelm or Charles
William de*→*see* Hamilton, Karl
Wilhelm de
Hamilton, Karl Willem de→*see*
Hamilton, Karl Wilhelm de
Hamilton, Kathleen (*Canadian
artist, 20th cent.*) WC
Hamilton, Lady Anne→*see* Hamilton,
Anne, Lady
Hamilton, Lady Sophia (*South
African artist, op.1800*) WC
Hamilton, Letitia Marion (*British
artist, 1878-1964*) WI
Bibl: ▶Waters, Brit. artists
Hamilton, Margaret (*British artist,
op.1910-*) WI
Hamilton, Maria, Miss→*see* Bell,
Maria
Hamilton, Mary F. (*British artist, op.
1807-1849*) WC WI
Hamilton, Maxwell JG
Hamilton, Mel (*American architect,
Chicago*) AV
Bibl: ▶AIA Pro File, 1983
Hamilton, Peter (*Canadian architect,
Toronto*) AV
Bibl: ▶Canad. arch. dir., 1985
**Hamilton, Philipp Ferdinand
de** GC PR WC
(*Flemish artist, c.1664(?)-1750*) WC
(*Flemish painter, 1664-1750*) PR
(*Flemish, 1664-1750*) GC
Bibl: ▶Thieme-Becker; ▶Witt
checklist
Hamilton, Phillip Ferdinand de PR
Philipp Ferdinand de Hamilton PR
Hamilton, Phillip Ferdinand de→*see*
Hamilton, Philipp Ferdinand de
Hamilton, R.A.→*see* Hamilton,
William
Hamilton, Richard (*British designer*) AV
Bibl: Architectural review, 1984
Apr., v.175, no.1046, p.62
Hamilton, Richard BA WC WI
(*British artist, 1922-*) WC
(*British artist, b.1922*) BA WI
Bibl: ▶Contemp. artists; ▶Oxford
comp. 20c. art; ▶Phaidon 20c. art
Hamilton, Richard W. (*American
architect*) AV
Bibl: ▶Avery period. idx.

Hamilton, Robert *(British photographer, 20th c.)* **BA**
Bibl: Glasgow (GBR), Print Studio Gallery, Charles Rennie Mackintosh; WW Academia, 1973-74

Hamilton, Ron *(Canadian painter, sculptor, b.1950)* **BA**
Bibl: ▶Artists Canada; Brodszky, Stones, bones

Hamilton, Thomas **AV BA**
(1784-1858) AV
(Scottish architect, 1784-1858) BA
Bibl: ▶Dict. natl. biog.; ▶Thieme-Becker

Hamilton, Wilber Dean→see Hamilton, Edward Wilbur Dean

Hamilton, Wilbur Dean→see Hamilton, Edward Wilbur Dean

Hamilton, William *(American potter, 19th c.)* **BA**
Bibl: Ceramics monthly, XXVIII (Sep. 1980) pp.30-36

Hamilton, William **BA GC PR WC WI**
(British artist, 1751-1801) WC WI
(British painter, 1750/51-1801) PR
(British painter, 1751-1801) BA
(British, 1751-1801) GC
Bibl: ▶Dict. natl. biog.; ▶RILA/BHA; ▶Thieme-Becker; ▶Witt checklist
Hamilton PR
Hamilton, R.A. PR
W. Hamilton, R. A. PR
W. Hamilton, R.A. PR
William Hamilton PR

Hamilton, William Osborne *(British artist, op.18th c.)* **WI**

Hamine [Unidentified] *(Unknown painter)* **PR**
Bibl: 1712 Hiel inventory

Hamlet Winstanley→see Winstanley, Hamlet

Hamlet, T. *(British artist, 1779-1815)* **WI**
Bibl: ▶Foskett, Brit. miniature ptrs.

Hamlin, A. *(American artist, op. 1841-1851)* **WI**

Hamlin, Alfred Dwight Foster *(American architect, 1855-1926)* **BA**
Bibl: ▶Macmillan encyc. archts.; ▶WWW Amer., v.1

Hamlin, Louise *(American painter, 20th c.)* **BA**
Bibl: Masters, G., in ARTS MAG LIX/10 (summer 1985) 17

Hamlin, Samuel *(American pewterer, 1746-1801)* **BA**
Bibl: Laughlin, Pewter Amer.

Hamlin, Talbot Faulkner *(American architect, 1889-1956)* **BA**
Bibl: ▶Macmillan encyc. archts.; ▶WWW Amer., v.3

Hamlin, William *(American printmaker, 1772-1869)* **BA**
Bibl: ▶Dict. Amer. biog.; ▶Groce, Artists Amer.

Hamm *(German artist, op.1806)* **WC**

Hamm, Eugen *(German artist, 1885-1930)* **WC**

Hamm, Henri *(French artist, 20th cent.)* **WC**

Hamm, Joseph G. *(American interior designer)* **AV**
Bibl: Interior design, 1989 Apr., v.60, no.6, p.276

Hamm, Manfred *(German photographer, b.1944)* **BA**
Bibl: Föhl, Marburger Jahrb. Kunst., XX (1981) pp.107-112; Hamm, GARES, FER ET STYLES (1990); ▶MoMA libr. cat.

Hammacher, Arno *(Dutch artist, photographer, b.1927)* **BA**
Bibl: ▶MoMA libr. cat.; ▶Parry, Photo idx.

Hamman, Edouard Jean Conrad *(Belgian artist, 1819-1888)* **WC**

Hamman, Edouard, Michel Ferdinand *(French artist, op.1880-1889)* **WC**

Hamman, Joe *(French painter, 20th century)* **GC**
Bibl: ▶Bénézit

Hamme→see Hamme, Alexis van

Hamme, Alexis van **GC PR WC**
(Belgian artist, 1818-1875) WC
(Belgian painter, 1818-1875) PR
(Belgian, 1818-1875) GC
Bibl: ▶Thieme-Becker; ▶Witt checklist
Alexis van Hamme PR
Hamme PR

Hamme, Johann Christoph van *(German artist, 1701-1755)* **WC**

Hammeil→see Flemal, Bertholet (I)

Hammel, Pietro *(Dutch architect, Rotterdam)* **AV**
Bibl: De Architect, 1986 Apr., v.17, no.4, p.78

Hammel, Richard F. *(American architect, Minneapolis, Minn, d. 1986)* **AV**
Bibl: ▶AIA Pro File, 1985

Hammenhog, V. *(Swedish artist, 19th cent.)* **WC**

Hammer family *(German wax modelers, 18th-20th cs.)* **BA**
Bibl: Rohrich, Ceroplastica, v.1, pp.433-441

Hammer, Christian Gottlob **GC**
(German artist, 1779-1864) WC
(German draughtsman, 1779-1864) GC
Bibl: ▶Thieme-Becker

Hammer, Christian Gottlob or Gottlieb **WC**

Hammer, Christian Gottlob or Gottlieb→see Hammer, Christian Gottlob

Hammer, Emil Eduard *(German sculptor, wax modeler, b.1865)* **BA**
Bibl: Rohrich, Ceroplastica, v.1, pp.433-441

Hammer, Franz *(German artist, op. 1700)* **WC**

Hammer, John J. *(German artist, 1842-1906)* **WC**

Hammer, Viktor **BA WC**
(Austrian painter, 1882-1967) BA
(German artist, 1882-) WC
Bibl: ▶Bénézit; ▶Fuchs, Öst. Maler 19. Jahrh.; ▶MoMA libr. cat.; NY Times obit.

Hammerbacher, Herta *(Landscape architect, born ca.1900)* **AV**
Bibl: ▶Avery period. idx.

Hammerbeck, Wanda *(American photographer, b.1945)* **BA**
Bibl: San Francisco, Museum of modern Art, PHOTOGRAPHIC WORKS: WANDA HAMMERBECK, LAURIE BROWN, 1978

Hammerich, Magdalene *(Danish painter, 1885-1967)* **BA**
Bibl: ▶Art Index, v.36

Hammerschmidt, W. **BA GC JG**
(German photographer, act. 1860s-1870s) GC
(German photographer, act. 1858-1862) BA
(German, d. 1869, active Egypt) JG
Bibl: ▶Idx. Amer. photog. colls.; ▶Natl. union cat., pre-1956; Witkin, Photograph collectors' guide, p.350

Hammershoi, Svend→see Hammershøi, Svend

Hammershøi, Svend **BA**
(Danish artist, 1873-1848) WC
(Danish painter, ceramist, 1873-1948) BA
Bibl: ▶Bénézit; ▶Vollmer, Künst.-Lex. 20. Jhr.; ▶Weilbach, Kunst.leks.

Hammershoi, Svend **WC**

Hammershøi, Vilhelm **BA**
(Danish artist, 1864-1916) WC
(Danish painter, 1864-1916) BA
Bibl: ▶Bénézit; ▶Weilbach, Kunst. leks.

Hammershoi, Wilhelm **WC**

Hammershoi, Wilhelm→see Hammershøi, Vilhelm

Hammersley, Frederick *(American painter, b.1919)* **BA**
Bibl: ▶Cummings, Contemp. Amer. artists, 1971; ▶MoMA libr. cat.; ▶WW Amer. Art, 1976

Hammersley, James Astbury *(British artist, 1815-1869)* **WC WI**

Hammill, Terence *(British artist, b.1941)* **WI**

Hammitt, Clawson Shakespeare *(American painter, 1857-1927)* **BA**
Bibl: ▶Bénézit; ▶Fielding's Amer. ptrs.; ▶Thieme-Becker; ▶Vollmer, Künst.-Lex. 20. Jhr.; ▶Young, Amer. artists

Hammock, Virgil G. *(Canadian painter, b.1938)* **BA**
Bibl: ▶Artists Canada; Sackville (NB, CAN), Mt. Allison Univ. Owens Gall., 5 faculty

Hammon, G.H. *(Australian artist, 19th cent.)* **WC**

Hammond→see Hammond, J.

Hammond, A. *(British artist, op. 1781-1803)* **WC WI**

Hammond, A.H.K.→see Hamond, A.H. Knighton

Hammond, Arthur *(British artist, op.1905-)* **WI**

Hammond, Clarence E. *(American landscape architect, retired, Green Belt, Md.; founder of Scruggs and Hammond)* **AV**
Bibl: Landscape architecture, 1988 June,v.78, no.4

Hammond, Edward Alan Charles *(British architect, London)* **AV**
Bibl: ▶RIBA members, 1984
Hammond, Ted **AV**

Hammond, Gertrude E. Demain *(British artist, 1862-1952)* **WI**
McMurdie, Gertrude DeMain, Mrs. **WI**

Hammond, Harmony Lynn *(American painter, sculptor, b.1944)* **BA**
Bibl: ▶NY art yrbk.; ▶WW Amer. Art, 1976

Hammond, J. *(British painter, act. 1800-1820)* **PR**
Bibl: ▶Graves Royal Acad. contribs.; ▶Thieme-Becker
Hammond **PR**
J. Hammond **PR**

Hammond, James *(American architect)* **AV**

Hammond, Jon *(Architect, Davis, CA)* **AV**
Bibl: Fine homebuilding, 1984-1985 Dec.-Jan., no.24, p.70

Hammond, Mrs. *(British artist, op. 1810-1826)* **WC WI**

Hammond, Natalie→see Hammond, Natalie Hays

Hammond, Natalie Hays *(American, b.1905)* **GC**
Bibl: ▶Fielding's Amer. ptrs.; Getty Photo Study Coll.; Juley coll., NMAA
Hammond, Natalie **GC**

Hammond, Robert John *(British artist, op.1879-1911)* **WI**

Hammond, Ted→see Hammond, Edward Alan Charles

Hammond, Thomas **WC WI**
(American artist, 20th cent.) **WC**
(American artist, op.20th c.) **WI**

Hammonds, Albert L. **WC WI**
(British artist, 20th cent.) **WC**
(British artist, op.20th c.) **WI**

Hammoutène, Franck *(French architect, Paris)* **AV**
Bibl: Architecture intérieure cree, 1986 Apr.-May, no.211, p.110

Hamnett, Nina **BA WI**
(British artist, 1890-1956) **WI**
(British painter, illustrator, 1890-1956) **BA**
Bibl: ▶Natl. union cat., pre-1956; ▶Vollmer, Künst.-Lex. 20. Jhr.

Hamon, Jean Louis **BA GC WC**
(French artist, 1821-1874) **WC**
(French painter, 1821-1874) **BA**
(French, 1821-1874) **GC**
Bibl: ▶Thieme-Becker

Hamon, Pierre Paul *(French artist, 1817-1860)* **WC**

Hamond, A.H. Knighton **WI**
(British artist, 1875-1970) **WI**
(British artist, 20th cent.) **WC**
Hammond, A.H.K. **WC**

Hamp, Christian Mary *(British architect, London)* **AV**
Bibl: ▶RIBA members, 1987

Hampe, Guido *(German artist, 1839-1875)* **WC**

Hampe, Karl Friedrich **BA WC**
(German artist, 1772-1848) **WC**
(German painter, printmaker, 1772-1848) **BA**
Bibl: ▶Bénézit; ▶Thieme-Becker; ▶Witt checklist

Hampel, Angela *(East German painter, b.1956)* **BA**
Bibl: Berlin (DEU), Nationalgalerie, Expressivität Heute (1985)

Hampel, Carl **WC WI**
(British artist, 1891-) **WC**
(British artist, 1891-op.1940) **WI**

Hampel, Charlotte *(German artist, 1863-)* **WC**

Hampel, Sigmund Walter *(German artist, 1868-1949)* **WC**

Hampeln, Carl von or Charles de *(Russian artist, 1808-p.1880)* **WC**

Hamper, Nicholas *(British artist, b.1956)* **WI**

Hamper, W. *(British artist, op.1793-1795)* **WC WI**

Hampl, Jiří Vaclav *(Czech sculptor, painter, b.1929)* **BA**
Bibl: Jihlava (CSK), Oblastni Galerie, Vysociny, Marie Uchytilova (1981)

Hampson, Roger Hanier *(British artist, b.1925)* **WI**

Hampton, Humphrey Arthur Parkington *(British architect, author, 1888-1974)* **BA**
Bibl: Trans. of the Worc. Archaeolog. Society V/1976 p.81; ▶Who's Who [GBR], 1974, 1975

Hampton, James *(American sculptor, 1909-1964)* **BA**
Bibl: Boston (MA, USA), Museum of Fine Arts, James Hampton: the throne of the third heaven of the nations millenium generally assembly, 1977

Hampton, Lucille→see Hampton, Lucille Charlotte

Hampton, Lucille Charlotte *(American sculptor, b.1922)* **GC**
Bibl: Getty Photo Study Coll.; ▶Opitz, Amer. sculptors
Hampton, Lucille **GC**

Hampton, Mark *(American interior designer)* **AV**
Bibl: Architectural digest, 1984 Oct., v.41, no.10

Hamrol, Lloyd *(American sculptor, b.1937)* **BA**
Bibl: UC Santa Barbara cat. sheets

Hamsík, Mojmír *(Czech painter, restorer, b.1921)* **BA**
Bibl: Mašin, J., in UMENI XXXI/4 (1983) 345

Hamson, T.B. *(British artist, 19th cent.)* **WC**

Hamza, Johann *(German artist, 1850-1927)* **WC**

Han Suess von Kulmbach→see Kulmbach, Hans Suess von

Han, Balthasar *(German artist, 1505-1578)* **WC**

Han, Franz *(German artist, op.1526-1528)* **WC**

Han, H.→see Han, H.N.

Han, H.N. **BA**
(American painter, b.1939) **BA**
(Oriental artist, 1939-) **WC**
Han, H. **WC**

Han, Hermann→see Hahn, Hermann

Han, Pao-Teh *(Nationalist Chinese architect, Taiwan)* **AV**
Bibl: Architectural digest, 1988 Jan., v.45, no.1, p.76

Han, Raymond *(American painter, 20th c.)* **BA**
Bibl: Arts mag LVII (4 Dec, 1982)

Han. Carrachi→see Carracci, Annibale

Hanaeman, W. *(Netherlands artist, 17th cent.)* **WC**

Hanan, Renée *(American painter, b.1954)* **BA**
Bibl: Ithaca (NY, USA), Cornell Univ., Johnson Mus. of Art, Ptg. up front (1981)

Hanappier, Jacques *(French silversmith, b.1704, master 1730)* **GC**
Bibl: ▶Mabille, Orfèv. fran.

Hanappier, Pierre IX *(French silversmith, 1707-1777, master 1730)* **GC**
Bibl: ▶Mabille, Orfèv. fran.

Hanauer, Wilhelm (*Swiss architect/renovation architect, 1854-1930*) **AV**
   Bibl: Unsere Kunstdenkmäler, 1988, v.39, no.2, p.169
Hanbury, W. **WC WI**
   (*British artist, op.1770-*) **WI**
   (*British artist, op.1770-1771*) **WC**
Hanbury, William (*British ecclesiastic, gardener, author, 1725-1778*) **BA**
   Bibl: ▶Dict. natl. biog.; ▶Libr. of Congr. Name Auth. File
Hanchett (*British painter, act. 1791-1800*) **PR**
   Bibl: ▶Thieme-Becker
   Capt. Hanchett PR
Hancock, Charles **BA WC WI**
   (*British artist, 1802-1877*) **WI**
   (*British artist, op.1819-1868*) **WC**
   (*British painter, 1802-1877*) **BA**
   Bibl: ▶Bénézit; Connoisseur CCI 809 July 1979 190-193; ▶Fisher, Watercolour ptrs.; ▶Mallalieu, Brit. watercolour artists; Paviere, Brit. sporting ptrs; ▶Thieme-Becker
Hancock, Daniel (*British glassworker, act.1873*) **BA**
   Bibl: ▶Newman, Glass; Polak, Glass, p.193; Rakow, JOURNAL OF GLASS STUDIES XXIV (1982), 52
Hancock, Ellen J. (*British artist, op. 1876-*) **WI**
Hancock, J.L. → *see* Hancock, Joseph Lane
Hancock, John (*British artist, 1808-1890*) **WI**
Hancock, Joseph Lane (*American painter, 1864-1925*) **PR**
   Bibl: ▶Fielding's Amer. ptrs., 1986; ▶WWW Amer. art
   Hancock, J.L. PR
   Joseph Lane Hancock PR
Hancock, K.B. (*British artist, op.20th c.*) **WI**
Hancock, Macklin (*Canadian city planner*) **AV**
   Bibl: Society for the Study of Architecture in Canada. Selected papers, 1985, v.6, p.32
Hancock, Mildred L. (*British artist, op.1890-1897*) **WI**
   Welsford, Mildred WI
Hancock, N. → *see* Hancock, Nathaniel
Hancock, Nathaniel **WI**
   (*American artist, op.1790-1809*) **WI**
   (*American artist, op.1792-1809*) **WC**
   Hancock, N. **WC**
Hancock, Peter (*British architect practicing in Lesotho, 1932-*) **AV**
   Bibl: UIA international architect, 1985, no.8, inside back cover

Hancock, Ralph (*British horticulturalist*) **AV**
   Bibl: Progressive architecture, 1987 Nov., v.68, no.12, p.27
Hancock, Robert **BA WC WI**
   (*British artist, 1730-1817*) **WC**
   (*British artist, 1731-1817*) **WI**
   (*British printmaker, painter, 1730-1817*) **BA**
   Bibl: ▶Dict. natl. biog.; Mackenzie; ▶Thieme-Becker
Hancock, Tom (*Consultant architect, Great Britain?*) **AV**
   Bibl: World of interiors, 1985 Apr., p.123
Hancock, Walker (*American sculptor, b.1901*) **GC**
   Bibl: Getty Photo Study Coll.; ▶Opitz, Amer. sculptors
   Hancock, Walker Kirtland GC
Hancock, Walker Kirtland → *see* Hancock, Walker
Hancock, Walter (*English mason, act.1589, d.ca.1599*) **BA**
   Bibl: Haslam: Powys, p.166; ▶Summerson, Arch. GBR, p.36
Hancock, William Lynett **WC WI**
   (*American artist, 1942-*) **WC**
   (*American artist, b.1942*) **WI**
Hancocks, Ben (*British artist, b.1951*) **WI**
Hand → *see* Hand, Thomas
Hand, Harland (*American landscape designer*) **AV**
   Bibl: Garden design, 1984 Autumn, p.51
Hand, Matthew Samuel (*British artist, op.19th c.*) **WI**
Hand, Richard (*British glass painter, act.1775, d.ca.1816*) **BA**
   Bibl: Marks, Crown in glory, (07), pp.65-66; ▶Redgrave, Engl. school; ▶Thieme-Becker
Hand, Thomas **GC PR WC WI**
   (*British artist, circa 1771-1804*) **WI**
   (*British artist, op.1790-m.1804*) **WC**
   (*British painter, act. 1790-1804*) **PR**
   (*British, act.1790-1804*) **GC**
   Bibl: ▶Thieme-Becker; ▶Witt checklist
   Hand PR
   Hands PR
   T. Hand PR
   T. Hands PR
   Thomas Hand PR
Handaguter → *see* Hondecoeter, Melchior d'
Handecoutre → *see* Hondecoeter, Melchior d'
Handekoeter → *see* Hondecoeter, Melchior d'
Handelbourg-Lescot → *see* Haudebourt, Antoinette Cécile Hortense Lescot
Handford, Martin (*British artist, b.1956*) **WI**

Handforth, Thomas (*American artist, 1897-1948*) **WI**
Handke, Johann Christoph (*German artist, 1694-1774*) **WC**
Handler, Richard (*German artist, 20th cent.*) **WC**
Handley, Roger (*British artist, op. 20th c.*) **WI**
Handley-Read, Captain Edward Henry → *see* Handley-Read, Edward Henry
Handley-Read, Edward Henry **WI**
   (*British artist, 1869-1935*) **WI**
   (*British artist, 1870-1935*) **WC**
   Bibl: Paviere, Landscape
Handley-Read, Captain Edward Henry **WC**
   Read, Edward Henry WI
Handlin, David P. (*American architect*) **AV**
Handmann, Abel (*Swiss goldsmith, 1715-1788*) **BA**
   Bibl: ▶Schweiz. Künst.-Lex.; ▶Thieme-Becker
Handmann, Emanuel (Jacob Emanuel) → *see* Handmann, Emmanuel Jakob
Handmann, Emmanuel Jakob **GC**
   (*Swiss artist, 1718-1781*) **WC**
   (*Swiss painter, 1718-1781*) **GC**
   Bibl: ▶Bénézit
Handmann, Emanuel (Jacob Emanuel) **WC**
Handrahan, George W. (*American artist, b.1949*) **WI**
Hands → *see* Hand, Thomas
Handschick, Heinz (*German artist, 20th cent.*) **WC**
Handschuh, Johann Franz (*German porcelain, painter, b.1761, act. 1789*) **BA**
   Bibl: Dostal, Weltkunst, LIII/19 (1 Oct. 1983) pp.2540-2543
Handville, Robert **WC WI**
   (*American artist, 20th cent.*) **WC**
   (*American artist, op.20th cent.*) **WI**
Handy, F.W. (*British artist, op.19th c.*) **WI**
Handy, John (*British artist, op.1787-1791*) **WC WI**
Handy, Levin C. (*American, active Washington, D.C., U.S. 1865-ca.1898*) **JG**
Handycoutre → *see* Hondecoeter, Melchior d'
Hane, Roger **WC WI**
   (*American artist, 20th cent.*) **WC**
   (*American artist, op.20th cent.*) **WI**
Hanebeck, Gerd (*German artist, 20th cent.*) **WC**
Hanedoes, Louwrens **GC WC**
   (*Dutch artist, 1822-1905*) **WC**
   (*Dutch painter, 1822-1905*) **GC**
   Bibl: ▶Thieme-Becker

Hanes, F.W. (British artist, 19th cent.) **WC**

Hanette, Lotars (French printmaker, d.1378?) **BA**
Bibl: TRANS OF THE MON BRASS SOC XII/3 (1977) 199-209

Haney, William H. (American painter, draftsman, b.1950) **BA**
Bibl: ▶WW Amer. Art

Haney, William L → see Haney, William L.

Haney, William L. **BA WI**
(American artist, 20th cent.) **WC**
(American artist, op.20th c.) **WI**
(American painter, 20th c.) **BA**
Bibl: Wallach, A., in ARTS MAG LVIII/10 (sumer 1984) 20

Haney, William L **WC**

Hanf, Bob (German artist, 20th cent.) **WC**

Hanfstaengel, Erwin → see Hanfstängel, Erwin

Hanfstaengel, Franz → see Hanfstaengl, Franz Seraph

Hanfstaengel, Hanns → see Hanfstängel, Hanns

Hanfstaengl, Ernst (German artist, 1840-1897) **WC**

Hanfstaengl, F. → see Hanfstaengl, Franz Seraph

Hanfstaengl, Franz Seraph **BA**
(German artist, 1804-1877) **WC**
(German photographer, 1804-1877) **GC**
(German printmaker, 1804-1877) **BA**
Bibl: ▶Bénézit; Getty Photo Study Coll.; ▶Idx. Amer. photog. colls.; ▶Libr. of Congr. Name Auth. File; ▶Thieme-Becker
F. Hanfstängel (Munich) **GC**
Hanfstaengel, Franz **GC**
Hanfstaengl, F. **GC**

Hanfstaengl, Hanfstangl or Hanfstingl, Franz Seraph **WC**

Hanfstängl, Franz **GC**

Hanfstaengl, Hanfstangl or Hanfstingl, Franz Seraph → see Hanfstaengl, Franz Seraph

Hanfstängel, Erwin **GC**
(b. Germany, active Paris, France 1860s) **JG**
(German photographer, act. 1860s) **GC**
Bibl: ▶Idx. Amer. photog. colls.

Hanfstaengel, Erwin **GC JG**

Hanfstängel, Hanns (German photographer, act. 1860s) **GC**
Bibl: ▶Idx. Amer. photog. colls.
Hanfstaengel, Hanns **GC**

Hanfstängl, Franz → see Hanfstaengl, Franz Seraph

Hanganu, Dan S. (Canadian architect, Montreal) **AV**
Bibl: ▶Canad. arch. dir., 1985

Hangen, Heijo (German artist, 1927-) **WC**

Hanger, Max (German artist, 1874-) **WC**

Hanhart family (Swiss gunsmiths, 17th-18th cs.) **BA**
Bibl: Waffen- u. Kostümkunde, XX/1 (1978) pp.41-46

Hanhart, Hans Heinrich (Swiss gunsmith, 1664-1737) **BA**
Bibl: Waffen- u. Kostümkunde, XX/1 (1978) pp.41-46

Hanias, Johannes (German artist, op.1650-1654) **WC**

Hanibal Caracci → see Carracci, Annibale

Hanicotte, Augustin (French artist, op.1900-1914) **WC**

Hanioti, Elise (French artist, 20th cent.) **WC**

Hanisch the Elder, Alois (German artist, op.1840) **WC**

Hanisch, Alois (German artist, 1866-) **WC**

Hanix, Robert (Netherlands(?) artist, op.1730) **WC**

Hankar, Paul **AV BA**
(Belgian architect, 1859-1901) **BA**
(Belgian architect, Brussels, 1859-1901) **AV**
Bibl: ▶Brockhaus Enzyk.; Brussels (BEL), École supérieur, Brussels 1900 (1972); ▶Encyc. world art; ▶Hitchcock, Arch. 19 & 20cs; ▶Libr. of Congr. Name Auth. File; ▶Thieme-Becker

Hanke, Hans (German artist, 19th cent.) **WC**

Hanke, Reinhold (German ceramist, 1839-1886) **BA**
Bibl: ▶Artist biog. master idx.; Reinhold, WELTKUNST, LVII/5 (1 Mar 87), p.583-585; Savage, 19c. antiques

Hankes, J.F. (British artist, op.1838-1859) **WI**

Hankey, Mabel Emily (British artist, d.1943) **WI**
Hobson, Mabel Emily, Miss **WI**
Lee-Hankey, William, Mrs., (Mabel Emily) **WI**

Hankey, William Lee **WI**
(British artist, 1869-1952) **WC WI**
Hankey, William, Lee **WC**
Lee-Hankey, William Lee **WI**
Hankey, William Lee, Mrs., (Edith Mary) → see Garner, Edith Mary
Hankey, William, Lee → see Hankey, William Lee
Hankins, P. Abraham → see Hankins, Peter Abraham

Hankins, Peter Abraham **WI**
(American artist, 20th cent.) **WC**
(American artist, op.20th c.) **WI**
Hankins, P. Abraham **WC**

Hankø, Ole (Norwegian architect) **AV**
Bibl: Byggekunst: the Norwegian review of architecture, 1985, v.67, no.4, p.186

Hanley, Liam (British artist, op.20th c.) **WI**

Hanlon, Jack P. (British artist, b.1913) **WI**

Hanmer, Thomas, baronet (English author, gardener, 1612-1678) **BA**
Bibl: ▶Burke's dormant & extinct; Cokayne, Complete peerage, v.1, p.152; ▶Dict. natl. biog.; ▶Natl. union cat., pre-1956; Robinson, GARDEN HISTORY, XVI/1 (Spring 1988), p. 1-7

Hann, Marlys (American architect, NYC) **AV**
Bibl: House & Garden, 1987 Jan., v.159, no.1, p.100

Hann, Sebastian (Czech goldsmith, 1644-1713) **BA**
Bibl: ▶Thieme-Becker

Hanna, Dan (American artist, b.1945) **BA**
Bibl: Columbia (SC, USA), Mus. Art & Sci., Carolinians in NY (1981)

Hanna, Jean Shuman (American, 20th c.) **BA**
Bibl: WW Amer., 1982-83

Hanna, Ronald C. (American architect, Hauppauge, N.Y) **AV**
Bibl: Design solutions, 1988 SPring, v.8, no.1, p.21

Hanna, Susan R. (American painter, b.1948) **BA**
Bibl: Columbia (SC, USA), Mus. Art & Sci., Carolinians in NY (1981); Greenville (SC, USA), County Mus. Art, 5 South Carolina artists (1975)

Hanna, Thomas King (American artist, 1872-1951) **WI**

Hannaford, Charles E. (British artist, 1863-1955) **WC WI**
Bibl: ▶Mallalieu, Brit. watercolour artists

Hannaford, Harvey E. (American architect, son of Samuel Hannaford, d. 1923) **AV**
Bibl: ▶Withey, Amer. archts.

Hannaford, Samuel (American architect, Cincinnati, Ohio; born in England, came to U.S. as a boy and set up his arch. practice in 1857, 1835-1910) **AV**
Bibl: ▶Withey, Amer. archts.

Hannah, B. **WC WI**
(British artist, 20th cent.) **WC**
(British artist, op.20th c.) **WI**
Hannah, Bruce → see Hannah, Bruce R.

Hannah, Bruce R.   BA
   (American furniture designer,
      20th c.)   BA
   (American industrial designer, b.
      ca.1942)   AV
      Bibl: ▶Art Index, lists art in
      Domus, May 1972; Metropolis,
      1985 July-Aug., v.5, no.1, p.18

Hannah, Bruce   AV
Hannah, George   WC WI
   (British artist, b.circa 1896)   WI
   (British artist, c.1896-)   WC
Hannam, Florence (British artist, op.
   circa 1887-)   WI
Hannaman→see Hanneman, Adriaen
Hannamann, William   WI
   (British artist, op.1786)   WC
   (British artist, op.1786-)   WI
Hannemann, William   WC
Hannan, William   GC WC WI
   (British artist, op.1757-, d.circa
      1775)   WI
   (British artist, op.1757-m.c.
      1775)   WC
   (British, d. ca.1775)   GC
      Bibl: ▶Thieme-Becker; ▶Witt
      checklist

Hannaux, Paul (French artist, 1899-
   1954)   WC
Hannay, Mrs. (British artist, op.20th
   c.)   WI
Hannebrink, Willem Albertus   GC
   (Dutch artist, 1762-1840)   WC
   (Dutch draughtsman, 1762-
      1840)   GC
      Bibl: ▶Thieme-Becker
Haanebrink, Willem Albertus   WC
Hanneman→see Hanneman, Adriaen
Hanneman, Adriaen   BA GC PR WC
   (Dutch artist, c.1601-1671)   WC
   (Dutch painter, ca.1601-
      1671)   BA GC PR
      Bibl: ▶Bénézit; ▶Encyc. world art;
      Kuile, O. ter ADRIAEN
      HANNEMAN... p.127; ▶RILA/BHA;
      ▶Wurzbach, NLD Künst.-Lex.
      A. Hanneman   PR
      Adriaen Hanneman   PR
      Adrien Hanneman   PR
      Hannaman   PR
      Hanneman   PR
      Henneman   PR
Hanneman, Christopher William→see
   Hunneman, Christopher William
Hannemann, William→see
   Hannamann, William
Hänni family (Swiss painters, 19th
   c.)   BA
      Bibl: Schaufelberger, A.: DIE
      THUNER VEDUTENMALER..., 1983
Hannibal Caracci→see Carracci,
   Annibale
Hannibal Carracci→see Carracci,
   Annibale

Hannibal, Martin (Hungarian painter
   in SWE, 1640-1720)   BA
      Bibl: ▶Svenskt konst.-lex.;
      ▶Thieme-Becker
Hannier, Guillaume-Claude (French
   silversmith, master 1773)   GC
      Bibl: ▶Nocq, Poinçon de Paris
Hannier, Jean (French silversmith,
   act.1685-1727)   GC
      Bibl: ▶Mabille, Orfèv. fran.
**Hannl, Handel, Händel, Hanel,
   Hannel or Hennel, Maximilian
   Joseph** (German artist,
   1694/6-1759)   WC
Hannong family (French ceramists,
   18th c.)   BA
      Bibl: ▶Honey, Euro. ceramic
*Hannong, Hannon or Hannung, Paul
   Anton→see* Hannong, Paul Anton
Hannong, Paul Anton   BA
   (French ceramist, 1700-1760)   BA
   (German artist, 1700-1760)   WC
      Bibl: ▶Honey, Euro. ceramic;
      ▶Thieme-Becker
**Hannong, Hannon or Hannung,
   Paul Anton**   WC
Hannosset, Lambertus (Flemish
   silversmith, act.1735, d.1770)   BA
      Bibl: Jansen, BULL. DE L'INST.
      ROYAL DU PATRIMOINE
      ARTISTIQUE, XIX (1982-83)p.34-52
Hannot→see Hannot, Johannes
Hannot, Johannes   GC PR WC
   (Dutch artist, op.1650-1683)   WC
   (Dutch painter, act. 1650, 1683)   PR
   (Dutch painter, act.1650-1683)   GC
      Bibl: Getty Photo Study Coll.;
      ▶Thieme-Becker; ▶Witt checklist
      Hannot   PR
      Honnot   PR
      Horot (?)   PR
      Johannes Hannot   PR
Hannotiau, M. (Belgian artist,
   19th/20th cent.)   WC
Hannotlau, Alexandre Auguste
   (Belgian artist, 1863-1901)   WC
**Hanns von Burghausen the
   younger** (German architect, act.
   1484-1489)   BA
      Bibl: ARS BAVARICA, 35-36 (1984)
      133-138
      Burghausen, Hanns von, the
         younger   BA
Hanntlas, Andre (German ceramist,
   act.1552)   BA
      Bibl: Anz. des Germ. Nationalmus.
      (1980) 93-104
Hannum, Richard C. (American
   architect, San Francisco, CA)   AV
      Bibl: ▶AIA Pro File, 1987-88
Hanoteau, Hector (French artist,
   1823-1890)   WC
Hanrahan, James C. (American
   interior designer)   AV
      Bibl: Architectural digest, 1987
      Aug., v.44, no.8, p.86

Hanrath, Johann Otto (Otto)
   (Dutch artist, 1882-1944)   WC
Hanray, Margaret Delisle, Miss→see
   Burns, Margaret Delisle
Hans Baldung→see Baldung, Hans
   (Hans Baldung Grien)
Hans Bol→see Bol, Hans
Hans Bollongier→see Bollongier,
   Hans
Hans Boulenger→see Bollongier,
   Hans
Hans Brosamer→see Brosamer, Hans
Hans Brunner→see Brunner, Hans
Hans Bulangier→see Bollongier, Hans
Hans Corvus→see Corvus, Hans
Hans Cranach→see Cranach, Hans
Hans de Jode→see Jode, Hans de
Hans der Krumenauer→see
   Krumenauer, Hans
Hans Durer→see Durer, Hans
Hans Ewouts→see Ewouts, Hans
Hans Goderis→see Goderis, Hans
Hans Goederen→see Goedaert,
   Johannes
Hans Goldschmid→see Goldschmid,
   Hans
Hans Graaf→see Graaf, Hans
Hans Graf→see Graf, Johann
Hans Hofmann→see Hofmann, Hans
Hans Holbein→see Holbein, Hans,
   the younger
Hans Holbein (II)→see Holbein, Hans,
   the younger
Hans Holbein (the elder)→see
   Holbein, Hans, the elder
Hans Holbein (the younger)→see
   Holbein, Hans, the younger
Hans Holbien→see Holbein, Hans,
   the younger
Hans Holzer→see Holzer, Hans
   [Unidentified]
Hans Hulsman→see Hulsman, Johann
Hans Hülsmann→see Hulsman,
   Johann
Hans Jordaens (I)→see Jordaens,
   Hans (I)
Hans Jordaens (IV)→see Jordaens,
   Hans (IV)
Hans Krell→see Krell, Hans
Hans Leonhard Schaufelein→see
   Schäufelein, Hans Leonhard
Hans Makart→see Makart, Hans
Hans Maler→see Maler, Hans
Hans Memling→see Memling, Hans
Hans Moultscher→see Multscher,
   Hans
Hans Müelich→see Müelich, Hans
Hans Multscher→see Multscher,
   Hans
Hans Muoltscher→see Multscher,
   Hans

Hans of Antwerp   **BA VO**
  (early Netherlandish goldsmith,
    merchant in England, act.
    1515-1547)   BA
  (German goldsmith, act.1532)   BA
  (Hanseatic merchant and
    goldsmith, collaborator and   VO
    sitter of Holbein, b. ca.
    1497)
    Bibl: Ganz, Paintings of Holbein,
    p. 240; Holman, in Met. Mus.
    Journal XIV (1979) p.144; Singer,
    Neuer Bildniskat.; ▶Thieme-Becker

Hans von Antwerp   **BA**
  John of Antwerp   VO
Hans Pleydenwurff →*see*
  Pleydenwurff, Hans
Hans Reichel →*see* Reichel, Hans
Hans Rottenhammer (I) →*see*
  Rottenhammer, Hans I
Hans Strigel →*see* Strigel, Hans
Hans Thoma →*see* Thoma, Hans
Hans [Unidentified] *(Unknown*
  painter)   **PR**
    Bibl: Lutzen inventory,
    Amsterdam, 1680
Hans van Aacken →*see* Aachen, Hans
  von
Hans van Acken →*see* Aachen, Hans
  von
Hans van Brugge →*see* Memling,
  Hans
Hans van Nes →*see* Nes, Johan (Jan)
  Dircksz.
Hans von Aachen →*see* Aachen, Hans
  von
Hans von Achen →*see* Aachen, Hans
  von
Hans von Antwerp →*see* Hans of
  Antwerp
Hans von Burghausen the elder   **BA**
  (German architect, ca.1370-
    1432)   BA
  (Gothic architect, Landshut,
    Germany. Also known as
    Meister Hans von
    Burghausen, 1360?-1432)   AV
    Bibl: ▶Allgem. Deut. Biog.; Ars
    Bavarica 35-36 (1984) 1-18;
    ▶Avery Libr. cat.; ▶Encyc. world
    art; Frankl, Gothic arch., pp.182-
    184; Reclams Bayern; Spitzberger,
    LANDSHUT,16,23; ▶Thieme-Becker
  Burghausen, Hans von (Hans
    Stethaimer, the elder)   BA
  Purghauser, Hanns   BA
  Stethaimer, Hans   **AV**
  Stethaimer, Hans, the elder   BA
  Stettheimer, Hans   BA
Hans von Coln *(German artist, op.*
  1520-1522)   **WC**
Hans von Frankfurt *(German artist,*
  op.1537)   **WC**

Hans von Judenburg *(Austrian*
  sculptor, act.1411-1424)   **BA**
    Bibl: ▶Encyc. world art; Kreuzer-
    Eccel, Hans von Judenburg;
    Müller, Sculpture NLD DEU FRA
    ESP, p.44
  Judenburg, Hans von   BA
Hans von Köln →*see* Johann von Köln
Hans von Marees →*see* Marées, Hans
  von
Hans von Metz   **GC WC**
  (German artist,
    op.1448-m.1462/3)   WC
  (German painter, act. mid-15th
    century)   GC
    Bibl: ▶Bénézit
Hans von Reutlingen *(German*
  goldsmith, ca.1465-ca.1547)   **BA**
    Bibl: Grimme, AACHENER
    KUNSTBLATTER, XLIX (1980-81),
    15; ▶Thieme-Becker
  Reutlingen, Hans von   BA
Hans von Tübingen   **BA**
  (Austrian painter, act.1433-
    1461)   BA
  (German artist, op.1433-m.a.
    1462)   WC
    Bibl: ▶Bénézit; ▶Thieme-Becker
Hans von Tubingen, Teubing,
  Teubingen, Tulbing or
  Twbing (possibly identified
  with Master of the S.
  Lambert Altar and with
  Master of the Linz
  Crucifixion)   **WC**
Hans von Tubingen, Teubing,
  Teubingen, Tulbing or Twbing
  (possibly identified with Master of
  the S. Lambert Altar and with
  Master of the Linz
  Crucifixion) →*see* Hans von
  Tübingen
Hans von Zürich   **BA WC**
  (Swiss artist, op.1456)   WC
  (Swiss painter in AUT, act.1451-
    1476)   BA
    Bibl: ▶Bénézit; Perger, Öster. Zeit.
    für Kunst u. Denk. 35/3-4 (1981)
    85-89; ▶Thieme-Becker; ▶Witt
    checklist
Hans Vredeman de Vries →*see*
  Vredeman de Vries, Hans
Hans Wertinger →*see* Wertinger,
  Hans
Hans, Josefus Gerardus   **GC WC**
  (Dutch artist, 1826-1891)   WC
  (Dutch painter and
    draughtsman, 1826-1891)   GC
    Bibl: ▶Thieme-Becker
Hansbergen →*see* Haensbergen,
  Johan van
Hansch, Anton *(German artist,*
  1813-1876)   **WC**

Hänsch, Klaus *(West German*
  architect, Stuttgart)   **AV**
    Bibl: ▶Bund Deut. Arch. Hdbch.,
    1987
Hänsch, Wolfgang *(German*
  architect, VEB Gesellschaftsbau
  Dresden)   **AV**
    Bibl: Bauwelt, 1985 Apr.5, v.76,
    no.13, p.522
Hansche, Jan Christiaen *(Flemish*
  stucco artist, act.1655-1677)   **BA**
    Bibl: Revue belge d'arch. et d'hist.
    del'art XLI (1972) 105-111;
    ▶Thieme-Becker
Hanselaere, Pieter van *(Belgian*
  painter, 1786-1862)   **GC**
    Bibl: ▶Bénézit
Hansell, Freya *(American painter,*
  20th c.)   **BA**
    Bibl: Martin, Arts mag., LIX/5
    (Jan. 1985) pp.13-18
Hanselmann, Urs *(Swiss artist,*
  b.1944)   **BA**
    Bibl: ▶Lex. zeitgen. Schweiz.
    Künstler, p.158
Hansen →*see* Hansen, Armin Carl
Hansen, Anton *(Danish artist, 1891-*
  1960)   **WC**
Hansen, Armin →*see* Hansen, Armin
  Carl
Hansen, Armin Carl *(American*
  painter, 1886-1957)   **BA PR**
    Bibl: ▶Dawdy, Artists Amer. West;
    ▶RILA/BHA
  Armin Carl Hansen   PR
  Hansen   PR
  Hansen, Armin   PR
Hansen, Asor *(Henrik Asor)*
  (Norwegian artist, 1862-1929)   **WC**
Hansen, C. F., (Christian
  Frederik) →*see* Hansen, Christian
  Frederik
Hansen, Carel Lodewijk   **GC WC**
  (Dutch artist, 1765-1840)   WC
  (Dutch painter and
    draughtsman, 1765-1840)   GC
    Bibl: Getty Photo Study Coll.;
    ▶Thieme-Becker; ▶Witt checklist
Hansen, Carl Christian Constantin   **BA**
  (Danish artist, 1804-1880)   WC
  (Danish painter, 1804-1880)   BA
    Bibl: ▶Bénézit; ▶Busse, Maler u.
    Bildhauer 19. Jahr.;
    ▶Thieme-Becker; ▶Weilbach,
    Kunst.leks.; ▶Witt checklist
Hansen, Constantin (Carl
  Christian Constantin)   **WC**
Hansen, Christian Frederik *(Danish*
  architect, 1756-1845)   **AV BA**
    Bibl: ▶Libr. of Congr. Name Auth.
    File; ▶Macmillan encyc. archts.;
    Reclams DNK, p.156
  Hansen, C. F., (Christian Frederik)   AV
Hansen, Christian Peter *(Danish*
  painter, 1889-1939)   **BA**
    Bibl: ▶Vollmer, Künst.-Lex. 20.
    Jhr.; ▶Weilbach, Kunst.leks.

Hansen, Constantin (Carl Christian Constantin) →see Hansen, Carl Christian Constantin

Hansen, Daryl E. *(American architect)*   **AV**
 Bibl: ▶AIA Pro File, 1983

Hansen, Ejnar   **PR WI**
 (American artist, 1884-1965)   WI
 (American painter, 1884-1965)   PR
 Bibl: ▶WWW Amer. art
 Ejnar Hansen   PR

Hansen, Ernst *(Danish artist, 1892-1968)*   **WC**

Hansen, Finn Karentius *(Danish cabinetmaker and furniture designer, 20th cent)*   **AV**
 Bibl: Arkitektur DK, 1988, v.32, no.5, p.216

Hansen, Frida *(Norwegian weaver, 1855-1931)*   **BA**
 Bibl: Jarry. LA TAPISSERIE, ART DU XXÈME SIÈCLE, pp.51-57

Hansen, Gaylen C. *(American artist, b.1921)*   **BA**
 Bibl: UC Santa Barbara cat. sheets

Hansen, Hans *(Danish artist, 1769-1828)*   **WC**

Hansen, Hans *(Danish architect, painter, printmaker, 1889-1966)*   **BA**
 Bibl: Cologne (DEU), Kunstverein, Max Ernst in Köln (1980); ▶Vollmer, Künst.-Lex. 20. Jhr.; ▶Weilbach, Kunst.leks.

Hansen, Hans Christian *(Danish architect, 1803-1883)*   **BA**
 Bibl: ▶Macmillan encyc. archts.; ▶Portoghesi, Diz. arch. e urbanistica; ▶Thieme-Becker; ▶Weilbach, Kunst.leks.

Hansen, Heinrich   **BA WC**
 (Danish artist, 1821-1890)   WC
 (German painter, printmaker dealer, 1821-1890)   BA
 Bibl: ▶Bénézit; ▶Thieme-Becker; ▶Vollmer, Künst.-Lex. 20. Jhr.; ▶Weilbach, Kunst.leks.

Hansen, Henning *(Danish architect, 1880-1945)*   **AV**

Hansen, Henry W. →see Hansen, Herman Wendelborg

Hansen, Herman Wendelborg   **BA WI**
 (American artist, 1853-1924)   WC WI
 (American painter, printmaker, 1854-1924)   BA
 Bibl: ▶Dawdy, Artists Amer. West, v.6; ▶Samuels, Artists Amer. West; ▶WWW Amer. art

Hansen, Henry W.   **WC**

Hansen, Holger Tangaa *(Danish architect, Lyngby, 1921-)*   **AV**
 Bibl: ▶Danske Arkitekters Landsforbund, 1984-85

Hansen, Hubert   **BA GC**
 (French cabinetmaker, act.1747, d.1756)   BA
 (French ébéniste, master 1747, d. 1756)   GC
 Bibl: Apollo, CXI/216 (Feb. 1980) pp.127-134; Packer, Paris furniture; ▶Salverte, Ébénistes 18e s.

Hansen, Jacob Gerard *(Dutch architect, painter, 1899-1960)*   **BA**
 Bibl: ▶Grote Winkler Prins, v.10; ▶Scheen, Ned. beeldende kunst.

Hansen, James *(American painter, 20th c.)*   **BA**
 Bibl: Arts Mag., (Feb. 1982) pp. 36-37

Hansen, Josef Theodor *(Danish artist, 1848-1912)*   **WC**

Hansen, Lambertus Johannes   **GC WC**
 (Dutch artist, 1803-1859)   WC
 (Dutch painter, 1803-1859)   GC
 Bibl: ▶Thieme-Becker.

Hansen, Lars *(Danish painter, 1813-1872)*   **BA**
 Bibl: ▶Thieme-Becker.

Hansen, Lilla *(Norwegian architect)*   **AV**

Hansen, Lys *(British artist, op.20th c.)*   **WI**

Hansen, Mogens *(Danish architect, Copenhagen)*   **AV**
 Bibl: ▶Danske Arkitekters Landsforbund, 1984-85

Hansen, Øivind *(Norwegian medalist, 1949-1979)*   **BA**
 Bibl: Ronning, ØIVIND HANSEN..., 1979

Hansen, Oskar *(Polish architect, 1922-)*   **AV**
 Bibl: ▶Contemp. archts.

Hansen, Osmund *(Danish painter, b.1908)*   **BA**
 Bibl: Petersen, Bent, NORTH /17/(1987), p.1-86

Hansen, Peter Marius   **BA WC**
 (Danish artist, 1868-1928)   WC
 (Danish painter, printmaker, 1868-1928)   BA
 Bibl: ▶Bénézit; ▶Encyc. world art; ▶Thieme-Becker; ▶Vollmer, Künst.-Lex. 20. Jhr.; ▶Weilbach, Kunst.leks.

Hansen, Preben *(Danish architect)*   **AV**

Hansen, Ragnar *(Norwegian silversmith in AUS, b.1945)*   **BA**
 Bibl: O'Callaghan, Art Bulletin of Victoria, 24 (1983) pp.67-71

Hansen, Robert   **WC WI**
 (American artist, 1924-)   WC
 (American artist, b.1924)   WI

Hansen, Sine *(Scandinavian artist, 20th cent.)*   **WC**

Hansen, Sven *(Danish landscape architect, 1910-1989)*   **AV**
 Bibl: Landskab, 1989 Oct., v.70, no.6, p.133

Hansen, Svend Wiig →see Wiig Hansen, Svend

Hansen, Theofilus Edvard, (Freiherr von Hansen) →see Hansen, Theophilus Edvard von

Hansen, Theophil →see Hansen, Theophilus Edvard von

Hansen, Theophilus Edvard von   **BA**
 (Danish architect, 1813-1891)   BA
 (Danish architect, active in Vienna, 1813-1891)   AV
 (Danish artist, 1813-1891)   WC
 Bibl: Arkitekturhistorisk 1 (1979) 88-108; ▶Encyc. world art; ▶Libr. of Congr. Name Auth. File; ▶Thieme-Becker

Hansen, Theofilus Edvard, (Freiherr von Hansen)   **WC**

Hansen, Theophil   **AV**

Hansen, Wiig →see Wiig Hansen, Svend

Hanser [Unidentified] *(Unknown painter)*   **PR**
 Bibl: (March 11, 1815, lot 79, Christie's)

Hansjacob, Anton *(West German landscape architect)*   **AV**
 Bibl: Deutsche Bauzeitung, 1989 June, v.123, no.6, p.48

Hansjacob, Gottfried →see Hansjakob, Gottfried

Hansjakob, Gottfried *(German landscape architect, Munich)*   **AV**
 Bibl: Deutsche Bauzeitung, 1989 June, v.123, no.6, p.48; Landscape architecture, 1985 Mar.-Apr., v.75, no.2, p.52
 Hansjacob, Gottfried   AV

Hansjakob, Toni *(West German architect, Munich)*   **AV**
 Bibl: Baumeister, 1987 Nov., v.84, no.11, p.48

Hanslip, Alice *(British artist, op.circa 1876-)*   **WI**

Hansom, Charles Francis *(British architect, act.1846-1851)*   **BA**
 Bibl: Burlington, Apr 1981, p.232; ▶Dict. natl. biog.; ▶Wodehouse, Brit. archts.

Hansom, Joseph Aloysius *(British architect, inventor of Hansom cab, 1803-1882)*   **AV**
 Bibl: ▶Colvin, Brit. archts.

Hanson Duvall Puthuff →see Puthuff, Hanson Duvall

Hanson or Hansonn, Christian Heinrich Johann *(German artist, 1790-1863)*   **WC**

Hanson, A. E. *(American landscape architect, 1893-)*   **AV**
 Bibl: ▶Libr. of Congr. Name Auth. File

Hanson, Duane   **BA GC WC WI**
(American artist, 1925-)   WC
(American artist, b.1925)   WI
(American sculptor, b.1925)   BA GC
Bibl: ▶MoMA libr. cat.;
▶RILA/BHA; ▶WW Amer. Art,
1976
Hanson, Halfdan   **BA**
(American architect, 1884-
1952)   AV BA
Bibl: Amer. Art Jrnl. XIII/1 (winter
1981) 69-89
Hanson, Halfdan M.   **AV**
Hanson, Halfdan M. →see Hanson,
Halfdan
Hanson, Joseph Mellor   **BA WI**
(American painter, 1900-1963)   BA
(British artist, 1900-1967)   WI
Bibl: ART DIGEST (May 15, 1945);
Burnham idx.; ▶MoMA libr. cat.;
UC Santa Barbara cat. sheets;
▶Vollmer, Künst.-Lex. 20. Jhr.
Hanson, Lawrence (American
sculptor, b.1936)   **BA**
Bibl: ▶WW Amer. Art
Hanson, Norman (South African
architect, 1909-)   **AV**
Bibl: ▶Contemp. archts.
Hanson, P. (American artist, op.
1886)   **WC**
Hanson, Peter (American artist,
1821-1887)   **WI**
Hanson, Philip   **BA WC WI**
(American artist, 20th cent.)   WC
(American artist, b.1943)   WI
(American painter, b.1943)   BA
Bibl: Whitney
Hanson, Rolf (Swedish artist,
b.1953)   **BA**
Bibl: Stockholm (SWE),
Nationalmuseum, Moderna
museet, ROLF HANSON, 1986
(RLIN)
Hanson, Victor F. (American, 20th
c.)   **BA**
Bibl: Detroit (MI, USA), Institute
of Arts, QUEBEC AND RELATED
SILVER AT THE DETROIT INSTITUTE
OF ARTS (1987)
Hanssen [Unidentified] (Unknown
painter)   **PR**
Bibl: (March 11, 1815, lot 105,
Christie's)
Hansson, Göran (Architect, West
Berlin)   **AV**
Bibl: Arkitekten, 1988 June 28,
v.90, no.12, p.337
Hansson, Holger (Swedish artist,
op.1586-1619)   **WC**
Hanstein, Hermann von (German
artist, 1809-1878)   **WC**
Hanswyck, Hans (Netherlandish
draughtsman, 17th century)   **GC**
Bibl: Getty Photo Study Coll.
(Duits coll.)

Hant [Unidentified] (Unknown
painter)   **PR**
Bibl: (April 8, 1815, lot 102,
Christie's)
Hantaï, Simon   **BA WC**
(French painter, b.1922)   BA
(Hungarian artist, 1922-)   WC
Bibl: ▶Bénézit; ▶Parry, Contemp.
art; ▶Vollmer, Künst.-Lex. 20. Jhr.
Häntler family (German architects,
15th-16th cs.)   **BA**
Bibl: Liedke, ARS BAVARICA XLIII-
XLIV (1986) 131-138
Hantzsch, Johann Gottlieb (German
artist, 1794-1848)   **WC**
Hanula, Jozsef (Hungarian artist,
1863-1944)   **WC**
Hanuscak, Michal (Architect, act. in
Poland)   **AV**
Bibl: Casabella, 1989 Oct., v.53,
no.561, p.38
Hanzik, Stanislav (Czech sculptor,
b.1931)   **BA**
Bibl: Roudnice nad Labem (CSK),
Gal. Vytvarneho Umění, Stanislav
Hanzik, 1979
Haorlem, Nycola van (early
Netherlandish in ESP, 16th c.)   **BA**
Bibl: Enciso, Archivum artis
louvaniense (1981), pp.250-263
Haozous, Bob (American sculptor,
20th c.)   **BA**
Hapke, Peter (West German
architect)   **AV**
Bibl: Deutsche Bauzeitschrift,
1989 Jan., no.1, p.14
Happel, Carl →see Happel, Karl
Happel, Karl   **BA**
(American artist, 19th cent.)   WC
(American artist, b.1819)   WI
(German painter, 1819-1914)   BA
Bibl: ▶Bénézit; Karlsruhe,
Kunsthalle; ▶Thieme-Becker
Happel, Carl   **WC WI**
Happelmann, Jacob Andreas
(Swiss artist, op.1738)   **WC**
Happold, Edmund →see Happold, Ted
Happold, Ted   **AV BA**
(Architect, professor)   AV
(British architect, b.1930)   BA
Bibl: ▶Avery period. idx., 1985;
RIBA Journal LXXXVII 6 Je 1980
46-48; RIBA journal, 1983 Apr.,
v.90, no.4, p.46
Happold, Edmund   **AV**
Haquette →see Haquette, Georges
Jean Marie
Haquette, G. →see Haquette, Georges
Jean Marie
**Haquette, Georges Jean
Marie**   **GC PR WC**
(French artist, 1854-1906)   WC
(French painter, 1854-1906)   GC PR
Bibl: ▶Bénézit; ▶Thieme-Becker
Georges Jean Marie Haquette   PR
Haquette   PR
Haquette, G.   PR

Hara, Hiroshi (Japanese architect,
1936-)   **AV**
Bibl: ▶Contemp. archts.
Hara, Shinichi (Japanese artist, 20th
c.)   **BA**
Bibl: Artforum, XXV/4 (Dec.
1986) pp.84-85
Hara, Teruo (Japanese architect in
U.S, 1928?-)   **AV**
Bibl: Architectural digest, 1985
May, v.42, no.5, p.176
Harada, Shizuo (Japanese architect)   **AV**
Bibl: L'Arca, 1989 Jan., no.23,
p.47
Harald-Gallen, Arthur (Finnish
artist, 1880-)   **WC**
Harari, Ralph (British, 1893-1969)   **BA**
Bibl: Boardman and Scarisbrick,
THE RALPH HARARI COLLECTION,
1977 book
Haraszty, Eszter (American interior
designer)   **AV**
Bibl: Architectural digest, 1985
Aug., v.42, no.8, p.114
Haraszty, István   **BA WC**
(Hungarian artist, 20th cent.)   WC
(Hungarian sculptor, b.1934)   BA
Bibl: ▶Art Index, 1975; Bonn
(DEU), Stadt. Kunstmus., Neue
ungarische Konstruktivisten
(1975)
Harbauer, Volker (West German
landscape architect,
Emmendingen)   **AV**
Bibl: Baumeister, 1986 Aug., v.83,
no.8, p.59
Harberton, Ernest Arthur George
Pomeroy, Viscountess,
(Fairlie) →see Harmar, Fairlie
Harberts, Mark A. (American
architect, Albuquerque, N.M)   **AV**
Bibl: ▶AIA Pro File, 1987-88
Harbeson, Benjamin (American
coppersmith, act.1766-after 1798)   **BA**
Bibl: ART & ART IV/1 (Jan-Feb
1981) 74-77
Harbord, Felix (British architect,
painter, 1906-1981)   **BA**
Bibl: COUNTRY LIFE, CLXXV, 4518
(22 Mar 1984) 762-763;
Guinness, Irish houses & castles,
pp.139-142
Harburger, Edmund   **BA WC**
(German artist, 1846-1906)   WC
(German painter, illustrator,
1846-1906)   BA
Bibl: ▶Thieme-Becker
Harbutt, Charles (American
photographer, b.1935)   **BA**
Bibl: ▶Image; ▶MoMA libr. cat.
Harbuz, Ann Alexandra (Canadian
painter, b.1908)   **BA**
Bibl: Artscanada XXXVI/3 (Oct-
Nov 1979) 5

Harcharik, Paul *(American
printmaker, painter, 20th c.)* **BA**
   Bibl: ▶Art Index, v.36; McGeevy,
   SECAC Review XI/2 (1987), 151-
   153
Harcourt, Countess → see Harcourt,
   Mary
Harcourt, Elizabeth, Lady *(British
artist, op.1761-, d.1811)* **WI**
   Hartwell, Elizabeth Lee, Baroness
   of   WI
   Lee, Elizabeth, Lady   WI
Harcourt, Francoise d' *(French
artist, op.1965)* **WC**
Harcourt, George **BA WC WI**
   (British artist, 1868-1947) WC WI
   *(British painter, 1869-after
   1923)*   BA
   Bibl: ▶Bénézit; ▶Johnson, Brit.
   artists; ▶Thieme-Becker
Harcourt, George Simon → see
   Harcourt, George Simon, 2nd Earl
*Harcourt, George Simon (not
Charles), Earl of → see* Harcourt,
   George Simon, 2nd Earl
Harcourt, George Simon, 2nd Earl **WI**
   (British artist, 1736-1809) WC WI
   (British painter, d. 1809) PR
   Bibl: ▶RILA/BHA
   George Simon Harcourt   PR
   George Simon, Earl Harcourt PR
   Harcourt, George Simon   PR
**Harcourt, George Simon (not
Charles), Earl of** **WC**
Harcourt, George Simon, Earl **PR**
Harcourt, George Simon, Earl → see
   Harcourt, George Simon, 2nd Earl
Harcourt, Mary **WC WI**
   (British artist, 1750-1833) WI
   (British artist, op.1760) WC
   (British artist, op.1760-1786) WC
D'Harcourt, Mary **WC**
   Danby, Mary, Miss   WI
   Harcourt, Countess   WI
Harcourt, Simon *(1661?-1727)* **AV**
   Bibl: Burlington magazine, 1985
   Apr., v.127, no.985, p.226
Harculus → see Segers, Hercules
   Pietersz.
Harculus Zegers → see Segers,
   Hercules Pietersz.
Hardacre, Charles **WC WI**
   (British artist, 20th cent.) WC
   (British artist, op.20th c.) WI
Hardacre, Martin *(British artist,
1875-1916)* **WI**
Hardame → see Hardimé, Pieter
Hardegger, August *(Swiss
architect, author, 1858-1927)* **BA**
   Bibl: ▶Natl. union cat.; ▶NYPL Art
   & Arch. Div., Dict. catalog;
   ▶Schweiz. Künst.-Lex.;
   ▶Thieme-Becker

Harden, John **BA WC WI**
   (British artist, 1772-1847) WC WI
   (British painter, 1772-1847) BA
   Bibl: ▶Libr. of Congr. Name Auth.
   File
Harden, Marvin *(American painter,
printmaker, b.1935)* **BA**
   Bibl: Fine, AFRO-AMERICAN
   ARTISTS; ▶WW Amer. Art, 1979
Hardenberg, Lambertus **GC WC**
   (Dutch artist, 1822-1900) WC
   (Dutch painter, 1822-1900) GC
   Bibl: ▶Thieme-Becker
Hardenberg, Wilhelm van → see
   Ehrenberg, Wilhelm van
*Hardenbergh or Hardenberg Cornelis
van → see* Hardenbergh, Cornelis
   van
Hardenbergh, Cornelis van **GC**
   (Dutch artist, 1755-1843) WC
   *(Dutch painter and
   draughtsman, 1755-1843)* GC
   Bibl: Getty Photo Study Coll.;
   ▶Thieme-Becker
**Hardenbergh or Hardenberg
Cornelis van** **WC**
Hardenbergh, Henry J. *(American
architect, 1847-1918)* **AV**
   Bibl: ▶Macmillan encyc. archts.
Harder, Johannes *(German
craftsman, decorative artist, 1877-
1948)* **BA**
   Bibl: Lühning, 'Der Kellinghusener
   Kabinettschrank von Johannes
   Harder' NORDELBINGEN LIV
   (1985) 183-192
Hardgrave, Charles *(British painter,
act.1885-1918)* **BA**
   Bibl: ▶Bénézit; ▶Johnson, Brit.
   artists; ▶Thieme-Becker
Hårdh, Carl Adolph *(Finnish
photographer, 1835-1875)* **BA**
   Bibl: Hist. photography, I/2 (Apr.
   1977) pp.135-152
Hardie, Charles Martin *(British
artist, 1858-1916)* **WC WI**
   Bibl: ▶Johnson, Brit. artists
Hardie, Gwen *(British artist, op.
1986-)* **WI**
Hardie, Martin **BA WC WI**
   (British artist, 1875-1952) WC WI
   (British printmaker, 1875-1952) BA
   Bibl: ▶Bénézit; Oxford (GB),
   Oxford University, Ashmolean
   Museum. Prints of Martin HArdie,
   1975; ▶Who was who [GBR],
   1951-60
Hardie-Condie, R. *(British artist, op.
20th c.)* **WI**
Hardime → see Hardimé, Pieter
Hardime, Paul *(Flemish artist, 17th
cent.)* **WC**
Hardime, Peter → see Hardimé, Pieter

Hardimé, Pieter **GC PR WC**
   (Dutch painter, 1677-1758) PR
   (Flemish artist, 1677/8-c.1758) WC
   (Flemish, 1677-1758) GC
   Bibl: ▶Thieme-Becker
   Hardame   PR
   Hardime   PR
   Hardime, Peter   PR
   Pieter Hardime   PR
Hardimé, Simon **GC WC**
   (Flemish artist, 1664/72-1737) WC
   (Flemish painter, 1672?-1737) GC
   Bibl: ▶Thieme-Becker
Hardin, Adlai → see Hardin, Adlai S.
Hardin, Adlai S. *(American sculptor,
b.1901)* **GC**
   Bibl: Getty Photo Study Coll.;
   ▶Opitz, Amer. sculptors
   Hardin, Adlai   GC
Harding → see Harding, Francis
Harding, Charlotte **BA WC WI**
   (American artist, 1873-1951) WI
   (American artist, 20th cent.) WC
   *(American illustrator, 1873-
   1951)* BA
   Bibl: ▶Bénézit; Chadds Ford (PA,
   USA), Brandywine River Mus.,
   Women artists (1975); ▶Havlice,
   Idx. art. bio.
   Brown, James A., Mrs., (Charlotte) WI
Harding, Chester **BA GC PR WI**
   (American artist, 1792-1866) WC WI
   (American painter, 1792-1866) BA PR
   (American, 1792-1866) GC
   Bibl: ▶Bénézit; ▶Fielding's Amer.
   ptrs.; ▶Natl. union cat., pre-1956;
   ▶RILA/BHA; ▶Thieme-Becker;
   ▶WWW Amer., 1607; ▶Young,
   Amer. artists
   Chester Harding   PR
Harding, Chester (not Charles) **WC**
Harding, Chester (not Charles) → see
   Harding, Chester
Harding, D. **WC WI**
   (British artist, 19th cent.) WC
   (British artist, op.19th c.) WI
   Bibl: ▶Waters, Brit. artists
Harding, David **BA WI**
   (British artist, 20th c.) BA
   (British artist, b.1944) WI
   Bibl: ARCH. REV., CLXVI (Aug
   1979) 125-129
Harding, Francis **BA PR WC WI**
   *(British artist, op.c.1730-m.a.
   1760)* WC
   (British artist, op.circa 1730-) WI
   (British painter, act. 1740-1766) PR
   (English painter, act.1740-1766) BA
   Bibl: ▶Bénézit; ▶RILA/BHA;
   ▶Thieme-Becker
   Francis Harding   PR
   Harding   PR
   Hardinge   PR
Harding, Frank *(British artist, op.
1885-1890)* **WI**

Harding, Frederick   WC WI
   (British artist, op.1814-1857)   WI
   (British artist, op.1825-1857)   WC
   Bibl: ▶Foskett, Brit. miniature ptrs.

Harding, George *(American artist, 1882-1959)*   WI

Harding, George Frederick Morris *(Irish sculptor, 1874-1964)*   BA
   Bibl: Hewitt, Art Ulster; ▶Johnson, Brit. artists; ▶Who was who [GBR], 1961-70

Harding, George Milford *(American architect, 1827-1910)*   AV
   Bibl: Landmarks observer, v.9, n.2, p.10

Harding, George Perfect   WC WI
   (British artist, circa 1780-1853)   WI
   (British artist, op.1797-m.1853)   WC

Harding, H.J. *(British artist, op.1818-1825)*   WC WI

Harding, I.W. *(British artist, op.18th c.)*   WI

Harding, J.L. → see Harding, John L.

Harding, J.W. *(English painter, 18th c.)*   BA

Harding, James → see Harding, James Duffield

Harding, James
   Duffield   AV BA GC PR WC WI
   (British artist, 1798-1863)   WC WI
   (British artist, 19th cent.)   WC
   (British illustrator, 1798-1863)   AV
   (British painter, 1798-1863)   PR
   (British painter, printmaker, 1798-1863)   BA
   (British, 1798-1863)   GC
   Bibl: ▶Bénézit; ▶Libr. of Congr. Name Auth. File; ▶RILA/BHA; ▶Thieme-Becker; ▶Witt checklist
   Duffield, Harding   WC
   Harding, James   PR
   James Duffield Harding   PR

Harding, John *(American architect, New York City)*   AV
   Bibl: Metropolis, 1983 Mar., v.2, no.7, p.5

Harding, John L.   WI
   (American artist, op.1830-1897)   WI
   (American artist, op.1835-1882)   WC

Harding, J.L.   WC

Harding, Lewis *(British photographer, act.1854-1875)*   BA
   Bibl: Hist. of Photography VIII/2 (Apr-June 1984) 89-98

Harding, Mary E., Miss *(British artist, op.circa 1880-)*   WI

Harding, Noel Robert *(Canadian artist, b.1945)*   BA
   Bibl: ▶Intl. dir. exh. artists, 1983; Paris, Centre cultural canadien, NOEL HARDING, 1977; ▶WW Amer. Art

Harding, Richard *(British ceramist, b.1957)*   BA
   Bibl: Arts Council GBR, Welsh Comm., Coming out (1979)

Harding, Robert *(American painter, 20th c.)*   BA
   Bibl: Arts Magazine LII/2 (Feb 1978) 17

Harding, Sylvester   GC WI
   (British artist, 1745-1809)   WC WI
   (British, 1745-1809)   GC
   Bibl: ▶Foskett, Brit. miniature ptrs.; ▶Thieme-Becker

Harding, Sylvester or Edward   WC
Harding, Sylvester or Edward → see Harding, Sylvester
Harding, T. → see Harding, Thomas

Harding, Thomas   WI
   (British artist, op.1788-1796)   WC WI
   (British artist, op.c.1800)   WC

Harding, T.   WC
Harding, Thomas(?)   WC
Harding, Thomas(?) → see Harding, Thomas

Harding, W.   WC WI
   (British artist, op.1787-1792)   WI
   (British artist, op.c.1790)   WC

Hardinge → see Harding, Francis

Hardinge, Charles Stewart, 2nd Viscount *(British artist, 1822-1894)*   WI

Hardiviller, Charles Achille d' *(French artist, 1795-p.1835)*   WC

Hardman, John *(British goldsmith, glass painter, 1811-1867)*   BA
   Bibl: Bury, S., Connoisseur CLXXIX/719 (Jan 1972) p.15-20; ▶Busse, Maler u. Bildhauer 19. Jahr.; ▶Thieme-Becker

Hardorff the Elder, Gerdt → see Hardorff, Gerdt, the elder
Hardorff, Gerdt I → see Hardorff, Gerdt, the elder

Hardorff, Gerdt, the elder   BA
   (German artist, 1769-1864)   WC
   (German draughtsman, 1769-1864)   GC
   (German painter, printmaker, 1769-1864)   BA
   Bibl: ▶Bénézit; Hamburg (DEU), Kunsthalle, Meister des 19 Jahrh. (1969); ▶Thieme-Becker

Hardorff the Elder, Gerdt   WC
Hardorff, Gerdt I   GC

Hardorff, Hermann Rudolf II *(German painter, 1816-1907)*   GC
   Bibl: ▶Bénézit

Hardouin-Mansart, Jules → see Mansart, Jules Hardouin

Hardouyn, Germain *(French illuminator, act.1505-1540)*   BA
   Bibl: ▶Thieme-Becker

Hardouyn, Gilles *(French painter, publisher, act.1497-1521)*   BA
   Bibl: ▶Thieme-Becker

Hardrick, Don W. *(American painter, b.1947)*   BA
   Bibl: Laguna Beach (CA, USA), Mus. Art, West Coast realism (1983)

Hards, Anthony *(British interior designer)*   AV
   Bibl: The world of interiors, 1987 May, p.119

Harduin, Louise *(French, 1816-1878)*   BA
   Bibl: Brunet, Gilbert. LE PORTRAIT DE L.H. PAR COROT, p.25

Hardwick of Bath, William N. → see Hardwick, William Noble, (of Bath)

Hardwick, John Jessop   BA WC WI
   (British artist, 1831-1917)   WC WI
   (British painter, 1831-1917)   BA
   Bibl: ▶Bénézit; ▶Mallalieu, Brit. watercolour artists; ▶Thieme-Becker

Hardwick, Melbourne H. *(American artist, 1857-1916)*   WI

Hardwick, Philip   AV BA
   (British architect, 1792-1870)   BA
   (British architect, younger son of Thomas Hardwick (1725-1798), 1792-1870)   AV
   Bibl: ▶Colvin, Brit. archts.; Fawcett, 7 Victorian archts., p. 32; Penguin dict. arch.; ▶Thieme-Becker; ▶WW Arch.

Hardwick, Philip Charles   AV BA
   (British architect, 1822-1892)   BA
   (British architect, son of Philip Hardwick (1792-1870), 1822-1892)   AV
   Bibl: ▶Avery obit. idx.; ▶Colvin, Brit. archts.; Fawcett, 7 Victorian archts., p. 32; Pelican Hist. of Art; ▶Thieme-Becker; ▶WW Arch.

Hardwick, Thomas   AV BA WC WI
   (British architect, 1752-1829)   BA
   (British architect, son of Thomas Hardwick (1725-1798), 1752-1829)   AV
   (British artist, 1752-1829)   WC WI
   Bibl: ▶Colvin, Brit. archts.; ▶Thieme-Becker

Hardwick, William Noble, (of Bath)   WI
   (British artist, 1805-1865)   WI
   (British artist, op.1829-m.1865)   WC

Hardwick of Bath, William N.   WC

Hardwicke, David Warren *(American designer)*   AV
   Bibl: Design solutions, 1985 Fall, v.5, no.3, p.38

Hardwicke, J. *(British artist, op.18th-19th c.)*   WI

Hardy → see Hardy, Dudley

Hardy Dejuinne, François Louis   BA
   (French artist, 1786-1844)   WC
   (French painter, 1784-1844)   BA
   (French painter, 1786-1844)   GC
   Bibl: ▶Bénézit; ▶Havlice, Idx. art. bio.; Master Drawings Aut. 75, p.261 XIII/3
   Dejuinne or De Juinne, Francois Louis   WC
   Dejuinne, François Louis   GC

Hardy family *(American painters, 19th-20th cs.)*   BA
   Bibl: ▶Groce, Artists Amer.

Hardy the Younger, James → *see* Hardy, James II

Hardy, Anna Eliza *(American artist, 1839-1934)* **WC WI**

Hardy, Bert *(British photographer, 20th c.)* **BA**

Hardy, Carel *(Dutch artist, op.1649-1651)* **WC**

Hardy, David **WC WI**
  (British artist, circa 1837-1870) **WI**
  (British artist, op.1855-1870) **WC**

Hardy, Deric, Mrs.(Florence) → *see* Small, Florence

Hardy, DeWitt *(American painter, b.1940)* **BA**
  Bibl: ▶WW Amer. Art, 1980

Hardy, Dorofield *(British artist, op. 1882-1920)* **WC WI**

Hardy, Dudley **BA PR WC WI**
  (British artist, 1866-1867-1922) **WI**
  (British artist, 1866/7-1922) **WC**
  (British painter, 1866-1922) **PR**
  (British painter, printmaker, 1866-1922) **BA**
  Bibl: ▶Johnson, Brit. artists; ▶RILA/BHA; ▶Thieme-Becker; ▶Waters, Brit. artists

  Dudley Hardy **PR**
  Hardy **PR**

Hardy, E. **WC WI**
  (British artist, 18th cent.) **WC**
  (British artist, op.18th c.) **WI**

Hardy, F. le *(British artist, op.1790-1802)* **WC WI**

Hardy, Frederick Daniel **BA WC WI**
  (British artist, 1826-1911) **WC WI**
  (British painter, 1826-1911) **BA**
  Bibl: ▶Thieme-Becker; ▶Waters, Brit. artists

Hardy, George **BA WI**
  (British artist, 1822-1909) **WI**
  (British painter, 1822-1909) **BA**
  Bibl: ▶Thieme-Becker; ▶Waters, Brit. artists

Hardy, Heywood **WC WI**
  (British artist, 1842-1933) **WI**
  (British artist, op.1861-1893) **WC**

Hardy, Hugh **AV BA**
  (American architect, 1932-) **AV**
  (American architect, 20th c.) **BA**
  Bibl: ▶Art Index, 1972-1973; ▶Avery period. idx.; Connaissance des Arts, no.263, Jan.1974, p.92; ▶Contemp. archts.

Hardy, J.P. *(British, 20th c.)* **BA**

Hardy, James I *(British artist, 1801-1879)* **WI**

Hardy, James II **WI**
  (British artist, 1832-1889) **WC WI**

Hardy the Younger, James **WC**

Hardy, James III *(British artist, op. 1973-)* **WI**

Hardy, Jean *(French sculptor, 1653-1737)* **BA GC**
  Bibl: ▶Bénézit; ▶RILA/BHA; ▶Thieme-Becker

Hardy, Jeremiah P. → *see* Hardy, Jeremiah Pearson

Hardy, Jeremiah Pearson **WI**
  (American artist, 1800-1885) **WI**
  (American artist, 1800-1887) **WC**

  Hardy, Jeremiah P. **WC**

Hardy, John *(American painter, 20th c.)* **BA**
  Bibl: ▶WW Amer. Art

Hardy, Muriel Ada *(British artist, op.20th c.)* **WI**
  Bibl: ▶Foskett, Brit. miniature ptrs.

Hardy, Norman H. *(British artist, circa 1864-1914)* **WI**

Hardy, Paul *(British artist, op.1890-1899)* **WI**

Hardy, Sydney *(British architect)* **AV**

Hardy, Thomas **WC WI**
  (British artist, 1757-circa 1805) **WI**
  (British artist, op.1777-1805) **WC**

Hardy, Thomas Bush *(British artist, 1842-1897)* **WC WI**

Hardy, Val *(British artist, op.19th c.)* **WI**

Hardy, W.H. *(British artist, op.1868-1892)* **WI**

Hare Pomare *(Maori, act.1863)* **BA**
  Bibl: Bell, Art History, 76

Hare, Alice, Miss → *see* Westlake, Alice

Hare, Augustus J.C. → *see* Hare, Augustus John Cuthbert

Hare, Augustus John Cuthbert **WI**
  (British artist, 1834-1903) **WI**
  (British artist, op.c.1860) **WC**

  Hare, Augustus J.C. **WC**

Hare, Augustus William *(British artist, 1792-1834)* **WC WI**

Hare, Channing *(American painter, d.1976)* **BA**
  Bibl: ART GALLERY, (Feb/Mar 1976); ▶WW Amer. Art, 1966, 1970

Hare, Chauncey *(American photographer, b.1934)* **BA**
  Bibl: ▶Parry, Photo idx.

Hare, David *(American sculptor, painter, b.1917)* **BA**
  Bibl: ▶NY art yrbk.; ▶WW Amer. Art, 1976

Hare, Henry Thomas *(British architect, 1860-1921)* **BA**
  Bibl: ▶Avery obit. idx.; ▶Thieme-Becker

Hare, Jeanette → *see* Hare, Jeanette R.

Hare, Jeanette R. *(American sculptor (b. Belgium), b.1898)* **GC**
  Bibl: Getty Photo Study Coll.; ▶Opitz, Amer. sculptors

  Hare, Jeanette **GC**

Hare, Julius *(British artist, 1859-1932)* **WI**

Hare, Richard V. *(American interior designer, New York, NY)* **AV**
  Bibl: Architectural digest, 1986 Aug., v.43, no.8, p.66

Hare, Sharon *(American sculptor, b.1950)* **BA**
  Bibl: Claremont (CA, USA), Galleries of the Claremont Colleges, Gallery as studio (1975)

Hare, St. George **PR WC WI**
  (British artist, 1857-1933) **WC WI**
  (Irish painter, 1857-1933) **PR**
  Bibl: ▶Fisher, Watercolour ptrs.; Nat Gal of Ireland catalogue; ▶Thieme-Becker

  St. George Hare **PR**

Hare-Hunt Painter **GC**
  Bibl: ▶Beazley, Attic red-fig. vase-ptrs.

Harebutle, Joseph *(British artist, op. 1847-)* **WI**

Harel de la Noë, Louis-Auguste-Marie *(French engineer, 1852-1931)* **BA**
  Bibl: ▶Dict. biog. fran.; Midant, J.-P., MON. HIST. DE LA FRANCE, 150-51 (Apr-June 1987), p.91-95

Harembourg family → *see* Hornebolt family

Harford the Younger, John Scandrett → *see* Harford, John Scandrett II

Harford, John Scandrett II **WI**
  (British artist, 1786-1866) **WC WI**
  Bibl: ▶Fisher, Watercolour ptrs.

Harford the Younger, John Scandrett **WC**

Hargitt, Edward *(British artist, 1835-1895)* **WC WI**

Hargrave, Jeremiah *(British architect, woodcarver, cabinetmaker, 1726-1786)* **BA**
  Bibl: JOURNAL OF FURNITURE HISTORY XII (1976), p. 51-58

Hargrave, Joseph *(British architect, woodcarver, cabinetmaker, act. 1776-1802)* **BA**
  Bibl: JOURNAL OF FURNITURE HISTORY XII (1976), p. 51-58

Hargreave, James *(British artist, op. 1693-1710)* **WI**

Hargreaves, Alice Pleasance Liddell *(British, 1852-1934)* **BA**
  Bibl: New York (NY, USA), Morgan Libr., Lewis Carroll & Alice (1982); RLIN BKS file

Hargreaves, George *(American landscape architect, San Francisco)* **AV**
  Bibl: Utah architect, 1984 Fall, p.4

Hargreaves, George **WC WI**
  (British artist, 1797-1870) **WI**
  (British artist, 1797-p.1834) **WC**
  Bibl: ▶Foskett, Brit. miniature ptrs.

Hargreaves, Jaci *(Brazilian architect)* **AV**
  Bibl: Projeto, 1985 Aug., no.78, p.90

Hargreaves, James *(British inventor, d.1778)* **BA**
  Bibl: ▶Dict. natl. biog.

Hargreaves, Sally *(British artist, b.1946)* **WI**

Hargreaves, Thomas (British artist, 1775-1846) **WC WI**
Bibl: ▶Waterhouse, Brit. 18c. ptrs.

Hari, Johannes I **GC**
(Dutch artist, 1772-1849) WC
(Dutch painter, 1772-1849) GC
Bibl: ▶Thieme-Becker

Hari, Johannes, I **WC**
Hari, Johannes, I → see Hari, Johannes I

Haring, H. (German artist, 17th cent.) **WC**

Häring, Hugo **AV BA**
(German architect, 1882-1958) BA
(West German architect, author, 1882-1958) AV
Bibl: ▶Contemp. archts.; ▶Libr. of Congr. Name Auth. File; ▶Macmillan encyc. archts.; ▶Portoghesi, Diz. arch. e urbanistica; ▶Vollmer, Künst.-Lex. 20. Jhr.

Haring, Keith **AV BA WI**
(American artist, b.1958) WI
(American artist, New York City, 1958-) AV
(American painter, 1958-1990) BA
Bibl: Arts Mag. LVI (Sept 1981), pp.164-165; ▶Intl. dir. exh. artists, 1982, 1983; Nadelman, Artnews, LXXXI/8 (Oct. 1982) p.76; National Public Radio, ALL THINGS CONSIDERED (16 Feb 1990); ULAN 1988

Haringer, Carl Joseph **BA WC**
(Austrian painter, architect, 18th c.) BA
(German artist, op.c.1716-1733) WC
Bibl: ▶Bénézit; ▶Thieme-Becker

Haringh or Haaring, Daniel → see Haringh, Daniel

Haringh, Daniel **GC**
(Dutch artist, c.1636-1706) WC
(Dutch painter, ca.1636-1706) GC
Bibl: ▶Getty Photo Study Coll.; Rijksmuseum; ▶Thieme-Becker

Haringh or Haaring, Daniel **WC**

Harington, John → see Harrington, John

Haritonoff, Nicholas (Russian artist, op.1930) **WC**

Harjula, Ruth (British interior designer) **AV**
Bibl: The world of interiors, 1989 July-Aug., p.86

Harkavy, Minna **BA GC**
(American sculptor (b. Estonia), b.1895) GC
(American sculptor, 1895-1987) BA
Bibl: ▶Collins, Women artists Amer.; Getty Photo Study Coll.; ▶MoMA libr. cat.; ▶Opitz, Amer. sculptors; ▶Vollmer, Künst.-Lex. 20. Jhr.; ▶WW Amer. Art, 1976; ▶WWW Amer. art, v.9

Harkavy, Minna R. **GC**

Harkavy, Minna R. → see Harkavy, Minna

Harker, Joseph Cunningham **WI**
(British artist, 1855-1927) WC WI

Harker, Joseph Cunninghan **WC**

Harker, Joseph Cunninghan → see Harker, Joseph Cunningham

Harker, Margaret (British artist, b.1920) **WI**

Harkins, George (American painter, 20th c.) **BA**
Bibl: ARTS MAG, LVIII, 9 (May 1984) 2; ▶Intl. dir. exh. artists, 1983

Harkness, Albert (American architect, 1886-1981) **AV BA**
Bibl: Jordy, H.-R. Hitchcock festschrift, p. 336, n. 3; ▶WWW Amer., v.8

Harkness, John C. (American architect, 1916-) **AV**

Harkness, Mary (American, 20th c.) **BA**
Bibl: ▶WWW Amer., v.1

Harkness, Sarah P. → see Harkness, Sarah Pillsbury

Harkness, Sarah Pillsbury **BA**
(American architect, 1914-) AV
(American architect, b.1914) BA
Bibl: WW Amer., 1977

Harkness, Sarah P. **AV**

Harlamoff, Alexei Alexeievich → see Charlamoff, Alexej Alexejewitsch

Harland, Peter J. B. → see Harland, Peter John Blundell

Harland, Peter John Blundell **BA**
(British architect, 1900-1973) AV BA
Bibl: ▶Avery period. idx.; Powers, Country Life CLXXVIII/4593 (29 Aug 1985) 559

Harland, Peter J. B. **AV**

Hårleman, Carl **AV BA**
(Swedish architect, 1700-1752) AV
(Swedish architect, 1700-1753) BA
Bibl: ▶Macmillan encyc. archts.; ▶RILA/BHA; ▶WW Arch.

Harleman, Karl **AV**

Harleman, Karl → see Hårleman, Carl

Harleston, Edwin Augustus (American painter, 1882-1931) **BA**
Bibl: ▶Cederholm, Afro-Amer. artists; Los Angeles (CA, USA), LACMA, Black Amer. art (1986), p.136

Harley (Engraver) **WI**

Harley, George (British artist, 1791-1871) **WC WI**

Harley, Herbert E. (British artist, op. 1884-1908) **WI**

Harley, Lilian, Mrs. → see Rowney, Lilian

Harley, Steve (American painter, 1863-1947) **BA**
Bibl: New York (NY, USA), Whitney Mus., Amer. folk ptrs. (1980)

Harley-Smith, R. (British artist, op. 1932-1939) **WI**

Harlez, Guillaume Joseph de (Flemish, 1691-1763) **BA**
Bibl: ▶Biog. Nat. Belgique; Collard, Art & Fact 1 (1982), p. 48-59; Genicot, Châteaux de plaisance... de Belgique

Harlfinger, Richard (Austrian painter, 1873-1948) **BA**
Bibl: ▶Bénézit; ▶Fuchs, Öst. Maler 19. Jahrh.; ▶Österr. biog. Lex. 1815-1950; ▶Thieme-Becker; ▶Vollmer, Künst.-Lex. 20. Jhr.

Harling, William Owen (British artist, op.1849-1878) **WI**

Harlingen, Pieter van → see Feddes, Pieter van (Pieter van Harlingen)

Harlingue, A. (French, active early 20th century) **JG**

Harloff, G. (German artist, 20th cent.) **WC**

Harloff, Guy (Italian painter, b.1933) **BA**

Harlow → see Harlow, George Henry

Harlow, Alfred B. (American architect, 1857-1927) **AV**
Bibl: ▶Withey, Amer. archts.

Harlow, George → see Harlow, George Henry

Harlow, George H. → see Harlow, George Henry

Harlow, George Henry **BA GC PR WC WI**
(British artist, 1787-1819) WC WI
(British painter, 1787-1819) BA PR
(British, 1787-1819) GC
Bibl: ▶Bénézit; ▶Dict. natl. biog.; ▶Redgrave, Engl. school; ▶RILA/BHA; ▶Thieme-Becker; ▶Witt checklist

George Henry Harlow PR
Harlow PR
Harlow, George PR
Harlow, George H. PR

Harlow, J.N. [Unidentified]
(Unknown painter) **PR**
Bibl: (May 26, 1812, lot 65, Robins)

J. N. Harlow PR

Harman Saghtleeven → see Saftleven, Herman

Harman, Maryann Whittemove (American painter, b.1935) **BA**
Bibl: ▶WW Amer. Art, 1976

Harmanns Hals → see Hals, Harmen

Harmar → see Harmar, Fairlie

Harmar or Harmer, Fairlie (Viscountess Harberton) → see Harmar, Fairlie

Harper, Johann *(Swedish, 1688-*
1746)   **GC**
   Bibl: ▶Thieme-Becker
Harper, John *(British photographer,*
sculptor, b.1946)   **BA**
   Bibl: ▶Babington Smith, Contemp.
   artists
Harper, John   **AV BA WC WI**
  (British architect, 1809-1842)   AV BA
  (British artist, 1809-1842)   WC WI
   Bibl: ▶Colvin, Brit. archts.; ▶Dict.
   natl. biog.
Harper, Michael   **AV**
Harper, Robert L. *(American*
architect, 1937-)   **AV**
Harper, T. *(British artist, op.1817-*
1843)   **WC WI**
   Bibl: ▶Foskett, Brit. miniature ptrs.
Harper, William *(American*
enamelist, b.1944)   **BA**
   Bibl: ▶WW Amer. Art, 1978
Harpignes → *see Harpignies, Henri-*
Joseph
Harpignies → *see Harpignies, Henri-*
Joseph
Harpignies, G. *(French artist, 19th*
cent.)   **WC**
Harpignies, Henri → *see Harpignies,*
Henri-Joseph
Harpignies, Henri Joseph → *see*
Harpignies, Henri-Joseph
Harpignies, Henri-Joseph   **BA PR**
  (French artist, 1819-1916)   WC
  (French painter, 1819-1916)   PR
  (French painter, printmaker,
  1819-1916)   BA
  (French, 1819-1916)   GC
   Bibl: ▶Dict. biog. fran.;
   ▶RILA/BHA; ▶Thieme-Becker;
   ▶Witt checklist
  Harpignes   PR
  Harpignies   PR
Harpignies, Henri   **PR**
Harpignies, Henri Joseph   **GC PR WC**
  Henri Harpignies   PR
Harpsau *(German artist, 19th cent.)*   **WC**
Harrach, Ferdinand Graf von
(German artist, 1832-1915)   **WC**
Harraden, Richard Banks *(British*
artist, 1778-1862)   **WC WI**
   Bibl: ▶Mallalieu, Brit. watercolour
   artists
Harrewijn or Harrevyn, Jacobus → *see*
Harrewijn, Jacobus
Harrewijn or Harrewyn, Francois
(Flemish artist, 1700-1764)   **WC**
Harrewijn, Jacob → *see Harrewijn,*
Jacobus

Harrewijn, Jacobus   **BA GC**
  (1660-1727)   AV
  (Dutch printmaker, 1660-1727)   BA
  (Dutch printmaker, 1662-d. aft.
  1732)   GC
  (Flemish artist, c.1660-p.1732)   WC
   Bibl: ▶Bénézit; Fogg Annual
   Report 1974-76, p. 84-96;
   ▶Thieme-Becker; ▶Waller, Noord
   NLD Graveurs; ▶Wurzbach, NLD
   Künst.-Lex.
Harrewijn or Harrevyn, Jacobus   **WC**
Harrewijn, Jacob   **AV**
Harrich or Harrisch, Jost or
Jobst → *see Harrich, Jobst*
Harrich, Jobst   **BA GC**
  (German artist, c.1580-1617)   WC
  (German painter, ca.1580-1617) BA GC
   Bibl: ▶Bénézit; ▶Thieme-Becker
Harrich or Harrisch, Jost or
Jobst   **WC**
Harries, Katrine *(South African*
illustrator, printmaker, 1914-1978)   **BA**
   Bibl: Cape Town (South Africa),
   South African Nat'l. Gallery,
   Katrine Harries 1914-1978 (1978);
   ▶Natl. union cat., 1968-1972
Harries, Mags *(American artist,*
b.1945)   **BA**
   Bibl: Lincoln (MA, USA),
   DeCordova and Dana Museum &
   Park, MAGS HARRIES (1982)
Harriet Blackstone → *see Blackstone,*
Harriet
Harriet Gouldsmith Arnold → *see*
Arnold, Harriet
Harriet Kirkpatrick → *see Kirkpatrick,*
Harriet
Harriet, Fulchran Jean   **BA GC WC**
  (French artist, op.1789-m.1805)   WC
  (French artist, op.1796)   WC
  (French painter, 1778-1805)   BA
  (French, act.1789-d.1805)   GC
   Bibl: ▶Bellier, Artistes fran.;
   ▶Bénézit; London, Wildenstein &
   Co., Ltd., CONSULAT-EMPIRE...
   1981 (UK); ▶Thieme-Becker; ▶Witt
   checklist
Fulchram, Jean Harriet   **WC**
Harring, Harro Paul *(German*
author, painter, 1798-1870)   **BA**
   Bibl: ▶Natl. union cat., pre-1956;
   Nordelbingen XLIX (1980), p.
   17-28
Harring, William *(American*
printmaker, act.1865)   **BA**
   Bibl: Marzio, Chromolithography
Harrington → *see Harrington, Joseph*
Harrington Fitzgerald → *see Fitzgerald,*
Harrington
Harrington, Addie A.   **WC WI**
  (American artist, op.1863)   WC
  (American artist, op.1863-)   WI
Harrington, Charles   **WC WI**
  (British artist, -1943)   WC
  (British artist, 1865-1943)   WI

Harrington, George *(American*
painter, 20th c.)   **BA**
   Bibl: New Haven (CT USA) phone
   book (1977?); Springfield (MA,
   USA), Smith Art Mus., George
   Harrington (1976)
Harrington, J. Brooke *(American*
architect, 1944-)   **AV**
   Bibl: Process: architecture, n.2,
   1977, p.41
Harrington, Jane *(British artist,*
d.1824)   **WI**
  Fleming, Jane   WI
Harrington, Joan *(English, act.1336)* **BA**
   Bibl: Cokayne, Complete peerage,
   v.2, p.315
  Haverington, Joan de   BA
Harrington, John *(English, ca.1281-*
1347)   **BA**
   Bibl: Cokayne, Complete peerage,
   v.2, pp.314-315; Pevsner, N.
   Lancs, 89
  Harington, John   BA
  Haverington, John de   BA
Harrington, Joseph *(American*
painter, 1841-1900)   **PR**
   Bibl: ▶WWW Amer. art
  Harrington   PR
  Joseph Harrington   PR
Harrington, R. → *see Harrington,*
Robert
Harrington, Robert   **WI**
  (British artist, 1805-1884)   WI
  (British artist, 19th cent.)   WC
Harrington, R.   **WC**
Harriott, William Henry   **WC WI**
  (British artist, op.1811-, d.1839) WI
  (British artist, op.1811-m.1839)   WC
Harriri, Gisue *(Architect)*   **AV**
   Bibl: AA files, 1987 Spring, no.14,
   p.24
Harriri, Nojgan *(Architect)*   **AV**
   Bibl: AA files, 1987 Spring, no.14,
   p.24
Harris *(American, active Washington,*
D.C. U.S. ca. 1916)   **JG**
Harris → *see Harris, Lawren Stewart*
Harris → *see Harris, Philip Spooner*
Harris the Elder, John → *see Harris,*
John II
Harris, Albert   **WC WI**
  (British artist, 19th cent.)   WC
  (British artist, op.1890-1900)   WI
Harris, Alfred Peter *(Canadian*
painter, b.1932)   **BA**
   Bibl: ▶Artists Canada; ▶Idx.
   Ontario artists; ▶MacDonald, Can.
   artists
Harris, Belle → *see Harris, Belle C.*

Harris, Belle C. *(American sculptor, nd)*   **GC**
  Bibl: Getty Photo Study Coll.; ▶Opitz, Amer. sculptors
  Harris, Belle   GC
  Harris, Mrs. Richard T.   GC
  Harriss, Belle   GC
  Harriss, Belle C.   GC
  Harriss, Mrs. Richard T.   GC
Harris, Carole *(American artist, 20th c.)*   **BA**
  Bibl: Chavis, 10 Michigan Afro-Amer. artists
Harris, Charles *(Irish silversmith)*   **BA**
  Bibl: Antiques, CXX/4 (Oct. 1981) pp.915-921
Harris, Charles X→see Harris, Charles X.
Harris, Charles X.   **WI**
  (American artist, 1856-)   WC
  (American artist, b.1856)   WI
  Harris, Charles X   **WC**
Harris, Daniel *(British artist, op. 1789-1799)*   **WC WI**
Harris, Edwin   **BA WC WI**
  (British artist, 1855-1906)   WC WI
  (British painter, 1855-1906)   BA
  Bibl: ▶Johnson, Brit. artists; ▶Waters, Brit. artists
Harris, Frances Elisabeth Louise nee. Rosenberg (Mrs. J. Dafter Harris)→see Harris, Frances Elizabeth Louise, (Fanny)
Harris, Frances Elizabeth Louise, (Fanny)   **WI**
  (British artist, 1822-1873)   WC WI
Harris, Frances Elisabeth Louise nee. Rosenberg (Mrs. J. Dafter Harris)   **WC**
  Rosenberg, Frances Elisabeth Louise, Miss   WI
Harris, George Walter *(British artist, op.1864-1893)*   **WC**
Harris, Harwell Hamilton   **AV BA**
  (American architect, 1903-)   AV
  (American architect, b.1903)   BA
  Bibl: ▶Contemp. archts.; ▶Macmillan encyc. archts.
Harris, Henry   **WC WI**
  (British artist, 1826-1878)   WI
  (British artist, op.1826-1878)   WC
Harris, Henry *(British, d.1764)*   **BA**
  Bibl: Russell, Burlington Mag. CXXV/958 (Jan 1983), 32
Harris, Ian *(Australian architect)*   **AV**
  Bibl: The Architect, W.A., 1988 summer, v.29, no.4, p.16
Harris, J.   **WC WI**
  (British artist, op.1760-1765)   WI
  (British artist, op.c.1760-1765)   WC
Harris, James   **WC WI**
  (British artist, 1810-1887)   WI
  (British artist, op.1847-1876)   WC
Harris, James Charles *(British artist, 1831-1904)*   **WI**

Harris, Jefferey   **WC WI**
  (British artist, 1932-)   WC
  (British artist, b.1932)   WI
Harris, Jeffrey *(New Zealander painter, b.1949)*   **BA**
  Bibl: Auckland (NZL), City Art Gall., Jeffrey Harris (1985); ▶Intl. dir. exh. artists, 1982, 1983
Harris, Joe *(American, contemporary)*   **JG**
Harris, John→see Harris, John I
Harris, John I   **WI**
  (British artist, op.1686-1740)   WC WI
  (Engraver, op.1686-1740)   WI
  Harris, John   **WC**
Harris, John I→see Harris, John II
Harris, John II *(British painter, printmaker, act.1750)*   **BA**
  Bibl: APOLLO, CVIII/197 (July 1978), p. 4-11
Harris, John II   **WI**
  (British artist, 1770-1834)   WC WI
  (British artist, a.1793-m.1834)   WC
  Harris the Elder, John   **WC**
  Harris, John I   **WC**
Harris, John III *(British artist, circa 1791-circa 1873)*   **WI**
Harris, Joseph M. *(American architect. Principal, Clark, Tribble, Harris & Li, Charlotte, N.C)*   **AV**
  Bibl: ▶AIA Pro File, 1978
Harris, Josephine *(British artist, op. 1975-)*   **WI**
Harris, Lawren Phillips *(Canadian painter, printmaker, b.1910)*   **BA**
  Bibl: ▶Artists Canada; ▶MacDonald, Can. artists
Harris, Lawren S.→see Harris, Lawren Stewart
Harris, Lawren Stewart   **BA PR**
  (British, b.1885)   GC
  (Canadian artist, 1885-)   WC
  (Canadian painter, 1885-1970)   BA PR
  Bibl: ▶Creative Canada; ▶Havlice, Idx. art bio.; ▶MacDonald, Can. artists; ▶RILA/BHA; ▶Witt checklist
  Harris   PR
Harris, Lawren S.   **GC PR WC**
  Lawren Stewart Harris   PR
Harris, Margo→see Harris, Margo Liebes
Harris, Margo Liebes *(American sculptor (b. Germany), b.1925)*   **GC**
  Bibl: Getty Photo Study Coll.; ▶Opitz, Amer. sculptors
  Harris, Margo   GC
Harris, Mark   **BA WI**
  (British artist, b.1954)   WI
  (British painter, 20th c.)   BA
  Bibl: London (GBR), Riverside Studios, 5 Painters (1984)
Harris, Michael M. *(American architect, d. 1982)*   **AV**
  Bibl: AIA Jrnl., LXXI/12 (Oct. 1982) p.103

Harris, Moses   **WC WI**
  (British artist, 1731-circa 1785)   WI
  (British artist, 1731-p.1785)   WC
Harris, Mrs. Richard T.→see Harris, Belle C.
Harris, P.S.→see Harris, Philip Spooner
Harris, Paul *(American sculptor, b.1925)*   **BA**
  Bibl: ▶Art Index, v.21; ▶Groce, Artists Amer.; Leon, PAUL HARRIS; ▶WW Amer. Art, 1976; ▶Young, Amer. artists
Harris, Philip Spoonen→see Harris, Philip Spooner
Harris, Philip Spooner   **PR WI**
  (American artist, 1824-1884)   WI
  (American painter, 1824-1884)   PR
  Harris   PR
  Harris, P.S.   PR
  Harris, Philip Spoonen   **PR**
  Philip Spoonen Harris   PR
Harris, Richard *(British sculptor, b.1954)*   **BA**
  Bibl: Davies, Studio intl., CXCVI/999 (Apr.-May 1983) pp. 10-13; ▶Intl. dir. exh. artists, 1983, v.2
Harris, Robert   **BA WC**
  (British artist, 1849-1919)   WC
  (Canadian painter, 1849-1919)   BA
  Bibl: ▶Creative Canada; ▶Thieme-Becker
Harris, Robert S. *(American architect, Los Angeles)*   **AV**
  Bibl: ▶AIA Pro File, 1987-88
Harris, Roberta *(American artist, b.1943)*   **BA**
  Bibl: Newport Beach (CA, USA), Newport Harbor Art Mus., Houston (1978)
Harris, Steven *(American architect, 1950-)*   **AV**
  Bibl: Ottagono, 1987 Sept., v.22, no.86, p.33
Harris, Suzanne *(American artist, 1940-1979)*   **BA**
  Bibl: Art in Amer. LXIV (Sept-Oct 1976), p. 100; Art in Amer. LXVIII/1 (Jan 1986), p. 15-17
Harris, Thomas *(British architect, 1830-1900)*   **BA**
  Bibl: ▶Avery period. idx.; Girouard, Henry-Russell Hitchcock festschrift, p. 366
Harris, Thomas M. *(American interior designer, El Dorado, Ark)*   **AV**
  Bibl: Southern accents, 1987 Nov.-Dec., v.10, no.6, p.96
Harris, Tomás   **BA WC WI**
  (British artist, 1908-)   WC
  (British artist, 1908-1964)   WI
  (British artist, dealer, art historian, 1908-1964)   BA
  Bibl: ▶Dict. natl. biog., 1961-1970

Harris, William Cornwallis *(British engineer, 1807-1848)* **BA**
Bibl: ▶Dict. natl. biog., v.25; Maitland, COUNTRY LIFE, CLXXXI/ (29 Aug.1987), 84-85; ▶Natl. union cat., pre-1956

Harris, William Critchlow *(Canadian architect, Prince Edward Island, 1856-1913)* **AV**
Bibl: Canadian heritage, 1986 May-June, v.12, no.2, p.33

Harris, William E. *(British artist, op. 1871-1910)* **WI**

Harrison B. Brown → *see* Brown, Harrison B.

Harrison [Unidentified] *(Unknown painter)* **PR**
Bibl: (March 20, 1813, lot 101, Del Vecchio)

Harrison, Alexander **BA PR**
(American artist, 1853-1930) **WC WI**
(American painter, 1853-1930) **BA PR**
Bibl: ▶Bénézit; ▶Fielding's Amer. ptrs.; ▶RILA/BHA; ▶Thieme-Becker; ▶Vollmer, Künst.-Lex. 20. Jhr.; ▶WWW Amer.

Alexander Harrison **PR**

Harrison, Alexander (Thomas Alexander) **WC**

Harrison, Thomas Alexander **PR WI**

Harrison, Alexander (Thomas Alexander) → *see* Harrison, Alexander

Harrison, Anthony **WC WI**
(British artist, 20th cent.) **WC**
(British artist, op.20th c.) **WI**

Harrison, Arthur P. *(British artist, op.1816-1821)* **WC WI**

Harrison, Bernard **WC WI**
(British artist, op.1893-c.1912) **WC**
(British artist, op.1893-circa 1912) **WI**

Harrison, Bernard J. *(American architect)* **AV**
Bibl: House & garden, 1984 Sept., v.156, no.9, p.198

Harrison, Birge **BA PR**
(American artist, 1854-1929) **WI**
(American artist, 1854-p.1904) **WC**
(American painter, 1854-1929) **BA PR**
Bibl: ▶Bénézit; ▶Fielding's Amer. ptrs.; ▶RILA/BHA; ▶Thieme-Becker; ▶WWW Amer.

Birge Harrison **PR**

Harrison, Lovell Birge **WC WI**

Harrison, C. *(British artist, op.1966-)* **WI**

Harrison, Charles *(British artist, art historian, 20th c.)* **BA**
Bibl: Harrison, Engl. art, (info. from back cover)

Harrison, Charles Harmony **BA WI**
(British artist, 1842-1902) **WI**
(British painter, 1842-1902) **BA**
Bibl: COUNTRY LIFE, CLVII 40 (Mar, 75), p. 542 ff; ▶Fisher, Watercolour ptrs.

Harrison, Christopher D. *(British artist, op.20th c.)* **WI**

Harrison, Christopher J. *(British artist, b.1945)* **WI**

Harrison, Claude William **BA WI**
(British artist, b.1922) **WI**
(British painter, b.1922) **BA**
Bibl: Kendall (GBR), Abbot Hall, Cumbrian portrait ptg. (1982); ▶Vollmer, Künst.-Lex. 20. Jhr.; ▶Waters, Brit. artists

Harrison, Colin *(British painter, b.1939)* **BA**
Bibl: London (GBR), Roundhouse Gallery, Irish art (1980)

Harrison, Dex *(English architect, 1909-1987)* **AV**
Bibl: Building design, 1988 Jan.8, no.867, p.2

Harrison, F.C. **WC WI**
(British artist, 20th cent.) **WC**
(British artist, op.20th c.) **WI**

Harrison, Gabriel *(American, 1818-1902, active Brooklyn, NY, U.S.)* **JG**

Harrison, George *(British artist, op. 1875-1920)* **WI**

Harrison, George Henry *(British artist, 1816-1846)* **WC WI**

Harrison, Harold Bertram *(British, 1855-1924)* **BA**
Bibl: Coventry (GBR), Herbert Art Gall. and Mus., ARTISTS AT APPLEHAYES... 1986 (RILA.GBR)

Harrison, Helen Mayer *(American artist, b.1927)* **BA**
Bibl: New Brunswick (NJ, USA), Rutgers U., Response to the environment (1975); ▶WW Amer. Art, 1976

Harrison, Henry G. *(American architect, 1813-1895)* **AV**
Bibl: ▶Macmillan encyc. archts.

Harrison, J.B. *(British artist, d.1958)* **WI**

Harrison, J.C. → *see* Harrison, John Cyril

Harrison, James *(British artist, op. 1827-1881)* **WC WI**

Harrison, James *(British architect, 1814-1866)* **BA**
Bibl: Howell, in CHESTER ARCHEOLOGICAL SOC. LXIII (1980); Pevsner, Cheshire

Harrison, John *(British artist, op. 1845-1865)* **WI**

Harrison, John Cyril **WI**
(British artist, op.1882-1891) **WC WI**
Bibl: Paviere, Brit. sporting ptrs

Harrison, J.C. **WC**

Harrison, John, Dr. *(British artist, 1810-1896)* **WI**

Harrison, Joseph *(American engineer, 1810-1874)* **BA**
Bibl: ▶WWW Amer.

Harrison, Kevin *(British sculptor, b.1953)* **BA**
Bibl: Cardiff (GBR), Oriel, KEVIN HARRISON, KEIR SMITH (1976)

Harrison, L.A. → *see* Harrison, Lawrence Alexander

Harrison, Lawrence Alexander **WI**
(British artist, -1937) **WC**
(British artist, 1866-1867-1937) **WI**

Harrison, L.A. **WC**

Harrison, Liz *(British artist, b.1947)* **BA**
Bibl: London, Whitechapel Art Gallery, LIZ HARRISON...1976

Harrison, Lorna, Miss → *see* Binns, Lorna

Harrison, Lovell Birge → *see* Harrison, Birge

Harrison, Margaret *(British artist, 20th c.)* **BA**
Bibl: Arts Council GBR, Lives (1979); Lucie Smith

Harrison, Mary Kent **WC WI**
(British artist, 1915-) **WC**
(British artist, b.1915) **WI**
Marryat, Mary, Miss **WI**

Harrison, Newton A. *(American sculptor, b.1932)* **BA**
Bibl: ▶WW Amer. Art, 1973, 1976

Harrison, Peter *(American architect, 1716-1775)* **AV**

Harrison, Sarah Cecilia *(British artist, 1863-1941)* **WI**

Harrison, Stephen *(English architect, joiner, act.1603)* **BA**
Bibl: ▶Dict. natl. biog.; ▶Thieme-Becker

Harrison, Thomas *(British architect, 1744-1829)* **AV BA**
Bibl: ▶Colvin, Brit. archts.; ▶Summerson, Arch. GBR; ▶Thieme-Becker

Harrison, Thomas Alexander → *see* Harrison, Alexander

Harrison, Thomas Erat **WC WI**
(British artist, 1853-1917) **WI**
(British artist, op.1875-1910) **WC**

Harrison, W.H. *(French, active 19th century)* **JG**

Harrison, Wallace K. → *see* Harrison, Wallace Kirkman

Harrison, Wallace Kirkman **BA**
(American architect, 1895-1981) **AV BA**
Bibl: ▶Contemp. archts.; Hanover, Dartmouth, Hood Mus. of Art, THANK YOU, WALLACE K. HARRISON (1985); ▶Libr. of Congr. Name Auth. File; WW Amer., 1980-81

Harrison, Wallace K. **AV**

Harrison, William Allan *(Canadian painter, b.1911)* **BA**
Bibl: ▶Artists Canada; ▶MacDonald, Can. artists

Harriss, Belle → *see* Harris, Belle C.

Harriss, Belle C. → *see* Harris, Belle C.

Harriss, David *(British architect, 20th c.)* **BA**
Bibl: Davies, Arch. review, CLXXVI/1049 (Jul. 1984) p.76

Harriss, Mrs. Richard T. → see Harris,
Belle C.

Harriton, Abraham (American
painter, 1893-1984/85)   **BA**
  Bibl: ▶Artist biog. master idx.;
  ▶Fielding's Amer. ptrs.; ▶WW
  Amer. Art, 1947, 1984; ▶WWW
  Amer. art

Harrouart (French artist, 19th cent.)   **WC**

Harrow Class   **GC**
  Bibl: Paralipomena

Harrow Painter   **GC JG**
  (vase-painter, ca. 500-475 BC)   GC
  Bibl: ▶Beazley, Attic red-fig. vase-
  ptrs.; Richter, Attic red-fig. vases

Harrowing, Walter (British artist,
  op.1877-1904)   **WI**

Harry Aiken Vincent → see Vincent,
  Harry Aiken

Harry B. Lachman → see Lachman,
  Harry B.

Harry Bless → see Bles, Herri met de

Harry Gottlieb → see Gottlieb, Harry

Harry Herman Roseland → see
  Roseland, Harry

Harry Humphrey Moore → see Moore,
  Harry Humphrey

Harry Leslie Hoffman → see Hoffman,
  Harry Leslie

Harry Phelan Gibb → see Gibb, Henry
  Phelan

Harry Russell Ballinger → see Ballinger,
  Harry Russell

Harry Willson Watrous → see
  Watrous, Harry Willson

Harry, Philip   **WC WI**
  (American artist, op.1835-1848)   WI
  (American artist, op.1843)   WC

Harsdorff, Caspar Frederik   **AV BA WC**
  (Danish architect, 1735-1799)   BA
  (Danish architect, 1753-1799)   AV
  (Danish artist, 1735-1799)   WC
  Bibl: ▶Macmillan encyc. archts.;
  ▶Portoghesi, Diz. arch. e
  urbanistica; ▶Thieme-Becker

Harssens, S.L. (Flemish artist, 17th
  cent.)   **WC**

Hart → see Hart, Alfred

Hart → see Hart, James McDougal

Hart → see Hart, William M.

Hart Nibbrig, Ferdinand   **BA**
  (Dutch artist, 1866-1915)   WC
  (Dutch painter, 1866-1915)   GC
  (Dutch painter, printmaker,
  1866-1915)   BA
  Bibl: ▶Grote Winkler Prins;
  ▶Scheen, Ned. beeldende kunst.;
  ▶Thieme-Becker; ▶Wright, Ptgs.
  Dutch museums
  Hart Nibbring, Ferdinand   GC

Nibbrig, Ferdinand Hart   **BA GC WC**

Hart Nibbring, Ferdinand → see Hart
  Nibbrig, Ferdinand

Hart, Abraham van der (Dutch
  architect, 1747-1820)   **AV BA**
  Bibl: ▶Avery Libr. cat.;
  ▶Portoghesi, Diz. arch. e
  urbanistica; ▶Thieme-Becker;
  ▶Wurzbach, NLD Künst.-Lex.

Hart, Alfred (American painter,
  1816-1908)   **PR**
  Bibl: catalogue; ▶Fielding's Amer.
  ptrs., 1983
  Alfred Hart   PR
  Hart   PR
  Hart, Alfred A.   PR

Hart, Alfred A. → see Hart, Alfred

Hart, C.E. (Engraver)   **WI**

Hart, C.H. (British artist, op.1856-
  1873)   **WI**

Hart, C.M. (British artist, op.20th c.) **WI**

Hart, Celeste (American interior
  designer)   **AV**
  Bibl: House beautiful, 1989 June,
  v.131, no.6, p.98

Hart, Cornelia van der (Dutch
  painter, 1851-1940)   **GC**
  Bibl: ▶Bénézit

Hart, Dick (British artist, b.1920)   **WI**

Hart, E.H. (American, active NY, U.S.
  ca. 1890)   **JG**

Hart, Elizabeth, Miss → see Polunin,
  Elizabeth V.

Hart, Emma → see Hamilton, Emma

Hart, Frank (British artist, 1878-
  1959)   **WI**

Hart, Frederick → see Hart, Frederick
  E.

Hart, Frederick E.   **BA**
  (American sculptor)   AV
  (American sculptor, 20th c.)   BA
  Bibl: Hess, E., in ART IN AMERICA
  LXXI/4 (Apr 1983) 120;
  Landscape, 1985, v.28, no.2, p.1;
  North, P., in NEW ART EXAMINER
  XII/7 (Apr 1985) 27

Hart, Frederick   **AV**

Hart, George Overbury   **BA GC PR**
  (American artist, 1868-1933)   WC WI
  (American painter, 1868-1933)   PR
  (American painter, printmaker,
  1868-1933)   BA
  (American, 1868-1933)   GC
  Bibl: ▶Bénézit; ▶Fielding's Amer.
  ptrs.; ▶RILA/BHA; ▶Witt checklist
  George Overbury Hart   PR

Hart, George Overbury (Pop)   **WC**

Hart, George Overbury, (Pop)   **WI**
  Hart, Pop   WI

Hart, George Overbury (Pop) → see
  Hart, George Overbury

Hart, George Overbury, (Pop) → see
  Hart, George Overbury

Hart, Glynn Boyd (British artist, op.
  20th c.)   **WI**

Hart, James MacDougal → see Hart,
  James McDougal

Hart, James McDougal   **BA PR WI**
  (American artist, 1828-1901)   WC WI
  (American painter, 1828-1901)   BA PR
  Bibl: ▶Dict. Amer. biog.; ▶Groce,
  Artists Amer.; ▶RILA/BHA;
  ▶Thieme-Becker
  Hart   PR

Hart, James MacDougal   **WC**
  Hart, James McDougald   PR
  James McDougal Hart   PR

Hart, James McDougald → see Hart,
  James McDougal

Hart, James Turpin (British artist,
  1835-1899)   **WC WI**

Hart, Joel Tanner (American artist,
  1810-1877)   **WC WI**

Hart, John (British artist, b.1921)   **WI**

Hart, Pop → see Hart, George
  Overbury

Hart, Pro (Kevin) (Australian artist,
  20th cent.)   **WC**

Hart, Robert J. (Australian
  landscape architect)   **AV**
  Bibl: Landscape Australia, 1984
  Nov., v.6, no.4, p.297

Hart, Robert Lamb (American
  architect, New York, NY)   **AV**
  Bibl: ▶AIA Pro File, 1985

Hart, Solomon Alexander   **BA WC WI**
  (British artist, 1806-1881)   WC WI
  (British painter, 1806-1881)   BA
  Bibl: ▶Dict. natl. biog.; ▶Johnson,
  Brit. artists; ▶Thieme-Becker

Hart, Thomas   **WC WI**
  (British artist, op.1776-, d.1785)   WI
  (British artist, op.1776-m.1785)   WC

Hart, Thomas Gray (British artist,
  1797-1881)   **WC WI**

Hart, van [Unidentified] (Unknown
  painter)   **PR**
  Bibl: (August 7, 1810, lot 27,
  Fisher)
  Van Hart   PR

Hart, William   **WC WI**
  (American artist, 1830-1908)   WI
  (British artist, 19th cent.)   WC

Hart, William → see Hart, William M.

Hart, William M.   **BA WC WI**
  (American artist, 1823-1894)   WC WI
  (American draughtsman, 1823-
  1894)   GC
  (American painter, 1823-1894)   BA PR
  Bibl: ▶Bénézit; Coral Gables (FL,
  USA), Lowe Art Mus., 19c. Amer.
  topographic ptrs. (1975); ▶Groce,
  Artists Amer.; ▶Thieme-Becker
  Hart   PR

Hart, William   **GC PR**
  William Hart   PR

Harta, Anton (Hungarian artist,
  1884-)   **WC**

Harta, Felix Albrecht (Hungarian
  artist, 1884-)   **WC**

Hartel, Hermann (German artist, op.
  1841-1843)   **WC**

Hartell, John Anthony   **BA WC WI**
  (American artist, 1902-) WC
  (American artist, b.1902) WI
  (American painter, educator,
    b.1902) BA
    Bibl: UC Santa Barbara cat.
    sheets; ▶Vollmer, Künst.-Lex. 20.
    Jhr.; ▶WW Amer. Art, 1976,
    1980, 1989-1990

Hartenkampfe, G.T. Kempfe von **WC**
  (German artist, 1871-) WC
  (German artist, 1876-1956) WC

Kempf-Hartenkampf, Gottlieb
  Theodor von **WC**

Härter, Joachim *(German architect,*
  engineer) **AV**
    Bibl: Architektur der DDR, 1985
    Sept., v.34, no.9, p.529

Hartgring, Johannes Hendricus **BA**
  (Dutch pottery painter, 1876-1951)
    Bibl: ▶Scheen, Ned. beeldende
    kunst.

Harth, Philipp *(German sculptor,*
  1885-1968) **BA**
    Bibl: Kinkel, WELTKUNST, LV/13
    (July 1985), pp.1895-1899; Roh,
    DEUT. PLASTIK VON 1900 BIS
    HEUTE (1963) p.19; Roh,
    KUNSTWERK XXIV/6 (Nov 1971),
    p.83; ▶Vollmer, Künst.-Lex. 20.
    Jhr.; Werner, DEUT.PLASTIK...
    (1940)p.207

Hartigan, Grace **BA GC WC WI**
  (American artist, 20th cent.) WC
  (American artist, b.1922) WI
  (American painter, 1922-1945) GC
  (American painter, b.1922) BA
    Bibl: ▶Bénézit; ▶Cummings,
    Contemp. Amer. artists; ▶WW
    Amer. Art, 1976

Hartigan, Paul *(New Zealander*
  painter, b.1953) **BA**
    Bibl: Auckland (NZL), City Art
    Gallery, New image (1983)

Hartill, Brenda *(British artist, op.*
  20th c.) **WI**

Harting, Dirk *(Dutch printmaker,*
  b.1884) **GC**
    Bibl: ▶Vollmer, Künst.-Lex. 20. Jhr.

Hartinger, Anton *(German artist,*
  1806-1890) **WC**

Hartl, Karl *(Austrian architect)* **AV**
    Bibl: Planen Bauen Wohnen,
    1987, no.119, p.34

Hartland, Henry Albert *(British*
  artist, 1840-1893) **WC WI**

Hartley → see Hartley, Marsden

Hartley, Alfred *(British artist, 1855-*
  1933) **WC WI**

Hartley, Charles Augustus *(British*
  engineer, 1825-1915) **BA**
    Bibl: ▶Dict. natl. biog., 1912-
    1921; ▶Libr. of Congr. Name
    Auth. File; ▶Who was who [GBR]

Hartley, Edmund → see Hartley,
  Marsden

Hartley, Jesse **AV BA**
  (British engineer, 1780-1860) BA
  (English civil engineer,
    Liverpool, 1780-1860) AV
    Bibl: ▶Avery obit. idx., 1980;
    ▶Dict. natl. biog., v.25, p.71;
    Pevsner, S. Lancs, p. 37

Hartley, Joan *(American sculptor,*
  nd) **GC**
    Bibl: ▶Opitz, Amer. sculptors

Hartley, Jonathan Scott **BA WI**
  (American artist, 1845-) WC
  (American artist, 1845-1912) WI
  (American sculptor, 1845-1912) BA
    Bibl: ▶Fielding's Amer. ptrs.;
    ▶WWW Amer., v.1

Hartley, Jonathon Scott **WC**
Hartley, Jonathon Scott → see Hartley,
  Jonathan Scott

Hartley, Marsden **BA GC PR WC WI**
  (American artist, 1877-1943) WI
  (American artist, 1878-1943) WC
  (American painter, 1877-1943) PR
  (American painter, poet, 1877-
    1943) BA
  (American, 1878-1943) GC
    Bibl: ▶Bénézit; ▶Encyc. world art;
    ▶Natl. union cat., pre-1956;
    ▶RILA/BHA; ▶Witt checklist
  Hartley PR
  Hartley, Edmund WI
  Marsden Hartley PR

Hartley, Mary *(British artist, op.*
  1761-1775) **WC WI**
    Bibl: ▶Mallalieu, Brit. watercolour
    artists
  Hartley, Mary, Miss WI
Hartley, Mary, Miss → see Hartley,
  Mary

Hartley, Ralph *(British artist, op.*
  20th c.) **WI**

Hartley, Roger *(American architect)* **AV**

Hartmacker [Unidentified]
  (Unknown painter) **PR**
    Bibl: (Friday, Feb. 12, 1802, lot 92
    & 93, Edwards)

Hartman, Bertram **WC WI**
  (American artist, 1882-) WC
  (American artist, b.1882) WI

Hartman, Craig W. *(American*
  architect, Houston, Tex) **AV**
    Bibl: ▶AIA Pro File, 1985

Hartman, George E. *(American*
  architect, partner in firm of
  Hartman-Cox Architects, 1936-) **AV**
    Bibl: ▶AIA Pro File, 1980;
    ▶Contemp. archts.

Hartman, Laura *(American architect,*
  Berkeley, Calif) **AV**
    Bibl: Progressive architecture,
    1981 Apr., v.62, no.4, p.138

Hartman, Mauno *(Finnish sculptor,*
  b.1930) **BA**
    Bibl: ▶Artist biog. master idx.;
    Goteborg, Konstmuseum, FINNISH
    WOOD SCULPTURE, 1977

Hartmann, Adolf *(German painter,*
  1900-1972) **GC**
    Bibl: ▶Schweers, Gemälde deut.
    Museen

Hartmann, Carl *(German artist,*
  1818-p.1857) **WC**

Hartmann, Erich *(German painter,*
  printmaker, 1886-1974) **BA**
    Bibl: ▶Bénézit; Hamburg, Altonaer
    Museum, ERICH HARTMANN
    (1976); ▶MoMA libr. cat.;
    ▶Thieme-Becker; ▶Vollmer,
    Künst.-Lex. 20. Jhr.

Hartmann, Ferdinand (Christian
  Ferdinand) *(German artist, 1774-*
  1852) **WC**

Hartmann, Franz *(German artist,*
  c.1697-1728) **WC**

Hartmann, Günter F. *(Architect,*
  Wiesbaden) **AV**
    Bibl: Architektur,
    Innenarchitektur, Technischer
    Ausbau, v.92, no.1, 1984, p.28

Hartmann, Johann Joseph **GC WC**
  (German painter, 1753-1830) GC
  (Swiss artist, 1753-1830) WC
    Bibl: ▶Bénézit

Hartmann, Johann or Johannes
  Jakob *(Czech artist, 1680-p.1728)* **WC**

Hartmann, Johannes *(German*
  artist, op.c.1480) **WC**

Hartmann, Joseph *(German artist,*
  op.1747-p.1788) **WC**

Hartmann, Jürgen *(West German*
  architect, Remscheid) **AV**
    Bibl: Die Kunst, 1985 Feb., v.97,
    no.2, p.135

Hartmann, Karl *(German artist,*
  1861-) **WC**

Hartmann, Ludwig **GC WC**
  (German artist, 1835-1902) WC
  (German painter, 1835-1902) GC
    Bibl: ▶Thieme-Becker

Hartmann, Matthaus Christoph
  (German artist, c.1791-a.1850) **WC**

Hartmann, Oluf **BA WC**
  (Danish artist, 1879-1910) WC
  (Danish painter, printmaker,
    1879-1910) BA
    Bibl: ▶Nørregård-Nielsen, Dansk
    kunst; ▶Witt checklist

Hartmann, Peter *(Austrian*
  architect) **AV**
    Bibl: Bauforum, 1987, v.20, no.
    119, p.52

Hartmann, Richard *(German*
  painter, 1868-1931) **BA**
    Bibl: ▶Bénézit; ▶Vollmer,
    Künst.-Lex. 20. Jhr.

Hartmann, William *(American*
  architect, 20th c.) **BA**
    Bibl: ▶AIA Pro File, 1978

Hartmann, Wolfgang or
  Wolffgang *(Swedish artist, op.*
  1640-54) **WC·**

Hartnell, Nathaniel *(British artist,*
  op.1829-1864) **WI**

Hartney, Mick (British artist, b.1946) **WI**
Hartog, A. den (Dutch architect) **AV**
  Bibl: Architecture and urbanism,
  1984 Oct., no.10(169), p.65
Hartop, Leonora [Unidentified]
  (Unknown painter) **PR**
  Bibl: 1706 De Letter inventory
  juffr. Hartop **PR**
  juffr. Leonora Hartman **PR**
  Leonora Hartop **PR**
Hartover, Peter (British artist, op.
  1674-) **WI**
Hartray, John F., Jr. (American
  architect, 1930-) **AV**
Hartrick, Archibald Standish **BA WC WI**
  (British artist, 1864-1950) **WC WI**
  (British painter, printmaker,
  1864-1950) **BA**
  Bibl: ▶Bénézit; ▶Johnson, Brit.
  artists; ▶Waters, Brit. artists;
  ▶Who was who [GBR], 1941-50
Hartrick, Archibald Standish, Mrs.,
  (Lily) → see Blatherwick, Lily
Hartshorne, Jane (British artist, op.
  18th c.) **WI**
Hartsook (American, active
  California, ca. 1914) **JG**
Hartsuyker, E. (Dutch architect) **AV**
  Bibl: Techniques et architecture,
  no.340, p.69
Hartsuyker-Curjel, L. (Dutch
  architect) **AV**
  Bibl: Techniques et architecture,
  no.340, p.69
Hartung, Hans **BA GC WC**
  (French painter and
  draughtsman, b.1904) **GC**
  (French painter, printmaker,
  1904-1989) **BA**
  (German artist, 1904-) **WC**
  Bibl: ▶Contemp. artists, 1989;
  Getty Photo Study Coll.; NEW
  YORK TIMES (10 Dec 1989);
  ▶RILA/BHA; ▶Witt checklist;
  ▶WW France, 1989
Hartung, Heinrich (German artist,
  1851-1919) **WC**
Hartung, Karl **GC WC**
  (German artist, 1908-) **WC**
  (German draughtsman, 1908-
  1967) **GC**
  Bibl: ▶Bénézit; Getty Photo Study
  Coll.; ▶Witt checklist
Hartung, Manfred (East German
  architect, Berlin) **AV**
  Bibl: Architektur der DDR, 1989
  Jan., v.38, no.1, p.18
Hartveit, Berit (Norwegian
  landscape architect, 1960-) **AV**
  Bibl: Byggekunst: the Norwegian
  review of architecture, 1988,
  v.70, no.5, p.360
Hartwell, Charles Leonard (British
  sculptor, 1873-1951) **BA**
  Bibl: ▶Bénézit; ▶Thieme-Becker;
  ▶Who was who [GBR], 1951-60

Hartwell, Elizabeth Lee, Baroness
  of → see Harcourt, Elizabeth, Lady
Hartwell, Richard (British artist,
  b.1946) **WI**
Hartwic (German ecclesiastic, scribe,
  11th c.) **BA**
  Bibl: Huglo, SCRIPTORIUM, XLII/2
  (1988), P.183-190
Hartwich, Herman (American artist,
  1853-1926) **WI**
Hartwick, George Gunther
  (American artist, op.1847-1857) **WC WI**
Hartwig, Cleo (American sculptor,
  b.1911) **GC**
  Bibl: ▶Opitz, Amer. sculptors
Hartwig, Emil Bert (German painter,
  printmaker, b.1907) **BA**
  Bibl: Wangler, Schüler des
  Bauhauses, p.26
Hartwig, Max (German artist, 1873-) **WC**
Hartz, Lauritz (Danish artist, 1903-) **WC**
Hartz, Louis **GC**
  (Dutch artist, 1869-1935) **WC**
  (Dutch painter, 1869-1935) **GC**
  Bibl: ▶Vollmer, Künst.-Lex. 20. Jhr.
Hartz, Louis Jacob **WC**
Hartz, Louis Jacob → see Hartz, Louis
Hartzer, Ferdinand Carl Emmanuel
  (German sculptor, 1838-1906) **BA**
  Bibl: Arndt, NIEDERDEUTSCH.
  BEITRAGE Z. KUNSTGESCHICHTE,
  XVI (1980), p. 199-233; ▶Bénézit;
  ▶Busse, Maler u. Bildhauer 19.
  Jahr.; ▶Thieme-Becker
Hartzsch, Günter (East German city
  planner) **AV**
  Bibl: Architektur der DDR, 1989
  Jan., v.38, no.1, p.9
Haru, Yoko (American painter, 20th
  c.) **BA**
Harvard Painter **GC**
  Bibl: ▶Beazley, Attic red-fig. vase-
  ptrs.
Harvell the Younger, J. → see Harvell,
  J. II
Harvell, J. II **WI**
  (British artist, op.1840) **WC**
  (British artist, op.1840-) **WI**
Harvell the Younger, J. **WC**
Harvest [Unidentified] (Unknown
  painter) **PR**
  Bibl: (June 28, 1810, lot 118,
  Smith)
Harvey T. Dunn → see Dunn, Harvey T.
Harvey, Don (American artist,
  b.1941) **BA**
  Bibl: Akron (OH, USA), Akron Art
  Mus., Ohio perspectives (1986),
  p.6; ▶Babington Smith, Contemp.
  artists; Guide exh. artists: N.
  Amer. ptrs.; New York (NY, USA),
  New Mus., Outside NY: Ohio
  (1980), p.36
Harvey, Douglas D. (British artist,
  op.1859-1872) **WI**
Harvey, Eli (American artist, b.1860) **WI**

Harvey, Elizabeth (British artist, op.
  1802-1812) **WC WI**
Harvey, Elsie M. (British artist,
  b.1893) **WI**
  Mackrow, Elsie, Miss **WI**
Harvey, George **BA GC**
  (British artist, 1806-1876) **WC WI**
  (British painter, 1806-1876) **BA**
  (Scottish draughtsman, 1806-
  1876) **GC**
  Bibl: ▶Harris, Scottish ptrs.;
  ▶RILA/BHA; ▶Thieme-Becker
Harvey, George II **WI**
Harvey, Sir George **WC**
Harvey, George → see Harvey, George
  I
Harvey, George I **WI**
  (British artist, 1799-p.1877) **WC**
  (British artist, 1800-1801-1878) **WI**
  Bibl: ▶Foskett, Brit. miniature ptrs.
Harvey, George **WC**
Harvey, George II → see Harvey,
  George
Harvey, Gertrude (British artist,
  1889-1966) **WI**
  Bodinar, Gertrude, Miss **WI**
Harvey, H.J. → see Harvey, Herbert
  Johnson
Harvey, H.W., Capt. (British artist,
  op.1797-) **WI**
Harvey, Harold C. **BA WC WI**
  (British artist, 1874-1941) **WC WI**
  (British painter, 1874-1941) **BA**
  Bibl: ▶Johnson, Brit. artists;
  ▶Waters, Brit. artists
Harvey, Henrietta **WC WI**
  (British artist, 19th cent.) **WC**
  (British artist, op.19th c.) **WI**
Harvey, Herbert Johnson **WI**
  (British artist, 1883-1928) **WC WI**
Harvey, H.J. **WC**
Harvey, Hilda Mary (British artist,
  op.1886-1939) **WI**
Harvey, J. **WC WI**
  (British artist, op.1827) **WC**
  (British artist, op.1827-) **WI**
Harvey, J.D.M. (British artist, op.
  1920's-) **WI**
Harvey, J.S. **WC WI**
  (British artist, 18th cent.) **WC**
  (British artist, op.1760-) **WI**
Harvey, Jake (British sculptor,
  b.1948) **BA**
  Bibl: Arts Council GBR, Scot.
  Comm., Objects & constructions
  (1978); ▶WW Art, 1977
Harvey, James **WC WI**
  (British artist, op.1789) **WC**
  (British artist, op.1789-1798) **WI**
Harvey, John (American architect) **AV**
Harvey, John Rabone (British artist,
  1862-1933) **WI**
Harvey, Meredith (British artist, op.
  20th c.) **WI**

Harvey, Michael *(British painter,*
b.1946)   **BA**
Harvey, Robert   **WC WI**
 (American artist, 1924-)   WC
 (American artist, b.1924)   WI
Harvey, Sir George → *see* Harvey,
 George
Harvey, W. Alexander *(British*
 architect, Bourneville)   **AV**
 Bibl: Architectural history, 1987,
 v.30, p.154
Harvey, William *(British artist, 1796-*
 1866)   **WC WI**
Harvey, William II   **WI**
 (British artist, op.1900-)   WI
 (British artist, op.c.1900)   WC
 Harvey, William, II   **WC**
Harvey, William, II → *see* Harvey,
 William II
Harvie, R.   **WC WI**
 (British artist, op.1751)   WC
 (British artist, op.1751-)   WI
Harwick of Bath → *see* Harwick, (of
 Bath)
Harwick, (of Bath)   **WI**
 (British artist, 19th cent.)   WC
 (British artist, op.19th c.)   WI
 Harwick of Bath   **WC**
Harwill, F., Mrs. *(British artist, op.*
 19th c.)   **WI**
Harwood, E. Lucy *(British painter,*
 1893-1972)   **BA**
 Bibl: Colchester, LUCY HARWOOD
 (1975) (not in CAI Library as of
 1/90)
Harwood, Edward   **WC WI**
 (British artist, 1814-op.1872)   WI
 (British artist, 1814-p.1872)   WC
 Bibl: Paviere, Brit. sporting ptrs
Harwood, Francis   **BA JG**
 (British sculptor in ITA, act.
 1748-1783)   BA
 (English (worked in Florence)
 active, 1748-1783)   JG
 Bibl: BURLINGTON, CXXII/922 (Jan
 80), p. 65-66; ▸Gunnis, Brit. sculp.
Harwood, Gillian *(British*
 architectural conservationist,
 London)   **AV**
 Bibl: RIBA journal, 1984 Feb.,
 v.91, no.2, p.4
Harwood, Henry   **WC WI**
 (British artist, 1803-1868)   WC
 (British artist, op.1892-1902)   WI
 Bibl: ▸Johnson, Brit. artists
Harwood, James *(British artist,*
 1816-1872)   **WC WI**
Harwood, James Taylor → *see* Taylor,
 Frederick Bourchier
Harwood, John   **WC WI**
 (British artist, op.1818-1829)   WI
 (British artist, op.1829)   WC
Harwood, Robert   **WC WI**
 (British artist, 1830-op.1879)   WI
 (British artist, 1830-p.1876)   WC

Háry, Gyula *(Hungarian painter,*
 printmaker, 1864-1946)   **BA**
Has, Haas, Hase or Hass, Georg
 (German artist, op.1571-1583)   **WC**
Hasbrouck, Wilbert R. *(American*
 architect, Chicago)   **AV**
 Bibl: ▸AIA Pro File, 1985
Hasch, Carl *(German artist, 1834-*
 1897)   **WC**
Hase, A.   **GC WC**
 (Dutch painter, act.1669)   GC
 (Netherlands artist, op.1669)   WC
 Bibl: ▸Bénézit
Hase, Conrad Wilhelm *(German*
 master mason and architect, 1818-
 1902)   **AV**
 Bibl: ▸Macmillan encyc. archts.;
 ▸Thieme-Becker
Hasegawa, Hiroshi *(Japanese*
 architect)   **AV**
 Bibl: Architecture and urbanism,
 1986 Apr., no.4(187), p.12
Hasegawa, Itsuko   **AV BA**
 (Japanese architect, 1941-)   AV
 (Japanese architect, b.1941)   BA
 Bibl: ▸Avery period. idx., suppl.
 7,6; GA houses, 1983 July, no.14,
 p.[194]; Kenchiku bunka, 1987
 Dec., v.42, no.494, p.226
Haselberg, Martin von *(Argentine*
 artist, b.1949)   **BA**
 Bibl: Berkeley (CA, USA), Univ. of
 Cal., Art Mus., Kipper Kids (1979)
Haselden, Celia Mary *(British, b.ca.*
 1908)   **BA**
 Bibl: Burlington, CXXVIII/994 (Jan
 1986) 35
Haselden, Ron *(British artist,*
 b.1944)   **BA WI**
 Bibl: ▸Art Index, v.28; ▸Babington
 Smith, Contemp. artists; ▸Intl. dir.
 exh. artists, 1983, v.1
Haselden, William Kerridge *(British*
 artist, 1872-1953)   **WC WI**
Haseler, H. → *see* Haseler, Henry
Haseler, Henry   **WI**
 (British artist, op.1814-1825)   WC WI
 Haseler, H.   **WC**
Haselhuhn, Werner *(East German*
 painter, b.1925)   **BA**
 Bibl: Fuhrmann, DRESDENER
 KUNSTBLATTER, XXIV/4 (1980),
 p. 121; Heinz, WERNER
 HASELHUHN (1979) (RILA-DDR);
 ▸Vollmer, Künst.-Lex. 20. Jhr.
Haseloff, Horst *(West German*
 architect, Berlin)   **AV**
 Bibl: Baumeister, 1989 Mar., v.86,
 no.3, p.50
Haseltine → *see* Haseltine, William
 Stanley
Haseltine, Herbert *(American*
 sculptor (b. Italy), 1877-1962)   **GC**
 Bibl: ▸Opitz, Amer. sculptors

Haseltine, William Stanley **BA PR WC WI**
 (American artist, 1835-1900)   WC WI
 (American painter, 1835-1900)   BA PR
 (American, 1835-1900)   GC
 Bibl: Coral Gables (FL, USA), Lowe
 Art Mus., 19c. Amer. topographic
 ptrs. (1975); ▸Dict. Amer. biog.;
 ▸Fielding's Amer. ptrs.; ▸Groce,
 Artists Amer.; ▸RILA/BHA;
 ▸Thieme-Becker
 Haseltine   PR
 Haseltine, William Stanley N.A.   **GC**
 William Stanley Haseltine   PR
Haseltine, William Stanley N.A. → *see*
 Haseltine, William Stanley
Hasemann, Arminius *(German*
 sculptor, printmaker, b.1888)   **BA**
 Bibl: ▸Bénézit; Ludwig,
 WELTKUNST, LIII (Jan 1983);
 ▸Thieme-Becker
Hasemann, Wilhelm   **GC**
 (German artist, 1850-1913)   WC
 (German painter, 1850-1913)   GC
 Bibl: ▸Thieme-Becker
Hasemann, Wilhelm Gustav
 Friedrich   **WC**
Hasemann, Wilhelm Gustav
 Friedrich → *see* Hasemann, Wilhelm
Hasen, Bert Stanly *(American*
 painter, b.1921)   **BA**
 Bibl: ▸WW Amer. Art, 1986
Hasenauer, Karl Freiherr von → *see*
 Hasenauer, Karl von
Hasenauer, Karl von   **BA**
 (Austrian architect, 1833-1894)   BA
 (German artist, 1833-1894)   WC
 Bibl: ▸Brockhaus Enzyk.;
 ▸Thieme-Becker
 Hasenauer, Karl Freiherr von   **WC**
Hasenclever → *see* Hasenclever,
 Johann Peter
Hasenclever, Johann
 Peter   **BA GC PR WC**
 (German artist, 1810-1853)   WC
 (German painter, 1810-
 1853)   BA GC PR
 Bibl: ▸Bénézit; ▸Brockhaus Enzyk.;
 ▸Natl. union cat., 1956;
 ▸RILA/BHA; ▸Thieme-Becker
 Hasenclever   PR
 Johann Peter Hasenclever   PR
Hasenpflug, Carl Georg
 Adolph   **BA GC WC**
 (German artist, 1802-1858)   WC
 (German painter, 1802-1858)   BA GC
 Bibl: ▸Bénézit; ▸Neue deutsche
 Biog.; ▸Thieme-Becker
Hasfelt, N. *(Dutch painter, 17th*
 century)   **GC**
 Bibl: Getty Photo Study Coll.
 (Duits coll.)
Hashagen, A.   **WC WI**
 (American artist, 19th cent.)   WC
 (American artist, op.1847-)   WI
Hashimoto, Fumitaka *(Japanese*
 architect, 1940-)   **AV**
 Bibl: GA houses, n.14, July 1983,
 p.114

Hashimoto, Yoshimi *(Japanese*
sculptor in DEU, b.1949)   **BA**
  Bibl: Coburg (DEU), Kunstsamm.
  Veste Coburg, Bildhauer d. 20.
  jahrh. (1982)
Hashmy, Kalija *(American architect)*   **AV**
Hasior, Wladyslaw *(Polish sculptor,*
b.1928)   **BA**
  Bibl: ▶Bénézit; ▶MoMA libr. cat.;
  Porto (PRT), Mus. Nac. de Soares
  des Reis, Pintura Polaca (1976)
Haske, Joseph *(American painter,*
20th c.)   **BA**
  Bibl: ▶Intl. dir. exh. artists, 1983;
  Madoff, S.H., in ARTS MAG
  LVIII/6 (Feb 1984) 138
Haskell, Ernest   **BA WC WI**
(American artist, 1876-1925)   **WC WI**
(American painter, printmaker,
1876-1925)   **BA**
  Bibl: ▶Fielding's Amer. ptrs.;
  Haskell, Permanent Collections,
  1948; ▶Vollmer, Künst.-Lex. 20.
  Jhr.
Haskell, John Gideon *(American*
architect, 1832-1907)   **BA**
  Bibl: Peterson, JOHN G. HASKELL,
  1984; ▶Thieme-Becker; ▶Withey,
  Amer. archts.
Haskell, Llewllyn S. *(1815-1872)*   **AV**
Haskell, Samuel Stevens *(Canadian*
architect, d. 1913)   **AV**
  Bibl: ARQ: Architecture/Quebec,
  1986 June, no.31, p.14
Haslam, Nicholas *(British interior*
designer)   **AV**
  Bibl: Architectural digest, 1986
  Feb., v.43, no.2, p.54
Haslbägck, Franz   **GC WC**
(German artist, op.1497)   **WC**
(German, act.1497)   **GC**
  Bibl: ▶Witt checklist
Hasledine, P. *(British artist, op.20th*
c.)   **WI**
Haslehurst, C. *(British artist, op.18th*
c.)   **WI**
Haslehurst, Ernest W. → see
  Haslehurst, Ernest William
Haslehurst, Ernest William   **WI**
(British artist, 1866-1949)   **WC WI**
Haslehurst, Ernest W.   **WC**
Hasler, Ottmar *(Austrian architect,*
Vienna and Lackendorf)   **AV**
  Bibl: Baumeister, 1986 Dec., v.83,
  no.12, p.46
Häsler, Rudolf *(Swiss painter,*
b.1927)   **BA**
  Bibl: RUDOLF HASLER: LIFE AND
  WORK (1982) (RILA-CHE)
Haslock, J.   **WC WI**
(British artist, 19th cent.)   **WC**
(British artist, b.1868)   **WI**
Haslund, Otto Carl Bentzon
(Danish artist, 1842-1917)   **WC**
Haspel von Biberach, Jorg *(German*
artist, 15th cent.)   **WC**

Hassall, John   **BA WC WI**
(British artist, 1868-1948)   **WC WI**
(British painter, illustrator,
designer, 1868-1948)   **BA**
  Bibl: ▶Thieme-Becker; ▶Waters,
  Brit. artists; ▶Who was who
  [GBR], 1941-50
Hassam → see Hassam, Childe
Hassam, Alfred *(British artist, op.*
1865-1897)   **WI**
Hassam, Childe   **BA GC PR WC**
(American artist, 1859-1935)   **WC WI**
(American painter, 1859-1935)   **PR**
(American painter, printmaker,
1859-1935)   **BA**
(American, 1859-1935)   **GC**
  Bibl: Baigell, Dict. Amer. art;
  ▶Britannica encyc. Amer. art;
  Clark Art Inst. Libr.; Hoopes,
  CHILDE HASSAM, p. 9; ▶Oxford
  comp. 20c. art; ▶Phaidon 20c.
  art; ▶RILA/BHA; ▶Thieme-Becker;
  ▶Witt checklist; ▶WWW Amer.
  art
    Childe Hassam   PR
    Hassam   PR
Hassam, Frederick Childe   **BA PR WI**
    Hassam, Frederick Childs   PR
Hassam, Frederick Childe → see
  Hassam, Childe
Hassam, Frederick Childs → see
  Hassam, Childe
Hasse, Christian *(East German*
painter, printmaker, b.1931)   **BA**
  Bibl: Claussnitzer, G.: CHRISTIAN
  HASSE, 1985
Hasse, Marquard, the elder
(Estonian sculptor, act.1426-1446)   **BA**
  Bibl: Bonsdorff, Konsthist.
  Tidskrift, LVI/3 (1987) pp.96-113
Hasse, Sella *(German painter,*
printmaker, 1878-1963)   **BA**
  Bibl: Berlin, East, Nat'l. Gal.;
  ▶Thieme-Becker; ▶Vollmer,
  Künst.-Lex. 20. Jhr.
Hassebrauk, Ernst   **BA WC**
(German artist, 1905-)   **WC**
(German painter, 1905-1974)   **BA**
  Bibl: Dresden (DDR), Staatl.
  Kunstsammlungen, exhib. Feb-Apr
  1979; ▶Kindlers Malerei Lex.;
  ▶Vollmer, Künst.-Lex. 20. Jhr.
Hassel or Hassells, Werner
(Warner) *(German artist, op.1674-*
1707)   **WC**
Hassel, William *(British artist, op.*
1770)   **WC**
Hasselbach, W. → see Hasselbach,
  Wilhelm
Hasselbach, Wilhelm *(German*
painter, 1846-aft.1919)   **PR**
  Bibl: ▶Thieme-Becker
    Hasselbach, W.   PR
    Wilhelm Hasselbach   PR

Hasselberg-Olsson, Elisabet
(Swedish weaver, b.1932)   **BA**
  Bibl: National museum Bulletin,
  I/3 (1977), p. 103-113
Hasselgren, Gustaf Erik *(Swedish*
artist, 1781-1827)   **WC**
Hasselhorst, Heinrich (Johann
Heinrich) *(German artist, 1825-*
1904)   **WC**
Hassell, Edward   **AV WC WI**
(British artist, 1777-1852)   **WC**
(British artist, 1811-1852)   **WI**
(British designer)   **AV**
  Bibl: Country life, 1984 Oct.11,
  v.176, no.4547, p.1028
Hassell, F. Colin *(Australian*
architect)   **AV**
Hassell, John   **WC WI**
(British artist, 1767-1825)   **WI**
(British artist, op.1789-m.1825)   **WC**
Hasselmann Painter   **GC**
  Bibl: ▶Beazley, Attic red-fig. vase-
  ptrs.
Hasselqvist, Arne *(Swedish*
architect, lives in Mustique)   **AV**
  Bibl: Architectural digest, 1985
  Oct., v.42, no.10, p.150
Hasselt → see Hasselt, Izak van
Hasselt, Bertha *(Dutch painter,*
1878-1932)   **GC**
  Bibl: ▶Vollmer, Künst.-Lex. 20. Jhr.
Hasselt, Isaak van → see Hasselt, Izak
  van
Hasselt, Izaak van → see Hasselt, Izak
  van
Hasselt, Izak van   **PR**
(Dutch painter, 17th century)   **GC**
(Dutch painter, act. mid 17th
cent.)   **PR**
  Bibl: George Goldner; Getty Photo
  Study Coll.; ▶Thieme-Becker
    Hasselt   PR
    Hasselt, Isaak van   PR
Hasselt, Izaak van   **GC PR**
    Izak van Hasselt   PR
Hasselt, J.C. van *(Netherlands artist,*
op.1659)   **WC**
Hasselt, Wilhelmus Josephus (Willem)
van → see Hasselt, Willem van
Hasselt, Willem van   **GC**
(Dutch artist, 1882-1963)   **WC**
(Dutch painter, 1882-1963)   **GC**
  Bibl: ▶Bénézit
Hasselt, Wilhelmus Josephus
(Willem) van   **WC**
Hassinger, Herman *(American*
architect)   **AV**
  Bibl: ▶AIA Pro File, 1985
Hassinger, Maren *(American*
sculptor, b.1947)   **BA**
  Bibl: Los Angeles (CA, USA),
  Municipal Art Gallery, Afro-Amer.
  abstraction (1982)

Hasslett, van [Unidentified]
(Unknown painter) **PR**
 Bibl: (June 9, 1804, lot 62,
  Christie's)
 Van Hasslett **PR**
Hasslwander, Josef *(German artist,*
1812-1878) **WC**
Hassunt, Giovan Battista
 [Unidentified] *(Unknown painter)* **PR**
 Bibl: Riccardi inventory dated
  1776
 Giovan Battista Hassunt **PR**
Hastain, Eugene **WC WI**
 (British artist, op.1907) **WC**
 (British artist, op.1907-) **WI**
Haste, David *(British artist, b.1938)* **WI**
Hasted, Edward *(British artist, op.*
1778-1799) **WC WI**
Hasted, Michael *(British painter,*
20th c.) **BA**
 Bibl: Hasted, LEONARDO, XIII/3
  (summer 1980), p. 186-191
Hasten, Frank **WC WI**
 (British artist, 19th cent.) **WC**
 (British artist, op.19th c.) **WI**
Hastenbergh **GC**
 (Dutch artist, op.1651-1660) **WC**
 (Dutch painter, act.1651-1660) **GC**
 Bibl: Getty Photo Study Coll.;
  ▶Witt checklist
Hastenbergh or Hastenburg **WC**
Hastenbergh or Hastenburg→see
 Hastenbergh
Hastenteufel, Dieter *(Canadian*
sculptor, b.1939) **BA**
 Bibl: ▶Artists Canada; ▶WW
  Amer. Art
Hastings, Amelia *(British sculptor,*
20th c.) **BA**
 Bibl: Cookham (GBR), Vicarage,
  Impact (1979)
Hastings, Diane *(American architect,*
San Antonio, Tex) **AV**
 Bibl: Texas architect, 1989 Mar.-
  Apr., v.39, no.2, p.54
Hastings, Edward **WC WI**
 (British artist, op.1804-1827) **WC**
 (British artist, op.1804-1861) **WI**
Hastings, Henry *(English, ca.1630-*
1649) **BA**
 Bibl: Approaches to Marvell
  Heininger: Marvell's 'Geometrick
  Year' p.87-107
Hastings, Hugh *(English, ca.1307-*
1347) **BA**
 Bibl: ▶Dict. natl. biog.; Pevsner
  NW & S Norfolk, 155
 Hastyngs, Hugh de **BA**
Hastings, I. **WC WI**
 (British artist, op.1829) **WC**
 (British artist, op.1829-) **WI**
Hastings, Rafael *(Peruvian artist,*
20th c.) **BA**
 Bibl: ▶Bénézit; Jrnl./So. Cal. Art
  Mag., (Nov.-Dec. 1979)

Hastings, Thomas **AV BA**
 (1860-1929) **AV**
 (American architect, 1860-1929) **BA**
 Bibl: ▶Avery obit. idx.;
  ▶Thieme-Becker
Hastings, Thomas **WI**
 (British artist, op.1804-1831) **WI**
 (British artist, op.1813-1831) **WC**
Hastings, Thomas (Captain
 Thomas) **WC**
Hastings, Thomas (Captain
 Thomas)→see Hastings, Thomas
Hastings, Warren *(British artist,*
1732-1818) **WI**
Hastner→see Hastner, Hieronymus
Hastner, Hieronymus **GC PR**
 (Italian artist, 1665-1729) **WC**
 (Italian painter, 1665-1729) **PR**
 (Italian, 1665-1729) **GC**
 Bibl: Getty Photo Study Coll.
  (Ptgs.); ▶Thieme-Becker
 Corazza **PR**
 Hastner **PR**
Hastner, Hieronymus (il
 Corazza) **GC WC**
 Hieronymus Hastner **PR**
 [N...] Corazza **PR**
Hastner, Hieronymus (il
 Corazza)→see Hastner,
 Hieronymus
Hastwell, Vincent Edward *(British*
architect) **AV**
Hastyngs, Hugh de→see Hastings,
 Hugh
Hasucha, Christian *(German artist,*
b.1955) **BA**
 Bibl: London (GBR), Goethe Inst.,
  Young German artists (1982)
Hata, Seiichi *(Japanese architect)* **AV**
 Bibl: Space design, 1985 Oct., no.
  253
Hatakeyama, Hiroshige *(Japanese*
architect) **AV**
 Bibl: Japan architect, 1982 Oct.,
  v.57, no.306, p.53
Hatch, C. **WC WI**
 (British artist, op.1855) **WC**
 (British artist, op.1855-) **WI**
Hatch, George W. *(Engraver, 1805-*
1867) **WI**
Hatch, Hatty **AV**
Hatch, John Davis *(American*
architect, 1826-1875) **BA**
 Bibl: ANTIQUES, Apr 1980, p.
  868-879
Hatch, John Woodsum *(American*
painter, b.1919) **BA**
 Bibl: Durham (NH, USA), Univ. of
  N.H., Univ. Art Galleries, JOHN W.
  HATCH..., 1985; ▶WW Amer. Art
Hatch, Louise E. *(American artist,*
b.1951) **WI**

Hatch, Tom *(American artist,*
b.1950) **BA**
 Bibl: ▶Artist biog. master idx.;
  New York (NY, USA), New Mus.,
  Outside NY (1978)
Hatch, Will A. *(American*
photographer, b.1875) **BA**
 Bibl: Buffalo (NY, USA), Albright-
  Knox, Photo-pictorialists (1981)
Hatcher, Gary C. *(American potter,*
20th c.) **BA**
 Bibl: Ceramics monthly, XXVIII
  (1980)
Hatcher, L. Brower *(American*
sculptor, 20th c.) **BA**
 Bibl: ▶Art Index, v.46, no.3
Hatcliffe, William *(English, 16th c.)* **BA**
Hateley, Edward→see Haytley,
 Edward
Hatfield, Charles *(American*
sculptor, 20th century) **GC**
 Bibl: Juley coll., NMAA
Hatfield, Robert *(English painter,*
17th c.) **BA**
 Bibl: Jrnl. Walters Art Gall.,
  XXXVIII (1980) pp.6-33
Hath **WC WI**
 (British artist, 18th cent.) **WC**
 (British artist, op.18th c.) **WI**
Hathaway→see Hathaway, George
 M.
Hathaway, Carl H. *(American artist,*
1858-1930) **WI**
Hathaway, George M. *(American*
painter, ca.1852-1903) **PR**
 Bibl: ▶WWW Amer. art
 George M. Hathaway **PR**
 Hathaway **PR**
Hathaway, John W. *(American*
stained glass artist, teacher and
lecturer, Philadelphia, Penn, 1906-
1987) **AV**
 Bibl: Stained glass, 1988 Winter,
  v.83, no.4, p.253
Hathaway, Rufus **BA PR WC WI**
 (American artist, 1770-1822) **WC WI**
 (American painter, 1770-1822) **BA PR**
 Bibl: ▶Groce, Artists Amer.;
  ▶RILA/BHA; ▶Young, Amer. artists
 Rufus Hathaway **PR**
Hatherell, William **WC WI**
 (British artist, 1855-) **WC**
 (British artist, 1855-1928) **WI**
Hatherly, Ana *(Portuguese poet,*
artist, cinematographer, b.1929) **BA**
 Bibl: ▶Tannock, Port. 20c. artists
Hathorn, George T. →see Hathorne,
 George
Hathorne, George **BA**
 (American architect) **AV**
 (American architect, d.1889) **BA**
 Bibl: ▶Avery obit. idx.; Dict.
  American Archs.; ▶WWW Amer.
Hathorn, George T. **AV**

Hatløy, Svein *(Norwegian architect,*
Bergen)   **AV**
   Bibl: Byggekunst, 1984, no.6,
   p.319

Hatmanu, Dan *(Rumanian artist,*
1926-)   **WC**

Hatt, Emilie Demant *(Danish*
painter, 1873-1958)   **BA**
   Bibl: ▶Bénézit; Dam, DANSKE
   MALER-SIGNATURER (1945);
   ▶Natl. union cat., pre-1956; Skive
   (DNK) Museum, EMILIE DEMANT
   HATT, 1983; ▶Thieme-Becker;
   ▶Vollmer, Künst.-Lex. 20. Jhr.;
   ▶Weilbach, Kunst.leks.

Hattemore, Archibald   **WC WI**
   (British artist, 20th cent.)   WC
   (British artist, op.1926-1930)   WI

Hatten, Tom *(American sculptor,*
20th c.)   **BA**

Hattich → see Hattich, Petrus van
Hattich or Hattick, Petrus or Pieter
van → see Hattich, Petrus van
Hattich, Petrus → see Hattich, Petrus
van

Hattich, Petrus van   **PR**
   (Dutch artist, op.1646-1665)   WC
   (Dutch painter, bef.1620-aft.
   1665)   PR
   (Dutch painter, ca.1620-aft.
   1665)   GC
     Bibl: Getty Photo Study Coll.;
     ▶Thieme-Becker
   Hattich   PR
Hattich or Hattick, Petrus or
Pieter van   **WC**
Hattich, Petrus   **GC**
   Hattick, Petrus van   PR
   Petrus van Hattich   PR
Hattick, Petrus van → see Hattich,
Petrus van

Hattingh, Peter *(South African*
architect)   **AV**
   Bibl: UIA international architect,
   1985, no.8, inside back cover

Hatton, Brian   **BA WC WI**
   (British artist, 1887-1916)   WC WI
   (British painter, 1887-1916)   BA
   Bibl: ▶Johnson, Brit. artists;
   ▶Waters, Brit. artists

Hatton, Helen Howard   **WI**
   (British artist, 1860-op.1904)   WI
   (British artist, op.1895)   WC
Hatton, Helen Howard (Helen
Margetson)   **WC**
   Margetson, William Henry, Mrs.,
   (Helen)   WI
Hatton, Helen Howard (Helen
Margetson) → see Hatton, Helen
Howard

Hattori, Fuyuki *(Japanese artist,*
b.1955)   **BA**
   Bibl: Geneva (CHE), Musée Rath,
   Art japonais d'aujourd'hui (1983)

Hátvany, Ferenc, baron *(Hungarian*
painter, 1881-1958)   **BA**
   Bibl: ▶Bénézit; ▶Met. Mus. Art
   libr. cat.; ▶Thieme-Becker;
   ▶Vollmer, Künst.-Lex. 20. Jhr.;
   Wethey, El Greco

Hatwell, Anthony *(British sculptor,*
b.1931)   **BA**
   Bibl: Arts Council GBR, Scot.
   Comm., Objects & constructions
   (1978); ▶Bénézit; ▶WW Art, 1977

Hatyseren, Segewyn *(early*
Netherlandish bell founder, act.
1507, d.1540-1547)   **BA**
   Bibl: Dubbe, ANTIEK, XVII/10
   (May 1983), p. 539-542;
   Fehrmann, Dekampfer Klokgieters
   (1967), p. 126-127;
   ▶Thieme-Becker; Wittopkoning,
   NEDERLANDSEVIJZDS (1953), p.
   56-59

Hatz, Felix *(Swedish artist, 1904-)* **WC**
Hatzl, Alexander → see Wasserburger,
C.A. (Alexander Hatzl)

Haub, Christian *(American painter,*
20th c.)   **BA**
   Bibl: ARTS MAG. LV/10 (June
   1981), p. 120-123

Hauben-Ross, Barbara *(American*
interior designer, NYC)   **AV**
   Bibl: Interior design, 1987 Aug.,
   v.58, no.10, p.212

Haubensak, Pierre *(Swiss painter in*
USA, b.1935)   **BA**
   Bibl: ▶Bénézit; ▶MoMA libr. cat.;
   ▶NY art yrbk.

Haubensak, René *(Swiss architect,*
Zurich)   **AV**
   Bibl: Archithese, 1988 Mar.-Par.,
   v.19, no.2, p.57

Hauber, Joseph   **BA GC WC**
   (German artist, 1766-1834)   WC
   (German painter, printmaker,
   1766-1834)   BA
   (German, 1766-1834)   GC
   Bibl: ▶Bénézit; ▶Thieme-Becker;
   ▶Witt checklist

Hauber, Wolfgang *(German artist,*
16th cent.)   **WC**
Hauberisser, Georg → see
Hauberrisser, Georg Ritter von

Hauberrisser, Georg Ritter von
(1841-1922)   **AV**
   Hauberisser, Georg   AV

Häublin, Nicolaus *(German*
printmaker, act.1650-1680)   **BA**
   Bibl: ▶Bénézit; ▶Hollstein, German;
   ▶Thieme-Becker

Hauch, J.M. *(German artist, 18th*
cent.)   **WC**

Hauck or Hauckh, Johann Veit
(German artist, op.1700-1746)   **WC**

Hauck, August Christian *(German*
draughtsman, 1742-1801)   **GC**
   Bibl: ▶Thieme-Becker

Hauck, Friedrich Ludwig *(German*
artist, 1718-1801)   **WC**

Hauck, Inigo Maurice *(British artist,*
op.1761-1767)   **WC WI**
Hauck, J.P.F. *(Swiss artist, op.1752-*
1760)   **WC**

Haudebourg Lescot → see
Haudebourt, Antoinette Cécile
Hortense Lescot
Haudebourt → see Haudebourt,
Antoinette Cécile Hortense Lescot
Haudebourt Lescot → see Haudebourt,
Antoinette Cécile Hortense Lescot

Haudebourt, Antoinette Cécile
Hortense Lescot   **BA GC PR**
   (French artist, 1784-1845)   WC
   (French painter, 1784-1845) BA GC PR
   Bibl: ▶Bellier, Artistes fran.;
   ▶Bénézit; ▶Busse, Maler u.
   Bildhauer 19. Jahr.; Getty Photo
   Study Coll. (Ptgs.); ▶RILA/BHA,
   1987; ▶Thieme-Becker; ▶Witt
   checklist
   Antoinette Cecile Hortense Lescot
   Haudebourt   PR
   Handelbourg-Lescot   GC
   Haudebourg Lescot   PR
   Haudebourt   PR
   Haudebourt Lescot   PR
   Haudebourt-Lescot, Antoine Cécile
   Hortense   GC
Haudebourt-Lescot, Antoine
Cecile Hortense (nee Lescot)   **WC**
   Mselle. Lescot   PR
Haudebourt-Lescot, Antoine Cécile
Hortense → see Haudebourt,
Antoinette Cécile Hortense Lescot
Haudebourt-Lescot, Antoine Cecile
Hortense (nee Lescot) → see
Haudebourt, Antoinette Cécile
Hortense Lescot

Hauduroy, Mark Anthony *(English*
painter, act.1694)   **BA**
   Bibl: ▶Colvin, Brit. archts.

Haueisen, Albert   **BA WC**
   (German artist, 1872-1954)   WC
   (German painter, 1872-1954)   BA
   Bibl: ▶Bénézit; ▶Brockhaus Enzyk.;
   ▶Thieme-Becker

Haueisen, Johannes *(East German*
architect)   **AV**
   Bibl: Architektur der DDR, 1989
   Feb., v.38, no.2, p.22

Hauenstein, Rolf *(Swiss painter,*
printmaker, b.1951)   **BA**
   Bibl: ▶Intl. dir. exh. artists, 1982,
   1983

Hauer family *(German gunsmiths,*
18th-19th cs.)   **BA**
   Bibl: ▶Thieme-Becker; Trenschel,
   KUNST & ANTIQUITATEN, III (May-
   June 1982), p. 62-65

Hauer, Andreas *(German gunsmith,*
1739-1807)   **BA**
   Bibl: ▶Thieme-Becker; Trenschel,
   KUNST UND ANTIQUITATEN, III
   (May-June 1982), p. 62-65

Hauer, Erwin (American sculptor, 20th c.) **BA**
Bibl: Montclair (NJ, USA), Art Mus., Albers (1981)

Hauer, J. Stephan (German gunsmith, 1740-1808) **BA**
Bibl: ▶Thieme-Becker; Trenschel, KUNST UND ANTIQUITATEN, III (May-June 1982), p. 62-65

Hauer, Jean Jacques **BA GC WC**
(French artist, 1751-1829) **WC**
(French painter, 1751-1829) **BA**
(French, 1751-1829) **GC**
Bibl: ▶Bénézit; ▶Thieme-Becker; ▶Witt checklist

Hauer, Stephan II (German gunsmith, 1777-1835) **BA**
Bibl: Trenschel, KUNST & ANTIQUITATEN, III (May-June 1982), p. 62-65

Haufs, Willi (West German architect, Trier) **AV**
Bibl: Der Architekt, 1989 Apr., no.4, p.174

Haufschild, Lutz (Canadian sculptor, originally from West Germany) **AV**
Bibl: Glass studio, 1984, no.34, p.6

Haug, Robert von **GC WC**
(German artist, 1857-1922) **WC**
(German painter, 1857-1922) **GC**
Bibl: ▶Thieme-Becker

Hauge, John Audun (Norwegian sculptor, b.1955) **BA**
Bibl: ▶Norsk Kunstner Leks.

Haugh, George **WC WI**
(British artist, 1756-1827) **WI**
(British artist, op.c.1777-1818) **WC**

Haughton →see Haughton, Moses I

Haughton, Benjamin **WC WI**
(British artist, 1865-1924) **WI**
(British artist, 19th cent.) **WC**

Haughton, David **WC WI**
(British artist, 20th cent.) **WC**
(British artist, b.1924) **WI**

Haughton, Matthew (British artist, 1768-1821) **WI**

Haughton, Moses (I) →see Haughton, Moses I

Haughton, Moses I **WI**
(British artist, 1734-1804) **WC WI**
(British painter, 1734-1804) **PR**
Bibl: ▶Thieme-Becker
Haughton **PR**
Haughton, Moses (I) **PR**
Haughton, Moses, I **WC**
M. Haughton **PR**
Moses Haughton **PR**
Moses Haughton (I) **PR**
Moses Houghton **PR**

Haughton, Moses II **WI**
(British artist, 1772-1774-1848) **WI**
(British artist, c.1772-p.1848) **WC**
Bibl: Mackenzie
Haughton, Moses, II **WC**

Haughton, Moses, I →see Haughton, Moses I
Haughton, Moses, II →see Haughton, Moses II

Haukeland, Alf (Norwegian landscape architect, 1955-) **AV**
Bibl: Byggekunst: the Norwegian review of architecture, 1988, v.70, no.5, p.360

Haul du Jardin →see Dujardin, Karel

Haunold, Karl (German artist, 1832-1911) **WC**

Haupers, Clement Bernard (American painter, printmaker, b.1900) **BA**
Bibl: ▶Bénézit; ▶Havlice, Idx. art. bio.; ▶Vollmer, Künst.-Lex. 20. Jhr.; ▶WW Amer. Art, 1947

Haupt, Friedrich (German artist, 1940-) **WC**

Haupt, Georg **BA GC JG**
(Swedish cabinetmaker, 1741-1784) **BA**
(Swedish ébéniste, 1741-1784) **GC**
(Swedish, 1741-1784) **JG**
Bibl: ▶Salverte, Ébénistes 18e s.; ▶Svenskt konst.-lex.; ▶Thieme-Becker
Haupt, Georges **GC**
Haupt, Georges →see Haupt, Georg

Haupt, Herman (American architect, engineer, 1817-1905) **AV**
Bibl: ▶Libr. of Congr. Name Auth. File

Haupt, Otto (German architect, 1891-1966) **BA**
Bibl: Karlsruhe (DEU), Staat. Kunsthalle, Fridericiana (1975), p.121

Haupt, Zygmunt (Polish artist, 20th cent.) **WC**

Hauptmann, Eugenie, (nee Sommer) (Austrian artist, 1865-) **WC**

Hauptmann, Georg Anton (German master builder, 19th cent) **AV**
Bibl: Architectur der DDR, 1989 Apr., v.38, no.4, p.14

Hauptmann, Ivo **BA WC**
(German artist, 1886-) **WC**
(German painter, printmaker, 1886-1973) **BA**
Bibl: ▶Bénézit; ▶Fogg Mus. Libr. cat.; Hamburg (BRD), Altonaer Museum, IVO HAUPTMANN (1886-1973): AQUARELLE UND ZEICHNUNGER (1976); Kunstwerk, XXVI (Nov. 1973), p.79; ▶Vollmer, Künst.-Lex. 20. Jhr.

Hauptmann, K. (German artist, op. 1931) **WC**

Hauptmann, Susette (nee Hummel) (French artist, 1811-1890) **WC**

Hauptner →see Hauptner, Ferdinand

Hauptner, Ferdinand (German painter, act. 1828-1846) **PR**
Bibl: ▶Thieme-Becker
Ferdinand Hauptner **PR**
Hauptner **PR**

Haure →see Hauré, Jean

Hauré, Jean (French sculptor, act. ca.1774-1796) **GC**
Bibl: Watson, Wallace Coll.
Haure **JG**

Hauron, Louis Ducos du →see Ducos du Hauron, Louis

Haus, H.M. (Dutch painter, act.1835-d.1841) **GC**
Bibl: ▶Wurzbach, NLD Künst.-Lex.

Haus, Rudolf (German artist, 20th cent.) **WC**

Hausbuchmeister →see Master of the Housebook

Hausch, Alexander Fjodorowitsch (Russian painter, b. 1873) **PR**
Bibl: ▶Thieme-Becker
Alexander Fjodorowitsch Hausch **PR**
Hausch, Alexandr F. **PR**
Hausch, Alexsandr F. **PR**

Hausch, Alexandr F. →see Hausch, Alexander Fjodorowitsch
Hausch, Alexsandr F. →see Hausch, Alexander Fjodorowitsch

Hauschild, Max (German artist, 1907-1961) **WC**

Hauschild, P. Moritz (American architect) **AV**

Hauschild, Wilhelm Ernst Ferdinand Franz (German artist, 1827-1887) **WC**

Häuselmayer, Otto (Austrian architect, Vienna, 1943-) **AV**
Bibl: Bauforum, 1985, v.18, no. 112, p.9

Hauseman (German(?) painter, 17th century(?)) **GC**
Bibl: Getty Photo Study Coll. (Duits coll.)

Hauser, Dieter (German architect, 1936-) **AV**
Bibl: Deutsche Bauzeitung, 1979 May, v.113, no.5, p.108

Hauser, Friedrich (German sculptor, 19th c.) **BA**

Hauser, Johann (Austrian artist, b.1926) **BA**
Bibl: Bremen (DEU), Kunsthalle, Aspekte der Zeichnung (1980)

Hauser, John (American artist, 1858-1913) **WI**

Hauserman, Charles (Swiss artist, 20th cent.) **WC**

Hausermann, Pascal (Swiss architect, b.1936) **BA**
Bibl: ▶Art Index, 1971-1973; ▶Avery period. idx.; ▶Oudin, Dict. architectes

Haushofer, Maximilian   **BA WC**
    (German artist, 1811-1866)   WC
    (German painter, 1811-1866)   BA
    Bibl: ▶Bénézit; ▶Thieme-Becker
Hauslab, Franz Edler von (German
    artist, 1749-1820)   WC
Häusler, Hans (Austrian architect,
    Vienna)   AV
    Bibl: ▶Verzeich. Öst. Ziviltech.
Hausman→see Huysmans, Cornelis
Hausmann→see Huysmans, Cornelis
Hausmann, Friedrich Karl (German
    artist, 1825-1886)   WC
Hausmann, Gustav (German artist,
    1827-1899)   WC
Hausmann, Raoul   **BA JG WC**
    (Austrian painter, sculptor,
      author, 1886-1971)   BA
    (Austrian, 1886-1971)   JG
    (French artist, 1886-1971)   WC
    Bibl: ▶Bénézit; ▶MoMA libr. cat.;
    ▶Vollmer, Künst.-Lex. 20. Jhr.
Hausmann, Ruprecht (German
    architect, 1936-)   AV
    Bibl: Deutsche Bauzeitung, 1981
    Oct., v.115, no.10, p.138
Hausmann-Kohlmann, Hanna
    (German painter, b.1897)   BA
    Bibl: ▶Vollmer, Künst.-Lex. 20. Jhr.
Hausner, Rudolf   **BA WC**
    (Austrian painter, b.1914)   BA
    (German artist, 1914-)   WC
    Bibl: ▶MoMA libr. cat.; ▶Vollmer,
    Künst.-Lex. 20. Jhr.; ▶WW Austria
Hauss, Gerhard (West German
    architect, Heidelberg)   AV
    Bibl: ▶Bund Deut. Arch. Hdbch.,
    1987
Haussard, Jean→see Haussard, Jean-
    Baptiste
Haussard, Jean Baptiste→see
    Haussard, Jean-Baptiste
Haussard, Jean-Baptiste   **WI**
    (Engraver, 1679-1749)   WI
    (Engraver, op.circa 1679-)   WI
    (French artist, 1679-1767)   WC
    Haussard, Jean   **WI**
    Haussard, Jean Baptiste   **WC**
Hausser von Aachen, Johann→see
    Hausser, Johann
Hausser von Ach, Johannes→see
    Hausser, Johann
Häusser, Elias David (German
    architect, 1687-1745)   BA
Hausser, Johann   **GC**
    (German artist, op.1603)   WC
    (German painter, act.1603)   GC
    Bibl: ▶Schweers, Gemälde deut.
    Museen; ▶Thieme-Becker
    Hausser von Aachen, Johann   **WC**
    Hausser von Ach, Johannes   GC
Häusser, Robert (German
    photographer, b.1924)   BA
    Bibl: ▶Contemp. photogs.
Haussman→see Huysmans, Cornelis

Haussmann or Hausmann, Elisa
    Gottlob or Gottlieb→see
    Haussmann, Elias Gottlob
Haussmann, Elias Gottlob   **BA GC**
    (German artist, 1695-1774)   WC
    (German painter, 1695-1774)   BA GC
    Bibl: ▶Bénézit; ▶Thieme-Becker;
    ▶Witt checklist

Haussmann or Hausmann, Elisa
    Gottlob or Gottlieb   **WC**
Haussmann, Georges Eugène,
    baron   **AV BA**
    (1809-1891)   AV
    (French public official, city
      planner, 1809-1891)   BA
    Bibl: ▶Columbia encyc.
Haussmann, Robert (German
    architect, 1931-)   AV
    Bibl: Bauwelt, 1985 Mar.15, v.76,
    no.11, p.373
Haussmann-Högl, Trix (German
    architect, 1933-)   AV
    Bibl: Bauwelt, 1985 Mar.15, v.76,
    no.11, p.373
Haussoullier, W. (French artist,
    1818-1891)   WC
Haussy, Arsene Desire di (French
    artist, 1830-p.1870)   WC
Hauteuil [Unidentified] (Unknown
    painter)   PR
    Bibl: Simon Cornu inventory,
    dated 1644 (item 54)
Hauth, Emil van (German artist,
    1899-)   WC
Hautreu [Unidentified] (Unknown
    painter)   PR
    Bibl: Clary inventory dated 1828
    Kautreu   PR
Hautt, David Nikolaus (Swiss
    engraver, printer, act.1636-1657)   BA
    Bibl: ▶Bénézit; ▶Schweiz.
    Künst.-Lex.; ▶Thieme-Becker
Hautt, Nikolaus (Swiss printmaker,
    cartographer, printer, 1641-after
    1675)   BA
    Bibl: ▶Bénézit; ▶Schweiz.
    Künst.-Lex.; ▶Thieme-Becker
Hauvette, Christian (French
    architect, 1944-)   AV
    Bibl: ▶Annuaire archts. fran.,
    1978
Hauwede, Herbert (German artist,
    1912-)   WC
Hauwiller, Joseph Wolfgang
    (Alsatian painter, 1709-1786)   BA
    Bibl: ▶Bénézit; Ludmann, CAHIERS
    ALSAC. D'ARCH. D'ART..., XXV
    (1982), p. 125; ▶Thieme-Becker
Hauxner, Jørgen (Danish architect,
    20th c.)   BA
    Bibl: Arkitekten LXXXV/2 (1983)
    25-32
Hauzinger or Hautzinger, Josef
    (German artist, 1728-c.1786)   WC

Havana Group (Sicilian vase-
    painters)   GC
    Bibl: ▶Trendall, Red-fig. vases
    Lucania
Havard, James Pinkney   **BA WI**
    (American artist, b.1937)   WI
    (American painter, b.1937)   BA
    Bibl: ▶NY art yrbk.; ▶WW Amer.
    Art, 1976
Havart, Adriana (Netherlandish(?),
    18th century)   GC
    Bibl: Sotheby's Amsterdam
Havas, Anikó Z. (Hungarian
    architect)   AV
    Bibl: Architektur + Wettbewerbe,
    1986 Dec., no.128, p.19
Havas, Heikki (Finnish
    photographer(?))   AV
    Bibl: Arkkitehti, 1989, v.86, no.2,
    p.72
Have, Henrik (Danish painter,
    b.1946)   BA
    Bibl: Hrymfaxe XIV, 2 (July 1984)
    15-21; ▶Intl. dir. exh. artists,
    1982
Havelaar, A. (Netherlands artist,
    17th/18th cent.)   WC
Havelka, Josef Ignac (Russian artist,
    1716-1788)   WC
Havelka, Roman (Czech painter,
    1877-1950)   BA
    Bibl: Hodonin (CSK), Galerie,
    ROMAN HAVELKS, 1977;
    ▶Vollmer, Künst.-Lex. 20. Jhr.
Havell→see Havell, William
Havell, Alfred Charles (British artist,
    1855-1928)   WI
Havell, Charles Richards (British
    artist, op.1858-1866)   WC WI
Havell, Daniel   **WC WI**
    (British artist, 1785-1826)   WI
    (British artist, op.1810-m.
      1826(?))   WC
Havell, Edmund I   **WI**
    (British artist, op.1814-, d.1853)   WI
    (British artist, op.1814-m.1853)   WC
    Havell, Edmund, I   **WC**
Havell, Edmund II   **WI**
    (British artist, 1819-1894)   WI
    (British artist, 1819-p.1895)   WC
    Bibl: ▶Foskett, Brit. miniature ptrs.
    Havell, Edmund, II   **WC**
Havell, Edmund, I→see Havell,
    Edmund I
Havell, Edmund, II→see Havell,
    Edmund II
Havell, George (British artist, op.
    1826-1833)   WC WI

Havell, Robert   **BA PR**
(American painter, 1793-1878)   PR
(American printmaker, painter,
    1793-1878)   BA
(British artist, 1793-1878)   WC
(British artist, engraver, 1793-
    1878)   WI
(Engraver, 1793-1878)   WI
    Bibl: Coral Gables (FL, USA), Lowe
    Art Mus., 19c. Amer. topographic
    ptrs. (1975); ▶Fielding's Amer.
    ptrs., suppl.; ▶Groce, Artists
    Amer.; ▶RILA/BHA; ▶Young,
    Amer. artists
Havell, Robert (Jr.)   PR
Havell, Robert II   **WI**
Havell, Robert, II   **WC**
Havell, Robert, Jr.   **WI**
Robert Havell   PR
Havell, Robert (Jr.) → see Havell,
    Robert
Havell, Robert I   **WI**
(British artist, 1769-1832)   WI
(British artist, a.1793-1832)   WC
(Engraver)   WI
Havell, Robert, I   **WC**
Havell, Robert, Sr.   **WI**
Havell, Robert II → see Havell, Robert
Havell, Robert, I → see Havell, Robert I
Havell, Robert, II → see Havell, Robert
Havell, Robert, Jr. → see Havell,
    Robert
Havell, Robert, Sr. → see Havell,
    Robert I
Havell, William   **BA PR WC WI**
(British artist, 1782-1857)   WC WI
(British painter, 1782-1857)   BA PR
    Bibl: ▶Dict. natl. biog.; ▶Redgrave,
    Engl. school; ▶RILA/BHA; ▶Witt
    checklist
Havell   PR
William Havell   PR
Havelock, Helen   **WC WI**
(British artist, 18th cent.)   WC
(British artist, op.18th c.)   WI
Haven, Frank de → see Haven, Franklin
    de
Haven, Franklin de   **WI**
(American artist, 1856-1934)   WC WI
(American painter, 1856-1934)   PR
    Bibl: ▶WWW Amer. art
De Haven   PR
De Haven, Franklin   **PR**
Dehaven, Franklin   PR
Franklin De Haven   PR
Haven, Frank de   **WC**

Haven, Lambert van   **BA**
(Danish architect, painter, 1630-
    1695)   AV
(Norwegian architect, painter in
    DNK, 1630-1695)   BA
(Norwegian artist, 1630-1695)   WC
(Scandinavian, 1630-1695)   GC
    Bibl: ▶Norsk Kunstner Leks.;
    ▶Thieme-Becker; ▶Weilbach,
    Kunst.leks.
Haven, Lambert von   **AV GC WC**
Haven, Lambert von → see Haven,
    Lambert van
Haven, Michael von   **GC WC**
(Norwegian artist, 1625-
    1683(?))   WC
(Norwegian, d. ca.1683)   GC
    Bibl: ▶Thieme-Becker; ▶Witt
    checklist
Havenhand, Andrew (British
    painter, b.1957)   BA
    Bibl: Arts Council GBR, Welsh
    Comm., Coming out (1979)
Havenith, Hugo (German artist,
    1853-)   WC
Haver, Jean Jacques (French, act.
    1795)   GC
    Bibl: ▶Thieme-Becker
Haverford Painter (Apulian vase-
    painter)   GC
    Bibl: Trendall, Attic red-fig. vases
    Apulia
Haverington, Joan de → see
    Harrington, Joan
Haverington, John de → see
    Harrington, John
Haverkamp, Gerhard   **GC**
(Dutch artist, 1872-1926)   WC
(Dutch draughtsman and
    printmaker, 1872-1926)   GC
    Bibl: ▶Vollmer, Künst.-Lex. 20. Jhr.
**Haverkamp, Gerhard Christiaan
    (Gerrit)**   **WC**
Haverkamp, Gerhard Christiaan
    (Gerrit) → see Haverkamp, Gerhard
Havermaet, Charles van (British
    artist, op.1895-1911)   WI
Haverman → see Haverman,
    Margareta
Haverman, Hendrick Johannes → see
    Haverman, Hendrik Johannes
Haverman, Hendrik Johannes   **BA GC**
(Dutch artist, 1857-1928)   WC
(Dutch draughtsman and
    printmaker, 1857-1928)   GC
(Dutch painter, printmaker,
    1857-1928)   BA
    Bibl: ▶Bénézit; ▶Scheen, Ned.
    beeldende kunst.;
    ▶Thieme-Becker; ▶Witt checklist
Haverman, Hendrick Johannes   **WC**

Haverman, Margareta   **GC PR**
(Dutch painter, act. 1716-1722)   PR
(Dutch painter, act.1716- d. ca.
    1795)   GC
    Bibl: ▶Thieme-Becker
Haverman   PR
Margareta Haverman   PR
Havers, Alice   **WI**
(British artist, 1850-1890)   WC WI
Havers, Alice (Alice Morgan)   **WC**
Morgan, Frederick, Mrs.(Alice
    Mary)   WI
Havers, Alice (Alice Morgan) → see
    Havers, Alice
Haverty, Joseph Patrick   **BA WC WI**
(British artist, 1794-1864)   WC WI
(Irish painter, 1794-1864)   BA
    Bibl: ▶Strickland, Irish artists
Havik, Torgeir (Norwegian
    architect)   AV
    Bibl: Byggekunst, 1988, v.70,
    no.2, p.106
Haviland, Charles Édouard (French
    porcelain manufacturer, 1839-
    1921)   BA
    Bibl: Lesur & Tardy, Poteries et
    faiences françaises (1969); ▶Libr.
    of Congr. Name Auth. File
Haviland, Harriet M., Miss   **WI**
(British artist, op.1864)   WC
(British artist, op.1864-)   WI
Haviland, Miss Harriet M.   **WC**
Haviland, John   **AV BA**
(American architect, 1792-1852)   BA
(American Greek Revival
    architect, 1792-1852)   AV
    Bibl: ▶Avery obit. idx.; ▶Libr. of
    Congr. Name Auth. File; ▶WWW
    Amer., 1607
Haviland, Miss Harriet M. → see
    Haviland, Harriet M., Miss
Haviland, Paul Burty   **BA JG**
(American, 1880-1950)   JG
(French photographer, editor,
    collector, 1880-1950)   BA
    Bibl: ART BULLETIN, March 75, p.
    110; Craig Bailey; Photo
    Secession; Sanowiller, PICABIA, I
Havill, Frederick   **WC WI**
(British artist, 1849-1874)   WC
(British artist, 1849-1884)   WI
Havinden, Ashley   **BA**
(British artist, 1903-)   WC
(British artist, b.1903)   WI
(British painter, designer,
    b.1903)   BA
    Bibl: DECORATIVE ARTS SOC., 3
    (1979); ▶MoMA libr. cat.
Havinden, Ashley Eldrid   **WC WI**
Havinden, Ashley Eldrid → see
    Havinden, Ashley
Havinden, John   **BA JG**
(British photographer, b.1909)   BA
(British, 1908-1987)   JG
    Bibl: Oxford (GBR), MoMA, Mod.
    British photog. (1980)

Havlicek or Hawlicek, Vincenz
(German artist, 1864-1900) **WC**
Havlíček, Josef (Czechoslovakian
architect, 1899-1961) **AV**
Bibl: ▶Contemp. archts.
Havlík, Zdeněk (Czech architect) **AV**
Bibl: Architektura ČSR, 1988,
v.47, no.2, p.52
Havner, John (American metalsmith,
b.1950) **BA**
Bibl: St. Petersburg (FL, USA),
MFA, Contemp. silversmiths
(1979)
Havrah (American, active Paris,
France 1920s) **JG**
Havránek, Bedřich **BA**
(Czech artist, 1821-1899) **WC**
(Czech painter, 1821-1899) **BA**
Bibl: ▶Busse, Maler u. Bildhauer
19. Jahr.; ▶Encyk. českého výtv.
umění; ▶Thieme-Becker; ▶Witt
checklist
Havranek, Friedrich **WC**
Havranek, Friedrich→see Havránek,
Bedřich
Havyatt, Richard (Australian painter,
b.1945) **BA**
Bibl: ▶Encyc. Australian art
Hawa, Eliane (French artist, 20th
cent.) **WC**
Haward, Birkin A. C. (British
architect, London) **AV**
Bibl: ▶Guide to RIBA practices,
1987
Haward, David (British architecture
student, Polytechnic of North
London) **AV**
Bibl: Building design, 1987 Sept.
4, no.851, p.8
**Hawarden, Clementina
Elphinstone** **BA**
(British photographer, 1822-
1865) **BA**
(British, 1822-1865) **JG**
Bibl: ▶Artist biog. master idx.;
▶ICP encyc. photog., p.582;
▶Macmillan photog. encyc.
**Hawarden, Lady Clementina
Elphinstone** **JG**
Hawarden, Lady Clementina
Elphinstone→see Hawarden,
Clementina Elphinstone
Haweis, Stephen **BA**
(British artist, op.1911-1914) **WI**
(British painter, photographer,
b.1878, act.1914) **BA**
Bibl: Elsen, Rodin's studio;
▶Johnson, Brit. artists; Pinet,
Rodin: Sculpteur et les
photographes (1985)
Haweis, Stephen George **WI**
Haweis, Stephen George→see
Haweis, Stephen
Hawes ((also Chase & Hawes, active
Boston, Massachusetts, USA)) **JG**
Hawes of Doncaster→see Hawes, (of
Doncaster)

Hawes, (of Doncaster) **WI**
(British artist, 18th cent.) **WC**
(British artist, op.18th c.) **WI**
Hawes of Doncaster **WC**
Hawes, Josiah Johnson **BA JG**
(American photographer, 1808-
1901) **BA**
(American, 1808-1901 (also
Southworth & Hawes,
daguerreotypist)) **JG**
Bibl: ▶Gernsheim, Hist. photog.;
▶Newhall, Photog.; PA
Hawes, Meredith William **BA WC WI**
(British artist, 1905-) **WC**
(British artist, b.1905) **WI**
(British painter, b.1905) **BA**
Bibl: ▶Witt checklist; ▶WW Art,
1982
Hawes, Philip B. (American
architect, Oracle, Ariz) **AV**
Bibl: ▶AIA Pro File, 1987-88
Hawke, Peter (British artist, 1801-
1887) **WI**
Hawke, Ron (Australian painter,
b.1933) **BA**
Bibl: Melbourne (AUS), Natl. Gall.
Victoria, New realism (1981)
Hawkeland, Lars (Norwegian
architect, Oslo) **AV**
Bibl: Norske Ark. Lands. Årbok
1987
Hawker, Edward (British artist, circa
1640-op.1722) **WI**
Hawker, Gareth Wyn **WC WI**
(British artist, 20th cent.) **WC**
(British artist, op.20th c.) **WI**
Wyn-Hawker, Gareth **WC**
Hawker, J. (British artist, op.1804-
1809) **WC WI**
Hawker, Susan (British artist, op.
20th c.) **WI**
Hawker, Thomas **WI**
(British artist, c.1640-a.1722) **WC**
(British artist, circa 1640-circa
1725) **WI**
Hawker, Thomas (not Edward) **WC**
Hawker, Thomas (not Edward)→see
Hawker, Thomas
Hawkes, Dean (British architect) **AV**
Bibl: ▶RIBA members, 1983
Hawkes, E. **WC WI**
(British artist, 19th cent.) **WC**
(British artist, op.19th c.) **WI**
Hawkes, Julian (British sculptor,
b.1944) **BA**
Bibl: ▶Artist biog. master idx.;
Norwich (GBR), School of Art,
Current Brit. sculp. (1979)
Hawkes, Pamela W. (American
architectural conservator) **AV**
Bibl: APT bulletin v.11, n.1, p.17
Hawkes, T.Leslie (British artist, op.
20th c.) **WI**
Hawkes, W. **WC WI**
(British artist, 19th cent.) **WC**
(British artist, op.19th c.) **WI**

Hawkes, William (British architect) **AV**
Bibl: Country life, v.176, no.4556,
p.1844
Hawkesmore, Nicholas→see
Hawksmoor, Nicholas
Hawkesworth, J. **WC WI**
(British artist, 18th cent.) **WC**
(British artist, op.18th c.) **WI**
Hawkesworth, J.H. **WC WI**
(British artist, op.1858) **WC**
(British artist, op.1858-) **WI**
Hawkesworth, William Thomas→see
Hawksworth, William Thomas
Martin
Hawking→see Hawking, van
[Unidentified]
Hawking, Van→see Hawking, van
[Unidentified]
Hawking, van [Unidentified]
(Unknown painter) **PR**
Bibl: (Friday, June 19th, 1801, lot
36, Graham & Hindle)
Hawking **PR**
Hawking, Van **PR**
Van Hawking **PR**
Hawkins, C. **WC WI**
(British artist, 19th cent.) **WC**
(British artist, op.19th c.) **WI**
Hawkins, Dennis **WC WI**
(British artist, 1925-) **WC**
(British artist, b.1925) **WI**
Hawkins, F.K. **WC WI**
(British artist, op.c.1841) **WC**
(British artist, op.circa 1841-) **WI**
Hawkins, George II (British artist,
1819-1852) **WC WI**
Bibl: Mackenzie
Hawkins, Henry (British artist, op.
circa 1820-) **WI**
Hawkins, Jane, Miss (British artist,
op.1871-1874) **WC WI**
Hawkins, Jene (British artist, op.
20th c.) **WI**
Hawkins, Louis Welden **GC**
(French artist, -1910) **WC**
(French painter, d.1910) **GC**
Bibl: ▶Thieme-Becker
Hawkins, Louis Weldon **WC**
Hawkins, Louis Weldon→see
Hawkins, Louis Welden
Hawkins, Louisa **WI**
(British artist, op.1839-1868) **WC WI**
**Hawkins, Louisa (Mrs. W.
Hawkins)** **WC**
Hawkins, Louisa (Mrs. W.
Hawkins)→see Hawkins, Louisa
Hawkins, Philip (British, act.1720-
1730) **BA**
Bibl: ▶Colvin, Brit. archts., pp.285,
817; CONNOISSEUR, CCVIII/837
(Nov 1981) p. 184
Hawkinson, Laurie (Architect?
associate of Henry Smith-Miller,
NYC) **AV**
Bibl: Interior design 1984 Dec.,
v.55, no.12, p.186

Hawks, John   **AV BA**
    (American architect, 1731-1790)   AV
    (British architect in USA, act.
       1766-1770)   BA
       Bibl: Herzog, EARLY
       ARCHITECTURE OF NEW BERN...
Hawksett, Samuel   **BA WI**
    (British artist, 1776-1851)   WI
    (Canadian painter, act.1856-
       1903)   BA
       Bibl: ▶Harper, Early ptrs. Canada
Hawksley, Arthur *(British artist,*
    1842-1915)   **WC WI**
Hawksley, Dorothy Webster
    (British artist, 1884-1970)   **WC WI**
       Bibl: ▶Fisher, Watercolour ptrs.
Hawksmoor, Nicholas   **AV BA FA**
    (1661-1736; Architect, England)   FA
    (British architect associated
       with Wren, 1661-1736)   AV
    (English architect, 1661-1736)   BA
       Bibl: ▶Avery Libr. cat.; ▶Colvin,
       Brit. archts., p.19; De la Ruffiniere
       du Prey, JOURNAL...SOC.OF
       ARCHITECT. HISTORIANS,
       48/1(Mar.1989); Fletcher's arch.,
       1975, p.982; ▶Libr. of Congr.
       Name Auth. File; London,
       Lambeth Palace Lib., THE QUEEN
       ANNE CHURCHES, p.xv; London,
       Whitechapel Art Gallery,
       HAWKSMOOR (1977); ▶Macmillan
       encyc. archts.; Meal;
       ▶Thieme-Becker
    Hawkesmore, Nicholas   FA
Hawksworth, W.T.M. → see
    Hawksworth, William Thomas
    Martin
Hawksworth, William Thomas
    Martin   **WI**
    (British artist, 1853-1935)   WI
    (British artist, 20th cent.)   WC
    (British artist, op.1881-1893)   WC
    Hawkesworth, William Thomas   **WC**
    Hawksworth, W.T.M.   **WC**
Hawley, Christine   **AV BA**
    (British architect, b.1949)   BA
    (British architect, London,
       1949-)   AV
       Bibl: ▶Arch. period. idx./RIBA,
       1983; ▶Avery period. idx., 7th
       suppl.; ▶Contemp. archts.; ▶RIBA
       members, 1987; RLIN BKS file
Hawley, Hughson   **WC WI**
    (American artist, 19th cent.)   WC
    (American artist, op.1877-1885)   WI
Hawley, Margaret Foote   **WC WI**
    (American artist, 1880)   WC
    (American artist, 1880-1963)   WI
Haworth, B. Cogill *(Canadian artist,*
    20th cent.)   **WC**
Haworth, E. Fanny, Miss   **WI**
    (British artist, op.1844-1855)   WC WI
       Bibl: ▶Johnson, Brit. artists
    Haworth, Miss E. Fanny   **WC**

Haworth, Jann *(American sculptor,*
    b.1942)   **BA**
       Bibl: ▶MoMA libr. cat.; ▶Parry,
       Contemp. art
Haworth, Miss E. Fanny → see
    Haworth, E. Fanny, Miss
Haworth, Peter *(British painter,*
    stained glass artist in CAN,
    b.1889)   **BA**
       Bibl: ▶MacDonald, Can. artists;
       ▶Vollmer, Künst.-Lex. 20. Jhr.;
       ▶WW Amer. Art
Haws   **WC WI**
    (British artist, op.c.1700)   WC
    (British artist, op.circa 1700-)   WI
Haws, Irving *(American architect)*   **AV**
       Bibl: Fine homebuilding, 1988
       Feb.-Mar., no.44, p.64
Hawthorne → see Hawthorne, Charles
    Webster
Hawthorne, Charles W. → see
    Hawthorne, Charles Webster
Hawthorne, Charles
    Webster   **BA PR WC WI**
    (American artist, 1872-)   WC
    (American artist, 1872-1930)   WI
    (American painter, 1872-1930)   BA PR
       Bibl: ▶Fielding's Amer. ptrs.,
       addendum; Provincetown (MA,
       USA), Chrysler Art Mus.,
       Hawthorne retrospective;
       ▶RILA/BHA; ▶Smith, Idx. Amer.
       artists
    Charles Webster Hawthorne   PR
    Hawthorne   PR
    Hawthorne, Charles W.   PR
Hawthorne, Elwin   **WC WI**
    (British artist, 20th cent.)   WC
    (British artist, b.1905)   WI
Haxton, David *(American*
    photographer, b.1943)   **BA**
       Bibl: Arts Mag. LIII/4 (Dec 1978),
       19; Chicago (IL, USA), MoCA,
       Concept, Narrative, Document
       (1979)
Haxton, Elaine *(Australian artist,*
    20th cent.)   **WC**
Hay, Alastair *(British architect,*
    London)   **AV**
       Bibl: Transactions/RIBA, 1987,
       v.5, no.2(10), p.53
Hay, Alex   **WC WI**
    (British artist, 1936-)   WC
    (British artist, b.1936)   WI
Hay, Andrew   **WC WI**
    (British artist, op.1710-1754)   WI
    (British(?) artist, op.1710)   WC
Hay, Anthony *(American*
    cabinetmaker, act.1751, d.1770)   **BA**
       Bibl: Antiques, CXIV/2 (Aug.
       1978) pp.282-293
Hay, Bernard → see Hay, Bernardo

Hay, Bernardo   **PR WI**
    (British artist, b.1864)   WI
    (British painter, b. 1864)   PR
       Bibl: ▶Thieme-Becker
    Bernardo Hay   PR
    Hay, Bernard   PR
Hay, Cecil George Jackson *(British*
    artist, b.1899)   **WI**
Hay, Chris *(British architect or*
    designer, London)   **AV**
       Bibl: Architects' journal, 1988
       Nov.30, v.188, no.48, p.24
Hay, D. *(Active Edinburgh, Scotland,*
    U.K.)   **JG**
Hay, David Ramsay   **AV BA**
    (British decorative artist, author,
       1798-1866)   BA
    (Scottish interior designer,
       1797-1866)   AV
       Bibl: Country life, 1987 July 30,
       v.181, no.31, p.127; ▶Dict. natl.
       biog.; ▶Natl. union cat., pre-1956;
       V & A libr. cat.
Hay, Dick *(American sculptor,*
    b.1942)   **BA**
       Bibl: Ceramics monthly, XXVIII/2
       (Feb. 1980) pp.40-43; ▶WW
       Amer. Art, 1978
Hay, G. *(Active Edinburgh, Scotland,*
    U.K. (also G. & D. Hay))   **JG**
Hay, George   **BA WC WI**
    (British artist, 1831-1913)   WC WI
    (British painter, 1831-1912/13)   BA
       Bibl: Harris, Scottish pictures;
       ▶Harris, Scottish ptrs.; ▶Johnson,
       Brit. artists; ▶Thieme-Becker
Hay, George *(Scottish architect and*
    architectural historian, 1911-1986)   **AV**
       Bibl: Antiquaries journal, 1987,
       v.67, pt.2, p.481
Hay, Helen   **WC WI**
    (British artist, op.1895)   WC
    (British artist, op.1895-1940)   WI
Hay, James   **WC WI**
    (British artist, op.1887-1892)   WC
    (British artist, op.1887-circa
       1920)   WI
Hay, James Hamilton *(British artist,*
    1874-1916)   **WC WI**
Hay, Jane Benham *(British artist,*
    op.1848-1862)   **WI**
Hay, John Arthur Machray *(British*
    artist, 1887-1960)   **WC WI**
Háy, Károly László *(Hungarian*
    painter, printmaker, 1907-1961)   **BA**
       Bibl: Budapest Magyar Nemzeti
       Galleria, ex. cat. for one-man
       show, 1975; ▶Vollmer, Künst.-Lex.
       20. Jhr., suppl.
Hay, Paul *(German artist, 1867-)*   **WC**
Hay, Peter Alexander *(British artist,*
    1866-1952)   **WC WI**
Hay, W. *(British artist, op.1776-*
    1797)   **WC WI**

Hay, William   **AV WI**
(British artist, op.1852-1881)   WI
(Canadian architect)   AV
   Bibl: Society for the Study of
   Architecture in Canada. Bulletin,
   1989 Mar., v.14, no.1, p.9
Hay, William (British architect in
   CAN, 1818-after 1861)   **BA**
   Bibl: Jrnl. of Canad. Art Hist. IV/2
   (1977-78), 98-110
Hay, William Hardie (British artist,
   b.1859)   **WI**
Haya, Maria Eugenia→see Marucha
   (Maria Eugenia Haya)
Hayakawa, Kunichiko   **BA**
(Japanese architect, 1941-)   AV
(Japanese architect, painter,
   b.1941)   BA
   Bibl: ▶Avery period. idx., suppl.
   7,6; GA houses, n.14, July 1983,
   p.180; Vorreiter-Wajed, G., in
   ARCHITECTURAL REVIEW,
   CLXXIX/1069 (Mar 1986), p. 78
Hayakawa, Kunihiko   **AV**
Hayakawa, Kunihiko→see Hayakawa,
   Kunichiko
Hayami, Shiro (Japanese artist,
   b.1927)   **BA**
   Bibl: Geneva (CHE), Musée Rath,
   Art japonais d'aujourd'hui (1983)
Hayard, Caroline (French,
   1810/11-1894)   **BA**
   Bibl: Cambridge (MA, USA),
   Harvard U. Fogg Art Museum,
   Ingres (1967); Naef, Gazette des
   B.-A., LXVII (1966)
Hayard, Jeanne Susanne Alliou
(French, 1775-1854)   **BA**
   Bibl: Cambridge (MA, USA),
   Harvard U. Fogg Art Museum,
   Ingres (1967); Naef, Gazette des
   B.-A., LXVII (1966), p.41
Hayashi, Kanji (Japanese architect,
   1936-)   **AV**
   Bibl: Kenchiku bunka, 1987 Dec.,
   v.42, no.494, p.234
Hayashi, Kenjiro (Architect, Japan)   **AV**
   Bibl: Space design, 1982 Dec., no.
   219, p.42
Hayashi, Kimiko (Japanese
   architect)   **AV**
   Bibl: Japan architect, 1982 Jan.,
   v.57, no.297, p.35
Hayashi, Masako (Japanese
   architect)   **AV**
Hayashi, Shoji (Japanese architect)   **AV**
Hayashi, Yasuyoshi (Japanese
   architect)   **AV**
   Bibl: Toshi-jutaka, 1985 Oct., no.
   216, p.70
Haycock, Edward (British architect,
   b.ca.1791, act.1835)   **BA**
   Bibl: Country Life CLXI (10 Feb
   1977), p.313; ECHLG, p.153
Hayden, Charles (American interior
   designer)   **AV**
   Bibl: Architectural digest, 1984
   Sept. v.41, no.9, p.180

Hayden, Charles Henry (American
   artist, 1856-1901)   **WC WI**
Hayden, Dolores (American
   architectural writer)   **AV**
   Bibl: Architectural record, 1984
   July, v.172, no.8
Hayden, Edward Parker (American
   painter, d. 1922)   **PR**
   Bibl: ▶WWW Amer. art
   Edward Parker Hayden   PR
Hayden, Henri   **BA PR WC**
(French artist, 1883-)   WC
(French painter, 1883-1970)   BA PR
   Bibl: ▶Bénézit; ▶RILA/BHA;
   ▶Vollmer, Künst.-Lex. 20. Jhr.
   Henri Hayden   PR
Hayden, Michael (Canadian
   sculptor, b.1943)   **BA**
   Bibl: ▶Artists Canada; ▶Natl. Gall.
   Canada libr. cat.
Hayden, Palmer C. (American
   painter, 1893-1973)   **BA**
   Bibl: ▶Cederholm, Afro-Amer.
   artists; Los Angeles (CA, USA),
   LACMA, Black Amer. art (1986),
   p.147
Hayden, Richard S. (American
   architect)   **AV**
Hayden, Sophia   **BA**
(American architect)   AV
(American architect, ca.1868-
   1953)   BA
   Bibl: Brooklyn (NY, USA), Brooklyn
   Mus., Women in arch. (1977)
Hayden, Sophia G.   **AV**
Hayden, Sophia G.→see Hayden,
   Sophia
Haydock, Richard   **WC WI**
(British artist, c.1570-c.1640)   WC
(British artist, circa 1570-circa
   1640)   WI
Haydon→see Haydon, Benjamin
   Robert
**Haydon, Benjamin
   Robert**   **BA GC PR WC WI**
(British artist, 1786-1846)   WC WI
(British painter, 1786-1846)   PR
(British painter, author, 1786-
   1846)   BA
(British, 1786-1846)   GC
   Bibl: ▶Bénézit; ▶RILA/BHA;
   ▶Thieme-Becker; ▶Witt checklist
   Benjamin Robert Haydon   PR
   Haydon   PR
Hayeck or Hayek, Hans von→see
   Hayek, Hans von
Hayek, Hans von   **BA**
(Austrian painter in Germany,
   1869-1940)   BA
(German artist, 1869-)   WC
   Bibl: ▶Bénézit; ▶Busse, Maler u.
   Bildhauer 19. Jahr.;
   ▶Thieme-Becker; ▶Vollmer,
   Künst.-Lex. 20. Jhr.
Hayeck or Hayek, Hans von   **WC**

Hayes, Albert (British artist, op.circa
   1909-)   **WI**
Hayes, Claude (British artist, 1852-
   1922)   **WC WI**
Hayes, Colin (British artist, b.1919)   **WI**
Hayes, David Vincent (American
   sculptor, b.1931)   **BA**
   Bibl: ▶Havlice, Idx. art. bio.; ▶WW
   Amer. Art, 1976
Hayes, Edward   **BA WC**
(British artist, 1797-1864)   WC WI
(Irish painter, 1797-1864)   BA
   Bibl: ▶Strickland, Irish artists
Hayes, Edward I   **WI**
Hayes, Edward I→see Hayes, Edward
Hayes, Edward II (British artist, op.
   20th c.)   **WI**
Hayes, Edwin   **BA GC WC WI**
(British artist, 1819-1904)   WC WI
(British painter, 1820-1904)   BA
(Irish painter, 1819-1904)   GC
   Bibl: ▶Bénézit; ▶Mallalieu, Brit.
   watercolour artists; ▶Wood,
   Victorian ptrs.
Hayes, Frederick William (British
   artist, 1848-1918)   **WC WI**
Hayes, George (British artist, 1823-
   1895)   **WC WI**
Hayes, George A.   **WC WI**
(American artist, 1854-1934)   WI
(American artist, op.c.1860)   WC
Hayes, Gerald (American artist,
   b.1940)   **BA**
   Bibl: ARTS MAGAZINE, LVI/3 (Nov
   1979), 127-129
Hayes, Henry Edgar (British artist,
   op.1879-1886)   **WI**
Hayes, I. (British painter, 19th c.)   **BA**
   Bibl: Connoisseur, CCII/811 (Sep.
   1979) pp.2-7
Hayes, John   **WC WI**
(British artist, c.1786-1866)   WC
(British artist, circa 1786-1866)   WI
Hayes, John F. (American architect,
   1932-)   **AV**
Hayes, Matilda   **WC WI**
(British artist, op.1821)   WC
(British artist, op.1821-)   WI
Hayes, Michael Angelo (British
   artist, 1820-1877)   **WC WI**
Hayes, Patricia (British artist,
   b.1951)   **WI**
Hayes, Randy (American painter,
   b.1944)   **BA**
   Bibl: Laguna Beach (CA, USA),
   Mus. Art, West Coast realism
   (1983)
Hayes, Ross E. (Canadian architect,
   Calgary, Alberta)   **AV**
   Bibl: Canadian architect, 1986
   Oct., v.31, no.10, p.36
Hayes, Sidney (British artist, d.circa
   1923)   **WI**
Hayes, Thad (American interior
   designer, New York City)   **AV**
   Bibl: NYC phone bk., 1987

Hayes, Vertis (American painter,
  b.1911)   **BA**
  Bibl: Arts Mag., LII/2 (Oct. 1977)
  pp.122-126
Hayes, William   **BA WC WI**
  (British artist, op.1773-1799)   WC WI
  (British painter, draftsman,
    printmaker, act.1775-1794)   BA
  Bibl: ▶Fisher, Watercolour ptrs.;
  ▶Mallalieu, Brit. watercolour
  artists; ▶Thieme-Becker
Hayet, Jacques (French artist,
  -1916)   **WC**
Hayet, Louis (French painter, 1864-
  1940)   **BA PR**
  Bibl: ▶Bénézit; Broudie, SEURAT IN
  PERSPECTIVE (1978); ▶Busse,
  Maler u. Bildhauer 19. Jahr.;
  Guggenheim, NEO-IMPRESSIONISM
  (1968); ▶Monneret,
  Impressionisme; Pontrise, Musee
  Pissarro, LOUIS HAYET, 1864-
  1940 (1983); ▶RILA/BHA; Sutter,
  LES NEO-IMPRESSIONISTES (1970)
  Louis Hayet   PR
Hayez, Francesco   **AV BA GC WC**
  (Italian artist, 1791-1881)   WC
  (Italian painter, 1791-1882) AV BA GC
  Bibl: ▶Bolaffi; ▶Comanducci, Diz.;
  ▶Libr. of Congr. Name Auth. File;
  ▶RILA/BHA, 1986;
  ▶Thieme-Becker
Hayles, John → see Hayls, John
Hayley Lever → see Lever, Hayley
Hayley, Thomas Alphonse (British
  artist, 1780-1800)   **WC WI**
Hayllar, Edith   **WC WI**
  (British artist, 1860-1948)   WI
  (British artist, op.1881-1897)   WC
Hayllar, James   **WC WI**
  (British artist, 1829-1920)   WI
  (British artist, 1829-c.1898)   WC
Hayllar, Jessica (British artist, 1858-
  1940)   **WC WI**
Hayllar, Kate (British artist, op.1883-
  1900)   **WI**
Hayllar, Mary (British artist, op.
  1880-1885)   **WI**
Hayls, Hayles or Hales, John → see
  Hayls, John
Hayls, John   **GC WI**
  (British artist, op.1651-, d.1679) WI
  (British artist, op.1651-m.1679)   WC
  (British painter, d.1679)   GC
  Bibl: ▶Brit. Mus. cat.; Sotheby's;
  ▶Witt checklist
  Hales, John   WI
  Hayles, John   GC WI
  Hayls, Hayles or Hales, John   WC
Haym, Niccolò Francesco   **BA WC**
  (Italian artist, c.1688-c.1729)   WC
  (Italian musician, collector,
    printmaker, author in GBR,
    1688/89-ca.1729)   BA
  Bibl: Arte veneta XXXII (1978),
  352-353; ▶Thieme-Becker
Hayman → see Hayman, Francis

Hayman, A. (Engraver, op.1850-)   **WI**
Hayman, Francis   **BA GC PR WC WI**
  (British artist, 1708-1776)   WC WI
  (British painter, 1708-1776)   BA PR
  (British, 1708-1776)   GC
  Bibl: ▶Dict. natl. biog.;
  ▶RILA/BHA; Thames & Hudson
  Brit. art; ▶Thieme-Becker; ▶Witt
  checklist
  Francis Hayman   PR
  Haiman   PR
  Hayman   PR
Hayman, Patrick   **BA WC WI**
  (British artist, 1915-)   WC
  (British artist, b.1915)   WI
  (British painter, sculptor,
    b.1915)   BA
  Bibl: ▶MoMA libr. cat.; ▶Vollmer,
  Künst.-Lex. 20. Jhr.
Haymans, A. (Engraver)   **WI**
Haymes, David A. (American
  architect, 1954-)   **AV**
  Bibl: ▶AIA Pro File, 1987-88
Hayne de Bruxelles   **GC PR WC**
  (Flanders painter, act.1440-
    1450)   GC
  (Netherlandish painter, act.
    1460)   PR
  (Netherlands artist, op.c.1460)   WC
  Bibl: Dupont; Dupont, L'Amour de
  l'Art, XVI (1938) 363ff; Getty
  Photo Study Coll. (Ptgs.); ▶Witt
  checklist
  Bruxelles, Hayne de   GC
Haynes, Arthur S.   **WC WI**
  (British artist, op.1885-1906)   WI
  (British artist, op.1887-1890)   WC
Haynes, Douglas Hector (Canadian
  painter, b.1936)   **BA**
  Bibl: Artists in Canada;
  ▶MacDonald, Can. artists; ▶Natl.
  Gall. Canada libr. cat.
Haynes, Edmund (Architect, worked
  in Barbados, 1830's)   **AV**
  Bibl: Maison française, 1987 July-
  Aug., no.408, p.96
Haynes, Frank Jay   **BA**
  (American photographer, ca.
    1860-ca.1920)   BA
  (American, 1853-1921)   JG
  Bibl: ▶Current, Photog. & Old
  West, p.164; ▶Eastman House
  database; Fort Worth. Amon
  Carter Mus of Western Art,
  PHOTOG IN 19TH C. AMERICA
  (1991) p.324; ▶MoMA libr. cat.;
  ▶Natl. union cat., pre-1956;
  Norfolk (VA, USA), Chrysler Mus.,
  19th ce. Mammoth Plates
  (1979/80); ▶Parry, Photo idx.;
  ▶WWW Amer. art
Haynes, Frederick Jay   **JG**
Haynes, Frederick (British artist, op.
  circa 1860-)   **WI**
Haynes, Frederick Jay → see Haynes,
  Frank Jay

Haynes, Irving B. (American
  architect)   **AV**
Haynes, John (American architect,
  partner in firm of Barnett, Haynes
  and Barnett)   **AV**
  Bibl: ▶Withey, Amer. archts.
Haynes, John (British artist, op.
  1730-1753)   **WC**
Haynes, John William (British artist,
  op.1852-1882)   **WC WI**
Haynes, Michael   **AV**
Haynes, Nancy   **BA WI**
  (American artist, 1947-op.1987)   WI
  (American painter, b.1947)   BA
Haynes-Williams, John → see Williams,
  John Haynes
Haynie, Hugh (American cartoonist,
  b.1927)   **BA**
  Bibl: Berkeley (CA, USA), UCB Art
  Mus., Amer. presidency political
  cartoons (1976); ▶WW Amer. Art,
  1976
Hayrapet (Armenian, active 1615-
  1680s)   **JG**
Hays, Audrey (American interior
  designer, Palm Beach, Fla)   **AV**
  Bibl: Southern accents, 1987 Nov.
  -Dec., v.10, no.6, p.106
Hays, Barton Stone (American
  painter, 1826-1914)   **BA**
  Bibl: ▶Groce, Artists Amer.,
  suppl.; Indianapolis (IN, USA),
  Mus. Art, Mirages of memory
  (1976)
Hays, William Jacob I (American
  painter, 1830-1875)   **BA**
  Bibl: ▶Fielding's Amer. ptrs.;
  ▶Groce, Artists Amer.;
  ▶Thieme-Becker
Hays, William Jacob II   **WI**
  (American artist, 1872-1934)   WC WI
  Hays, William Jacob, II   WC
Hays, William Jacob, II → see Hays,
  William Jacob II
Hayter → see Hayter, George
Hayter, Charles (British artist, 1761-
  1835)   **WC WI**
Hayter, Edwin   **WC WI**
  (British artist, 19th cent.)   WC
  (British artist, op.19th c.)   WI
Hayter, George   **BA PR WI**
  (British artist, 1792-1871)   WC WI
  (British painter, 1792-1871)   PR
  (British painter, printmaker,
    1792-1871)   BA
  Bibl: ▶Thieme-Becker; ▶Wood,
  Victorian ptrs.
  George Hayter   PR
  Hayter   PR
  Hayter, George, Sir   PR
  Hayter, Sir George   WC
Hayter, George, Sir → see Hayter,
  George

Hayter, John   **WC WI**
  (British artist, 1800-1891)   WC
  (British artist, 1800-1891-1895)   WI
  Bibl: ▶Foskett, Brit. miniature ptrs.
Hayter, Sir George→see Hayter,
George
Hayter, Stanley William   **BA WC WI**
  (British artist, 1901-)   WC
  (British artist, b.1901)   WI
  (British painter, printmaker,
    1901-1988)   BA
  Bibl: ▶ARTbibl. mod., v.20, #2,
    p.220; ▶Artist biog. master idx.;
    ▶Bénézit; ▶Encyc. world art;
    ▶Phaidon 20c. art; ▶Waters, Brit.
    artists; ▶Who's Who [GBR]
Haytley or Hateley, Edward→see
Haytley, Edward
Haytley, Edward   **BA WI**
  (British artist, 1746-1761)   WC WI
  (British painter, act.1740, d.ca.
    1762)   BA
  Bibl: ▶Dict. natl. biog.; ▶Redgrave,
    Engl. school; ▶Thieme-Becker
  Hateley, Edward   WI
Haytley or Hateley, Edward   **WC**
Hayward [Unidentified] (Unknown
  painter)   PR
  Bibl: (June 15, 1812, lot 5[a],
    Philipe)
Hayward, Alfred (American painter,
  20th century)   GC
  Bibl: ▶Bénézit
**Hayward, Alfred Frederick
  William**   **WC WI**
  (British artist, 1856-)   WC
  (British artist, 1856-1939)   WI
Hayward, Alfred Robert (British
  artist, 1875-1971)   **WC WI**
Hayward, Arthur   **WC WI**
  (British artist, 1889-)   WC
  (British artist, b.1889)   WI
Hayward, Franklyn Harold
  (American painter, 1861/67-1945) BA
Hayward, George   **WC WI**
  (American artist, 1800-1872)   WI
  (American artist, op.c.1834-72)   WC
  (Engraver, New York, NY., 1800-
    1872)   WI
Hayward, Henry W. (Australian
  architect)   AV
Hayward, James (American painter,
  b.1943)   BA
Hayward, Jim (American interior
  designer, New York City(?))   AV
  Bibl: Interiors, 1987 July, v.146,
    no.12, p.64
Hayward, John Samuel (British
  artist, 1778-1822)   **WC WI**
Hayward, Mrs.   **WC WI**
  (British artist, 19th cent.(?))   WC
  (British artist, op.19th c.)   WI
Hayward, Richard (British sculptor,
  1728-1800)   BA
Hayward, Tony (British sculptor,
  20th c.)   BA

Hayward, William   **AV BA**
  (British architect, engineer, ca.
    1740-1782)   BA
  (English architect, c.1740-1782)   AV
  Bibl: ▶Colvin, Brit. archts., p.410
Hayward-Baird, Lynda (Canadian
  textile artist, b.1941)   BA
Haywood, William (British artist,
  op.1844-1867)   **WC WI**
Hayworth, Samuel (British
  woodcarver, act.1754-1766)   BA
Ḥayyim ben Asher Anshel (Austrian
  scribe, illuminator, act.1725,
    d.1784)   BA
  Bibl: Barnett, CAT. OF JEWISH
    MUS., LONDON, p.121-22;
    Schreiber, Jrnl. Jewish art, VII
    (1980) pp.44-49
Hayyim, Joseph Ibn→see Ibn Hayyim,
Joseph
Hazan, Jack (film director, 20th c.) BA
Hazard, John Bevan (British, d.
    1892)   JG
Hazard, Simeon (American
  cabinetmaker, act.1840-1850)   BA
Hazelgrove, Albert James (1884-
    1958; Architect, Ottawa)   FA
  Bibl: ▶Hill, Archts. Canada, 1986
Hazelgrove, Nancy Ann (Canadian
  painter, printmaker, sculptor,
    b.1945)   BA
Hazelton→see Hazelton, Isaac
Brewster
Hazelton, Isaac Brewster (American
  painter, 1875-1943)   PR
  Bibl: ▶WWW Amer. art
  Hazelton   PR
  Isaac Brewster Hazelton   PR
Hazenplug, Frank   **WC WI**
  (American artist, 1873-)   WC
  (American artist, b.1873)   WI
  (Engraver, Chicago, IL., b.1873)   WI
Hazes, Ruud (Dutch architect)   AV
  Bibl: Archis, 1988 Dec., no.12,
    p.2
Hazlehurst, Thomas   **WC WI**
  (British artist, circa 1740-circa
    1821)   WI
  (British artist, op.1760-1818)   WC
Hazlewood, David (British artist,
  op.20th c.)   WI
Hazlitt, Don Robert (American
  painter, b.1948)   BA
Hazlitt, John (British artist, 1769-
    1837)   **WC WI**
Hazlitt, William (British artist, 1778-
    1830)   **WC WI**
Hazon, Michel Barthelemy (French
  painter, 1722-1818)   GC
  Bibl: ▶Thieme-Becker
Hbens→see Holbein, Hans, the
younger
He Heem→see Heem, Jan Davidsz.
de
Head→see Head, Guy

Head, Charles   **WC WI**
  (British artist, op.c.1904)   WC
  (British artist, op.circa 1904-)   WI
Head, Charles Franklin, Major
  (British artist, d.1850)   WI
Head, Edith (American fashion
  designer, d.1981)   BA
Head, Guy   **BA GC PR WC WI**
  (British artist, 1753-1800)   WC
  (British artist, 1758-1800)   WI
  (British painter, 1753-1800)   BA
  (British painter, 1762-1800)   PR
  (British, 1762-1800)   GC
  Bibl: ew; ▶RILA/BHA;
    ▶Thieme-Becker; ▶Waterhouse,
    Brit. 18c. ptrs.
  G. Head   PR
  [Guy Head]   PR
  Guy, Head   PR
  Guyhead   PR
  Head   PR
  Head?   PR
Head, Jonathan   **WC WI**
  (British artist, 20th cent.)   WC
  (British artist, op.20th c.)   WI
Head, Tim   **BA WI**
  (British artist, b.1946)   WI
  (British photographer, artist,
    b.1946)   BA
Head?→see Head, Guy
Headborg, Jarret (American interior
  designer)   AV
  Bibl: Metropolitan home, 1989
    Aug., v.21, no.8, p.117
Heade→see Heade, Martin Johnson
Heade, Martin J.→see Heade, Martin
Johnson
**Heade, Martin
  Johnson**   **BA GC PR WC WI**
  (American artist, 1814-1904)   WC
  (American artist, 1819-1904)   WI
  (American painter, 1819-1904)   BA PR
  (American, 1814-1904)   GC
  Bibl: ▶RILA/BHA; ▶Witt checklist
  Heade   PR
  Heade, Martin J.   PR
  Martin Johnson Heade   PR
Headley or Hidley, Joseph H.→see
Hidley, Joseph H.
Headley, David (American painter,
  b.1946)   BA
Heady, A. (American artist, op.1900-
    1928)   WI
Heakwell (Engraver)   WI
Heal, Ambrose (British
  cabinetmaker, designer, author,
    1872-1959)   BA
Heald, Louisa Mary, Miss→see
Bancroft, Louisa Mary
Heald, Paul (American painter,
  b.1936)   BA
Heale, Jonathan   **BA WI**
  (British artist, op.20th c.)   WI
  (British painter, printmaker,
    b.1949)   BA

Healey →see Healy, George Peter
Alexander

Healey, David *(American
photographer, 20th c.)* **BA**
Bibl: Norfolk (VA, USA), Chrysler
Mus, Not Fade Away (1980)

Healey, Edward Hopkins *(American
architect, Cedar Rapids, Iowa)* **AV**
Bibl: ▶AIA Pro File, 1987-88

Healey, G.R. *(British artist, op.1840-
1852)* **WC WI**

Healey, George →see Healy, George
Peter Alexander

Healey, George Peter Alexander →see
Healy, George Peter Alexander

Healy or Haly, Robert →see Healy,
Robert

Healy, Anne Laura *(American
sculptor, b.1939)* **BA**

Healy, Brian *(American architect)* **AV**
Bibl: ▶AIA Pro File, 1985

Healy, G.P.A. →see Healy, George
Peter Alexander

Healy, George P.A. →see Healy,
George Peter Alexander

Healy, George Peter →see Healy,
George Peter Alexander

**Healy, George Peter
Alexander** **BA GC PR WC WI**
(American artist, 1808-1894) **WC**
(American artist, 1813-1894) **WI**
*(American painter, 1813-
1894)* **BA GC PR**
Bibl: ▶RILA/BHA
George Peter Alexander Healey **PR**
Healey **PR**
Healey, George **PR**
Healey, George Peter Alexander **PR**
Healy, G.P.A. **PR**
Healy, George P.A. **PR**
Healy, George Peter **PR**

Healy, Julia Schmitt *(Canadian
painter, printmaker, b.1947)* **BA**

Healy, Michael *(Irish stained glass
artist, Dublin, 1873-1941)* **AV**
Bibl: Historic places in New
Zealand, 1989 June, no.25, p.24

Healy, Nada *(Yugoslav artist in CAN,
b.1947)* **BA**

Healy, Robert **BA WI**
(British artist, op.1765-1771) **WC WI**
(Irish painter, 1743-1771) **BA**
Haly, Robert **WI**
Healy or Haly, Robert **WC**

Hean, J. de *(Netherlands artist, 18th
cent.)* **WC**

Heap of Birds, Edgar *(American
artist, b.1954)* **BA**

Heaphy, Charles *(British artist,
1822-1881)* **WC WI**

Heaphy, Elizabeth, Miss →see Murray,
Elizabeth, (GBR)

Heaphy, Mary Ann **WI**
(British artist, op.1821-1847) **WC WI**
Bibl: ▶Foskett, Brit. miniature ptrs.

**Heaphy, Miss M.A. (Mrs W.
Musgrave)** **WC**
Musgrave, William, Mrs., (Mary
Ann) **WI**

*Heaphy, Miss M.A. (Mrs W.
Musgrave) →see* Heaphy, Mary
Ann

Heaphy, Thomas **BA**
(British artist, 1775-1835) **WC WI**
(British painter, 1775-1835) **BA**
Bibl: ▶Redgrave, Engl. school;
▶Thieme-Becker; ▶Yale Brit. artists
list

Heaphy, Thomas I **WI**
Heaphy, Thomas, I **WC**
Heaphy, Thomas Frank **WI**
(British artist, 1813-1873) **WC WI**
Heaphy, Thomas, II **WC**

Heaphy, Thomas I →see Heaphy,
Thomas

Heaphy, Thomas, I →see Heaphy,
Thomas

Heaphy, Thomas, II →see Heaphy,
Thomas Frank

Heard, J. →see Heard, Joseph

Heard, Joseph **WI**
(British artist, 1799-1859) **WI**
(British artist, op.c.1850) **WC**

Heard, J. **WC**

Heard, T.H. *(Engraver, op.circa
1879-)* **WI**

Hearn, Joseph **WC WI**
(British artist, 18th cent.) **WC**
(British artist, op.18th c.) **WI**

Hearn, Richard **BA WI**
(British artist, op.circa 1847-) **WI**
*(Irish painter in FRA, act.1847-
1870)* **BA**

Hearnden, Anthony **WC WI**
(British artist, 20th cent.) **WC**
(British artist, op.20th c.) **WI**

Hearne →see Hearne, Thomas

Hearne, Thomas **BA GC PR WC WI**
(British artist, 1744-1817) **WC WI**
(British painter, 1744-1817) **BA PR**
(British, 1744-1817) **GC**
Bibl: ▶RILA/BHA; ▶Thieme-Becker;
▶Witt checklist
Hearne **PR**
Thomas Hearne **PR**

Hearsey, Captain Hyder →see
Hearsey, Hyder Young

Hearsey, Hyder Young **BA**
(British artist, 1782-1840) **WI**
(British artist, op.1808) **WC**
*(British soldier, painter in IND,
1782-1840)* **BA**

Hearsey, Captain Hyder **WC**
Hearsey, Hyder, Capt. **WI**

Hearsey, Hyder, Capt. →see Hearsey,
Hyder Young

Hearst Master *(Spanish, 16th
century)* **GC**
Bibl: ▶Thieme-Becker

Hearst Painter *(Apulian vase-
painter)* **GC**
Bibl: Trendall, Attic red-fig. vases
Apulia

Hearst, Nan *(American achitect, San
Francisco, Calif)* **AV**
Bibl: ▶AIA Pro File, 1987-88

Heartfield, John **BA WC**
(German artist, 1891-1968) **WC**
*(German painter, printmaker,
filmmaker, journalist, 1891-
1968)* **BA**

Heaten, John *(American painter, act.
1737)* **BA**

Heath →see Heath, James

Heath, Adrian **BA WC WI**
(British artist, 1920-) **WC**
(British artist, b.1920) **WI**
(British painter, b.1920) **BA**

Heath, C. *(British artist, op.19th c.)* **WI**
Bibl: ▶Houfe, Brit. book illus.

Heath, Charles **BA WI**
*(British printmaker, publisher,
1785-1848)* **BA**
*(Engraver, London, GTL., 1785-
1848)* **WI**

Heath, David Martin *(American
photographer, b.1931)* **BA**

Heath, Edda Maxwell **WC WI**
(American artist, 20th cent.) **WC**
(American artist, op.1897-1935) **WI**

Heath, Ellen **WC WI**
(British artist, 19th cent.) **WC**
(British artist, op.19th c.) **WI**

Heath, Ernest Dudley **WC WI**
(British artist, 19th cent.) **WC**
*(British artist, op.1886-circa
1930)* **WI**

Heath, Frank Gasgoyne *(British
artist, 1873-1936)* **WI**

Heath, Frank L. *(American artist,
1857-1921)* **WC WI**

Heath, H. **WC WI**
(British artist, 19th cent.) **WC**
(British artist, op.19th c.) **WI**

Heath, James **PR WC WI**
(British artist, 1757-1834) **WC WI**
(British painter, 1757-1834) **PR**
Bibl: ▶Thieme-Becker
Heath **PR**
James Heath **PR**

Heath, Joshua *(British ceramist, act.
1770-1800)* **BA**

Heath, Margaret A. **WC WI**
(British artist, op.1886-1893) **WC**
*(British artist, op.1886-circa
1920)* **WI**

Heath, Margery *(British artist, op.
20th c.)* **WI**

Heath, William (*British artist, 1795-1840*) **WC WI**
    Bibl: Paviere, Brit. sporting ptrs
    Pry, Paul   WI
Heathcote, Charles Gilbert (*British painter, 1841-1913*) **BA**
Heathcote, H.M.   **WC WI**
    (*British artist, 19th cent.*)   WC
    (*British artist, op.19th c.*)   WI
Heathcote, John Moyer (*British artist, 1800-1890*) **WI**
Heathcote, Norman (*British artist, op.1897-*) **WI**
Heatherley, Thomas (*British artist, 1824-1913*) **BA**
Heaton, Augustus George→see Heaton, Augustus Goodyear
Heaton, Augustus Goodyear (*American artist, 1844-1931*) **WI**
    Heaton, Augustus George   WI
Heaton, E.   **WC WI**
    (*British artist, 19th cent.*)   WC
    (*British artist, op.19th c.*)   WI
Heaton, Jack (*British artist, b.1907*) **WI**
Heaton, John Aldan   **WC WI**
    (*British artist, 1830(?)-1897*)   WC
    (*British artist, 1830-1897*)   WI
Heaton, Robert (*British architect*) **AV**
    Bibl: Building, 1985 Oct.4, v.249, no.40, p.42
Heavey, Derek (*British architect*) **AV**
    Bibl: Architects' journal, 1980 Aug.6, v.172, no.32, p.251
Hebald, Milton Elting (*American sculptor, printmaker, b. 1917*) **BA**
Hebald-Heymann, Margo (*American architect, Santa Monica, Calif*) **AV**
    Bibl: ▶AIA Pro File, 1987-88
Hebbe (*German(?) artist, 18th cent.(?)*) **WC**
Hebborn, E.→see Hebborn, Eric
Hebborn, Eric   **WI**
    (*British artist, 20th cent.*)   WC
    (*British artist, op.20th c.*)   WI
    Hebborn, E.   **WC**
Hebeisen, Res (*Architect Bern*) **AV**
    Bibl: Baumeister 1985 Feb, v.82, no.2, p.56
Hebenstreit, Sigmund (*German draughtsman, bef.1580-1611*) **GC**
    Bibl: Getty Photo Study Coll.; ▶Thieme-Becker
Heber-Percy, Michael David (*British architect*) **AV**
Heberlin, Hanns (*German woodcarver, act.1513-1521*) **BA**
    Bibl: Brandl. MET. MUS. J XIX-XX/1984-85 p.39-62; ▶Thieme-Becker
Hebert→see Hébert, Antoine Auguste Ernest
Hebert (Martinez de), Pedro (*French*) **JG**
Hébert, Adrien (*Canadian painter, 1890-1967*) **BA**

Hébert, Antoine Auguste Ernest   **BA PR**
    (*French artist, 1817-1908*)   WC
    (*French painter, 1817-1908*)   PR
    (*French painter, sculptor, printmaker, 1817-1908*)   BA
    (*French, 1817-1908*)   GC
    Bibl: ▶Bénézit; Getty Photo Study Coll. (Ptgs.); ▶Thieme-Becker; ▶Witt checklist
    Antoine Auguste Ernest Hebert   PR
    Hebert   PR
    Hebert, Ernest   **GC PR**
    Hebert, Ernest-Antoine-Auguste   GC
    Herbert, Ernest   PR
    Herbert, Ernest Auguste Antoine   **GC WC**
Hebert, Ernest→see Hébert, Antoine Auguste Ernest
Hebert, Ernest-Antoine-Auguste→see Hébert, Antoine Auguste Ernest
Hébert, Héléne→see Bertaux, Mme. Leon
Hebert, Jules (*Swiss artist, 1812-1897*) **WC**
Hébert, Louis-Philippe (*Canadian sculptor, 1850-1917*) **BA**
    Bibl: ▶Artists Canada; Canad. encyc.; ▶Creative Canada; ▶Natl. Gall. Canada libr. cat.; ▶Thieme-Becker
Hébert, Pierre Eugène Emile (*French sculptor, 1828-1893*) **BA**
Hebert, Theodore Martin (*French, 1829-1913*) **GC**
    Bibl: ▶Thieme-Becker
Hebey, Isabelle (*French designer*) **AV**
    Bibl: L'Oeil, 1989 Mar., no.404, p.68
Hebler, Herman (*Norwegian printmaker, painter, b.1911*) **BA**
Hebuli, Hanz de→see De Vals, Hans
Hebuterne, Andre (*French artist, 20th cent.*) **WC**
Hébuterne, Jeanne (*French artist, 1898-1920*) **BA**
Hecate Painter (*South Italian vase-painter, 4th century BC*) **GC**
    Bibl: ▶Trendall, Red-fig. vases Lucania
Hecht, Guillaume van der (*Belgian artist, op.1851-1863*) **WC**
Hecht, Hendrik (Henri) van der (*Belgian artist, 1841-1901*) **WC**
Hecht, J. Christopher (*American craftsman, b.1950*) **BA**
Hecht, Joseph (*Polish artist, 1891-*) **WC**
Heck, Claes (Nicolaas) Jacobsz. van der→see Heck, Claes Jacobsz. van der
Heck, Claes Dircksz. van der   **GC**
    (*Dutch artist, op.1604-m.1649*)   WC
    (*Dutch painter, 1571-1648*)   GC
    Bibl: ▶Bénézit; ▶Thieme-Becker; ▶Witt checklist
Heck, Claes Dirksz. van der   **WC**

Heck, Claes Dirksz. van der→see Heck, Claes Dircksz. van der
Heck, Claes Jacobsz. van der   **GC PR**
    (*Dutch artist, c.1575/81-1652*)   WC
    (*Dutch painter, 1575/81-1652*)   GC
    (*Dutch painter, d. 1652*)   PR
    Bibl: Rijksmuseum; ▶Thieme-Becker; ▶Witt checklist
    Claes Jacobsz. van der Heck   PR
    Heck, Claes (Nicolaas) Jacobsz. van der   PR
    Heck, Nicolaes (Claes) Jacob van der   **WC**
Heck, Nicolaes (Claes) Jacob van der→see Heck, Claes Jacobsz. van der
Hecke→see Hecke, Jan van den (I)
Hecke, Clara van (*Flemish, b.1593, act.1631*) **BA**
Hecke, Jan François van den (*Flemish weaver, act.1660-1695*) **BA**
    Bibl: Denuce, Antwerp. tapijtkunst en Handel, p.150, p.384; Gobel, Lowlands Tapestries; ▶Thieme-Becker
Hecke, Jan I van den→see Hecke, Jan van den (I)
Hecke, Jan van den (*Flemish weaver, d.ca.1633*) **BA**
Hecke, Jan van den (I)   **PR**
    (*Dutch painter, 1620-1684*)   PR
    (*Flemish artist, 1620-1684*)   WC
    (*Flemish, 1620-1684*)   GC
    Bibl: ▶Thieme-Becker
    Eckel, van   PR
    Hecke   PR
    Hecke, Jan I van den   **GC**
    Hecke, Jan, I van den   **WC**
    J. van der Hecke   PR
    Jan van den Hecke (I)   PR
    John van Heck   PR
Hecke, Jan, I van den→see Hecke, Jan van den (I)
Hecke, Peter van den (*Flemish artist, op.1711-m.1752*) **WC**
Heckel→see Heckel, Erich
Heckel→see Hickel, Anton
Heckel, Abraham   **GC WC**
    (*German draughtsman, act. 2nd half 18th c.*)   GC
    (*German(?) artist, 18th cent.*)   WC
    Bibl: ▶Thieme-Becker
Heckel, Augustin (*German artist, 1690-1770*) **WC**
Heckel, Catharina   **GC**
    (*German artist, 1699-1741*)   WC
    (*German draughtsman, 1699-1741*)   GC
    Bibl: ▶Thieme-Becker
    Sperling, Catharina   GC
    Sperling, Catherina, nee Heckel   **WC**

Heckel, Erich   **BA GC PR WC**
   (German artist, 1883-)   WC
   (German painter, 1883-1970)   PR
   (German painter, draughtsman,
     and printmaker, 1883-1970)   GC
   (German painter, printmaker,
     1883-1970)   BA
     Bibl: Getty Photo Study Coll.;
      ▶RILA/BHA; ▶Witt checklist
   Erich Heckel   PR
   Heckel   PR
Heckele, Jan van→see Eeckele, Jan
van
Heckell, van [Unidentified]
   (Unknown painter)   **PR**
     Bibl: (June 1, 1813, lot 58, Coxe)
   Van Heckell   PR
Hecken, Abraham I van den
   (Dutch, 17th century)   **GC**
     Bibl: ▶Thieme-Becker
Hecken, Abraham II van den→see
Hecken, Abraham van den (II)
Hecken, Abraham van den (II)   **PR**
   (Dutch painter, d. 1639)   PR
   (Flemish artist, op.1635-1655)   WC
   (Flemish, 17th century)   GC
     Bibl: ▶Thieme-Becker; ▶Witt
     checklist
   AB VD HECKEN   PR
   Abraham van den Hecken (II)   PR
   Hecken, Abraham II van den   **GC**
   Hecken, Heck or Hecke,
     Abraham, II Van den   **WC**
   Van der Hecken   PR
Hecken, Heck or Hecke, Abraham, II
Van den→see Hecken, Abraham
van den (II)
Hecken, Samuel van den   **GC WC**
   (Flemish artist, op.1616-1637)   WC
   (Flemish painter, act.1616-1637)   GC
     Bibl: ▶Thieme-Becker
Heckenauer, Leonard II (German
   printmaker, b.1650-1660, d.ca.
   1704)   **BA**
     Bibl: ▶Hollstein, German, v.13;
     ▶Thieme-Becker
   Heggenauer, Leonhard II   BA
Heckendorf, Franz   **GC WC**
   (German artist, 1888-)   WC
   (German painter, 1888-1962)   GC
     Bibl: ▶Thieme-Becker
Hecker, C.   **WC WI**
   (American artist, 19th cent.)   WC
   (American artist, op.1865-)   WI
Hecker, Christian Friedrich
   (Austrian gem carver in ITA, ca.
   1754-1795)   **BA**
     Bibl: ▶Bulgari, Argentieri d'Italia;
     Sattel Bernardini, Xenia 15
     (1988), p. 73-98; ▶Thieme-Becker
Hecker, Franz (German painter,
   printmaker, 1870-1944)   **BA**
Hecker, Hans-Dieter (West German
   architect, Freiburg, 1934-)   **AV**
     Bibl: Architecture & urbanism,
     1989 Apr., no.4(223), p.30

Hecker, Peter (German painter,
   b.1884)   **BA**
Hecker, Zvi   **AV BA**
   (Israeli architect, 1931-)   AV
   (Israeli architect, designer,
     painter, sculptor, b.1931)   BA
     Bibl: ▶Contemp. archts.
Heckmann, Hans (German ceramist,
   b.1935)   **BA**
Heckmann, Renate (German
   ceramist, b.1937)   **BA**
Heckmanns, Jürgen (German
   printmaker, sculptor, b.1939)   **BA**
Heckroth, Hein→see Heckroth,
   Heinrich
Heckroth, Heinrich   **BA**
   (German artist, 1901-)   WC
   (German scenographer, 1901-
     1970)   BA
   Heckroth, Hein   **WC**
Heckrott, Veit (West German
   architect)   **AV**
Hecquet, F. (French artist, op.1822-
   1824)   **WC**
Hectenburgh→see Huchtenburgh, Jan
van
Hector Joseph Lemaire→see Lemaire,
Hector Joseph
Hector Leroux→see Leroux, Hector
Hector Painter (vase-painter, ca.
   450-420 BC)   **GC**
     Bibl: ▶Beazley, Attic red-fig. vase-
     ptrs.; Richter, Attic red-fig. vases
Hector Painter, Circle of
   Polygnotos   **JG**
Hector Painter, Circle of
Polygnotos→see Hector Painter
Heda→see Heda, Gerrit Willemsz.
Heda→see Heda, Willem Claesz.
Heda, Gerrit→see Heda, Gerrit
Willemsz.
Heda, Gerrit Willemsz.   **GC PR WC**
   (Dutch artist, c.1620-a.1702)   WC
   (Dutch painter, ca.1620-bef.
     1702)   GC
   (Dutch painter, d. 1702)   PR
     Bibl: Getty Photo Study Coll.;
     ▶Thieme-Becker; ▶Witt checklist
   Gerrit van Heda   PR
   Gerrit Willemsz. Heda   PR
   Heda   PR
   Heda, Gerrit   PR
Heda, Pieter Claesz. (Dutch, 17th
   century)   **GC**
     Bibl: Christie's; Getty Photo Study
     Coll. (Duits coll.)
Heda, Willem Claesz→see Heda,
Willem Claesz.

Heda, Willem Claesz.   **BA GC PR WC**
   (Dutch artist, 1594-1680)   WC
   (Dutch painter and
     draughtsman, 1594-1680/82)   GC
   (Dutch painter, 1594-1680/82)   BA PR
     Bibl: ▶Bénézit; Getty Photo Study
     Coll.; ▶Nieuw NLD biog. woord.;
     ▶Petit Robert 2; ▶RILA/BHA;
     ▶Thieme-Becker; ▶Wurzbach, NLD
     Künst.-Lex.
   Heda   PR
   Heda, Willem Claesz   PR
   Heder   PR
   Heeda   PR
   Willem Claesz. Heda   PR
Hedberg, Kalle (Swedish artist,
   1894-)   **WC**
Hedborg, Jarrett (American
   architect, Hollywood, Calif)   **AV**
     Bibl: House & garden, 1988 Mar.,
     v.160, no.3, p.136
Hedderly, James (British, ca. 1815-
   1885)   **JG**
Hedegaard, Peter (Dutch artist,
   20th cent.)   **WC**
Hedel, Jan (Polish sculptor, act.
   1745-1748)   **BA**
     Bibl: Drema, Biuletyn Hist. Sztuki
     XLII/1 (1980) 63-75
Hedemann, Volker (East German
   photographer, b.1942)   **BA**
     Bibl: BILDENDE KUNST 4 (1984)
     166
Heder→see Heda, Willem Claesz.
Hederich, D.   **GC WC**
   (German artist, op.1597)   WC
   (German draughtsman, act.
     1597)   GC
     Bibl: ▶Witt checklist
Hedgeland, George (English glass-   **AV**
   painter, fl. mid-19th cent., London)
     Bibl: Apollo, 1989 Mar., v.129,
     no.325, p.162
Hedges, Janet (British sculptor,
   b.1955)   **BA**
     Bibl: ▶Babington Smith, Contemp.
     artists; ▶Intl. dir. exh. artists,
     1983
Hedges, Nick (British photographer,
   b.1943)   **BA**
     Bibl: ▶Contemp. photogs.; ▶Intl.
     dir. exh. artists, 1982
Hedley, H.   **WC WI**
   (British artist, op.1738)   WC
   (British artist, op.1738-)   WI
Hedley, Ralph (British artist, 1851-
   1913)   **WC WI**
Hedlinger, Johann Karl   **BA GC WC**
   (Swiss artist, 1691-1771)   WC
   (Swiss medalist in SWE, 1691-
     1771)   BA
   (Swiss, 1691-1771)   GC
     Bibl: ▶Svenskt konst.-lex.;
     ▶Thieme-Becker; ▶Witt checklist
Hedlund, Borje (Swedish artist, 20th
   cent.)   **WC**

Hedlund, Hans →see Hedlund, Hans
Fredrik
Hedlund, Hans Fredrik   **BA**
(Swedish architect)   AV
(Swedish architect, 1855-1931)   BA
  Bibl: Konsthistorisk tidskrift,
  1986, v.55, no.1, p.20; ▶Svenska
  konstnärer; ▶Svenskt konst.-lex.;
  ▶Thieme-Becker
Hedlund, Hans   **AV**
Hedman, R.   **WC WI**
(British artist, 19th cent.)   WC
(British artist, op.19th c.)   WI
Hedman, Richard *(City planner)*   **AV**
  Bibl: Planning, 1984 Oct., v.50,
  no.10, p.17
Hédouin, Jean Baptiste   **BA**
*(French cabinetmaker, act.1738,
  d.1783)*   BA
*(French ébéniste, master 1738,
  d. 1783)*   GC
  Bibl: ▶Salverte, Ébénistes 18e s.;
  ▶Thieme-Becker; ▶Vial, Artistes
  décorateurs
Hédouin, Jean-Baptiste   **GC**
Hédouin, Jean-Baptiste →see Hédouin,
Jean Baptiste
*Hedouin, Pierre Edmund
Alexandre →see* Hedovin, Edmond
Hedovin, Edmond   **GC**
(French artist, 1820-1889)   WC
(French painter, 1820-1889)   GC
  Bibl: ▶Thieme-Becker
**Hedouin, Pierre Edmund
Alexandre**   **WC**
Hedrick, Wally Bill *(American
  sculptor, painter, b.1928)*   **BA**
  Bibl: ▶WW Amer. Art, 1976
Hedrick, Wyatt C. *(American
  architect, active in Texas, 1888-
  1964)*   **AV**
Heebner, Mary *(American artist,
  b.1951)*   **BA**
  Bibl: Santa Barbara (CA, USA),
  Mus. Art, Mary Heebner (1980)
Heeda →see Heda, Willem Claesz.
Heede, Vigor van *(Flemish artist,
  1661-1708)*   **WC**
Heeks, Willy *(American painter, 20th
  c.)*   **BA**
  Bibl: Cameron, Arts mag., LXI
  (Sep. 1986) pp.40-46
Heel, Johanin *(German artist, op.
  1738-1759)*   **WC**
Heel, L. van *(Flemish artist, 17th
  cent.)*   **WC**
Heem →see Heem, Cornelis de
Heem →see Heem, David Davidsz. de
(II)
Heem →see Heem, David de (I)
Heem →see Heem, Jan Davidsz. de

Heem, Cornelis de   **BA GC PR WC**
(Dutch artist, 1631-1695)   WC
(Dutch painter, 1631-1695)   GC PR
(Flemish painter, 1631-1695)   BA
  Bibl: ▶Bénézit; Getty Photo Study
  Coll.; ▶Seyn, Écoles flam. et holl.;
  ▶Thieme-Becker; ▶Witt checklist;
  ▶Wurzbach, NLD Künst.-Lex.
C. de Heem   PR
C. de Hemm   PR
C. Deheem   PR
Cornelis de Heem   PR
Heem   PR
Heem, David (III) Cornelisz. de
(Dutch painter, 1663-aft.1729)   **PR**
  Bibl: ▶Thieme-Becker
David (III) Cornelisz. de Heem   PR
Jan de Heem   PR
Heem, David Davidsz. (II) →see
Heem, David Davidsz. de (II)
Heem, David Davidsz. de →see Heem,
David Davidsz. de (II)
Heem, David Davidsz. de (II)   **PR**
(Dutch artist, op.1668)   WC
(Dutch painter, 1610-aft.1668)   GC
(Dutch painter, act. 1668)   PR
  Bibl: ▶Bénézit; Getty Photo Study
  Coll.; ▶Thieme-Becker
David Davidsz. Heem (II)   PR
David II Davidsz. Heem   PR
Heem   PR
Heem, David Davidsz. (II)   PR
Heem, David Davidsz. de   **PR WC**
Heem, David II Davidsz.   PR
Heem, David II Davidsz. de   **GC**
Heem, David de →see Heem, David
de (I)
Heem, David de (I)   **PR**
(Dutch artist, c.1570-c.1632)   WC
(Dutch painter, 1570-1632)   PR
*(Dutch painter, ca.1570-ca.
  1632)*   GC
  Bibl: Getty Photo Study Coll.;
  ▶Thieme-Becker; ▶Witt checklist
David de Heem (I)   PR
Heem   PR
Heem, David de   PR
Heem, David de I   **GC**
Heem, David I de   PR
Heem, David, I de   **WC**
Heem, David de I →see Heem, David
de (I)
Heem, David I de →see Heem, David
de (I)
Heem, David II Davidsz. →see Heem,
David Davidsz. de (II)
Heem, David II Davidsz. de →see
Heem, David Davidsz. de (II)
Heem, David, I de →see Heem, David
de (I)
Heem, Jan Davidsz de →see Heem,
Jan Davidsz. de

Heem, Jan Davidsz. de   **BA PR WC**
(Dutch artist, 1606-1683/4)   WC
*(Dutch painter and
  draughtsman, 1606-1683/84)*   GC
(Dutch painter, 1606-1683/84)   PR
(Dutch painter, 1606-ca.1684)   BA
  Bibl: ▶Bénézit; Getty Photo Study
  Coll.; ▶RILA/BHA;
  ▶Thieme-Becker; ▶Wurzbach, NLD
  Künst.-Lex.
D. de Heem   PR
D. Heem   PR
Dahem   PR
De Heem   PR
De Heeme   PR
De Heen   PR
De Hem   PR
De Heme   PR
De Hemee   PR
De Hum   PR
De Hume   PR
de oude D'Heem   PR
de oude de Heem   PR
Deheem   PR
Deheim   PR
Deheme   PR
Ditteems   PR
Du Hem   PR
He Heem   PR
Heem   PR
Heem, Jan Davidz de   PR
Heem, Jan I Davidsz. de   **GC**
I. D. De Heem   PR
I.D. De Heem   PR
J. D. Deehem   PR
J. De Heem   PR
J.D. De Heem   PR
J.D. de Hemm   PR
J.D. Heem   PR
Jan Davidsz. de Heem   PR
Jan Davidts de Heem   PR
Jan de Heem   PR
Jan van Heem   PR
Johan de Heem   PR
John David de Haeem   PR
John David de Haem   PR
John David de Heem   PR
Monsu' Gem Fiammengo   PR
Van Heem.   PR
vander Eem   PR
Heem, Jan I Davidsz. de →see Heem,
Jan Davidsz. de
Heem, Jan II Jansz. de *(Dutch
  painter, 1650-1683/84)*   **GC**
  Bibl: ▶Thieme-Becker
Heem, Nicolaas de [Unidentified]
(Unknown painter)   **PR**
  Bibl: 1724 Trip inventory
Nicolaas de Heem   PR
Heems →see Huens [Unidentified]
Heemskerck →see Heemskerck,
Egbert van (the elder)
Heemskerck →see Heemskerck,
Egbert van (the younger)

Heemskerck → *see Heemskerck, Maerten van*

Heemskerck or Heemskerk, Bastiaan or Sebastiaan → *see Heemskerck, Bastiaan*

Heemskerck or Heemskerk, Egbert, I van → *see Heemskerck, Egbert van (the elder)*

Heemskerck or Heemskerk, Egbert, II van → *see Heemskerck, Egbert van (the younger)*

Heemskerck or Heemskerk, Maarten van → *see Heemskerck, Maerten van*

Heemskerck van Beest, Jacob Eduard   **GC**
   (Dutch artist, 1828-1894)   WC
   (Dutch painter and draughtsman, 1824-1894)   GC
     Bibl: ▶Thieme-Becker

Heemskerk van Beest, Jacob Eduard van   **WC**

Heemskerck van Beest, Jacoba Berendina van   **BA GC**
   (Dutch artist, 1876-1923)   WC
   (Dutch painter, 1876-1923)   GC
   (Dutch painter, printmaker, 1876-1923)   BA
     Bibl: ▶Scheen, Ned. beeldende kunst.; ▶Thieme-Becker; ▶Vollmer, Künst.-Lex. 20. Jhr.; ▶Witt checklist

Heemskerk van Beest, Jacoba Berendina van   **WC**

Heemskerck, Bastiaan   **GC**
   (Dutch artist, op.1691-m.1748)   WC
   (Dutch painter, act.1691-d. 1748)   GC
     Bibl: ▶Thieme-Becker

Heemskerck or Heemskerk, Bastiaan or Sebastiaan   **WC**
Heemskerck, Sebastiaan   GC

Heemskerck, Egbert I van → *see Heemskerck, Egbert van (the elder)*

Heemskerck, Egbert van → *see Heemskerck, Egbert van (the elder)*

Heemskerck, Egbert van (I) → *see Heemskerck, Egbert van (the elder)*

Heemskerck, Egbert van (the elder)   **PR**
   (Dutch artist, c.1634-1704)   WC
   (Dutch painter and draughtsman, 1634/35-1704)   GC
   (Dutch painter, 1634/35-1704)   PR
     Bibl: Getty Photo Study Coll.; ▶Thieme-Becker

A. Heemskirk   PR
E. Heemskirk   PR
E. Hemskerck   PR
E. Hemskirk   PR
E. Humskirk   PR
Egb, Hemskerck   PR
Egb. Hemskerck   PR
Egb. Hemskirk   PR
Egbert Heemskerck   PR
Egbert Heemskirk   PR
Egbert Hemskerck   PR
Egbert Hemskerk   PR
Egbert Hemskirk   PR
Egbert Hermskerck   PR
Egbert van Heemskerck (I)   PR
Heemskerck   PR

Heemskerck or Heemskerk, Egbert, I van   **WC**
Heemskerck, Egbert I van   **GC**
Heemskerck, Egbert van   PR
Heemskerck, Egbert van (I)   PR
Heemskerk   PR
Heemskerk, Egbert I van   GC
Heemskerk, Egbert van   PR
Heemskirk   PR
Hemnskirk   PR
Hemokerk   PR
Hemskerck   PR
Hemskercke   PR
Hemskerk   PR
Hemskerke   PR
Hemskirck   PR
Hemskirk   PR
Hemskirke   PR
Hiemskirk   PR
Kemskerck   PR
marked Egb. Hemskerck 1661   PR
Old Hemskerck   PR
Old Hemskirk   PR

Heemskerck, Egbert van (the younger)   **PR**
   (Dutch artist, -1744(?))   WC
   (Dutch painter, d. 1744)   PR
     Bibl: ▶Bénézit, [dates 1634-1704 are incorrect]; ▶Thieme-Becker; ▶Witt checklist
Egbert van Heemskerck (the younger)   PR
Heemskerck   PR

Heemskerck or Heemskerk, Egbert, II van   **WC**
Hemskerk, Egbert (the Younger)   PR
Hemskirk, jun.   PR

Heemskerck, Maarten Jacobsz. van → *see Heemskerck, Maerten van*

Heemskerck, Maarten van → *see Heemskerck, Maerten van*

Heemskerck, Maerten van   **BA CE FA PR**
   (1498-1574; Draftsman, Painter, Netherlands)   FA
   (early Netherlandish painter, printmaker, 1498-1574)   BA
   (Netherlandish painter, 1498-1574)   PR
   (Netherlands artist, 1498-1574)   WC
   (North Netherlandish painter, draughtsman, and printmaker, 1498-1574)   GC
   (Painter, engraver, draughtsman, 1498-1574)   CE
     Bibl: Getty Photo Study Coll. (Ptgs.); Grosshans, MAERTEN VAN HEEMSKERCK, DIE GEMALDE (1980); ▶Osten, Ptg. & sculp. DEU & NLD; ▶RILA/BHA, Subject, 1988; ▶Thieme-Becker, v.16, p.227 ff.; ▶Wurzbach, NLD Künst.-Lex.
Heemskerck   PR

Heemskerck or Heemskerk, Maarten van   **WC**
Heemskerck, Maarten Jacobsz. van   PR
Heemskerck, Maarten van   CE GC PR
Heemskerck, Marten van   **GC PR**
Heemskerck, Martinus   CE
Heemskerk   PR
Heemskerk, Maarten van   FA
Heemskirk   PR
Heemskirke   PR
Hemskerck   PR
Hemskerk   PR
Hemskirck   PR
Hemskirk   PR
M. Heemskirck   PR
M. Heemskirke   PR
M. Hemskirck   PR
M. Hemskirk   PR
Maarten van Heemskerck   PR
Maerten van Heemskerck   PR
Martin Heemskirke   PR
Martin Hemskirk   PR
[Martin] van Veen   PR
Martino Hemskerck   PR
Van Heemskerck, Maarten   CE
Van Heemskerck, Maerten   CE
Van Heemskerck, Marten   **CE**
Van Heemskerck, Martinus   CE
Van Heemskerk, Maarten   CE
Van Heemskerk, Marten   CE
Van Heemskerk, Martinus   CE
van Veen   PR

Heemskerck, Marten van → *see Heemskerck, Maerten van*

Heemskerck, Martinus → *see Heemskerck, Maerten van*

Heemskerck, Sebastiaan → *see Heemskerck, Bastiaan*

Heemskerk → *see Heemskerck, Egbert van (the elder)*

Heermann, L. (German artist, 1811-
1881)   **WC**
Heermann, Norbert→see Heerman,
Norbert
Heermans, Augustyn→see Herrmann,
Augustin
Heerschop or Herschop,
Hendrick→see Heerschop, Hendrik
Heerschop, Hendrick→see
Heerschop, Hendrik
Heerschop, Hendrik   **BA**
(Dutch artist, 1620/1-p.1672)   **WC**
(Dutch painter, 1620/21-d. aft.
1672)   **GC**
(Dutch painter, printmaker,
1627-after 1672)   **BA**
Bibl: ▶Thieme-Becker; ▶Wurzbach,
NLD Künst.-Lex.
Heerschop or Herschop,
Hendrick   **WC**
Heerschop, Hendrick   **GC**
Heerstal, Gerrit van *(Dutch*
sculptor, act.1710-1750)   **BA**
Bibl: ▶Thieme-Becker; ▶Wurzbach,
NLD Künst.-Lex.
Heerup, Henry   **BA WC**
(Danish painter, sculptor,
printmaker, b.1907)   **BA**
(Dutch artist, 20th cent.)   **WC**
Bibl: ▶Bénézit; ▶Vollmer,
Künst.-Lex. 20. Jhr., v.2
Heery, George T. *(American*
architect)   **AV**
Bibl: ▶AIA Pro File, 1983
Hees, F. van   **GC WC**
(Netherlandish painter, act.
1656)   **GC**
(Netherlands artist, op.1656)   **WC**
Bibl: ▶Witt checklist
Hees, Gerrit van   **GC PR WC**
(Dutch artist, op.1650-m.1670)   **WC**
(Dutch painter, act. 1650, d.
1670)   **PR**
(Dutch painter, act.1660-d.
1670)   **GC**
Bibl: Getty Photo Study Coll.;
▶Thieme-Becker
Gerrit Hees   **PR**
Gerrit van Hees   **PR**
Hees, Maria *(Dutch designer,*
b.1948)   **BA**
Bibl: Dutch Art & Arch. Today, 8
(May 1981) 26-31
Heesbeen, Petra van *(Dutch potter,*
20th c.)   **BA**
Bibl: Ceramics monthly, XXVIII/5
(May 1980) pp.32-37
Heesche, Franz *(German artist,*
1806-1876)   **WC**
Heeser, Peter M. *(German artist,*
b.1938)   **BA**
Bibl: Krefeld (BRD), Kaiser Wilhelm
Museum, PETER M. HEESER (1978)
Heest, Jaap van *(Dutch architect)*   **AV**
Bibl: Architecture & urbanism,
1988 Oct., no.10(217), p.158

Heeswijk, Hans van *(Dutch*
architect, 1952-)   **AV**
Bibl: Casabella, 1984 July-Aug.,
v.48, no.504, p.16
Heeusman, P.T. *(Netherlands artist,*
17th/18th cent.)   **WC**
Hefele, J.F.   **GC WC**
(German artist, -c.1710)   **WC**
(German painter, d. ca.1710)   **GC**
Bibl: ▶Witt checklist
Hefele, Melchior *(Austrian architect,*
1716-1799)   **BA**
Bibl: ▶Portoghesi, Diz. arch. e
urbanistica; ▶Thieme-Becker
Häfele, Melchior   **BA**
Heverle, Melchior   **BA**
Höferle, Melchior   **BA**
Hefernan, J. P. *(American architect,*
Boston, Mass., fl. 1930's)   **AV**
Bibl: Boston Preservation Alliance
letter, 1988 Aug., v.9, no.7, p.1
Heffernan, Joanna *(Irish, act.ca.*
1855-ca.1903)   **BA**
Bibl: Fermigier, COURBET, p.9, 95,
98; Gregory, JAMES MCNEILL
WHISTLER, p.84 ff, p.228;
Havlice, World ptg. idx.; Mack,
GUSTAVE COURBET, p.204
Heffner, Karl   **GC WC**
(German artist, 1849-p.1889)   **WC**
(German painter, 1849-1925)   **GC**
Bibl: ▶Thieme-Becker
Hefft, Anton *(Austrian architect,*
1815-1900)   **BA**
Bibl: ▶Österr. biog. Lex. 1815-
1950; ▶Thieme-Becker
Heft, Carol *(American painter, 20th*
c.)   **BA**
Bibl: Arts Mag. LVII (2 Oct 1982),
p.17
Heftel, Daniel L. *(Central and South*
American artist, 20th cent.)   **WC**
Hefti, Anja *(Swiss artist, 20th cent.)*   **WC**
Heftler-Louiche, Jean-Marc *(French*
architect)   **AV**
Bibl: Country life, 1989 Jan.12,
v.183, no.2, p.72
Hegar, Milan *(Czech graphic*
designer, 20th c.)   **BA**
Hege, Walter *(German*
photographer, 1893-1955)   **GC**
Bibl: ▶Idx. Amer. photog. colls.
Hegedüs, Béla *(Hungarian painter,*
20th c.)   **BA**
Hegedušič, Krsto   **BA WC**
(Yugoslav artist, 1901-)   **WC**
(Yugoslav painter, b.1901)   **BA**
Bibl: Hague, Gemeentemuseum,
KRSTO HEGEDUSIC (1960);
▶Vollmer, Künst.-Lex. 20. Jhr.
Hegel, Konstanty *(Polish sculptor,*
1799-1876)   **BA**
Bibl: ▶Bénézit; BIULETYN HISTORII
SZTUKI, XL/3 (1978) 319;
▶Thieme-Becker

Hegemann, Werner *(German-born*
American urban planner, author,
educator, 1881-1936)   **AV**
Bibl: ▶Macmillan encyc. archts.
Hegenbart, Fritz *(German artist,*
1864-)   **WC**
Hegenbarth, Emanuel *(German*
painter, 1868-1923)   **BA**
Bibl: ▶Thieme-Becker; ▶Vollmer,
Künst.-Lex. 20. Jhr.
Hegenbarth, Josef   **BA WC**
(German artist, 1884-)   **WC**
(German painter, printmaker,
1884-1962)   **BA**
Bibl: ▶Bénézit; ▶Vollmer,
Künst.-Lex. 20. Jhr.
Hegesiboulos Painter *(vase-painter,*
ca. 530-500 BC)   **GC**
Bibl: ▶Beazley, Attic red-fig. vase-
ptrs.; Richter, Attic red-fig. vases
Hegewald, Ulf *(German painter,*
b.1942)   **BA**
Bibl: Aachen (BRD), Nene Galerie,
ULF HEGEWALD (1976); ▶WW
Arts DEU
Hegg, Eric A. *(American*
photographer, 1868-1955)   **BA**
Bibl: HISTORIC PRESERVATION, II
(Apr-June 1977) 14-21
Hegg, Theresa Maria, (nee de
Landerset) *(Swiss artist, 1829-p.*
1875)   **WC**
Heggenauer, Leonhard II→see
Heckenauer, Leonard II
Heggli, Hans II→see Jegli, Hans II
Hegi, Franz *(Swiss artist, 1774-1850)*   **WC**
Hegi, Salomon *(Swiss artist, 1783-*
1837)   **WC**
Hegias of Athens *(Greek sculptor,*
5th c BC (1st half))   **GC**
Bibl: ▶Robertson, Greek art, p.197
Hegylos of Laconia *(Greek sculptor,*
6th c BC)   **GC**
Bibl: Getty Photo Study Coll.;
▶Robertson, Greek art, p.59
Hehl, Josef *(German sculptor,*
ceramist, 1885-1953)   **BA**
Bibl: ▶Vollmer, Künst.-Lex. 20. Jhr.
Heiber, Heinz *(German sculptor,*
architect, b.1928)   **BA**
Bibl: ▶Libr. of Congr. Name Auth.
File; UC Santa Barbara cat. sheets;
▶WW Arts DEU
Heiberg, Astri Welhaven
(Norwegian artist, 1883-)   **WC**
Heiberg, Bernt *(Norwegian*
architect)   **AV**
Bibl: Byggekunst, 1984, no.5,
p.253
Heiberg, Edvard   **AV BA**
(Danish architect, 1897-1958)   **BA**
(Norwegian architect)   **AV**
Bibl: ▶Avery Libr. cat.; ▶Avery
obit. idx.; Ravn, ARKITEKT
EDVARD HEIBERG
Heiberg, Jean Hjalmar *(Norwegian*
artist, 1883-)   **WC**

Heiberg, Kasper *(Danish artist, 1928-1984)* **BA**
    Bibl: ▶Nørregård-Nielsen, Dansk kunst; Odense (DNK), Brandts Klaedefabrik, Trade de Kasper Heidberg, 1987

Heicke, Joseph *(German artist, 1811-1861)* **WC**

Heidacker, Stephanus *(West German painter, b.1959)* **BA**
    Bibl: Guide exh. artists: N. Amer. ptrs.

Heidbrinck, Oswald *(French artist, 1850-1914)* **WC**

Heide, Henning von der **BA**
    (German artist, op.1487-1520) **WC**
    (German sculptor, ca.1460-1521) **BA**
    Bibl: ▶Allgem. Deut. Biog.; Baedekers Lübeck (1971), 28; ▶Thieme-Becker; Wallraf-Richartz JB (1975), p.65-84

    Heyde or Heide, Henning von der **WC**

Heideck, Carl Wilhelm, Freiherr von **BA**
    (German artist, 1788-1861) **WC**
    (German painter, 1788-1861) **BA GC**
    Bibl: ▶Bénézit; ▶Kindlers Malerei Lex.; ▶Thieme-Becker

    Heideck, Heidegger or Heydeck, Karl Wilhelm Freiherr von **WC**
    Heideck, Karl Wilhelm von **GC**
    Heidegger, Karl Wilhelm von **GC**
    Heideck, Heidegger or Heydeck, Karl Wilhelm Freiherr von →see Heideck, Carl Wilhelm, Freiherr von
    Heideck, Karl Wilhelm von →see Heideck, Carl Wilhelm, Freiherr von

Heidegger or Heid, Johann (Hans) Ulrich *(Swiss artist, 1700-1747)* **WC**
    Heidegger, Karl Wilhelm von →see Heideck, Carl Wilhelm, Freiherr von

Heidelbach, Karl *(German artist, 20th cent.)* **WC**

Heidelberg Painter **GC JG**
    (vase-painter, ca. 575-555 BC) **GC**
    Bibl: ▶Beazley, Attic bl.-fig. vase-ptrs.; Boardman, Attic Bl.-fig. Vases

Heidelberger, Herbert *(American, 20th c.)* **BA**

Heideloff or Heydeloff, Carl Alexander von →see Heideloff, Karl Alexander von

Heideloff, Karl Alexander von **BA**
    (German architect, historian, sculptor, 1789-1865) **BA**
    (German artist, 1789-1865) **WC**
    Bibl: ▶Brockhaus Enzyk.; ▶Neue deutsche Biog.; ▶Thieme-Becker

    Heideloff or Heydeloff, Carl Alexander von **WC**

Heideloff, Nicolaus Innocentius Wilhelm. Clemens van *(German artist, c.1761-1837)* **WC**

Heideloff, Victor Wilhelm, Peter *(German artist, 1757-1817)* **WC**

Heidelsberger, Heinrich *(German, 1906 -)* **JG**

Heideman, Susan *(American painter, b.1950)* **BA**
    Bibl: ▶Intl. dir. exh. artists, 1983; Northampton, Smith College Mus of Art, SUSAN HEIDEMAN (1985)

Heidemens, Henri *(Engraver, 1801-1846)* **WI**

Heidenreich, Theo *(German ceramist, b.1915)* **BA**

Heider, Klaus *(German painter, printmaker, filmmaker, b.1936)* **BA**
    Bibl: Tubingen, Kunsthalle, KLAUS HEIDER (1975), p.110

Heidergerken, Manfred *(West German architect)* **AV**
    Bibl: Bauwelt, 1989 July 14, v.80, no.27, p.1299

Heidland, R. *(German artist, op.c. 1850)* **WC**

Heidorn, M. *(W. German architect)* **AV**
    Bibl: Deutsche Bauzeitschrift, 1986 Nov., v.34, no.11, p.1391

Heidtmann, Hans Christopher *(German goldsmith, 1728-1804)* **BA**
    Bibl: Schönfeld, Kunst u. Antiquitäten 2 (Mar-Apr 1983) 42; ▶Thieme-Becker

Heier or Hoeur, Johann *(German artist, op.1737)* **WC**

Heigel, Franz Napoleon **GC WC**
    (French artist, 1813-1888) **WC**
    (German draughtsman, 1813-1888) **GC**
    Bibl: ▶Bénézit

Heigel, Joseph **GC WC**
    (German artist, 1780-1837) **WC**
    (German painter, 1780-1837) **GC**
    Bibl: ▶Bénézit

Heighway, Richard *(British artist, op.1787-1793)* **WC WI**

Heij, Johanna Catharina *(Dutch sculptor, painter, b.1932)* **BA**
    Bibl: ▶Scheen, Ned. beeldende kunst.

Heijboer or Heyboer, Anton →see Heyboer, Anton
Heijboer, Anton →see Heyboer, Anton
Heijde, Herman Henry op der →see Heyde, Herman Henry op der
Heijden, Jacobus Cornelis Johannes van der →see Heyden, J.C.J. van der
Heijl, Marinus →see Heyl, Marinus
Heijligers or Heyligers, Antoon Francois →see Heyligers, Antoon Francois
Heijligers, Antoon Francois →see Heyligers, Antoon Francois

Heijmans, Eduard Hendrick *(Dutch artist, 1912-)* **WC**

Heikel, Elia *(Finnish architect)* **AV**
    Bibl: Arkkitehti, 1986, no.1, p.54

Heiken, Ulrich *(West German architect)* **AV**
    Bibl: Architekture & Wohnen, 1988 Nov.-Dec., no.6, p.136

Heikkinen, Mikko *(Finnish architect)* **AV**
    Bibl: Arkkitehti, 1985, no.5, p.72

Heil, Daniel van **GC PR WC**
    (Flemish artist, 1604-1662(?)) **WC**
    (Flemish painter, 1604-1662) **PR**
    (Flemish, 1604-1662) **GC**
    Bibl: ▶Thieme-Becker; ▶Witt checklist
    Daniel van Heil **PR**
    Van Heil **PR**

Heil, Jan Baptist van *(Flemish artist, 1609-p.1661)* **WC**

Heil, Richard *(West German architect, Frankfurt)* **AV**
    Bibl: Deutsche Bauzeitung, 1989 Apr., v.123, no.4, p.56

Heil, Theodore van **GC WC**
    (Flemish artist, op.1668) **WC**
    (Flemish, act.1668) **GC**
    Bibl: ▶Witt checklist

Heilbuth →see Heilbuth, Ferdinand

Heilbuth, Ferdinand **BA GC PR WC**
    (French artist, 1826-1889) **WC**
    (French painter, 1826-1889) **BA PR**
    (French, 1826-1889) **GC**
    Bibl: ▶RILA/BHA; ▶Thieme-Becker
    Ferdinand Heilbuth **PR**
    Heilbuth **PR**

Heilemann, Ernst *(German artist, 1870-)* **WC**

Heiliger, Bernhard **BA WC**
    (German artist, 1915-) **WC**
    (German sculptor, painter, b.1915) **BA**
    Bibl: ▶Encyc. world art; ▶Gorenflo, Bild. Künstler; ▶Havlice, Idx. art. bio.; ▶Vollmer, Künst.-Lex. 20. Jhr.; ▶WW Arts DEU

Heilmair, Emil *(German artist, 1802-1836)* **WC**

Heilmann, Anton *(German artist, 1830-1912)* **WC**

Heilmann, J.J. *(French, active 1852-1857)* **JG**

Heilmann, Jean Gaspard →see Heilmann, Johann Kaspar

Heilmann, Johann Kaspar **PR WC**
    (French painter, 1718-1760) **GC**
    (German artist, 1718-1760) **WC**
    (German painter, 1718-1760) **PR**
    Bibl: ▶Bénézit; ▶Thieme-Becker

Heilmann, Jean Gaspard **GC PR**
    Johann Kaspar Heilmann **PR**

Heilmann, Mary *(American painter, b.1940)* **BA**
    Bibl: ▶Art Index, v.38; ▶ARTbibl. mod., 11 (1980-84) #1804; ▶Intl. dir. exh. artists, 1982; ▶NY art yrbk.

Heilmayer, Karl (German artist, 1829-1908) **WC**

Heim, Francois Joseph **GC WC**
(French artist, 1787-1865) WC
(French, 1787-1865) ·GC
Bibl: ▶Thieme-Becker; ▶Witt checklist

Heim, Heinz (German artist, 1859-1895) **WC**

Heim, Jacques (French couturier, 20th c.) **BA**

Heim, Jean-Pierre **AV BA**
(French architect, 20th c.) BA
(French architect, Paris) AV
Bibl: Architectes architecture, 1988 Mar., no.185, p.25; ▶Avery period. idx., 4th suppl.; Paris phone book, 1988

Heim, Régine (Swiss artist, b.1908) **BA**
Bibl: ▶Künst.-Lex. Schweiz 20. Jahrh.; ▶Lex. zeitgen. Schweiz. Künstler

Heimarmene Painter **GC**
Bibl: ▶Beazley, Attic red-fig. vase-ptrs.

Heimbach → see Heimbach, Wolfgang
Heimbach, Christian Wolfgang → see Heimbach, Wolfgang

Heimbach, Wolfgang **BA GC PR**
(German artist, c.1615-p.1678) WC
(German painter, ca.1610-aft. 1678) PR
(German painter, ca.1610-after 1678) BA
(German, ca.1615-ca.1678) GC
Bibl: Getty Photo Study Coll. (Ptgs.); ▶RILA/BHA; ▶Thieme-Becker; ▶Witt checklist
Heimbach PR
Heimbach, Christian Wolfgang GC

Heimbach, Wolfgang (not Christian) **WC**
Wolfgang Heimbach PR
Heimbach, Wolfgang (not Christian) → see Heimbach, Wolfgang

Heimberg, Theodor (German artist, 19th cent.) **WC**

Heimerdinger → see Heimerdinger, Friedrich

Heimerdinger, Friedrich (German painter, 1817-1882) **PR**
Bibl: ▶Thieme-Becker
Friedrich Heimerdinger PR
Heimerdinger PR

Heimig, Walter (German artist, 1881-) **WC**

Heimlich, Johann Daniel **GC WC**
(French artist, 1740-1796) WC
(French painter, 1740-1796) GC
Bibl: ▶Bénézit

Heimsath, Clovis (American architect, 1930-) **AV**
Bibl: ▶Amer. archts. dir., 1970

Heimsener Master (German woodcarver, act.1510-1520) **BA**
Bibl: Karrenbrock, NEIDERDEUTSCHE BEITRAGE ZUR KUNSTGESCHICHTE, XXVI(1987), 63-82

Hein → see Heins, D.

Hein, Brigit (German artist, b.1942) **BA**

Hein, Christianus Hendricus (Dutch painter, 1815-aft.1858) **GC**
Bibl: ▶Thieme-Becker

Hein, Eugen (Austrian architect, 1956-) **AV**
Bibl: Kenchiku bunka, 1984 Dec., v.39, p.458, p.84

Hein, Frank (American painter, b.1942) **BA**

Hein, Franz **BA WC**
(German artist, op.1863) WC
(German painter, printmaker, 1863-1927) BA

Hein, Hendrik Jan **GC WC**
(Dutch artist, 1822-1866) WC
(Dutch painter, 1822-1866) GC
Bibl: ▶Thieme-Becker

Hein, M. (Dutch artist, 17th cent.) **WC**

Hein, Wilhelm (German artist, b.1940) **BA**

Heince, Haentz, Hainsse, Heins, Heintze, Hinse or Hintz, Zacharie (French artist, 1611-1669) **WC**

Heindl or Heintl, Wolfgang Andreas (Austrian artist, 1683/4-1757) **WC**

Heindorff, Michael **BA WI**
(British artist, b.1949) WI
(British painter, printmaker, b.1949) BA

Heine → see Heine, Friedrich Wilhelm

Heine, Adalbert (German artist, 1769-1831) **WC**

Heine, Carl (German artist, 1842-1882) **WC**

Heine, Fredrich-Wilhelm → see Heine, Friedrich Wilhelm

Heine, Friedrich Wilhelm (German painter, 1845-1921) **PR**
Bibl: ▶Thieme-Becker
Friedrich Wilhelm Heine PR
Heine PR
Heine, Fredrich-Wilhelm PR

Heine, Johann Adalbert (German artist, op.1885-1890) **WC**

Heine, Ludwig (Friedrich Ludwig) (German artist, op.1816-1834) **WC**

Heine, Thomas Theodor **BA WC**
(German artist, 1867-) WC
(German painter, printmaker, author, 1867-1948) BA

Heine, Wilhelm (Peter Bernhard Wilhelm) (German artist, 1827-1885) **WC**

Heine, Wilhelm Joseph (German artist, 1813-1839) **WC**

Heinecken, Robert (American photographer, b.1931) **BA**
Bibl: ▶Auer, Encyc. photographes; ▶Contemp. photogs.; ▶ICP encyc. photog.

Heinefetter, Johann Baptist (German painter, 1815-1902) **BA**

Heinemann, Alo (Belgian architect) **AV**
Bibl: Deutsche Bauzeitung, 1986 Aug., v.120, no.8, p.24

Heinemann, Ernst **BA WI**
(American printmaker, 1848-1912) BA
(Engraver, Fort Wadsworth, NY., 1848-1912) WI
Bibl: ▶Thieme-Becker; ▶WWW Amer., v.1

Heinemann, Georg (West German architect) **AV**
Bibl: Deutsches Architektenblatt, 1987 Sept., v.19, no.9, p.993

Heinemann-Perliz, Annemarie (Belgian architect) **AV**
Bibl: Deutsche Bauzeitung, 1986 Aug., v.120, no.8, p.24

Heiner, Eugene (American architect, Galveston, Tex., fl. ca.1880) **AV**
Bibl: Texas architect, 1988 Nov.-Dec., p.40

Heiner, Wilhelm (German artist, 1902-) **WC**

Heinersdorff, Gottfried (German manufacturer, act.1911) **BA**

Heiney, Alison (British landscape architect, London) **AV**
Bibl: Building design, 1989 Sept.22, no.954, p.18

Heinig, Ilja (German painter, b.1950) **BA**
Bibl: ▶Art Index, v.36; Ohff, Kunstwerk, XXXVIII (Sep 1985) pp.56-69

Heinigke, Otto W. (American stained glass designer, 1850-1915) **AV**
Bibl: Stained glass, 1986 Summer, v.81, no.2, p.90

Heinisch, Barbara (West German painter, performance artist, b.1944) **BA**

Heinisch, Karl Adam (German artist, 1847-1927) **WC**

Heinkel, G. van der **GC WC**
(Dutch artist, 18th cent.) WC
(Dutch draughtsman, 18th century) GC
Bibl: ▶Witt checklist

Heinlein, Heinrich **GC WC**
(German artist, 1803-1885) WC
(German draughtsman, 1803-1885) GC
Bibl: ▶Bénézit

Heino, Marja (Finnish architect) **AV**
Bibl: Arkkitehtuurikilpailuja, 1989, no.2, p.1

Heino, Raimo (Finnish medalist, b.1932) **BA**
Bibl: Passi, MEDAL 8 (summer 1986) 26-29

Heino, Steve *(American painter, 20th c.)* **BA**

Heinrich Aldegrever → see Aldegrever, Heinrich

Heinrich Andreas Sophus Petersen → see Petersen, Heinrich Andreas Sophus

Heinrich Burkel → see Bürkel, Heinrich

Heinrich Campendonck → see Campendonk, Heinrich

Heinrich de Aldegrever → see Aldegrever, Heinrich

Heinrich Füger → see Füger, Heinrich

Heinrich Johann Vogeler → see Vogeler, Heinrich Johann

Heinrich Nauen → see Nauen, Heinrich

Heinrich Rieter → see Rieter, Heinrich

Heinrich Schaumann → see Schaumann, Heinrich

Heinrich Schlesinger → see Schlesinger, Heinrich

[Heinrich] Snellinck → see Snellinck, Jan I

Heinrich von Angeli → see Angeli, Heinrich von

Heinrich Wilhelm Schweickardt → see Schweickardt, Heinrich Wilhelm

Heinrich Wuest → see Wüst, Johann Heinrich

Heinrich, August **BA GC**
  (German artist, 1794-1822) WC
  (German painter, 1794-1822) BA
  (German, 1794-1822) GC
    Bibl: ▶Thieme-Becker; ▶Witt checklist

Heinrich, August (Johann August) **WC**
Heinrich, August (Johann August) → see Heinrich, August

Heinrich, C. **GC WC**
  (German artist, 17th/18th cent.) WC
  (German, 17th/18th centuries) GC
    Bibl: ▶Thieme-Becker

Heinrich, Eduard *(Hungarian artist, 1819-1885)* **WC**

Heinrich, Erwin *(German)* **GC**
    Bibl: Gernsheim, Corpus Photog. of Drawings, 1435

Heinrich, Franz *(German artist, 1802-1890)* **WC**

Heinrich, George *(American architectural photographer)* **AV**
    Bibl: Architecture Minnesota, 1989 Mar.-Apr., v.15, no.2, p.36

Heinrich, Hans *(German artist, 17th cent.)* **WC**

Heinrich, Karl *(Austrian architect, Weis)* **AV**
    Bibl: ▶Verzeich. Öst. Ziviltech.

Heinrich, Olivier *(German artist, op. 1815)* **WC**

Heinrich, P.S. or T *(German(?) artist, 18th cent.)* **WC**

Heinrich, Richard *(American sculptor, b.1941)* **BA**

Heinrich, Thugut **GC WC**
  (Austrian painter, act.1828-1859) GC
  (German artist, op.1828-1859) WC
    Bibl: ▶Thieme-Becker; ▶Witt checklist

Heinrichs, Georg **AV BA**
  (1926-) AV
  (German architect, b.1926) BA

Heinrichs, Victor *(Architect, Canada ?)* **AV**
    Bibl: Women and environments, 1985 Winter, v.7, no.1, p.18

Heinrichsmeyer, Reinhard *(West German artist, 20th c.)* **BA**

Heinrici, Alexander *(American printer, 20th c.)* **BA**

Heinrici, Johann Martin *(Swiss artist, 1711-1786)* **WC**

Heinrici, Klaus Peter *(West German architect, Frankfurt)* **AV**
    Bibl: Bauwelt, 1989 May 5, v.80, no.18, p.804

Heins → see Heins, D.
Heins → see Heins, John Theodore

Heins, D. **PR WC WI**
  (British artist, 1697-1756) WI
  (British artist, op.c.1725-p.1779) WC
  (German painter, 1697-1756) PR
    Bibl: ▶Waterhouse, Brit. 18c. ptrs.
  D. Heins PR
  Dirck (John Theodore) Heins, Sr. PR
  Haine PR
  Hein PR
  Heins PR

Heins, Dirck (John Theodore, Sr.) **PR**
  John Theodore Heins, Sr. PR
Heins, Dirck (John Theodore, Sr.) → see Heins, D.

Heins, George Louis *(American architect, 1860-1907)* **AV**
    Bibl: ▶Macmillan encyc. archts.; ▶Withey, Amer. archts.

Heins, John Theodore **WC WI**
  (British artist, 1732-1771) WC WI
  (British painter, 1732-1771) PR
    Bibl: ▶Thieme-Becker
  Haine PR
  Heins PR

Heins, John Theodore, Jr. **PR**
  John Theodore Heins, Jr. PR
Heins, John Theodore, Jr. → see Heins, John Theodore

Heinsbergen, Anthony B. *(American interior designer)* **AV**
    Bibl: Marquee, 1987 Fourth quarter, v.19, no.2, p.3; old Avery Index

Heinsch, Jan Jiri → see Heintsch, Jan Jiří

Heinsdorff, Markus *(West German artist, b.1957)* **BA**
    Bibl: Munich (DEU), Galerie der Künstler. LUFTEK; MARKUS... (1986)

Heinsen, Hein Olaf *(Danish sculptor, b.1935)* **BA**
    Bibl: ▶Art diary int'l., 1990; ▶Køie, Kunst.leks.; Lyngby (DNK), Sophienholm, HEIN HEINSEN (1985) RILA/DNK; ▶Nørregård-Nielsen, Dansk kunst

Heinsius → see Heinsius, Johann Ernst

Heinsius, Johann Ernst **BA GC PR WC**
  (German artist, 1740-1812) WC
  (German painter, 1740-1812) BA PR
  (German, 1740-1812) GC
    Bibl: ▶RILA/BHA; ▶Witt checklist
  Heinsius PR
  Johann Ernst Heinsius PR

Heintsch, Jan Jiří **BA**
  (Czech artist, 19th cent.) WC
  (Czech painter, 1647-1712) BA

Heinsch, Jan Jiri **WC**

Heintz → see Heintz, Joseph, the elder
Heintz → see Heintz, Joseph, the younger

Heintz, Abraham **GC WC**
  (German artist, op.1650) WC
  (German draughtsman, act. 1650) GC
    Bibl: ▶Witt checklist

Heintz, Adam *(German painter in ITA, 17th c.)* **BA**

Heintz, Carl Egon *(West German architect, city architect for Munich)* **AV**
    Bibl: Deutsche Bauzeitung, 1988 June, v.122, no.6, p.38

Heintz, Daniel → see Heintz, Daniel, the elder

Heintz, Daniel, the elder **BA**
  (Swiss architect, born in Basel, died in Bern, 1550(?)-1596) AV
  (Swiss architect, sculptor, act. 1550, d.1596) BA
    Bibl: ▶Bénézit; ▶Portoghesi, Diz. arch. e urbanistica; ▶Schweiz. Künst.-Lex.; ▶Thieme-Becker

Heintz, Daniel **AV**

Heintz, Daniel, the younger *(Swiss architect, 1574-1633)* **BA**
    Bibl: ▶Encyc. world art; ▶Portoghesi, Diz. arch. e urbanistica; ▶Schweiz. Künst.-Lex.; ▶Thieme-Becker

Heintz, Daniele *(Italian painter, ca. 1639-1709)* **BA**

Heintz, Ens or Enzo Johann (Giovanni) *(Italian artist, op.1611-1656)* **WC**

Heintz, Enz, Enzo, Heintius, Heinz or Henz, Joseph, II → see Heintz, Joseph, the younger

Heintz, Hainz or Heinz, Joseph, I → see Heintz, Joseph, the elder

Heintz, Johann **GC**
  (German artist, op.1622) WC
  (German painter, 17th century) GC
    Bibl: ▶Bénézit

Heinz, Johannes **WC**

Heintz, Josef (the elder) → see Heintz, Joseph, the elder
Heintz, Joseph → see Heintz, Joseph, the younger
Heintz, Joseph (the elder) → see Heintz, Joseph, the elder
Heintz, Joseph (the younger) → see Heintz, Joseph, the younger
Heintz, Joseph II → see Heintz, Joseph, the younger

Heintz, Joseph, the elder   BA PR
  (German painter, 1564-1609)   PR
  (Swiss artist, 1564-1609)   WC
  (Swiss painter and architect, 1564-1609)   GC
  (Swiss painter, architect, 1564-1609)   BA
  Bibl: ▶Allgem. Deut. Biog.; ▶RILA/BHA; ▶Schweiz. Künst.-Lex.; ▶Thieme-Becker
  Hainz, Josef   GC
  Heintz   PR
Heintz, Hainz or Heinz, Joseph, I   WC
  Heintz, Josef (the elder)   PR
Heintz, Joseph (the elder)   GC PR
  Heinz   PR
  Heinz, Josef   GC
  Heinz, Joseph   PR
  Josef Heintz (the elder)   PR
  Joseph Heintz (the elder)   PR
Heintz, Joseph, the younger   BA
  (ca.1600-ca.1678)   AV
  (German artist, c.1600-p.1678)   WC
  (German painter in ITA, ca.1600-after 1678)   BA
  (German painter, ca.1600-aft. 1678)   GC PR
  Bibl: ▶RILA/BHA; Sotheby's
  Heintz   PR
Heintz, Enz, Enzo, Heintius, Heinz or Henz, Joseph, II   WC
Heintz, Joseph   AV
Heintz, Joseph (the younger)   GC PR
Heintz, Joseph II   GC
  Heinz, Joseph   GC
  Heinz, Joseph (the younger)   PR
  Joseph Heintz (the younger)   PR
Heintz, Richard *(Belgian artist, 1871-1929)*   WC
Heintze, Johann Georg *(German porcelain painter, 1707-after 1749)*   BA
Heintzelman, Arthur William *(American artist, 1891-1965)*   WI
Heinz → see Heintz, Joseph, the elder
Heinz(?) *(German(?) artist, 17th cent.)*   WC
Heinz, Arno *(Tunisian (?) architect)*   AV
  Bibl: Architectural record, 1983 Sept.II, v.171, no.11, p.80
Heinz, Johannes → see Heintz, Johann
Heinz, Josef → see Heintz, Joseph, the elder
Heinz, Joseph → see Heintz, Joseph, the elder

Heinz, Joseph → see Heintz, Joseph, the younger
Heinz, Joseph (the younger) → see Heintz, Joseph, the younger
Heinz, Karl *(Austrian architect, Innsbruck)*   AV
  Bibl: ▶Verzeich. Öst. Ziviltech.
Heinzlmann, Anton *(German artist, 1798-1829)*   WC
Heinzmann, Carl Friedrich *(German artist, 1795-1846)*   WC
Heise, Myron *(American painter, 20th c.)*   BA
Heise, Wilhelm *(German artist, 1892-1965)*   WC
Heisig, Bernhard *(German painter, printmaker, b.1925)*   BA
  Bibl: ▶DuMonts Künst.-Lex.; ▶Gorenflo, Bild. Künstler, v.2; Knaurs DDR 1989-90, p.225; ▶Lex. Kunst, v.2, p.248; ▶Vollmer, Künst.-Lex. 20. Jhr.
  Hajzig, Bernhard   BA
Heisig, Johannes *(East German painter, printmaker, b.1953)*   BA
  Bibl: Berlin (DEU), Nationalgalerie, Expressivität Heute (1985); Schumann, Bindende Kunst, 7 (1983) pp.324-326
Heisler, H.G. *(German printmaker, 19th c.)*   BA
Heisler, Jindřich *(Czech artist, poet, 1914-1953)*   BA
Heiss → see Heiss, Johann
Heiss, Elias Christoph   BA WC
  (German artist, c.1660-1731)   WC
  (German painter, printmaker, publisher, 1660-1731)   BA
  Bibl: ▶Hollstein, German, v.13; ▶Thieme-Becker; ▶Witt checklist
Heiss, Ernst *(Austrian architect)*   AV
  Bibl: Bauforum, 1987, v.20, no. 124, p.56
Heiss, Gottlieb, I *(German artist, 1684-1740)*   WC
Heiss, Johann   BA GC PR WC
  (German artist, 1640-1704)   WC
  (German painter, 1640-1704)   BA PR
  (German, 1640-1704)   GC
  Bibl: ▶RILA/BHA; ▶Thieme-Becker
  Heiss   PR
  J. Heiss   PR
  Johann Heiss   PR
Heiss, Thomas *(Architect, Berlin)*   AV
  Bibl: Bauwelt, 1984 Nov. 9, v.75, no.42, p.1808
Heister, C. *(German artist, 19th cent.)*   WC
Heitinger *(German artist, 19th cent.)*   WC
Heitland, Ivy *(British artist, 1875-1895)*   WC WI
Heitzig, Fred *(American architectural photographer, Jersey Co., Ill., fl. 1930's)*   AV
  Bibl: Historic Illinois, 1989 Apr., v.11, no.6, p.7

Heitzinger, Jakob *(German artist, op.c.1500-1510)*   WC
Heiz, André Vladimir *(Swiss artist, author, b.1951)*   BA
Heizer, Michael   AV BA WC WI
  (American artist, 1944-)   AV
  (American artist, 20th cent.)   WC
  (American artist, b.1944)   WI
  (American painter, sculptor, printmaker, b.1944)   BA
  Bibl: Artspeak, p.71-72, 137; ▶Babington Smith, Contemp. artists; ▶Contemp. artists, 1989; Contemporary art and artists; ▶Gorenflo, Bild. Künstler; ▶Intl. dir. exh. artists, 1982, 1983
Heizer, R. (Professor) *(American, active 20th century)*   JG
Hejduk, John → see Hejduk, John Quentin
Hejduk, John Quentin   BA
  (American architect and educator, 1929-)   AV
  (American architect, b.1929)   BA
  Bibl: ▶AIA Pro File; ▶Libr. of Congr. Name Auth. File; Oxford UP, 5 archts.
Hejduk, John   AV
Hek, Ronald van *(Dutch architect)*   AV
  Bibl: De Architect, 1989 May, v.20, no.5, p.105
Hekking → see Hekking, William M.
Hekking, J. Antonio *(American painter, act. 1859)*   PR
  Bibl: ▶Young, Amer. artists
  J. Antonio Hekking   PR
Hekking, W. Junior → see Hekking, William M.
Hekking, Willem   GC
  (Dutch artist, 1796-1862)   WC
  (Dutch painter and draughtsman, 1796-1862)   GC
  Bibl: ▶Thieme-Becker
Hekking, Willem, I   WC
Hekking, Willem II → see Hekking, Willem, Jr.
Hekking, Willem Jr. → see Hekking, Willem, Jr.
Hekking, Willem, I → see Hekking, Willem
Hekking, Willem, Jr.   WI
  (Dutch artist, 1825-1904)   WI
  (Dutch draughtsman, 1825-1904)   GC
  Bibl: Getty Photo Study Coll.; Getty Photo Study Coll. (Douwes coll.)
Hekking, Willem II   GC
  Hekking, Willem Jr.   GC
Hekking, William M.   PR
  (American artist, 1885-)   WC
  (American painter, 1885-1970)   PR
  Bibl: ▶WWW Amer. art
  Hekking   PR
Hekking, W. Junior   WC
  William M. Hekking   PR

Hektoridas *(Greek sculptor, 4th c BC (1st half))* **GC**
    Bibl: ▶Robertson, Greek art, p.397

Hel, Abraham del → see Hele, Abraham del

Heland, Martin Rudolf *(Swedish artist, 1765-1814)* **WC**

Helant or Heland, Anthonie Joseph *(Dutch artist, c.1752-c. 1837)* **WC**

Helbig Painter *(Apulian vase-painter)* **GC**
    Bibl: Trendall, Attic red-fig. vases Apulia

Helbig Reverse-Group **GC**
    Bibl: ▶Beazley, Attic red-fig. vase-ptrs.

Helbig, Jules Chretien Charles Joseph Henri *(Belgian artist, 1821-1906)* **WC**

Helbig, Peter *(German artist, 1841-1896)* **WC**

Helbigk or Helwick, Jacob Heinrich → see Helbigk, Jacob Heinrich

Helbigk, Jacob Heinrich **GC**
    (German artist, -1746) **WC**
    (German painter, d.1746) **GC**
    Bibl: ▶Thieme-Becker

Helbigk or Helwick, Jacob Heinrich **WC**

Helbling, Franz Thaddäus **GC WC**
    (German artist, op.1776) **WC**
    (German painter, act.1776) **GC**
    Bibl: ▶Thieme-Becker

Helcke, Arnold **WC WI**
    (British artist, op.1865-1898) **WC**
    (British artist, op.1865-1911) **WI**

Held *(Engraver, op.1850-)* **WI**

Held → see Held, Andreas

Held, Al **BA WC WI**
    (American artist, 20th cent.) **WC**
    (American artist, b.1928) **WI**
    (American painter, b.1928) **BA**

Held, Andreas *(German painter, 1661-1745)* **PR**
    Bibl: ▶Thieme-Becker
    Andreas Held **PR**
    Held **PR**

Held, Johann Markus *(German painter, ca.1743-1772)* **BA**

Held, John II **BA**
    (American artist, 1889-) **WC**
    (American artist, 1889-1958) **WI**
    (American painter, 1889-1958) **BA**
    Held, John, II **WC**
    Held, John, Jr. **WI**

Held, John, II → see Held, John II
Held, John, Jr. → see Held, John II

Held, Julie *(British artist, b.1958)* **WI**

Held, M. von *(German artist, 19th cent.)* **WC**

Held, Marc **AV BA**
    (French designer, b.1932) **BA**
    (Interior architect, France) **AV**
    Bibl: Interiors, 1984 Aug., v.144, no.1, p.140

Held-Schäffer, Andrea *(West German architect)* **AV**
    Bibl: Architettura; cronache e storia, 1988 Mar., v.34, no.3, p.205

Heldt, A. *(German artist, op.1712)* **WC**

Heldt, Werner **BA WC**
    (German artist, 1904-1954) **WC**
    (German painter, printmaker, 1904-1954) **BA**
    Bibl: ▶Art Index, 1991; ▶Bénézit; ▶Brockhaus Enzyk.; ▶Castagno, Eur. Sigs.; ▶Gorenflo, Bild. Künstler; ▶Phaidon 20c. art; ▶Vollmer, Künst.-Lex. 20. Jhr.

Hele, Abraham del *(Flemish painter, 1534-1598)* **BA**
    Bibl: ▶Bénézit; ▶Thieme-Becker; ▶Wurzbach, NLD Künst.-Lex.
    Delhel, Abraham **BA**
    Hel, Abraham del **BA**
    Hell, Abraham del **BA**

Hele, Ivar **GC WC**
    (Australian artist, 1912-) **WC**
    (British, b.1912) **GC**
    Bibl: ▶Witt checklist

Hele, Izaak del *(early Netherlandish painter, ca.1536-after 1573)* **BA**

Helen *(Greek painter, 4th c BC(?))* **GC**
    Bibl: Getty Photo Study Coll.; ▶Robertson, Greek art, p.502

Helen Maria Turner → see Turner, Helen Maria
Helen Torr → see Torr, Helen

Helena, Princess *(British artist, 1846-1923)* **WI**

Helenyi, Tibor *(Hungarian artist, 20th cent.)* **WC**

Helfant, Nancy *(American textile artist, 20th c.)* **BA**

Helfer, Hans *(German artist, 1908-)* **WC**

Helfferich, Franz *(Dutch painter, 1871-1941)* **GC**
    Bibl: ▶Vollmer, Künst.-Lex. 20. Jhr.

Helfgott, Myron *(American sculptor, b.1936)* **BA**
    Bibl: Richmond (VA, USA), Virginia MFA, Process, image, portrait (1986), pp.17-19

Helfond, Riva *(American printmaker, painter, b.1910)* **BA**
    Bibl: Beall, Amer. prints LC, p.206; O'Connor, New Deal art projects (1972), p.284; ▶WW Amer. Art, 1989

Helg, Franca *(Italian (?) architect)* **AV**
    Bibl: ▶Avery period. idx.

Helgueros, Andrés de los *(Spanish sculptor, act.1726-1742)* **BA**
    Bibl: Tárraga, Arch. esp. de arte, LIX/236 (Oct-Dec 1986) 386-400
    Gómez de los Elgueros, Andrés **BA**

Helhafen, Ignaz → see Elhafen, Ignaz

Helie de Borron **JG**

Helie, A. *(Swedish(?) artist, op. 1783)* **WC**

Heligoland Group *(South Italian vase-painters, 350-325 BC)* **GC**
    Bibl: McPhee & Trendall, Fish-Plates

Heligoland Painter *(South Italian vase-painter, 350-325 BC)* **GC**
    Bibl: McPhee & Trendall, Fish-Plates

Heliker, John → see Heliker, John Edward

Heliker, John Edward **BA WI**
    (American artist, 1909-) **WC**
    (American artist, b.1909) **WI**
    (American painter, b.1909) **BA**

Heliker, John **WC**

Helin, Pekka *(Finnish architect, 1945-)* **AV**
    Bibl: Process: architecture, n.37, 1983, p.58

Heliodoros → see Heliodoros of Rhodes

Heliodoros of Rhodes **GC**
    (Greek sculptor, 2nd/1st c BC) **GC**
    (Sculptor, 2nd cent. BC-post 100 BC/ante 50 BC) **CE**
    Bibl: Getty Photo Study Coll.
    Heliodoros **CE**
    Heliodorus **CE**

Heliodorus from Rhodes **CE**

Heliodorus → see Heliodoros of Rhodes
Heliodorus from Rhodes → see Heliodoros of Rhodes

Hélion, Jean *(French painter, 1904-1987)* **BA**
    Bibl: ▶Art Index, v.36; ▶ARTbibl. mod., 20/2; ▶Bénézit; PHAIDON; ▶WW France

Helios Group *(Apulian vase-painters)* **GC**
    Bibl: Trendall, Attic red-fig. vases Apulia

Hell Breughel → see Brueghel, Pieter, the younger
Hell, Abraham del → see Hele, Abraham del

Hell, Johan van **GC**
    (Dutch artist, 1889-) **WC**
    (Dutch painter, 1889-1952) **GC**
    Bibl: ▶Vollmer, Künst.-Lex. 20. Jhr.

Hell, Johannes Gerardus Diederik (Johan) van **WC**

Hell, Johannes Gerardus Diederik (Johan) van → see Hell, Johan van

Hell, Ter *(West German painter, b.1954)* **BA**

Hell, Willy ter *(German artist, 1883-)* **WC**

Helland-Hansen, Peter *(Norwegian architect)* **AV**
    Bibl: Byggekunst, 1986, v.68, no.2, p.104

Hellart or Helart, Jacques *(French artist, 1664-1719)* **WC**

Hellart, Louis Charles or Louis *(French artist, 1696/9(?)-1757(?))* **WC**

Hellawell, John *(Engraver, New York, NY., 1837-1919)* **WI**

Helldén, David *(Swedish architect, 1905-)*   **AV**
    Bibl: ▶Svenska Ark. Riks., 1984
Helle *(French, active 1870s)*   **JG**
Helle, Louis →see Elle, Louis
Hellebranth, Bertha de →see Hellenbrath, Bertha de
Hellemans, Pierre Jean *(Belgian artist, 1787-1845)*   **WC**
Hellenbrath, Bertha de   **WI**
    (American artist, op.1929-)   WI
    (American(?) artist, op.1929)   WC
    Hellebranth, Bertha de   **WC**
Heller, Bert *(German artist, 1912-)*   **WC**
Heller, G. *(Israeli architect, Tel Aviv)*   **AV**
    Bibl: Architettura; cronache e storia, 1988 Nov., v.34, no.11, p.786
Heller, Louis Herman *(American photographer, 1839-1928)*   **BA**
Heller, Ruprecht *(German artist, op. 1529)*   **WC**
Heller, Wolfgang *(German architect, 1942-)*   **AV**
    Bibl: Deutsche Bauzeitung, 1985 Apr., v.119, no.4, p.128
Hellesen, Julius (Lars Julius August) *(Danish artist, 1823-1877)*   **WC**
Helleu →see Helleu, Paul César
Helleu, J. *(French artist, 1894-)*   **WC**
Helleu, Paul →see Helleu, Paul César
Helleu, Paul César   **BA GC PR**
    (French artist, 1859-1927)   WC
    (French painter, 1859-1927)   PR
    (French painter, printmaker, 1859-1927)   BA
    (French, 1859-1927)   GC
    Bibl: ▶Bénézit; George Goldner; ▶Petit Robert 2; ▶RILA/BHA; ▶Thieme-Becker; ▶Witt checklist
    Helleu   PR
    Helleu, Paul   **WC**
    Helleu, Paul-Cesar   PR
    Paul Cesar Helleu   PR
Helleu, Paul-Cesar →see Helleu, Paul César
Helley, Peter *(American painter, critic, 20th c.)*   **BA**
    Bibl: ARTS MAGAZINE, LX/1 (Sept 1985) 72-79
Hellier, Jean-Yves   **AV**
Hellin de Burchgrave *(Flemish scribe, act.1476)*   **GC**
    Bibl: Shailor, Yale, p.226
Hellingrath, Berthold *(German painter, sculptor, printmaker, 1877-1954)*   **BA**
Hellman, Glenn *(British sculptor, b.1938)*   **BA**
Hellman, Louis *(Austrian architect and cartoonist, b. in London, lives in Austria, 1936-)*   **AV**
    Bibl: ▶Libr. of Congr. Name Auth. File

Hellmann, Elma *(American, active ca. 1903)*   **JG**
Hellmer, Edmund von *(Austrian sculptor, 1850-1935)*   **BA**
Hellmuth, George F. *(American architect. Principal, Hellmuth, Yamasaki & Leinweber, 1949-55. Principal, Hellmuth, Obata & Kassabaum, St. Louis, 1955-, 1907-)*   **AV**
    Bibl: ▶Amer. archts. dir., 1970
Hellmuth, Suzanne *(American artist, b.1947)*   **BA**
Hellner, Franz Xaver *(German goldsmith, silversmith, 1819-1901)*   **BA**
    Bibl: Clasen, RHEIMISCHE SILBERMARKEN, 25; Köln (DEU), Stadt. Mus., Köln Goldschmiede (1980), p.129
Hellqvist, Carl Gustaf *(Swedish artist, 1851-1890)*   **WC**
Hellwag, Rudolf   **GC WC**
    (Austrian painter, b.1867)   GC
    (German artist, 1867-1942)   WC
    Bibl: ▶Bénézit
Hellwegen →see Hellwegen, H.A.
Hellwegen, H. →see Hellwegen, H.A.
Hellwegen, H.A. *(American painter, act. 1880's)*   **PR**
    Bibl: ▶Hughes, Artists California
    H.A. Hellwegen   PR
    Hellwegen   PR
    Hellwegen, H.   PR
Hellweger, Franz *(German painter, 1812-1880)*   **BA**
    Bibl: ▶Busse, Maler u. Bildhauer 19. Jahr.; ▶Thieme-Becker
Hellwig, Norbert *(German architect, Bremen)*   **AV**
    Bibl: Deutsche Bauzeitung, 1985 July, v.119, no.7, p.48
Hellyer, Jeff *(British artist, b.1947)*   **BA WI**
Hellyer, Thomas   **WC WI**
    (British artist, op.1800)   WC
    (British artist, op.1800-)   WI
Helm, Katherine   **WC WI**
    (American artist, 19th cent.)   WC
    (American artist, op.1842-)   WI
Helm, Robert *(American artist, b.1943)*   **BA**
    Bibl: ARTFORUM XXIII/3 (Nov 1984) 74-76; New York (NY, USA), Whitney Mus., Biennial (1987)
Helm, Stewart *(British artist, b.1960)*   **WI**
Helman, Harold H. *(American architect, Chicago)*   **AV**
    Bibl: ▶AIA Pro File, 1985
Helman, Phoebe *(American sculptor, painter, b.1929)*   **BA**
Helman, Robert *(French artist, 20th cent.)*   **WC**
Helmberger, Adolf *(German artist, 1885-)*   **WC**
Helmbraker →see Helmbreker, Dirk
Helmbrecker →see Helmbreker, Dirk

Helmbreker →see Helmbreker, Dirk
Helmbreker, Dirk   **BA GC PR**
    (Dutch artist, 1633-1696)   WC
    (Dutch painter and draughtsman, 1633-1696)   GC
    (Dutch painter in ITA, 1633-1696)   BA
    (Dutch painter, 1633-1696)   PR
    Bibl: ▶RILA/BHA; ▶Thieme-Becker
    Dirk Helmbreker   PR
    Elembrech, Theodoor   GC
    Helmbraker   PR
    Helmbrecker   PR
    Helmbreker   PR
    Helmbreker, Helmbreecker or Elembrech, Dirk, Theodor or Teodoro   **WC**
    M.o Teodoro   PR
    Monsieur Teodoro   PR
    Monsieur Teodoro Hembrecker Fiammingo   PR
    Monsu Teodoro Helmbreecherr   PR
    Monsu Teodoro Velmbrecker   PR
    Monsu' Teodoro   PR
    Monsu' Teodoro fiammingo   PR
    Monsu' Teodoro Helmbreecherr   PR
    Monsu' Teodoro Velmbreccker   PR
    Teodoro   PR
    Teodoro Helbrecker   PR
    Teodoro Helmbrecker   PR
    Theo: Helmbreker   PR
    Theod. Helmbrecker   PR
Helmbreker, Helmbreecker or Elembrech, Dirk, Theodor or Teodoro →see Helmbreker, Dirk
Helmer, Hermann   **AV BA**
    (Austrian architect, 1849-1919)   BA
    (Austrian architect, Vienna, 1849-1919)   AV
    Bibl: ▶Österr. biog. Lex. 1815-1950; ▶Thieme-Becker
Helmer, Philipp *(German painter, 1846-1912)*   **GC**
    Bibl: ▶Thieme-Becker
Helmet Painter *(Apulian vase-painter)*   **GC**
    Bibl: Trendall, Attic red-fig. vases Apulia
Helmhack, Abraham *(German glass painter, printmaker, Hausmaler, 1654-1724)*   **BA**
Helmick →see Helmick, Howard
Helmick, Howard   **PR WC WI**
    (American artist, 1845-1907)   WC WI
    (American painter, 1845-1907)   PR
    Bibl: ▶Thieme-Becker
    Helmick   PR
    Howard Helmick   PR
Helmick, Ralph *(American artist, 20th c.)*   **BA**
Helmle or Helmlin, Sebastian *(German artist, 1799-p.1841)*   **WC**
Helmle, Frank J. *(American architect, 1869-1939)*   **BA**

Helmon, Marcel *(Netherlandish painter)* **GC**
> Bibl: Getty Photo Study Coll. (Douwes coll.)

Helmond, Lucas van → see Gassel, Lucas

Helmont → see Helmont, Mattheus van

Helmont → see Helmont, Zeger Jacob van

Helmont or Hellemont, Mattheus van → see Helmont, Mattheus van

Helmont or Hellemont, Zeger Jacob van → see Helmont, Zeger Jacob van

Helmont, Johann Franz van *(Dutch sculptor in Germany, act.1715, d. before 1756)* **BA**
> Bibl: ▶Bénézit; ▶Thieme-Becker

Helmont, Mattheus van **GC PR**
> *(Flemish artist, 1623-p.1674)* **WC**
> *(Flemish painter, 1623-aft.1674)* **PR**
> *(Flemish, 1623-aft.1674)* **GC**
> Bibl: ▶Thieme-Becker; ▶Witt checklist

Helmont **PR**

Helmont or Hellemont, Mattheus van **WC**

M. Van Holmont **PR**
Mattheus van Helmont **PR**
V. Hallmont **PR**
V. Helmont **PR**
Van Hallemont **PR**
Van Hellemont **PR**
Van Hellmont **PR**
Van Helmont **PR**

Helmont, Theodor *(Dutch(?) artist, op.1656)* **WC**

Helmont, Zeger Jacob van **GC PR**
> *(Flemish artist, 1683-1726)* **WC**
> *(Flemish painter, 1683-1726)* **GC PR**
> Bibl: ▶Thieme-Becker

Helmont **PR**

Helmont or Hellemont, Zeger Jacob van **WC**

Van Helmont **PR**
Zeger Jacob van Helmont **PR**

Helmore, Heathcote *(Architect, New Zealand)* **AV**
> Bibl: Ville giardini, 1985 June, no. 197, p.50

Helmschmied, Kolman **BA**
> *(German armorer, 1470/71-1532)* **BA**
> *(German artist, 1471-1532)* **WC**

Kolman, Colman or Koloman **WC**

Helmsdorf, Friedrich (Johann Friedrich) *(German artist, 1783-1852)* **WC**

Helpinen, Harto *(Finnish architect)* **AV**
> Bibl: Ville giardini, 1984 Nov., no. 191, p.24

Helpman, John Robert Crichton *(British artist, b.1814)* **WI**

Helps, Francis *(British artist, op. 1920-1950)* **WI**

Helsby, Alfredo *(South American artist, op.c.1889)* **WC**

Helscher, David → see Heschler, David

Helsdingh → see Hulsdonck, Jacob

helsen Breugel → see Brueghel, Pieter, the younger

Helst → see Helst, Bartholomeus van der

Helst or Elst, Bartholomeus, Bartelmeus or Bartel van der, or Bartholomeus Verelst or Verhelst → see Helst, Bartholomeus van der

Helst or Elst, Lodevyk van der *(Dutch artist, 1642-p.1682)* **WC**

Helst, Bartholomeus van der **BA GC JG PR**
> *(Dutch artist, 1613(?)-1670)* **WC**
> *(Dutch painter, 1613-1670)* **PR**
> *(Dutch painter, ca.1613-1670)* **BA**
> *(Dutch painter, draughtsman, and printmaker, 1613-1670)* **GC**
> *(Dutch, 1613-1670)* **JG**
> Bibl: (April 2, 1813, lot 145, Christie's), ▶Bénézit; ▶Getty Photo Study Coll., ▶RILA/BHA; ▶Thieme-Becker; ▶Wurzbach, NLD Künst.-Lex.

Aelst, van der **PR**
B. van der Helst **PR**
Barthélemy van der Helst **PR**
Bartholomeus van der Helst **PR**
Elst, Bartholomeus van der **GC**
Helst **PR**

Helst or Elst, Bartholomeus, Bartelmeus or Bartel van der, or Bartholomeus Verelst or Verhelst **WC**

Helst, Bartolomeus van der **PR**
V. der Helst **PR**
V. Helst **PR**
van der Haelst **PR**
van der Helst **PR**
Van Helst **PR**
Vander Elst **PR**
Vander Helst **PR**
Vander Helst. B. **PR**
Vander Hest **PR**
Vanderelst **PR**
Vanderheldst **PR**
Vanderhelst **PR**
Vandevelst **PR**
Verelst, Bartholomeus **GC**
Verhelst, Bartholomeus **GC**

Helst, Bartolomeus van der → see Helst, Bartholomeus van der

Helst, G. van *(Netherlands artist, 17th/18th cent.)* **WC**

Helst, Jeronimus van der *(Dutch artist, c.1629-p.1671)* **WC**

Helst, Lodewyk van der **GC PR**
> *(Dutch painter, 1642-1684)* **PR**
> *(Dutch painter, 1642-ca.1690)* **GC**
> Bibl: Getty Photo Study Coll.; ▶Thieme-Becker

L.V. Elst **PR**
Lodewijck van der Helst **PR**
Lodewyk van der Helst **PR**

Helsted, Axel Theofilus *(Danish artist, 1847-1907)* **WC**

Helsted, Frederik Ferdinand *(Danish artist, 1809-1875)* **WC**

Helstocade → see Helt Stockade, Nicolaes van

Helt Stockade → see Helt Stockade, Nicolaes van

Helt Stockade, Nicolaes van **GC PR WC**
> *(Dutch artist, 1614-1669)* **WC**
> *(Dutch painter, 1614-1669)* **GC PR**
> Bibl: Getty Photo Study Coll.; ▶Thieme-Becker; ▶Witt checklist

H. Stoccade **PR**
Helstocade **PR**
Helt Stockade **PR**
Helt Stokade **PR**
Helt-Stocaden **PR**
Helt-Stockade, Nicolaes van **PR**
Heltstocade **PR**
N. V. Stocade **PR**
[Niclas van] Heltstocade **PR**
Nicolaes van Helt Stockade **PR**
Stocade **PR**
Stockade **PR**

Helt Stokade → see Helt Stockade, Nicolaes van

Helt-Stocaden → see Helt Stockade, Nicolaes van

Helt-Stockade, Nicolaes van → see Helt Stockade, Nicolaes van

Heltewig, Gudrun *(West German architect)* **AV**
> Bibl: Architektur + Wettbewerbe, 1988 Dec., no.136, p.50

Heltius, J. *(Netherlands artist, 17th cent.)* **WC**

Helton, Jean or Jesu *(French artist, 1904-)* **WC**

Heltstocade → see Helt Stockade, Nicolaes van

Helvig, Amalia von *(Swedish artist, op.1805)* **WC**

Helyer, Nigel *(British artist, op.20th c.)* **WI**

Helzel, Bonaventura *(Italian printmaker, 18th c.)* **BA**

Hem, Hermann van der **GC WC**
> *(Dutch artist, op.1638-m.1649)* **WC**
> *(Dutch draughtsman, 1619-1649)* **GC**
> Bibl: ▶Thieme-Becker

Hem, Pieter (Piet) van der → see Hem, Pieter van der

Hem, Pieter van der BA GC
(Dutch artist, 1885-1961) WC
(Dutch painter, 1885-1961) GC
(Dutch painter, printmaker,
1885-1961) BA
Bibl: ▶Scheen, Ned. beeldende
kunst.; ▶Thieme-Becker; ▶Witt
checklist

Hem, Pieter (Piet) van der WC
Hemelaer, Catherina (Flemish, act.
1634, d.1662) BA
Bibl: Scott, CINCINNATI ART
MUSEUM BULLETIN XIII/4 (Dec
1987) 4-10; ▶Wurzbach, NLD
Künst.-Lex.

Hemeling, Johann Carl (Swiss(?)
architect and engineer, fl. first half
of 18th cent., act. in Switzerland
and Germany, 18th cent.) AV
Bibl: ▶Thieme-Becker
Hemelingh, Jean Charles AV
Hemmeling, Johann Carl AV
Hemelingh, Jean Charles → see
Hemeling, Johann Carl

Hemelman, Albert (Dutch painter
and printmaker, 1883-1951) GC
Bibl: ▶Vollmer, Künst.-Lex. 20. Jhr.

Hemenway, Nancy (American
painter, designer, b.1920) BA

Hemert, Frank van (Dutch painter,
b.1956) BA
Bibl: Kassel (DEU), Documenta 7, I
(1982), p. 426

Hemert, Jan van GC WC
(Dutch artist, op.1645) WC
(Dutch painter, act.1645) GC
Bibl: ▶Thieme-Becker

Hemery, Mlle. (French artist, op.
1797) WC
Hemery, Thérèse Eléonore → see
Lingée, Thérèse Eléonore
Hemessen → see Hemessen, Jan van
Hemessen → see Hemessen, Katharina
van
Hemessen, Catharina van → see
Hemessen, Katharina van
Hemessen, Catharina van
(Sanders) → see Hemessen,
Katharina van
Hemessen, J.S. van → see Hemessen,
Jan van
Hemessen, Jan Sanders van → see
Hemessen, Jan van
Hemessen, Jan Sanders van or de
(Also identified with Master of the
Brunswick Monogram) → see
Hemessen, Jan van

Hemessen, Jan van BA GC PR
(early Netherlandish painter, ca.
1500-1575?) BA
(Flanders painter, ca.1504-ca.
1566) GC
(Netherlandish painter, ca.1500-
1575?) PR
(Netherlands artist, op.1519-m.
a.1566) WC
Bibl: ▶Bénézit; ▶Encyc. world art;
▶Friedländer, Early Neth. ptg., XII,
p.44; Genaille, REVUE BELGE
D'ARCH. ET D'HISTOIRE DE L'ART,
68 (1989), 137-138; ▶RILA/BHA;
▶Thieme-Becker; ▶Wurzbach, NLD
Künst.-Lex.

Hemessen PR
Hemessen, J.S. van PR
Hemessen, Jan Sanders van PR
Hemessen, Jan Sanders van or
de (Also identified with
Master of the Brunswick
Monogram) WC
Hernesen PR
J. de Hemessen, 1557 PR
Jan de Hemessen PR
Jan van Hemessen PR
Hemessen, Katharina de → see
Hemessen, Katharina van

Hemessen, Katharina van BA PR
(early Netherlandish painter,
b.ca.1527) BA
(Flanders painter, 1528-aft.
1587) GC
(Netherlandish painter,
1527/28-aft.1566) PR
(Netherlands artist,
1527/8-1587) WC
Bibl: Getty Photo Study Coll.;
▶Petteys, Women artists;
▶Thieme-Becker
H., Caterina van PR
Hemessen PR
Hemessen, Catharina van PR
Hemessen, Catharina van
(Sanders) GC
Hemessen, Katharina de PR
Hemessen, Katharina van or de WC
Katharina van Hemessen PR
Hemessen, Katharina van or de → see
Hemessen, Katharina van
Hemgård, Gretel (Finnish(?)
landscape architect) AV
Bibl: Arkkitehti, 1989, v.86, no.3,
p.47

Heming, Matilda WI
(British artist, 1808-1855) WC
(British artist, op.1796-1855) WI
Heming, Matilda, (nee Lowry) WC
Lowry, Matilda, Miss WI
Heming, Matilda, (nee Lowry) → see
Heming, Matilda

Heming, Thomas BA GC
(British goldsmith, act.1745-
1782) BA
(British silversmith, act. from
1745, d.1795/1781) GC
Bibl: ▶Grimwade, London
goldsmiths, 1982
Hemington, Charlotte, Miss → see
Avarne, Charlotte
Hemingway, Andrew (British artist,
op.20th c.) WI
Hemingway, Peter AV BA
(Canadian architect, 1929-) AV
(Canadian architect, 20th c.) BA
Bibl: Building with words..., 1981,
p.56
Hemken, Willem (de Haas) GC
(Dutch artist, 1831-1911) WC
(Dutch painter, 1831-1911) GC
Bibl: ▶Scheen, Ned. beeldende
kunst.
Hemken, Willem de Haas WC
Hemken, Willem de Haas → see
Hemken, Willem (de Haas)
Hemmel, Peter (Pierre d'Andlau)
(Alsatian glazier, ca.1420-ca.1505) BA
Hemmeling, Johann Carl → see
Hemeling, Johann Carl
Hemming, Adrian (British artist,
b.1945) WI
Hemmler, David (American
architect) AV
Hemnskirk → see Heemskerck, Egbert
van (the elder)
Hemokerk → see Heemskerck, Egbert
van (the elder)
Hempel, Andreas (German
architect, Munich) AV
Bibl: Detail, 1981 Mar.-Apr., no.2,
p.168
Hempel, Brigitte (Austrian designer
or architect) AV
Bibl: Bauforum, 1988, v.21, no.
128, p.42
Hempel, Helmut (Austrian architect
and educator, Vienna, 1949-) AV
Bibl: Ottagono, 1988 Mar., p.24
Hempel, Joseph Ritter von
(German artist, 1800-p.1862) WC
Hempfing, Wilhelm (German artist,
1886-1951) WC
Hemphill, M.D, William Despard
(British, active 1860s) JG
Hemple, Anouska (British fashion
designer) AV
Bibl: Architectural digest, 1989
Sept., v.46, no.9, p.138
Hempton, Paul BA WC WI
(British artist, 1946-) WC
(British artist, b.1946) WI
(British painter, b.1946) BA
Bibl: ▶Art Index, v.36; ▶Spalding,
20c. ptrs. & sculpt.; Sunderland
(GBR), Arts Ctr., Working process
(1978); ▶WW Art, 1988
Hempton, Paul Andrew Keates BA

Hempton, Paul Andrew Keates → *see* Hempton, Paul

Hemskerck → *see* Heemskerck, Egbert van (the elder)

Hemskerck → *see* Heemskerck, Maerten van

Hemskercke → *see* Heemskerck, Egbert van (the elder)

Hemskerk → *see* Heemskerck, Egbert van (the elder)

Hemskerk → *see* Heemskerck, Maerten van

Hemskerk, Egbert (the Younger) → *see* Heemskerck, Egbert van (the younger)

Hemskerke → *see* Heemskerck, Egbert van (the elder)

Hemskirck → *see* Heemskerck, Egbert van (the elder)

Hemskirck → *see* Heemskerck, Maerten van

Hemskirk → *see* Heemskerck, Egbert van (the elder)

Hemskirk → *see* Heemskerck, Maerten van

Hemskirk, jun. → *see* Heemskerck, Egbert van (the younger)

Hemskirke → *see* Heemskerck, Egbert van (the elder)

Hemsley, J.   **WC WI**
  (British artist, 19th cent.)   WC
  (British artist, op.19th c.)   WI

Hemsley, William   **WC WI**
  (British artist, 1819-1906)   WI
  (British artist, 1819-p.1893)   WC
  Bibl: Paviere, Brit. sporting ptrs

Hemsworth, Gerard   **BA WI**
  (British artist, b.1945)   WI
  (British painter, b.1945)   BA

Hemy, Bernard Benedict *(British artist, circa 1855-1913)*   **WI**

Hemy, Charles Napier   **BA WC WI**
  (British artist, 1841-1917)   WC WI
  (British painter, 1841-1917)   BA
  Bibl: ▶Bénézit; ▶Johnson, Brit. artists; ▶Thieme-Becker

Hemy, Thomas Marie Madawaska   **WC WI**
  (British artist, 1852-1937)   WI
  (British artist, op.c.1873)   WC

Hen, Catharina de → *see* Knibbergen, Catharina van

Henard, C. *(French artist, op.1785-1812)*   **WC**

Hénard, Eugène *(French city planner, Paris, 1849-1923)*   **AV**
  Bibl: ▶Libr. of Congr. Name Auth. File, dates from field 678 of NAF added

Henave [Unidentified] *(Unknown painter)*   **PR**
  Bibl: Feb. 11, 1804, lot 114, Christie's; June 23, 1804, lot 79 Christie's

Henchman, Daniel *(American silversmith, 1730-1775)*   **BA**

Hencke, Peter *(German sculptor, d.1777)*   **BA**
  Bibl: Lübeck (DEU), Mus. Kunst u. Kulturges., Euro. Kleinplastik (1976)
  Monogrammist PH   BA

Henckel, Anton *(Swiss artist, op. 1525-1538)*   **WC**

Hencze, Tamás *(Hungarian painter, b.1938)*   **BA**

Hendel, Klaus *(West German architect, Berlin)*   **AV**
  Bibl: Baumeister, 1989 Mar., v.86, no.3, p.56

Henderikse, Jan Jozias *(Dutch artist, b.1937)*   **BA**
  Bibl: ▶Scheen, Ned. beeldende kunst.

Hendershot, Janet *(Canadian painter, b.1945)*   **BA**

Henderson → *see* Henderson, Peter Charles

Henderson the Elder, John → *see* Henderson, John I

Henderson [Unidentified] *(Unknown painter)*   **PR**
  Bibl: (February 27, 1807, lot 10, Christie's)

Henderson, Alexander *(Canadian (b. Scotland, UK), 1831-1913)*   **JG**

Henderson, Andrew *(British artist, 1783-1835)*   **WC WI**

Henderson, Arn *(American architect, Norman, OK, 1934-)*   **AV**
  Bibl: ▶AIA Pro File, 1985; Architecture and urbanism, no. 174, p.122

Henderson, Arthur Edward *(British artist, 1870-1956)*   **WC WI**

Henderson, Brian *(Irish painter, b.1950)*   **BA**

Henderson, Charles Cooper   **BA WC WI**
  (British artist, 1803-1877)   WC WI
  (British painter, printmaker, 1803-1877)   BA
  Bibl: ▶Dict. natl. biog.; ▶Thieme-Becker; ▶Witt checklist

Henderson, Cornelius   **WC WI**
  (British artist, 1799-)   WC
  (British artist, b.1799)   WI

Henderson, Curtis *(American interior designer, New York City and Bath, Me)*   **AV**
  Bibl: Colonial homes, 1989 Apr., v.15, no.2, p.82

Henderson, Elsie Marian   **WC WI**
  (British artist, 1880-)   WC
  (British artist, b.1880)   WI
  Coudenhove, Elsie Marian, Baroness de   WI

Henderson, Ewen *(British artist, op. 1989-)*   **WI**

Henderson, F.   **WC WI**
  (British artist, 19th cent.)   WC
  (British artist, op.19th c.)   WI

Henderson, Fiona *(British artist, b.1955)*   **WI**

Henderson, George *(Australian architect, 1936-)*   **AV**

Henderson, Jack *(American artist, op.1975-)*   **WI**

Henderson, James *(British photographer, act.1851-1855)*   **BA**

Henderson, Jan *(American artist, 20th cent.)*   **WC**

Henderson, Jeremy *(Irish painter, b.1952)*   **BA**

Henderson, John *(British architect, 1804-1862)*   **AV**
  Bibl: Country life, 1985 Sept.19, v.178, no.4596, p.811

Henderson, John → *see* Henderson, John II

Henderson, John I   **BA WI**
  (British artist, 1764-1834)   WC WI
  (British collector, painter, 1764-1843)   BA
  Bibl: ▶Fisher, Watercolour ptrs.; ▶Thieme-Becker; ▶Witt checklist; Witton, TURNER STUDIES IV 12 (Winter 1984) 8-23

Henderson the Elder, John   **WC**

Henderson, John II   **WI**
  (British artist, 1860-1924)   WC WI

Henderson, John   **WC**

Henderson, Jon *(American artist, op.1930-)*   **WI**

Henderson, Joseph *(British artist, 1832-1908)*   **WC WI**

Henderson, Joseph Morris *(British artist, 1863-1936)*   **WC WI**

Henderson, Keith   **BA WC WI**
  (British artist, 20th cent.)   WC
  (British artist, b.1883)   WI
  (British painter, 1883-1982)   BA

Henderson, Ken *(British artist, b.1945)*   **WI**

Henderson, Mel *(American artist, b.1922)*   **BA**

Henderson, Nigel   **BA WC WI**
  (British artist, b.1917)   WI
  (British artist, op.1949)   WC
  (British photographer, b.1917)   BA

Henderson, P. → *see* Henderson, Peter Charles

Henderson, Paul *(American architect, St. Louis, MO, 1947-)*   **AV**
  Bibl: Inland architect, 1985 Nov.-Dec., v.29, no.6, p.36

Henderson, Peter Charles *(British painter, act. 1799-1829, d. 1829)*   **PR**
  Bibl: Dictionary of British Flower Painters, vol. 1; ▶Thieme-Becker
  Henderson   PR
  Henderson, P.   PR
  P. Henderson   PR
  Peter Charles Henderson   PR

Henderson, Philip *(American architect)* **AV**

Henderson, T. **WC WI**
(British artist, op.1864) WC
(British artist, op.1864-) WI

Henderson, Tom *(American sculptor in CAN, b.1936)* **BA**

Henderson, Victor Lance *(American painter, b.1939)* **BA**

Henderson, W.B. *(British artist, op. 1951-)* **WI**

Henderson, W.S.P. **WC WI**
(British artist, op.1836-1874) WI
(British artist, op.c.1836-1874) WC

Henderson, William **BA**
(British artist, b.1941) WI
(British painter, printmaker, b.1941) BA

Henderson, William I **WI**

Henderson, William **AV BA**
(British architect, ca.1737-1824) BA
(ca.1737-1824) AV

Henderson, William → see Henderson, William II

Henderson, William I → see Henderson, William

Henderson, William II **WI**
(British artist, 20th cent.) WC
(British artist, op.20th c.) WI

Henderson, William **WC**

Henderson, William Penhallow **BA WI**
(American artist, 1877-1943) WI
(American painter, printmaker, architect, 1877-1943) BA

Hendius → see Hondius, Abraham

Hendler, Maxwell **BA WC WI**
(American artist, 20th cent.) WC
(American artist, b.1938) WI
(American painter, b.1938) BA

Hendler, Raymond **WC WI**
(American artist, 20th cent.) WC
(American artist, op.20th c.) WI

Hendon, Cham *(American painter, 20th c.)* **BA**
Bibl: Arts Magazine, LIII/ 8 (1979), 19; Guide exh. artists: N. Amer. ptrs.; ▶Intl. dir. exh. artists, 1982

Hendrich, Antal *(Hungarian artist, 1878-)* **WC**

Hendrick Andriesz. → see Andriesz., Hendrick

Hendrick Anthonis → see Antonissen, Henricus Josephus

Hendrick Arentsen Vapour → see Vapour, Hendrick Arentsen

Hendrick Avercamp → see Avercamp, Hendrick

Hendrick Bloemaert → see Bloemaert, Hendrick

Hendrick Blom → see Blom, Hendrick [Unidentified]

Hendrick Bogaert → see Bogaert, Hendrick Hendricksz.

Hendrick Coops → see Coops, Hendrick

Hendrick Cornelisz. Vroom → see Vroom, Hendrick Cornelisz.

Hendrick Coster → see Coster, Hendrick

Hendrick Cuyper → see Cuyper, Hendrick

Hendrick Danckerts → see Danckerts, Hendrick

Hendrick de Keyser → see Keyser, Hendrik de

Hendrick Dubbelt → see Dubbels, Hendrik Jacobsz.

Hendrick Goltius → see Goltzius, Hendrik

Hendrick Goltzius → see Goltzius, Hendrik

Hendrick Hendricksz. Bogaert → see Bogaert, Hendrick Hendricksz.

Hendrick Martensz. Sorgh → see Sorgh, Hendrik Martensz.

Hendrick Momber → see Mommers, Hendrik

Hendrick Mommers → see Mommers, Hendrik

Hendrick Schoock → see Schoock, Hendrick

Hendrick ten Oever → see Oever, Hendrick ten

Hendrick Terbruggen → see Terbrugghen, Hendrick

Hendrick Terbrugghen → see Terbrugghen, Hendrick

Hendrick van Anthonissen → see Anthonissen, Hendrick van

Hendrick van Anthonisz. → see Antonissen, Henricus Josephus

Hendrick van Balen → see Balen, Hendrik I van

Hendrick van Cleef III → see Cleve, Hendrick III van

Hendrick van Cleve (III) → see Cleve, Hendrick III van

Hendrick van den Broeck → see Broeck, Hendrick van den

Hendrick van der Burch → see Burch, Hendrick van der

Hendrick van der Burgh → see Burch, Hendrick van der

Hendrick van Steenwyck (II) → see Steenwyck, Hendrik van, the younger

Hendrick van Vliet → see Vliet, Hendrik Cornelisz. van

Hendrick Vapoor → see Vapour, Hendrick Arentsen

Hendrick, Don W. *(American painter, b.1947)* **BA**

Hendrick, Nicolas → see Broeck, Hendrick van den

Hendricks A. Hallett → see Hallett, Hendricks A.

Hendricks, Ahasuerus *(American silversmith, ca.1640-1727)* **BA**
Bibl: Fales, Early Amer. silver; NY state silversmiths; ▶Thieme-Becker

Hendricks, David Charles *(American painter, printmaker, b.1948)* **BA**
Bibl: ▶WW Amer. Art, 1989

Hendricks, Edward Lee *(American sculptor, b.1952)* **BA**
Bibl: ▶Art Index, Jan. 1989; ▶Artist biog. master idx.; ▶WW Amer. Art, 1989-1990

Hendricks, Geoffrey *(American artist, b.1931)* **BA**
Bibl: ▶Contemp. artists; ▶WW Amer. Art, 1989-1990

Hendricks, Jon *(American artist, b. 1940)* **BA**
Bibl: ▶Contemp. artists

Hendrickson, Ken *(American painter, b.1952)* **BA**
Bibl: Guide exh. artists: N. Amer. ptrs.; ▶Intl. dir. exh. artists, 1983

Hendrickson, Warren J. *(American architect)* **AV**
Bibl: Chicago architectural journal, 1985, v.5, p.152

Hendricksz, Dirck → see Hendricksz., Dirck, Teodoro d'Errico

Hendricksz. Bogaert → see Bogaert, Hendricksz.

Hendricksz. or Heyndricsx, Dirck (Enrico or Teodoro (d'Errico) Fiammingo; possibly identified with Teodoro Gerrico) → see Hendricksz., Dirck, Teodoro d'Errico

Hendricksz., Dirck (Teodoro d'Errico) → see Hendricksz., Dirck, Teodoro d'Errico

Hendricksz., Dirck, Teodoro
d'Errico **BA**
(Flemish painter in ITA, ca.1550-
1618) BA
(Flemish painter, act. ca.1574) PR
(Flemish, op.1574-m.1618) WC
Bibl: ▶Bolaffi; De Martini, Boll.
d'arte LXX, 29, 1985; Previtali,
Cinquecento a Napoli, p.100;
▶Thieme-Becker; ▶Wilenski, Flem.
ptrs.
Dirck Hendricksz PR
Dirck Hendricksz. PR
Enrico fiamenco PR
Enrico Fiamengho PR
Enrico Fiamengo PR
Enrico Fiammingo PR
Enrigo Fiammingo PR
Errico Fiamenco PR
Errico Fiamengo PR
Errico Fiammingo PR
Hendricksz, Dirck PR
Hendricksz. or Heyndricsx, Dirck
(Enrico or Teodoro (d'Errico)
Fiammingo; possibly
identified with Teodoro
Gerrico) **WC**
Hendricksz., Dirck (Teodoro
d'Errico) **PR**
Teodoro d'Errico PR
Teodoro Fiamengo PR
Hendrickx, Joseph (Belgian painter,
printmaker, 1906-1971) **BA**
Bibl: Clark Art Inst. Libr.; ▶Dict.
biog. artistes belges; ▶Grote
Winkler Prins; ▶MoMA libr. cat.;
▶Vollmer, Künst.-Lex. 20. Jhr.
Hendrie, John **WC WI**
(British artist, op.1677) WC
(British artist, op.1677-) WI
Hendrik Anton Hage→see Hage,
Hendrik Anton
Hendrik Carree→see Carree, Hendrik
Hendrik Cornelisz. van Vliet→see
Vliet, Hendrik Cornelisz. van
Hendrik de Clerck→see Clerck,
Hendrik de
Hendrik de Fromantiou→see
Fromantiou, Hendrik de
Hendrik de Keyser (I)→see Keyser,
Hendrik de
Hendrik de Meijer→see Meijer,
Hendrik de
Hendrik de Valk→see Valk, Hendrik
de
Hendrik Dirk Kruseman van
Elten→see Kruseman van Elten,
Hendrik Dirk
Hendrik Dubbels→see Dubbels,
Hendrik Jacobsz.
Hendrik Frans de Cort→see Cort,
Hendrik Frans de
Hendrik Frans van Lint→see Lint,
Hendrik Frans van

Hendrik Gerritsz. Pot→see Pot,
Hendrik Gerritsz.
Hendrik Goltsius→see Goltzius,
Hendrik
Hendrik Goltzius→see Goltzius,
Hendrik
Hendrik Jacobsz. Dubbels→see
Dubbels, Hendrik Jacobsz.
Hendrik Leys→see Leys, Hendrik,
baron
Hendrik Lofvers→see Lofvers,
Hendrik
Hendrik Martenze Zorgh→see Sorgh,
Hendrik Martensz.
Hendrik Mommers→see Mommers,
Hendrik
Hendrik Pietersz. de Hondt→see
Hondt, Hendrik Pietersz. de
Hendrik Rietschoof→see Rietschoof,
Hendrik
Hendrik van Balen (I)→see Balen,
Hendrik I van
Hendrik van Balen (II)→see Balen,
Hendrik van (II)
Hendrik van der Borcht (the
elder)→see Borcht, Hendrik van
der (the elder)
Hendrik van Kleef→see Cleve,
Hendrick III van
Hendrik van Limborch→see
Limborch, Hendrik van
Hendrik Van Lint→see Lint, Hendrik
Frans van
Hendrik van Minderhout→see
Minderhout, Hendrik van
Hendrik van Schoel→see Schoel,
Hendrick van
Hendrik van Somer→see Somer,
Hendrick van
Hendrik van Steenwyck (I)→see
Steenwyck, Hendrik van, the elder
Hendrik van Streeck→see Streeck,
Hendrik van
Hendrik van Vliet→see Vliet, Hendrik
Cornelisz. van
Hendrik Verschuring→see
Verschuring, Hendrik
Hendrik Willem Mesdag→see
Mesdag, Hendrik Willem
Hendriks→see Hendriks, Wybrand
Hendriks, Axend (Dutch artist,
1901-1951) **WC**
Hendriks, Frederik Hendrik **GC WC**
(Dutch artist, 1808-1865) WC
(Dutch painter, 1808-1865) GC
Bibl: ▶Thieme-Becker
Hendriks, G. (Gerardus) **GC**
(Dutch artist, 19th cent.) WC
(Dutch painter, act.19th century
(first half)) GC
Bibl: ▶Scheen, Ned. beeldende
kunst.
Hendriks, Gerardus **WC**
Hendriks, Gerardus→see Hendriks, G.
(Gerardus)

Hendriks, Jurrian (Dutch
draughtsman, 1859-1952) **GC**
Bibl: ▶Scheen, Ned. beeldende
kunst.
Hendriks, Roelof (French(?)
architect) **AV**
Bibl: Architecture intérieure créé,
1988 Oct.-Nov., no.226, p.168
Hendriks, Sara Fredricka (Dutch
artist, 1846-1925) **WC**
Hendriks, Wijbrand→see Hendriks,
Wybrand
Hendriks, Wybrand **BA GC PR WC**
(Dutch artist, 1744-1831) WC
(Dutch painter and
draughtsman, 1744-1831) GC
(Dutch painter, 1744-1831) BA PR
Bibl: Getty Photo Study Coll.;
▶Rosenberg, Dutch art & arch.;
▶Thieme-Becker; ▶Witt checklist;
▶Wurzbach, NLD Künst.-Lex.
Hendriks PR
Hendriks, Wijbrand **PR**
Wijbrand Hendriks PR
Wybrand Hendriks PR
Hendrikus Alexander van Ingen→see
Ingen, Hendrikus Alexander van
Hendrix, Illya (American interior
designer) **AV**
Bibl: Architectural digest, 1986
Mar., v.43, no.3, p.182
Hendrix, Liz (American interior
designer, Seattle, Wash) **AV**
Bibl: Restaurant/hotel design,
1988 Nov., v.10, no.11, p.72
Hendschel, Albert Louis Ulrich
(German artist, 1834-1883) **WC**
Hendtzschel, Gottfried (Norwegian
artist, op.1625-p.1648) **WC**
Hendy, Stuart (British architect) **AV**
Hendy, W. **WC WI**
(British artist, 19th cent.) WC
(British artist, op.19th c.) WI
Heneghan, George E. (American
architect, Hawaii) **AV**
Bibl: ▶AIA Pro File, 1985
Heng, G. S. (British architect) **AV**
Bibl: Architects' journal, 1989
Aug.23, v.190, no.8-9, p.24
Hengeler, Adolf **GC WC**
(German artist, 1863-) WC
(German painter, 1863-1927) GC
Bibl: ▶Schweers, Gemälde deut.
Museen; ▶Thieme-Becker
Hengeveld, Jan (Dutch
businessman, Amsterdam) **AV**
Bibl: Monumentum, 1984 Dec.,
v.27, no.4, p.261
Hengstenburgh, Hermann→see
Henstenburgh, Herman
Heniker [Unidentified] (Unknown
painter) **PR**
Bibl: (May 13, 1813, lot 6, Coxe)
Henke, Dieter (Austrian architect) **AV**
Bibl: Bauforum, 1987, v.20, no.
124, p.11
Henke, G.→see Henkes, Gerke

Henkel, August *(American painter, .1881-1961)* **BA**
Bibl: Archives Amer. Art Jrnl., XVI/3 (1976) pp.8-11; ▶Artist biog. master idx.; NY Times obit.

Henkel, Friedrich B. *(German sculptor, 20th c.)* **BA**
Bibl: Protzmann, Dresdener Kunst., XXX, 2, (1986) pp. 34-41

Henkel, James *(American photographer, b.1947)* **BA**
Bibl: SITES, The Photographer's Hand (1980-82)

Henkels, George J. *(American cabinetmaker, 19th c.)* **BA**
Bibl: NUR pre 56; WINTERTHUR PORTFOLIO, 1977, 103-114

Henkes → see Henkes, Gerke

Henkes, Désirée *(Dutch artist, b.1956)* **BA**
Bibl: Guide exh. artists: N. Amer. ptrs.; Rotterdam (NLD), Mus. Boymans-van Beuningen, Veertien Kunstenaars (1983)

Henkes, Gerke **GC PR WC**
(Dutch artist, 1844-1927) WC
(Dutch painter and draughtsman, 1844-1927) GC
(Dutch painter, 1844-1927) PR
Bibl: ▶Bénézit; ▶Witt checklist
Gerke Henkes PR
Henke, G. PR
Henkes PR

Henkes, Roelof Lucas Johannes **GC**
(Dutch artist, 1903-) WC
(Dutch painter and draughtsman, b.1903) GC
Bibl: ▶Vollmer, Künst.-Lex. 20. Jhr.

Henkes, Roelof Lucas Johannes (Dolf) **WC**
Henkes, Roelof Lucas Johannes (Dolf) → see Henkes, Roelof Lucas Johannes

Henket, Hubert-Jan **AV BA**
(Dutch architect, 20th c.) BA
(Dutch architect, Buxtel) AV
Bibl: ▶Avery period. idx., 4th suppl.; Detail, 1981 May-June, no.3, p.326

Henkle, James Lee *(American sculptor, b.1927)* **BA**
Bibl: ▶Artist biog. master idx.; ▶WW Amer. Art, 1989-1990

Henle, Fritz **BA JG**
(American (b. Germany), 1909 -) JG
(German photographer, b.1909) BA
Bibl: Afterimage, VIII/5 (Dec. 1980); ▶Artist biog. master idx.; ▶Contemp. photogs.; ▶MoMA libr. cat.; Munich (BRD), Stadtmus., Fotomuseum; SAMMLUNG JOS. BREITERBACH... 1979 (cat); ▶WW Amer. Art, 1989-1990

Henle, Jan *(Polish sculptor, 17th c.)* **BA**
Bibl: Kaczmarzyk in Biuletyn historii szturki, XLI, 4, 1979, 347-62

Henley, Henry W. *(British artist, op. 1871-1895)* **WI**

Henley, Lionel Charles **WC WI**
(British artist, 1843-circa 1893) WI
(British artist, op.1862-93) WC

Henman, William *(British architect, d.1917)* **BA**
Bibl: ▶Avery obit. idx.

Henn, Ewald *(East German architect, professor and President of the Bund der Architekten der DDR, 1987)* **AV**
Bibl: Architektur der DDR, 1987 Sept., v.36, no.9, p.6

Henn, Rudolph *(American sculptor, 20th century)* **GC**
Bibl: Juley coll., NMAA

Henn, Ulrich *(German artist, op.c. 1957)* **WC**

Henn, Walter *(German architect, Braunschweig)* **AV**
Bibl: Detail, 1982 Sept.-Oct., no.5, p.537

Henne, Eberhard Siegfried *(German artist, 1759-1828)* **WC**

Henne, Joachim **BA WC**
(German artist, op.1702) WC
(German sculptor, painter, ca.1630/40-after 1707) BA
Bibl: Schidlof, Miniature in Europe; ▶Thieme-Becker

Henneberg, Georg or Jorg, II *(German artist, op.1556-1590)* **WC**

Henneberg, Hugo *(Austrian, 1863-1910)* **JG**

Henneberg, Jes *(Danish architect, Aarhus)* **AV**
Bibl: Arkitektur DK, 1988, v.32, no.5, p.238

Henneberg, Rudolf Friedrich August *(German artist, 1826-1876)* **WC**

Henneberger, Hans *(German artist, op.1593-m.1601)* **WC**

Hennebicq, Andre *(Belgian artist, 1836-1904)* **WC**

Hennebique, François **AV BA**
(1842-1921) AV
(French engineer, 1842-1921) BA
Bibl: ▶Larousse grande encyc.

Hennebo, Dieter *(West German landscape architect)* **AV**
Bibl: Garten und Landschaft, 1988, v.98, no.5, p.22; ▶Libr. of Congr. Name Auth. File

Hennecart, Hannequart or Hennequart, Jean *(Netherlands artist, op.1454-1475)* **WC**
Hennekijn → see Hennekyn, Paulus

Hennekin, Simon *(British woodcarver, act.1776)* **BA**
Bibl: Furniture hist., XI (1975) pp. 53-55

Hennekyn → see Hennekyn, Paulus
Hennekyn or Hennekin, Paulus → see Hennekyn, Paulus

Hennekyn, Paulus **GC JG PR**
(Dutch artist, 1611/14-1672) WC
(Dutch painter, 1611/14-1672) GC PR
(Dutch, ca. 1611-1672) JG
Bibl: Getty Photo Study Coll.; ▶Thieme-Becker
Hennekijn PR
Hennekyn PR
Hennekyn or Hennekin, Paulus **WC**
Paulus Hennekyn PR

Hennell family *(British goldsmiths, 18th-20th cs.)* **BA**
Bibl: ▶Thieme-Becker

Hennell, David **JG**
Hennell, Robert **JG WC WI**
(British artist, 1826-1892) WC WI
Hennell, Samuel **JG**
Hennell, Thomas → see Hennell, Thomas Barclay

Hennell, Thomas Barclay **BA WI**
(British artist, 1903-1944) WC
(British artist, 1903-1945) WI
(British painter, 1903-1945) BA
Bibl: ▶Artist biog. master idx.; ▶Johnson, Brit. artists; ▶Peppin, Bk. illus. 20c.; ▶Waters, Brit. artists

Hennell, Thomas **WC**
Henneman → see Hanneman, Adriaen

Henneman, Jeroen *(Dutch painter, printmaker, b.1942)* **BA**
Bibl: ▶Grote Winkler Prins; Paris (FRA), Inst. néerlandais, L'Atelier de Piet Clement (1976); ▶Scheen, Ned. beeldende kunst.

Henneman, Nicholas **BA**
(British (b. Netherlands), 1813-1893) JG
(Dutch photographer in GBR, 1813-1893) BA
Bibl: Arnold, WILLIAM HENRY FOX TALBOT; ▶Art Index, v.37; ▶Artist biog. master idx.; Arts Council of GB, FROM TODAY PAINTING IS DEAD...; HIST. OF PHOTOG IV/4 (Oct 1980) 313-322; ▶ICP encyc. photog.

Henneman, Nikolas **JG**
Henneman, Nikolas → see Henneman, Nicholas

Hennequin de Bruges → see Bondol, Jean

Hennequin du Vivier → see Duvivier, Jehan

Hennequin, Jean *(French gunsmith, 17th c.)* **BA**
Bibl: ▶Thieme-Becker; WAFFEN UND KOSTÜNKUNDE XIX 2 1977 151-156

**Hennequin, Philippe
Auguste**   **BA GC WC**
   (French artist, 1762-1833)   **WC**
   (French painter, printmaker,
      1762-1833)   **BA**
   (French, 1762-1833)   **GC**
   Bibl: ▶Artist biog. master idx.;
      ▶Busse, Maler u. Bildhauer 19.
      Jahr.; ▶Encyc. Britannica;
      ▶Larousse grande encyc.;
      ▶Thieme-Becker; ▶Witt checklist
Henner → see Henner, Jean Jacques
Henner, George P. (German artist,
   op.1784)   **WC**
*Henner, Jean → see Henner, Jean
   Jacques*
Henner, Jean Jacques   **BA PR WC**
   (French artist, 1829-1905)   **WC**
   (French painter, 1829-1905) **BA GC PR**
   Bibl: ▶Artist biog. master idx.;
      ▶Brockhaus Enzyk.; ▶Busse, Maler
      u. Bildhauer 19. Jahr.; ▶Larousse
      grande encyc.; ▶RILA/BHA;
      ▶Thieme-Becker
   Henner   PR
   Henner, Jean   PR
   Henner, Jean-Jacques   **GC PR**
   Jean Jacques Henner   PR
*Henner, Jean-Jacques → see Henner,
   Jean Jacques*
Hennes, Hilary (British artist, op.
   20th c.)   **WI**
Hennessy, Patrick (British artist,
   1920-1980)   **WI**
Hennessy, Richard (American
   painter, 20th c.)   **BA**
   Bibl: ART IN AMERICA, vol 65,
      May 1977, p.113; Arts Magazine,
      vol 52, June 1978; ▶Intl. dir. exh.
      artists, 1983
Hennessy, William John   **WC WI**
   (British artist, 1839-1917)   **WI**
   (British artist, 1839-c.1920)   **WC**
   Bibl: ▶Johnson, Brit. artists
**Hennezel d'Essert, Béat-Antoine-
   François de** (Swiss architect,
   1733-1810)   **BA**
   Bibl: Hajjar, GENAVA, XXXI (1983)
      89-99; Kunstdenkmäler der
      Schweiz, Canton de Vaud, IV, 312
   Essear, Béat-Antoine-François de
      Hennezel d'   BA
Hennies, Ehrenfried (West German
   architect, Braunschweig, 1947-)   **AV**
   Bibl: Deutsche Bauzeitung,
      CXXII/9 (Sep. 1988) p.194
Hennig, Albert (German, 1907-)   **JG**
Hennig, Artur Bruno Kurt (German
   painter, b.1880)   **GC**
   Bibl: ▶Thieme-Becker
Hennig, Bernd (German sculptor,
   b.1952)   **BA**
   Bibl: Baden-Baden (DEU),
      Staatliche Kunsthalle, Bernd
      Hennig (1978)

Hennig, Gustav Adolph   **GC WC**
   (German artist, 1797-1869)   **WC**
   (German draughtsman, 1797-
      1869)   **GC**
   Bibl: ▶Thieme-Becker
Hennig, Johann Friedrich (German
   artist, c.1778-p.1806)   **WC**
Hennig, Karl (German artist, 1871-)   **WC**
**Hennigs, Gusta (Carl Gustaf
   Albert) von** (Swedish artist, 1866-
   1941)   **WC**
Henniker, Annie L. (British artist,
   op.1897-1925)   **WI**
Hennin → see Hennin, Adriaen de
Hennin, Adriaen de   **GC PR**
   (Dutch artist, op.1664-m.1710)   **WC**
   (Dutch painter, act. 1664, d.
      1710)   **PR**
   (Dutch painter, act.1664-d.
      1710)   **GC**
   Bibl: ▶Bénézit; Getty Photo Study
      Coll.; ▶Thieme-Becker; ▶Witt
      checklist
   Adriaen de Hennin   PR
   Heenij   PR
   Hennin   PR
   **Hennin, Henny or Henyn,
      Adriaen de**   **WC**
   Hennj   PR
   Henny   PR
   Henny, Adriaen de   GC
*Hennin, Henny or Henyn, Adriaen
   de → see Hennin, Adriaen de*
Hennin, Jacob de   **GC WC**
   (Dutch artist, 1629-c.1688)   **WC**
   (Dutch draughtsman, 1629-d.
      aft.1688)   **GC**
   Bibl: ▶Thieme-Becker
Hénnin, Jean-Marie (French
   architect, Paris)   **AV**
   Bibl: ▶Annuaire archts. fran.,
      1987
Henning, Adolf (German
   draughtsman, 1809-1900)   **GC**
   Bibl: ▶Thieme-Becker
*Henning, Archibald S. → see Henning,
   Archibald Samuel*
Henning, Archibald Samuel   **WI**
   (British artist, op.1825-, d.1864)   **WI**
   (British artist, op.1825-1834)   **WC**
   Henning, Archibald S.   **WC**
Henning, Christian   **GC WC**
   (German artist, 1741-1822)   **WC**
   (German draughtsman, 1741-
      1822)   **GC**
   Bibl: ▶Thieme-Becker
Henning, Gerhard   **BA GC WC**
   (Danish sculptor, 1880-1967)   **BA GC**
   (Swedish artist, 1880-1967)   **WC**
   Bibl: ▶Bénézit; Borgens Danmark;
      ▶MoMA libr. cat.; ▶RILA/BHA;
      Rostrup, H., GERHARD HENNING:
      EN MINDEBOG; ▶Vollmer,
      Künst.-Lex. 20. Jhr.; ▶Weilbach,
      Kunst.leks.
Henning, John → see Henning, John I

Henning, John I   **BA**
   (British artist, 1771-1851)   **WC WI**
   (British sculptor, 1771-1851)   **BA**
   Bibl: ▶Bénézit; ▶Dict. natl. biog.;
      ▶Gunnis, Brit. sculp.;
      ▶Thieme-Becker
Henning, John   **WC WI**
Henninger, John (American artist,
   b.1942)   **BA**
   Bibl: New York (NY, USA), New
      Mus., Extended sensibilities
      (1982)
Henninger, Manfred (German
   painter, b.1894)   **BA**
   Bibl: Guide exh. artists: N. Amer.
      ptrs.; ▶Intl. dir. exh. artists, 1983;
      ▶Vollmer, Künst.-Lex. 20. Jhr.;
      ▶WW Arts DEU
Henninger-Thoma, Gabriela
   (German architect, Freiburg)   **AV**
   Bibl: Bauwelt, 1986 June 6, v.77,
      no.22, p.789
Hennings, Emmy (German artist,
   author, 1885-1948)   **BA**
   Bibl: Deutsches Dichterlexikon;
      ▶Natl. union cat., pre-1956;
      WOMAN'S ART JOURNAL,
      II/1(1981)
Hennings, Ernest Martin   **BA WI**
   (American artist, 1886-1956)   **WI**
   (American painter, 1886-1956)   **BA**
   Bibl: ▶Bénézit; Currier's guide
      1645-1945; ▶WWW Amer.
Hennings, Johann Friedrich
   (German artist, 1838-1899)   **WC**
Henningsen, Erik Ludvig   **BA WC**
   (Danish artist, 1855-1930)   **WC**
   (Danish painter, 1855-1930)   **BA**
   Bibl: ▶Busse, Maler u. Bildhauer
      19. Jahr.; ▶Thieme-Becker;
      ▶Vollmer, Künst.-Lex. 20. Jhr.
Henningsen, Paul (Danish designer,
   1894-1967)   **AV**
   Bibl: ▶Libr. of Congr. Name Auth.
      File
*Henningsen, Thorkild → see
   Henningsen, Thorkild Gustav*
Henningsen, Thorkild Gustav   **BA**
   (Danish architect, 1884-1931)   **AV**
   (Danish architect, author, 1884-
      1931)   **BA**
   Bibl: ▶Vollmer, Künst.-Lex. 20.
      Jhr.; ▶Weilbach, Kunst.leks.
Henningsen, Thorkild   **AV**
Hennj → see Hennin, Adriaen de
Henny → see Hennin, Adriaen de
*Henny, Adriaen de → see Hennin,
   Adriaen de*
Henny, Franco (Italian architect)   **AV**
   Bibl: Ville giardini, 1987 Dec., no.
      222 suppl., p.38
Henocq, Tony (British architect)   **AV**
   Bibl: RIBA journal, 1982 Feb.,
      v.89, no.2, p.[21]
Henri → see Henri, Robert

Henri Auguste d'Ainecy
  Montpezat→see Montpezat, Henri
  Auguste d'Ainecy
Henri Baptiste Lebasque→see
  Lebasque, Henri Baptiste
Henri Brispot→see Brispot, Henri
Henri Chanet→see Chanet, Henri
Henri Charles Manguin→see
  Manguin, Henri Charles
Henri Cleenewerck→see
  Cleenewerck, Henri
Henri de Beul→see Beul, Henri de
Henri de Saint-Jean→see Saint-Jean,
  Henri de
Henri de Vulcop→see Master of
  Coëtivy
Henri Edmond Cross→see Cross,
  Henri Edmond
Henri Eugene Callot→see Callot,
  Henri Eugène
Henri Eugene Le Sidaner→see Le
  Sidaner, Henri Eugène
Henri Evenepoel→see Evenepoel,
  Henri
Henri Fantin-Latour→see Fantin-
  Latour, Henri
Henri Francois Riesener→see
  Riesener, Henri Francois
Henri Francois van Lint→see Lint,
  Hendrik Frans van
Henri Gascard→see Gascard, Henri
Henri Gaudier-Brzeska→see Gaudier-
  Brzeska, Henri
Henri Goltz→see Goltzius, Hendrik
Henri Harpignies→see Harpignies,
  Henri-Joseph
Henri Hayden→see Hayden, Henri
Henri Horace Roland de la
  Porte→see Roland de la Porte,
  Henri Horace
Henri Jacquier→see Jacquier, Henri
Henri Jean Guillaume Martin→see
  Martin, Henri Jean Guillaume
Henri Lehmann→see Lehmann, Henri
Henri Marie Raymond de
  Toulouse-Lautrec→see Toulouse-
  Lautrec, Henri de
Henri Matisse→see Matisse, Henri
Henri Ottmann→see Ottmann, Henri
Henri Pierre Danloux→see Danloux,
  Henri-Pierre
Henri Pierre Picou→see Picou, Henri
  Pierre
Henri Rousseau→see Rousseau, Henri
  (le Douanier)
Henri Verge-Sarrat→see Vergé-Sarrat,
  Henri
Henri, Adrian→see Henri, Adrian
  Maurice

Henri, Adrian Maurice   **BA**
  (British artist, 20th cent.)   WC
  (British artist, op.1989-)   WI
  (British painter, author,
    musician, b.1932)   BA
    Bibl: ▶Intl. dir. exh. artists, 1983;
    ▶MoMA libr. cat.; ▶Natl. union
    cat., pre-1956; ▶Who's Who
    [GBR], 1989
Henri, Adrian   **WC WI**
Henri, Florence   **BA JG WC**
  (American, 1895-1982, active
    France and Germany)   JG
  (French artist, 20th cent.)   WC
  (French photographer, painter,
    1893-1982)   BA
    Bibl: ▶Contemp. photogs.;
    Geneva, Musée d'Art et d'Hist.,
    FLORENCE HENRI (1981);
    Molderings, KUNSTFORUM INTL.,
    52 (Aug 1982) 137-139; ▶MoMA
    libr. cat.; ▶Parry, Photo idx.;
    ▶Witt checklist
Henri, Pierre (French artist, 18th
  cent.)   **WC**
Henri, Robert   **BA GC PR WC WI**
  (American artist, 1865-1929)   WC WI
  (American painter, 1865-1929)   BA PR
  (American, 1865-1929)   GC
    Bibl: ▶Art Index, 1989; ▶Busse,
    Maler u. Bildhauer 19. Jahr.;
    ▶Dict. Amer. biog.; ▶Natl. union
    cat., pre-1956; ▶RILA/BHA;
    ▶Who's Who [GBR], 1897-1980
    index; ▶Witt checklist; ▶Young,
    Amer. artists
  Cozad, Robert Henry   WI
  Henri   PR
  Robert Henri   PR
Henrich, Albert (German artist,
  1899-)   **WC**
Henrich, Biff (American
  photographer, b.1953)   **BA**
    Bibl: ▶Intl. dir. exh. artists
Henrichsen, Carsten (Danish artist,
  1824-1897)   **WC**
Henrichsen, Johann Georg
  (Swedish artist, 1707-1779)   **WC**
Henrici or Henrizi, Johann Josef
  Karl→see Henrici, Johann Josef
  Karl
Henrici, Carlo→see Henrici, Johann
  Josef Karl
Henrici, Johann Josef Karl   **BA GC**
  (German artist, 1737-1823)   WC
  (German painter, 1737-1823)   BA GC
    Bibl: ▶Bénézit; ▶Fogg Mus. Libr.
    cat.; ▶Thieme-Becker
**Henrici or Henrizi, Johann Josef
  Karl**   **WC**
  Henrici, Carlo   BA
  Henrizi, Johann Josef Karl   BA
Henrick Antonisz.→see Anthonissen,
  Hendrick van
Henricksen, Ralf Christian
  (American painter, 1907-1975)   **BA**
    Bibl: ▶WW Amer. Art, 1973, 1978

Henricus (French illuminator, act.
  1285)   **GC**
    Bibl: Segre, Bestiaire, xxxvii
Henricus de Nemosio (French
  scribe, act. 1248)   **GC**
    Bibl: ▶Branner, Ms. ptg. Paris,
    p.220
Henricus Engelbertus Reyntjens→see
  Reyntjens, Henricus Engelbertus
Henricus Josephus Antonissen→see
  Antonissen, Henricus Josephus
Henricus Turken→see Turken,
  Henricus
Henricus van Mecheln→see Broeck,
  Hendrick van den
Henricus van Weerts→see Weerts,
  Henricus van
Henricus, Ludovico de→see Arrighi,
  Ludovico
Henriet, Claude, the younger
  (French painter, ca.1540-1603/04)   **BA**
    Bibl: ▶Bénézit; ▶Thieme-Becker
Henriet, Israël (French painter,
  printmaker, publisher, 1590-1661)   **BA**
    Bibl: ▶Bénézit; ▶Nouv. biog. gén.;
    ▶Thieme-Becker
Henriette Browne→see Browne,
  Henriette, (Sophie)
Henriette Lewis Jamison→see
  Jamison, Henriette Lewis
Henriette Ronner→see Ronner,
  Henriette
Henriette Wolters→see Wolters,
  Henriette (née van Pee)
Henrigo Spagnuolo, D.
  [**Unidentified**] (Unknown painter)   **PR**
    Bibl: (May 9, 1803, lot 29, James
    Vallance)
  D. Henrigo Spagnuolo   PR
Henrik Louis Lund→see Lund, Henrik
  Louis
Henriksen, Arne (Norwegian
  architect, Oslo, 1944-)   **AV**
    Bibl: Norske Ark. Lands. Årbok
    1987
Henriod, Gus. (French, ca.1832-after
  1901)   **BA**
Henrion→see Henrion, Armand
  François Joseph
Henrion, Armand François Joseph
  (French painter, b. 1875)   **PR**
  Armand Francois Joseph Henrion   PR
  Henrion   PR
  Henrion, Armand-Francois-Joseph   PR
Henrion,
  Armand-Francois-Joseph→see
  Henrion, Armand François Joseph
Henrion, Patricia (French architect)   **AV**
    Bibl: Techniques et architecture,
    1989 Aug.-Sept., no.385, p.104
Henriot (Jean Henri Maigrot)
  (French illustrator, 1857-1933)   **BA**
    Bibl: ▶Bénézit; ▶Natl. union cat.;
    ▶Thieme-Becker
Henriot, Richard (French architect)   **AV**

*Henriquel, Louis Pierre (Henriquel
Dupont)→see* Henriquel-Dupont,
Louis Pierre

Henriquel-Dupont, Louis Pierre   **GC**
  (French artist, 1797-1892)   **WC**
  (French painter, 1797-1892)   **GC**
  Bibl: ▶Thieme-Becker

**Henriquel, Louis Pierre
(Henriquel Dupont)**   **WC**

Henriques or Anriques, Francisco
  (Portuguese artist, -c.1519)   **WC**

Henriques, Ethel Quixano *(British
artist, 1868-1936)*   **WI**

Henriques, Lady Rose L.→see
Henriques, Rose L.

Henriques, Rose L.   **WI**
  (British artist, 20th cent.)   **WC**
  (British artist, op.1937-1940)   **WI**

Henriques, Lady Rose L.   **WC**

Henriquez, Benott Louis *(French
artist, 1732-1806)*   **WC**

Henriquez, Emmanuel *(Spanish
artist, 1593-1653)*   **WC**

Henriquez, Richard   **AV BA**
  (Canadian architect, 20th c.)   **BA**
  *(Canadian architect, partner in
firm of Henriquez & Partners,
Vancouver, 1941-)*   **AV**
  Bibl: Building with words..., 1981,
p.60; White, Vanguard, XIII/4
(May 1984) p.26

Henrizi, Johann Josef Karl→see
Henrici, Johann Josef Karl

Henry→see Henry, Edward Lamson

Henry→see Henry, Paul

Henry Albert Botkin→see Botkin,
Henry Albert

Henry Alexander→see Alexander,
Henry

Henry Bacon→see Bacon, Henry

Henry Benbridge→see Benbridge,
Henry

Henry Bernard Chalon→see Chalon,
Henry Bernard

Henry Bright→see Bright, Henry

Henry Carré→see Carree, Hendrik

Henry Cheeves Pratt→see Pratt,
Henry Cheever

Henry Cleef→see Cleve, Hendrick III
van

Henry Collins Bispham→see Bispham,
Henry Collins

Henry du Bles→see Bles, Herri met
de

Henry Dutton Morse→see Morse,
Henry Dutton

Henry Elis Mattson→see Mattson,
Henry Elis

Henry Fuseli→see Fuseli, Henry

Henry Goltzius→see Goltzius,
Hendrik

Henry Gritten→see Gritten, Henry C.

Henry Hammond Ahl→see Ahl, Henry
Hammond

Henry Howard→see Howard, Henry

Henry Inman→see Inman, Henry

Henry John Boddington→see
Boddington, Henry John, (Williams)

Henry John Dobson→see Dobson,
Henry John

Henry Joseph Breuer→see Breuer,
Henry Joseph

Henry Lamb→see Lamb, Henry

Henry Lee McFee→see McFee, Henry
Lee

Henry Lerolle→see Lerolle, Henry

Henry Marriott Paget→see Paget,
Henry Marriott

Henry Milbourne→see Milbourne,
Henry

Henry Moore→see Moore, Henry

Henry Moret→see Moret, Henry

Henry Mosler→see Mosler, Henry

Henry Oliver Walker→see Walker,
Henry Oliver

Henry Ossawa Tanner→see Tanner,
Henry Ossawa

Henry Pember Smith→see Smith,
Henry Pember

Henry Perronet Briggs→see Briggs,
Henry Perronet

Henry Raeburn→see Raeburn, Henry

Henry Rankin Poore→see Poore,
Henry Rankin

Henry Robert Morland→see Morland,
Henry Robert

Henry Scheffer→see Scheffer, Henry

Henry Schnakenberg→see
Schnakenberg, Henry

Henry Siddons Mowbray→see
Mowbray, Henry Siddons

Henry Singleton→see Singleton,
Henry

Henry Stone→see Stone, Henry

Henry Strater→see Strater, Henry

Henry Stull→see Stull, Henry

Henry Swinburne→see Swinburne,
Henry

Henry Tanworth Wells→see Wells,
Henry Tanworth

Henry Thompson→see Thomson,
Henry

Henry Thompson, Esq. R.A.→see
Thomson, Henry

Henry Thomson→see Thomson,
Henry

Henry Tilson→see Tilson, Henry

Henry Tonks→see Tonks, Henry

Henry Tresham→see Tresham, Henry

Henry Tresham, R. A.→see Tresham,
Henry

Henry Tresham, R.A.→see Tresham,
Henry

Henry Turner Munns→see Munns,
Henry Turner

Henry Van Streek→see Streeck,
Hendrik van

Henry Varnum Poor→see Poor, Henry
Varnum

Henry Walter→see Walter, Henry

Henry Walton→see Walton, Henry

Henry Ward Ranger→see Ranger,
Henry Ward

Henry Willard→see Willard, Henry

Henry William Bunbury→see
Bunbury, Henry William

Henry William Pickersgill→see
Pickersgill, Henry William

Henry Wyatt→see Wyatt, Henry

Henry, A.   **WC WI**
  (British artist, op.19th c.)   **WI**
  (British(?) artist, 19th cent.)   **WC**

Henry, Aime *(French artist, 20th
cent.)*   **WC**

Henry, Dale *(American painter,
b.1931)*   **BA**
  Bibl: ▶Artist biog. master idx.;
▶NY art yrbk.

Henry, David *(British architect,
1935-1989)*   **AV**
  Bibl: ▶RIBA members, 1987

Henry, E. *(American artist, op.1862-)*   **WI**

Henry, E. Grace Mitchell→see Henry,
Grace

Henry, Eduard Lamson→see Henry,
Edward Lamson

Henry, Edward→see Henry, Edward
Lamson

**Henry, Edward
Lamson**   **BA GC PR WC WI**
  (American artist, 1841-1919)   WC WI
  *(American painter, 1841-
1919)*   BA GC PR
  Bibl: ▶Busse, Maler u. Bildhauer
19. Jahr.; ▶Dict. Amer. biog.;
Getty Photo Study Coll.;
▶RILA/BHA; ▶Thieme-Becker;
▶Witt checklist

  Edward Lamson Henry   PR
  Henry   PR

Henry, Eduard Lamson   **GC**
  Henry, Edward   PR
  Henry, Edward Lawson   PR

Henry, Edward Lawson→see Henry,
Edward Lamson

Henry, George→see Henry, George F.

Henry, George F.   **BA**
  (British artist, 1859-1943)   WC WI
  (British painter, 1858-1943)   BA
  Bibl: ▶Bénézit; Billcliffe; ▶Busse,
Maler u. Bildhauer 19. Jahr.;
▶Harris, Scottish ptrs.;
▶Thieme-Becker; ▶Vollmer,
Künst.-Lex. 20. Jhr.

Henry, George   **WC WI**

Henry, Ghislain-Joseph *(Belgian
architect, 1754-1820)*   **BA**
  Bibl: ▶Biog. Nat. Belgique;
▶Portoghesi, Diz. arch. e
urbanistica; ▶Thieme-Becker

Henry, Grace   PR **WC WI**
   (British artist, 1868-1953)   WI
   (British artist, op.c.1930)   WC
   (British painter, 1868-1953)   PR
     Bibl: ▶Johnson, Brit. artists; Nat
     Gal of Ireland catalogue; ▶Waters,
     Brit. artists
   E. Grace Mitchell Henry   PR
   Grace Henry   PR
  Henry, E. Grace Mitchell   **PR**
   Mitchell, Emily Grace, Miss   WI
Henry, Guy *(French architect)*   AV
     Bibl: Casabella, 1985 May, v.49,
     no.513, p.14
Henry, James → see Henry, James
  Levin
Henry, James Levin   **WI**
   (British artist, 1855-circa 1929)   WI
   (British artist, 19th cent.)   WC
     Bibl: ▶Mallalieu, Brit. watercolour
     artists
  Henry, James   **WC**
Henry, Jean   **GC**
   (French artist, 1734-1784)   WC
   (French, 1734-1784)   GC
     Bibl: ▶Thieme-Becker; ▶Witt
     checklist
  Arles, Jean Henry d'   **WC**
  Henry, Jean (Henry d'Arles)   **WC**
Henry, Jean (Henry d'Arles) → see
  Henry, Jean
Henry, John *(American*
  photographer, b.1947)   **BA**
     Bibl: San Antonio (TX, USA),
     Witte Mem. Mus., What's up in
     Texas (1978); Springfield (MA,
     USA), Art Museum, John Henry
     (1977); ▶WW Amer. Art, 1976
Henry, John   **WC WI**
   (British artist, 19th cent.)   WC
   (British artist, op.1837-)   WI
Henry, John Raymond *(American*
  sculptor, b.1943)   **BA**
Henry, Maurice *(French artist,*
  1907-)   **WC**
Henry, Michel *(French painter, 19th*
  century)   **GC**
     Bibl: ▶Bénézit
Henry, Moses H *(American painter,*
  act.1850)   **BA**
     Bibl: Greenwald, A.M., JOURNAL
     OF JEWISH ART X (1984) 87-101
Henry, Paul   **BA PR WC WI**
   (British artist, 1876-1958)   WC WI
   (Irish painter, 1876-1958)   BA PR
     Bibl: Ireland: cult. encyc., p.105;
     ▶Johnson, Brit. artists;
     ▶RILA/BHA; ▶Vollmer, Künst.-Lex.
     20. Jhr.; ▶Waters, Brit. artists
   Henry   PR
   Paul Henry   PR
Henry, Paul Edmond *(French*
  painter, d.1904)   **GC**
     Bibl: ▶Bénézit

Henry, Pedro *(Spanish architect,*
  18th cent)   **AV**
     Bibl: Arch. esp. de arte, LXII/245
     (Jan-Mar 1989) 87
Henry, Robert *(American painter,*
  b.1933)   **BA**
     Bibl: ▶Intl. dir. exh. artists, 1983;
     ▶WW Amer. Art, 1989-1990
Henry, S. *(British artist, op.20th c.)*   **WI**
Henry, T. Charlton, Mrs. *(American,*
  20th c.)   **BA**
     Bibl: Philadelphia telephone book
Henry, T.M.   **WC WI**
   (British artist, 19th cent.)   WC
   (British artist, op.19th c.)   WI
Henry, William *(British artist, op.*
  1847-1883)   **WC WI**
Henryk Gotlib → see Gotlib, Henryk
Henryk Stazewski → see Stażewski,
  Henryk
Hens, Carlos [Unidentified]
   (Unknown painter)   **PR**
     Bibl: 1651 Carpio inventory
   Carlos hens   PR
Hens, Frans *(Belgian artist, 1856-*
  1928)   **WC**
Hens, Juan [Unidentified]
   (Unknown painter)   **PR**
     Bibl: 1651 Carpio inventory
   Juan hens   PR
Hensberch → see Haensbergen, Johan
  van
Hensbergen → see Haensbergen,
  Johan van
Hensch, Gotthilf Friedrich *(German*
  artist, 1732-1785)   **WC**
Henschel, Moritz *(German artist,*
  op.1809-1818)   **WC**
Henschel, Wilhelm *(German artist,*
  1781-1865)   **WC**
Hensel, Hermann *(German artist,*
  1898-)   **WC**
Hensel, Wilhelm   **BA WC**
   (German artist, 1794-1861)   WC
   (German painter, printmaker,
   1794-1861)   BA
     Bibl: ▶Bénézit; ▶Thieme-Becker
Henseler, Ernest *(German artist,*
  1852-p.1900)   **WC**
Henseler, Franz *(German painter,*
  draftsman, 1885-1918)   **BA**
     Bibl: LC slip; ▶Vollmer, Künst.-Lex.
     20. Jhr.
Henselmann, Hermann   **AV BA**
   (Architect, East Germany, 1905-)   AV
   (German architect, author,
   b.1905)   BA
     Bibl: Architektur der DDR, 1985
     Jan, v.34, no.1, p.66; ▶Avery
     period. idx.; ▶Vollmer, Künst.-Lex.
     20. Jhr.
Hensett, J.   **WC WI**
   (British artist, 19th cent.)   WC
   (British artist, op.19th c.)   WI
Henshall, Henry (John Henry) → see
  Henshall, Henry, (John Henry)

Henshall, Henry, (John Henry)   **WI**
   (British artist, 1856-1928)   WC WI
  Henshall, Henry (John Henry)   **WC**
Henshaw, Frederick Henry *(British*
  artist, 1807-1891)   **WC WI**
Henshaw, Henry Wetherbee
  (American naturalist,
  photographer, 1850-1930)   **BA**
     Bibl: HIST OF PHOTOG, VIII/3
     (July-Sept 1984) 169-174; ▶WWW
     Amer., v.1
Henshaw, I.N.   **WC WI**
   (British artist, 19th cent.)   WC
   (British artist, op.19th c.)   WI
Henson, Bill *(Australian*
  photographer, b.1955)   **BA**
     Bibl: ▶Idx. Amer. photog. colls.;
     ▶Intl. dir. exh. artists, 1983; New
     York (NY, USA), Guggenheim
     Mus., Australian visions (1984)
Henson, Edward *(British artist, op.*
  20th c.)   **WI**
Henson, S. or L. or T.   **WC WI**
   (British artist, op.1799)   WC
   (British artist, op.1799-)   WI
Henstenburgh or Henstenburg,
  Anton → see Henstenburgh, Anton
Henstenburgh, Anton   **GC**
   (Dutch artist, 18th cent.)   WC
   (Dutch draughtsman, 18th
   century)   GC
     Bibl: ▶Thieme-Becker
  Henstenburgh or Henstenburg,
  Anton   **WC**
Henstenburgh, Hengstenburg, or
  Henstenburg, Herman → see
  Henstenburgh, Herman
Henstenburgh, Herman   **GC PR**
   (Dutch artist, 1667-1726)   WC
   (Dutch draughtsman, 1667-
   1726)   GC
   (Dutch painter, 1667-1726)   PR
     Bibl: Getty Photo Study Coll.;
     Getty Photo Study Coll. (Ptgs.);
     ▶Thieme-Becker; ▶Witt checklist
   Hengstenburgh, Hermann   GC
  Henstenburgh, Hengstenburg,
  or Henstenburg, Herman   **WC**
   Hensterberg   PR
   Herman Henstenburgh   PR
Hensterberg → see Henstenburgh,
  Herman
Henthorst → see Honthorst, Gerrit van
Henton, George W.Moore *(British*
  artist, circa 1861-1924)   **WI**
Hentrich, Helmut   **AV BA**
   (German architect, b.1905)   BA
   (West German architect, 1905-)   AV
     Bibl: ▶Artist biog. master idx.;
     ▶Avery period. idx.; ▶Contemp.
     archts.; ▶WW Arts DEU
Hentsch, J. *(Swiss architect,*
  Geneva)   **AV**
     Bibl: Archithese, 1987 Sept.-Oct.,
     v.17, no.5, p.28
Hentschel, C. *(Engraver, op.1850-)*   **WI**

Hentschel, Gustav (German architect, Bonn-Bad Godesberg, 1872-1944)   AV
    Bibl: Der Architekt, 1987 Sept., no.9, p.402

Hentschel, Karl (German ceramist, painter, printmaker, 1884-1959)   BA
    Bibl: Stahlke, W., in KERAMOS 99 (Jan 1983) 83; ▶Vollmer, Künst.-Lex. 20. Jhr.

Hentschel, Konrad (German ceramist, sculptor, 1872-1907)   BA
    Bibl: ▶Bénézit; ▶Penguin dec. arts; ▶Thieme-Becker

Hentz, Richard (American artist, op. 1970-1980)   WI

Hentze, Gudmund Herman Peter (Danish painter, printmaker, 1875-1948)   BA
    Bibl: Martensen-Larsen, B., TIDSSKRIFT FOR KUNST OG KULTUR, 38 (1984) 58-65; ▶Vollmer, Künst.-Lex. 20. Jhr.

Hentzschel, Christian Gottlieb (German porcelain painter, act. 1737-1761)   BA
    Bibl: ▶Honey, Euro. ceramic; ▶Thieme-Becker

Henwood, J.   WC WI
    (British artist, 19th cent.)   WC
    (British artist, op.19th c.)   WI
Henwood, Th. → see Henwood, Thomas

Henwood, Thomas   AV WI
    (British artist, 19th cent.)   WC
    (British artist, op.1842-1855)   WI
    (English watercolorist, 1797-1861)   AV
    Bibl: Sussex Archaeological Society. Newsletter, 1988 Apr., no.54, p.14

Henwood, Th.   WC

Henzel, James (Irish silversmith, act. 1808-1818)   BA
    Bibl: Antiques, CXX/4 (Oct. 1981) pp.915-921

Henzell, Isaac (British artist, op. 1854-1875)   WC WI

Henzi, Hentzi or Hentzy, Rudolf (Swiss artist, 1731-1803)   WC

Hepburn, Andrew (American architect, 1910-)   AV
    Bibl: ▶Amer. archts. dir., 1970

Hephaisteion (Greek architect, 5th c BC(?))   GC
    Bibl: Getty Photo Study Coll.; ▶Robertson, Greek art, p.669

Hephaisteion Painter   GC
    Bibl: ▶Beazley, Attic red-fig. vase-ptrs.

Hephaistion (Greek mosaicist, 2nd c BC)   GC
    Bibl: ▶Robertson, Greek art, p.580

Hephaistos Painter   GC
    Bibl: ▶Beazley, Attic red-fig. vase-ptrs.

Hepher, David   BA WC WI
    (British artist, 20th cent.)   WC
    (British artist, b.1935-1945)   WI
    (British painter, b.1935)   BA
    Bibl: ▶Artist biog. master idx.; ▶Bénézit; Sunderland (GBR), Arts Ctr., Working process (1978)

Hepman (British artist, op.1826-1839)   WC

Heppener, Johannes Jacobus (Dutch painter, 1826-1898)   GC
    Bibl: ▶Thieme-Becker

Heppenheimer, F. (Engraver, op. 19th c.)   WI

Hepper, (of Doncaster) (British artist, op.19th c.)   WI

Hepper, Carol (American sculptor, b.1953)   BA
    Bibl: New York (NY, USA), Guggenheim Mus., New perspectives (1983)

Hepper, G. (British artist, op.1855-1868)   WI

Hepple, Norman   BA
    (British artist, 1908-)   WC
    (British artist, b.1908)   WI
    (British painter, b.1908)   BA
    Bibl: ▶Art Index, Oct. 1935-Sep. 1938; ▶Artist biog. master idx.; ▶Vollmer, Künst.-Lex. 20. Jhr.; ▶WW Art, 1977, 1980-88

Hepple, Robert Norman   WC WI
Hepple, Robert Norman → see Hepple, Norman

Hepple, William (British artist, 1854-1937)   WI
    Bibl: ▶Waters, Brit. artists
Hepplewhite, A. → see Hepplewhite, Alice

Hepplewhite, Alice   BA
    (British artist, 18th cent.)   WC
    (British, 18th c.)   BA
    Bibl: Peck, Woman's Art Jrnl. VIII (Fall-Win 1987-88), p.25-27

Hepplewhite, A.   WC

Hepplewhite, George (English cabinetmaker, designer, d.1786)   BA
    Bibl: ▶Boger, World pott. & porc.; ▶New Columbia encyc.; ▶Penguin dec. arts

Hepworth, Anthony (British sculptor, 20th c.)   BA
    Bibl: ▶Intl. dir. exh. artists

Hepworth, Barbara   BA GC WC WI
    (British artist, 1903-1975)   WC WI
    (British sculptor, 1903-1975)   BA GC
    Bibl: ▶Havlice, Idx. art. bio.; ▶McGraw-Hill dict. art; ▶RILA/BHA; ▶Vollmer, Künst.-Lex. 20. Jhr.; Wakefield Art Gallery and Museums, Barbara Hepworth: Early Life (1985)
Nicholson, Ben, Mrs., (Barbara)   WI
Skeaping, John Rattenbury, Mrs. (Barbara)   WI

Hepworth, Dorothy Mary (British artist, 1898-1978)   WI

Hepworth-Nicholson, Simon (British artist, b.1934)   WI

Her, Theodor (German artist, 1838-1892)   WC

Herail, Jean Baptiste (French artist, 19th cent.)   WC

Heraion Painter   GC
    Bibl: ▶Beazley, Attic red-fig. vase-ptrs.

Herakleidas (Greek coin engraver, 5th c BC (late))   GC
    Bibl: Getty Photo Study Coll.

Herakles Painter   GC
    Bibl: ▶Beazley, Attic red-fig. vase-ptrs.

Heraklitos (Roman mosaicist)   GC
    Bibl: Getty Photo Study Coll.

Herald, James Watterston   WC WI
    (British artist, -1914)   WC
    (British artist, 1859-1914)   WI

Heramb, Thore (Norwegian painter, b.1916)   BA
    Bibl: London (GBR), Royal College of Art, Advocaat, Heramb, Thurman (1985); ▶Norsk Kunstner Leks.

Hérard, Léonard (Flemish sculptor, 1630/1637-1675)   GC
    Bibl: ▶Thieme-Becker
Errard, Léonard   GC
Herrard, Léonard   GC

Heraud, Bernard   AV

Herault, Charles Antoine (French, 1644-1718)   GC
    Bibl: Getty Photo Study Coll. (Ptgs.); ▶Thieme-Becker
Herault, Ferdinand   GC
Herault, Ferdinand → see Herault, Charles Antoine

Herault, Jacques (French, b.1679)   GC
    Bibl: ▶Thieme-Becker

Hérault, Jean (Eighteenth-century architect associated with the restoration of Saint-Lucien at Beauvais)   AV

Herbach, H.F. (German(?) artist, 17th cent.)   WC

Herbault family (French architects, act. late 19th c.)   BA
    Bibl: ▶Bauchal, Archtes. fran.

Herbecq, Anne (Belgian architect)   AV
    Bibl: Architecture d'aujourd'hui, 1983 Feb., no.225, p.XX

Herbecq, Bernard (Belgian architect, 1950-)   AV
    Bibl: Das Kunstwerk, n.3-4, Sept. 1983, p.72

Herbel, Charles   BA WC
    (French artist, c.1656-1703)   WC
    (French painter, ca.1656-1703)   BA
    Bibl: ▶Bénézit; ▶Nouv. biog. gén.; ▶Thieme-Becker

Herberger, Dominikus Hermenegild (German sculptor, 1694-1760)   BA
    Bibl: Dehio, Östl. Schwaben (1935)

Herbert H. Newton→see Newton,
Herbert H.

Herbert Meyer→see Meyer, Herbert

Herbert Nelson Hoven→see Hoven,
Herbert Nelson

Herbert Pugh→see Pugh, Herbert

Herbert, Albert C.   **WC WI**
(British artist, 20th cent.)   WC
(British artist, op.1956-)   WI

Herbert, Alfred   **WC WI**
(British artist, circa 1820-1861)   WI
(British artist, op.1844-m.1861)   WC

Herbert, Arthur John (British artist,
1834-1856)   **WC WI**

Herbert, Charles E. (American
architect)   **AV**
Bibl: ▶AIA Pro File, 1985

Herbert, Cyril Wiseman Rogers
(British artist, 1847-1882)   **WI**

Herbert, Eduard (German architect,
Munich, fl. 1912)   **AV**
Bibl: Der Architekt, 1987 July-
Aug., no.7-8, p.358

Herbert, Ernest→see Hébert, Antoine
Auguste Ernest

Herbert, Ernest Auguste
Antoine→see Hébert, Antoine
Auguste Ernest

Herbert, Henry→see Pembroke,
Henry Herbert, 9th Earl of

Herbert, James→see Herbert, James
Drummond

Herbert, James Dowling   **WC WI**
(British artist, c.1762-1837)   WC
(British artist, circa 1762-1837)   WI

Herbert, James Drummond
(American sculptor, b.1896)   **GC**
Bibl: Getty Photo Study Coll.;
▶Opitz, Amer. sculptors
Herbert, James   GC

Herbert, John (British landscape
architect, d. 1988?)   **AV**
Bibl: Landscape design, 1989
Feb., no.177, p.IV

Herbert, John Rogers (British artist,
1810-1890)   **WC WI**

Herbert, Magdalen (English, act.
1596, d. 1627)   **BA**
Bibl: Haslam: Powys, p.166

Herbert, Oskar (German architect,
Bad Neustadt)   **AV**
Bibl: Architektur,
Innenarchitektur, Technischer
Ausbau, 1985 Sept., v.93, no.6,
p.68

Herbert, Peggy (Canadian painter,
20th c.)   **BA**
Bibl: ▶Artists Canada; Halifax (NS,
CAN), Centennial Art Gallery,
PEGGY HERBERT (1976); ▶Natl.
Gall. Canada libr. cat.

Herbert, Richard (English, d. 1596)   **BA**
Bibl: Blue guide: Wales, p.212;
Haslam: Powys, p.166

Herbert, Sydney (British artist,
1854-1914)   **WI**

Herbert, Wilfred Vincent   **WC WI**
(British artist, op.1863-1891)   WI
(British artist, op.c.1863-1891)   WC

Herberte, E.B.   **WC WI**
(British artist, 1857-1893)   WI
(British artist, 19th cent.)   WC

Herbette, Maurice (French, 20th c.)   **BA**

Herbig, Otto   **GC WC**
(German artist, 1889-)   WC
(German painter, 1889-1971)   GC
Bibl: ▶Schweers, Gemälde deut.
Museen

**Herbig, Wilhelm (Friedrich
Wilhelm Heinrich)** (German artist,
1787-1861)   **WC**

Herbin→see Herbin, Auguste

Herbin, Auguste   **BA PR WC**
(French artist, 1882-1960)   WC
(French painter, 1882-1960)   BA PR
Bibl: ▶Art Index, v.14; ▶Bénézit;
▶Encyc. world art; ▶Petit
Larousse; ▶Phaidon 20c. art;
▶RILA/BHA; ▶Vollmer, Künst.-Lex.
20. Jhr.
Auguste Herbin   PR
Herbin   PR

Herbin, Girard (French artist, op.c.
1600-1658(?))   **WC**

Herbo, Fernand (French artist, 19th
cent.)   **WC**

Herbo, Leon (Belgian artist, 1850-
1907)   **WC**

Herbrich, Peter   **AV BA**
(German artist, b.1939)   BA
(West German sculptor)   AV
Bibl: Garten und Landschaft,
1989, v.99, no.1, p.11;
Kunstwerk XXVI, Jan 1973, p.58;
▶Natl. union cat., 1976

Herbst or Herbster, Hans→see
Herbst, Hans

Herbst, Hans   **BA**
(German artist, 1468-1550)   WC
(Swiss painter, 1470-1552)   BA
Bibl: ▶Bénézit; ▶Schweiz.
Künst.-Lex.; ▶Thieme-Becker;
ZEITSCH. FÜR SCHW. ARCH. UND
KUNST. XXXV/3 (1978) p.170

Herbst or Herbster, Hans   **WC**

Herbst, Johannes (French
silversmith, master 1631)   **GC**
Bibl: ▶Mabille, Orfèv. fran.

Herbst, Marion (Dutch weaver,
b.1944)   **BA**
Bibl: Amsterdam (NLD), Stedelijk
Museum, Atelier 16 (1980)

Herbst, Thomas Ludvig→see Herbst,
Thomas Ludwig

Herbst, Thomas Ludwig   **GC**
(German artist, 1848-1915)   WC
(German painter, 1848-1915)   GC
Bibl: ▶Thieme-Becker

Herbst, Thomas Ludvig   **WC**

Herbsthoffer→see Herbsthoffer, Karl

Herbsthoffer, Karl   **PR**
(German artist, 1821-1876)   WC
(German painter, 1821-1876)   PR
Bibl: ▶Thieme-Becker
Herbsthoffer   PR

**Herbsthoffer, Karl (Peter Rudolf
Karl)**   **WC**
Karl Herbsthoffer   PR

Herbsthoffer, Karl (Peter Rudolf
Karl)→see Herbsthoffer, Karl

Herbulis, Albert von (1860-1928)   **AV**

Herci, Hans (German potter, act.ca.
1620-1630)   **BA**
Bibl: KERAMOS, 102 (Oct 1983)
45-54

Herčík, Josef (Czech artist, 20th c.)   **BA**
Bibl: Šindelář, Umění, XXVIII/4
(1980) pp.289-304

Herck, Jan (Flemish goldsmith, act.
1627-1647)   **BA**
Bibl: Connoisseur CXCIV/782 (Apr
1977) p.253; GEORGE PETEL
CATALOGUE 1973; RUBENS I
SVERIGE, p.131-140

Herck, Melchior (Flemish, act.1691-
1735)   **GC**
Bibl: Getty Photo Study Coll.
(Ptgs.); ▶Thieme-Becker
Arckens, Jacobus Melchior   GC

Hercle Painter (Etruscan vase-
painter)   **GC**
Bibl: ▶Szilagyi, Etruszko-korinthosi

Hercolani, Marcantonio (Italian
ceramist, d.1772)   **BA**
Bibl: Bertocchi, Carrobbio, XIV
(1988) (docs)

Hercules→see Segers, Hercules
Pietersz.

Hercules Master (Italian sculptor,
13th c.)   **BA**
Bibl: COMMENTARI, XII (1961)
p.13ff; Demus, San Marco, p.125
ff

Hercules Pietersz. Segers→see
Segers, Hercules Pietersz.

Hercules Sanders→see Sanders,
Hercules

Hercules Seger→see Segers, Hercules
Pietersz.

Hercules Segers→see Segers,
Hercules Pietersz.

Herczeg, Klára (Hungarian sculptor,
b.1906)   **BA**
Bibl: ▶Vollmer, Künst.-Lex. 20. Jhr.

Herd, Samuel (British artist, op.18th
c.)   **WI**

Herdebout, H. (Flemish artist, 17th
cent.)   **WC**

Herdeg, Klaus (American architect,
New York)   **AV**
Bibl: ▶Libr. of Congr. Name Auth.
File

Herdeg, Martin (West German
architecture student,
Kunstakademie Stuttgart, 1988)   **AV**
Bibl: Deutsche Bauzeitschrift,
1988 May, v.36, no.5, p.610

Herdegen, Ray *(American painter,*
20th c.)   **BA**
    Bibl: Minneapolis (MN, USA),
    Walker Art Ctr., Akagawa et al.
    (1975)
Herdegen, Seitz *(German goldsmith,*
act.1446, d.1471)   **BA**
    Bibl: Anz. des Germ. Nationalmus.
    (1978) 24-34; Kohlhaussen,
    Nürnberger Goldschmiedekunst
Herdenberg, Wilhelm van → see
    Ehrenberg, Wilhelm van
Herder van Gröningen   **GC WC**
    (Netherlands artist, c.1550(?)-c.
    1609(?))   **WC**
    (North Netherlandish painter,
    ca.1550-1609)   **GC**
    Bibl: ▶Thieme-Becker
Herder, Adeline *(American sculptor,*
20th c.)   **BA**
    Bibl: ▶Art Index, v.29; Art News
    60, Dec 1961, p.18
Herdincg, Hermann A. *(German*
artist, op.1663)   **WC**
Herdman, J.Innes *(British artist, op.*
19th c.)   **WI**
Herdman, Robert   **BA GC WC WI**
    (British artist, 1829-1888)   **WC WI**
    (British painter, 1829-1888)   **BA**
    (Scottish draughtsman, 1829-
    1888)   **GC**
    Bibl: ▶Bénézit; ▶Harris, Scottish
    ptrs.; ▶Johnson, Brit. artists;
    ▶Thieme-Becker
Herdman, Robert Duddingstone
    (British artist, 1863-1922)   **WC WI**
Herdman, Stanley *(British artist, op.*
1882-)   **WI**
Herdman, William Gavin → see
    Herdman, William Gawin
Herdman, William Gawin   **AV WI**
    (British artist, 1805-1882)   **WC WI**
    (British artist, astronomer,
    author, 1805-1882)   **AV**
    Bibl: ▶Dict. natl. biog.
Herdman, William Gavin   **WC**
Herdt, Friedrich Wilhelm *(German*
artist, c.1790-p.1840)   **WC**
Herdt, Herde or Hert Jan de → see
    Herdt, Jan de
Herdt, Jan de   **BA**
    (Flemish artist, op.1646-1668)   **WC**
    (Flemish painter, printmaker,
    act.1646-1668)   **BA**
    Bibl: ▶Bénézit; BULLETIN DE
    MUSÉE NATIONAL DE VARSOVIE
    XVIII/2 (1977) p.45;
    ▶Thieme-Becker
Herdt, Herde or Hert Jan de   **WC**
Héré de Corny, Emmanuel   **AV BA**
    (1705-1763)   **AV**
    (French architect, city planner,
    1705-1763)   **BA**
    Bibl: ▶Columbia encyc.; ▶Encyc.
    world art; ▶Thieme-Becker

Hereau, Jules *(French artist, 1839-*
1879)   **WC**
Heredia, Pedro de *(Spanish*
sculptor, act.1549-1571)   **BA**
    Bibl: ▶Ceán Bermúdez, Bellas artes
    ESP; ▶Thieme-Becker
Hereman → see Heeremans, Thomas
Heremans, Walter *(Belgian*
architect)   **AV**
    Bibl: Abitare, 1989 Jan.-Feb.,
    p.128
Heremias de Montagnone *(Italian*
(Paduan), ca. 1250/60-1321)   **JG**
Herford or Hereford, Laura A. → see
    Herford, Laura A.
Herford, Laura A.   **WI**
    (British artist, circa 1831-1870) **WI**
    (British artist, op.c.1861-m.
    1870)   **WC**
Herford or Hereford, Laura A.   **WC**
Herford, Wilhelm von *(German*
diplomat, photographer, 1814-
1866)   **BA**
    Bibl: Adam. H.P. IX, 4, Oct-Dec
    '85 p. 321-324
Hergau, Hector *(French painter,*
1801-1872)   **GC**
    Bibl: ▶Bénézit
Hergé (Georges Remy) *(Belgian*
author, cartoonist, illustrator,
1907-1983)   **BA**
    Bibl: ARTFORUM, XXII/9 (May
    1984) 71-75; ▶Dict. biog. artistes
    belges; ▶Natl. union cat., pre-
    1956
    Remy, Georges   **BA**
Hergenröder, Georg Heinrich   **GC**
    (German artist, 1736-c.1794)   **WC**
    (German, 1736-ca.1794)   **GC**
    Bibl: ▶Thieme-Becker; ▶Witt
    checklist
Hergenroeder, Herchenroder or **WC**
Hergenruder, George Heinrich
Hergenroeder, Herchenroder or
    Hergenruder, George
    Heinrich → see Hergenröder, Georg
    Heinrich
Herholdt, Johan Daniel *(Danish*
architect, 1818-1902)   **AV BA**
    Bibl: ▶Portoghesi, Diz. arch. e
    urbanistica; ▶Weilbach, Kunst.
    leks.
Heric, John F. *(American sculptor,*
b.1942)   **BA**
    Bibl: Montgomery (Ala, USA),
    Museum of Fine Arts, John Heric:
    Sculptor 1976; ▶WW Amer. Art,
    1976
Herich, Reinhard *(West German*
architect)   **AV**
    Bibl: Architektur + Wettbewerbe,
    1987 Sept., no.131, p.13
Héricourt, Claude *(French*
silversmith, master 1763)   **GC**
    Bibl: ▶Nocq, Poinçon de Paris
Herigelandt, Pieter van
    (Netherlands artist, op.1691)   **WC**

Herigoyen, Emmanuel Josef von
(Portuguese architect in Germany,
1746-1817)   **BA**
    Bibl: Baedeker's Nordbayern-
    Ostbayern; Dehio: Bayern; ▶Neue
    deutsche Biog.; ▶Portoghesi, Diz.
    arch. e urbanistica;
    ▶Thieme-Becker
Heriman *(German scribe, illuminator,*
act.1160-1175)   **BA**
    Bibl: ▶Allgem. Deut. Biog.; Cohen-
    Muhlin, BURLINGTON, CXXVII/993
    (Dec 1985) 880-887;
    ▶Thieme-Becker
Herimundus *(German scribe and*
rubricator (?), 8th or 9th
centuries)   **GC**
    Bibl: Lowe, Codices, I, 97
Hering family *(British bookbinders,*
18th-19th cs.)   **BA**
    Bibl: Ramsden, London
    bookbinders
Hering or Haering, Hans (Johann
    Georg) → see Hering, Hans
Hering, Georg *(German sculptor, ca.*
1521-1554)   **BA**
    Bibl: ▶Bénézit; Reindl, Loy Hering;
    ▶Thieme-Becker
Hering, George Edwards *(British*
artist, 1805-1879)   **WC WI**
Hering, Hans   **GC**
    (German artist, op.1587-1635)   **WC**
    (German draughtsman, act.
    1587-1635)   **GC**
    Bibl: ▶Thieme-Becker
    Haering, Johann Georg   **GC**
Hering or Haering, Hans (Johann
Georg)   **WC**
Hering, Loy   **BA GC**
    (German sculptor, ca.1484-after
    1554)   **BA**
    (German sculptor, ca.1521-
    1554)   **GC**
    Bibl: ▶Art Index, v.32; Reindl, Loy
    Hering; ▶RILA/BHA;
    ▶Thieme-Becker
Hering, Martin *(German sculptor,*
ca.1515-ca.1560)   **BA**
    Bibl: ▶Bénézit; Reindl, Loy Hering;
    ▶Thieme-Becker
Hering, P. *(Dutch artist, 20th cent.)* **WC**
Hering, Thomas *(German sculptor,*
act.1541-1549)   **BA**
    Bibl: Münchner Jahrb. der
    bildenden Kunst XXVI 1975
    p.162; ▶Neue deutsche Biog.;
    ▶Thieme-Becker

Heriot, George　　　　　BA WC WI
　(British artist, 1766-1844)　　　WI
　(British artist, op.1789-1820)　WC
　(British painter in CAN, 1766-
　　1844)　　　　　　　　　　BA
　Bibl: ▶Artist biog. master idx.;
　　▶Dict. natl. biog.; ▶Groce, Artists
　　Amer.; ▶Harper, Ptg. Canada;
　　Hubbard, 300 yrs. of Canadian
　　art; Kingston (Ont, CND) Qu. U.,
　　A.E. Art Centre, GEORGE
　　HERIOT..., 1978; ▶MacDonald,
　　Can. artists; ▶Thieme-Becker;
　　▶Wood, Victorian ptrs., v.2

Heriot, J. C. A. (Canadian architect,
　1862-1921)　　　　　　　　AV
　Bibl: Journal of the Society for
　　the Study of Architecture in
　　Canada, 1987 Mar., v.12, no.1,
　　p.16

Heriot, Jean (Canadian painter,
　b.1946)　　　　　　　　　BA
　Bibl: Vancouver (BC, CAN), Art
　　Gallery, Current pursuits (1976)

Hérisset, Antoine (French
　printmaker, 1685-1769)　　BA
　Bibl: ▶Bénézit; Fonds Français XI;
　　▶Thieme-Becker

Herisson, Jean Louis (French artist,
　19th cent.)　　　　　　　WC

Heritage, Robert (British designer,
　b.1927)　　　　　　　　　BA
　Bibl: ▶Artist biog. master idx.;
　　▶Who's Who [GBR]

Herk, Arne van (Dutch architect)　AV
　Bibl: Architectural review, 1985
　　Jan., v.177, no.1055, p.14
　van Herk, Arne　　　　　　AV

Herkenrath, Peter　　　　BA WC
　(German artist, 1900-)　　　WC
　(German painter, printmaker,
　　b.1900)　　　　　　　　BA
　Bibl: ▶Bénézit; ▶Vollmer,
　　Künst.-Lex. 20. Jhr.; ▶WW Arts
　　DEU

Herkomer→see Herkomer, Herman
　Gustave
Herkomer→see Herkomer, Hubert
　von
Herkomer, H.→see Herkomer,
　Herman Gustave
Herkomer, H.→see Herkomer, Hubert
　von
Herkomer, Herman G.→see
　Herkomer, Herman Gustave

Herkomer, Herman Gustave　WC WI
　(American artist, 1863-1935)　WC WI
　(American painter, 1863-1935)　PR
　Bibl: ▶Thieme-Becker
　Herkomer　　　　　　　　PR
　Herkomer, H.　　　　　　PR
　Herkomer, Herman G.　　　PR
　Herman G. Herkomer　　　PR

Herkomer, Hubert von　BA GC PR WI
　(British artist, 1849-1914)　WC WI
　(British painter, 1849-1914)　PR
　(British painter, printmaker,
　　1849-1914)　　　　　　BA
　(British, 1849-1914)　　　GC
　(English artist, born in Bavaria,
　　1849-1914)　　　　　　AV
　Bibl: ▶Art Index, v.36; Knaurs:
　　Deutschland; ▶Libr. of Congr.
　　Name Auth. File; ▶McGraw-Hill
　　dict. art; ▶RILA/BHA;
　　▶Thieme-Becker; ▶Witt checklist
　Herkomer　　　　　　　　PR
　Herkomer, H.　　　　　　PR
　Herkomer, Hubert von, Sir　AV PR
　Herkomer, Sir Hubert von　WC
　Hubert von Herkomer　　　PR
　Herkomer, Hubert von, Sir→see
　　Herkomer, Hubert von
　Herkomer, Sir Hubert von→see
　　Herkomer, Hubert von

Herkommer, Johann Georg
　(German goldsmith, act.1712,
　　d.1754)　　　　　　　　BA
　Bibl: Rosenberg, Goldschmiede
　　Merkzeichen, v.2, pp.202-203;
　　▶Seling, Augsburger
　　Goldschmiede, v.3, p.317;
　　▶Thieme-Becker

Herland, Hugh　　　　　　AV BA
　(British carpenter, d.1405)　AV
　(English carpenter, 1330-1405)　BA
　Bibl: Huang, WESTMINSTER HALL..
　　.(1987)diss.; Pevsner, London, v.1,
　　p.530; SAH journal, 1984 Dec.,
　　v.43, no.4, p.300

Herland, Mlle. Emma (French artist,
　1856-p.1901)　　　　　　WC
Herle, F. van (Dutch artist, op.1857)　WC
Herlein, Johann Andreas→see
　Herrlein, Johann Andreas
Herlein, P. (German(?) artist, 18th
　cent.)　　　　　　　　　WC
Herlin, Auguste Joseph (French
　artist, 1815-1900)　　　　WC
Herlin, Friedrich　　　　　BA GC
　(German artist, c.1435-c.1500)　WC
　(German painter,
　　ca.1425/30-ca.1500)　　GC
　(German painter, ca.1435-ca.
　　1500)　　　　　　　　BA
　Bibl: ▶Artist biog. master idx.;
　　▶Caplan, Artists' sigs.; Dehio:
　　Bayern; Getty Photo Study Coll.;
　　▶McGraw-Hill dict. art;
　　▶Schweers, Gemälde deut.
　　Museen; ▶Thieme-Becker
**Herlin, Herleinn, Herlen, Horlein
　or Horlin 'the Elder' Friedrich**　WC
Herlin, Herleinn, Herlen, Horlein or
　Horlin 'the Elder' Friedrich→see
　Herlin, Friedrich
Herlin, Martin (German, 16th c.)　BA
Herluison, Louis (French artist,
　1667-1706)　　　　　　WC
Hermafrodito→see Linsen, Jan

Hermaios　　　　　　　　GC
　Bibl: ▶Beazley, Attic red-fig. vase-
　　ptrs.
Hermaios Painter　　　　GC JG
　(vase-painter, ca. 530-500 BC)　GC
　Bibl: ▶Beazley, Attic red-fig. vase-
　　ptrs.; Richter, Attic red-fig. vases
Herman (British artist, op.1826-
　1839)　　　　　　　　　WI
herman→see Swanevelt, Herman van
herman d'Italie→see Swanevelt,
　Herman van
Herman Fuechsel→see Fuechsel,
　Hermann
Herman G. Herkomer→see Herkomer,
　Herman Gustave
Herman Gillis→see Gillis, Herman
Herman Henstenburgh→see
　Henstenburgh, Herman
Herman Herzog→see Herzog,
　Herman
Herman Irranevelt→see Swanevelt,
　Herman van
Herman Jean Joseph Richir→see
　Richir, Herman Jean Joseph
Herman Johannes van der
　Weele→see Weele, Herman
　Johannes van der
Herman Lin→see Lin, Herman
Herman Naiwinx→see Nauwincz,
　Herman
Herman of Cologne (German
　painter, act.1401)　　　　BA
　Bibl: ▶Bénézit; ▶Encyc. world art;
　　▶Thieme-Becker
Herman R. Dietz→see Dietz, Herman
　R.
Herman Sachleven→see Saftleven,
　Herman
Herman Saftleven→see Saftleven,
　Herman
Herman Svanefeld→see Swanevelt,
　Herman van
Herman Swamfeld→see Swanevelt,
　Herman van
Herman Swanefeld→see Swanevelt,
　Herman van
Herman Swanefeld, Called, the
　Hermit of Italy→see Swanevelt,
　Herman van
Herman Terborch→see Terborch,
　Harmen
Herman van der Myn→see Myn,
　Herman van der
Herman van Swaneveldt→see
　Swanevelt, Herman van
Herman van Swanevelt→see
　Swanevelt, Herman van
Herman Vander Myn→see Myn,
　Herman van der
Herman Verelst→see Verelst, Herman
Herman Willem Koekkoek→see
　Koekkoek, Herman Willem

Herman, J. (Dutch painter, 17th
century)   **GC**
   Bibl: ▶Thieme-Becker
Hermans, Jan   GC
Herman, Josef   **BA WC WI**
   (British artist, 1911-)   WC
   (British artist, b.1911)   WI
   (British painter, b.1911)   BA
   Bibl: ▶Bénézit; Phaidon; ▶Vollmer,
   Künst.-Lex. 20. Jhr.; ▶WW Art,
   1982

Herman, Larry (British
photographer, 20th c.)   **BA**
   Bibl: Arts Council GBR, Scot.
   Comm., Photographer's image
   (1978)

Herman, Lipót (Hungarian painter,
b.1884)   **BA**
   Bibl: Budapest, Magyar Nemzeti
   Galéria, LIPOT HERMAN
   RETROSPECTIE (1974);
   ▶Thieme-Becker; ▶Vollmer,
   Künst.-Lex. 20. Jhr.

Herman, Marvin (American
architect, working in Chicago)   **AV**
   Bibl: ▶AIA Pro File, 1985

Herman, Robert (American
architect)   **AV**
   Bibl: ▶AIA Pro File, 1985

Herman, Roger (West German
painter, printmaker in USA,
b.1947)   **BA**
   Bibl: ▶Art Index, v.36; Brody, J., in
   PRINT COLLECTOR'S NEWSLETTER
   XV/6 (Jan-Feb) 1985 200; ▶Intl.
   dir. exh. artists, 1983; Santa
   Barbara (CA, USA), UCSB Art
   Mus., Figuration (1982)

Herman, Ron (American landscape
architect, 1941-)   **AV**
   Bibl: Process: architecture, 1985
   Aug., no.61, p.113

Herman, Sali   **BA WC**
   (Australian(?) artist, 1898-)   WC
   (Swiss painter in AUS, b.1898)   BA
   Bibl: ▶Artist biog. master idx.;
   NN; ▶Vollmer, Künst.-Lex. 20. Jhr.;
   ▶WW Austria
Herman, Stephan → see Hermann,
   Stephan

Hermanjat, Jacques Elie Abraham
(Swiss painter, 1862-1932)   **BA**
   Bibl: ▶Künst.-Lex. Schweiz 20.
   Jahrh.; ▶Vollmer, Künst.-Lex. 20.
   Jhr.

Hermann (German artist, 16th cent.) **WC**
Hermann A. Plathner → see Plathner,
   Hermann A.
Hermann Dudley Murphy → see
   Murphy, Hermann Dudley
Hermann Dyck → see Dyck, Hermann
Hermann Freihold Pluddemann → see
   Plüddemann, Hermann Freihold
Hermann Kaulbach → see Kaulbach,
   Hermann
Hermann Muller → see Muller,
   Hermann [Unidentified]

**Hermann or Hormann, Joseph
Markus** (German artist, 1732-
1811)   **WC**
Hermann Satchleven → see Saftleven,
   Herman
Hermann the Elder, Franz Georg
(German artist, op.1665-m.1735)   **WC**
Hermann [Unidentified] (Unknown
painter)   **PR**
   Bibl: (January 28, 1803, lot 25A,
   Christie's)
Hermann von Münster (stained
glass artist, act.1381, d.1392)   **BA**
   Bibl: Herold PAYS LORRAIN LXVI,
   1, 1985 p.34-39; ▶Thieme-Becker
Hermann, Carl Heinrich (German
painter, 1802-1880)   **BA**
   Bibl: ▶Bénézit; ▶Thieme-Becker
Hermann, Christian Gottfried
(German artist, 1743-1813)   **WC**
Hermann, Dieter   **AV**
   (German architect, Stuttgart)   AV
   (West German architect,
   Stuttgart)   AV
   Bibl: AIT, 1984 Sept., v.92, no.6,
   p.36; Detail, 1989 Mar.-Apr.,
   v.29, no.2, p. SI
Herrmann, Dieter   **AV**
Hermann, Franz Georg II (German
painter, 1692-1768)   **BA**
   Bibl: ▶Bénézit; ▶Thieme-Becker
Hermann, Franz Ludwig   **BA WC**
   (German mural painter, son of
   Franz Benedikt Herrmann;
   born in Wangen, died in
   Konstanz, 1710-1791)   AV
   (German painter, 1710-1791)   BA
   (Swiss artist, 1710-1791)   WC
   Bibl: ▶Bénézit; Dehio:
   Baden-Württemberg; Knaurs:
   Schweiz; ▶Neue deutsche Biog.;
   ▶Schweiz. Künst.-Lex.;
   ▶Thieme-Becker; Unsere
   Kunstdenkmäler, 1987, v.38,
   no.4, p.499, gives birth date as
   1723; ▶Witt checklist
Herrmann, Franz Ludwig   **AV**
Hermann, Georg (German
goldsmith, printmaker, 1579-ca.
1603)   **BA**
   Bibl: ▶Hollstein, German, v.13;
   ▶Nagler, Neues Künst.-Lex.;
   ▶Strutt, Dict. engravers;
   ▶Thieme-Becker
Hermann, Günter (West German
architect, Stuttgart)   **AV**
   Bibl: Detail, 1982 July-Aug., no.4,
   p.397
Hermann, Hans → see Herrmann, Hans
Hermann, Heinrich (American
architect)   **AV**
   Bibl: Montana state architectural
   review, 1986 Spring, v.4, p.6

Hermann, Heinrich Wilhelm   **BA**
   (South African artist, 19th cent.) WC
   (South African painter, 1841-
   1916)   BA
   Bibl: Cape Town (SA), South
   African National Gallery. One
   hundred years ago: an exhib......
   (now Queen Victoria Street),
   1975
Hermann, W.   **WC**
Hermann, Henry (American
furniture manufacturer, 1837-
1896)   **BA**
   Bibl: ANTIQUES, CXIX (MAy 1981)
   1174-1177
Hermann, Herbert Z. (British artist,
op.1886-)   **WI**
Hermann, Hubert (Austrian
architect, Vienna and Luxembourg,
1955-)   **AV**
   Bibl: Deutsche Bauzeitung, 1988
   July, v.122, no.7, p.138
Hermann, Leo   **WI**
   (British artist, op.19th c.)   WI
   (French artist, 1853-)   WC
Herrmann, Leo   **WC**
Hermann, Ludwig   **GC WC**
   (German artist, 1812-81)   WC
   (German painter, 1812-1881)   GC
   Bibl: ▶Bénézit
Hermann, Paul (French artist, 1865-) **WC**
Hermann, Stephan   **BA**
   (German artist, op.1568-
   1609(?))   WC
   (German draughtsman, act.
   1568-1596)   GC
   (German goldsmith, printmaker,
   publisher, act.1568-1596)   BA
   Bibl: Getty Photo Study Coll.;
   Getty Photo Study Coll. (Duits
   coll.); ▶Hollstein, German, v.13;
   ▶Nagler, Neues Künst.-Lex.;
   ▶Thieme-Becker, v.16, pp.503-
   504; ▶Witt checklist
Herman, Stephan   **GC WC**
   Monogrammist H S   GC
Hermann, W. → see Hermann,
   Heinrich Wilhelm
Hermann-Leon, Charles   **WC**
   (French artist, 1838-1907)   WC
   (French artist, 1838-1908)   WC
Herrmann, Leon Charles   **WC**
Hermann-Paul (German artist, 1874-
1940)   **WC**
Hermanns, Ernst (German sculptor,
b.1914)   **BA**
   Bibl: ▶Bénézit; Knaurs Lex. mod.
   Plastik; ▶Vollmer, Künst.-Lex. 20.
   Jhr.
Hermanns, Heinrich   **GC WC**
   (German artist, 1862-)   WC
   (German artist, 1862-1942)   WC
   (German painter, 1862-1942)   GC
   Bibl: ▶Bénézit

Hernandez y Amores, German
(Spanish artist, 1823-1804) **WC**
Hernández, Agustín → see Hernández Navarro, Agustín
Hernández, Alejo → see Fernández, Alejo
Hernandez, Anthony *(American photographer, b.1947)* **BA**
Bibl: ▶Auer, Encyc. photographes; Lawrence (KS, USA), U. Kansas Mus. Art, Language of light (1974)
Hernandez, Daniel **PR WC**
(Peruvian painter, 1856-1932) **PR**
(South and Central American artist, 1856-1932) **WC**
Bibl: ▶Thieme-Becker
Daniel Hernandez **PR**
Hernandez **PR**
Hernandez, Francisco **GC WC**
(Spanish artist, 17th cent.) **WC**
(Spanish painter, act. early 17th century) **GC**
Bibl: ▶Bénézit
Hernández, Gregorio → see Fernández, Gregorio
Hernández, Jerónimo *(Spanish sculptor, 1541-1586)* **BA**
Bibl: Arch. esp. de arte, LIV/216 (Oct-Dec 1981) 405; ▶Kubler, Art & arch. ESP & PRT
Hernández, José *(Spanish painter, b.1944)* **BA**
Bibl: ▶Campoy, Español contemp.; ▶MoMA libr. cat.
Hernandez, Patrick *(French architect, Bordeaux)* **AV**
Bibl: Deutsche Bauzeitung, 1989 Feb., v.123, no.2, p.44
Hernández, Pedro *(Spanish stonecutter, act.1565)* **BA**
Bibl: España entre el Mediterraneo y el Atlántico (1973), v.2, pp.410-418
Hernandez, Santiago *(Mexican artist, 1833-1908)* **WC**
Hernández, Sebastián *(Spanish armorer, act.ca.1560-1600)* **BA**
Bibl: ▶Ceán Bermúdez, Bellas artes ESP; Martin, Fernando A., REALES SITIOS, XXII, 86, p.14; REAL ARMERIA DE MADRID; ▶Thieme-Becker
Hernández, Tomás *(Spanish painter, act.ca.1602-1608)* **BA**
Bibl: ▶Aldana Fernández, Artistas valencianos; ▶Bénézit; ▶Ceán Bermúdez, Bellas artes ESP; Guias artisticas, Valencia, p.92; ▶O'Neil, Spanish ptrs.; Valencia (ESP), Colegio del Corpus Christi, Pintura y pintores (1980)
Hernando de Ávila → see Ávila, Hernando de
Hernando Del Mudo → see Fernández de Navarrete, Juan (el Mudo)

Hernao de Bruselas → see Bruselas, Arnau de
Herncunnan *(European, active 1850s)* **JG**
Herndon, Joseph L. *(American architectural conservator)* **AV**
Bibl: Historic preservation, 1987 May-June, v.39, no.3, p.27
Herneisen, Andreas **BA GC**
(German artist, 1538-1610) **WC**
(German painter, 1538-1610) **BA GC**
Bibl: ▶Bénézit; Getty Photo Study Coll.; Pelican Hist. of Art; ▶Thieme-Becker; ▶Witt checklist
Herneisen, Herneissen, Herneyssen or Horneiser, Andreas or Endres **WC**
Herneisen, Herneissen, Herneyssen or Horneiser, Andreas or Endres → see Herneisen, Andreas
Herner, Adolphe → see Hervier, Louis Adolphe
Hernesen → see Hemessen, Jan van
Hernmarck, Helena *(Swedish tapestry maker, b.1941)* **BA**
Bibl: ▶Art Index, Nov. 1973-Oct. 1974; Nov. 1987-Oct. 1988; ▶Intl. dir. exh. artists, 1982; Los Angeles, County Museum of Art, TAPESTRIES OF HELENA HERNMARCK (1974-75)
Herold or Herolt, Johanna Helena, (nee Graff) *(German artist, 1668-p.1702)* **WC**
Herold, Christian Frederich *(German, 1700-1779)* **JG**
Herold, Georg *(German painter, b.1947)* **BA**
Bibl: Catón, B., in ARTSCRIBE INT. 57 (Apr-May 1986) 48
Herold, Heroldt or Horoldt, Johann Gregor → see Höroldt, Johann Gregor
Hérold, Jacques **BA WC**
(French artist, 1910-) **WC**
(Romanian painter, printmaker in FRA, b.1910) **BA**
Bibl: ▶Artist biog. master idx.; ▶Bénézit; ▶Encyc. world art; Guide exh. artists: N. Amer. ptrs.; ▶MoMA libr. cat.; ▶Phaidon 20c. art; ▶Vollmer, Künst.-Lex. 20. Jhr.
Herold, Rainer *(German artist, 20th c.)* **BA**
Bibl: Altenburg (DEU), Staat. Lindenau-Mus., Etching & engraving (1979); Guide exh. artists: N. Amer. ptrs.
Heron, James *(British artist, op. 1880-1919)* **WI**

Heron, Patrick **BA WC WI**
(British artist, 1920-) **WC**
(British artist, b.1920) **WI**
(British painter, b.1920) **BA**
Bibl: ▶Contemp. artists; ▶DuMonts Künst.-Lex.; ▶Encyc. world art; Guide exh. artists: N. Amer. ptrs.
Heron, Susanna *(British sculptor, b.1949)* **BA**
Bibl: ▶Intl. dir. exh. artists, 1982-1983; London (GBR), Whitechapel Art Gall., SUSANNA HERON: SCULPTURE, 1985, 6 (RILA/GBR)
Heron, Tom *(British textile manufacturer, b.1890)* **BA**
Bibl: Dec Arts Soc IV (1980) 34-39
Heroux, James M. *(American landscape architect, Excelsior, Minn)* **AV**
Bibl: ▶AIA Pro File, 1989-90
Heroy, John N. *(American photographer, 20th c.)* **BA**
Bibl: ▶Intl. dir. exh. artists, 1983; ▶Natl. Faculty Dir.
Herp → see Herp, Willem I van
Herp, Guilliam van, I → see Herp, Willem I van
Herp, Willem (I) van → see Herp, Willem I van
Herp, Willem I van **BA GC**
(Flemish artist, 1614-1677) **WC**
(Flemish painter, 1614-1667) **BA**
(Flemish painter, 1614-1677) **PR**
(Flemish, 1614-1677) **GC**
Bibl: ▶RILA/BHA; ▶Thieme-Becker; ▶Wurzbach, NLD Künst.-Lex.
G. van Herp **PR**
Herp **PR**
Herp, Guilliam van, I **PR**
Herp, Willem (I) van **PR**
Herp, Willem or Guilliam, I van **WC**
Herp, Willem van **PR**
Herp, Willem van (I) **PR**
V Harp **PR**
V. Harp **PR**
van Harp **PR**
Van Harpe **PR**
Van Herp **PR**
Vanharp **PR**
Willem van Herp (I) **PR**
Herp, Willem or Guilliam, I van → see Herp, Willem I van
Herp, Willem van → see Herp, Willem I van
Herp, Willem van (I) → see Herp, Willem I van
Herpfer, Carl **GC WC**
(German artist, 1836-1897) **WC**
(German painter, 1836-1897) **GC**
Bibl: ▶Thieme-Becker

Herpin Master   **BA**
  (German artist, op.c.1480)   WC
  (German artist, op.c.1480-1490)   WC
  (German painter and
    draughtsman, act. ca.1500)   GC
  (German painter, printmaker,
    act.1483-1500)   BA
  (German painter, printmaker,
    act.ca.1480-1490)   BA
    Bibl: Jahrb. der Berliner Museen
    XXVII (1985) 45; Lehrs VI, 343;
    ▶Nagler, Neues Künst.-Lex.;
    Shestack, MASTER LCz AND
    MASTER W'B (1971), 51;
    ▶Thieme-Becker; ▶Witt checklist
  Master of the Herpinhandschrift **WC**
  Master W B   **GC**
  Master WB   **BA**
  Monogrammist W.B.   **WC**
Herpin, Leon Pierre *(French artist,*
  1841-1880)   **WC**
Herr or Heer, Michael → see Herr,
  Michael
Herr, Claudius (Johann Claudius)
  (German artist, 1775-p.1838)   **WC**
Herr, François *(French architect,*
  painter, b.1909)   **BA**
    Bibl: Rouen (FRA), Musée des
    B.-A., Rouen-Madrid (1981)
Herr, Laurenz *(German artist, 1787-*
  p.1850)   **WC**
Herr, Michael   **GC**
  (German artist, 1591-1661)   WC
  (German draughtsman, 1591-
  1661)   GC
    Bibl: ▶Bénézit
  Heer, Michael   GC
  Herr or Heer, Michael   **WC**
Herrad von Landsberg *(German*
  abbess, author, illuminator, act.
  1160, d.1195)   **BA**
    Bibl: Bachmann, Women artists,
    p.51; ▶Bénézit; ▶Bradley,
    Miniaturists, v.2, pp.98-100;
    ▶D'Ancona, Miniaturistes; ▶Encyc.
    world art, v.6, p.161; Green,
    HERRAD OF HOHENBOURG,
    HORTUS DELICIARUM (1979);
    ▶Petteys, Women artists; RLIN
    BKS file; ▶Thieme-Becker
Herran, Saturnino *(Mexican artist,*
  20th cent.)   **WC**
Herrant, Crispin *(German artist, op.*
  1529-m.1549)   **WC**
Herrara, Alberto *(Colombian*
  architect)   **AV**
    Bibl: Escala, 1989, v.20, no.141,
    p.29
Herrara, Francisco (the
  Younger) → see Herrera, Francisco
  II
Herrard, Léonard → see Hérard,
  Léonard
Herregoudts, Pieter *(German artist,*
  17th cent.)   **WC**
Herregouts, Hendrik *(Flemish artist,*
  1633-1704)   **WC**

Herregouts, Jan Baptist *(Flemish*
  artist, c.1640-1721)   **WC**
Herregouts, Maximilian *(Flemish*
  artist, op.1674)   **WC**
Herrenberger, Justus *(German*
  architect, Brunswick)   **AV**
    Bibl: Deutsche Bauzeitschrift,
    1985 Mar., v.33, no.3, p.276
Herrenburg, Johann Andreas
  (German artist, 1824-1906)   **WC**
Herrera → see Herrera, Francisco I de
Herrera → see Herrera, Francisco II
Herrera Barnuevo, Sebastián de   **BA**
  (Spanish artist, 1619-1671)   WC
  (Spanish painter, sculptor,
  architect, 1619-1671)   BA
    Bibl: ▶Art Index, Nov. 1987-Oct.
    1988; ▶Ceán Bermúdez, Bellas
    artes ESP; ▶Encyc. world art;
    Reclams Madrid u. Zentral-
    Spanien; ▶Thieme-Becker
Herrera Barnuevo, Sebastiano
  de   **WC**
Herrera Barnuevo, Sebastiano
  de → see Herrera Barnuevo,
  Sebastián de
Herrera el Viejo → see Herrera,
  Francisco I de
Herrera le jeune → see Herrera,
  Francisco II
Herrera le vieux → see Herrera,
  Francisco I de
Herrera Mendoza, Hernan
  (Colombian architect)   **AV**
    Bibl: Escala, 1988, no.138, p.13
Herrera Sen → see Herrera, Francisco I
  de
Herrera the elder → see Herrera,
  Francisco I de
Herrera, A. Miguel de → see Herrera,
  Fray Miguel de
Herrera, Alonso de   **BA WC**
  (Spanish artist, op.1579-1611)   WC
  (Spanish painter, 1555-1624)   BA
Herrera, Antonio de *(Spanish*
  sculptor, act.1631)   **BA**
    Bibl: ▶Ceán Bermúdez, Bellas artes
    ESP
Herrera, Carlos Maria *(South and*
  Central American artist, 1875-
  1914)   **WC**
Herrera, Francesco I → see Herrera,
  Francisco I de
Herrera, Francisco (the elder) → see
  Herrera, Francisco I de
Herrera, Francisco (the
  younger) → see Herrera, Francisco II
Herrera, Francisco de (the
  elder) → see Herrera, Francisco I de

Herrera, Francisco I de   **BA**
  (Spanish artist, 1576-1656)   WC
  (Spanish painter, 1576-1656)   PR
  (Spanish painter, ca.1576-ca.
  1654)   BA
  (Spanish, 1576-1656)   GC
    Bibl: ▶Art Index; ▶Artist biog.
    master idx.; ▶Bénézit; ▶Encic.
    univ. ilus.; ▶Havlice, Idx. art. bio.;
    Ripoll, Martinez Francisco de
    Herrera; ▶Thieme-Becker; ▶Witt
    checklist
  Francisco Herrera (the elder)   PR
  Herrera   PR
  Herrera el Viejo   PR
  Herrera le vieux   PR
  Herrera Sen   PR
  Herrera the elder   PR
  Herrera, Francesco I   **GC**
  Herrera, Francisco (the elder)   **PR**
  Herrera, Francisco de (the elder)   PR
  Herrera, Francisco, I   **WC**
Herrera, Francisco II   **BA**
  (Spanish artist, 1622-1685)   WC
  (Spanish painter, 1622-1685)   PR
  (Spanish painter, architect,
  1622-1685)   BA
    Bibl: Apollo XXXV, July 1966,
    p.34; ▶Ceán Bermúdez, Bellas
    artes ESP; ▶Encic. univ. ilus.;
    ▶Encyc. world art; Enggass,
    Hortus imaginum, p.135;
    ▶RILA/BHA; ▶Thieme-Becker;
    ▶Witt checklist
  Francisco Herrera (the younger)   PR
  François Herrera (le jeune)   PR
  Herrara, Francisco (the Younger)   PR
  Herrera   PR
  Herrera le jeune   PR
  Herrera, Francisco (the
  younger)   **PR**
  Herrera, Francisco, II   **WC**
Herrera, Francisco, I → see Herrera,
  Francisco I de
Herrera, Francisco, II → see Herrera,
  Francisco II
Herrera, Frank *(American*
  photographer, b.1940)   **BA**
    Bibl: Baltimore (MD, USA), Mus.
    Art, 5 Maryland photogs. (1980)
Herrera, Fray Miguel de   **PR WC**
  (Spanish artist, op.1725-1778)   WC
  (Spanish painter, act. 1725-
  1778)   PR
    Bibl: ▶Witt checklist
  Fray Miguel de Herrera   PR
  Herrera, A. Miguel de   PR
  Herrera, Miguel de   PR

Herrera, Juan de   **AV BA**
(Spanish architect, 1530-1597)   BA
(Spanish soldier, courtier,
    architect, ca.1530-1597)   AV
    Bibl: ▶Avery period. idx.; ▶Encyc.
    Britannica; ▶Encyc. world art; Lex.
    für Theol. u. Kirche; ▶Macmillan
    encyc. archts.; Phaidon, Spain
    (1985); ▶Portoghesi, Diz. arch. e
    urbanistica; ▶Thieme-Becker
Herrera, Juan de   **BA**
(Spanish artist, 18th cent.)   WC
(Spanish painter, ca.1750-1802)   BA
    Bibl: Banda Vargas, Arch. esp. de
    arte, LVII/226 (Apr-Jun 1984),
    138
Herrera, Juan M   **WC**
Herrera, Juan M → see Herrera, Juan
de
Herrera, Miguel de → see Herrera,
Fray Miguel de
Herrero Pintó, Pedro (Spanish
architect)   **AV**
    Bibl: Bauwelt, 1988 Feb.19, v.79,
    no.7-8, p.296
Herrero, Jesús María (Spanish
architect)   **AV**
    Bibl: A & V, 1987, no.12, p.74
Herreros de Tejada, Luis (Spanish
painter, b.1867, act.1889)   **BA**
    Bibl: Arch. esp. de arte, LVIII/232
    (Oct-Dec 1985) 406-412;
    MADRID, I, 111
Herreros, Juan (Spanish architect,
Madrid)   **AV**
    Bibl: El croquis, 1988 Oct.-Nov.,
    v.7, no.36, p.90
Herreros, Ramón (Spanish painter,
b.1947)   **BA**
    Bibl: Combalía, Studio intl.,
    CXCVII/1007 (1984) p.19
Herreshoff, Louise → see Herreshoff,
Louise C.
Herreshoff, Louise C.   **BA**
(American artist, 1876-1967)   WI
(American painter, 1876-1967)   BA
    Bibl: Art News. Jan 1977, pp.100-
    101; ▶Artist biog. master idx.;
    Washington, DC, Corcoran
    Gallery. Louis Herreshoff: an
    American artist discovered, 1976
Eaton, C.C., Mrs., (Louise)   WI
Herreshoff, Louise   **WI**
Reeves, E.D., Mrs., (Louise)   WI
Herreyns, Willem Jacob (Flemish
artist, 1743-1827)   **WC**
Herrfurth, Oskar (German artist,
1862-)   **WC**
Herri Bles → see Bles, Herri met de
Herri Met de Bles → see Bles, Herri
met de
Herribles → see Bles, Herri met de
Herrick, Fred C. (British artist, 1887-
1970)   **AV**
    Bibl: Architects' journal,1988 June
    8, v.187, no.23, p.80

Herrick, Henry Walker (American
printmaker, 1824-1906)   **BA**
    Bibl: ▶Artist biog. master idx.;
    ▶WWW Amer. art
Herrick, William Salter (British
artist, op.1852-1888)   **WC WI**
Herries, William Robert (British
artist, circa 1818-1845)   **WI**
Herriman, George   **AV BA**
(American cartoonist, 1881-
    1944)   BA
(American comic strip artist,
    inventor of Krazy Kat, 1880-
    1944)   AV
    Bibl: Arts Mag Mar '82, p.3;
    ▶Encyc. Britannica; ▶Libr. of
    Congr. Name Auth. File
Herring → see Herring, John Frederick
I
Herring, Benjamin → see Herring,
Benjamin II
Herring, Benjamin I (British painter,
1806-1830)   **BA**
    Bibl: ▶Artist biog. master idx.;
    Beckett, J.F. Herring & sons, 91
Herring, Benjamin II   **BA**
(British artist, 1830-1871)   WI
(British artist, op.c.1861-1871)   WC
(British painter, 1830-1871)   BA
    Bibl: Beckett, J.F. Herring & sons,
    91; ▶Dict. natl. biog.;
    ▶Thieme-Becker
Herring, Benjamin   **WC WI**
Herring, Charles   **BA WI**
(British artist, 1828-1856)   WI
(British painter, 1828-1856)   BA
    Bibl: Beckett, J.F. Herring & sons,
    91; ▶Dict. natl. biog.;
    ▶Thieme-Becker
Herring, Fred (American architect)   **AV**
    Bibl: Marquee, 1988, v.20, no.4,
    p.10
Herring, James   **BA WC WI**
(American artist, 1794-1867)   WI
(American artist, 1796-1867)   WC
(American painter, 1794-1867)   BA
    Bibl: ANTIQUES CXIII/1 Jan 1978,
    p.212-220; ▶Bénézit; ▶Busse,
    Maler u. Bildhauer 19. Jahr.;
    ▶Dict. Amer. biog.; ▶Fielding's
    Amer. ptrs.; ▶Thieme-Becker
Herring, John → see Herring, John
Frederick I
Herring, John Frederick → see Herring,
John Frederick I
Herring, John Frederick (I) → see
Herring, John Frederick I
Herring, John Frederick (II) → see
Herring, John Frederick II
Herring, John Frederick (the
younger) → see Herring, John
Frederick II

Herring, John Frederick I   **BA GC WI**
(British artist, 1795-1865)   WC WI
(British painter, 1795-1865)   BA PR
(British, 1795-1865)   GC
    Bibl: ▶Bénézit; ▶RILA/BHA;
    ▶Thieme-Becker
Herring   PR
Herring, John   PR
Herring, John Frederick   PR
Herring, John Frederick (I)   **PR**
Herring, John Frederick, I   **WC**
Herring, John Frederick, Sr.   PR
John Frederick Herring (I)   PR
Herring, John Frederick II   **BA WI**
(British artist, 1815-1907)   WC WI
(British painter, 1815-1907)   BA PR
    Bibl: Beckett, J.F. Herring & sons,
    91; ▶Dict. natl. biog.; ▶Houfe,
    Brit. book illus.; ▶RILA/BHA;
    ▶Thieme-Becker
Herring, John Frederick (II)   **PR**
Herring, John Frederick (the
    younger)   PR
Herring, John Frederick, II   **WC**
John Frederick Herring (II)   PR
Herring, John Frederick, I → see
Herring, John Frederick I
Herring, John Frederick, II → see
Herring, John Frederick II
Herring, John Frederick, Sr. → see
Herring, John Frederick I
Herriton, Christine N. (British
sculptor, b.1955)   **BA**
    Bibl: Nottingham (GBR), City
    Mus., Said with feeling (1979)
Herrlein or Horlein, Johann Peter
(German artist, op.1750-1803)   **WC**
Herrlein, Johann Andreas   **GC**
(German artist, 1720-1796)   WC
(German painter, 1720-1796)   GC
    Bibl: ▶Thieme-Becker
Herlein, Johann Andreas   GC
Herrlein, Johann Andreas(?)   **WC**
Herrlein, Johann Andreas(?) → see
Herrlein, Johann Andreas
Herrliberger, David   **BA WC**
(Swiss artist, 1697-1777)   WC
(Swiss printmaker, publisher,
    1697-1777)   BA
    Bibl: ▶Schweiz. Künst.-Lex.;
    ▶Thieme-Becker
Herrlich, Philipp (German painter,
1818-1868)   **GC**
    Bibl: ▶Thieme-Becker
Herrmann, Alexander (German
artist, 1814-1845)   **WC**
Herrmann, Augustin   **WC WI**
(American artist, 1608-1686)   WI
(American artist, op.c.1685)   WC
Heermans, Augustyn   WI
Herrmann, Carl Gustav (German
artist, 1857-)   **WC**

Herrmann, Curt   BA GC WC
  (German artist, 1854-1929)   WC
  (German painter, 1854-1929)   BA GC
  Bibl: Barthelmess,
  KUNSTCHRONIK, 42/10 (Oct
  1989) p.582-585; ▶Brockhaus
  Enzyk.; ▶Busse, Maler u. Bildhauer
  19. Jahr.; ▶Thieme-Becker;
  ▶Vollmer, Künst.-Lex. 20. Jhr.;
  ▶Witt checklist
Herrmann, Dieter→see Hermann,
  Dieter
Herrmann, Frank Simon *(American*
  artist, 1866-1942)   WI
Herrmann, Franz Ludwig→see
  Hermann, Franz Ludwig
Herrmann, Hans   GC
  (German artist, 1858-1942)   WC
  (German painter, 1858-1942)   GC
  Bibl: ▶Schweers, Gemälde deut.
  Museen; ▶Thieme-Becker
  Hermann, Hans   GC
Herrmann, Hans (Johann Emil
  Rudolf)   WC
  Herrmann, Johann Emil Rudolf   GC
Herrmann, Hans *(German artist,*
  1813-1890)   WC
Herrmann, Hans (Johann Emil
  Rudolf)→see Herrmann, Hans
Herrmann, Johann Emil Rudolf→see
  Herrmann, Hans
Herrmann, Karl Ernst *(German*
  scenographer, b.1936)   BA
  Bibl: ▶Artist biog. master idx.;
  Hamburg (DEU), Kunstverein,
  Inszenierte Räume..., 1979
Herrmann, Leo→see Hermann, Leo
Herrmann, Leon Charles→see
  Hermann-Leon, Charles
Herrmanstorfer, Josef or Joseph
  (German artist, 1817-1901)   WC
Herron, Donald Lawrence
  (American painter, printmaker,
  photographer, 20th c.)   BA
  Bibl: Arts Mag. LVII (2 Oct 1982),
  "Don L. Herron," p.4
Herron, Gaylord Oscar *(American*
  photographer, painter, b.1942.)   BA
  Bibl: ▶Artist biog. master idx.;
  ▶Natl. union cat., Apr 1977; New
  Art Examiner, v. IV, no. 1
Herron, Ron   AV BA
  (British architect, 1930-)   AV
  (British architect, b.1930)   BA
  Bibl: ▶Avery period. idx., 1986
  suppl. as Ron, b.1930; ▶Contemp.
  archts., (as Ronald James, b.1930)
  Herron, Ronald James   AV
Herron, Ronald James→see Herron,
  Ron
Herry Bles→see Bles, Herri met de
Hers, François *(Belgian*
  photographer, in France since
  1968, 1943-)   AV
  Bibl: Architecture d'aujourd'hui,
  1987 sept., no.252, p.25

Hersberger, Marguerite *(Swiss*
  sculptor, b.1943)   BA
  Bibl: ▶Lex. zeitgen. Schweiz.
  Künstler
Hersch→see Hersch, Lee
Hersch, Eugen *(German artist,*
  1887-)   WC
Hersch, Lee *(American painter, b.*
  1896)   PR
  Bibl: ▶WWW Amer. art
  Hersch   PR
  Lee Hersch   PR
Hersch, Stefan   WC WI
  (American artist, 20th cent.)   WC
  (American artist, op.20th c.)   WI
Hersche, Johann Sebastian *(Swiss*
  painter, 1619-after 1691)   BA
  Bibl: Duft. DIE GALLUS-KAPELLE...,
  p.30; ▶Schweiz. Künst.-Lex.;
  ▶Thieme-Becker
Herschel, John (Sir) Frederick
  William *(British, 1792-1871)*   JG
Herscoe, Robert *(American*
  architect)   AV
  Bibl: Building, 1989 Jan.20, v.254,
  no.3, p.60
Herselle, Joost II van *(Flemish*
  tapestry maker, act.1586)   BA
  Bibl: ▶Thomson, Tapestry
Hersent→see Hersent, Louis
Hersent, Louis   AV BA GC PR WC
  (French artist, 1777-1860)   WC
  (French painter and
  lithographer, Paris, 1777-
  1860)   AV
  (French painter, 1777-1860)   GC PR
  (French painter, printmaker,
  1777-1860)   BA
  Bibl: ▶Bénézit; ▶RILA/BHA;
  ▶Thieme-Becker
  Hersent   PR
  Louis Hersent   PR
Hersent, Mme. Louise Marie-
  Jeanne, (nee Mauduit) *(French*
  artist, 1784-1862)   WC
Hersey, Bill→see Hersey, William K.
Hersey, John   WC WI
  (British artist, 20th cent.)   WC
  (British artist, op.20th c.)   WI
Hersey, William K. *(American*
  architect, Los Angeles, Calif, 1940-
  1989)   AV
  Bibl: L.A. architect, 1989 June,
  p.4
  Hersey, Bill   AV
Hershey, Nona *(American*
  printmaker, painter, b.1946)   BA
  Bibl: Guide exh. artists: N. Amer.
  ptrs.; ▶WW Amer. Art, 1986
Hershman, Lynn Lester *(American*
  artist, b.1941)   BA
  Bibl: ▶Art Index, Nov. 1983-Oct.
  1984; ▶Intl. dir. exh. artists,
  1983; New York (NY, USA), New
  Mus., Persona (1981); ▶WW
  Amer. Art

Hershman, Salo *(Israeli architect)*   AV
  Bibl: Architecture & urbanism,
  1983 Nov., no.9(158), p.85
Hershom, Eliza *(German artist, 20th*
  cent.)   WC
Herson, Emile Antoine François
  (French painter, b.1805)   GC
  Bibl: ▶Bénézit
Herssens, Ida *(20th c.)*   BA
Herst, Auguste Clement Joseph
  (French artist, 1825-p.1861)   WC
Herstel→see Erstet, Jean-Ulrich
Hertel, Albert   BA WC
  (German artist, 1843-1912)   WC
  (German painter, 1843-1912)   BA
  Bibl: ▶Bénézit; ▶Thieme-Becker
Hertel, Gottlieb *(German artist,*
  1683-1743)   WC
Hertel, Johann Georg *(German*
  print publisher, act.1750-1760)   BA
  Bibl: ▶Bénézit; Le Stampe e la
  diffusione delle immagini ... (CIHA
  24, Bologna 1979), 94;
  ▶Thieme-Becker
Hertel, Karl Konrad Julius *(German*
  artist, 1837-1895)   WC
Herter→see Herter, Albert
Herter, Albert   PR WC WI
  (American artist, 1871-1950)   WC WI
  (American painter, 1871-1950)   PR
  Bibl: ▶WWW Amer. art
  Albert Herter   PR
  Herter   PR
Herter, Christian   AV BA
  (American decorator, furniture
  designer, architect, 1840-
  1883)   BA
  (Designer and architect)   AV
  Bibl: ▶Artist biog. master idx.;
  Boger, Furn. Styles; House +
  garden, 1985 May, v.157, no.5,
  p.17; ▶Penguin dec. arts;
  ▶Thieme-Becker; ▶WWW Amer.,
  1607
Herter, D. *(German, active 1880s)*   JG
Herter, Gustave *(Designer and*
  architect)   AV
  Bibl: House + garden, 1985 May,
  v.157, no.5, p.17
Herterich, Eduard *(German painter,*
  printmaker, b.1905)   BA
  Bibl: ▶WW Arts DEU
Herterich, Heinrich Joachim
  (German artist, 1772-1852)   WC
Herterich, Johann Kaspar *(German*
  artist, 1843-1905)   WC
Herterich, Ludwig→see Herterich,
  Ludwig von
Herterich, Ludwig von   BA
  (German artist, 1856-1932)   WC
  (German painter, 1856-1932)   BA
  Bibl: ▶Busse, Maler u. Bildhauer
  19. Jahr.; ▶Thieme-Becker;
  ▶Vollmer, Künst.-Lex. 20. Jhr.
Herterich, Ludwig   WC
Hertervig or Hertewik, Lars
  (Norwegian artist, 1830-1902)   WC

Hertig, Heinz *(Swiss architect, Zurich)* **AV**
  Bibl: ▶Schweiz. Ingen. u. Archit., 1984-1985
Hertig, Walter *(Swiss architect, Zurich)* **AV**
  Bibl: ▶Schweiz. Ingen. u. Archit., 1984-1985
Hertlein, Hans *(German architect, 1881-1963)* **BA**
Hertochs or Hertocks, A. *(Dutch artist, op.1626-1672)* **WC**
Hertochvelt → see Hertochvelt, Christoffel [Unidentified]
Hertochvelt, Christoffel [Unidentified] *(Unknown painter, act. 17th century)* **PR**
  Bibl: Hartogvelt inventory 1666
  Christoffel Hertochvelt **PR**
  Hertochvelt **PR**
Hertoft, Nanna *(Danish artist, 20th c.)* **BA**
  Bibl: Hertoft, N., in HERNING KUNSTMUSEUMS BULLETIN 2 (autumn 1985) 14 (RILA/DNK)
Herts, Henry Beaumont *(American architect, 1871-1933)* **AV**
Hertul *(Hungarian illuminator, act. 1326-1331)* **BA**
  Bibl: Acta historiae artium, XXIII/3-4 (1977) pp.287-289
Hertz, Betti-Sue *(American artist, art administrator, 20th c.)* **BA**
  Bibl: ▶Art Index, Nov. 1987-Oct. 1988; Van Wagner, J.K., ARTS MAGAZINE/ LXIII/ 2/ (Oct. 1988), 82
Hertz, Mogens M. *(American architect)* **AV**
Hertzberg, Benjamin *(American photographer, b.1910.)* **BA**
  Bibl: ▶Artist biog. master idx.; Ithaca (NY, USA), Cornell Univ., Herbert F. Johnson Museum of Art, THE SELECTIVE EYE; photos. by Benjamin Hertzberg, 1977
Hertzberger, Herman **AV BA**
  (Dutch architect, Amsterdam, 1932-) **AV**
  (Dutch architect, b.1932) **BA**
  Bibl: ▶Avery period. idx.; ▶Contemp. archts., 1987; DUTCH ART AND ARCHITECTURE TODAY, 6 (Dec 1979) p.25-35
Hertzen, Heikki S. von *(Finnish city planner, 1942-)* **AV**
  Bibl: ▶Libr. of Congr. Name Auth. File
Hertzer, Carol *(American painter, 20th c.)* **BA**
  Bibl: Breslow, Arts mag., LVII/1 (Sep. 1982) p.13
Hertzog von Brin *(Bohemian goldsmith, printmaker, act.1589-1606)* **BA**
  Bibl: Bukovinska, Leids Kunsthist. Jrbk., I (1982) pp.71-82; ▶Thieme-Becker

Hertzog, Anton *(Austrian painter, 1692-1740)* **BA**
  Bibl: Dehio: Österreich, II (1935); Koller, Öster. Zeit. für Kunst u. Denk. 34/1-2 (1980), 48-51; ▶Thieme-Becker
Hervai, Zoltán *(Hungarian painter, b.1919)* **BA**
  Bibl: Müvészettörténeti Értesítö, XXIV/ 4 (1975),293
Herve, Francis de la Monniere *(British artist, op.1818-1840)* **WI**
Hervé, François *(French cabinetmaker in GBR, act.1770-1790)* **BA**
  Bibl: Burlington, CXXII (June 1980), 400-414; ▶Salverte, Ébénistes 18e s.
Herve, Gabriel *(French artist, 1868-p.1907)* **WC**
Herve, Jules *(French artist, 1887-)* **WC**
Hervé, Lucien *(French photographer, 1910-)* **AV**
  Bibl: ▶Libr. of Congr. Name Auth. File, date from 678 field
Hervens, Jacques *(Belgian artist, 1890-1928)* **WC**
Hervey, Antoinette B. *(American, active New York, 1930's)* **JG**
Hervey, Elizabeth, Miss → see Devonshire, Elizabeth, Duchess of
Hervey, Frederick *(1730-1803)* **AV**
Hervey, John Augustus **AV**
Hervey-Bathurst, Caroline **WC WI**
  (British artist, 20th cent.) **WC**
  (British artist, op.1975-) **WI**
Hervier → see Hervier, Louis Adolphe
Hervier, Adolphe (Louis Henri Victor Jules Francois Adolphe) → see Hervier, Louis Adolphe
Hervier, Louis → see Hervier, Louis Adolphe
Hervier, Louis Adolphe **BA PR**
  (French artist, 1818-1879) **WC**
  (French painter, 1818-1879) **GC PR**
  (French painter, printmaker, 1818-1879) **BA**
  Bibl: ▶Bénézit; ▶Bryan, Ptrs. & engravers; ▶Dict. biog. fran.; ▶Encyc. world art; ▶RILA/BHA; ▶Witt checklist
Herner, Adolphe **GC**
  Hervier **PR**
Hervier, Adolphe (Louis Henri Victor Jules Francois Adolphe) **WC**
  Hervier, Louis **PR**
  Louis Adolphe Hervier **PR**
Hervieu, August → see Hervieu, Auguste

Hervieu, Auguste **BA**
  (British artist, op.1819-1858) **WC WI**
  (French painter, illustrator, 1794-1858) **BA**
  Bibl: ▶Bénézit; Cincinnati (OH, USA), Art Museum, FRENCH DRAWINGS...(1979); ▶Groce, Artists Amer.; London. National Portrait Gallery. Concise catalog (Augustus); ▶Thieme-Becker
Hervieu, August **WC WI**
Hervieu, Louise Jeanne Aimee *(French artist, 1878-1954)* **WC**
Hervy, Jehan de, the elder *(early Netherlandish painter, act.1472-1507)* **BA**
  Bibl: ▶Bénézit; Roberts, THE MASTER OF THE LEGEND OF S. LUCY (1982); ▶Thieme-Becker; ▶Wurzbach, NLD Künst.-Lex.
Herweegen [Unidentified] *(Unknown painter)* **PR**
  Bibl: (Thursday, Feb. 5, 1801, lot 49, Christie's)
Herwegen or Herwegen-Manini, Veronik Maria *(German artist, 1851-)* **WC**
Herwijck, Steven Cornelisz. van *(early Netherlandish sculptor, medalist, ca.1530-ca.1565)* **BA**
  Bibl: ▶Bénézit; ▶Thieme-Becker
Herwijnen, Jan van *(Dutch painter and draughtsman, 1889-1965)* **GC**
  Bibl: ▶Vollmer, Künst.-Lex. 20. Jhr.
Herz or Hertz the Younger, Johann Daniel (von Herzburg) → see Herz, Johann Daniel, the younger
Herz or Hertz, Johann *(German artist, 1599-1635)* **WC**
Herz, Christoph *(German artist, op. 1658)* **WC**
Herz, Gottlieb *(German(?) painter, 1810-1897)* **GC**
  Bibl: Foucault
Herz, Jacob *(German painter, d.1753)* **GC**
  Bibl: ▶Thieme-Becker
Herz, Johann Daniel, the younger **BA**
  (German artist, 1720-1793) **WC**
  (German printmaker, critic, publisher, 1720-1793) **BA**
  Bibl: ▶Bénézit; ▶Thieme-Becker
Herz or Hertz the Younger, Johann Daniel (von Herzburg) **WC**
  Herzberg, Johann Daniel Herz von **BA**
Herzberg, Henry Joseph *(British architect, London)* **AV**
  Bibl: ▶RIBA members, 1987
Herzberg, Johann Daniel Herz von → see Herz, Johann Daniel, the younger
Herzberg, Robert → see Herzberg, Robert A.

Herzberg, Robert A. *(German
painter, 1886-1955)* **PR**
    Bibl: Detroit Inst of Arts
    catalogue; ▶WWW Amer. art
  Herzberg, Robert **PR**
  Robert A. Herzberg **PR**
Herzelt, Friedrich *(German architect,
Berlin)* **AV**
    Bibl: Werk, Bauen + Wohnen,
    1988 Sept., no.9, p.14
Herzfeld, Anatol → see Anatol (Anatol
Herzfeld)
Herzger, Walter *(German painter,
b.1903)* **BA**
    Bibl: ▶Bénézit; Deutsche
    Künstlerkolonien u. Künstlerorte;
    ▶Vollmer, Künst.-Lex. 20. Jhr.
Herzig, Franz *(West German
architect, Darmstadt)* **AV**
    Bibl: Detail, 1989 Aug.-Sept.,
    v.29, no.4, p.349
Herzig, Johannes → see Herzog,
Johannes
Herzlein, Kiliane de *(German artist,
18th cent.)* **WC**
Herzmanovsky-Orlando, Fritz von
(Austrian artist, 1877-1954) **WC**
Herzog → see Herzog, Herman
Herzog, Charlotte *(German painter,
b.1936)* **BA**
    Bibl: ▶Art Index, Nov. 1978-Oct.
    1979; Galerie 66. Herzog. 1971;
    ▶WW Arts DEU
Herzog, Frank *(West German
architecture student, Universität
Dortmund, 1986)* **AV**
    Bibl: Architektur + Wettbewerbe,
    1988 Mar., no.133, p.88
Herzog, Fülöp Ferenc *(Austrian
architect, 1860-1925)* **BA**
    Bibl: ▶Portoghesi, Diz. arch. e
    urbanistica; ▶Thieme-Becker;
    ▶Vollmer, Künst.-Lex. 20. Jhr.
Herzog, Herman **BA PR WC**
  (German artist, 1832-1832) **WC**
  *(German painter in USA, 1831-
1932)* **BA**
  (German painter, 1831-1932) **PR**
  (German painter, 1832-1932) **GC**
    Bibl: Amer. Art Rev. III, 4 (1976),
    52; ▶Bénézit; ▶RILA/BHA;
    ▶Thieme-Becker; ▶Vollmer,
    Künst.-Lex. 20. Jhr.
  Herman Herzog **PR**
  Herzog **PR**
Herzog, Hermann **GC PR**
Herzog, Hermann → see Herzog,
Herman
Herzog, Jacques *(Swiss architect,
Basel)* **AV**
    Bibl: ▶Schweiz. Ingen. u. Archit.,
    1984-1985
Herzog, Jakob *(Swiss artist, 1867-
1959)* **WC**
Herzog, Jean → see Herzog, Johannes

Herzog, Johannes **AV BA**
  (Swiss engineer, act.1779) **BA**
  *(Swiss engineer, from
Appenzell, 18th century)* **AV**
    Bibl: Genava, 1977, n.s. v.25, pp.
    199, 202
  Herzig, Johannes **AV**
Herzog, Jean **AV**
Herzog, Lewis *(American artist,
1868-1943)* **WI**
Herzog, Thomas **AV BA**
  (German architect, 20th c.) **BA**
  (German architect, Munich) **AV**
    Bibl: ▶Avery period. idx., suppl.
    6,7; Bauwelt, 1985 Jan.25, v.76,
    no.4, p.145
Herzog, Wolfgang Werner *(German
artist, 1933-)* **WC**
Heschler, David **BA GC**
  *(German draughtsman, act.
1640-1651)* **GC**
  *(German sculptor, act.1600-
1651)* **BA**
    Bibl: ▶Encyc. world art;
    ▶Thieme-Becker
  Helscher, David **GC**
*Hesdin, Esdin or Odin, Jacquemart
de → see* Hesdin, Jacquemart de
Hesdin, Jacquemart de **BA GC**
  *(French artist, op.1384-m.c.
1409)* **WC**
  *(French illuminator, act. ca.
1384-1409)* **GC**
  *(French illuminator, act.1380-
1411)* **BA**
    Bibl: ▶Bénézit; ▶Bradley,
    Miniaturists; ▶Thieme-Becker
**Hesdin, Esdin or Odin,
Jacquemart de** **WC**
Hesdin, Pseudo-Jacquemart de → see
Pseudo-Jacquemart
Heseltine, Anna Katrina, Mrs. → see
Zinkeisen, Anna Katrina
Heseltine, John Postle **BA WC WI**
  (British artist, 1843-1929) **WC WI**
  *(British printmaker, art
administrator, collector,
1843-1929)* **BA**
    Bibl: ▶Artist biog. master idx.;
    ▶Havlice, Idx. art. bio.;
    ▶Thieme-Becker; ▶Who was who
    [GBR], 1929-40
Heseltine, Michael *(British artist,
b.1961)* **WI**
Hesiod Painter **GC**
    Bibl: ▶Beazley, Attic red-fig. vase-
    ptrs.
Hesione Painter *(Etruscan vase-
painter)* **GC**
    Bibl: Beazley, Etruscan vase-ptrs.
Hesius, Willem *(Flemish priest, poet,
architect, 1601-1690)* **BA**
Heskia, Yves *(French architect,
Caluire)* **AV**
    Bibl: ▶Annuaire archts. fran.,
    1978

Hesler, Alexander *(American (b.
Canada), 1823-1895,
daguerreotypist)* **JG**
Heslewood, Tom **WC WI**
  (British artist, 20th cent.) **WC**
  (British artist, op.20th c.) **WI**
Heslop, Arthur *(British artist, 1881-
1955)* **WC WI**
Hesperia Painter *(Etruscan vase-
painter)* **GC**
    Bibl: ▶Szilagyi, Etruszko-korinthosi
Hess → see Hess, Peter Heinrich
Lambert von
Hess, Alan *(American architect and
author, active in Calif)* **AV**
Hess, Anton Heinrich *(German
sculptor, 1838-1909)* **BA**
    Bibl: ▶Busse, Maler u. Bildhauer
    19. Jahr.; ▶Thieme-Becker
Hess, Berthe *(French artist, 20th
cent.)* **WC**
Hess, Carl Adolph Heinrich
(German artist, 1769-1849) **WC**
Hess, Carl Ernst Christoph *(German
artist, 1755-1828)* **WC**
Hess, Christian *(Austrian painter,
1895-1944)* **BA**
Hess, David *(Swiss artist, 1770-
1843)* **WC**
Hess, Emil John *(American painter,
sculptor, b.1913)* **BA**
    Bibl: ▶Havlice, Idx. art. bio.; ▶WW
    Amer. Art, 1976
Hess, Eugene *(German artist, 1824-
1862)* **WC**
Hess, Florence *(British artist, 1891-
1974)* **WI**
Hess, Georg Friedrich *(German
artist, 1697-1782)* **WC**
Hess, Heinrich Maria von **BA GC WC**
  (German artist, 1798-1863) **WC**
  (German painter, 1798-1863) **GC**
  *(German painter, printmaker,
1798-1863)* **BA**
    Bibl: ▶Artist biog. master idx.;
    ▶Bénézit; ▶Brockhaus Enzyk.;
    ▶Neue deutsche Biog.;
    ▶Thieme-Becker; ▶Witt checklist
Hess, Hieronymous → see Hess,
Hieronymus
Hess, Hieronymus **BA**
  (Swiss artist, 1799-1850) **WC**
  *(Swiss painter, printmaker,
1799-1850)* **BA**
    Bibl: ▶Bénézit; ▶Schweiz.
    Künst.-Lex.; ▶Thieme-Becker
Hess, Hieronymous **WC**
Hess, Ignatius → see Hess, Johann
Ignaz
Hess, James **WC WI**
  (American artist, op.1874-1884) **WI**
  (American artist, op.c.1879) **WC**

Hess, Jaro (American painter, 1889-
1977)   **BA**
> Bibl: Grand Rapids (MI, USA), Art
> Mus., Artists of Grand Rapids
> (1981)

Hess, Johann Ignaz   **BA**
> (German artist, op.1748-m.
> 1784)   WC
> (German porcelain painter, act.
> 1748, d.1784)   BA
> Bibl: ▶Boger, World pott. & porc.;
> ▶Bruckmann's Fayence-Lex.;
> Dostal, Weltkunst, LIII/19 (1 Oct.
> 1983) pp.2540-2543; ▶Honey,
> Euro. ceramic

Hess, Ignatius   **WC**

Hess, Julius (German painter, 1878-
1957)   **GC**
> Bibl: ▶Thieme-Becker

Hess, Ludwig   **BA WC**
> (Swiss artist, 1760-1800)   WC
> (Swiss painter, printmaker,
> 1760-1800)   BA
> Bibl: KDS, ZÜRICH STADT, Bd.1,
> p.358; ▶Schweiz. Künst.-Lex.;
> ▶Thieme-Becker

Hess, Ludwig Ferdinand (German
architect, painter, 1795-1876)   **BA**
> Bibl: ▶Macmillan encyc. archts.;
> ▶Thieme-Becker

Hess, Max (German artist, 1825-
1868)   **WC**

**Hess, Peter Heinrich Lambert
von**   **BA GC**
> (German artist, 1792-1871)   WC
> (German draughtsman, 1792-
> 1871)   GC
> (German painter, 1792-1871)   BA PR
> Bibl: ▶Bénézit; ▶Thieme-Becker
> Hess   PR

Hess, Peter von   **GC PR WC**
> Peter von Hess   PR
> Hess, Peter von→see Hess, Peter
> Heinrich Lambert von

Hess, Richard (German sculptor,
b.1937)   **BA**
> Bibl: ▶Intl. dir. exh. artists, 1982;
> ▶WW Arts DEU

Hess, Wilhelm (Austrian architect,
act.1885)   **BA**
> Bibl: Dehio Karnten, 293

Hesse Group (Etruscan vase-
painters)   **GC**
> Bibl: Beazley, Etruscan vase-ptrs.

Hesse, Alexandre   **GC**
> (French artist, 1806-1879)   WC
> (French, 1806-1879)   GC
> Bibl: George Goldner;
> ▶Thieme-Becker; ▶Witt checklist

Hesse, Alexandre Jean Baptiste   **WC**
Hesse, Alexandre Jean Baptiste→see
Hesse, Alexandre

Hesse, Carl Johann Paul (German
architect, 1827-1895)   **BA**
> Bibl: Börsch-Supan, Berliner
> Baukunst nach Schinkel, pp.582-
> 583; Jahrb. Preussischer
> Kulturbesitz XIX (1982), 364

Hesse, Eva   **BA WI**
> (American artist, 1936-1970)   WI
> (American sculptor, 1936-1970)   BA
> Bibl: ▶Art Index, v.19, 20; Art
> News LXIX/ 5 (Sept.1970), 8;
> ▶Contemp. artists; ▶Darmstädter,
> Künstlerlex.; ▶DuMonts
> Künst.-Lex.; ▶WW Amer. Art,
> 1970

Hesse, Hans   **BA WC**
> (German artist, op.1497-1521)   WC
> (German painter, act.1497-1521)   BA
> Bibl: ▶Bénézit; Sander, HANS
> HESSE; ▶Thieme-Becker

Hesse, Henri Joseph   **GC WC**
> (French artist, 1781-1849)   WC
> (French painter, 1781-1849)   GC
> Bibl: ▶Bénézit

Hesse, Hermann   **AV BA**
> (German author, painter, 1877-
> 1962)   BA
> (West German architect,
> Lippstadt)   AV
> Bibl: ▶Bénézit; ▶Brockhaus Enzyk.;
> Deutsche Bauzeitschrift, 1988
> Dec., no.12, p.1679; Frenzel,
> Daten Deutscher Dichtung, p.492;
> ▶Thieme-Becker; ▶Vollmer,
> Künst.-Lex. 20. Jhr.; Wilpert,
> DEUTSCHES DICHTERLEXIKON,
> p.252

Hesse, Nicolas Auguste   **BA GC WC**
> (French artist, 1795-1869)   WC
> (French painter, 1795-1869)   BA GC
> Bibl: ▶Bénézit; ▶Larousse, Grand
> dict. 19e s.; ▶Thieme-Becker

Hesse, Roland (Architect, East
Germany)   **AV**
> Bibl: Architektur der DDR, 1985
> Jan, v.34, no.1, p.38

Hesse, Rudolf (German artist, 1871-)   **WC**

Hesselberger, Wolfgang (German
architect, Munich)   **AV**
> Bibl: Baumeister, 1985 Jan., v.82,
> no.1, p.52

Hesselbom, Otto (Johan Otto)
(Swedish artist, 1848-1913)   **WC**
Hesselius, Gustaf→see Hesselius,
Gustavus
Hesselius, Gustaf, I→see Hesselius,
Gustavus

Hesselius, Gustaf, II (Swedish artist,
1727-1775)   **WC**
Hesselius, Gustav (the elder)→see
Hesselius, Gustavus

Hesselius, Gustavus   **BA GC PR**
> (American artist, 1682-1755)   WC WI
> (American painter and organ
> builder, 1682-1755)   GC
> (American painter, 1682-1755)   PR
> (American painter, organ
> builder, 1682-1755)   BA
> Bibl: ▶Dict. Amer. biog.; ▶Encyc.
> world art; ▶Fielding's Amer. ptrs.;
> ▶Groce, Artists Amer.;
> ▶RILA/BHA; ▶Thieme-Becker

> Gustav Hesselius (the elder)   PR
> Hesselius, Gustaf   GC

Hesselius, Gustaf, I   **WC**
Hesselius, Gustav (the elder)   **PR**
Hesselius, Gustavus I   **WI**
Hesselius, Gustavus I→see Hesselius,
Gustavus
Hesselius, Johan→see Hesselius, John
Hesselius, Johann→see Hesselius,
John

Hesselius, John   **BA**
> (American artist, 1728-1778)   WC WI
> (American painter, 1728-1778)   BA
> (American, 1728-1778)   GC
> Bibl: ▶Dict. Amer. biog.;
> ▶McGraw-Hill dict. art;
> ▶Thieme-Becker; ▶Witt checklist;
> ▶WWW Amer., 1607

Hesselius, Johan   **GC WC**
Hesselius, Johann   **WI**

Hessemer, Friedrich Maximilian
(German artist, 1800-1860)   **WC**

Hessen, Tatiana von (West German
interior designer)   **AV**
> Bibl: Architektur & Wohnen, 1989
> Jan.-Feb., no.1, p.34

Hessing, Leonard (Australian artist,
1931-)   **WC**

Hessing, Perle (painter, b.1908)   **BA**
> Bibl: ▶Bihalji-Merin, Naive art;
> Guide exh. artists: N. Amer. ptrs.;
> Leonardo XII/4 (Autumn 1979)
> 306-307

Hester, Gene (American stained
glass artist, Houston, Tex)   **AV**
> Bibl: Stained glass quarterly, 1989
> Summer., v.84, no.2, p.117

Hester, Joy (Australian painter,
draftsman, 1920-1960)   **BA**
> Bibl: ▶Encyc. Australian art;
> Melbourne, Nat'l Gall. of Victoria,
> JOY HESTER 1981

Hester, Randolph T. (American
landscape architect, Berkeley,
Calif)   **AV**
> Bibl: Landscape architecture,
> 1986 Nov.-Dec., v.76, no.6, p.58

Hester, Wilhelm   **BA JG**
> (American (b. Germany), active
> Seattle, WA, U.S. 1893-1920)   JG
> (German photographer in USA,
> act.1893-1915)   BA
> Bibl: ▶Parry, Photo idx.

Hesterberg, Hesto (German artist,
1895-)   **WC**

Hesterman, H.A. (Dutch artist, 17th cent.) **WC**

Hesterman, Johannes Albertus II (Dutch draughtsman, 1877-1955) **GC**
Bibl: ▶Scheen, Ned. beeldende kunst.

Hesters, Jacques (French architect, Paris) **AV**
Bibl: ▶Annuaire archts. fran., 1987

Hesters, Jean-Luc (French architect) **AV**
Bibl: AMC, 1986 Oct., no.13, p.62

Hestnes Ferreira, Raul (Portuguese architect, 1931-) **AV**
Bibl: Arquitectura, 1984 May-June, v.4, no.152, p.34

Hesz, János Mihály **BA WC**
(Hungarian artist, 1768-1833) **WC**
(Hungarian painter, 1768-ca. 1833) **BA**
Bibl: Prokopp, MURESZETT. ERTESITO, XXX, 3 (1981) 200-205; ▶Thieme-Becker; ▶Witt checklist

Hetlie, M.(?) (Dutch(?) artist, op. 1683) **WC**

Hetmanek, Alfons (Austrian architect, Vienna, in school of Otto Wagner) **AV**
Bibl: RLIN BKS file

Hetreau, Remy (French artist, 1913-) **WC**
Hetsch, G. F. → see Hetsch, Gustav Friedrich

Hetsch, Gustav Friedrich **BA**
(Danish architect, 1788-1864) **BA**
(German architect, b. Stuttgart, trained in Germany and France, practiced in Copenhagen 1815-1864, 1788-1864) **AV**
Bibl: ▶Macmillan encyc. archts.; ▶Thieme-Becker; ▶Weilbach, Kunst.leks.

Hetsch, G. F. **AV**
Hetsch, Philipp Friedrich von **BA GC WC**
(German artist, 1758-1838) **WC**
(German painter, 1758-1838) **BA GC**
Bibl: ▶Neue deutsche Biog.; ▶Thieme-Becker; ▶Witt checklist

Hett, Leonard Keir (1887-1978) **AV**
Hettinga Tromp, Tijtske Geertruida Maria van (Dutch painter, 1872-1962) **GC**
Bibl: ▶Vollmer, Künst.-Lex. 20. Jhr.

Hettner, Otto (Hermann Otto) (German artist, 1875-1931) **WC**
Hetz → see Hetz, Karl
Hetz, Carl → see Hetz, Karl
Hetz, Karl (German painter, 1828-1899) **PR**
Bibl: ▶Thieme-Becker
Hetz **PR**
Hetz, Carl **PR**
Karl Hetz **PR**

Hetzel, George (American painter, 1826-1899) **BA**
Bibl: ▶Artist biog. master idx.; Currier's guide 1645-1945; ▶Groce, Artists Amer.; ▶Thieme-Becker; ▶Young, Amer. artists
Hetzendorf von Hohenberg → see Hohenberg, Johan Ferdinand von
Hetzendorf von Hohenberg, Johann Ferdinand → see Hohenberg, Johan Ferdinand von
Hetzendorfer, Johann Ferdinand → see Hohenberg, Johan Ferdinand von
Heubacher, Margarethe (Austrian architect) **AV**
Bibl: ▶Verzeich. Öst. Ziviltech.
Heubacher-Sentobe, Margarethe **AV**
Heubacher-Sentobe, Margarethe → see Heubacher, Margarethe
Heubel, Jakob (German artist, op.c. 1676-1680) **WC**
Heuberger family (Swiss wax modelers, 18th-19th cs.) **BA**
Bibl: Oberholzer, Zeit für Schweiz. Arch. u. Kunstges. XXXVIII/3 (1981), pp. 202-219; ▶Pyke, Wax modellers; ▶Thieme-Becker
Heuberger, Anton (Swiss wax modeler, b.1794, act.1821) **BA**
Bibl: Oberholzer, Zeit für Schweiz. Arch. u. Kunstges. XXXVIII/3 (1981), pp. 205-206; ▶Pyke, Wax modellers; ▶Thieme-Becker
Heuberger, Franz Xaver (Swiss wax modeler, 1791-1863?) **BA**
Bibl: Oberholzer, Zeit für Schweiz. Arch. u. Kunstges. XXXVIII/3 (1981), pp. 202-204; ▶Pyke, Wax modellers; ▶Thieme-Becker
Heuberger, Josef Gregor (Swiss wax modeler, 1779-1855) **BA**
Bibl: Oberholzer, Zeit für Schweiz. Arch. u. Kunstges. XXXVIII/3 (1981), pp. 204-205; ▶Pyke, Wax modellers; ▶Thieme-Becker
Heuberger, Karl Friedrich (Swiss wax modeler, 1817-1887) **BA**
Bibl: Oberholzer, Zeit für Schweiz. Arch. u. Kunstges. XXXVIII/3 (1981), pp. 205-206
Heude, Nicholas → see Heude, Nicolas
Heude, Nicolas **VO**
(British painter, d. 1703) **VO**
(French artist, op.1672-p.1682) **WC**
Bibl: Croft-Murray, Dec. ptg. England, v.1, p.248; ▶Libr. of Congr. Name Auth. File, NAFR9233246
Eude, Nicolas **VO**
Heude, Nicholas **WC**
Heuens → see Huens [Unidentified]
Heuer, Barlach (German painter, printmaker in FRA, b.1930) **BA**
Heuer, Christian Ludwig Wilhelm (German printmaker, 1813-1890) **BA**
Bibl: Deutsche Künstlerkolonien u. Künstlerorte; ▶Thieme-Becker

Heuffer, Klaus (German-born Venezuelan architect) **AV**
Bibl: Interior design, 1984 Jan., v.55, no.1, p.183
Heukelom, Jan Bertus (Dutch painter, 1875-1965) **GC**
Bibl: ▶Vollmer, Künst.-Lex. 20. Jhr.
Heumann, Georg Daniel (German artist, 1691-1759) **WC**
Heunert, Friedrich (German painter, 1808-1876) **GC**
Bibl: ▶Bénézit
Heuns → see Huens [Unidentified]
Heupel, G. (Greek architect, 1938-) **AV**
Bibl: Architektonika Themata — Architecture in Greece, 1989, no.23, p.144
Heupel, X. (Greek architect, 1938-) **AV**
Bibl: Architektonika Themata — Architecture in Greece, 1989, no.23, p.144
Heur, Cornelis Joseph d' → see Heurs, Cornelis Joseph d'
Heurn, Cornelis van (Netherlandish draughtsman, act. late 17th c.?) **GC**
Bibl: Sotheby's
Heurs, Cornelis Joseph d' **GC**
(Flemish artist, 1707-1762) **WC**
(Flemish painter, 1707-1762) **GC**
Bibl: ▶Bénézit; Sotheby's
Heur, Cornelis Joseph d' **WC**
Heurs, Joseph van **GC**
Heurs, Joseph van → see Heurs, Cornelis Joseph d'
Heurt, Forrest → see Hewit, Forrest
Heurtault, Nicolas → see Heurtaut, Nicolas (menuisier)
Heurtaut, Nicolas → see Heurtaut, Nicolas (menuisier)
Heurtaut, Nicolas (menuisier) **GC**
(French menuisier, 1720-1771?, master 1755) **GC**
(French, 1720-1771) **JG**
Bibl: ▶Salverte, Ébénistes 18e s.; ▶Vial, Artistes décorateurs
Heurtault, Nicolas **GC**
Heurtaut, Nicolas **JG**
Heusch or Heus, Abraham de (Dutch artist, c.1650-1712(?)) **WC**
Heusch or Heus, Willem, Guilliam or Guglielmo de → see Heusch, Willem de
Heusch, Giacomo → see Heusch, Jacob de
Heusch, Jacob de **GC PR**
(Dutch artist, 1657-1701) **WC**
(Dutch painter, 1657-1701) **PR**
(Dutch painter, draughtsman, and printmaker, 1657-1701) **GC**
Bibl: Getty Photo Study Coll.; ▶Thieme-Becker
Heusch, Giacomo **GC**
Heusch, Jacob or Giacomo de (Afdruk) **WC**
Jacob de Heusch **PR**

Hewitt, Charles (*American painter, 20th c.*) **BA**
    Bibl: ▶Art Index, v.36; Waits, ARTS MAGAZINE, LXII/9 (May 1988), p. 90

Hewitt, David (*British artist, op. 1839-, d.1939*) **WI**

Hewitt, Edwin Hawley (*American architect, Minneapolis, Minn, 1874-1939*) **AV**
    Bibl: ▶Avery obit. idx.

Hewitt, Francis Ray (*American painter, b.1936*) **BA**
    Bibl: ▶Artist biog. master idx.; ▶WW Amer. Art, 1989

Hewitt, George W.→*see Hewitt, George Watson*

Hewitt, George Watson **AV**
    (*American architect, 1841-1916*) AV
    (*American, 1841-1917*) JG
    Bibl: ▶Withey, Amer. archts.

Hewitt, George W. **JG**

Hewitt, H. (*American artist, op.1845-1870*) **WI**

Hewitt, Henry (*British artist, 1818-1875*) **WI**

Hewitt, I. (*American artist, 19th cent.*) **WC**

Hewitt, John M. (*American, active Louisville, KY, U.S. 1848, daguerreotypist*) **JG**

Hewitt, M.K. (*Engraver, op.1800-1836*) **WI**

Hewitt, Mark Alan (*American architect, Bergenfield, N.J, 1953-*) **AV**
    Bibl: phone call to office 3/89

Hewitt, William D. (*1848-1924*) **AV**

Hewitt, William Graily (*English, 1864-1952*) **JG**

Hewitt, William K. (*American painter, 1818-1892*) **PR**
    Bibl: ▶Fielding's Amer. ptrs., 1986
    Hewitt, William Keesey PR
    William K. Hewitt PR
Hewitt, William Keesey→*see Hewitt, William K.*

Hewland, Elise Dalton (*British artist, b.1901*) **WI**

Hewlet→*see Hewlett, James*

Hewlett, Francis **BA WI**
    (*British artist, op.1978-*) WI
    (*British painter, b.1930*) BA
    Bibl: Arts Council of GB, Welsh Com., FRANCIS HEWLETT, 1978; ▶Natl. union cat., 1977-1986

Hewlett, James **PR WC WI**
    (*British artist, 1789-1836*) WI
    (*British artist, op.1799-m.1836*) WC
    (*British painter, d. 1836*) PR
    Bibl: ▶Fisher, Watercolour ptrs.; ▶Thieme-Becker
    Hewlet PR
    James Hewlett PR

Hewlings, Charles (*British sculptor, b.1948*) **BA**
    Bibl: ▶Art Index, v.49, no.3; Artforum, XVI/8 (Apr. 1978) pp. 27-31; Bristol (GBR), Arnolfini Gallery, Style in the 70s (1979)

Hewson→*see Hewson, Stephen*

Hewson, Stephen (*British painter, act. 1768-1800/05*) **PR**
    Bibl: ▶Bénézit; ▶Thieme-Becker
    Hewson PR
    Stephen Hewson PR

Hey, Jean (*early Netherlandish painter in FRA, act.ca.1480-ca.1504*) **BA**
    Bibl: ▶Bénézit; REVUE DE L'ART, 1-2 (1968) 27-33; Sterling, in Ars Auro Prior: Studia Ioanni Białosticki (1981) 212-215; ▶Thieme-Becker; ▶Witt checklist

Hey, Jean→*see Master of Moulins*

Heyberger, G. W. **AV**
    (*German architect, 1880-1914*) AV
    (*German archtiect, Bremen, fl. 1912*) AV
    Bibl: Der Architekt, 1988 Apr., no.4, p.234; ▶Thieme-Becker

Heyberger, Gregor Werner **AV**
Heyberger, Gregor Werner→*see Heyberger, G. W.*

Heyboer, Anton **BA GC**
    (*Dutch artist, 1924-*) WC
    (*Dutch printmaker, 1924-d. aft. 1962*) GC
    (*Dutch printmaker, painter, b.1924*) BA
    Bibl: ▶Art Index, vs.16, 18, 35; ▶Artist biog. master idx.; ▶Natl. union cat., 1977-1986; ▶Scheen, Ned. beeldende kunst., p.476

Heijboer or Heyboer, Anton **WC**
    Heijboer, Anton GC

Heydanus, Thomas Johannus (*Dutch cabinetmaker, 1789-1857*) **BA**
    Bibl: J. Verbeek, in ANTIEK, XX/8 (Mar. 1,1986), p. 464-470

Heyde or Heide, Henning von der→*see Heide, Henning von der*

Heyde, Herman Henry op der (*Dutch painter, 1813-1857*) **GC**
    Bibl: ▶Scheen, Ned. beeldende kunst.
    Heijde, Herman Henry op der GC
Heyde, Jan van der→*see Heyden, Jan van der*

Heydeck, Adolf von **GC**
    (*German artist, 1787-1856*) WC
    (*German draughtsman, 1787-1856*) GC
    Bibl: ▶Thieme-Becker

Heydeck, Adolf von (Poussin Heydeck) **WC**
    Poussin-Heydeck, Adolf von GC
Heydeck, Adolf von (Poussin Heydeck)→*see Heydeck, Adolf von*

Heydehoper, G.M.J. van (*Netherlands artist, 17th cent.(?)*) **WC**
Heyden→*see Heyden, Jan van der*
Heyden or Heyde, Jan van der→*see Heyden, Jan van der*

Heyden, August Jakob Theodor von (*German artist, 1827-1897*) **WC**

Heyden, J.C.J. van der (*Dutch painter, printmaker, photographer, b.1928*) **BA**
    Bibl: ▶Art diary int'l., 1990; ▶Bénézit; Eindhoven (NLD), Stedelijk van Abbenmuseum, J.C.J. VAN DER HEYDEN (1983); ▶Scheen, Ned. beeldende kunst.
    Heijden, Jacobus Cornelis Johannes van der BA

Heyden, J.H. von (*German artist, 19th cent.*) **WC**

Heyden, Jacob van der **BA GC**
    (*French draughtsman, 1573-1645*) GC
    (*German painter, sculptor, printmaker, publisher, 1573-1645*) BA
    Bibl: Getty Photo Study Coll.; ▶Hollstein, German, v.13a; ▶Thieme-Becker, v.17

Heyden, Jacob van der (*Flemish, act. ca.1678*) **GC**
    Bibl: ▶Thieme-Becker

Heyden, Jan van der BA GC JG PR
(Dutch artist, 1637-1712) WC
(Dutch painter and printmaker, 1637-1712) GC
(Dutch painter, 1637-1712) PR
(Dutch painter, printmaker, inventor, 1637-1712) BA
(Dutch, 1637-1712) JG
Bibl: ▶Bénézit; ▶Grote Winkler Prins; ▶RILA/BHA; ▶Thieme-Becker; Wurgbach
Gio: Vandaneinden PR
Giovanni Vandaneinden PR
Heyde, Jan van der GC
Heyden PR
Heyden or Heyde, Jan van der WC
Hyde, Jan van der GC
J. van der Heijde PR
Jan van der Heide PR
Jan van der Heijden PR
Jan van der Heyden PR
Jean van der Heyden PR
John Vander Heyden PR
Monsu' Gio: Vandaneinden PR
Monsu' Giov. Vandaneinden PR
Monsu' Giovanni Vandaneinden PR
V der Heyde PR
V. de Heyde PR
V. der Heyde PR
V. der Heyden PR
V. der Hyde PR
V. Heyden PR
Van den Heijde PR
Van der Heiden PR
van der Heijden PR
Van der Heyde PR
van der Heyden PR
Vandaneinden PR
Vander Hayden PR
Vander Heiden PR
Vander Heijden PR
Vander Heyde PR
Vander Heyden PR
Vander Hyde PR
Vanderhayden PR
Vanderheyde PR
Vanderheyden PR
Vanderhyde PR
Vender Heyde PR
Wander Heiden PR
Heyden, Karl (German artist, 1845-1933) WC
Heyden, Otto Johann Heinrich
(German, 1820-1897) GC
Bibl: ▶Thieme-Becker

Heyden, Pieter van der BA GC
(early Netherlandish printmaker, ca.1530-ca.1575) BA
(Netherlandish, ca.1530-aft. 1572) GC
(Netherlands artist, c.1530-p. 1572) WC
Bibl: ▶Bénézit; ▶Hollstein, Dutch & Flemish; ▶McGraw-Hill dict. art; ▶Thieme-Becker; ▶Winkler Prins van de kunst
Heyden, Pieter van der, or Pieter Verheyden (Petrus a Merica, Ameringius, Mericinus, Miricenys, Miricinus, Miriginus or Myricenis) WC
Heyden, Pieter van der, or Pieter Verheyden (Petrus a Merica, Ameringius, Mericinus, Miricenys, Miricinus, Miriginus or Myricenis) → see Heyden, Pieter van der
Heydendahl, Joseph (German artist, 1844-1906) WC
Heyder, Otto (German painter, b.1863) GC
Bibl: ▶Thieme-Becker
Heyderdahl, Hans Olaf (Norwegian artist, 1857-1913) WC
Heyduck, Georg Paul (German painter, 1898-1962) BA
Bibl: Regensburg (BRD), Ostdeusche Galerie, GEORG PAUL HEYDUCH..., 1978; ▶Vollmer, Künst.-Lex. 20. Jhr.
Heyenbrock or Heijenbrock Johan Coenraad Herman (Herman) → see Heyenbrock, Johan Coenraad Hermann
Heyenbrock, Herman → see Heyenbrock, Johan Coenraad Hermann
Heyenbrock, Johan Coenraad Hermann BA
(Dutch artist, 1871-1948) WC
(Dutch painter, 1871-1948) GC
(Dutch painter, printmaker, 1871-1948) BA
Bibl: ▶Scheen, Ned. beeldende kunst.; ▶Thieme-Becker; ▶Vollmer, Künst.-Lex. 20. Jhr.
Heyenbrock or Heijenbrock Johan Coenraad Herman (Herman) WC
Heyenbrock, Herman GC
Heyer, Paul (American architect, 1936-) AV
Bibl: Architecture & urbanism, 1987 Apr., no.4(199), p.12
Heyer, Pieter (German artist, 18th cent.) WC
Heygendorf, Caroline von, (nee Jagemann) (German artist, 19th cent.(?)) WC

Heyl or Heijl, Marinus → see Heyl, Marinus
Heyl, Marinus GC
(Dutch artist, 1836-1931) WC
(Dutch painter, 1836-1931) GC
Bibl: ▶Scheen, Ned. beeldende kunst.
Heijl, Marinus GC
Heyl or Heijl, Marinus WC
Heyl, Werner (West German architect, Kaiserslautern, 1914?-1989) AV
Bibl: Deutsches Architektenblatt, 1989 Apr.1, v.21, no.4, p.110
Heylan family (Flemish printmakers in ESP, 17th c.) BA
Bibl: Moreno Garrido, Grabado en Granada, p.56; ▶Thieme-Becker
Heyland, Francesco (Francis)
(Active Italy 19th century (also Mathieu Deroche & Heyland)) JG
Heylbroeck, Heilbroeck, Heylbrouck etc., Norbert, II
(Flemish artist, c.1735/40-1785) WC
Heylbrouck, Norbert I (Flemish printmaker, medalist, goldsmith, 1700-1762) BA
Bibl: ▶Bénézit; ▶Biog. Nat. Belgique; Schoonhovens, A.L., ANTIEK, XXI/9 (April 1987), 545; ▶Seyn, Écoles flam. et holl.; ▶Thieme-Becker
Heyligers, Antoon Francois GC
(Dutch artist, 1828-1897) WC
(Dutch painter, 1828-1897) GC
Bibl: ▶Scheen, Ned. beeldende kunst.
Heijligers or Heyligers, Antoon Francois WC
Heijligers, Antoon Francois GC
Heylmann, Friedrich Christian II
(German architect, 1771-1837) BA
Bibl: Spallek NORDELBINGEN, LIII/1984 p.85-95; ▶Thieme-Becker
Heyman Dullaert → see Dullaert, Heyman
Heyman, Abigail (American photographer, b.1942) BA
Bibl: ▶Artist biog. master idx.; ▶Auer, Encyc. photographes; ▶Contemp. artists; Kalamazoo (MI, USA), Inst. Art, Young Amer. photogs. (1975)
Heymann, Mario AV
Heymans, Adriaan Joseph BA
(Belgian artist, 1839-1921) WC
(Belgian painter, 1839-1921) BA
Bibl: ▶Artist biog. master idx.; Blue guide: Belgium & Luxembourg; ▶Dict. biog. artistes belges; ▶Thieme-Becker
Heymans, Adriaan Jozef (Jozef) WC
Heymans, Adriaan Jozef (Jozef) → see Heymans, Adriaan Joseph
Heymark, Gustave (German artist, 19th cent.) WC

Heyn, Augustus *(German artist, 1837-)*   **WC**

Heyne, Johann Christoph
(American pewterer, 1715-1781)   **BA**
Bibl: ANTIQUES CXVII 1 Jan 1980 p.222; Meyer, Folk artists biog. idx.; Montgomery, HISTORY OF PEWTER IN AMERICA

Heynold-von Graefe, Blida *(German artist, 20th c.)*   **BA**
Bibl: Baden (DEU), Gal. Trudelhaus, Aus der Ittenschule (1984), 1926-34

Heynrick Dubbels→see Dubbels, Hendrik Jacobsz.

Heyrault, Louis Robert   **GC WC**
(French artist, op.1847-1880)   WC
(French, act.1847-1880)   GC
Bibl: ▶Thieme-Becker

Heysen, Hans   **BA GC WC**
(Australian artist, 1871-1968)   WC
(Australian painter, 1877-1968)   BA
(British, 1871-1968)   GC
Bibl: ▶Art Index, v.23; ART INTERNATIONAL XXIII 3-4 summer 1979, 46-51; ▶Encyc. Australian art; ▶Witt checklist

Heywood, J. Carl *(Canadian painter, printmaker, b.1941)*   **BA**
Bibl: ▶Art Index, v.32; ▶Artists Canada, 1975; ▶Intl. dir. exh. artists, 1982; Kingston (Ont, CAN), Queen's U. Etherington Art Ctr., 5 Kingston printmkrs. (1975); ▶Natl. Gall. Canada libr. cat., index, 1967-1974

Heywood, John *(British architect)*   **AV**

Heywood, John D. *(American, active Boston, MA, U.S. 1850s-1860s, daguerreotypist)*   **JG**

Heywood, Tom *(British artist, op. circa 1882-)*   **WI**

Heyworth, Alfred *(British artist, 1926-1976)*   **WI**

[Hiacinthe Collin de] Vermont→see Collin de Vermont, Hyacinthe

Hibbard, Aldro Thompson *(American artist, 1886-1972)*   **WI**

Hibbard, C.P. *(American, active 19th century)*   **JG**

Hibbart, William   **WC WI**
(British artist, op.1760-1800)   WI
(British artist, op.c.1760-c.1800)   WC

Hibberd, Shirley *(1825-1890)*   **AV**

Hibbert, J.   **WC WI**
(British artist, 19th cent.)   WC
(British artist, op.19th c.)   WI
Bibl: Mackenzie

Hibbert, Sophia *(British, 1760-1827)*   **BA**
Bibl: PANTHEON, XXXVI, July-Sept. 1978, 222-230

Hibon, Auguste *(French painter, 1780-1857)*   **GC**
Bibl: ▶Bénézit

Hick, Allanson *(British artist, b.1898)*   **WI**

Hickel→see Hickel, Anton

Hickel→see Hickel, van [Unidentified]

Hickel, Anton   **GC PR**
(Austrian painter, 1745-1798)   GC
(German artist, 1745-1798)   WC
(German painter, 1745-1798)   PR
Bibl: ▶Bénézit; Getty Photo Study Coll.; ▶Thieme-Becker
Anton Hickel   PR
Heckel   PR
Hickel   PR
Hickel, Anton or Carl Anton   **WC**
Huckel   PR
Hickel, Anton or Carl Anton→see Hickel, Anton

Hickel, Hickl or Hikl, Joseph
(German artist, 1736-1807)   **WC**

Hickel, van [Unidentified]
(Unknown painter)   **PR**
Bibl: (June 2, 1810, lot 95, Farebrother)
Hickel   PR
Van Hickel   PR

Hicken, John   **WC WI**
(British artist, 18th cent.)   WC
(British artist, op.18th c.)   WI

Hickey, Dale *(Australian painter, b.1937)*   **BA**
Bibl: ▶Art Index, v.26; ▶Encyc. Australian art; Melbourne (AUS), Natl. Gall. Victoria, New realism (1981)

Hickey, Margarit *(Irish, d.1830)*   **BA**
Bibl: De hOir, in FIGURES FROM THE PAST (1987) 314-323

Hickey, Patrick *(British artist, b.1927)*   **WI**

Hickey, Thomas   **BA PR WC WI**
(British artist, 1741-1824)   WC WI
(Irish painter, 1741-1824)   BA PR
Bibl: Apollo CII/161 July 1975 p.30; ▶Busse, Maler u. Bildhauer 19. Jahr.; ▶Dict. natl. biog.; ▶RILA/BHA; ▶Strickland, Irish artists; ▶Thieme-Becker
Thomas Hickey   PR

Hickin, George *(British artist, op. 1858-1877)*   **WC WI**
Bibl: Morris

Hickinbottom, Clive *(British ceramist, b.1952)*   **BA**
Bibl: Sunderland (GBR), Arts Ctr., State of clay (1978)

Hickman, Craig *(American photographer, b.1948)*   **BA**
Bibl: Pullman (WA, USA), Washington St. Univ. Mus. Art, A partial view (1979)

Hickman, David   **WC WI**
(American artist, 1937-)   WC
(American artist, b.1937)   WI

Hickman, Helen Carew *(American glass artist, New Berlin, Wisc)*   **AV**
Bibl: Stained glass, 1982 Spring, v.77, no.1, p.23

Hickman, Ian *(British artist, b.1952)*   **WI**

Hickman, John *(American architect, Kinston, N.C)*   **AV**
Bibl: ▶AIA Pro File, 1985

Hickman, Steven *(American interior designer)*   **AV**
Bibl: Southern accents, 1986 Mar. -Apr., v.9, no.2, p.70

Hickmann *(German artist, 19th cent.)*   **WC**

Hickok, Conde Wilson *(American artist, op.1850-)*   **WI**

Hickox, Patrick *(American architect)*   **AV**

Hicks, Anne *(British painter, b.1928)*   **BA**
Bibl: Bristol (GBR), Arnolfini Gallery, Bristol sample (1979); ▶Intl. dir. exh. artists, 1982-1983; ▶WW Art

Hicks, David→see Hicks, David Nightingale

Hicks, David Nightingale   **BA**
(British interior decorator, designer, author, b.1929)   BA
(British interior designer)   AV
Bibl: Arch. digest, 1986 May, v.43, no.5, p.127; COUNTRY LIFE CLXVI (July 79) 86-89; 162-165; 232-235; ▶Who's Who [GBR], 1979

Hicks, David   **AV**

Hicks, Edward   **BA GC WC WI**
(American artist, 1780-1849)   WC WI
(American painter, 1780-1849)   BA
(American, 1780-1849)   GC
Bibl: ▶Art Index, Oct. 1941-Sep. 1944, p.401; ▶Artist biog. master idx.; ▶Busse, Maler u. Bildhauer 19. Jahr.; Currier's guide 1645-1945; ▶Witt checklist

Hicks, Frederick *(American artist, 20th c.)*   **BA**
Bibl: Stony Brook, Museums, HIGHLIGHTS OF THE COLLECTION (1982)

Hicks, George→see Hicks, George Elgar

Hicks, George Edgar→see Hicks, George Elgar

Hicks, George Elgar   **BA PR WI**
(British artist, 1824-1914)   WC WI
(British painter, 1824-1914)   BA PR
Bibl: ▶Bénézit; ▶Havlice, Idx. art. bio.; ▶Johnson, Brit. artists; ▶Mallalieu, Brit. watercolour artists; ▶RILA/BHA; ▶Thieme-Becker; ▶Wood, Victorian ptrs.
George Elgar Hicks   PR
Hicks, George   PR
Hicks, George Edgar   **WC**

Hicks, Howard *(British engineer; pioneered the design and build concept, 1915-1989)*   **AV**
Bibl: Building design, 1989 Jan.13, no.919, p.2

Hicks, Jerry *(British painter, b.1927)*   **BA**
Bibl: Bristol (GBR), Arnolfini Gallery, Bristol sample (1979); ▶WW Art, 1977

Hicks, John *(British architect, act.*
1856-1862)   **BA**
  Bibl: ▶Artist biog. master idx.;
  Beatty, TH. HARDY AND THE
  RESTORATION OF ST. PETER'S CH.
  1978; ▶Encyc. Britannica
Hicks, Lilburne   **WC WI**
(British artist, op.1830-, d.1861)   WI
(British artist, op.1830-1861)   WC
  Bibl: ▶Mallalieu, Brit. watercolour
  artists
Hicks, Mary *(American artist, 20th*
c.)   **BA**
  Bibl: ▶Artweek idx.; Los Angeles
  (CA, USA), LAICA, Architectural
  sculp. (1980)
Hicks, Robert   **WC WI**
(British artist, 19th cent.)   WC
(British artist, op.19th c.)   WI
Hicks, Sheila *(American textile artist*
in FRA, b.1934)   **BA**
  Bibl: ▶Art Index, v.34; Kiang, DU
  9 (1985) p.80-81
Hicks, Thomas   **BA PR WC WI**
(American artist, 1823-1890)   WC WI
(American painter, 1823-1890)   BA PR
  Bibl: ▶RILA/BHA; ▶Thieme-Becker;
  ▶WWW Amer., 1967
  Thomas Hicks   PR
Hicks, William Searle *(British*
architect, 1849-1902)   **BA**
  Bibl: ▶Gray, Edwardian arch.,
  p.141
Hidalgo, Maria →see Fontana
  Hidalgo, Maria José
Hidalgo, Maria José Fontana →see
  Fontana Hidalgo, Maria José
Hiddeman →see Hiddeman, Friedrich
  Peter
Hiddeman, Friedrich Peter   **PR**
(German artist, 1829-1892)   WC
(German painter, 1829-1892)   PR
  Bibl: ▶Thieme-Becker
  Friedrich Peter Hiddeman   PR
  Hiddeman   PR
Hiddemann, Friedrich Peter   **PR WC**
Hiddemann, Friedrich Peter →see
  Hiddeman, Friedrich Peter
Hide, Peter *(British sculptor in CAN,*
b.1944)   **BA**
  Bibl: ▶Art Index, Nov. 1973,
  1974; Arts Council GBR,
  Condition of sculp. (1975), p.34;
  Fenton VANGUARD XIII/4/May
  1984, p.15; London (GBR), Marble
  Hill House, Sculp. in landscape
  (1975)
Hidemark, Bengt *(Swedish*
architect, Stockholm)   **AV**
  Bibl: ▶Svenska Ark. Riks., 1984
Hidemarkin, Ove *(Finnish architect)* **AV**
  Bibl: Arkkitehti, 1985, no.2, p.24
Hider, F.   **WC WI**
(British artist, 19th cent.)   WC
(British artist, circa 1861-1933)   WI

Hidley, Joseph H.   **BA GC WC WI**
(American artist, 1830-1872)   WC WI
(American painter, 1830-1872)   BA GC
  Bibl: ▶Art Index, Jan. 1990;
  Garbisch coll., pp.77-81; ▶Groce,
  Artists Amer.; Meyer, Folk artists
  biog. idx.; ▶RILA/BHA; ▶Young,
  Amer. artists
Headley or Hidley, Joseph H.   **WC**
Hidy, Lance *(American printmaker,*
designer, 20th c.)   **BA**
  Bibl: Catonville (Md, USA), Univ.
  od Md., Baltimore Co., Albin O.
  Kuhn Library & Gall., L.H.'S
  POSTERS..., 1983
Hie, G. Le *(French artist, 19th cent.)* **WC**
Hiegel, Hans R. *(German architect,*
1954-)   **AV**
  Bibl: Architecture and urbanism,
  1986 Mar., no.3(186), p.48
Hieger, Simon   **WC WI**
(British artist, 20th cent.)   WC
(British artist, op.20th c.)   WI
Hiels, T.(?) *(Netherlands(?) artist,*
17th/18th cent.)   **WC**
Hielscher, Horst *(West German*
architect, Berlin)   **AV**
  Bibl: Bauwelt, 1987 Aug.28, v.78,
  no.33, p.1197
Hiem, Pham *(Oriental artist, 20th*
cent.)   **WC**
Hiemskirk →see Heemskerck, Egbert
  van (the elder)
Hien, Albert *(West German artist,*
b.1956)   **BA**
  Bibl: ▶Intl. dir. exh. artists, 1983;
  Pohlen, A., in ARTSFORUM
  XXIV/9 (May 1986) 102
Hien, Daniel *(German artist, 1725-*
1773)   **WC**
Hier. Galle →see Galle, Hieronymus (I)
Hiere, Laurent de →see La Hyre,
  Laurent de
Hière, Nicolas →see La Hire, Nicolas
Hierl, Fritz *(German architect,*
Murnau)   **AV**
  Bibl: Detail, 1981 May-June, no.3,
  p.370
Hierl-Deronco, Otto *(German artist,*
1859-1935)   **WC**
Hiernle, Franz Matthias *(German*
sculptor, 1677-1732)   **BA**
  Bibl: Dehio: Hessen;
  ▶Thieme-Becker
Hiernle, Johann Kaspar *(German*
sculptor, 1710-1755)   **BA**
  Bibl: ▶Neue deutsche Biog.;
  ▶Thieme-Becker
Hiernle, Sebastian *(German*
sculptor, 1705-1755)   **BA**
  Bibl: ▶Neue deutsche Biog.;
  ▶Thieme-Becker

Hiernøe, Jens Rasmussen *(Danish*
sculptor, architect, 1748-1801)   **BA**
  Bibl: ▶Portoghesi, Diz. arch. e
  urbanistica; ▶Thieme-Becker; Trap,
  Kongeriget DNK: personalregister;
  ▶Weilbach, Kunst.leks.
Hieron   **GC**
  Bibl: ▶Beazley, Attic red-fig. vase-
  ptrs.
Hieroni *(Polish artist, 1916-)*   **WC**
Hieronymous Bosch →see Bosch,
  Hieronymus (Hieronymus van
  Aken)
Hieronymus Bosch →see Bosch,
  Hieronymus (Hieronymus van
  Aken)
Hieronymus Francken (I) →see
  Francken, Hieronymus I
Hieronymus Galle (I) →see Galle,
  Hieronymus (I)
Hieronymus Hastner →see Hastner,
  Hieronymus
Hieronymus Janssens →see Janssens,
  Hieronymus
Hieronymus van Aken →see Bosch,
  Hieronymus (Hieronymus van
  Aken)
Hieronymus van Kessel →see Kessel,
  Hieronymus van
Hierschl-Minerbi, Joachim van
(Joachim van Hier) *(Austrian*
artist, 1834-)   **WC**
Hierzegger, Heiner *(Austrian*
architect)   **AV**
  Bibl: Bauforum, 1987, v.20, no.
  124, p.63
Hiesmayr, Ernst *(Engineer)*   **AV**
  Bibl: Bauforum, 1984, v.17, no.
  104, p.49
Hietala, Lasse *(Finnish artist, 20th*
cent.)   **WC**
Hietanen, Reino *(Finnish painter,*
b.1932)   **BA**
  Bibl: Arts Council GBR, Scot.
  Comm., 6 Finnish artists (1978);
  ▶Bénézit
Higby, Beecher *(American architect,*
fl. 19th cent)   **AV**
  Bibl: Antiques, 1988 July, v.134,
  no.1, p.130
Higby, Wayne *(American ceramist,*
painter, sculptor, b.1943)   **BA**
  Bibl: ▶Art Index, v.37; ▶Artist
  biog. master idx.; ▶Contemp.
  artists; Hanover (NH, USA),
  Dartmouth College, Contemp.
  clay (1976); ▶Intl. dir. exh. artists,
  1983
Higginbotham *(American*
(commercial), active Dallas, 1923)   **JG**
Higgins   **WC WI**
(British artist, op.1803-)   WI
(British artist, op.c.1803)   WC
Higgins →see Higgins, Victor

Higgins, Charles S., (Pic) WI
   (British artist, 1893-) WC
   (British artist, b.1893) WI
   Bibl: ▶Waters, Brit. artists
Dall, Ian WI
Pic, Charles S. Higgins WC
Higgins, Daniel Paul (12.IX.1886-26
?.XII.1953; Architect, United States
of America) FA
   Bibl: ▶Macmillan encyc. archts.,
   v.2
Higgins, Dick (American artist,
b.1938) BA
   Bibl: ▶Art Index, v.37; ▶Artist
   biog. master idx.; ▶Contemp.
   artists; ▶MoMA libr. cat.; ▶WW
   Amer. Art, 1976
Higgins, Doria (American
psychologist, painter, b.1921) BA
   Bibl: North Bennington (Vt, USA),
   Park-McCullough House
Higgins, Douglas (American painter,
20th c.) BA
   Bibl: ▶Art Index, Jan. 1990; Guide
   exh. artists: N. Amer. ptrs.; Silk,
   G.D., in ARTS MAG LVII/5 (Jan.
   1983) 2
Higgins, Edward Leander
(American architect, 1879-1936) AV
   Bibl: ▶Archts. Maine, v.3, no.6,
   p.1
Higgins, Eugene PR WC WI
   (American artist, 1874-1958) WC WI
   (American painter, 1874-1958) PR
   Bibl: ▶WWW Amer. art
Eugene Higgins PR
Higgins, Hal (British architect) AV
   Bibl: RIBA journal, 1983 July, v.90,
   no.7, p.4
Higgins, J.C. (American, active
Boston, MA, U.S. 1880s and ME,
U.S. 1890s (J.C.) JG
Higgins, Kate Elizabeth, Mrs. → see
   Olver, Kate Elizabeth
Higgins, O.T. (Active Boston, MA,
U.S. 1854-1864, daguerreotypist) JG
Higgins, Sharon (American painter,
20th c.) BA
   Bibl: Lally, H.G., in WOMEN
   ARTISTS NEWS, IX/2 (winter
   1983-84) 24
Higgins, Steve (Canadian sculptor,
20th c.) BA
   Bibl: WAG May 1982
Higgins, Victor BA PR WI
   (American artist, 1884-) WC
   (American artist, 1884-1949) WI
   (American painter, 1884-1949) BA PR
   Bibl: ▶Havlice, Idx. art. bio.; NY
   Times obit.; ▶RILA/BHA;
   ▶Vollmer, Künst.-Lex. 20. Jhr.;
   ▶WWW Amer., 1943
Higgins PR
Higgins, W.Victor WC
Higgins, William Victor WI
Victor Higgins PR

Higgins, W.Victor → see Higgins,
   Victor
Higgins, William Victor → see Higgins,
   Victor
Higginson, Harry Pasley (New
Zealand engineer, bridge designer,
Dunedin, fl. 1880's) AV
   Bibl: Historic places in New
   Zealand, 1987 Dec., no.19, p.12
Higgs, Cecil (South African painter,
b.1900) BA
   Bibl: Cape Town (SA), South
   African National Gallery, CECIL
   HIGGS : OORSIGTENTOONSTILLING
   1975. A RETROSPECTIVE
   EXHIBITION 1975. (1975)
High, Timothy Griffin (American
printmaker, b.1949) BA
   Bibl: ▶Intl. dir. exh. artists; ▶WW
   Amer. Art
Higham, Alice (British textile artist,
b.1929) BA
   Bibl: Oshawa (Ont, CAN),
   McLaughlin Gallery, Christmas:
   another dimension (1980)
Higham, J.W. (British artist, op.
1821-1835) WC WI
   Bibl: ▶Foskett, Brit. miniature ptrs.
Higham, Thomas (British artist,
1796-1844) WC WI
Highmore → see Highmore, Joseph
Highmore, Anthony (British artist,
1719-1799) WC WI
Highmore, J. → see Highmore, Joseph
Highmore, Joseph BA GC PR WC WI
   (British artist, 1692-1780) WC WI
   (British painter, 1692-1780) BA PR
   (British, 1692-1780) GC
   Bibl: ▶Artist biog. master idx.;
   ▶Dict. natl. biog.; ▶Petit Larousse;
   ▶RILA/BHA; ▶Thieme-Becker
Highmore PR
Highmore, J. PR
Joseph Highmore PR
Highmore, Susanna, Miss → see
   Duncombe, Susanna
Highmore, Thomas (English painter,
1660-1720) BA
   Bibl: ▶Dict. natl. biog.;
   ▶Thieme-Becker; ▶Waterhouse,
   Brit. 18c. ptrs.
Highstein, Jene (American sculptor,
painter, b.1942) BA
   Bibl: ▶Art Index; ▶Intl. dir. exh.
   artists, 1983; ▶NY art yrbk.
Highwood, George (British artist,
op.19th c.) WI
Higi, Anton (Swiss architect, Zurich,
1885-1951) AV
   Bibl: ▶Avery period. idx.
Higonnet, Léon (French architect,
act.1883) BA
   Bibl: ▶Jenny, Kunstführer Schweiz,
   v.1; Müller in UNSERE
   KUNSTDENKMÄLER, XXXIII, 4
   (1982) 445-450

Higson, Pirkko (British indoor
garden expert) AV
   Bibl: Architects' journal, 1985
   May 8, v.181, no.19, p.82
Higton → see Higton, T.
Higton, T. (British painter, act. 1801) PR
   Bibl: ▶Thieme-Becker
Higton PR
Higtow PR
T. Higton PR
Higtow → see Higton, T.
Higueras Diaz, Fernando (Spanish
architect) AV
   Bibl: Architecture and urbanism,
   1985 Aug., no.8(179), p.49
Diaz, Fernando Higueras AV
Hiibrer [Unidentified] (Unknown
painter) PR
   Bibl: (July 23, 1803, lot 12,
   Farebrother)
Hijjas bin Kasturi (Malaysian
architect) AV
   Bibl: Pertubuhan Akitek Malaysia,
   1984 membership list, 4
Kasturi, Hijjas bin AV
hijo del Bacan → see Bassano,
   Francesco II (Francesco II da Ponte)
Hikosaka, Yutaka (Japanese
architect, 1952-) AV
   Bibl: Japan architect, 1988 Nov.-
   Dec., v.63, no.11-12, p.20
Hilair → see Hilair, Jean-Baptiste
Hilair, Jean Baptiste → see Hilair, Jean-
   Baptiste
Hilair, Jean-Baptiste BA GC PR
   (French artist, 1753-1822) WC
   (French painter, 1753-aft.
   1822) GC PR
   (French painter, 1753-after
   1822) BA
   Bibl: ▶Bénézit; ▶Busse, Maler u.
   Bildhauer 19. Jahr.; Chicago Art
   Inst. cat.; ▶Dict. biog. fran.; ▶Petit
   Larousse; ▶Thieme-Becker; ▶Witt
   checklist
Hilair PR
Hilair, Jean Baptiste PR WC
Hilaire, Jean-Baptiste GC
Jean Baptiste Hilair PR
Hilaire (Spanish sculptor, carver,
probably born in France, fl. 1519-
1523) AV
   Bibl: ▶Thieme-Becker
Hilario AV
Maestro Hilario AV
Hilaire Hiler → see Hiler, Hilaire
Hilaire, Camille (French artist, 1916-) WC
Hilaire, Jean-Baptiste → see Hilair,
   Jean-Baptiste
Hilarie Germain Edgar Degas → see
   Degas, Edgar
Hilario (French metalworker in ESP,
act.1510-1526) BA
   Bibl: ▶Ars Hispaniae, v.11, p.74;
   Gallego de Miguel, GOYA, 216
   (1990), 322-327; Lozoya, Historia
   del Arte Espánico v.3 (1940) 36;
   ▶Thieme-Becker

Hilario → *see* Hilaire

Hilarión Ibarra, José *(Venezuelan mural painter)*   **AV**
Bibl: Armitano Arte, 1984 Feb., no.7, p.81

Hilberseimer, Ludwig → *see* Hilberseimer, Ludwig Karl

Hilberseimer, Ludwig Karl   AV **BA**
(Architect and city planner, born Karlsruhe, Germany, emigrated to Chicago, 1938, 1885-1967)   AV
(German architect, city planner, critic, 1885-1967)   BA
Bibl: ▶Avery obit. idx.; ▶Libr. of Congr. Name Auth. File; ▶Macmillan encyc. archts.; ▶Portoghesi, Diz. arch. e urbanistica

Hilberseimer, Ludwig   AV

Hilbert, Kamil *(Czech architect, 1869-1933)*   BA
Bibl: ▶Portoghesi, Diz. arch. e urbanistica; ▶Vollmer, Künst.-Lex. 20. Jhr.

Hild, Andreas *(West German architect)*   AV
Bibl: Werk, Bauen + Wohnen, 1988 May, no.5, p.23

Hild, Johann Kaspar *(German painter, 1676-1716)*   GC
Bibl: ▶Thieme-Becker

Hild, Johannes *(in HUN architect, act.1789, d.1811)*   BA
Bibl: ▶Portoghesi, Diz. arch. e urbanistica; ▶Thieme-Becker

Hild, Jósef *(Hungarian architect, 1789-1867)*   BA
Bibl: ▶Portoghesi, Diz. arch. e urbanistica; ▶Thieme-Becker

Hilda Fearon → *see* Fearon, Hilda
Hilda Lucy Milne → *see* Milne, Hilda Lucy

Hilda, E.Baily, Mlle. *(Austrian artist, op.c.1895)*   WC

Hildebert *(German illuminator, 12th c.)*   BA
Bibl: ▶Encyc. world art; Paris (FRA), Musée arts décoratifs, L'Art ancien en CSK; Umeni XXIV-5(1976) p.407

Hildebrand, Adolf Ernst Robert → *see* Hildebrand, Adolf von

Hildebrand, Adolf von   BA GC JG
(German artist, 1847-1921)   WC
(German sculptor, 1847-1921)   GC
(German sculptor, art historian, 1847-1921)   BA
(German, b. Marburg 1847, d. Munich 1921)   JG
Bibl: ▶Encyc. world art; Getty Photo Study Coll. (Sculp.); Knours; ▶RILA/BHA; ▶Thieme-Becker

Hildebrand, Adolf Ernst Robert   WC
Von Hildebrand, Adolf   GC

Hildebrand, Ernst *(Architect)*   **AV**
Bibl: DBZ, 1984 Oct., v.32, no.10, p.1343

Hildebrand, Franz Anton → *see* Hillebrandt, Franz Anton

Hildebrandt, Eduard   GC WC
(German artist, 1818-1869)   WC
(German painter, 1818-1869)   GC
Bibl: ▶Bénézit

Hildebrandt, Ferdinand Theodor   BA GC
(German artist, 1804-1874)   WC
(German painter, 1804-1874)   BA GC
Bibl: ▶Bénézit; ▶Bryan, Ptrs. & engravers; Düsseldorf (DEU), Kunstmus., The Hudson and the Rhine (1976); ▶Thieme-Becker

Hildebrandt, Theodor *(Ferdinand Theodor)*   WC

Hildebrandt, Friedrich Fritz   GC
(German artist, 1819-1855)   WC
(German painter, 1819-1885)   GC
Bibl: ▶Bénézit

Hildebrandt, Fritz   WC
Hildebrandt, Fritz → *see* Hildebrandt, Friedrich Fritz

Hildebrandt, Henry O. *(American architect, Cincinnati, Ohio)*   AV
Bibl: Oculus, 1988 Oct., p.14

Hildebrandt, Jean Lucas von → *see* Hildebrandt, Johann Lucas von

Hildebrandt, Johann Lucas von   AV BA WC
(Austrian architect, 1668-1745)   AV BA
(German artist, 1668-1745)   WC
Bibl: ▶Art Index, v.24; ▶Avery period. idx.; Dehio: Wien (1960); Knaurs: Deutschland; Lex. für Theol. u. Kirche; ▶Macmillan encyc. archts.; Phaidon Austria 1985; Reclams Österreich, I; ▶Thieme-Becker

Hildebrandt, Jean Lucas von   AV

Hildebrandt, Lily *(German painter, 1887-1974)*   PR
Bibl: ▶Caplan, Artists' sigs.; Yale UAG catalogue
Hildebrandt, Lily Uhlmann   PR
Lily Hildebrandt   PR

Hildebrandt, Lily Uhlmann → *see* Hildebrandt, Lily

Hildebrandt, Theodor (Ferdinand Theodor) → *see* Hildebrandt, Ferdinand Theodor

Hildegardus, Master → *see* Master Hilgardus

Hildenbrand, Adolf *(German painter, printmaker, enamelist, 1881-1944)*   BA
Bibl: ▶Thieme-Becker; ▶Vollmer, Künst.-Lex. 20. Jhr.

Hilder, J.J. *(Australian artist, 1881-1916)*   WC

Hilder, P. John   WI
(British artist, 1811-1839)   WC WI

Hilder, P.John   WC
Hilder, P.John → *see* Hilder, P. John

Hilder, Richard H. *(British artist, 1813-1852)*   WC WI

Hilder, Rowland   WC WI
(British artist, 1905-)   WC
(British artist, b.1905)   WI

Hildesheim Group *(vase-painters, ca. 450-400 BC)*   GC
Bibl: ▶Beazley, Attic bl.-fig. vase-ptrs.; Boardman, Attic Bl.-fig. Vases

Hilditch, George *(British artist, 1803-1857)*   WC WI

Hilditch, Richard H. *(British artist, op.1823-1865)*   WI

Hildner, Jeffrey S. *(American architect, Princeton, NJ)*   AV
Bibl: ▶AIA Pro File, 1985

Hildrew, George *(American painter, 20th c.)*   BA

Hileken *(French porcelain painter, act.1769-1774)*   GC
Bibl: ▶Brunet, Sèvres

Hiler → *see* Hiler, Hilaire

Hiler, Hilaire *(American painter, 1898-1966)*   PR
Bibl: ▶WWW Amer. art
Hilaire Hiler   PR
Hiler   PR

Hilf, Rainer *(German interior design architect, Nurnberg)*   AV
Bibl: Architektur, Innenarchitektur, Technischer Ausbau, v.92, no.6, 1984, p.54

Hilfgatt, Brand Christian → *see* Brand, Christian Hilfgott

Hilfiker, Hans   AV BA
(Swiss engineer, 1901-)   AV
(Swiss engineer, designer, b.1901)   BA
Bibl: Archithese, 1986 May-June, v.15, no.3, p.12

Hilgardus, Master → *see* Master Hilgardus

Hilgemann, Ewerdt *(German sculptor in NLD, b.1938)*   BA
Bibl: ▶Art Index, v.22; Guide exh. artists: N. Amer. ptrs.; ▶Intl. dir. exh. artists, 1982; ▶MoMA libr. cat.

Hilgenhurst, Charles G. *(American architect, 1929?-1980)*   AV
Bibl: ▶AIA Pro File, 1985

Hilger, Charles *(American artist, b.1938)*   BA
Bibl: Sacramento (CA, USA), Crocker Art Museum, Paper/art (1981)

Hilger, Wilfred *(German architect, Wiesbaden)*   AV
Bibl: Architektur, Innenarchitektur, technischer Ausbau, 1984 Mar., v.92, no.2, p.50

Hilgers, Carl   GC WC
(German artist, 1818-1890)   WC
(German painter, 1818-1890)   GC
Bibl: ▶Thieme-Becker

Hilgert, Ludvík — AV
Hilker, Georg Christian *(Danish painter, 1807-1875)* — BA
Hill *(American, active Brooklyn, NY, U.S.)* — JG
Hill → see Hill, Andrew Putnam
Hill → see Hill, Thomas
Hill, Adrian Keith Graham — WC WI
  (British artist, 1895-) — WC
  (British artist, 1895-1977) — WI
    Bibl: ▶Johnson, Brit. artists
Hill, Albert Henry *(American architect, 1913?-1985)* — AV
    Bibl: Architecture: the AIA journal, 1985 Apr., v.74, no.4, p.34,39
Hill, Amelia Robertson — WI
  (British artist, 1820-1904) — WI
  (British artist, op.1863-p.1891) — WC
Hill, Amelia Robertson, (nee Paton) — WC
  Paton, Amelia Robertson, Miss — WI
Hill, Amelia Robertson, (nee Paton) → see Hill, Amelia Robertson
Hill, Andrew P. → see Hill, Andrew Putnam
Hill, Andrew Putnam *(American painter, act. 1867-1922)* — PR
    Bibl: ▶Dawdy, Artists Amer. West
  Andrew Putnam Hill — PR
  Hill — PR
  Hill, Andrew P. — PR
Hill, Anthony — BA WC WI
  (British artist, 1930-) — WC
  (British artist, b.1930) — WI
  (British painter, b.1930) — BA
Hill, Arthur — WC WI
  (British artist, circa 1830-op. 1893) — WI
  (British artist, op.1858-1893) — WC
Hill, Carl Frederik → see Hill, Carl Fredrik
Hill, Carl Fredrik — BA GC
  (Scandinavian, 1849-1911) — GC
  (Swedish artist, 1849-1911) — WC
  (Swedish painter, 1849-1911) — BA
    Bibl: ▶Thieme-Becker
Hill, Carl Frederik — WC
Hill, Charles Christopher *(American collagist, painter, b.1948)* — BA
    Bibl: ▶Art Index, v.26; ARTS MAG, 50 (Jan 1976) p.23; CONNAISSANCE DES ARTS, 295 (Sept 1976) p.95; ▶Intl. dir. exh. artists, 1983; ▶WW Amer. Art, 1989
Hill, Chris — BA WI
  (British artist, 20th c.) — BA
  (British artist, op.20th c.) — WI
    Bibl: Morgan, S., in STUDIO INTERNATIONAL, CXCVI/1001 (Aug 1983) 40
Hill, Clinton J. *(American painter, printmaker, b.1922)* — BA

Hill, David Octavius — BA GC JG WC WI
  (British artist, 1802-1870) — WC WI
  (British painter, photographer, 1802-1870) — BA
  (Scottish draughtsman, 1802-1870) — GC
  (Scottish, 1802-1870 (also David Octavius Hill and Robert Adamson)) — JG
    Bibl: ▶Bénézit; ▶Encyc. world art; ▶Gernsheim, Hist. photog.; ▶Newhall, Photog.
Hill, Derek — BA WC WI
  (British artist, 1916-) — WC
  (British artist, b.1916) — WI
  (British painter, stage designer, b.1916) — BA
    Bibl: ▶Art Index, v.26; WW Amer., 1988; ▶WW Art
Hill, Diana — WI
  (British artist, op.1785) — WC
  (British artist, op.1785-) — WI
  Dietz, Diana, Miss — WI
Hill, Diana, (nee Dietz) — WC
Hill, Diana, (nee Dietz) → see Hill, Diana
Hill, Draper *(American cartoonist, b.1935)* — BA
    Bibl: WW Amer.; ▶WW Amer. Art
Hill, Ed *(American photographer, draftsman, b.1935)* — BA
Hill, Edward *(American painter, 1843-1923)* — PR
    Bibl: ▶Hughes, Artists California
  Edward Hill — PR
Hill, Edward Rufus *(American artist, 1852-1908)* — WI
Hill, Ellen G. *(British artist, op.1864-1893)* — WI
Hill, Friedrich Jakob *(German artist, 1758-1846)* — WC
Hill, Gary *(American video artist, sculptor, b.1951)* — BA
Hill, Gillian *(Canadian painter, printmaker, 20th c.)* — BA
Hill, Howard — WC WI
  (American artist, op.1860) — WC
  (American artist, op.1860-1877) — WI
Hill, I. *(Engraver)* — WI
Hill, Ira L. *(American, active NY, U.S. early 20th century (Ira L. Hill Studio))* — JG
Hill, J. *(British artist, op.19th c.)* — WI
    Bibl: ▶Foskett, Brit. miniature ptrs.
Hill, J. G. *(British architect)* — AV
    Bibl: Architects' journal, 1980 Sept.24, v.172, no.39, p.576
Hill, James G. *(1814-19.XII.1913; Architect, United States of America)* — FA
    Bibl: ▶Lowry, Building natl. image; ▶Withey, Amer. archts., p.287
Hill, James Jerome *(American filmmaker, 1905-1972)* — BA
Hill, James John *(British artist, 1811-1882)* — WC WI

Hill, James R. *(American performance artist, b.1945)* — BA
    Bibl: ▶Art Index, v.27; Artweek (March 10, 1979); ▶Intl. dir. exh. artists; New York (NY, USA), New Mus., Outside NY (1978); Tallahassee (FL, USA), FSU, Art Gallery, 4 Houston Artists (1978)
Hill, James Stevens *(British artist, 1854-1921)* — WC WI
    Bibl: ▶Johnson, Brit. artists
Hill, Jockey — WC WI
  (British artist, 1753-1795) — WI
  (British artist, 1753-p.1795) — WC
Hill, Joe *(British master craftsman of dry-stone walls)* — AV
    Bibl: World of interiors, 1989 Apr., p.37
Hill, John — BA WC WI
  (British artist, 1770-1850) — WC WI
  (British printmaker in USA, 1770-1850) — BA
  (Engraver, 1770-1850) — WI
Hill, John I — WI
Hill, John Henry — BA WC WI
  (American artist, 1839-1922) — WC WI
  (American painter, printmaker, 1839-1922) — BA
Hill, John I → see Hill, John
Hill, John II *(British artist, op.1970-)* — WI
Hill, John William — BA WC WI
  (American artist, 1812-1879) — WI
  (American painter, 1812-1879) — BA
  (British artist, 1812-1879) — WC
Hill, Kate E. *(British artist, op.1895-1898)* — WI
Hill, L.M., Miss *(British artist, 1886-1895)* — WI
Hill, Nathaniel *(British artist, 1861-1934)* — WI
    Bibl: ▶Johnson, Brit. artists
Hill, Norman — WC WI
  (British artist, 19th cent.) — WC
  (British artist, op.19th c.) — WI
Hill, Oliver *(British architect, 1887-1968)* — AV BA
    Bibl: ▶Libr. of Congr. Name Auth. File; RIBA journal, 1968 June, v.75, p.279 [dates]
Hill, Pamela *(American artist, 1803-1860)* — WC WI
Hill, Pati *(American artist, 20th c.)* — BA
Hill, Robert — WC WI
  (British artist, op.1750) — WC
  (British artist, op.1750-) — WI
Hill, Robert W. *(British artist, op. 20th c.)* — WI
Hill, Robin — BA WC WI
  (Australian painter, illustrator, b.1932) — BA
  (British artist, 20th cent.) — WC
  (British artist, op.20th c.) — WI
Hill, Roderic *(British artist, b.1944)* — WI
Hill, Rowland H. → see Hill, Rowland Henry

Hill, Rowland Henry   **WI**
  (British artist, 1873-)   WC
  (British artist, 1873-1952)   WI
Hill, Rowland H.   **WC**
Hill, S. (British artist, op.18th c.)   **WI**
  Bibl: ▶Waterhouse, Brit. 18c. ptrs.
Hill, Samuel   **WC WI**
  (American artist, op.1789-
   1803)   WC WI
  (Engraver, Boston, MA., op.
   1789-1803)   WI
Hill, Stuart (British sculptor, b.1943) **BA**
Hill, T. (British artist, op.1839)   **WC**
Hill, Thomas   **BA GC PR WC**
  (American artist, 1829-1908) WC WI
  (American painter, 1829-
   1908)   BA GC PR
  Bibl: ▶RILA/BHA
  Hill   PR
Hill, Thomas, (USA.)   **WI**
  Thomas Hill   PR
Hill, Thomas → see Hill, Thomas,
  (GBR.)
Hill, Thomas, (GBR.)   **WI**
  (British artist, 1661-1734)   WC WI
Hill, Thomas   **WC**
Hill, Thomas, (USA.) → see Hill,
  Thomas
Hill, Vernon   **BA WC WI**
  (British artist, 1887-)   WC
  (British artist, b.1887)   WI
  (British sculptor, printmaker,
   b.1887)   BA
Hill, Walter Guy (British artist, op.
  20th c.)   **WI**
Hill, William (American politician,
  iron manufacturer, 1741-1816)   **BA**
  Bibl: Cowan, Jrnl. of Early
   Southern Dec. Arts XIII (Nov
   1987), 1-31; ▶Dict. Amer. biog.;
   ▶WWW Amer.
Hill, William (British artist, op.19th
  c.)   **WI**
  Bibl: Paviere, Landscape
Hill-Montgomery, Candace
  (American painter, sculptor,
  photographer, b.1945)   **BA**
  Bibl: ▶Art Index, v.31; ▶Intl. dir.
   exh. artists, 1983; New York (NY,
   USA), New Mus, CANDACE HILL-
   MONTGOMERY (1982)
Hillairet, Anatole-Eugene (French
  artist, 19th cent.)   **WC**
Hillblom, Henrik (American artist,
  1863-1928)   **WI**
Hille, Henrik (Norwegian architect)   **AV**
  Bibl: Architects' journal, 1988
   Nov.9, p.38
Hille, Hubertus van (Dutch painter,
  b.1903)   **BA**
Hille, Werner H. (West German
  architect, Arnsberg)   **AV**
  Bibl: ▶Bund Deut. Arch. Hdbch.,
   1987

Hilleberghe or Hulleberghe(?),
  Antoine van → see Hilleberghe,
  Antoine van
Hilleberghe, Antoine van   **GC**
  (Netherlandish painter, act.
   1552-1556)   GC
  (Netherlands artist, op.1552-
   1556)   WC
  Bibl: ▶Thieme-Becker
Hilleberghe or Hulleberghe(?),
  Antoine van   **WC**
  Hulleberghe   GC
Hillebrand, Elmar (German sculptor,
  b.1925)   **BA**
  Bibl: Hofmann, KOLNER
   DOMBLATT, LIII (1988), p. 195-
   198; ▶Wer ist wer, 1989
Hillebrand, Franz Anton → see
  Hillebrandt, Franz Anton
Hillebrand, Lucy   **AV BA**
  (German architect, 20th c.)   BA
  (West German architect, author)   AV
  Bibl: ▶Avery period. idx., 6th
   suppl.; Daidalos 15 (15 Mar.
   1985)
Hillebrandt, Franz Anton (Austrian
  architect, 1719-1797)   **AV BA**
  Bibl: ▶Encyc. world art
  Hildebrand, Franz Anton   AV
  Hillebrand, Franz Anton   AV
Hillebrandt, Master (German artist,
  op.1528)   **WC**
Hillebrecht, Rudolf (German
  architect, 1910-)   **AV**
  Bibl: Bauwelt, 1987 Dec.23, v.78,
   no.48. p.1804
Hillegaert → see Hillegaert, Pauwels I
  van
Hillegaert or Hilligaert, Pauwels, I
  van → see Hillegaert, Pauwels I van
Hillegaert, Pauwels I van   **BA GC**
  (Dutch artist, 1595/6-1640)   WC
  (Dutch painter,
   1595/96-1640)   BA GC PR
  Bibl: Getty Photo Study Coll.;
   ▶Thieme-Becker
  Hillegaert   PR
Hillegaert or Hilligaert, Pauwels,
  I van   **WC**
Hillegaert, Pauwels van (I)   **PR**
  Paulus Hillegaert   PR
  Pauwels van Hillegaert (I)   PR
  Pauwls van Hillegaert   PR
  Pouwlus Hillegart   PR
Hillegaert, Pauwels II van (Dutch
  draughtsman, 1631-1658)   **GC**
  Bibl: ▶Bénézit
Hillegaert, Pauwels van (I) → see
  Hillegaert, Pauwels I van
Hillemacher, Ernest (Eugene
  Ernest) (French artist, 1818-1887) **WC**

Hillenbrand, Uta (W. German
  architectural student, Darmstadt) **AV**
  Bibl: Architektur,
   Innenarchitektur, Technischer
   Ausbau, 1986 Nov., v.94, no.11,
   p.46
Hiller von Gaertringen, Johann
  Christian (German, 20th c.)   **BA**
Hiller, Anton (German sculptor,
  b.1893)   **BA**
Hiller, H. (German artist, op.1865-
  1894)   **WC**
Hiller, Karol (Polish painter,
  printmaker, 1891-1939)   **BA**
Hiller, Susan   **BA WI**
  (American artist in GBR, b.1940) BA
  (British artist, b.1940)   WI
  Bibl: ▶Art Index, v.34, v.36;
   ▶Artist biog. master idx.;
   ▶Dolman, Contemp. Brit. artists;
   Guide exh. artists: Sculp.
Hillerns, Hero Dietrich (German
  architect, 1807-1885)   **BA**
Hillers, John K.   **BA JG**
  (American (b. Germany), 1843-
   1925)   JG
  (American photographer, 1843-
   1925)   BA
Hillestrom the Elder, Per (Swedish
  artist, 1732-1816)   **WC**
Hilleveld, Adrianus David   **GC WC**
  (Dutch artist, 1836-)   WC
  (Dutch painter, 1838-ca.1869?)   GC
  Bibl: ▶Thieme-Becker
Hillfon, Maria (Swedish weaver,
  printmaker, painter, b.1945)   **BA**
  Bibl: ▶Intl. dir. exh. artists, 1983;
   Nationalmus. Bull., I/3 (1977) pp.
   103-113
Hillhouse, May (South African
  painter, printmaker, b.1908)   **BA**
Hilliard → see Hilliard, Nicholas
Hilliard, John   **BA WC WI**
  (British artist, 20th cent.)   WC
  (British artist, b.1945)   WI
  (British artist, photographer,
   b.1945)   BA
Hilliard, Laurence   **BA WC WI**
  (British artist, 1581-1582-1647-
   1648)   WI
  (British artist, c.1581-p.1640)   WC
  (English miniaturist, goldsmith,
   ca.1581-1640)   BA
  Bibl: Thames & Hudson Brit. art

Himmel, Richard *(American designer)*   **AV**
    Bibl: Interior design, 1986 Feb., v.57, no.2, p.186

Himmel, Scott *(American architect, interior designer)*   **AV**
    Bibl: ▶AIA Pro File, 1987-88

Himmelfarb, John   **BA WI**
    (American artist, b.1946)   **WI**
    (American painter, printmaker, b.1946)   **BA**
    Bibl: Guide exh. artists: N. Amer. ptrs.; ▶Intl. dir. exh. artists, 1982; ▶WW Amer. Art

Himmelsbach, Emil *(Active Switzerland 1930s)*   **JG**

Himpel, Aarnout ter   **GC PR WC**
    (Dutch artist, 1634-1686)   **WC**
    (Dutch draughtsman, 1634-1686)   **GC**
    (Dutch painter, 1634-1686)   **PR**
    Bibl: ▶Bénézit; Getty Photo Study Coll.; ▶Thieme-Becker; ▶Witt checklist
    Aarnout ter Himpel   **PR**
    Ten Himpel   **PR**
    Ter Himpel   **PR**
    Ter Himpel, Aarnout   **GC**

Hims [Unidentified] *(Unknown painter)*   **PR**
    Bibl: (April 6, 1815, lot 46, Hoggart and Phillips)

Hinchcliffe, Richard George   **WC WI**
    (British artist, 1868-)   **WC**
    (British artist, 1868-1942)   **WI**

Hinchey, William J.   **BA WC WI**
    (American artist, 1829-1893)   **WC WI**
    (American painter, illustrator, 1829-1893)   **BA**

Hinckley, Robert *(American artist, 1853-1941)*   **WI**

Hinckley, Thomas Hewer→see Hinckley, Thomas Hewes

Hinckley, Thomas Hewes   **PR WI**
    (American artist, 1813-1896)   **WC WI**
    (American painter, 1813-1896)   **PR**
    Bibl: ▶Fielding's Amer. ptrs., 1986

Hinckley, Thomas Hewer   **WC**
    Thomas Hewes Hinckley   **PR**

Hincks, William   **WC WI**
    (British artist, 1752-1797)   **WI**
    (British artist, op.1773-1788)   **WC**

Hind, Arthur Mayger   **WI**
    (British artist, 1880-1957)   **WC WI**
    Bibl: ▶Johnson, Brit. artists

Hind, Arthur N.   **WC**

Hind, Arthur N.→see Hind, Arthur Mayger

Hind, Frank *(British artist, op.1884-1904)*   **WI**

Hind, R. *(British artist, op.19th c.)*   **WI**

Hind, William→see Hind, William George Richardson

Hind, William George Richardson   **BA**
    (Canadian artist, op.1862)   **WC**
    (Canadian painter, 1833-1889)   **BA**
    Bibl: ▶Artist biog. master idx.; ▶Artists Canada; Canad. encyc.; ▶Harper, Ptg. Canada; ▶Havlice, Idx. art. bio.

Hind, William   **WC**

Hinde, Jean *(British artist, op.20th c.)*   **WI**

Hindenlang, Charles *(Swiss artist, 1894-1960)*   **WC**

Hinder, Frank   **GC WC**
    (Australian artist, 1906-)   **WC**
    (British, b.1906)   **GC**
    Bibl: ▶Witt checklist

Hindley, Frank *(French architect, Paris)*   **AV**
    Bibl: ▶Annuaire archts. fran., 1978

Hindley, Godfrey C.   **WC WI**
    (British artist, op.1876-1903)   **WC**
    (British artist, op.1876-1914)   **WI**

Hindorf, Heinz *(Artist)*   **AV**
    Bibl: Das Münster, 1984, v.37, no.2, p.128

Hinds, George A.   **AV BA**
    (American architect, 1922-)   **AV**
    (American architect, b.1922)   **BA**

Hine, F.S. *(Engraver)*   **WI**

Hine, Harry T.   **WI**
    (British artist, 1845-1941)   **WI**
    (British artist, op.1887-1892)   **WC**

Hime, Harry   **WC**

Hine, Harry, Mrs., (Victoria Susanna)→see Colkett, Victoria Susanna

Hine, Henry George *(British artist, 1811-1895)*   **WC WI**

Hine, Lewis Wickes   **BA JG**
    (American photographer, 1874-1940)   **BA**
    (American, 1874-1940)   **JG**

Hine, Thomas Chambers   **AV BA**
    (1853-1899)   **AV**
    (British architect, ca.1813-1899)   **BA**

Hines, Francis *(American sculptor, 20th c.)*   **BA**
    Bibl: ▶Art Index, v.29; ▶Intl. dir. exh. artists, 1982; NY TIMES (28 May 1979) p.B1

Hines, Frederick   **WC WI**
    (British artist, op.1875-1897)   **WI**
    (British artist, op.1875-97)   **WC**

Hines, Gerald *(American real estate developer)*   **AV**
    Bibl: Metropolis, 1987 Mar., v.6, no.7, p.38

Hines, Gladys   **BA WI**
    (British artist, 19th-20th cs.)   **BA**
    (British artist, op.1922-)   **WI**
    Bibl: Anscombe, Omega & after

Hines, Theodore *(British artist, op. 1876-1889)*   **WC WI**

Hines, Thomas S. *(American architect and author)*   **AV**

Hingeland, Pieter van *(Dutch artist, 17th cent.)*   **WC**

Hingston, David *(American architect, Portland, Me)*   **AV**
    Bibl: Landmarks observer, 1986 Sept.-Oct., v.13, no.5, p.16

Hingston, James *(British landscape architect and teacher, York, d. 1988)*   **AV**
    Bibl: Annual report of the York Georgian Society, 1988, p.12

Hinkle→see Hinkle, Clarence K.

Hinkle, Clarence→see Hinkle, Clarence K.

Hinkle, Clarence K.   **PR WI**
    (American artist, 1880-1960)   **WI**
    (American painter, 1880-1960)   **PR**
    Bibl: ▶WWW Amer. art
    Clarence K. Hinkle   **PR**
    Hinkle   **PR**
    Hinkle, Clarence   **PR**

Hinman, Charles→see Hinman, Charles B.

Hinman, Charles B.   **BA WI**
    (American artist, 20th cent.)   **WC**
    (American artist, b.1932)   **WI**
    (American painter, sculptor, b.1932)   **BA**

Hinman, Charles   **WC**

Hinnerk, Joachim→see Wrage, Hinrich

Hinrichsen, Helen Johnson *(American painter, 20th c.)*   **BA**

Hinrichsen, Lorens Vilhelm *(Danish artist, 1865-p.1900)*   **WC**

Hinrichsmeyer, Ulrich *(West German architect)*   **AV**
    Bibl: Japan architect, 1988 Feb., v.63, no.2(370), p.61

Hinrick Levenstede→see Levenstede, Hinrick

Hins(?), D. *(Netherlands(?) artist, op. 1758)*   **WC**

Hinschelwood, Robert→see Hinshelwood, Robert

Hinshelwood, Robert *(Engraver, 1812-circa 1875)*   **WI**
    Hinschelwood, Robert   **WI**

Hinslow, Phil *(British artist, op.20th c.)*   **WI**

Hinterreiter, Hans *(Swiss painter, b.1902)*   **BA**

Hinterwirth, Gerhart *(Austrian architect)*   **AV**
    Bibl: Bauforum, 1988, v.21, no. 126, p.57

Hinton, Alfred *(American artist, 20th c.)*   **BA**
    Bibl: Chavis, 10 Michigan Afro-Amer. artists

Hinton, Alfred Horsley   **BA JG**
    (British photographer, 1863-1908)   **BA**
    (British, 1863-1908)   **JG**

Hinton, Kem Gardner *(American architect, Nashville, TN)*   **AV**
  Bibl: ▶AIA Pro File, 1987-88

Hintz, Julius *(German artist, 1805-1862)*   **WC**

Hintz, Skip *(American architect, Los Angeles)*   **AV**
  Bibl: L.A. architect, 1987 Jan., p.10

Hintze, Heinrich (Johann Heinrich)→see Hintze, Johann Heinrich

Hintze, Jedrzej (Andreas) *(Polish artist, op.1814-1826)*   **WC**

Hintze, Johann Heinrich   **BA GC**
  (German artist, 1800-a.1862)   **WC**
  (German painter, 1800-ca. 1862)   **BA GC**
  Bibl: ▶Bénézit

Hintze, Heinrich (Johann Heinrich)   **WC**

Hinz, Georg   **BA**
  (German artist, op.1666-1700)   **WC**
  (German painter, act.1666-1700)   **BA GC**
  Bibl: ▶Bénézit; Frese, WELTKUNST, 58/7(1989). 1045-1047; George Goldner; Getty Photo Study Coll.; Getty Photo Study Coll. (Ptgs.); ▶Havlice, Idx. art. bio.; Hentzen, HAMBURGER KUNSTHALLE(1969); ▶Schweers, Gemälde deut. Museen; ▶Thieme-Becker; ▶Witt checklist

  Hainz, Georg   **GC**

Hainz, Heintz, Hinz or Hintzsch, Georg (Johann Georg)   **WC**
  Hainz, Johann Georg   **GC**

Hinz, Johann Georg   **GC**

Hinz, Gerhard *(E. German city planner, Stralsund)*   **AV**
  Bibl: Architektur der DDR, 1986 Dec., v.35, no.12, p.745

Hinz, Gerrit *(Netherlands artist, 17th cent.(?))*   **WC**
Hinz, Johann Georg→see Hinz, Georg
Hiob Berckheyde→see Berckheyde, Job Adriaensz.

Hiolle, Ernest Eugène *(French sculptor, 1834-1886)*   **BA**

Hioolen, Cornelia (Cornelia Baumann Hioolen) *(Dutch artist, 1885-)*   **WC**

Hiorne, David *(British architect, d.1758)*   **BA**
  Bibl: ▶Colvin, Brit. archts.; ▶Macmillan encyc. archts.; RIBA Idx. archts.

Hiorne, Francis *(English architect, 1744-1789)*   **BA**
  Bibl: ▶Colvin, Brit. archts.; Pelican Hist. of Art; ▶Thieme-Becker

Hiorne, William *(British architect, ca.1712-1776)*   **BA**
  Bibl: ▶Colvin, Brit. archts.; ▶Macmillan encyc. archts.

Hipkins, Edith J.   **WC WI**
  (British artist, 19th cent.)   **WC**
  (British artist, op.1879-1911)   **WI**

Hipolite or Hyppolite, Auguste *(French artist, op.1799-1845)*   **WC**
Hipolite, Auguste→see Desbuissons, Joseph Auguste (Auguste Hipolite)

Hippacontist Painter   **GC**
  Bibl: ▶Beazley, Attic red-fig. vase-ptrs.

Hippius, Gustave Adolf *(Russian artist, 1792-1856)*   **WC**

Hippocamp Group *(South Italian vase-painters, 350-300 BC)*   **GC**
  Bibl: McPhee & Trendall, Fish-Plates

Hippocamp Painter *(Etruscan vase-painter)*   **GC**
  Bibl: ▶Szilagyi, Etruszko-korinthosi

Hippocamp Painter   **GC JG**
  (South Italian vase-painter, 350-300 BC)   **GC**
  Bibl: McPhee & Trendall, Fish-Plates

Hippocrates *(Greek, 4th century B.C.)*   **JG**

Hippodamos of Miletos *(Greek city planner, 5th c BC)*   **GC**
  Bibl: ▶Bowder, WWW Greek, p.124

Hippolyta Master→see Binasco, Francesco

Hippolyte Bellange→see Bellangé, Joseph-Louis-Hippolyte

Hippolyte Painter *(Apulian vase-painter)*   **GC**
  Bibl: Trendall, Attic red-fig. vases Apulia

Hippolyte Petitjean→see Petitjean, Hippolyte

Hippolyte Scarsellin→see Scarsellino (Ippolito Scarsella)

Hippolyte-Jean Flandrin→see Flandrin, Hippolyte-Jean

Hippolyte-Lucas, Marie Félix   **GC**
  (French artist, 1854-1925)   **WC**
  (French painter, 1854-1925)   **GC**
  Bibl: ▶Bénézit

  Lucas, Hippolyte Felix Marie   **WC**

Hipwell, W.   **WC WI**
  (British artist, 19th cent.)   **WC**
  (British artist, op.19th c.)   **WI**

Hirakura, Naoko *(Japanese architect, 1950-)*   **AV**
  Bibl: Japan architect, 1988 Nov.-Dec., v.63, no.11-12, p.64

Hiral, J. *(American architect)*   **AV**
  Bibl: Iowa architect, 1985 Summer, v.33, no.3, p.12

Hiram Reynolds Bloomer→see Bloomer, Hiram Reynolds

Hirayama, Akiyoshi *(Japanese architect, 1947-)*   **AV**
  Bibl: Kenchiku bunka, 1987 Dec., v.42, no.494, p.240

Hirche, Bernhard *(German architect)*   **AV**
  Bibl: Kunst und Kirche, 1985, no.1, p.33

Hirche, Herbert   **AV BA**
  (German architect, designer, b.1910)   **BA**
  (West German architect, designer and professor)   **AV**
  Bibl: Der Architekt, 1988 May, no.5, p.332; ▶Wer ist wer

Hird, Robert *(British shoemaker, author, 1768-1841)*   **BA**
  Bibl: COUNTRY LIFE, 4,11,18 Mar 1971; Lewis, L., COLLECTANEA HISTORICA: ESSAYS IN MEMORY OF STUART RIGOLD

Hire, Brian *(American lighting designer)*   **AV**
  Bibl: Architectural lighting, 1988 June, v.2, no.6, p.20

Hirémy-Hirschl, Adolph *(Hungarian painter, 1860-1933)*   **BA**
  Bibl: ▶Österr. biog. Lex. 1815-1950; ▶Thieme-Becker; ▶Vollmer, Künst.-Lex. 20. Jhr.

Hirmer, Max *(German photographer and publisher, b.1893)*   **GC**
  Bibl: ▶Libr. of Congr. Name Auth. File

Hirmer, Verlag   **GC**
  Bibl: Getty Photo Study Coll.

Hirn, Jean Georges *(French painter, 1777-1839)*   **GC**
  Bibl: ▶Thieme-Becker

Hiro (Yasuhiro Wakabayashi) *(American photographer, b.1930)*   **BA**
  Bibl: ▶Hall-Duncan, Fashion photog.; ▶Parry, Photo idx.

Hirose, Kenji *(Japanese architect, 1922-)*   **AV**
  Bibl: Kenchiku bunka, 1987 Dec., v.42, no.494, p.242

Hiroshige   **BA**
  (Japanese artist, 1797-1858)   **AV**
  (Japanese printmaker, 1797-1858)   **BA**
  Bibl: ▶Bénézit; Dict. univ. peinture; ▶Encyc. world art; ▶Libr. of Congr. Name Auth. File; NY. MMA. Pr Dept. GREAT WAVE; ▶Oxford comp. art; Paine, Art & arch. Japan; RLIN BKS file, DCLC862257-b; ▶Thieme-Becker; Williams Coll. Libr.

Andō, Hiroshige   **AV**

Hirsch, Alphonse *(French artist, 1843-1884)*   **WC**

Hirsch, Auguste Alexandre *(French artist, 1833-1912)*   **WC**

Hirsch, Gilah Yelin *(American painter, b.1944)*   **BA**
  Bibl: ▶WW Amer. Art

Hirsch, Howard *(American interior designer)*   **AV**
  Bibl: Interior design, 1986 Dec., v.57, no.12, p.160

Hirsch, J.M.(?)→see Hirsch, Joseph M.

Hirsch, Joseph   **BA WC WI**
  (American artist, 1910)   WC
  (American artist, 1910-1981)   WI
  (American painter, 1910-1981)   BA
  Bibl: ▶Cummings, Contemp.
    Amer. artists; NY Times 22 Sept
    1981
Hirsch, Joseph M.   **WI**
  (American artist, op.1908)   WC
  (American artist, op.1908-)   WI
   Hirsch, J.M.(?)   **WC**
Hirsch, Karl Georg (German
  printmaker, b.1938)   BA
  Bibl: Altenburg (DEU), Staat.
    Lindenau-Mus., Etching &
    engraving (1979); Arta, 28/4-5
    (Apr-May 1980) 58-76
Hirsch, Sanford (American sculptor,
  b.1951)   BA
  Bibl: Muncie (IN, USA), Ball State
    University, Art Gallery, SANFORD
    HIRSCH..., 1985, 8
Hirsch, Stefan   **BA PR WI**
  (American artist, 1899-1964)   WI
  (American painter, 1899-1964)   BA PR
  Bibl: ▶Bénézit; ▶MoMA libr. cat.;
    ▶RILA/BHA
  Stefan Hirsch   PR
Hirsch, Ursula (German artist, 1929-) **WC**
Hirschberg, Martin (Canadian
  sculptor, b.1937)   BA
  Bibl: ▶Artists Canada; ▶Natl. Gall.
    Canada libr. cat.; New Brunswick
    (NJ, USA), Rutgers U., Response
    to the environment (1975)
Hirsche, Herbert Lee (American
  painter, sculptor, b.1927)   BA
Hirschegger-Ramser, Franz
  (Austrian architect)   AV
  Bibl: ▶Verzeich. Öst. Ziviltech.
Hirscheli or Hirschely, Caspar
  (German artist, 1698-1743)   WC
Hirschenberg, Samuel (Polish artist,
  1865-1908)   WC
Hirscher, Heinz E. (German artist,
  1927-)   WC
Hirschfeld, Emil Benediktoff
  (Russian artist, 1867-1922)   WC
Hirschfelder, Salomon (German
  artist, 1832-1903)   WC
Hirschfield, Alan (American
  architect)   AV
  Bibl: Cite: a publication of the
    Rice Design Alliance, 1985-1986,
    p.17
Hirschfield, James (American artist,
  20th c.)   BA
  Bibl: ▶Art Index; Artweek JA 31
    '81, p.16; Vanguard, X/8 (Oct.
    1981) pp.10-15
Hirschfield, Morris → see Hirshfield,
  Morris
Hirschhorn, Engelhard I von
  (German, d.1361)   BA
  Bibl: ZEIT. D. DEUT. VER. F.
    KUNSTW., XXXII, 1978

Hirschmann, Johann Baptist
  (German artist, 1770-p.1821)   **WC**
Hirschmann, Johann Leonhard
  (German artist, 1672-1750)   **WC**
Hirschmann, Thomas   **BA WC**
  (German artist, op.1670-1691)   WC
  (German printmaker, act.1670-
    1691)   BA
  Bibl: ▶Hollstein, German, v.13a;
    ▶Thieme-Becker, v.27; ▶Witt
    checklist
Hirschnaer, J. (German artist, op.
  1764)   **WC**
Hirschsprung, Pauline (Danish,
  1845-1912)   **BA**
  Bibl: København (DNK),
    Hirschsprung samlung, Danske
    Kunstneres Arbejder (1957)
Hirschvogel the Elder, Veit → see
  Hirschvogel, Veit (the Elder)
Hirschvogel, Augustin   **BA GC**
  (German artist, 1503-1553)   WC
  (German printmaker, glass
    painter, medalist,
    cartographer, 1503-1553)   BA
  (German, 1503-1553)   GC
  Bibl: ▶Allgem. Deut. Biog.;
    ▶Brockhaus Enzyk.; ▶Forrer,
    Medallists; ▶Hollstein, German;
    ▶Neue deutsche Biog.;
    ▶Thieme-Becker
Hirschvogel, Hirsfogel or
  Hirsvogel, Augustin   **WC**
  Hirsfogel, Augustin   BA
  Hirsvogel, Augustin   BA
Hirschvogel, Hirsfogel or Hirsvogel,
  Augustin → see Hirschvogel,
  Augustin
Hirschvogel, Veit (the Elder)   **GC**
  (German artist, 1461-1525)   WC
  (German draughtsman, 1461-
    1525)   GC
  Bibl: ▶Bénézit
Hirschvogel the Elder, Veit   **WC**
Hirschvogel, Veit, the younger
  (German glass painter, 1485-1553)   BA
  Bibl: ▶Bénézit; ▶Thieme-Becker
Hirsfogel, Augustin → see Hirschvogel,
  Augustin
Hirsh, Hy (American, d. 1961)   **JG**
Hirshen, Sanford (American
  architect and educator)   **AV**
  Bibl: ▶AIA Pro File, 1983
Hirshfield, Morris   **BA WI**
  (American artist, 1872-1946)   WC WI
  (American painter, 1872-1946)   BA
  Bibl: ▶Bénézit; Dict. mod. ptg.;
    ▶Jakovsky, Peintres naïfs;
    ▶Kindlers Malerei Lex.; ▶MoMA
    libr. cat.
  Hirschfield, Morris   **WC**
Hirshfield, Pearl (American sculptor,
  painter, 20th c.)   **BA**
  Bibl: LEONARDO, XVIII/3 (1985)
    153-153 (sic); ▶WW Amer. Art

Hirsig, Horst (German painter,
  b.1929)   **BA**
  Bibl: Berlin. Staatliche Museen.
    Nationalgalerie.Horst Hirsig,
    Ursula Sax, Gerd van Dülmen
    1974
Hirst, Brian (British surveyor;
  Director of land and buildings for
  Warwickshire Co. Council)   **AV**
  Bibl: Building, 1988 June 26,
    v.253, no.26, p.36
Hirst, Claude Raguet   **WI**
  (American artist, 1855-1942)   WC WI
  Fitler, William Crothers, Mrs.,
    (Claude Raguet)   WI
  Hirst, Claude Raquet   **WC**
Hirst, Claude Raquet → see Hirst,
  Claude Raguet
Hirst, Derek   **BA WC WI**
  (British artist, 20th cent.)   WC
  (British artist, b.1930)   BA
  (British artist, op.20th c.)   WI
  Bibl: London (GBR), Tate Gallery,
    Series (1977); ▶MoMA libr. cat.
Hirst, Peter (Australian architect,
  1940-)   **AV**
Hirst, Philip E.D. (British architect,
  20th c.)   **BA**
  Bibl: London (GBR), Building Ctr.,
    Brit. arch. (1982)
Hirst, T. J. (British architect)   **AV**
  Bibl: Architects' journal, 1988
    May 25, v.187, no.21, p.59
Hirst, William (British artist, op.
  1766-1783)   **WC WI**
Hirsvogel, Augustin → see
  Hirschvogel, Augustin
Hirt, Aloys Ludwig (German
  archaeologist, author, 1759-1837) **AV**
  Bibl: ▶Thieme-Becker
Hirt, Donna Rae (American
  printmaker, b.1946)   **BA**
  Bibl: Art News, Vol. 76, Mar
    1977, p.116; Boston (MA, USA),
    MFA, New England Works on
    Paper (1976-77)
Hirt, Friedrich Christoph (German
  painter, 1685-1763)   **GC**
  Bibl: ▶Thieme-Becker
Hirt, Friedrich Wilhelm   **GC**
  (German artist, 1721-1772)   WC
  (German painter, 1721-1772)   GC
  Bibl: ▶Thieme-Becker
  Hirt, Wilhelm Friedrich   **WC**
Hirt, Joseph Conrad (German artist,
  op.1673-1687)   **WC**
Hirt, M.G. (German artist, op.1748)   **WC**
Hirt, Michael Conrad (German,
  1615-aft.1694)   **GC**
  Bibl: ▶Thieme-Becker
Hirt, Wilhelm Friedrich → see Hirt,
  Friedrich Wilhelm
Hirth du Frênes, Rudolf   **BA WC**
  (German artist, 1846-1916)   WC
  (German painter, 1846-1916)   BA
  Bibl: ▶Neue deutsche Biog.;
    ▶Thieme-Becker

Hirtz, Hans *(German artist, op.1558-m.a.1582)* **WC**

Hirzel, Heinrich *(Swiss artist, 1729-1790)* **WC**

Hirzel, Susette (Ott) *(Swiss artist, 1769-1858)* **WC**

Hirzel, William *(American potter, b.1856)* **BA**

His, Andreas *(Swiss painter, b.1928)* **BA**
Bibl: ▶Lex. zeitgen. Schweiz. Künstler

His, Rene Charles Edmond *(French artist, 1877-)* **WC**

Hisaka, Don M. *(American architect)* **AV**
Bibl: ▶AIA Pro File, 1983

Hischbein or Hichsbein *(German artist, op.1762)* **WC**

Hischylos **GC JG**
Bibl: ▶Beazley, Attic red-fig. vase-ptrs.

Hischylos Painter *(vase-painter, ca. 530-500 BC)* **GC**
Bibl: ▶Beazley, Attic red-fig. vase-ptrs.; Richter, Attic red-fig. vases

Hisey, Sunnye H. *(American architect)* **AV**

Hiski, Jean Charles *(French architect, act.1749)* **BA**
Bibl: Cahiers alsaciens XXIV '81 169-175

Hislop, Andrew Healey *(British artist, 1887-1954)* **WI**

Hislop, Margaret Ross *(British artist, 1894-1972)* **WI**
Grant, Margaret Ross **WI**

Hislop, Walter Balmer **WC WI**
(British artist, 19th cent.) **WC**
(British artist, op.1912-, d.1915) **WI**

Hispalense→see Hispalense, Juan

Hispalense, Juan **BA PR**
(Spanish artist, op.c.1420) **WC**
(Spanish painter, 15th c.) **BA**
(Spanish painter, act. 15th century) **PR**
Bibl: ▶Encyc. world art; ▶RILA/BHA
Hispalense **PR**
Juan Hispalense **PR**
Juan Hispalense or Hispalensis **WC**
Sevilla, Juan de **PR**

Hispano Dutch Master *(Hispanic, 15th century)* **GC**
Bibl: Washington (DC, USA), Natl. Gall. cat.

Histed, Ernest Walter *(American (b. England, UK), 1860-1947)* **JG**

Hita, Miguel de *(Spanish mason, act.1533-1538)* **BA**
Bibl: Estella, Arch. esp. de arte, LVIII/229 (Jan-Mar 1985) 58-65

Hitch, Stewart *(American painter, b.1940)* **BA**
Bibl: ARTFORUM XVIII/1 Sept 1979, p.49-53; Ithaca (NY, USA), Cornell Univ., Johnson Mus. of Art, Ptg. up front (1981)

Hitchcock, Alfred Joseph *(British film director, 1899-1980)* **BA**
Bibl: ▶Who was who [GBR]; ▶WWW Amer., v.7

Hitchcock, Charlotte *(American architect)* **AV**
Bibl: ▶Architecture: the AIA journal, 1985 Oct., v.74, no.10, p.18

Hitchcock, George **BA WC WI**
(American artist, 1850-1913) **WC WI**
(American painter, illustrator, 1850-1913) **BA**
Bibl: ▶Bénézit; Dayton (OH, USA), Amer. expatriate ptrs. (1976); ▶Fielding's Amer. ptrs.; ▶WWW Amer., 1897

Hitchcock, Harold **WC WI**
(American artist, 20th cent.) **WC**
(American artist, b.1914) **WI**

Hitchcock, John Thomas *(1812-1846)* **AV**

Hitchcock, Lambert *(American cabinetmaker, 1795-1852)* **BA**
Bibl: ▶Penguin dec. arts; ▶Savage, Ceramics

Hitchcock, Lucius Wolcott **WC WI**
(American artist, 1868-) **WC**
(American artist, 1868-1942) **WI**

Hitchcock, Malcolm *(British artist, op.20th c.)* **WI**

Hitchcock, Miriam *(American painter, b.1953)* **BA**
Bibl: Waltham (MA, USA), Brandeis Univ., Rose Art Museum, Ardent Gestures (1985)

Hitchcock, Ray *(American sculptor, b.1937)* **BA**

Hitchens→see Hitchens, Ivon

Hitchens, Ivon **BA PR WC WI**
(British artist, 1893-) **WC**
(British artist, 1893-1979) **WI**
(British painter, b. 1893) **PR**
(British painter, b.1893) **BA**
Bibl: ▶Encyc. world art; ▶Fogg Mus. Libr. cat.; Mc-Graw; ▶RILA/BHA; ▶Vollmer, Künst.-Lex. 20. Jhr.; ▶Who was who [GBR], 1971-80; ▶Who's Who [GBR], 1975; ▶WW Art
Hitchens **PR**
Ivon Hitchens **PR**

Hitchmough, Colin *(British painter, b.1943)* **BA**
Bibl: UC Santa Barbara cat. sheets

Hite, Eleanor *(American sculptor, 20th century)* **GC**
Bibl: Juley coll., NMAA

Hittorf, Jacques Ignace→see Hittorff, Jacques Ignace

Hittorf, Jakob Ignaz→see Hittorff, Jacques Ignace

Hittorff, Jacob Ignaz→see Hittorff, Jacques Ignace

Hittorff, Jacques Ignace **BA**
(French architect, 1792-1867) **BA**
(German architect in France, 1792-1867) **AV**
(German artist, 1792-1867) **WC**
(German draughtsman, 1792-1867) **GC**
Bibl: ▶Larousse grande encyc.; ▶Macmillan encyc. archts.; ▶Oudin, Dict. architectes; ▶Thieme-Becker; ▶WW Arch.
Hittorf, Jacques Ignace **AV**
Hittorf, Jakob Ignaz **GC WC**
Hittorf, Jacob Ignaz **AV**

Hitz, Conrad *(Swiss artist, 1798-1866)* **WC**

Hitz, Dora **GC WC**
(German artist, 1856-p.1891) **WC**
(German painter, 1856-1924) **GC**
Bibl: ▶Thieme-Becker

Hitzelberger, Johann Georg *(German architect, 1714-1792)* **BA**
Bibl: Hitchcock, Rococo arch. So. Germany, p.250 (J.G. Hitzelsberger); Jahrb. des Hist. Vereins Dillingen LXXXV (1983) 213-239 (Johann Georg Hitzelberger, 1714-92)

Hitzig, Friedrich *(German architect, 1811-1881)* **BA**
Bibl: ▶Brockhaus Enzyk.; ▶Neue deutsche Biog.

Hitzl, Franz de Paula *(Austrian sculptor, 1738-1819)* **BA**
Bibl: ▶Österr. biog. Lex. 1815-1950; ▶Thieme-Becker

Hitzler, Franz *(West German painter, b.1946)* **BA**
Bibl: Munich (BRD), Stadtische Galerie im Lenbachhaus, FRANZ HITZLER, 1979

Hix, John *(Canadian architect)* **AV**
Bibl: Canadian architect, 1984 Dec., v.29, no.12, p.36

Hixon, R. **WC WI**
(British artist, op.1813) **WC**
(British artist, op.1813-) **WI**

Hixon, William J. *(British artist, op. 1825-1857)* **WI**

Hižinskij, Leonid Semenovič *(Russian illustrator, b.1896)* **BA**
Bibl: ▶Natl. union cat., pre-1956

Hjelholt, Berit *(Finnish weaver weaver in DNK, b.1920)* **BA**
Bibl: ▶Dansk kunst. leks.; Lium, CRASI,48(1987)pp.40-48

Hjerten, Sigrid (Grunewald)→see Hjertén, Sigrid Maria

Hjertén, Sigrid Maria **BA**
(Swedish artist, 1885-1948) **WC**
(Swedish painter, 1885-1948) **BA**
Bibl: ▶Svenskt konst.-lex.; ▶Vollmer, Künst.-Lex. 20. Jhr.; ▶Witt checklist

Hjerten, Sigrid (Grunewald) **WC**

Hjertholm, Helge *(Scandinavian architect)* **AV**
    Bibl: Byggekunst, 1984, v.66, no.7, p.348
Hjort, Bror → see Hjorth, Bror
Hjorth Nielsen, Søren **BA**
    (Danish artist, 1901-) **WC**
    (Danish painter, printmaker, b.1901) **BA**
    Nielsen, Soren Hjorth **WC**
Hjorth, Brer → see Hjorth, Bror
Hjorth, Bror **GC**
    (Scandinavian artist, op.1958) **WC**
    (Swedish draughtsman and sculptor, b.1894) **GC**
    Bibl: ▶Bénézit; Gernsheim, Corpus Photog. of Drawings
    Hjort, Bror **WC**
    Hjorth, Brer **GC**
Hjorth, Ragnar *(Swedish architect, 1887-)* **AV**
    Bibl: ▶Libr. of Congr. Name Auth. File
Hjorth, Vagn *(Danish architect, Charlottenlund, 1936-)* **AV**
    Bibl: ▶Danske Arkitekters Landsforbund, 1984-85
Hjortzberg, Olle (Gustav Olaf)
    (Swedish artist, 1872-p.1929) **WC**
Hlamov, V. *(Russian photographer, 19th c.)* **BA**
Hlavacek, Anton (Avlov?) *(German artist, op.1842)* **WC**
Hlaváček, Karel *(Czech poet, painter, printmaker, 1874-1898)* **BA**
Hlavács, Károly *(Hungarian architect)* **AV**
    Bibl: Architektur + Wettbewerbe, 1986 Dec., no.128, p.19
Hlaweniczka, Kurt *(Austrian architect, Vienna)* **AV**
    Bibl: Planen Bauen Wohnen, 1986, no.115, p.11
Hlebnikova, Vera Vladimirovna *(Russian painter, 1891-1941)* **BA**
Hložník, Ferdinand *(Czech painter, printmaker, b.1921)* **BA**
Hložník, Vincent *(Czech painter, printmaker, b.1919)* **BA**
Hnens → see Huens [Unidentified]
Hník, Jaromir *(Czech designer(?), Prague)* **AV**
    Bibl: Bauwelt, 1987 Apr.24, v.78, no.16, p.584
Hnizdovsky, Jacques **BA**
    (American painter, printmaker, b.1915) **BA**
    (Czech artist, op.1915) **WC**
    Hnizdovsky, Yakiv **WC**
Hnizdovsky, Yakiv → see Hnizdovsky, Jacques
Ho bein → see Holbein, Hans, the younger
Ho Vecelli (Son of Titian) → see Vecellio, Orazio

Ho, Angela *(Chinese sculptor in USA, 20th c.)* **BA**
    Bibl: ▶Intl. dir. exh. artists, 1982
Ho, Francis *(American photographer, b.1938)* **BA**
Ho, Kar Hwa *(British architect)* **AV**
    Bibl: AA files 1986 Spring, no.11, p.93
Ho, Mui *(American(?) architect, Calif)* **AV**
    Bibl: Architecture, the AIA journal, 1983 Oct., v.72, no.10, p.60
Ho, Tao *(British architect, 1936-)* **AV**
    Bibl: ▶Contemp. archts.
Hoadley, David *(American architect, 1774-1839)* **BA**
Hoadley, Peter *(British artist, b.circa 1700)* **WI**
Hoadly, Sarah → see Hoadly, Sarah Curtis
Hoadly, Sarah Curtis **BA**
    (British artist, 1676-1742-1743) **WI**
    (British artist, op.1700-m.1743) **WC**
    (English painter, d.1743) **BA**
    Bibl: ▶Dict. natl. biog.; ▶Thieme-Becker
    Curtis, Sarah, Miss **WI**
    Hoadly, Sarah **WI**
    Hoadly, Sarah, (nee Curtis) **WC**
Hoadly, Sarah, (nee Curtis) → see Hoadly, Sarah Curtis
Hoagland, John *(American photographer, 1947-1984)* **BA**
    Bibl: AFTERIMAGE, XII (summer 1984), 7 (obit); ▶Art Index, v.32
Hoak, Edward Warren **AV**
Hoar, Frank **WC WI**
    (British artist, 1898-op.1989) **WI**
    (British artist, 20th cent.) **WC**
Hoare → see Hoare, William
Hoare of Bath → see Hoare, William
Hoare, Alda *(British, 1861-1947)* **BA**
    Bibl: NATL. TRUST STUDIES (1979) 99-111
Hoare, George T. *(British artist, 1888-1895)* **WI**
Hoare, Henry *(British amateur garden designer, 1705-1785)* **AV**
    Bibl: Garden design, 1986 Autumn, v.5, no.3, p.54
Hoare, Mary *(British artist, circa 1753-1820)* **WI**
Hoare, Peter Richard **WC WI**
    (British artist, 1772-1849) **WI**
    (British artist, 18th cent.) **WC**

Hoare, Prince **BA WC WI**
    (British artist, 1755-1834) **WC WI**
    (British painter, author, 1755-1834) **BA**
    (British, 1755-1834) **GC**
    Bibl: ▶Dict. natl. biog.; ▶Fisher, Watercolour ptrs.; ▶Mallalieu, Brit. watercolour artists; ▶Natl. union cat., pre-1956; ▶Thieme-Becker; ▶Waterhouse, Brit. 18c. ptrs.; ▶Witt checklist
    Hoare, Prince II **GC**
Hoare, Prince I *(British, 1707-1792)* **GC**
    Bibl: ▶Dict. natl. biog.; ▶Thieme-Becker
Hoare, Prince II → see Hoare, Prince
Hoare, Richard Colt, baronet **BA**
    (British antiquary, draftsman, 1758-1838) **BA**
    (British artist, 1758-1838) **WC WI**
    Bibl: ▶Dict. natl. biog.; ▶Redgrave, Engl. school; ▶Thieme-Becker
    Hoare, Richard Colt, Sir **WI**
    Hoare, Sir Richard Colt **WC**
Hoare, Richard Colt, Sir → see Hoare, Richard Colt, baronet
Hoare, Sir Richard Colt → see Hoare, Richard Colt, baronet
Hoare, William **BA GC PR**
    (British artist, 1706-1799) **WC WI**
    (British painter, 1707-1792) **PR**
    (British painter, ca.1707-1792) **BA**
    (British, ca.1707-1799) **GC**
    Bibl: ▶Dict. natl. biog.; ▶Redgrave, Engl. school; ▶RILA/BHA; ▶Thieme-Becker; ▶Witt checklist; ▶Yale Brit. artists list
    Hoare **PR**
    Hoare of Bath **PR**
    Hoare, William (Hoare of Bath) **WC**
    Hoare, William, (of Bath) **WI**
    William Hoare **PR**
Hoare, William (Hoare of Bath) → see Hoare, William
Hoare, William J. K. *(American landscape architect)* **AV**
    Bibl: Garden design, 1986 Autumn, v.5, no.3, p.77
Hoare, William, (of Bath) → see Hoare, William
Hoban, James **AV BA FA**
    (American architect and builder, 1762-1831) **AV**
    (American architect, 1762-1831) **BA**
    (ca. 1756-2.XII.1821; Architect, District of Columbia, Philadelphia, South Carolina) **FA**
    Bibl: ▶Withey, Amer. archts., p.291; ▶WWW Amer.
Hobart → see Hobart, Clark
Hobart Painter **GC**
    Bibl: ▶Beazley, Attic red-fig. vase-ptrs.

Hobart, Clark (American painter, ca.
1870-1928) **PR**
    Bibl: De Young Mus. cat.; ▶WWW
    Amer. art
    Clark Hobart **PR**
    Hobart **PR**
Hobart, John R. (British artist, op.
1823-1839) **WI**
Hobbeheydar, Christine (British
photographer, b.1948) **BA**
    Bibl: Arts Council GBR, 3
    perspectives photography (1979)
Hobbema →see Hobbema, Meindert
Hobbema, Meindert **BA GC JG PR**
    (Dutch artist, 1638-1709) **WC**
    (Dutch painter and
        draughtsman, 1638-1709) **GC**
    (Dutch painter, 1638-1709) **BA PR**
    (Dutch, 1638-1709) **JG**
    Bibl: (November 3, 1812, lot 320,
    Halse); ▶Encyc. world art;
    ▶RILA/BHA; ▶Thieme-Becker;
    ▶Wurzbach, NLD Künst.-Lex.
    After Hobbima **PR**
    Habbima **PR**
    Hobbema **PR**
    Hobbema, Meyndert **PR**
Hobbema, Meyndert Lubbertsz **WC**
    Hobbima **PR**
    Hobbimer **PR**
    Hobbimma **PR**
    Hobbina **PR**
    Hobbyme **PR**
    Hobdoma **PR**
    Hobema **PR**
    Hobima **PR**
    Holbimer **PR**
    Holbina **PR**
    M. Hobbema **PR**
    M. Hobbima **PR**
    Meindert Hobbema **PR**
    Minderhoot Hobima **PR**
    Minderhout Hobbima **PR**
Hobbema, Meyndert →see Hobbema,
    Meindert
Hobbema, Meyndert Lubbertsz →see
    Hobbema, Meindert
Hobbes, Isaac H. (American
architect, act.ca.1868) **BA**
    Bibl: Carnegie mag., LVI/3 (May-
    Jun. 1982) pp.6-9
Hobbima →see Hobbema, Meindert
Hobbimer →see Hobbema, Meindert
Hobbimma →see Hobbema, Meindert
Hobbina →see Hobbema, Meindert
Hobbing, Edzard (German sculptor,
1909-1974) **BA**
    Bibl: Riedl. EDZARD HOBBING-
    SMALL BRONZES...; ▶Vollmer,
    Künst.-Lex. 20. Jhr.
Hobble Group (vase-painters, ca.
350 BC) **GC**
    Bibl: ▶Beazley, Attic bl.-fig. vase-
    ptrs.

Hobbs, Frederick H. (American
architect, 1909-1985) **AV**
    Bibl: ▶Amer. archts. dir.;
    Architecture: the AIA journal,
    1985 Sept., v.74, no.9, p.168
Hobbs, George T. →see Hobbs,
    George Thompson
Hobbs, George Thompson **WI**
    (American artist, 1846-) **WC**
    (American artist, b.1846) **WI**
    Hobbs, George T. **WC**
Hobbs, Jean (British artist, op.20th
c.) **WI**
Hobbs, Joe Ferrell (American artist,
20th c.) **BA**
    Bibl: ART NEWS, V. 72, May
    1973, p.45; ARTS MAGAZINE,
    v.47, Mar 1973, p.51; Fort Worth
    (TX, USA), Art Museum, Great
    Amer. rodeo (1976)
Hobbs, Peter **WC WI**
    (British artist, 1930-) **WC**
    (British artist, b.1930) **WI**
Hobbs, R.E., Capt. (British artist, op.
1804-) **WI**
Hobbs, Richard (American architect,
Seattle, WA) **AV**
    Bibl: ▶AIA Pro File, 1987-88
Hobbyme →see Hobbema, Meindert
Hobday, William Armfield (British
artist, 1771-1831) **WC WI**
Hobden, Frank **WC WI**
    (British artist, op.1879-1930) **WI**
    (British artist, op.c.1879-c.1930) **WC**
Hobdoma →see Hobbema, Meindert
Hobema →see Hobbema, Meindert
Hobima →see Hobbema, Meindert
Hobley, Edward G. →see Hobley,
    Edward George
Hobley, Edward George **WI**
    (British artist, 1866-1916) **WI**
    (British artist, op.1893-1916) **WC**
    Hobley, Edward G. **WC**
Hobrecht, James L. **AV**
Hobson, Alice Mary (British artist,
1860-1954) **WI**
Hobson, Anthony (British artist, op.
20th c.) **WI**
Hobson, Cecil J. →see Hobson, Cecil
    James
Hobson, Cecil James **WI**
    (British artist, 1874-1915) **WI**
    (British artist, 19th cent.) **WC**
    Bibl: ▶Johnson, Brit. artists
    Hobson, Cecil J. **WC**
Hobson, Diana (American
printmaker, b.1942) **BA**
    Bibl: Long Beach (CA, USA), CSU,
    Black dolphin prints (1978)
Hobson, Henry E. (British artist, op.
1857-1866) **WC WI**
Hobson, Henry I (British artist,
b.1814) **WI**
Hobson, Jonathan Scott (British
architect, Beverly, N. Humberside) **AV**
    Bibl: ▶RIBA members, 1987

Hobson, Katherine →see Hobson,
    Katherine Thayer
Hobson, Katherine Thayer
(American sculptor, 1889-1982) **GC**
    Bibl: Getty Photo Study Coll.;
    ▶Opitz, Amer. sculptors
    Hobson, Katherine **GC**
    Hobson-Kraus, Mrs. **GC**
Hobson, Kenneth **WC WI**
    (British artist, 1897-) **WC**
    (British artist, b.1897) **WI**
Hobson, Mabel Emily, Miss →see
    Hankey, Mabel Emily
Hobson-Kraus, Mrs. →see Hobson,
    Katherine Thayer
Hoc, Giovanni [Unidentified]
    (Unknown painter) **PR**
    Bibl: Lumaga inventory, Naples,
    102
    Giovanni Hoc **PR**
Hoch, Friedrich (Georg Friedrich)
(German artist, 1751-1812) **WC**
Höch, Hannah **BA JG WC**
    (German artist, 1889-) **WC**
    (German artist, 1889-1978) **BA**
    (German, b. 1889) **JG**
    Bibl: Hannover (DEU), Kestner
    Gesellschaft, DADA:
    PHOTOGRAPHIE UND
    PHOTOCOLLAGE, 1979, p.167
Hoch, Johann Jacob **BA**
    (German artist, 1750-1829) **WC**
    (German draughtsman, 1750-
        1829) **GC**
    (German painter, 1750-1829) **BA**
    Bibl: Reber, H., in STUDIEN ZUM
    EUROPAISCHEN
    KUNSTHANDWERK... (1983) 266;
    ▶Thieme-Becker; ▶Witt checklist
Hoch, Johann Jakob **GC WC**
Hoch, Johann Jakob →see Hoch,
    Johann Jacob
Hoch, Kate (German artist, 20th
cent.) **WC**
Hochard, Gaston (French artist,
1863-1913) **WC**
Hochecker, Franz (German painter,
1730-1782) **GC**
    Bibl: ▶Bénézit
Hochfeld or Hocfeld, Cristoph
(German artist, op.1728-1767) **WC**
Hochfeld, Ernst (German architect,
fl. 1920's) **AV**
    Bibl: Archis, 1988 Dec., no.12,
    p.4
Hochhausen, William (American
sculptor, 20th c.) **BA**
    Bibl: Arts Magazine Apr 1973,
    p.82; Arts Magazine OCt 1977,
    p.17
Hochl, Anton (German artist, 1820-
1897) **WC**
Hochmann, Franz Gustav (German
artist, 1861) **WC**
Hochstetter, Sebastian (Austrian,
active ca. 1540-1569) **JG**

Hock, Johann (German)   GC
  Bibl: Gernsheim, Corpus Photog.
    of Drawings, 1427
Hock, Louis (American artist, 20th
  c.)   BA
  Bibl: ▶Art Index, v.36;
    Freudenheim, Artforum,
    XXVI/155; Marks, Afterimage, XV
    (Apr. 1988) p.3; Seld, ARTWEEK
    (10 Oct. 1987), 8-9
Hock-Aun, Teh (British painter,
  b.1949)   BA
Höckelmann, Antonius (West
  German sculptor, painter, b.1937)   BA
  Bibl: ▶DuMonts Künst.-Lex.; ▶WW
    Arts DEU
Höcker, Paul   BA
  (German artist, 1854-1910)   WC
  (German painter, 1854-1910)   BA GC
  Bibl: ▶Busse, Maler u. Bildhauer
    19. Jahr.; Ludwig, H., in
    WELTKUNST, LIV/8 (15 Apr 1984)
    1115; ▶Thieme-Becker
  Hoecker, Paul   GC WC
Höckert, Johan Fredrik   BA WC
  (Swedish artist, 1826-1866)   WC
  (Swedish painter, 1826-1866)   BA
  Bibl: ▶Svenskt konst.-lex.;
    ▶Thieme-Becker; ▶Witt checklist
Höckert, Joseph (Swedish
  cabinetmaker, act.1799-1829)   BA
  Bibl: Nationalmuseum Bull. II/2
    (1978) 62
Hocking, Ralph (American artist,
  20th c.)   BA
  Bibl: Furlong, L., in ART JOURNAL
    XLV/3 (fall 1985) 233
Höckner, Johann Caspar (German
  printmaker, 1629-ca.1670)   BA
  Bibl: ▶Hollstein, German, v.13a;
    ▶Thieme-Becker, v.17
Hockney, David   AV BA WC WI
  (Artist)   AV
  (British artist, 1937-)   WC
  (British artist, b.1937)   WI
  (British painter, printmaker,
    photographer, collagist,
    b.1937)   BA
  Bibl: ▶Babington Smith, Contemp.
    artists; ▶Bénézit; ▶Contemp.
    artists; ▶Intl. dir. exh. artists;
    ▶Libr. of Congr. Name Auth. File;
    ▶MoMA libr. cat.; ▶Oxford comp.
    20c. art
Hod, Edmund (German artist, 19th
  cent.)   WC
Hodasevič, Valentina Mihajlovna
  (Russian painter, scenographer,
  1894-1970)   BA
  Bibl: DEK. ISKUST. SSSR, 264 (Nov
    1979) 34-37
Hode, Pierre (French artist, 1899-
  1942)   WC
Hodé, René (French architect, 1811-
  1874)   BA
  Bibl: Ann. artistes fran., 1860-61;
    Paris, Hôtel Sully, L'OEUVRE DE
    RENÉ HODÉ..., 1976

Hodeckgeest → see Houckgeest,
  Gerard
Hodes, Fran (American artist, 20th
  c.)   BA
  Bibl: Brooklyn (NY, USA), Brooklyn
    Mus., Woman's Place (1982)
Hodge, Francis Edwin (British artist,
  1883-1949)   WC WI
Hodge, Maureen (British artist,
  b.1941)   BA
  Bibl: Arts Council GBR, Scot.
    Comm., Small tapestries (1976)
Hodge, Simon Prince (British artist,
  b.1903)   WI
  Bibl: ▶Waters, Brit. artists
Hodges → see Hodges, William
Hodges, C.M.   WC WI
  (British artist, 1858-1916)   WI
  (British artist, 19th cent.)   WC
Hodges, Charles H. → see Hodges,
  Charles Howard
Hodges, Charles Howard   BA WC WI
  (British artist, 1764-1837)   WC WI
  (British painter, printmaker in
    NLD, 1764-1837)   BA
  (Engraver)   WI
  Bibl: ▶Dict. natl. biog.; Feltz, A.C.
    A.W. van der, CHARLES HOWARD
    HODGES... (1837); ▶Scheen, Ned.
    beeldende kunst.; ▶Thieme-Becker
Hodges, Charles H.   WI
Hodges, R. A. → see Hodges, William
Hodges, R.A. → see Hodges, William
Hodges, Sidney   WI
  (British artist, 1829-1900)   WC WI
Hodges, Sidney (J.S. Willis)   WC
  Willis, J.S.   WI
Hodges, Sidney (J.S. Willis) → see
  Hodges, Sidney
Hodges, Theo (British interior
  designer, London)   AV
  Bibl: The world of interiors, 1989
    Feb., p.108
Hodges, Walter Parry (British artist,
  1760-1845)   WC WI
Hodges, William   BA GC PR WC WI
  (British artist, 1744-1797)   WC WI
  (British painter, 1744-1797)   PR
  (British painter, printmaker,
    1744-1797)   BA
  (British, 1744-1797)   GC
  Bibl: ▶Bénézit; ▶Redgrave, Engl.
    school; ▶RILA/BHA;
    ▶Thieme-Becker; ▶Witt checklist
  Hodges   PR
  Hodges, R. A.   PR
  Hodges, R.A.   PR
  J. Hodges, Esq. R.A.   PR
  S. Hodges, Esq. R.A.   PR
  W. Hodges   PR
  W. Hodges, Esq. R.A.   PR
  William Hodges   PR
Hodges, William Merrett (British
  artist, op.1891-1961)   WI

Hodgeson, William (Canadian
  builder and designer, Ottawa, fl.
  1883)   AV
  Bibl: ARQ: Architecture/Quebec,
    1989 Apr., no.48, p.38
Hodgetts, Craig (American
  architect, 1937-)   AV
  Bibl: Institute for Architecture and
    Urban Studies. Catalogue, n.18,
    1982, p.104
Hodgetts, Emily   WC WI
  (British artist, op.1820)   WC
  (British artist, op.1820-)   WI
Hodgins, Henry   WC WI
  (British artist, op.1760-, d.1796)   WI
  (British artist, op.1760-m.1796)   WC
Hodgins, William (American interior
  designer)   AV
  Bibl: Architectural digest, 1983
    May, v.40, no.5
Hodgkin, C. Eliot   WC WI
  (British artist, 1905-)   WC
  (British artist, b.1905)   WI
Hodgkin, Howard   AV BA WC WI
  (British artist, 1932-)   WC
  (British artist, b.1932)   WI
  (British designer, painter, 1932-)   AV
  (British painter, b.1932)   BA
  Bibl: ▶Bénézit; ▶Libr. of Congr.
    Name Auth. File; ▶Who's Who
    [GBR], 1976
Hodgkin, Jonathan Edward (British
  artist, 1875-1953)   WC WI
  Bibl: ▶Waters, Brit. artists
Hodgkins, E.M. (British, act.1909-
  1911)   BA
  Bibl: ▶Natl. union cat., pre-1956
Hodgkins, Frances   BA WC WI
  (British artist, 1870-1947)   WI
  (British artist, 1871-1947)   WC
  (British painter, designer, 1869-
    1947)   BA
  Bibl: ▶Bénézit; dd McCormick,
    E.H., Portrait of Frances Hodgkins,
    1981; ▶Johnson, Brit. artists;
    ▶Libr. of Congr. Name Auth. File;
    ▶Vollmer, Künst.-Lex. 20. Jhr.;
    ▶Waters, Brit. artists
Hodgkins, Thomas F.   WC WI
  (British artist, -1903)   WC
  (British artist, op.1803-, d.1903)   WI
Hodgkins, William, Mathew (New
  Zealand artist, 1833-1898)   WC
Hodgkinson, Edward A. (Canadian
  painter, 20th c.)   BA
  Bibl: ▶Artists Canada; Windsor
    (Ont, CND), Art Gallery of W.,
    Hodgkinson/Meanwell (1977)
Hodgkinson, Frank   GC WC
  (Australian artist, 1919-)   WC
  (British, b.1913)   GC
  Bibl: ▶Witt checklist
Hodgkinson, John   WC WI
  (British artist, 1883-)   WC
  (British artist, b.1883)   WI

Hodgkinson, Patrick (*British architect*)   **AV**
   Bibl: AA files, 1989 Spring, no.17, p.112

Hodgkinson, Peter   **AV BA**
  (*British architect and author, head of design in office of Taller de Arquitectura, Barcelona*)   **AV**
  (*in ESP architect, b.1940*)   **BA**
   Bibl: ▶Avery period. idx., 2nd suppl.; Glancey, J., in ARCHITECTURAL REVIEW CLXXI/1024 (June 1982) p.30-32; Transactions 3, v.2, n.1, 1982-83, p.67

Hodgson, Barry (*Canadian painter, b.1954*)   **BA**
   Bibl: Kitchener (Ont, CND), Kitchener-Waterloo Art Gallery BARRY HODGSON..., 1983

Hodgson, Brian Houghton (*British naturalist, painter, 1800-1894*)   **BA**
   Bibl: Head, Country Life CLXXIX/4627 (24 Apr 1986) 1128; ▶Natl. union cat., pre-1956

Hodgson, Carole   **BA WI**
  (*British artist, 1940-op.1984*)   **WI**
  (*British sculptor, b.1940*)   **BA**
   Bibl: Milwaukee (WI, USA), U. of W., Fine Arts Galleries, CAROLE HODGSON..., 1980

Hodgson, Charles   **WC WI**
  (*British artist, 1769-1825*)   **WI**
  (*British artist, op.1802-1825*)   **WC**
   Bibl: Moore

Hodgson, David (*British artist, 1798-1864*)   **WC WI**

Hodgson, George (*British artist, 1847-1921*)   **WI**

Hodgson, John Evan   **WC WI**
  (*British artist, 1831-1895*)   **WI**
  (*British artist, 1856-1895*)   **WC**
   Bibl: ▶Wilson, Brit. marine ptrs.

Hodgson, John James (*British artist, 1871-1906*)   **WI**

Hodgson, Leslie (*American architect, 1879-1947*)   **BA**
   Bibl: Prairie School Review, XII/1 (1975) pp.5-22

Hodgson, Louisa (*British artist, op. 1934-1950*)   **WI**

Hodgson, Thomas Sherlock (*Canadian painter, b.1924*)   **BA**
   Bibl: ▶Artists Canada; ▶Intl. dir. exh. artists

Hodgson, W.T. (*British artist, op. 19th c.*)   **WI**

Hodgson, Walker (*British artist, op. 19th c.*)   **WI**

Hödicke, Karl Horst   **BA WC**
  (*German artist, 20th cent.*)   **WC**
  (*German painter, photographer, filmmaker, b.1938*)   **BA**
   Bibl: ▶Art Index, 1976; ▶Babington Smith, Contemp. artists; Berlin. Neuer Berliner Kunstverein; Hicks, E., in ARTWEEK XIV/5 (5 Feb 1983), p.5; ▶Intl. dir. exh. artists, 1982; KUNST IN BERLIN, p.379; Larsen, S.C., in ART NEWS LXXXII/4 (Apr 1983) p.120; Studio 19 November 1975, p.250; ▶WW Arts DEU

Hodler→see Hodler, Ferdinand

Hodler, Ferdinand   **BA GC PR WC**
  (*Swiss artist, 1853-1918*)   **WC**
  (*Swiss painter, 1853-1918*)   **BA GC PR**
   Bibl: ▶Encyc. world art; ▶RILA/BHA; ▶Thieme-Becker; ▶Witt checklist
  Ferdinand Hodler   **PR**
  Hodler   **PR**

Hodne, Thomas H., Jr. (*American architect, Minneapolis, MN*)   **AV**
   Bibl: ▶AIA Pro File, 1983

Hodnick, Holly (*American architect*)   **AV**
   Bibl: Architecture: the AIA journal, 1986 June, v.75, no.6, p.87

Hödrich, Johan Gottfried (*Danish architect, 1697-1745*)   **BA**
   Bibl: ▶Natl. union cat., 1975

Hodshon, Cornelia Catharina (*Dutch, 1768-1829*)   **BA**
   Bibl: Swigchem, Nederlands Kunsthist. Jaarb., XXXI (1980), 439-455

Hodson, Frederik John (*British artist, 1806-1888*)   **WI**

Hodson, Haro (*British artist, op. 1989-*)   **WI**

Hodson, John   **WC WI**
  (*British artist, 1945-*)   **WC**
  (*British artist, b.1945*)   **WI**

Hodson, S.J.→see Hodson, Samuel John

Hodson, Samuel John   **WI**
  (*British artist, 1836-1908*)   **WC WI**

Hodson, S.J.   **WC**

Hodson, Shirley (*British artist, 1872-1882*)   **WI**

Hoeber, Arthur (*American painter, 1854-1915*)   **BA**
   Bibl: ▶Fielding's Amer. ptrs.; ▶WWW Amer., v.1

Hoechel, Arnold (*Swiss architect and city planner, Geneva, fl. 1920s*)   **AV**
   Bibl: Archithese, 1986 Sept.-Oct., v.15, no.5, p.79

Hoechle, Hochle or Hochle, Johann Baptist→see Hoechle, Johann Baptist

Hoechle, Johann Baptist   **GC**
  (*Swiss artist, 1754-1832*)   **WC**
  (*Swiss painter, 1754-1832*)   **GC**
   Bibl: Getty Photo Study Coll.; ▶Thieme-Becker

Hoechle, Hochle or Hochle, Johann Baptist   **WC**

Hoechle, Johann Nepomuk (*German artist, 1790-1835*)   **WC**

Hoechstetter, Rolf (*West German architect, Darmstadt*)   **AV**
   Bibl: ▶Bund Deut. Arch. Hdbch., 1987

Hoeck or Houck, Peter Cornelisz. van den→see Houck, Peter

Hoeck, F.V. [**Unidentified**]
  (*Unknown painter*)   **PR**
   Bibl: (March 25, 1813, lot 40, Del Vecchio)
  F.V. Hoeck   **PR**

Hoeck, Hinrich van (*Belgian artist, 19th cent.*)   **WC**

Hoeck, Peter Cornelisz. van den→see Houck, Peter

Hoecke→see Hoecke, Jan van den

Hoecke→see Hoecke, Robert van den

Hoecke, Jan van den   **BA GC PR WC**
  (*Flemish artist, 1611-1651*)   **WC**
  (*Flemish painter, 1611-1651*)   **BA PR**
  (*Flemish, 1611-1651*)   **GC**
   Bibl: ▶Artist biog. master idx.; ▶Bénézit; ▶RILA/BHA; ▶Thieme-Becker
  Hoecke   **PR**
  I. Vanhoek   **PR**
  J. V. Hoeck   **PR**
  J. van Hoeck   **PR**
  J.V. Hoeck   **PR**
  Jan van den Hoecke   **PR**
  Johannes Hoek   **PR**
  Van Hoeck   **PR**
  Van Hoek   **PR**

Hoecke, Jasper van den→see Hoecke, Kaspar van den

Hoecke, Kaspar or Jasper van den→see Hoecke, Kaspar van den

Hoecke, Kaspar van den   **GC**
  (*Flemish artist, op.1595-1648*)   **WC**
  (*Flemish painter, act.1595-d. aft. 1648*)   **GC**
   Bibl: ▶Thieme-Becker
  Hoecke, Jasper van den   **GC**

Hoecke, Kaspar or Jasper van den   **WC**

Hoecke, Robert van den   **BA GC PR WC**
    (Flemish artist, 1622-1668)   WC
    (Flemish painter, 1622-1668)   PR
    (Flemish painter, printmaker,
      1622-1668)   BA
    (Flemish, 1622-1668)   GC
    Bibl: ▶Bernt, Neth. ptrs. 17c.;
    ▶RILA/BHA; ▶Thieme-Becker;
    ▶Wilenski, Flem. ptrs.; ▶Witt
    checklist; ▶Wurzbach, NLD
    Künst.-Lex.
    Hoecke   PR
    R. Van Hoeck   PR
    Robert van den Hoecke   PR
    Van Hoek   PR
    Van Houk   PR
Hoecker, Paul→see Höcker, Paul
Hoeckgeest→see Houckgeest, Gerard
Hoeckl, Herbert *(German artist,*
    20th cent.)   **WC**
Hoef, A. van der   **PR WC**
    (Dutch artist, op.1642-1659)   WC
    (Dutch painter, act. 1642-1659)   PR
    Bibl: ▶Thieme-Becker
    A. van der Hoef   PR
    Abraham Verhoeven   PR
Hoef, Abraham van der *(Dutch*
    painter, act.1613-1649)   **GC**
    Bibl: ▶Thieme-Becker
    Hoeff, A. van   GC
Hoef, C.J. van der *(Netherlandish*
    ceramic designer, 1875-1933)   **BA**
    Bibl: Blaauwen, A.L. den,
    BULLETIN VAN HET
    RIJKSMUSEUM, XX/1 (Mar 1972),.
    33-46
Hoeff, A. van→see Hoef, Abraham
    van der
Hoeffius   **GC WC**
    (Netherlandish painter, act.
      1650-1660)   GC
    (Netherlands artist, 17th cent.)   WC
    Bibl: ▶Thieme-Becker
Hoefnagel or Hufnagel, Georg or
    Joris→see Hoefnagel, Joris
Hoefnagel, Georg→see Hoefnagel,
    Joris
Hoefnagel, Georg (Joris)→see
    Hoefnagel, Joris
Hoefnagel, Jacob   **GC**
    (Flemish artist, 1575-c.1630)   WC
    (Flemish, 1575-ca.1630)   GC
    Bibl: ▶Thieme-Becker; ▶Witt
    checklist
Hoefnagel, Jacob (also,
    erroneously, Jan)   **WC**
Hoefnagel, Jacob (also, erroneously,
    Jan)→see Hoefnagel, Jacob

Hoefnagel, Joris   **BA GC**
    (early Netherlandish painter,
      1542-1600)   BA
    (Flanders painter and
      draughtsman, 1542-1600)   GC
    (Flemish/Hungarian, b. Antwerp
      1542, d. Vienna)   JG
    (German painter, 1542-1600)   PR
    (Netherlands artist, 1542-1600)   WC
    Bibl: ▶Bénézit; ▶Encyc. world art;
    Getty Photo Study Coll. (Ptgs.);
    ▶RILA/BHA; ▶Thieme-Becker;
    ▶Wilenski, Flem. ptrs.; ▶Witt
    checklist
    Georg Hoefnagel   PR
Hoefnagel or Hufnagel, Georg
    or Joris   **WC**
Hoefnagel, Georg   **GC PR**
Hoefnagel, Georg (Joris)   **JG**
    Hufnagel, Georg   GC
Hoefslach [Unidentified] *(Unknown*
    painter, act. 17th century)   **PR**
    Bibl: Giallard inventory 1639
Hoegarde [Unidentified] *(Unknown*
    painter)   **PR**
    Bibl: 1740 Rijp inventory
Hoehenrieder, Johann *(German*
    artist, 1790-1866)   **WC**
Hoehme, Gerhard   **BA WC**
    (German artist, 1920-)   WC
    (German painter, printmaker,
      b.1920)   BA
    Bibl: ▶Art Index, vs.38-39;
    ▶Bénézit; Guide exh. artists:
    Sculp.; Kiel (DEU), Kunsthalle zu
    Kiel, IN MEMORIAM GERHARD
    HOEHME 1920-1989...(1989)
    BHA/FRA; ▶Vollmer, Künst.-Lex.
    20. Jhr., suppl.
Hoek, Hans van *(Dutch painter in*
    CAN, b.1947)   **BA**
    Bibl: Amsterdam (NLD), Stedelijk
    Museum, 11 Schilders (1976);
    ▶Natl. Gall. Canada libr. cat.;
    ▶RILA/BHA
Hoelloff, Curt *(German artist, 1887-)*   **WC**
Hoelscher, Richard *(German artist,*
    1867-)   **WC**
Hoeltzel, Susan *(American painter,*
    20th c.)   **BA**
    Bibl: Moss, J., in ARTS MAGAZINE,
    LIX/5 (Jan 1985) 8
Hoeltzer, Ernst *(German engineer,*
    photographer in IRN, 1835-1911)   **BA**
Hoelzel, Adolf→see Hölzel, Adolf
Hoem, Knut *(Norwegian architect,*
    Stavenger, 1929-)   **AV**
    Bibl: Byggekunst: the Norwegian
    review of architecture, 1985,
    v.67, no.8, p.432
Hoendermans, Joannes *(Dutch*
    painter, act.1679)   **GC**
    Bibl: ▶Thieme-Becker

Hoenich, Paul Konrad *(Israeli artist,*
    b.1907)   **BA**
    Bibl: Hoenich, P.K., LEONARDO,
    XIX/2 (1986) p.123-126; RLIN BKS
    file
Hoeniger, Paul *(German painter,*
    1865-1924)   **BA**
    Bibl: ▶Bénézit; ▶Thieme-Becker;
    ▶Vollmer, Künst.-Lex. 20. Jhr.
Hoening, Margaret→see French,
    Margaret
Hoenow, Max *(German artist, 1851-*
    1909)   **WC**
Hoensbroek, van *(Netherlands*
    artist, 18th cent.(?))   **WC**
Hoentschel, Georges *(French*
    architect, sculptor, ceramist,
    1860?-1915)   **BA**
    Bibl: ▶Met. Mus. Art libr. cat.;
    ▶Thieme-Becker
Hoepiner, Franz *(German artist,*
    19th cent.)   **WC**
Hoeppe or Hoppe, Ferdinand
    Bernhard→see Hoppe, Ferdinand
    Bernhard
Hoerle, Heinrich   **BA WC**
    (German artist, 20th cent.)   WC
    (German painter, 1895-1936)   BA
    Bibl: ▶Bénézit; ▶MoMA libr. cat.;
    ▶Phaidon 20c. art; ▶Vollmer,
    Künst.-Lex. 20. Jhr.
Hoernes-Kasimir, Tanna *(German*
    artist, op.1887)   **WC**
Hoesch, Hans *(German painter,*
    1855-1902)   **GC**
    Bibl: ▶Bénézit
Hoese, Jean de la *(Belgian artist,*
    1846-1917)   **WC**
Hoesli, Bernhard *(1923-)*   **AV**
Hoess, Eugen Ludwig *(German*
    artist, 1866-)   **WC**
Hoesslin→see Hoesslin, Georg von
Hoesslin, Georg von   **PR**
    (German painter, 1851-1923)   PR
    (Hungarian artist, 1831-1923)   WC
    Bibl: ▶Thieme-Becker
    Georg von Hoesslin   PR
    Hoesslin   PR
Hoesslin, George von   **WC**
Hoesslin, George von→see Hoesslin,
    Georg von
Hoet→see Hoet, Gerard I
Hoet, Gerard→see Hoet, Gerard I
Hoet, Gerard (I)→see Hoet, Gerard I

Hoet, Gerard I | BA GC
  (Dutch artist, 1648-1733) | WC
  (Dutch painter and
    draughtsman, 1648-1733) | GC
  (Dutch painter, 1648-1733) | PR
  (Dutch painter, printmaker,
    1648-1733) | BA
  (Dutch, 1648-1733) | JG
  Bibl: Getty Photo Study Coll.;
    ▶RILA/BHA; ▶Seyn, Écoles flam. et
    holl.; ▶Thieme-Becker; ▶Witt
    checklist; Wurzbach, NLD
    Künst.-Lex.
  De Hoet | PR
  G. Hoet | PR
  G. Hoor | PR
  G. Houet | PR
  Gerard Hoet | PR
  Gerard Hoet (I) | PR
  Gerard Huet | PR
  Gerrard Hoed | PR
  Gerrit Hoet | PR
  Hoet | PR
  Hoet, Gerard | JG PR
  Hoet, Gerard (I) | PR
  Hoet, Gerard, I | WC
Hoet, Gerard II (Dutch painter,
  d.1760) | GC
  Bibl: ▶Thieme-Becker
Hoet, Gerard, I → see Hoet, Gerard I
Hoet, H. (Dutch draughtsman, act.
  ca.1649-1659) | GC
  Bibl: ▶Thieme-Becker
Hoet, Hendrik Jacob | GC WC
  (Dutch artist, 1693-1733) | WC
  (Dutch painter, 1693-1733) | GC
  Bibl: ▶Thieme-Becker
Hoet, Johan (Dutch artist, op.1673) | WC
Hoet, Leon Geronimo (Venezuelan
  engineer and architect, fl. 1932) | AV
  Bibl: Preservation news, 1989
    Mar., v.29, no.3, p.5
Hoetger, Bernhard | AV BA
  (German architect, sculptor and
    engineer, 1874-1949) | AV
  (German sculptor, architect,
    painter, printmaker, 1874-
    1949) | BA
  Bibl: ▶Macmillan encyc. archts.;
    ▶Neue deutsche Biog.; ▶Vollmer,
    Künst.-Lex. 20. Jhr.
Hoeve, Abraham van der → see
  Houve, Abraham van der
Hoeven, Abraham van der → see
  Houve, Abraham van der
Hoeven, Jan van (Dutch artist, op.
  1655) | WC
Hoevenaar, Jozef (Dutch painter
  and draughtsman, 1840-1926) | GC
  Bibl: ▶Thieme-Becker
Hoever, Kees van der (Dutch
  public, Hague) | AV
  Bibl: De Architect, 1989 Apr.,
    v.20, no.4, p.106

Hoewaer, Lidy (Belgian ceramist,
  sculptor, b.1943) | BA
  Bibl: Szenassy, Met Eigen Ogen,
    318-323
Hoey, Jan Dammerts van | BA
  (Dutch painter, printmaker in
    FRA, 1545-1615) | BA
  (Netherlandish painter, 1545?-
    1615) | GC
  (Netherlands artist, 1545(?)-
    1615) | WC
  Bibl: ▶Bénézit; Getty Photo Study
    Coll.; ▶Thieme-Becker; ▶Witt
    checklist; ▶Wurzbach, NLD
    Künst.-Lex.
  Dhoey, Jean | GC
  Doué, Jean I de | BA
  Hoey, Jean de | GC
  Hoey, Jean de, or Jean Dhoey
    or Doe (Jan Dammesz.) | WC
  Hoey, Jean de → see Hoey, Jan
    Dammerts van
  Hoey, Jean de, or Jean Dhoey or Doe
    (Jan Dammesz.) → see Hoey, Jan
    Dammerts van
Hoey, Nicolas d' | BA
  (Flemish painter, printmaker in
    FRA, act.1564, d.1611/12) | BA
  (Netherlands artist, op.c.1590-
    1611) | WC
  Bibl: Guillaume, in SCRITTI DI
    STORIA DELL'ARTE IN ONORE DI
    FED. ZERI (1984 (docs) 472-473;
    ▶Illus. Bartsch, v.16; Paris (FRA),
    Grand Palais, Fontainebleau
    (1972); ▶Thieme-Becker; ▶Witt
    checklist
  Hoey, Nicolas de, or Nicolas | WC
    Dhioey, Douay, Doue or Douy
  Hoey, Nicolas de, or Nicolas Dhioey,
    Douay, Doue or Douy → see Hoey,
    Nicolas d'
Hoey, Pat (Canadian painter,
  sculptor, b.1938) | BA
  Bibl: Kingston (Ont, CND),
    Queen's University, Agnes
    Ethington Art Centre, PAT HOEY,
    1978
Hoeydonck, Paul van | BA WC
  (Belgian artist, 1925-) | WC
  (Belgian sculptor, painter,
    b.1925) | BA
  Bibl: ▶Dict. biog. artistes belges;
    ▶Intl. dir. exh. artists, 1982
Hoeye or Hoye, Rombout van den
  (Dutch artist, 1622-) | WC
Hof, F. (German artist, 18th cent.) | WC
Hofbauer, Ferdinand (German
  artist, 1801-1864) | WC
Hofbauer, Ludwig (German artist,
  1843-) | WC
Hofelich, Ludwig Friedrich (German
  artist, 1842-1903) | WC
Hofer → see Hofer, Karl
Hofer, Adolf (German artist, 1869-) | WC

Hofer, Andreas (Swiss painter,
  b.1956) | BA
  Bibl: Olten (CHE), Kunstmuseum,
    ANDREAS HOFER, 1986
Hofer, Anton (Italian designer,
  painter, 1888-1979) | BA
  Bibl: FESTSCHRIFT NICOLO
    RASMO, p.426; ▶Vollmer,
    Künst.-Lex. 20. Jhr.
Hofer, Carl → see Hofer, Karl
Hofer, Evelyn | AV BA
  (American architectural
    photographer) | AV
  (American photographer, 20th
    c.) | BA
  Bibl: Du, XXXVII/439 (Sep. 1977)
    pp.30-83; ▶MoMA libr. cat.
Hofer, Frances L. (American,
  d.1978) | BA
  Bibl: Cambridge (MA, USA),
    Harvard U., Fogg Art Mus.,
    MASTER DRAWINGS... 1984, p.8;
    Cambridge (MA, USA), Harvard,
    Houghton Lib., Drawings for
    books..., 1980
Hofer, Hans (Swiss artist, op.1580) | WC
Höfer, Heinrich | BA GC WC
  (German artist, 1825-1878) | WC
  (German painter, 1825-1878) | BA GC
  Bibl: ▶Busse, Maler u. Bildhauer
    19. Jahr.; Ludwig, Weltkunst,
    LVII/20 (15 Oct. 1987) pp.2888-
    2891; ▶Thieme-Becker
Hofer, Ignaz (German artist, 1790-
  1862) | WC
Hofer, Karl | BA GC PR WC
  (German artist, 1878-1955) | WC
  (German painter, 1878-1955) | PR
  (German painter, printmaker, art
    historian, 1878-1955) | BA
  (German, 1878-1955) | GC
  Bibl: ▶Bénézit; ▶Brockhaus Enzyk.,
    p.579; ▶Darmstädter, Künstlerlex.,
    p.291; ▶Libr. of Congr. Name
    Auth. File; ▶Neue deutsche Biog.,
    p.381; Reclams KUNSTFUHRER,
    p.326; ▶RILA/BHA; ▶Vollmer,
    Künst.-Lex. 20. Jhr.; ▶Witt
    checklist
  Carl Hofer | PR
  Hofer | PR
  Hofer, Carl | PR
Hofer, Konrad (Swiss artist, 1928-) | WC
Hofer, Otto (Austrian architect,
  1847-1901) | BA
  Bibl: ▶Österr. biog. Lex. 1815-
    1950; ▶Thieme-Becker
Höfer, Werner (Austrian architect,
  Vienna) | AV
  Bibl: ▶Verzeich. Öst. Ziviltech.
Höferle, Melchior → see Hefele,
  Melchior
Hoff → see Hoff, Carl Heinrich (I)
Hoff the Elder, Karl → see Hoff, Carl
  Heinrich (I)

Hoff, Carl Heinrich (I)	**PR**
(German artist, 1838-1890)	WC
(German painter, 1838-1890)	PR
Bibl: ▶Thieme-Becker	
Carl Heinrich Hoff (I)	PR
Carl Hoff	PR
Hoff	PR
Hoff the Elder, Karl	**WC**
Hoff, Carsten	**AV BA**
(Architect, Denmark)	AV
(Danish architect, 20th c.)	BA

Bibl: AC, 1984 Oct, v.29, no.
2(110), p.78; ▶Avery period. idx.,
2nd suppl.; Dirckinck-Holmfeld,
Arkitektur DK, XXVII (3 May
1983) p.97; ▶Libr. of Congr.
Name Auth. File

Hoff, Margo	**WC WI**
(American artist, 1912-)	WC
(American artist, b.1912)	WI
Hoff, Robert van't (Dutch architect, 1887-1979)	**BA**

Bibl: ▶Macmillan encyc. archts.;
▶Portoghesi, Diz. arch. e
urbanistica

Hoff, Simon Simonson (Norwegian
artist, op.1770)   **WC**

Hoffacker, Michael (American
designer, Cincinnati, Ohio)   **AV**

Bibl: Builder, 1987 Nov., v.10,
no.11, p.91

Hoffbauer, Charles C.J. (French
artist, 1875-p.1906)   **WC**

Hoffbauer, J. H. Feodor → see
Hoffbauer, Théodore Joseph
Hubert

Hoffbauer, Theodor Josef
Hubert → see Hoffbauer, Théodore
Joseph Hubert

Hoffbauer, Théodore Joseph Hubert	**AV**
(French painter of architecture, 1839-1922)	AV
(German artist, 1839-p.1892)	WC

Bibl: ▶Libr. of Congr. Name Auth.
File

Hoffbauer, J. H. Feodor	AV
Hoffbauer, Theodor Josef Hubert	**WC**
Hoffbro, Peter Lorens (Swedish painter, printmaker, 1710-1759)	**BA**

Bibl: ▶Svenskt konst.-lex.

Hoffenrichler, Jean → see Potarange,
Jean

Hoffer, E. (Architect)   **AV**

Bibl: Baumeister, 1989 Apr., v.86,
no.4, p.62

Hoffer, Georg (Austrian sculptor,
act.1690-1699)   **BA**

Bibl: Bovos, Művészettörténeti
Értésítő, XXXII/1-2 (1983), pp.17,
33

Hoffers, Carl Eugen (Finnish
photographer, 1832-1893)   **BA**

Bibl: Hist. photography, I/2 (Apr.
1977) pp.135-152

Hoffland → see Hofland, Thomas
Christopher

Hoffman → see Hoffman, Martin

Hoffman, Anton → see Hoffmann,
Anton

Hoffman, David (American architect)	**AV**
Hoffman, Edward Fenno III	
(American sculptor, b.1916)	**BA**

Bibl: Guide exh. artists: N. Amer.
ptrs.; NY Times obit., 24 Sep
1991; ▶WW Amer. Art

Hoffman, Eric (American painter,
20th c.)   **BA**

Bibl: Arts Mag LVI, 10 June '82,
p.5

Hoffman, Ernst Theodor Wilhelm.
(Amadeus) → see Hoffmann, Ernst
Theodor Amadeus

Hoffman, F. Burrall → see Hoffman, F.
Burrall II

Hoffman, F. Burrall II	**BA**
(American architect, 1883-1980)	AV
(American architect, act.1914-1946)	BA

Bibl: Abitare 1989 July-Aug., no.
276, p.124; Antiques, CXXI/1
(1982) p.312; ▶Avery Libr. cat.;
▶Avery period. idx.; Nat'l Reg,
p.143

Hoffman, F. Burrall	**AV**
Hoffman, Francis Burrall	AV
Hoffman, F.G. (German artist, op.c. 1790)	**WC**
Hoffman, Fels Char (Swiss artist, op.1651)	**WC**

Hoffman, Francis Burrall → see
Hoffman, F. Burrall II

Hoffman, Georg Andreas → see
Hoffmann, Georg Andreas

Hoffman, Georges Johannes → see
Hoffmann, Georg Jan

Hoffman, Hans → see Hofmann, Hans

Hoffman, Harry Leslie (American
painter, 1874-1966)   **PR**

Bibl: ▶WWW Amer. art

Harry Leslie Hoffman   PR

Hoffman, Heinrich → see Hoffmann,
Heinrich

Hoffman, Irene (German, active
1920s)   **JG**

Hoffman, Irwin David (American
painter, printmaker, sculptor,
b.1901)   **BA**

Bibl: Boston, Public Library, IRWIN
D. HOFFMAN (1981); ▶Vollmer,
Künst.-Lex. 20. Jhr.

Hoffman, Johan Franz (German
artist, 1701-c.1766)   **WC**

Hoffman, Jonas (Swedish artist,
1731-1780)   **WC**

Hoffman, Josef	**GC**
(Austrian painter, 1831-1904)	GC
(German artist, 1831-1904)	WC
Bibl: ▶Thieme-Becker	
Hoffmann, Josef	**WC**

Hoffman, Josef → see Hoffmann, Josef
Franz Maria

Hoffman, M. (Netherlands artist,
1914-)   **WC**

Hoffman, Malvina	**BA GC**
(American artist, 1887-)	WC
(American artist, 1887-1966)	WI
(American sculptor, 1887-1966)	BA GC

Bibl: ▶Bénézit; ▶Britannica encyc.
Amer. art; ▶Collins, Women
artists Amer.; ▶Petteys, Women
artists; ▶RILA/BHA; ▶Schwab, Life
& death; ▶Vollmer, Künst.-Lex.
20. Jhr.; ▶WWW Amer., 1966

Grimson, Samuel Grimson, Mrs.,
(Malvina Cornell)   WI

Hoffman, Malvina (Grimson)	**WC**
Hoffman, Malvina Cornell	**WI**

Hoffman, Malvina (Grimson) → see
Hoffman, Malvina

Hoffman, Malvina Cornell → see
Hoffman, Malvina

Hoffman, Martin	**BA WC WI**
(American artist, 1935-)	WC
(American artist, b.1935)	WI
(American painter, illustrator, b.1935)	BA

Bibl: ▶WW Amer. Art

Hoffman, Martin (Dutch painter,
act. 1737)   **PR**

Bibl: Dictionary of Swedish Artists

Hoffman	PR
Martin Hoffman	PR

Hoffman, Samuel → see Hofmann,
Samuel

Hoffman, Vlastimil → see Hofman,
Vlastimil

Hoffmann, Alfred (East German
architect, 1929-)   **AV**

Bibl: Architektur der DDR, 1989
Mar., v.38, no.3, p.41

Hoffmann, Alfred (West German
landscape architect)   **AV**

Bibl: Garten und Landschaft,
1988, v.98, no.5, p.22

Hoffmann, Anker (Danish sculptor,
1904-1985)   **BA**

Bibl: ▶Køie, Kunst.leks.;
▶Nørregård-Nielsen, Dansk kunst;
▶Weilbach, Kunst.leks.

Hoffmann, Anton	**GC**
(German artist, 1863-1938)	WC
(German painter, 1863-1938)	GC
Bibl: ▶Thieme-Becker	
Hoffman, Anton	**WC**

Hoffmann, Carl Heinrich (German
goldsmith, silversmith, b.1784, act.
1840)   **BA**

Bibl: Scheffler, Berliner
Goldschmiede; Scheffler, W.,
KUNST UND ANTIQUITÄTEN
(1982) 1, 56-58

Hoffmann, Dan (*American architect, as of 1987, Director of graduate program in architecture at the Cranbrook Academy of Art*) **AV**
Bibl: Inland architect, 1987 Sept.-Oct., v.31, no.5, p.54

Hoffmann, Egon (*East German architect, Greifswald*) **AV**
Bibl: Architektur der DDR, 1987 Dec., v.36, no.12, p.24

Hoffmann, Emmanuel (*German glass cutter, 1819-1878*) **BA**
Bibl: Anz. des Germ. Nationalmus. (1979) 153-165; ▶Thieme-Becker

Hoffmann, Ernest (*American architect, Albany, N.Y., fl. 1892*) **AV**
Bibl: Albany preservation report, 1988 Spring, v.7, no.2, p.3

Hoffmann, Ernst (*Austrian architect, Vienna, 1949-*) **AV**
Bibl: Ottagono, 1988 Mar., p.24

Hoffmann, Ernst Theodor Amadeus **BA**
(*German artist, 1776-1822*) WC
(*German author, composer, artist, lawyer, 1776-1822*) BA
(*German draughtsman, 1776-1822*) GC
Bibl: ▶Bénézit; ▶New Columbia encyc.

Hoffman, Ernst Theodor Wilhelm. (Amadeus) **WC**

Hoffmann, Ernst Theodor Amedeus **GC**

Hoffmann, Ernst Theodor Amedeus→see Hoffmann, Ernst Theodor Amadeus

Hoffmann, Eugen (*German painter, sculptor, 1892-1955*) **BA**
Bibl: ▶Libr. of Congr. Name Auth. File; ▶Vollmer, Künst.-Lex. 20. Jhr.

Hoffmann, Felicità **BA GC**
(*Italian artist, d.1760*) BA
(*Italian artist, op.1728-m.1760*) WC
(*Italian painter, act.1728-d. 1760*) GC
Bibl: ▶Bénézit, sv. Hoffmann; ▶Bolaffi, (as Hoffmann Sarton, Felicia); ▶Thieme-Becker, sv. Hoffmann; ▶Witt checklist, sv. Hoffmann

Hoffmann, Felicita (nee Sartori) **WC**
Sartori, Felicita GC
Hoffmann, Felicita (nee Sartori)→see Hoffmann, Felicità

Hoffmann, Felix (*Swiss painter, glass painter, printmaker, b.1911*) **BA**
Bibl: ▶Künst.-Lex. Schweiz 20. Jahrh.; ▶Vollmer, Künst.-Lex. 20. Jhr.

Hoffmann, Georg (*Swiss painter, printmaker, 1808-1858*) **BA**
Bibl: Meles, B., in 07 PANORAMA: KOLLOQUIUM...316

Hoffmann, Georg Andreas **GC**
(*German artist, 1752-1808*) WC
(*German painter, 1752-1808*) GC
Bibl: ▶Thieme-Becker

Hoffman, Georg Andreas **WC**

Hoffmann, Georg Jan **GC**
(*Dutch artist, 1833-1873*) WC
(*Dutch painter, 1833-1873*) GC
Bibl: ▶Thieme-Becker

Hoffman, Georges Johannes **WC**

Hoffmann, Hans **BA GC JG WC**
(*German artist, op.1568-m.1591/2*) WC
(*German painter in Bohemia, ca. 1530-ca.1591*) BA
(*German, ca. 1530-1591/2*) JG
(*German, d. ca.1592*) GC
Bibl: ▶Neue deutsche Biog.; ▶Thieme-Becker; ▶Witt checklist

Hoffmann, Heinrich **BA**
(*German, active Munich, Germany 1930s-1940s (Nazi)*) JG

Hoffman, Heinrich **JG**

Hoffmann, Heinrich-Adolf-Valentin
(*German artist, 1814-1896*) **WC**

Hoffmann, Hubert (*German architect, city planner, painter in AUT, b.1904*) **BA**
Bibl: Neumann, Bauhaus, p.242; Wangler, Schüler des Bauhauses, p.30

Hoffmann, Jan Eliasz (*Polish sculptor, 18th c.*) **BA**
Bibl: ▶Bénézit; Biul. Hist. Sztuki XL, 1978; ▶Thieme-Becker

Hoffmann, Johann F. (*German glass cutter, 1840-1900*) **BA**
Bibl: ▶Thieme-Becker

Hoffmann, Johann Gottfried
(*Polish architect, act.1771-1792*) **BA**
Bibl: BILDHNDBCH. KUNST IN DER USSR, 441; ▶Hempel, Baroque central Euro., p.308; POLISH ART STUDIES, V (1984) 26; ▶Thieme-Becker

Hoffmann, Josef→see Hoffman, Josef
Hoffmann, Josef→see Hoffmann, Josef Franz Maria

Hoffmann, Josef Franz Maria **AV BA**
(*Austrian architect, designer, 1870-1956*) AV BA
(*German artist, 1870-1956*) WC
Bibl: ▶Contemp. archts.; ▶Encyc. world art; ▶Libr. of Congr. Name Auth. File; ▶Macmillan encyc. archts.; ▶Thieme-Becker; ▶Vollmer, Künst.-Lex. 20. Jhr.

Hoffman, Josef **WC**
Hoffmann, Josef AV
Hoffmann, Joseph AV
Hoffmann, Joseph→see Hoffmann, Josef Franz Maria

Hoffmann, Karl (*German painter, 1838-aft.1900*) **PR**
Bibl: ▶Thieme-Becker
Hoffmann, Karl (the Younger) PR
Hoffmann, Karl, the Younger PR
Karl Hoffmann PR

Hoffmann, Karl (*1806-1889*) **AV**
Hoffmann, Karl (the Younger)→see Hoffmann, Karl
Hoffmann, Karl, the Younger→see Hoffmann, Karl

Hoffmann, L. (*German artist, 19th cent.*) **WC**

Hoffmann, Ludwig Ernst Emil
(*German architect, 1852-1932*) **AV BA**
Bibl: ▶Brockhaus Enzyk.; ▶Portoghesi, Diz. arch. e urbanistica; ▶Thieme-Becker

Hoffmann, Martin (*Swiss sculptor, act.1507, d. before 1532*) **BA**
Bibl: KUNSTDENKMALER DES KANTONS BASEL-STADT vol. 4 p.308; ▶Schweiz. Künst.-Lex.; ZEITSCHRIFT FÜR SCHW ARCH UND KUNST XXXV/2 (1978) p.108

Hoffmann, Peter (*West German architect, Oberursel*) **AV**
Bibl: Deutsche Bauzeitung, 1986 May, v.120, no.5, p.172

Hoffmann, Philipp (*German architect, 1806-1889*) **BA**
Bibl: ▶Neue deutsche Biog.; Wiesbaden, Nassauischer kunstv., PHILIPP HOFFMANN (1982)

Hoffmann, Romain (*Architect, Luxembourg, 1949-*) **AV**
Bibl: Deutsche Bauzeitung, 1988 July, v.122, no.7, p.138

Hoffmann, Samuel→see Hofmann, Samuel

Hoffmann, Werner F. (*German architect, Freiburg*) **AV**
Bibl: Deutsche Bauzeitung, 1986 Aug., v.120, no.8, p.58

Hoffmann-Fallersleben, Franz **GC WC**
(*German artist, 1855-1927*) WC
(*German painter, 1855-1927*) GC
Bibl: ▶Thieme-Becker

Hoffmeister, Adolf **BA WC**
(*Czech artist, 1902-*) WC
(*Czech author, draftsman, b.1902*) BA
Bibl: ▶Bénézit; ▶Vollmer, Künst.-Lex. 20. Jhr.

Hoffmeister, J. H. (*Dutch printmaker, act.1857-62*) **GC**
Bibl: ▶Thieme-Becker

Hoffmeister, Johann Peter
(*German artist, 1740-1772*) **WC**

Hoffmeister, Johann Philipp
(*German artist, -1771*) **WC**

Hoffnas→see Hoffnas, Johann Wilhelm

Hoffnas, Hoffnaass or Hofhaas, Lorenz (*German artist, 1772-1837*) **WC**

---

*Hoffnas, Hoffnass, Hofnaas, Hofnass
etc., Johann Wilhelm→see*
Hoffnas, Johann Wilhelm

Hoffnas, Johann Wilhelm   **PR**
   (German artist, 1727-1795)   WC
   (German painter, 1727-1795)   PR
      Bibl: ▶Thieme-Becker
   Hoffnas   PR
   **Hoffnas, Hoffnass, Hofnaas,
      Hofnass etc., Johann Wilhelm WC**
   Hofnaas   PR
   Johann Wilhelm Hoffnas   PR
Hoffnung, Gerard *(British artist,
   1925-1959)*   **WC WI**
Hoffstadt, Friedrich *(German
   collector, artist, author, 1802-
   1846)*   **BA**
      Bibl: GOTHISCHES A B C BUCH,
      DAS IST: GRUNDIEGELN DES
      BOTHISCHEN STYLS FÜR
      KÜNSTLER UND WEIKLEUTE;
      ▶Natl. union cat.; ▶Thieme-Becker
Hoffstadter, Friedrich *(Czech artist,
   1910-)*   **WC**
Hoffy, Alfred→see Hoffy, Alfred M.
Hoffy, Alfred M.   **WC WI**
   (American artist, 1790-op.1860)   WI
   (American artist, c.1790-1860)   WC
   *(Engraver, Philadelphia, PA., op.
      1750-1864)*   WI
   Hoffy, Alfred   **WI**
Hofker, Willem Gerard *(Dutch
   draughtsman, 1902-d. aft.1946)*   **GC**
      Bibl: ▶Scheen, Ned. beeldende
      kunst.
Hofkunst, Alfred   **BA WC**
   *(Austrian painter in CHE,
      b.1942)*   BA
   (Swiss artist, op.1971)   WC
      Bibl: ▶Art Index, v.23; ▶Bénézit;
      Thames
*Hofland→see Hofland, Thomas
Christopher*
**Hofland, Thomas
   Christopher**   **BA PR WC WI**
   (British artist, 1777-1843)   WC WI
   (British painter, 1777-1843)   BA PR
      Bibl: ▶Dict. natl. biog.;
      ▶RILA/BHA; ▶Thieme-Becker
   Hoffland   PR
   Hofland   PR
   Thomas Christopher Hofland   PR
Hoflehner, Rudolf   **BA WC**
   *(Austrian sculptor, painter,
      printmaker, b.1916)*   BA
   (German artist, -1916)   WC
      Bibl: ▶Bénézit; ▶Vollmer,
      Künst.-Lex. 20. Jhr.
Höfler, Horst *(West German
   architect, Stuttgart)*   **AV**
      Bibl: Garten + Landschaft, 1986
      Aug., v.96, no.8, p.15
Hofler, Johann Wolfgang *(Austrian
   painter, d.1702)*   **BA**
      Bibl: ▶Bénézit; ▶Thieme-Becker

Hofler, Max *(German artist, 19th
   cent.)*   **WC**
Hofling, Salomon *(Swedish artist,
   1778-1827)*   **WC**
Hoflinger, Christan Jacob   **GC**
   (German artist, 1759-1837)   WC
   (German painter, 1759-1837)   GC
      Bibl: ▶Scheen, Ned. beeldende
      kunst.
Hoflinger, Christian Jacob   **WC**
Hoflinger, Christian Jacob→see
   Hoflinger, Christan Jacob
*Hofman, Charles→see Hofmann,
   Charles C.*
Hofman, Jiří *(Czech architect, 20th
   c.)*   **BA**
      Bibl: Margolius: Cubism in Arch
*Hofman, Pieter→see Hofman, Pieter
(Giannizzero)*
Hofman, Pieter (Giannizzero)   **BA**
   *(Flemish painter in ITA, 1642-
      1692)*   BA
   (Flemish painter, ca.1642-1692)   PR
      Bibl: De Angelis, Boll. Pontifici VII
      (1987), p.73; ▶Thieme-Becker;
      ▶Wurzbach, NLD Künst.-Lex.
   Giannizzero   PR
   Giannizzero d'Anversa   PR
   Hofman, Pieter   **PR**
   Pieter Hofman   PR
*Hofman, Samuel→see Hofmann,
   Samuel*
Hofman, Vlastimil   **BA**
   (Czech painter, 1881-1970)   BA
   (Polish artist, 1881-p.1921)   WC
      Bibl: ▶Bénézit; Biuletyn historii
      sztuki XLI, 3 79, 263-74;
      ▶Vollmer, Künst.-Lex. 20. Jhr., v.1
   Hoffman, Vlastimil   **WC**
Hofman, Vlastislav   **BA**
   *(Czech architect, scenographer,
      painter, printmaker, 1884-
      1964)*   BA
   *(Czechoslovakian architect,
      1884-1964)*   AV
      Bibl: Berlin, Int. Design Zentrum,
      VLASTISLAV HOFMAN (1982);
      ▶Encyk. českého výtv. umění;
      ▶Natl. union cat., pre-1956; RLIN
      BKS file; ▶Thieme-Becker; UC
      Santa Barbara cat. sheets
   Hofman, Vlatislav   **AV**
*Hofman, Vlatislav→see Hofman,
   Vlastislav*
Hofmann→see Hofmann, Hans
Hofmann, A. *(German artist, 19th
   cent.)*   **WC**
Hofmann, Armin *(Swiss artist,
   1920-)*   **WC**

Hofmann, Charles C.   **BA WI**
   (American artist, 1820-1882)   WI
   (American artist, op.1878)   WC
   (American painter, 1821-1882)   BA
      Bibl: New York (NY, USA),
      Whitney Mus., Amer. folk ptrs.
      (1980)
   Hofman, Charles   **WC**
Hofmann, Egon *(German artist,
   1884-1972)*   **WC**
Hofmann, Frank *(New Zealander
   photographer, 1916-1989)*   **BA**
      Bibl: Ensing, ART NEW ZEALAND,
      LII (spring 1989), 51
Hofmann, G.W. *(German painter,
   18th century)*   **GC**
      Bibl: ▶Bénézit
Hofmann, Hans   **BA GC PR WC WI**
   (American artist, 1880-)   WC
   (American painter, 1880-1966)   GC
   (German artist, 1880-)   WC
   (German artist, 1880-1966)   WI
   *(German painter in USA, 1880-
      1966)*   BA
   (German painter, 1880-1966)   PR
      Bibl: ▶Britannica encyc. Amer. art;
      ▶Encyc. world art, Ger-Amer;
      McG-H-Ger-Amer; ▶RILA/BHA
   Hans Hofmann   PR
   Hoffman, Hans   **WC**
   Hofmann   PR
**Hofmann, Heinrich Johann Michael
   Ferdinand Heinrich)** *(German
   artist, 1824-1911)*   **WC**
Hofmann, Julius   **AV BA**
   (1840-1896)   AV
   (German architect, 1840-1896)   BA
      Bibl: ▶Neue deutsche Biog.;
      ▶Thieme-Becker
*Hofmann, Ludvig von→see Hofmann,
   Ludwig von*
Hofmann, Ludwig von   **BA GC**
   (German artist, 1861-1945)   WC
   (German painter, 1861-1945)   GC
   *(German painter, printmaker,
      illustrator, 1861-1945)*   BA
      Bibl: ▶Neue deutsche Biog.;
      ▶Thieme-Becker; ▶Vollmer,
      Künst.-Lex. 20. Jhr.; ▶Witt
      checklist
   Hofmann, Ludvig von   **WC**
Hofmann, Michael *(East German
   architect)*   **AV**
      Bibl: Architektur der DDR, 1989
      Aug., v.38, no.8, p.28

Hofmann, Samuel   **BA PR**
  (*Swiss artist, c.1592-1648*)   WC
  (*Swiss artist, op.1619-1645*)   WC
  (*Swiss painter, 1591/92-1648*)   PR
  (*Swiss painter, ca.1592-1648*)   GC
  (*Swiss painter, ca.1595-1649*)   BA
  Bibl: ▶Bénézit; Schlégl, SAMUEL
    HOFMANN (1980); ▶Schweiz.
    Künst.-Lex.; ▶Thieme-Becker
  Hoffman, Samuel   GC PR
Hoffmann, Samuel   **GC PR WC**
Hofman, Samuel   **WC**
  Samuel Hoffmann   PR
Hofmann, Werner (*German artist,*
  1897-)   **WC**
Hofmann, Werner (*German painter,*
  printmaker, 1907-1983)   **BA**
  Bibl: Quinger, BILDENDE KUNST
    (5) 1984, p.214-216; ▶Vollmer,
    Künst.-Lex. 20. Jhr.
Hofmeister, Eugen   **GC WC**
  (*German artist, 1843-*)   WC
  (*German, b.1843*)   GC
  Bibl: ▶Thieme-Becker
Hofmeister, Henry (*American*
  architect, 1891?-1962)   **BA**
  Bibl: ▶Wodehouse, Amer. archts.
    WWI-pres.
Hofmeister, Johannes (*German*
  artist, 20th cent.)   **WC**
Hofmeister, Oskar (*German*
  photographer, 1871-1937)   **BA**
  Bibl: ▶Gernsheim, Hist. photog.;
    ▶Rosenblum, World hist. photog.
Hofmeister, Theodor (*German*
  photographer, 1868-1943)   **BA**
  Bibl: ▶Gernsheim, Hist. photog.;
    ▶Rosenblum, World hist. photog.
Hofnaas→see Hoffnas, Johann
  Wilhelm
Hofreiter or Hofreuter, Karl
  (*German artist, op.1724-1736*)   **WC**
Hofrichter, József   **AV BA**
  (*Hungarian architect, 1779-*
  1835)   AV
  (*Hungarian architect, 1779-*
  1853)   BA
  Bibl: Bildhdbch. Kunst Ungarn,
    p.369; Kampis, Art Hungary;
    Muveszettorteneti ertesito, 1983,
    v.32, no.3, p.176; ▶Thieme-Becker
Hofschen, Edgar (*German painter,*
  b.1941)   **BA**
  Bibl: ▶Art Index, Nov. 1974-Oct.
    1975; ▶Bénézit; ▶MoMA libr. cat.
Hofstadt or Hoffstadt, Pieter van
  der (Pieter de Vocht)
  (*Netherlands artist, op.1523-1569*) **WC**
Hofsted or Hofstede van Essen, G.
  (*German artist, op.1693-1703*)   **WC**
Hofstetten, Franz Xaver von
  (*German artist, 1811-1883*)   **WC**
Hofstetter, William Alfred
  (*American artist, b.1884*)   **WI**
Hofstotter, Franz (*German artist,*
  1871-)   **WC**

Hofwerberg, Carl (*Swedish artist,*
  op.1737)   **WC**
Hogan, Eileen (*British artist, b.1946*) **WI**
Hogan, João Navarro (*Portuguese*
  painter, b.1914)   **BA**
  Bibl: ▶Pamplona, Pint. escult. PRT;
    ▶Tavares Chicó, Pint. portuguesa
Hogan, John (*Irish sculptor, 1800-*
  1858)   **BA**
  Bibl: ▶Strickland, Irish artists
Hogan, Maurice (*Irish architect*)   **AV**
  Bibl: Irish Architect, 1989 Mar.-
    Apr., no.70, p.26
Hogan, Patrick (*American painter,*
  b.1947)   **BA**
  Bibl: New York (NY, USA),
    Guggenheim Mus., 19 artists
    (1981)
Hogarth→see Hogarth, William
Hogarth,→see Hogarth, William
Hogarth, Arthur Paul   **BA WI**
  (*British artist, 1917-*)   WC
  (*British artist, b.1917*)   WI
  (*British painter, illustrator,*
  author, b.1917)   BA
  Bibl: ▶Peppin, Bk. illus. 20c.
Hogarth, Paul   **WC**
Hogarth, Paul→see Hogarth, Arthur
  Paul
Hogarth, William   **AV BA GC JG PR WC WI**
  (*1697-1764*)   AV
  (*British artist, 1697-1764*)   WC WI
  (*British painter, 1697-1764*)   PR
  (*British, 1697-1764*)   GC
  (*English painter, printmaker,*
  1697-1764)   BA
  (*English, 1697-1764*)   JG
  Bibl: ▶Artist biog. master idx.;
    ▶Bénézit; ▶Darmstädter,
    Künstlerlex.; ▶McGraw-Hill dict.
    art; ▶RILA/BHA; ▶Thieme-Becker
  Hogarth   PR
  Hogarth,   PR
  Horarth   PR
  W. Hogarth   PR
  William Hogarth   PR
Hogben, Gavin (*British architect,*
  1954-)   **AV**
  Bibl: Ottagono, 1987 Sept., v.22,
    no.86, p.38
Hogenberg, Franz   **BA GC**
  (*early Netherlandish painter,*
  printmaker, publisher, before
  1540-1590?)   BA
  (*Flanders painter, bef.1540-ca.*
  1590)   GC
  (*Netherlands artist, a.1540-c.*
  1590(?))   WC
  Bibl: ▶Aa, Biog. woordenboek
    NLD; ▶Bénézit; ▶Thieme-Becker
Hogenberg, Hogenbergh,
  Hohenberg, Hoochberg,
  Hoogenberg, Hougenberghe
  or van Hooberg, Franz   **WC**
  Master Francis   BA
  Pan Francis   BA

Hogenberg, Hogenbergh, Hohenberg,
  Hoochberg, Hoogenberg,
  Hoogenberghe or van Hooberg the
  Elder, Nikolaus (Johann
  Nicolaus)→see Hogenberg,
  Nikolaus
Hogenberg, Hogenbergh, Hohenberg,
  Hoochberg, Hoogenberg,
  Hougenberghe or van Hooberg,
  Franz→see Hogenberg, Franz
Hogenberg, Hogenbergh,
  Hohenberg, Hoochbergh,
  Hoogenberg, Hoogenberghe or
  van Hooberg the Younger,
  Johann or Hans (*German artist,*
  op.1594-1614)   **WC**
Hogenberg, Hogenbergh,
  Hohenberg, Hoochbergh,
  Hoogenberg, Hoogenberghe or
  van Hooberg, Remigius
  (*Netherlands artist, c.1536-p.1587*) **WC**
Hogenberg, Nikolaus   **BA GC**
  (*German artist, op.1523-m.*
  1539)   WC
  (*German painter, printmaker, ca.*
  1500-1539)   BA
  (*German, d.1539*)   GC
  Bibl: ▶Encyc. world art; ▶Hollstein,
    German, v.13a; ▶Met. Mus. Art
    libr. cat.; ▶Thieme-Becker; ▶Witt
    checklist

Hogenberg, Hogenbergh,
  Hohenberg, Hoochberg,
  Hoogenberg, Hoogenberghe
  or van Hooberg the Elder,
  Nikolaus (Johann Nicolaus)   **WC**
Höger, Fritz   **AV BA**
  (*German architect, 1877-1949*)   BA
  (*German architect, Hamburg,*
  1877-1949)   AV
  Bibl: ▶Avery Libr. cat.; ▶Avery
    obit. idx.; ▶Macmillan encyc.
    archts.; ▶Neue deutsche Biog.;
    ▶Thieme-Becker
Hoger, Joseph (*German artist, 1801-*
  1877)   **WC**
Hoger, R.A. (*German artist, 19th*
  cent.)   **WC**
Hogers, Jacob   **GC WC**
  (*Dutch artist, 1614-p.1655*)   WC
  (*Dutch painter and*
  draughtsman, 1614-aft.1655)   GC
  Bibl: Getty Photo Study Coll.;
    ▶Thieme-Becker; ▶Witt checklist
Hogerwaard, Frans (*Dutch painter,*
  1882-1921)   **GC**
  Bibl: ▶Thieme-Becker
Hogg, Herbert W. (*British artist, op.*
  1883-1885)   **WC WI**
Hogg, Jabez (*British, 1817-1899,*
  daguerreotypist)   **JG**
Hoggatt, William (*British artist,*
  1880-1961)   **WI**

Högler, Wolfgang   **GC WC**
   (German artist, 1674-1754)   WC
   (German painter, 1674-1754)   GC
   Bibl: ▶Witt checklist
Hogley, Stephen E. *(British artist,*
op.1874-1893)   **WI**
Hoglund, J. David *(Architect, 1955-)*   **AV**
   Bibl: ▶Libr. of Congr. Name Auth.
   File
Hogrefe, Robert *(American*
architect)   **AV**
   Bibl: Architectural digest, 1986
   May, v.43, no.5, p.155
Hogue → see Hogue, Alexandre
Hogue, Alexandre   **BA PR WC**
   (American painter, b. 1898)   PR
   (American painter, calligrapher,
   b.1898)   BA
   (French artist, op.1936)   WC
   Bibl: ▶RILA/BHA; ▶WW Amer. Art,
   1976
   Alexandre Hogue   PR
   Hogue   PR
Hogue, Gwendolyn *(American*
artist, 20th c.)   **BA**
   Bibl: Chavis, 10 Michigan Afro-
   Amer. artists
Hoguet, Charles   **GC WC**
   (German artist, 1821-1870)   WC
   (German painter, 1821-1870)   GC
   Bibl: ▶Thieme-Becker
Hoguet, Louis *(German painter, act.*
1856-1881)   **GC**
   Bibl: ▶Thieme-Becker
Hohanes → see Yovhannēs
Hohauser, Henry *(American*
architect, Miami Beach, FL)   **AV**
   Bibl: Landscape, 1983, v.27, no.1,
   p.43
Hohauser, Sanford *(American*
architect, b.1933)   **BA**
   Bibl: ▶Avery period. idx., H-S;
   ▶NYPL Art & Arch. Div., Dict.
   catalog
Hohe, Christian Nikolaus *(German*
artist, 1798-1868)   **WC**
Hohenbaum, Hans *(Swiss painter in*
AUT, 15th c.)   **BA**
   Bibl: Perger, Öster. Zeit. für Kunst
   u. Denk. 35/3-4 (1981) 85-89

Hohenberg, Johan Ferdinand von   **BA**
   (Austrian architect, 1732-
   1816)   AV BA
   (Austrian draughtsman, 1732-
   1816)   GC
   (German artist, 1732-1816)   WC
   Bibl: Ancient Monuments Society.
   Transactions, 1986, new ser.,
   v.30, p.70; ▶Avery period. idx.;
   Getty Photo Study Coll.;
   ▶RILA/BHA; ▶Thieme-Becker
   Hetzendorf von Hohenberg   GC
   Hetzendorf von Hohenberg,
   Johann Ferdinand   AV
   Hetzendorfer, Johann Ferdinand   AV
Hohenberg, Johann Ferdinand
Hetzendorf von   **AV**
Hohenberg, Johann Ferdinand
von   **GC**
Hohenberg, Johann Ferdinand
von (Hetzendorf, Hezendorf,
Hotzendorf or Hozendorf von
Hohenberg)   **WC**
Hohenberg, Johann Ferdinand
Hetzendorf von → see Hohenberg,
Johan Ferdinand von
Hohenberg, Johann Ferdinand
von → see Hohenberg, Johan
Ferdinand von
Hohenberg, Johann Ferdinand von
(Hetzendorf, Hezendorf,
Hotzendorf or Hozendorf von
Hohenberg) → see Hohenberg,
Johan Ferdinand von
Hohenberger, Franz *(Austrian artist,*
1867-)   **WC**
Hohenegger, Johann *(Austrian (?)*
architect)   **AV**
   Bibl: Planen bauen wohnen, no.
   105, p.13
Hohenstein, Adolf   **GC**
   (Russian artist, 1854-)   WC
   (Russian painter, 1854-aft.1917)   GC
   Bibl: ▶Thieme-Becker
Hohenstein, Adolfo   **WC**
Hohenstein, Adolfo → see Hohenstein,
Adolf
Höher, Inge *(German painter,*
b.1941)   **BA**
   Bibl: Berlin (BRD), Neuer Berliner
   Kunstv., Inge Höher..., 1980
Hohlt, Albrecht *(German ceramist,*
20th c.)   **BA**
   Bibl: KERAMOS 83 Jan 1979
   81-88
Hohlwein, Ludwig *(German*
architect, painter, designer, 1874-
1949)   **BA**
   Bibl: ▶Neue deutsche Biog.;
   ▶Thieme-Becker; ▶Vollmer,
   Künst.-Lex. 20. Jhr.
Höhn, Johann II *(Polish medalist, ca.*
1642-1693)   **BA**
   Bibl: ▶Forrer, Medallists; Jones,
   Medal; ▶Slownik artystów
   polskich; Topolnicka-Niemcewicz,
   MEDAL, 13 (autumn 1988), 39-42

Hohnbaum, Carl Franz *(German*
artist, 1825-1867)   **WC**
Hohr, Franz Xaver Ludwig *(French*
artist, 1766-1848)   **WC**
Hohstein, Edward *(American artist,*
op.20th c.)   **WI**
Hoijer, Carl Theodor *(Finnish*
architect, 1843-1910)   **AV**
   Bibl: ▶Portoghesi, Diz. arch. e
   urbanistica, v.3, p.109
Hoijtema, Theodoor (Theo) van → see
Hoijtema, Theodoor van
Hoijtema, Theodoor van   **BA GC**
   (Dutch artist, 1863-1917)   WC
   (Dutch painter and
   draughtsman, 1863-1917)   GC
   (Dutch painter, printmaker,
   1863-1917)   BA
   Bibl: ▶Bénézit; ▶RILA/BHA;
   ▶Scheen, Ned. beeldende kunst.;
   ▶Thieme-Becker
   Hoijtema, Theodoor (Theo) van   **WC**
   Hoytema, Theodoor van   **GC**
Hoile, H. *(Australian artist, op.1835)*   **WC**
Hoin, Claude → see Hoin, Claude Jean
Baptiste
Hoin, Claude Jean Baptiste   **BA WC**
   (French artist, 1750-1817)   WC
   (French painter, printmaker,
   1750-1817)   BA
   (French, 1750-1817)   GC
   Bibl: ▶Bellier, Artistes fran.;
   ▶Bénézit; ▶Thieme-Becker; ▶Witt
   checklist
   Hoin, Claude   **GC**
Hoinka, Manfred *(German sculptor,*
b.1939)   **BA**
   Bibl: ▶WW Arts DEU
Hoit → see Hoit, Albert Gallatin
Hoit, Albert Gallatin   **PR WC WI**
   (American artist, 1809-1856)   WC WI
   (American painter, 1809-1856)   PR
   Bibl: ▶Witt checklist
   Albert Gallatin Hoit   PR
   Hoit   PR
Højholt, Per *(Danish artist, author,*
b.1928)   **BA**
   Bibl: Dansk biog. leks.; ▶Natl.
   union cat., pre-1956; Wang
   Hansen, KRITIK, XVII/68 (1984)
   104-128
Hokanson, Hans *(American sculptor,*
printmaker, b.1925)   **BA**
   Bibl: Arts Mag. CII/3 (Nov 1977),
   p.25; Arts Magazine 51 (Sept
   1976) p.24; ▶Locus; ▶MoMA libr.
   cat.; ▶NY art yrbk.
Hokanson, Lars *(Scandinavian artist,*
20th cent.)   **WC**
Hoke, Giselbert *(German artist,*
1927-)   **WC**

Hokkanen, Pertti *(Finnish architect, Espoo)* AV
Bibl: Arkkitehti, 1984, no.5; Arkkitehti, 1987, v.84, no.4-5, p.95

Hokner [Unidentified] *(Unknown painter)* PR
Bibl: (July 11, 1815, lot 35, Foster)

Hokusai, Katsushika *(Japanese printmaker, 1760-1849)* BA
Bibl: ▶Encyc. world art; ▶New Columbia encyc.

Holabird, John A *(American architect, 1920-)* AV
Bibl: Process: architecture, n.35, Dec. 1982, p.147

Holabird, John Augur *(American architect, 1886-1945)* BA
Bibl: ▶Hitchcock, Arch. 19 & 20cs; Peisch, The Chicago School of Arch.; ▶WWW Amer.

Holabird, William *(American architect, 1854-1923)* AV

Holan, Karel *(Czech painter, 1893-1953)* BA
Bibl: ▶Bénézit; ▶Vollmer, Künst.-Lex. 20. Jhr.

Holand, Johann *(German, b. Eggenfelden ca. 1390)* JG

Holanda, Francisco de → *see* Hollanda, Francisco de

Holarek, Emil *(Czech artist, 1867-1919)* WC

Holbe → *see* Holbein, Hans, the younger

Holbeen → *see* Holbein, Hans, the younger

Holbein → *see* Holbein, Hans, the younger

Holbein (Olpeius Olpenus, Holby, Holben etc.,) Hans, II → *see* Holbein, Hans, the younger

Holbein (the elder) → *see* Holbein, Hans, the elder

Holbein the Younger, Hans → *see* Holbein, Hans, the elder

Holbein, Ambrosius BA GC PR
(German artist, c.1494-c.1520) WC
(German painter, ca.1494-ca. 1520) BA PR
(German, ca.1494-ca.1520) GC
Bibl: ▶Encyc. world art; ▶RILA/BHA; ▶Thieme-Becker
Ambrosius Holbein PR

Holbein, Ambrosius Prosy, Ambrose or Ambrosy WC

Holbein, Ambrosius Prosy, Ambrose or Ambrosy → *see* Holbein, Ambrosius

Holbein, Hans (II) → *see* Holbein, Hans, the younger

Holbein, Hans (the elder) → *see* Holbein, Hans, the elder

Holbein, Hans (the younger) → *see* Holbein, Hans, the younger

Holbein, Hans, I → *see* Holbein, Hans, the elder

Holbein, Hans, the elder BA
(German artist, 1460/5-1524) WC
(German painter and draughtsman, ca.1465-1524) GC
(German painter, 1460-1524) PR
(German painter, ca.1465-1524) BA
(Swiss, 1497-1543) JG
Bibl: ▶Allgem. Deut. Biog.; ▶Artist biog. master idx.; ▶Bénézit; ▶Darmstädter, Künstlerlex.; ▶McGraw-Hill dict. art; ▶Neue deutsche Biog.; ▶Petit Larousse; ▶RILA/BHA; ▶Thieme-Becker; ▶Winkler Prins van de kunst
Hans Holbein (the elder) PR
Holbein (the elder) PR
Holbein the Younger, Hans JG
Holbein, Hans (the elder) GC PR
Holbein, Hans, I WC

Holbein, Hans, the younger BA PR
(German artist, c.1497-1543) WC
(German painter and draughtsman, 1497/98-1543) GC
(German painter, 1497/98-1543) PR
(German painter, printmaker, ca. 1497-1543) BA
Bibl: ▶Allgem. Deut. Biog.; ▶Artist biog. master idx.; ▶Bénézit; ▶Darmstädter, Künstlerlex.; ▶McGraw-Hill dict. art; ▶Neue deutsche Biog.; ▶RILA/BHA; ▶Thieme-Becker
Albens fiammingo PR
Giovanni Holben PR
Giovanni Holbeno PR
Giovanni Holbense PR
H. Holbein PR
H. Holbien PR
Hans Holbein PR
Hans Holbein (II) PR
Hans Holbein (the younger) PR
Hans Holbien PR
Hbens PR
Ho bein PR
Holbe PR
Holbeen PR
Holbein PR
Holbein (Olpeius Olpenus, Holby, Holben etc.,) Hans, II WC
Holbein, Hans (II) PR
Holbein, Hans (the younger) GC PR
Holbeins PR
Holben PR
Holbeni PR
Holbens PR
Holber PR
Holbien PR
Hollebeen PR
Jean Holbein PR
John, or Hans, Holbein PR
Oelbren PR
Olbeius PR
Olbeni PR
Olbens PR
Orbens PR
Orbens Svizzero PR
Ubeno PR
Ulbens PR
Ulbens fiammengo PR
Holbein, Sigismund → *see* Holbein, Sigmund

Holbein, Sigmund GC PR
(German artist, 1465/70-1540) WC
(German painter, d. 1540) PR
(German, 1465/70-1540) GC
Bibl: ▶Thieme-Becker; ▶Witt checklist

Holbein, Sigismund WC
Sigmund Holbein PR

Holbein, Therese *(German artist, c.1785-1859)* WC

Holbeins → *see* Holbein, Hans, the younger

Holbek, Johannes *(Danish painter,*
author, 1872-1903)   **BA**
   Bibl: ▶Nørregård-Nielsen, Dansk
   kunst; ▶Thieme-Becker
Hölbeling, Johann Andreas
(German goldsmith, act.1792,
d.1826)   **BA**
   Bibl: Scheffler, Goldschmiede
   Niedersachsens
Holben→see Holbein, Hans, the
   younger
Holbeni→see Holbein, Hans, the
   younger
Holbens→see Holbein, Hans, the
   younger
Holber→see Holbein, Hans, the
   younger
Holberton, Wakeman *(American*
artist, 1839-1898)   **WI**
Holbien→see Holbein, Hans, the
   younger
Holbimer→see Hobbema, Meindert
Holbina→see Hobbema, Meindert
Holblock→see Holblock, Jan
   Cornelisz.
Holblock, Jan Cornelisz. *(Dutch*
painter, ca.1612-1679)   **PR**
   Bibl: ▶Thieme-Becker
   Holblock   PR
   Jan Cornelisz. Holblock   PR
Holbo, Kristen *(Norwegian artist,*
1869-p.1900)   **WC**
Holbrook, Bill *(American interior*
designer, Long Beach, Calif)   **AV**
   Bibl: House beautiful, 1987 Feb.,
   v.130, no.2, p.58
Holbrook, Peter   **WC WI**
   (American artist, 1940-)   WC
   (American artist, b.1940)   WI
Holcombe, James W. *(British, active*
Venice, Italy 1890s)   **JG**
Hold, Abel *(British artist, 1815-1891)*   **WI**
Holdanowicz, Leszek *(Polish artist,*
20th cent.)   **WC**
Holdcroft, John   **WC WI**
   (British artist, 1926-)   WC
   (British artist, b.1926)   WI
Holden, Ann *(American interior*
designer, New Orleans, La)   **AV**
   Bibl: House beautiful, 1985 Oct.,
   v.127, no.11, p.52
Holden, Barry   **AV BA**
   (American artist, 20th c.)   BA
   (American sculptor)   AV
   Bibl: Cameron, Arts mag., LXI
   (Sep. 1986) pp.40-46; Fine
   homebuilding, 1989 Apr.-May,
   no.53, back cover
Holden, Charles Henry   **BA**
   (British architect, 1875-1960)   AV BA
   Bibl: ▶Avery obit. idx.; ▶Contemp.
   archts.
Holden, Charles, Sir   **AV**
Holden, Charles, Sir→see Holden,
   Charles Henry

Holden, Clifford   **WC WI**
   (British artist, 1919-)   WC
   (British artist, b.1919)   WI
   Bibl: ▶Waters, Brit. artists
Holden, Colin *(British artist, b.1957)*   **BA**
   Bibl: Arts Council GBR, Welsh
   Comm., Coming out (1979)
Holden, Harold→see Holden, Harold
   Henry
Holden, Harold Henry   **WI**
   (British artist, 1885-)   WC
   (British artist, b.1885)   WI
Holden, Harold   **WC**
Holden, Hyla *(British enamelist,*
1723-1766)   **BA**
   Bibl: Benjamin, Engl. enamels;
   English ceramic circle, X/2 (1977)
   pp.118-129
Holden, Jean S.→see Holden, Jean
   Stansbury
Holden, Jean Stansbury *(American*
painter, ca.1842-1934)   **PR**
   Bibl: ▶Petteys, Women artists
   Holden, Jean S.   PR
   Jean Stansbury Holden   PR
Holden, John N. *(British artist, op.*
1949-)   **WI**
Holden, Richard *(American*
architect)   **AV**
   Bibl: Architectural digest, v.41,
   n.8, 1984, p.84
Holdensen, Annette *(Danish textile*
artist, b.1934)   **BA**
   Bibl: Lium, Fynske
   Kunsthåndvaerkere; Lium, R.N.,
   CRAS:..., 51 (1987) p.82-95
Holdensen, Peter *(American*
architect, Boston, Mass.; fl. ca.
1930)   **AV**
   Bibl: Landmarks observer, 1989
   spring, v.15, no.4, p.5
Holder, Edward Henry   **WC WI**
   (British artist, circa 1864-op.
   circa 1922)   WI
   (British artist, op.1864-m.1917)   WC
Holder, Edwin *(British artist, op.*
1856-1864)   **WI**
Holder, Franz van *(Belgian artist,*
1882-1919)   **WC**
Holder, Wayne Brinson *(American*
interior designer, Mobile, Ala)   **AV**
   Bibl: Southern accents, 1988
   Sept.-Oct., v.11, no.5, p.230
Holdermann, Georg *(German wax*
modeler, 1585-1629)   **BA**
   Bibl: Anz. des Germ. Nationalmus.
   (1979) 121; ▶Thieme-Becker
Holding, Carol *(American artist, op.*
20th c.)   **WI**
Holding, Edgar Thomas   **WC WI**
   (British artist, 1870-1952)   WI
   (British artist, 19th cent.)   WC
Holding, Henry James G. *(British*
artist, 1833-1872)   **WI**

Holding, John   **WC WI**
   (British artist, 19th cent.)   WC
   (British artist, op.19th c.)   WI
Holdredge→see Holdredge, Ransome
   Gillet
Holdredge, Ransom Gillet→see
   Holdredge, Ransome Gillet
Holdredge, Ransome G. →see
   Holdredge, Ransome Gillet
Holdredge, Ransome Gillet   **WI**
   (American artist, 1836-1899)   WC WI
   (American painter, 1836-1899)   PR
   Bibl: ▶WWW Amer. art
   Holdredge   PR
Holdredge, Ransom Gillet   **PR**
Holdredge, Ransome G.   **WC**
   Holdridge, Ransom G.   PR
   Ransom Gillet Holdredge   PR
Holdridge, Ransom G. →see
   Holdredge, Ransome Gillet
Holdship, Richard *(British*
printmaker, pottery manufacturer,
act.1751-1764)   **BA**
   Bibl: ▶Mankowitz, Encyc. pott. &
   porc.
Holdstock, Arthur Worsley
(Canadian artist, op.1850)   **WC**
Hole, Henry Fulke Plantaganet
   Woolcombe→see Hole, Henry
   Fulke Plantagenet Woolcombe
Hole, Henry Fulke Plantagenet
Woolcombe   **BA**
   (British artist, op.1798-, d.1820)   WI
   (British artist, op.1798-m.1820)   WC
   (British printmaker, ca.1781-
   1820)   BA
   Bibl: ▶Dict. natl. biog.; ▶Redgrave,
   Engl. school; ▶Thieme-Becker
Hole, Henry Fulke Plantaganet
Woolcombe   **WC**
Hole, Henry Plantaganet
Woolcombe   **WI**
Hole, Henry Plantaganet
   Woolcombe→see Hole, Henry
   Fulke Plantagenet Woolcombe
Hole, William *(British artist, op.*
1607-1624)   **WC WI**
Hole, William B. →see Hole, William
   Brassey
Hole, William Brassey   **WC WI**
   (British artist, 1846-1917)   WC WI
   (Engraver, London, GTL., 1846-
   1917)   WI
Hole, William B.   **WI**
Holéczyová, Elena *(Czech*
lacemaker, b.1906)   **BA**
   Bibl: Fuhrmann, Brigitta
Holemans, Henri Joseph *(Belgian*
goldsmith, 1894-1973)   **BA**
   Bibl: Ogonovszky, ANNALES
   D'HISTOIRE DE L'ART ET
   D'ARCHEOLOGIE, X (1988), p.
   51-66
Holfeld, Anke *(German artist, 20th*
cent.)   **WC**

Holfeld, Hippolyte Dominique   **GC WC**
(French artist, 1804-1872)   WC
(French painter, 1804-1872)   GC
Bibl: ▶Bénézit

Holford, Robert Stayner (British
   gardener, 1808-1892)   **AV**
Bibl: ▶Libr. of Congr. Name Auth.
File

Holford, W.G., Mrs., (Margorie) → see
Brooks, Marjorie

**Holford, William Graham Holford,
Baron** (British architect, city
   planner, 1907-1975)   **AV**
Bibl: ▶Libr. of Congr. Name Auth.
File

Holgate, Edwin Headley   **BA WC**
(Canadian artist, 1892-)   WC
(Canadian painter, printmaker,
   1892-1977)   BA
Bibl: ▶Artists Canada;
▶MacDonald, Can. artists; Ottawa
(Ont, CAN), Natl. Gall.,
Modernism in Quebec art (1982)

Holgate, Thomas W. (British artist,
   1899-1910)   **WI**

Holguín, Melchor Pérez → see Pérez
Holguín, Melchor

Holhtz, Jacob [Unidentified]
(Unknown painter)   **PR**
Bibl: (March 2, 1805, lot 69,
Christie's)
Jacob Holhtz   PR

Holiday, Gilbert Joseph (British
   artist, 1879-1937)   **WI**
Bibl: Paviere, Brit. sporting ptrs

Holiday, Henry   **BA WC**
(British artist, 1839-1927)   BA WC WI
Bibl: ▶Johnson, Brit. artists;
▶Thieme-Becker; ▶Vollmer,
Künst.-Lex. 20. Jhr.

Holiday, Henry James   **WI**
Holiday, Henry James → see Holiday,
Henry

Holik, Franz (Austrian architect, act.
   ca.1900)   **BA**

Holis, Doug (American artist, 20th
   c.)   **BA**
Bibl: Dayton (O, USA), Wright
State U., Dept. of Art,
QUINTESSANCE, 1979

Holk, Lois (Austrian architect)   **AV**
Bibl: Der Aufbau, 1986, v.41,
no.8, p.424

Holker, John (British textile
   manufacturer, 1719-1786)   **BA**
Holl → see Holl, Frank

Holl, Barth. (German)   **GC**
Bibl: Gernsheim, Corpus Photog.
of Drawings, 1774

Holl, Benjamin (Engraver, 1808-
   1884)   **WI**

Holl, Edward   **AV BA**
(British architect, act.1804,
   d.1824)   BA
(British architect, d.1824)   AV
Bibl: ▶Colvin, Brit. archts.
Holl, Elias → see Holl, Elias I

Holl, Elias I   **BA**
(1573-1646)   AV
(German architect, 1573-1646)   BA
(German artist, 1573-1646)   WC
Bibl: ▶Brockhaus Enzyk.; ▶Encyc.
world art; Penguin dict. arch.;
▶Thieme-Becker

Holl, Elias   **AV WC**

Holl, Elias II (German painter,
   printmaker, 1611-1657)   **BA**
Bibl: ▶Hollstein, German, v.15;
▶Thieme-Becker, v.17, p.368

Holl, Francis I (British artist, 1815-
   1884)   **WI**
Holl, Francis Montague (Frank) → see
Holl, Frank

Holl, Frank   **BA PR WI**
(British artist, 1845-1888)   WC WI
(British painter, 1845-1888)   BA PR
Bibl: ▶Dict. natl. biog.; ▶RILA/BHA
Frank Holl   PR
Holl   PR

Holl, Francis Montague (Frank)   **WC**
Holl, Hieronymus I   **BA**
Holl, Matthäus (German architect,
   1620-1681)   **BA**
Bibl: ▶Neue deutsche Biog.;
Reclams Schweden, pp.277, 409

Holl, Steven   **AV BA**
(American architect, b.1947)   BA
(American architect, New York,
   N.Y, 1947-)   AV
Bibl: ▶Avery period. idx., 1986
suppl.; Holl, AA Files, XIV (Spr
1987) 18-24; New York (NY,
USA), MOMA, Emilio Ambasz,
Steven Holl... (1989) p.14; NYC
phone bk., 1987

Holl, William I   **WI**
(British artist, 1771-1838)   WC WI
Holl, William, I   **WC**
Holl, William, I → see Holl, William I
Holl, William, II (Engraver, 1807-
   1871)   **WI**

Hollagan, M.J.   **WC WI**
(British artist, op.1790-1809)   WI
(British artist, op.1795-1809)   WC
Bibl: ▶Waterhouse, Brit. 18c. ptrs.

Hollams, F. Mabel   **WC WI**
(British artist, op.1897-1912)   WC
(British artist, op.1897-1929)   WI
Hollams, F.Mabel, Miss   WI
Hollams, F.Mabel, Miss → see Hollams,
F. Mabel

Holland, Clifford M. (American
   engineer)   **AV**
Bibl: Lotus international, 1988,
no.56, p.87

Holland, Francis Raymond
(American painter, 1886-1934)   **PR**
Bibl: ▶WWW Amer. art
Francis Raymond Holland   PR
Holland, George → see Holland, John
Joseph
Holland, George (John Joseph) → see
Holland, John Joseph

**Holland, George Herbert
Buckingham** (British artist,
   b.1901)   **WI**
Holland, H.   **WC WI**
(British artist, 17th cent.)   WC
(British artist, op.17th c.)   WI
Holland, Harry   **BA WI**
(British artist, b.1941)   WI
(British painter, printmaker,
   b.1941)   BA
Bibl: ▶Babington Smith, Contemp.
artists

Holland, Henry   **AV BA FA WC WI**
(1745-1806; Architect, England)   FA
(British architect, 1745-1806)   AV BA
(British artist, c.1740-1806)   WC
(British artist, circa 1740-1806)   WI
Bibl: ▶Colvin, Brit. archts.; ▶Dict.
natl. biog.; ▶Encyc. world art;
▶Macmillan encyc. archts., v.2,
p.409 ff.; ▶Thieme-Becker

Holland, James   **BA GC PR WC WI**
(British artist, 1800-1870)   WC WI
(British painter, 1800-1870)   BA PR
(British, 1800-1870)   GC
Bibl: ▶Dict. natl. biog.; ▶Redgrave,
Engl. school; ▶RILA/BHA;
▶Thieme-Becker; ▶Witt checklist
James Holland   PR
Holland, John → see Holland, John I
Holland, John → see Holland, John II

Holland, John I   **WI**
(British artist, 18th cent.)   WC
(British artist, op.18th c.)   WI
Bibl: Hall, Nottinghamshire
Holland, John   **WC**
Holland, John II   **WI**
(British artist, 1830-1886)   WI
(British artist, op.1831-1879)   WC
Holland, John   **WC**
Holland, John Joseph   **WI**
(American artist, c.1776-1820)   WC
(American artist, circa 1776-
   1820)   WI
Holland, George   WI
Holland, George (John Joseph)   **WC**
Holland, Juliet (American artist,
   20th c.)   **BA**
Bibl: ▶Intl. dir. exh. artists, 1982-
1983

Holland, Lindsay (Australian
   architect, Melbourne)   **AV**
Bibl: Transition, 1988 Autumn,
no.24, p.52

Holland, Margaret (English, d.1439)   **BA**
Bibl: Blue guide, p.27; ▶Burke's
dormant & extinct; Canterbury:
The Cath., p.15

Holland, Nathaniel Dance → see
Dance-Holland, Nathaniel

Holland, Neil John (British architect)   **AV**
Bibl: ▶RIBA members, 1983

Holland, Peter   **WC WI**
(British artist, 1757-op.1812)   WI
(British artist, op.1781-1812)   WC

Holland, Sebastopol Samuel
(British artist, op.1880-1911)   **WI**

Holland, Tom   **BA WC WI**
(American artist, 20th cent.)   WC
(American artist, b.1936)   WI
(American painter, b.1936)   BA
Bibl: ▶Intl. dir. exh. artists, 1983;
▶WW Amer. Art, 1984

Holland, William   **WC WI**
(British artist, op.1798)   WC
(British artist, op.1798-)   WI

Hollanda, António de   **BA**
(early Netherlandish painter,
illuminator in PRT, act.1518-
1551)   BA
(Portuguese artist, 16th cent.)   WC
Bibl: ▶Pamplona, Pint. escult. PRT;
▶Thieme-Becker

Antonio de Hollanda   **WC**

Hollanda, Francisco de   **AV BA FA**
(1517-1584)   AV
(ca. 1517/1518-19.VI.1584;
Artist, Portugal)   FA
(Miniaturist, painter,
draughtsman, writer, post
1516/ante 1519-1584)   CE
(Portuguese artist, architect,
author, 1517-1584)   BA
(Portuguese artist,
c.1517/18-1584)   WC
Bibl: ▶Bénézit; De Aetatibus
Mundi Imagines, Madrid (ESP),
Biblioteca Nacional, scenes from
Genesis; ▶Encyc. world art; ▶Natl.
union cat., pre-1956; ▶RILA/BHA,
Subject, 1988; Segurado, F
d'Ollanda; Smith, Art Portugal;
▶Thieme-Becker, v.12, p.331 ff,
and p.614

D'Ollanda, Francisco   CE
Da Holanda Francisco   CE
De Holanda, Francisco   **CE**
De Holanda, Francisco   CE
Dolanda, Francisco   CE FA
Francisco d'Ollanda   FA
Francisco de Hollanda   AV CE
Francisco de Hollanda d'Ollanda
or Dolanda   **WC**
Francisco Dolanda   FA
Francisco Dollanda   CE
Holanda, Francisco de   AV
Ollanda, Francisco d'   AV
Hollander Cz., Hendrik   **GC**
(Dutch artist, 1823-1884)   WC
(Dutch painter, 1823-1884)   GC
Bibl: ▶Thieme-Becker

Hollander, Cz., Hendrik   **WC**
Hollander, Cz., Hendrik → see
Hollander Cz., Hendrik

Hollander, Elizabeth (Commissioner
of Planning, Chicago, Ill)   **AV**
Bibl: Inland architect, 1987 Jan.-
Feb., v.31, no.1, p.20; Inland
architect, 1989 Sept.-Oct., v.33,
no.5, p.78
Hollender, Elizabeth   AV

Hollander, Fenton (American
architect, Cambridge, Mass)   **AV**
Bibl: ▶AIA Pro File, 1987-88

Hollander, Irwin   **BA WI**
(American printer, b.1927)   BA
(Engraver, b.1927)   WI
Bibl: ▶Archives Amer. Art Jrnl.,
XI/1-4 (1971)

Hollander, Jord den (Dutch
architect)   **AV**
Bibl: De Architect, 1988 July-Aug.,
v.19, no.7-8. p.57

Hollander, Paul den (Dutch
photographer, b.1950)   **BA**
Bibl: Naples (ITA), Museo
Capodimonte, Napoli '82 (1982)

Hollanders, Johannes (Belgian
artist, 1821-)   **WC**

Hollar, Wenceslaus   **BA**
(Bohemian printmaker, 1607-
1677)   BA
(Czech draughtsman, 1607-
1677)   GC
(German artist, 1607-1677)   WC
Bibl: ▶Bénézit; ▶Brockhaus Enzyk.;
Getty Photo Study Coll.; ▶Lex.
Kunst; ▶Thieme-Becker

Hollar, Wenzel   **GC**
Hollar, Wenzel (Wenceslas von
Pracha)   **WC**
Hollar, Wenzel → see Hollar,
Wenceslaus
Hollar, Wenzel (Wenceslas von
Pracha) → see Hollar, Wenceslaus
Hollebeen → see Holbein, Hans, the
younger

Hollebeke, Bruno Jean Charles van
(Belgian artist, 1817-1892)   **WC**

Hollegha, Wolfgang (German artist,
1929-)   **WC**

Hollein, Hans   **AV BA**
(Austrian architect, 1934-)   AV
(Austrian architect, designer,
artist, b.1934)   BA
Bibl: ▶Contemp. archts.; ▶MoMA
libr. cat.; ▶WW Austria

Hollenbeck, Frank Bradbury
(American architect, East
Hampton, N.Y.; principal of Morey
& Hollenbeck, 1932-)   **AV**
Bibl: ▶AIA Pro File, 1987-88
Hollender, Elizabeth → see Hollander,
Elizabeth

Hollerbach, Serge (American
painter, b.1923)   **BA**
Bibl: ▶WW Amer. Art, 1980

Holliday, Edward (British artist, op.
1877-1884)   **WI**

Holliday, J. Michael (American
architect, Sarasota, Fla)   **AV**
Bibl: Fine homebuilding, 1988
Oct.-Nov., no.49, p.back cover

Holliday, Jessie (British artist, op.
1905-1908)   **WI**

Hollier, Jean Francois (French artist,
1772-1845)   **WC**

Hollin [Unidentified] (Unknown
painter)   **PR**
Bibl: (April 3, 1806, lot 23,
Greenwood)
Hollingdale, B. → see Hollingdale, R.

Hollingdale, Horatio R. (British
artist, op.1881-1899)   **WI**
Hollingdale, R.   **WI**
(British artist, op.1850-1899)   WC
(British artist, op.19th c.)   WI
Hollingdale, B.   WI
Hollingdale, Richard   **WC**
Hollingdale, Richard → see
Hollingdale, R.

Hollinger (American, active NY, U.S.
ca. 1900 (Hollinger & Co.))   **JG**

Hollingsworth, George (American
artist, 1813-1882)   **WC WI**

Hollingsworth, William Robert
(American artist, 1910-1944)   **BA**
Bibl: Hollingsworth: Hollingsworth
Hollingworth Magniac
Collection → see Magniac,
Hollingworth

Hollingworth, John (Canadian
photographer, act.1861-1867)   **BA**
Bibl: HIST. OF PHOTOG. II, July
1978
Hollingworth, T. → see Hollingworth,
Thomas

Hollingworth, Thomas   **WI**
(British artist, 19th cent.)   WC
(British artist, op.1857-1885)   WI
Hollingworth, T.   **WC**

Hollins, John (British artist, 1798-
1855)   **WC WI**

Hollins, Peter (British sculptor, 1800-
1886)   **BA**
Bibl: ▶Dict. natl. biog.; ▶Grant,
Brit. sculptors; ▶Gunnis, Brit.
sculp.; ▶Thieme-Becker

Hollins, R. S. (British building
surveyor, architect, Framingham)   **AV**
Bibl: RIBA journal, 1984 Apr.,
v.91, no.4, p.39

Hollins, T.   **WC WI**
(British artist, 18th cent.)   WC
(British artist, op.18th c.)   WI

Hollis, Douglas   **AV BA**
(American artist, designer of
''site-sensitive structures,''
San Francisco, Calif)   AV
(American sculptor, b.1948)   BA
Bibl: Buffalo (NY, USA), Albright-
Knox, MADE FOR BUFFALO...,
1980; Landscape architecture,
1987 May-June, v.77, no.3, p.52

Hollis, George (British artist, 1792-
1842)   **WC WI**
Bibl: ▶Engen, Victorian engravers

Hollis, Thomas (British artist, 1818-
1843)   **WC WI**

Hollister (Active Niagara Falls,
Ontario, Canada, daguerreotypist)   **JG**

Holló, László (*Hungarian painter, 1887-1976*) **BA**
Bibl: Biro, B., A MAGYAR MUVES.. ..BIBLIOGRAFIAJA (1955), p.297; Kovacs, P., DEBRECENI MUZEUM EVKONYUE (1987), pp.421-425; ▶Libr. of Congr. Name Auth. File, 1987-88

Hollósy, Simon **BA WC**
(*Hungarian artist, 1857-1918*) WC
(*Hungarian painter, 1857-1918*) BA
Bibl: ▶Bénézit; ▶Thieme-Becker; ▶Uj magyar lexikon

Hollow, Geoffrey (*British artist, b.1944*) **WI**

Holloway, Charles (*American artist, 1859-1941*) **AV**
Bibl: ▶WWW Amer. art

Holloway, Charles Edward (*British artist, 1838-1897*) **WC WI**

Holloway, Christopher (*British artist, b.1957*) **WI**

Holloway, J. **WC WI**
(*British artist, 19th cent.*) WC
(*British artist, op.19th c.*) WI
Bibl: Morris

Holloway, John Henry (*British artist, 20th c.*) **BA**
Bibl: Leonardo XI/1 (winter 1978) p.9-12

Holloway, Louis C. (*American architect*) **AV**
Bibl: Southern accents, 1985 Nov. -Dec., v.8, no.6, p.116

Holloway, Thomas (*British artist, 1748-1827*) **WC WI**
Bibl: ▶Waterhouse, Brit. 18c. ptrs.

Hollweg, Alexander (*British artist, op.20th c.*) **WI**

Hollyer, Eva **WC WI**
(*British artist, op.1889-1902*) WI
(*British artist, op.1891-1892*) WC

Hollyer, Frederick (*British, 1837-1933*) **JG**

Hollyhead, Brian (*British illustrator, 20th c.*) **BA**
Bibl: Arts Council GBR, Welsh Comm., Images to order (1979)

Hollywood, Elias (*British painter, b.1936*) **BA**
Bibl: Bristol (GBR), Arnolfini Gallery, Bristol sample (1979)

Holm (*Unknown artist*) **GC**
Bibl: Gernsheim, Corpus Photog. of Drawings, 1739

Holm → see Holm, Emil

Holm → see Holm, Per Daniel

Holm, Anders (*Swedish artist, c.1770-p.1822*) **WC**

Holm, Christian Frederik Carl (*Danish artist, 1804-1846*) **WC**

Holm, Emil (*Danish painter, 1823-1863*) **PR**
Bibl: ▶Thieme-Becker
Emil Holm PR
Holm PR
Holm, Niels Emil Severin PR

Holm, Erik Einar (*Danish architect*) **AV**
Bibl: ▶Danske Arkitekters Landsforbund

Holm, Hans Jørgen (*Danish architect, 1835-1916*) **BA**

Holm, Harald Martin Hansen (*Danish artist, 1866-1920*) **WC**

Holm, Heinrich Gustav Ferdinand (*Danish artist, 1816-1861*) **WC**

Holm, Jesper Johansen (*Danish, 1748-1828*) **GC**
Bibl: ▶Bénézit

Holm, Niels **VO**
(*Danish sculptor, b. 1860*) VO
(*Scandinavian artist, 1860-*) WC
Bibl: ▶Thieme-Becker, v. 17, p. 389

Holm, Niels Emil Severin **WC**
Holm, Niels Emil Severin → see Holm, Emil
Holm, Niels Emil Severin → see Holm, Niels

Holm, O. (*Scandinavian artist, 19th cent.*) **WC**
Holm, P.D. → see Holm, Per Daniel

Holm, Per Daniel **PR**
(*Scandinavian artist, 1835-1903*) WC
(*Swedish painter, 1835-1903*) PR
Bibl: ▶Thieme-Becker
Holm PR

Holm, P.D. **WC**
Per Daniel Holm PR

Holm, Thomas Campanius (*Swedish printmaker, ca.1670-1702*) **BA**
Bibl: ▶Svenskt konst.-lex.

Holm-Moller, Olivia → see Holm-Møller, Olivia

Holm-Møller, Olivia **BA**
(*Danish artist, 1875-*) WC
(*Danish painter, sculptor, printmaker, 1875-1970*) BA
Bibl: Lyngby (DNK), Sophienholm, OLIVIA HOLM-MØLLER, SOPHIENHOLM, 1978; ▶Vollmer, Künst.-Lex. 20. Jhr.; ▶Weilbach, Kunst.leks.

Holm-Moller, Olivia **WC**

Holman, Donald R. (*Canadian printmaker, b.1946*) **BA**

Holman, Francis **BA WC WI**
(*British artist, op.1760-, d.1790*) WI
(*British artist, op.1767-1784*) WC
(*English painter, act.1774-1784*) BA
Bibl: ▶Bénézit; ▶Thieme-Becker

Holman, G.P. (*American, active ca. 1910*) **JG**

Holman, Louis Arthur (*American author, dealer, illustrator, 1866-1939*) **BA**
Bibl: ▶Fielding's Amer. ptrs.; ▶WWW Amer., v.1

Holman, R. **WC WI**
(*British artist, op.1765*) WC
(*British artist, op.1765-*) WI

Holman-Hunt, William, Mrs. (Marion Edith) → see Hunt, Marion Edith

Holmberg, August Johann (*German artist, 1851-1911*) **WC**

Holmberg, Gustaf Werner **BA WC**
(*Finnish artist, 1830-1860*) WC
(*Finnish painter, 1830-1860*) BA
Bibl: Düsseldorf (DEU), Kunstmus., Düsseldorf u. Norden (1976); ▶Encyc. world art; ▶Thieme-Becker

Holmbergsson, Johan (*Swedish artist, 1804-1835*) **WC**

Holmboe, Thorolf (*Norwegian artist, 1866-1935*) **WC**

Holme, Rathbone **WC WI**
(*British artist, 20th cent.*) WC
(*British artist, op.20th c.*) WI

Holmead Phillips → see Phillips, Holmead

Hølmebakk, Carl-Viggo (*Norwegian architect, 1958-*) **AV**
Bibl: Byggekunst: the Norwegian review of architecture, 1988, v.70, no.5, p.348

Holmer, Kerstin (*Swedish landscape architect, Sölvesborg(?)*) **AV**
Bibl: Arkitektur: the Swedish review of architecture, 1988 Jan.-Feb., v.88, no.1, p.48

Holmer, Lars A. (*Swedish architect, Sölvesborg, 1929-*) **AV**
Bibl: ▶Svenska Ark. Riks., 1984

Holmes (*daguerreotypist*) **JG**

Holmes (*British artist, 19th cent.*) **WC**

Holmes, Andrew **AV BA**
(*British architect, artist*) AV
(*British architect, b.1947*) BA
Bibl: ▶Arch. period. idx./RIBA; ▶Art Index, v.34; ▶Avery period. idx., suppl. 7,8; Design, 1985 Apr., no.436, p.44

Holmes, Arthur W. → see Holmes, Arthur William

Holmes, Arthur William **BA**
(*Canadian architect, 1863-*) AV
(*Canadian architect, 1863-1944*) BA
Bibl: Bulletin of the Society for the Study of Architecture in Canada, 1985 Mar., v.10, no.1, p.4; Thomas, Racar, XIII/2 (1986) p.97

Holmes, Arthur W. **AV**

Holmes, Basil (*British artist, op. 1844-1850*) **WI**

Holmes, Bob (*Scottish architect*) **AV**
Bibl: Building design, 1987 Aug. (suppl.), p.49

Holmes, Charles John   **BA PR WI**
    (British artist, 1868-1936)   WC WI
    (British painter, 1868-1936)   PR
    (British painter, printmaker,
      critic, 1868-1936)   BA
    Bibl: ▶Bénézit; ▶RILA/BHA;
      ▶Vollmer, Künst.-Lex. 20. Jhr.;
      ▶Waters, Brit. artists; ▶Who was
      who [GBR], 1929-40
    Charles John Holmes   PR
    Holmes, Charles John, Sir   PR
Holmes, Sir Charles John   WC
Holmes, Charles John, Sir → see
  Holmes, Charles John
Holmes, David Valentine *(American*
    sculptor, painter, b.1945)   **BA**
    Bibl: ▶WW Amer. Art
Holmes, Dwight E. *(American*
    architect)   **AV**
Holmes, Edward   WC WI
    (British artist, op.1841-, d.circa
      1893)   WI
    (British artist, op.1841-1891)   WC
Holmes, Emily R., Miss *(British*
    artist, op.1898-)   WI
Holmes, Frank *(American painter,*
    20th c.)   BA
    Bibl: ▶Art Index, Jan. 1978
Holmes, George   WC WI
    (British artist, op.1789-1802)   WC
    (British artist, op.1789-1804)   WI
Holmes, George Augustus   WC WI
    (British artist, op.1852-, d.1911)   WI
    (British artist, op.c.1852-m.
      1911)   WC
Holmes, Hendrik S. *(American*
    architect)   AV
    Bibl: Architecture, the AIA
      journal, 1983 Oct., v.72, no.10,
      p.76
Holmes, James   **BA WC WI**
    (British artist, 1777-1860)   WC WI
    (British painter, printmaker,
      1777-1860)   BA
    Bibl: ▶Dict. natl. biog.; ▶Redgrave,
      Engl. school; ▶Thieme-Becker
Holmes, Jess *(American architect,*
    Albuquerque, N.M.)   AV
    Bibl: ▶AIA Pro File, 1985
Holmes, Madeline Rachel, Miss → see
  Wells, Madeline Rachel
Holmes, Marcus *(South African*
    architect, 1952-)   AV
    Bibl: UIA international architect,
      1985, no.8, inside back cover
Holmes, Nicholas H. *(American*
    artist, Mobile, AL)   AV
    Bibl: ▶AIA Pro File, 1983
Holmes, Oliver Wendell *(American*
    artist, 1809-1894)   WC WI
Holmes, Randle [Unidentified]
    (Unknown painter)   PR
    Bibl: (1810, lot 9, Broster (John))
    Randle Holmes   PR
Holmes, Reg *(Canadian artist, 20th*
    cent.)   WC

Holmes, Richard Rivington *(British*
    artist, 1835-1911)   WI
Holmes, Robert *(Canadian painter,*
    1861-1930)   BA
    Bibl: ▶Artists Canada;
      ▶MacDonald, Can. artists
Holmes, S. *(British artist, op.1821-)*   WI
Holmes, Sir Charles John → see
  Holmes, Charles John
Holmes, William *(British silversmith,*
    act.1762-ca.1805)   BA
    Bibl: SAINT LOUIS ART MUSEUM
      BULLETIN XV/2 (Apr-June) 1979,
      174-175
Holmes, William Henry   **BA WI**
    (American artist, 1846-1933)   WI
    (American painter, 1846-1933)   BA
Holmgren, Eric *(American architect,*
    New York City)   AV
    Bibl: Sites, 1989, no.21-22, p.33
Holmlund, Josefina *(Scandinavian*
    artist, 1827-1905)   WC
Holmskov, Helge *(Danish sculptor,*
    b.1925)   BA
    Bibl: ▶Bénézit; Jensen: HELGE
      HOLMSKOV, 1982
Holmström family *(Russian*
    jewelers, 19th-20th cs.)   BA
    Bibl: Bainbridge, PETER CARL
      FABERGE... (1979) index; Munich
      (DEU), Kunsthalle, Faberge (1987),
      pp.328-329, 356
Holodilina, Elena Nikolaevna
    (Russian artist, 20th cent.)   WC
Holpein *(Russian artist, op.c.1850-*
    1854)   WC
Holper, Hieronymus *(German*
    goldsmith, act.1435-1476)   BA
    Bibl: Anz. des Germ. Nationalmus.
      (1978) 24-34; ▶Thieme-Becker
Holperl, Antonin *(Czech artist,*
    1820-1888)   WC
Holroyd, Charles   **PR WI**
    (British artist, 1861-1917)   WC WI
    (British painter, 1861-1917)   PR
    Bibl: ▶Thieme-Becker
    Charles Holroyd   PR
    Holroyd, Charles, Sir   PR
Holroyd, Sir Charles   WC
Holroyd, Charles, Sir → see Holroyd,
  Charles
Holroyd, Sir Charles → see Holroyd,
  Charles
Holroyd, T. *(British artist, op.1860-*
    1878)   WI
Holscher, Knud *(Danish architect,*
    Virum, 1930-)   AV
    Bibl: ▶Danske Arkitekters
      Landsforbund, 1987-88
Holse → see Holzer, Hans
  [Unidentified]
Holsoe, Carl Vilhelm *(Danish artist,*
    1863-1935)   WC
Holsøe, N. P. → see Holsøe, Niels
  Peter Christian

Holsøe, Niels Peter Christian   **BA**
    (Danish architect, 1826-1895)   BA
    (Danish architect, fl. l. 19th
      cent)   AV
    Bibl: Abitare, 1989 Oct., no.278,
      p.212; ▶Thieme-Becker;
      ▶Weilbach, Kunst.leks.
Holsøe, N. P.   AV
Holsøe, Poul *(Danish architect)*   AV
    Bibl: Arkitektur DK, 1986 Nov.,
      v.30, no.6-7, p.245
Holst Roland, Richard Nicolaus → see
  Holst, Roland
Holst [Unidentified] *(Unknown*
    painter)   PR
    Bibl: (April 23, 1807, lots 22 &
      23, Robins)
Holst, Aage *(Danish architect)*   AV
    Bibl: ▶Danske Arkitekters
      Landsforbund, 1984-85
Holst, Anne Crawford Allen
    (American, 20th c.)   **BA**
    Bibl: Binney, Country Life,
      CLXXIX/4624 (3 Apr. 1986)
      p.861
Holst, Anni de → see Meester, Annie
  de
Holst, Christian *(Danish architect)*   AV
    Bibl: ▶Danske Arkitekters
      Landsforbund, 1984-85
Holst, Erik *(Danish architect)*   AV
    Bibl: ▶Danske Arkitekters
      Landsforbund, 1984-85
Holst, Herman Valentin von
    (German born architect,
      immigrated to Chicago in 1891)   AV
    Bibl: Historic Illinois, 1985 Dec.,
      v.8, no.4, p.12
Holst, Johan Gustaf von *(Swedish*
    artist, 1841-1917)   WC
Holst, Johann   GC
    (Dutch artist, op.1689-1725)   WC
    (German painter, act.1689-aft.
      1725)   GC
    Bibl: ▶Thieme-Becker
Holst, Johann van   WC
Holst, Johann van → see Holst, Johann
Holst, Laurits Bernhard *(Danish*
    artist, 1848-p.1878)   WC
Holst, Peter *(Danish city planner)*   AV
    Bibl: Landskab, 1984 Sept., v.65,
      no.6, p.134
Holst, Richard Nicolaus Roland → see
  Holst, Roland
Holst, Roland   **BA**
    (Dutch artist, 1868-1938)   WC
    (Dutch draughtsman, 1868-
      1938)   GC
    (Dutch painter, critic, 1868-
      1938)   BA
    Bibl: ▶Bénézit; ▶Busse, Maler u.
      Bildhauer 19. Jahr.; ▶Natl. union
      cat., pre-1956; ▶Scheen, Ned.
      beeldende kunst.;
      ▶Thieme-Becker; ▶Vollmer,
      Künst.-Lex. 20. Jhr.
    Holst Roland, Richard Nicolaus   GC
    Holst, Richard Nicolaus Roland   WC
    Roland Holst, Richard   GC

Holst, Theodor M. von → *see* Von Holst, Theodor M.

Holst, Theodore M. von → *see* Von Holst, Theodor M.

Holstayn, Josef (*German artist, 20th cent.*) **WC**

Holste, Thomas James (*American painter, b.1943*) **BA**
Bibl: San Diego (CA, USA), San Diego State Univ., Gallery, NEWSPAU IN SAN DIEGO (1979); ▶WW Amer. Art

Holsteijn → *see* Holsteijn, Cornelis

Holsteijn → *see* Holsteijn, Pieter (I)

Holsteijn → *see* Holsteijn, Pieter (II)

Holsteijn or Holsteyn, Cornelis → *see* Holsteijn, Cornelis

Holsteijn or Holsteyn, Pieter, I → *see* Holsteijn, Pieter (I)

Holsteijn or Holsteyn, Pieter, II → *see* Holsteijn, Pieter (II)

Holsteijn, Cornelis **GC PR**
(*Dutch artist, 1618-1658*) WC
(*Dutch painter and draughtsman, 1618-1658*) GC
(*Dutch painter, 1618-1658*) PR
Bibl: Getty Photo Study Coll.; Getty Photo Study Coll. (Ptgs.); ▶Thieme-Becker; ▶Witt checklist
C. Holsteijn PR
C. Holstein PR
C. Holstien PR
Cornelis Holsteijn PR
Cornelis Holsteyn PR
Halstijn PR
Holsteijn PR
Holsteijn or Holsteyn, Cornelis **WC**
Holstein PR
Holsteyn PR
Holsteyn, Cornelis GC
van Holsteyn PR
Holsteijn, Pieter (I) **PR**
(*Dutch artist, c.1580/90-1662*) WC
(*Dutch draughtsman, ca.1580-1662*) GC
(*Dutch painter, 1580/90-1662*) PR
Bibl: ▶Bénézit; Gaillard inventory 1639; Getty Photo Study Coll.; ▶Thieme-Becker; ▶Witt checklist
Holsteijn PR
Holsteijn or Holsteyn, Pieter, I **WC**
Holsteijn, Pieter I **GC**
Holsteyn, Pieter (the Elder) GC
Pieter Holsteyn (I) PR
Pr. Holsteyn PR

Holsteijn, Pieter (II) **PR**
(*Dutch artist, c.1614-1673/83*) WC
(*Dutch draughtsman, ca.1614-1683 or 1687*) GC
(*Dutch painter, 1614-1673*) PR
Bibl: ▶Bénézit; Gaillard inventory 1639; Getty Photo Study Coll.; ▶Thieme-Becker; ▶Witt checklist
Holsteijn PR
Holsteijn or Holsteyn, Pieter, II **WC**
Holsteijn, Pieter II **GC**
Holsteyn, Pieter II GC
Pieter Holsteyn (II) PR
Pr. Holsteyn PR
Holsteijn, Pieter I → *see* Holsteijn, Pieter (I)
Holsteijn, Pieter II → *see* Holsteijn, Pieter (II)
Holstein → *see* Holsteijn, Cornelis
Holstein, A. van (*Netherlands artist, 17th cent.*) **WC**
Holstein, Pieter (*Dutch painter, printmaker, sculptor, b.1934*) **BA**
Bibl: Paris (FRA), Inst. néerlandais, L'Atelier de Piet Clement (1976); ▶Scheen, Ned. beeldende kunst.
Holsteyn → *see* Holsteijn, Cornelis
Holsteyn, Cornelis → *see* Holsteijn, Cornelis
Holsteyn, J. **GC WC**
(*Dutch artist, 18th cent.*) WC
(*Dutch painter, 18th century*) GC
Bibl: ▶Witt checklist
Holsteyn, Pieter (the Elder) → *see* Holsteijn, Pieter (I)
Holsteyn, Pieter II → *see* Holsteijn, Pieter (II)
Holstock, J. van (*Dutch artist, op. 1806*) **WC**
Holswilder, Jan Pieter (*Dutch draughtsman, 1850-1890*) **GC**
Bibl: ▶Thieme-Becker
Holt, E.F. → *see* Holt, Edwin Frederick
Holt, Edwin Frederick **WI**
(*British artist, op.1850-1897*) WI
(*British artist, op.c.1850-1865*) WC
Holt, E.F. **WC**
Holt, Eric **BA WC WI**
(*British artist, 1944-*) WC
(*British artist, b.1944*) WI
(*designer, 20th c.*) BA
Bibl: "Furniture System", Arch. Review CLXXXII (Sept 1987), 87-9
Holt, G. H. M. (*Dutch architect, 1904-1988*) **AV**
Bibl: Archis, 1988 Mar., no.3, p.5 [death date]; ▶Libr. of Congr. Name Auth. File
Holt, Gertrude M. (*British artist, op. 1908-1913*) **WI**
Holt, Henri Friso ten **GC**
(*Dutch artist, 1921-*) WC
(*Dutch painter, 1884-1968*) GC
Bibl: ▶Vollmer, Künst.-Lex. 20. Jhr.
Holt, Henri Friso ten (Friso) **WC**

Holt, Henri Friso ten (Friso) → *see* Holt, Henri Friso ten
Holt, Herbert **WC WI**
(*British artist, 1894-op.1958*) WI
(*British artist, 1894-p.1958*) WC
Bibl: ▶Johnson, Brit. artists
Holt, Herbert (*Canadian planner, Montreal*) **AV**
Bibl: Urban design international, 1983 Winter, v.4, no.2, p.24
Holt, J. **WC WI**
(*British artist, op.1855*) WC
(*British artist, op.1855-*) WI
Holt, Jacob W. **AV BA**
(*American architect, builder, 1811-1880*) BA
(*American builder who worked in North Carolina and Virginia, 1811-1880*) AV
Bibl: NATL. REGISTER OF HIST. PLACES, 556; WINTERTHUR PORTFOLIO, XVI (1981) 2
Holt, Lilian **BA WI**
(*British artist, op.20th c.*) WI
(*British painter, b.1898*) BA
Bibl: Art Monthly 44 (Mar 1981) 3-7
Holt, Martha A. (*American ceramist, sculptor, b.1945*) **BA**
Bibl: ▶Intl. dir. exh. artists, 1983; ▶WW Amer. Art
Holt, Nancy → *see* Holt, Nancy Louise
Holt, Nancy Louise **BA**
(*American artist, 1938-*) AV
(*American sculptor, filmmaker, b.1938*) BA
Bibl: ▶Contemp. artists; New Brunswick (NJ, USA), Rutgers U., Response to the environment (1975); ▶WW Amer. Art, 1976
Holt, Nancy **AV**
Holt, Philetus H. (*American architect*) **AV**
Bibl: ▶AIA Pro File, 1987-88
Holt, Richard (*British manufacturer, act.1722-1732*) **BA**
Bibl: Valpy,ENGLISH CERAMIC CIRCLE TRANS.,XXII/3/(1986),pp.206-226
Holt, Sara Barton **WC WI**
(*American artist, op.1881*) WC
(*American artist, op.1881-*) WI
Holte, Frank Augustus Brandish **WC WI**
(*British artist, 1869-*) WC
(*British artist, b.1869*) WI
Holtermann, Anton (*Austrian architect, Vienna*) **AV**
Bibl: ▶Verzeich. Öst. Ziviltech.
Holtermann, Peter Hoyer (*Norwegian artist, 1820-1865*) **WC**
Holthausen, Jean (*French ébéniste, master 1764, act. to 1782*) **GC**
Bibl: ▶Salverte, Ébénistes 18e s.; Theunissen, Meubles
Holthausen, Ludwig (*German artist, 1807-1890*) **WC**

Holthuys, Andreas →see Holthuys, Dries

Holthuys, Dries *(German sculptor, act.1496)*   **BA** GC
Bibl: ▶Bénézit; Dehio: Rheinland-Pfälz, pp.292, 660-661; Getty Photo Study Coll. (Medieval); Müller, Sculpture NLD DEU FRA ESP, p.164; ▶Thieme-Becker, (var)

Holthuys, Andreas   GC

Holthuys, Driess   GC
Holthuys, Driess →see Holthuys, Dries

Holtman *(German artist, 18th cent.)*   **WC**

Holton, Nina *(American sculptor, 20th c.)*   **BA**
Bibl: Leonardo XIV/2 (spring 1981) 125

Holtorf, Hans *(German painter, b.1899)*   **BA**
Bibl: ▶Vollmer, Künst.-Lex. 20. Jhr.

Holtswijller, Peter *(Flemish goldsmith, act.1553-1574)*   **BA**
Bibl: Berliner Museen: XXIII/2 (1973) p.55-57

Holty, Carl Robert   **BA WC WI**
(American artist, 1900-)   WC
(American artist, 1900-1973)   WI
(American painter, author, 1900-1973)   BA
Bibl: ▶Cummings, Contemp. Amer. artists; ▶Vollmer, Künst.-Lex. 20. Jhr.; ▶WW Amer. Art, 1975, 1976

Holtz, Franz Viktor *(German artist, 1859-)*   **WC**

Holtz, Karl *(German illustrator, cartoonist, 1899-1978)*   **BA**
Bibl: Altenburg, staat. Lindenau-Mus., KARL HOLZ (1981); ▶Bénézit; BILDENDE KUNST, 10 (1980) 497-499; Geipel, The cartoon; ▶Natl. union cat., pre-1956; ▶Vollmer, Künst.-Lex. 20. Jhr.

Holtzbecher, Johann Christoph *(German, 1700-1762)*   GC
Bibl: ▶Thieme-Becker

Holtzenberger, Johann Christoph *(Austrian painter in CSK, 17th c.)*   **BA**
Bibl: Plichta, Umění XXVIII, 2 (1980) 151-167

Holtzhey, Johann George *(Dutch medalist, 1726-1808)*   **BA**
Bibl: ▶Forrer, Medallists; MEDAL, 10 (winter 1986), p. 11-17; ▶Thieme-Becker

Holtzman, Harry *(American painter, author, b.1912)*   **BA**
Bibl: ▶Art Index, Jan. 1974; ▶Natl. union cat., 1968-1972; ▶Seuphor, Abstract ptg.

Holtzman, Joseph *(American furniture designer)*   **AV**
Bibl: House & garden, 1989 Nov., v.161, no.11, p.66

Holtzmann, Hans   **GC WC**
(German artist, 16th cent.)   WC
(German draughtsman, 16th century)   GC
Bibl: ▶Witt checklist

Holtzwart, F.A.   **WC WI**
(American artist, op.1838)   WC
(American artist, op.1838-)   WI

Holub, Georg *(Czech artist, 1861-1919)*   **WC**

Holub, Leo *(American photographer, b.1916)*   **BA**
Bibl: Murray in ARTWEEK 13, 17, 1 May (1982) p.12

Holworthy, James   **BA WC WI**
(British artist, 1781-1841)   WC WI
(British painter, 1780-1841)   BA
Bibl: ▶Fisher, Watercolour ptrs.; ▶Mallalieu, Brit. watercolour artists; ▶Redgrave, Engl. school; ▶Thieme-Becker; Timms, r.C., in OLD WATERCOLOUR SOCIETY's CLUB LVIII (1983) 9-

Holy, Adrien *(French artist, 1898-)*   **WC**

Holý, Miloslav *(Czech painter, printmaker, 1897-1974)*   **BA**
Bibl: ▶Bénézit; UMĚNÍ, XXIII/1 (1975), pp.58-63; ▶Vollmer, Künst.-Lex. 20. Jhr.

Holyoake, Rowland *(British artist, op.1880-1911)*   **WI**

Holyoake, William *(British artist, 1834-1894)*   **WC WI**

Holz, Johann Daniel *(German artist, 1867-1945)*   **WC**

Holz, Paul *(German draftsman, 1883-1938)*   **BA**
Bibl: Berlin, East, Nat'l. Gal.

Holzalb, Johann Rudolf *(Swiss artist, 1723-1806)*   **WC**

Holzbauer, Wilhelm *(Austrian architect, 1930-)*   **AV**
Bibl: ▶Contemp. archts.

Holzel →see Hölzel, Adolf

Hölzel, Adolf   **BA GC PR WC**
(German artist, 1853-)   WC
(German artist, 1853-1934)   WC
(German painter, 1853-1934)   BA PR
(German, 1853-1934)   GC
Bibl: ▶Bénézit; ▶Brockhaus Enzyk.; ▶Busse, Maler u. Bildhauer 19. Jahr.; ▶Lex. Kunst; ▶Neue deutsche Biog.; ▶Österr. biog. Lex. 1815-1950; ▶RILA/BHA; ▶Thieme-Becker; ▶Vollmer, Künst.-Lex. 20. Jhr.; ▶Witt checklist

Adolf Holzel   PR
Hoelzel, Adolf   **BA WC**
Holzel   PR

Hölzel, Jean Baptiste von   **GC WC**
(German artist, op.1770-1780)   WC
(German painter, act.1770-1780)   GC
Bibl: ▶Witt checklist

Hölzel, Ken *(West German(?) architect)*   **AV**
Bibl: Forum, 1988 Oct., v.32, no.4, p.16

Holzer →see Holzer, Hans [Unidentified]

Holzer →see Holzer, Johann Evangelist

Holzer, Hans [Unidentified]   **PR**
(Unknown painter)
Bibl: (May 14 & ff., 1804, lot 791, Truchsessian Gallery; July 30, 1806, lot 115, King)

Hans Holzer   PR
Holse   PR
Holzer   PR

Holzer, J. A. *(Swiss born, American painter and sculptor, 1858-1938)*   **AV**
Bibl: ▶Amer. art annual, v.5, 1905-06; ▶Thieme-Becker; ▶Vollmer, Künst.-Lex. 20. Jhr., v.6 (death date; name cited as Jakob Adolf)

Holzer, Jenny *(American conceptual artist, sculptor, b.1950)*   **BA**
Bibl: ▶Intl. dir. exh. artists, 1983; ▶WW Amer. Art, 1984

Holzer, Johann Evangelist   **BA GC PR**
(German artist, 1709-1740)   WC
(German painter, 1709-1740)   PR
(German painter, printmaker, 1709-1740)   BA
(German, 1709-1740)   GC
Bibl: ▶Bénézit; ▶Encyc. world art; ▶RILA/BHA; ▶Thieme-Becker

Holzer   PR
Holzer, Johann Evangelist (Elias)   **WC**
Johann Evangelist Holzer   PR
Holzer, Johann Evangelist (Elias) →see Holzer, Johann Evangelist

Holzer, Joseph *(German artist, 1824-1876)*   **WC**

Holzer, Sasha *(British artist, b.1959)*   **WI**

Holzer-Defanti, Constantin *(Austrian ceramist, b.1881)*   **BA**
Bibl: KERAMOS, 99 (Jan 1983) 61-66

Holzhammer, Franz Xaver *(German architect, 20th c.)*   **BA**
Bibl: Hederer, BAUTEN U. PLÄTZE IN MÜNCHEN, 166

Holzhausen, Klaus *(Swiss landscape architect, Zurich)*   **AV**
Bibl: Anthos, 1985, v.24, no.1, p.3

Holzinger, Franz Joseph Ignaz   **BA GC**
(Austrian sculptor, 1691-1775)   GC
(Austrian sculptor, stucco artist, 1691-1775)   BA
Bibl: KUNSTJAHRBUCH DER STADT LINZ 1974-75, p.51-59; ▶RILA/BHA; ▶Thieme-Becker

Hölzinger, Johannes Peter *(West German architect, 1936-)*   **AV**
Bibl: Botta, M. in Daidalos 13 (15 Sept. 1984)

Holzl, G.E. (Giovanni?
  Evangelista?) (German artist, op.
  1755-1759)   WC
Holzl, Johann Felix (German artist,
  18th cent.)   WC
Hölzle, Franz (German painter, act.
  ca.1760)   BA
  Bibl: Vollmer, Ars bavarica, 15-16
  (1980) pp.97-104
Holzmair, Hans (German
  draughtsman, act.1591-1602)   GC
  Bibl: ▶Thieme-Becker
Holzman, Bernardo (Italian
  goldsmith, act.1700-1721)   BA
  Bibl: Fock, Burlington mag.,
  CXIV/826 (Jan. 1972), pp.11-17;
  ▶Thieme-Becker
Holzman, Malcolm   AV BA
  (American architect)   AV
  (American architect, 20th c.)   BA
  Bibl: ▶Avery period. idx., 4th
  suppl.; ▶Contemp. archts.;
  ▶Wodehouse, Amer. archts. WWI-
  pres.
Holzmann, Adolf (Swiss artist,
  1890-)   WC
Holzmann, Carl Friedrich (German
  artist, 1740-1811)   WC
Holzmann, Johann→see Hulsman,
  Johann
Holzmeister, Clemens (Austrian
  architect, 1886-1983)   AV BA
  Bibl: Baumeister, 1986 Mar., v.83,
  no.3, p.60; ▶Contemp. archts.;
  ▶Encyc. world art; NYT 14 June
  83 p.88; ▶WW Austria
Holzmüller, Walter (Austrian
  architect, 1946-)   AV
  Bibl: Ottagono, 1988 Mar., p.20
Høm, Paul Brieghel (Danish painter,
  b.1905)   BA
  Bibl: ▶Nørregård-Nielsen, Dansk
  kunst; ▶Vollmer, Künst.-Lex. 20.
  Jhr., suppl.
Homan, Reinder (Dutch printmaker,
  painter, b.1950)   BA
  Bibl: Blom, A. van der, Grafiek Nu
  (1984), p.154; ▶Intl. dir. exh.
  artists, 1983
Homann, Alfred (Danish architect,
  Copenhagen)   AV
  Bibl: ▶Danske Arkitekters
  Landsforbund, 1984-85
Homann, Henry William (British
  artist, op.1864-)   WI
Homar, Gaspar (Spanish designer,
  Barcelona, fl. early 1900's)   AV
  Bibl: Interiors, 1989 July, v.148,
  no.12, p.100
Homar, Lorenzo   WC WI
  (American artist, 20th cent.)   WC
  (American artist, op.20th c.)   WI
Homburg, Hans (Dutch architect,
  Amsterdam)   AV
  Bibl: Deutsche Bauzeitung, 1989
  May, v.123, no.5, p.110

Homburger, Freddy (American
  painter, physician, b.1916)   BA
Home→see Home, Robert
Home, Mary (British interior
  designer)   AV
  Bibl: Restaurant and hotel design,
  1986 Nov., v.8, no.9, p.78
Home, Robert   BA PR WC WI
  (British artist, 1752-1834)   WC WI
  (British painter, 1752-1834)   BA PR
  Bibl: ▶Redgrave, Engl. school;
  ▶RILA/BHA; ▶Thieme-Becker
  Home   PR
  Robert Home   PR
Homeier, Jörg   AV
Homer→see Homer, Winslow
Homer Dodge Martin→see Martin,
  Homer Dodge
Homer, Henrietta Benson
  (American artist, 1809-1884)   WI
Homer, Winslow   BA GC PR WC WI
  (American artist, 1836-1910)   WC WI
  (American painter, 1836-1910)   BA PR
  (American, 1836-1910)   GC
  (Engraver, 1836-1910)   WI
  Bibl: ▶Artist biog. master idx.;
  ▶Bénézit; ▶Darmstädter,
  Künstlerlex.; ▶McGraw-Hill dict.
  art; ▶RILA/BHA; ▶Thieme-Becker
  Homer   PR
  Winslow Homer   PR
Homfray, Jeston (British artist,
  1797-1851)   WC WI
Homma, Toshio (Japanese architect,
  1931-)   AV
  Bibl: Kenchiku bunka, 1987 Dec.,
  v.42, no.494, p.262
Hommel, George P. (American,
  active Hollywood 1920s)   JG
Hommel, Hendrik Alois (West
  German architect, Frankfurt)   AV
  Bibl: ▶Bund Deut. Arch. Hdbch.,
  1987
Homogalakto→see Pückler-Muskau,
  Hermann, Fürst von
Homoky, Nicholas (Hungarian
  ceramist in GBR, b.1950)   BA
  Bibl: Düsseldorf (BRD), Hetjens-
  Mus., Deutsches Keramik.,
  NICHOLAS HOMOKY, 1981; ▶Intl.
  dir. exh. artists
Homolatsch, Otto (German artist,
  1883-)   WC
Hompel, Ludwig ten (German
  artist, 1887-1932)   WC
Hompson, Davi Det (American
  artist, b.1939)   BA
  Bibl: ▶WW Amer. Art, 1976
Homsey, George W. (American
  architect)   AV
Homsey, Samuel Eldon (American
  architect, Wilmington, Del, 1904-) AV
  Bibl: ▶Amer. archts. dir., 1970

Homsey, Victorine   BA
  (American architect, b.1900)   BA
  (American architect,
  Wilmington, Del, 1900-)   AV
  Bibl: ▶Amer. archts. dir., 1970;
  WW Amer., 1976
Homsey, Victorine Du Pont   AV
Homsey, Victorine Du Pont→see
  Homsey, Victorine
Hon, Henri le (Belgian painter, 1809-
  1872)   GC
  Bibl: ▶Bénézit
Honbraken→see Houbraken, Arnold
Hond, Abraham Danielsz.→see
  Hondius, Abraham
Honde Kooter→see Hondecoeter,
  Melchior d'
Hondecoeter→see Hondecoeter,
  Gillis Claesz. d'
Hondecoeter→see Hondecoeter,
  Gysbert Gillisz. de
Hondecoeter→see Hondecoeter,
  Melchior d'
Hondecoeter, Gijsbert Gillisz. d'→see
  Hondecoeter, Gysbert Gillisz. de
Hondecoeter, Gillis Claesz. d'   BA PR
  (Dutch artist, c.1580-1638)   WC
  (Dutch painter and
  draughtsman, 1575-1638)   GC
  (Dutch painter, d. 1638)   PR
  (Dutch painter, d.1638)   BA
  Bibl: ▶Bénézit; Getty Photo Study
  Coll.; ▶RILA/BHA; Schoonsteen
  inventory 1647; Stechow DUTCH
  LANDSCAPE PAINTINGS OF THE
  17TH C.; ▶Thieme-Becker;
  ▶Wurzbach, NLD Künst.-Lex.
  Gillis Claesz. d' Hondecoeter   PR
  Gillis Hondecoeter   PR
  Hondecoeter   PR
Hondecoeter, Gillis Claesz. de   GC
Hondecoeter, Hondecoutre or
  Hondekoeter, Gillis Claesz. de
  or d'   WC
  Hondecoutre, Gillis Claesz. de   GC
  Hondekoeter, Gillis Claesz. de   GC
  Jillis Handekoeter   PR
  Jillis Handekooter   PR
  Jillis Hondekoter   PR
Hondecoeter, Gillis Claesz. de→see
  Hondecoeter, Gillis Claesz. d'

Hondecoeter, Gysbert Gillisz. de GC PR
   (Dutch artist, 1604-1653) WC
   (Dutch painter and
      draughtsman, 1604-1653) GC
   (Dutch painter, 1604-1653) PR
      Bibl: Getty Photo Study Coll.;
      ▶Thieme-Becker
   de oude Gillis Hondecoeter PR
   de oude Hondekoeter PR
   den oude Hondekoeter PR
   den ouden Hondekoeter PR
   G. Hondekoeter PR
   Gilles Hondekoeter PR
   Gillis de Hondekoutere PR
   Gillis Hondekoeter PR
   Gysbert Gillisz. de Hondecoeter PR
   Gysbrecht Hondekoeter PR
   Hondecoeter PR
   Hondecoeter, Gijsbert Gillisz. d' PR
Hondecoeter, Hondecoutre or
   Hondekoeter, Gysbert Gillisz.
   or Jillisz. de or d' WC
   Hondecoutre, Gysbert Gillisz. de GC
   Hondekoeter, Gysbert Gillisz. de GC
Hondecoeter, Hondecoutre or
   Hondekoeter, Gillis Claesz. de or
   d'→see Hondecoeter, Gillis Claesz.
   d'
Hondecoeter, Hondecoutre or
   Hondekoeter, Gysbert Gillisz. or
   Jillisz. de or d'→see Hondecoeter,
   Gysbert Gillisz. de
Hondecoeter, Hondecoutre or
   Hondekoeter, Melchior de or
   d'→see Hondecoeter, Melchior d'
Hondecoeter, Melchior→see
   Hondecoeter, Melchior d'

Hondecoeter, Melchior d' BA PR
   (Dutch artist, 1636-1695) WC
   (Dutch painter and
      draughtsman, 1636-1695) GC
   (Dutch painter, 1636-1695) BA PR
      Bibl: ▶Bénézit; ▶Encyc. world art;
      Getty Photo Study Coll.;
      ▶McGraw-Hill dict. art;
      ▶RILA/BHA; ▶Rosenberg, Dutch
      art & arch.; ▶Thieme-Becker;
      ▶Wurzbach, NLD Künst.-Lex.
   Eondekoeter, Melchior de GC
   Handaguter PR
   Handecoutre PR
   Handekoeter PR
   Handycoutre PR
   Honde Kooter PR
   Hondecoeter PR
Hondecoeter, Hondecoutre or
   Hondekoeter, Melchior de or
   d' WC
   Hondecoeter, Melchior PR
Hondecoeter, Melchior de GC PR
   Hondecooter PR
   Hondecoutre, Melchior de GC
   Hondekoeter PR
   Hondekoeter, Melchior de GC
   Hondekoote PR
   Hondekooter PR
   Hondekoter PR
   Hondekr PR
   Hondicator PR
   Hondichooter PR
   Hondicoeter PR
   Hondicooter PR
   Hondicuter PR
   Hondikoeter PR
   Hondikoetor PR
   Hondikooter PR
   Hondikuter PR
   Hondiscooter PR
   Hundercutter PR
   M. de Hondekoet PR
   M. Hondecooter PR
   M. Hondekoeter PR
   M. Hondikoeter PR
   M. Hondikooter PR
   Melchior d'Hondecoeter PR
   Melchior de Hondecoeter PR
   Melchior de Hondekoeter PR
   Melchior Hondekoeter PR
   Milchior Hondekoeter PR
Hondecoeter, Melchior de→see
   Hondecoeter, Melchior d'
Hondecooter→see Hondecoeter,
   Melchior d'
Hondecoutre, Gillis Claesz. de→see
   Hondecoeter, Gillis Claesz. d'
Hondecoutre, Gysbert Gillisz.
   de→see Hondecoeter, Gysbert
   Gillisz. de
Hondecoutre, Melchior de→see
   Hondecoeter, Melchior d'
Hondekoeter→see Hondecoeter,
   Melchior d'

Hondekoeter, Gillis Claesz. de→see
   Hondecoeter, Gillis Claesz. d'
Hondekoeter, Gysbert Gillisz.
   de→see Hondecoeter, Gysbert
   Gillisz. de
Hondekoeter, Melchior de→see
   Hondecoeter, Melchior d'
Hondekoote→see Hondecoeter,
   Melchior d'
Hondekooter→see Hondecoeter,
   Melchior d'
Hondekoter→see Hondecoeter,
   Melchior d'
Hondekr→see Hondecoeter, Melchior
   d'
Hondelatte, Jacques *(French*
   architect) AV
      Bibl: Architecture d'aujourd'hui,
      no.236, p.70
Hondeous→see Hondius, Abraham
Hondhorst→see Honthorst, Gerrit
   van
Hondicator→see Hondecoeter,
   Melchior d'
Hondichooter→see Hondecoeter,
   Melchior d'
Hondicoeter→see Hondecoeter,
   Melchior d'
Hondicooter→see Hondecoeter,
   Melchior d'
Hondicuter→see Hondecoeter,
   Melchior d'
Hondiest→see Hondius, Abraham
Hondikoeter→see Hondecoeter,
   Melchior d'
Hondikoetor→see Hondecoeter,
   Melchior d'
Hondikooter→see Hondecoeter,
   Melchior d'
Hondikuter→see Hondecoeter,
   Melchior d'
Hondiscooter→see Hondecoeter,
   Melchior d'
Hondius→see Hondius, Abraham
Hondius or de Hondt, Abraham→see
   Hondius, Abraham

Hondius, Abraham   GC PR
(Dutch artist, c.1625/30-1695)   WC
(Dutch painter and
    draughtsman, 1625-1695)   GC
(Dutch painter,
    ca.1625/30-aft.1695)   PR
Bibl: (February 27, 1813, lot 93,
    Del Vecchio); ▶Bénézit; ▶Bernt,
    Neth. ptrs. 17c.; Getty Photo
    Study Coll.; Rijksmuseum;
    ▶Thieme-Becker
    A. Hondes   PR
    A. Hondius   PR
    Abr. Hondius   PR
    Abraham Hondius   PR
    Abram Hondius   PR
    H. Hondius   PR
    Hendius   PR
    Hond, Abraham Danielsz.   GC
    Hondeous   PR
    Hondiest   PR
    Hondius   PR
Hondius or de Hondt, Abraham   WC
    Hondius, Abraham Danielsz.   GC PR
    Hondt, Abraham de   GC
    Hont, Abraham Danielsz.   GC
    Hungeois   PR
    Uondius   PR
Hondius, Abraham Danielsz. →see
    Hondius, Abraham
Hondius, Gerrit   BA PR
(Dutch painter in USA, 1891-
    1970)   BA
(Dutch painter, 1891-1970)   PR
Bibl: ▶Art Index, Nov.; ▶Havlice,
    Idx. art. bio.; ▶RILA/BHA; Storrs
    (CAN, USA), University, William
    Benton Museum of Art, GERRIT
    HONDIUS 1891-1970 (1976);
    ▶Vollmer, Künst. 20. Jhr.
    Gerrit Hondius   PR
    Hondius, Gerritt   PR
Hondius, Gerritt →see Hondius, Gerrit
Hondius, Hendrik I   BA GC
(Dutch printmaker, 1573-after
    1649)   BA
(Flemish artist, 1573-p.1649)   WC
(Flemish, 1573-aft.1649)   GC
Bibl: ▶Aa, Biog. woordenboek
    NLD; Hollstein; ▶RILA/BHA;
    ▶Strutt, Dict. engravers;
    ▶Thieme-Becker; ▶Waller, Noord
    NLD Graveurs; ▶Wurzbach, NLD
    Künst.-Lex.
Hondius, Hendrik, I   WC
Hondius, Hendrik II (Dutch, ca.
    1597)   GC
Bibl: ▶Thieme-Becker
Hondius, Hendrik, I →see Hondius,
    Hendrik I
Hondius, Jodocus   JG
(Dutch, 1567-1611)   JG
(Netherlands artist, 1563-c.
    1611)   WC
Hondius, Jodocus or Joos, I   WC

Hondius, Jodocus or Joos, I →see
    Hondius, Jodocus
Hondius, Willem   BA GC
(Dutch artist, c.1597-c.1660)   WC
(Dutch draughtsman, ca.1597-
    ca.1660)   GC
(Dutch printmaker, ca.1597-ca.
    1660)   BA
Bibl: ▶Bénézit; ▶Bryan, Ptrs. &
    engravers; ▶Encyc. world art;
    ▶Hollstein, Dutch & Flemish;
    ▶Thieme-Becker; ▶Wurzbach, NLD
    Künst.-Lex.
Hondius, Willem.   WC
Hondius, Willem. →see Hondius,
    Willem
Hondorp, Rick   AV
Hondt →see Hondt, Hendrik Pietersz.
    de
Hondt or Hont, Hendrik de →see
    Hondt, Hendrik Pietersz. de
Hondt, Abraham de →see Hondius,
    Abraham
Hondt, Hendrick de →see Hondt,
    Hendrik Pietersz. de
Hondt, Hendrik de →see Hondt,
    Hendrik Pietersz. de
Hondt, Hendrik Pietersz. de   PR
(Dutch painter, act. 1637-1645)   PR
(Flemish artist, 17th cent.)   WC
(Flemish, 17th century)   GC
Bibl: ▶Thieme-Becker; ▶Witt
    checklist
    De Hondt   PR
    Hendrik Pietersz. de Hondt   PR
    Hondt   PR
Hondt or Hont, Hendrik de   WC
    Hondt, Hendrick de   PR
Hondt, Hendrik de   GC
Hondt, Lambert de   GC WC
(Flemish artist, op.1679)   WC
(Flemish, act.1679)   GC
Bibl: ▶Witt checklist
Hondt, Philipp de   BA GC WC
(Flemish artist, op.1739)   WC
(Flemish painter, d. bef.1743)   GC
(Flemish painter, d.ca.1743)   BA
Bibl: ▶Bénézit; ▶Thieme-Becker
Hone →see Hone, Nathaniel I
Hone, David (British artist, op.1964-)   WI
Hone, Evie →see Hone, Evie S.
Hone, Evie S.   WI
(British artist, 1894-1955)   WC WI
Bibl: ▶Waters, Brit. artists
Hone, Evie   WC
Hone, Horace   WC WI
(British artist, 1754-1756-1825)   WI
(British artist, 1756-1825)   WC
Hone, Keith (American architect,
    New York City)   AV
Bibl: Metropolis, 1987 Apr., v.6,
    no.8, p.47
Hone, Nathaniel →see Hone,
    Nathaniel I
Hone, Nathaniel (I) →see Hone,
    Nathaniel I

Hone, Nathaniel I   BA GC WI
(British artist, 1718-1784)   WC WI
(British painter, 1718-1784)   PR
(Irish painter, 1718-1784)   BA GC
Bibl: Crookshank, Ptrs. Ireland;
    Getty Photo Study Coll.;
    ▶RILA/BHA; ▶Strickland, Irish
    artists; ▶Thieme-Becker; ▶Witt
    checklist
    Hone   PR
Hone, Nathaniel   GC PR
Hone, Nathaniel (I)   PR
Hone, Nathaniel, I   WC
    N. Hone   PR
    Nath. Home, R.A.   PR
    Nath. Hone, R A.   PR
    Nath. Hone, R.A.   PR
    Nathaniel Hone   PR
Hone, Nathaniel II   BA WI
(British artist, 1831-1917)   WC WI
(Irish painter, 1831-1917)   BA
Bibl: Crookshank, Ptrs. Ireland;
    ▶Johnson, Brit. artists;
    ▶Thieme-Becker; ▶Waters, Brit.
    artists; ▶Witt checklist
Hone, Nathaniel, II   WC
Hone, Nathaniel, I →see Hone,
    Nathaniel I
Hone, Nathaniel, II →see Hone,
    Nathaniel II
Honegger, Gottfried   BA WC
(Swiss artist, 1917-)   WC
(Swiss painter, sculptor,
    printmaker, b.1917)   BA
Bibl: ▶Künst.-Lex. Schweiz 20.
    Jahrh.; ▶Lex. zeitgen. Schweiz.
    Künstler; Zug (CHE), Kunsthaus
    Zug, Gottfried Honegger..., 1984
Honer, Nigel Patrick Stentiford
(English architect, Swindon)   AV
Bibl: ▶RIBA members, 1983
Honeyman, John   AV BA
(British architect, 1831-1914)   BA
(Scottish architect, 1831-1914)   AV
Bibl: ▶Arch. period. idx./RIBA;
    ▶Avery obit. idx.; ▶Macmillan
    encyc. archts.; ▶Wodehouse, Brit.
    archts.
Hong, James (American architect,
    designer, 20th c.)   BA
Bibl: ▶Arch. period. idx./RIBA
Hongre, Étienne le →see Le Hongre,
    Étienne
Honich, Adriaen →see Honing,
    Adriaen
Honich, Heinrich (German artist,
    1875-1957)   WC
Honig, Mervin (American painter,
    b.1920)   BA
Bibl: ▶Intl. dir. arts, 1985-1986;
    ▶WW Amer. Art
**Honing or Honich, Adriaen
(Lossenbruy)** (Dutch artist, op.
    1663-1683)   WC

Honing, Adriaen *(Dutch draughtsman, act.1663-d. aft. 1673)* GC
    Bibl: ▶Bénézit; ▶Thieme-Becker
    Honich, Adriaen   GC

Honingh, Ronno *(Dutch architect, Amsterdam)* AV
    Bibl: De Architect, 1989 May, v.20, no.5, p.83

Honnecourt, Villard de →see Villard de Honnecourt

Honnet, Gabriel *(French artist, 17th cent.)* WC

Honnot →see Hannot, Johannes

Honold, Reinhardt   AV BA
    (architect, 20th c.)   BA
    (Austrian architect)   AV
    Bibl: Arch. review, CLXXX/1074 (Aug. 1986) pp.52-53; ▶Avery period. idx., 7th suppl.

Honolulu Class   GC
    Bibl: Paralipomena

Honolulu Master *(Italian painter, act. late 15th c.)*   BA
    Bibl: APOLLO CIX/204 (Feb 1979) p.88

Honorato [Unidentified] *(Unknown painter)*   PR
    Bibl: Doria inventory, Naples, 1690; ▶Thieme-Becker, cites Pelle, Honoré (Onorato), sculp. Genoa 17/18th c.

Honoratus →see Honoré

Honoré *(French illuminator, act. 1288-1296)*   BA GC
    Bibl: ▶Bénézit; ▶D'Ancona, Miniaturistes; ▶Encyc. world art; Getty Photo Study Coll. (Medieval); ▶RILA/BHA; ▶Thieme-Becker
    Honoratus   GC
    Maître Honoré   GC

Honore Marius Berard →see Berard, Honore Marius

Honore Victorin Daumier →see Daumier, Honoré Victorin

Honsem, Anna Maria van [Unidentified] *(Unknown painter)*   PR
    Bibl: 1706 De Letter inventory
    juffr. Anna Maria van Honsem   PR

Hont, Abraham Danielsz. →see Hondius, Abraham

Hontañón, Rodrigo Gil de →see Gil de Hontañón, Rodrigo

Honthorst →see Honthorst, Gerrit van
Honthorst, Gerard van →see Honthorst, Gerrit van
Honthorst, Gerhard →see Honthorst, Gerrit van
Honthorst, Gerrit →see Honthorst, Gerrit van
Honthorst, Gerrit or Gerard van (Gherardo della Notte or delle Notti, or Gherardo Fiammingo) →see Honthorst, Gerrit van

Honthorst, Gerrit van   BA GC JG PR
    (Dutch artist, 1590-1656)   WC
    (Dutch painter and draughtsman, 1590-1656)   GC
    (Dutch painter, 1590-1656)   BA PR
    (Dutch, 1590-1656)   JG
    Bibl: ▶Encyc. world art; Getty Photo Study Coll.; ▶RILA/BHA; ▶Thieme-Becker
    C. della Notte   PR
    G. de la Notte   PR
    G. del Notta   PR
    G. Della Notte   PR
    G. della Notti   PR
    G. Hontherst   PR
    G. Honthorst   PR
    G. Honthurst   PR
    G. Notti   PR
    Ger. de la Notte   PR
    Ger. Del Notti   PR
    Gerard de la Notte   PR
    Gerard Honthorst   PR
    Gerard Honthurst   PR
    Gerard Hontorst   PR
    Gerardo delle notti   PR
    Gerardo fiamengo   PR
    Gerrit van Honthorst   PR
    Gherard Honthorst   PR
    Gherardo della Notte   GC PR
    Gherardo delle Notti   PR
    Gherardo Fiamengo   PR
    Gherardo Fiammingo   GC
    Ghirardo   PR
    Ghirardo fialdengo   PR
    Ghirardo fiamengo   PR
    Henthorst   PR
    Hondhorst   PR
    Honthorst   PR
    Honthorst, Gerard van   PR
    Honthorst, Gerhard   PR
    Honthorst, Gerrit   PR

Honthorst, Gerrit or Gerard van (Gherardo della Notte or delle Notti, or Gherardo Fiammingo)   WC
    Honthoust   PR
    Hornthorst   PR
    Horthorst   PR
    Houthorst   PR
    Monsù Gherardo Fiamengo   PR
    Monsu' Geraldi   PR
    Monsu' Geraldo   PR
    Monsu' Gherardo Fiamengo   PR
    Monsu' Giraud della notte   PR

Honthorst, Willem or Guglielmo van →see Honthorst, Willem van

Honthorst, Willem van   GC PR
    (Dutch artist, 1594-1666)   WC
    (Dutch painter, 1594-1666)   GC PR
    Bibl: Getty Photo Study Coll.; ▶Thieme-Becker

Honthorst, Willem or Guglielmo van   WC
    Willem van Honthorst   PR

Honthoust →see Honthorst, Gerrit van
Honufriis, Crescenzio de →see Onofri, Crescenzio

Honzík, Karel   AV

Honzinti →see Bloemen, Jan Frans van (Orizonte)

Hoo, Thomas →see Thomas of Hoo
Hooch →see Hooch, Carel Cornelisz. de
Hooch →see Hooch, Horatius de
Hooch →see Hooch, Pieter de

Hooch or Hoogh, Gerrit de *(Dutch artist, op.1660-1679)*   WC

Hooch or Hoogh, Horatius de →see Hooch, Horatius de

Hooch, Carel Cornelisz. de   BA GC PR
    (Dutch artist, op.1627-m.1638)   WC
    (Dutch painter and draughtsman, act.1627-d. 1638)   GC
    (Dutch painter, act. 1627, d. 1638)   PR
    (Dutch painter, printmaker, act. 1627, d.1638)   BA
    Bibl: ▶Bénézit; ▶Bernt, Neth. ptrs. 17c.; Getty Photo Study Coll.; Getty Photo Study Coll. (Ptgs.); ▶Thieme-Becker; ▶Witt checklist; ▶Wurzbach, NLD Künst.-Lex.
    Carel Cornelisz. de Hooch   PR
    Carel de Hooch   PR
    Carel de Hoogh   PR
    De Hooch   PR
    De Hoock   PR
    Hooch   PR

Hooch, Hoogh or Hooghe, Carel or Charles Cornelisz. de   WC
    Hoogh, Charles Cornelisz. de   GC

Hooch, David de *(Dutch painter, 17th century)*   GC
    Bibl: Getty Photo Study Coll. (Duits coll.)

Hooch, Hoogh or Hooghe Pieter Hendricksz. de →see Hooch, Pieter de

Hooch, Hoogh or Hooghe, Carel or Charles Cornelisz. de →see Hooch, Carel Cornelisz. de

Hooch, Horatius de   GC PR
    (Dutch artist, op.1652-1692(?))   WC
    (Dutch painter, act. 1642-1686)   PR
    (Dutch painter, act.1652-1686)   GC
    Bibl: Getty Photo Study Coll.; ▶Thieme-Becker
    Hooch   PR

Hooch or Hoogh, Horatius de   WC
    Hoogh, Horatius de   GC
    Horatius de Hooch   PR
    Oratius de Hoogh   PR

Hooch, Pieter de   BA GC JG PR
    (Dutch artist, 1629-p.1683)   WC
    (Dutch painter and
        draughtsman, 1629-aft.1683)   GC
    (Dutch painter, 1629-aft.1683)   PR
    (Dutch painter, 1629-after 1683)   BA
    (Dutch, 1629-after 1684)   JG
    Bibl: ▶Artist biog. master idx.;
        ▶Bénézit; ▶Bernt, Neth. ptrs. 17c.;
        Getty Photo Study Coll.; ▶Lex.
        Kunst; ▶McGraw-Hill dict. art;
        ▶RILA/BHA; ▶Thieme-Becker;
        ▶Winkler Prins van de kunst;
        ▶Wurzbach, NLD Künst.-Lex.

    De Hoog   PR
    De Hooge   PR
    De Hoogh   PR
    De Hoogt   PR
    Dehooge   PR
    Hooch   PR
Hooch, Hoogh or Hooghe Pieter
    Hendricksz. de   WC
    Hooch, Pieter Hendricksz. de   PR
    Hoogh, Pieter de   GC PR
    Hooghe, Pieter de   GC
    P. de Hooge   PR
    P. de Hoogh   PR
    P. de Hooghe   PR
    Peter d. Hooge   PR
    Peter de Hoage   PR
    Peter De Hoog   PR
    Pierre de Hoogh   PR
    Pieter de Hog   PR
    Pieter de Hoge   PR
    Pieter de Hooch   PR
    Pieter de Hoog   PR
    Pieter de Hooge   PR
    Pietre de Hooge   PR
    Vander Hoogh   PR
Hooch, Pieter Hendricksz. de→see
    Hooch, Pieter de
Hood, Dorothy *(American painter,*
    b.1919)   BA
    Bibl: Syracuse (NY, USA), Everson
        Mus., New works in clay (1981);
        ▶WW Amer. Art, 1976
Hood, Henry *(English illuminator,*
    act.1384-1389)   BA
    Bibl: Sandler, Speculum, LX/2
        (Apr. 1985) p.365
Hood, James   WC WI
    (British artist, 18th cent.)   WC
    (British artist, op.18th c.)   WI
Hood, John *(British artist, op.1762-*
    1771)   WC WI
Hood, P.H. *(Active 19th century)*   JG
Hood, Raymond M.   BA
    (American architect, 1881-
        1934)   AV BA
    Bibl: ▶Avery obit. idx.; ▶Contemp.
        archts.; ▶Libr. of Congr. Name
        Auth. File; ▶Withey, Amer. archts.
Hood, Raymond Mathewson   AV
Hood, Raymond Mathewson→see
    Hood, Raymond M.

Hood, Robert *(Canadian*
    topographer, draftsman, 1796-
    1821)   BA
    Bibl: ▶Harper, Ptg. Canada;
        ▶Havlice, Idx. art. bio.; ▶Natl.
        union cat., 1975
Hood, Sallie *(American architect)*   AV
    Bibl: Fine homebuilding, 1987
        spring, no.38, p.20
Hood, Thomas *(British artist, 1835-*
    1874)   WC WI
    Bibl: Mackenzie
Hoodegist→see Houckgeest, Gerard
Hoodless, H.E. (Harry Taylor?)→see
    Hoodless, H.E., (Harry Taylor)
Hoodless, H.E., (Harry Taylor)   WI
    (British artist, 1913-)   WC
    (British artist, b.1913)   WI
Hoodless, H.E. (Harry Taylor?)   WC
Hoof, P. *(German artist, op.1781)*   WC
Hooft, Cornelis Gerardus→see Hooft,
    Cornelis Gerardus 't
Hooft, Cornelis Gerardus 't   GC
    (Dutch artist, 1866-1936)   WC
    (Dutch painter, 1866-1936)   GC
    Bibl: ▶Wright, Ptgs. Dutch
        museums
Hooft, Cornelis Gerardus   WC
Hooft, J. *(Dutch artist, 17th cent.)*   WC
Hooft, Jan *(Dutch painter, act. 2nd*
    half 17th cent.)   PR
    Bibl: ▶Thieme-Becker
    Jan Hooft   PR
Hooft, Nicolas   GC WC
    (Dutch artist, 1664-1748)   WC
    (Dutch painter, 1664-1748)   GC
    Bibl: ▶Thieme-Becker
Hoog, Bernard de   GC PR
    (Dutch artist, 1866-1943)   WC
    (Dutch painter, 1867-1943)   GC PR
    Bibl: ▶Bénézit; ▶Thieme-Becker;
        ▶Witt checklist
    Bernard de Hoog   PR
    De Hoog, Bernard   PR
    DeHoog, Bernard   PR
Hoog, Johan Bernard (Bernard)
    de   WC
Hoog, J.   GC WC
    (Dutch artist, op.c.1650)   WC
    (Dutch draughtsman, act. ca.
        1650)   GC
    Bibl: ▶Witt checklist
Hoog, Johan Bernard (Bernard)
    de→see Hoog, Bernard de
Hooger, F. *(Netherlands artist, 17th*
    cent.)   WC
Hoogerbeets, Gerrit *(German artist,*
    b.1948)   BA
    Bibl: ▶WW Arts DEU
Hoogerheyden, Engel   GC WC
    (Dutch artist, 1740-1809)   WC
    (Dutch painter, 1740-1809)   GC
    Bibl: ▶Thieme-Becker

Hoogers, Hendrick   GC
    (Dutch artist, 1747-1814)   WC
    (Dutch painter and
        draughtsman, 1747-1814)   GC
    Bibl: Getty Photo Study Coll.;
        ▶Thieme-Becker
Hoogers, Hendrik   WC
Hoogers, Hendrik→see Hoogers,
    Hendrick
Hoogestraten, Samuel Dircksz.
    van→see Hoogstraten, Samuel van
Hoogevest, T. van *(Dutch architect)*   AV
    Bibl: ▶Federatie O jrbk., 1984
Hoogh, Charles Cornelisz. de→see
    Hooch, Carel Cornelisz. de
Hoogh, Horatius de→see Hooch,
    Horatius de
Hoogh, Pieter de→see Hooch, Pieter
    de
Hooghe→see Hooghe, Romeyn de
Hooghe, Balthasar Richard de
    (Flemish artist, 1636-1697)   WC
Hooghe, Hooch, Hooge or Hoogh,
    Romeyn de→see Hooghe, Romeyn
    de
Hooghe, Pieter de→see Hooch,
    Pieter de
Hooghe, Romeyn de   BA GC PR
    (Dutch artist, 1645-1708)   WC
    (Dutch painter, 1645-1708)   PR
    (Dutch painter, draughtsman,
        sculptor, and printmaker,
        1645-1708)   GC
    (Dutch painter, sculptor,
        printmaker, 1645-1708)   BA
    Bibl: ▶Encyc. world art;
        ▶RILA/BHA
    Hooghe   PR
Hooghe, Hooch, Hooge or
    Hoogh, Romeyn de   WC
    R.D. Hoodge   PR
    Romeyn de Hooghe   PR
Hooghstoel or Hoogstoel,
    Emmanuel Bernard *(French artist,*
    op.c.1766)   WC
Hoogkamer, Willem H.   GC
    (Dutch artist, 1790-1864)   WC
    (Dutch draughtsman, d.1864)   GC
    Bibl: ▶Bénézit
Hoogkamer, Willem Hendrik   WC
Hoogkamer, Willem Hendrik→see
    Hoogkamer, Willem H.
Hoogland, William *(Engraver,*
    Boston, MA., circa 1795-1832)   WI
Hoogs, Lorraine *(American ceramist,*
    b.1941)   BA
    Bibl: Syracuse (NY, USA), Everson
        Mus., New works in clay (1981)
Hoogsaat, Hooghseet or Hoogzaat,
    Jan Cornelisz.→see Hoogsaat, Jan
    Cornelisz.

Hoogsaat, Jan Cornelisz.   GC
(Dutch artist, 1654-p.1730)   WC
(Dutch painter and
draughtsman, 1654-aft.1730)   GC
Bibl: Getty Photo Study Coll.;
▶Thieme-Becker
Hoogsaat, Hooghseet or
Hoogzaat, Jan Cornelisz.   WC
Hoogstad, Jan   AV BA
(Dutch architect, b.1930)   BA
(Dutch architect, Rotterdam)   AV
Bibl: Architect, 1984 Oct., v.15,
no.10, p.85; ▶Avery period. idx.;
R. Bullhorst, in DUTCH ART &
ARCHITECTURE TODAY 15 (1984),
20-25
Hoogstarten→see Hoogstraten,
Samuel van
Hoogstraaten→see Hoogstraten,
Samuel van
Hoogstraaten, Samuel van→see
Hoogstraten, Samuel van
Hoogstraeten, Samuel van→see
Hoogstraten, Samuel van
Hoogstraten→see Hoogstraten,
Samuel van
Hoogstraten or Hoogstraaten,
Abraham van *(Dutch artist, op.*
1685-m.1736)   WC
Hoogstraten, Dirck van   GC
(Dutch artist, c.1595/6-1640)   WC
(Flemish painter, ca.1595-1640)   GC
Bibl: ▶Thieme-Becker
Hoogstraten, Dirk or Theodor
van   WC
Hoogstraten, Dirk or Theodor
van→see Hoogstraten, Dirck van
Hoogstraten, G. van *(Unknown*
artist)   GC
Bibl: Gernsheim, Corpus Photog.
of Drawings, 1529
Hoogstraten, J. van *(Dutch(?)*
artist, op.1789)   WC
Hoogstraten, Jan van   GC WC
(Dutch artist, c.1627/32-1654)   WC
(Dutch draughtsman,
1627/32-1654)   GC
Bibl: ▶Thieme-Becker
Hoogstraten, Samuel van   BA GC PR
(Dutch artist, 1627-1678)   WC
(Dutch painter, 1627-1678)   PR
(Dutch painter, draughtsman,
and printmaker, 1627-1678)   GC
(Dutch painter, printmaker,
poet, 1627-1678)   BA
Bibl: ▶Encyc. world art;
▶RILA/BHA; ▶Thieme-Becker
Hoogestraten, Samuel Dircksz.
van   WC
Hoogstarten   PR
Hoogstraaten   PR
Hoogstraaten, Samuel van   PR
Hoogstraeten, Samuel van   GC
Hoogstraten   PR
Samuel van Hoogstraten   PR
Van Hoogstraten   PR

Hooijberg, Elbert *(Dutch painter,*
1903-d. aft.1965)   GC
Bibl: ▶Scheen, Ned. beeldende
kunst.
Hook, Allan J. *(British artist, 1853-*
op.1900)   WI
Hook, Bryan→see Hook, Bryan H.
Hook, Bryan H.   WI
(British artist, 1856-1916)   WC WI
Bibl: ▶Johnson, Brit. artists
Hook, Bryan   WC
Hook, James Clarke   BA WC WI
(British artist, 1819-1907)   WC WI
(British painter, printmaker,
1819-1907)   BA
Bibl: ▶Bénézit; Champlin, Cycl.
ptrs.; Di. of Brit. Etchers; ▶Dict.
natl. biog., 1901; ▶Havlice, Idx.
art. bio.; ▶Johnson, Brit. artists;
▶Mallalieu, Brit. watercolour
artists; ▶Thieme-Becker; ▶Who
was who [GBR], 1897; ▶Wood,
Victorian ptrs.
Hook, William E. *(American, active*
Manitou Springs, CO, U.S. 1870s-
1880s)   JG
Hooke, Richard *(Irish painter, 1823-*
1887)   PR
Bibl: ▶Thieme-Becker
Richard Hooke   PR
Hooke, Robert   AV BA
(British architect, 1635-1703)   AV
(English scientist, architect,
inventor, 1635-1703)   BA
Bibl: ▶Libr. of Congr. Name Auth.
File; ▶Portoghesi, Diz. arch. e
urbanistica; ▶Thieme-Becker
Hooker, Charlie *(British artist,*
b.1953)   BA
Bibl: London (GBR), Tate Gallery,
Artists & performance (1981)
Hooker, George E. *(American*
architect, Chicago, 1861-1928)   AV
Bibl: Harvard architecture review,
1981, p.77
Hooker, Helen *(American sculptor,*
20th century)   GC
Bibl: Juley coll., NMAA
Hooker, Joseph Dalton   WI
(British artist, 1817-1911)   WC WI
Hooker, Sir Joseph Dalton   WC
Hooker, Philip *(American architect,*
1766-1836)   AV BA
Bibl: ▶Portoghesi, Diz. arch. e
urbanistica; ▶Thieme-Becker;
▶Withey, Amer. archts.
Hooker, Sir Joseph Dalton→see
Hooker, Joseph Dalton
Hooker, Tish Fort *(American interior*
designer, Nashville, TN)   AV
Bibl: Architectural digest, 1985
Dec., v.42, no.12, p.110
Hoolaart, Gillis Hendricus *(Dutch*
glass engraver, 1731-1816)   BA
Bibl: ?Wurzbach; ▶Newman,
Glass; ▶Penguin dec. arts; Smith,
Weltkunst LII, 19 (Oct 1982)
2620-24; ▶Thieme-Becker

Hoole, Elijah   AV BA
(British architect, act.1857-
1882)   BA
(British architect, London, 19th
cent)   AV
Bibl: Wetter, Zeitschr. für
schweiz. Arch. und Kunstgesch.,
XLIV/3 (1987) 217
Hoop, A. van der *(Dutch*
draughtsman, 1782-1854)   GC
Bibl: ▶Kraam, Holl. en Vlaamsche
kunst.
Hoop, Wouter   GC WC
(Dutch artist, op.1643/4)   WC
(Dutch painter, act.1643/44)   GC
Bibl: ▶Witt checklist
Hoope, Cornelis Jan ten (Bob)
(Dutch painter, b.1920)   GC
Bibl: ▶Scheen, Ned. beeldende
kunst.
Hooper, E.Lancaster *(British artist,*
op.19th c.)   WI
Hooper, Frances *(American, 20th c.)*   BA
Hooper, George *(British artist,*
b.1910)   WI
Hooper, Henry Andrew *(British*
artist, op.19th c.)   WI
Hooper, John Horace *(British artist,*
op.1877-1899)   WC WI
Hooper, Lesley *(English interior*
designer)   AV
Bibl: Building design, 1988 Aug.
suppl., p.22
Hooper, Robert *(American painter,*
b.1952)   BA
Bibl: Waltham (MA, USA),
Brandeis Univ., Rose Art Museum,
Ardent Gestures (1985)
Hooper, Samuel *(1851-1911;*
Architect, Winnipeg)   FA
Bibl: CAAD Finding Aid RG 11M
79003/36 Items 2211-2231; ▶Hill,
Archts. Canada, 1986
Hooper, William G. *(British artist,*
op.1870-1898)   WI
Hooper, William Willoughby
(Colonel) *(British, 1837-1912,*
active India 1876-1877)   JG
Hooren, G. van *(Dutch artist, 18th*
cent.(?))   WC
Hooren, Isaack Jacobsz. van   GC WC
(Dutch artist,
op.1646-m.1651/2)   WC
(Dutch painter, d.1651/52)   GC
Bibl: ▶Thieme-Becker
Hoorenbault family→see Hornebolt
family
Hoorn→see Hoorn, Jordanus
Hoorn, Jordanus   GC PR WC
(Dutch artist, 1753-1833)   WC
(Dutch painter, 1753-1833)   GC PR
Bibl: Getty Photo Study Coll.;
▶Thieme-Becker; ▶Witt checklist
Hoorn   PR
Jordanus Hoorn   PR

Hoornik, Clasina (*Dutch seamstress, prostitute, b.1850, act.1883*) **BA**
Bibl: Zernel, ART HISTORY, X/3 (SEPT 1987) p.351-368

Hooven, Herbert → see Hoven, Herbert Nelson

Hoover, George (*American architect, Denver*) **AV**
Bibl: ▶AIA Pro File, 1983

Hoover, L.F. (*American, active, 1920s New York*) **JG**

Hoover, Nan (*American photographer, performance artist, filmmaker, b.1931*) **BA**
Bibl: Amsterdam (NLD), Stedelijk Museum, Nan Hoover (1979); ▶Intl. dir. exh. artists; Montreal (Que, CND), Mus. d'Art Contemp., NAN HOOVER..., 1982y; UC Santa Barbara cat. sheets

Hoover, Norman G. (*American architect*) **AV**

Hoover, Ron (*American painter, b.1944*) **BA**
Bibl: Albuquerque (NM, USA), UNM Art Mus., Certain realities (1983)

Hoøyer, Cornelius → see Höyer, Cornelius

Hope, James (*American artist, 1818-1892*) **WC WI**

Hope, James Archibald, Sir **WI**
(*British artist, 1785-1871*) **WC WI**

Hope, Sir James Archibald **WC**

Hope, James Douglas (*American, 1846-1929*) **JG**

Hope, James, Mrs. **WI**
(*British artist, 19th cent.*) **WC**
(*British artist, op.19th c.*) **WI**

Hope, Mrs. James **WC**

Hope, John (*British architect, 1734-1808*) **AV BA**
Bibl: ▶Avery period. idx.; ▶Colvin, Brit. archts.

Hope, John (*Scottish, d.1682*) **BA**
Bibl: ▶Burke's dormant & extinct, p.570; ▶Dict. natl. biog.

Hope, John Edward (*fl.1845; draftsman (technical), Woolwich*) **FA**
Bibl: NA objects; Natl. Arch. of Canada, CAAD Finding Aid

Hope, Mrs. James → see Hope, James, Mrs.

Hope, Robert (*British artist, 1869-1936*) **WC WI**

Hope, Sir James Archibald → see Hope, James Archibald, Sir

Hope, T.H. → see Hope, Thomas H.

Hope, Thomas **AV BA**
(*1769-1831*) **AV**
(*British painter, architect, author, collector, 1769-1831*) **BA**
Bibl: ▶Bénézit; ▶BURLINGTON, CXXII (June 1980) 427-428; ▶Dict. natl. biog.; ▶Encyc. Britannica; ▶Thieme-Becker

Hope, Thomas H. **WI**
(*American artist, 19th cent.*) **WC**
(*American artist, op.1826-, d.1926*) **WI**

Hope, T.H. **WC**

Hopea, Saara (*Finnish craftsman, b.1925*) **BA**
Bibl: Sunderland (GBR), Arts Ctr., Suomen Lasi--Finnish glass (1979)

Hopetown, Eliza, Countess of → see Carnegie, Eliza, Countess of Hopetown

Hopewell, Barry (*British artist, op. 20th c.*) **WI**

Hopf, Peter S. (*American architect, 1929-*) **AV**
Bibl: ▶Libr. of Congr. Name Auth. File

Hopfer or Hopffer, Bartholomaus, II (*German artist, op.c.1650-1698*) **WC**

Hopfer or Hopffer, Daniel, I → see Hopfer, Daniel I

Hopfer or Hopffer, Hieronymus → see Hopfer, Hieronymus

Hopfer, C.B. (*German, act.1531*) **GC**
Bibl: ▶Thieme-Becker

Hopfer, Daniel (the Elder) → see Hopfer, Daniel I

Hopfer, Daniel I **BA GC**
(*German artist, c.1470-1536*) **WC**
(*German painter and draughtsman, ca.1470-1536*) **GC**
(*German painter, printmaker, ca. 1470-1536*) **BA**
Bibl: Getty Photo Study Coll.; ▶Thieme-Becker

Hopfer or Hopffer, Daniel, I **WC**
Hopfer, Daniel (the Elder) **GC**

Hopfer, Hieronymus **BA GC**
(*German artist, op.1528-1550*) **WC**
(*German painter and draughtsman, act. ca.1520-1550*) **GC**
(*German printmaker, act.ca. 1520-after 1550*) **BA**
Bibl: Getty Photo Study Coll.; ▶RILA/BHA; ▶Thieme-Becker

Hopfer or Hopffer, Hieronymus **WC**

Hopfer, Johann Berhard Gottfried (*German artist, c.1716-1789*) **WC**

Hopfer, Lambert **BA GC WC**
(*German artist, 16th cent.*) **WC**
(*German printmaker, act.ca. 1525-1550*) **BA**
(*German, 16th century*) **GC**
Bibl: ▶Hollstein, German, v.15a; ▶Thieme-Becker, v.17

Hopfer, Wolfgang Ludwig (*German artist, 1648-1698*) **WC**

Hopfgarten, August Ferdinand **GC WC**
(*German artist, 1807-1896*) **WC**
(*German, 1807-1896*) **GC**
Bibl: ▶Thieme-Becker

Höpfner, Christian (*German sculptor, b.1939*) **BA**
Bibl: ▶WW Arts DEU

Höpfner, Wilhelm (*German printmaker, painter, 1899-1968*) **BA**
Bibl: Cottbus (DDR), Galerie Kunstsamm., Wilhelm Hopfner (1979); ▶Vollmer, Künst.-Lex. 20. Jhr.

Hopkin → see Hopkin, Robert

Hopkin, Robert (*American painter, 1832-1909*) **BA PR**
Bibl: East Lansing (MI, USA), MSU, Kresge Gallery, Early Michigan ptgs. (1977); Gibson; ▶Groce, Artists Amer.; ▶RILA/BHA

Hopkin **PR**
Robert Hopkin **PR**

Hopkins → see Hopkins, W.

Hopkins, Arthur (*British artist, 1848-1930*) **WC WI**

Hopkins, Asa (*American musical instrument maker, 1799-1838*) **BA**
Bibl: Antiques, CXVII/6 (Jun. 1980) pp.1333-1335

Hopkins, Budd **BA WC WI**
(*American artist, 1931-*) **WC**
(*American artist, b.1931*) **WI**
(*American painter, b.1931*) **BA**
Bibl: ▶Archives Amer. Art Jrnl., XI/1-4 (1971); ▶WW Amer. Art, 1976

Hopkins, Charles Benjamin (*American painter, 1882-aft.1941*) **PR**
Bibl: ▶Hughes, Artists California
Charles Benjamin Hopkins **PR**

Hopkins, Clive (*British painter, printmaker, b.1946*) **BA**
Bibl: Kingston-upon-Hull (GBR), Ferens Art Gallery, Drawing in action (1978)

Hopkins, Clyde **BA WI**
(*British artist, b.1946*) **WI**
(*British painter, b.1946*) **BA**
Bibl: Cambridge (GBR), Cambridge Univ., Kettle's Yard, Ptgs. & drawings (1980); Oxford (GBR), MoMA, Open Attitudes (1979)

Hopkins, Edna Boies (*American printmaker, 1878-1935*) **BA**
Bibl: ▶Bénézit; ▶Collins, Women artists Amer.; Gibson; ▶WWW Amer., 1897

Hopkins, Frances Ann **WI**
(*British artist, 1838-1918*) **WC WI**
Bibl: ▶Johnson, Brit. artists
Beechey, Frances Ann, Miss **WI**

Hopkins, Frances Ann, (nee Beechey) **WC**

Hopkins, Frances Ann, (nee Beechey) → see Hopkins, Frances Ann

Hopkins, George (*American architect*) **AV**

Hopkins, George Edward (*American artist, 1855-op.1880*) **WI**

Hopkins, James Cleveland (*American architect, Boston, Mass, 1873-1938*) **AV**
Bibl: ▶Withey, Amer. archts.

Hopkins, James R. →*see* Hopkins,
James Roy
Hopkins, James Roy   **BA PR WI**
    (American artist, 1877-1969)   WI
    (American artist, 1878-p.1937)   WC
    (American painter, 1877-1969) BA PR
    Bibl: ▶Bénézit; ▶Fielding's Amer.
    ptrs.; ▶RILA/BHA; Springfield (O,
    USA), Art Center, JAMES ROY
    HOPKINS, OHIO ARTIST, 1977;
    ▶Vollmer, Künst.-Lex. 20. Jhr.;
    ▶WWW Amer., 1969-1973
  Hopkins, James R.   **PR WC**
    James Roy Hopkins   PR
Hopkins, John *(British, 1858-1871)* **BA**
    Bibl: Hallett, Hist. photo., XI (Apr.-
    Jun. 1987) pp.119-122
Hopkins, John William *(Canadian
    architect, 19th century)*   **AV**
    Bibl: ARQ: Architecture/Quebec,
    1986 Apr., no.30, p.26
Hopkins, Merina Lujan →*see* Chalee,
Pop
Hopkins, Michael   **AV BA**
    (British architect, 1935-)   AV
    (British architect, b.1935)   BA
    Bibl: AMC: revue d'architecture,
    1985 Oct., no.9, p.28; ▶Arch.
    period. idx./RIBA, 1988; ▶Who's
    Who [GBR], 1990
Hopkins, Thurston *(British, 1913 -)* **JG**
Hopkins, W.   **PR WC WI**
    (British artist, op.c.1790-1820)   WC
    (British artist, op.circa 1790-)   WI
    (British painter, act. 1790s)   PR
    Bibl: ▶Waterhouse, Brit. 18c. ptrs.
    Hopkins   PR
    W. Hopkins   PR
Hopkins, William H.   **WC WI**
    (British artist, op.1853-, d.1892) WI
    (British artist, op.1853-m.1892)   WC
Hopkins-Hughes, Diane *(American
    photographer, b.1935)*   **BA**
    Bibl: San Antonio (TX, USA),
    Witte Mem. Mus., What's up in
    Texas (1978)
Hopkinson →*see* Hopkinson, Charles
Hopkinson, Charles   **PR WI**
    (American artist, 1869-1962)   WI
    (American artist, 1869-p.1952)   WC
    (American painter, 1869-1962)   PR
    Bibl: ▶Fielding's Amer. ptrs.,
    1983; ▶WWW Amer. art
    Charles Sydney Hopkinson   PR
    Hopkinson   PR
    Hopkinson, Charles Sidney   PR
  Hopkinson, Charles Sydney   **PR WC**
Hopkinson, Charles Sidney →*see*
Hopkinson, Charles
Hopkinson, Charles Sydney →*see*
Hopkinson, Charles
Hopkinson, Francis *(American artist,
    1737-1791)*   **WC WI**
Hopkinson, John *(British artist, op.
    1975-1978)*   **WI**
Hopley, Edward William John
    (British artist, 1816-1869)   **WC WI**

Hopner →*see* Hoppner, John
Hoppania, Heikki *(Finnish architect)* **AV**
    Bibl: Arkkitehti, 1985, no.5, p.34
Hoppé, Emil Otto   **BA**
    *(British photographer, 1878-
    1972)*   BA
    (British, b. Germany, 1878-1972)   JG
    Bibl: Beaton, Magic image; ▶Fogg
    Mus. Libr. cat.; ▶Who's Who
    [GBR], 1974
  Hoppe, Emile Otto   **JG**
Hoppe, Emile Otto →*see* Hoppé, Emil
Otto
Hoppe, Erik *(Danish artist, 1896-
    1968)*   **WC**
Hoppe, Ferdinand Bernhard   **GC**
    *(Dutch painter and
    draughtsman, 1841-1922)*   GC
    (German artist, 1831-1922)   WC
    Bibl: ▶Wright, Ptgs. Dutch
    museums
  **Hoeppe or Hoppe, Ferdinand
    Bernhard**   **WC**
Hoppe, Ferdinand Theodor
    (German artist, 1848-1890)   **WC**
Hoppe, Theodor *(Austrian architect,
    act.1874-1876)*   **BA**
    Bibl: Dehio: Wien (1960); ▶Österr.
    biog. Lex. 1815-1950; Österr.
    Kunsttopographie XLIV, 22 416,
    428; Vancsa, Öster. Zeit. für
    Kunst u. Denk. 35/1-2 (1981) 29
Hoppen →*see* Hoppen, Karol
Hoppen, Donald *(Architect)*   **AV**
    Bibl: UIA International architect,
    1984. no.6, p.50
Hoppen, Jerzy *(Polish painter,
    printmaker, 1891-1969)*   **BA**
    Bibl: Rocznik Muzeum
    Narodowego w Warszawie
    XXI/1977, p.293-300; ▶Vollmer,
    Künst.-Lex. 20. Jhr.
Hoppen, Karl →*see* Hoppen, Karol
Hoppen, Karol *(Polish painter, 1798-
    1849)*   **PR**
    Bibl: ▶Thieme-Becker
    Hoppen   PR
    Hoppen, Karl   PR
    Karol Hoppen   PR
Hoppenbrouwers, J.F. →*see*
Hoppenbrouwers, Johannes
Franciscus
**Hoppenbrouwers, Johannes
    Franciscus**   **GC PR WC**
    (Dutch artist, 1819-1866)   WC
    (Dutch painter, 1819-1866)   GC PR
    Bibl: ▶Thieme-Becker
    Hoppenbrouwers, J.F.   PR
    Johannes Franciscus
    Hoppenbrouwers   PR
Hoppenfeld, Morton *(American
    architect, Albuquerque, NM and
    Columbus, OH, d.1985)*   **AV**
    Bibl: New Mexico architecture,
    1985 Mar.-Apr., v.26, no.2, p.17

**Hoppenhaupt the Elder, Johann
    Michel II** *(German artist, 1709-c.
    1750)*   **WC**
**Hoppenhaupt, Johann Christian,
    the younger** *(German sculptor,
    decorator, act.1746, d.1778-1786)*   **BA**
    Bibl: ▶Bénézit; ▶Encyc. world art;
    ▶Thieme-Becker
Hopper →*see* Hopper, Edward
Hopper, Edward   **AV BA GC PR WC WI**
    (American artist, 1882-)   WC
    (American artist, 1882-1967)   AV WI
    *(American painter, 1882-
    1967)*   BA GC PR
    (Engraver, 1882-1967)   WI
    Bibl: ▶Bénézit; ▶Britannica encyc.
    Amer. art; ▶Fielding's Amer. ptrs.;
    ▶RILA/BHA; ▶Young, Amer. artists
    Edward Hopper   PR
    Hopper   PR
**Hopper, Josephine Verstille
    Nivison** *(American painter,
    b.1883)*   **BA**
    Bibl: Woman's Art Journal I, 1980
    28-32
Hopper, Leonard *(American
    landscape architect, New York,
    N.Y)*   **AV**
    Bibl: Landscape architecture,
    1988 Nov., p.46
Hopper, Pegge *(American artist, op.
    20th c.)*   **WI**
Hopper, Thomas   **AV BA WC WI**
    (British architect, 1776-1856)   AV BA
    (British artist, 1776-1856)   WC WI
    Bibl: ▶Colvin, Brit. archts.; ▶Dict.
    natl. biog.
Hoppesteyn, Jacob Wemmersz.
    *(Dutch pottery manufacturer,
    1627-1671)*   **BA**
    Bibl: ▶Penguin dec. arts;
    ▶Thieme-Becker
Hoppin Group   **JG**
Hoppin Painter   **GC JG**
    (Apulian vase-painter)   GC
    Bibl: Trendall, Attic red-fig. vases
    Apulia
Hoppin, Augustus *(American
    painter, illustrator, 1828-1896)*   **BA**
    Bibl: ▶Fielding's Amer. ptrs.;
    ▶Groce, Artists Amer.; ▶Young,
    Amer. artists
Hoppin, Francis Laurens Vinton
    *(American architect, New York,
    NY, 1867-1941)*   **AV**
    Bibl: ▶Francis, Archts. NYC 1840-
    1900
Hoppin, Thomas Frederick
    (American artist, 1816-1872)   **WC WI**
Hoppin-Lecce Group   **JG**
Hoppner →*see* Hoppner, John

Hoppner, John   **BA GC PR WC WI**
  (British artist, 1758-1810)   WC WI
  (British painter, 1758-1810)   BA PR
  (British, 1758-1810)   GC
    Bibl: ▶Dict. natl. biog.; ▶Redgrave,
    Engl. school; ▶RILA/BHA;
    ▶Thieme-Becker
  Hopner   PR
  Hoppner   PR
  John Hoppner   PR
Hoppner, Lascelles H.   **WI**
  (British artist, 1788-op.1833)   WI
  (British artist, 1788-p.1833)   WC
  Hoppner, Lascelles H. (William
  H. Lascelles)   **WC**
  Lascelles, William H.   WI
  Hoppner, Lascelles H. (William H.
    Lascelles) →see Hoppner, Lascelles
    H.
Hoppner, Peter *(American architect)*   **AV**
Hoppner, Richard (not Robert)
  Belgrave →see Hoppner, Richard
  Belgrave
Hoppner, Richard Belgrave   **WI**
  (British artist, 1786-1872)   WC WI
  Hoppner, Richard (not Robert)
  Belgrave   **WC**
Hopstock, Bitten *(Norwegian*
  interior architect)   **AV**
    Bibl: Byggekunst, 1985, v.67,
    no.3, p.118
Hoptpon, Frank *(British artist, op.*
  19th c.)   **WI**
Hopwood, Henry Silkstone *(British*
  artist, 1860-1914)   **WC WI**
Hopwood, James, the elder *(British*
  printmaker, ca.1752-1819)   **BA**
    Bibl: ▶Dict. natl. biog.;
    ▶Thieme-Becker
Hopwood, William *(British artist,*
  op.1801-1807)   **WC WI**
Hoquet, Charles *(French painter,*
  1821-1870)   **GC**
    Bibl: ▶Bénézit
Hor, Andreas *(Swiss artist, op.1558-*
  1575)   **WC**
Hora, Coriolan *(Romanian painter,*
  b.1928)   **BA**
    Bibl: ARTA, XXVI (1979) 44-45;
    ▶Barbosa, Art. romani contemp.
Hora, Frantisek *(Czech painter,*
  b.1913)   **BA**
    Bibl: Liberec (CS), Oblastini
    Galerie, FRANTISEK HORA
    VYBERZDILA (9 Mar-16 Apr 1978)
Horace Bundy →see Bundy, Horace
Horace Duesbury →see Duesbury,
  Horace
Horace Gentileschi →see Gentileschi,
  Orazio
Horace Pippin →see Pippin, Horace
Horace Vernet →see Vernet, Horace
Horacio Borgian →see Borgianni,
  Orazio
Horam →see Oram, William, (Old
  Oram)

Horarth →see Hogarth, William
Horatio Nelson Poole →see Poole,
  Horatio Nelson
Horatio W. Shaw →see Shaw, Horatio
  W.
Horatio Walker →see Walker, Horatio
Horatius de Hooch →see Hooch,
  Horatius de
Horatius Paulin →see Paulyn, Horatius
Horatius Paulyn →see Paulyn,
  Horatius
Horazio, Bernardus *(Italian artist,*
  17th cent.)   **WC**
Horberg, J. *(German artist, 19th*
  cent.)   **WC**
Hörberg, Pehr   **BA WC**
  (Swedish artist, 1746-1816)   WC
  (Swedish painter, printmaker,
    1746-1816)   BA
    Bibl: ▶Bénézit; ▶Thieme-Becker
Hørbov, Emil *(Danish painter,*
  b.1915)   **BA**
    Bibl: ▶Vollmer, Künst.-Lex. 20.
    Jhr.; ▶Weilbach, Kunst.leks.
Horchler, Anton *(German sculptor,*
  act.1844)   **BA**
    Bibl: Kultzen, R., in (07)
    SCHLÖSSER, Gärten, Berlin...,
    p.296
Horčička, František *(Czech painter,*
  restorer, 1776-1856)   **BA**
    Bibl: ▶Busse, Maler u. Bildhauer
    19. Jahr.; ▶Encyk. českého výtv.
    uměni; ▶Thieme-Becker
Hord, Donal *(American sculptor,*
  1902-1966)   **BA**
    Bibl: ▶Samuels, Artists Amer.
    West; ▶Young, Amer. artists
Horden, Richard   **AV BA**
  (British architect)   AV
  (British architect, 20th c.)   BA
    Bibl: ▶Arch. period. idx./RIBA,
    1988; Architecture: the AIA
    journal, 1986 Oct., v.75, no.10,
    p.56; ▶Avery period. idx., 1986
    suppl.
Horder *(Danish sculptor, mason,*
  d.1175)   **BA**
    Bibl: ▶Encyc. world art; Hein,
    HORDER, EN ROMANSK
    STENMESTER (1986); Reclams
    DNK, p.338; ▶Weilbach, Kunst.
    leks.
  Master Horder   BA
Hordijk, Gerardus (Gerard) →see
  Hordyk, Gérard
Hordyk, Gérard   **GC**
  (Dutch artist, 1899-1958)   WC
  (Dutch painter, 1899-1958)   GC
    Bibl: ▶Bénézit
Hordijk, Gerardus (Gerard)   **WC**

Hore, James   **BA WC WI**
  (British artist, op.c.1829-1837)   WC
  (British artist, op.circa 1829-)   WI
  (British painter, act.1829-1837)   BA
    Bibl: STUDIES: AN IRISH
    QUARTERLY REV., Vol LXV, spring
    1976, p.46-51
Hore, Somnath *(Indian printmaker,*
  b.1921)   **BA**
    Bibl: ▶Intl. dir. exh. artists, 1982-
    1983; Lewin, E., in MET EIGEN
    OGEN: OPSTELLEN AANGEBODEN
    DOOR LEERLINGEN EN
    MEDEWERKERS AAN HANS L.C.
    JAFFÉ, Amsterdam, 1984, 296-
    303; ▶Vollmer, Künst.-Lex. 20.
    Jhr.
Horeau, Hector   **AV BA WC**
  (French architect, 1801-1872)   AV BA
  (French artist, 1801-1872)   WC
    Bibl: ▶Thieme-Becker
Horejc, Jaroslav *(Czech sculptor,*
  1886-1983)   **BA**
    Bibl: ▶Bénézit; ▶Encyk. českého
    výtv. uměni; ▶Vollmer, Künst.-Lex.
    20. Jhr.; VYTRARNA KULTURA,
    VII, 3 (1983) 31-34
Hořejší, Ivan *(Czech architect)*   **AV**
    Bibl: Architektura ČSR, 1988,
    v.47, no.1, p.42
Horeman →see Horemans, Jan Joseph
  I
Horemans →see Horemans, Jan
  Joseph I
Horemans →see Horemans, Peter
  Jakob
Horemans, F. [Unidentified]
  (Unknown painter)   **PR**
    Bibl: (April 8, 1815, lots 105[a] &
    105[b], Christie's)
  F. Horemans   PR
Horemans, Jan →see Horemans, Jan
  Joseph I
Horemans, Jan Josef (the Elder) →see
  Horemans, Jan Joseph I
Horemans, Jan Josef I →see
  Horemans, Jan Joseph I
Horemans, Jan Josef II →see
  Horemans, Jan Joseph II
Horemans, Jan Josef, I →see
  Horemans, Jan Joseph I
Horemans, Jan Josef, II →see
  Horemans, Jan Joseph II
Horemans, Jan Joseph →see
  Horemans, Jan Joseph II
Horemans, Jan Joseph (I) →see
  Horemans, Jan Joseph I
Horemans, Jan Joseph (II) →see
  Horemans, Jan Joseph II
Horemans, Jan Joseph (the
  Elder) →see Horemans, Jan Joseph
  I

Horemans, Jan Joseph I   **BA**
    (Flemish artist, 1682-1759)   WC
    (Flemish painter, 1682-1759)   BA PR
    (Flemish, 1682-1759)   GC
      Bibl: Biog Woodenbock; ▶Encyc.
      world art; ▶Nagler, Neues
      Künst.-Lex.; ▶RILA/BHA;
      ▶Thieme-Becker; ▶Witt checklist;
      ▶Wurzbach, NLD Künst.-Lex.
    Horeman   PR
    Horemans   PR
    Horemans, Jan   PR
    Horemans, Jan Josef (the Elder)   PR
Horemans, Jan Josef I   GC
Horemans, Jan Josef, I   WC
Horemans, Jan Joseph (I)   PR
    Horemans, Jan Joseph (the Elder)   PR
    Horman   PR
    Hormnns   PR
    Hoveman   PR
    Jan Joseph Horemans (I)   PR
    Johann Horemans   PR
Horemans, Jan Joseph II   **BA**
    (Flemish artist, 1714-p.1790)   WC
    (Flemish painter, 1714-ca.1790) BA PR
    (Flemish, 1714-aft.1790)   GC
      Bibl: ▶Encyc. world art;
      ▶RILA/BHA; ▶Witt checklist;
      ▶Wurzbach, NLD Künst.-Lex.
Horemans, Jan Josef II   GC
Horemans, Jan Josef, II   WC
    Horemans, Jan Joseph   PR
Horemans, Jan Joseph (II)   **PR**
    Jan Joseph Horemans (II)   PR
Horemans, Peter Jacob→see
    Horemans, Peter Jakob
Horemans, Peter Jakob   **BA PR**
    (Flemish artist, 1700-1776)   WC
    (Flemish, 1700-1776)   GC
    (German painter, 1700-1776) BA PR
      Bibl: ▶Bryan, Ptrs. & engravers;
      Munich (DEU), Alte Pinakothek,
      Peter Jakob Horemans;
      ▶RILA/BHA; ▶Thieme-Becker;
      ▶Witt checklist
    Horemans   PR
    Horemans, Peter Jacob   PR
Horemans, Pieter Jacob   **GC PR WC**
    Peter Jakob Horemans   PR
Horemans, Pieter Jacob→see
    Horemans, Peter Jakob
Horenbant, Joseph *(Belgian artist,*
    1863-)   WC
Horenbeeck, Anne van *(Belgian*
    interior designer)   AV
      Bibl: Abitare, 1985 Nov., no.239,
      p.8
Horenbout family→see Hornebolt
    family
Horenbout, Gerard→see Hornebolt,
    Gerard
Horenbout, Harembourg,
    Hoorenbault, Hornebout etc.,
    Gerard→see Hornebolt, Gerard

Horenbout, Harembourg,
    Hoorenbault, Hornebout etc.,
    Lukas→see Hornebolt, Lucas
Horevicz, Luis Carlos *(Brazilian*
    architect)   AV
      Bibl: Projeto, 1988 May, no.110,
      p.98
Horgnies, Norbert Joseph *(Belgian*
    artist, op.1830-1870)   WC
Horiba, Hiroshi *(Japanese architect,*
    1960-)   AV
      Bibl: Space design, 1986 Dec., no.
      267, p.58
Horiguchi, Sutemi *(Japanese*
    architect, 1895-)   AV
      Bibl: ▶Contemp. archts.
    Horiguti, Sutemi   AV
Horiguti, Sutemi→see Horiguchi,
    Sutemi
Horiike, Hideto *(Japanese architect,*
    1949-)   AV
      Bibl: Space design, 1986 Dec., no.
      267, p.56
Horinckh, Erasmus→see Horninck,
    Erasmus
Horion→see Horions, Johan
Horion, Alexander de→see Horion,
    Alexandre de
Horion, Alexandre de   GC
    (Flemish artist, 1590-1659)   WC
    (Flemish, ca.1590-1659)   GC
      Bibl: ▶Thieme-Becker; ▶Witt
      checklist
Horion, Alexander de   WC
Horion, Johan→see Horions, Johan
Horions, Johan   **GC PR**
    (Dutch painter and
    draughtsman, act.1655-1662)   GC
    (Dutch painter, act. ca.1655)   PR
      Bibl: ▶Thieme-Becker
    Horion   PR
    Horion, Johan   GC
    Johan Horions   PR
    Orions, Johan   GC
Hörislamb, A. *(German)*   GC
      Bibl: Gernsheim, Corpus Photog.
      of Drawings, 1733
Horisonte→see Bloemen, Jan Frans
    van (Orizonte)
Horisonti→see Bloemen, Jan Frans
    van (Orizonte)
Horizonte→see Bloemen, Jan Frans
    van (Orizonte)
Horizonti→see Bloemen, Jan Frans
    van (Orizonte)
Hörl, Ottmar *(West German*
    architect, 1950-)   AV
      Bibl: AMC, 1988 Dec.-1989 Jan.,
      no.23-24, p.136
Horlbeck, Günter *(German*
    printmaker, b.1927)   BA
      Bibl: ▶Vollmer, Künst.-Lex. 20. Jhr.

Horlbeck-Kappler, Irmgard   **BA WC**
    (German artist, 20th cent.)   WC
    (German printmaker, b.1925)   BA
      Bibl: Leipzig, Mus. der bildenden
      ϗ. exh., 1975
Horleman *(Swedish artist, 18th*
    cent.(?))   WC
Horler, Miklós *(Hungarian architect,*
    Budapest, 1923-)   AV
      Bibl: Magyar építőművészet,
      1987, v.78, no.4-5., p.7
Horlin, Tor *(Swedish artist, 1899-)*   WC
Horling, Johan Frederik *(Swedish*
    artist, 1718-1786)   WC
Horlor→see Horlor, George W.
Horlor, George W.   **PR WC WI**
    (British artist, op.1849-1891)   WI
    (British artist, op.c.1849-1890)   WC
    (British painter, act. 1849-1890)   PR
      Bibl: ▶Thieme-Becker
    George W. Horlor   PR
    Horlor   PR
Horlor, Joseph   **WC WI**
    (British artist, 1809-1887)   WI
    (British artist, op.1830-1866)   WC
Hormai, Mikko *(Finnish architect)*   AV
      Bibl: Arkkitehtuurikilpailuja, 1989,
      no.8, p.3
Horman→see Horemans, Jan Joseph I
Hörmann, Eckart *(German architect)* AV
      Bibl: Deutsche Bauzeitschrift 1985
      Apr., v.33, no.4, p.445
Hörmann, Johannes *(German*
    clergyman, cabinetmaker, 1651-
    1699)   BA
      Bibl: Dettelbacher, OBERFALZ...
      (1980), p.106; ▶Neue deutsche
      Biog.; RECLAMS KUNSTFUHRER
      DEUTSCHLAND, v.1,p.36
Hörmann, Theodor von   **BA WC**
    (Austrian painter, 1840-1895)   BA
    (German artist, 1840-1895)   WC
      Bibl: ▶Bénézit; Fuch;
      ▶Thieme-Becker
Hormnns→see Horemans, Jan Joseph
    I
Horms, Johann Oswald→see Harms,
    Johann Oswald
Hormuth-Kallmorgen, Margarethe
    (German painter, 1858-1916)   BA
      Bibl: ▶Bénézit; ▶Thieme-Becker
Horn, B. d' *(Dutch painter, 17th*
    century)   GC
      Bibl: ▶Thieme-Becker
Horn, Carl Gottlob *(Danish*
    architect, 1734-1807)   BA
      Bibl: Dehio: Hamburg Schleswig-
      Holstein; ▶Neue deutsche Biog.;
      ▶Weilbach, Kunst.leks.
Horn, Clement *(German armorer,*
    act.ca.1580-ca.1625/30)   BA
      Bibl: Martin, Fernando A., REALES
      SITIOS, XXII, 86, p.14; REAL
      ARMERIA DE MADRID;
      ▶Thieme-Becker

Horn, Dirck de *(Dutch painter, 1626-1681)* **GC**
    Bibl: Laurens Bol
Horn, Gerald *(American architect, 1934-)* **AV**
    Bibl: New Chicago architecture, 1981, p.136
Horn, R. *(Dutch artist, op.1648)* **WC**
Horn, Rebecca *(West German artist, b.1944)* **BA**
    Bibl: ▶DuMonts Künst.-Lex.; ▶Intl. dir. exh. artists, 1983; Philadelphia (PA, USA), ICA, Video art (1975); Studio International, vol. 191, no.981, May-June 1978, p.220; Studio International, vol. 192, no.982, June-Aug 1976, p.60
Horn, Richard *(German sculptor, b.1898)* **BA**
    Bibl: ▶Vollmer, Künst.-Lex. 20. Jhr.
Horn, Roni *(American artist, b.1955)* **BA**
    Bibl: Munich (DEU), Kunstraum München, Roni Horn, 1983 (RILA/DEU)
Horn, W. *(German artist, 19th cent.)* **WC**
Horn, Werner *(German, 20th c.)* **BA**
Horna, Juan de *(Spanish silversmith, act.1526-1550)* **BA**
    Bibl: Hernmarck, Euro. silversmith; Maldonado Nieto, Arch. esp. de arte, LIX/235 (Jul-Sep 1986) 304-319; ▶Thieme-Becker
    Orna, Juan de **BA**
Hornak, Ian *(American painter, b.1944)* **BA**
    Bibl: ▶NY art yrbk.
Hornay, Erasmus → see Horninck, Erasmus
Hornbacher, Sara *(American artist, 20th c.)* **BA**
    Bibl: Collins, Art Jrnl., XLV/3 (Fall 1985) p.244
Hornback, Ann *(American painter, b.1945)* **BA**
    Bibl: New Orleans (LA, USA), Mus. Art, New Orleans triennial (1983)
Hornblower, Joseph Coerten *(American architect, 1848-1908)* **BA**
    Bibl: ▶WWW Amer., 1897+
Hornbostel, Henry *(American architect, 1867-1961)* **AV**
    Bibl: ▶Macmillan encyc. archts.
Hornbrook, T.L. → see Hornbrook, Thomas Lyde
Hornbrook, Thomas Lyde **BA WI**
    (British artist, 1780-1850) **WI**
    (British artist, op.1814-1844) **WC**
    (British painter, 1780-1850) **BA**
    Bibl: Aa/VII, 3, July-Sept'85 p.22; ▶Archibald, Sea ptrs.; ▶Thieme-Becker
Hornbrook, T.L. **WC**
Hornby, Anna *(British artist, op.20th c.)* **WI**

Hornby, Lester George **WC WI**
    (American artist, 1882-) **WC**
    (American artist, 1882-1956) **WI**
Horndash, Ulrich *(German painter, b.1951)* **BA**
    Bibl: Munich (BRD), Städt. Galerie im LEnbachhaus, Kunstforum Maximilianstrasse, ULRICH HORNDASH..., 1982-83
Horne, Cleeve *(Canadian artist, 1912-)* **WC**
Horne, Herbert Percy **BA WI**
    (British architect, author, collector, 1864-1916) **BA**
    (British artist, 1864-1916) **WI**
    Bibl: ▶Portoghesi, Diz. arch. e urbanistica; ▶Thieme-Becker; ▶Who was who [GBR]
Horne, Trevor **AV BA**
    (British architect, 20th c.) **BA**
    (British architect, London) **AV**
    Bibl: ▶Avery period. idx., suppl. 4,6; ▶RIBA members, 1983
Hornebolt family *(early Netherlandish painters in England, 15th-17th cs.)* **BA**
    Bibl: Campbell, Burlington mag., LXXVIII/1003 (Oct. 1986) pp.719-727; ▶Dict. natl. biog.; ▶Seyn, Écoles flam. et holl.; ▶Thieme-Becker; ▶Wurzbach, NLD Künst.-Lex.
    Harembourg family **BA**
    Hoorenbault family **BA**
    Horenbout family **BA**
Hornebolt, Gerard **BA**
    (early Netherlandish painter, illuminator, ca.1465-1540/41) **BA**
    (Flanders painter and illuminator, ca.1465-ca.1540) **GC**
    (Flemish, active 1487-ca. 1520) **JG**
    (Netherlands artist, op.1487-m.1540/1) **WC**
    Bibl: ▶Bénézit; BN; Bultema; Campbell, Burlington mag., LXXVIII/1003 (Oct. 1986) pp.719-727; De Winter, Bull. Cleve. Mus. 68 (1981), pp.342-427; ▶Dict. natl. biog.; ▶Encyc. world art; ▶Foskett, Brit. miniature ptrs.; Genaille, Belgique; ▶RILA/BHA; ▶Seyn, Écoles flam. et holl.; ▶Thieme-Becker; ▶Wurzbach, NLD Künst.-Lex.
Horenbout, Gerard **GC JG**
Horenbout, Harembourg, Hoorenbault, Hornebout etc., Gerard **WC**

Hornebolt, Lucas **BA**
    (early Netherlandish painter in England, 1490/95-1544) **BA**
    (Netherlands artist, op.1534-m. 1544) **WC**
    Bibl: ▶Bénézit; BN; ▶Dict. natl. biog.; London (GBR), V & A Mus., Tudor court (1983); Paget, Burlington mag. (1959); Schidlof, Miniature in Europe; ▶Seyn, Écoles flam. et holl.; ▶Thieme-Becker; ▶Wurzbach, NLD Künst.-Lex.
Horenbout, Harembourg, Hoorenbault, Hornebout etc., Lukas **WC**
Hornebolt, Susanna *(early Netherlandish painter in England, ca.1503-ca.1554)* **BA**
    Bibl: ▶Bénézit; Campbell, Burlington mag., LXXVIII/1003 (Oct. 1986) pp.719-727; ▶Dict. natl. biog.; ▶Foskett, Brit. miniature ptrs.; Paget, Burlington mag. (1959), p. 396; ▶Seyn, Écoles flam. et holl.; ▶Thieme-Becker; ▶Wurzbach, NLD Künst.-Lex.
Hornebrook, George Hamilton *(British artist, op.1877-)* **WI**
Horneck, Erasmus → see Horninck, Erasmus
Hornecker, Joseph *(French architect, Nancy, 1873-1942)* **AV**
    Bibl: Cahiers de la recherche architecturale, 1989, no.24-25, p.30
Hornecker, Leon *(German artist, 1864-1924)* **WC**
Hornel, Edward Atkinson **BA GC WC WI**
    (British artist, 1864-1933) **WC WI**
    (British painter, 1864-1933) **BA**
    (British, 1863-1933) **GC**
    Bibl: Brit per JK; ▶Thieme-Becker; ▶Vollmer, Künst.-Lex. 20. Jhr.
Hornell, James *(British, active 1890s)* **JG**
Hornell, Taffy *(Canadian painter, b.1951)* **BA**
    Bibl: Windsor (Ont, CND), Art Gall., William C. Law/Taffy Hornell (1982)
Horneman, Christian *(Danish artist, 1765-1844)* **WC**
Hornemann, Jurgen *(West German architect, Greven)* **AV**
    Bibl: Deutsche Bauzeitschrift, 1985 Aug., v.33, no.8, p.1003
Horner **WC WI**
    (British artist, 19th cent.) **WC**
    (British artist, op.19th c.) **WI**
Horner → see Horner, Friedrich

Horner, Friedrich PR WC
   (Swiss artist, 1800-1864) WC
   (Swiss painter, 1800-1864) PR
   Bibl: ▶Thieme-Becker
   Friedrich Horner PR
   Horner PR
Horner, G.(?) Christopher→see
   Horner, George Christopher
Horner, George *(American artist,*
   20th c.) BA
   Bibl: McCormick, ARTFORUM
   XXV/8 (Apr 1987) 92-93
Horner, George Christopher WI
   (British artist, 1829-1881) WI
   (British artist, op.1857-1867) WC
   Horner, G.(?) Christopher WC
Horner, Johan *(Swedish artist, 1711-*
   1763) WC
Horner, John *(British artist, 1876-*
   1891) WI
Horner, Rev. W.→see Horner, W.
Horner, Susanna Strangways
   (British, act.1732, d.1758) BA
   Bibl: Pevsner, Dorset, p. 278;
   Russell, Burlington Mag.
   CXXV/958 (Jan 1983), 32
Horner, Thomas→see Hornor,
   Thomas
Horner, W. WI
   (British artist, op.1808-1820) WC WI
   Horner, Rev. W. WC
Hornick, Erasmus→see Horninck,
   Erasmus
Hörnickh, Erasmus→see Horninck,
   Erasmus
Horninck, Erasmus BA GC
   (Flanders draughtsman, act.ca.
   1550-d. ca.1583) GC
   (German artist, op.c.1550) WC
   (German goldsmith, printmaker,
   d.1583) BA
   Bibl: Getty Photo Study Coll.;
   ▶Hollstein, German, v.15a;
   ▶RILA/BHA; ▶Thieme-Becker, v.17;
   ▶Witt checklist
   Horinckh, Erasmus GC
   Hornay, Erasmus GC
   Horneck, Erasmus GC
   Hornick, Erasmus GC WC
   Hörnickh, Erasmus GC
   Hornlein, Erasmus GC
Hörning, Jürgen *(West German*
   architect, Düsseldorf) AV
   Bibl: Architektur,
   Innenarchitektur, Technischer
   Ausbau, 1988 Jan.-Feb. v.96, no.
   1-2, p.38
Hørning, Tonny *(Danish artist,*
   b.1941) BA
   Bibl: ▶Art diary int'l., 1990;
   Billedkunst: Broer, Motorveje
   (1985)
Horniz (German artist, op.1795) WC
Hornlein, Erasmus→see Horninck,
   Erasmus

Hornöck, Franz Xaver *(German*
   painter, collector, 1752-1822) BA
   Bibl: ▶Bénézit; Markmiller,
   Barockmaler; ▶Thieme-Becker
Hornor or Horner, Thomas→see
   Hornor, Thomas
Hornor, Thomas BA WI
   (British artist, op.1823-1844) WC WI
   (British topographer,
   printmaker, 1785-1844) BA
   Bibl: ▶Bénézit; ▶Fielding's Amer.
   ptrs.; ▶Groce, Artists Amer.;
   Hyde, REGENT'S PARK
   COLOSSEUM, 1982;
   ▶Thieme-Becker; ▶Witt checklist
   Horner, Thomas WI
   Hornor or Horner, Thomas WC
Hornsey, J. *(British artist, op.1795-*
   1800) WC WI
Hornstain, Gabriel GC WC
   (German artist, op.1640) WC
   (German draughtsman, act. ca.
   1639) GC
   Bibl: ▶Thieme-Becker
Hornstein, Michal *(Canadian, 20th*
   c.) BA
   Bibl: Winterthur (CH),
   Kunstmuseum, FERDINAND
   HODLER (1983)
Hornthorst→see Honthorst, Gerrit
   van
Hornung, David *(German artist, op.*
   1671) WC
Hornung, Emile Charles *(Swiss*
   artist, 1883-) WC
Hornung, Joseph *(Swiss artist,*
   1792-1870) WC
Hornung, Preben *(Danish painter,*
   b.1919) BA
   Bibl: BHA/DNK; Hjort: Hornung;
   ▶Køie, Kunst.leks.;
   ▶Nørregård-Nielsen, Dansk kunst
Horny, Franz→see Horny, Franz
   Theobald
Horny, Franz Theobald BA WC
   (German artist, 1798-1824) WC
   (German painter, 1798-1824) BA
   (German, 1798-1824) GC
   Bibl: ▶Bénézit; ▶Brockhaus Enzyk.;
   George Goldner; ▶Neue deutsche
   Biog.; ▶Thieme-Becker; ▶Witt
   checklist
   Horny, Franz GC
Höroldt, Johann Gregor BA JG
   (German artist, 1696-1775) WC
   (German porcelain painter,
   porcelain manufacturer, 1696-
   1775) BA
   (German, 1696-1775, active
   1720-1756 and 1763-1765) JG
   Bibl: ▶Boger, World pott. & porc.;
   ▶Honey, Euro. ceramic; ▶Neue
   deutsche Biog.; ▶Thieme-Becker;
   ▶Witt checklist
   Herold, Heroldt or Horoldt,
   Johann Gregor WC

Horologi, Francesco→see Orologgi,
   Francesco
Horot (?)→see Hannot, Johannes
Horovitz or Horovicz, Leopold (Lipot)
   Stefan→see Horowitz, Leopold
Horowitz, Ida→see Applebroog, Ida
Horowitz, Leopold GC
   (Hungarian artist, 1838-1917) WC
   (Hungarian painter, 1838-1917) GC
   Bibl: ▶Thieme-Becker
   Horovitz or Horovicz, Leopold
   (Lipot) Stefan WC
Horozonte→see Bloemen, Jan Frans
   van (Orizonte)
Horozonti→see Bloemen, Jan Frans
   van (Orizonte)
Hörr, Joseph *(German sculptor,*
   1732-1785) BA
   Bibl: Morath, Zum Leben und
   Werk des Bildhauers;
   ▶Thieme-Becker
Horrix, Matthijs *(Dutch furniture*
   manufacturer, 1815-1889) BA
Horrix, Willem *(Dutch furniture*
   manufacturer, 1816-1881) BA
Horriz (German(?) artist, op.1795) WC
Horrozonti→see Bloemen, Jan Frans
   van (Orizonte)
Horsburgh, J. WC WI
   (British artist, op.1888-) WI
   (British(?) artist, op.1888) WC
Horschelt, Theodor (Fedor
   Fedorowitsch) *(German artist,*
   1829-1871) WC
Horse-Bird Group *(vase-painters, ca.*
   590-570 BC) GC
   Bibl: ▶Beazley, Attic bl.-fig. vase-
   ptrs.; Boardman, Attic Bl.-fig.
   Vases
Horse-head Amphorae *(vase-*
   painter, ca. 600-550 BC) GC
   Bibl: ▶Beazley, Attic bl.-fig. vase-
   ptrs.; Boardman, Attic Bl.-fig.
   Vases
Horseman Group *(South Italian*
   vase-painters, 4th century BC) GC
   Bibl: ▶Trendall, Red-fig. vases
   Lucania
Horseman Painter *(South Italian*
   vase-painter, 4th century BC) GC
   Bibl: ▶Trendall, Red-fig. vases
   Lucania
Horsey, Henry Hodge *(1830-1911;*
   Architect, Kingston, Ottawa) FA
   Bibl: ▶Hill, Archts. Canada, 1986;
   Kalman, Exploring Ottawa
Horsfall, Charles M. WC WI
   (British artist, 19th cent.) WC
   (British artist, op.1899-1907) WI
Horsfield, Dr. Thomas→see Horsfield,
   Thomas, Dr.
Horsfield, Kate *(American painter,*
   20th c.) BA
   Bibl: ▶Amer. archts. dir.; Weiss,
   New art examiner, X/2 (Nov.
   1982) p.10

Horsfield, Nicholas *(British artist,*
b.1917) **WI**
Horsfield, Ron *(British architect)* **AV**
    Bibl: Building design, 1987 Aug.
    (suppl.), p.8
Horsfield, Thomas, Dr. **WI**
    (British artist, op.1800-1818) WC WI
Horsfield, Dr. Thomas **WC**
Horsley → see Horsley, John Callcott
Horsley, G.H. **WC WI**
    (British artist, 19th cent.) WC
    (British artist, op.19th c.) WI
Horsley, Gerald *(British architect,*
1865-1917) **BA**
    Bibl: ▶Avery obit. idx.; ▶Avery
    period. idx.
Horsley, Hopkins Horsley Hobday
(British artist, 1807-1890) **WC WI**
    Bibl: Paviere, Landscape
Horsley, J. *(British artist, op.1797-)* **WI**
Horsley, John Calcott → see Horsley,
John Callcott
Horsley, John Callcott **BA PR WI**
    (British artist, 1817-1903) WC WI
    (British painter, 1817-1903) BA PR
    (British, 1817-1903) GC
    (English, 1817-1903) JG
    Bibl: ▶Johnson, Brit. artists;
    ▶RILA/BHA; ▶Thieme-Becker;
    ▶Who was who [GBR], 1897
    Horsley PR
Horsley, John Calcott **GC JG PR WC**
    John Callcott Horsley PR
Horsley, Walter Charles **WC WI**
    (British artist, 1855-1934) WI
    (British artist, 1855-p.1911) WC
    Bibl: ▶Johnson, Brit. artists
Horst → see Horst, Gerritt Willemsz.
Horst → see Horst, Horst P.
Horst, Gerard van der *(German*
painter, act.1610-1628) **GC**
    Bibl: ▶Thieme-Becker
Horst, Gerrit Willemsz. → see Horst,
Gerritt Willemsz.
Horst, Gerritt Willemsz. **BA PR**
    (Dutch artist, c.1612-1652) WC
    (Dutch painter and
    draughtsman, c.1612-1652) GC
    (Dutch painter, 1612-1652) PR
    (Dutch painter, ca.1612-1652) BA
    Bibl: ▶Bénézit; Hofstede de Groot,
    Dutch ptrs.; ▶Thieme-Becker
    Gerrit Willemsz. Horst PR
    Gerritt Willemsz. Horst PR
    Horst PR
Horst, Gerrit Willemsz. **GC PR WC**
Horst, Henk ter *(Dutch painter,*
b.1917) **BA**
    Bibl: Rotterdam (NLD), Mus.
    Boymans-van Beuningen, Veertien
    Kunstenaars (1983)

Horst, Horst P. **BA**
    (American (b. Germany), 1906 ·) JG
    (American photographer,
    b.1906) BA
    (German photographer, 1906-) AV
    Bibl: Beaton, Magic image; ▶Fogg
    Mus. Libr. cat.; ▶Hall-Duncan,
    Fashion photog.; ▶Libr. of Congr.
    Name Auth. File; ▶MoMA libr.
    cat.; ▶Parry, Photo idx.
Horst **AV**
Horst, Horst Paul **JG**
Horst, Horst Paul → see Horst, Horst
P.
Horst, J. var *(Dutch artist, 18th*
cent.(?)) **WC**
Horst, Jan van *(North Netherlandish*
painter, act. ca.1572) **GC**
    Bibl: ▶Thieme-Becker
Horst, Nicolaus van der **GC WC**
    (Flemish artist, 1587/98-1646) WC
    (Flemish painter, 1587/96-1646) GC
    Bibl: ▶Witt checklist
Horst, P. van der *(Dutch artist, op.*
c.1660) **WC**
Horst, S. **GC PR WC**
    (Dutch artist, op.1662) WC
    (Dutch painter, act. 1662) PR
    (Dutch painter, act.1662) GC
    Bibl: Getty Photo Study Coll.;
    ▶Thieme-Becker
    S. Horst PR
Horst, Uwe *(Architect, BRD)* **AV**
    Bibl: DBZ, 1985 Jan., v.33, no.1,
    p.53
Horst-Schulze, Paul *(German artist,*
1876-1937) **WC**
Horstig, Eugen *(German artist,*
1843-1901) **WC**
Horstink, Warner *(Dutch, 1756-*
1815) **GC**
    Bibl: ▶Thieme-Becker
Horstmeier, Albert *(American artist,*
1865-1940) **WI**
Horstok → see Horstok, Johannes
Petrus van
Horstok, Johannes Petrus → see
Horstok, Johannes Petrus van
Horstok, Johannes Petrus van **PR WC**
    (Dutch artist, 1745-1825) WC
    (Dutch painter, 1745-1825) GC PR
    Bibl: George Goldner; Getty Photo
    Study Coll.; ▶Thieme-Becker;
    ▶Witt checklist
    Horstok PR
Horstok, Johannes Petrus **GC PR**
    Johannes Petrus van Horstok PR
Hort, Aert van → see Arnoult de
Nimègue

Horta, Victor **BA**
    (Belgian architect, 1861-1947) BA
    (Belgian Art Nouveau architect
    and designer, 1861-1947) AV
    Bibl: ▶Contemp. archts.; ▶Libr. of
    Congr. Name Auth. File; ▶Vollmer,
    Künst.-Lex. 20. Jhr.
Horta, Victor, Baron **AV**
Horta, Victor, Baron → see Horta,
Victor
Hortenburg [Unidentified]
(Unknown painter) **PR**
    Bibl: (November 18, 1808, lot 90,
    Christie's)
Hortense, Queen of Holland
(French artist, 1783-1837) **WC**
Horter → see Horter, Earl
Horter, Earl **PR WC WI**
    (American artist, 1881-1940) WC WI
    (American painter, 1881-1940) PR
    Bibl: ▶Fielding's Amer. ptrs., 1986
    Earl Horter PR
    Horter PR
Horthemels, Louise-Magdeleine
(French printmaker, 1686-1767) **BA**
    Bibl: ▶Bénézit; ▶Petteys, Women
    artists; ▶Strutt, Dict. engravers;
    WOMENS ART JOURNAL, VI/2
    (Fall-Winter, 1985-86) 20-23
Horthorst → see Honthorst, Gerrit van
Horti, Pal *(Hungarian artist, 1865-*
1907) **WC**
Hortolani family → see Ortolani family
Hortolano → see Ortolano (Giovanni
Battista Benvenuti)
Hortolano da Ferrara → see Ortolano
(Giovanni Battista Benvenuti)
Hortolano di ferrara → see Ortolano
(Giovanni Battista Benvenuti)
Horton [Unidentified] *(Unknown*
painter) **PR**
    Bibl: (May 9, 1803, lot 53,
    Vallance)
Horton, E. **WC WI**
    (British artist, 19th cent.) WC
    (British artist, op.19th c.) WI
Horton, George Edward *(British*
artist, 1859-1950) **WC WI**
Horton, Percy Frederick **BA PR WI**
    (British artist, 1897-1970) WI
    (British painter, 1897-1970) BA PR
    Bibl: ▶Johnson, Brit. artists;
    ▶RILA/BHA; ▶Vollmer, Künst.-Lex.
    20. Jhr.; ▶Who was who [GBR],
    v.6
    Percy Frederick Horton PR
Horton, Ronald **BA WI**
    (British artist, 1902-1981) WI
    (British painter, 20th c.) BA
    Bibl: ▶Johnson, Brit. artists
Horton, William Samuel **BA WC WI**
    (American artist, 1865-1936) WC WI
    (American painter, author, 1865-
    1936) BA
    Bibl: ▶Fielding's Amer. ptrs.;
    Gibson, Artists of early Michigan

Horvat, Miljenko *(Yugoslav painter, printmaker in CAN, b.1935)* **BA**
Bibl: ▶MoMA libr. cat.; Paris (FRA), Centre culturel canadien, MILJENKOHORVAT, 1981

Horvat-Zdalski, Josef *(Yugoslav artist, op.1923-1966)* **WC**

Horváth, Lajos *(Hungarian architect)* **AV**
Bibl: Magyar Építőművészet, 1984, no.2, p.41

Horváth, Zoltán *(Hungarian architect, Budapest, 1953-)* **AV**
Bibl: Magyar építőművészet, 1988, v.79, no.2, p.40

Horvitz, Robert Joseph *(American critic, artist, 20th c.)* **BA**
Bibl: Artforum 13, Sept 74, p.34

Horvitz, Shelah *(American artist, 20th c.)* **BA**
Bibl: JOURNAL OF PRE-RAPHAELITE STUDIES, III/2 (May 1983) 131

Horvitz, Suzanne Joan *(American painter, printmaker, 20th c.)* **BA**
Bibl: ▶Intl. dir. exh. artists, 1983; ▶WW Amer. Art

Horwert, Nikolaus *(German painter, act. ca.1480)* **GC**
Bibl: Stewart, Unequal lovers

Horwitt, Will *(American sculptor, b.1934)* **BA**
Bibl: ▶MoMA libr. cat.; New York (NY, USA), Gruenebaum Gallery, Constructivism (1975); ▶WW Amer. Art, 1976

Horwitz, Channa *(American artist, 20th c.)* **BA**
Bibl: Artweek v.VIII, MAy 1 1979, p.9; Newport Beach (CA, USA), Newport Harbor Art Mus., Three directions: Agnes Denes, Channa Horwitz, Joyce Cutler, Shaw, 1976

Horwitz, Herbert A. *(British artist, op.1892-1925)* **WI**

Horwood, Edgar Lewis *(1868-1957; Architect, Government architect, Ottawa)* **FA**
Bibl: CAAD Finding Aids, Ewart, J. Albert, 76703/13; ▶Hill, Archts. Canada, 1986

Hory, Elmyr de *(Hungarian art forger in ESP, 1906-1976)* **BA**
Bibl: Clifford Irving, Fakes; ▶MoMA libr. cat.; NY Times obit., 13 Dec 1976

Horydczak, Theodor *(American photographer, act.1920, d.1971)* **BA**
Bibl: ▶Bénézit; QUARTERLY JOURNAL OF THE LIBRARY OF CONGRESS XXXVI/1 winter 1979 p.38-67; ▶Vollmer, Künst.-Lex. 20. Jhr.

Hosak, Bärbel *(German designer, b.1955)* **BA**
Bibl: London (GBR), Goethe Inst., DAAD Scholarship-holders (1983)

Hosaka, Yoichiro *(Japanese architect, 1934-)* **AV**
Bibl: Kenchiku bunka, 1987 Dec., v.42, no.494, p.260

Hoschede-Monet, Blanche **WC**
(French artist, 1865-1947) **WC**
(French artist, 20th cent.) **WC**

Monet, Blanche Hoschede **WC**

Höscheler, Samuel→*see* Höscheller, Samuel

Höscheller, Samuel *(Swiss stucco artist, 1630-1713/15)* **BA**
Bibl: ▶Schweiz. Künst.-Lex., v.2; Wipf, NOS MONUMENTS D'ART ET D'HISTOIRE XXXVII 91986) 146-54

Höscheler, Samuel **BA**

Hosemann, Friedrich Wilhelm Heinrich Theodor→*see* Hosemann, Theodor

Hosemann, Theodor **BA GC**
(German artist, 1807-1875) **WC**
(German painter and draughtsman, 1807-1895) **GC**
(German painter, printmaker, 1807-1875) **BA**
Bibl: ▶Bénézit; ▶Neue deutsche Biog.; ▶Thieme-Becker

Hosemann, Friedrich Wilhelm Heinrich Theodor **GC**

Hosemann, Theodor (Friedrich Wilhelm Heinrich Theodor) **WC**

Hosemann, Theodor (Friedrich Wilhelm Heinrich Theodor)→*see* Hosemann, Theodor

Hosenfelder, Christian Friedrich *(German artist, 1706-1780)* **WC**

Hosennestel, Sabina Auffenwerth *(German porcelain painter, 1706-1782)* **BA**
Bibl: Clarke, Keramos, 109 (Jul. 1985) pp.3-16; Ducret, Meissner Porzellan, v.2, 10ff; ▶Honey, Euro. ceramic

Aufenwerth, Sabina **BA**

Hosford, Ray *(American painter, 20th c.)* **BA**
Bibl: Shreveport (LA, USA), Norton Art Gallery, America the beautiful (1975)

Hoshina, Fuminori *(Japanese architect)* **AV**
Bibl: Japan architect, 1988 Mar., v.63, no.3(371), p.41

Hoshina, Takayuki *(Japanese architect)* **AV**
Bibl: Japan architect, 1986 Oct., v.61, no.10, p.58

Hoshina, Toyomi *(Japanese artist, b.1953)* **BA**
Bibl: Geneva (CHE), Musée Rath, Art japonais d'aujourd'hui (1983)

Hoshino, Satoru *(Japanese artist, b.1945)* **BA**
Bibl: Geneva (CHE), Musée Rath, Art japonais d'aujourd'hui (1983)

Hosiasson→*see* Hosiasson, Philippe

Hosiasson, Philippe **BA PR WC**
(French artist, 1898-) **WC**
(French painter, 1898-1978) **BA PR**
Bibl: Emmerich Gallery, PHILIPPE HOSIASSON(1978); ▶RILA/BHA; ▶WW France, 1975-76

Hosiasson **PR**

Philippe Hosiasson **PR**

Hosidius [Unidentified] *(Unknown painter)* **PR**
Bibl: (May 24, 1810, lot 27, Smith (John))

Hosironti→*see* Bloemen, Jan Frans van (Orizonte)

Hoskin, Robert *(Engraver, b.1842)* **WI**

Hosking, Eric *(British artist, b.1909)* **WI**

Hosking, Knighton **BA WC WI**
(British artist, 1944-) **WC**
(British artist, b.1944) **WI**
(British painter, b.1944) **BA**
Bibl: Sunderland (GBR), Arts Ctr., Working process (1978)

Hoskins, Gayle Porter *(American painter, illustrator, 1887-1962)* **BA**
Bibl: ▶Artist biog. master idx.; ▶Collins, Women artists Amer.; ▶Fielding's Amer. ptrs.; ▶Vollmer, Künst.-Lex. 20. Jhr.; ▶WWW Amer. art

Hoskins, John *(British sculptor, b.1921)* **BA**
Bibl: London (GBR), Marble Hill House, Sculp. in landscape (1975); ▶Phaidon 20c. art

Hoskins, John E. *(Canadian architect, St. John's, Nfld, fl. 1920's)* **AV**
Bibl: Canadian architect, 1989 Oct., v.34, no.10, p.55

Hoskins, John I **BA WI**
(British artist, 1590's-1664-1665) **WI**
(British artist, op.1620-m.1665) **WC**
(English painter, act.1620, d.ca. 1664) **BA**
Bibl: ▶Foskett, Brit. miniature ptrs.; Foster, Ptrs. miniature; ▶Thieme-Becker; ▶Witt checklist

Hoskins, John, I **WC**

Hoskins, John II **BA WI**
(British artist, circa 1630-op. 1693) **WI**
(British artist, op.1658-1686) **WC**
(English painter, b.ca.1630, act. 1693) **BA**
Bibl: BURLINGTON CXXVII/983 (Feb 1985) 84; ▶Dict. natl. biog.; Edmond, M., WALPOLE SOCIETY, XLVII (1980) 114; Foster, Ptrs. miniature; ▶Thieme-Becker; ▶Witt checklist

Hoskins, John, II **WC**

Hoskins, John, I→*see* Hoskins, John I
Hoskins, John, II→*see* Hoskins, John II

Hoskins, Michael *(American painter,* BA
20th c.)
Bibl: Douglas, New art examiner,
XI/9 (Jun. 1984) p.12

Hoslwanger, Wolfganger *(German*
artist, op.1600) **WC**

Hosmer, Harriet Goodhue
(American sculptor in ITA, 1830-
1908) BA
Bibl: ▶Petteys, Women artists

Hosmer, Joseph *(American*
cabinetmaker, 1735-1821) BA
Bibl: Dodge, Antiques, CVI/6
(Dec. 1974) pp.1014-1023

Hosoe, Eikoh *(Japanese*
photographer, b.1933) BA
Bibl: ▶Contemp. photogs.; ▶Intl.
dir. exh. artists, 1983; ▶Parry,
Photo idx.

Hosoe, Isao *(Japanese architect,*
1942-) AV
Bibl: Modo, 1985 Sept., v.9,
no.82, p.41

Hospitaller Master *(French*
illuminator, act.ca.1282) BA

Hoss, Peter *(American artist, 20th*
c.) BA
Bibl: Boston (MA, USA), ICA,
Boston now (1982)

Hosson, F.C. **GC WC**
(Dutch artist, 1717-1799) WC
(German painter, 1717-1799) GC
Bibl: ▶Thieme-Becker; ▶Wright,
Ptgs. Dutch museums
Hosson, Hermanus Fridericus
Carolus de GC
Hosson, Hermanus Fridericus Carolus
de→see Hosson, F.C.
Host, Oluf→see Høst, Oluf Kristian
Alexander

Høst, Oluf Kristian Alexander BA
(Danish painter, 1884-1966) BA
(Danish(?) artist, 20th cent.) WC
Bibl: ▶Busse, Maler u. Bildhauer
19. Jahr.; Ernst,
BORNHOLMERMALERNE...(1984);
Meister, OLUF HOEST; ▶Vollmer,
Künst.-Lex. 20. Jhr.; ▶Weilbach,
Kunst.leks.; ▶Witt checklist

Host, Oluf **WC**

Hostettler, Emil *(Swiss architect,*
early 20th c) AV
Bibl: Werk, Bauen + Wohnen,
1989 June, no.6, p.8

Hostman, Hugo *(Swiss ecclesiastic,*
cabinetmaker, act.1763-1767) BA
Bibl: Fruh, Zeits. Schweiz. Arch. u.
Kunst, XXXVIII/1 (1981) pp.59-79;
▶Jenny, Kunstführer Schweiz, v.1,
p.630; Kunstdenkmäler Thurgau,
v.1, pp.230, 260

Hotchkiss, Almerin *(American*
landscape architect, d.1896) AV
Bibl: Winterthur portfolio, v.18,
n.4 1983, p.252

Hotchkiss, Frank E. *(American city*
planner, Pacific Palisades, Calif) AV
Bibl: ▶AIA Pro File, 1987-88

Hotchkiss, Thomas H. **WC WI**
(American artist, circa 1834-
1869) WI
(American artist, op.c.1856-m.
1869) WC

Hotchkiss, Wales *(American painter,*
b. 1826) **PR**
Bibl: ▶Fielding's Amer. ptrs., 1986
Wales Hotchkiss PR

Hotene, José Sanc *(Brazilian*
architect) AV
Bibl: Projeto, 1988 Feb., no.107,
p.79

Hotere, Ralph *(New Zealander*
painter, b.1931) BA
Bibl: Art Intl. XIX/1 (Jan 1975),
18 ff

Hoth, Sue Robinson *(American*
sculptor, b.1946) BA
Bibl: Montgomery(AL, USA),
Museum Of Fine Arts. SUE
ROBINSON HOTH(1979)

Hotham, Amelia **WC WI**
(British artist, op.1793) WC
(British artist, op.1793-, d.1812) WI
Woodcock, J., Hon.Mrs., (Amelia) WI

Hotshkis, Mary **WC WI**
(British artist, 17th cent.(?)) WC
(British artist, op.17th c.) WI

Hotson, Norman *(Canadian*
architect, Vancouver, B.C) AV
Bibl: Section a, 1985 Jan., v.2, no.
5-6, p.18

Hottenroth, Edmund *(German*
painter, 1804-1889) BA
Bibl: ▶Bénézit; ▶Neue deutsche
Biog.; ▶Thieme-Becker

Hottinger, William A. *(American*
artist, b.1890) WI

Hotz, Theo *(Swiss architect, 1928-)* AV
Bibl: Deutsche Bauzeitung, 1988
Dec., v.122, no.12, p.146

Hotzen, Adalbert *(German*
architect, act.1893-1894) BA
Bibl: Rauterberg, NORDELBINGEN,
LIII (1984) 49-76

Hotzendorff, Conrad von *(German*
artist, op.1820) **WC**

Hötzendorff, Theodor von *(German*
painter, b.1898) GC
Bibl: ▶Vollmer, Künst.-Lex. 20. Jhr.

Hötzl, Josef *(Austrian architect,*
1866-1947) AV
Bibl: Planen Bauen Wohnen,
1987, no.119, p.11

Houasse→see Houasse, Michel Ange
Houasse or Ouasse, Michel
Ange→see Houasse, Michel Ange
Houasse or Ouasse, Rene
Antoine→see Houasse, René
Antoine

Houasse, Michel Ange **BA PR**
(French artist, c.1680-1730) WC
(French painter, 1680-1730) BA PR
Bibl: (April 20, 1812, lot 8,
Robins); ▶Bénézit; Clark Art Inst.
Photo & Slide Dept.; ▶RILA/BHA;
▶Thieme-Becker
Houasse PR

Houasse or Ouasse, Michel
Ange **WC**
Michel Ange Houasse PR
Ovase, M. Angelo PR

Houasse, René Antoine **BA GC PR**
(French artist, 1644/5-1710) WC
(French painter, ca.1645-1710) BA PR
(French, 1644/45-1710) GC
Bibl: ▶Havlice, Idx. art. bio.;
▶RILA/BHA; ▶Thieme-Becker;
▶Witt checklist

Houasse or Ouasse, Rene
Antoine **WC**
Rene Antoine Houasse PR

Houben, Francine *(Dutch architect,*
1955-) AV
Bibl: Tableau: Tijdschrift voor
beelende kunst, 1987 Dec., v.10,
no.3, p.44

Houben, Henri *(Belgian artist, op.*
1885-1898) **WC**

Houbigant, Armand Gustave
(French artist, 1789-1862) **WC**

Houbolt, Eduard Johannes
Fredericus **BA GC WC**
(Dutch artist, 1885-1954) WC
(Dutch draughtsman, 1885-
1954) GC
(Dutch painter, printmaker,
1885-1954) BA
Bibl: ▶Bénézit; ▶Thieme-Becker;
Venema, NEDERLANDSE
SCHILDERS...(1980), 163;
▶Vollmer, Künst.-Lex. 20. Jhr.

Houbrachen→see Houbraken, Arnold
Houbracken→see Houbraken, Arnold
Houbracken, Arnold→see Houbraken,
Arnold
Houbraken→see Houbraken, Arnold

Houbraken, Arnold **BA GC PR WC**
(Dutch art historian, painter,
printmaker, 1660-1719) BA
(Dutch artist, 1660-1719) WC
(Dutch painter and
draughtsman, 1660-1719) GC
(Dutch painter, 1660-1719) PR
Bibl: ▶Encyc. world art; Getty
Photo Study Coll.; ▶Nieuw NLD
biog. woord.; ▶Oxford comp. art;
▶RILA/BHA; ▶Thieme-Becker
Arnold Houbracken PR
Arnold Houbraken PR
Honbraken PR
Houbrachen PR
Houbracken PR
Houbracken, Arnold PR
Houbraken PR
marked A. Houbraken PR

**Houbraken, Giovanni van, or
Giovanni Vanderbrach or
Vanhoubraken** *(Flemish artist, op.
c.1635-1674)* WC
Houbraken, Jacobus GC WC
  (Dutch artist, 1698-1780) WC
  *(Dutch draughtsman and
    printmaker, 1698-1780)* GC
  Bibl: Getty Photo Study Coll.;
    ▶Thieme-Becker; ▶Witt checklist
Houbraken, Niccolino van GC PR
  (Flemish artist, op.1706-1724) WC
  *(Flemish painter, act. 1706-
    1724)* PR
  (Flemish, act.1706-1724) GC
  Bibl: ▶Thieme-Becker

**Houbraken, Niccolino van, or
  Niccolino Vanderbrach or
  Vanhoubraken** WC
  Houbraken, Nicola van PR
  Niccolino van Houbraken PR
  Valdubrochen PR
  Vanhoubrachen PR
*Houbraken, Niccolino van, or
  Niccolino Vanderbrach or
  Vanhoubraken → see* Houbraken,
  Niccolino van
Houbraken, Nicola van → see
  Houbraken, Niccolino van
Houbron, Frederic Anatole GC WC
  (French artist, c.1851-1901) WC
  (French painter, 1851-1908) GC
  Bibl: ▶Bénézit

Houck, Peter BA
  *(Dutch draftsman, act.1603-
    1626)* BA
  (Flemish artist, op.1603-1626) WC
  (Flemish painter, act.1603-1626) GC
  Bibl: ▶Bénézit; Spicer, MASTER
    DRAWINGS, XXVI(WINTER 1988),
    351-356; ▶Thieme-Becker; ▶Witt
    checklist

  **Hoeck or Houck, Peter
    Cornelisz. van den** WC
  Hoeck, Peter Cornelisz. van den GC
Houck, Van → see Houck, van
  [Unidentified]
Houck, van [Unidentified]
  (Unknown painter) PR
  Bibl: (March 1, 1805, lot 31,
    Christie's)
  Houck, Van PR
  Van Houck PR
Houckgeest → see Houckgeest, Gerard
*Houckgeest or Hoeckgeest, Gerard,
  Geraert or Gerrit → see*
  Houckgeest, Gerard

Houckgeest, Gerard BA GC PR
  (Dutch artist, c.1600-1661) WC
  *(Dutch painter and
    draughtsman, ca.1600-1661)* GC
  (Dutch painter, ca.1600-1661) BA PR
  Bibl: ▶Bénézit; Brul inventory
    1653; Getty Photo Study Coll.;
    ▶Thieme-Becker;
  Gerard Houckgeest PR
  Hodeckgeest PR
  Hoeckgeest PR
  Hoodegist PR
  Houckgeest PR
**Houckgeest or Hoeckgeest,
  Gerard, Geraert or Gerrit** WC
  Houckvelt PR
Houckgeest, Joachim Ottensz. GC
  (Dutch artist, c.1580/90-a.1645) WC
  *(Dutch painter,
    ca.1580/90-bef.1645)* GC
  Bibl: Getty Photo Study Coll.;
    ▶Thieme-Becker
**Houckgeest. or Hoeckgeest,
  Joachim Ottensz.** WC
*Houckgeest. or Hoeckgeest, Joachim
  Ottensz. → see* Houckgeest,
  Joachim Ottensz.
Houckvelt → see Houckgeest, Gerard
Houdan, J. *(French designer, act.
  1764-1770)* BA
  Bibl: ▶Bénézit; Jervis,
    BURLINGTON MAGAZINE,
    CXXVI/975 (June 1984) p.343-
    347; ▶Nagler, Neues Künst.-Lex.;
    Roberts, BURLINGTON MAGAZINE,
    1034/131 (May 1989) p.350-353;
    ▶Thieme-Becker
Houdard, Charles-Louis-M. *(French
  artist, 19th cent.)* WC
Houdetot, Comte Frederic d'
  (French artist, 19th cent.) WC
Houdoit, J. *(French, active 1840s-
  1870s)* JG
Houdon, Jean Antoine → see Houdon,
  Jean-Antoine
Houdon, Jean-Antoine BA GC JG
  (French artist, 1741-1828) WC
  (French sculptor, 1741-1828) BA GC
  (French, 1741-1828) JG
  Bibl: ▶Bénézit; ▶Larousse grande
    encyc.; ▶RILA/BHA;
    ▶Thieme-Becker; ▶Witt checklist
Houdon, Jean Antoine WC
Houdrie of Paris → see Oudry, Jean-
  Baptiste
**Houel, Jean Pierre Louis
  Laurent** BA GC WC
  (French artist, 1735-1813) WC
  *(French painter and engraver,
    1735-1813)* GC
  *(French painter, printmaker,
    1735-1813)* BA
  Bibl: ▶Bénézit; ▶Thieme-Becker;
    ▶Witt checklist
Houel, Nicholas *(French artist, 16th
  cent.)* WC

Houet → see Huet, Jean Baptiste
Houez, Charles François *(French
  painter, 1819-1849)* GC
  Bibl: ▶Bénézit
Houff, Abraham van der → see Houve,
  Abraham van der
Houfton, Percy *(British architect,
  Chesterfield)* AV
  Bibl: Architectural history, 1987,
    v.30, p.150
Hough, van [Unidentified]
  (Unknown painter) PR
  Bibl: (July 23, 1803, lot 20,
    Farebrother)
  Van Hough PR
Hough, William *(British artist, op.
  1857-1894)* WC WI
Houghton, Arthur Boyd BA PR WC WI
  (British artist, 1836-1875) WC WI
  (British painter, 1836-1875) PR
  *(British painter, illustrator, 1836-
    1875)* BA
  Bibl: ▶Dict. natl. biog.;
    ▶RILA/BHA; ▶Wood, Victorian
    ptrs.
  Arthur Boyd Houghton PR
Houghton, Elizabeth Ellen *(British
  artist, 1853-1922)* WI
Houghton, J.R. *(British designer,
  act.1898-1901)* BA
  Bibl: London (GBR), Mus. London,
    London design studio (1980)
Houghton, John *(American
  carpenter, 1624-1684)* BA
  Bibl: WINTERTHUR PORTFOLIO,
    XIII(1979),1-46
Houghton, Matthew WC WI
  (British artist, 18th cent.) WC
  (British artist, op.18th c.) WI
Houghton, Stanley *(British artist,
  op.20th c.)* WI
Houlditch, John *(British artist, op.
  1784-1791)* WI
Houle, Robert *(Canadian artist,
  b.1947)* BA
  Bibl: Regina (Sask, CAN), U.Sask.
    Gallery, A new generation (1982)
Houlès, Suzanne *(French interior
  designer)* AV
  Bibl: Maison Française, 1985 May,
    no.387, p.130
Houliere → see Houlière, R. de la
Houlière, R. de la PR
  (French artist, op.1789-1791) WC
  (French painter, act. 1789-91) PR
  Bibl: ▶Thieme-Becker
  Houliere PR
  Houlieres PR
  La Houliere, R. de WC
  la Houlieres PR
  R. de la Houliere PR
Houlieres → see Houlière, R. de la
Hound-and-Hare Group GC
  Bibl: ▶Beazley, Attic bl.-fig. vase-
    ptrs.
Hounsom, G. → see Hounsom, George

Hounsom, George   **WI**
(British artist, op.1796-1806)   WC WI
Hounsom, G.   **WC**
Houra, Miroslav (Czech painter,
printmaker, b.1933)   **BA**
Bibl: Litomerice (CSK), Gal.
Vytvarneho Uměni, Miroslav
Houra: Obrazy, Grafika, Tapiserie
(Nov. 1978-Jan. 1979)
Houry, Pierre (French porcelain
painter, act.1754-1755)   **GC**
Bibl: ▶Brunet, Sèvres
House, Gordon   **BA WC WI**
(British artist, 1932-)   WC
(British artist, b.1932)   BA WI
Bibl: ▶Babington Smith, Contemp.
artists
House, Harlan (Canadian ceramist,
b.1943)   **BA**
House, R. (British artist, op.1863-)   **WI**
House, Timothy (Engraver,
Newtonville, MA., op.circa 1836-,
d.1865)   **WI**
Housebook Master → see Master of
the Housebook
Houseman → see Huysmans, Cornelis
Houser, Allan C. (American sculptor,
painter, b.1914)   **BA**
Bibl: ▶WW Amer. Art, 1978
Houser, Jim (American painter,
b.1928)   **BA**
Bibl: ▶WW Amer. Art, 1980
Houseworth, Marvin (American
architect)   **AV**
Bibl: ▶AIA Pro File, 1989-90
Houseworth, Thomas (American,
1829-1915 (Houseworth & Co.))   **JG**
Housez, Charles (French artist,
1822-1888)   **WC**
Houshiary, Shirazeh (Iranian
sculptor in GBR, b.1955)   **BA**
Bibl: Edinburgh(GBR), Fruit Market
Gallery. OBJECTS AND FIGURES...
(1983); ▶Intl. dir. exh. artists
Houska, Marek (Czech architect)   **AV**
Bibl: Architektura ČSR, 1988,
v.47, no.2, p.63
Housman → see Huysmans, Cornelis
Housman, Laurence   **BA GC WI**
(British artist, 1867-1959)   WC WI
(British illustrator, author, 1865-
1959)   BA
(British, 1867-1959)   GC
Bibl: ▶Dict. natl. biog.; ▶Johnson,
Brit. artists; ▶Thieme-Becker;
▶Witt checklist
Housman, Laurenee   **WC**
Housman, Laurenee → see Housman,
Laurence
Houssaye, Josephine (French artist,
1840-p.1900)   **WC**
Houssin (French photographer, act.
1863)   **BA**
Bibl: Rice, AFTERIMAGE XIV (May
1987)

Houst [Unidentified] (Unknown
painter)   **PR**
Bibl: (May 27, 1807, lot 11,
Phillips (Harry))
Houston Painter   **GC**
Bibl: ▶Beazley, Attic red-fig. vase-
ptrs.
Houston, Bruce (American sculptor,
b.1937)   **BA**
Bibl: ▶WW Amer. Art, 1989
Houston, Frances C. (American
artist, 1867-1906)   **WI**
Houston, George   **GC WC WI**
(British artist, 1869-1947)   WC WI
(Scottish painter and
draughtsman, b.1869)   GC
Bibl: ▶Bénézit
Houston, H.H. (British artist, op.
1791-1798)   **WC WI**
Houston, Ian (British artist, op.20th
c.)   **WI**
Houston, John   **WC WI**
(British artist, b.1930)   WI
(British artist, op.1930-34)   WC
Houston, John Adam (British artist,
1812-1884)   **WC WI**
Houston, John Rennie McKenzie
(British artist, 1856-1932)   **WI**
Houston, John, Mrs., (Elizabeth) → see
Blackadder, Elizabeth V.
Houston, Nora (American painter,
act. 19th-20th centuries)   **PR**
Bibl: ▶WWW Amer. art
Nora Houston   PR
Houston, Richard   **BA WC WI**
(British artist, c.1721-1775)   WC
(British artist, circa 1721-1775)   WI
(Engraver, circa 1721-1775)   WI
(Irish printmaker, painter, 1721-
1775)   BA
Bibl: ▶Dict. natl. biog.;
▶Strickland, Irish artists;
▶Thieme-Becker
Houston, Robert   **WC WI**
(British artist, 1891-c.1942)   WC
(British artist, 1891-circa 1942)   WI
Bibl: ▶Johnson, Brit. artists
Houston, Thomas   **WC WI**
(British artist, op.18th c.)   WI
(British(?) artist, 18th cent.)   WC
Houstoun, D. Mackay (Canadian
artist, 20th cent.)   **WC**
Hout, H. J. van den (Dutch
printmaker, act. mid-19th century)   **GC**
Bibl: ▶Thieme-Becker
Hout, Jan van   **GC WC**
(Netherlandish painter, act.
1506)   GC
(Netherlands artist, op.1506)   WC
Bibl: ▶Witt checklist
Houte, Adrian van den, the elder
(early Netherlandish glass painter,
act.1513-1519)   **BA**
Bibl: ▶Bénézit; ▶Thieme-Becker
Houte, C. ten (Dutch artist, op.
1644)   **WC**

Houte, Rombout van den (Dutch
artist, op.1613)   **WC**
Houten → see Houten, Pr. van
[Unidentified]
Houten or Hout, T. van (Flemish(?)
artist, 17th cent.)   **WC**
Houten, Alida van (Dutch painter,
1868-1960)   **GC**
Bibl: ▶Wright, Ptgs. Dutch
museums
Houten, Barbara Elisabeth van
(Dutch artist, 1862-1950)   **WC**
Houten, F. van (Flemish artist, 17th
cent.)   **WC**
Houten, Gerard van   **GC WC**
(Dutch artist, op.1675-m.1706)   WC
(Dutch draughtsman, act.1675-
d.1706)   GC
Bibl: ▶Witt checklist
Houten, H.L. van den (Australian
artist, op.1876)   **WC**
Houten, Hans van (Flemish artist,
1578(?)-p.1625)   **WC**
Houten, Hans van den (Dutch
artist, b.1944)   **BA**
Bibl: Amsterdam (NLD), Stedelijk
Museum, Atelier 16 (1980)
Houten, Pr. van [Unidentified]
(Unknown painter, act. 17th
century)   **PR**
Bibl: Gaillard inventory 1639
Houten   PR
Pr. van Houten   PR
Houten, Sina van → see Mesdag van
Houten, Sina
Houthorst → see Honthorst, Gerrit van
Houthuensen, Albertus
Antonius → see Houthuesen, Albert
Anthony
Houthuesen, Albert Anthony   **BA**
(British artist, 1903-)   WC
(British artist, b.1903)   WI
(British painter, printmaker,
1903-1979)   BA
Bibl: ▶Bénézit; ▶Johnson, Brit.
artists; ▶Waters, Brit. artists;
▶Who was who [GBR], 1971-80
**Houthuensen, Albertus
Antonius**   **WC**
Houthuesen, Albertus Antonius   **WI**
Houthuesen, Albertus Antonius → see
Houthuesen, Albert Anthony
Houthuesen, Catherine → see Dean,
Catherine
Houthuijsen, Houthuijse or
Houthuysen, Jan Jansz. van → see
Houthuijsen, Jan Jansz. van
Houthuijsen, Jan Jansz. van   **GC**
(Dutch artist, op.1648-m.1662)   WC
(Dutch painter, act.1648-d.
1662)   GC
Bibl: ▶Thieme-Becker
**Houthuijsen, Houthuijse or
Houthuysen, Jan Jansz. van**   **WC**
Houtman, Maerten (Dutch artist,
op.1766-1790)   **WC**

Houtman, Martinus *(Dutch painter, 1782-1863)* **GC**
Bibl: ▶Thieme-Becker

Houtryve, Erasmus van *(Flemish tin founder, 1704-1743)* **BA**
Bibl: Dijkmans, ANTIEK XIX/3 (Oct 1984), 137-139

Houve or Hoeven, Abraham van der → *see* Houve, Abraham van der

Houve, Abraham van der **GC**
(Dutch artist, op.1615-m.1621) WC
(Dutch painter, ca.1575-1621) GC
Bibl: ▶Schweers, Gemälde deut. Museen; ▶Witt checklist

Houve, Abraham van der GC
Hoeven, Abraham van der GC
Houff, Abraham van der GC

Houve or Hoeven, Abraham van der **WC**

Houve, Paul de la → *see* De la Houve, Paul

Houve, Salomon de la *(French(?) artist, 17th cent.)* **WC**

Houwen, Joris *(Belgian artist, 20th cent.)* **WC**

Hovadik, Jaroslav *(Canadian artist, 20th cent.)* **WC**

Hovara, Filippo → *see* Juvara, Filippo

Hove *(Netherlands(?) artist, op.1784-1791)* **WC**

Hove → *see* Hove, Hubertus van

Hove, Bartholomeus Johannes van **BA GC WC**
(Dutch artist, 1790-1880) WC
(Dutch painter, printmaker, 1790-1880) BA
(Dutch, 1790-1880) GC
Bibl: ▶Thieme-Becker

Hove, Edmond Theodor van **GC WC**
(Belgian artist, 1853-1913) WC
(Belgian painter, 1853-1913) GC
Bibl: ▶Bénézit

Hove, Hoove or Hoven, Frederick Hendrick van, or Frederick Hendrick van den Hooven *(Dutch artist, c.1628-1698)* **WC**

Hove, Hubertus van **GC PR WC**
(Dutch artist, 1814-1864) WC
(Dutch painter, 1814-1865) PR
(Dutch, 1814-1865) GC
Bibl: ▶Thieme-Becker

Hove PR
Hubertus van Hove PR

Hove, Johannes Huybertus van *(Dutch artist, 1827-1881)* **WC**

Hove, Victor François Guillaume van **GC WC**
(Belgian artist, 1826-1891) WC
(Belgian painter, 1826-1891) GC
Bibl: Getty Photo Study Coll. (Ptgs.); ▶Thieme-Becker

Hove, Victor van GC
Hove, Victor van → *see* Hove, Victor François Guillaume van

Hovel, A. van *(Flemish(?) artist, 17th cent.)* **WC**

Hövel, Dierk van den *(West German architect, Düsseldorf)* **AV**
Bibl: Architektur, Innenarchitektur, Technischer Ausbau, 1989 Mar., v.97, no.3, p.38

Hoveman → *see* Horemans, Jan Joseph I

Hovemeyer, August *(German artist, 1824-1878)* **WC**

Hoven → *see* Hoven, Herbert Nelson

Hoven, H. ten *(Dutch artist, 20th cent.)* **WC**

Hoven, H. van [Unidentified] *(Unknown painter)* **PR**
Bibl: (February 23, 1808, Dublin)

H. Vanhoven PR

Hoven, Herbert Nelson *(American painter, b. 1898)* **PR**
Bibl: ▶WWW Amer. art

Herbert Nelson Hoven PR
Hooven, Herbert PR
Hoven PR

Hovenden → *see* Hovenden, Thomas

Hovenden, Thomas **BA GC PR WC WI**
(American artist, 1840-1895) WC WI
(American painter, 1840-1895) BA GC PR
Bibl: ▶Fielding's Amer. ptrs.; ▶RILA/BHA; ▶Thieme-Becker; ▶WWW Amer., 1607; ▶Young, Amer. artists

Hovenden PR
Hovendon, Thomas PR
Thomas Hovenden PR
Hovendon, Thomas → *see* Hovenden, Thomas

Hovens Greve, Hans J. A. *(Dutch city planner, d.1984)* **AV**
Bibl: Stedebouw en Volkshuisvesting, 1984 Oct., v.65, no.10

Hoversland, Beverly **AV**

Hovey, David *(American architect)* **AV**

Hovich, de [Unidentified] *(Unknown painter)* **PR**
Bibl: (June 24, 1813, lot 99, Del Vecchio)

De Hovich PR

How → *see* How, Julia Beatrice

How, B.A. [Unidentified] *(British painter, act. 1st half 19th cent.)* **PR**
Bibl: Boston MFA catalogue

B.A. How PR

How, Beatrice → *see* How, Julia Beatrice

How, F. **WC WI**
(British artist, op.1648) WC
(British artist, op.1648-1650-1660) WI

How, Julia Beatrice **BA PR WI**
(British artist, 1867-1932) WC WI
(British painter, 1867-1932) BA PR
Bibl: ▶Bénézit; ▶RILA/BHA; ▶Vollmer, Künst.-Lex. 20. Jhr.; ▶Waters, Brit. artists

How PR

How, Beatrice **PR WC**
Julia Beatrice How PR

Howard → *see* Howard, Henry
Howard Chandler Christy → *see* Christy, Howard Chandler
Howard E. Smith → *see* Smith, Howard Everett
Howard Gardiner Cushing → *see* Cushing, Howard Gardiner
Howard Giles → *see* Giles, Howard Everett
Howard Helmick → *see* Helmick, Howard
Howard R.A. → *see* Howard, Henry

Howard, A.B. *(British artist, op.19th c.)* **WI**

Howard, A.R.A. → *see* Howard, Henry

Howard, Alan *(American architect, Chicago, IL, 1931-)* **AV**
Bibl: Architecture and urbanism, no.174, p.123

Howard, Anthony Christian **WC WI**
(British artist, 20th cent.) WC
(British artist, b.1945) WI

Howard, Cecil de Blaquiere *(American sculptor, 1888-1956)* **GC**
Bibl: ▶Opitz, Amer. sculptors

Howard, Charles → *see* Howard, Charles Houghton

Howard, Charles Houghton **BA PR**
(American painter in GBR, 1899-1978) BA
(American painter, 1899-1978) PR
(British artist, 1899-) WC
(British artist, b.1899) WI
Bibl: ▶Bénézit; ▶RILA/BHA; Sacramento (CA, USA), Crocker Art Museum, From exposition (1981); ▶Vollmer, Künst.-Lex. 20. Jhr.; ▶WW Amer. Art, 1956, 1966

Charles Houghton Howard PR

Howard, Charles **PR WC WI**

Howard, Coy **AV BA**
(American architect, active in Los Angeles, 1943-) AV
(American architect, b.1943) BA
Bibl: Art in Amer., LXIX/6 (Sum. 1981) pp.114-123; ▶Avery period. idx.

Howard, E. Stirling **WI**
(British artist, op.1834-1870) WC WI

Howard, E.Stirling **WC**
Howard, E.Stirling → *see* Howard, E. Stirling

Howe, Wallis Eastburn *(American architect, 1868-1960)*   **BA**
  Bibl: Jordy, H.-R. Hitchcock festschrift, pp. 324, 330, 333; ▶WWW Amer., v.4

Howe, Will → see Howe, William Henry

Howe, William *(American civil engineer, 1803-1952)*   **AV**
  Bibl: A biographical dictionary of American civil engineers. 1972, p.63

Howe, William Henry   **BA PR WC WI**
  (American artist, 1846-)   **WC**
  (American artist, 1846-1929)   **WI**
  (American painter, 1846-1929)   **BA PR**
  Bibl: ▶Fielding's Amer. ptrs.; ▶RILA/BHA; ▶WWW Amer. art
  Howe, Will   **PR**
  William Henry Howe   **PR**

Höweler, Gerard *(Dutch sculptor, b.1940)*   **BA**
  Bibl: Amsterdam (NLD), Museum Fodor, GERARD HOWELER (1975-76)

Howell, Claude Flynn *(American painter, b.1915)*   **BA**
  Bibl: ▶WW Amer. Art, 1989

Howell, Daniel *(American lighting designer, Los Angeles, Calif)*   **AV**
  Bibl: Architectural lighting, 1989 Oct., v.3, no.10, p.16

Howell, Douglass Morse *(American painter, historian, b.1906)*   **BA**
  Bibl: ▶MoMA libr. cat.; ▶WW Amer. Art, 1983

Howell, Elwood *(American painter, 20th c.)*   **BA**
  Bibl: Huntington (NY, USA), Heckscher Mus., 4 II: Shifting focus (1981)

Howell, Felice Waldo → see Howell, Felicie Waldo

Howell, Felicie → see Howell, Felicie Waldo

Howell, Felicie Waldo   **GC WC WI**
  (American artist, 1897-)   **WC**
  (American artist, 1897-1968)   **WI**
  (American painter, 1897-1968)   **PR**
  (American painter, b.1897)   **GC**
  Bibl: ▶Bénézit; ▶WWW Amer. art
  Felice Howell   **PR**
  Howell, Felice Waldo   **PR**
  Howell, Felicie   **PR**
  Mixter, George W., Mrs., (Felice Waldo)   **WI**

Howell, Luke   **WC WI**
  (British artist, 18th cent.)   **WC**
  (British artist, op.18th c.)   **WI**

Howell, Samuel *(British artist, op. 1828-1854)*   **WC WI**

Howell, William G. → see Howell, William Gough

Howell, William Gough   **BA**
  (British architect, 1922-1974)   **AV BA**
  Bibl: ▶Contemp. archts.
  Howell, William G.   **AV**

Howell, William T. *(American early 20th century, Hudson River Valley)*   **JG**

Howells, John Mead   **AV BA**
  (1868-1959)   **AV**
  (American architect, 1868-1959)   **BA**
  Bibl: ▶Avery Libr. cat.; Chicago on foot

Howells, Michael D. *(British artist, b.1957)*   **WI**

Howes, John   **WC WI**
  (British artist, op.1770-1795)   **WI**
  (British artist, op.1772-1795)   **WC**

Howes, Royce *(American painter, 20th c.)*   **BA**
  Bibl: ▶Art Index, v.36; Toepp, Arts Mag. LXII/5 (Jan. 1988) 54-55

Howeson, Ann *(British artist, b.1952)*   **WI**

Howey, Mary G.O. *(British artist, op.1907-1914)*   **WI**

Howgate, William → see Howgate, William Arthur

Howgate, William Arthur   **WI**
  (British artist, op.1884-1904)   **WC**
  (British artist, op.1884-1906)   **WI**
  Howgate, William   **WC**

Howieson, William → see Howison, William

Howis, William *(British artist, 1804-1882)*   **WI**

Howison or Howieson, William → see Howison, William

Howison, William   **WI**
  (British artist, 1798-1850)   **WC WI**
  Howieson, William   **WI**
  Howison or Howieson, William   **WC**

Howitt → see Howitt, Samuel

Howitt, John Newton *(American artist, b.1885)*   **WI**

Howitt, Samuel   **PR WC WI**
  (British artist, 1756-1822)   **WI**
  (British artist, c.1765-1822)   **WC**
  (British painter, ca.1765-1822)   **PR**
  Bibl: Paviere, Brit. sporting ptrs; ▶Thieme-Becker; ▶Witt checklist
  Howitt   **PR**
  Samuel Howitt   **PR**

Howland, Alfred Cornelius   **BA WI**
  (American artist, 1838-1909)   **WI**
  (American painter, 1838-1909)   **BA**
  Bibl: ▶Fielding's Amer. ptrs.; ▶Groce, Artists Amer.; ▶Young, Amer. artists

Howland, Hortense *(French, 1835-1920)*   **BA**
  Bibl: BURLINGTON MAGAZINE(MAY 1974), 275

Howland, Isabella *(American sculptor, 20th century)*   **GC**
  Bibl: Juley coll., NMAA

Howland, John D. → see Howland, John Dare

Howland, John Dare   **WI**
  (American artist, 1842-1914)   **WC WI**
  Howland, John D.   **WC**

Howland, Rebecca *(American sculptor, 20th c.)*   **BA**
  Bibl: ▶Intl. dir. exh. artists, 1983; McCormick, C., in ARTFORUM XXIV/8 (Apr 1986) 98

Howlett, Bartholomew *(British artist, 1767-1827)*   **WC WI**

Howlett, Robert *(British photographer, d.1858)*   **BA**

Howley, James *(British architect, London)*   **AV**
  Bibl: ▶RIBA members, 1987

Howlin, John   **BA WC WI**
  (British artist, 1940-)   **WC**
  (British artist, b.1940)   **WI**
  (Canadian painter, printmaker, b.1941)   **BA**
  Bibl: ▶Artists Canada; Toronto(ONT, USA), York Univ., Art Gallery. JOHN HOWLIN(1976)

Howling Wolf *(American Indian painter, b.1849, act.1881)*   **BA**
  Bibl: Szabo, ART JOURNAL XLIV/4 (winter 1984) 368, 373, n. 10 & 11

Howman, A.E., Rev.   **WI**
  (British artist, op.1827)   **WC**
  (British artist, op.1827-)   **WI**
  Howman, Rev. A.E.   **WC**

Howman, Margaret *(British painter, b.1915)*   **BA**
  Bibl: Bristol (GBR), Arnolfini Gallery, Bristol sample (1979)

Howman, Rev. A.E. → see Howman, A.E., Rev.

Howorth, E.J. *(Canadian artist, b.1943)*   **BA**
  Bibl: Paris (FRA), Ctr culturel canadien, The grand western Canadian screen shop (1977)

Howorth, Tom *(American architect, Jackson, Miss)*   **AV**
  Bibl: Architecture: the AIA journal, 1987 Mar., v.76, no.3, p.133; phone call to office 3/30/88

Howse, George   **WC WI**
  (British artist, op.1830-, d.circa 1860)   **WI**
  (British artist, op.1830-m.c. 1860)   **WC**
  Bibl: ▶Wilson, Brit. marine ptrs.

Howson, Peter *(British artist, op. 20th c.)*   **WI**

Howzer, Wolfgang *(British, active 1652-ca. 1682)*   **JG**

Hoxie, Elizabeth *(American artist, 1947-1983)*   **BA**
  Bibl: Zurcher&Kalister, NEW ART EXAMINER, XI/6(MAR 1984), 6

Hoxie, Joseph C. *(American architect, 1814-1870)*   **AV**
  Bibl: SAH journal, v.26, n.2, 1967, p.149; ▶Withey, Amer. archts.

Hoxie, Vinnie Ream → see Ream, Vinnie

Hoy or Hoey, Nikolaus van → *see* Hoy, Nikolaus van

Hoy, Nikolaus van GC
  (Flemish artist, 1631-1679) WC
  (Flemish, 1631-1679) GC
  Bibl: ▶Thieme-Becker

Hoy or Hoey, Nikolaus van WC

Hoyau, Germain *(French city planner, Paris)* AV
  Bibl: ▶Libr. of Congr. Name Auth. File

Høydahl, Per *(Norwegian architect, Oslo)* AV
  Bibl: Byggekunst, 1987, v.69, no.7, p.464

Høyer, Christian Faedder *(Danish painter, 1775-1855)* BA
  Bibl: ▶Weilbach, Kunst.leks.

Höyer, Cornelius GC
  (Danish, 1741-1804) GC
  (Scandinavian artist, 1741-1804) WC
  Bibl: ▶Thieme-Becker

Hoøyer, Cornelius WC

Hoyer, David *(German artist, 1670-1720)* WC

Hoyer, Edward WC WI
  (British artist, 19th cent.) WC
  (British artist, op.19th c.) WI

Hoyer, Jean Louis Joseph GC
  (Swiss artist, 1762-1829) WC
  (Swiss painter, 1762-1829) GC
  Bibl: ▶Bénézit

Hoyer, Joseph (Jean Louis Joseph) WC

Hoyer, Joseph (Jean Louis Joseph) → *see* Hoyer, Jean Louis Joseph

Høyer, Karsten *(Danish architect)* AV
  Bibl: Living architecture, 1989, no.8, p.121

Hoyer, Peter *(British artist, op.circa 1875-)* WI

Hoyland, Francis WC WI
  (British artist, b.1930) WI
  (British artist, op.1965-66) WC

Hoyland, Henry G. *(British artist, 1894-1948)* WC WI

Hoyland, John BA WC WI
  (British artist, 1934-) WC
  (British artist, b.1934) WI
  (British painter, b.1934) BA
  Bibl: ▶Bénézit; ▶Vollmer, Künst.-Lex. 20. Jhr.

Hoyland, Philipa *(British artist, op. 20th c.)* WI

Hoyle, Walter WC WI
  (British artist, 1922-) WC
  (British artist, b.1922) WI

Hoyles, Ben *(British artist, op.19th-20th c.)* WI

Hoynck van Papendrecht, Jan → *see* Hoynk van Papendrecht, Jan

Hoynck, Otto *(Dutch artist, c.1630-p.1686)* WC

Hoyningen-Huene, George BA JG
  (American (b. Russia, now USSR), 1900-1968) JG
  (Russian photographer in USA, 1900-1968) BA
  Bibl: ▶Fogg Mus. Libr. cat.; ▶MoMA libr. cat.; ▶Parry, Photo idx.

Hoynk van Papendrecht, Jan BA
  (Dutch artist, 1858-1933) WC
  (Dutch painter and draughtsman, 1858-1933) GC
  (Dutch painter, 1858-1933) BA
  Bibl: ▶Bénézit; ▶Scheen, Ned. beeldende kunst.; ▶Witt checklist

Hoynck van Papendrecht, Jan GC WC

Hoyoll, Philipp *(German artist, 1816-p.1875)* WC

Hoyrup, Paul *(Danish artist, 20th cent.)* WC

Hoys, Leopold *(German clockmaker, 1713-1797)* BA
  Bibl: ▶Baillie, Watch- & clockmkrs.; ▶Britten, Old clocks; ▶Thieme-Becker

Hoyt, Burnham *(American architect, Denver, Colo., fl. 1940's)* AV
  Bibl: ▶Withey, Amer. archts.

Hoyt, Robert Ingle *(American architect, 1913-1985?)* AV
  Bibl: ▶Amer. archts. dir.; Architecture: the AIA journal, 1986 Feb., v.75, no.2, p.79

Hoyte, John Clarke B.C. *(British artist, 1835-1913)* WC WI

Hoytema, Theodoor van → *see* Hoijtema, Theodoor van

Hoz Arderius, Rafael de la *(Spanish architect)* AV
  Bibl: L'Arca, 1989 Mar., no.25, p.31

Hoz Castanys, Rafael de la *(Spanish architect)* AV
  Bibl: L'Arca, 1989 Mar., no.25, p.31

Hozzetenti [Unidentified]
  (Unknown painter) PR
  Bibl: (June 28, 1811, lot 57, Crook)

Hradil, Rudolf *(German artist, 1925-)* WC

Hrankovicova, Katarina → *see* Hrankovicova, Katja

Hrankovicova, Katja *(West German architect)* AV
  Bibl: Abitare, 1986 June, no.245, p.170

Hrankovicova, Katarina AV

Hrdlicka, Alfred AV BA WC
  (Austrian artist, 1928-) WC
  (Austrian sculptor, printmaker, painter, b.1928) BA
  (Sculptor, act. in Austria, 1928-) AV
  Bibl: ▶Artist biog. master idx.; ▶Bénézit; Guide exh. artists: N. Amer. ptrs.; ▶Havlice, Idx. art. bio.; ▶Intl. dir. exh. artists, 1982-1983; ▶Libr. of Congr. Name Auth. File; ▶MoMA libr. cat.; Schmied, Nach Klimt

Hristov, Ivan *(Bulgarian painter, b.1900)* BA
  Bibl: Koleva, IVAN HRISTOV(1981)

Hrošecký, Jan → *see* Woczasek, Jan Antonín

Hrvacki, Drago *(Yugoslav sculptor, painter, printmaker, b.1936)* BA
  Bibl: ▶ARTbibl. mod., 13; Ljubljana(YUG), Mala Galerija. DRAGO HRVACKI(1975)

HS → *see* Sambin, Hugues

Hsia, Ken *(Interior designer, Toronto)* AV
  Bibl: Interior design, 1988 Dec., v.59, no.16, p.168

Hsieh, Tehching *(American artist, 20th c.)* BA
  Bibl: ART IN AMERICA LXXII/8 (Sept 1984), 176-179

Hsu, Ti Shan → *see* Hsu, Tishan

Hsu, Tishan BA
  (American artist, b.1951) WI
  (American painter, b.1951) BA
  Bibl: Wei, L., ART IN AMERICA, LXXV/7 (July 1987), pp.80-97, 112-129, 171

Hsu, Ti Shan WI

Hualla, Emanuela *(Austrian architect)* AV
  Bibl: Bauforum, 1987, v.20, no. 122, p.58

Huang, Nancy *(American interior designer, New York City)* AV
  Bibl: Area, July-Aug., v.6, no.29, p.24

Huard, Charles *(French artist, 1875-1965)* WC

Huard, E. *(French, active Russia ca. 1862)* JG

Huard, Frances Wilson WC WI
  (American artist, 19th cent.) WC
  (American artist, op.19th c.) WI

Huas, Pierre Adolphe → *see* Huas, Pierre-Adolphe

Huas, Pierre-Adolphe GC
  (French artist, 1838-1900) WC
  (French, 1838-1900) GC
  Bibl: ▶Thieme-Becker

Huas, Pierre Adolphe WC

Huaud family *(Swiss enamelists, 17th-18th cs.)* BA

Huaud, Amy   **BA WC**
   (Swiss artist, 1657-1724)   WC
   (Swiss enamelist, 1657-1724)   BA
   Bibl: Boeckh, Genava, XXXIII
   (1985) pp.75-81; ▶Schweiz.
   Künst.-Lex.; ▶Thieme-Becker
Huaud, Huault or Huaugt, Jean
Pierre → see Huaud, Jean-Pierre
Huaud, Jean-Pierre   **BA**
   (Swiss artist, 1655-1723)   WC
   (Swiss enamelist, 1655-1723)   BA
   Bibl: ▶Schweiz. Künst.-Lex.;
   ▶Thieme-Becker

Huaud, Huault or Huaugt, Jean
Pierre   **WC**
Huaud, Pierre I *(Swiss goldsmith,*
   enamelist, 1612-1680)   **BA**
   Bibl: ▶Schweiz. Künst.-Lex.;
   ▶Thieme-Becker
Huaud, Pierre II   **BA**
   (Swiss artist, 1647-c.1698)   WC
   (Swiss enamelist, 1647-1696/98)   BA
   Bibl: Boeckh, Genava, XXXIII
   (1985) pp.75-81; ▶Bradley,
   Miniaturists, v.2, pp.98-100;
   Reclams Baden-Würtemberg,
   p.672; ▶Schweiz. Künst.-Lex.;
   ▶Thieme-Becker
Huaud, Pierre, II   **WC**
Huaud, Pierre, II → see Huaud, Pierre II
Hubacek, Karel *(Architect,*
   Czechoslovakia, 1924-)   **AV**
   Bibl: Architektur,
   Innenarchitektur, Technischer
   Ausbau, 1985 Jan.-Feb., v.93,
   no.1, p.10
Hubacher, Simon *(Canadian*
   architect)   **AV**
   Bibl: ARQ: Architecture/Quebec,
   1989 Apr., no.48, p.30
Hubard, William James *(American*
   artist, 1807-1862)   **WC WI**
Hubay, Anton von *(Hungarian*
   artist, 1898-)   **WC**
Hubbard, B. *(British artist, op.1839-*
   1864)   **WC WI**
Hubbard, Charles Daniel *(Engraver,*
   1876-1951)   **WI**
Hubbard, Eleanor *(American artist,*
   20th c.)   **BA**
   Bibl: Purchase (NY, USA), SUNY,
   Neuberger Mus, Seven artists...,
   1981
Hubbard, Eric Hesketh   **WC WI**
   (British artist, 1892-)   WC
   (British artist, 1892-1957)   WI
Hubbard, Frank McKinney (Kin)
   (American cartoonist, 1868-1930)   **BA**
   Bibl: ▶Dict. Amer. biog.;
   ▶Fielding's Amer. ptrs.; ▶WWW
   Amer., 1897

Hubbard, John   **BA WC WI**
   (American artist, 20th cent.)   WC
   (American artist, b.1931)   WI
   (American painter in GBR,
   b.1931)   BA
   Bibl: ▶MoMA libr. cat.; ▶WW
   Amer. Art, 1987
Hubbard, Richard William   **WC WI**
   (American artist, 1816-1888)   WI
   (American artist, 1817-1888)   WC
Hubbard, W. *(British artist, op.1809-*
   1867)   **WC WI**
   Bibl: Paviere, Brit. sporting ptrs
Hubbard, William *(American*
   architect and author, 1947-)   **AV**
   Bibl: Modulus, (1980-1981) p.113
Hubbell, Henry Salem   **BA WC WI**
   (American artist, 1870-)   WC
   (American artist, 1870-1949)   WI
   (American painter, 1870-1949)   BA
   Bibl: ▶Fielding's Amer. ptrs.;
   ▶Fogg Mus. Libr. cat.; ▶Havlice,
   Idx. art. bio.; ▶Vollmer,
   Künst.-Lex. 20. Jhr.
Hubbell, James *("Painter, sculptor,*
   stained-glass artist, poet,
   architect")   **AV**
   Bibl: ▶Libr. of Congr. Name Auth.
   File
Hubbell, Kent *(American architect)* **AV**
   Bibl: Techniques et architecture,
   1980 Dec., no.333, p.105
Hubbert   **WC WI**
   (British artist, 16th cent.)   WC
   (British artist, op.1583-1586)   WI
Hubbuch, Karl   **BA WC**
   (German artist, 1891-)   WC
   (German painter, printmaker,
   1891-1979)   BA
   Bibl: Karlsruhe(DEU), Badischer
   Kunstverein. KARL HUBBUCH,
   1891-1979; ▶Vollmer, Künst.-Lex.
   20. Jhr.
Hubbuck, Hilde *(German, active*
   1920s, Bauhaus)   **JG**
Hubbuck, Rodney *(British artist,*
   b.1940)   **WI**
Hübenbecker, Klaus *(German*
   architect, Hamburg)   **AV**
   Bibl: Deutsche Bauzeitschrift,
   1986 June, v.34, no.6, p.737
Huber or Hubert, Thomas *(German*
   artist, 1700-1779)   **WC**
Huber or Hueber, Joseph (Johann
   Joseph Anton) *(Swiss artist,*
   1737-1815)   **WC**
Huber the Elder, Johann Rudolf → see
   Huber, Johann Rudolf, the elder
Huber von Weissenhorn,
   Conrad → see Huber, Conrad
Huber, Achilles *(Swiss architect,*
   1776-1860)   **BA**
   Bibl: ▶Schweiz. Künst.-Lex.;
   ▶Thieme-Becker
Huber, Benedikt *(Architect, Zurich)* **AV**
   Bibl: Deutsche Bauzeitschrift,
   1984, v.32, p.1019

Huber, Conrad   **GC WC**
   (German artist, 1752-1830)   WC
   (German painter, 1752-1830)   GC
   Bibl: ▶Thieme-Becker
   Huber von Weissenhorn, Conrad   GC
Huber, Ernst *(German artist, 1895-)* **WC**
Huber, Hans (Monogrammist h.h.)
   (German artist, op.1491-1501)   **WC**
Huber, Hans Rudolf *(French painter,*
   b.1936)   **BA**
   Bibl: Geneva(CHE), Musee d'art et
   d'histoire. NEUF PEINTURES...
   (1978)
Huber, Hermann   **BA WC**
   (Swiss artist, 1888-)   WC
   (Swiss painter, printmaker,
   1888-1968)   BA
   Bibl: ▶Bénézit; ▶Thieme-Becker;
   ▶Vollmer, Künst.-Lex. 20. Jhr.
Huber, István Dési → see Dési-Huber,
   István
Huber, J. Whitney *(American*
   architect, Essex, Conn)   **AV**
   Bibl: ▶AIA Pro File, 1987-88
Huber, Jacob Wilhelm *(German*
   artist, 1787-1871)   **WC**
Huber, Jean   **BA GC**
   (Swiss artist, 1721-1786)   WC
   (Swiss painter, printmaker,
   1721-1786)   BA
   (Swiss, 1721-1786)   GC
   Bibl: ▶Bénézit; ▶Larousse grande
   encyc.; ▶Thieme-Becker; ▶Witt
   checklist
Huber, Jean ('Huber Voltaire')   **WC**
Huber, Jean ('Huber Voltaire') → see
   Huber, Jean
Huber, Jean Daniel   **BA WC**
   (German artist, 1754-1845)   WC
   (German painter, 1754-1845)   PR
   (Swiss painter, printmaker,
   1754-1845)   BA
   Bibl: ▶Thieme-Becker
Huber, Jean-Daniel   **PR**
   Jean-Daniel Huber   PR
Huber, Jean-Daniel → see Huber, Jean
   Daniel
Huber, Johann Kaspar *(Swiss artist,*
   1752-1827)   **WC**
Huber, Johann Rudolf, the elder   **BA**
   (Swiss artist, 1668-1748)   WC
   (Swiss painter, 1668-1748)   BA GC
   Bibl: ▶Bénézit; ▶Thieme-Becker
Huber the Elder, Johann Rudolf   **WC**
Huber, Johann Rudolph I   **GC**
Huber, R.   **WC**
Huber, Johann Rudolph I → see Huber,
   Johann Rudolf, the elder
Huber, Kurt *(Swiss architect,*
   Fravenfeld)   **AV**
   Bibl: ▶Schweiz. Ingen. u. Archit.,
   1984-1985
Huber, Ludwig *(German artist, op.*
   1837)   **WC**
Huber, Max → see Huber, Max
   Emmanuel

Huber, Max Emmanuel   **BA**
  (Swiss artist, 1903-)   **WC**
  (Swiss painter, printmaker,
   illustrator, b.1903)   **BA**
   Bibl: ▶Künst.-Lex. Schweiz 20.
   Jahrh.; ▶Lex. zeitgen. Schweiz.
   Künstler; ▶Vollmer, Künst.-Lex.
   20. Jhr.

Huber, Max   **WC**

Huber, Patrick *(Swiss architect)*   **AV**
   Bibl: Abitare, 1982 July-Aug., no.
   206, p.65

Huber, Patriz *(German designer,*
  architect, 1878-1902)   **BA**
   Bibl: ▶Thieme-Becker; Ulmer,
   Weltkunst LV/23 (Dec 1985)
   3709-3913

Huber, R. → see Huber, Johann Rudolf,
  the elder

Huber, Rudolf *(Swiss artist, 1770-*
  1844)   **WC**

Huber, Rudolf Carl *(German artist,*
  1839-1896)   **WC**

Huber, Stephan *(West German*
  artist, b.1952)   **BA**
   Bibl: Guide exh. artists: Sculp.;
   ▶Intl. dir. exh. artists, 1983

Huber, Thomas *(West German*
  artist, b.1955)   **BA**
   Bibl: Bern (CHE), Kunsthalle Bern,
   Konstruierte Orte (1983)

Huber, Wilhelm *(West German*
  architect, Eichstätt)   **AV**
   Bibl: Detail, 1987 Sept.-Oct., v.27,
   no.5, p.463

Huber, Wolf → see Huber, Wolfgang

Huber, Wolfgang   **BA PR**
  (German artist, c.1490-1553)   **WC**
  (German painter, 1485/90-1553)   **PR**
  (German painter, draughtsman,
   and printmaker,
   ca.1480/85-1553)   **GC**
  (German painter, printmaker,
   1485/90-1553)   **BA**
  (German, 1480/1485-1553)   **JG**
   Bibl: ▶Brockhaus Enzyk.; ▶Encyc.
   world art; Getty Photo Study
   Coll.; Nagler, Monogrammisten,
   V.1707; ▶RILA/BHA; ▶Schweers,
   Gemälde deut. Museen;
   ▶Thieme-Becker; ▶Witt checklist

Huber, Wolf   **GC JG PR**

Huber, Wolfgang or Wolf   **WC**
  Master WH   **BA**
  Monogrammist WH   **BA**
  Wolfgang Huber   **PR**

Huber, Wolfgang or Wolf → see
  Huber, Wolfgang

Hubernis Frecketter → see Frecketter,
  Hubernis [Unidentified]

Hubers, Hans *(Dutch architect or*
  designer)   **AV**
   Bibl: Bouw, 1988 Apr.15, v.43,
   no.8, p.17

Hubert → see Robert, Hubert

Hubert Descours, Michel → see
  Descours, Michel

Hubert Drouais → see Drouais, Hubert

Hubert Goltzius → see Goltzius,
  Hubertus

Hubert Lindsay Wellington → see
  Wellington, Hubert Lindsay

Hubert Quilinus → see Quellinus,
  Hubertus

Hubert Robert → see Robert, Hubert

Hubert van Ravesteyn → see
  Ravesteyn, Hubert van

Hubert von Herkomer → see
  Herkomer, Hubert von

Hubert, Auguste *(French architect,*
  1755-1798)   **BA**
   Bibl: ▶Bauchal, Archtes. fran.;
   ▶Lance, Dict. archts. fran.;
   ▶Macmillan encyc. archts.;
   ▶Thieme-Becker

  Cheval de Saint Hubert, Auguste   **BA**

Hubert, Bruno *(French architect)*   **AV**
   Bibl: Techniques et architecture,
   1984 Aug.-Sept., p.113

Hubert, Edgar   **WC WI**
  (British artist, 1906-)   **WC**
  (British artist, b.1906)   **WI**

Hubert, F. *(German artist, 19th*
  cent.)   **WC**

Hubert, Jean Baptiste Louis → see
  Hubert, Jean-Baptiste Louis

Hubert, Jean-Baptiste Louis   **GC**
  (French artist, 1801-)   **WC**
  (French painter, b.1801)   **GC**
   Bibl: Getty Photo Study Coll.;
   ▶Thieme-Becker; ▶Witt checklist

Hubert, Jean Baptiste Louis   **GC WC**

Hubert, Laurent *(Swiss artist,*
  b.1960)   **BA**
   Bibl: Lausanne (CHE), Musée
   Cantonal B.-A., Jeunes vaudois
   (1983)

Hubert, Laurent *(French artist,*
  op.1749-m.1776/86)   **WC**

Hubert, Odile *(French architect)*   **AV**
   Bibl: Architecture & urbanism,
   1986 Oct., no.10, p.54

Huberti, Edouard Jules Joseph   **BA WC**
  (Belgian artist, 1818-1880)   **WC**
  (Belgian painter, composer,
   1818-1880)   **BA**
   Bibl: ▶Dict. biog. artistes belges;
   ▶Thieme-Becker

Hubertus van Hove → see Hove,
  Hubertus van

Hubka, Thomas *(American architect,*
  Portland, Me)   **AV**
   Bibl: Landmarks observer, 1986
   Jan.-Feb., v.13, no.1, p.9

Hublin, Auguste   **GC**
  (French artist, 1830-1891)   **WC**
  (French, 1830-1891)   **GC**
   Bibl: Getty Photo Study Coll.
   (Ptgs.); ▶Thieme-Becker

Hublin, Auguste (Emile
  Auguste)   **WC**
  Hublin, Emile-Auguste   **GC**

Hublin, Auguste (Emile
  Auguste) → see Hublin, Auguste

Hublin, Emile-Auguste → see Hublin,
  Auguste

Hubner → see Hubner, Louis

Hubner, Carl *(German artist, 1797-*
  1831)   **WC**

Hubner, Carl → see Hübner, Carl
  Wilhelm

Hübner, Carl Wilhelm   **BA GC PR**
  (German artist, 1814-1879)   **WC**
  (German painter, 1814-
   1879)   **BA GC PR**
   Bibl: ▶Bénézit; ▶Bryan, Ptrs. &
   engravers; ▶Thieme-Becker; ▶Witt
   checklist

  Carl Wilhelm Hubner   **PR**
  Hubner, Carl   **PR**

Hubner, Carl-Wilhelm   **WC**
  Hubner, Karl Wilhelm   **PR**

Hubner, Carl-Wilhelm → see Hübner,
  Carl Wilhelm

Hübner, Hannes   **AV**

Hubner, Heinrich *(German artist,*
  1869-)   **WC**

Hubner, J.M. *(German artist, 19th*
  cent.)   **WC**

Hübner, Julius   **BA GC**
  (German artist, 1806-1882)   **WC**
  (German painter and
   draughtsman, 1806-1882)   **GC**
  (German painter, printmaker,
   1806-1882)   **BA**
   Bibl: ▶Brockhaus Enzyk.; Getty
   Photo Study Coll.; Renger in DE
   ARTE ET LIBRIS; FESTSCHRIFT
   ERASMUS (1984), p.369-386;
   ▶Thieme-Becker

Hubner, Julius Rudolf Julius-
  Benno   **WC**

Hubner, Julius Rudolf
Julius-Benno → see Hübner, Julius

Hubner, Karl Wilhelm → see Hübner,
  Carl Wilhelm

Hübner, L.   **GC WC**
  (German(?) artist, op.1752)   **WC**
  (German(?) painter, act.1752)   **GC**
   Bibl: ▶Witt checklist

Hubner, Louis *(German painter, act.*
  1740-1769)   **PR**
   Bibl: ▶Waterhouse, Brit. 18c. ptrs.

  Hubner   **PR**
  Louis Hubner   **PR**

Hübner, Peter   **AV BA**
  (West German architect, 1939-)   **AV**
  (West German architect, 20th
   c.)   **BA**
   Bibl: ▶Avery period. idx.;
   Deutsche Bauzeitung, 1985 Mar.,
   v.119, no.3, p.114

Hübner, Stefan *(Austrian architect)*   **AV**
   Bibl: Architettura; cronache e
   storia, 1987 Oct.,v.33, no.10,
   p.726

Hübner, Tibor *(Hungarian architect, Budapest, fl. 1930's)*   **AV**
   Bibl: Magyar építőművészet, 1987, v.78, no.6, p.26

Hübner, Ulrich   **GC WC**
   (German artist, 1872-1932)   WC
   (German painter, 1872-1932)   GC
   Bibl: ▶Thieme-Becker

Hubrecht, Martin *(French painter, b.1892)*   **GC**
   Bibl: ▶Bénézit

Hübsch, Heinrich   **AV BA WC**
   (1795-1863)   AV
   (German architect, 1795-1863)   BA
   (German artist, 1795-1863)   WC
   Bibl: ▶Thieme-Becker

Hübschmannová, Anna *(Czech architect, Prague)*   **AV**
   Bibl: Architecture, the AIA journal, 1983 Aug., v.72, no.8, p.156

Huby, Peter *(British artist, b.ca. 1946)*   **BA**
   Bibl: Kingston-upon-Hull (GBR), Ferens Art Gallery, 4 one-man shows (1974)

Huchtenberg → *see* Huchtenburgh, Jan van
Huchtenborgh → *see* Huchtenburgh, Jan van
Huchtenburg → *see* Huchtenburgh, Jan van
Huchtenburg, Huchtenburgh, Hughtenburgh, Hugtenburg or Hugtenburgh, Johann or Jan van → *see* Huchtenburgh, Jan van

Huchtenburg, Jacob van   **GC WC**
   (Dutch artist, c.1640/5-1675)   WC
   (Dutch painter, ca.1639-1675)   GC
   Bibl: ▶Bénézit

Huchtenburg, Jan van → *see* Huchtenburgh, Jan van
Huchtenburgh → *see* Huchtenburgh, Jan van

Huchtenburgh, Jan van   **GC PR**
   (Dutch artist, 1647-1733)   WC
   (Dutch painter and draughtsman, 1647-1733)   GC
   (Dutch painter, 1647-1733)   PR
   Bibl: ▶Bénézit; ▶Thieme-Becker

   Haickenburg   PR
   Hectenburgh   PR
   Huchtenberg   PR
   Huchtenborgh   PR
   Huchtenburg   PR

Huchtenburg, Huchtenburgh, Hughtenburgh, Hugtenburg or Hugtenburgh, Johann or Jan van   **WC**

Huchtenburg, Jan van   **GC**
   Huchtenburgh   PR
   Hucktenberg   PR
   Hucktenburg   PR
   Hucktenburgh   PR
   Huctenberg   PR
   Huctenbergh   PR
   Huctenbourg   PR
   Huctenburg   PR
   Huctenburgh   PR
   Hughtenberg   PR
   Hughtenbnrgh   PR
   Hughtenborg   PR
   Hughtenburg   PR
   Hughtenburgh, Jan van   GC
   Hughtenburgh, Johan van   PR
   Hugtelenburg   PR
   Hugtemburg   PR
   Hugtenberg   PR
   Hugtenbergh   PR
   Hugtenbugh   PR
   Hugtenburg   PR
   Hugtenburg, Jan van   GC
   Hugtenburgh   PR
   Huiehmberg   PR
   Hutchenberg   PR
   Hutchenburgh   PR
   Hutchtenberg   PR
   Hutehmberg   PR
   Hutenburg   PR
   Hutenburgh   PR
   Hutherberg   PR
   Jan Hugtenburg   PR
   Jan van Huchtenburgh   PR
   Johann van Hugtenburgh   PR
   John Van Hugtenburg   PR
   Luchenburg   PR
   Luchtenburg   PR
   Lughtenburgh   PR
   marked Hurtemburgh   PR
   Uchtenbroeck   PR
   Uchtenburgh   PR
   Ugtenburg   PR

Huck, Johann Gerhard   **BA WC**
   (German artist, c.1759-1811)   WC
   (German painter, printmaker, ca. 1759-1811)   BA
   Bibl: ▶Bénézit; ▶Thieme-Becker

Huckel → *see* Hickel, Anton

Hückstädt, Eberhard *(German painter, b.1936)*   **BA**
   Bibl: DRESDENER KUNSTBLATTER, XX/6(1976), 162-168

Hucktenberg → *see* Huchtenburgh, Jan van
Hucktenburg → *see* Huchtenburgh, Jan van
Hucktenburgh → *see* Huchtenburgh, Jan van

Huckvale, William *(British architect, late 19th cent)*   **AV**
   Bibl: Country life, 1989 Feb.23, v.183, no.8, p.115

Hucleux, Jean Olivier *(French artist, b.1923)*   **BA**
   Bibl: LACMA, EUROPEAN PAINTING IN THE SEVENTIES(1975)

Huctenberg → *see* Huchtenburgh, Jan van
Huctenbergh → *see* Huchtenburgh, Jan van
Huctenbourg → *see* Huchtenburgh, Jan van
Huctenburg → *see* Huchtenburgh, Jan van
Huctenburgh → *see* Huchtenburgh, Jan van

Huddesford → *see* Huddesford, George

Huddesford, George   **PR WC WI**
   (British artist, 1749-1809)   WC WI
   (British painter, 1749-1809)   PR
   Bibl: ▶Bénézit; ▶Thieme-Becker; ▶Waterhouse, Brit. 18c. ptrs.

   George Huddesford   PR
   Huddesford   PR
   M. Huddesford   PR
   Mr. Huddesford   PR

Huddle, R.J. *(American artist, op. 1835-1845)*   **WI**

Hude, von der *(German artist, op.c. 1750)*   **WC**

Hudecek, Antonin *(Czech artist, 1872-1941)*   **WC**

Hudeček, František *(Czech painter, printmaker, b.1909)*   **BA**
   Bibl: ▶Encyc. world art; ▶Encyk. českého výtv. umění; ▶Vollmer, Künst.-Lex. 20. Jhr.

Hudjakov, K.V. *(Russian artist, 20th c.)*   **BA**
   Bibl: Moscow (RUS), Assc. Comm. Graphic Artists, 2nd exh. (1979)

Hudon, Wieslaw *(Polish artist, 20th cent.)*   **WC**

Hudson *(American artist, choreographer, b.1950)*   **BA**
   Bibl: Oberlin (OH, USA), Oberlin Coll., Allen Mem. Art Mus., Young Americans (1981)

Hudson → *see* Hudson, Charles Bradford
Hudson → *see* Hudson, Elmer Forrest
Hudson → *see* Hudson, Thomas

Hudson [Unidentified] *(Unknown painter)* **PR**
  Bibl: (September 26, 1812, lot 564, Phillips)
Hudson, Andrew *(American painter, b.1935)* **BA**
  Bibl: ▶Intl. dir. exh. artists, 1983; Washington(DC, USA), Corcoran. ONGOING DIALOGUES(1982)-UCSB
Hudson, Anna Hope **BA**
  (American artist, 1869-1957) **WC WI**
  (American painter in GBR, 1869-1957) **BA**
  Bibl: Fine Arts Soc., Camden Town Recalled (1976), p.33; ▶Young, Amer. artists
  Hudson, Anna Hope (Nan) **WC**
  Hudson, Anne Hope **WI**
  Hudson, Nan **WI**
Hudson, Anna Hope (Nan) → see Hudson, Anna Hope
Hudson, Anne Hope → see Hudson, Anna Hope
Hudson, Charles Bradford
  (American painter, 1865-1938) **PR**
  Bibl: ▶WWW Amer. art
  Charles Bradford Hudson **PR**
  Hudson **PR**
Hudson, Eleanor Erlund **WI**
  (British artist, 20th cent.) **WC**
  (British artist, b.1912) **WI**
  Hudson, Erlund **WC**
Hudson, Elmer Forrest *(American painter, 1862-1932)* **PR**
  Bibl: ▶WWW Amer. art
  Elmer Forrest Hudson **PR**
  Hudson **PR**
  Hudson, Elmer L. **PR**
Hudson, Elmer L. → see Hudson, Elmer Forrest
Hudson, Erlund → see Hudson, Eleanor Erlund
Hudson, Grace Carpenter **BA WC WI**
  (American artist, 1865-1937) **WC WI**
  (American painter, 1865-1937) **BA**
  Bibl: ▶Dawdy, Artists Amer. West; ▶Samuels, Artists Amer. West
Hudson, Gwynedd M. *(British artist, op.1909-1935)* **WI**
Hudson, Henry John *(British artist, op.1881-1910)* **WI**
Hudson, Henry M. *(British artist, op. 1782-1800)* **WC WI**
Hudson, Jeff *(American artist, 20th c.)* **BA**
  Bibl: Framingham (MA, USA), Danforth Mus., Homage (1981)
Hudson, Jules → see Hudson, Julien

Hudson, Julien **BA WI**
  (American artist, op.1830-1840) **WC WI**
  (American painter, act.1831, d.1844) **BA**
  Bibl: ▶Cederholm, Afro-Amer. artists; ▶Fielding's Amer. ptrs.; ▶Groce, Artists Amer.; New York (NY, USA), Met. Mus., 19c. Afro-American art (1976)
  Hudson, Jules **WI**
  Hudson, Julien (Jules) **WC**
Hudson, Julien (Jules) → see Hudson, Julien
Hudson, N. **WC WI**
  (British artist, op.1782) **WC**
  (British artist, op.1782-) **WI**
Hudson, Nan → see Hudson, Anna Hope
Hudson, Richard Everett *(British architect, Eastbourne, England)* **AV**
  Bibl: ▶RIBA members, 1987
Hudson, Robert H. *(American sculptor, b.1938)* **BA**
  Bibl: Guide exh. artists: N. Amer. ptrs.; ▶WW Amer. Art, 1989
Hudson, Robert II **WI**
  (British artist, -1884) **WC**
  (British artist, d.1884) **WI**
  Hudson, Robert, II **WC**
Hudson, Robert, II → see Hudson, Robert II
Hudson, Sean *(British filmmaker, 20th c.)* **BA**
  Bibl: STUDIO INTERNATIONAL, CLXXXIX(1974)(MAR-APR 1975)p. 116
Hudson, Stephen *(British woodcarver, act.1776)* **BA**
  Bibl: Furniture hist., XI (1975) pp. 53-55
Hudson, Thomas **BA GC PR WC WI**
  (British artist, 1701-1779) **WC WI**
  (British painter, 1701-1779) **PR**
  (British, 1701-1779) **GC**
  (English painter, 1701-1779) **BA**
  Bibl: ▶Bénézit; ▶RILA/BHA; ▶Thieme-Becker
  Hudson **PR**
  Mr. Hudson **PR**
  Thomas Hudson **PR**
Hudson, W.A. *(American, active Northern California, USA 1900-1926, d. 1939)* **JG**
Hudson, William → see Hudson, William C.
Hudson, William C. **WI**
  (British artist, 1782-1850) **WI**
  (British artist, op.1813-m.1847) **WC**
  Bibl: ▶Foskett, Brit. miniature ptrs.
Hudson, William **WC**
Hudson, William, Jr. *(American artist, b.1787)* **WI**
Hue → see Hue, Jean Francois
Hue, Alexandre *(French artist, op. 1810-1842)* **WC**

Hue, Charles Desire → see Hue, Charles-Desire
Hue, Charles-Desire **GC**
  (French artist, op.1883) **WC**
  (French, act.1879) **GC**
  Bibl: ▶Thieme-Becker
Hue, Charles Desire **WC**
Hue, Jean Francois **GC PR WC**
  (French artist, 1751-1823) **WC**
  (French painter, 1751-1823) **PR**
  (French, 1751-1823) **GC**
  Bibl: ▶Bénézit; ▶Thieme-Becker; ▶Witt checklist
  Hue **PR**
  Jean Francois Hue **PR**
  Mons. Hue **PR**
Hue, Lambertus Jansz. de **PR WC**
  (Dutch artist, 1623-1681) **WC**
  (Dutch painter, 1623-1681) **PR**
  Bibl: ▶Thieme-Becker
  de Hue **PR**
  Lambertus Jansz. de Hue **PR**
Hueber, Franz Michael *(Austrian painter, d.1746)* **BA**
  Bibl: Dehio; ▶Thieme-Becker
Huebler, Douglas **BA WC WI**
  (American artist, 20th cent.) **WC**
  (American artist, b.1924) **BA WI**
  Bibl: ▶Babington Smith, Contemp. artists; ▶WW Amer. Art, 1989
Hueffer, Francis, Mrs. *(British artist, 1852-1927)* **WI**
  Brown, Cathy Madox, Miss **WI**
Hueller, Otto *(German artist, op. 1920)* **WC**
Huelsenbeck, Richard *(German physician, painter, author in USA, 1892-1974)* **BA**
  Bibl: ▶Bénézit; ▶Encyc. world art; ▶Havlice, Idx. art. bio.; Huelsenback, Dada drummer, intro.
Huemer, Franz *(Swiss sculptor, b.1924)* **BA**
  Bibl: Aarau (CHE), Kunsthaus, FRANZ HUEMER (1983)
Huen → see Huens [Unidentified]
Huens *(Flemish(?) artist, op.c.1620)* **WC**
Huens of Antwerp → see Huens [Unidentified]

Huens [Unidentified] (*Unknown painter*)   **PR**

> Bibl: April 2, 1801, lot 15, Christie's; April 21, 1804, lot 47, Christie's; April 28, 1809, lot 35, Christie's; April 4, 1801, lot 19, Christie's; April 7, 1802, lot 27, Edwards; December 14, 1802, lot 36, Christie's; December 14, 1804, lot 18, Christie's; February 12, 1802, lot 36b, Edwards; February 22, 1804, lot 31, Edwards; February 3, 1803, lot 40, Farebrother; February 5, 1802, lot 52, Christie's; June 15, 1805, lot 43, Christie's; June 15, 1805, lot 50, Christie's; June 18, 1805, lot 57, Christie's; March 21, 1805, lot 45, King Junior; March 31, 1801, lot 76, Edwards; May 1, 1802, lot 11, Christie's; May 29, 1805, lot 63, Skinner and Dyke; May 30, 1804, lot 211, Sotheby's; May 7, 1806, lot 5, Christie's; May 8, 1801, lot 54, Christie's; November 26, 1802, lot 103, Edwards; October 10, 1809, lot 76, Winstanley

> D. Huens   **PR**
> Heems   **PR**
> Heuens   **PR**
> Heuns   **PR**
> Hnens   **PR**
> Huen   **PR**
> Huens of Antwerp   **PR**

Huerchino → *see* Guercino (Giovanni Francesco Barbieri)

Huerta, Gaspar de la (*Spanish artist, 1645-1714*)   **WC**

Huerta, Juan de la → *see* Juan de la Huerta

Huesch → *see* Heusch, Willem de

Huet → *see* Huet, Jean Baptiste

Huet the Elder, Nicolas → *see* Huet, Nicolas (the Elder)

Huet, Bernard   **AV BA**
> (*French architect, b.1932*)   **BA**
> (*French architect, member of T.A.U, 1932-*)   **AV**
> Bibl: ▶Avery period. idx., 6th suppl.; International architect, issue 1, 1983, p.[1]

Huet, Christophe   **GC**
> (*French artist, op.1735-m.1759*)   **WC**
> (*French, d.1759*)   **GC**
> Bibl: ▶Thieme-Becker

Huet, Christophe (not Charles)   **WC**

Huet, Christophe (not Charles) → *see* Huet, Christophe

Huet, François   **GC**
> (*French artist, 1772-1813*)   **WC**
> (*French, 1772-1813*)   **GC**
> Bibl: ▶Thieme-Becker

Huet, Huet-Villiers or Villiers-Huet, Francois, (Jean Francois Marie)   **WC**

Huet, Hippolyte (*French artist, op.c. 1831*)   **WC**

Huet, Huet-Villiers or Villiers-Huet, Francois, (Jean Francois Marie) → *see* Huet, François

Huet, Jean Baptiste   **BA GC PR WC**
> (*French artist, 1745-1811*)   **WC**
> (*French painter, 1745-1811*)   **BA PR**
> (*French, 1745-1811*)   **GC**
> Bibl: ▶Bénézit; ▶RILA/BHA; ▶Thieme-Becker; ▶Witt checklist

> De Houet   **PR**
> Houet   **PR**
> Huet   **PR**
> Huette   **PR**
> Jean Baptiste Huet   **PR**
> Jean-Baptiste Marie Huet   **PR**

Huet, Nicolas (the Elder)   **GC**
> (*French artist, c.1718-p.1788*)   **WC**
> (*French, ca.1718-aft.1788*)   **GC**
> Bibl: ▶Witt checklist

Huet the Elder, Nicolas   **WC**

Huet, Paul   **BA GC WC**
> (*French artist, 1803-1869*)   **WC**
> (*French painter, printmaker, 1803-1869*)   **BA**
> (*French, 1803-1869*)   **GC**
> Bibl: Miguel, Paul Huet; ▶Thieme-Becker

Huette → *see* Huet, Jean Baptiste

Huetter, Sigmund → *see* Master of the Freising Visitation (Sigmund Huetter)

Huf, Paul (*Dutch photographer, b.1924*)   **BA**
> Bibl: ▶MoMA libr. cat.; Nijmegen (NLD), Nijmeegs Mus., Zien en Gezien Worden (1983)

Huffam, A.W.   **WC WI**
> (*British artist, op.1825-1859*)   **WI**
> (*British artist, op.1828-1832*)   **WC**

Huffel, Pieter van (*Flemish painter, 1769-1844*)   **BA**
> Bibl: ▶Kraam, Holl. en Vlaamsche kunst.; ▶Thieme-Becker; Vlieghe, in JAARBOEK VAN HET KONINKLIJK MUSEUM VOOR SCHONE KUNSTEN-ANTWERPEN (1987), p. 237-242 (RILA-WLD); ▶Wurzbach, NLD Künst.-Lex.

Huffman, Brenda (*American graphic designer, Ivoryton, Conn*)   **AV**
> Bibl: Architecture, the AIA journal, Dec., v.75, no.12, p.76

Huffman, Laton Alton   **BA JG**
> (*American photographer, 1854-1931*)   **BA**
> (*American, 1854-1931*)   **JG**
> Bibl: ▶Current, Photog. & Old West; ▶Parry, Photo idx.

Huffsey, Samuel (*American glass worker, 1801-1860*)   **BA**
> Bibl: McKearin, Amer. glass; Mucha, M.E., JOURNAL OF GLASS STUDIES, XXVI (1984), 113; Pepper, GLASS GAFFERS OF NEW JERSY (1971)

Hüfftlein-Otto, Ursula (*West German architect, Stuttgart*)   **AV**
> Bibl: Deutsches Architektenblatt, 1988 Oct.1, v.20, no.10, p.1375

Hufnagel, Georg → *see* Hoefnagel, Joris

Hufnagl, Viktor (*Austrian architect, Vienna*)   **AV**
> Bibl: ▶Verzeich. Öst. Ziviltech., 1984

Hug, Susan (*American architect*)   **AV**
> Bibl: Interior design, 1989 Oct., v.60, no.14, p.258

Hugard de la Tour, Claude-Sebastien (*French artist, 1818-1886*)   **WC**

Huge → *see* Huge, Jurgan Frederick

Huge, Jurgan Frederick (*American painter, 1809-1878*)   **BA PR**
> Bibl: Lipman, Rediscovery: Jurgan Frederick Huge (1973); ▶RILA/BHA

> Huge   **PR**
> Jurgan Frederick Huge   **PR**

Hugé, Pierre II (*French silversmith, d.1765, master 1742*)   **GC**
> Bibl: ▶Mabille, Orfèv. fran.

> Huger, Pierre II   **GC**

Hügel, Helmut vom (*German painter, printmaker, 1899-1931*)   **BA**
> Bibl: ▶Bénézit; ▶Kindlers Malerei Lex.; ▶Vollmer, Künst.-Lex. 20. Jhr.

Hugensz. or Huygensz., Dirck → *see* Hugenz., Dirck

Hugenz. van Cloetinge, Pieter → *see* Cloetinge, Pieter Hugenz. van

Hugenz., Dirck   **BA**
> (*early Netherlandish painter, act.1521-1538*)   **BA**
> (*Netherlands artist, op.1521-1538*)   **WC**
> Bibl: ▶Bénézit; ▶Thieme-Becker; ▶Wurzbach, NLD Künst.-Lex.

Hugensz. or Huygensz., Dirck   **WC**

Huger, Pierre II → *see* Hugé, Pierre II

Huget (*French sculptor, 16th century*)   **GC**
> Bibl: Getty Photo Study Coll. (Sculp.); ▶Thieme-Becker

> Hughes Lallement   **GC**

Hugford, Ferdinand Enrico (*Italian artist, 1659-1771*)   **WC**

Hugford, Hughford, Hugsford, Hoxford or Oxford, Ignazio Enrico → *see* Hugford, Ignazio Enrico

---

Hugford, Ignazio Enrico   **BA GC PR**
   (Italian artist, 1703-1778)   WC
   (Italian painter and printmaker,
    1703-1778)   GC
   (Italian painter, 1703-1778)   PR
   (Italian painter, printmaker,
    author, 1703-1778)   BA
    Bibl: ▶Bolaffi; ▶Dict. natl. biog.;
    ▶RILA/BHA, 1986;
    ▶Thieme-Becker; ▶Witt checklist
Hugford, Hughford, Hugsford,
  Hoxford or Oxford, Ignazio
  Enrico   **WC**
  Ignazio Enrico Hugford   PR
  Ignazio Hugford   PR
  Ugford   PR
Huggill, Henry Percy *(British artist,*
  1886-1957)   **WI**
Huggins, J.M. II *(British artist, op.*
  1827-1842)   **WC WI**
Huggins, Wilfred *(British artist, op.*
  1912-1938)   **WI**
Huggins, William *(British artist,*
  1820-1884)   **WC WI**
Huggins, William John   **BA WC WI**
  (British artist, 1781-1845)   WC WI
  (British painter, 1781-1845)   BA
   Bibl: ▶Archibald, Sea ptrs.;
   ▶Thieme-Becker; ▶Witt checklist
Hugh Bolton Jones→see Jones, Hugh
  Bolton
Hugh Capet, King of France *(ca.*
  938-996)   **AV**
   Bibl: ▶Libr. of Congr. Name Auth.
   File
  Capet, Hugh   AV
  Hugues Capet   AV
Hugh de Tennach *(Swiss scribe, act.*
  ca.1338-1340)   **GC**
   Bibl: Kat. datierten Handschriften
   (1983), n.451; Scriptoria Helvetica
   IX (1964), pp.89-90
Hugh Douglas Hamilton→see
  Hamilton, Hugh Douglas
Hugh Henry Breckenridge→see
  Breckenridge, Hugh Henry
Hugh Irvine→see Irvine, Hugh
Hugh Primrose Dean→see Dean,
  Hugh Primrose
Hugh Reinagle→see Reinagle, Hugh
Hugh, of Northwold, Bishop of Ely
  (Abbot of Bury St. Edmunds, 1213-
  1229; Bishop of Ely, 1229-1254;
  builder of the presbytery of Ely
  Cathedral, d. 1254)   **AV**
   Bibl: ▶Dict. natl. biog.
Hughes→see Hughes, Arthur
Hughes→see Hughes, Jerome A.
Hughes→see Hughes, Trajan
Hughes Lallement→see Huget
Hughes Sambim→see Sambin,
  Hugues

Hughes, Arthur   **BA GC PR WC**
  (British artist, 1832-1915)   WC WI
  (British painter, 1832-1915)   BA PR
  (British, 1832-1915)   GC
   Bibl: ▶Encyc. world art;
   ▶RILA/BHA; Thames & Hudson
   Brit. art; ▶Thieme-Becker; ▶Witt
   checklist; ▶Wood, Victorian ptrs.
  Arthur Hughes   PR
  Hughes   PR
Hughes, Arthur II   **WI**
Hughes, Arthur→see Hughes, Arthur I
Hughes, Arthur Foord *(British*
  artist, 1856-1914)   **WI**
   Bibl: ▶Fisher, Watercolour ptrs.
Hughes, Arthur I   **WI**
  (British artist, 1805-1838)   WC WI
Hughes, Arthur   **WC**
Hughes, Arthur II→see Hughes,
  Arthur
Hughes, C.E.   **WC WI**
  (British artist, 19th cent.)   WC
  (British artist, op.19th c.)   WI
Hughes, Cornelius Jabez *(British,*
  1819-1884, active Glasgow,
  Scotland, U.K.)   **JG**
Hughes, D. Marguerite→see Hughes,
  Daisy Marguerite
Hughes, Daisy Marguerite
  (American painter, 1883-1968)   **PR**
   Bibl: ▶Hughes, Artists California
  Daisy Marguerite Hughes   PR
  Hughes, D. Marguerite   PR
Hughes, Dick *(Architect, Las Vegas,*
  NM)   **AV**
   Bibl: Earthbuilder, no.44, p.24
Hughes, Edward *(British artist,*
  1829-1908)   **WC WI**
Hughes, Edward John   **BA WC**
  (Canadian artist, 1913-)   WC
  (Canadian painter, b.1913)   BA
   Bibl: ▶MacDonald, Can. artists
Hughes, Edward Robert   **BA WC WI**
  (British artist, 1851-1914)   WC WI
  (British painter, 1851-1914)   BA
   Bibl: ▶Bénézit; ▶Johnson, Brit.
   artists
Hughes, Edwin   **WC WI**
  (British artist, 19th cent.)   WC
  (British artist, op.1872-1892)   WI
Hughes, Eleanor Mary *(British*
  artist, 1882-1959)   **WI**
  Waymouth, Eleanor Mary, Miss   WI
Hughes, Elfrida *(British artist, op.*
  1918-)   **WI**
Hughes, Ethel *(British artist, op.*
  1896-1924)   **WI**
Hughes, George *(British artist, op.*
  1813-1858)   **WC WI**
Hughes, George Frederick *(British*
  artist, op.1859-1883)   **WI**
Hughes, Hugh *(British artist, 1790-*
  1863)   **WC WI**
Hughes, Ian *(British artist, op.20th*
  c.)   **WI**
Hughes, J.A.→see Hughes, Jerome A.

Hughes, Jane *(British, d.1869)*   **BA**
   Bibl: Mongomeryshire Collections,
   LXXIV (1986) 90
Hughes, Jerome A. *(American*
  painter, act. 1895)   **PR**
   Bibl: ▶Hughes, Artists California
  Hughes   PR
  Hughes, J.A.   PR
  Jerome A. Hughes   PR
Hughes, John *(British artist, 1790-*
  1857)   **WC WI**
Hughes, John Joseph *(British artist,*
  op.1838-, d.circa 1909)   **WI**
Hughes, Kate Elizabeth, Mrs.→see
  Gilbert, Kate Elizabeth
Hughes, Leda→see
  Papaconstantinou-Hughes, Leda
Hughes, Luke *(British cabinetmaker,*
  20th c.)   **BA**
   Bibl: Hill, COUNTRY LIFE CLXXX
   (30 Oct 1986), p.1352-1353
Hughes, Lynn *(Canadian painter,*
  b.1951)   **BA**
   Bibl: ▶Intl. dir. exh. artists, 1983;
   Vancouver(BC, CAN), Emily Carr
   College of Art and Design.Chas.H.
   Scott Gallery. MEAT AND
   MYSTERY(1982)
Hughes, Malcolm   **BA WC WI**
  (British artist, 1920-)   WC
  (British artist, b.1920)   BA WI
   Bibl: ENCY.OF BRTISH ART; WW
   Amer., 1988
Hughes, Margaret   **WC WI**
  (British artist, 20th cent.)   WC
  (British artist, op.20th c.)   WI
Hughes, Mrs. Philippa
  Swinnerton→see Hughes, Philippa
  Swinnerton
Hughes, Myra Kathleen *(British*
  artist, 1877-1918)   **WC WI**
Hughes, Patrick   **BA WC WI**
  (British artist, 20th cent.)   WC
  (British artist, b.1939)   WI
  (British painter, b.1939)   BA
   Bibl: ▶Dolman, Contemp. Brit.
   artists
Hughes, Philippa Swinnerton   **WI**
  (British artist, 1824-1917)   WI
  (British artist, 19th cent.)   WC
Hughes, Mrs. Philippa
  Swinnerton   **WC**
Hughes, R. *(British artist, op.1793-*
  1799)   **WC WI**
Hughes, R. Gordon *(fl.1935;*
  Architect, Ottawa)   **FA**
   Bibl: CAAD Finding Aid RG 11M
   79003/36; Natl. Arch. of Canada,
   CAAD Finding Aid; Ottawa City
   Directories
Hughes, Robert *(American sculptor,*
  b.1915)   **BA**
   Bibl: ▶Artweek idx.; Manchester
   (NH, USA), Currier Gallery, Large
   scale (1979); ▶MoMA libr. cat.

Hughes, Robert Ball *(American sculptor, 1806-1868)* **BA**
  Bibl: ▶Groce, Artists Amer.;
  ▶Young, Amer. artists
Hughes, Robert Morson *(British artist, 1873-1953)* **WI**
Hughes, S. **WC WI**
  (British artist, 19th cent.) WC
  (British artist, op.19th c.) WI
Hughes, S.G. *(Engraver)* **WI**
Hughes, Sydney **WC WI**
  (British artist, 20th cent.) WC
  (British artist, op.20th c.) WI
Hughes, T.J.→see Hughes, Thomas John
Hughes, Talbot *(British artist, 1869-1942)* **WC WI**
Hughes, Terry *(Scottish architect, Edinburgh)* **AV**
  Bibl: Building design, 1989 May 19, no.937, p.10
Hughes, Thomas John **WI**
  (British artist, op.1851-1865) WC WI
Hughes, T.J. **WC**
Hughes, Trajan **PR WI**
  (British artist, op.1709-1712) WC WI
  (British painter, act. 1709-1712) PR
  Bibl: ▶Waterhouse, Brit. 18c. ptrs.
  Hughes PR
Hughes, Trajan (Tregan) **WC**
  Trajan Hughes PR
Hughes, Trajan (Tregan)→see Hughes, Trajan
Hughes, Vernon *(British artist, op. 1852-1855)* **WC WI**
Hughes, W.A. *(British designer, 20th c.)* **BA**
  Bibl: London (GBR), Mus. London, London design studio (1980)
Hughes, William **PR WC WI**
  (British artist, 1842-1901) WC WI
  (British painter, 1842-1901) PR
  Bibl: Paviere, Brit. sporting ptrs;
  ▶Thieme-Becker
  William Hughes PR
Hughes-Davies, Patricia *(British sculptor, b.1944)* **BA**
  Bibl: Arts Council GBR, Welsh Comm., Coming out (1979)
Hughes-Stanton→see Hughes-Stanton, Herbert Edwin Pelham
Hughes-Stanton, Blair Rowlands **BA WC WI**
  (British artist, 1902-) WC
  (British artist, 1902-1981) WI
  (British painter, printmaker, b.1902) BA
  Bibl: ▶Johnson, Brit. artists;
  ▶Who's Who [GBR], 1978
Hughes-Stanton, Blair Rowlands, Mrs. (Gertrude Anna Bertha)→see Hermes, Gertrude

Hughes-Stanton, Herbert Edwin Pelham **WI**
  (British artist, 1870-1937) WC WI
  (British painter, 1870-1937) PR
  Bibl: ▶Thieme-Becker
  Hughes-Stanton PR
Hughes-Stanton, Herbert Edwin Pelham, Sir **PR**
Hughes-Stanton, Sir Herbert Edwin Pelham **PR WC**
  Sir Herbert Edwin Pelham Hughes-Stanton PR
Hughes-Stanton, Herbert Edwin Pelham, Sir→see Hughes-Stanton, Herbert Edwin Pelham
Hughes-Stanton, Sir Herbert Edwin Pelham→see Hughes-Stanton, Herbert Edwin Pelham
Hughtenberg→see Huchtenburgh, Jan van
Hughtenbnrgh→see Huchtenburgh, Jan van
Hughtenborg→see Huchtenburgh, Jan van
Hughtenburg→see Huchtenburgh, Jan van
Hughtenburgh, Jan van→see Huchtenburgh, Jan van
Hughtenburgh, Johan van→see Huchtenburgh, Jan van
Hughto, Darryl *(American painter, b.1943)* **BA**
  Bibl: ▶Art Index, vs.22, 23; ▶Intl. dir. exh. artists, 1982-1983
Hughto, Margie *(American ceramist, 20th c.)* **BA**
  Bibl: CERAMICS MONTHLY, XXVIII/5 (MAY 1980), 40-46; ▶MoMA libr. cat.
Hugin, Karl→see Hügin, Karl Otto
Hügin, Karl Otto **BA**
  (Swiss artist, 1887-) WC
  (Swiss painter, printmaker, 1887-1963) BA
  Bibl: ▶Bénézit; ▶Künst.-Lex. Schweiz 20. Jahrh.; ▶Lex. zeitgen. Schweiz. Künstler
Hugin, Karl **WC**
Hugle, Reinhard *(German architect, Munich)* **AV**
  Bibl: Detail, 1981 Nov.-Dec., no.6, p.799
Hugman, Robert H. *(American architect, 1902?-1980)* **AV**
Hugnet, Georges **BA WC**
  (French artist, 20th cent.) WC
  (French photographer, 1870-1936) BA
  Bibl: Ades, PHOTOMONTAGE, 170,n.165; ▶Encyc. world art; ▶MoMA libr. cat.
Hugo Ballin→see Ballin, Hugo
Hugo Charlemont→see Charlemont, Hugo

Hugo d'Oignies *(early Netherlandish goldsmith, act.1187-1228)* **BA**
  Bibl: ▶Aa, Biog. woordenboek NLD; ▶Thieme-Becker
Hugo Mieth→see Mieth, Hugo
Hugo of Fouilloy *(French, b. Fouilloy, near Corbie, ca. 1110; d. ca. 1173-1174)* **JG**
Hugo van der Goes→see Goes, Hugo van der
Hugo von Habermann→see Habermann, Hugo von
Hugo Wilhelm Kauffmann→see Kauffmann, Hugo Wilhelm
Hugo, Charles Victor **BA**
  (French photographer, 1826-1871) BA
  (French, 1826-1871) JG
  Bibl: ▶Gernsheim, Hist. photog.; ▶Newhall, Photog.
Hugo, Charles-Victor **JG**
Hugo, Charles-Victor→see Hugo, Charles Victor
Hugo, Freiherr von Habermann→see Habermann, Hugo von
Hugo, Harold *(American printer, d.1985)* **BA**
  Bibl: Biog. idx., v.14, 1984-86; McLean, PRINT QUARTERLY, IV/MAR.1987)p.40-45; NY TIMES, OCT.5,1985,p.28; Storrs (CT, USA), Univ. of CT. Mus. of Art, HAROLD HUGO (1989)
Hugo, Jean **BA WC**
  (French artist, 1894-) WC
  (French painter, designer, 1894-1984) BA
  Bibl: ▶Bénézit; ▶Dict. biog. fran.; ▶MoMA libr. cat.; ▶Vollmer, Künst.-Lex. 20. Jhr.
Hugo, Leopold *(American, active northern CA, U.S. 1900-1926, died 1933)* **JG**
Hugo, Melchior von *(German painter, sculptor, printmaker, b.1872)* **BA**
  Bibl: ▶Bénézit; Jahrb. der Staatl. Kunstsamml. Baden-Württemberg XXI (1984) pp.151-161
Hugo, Nana von *(W. German architect, 1936-)* **AV**
  Bibl: Domus, 1986 Dec., no.678, p.IV
Hugo, Valentine, (nee Gross) *(French artist, 1890-)* **WC**
Hugo, Verena von *(German artist, b.1943)* **BA**
  Bibl: ▶Art Index, v.25; Kunstwerk, XXX/2 (Apr. 1977) pp.3-33
Hugo, Victor→see Hugo, Victor Marie, comte
Hugo, Victor Marie→see Hugo, Victor Marie, comte

Hugo, Victor Marie, comte   **BA**
  (*French artist, 1802-1885*)   WC
  (*French author, draftsman,
    1802-1885*)   BA
  (*French novelist, dramatist,
    poet, painter, and
    draughtsman, 1802-1885*)   GC
  (*French poet, novelist,
    dramatist, 1802-1885*)   AV
     Bibl: ▶Bénézit; ▶Encyc. world art;
       ▶Larousse grande encyc.; ▶Libr. of
       Congr. Name Auth. File; ▶Witt
       checklist
Hugo, Victor   **AV WC**
Hugo, Victor Marie   **GC**
Hugonnet, Aloys (*Swiss artist,
  1879-1938*)   **WC**
Hugoulin, Emile (*French sculptor,
  1848-1923*)   **BA**
     Bibl: ▶Bénézit; ▶Camard, Ptrs. &
       sculps. provençaux; NBF
Hugrel, Pierre Honore (*French
  artist, 1827-p.1868*)   **WC**
Hugtelenburg→see Huchtenburgh,
  Jan van
Hugtemburg→see Huchtenburgh, Jan
  van
Hugtenberg→see Huchtenburgh, Jan
  van
Hugtenbergh→see Huchtenburgh, Jan
  van
Hugtenbugh→see Huchtenburgh, Jan
  van
Hugtenburg→see Huchtenburgh, Jan
  van
Hugtenburg, Jan van→see
  Huchtenburgh, Jan van
Hugtenburgh→see Huchtenburgh,
  Jan van
Hugue, Manuel Martinez (Manolo)
  (*Spanish artist, c.1876-m.1945*)   **WC**
Huguenet, Jacques Joseph (*French
  artist, 1815-p.1864*)   **WC**
Huguenin, Gustave (*French
  architect, act.1881*)   **BA**
     Bibl: Lemoine, MON. HIST. DE LA
       FRANCE 147 (Oct-Nov 1986) 64
**Huguenin-Lassanguette, Fritz
  Edouard** (*Swiss artist, 19th cent.*) **WC**
Huguenin-Panchaud, Augustin
  (*Swiss artist, c.1806-p.1857*)   **WC**
Hugues Capet→see Hugh Capet,
  King of France
Hugues de Beaumont→see
  Beaumont, Hugues de
Hugues Merle→see Merle, Hugues
Hugues Taraval→see Taraval, Hugues
Hugues, Patrice (*French artist, 20th
  c.*)   **BA**
     Bibl: Paris,
       COLOQUIO:ARTES/51(DEC 1981),
       32-41
Hugues, Theodor (*Architect, BRD?*) **AV**
     Bibl: Detail, 1985 Jan.-Feb., v.25,
       no.1, p.57
Huguet→see Huguet, Victor Pierre

Huguet, Enric (*Spanish artist, 20th
  cent.*)   **WC**
Huguet, Jaime   **GC WC**
  (*Spanish artist, op.1448-1489*)   WC
  (*Spanish, act.1448-1487*)   GC
     Bibl: ▶Thieme-Becker
Huguet, Jean Charles (*French artist,
  1815-p.1861*)   **WC**
Huguet, Pere or Pedro (*Spanish
  artist, op.1439*)   **WC**
Huguet, Philippe Jean Baptiste
  (*French goldsmith, act.1798-after
  1810*)   **BA**
     Bibl: ARTS UNDER NAPOLEON,
       160; Dennis, Fr. silver, p.73;
       Verdier, NATL.GALLERY OF CAN
       BULLETIN, II(1978-79), 58-59
Huguet, Pierre (Pierre Latour)
  (*Canadian silversmith, 1749-1817*) **BA**
     Bibl: Langdon, Can. silversmiths;
       Winnipeg (Man, CAN), Art
       Gallery, Canadian silver (1974)
Huguet, Victor Pierre   **PR WC**
  (*French artist, 1835-1902*)   WC
  (*French painter, 1835-1902*)   PR
     Bibl: ▶Thieme-Becker
  Huguet   PR
  Victor Pierre Huguet   PR
*Huhn, Carl Theodor
  Fjodorawitsch→see* Goun, Karl
  Theodor Fiodorovitch
Hühn, Julius (*Yugoslav
  photographer, act.1850s*)   **BA**
     Bibl: Hist. photography, I/2 (Apr
       1977), 153-167
Huhtiniemi, Reino (*Finnish architect,
  Helsinki*)   **AV**
     Bibl: SAFA 87: Suomen Arkkit.
Huibers, Jan Derk (*Dutch painter,
  1829-1919*)   **GC**
     Bibl: ▶Scheen, Ned. beeldende
       kunst.
**Huidekoper or Huidekoper,
  Christiaan (Chris)** (*Dutch artist,
  1878-1939*)   **WC**
Huidobro, Borja (*French architect,
  born in Chile, 1936-*)   **AV**
     Bibl: International architect, issue
       1, 1983, p.[1]
Huie, Chris (*American photographer,
  b.1941*)   **BA**
     Bibl: San Francisco (CA, USA),
       SFMoMA, Jim Dong (1979)
Huiehmberg→see Huchtenburgh, Jan
  van
Huijsman→see Huysmans, Cornelis
Huillard, Paul (*French architect,
  1875-1966*)   **BA**
     Bibl: ▶Thieme-Becker
Huillier, Jacques (*French artist, 19th
  cent.*)   **WC**
Huilliot, C.→see Huilliot, Claude

Huilliot, Claude   **GC PR**
  (*French artist, 1632-1702*)   WC
  (*French painter, 1632-1702*)   GC
  (*French painter, ca.1631-1702*)   PR
     Bibl: ▶Bénézit; Sotheby's;
       ▶Thieme-Becker; ▶Witt checklist
  Claude Huilliot   PR
  Huilliot, C.   GC
  Hulitt   PR
Hulliot or Huillot, Claude   **WC**
  Hulliot, Claude   GC
Huilliot, Pierre Nicolas   **BA**
  (*French artist, 1674-1751*)   WC
  (*French painter, 1674-1751*)   BA
Huillot, Pierre Nicolas   **WC**
Huillot, Pierre Nicolas→see Huilliot,
  Pierre Nicolas
Huin (*Swiss artist, op.1790*)   **WC**
Huin, Giuseppe (*Italian architect,
  19th c.*)   **BA**
     Bibl: Zanni, ARTE IN FRIULI-ARTE A
       TRIESTE, X (1988), pp.83-90
Huisman→see Huysmans, Cornelis
Huisman, Hetty (*Dutch artist,
  b.1941*)   **BA**
     Bibl: Amsterdam (NLD), Sted.
       Museum, HETTY HUISMAN...
       (1974); ▶Intl. dir. exh. artists,
       1983
Huisman, Nele (*Belgian architect*) **AV**
     Bibl: Architektur & Wohnen, 1989
       Sept.-Oct., no.5, p.60
Huismans, Sipke (*Dutch artist,
  1938-*)   **WC**
Huizinga, Menno (*Dutch
  photographer, 1907-1947*)   **BA**
     Bibl: Hague, FOTOGRAFIE IN NLD
       1920-40, 151; Hague,
       Gemeentemuseum, MENNO
       HUIZINGA(1984)
Hujar, Peter   **BA JG**
  (*American photographer,
    b.1934*)   BA
  (*American, 1934 -*)   JG
     Bibl: ▶Art Index, vs.37-38;
       ARTFORUM, 15/p.68-9;
       ▶Contemp. photogs.; ▶Intl. dir.
       exh. artists, 1983
Huklenbrok, Henri J.H. (*German
  artist, op.c.1893-1903*)   **WC**
Hulbert, Fanny   **WC WI**
  (*British artist, op.1841*)   WC
  (*British artist, op.1841-*)   WI
Hulbert, Thelma   **WC WI**
  (*British artist, 1913-*)   WC
  (*British artist, b.1913*)   WI
Hulde (*Swiss artist, 19th cent.*)   **WC**
Hule, P. van (*Netherlands artist, op.
  1656*)   **WC**
Hulen [Unidentified] (*Unknown
  painter*)   **PR**
     Bibl: (April 10, 1813, lot A47,
       Christie's)
Hulett or Hulet, James→see Hulett,
  James

Hulett, James   **WI**
    (British artist, op.1740-, d.1771)   WI
    (British artist, op.1740-m.1771)   WC
      Bibl: ▶Witt checklist
    Hulett or Hulet, James   **WC**
Hulft, T.→see Hulst, T. [Unidentified]
Hulier [Unidentified] *(Unknown
    painter)*   **PR**
      Bibl: (March 28, 1811, lot 17,
      Christie's)
Hulitt→see Huilliot, Claude
Hulk, Abraham→see Hulk, Abraham II
Hulk, Abraham II   **WI**
    (British artist, 1813-1897)   WI
    (British artist, op.1876-1898)   WC
    (Dutch artist, 1813-1897)   WC
    (Dutch painter, 1813-1897)   GC
      Bibl: ▶Thieme-Becker
    Hulk, Abraham   **GC**
    Hulk, Abraham, I   **WC**
    Hulk, Abraham, II   **WC**
Hulk, Abraham, I→see Hulk, Abraham
    II
Hulk, Abraham, II→see Hulk,
    Abraham II
Hulk, Hendrik   **GC WC**
    (Dutch artist, 1842-1937)   WC
    (Dutch painter, 1842-1937)   GC
      Bibl: ▶Bénézit
Hulk, J.F.   **GC**
    (Dutch artist, 1829-1911)   WC
    (Dutch painter, 1829-1911)   GC
      Bibl: ▶Thieme-Becker
Hulk, Johannes Frederik, I   **WC**
*Hulk, Johannes (John) Frederik,
    II→see* Hulk, John Frederik
Hulk, Johannes Frederik, I→see Hulk,
    J.F.
Hulk, John Frederik   **GC**
    (Dutch artist, 1855-1913)   WC
    (Dutch painter and
      draughtsman, 1855-1913)   GC
      Bibl: ▶Thieme-Becker
**Hulk, Johannes (John) Frederik,
    II**   **WC**
Hulk, William Frederik   **WI**
    (British artist, 1852-)   WC
    (British artist, 1852-op.1906)   WI
    Hulk, William Frederik   **WC**
Hulk, William Frederik→see Hulk,
    William Frederik
Hull, Arundel C. *(American
    photographer, 1846-1908)*   **BA**
      Bibl: ▶Current, Photog. & Old
      West
Hull, Edward   **WC WI**
    (British artist, 1810-1877)   WI
    (British artist, op.1827-1877)   WC
Hull, Gert *(Norwegian, ca.1760-
    1810)*   **GC**
      Bibl: ▶Thieme-Becker
Hull, John *(American silversmith,
    1624-1683)*   **BA**
      Bibl: ▶Penguin dec. arts;
      ▶Thieme-Becker

Hull, John *(American painter, b.ca.
    1952)*   **BA**
      Bibl: Guide exh. artists: N. Amer.
      ptrs.; NEW ART EXAMINER XIII/2
      (Oct 1985) 38-41
Hull, Richard *(American painter,
    b.1955)*   **BA**
      Bibl: ▶Intl. dir. exh. artists, 1983
Hull, Thomas→see Hull, Thomas H.
Hull, Thomas H.   **WI**
    (British artist, op.1775-, d.1800)   WI
    (British artist, op.1775-m.1800)   WC
      Bibl: ▶Foskett, Brit. miniature ptrs.
    Hull, Thomas   **WC**
Hull, William *(British artist, 1820-
    1880)*   **WC WI**
Hulle, Anselmus van *(Dutch
    painter, ca.1601-ca.1674)*   **BA**
    (Dutch painter, ca.1601-ca.
      1674)   BA
    (Flemish artist, 1601-p.1674)   WC
      Bibl: ▶Bénézit; ▶Thieme-Becker;
      ▶Wurzbach, NLD Künst.-Lex.
    **Hulle, Anselmus von (Anselmus
    Hebbelynck)**   **WC**
*Hulle, Anselmus von (Anselmus
    Hebbelynck)→see* Hulle, Anselmus
    van
Hulle, Robert   **AV BA**
    (British architect, master mason,
      d.1442)   AV
    (English mason, act.1400-1442)   BA
      Bibl: British Archaeological
      Association. Journal, 1985, v.138,
      p.102; Harvey, Perpendicular style
Hulleberghe→see Hilleberghe,
    Antoine van
*Hullegarden or Hullegaerde, Carel
    van→see* Hullegarden, Carel van
Hullegarden, Carel van   **GC**
    (Dutch artist, op.1647-1669)   WC
    (Dutch painter, act.1647-1669)   GC
      Bibl: Getty Photo Study Coll.;
      ▶Thieme-Becker; ▶Witt checklist
    **Hullegarden or Hullegaerde,
    Carel van**   **WC**
Hulley→see Hulley, H.
Hulley the Elder, Thomas→see
    Hulley, Thomas I
Hulley, H.   **BA PR WC WI**
    (British artist, op.1783-1800)   WC WI
    (British painter, act. 1783-1800)   PR
    (Irish painter, act.1783-1790)   BA
      Bibl: ▶Bénézit; ▶Strickland, Irish
      artists; ▶Thieme-Becker;
      ▶Waterhouse, Brit. 18c. ptrs.;
      ▶Witt checklist
    H. Hulley   PR
    Hulley   PR
    Hully   PR
    Hutley   PR
Hulley, Thomas I   **WI**
    (British artist, op.1798-1817)   WC WI
    Hulley the Elder, Thomas   **WC**
Hullgren, Oscar *(Swedish artist,
    1869-1948)*   **WC**

Hulliot or Huillot, Claude→see
    Huilliot, Claude
Hulliot, Claude→see Huilliot, Claude
Hullmandel, Charles Joseph *(British
    printmaker, 1789-1850)*   **BA**
      Bibl: ▶Bénézit; ▶Dict. natl. biog.;
      ▶Redgrave, Engl. school;
      ▶Thieme-Becker
Hullner, C. *(German artist, 19th
    cent.)*   **WC**
Hully→see Hulley, H.
Hulmans, J. *(Flemish artist, 17th
    cent.)*   **WC**
Hulme, F. Edward→see Hulme,
    Frederick Edward
Hulme, Frederick Edward   **BA**
    (British artist, op.19th c.)   WI
    (British botanist, printmaker,
      1841-1909)   BA
      Bibl: ▶Thieme-Becker
    Hulme, F. Edward   **WI**
Hulme, Frederick William *(British
    artist, 1816-1884)*   **WC WI**
Hulme, J. Henry   **WC WI**
    (British artist, 18th cent.)   WC
    (British artist, op.18th c.)   WI
Hulot, Guillaume *(French sculptor,
    act.1685-1722)*   **BA**
      Bibl: ▶Lami, Sculp. fran. 19e s.;
      ▶Thieme-Becker
Hulsberg, Henry   **WC WI**
    (British artist, -1729)   WC
    (British artist, d.1729)   WI
Hulsdonck→see Hulsdonck, Jacob
Hulsdonck, Gillis van   **GC WC**
    (Flemish artist, c.1625-p.1669)   WC
    (Flemish painter, ca.1625-aft.
      1669)   GC
      Bibl: ▶Thieme-Becker
Hulsdonck, Jacob   **PR**
    (Dutch painter, 1582-1647)   PR
    (Flemish artist, 1582-1647)   WC
    (Flemish, 1582-1647)   GC JG
      Bibl: ▶Thieme-Becker
    Helsdingh   PR
    Hulsdonck   PR
    **Hulsdonck, Jacob (also,
    erroneously, Jan) van**   **WC**
    Hulsdonck, Jacob van   **GC JG PR**
    Jacob Hulsdonck   PR
    Visdonck   PR
*Hulsdonck, Jacob (also, erroneously,
    Jan) van→see* Hulsdonck, Jacob
Hulsdonck, Jacob van→see
    Hulsdonck, Jacob
Hulseboom, Gerrit   **GC WC**
    (Dutch artist, 1784-1863)   WC
    (Dutch draughtsman, 1784-
      1863)   GC
      Bibl: ▶Thieme-Becker
Hulsebos, R. *(Dutch(?) artist, op.
    1800-1819)*   **WC**
Hulsebosch, J. *(Dutch architect,
    Rotterdam)*   **AV**
      Bibl: Assemblage, 1987 July, no.3,
      p.122

Hulsen, Esaias van (Esaias Hulsius)
(Dutch artist, 1570(?)-a.1627) **WC**
Hulsen, Friedrich van **GC**
(Dutch artist, c.1580(?)-c.1660) **WC**
(German, ca.1580-ca.1660) **GC**
   Bibl: ▶Thieme-Becker
Hulsen, Friedrich van (Federicus
  Hulsius) **WC**
Hulsen, Friedrich van (Federicus
  Hulsius)→see Hulsen, Friedrich van
Hülser, Angelika *(German architect,*
  Düsseldorf) **AV**
   Bibl: Die Kunst, 1985 Oct., v.96,
   no.10, p.835
Hülser, Ingo *(German architect,*
  Düsseldorf) **AV**
   Bibl: Die Kunst, 1985 Oct., v.96,
   no.10, p.835
Hulshoff-Pol, Albertus Gerhard
  (Dutch draughtsman, b.1883) **GC**
   Bibl: ▶Vollmer, Künst.-Lex. 20. Jhr.
Hulsman→see Hulsman, Johann
Hulsman or, Hulsmann (not
  Holzmann) Johann→see Hulsman,
  Johann
Hulsman, Johann **GC PR**
  (German artist, op.1634-1644) **WC**
  (German painter and
  draughtsman, act.1632-d. bef.
  1652) **GC**
  (German painter, act. 1634-
  1644) **PR**
   Bibl: Getty Photo Study Coll.;
   ▶Schweers, Gemälde deut.
   Museen; ▶Thieme-Becker; ▶Witt
   checklist
  H. Hulsman **PR**
  Hans Hulsman **PR**
  Hans Hülsmann **PR**
  Holzmann, Johann **GC**
  Hulsman **PR**
Hulsman or, Hulsmann (not
  Holzmann) Johann **WC**
  Hulsmann, Jan **GC**
  J. Hulsman **PR**
  J. Hulsmann **PR**
  Johann Hulsman **PR**
Hulsmann, Dirk *(German architect,*
  Krefeld) **AV**
   Bibl: Bauwelt, 1985 May 31, v.76,
   no.20-21, p.799
Hülsmann, Gisberth *(Architect,*
  Bonn) **AV**
   Bibl: Detail, 1981 MAr.-Apr., no.2,
   p.181
Hulsmann, Jan→see Hulsman, Johann
Hülsmeier, Werner *(Architect,*
  Germany(?)) **AV**
   Bibl: Detail, 1982 Mar.-Apr., no.2,
   p.149
Hulst→see Hulst, Franz de
Hulst or Hult, Pieter van der, or
  Pieter Verhulst (Zonnebloom)→see
  Hulst, Pieter van der
Hulst, Frans de or van der→see
  Hulst, Franz de

Hulst, Franz de **GC PR**
  (Dutch artist, c.1610-1661) **WC**
  (Dutch painter, 1610-1661) **PR**
  (Dutch painter, ca.1610-1661) **GC**
   Bibl: Getty Photo Study Coll.;
   ▶Thieme-Becker
  Frans de Hulst **PR**
  Franz de Hulst **PR**
  Hulst **PR**
Hulst, Frans de or van der **WC**
  Hulst, Franz van der **GC**
Hulst, Franz van der→see Hulst,
  Franz de
Hulst, Hendrik van *(Dutch artist,*
  1685-1754) **WC**
Hulst, Hulft or Ulst, Maerten Fransz.
  van der→see Hulst, Maerten
  Fransz. van der
Hulst, Jan Baptist van der **BA WC**
  (Belgian artist, 1790-1862) **WC**
  (Belgian painter, printmaker,
  1790-1862) **BA**
   Bibl: ▶Bénézit; ▶Scheen, Ned.
   beeldende kunst.; ▶Thieme-Becker
Hulst, Maerten Fransz. van der **GC PR**
  (Dutch artist, op.c.1630-1645) **WC**
  (Dutch painter, act. 1630-1645) **PR**
  (Dutch, act. ca.1630-1645) **GC**
   Bibl: ▶Thieme-Becker
Hulst, Hulft or Ulst, Maerten
  Fransz. van der **WC**
  Maerten Fransz. van der Hulst **PR**
Hulst, Pieter van der **GC**
  (Dutch artist, 1651-1727) **WC**
  (Dutch painter and
  draughtsman, 1651-1727) **GC**
   Bibl: ▶Thieme-Becker
Hulst or Hult, Pieter van der, or
  Pieter Verhulst (Zonnebloom) **WC**
  Hult, Pieter van der **GC**
  Verhulst, Pieter van der **GC**
Hulst, Pieter van der→see Hulst,
  Pieter van der (I)
Hulst, Pieter van der (I) **PR**
  (Dutch painter, 1575-1628) **PR**
  (Flemish artist, op.1583-m.c.
  1628) **WC**
   Bibl: ▶Thieme-Becker; Worcester
   Art Museum catalogue
  Hulst, Pieter van der **PR**
Hulst, Pieter, I van der, or Pieter
  Verhulst **WC**
  Pieter van der Hulst (I) **PR**
Hulst, Pieter, I van der, or Pieter
  Verhulst→see Hulst, Pieter van der
  (I)
Hulst, Pieter, II van der, or Pieter
  Verhulst *(Flemish artist, op.1623-*
  1637) **WC**
Hulst, T. **[Unidentified]** *(Dutch*
  painter) **PR**
  Hulft, T. **PR**
  T. Hulft **PR**

Hulstijn, Cornelis Johannes van **GC WC**
  (Dutch artist, 1813-1879) **WC**
  (Dutch painter, 1813-d. aft.
  1887) **GC**
   Bibl: ▶Thieme-Becker
Hulswit→see Hulswit, Jan
Hulswit, Jan **GC PR WC**
  (Dutch artist, 1766-1822) **WC**
  (Dutch draughtsman, 1766-
  1822) **GC**
  (Dutch painter, 1766-1822) **PR**
   Bibl: ▶Thieme-Becker
  Hulswit **PR**
  Jan Hulswit **PR**
Hult, Pieter van der→see Hulst,
  Pieter van der
Hultberg, John **WC WI**
  (American artist, 1922-) **WC**
  (American artist, b.1922) **WI**
Hulten, Peter van *(Dutch architect)* **AV**
   Bibl: De Architect, 1988 Nov.,
   v.19, no.11, p.92
Hulton, William **BA PR**
  (British artist, 1852-1921) **WI**
  (British painter, 1851-1921) **PR**
  (British painter, act.1882,
  d.1921) **BA**
   Bibl: Ashmolean Museum
   catalogue; ▶Johnson, Brit. artists;
   ▶Thieme-Becker; ▶Waters, Brit.
   artists; ▶Wood, Victorian ptrs.
Hulton, William S. **WI**
  Hulton, William Stokes **PR**
  William Hulton **PR**
Hulton, William S.→see Hulton,
  William
Hulton, William Stokes→see Hulton,
  William
Humair, Daniel *(French artist, 20th*
  cent.) **WC**
Humann→see Humann, O. Victor
Humann, O. Victor *(American*
  painter, 1874-1951) **PR**
   Bibl: Worcester Art Museum
   catalogue; ▶WWW Amer. art
  Humann **PR**
  O. Victor Humann **PR**
Humbaire, Jean-Pierre *(French*
  architect) **AV**
   Bibl: ▶Annuaire archts. fran.,
   1978
Humbert De Molard, Baron Louis-
  Adolphe *(French, 1800-1874)* **JG**
Humbert de Superville, David Pierre
  Giottino→see Humbert de
  Superville, David Pierre Giottino
Humbert de Superville, David
  Pierre Giottino **BA GC**
  (Dutch artist, 1770-1849) **WC**
  (Dutch draughtsman, 1770-
  1849) **GC**
  (Dutch painter, printmaker,
  1770-1849) **BA**
   Bibl: ▶Bénézit; ▶Thieme-Becker
Humbert de Superville, David
  Pierre Giottino **WC**

Humbert, Albert Jenkins (British
architect, 1822-1877)   **BA**
  Bibl: ▶Portoghesi, Diz. arch. e
  urbanistica; ▶Thieme-Becker
Humbert, Andre Louis Maxime
(French artist, 1879-)   **WC**
Humbert, Charles   **GC**
  (Swiss artist, 1813-1881)   WC
  (Swiss painter, 1813-1881)   GC
  Bibl: ▶Thieme-Becker
**Humbert, Charles (Jean Charles
  Ferdinand)**   **WC**
Humbert, Charles (Jean Charles
Ferdinand) →see Humbert, Charles
Humbert, Ferdinand   **BA PR**
  (French artist, 1842-1934)   WC
  (French painter, 1842-1934) BA GC PR
  Bibl: ▶Bénézit; ▶Larousse grande
  encyc.; ▶RILA/BHA;
  ▶Thieme-Becker
  Ferdinand Humbert   PR
Humbert, Jacques Fernand   **GC PR**
Hymbert, Jacques Fernand   **WC**
Humbert, Frederic (French artist,
  19th/20th cent.)   **WC**
Humbert, Jacques Fernand →see
  Humbert, Ferdinand
Humbert, Jean   **BA WC**
  (Dutch artist, 1734-1794)   WC
  (Dutch painter, 1734-1794)   BA
  Bibl: ▶Thieme-Becker; ▶Witt
  checklist; ▶Wurzbach, NLD
  Künst.-Lex.
Humbert, Jean George (German
  silversmith, goldsmith, 1770-1837)   **BA**
  Bibl: Scheffler, Berliner
  Goldschmiede; Scheffler,
  KUNSTUND ANTIQUITATER(1982),
  56-58
Humblot, Antoine   **GC**
  (French artist, op.1720-m.1758)   WC
  (French painter, d.1758)   GC
  Bibl: ▶Bénézit
**Humblot, Humbelot or
  Humblau, Antoine**   **WC**
Humblot, Humbelot or Humblau,
  Antoine →see Humblot, Antoine
Humblot, Robert   **GC**
  (French artist, 1907-1962)   WC
  (French painter, 1907-1962)   GC
  Bibl: ▶Bénézit
Humblot, Roberto   **WC**
Humblot, Roberto →see Humblot,
  Robert
Humboldt, Alexander Freiherr
  von →see Humboldt, Alexander,
  Freiherr von
Humboldt, Alexander von →see
  Humboldt, Alexander, Freiherr von

**Humboldt, Alexander, Freiherr
  von**   **BA**
  (German artist, 1769-1859)   WC
  (German naturalist, traveler,
  statesman, 1769-1859)   AV
  (German scientist, draftsman,
  geographer, 1769-1859)   BA
  Bibl: ▶Brockhaus Enzyk.;
  ▶Gernsheim, Hist. photog.; ▶Libr.
  of Congr. Name Auth. File; ▶Neue
  deutsche Biog.; ▶Thieme-Becker
**Humboldt, Alexander Freiherr
  von**   **WC**
Humboldt, Alexander von   **AV**
Humborg, Adolf (German artist,
  1847-)   **WC**
Hume →see Hume, Abraham
Hume, Abraham (British painter,
  1749-1838)   **PR**
  Bibl: ▶RILA/BHA
  Abraham Hume   PR
  Hume   PR
  Sir Abraham Hume   PR
Hume, Amelia, Miss →see Long,
  Amelia
Hume, Edith   **WI**
  (British artist, op.1862-1896)   WC
  (British artist, op.1862-1906)   WI
  Dunn, Edith, Miss   WI
**Hume, Edith, (nee Dunn, wife
  of Thomas Hume)**   **WC**
Hume, Edith, (nee Dunn, wife of
  Thomas Hume) →see Hume, Edith
Hume, Thomas O. (British artist, op.
  1864-1894)   **WI**
Hume, William (British artist, op.
  19th c.)   **WI**
Humek, Gabrijel (Yugoslav painter,
  b.1907)   **BA**
  Bibl: Ljubljana (YUG), Moderna
  Galerija, GABRIJEL HUMEK, 1986
Humelsine, Carlisle H. (American
  preservationist, Va.; former pres.
  of the National Trust for Historic
  Preservation, d. 1989)   **AV**
  Bibl: Preservation news, 1989
  Mar., v.29, no.3, p.3
Humes, Richard →see Humes, Richard
  Howard
Humes, Richard Howard (American
  sculptor, b.1935)   **GC**
  Bibl: Getty Photo Study Coll.;
  ▶Opitz, Amer. sculptors
  Humes, Richard   GC
Hummel →see Hummel, Theodor
Hummel, Carl (German artist,
  c.1769-1840)   **WC**
Hummel, Carl Maria Nicolaus   **GC WC**
  (German artist, 1821-1907)   WC
  (German, 1821-1907)   GC
  Bibl: ▶Thieme-Becker; ▶Witt
  checklist
Hummel, Erdmann (Johann
  Erdmann) →see Hummel, Johann
  Erdmann

Hummel, Gustav Adolf (Swiss
  artist, 1850-p.1893)   **WC**
Hummel, Johann Erdmann   **BA**
  (German artist, 1769-1852)   WC
  (German painter, printmaker,
  1769-1852)   BA
  (German, 1769-1852)   GC
  Bibl: ▶Neue deutsche Biog.;
  ▶Thieme-Becker; ▶Witt checklist
**Hummel, Erdmann (Johann
  Erdmann)**   **GC WC**
Hummel, Ludwig (Luigi) (Italian
  artist, 1770-1840)   **WC**
Hummel, Morus (Canadian sculptor,
  b.1936)   **BA**
  Bibl: ▶Artists Canada;
  Kingston(ONT, CAN), Q.U. Aagnes
  Eth.ArtC., STANDBILDER...(1978)
Hummel, Theodor   **PR WC**
  (German artist, 1864-1939)   WC
  (German painter, 1864-aft.1914)   PR
  Bibl: ▶Thieme-Becker
  Hummel   PR
  Hummel, Theodore   PR
  Theodor Hummel   PR
Hummel, Theodore →see Hummel,
  Theodor
Hummerston, Effie (British artist,
  b.1891)   **WI**
Humpert, Klaus   **AV BA**
  (1929-)   AV
  (German architect, b.1929)   BA
  Bibl: KUNSTWERK,
  XXXII/2-3(APR-JUNE 1979), 72
Humphrey, David Aiken (American
  painter, printmaker, b.1955)   **BA**
  Bibl: ▶WW Amer. Art
Humphrey, Jack Waldon →see
  Humphrey, Jack Weldon
Humphrey, Jack Weldon   **BA**
  (Canadian artist, 1901-)   WC
  (Canadian painter, 1901-1967)   BA
  Bibl: ▶Artists Canada;
  ▶MacDonald, Can. artists
Humphrey, Jack Waldon   **WC**
Humphrey, Margo (American artist,
  b.1942)   **BA**
  Bibl: San Francisco (CA, USA),
  SFMoMA, Carmen Lomas Garzan
  (1980)
Humphrey, Nene (American
  sculptor, b.1947.)   **BA**
  Bibl: ▶WW Amer. Art, 1989
Humphrey, Ralph   **BA WC WI**
  (American artist, 1932-)   WC
  (American artist, b.1932)   WI
  (American painter, b.1932)   BA
  Bibl: NY Times obit., 17 Jul 1990;
  ▶WW Amer. Art, 1989
Humphrey, Walter Beach
  (American painter, b. 1892)   **PR**
  Bibl: ▶WWW Amer. art
  Walter Beach Humphrey   PR
Humphreys →see Humphry, Ozias

Humphreys, Cécilia *(Canadian architect, Ottawa, Ont)* **AV**
Bibl: ▶Canad. arch. dir., 1987

Humphreys, Charles S. **WC WI**
(American artist, op.1854-1870) WC
(American artist, op.1854-1876) WI

Humphreys, Henry Noel **BA WI**
(British artist, 1810-1879) WI
(British draftsman, naturalist, numismatist, 1810-1879) BA
Bibl: ▶Dict. natl. biog.; ▶Thieme-Becker

Humphries, Henry Noel **WI**

Humphreys, James *(American printer, 1748-1810)* **BA**
Bibl: ▶WWW Amer., 1607

Humphreys, John *(British artist, op. 20th c.)* **WI**

Humphreys, Richard *(American silversmith, 1750-1832)* **BA**
Bibl: ANTIQUES, CXVIII(AUG 1980), 285-289; Philadelphia silver

Humphreys, W. *(Engraver)* **WI**

Humphreys-Johnstone, John *(British artist, 1857-1941)* **WI**

Humphries → see Humphry, Ozias

Humphries, Henry Noel → see Humphreys, Henry Noel

Humphry → see Humphry, Ozias

Humphry, Ozias **BA GC PR WC WI**
(British artist, 1742-1810) WC WI
(British painter, 1742-1810) PR
(British painter, miniaturist, 1742-1810) BA
(British, 1742-1810) GC
Bibl: (November 27, 1813, lots 43 & 44, Christie's); ▶Bénézit; ▶Dict. natl. biog.; ▶RILA/BHA; ▶Thieme-Becker
Humphreys PR
Humphries PR
Humphry PR
Humphry, R.A. PR
Mr. Humphry, R.A. PR
O. Humphreys PR
Ozias Humphrey, R.A. PR
Ozias Humphreys PR
Ozias Humphry PR

Humphry, R.A. → see Humphry, Ozias

Humphry, Richard *(British painter, b.1942)* **BA**
Bibl: Arts Council GBR, Welsh Comm., Richard Humphry & Eric Paet (1977); ▶MoMA libr. cat.

Humphrys *(Engraver)* **WI**

Humrich, Edward Robert *(American architect)* **AV**
Bibl: Chicago architectural journal, 1985, v.5, p.127

Hums, Josef *(Austrian architect)* **AV**
Bibl: Planen Bauen Wohnen, 1988, no.122, p.20

Hun, J.C. *(Dutch(?) artist, op.1708)* **WC**

Hunaeus, Andreas Herman *(Danish painter, 1814-1866)* **BA**
Bibl: ▶Bénézit; ▶Thieme-Becker

Hund, Hans-Peter *(East German painter, b.1940)* **BA**
Bibl: George, M., BILDENDE KUNST, 4 (1984), 184-185

Hundercutter → see Hondecoeter, Melchior d'

Hundertpfund, Liberat *(German artist, 1806-1878)* **WC**

Hundertwasser → see Hundertwasser, Friedensreich (Friedrich Stowasser)

Hundertwasser, Friedensreich (Friedrich Stowasser) **BA**
(Austrian artist, designer, 1928-) AV
(Austrian painter, printmaker, b.1928) BA
(German artist, 1928-) WC
Bibl: ▶Contemp. artists; Koschatzky & Kertesz, HUNDERTWASSER:THE COMPLETE GRAPHIC WORK...(1986)p. 8; ▶Libr. of Congr. Name Auth. File
Friedensreich Hundertwassser AV
Hundertwasser **AV**
Hundertwasser, Fritz **WC**
Hundertwasssser, Friedrich AV
Stowasser, Friedrich AV

Hundertwasser, Fritz → see Hundertwasser, Friedensreich (Friedrich Stowasser)

Hundertwasssser, Friedrich → see Hundertwasser, Friedensreich (Friedrich Stowasser)

Hundrieser, Emil *(German sculptor, 1846-1911)* **BA**
Bibl: ▶Bénézit; ▶Thieme-Becker

Hune or Huhne, Andreas Caspar *(German artist, c.1758-1813)* **WC**

Hüneche, Bernhard *(Danish carpenter, act.1736-1737)* **BA**
Bibl: Toennesen, ANTIKV STUDIER:FORT.OG BYG.,5(1982), 190-219

Huneman → see Hunneman, Christopher William

Hünerwadel, Peter S. *(Swiss architect, Basel)* **AV**
Bibl: ▶Schweiz. Ingen. u. Archit., 1984-1985

Hung, Chung *(Chinese sculptor in CAN, b.1946)* **BA**
Bibl: Vancouver (BC, CAN), Carr Coll. Art & Design Scott Gallery, Chung Hung (1982)

Hungeois → see Hondius, Abraham

Hungerbühler, Emil **BA WC**
(Swiss artist, 1914-) WC
(Swiss painter, printmaker, b.1914) BA
Bibl: ▶Künst.-Lex. Schweiz 20. Jahrh.; ▶Lex. zeitgen. Schweiz. Künstler

Hungerford, Cyrus Cotton *(American cartoonist, 20th c.)* **BA**
Bibl: WW Amer., 1976; ▶WW Amer. Art, 1976

Hunin, Pierre Paul Alouis (Alouis) *(Belgian artist, 1808-1855)* **WC**

Hunn, Thomas H. *(British artist, op. 1878-1910)* **WI**

Hunneman → see Hunneman, Christopher William

Hunneman, Christopher William **PR WC WI**
(British artist, 1730-1793) WC WI
(British painter, ca.1730-1793) PR
Bibl: ▶Thieme-Becker; ▶Waterhouse, Brit. 18c. ptrs.
Christopher William Hunneman PR
Hanneman, Christopher William WI
Huneman PR
Hunneman PR

Hunsinger, Jason *(American sculptor, 20th c.)* **BA**
Bibl: Arts Mag., 3 Nov 1982, p.54

Hunsley, William **WC WI**
(British artist, op.1837-1843) WI
(British artist, op.1841) WC

Hunsruck, Hans von (Duke Johann II of Bavaria) *(German artist, 15th cent.)* **WC**

Hunt → see Hunt, E. Aubrey

Hunt → see Hunt, William Holman

Hunt Painter **GC JG**
(Greek vase-painter and potter, act. ca.565-530 BC) GC
Bibl: Stibbe, Lak. Vases

Hunt, Alfred *(British artist, op.1860-1884)* **WI**

Hunt, Alfred William **BA GC PR WC WI**
(British artist, 1830-1896) WC WI
(British painter, 1830-1896) BA PR
(British, 1830-1896) GC
Bibl: ▶RILA/BHA; ▶Thieme-Becker; ▶Witt checklist
Alfred William Hunt PR

Hunt, Angela *(British textile artist, b.1957)* **BA**
Bibl: ▶Intl. dir. exh. artists, 1983; Sunderland(GBR), Arts Centre. DICK WOOD...(1982)(UK)

Hunt, Anthony *(British structural engineer)* **AV**
Bibl: Architects' journal, 1984 Nov.7, v.180, no.45, p.36

Hunt, Arthur Ackland **WC WI**
(British artist, op.1863-1913) WI
(British artist, op.1865-1902) WC

Hunt, Bernard Andrew *(British architect)* **AV**

Hunt, Bryan **BA WI**
(American artist, b.1947) WI
(American sculptor, b.1947) BA
Bibl: ▶Locus; ▶WW Amer. Art, 1989

Hunt, C.H. *(Australian artist, 1857-1938)* **WC**

Hunt, C.L. *(American, active New
Hampshire, 1870s)*   **JG**
Hunt, Cecil Arthur *(British artist,
1873-1965)*   **WC WI**
Hunt, Charles → *see* Hunt, Charles I
Hunt, Charles D. *(American painter,
1840-1914)*   **BA**
   Bibl: ▶Groce, Artists Amer.;
   ▶Young, Amer. artists
Hunt, Charles I   **WI**
   (British artist, 1803-1877)   WC WI
   (British, 1803-1877)   GC
   Bibl: Mackenzie; ▶Witt checklist
Hunt, Charles   **GC WC**
Hunt, Charles II *(British artist,
b.1830)*   **WI**
Hunt, Daysy Vere *(Unknown artist)* **GC**
   Bibl: Gernsheim, Corpus Photog.
   of Drawings, 1716
Hunt, E. Aubrey   **PR WI**
   (American artist, 1855-1922)   WC
   (American painter, 1855-1922)   PR
   (British artist, 1855-1922)   WI
   Bibl: ▶Thieme-Becker
   E. Aubrey Hunt   PR
   Hunt   PR
Hunt, E. Aubry   **WC**
   Hunt, Edward Aubrey   WI
Hunt, E. Aubry → *see* Hunt, E. Aubrey
Hunt, Edgar   **WC WI**
   (British artist, 1876-1953)   WI
   (British artist, 19th cent.)   WC
   Bibl: Wood, Brit. animal ptrs.
Hunt, Edward Aubrey → *see* Hunt, E.
Aubrey
Hunt, Emily *(British artist, 1836-op.
1862)*   **WI**
Hunt, G.   **WC WI**
   (British artist, op.1823)   WC
   (British artist, op.1823-)   WI
Hunt, Gerry *(British painter, b.1927)* **BA**
   Bibl: Cambridge (GBR), Cambridge
   Univ., Kettle's Yard, Verbiage
   (1979)
Hunt, Harry Millson *(British artist,
op.1866-)*   **WI**
Hunt, Henry *(Canadian sculptor,
b.ca.1914)*   **BA**
   Bibl: ▶Artists Canada; Brodszky,
   Stones, bones
Hunt, Holman → *see* Hunt, William
Holman
Hunt, J. *(British artist, op.1865-)*   **WI**
Hunt, James   **WC WI**
   (British artist, 19th cent.)   WC
   (British artist, op.19th c.)   WI
Hunt, Jarvis *(American architect,
Chicago, Ill. ; nephew of Richard
Morris Hunt, 1859-1941)*   **AV**
   Bibl: ▶Withey, Amer. archts.
Hunt, John *(Irish, 20th c.)*   **BA**

Hunt, John Horbury   **AV BA**
   *(American architect in AUS,
   1838-1904)*   BA
   *(Australian architect, 1838-
   1904)*   AV
   Bibl: ▶Avery period. idx.; ▶Tanner,
   Archts. Australia; ▶Withey, Amer.
   archts.
Hunt, Joseph Rowland *(American
architect, son of Richard Morris
Hunt (1827-1895), worked in
partnership with his brother
Richard H. Hunt (1862-1931) under
the name of Hunt & Hunt, New
York City, 1901-, 1870-1924)*   **AV**
   Bibl: ▶Withey, Amer. archts.
Hunt, Maria *(British artist, op.1856-
1866)*   **WI**
Hunt, Marion Edith   **WI**
   (British artist, 1846-1931)   WI
   (British artist, 19th cent.)   WC
   Holman-Hunt, William, Mrs.
   (Marion Edith)   WI
**Hunt, Marion Elizabeth (Mrs.
William)**   **WC**
   Waugh, Marion Edith, Miss   WI
*Hunt, Marion Elizabeth (Mrs.
William)* → *see* Hunt, Marion Edith
Hunt, Myron   **AV BA**
   (American architect, 1868-1952) BA
   (American architect, California) AV
   Bibl: ▶Avery obit. idx.; LA
   Architect 1984 Dec., p.2; ▶WWW
   Amer., v.3
Hunt, Reuben *(British artist, op.
1881-)*   **WI**
Hunt, Rhoda H. *(British artist, op.
1884-1904)*   **WI**
Hunt, Richard → *see* Hunt, Richard I
Hunt, Richard Howard *(American
sculptor, b.1935)*   **BA**
   Bibl: ▶Cummings, Contemp.
   Amer. artists; ▶Havlice, Idx. art.
   bio.; ▶WW Amer. Art, 1976
Hunt, Richard Howland *(American
architect, eldest son of Richard
Morris Hunt (1827-1895), worked
in partnership with his brother
Joseph Rowland Hunt (1870-1924)
under the name of Hunt & Hunt,
New York City, 1901-, 1862-1931)*   **AV**
   Bibl: ▶Withey, Amer. archts.
Hunt, Richard I   **WI**
   (British artist, op.1640)   WC
   (British artist, op.1640-1642) WI
Hunt, Richard   **WC**
Hunt, Richard II *(British artist, op.
1882-)*   **WI**
Hunt, Richard Morris *(American
architect, 1827-1895)*   **AV BA**
   Bibl: ▶Dict. Amer. biog.; ▶Encyc.
   world art; ▶Macmillan encyc.
   archts.; ▶Withey, Amer. archts.

Hunt, Robert *(British scientific
author, photographer, 1807-1887)*   **BA**
   Bibl: ▶Dict. natl. biog.;
   ▶Gernsheim, Hist. photog.
Hunt, Ross *(American stonemason
and restorationist, San Antonio,
Tex)*   **AV**
   Bibl: Preservation news, 1988
   June, v.28, no.5, p.13
Hunt, S.V. → *see* Hunt, Samuel
Valentine
Hunt, Samuel Valentine   **WI**
   (British artist, 1803-)   WC
   (British artist, 1803-1892)   WI
   (Engraver, op.1853-1863)   WI
Hunt, S.V.   **WC WI**
Hunt, Sidney *(British painter, 1896-
1940)*   **BA**
   Bibl: ▶Johnson, Brit. artists;
   Southport (GBR), Atkinson Art
   Gall., Seven & Five Society (1979)
Hunt, Thomas *(British artist, 1854-
1929)*   **WC WI**
Hunt, Tom Greenwood *(British
artist, op.1875-1878)*   **WI**
Hunt, Tony *(British structural
engineer, London)*   **AV**
   Bibl: Blueprint (London), 1989
   Mar., no.55, p.34
Hunt, Violet   **WC WI**
   (British artist, 1856-)   WC
   (British artist, b.1856)   WI
Hunt, Wallace *(British architect,
d.1985)*   **AV**
   Bibl: RIBA journal, 1986 Jan., v.93,
   no.1, p.49
Hunt, Walter *(British artist, 1861-
1941)*   **WC WI**
Hunt, William → *see* Hunt, William
Henry
Hunt, William H.Thurlow *(British
artist, op.1883-1904)*   **WI**
Hunt, William Henry   **BA GC PR WC WI**
   (British artist, 1790-1864)   WC WI
   (British painter, 1790-1864)   BA PR
   (British, 1790-1864)   GC
   Bibl: ▶Fogg Mus. Libr. cat.;
   ▶Havlice, Idx. art. bio.; ▶Met.
   Mus. Art libr. cat.; ▶RILA/BHA;
   ▶Thieme-Becker; ▶Witt checklist
   Hunt, William   PR
   William Henry Hunt   PR
Hunt, William Holman   **BA GC PR WC WI**
   (British artist, 1827-1910)   WC WI
   (British painter, 1827-1910)   BA GC PR
   Bibl: ▶RILA/BHA; ▶Thieme-Becker;
   ▶Witt checklist
   Hunt   PR
   Hunt, Holman   GC
   William Holman Hunt   PR
Hunt, William Howes   **WI**
   (British artist, 1806-1879)   WI
   (British artist, 19th cent.)   WC
   Bibl: ▶Mallalieu, Brit. watercolour
   artists
Hunt, William Hoyes   **WC**

Hunt, William Hoyes → *see* Hunt,
William Howes

Hunt, William Morris **BA GC PR WC WI**
  (American artist, 1824-1879) WC WI
  (American painter, 1824-1879) BA PR
  (American, 1824-1879) GC
    Bibl: ▶Columbia encyc.;
      ▶RILA/BHA; ▶Witt checklist
  William Morris Hunt PR
Hünten, Emil **GC WC**
  (French artist, 1827-1902) WC
  (German painter, 1827-1903) GC
    Bibl: ▶Thieme-Becker
  Hünten, Johann Emil GC
Hunten, Franz Johann *(German*
  artist, 1822-1887) WC
Hünten, Johann Emil → *see* Hünten,
  Emil
Hunter → *see* Hunter, Robert I
Hunter [Unidentified] *(Irish painter)* PR
    Bibl: Jan.16, 1805, lot 15, and
      May 30, 1805, lot 12, and Mar.2,
      1812, lot A4. All sales were in
      Dublin.
Hunter, A. *(British artist, op.1842-)* WI
Hunter, Alexis **BA WI**
  (British artist, op.1977-1981) WI
  (New Zealander photographer,
    b.1948) BA
    Bibl: Hunter & Eastmond, ART
      NEW ZEALAND, 54 (1990)
      p.50-54, 92; London (GBR), ICA,
      ALEXIS HUNTER...(1978);
      London(GBR), Institute of Cont.
      Arts, ALEXIS HUNTER...(1978)
Hunter, B.F. → *see* Hunter, Blanche F.
Hunter, Blanche F. **WI**
  (British artist, 19th cent.) WC
  (British artist, op.1889-1907) WI
  Hunter, B.F. **WC**
Hunter, Carl J. *(American architect)* AV
    Bibl: Architecture: the AIA
      journal, 1987 May, v.76, no.5,
      p.184
Hunter, Clementine *(American*
  painter, ca.1883-1988) BA
    Bibl: ▶Cederholm, Afro-Amer.
      artists; Los Angeles (CA, USA),
      LACMA, Black Amer. art (1986);
      NPR; ▶Petteys, Women artists
Hunter, Colin *(British artist, 1841-*
  1904) WC WI
Hunter, Dard *(American designer,*
  1883-1966) BA
    Bibl: ▶Who was who [GBR], v.4
Hunter, Debora *(American*
  photographer, b.1950) BA
    Bibl: ▶WW Amer. Art, 1980
Hunter, Frederick Leo *(American*
  artist, 1863-1943) WI
Hunter, George *(Superintendent of*
  Elgin Watch Company and
  designer of First Universalist
  Church of Elgin, IL) AV
    Bibl: Historic Illinois, 1981 Oct.,
      v.4, no.3, p.8
Hunter, George **JG**

Hunter, George Leslie **BA WC WI**
  (British artist, 1879-1931) WC WI
  (British painter, 1877-1931) BA
    Bibl: ▶Harris, Scottish ptrs.;
      ▶Johnson, Brit. artists; ▶Waters,
      Brit. artists
  Hunter, Leslie **WC**
Hunter, George Sherwood **WC WI**
  (British artist, op.1855-, d.1920) WI
  (British artist, op.c.1882-m.
    1920) WC
    Bibl: ▶Waters, Brit. artists
Hunter, Henry *(Australian architect)* AV
Hunter, Ian *(British artist, b.1939)* WI
Hunter, J. **WC WI**
  (British artist, 19th cent.) WC
  (British artist, op.19th c.) WI
Hunter, James → *see* Hunter, James I
Hunter, James I **WI**
  (British artist, 1715-1745) WC WI
  Hunter, James **WC**
Hunter, James II *(British artist,*
  d.1792) WI
Hunter, John Kelso *(British artist,*
  1802-1873) WI
Hunter, John Young **PR WC WI**
  (British artist, 1874-1955) WC WI
  (British painter, 1874-1955) PR
    Bibl: Allen AM catalogue;
      ▶Thieme-Becker
  John Young Hunter PR
  Young-Hunter, John PR
Hunter, John, Mrs., (Mary
  Ethel) → *see* Hunter, Mary Ethel
Hunter, Leonard *(American*
  sculptor, 20th c.) BA
    Bibl: Hanover (NH, USA),
      Dartmouth College, Hopkins
      Center, Woodworks (1974)
Hunter, Leslie → *see* Hunter, George
  Leslie
Hunter, Mary Ethel *(British artist,*
  1878-1936) WI
  Hunter, John, Mrs., (Mary Ethel) WI
Hunter, Mary Sutherland *(British*
  artist, b.1899) WI
Hunter, Mary Young **WC WI**
  (British artist, 1878-1936) WI
  (British artist, op.c.1899-1914) WC
Hunter, Richard *(British artist, op.*
  20th c.) WI
Hunter, Robert *(Australian artist,*
  b.1947) BA
    Bibl: New York (NY, USA), Mus. of
      Mod. Art, 8 Contemp. Artists
      (1974)
Hunter, Robert → *see* Hunter, Robert I

Hunter, Robert I **WI**
  (British artist, op.1745-1803) WC WI
  (British, act.1752-1803) GC
  (Irish painter, act. 1752-1803) PR
    Bibl: ▶Dict. natl. biog.;
      ▶Thieme-Becker; ▶Waterhouse,
      Brit. 18c. ptrs.
  Hunter PR
  Hunter, Robert **GC PR WC**
  Robert Hunter PR
Hunter, Robert II *(British artist,*
  b.1920) WI
Hunter, Russell Vernon *(American*
  painter, museum administrator,
  author, 1900-1955) BA
    Bibl: ▶Samuels, Artists Amer.
      West
Hunting, Leonard **WC WI**
  (British artist, 20th cent.) WC
  (British artist, op.20th c.) WI
Huntington, Alonzo St. George
  (American artist, 1868-1941) WI
Huntington, Anna → *see* Huntington,
  Anna Hyatt
Huntington, Anna Hyatt *(American*
  sculptor, 1876-1973) AV BA GC
    Bibl: ▶Fielding's Amer. ptrs.; Getty
      Photo Study Coll.; ▶Libr. of
      Congr. Name Auth. File;
      ▶RILA/BHA; ▶WW Amer. Art,
      1966; ▶Young, Amer. artists
  Huntington, Anna GC
  Hyatt-Huntington, Anna **AV**
Huntington, Daniel **BA GC PR WC WI**
  (American artist, 1816-1906) WC WI
  (American painter, 1816-
    1906) BA GC PR
    Bibl: ▶Groce, Artists Amer.;
      ▶RILA/BHA; ▶Thieme-Becker
  Daniel Huntington PR
Huntington, Jim **BA WI**
  (American artist, op.20th c.) WI
  (American sculptor, b.1941) BA
    Bibl: Guide exh. artists: N. Amer.
      ptrs.; ▶WW Amer. Art
Huntington, Roswell *(American*
  silversmith, 1763-1836) BA
    Bibl: Bohen, EARLY CONN.SILVER;
      Kovel, Amer. silver
Huntington, Wallace *(American*
  landscape architect, Oregon) AV
    Bibl: House & garden, 1986 Sept.,
      v.158, no.9, p.140
Huntington, William *(American*
  silversmith, 1792-1874) BA
    Bibl: Kovel, Amer. silver
Huntly, Maria Antoinetta,
  Marchioness of *(British artist, op.*
  1830-1893) WI
Hunziker, Christian *(Swiss architect,*
  1926-) AV
    Bibl: Deutsche Bauzeitung, 1986
      July, v.120, no.7, p.10

Hunziker, Frieda (*Dutch painter,*
1908-1966)   **BA**
  Bibl: ▶Scheen, Ned. beeldende
    kunst.; ▶Vollmer, Künst.-Lex. 20.
    Jhr.
Hunziker, Hermann (*Swiss painter,*
1840-1910)   **BA**
  Bibl: Aarau (CHE), Galerie 6,
    Hermann Hunziker 1840-1910
Hunziker, Max (*German(?) artist,*
1901-)   **WC**
Hunziker, Rudy (*Architect, 1946-*)   **AV**
  Bibl: Architecture d'aujourd'hui,
    1985 Oct., no.241, p.87
Hunziker, Terry (*American interior*
designer, Seattle, Wash)   **AV**
  Bibl: House & garden, 1987 Feb.,
    v.159, no.2, p.112
Hunziker, Walter (*Swiss architect,*
1948-)   **AV**
Hunziker, Wolf (*Swiss*
architect/landscape architect,
Reinach)   **AV**
  Bibl: Anthos, 1987, v.26, no.3,
    p.1
Hunzinger, George Jakob   **AV BA**
  (*American cabinetmaker, 1835-*
  ca.1898)   **BA**
  (*American furniture*
  manufacturer and designer,
  1835-1899?)
                                          AV
  Bibl: ART AND ANTIQUES,
    III/1(JAN-FEB'80), 116-123;
    Nineteenth century, 1982, v.8,
    no.3-4, p.115; ▶Penguin dec. arts
Hunzinger, Werner   **WC WI**
  (*American artist, 1816-1861*)   **WI**
  (*American artist, 1816-p.1861*) **WC**
Huomi → see Lomi, Aurelio
Huot, Charles (*Canadian painter,*
1855-1930)   **BA**
  Bibl: ▶MacDonald, Can. artists
Huot, Francois (*French artist,*
c.1782)   **WC**
Huot, Robert   **BA WC WI**
  (*American artist, 1935-*)   **WC**
  (*American artist, b.1935*)   **WI**
  (*American painter, b.1935*)   **BA**
  Bibl: ▶Cummings, Contemp.
    Amer. artists; ▶MoMA libr. cat.
Huotelin, Paula (*Finnish architect*) **AV**
  Bibl: Arkkitehtuurikilpailuja, 1988,
    no.8, p.2
Hüpeden, Ernest (*American painter,*
act.1899, d.1911)   **BA**
  Bibl: Meyer, Folk artists biog. idx.;
    Stone, Clarion (winter 1985),
    54-63
Huppi → see Hüppi, Alfonso
Hüppi, Alfonso   **BA**
  (*German artist, op.1970*)   **WC**
  (*W.German painter, b.1935*)   **BA**
  Bibl: ▶MoMA libr. cat.; ▶WW Arts
    DEU
Huppi   **WC**

Huquier, Gabriel (*French painter,*
printmaker, dealer, 1695-1772) **BA**
  Bibl: ▶Bénézit; Clark Art Inst.
    Photo & Slide Dept.;
    ▶Thieme-Becker
Huquier, Jacques Gabriel   **GC WC**
  (*French artist, 1725-1805*)   **WC**
  (*French, 1725-1805*)   **GC**
  Bibl: ▶Witt checklist
Huquier, Nicolas (*French painter,*
17th c.)   **BA**
  Bibl: ▶Thieme-Becker
Hurd (*American, active late 19th*
century North Adams,
Massachusetts)   **JG**
Hurd, Jacob (*American silversmith,*
1702/03-1758)   **BA**
  Bibl: Kovel, Amer. silver; ▶Penguin
    dec. arts
Hurd, Kenneth E. (*American*
architect, Boston, MA)   **AV**
  Bibl: ▶AIA Pro File, 1985
Hurd, Mick (*British interior designer*) **AV**
  Bibl: World of interiors, 1988
    July-Aug., p.86
Hurd, Nathaniel   **WC WI**
  (*American artist, 1729-1777*)   **WI**
  (*American artist, 1730-1770*)   **WC**
  (*Engraver, 1729-1777*)   **WI**
Hurd, Peter   **BA WC WI**
  (*American artist, 1904-*)   **WC**
  (*American artist, 1904-1984*)   **WI**
  (*American painter, author, 1904-*
  1984)   **BA**
  Bibl: ▶Art Index, v.33; ▶WW
    Amer. Art, 1976
Hurd, Philip (*British artist, op.19th*
c.)   **WI**
Hurd, William (*British artist, op.*
1781-)   **WI**
Hurel, Suzanne (*French artist,*
1876-)   **WC**
Huret, Francois (*French, act. ca.*
1640)   **GC**
  Bibl: ▶Thieme-Becker
Huret, Grégoire   **BA GC WC**
  (*French artist, 1606-1670*)   **WC**
  (*French painter, 1606-1670*)   **GC**
  (*French printmaker, 1606-1670*) **BA**
  Bibl: ▶Bénézit; Lippincott's Dict.
    Biog.; ▶Thieme-Becker
Hurier, P.C. (*French ébéniste, act.*
ca.1770)   **GC**
  Bibl: French & Co; French & Co,
    stock #55675
Hurkmans, Jo. A. (*Dutch architect,*
Tilburg)   **AV**
  Bibl: ▶Federatie O jrbk., 1987
Hurlbring, Rolf (*Architect, Rheda-*
Wiedenbrück BRD)   **AV**
  Bibl: Bauwelt, 1984 Dec.7, v.75,
    no.46, p.1966
Hurlbut, Spring (*Canadian artist,*
b.1952)   **BA**
  Bibl: Toronto(ONT, CAN), Art
    Gallery of Ontario. SPRING
    HURLBUT...(1981)

Hurlbutt, Roger   **AV BA**
  (*17th century master carpenter,*
  active in Warwickshire)   **AV**
  (*English architect, act.1669-*
  1692)   **BA**
  Bibl: ▶Colvin, Brit. archts., 1978,
    p.440; Worsley, Country Life
    CLXXXII (4 Feb. 1988), 81
Hurlbutt, William   **AV BA**
  (*Carpenter active in*
  Warwickshire in latter part of
  17th century)   **AV**
  (*English architect, act.1670-*
  1684)   **BA**
  Bibl: ▶Colvin, Brit. archts., 1978,
    p.440
Hurle, Wolfgang (*West German*
photographer, b.1955)   **BA**
  Bibl: Munich (DEU), Galerie der
    Künstler, Fotografie: Porträt
    (1985)
Hurley → see Hurley, Edward Timothy
Hurley, Edward Timothy   **BA PR**
  (*American painter, 1869-1950*)   **PR**
  (*American painter, printmaker,*
  1869-1950)   **BA**
  Bibl: ▶RILA/BHA; ▶WWW Amer.
  Edward Timothy Hurley   **PR**
  Hurley   **PR**
Hurley, Robert Newton (*Canadian*
painter, 1894-1980)   **BA**
  Bibl: ▶MacDonald, Can. artists;
    ▶Natl. Gall. Canada libr. cat.,
    suppl.
Hurley, Wilson (*American painter,*
b.1924)   **BA**
  Bibl: ▶ARTbibl. mod., 5 #1728,
    12 #6294; ▶WW Amer. Art,
    1976, 1991-92
Hurlstone → see Hurlstone, Frederick
Yeates
Hurlstone Fairchild → see Fairchild,
Hurlstone
Hurlstone, Frederick Yeates   **PR WC WI**
  (*British artist, 1801-1869*)   **WC WI**
  (*British painter, 1801-1869*)   **PR**
  Bibl: ▶Yale Brit. artists list
  Frederick Yeates Hurlstone   **PR**
  Hurlstone   **PR**
Hurlstone, Richard   **WC WI**
  (*British artist, op.1764-, d.1777-*
  1780)   **WI**
  (*British artist, op.1764-1780*) **WC**
Hurn, David (*British photographer,*
b.1934)   **BA**
  Bibl: ▶Auer, Encyc. photographes;
    ▶Intl. dir. exh. artists, 1983
Hurn, P.S.   **WC WI**
  (*British artist, 19th cent.*)   **WC**
  (*British artist, op.19th c.*)   **WI**
Hurni, Peter (*Swiss engineer,*
Director of Bau, Betrieb und
Unterhalt der Nationalstrassen,
1929-)   **AV**
  Bibl: ▶Schweiz. Ingen. u. Archit.,
    1984-1985

Hurok Painter *(Etruscan vase-painter)*   GC
   Bibl: ▶Szilagyi, Etruszko-korinthosi

Hurrell, George *(American, 1904 -)*   JG

Hurrell, John *(British painter in NZL, b.1950)*   BA
   Bibl: Auckland (NZL), City Art Gallery, Recent NZL art (1983)

Hurry, Leslie   BA WC WI
   (British artist, 1909-)   WC
   (British artist, 1909-1978)   WI
   (British painter, scenographer, 1909-1978)   BA
   Bibl: LONDON(ENG), Imperial War Museum. NEO-ROMANTIC WATERCOLOURS(1981-82); ▶Met. Mus. Art libr. cat.; ▶MoMA libr. cat.

Hurson, Michael *(American painter, sculptor, b.1941)*   BA
   Bibl: ▶WW Amer. Art, 1989

Hurst, A.H. *(British, 18th century)*   GC
   Bibl: ▶Thieme-Becker

Hurst, Henry William Lowe (Hal) → see Hurst, Henry William Lowe, (Hal)

Hurst, Henry William Lowe, (Hal)   WI
   (British artist, 1865-1938)   WC WI

Hurst, Henry William Lowe (Hal)   WC

Hurst, Sam T. *(American architect, Montecito, Calif)*   AV
   Bibl: ▶AIA Pro File, 1987-88

Hurt, Louis Bosworth *(British artist, 1856-1929)*   WI

Hurtado de Mendoza, Esteban *(Spanish artist, op.1630)*   WC

Hurtado Izquierdo, Francisco *(Spanish architect, 1669-1725)*   BA
   Bibl: ▶Encyc. world art; ▶Portoghesi, Diz. arch. e urbanistica; ▶Thieme-Becker

Hurtado, Eva *(Spanish architect, Madrid)*   AV
   Bibl: El croquis, 1988 Oct.-Nov., v.7, no.36, p.90

Hurtador, Abel *(Peruvian architect, 20th cent)*   AV
   Bibl: Documentos de arquitectura y urbanismo: DAU, 1988 Aug., v.1, no.4, p.68

Hurter, Hans *(Swiss artist, 20th cent.)*   WC

Hurter, Johann Heinrich → see Hurter, Johann Heinrich von

Hurter, Johann Heinrich von   BA
   (Swiss artist, 1734-1799)   WC
   (Swiss painter, enamelist, 1734-1799)   BA
   Bibl: ▶Schweiz. Künst.-Lex.; ▶Thieme-Becker; ▶Witt checklist

Hurter, Johann Heinrich   WC

Hurtig, Martin Russell *(American painter, sculptor, b.1929)*   BA
   Bibl: ▶WW Amer. Art, 1981

Hurtrel, Georges *(French printer, publisher, act.1870-1887)*   BA
   Bibl: Wieck, OUD HOLLAND, XCV/3(1981), 155-161

Hurtrel, Simon   BA GC
   (French sculptor, 1648-1724)   BA GC
   (French, 1648-1724)   JG
   Bibl: ▶Bénézit; ▶Dict. biog. fran.; Getty Photo Study Coll. (Sculp.); ▶Lami, Sculp. fran. 18e s.; ▶RILA/BHA; ▶Thieme-Becker

Hurtrelle, Simon   GC JG
   Urtrel, Simon   GC

Hurtrelle, Simon → see Hurtrel, Simon

Hurtu, Jacques *(French artist, op. 1614-1619)*   WC

Hurtubise, Jacques   BA WC
   (Canadian artist, 20th cent.)   WC
   (Canadian painter, printmaker, b.1939)   BA
   Bibl: ▶Artists Canada; ▶Natl. Gall. Canada libr. cat.

Hurwitz, Sidney *(American artist, op.20th c.)*   WI

Husain, Rabiul *(Architect, Bangladesh)*   AV
   Bibl: Architecture + design, 1988 May-June, v.4, no.4, p.23

Husebye, Terry *(American photographer, b.1945)*   BA
   Bibl: Afterimage, VIII/5 (Dec. 1980)

Husemann, Dieter *(Architect, Germany?)*   AV
   Bibl: Detail, 1982 Sept.-Oct., no.5, p.537

Hushlak, Gerald *(British artist, b.1945)*   WI

Hüsing, Waldemar *(West German architect, d.1979)*   AV

Hüske, H. *(West German architect, Bielefeld)*   AV
   Bibl: Deutsche Bauzeitschrift, 1986 Oct., v.34, no.10, p.1231

Huskinson   WC WI
   (British artist, 19th cent.)   WC
   (British artist, op.19th c.)   WI

Huskinson or Huskisson, R. → see Huskisson, Robert

Huskinson, L.   WI
   (British artist, op.1839-1859)   WC WI

Huskisson or Huskinson, L.   WC

Huskinson, R. → see Huskisson, Robert

Huskinson, Thomas L.B. *(British artist, op.1927-1938)*   WI

Huskisson or Huskinson, L. → see Huskinson, L.

Huskisson, Robert   WI
   (British artist, 1820-1861)   WI
   (British artist, op.1832-m.c. 1854)   WC
   Bibl: Hall, Nottinghamshire

Huskinson or Huskisson, R.   WC
   Huskinson, R.   WI

Hüsler, Urs *(Swiss architect, St. Moritz)*   AV
   Bibl: l'Arca, 1989 Mar. suppl. arca 2, no.25, p.98

Husnik, Jakub *(German artist, 1837-1916)*   WC

Huson, Thomas *(British artist, 1844-1920)*   WC WI

Huss, Ernst H. *(Austrian architect, Vienna)*   AV
   Bibl: Planen Bauen Wohnen, 1989, no.127, p.31

Huss, Jozef *(Polish architect, 1846-1904)*   AV
   Bibl: Kwartalnik architektury i urbanistyki 1984, v.29, no.3-4, p.353-354

Hussem, Willem Frans Karel   BA
   (Dutch artist, 1900-)   WC
   (Dutch painter, sculptor, poet, 1900-1974)   BA
   Bibl: ▶Grote Winkler Prins; ▶Scheen, Ned. beeldende kunst.; ▶Vollmer, Künst.-Lex. 20. Jhr.

Hussem, William Frans Karel   WC

Hussem, William Frans Karel → see Hussem, Willem Frans Karel

Hussey → see Hussey, Philip

Hussey, Giles   BA WC WI
   (British artist, 1710-1788)   WC WI
   (British painter, 1710-1788)   BA
   Bibl: ▶Dict. natl. biog.; ▶Thieme-Becker; ▶Witt checklist

Hussey, James *(British artist, b.1949)*   WI

Hussey, Mary Rosamund *(British, act.1900-1910)*   BA
   Bibl: Cornforth, NATIONAL TRUST STUDIES(1981), 85; ▶Who was who [GBR], v.5

Hussey, Philip   PR WC WI
   (British artist, 1713-1783)   WC WI
   (British painter, 1713-1783)   PR
   (British, 1713-1783)   GC
   Bibl: ▶Thieme-Becker

   Hussey   PR

Hussey, Phillip   GC
   Philip Hussey   PR

Hussey, Phillip → see Hussey, Philip

Husson, Honoré Jean Aristide *(French sculptor, 1803-1864)*   BA
   Bibl: ▶Bénézit; ▶Thieme-Becker

Husson, Jerome Elisabeth *(French painter, 1767-1832)*   GC
   Bibl: ▶Bénézit

Hustwick, F.   WC WI
   (British artist, op.1800)   WC
   (British artist, op.1800-)   WI
   Bibl: ▶Wilson, Brit. marine ptrs.

Husum, Peter   **AV BA**
    (Danish copper-founder and
      sculptor, Copenhagen, d. ca.
      1619)   AV
    (Danish sculptor, bronze
      founder, act.1612-1619)   BA
    Bibl: ▶Encyc. world art; Münchner
      jahrb. der bildenden Kunst, XXVI
      (1975), 177-192; ▶Thieme-Becker
Huszar→see Huszar, Vilmos

Huszar, Vilmos   **BA GC PR WC**
    (Dutch artist, 1884-1960)   WC
    (Hungarian painter in NLD,
      1884-1960)   BA
    (Hungarian painter, 1884-1960) GC PR
    Bibl: ▶Bénézit; ▶RILA/BHA;
      ▶Scheen, Ned. beeldende kunst.;
      ▶Vollmer, Künst.-Lex. 20. Jhr.
    Huszar   PR
    Vilmos Huszar   PR
Hutchenberg→see Huchtenburgh, Jan
    van
Hutchenburgh→see Huchtenburgh,
    Jan van

Hutcheson, Walter *(British artist,*
    d.1910)   WI
Hutchings, Frank Townsend
    (American artist, 1869-1937)   WI
Hutchings, George *(Active New*
    York, NY, U.S. ca. 1846-1847,
    daguerreotypist)   JG
Hutchings, James *(British artist, op.*
    1849-1893)   WI
Hutchins, Robert S. *(American*
    architect, New York City)   AV
    Bibl: Architectural digest, 1989
      June, v.46, no.6, p.118
Hutchinson, D.C. *(American artist,*
    b.1869)   WI
Hutchinson, George W.C. *(British*
    artist, op.1875-1890)   WI
Hutchinson, Henry *(British artist,*
    1800-1831)   **WC WI**
Hutchinson, Jaqueth *(American*
    sculptor, b.1942)   BA
    Bibl: Framingham (MA, USA),
      Danforth Mus., Abstract art New
      Engl. (1983)
Hutchinson, John Maxwell *(British*
    architect, London)   AV
    Bibl: ▶RIBA members, 1984
    Hutchinson, Max   AV
Hutchinson, Leonard *(Canadian*
    painter, printmaker, b.1896)   BA
    Bibl: ▶Artists Canada; ▶Idx.
      Ontario artists; ▶Natl. Gall.
      Canada libr. cat., suppl.
Hutchinson, Max→see Hutchinson,
    John Maxwell
Hutchinson, Peter Arthur *(British*
    artist in USA, b.1930)   BA
    Bibl: ▶WW Amer. Art, 1976
Hutchinson, Robert *(Designer, San*
    Francisco)   AV
    Bibl: Interior design, 1984 Apr.,
      v.56, no.4, p.174

Hutchinson, Ron L. *(American*
    architect, partner in Kruger, Lake
    and Pogue, and Hutchinson,
    Brown and Partners, Albuquerque,
    NM, ca.1948-1984)   AV
    Bibl: New Mexico architecture,
      1985 Mar.-Apr., v.26, no.2, p.5
Hutchinson, Samuel *(British artist,*
    op.1770-1802)   WI
Hutchinson, Suzanne *(British artist,*
    op.20th c.)   WI
Hutchison, Frederick William
    (Canadian artist, 1871-1953)   WC
Hutchison, James   **WC WI**
    (British artist, 18th cent.)   WC
    (British artist, op.18th c.)   WI
Hutchison, Robert Gemmell *(British*
    artist, 1855-1936)   **WC WI**
    Bibl: ▶Mallalieu, Brit. watercolour
      artists
Hutchison, William Oliphant
    (British artist, 1889-1970)   **WC WI**
Hutchisson→see Hutchisson, William
    Henry F.
Hutchisson, William Henry F.   **WI**
    (British artist, 1815-1861)   WI
    (British artist, 19th cent.)   WC
Hutchisson   **WC**
Hutchtenberg→see Huchtenburgh,
    Jan van
Hutehmberg→see Huchtenburgh, Jan
    van
Hutenburg→see Huchtenburgh, Jan
    van
Hutenburgh→see Huchtenburgh, Jan
    van
Huter, Urbanus *(German painter,*
    act. ca.1500)   GC
    Bibl: Getty Photo Study Coll.
      (Douwes coll.)
Huth, Eilfried *(Austrian architect, b.*
    in Indonesia, lives in Graz, 1930-)   AV
    Bibl: ▶Libr. of Congr. Name Auth.
      File
Huth, Franz *(German painter, 1876-*
    1970)   GC
    Bibl: ▶Thieme-Becker
Hüther, Julius   **BA WC**
    (German artist, 1881-1954)   WC
    (German painter, 1881-1954)   BA
    Bibl: ▶Thieme-Becker; ▶Vollmer,
      Künst.-Lex. 20. Jhr.
Hüther, Tom *(West German*
    architect)   AV
    Bibl: Ville giardini, 1989 May, no.
      237, p.2
Hutherberg→see Huchtenburgh, Jan
    van
Hutin→see Hutin, Charles François

Hutin, Charles François   **BA GC PR WC**
    (French artist, 1715-1776)   WC
    (French painter, 1715-1776)   PR
    (French sculptor, painter, 1715-
      1776)   BA
    (French, 1715-1776)   GC
    Bibl: ▶Bénézit; ▶Neue deutsche
      Biog.; ▶RILA/BHA;
      ▶Thieme-Becker; ▶Witt checklist
    Charles Francois Hutin   PR
    Hutin   PR
Hutin, Pierre *(French artist, c.1720-*
    1763)   WC
Hutinot, Pierre *(French sculptor,*
    1616-1679)   GC
    Bibl: ▶Thieme-Becker
Hutler, Walter *(Austrian architect,*
    Linz)   AV
    Bibl: ▶Verzeich. Öst. Ziviltech.
Hutley→see Hulley, H.
Hutner, Paul *(Canadian painter,*
    b.ca.1948)   BA
    Bibl: ▶Artists Canada
Hutschenreuther, Lorenz *(German*
    porcelain manufacturer, 1817-
    1886)   BA
    Bibl: ▶Boger, World pott. & porc.;
      ▶Danckert, Euro. Porzellans;
      ▶Neue deutsche Biog.
Hutsebaut, Achiel *(Belgian*
    architect)   AV
    Bibl: Architecture d'aujourd'hui,
      1983 June, no.227, p.XIV
Hutson, B. *(Australian (?))*   GC
    Bibl: Gernsheim, Corpus Photog.
      of Drawings, 1418
Hutson, William Richard *(American*
    painter, b.1936)   BA
    Bibl: ▶Cederholm, Afro-Amer.
      artists; Cleveland (OH, USA), Mus.
      Art, 7 Amer. Artists (1983)
Hutt, Henry   **WC WI**
    (American artist, 20th cent.)   WC
    (American artist, b.1875)   WI
Hütte, Axel *(German photographer,*
    b.1951)   BA
    Bibl: ▶Babington Smith, Contemp.
      artists
Hutter, Albrecht *(German porcelain*
    painter, 1754-ca.1805)   BA
    Bibl: ▶Honey, Euro. ceramic;
      Kreiger, KEROMOS, 65(SEPT
      1974), 17-20
Hutter, Elizabeth *(Swiss (?)*
    architect)   AV
    Bibl: Progressive architecture,
      1982 July, v.63, no.7, p.54
Hutter, Emil *(German artist, 1835-*
    1886)   WC
Hutter, Franz Xaver *(German*
    printmaker, act.ca.1780)   BA
    Bibl: Pantheon XLI/4 (Oct-Dec
      1983) 335, 400; ▶Thieme-Becker
Hutter, Joos *(Swiss artist, 1914-)*   WC
Hutter, Sergio *(Italian architect)*   AV
    Bibl: Baumeister, 1989 Apr., v.86,
      no.4, p.62

Hutter, Wolfgang   **BA WC**
(Austrian painter, printmaker,
    b.1928)   BA
(German artist, 1928-)   WC
Bibl: ▶MoMA libr. cat.; ▶Vollmer,
Künst.-Lex. 20. Jhr.; ▶WW Austria

Huttinger, Peter (American painter,
printmaker, b.1953)   **BA**
Bibl: New York (NY, USA), New
Mus., Outside NY: Ohio (1980);
Oberlin (OH, USA), Oberlin Coll.,
Allen Mem. Art Mus., Art & social
change (1983); Washington, DC
(USA), Corcoran Gallery, 39th
biennial (1985)

Hutton, Dorothy (British artist,
b.1889)   **WI**

Hutton, Edward T. (British artist,
op.1879-)   **WI**

Hutton, Gary (Interior design)   **AV**
Bibl: Interior design, 1984 Nov.,
v.55, no.11, p.246

Hutton, John → see Hutton, John
Campbell

Hutton, John Campbell   **BA**
(British artist, 1906-)   WC
(New Zealander painter, glass
    engraver, b.1906)   BA
Bibl: ▶Libr. of Congr. Name Auth.
File; National Library of Canada,
JOHN HUTTON'S GLASS
ENGRAVINGS; ▶Who's Who [GBR],
1978

Hutton, John   **WC**

Hutton, Louisa (British architect)   **AV**
Bibl: Building design, 1988 July 1,
no.892, p.10

Hutton, R.L. (British artist, op.1912-
1917)   **WI**

Hutton, Stan (Canadian architect)   **AV**
Bibl: Fine homebuilding, 1989
Aug., no.55, p.42

Hutton, W.   **WC WI**
(British artist, op.1821)   WC
(British artist, op.1821-)   WI

Hutton, William Rich (American
artist, 1826-1901)   **WI**

Huttunen, Hannu (Finnish architect)   **AV**
Bibl: Arkkitehtuurikilpailuja, 1989,
no.7, p.2

Huusko, Jorma (Finnish architect)   **AV**
Bibl: Arkkitehti, 1985, no.4, p.52

Huut, Max van (Dutch architect,
Amsterdam, 1947-)   **AV**
Bibl: Deutsche Bauzeitschrift,
1988 Oct., p.208

Huvé, Jean Jacques (French
architect, 1742-1808)   **BA**
Bibl: ▶Lance, Dict. archts. fran.;
▶Thieme-Becker

Huwendiek, Klaus (West German
architect, Hamburg)   **AV**
Bibl: Deutsches Architektenblatt,
1985 Jan.1, v.17, no.1, p.83

Hux, William (English pewterer, act.
1700-1729)   **BA**
Bibl: Horst, A.J. van der, Antiek
XX/I (June-July 1985), 28; R.
Jackson, ENGLISH PEWTER
TOUCHMARKS, London 1970, 63

Huxley, Marion (British artist, op.
19th c.)   **WI**

Huxley, Paul   **BA WC WI**
(British artist, 1938-)   WC
(British artist, b.1938)   WI
(British painter, b.1938)   BA
Bibl: ▶Bénézit; ▶MoMA libr. cat.

Huybert van Westhoven → see
Westhoven, Huybert van

Huyberts or Huybrechts, Cornelis
(Dutch artist, 1669/70-c.1712)   **WC**

Huybrechts, Peeter (Flemish artist,
1614-c.1660)   **WC**

Huygens, Christiaan   **GC**
(Dutch artist, 1629-1695)   WC
(Dutch draughtsman, 1629-
    1695)   GC
Bibl: ▶Bénézit

Huygens, Christian   **WC**

Huygens, Christian → see Huygens,
Christiaan

Huygens, Constantijn I   **BA**
(Dutch draughtsman, 1596-
    1687)   GC
(Dutch statesman and humanist,
    1596-1687)   AV
(Dutch statesman, poet,
    draftsman, 1596-1687)   BA
Bibl: ▶Columbia encyc.; ▶Encyc.
world art; Getty Photo Study
Coll.; ▶Grote Winkler Prins;
▶Thieme-Becker

**Huygens, Constantijn, heer van
Zuilichen**   **AV**

Huygens, Constantin I   **GC**

Huygens, Constantijn II   **BA**
(Dutch artist, 1628-1697)   WC
(Dutch artist, statesman, 1628-
    1697)   BA
(Dutch draughtsman, 1628-
    1697)   GC
Bibl: ▶Bénézit; Getty Photo Study
Coll.; ▶RILA/BHA;
▶Thieme-Becker; ▶Wurzbach, NLD
Künst.-Lex.

Huygens, Constantin II   **GC**

Huygens, Constantin, II   **WC**

Huygens, Constantijn, heer van
Zuilichen → see Huygens,
Constantijn I

Huygens, Constantin I → see
Huygens, Constantijn I

Huygens, Constantin II → see
Huygens, Constantijn II

Huygens, Constantin, II → see
Huygens, Constantijn II

Huygens, Francois Joseph   **GC WC**
(Belgian artist, 1820)   WC
(Belgian painter, 1820-1908)   GC
Bibl: ▶Thieme-Becker

Huygens, Frederik Lodewijk   **GC WC**
(Dutch artist, 1802-1887)   WC
(Dutch painter, 1802-1887)   GC
Bibl: ▶Thieme-Becker

Huygens, Henriëtte Adriana (Dutch
draughtsman, 1835-1896)   **GC**
Bibl: ▶Scheen, Ned. beeldende
kunst.

Huygens, Philips (Dutch artist,
1633-1657)   **WC**

Huygens, Remmert W. (American
architect, Boston, Mass, 1932-)   **AV**
Bibl: Process: architecture, n.7,
1978, p.212

Huynet (French, active Nimes,
1870s)   **JG**

Huyot, Jean Georges → see Auriol,
George

Huys → see Huys, Pieter

Huys, Frans   **BA GC WC**
(early Netherlandish printmaker,
    1522-1562)   BA
(Netherlandish, 1522-1562)   GC
(Netherlandish artist, 1522-1562)   WC
Bibl: ▶Bénézit; HOLLSTEIN;
▶Thieme-Becker; ▶Wurzbach, NLD
Künst.-Lex.

Huys, Jan van (Dutch(?) artist,
17th/18th cent.)   **WC**

Huys, Pieter   **BA GC PR WC**
(early Netherlandish painter,
    printmaker, ca.1519-1584)   BA
(Flanders painter and
    printmaker, ca.1519-1584)   GC
(Netherlandish painter, ca.1519-
    1584)   PR
(Netherlands artist, op.1545-
    1577)   WC
Bibl: ▶Bénézit; ▶RILA/BHA;
▶Thieme-Becker

Huys   PR
Pieter Huys   PR

Huyschman → see Huysmans, Cornelis

Huysen, Hans (Dutch artist, 20th
cent.)   **WC**

Huysman → see Huysmans, Cornelis
Huysmann → see Huysmans, Cornelis
Huysmans → see Huysmans, Cornelis
Huysmans → see Huysmans, Jan
Baptiste

Huysmans, Cornelis   **GC PR WC**
  (Flemish artist, 1648-1727)   WC
  (Flemish painter, 1648-1727)   PR
  (Flemish, 1648-1727)   GC
    Bibl: ▶Thieme-Becker
  Corneille Huysmanns   PR
  Corneille Huysmans   PR
  Cornelis Huysmans   PR
  Hausman   PR
  Hausmann   PR
  Haussman   PR
  Houseman   PR
  Housman   PR
  Huijsman   PR
  Huisman   PR
  Huyschman   PR
  Huysman   PR
  Huysmann   PR
  Huysmans   PR
  Huysmans, Cornelisz   PR
  Michael van Huysman   PR
Huysmans, Cornelisz→see Huysmans,
  Cornelis
Huysmans, Houseman, Huisman or
  Huysman, Jacob→see Huysmans,
  Jacob
Huysmans, Jacob   **GC**
  (Flemish artist, c.1633-1696)   WC
  (Flemish, ca.1633-1696)   GC
    Bibl: ▶Thieme-Becker
  Huysmans, Houseman, Huisman
  or Huysman, Jacob   WC
Huysmans, Jan Baptist (Belgian
  artist, 1826-)   WC
Huysmans, Jan Baptist→see
  Huysmans, Jan Baptiste
Huysmans, Jan Baptiste   **BA PR**
  (Flemish artist, 1654-1716)   WC
  (Flemish painter, 1654-1716)   BA PR
  (Flemish, 1654-1716)   GC
    Bibl: ▶RILA/BHA; ▶Thieme-Becker;
      ▶Witt checklist; ▶Wurzbach, NLD
      Künst.-Lex.
  Huysmans   PR
  Huysmans, Jan Baptist   WC
  Huysmans, Jan-Baptist   GC PR
  J.B. Huijsmans   PR
  Jan Baptiste Huysmans   PR
  Jan Battista Huijsmans   PR
  Jean Hulsman   PR
Huysmans, Jan-Baptist→see
  Huysmans, Jan Baptiste
Huysmans, P.J. (Flemish artist, op.c.
  1800)   WC
Huyssen, Margareta (Dutch, act.
  1688-1706)   GC
    Bibl: ▶Thieme-Becker
Huyssen, van (Dutch(?))   GC
    Bibl: Giraudon; Gouradon
Huyssens, Peter (Flemish architect,
  1577-1637)   BA
    Bibl: ▶Oudin, Dict. architectes;
      ▶Portoghesi, Diz. arch. e
      urbanistica; ▶Thieme-Becker
Huyssum→see Huysum, Jan van
Huysum→see Huysum, Jan van

Huysum or Huijsum, Jacob van→see
  Huysum, Jacob van
Huysum or Huijsum, Jan van→see
  Huysum, Jan van
Huysum, Ad. (Dutch artist, op.1704) **WC**
Huysum, Jacob van   **GC PR**
  (Dutch artist, c.1687/9-1740(?))   WC
  (Dutch painter,
    1687/89-1741(?))   PR
  (Dutch, ca.1687-1740)   GC
    Bibl: ▶Thieme-Becker
  Huysum or Huijsum, Jacob van   WC
  Jacob V. Huysum   PR
  Jacob van Huysum   PR
Huysum, Jan van   **BA GC JG PR**
  (Dutch artist, 1682-1749)   WC
  (Dutch painter and
    draughtsman, 1682-1749)   GC
  (Dutch painter, 1682-1749)   BA PR
  (Dutch, 1682-1749)   JG
    Bibl: Getty Photo Study Coll.;
      ▶RILA/BHA; ▶Thieme-Becker;
      White, THE FLOWER DRAWINGS
      OF JAN VAN HUYSUM
  d'Oude van Huyssum   PR
  Huyssum   PR
  Huysum   PR
  Huysum or Huijsum, Jan van   WC
  J. V. Huysem   PR
  J. V. Huysum   PR
  J. van Huysem   PR
  J. Van Huysum   PR
  J. Van Huysun   PR
  J. Vanhuysum   PR
  J.V. Huysem   PR
  J.V. Huysen   PR
  Jan V. Huysum   PR
  Jan van Huijsum   PR
  Jan van Huysum   PR
  Jean Hulsman   PR
  John Van Huysum   PR
  Jonge van Huysen   PR
  San Van Huysum fecit 1720   PR
  V. Huysem   PR
  V. Huysen   PR
  V. Huysum   PR
  Van Hesen   PR
  van Huijssen   PR
  Van Huysem   PR
  Van Huysen   PR
  Van Huysman   PR
  Van Huysom   PR
  Van Huyson   PR
  Van Huyssum   PR
  Van Huysum   PR
  Van Huysun   PR
  Van Huyusm   PR
  Vanheysum   PR
  Vanhuysen   PR
  Vanhuyson   PR
  Vanhuysum   PR
  Vanhysom   PR
Huysum, Justus van→see Huysum,
  Justus van (I)

Huysum, Justus van (I)   **PR**
  (Dutch artist, 1659-1716)   WC
  (Dutch painter, 1659-1716)   GC PR
    Bibl: Getty Photo Study Coll.;
      ▶Thieme-Becker; ▶Witt checklist
  Huysum, Justus van   PR
  Huysum, Justus van I   GC
  Huysum, Justus, I van   WC
  Justus van Huijsum   PR
  Justus van Huysum (I)   PR
Huysum, Justus van I→see Huysum,
  Justus van (I)
Huysum, Justus van II (Dutch
  painter, ca.1685-1707)   GC
    Bibl: ▶Thieme-Becker
Huysum, Justus, I van→see Huysum,
  Justus van (I)
Huysum, Michiel van   **GC WC**
  (Dutch artist, op.1729-1760)   WC
  (Dutch painter and
    draughtsman, act.1729-1759)   GC
    Bibl: ▶Bénézit
Huzeshvili, Jemal Nikolaevich
  (Russian artist, 20th cent.)   WC
Huzjan, Zdenko (Yugoslav painter,
  b.1948)   BA
    Bibl: ▶Babington Smith, Contemp.
      artists; Ljubljana(YUG), Mala
      galerija, ZDENKO HUZJAN(1981)
Hvoslef-Eide, Didrik (Norwegian
  architect)   AV
    Bibl: Byggekunst: the Norwegian
      review of architecture, 1985,
      v.67, no.4, p.182
Hwa, Eng Thian (Architect, London) **AV**
    Bibl: Building design, 1989 Mar.3,
      no.926, p.24
Hyacinta Brandi→see Brandi,
  Giacinto
Hyacinth de La Pegna→see La Pegna,
  Hyacinth de
Hyacinthe Collin de Vermont→see
  Collin de Vermont, Hyacinthe
Hyacinthe Rigaud→see Rigaud,
  Hyacinthe
Hyams, Harriet (American stained
  glass artist, Palisades, N.Y)   AV
    Bibl: Stained glass, 1982-83 Fall,
      v.77, no.3, p.242
Hyams, William (British artist, 1878-
  op.1960)   WI
Hyatt, Alpheus, Mrs. →see Hyatt,
  Audella
Hyatt, Audella (American painter,
  1839-1932)   PR
    Bibl: ▶WWW Amer. art
  Audella Hyatt   PR
  Hyatt, Alpheus, Mrs.   PR
  Hyatt, Mrs.   PR
Hyatt, Derek   **WC WI**
  (British artist, 1931-)   WC
  (British artist, b.1931)   WI
Hyatt, Mrs.→see Hyatt, Audella
Hyatt, Thaddeus (1816-1901)   **AV**
Hyatt-Huntington, Anna→see
  Huntington, Anna Hyatt

Iacopo da Pontormo → *see* Pontormo
(Jacopo Carrucci)

Iacopo da Puntormo → *see* Pontormo
(Jacopo Carrucci)

Iacopo da Puntorno → *see* Pontormo
(Jacopo Carrucci)

Iacopo Ligozzi → *see* Ligozzi, Jacopo

Iacopo Ligozzi Veronese → *see*
Ligozzi, Jacopo

Iacopo Tintoretto → *see* Tintoretto,
Jacopo (Jacopo Robusti)

Iacopus Antonius Siverinus → *see*
Siverinus, Iacopus Antonius

*Iacovleff or Iakovieff, Alexander
Ievgienievitch* → *see* Jakovlev,
Aleksandr Evgen'evič

Iacovleff, Alexandre E. → *see* Jakovlev,
Aleksandr Evgen'evič

*Iacovleff, Alexandre
Evguenievitch* → *see* Jakovlev,
Aleksandr Evgen'evič

Iacucci, Paola *(Architect)*   AV
Bibl: Archetype, 1982 Fall, v.2,
no.4, p.26

Iacurto, Francesco *(Canadian artist,
1908-)*   WC

Iakobii, Valerian Ivanovich → *see*
Jakobij, Valerjan Ivanovič

Iakovlev → *see* Jakovlev, Aleksandr
Evgen'evič

Iakulov, Georgii → *see* Jakulov, Georgij
Bogdanovič

Iams, J. Howard → *see* Iams, John
Howard

Iams, John Howard *(American
painter, b. 1897)*   PR
Bibl: ▶WWW Amer. art
Iams, J. Howard   PR
John Howard Iams   PR

Ianelli, Arcangelo *(Brazilian painter,
b.1922)*   BA
Bibl: ▶Pontual, Artes plásticas
Brasil; Toronto (Ont, CAN), Art
Gal. of Ont., 10 Brazilian artists
(1975)

Iannelli, Alfonso   AV BA
*(Italian artist, monument
designer, 1888-1965)*   AV
*(Italian sculptor, designer in
USA, b.1888)*   BA
Bibl: ▶Bénézit; Chicago
architectural journal, 1985, v.5,
p.34; ▶Vollmer, Künst.-Lex. 20.
Jhr.; ▶WWW Amer. art

Iasos of Kollytos *(Greek sculptor,
2nd c BC (end))*   GC
Bibl: ▶Robertson, Greek art, p.364

Iavelli, Rita Catterina Maria Teresa
(Italian, b.1869, act.1890)   BA
Bibl: Comoli Mandracci, V., in
RAIMONDO D'ARONCO, 1981,
97, 101

Ibarra, Jose *(Spanish artist, 1688-
1756)*   WC

Ibarreche, Antonio *(Argentine
architect)*   AV
Bibl: Summa, 1985 Jan.-Feb., no.
208-209, p.92

Ibbertson → *see* Ibbetson, Julius
Caesar

Ibbeson, Graham *(British sculptor,
b.1951)*   BA
Bibl: Cambridge (GBR), Camb.
Univ., Fitzwilliam Mus., Bernard
Meadows (1980)

Ibbetson → *see* Ibbetson, Julius Caesar

Ibbetson, Denzil   WC WI
(British artist, op.1821)   WC
(British artist, op.1821-)   WI

Ibbetson, Julius → *see* Ibbetson, Julius
Caesar

Ibbetson, Julius Caesar BA GC PR WC WI
(British artist, 1759-1817)   WC WI
(British painter, 1759-1817)   PR
*(British painter, printmaker,
1759-1817)*   BA
(British, 1759-1817)   GC
Bibl: ▶Dict. natl. biog.;
▶RILA/BHA; ▶Thieme-Becker;
▶Witt checklist

Ebetson   PR
Ibbertson   PR
Ibbetson   PR
Ibbetson, Julius   PR
Ibbettson   PR
Ibbotson   PR
Ibbottson   PR
Ibbstston   PR
Ibetson   PR
Ibitson   PR
J. Ibbetson   PR
Julius Caesar Ibbetson   PR
Julius Ibbetson   PR

Ibbettson → *see* Ibbetson, Julius
Caesar

Ibbotson → *see* Ibbetson, Julius Caesar

Ibbotson, Steve *(British architect)*   AV
Bibl: Architects' journal, 1981
Nov.25, v.174, no.47, p.1034

Ibbott, Terence   WC WI
(British artist, 1941-)   WC
(British artist, b.1941)   WI

Ibbottson → *see* Ibbetson, Julius
Caesar

Ibbstston → *see* Ibbetson, Julius Caesar

Ibels, Henri Gabriel   BA GC WC
(French artist, 1867-1936)   WC
*(French printmaker, painter,
author, 1867-1936)*   BA
(French, 1867-1936)   GC
Bibl: ▶Bénézit; ▶Encyc. world art;
▶Witt checklist

Ibens, Paul *(French(?) interior
designer)*   AV
Bibl: Maison français, 1989 June,
no.427, p.94

Ibetson → *see* Ibbetson, Julius Caesar

Ibi, Sinibaldo   GC PR WC
(Italian artist, c.1475-c.1550)   WC
(Italian painter, 1475-1550)   PR
(Italian, ca.1475-ca.1550)   GC
Bibl: ▶Thieme-Becker; ▶Witt
checklist
Sinibaldo Ibi   PR

Ibitson → *see* Ibbetson, Julius Caesar

Ibn Hayyim, Joseph   BA
*(Hebrew illuminator in ESP, 15th
c.)*   BA
(Illuminator)   GC
Bibl: Bodleian Libr. facsim. ed. of
Kennicott Bible; Encyc. Judaica;
Getty Photo Study Coll.
(Medieval); Le Stampe e la
diffusione delle immagini ... (CIHA
24, Bologna 1979), 23-29; Roth,
Kennicott Bible
Hayyim, Joseph Ibn   GC
Joseph Ibn Hayyim   GC

Ibn Zabara, Moses ben Jacob
*(Hebrew scribe in ESP, act.1476-
1482)*   BA
Bibl: Encyc. Judaica; Le Stampe e
la diffusione delle immagini ...
(CIHA 24, Bologna 1979), 23-27;
Roth, Kennicott Bible, p.3

*Ibn Zayn al-Dīn Shīrāzī, Qaram
al-Dīn* → *see* Qaram al-Dīn ibn Zayn
al-Dīn Shīrāzī

Ibos, Jean-Marc *(French architect)*   AV
Bibl: Architecture d'aujourd'hui,
1985 June, no.239, p.22

Ibsen, Immanuel   BA WC
*(Danish painter, sculptor, 1887-
1944)*   BA
(Scandinavian artist, 1887-1944)   WC
Bibl: ▶Nørregård-Nielsen, Dansk
kunst; ▶Vollmer, Künst.-Lex. 20.
Jhr.; ▶Weilbach, Kunst.leks.

Icart, Louis *(French painter, 20th
century)*   GC
Bibl: ▶Bénézit

Icarus Painter *(vase-painter, ca. 475-
450 BC)*   GC
Bibl: ▶Beazley, Attic red-fig. vase-
ptrs.; Richter, Attic red-fig. vases

Icaza, Francisco *(Mexican artist,
20th c.)*   BA
Bibl: Diss. Abstracts Intl. (Dec
1977), 3111-A

Ichiura, Ken *(Japanese architect, act.
1940s-1950s)*   AV
Bibl: ▶Avery period. idx.

Ichter, Paul *(French architect)*   AV
Bibl: Technique et architecture,
1982 Dec.-1983 Jan., no.34, p.94

Iciar or Yciar, Juan de *(Spanish
artist, 1525-p.1550)*   WC

Ictinos → *see* Iktinos

Ida, Shoichi *(Japanese artist, b.1941)*   BA
Bibl: ARTFORUM XXV/3 (Nov
1986) p.102-107; ▶Babington
Smith, Contemp. artists; Guide
exh. artists: N. Amer. ptrs.; ▶Intl.
dir. exh. artists, 1982-1983

Idanoff *(Russian artist, 18th cent.)*   WC

Idé, Kazunari (Japanese architect) **AV**
Ides Reyniersz., Ide Reynier
(Dutch, 1739-1822) **BA**
Bibl: Belonje, TRANSACTIONS OF
THE MONUMENTAL BRASS
SOCIETY, XII/4(1978), 312-313
Ides, Cornelia Reynier (Dutch,
d.1807) **BA**
Bibl: Belonje, TRANSACTIONS OF
THE MONUMENTAL BRASS
SOCIETY, XII/4(1978), 312-313
Idrac, Jean Marie Antoine (French
sculptor, 1849-1884) **GC**
Bibl: ▶Thieme-Becker
Idromeno, Kolë (Albanian
photographer, 1860-1939) **BA**
Bibl: Girard, Hist. photography,
VI/3 (Jul. 1982) pp.241-256
*Idserts, Idserdts or Idsertz,
Pieter* → see Idserts, Pieter
Idserts, Pieter **GC**
(Dutch artist, op.1727-1771) **WC**
(Dutch draughtsman, 1698-
1781) **GC**
Bibl: Getty Photo Study Coll.;
▶Thieme-Becker; ▶Wright, Ptgs.
Dutch museums
**Idserts, Idserdts or Idsertz,
Pieter** **WC**
**Idsinga, Wilhelmina Geertruida
van** (Dutch artist, 1788-1819) **WC**
Ieperen, Johan Hendrik van (Dutch
painter, 1909-d. aft.1946) **GC**
Bibl: ▶Scheen, Ned. beeldende
kunst.
Ievan (Welsh scribe and illuminator,
2nd half 11th century) **GC**
Bibl: Alexander, Insular mss., p.89
Ifield, John (English potter, act.
1674, d.1716) **BA**
Bibl: Rackham, ENG.POTTERY;
Schmitzer, POST-MEDIEVAL
ARCHAEOLOGY, XI(1977), 103-
105
Ifold, Frederick (British artist, op.
1846-1867) **WC WI**
Igdirligil, Ahmed (Austrian
architect) **AV**
Bibl: Bauforum, 1987, v.20, no.
124, p.34
Igel, Peter (German artist,
op.1496-1515/16) **WC**
Igelsrud, Ann (American ceramist,
b.1953) **BA**
Bibl: Syracuse (NY, USA), Everson
Mus., New works in clay (1981)
Igin, Josif Il'ič (Russian caricaturist,
20th c.) **BA**
Bibl: ▶Natl. union cat., Jul-Sep
1976
Igler, Gustav (German artist, 1842-
1908) **WC**
Iglesias, Cristina (Spanish sculptor,
b.1956) **BA**
Bibl: Eindhoven (NLD), Stedelijk
van Abbemuseum, Christa
Dichgans, Lili Dujourie (1985)

Iglesias, Pedro (Spanish architect,
Madrid) **AV**
Bibl: 1988 June, v.52, no.547,
p.54
Ignace Duvivier → see Duvivier, Ignace
Ignacio de Iriarte → see Iriarte,
Ignacio de
Ignacio de Léon y Escoura → see Léon
y Escoura, Ignacio de
Ignacio Zuloaga → see Zuloaga,
Ignacio
Ignatius Sterne → see Stern, Ignaz
Ignatius van der Stock → see Stock,
Ignatius van der
Ignatov, Nikolaj (Russian painter,
20th c.) **BA**
Bibl: Dek. Iskusstvo SSSR (June
1974), 1-4, 56
Ignaz Marcel Gaugengigl → see
Gaugengigl, Ignaz Marcel
Ignaz Stern → see Stern, Ignaz
Ignazio Enrico Hugford → see
Hugford, Ignazio Enrico
Ignazio Hugford → see Hugford,
Ignazio Enrico
Ignazio Sterner → see Stern, Ignaz
Ignazio Sterni → see Stern, Ignaz
Ignazio Unterberger → see
Unterberger, Ignazio
Igounet de Villers, Charles-Andre
(French artist, 1881-1944) **WC**
Igton [Unidentified] (Unknown
painter) **PR**
Bibl: (June 24, 1813, lot 53, Del
Vecchio)
Iguel, Charles François Marie
(French sculptor, 1827-1893) **BA**
Bibl: ▶Bénézit; ▶Thieme-Becker
Ihara, Hidemi (Japanese architect) **AV**
Bibl: Progressive architecture,
1989 Dec., v.70, no.13, p.26)
Ihara, Michio (Japanese sculptor,
b.1928) **BA**
Bibl: ▶WW Amer. Art, 1976
Ihle, Hans Joachim (German
sculptor, b.1919) **BA**
Bibl: ▶Vollmer, Künst.-Lex. 20.
Jhr.; ▶WW Arts DEU
Ihle, Johann Eberhard (German
painter, 1727-1814) **GC**
Bibl: ▶Thieme-Becker
Ihle, John (American printmaker,
b.1925) **BA**
Bibl: Grand Forks(ND, USA),
Univ.of ND Art Gallery. IHLE,
SURVEY OF WORK (1976);
▶MoMA libr. cat.; ▶WW Amer.
Art, 1989
Ihlee, Eduard (German artist, 1812-
1885) **WC**
Ihlee, R. → see Ihlee, Rudolf
Ihlee, Rudolf **WI**
(British artist, op.1910-1955) **WI**
(German artist, 19th cent.) **WC**
Ihlee, R. **WC**
Ihly, Daniel (Swiss artist, 1854-1910) **WC**

Ihnatowicz, Maria (Polish artist,
20th cent.) **WC**
Ihriský, Vojtech (Czech sculptor,
20th c.) **BA**
Bibl: Rollerova, VOJTECH
IHRISKY(1978)
Iida, Yoshiko (Japanese architect,
1950-) **AV**
Bibl: Kenchiku bunka, 1987 Dec.,
v.42, no.494, p.22
Iijima, Naoki (Japanese designer,
Tokyo, 1949-) **AV**
Bibl: Ottagono, 1987 June, v.22,
no.85, p.36
Iimura, Taka (Japanese artist in USA,
b.1937) **BA**
Bibl: ▶MoMA libr. cat.;
Philadelphia (PA, USA), ICA, Video
art (1975)
Iisakkila, Leena (Finnish landscape
architect) **AV**
Bibl: Baumeister, 1989 Oct., v.86,
no.10, p.39
Ijkens → see Ijkens, Frans
Ijkens, Frans **BA PR**
(Flemish artist, 1601-c.1693) **WC**
(Flemish painter, 1601-1693) **BA PR**
(Flemish, 1601-1693) **GC**
Bibl: Champlin, Cycl. ptrs.;
▶RILA/BHA; ▶Thieme-Becker;
▶Witt checklist; ▶Wurzbach, NLD
Künst.-Lex.
F. Eijkens **PR**
Francoijs Eyckens **PR**
Frans Ijkens **PR**
Ijkens **PR**
Ykens, Eyckens or Ijkens, Frans **WC**
Ykens, Frans **GC PR**
Ijkens, Pieter → see Ykens, Pieter
IJlstra, Bouke Johan → see Ylstra,
Bouke Johan
Ijsenbrandt, Adriaen van → see
Isenbrant, Adriaen
Ikebe, Kiyoshi (Architect, Japan) **AV**
Bibl: Space design, 1985 Jan., no.
244, p.26
Ikeda, Sue Lung Li **AV**
Ikegami, Toshiroh (Japanese
architect) **AV**
Bibl: Domus, 1984 Sept., no.653,
p.69
Ikegawa, Shiro (Japanese artist in
USA, b.1933) **BA**
Bibl: Long Beach (CA, USA), CSU,
Black dolphin prints (1978);
▶MoMA libr. cat.
Ikegaya, Hajime (Japanese artist,
b.1955) **BA**
Bibl: Geneva (CHE), Musée Rath,
Art japonais d'aujourd'hui (1983)
Ikehara, Kenichiro (Japanese
landscape architect, environmental
designer, 1928-) **AV**
Bibl: Process: architecture, 1985
June, no.59, p.142

Il'ina, Lidija Aleksandrovna
(Russian printmaker, illustrator,
b.1915) **BA**
   Bibl: ▶Gorenflo, Bild. Künstler;
   ▶Intl. dir. exh. artists, 1983;
   ▶Vollmer, Künst.-Lex. 20. Jhr.
Ilan, Eli *(Israeli sculptor, b.1928)* **BA**
   Bibl: Cape Town (ZAF), S. African
   Natl. Gallery, Israeli art (1980)
Ilario Bonacolsi, Pier Giacomo → see
   Antico (Pier Jacopo Alari
   Bonacolsi)
Ilario Bonacolsi, Pier Jacopo → see
   Antico (Pier Jacopo Alari
   Bonacolsi)
Ilario da Viterbo **GC WC**
   (Italian artist, op.1393) **WC**
   (Italian painter, act. late 14th ·
   early 15th c) **GC**
   Bibl: TCI Umbria
Ilario Spolverini → see Spolverini, Ilario
Ilavský, Ján *(Czech painter, 20th c.)* **BA**
   Bibl: VTTVARNA KULTURA v.6
   (1981), 53-55
Ilcott, Terry *(British artist, b.1945)* **WI**
Ildibrandino, ser Cecco di → see Ser
   Cecco di Ildibrandino
Ilg, Fritz *(German artist, 19th cent.)* **WC**
Ilg, Gus *(Engraver)* **WI**
Ilgerl, Hans → see Ilgerl, Johann
Ilgerl, Johann **AV**
   Ilgerl, Hans **AV**
Iliazd *(Russian artist, author in FRA,*
   1894-1975) **BA**
   Bibl: ▶Bowlt, Russian avant-garde;
   ▶Fogg Mus. Libr. cat.; NOUVELLES
   DE L'ESTAMPE, 15 (May-June
   1974) p.18-20; NOUVELLES DE
   L'ESTAMPE, 26 (Mar-Apr 1976)
   p.28-29 [obit]
   Eganbyuri, Eli **BA**
   Il'iazd **BA**
Iligan → see Iligan, Ralph W.
Iligan, Ralph → see Iligan, Ralph W.
Iligan, Ralph W. *(American painter,*
   1894-1960) **PR**
   Bibl: ▶WWW Amer. art
   Iligan **PR**
   Iligan, Ralph **PR**
   Ralph W. Iligan **PR**
Iliprandi, Giancarlo *(Italian artist,*
   1925-) **WC**
Iliupersis Painter **GC JG**
   (Apulian vase-painter) **GC**
   Bibl: Trendall, Attic red-fig. vases
   Apulia
Ilja Efimovic Repin → see Repin, Il'ja
   Efimovič
Iller, Johann Heinrich *(Russian*
   painter, 18th century) **GC**
   Bibl: ▶Bénézit
Illgenfitz, Fritz *(German artist, 20th*
   c.) **BA**
   Bibl: Altenburg (DEU), Staat.
   Lindenau-Mus., Etching &
   engraving (1979)

Illidge, Thomas Henry *(British artist,*
   1799-1851) **WC WI**
Illies, Arthur Karl Wilhelm → see Illies,
   Karl Wilhelm Arthur
Illies, Karl Wilhelm Arthur **BA**
   (German artist, 1870-1953) **WC**
   (German painter, printmaker,
   1870-1952) **BA**
   Bibl: ▶Bénézit; ▶Neue deutsche
   Biog.; ▶Vollmer, Künst.-Lex. 20.
   Jhr.
Illies, Arthur Karl Wilhelm **WC**
Illig, Wolfgang *(German architect,*
   Munich, 1935-) **AV**
   Bibl: Deutsche Bauzeitung, 1985
   Sept., v.119, no.9, p.158
Illingworth → see Illingworth, Leslie
   Gilbert
Illingworth, Leslie Gilbert **WI**
   (British artist, 19th cent.) **WC**
   (British artist, b.1902) **WI**
   Bibl: ▶Waters, Brit. artists
Illingworth **WC**
Illingworth, Michael *(New Zealand*
   artist, 1932-) **WC**
Illman, Thomas *(Engraver, op.1824-,*
   d.1860) **WI**
Illustratore, L' *(Italian illuminator,*
   14th c.) **BA**
   Bibl: Rotili, LA MINIATURA
   GOTICA IN ITALIA
Ilonen, Pia *(Finnish architect(?))* **AV**
   Bibl: Arkkitehti, 1988, v.85, no.1,
   p.74
Ilse, Michael *(American landscape*
   architect, Houston, Tex) **AV**
   Bibl: Garden design, 1989
   Autumn, v.8, no.3, p.50
Ilsted or Ilstedt, Peter Vilhelm
   (Danish artist, 1861-1933) **WC**
Ilsted, Ida *(Danish, 19th c.)* **BA**
   Bibl: Wang Hansen, ARGOS, III
   (1988), p.7-22
Imagawa, Norihide *(Japanese*
   architect) **AV**
   Bibl: Space design, 1987 Jan., no.
   268, p.97)n encyclopedia of
   architects
Image, Selwyn **BA WC WI**
   (British artist, 1849-1930) **WC WI**
   (British painter, illustrator, 1849-
   1930) **BA**
   Bibl: ▶Busse, Maler u. Bildhauer
   19. Jahr.; ▶Johnson, Brit. artists;
   ▶Vollmer, Künst.-Lex. 20. Jhr.;
   ▶Who was who [GBR], 1929-40
Imai, Kenji *(Japanese architect)* **AV**
   Bibl: Kenchiku bunka, 1989 Apr.,
   v.44, no.510, p.135
Imbach, Walter *(Swiss architect,*
   Lucerne) **AV**
   Bibl: ▶Schweiz. Ingen. u. Archit.,
   1984-1985
Imbachhausen, Siegmund Haffner
   von *(German artist, 18th cent.)* **WC**
Imbault, Leonce Edouard *(French*
   artist, 1845-) **WC**

Imber, Jonathan *(American painter,*
   20th c.) **BA**
   Bibl: Boston (MA, USA), ICA,
   Boston now (1982)
Imbert, Anthony *(French artist, op.*
   1825) **WC**
Imbert, Hugnes-Eugène *(1807-*
   1875) **AV**
Imbert, J.F. *(French artist, op.1779-*
   m.1787) **WC**
Imbert, Jacques **AV**
Imer, Edouard Auguste *(French*
   artist, 1820-1881) **WC**
Imes, Birney *(American*
   photographer, 20th c.) **BA**
   Bibl: ▶Intl. dir. exh. artists, 1983;
   Rubinstein, Arts mag., LXIII (3
   Nov. 88) pp.72-75
Imhof, Eduard *(Swiss cartographer,*
   painter, b.1895) **BA**
   Bibl: Steffisburg, Kunsthaus, EIN
   SCHOPFERISCHES LEBENSWERK...
   (1985)
Imhof, Joseph A. *(American artist,*
   1871-1955) **WI**
Imhoff, Carl C.A. Baron von
   (German artist, op.1771-1777) **WC**
Imitation of the KX Painter *(vase-*
   painter, ca. 585-570 BC) **GC**
   Bibl: ▶Beazley, Attic bl.-fig. vase-
   ptrs.; Boardman, Attic Bl.-fig.
   Vases, (Komast Group)
Imkamp, 'Wilhelm *(German artist,*
   1906-) **WC**
Imlin, Jean-Louis III *(French*
   silversmith, d.1768, master 1746) **GC**
   Bibl: ▶Mabille, Orfèv. fran.
Immanratt → see Immenraet, Philips
   Augustyn
Immendorff, Jörg *(West German*
   painter, b.1945) **BA**
   Bibl: ▶Art Index, v.29; ▶Intl. dir.
   exh. artists, 1983; ▶MoMA libr.
   cat.; ▶Natl. union cat.; ▶WW Arts
   DEU
Immenraet → see Immenraet, Philips
   Augustyn
Immenraet, Emmelraet,
   Emmenraet etc., Michael
   Angelo *(Flemish artist, 1621-1683)* **WC**
Immenraet, Emmelraet, Emmenraet
   etc., Philips Augustyn → see
   Immenraet, Philips Augustyn
Immenraet, Philips Augustin → see
   Immenraet, Philips Augustyn

Immenraet, Philips Augustyn　　**GC PR**
　　(Flemish artist, 1627-1679)　　WC
　　(Flemish painter, 1627-1679)　　PR
　　(Flemish, 1627-1679)　　GC
　　　Bibl: Getty Photo Study Coll.
　　　(Ptgs.); ▶Thieme-Becker; ▶Witt
　　　checklist
　　Emmelraet, Philip Augustyn I　　GC
　　Immanratt　　PR
　　Immenraet　　PR
Immenraet, Emmelraet,
**　　Emmenraet etc., Philips**
**　　Augustyn**　　**WC**
　　Immenraet, Philips Augustin　　GC
　　Philips Augustyn Immenraet　　PR
Immerzeel, Anna Maria *(Dutch*
　　printmaker, 1817-1883)　　**GC**
　　　Bibl: ▶Scheen, Ned. beeldende
　　　kunst.
Immerzeel, Christiaan　　**GC WC**
　　(Dutch artist, 1808-1886)　　WC
　　(Dutch painter and printmaker,
　　1808-1886)　　GC
　　　Bibl: ▶Thieme-Becker
Immerzeel, J. *(Dutch artist, 1808-*
　　1858)　　**WC**
Imof, Gerard *(Swiss artist, 1940-)*　　**WC**
Imola, Innocenzo da→*see* Francucci,
　　Innocenzo (Innocenzo da Imola)
Imparato, Bernardino *(Italian*
　　painter, act. ca.1599)　　**PR**
　　　Bibl: ▶Thieme-Becker
　　Bernardino Imparato　　PR
　　Bernardo Imparato　　PR
　　Imparato, Bernardo　　PR
Imparato, Bernardo→*see* Imparato,
　　Bernardino
Imparato, Francesco *(Italian artist,*
　　op.1603)　　**WC**
Imparato, Girolamo　　**BA GC**
　　(Italian artist, op.1573-1621)　　WC
　　(Italian painter, act.1573-1621)　　GC
　　(Italian painter, ca.1550-ca.
　　1620)　　BA
　　　Bibl: ▶Bénézit; ▶Bolaffi; ▶Encyc.
　　　world art; ▶Thieme-Becker
Imparto, Girolamo　　**WC**
Imparto, Girolamo→*see* Imparato,
　　Girolamo
Imperiale→*see* Fernandi, Francesco
　　(Imperiali)
Imperiale, Gerolamo→*see* Imperiale,
　　Girolamo
Imperiale, Girolamo　　**BA**
　　(Italian artist, -c.1660(?))　　WC
　　(Italian painter, printmaker, act.
　　1622, d.ca.1639)　　BA
　　(Italian, d. ca.1660?)　　GC
　　　Bibl: ▶Bénézit; ▶Bolaffi;
　　　▶Thieme-Becker; ▶Witt checklist
Imperiale, Gerolamo　　**GC WC**
Imperiali→*see* Fernandi, Francesco
　　(Imperiali)
Imperiali, Fernandi→*see* Fernandi,
　　Francesco (Imperiali)

Imperiali, Francesco→*see* Fernandi,
　　Francesco (Imperiali)
Imperiali, Francesco (also Fernandi or
　　Ferrando)→*see* Fernandi,
　　Francesco (Imperiali)
Impey, Eugene Clutterbuck *(British*
　　army officer, photographer, 1830-
　　1904)　　**BA**
　　　Bibl: Thomas, Hist. of Photog. VII
　　　(1983), p.239; ▶Who was who
　　　[GBR], v.1
Imrie, Archibald Brown　　**WC WI**
　　(British artist, 1900-)　　WC
　　(British artist, b.1900)　　WI
Imsand, Marcel *(Swiss*
　　photographer, b.1929)　　**BA**
　　　Bibl: ▶Auer, Encyc. photographes
In the manner of Claude→*see* Claude
　　Lorrain
Incandela, Gérald　　**BA JG**
　　(American (b. Tunisia), 1952 -)　　JG
　　(Tunisian photographer, 20th c.)　　BA
　　　Bibl: PRINT COLLECTOR'S
　　　NEWSLETTER, IX/6(JAN-FEB 1979),
　　　180ff
Ince, A.C.　　**WC WI**
　　(British artist, 1868-)　　WC
　　(British artist, b.1868)　　WI
　　　Bibl: ▶Johnson, Brit. artists
Ince, Capt.　　**WI**
　　(British artist, op.1758-)　　WI
　　(British(?) artist, op.1758)　　WC
Ince, Captain　　**WC**
Ince, Captain→*see* Ince, Capt.
Ince, Charles Percy *(British artist,*
　　1875-1952)　　**WI**
Ince, E.S. *(British artist, op.1860-)*　　**WI**
Ince, Evelyn Grace　　**WC WI**
　　(British artist, a.1886-1941)　　WC
　　(British artist, circa 1886-1941)　　WI
Ince, Joseph Murray *(British artist,*
　　1806-1859)　　**WC WI**
Ince, William　　**AV BA WC WI**
　　(British artist, op.1754-1762)　　WC WI
　　(British cabinetmaker, d.1804)　　BA
　　(British cabinetmaker, fl. 1758-
　　1802)　　AV
　　　Bibl: FURNITURE HISTORY(1974),
　　　57; ▶Natl. union cat., 1956;
　　　▶Salverte, Ébénistes 18e s.;
　　　▶Thieme-Becker
Incerti, Achille *(Italian artist, 1907-p.*
　　1965)　　**WC**
Inchbold→*see* Inchbold, John William
Inchbold, John→*see* Inchbold, John
　　William
Inchbold, John William　　**PR WC WI**
　　(British artist, 1830-1888)　　WC WI
　　(British painter, 1830-1888)　　PR
　　　Bibl: ▶Thieme-Becker
　　Inchbold　　PR
　　Inchbold, John　　PR
　　John William Inchbold　　PR
Inchbold, Stanley *(British artist,*
　　1856-op.1921)　　**WI**

Incontri, Camillo　　**GC WC**
　　(Italian artist, 17th cent.)　　WC
　　(Italian, 17th century)　　GC
　　　Bibl: ▶Witt checklist
Incorpora, Giuseppe *(Italian, active*
　　Sicily ca. 1860-ca. 1873)　　**JG**
Incze, István *(Hungarian painter,*
　　b.1905)　　**BA**
　　　Bibl: MUVESZETTORENETI
　　　ERTESITO, xxiv/2 (1975), 145-146
Inczéné Sárkány, Ilona *(Hungarian*
　　craftsman, b.1918)　　**BA**
　　　Bibl: MUVESZETTORTENETI
　　　ERTESITO, XXIV/2(1975), 147
Indemio, Giovanni→*see* Fratino,
　　Giovanni (Giovanni de' Mio)
Indermaur, Robert *(American artist,*
　　op.1986-)　　**WI**
InderMühle, Karl Arnold *(Swiss*
　　architect, 1877-1933)　　**BA**
　　　Bibl: ▶Portoghesi, Diz. arch. e
　　　urbanistica; ▶Schweiz. Künst.-Lex.
India the Elder, Bernardino→*see*
　　India, Bernardino
India, Bernardino　　**BA GC**
　　(Italian artist, c.1528-1590)　　WC
　　(Italian painter, 1528-1590)　　BA GC
　　　Bibl: ▶Bolaffi; ▶Encyc. world art;
　　　▶RILA/BHA, 1986;
　　　▶Thieme-Becker; ▶Witt checklist
India the Elder, Bernardino　　**WC**
India, Bernardino (the Elder)　　**GC**
India, Bernardino (the Elder)→*see*
　　India, Bernardino
India, the Younger, Tullio→*see* India,
　　Tullio
India, Tullio　　**PR**
　　(Italian artist, p.1550-p.1624)　　WC
　　(Italian painter, aft.1550-ca.
　　1624)　　PR
　　　Bibl: ▶Thieme-Becker
India, the Younger, Tullio　　**WC**
　　Tullio India　　PR
Indiana, Robert　　**BA WC WI**
　　(American artist, 1928-)　　WC
　　(American artist, b.1928)　　WI
　　(American painter, sculptor,
　　b.1928)　　BA
　　　Bibl: ▶Contemp. artists; ▶WW
　　　Amer. Art, 1984
　　Clark, Robert　　WI
Indoni→*see* Indoni, Filippo
Indoni, Filippo　　**PR WC**
　　(Italian artist, op.c.1883)　　WC
　　(Italian painter, act. 1883)　　PR
　　　Bibl: ▶Thieme-Becker
　　Filippo Indoni　　PR
　　Indoni　　PR
Indrio, Anna Maria *(Danish*
　　architect)　　**AV**
　　　Bibl: Arkitekten, 1984 Dec.4,
　　　v.86, no.22, p.474
Induno, Domenico *(Italian artist,*
　　1815-1878)　　**WC**

Induno, Gerolamo   **GC WC**
  (*Italian artist, 1827-1890*)   WC
  (*Italian painter, 1827-1890*)   GC
    Bibl: ▶Thieme-Becker
Indyk, Shelley (*Australian architect*)   **AV**
    Bibl: Architectural review, 1988
    Oct., v.184, no.1100, p.94
Ineichen, Hannes (*Swiss architect,*
  Lucerne)   **AV**
    Bibl: ▶Schweiz. Ingen. u. Archit.,
    1984-1985, p.168
Ineichen-Meier, Irma (*Swiss painter,*
  b.1929)   **BA**
    Bibl: ▶Künst.-Lex. Schweiz 20.
    Jahrh.; ▶Lex. zeitgen. Schweiz.
    Künstler
Infante, Francisco (*Soviet artist,*
  b.1943)   **BA**
    Bibl: ▶Bénézit; Goya, 155 (Mar.-
    Apr. 1980) pp.286-291; ▶Intl. dir.
    exh. artists, 1982
Infield, Marinna Matricardi
  (*American sculptor, 20th c.*)   **BA**
    Bibl: Philadelphia (PA, USA),
    Temple University, Samuel Paley
    Library, The Tyler show (1974)
Inforette [**Unidentified**] (*Unknown*
  painter)   **PR**
    Bibl: Caiafa inventory dated 1676
Ingalls, Eve (*American painter,*
  printmaker, b.1936)   **BA**
    Bibl: ▶WW Amer. Art, 1978
Ingalls, Walter (*American painter,*
  1805-1874)   **BA PR**
    Bibl: ▶Groce, Artists Amer.;
    ▶RILA/BHA; ▶Young, Amer. artists
  Walter Ingalls   PR
Ingalton→see Ingalton, William
Ingalton, William   **PR WC WI**
  (*British artist, 1794-1866*)   WC WI
  (*British painter, 1794-1866*)   PR
    Bibl: Paviere, Brit. sporting ptrs;
    ▶Thieme-Becker
  Ingalton   PR
  William Ingalton   PR
Ingannati→see Ingannati, Pietro degli
Ingannati, Pietro degli   **BA GC PR WC**
  (*Italian artist, op.1529-1548*)   WC
  (*Italian painter, act. 1529-1548*)   PR
  (*Italian painter, act.1530-1548*)   BA GC
    Bibl: ▶Bolaffi; ▶Fredericksen &
    Zeri, Census; ▶RILA/BHA, 1986
  Ingannati   PR
  Pietro degli Ingannati   **PR**
Inganni, Angelo   **GC WC**
  (*Italian artist, 1807-c.1880*)   WC
  (*Italian painter, 1807-ca.1880*)   GC
    Bibl: ▶Thieme-Becker
Ingaramo, Ezio (*Italian architect,*
  Turin)   **AV**
    Bibl: Bauwelt, 1987 Apr.10, v.78,
    no.14, p.514
Ingber, S. (*Belgian interior designer,*
  Brussels(?))   **AV**
    Bibl: Restaurant and hotel design,
    1986 Nov., v.8, no.9, p.84

Ingeborg Psalter atelier (*French*
  illuminators, act. late 12th c.)   **GC**
    Bibl: Deuchler, Ingeborgpsalter,
    180-182
  Ingeborg Psalter shop   GC
  Ingeborg Psalter workshop   GC
Ingeborg Psalter shop→see Ingeborg
  Psalter atelier
Ingeborg Psalter workshop→see
  Ingeborg Psalter atelier
Ingegno→see Ingegno d'Assisi
Ingegno (Andrea di Luigi da
  Assisi)→see Ingegno d'Assisi
Ingegno (Andrea di Luigi)→see
  Ingegno d'Assisi
Ingegno d'Assisi   **WI**
  (*Italian artist, 1465-1516*)   WI
  (*Italian artist, c.1470-1516*)   WC
  (*Italian painter, act. 1484-1516*)   PR
  (*Italian painter, ca.1470-1516*)   GC
    Bibl: Getty Photo Study Coll.
    (Douwes coll.); Nat. Gall. cat.
    (GBR); ▶Thieme-Becker; ▶Witt
    checklist
  Alovigi Assisi   GC
  Aloysii d'Assissi   WI
  Andrea di Aloigi   PR
  Andrea di Luigi   PR
  Ingegno   PR
Ingegno (Andrea di Luigi da
  Assisi)   **GC**
Ingegno (Andrea di Luigi)   **PR**
  Ingegno, Andrea Alovigi   GC
Ingegno, Andrea Alovigi or
  Aloysii (d'Assisi)   **WC**
  Ingegno, Andrea di Luigi   GC
  L'Ingegno   PR
  Luigi, Andrea di   GC
Ingegno, Andrea Alovigi→see
  Ingegno d'Assisi
Ingegno, Andrea Alovigi or Aloysii
  (d'Assisi)→see Ingegno d'Assisi
Ingegno, Andrea di Luigi→see
  Ingegno d'Assisi
Ingelback→see Lingelbach, Johannes
Ingemann, Poul (*Danish architect,*
  Copenhagen, 1952-)   **AV**
    Bibl: ▶Danske Arkitekters
    Landsforbund, 1987-88
Ingemney, Franz-Maria→see
  Ingenmey, Franz Maria
Ingen→see Ingen, Hendrikus
  Alexander van
Ingen, E.   **WC WI**
  (*British artist, 19th cent.*)   WC
  (*British artist, op.19th c.*)   WI
Ingen, Hendrik van (*Dutch painter*
  and printmaker, 1833-1898)   **GC**
    Bibl: ▶Scheen, Ned. beeldende
    kunst.
Ingen, Hendrikus Alexander van
  (*Dutch painter, 1846-1920*)   **PR**
    Bibl: ▶Thieme-Becker
  Hendrikus Alexander van Ingen   PR
  Ingen   PR
  Ingen, Hendrikus Alexander von   PR

Ingen, Hendrikus Alexander von→see
  Ingen, Hendrikus Alexander van
Ingen, Jennifer van (*Dutch(?) artist,*
  20th cent.)   **WC**
Ingen, Johan van (*Dutch*
  draughtsman, 1918-d. aft.1965)   **GC**
    Bibl: ▶Scheen, Ned. beeldende
    kunst.
Ingen, Willem or Guillelmo van
  (*Dutch artist, 1651-1708*)   **WC**
Ingen, William Brantley van   **WC WI**
  (*American artist, 1858-*)   WC
  (*American artist, 1858-op.1928*)   WI
Ingenhoven, Robert (*German*
  architect, Neuss)   **AV**
    Bibl: Die Kunst, 1986 Jan., v.96,
    no.1, p.62
Ingenmey→see Ingenmey, Franz
  Maria
Ingenmey, Franz Maria (*German*
  painter, 1830-1878)   **PR**
    Bibl: ▶Thieme-Becker
  Franz Maria Ingenmey   PR
  Ingemney, Franz-Maria   PR
  Ingenmey   PR
Ingerle→see Ingerle, Rudolph F.
Ingerle, Rudolph F. (*American*
  painter, 1879-1950)   **PR**
    Bibl: ▶Thieme-Becker; ▶WWW
    Amer. art
  Ingerle   PR
  Rudolph F. Ingerle   PR
Ingham, Charles Cromwell   **WC WI**
  (*American artist, 1796-1863*)   WI
  (*British artist, 1796-1863*)   WC
Ingham, Elizabeth Howell
  (*American artist, op.1909-1933*)   **WI**
Ingham, Gillian (*British painter, 20th*
  c.)   **BA**
    Bibl: ARTSCRIBE, 16(FEB 1979)
Ingham, John Q. (*American*
  architect, cabinetmaker, and
  partner in Ingham and Veazie,
  Elmira, NY, 1838-ca.1918)   **AV**
    Bibl: Preservation League of New
    York State. Newsletter, 1984
    Sept.-Oct., p.4
Inghirami, Francesco (*Italian*
  painter, 1772-1846)   **GC**
    Bibl: ▶Thieme-Becker
Ingilby, William Amcotts, Sir
  (*British architect, 19th cent*)   **AV**
    Bibl: Country life, 1988 Aug.25,
    v.182, no.34, p.118
Ingle, John Stuart (*American*
  painter, b.ca.1932)   **BA**
    Bibl: ▶Art Index; ▶Intl. dir. exh.
    artists
Ingle, Laura (*British artist, op.1896-*
  1925)   **WI**
Ingleby, J.→see Ingleby, John

Ingleby, John   **BA. WI**
(British artist, 1749-1808)   **WI**
(British artist, 18th cent.)   **WC**
(British painter, act.1770-1790)   **BA**
Bibl: ▶Fisher, Watercolour ptrs.;
Llandudno (GBR), Mostyn Art
Gallery, The native land (1979)
Ingleby, J.   **WC**
Inglefield, Charlotte (British artist,
op.circa 1855-circa 1857)   **WI**
Inglefield, E.A. →see Inglefield,
Edward Augustus
Inglefield, Edward Augustus   **WI**
(British artist, 1820-1894)   **WI**
(British artist, op.1845-1870)   **WC**
Inglefield, E.A.   **WC**
Ingles, David N.   **WC WI**
(British artist, op.c.1810-1820)   **WC**
(British artist, op.circa 1910-
circa 1920)   **WI**
Ingles, George Scott (British artist,
1874-op.1934)   **WI**
Inglés, Jorge   **BA PR WC**
(Spanish artist, op.1455)   **WC**
(Spanish painter, act. 1455)   **PR**
(Spanish painter, act.1455)   **BA**
(Spanish, act.ca.1455)   **GC**
Bibl: ▶Bénézit; ▶Ceán Bermúdez,
Bellas artes ESP; ▶Encic. univ.
ilus.; ▶Post, Spanish ptg., v.4,
p.65 ff.; ▶Thieme-Becker
Jorge Ingles   **GC PR**
Inglese, Gaspare (Italian architect)   **AV**
Bibl: ▶L'Industria delle costruzioni,
1989 Apr., v.2, no.210, p.24
Inglis, Clarissa (Canadian artist,
20th c.)   **BA**
Bibl: ▶Intl. dir. exh. artists, 1983;
Windsor (Ont, CAN), Art Gallery
of Windsor, CLARISSA INGLIS...,
1986
Inglis, Esther   **WC WI**
(British artist, 16th cent.)   **WC**
(British artist, circa 1571-1624-
1625)   **WI**
Bibl: ▶Fisher, Watercolour ptrs.
Kello, Esther, Mrs.   **WI**
Ingold, Otto (Swiss architect, 1883-
1943)   **BA**
Bibl: ▶Portoghesi, Diz. arch. e
urbanistica; ▶Thieme-Becker;
▶Vollmer, Künst.-Lex. 20. Jhr.
Ingoli, Matteo   **BA GC**
(Italian artist, 1587-1631)   **WC**
(Italian painter, architect, ca.
1587-1631)   **BA**
(Italian painter,
ca.1585/87-1631)   **GC**
Bibl: ▶Bolaffi; ▶Thieme-Becker;
▶Witt checklist
Ingoli, Matteo (Il Ravennate)   **WC**
Ingoli, Matteo (Il Ravennate) →see
Ingoli, Matteo
Ingoni, Giovanni Battista (Italian
painter, 1528-1608)   **BA**
Bibl: ▶Bolaffi; ▶Thieme-Becker

Ingouf, Francois Robert, I (French
artist, 1747-1812)   **WC**
Ingpen, Robert Roger (Australian
artist, designer, author, b.1936)   **BA**
Bibl: ▶Encyc. Australian art
Ingram, C.   **WC WI**
(British artist, 19th cent.)   **WC**
(British artist, op.early 19th c.)   **WI**
Ingram, Earle (fl.1965; Architect,
draftsman, Ottawa)   **FA**
Bibl: Kalman, Noffke
Ingram, John (British in ITA, 1767-
1841)   **BA**
Bibl: MASTER DRAWINGS, XV/1
(spring 1977), 3-15
Ingram, Judith (American artist,
b.1926)   **BA**
Bibl: ▶WW Amer. Art
Ingram, Virginia (American sculptor,
printmaker, b.1929)   **BA**
Bibl: Shewmake, Woman's Art
Jrnl., V/1 (Spr.-Sum. 1984) pp.
40-46
Ingram, Whit (American sculptor,
b.1948)   **BA**
Bibl: New York (NY, USA),
Guggenheim Mus., New
perspectives (1983)
Ingram, William (American artist,
op.1858-1861)   **WI**
Ingram, William Ayerst (British
artist, 1855-1913)   **WC WI**
Ingres →see Ingres, Jean Auguste
Dominique
Ingres, J.A.D. →see Ingres, Jean
Auguste Dominique
**Ingres, Jean Auguste
Dominique**   **AV BA GC PR WC**
(1780-1867)   **AV**
(French artist, 1780-1867)   **WC**
(French painter, 1780-1867)   **BA GC PR**
(French, 1780-1867)   **JG**
Bibl: ▶RILA/BHA; ▶Thieme-Becker
Ingres   **PR**
Ingres, J.A.D.   **PR**
**Ingres, Jean-Auguste-
Dominique**   **JG PR**
Jean Auguste Dominique Ingres   **PR**
Ingres, Jean Marie Joseph   **BA**
(French artist, 1755-1814)   **WC**
(French painter, sculptor, 1755-
1814)   **BA**
Bibl: ▶Bénézit; ▶Thieme-Becker
**Ingres, Joseph (Jean Marie
Joseph)**   **WC**
Ingres, Jean-Auguste-Dominique →see
Ingres, Jean Auguste Dominique
Ingres, Joseph (Jean Marie
Joseph) →see Ingres, Jean Marie
Joseph
Ingvartsen, Marianne (Danish
architect, Copenhagen)   **AV**
Bibl: ▶Danske Arkitekters
Landsforbund, 1984-85

Inha, Into Konrad (Finnish
journalist, photographer, 1865-
1930)   **BA**
Bibl: Hist. photography, I/2 (Apr.
1977) pp.135-152
Iñiguez de Onzoño, José Luís
(Spanish architect)   **AV**
Bibl: Arquitectura, 1987 July-Aug.,
v.68, no.267, p.92
De Onzoño, José Luís Iñiguez   **AV**
Onzoño, José Luís Iñiguez de   **AV**
Iñiguez, Francisco (Spanish
architect, fl. early 1900's)   **AV**
Bibl: Seminario de arte aragones,
1985, v.39, p.229
Iñiguez, Manuel (Spanish architect,
1948-)   **AV**
Bibl: Das Kunstwerk, n.3-4, Sept.
1983, p.18
Injalbert, Antoine (French sculptor,
b.1845)   **GC**
Bibl: Getty Photo Study Coll.
(Sculp.); ▶Thieme-Becker
Injalbert, Jean Antoine   **GC**
Injalbert, Jean Antoine →see Injalbert,
Antoine
Inkret, Lovro (Yugoslav sculptor,
b.1949)   **BA**
Bibl: ▶Intl. dir. exh. artists
Inlander, Henry →see Inlander, Vienna
Inlander, Vienna   **WI**
(British artist, 1925-)   **WC**
(British artist, b.1925)   **WI**
Inlander, Henry   **WC**
Inman →see Inman, Henry
Inman or Inmann, Henry →see Inman,
Henry
Inman, Henry   **BA GC PR WI**
(American artist, 1801-1846)   **WC WI**
(American painter, 1801-1846)   **BA PR**
(American, 1801-1846)   **GC**
Bibl: ▶Britannica encyc. Amer. art;
▶Dict. Amer. biog.; ▶Encyc. world
art; ▶RILA/BHA; ▶Witt checklist
Henry Inman   **PR**
Inman   **PR**
Inman or Inmann, Henry   **WC**
Inman, John O'Brien (American
artist, 1828-1896)   **WC WI**
Inman, William Southcote (British
architect, 1798-1879)   **BA**
Bibl: ▶Colvin, Brit. archts.
Innder [Unidentified] (Unknown
painter)   **PR**
Bibl: (April 23, 1802, lot 62, Evill)
Innerst, Mark (American painter,
b.1957)   **BA**
Bibl: ARTS MAGAZINE LIX/2 (Oct
1984), p.2; New York (NY, USA),
Guggenheim Mus., New horizons
(1985)
Innes, George →see Inness, George
Innes, Here (Dutch artist, 17th
cent.)   **WC**

Innes, James Dickson **BA GC**
(British artist, 1887-1914) WC WI
(British painter, 1887-1914) BA
(British, 1887-1914) GC
Bibl: ▶Johnson, Brit. artists;
▶Thieme-Becker; ▶Waters, Brit.
artists; ▶Witt checklist

Innes, James Dixon **WC WI**
Innes, James Dixon→see Innes, James
Dickson

Innes, Michael William (British
architect) **AV**

Innes, Robert **WC WI**
(British artist, op.1833) WC
(British artist, op.1833-) WI

Innes, William T. (American, active
Philadelphia, PA, U.S. ca. 1900) **JG**
Inness→see Inness, George
Inness the Younger, George→see
Inness, George II

Inness, George **BA GC PR WC WI**
(American artist, 1825-1894) WC WI
(American painter, 1825-1894) BA PR
(American, 1825-1894) GC
Bibl: ▶RILA/BHA; ▶Thieme-Becker;
▶Witt checklist
George Inness PR
Inness, George PR
Inness PR
Inness, George, Jr. PR
Inness, Georges, Jr. PR

Inness, George II **BA**
(American artist, 1853-) WC
(American artist, 1854-1926) WI
(American painter, 1853-1926) BA
Bibl: ▶Busse, Maler u. Bildhauer
19. Jahr.; ▶Thieme-Becker;
▶Vollmer, Künst.-Lex. 20. Jhr.

Inness the Younger, George **WC**
Inness, George, Jr. **WI**
Inness, George, Jr.→see Inness,
George
Inness, George, Jr.→see Inness,
George II
Inness, Georges, Jr.→see Inness,
George

Innis, David (British artist, op.20th
c.) **WI**

Innis, J.P. (Engraver) **WI**
Innoc.o da Imola→see Francucci,
Innocenzo (Innocenzo da Imola)

Innocent **JG**
Innocent d'Imola→see Francucci,
Innocenzo (Innocenzo da Imola)
Innocent Francucci→see Francucci,
Innocenzo (Innocenzo da Imola)

Innocenti, Bruno (Italian sculptor,
b.1906) **BA GC**
Bibl: ▶Bénézit; ▶RILA/BHA;
▶Vollmer, Künst.-Lex. 20. Jhr.

Innocenti, Camillo (Italian artist,
1871-) **WC**

Innocenti, Roberto (Italian
engineer, 20th c.) **BA**
Bibl: Armstrong, ART NEWS,
LXXXVII/3 (Mar 1988), p. 162-
167
Innocenza da Imola→see Francucci,
Innocenzo (Innocenzo da Imola)
Innocenzio Ansaldi→see Ansaldi,
Innocenzo
Innocenzio Spinazzi→see Spinazzi,
Innocenzo
Innocenzo Ansaldi→see Ansaldi,
Innocenzo
Innocenzo da Imola→see Francucci,
Innocenzo (Innocenzo da Imola)
Innocenzo da Imola (Francucci)→see
Francucci, Innocenzo (Innocenzo
da Imola)
Innocenzo da Imola (Innocenzo
Francucci)→see Francucci,
Innocenzo (Innocenzo da Imola)

Innocenzo da Palermo (Fra) (Italian
sculptor, ca.1592-ca.1648) **GC**
Bibl: TCI Umbria
Fra Innocenzo da Palermo GC
Innocenzo Francucci→see Francucci,
Innocenzo (Innocenzo da Imola)
Innocenzo Francucci da Imola→see
Francucci, Innocenzo (Innocenzo
da Imola)
Innocenzo Tacconi→see Tacconi,
Innocenzo
Innoco da Imola→see Francucci,
Innocenzo (Innocenzo da Imola)

Ino, Pierre (French artist, 1909-) **WC**
...inos (Euboean? potter, ca. 700 BC) **GC**
Bibl: Boardman, Greeks Overseas

Inoue, Bukichi (Japanese architect) **AV**
Inoue, Yoko (Architect, Japan) **AV**
Bibl: Space design, 1984 Dec., no.
243, p.16

Insall, Donald William (British
architect) **AV**

Inscription Painter (vase-painter, ca.
475-450 BC) **GC**
Bibl: ▶Beazley, Attic red-fig. vase-
ptrs.; Richter, Attic red-fig. vases

Insetta, Michael (American artist,
N.J) **AV**
Bibl: Architecture, the AIA
journal, 1984 Jan., v.73, no.1,
p.51

Inshaw, David **BA WI**
(British artist, b.1943) WI
(British painter, b.1943) BA
Bibl: Brighton (GBR), Art Gall and
Mus, DAVID INSHAW (1978)

Insius [Unidentified] (Unknown
painter) **PR**
Bibl: Etienne Delessert inventory,
dated 1816, item 176

Inskip, Peter (British architect,
London) **AV**
Bibl: ▶RIBA members, 1983

Inskipp, James **GC WC WI**
(British artist, 1790-1868) WC WI
(British, 1790-1868) GC
Bibl: ▶Witt checklist

Insley, Albert Babb (American
artist, 1842-1937) **WI**

Insley, Henry E. (American
photographer, 1811-1894) **BA**
Bibl: HISTORY OF PHOTOGRAPHY,
VIII/4 (Oct-Dec 1984) 276; ▶Idx.
Amer. photog. colls.; Rinhart,
AMERICAN DAGUERREOTYPE

Insley, Will **AV BA WC WI**
(American architect, 1929-) AV
(American artist, 20th cent.) WC
(American artist, b.1929) WI
(American painter, b.1929) BA
Bibl: ▶Libr. of Congr. Name Auth.
File; ▶WW Amer. Art, 1976

Institoris (German artist, op.c.1830) **WC**

Inston, Peter Robert (English
architect, Belbroughton) **AV**
Bibl: ▶RIBA members, 1987

Instone, Jeff (British artist, b.1941) **WI**

Interguglielmi, Elia **BA WC**
(Italian artist, -1773) WC
(Italian painter, d.1773) BA
Bibl: ▶Bénézit; ▶Thieme-Becker

Intermediate Group **GC JG**
(South Italian vase-painters, 4th
century BC) GC
Bibl: ▶Trendall, Red-fig. vases
Lucania

Internari, Giovanni Battista (Italian
artist, op.1749-m.1761) **WC**

Introini, Vittorio (Italian architect) **AV**
Bibl: Ville giardini, 1988 Apr., no.
225, p.36
Intrombatore Padre→see
Trombatore, Giuseppe

Invernizzi, Enrica (Italian architect) **AV**
Bibl: Casabella, 1986 July-Aug.,
no.526, p.56

Invrea, Irene (French artist, 20th
cent.) **WC**

Inwood, Henry William (British
architect, 1794-1843) **AV**
Bibl: ▶Macmillan encyc. archts.
Inza→see Inza, Joaquin X.
Inza or Ynza, Joaquin X.→see Inza,
Joaquin X.

Inza, Joaquin X. **BA GC PR**
(Spanish artist, op.1784) WC
(Spanish painter, 1736-1811) BA
(Spanish painter, 1736-1811,
act. 1784) PR
(Spanish, act.1784) GC
Bibl: Getty Photo Study Coll.
(Ptgs.); GOYA, 152(SEPT-OCT
1979), 90-93; ▶Ossorio y Bernard,
Artistas españoles 19s.;
▶Thieme-Becker; ▶Witt checklist
Inza PR

Inza or Ynza, Joaquin X. **WC**
Joaquin X. Inza PR
Ynza, Joaquin X. GC

Io Painter *(Campanian vase-painter)* **GC**
Bibl: ▶Beazley, Attic red-fig. vase-ptrs.; ▶Trendall, Red-fig. vases Lucania

Ioachino [Unidentified] *(Unknown painter)* **PR**
Bibl: Botteri inventory, Milan, 1697

Ioan *(Romanian archimandrite, artist, 17th c.)* **BA**
Bibl: ARTA, XXVIII/9(1981), 3-4
Ioan Brixia →see Giovanni Antonio da Brescia

Ioan Iveropoulos *(Georgian painter in BGR, 11th c.)* **BA**
Bibl: Panayetova-Piguet, in L'ARTE GEORGIANA DAL IX AL XIV S. 187-197
Iveropoulos, Ioan BA

Ioannes *(Spanish illuminator and scribe, act. ca.920)* **GC**
Bibl: Williams, Early Span. mss. illum., pp.44-47

Ioannes Fiorentinus *(Italian sculptor in HUN, 16th c.)* **BA**
Bibl: Balogh, Ars Hungarica, II/1 (1974) pp.27-58

Iobates Painter *(South Italian vase-painter, 4th century BC)* **GC**
Bibl: ▶Trendall, Red-fig. vases Lucania
Iohannes Maria Falconetus →see Falconetti, Gian Maria

Iohanni di Niccolò *(Italian scribe, 15th century)* **GC**
Bibl: Brieger, Divine comedy, v.1, pp.240-322

Ionescu, Alexandru Dan *(Rumanian artist, 20th cent.)* **WC**

Ionescu, Gheorghe *(Rumanian artist, 1912-)* **WC**

Ionescu, Nicolae *(Romanian photographer, 1903-1974)* **BA**
Bibl: STUDII SI CEREFARI DE ISTORIA ARTEI, XXII(1975)

Ioni, G.Frederigo *(Italian artist, op. 19th c.)* **WI**

Ionides, Basil *(British architect)* **AV**

Iosa-Ghini, Massimo *(Italian architect)* **AV**
Bibl: Interiors, 1989 May, v.148, no.10, p.28
Iovene →see Iovene, Bernardo [Unidentified]

Iovene, Bernardo [Unidentified] *(Unknown painter)* **PR**
Bibl: Inventory of Giovanni Montoya de Cardona from 1718/06/28
Bernardo Giovenne ,PR
Bernardo Iovene PR
Iovene PR

Iovine, Giuseppe *(Italian painter, act. 17th century)* **PR**
Bibl: Giuseppe Iovine inventory dated 1634;
Gioseppe PR
Giuseppe Iovine PR
Iovino PR
Iovino →see Iovine, Giuseppe

Iovino, Giovanni Antonio [Unidentified] *(Italian painter, act. bef.1648)* **PR**
Bibl: Salernitano inventory, Naples, 1648
Giov. Antonio Iovino PR

Iphigeneia Painter **GC**
Bibl: ▶Beazley, Attic red-fig. vase-ptrs.
Ipousteguy, Jean →see Ipoustéguy, Jean Robert

Ipoustéguy, Jean Robert **BA**
(French artist, 1920-) WC
(French sculptor, painter, b.1920) BA
Bibl: ▶Bénézit; ▶Vollmer, Künst.-Lex. 20. Jhr.; ▶Witt checklist

Ipousteguy, Jean **WC**
Ippolito Borghese →see Borghese, Ippolito
Ippolito Casoli →see Casoli, Ippolito
Ippolito Costa →see Costa, Ippolito
Ippolito Scarsella →see Scarsellino (Ippolito Scarsella)
Ippolito Scarsella di Ferrara →see Scarsellino (Ippolito Scarsella)
Ippolito Scarsella Ferrarese, detto Scarsellino →see Scarsellino (Ippolito Scarsella)
Ippolito Scarsella, detto Scarsellino →see Scarsellino (Ippolito Scarsella)
Ippolito Scarsellino →see Scarsellino (Ippolito Scarsella)
Ippolito Scarsellino da Ferrara →see Scarsellino (Ippolito Scarsella)

Ippolito, Angelo **BA WC WI**
(American artist, 1922-) WC
(American artist, b.1922) WI
(American painter, b.1922) BA
Bibl: ▶NY art yrbk.; ▶Parry, Contemp. art; ▶WW Amer. Art
Ipsen →see Ipsen, Ernest Ludwig
Ipsen, Ernest L. →see Ipsen, Ernest Ludwig
Ipsen, Ernest Ludvig →see Ipsen, Ernest Ludwig

Ipsen, Ernest Ludwig **WI**
(American artist, 1869-) WC
(American artist, 1869-1951) WI
(American painter, 1869-1951) PR
Bibl: ▶WWW Amer. art
Ernest L. Ipsen PR
Ipsen PR
Ipsen, Ernest L. **PR**
Ipsen, Ernest Ludvig **WC**

Ipsen, Jacob *(Danish, 1756-aft.1781)* **GC**
Bibl: ▶Thieme-Becker; ▶Witt checklist

Ipsen, Paul **GC WC**
(Swedish artist, 1746-p.1781) WC
(Swedish, b.1746) GC
Bibl: ▶Thieme-Becker; ▶Witt checklist

Ira Jean Belmont →see Belmont, Ira Jean

Irace, Severo *(Italian painter, 16th c.)* **BA**
Bibl: ▶Bénézit; ▶Bolaffi; PROSPETTIVA, 46 (July 1986), p. 66-79; ▶Thieme-Becker

Irala Yuso, Matías Antonio de *(Spanish painter, printmaker, ecclesiastic, 1680-1753)* **BA**
Bibl: ▶Ceán Bermúdez, Bellas artes ESP; ▶Encic. univ. ilus.; ▶Thieme-Becker

Iranzo, Ubaldo *(Spanish architect, 19th cent)* **AV**
Bibl: El croquis, 1988 Aug.-Sept., v.7, no.35, p.54

Irelan, John Peters *(American interior designer, Washington, D.C)* **AV**
Bibl: Southern accents, 1988 Mar.-Apr., v.11, no.2, p.160
Ireland →see Ireland, A.M. [Unidentified]

Ireland, A.M. [Unidentified] *(Unknown painter)* **PR**
Bibl: (May 12, 1801, lots 397 & 401, Sotheby's)
A.M. Ireland PR
Ireland PR

Ireland, David **AV BA**
(American artist, b.1930) BA
(Architect-artist, San Francisco, CA) AV
Bibl: ▶Art Index, 1983; San Francisco (CA, USA), Capp Street, 65 Capp Street project (1984)

Ireland, Denise *(British painter in CAN, b.1949)* **BA**
Bibl: ▶Babington Smith, Contemp. artists

Ireland, Samuel **BA WC**
(British artist, op.1760-, d.1800) WI
(British artist, op.1760-m.1800) WC
(British author, printmaker, collector, act.1760, d.1800) BA
Bibl: ▶Dict. natl. biog.; ▶Redgrave, Engl. school; ▶Thieme-Becker

Ireland, Samuel I **WI**
Ireland, Samuel I →see Ireland, Samuel

Ireland, Samuel II *(British artist, op. 1882-1928)* **WI**
Ireland, Thomas →see Ireland, Thomas Taylor

Ireland, Thomas Taylor **WI**
(British artist, 19th cent.) WC
(British artist, op.1880-1927) WI
Ireland, Thomas **WC**

Iren, M. [**Unidentified**] *(Unknown painter)* **PR**
    Bibl: (March 8, 1810, lot 45, Jaubert)
    M. Iren **PR**

Ireson, Nathaniel **AV BA**
    (British architect, 1686-1769) **AV**
    (English architect, mason, 1686-1769) **BA**
    Bibl: ▶Colvin, Brit. archts.; ▶Thieme-Becker

Iriarte→see Iriarte, Ignacio de

Iriarte, Ignacio de **GC PR WC**
    (Spanish artist, 1621-1685) **WC**
    (Spanish painter, 1621-1685) **PR**
    (Spanish, 1621-1685) **GC**
    Bibl: ▶Thieme-Becker; ▶Witt checklist
    Ignacio de Iriarte **PR**
    Iriarte **PR**
    Yriarte **PR**
    Yriarte, Ignacio **PR**

Iriarte, Jose Maria *(Mexican artist, op.1852)* **WC**

Iriarte, Juan de *(Spanish wood carver, San Sebastian, 16th cent)* **AV**
    Bibl: ▶Thieme-Becker
    De Iriarte, Juan **AV**

Iriarte, Valerio *(Spanish painter, 1680/90-ca.1744)* **BA**
    Bibl: ▶Ceán Bermúdez, Bellas artes ESP, v.2, p.314; Perez Sanchez, BOLETÍN DEL MUSEO DEL PRADO, III (1982), 9, 147-156; ▶Thieme-Becker

Iribe, Paul **AV BA WC**
    (French architect, designer, 1883-1935) **AV**
    (French artist, -1935) **WC**
    (French caricaturist, decorator, designer, 1883-1935) **BA**
    Bibl: ▶Bénézit; ▶Libr. of Congr. Name Auth. File; ▶Penguin dec. arts; RLIN BKS file

Irie, Kei'ichi *(Japanese architect, 1950-)* **AV**
    Bibl: Japan architect, 1988 Nov.-Dec., v.63, no.11-12, p.36

Irinouchi, Akira *(Japanese architect, 1946-)* **AV**
    Bibl: Kenchiku bunka, 1987 Dec., v.42, no.494, p.52

Irion, Louis *(American cabinetmaker, Paoli, Penn)* **AV**
    Bibl: Colonial homes, 1989 Aug., v.15, no.4, p.65

Iris Marie Andrews Miller→see Miller, Iris Marie Andrews

Iris Painter *(Apulian vase-painter)* **GC**
    Bibl: Trendall, Attic red-fig. vases Apulia

Irish, Anthony Owen **AV**

Irland, Basia *(American artist, poet in CAN, b.1946)* **BA**
    Bibl: Stratford (Ont, CAN), Gallery/Stratford, The Ephemeris (1981)

Irmer, Carl **BA GC WC**
    (German artist, 1834-1900) **WC**
    (German painter, 1834-1900) **GC**
    (German painter, printmaker, 1834-1900) **BA**
    Bibl: ▶Bénézit; ▶Thieme-Becker

Irminger, Valdemar Henrik Nicolai *(Danish artist, 1850-1938)* **WC**

Irmisch, Hans *(German architect, act.1565, d.1597)* **BA**
    Bibl: ▶Portoghesi, Diz. arch. e urbanistica; ▶Thieme-Becker

Irolli, Vincenzo **GC WC**
    (Italian artist, 1860-1945) **WC**
    (Italian painter, b.1860) **GC**
    Bibl: ▶Thieme-Becker

Ironside, Robin **BA WC WI**
    (British art historian, painter, author, 1912-1965) **BA**
    (British artist, 1912-) **WC**
    (British artist, 1912-1965) **WI**
    Bibl: ▶Who was who [GBR]

Irton, Major→see Irton, Richard

Irton, Richard **WI**
    (British artist, op.1815-1841) **WI**
    (British artist, op.1820-1830) **WC**

Irton, Major **WC**

Irvin, Albert **BA WC WI**
    (British artist, 1922-) **WC**
    (British artist, b.1922) **WI**
    (British painter, b.1922) **BA**
    Bibl: ▶Bénézit; ▶Contemp. artists

Irvin, Willis *(American architect, 1819?-1950)* **AV**
    Bibl: ▶Avery obit. idx.

Irvine→see Irvine, Hugh

Irvine, Alan Montgomery *(British architect, London)* **AV**
    Bibl: ▶RIBA members, 1987

Irvine, Flavia *(British artist, op.20th c.)* **WI**

Irvine, Hugh **PR WC WI**
    (British artist, op.1808-1829) **WC WI**
    (British painter, act. 1808-1829) **PR**
    Bibl: ▶Graves Royal Acad. contribs.; ▶Thieme-Becker
    Hugh Irvine **PR**
    Irvine **PR**

Irvine, James Thomas *(British artist, 1826-circa 1900)* **WI**

Irvine, John/James **WI**
    (British artist, 1757-op.1834) **WI**
    (British artist, op.1787-1834) **WC**
    Bibl: ▶Waterhouse, Brit. 18c. ptrs.

Irvine, John/James? **WC**

Irvine, John/James?→see Irvine, John/James

Irvine, Keith *(American interior designer, New York City)* **AV**
    Bibl: NYC phone bk., 1987

Irvine, Wilson Henry *(American artist, 1869-1936)* **WC WI**

Irvine-Boswell, Margaret Christie *(British, d.1875)* **BA**
    Bibl: Bull. Detroit Inst. Arts, LVII/1 (1979) pp.41-45

Irving Ramsay Wiles→see Wiles, Irving Ramsay

Irving, J. Beaufain→see Irving, John Beaufain

Irving, J.Thwaite *(British artist, op. 1888-1909)* **WI**

Irving, John Beaufain **BA WI**
    (American artist, 1825-1877) **WI**
    (American artist, 1826-1877) **WC**
    (American painter, 1825/26-1877) **BA**
    Bibl: ▶Fielding's Amer. ptrs.; ▶Groce, Artists Amer.; ▶Thieme-Becker

Irving, J. Beaufain **WC**

Irving, Laurence Henry Forster **WC WI**
    (British artist, 1897-) **WC**
    (British artist, b.1897) **WI**

Irving, William *(British artist, 1866-1943)* **WI**

Irwin *(Engraver, op.1850-)* **WI**

Irwin→see Irwin, Benoni

Irwin, Benoni *(American painter, 1840-1896)* **PR**
    Bibl: ▶Thieme-Becker
    Benoni Irwin **PR**
    Irwin **PR**

Irwin, Gvyther→see Irwin, Gwynther

Irwin, Gwynther **BA**
    (British artist, 1931-) **WC**
    (British artist, b.1931) **BA WI**
    Bibl: ▶Dolman, Contemp. Brit. artists

Irwin, Gvyther **WC**
Irwin, Gwyther **WI**

Irwin, Gwyther→see Irwin, Gwynther

Irwin, Harriet Morrison *(American architect, 1828-1897)* **BA**
    Bibl: ▶Natl. union cat., pre-1956

Irwin, Leighton *(Australian architect and educator)* **AV**
    Bibl: Transition, 1988 Spring, no.26, p.101

Irwin, Leslie Chamberlain *(British artist, op.1886-)* **WI**

Irwin, Robert **AV BA WC WI**
    (American artist, 20th cent.) **WC**
    (American artist, b.1928) **WI**
    (American environmental artist, sculptor, 1928-) **AV**
    (American painter, sculptor, b.1928) **BA**
    Bibl: ART IN AMERICA, LXIV(MAR-APR 1976), 68; Clark Art Inst. Libr.; ▶WW Amer. Art

Is. Ostade→see Ostade, Isack van

Is. Vecchio→see Eismann, Johann Anton

Is: Ostade→see Ostade, Isack van

Isa'eva, Vera Vasil'evna *(Russian sculptor, b.1898)* **BA**
    Bibl: Ardentovo, V.V. ISA'EVA(1977); ▶Thieme-Becker

Isaac Brewster Hazelton→see Hazelton, Isaac Brewster

Isaac de Jouderville→see Joudreville, Isaac de

Isaac de Moucheron→see Moucheron, Isaac de

Isaac Elias→see Elias, Isaac

Isaac Fuller→see Fuller, Isaac

Isaac H. Keely→see Keeley, Isaac H.

Isaac Isaacsz.→see Isaacsz., Isaac

Isaac Koedijck→see Koedijck, Isaac

Isaac Koene→see Koene, Isaac

Isaac Master BA
 (Italian artist, 13th cent.) WC
 (Italian painter, 13th c.) BA
  Bibl: ▶Artist biog. master idx.;
  ▶Encyc. world art

Master of the Isaac Frescoes WC

Isaac Moucheron→see Moucheron, Isaac de

Isaac Oliver→see Oliver, Isaac I

Isaac Oliver (I)→see Oliver, Isaac I

Isaac Ostade→see Ostade, Isack van

Isaac Pocock→see Pocock, Isaac

Isaac Sailmaker→see Sailmaker, Isaac

Isaac Sheffield→see Sheffield, Isaac

Isaac van Duynen→see Duynen, Isaac van

Isaac van Ostade→see Ostade, Isack van

Isaac Vogelsang→see Vogelsang, Isaac

Isaac, Isaacs, Isac etc., Jaspar de→see Isaac, Jaspar de

Isaac, Jaspar de BA GC
 (Dutch printmaker, d.1654) GC
 (Dutch printmaker, publisher in FRA, act.1612, d.1654) BA
 (Flemish artist, op.1612-m.1654) WC
  Bibl: ▶Bénézit; ▶Thieme-Becker;
  ▶Witt checklist; ▶Wurzbach, NLD Künst.-Lex.

Isaac, Isaacs, Isac etc., Jaspar de WC
Isac, Gaspard de GC

Isaac, John R. (British artist, op. 1847-m.1871) WC

Isaac, Richard (Canadian architect) AV
  Bibl: Canadian architect, 1987 Dec., v.32, no.12, p.22

Isaac-Rose, Edith (American artist, 20th c.) BA
  Bibl: Langer, C.,ARTS, LXII (Dec 1987), p.98

Isaace Ostade→see Ostade, Isack van

Isaachsen, Olaf Wilhelm (Norwegian artist, 1835-1893) WC

Isaack Iacksz.→see Isaacsz., Isaac

Isaack Luttichuijs→see Luttichuijs, Isaack

Isaack Ostade→see Ostade, Isack van

Isaack Speeck→see Speeck, Isaack

Isaack van Ostade→see Ostade, Isack van

Isaacq Jansz. [Unidentified]
 (Unknown painter, act. 17th century) PR
  Bibl: Blaeuw inventory 1648

Isaacs, Esther S.→see Sutro, Esther Stella

Isaacs, Esther Stella, Miss→see Sutro, Esther Stella

Isaacs, Ron (American painter, b.1941) BA
  Bibl: ▶WW Amer. Art, 1978

Isaacson, Joseph Jacob (Dutch draughtsman, 1859-1942) GC
  Bibl: ▶Scheen, Ned. beeldende kunst.

Isaacson, Lynn (American artist, 20th c.) BA
  Bibl: Klein, E.L., in ARTS MAGAZINE LVIII/1 (Sept 1983) 12

Isaacsz, Isacs, Isacson etc., Isaac→see Isaacsz., Isaac

Isaacsz.→see Isaacsz., Pieter Fransz.

Isaacsz., Isaac GC PR
 (Dutch artist, 1599-p.1665) WC
 (Dutch painter, 1599-1665) PR
 (Dutch painter, 1599-aft.1665) GC
  Bibl: Getty Photo Study Coll.;
  ▶Thieme-Becker; ▶Witt checklist
Isaac Isaacsz. PR
Isaack Iacksz. PR

Isaacsz, Isacs, Isacson etc., Isaac WC

Isaacsz., Isaachsen, Isacs or Isaksen, Pieter Fransz.→see Isaacsz., Pieter Fransz.

Isaacsz., Pieter Fransz. BA GC PR
 (Belgian painter, 1569-1625) PR
 (Danish artist, 1569-1625) WC
 (Danish, 1569-1625) GC
 (Dutch painter, 1569-1625) BA
  Bibl: ▶Thieme-Becker; ▶Witt checklist; ▶Wurzbach, NLD Künst.-Lex.
Isaacsz. PR

Isaacsz., Isaachsen, Isacs or Isaksen, Pieter Fransz. WC
Pieter Fransz. Isaacsz. PR
Pieter Isaacx PR

Isaak Il'ic Levitan→see Levitan, Isaak Il'ič

Isaak Kleynhens→see Kleynhens, Isaak

Isaak Major→see Major, Isaak

Isaak Nickelen→see Nickelen, Isaak

Isaak Ouwater→see Ouwater, Isaak

Isaak Soreau→see Soreau, Isaak

Isaak Van Nikkelen→see Nickelen, Isaak

Isaak Vromans→see Vromans, Isaak

Isabella Siras→see Siras, Isabella [Unidentified]

Isabelli [Unidentified] (Unknown painter) PR
  Bibl: Botteri inventory, Milan, 1697

Isabello, Leonardo (Italian architect, act.1544-1556) BA
  Bibl: Caciagli, ARCHIVIO STORICO BERGAMASCO, IV/2 (1984), 265; ▶Thieme-Becker

Isabey→see Isabey, Eugène

Isabey, Eugène BA GC PR
 (French artist, 1803-1886) WC
 (French painter, 1803-1886) PR
 (French painter, printmaker, 1803-1886) BA
 (French, 1803-1886) GC
  Bibl: ▶Bénézit; ▶Encyc. world art; Getty Photo Study Coll. (Ptgs.); ▶Petit Robert 2; ▶RILA/BHA; ▶Thieme-Becker; ▶Witt checklist
Isabey PR

Isabey, Eugene (Louis Gabriel Eugene) WC
Isabey, Eugene Louis Gabriel PR
Isabey, Eugene-Louis-Gabriel PR

Isabey, Louis Gabriel Eugène BA GC PR
Isabey, Louis-Gabriel-Eugene PR
Louis Gabriel Eugene Isabey PR

Isabey, Eugene (Louis Gabriel Eugène)→see Isabey, Eugène

Isabey, Eugene Louis Gabriel→see Isabey, Eugène

Isabey, Eugene-Louis-Gabriel→see Isabey, Eugène

Isabey, Jean Baptiste BA WC
 (French artist, 1767-1855) WC
 (French painter, 1767-1855) GC
 (French painter, printmaker, 1767-1855) BA
  Bibl: ▶Bénézit; ▶Dict. biog. fran.; ▶Larousse grande encyc.; ▶Thieme-Becker; ▶Witt checklist

Isabey, Jean-Baptiste GC
Isabey, Jean-Baptiste→see Isabey, Jean Baptiste

Isabey, Louis Gabriel Eugène→see Isabey, Eugène

Isabey, Louis-Gabriel-Eugène→see Isabey, Eugène

Isac, Gaspard de→see Isaac, Jaspar de

Isacco or Isaach de Imbonate (Italian artist, op.1402-1423) WC

Isack van Ostade→see Ostade, Isack van

Isacq van Ostade→see Ostade, Isack van

Isager, Kristian (Danish architect) AV
  Bibl: Arkitektur DK, 1986 Aug., v.30, no.4, p.158

Isaia da Pisa BA GC
 (Italian sculptor, act. ca. 1450) GC
 (Italian sculptor, act.1450) BA
  Bibl: ▶Encyc. world art; Pelican Hist. of Art; ▶RILA/BHA; ▶Thieme-Becker

Isaiah Master (French stained glass worker, 13th c.) BA
  Bibl: ART BULLETIN, LIX(4 DEC. 1977), 483-493

Isaias van de Velde→see Velde, Esaias I van de

Isaksen, Rune Fink (Danish architect) AV
  Bibl: Arkitektur DK, 1984 Sept., v.28, no.5, p.199

Isakson, Karl Oscar **BA GC**
    (Scandinavian, 1878-1922) GC
    (Swedish artist, 1878-1922) WC
    (Swedish painter, 1878-1922) BA
    Bibl: ▶Thieme-Becker; ▶Weilbach,
    Kunst.leks.; ▶Witt checklist
Isaksons, Karl Oscar **WC**
Isaksons, Karl Oscar → see Isakson,
Karl Oscar
Isarecker, Ulrich (German architect,
    act.1433-1458) **BA**
    Bibl: Ars Bavarica, 35-36 (1984)
    pp.119-127
Isbrand, Victor (Danish painter,
    b.1897) **BA**
    Bibl: ▶Nørregård-Nielsen, Dansk
    kunst; ▶Thieme-Becker;
    ▶Weilbach, Kunst.leks.
Iscelenov, Nikolaj (Russian architect,
    20th c.) **BA**
    Bibl: Dek. Iskusstvo SSSR, 246
    (May 1978) p.32
Ischelan, Hans (German artist, 1873-
    1964) **WC**
Isefjord Master (Danish painter, act.
    1450-1475) **BA**
    Bibl: Reinholdt, GRAS 35 (1983),
    4-7; Trap, Kongeriget DNK:
    personalregister, v.3, p.133;
    ▶Weilbach, Kunst.leks.
Iseli, Rolf **BA WC**
    (Swiss artist, 20th cent.) WC
    (Swiss artist, b.1934) BA
    Bibl: ▶Babington Smith, Contemp.
    artists; Guide exh. artists: N.
    Amer. ptrs.; ▶RILA/BHA, 15/1
Iselin, Henri Frédéric (French
    sculptor, 1825-1905) **GC**
    Bibl: ▶Thieme-Becker
Iselin, Lewis (American sculptor,
    20th century) **GC**
    Bibl: Juley coll., NMAA
Isenbart, Emile **GC**
    (French artist, 1846-1921) WC
    (French painter, 1846-1921) GC
    Bibl: ▶Bénézit
Isenbart, Marie Victor Emile **WC**
Isenbart, Marie Victor Emile → see
Isenbart, Emile
Isenbrandt, Adriaen → see Isenbrant,
Adriaen
Isenbrant → see Isenbrant, Adriaen

Isenbrant, Adriaen **BA GC PR**
    (early Netherlandish painter,
    d.1551) BA
    (Flanders painter, ca.1490-1551) GC
    (Flemish, active 1510-1551) JG
    (Netherlandish painter, d. 1551) PR
    (Netherlands artist, op.1510-m.
    1551) WC
    Bibl: ▶Bénézit; Getty Photo Study
    Coll. (Ptgs.); ▶RILA/BHA;
    ▶Thieme-Becker; ▶Wurzbach, NLD
    Künst.-Lex.
    Adriaen Isenbrant PR
    Ijsenbrandt, Adriaen van PR
    Isenbrandt, Adriaen PR
    Isenbrant PR
Isenbrant, Isebrant, Ysenbaert
    or Ysenbrant, Adriaen **WC**
    Ysenbrandt, Adriaan PR
    Ysenbrandt, Adriaen GC PR
    Ysenbrandt, Adrien **JG** PR
Isenbrant, Isebrant, Ysenbaert or
Ysenbrant, Adriaen → see Isenbrant,
Adriaen
Isenmann, Caspar **GC WC**
    (German artist, op.1433-m.
    1472) WC
    (German painter, d.1472) GC
    Bibl: ▶Thieme-Becker
Isenrath, Paul (German sculptor,
    b.1936) **BA**
    Bibl: ▶MoMA libr. cat.; ▶WW Arts
    DEU
Isenring, Johann Baptist **BA WC**
    (Swiss artist, 1796-1860) WC
    (Swiss painter, printmaker,
    1796-1860) BA
    (Swiss, 1796-1860,
    daguerreotypist) JG
    Bibl: ▶Schweiz. Künst.-Lex.; ▶Witt
    checklist
    Isenring, Johann Baptiste **JG**
Isenring, Johann Baptiste → see
Isenring, Johann Baptist
Isepp, Sebastian (Austrian painter,
    1884-1954) **BA**
    Bibl: ▶Bénézit; ▶London Times
    obit.; ▶Thieme-Becker
Iser, Iosif **BA WC**
    (Romanian painter, printmaker,
    1881-1958) BA
    (Rumanian artist, 1881-) WC
    Bibl: ▶Bénézit; ▶Thieme-Becker;
    ▶Vollmer, Künst.-Lex. 20. Jhr.
Isermann, Jim (American artist,
    b.1955) **BA**
    Bibl: Bowsher, J., et al. in
    JOURNAL: A CONTEMPORARY
    ARTS MAGAZINE, 36 (spring
    1983) 60; Providence (RI, USA),
    RISD, Museum of Art, FURNITURE,
    FURNISHINGS..., 1984
Isgrò, Emilio (Italian painter, poet,
    b.1937) **BA**
    Bibl: ▶Art Index, v.22; ▶Bénézit;
    ▶Bolaffi

Isham, Samuel **BA WI**
    (American artist, 1855-1914) WI
    (American painter, author, 1855-
    1914) BA
    Bibl: Clark Art Inst. Libr.;
    ▶Fielding's Amer. ptrs.; ▶WWW
    Amer., v.1
Isham, Sheila Eaton (American
    painter, printmaker, b.1927) **BA**
    Bibl: ▶WW Amer. Art
Ishibashi, Toshihiko (Japanese
    architect, since 1985 in practice
    wilth Kotoko Tokugawa, 1947-) **AV**
    Bibl: Ottagono, 1987 June, v.22,
    no.85, p.23
Ishida, Nobuo (Japanese architect) **AV**
    Bibl: Japan architect, 1983 Oct.,
    v.58, no.10(318), p.50
Ishida, Toshiaki (Japanese architect,
    1950-) **AV**
    Bibl: Japan architect, 1988 Nov.-
    Dec., v.63, no.11-12, p.60
Ishida, Toshikazu (Japanese
    architect, 1958-) **AV**
    Bibl: Japan architect, 1989 Mar.,
    v.64, no.3(383), p.7
Ishii, Ben (Japanese architect) **AV**
    Bibl: Japan architect, 1985 Jan.,
    v.60, no.1(333), p.52
Ishii, Kazuhiro (Japanese architect,
    1944-) **AV**
    Bibl: ▶Contemp. archts.
Ishii, Motoko (Japanese lighting
    designer) **AV**
    Bibl: Japan architect, 1989 Oct.,
    v.64, no.10(390), p.4
Ishii, Osamu (Japanese architect,
    1922-) **AV**
    Bibl: Japan architect, 1982 Mar.,
    v.57, no.299, p.7
Ishii, Tsutomu (Japanese architect) **AV**
    Bibl: Space design, 1987 Jan., no.
    268, p.97)n encyclopedia of
    architects
Ishii, Yoshiyasu (Japanese designer,
    1931-) **AV**
    Bibl: Process: architecture, n.30,
    1982, p.163
Ishioka, Eiko (Japanese graphic
    artist, 20th c.) **BA**
    Bibl: Sischy, I., in ARTFORUM
    XXII/7 (Mar 1984) 80
Ishiyama, Osamu (Japanese
    architect, 1944-) **AV**
    Bibl: De Architect, 1988 Dec.,
    v.19, no.12, p.54
Isias vande Velde → see Velde, Esaias I
van de
Isidor of Seville (Spanish, ca. 560-
    636) **JG**
Isidore → see Isidoros of Miletus
Isidore Levy → see Levy, Isidore
Isidore, Raymond (French naive
    artist, mosaicist, and builder,
    Chartres, 1900-1964) **AV**
    Bibl: ▶Libr. of Congr. Name Auth.
    File
    Picassiette AV

Isidoro Fiammingo [Unidentified]
(Unknown painter)   **PR**
    Bibl: Belprato inventory, Naples,
    1667
Isidoro Milesio → see Isidoros of
    Miletus
Isidoros of Miletus *(Engineer,*
geometer, scholar, architect, post
442/ante 512-post 537/ante 612)   **CE**
    Isidore   CE
    Isidoro Milesio   CE
Isidorus *(Italian scribe, act.1170)*   **GC**
    Bibl: Barzon, Codici Miniati
    Capitolare Padova, p.5; Padua,
    Codici Miniati (1967), pp.11-13
Iskowitz, Gershon *(Canadian*
painter, b.1921)   **BA**
    Bibl: ▶Artists Canada; ▶Bénézit;
    ▶Havlice, Idx. art. bio.;
    ▶MacDonald, Can. artists
Islam, Muzharul *(Architect,*
Bangladesh)   **AV**
    Bibl: Architecture + design, 1988
    May-June, v.4, no.4, p.23
Isler, A.F. *(American, active*
Michigan, 1890s)   **JG**
Isler, Heinz *(Swiss engineer, b.1926)*   **BA**
    Bibl: Princeton (NJ, USA),
    Princeton Univ., Art Mus., HEINZ
    ISLER..(1980)
Ismael, Antonio *(Indonesian*
architect)   **AV**
    Bibl: Architectural review, 1989
    Nov., v.186, no.113, p.109
Isman Vacchio → see Eismann, Johann
    Anton
Isman Vecchia → see Eismann, Johann
    Anton
Isman Vecchio → see Eismann, Johann
    Anton
Isman Veccio → see Eismann, Johann
    Anton
Isman, Johann → see Eismann, Johann
    Anton
Isnard, Pierre Francois *(French*
artist, op.1776-1781)   **WC**
Isnard, Vivien *(French painter,*
b.1946)   **BA**
    Bibl: ▶Art Index, v.51; Arts
    Council GBR, French art (1979)
Isogonos *(Greek sculptor, 3rd c BC)*   **GC**
    Bibl: ▶Brilliant, Anc. Greeks, p.341
Isola, Aimaro *(Italian architect,*
Turin, 1931-)   **AV**
    Bibl: Arkkitehti, 1987, v.84, no.3,
    p.52
    Oreglia d'Isola, Aimaro   AV
Isola, Emma   **WC WI**
    (British artist, 19th cent.)   WC
    (British artist, op.19th c.)   WI
Isola, Giuseppe   **GC WC**
    (Italian artist, 1808-1893)   WC
    (Italian painter, 1808-1893)   GC
    Bibl: ▶Bénézit
Isolated Manuscripts atelier → see
    Isolated Manuscripts ateliers

Isolated Manuscripts ateliers
(French illuminators, act. ca.1250-
1270)   **GC**
    Bibl: ▶Branner, Ms. ptg. Paris, pp.
    80-82, 220; Getty Photo Study
    Coll. (Medieval)
    Isolated Manuscripts atelier   GC
    Isolated Manuscripts workshop   GC
Isolated Manuscripts workshop → see
    Isolated Manuscripts ateliers
Isoré, Irina *(French interior designer,*
Paris)   **AV**
    Bibl: Maison française, 1985 Dec.-
    1986 Jan., no.393, p.95
Isotta degli Atti → see Atti, Isotta
    degli
Isou, Isidore *(French author, artist,*
20th c.)   **BA**
    Bibl: ▶MoMA libr. cat.; ▶Natl.
    union cat., 1973-1977
Isoz, Emil *(Swiss architect,*
Rehetobel)   **AV**
    Bibl: Schweizer Baumarkt, 1988
    May 2, no.9, p.viii
Isozaki, Arata   **AV BA FA**
    (born ca. 1930; Architect,
    Japan)   FA
    (Japanese architect, 1931-)   AV
    (Japanese architect, b.1931)   BA
    Bibl: ▶Avery Libr. cat.; ▶Contemp.
    archts., 1987; DAM object
    records; GA houses, n.14, July
    1983, p.24; Joedicke,
    Architecture since 1945; Tempel,
    New Japanese Architecture, p. 25
Israel *(American, active Baltimore,*
MD, U.S. 1865-1875)   **JG**
[Israel] van Mecheln → see Meckenem,
    Israhel van, the younger
Israel, Franklin David *(American*
architect, Los Angeles, Calif,
1945-)   **AV**
    Bibl: Architectural review, 1987
    Dec., v.182, no.1090, p.61
Israel, Laurent *(French architect,*
1948-)   **AV**
    Bibl: Intl. archt., 1 (1983) p.[61]
Israel, Lawrence *(British architect,*
1909-)   **AV**
    Bibl: ▶Contemp. archts.
Israel, Margaret *(American artist,*
b.1929)   **BA**
    Bibl: ▶NY art yrbk.
Israel, Marvin   **WC WI**
    (American artist, 20th cent.)   WC
    (American artist, op.20th c.)   WI
Israel, Robert *(American sculptor,*
scenographer, b.1939)   **BA**
    Bibl: ▶Art Index, vs.16, 18, 19;
    Minneapolis(MN, USA), Walker
    Art Center, ROBERT ISRAEL...
    (1975)
Israels → see Israëls, Jozef

Israels, Isaac Lazerus   **BA GC WC**
    (Dutch artist, 1865-1934)   WC
    (Dutch painter and
    draughtsman, 1865-1934)   GC
    (Dutch painter, printmaker,
    1865-1934)   BA
    Bibl: Getty Photo Study Coll.;
    ▶Scheen, Ned. beeldende kunst.;
    ▶Vollmer, Künst.-Lex. 20. Jhr.;
    ▶Witt checklist
Israels, Josef → see Israëls, Jozef
Israels, Joseph → see Israëls, Jozef
Israëls, Jozef   **BA GC PR WC**
    (Dutch artist, 1824-1911)   WC
    (Dutch painter, 1824-1911)   BA PR
    (Dutch painter, draughtsman,
    and printmaker, 1824-1911)   GC
    Bibl: Getty Photo Study Coll.;
    ▶RILA/BHA; ▶Scheen, Ned.
    beeldende kunst.;
    ▶Thieme-Becker; ▶Witt checklist
    Israels   PR
    Israels, Josef   PR
    Israels, Joseph   PR
    Israïls, Jozef   **PR**
    Jozef Israels   PR
Israelyan, R. *(Russian architect)*   **AV**
    Bibl: Process: architecture, 1985
    Jan., no.54, p.152
Israhel van Meckenem → see
    Meckenem, Israhel van, the
    younger
Israïls, Jozef → see Israëls, Jozef
Issel, Georg Wilhelm   **BA GC WC**
    (German artist, 1785-1870)   WC
    (German painter, patron, 1785-
    1870)   BA
    (German, 1785-1870)   GC
    Bibl: ▶Brockhaus Enzyk.;
    ▶Thieme-Becker; ▶Witt checklist
Isselburg, Peter   **BA GC**
    (German draughtsman,
    1568/80-1630)   GC
    (German printmaker, publisher,
    1568/80-ca.1630)   BA
    Bibl: ▶Bénézit; Getty Photo Study
    Coll.; ▶Neue deutsche Biog.;
    ▶Strutt, Dict. engravers;
    ▶Thieme-Becker
    Eisselburg, Peter   GC
    Yselburg, Peter   GC
Isselsteyn, Adrianus → see Ysselstein,
    Adrianus
Isser, Johanna von, (nee
Grossrubatscher) *(German artist,*
1802-1880)   **WC**
Isserman, Yves *(French architect)*   **AV**
Issigonis, Alec Arnold Constantine
(British designer, 1906-1988)   **BA**
    Bibl: ▶Art Index, Apr. 1989;
    ROYAL SOC. OF ARTS JOURNAL,
    CXXXVI(NOV1988), 914-15;
    ▶Who's Who [GBR], 1989
Issitt, Peter *(British artist, op.20th*
c.)   **WI**

Issod, Thomas *(English goldsmith, act.1668, d. before 1702)* **BA**
Bibl: ▶Grimwade, London goldsmiths; Heal, London goldsmiths 1200-1800; ▶Thieme-Becker

Isstomin, Konstantin → see Istomin, Konstantin Nikolaevič

Issupoff, Alessio *(Italian artist, 19th cent.)* **WC**

Ista, Ernest *(French artist, op.c. 1877)* **WC**

Isted, Ambrose **WC WI**
(British artist, 19th cent.) WC
(British artist, op.19th c.) WI

Istomin, Konstantin Nikolaevič **BA**
(Russian artist, 1887-) WC
(Russian painter, 1887-1942) BA
Bibl: ▶Fogg Mus. Libr. cat.; ▶Vollmer, Künst.-Lex. 20. Jhr.

Isstomin, Konstantin **WC**

Istrati, Alexander *(Rumanian artist, 1915-)* **WC**

Istvan Farkas → see Farkas, István

István, Master → see Stephen of Košice

Itai, Hoichiro *(Japanese architect, 1948-)* **AV**
Bibl: Kenchiku bunka, 1987 Dec., v.42, no.494, p.40

Italia, Angelo *(Italian architect, ecclesiastic, 1628-1700)* **BA**
Bibl: Blunt, Sicilian baroque, p.150, no.93; LE ARTI IN SICILIA NEL SETTECENTO, ACCASCINA FESTSCHR., p. 75; ▶Macmillan encyc. archts.; TCI Sicilia; ▶Wittkower, Art & arch. Italy

Italia, Shalom *(Italian printmaker, ca.1619-ca.1655)* **BA**
Bibl: Encyc. Judaica; Israel Mus. Jrnl. V (spring 1986) 107-108; ▶Thieme-Becker

Italico Brass → see Brass, Italico

Italus in Pesth *(Italian sculptor in HUN, 16th c.)* **BA**
Bibl: Balogh, Ars Hungarica, II/1 (1974) pp.27-58

Itami, Jun *(Japanese architect, 1937-)* **AV**
Bibl: Architecture & urbanism, 1987 Oct., no.10(205), p.78

Itaya, Ryoki *(Japanese architect)* **AV**
Bibl: Progressive architecture, 1989 Dec., v.70, no.13, p.26)

Itchkawich, David Michael **BA WI**
(American artist, b.1937) WI
(American printmaker, b.1937) BA
Bibl: ▶WW Amer. Art, 1976

Item, Georges *(Swiss artist, 1927-)* **WC**

Itier, Alphonse Eugène Jules **BA**
(French customs official, photographer, 1802-1877) BA
(French, 1802-1877, daguerreotypist) JG
Bibl: HISTORY OF PHOTOGRAPHY, V (JULY 1981), 225-244

Itier, Jules **JG**

Itier, Jules → see Itier, Alphonse Eugène Jules

Ito, Kazutoshi *(Japanese architect)* **AV**
Bibl: Places, 1988, v.5, no.3, p.39

Ito, Miyoko *(American painter, 1918-1983)* **BA**
Bibl: ▶Babington Smith, Contemp. artists; ▶Intl. dir. exh. artists; NEW ART EXAMINER, XI/2(NOV 1983), 6

Ito, Takashi → see Itoh, Takashi

Ito, Tetsuo *(Architect, Japan, 1942-)* **AV**
Bibl: Kenchiku bunka, 1987 Dec., v.42, no.494, p.46

Ito, Toyo **AV BA**
(Japanese architect, 1941-) AV
(Japanese architect, b.1941) BA
Bibl: Art in Amer., LXIX/6 (Sum. 1981) pp.114-123; ▶Avery period. idx.; GA houses, 1983 July, no.14, p.142

Itoh, Toyoo AV

Ito, Yoshiyasu *(Japanese artist, Tokyo, 1953-)* **AV**
Bibl: Process: architecture, 1988 Aug., no.74, p.158

Itoh, Takashi *(Japanese architect)* **AV**
Bibl: Japan architect, 1987 May, no.361, p.62

Ito, Takashi AV

Itoh, Toyoo → see Ito, Toyo

Itschner, Carl *(Swiss artist, 1813-1879)* **WC**

Ittar, Sebastiano *(Italian artist, op. 1800)* **WC**

Itten, Johannes **BA WC**
(Swiss artist, 1888-) WC
(Swiss painter, sculptor, 1888-1967) BA
Bibl: ▶Art Index; ▶Bénézit; ▶Fogg Mus. Libr. cat.; ▶MoMA libr. cat.

Ittenbach, Franz *(German artist, 1813-1879)* **WC**

Itting, Gotthardt *(German, active 1920s, Bauhaus)* **JG**

Ittner, H. Curtis *(American architect, St. Louis, Mo)* **AV**
Bibl: ▶AIA Pro File, 1987-1988

Iturrino, Francesco de → see Iturrino, Francisco de

Iturrino, Francisco de **BA**
(Spanish artist, 1864-1924) WC
(Spanish painter, 1864-1924) BA
Bibl: Barañano Letamendía, Goya 205-206 (July-Oct) 1988, 94-98; ▶Witt checklist

Iturrino, Francesco de **WC**

Itz, G. N. → see Itz, George Nicolaas

Itz, George Nicolaas **BA**
(Dutch architect, 1799-1869) BA
(Dutch architect, Dordrecht, 1799-1869) AV
Bibl: Annèt Meffert and Ruud Schook, G.N. ITZ, STADSBOUWMEESTER VAN DORDRECT: 1832-1867, Delft 1985; Domus, 1984 Apr., no.649, p.52; ▶Nieuw NLD biog. woord.

Itz, G. N. **AV**

Itzkowitz, Lynn *(American printmaker, b.1947)* **BA**
Bibl: Hamilton(NY, USA), Colgate Univ., Picker Art Gallery. DRAWINGS BY LYNNITZKOWITZ(1976)

Itzlfeldner, Johann Georg *(Austrian sculptor in Germany, 1704/05-1790)* **BA**
Bibl: Dehio: Oberbayern, pp.411, 412, 456; Preiss, R., JOHANN GEORG ITZLFELDNER, 1704/05-1790..., 1983; ▶Thieme-Becker

Iudica Painter *(Sicilian vase-painter)* **GC**
Bibl: ▶Trendall, Red-fig. vases Lucania

Iudica, Mario *(Italian artist)* **AV**
Bibl: Arca, 1989 Mar.-Apr., v.9, no.45, p.30

Iunker, Carl → see Junker, Carl

Ivan Choultse → see Choultsé, Ivan

Ivan Dabrowski → see Graham, John D.

Ivan Elven → see Elven, Ivan

Ivan Gregorovitch Olinsky → see Olinski, Ivan Gregorovitch

Ivan Konstantinovic Ajvazovskij → see Ajvazovskij, Ivan Konstantinovič

Ivan Le Lorraine Albright → see Albright, Ivan Le Lorraine

Ivan Pokitonov → see Pokitonov, Ivan

Ivan Swift → see Swift, Ivan

Ivancenco, Gheorghe *(Rumanian artist, 1914-)* **WC**

Ivančić, Nina *(Yugoslav painter, b.1953)* **BA**
Bibl: Graz (AUT), Kunstlerhaus, Eros, Mythos (1983)

Ivanitskij, A. *(Russian mining engineer, photographer, act.1858-1863)* **BA**
Bibl: HISTORY OF PHOTOGRAPHY, II/1(JAN 1978)

Ivánka, András *(Hungarian artist or architect, 1911-)* **AV**
Bibl: Magyar építőművészet, 1987, v.78, no.4-5, p.62

Ivanoff, Alexandre → see Ivanov, Aleksandr Andreevič

Ivanoff, Michail Matveievitch **GC**
(Russian artist, 1748-1823) WC
(Russian painter, 1748-1823) GC
Bibl: ▶Bénézit

Iwanoff, Michail Matwejewitsch **WC**

Iwonski, Carl G. von *(American painter, 1830-1922)*   **BA**
Bibl: ▶Dawdy, Artists Amer. West; ▶Groce, Artists Amer.

Ixion Group *(South Italian vase-painters, 4th century BC)*   **GC**
Bibl: ▶Trendall, Red-fig. vases Lucania

Ixion Painter   **GC JG**
(Campanian vase-painter)   **GC**
Bibl: ▶Trendall, Red-fig. vases Lucania

Ixnard, Michel d'→see Ixnard, Pierre Michel d'

Ixnard, Pierre Michel d'   **AV BA GC WC**
(1723-1795)   AV
(French architect, 1723-1795)   BA
(French artist, 1723-1795)   WC
(French, 1723-1795)   GC
Bibl: Congrès archéologique de France, 1978, pp. 62, 73, note 28; ▶Encyc. world art; ▶Lance, Dict. archts. fran.; ▶Thieme-Becker; ▶Witt checklist

Dixnard, Pierre Michel   GC

Ixnard, Michel d'   GC

Iyall, Bob *(American photographer, b.1952)*   **BA**
Bibl: Pullman (WA, USA), Washington St. Univ. Mus. Art, A partial view (1979)

Iz the Wiz *(American artist, 20th c.)*   **BA**
Bibl: ▶Art Index; Arts Mag., Lightning strikes, (3 Nov. 1982)

Izaak van Oosten→see Oosten, Izaac van

Izak van Hasselt→see Hasselt, Izak van

Izaks, Wim *(Dutch artist, b.1950)*   **BA**
Bibl: Amsterdam (NLD), Stedelijk Museum, Ansuya Blom (1978)

Izant, Herbert *(British artist, op. 1880-1900)*   **WI**

Izenour, Steven   **AV BA**
(American architect, 20th c.)   BA
(American architetct, author)   AV
Bibl: ▶Avery period. idx., suppl. 4,6,7

Izewski, Dorothy *(American architect)*   **AV**
Bibl: GA houses, 1989 July, no.26, p.90

Izis *(French (b. Lithuania, Russia, now USSR), 1911-1980)*   **JG**

Izmiroglu, Esen *(Middle Eastern artist, 20th cent.)*   **WC**

Izquierdo Wachholtz, Luis
(Architect, Chile)   **AV**
Bibl: AC: the fibrecement review, 1985 Oct., v.30, no.2(112), p.18

Izquierdo, Begona *(Spanish artist, op.1957-1964)*   **WC**

Izquierdo, Manuel *(American sculptor, printmaker, b.1925)*   **BA**
Bibl: ▶Art Index, v.11; ARTFORUM, 2/8(FEB 1964), 16; Washington, DC (USA), NCFA, Art of the Pacific Northwest (1974), p.112

Izue, Kan *(Japanese architect, 1931-)*   **AV**
Bibl: Japan architect, 1988 Nov.-Dec., v.63, no.11-12, p.5

Izue, Yutaka *(Japanese architect)*   **AV**

Izzard, Colin *(British builder(?))*   **AV**
Bibl: Building, 1989 Aug.4, v.254, no.31, p.36

Izzo, Alberto *(Italian architect)*   **AV**
Bibl: Abitare, 1982 Nov., no.209, p.76

Izzo, Charles *(American architect)*   **AV**

J Steen→see Steen, Jan
J. A. Marienhof→see Marienhof, J.A.
J. A. Moore→see Mor, Anthonis
J. Andre Castaigne→see Castaigne, J. Andre
J. Antonio Hekking→see Hekking, J. Antonio
J. Asselijn→see Asselyn, Jan
J. Asselin→see Asselyn, Jan
J. Asselyn→see Asselyn, Jan
J. Asseylyn→see Asselyn, Jan
J. Astlin→see Asselyn, Jan
J. B. di Coneglia→see Cima da Conegliano, Giovanni Battista
J. B. Innocenti Collomba→see Colombo, Giovanni Battista Innocenzo
J. B. Malchary→see Malchair, John Baptist
J. B. Weenix→see Weenix, Jan Baptist
J. Backer→see Backer, Jacob Adriaensz.
J. Baffano→see Bassano, Jacopo (Jacopo da Ponte)
J. Baker→see Baker, J. [Unidentified]
J. Baptiest→see Monnoyer, Jean-Baptiste I
J. Baptist→see Monnoyer, Jean-Baptiste I
J. Baptista Lama→see Lama, Giovanni Battista
J. Barber→see Barber, Joseph
J. Bassan→see Bassano, Jacopo (Jacopo da Ponte)
J. Bassano→see Bassano, Jacopo (Jacopo da Ponte)
J. Beich→see Beich, Joachim Franz
J. Belin→see Bellini, Giovanni
J. Bellini→see Bellini, Giovanni
J. Bellino→see Bellini, Giovanni
J. Berkheyde→see Berckheyde, Job Adriaensz.
J. Biech→see Beich, Joachim Franz
J. Biscop→see Bisschop, Jan de
J. Bleker→see Bleker, Gerrit Claesz
J. Blom→see Blom, Jan
J. Bluck→see Bluck, J.

J. Bockhorst→see Boeckhorst, Jan
J. Bol→see Bol, Hans
J. Bonnemaison→see Bonnemaison, J.
J. Bos→see Bosch, Hieronymus (Hieronymus van Aken)
J. Both→see Both, Jan
J. Bourdon→see Bourdon, Sébastien
J. Bouwerman→see Wouwerman, Jan
J. Breughel→see Brueghel, Jan, the elder
J. Brughel→see Brueghel, Jan, the elder
J. Bryant→see Bryant, Joshua
J. Burden→see Burden, J.
J. Burnet→see Burnet, John
J. Buttnew→see Buttner, Jurriaan
J. Chiara→see Chiari, Giuseppe Bartolomeo
J. Chiari→see Chiari, Giuseppe Bartolomeo
J. Collet→see Collet, John
J. Collins→see Collins, John
J. Constable→see Constable, John
J. Constantin→see Constantin, Jean-Antoine
J. D. Deehem→see Heem, Jan Davidsz. de
J. da Bellini→see Bellini, Giovanni
J. da Bellino→see Bellini, Giovanni
J. da Udini→see Martini, Giovanni (Giovanni da Udine)
J. dd Mabeuse→see Gossaert, Jan
J. de Bellini→see Bellini, Giovanni
J. De Bellino→see Bellini, Giovanni
J. de Bischop→see Bisschop, Jan de
J. De Heem→see Heem, Jan Davidsz. de
J. de Hemessen, 1557→see Hemessen, Jan van
J. De Koeninck→see Koninck, Jacob (II)
J. De Koeninck→see Koninck, Jacob I
J. de Landsheer→see Landtsheer, Jan de
J. de Langhe→see Langhe, J. de
J. de Mabeuge→see Gossaert, Jan
J. De Mabeuse→see Gossaert, Jan
J. de Mabuge→see Gossaert, Jan
J. de Mabuse→see Gossaert, Jan
J. de Mabuze→see Gossaert, Jan
J. de Maubege→see Gossaert, Jan
J. de Maubeuge→see Gossaert, Jan
J. De Maubeuse→see Gossaert, Jan
J. de Maubuse→see Gossaert, Jan
J. de Maugeuge→see Gossaert, Jan
J. de Pezaro→see Cantarini, Simone
J. De Ponte il Bassano→see Bassano, Jacopo (Jacopo da Ponte)
J. de Roor→see Roore, Jacobus Ignatius de
J. de Roore→see Roore, Jacobus Ignatius de
J. de Wit→see Wit, Jacob de
J. de Witt→see Wet, Jacob Willemsz. de

J. De Witt →see Wit, Jacob de
J. Di Bellini →see Bellini, Giovanni
J. Duijts →see Duyts, Jan de
J. Eckels →see Ekels, Jan (the elder)
J. F. Rigaud, R. A. →see Rigaud, John Francis
J. Felpacker →see Felpacher
J. Ferdinand →see Ferdinandus, J. [Unidentified]
J. Fouquieres →see Fouquières, Jacques
J. Fr. Mieris →see Mieris, Jan van
J. Fr. Morales →see Morales, J.Fr. [Unidentified]
J. Fris →see Fris, Jan (Johannes)
J. Fyt →see Fyt, Jan
J. Fytt →see Fyt, Jan
J. G. Cuyp →see Cuyp, Jacob Gerritsz.
J. G. Sluijes →see Sluis, Jacob van der
J. Girtin →see Girtin, James
J. Glauber →see Glauber, Johannes (Polidoro)
J. Greffier →see Griffier, Jan I
J. Griffier →see Griffier, Jan I
J. H. Roos →see Roos, Johann Heinrich
J. Hackert →see Hackaert, Jan
J. Hals →see Hals, Johannes
J. Hammond →see Hammond, J.
J. Heiss →see Heiss, Johann
J. Hodges, Esq. R.A. →see Hodges, William
J. Hulsman →see Hulsman, Johann
J. Hulsmann →see Hulsman, Johann
J. Ibbetson →see Ibbetson, Julius Caesar
J. J. Russell →see Russell, John
J. Janson →see Janson, Johannes
J. Jeffrey Grant →see Grant, J. Jeffery
J. Jordaen →see Jordaens, Jacob
J. Jordaens →see Jordaens, Jacob
J. Jordeans →see Jordaens, Jacob
J. Koenig →see König, Johann
J. Kreugher →see Kreugher, J. [Unidentified]
J. Kuhn (Paris) →see Kuhn, B.
J. L. →see Levy, J.
J. La Duc →see Ducq, Johan le
J. Labrador →see Labrador, Juan
J. Lastman →see Lastman, Pieter Pietersz.
J. Le Roy →see Roy, Jean-Baptiste de
J. Leevens →see Lievens, Jan
J. Lievens →see Lievens, Jan
J. Lingelbag →see Lingelbach, Johannes
J. Lois →see Lois, Jacob
J. Lys →see Liss, Johann (Pan)
J. M. Wright →see Wright, John Michael
J. Mabuse →see Gossaert, Jan
J. Major →see Major, Isaak
J. Maubeuge →see Gossaert, Jan
J. Meil →see Miel, Jan
J. Miel →see Miel, Jan

J. Mieris →see Mieris, Jan van
J. Mill →see Miel, Jan
J. Milton →see Milton, John
J. Mola →see Mola, Pier Francesco
J. Molenaer →see Molenaer, Jan Miense
J. Moor →see More, Jacob
J. Moore →see More, Jacob
J. Moore, of Rome →see More, Jacob
J. More →see More, Jacob
J. Moucheron →see Moucheron, Isaac de
J. Mytens →see Mytens, Jan
J. N. Harlow →see Harlow, J.N. [Unidentified]
J. Niels →see Niels, J.
J. Noortrijs →see Noortig (Noortrys), Jan
J. Northcote →see Northcote, James
J. Northcote, R. A. →see Northcote, James
J. Northcote, R.A. →see Northcote, James
J. of Maubeuge →see Gossaert, Jan
J. Olaf Olson →see Olson, J. Olaf
J. Olib →see Olib, J. [Unidentified]
J. Oliver →see Oliver, Isaac I
J. Opie, Esq. →see Opie, John
J. Opie, R. A. →see Opie, John
J. Opie, R.A. →see Opie, John
J. Os →see Os, Jan van
J. Ostade →see Ostade, Isack van
J. Ouvater →see Ouwater, Isaak
J. Ouwater →see Ouwater, Isaak
J. Pereiro →see Pereiro, J. [Unidentified]
J. Pereja →see Pareja, Juan de
J. Pocue →see Pocue, J. [Unidentified]
J. Pringle →see Pringle, J.
J. R. Smith →see Smith, John Raphael
J. Reyn →see Rijn, Jan van
J. Reynolds →see Reynolds, Joshua
J. Ribera →see Ribera, Jusepe de (lo Spagnoletto)
J. Romano →see Giulio Romano (Giulio Pippi)
J. Rosa →see Roos, Joseph (I)
J. Rosa: →see Roos, Joseph (I)
J. Runciman →see Runciman, John
J. Ruysdaal →see Ruisdael, Jacob van
J. Ruysdae →see Ruisdael, Jacob van
J. Ruysdael →see Ruisdael, Jacob van
J. Ruysdale →see Ruisdael, Jacob van
J. S. Copley, R. A. →see Copley, John Singleton
J. Savary →see Savery, Jacob I
J. Scott →see Scott, Samuel
J. Seyers →see Seghers, Jan Baptiste
J. Solemacker →see Soolmaker, Jan Frans
J. Steen →see Steen, Jan
J. Stein →see Steen, Jan
J. Stella →see Stella, Jacques
J. Stern →see Stern, Ignaz
J. Strigel →see Strigel, Ivo

J. T. Serres →see Serres, John Thomas
J. Tensfeld →see Tensfeld, J.
J. V. Baelen →see Balen, Jan van
J. V. Bemmel →see Bemmel, J.V.
J. V. Eycke →see Eyck, Jan van
J. V. Hoeck →see Hoecke, Jan van den
J. V. Huysem →see Huysum, Jan van
J. V. Huysum →see Huysum, Jan van
J. V. Nickop →see Nickelen, Jan
J. V. Os →see Os, Jan van
J. V. Ostade →see Ostade, Isack van
J. Van Asslin →see Asselyn, Jan
J. van Capelle →see Cappelle, Jan van de
J. Van Daele →see Daele, Jan van [Unidentified]
J. van de Velde →see Velde, Jan II van de
J. van der Hecke →see Hecke, Jan van den (I)
J. van der Heijde →see Heyden, Jan van der
J. van der Meer →see Vermeer, Jan (III)
J. Van Eyck →see Eyck, Jan van
J. van Hoeck →see Hoecke, Jan van den
J. van Huysem →see Huysum, Jan van
J. Van Huysum →see Huysum, Jan van
J. Van Huysun →see Huysum, Jan van
J. van Kessel →see Kessel, Jan van
J. van Necklen →see Nickelen, Jan
J. van Nieuland →see Nieulandt, Jacob van
J. Van Os →see Os, Jan van
J. van Streeck →see Streeck, Juriaen van
J. Van Stry →see Strij, Jacob van
J. Van Tulden →see Thulden, Theodoor van
J. Vandervester →see Vester, J. van der [Unidentified]
J. Vandyck →see Dyck, J. van [Unidentified]
J. Vanhuysum →see Huysum, Jan van
J. Vanloo →see Vanloo, Jean Baptiste
J. Veccio →see Eismann, Johann Anton
J. Vender Does →see Does, Jacob van der (the elder)
J. Verkolie →see Verkolje, Jan I
J. Vermeer →see Vermeer, Jan (II)
J. Vernet →see Vernet, Joseph
J. Vonck →see Vonck, Jan
J. W. Turner →see Turner, Joseph Mallord William
J. Wade →see Wade, J.
J. Ward →see Ward, James
J. Ward, R.A. →see Ward, James
J. Whitcomb →see Whitcombe, Thomas
J. Wijnants →see Wijnants, Jan
J. Wilkins →see Wilkins, J.

J. William Jennys → *see* Jennys, William

J. Wills → *see* Wills, James

J. Wouvermans → *see* Wouwerman, Jan

J. Wright → *see* Wright, Joseph (Wright of Derby)

J. Wte. Wael → *see* Wtewael, Joachim Antonisz.

J. Wyatt → *see* Wyatt, James

J. Wyck → *see* Wyck, Jan

J. Wynants → *see* Wijnants, Jan

J., E. *(fl.1955; draftsman (technical), Toronto)*   **FA**
    Bibl: NA objects; Natl. Arch. of Canada, CAAD Finding Aid

E.J.   FA

[J...] Toussin → *see* Toussyn, Johann

J.A. Winck → *see* Wink, Johann Amandus

J.A.C *(American, contemporary)*   **JG**

J.B. → *see* Monogrammist J.B.

J.B. Huijsmans → *see* Huysmans, Jan Baptiste

J.B. Lama → *see* Lama, Giovanni Battista

J.B. Lenardi → *see* Lenardi, Giovanni Battista

J.B. Paterre → *see* Pater, Jean-Baptiste Joseph

J.B. Vandermeulen → *see* Meulen, Adam Frans van der

J.B. Vivian → *see* Vivian, J.B. [Unidentified]

J.B. Weeninx → *see* Weenix, Jan Baptist

J.B. Weenix → *see* Weenix, Jan Baptist

J.B. Weninx → *see* Weenix, Jan Baptist

J.B. Wenix → *see* Weenix, Jan Baptist

J.B.D. → *see* Monogrammist J.B.D.

J.C. → *see* Monogrammist J.C.

J.C. Biedermann → *see* Biedermann, J.C.

J.C. Brand → *see* Brand, Johann Christian

J.C. Morris → *see* Morris, J.C.

J.C. van der Hagen → *see* Hagen, J.C. van der

J.D *(French, active Paris, 1889)*   **JG**

J.D. De Heem → *see* Heem, Jan Davidsz. de

J.D. de Hemm → *see* Heem, Jan Davidsz. de

J.D. Heem → *see* Heem, Jan Davidsz. de

J.D. Mabuge → *see* Gossaert, Jan

J.D.S. → *see* Monogrammist J.D.S.

J.E. Morel → *see* Morel, Jan Evert

J.E.H. Robinson → *see* Robinson, J.E.H.

J.F Gont → *see* Gont, J.F. [Unidentified]

J.F. Barry Pittar → *see* Pittar, J.F. Barry

J.F. Beich → *see* Beich, Joachim Franz

J.F. Rigaud → *see* Rigaud, John Francis

J.F. Rigaud, R.A. → *see* Rigaud, John Francis

J.F. Solemaker → *see* Soolmaker, Jan Frans

J.F. van Bloemen → *see* Bloemen, Jan Frans van (Orizonte)

J.F. van Capelle → *see* Cappelle, Jan van de

J.Fr. Mieris → *see* Mieris, Jan van

J.G *(French, active 19th century)*   **JG**

J.G.L. → *see* Monogrammist J.G.L.

J.H. Prins, 1784 → *see* Prins, Johannes Huibert

J.H. Roos → *see* Roos, Johann Heinrich

J.K. Porter → *see* Porter, Robert Kerr, Sir

J.L. → *see* Laurent, Juan

J.L. Condit → *see* Condit, J.L.

J.L. Keaft → *see* Keaft, J.L. [Unidentified]

J.L. Mourier → *see* Mourier, J.L. [Unidentified]

J.M. Molenaar → *see* Molenaer, Jan Miense

J.M.W. Turner, R.A. → *see* Turner, Joseph Mallord William

J.P. Lely → *see* Lely, Peter

J.P. Panini 1729 → *see* Pannini, Giovanni Paolo

J.P. van Wyck → *see* Wyck, J.P. van

J.R. Smith → *see* Smith, John Raphael

J.R. Symth → *see* Smith, John Raphael

J.S. Copley → *see* Copley, John Singleton

J.S. Copley, R.A. → *see* Copley, John Singleton

J.S. Keller → *see* Keller, Johann Sigmund

J.T. Van Meiris → *see* Mieris, Jan van

J.V. Barber → *see* Barber, John Vincent

J.V. Bemmel → *see* Bemmel, J.V.

J.V. Daele → *see* Daele, Jan van [Unidentified]

J.V. der Meer → *see* Vermeer, Jan (III)

J.V. Eyck → *see* Eyck, Jan van

J.V. Geel → *see* Geel, Jacob Jacobsz. van

J.V. Goal → *see* Gool, Jan van

J.v. Goijen → *see* Goyen, Jan Josephsz. van

J.V. Gool → *see* Gool, Jan van

J.V. Hoeck → *see* Hoecke, Jan van den

J.V. Huysem → *see* Huysum, Jan van

J.V. Huysen → *see* Huysum, Jan van

J.V. Streek → *see* Streeck, Juriaen van

J.W. Frank → *see* Franck, Johan Willem

J.W.M. Turner, R.A. → *see* Turner, Joseph Mallord William

J: C: Powell → *see* Powell, C.M.

J:Battista Buser → *see* Busiri, Giovanni Battista

Jaar, Alfredo *(Chilean artist in USA, b.1956)*   **BA**
    Bibl: ▶Art Index, vs.35-37; ▶WW Amer. Art, 1989

Jaaster → *see* Jaaster, Jochem

Jaaster, Jochem   **PR WC**
    (Dutch artist, op.1647)   WC
    (Dutch painter, act. ca.1646)   PR
    Bibl: ▶Thieme-Becker

Jaaster   PR

Jochem Jaaster   PR

Jaatinen, Marjatta *(Finnish architect)*   **AV**
    Bibl: Arkkitehti, 1985, no.8, p.58

Jaatinen, Martti *(Finnish architect)*   **AV**
    Bibl: Arkkitehti, 1985, no.8, p.58

Jaatinen, Osmo *(Finnish architect)*   **AV**
    Bibl: Arkkitehti, 1989, v.86, no.1, p.37

Jablonskaja, Tat'jana Nilovna   **BA**
    (Russian artist, 1917-)   WC
    (Russian painter, b.1917)   BA
    Bibl: ▶Encyc. world art; ▶Vollmer, Künst.-Lex. 20. Jhr.; Vronskaya, Biog. dict. USSR

Jablonskaja, Tatiana   **WC**

Jablonskaja, Tatiana → *see* Jablonskaja, Tat'jana Nilovna

Jablonsky, Stephen *(American composer, educator, artist, 20th c.)*   **BA**
    Bibl: LEONARDO, XII/4(AUTUMN 1979), 308-10

Jac Bassano → *see* Bassano, Jacopo (Jacopo da Ponte)

Jac Jordaens → *see* Jordaens, Jacob

Jac. Bassan → *see* Bassano, Jacopo (Jacopo da Ponte)

Jac. Bassano → *see* Bassano, Jacopo (Jacopo da Ponte)

Jac. Jordaens → *see* Jordaens, Jacob

Jac. Jordeans → *see* Jordaens, Jacob

Jac. Ruijsdael → *see* Ruisdael, Jacob van

Jac. Ruysdael → *see* Ruisdael, Jacob van

Jac. Stella → *see* Stella, Jacques

Jaccard, Christian *(French artist, b.1939)*   **BA**
    Bibl: ▶Art Index, Nov. 1973-Oct. 1974; Los Angeles (CA, USA), LAICA, Unstretched surfaces (1977)

Jachimo Bassan → *see* Bassano, Jacopo (Jacopo da Ponte)

Jachimo Bassano → *see* Bassano, Jacopo (Jacopo da Ponte)

Jachimowicz, Theodor *(Polish artist, 1800-1889)*   **WC**

Jachmann, Christine *(West German architect)*   **AV**

Jachna, Joseph David *(American photographer, b.1935)*   **BA**
    Bibl: ▶WW Amer. Art, 1989

Jachtmann, Johann Ludwig *(German medalist, sculptor, gem carver, 1776-1842)*   **BA**
    Bibl: ▶Bénézit; ▶Thieme-Becker

Jacimo Bassan → *see* Bassano, Jacopo (Jacopo da Ponte)

Jack Butler Yeats→see Yeats, Jack
   Butler
Jack Gage Stark→see Stark, Jack
   Gage
Jack Wilkinson Smith→see Smith,
   Jack Wilkinson
Jack, George (British architect,
   furniture designer, 1855-1932)   **BA**
   Bibl: ▶Penguin dec. arts
Jack, Kenneth   **WI**
   (Australian draughtsman,
   b.1924)   **GC**
   (British artist, op.20th c.)   **WI**
   Bibl: ▶Encyc. Australian art
   Jack, Kenneth William David   **GC**
Jack, Kenneth William David→see
   Jack, Kenneth
Jack, Richard (British artist, 1866-
   1952)   **WC WI**
Jack, Russell C. (Australian
   architect, 1925-)   **AV**
Jack, William (English architect,
   London)   **AV**
   Bibl: Architects' journal, 1984 July
   11, v.180, no.28, p.20
Jack, William Murray (Scottish
   architect, St. Andrews, Fife)   **AV**
   Bibl: ▶RIBA members, 1987
Jackli, Hans→see Jegli, Hans II
Jacklin, Bill   **BA WC WI**
   (British artist, 1943-)   **WC**
   (British artist, b.1943)   **WI**
   (British painter, b.1943)   **BA**
   Bibl: ▶Bénézit; ▶Dolman,
   Contemp. Brit. artists
Jackman, P.   **WC WI**
   (British artist, 19th cent.)   **WC**
   (British artist, op.1867-1870)   **WI**
Jackman, William G.   **WC WI**
   (British artist, op.1841-1860)   **WI**
   (British artist, op.c.1841-1860)   **WC**
Jackowski, Andrzej   **BA WI**
   (British artist, b.1947)   **WI**
   (British painter, b.1947)   **BA**
   Bibl: ▶Babington Smith, Contemp.
   artists
Jackowski, Stanisław (Polish
   sculptor, collector, 1887-1951)   **BA**
Jacks, Robert (American painter,
   20th c.)   **BA**
   Bibl: Toronto(ONT, CAN), Art
   Gallery of Ontario. FOUR
   PAINTERS...(1975)
Jackson→see Jackson, John
Jackson→see Jackson, Will F.
Jackson→see Jackson, William
Jackson, Albert Edward (British
   artist, 1873-1952)   **WI**
Jackson, Alexander Brooks   **BA WI**
   (American artist, 1925-1981)   **WI**
   (American painter, 1925-1981)   **BA**
   Bibl: Norfolk(VA, USA), Chrysler
   Museum. A.B.JACKSON...(1981);
   ▶WW Amer. Art

Jackson, Alexander Young   **BA GC WC**
   (Canadian artist, 1883-)   **WC**
   (Canadian painter, 1882-1974)   **BA**
   (Canadian, b.1883)   **GC**
   Bibl: ▶MacDonald, Can. artists;
   ▶MoMA libr. cat.; ▶Witt checklist
Jackson, Arthur   **WC WI**
   (British artist, 1911-)   **WC**
   (British artist, b.1911)   **WI**
Jackson, Bruce (American educator,
   photographer, filmmaker, author,
   20th c.)   **BA**
   Bibl: ▶Natl. Faculty Dir.; ▶Natl.
   union cat.
Jackson, Daryl   **AV BA**
   (Australian architect, 1937-)   **AV**
   (Australian architect, b.1937)   **BA**
   Bibl: ▶Avery period. idx., 6th
   suppl.; ▶Contemp. archts.
Jackson, David (Australian architect,
   1931-)   **AV**
   Bibl: ▶Contemp. archts.
Jackson, Day (British artist, op.
   1856-)   **WI**
Jackson, Edwin (English architect,
   Ashford, now deceased)   **AV**
   Bibl: Traditional homes, 1988
   July, v.4, no.10, p.32
Jackson, Edwin W. (American artist,
   1825-op.1857)   **WI**
Jackson, Emily H. (British artist, op.
   1870-1884)   **WI**
   Bibl: ▶Fisher, Watercolour ptrs.
Jackson, Emmet T. (American
   architect)   **AV**
   Bibl: Texas architect, 1985 Sept.-
   Oct., v.35, no.5, p.78
Jackson, Errol (British photographer,
   20th c.)   **BA**
   Bibl: AFTERIMAGE, VII(1980)
Jackson, F.J.   **WC WI**
   (American artist, 19th cent.)   **WC**
   (American artist, op.19th c.)   **WI**
Jackson, Francis Ernest   **BA WC WI**
   (British artist, 1872-1945)   **WC WI**
   (British painter, printmaker,
   1872-1945)   **BA**
   Bibl: ▶Engen, Victorian engravers;
   ▶Johnson, Brit. artists; ▶Waters,
   Brit. artists; ▶Wood, Victorian
   ptrs.
Jackson, Frederick Hamilton
   (British artist, 1848-1923)   **WI**
Jackson, Frederick William (British
   artist, 1859-1918)   **WC WI**
Jackson, G.→see Jackson, George I
Jackson, George I   **WI**
   (British artist, op.1839-1844)   **WC WI**
   Bibl: Paviere, Brit. sporting ptrs
   Jackson, G.   **WC**
Jackson, Gilbert   **WC WI**
   (British artist, c.1622-c.1642)   **WC**
   (British artist, op.1622-1658)   **WI**
Jackson, H. (British artist, op.19th
   c.)   **WI**

Jackson, Harry→see Jackson, Harry
   Andrew
Jackson, Harry Andrew   **BA GC**
   (American painter, sculptor,
   b.1924)   **BA**
   (American sculptor and painter,
   b.1924)   **GC**
   Bibl: Getty Photo Study Coll.
   (Sculp.); ▶RILA/BHA; ▶WW Amer.
   Art, 1978
   Jackson, Harry   **GC**
**Jackson, Henry Alexander
   Carmichael** (Canadian artist,
   naturalist, 1877-1961)   **BA**
   Bibl: ▶Artists Canada; Cazort, MR.
   JACKSON'S MUSHROOMS(1979);
   ▶MacDonald, Can. artists
Jackson, Herb (American painter,
   printmaker, b.1945)   **BA**
   Bibl: ▶WW Amer. Art, 1980
Jackson, Herbert (British architect,
   1910-1989)   **AV**
   Bibl: ▶RIBA members, 1987
Jackson, Huson (American architect)   **AV**
   Bibl: ▶Contemp. archts.
Jackson, J.G. (British artist, op.1817-
   1844)   **WC WI**
   Bibl: ▶Houfe, Brit. book illus.
Jackson, John   **PR WC WI**
   (British artist, 1778-1831)   **WC WI**
   (British painter, 1778-1831)   **PR**
   Bibl: ▶Bénézit; ▶Dict. natl. biog.;
   ▶Thieme-Becker
   Jackson   **PR**
   John Jackson   **PR**
Jackson, John (British sculptor,
   b.1938)   **BA**
   Bibl: Colchester(GBR), Minories.
   SCULPTOR'S DRAWINGS(19790
Jackson, John Baptist (Jackson of
   Battersea)   **BA WC**
   (British artist, 1701-c.1780)   **WC**
   (British artist, 1701-circa 1780)   **WI**
   (British printmaker, designer,
   1701-ca.1780)   **BA**
   Bibl: ▶Dict. natl. biog.; ▶Redgrave,
   Engl. school; Teynac,
   WALLPAPER; ▶Thieme-Becker
**Jackson, John Baptist, (of
   Battersea)**   **WI**
Jackson, John Baptist, (of
   Battersea)→see Jackson, John
   Baptist (Jackson of Battersea)
Jackson, John Edwin (American
   artist, 1876-circa 1950)   **WI**
Jackson, John Richardson   **BA WC WI**
   (British artist, 1819-1877)   **WC WI**
   (British printmaker, 1819-1877)   **BA**
   Bibl: ▶Bénézit; ▶Thieme-Becker
Jackson, Joseph II (British artist, op.
   1816-, d.1850)   **WI**
Jackson, Karen (British interior
   designer)   **AV**
   Bibl: The world of interiors, 1989
   Sept., p.144

Jackson, Mark *(American painter,*
  b.ca.1952)   **BA**
    Bibl: ▶Art Index, v.35; ▶Intl. dir.
    exh. artists
Jackson, Oliver Lee *(American*
  painter, b.1935)   **BA**
    Bibl: Seattle(WA, USA), Art
    Museum. OLIVER JACKSON(1982);
    ▶WW Amer. Art, 1989
Jackson, Percy *(British architect,*
  d.1985)   **AV**
    Bibl: RIBA journal, 1986 Jan., v.93,
    no.1, p.49
Jackson, R. Graham *(American*
  architect, Houston, Tex)   **AV**
    Bibl: ▶AIA Pro File, 1987-88
Jackson, Richard   **BA WC WI**
    (American artist, 1939-)   WC
    (American artist, b.1939)   WI
    (American painter, b.1939)   BA
    Bibl: ▶Intl. dir. exh. artists, 1983
Jackson, Samuel *(British artist,*
  1794-1869)   **WC WI**
Jackson, Samuel Phillips *(British*
  artist, 1830-1904)   **WC WI**
Jackson, Stephen *(British artist,*
  b.1953)   **WI**
Jackson, T. G., (Thomas
  Graham) → *see* Jackson, Thomas
  Graham
Jackson, Thomas Graham   **BA**
    (British architect, author, 1835-
    1924)   BA
    (British architect, educator,
    1835-1924)   AV
    Bibl: ▶Libr. of Congr. Name Auth.
    File; ▶Macmillan encyc. archts.;
    ▶Who was who [GBR], v.1
    Jackson, T. G., (Thomas Graham)   AV
Jackson, Thomas Graham, Sir   **AV**
Jackson, Thomas Graham, Sir → *see*
  Jackson, Thomas Graham
Jackson, Thomas R. *(American*
  architect, New York City, 1826-
  1901)   **AV**
    Bibl: ▶Withey, Amer. archts.
Jackson, Vanessa *(British artist,*
  b.1953)   **WI**
Jackson, Welby   **WC WI**
    (British artist, 19th cent.)   WC
    (British artist, op.19th c.)   WI
Jackson, Will F. *(American painter,*
  1851-1936)   **PR**
    Bibl: ▶WWW Amer. art
    Jackson   PR
    Jackson, William F.   PR
    Will F. Jackson   PR
Jackson, William   **PR WC WI**
    (British artist, 1730-1803)   WC WI
    (British painter, 1730-1803)   PR
    Bibl: ▶Thieme-Becker;
    ▶Waterhouse, Brit. 18c. ptrs.
    Jackson   PR
    William Jackson   PR
Jackson, William F. → *see* Jackson,
  Will F.

Jackson, William Henry   **BA JG**
    (American photographer, 1843-
    1942)   BA
    (American, 1843-1942)   JG
    Bibl: ▶Gernsheim, Hist. photog.;
    ▶Newhall, Photog.
Jackson-Jarvis, Martha *(American*
  artist, b.1952)   **BA**
    Bibl: ART MAGAZINE(3 NOV
    1983); New York (NY, USA), Mus.
    Contemp. Hispanic Art, Decade
    show (1990)
Jackus, Paul *(British artist, op.20th*
  c.)   **WI**
Jacob A. Duck → *see* Duck, Jacob A.
Jacob Adriaensz. Backer → *see* Backer,
  Jacob Adriaensz.
Jacob Adriaensz. Bellevois → *see*
  Bellevois, Jacob Adriaensz.
Jacob Asselijn → *see* Asselyn, Jan
Jacob Backer → *see* Backer, Jacob
  Adriaensz.
Jacob Bassan → *see* Bassano, Jacopo
  (Jacopo da Ponte)
Jacob Campo Weyerman → *see*
  Weyerman, Jacob Campo
Jacob Christof Le Blon → *see* Le Blon,
  Jakob Christof
Jacob Coninx → *see* Koninck, Jacob I
Jacob Cornelisz van Oostsanen → *see*
  Cornelisz. van Oostsanen, Jacob
Jacob Cornelisz. van
  Amsterdam → *see* Cornelisz. van
  Oostsanen, Jacob
Jacob Cornelisz. van Oostsanen → *see*
  Cornelisz. van Oostsanen, Jacob
Jacob de Backer → *see* Backer, Jacob
  de
Jacob de Gheyn (II) → *see* Gheyn,
  Jacob II de
Jacob de Gheyn (III) → *see* Gheyn,
  Jacob III de
Jacob de Heusch → *see* Heusch, Jacob
  de
Jacob de Roor → *see* Roore, Jacobus
  Ignatius de
Jacob de Wet → *see* Wet, Jacob
  Willemsz. de
Jacob de Wit → *see* Wit, Jacob de
Jacob Esselen → *see* Esselens, Jacob
Jacob Esselens → *see* Esselens, Jacob
Jacob Fopsen van Es → *see* Es, Jacob
  Fopsen van
Jacob Fransz. van der Merck → *see*
  Merck, Jacob Fransz. van der
Jacob frères → *see* Jacob, Georges II
Jacob Gerritsz. Cuyp → *see* Cuyp,
  Jacob Gerritsz.
Jacob Getlar Smith → *see* Smith, Jacob
  Getlar
Jacob Grimmer → *see* Grimmer, Jacob
Jacob Grimmer, 1587 → *see* Grimmer,
  Jacob
Jacob Grooth → *see* Grooth, Jacob

Jacob Henricus Maris → *see* Maris,
  Jacob Henricus
Jacob Holhtz → *see* Holhtz, Jacob
  [Unidentified]
Jacob Hulsdonck → *see* Hulsdonck,
  Jacob
Jacob Jacobsz. van Geel → *see* Geel,
  Jacob Jacobsz. van
Jacob Jansz. van Velsen → *see* Velsen,
  Jacob Jansz. van
Jacob Jordaens → *see* Jordaens, Jacob
Jacob Koninck → *see* Koninck, Jacob I
Jacob Koninck (I) → *see* Koninck,
  Jacob I
Jacob Koninck (II) → *see* Koninck,
  Jacob (II)
Jacob l'aîné → *see* Jacob, Georges II
Jacob Lois → *see* Lois, Jacob
Jacob Lyon → *see* Lyon, Jacob
Jacob Marrel → *see* Marrel, Jacob
Jacob Matham → *see* Matham, Jacob
Jacob Moore → *see* More, Jacob
Jacob More → *see* More, Jacob
Jacob Ochtervelt → *see* Ochtervelt,
  Jacob
Jacob of Strasbourg (Jacobus
  Argentoratensis) → *see* Jacob von
  Strassburg (Jacobus
  Argentoratensis)
Jacob Oliviers → *see* Oliviers, Jacobus
Jacob Pinas → *see* Pynas, Jacob
  Symonsz.
Jacob Pynas → *see* Pynas, Jacob
  Symonsz.
Jacob Ruijschdael → *see* Ruisdael,
  Jacob van
Jacob Ruijsdaal → *see* Ruisdael, Jacob
  van
Jacob Ruisdael → *see* Ruisdael, Jacob
  van
Jacob Ruysdaal → *see* Ruisdael, Jacob
  van
Jacob Ruysdael → *see* Ruisdael, Jacob
  van
Jacob Ruysdal → *see* Ruisdael, Jacob
  van
Jacob Ruysdale → *see* Ruisdael, Jacob
  van
Jacob Ruysdall → *see* Ruisdael, Jacob
  van
Jacob Salomonsz. van Ruysdael → *see*
  Ruysdael, Jacob Salomonsz. van
Jacob Savery (I) → *see* Savery, Jacob I
Jacob Savery (II) → *see* Savery, Jacob
  (II)
Jacob Symonsz. Pynas → *see* Pynas,
  Jacob Symonsz.
Jacob Toorenvliet → *see* Toorenvliet,
  Jacob
Jacob Toornvliet → *see* Toorenvliet,
  Jacob
Jacob Ugtervelt → *see* Ochtervelt,
  Jacob
Jacob V. Huysum → *see* Huysum,
  Jacob van

Jacob van Amsterdam→see
Cornelisz. van Oostsanen, Jacob

Jacob van Campen→see Campen,
Jacob van

Jacob van der Croos→see Croos,
Jacob van der

Jacob van der Does (I)→see Does,
Jacob van der (the elder)

Jacob van der Lamen→see Lamen,
Jacob van der

Jacob van der Lanen→see Lamen,
Jacob van der

Jacob van der Sluis→see Sluis, Jacob
van der

Jacob van der Ulft→see Ulft, Jacob
van der

Jacob van Huysum→see Huysum,
Jacob van

Jacob van Loo→see Loo, Jacob van

Jacob van Mosscher→see Mosscher,
Jacob van

Jacob van Nieulandt→see Nieulandt,
Jacob van

Jacob van Oost (I)→see Oost, Jacob
I van

Jacob van Oost (the younger)→see
Oost, Jacob van (the younger)

Jacob van Ruisdael→see Ruisdael,
Jacob van

Jacob van Spreeuwen→see
Spreeuwen, Jacob van

Jacob van Stry→see Strij, Jacob van

Jacob van Utrecht→see Claessens,
Jacobus Trajectensis (Jacob van
Utrecht)

Jacob van Walscapelle→see
Walscapelle, Jacob van

Jacob Verdoes→see Does, Jacob van
der (the elder)

**Jacob von Strassburg (Jacobus
Argentoratensis)**   **BA**
(German artist, op.1494-1530)   WC
(German printmaker, act.1494-
1530)   BA
Bibl: ▶Bénézit; ▶Thieme-Becker

**Jacob of Strasbourg (Jacobus
Argentoratensis)**   **WC**

Jacob von Utrecht (Jacob Claesz. or
Klaesz. Trajectensis)→see
Claessens, Jacobus Trajectensis
(Jacob van Utrecht)

Jacob Weyer→see Weyer, Jacob

Jacob Willemsz. de Wet→see Wet,
Jacob Willemsz. de

Jacob Willemsz. Delff (I)→see Delff,
Jacob Willemsz. (I)

Jacob Willemsz. Delff (II)→see Delff,
Jacob Willemsz. II

Jacob Woutersz. Vosmaer→see
Vosmaer, Jacob Woutersz.

Jacob Xavery (IV)→see Xavery, Jacob
(IV)

Jacob, François-Honoré-Georges→see
Jacob-Desmalter, François Honoré
Georges

Jacob, Frank van (German(?) artist,
16th cent.)   **WC**

Jacob, Georges   **BA JG**
(French cabinetmaker, 1739-
1814)   BA
(French menuisier, 1739-1814,
master 1765)   GC
(French, 1739-1814, master
1765)   JG
Bibl: DADA; ▶Salverte, Ébénistes
18e s.

Jacob, Georges I   **GC**
Jacob, Georges I→see Jacob,
Georges

Jacob, Georges II (French menuisier,
1768-1803)   **GC**
Bibl: ▶Salverte, Ébénistes 18e s.;
▶Vial, Artistes décorateurs

Jacob frères   GC
Jacob l'aîné   GC

Jacob, Georges-Alphonse (French
menuisier, 1799-1870)   **GC**
Bibl: ▶Salverte, Ébénistes 18e s.;
▶Vial, Artistes décorateurs

Jacob-Desmalter   GC

Jacob, Guillaume (French goldsmith,
act.1685)   **BA**
Bibl: ▶Thieme-Becker

Jacob, H.H.   **WC WI**
(British artist, op.1817)   WC
(British artist, op.1817-)   WI

Jacob, Harro (German sculptor,
b.1939)   **BA**
Bibl: ▶Bénézit

Jacob, Henri (French menuisier,
master 1779)   **GC**
Bibl: ▶Salverte, Ébénistes 18e s.

Jacob, Isaak→see Jacob, Julius I

Jacob, Jean Gilles (Belgian architect,
1714-1781)   **BA**
Bibl: Genicot, ETUDES SUR DES
CONSTRUCTIOUS..., p.9

Jacob, Julius I   **GC**
(German artist, 1811-1882)   WC
(German draughtsman, 1811-
1882)   GC
Bibl: ▶Bénézit

Jacob, Isaak   GC

Jacob, Julius, I   **WC**
Jacob, Julius II→see Jacob, Julius, the
younger

Jacob, Julius, I→see Jacob, Julius I

Jacob, Julius, II→see Jacob, Julius,
the younger

Jacob, Julius, the younger   **BA**
(German artist, 1842-1929)   WC
(German painter, 1842-1929)   BA GC
Bibl: ▶Bénézit; ▶Neue deutsche
Biog.; ▶Thieme-Becker

Jacob, Julius II   **GC**
Jacob, Julius, II   **WC**

Jacob, Max   **BA**
(French artist, 1876-1944)   WC
(French painter, author, 1876-
1944)   BA
Bibl: ▶Bénézit; ▶Encyc. world art;
▶Vollmer, Künst.-Lex. 20. Jhr.

Jacob, Max Cyprien   **WC**
Jacob, Max Cyprien→see Jacob, Max

Jacob, Nicolas Henri   **GC**
(French artist, 1782-1871)   WC
(French, 1782-1871)   GC
Bibl: ▶Thieme-Becker; ▶Witt
checklist

Jacob, Nicolas-Henri   **WC**
Jacob, Nicolas-Henri→see Jacob,
Nicolas Henri

Jacob, Philip (British artist, op.20th
c.)   **WI**

Jacob, Ronald (American architect) **AV**
Bibl: GA houses, 1987 Feb.,
no.21, p.113

Jacob, Walter Friedrich Richard   **BA**
(German artist, 1893-)   WC
(German painter, printmaker,
1893-1964)   BA
Bibl: Arnold, WELTKUNST, LVII
(1987); ▶Bénézit; ▶Thieme-Becker

**Jacob, Walter Friedrich Richard
Walter)**   **WC**
Jacob, Walter Friedrich Richard
Walter)→see Jacob, Walter
Friedrich Richard

Jacob-Desmalter→see Jacob,
Georges-Alphonse

Jacob-Desmalter→see Jacob-
Desmalter, François Honoré
Georges

**Jacob-Desmalter, François Honoré
Georges**   **BA**
(French cabinetmaker, 1770-
1841)   BA
(French menuisier, 1770-1841)   GC
Bibl: ▶Penguin dec. arts;
▶Salverte, Ébénistes 18e s.;
▶Thieme-Becker

Jacob, François-Honoré-Georges   **GC**
Jacob-Desmalter   GC

Jacobelli, Paolo (Italian architect,
1936-)   **AV**
Bibl: Architettura, 1989 Sept.,
v.35, no.9, p.606

Jacobello Alberegno→see Alberegno,
Jacobello

Jacobello d'Antonello→see Jacopo di
Antonello

Jacobello da Messina→see Jacopo di
Antonello

Jacobello da Venezia→see Masegne,
Jacobello dalle

Jacobello dalle Masegne→see
Masegne, Jacobello dalle

Jacobello del Fiore BA GC JG PR WC
 (Italian artist, op.1401-m.1439) WC
 (Italian painter, 1370-1439) BA
 (Italian painter, d. 1439) PR
 (Italian painter, doca.1394-d. 1439) GC
 (Italian, active 1394-1439) JG
 Bibl: ▶Bénézit; Berenson, Venetian, v.1, p.93; ▶Bolaffi; ▶Encic. italiana; JPG Museum; ▶RILA/BHA; ▶Thieme-Becker; ▶White, Art & arch. Italy; ▶Witt checklist

Jacobello di Bonomo BA GC WC
 (Italian artist, op.c.1378-1385) WC
 (Italian painter, act.1375-1385) BA GC
 Bibl: ▶Bénézit; ▶Bolaffi; ▶RILA/BHA, 1986; ▶Thieme-Becker

Jacobellus GC JG
 (Italian scribe and illuminator, act. ca.1270) GC
 Bibl: ▶Euw, Ludwig mss., v.1, pp. 262-265
 Muriolus of Salerno GC

Jacober, Aldo (Italian architect) AV
 Bibl: Abitare, 1983 Oct., no.218, p.8
Jacobi→see Jacobi, Eduard
Jacobi [Unidentified] (Unknown painter) PR
 Bibl: January 27, 1809, lot 69, Christie's; March 14, 1806, lot 23, Christie's
Jacobi, Carlo (Italian photographer, 19th c.) BA
 Bibl: HISTORY OF PHOTOGRAPHY, VIII/4 (Oct-Dec 1984) 315-328
Jacobi, Eduard (German painter, act. 1860-1876) PR
 Bibl: ▶Thieme-Becker
 Eduard Jacobi PR
 Jacobi PR
Jacobi, Eli (American illustrator, painter, printmaker, 1898-1984) BA
 Bibl: Sullivan, Arts Mag. LXI/3 (Nov 1986) 109; ▶WWW Amer. art
Jacobi, F. C. (Italian(?) artist, op. 1771) WC
Jacobi, Jacques (Swiss artist, 1877-1922/32) WC
Jacobi, Lotte BA JG
 (American photographer, 1896-1990) BA
 (American, b. Germany 1896) JG
 Bibl: Clark Art Inst. Libr.; ▶Contemp. photogs., 1988; NY Times obit., 5 May 1990
Jacobi, Otto R.→see Jacobi, Otto Reinhold

Jacobi, Otto Reinhold BA
 (Canadian artist, 19th cent.) WC
 (German painter in CAN, 1812-1901) BA
 Bibl: ▶Artists Canada; ▶Bénézit; ▶Harper, Ptg. Canada; ▶MacDonald, Can. artists
Jacobi, Otto R. WC
Jacobi, Peter (West German artist, b.1935) BA
 Bibl: ▶Intl. dir. exh. artists, 1983
Jacobi, Ritzi (West German artist, b.1941) BA
 Bibl: ▶Babington Smith, Contemp. artists; ▶Intl. dir. exh. artists, 1983
Jacobo (Jacobus) da Fabriano (Italian artist, op.1460-1474) WC
Jacobo Basan→see Bassano, Jacopo (Jacopo da Ponte)
Jacobo da Puntormo→see Pontormo (Jacopo Carrucci)
Jacobs of Rotterdam, Gerrit GC WC
 (Dutch artist, op.1652) WC
 (Dutch, act.1652) GC
 Bibl: ▶Witt checklist
Jacobs, Edward (Active New Orleans, LA, U.S. 1845-1859, daguerreotypist) JG
Jacobs, Emil PR
 (German artist, 1802-1866) WC
 (German painter, 1802-1866) PR
 Bibl: ▶Thieme-Becker
 Emil Jacobs PR
Jacobs, Emil (Paul Emil) WC
 Jacobs, Paul Emil PR
Jacobs, Emil (Paul Emil)→see Jacobs, Emil
Jacobs, F. G. (German architect) AV
 Bibl: Deutsche Bauzeitschrift, 1986 May, v.34, no.5, p.571
Jacobs, Francois (German artist, 19th cent.) WC
Jacobs, Fred (Dutch architect, Breda) AV
 Bibl: Bouw, 1989 Sept.8, v.44, no.18, p.36
Jacobs, Gail (American interior designer) AV
 Bibl: Architectural digest, 1984 Sept. v.41, no.9, p.135
Jacobs, Harold (American painter, sculptor, b.1932) BA
 Bibl: Philadelphia (PA, USA), Moore College of Art...HAROLD JACOBS; SELECTED WORKS 1966-1985 22 Mar-3 May 1985; ▶WW Amer. Art
Jacobs, Hieronymus (early Netherlandish goldsmith, 16th c.) BA
 Bibl: Molle, REVUE BELGE D'ARCHEOLOGIE ET D'HISTOIRE DE L'ART, XLI(1972), 3-20
Jacobs, J. (British artist, op.1816-1864) WC
Jacobs, Jacobus Albertus Michael (Jacob) (Belgian artist, 1812-1879) WC

Jacobs, Jane (American city planner?, 1916-) AV
 Bibl: ▶Libr. of Congr. Name Auth. File
Jacobs, Jim (American painter, printmaker, b.1945) BA
 Bibl: ▶WW Amer. Art, 1989
Jacobs, Johannes (Flemish goldsmith in ITA, 1574/75-1650) BA
 Bibl: Kiene, M., BULLETIN DE L'INSTITUT HISTORIQUE BELGE DE ROME/LIII-LIV (1983-84), 177-191; ▶Thieme-Becker
Jacobs, John (British artist, op.1816-1864) WI
Jacobs, Lazarus (German glass maker in GBR, 1709-1796) BA
 Bibl: Josephs, BRISTOL AND GLOUCS., XCV (1977) 98-101; ▶Newman, Glass
Jacobs, Paul Emil→see Jacobs, Emil
Jacobs, Peter Frans (Belgian painter, 1780-1808) GC
 Bibl: ▶Thieme-Becker
Jacobs, R. C. L. M. (Belgian architect, Hasselt) AV
 Bibl: Bouw, 1987 Sept.4, v.42, no.18, p.35
Jacobs, René (Belgian architect, Hasselt) AV
 Bibl: De Architect, 1986 Apr., v.17, no.4, p.26
Jacobs, Stephen B. (American architect) AV
 Bibl: ▶AIA Pro File, 1985
Jacobs, William Leroy (American artist, 1869-1917) WI
Jacobsen→see Jacobsen, Antonio
Jacobsen, Anthony (American artist, op.c.1850-1890) WC
Jacobsen, Antonio BA PR WI
 (American artist, 1850-1921) WI
 (American painter, 1849-1921) BA PR
 Bibl: ART & ANTIQUES, III/4(JULY-AUG 1980), p.62; ▶RILA/BHA
 Antonio Jacobsen PR
 Jacobsen PR
 Jacobsen, Antonio Nicolo Gasparo PR
Jacobsen, Antonio Nicolo Gasparo→see Jacobsen, Antonio
Jacobsen, Arne (Danish architect, 1902-1971) AV BA
 Bibl: ▶Contemp. archts.; ▶London Times obit.; ▶Macmillan encyc. archts.; ▶Portoghesi, Diz. arch. e urbanistica; ▶Vollmer, Künst.-Lex. 20. Jhr.; ▶Weilbach, Kunst.leks.
Jacobsen, David BA WC
 (Danish artist, 1821-1871) WC
 (Danish painter, 1821-1871) BA
 Bibl: ▶Bénézit; ▶Thieme-Becker

Jacobsen, Egill   **BA**
  (Danish artist, 20th cent.)   **WC**
  (Danish painter, b.1910)   **BA**
    Bibl: ▶Bénézit; ▶Havlice, Idx. art.
    bio.

Jacobsen, Egille   **WC**
Jacobsen, Egille→*see* Jacobsen, Egill

Jacobsen, Eigil Smith *(Danish
  architect, Aarhus)*   **AV**
    Bibl: ▶Danske Arkitekters
    Landsforbund, 1984-85

Jacobsen, Georg *(Danish painter,
  b.1887)*   **BA**
    Bibl: ▶Bénézit; ▶MoMA libr. cat.;
    ▶Vollmer, Künst.-Lex. 20. Jhr.;
    ▶Weilbach, Kunst.leks.

Jacobsen, Holger *(Danish architect,
  b.1876)*   **BA**
    Bibl: ▶Vollmer, Künst.-Lex. 20.
    Jhr.; ▶Weilbach, Kunst.leks.

Jacobsen, Hugh Newell *(American
  architect, 1929-)*   **AV**
    Bibl: ▶Amer. archts. dir., 1970

Jacobsen, Lorentz *(Danish architect,
  18th c.)*   **BA**
    Bibl: Paulsen, Augustenborg

Jacobsen, Michael *(American
  painter, b.1957)*   **BA**
    Bibl: Milwaukee (WI, USA), Art
    Mus., Emerging imagists (1983)

Jacobsen, Nils *(Norwegian architect,
  Stavenger, 1940-)*   **AV**
    Bibl: Byggekunst: the Norwegian
    review of architecture, 1985,
    v.67, no.8, p.432

Jacobsen, Robert *(Danish sculptor,
  b.1912)*   **BA**
    Bibl: ▶Bénézit; ▶Vollmer,
    Künst.-Lex. 20. Jhr.; ▶Weilbach,
    Kunst.leks.

Jacobsen, Robin *(American interior
  designer, New York, NY, 1941?-
  1986)*   **AV**
    Bibl: Interior design, 1986 Oct.,
    v.57, no.10A, p.65

Jacobsen, Sophus *(Norwegian
  artist, 1833-1912)*   **WC**

Jacobsen, Svein *(Norwegian
  architect, Oslo)*   **AV**
    Bibl: Byggekunst: the Norwegian
    review of architecture, 1988,
    v.70, no.7, p.524

Jacobsgaard, Karl *(West German
  architect, Hamburg)*   **AV**
    Bibl: Werk Bauen + Wohnen,
    1989 Sept., no.9, p.85

Jacobshagen, N. Keith *(American
  painter, photographer, b.1941)*   **BA**
    Bibl: ARTFORUM, XXV/2 (Oct
    1986) 112-115; Guide exh.
    artists: N. Amer. ptrs.; ▶WW
    Amer. Art, 1986

Jacobson, Carl *(in USA painter, 20th
  c.)*   **BA**
    Bibl: Matlock, STUDIO INT., CCI
    (Apr 1988), p. 34-37; NYC phone
    bk.

Jacobson, David *(American
  architect, Owatonna, Minn., fl.
  1920's)*   **AV**
    Bibl: Architecture Minnesota,
    1989 Sept.-Oct., v.15, no.5, p.28

Jacobson, Edward L. Z.   **AV**

Jacobson, Karen *(American
  architect, New York, NY)*   **AV**
    Bibl: House beautiful, 1985 Mar.,
    v.127, no.3, p.86

Jacobson, Lynn *(American interior
  designer, NYC)*   **AV**
    Bibl: Architectural digest, 1988
    Mar., v.45, no.3, p.150

Jacobson, Nels *(American architect,
  Owatonna, Minn., fl. 1920's)*   **AV**
    Bibl: Architecture Minnesota,
    1989 Sept.-Oct., v.15, no.5, p.28

Jacobson, Phillip L. *(American
  architect, Seattle, Wash)*   **AV**
    Bibl: ▶AIA Pro File, 1987-88

*Jacobsz or Jacobsen, Juriaen or
  Jurgen*→*see* Jacobsz., Juriaen

Jacobsz, Dirck→*see* Jacobsz., Dirk

Jacobsz.→*see* Jacobsz., Dirk

**Jacobsz. or Jacobs, Huybrecht or
  Hubertus (Grimani)** *(Dutch artist,
  c.1562-1631)*   **WC**

Jacobsz., Dirck→*see* Jacobsz., Dirk

Jacobsz., Dirk   **BA GC PR WC WI**
  (Dutch, ca. 1497-1567)   **JG**
  *(early Netherlandish painter,
  1497-1567)*   **BA**
  *(Netherlandish painter, 1497-
  1567)*   **PR**
  *(Netherlands artist, c.1497-
  1567)*   **WC**
  *(Netherlands artist, circa 1497-
  1567)*   **WI**
  *(North Netherlandish painter,
  1497-1567)*   **GC**
    Bibl: ▶RILA/BHA; ▶Thieme-Becker;
    ▶Witt checklist
  Dirk Jacobsz.   **PR**

Jacobsz, Dirck   **JG**
  Jacobsz.   **PR**
  Jacobsz., Dirck   **PR**

Jacobsz., Hughe   **BA**
  *(early Netherlandish painter,
  1480-1538)*   **BA**
  *(Netherlands artist,
  op.1494-m.c.1534/8)*   **WC**
    Bibl: ▶Bénézit; ▶Encyc. world art;
    ▶Thieme-Becker; ▶Wurzbach, NLD
    Künst.-Lex.

**Jacobsz., Hughe, Huge, Hugo or
  Huygh (possibly identified
  with Master of the St. John
  Altarpiece)**   **WC**
*Jacobsz., Hughe, Huge, Hugo or
  Huygh (possibly identified with
  Master of the St. John
  Altarpiece)*→*see* Jacobsz., Hughe

Jacobsz., Juriaen   **BA GC**
  (Flemish painter, 1625/6-1685)   **GC**
  (Flemish painter, ca.1625-1685)   **BA**
  (German artist, 1625/6-1685)   **WC**
    Bibl: ▶Bénézit; ▶Encyc. world art;
    Getty Photo Study Coll.;
    ▶RILA/BHA; ▶Thieme-Becker;
    ▶Witt checklist

**Jacobsz or Jacobsen, Juriaen or
  Jurgen**   **WC**

Jacobsz., Lambert   **BA GC WC WI**
  (Dutch artist, 1592-1637)   **WI**
  (Dutch artist, c.1598-1636)   **WC**
  *(Dutch painter, before 1600 -
  1637)*   **BA**
  (Dutch, ca.1598-1636)   **GC**
    Bibl: ▶Thieme-Becker; ▶Witt
    checklist; ▶Wurzbach, NLD
    Künst.-Lex.

Jacobsz., Simon *(Dutch, b.1520)*   **GC**
    Bibl: ▶Thieme-Becker

Jacobus *(Spanish artist, 15th cent.)*   **WC**

Jacobus   **BA**
  *(Italian marbleworker and
  mosaicist, act.1185-1217)*   **GC**
  (Italian mason, 13th c.)   **BA**
    Bibl: Getty Photo Study Coll.
    (Medieval); Glass, Pavements;
    Hutton, Cosmati, p.7; Römisches
    Jahrb. für Kunstgesch. (1976), 15

Jacobus (elder)   **GC**
  Jacobus I   **GC**
  Jacobus Romanus (elder)   **GC**
Jacobus (elder)→*see* Jacobus

Jacobus (younger) *(Italian
  marbleworker and mosaicist, act.
  1231-1235)*   **GC**
    Bibl: Getty Photo Study Coll.
    (Medieval); Hutton, Cosmati, p.7
  Jacobus Romanus (younger)   **GC**

Jacobus Biltius→*see* Biltius, Jacobus
Jacobus Broekerhoff→*see*
  Broekerhoff, Jacobus
*Jacobus Cornelis Wyand
  Cossaar*→*see* Cossaar, Jacobus
  Cornelis Wyand

Jacobus de Albona *(French scribe,
  act.1270)*   **GC**
    Bibl: ▶Branner, Ms. ptg. Paris, pp.
    137-138

Jacobus de Cessolis *(Probably
  French, flourished 1290)*   **JG**

Jacobus de Lucha *(Italian scribe,
  14th century)*   **GC**
    Bibl: Conti, Miniatura bolognese,
    p.85

Jacobus Esselens→*see* Esselens,
  Jacob
Jacobus I→*see* Jacobus
Jacobus Ignatius de Roore→*see*
  Roore, Jacobus Ignatius de
Jacobus Leisten→*see* Leisten,
  Jacobus
Jacobus Oliviers→*see* Oliviers,
  Jacobus
Jacobus Packee→*see* Packee, Jacobus

Jacobus Pictor *(Italian painter, act. 1286-1288)* **BA**
    Bibl: Carta ROMA ANNO 1300, p.457

Jacobus Romanus (elder) →see Jacobus

Jacobus Romanus (younger) →see Jacobus (younger)

Jacobus Simon Hendrik Kever →see Kever, Jacobus Simon Hendrik

Jacobus Uchtervelt →see Ochtervelt, Jacob

Jacobus van der Hagen →see Hagen, Jacobus van der

Jacobus Victor →see Victors, Jacomo

Jacobus Victors →see Victors, Jacomo

Jacobus Vrel →see Vrel, Jacobus

Jacoby, Alfred *(German architect, Frankfurt)* **AV**
    Bibl: Deutsche Bauzeitschrift, 1984 Dec., v.32, no.12, p.1679

Jacoby, Helmut **AV BA**
    (German architect, b.1926) BA
    (German(?) architect, 1926-) AV
    Bibl: ▶Avery Libr. cat.; Clark Art Inst. Libr., Daidalos, 1987 Sept., no.25, p. 92ff; ▶RILA/BHA

Jacoby, Nicolas *(French architect, act.1759)* **BA**
    Bibl: Ars Hungarica, V/2 (1977) pp.241-249

Jacoby, V. *(Russian artist, 1834-1905)* **WC**

Jacomart (Jaime Baçó) **BA**
    (Spanish artist, op.1440-m.1461) WC
    (Spanish painter, 1409?-1461) PR
    (Spanish painter, ca.1413-1461) BA
    Bibl: ▶Aldana Fernández, Artistas valencianos; ▶Bénézit; Detroit Inst of Arts catalogue; ▶Encyc. world art; ▶Rafols, Artistas Cataluña; ▶Thieme-Becker

Baco PR
Baco, Jacomart **PR**
Baco, Jaime (Jacomart) **WC**
Jacomart Baco PR
Jacomart Baco →see Jacomart (Jaime Baçó)

Jacomb-Hood →see Jacomb-Hood, George Percy

Jacomb-Hood, George Percy **PR WC WI**
    (British artist, 1857-1929) WC WI
    (British painter, 1857-1930) PR
    Bibl: Ashmolean Museum catalogue; ▶Thieme-Becker

George Percy Jacomb-Hood PR
Jacomb-Hood PR
Jacome Bazan →see Bassano, Jacopo (Jacopo da Ponte)

Jacome Vazan →see Bassano, Jacopo (Jacopo da Ponte)

Jacometti, Ignazio *(Italian sculptor, 1819-1883)* **GC**
    Bibl: TCI Roma e dintorni

Jacometti, Pietro Paolo *(Italian sculptor, bronze founder, painter, architect, 1580-ca.1655)* **BA**
    Bibl: ▶Bénézit; ▶Thieme-Becker

Jacometti, Tarquinio *(Italian sculptor and architect, act.late 16th - early 17th century)* **GC**
    Bibl: TCI Marche

Jacometto **BA PR**
    (Italian artist, -a.1497) WC
    (Italian painter, act. ca.1472-1494, d. 1497) PR
    (Italian painter, act.1472-1494) BA
    (Italian, d. bef.1497) GC
    Bibl: ▶Bolaffi; ▶Fredericksen & Zeri, Census; Getty Photo Study Coll. (Ptgs.); ▶Thieme-Becker; ▶Witt checklist

Jacometto Veneziano **GC PR WC**
Veneziano, Jacometto GC PR
Jacometto Veneziano →see Jacometto

Jacomin →see Jacomin, Jean Marie

Jacomin, Alfred **GC WC**
    (French artist, 1842-1913) WC
    (French, 1842-1913) GC
    Bibl: ▶Thieme-Becker

Jacomin, Jean Marie *(French painter, 1789-1858)* **PR**
    Bibl: ▶Thieme-Becker

Jacomin PR
Jacomin, Jean-Marie PR
Jean Marie Jacomin PR
Jacomin, Jean-Marie →see Jacomin, Jean Marie

Jacomin, Marie Ferdinand *(French artist, 1843-1902)* **WC**

Jacomini, Beverly *(American interior designer, Houston, Tex)* **AV**
    Bibl: Southern accents, 1988 July-Aug., v.11, no.4, p.76

Jacomo Bassan →see Bassano, Jacopo (Jacopo da Ponte)

Jacomo Bassano →see Bassano, Jacopo (Jacopo da Ponte)

Jacomo da Pesaro *(Italian ceramist, act.1507, d.1547)* **BA**
    Bibl: Alvera, ARTE VENETA, XXXVII(1983), 219; ▶Honey, Euro. ceramic; ▶Thieme-Becker

Jacomo da Pontormo →see Pontormo (Jacopo Carrucci)

Jacomo da Puntormo →see Pontormo (Jacopo Carrucci)

Jacomo del Pisano →see Giacomo del Pisano

Jacomo di Giovanni (di Onofrio) *(Italian artist, op.c.1515-1522)* **WC**

Jacomo Pontorno →see Pontormo (Jacopo Carrucci)

Jacomo Victor →see Victors, Jacomo

Jacono, Jan **WC WI**
    (British artist, 1949-) WC
    (British artist, b.1949) WI

Jacope Bassano →see Bassano, Jacopo (Jacopo da Ponte)

Jacopino d'Arezzo *(Italian illuminator, 15th century)* **GC**
    Bibl: ▶Bénézit; Fava, Biblioteca Estense, v.2, p.131

Jacopino da Arezzo GC
Jacopino da Arezzo →see Jacopino d'Arezzo

Jacopino da Tradate **BA**
    (Italian sculptor, act.1401-1425) BA
    (Italian sculptor, doca.1401-1425) GC
    Bibl: ▶Bessone-Aurelj, Scult. & arch. ital.; TCI Lombardia; TCI Milano e laghi; ▶Thieme-Becker

Iacopino da Tradate **GC**
Jacopino dal Conte →see Jacopino del Conte

Jacopino de' Bavosi →see Jacopino di Francesco de' Bavosi

Jacopino del Conte **BA GC PR**
    (Italian artist, 1510-1598) WC
    (Italian painter, 1510-1598) BA GC PR
    Bibl: ▶Bolaffi; ▶Encic. italiana; ▶Encyc. world art; ▶Freedberg, Ptg. Italy; ▶RILA/BHA; ▶Thieme-Becker

Conte, Jacopino del PR
Conte, Jacopo del GC
Conte, Jacopo or Jacopino del **WC**
Jacopino dal Conte PR
Jacopino di Francesco →see Jacopino di Francesco de' Bavosi

Jacopino di Francesco de' Bavosi **BA**
    (Italian artist, 14th cent.) WC
    (Italian artist, op.1350-1385) WC
    (Italian painter, 14th century) GC
    (Italian painter, act. ca.1350-ca.1383) PR
    (Italian painter, act.1360-1383) BA
    (Italian, act.1350-1385) GC
    Bibl: ▶Bénézit; ▶Bolaffi; ▶Fredericksen & Zeri, Census; TCI Emilia-Romagna; ▶Thieme-Becker; ▶Witt checklist

Avanzo, Pseudo-Jacopo (Jacopo de' Bavosi or Jacopo da Bologna) GC
Avanzo, Pseudo-Jacopo (Jacopo dei Bavosi or Jacopo da Bologna) **WC**
Jacopino de' Bavosi GC
Jacopino di Francesco **PR WC**
Jacopo di Francesco **GC**
Pseudo Avanzo **GC**

Jacopo Amigoni →see Amigoni, Jacopo

Jacopo Bambini →see Bambini, Giacomo

Jacopo Bassano →see Bassano, Jacopo (Jacopo da Ponte)

Jacopo Bellini →see Bellini, Jacopo

Jacopo Carucci da Pontormo →see Pontormo (Jacopo Carrucci)

Jacopo Cavedone →see Cavedone, Giacomo

Jacopo Chimenti → *see* Jacopo da Empoli (Jacopo Chimenti)

Jacopo Cortese, Called, Il Borgognone → *see* Courtois, Jacques (le Bourguignon)

Jacopo d'Antonello → *see* Jacopo di Antonello

Jacopo d'Antonio Tatti → *see* Sansovino, Jacopo (Jacopo d'Antonio Tatti)

Jacopo da Bologna *(Italian painter, act.1516)* **BA**

    Bibl: Faietti, Bologna e l'umanesimo, pp.231-237; TCI Emilia-Romagna, artist idx.

Jacopo da Bologna → *see* Ripanda, Jacopo

Jacopo da Camerino *(Italian artist, 15th cent.)* **WC**

Jacopo da Campli → *see* Giacomo da Campli

Jacopo da Cassola *(Italian scribe, 15th century)* **GC**

    Bibl: Fava, Biblioteca Estense, v.2, p.131

Jacopo da Empoli → *see* Jacopo da Empoli (Jacopo Chimenti)

Jacopo da Empoli (Jacopo Chimenti) **BA PR**

    (Italian artist, c.1554-1640) **WC**

    (Italian painter, ca.1554-1640) **BA GC PR**

    Bibl: ▶Bolaffi; ▶Encic. italiana; ▶Encyc. world art; Getty Photo Study Coll. (Ptgs.); ▶RILA/BHA; ▶Thieme-Becker

    Chimenti **PR**

    Chimenti, Jacopo **PR**

Chimenti, Jacopo (Jacopo da Empoli) **GC WC**

    Empoli **PR**

    Empoli, Jacopo da **GC PR**

    Iacopo Chimenti da Iacopo **PR**

    Iacopo da Empoli **PR**

    Jacopo Chimenti **PR**

    Jacopo da Empoli **GC PR**

Jacopo da Firenze **GC WC**

    (Italian artist, op.1410) **WC**

    (Italian, act.1410) **GC**

    Bibl: ▶Witt checklist

Jacopo da Milano → *see* Jacopo di Domenico da Milano

Jacopo da Monselice *(Italian painter, act.1381-1406)* **BA**

    Bibl: ▶Bolaffi; ▶Thieme-Becker

Jacopo da Montagnana **BA GC PR**

    (Italian artist, c.1440/3-p.1499) **WC**

    (Italian painter, 1440/43-1499/1508) **BA PR**

    (Italian, 1440/43-1499/1508) **GC**

    Bibl: ▶Bénézit; ▶Bolaffi; ▶Encic. italiana; ▶Encyc. world art; ▶RILA/BHA; ▶Thieme-Becker; ▶Witt checklist

    Montagnana, Jacopo da **PR**

Montagnana, Jacopo di Paride Parisati da **GC WC**

Jacopo da Norcia (Jacopo Siciliano) *(Italian artist, op.1524-m.1544)* **WC**

Jacopo da Pergola *(Italian scribe, act.1452)* **GC**

    Bibl: Zazzeri, Codici Malatestiana, p.46

Jacopo da Ponte → *see* Bassano, Jacopo (Jacopo da Ponte)

Jacopo da Ponte, Called, Il Bassano, and Il Bassan Vecchio → *see* Bassano, Jacopo (Jacopo da Ponte)

Jacopo da Reggio *(Italian illuminator, 13th c.)* **BA**

    Bibl: ▶Thieme-Becker

Jacopo da Riva *(Italian artist, op. 1372-m.a.1418)* **WC**

Jacopo da Roccantica *(Italian artist, 15th cent.)* **WC**

Jacopo da San Polo *(Italian artist, op.1451)* **WC**

Jacopo da San Severino *(Italian artist, 15th cent.)* **WC**

Jacopo da Valenza **GC PR WC**

    (Italian artist, op.1485-1509) **WC**

    (Italian painter, act. 1485-1509) **PR**

    (Italian, act.1485-1509) **GC**

    Bibl: ▶Thieme-Becker; ▶Witt checklist

Jacopo da Verona **BA GC WC**

    (Italian artist, 1355-p.1442) **WC**

    (Italian painter, 1355-1436/42) **GC**

    (Italian painter, b.1355, d.1436-1442) **BA**

    Bibl: ▶Bolaffi; ▶RILA/BHA, 1986; ▶Thieme-Becker; ▶Witt checklist

Jacopo dal Casentino (Landini) → *see* Jacopo del Casentino

Jacopo de Barbari → *see* Barbari, Jacopo de'

Jacopo de'Barbari → *see* Barbari, Jacopo de'

Jacopo de'Boateri **GC**

    (Italian artist, op.c.1500) **WC**

    (Italian painter, act. ca.1500) **GC**

    Bibl: Ciaranfi, Pitti, p.92; Getty Photo Study Coll. (Ptgs.)

    Boateri, Jacopo **WC**

    Boateri, Jacopo de' **GC**

Jacopo del Arcangelo → *see* Sellaio, Jacopo del

Jacopo del Casentino **BA GC PR**

    (Italian artist, 1279-1358) **WC**

    (Italian painter and illuminator, 1279-1358) **GC**

    (Italian painter, 1278/70-1358(?)) **PR**

    (Italian painter, 1297-ca.1358) **BA**

    Bibl: ▶Bolaffi; COMMENTARI, XXIX/1-4 (Jan-Dec 1978) 165-168; ▶Fredericksen & Zeri, Census; Getty Photo Study Coll. (Medieval); TCI Firenze; ▶Thieme-Becker; ▶Witt checklist

Jacopo dal Casentino (Landini) **WC**

Jacopo del Sellaio → *see* Sellaio, Jacopo del

Jacopo del Tonghi → *see* Giacomo del Tonghio

Jacopo del Tonghio → *see* Giacomo del Tonghio

Jacopo della Pila **BA GC**

    (Italian sculptor, act.1471-1502) **BA**

    (Italian sculptor, doc.a.1471-1502) **GC**

    Bibl: TCI Napoli e dintorni; ▶Thieme-Becker

Jacopo della Quercia → *see* Della Quercia, Jacopo

Jacopo di Alessandro del Tedesco *(Italian artist, op.1503)* **WC**

Jacopo di Antonello **BA GC**

    (Italian artist, c.1455-p.1490) **WC**

    (Italian painter, b.ca.1455, act. 1479-1482) **BA**

    (Italian painter, ca.1455-act. 1479-1482) **GC**

    Bibl: ▶Bolaffi; Getty Photo Study Coll. (Ptgs.); ▶RILA/BHA, 1986; ▶Thieme-Becker; ▶Witt checklist

    Jacobello d'Antonello **GC**

    Jacobello da Messina **GC**

Jacopo d'Antonello **GC**

Jacopo or Jacobello d'Antonello **WC**

Jacopo di Bartolomeo *(Italian painter, act.1430)* **BA**

    Bibl: Corbo, Commentary XXVIII/1-3 (Jan-Sept 1977), 162-171

Jacopo di Bedo di Benedetto da Gubbio *(Italian, act.1434-1475)* **GC**

    Bibl: ▶Thieme-Becker

Jacopo di Cione **BA GC PR WC WI**

    (Italian artist, op.1365-1398) **WI**

    (Italian artist, op.c.1365-1398) **WC**

    (Italian painter, act. 1362-1398) **PR**

    (Italian painter, act.1362-1398) **BA GC**

    Bibl: ▶Bolaffi; ▶Encyc. world art; ▶RILA/BHA, 1986; ▶Thieme-Becker; ▶White, Art & arch. Italy, p.370

Jacopo di Domenico da Milano **GC**

    (Italian artist, op.1511-1535) **WC**

    (Italian, act.1525-1538) **GC**

    Bibl: ▶Thieme-Becker

Jacopo da Milano **WC**

Jacopo di Domenico di Nuccio
(Italian painter, b.ca.1382, act.
1427) **BA**
Bibl: ANTICHITÀ VIVA, XXVI/2
(Mar-June, 1987) 5-7; ▶Bolaffi;
▶Fremantle, Florentine Gothic,
p.593; ▶Thieme-Becker
Jacopo di Francesco → see Jacopino di
Francesco de' Bavosi
Jacopo di Giovanni di Francesco **BA**
(Italian artist, -1553) **WC**
(Italian painter, 1495-1553) **BA**
Bibl: ▶Bénézit; ▶Bolaffi; Ciatti,OPD
RESTAURO,II(1987),p.122;
▶Thieme-Becker; ULAN 1988;
▶Witt checklist
**Jacopo di Giovanni di Francesco
(Jacone)** **WC**
*Jacopo di Giovanni di Francesco
(Jacone) → see* Jacopo di Giovanni
di Francesco
Jacopo di Lorenzo di Tebaldo
(Italian sculptor, mosaicist, 13th
c.) **BA**
Bibl: ▶Bénézit; ▶Encyc. world art;
▶Thieme-Becker
Jacopo di Michele, Il Gera **GC**
(Italian artist, op.1389-1390) **WC**
(Italian, act. ca. 1389) **GC**
Bibl: George Goldner; Getty Photo
Study Coll. (Ptgs.);
▶Thieme-Becker; ▶Witt checklist
Gera **GC**
Gera, Jacopo di Michele, Il **WC**
Jacopo di Mino del Pellicciaio **BA GC**
(Italian artist, -a.1396) **WC**
(Italian artist, op.1342-m.a.
1396) **WC**
(Italian painter, act.1344-1389) **BA**
(Italian painter, doca.1342-d.ca.
1396) **GC**
Bibl: ▶Bolaffi; TCI Toscana;
▶Thieme-Becker
Giacomo di Mino di Neri del
Pellicciaio **GC**
**Jacopo or Giacomo di Minto or
Mino del Pellicciaio** **WC**
Pellicciaio, Giacomo di Mino del **WC**
Jacopo di Paolo **BA GC PR**
(Italian artist, op.1390-1426) **WC**
(Italian painter, act. 1378-1426) **PR**
(Italian painter, act.1378-
1426) **BA GC**
Bibl: ▶Bolaffi; ▶Encyc. world art;
▶Fredericksen & Zeri, Census;
▶RILA/BHA, 1986
Jacopo di Paolo da Bologna **WC**
Jacopo di Paolo da Bologna → see
Jacopo di Paolo
Jacopo di Paolo di Pomposa
(Italian artist, 14th cent.) **WC**
Jacopo di Paolo Marieschi → see
Marieschi, Jacopo di Paolo
Jacopo di Piero Guidi (Italian
sculptor, architect, act.1370-1405) **BA**
Bibl: ▶Portoghesi, Diz. arch. e
urbanistica; ▶Thieme-Becker

Jacopo di Rosa → see Jacopo di Rosa
[Unidentified]
Jacopo di Rosa [Unidentified]
(Unknown painter) **PR**
Bibl: Tuttavilla inventory, Naples,
1681: possibly same as Giacomo
Russo?
Jacopo di Rosa **PR**
Jacovo di Rosa **PR**
**Jacopo di Ser Michele da Citta di
Castello** (Italian painter, act.1412) **GC**
Bibl: ▶Thieme-Becker
Jacopo di Stefano di Filippo
(Italian, 1490) **JG**
Jacopo di Vinciolo (Italian painter,
before 1430-1495) **BA**
Bibl: Prospettiva, 33-36 (Apr
1983-Jan 1984) 62-75
Jacopo Filippo d'Argenta → see
Argenta, Iacopo Filippo
Jacopo Francia → see Francia,
Giacomo
Jacopo Guarana → see Guarana,
Jacopo
Jacopo Ligozzi → see Ligozzi, Jacopo
Jacopo Moore → see More, Jacob
Jacopo Nizzola da Trezzo (Italian
medalist, sculptor, architect,
goldsmith, gem engraver, ca.1515-
1589) **BA**
Bibl: ▶Encic. italiana; ▶Encic. univ.
ilus.; ▶Forrer, Medallists;
▶Thieme-Becker
*Jacopo or Giacomo di Minto or Mino
del Pellicciaio → see* Jacopo di
Mino del Pellicciaio
Jacopo or Jacobello d'Antonello → see
Jacopo di Antonello
Jacopo Palma (il Giovane) → see
Palma Giovane (Jacopo Negretti)
Jacopo Palma (il Vecchio) → see
Palma, Jacopo il Vecchio
Jacopo Palma Giovane → see Palma
Giovane (Jacopo Negretti)
Jacopo Palma seniore → see Palma,
Jacopo il Vecchio
*Jacopo Palma Vecchio (Jacopo
Negreti) → see* Palma, Jacopo il
Vecchio
Jacopo Pontormo → see Pontormo
(Jacopo Carrucci)
Jacopo Ripanda → see Ripanda,
Jacopo
Jacopo Robusti → see Tintoretto,
Jacopo (Jacopo Robusti)
*Jacopo Robusti detto il
Tintoretto → see* Tintoretto, Jacopo
(Jacopo Robusti)
Jacopo Russo → see Russo, Jacopo
Jacopo Siciliano → see Del Duca,
Giacomo
Jacopo Tedesco (German architect
in ITA, act.1228) **BA**
Bibl: ▶Macmillan encyc. archts.;
▶Portoghesi, Diz. arch. e
urbanistica; ▶Thieme-Becker

Jacopo Tintoretto → see Tintoretto,
Jacopo (Jacopo Robusti)
Jacopo Veneziano (Italian artist, op.
1516) **WC**
Jacopo Vignali → see Vignali, Jacopo
Jacopo Zoboli → see Zoboli, Giacomo
Jacopo Zucchi → see Zucchi, Jacopo
Jacopo, Fra (Italian mosaicist, act.
1225) **BA**
Bibl: ▶Encyc. world art;
▶Thieme-Becker
Jacops, Joseph (Belgian artist,
1808-) **WC**
Jacopsz., Floris (early Netherlandish
painter, act.1471-1506) **BA**
Bibl: Bangs, J.D., TRIBUTE TO
LOTTE BRAND PHILIP...(1985)
p.21-27
Jacopus de Turchlarius (Italian
artist, 17th cent.) **WC**
Jacot, Antoine-Pierre (French
ébéniste, master 1766) **GC**
Bibl: ▶Salverte, Ébénistes 18e s.
Jacot, Pierre-Martin (French artist) **AV**
Bibl: Architecture intérieure créé,
1985 Dec.-1986 Jan., no.209,
p.52
Jacotot, Pascale (French landscape
architect) **AV**
Bibl: Architecture d'aujourd'hui,
1989 Apr., no.262, p.44
Jacottet, Jean (Swiss artist, 1806-p.
1843) **WC**
Jacovacci, Francesco **GC WC**
(Italian artist, 1838-1908) **WC**
(Italian painter, 1838-1908) **GC**
Bibl: ▶Witt checklist
Jacovo di Castro → see Castro,
Giacomo di
Jacovo di Rosa → see Jacopo di Rosa
[Unidentified]
Jacovo Tintoretto → see Tintoretto,
Jacopo (Jacopo Robusti)
Jacquand → see Jacquand, Claude
(Claudius)
Jacquand, Claude → see Jacquand,
Claude (Claudius)
Jacquand, Claude (Claudius) **BA PR**
(French artist, 1804-1878) **WC**
(French painter, 1804-1878) **BA PR**
(French, 1804-1878) **GC**
Bibl: ▶Bénézit; ▶RILA/BHA;
▶Thieme-Becker; ▶Witt checklist
Claude Jacquand **PR**
Jacquand **PR**
Jacquand, Claude **GC**
Jacquand, Claude or Claudius **WC**
Jacquand, Claude or Claudius → see
Jacquand, Claude (Claudius)
Jacquand, Mlle (French artist, op.
1810-1818) **WC**
Jacquard → see Jacquard, Claude II
Jacquard, Antoine (French artist,
op.1616-m.c.1640) **WC**
Jacquard, Claude → see Jacquard,
Claude II

Jacquard, Claude (II) → see Jacquard,
  Claude II
Jacquard, Claude II   **BA**
   (French artist, 1686-1736) **WC**
   (French painter, 1686-1736) **BA PR**
   Bibl: ▶Bénézit; Clark Art Inst.
    Libr.; ▶RILA/BHA; ▶Thieme-Becker
  Claude Jacquard **PR**
  Claude Jacquard (II) **PR**
  Jacquard **PR**
  Jacquard, Claude **PR**
  Jacquard, Claude (II) **PR**
  Jacquart or Jacquard, Claude, II **WC**
Jacquard, Joseph Marie (French
   inventor, 1752-1834) **BA**
   Bibl: ▶New Columbia encyc.
Jacquart (French artist, 19th cent.) **WC**
Jacquart or Jacquard, Claude, II → see
  Jacquard, Claude II
Jacque → see Jacque, Charles Émile
Jacque, Charles → see Jacque, Charles
  Émile
Jacque, Charles Émile **BA GC PR WC**
   (French artist, 1813-1894) **WC**
   (French painter, 1813-1894) **GC PR**
   (French painter, printmaker,
    1813-1894) **BA**
   Bibl: ▶Bénézit; ▶RILA/BHA;
    ▶Thieme-Becker; ▶Witt checklist
  Charles Émile Jacque **PR**
  Jacque **PR**
  Jacque, Charles **PR**
  Jacque, Charles-Emile **PR**
  Jacques, Charles **PR**
  Jacques, Charles Emile **PR**
Jacque, Charles-Emile → see Jacque,
  Charles Émile
Jacque, Louis (Canadian artist,
   1919-) **WC**
Jacquemart, Alfred (French
   sculptor, 1824-1896) **GC**
   Bibl: Getty Photo Study Coll.
    (Sculp.); ▶Thieme-Becker
  Jacquemart, Henri Marie Alfred **GC**
Jacquemart, Henri Marie Alfred → see
  Jacquemart, Alfred
Jacquemart, Jules Ferdinand **BA GC**
   (French artist, 1837-1880) **WC**
   (French painter, 1837-1880) **GC**
   (French painter, printmaker,
    1837-1880) **BA**
   Bibl: ▶Bénézit; ▶Thieme-Becker
  Jacquemart, Jules Ferdinand. **WC**
Jacquemart, Jules Ferdinand. → see
  Jacquemart, Jules Ferdinand
Jacquemart, Mme. Edouard **GC**
   (French artist, 1841-1912) **WC**
   (French painter, 1841-1912) **GC**
   Bibl: ▶Bénézit
  Jacquemart, Nelie, (nee Andre) **WC**
Jacquemart, Nelie, (nee Andre) → see
  Jacquemart, Mme. Edouard
Jacquemin (French artist, 17th cent.) **WC**
Jacquemin, Andre (French artist,
   1904) **WC**

Jacquemin, Emile (French architect,
   builder, and founder of weekly
   newspaper L'Immeuble et la
   construction dans l'Est, 1850-
   1907) **AV**
   Bibl: Cahiers de la recherche
    architecturale, 1989, no.24-25,
    p.100
Jacquemin, Gary (American
   architect) **AV**
Jacquemin, Jeanne (French artist,
   19th cent.) **WC**
Jacquemot, Giles (French architect,
   Paris) **AV**
   Bibl: Techniques et architecture,
    1984 Dec., no.357, p.111
Jacques Albert Senave → see Sénave,
  Jacques Albert
Jacques Almand → see Griesinger,
  Jakob
Jacques Antoine Arlaud → see Arlaud,
  Jacques Antoine
Jacques Antoine Beaufort → see
  Beaufort, Jacques Antoine
Jacques Antoine Vallin → see Vallin,
  Jacques Antoine
Jacques Augustin Pajou → see Pajou,
  Jacques Augustin
Jacques Backereel → see Backereel,
  Jacques
Jacques Bassan → see Bassano, Jacopo
  (Jacopo da Ponte)
Jacques Blanchard → see Blanchard,
  Jacques
Jacques Callot → see Callot, Jacques
Jacques Cavedon → see Cavedone,
  Giacomo
Jacques Chapiro → see Chapiro,
  Jacques
Jacques Coignet → see Coignet,
  Jacques
Jacques Courtois → see Courtois,
  Jacques (le Bourguignon)
Jacques d'Angouleme → see Jacques,
  Pierre (Jacques d'Angoulême)
Jacques d'Arthois → see Arthois,
  Jacques d'
Jacques D'Artois → see Arthois,
  Jacques d'
Jacques de Chartres → see Collet,
  Jacques
Jacques de Lajoue (II) → see Lajoue,
  Jacques II de
Jacques de Reims → see Jacques,
  Pierre (Jacques d'Angoulême)
Jacques de Ville → see Ville, Jacques
  de
Jacques de Wiellier → see Ville,
  Jacques de
Jacques du Pont → see Bassano,
  Jacopo (Jacopo da Ponte)
Jacques Dumont → see Dumont,
  Jacques
Jacques Eschot → see Eschot, Jacques

Jacques Fouquieres → see Fouquières,
  Jacques
Jacques Francois Carabain → see
  Carabain, Jacques François
Jacques Francois Joseph
  Swebach → see Swebach, Jacques
  François Joseph
Jacques Grief Claeuw → see Claeuw,
  Jacques Grief
Jacques Jordaens → see Jordaens,
  Jacob
Jacques Jordans → see Jordaens,
  Jacob
Jacques Laudin (I) → see Laudin,
  Jacques I
Jacques Laurent Agasse → see Agasse,
  Jacques Laurent
Jacques le Maçon → see Collet,
  Jacques
Jacques le Saige de Douai → see Le
  Saige, Jacques
Jacques Linard → see Linard, Jacques
Jacques Lipchitz → see Lipchitz,
  Jacques
Jacques Louis David → see David,
  Jacques-Louis
Jacques Louis Francois Touze → see
  Touzé, Jacques Louis François
Jacques Mauny → see Mauny, Jacques
Jacques Palme → see Palma, Jacopo il
  Vecchio
Jacques Parmentier → see Parmentier,
  James
Jacques Pontormo → see Pontormo
  (Jacopo Carrucci)
Jacques Raymond Brascassat → see
  Brascassat, Jacques Raymond
Jacques Robusti → see Tintoretto,
  Jacopo (Jacopo Robusti)
Jacques Roger Simon → see Simon,
  Jacques Roger
Jacques Rousseau → see Rousseau,
  Jacques
Jacques Ruysdael → see Ruisdael,
  Jacob van
Jacques Sarrazin → see Sarrazin,
  Jacques
Jacques Savery → see Savery, Jacob (II)
Jacques Sebastien Le Clerc → see Le
  Clerc, Jacques Sébastien
Jacques Stella → see Stella, Jacques
Jacques van Schuppen → see
  Schuppen, Jacques van
Jacques Villon → see Villon, Jacques
  (Gaston Duchamp)
Jacques Wilbaut → see Wilbaut,
  Jacques
Jacques Yverni → see Yverni, Jacques
Jacques, Andre (French artist,
   1880-) **WC**
Jacques, Charles → see Jacque,
  Charles Émile
Jacques, Charles Emile → see Jacque,
  Charles Émile

Jacques, Herbert *(American architect, partner in firm of Andrews, Jacques & Rantoul, Boston, Mass, 1857-1916)* **AV**
    Bibl: ▶Withey, Amer. archts.

Jacques, Maurice **JG WC**
    (French artist, 1712-1784) WC
    (French, 1712-1784) JG

Jacques, Nicolas *(French sculptor, ca.1578-1649)* **BA**
    Bibl: ▶Bénézit; DICT.SCULP.DE L'ECOLE FRANCAIS; ▶Thieme-Becker;

Jacques, Nicolas *(French artist, 1780-1844)* **WC**

Jacques, Norman Christopher→see Jaques, Norman Christopher

Jacques, Pierre→see Jacques, Pierre (Jacques d'Angoulême)

Jacques, Pierre *(Jacques d'Angoulême)* **BA WC**
    (Draughtsman, sculptor, c.1545-1596) CE
    (French artist, 1516/20-1596) WC
    (French sculptor, ca.1520-1596) BA
    Bibl: BELAS ARTES, 31(1977), 65-69; ▶Bénézit; ▶Thieme-Becker
    Jacques d'Angouleme CE
    Jacques de Reims CE

Jacques, Pierre **CE**

Jacques-Andre-Joseph-Camelot Aved→see Aved, Jacques André Joseph Camelot

Jacquet→see Jacquet, Gustave Jean

Jacquet de Grenoble, Mathieu→see Jacquet, Mathieu

Jacquet, Achille *(French artist, 1846-1908)* **WC**

Jacquet, Alain **BA**
    (French artist, 1939-) WC
    (French painter, sculptor, b.1939) BA
    Bibl: ▶Bénézit; ▶MoMA libr. cat.

Jacquet, Alain G.F. **WC**

Jacquet, Alain G.F.→see Jacquet, Alain

Jacquet, Clement *(French artist, 1895-)* **WC**

Jacquet, Eugene *(French, active Algeria 1880s)* **JG**

Jacquet, François Henri *(French sculptor, b.1798, act.1826)* **BA**
    Bibl: Pinatel, REVUE DU LOUVRE, XXXI/1(1982)

Jacquet, Germain *(French sculptor, act.1597-1636)* **BA**
    Bibl: ▶Bénézit; ▶Larousse grande encyc.; ▶Thieme-Becker

Jacquet, Gustave→see Jacquet, Gustave Jean

Jacquet, Gustave Jean **BA GC PR**
    (French artist, 1846-1909) WC
    (French painter, 1846-1909) BA PR
    (French, 1846-1909) GC
    Bibl: ▶Bénézit; ▶Thieme-Becker; ▶Witt checklist
    Gustave Jean Jacquet PR
    Jacquet PR
    Jacquet, Gustave PR

Jacquet, Jean Gustave **WC**
    Jacquets, G. PR
    Jaquet, Gustave Jean PR

Jacquet, Jean Gustave→see Jacquet, Gustave Jean

Jacquet, Jean-Michel *(Swiss painter, printmaker, b.1950)* **BA**
    Bibl: La Chaux-de-Fonds (FRA), Musée des B.-A., Reise um den Spiegel (1986)

Jacquet, Mathieu **GC WC**
    (French artist, op.1590-m.a. 1610) WC
    (French sculptor, ca.1545-aft. 1611) GC
    Bibl: Getty Photo Study Coll. (Sculp.); ▶RILA/BHA
    Grenoble, Mathieu Jacquet de GC
    Jacquet de Grenoble, Mathieu GC
    Mathieu, Jaquet (Grenoble) GC

Jacquets, G.→see Jacquet, Gustave Jean

Jacquette, Yvonne→see Jacquette, Yvonne Helene

Jacquette, Yvonne Helene **BA WI**
    (American artist, 1934-) WC
    (American artist, b.1934) WI
    (American painter, b.1934) BA
    Bibl: ▶WW Amer. Art, 1978

Jacquette, Yvonne **WC**

Jacquier→see Jacquier, Henri

Jacquier, Henri **PR**
    (French painter, 1878-1921) GC PR
    Bibl: ▶Bénézit; ▶Thieme-Becker
    Henri Jacquier PR
    Jacquier PR

Jacquier, Henry **GC**

Jacquier, Henry→see Jacquier, Henri

Jacquies, Jean *(Leblond)* *(Canadian sculptor, act.1713-1718)* **BA**
    Bibl: Porter, Annunciation Quebec sculp.

Jacquin, Francois Xavier Joseph *(Belgian artist, 1756-1826)* **WC**

Jacquin, Jean Claude *(French sculptor, act.1713-1719)* **BA**
    Bibl: Michel, PAYS LORRAIN, LXIV(1983), 179

Jacquin, Nicolaus Joseph von *(Dutch artist, 1727-1817)* **WC**

Jacquotot, Marie Victoire→see Jaquotot, Marie Victoire

Jacquotot, Marie-Victoire→see Jaquotot, Marie Victoire

Jadin, Godefroy *(Louis Godefroy)*→see Jadin, Louis Godefroy

Jadin, Louis Godefroy **GC**
    (French artist, 1805-1882) WC
    (French painter, 1805-1882) GC
    Bibl: ▶Bénézit

Jadin, Godefroy *(Louis Godefroy)* **WC**

Jadot, Jean Nicolas→see Jadot, Jean Nicolas, baron de Ville-Issey

Jadot, Jean Nicolas, baron de Ville-Issay→see Jadot, Jean Nicolas, baron de Ville-Issey

Jadot, Jean Nicolas, baron de Ville-Issey **BA**
    (French architect and sculptor, 1710-1761) GC
    (French architect from Lorraine, worked in Tuscany, 1710-1761) AV
    (French architect, 1710-1761) BA
    Bibl: ▶Encyc. world art; Getty Photo Study Coll. (Sculp.); ▶Larousse grande encyc.; ▶Macmillan encyc. archts.; ▶Oudin, Dict. architectes; ▶Portoghesi, Diz. arch. e urbanistica; ▶RILA/BHA; ▶Thieme-Becker

Jadot, Jean Nicolas **AV**

Jadot, Jean Nicolas, baron de Ville-Issay **GC**
    Jadot, Jean-Nicolas GC

Jadot, Jean-Nicolas→see Jadot, Jean Nicolas, baron de Ville-Issey

Jaeckel, Karl Heinrich *(Jackel Henry)* *(German artist, op.1853)* **WC**

Jaeckel, Willy **BA GC WC**
    (German artist, 1888-1944) WC
    (German painter and draughtsman, 1888-1944) GC
    (German painter, printmaker, 1888-1944) BA
    Bibl: ▶MoMA libr. cat.; ▶Neue deutsche Biog.; ▶Thieme-Becker; ▶Vollmer, Künst.-Lex. 20. Jhr.

Jaeger, Carl **BA WC**
    (German artist, 1833-1887) WC
    (German painter, printmaker, 1833-1887) BA
    Bibl: ▶Bénézit; Nürnberg (DEU), Stadtgesch. Mus., Wirkung u. Nachleben Durers (1976); ▶Thieme-Becker

Jaeger, Joh *(Swedish, active Stockholm, Sweden, 1880's)* **JG**

Jaeger, Manfred *(German architect, Aachen)* **AV**
    Bibl: Architektur + Wettbewerbe, 1985 Mar., no.121, p.10

Jaeger, Peter **AV BA**
    (German architect, b.1935) BA
    (West German architect, 1935-) AV
    Bibl: KUNSTWERK, XXXII/2-3(APR-JUNE 1979), 16-17

Jaeger, Wilhelm *(Swiss painter,*
b.1941)   **BA**
   Bibl: Munich(DEU), Stadt.Gal.,
   Kunstf.Max. WILHELM
   JAEGER(1981)
Jaegher, de *(Belgian, 20th c.)*   **BA**
Jael, T.F. von *(German(?) artist,*
19th cent.(?))   **WC**
Jaen Marsen → *see* Martszen, Jan (the
   younger)
Jaenisch, Hans *(German artist,*
1907-)   **WC**
Jaersvelt, Reiner van *(early*
Netherlandish goldsmith, 16th c.)   **BA**
   Bibl: Hayward, Goldsmiths &
   Mannerism
Jaffan, Ahmad *(Middle Eastern*
artist, 20th cent.)   **WC**
Jaffe, Lee *(American painter, poet,*
b.1950)   **BA**
   Bibl: Heit, J‡ in ARTS MAG LVIII/7
   (Mar, 1984) 11; Morgan, S., in
   ARTSCRIBE INT. 59 (Sept-Oct,
   1986) 35
Jaffe, Norman *(American architect,*
1932-)   **AV**
   Bibl: Process: architecture, n.7,
   1978, p.210
Jaffe, Shirley *(American painter,*
b.1923)   **BA**
   Bibl: ▶Bénézit; ▶MoMA libr. cat.;
   ▶Vollmer, Künst.-Lex. 20. Jhr.
Jaffe, Steven *(American painter,*
b.1942)   **BA**
   Bibl: Philadelphia (PA, USA),
   College of Art, Words and Images
   (1979)
Jaffee, N. Jay *(American*
photographer, b.1921)   **BA**
   Bibl: Brooklyn(NY, USA), Brooklyn
   Museum. INWARD IMAGE...
   (1981); ▶Natl. union cat., 1973-
   1977
Jaffray, Alexander   **AV WI**
(1677-)   **AV**
(British artist, op.1730-)   **WI**
Jaga, Gaspare da → *see* Da Jaga,
   Gaspare
Jagemann, Ferdinand *(German*
artist, 1780-1820)   **WC**
Jager, Bert *(German artist, 1919-)*   **WC**
Jäger, Bodo *(German architect,*
Hildesheim)   **AV**
   Bibl: Detail, 5 (Sep.-Oct. 1980)
   p.683
Jager, Carl *(German artist, 18th*
cent.)   **WC**
Jäger, Elias *(German goldsmith,*
1653-1709)   **BA**
   Bibl: ▶Thieme-Becker
Jäger, Franz II *(Austrian architect,*
1780-1839)   **BA**
   Bibl: ▶Österr. biog. Lex. 1815-
   1950; ▶Thieme-Becker
Jager, Franz, I *(German artist, 1743-*
1809)   **WC**

Jager, Friedrich Wilhelm Johannes
(German artist, 1833-1888)   **WC**
Jäger, Gottfried *(West German*
photographer, b.1937)   **BA**
   Bibl: ▶Auer, Encyc. photographes;
   ▶Wer ist wer, 1988-89; ▶WW
   Arts DEU
Jager, Gustav *(German artist, 1808-*
1871)   **WC**
Jager, Herbert de *(Dutch artist,*
1642-1705)   **WC**
Jäger, Jakob *(German goldsmith,*
1626-ca.1673)   **BA**
   Bibl: ▶Thieme-Becker
Jager, John *(American architect and*
city planner, active in Minneapolis,
1871-1959)   **AV**
   Bibl: "Architecture Minnesota,"
   1981 Apr.-May, v.7, n.2, p.148-
   150
Jager, Julius *(German artist, -1887)*   **WC**
Jagger, Charles   **WC WI**
(British artist, c.1770-1827)   **WC**
(British artist, circa 1770-1827)   **WI**
Jagger, Charles Sargeant *(British*
sculptor, 1885-1934)   **BA**
   Bibl: ▶Bénézit; ▶Grant, Brit.
   sculptors; ▶Thieme-Becker; ▶Who
   was who [GBR], v.3
Jagger, David   **BA WC WI**
(British artist, -1958)   **WC**
(British artist, d.1958)   **WI**
(British painter, d.1958)   **BA**
   Bibl: ▶Vollmer, Künst.-Lex. 20.
   Jhr.; ▶Waters, Brit. artists; ▶Who
   was who [GBR], 1951-60
Jagger, Gillian *(American painter,*
sculptor, b.1930)   **BA**
   Bibl: ▶WW Amer. Art, 1978
Jagu, Francine Morin *(French artist,*
20th cent.)   **WC**
Jahan, Eric *(American architect)*   **AV**
   Bibl: Progressive architecture,
   1985 Aug., v.66, no.8, p.103
Jahan, Pierre   **BA JG**
(French photographer,
illustrator, b.1909)   **BA**
(French, 1909 -)   **JG**
   Bibl: ▶Auer, Encyc. photographes;
   Qui est Qui en France
Jahn, Gustave *(German artist, 1850-*
1904)   **WC**
Jahn, Helmut   **AV BA**
(American architect, 1940-)   **AV**
(West German architect in USA,
b.1940)   **BA**
   Bibl: ▶AIA Pro File, 1985;
   ▶Contemp. archts.; WW Amer.
Jahn, Jan Quirin   **BA**
(Bohemian painter, art historian,
1739-1802)   **BA**
(German artist, 1739-1802)   **WC**
   Bibl: ▶Allgem. Deut. Biog.; ▶Neue
   deutsche Biog.; ▶Thieme-Becker
Jahn, Quirin (John Quirin)   **WC**
Jahn, Quirin (John Quirin) → *see* Jahn,
   Jan Quirin

Jahn-Heilegenstadt, Albert
(German artist, 1885-1961)   **WC**
Jahncke, Davis *(American architect,*
partner in Jahncke Spooner
Associates, Architects Planners)   **AV**
   Bibl: ▶AIA Pro File, 1983, p.386
Jahnke, Helga *(German painter,*
printmaker, b.1939)   **BA**
   Bibl: ▶Intl. dir. exh. artists;
   Munich (DEU), Kunstverein,
   Stadt-Landschaft-München (1980);
   ▶WW Arts DEU
Jahns, Rudolf   **BA WC**
(German artist, 1896-)   **WC**
(German painter, printmaker,
1896-1983)   **BA**
   Bibl: ▶Fogg Mus. Libr. cat.; LC
   Slip; ▶Schweers, Gemälde deut.
   Museen; ▶Vollmer, Künst.-Lex. 20.
   Jhr.; Winter, Kunstwerk,
   XXXVI/3-4 (1983) pp.177-179
Jahoda, Susan Eve *(American*
photographer, 20th c.)   **BA**
   Bibl: Kuhn, J., ARTS MAGAZINE,
   LIX/9 (May 1985) 2
Jahyer *(Engraver, op.1850-)*   **WI**
Jai Bassan → *see* Bassano, Jacopo
   (Jacopo da Ponte)
Jai Singh, II, maharaja of Jaipur
(Astronomer, 1686-1743)   **AV**
   Bibl: ▶Libr. of Congr. Name Auth.
   File
   Sawai Jai Singh   **AV**
Jaime Cirera → *see* Cirera, Jaime
Jaime Ferrer → *see* Ferrer, Jaime
Jaime Lana → *see* Lana, Jaime
Jaime, Jean François   **GC WC**
(French artist, 1804-p.1831)   **WC**
(French painter, 19th century)   **GC**
   Bibl: ▶Bénézit
Jain, Uttam C. *(Indian architect,*
1934-)   **AV**
   Bibl: ▶Contemp. archts.
Jak *(British artist, op.20th c.)*   **WI**
Jakab, Dezsó *(1864-1932)*   **AV**
Jakab, Károly *(Hungarian painter,*
b.1904)   **BA**
   Bibl: Szíj, Jakob Károly..., p.8
Jakac, Božidar *(Yugoslav painter,*
illustrator, b.1899)   **BA**
   Bibl: ▶Bénézit; ▶Vollmer,
   Künst.-Lex. 20. Jhr.
Jäkkel, Gerhard *(German architect)*   **AV**
   Bibl: Bauwelt, 1985 Oct.4, v.76,
   no.37, p.1514
Jakl, Hermann *(Swiss painter,*
printmaker, b.1915)   **BA**
   Bibl: ▶Künst.-Lex. Schweiz 20.
   Jahrh.; ▶Lex. zeitgen. Schweiz.
   Künstler
Jakob Bogdany → *see* Bogdany, Jakob
Jakob Gillig → *see* Gillig, Jakob
Jakob Griesinger → *see* Griesinger,
   Jakob
Jakob Josef Eeckhout → *see* Eeckhout,
   Jakob Josef
Jakob Roos → *see* Roos, Jakob

Jakob Seisenegger → see Seisenegger, Jakob

Jakob von Landshut (German architect, act.1495-1509) BA
Bibl: Ars Bavarica, 35-36 (1984) pp.119-127; Barth, HANDBUCH DER ELSÄSSISCHEN KIRCHEN IM MITTELALTER; Hotz, Hdbch. Künstdenk. Elsass u. Lothringen; ▶Thieme-Becker

Jakob Wabbe → see Wabbe, Jakob

Jakob Wilhelm Christian Roux → see Roux, Jakob Wilhelm Christian

Jakob, Josef (South American artist, 20th cent.) WC

Jakob, Karl-Heinz (German artist, 1929-) WC

Jakobij, Valerjan Ivanovič (Russian painter, 1834-1902) BA
Bibl: ▶Hamilton, Art & arch. Russia, p.249; Valk
Iakobii, Valerian Ivanovich BA
Yacobi, Valerian Ivanovich BA

Jakobovits, Marta (Romanian ceramist, sculptor, 20th c.) BA
Bibl: Arta, XXVIII/10-11 (1981)

Jakoby, Július (Czech painter, b.1903) BA
Bibl: ▶Bénézit; ▶Váross, Slovenska

Jakoulov, Georges (Yuri Bogdanovitch) → see Jakulov, Georgij Bogdanovič

Jakovlev → see Jakovlev, Aleksandr Evgen'evič

Jakovlev, Aleksandr Evgen'evič BA PR
(Russian artist, 1887-) WC
(Russian artist, 1887-1938) WC
(Russian draughtsman and painter, 1887-1938) GC
(Russian painter, 1887-1938) PR
(Russian painter, illustrator in FRA, 1887-1938) BA
Bibl: ▶Bénézit; ▶RILA/BHA
Aleksandr Evgen'evic Jakovlev PR
Iacoleef, Alexander PR
Iacoleff, Alexander PR
Iacovleff or Iakovieff, Alexander Ievgienievitch WC
Iacovleff, Alexandre E. PR
Iacovleff, Alexandre Evguenievitch PR
Iakovlev PR
Jakovlev PR
Jakovlev, Aleksandr Evgenevic GC
Jakovlev, Alexander Yevgenevitch WC
Jakowleff, Alexander Jewgjenjewitsch PR
Jakovlev, Aleksandr Evgenevic → see Jakovlev, Aleksandr Evgen'evič
Jakovlev, Alexander Yevgenevitch → see Jakovlev, Aleksandr Evgen'evič

Jakovljevic, Nada (French (?) architect) AV
Bibl: Archives d'architecture moderne, 1988, no.38, p.67

Jakowleff, Alexander Jewgjenjewitsch → see Jakovlev, Aleksandr Evgen'evič

Jakuba, János (Hungarian painter, 1909-1974) BA
Bibl: Budapest, Magyar Nemz. Gal., JAKUBA JÁNOS..., 1980; ▶Vollmer, Künst.-Lex. 20. Jhr.

Jakubeit, Heinz (West German architect, Karlsruhe) AV
Bibl: ▶Bund Deut. Arch. Hdbch., 1987
Jakubeit, J. A. Heinz AV
Jakubeit, J. A. Heinz → see Jakubeit, Heinz

Jakulov, Georgij Bogdanovič BA
(Russian artist, 1884-1928) WC
(Russian painter, stage designer, 1884-1928) BA
Bibl: ▶Encic. spettacolo
Iakulov, Georgii BA

Jakoulov, Georges (Yuri Bogdanovitch) WC
Yakulov, Georgii BA

Jakunčikova, Marija Vasil'evna (Russian painter, designer, 1870-1902) BA
Bibl: Kiselev. MARIJA JAKUNČIKOVA; ▶Thieme-Becker

Jakupow, W. (Polish artist, 20th cent.) WC

Jalabert, Charles François BA GC WC
(French artist, 1819-1901) WC
(French painter, 1819-1901) BA
(French, 1819-1901) GC
Bibl: ▶Bénézit; ▶Witt checklist

Jalabert, Jean GC WC
(French artist, 1815-) WC
(French, b.1815) GC
Bibl: ▶Witt checklist

Jalabert, Paulette Eliane (French artist, 1904-) WC

Jalapeeno, Jimmy (American painter, performance, b.1947) BA
Bibl: New Orleans (LA, USA), Mus. Art, New Orleans triennial (1983)

Jalavisto, Mikko (Finnish painter, b.1937) BA

Jalea, Ton (Rumanian artist, 1887-) WC

Jaley, Jean Louis Nicolas (French sculptor, 1802-1866) BA GC
Bibl: ▶Bénézit; ▶RILA/BHA; ▶Thieme-Becker

Jalland, G.H. WC WI
(British artist, 19th cent.) WC
(British artist, op.1888-1908) WI

Jallier de Savault, Claude Jean Baptiste → see Jallier, Claude Jean Baptiste

Jallier, Claude Jean Baptiste BA GC
(French architect, 1740-1806) BA
(French artist, 1738-1806) WC
(French painter, 1738-1806) GC
Bibl: ▶Bénézit; BULLETIN DE LA SOCIÉTÉ DE L'HISTOIRE DE L'ART FRANÇAIS, 1976, 255-160; ▶Lance, Dict. archts. fran.; ▶Thieme-Becker

Jallier de Savault, Claude Jean Baptiste WC

Jallier, Noël BA WC
(French artist, op.1549) WC
(French painter, act.1549) BA
Bibl: Monuments hist. 101 (Feb 1979) 77-94; ▶Thieme-Becker

Jallinoja, Reijo (Finnish architect) AV
Bibl: Architektur + Wettbewerbe, 1985 Dec., no.124, p.22

Jamacois, E. (French artist, 19th cent.) WC

Jamar, Armand Gustave Gerard (Belgian artist, 1870-1946) WC

Jamar, Louis Alexis (French, act. 1842-1850) GC
Bibl: ▶Thieme-Becker

Jame, Alphonse (French artist, op. 1839-1880) WC

Jame, Jean (French silversmith, act. 2nd half 17th century) GC
Bibl: ▶Mabille, Orfèv. fran.

James (American, active Seattle, 1920's (James & Bushnell)) JG

James → see James, Alexander
James → see James, George, (GBR.)
James → see James, Will
James → see James, William (British)
James A. Cleveland → see Cleveland, James A.
James Abbott McNeill Whistler → see Whistler, James Abbott McNeill
James Alfred Aitkin → see Aitken, James Alfred
James Anthony Arlaud → see Arlaud, Jacques Antoine
James Archer → see Archer, James
James Arthur O'Connor → see O'Connor, James Arthur
James Baker Pyne → see Pyne, James Baker
James Barenger → see Barenger, James II
James Barry → see Barry, James
James Bisset → see Bisset, James
James Bolivar Manson → see Manson, James Bolivar
James Bowman → see Bowman, James
James Bridges → see Bridges, James
James Bunck → see Bunk, James H.
James Carroll Beckwith → see Beckwith, James Carroll
James Clarke → see Clarke, James
James Duffield Harding → see Harding, James Duffield
James Durno → see Durno, James
James Earl → see Earl, James

James Ensor→see Ensor, James
James Everett Stuart→see Stuart, James Everett
James Fitzgerald→see Fitzgerald, James Edward
James Francis Danby→see Danby, James Francis
James Frothingham→see Frothingham, James
James G. Forbes→see Forbes, James G.
James Gale Tyler→see Tyler, James Gale
James Girtin→see Girtin, James
James Green→see Green, James
James H. Anderson→see Anderson, James H.
James H. Cafferty→see Cafferty, James H.
James Hamilton Shegogue→see Shegogue, James Hamilton
James Harvey Young→see Young, James Harvey
James Heath→see Heath, James
James Henry Beard→see Beard, James Henry
James Henry Daugherty→see Daugherty, James Henry
James Hewlett→see Hewlett, James
James Holland→see Holland, James
James Jacques Joseph Tissot→see Tissot, James
James Jefferys→see Jefferys, James
James Lambert (II)→see Lambert, James (II)
James Lonsdale→see Lonsdale, James
James Mannin→see Mannin, James
James Maubert→see Maubert, James
James McDougal Hart→see Hart, James McDougal
James Millar→see Millar, James C.
James N. Rosenberg→see Rosenberg, James N.
James Nixon→see Nixon, James
James Norie→see Norie, James
James Northcote→see Northcote, James

James of Saint George (English master mason, act.1270) **BA**
    Bibl: Kidson, Engl. arch., p.108; Taylor, Castles 13c. Wales & Savoy
James Ormsbee Chapin→see Chapin, James Ormsbee
James Paterson→see Paterson, James
James Peale→see Peale, James
James Pollard→see Pollard, James
James Pryde→see Pryde, James
James Rannie Swinton→see Swinton, James Rannie
James Rawlinson→see Rawlinson, James, (of Derby)
James Roberts→see Roberts, James
James Roy Hopkins→see Hopkins, James Roy

James Sant→see Sant, James
James Seymour→see Seymour, James
James Smetham→see Smetham, James
James Stark→see Stark, James
James Swinnerton→see Swinnerton, James G.
James Torrance→see Torrance, James
James Ward→see Ward, James
James Wells Champney→see Champney, James Wells
James Wills→see Wills, James
James Worsdale→see Worsdale, James

James, Alexander (American painter, 1890-1946) **PR**
    Bibl: ▶WWW Amer. art
Alexander James   PR
James   PR
James, Burke (American architect, b.1926) **BA**
James, Charles (American couturier, 1906-1978) **BA**
    Bibl: Brooklyn (NY, USA), Mus., GENIUSOF CHAS. JAMES (1982)
James, Christopher (American, 1947-) **JG**
James, David   **WC WI**
    (British artist, op.1853-1904) WI
    (British artist, op.1881-1892) WC
James, Edith Augusta (British artist, 1857-1898) **WC WI**
James, Edward (British artist, op. 1867-) **WI**
James, Edward (British surrealist architect, lived in Mexico) **AV**
    Bibl: House & garden, 1987 June, v.159, no.6, p.198
James, Esta (American potter, 20th c.) **BA**
    Bibl: ▶Art Index
James, Francis (British artist, op. 1832-1845) **WC WI**
James, Francis Edward (British artist, 1849-1920) **WC WI**
James, Frederick (American artist, 1845-1907) **WI**
James, Geoffrey (Canadian photographer, 20th c.) **BA**
    Bibl: ▶Artists Canada; ▶Eastman House database; London (GBR), RIBA, Heinz Gall., Landscape with Ruins...(1986)
James, George→see James, George, (GBR.)
James, George→see James, George, (USA.)
James, George Watson, Jr. (American painter, b. 1887) **PR**
    Bibl: Richmond catalogue; ▶WWW Amer. art
George Watson James, Jr.   PR

James, George, (GBR.) **WI**
    (British artist, op.1755-, d.1795) WI
    (British artist, op.1761-m.1795) WC
    (British painter, act. 1755, d. 1795) PR
    Bibl: ▶Thieme-Becker
G. James   PR
George James   PR
James   PR
James, George **PR WC**
James, George, (USA.) **WI**
    (American artist, 20th cent.) WC
    (American artist, op.20th c.) WI
James, George **WC**
James, Gilbert **WC WI**
    (British artist, 19th cent.) WC
    (British artist, op.1886-1950) WI
James, H. **WC WI**
    (British artist, op.c.1810) WC
    (British artist, op.circa 1810-) WI
James, Harry E. (British artist, op. 1882-1912) **WI**
    Bibl: ▶Mallalieu, Brit. watercolour artists
James, Henry (American architect, Greenwich, CT) **AV**
    Bibl: Garden design, 1986 Summer, v.5, no.2, p.27
James, John **AV BA**
    (British architect, ca.1672-1746) AV
    (English architect, ca.1672-1746) BA
    Bibl: ▶Colvin, Brit. archts.; ▶Macmillan encyc. archts.; ▶Thieme-Becker
James, John (Australian architect and Medieval French buildings scholar, 1931-) **AV**
    Bibl: Art bulletin, v.66, n.1, p.[15]ff; ▶Avery Libr. cat.
James, Keith (American interior designer) **AV**
    Bibl: Southern accents, 1986 Sept.-Oct., v.9, no.5, p.114
James, Kim **WC WI**
    (British artist, 20th cent.) WC
    (British artist, op.20th c.) WI
James, Laura Gwenllian (British artist, op.1897-1907) **WI**
Rice, Laura Gwenllian, Miss   WI
James, Laurace (American sculptor, 20th c.) **BA**
    Bibl: Arts Mag. LIV/7 (Mar 1980), p.10
James, Lisa (British artist, op.20th c.) **WI**
James, Lord Walter John (3rd Baron Northbourne)→see James, Walter John
James, Louis **GC WC**
    (Australian artist, 1920-) WC
    (British, b.1920) GC
    Bibl: ▶Witt checklist
James, Peter **WC WI**
    (British artist, op.1874) WC
    (British artist, op.1874-) WI

James, R. (British artist, op.1841-
1851)   WC WI
James, Richard   WC WI
(British artist, 1937-)   WC
(British artist, b.1937)   WI
James, Richard S. (British artist, op.
1860-1900)   WI
James, Robert S.   AV
James, Rosalie (American artist, op.
20th c.)   WI
James, Tzena (British architect,
Islesworth)   AV
Bibl: ▶RIBA members, 1984
James, Vince (American architect)   AV
Bibl: Architecture & urbanism,
1983 Sept., no.9(156), p.68
James, Walter John   BA
(British artist, 1869-1932)   WI
(British artist, 1869-1933)   WC
(British painter, printmaker,
1869-1932)   BA
Bibl: ▶Johnson, Brit. artists;
▶Waters, Brit. artists
James, Lord Walter John (3rd
Baron Northbourne)   WC
Northbourne, Lord (Hon. Walter
John James)   WC
Northbourne, Walter John
James, Lord   WI
James, Will   WC WI
(American artist, 1882-)   WC
(American artist, 1882-1961)   WI
(American painter, 1882-1961)   PR
Bibl: ▶WWW Amer. art
James   PR
James, William   PR
William James   PR
James, William (Canadian
photographer, 1870-1944)   BA
Bibl: Saskatoon, Mendel Art
Gallery, WILLIAM JAMES...(1986)
James, William → see James, Will
James, William → see James, William I
James, William (British) (British
painter, act. 1750-1800)   PR
Bibl: ▶Thieme-Becker
James   PR
William James   PR
James, William I   WI
(British artist, op.1754-1771)   WI
(British artist, op.1761-1771)   WC
(British, act.1761-1771)   GC
Bibl: ▶Witt checklist
James, William   GC WC
James, William II (British artist, op.
20th c.)   WI
Jameson → see Jamesone, George
Jameson, Arthur E. (American
artist, b.1872)   WI
Jameson, Cecil → see Jameson, Cecil
Stuart
Jameson, Cecil Stuart   WI
(British artist, 1883-op.1937)   WI
(British artist, 20th cent.)   WC
Bibl: ▶Waters, Brit. artists
Jameson, Cecil   WC

Jameson, Demetrios (American
artist, b.1919)   WI
Jameson, Frank (British artist, 1899-
1968)   WI
Bibl: ▶Johnson, Brit. artists
Jameson-Smith, Frank   WI
Jameson, John (British toymaker,
turner, act.1780-1830)   BA
Jameson, John S.   BA WI
(American artist, 1842-1864)   WI
(American painter, 1842-1864)   BA
Bibl: Everett, AMER ART
JOURNAL, XV, 2 (spring 1983)
53-59
Jameson, Middleton (British artist,
op.1877-, d.1919)   WI
Jameson, Norma   WC WI
(British artist, 20th cent.)   WC
(British artist, b.1933-1941)   WI
Jameson, T. (British artist, op.early
19th c.)   WI
Jameson, William (American artist,
b.1944)   BA
Bibl: Columbia (SC, USA), Mus.
Art & Sci., Carolinians in NY
(1981)
Jameson-Smith, Frank → see Jameson,
Frank
Jamesone → see Jamesone, George
Jamesone, George   BA GC PR WC WI
(British artist, 1587-1588-1644)   WI
(British artist, 1587/8-1644)   WC
(British painter, 1588?-1644)   PR
(Scottish painter, 1587-1644)   GC
(Scottish painter, 1588?-1644)   BA
Bibl: ▶Allgem. Künst.-Lex.;
▶Bénézit; ▶Dict. natl. biog.; ▶Fogg
Mus. Libr. cat.; ▶RILA/BHA;
▶Thieme-Becker; Thomson, D. ART
OF G.J. '74
George Jamesone   PR
Jameson   PR
Jamesone   PR
Jamieson   PR
Jamete, Esteban (Spanish sculptor,
architect, act.1537-1561)   BA
Bibl: Blue guide: Spain, p.437;
▶Ceán Bermúdez, Bellas artes ESP;
▶Encic. univ. ilus.; Rokiski, Wad-al-
Hayara, X (1983) pp.419-426;
▶Thieme-Becker
Jami, Domenico → see Aimo,
Domenico (Varignana)
Jamieson → see Jamesone, George
Jamieson, Alexander   PR VO WC WI
(British artist, 1873-1939)   WC WI
(British painter, 1873-1937)   VO
(British painter, 1873-1939)   PR
Bibl: Ashmolean Museum
catalogue; ▶Libr. of Congr. Name
Auth. File, NAFR932047;
▶Thieme-Becker; ▶Waters, Brit.
artists, p. 180
Alexander Jamieson   PR
Jamieson, Alexander, Mrs.,
(Biddy) → see MacDonald, Biddy

Jamieson, Andrew (British interior
designer, London)   AV
Bibl: Building design, 1988 Apr.
(suppl.), p.26
Jamieson, Elizabeth   WC WI
(British artist, 1924-)   WC
(British artist, b.1924)   WI
Jamieson, F.E.   WC WI
(British artist, circa 1895-op.
circa 1950)   WI
(British artist, op.c.1920-1950)   WC
Jamieson, Gil (Australian artist,
1938-)   WC
Jamieson, Mitchell   BA WC WI
(American artist, 1915-)   WC
(American artist, 1915-1976)   WI
(American painter, 1915-1976)   BA
Bibl: ▶MoMA libr. cat.; ▶Vollmer,
Künst.-Lex. 20. Jhr.; Wash., D.C.,
Corcoran Gallery of Art,
mITCHELL JAMIESON, TWO
WARS, 1980 (LC)
Jamieson, Peter   WC WI
(British artist, 20th cent.)   WC
(British artist, b.1945)   WI
Jamieson, Peter (British architect,
London)   AV
Bibl: ▶RIBA members
Jamieson, Philip   WC WI
(American artist, 1925-)   WC
(American artist, b.1925)   WI
Jamieson, R.Kirkland, Mrs., (Dorothea
Medley) → see Selous, Dorothea
Jamin, Diederik Franciscus   GC WC
(Dutch artist, 1838-1865)   WC
(Dutch painter, 1838-1865)   GC
Bibl: ▶Thieme-Becker
Jamin, Paul Joseph   GC
(French artist, 1853-1903)   WC
(French painter, 1853-1903)   GC
Bibl: ▶Bénézit
Jamin, Paul-Joseph   WC
Jamin, Paul-Joseph → see Jamin, Paul
Joseph
Jamin, Philip   BA GC
(Swiss printmaker, 1848-1918)   GC
(Swiss printmaker, historian,
mycologist, 1848-1918)   BA
Bibl: Fulpius, MUSées de Genève,
227 (July-Aug 1982) 5-7; ▶Natl.
union cat., pre-1956; ▶RILA/BHA
Jamin, Raymond (French engineer,
architect, 20th c.)   BA
Bibl: ▶Larousse grande encyc.;
Trousseau, Mon. Hist. de la
France 134 (Aug-Sept 1984)
Jamis, Fayad (Spanish artist, 20th
cent.)   WC
Jamison → see Jamison, Henriette
Lewis
Jamison, Henrietta Lewis → see
Jamison, Henriette Lewis

Jamison, Henriette Lewis
  (American painter, 1862-1895)   **PR**
      Bibl: Columbus M of A catalogue;
      ▶Petteys, Women artists
    Henriette Lewis Jamison   PR
    Jamison   PR
    Jamison, Henrietta Lewis   PR
Jamitzer, Christoph → see Jamnitzer,
  Christoph
Jamnitzer, Christoph   **BA GC WC**
  (German artist, 1563-1618)   WC
  (German draughtsman, 1563-
    1618)   GC
  (German goldsmith, 1563-1618)   BA
      Bibl: ▶Allgem. Deut. Biog.;
      ▶Bénézit; ▶Forrer, Medallists;
      ▶Oxford dec. arts;
      ▶Thieme-Becker
    Gamiczer, Christoph   GC
    Jamitzer, Christoph   GC
Jamnitzer, Hans II *(German*
  goldsmith, medalist, ca.1538-1603)   **BA**
      Bibl: ▶Forrer, Medallists;
      Pechstein, Anz. des Germ.
      Nationalmus. (1984) 71-76;
      ▶Thieme-Becker
Jamnitzer, Wenzel (the Elder) → see
  Jamnitzer, Wenzel I
Jamnitzer, Wenzel I   **BA** GC
  (German artist, 1508-1585)   WC
  (German draughtsman, 1508-
    1585)   GC
  (German goldsmith, medalist,
    1508-1585)   BA
      Bibl: ▶Allgem. Deut. Biog.;
      ▶Forrer, Medallists; Getty Photo
      Study Coll.; ▶Oxford dec. arts;
      ▶Thieme-Becker; ▶Witt checklist
    Jamnitzer, Wenzel (the Elder)   **GC**
    Jamnitzer, Wenzel, I   **WC**
Jamnitzer, Wenzel, I → see Jamnitzer,
  Wenzel I
Jamois, Edmund Victor *(French*
  artist, 1876-)   **WC**
Jampol, Glenn *(American painter,*
  b.1950)   **BA**
      Bibl: ▶Intl. dir. exh. artists;
      Mission Viejo (CA, USA),
      Saddleback Art Gallery, Sheila
      Elias et al. (1981)
Jamyn → see Brooks, Henry Jermyn
Jan Abrahamsz. Beerstraten → see
  Beerstraten, Jan Abrahamsz.
Jan Adriaensz. Man → see Man, Jan
  Adriaensz.
Jan Adriaensz. van Staveren → see
  Staveren, Jan Adriaensz. van
Jan Albertsz. Rootius → see Rootius,
  Jan Albertsz.
Jan Andrea Lievens (II) → see Lievens,
  Jan Andrea (II)
Jan Anthonie van der Leepe → see
  Leepe, Jan Anthonie van der
Jan Anthonisz. van Ravesteyn → see
  Ravesteyn, Jan Anthonisz. van
Jan Asselijn → see Asselyn, Jan

Jan Asselyn → see Asselyn, Jan
Jan Asselyn, called Crabbetie → see
  Asselyn, Jan
Jan Asslyn → see Asselyn, Jan
Jan Baegert → see Baegert, Jan
Jan Baptist Brueghel → see Brueghel,
  Jan Baptist
Jan Baptist Francken → see Francken,
  Jan Baptist
Jan Baptist Lambrechts → see
  Lambrechts, Jan Baptist
Jan Baptist van der Meiren → see
  Meiren, Jan Baptist van der
Jan Baptist Wans → see Wans, Jan
  Baptist
Jan Baptist Weenix → see Weenix, Jan
  Baptist
Jan Baptist Wenings → see Weenix,
  Jan Baptist
Jan Baptist Wolfaerts → see
  Wolfaerts, Jan Baptist
Jan Baptiste Huysmans → see
  Huysmans, Jan Baptiste
Jan Baptiste Seghers → see Seghers,
  Jan Baptiste
Jan Battista Huijsmans → see
  Huysmans, Jan Baptiste
Jan Blom → see Blom, Jan
Jan Bogt → see Both, Jan
Jan Bol → see Bol, Hans
Jan Borens → see Borens, Jan
  [Unidentified]
Jan Borrensz. Smit → see Smit, Jan
  Borritsz.
Jan Borritsz. Smit → see Smit, Jan
  Borritsz.
Jan Bot → see Both, Jan
Jan Both → see Both, Jan
Jan Bott → see Both, Jan
Jan Breughel → see Brueghel, Jan, the
  elder
Jan Brueghel → see Brueghel, Jan, the
  elder
Jan Brueghel (the elder) → see
  Brueghel, Jan, the elder
Jan Brueghel (the younger) → see
  Brueghel, Jan, the younger
Jan Brughel → see Brueghel, Jan, the
  elder
Jan Carel Vierpeyl → see Vierpeyl, Jan
  Carel
Jan Chelminski → see Chelminski, Jan
Jan Christiaen Sepp → see Sepp, Jan
  Christiaen
Jan Claes Rietschoof → see
  Rietschoof, Jan Claes
Jan Colaert → see Colaert, Johannes
Jan Coningh → see Koninck, Jacob I
Jan Cornelis Vermeyen → see
  Vermeyen, Jan Cornelis
Jan Cornelisz. Holblock → see
  Holblock, Jan Cornelisz.
Jan Cossiers → see Cossiers, Jan
Jan Davidsz. de Heem → see Heem,
  Jan Davidsz. de

Jan Davidts de Heem → see Heem, Jan
  Davidsz. de
Jan de Baen → see Baen, Jan de
Jan de Beer → see Beer, Jan de
Jan de Bellini → see Bellini, Giovanni
Jan de Bisschop → see Bisschop, Jan
  de
Jan de Bondt → see Bont, Jan de
Jan de Bray → see Bray, Jan de
Jan de Bruxelles → see Roome, Jan
  van
Jan de Cock → see Cock, Jan de
Jan de Coninck → see Koninck, Jacob I
Jan de Duyts → see Duyts, Jan de
Jan de Esel → see Hals, Johannes
Jan de Heem → see Heem, David (III)
  Cornelisz. de
Jan de Heem → see Heem, Jan
  Davidsz. de
Jan de Hemessen → see Hemessen,
  Jan van
Jan de Hollander → see Amstel, Jan
  van
Jan de Landtsheer → see Landtsheer,
  Jan de
Jan de Lis → see Liss, Johann (Pan)
Jan de Mabeuge → see Gossaert, Jan
Jan de Mabuse → see Gossaert, Jan
Jan de Rhyn → see Rijn, Jan van
Jan de Vlieger → see Vlieger, Jan de
  [Unidentified]
Jan de Vos → see Vos, Jan de
Jan de Vos (I) → see Vos, Jan de
Jan de Vries → see Vredeman de Vries,
  Hans
Jan de Wett → see Wet, Jacob
  Willemsz. de
Jan Decker → see Decker, Jan
Jan Denys → see Denys, Jan
Jan Duijster → see Duijster, Jan
  [Unidentified]
Jan Ekels (the elder) → see Ekels, Jan
  (the elder)
Jan Ekels (the younger → see Ekels,
  Jan (the younger)
Jan Emons → see Emons, Jan
  [Unidentified]
Jan Engels Carroselli → see Caroselli,
  Angelo
Jan Erasmus Quellinus → see
  Quellinus, Jan Erasmus
Jan Esel → see Hals, Johannes
Jan Evert Morel → see Morel, Jan
  Evert
Jan Frans Beschey → see Beschey, Jan
  Frans
Jan Frans Soolmaker → see Soolmaker,
  Jan Frans
Jan Frans van Bloemen → see
  Bloemen, Jan Frans van (Orizonte)
Jan Frans van Bredael → see Bredael,
  Jan Frans van
Jan Frans van Dael → see Dael, Jan
  Frans van

Jan Frederick Pieter Portielje→*see* Portielje, Jan Frederick Pieter

Jan Fris→*see* Fris, Jan (Johannes)

Jan Fyt→*see* Fyt, Jan

Jan Fytt→*see* Fyt, Jan

Jan Gabrielsz. Sonje→*see* Sonje, Jan Gabrielsz.

Jan Georg van Vliet→*see* Vliet, Jan Georg van

Jan Gerrit Grasdorp→*see* Grasdorp, Jan Gerrit

Jan Gerritsz. van Bronchorst→*see* Bronchorst, Jan Gerritsz. van

Jan Gerritsz. van Bronckhorst→*see* Bronchorst, Jan Gerritsz. van

Jan Gooijen→*see* Goyen, Jan Josephsz. van

Jan Gossaert→*see* Gossaert, Jan

Jan Griffier (I)→*see* Griffier, Jan I

Jan Guldenwagen→*see* Guldewagen, Jan Jacobsz.

Jan Hackaert→*see* Hackaert, Jan

Jan Hacker→*see* Hackaert, Jan

Jan Hackert→*see* Hackaert, Jan

Jan Hals→*see* Hals, Johannes

Jan Hooft→*see* Hooft, Jan

Jan Hugtenburg→*see* Huchtenburgh, Jan van

Jan Hulswit→*see* Hulswit, Jan

Jan Jacobsz. Guldewagen→*see* Guldewagen, Jan Jacobsz.

Jan Jacobsz. van der Stoffe→*see* Stoffe, Jan Jacobsz. van der

Jan Jansz. Buesem→*see* Buesem, Jan Jansz.

Jan Jansz. den Uyl→*see* Uyl, Jan Jansz. den

Jan Jansz. Treck→*see* Treck, Jan Jansz.

Jan Joest→*see* Joest, Jan

Jan Joest von Calcar or van Haarlem (Juan de Holanda)→*see* Joest, Jan

Jan Joost van Cossiau→*see* Cossiau, Jan Joost van

Jan Jordaens→*see* Jordaens, Hans (IV)

Jan Joseph Horemans (I)→*see* Horemans, Jan Joseph I

Jan Joseph Horemans (II)→*see* Horemans, Jan Joseph II

Jan Josephsz. van Goyen→*see* Goyen, Jan Josephsz. van

Jan Juriaensz. van Baden→*see* Baden, Jan Juriaensz. van

Jan Karel Donatus van Beecq→*see* Beecq, Jan Karel Donatus van

Jan Kessel→*see* Kessel, Jan van

Jan Kobell (II)→*see* Kobell, Jan (II)

Jan Lap→*see* Lapp, Jan Willemsz.

Jan Lapp→*see* Lapp, Jan Willemsz.

Jan Lieuwesz→*see* Lievens, Jan

Jan Lieven→*see* Lievens, Jan

Jan Lievens→*see* Lievens, Jan

Jan Lievens (I)→*see* Lievens, Jan

Jan Lievens d'oude→*see* Lievens, Jan

Jan Lievense d'oude→*see* Lievens, Jan

Jan Lievensz.→*see* Lievens, Jan

Jan Lievents→*see* Lievens, Jan

Jan Lievenz. de Oude→*see* Lievens, Jan

Jan Lievesse→*see* Lievens, Jan

Jan Lievesz. d'oude→*see* Lievens, Jan

Jan Lins→*see* Linsen, Jan

Jan Linsen→*see* Linsen, Jan

Jan Linssen→*see* Linsen, Jan

Jan Lis→*see* Liss, Johann (Pan)

Jan Liss→*see* Liss, Johann (Pan)

Jan Looten→*see* Looten, Jan

Jan Loten→*see* Looten, Jan

Jan Ludik→*see* Ludik, Jan [Unidentified]

Jan Luijcken→*see* Luyken, Jan

Jan Luissen→*see* Luissen, Jan [Unidentified]

Jan Luyken→*see* Luyken, Jan

Jan M. Molenaar→*see* Molenaer, Jan Miense

Jan Maas→*see* Maas, Jan (Johannes)

Jan Maat→*see* Blankerhoff, Jan

Jan Maet→*see* Blankerhoff, Jan

Jan Mandyn→*see* Mandyn, Jan

Jan Mari ten Kate→*see* Kate, Jan Mari ten

Jan Marsen→*see* Martszen, Jan (the younger)

Jan Marsse de Jonge→*see* Martszen, Jan (the younger)

Jan Marts→*see* Martszen, Jan (the younger)

Jan Martse de jonge→*see* Martszen, Jan (the younger)

Jan Martsen de jonge→*see* Martszen, Jan (the younger)

Jan Martsz→*see* Martszen, Jan (the younger)

Jan Martsz. de Jonge→*see* Martszen, Jan (the younger)

Jan Martszen (II)→*see* Martszen, Jan (the younger)

Jan Martszen (the younger)→*see* Martszen, Jan (the younger)

Jan Marz. de Jonge→*see* Martszen, Jan (the younger)

Jan Massys→*see* Massys, Jan

Jan Maurits Quinkhard→*see* Quinkhard, Jan Maurits

Jan Menisse Molenaer→*see* Molenaer, Jan Miense

Jan Miel→*see* Miel, Jan

Jan Miel, Called, Giovanni della Vite→*see* Miel, Jan

Jan Miele→*see* Miel, Jan

Jan Miell→*see* Miel, Jan

Jan Mienisse Molenaar→*see* Molenaer, Jan Miense

Jan Miens Molenaer→*see* Molenaer, Jan Miense

Jan Miense Molenaar→*see* Molenaer, Jan Miense

Jan Miense Molenaer→*see* Molenaer, Jan Miense

Jan Miensz. Molenaer→*see* Molenaer, Jan Miense

Jan Mienze Molenaer→*see* Molenaer, Jan Miense

Jan Mieris→*see* Mieris, Jan van

Jan Mieus Molenaer→*see* Molenaer, Jan Miense

Jan Minse Molenaer→*see* Molenaer, Jan Miense

Jan Miris→*see* Mieris, Jan van

Jan Molenaer→*see* Molenaer, Jan Miense

Jan Molinaer→*see* Molenaer, Jan Miense

Jan Mortel→*see* Mortel, Jan

Jan Mostaert→*see* Mostaert, Jan

Jan Mynse Molenaar→*see* Molenaer, Jan Miense

Jan Mynssen→*see* Molenaer, Jan Miense

Jan Mytens→*see* Mytens, Jan

Jan Nagel→*see* Nagel, Jan

Jan Nickelen→*see* Nickelen, Jan

Jan Olis→*see* Olis, Jan

Jan Peeter Verdussen→*see* Verdussen, Jan Peeter

Jan Peeters (I)→*see* Peeters, Jan I

Jan Persellis→*see* Porcellis, Jan

Jan Peters→*see* Peeters, Jan I

Jan Philip van Thielen→*see* Thielen, Jan Philip van

Jan Pieter Stoop→*see* Stoop, Jan Pieter

Jan Pietersz.→*see* Peeters, Jan I

Jan Pinas→*see* Pynas, Jan Symonsz.

Jan Polack→*see* Polack, Jan

Jan Porcellis→*see* Porcellis, Jan

Jan Provost (the younger)→*see* Provost, Jan, the younger

Jan Pynas→*see* Pynas, Jan Symonsz.

Jan Roos (I)→*see* Roos, Jan (I)

Jan Ruijscher→*see* Ruischer, Johannes (Jonge Hercules)

Jan Saenredam→*see* Saenredam, Jan

Jan Siberechts→*see* Siberechts, Jan

Jan Sierkes→*see* Sierkes, Jan [Unidentified]

Jan Snellinck (I)→*see* Snellinck, Jan I

Jan Sons→*see* Soens, Jan

Jan Soreau→*see* Soreau, Jan

Jan Steen→*see* Steen, Jan

Jan Stein→*see* Steen, Jan

Jan Stephan von Calcar→*see* Calcar, Jan Stephan van

Jan Stien→*see* Steen, Jan

Jan Swart→*see* Swart van Groningen, Jan

Jan Swart of Groningen→*see* Swart van Groningen, Jan

Jan Swart van Groningen→*see* Swart van Groningen, Jan

Jan Swart, van Groningen→*see* Swart van Groningen, Jan

Jan Symonsz. Pynas→see Pynas, Jan Symonsz.
Jan ten Compe→see Compe, Jan ten
Jan Tengnagel→see Tengnagel, Jan
Jan Theunisz. Blanckerhoff→see Blankerhoff, Jan
Jan Thomas van Kessel→see Kessel, Jan Thomas van
Jan Treck→see Treck, Jan Jansz.
Jan V. Huysum→see Huysum, Jan van
Jan van Amstel→see Amstel, Jan van
Jan van Assen→see Asselyn, Jan
Jan van Balen→see Balen, Jan van
Jan van Bassen→see Bassen, Jan van [Unidentified]
Jan van Beers→see Beers, Jan van
Jan van Bijlert→see Bijlert, Jan Hermansz. van
Jan van Brussel→see Roome, Jan van
Jan Van Bylert→see Bijlert, Jan Hermansz. van
Jan van Capelle→see Cappelle, Jan van de
Jan van Coninxloo (II)→see Coninxloo, Jan van (II)
Jan van Daele→see Daele, Jan van [Unidentified]
Jan van Dalen (II)→see Dalen, Jan van (II)
Jan van de Cappelle→see Cappelle, Jan van de
Jan van de Velde→see Velde, Jan II van de
Jan van de Velde→see Velde, Jan van de (III)
Jan van de Velde (II)→see Velde, Jan II van de
Jan van de Velde (III)→see Velde, Jan van de (III)
Jan van den Hecke (I)→see Hecke, Jan van den (I)
Jan van den Hoecke→see Hoecke, Jan van den
Jan van der Banck→see Banck, Jan van der
Jan van der Borght→see Borght, Jan van der
Jan van der Bruggen→see Bruggen, Jan van der
Jan van der Heide→see Heyden, Jan van der
Jan van der Heijden→see Heyden, Jan van der
Jan van der Heyden→see Heyden, Jan van der
Jan van der Meer→see Vermeer, Jan (II)
Jan van der Straet→see Straet, Jan van der (Giovanni Stradano)
Jan van der Vinne (I)→see Vinne, Jan van der (I)
Jan van Everdingen→see Everdingen, Jan van
Jan van Eyck→see Eyck, Jan van

Jan van Goien→see Goyen, Jan Josephsz. van
Jan van Goijen→see Goyen, Jan Josephsz. van
Jan van Gojen→see Goyen, Jan Josephsz. van
Jan van Gool→see Gool, Jan van
Jan van Goyen→see Goyen, Jan Josephsz. van
Jan van Heem→see Heem, Jan Davidsz. de
Jan van Hemessen→see Hemessen, Jan van
Jan van Huchtenburgh→see Huchtenburgh, Jan van
Jan van Huijsum→see Huysum, Jan van
Jan van Huysum→see Huysum, Jan van
Jan van Kalcker→see Calcar, Jan Stephan van
Jan van Kessel→see Kessel, Jan van
Jan van Kessel (I)→see Kessel, Jan van I
Jan van Kessel (II)→see Kessel, Jan van II
Jan van Leyden (possibly identified with Johann, van Leyden)→see Leyden, Jan van
Jan van Mieris→see Mieris, Jan van
Jan van Neck→see Neck, Jan van
Jan van Noort→see Noort, Joan van
Jan van Oort→see Noort, Joan van
Jan van Os→see Os, Jan van
Jan van Pee→see Pee, Jan van
Jan van Peene→see Pee, Jan van
Jan van Rijn→see Rijn, Jan van
Jan van Rillaert (the elder)→see Rillaert, Jan van (the elder)
Jan van Rintel→see Rintel (Rinzel), Jan van
Jan van Rossum→see Rossum, Jan van
Jan van Scorel→see Scorel, Jan van
Jan Van Thielen→see Thielen, Jan Philip van
Jan van Voordt→see Voordt, Jan van
[Jan] van Voort→see Voordt, Jan van
Jan van Wechelen→see Wechelen, Jan van
Jan vande Velde→see Velde, Jan van de (III)
Jan vanden Velde→see Velde, Jan II van de
Jan vander Does→see Does, Jacob van der (the elder)
Jan Verbruggen→see Verbruggen, Jan
Jan Verkolje→see Verkolje, Jan I
Jan Verkolje (I)→see Verkolje, Jan I
Jan Vermeer→see Vermeer, Jan
Jan Vermeer (II)→see Vermeer, Jan (II)
Jan Vermeer (III)→see Vermeer, Jan (III)

Jan Victors→see Victors, Jan
Jan Vonck→see Vonck, Jan
Jan Vroom→see Vroom, Jan [Unidentified]
Jan Weenix→see Weenix, Jan
Jan Weenix→see Weenix, Jan Baptist
Jan Weininx→see Weenix, Jan Baptist
Jan Weninx→see Weenix, Jan
Jan Wenix→see Weenix, Jan
Jan Wijnands→see Wijnants, Jan
Jan Wijnants→see Wijnants, Jan
Jan Wijnings→see Weenix, Jan Baptist
Jan Wildens→see Wildens, Jan
Jan Willemsz. Lapp→see Lapp, Jan Willemsz.
Jan Wils→see Wils, Jan
Jan Withoos→see Withoos, Johannes
Jan Wolffertsz. →see Wolfaerts, Jan Baptist
Jan Wolvertsz. →see Wolfaerts, Jan Baptist
Jan Wouwerman→see Wouwerman, Jan
Jan Wyck→see Wyck, Jan
Jan z Nysy (Polish painter, act.1468-1477)   **BA**
    Bibl: ▶Slownik artystów polskich; ▶Thieme-Becker; ▶Wielka ilustr. encyk.
Jan, Elvire (Bulgarian artist, 1904-)   **WC**
Jan. Assellyn→see Asselyn, Jan
Jan. Bol→see Bol, Hans
Jan. Hackert→see Hackaert, Jan
Jan. Jordaens→see Jordaens, Hans (IV)
Jan. Miel→see Miel, Jan
Jan. Peters→see Peeters, Jan I
Jan. Sepp→see Sepp, Jan Christiaen
Jan. Steen→see Steen, Jan
Jan. Van Eyck→see Eyck, Jan van
Janaig (French artist, 17th cent.)   **WC**
Janák, Pavel   **AV BA**
    (Czech architect, 1882-1956)   **BA**
    (Czechoslovak architect, 1882-1956)   **AV**
    Bibl: Architectural review, l966 Mar., v.139, no.829, p.229; ▶Thieme-Becker; ▶Vollmer, Künst.-Lex. 20. Jhr., v.1, v.2
Jancke, August (Martin Heinrich August) (German artist, 1810-1840)   **WC**
Janco, M. (American artist, 20th cent.)   **WC**
Janco, Marcel   **BA WI**
    (Romanian painter, architect, b.1895)   **BA**
    (Rumanian artist, 1895-)   **WC**
    (Rumanian artist, b.1895)   **WI**
    Bibl: ▶Artist biog. master idx.; ▶Babington Smith, Contemp. artists; ▶Bénézit; ▶Vollmer, Künst.-Lex. 20. Jhr.
Jancu, Marcel   **WC**

Jancsó, Miklós (Hungarian architect,
Tapolca) **AV**
　　Bibl: Magyar építőművészet,
　　1987, v.78, no.2, p.10
Jancu, Marcel→see Janco, Marcel
Janda, Charles (American
photographer, 20th c.) **BA**
　　Bibl: Oakland (CA, USA), Mus. of
　　Art, Amer. photog. natl parks
　　(1981)
Janda, Hermine von (German artist,
1854-1925) **WC**
Jandi, David (Hungarian artist, 1893-
1944) **WC**
Jandl, Jannt or Jantl, Anton
(German artist, 1723-1805) **WC**
Jandl, Robert (Architect,
Regensburg) **AV**
　　Bibl: Detail, 1981 Mar.-Apr., no.2,
　　p.171
Jane Berlandina→see Berlandina, Jane
Jane Steen→see Steen, Jan
Jane Stuart→see Stuart, Jane
Janeček, Ota **BA WC**
　　(Czech artist, 1919-) **WC**
　　(Czech painter, b.1919) **BA**
　　Bibl: Umení XXIX 1 1981 p.59-72
Janensch, Gerhard Adolf (German
sculptor, 1860-ca.1930) **BA**
　　Bibl: Columbia (SC, USA), Mus.
　　Art & Sci., Mandell coll. (1982);
　　Jahrb. Preussischer Kulturbesitz
　　XX (1983) 114; ▶Mackay,
　　Western sculp. bronze;
　　▶Thieme-Becker
Janes, Norman **BA**
　　(British artist, 1892-1980) **WI**
　　(British artist, 20th cent.) **WC**
　　(British painter, printmaker,
　　1892-1980) **BA**
　　Bibl: ▶Johnson, Brit. artists; Old
　　Watercolours, LV '80 p.44;
　　▶Vollmer, Künst.-Lex. 20. Jhr., v.1
Janes, Norman Thomas **WI**
Nanes, Norman **WC**
Janes, Norman Thomas→see Janes,
Norman
Janes, P. (Estonian architect) **AV**
　　Bibl: Process: architecture, 1985
　　Jan., no.54, p.153
Janet→see Clouet, Jean
Janet, Ange Louis **GC**
　　(French artist, 1815-1872) **WC**
　　(French painter, 1815-1872) **GC**
　　Bibl: ▶Bénézit
Janet, Ange Louis (Janet-Lange) **WC**
Janet, Ange Louis (Janet-Lange)→see
Janet, Ange Louis
Janety, Marc-Etienne (French
silversmith, master 1777) **GC**
　　Bibl: ▶Mabille, Orfèv. fran.
Janga, Mike (Dutch architect, b. in
Curaçao, 1944-) **AV**
　　Bibl: Deutsche Bauzeitung, 1989
　　Jan., v.123, no.1, p.130

Jänggl, Franz (Austrian architect,
1650-1734) **BA**
　　Bibl: Bildhandbch OSTER.; Czeike,
　　Wien Kunst & Kultur; Dehio: Wien
　　(1960); Jelonek, M.A., FRANZ
　　JÄNGGL... (1984); ▶Portoghesi,
　　Diz. arch. e urbanistica;
　　▶Thieme-Becker
Janiak, Grazyna (French architect) **AV**
Janikowski, Mieczyslaw Tadeusz
(Polish artist, 1912-1968) **WC**
Janin, Fernand (French architect,
painter, 1880-1912) **BA**
　　Bibl: ▶Thieme-Becker
Janin, Jean (French artist, 1899-) **WC**
**Janin, Louise (Jeanne Louise
Sophie)** (Swiss artist, 1781-1842) **WC**
Janinet, Jean Francois→see Janinet,
Jean-François
Janinet, Jean-François **GC**
　　(French artist, 1752-1814) **WC**
　　(French painter, 1752-1814) **GC**
　　Bibl: ▶Witt checklist
Janinet, Jean Francois **WC**
Janis Valters→see Valters, Jānis
Janis, Richard (American painter,
20th c.) **BA**
　　Bibl: (07) Celetic consciousness,
　　p.553
Janitch, Mary (Canadian artist,
b.1949) **BA**
　　Bibl: ▶Idx. Ontario artists
**Janjenko or Ianenko, Feodossij
Iwanowitsch** (Russian artist,
1762-1809) **WC**
Jank, Angelo (German artist, 1868-
1940) **WC**
Jank, Christian **AV BA WC**
　　(1833-) **AV**
　　(German artist, 1833-1888) **WC**
　　(German painter, printmaker,
　　1833-1888) **BA**
　　Bibl: ▶Bénézit; ▶Thieme-Becker
Jankel Adler→see Adler, Jankel
Jankes, Philip J. (South African
architect) **AV**
　　Bibl: Architect & builder, 1988
　　Feb., p.10
Jankó, János (Hungarian painter,
printmaker, 1833-1896) **BA**
　　Bibl: ▶Bénézit; ▶Thieme-Becker
Jankovic, Ivan (French architect,
1923-1984) **AV**
　　Bibl: Urbanisme, 1984 Oct.-Nov.,
　　v.204, p.43
Jankovič, Jozef (Czech artist,
b.1937) **BA**
　　Bibl: Bertók, I., LEONARDO XIX/1
　　(summer 1986) p.27-30; Guide
　　exh. artists: N. Amer. ptrs.
Jankovics, Tibor (Hungarian
architect) **AV**
Jankowska, Bogena (Polish artist,
20th cent.) **WC**
Jankowsky, F.W. (or J.W.) (German
artist, op.1825-1861) **WC**

Janku, Michal (Czech architect) **AV**
　　Bibl: Architektura ČSR, 1988,
　　v.47, no.3, p.60
Janmaat→see Blankerhoff, Jan
Janmot, Anne Francois Louis→see
Janmot, Louis
Janmot, Louis **BA GC**
　　(French artist, 1814-1892) **WC**
　　(French painter, 1814-1892) **GC**
　　(French painter, author, 1814-
　　1892) **BA**
　　Bibl: ▶Bénézit; ▶Larousse grande
　　encyc.; ▶Natl. union cat., pre-
　　1956; ▶RILA/BHA, 1987;
　　▶Thieme-Becker
Janmot, Anne Francois Louis **WC**
Janne Maria de Capua (Italian
potter in Low Countries, act.1513) **BA**
　　Bibl: Dumortier, Faenza,
　　LXXIII/4-5 (1987) pp.161-172
Janneck→see Janneck, Franz
Christoph
Janneck, Franz Christoph **GC PR WC**
　　(Austrian painter, 1703-1761) **GC PR**
　　(German artist, 1703-1761) **WC**
　　Bibl: ▶Bénézit; Getty Photo Study
　　Coll.; ▶Thieme-Becker; ▶Witt
　　checklist
　　Franz Christoph Janneck **PR**
　　Janneck **PR**
Jannello, Cesar (Argentine architect,
d.1985) **AV**
　　Bibl: Summa, 1985 Sept., no.217,
　　p.20
Jannini [Unidentified] (Unknown
painter) **PR**
　　Bibl: Orsini inventory, Naples,
　　1704, possibly Giannini
Jannini, Paulo Giacomo (Brazilian
architect) **AV**
　　Bibl: Projeto, 1985 July, no.77,
　　p.92
Janniot, Alfred Auguste **BA GC**
　　(French painter and sculptor,
　　1889-1969) **GC**
　　(French sculptor, painter, 1889-
　　1969) **BA**
　　Bibl: ▶Bénézit; ▶RILA/BHA;
　　▶Vollmer, Künst.-Lex. 20. Jhr.
Jannot, Henri (French artist, 1909-) **WC**
Janofske, Eckehard (West German
architect, 1950-) **AV**
　　Bibl: Daidalos, no.3, p.118
Janos, Czencz (Czech artist, 1885-) **WC**
Janosco, Jerry (American artist,
b.1947) **BA**
　　Bibl: New York (NY, USA), New
　　Mus., Extended sensibilities
　　(1982)
Janoušek, František (Czech painter,
1890-1943) **BA**
　　Bibl: ▶Encyk. českého výtv. umění
Janowich, Ron (American painter,
20th c.) **BA**
　　Bibl: Bell, T., in ARTS MAGAZINE
　　LIX/9 (May 1985) 3

Janowitz, Joel *(American painter, b.1945)* **BA**
    Bibl: ▶MoMA libr. cat.; ▶Whitney Mus. cat.

Janowski, Mikołaj *(Polish painter, 18th c.)* **BA**
    Bibl: ▶Bénézit; Michalowski, Biuletyn Historii Sztuki, XXXVII/3 (1975) pp.251-255; ▶Thieme-Becker; ▶Wielka ilustr. encyk.

Janowski, Witold *(Polish artist, 20th cent.)* **WC**

Jans, Edouard de *(Belgian artist, 1855-1919)* **WC**

Jans, Jean I *(Flemish tapestry weaver in FRA, ca.1618-1668)* **BA**
    Bibl: ▶Larousse grande encyc.; ▶Thieme-Becker; ▶Thomson, Tapestry, p.428; Weigert, French tapestry, pp. 113-14

Jans, Jean II *(Flemish tapestry weaver in FRA, ca.1644-1723)* **BA**
    Bibl: ▶Larousse grande encyc.; ▶Thieme-Becker; Weigert, French tapestry, pp. 113-14

Jans, Jean Jacques *(Flemish tapestry weaver in FRA, 1671-1731)* **BA**
    Bibl: Burnham Festschrift; ▶Larousse grande encyc.; ▶Thieme-Becker; Weigert, French tapestry, p. 114

Jansana, Imma *(Spanish architect)* **AV**
    Bibl: Architecture and urbanism, 1987 Feb., no.197, p.125

Janscha, Jantscha or Janza (not Janschka), Lorenz or Laurent →see Janscha, Laurenz

Janscha, Laurenz **BA**
    (Austrian painter, printmaker, collector, 1749-1812) BA
    (German artist, 1749-1812) WC
    Bibl: ▶Bénézit; ▶Thieme-Becker; ▶Witt checklist

Janscha, Jantscha or Janza (not Janschka), Lorenz or Laurent **WC**

Janschka, Fritz *(Austrian painter, graphic artist, b.1919)* **BA**
    Bibl: ▶MoMA libr. cat.; ▶Vollmer, Künst.-Lex. 20. Jhr.

Janseens →see Johnson, Cornelius I

Jansem, Jean *(Rumanian artist, 1920-)* **WC**

Jansen →see Janssens, Victor Honoré

Jansen →see Johnson, Cornelius I

Jansen, Angela Bing *(American printmaker, photographer, b.1929)* **BA**
    Bibl: ▶WW Amer. Art, 1978

Jansen, Bernd **AV BA**
    (German architect, b.1943) BA
    (West German architect, 1943-) AV
    Bibl: Das Kunstwerk, n.3-4, Sept. 1983, p.118; Kunstwerk, XXXII/2-3 (Apr.-Jun. 1979) pp. 18-20

Jansen, Catherine *(American sculptor, 20th c.)* **BA**

Jansen, F. *(Dutch painter, act.1635-1640)* **GC**
    Bibl: ▶Bénézit

Jansen, P. **GC**

Jansen, Franz M. *(German painter, printmaker, 1885-1958)* **BA**
    Bibl: ▶Art Index, 1974; ▶Bénézit; Bonn (BRD), Städtische Kunstsammlungen. Kunstmuseum Bonn. 1972; ▶Encyc. world art; ▶Fogg Mus. Libr. cat.; ▶Met. Mus. Art libr. cat.; ▶MoMA libr. cat.; ▶Natl. union cat.; ▶Vollmer, Künst.-Lex. 20. Jhr.; Wallraf-Richart-Jahrb. 36, 1974, p.371

Jansen, Frederik Johannes (Frits) *(Dutch painter, 1856-1928)* **GC**
    Bibl: ▶Wright, Ptgs. Dutch museums

Jansen, Georges *(French ébéniste, 1726, master 1767)* **GC**
    Bibl: ▶Salverte, Ébénistes 18e s.

Jansen, Heinrich **BA GC WC**
    (Danish artist, 1625-1667) WC
    (Danish, 1625-1667) GC
    (German painter, 1625-1667) BA
    Bibl: ▶Bénézit; ▶Thieme-Becker; ▶Witt checklist

Jansen, Hendrik Willebror →see Jansen, Hendrik Willebrord

Jansen, Hendrik Willebrord **GC**
    (Dutch artist, 1855-1908) WC
    (Dutch painter, 1855-1908) GC
    Bibl: ▶Thieme-Becker

Jansen, Hendrik Willebror **WC**

Jansen, Jan *(Norwegian architect)* **AV**
    Bibl: Byggekunst, 1984, no.5, p.198

Jansen, Jan *(Dutch goldsmith, act. 1661)* **BA**
    Bibl: Frederiks, Dutch silver, v.3, n.308; J.C.A. Estié, in ANTIEK XVII/1 (1982), 22-23

Jansen, Johan Wilhelm *(Dutch(?) artist, 18th cent.(?))* **WC**

Jansen, Johannes Mauritz *(Dutch artist, 1811-1857)* **WC**

Jansen, Joseph *(German artist, 1829-1905)* **WC**

Jansen, Lambertus Mattheus *(Dutch artist, 1891-1965)* **WC**

Jansen, Louise, (nee Siebke) *(German artist, 1835-1912)* **WC**

Jansen, M. Rob. *(Dutch painter, b.1878)* **GC**
    Bibl: ▶Vollmer, Künst.-Lex. 20. Jhr.

Jansen, Marit *(Norwegian architect)* **AV**
    Bibl: Byggekunst, 1984, no.5, p.198

Jansen, Martien **AV BA**
    (Dutch architect, 1950-) AV
    (Dutch architect, b.1950) BA
    Bibl: Casabella, 1984 July-Aug., v.48, no.504, p.16; J. Bosman, in DUTCH ART & ARCHITECTURE TODAY 13 (1983), 16-23

Jansen, P. →see Jansen, F.

Jansen, Peter *(Australian architect, 1938-)* **AV**
    Bibl: A + U, no.174, p.120

Jansen, W. *(Dutch painter, act.1830-1834)* **GC**
    Bibl: ▶Scheen, Ned. beeldende kunst.

Jansen, W. [Unidentified]
    (Unknown painter) **PR**
    Bibl: (June 16, 1806, lot 17, Coxe (Peter))

W. Jansen **PR**

Jansen, Wibrant *(Flemish(?) artist, op.1666)* **WC**

Jansen, Willem *(Dutch artist, 1892-)* **WC**

Jansen, Willem George Frederik **BA GC WC**
    (Dutch artist, 1871-1949) WC
    (Dutch painter, 1871-1949) GC
    (Dutch painter, ceramic designer, b.1871) BA
    Bibl: ▶Thieme-Becker

Jansenni, C.H. [Unidentified]
    (Unknown painter) **PR**
    Bibl: (January 16, 1805, lot 65, Vallance (James))

C.H. Jansenni **PR**

Jansens →see Janson, Johannes

Jansens →see Johnson, Cornelius I

Jansens, A. →see Janssens, Abraham I

Jansens, Francesco *(Flemish sculptor in ITA, 1702-after 1780)* **BA**
    Bibl: Lankheit, Floren. Barockplastik, p.227; PARAGONE, XXXVII/437 (July 1986), p. 65, note 31; ▶Thieme-Becker

Janson →see Jansón, Johannes

Janson, Agnes *(American painter, printmaker, 20th c.)* **BA**
    Bibl: ▶Intl. dir. exh. artists, 1982; ▶WW Amer. Art

Janson, Jakob *(German artist, op. 1806-1832)* **WC**

Janson, Johannes **BA GC JG PR**
    (Dutch artist, 1729-1784) **WC**
    (Dutch painter and
        draughtsman, 1729-1784) **GC**
    (Dutch painter, 1729-1784) **PR**
    (Dutch painter, printmaker,
        1729-1784) **BA**
    (Dutch, 1729-1784) **JG**
    Bibl: ▶Bénézit; Getty Photo Study
    Coll.; ▶RILA/BHA;
    ▶Thieme-Becker; ▶Witt checklist;
    ▶Wurzbach, NLD Künst.-Lex.
    J. Janson **PR**
    Jansens **PR**
    Janson **PR**
Janson, Johannes (sometimes
    also Jacobus) **WC**
    Johannes Janson **PR**
Janson, Johannes (sometimes also
    Jacobus) → see Janson, Johannes
Janson, Johannes Christiaan → see
    Janson, Johannes Christianus
Janson, Johannes Christianus **GC**
    (Dutch artist, 1763-1823) **WC**
    (Dutch draughtsman, 1763-
        1823) **GC**
    Bibl: ▶Thieme-Becker
Janson, Johannes Christiaan **WC**
Janson, Mark *(American architect)* **AV**
    Bibl: Architecture and urbanism,
    1986 Aug., no.81(191), p.70
Janson, Pieter *(Dutch artist, 1765-*
    1851) **WC**
Jansons, Andrew *(American painter,*
    b.1945) **BA**
    Bibl: ▶Art Index, vs.36, 37;
    Robins, ARTS MAGAZINE, LXIII/2
    (Oct. 1988), p. 44-47
Janssen → see Johnson, Cornelius I
Janssen or Jansen. Gerhard → see
    Janssen, Gerhard
Janssen van Ceulen, Cornelius → see
    Johnson, Cornelius I
Janssen, Bernard **AV**
Janssen, Bernardus Antonius
    Maria *(Dutch painter, b.1874)* **GC**
    Bibl: ▶Scheen, Ned. beeldende
    kunst.
Janssen, C. A. *(Dutch architect)* **AV**
    Bibl: Gemeentewerken, 1985
    Feb., v.14, no.2, p.45
Janssen, Cornelius → see Johnson,
    Cornelius I
Janssen, Ewert **AV BA**
    (Dutch architect in DNK, act.
        1662, d.ca.1692) **BA**
    (Dutch architect, worked 1662-
        1677 in Denmark) **AV**
    Bibl: ▶Portoghesi, Diz. arch. e
    urbanistica; Reclams DNK, p.300;
    ▶Thieme-Becker
Janssen, Gerhard *(German artist,*
    1863-1931) **WC**

Janssen, Gerhard **BA**
    (Dutch glass painter,
        printmaker, 1636-1725) **BA**
    (German artist, 1636-1725) **WC**
    Bibl: ▶Thieme-Becker; ▶Waller,
    Noord NLD Graveurs, p.63;
    ▶Weilbach, Kunst.leks.
    Janssen or Jansen. Gerhard **WC**
Janssen, Henri Adelbert
    (pseudonym) → see Kruiningen,
    Harry van (Henri Adelbert Janssen)
Janssen, Horst **BA WC**
    (German artist, 20th cent.) **WC**
    (German painter, printmaker,
        b.1929) **BA**
    Bibl: ▶Vollmer, Künst.-Lex. 20.
    Jhr.; ▶WW Arts DEU
Janssen, K.A. *(German artist,*
    b.1937) **BA**
Janssen, Peter Johann Theodor **BA WC**
    (German artist, 1844-1908) **WC**
    (German painter, 1844-1908) **BA**
    Bibl: ▶Busse, Maler u. Bildhauer
    19. Jahr.; ▶Thieme-Becker
Janssen, Servie *(Dutch artist,*
    b.1949) **BA**
    Bibl: Maastricht (NLD),
    Bonnefantenmuseum,
    WAYPASSER NORTH FEEL LAND
    (NFL)...1978
Janssen, Stephen Theodore *(British*
    enamelist, act.1747-1777) **BA**
    Bibl: Benjamin, Engl. enamels;
    ▶Thieme-Becker
Janssen, Victor Emil **BA GC WC**
    (German artist, 1807-1845) **WC**
    (German painter, 1807-1845) **BA**
    (German, 1807-1845) **GC**
    Bibl: ▶Bénézit; ▶Busse, Maler u.
    Bildhauer 19. Jahr.;
    ▶Thieme-Becker; ▶Witt checklist
Janssens → see Janssens, Abraham I
Janssens → see Janssens, Hieronymus
Janssens → see Janssens, Pieter
Janssens → see Janssens, Victor
    Honoré
Janssens → see Johnson, Cornelius I
Janssens Elinga, Pieter → see Janssens,
    Pieter
Janssens van Ceulen → see Johnson,
    Cornelius I
Janssens van Ceulen, Cornelius → see
    Johnson, Cornelius I
Janssens van Nuyssen, Abraham
    I → see Janssens, Abraham I
Janssens van Nuyssen, Abraham,
    I → see Janssens, Abraham I
Janssens, Abraham → see Janssens,
    Abraham I
Janssens, Abraham (I) → see Janssens,
    Abraham I

Janssens, Abraham I **BA GC**
    (Flemish artist, c.1575-1632) **WC**
    (Flemish painter, 1575-1632) **BA**
    (Flemish painter, ca.1575-1632) **PR**
    (Flemish, ca.1575-1632) **GC**
    Bibl: ▶Bénézit; Getty Photo Study
    Coll. (Ptgs.); ▶Kraam, Holl. en
    Vlaamsche kunst.; ▶RILA/BHA;
    ▶Thieme-Becker; ▶Wilenski, Flem.
    ptrs.; ▶Witt checklist; ▶Wurzbach,
    NLD Künst.-Lex.
    A. Janssens **PR**
    Abraham Janssens **PR**
    Abraham Janssens (I) **PR**
    Jansens, A. **PR**
    Janssens **PR**
Janssens van Nuyssen,
    Abraham I **GC**
Janssens van Nuyssen,
    Abraham, I **WC**
    Janssens, Abraham **PR**
Janssens, Abraham (I) **PR**
Janssens, Anna Maria *(Flemish*
    artist, op.1645-1668) **WC**
Janssens, Cornelis → see Johnson,
    Cornelius I
Janssens, Cornelius → see Johnson,
    Cornelius I
Janssens, Daniel *(Flemish painter,*
    tapestry designer, 1636-1682) **BA**
    Bibl: ▶Bénézit; ▶Thieme-Becker;
    ▶Wurzbach, NLD Künst.-Lex.
Janssens, Hendrik *(Dutch artist, op.*
    1673) **WC**
Janssens, Hieronymus **GC PR**
    (Flemish artist, 1624-1693) **WC**
    (Flemish painter, 1624-1693) **PR**
    (Flemish, 1624-1693) **GC**
    Bibl: Getty Photo Study Coll.
    (Ptgs.); ▶Thieme-Becker; ▶Witt
    checklist
    Hieronymus Janssens **PR**
    Janssens **PR**
Janssens, Hieronymus or
    Jeroom (den Danser) **WC**
    Janssens, Jeroom (den Danser) **GC**
Janssens, Hieronymus or Jeroom (den
    Danser) → see Janssens,
    Hieronymus
Janssens, Jan **GC**
    (Flemish artist, 1590-p.1646) **WC**
    (Flemish, 1590-aft.1646) **GC**
    Bibl: ▶Witt checklist
Janssens, Jan or Joannes **WC**
Janssens, Jan or Joannes → see
    Janssens, Jan
Janssens, Jeroom (den Danser) → see
    Janssens, Hieronymus
Janssens, Johan *(Belgian artist,*
    1809-) **WC**
Janssens, Jozef Marie Louis
    (Belgian artist, 1854-1930) **WC**

Janssens, Pieter   PR
(Dutch artist, 1623-a.1683)   WC
(Dutch painter and   GC
draughtsman, 1623-bef.1683)
(Dutch painter, d. bef.1682)   PR
Bibl: Getty Photo Study Coll.;
▶Thieme-Becker; ▶Witt checklist;
▶Wright, Ptgs. Dutch museums
Elinga, Pieter Janssens   GC
Janssens   PR
Janssens Elinga, Pieter   GC PR **WC**
P. Jansen   PR
Pieter Janssens   PR
Janssens, Victor Honoré   BA GC PR WC
(Flemish artist, 1658-1736)   WC
(Flemish painter, 1658-1736)   BA PR
(Flemish, 1658-1736)   GC
Bibl: ▶Bénézit; ▶RILA/BHA;
▶Thieme-Becker; ▶Witt checklist;
▶Wurzbach, NLD Künst.-Lex.
Jansen   PR
Janssens   PR
Victor Honore Janssens   PR
Victor Jansens   PR
Jansson, Eugene Frederik (Swedish
artist, 1862-1915)   WC
Jansson, F. (Scandinavian artist,
c.1825)   WC
Jansson, Jan (Dutch printmaker,
map dealer, 1588-1664)   BA
Bibl: LC slip; Skelton, R.A.,
DECORATIVE PRINTED MAPS...
Jansson, Karl Emanuel (Finnish
artist, 1846-1874)   WC
Jansteen → see Steen, Jan
Janstein → see Steen, Jan
Jansz, Frans (Netherlands artist, op.
1523-m.a.1542)   WC
Jansz. → see Jansz., Govert
Jansz., Govert (Dutch painter, 1578-
1619)   PR
Bibl: ▶Thieme-Becker
Govert Jans Mijnheer   PR
Govert Jansz.   PR
Jansz.   PR
Mynheer   PR
Jansz., Govert (Mijnheer)   GC WC
(Dutch artist, op.c.1655)   WC
(Dutch, act. ca.1655)   GC
Bibl: ▶Witt checklist
Jansz., Jacob (early Netherlandish
painter, act.1474-1509)   BA
Bibl: Boon, Ars auro prior, (1981)
pp.313-320; ▶Thieme-Becker;
▶Wurzbach, NLD Künst.-Lex.
Jansz., Pieter (Dutch glass painter,
1602-1672)   BA
Bibl: Bull. van het Rijksmuseum,
XXXIII/2 (1985) 71-72; Jaarboek
Amstelodamum, LXIX (1977)
91-92; ▶Thieme-Becker
Jansz., Pieter (Dutch draughtsman,
17th century)   GC
Bibl: Getty Photo Study Coll.
(Duits coll.)

Janszoen van Woerden, Hugo
(early Netherlandish printer, act.
1494-1526)   BA
Bibl: ▶Nieuw NLD biog. woord.;
▶Wurzbach, NLD Künst.-Lex.
Janszoen van Woerden, Pieter
(early Netherlandish printer, 15th-
16th cs.)   BA
Bibl: Quaerendo, VII/4 (1977) pp.
316-325
Woerden, Pieter Jansz. van   BA
Jantje van Emenes → see Emenes,
Jantje van [Unidentified]
Jantzen, Michael E.   AV
Jantzen, Michel (French architect,
Paris)   AV
Bibl: ▶Annuaire archts. fran.,
1978
Januarius Zick → see Zick, Januarius
Janus, Allan (American
photographer, b.1951)   BA
Bibl: Baltimore (MD, USA), Mus.
Art, 5 Maryland photogs. (1980)
Januška, Hieronymus (Austrian
goldsmith, 18th c.)   BA
Bibl: Simoniti, Zbornik za
umetnostno zgodovino XIV-XV
(1978-1979) 199-209
Janvier, Alex Simeon (Canadian
painter, b.1935)   BA
Bibl: ▶Artists Canada; ▶Canad.
artists exh., 1972-1973;
▶MacDonald, Can. artists
Janvrin, Elizabeth (American, 1687-
1757)   BA
Bibl: Antiques CXX 6 Dec '81
1422-23
Janvry, H. de (French artist, op.
1798-1800)   WC
Janz, Philipp (German artist, 1813-
1885)   WC
Janz, Robert (British artist, b.1932)   BA
Bibl: ▶Art Index, vs.29, 35; ART
INT'L, XXIII/9 (1980) p.48; Art Int,
XXIII, 9 (1980), p.48; ▶ARTbibl.
mod.; ARTWEEK (14 Feb 1987)
p.5; ▶Intl. dir. arts; London (GBR),
Goethe Inst., Brit. artists Berlin
(1981)
Janzer, Frigyes (Hungarian sculptor,
b.1939)   BA
Bibl: ex cat. 1975 Budapest,
Magyar Nemeti Galéria-one man
show
Japelli, Giuseppe → see Jappelli,
Giuseppe
**Japhet or Jazet, Alexandre Jean
Louis** (French artist, 1814-a.1864)   WC
Jappelli, Giuseppe   AV BA
(Italian architect, 1783-1852)   BA
(Italian architect, engineer,
1783-1852)   AV
Bibl: ▶Encyc. world art;
▶Macmillan encyc. archts.;
▶Portoghesi, Diz. arch. e
urbanistica
Japelli, Giuseppe   AV

Japy, Louis Aime (French artist,
1840-1916)   WC
Jaque, Louis (Canadian painter,
b.1919)   BA
Bibl: ▶Artists Canada; ▶Bénézit;
▶MacDonald, Can. artists
Jaquemin or Jacquemin, Francois
(French artist, op.1787-1836)   WC
Jaquerio, Giacomo I   BA GC
(Italian artist, op.1404-m.1453)   WC
(Italian painter, act.1403-1453)   BA
(Italian painter, act.1403-d.
1453)   GC
Bibl: ▶Bolaffi; ▶RILA/BHA, 1986;
TCI Piemonte; ▶Thieme-Becker
Jaquerio, Giacomo, I   WC
Jaquerio, Giacomo, I → see Jaquerio,
Giacomo I
Jaquerio, Matteo (Italian artist, op.
1404-1453)   WC
Jaques Jordans → see Jordaens, Jacob
Jaques Prevost → see Prevost, Jacques
Jaques Savrij → see Savery, Jacob (II)
Jaques, Norman Christopher   WI
(British artist, 20th cent.)   WC
(British artist, op.20th c.)   WI
Jacques, Norman Christopher   WC
Jaques, Peter (British artist, op.20th
c.)   WI
Jaques, Pierre (Swiss artist, 1913-)   WC
Jaques, Robin (British illustrator,
20th c.)   BA
Bibl: Arts Council GBR, Welsh
Comm., Images to order (1979)
Jaquet (French artist, 20th cent.)   WC
Jaquet, Gustave Jean → see Jacquet,
Gustave Jean
Jaquet, Jan Jozef (Belgian sculptor,
1822-1898)   BA
Bibl: ▶Bénézit; ▶Thieme-Becker
Jaquet, Jean Michel (Swiss painter,
printmaker, b.1950)   BA
Bibl: ▶Intl. dir. exh. artists, 1983;
▶Lex. zeitgen. Schweiz. Künstler
Jaquith, Nathaniel C. (American,
1818-1858, active New York, NY,
U.S. 1848-1858)   JG
Jaquotot, Marie Victoire   BA
(French artist, 1772-1855)   WC
(French artist, 1778-1855)   WC
(French porcelain painter,
musician, 1772-1855)   BA
Bibl: ▶Bénézit; ▶Brunet, Sèvres,
p.369; Sevres (FRA), Musee...
ceramique, PORCELAINES DE
SEVRES...(1975) p.6. (Mme. only;
no dates); ▶Thieme-Becker
Jacquotot, Marie Victoire   BA
Jacquotot, Marie-Victoire   WC
**Jaquotot, Marie Victoire (Le
Guay and Pinet)**   WC
Jaquotot, Marie Victoire (Le Guay
and Pinet) → see Jaquotot, Marie
Victoire

Jaray, Tess BA WC WI
(British artist, 1937-) WC
(British artist, b.1937) WI
(British painter, b.1937) BA
Bibl: ▶ARTbibl. mod., 21/1;
▶Dolman, Contemp. Brit. artists;
▶WW Art, 1988
Jardaeno → see Giordano, Luca
Jardel, Bernard (French artist,
1932-) WC
Jardin, Karel du → see Dujardin, Karel
Jardin, Nicolas Henri AV BA GC
(French architect, 1720-1799) AV BA
(French, 1720-1799) GC
Bibl: ▶Bauchal, Archtes. fran.;
Larusse; ▶Macmillan encyc.
archts.; ▶Thieme-Becker
Jardine, George (British artist,
b.1920) BA
Bibl: Arts Council GBR, A cold
wind (1979)
Jardines → see Jardines, José Maria
Jardines, José Maria PR WC
(Spanish artist, 1862-) WC
(Spanish painter, 1862-aft.1924) PR
Jardines PR
Jose Maria Jardines PR
Jardyn → see Dujardin, Karel
Jarema, Maria (Polish artist, 1908-
1958) WC
Jaremič, Stepan Petrovič BA
(Russian artist, 19th cent.) WC
(Russian painter, art historian,
1869-1939) BA
Bibl: ▶Bowlt, Russian avant-garde;
▶Great Soviet encyc.; ▶Natl. union
cat., pre-1956; ▶Thieme-Becker;
▶Witt checklist; ▶WWW USSR
Jaremitsch, Stepan Petrovitch WC
Jaremitsch, Stepan Petrovitch → see
Jaremič, Stepan Petrovič
Jaretti Sodano, Sergio (Italian
architect) AV
Bibl: Abitare, 1983 May, no.214,
p.88
Jarke, Hedwig (German artist,
1882-) WC
Jarl, Viggo (Danish sculptor in FRA,
1879-1979) BA
Bibl: Kaufmann, Kunstneren,
Maecenen Viggo Jarl (1979);
▶Vollmer, Künst.-Lex. 20. Jhr.;
▶Weilbach, Kunst.leks.
Jarman, Gerald (British artist,
b.1930) WI
Jarman, Henry Thomas (British
artist, op.1899-1938) WI
Jarman, Tom (Architect, New
Zealand, 1932?-1985) AV
Bibl: RIBA journal, 1986 Jan., v.93,
no.1, p.49
Jarmorini, Giovanni Giuseppe → see
Jarmorini, Giuseppe

Jarmorini, Giuseppe GC
(Italian artist, 1732-1816) WC
(Italian, ca.1732-1816) GC
Bibl: ▶Thieme-Becker; ▶Witt
checklist
Jarmorini, Giovanni Giuseppe WC
Jarmund, Kristin (Norwegian
architect, 1954-) AV
Bibl: Byggekunst: the Norwegian
review of architecture, 1988,
v.70, no.5, p.330
Jarnefelt or Jaernefelt, Eero
Nikolai → see Järnefelt, Eero Nikolai
Järnefelt, Eero Nikolai BA
(Danish artist, 1863-) WC
(Finnish painter, 1863-1937) BA
Bibl: ▶Bénézit; ▶Vollmer,
Künst.-Lex. 20. Jhr.
**Jarnefelt or Jaernefelt, Eero
Nikolai** WC
Jarnow, Al (American painter, 20th
c.) BA
Bibl: Martin, R., in ARTS
MAGAZINE LVIII/7 (Mar 1984) 12
Jarnuszkiewicz, Jerzy (Polish
sculptor, b.1919) BA
Bibl: Paris (FRA), Mus. d'art mod
de la ville, Sculptures polonaises
(1980); ▶Vollmer, Künst.-Lex. 20.
Jhr.
Jarnuszkiewicz, Krystian (Polish
sculptor, b.1930) BA
Bibl: Paris (FRA), Mus. d'art mod
de la ville, Sculptures polonaises
(1980)
Jarocki → see Jarocki, Wladyslaw
Jarocki, Wladyslav → see Jarocki,
Wladyslaw
Jarocki, Wladyslaw PR WC
(Polish artist, 1879-) WC
(Polish painter, b. 1879) PR
Bibl: ▶Thieme-Becker
Jarocki PR
Jarocki, Wladyslav PR
Wladyslaw Jarocki PR
Jaroschenko, Nikolai
Alexandrovich → see Jarošenko,
Nikolaj Aleksandrovič
Jarošenko, Nikolaj Aleksandrovič BA
(Russian artist, 1846-1898) WC
(Russian painter, 1846-1898) BA
Bibl: ▶Bénézit; ▶Bowlt, Russian
avant-garde; ▶Encyc. world art;
▶Fogg Mus. Libr. cat.; ▶Hamilton,
Art & arch. Russia; ▶Libr. of
Congr. Name Auth. File; ML;
▶Thieme-Becker
**Jaroschenko, Nikolai
Alexandrovich** WC
Jaroslav Cermak → see Čermák,
Jaroslav
Jarossay, Urbain (French
clockmaker, act.1788) BA

Jarratt, Joseph AV BA
(Irish architect, act.1753-1763) BA
(Irish architect, Dublin, fl. 1750) AV
Bibl: Bulletin of the Irish Georgian
Society, 1986 July-Dec., v.29, no.
1-2, p.25; Maguire, JOURNAL OF
THE ROYAL SOCIETY OF
ANTIQUARIES OF IRELAND, CXV
1985 p.13-39
Jarratt, Mrs. → see Berners, Miss
Jarraud, Leonard Antoine (French
artist, 1848-) WC
Jarret, Bruno (French photographer,
b.1946) BA
Bibl: Paris (FRA), Musée Rodin,
Rodin: 5 photographes (1985),
p.64
Jarrett, Clare (British artist, op.20th
c.) WI
Jarrin, Pierre (French silversmith,
d.1764, master 1712) GC
Bibl: ▶Nocq, Poinçon de Paris
Jarrin, Quentin (French silversmith,
b.1739, master 1764) GC
Bibl: ▶Mabille, Orfèv. fran.
Jarry, Nicolas GC JG WC
(French artist, 1620-c.1674) WC
(French painter and calligrapher,
1620-1670) GC
(French, b. ca. 1610-1615, d. ca.
1666 or 1674) JG
Bibl: ▶Bénézit
Jarsky, Paul H. (British artist, op.
20th c.) WI
Jarves, Deming (American glass
manufacturer, inventor, 1790-
1869) BA
Bibl: Barlow, Glass industry; Lee,
Sandwich glass, p.5; ▶WWW
Amer. hist.
Jarvie, Robert Riddle (American
silversmith, 1865-1941) BA
Bibl: Chicago Art Inst. Bull., May-
June '74; Chicago art per. idx.
Järvinen, Kari (Finnish architect,
1940-) AV
Bibl: Process: architecture, n.37,
1983, p.53
Järvinen, Simo (Finnish architect) AV
Bibl: Arkkitehti, 1985, no.1, p.58
Jarvis → see Jarvis, John Wesley
Jarvis → see Jervas, Charles
Jarvis, Charles → see Jervas, Charles
Jarvis, Charles Wesley (American
artist, 1812-1868) WC WI
Jarvis, Donald → see Jarvis, Donald
Alvin
Jarvis, Donald Alvin BA
(Canadian artist, 1923-) WC
(Canadian painter, b.1923) BA
Bibl: ▶Artists Canada;
▶MacDonald, Can. artists
Jarvis, Donald WC
Jarvis, Donald Edward (American
architect, Dallas, TX, 1928-1982) AV
Bibl: ▶Amer. archts. dir., 3rd ed.,
1970

Jarvis, Geoffrey *(Scottish architect)*   **AV**
Bibl: Country life, 1987 Aug.13,
v.181, no.33, p.87

Jarvis, H. Duane *(American
architect, 1932-1985)*   **AV**
Bibl: Texas architects, 1985 Mar.-
Apr., v.35, no.2, p.75

Jarvis, John Wesley   **BA GC PR WC WI**
(American artist, 1780-1840)   WC WI
*(American painter,
1780/81-1839/40)*   GC PR
*(American painter, printmaker,
sculptor, 1780/81-1839/40)*   BA
Bibl: ▶Dict. Amer. biog.; ▶Groce,
Artists Amer.; ▶RILA/BHA;
▶Smith, Idx. Amer. artists;
▶WWW Amer.
Jarvis   PR
John Wesley Jarvis   PR

Jarvis, Lewis *(American artist, 1845-
1900)*   **WC WI**

Jarvis, Thomas   **BA PR**
*(British painter, act. 1760, d.
1799)*   PR
(Irish glazier, act.1760, d.1799)   BA
Bibl: Gaunt: Oxford p.51; Marks,
Crown in glory, (07), p.58; New
College Record 1981 pp.15-20;
▶RILA/BHA; ▶Thieme-Becker
Thomas Jarvis   PR

Jas, Maria *(Polish artist, 20th cent.)*   **WC**

Jasberg, Unto *(Finnish artist, 20th
cent.)*   **WC**

Jascha, Johann *(Austrian artist,
b.1942)*   **BA**
Bibl: Bremen (DEU), Kunsthalle,
Aspekte der Zeichnung (1980)

Jaschke, Franz *(German artist, 1775-
1842)*   **WC**

Jasenský, Rudolf   **AV**

Jasiński, Ignacy *(Polish painter,
1833-1878)*   **BA**
Bibl: ▶Wielka ilustr. encyk.

Jason Painter *(Apulian vase-painter)*   **GC**
Bibl: Trendall, Attic red-fig. vases
Apulia

Jaspar, Paul *(Belgian architect, 1859-
1945)*   **BA**
Bibl: Brussels (BEL), École
supérieur, Brussels 1900 (1972);
▶Portoghesi, Diz. arch. e
urbanistica

Jasper Broers→see Broers, Jasper
Jasper Francis Cropsey→see Cropsey,
Jasper Francis
Jasper Gerardi→see Gerardi, Jasper
Jasper Van Lanen→see Lanen, Jasper
van [Unidentified]

Jasper, Joan *(American architect,
New York City)*   **AV**
Bibl: Architecture & urbanism,
1989 Apr., no.4, p.131

Jasper, Wolfgang *(W. German
architect)*   **AV**
Bibl: Arch Plus, 1986 Nov., no.87,
p.47

*Jaspers, Caspers, Gaspers or Jaspars,
Jan Baptist→see* Jaspers, Jan
Baptist

Jaspers, Jan Baptist   **GC**
(Flemish artist, 16?o(?)-1691)   WC
(Flemish, 1620(?)-1691)   GC
Bibl: Getty Photo Study Coll.
(Ptgs.); ▶Witt checklist
Caspers, Jan Baptist   GC
Gaspers, Jan Baptist   GC
**Jaspers, Caspers, Gaspers or
Jaspars, Jan Baptist**   **WC**

Jaspers, M. *(Belgian architect,
Brussels)*   **AV**
Bibl: Nieuw-neuf, 1989, no.140,
p.36

Jaspersen, Elisabeth *(German
painter, b.1900)*   **BA**
Bibl: ▶WW Arts DEU

Jassaud, Baron de *(French artist,
op.1834-1839)*   **WC**

Jastram, Joachim *(German sculptor,
b.1928)*   **BA**
Bibl: ▶Vollmer, Künst.-Lex. 20. Jhr.

Jastrau, Viggo *(Danish artist, 1857-
1946)*   **WC**

Jastrebzoff, Serge→see Ferat, Serge

Jaudon, Valerie   **BA WI**
(American artist, b.1943)   WI
(American painter, b.1945)   BA
Bibl: Artforum XV 4 Dec 1976,
p.26-30; ▶WW Amer. Art, 1980

Jauhiainen, Juliani *(Finnish
architect)*   **AV**
Bibl: Arkkitehti, 1985, v.82, no.
6-7, p.72

Jaulmes, Gustave Louis   **BA GC WC**
(French painter, 1873-1959)   GC
(Swiss artist, 1873-)   WC
*(Swiss painter, interior
decorator, designer, 1873-
1959)*   BA
Bibl: ▶Bénézit; ▶Thieme-Becker;
▶Vollmer, Künst.-Lex. 20. Jhr.;
▶Witt checklist

Jaumann, Rudolf Alfred *(German
artist, 1859-)*   **WC**

Jaunez, Lina→see Jaunez, Melle Lina
Jaunez, Melle Lina   **GC**
(French artist, op.1833-1834)   WC
(French painter, 19th century)   GC
Bibl: ▶Bénézit

Jaunez, Lina   **WC**

Jauran→see Jauran (Rodolphe de
Repentigny)
Jauran (Rodolphe de Repentigny)   **BA**
(Canadian artist, 1926-)   WC
*(Canadian painter,
photographer, author, 1926-
1959)*   BA
Bibl: ▶Artists Canada; ▶Bénézit;
▶MacDonald, Can. artists

Jauran   **WC**

Jáuregui y Aguilar, Juan de   **BA**
(Spanish artist, 1566/83-1641)   WC
*(Spanish painter, poet, 1583-
1641)*   BA
Bibl: ▶Encic. univ. ilus.; ▶Natl.
union cat., pre-1956; Oxford
comp. Spanish lit.;
▶Thieme-Becker; ▶Witt checklist

**Jauregui, Xauregui or Jaurigui y
Aguilar, Juan de**   **WC**
*Jauregui, Xauregui or Jaurigui y
Aguilar, Juan de→see* Jáuregui y
Aguilar, Juan de

Jauslin, Karl *(Swiss painter, 1842-
1904)*   **BA**
Bibl: ▶Schweiz. Künst.-Lex.;
▶Thieme-Becker

Jaussely, Léon *(French architect,
1875-1933)*   **BA**
Bibl: ▶Vollmer, Künst.-Lex. 20. Jhr.

Javacheff, Christo→see Christo
(Christo Vladimirov Javacheff)
Javacheff, Christo Vladimirov→see
Christo (Christo Vladimirov
Javacheff)
Javatcheff, Christo→see Christo
(Christo Vladimirov Javacheff)

Javier de Goribar, Nicolas *(Spanish
artist, 17th cent.)*   **WC**

Javier y Manubens, Francisco
(Brazilian architect)   **AV**
Bibl: Projeto, 1986 Mar., no.85,
p.27

Javorka, Tomas *(Architect, act. in
Poland)*   **AV**
Bibl: Casabella, 1989 Oct., v.53,
no.561, p.38

Javoy, Claude *(French menuisier,
master 1779, act. to 1787)*   **GC**
Bibl: ▶Salverte, Ébénistes 18e s.

Jawar (James Rannefeld)
(American craftsman, b.1948)   **BA**
Bibl: Colorado Springs (CO, USA),
Fine Arts Ctr., Woodworking in
the Rockies (1982)

Jawer, Rinagai Stanley *(American
printmaker, 20th c.)*   **BA**
Jawlensky→see Jawlensky, Alexej
von
Jawlensky, Aleksej→see Jawlensky,
Alexej von
Jawlensky, Alex von→see Jawlensky,
Alexej von
Jawlensky, Alexei→see Jawlensky,
Alexej von
Jawlensky, Alexei von→see
Jawlensky, Alexej von
Jawlensky, Alexej→see Jawlensky,
Alexej von

Jawlensky, Alexej von   BA PR
  (Russian artist, 1867-1941)   WC
  (Russian painter, 1867-1941)   BA PR
  (Russian, 1867-1941)   GC
  Bibl: ▶Art Index; ▶Fogg Mus. Libr.
    cat.; ▶Libr. of Congr. Name Auth.
    File; ▶Met. Mus. Art libr. cat.;
    ▶RILA/BHA; ▶Thieme-Becker;
    ▶Vollmer, Künst.-Lex. 20. Jhr.;
    ▶Witt checklist
  Alexej von Jawlensky   PR
  Jawlensky   PR
  Jawlensky, Aleksej   PR
  Jawlensky, Alex von   PR
  Jawlensky, Alexei   PR
Jawlensky, Alexei von   GC PR WC
  Jawlensky, Alexej   PR
  Jawlensky, Alexey   PR
Jawlensky, Alexey → see Jawlensky,
  Alexej von
Jaworoski, Jerzy *(Polish graphic
  artist, 1919-1975)*   BA
  Bibl: ▶Fogg Mus. Libr. cat.;
    Warsaw, Centralne Biuro Wystaw
    Art., JERZY JAWORSKI, 1977
Jaworska, Tamara *(Canadian
  tapestry artist, b.1926)*   BA
  Bibl: ▶Artists Canada; ▶Idx.
    Ontario artists; ▶WW Amer. Art
Jawurek, Karel *(Czech artist, 1815-
  1909)*   WC
Jay Van Everen → see Van Everen, Jay
Jay, Florence *(British artist, op.1905-
  1920)*   WI
Jay, Hamilton *(British artist, op.
  1875-1913)*   WI
Jay, Isabella Lee → see Jay, Jane
  Isabella Lee
Jay, Jane Isabella Lee   WI
  (British artist, op.1873-, d.1919)   WI
  (British artist, op.1882-1896)   WC
Jay, Isabella Lee   WC
Jay, Louis Joseph *(French painter,
  conservator, author, 1755-1836)*   BA
  Bibl: ▶Bellier, Artistes fran.; ▶Natl.
    union cat., pre-1956;
    ▶Thieme-Becker
Jay, W.   WC WI
  (British artist, op.1809-1817)   WC
  (British artist, op.1809-1926)   WI
Jay, William   AV BA
  *(British architect in USA, 1792-
  1837)*   BA
  (British architect, 1793-1837)   AV
  Bibl: ▶Colvin, Brit. archts.
Jay, William Samuel *(British artist,
  1843-1933)*   WC WI
Jazet, Jean Pierre Marie   BA GC WC WI
  *(Engraver, Paris, FRA., 1788-
  1871)*   WI
  (French artist, 1788-1871)   WC
  (French painter, 1788-1871)   GC
  (French printmaker, 1788-1871)   BA
  Bibl: ▶Bénézit; ▶Thieme-Becker

Jazet, Paul Léon   GC WC
  (French artist, 1848-)   WC
  (French painter, b.1848)   GC
  Bibl: ▶Bénézit
Jdanoff, Andrei Onnipovitch
  (Russian artist, op.1775-1811)   WC
Jeakes, Joseph   WC WI
  *(British artist, op.1796-, d.circa
  1829)*   WI
  (British artist, op.1796-1815)   WC
Jeal, Douglas *(British artist, b.1944)*   WI
Jean *(French scribe, act.1313-1316)*   BA
  Bibl: Collin-Roset, S., in PAYS
    LORRAIN LXIV/4 (1983) 220
Jean Achille Benouville → see
  Benouville, Jean Achille
Jean Adrien Guignet → see Guignet,
  Jean Adrien
Jean André Donducci → see Donducci,
  Giovanni Andrea (Mastelletta)
Jean Antoine Régillo → see Pordenone
  (Giovanni Antonio de Sacchis)
Jean Antoine Watteau → see Watteau,
  Jean Antoine
Jean Arp → see Arp, Hans
Jean Assellyn → see Asselyn, Jan
Jean Aubert → see Aubert, Jean
Jean Auguste Dominique Ingres → see
  Ingres, Jean Auguste Dominique
Jean Augustin Franquelin → see
  Franquelin, Jean Augustin
Jean Baglione → see Baglione,
  Giovanni
Jean Baptiste Antoine Guillemet → see
  Guillemet, Jean Baptiste Antoine
Jean Baptiste Audry → see Oudry,
  Jean-Baptiste
Jean Baptiste Belin → see Belin, Jean
  Baptiste I (Blin de Fontenay)
Jean Baptiste Berre → see Berre, Jean
  Baptiste
Jean Baptiste Blanchard → see
  Blanchard, Jean-Baptiste
Jean Baptiste Boel → see Boel, Jan
  Baptiste
Jean Baptiste Camille Corot → see
  Corot, Jean Baptiste Camille
Jean Baptiste Carpeaux → see
  Carpeaux, Jean-Baptiste
Jean Baptiste Charpentier (I) → see
  Charpentier, Jean Baptiste (I)
Jean Baptiste Clesinger → see
  Clésinger, Jean Baptiste
Jean Baptiste Descamps → see
  Descamps, Jean Baptiste
Jean Baptiste Edouard Detaille → see
  Detaille, Jean Baptiste Edouard
Jean Baptiste Fauvelet → see Fauvelet,
  Jean Baptiste
Jean Baptiste Francois Desoria → see
  Désoria, Jean Baptiste François
Jean Baptiste Greuze → see Greuze,
  Jean Baptiste
Jean Baptiste Henri Deshays → see
  Deshays, Jean Baptiste Henri

Jean Baptiste Hilair → see Hilair, Jean-
  Baptiste
Jean Baptiste Huet → see Huet, Jean
  Baptiste
Jean Baptiste Joseph Pater → see
  Pater, Jean-Baptiste Joseph
Jean Baptiste Jouvenet → see
  Jouvenet, Jean Baptiste
*Jean Baptiste le Monnoyer
  Junior → see* Monnoyer, Antoine
Jean Baptiste Le Prince → see Le
  Prince, Jean Baptiste
Jean Baptiste Mallet → see Mallet,
  Jean Baptiste
Jean Baptiste Marie Pierre → see
  Pierre, Jean Baptiste Marie
Jean Baptiste Mole → see Mole, Jean
  Baptiste
Jean Baptiste Monnoyer → see
  Monnoyer, Jean-Baptiste I
Jean Baptiste Oudry → see Oudry,
  Jean-Baptiste
Jean Baptiste Pillement → see
  Pillement, Jean Baptiste
Jean Baptiste Regnault → see
  Regnault, Jean-Baptiste, baron
Jean Baptiste Robie → see Robie, Jean
  Baptiste
Jean Baptiste Santerre → see Santerre,
  Jean-Baptiste
Jean Baptiste Simeon Chardin → see
  Chardin, Jean Baptiste Siméon
Jean Baptiste VanLoo → see Vanloo,
  Jean Baptiste
Jean Belin → see Belin, Jean Baptiste I
  (Blin de Fontenay)
Jean Bellegambe → see Bellegambe,
  Jean
Jean Béllin → see Bellini, Giovanni
Jean Bellineau → see Bellini, Giovanni
Jean Bellino → see Bellini, Giovanni
Jean Benedette Castiglione → see
  Castiglione, Giovanni Benedetto (il
  Grechetto)
Jean Béraud → see Béraud, Jean
Jean Bonvoisin → see Bonvoisin, Jean
Jean Both → see Both, Jan
Jean Boulanger → see Boulanger, Jean
Jean Boulogne → see Giambologna
  (Jean Boulogne)
Jean Bourdichon → see Bourdichon,
  Jean
Jean Breugle → see Brueghel, Jan, the
  elder
Jean Bylert → see Bijlert, Jan
  Hermansz. van
Jean Charles Cazin → see Cazin, Jean
  Charles
Jean Charles Langlois → see Langlois,
  Jean Charles
Jean Charles Meissonier → see
  Meissonier, Jean Charles
Jean Charlot → see Charlot, Jean
Jean Claude Naigeon → see Naigeon,
  Jean Claude

Jean Clouet→see Clouet, Jean

Jean Colombe→see Colombe, Jean

Jean d'Orbais   AV BA

(French architect, 13th cent.,
Reims Cathedral)   AV

(French master builder, act.
1210-1220)   BA

Bibl: Bull. Monumental,
CXXXVII/1 (1979) p.7; ▶Encyc.
world art; ▶Thieme-Becker

Orbais, Jean d'   AV

Jean d'Orléans   BA WC

(French artist, op.1361-1420)   WC

(French painter, act.1361-1407)   BA

Bibl: ▶Bénézit; ▶Thieme-Becker

Jean d'Ypres (Flemish sculptor, act.
1508-1510)   BA

Bibl: Dias, Coimbra no
Renascimento, pp.98-99;
Inventario artistico de Portugal,
Cidade de Coimbra (Lisbon:
Academia Nacional de Bellas
Artes, 1947); KRF Portugal;
▶Pamplona, Pint. escult. PRT

Jean de Beaumetz→see Beaumetz,
Jean de

Jean de Bologne→see Giambologna
(Jean Boulogne)

Jean de Bondolf→see Bondol, Jean

Jean de Bruges→see Bondol, Jean

Jean de Cambrai (French sculptor,
d.1438)   BA

Bibl: ▶Bénézit; ▶Encyc. world art

Jean de Dieu→see Dieu, Jean de

Jean de la Huerta→see Juan de la
Huerta

Jean de Liège (early Netherlandish
sculptor, d.1382)   BA

Bibl: ▶Bénézit; ▶Thieme-Becker

**Jean de Luca (or Nucci or Nuchii)
of Siena** (Italian artist, op.1347)   WC

Jean de Mabeuse→see Gossaert, Jan

Jean de Marville (early
Netherlandish sculptor, d.1389)   BA

Bibl: ▶Bénézit; ▶Encyc. world art;
▶Thieme-Becker

Jean de Maubeuge→see Gossaert,
Jan

**Jean de Montlucon, Molisson or
Molusson** (French artist, op.c.
1477-1492)   WC

Jean de Paris→see Perréal, Jean (Jean
de Paris)

Jean de Portugal→see Giovanni di
Consalvo

Jean de Rouen (French sculptor,
architect in PRT, b.1495-1500,
d.1580)   BA

Bibl: ▶Bénézit; ▶Encyc. world art;
▶Pamplona, Pint. escult. PRT;
Pelican Hist. of Art;
▶Thieme-Becker

Jean de Vignay (French, ca.
1282/85-1348)   JG

Jean Denis Maillard→see Maillard,
Jean Denis

Jean du Quesne   GC

(French scribe, act. 2nd half
15th c.)   GC

(French, active 1473-1474)   JG

Bibl: ▶Euw, Ludwig mss., v.4, pp.
240-255

Quesne, Jean du   JG

Jean Ducamps→see Ducamps, Jean

Jean Dupas→see Dupas,
Jean-Théodore

Jean Etienne Le Bel→see Le Bel, Jean
Étienne

Jean Etienne Liotard→see Liotard,
Jean-Etienne

Jean Faber→see Faber, Jean

Jean Ferdinand Chaigneau→see
Chaigneau, Jean Ferdinand

Jean François Barbieri→see Guercino
(Giovanni Francesco Barbieri)

Jean Francois Bredael→see Bredael,
Jan Frans van

Jean Francois Bremond→see
Brémond, Jean François

Jean Francois Colson→see Colson,
Jean François

Jean Francois de Troy→see Troy,
Jean François de

Jean Francois Hue→see Hue, Jean
Francois

Jean Francois Legillon→see Legillon,
Jean François

Jean François Millet→see Millet, Jean
François

Jean François Millet→see Millet, Jean
François II (Francisque Millet)

Jean Francois Millet (I)→see Millet,
Jean François I (Francisque Millet)

Jean Francois Pierre Peyron→see
Peyron, Jean François Pierre

Jean Francois Raffaelli→see Raffaëlli,
Jean François

Jean Francois Sablet→see Sablet,
Jean François (le Romain)

Jean Francois Xavier Roffiaen→see
Roffiaen, Jean François Xavier

Jean Frederic Bazille→see Bazille,
Frédéric

Jean Frederic Schall→see Schall, Jean
Frédéric

Jean Frelaut→see Frélaut, Jean

Jean Gabriel Domergue→see
Domergue, Jean Gabriel

[Jean] Grimoux→see Grimou, Alexis

Jean Hackaert→see Hackaert, Jan

Jean Hierosme Bressan→see Savoldo,
Giovanni Girolamo

Jean Hippolyte Marchand→see
Marchand, Jean Hippolyte

Jean Holbein→see Holbein, Hans, the
younger

Jean Honore Fragonard→see
Fragonard, Jean Honoré

Jean Hulsman→see Huysmans, Jan
Baptiste

Jean Hulsman→see Huysum, Jan van

Jean Isy de Botton→see Botton, Jean
Isy de

Jean Jacques Bachelier→see
Bachelier, Jean Jacques

Jean Jacques Boissard→see Boissard,
Jean Jacques

Jean Jacques Henner→see Henner,
Jean Jacques

Jean Jacques Lagrenee (the
younger)→see Lagrenée, Jean
Jacques II

Jean Jacques Pfister→see Pfister,
Jean Jacques

Jean Jacques Spoede→see Spoede,
Jean Jacques

Jean Joannès→see Juanes, Juan de
(Vicente Juan Macip)

Jean Joseph Benjamin Constant→see
Constant, Jean Joseph Benjamin

Jean Joseph Crotti→see Crotti, Jean
Joseph

Jean Joseph Taillasson→see
Taillasson, Jean Joseph

Jean Joseph Xavier Bidauld→see
Bidauld, Jean Joseph Xavier

Jean Julien Lemordant→see
Lemordant, Jean Julien

Jean Lanfranc→see Lanfranco,
Giovanni

Jean Laurent Bernin→see Bernini,
Gian Lorenzo

Jean Laurent Mosnier→see Mosnier,
Jean Laurent

Jean le Loup (French master builder,
act.1221-1237)   BA

Bibl: Bull. Monumental,
CXXXVII/1 (1979) p.7; ▶Encyc.
world art; ▶Thieme-Becker

Jean Lemaire→see Lemaire, Jean (Le
gros Lemaire)

Jean Leon Gerome→see Gérôme,
Jean Léon

Jean Louis Andre Theodore
Gericault→see Géricault, Jean
Louis André Théodore

Jean Louis Charbonnel→see
Charbonnel, Jean Louis

Jean Louis Ducis→see Ducis, Jean
Louis

Jean Louis Ernest Meissonier→see
Meissonier, Jean Louis Ernest

Jean Louis Forain→see Forain, Jean
Louis

Jean Louis Laneuville→see Laneuville,
Jean Louis

Jean Louis Prevost→see Prévost, Jean
Louis

Jean Lurcat→see Lurçat, Jean

Jean Mannheim→see Mannheim,
Jean

Jean Marie Jacomin→see Jacomin,
Jean Marie

Jean Metzinger→see Metzinger, Jean

Jean Michelin→see Michelin, Jean

Jean Miel→see Miel, Jan

Jean of Maubeuge→see Gossaert, Jan

Jean Paul Laurens→see Laurens, Jean Paul

Jean Perreal→see Perréal, Jean (Jean de Paris)

Jean Petitot→see Petitot, Jean

Jean Pierre Alexandre Antigna→see Antigna, Jean Pierre Alexandre

Jean Pierre Norblin→see Norblin, Jean Pierre (de la Gourdaine)

Jean Pierre Saint-Ours→see Saint-Ours, Jean Pierre

Jean Pierre Tassaert→see Tassaert, Jean Pierre

Jean Pillmant→see Pillement, Jean Baptiste

Jean Pougny→see Pougny, Jean

Jean Raoux→see Raoux, Jean

Jean Restout (II)→see Restout, Jean II

Jean Richard Goubie→see Goubie, Jean Richard

Jean Roller→see Roller, Jean

Jean Rotenhamer→see Rottenhammer, Hans I

Jean Schooreel→see Scorel, Jan van

Jean Simon Berthelemy→see Berthélemy, Jean Simon

Jean Souverbie→see Souverbie, Jean

Jean Stansbury Holden→see Holden, Jean Stansbury

Jean Stean→see Steen, Jan

Jean Steen→see Steen, Jan

Jean Stein→see Steen, Jan

Jean Stien→see Steen, Jan

Jean Tassel→see Tassel, Jean

Jean Thomas Thibault→see Thibault, Jean Thomas

Jean van de Kerkhove→see Kerkhove, Jean van de

Jean van der Heyden→see Heyden, Jan van der

Jean Van Eck→see Eyck, Jan van

Jean van Eick→see Eyck, Jan van

Jean van Eyk→see Eyck, Jan van

Jean Van Kessel père→see Kessel, Jan van I

Jean Victor Bertin→see Bertin, Jean Victor

Jean Wynants→see Wijnants, Jan

Jean Xceron→see Xceron, Jean

Jean, Felix (Haitian artist, 1930-) **WC**

Jean, Georges (Haitian artist, 1945-) **WC**

Jean, Jocelyn (Canadian artist, 20th c.) **BA**
  Bibl: Montreal (Que, CND), Mus. d'Art Contemp., Luc Béland, Lucio de Heusch, Jocelyn Jean... (1977)

Jean, L.S. (French artist, 19th cent.) **WC**

Jean, Marcel **BA WC**
  (French artist, 1900-) **WC**
  (French painter, author, b.1900) **BA**
    Bibl: ▶Bénézit; Guide exh. artists: N. Amer. ptrs.; ▶Witt checklist

Jean, Philip (British artist, 1755-1802) **WC WI**

Jean, Roger (British artist, circa 1783-1828) **WI**

Jean-Baptist Perroneau→see Perroneau, Jean-Baptiste

Jean-Baptiste Bonnart→see Bonnart, Jean-Baptiste

Jean-Baptiste Charles Desgrange→see Desgrange, Jean-Baptiste Charles

Jean-Baptiste de Roy→see Roy, Jean-Baptiste de

Jean-Baptiste Frederic Desmarais→see Desmarais, Jean-Baptiste Frederic

Jean-Baptiste Greuze→see Greuze, Jean Baptiste

Jean-Baptiste Marie Huet→see Huet, Jean Baptiste

Jean-Baptiste Morel→see Morel, Jean-Baptiste

Jean-Baptiste Oudry→see Oudry, Jean-Baptiste

Jean-Baptiste Perroneau→see Perroneau, Jean-Baptiste

Jean-Baptiste Santerre→see Santerre, Jean-Baptiste

Jean-Baptiste Sarazin→see Sarazin, Jean-Baptiste

Jean-Claude Bonnefond→see Bonnefond, Jean-Claude

Jean-Daniel Huber→see Huber, Jean Daniel

Jean-Francois Bredael→see Bredael, Jan Frans van

Jean-Louis Marnette) Marne→see Marne, Jean Louis de (Marnet)

Jean-Marc Nattier→see Nattier, Jean-Marc

Jean-Pierre Sudre (Paris)→see Sudre, Jean-Pierre

Jean-Robert, Andre (French artist, 1921-) **WC**

Jeanes, Sigismond J.E. (French artist, op.1906-) **WC**

Jeanet→see Clouet, François

Jeanet→see Clouet, Jean

Jeanmaire, Edouard (Swiss artist, 1847-1916) **WC**

Jeanne de Mayenne (French, act. 1220-1246) **BA**
  Bibl: Art Bulletin LXV/1 (Mar 1983) 23-33

Jeanne Philiberte Ledoux→see Ledoux, Jeanne Philiberte

Jeanneau, Hubert (French architect) **AV**
  Bibl: Architecture d'aujourd'hui, 1980 Apr., no.208, p.51

Jeanneret, Charles Edouard→see Le Corbusier (Charles Edouard Jeanneret)

Jeanneret, Charles Edouard (Le Corbusier)→see Le Corbusier (Charles Edouard Jeanneret)

Jeanneret, Charles-Edouard→see Le Corbusier (Charles Edouard Jeanneret)

Jeanneret, Gustave (Swiss artist, 1847-1927) **WC**

Jeanneret, Pierre **AV BA FA**
  (1896-1965; Architect, France) **FA**
  (French architect, 1896-1965) **BA**
  (Swiss architect, 1896-1967) **AV**
    Bibl: Le Corbusier, Sketchbooks, v.3; ▶Macmillan encyc. archts.; ▶MoMA libr. cat.; ▶Portoghesi, Diz. arch. e urbanistica; Rome, Pal. dei Convegni Le Corbusier, 1976

Jeanneret-Gris, Charles Édouard→see Le Corbusier (Charles Edouard Jeanneret)

Jeanneret-Gris, Charles-Edouard→see Le Corbusier (Charles Edouard Jeanneret)

Jeannet, Jacques (French artist, 1931-) **WC**

Jeanneteau, Marc (French photographer, 20th century) **GC**
  Bibl: Getty Photo Study Coll.

Jeannin→see Jeannin, Georges

Jeannin, Georges **PR WC**
  (French artist, 1841-1925) **WC**
  (French painter, 1841-1925) **PR**
    Bibl: ▶Thieme-Becker

Georges Jeannin **PR**

Jeannin **PR**

Jeanniot→see Jeanniot, Georges

Jeanniot, Georges **PR**
  (French artist, 1848-1934) **WC**
  (French painter, 1848-1934) **GC PR**
    Bibl: ▶Bénézit; ▶Thieme-Becker

Georges Jeanniot **PR**

Jeanniot **PR**

Jeanniot, Georges (Pierre Georges) **WC**

Jeanniot, Pierre Georges **GC PR**

Jeanniot, Georges (Pierre Georges)→see Jeanniot, Georges

Jeanniot, Pierre Alexandre (French artist, 1826-1892) **WC**

Jeanniot, Pierre Georges→see Jeanniot, Georges

Jeanrenaud, A. (French, 1835-1895) **JG**

Jeanron, Philippe Auguste **BA GC WC**
  (French artist, 1809-1877) **WC**
  (French painter, 1809-1877) **GC**
  (French painter, printmaker, museum administrator, 1809-1877) **BA**
    Bibl: ▶Bénézit; ▶Encyc. world art; Harambourg, Ptrs. paysagistes; ▶Thieme-Becker

Jeanselme frères→see Jeanselme, Jean-Arnoux

Jeanselme, Charles-Joseph Marie
(*French menuisier, b.1827, act. to 1871*) **GC**
Bibl: Ledoux-Lebard, Ébénistes

Jeanselme, Jean-Arnoux (*French menuisier, act.1824-1840*) **GC**
Bibl: Getty Photo Study Coll. (Dec. arts); Ledoux-Lebard, Ébénistes
Jeanselme frères **GC**

Jeanselme, Joseph-Pierre-François
(*French menuisier, act.1824-1840, d. 1860*) **GC**
Bibl: Ledoux-Lebard, Ébénistes

Jeanson, Barthélemy (*French architect, engineer, 1760-1820/28*) **BA**
Bibl: ▶Bauchal, Archtes. fran., suppl.; ▶Larousse, Grand dict. 19e s.; ▶Nouv. biog. gén.; ▶Portoghesi, Diz. arch. e urbanistica; Saddy in sOUFFLOT ET L'ARCHITECTURE DES LUMIÈRES pp.192-203; ▶Thieme-Becker

Jearrad, Robert William (*British architect, d.1861*) **AV**
Bibl: ▶Colvin, Brit. archts.
Jeaurat → see Jeaurat, Etienne

Jeaurat de Bertry, Nicholas Henry **BA**
(*French artist, 1728-1796*) **WC**
(*French painter, 1728-1796*) **GC**
(*French painter, 1728-after 1796*) **BA**
Bibl: ▶Bénézit; ▶Larousse grande encyc.; ▶Thieme-Becker

Jeaurat de Bertry, Nicolas Henry **GC**
Jeaurat, Nicolas Henry (Jeaurat de Bertry or Bertrix) **WC**
Jeaurat de Bertry, Nicolas Henry → see Jeaurat de Bertry, Nicholas Henry

Jeaurat, Edme **BA WC**
(*French artist, 1688-1738*) **WC**
(*French printmaker, 1688-1738*) **BA**
Bibl: ▶Bénézit; Fonds Française XII; ▶Thieme-Becker; ▶Witt checklist

Jeaurat, Etienne **BA GC PR WC**
(*French artist, 1699-1789*) **WC**
(*French painter, 1699-1789*) **PR**
(*French painter, printmaker, 1699-1789*) **BA**
(*French, 1699-1789*) **GC**
Bibl: ▶Bénézit; ▶RILA/BHA; ▶Thieme-Becker; ▶Witt checklist
Etienne Jeaurat **PR**
Jeaurat **PR**
Jeurat, Etienne **PR**
Jeaurat, Nicolas Henry (Jeaurat de Bertry or Bertrix) → see Jeaurat de Bertry, Nicholas Henry

Jeayes, Henry **PR WC WI**
(*British artist, op.1808*) **WC**
(*British artist, op.1808-*) **WI**
(*British painter, fl. 1808*) **PR**
Bibl: (March 30, 1807, Tregoning (J.)); ▶Witt checklist

Jebens, Adolf (*German painter, 1819-1888*) **GC**
Bibl: ▶Bénézit

Jebens, Peter (*West German architect, Hamburg*) **AV**
Bibl: Architektur & Wohnen, 1989 Sept.-Oct., no.5, p.22

Jech, František **AV**

Jecker, Werner (*Swiss printmaker, b.1944*) **BA**
Bibl: Lausanne (CHE), Musée arts déc., 4 expressions graphiques (1985)

Jeckyll, Thomas **BA WI**
(*British artist, op.19th c.*) **WI**
(*British designer, 1827-1881*) **BA**
Bibl: ▶Avery period. idx.; London (GBR), Royal Acad., Vict. & Edward. Dec. Art: Handley-Read Coll. (1972)

Jedberg [Unidentified] (*Unknown painter*) **PR**
Bibl: (May 4, 1803, lot 23, Edwards)

Jeff (Jeff Russell) (*American artist, b.1942*) **BA**
Bibl: ▶Intl. dir. exh. artists, 1983; New York (NY, USA), Pratt Inst. Manhattan Ctr. Gall., The destroyed print (1982)

Jefferson → see Jefferson, Joseph
Jefferson David Chalfant → see Chalfant, Jefferson David

Jefferson, J. (*British artist, 18th cent.*) **WC**

Jefferson, John (*British artist, op. 1811-1815*) **WI**

Jefferson, John Bryan (*British architect, director pf Design Services at Property Services Agency*) **AV**
Bibl: ▶RIBA members, 1987

Jefferson, Joseph **PR WC WI**
(*American artist, 1829-1905*) **WC WI**
(*American painter, 1829-1905*) **PR**
Bibl: ▶RILA/BHA
Jefferson **PR**
Joseph Jefferson **PR**

Jefferson, Thomas **AV FA GC WC WI**
(*13.IV (2.IV old style).1743-4.VII.1826, president 1801-1809; Architect, President, Scientist, Virginia, Washington*) **FA**
(*American artist, 1743-1826*) **WC WI**
(*American draughtsman, 1743-1826*) **GC**
(*Third President of the U.S, 1743-1826*) **AV**
Bibl: ▶Encyc. Britannica, v.6, p.522; ▶Libr. of Congr. Name Auth. File; Nichols, F. D., and Bear Jr., James A., Monticello, 1982; ▶RILA/BHA, Subject, 1988

Jefferson, William (*American artist, op.1864-*) **WI**
Jeffery John Archer Amherst, 5th Earl Amherst → see Amherst, Jeffery John Archer Amherst, 5th Earl of
Jefferys → see Jefferys, James

Jefferys, Charles W. → see Jefferys, Charles William

Jefferys, Charles William **BA**
(*British artist, 1869-1951*) **WC WI**
(*Canadian painter, 1869-1951*) **BA**
Bibl: ▶Artists Canada; ▶MacDonald, Can. artists

Jefferys, Charles W. **WC WI**

Jefferys, James **BA PR WC WI**
(*British artist, 1751-1784*) **WC WI**
(*British draftsman, painter, 1751-1784*) **BA**
(*British painter, 1751-1784*) **PR**
Bibl: Burl. Mag. CXVIII Mar 1976, p.151; ▶Dict. natl. biog.; ▶Fisher, Watercolour ptrs.; ▶RILA/BHA; ▶Thieme-Becker
James Jefferys **PR**
Jefferys **PR**
Jeffries **PR**

Jefferys, Marcel (*Belgian artist, 1872-1924*) **WC**

Jefferys, William **WC WI**
(*British artist, 1723-1730-1805*) **WI**
(*British artist, op.1766-1775*) **WC**

Jeffreson, J.W. **WC WI**
(*British artist, op.1850-1861*) **WI**
(*British artist, op.c.1850-1861*) **WC**
Jeffrey Raigersfield → see Raigersfield, Capt. J .de
Jeffrey, Earl Amherst → see Amherst, Jeffery John Archer Amherst, 5th Earl of

Jeffrey, Noel (*American designer*) **AV**
Bibl: House beautiful, 1985 Feb., v.127, no.2, p.85
Jeffries → see Jefferys, James

Jeffries, William (*British artist, b.1953*) **BA**
Bibl: Arts Council GBR, Scot. Comm., Small tapestries (1976)

Jeffs, Howard (*British photographer, b.1944*) **BA**
Bibl: Arts Council GBR, Summer Show 4 (1977)

Jegal, Ferdinand (*West German architect*) **AV**

Jegen, Henri (*Architect, Luxembourg(?)*) **AV**
Bibl: Architectural design, 1987, v.57, no.5-6, p.67
Jegers, Christophel → see Jegher, Christoffel

Jegers, Julijs **WC WI**
(*American artist, 1910-*) **WC**
(*American artist, b.1910*) **WI**

Jeggli, Johann Heinrich (*Swiss artist, op.1564*) **WC**
Jegher or Jeghers, Christoffel → see Jegher, Christoffel

Jemelkova, Jana *(Czech painter, printmaker, b.1928)*   **BA**
    Bibl: Brno (CS), Dŭmpanú z Kunštátu, JANA JEMELKOVA..., 1979

Jemison, Noah *(American painter, 20th c.)*   **BA**
    Bibl: Arts Mag. LI (Jan 1977), p.14; ▶Locus

Jemison, Richard *(American painter, b.1942)*   **BA**
    Bibl: Birmingham, Museum of Art, catalogue

Jena Painter *(vase-painter, ca. 400-366 BC)*   **GC**
    Bibl: ▶Beazley, Attic red-fig. vase-ptrs.; Richter, Attic red-fig. vases

Jena Workshop   **GC**
    Bibl: ▶Beazley, Attic red-fig. vase-ptrs.

Jenckell [Unidentified] *(Unknown painter)*   **PR**
    Bibl: (June 7, 1815, lot 67, Stanley)

Jencks, Charles *(British architect, author, b.1939)*   **BA**
    Bibl: ▶Avery period. idx., suppl. 4,6,7; Hill, R., in COUNTRY LIFE CLXXIX/4614 (23 Jan 1986) 192; ▶Who's Who [GBR], 1988

Jené, Edgar   **BA WC**
    (German artist, 1904-)   WC
    (German painter, b.1904)   BA
    Bibl: Költzsch, in SCHON IS NUR DAS WUNDERBARE, 1984; ▶Vollmer, Künst.-Lex. 20. Jhr.; ▶Witt checklist

Jenet, Johann *(German printmaker, editor, act.1623-1627)*   **BA**
    Bibl: ▶Hollstein, German, v.15a, p.215; ▶Thieme-Becker

Jenet, Sebastian *(German printmaker, publisher, act.ca.1640-1660)*   **BA**
    Bibl: ▶Hollstein, German, v.15a; ▶Thieme-Becker, v.18

Jenewien or Jennewien, Felix *(Czech artist, 1857-1905)*   **WC**

Jenichen, Balthasar   **BA GC**
    (German artist, op.1563-m.a. 1621)   WC
    (German printmaker, goldsmith, publisher, act.ca.1560, d. before 1621)   BA
    (German, act.1563-aft.1621)   GC
    Bibl: ▶Hollstein, German, v.15b, p.9; ▶Thieme-Becker; ▶Witt checklist

Jenichen, Jenich Jenisch or Jenitsch (not Jenckel) Balthasar   **WC**
Jenichen, Jenich Jenisch or Jenitsch (not Jenckel) Balthasar → see Jenichen, Balthasar

Jenkin, W.   **WC WI**
    (British artist, 19th cent.)   WC
    (British artist, op.1866-)   WI
    Bibl: Paviere, Landscape

Jenkins Sub-Group *(Apulian vase-painters)*   **GC**
    Bibl: Trendall, Attic red-fig. vases Apulia

Jenkins, Arthur Henry *(British artist, b.1871)*   **WI**

Jenkins, Blanche *(British artist, op. 1872-1915)*   **WI**

Jenkins, Charles Waldo *(American artist, 1820-op.1900)*   **WI**

Jenkins, Connie *(American painter, b.1945)*   **BA**
    Bibl: ▶Artweek idx.; Laguna Beach (CA, USA), Mus. Art, West Coast realism (1983)

Jenkins, David C. *(British artist, op. 1884-, d.1916)*   **WI**
    Bibl: Hall, Nottinghamshire

Jenkins, Dennis *(American architect, 1939-)*   **AV**

Jenkins, Edward   **WC WI**
    (British artist, op.c.1826)   WC
    (British artist, op.circa 1826-)   WI

Jenkins, Frank Lynn *(British sculptor, 1870-1927)*   **BA**
    Bibl: London (GBR), Fieldborne Galleries, London art schools (1979); ▶Thieme-Becker; ▶Vollmer, Künst.-Lex. 20. Jhr.

Jenkins, G.H.   **WC WI**
    (British artist, 19th cent.)   WC
    (British artist, op.1881-)   WI

Jenkins, J. *(British artist, 1788-1832)*   **WC WI**

Jenkins, Joseph John *(British artist, 1811-1885)*   **WC WI**

Jenkins, Julian *(American architect, AL)*   **AV**
    Bibl: Southern accents, 1986 Nov. -Dec., v.9, no.6, p.188

Jenkins, Karen Jean *(American artist, b.1944)*   **BA**
    Bibl: Sacramento (CA, USA), Crocker Art Museum, Paper/art (1981)

Jenkins, Keily *(American sculptor, 20th c.)*   **BA**
    Bibl: Cameron, D., in ARTS MAGAZINE LVIII/2 (Oct 1983) 7

Jenkins, Lawrence *(British artist, op.1978-1981)*   **WI**

Jenkins, Mary, Miss → see Brewer, Mary

Jenkins, Nicholas   **WC WI**
    (British artist, 20th cent.)   WC
    (British artist, op.1970-)   WI

Jenkins, Paul   **BA WC WI**
    (American artist, 1923-)   WC
    (American artist, b.1923)   WI
    (American painter, b.1923)   BA
    Bibl: Arts Mag. Oct. 1975; ▶MoMA libr. cat.; ▶NY art yrbk.; UC Santa Barbara cat. sheets; ▶WW Amer. Art, 1976

Jenkins, Paul Ripley *(American sculptor, painter, 1940-1974)*   **BA**
    Bibl: Univ. of Washington Gallery; ▶WW Amer. Art

Jenkins, Peter David *(British architect, London)*   **AV**
    Bibl: ▶RIBA members, 1983

Jenkins, Rhys *(British artist, op.20th c.)*   **WI**

Jenkins, Ronald Stewart *(Engineer)*   **AV**
    Bibl: The Arup journal, 1985 Summer, v.20, no.2, p.9

Jenkins, Thomas *(English goldsmith, act.1668, d.before 1707)*   **BA**
    Bibl: Connoisseur CXCV/785 (July 1977), p.172; Heal, London goldsmiths 1200-1800; Jackson, Engl. goldsmiths; ▶Thieme-Becker

Jenkins, Thomas   **BA WC WI**
    (British artist, 1722-1798)   WI
    (British artist, c.1720-1798)   WC
    (English painter, dealer, collector, ca.1720-1798)   BA
    Bibl: ▶Dict. natl. biog.; ▶Thieme-Becker

Jenkins, Tom *(American artist, b.1943)*   **BA**
    Bibl: Pasadena (CA, USA), Cal Tech, Baxter Art Gall., Barry Fahr (1981)

Jenkins, Wilfred   **WC WI**
    (British artist, 19th cent.)   WC
    (British artist, op.1875-1888)   WI

Jenkinson [Unidentified] *(Unknown painter)*   **PR**
    Bibl: (November 26, 1812, lot 10, Herbert)

Jenkinson, J.   **WC WI**
    (British artist, op.c.1780)   WC
    (British artist, op.circa 1780-)   WI

Jenks → see Jenks, Albert

Jenks, Albert *(American painter, 1824-1901)*   **PR**
    Bibl: ▶WWW Amer. art
    Albert Jenks   PR
    Jenks   PR

Jenlis [Unidentified] *(Unknown painter)*   **PR**
    Bibl: Simon Cornu inventory, dated 1644 (item 45)

Jennelle, Ernest M. *(American architect)*   **AV**

Jennens & Bettridge *(Canadian artist, op.c.1850)*   **WC**

Jenner, Isaac Walter   **WI**
    (British artist, 1836-1901)   WI
    (British artist, op.1855-1874)   WC
    Bibl: ▶Wood, Victorian ptrs.

Jenner, W.   **WC**

Jenner, Isaak → see Jehner, Isaak
Jenner, Michael (British architect)   **AV**
Jenner, Ross (Architect, Auckland,
New Zealand)   **AV**
  Bibl: New Zealand architect,
  1986, no.1, p.24
Jenner, S.   **WC WI**
  (British artist, op.c.1826)   WC
  (British artist, op.circa 1826-)   WI
  Bibl: ▶Houfe, Brit. book illus.
Jenner, Thomas   **WC WI**
  (British artist, op.1631-, d.1673)   WI
  (British artist, op.1631-1656)   WC
Jenner, W. → see Jenner, Isaac Walter
Jennesson, Jean Nicolas (French
architect, 1686-1755)   **AV BA**
  Bibl: ▶Bauchal, Archtes. fran.;
  ▶Lance, Dict. archts. fran.;
  ▶Portoghesi, Diz. arch. e
  urbanistica; ▶Thieme-Becker
Jennewein, Carl Paul (American
sculptor, 1890-1978)   **BA**
  Bibl: NY Times obit., 25 Feb
  1978, p.24; ▶Vollmer, Künst.-Lex.
  20. Jhr.; WW Amer., 1977; ▶WW
  Amer. Art, 1976
Jenney, Neil   **BA WI**
  (American artist, b.1945)   WI
  (American sculptor, painter,
  b.1945)   BA
  Bibl: Hartford (Conn, USA),
  Wadsworth Atheneum. Neil
  Jenney; Matrix 14
Jenney, William LeBaron   **AV BA**
  (American architect, 1832-1907)   BA
  (American architect, Chicago,
  Ill, 1832-1907)   AV
  Bibl: ▶Encyc. world art; ▶Withey,
  Amer. archts.
Jennie E. Bartlett → see Bartlett,
Jennie E.
Jennings or Jennys, Richard → see
Jennings, Richard
Jennings, E. Owen   **WI**
  (British artist, 1899-)   WC
  (British artist, b.1899)   WI
Jennings, E.Owen   **WC**
Jennings, E.Owen → see Jennings, E.
Owen
Jennings, Humphrey   **BA WC WI**
  (British artist, 1907-1950)   WC WI
  (British painter, photographer,
  filmmaker, 1907-1950)   BA
  Bibl: ▶Bénézit; ▶MoMA libr. cat.;
  ▶Vollmer, Künst.-Lex. 20. Jhr.
Jennings, J. Payne (British, active
1870s)   **JG**
Jennings, J.J.   **WC WI**
  (British artist, op.c.1845)   WC
  (British artist, op.circa 1845-)   WI
Jennings, Jamillah (American
sculptor, painter, dancer, 20th c.)   **BA**
  Bibl: Los Angeles (CA, USA),
  Municipal Art Gallery, Afro-Amer.
  abstraction (1982)

Jennings, Maurice J. (American
architect, Fayetteville, Ar)   **AV**
  Bibl: ▶AIA Pro File, 1985
Jennings, Philip O. (British
printmaker, painter, b.1921)   **BA**
  Bibl: ▶WW Art
Jennings, Richard   **WI**
  (American artist, op.1777-
  1783)   WC WI
Jennings or Jennys, Richard   **WC**
  Jennys, Richard   WI
Jennings, Samuel (British artist, op.
1789-1834)   **WC WI**
Jennings, W.G.   **WC WI**
  (British artist, 1797-1843)   WI
  (British artist, op.1797-1830)   WC
Jennings, W.R.   **WC WI**
  (British artist, 19th cent.)   WC
  (British artist, op.19th c.)   WI
  Bibl: ▶Waters, Brit. artists
Jennis, Gurnell C. → see Jennis,
Gurnell Charles
Jennis, Gurnell Charles   **WI**
  (British artist, 1874-1943)   WI
  (British artist, op.c.1910-1936)   WC
Jennis, Gurnell C.   **WC**
Jennis, Stevan (American sculptor,
painter, b.1945)   **BA**
  Bibl: ▶NY art yrbk.
Jenny, Arnold (British artist, 1831-
1881)   **WC WI**
Jenny, Jean-Marc (Swiss architect,
Vaud)   **AV**
  Bibl: ▶Schweiz. Ingen. u. Archit.,
  1988-1989
Jennys → see Jennys, William
Jennys, J. William → see Jennys,
William
Jennys, Richard → see Jennings,
Richard
Jennys, William   **BA PR WI**
  (American artist, op.1790-1805)   WI
  (American artist,
  op.c.1795-1797/8)   WC
  (American painter, act. 1802)   PR
  (American painter, act.ca.1795-
  1807)   BA
  Bibl: ▶Ebert, Amer. folk ptrs.,
  p.66; ▶Fielding's Amer. ptrs.;
  ▶Groce, Artists Amer.; ▶Young,
  Amer. artists
  J. William Jennys   PR
  Jennys   PR
Jennys, J. William   **PR**
Jennys, William (or J. William)   **WC**
Jennys, William (or J. William) → see
Jennys, William
Jenö, Szervatiusz (Romanian
sculptor, b.1903)   **BA**
  Bibl: ARTS XXI/2 p.14
Jensen, Albert (Danish architect,
Rødovre, 1918-1988)   **AV**
  Bibl: ▶Danske Arkitekters
  Landsforbund, 1984-85

Jensen, Albert (Danish architect,
1847-1913)   **BA**
  Bibl: ▶Thieme-Becker; Wielbach
Jensen, Alfred   **BA WC WI**
  (American artist, 1903-)   WC
  (American artist, 1903-1981)   WI
  (American painter, 1903-1981)   BA
  Bibl: NY Times, Apr. 1981; ▶WW
  Amer. Art
Jensen, Axel P. (Scandinavian artist,
20th cent.)   **WC**
Jensen, Bill (American painter,
b.1945)   **BA**
  Bibl: Art in Amer. LXVIII/9 (Nov
  1980) 109-113; Santa Barbara
  (CA, USA), UCSB Art Mus.,
  Contemp. drawings (1981)
Jensen, Carl (Danish artist, 1851-
1933)   **WC**
Jensen, Christian Albrecht   **BA WC**
  (Danish artist, 1792-1870)   WC
  (Danish painter, 1792-1870)   BA
  Bibl: ▶Bénézit; ▶Thieme-Becker;
  ▶Weilbach, Kunst.leks.
Jensen, Georg (Danish silversmith,
1866-1935)   **BA**
  Bibl: ▶Penguin dec. arts
Jensen, George (American artist,
b.1878)   **WI**
Jensen, Gerritt (Dutch
cabinetmaker, designer in GBR,
act.1680-1714)   **BA**
  Bibl: ▶Salverte, Ébénistes 18e s.;
  ▶Thieme-Becker
Jensen, Holger   **AV BA**
  (Danish architect, b.1918)   BA
  (Danish architect, Copenhagen,
  1918-)   AV
  Bibl: ▶Danske Arkitekters
  Landsforbund, 1984-85; Viborg
  (DNK), Skovgaard Museet,
  ARCHITECT HOLGER JENSEN, 1978
Jensen, Holger J. (Danish artist,
1900-1967)   **WC**
Jensen, Jacob (Norwegian ivory
carver, goldsmith in DNK, 1614-ca.
1695)   **BA**
  Bibl: ▶Thieme-Becker
Jensen, Jan Olav (Norwegian
architect, 1959-)   **AV**
  Bibl: Byggekunst, 1988, v.70,
  no.5, p.336
Jensen, Jens   **BA**
  (American landscape architect,
  1860?-1951)   BA
  (Danish architect)   AV
  Bibl: ▶Avery obit. idx.; ▶Danske
  Arkitekters Landsforbund,
  1984-85
Jensen, Jens-Erik   **AV**
Jensen, Jens-Erik → see Jensen, Jens
Jensen, Jeppe Juel (Danish artist,
1930-)   **WC**
Jensen, Johan Laurents → see Jensen,
Johan Laurentz

Jensen, Johan Laurentz　**BA PR**
　(Danish artist, 1800-1856)　WC
　(Danish painter, 1800-1856)　BA PR
　Bibl: ▶Bénézit; ▶RILA/BHA;
　▶Thieme-Becker; ▶Weilbach,
　Kunst.leks.
Jensen, Johan Laurents　**PR WC**
　Johan Laurentz Jensen　PR
Jensen, Marvin *(American
　craftsman, b.1945)*　BA
　Bibl: Raleigh (NC, USA), NC Mus.
　Art, Living with Baughman (1985)
Jensen, Max *(German artist, op.c.
　1885)*　WC
Jensen, Monique Kyhl *(Danish
　architect, Copenhagen)*　AV
　Bibl: Architektur + Wettbewerbe,
　1988 Mar., no.133, p.44
　Kyhl Jensen, Monique　AV
Jensen, Niels *(Danish painter,
　b.1907)*　BA
　Bibl: Damgaard Rasmussen
Jensen, Pamela *(American interior
　designer, Calif)*　AV
　Bibl: Restaurant and hotel design,
　1988 Mar., v.10, no.3, p.62
Jensen, Paule *(French interior
　designer)*　AV
　Bibl: Maison Française, 1985 Feb.,
　no.384, p.126
Jensen, Poul *(Danish architect)*　AV
　Bibl: Arkitekten, 1984 Dec.4,
　v.86, no.22, p.474
Jensen, Rolf A. *(Australian architect,
　Avalon Bay)*　AV
　Bibl: ▶RIBA members, 1984
Jensen, Søren Georg *(Danish artist,
　1917-1982)*　BA
　Bibl: ▶Nørregård-Nielsen, Dansk
　kunst, v.2; Petersen, NORTH-
　INFORMATION 141-142 (1986)
　1-70
Jensen, Theodor *(British artist, op.
　1853-1864)*　WI
Jensen, Thomas Martin *(American
　artist, 1831-1916)*　**WC WI**
Jensen-Klint, Peder Vilhelm　**AV BA**
　(Danish architect, 1853-1930)　AV
　*(Danish architect, painter, 1853-
　1930)*　BA
　Bibl: ▶Busse, Maler u. Bildhauer
　19. Jahr.; ▶Macmillan encyc.
　archts.; ▶Portoghesi, Diz. arch. e
　urbanistica; ▶Thieme-Becker;
　▶Weilbach, Kunst.leks.
　Klint, Pedar Vilhelm Jensen　AV
　Klint, Peter Vilhelm Jensen　AV
Jenshel, Len *(American
　photographer, b.1949)*　BA
　Bibl: ▶Intl. dir. exh. artists, 1982;
　London (GBR), ICA, New Amer.
　colour photog.
Jenson, Nikolaus *(French printer in
　ITA, ca.1420-1480)*　BA
　Bibl: ▶Brockhaus Enzyk.; ▶Natl.
　union cat., pre-1956

**Jentsch, Adolph Stephan
　Friedrich**　**BA GC**
　(German painter, b.1888)　GC
　*(German painter, lithographer,
　b.1888)*　BA
　Bibl: ▶Bénézit; ▶Thieme-Becker
Jentz, Thies *(German architect,
　b.1941)*　BA
　Bibl: Kunstwerk, XXXII/2-3 (Apr.-
　Jun. 1979) p.104
Jentzen, Friedrich *(German artist,
　1815-1901)*　WC
**Jentzsch, Jentsch or Jenzsch,
　Johann Gottfried** *(German artist,
　1759-1826)*　WC
Jentzsch, Johannes Gabriel (Hans)
　(German artist, 1862-p.1903)　WC
Jentzsch, Rolf *(German architect,
　Kassel, 1940-)*　AV
　Bibl: Deutsche Bauzeitung, 1985
　Nov., v.119, no.11, p.126
Jenzsch, Gustav *(German artist, op.
　1804)*　WC
Jepperson, Samuel Hans *(American
　artist, 1855-1931)*　WI
Jeppesen, Peter Juel *(Danish
　architect, Farum, 1947-)*　AV
　Bibl: ▶Danske Arkitekters
　Landsforbund, 1984-85
Jequier, Jules *(Swiss artist, 1834-
　1898)*　WC
Jer. Bos → see Bosch, Hieronymus
　(Hieronymus van Aken)
Jer. Mutiano → see Muziano, Girolamo
Jerace, Francesco *(Italian sculptor,
　1854-1937)*　GC
　Bibl: TCI Lombardia
Jeraj, Zmago *(Yugoslav painter,
　sculptor, printmaker, b.1937)*　BA
　Bibl: Ljubljana (YUG), Mala
　Galerija, ZMAGO JERAJ 1975
Jerde, Jon *(American architect)*　AV
　Bibl: ▶AIA Pro File, 1985
Jerdon, Thomas Claverhill *(British
　artist, op.1843-1847)*　WI
Jereb, James *(American house
　painter, head of Aesthetic Painting
　Co., Chicago, Ill)*　AV
　Bibl: Victorian homes, 1988
　Spring, v.7, no.2, p.76
Jeremiah Barrett → see Barrett,
　Jeremiah
Jeremiah Davison → see Davison,
　Jeremiah
Jeremiah Van Winghen → see Winghe,
　Jeremias van
Jeremias Majer → see Majer, Jeremias
Jerichau family *(Danish artists, 19th-
　20th cs.)*　BA
　Bibl: ▶Nørregård-Nielsen, Dansk
　kunst; ▶Weilbach, Kunst.leks.

Jerichau, Emil Jens Adolf Baumann
　(Danish painter, 1890-1916)　BA
　Bibl: ▶Bénézit; ▶Nørregård-Nielsen,
　Dansk kunst, Jerichau, Emil Jens
　Adolf Baumann, 1890-1916,
　maler; ▶Thieme-Becker;
　▶Weilbach, Kunst.leks.
Jerichau, Harald Adolf Nikolas
　(Danish artist, 1851-1878)　WC
Jerichau, Jens Adolf　**BA**
　(Danish sculptor, 1816-1883)　BA
　(Scandinavian artist, 1816-1883)　WC
　Bibl: ▶Thieme-Becker; ▶Weilbach,
　Kunst.leks.
Jerichau, Jens Adolph　**WC**
Jerichau, Jens Adolph → see Jerichau,
　Jens Adolf
*Jerichau-Baumann, Anna Maria
　Elisabeth → see* Jerichau-Baumann,
　Elisabeth Maria Anna
**Jerichau-Baumann, Elisabeth Maria
　Anna**　**BA**
　(Danish artist, 1819-1881)　WC
　(Danish painter, 1819-1881)　BA
　Bibl: ▶Nørregård-Nielsen, Dansk
　kunst, v.1; ▶Thieme-Becker;
　▶Weilbach, Kunst.leks.
**Jerichau-Baumann, Anna Maria
　Elisabeth**　**WC**
Jerman, Hugh *(British musician,
　painter, 1836-1895)*　BA
　Bibl: MONTGOMERYSHIRE
　COLLECTIONS, LXXII (1984) 45-52
Jermyn, H.　**WI**
　(British artist, op.1810)　WC
　(British artist, op.1810-)　WI
Jermyn, Miss H.　**WC**
Jermyn, Miss H. → see Jermyn, H.
Jernberg, August *(Swedish artist,
　1826-1896)*　WC
Jernberg, Olof August Andreas
　(Swedish artist, 1855-)　WC
Jerndorff, August Andreas　**BA WC**
　(Danish artist, 1846-1906)　WC
　(Danish painter, 1846-1906)　BA
　Bibl: ▶Nørregård-Nielsen, Dansk
　kunst; ▶Thieme-Becker; ▶Vollmer,
　Künst.-Lex. 20. Jhr.
Jernejec, Mladen *(Yugoslav painter,
　b.1950)*　BA
　Bibl: ▶Babington Smith, Contemp.
　artists
Jerningham, William *(British, act.
　1790s)*　BA
　Bibl: Antologia di B-A I/2 (June
　1977) 203-205; DANLOUX ET
　SON JOURNAL; ▶Dict. natl. biog.
Jeroaiacon, Germano *(Greek artist,
　16th cent.)*　WC
Jerome A. Hughes → see Hughes,
　Jerome A.
Jerome B. Thompson → see
　Thompson, Jerome B.
Jerome Colomes → see Colomes,
　Jerome

Jerome Martin Langlois (the younger) → see Langlois, Jérôme Martin, the younger

Jerome Myers → see Myers, Jerome

Jerome S. Blum → see Blum, Jerome S.

Jerome, Aimbrosini (French artist, op.1840-1871) WC

Jérôme, Jean Paul (Canadian painter, b.1928) BA
  Bibl: ▶Artists Canada; ▶MacDonald, Can. artists; Montreal (Que, CAN), Mus. d'art contemp., Dix ans (1979); ▶Vollmer, Künst.-Lex. 20. Jhr.

Jerome, P. WC WI
  (American artist, op.1942-1952) WI
  (American artist, op.c.1947) WC

Jeronimo Jacinto Espinosa → see Espinosa, Jerónimo Jacinto

Jeronimo Rodriguez de Espinosa → see Espinosa, Jeronimo Rodriguez de

Jeronimus Bosch → see Bosch, Hieronymus (Hieronymus van Aken)

Jeronymo [Unidentified] (Unknown painter) PR
  Bibl: (June 18, 1811, lot 12, Jones)

Jeronymus van Diest → see Diest, Jeronymus van

Jerosme Mutian → see Muziano, Girolamo

Jerrigh or Jerigh, E. (Flemish artist, op.1601) WC

Jerry Farnsworth → see Farnsworth, Jerry

Jersey Clere, Frederick de → see Clere, Frederick de Jersey

Jervais → see Jervas, Charles

Jervaise → see Jervas, Charles

Jervas → see Jervas, Charles

Jervas, Charles BA GC PR WI
  (British artist, c.1675-1739) WC
  (British artist, circa 1675-1739) WI
  (British painter, ca.1675-1739) PR
  (British, ca.1675-1739) GC
  (Irish painter, printmaker, ca. 1675-1739) BA
  Bibl: Burlingtn CXX/898 (Jan 1978) p.6; ▶Dict. natl. biog.; Getty Photo Study Coll. (Ptgs.); ▶RILA/BHA; ▶Strickland, Irish artists; ▶Thieme-Becker; Whinney, Engl. art 1625-1714; ▶Witt checklist; ▶Yale Brit. artists list
  Charles Jervas PR
  Gervais, Charles GC
  Jarvis PR
  Jarvis, Charles GC
  Jervais PR
  Jervaise PR
  Jervas PR

Jervas, Gervais, Gervase or Jarvis, Charles WC
  Jerves PR

Jervas, Gervais, Gervase or Jarvis, Charles → see Jervas, Charles

Jerves → see Jervas, Charles

Jervis McEntee → see McEntee, Jervis

Jervis, Elizabeth (English, ca.1700-after 1779) BA
  Bibl: Cokayne, Complete peerage; ▶Dict. natl. biog.; Hayden, P., COSTUME/XXII (1988), 32-38

Jervis, John (British artist, op.1765-) WI
  Bibl: ▶Strickland, Irish artists

Jervis, Kimberley (British architect, Sherborne, England) AV
  Bibl: Architects' journal, 1988 Apr.27, v.187, no.17, p.15

Jervis, William Percival (British ceramist, author in USA, 1850-after 1908) BA
  Bibl: Amer Art Pott. 1875-1930; Chadds Ford, Brandywine, POOR SORT OF HEAVEN...(1983)

Jervois, William Francis Drummond, Sir (Australian colonel and military engineer, late 19th cent) AV
  Bibl: Fort, 1987, v.15, p.105

Jes Jessen → see Jessen, Jes

Jes Wilhelm Schlaikjer → see Schlaikjer, Jes Wilhelm

Jeschin, Jaroslav (Czech artist, 19th cent.) WC

Jesias van de Velde → see Velde, Esaias I van de

Jespers, Floris BA WC
  (Belgian artist, 1889-1966) WC
  (Belgian painter, printmaker, 1889-1965) BA
  Bibl: ▶Bénézit; ▶Vollmer, Künst.-Lex. 20. Jhr.

Jespers, Oscar (Belgian artist, 1887-1970) WC

Jess (Jess Collins) BA
  (American artist, 20th cent.) WC
  (American artist, op.20th c.) WI
  (American painter, collagist, sculptor, b.1923) BA
  Bibl: ▶Intl. dir. exh. artists, 1983; ▶MoMA libr. cat.; ▶WW Amer. Art, 1982

Collins, Jess WC WI

Jessel, Jeremy WC WI
  (British artist, 1939-) WC
  (British artist, b.1939) WI

Jessel, Robert WC WI
  (British artist, 1899-) WC
  (British artist, b.1899) WI

Jessen, Carl Ludwig BA
  (German painter, 1833-1917) BA
  (Scandinavian artist, 1833-1917) WC
  Bibl: ▶Bénézit; ▶Thieme-Becker

Jessen, Karl Ludwig WC

Jessen, Jes (Danish painter, 1743-1807) PR
  Bibl: ▶Thieme-Becker
  Jes Jessen PR

Jessen, Karl Ludwig → see Jessen, Carl Ludwig

Jessie Arms Botke → see Botke, Jesse Arms

Jessie Henderson Drew-Bear → see Drew-Bear, Jessie Henderson

Jesson [Unidentified] (Unknown painter) PR
  Bibl: (May 20, 1809, lot 3[a], Christie's)

Jessop, Anne Phyllis, Miss → see Beechey, Anne Phyllis

Jessop, William (British artist, op. 1802-1836) WI

Jessor, Herman (American architect, New York City) AV
  Bibl: Sites, 1989, no.21-22, p.38

Jessup, Philippa (British artist, op. 20th c.) WI

Jessup, Robert (American artist, b.1952) WI

Jessup, Sam P. (American artist, op. 19th c.) WI

Jessurun de Mesquita, Samuel BA WC
  (Dutch artist, 1868-1944) WC
  (Dutch printmaker, 1868-1944) BA
  Bibl: ▶Scheen, Ned. beeldende kunst.; ▶Witt checklist

Jesus, Pablo de (Mexican artist, op. 1796) WC

Jetelová, Magdalena (Czech sculptor, b.1946) BA
  Bibl: Guide exh. artists: N. Amer. ptrs.; London (GBR), Riverside Studios MAGDALENA JETELOVÁ... 4 Sept-6 Oct 1985

Jettel → see Jettel, Eugen

Jettel, Eugen PR
  (Austrian painter, 1845-1901) PR
  (German artist, 1845-1901) WC
  Bibl: ▶Thieme-Becker
  Eugen Jettel PR
  Jettel PR

Jettel, Eugene PR WC
  Jettle, Eugene PR

Jettel, Eugene → see Jettel, Eugen

Jettle, Eugene → see Jettel, Eugen

Jettmar, Rudolf (German artist, 1869-) WC

Jeuffrain, Paul (French, d. 1916, active Naples, Italy and Algeria ca. 1852) JG

Jeurat, Etienne → see Jeaurat, Etienne

Jewell, D.B. WC WI
  (American artist, 19th cent.) WC
  (American artist, op.19th c.) WI

Jewell, Dick (British photographer, printmaker, b.1951) BA
  Bibl: Arts Council GBR, Lives (1979)

Jewell, Milton Walker (Canadian painter, b.1938) BA
  Bibl: ▶Intl. dir. arts

Jewell, Richard Roach (Australian architect, 1810-1891) AV
  Bibl: ▶Tanner, Archts. Australia

Jewels, Mary (British artist, op. 1940-1965) **WI**

Jewett → see Jewett, William

Jewett, William **GC PR VO WC WI**
(American artist, 1789-1874) **WI**
(American artist, 1795-1873) **WC**
(American painter, 1789-1874) **GC**
(American painter, 1790-1874) **PR**
(American painter, ca. 1790-1874) **VO**
Bibl: ▶Bénézit; ▶Fielding's Amer. ptrs., 1983; ▶Groce, Artists Amer.; ▶Libr. of Congr. Name Auth. File, NAFR9127438; ▶Witt checklist

Jewett **PR**
Jewett, William T. **PR**
William Jewett **PR**

Jewett, William S. (Smith) **VO**
(American artist, 1812-1873) **WI**
(American painter, 1812-1873) **VO**
Bibl: ▶Groce, Artists Amer.; ▶Libr. of Congr. Name Auth. File, NAFR929393

Jewett, William Smith **WI**

Jewett, William Smith → see Jewett, William S. (Smith)

Jewett, William T. → see Jewett, William

Jewitt, Thomas Orlando Sheldon → see Jewitt, Thomas Orlando Shelton

Jewitt, Thomas Orlando Shelton **WI**
(British artist, 1799-1869) **WC WI**

Jewitt, Thomas Orlando Sheldon **WC**

Jewreinoff, Dmitrij Iwanowitsch → see Evreinov, Dmitrij Ivanovič

Jezbara, August (Austrian goldsmith, act.1778, d.1802) **BA**
Bibl: Simoniti, Zbornik za umetnostno zgodovino XVII (1981) 75-87; ▶Thieme-Becker

Ježek, Stanislav (Czech painter, printmaker, b.1906) **BA**
Bibl: ▶Vollmer, Künst.-Lex. 20. Jhr.

Jiardano → see Giordano, Luca

Jichák, Eisik (Hungarian painter, act. 1792) **BA**
Bibl: Schoner, MUVESZETTORTENETI ERTESITO XXXIII/4 (1984) 271

Jicinsy, Karel (Czech, 20th century, active 1920s) **JG**

Jill, Rome (British artist, op.19th-20th c.) **WI**

Jillis Handekoeter → see Hondecoeter, Gillis Claesz. d'

Jillis Handekooter → see Hondecoeter, Gillis Claesz. d'

Jillis Hondekoter → see Hondecoeter, Gillis Claesz. d'

Jiménez Aranda, José **BA**
(Spanish artist, 1837-1903) **WC**
(Spanish painter, 1837-1903) **BA PR**
Bibl: Arch. esp. de arte, XLVII/186 (Apr-Jun 1974) 171-172; ▶Encic. univ. ilus.; ▶Thieme-Becker

Aranda **PR**
Aranda, José Jimenes **PR**
Aranda, Jose Jimenez **PR**
Aranda, Jose Jimines **WC**
Jimenez y Aranda, Jose **WC**
Jose Jimenes Aranda **PR**

Jiménez Donoso, José → see Donoso, José Jiménez

Jiménez y Aranda, Jose → see Jiménez Aranda, José

Jimenez y Aranda, Luis → see Aranda, Luis Jimines

Jiménez y Garcia, Miguel → see Ximénez, Miguel

Jimenez y Martin, Juan (Spanish artist, 1858-) **WC**

Jiménez, Carlos (American architect, Houston, Tex.; born in Costa Rica) **AV**
Bibl: House beautiful, 1987 Nov., v.129, no.11, p.104

Jiménez, Juan → see Ximénez, Juan

Jimenez, Luis (Spanish artist, 20th cent.) **WC**

Jimenez, Luis Alfonso (American sculptor, b.1940) **BA**
Bibl: ▶Parry, Contemp. art; ▶WW Amer. Art

Jiménez, Miguel → see Ximénez, Miguel

Jimenez, Prieto, Manuel (Spanish artist, 19th cent.) **WC**

Jimeno y Planes, Rafael **BA**
(Spanish artist, 1759-1802) **WC**
(Spanish painter, printmaker, 1759-ca.1802) **BA**
Bibl: ▶Encic. univ. ilus.; ▶Kubler, Art & arch. ESP & PRT; ▶Ossorio y Bernard, Artistas españoles 19s.; ▶Thieme-Becker

Ximeno, Raphael y Planes **WC**

Jimeno, Matías (Spanish painter, act.1654-1656) **BA**
Bibl: ▶Encic. univ. ilus.; ▶Thieme-Becker

Jingua → see Cinque, Joseph

Jiordano → see Giordano, Luca

Jiquidi, Aurel **BA WC**
(Romanian artist, 1896-1969) **BA**
(Rumanian artist, 1896-) **WC**
Bibl: Driscu, M., ARTE, I (1982), 25-27

Jira, Josef (Czech painter, b.1929) **BA**
Bibl: ▶Bénézit

Jíra, Lubos (Czech designer(?), Prague) **AV**
Bibl: Bauwelt, 1987 Apr.24, v.78, no.16, p.584

Jiránek, Miloš **BA WC**
(Czech artist, 1874-1911) **WC**
(Czech painter, printmaker, critic, 1875-1911) **BA**
Bibl: ▶Encyk. českého výtv. umění; ▶Fogg Mus. Libr. cat.; Ljubljana (YUG), Narodna Galerija, Česko slikarstvo 19. in začetka 20. stoletja (1975); ▶Met. Mus. Art libr. cat.; ▶Thieme-Becker; ▶Vollmer, Künst.-Lex. 20. Jhr.

Jirásek, Michal (Czech architectural student, 1988) **AV**
Bibl: Architektura ČSR, 1988, v.47, no.3, p.6

Jirásková, Marta (Czech sculptor, 1898-1981) **BA**
Bibl: Volavková, MARTA JIRÁSKOVÁ (1981); Výtvarná Kultura, VI/6 (1982) 25 (suppl)

Jirby, Inger (American artist, op. 1987-) **WI**

Jiricna, Eva **AV BA**
(Czech architect, designer in GBR, b.1939) **BA**
(Czech-born British architect, London, 1939-) **AV**
Bibl: ▶Avery period. idx., suppl. 6,7; Avery Ref. File (RLIN); Davies, Arch. review, CLXXVI/1049 (Jul. 1984) p.76; London phone bk.; ▶RIBA members, 1987

Jirou, Hugues **AV**

Jiroudek, František (Czech painter, b.1914) **BA**
Bibl: ▶Encyk. českého výtv. umění; ▶Vollmer, Künst.-Lex. 20. Jhr.

Jlanis Valters → see Valters, Jānis

Jń Stefánsson **BA**
(Icelandic painter, 1881-1962) **BA**
(Scandinavian artist, 1881-) **WC**
Bibl: Reykjavik (ISL), Natl. Gall., Fjórirfrumberjar (1985); ▶Vollmer, Künst.-Lex. 20. Jhr.; ▶Weilbach, Kunst.leks.

Stefansson, Jon **WC**

Jn. Bellini → see Bellini, Giovanni

Jn. Darbin → see Darbin, Jn. [Unidentified]

Jn. Miel → see Miel, Jan

Jnnocentio d'Agostino → see Agostino, Innocenzo d'

Jno. Asselyn → see Asselyn, Jan

Jno. de Bellino → see Bellini, Giovanni

Jno. R. Smith → see Smith, John Raphael

Jo, Leo → see Jo, Léo (Léontine Joris)

Jo, Léo (Léontine Joris) **BA**
(Belgian painter, caricaturist, 1870-1962) **BA**
(French artist, 19th cent.) **WC**
Bibl: San Francisco (CA, USA), Palace of FA, La Belle Époque (1980)

Jo, Leo **WC**

Joachim Antonisz. Wtewael → see Wtewael, Joachim Antonisz.

Joachim Beuckelaer →*see* Beuckelaer, Joachim

Joachim Beukelaer →*see* Beuckelaer, Joachim

Joachim Camphuysen →*see* Camphuysen, Joachim

Joachim de Patinir →*see* Patinir, Joachim

Joachim Ferdinand Richardt →*see* Richardt, Joachim Ferdinand

Joachim Franz Beich →*see* Beich, Joachim Franz

Joachim Patinir →*see* Patinir, Joachim

Joachim von Sandrart (I) →*see* Sandrart, Joachim I von

Joachim von Sandrart (II) →*see* Sandrart, Joachim von (II)

Joachim Wten Wael →*see* Wtewael, Joachim Antonisz.

Joachim Wten Wael 1600. →*see* Wtewael, Joachim Antonisz.

Joachims, Joachim, Joachimus, Joachmus or Jochmuss, Jeronimus or Hieronymus *(Dutch artist, c.1619(?)-1660)* **WC**

Joaillier *((Also Sebah & Joaillier) Turkey, active Constantinople 1860s-1870s)* **JG**

Joan Miro →*see* Miró, Joán

Joan van Noort →*see* Noort, Joan van

Joanes, Joan de →*see* Juanes, Juan de (Vicente Juan Macip)

Joanes, Vincente →*see* Macip, Vicente II

Joannes →*see* Juanes, Juan de (Vicente Juan Macip)

Joannes Buns →*see* Buns, Joannes

Joannes Philippus Spalthoven →*see* Spalthoven, Joannes Philippus

Joannes Pieters →*see* Pieters, Joannes [Unidentified]

Joannes van Dale →*see* Dale, Joannes van

Joannes, Fra (Frater Johannes) *(Italian artist, 15th cent.)* **WC**

Joannis de lo Prete *(Italian artist, op.1642)* **WC**

Joannon-Navier, Etienne Albert Eugene *(French artist, 1857-)* **WC**

Joanowich, Paul →*see* Joanowitch, Paul

Joanowitch →*see* Joanowitch, Paul

Joanowitch, Joannovics or Joannovits, Paul or Pal →*see* Joanowitch, Paul

Joanowitch, Paul **PR**
  (Austrian painter, 1859-aft. 1910) **PR**
  (Yugoslav artist, 1859-) **WC**
    Bibl: ▶Thieme-Becker
  Ivanovitch, Paul **PR**
  Joanowich, Paul **PR**
  Joanowitch **PR**

Joanowitch, Joannovics or Joannovits, Paul or Pal **WC**
  Paul Joanowitch **PR**

Joaquin Sorolla y Bastida →*see* Sorolla y Bastida, Joaquín

Joaquin Torres-Garcia →*see* Torres-García, Joaquín

Joaquin X. Inza →*see* Inza, Joaquin X.

Joass, John James *(British architect, 1868-1952)* **BA**
    Bibl: ▶Avery obit. idx.; ▶Thieme-Becker

Job Adriaensz. Berckheyde →*see* Berckheyde, Job Adriaensz.

Job Bercheyde →*see* Berckheyde, Job Adriaensz.

Job Berkheide →*see* Berckheyde, Job Adriaensz.

Job Berkhijden →*see* Berckheyde, Job Adriaensz.

Job, Charles *(British photographer, ca.1853-1930)* **BA**
    Bibl: Arts Council GBR, Pictorial photog. GBR (1978)

Jobard, Hippolyte Henri (Henri Job) *(French artist, 1857-1885)* **WC**

Jobart, Jean-François *(French silversmith, ca.1681-1757, master 1711)* **GC**
    Bibl: ▶Mabille, Orfèv. fran.

Jobbe-Duval, Felix Armand Marie *(French artist, 1821-1889)* **WC**

Jobbe-Duval, Gaston *(French painter, 20th century)* **GC**
    Bibl: ▶Bénézit

Jobbins, William H. *(British artist, op.circa 1872-)* **WI**

Jobert →*see* Jobert, Paul

Jobert, Paul **GC PR**
  (French painter, 1863-aft.1924) **PR**
  (French painter, b.1863) **GC**
    Bibl: ▶Bénézit; ▶Thieme-Becker
  Jobert **PR**
  Paul Jobert **PR**

Jobin, Bernard *(Swiss architect)* **AV**
    Bibl: Archithese, 1985 May, v.15, no.3, p.112

Jobin, Bernhard *(German artist, op. 1560-m.1597)* **WC**

Jobin, Louis *(Canadian sculptor, 1844-1928)* **BA**
    Bibl: ▶ARTbibl. mod., 19/1; ▶Artists Canada; Canad. encyc.; ▶Natl. Gall. Canada libr. cat.; ▶Vollmer, Künst.-Lex. 20. Jhr.

Jobling, J. *(British artist, 19th cent.)* **WC**

Jobling, Louise →*see* Jopling, Louise

Jobling, Robert *(British artist, 1841-1923)* **WC WI**

Jobmann, Oscar *(Architect)* **AV**
    Bibl: Progressive architecture, 1980 Apr., v.61, no.4, p.136

Jobnob. Eyck →*see* Eyck, Jan van

Jobse, J. W. *(Architect, Vlissingen)* **AV**
    Bibl: Detail, 1980 Nov.-Dec., no.1, p.864

Jobson, Frederick James *(British artist, 1812-1881)* **WC WI**

Jobst, Christoph *(German artist, 1557-1630)* **WC**

Jocelyn or Joscelyn, Nathaniel →*see* Jocelyn, Nathaniel

Jocelyn, Nathaniel **BA WI**
  (American artist, 1796-1881) **WC WI**
  (American painter, printmaker, 1796-1881) **BA**
  (Engraver, 1796-1881) **WI**
    Bibl: ▶Dict. Amer. biog.; ▶Groce, Artists Amer.; ▶WWW Amer., 1607

Jocelyn or Joscelyn, Nathaniel **WC**
  Joscelyn, Nathaniel **WI**

Jocelyn, Simeon S. →*see* Jocelyn, Simeon Smith

Jocelyn, Simeon Smith **BA**
  (American printmaker, 1799-1879) **BA**
  (Engraver, op.1830-) **WI**
    Bibl: ▶Groce, Artists Amer.; ▶WWW Amer.

Jocelyn, Simeon S. **WI**

Jochem Jaaster →*see* Jaaster, Jochem

Jochems, Herbert **GC WC**
  (Dutch artist, 1912-) **WC**
  (Dutch painter, 1912-d. aft. 1963) **GC**
    Bibl: ▶Scheen, Ned. beeldende kunst.

Jochims, Raimer *(German painter, b.1935)* **BA**
    Bibl: ▶Art Index, 1973; Lyon (FRA), Mus. des B.-A., Artistes francofortois contemp. (1975); ▶Wer ist wer; ▶Who's Who [GBR]; ▶WW Arts DEU

Jochum Beuckelaer →*see* Beuckelaer, Joachim

Jockel, Miss *(American artist, op. 1900-1928)* **WI**

Jocobellus de Masignis →*see* Masegne, Jacobello dalle

Jocys, Carlos *(Brazilian architect)* **AV**
    Bibl: Projeto, 1987 Dec.-1988 Jan., no.106, p.104

Joddrell, Vertue Hase *(British, 1756-1806)* **BA**
    Bibl: Bull. of the Detroit Inst. of Arts LVII/1 (1979) 49-45

Jode →*see* Jode, Hans de

Jode, Abraham de *(Dutch painter, 17th century)* **GC**
    Bibl: Getty Photo Study Coll. (Douwes coll.)

Jode, C. de →*see* Jode, Cornelis de

Jode, Cornelis de *(Flanders painter,*
1568-1600)   **GC**
    Bibl: Getty Photo Study Coll.
    (Ptgs.); ▶Thieme-Becker
    Jode, C. de   GC
Jode, Gerard de   **BA WC**
    (Dutch artist, 1509/17-1591)   WC
    (Flemish engraver, cartographer,
    publisher, 1509?-1591)   BA
    Bibl: ▶Bénézit; ▶Encyc. world art;
    ▶Hollstein, Dutch & Flemish;
    ▶Thieme-Becker
Jode, Hans de   **BA GC PR WC**
    (Dutch artist, op.1647-1662)   WC
    (Dutch painter, act. 1647-1662)   PR
    (Dutch painter, ca.1630-after
    1662)   BA
    (Dutch, act.1647-1662)   GC
    Bibl: Paragone XXVIII/33 (Sept
    1977) 24-33; ▶Thieme-Becker;
    ▶Witt checklist; ▶Wurzbach, NLD
    Künst.-Lex.
    de Jode   PR
    Hans de Jode   PR
    Jode   PR
Jöde, Jan *(Polish goldsmith, 1678-*
1743)   **BA**
    Bibl: Biuletyn historii sztuki
    XXXVIII (3) 1976, p.239;
    ▶Thieme-Becker
Jode, Pieter I de   **GC**
    (Flemish artist, 1570-1634)   WC
    (Flemish, 1570-1634)   GC
    Bibl: ▶Thieme-Becker; ▶Witt
    checklist
Jode, Pieter, I de   **WC**
Jode, Pieter II de   **GC**
    (Flemish artist, 1606-c.1674)   WC
    (Flemish, 1606-aft.1674)   GC
    Bibl: ▶Thieme-Becker; ▶Witt
    checklist
Jode, Pieter, II de   **WC**
Jode, Pieter, I de→see Jode, Pieter I
    de
Jode, Pieter, II de→see Jode, Pieter II
    de
Jodelet, Emmanuel *(French artist,*
1883-)   **WC**
Jodl, Ferdinand *(German artist,*
1805-1882)   **WC**
Jodlowski, Tadeusz *(Polish artist,*
20th cent.)   **WC**
Jodocus van Gent→see Joos van
    Gent (Joos van Wassenhove)
Jodocus van Winghe→see Winghe,
    Jodocus van
Jodrell, Peter *(Australian architect)* **AV**
    Bibl: The Architect, W.A., 1985,
    v.25, no.1, p.27
Jodry, Jean-François *(French*
architect)   **AV**
Joe Duncan Gleason→see Gleason,
    Joe Duncan

Joe, Mendelson *(Canadian painter,*
b.1944)   **BA**
    Bibl: Paris, Centre cultural
    canadien, MENDELSON JOE...,
    1981
Joedicke, Jürgen *(West German*
architect. Professor at Univ. of
Stuttgart, director of Institute for
Basic Research on Modern
Architecture, 1925-)   **AV**
    Bibl: Daidalos, no.12, p.119
Joel ben Simeon *(German scribe,*
illuminator in ITA, act.1449-1485)   **BA**
    Bibl: Edmunds, in JOURNAL OF
    JEWISH ART, 7 (1980) p.25;
    Gutmann in AB Sept (1976)
    p.442; Gutmann, Hebrew ms. ill.;
    Metzger in MITTEILUNGEN DES
    KUNSTHISTORISCHEN XX (1976)
    p.187 n.53
Joel, Grace *(New Zealand artist,*
1865-1924)   **WC**
Joel, J.B.   **WC WI**
    (British artist, 19th cent.)   WC
    (British artist, op.1890-1913)   WI
    Bibl: ▶Wood, Victorian ptrs.
Joelson, Suzanne *(American painter,*
20th c.)   **BA**
    Bibl: Falcon, S., in ARTS MAG
    LVIII/1 (Sept 1983) 6
Joensen-Mikines, S.→see Joensen-
    Mikines, Samuel
Joensen-Mikines, Samuel   **BA**
    (Danish painter, b.1906)   BA
    (Scandinavian artist, 20th cent.) WC
    Bibl: ▶Dict. Scand. biog.; ▶Libr. of
    Congr. Name Auth. File
Joensen-Mikines, S.   **WC**
Joerdaens→see Jordaens, Jacob
Joerdens, Felix A. *(German artist,*
-1883)   **WC**
Joest→see Joest, Jan
Joest Van Kalkar, Jan→see Joest, Jan
Joest, Jan   **BA GC PR**
    (early Netherlandish painter, ca.
    1450-1519)   BA
    (Netherlandish painter, ca.1450-
    1519)   PR
    (Netherlands artist, op.1474-m.
    1519)   WC
    (North Netherlandish painter,
    1460-1519)   GC
    Bibl: ▶Bénézit; ▶Encyc. world art;
    ▶Friedländer, Early Neth. ptg.,
    v.9a, pp.11-16; George Goldner;
    Getty Photo Study Coll. (Ptgs.);
    ▶Osten, Ptg. & sculp. DEU & NLD,
    pp.137-138; ▶RILA/BHA;
    ▶Thieme-Becker; ▶Wilenski, Flem.
    ptrs.; ▶Witt checklist; ▶Wurzbach,
    NLD Künst.-Lex.
    Jan Joest   GC PR
Jan Joest von Calcar or van
Haarlem (Juan de Holanda)   **WC**
    Joest   PR
    Joest Van Kalkar, Jan   PR
    Kalkar, Jan Joest von   GC

Joets, Jules Arthur *(French artist,*
1884-)   **WC**
Jofan, Boris Mihajlovič *(Russian*
architect, b.1891)   **BA**
    Bibl: ▶Encyc. world art; ▶Vollmer,
    Künst.-Lex. 20. Jhr.
Joganson, Boris Vladimirovič   **BA**
    (Russian artist, 1893-1973)   WC
    (Russian painter, 1893-1973)   BA
    Bibl: ▶Bowlt, Russian avant-garde,
    p.265; ▶Encyc. world art;
    ▶Vollmer, Künst.-Lex. 20. Jhr.
Johanson, Boris Vladimirovich
(Joganson)   **WC**
Joh, Sung-Yong *(Korean architect,*
Seoul)   **AV**
    Bibl: Kenchiku bunka, 1989 May,
    v.44, no.511, p.158
Joh. Voorhout→see Voorhout,
    Johannes
Johan Barthold Jongkind→see
    Jongkind, Johan Barthold
Johan Carl Loth→see Loth, Johann
    Carl (Carlotto)
Johan Contrafeier (perhaps Johan
Maler aus Flensburg, Johan dan
Maler or Johan or Johan
Jorgen) *(Norwegian artist, op.*
1640-1660)   **WC**
Johan Danckerts→see Danckerts,
    Johan
Johan de Heem→see Heem, Jan
    Davidsz. de
Johan Frederik Cornelis
    Scherrewitz→see Scherrewitz,
    Johan Frederik Cornelis
Johan Horions→see Horions, Johan
Johan Jakob Biedermann→see
    Biedermann, Johan Jakob
Johan Lagoor→see Lagoor, Johan
Johan Laurentz Jensen→see Jensen,
    Johan Laurentz
Johan le Ducq→see Ducq, Johan le
Johan Molenaer→see Molenaer, Jan
    Miense
Johan Richter→see Richter, Johan
Johan van Haensbergen→see
    Haensbergen, Johan van
Johan Willem Franck→see Franck,
    Johan Willem
Johan, Pere *(Spanish sculptor, act.*
1398-ca.1458)   **BA**
    Bibl: ▶Bénézit; Blue guide: Spain;
    ▶Ceán Bermúdez, Bellas artes ESP;
    Durancy Sampcre: ARS HISP:
    ESCULTURA GOTICA; Janke in
    SEMINANO DE ARTE ARAGONESE
    XXXIV 1981 111-20;
    ▶Thieme-Becker
Johana Mantuani→see Mantuani,
    Johana [Unidentified]
Johann (Jan) Dircksz. Nes→see Nes,
    Johan (Jan) Dircksz.
Johann Adalbert Angermayer→see
    Angermayer, Johann Adalbert

Johann Amandus Wink→see Wink,
Johann Amandus

Johann Anton Eismann→see Eismann,
Johann Anton

Johann Antonini of Třebíč *(Czech
stonemason, 17th c.)* **BA**
Bibl: Plichta, Umění XXVIII, 2
(1980) 151-167

Johann Bernard Klombeck→see
Klombeck, Johann Bernard

Johann Berthelsen→see Berthelsen,
Johann

Johann Boeckhorst→see Boeckhorst,
Jan

Johann Carl Loth→see Loth, Johann
Carl (Carlotto)

Johann Christian Brand→see Brand,
Johann Christian

Johann Christian Klengel→see
Klengel, Johann Christian

Johann Christian Thomas Wink→see
Wink, Christian

Johann Christian Vollerdt→see
Vollerdt, Johann Christian

Johann Christoph Dietzsch→see
Dietzsch, Johann Christoph

Johann Christoph Storer→see Storer,
Johann Christoph

Johann Conrad Gessner→see
Gessner, Johann Conrad

Johann Conrad Seekatz→see Seekatz,
Johann Conrad

Johann Cornelius Mertz→see Mertz,
Johann Cornelius

Johann Daniel Bager→see Bager,
Johann Daniel

Johann Daniel Preissler→see Preissler,
Johann Daniel

Johann Eleazar Schenau→see
Schenau, Johann Eleazar

Johann Elias Ridinger→see Ridinger,
Johann Elias

Johann Ernst Heinsius→see Heinsius,
Johann Ernst

Johann Evangelist Holzer→see
Holzer, Johann Evangelist

Johann Falch→see Falch, Johann

Johann Franz Nepomuk Lauterer→see
Lauterer, Johann Franz Nepomuk

Johann Friedrich Overbeck→see
Overbeck, Johann Friedrich

Johann Georg de Hamilton→see
Hamilton, Johann Georg de

Johann Georg Lederer→see Lederer,
Johann Georg

Johann Georg Meyer→see Meyer,
Johann Georg

Johann Georg Paul Mohr→see Mohr,
Johann Georg Paul

Johann Georg Pforr→see Pforr,
Johann Georg

Johann Georg Platzer→see Platzer,
Johann Georg

Johann Georg Stuhr→see Stuhr,
Johann Georg

Johann Georg Trautmann→see
Trautmann, Johann Georg

Johann Georg von Bemmel→see
Bemmel, Johann Georg von

Johann Georg Wagner→see Wagner,
Johann Georg

Johann Goerge Preissler→see
Preissler, Johann George

Johann Gottlieb Hackert→see
Hackert, Johann Gottlieb

Johann Graf→see Graf, Johann

Johann Gruembroech→see
Gruembroech, Johann

Johann Heinrich Keller (II)→see
Keller, Johann Heinrich (II)

Johann Heinrich Ramberg→see
Ramberg, Johann Heinrich

Johann Heinrich Roos→see Roos,
Johann Heinrich

Johann Heinrich Schönfeld→see
Schönfeld, Johann Heinrich

*Johann Heinrich Tischbein (the
elder)→see* Tischbein, Johann
Heinrich I

Johann Heiss→see Heiss, Johann

Johann Hendrik Mastenbroek→see
Mastenbroek, Johann Hendrik

Johann Horemans→see Horemans,
Jan Joseph I

Johann Hulsman→see Hulsman,
Johann

Johann Jakob Mettenleiter→see
Mettenleiter, Johann Jakob

Johann Jakob Schalch→see Schalch,
Johann Jakob

Johann Joseph Zoffany→see Zoffany,
Johann Joseph

Johann Justin Preissler→see Preissler,
Johann Justin

Johann Karl Baehr→see Baehr,
Johann Karl

Johann Kaspar Heilmann→see
Heilmann, Johann Kaspar

Johann Koerbecke→see Koerbecke,
Johann

Johann König→see König, Johann

Johann Kupezky→see Kupezky,
Johann

Johann Liss→see Liss, Johann (Pan)

*Johann Ludwig Ernst
Morgenstern→see* Morgenstern,
Johann Ludwig Ernst

Johann Mari Henri ten Kate→see
Kate, Johann Mari Henri ten

Johann Martin Stock→see Stock,
Johann Martin

Johann Melchior Roos→see Roos,
Johann Melchior

Johann Michael Rottmayr→see
Rottmayr, Johann Michael

Johann Nepomuk Ender→see Ender,
Johann Nepomuk

Johann Nepomuk Salvator *(Italian,
1852-ca.1910)* **BA**
Bibl: ▶Brockhaus Enzyk.;
Oberhammer, M., in FESTSCHRIFT
RICHARD MILESI, 194, 197;
Phaidon Austria 1985

Johann Nikolaus Grooth→see Grooth,
Johann Nikolaus

Johann Paul Schor→see Schor,
Johann Paul (Giovanni Paolo
Tedesco)

Johann Paul Waxschlunger→see
Waxschlunger, Johann Paul

Johann Peter Hasenclever→see
Hasenclever, Johann Peter

Johann Philip Lemke→see Lemke,
Johann Philip

Johann Philipp Eduard Gartner→see
Gärtner, Johann Philipp Eduard

Johann Sigmund Keller→see Keller,
Johann Sigmund

Johann Spilberg (the younger)→see
Spilberg, Johann II

Johann Spillenberger→see
Spillenberger, Johann

[Johann] Strigel→see Strigel, Hans

Johann Toussyn→see Toussyn,
Johann

Johann van Hugtenburgh→see
Huchtenburgh, Jan van

Johann von Aachen→see Aachen,
Hans von

Johann von Köln *(German, act.1501-
1522)* **GC**
Bibl: ▶Thieme-Becker
Hans von Köln **GC**

Johann von Schaffhausen *(Swiss
bell-founder, 14th c.)* **BA**
Bibl: Zeit. Schw. Arch. u. Kunst.,
XXXIII/2 (1976) pp.112-118

Johann von Troppau *(Bohemian
scribe, illuminator, act.1368)* **BA**
Bibl: ▶Thieme-Becker; Umění,
XXXIII/6 (1985) pp.508-519

Johann Wilhelm Baur→see Baur,
Johann Wilhelm

Johann Wilhelm Hoffnas→see
Hoffnas, Johann Wilhelm

Johann Wilhelm Preyer→see Preyer,
Johann Wilhelm

Johann Zoffany→see Zoffany, Johann
Joseph

Johann, Jakob Greg *(German artist,
1813-1865)* **WC**

Johann, Velvet Breughel→see
Brueghel, Jan, the elder

Johanna K. Woodwell Hailman→see
Hailman, Johanna K.Woodwell

Johanneau, E. *(French artist, 18th
cent.)* **WC**

Johannes *(Italian scribe, 14th
century)* **GC**
Bibl: Meer, Apocalypse, p.360

Johannes Stephan von Calcar→see
Calcar, Jan Stephan van

Johannes Aurifex de Venetiis → see
Frater Iohannes Aurifex de Venetiis
Johannes Beeldemaker → see
Beeldemaker, Johannes
Johannes Beens → see Beens,
Johannes [Unidentified]
Johannes Borman → see Borman,
Johannes
Johannes Bosboom → see Bosboom,
Johannes
Johannes Buns → see Buns, Joannes
Johannes Claesz. van der Aack → see
Aack, Johannes Claesz. van der
Johannes Colaert → see Colaert,
Johannes
Johannes Cornelis Haccou → see
Haccou, Johannes Cornelis
Johannes Cornelisz. Verspronck → see
Verspronck, Johannes Cornelisz.
Johannes Cristoffel Schultz → see
Schultz, Johannes Christoffel
Johannes de Haes → see Haes,
Johannes de
Johannes de Nuxigia *(Italian scribe,
14th century)*   **GC**
    Bibl: Paris, 10 siècles, p.78
*Johannes Duknowich de
Tragusia* → see Giovanni Dalmata
Johannes Episcopius → see Bisschop,
Jan de
*Johannes Franciscus
Hoppenbrouwers* → see
Hoppenbrouwers, Johannes
Franciscus
Johannes Glauber → see Glauber,
Johannes (Polidoro)
Johannes Goedart → see Goedaert,
Johannes
Johannes Grusch atelier *(French
illuminators, act. ca.1250-1275)*   **GC**
    Bibl: ▶Branner, Ms. ptg. Paris,
    p.222; Getty Photo Study Coll.
    (Medieval)
    Johannes Grusch shop   GC
    Johannes Grusch workshop   GC
Johannes Grusch shop → see Johannes
Grusch atelier
Johannes Grusch workshop → see
Johannes Grusch atelier
Johannes Hannot → see Hannot,
Johannes
Johannes Hendricus Jurres → see
Jurres, Johannes Hendricus
Johannes Hendrik Weissenbruch → see
Weissenbruch, Jan Hendrik
Johannes Hispanus   **BA GC WC**
    (Spanish artist, 15th cent.)   WC
    *(Spanish painter in ITA, 15th-
    16th c.)*   BA
    (Spanish, 15th century)   GC
    Bibl: ▶Ars Hispaniae, v.13;
    ▶Bolaffi; ▶Post, Spanish ptg.,
    v.11, pp.83-86; Tanzi, RICERCHE,
    17 (1982) 49; ▶Thieme-Becker;
    ▶Witt checklist

Johannes Hoek → see Hoecke, Jan van
den
Johannes Huibert Prins → see Prins,
Johannes Huibert
Johannes Janson → see Janson,
Johannes
Johannes Lingelbach → see Lingelbach,
Johannes
Johannes Magno de Veneciis → see
Frater Iohannes Magno de Veneciis
Johannes Molzahn → see Molzahn,
Johannes
Johannes Natus → see Natus,
Johannes
Johannes Nydenna de Confluentia
(Italian scribe, act.1472)   **GC**
    Bibl: Canova, Miniatura Veneta,
    p.55; Getty Photo Study Coll.
    (Medieval)
    Nydenna de Confluentia, Johannes GC
Johannes Petrus van Horstok → see
Horstok, Johannes Petrus van
Johannes Priwitzer → see Priwitzer,
Johannes
Johannes Rombouts → see Rombouts,
Johannes
Johannes Rosierse → see Rosierse,
Johannes
Johannes Schiefer → see Schiefer,
Johannes
Johannes Sculptor → see Johannes
Snickares
Johannes Snickares *(Swedish
altarpiece sculptor)*   **AV**
    Bibl: Antikvariskt arkiv, 1985,
    v.72, p.41
    Johannes Sculptor   AV
Johannes Spruyt → see Spruyt,
Johannes
Johannes Symoonisz. Torrentius → see
Torrentius, Jan Symoonisz.
Johannes Urselincx → see Urselincx,
Johannes
Johannes van der Bent → see Bent,
Johannes van der
Johannes van Somer → see Somer,
Johannes van
Johannes Vermeer → see Vermeer, Jan
(II)
Johannes von Bruneck → see Da
Brunico, Giovanni
Johannes von Gmünd → see Parler,
Johannes von
Johannes von Valkenburg *(German
scribe, miniaturist, monk, act.
1299)*   **BA**
    Bibl: ▶D'Ancona, Miniaturistes;
    ▶Thieme-Becker
Johannes Voorhout → see Voorhout,
Johannes
Johannes Vorsterman → see
Vorsterman, Johannes
Johannes Weiland → see Weiland,
Johannes

Johannes Withoos → see Withoos,
Johannes
Johannes, A. *(German artist, 15th
cent.)*   **WC**
Johannes, Godefridus *(Netherlands
artist, op.1585)*   **WC**
Johannes, Jeffrey G. *(American
painter, b.1951)*   **BA**
    Bibl: Milwaukee (WI, USA), Art
    Mus., Emerging imagists (1983)
Johannes, Rudolf *(West German
architect, Erlangen)*   **AV**
    Bibl: Baumeister, 1989 Aug., v.86,
    no.8, p.32
Johannessen, Arne *(Danish painter,
printmaker, b.1908)*   **BA**
    Bibl: ▶Vollmer, Künst.-Lex. 20.
    Jhr.; ▶Weilbach, Kunst.leks.
Johannessen, Ottar Helge
*(Norwegian painter, graphic artist,
b.1929)*   **BA**
    Bibl: NLK; Opstad, HRYMFAXE,
    XIX (JUN 1989), 19-26
Johannot → see Johannot, Alfred
Johannot, Alfred   **BA GC PR**
    (French painter, 1800-1837)   GC PR
    *(French painter, printmaker,
    1800-1837)*   BA
    (German artist, 1800-1837)   WC
    Bibl: ▶Bénézit; Getty Photo Study
    Coll.; ▶Thieme-Becker; ▶Witt
    checklist
    A. Johannot   PR
    Alfred Johannot   PR
    Johannot   PR
**Johannot, Alfred (Charles Henri
Alfred)**   **WC**
*Johannot, Alfred (Charles Henri
Alfred)* → see Johannot, Alfred
Johannot, Tony   **BA GC WC**
    *(French painter and printmaker,
    1803-1852)*   GC
    *(French printmaker, painter,
    1803-1852)*   BA
    (German artist, 1803-1852)   WC
    Bibl: ▶Bénézit; Getty Photo Study
    Coll.; ▶Thieme-Becker
Johannsen, H. *(German architect,
Osnabrück)*   **AV**
    Bibl: Deutsche Bauzeitschrift,
    1986 Aug., v.34, no.8, p.979
Johannsen, Lym *(German architect,
Hamburg)*   **AV**
    Bibl: Architektur + Wettbewerbe,
    1984 June, no.118, p.72
Johannsen, Theodor *(German artist,
1868-)*   **WC**
Johansen → see Johansen, John
Christen
Johansen, Carl *(American painter,
b.1946)*   **BA**
    Bibl: ▶Babington Smith, Contemp.
    artists
Johansen, Jean Myrtle MacLane
(American artist, 1878-1964)   **WI**
    MacLane, Jean Myrtle, Miss   WI

Johansen, John C. →see Johansen, John Christen

Johansen, John Christen GC PR WC
  (American painter,
    1876-ca.1964/66) PR
  (American painter, b.1876) GC
  (Danish artist, 1876-) WC
    Bibl: ▶Bénézit; ▶Fielding's Amer.
    ptrs.; ▶Thieme-Becker; ▶WWW
    Amer. art
  Johansen PR
  Johansen, John C. PR
  Johansen, John Christian PR
  John Christen Johansen PR
Johansen, John Christian →see
  Johansen, John Christen
Johansen, John MacLane →see
  Johansen, John McLane

Johansen, John McLane BA
  (American architect, b.1916) BA
  (American architect, painter,
    partner in firm of Johansen
    and Bhavani, 1916-) AV
    Bibl: ▶AIA Pro File; Brown, New
    Haven arch.; ▶Libr. of Congr.
    Name Auth. File

Johansen, John MacLane AV
Johansen, Otto Emil (Norwegian
  artist, 1886-1934) WC
Johansen, Viggo PR WC
  (Danish painter, 1851-1935) PR
    Bibl: ▶Witt checklist
  Viggo Johansen PR
Johanson, Boris Vladimirovich
  (Joganson) →see Joganson, Boris
  Vladimirovič

Johanson, Patricia AV BA WC WI
  (American artist, 1940-) WC
  (American artist, b.1940) WI
  (American sculptor, painter,
    b.1940) BA
  (Landscape architect) AV
    Bibl: Arts + architecture, 1985,
    new ser., v.3, no.4, p.59; ▶MoMA
    libr. cat.; ▶WW Amer. Art, 1976

Johanson, Perry B. (American
  architect, 1910?-1981) AV
**Johanson-Thor, Emil Nils (Thor
  Emil Nils Johanson)** (Swedish
  artist, 1889-) WC
Johansson, Aron (Swedish
  architect, 1860-1936) BA
    Bibl: Knutsson, Konsthist.
    Tidskrift, LIII/3 (1984), p.2;
    ▶Svenska konstnärer; ▶Svenskt
    konst.-lex.

Johansson, Arvid Claes William
  (Swedish artist, 1862-1923) WC
Johansson, Carl (Scandinavian artist,
  1863-1944) WC
Johansson, Eric (German artist,
  1913) WC

Johansson, Gerry (Swedish
  photographer, Höganäs) AV
    Bibl: Arkitektur; the Swedish
    review of architecture, 1984,
    v.84, no.8, p.30
Johansson, Johan (Swedish artist,
  1879-1951) WC
John (Spanish scribe, act.954) GC
    Bibl: Domínguez Bordona, Mss.,
    v.2, p.7, no.156
John (English master mason, act.
  1260) BA
    Bibl: Prior, ENGLISH MEDIEVAL
    ARCHITECTURE; Taylor, Castles
    13c. Wales & Savoy;
    ▶Thieme-Becker
John →see John, Augustus Edwin
John A. Stanton →see Stanton, John
  A.
John Alexander Gresse →see Gresse,
  John Alexander
John Altham →see Altham, John
John Asslyn →see Asselyn, Jan
John Astley →see Astley, John
John at Arch →see Aachen, Hans von
John Atkinson Grimshaw →see
  Grimshaw, John Atkinson
John Augustus Atkinson →see
  Atkinson, John Augustus
John Baker →see Baker, John, (GBR.)
John Baptist de Medina →see Medina,
  John Baptist de
John Baptist Malchair →see Malchair,
  John Baptist
John Baptiste Franck →see Francken,
  Jan Baptist
John Bellini →see Bellini, Giovanni
John Bellini Master of Titian →see
  Bellini, Giovanni
John Booth →see Both, Jan
John Both →see Both, Jan
John Boultbee →see Boultbee, John
John Bradley Storrs →see Storrs, John
  Bradley
John Brett →see Brett, John
John Breughel →see Brueghel, Jan,
  the elder
John Bridges →see Bridges, John
John Britton Matthew →see
  Matthew, John Britton
John Bromley →see Bromley, John
John Brueghel →see Brueghel, Jan,
  the elder
John Brueghel, called the Old →see
  Brueghel, Jan, the elder
John Brueghel, Called, Velvet
  Brueghel →see Brueghel, Jan, the
  elder
John Burnet →see Burnet, John
John Burney Ladbrooke →see
  Ladbrooke, John Burney
John Butler Yeats →see Yeats, John
  Butler
John Butts →see Butts, John
John Califano →see Califano, John

John Callcott Horsley →see Horsley,
  John Callcott
John Carroll →see Carroll, John
John Cawse →see Cawse, John
John Chapman →see Chapman, John
John Christen Johansen →see
  Johansen, John Christen
John Cleveley →see Cleveley, John I
John Cleveley →see Cleveley, John II
John Cleveley (I) →see Cleveley, John
  I
John Cleveley (II) →see Cleveley,
  John II
John Closterman →see Closterman,
  John
John Collet →see Collet, John
John Collier →see Collier, John
John Constable →see Constable, John
John Cooper →see Cooper, John
John Cordrey →see Cordrey, J.
John Covert →see Covert, John
John Cranch →see Cranch, John, (of
  Bath)
John Crome →see Crome, John
John D. Graham →see Graham, John
  D.
John da Bellino →see Bellini, Giovanni
John David de Haeem →see Heem,
  Jan Davidsz. de
John David de Haem →see Heem, Jan
  Davidsz. de
John David de Heem →see Heem, Jan
  Davidsz. de
John de Bellini →see Bellini, Giovanni
John de Bellino →see Bellini, Giovanni
John de Bischop →see Bisschop, Jan
  de
John De Critz →see De Critz, John,
  the elder
John de Mabeuse →see Gossaert, Jan
John de Mabuse →see Gossaert, Jan
John de Wael →see Wael, Jan de
John Decritz I →see De Critz, John,
  the elder
John Dixon →see Dixon, John
John Dominique →see Desiderii,
  Giovanni Domenico
John Dow →see Douw, Simon
  Johannes van
John Downman →see Downman,
  John
John E. Costigan →see Costigan, John
  Edward
John E. Ferneley →see Ferneley, John
  E.
John Eagles →see Eagles, John
John Eckstein →see Eckstein, John II
John Ellsworth Weis →see Weis, John
  Ellsworth
John Esslyn →see Asselyn, Jan
John Everett Millais →see Millais,
  John Everett
John F. Carlson →see Carlson, John
  Fabian
John Faed →see Faed, John

John Faulkner → *see* Faulkner, John
John Feary → *see* Feary, John
John Francis Barbieri, called Guercino → *see* Guercino (Giovanni Francesco Barbieri)
John Francis Murphy → *see* Murphy, John Francis
John Francis Rigaud → *see* Rigaud, John Francis
John Franklin Stacey → *see* Stacey, John Franklin
John Frederick Herring (I) → *see* Herring, John Frederick I
John Frederick Herring (II) → *see* Herring, John Frederick II
John Frederick Kensett → *see* Kensett, John Frederick
John Frederick Lewis → *see* Lewis, John Frederick
John Frederick Peto → *see* Peto, John Frederick
John Frost → *see* Frost, John
John Fytt → *see* Fyt, Jan
John Gardnor → *see* Gardnor, John
John George Brown → *see* Brown, John George
John Glover → *see* Glover, John
John Graham → *see* Graham, John
John Greenhill → *see* Greenhill, John
John Greville Fennell → *see* Fennell, John Greville
John Griffiths → *see* Griffiths, John I
John H. Grout → *see* Grout, John H.
John Haberle → *see* Haberle, John
John Hall → *see* Hall, John
John Hamilton Mortimer → *see* Mortimer, John Hamilton
John Harrison Mills → *see* Mills, John Harrison
John Hemming Fry → *see* Fry, John Hemming
John Hendrick Roos → *see* Roos, Johann Heinrich
John Henry Dolph → *see* Dolph, John Henry
John Henry Twachtman → *see* Twachtman, John Henry
John Henry Witt → *see* Witt, John Henry Harrison
John Herbert Evelyn Partington → *see* Partington, John H.E.
John Hodges Benwell → *see* Benwell, John Hodges
John Hoppner → *see* Hoppner, John
John Howard Iams → *see* Iams, John Howard
John Hubbard Rich → *see* Rich, John Hubbard
John Inigo Richards → *see* Richards, John Inigo
John Jackson → *see* Jackson, John
John James Audubon → *see* Audubon, John James
John James Barralet → *see* Barralet, John James

John James Masquerier → *see* Masquerier, John James
John Jay Barber → *see* Barber, John Jay
John Jay Baumgartner → *see* Baumgartner, John Jay
John Joseph Enneking → *see* Enneking, John Joseph
John K. McLaughlin → *see* McLaughlin, John D.
John Kane → *see* Kane, John
John Keyse Sherwin → *see* Sherwin, John Keyse
John Knox → *see* Knox, John
John Konig → *see* König, Johann
John L. Pappas → *see* Pappas, John L.
John La Farge → *see* La Farge, John
John Lambert (I) → *see* Lambert, John (I)
John Lange → *see* Lange, John
John Laporte → *see* Laporte, John
John Laurie-Wallace → *see* Laurie-Wallace, John
John Lewis Brown → *see* Brown, John Lewis
John Linnell → *see* Linnell, John
John Lucas → *see* Lucas, John
John Ludlow Morton → *see* Morton, John Ludlow
John Marin → *see* Marin, John
John Marshall Gamble → *see* Gamble, John Marshall
John Martin → *see* Martin, John
John Melchior Roos → *see* Roos, Johann Melchior
John Michael Wright → *see* Wright, John Michael
John Miel → *see* Miel, Jan
John Milton → *see* Milton, John
John Mix Stanley → *see* Stanley, John Mix
John Mortimer → *see* Mortimer, John Hamilton
John Neagle → *see* Neagle, John
John Nixon → *see* Nixon, John
John Noble → *see* Noble, John
John Northcote Nash → *see* Nash, John Northcote
John Nost Sartorius → *see* Sartorius, John Nost
John of Antwerp → *see* Hans of Antwerp
John of Bruges → *see* Memling, Hans
John of Glaston *(English cabinetmaker, 14th c.)*   **BA**
    Bibl: Tracy, Burl. Mag. CXXVIII/995 (Feb. 1986) p.92
John of Holywood *(English, d. 1244 or 1256)*   **JG**
John Opie → *see* Opie, John
John Partridge → *see* Partridge, John
John Pennington → *see* Pennington, John
John Pettie → *see* Pettie, John
John Pope → *see* Pope, John

John Powell → *see* Powell, John
John Quidor → *see* Quidor, John
John R. Grabach → *see* Grabach, John R.
John R.H. Lavery → *see* Lavery, John R.H.
John Ralston → *see* Ralston, John
John Raphael Smith → *see* Smith, John Raphael
John Rathbone → *see* Rathbone, John
John Read → *see* Reade, John R.
John Reitschoof → *see* Rietschoof, Jan Claes
John Riley → *see* Riley, John
John Rising → *see* Rising, John
John Ritchie → *see* Ritchie, John
John Ritto Penniman → *see* Penniman, John Ritto
John Robert Cozens → *see* Cozens, John Robert
John Robert Dicksee → *see* Dicksee, John Robert
John Rollin Tilton → *see* Tilton, John Rollin
John Roos → *see* Roos, Johann Heinrich
John Ross Key → *see* Key, John Ross
John Rothenamer → *see* Rottenhammer, Hans I
John Rowson Smith → *see* Smith, John Rowson
John Runcman → *see* Runciman, John
John Runiciman → *see* Runciman, John
John Russell → *see* Russell, John
John Sargeant Noble → *see* Noble, John Sargent
John Sell Cotman → *see* Cotman, John Sell
John Simpson → *see* Simpson, John
John Singer Sargent → *see* Sargent, John Singer
John Singleton Copley → *see* Copley, John Singleton
John Skippe → *see* Skippe, John
John Sloan → *see* Sloan, John
John Smibert → *see* Smibert, John
John Steen → *see* Steen, Jan
John Steuart Curry → *see* Curry, John Steuart
John Stump → *see* Stump, John Samuel
John T. Blankof → *see* Blankerhoff, Jan
John T. Young Gilroy → *see* Gilroy, John T. Young
John Theodore Heins, Jr. → *see* Heins, John Theodore
John Theodore Heins, Sr. → *see* Heins, D.
John Thomas Peele → *see* Peele, John Thomas
John Thomas Serres → *see* Serres, John Thomas
John Trumbull → *see* Trumbull, John
John Van Echen → *see* Aachen, Hans von

John van Eck→*see* Eyck, Jan van

John van Eyck→*see* Eyck, Jan van

John van Eycke→*see* Eyck, Jan van

John Van Goyen→*see* Goyen, Jan
  Josephsz. van

John Van Hagen→*see* Hagen, Joris
  van der

John van Heck→*see* Hecke, Jan van
  den (I)

John Van Hugtenburgh→*see*
  Huchtenburgh, Jan van

John Van Huysum→*see* Huysum, Jan
  van

John Van Kessel→*see* Kessel, Jan van
  II

John Van Kessel, 1682→*see* Kessel,
  Jan van II

John Van Lis→*see* Liss, Johann (Pan)

John Van Ravesteyn→*see* Ravesteyn,
  Jan Anthonisz. van

John Vander Heyden→*see* Heyden,
  Jan van der

John Vanderbank→*see* Banck, Jan
  van der

John Vanderlyn→*see* Vanderlyn, John

John Vanderveld→*see* Velde, Jan II
  van de

John Varley (I)→*see* Varley, John

John Vincent Barber→*see* Barber,
  John Vincent

John von Wicht→*see* Wicht, John
  von

John Voorhout→*see* Voorhout,
  Johannes

John Vorhoort→*see* Voorhout,
  Johannes

John Warner Norton→*see* Norton,
  John Warner

John Watson Gordon→*see* Gordon,
  John Watson

John Webb→*see* Webb, John

John Webber→*see* Webber, John

John Wesley Jarvis→*see* Jarvis, John
  Wesley

John Westbrooke Chandler→*see*
  Chandler, John Westbrooke

John White Abbott→*see* Abbott,
  John White

John White Alexander→*see*
  Alexander, John White

John White Allen Scott→*see* Scott,
  John White Allen

John William Buxton Knight→*see*
  Knight, John William Buxton

John William Edy→*see* Edy, John
  William

John William Godward→*see*
  Godward, John William

John William Inchbold→*see* Inchbold,
  John William

John Williamson→*see* Williamson,
  John, (GBR)

John Wolcot→*see* Wolcott, John,
  (Peter Pindar)

John Wollaston→*see* Wollaston, John

John Wootton→*see* Wootton, John

John Wouvermans→*see*
  Wouwerman, Jan

John Wouwermans→*see*
  Wouwerman, Jan

John Wyck→*see* Wyck, Jan

John Wycke→*see* Wyck, Jan

John Wynants→*see* Wijnants, Jan

John Young Hunter→*see* Hunter,
  John Young

John, Allen (*British artist, op.20th
  c.*)   **WI**

John, August   **BA**

  (*German artist, 1602-p.1678*)   WC

  (*German painter, printmaker,
  medalist, 1602-after 1678*)   BA
  Bibl: ▶Thieme-Becker; ▶Witt
  checklist

  John, August (Augustin)   **WC**

John, August (Augustin)→*see* John,
  August

John, Augustin Edwin→*see* John,
  Augustus Edwin

John, Augustus→*see* John, Augustus
  Edwin

John, Augustus Edwin   **BA PR WC WI**

  (*British artist, 1879-1961*)   WC WI

  (*British painter, 1878-1961*)   BA PR

  (*British, 1879-1961*)   GC
  Bibl: ▶Dict. natl. biog.; George
  Goldner; ▶RILA/BHA;
  ▶Thieme-Becker; ▶Vollmer,
  Künst.-Lex. 20. Jhr.; ▶Who was
  who [GBR], 1961-70; ▶Witt
  checklist

  Augustus Edwin John   PR

  John   PR

  John, Augustin Edwin   PR

  John, Augustus   **GC PR**

John, Dorelia (*American, 1881-1970*) **BA**
  Bibl: ▶Dict. natl. biog.; Holroyd,
  Augustus John

John, Gwen   **BA**

  (*British artist, 1876-1939*)   WC WI

  (*British painter, 1876-1939*)   BA
  Bibl: ▶Johnson, Brit. artists; RLIN
  BKS file; Thames & Hudson Brit.
  art; ▶Vollmer, Künst.-Lex. 20. Jhr.;
  ▶Waters, Brit. artists; ▶Witt
  checklist; ▶WW Art, 1929

  John, Gwendolyn Mary   **WC WI**

John, Gwendolyn Mary→*see* John,
  Gwen

John, Jiří (*Czech painter, printmaker,
  1923-1972*)   **BA**
  Bibl: ▶Bénézit; ▶Havlice, Idx. art.
  bio.; ▶Parry, Contemp. art; ▶Parry,
  Print idx.

John, or Hans, Holbein→*see* Holbein,
  Hans, the younger

John, otherwise Velvet Breughel→*see*
  Brueghel, Jan, the elder

John, Romilly (*British, b.1904*)   **BA**
  Bibl: Holroyd, Augustus John

John, Vivien (*British artist, op.1970-*) **WI**

John, Wilhelm (August Wilhelm)
  (*German artist, 1813-p.1837*)   **WC**

John, William Goscombe (*British
  sculptor, 1860-1952*)   **BA**
  Bibl: ▶Vollmer, Künst.-Lex. 20.
  Jhr.; ▶Who was who [GBR],
  1951-60

Johnab. Eyck→*see* Eyck, Jan van

Johnen, Jörg (*German critic, artist,
  b.1948*)   **BA**
  Bibl: Rotterdam (NLD),
  Lijnbaancentrum, DE VEREGELDE
  BRON. DER VERSIEGELTE
  BRUNNEN (1984)

Johnes, Thomas→*see* Johnson,
  Thomas

Jöhnk, Peter (*German interior
  architect, Hamburg*)   **AV**
  Bibl: Deutsche Bauzeitschrift,
  1986 Apr., v.34, no.4, p.442

Johns, Ambrose Bowden   **WC WI**

  (*British artist, 1776-1777-1858*)   WI

  (*British artist, 1776/7-1858*)   WC
  Bibl: ▶Fisher, Watercolour ptrs.

Johns, Barry   **AV BA**

  (*Canadian architect, 20th c.*)   BA

  (*Canadian architect, Edmonton,
  Alta*)   AV
  Bibl: ▶Avery period. idx., 1986
  suppl.; Canadian architect, 1985
  sept., v.30, no.9, p.18; Davey,
  ARCHITECTURAL REVIEW CLXXXI
  (May 1987) 82-85

Johns, Edwin Thomas (*British artist,
  1862-1947*)   **WI**

Johns, H. (*Netherlands artist, op.
  1791-1816*)   **WC**

Johns, J.   **WC WI**

  (*British artist, op.c.1798*)   WC

  (*British artist, op.circa 1798-*)   WI

Johns, Jasper   **BA GC WC WI**

  (*American artist, 1930-*)   WC

  (*American artist, b.1930*)   WI

  (*American painter, b.1930*)   GC

  (*American painter, printmaker,
  b.1930*)   BA
  Bibl: ▶Babington Smith, Contemp.
  artists; ▶RILA/BHA; ▶WW Amer.
  Art, 1989-1990

Johnsan Carr→*see* Carr, Johnson

Johnsen, Johan→*see* Johnsen, Johann

Johnsen, Johann   **GC**

  (*German artist, 1652-1708*)   WC

  (*German, 1652-1708*)   GC
  Bibl: ▶Witt checklist

Johnsen, Johan   **WC**

Johnson (*Engraver*)   **WI**

Johnson→*see* Johnson, Cornelius I

Johnson→*see* Johnson, David

Johnson→*see* Johnson, Eastman

Johnson Carr→*see* Carr, Johnson

Johnson, A. (*British artist, op.1848-
  1852*)   **WC**

Johnson, Alfred George (*British
  artist, circa 1820-op.1886*)   **WI**

Johnson, Arthur *(American artist, 1874-1954)* **WI**

Johnson, Arthur, (GBR.) *(British artist, op.1851-)* **WI**
Bibl: Cornish Artist

Johnson, Avery F. *(American artist, b.1906)* **WI**

Johnson, Barbara *(British, 1738-1825)* **BA**
Bibl: Rothenstein, APOLLO CXXVI/309 (Nov 1987) 375

Johnson, Ben **BA WI**
(American artist, op.20th c.) **WI**
(American painter, 1902-1967) **BA**
Bibl: ▶Cummings, Contemp. Amer. artists; NY Times obit.; ▶WW Amer. Art, necrol.

Johnson, Ben **AV BA**
(British painter of architectural subjects, 1946-) **AV**
(British painter, printmaker, b.1946) **BA**
Bibl: ▶Art Index, [date]; Building design, 1986 Dec.5, no.815, p.20; Guide exh. artists: N. Amer. ptrs.

Johnson, Bradbury *(American architect, 1766-1819)* **AV**
Bibl: ▶Archts. Maine, v.1, no.2, p.1

Johnson, Brian *(Architect, South African, born in England, 1941-)* **AV**
Bibl: UIA international architect, 1985, no.8, inside front cover

Johnson, Buffie *(American painter, b.1912)* **BA**
Bibl: ▶WW Amer. Art, 1976

Johnson, C. *(American artist, op. 19th c.)* **WI**

Johnson, Carla Rae *(American artist, 20th c.)* **BA**
Bibl: Huntington (NY, USA), Heckscher Mus., Kindred spirits (1981)

Johnson, Carol R. *(American landscsape architect, Cambridge, MA)* **AV**
Bibl: Dir. Amer. landscape arch. firms, 1986/87

Johnson, Charles Edward *(British artist, 1832-1913)* **WC WI**

Johnson, Charles Foreman
(American architect) **AV**

Johnson, Charles H. **WC WI**
(American artist, 19th cent.) **WC**
(American artist, op.19th c.) **WI**

Johnson, Charles William Heaton
(British artist, 1896-op.1924) **WI**

Johnson, Cheryl L. *(American lighting designer)* **AV**
Bibl: Architectural lighting, 1988 July, v.2, no.7, p.38

Johnson, Clarence R. *(American artist, 1894-1981)* **WI**

Johnson, Cletus *(American artist, b.1941)* **BA**
Bibl: ▶NY art yrbk.

Johnson, Clive → see Johnson, Frederick Clive

Johnson, Cornelis → see Johnson, Cornelius I

Johnson, Cornelis (II) → see Jonson, Cornelius II

Johnson, Cornelius → see Johnson, Cornelius I

Johnson, Cornelius (I) → see Johnson, Cornelius I

Johnson, Cornelius I **BA GC**
(British artist, 1593-1661-1662) **WI**
(British artist, 1593-1661/2) **WC**
(British painter, 1593-1661/62) **PR**
(British, 1593-1661/62) **GC**
(English painter, 1593-1661) **BA**
Bibl: Auckland City Art Gal. Qtrly 64 (May 1977), p.2; ▶Dict. natl. biog.; ▶Encyc. world art; George Goldner; Getty Photo Study Coll. (Wm. Suhr file); ▶Redgrave, Engl. school; ▶RILA/BHA; ▶Thieme-Becker; ▶Waterhouse, Brit. 18c. ptrs.; ▶Waterhouse, Brit. ptrs. 16-17cs.; ▶Yale Brit. artists list

A. Johnson **PR**
C Jansen **PR**
C. Iansens **PR**
C. Jan sn **PR**
C. Jansans **PR**
C. Janseen **PR**
C. Jansen **PR**
C. Jansens **PR**
C. Jansin **PR**
C. Janson **PR**
C. Janssen **PR**
C. Janssens **PR**
C. Johnson **PR**
Ceulen, Cornelis Janssen van **PR**
Ceulen, Cornelis van **BA**
Con. Jansen **PR**
Cor. Jansen **PR**
Cor. Jansens **PR**
Cor. Janssens **PR**
Cor. Johnson **PR**
Corn. Gansen **PR**
Corn. Jansen **PR**
Corn. Jansen Van Cuyln **PR**
Corn. Jansens **PR**
Corn. Janson **PR**
Corn: Jansen **PR**
Cornelian Jansen **PR**
Cornelious Jansens **PR**
Cornelis Jansen **PR**
Cornelis Jonson (I) **PR**
Cornelius Jansen **PR**
Cornelius Jansens **PR**
Cornelius Janson **PR**
[Cornelius Janson] van Keulen **PR**
Cornelius Janssen **PR**
Cornelius Johnson **PR**
Corns. Jansen **PR**
G. Jansens **PR**
Janseens **PR**
Jansen **PR**
Jansens **PR**
Janssen **PR**
Janssen van Ceulen, Cornelius **PR**
Janssen, Cornelius **BA**
Janssens **PR**
Janssens van Ceulen **PR**
Janssens van Ceulen, Cornelius **BA**
Janssens, Cornelis **PR**
Janssens, Cornelius **PR**
Johnson **PR**

Johnson, Cornelis   PR
Johnson, Cornelius   PR
Johnson, Cornelius (I)   **PR**
Jonson   PR
Jonson van Ceulen, Cornelis   PR
Jonson van Ceulen, Cornelis I   GC
Jonson van Ceulen, Cornelis, the
    elder   PR
Jonson van Ceulen, Cornelius   BA PR
Jonson, Cornelis (I)   PR
Jonson, Cornelis I   **GC**
Jonson, Cornelius   BA
Jonson, Cornelius I   **WI**
**Jonson, Johnson, Jansen or
    Janssens van Ceulen, (Koln)
    Cornelis, I**   **WC**
Jonssens, Cornelius   PR
Van Keulen   PR
Johnson, Cyrus (British artist, 1848-
    1925)   **WI**
Johnson, Dana (Designer)   **AV**
    Bibl: Interior design, 1984 Nov.,
    v.55, no.11, p.270
Johnson, David   **BA GC PR WC WI**
    (American artist, 1827-1908)   WC WI
    (American painter, 1827-
    1908)   BA GC PR
    Bibl: ▶Fielding's Amer. ptrs.;
    ▶Groce, Artists Amer.;
    ▶RILA/BHA; ▶Thieme-Becker
    David Johnson   PR
    Johnson   PR
Johnson, Derek Christopher
    (British artist, op.20th c.)   **WI**
Johnson, Don (American sculptor,
    b.1941)   **BA**
    Bibl: Santa Barbara (CA, USA),
    UCSB Art Mus., Sculptural
    perspectives (1979)
Johnson, Douglas Walter
    (American painter, printmaker,
    b.1946)   **BA**
    Bibl: ▶WW Amer. Art
Johnson, E. (British artist, op.19th
    c.)   **WI**
Johnson, E. Verner (American
    architect)   **AV**
    Bibl: ▶AIA Pro File, 1985
Johnson, Eastman   **BA GC PR WC WI**
    (American artist, 1824-1906)   WC WI
    (American painter, 1824-1906) BA PR
    (American, 1824-1906)   GC
    Bibl: ▶Fielding's Amer. ptrs.,
    1983; ▶RILA/BHA; ▶Witt
    checklist; ▶WWW Amer., 1897-
    1942; ▶Young, Amer. artists
    Eastman Johnson   PR
    Johnson   PR
    Johnson, Jonathan-Eastman   WI
Johnson, Edward Killingworth   **WC WI**
    (British artist, 1825-1896)   WC
    (British artist, 1825-1923)   WI
    Bibl: ▶Fisher, Watercolour ptrs.
Johnson, Elaine   **WC WI**
    (British artist, 1945-)   WC
    (British artist, b.1945)   WI

Johnson, Eric (American
    photographer, b.1949)   **BA**
    Bibl: Carmel (CA, USA), Friends of
    Photo., New landscapes (1981)
Johnson, Ernest & Esther Borough
    (British artist, 1867-1949)   **WI**
    George, Esther, Miss   WI
Johnson, Ernest Borough (British
    artist, 1866-1949)   **WC**
Johnson, Federico (Italian
    metalwork manufacturer, medalist,
    1855-1937)   **BA**
    Bibl: ▶Forrer, Medallists; Johnson,
    Jrnl. of Dec. & Propaganda Arts 9
    (summer 1988), p. 68-85
Johnson, Francis → see Johnson,
    Francis F.
Johnson, Francis F.   **BA**
    (British architect working in
    Yorkshire, 1911-)   AV
    (British architect, b.1911)   BA
    Bibl: Cornforth, Country Life
    CLXXVI (Oct. 1984); Period
    homes, 1985 Oct., v.6, no.10,
    p.32; Pevsner, Yorkshire E. Riding
Johnson, Francis   **AV**
Johnson, Frank Tenney → see Johnson,
    Frank Tenny
Johnson, Frank Tenny   **BA**
    (American artist, 1874-1939)   WC WI
    (American painter, 1874-1939)   BA
    Bibl: ▶Bénézit; ▶Dawdy, Artists
    Amer. West; ▶Fielding's Amer.
    ptrs.; ▶NY Times obit.; ▶WW
    Amer. Art, 1940-1941; ▶Young,
    Amer. artists
Johnson, Frank Tenney   **WC WI**
Johnson, Frederick Clive (British
    architect)   **AV**
    Bibl: ▶Guide to RIBA practices,
    1984
    Johnson, Clive   AV
Johnson, G.E. (Engraver)   **WI**
Johnson, George H. (American, b.
    1823, active CA, U.S. 1849-1852
    and NY, U.S.)   **JG**
Johnson, George P. (American
    architect)   **AV**
    Bibl: Architectural lighting, 1989
    Mar., v.3, no.3, p.22
Johnson, Glenys (British painter,
    sculptor, b.1952)   **BA**
    Bibl: ▶Intl. dir. exh. artists, 1983;
    London (GBR), ICA, Before it hits
    the floor (1983)
Johnson, Guy   **BA WC WI**
    (American artist, 1927-)   WC
    (American artist, b.1927)   WI
    (American painter, b.1927)   BA
    Bibl: ▶Parry, Contemp. art; West
    Palm Beach (FL, USA), Norton
    Gallery, Imagist realism (1974-
    1975)
Johnson, Harry John (British artist,
    1826-1884)   **WC WI**
Johnson, Henry (British artist, op.
    1824-1847)   **WC WI**

Johnson, Henry Denny (1842-1933;
    Architect, Edmonton)   **FA**
    Bibl: CAAD Finding Aid RG11M
    79003/36 Items 435-437;
    Edmonton City Directories; ▶Hill,
    Archts. Canada, 1986
Johnson, Herbert (British artist,
    1848-1906)   **WC WI**
Johnson, Isaac (British artist, 1754-
    1835)   **WC WI**
Johnson, J.A. (American, active ca.
    1914)   **JG**
Johnson, James (British artist, 1803-
    1834)   **WC WI**
Johnson, James (British architect, d.
    1807)   **AV**
    Bibl: ▶Colvin, Brit. archts.
Johnson, Jed (American interior
    designer, NYC)   **AV**
    Bibl: House & garden, 1988 Apr.,
    v.160, no.4, p.94
Johnson, John (American
    photographer, act.1839, d.1871)   **BA**
    Bibl: ▶Gernsheim, Hist. photog.;
    HISTORY OF PHOTOGRAPHY
    I/2(Apr 1977), p.129-134;
    ▶Newhall, Photog.
Johnson, John   **WC WI**
    (British artist, -c.1797)   WC
    (British artist, op.circa 1797-)   WI
    Bibl: Hall (Northumbria)
Johnson, John (British architect,
    partner of Alfred Meeson)   **AV**
    Bibl: Country life, 1985 Jan.10,
    v.177, no.4560, p.54
Johnson, John (British printer, 1882-
    1956)   **BA**
    Bibl: ▶Dict. natl. biog.; ▶Who was
    who [GBR], 1951-60
Johnson, John (British, 1754-1814)   **GC**
    Bibl: ▶Thieme-Becker
Johnson, Jonathan-Eastman → see
    Johnson, Eastman
Johnson, Joshua   **BA GC WC**
    (American artist, 18th cent.)   WC
    (American painter, act.1789-
    1832)   BA
    (American, 18th century)   GC
    Bibl: ▶Britannica encyc. Amer. art;
    ▶Cederholm, Afro-Amer. artists;
    Locke, Negro in art; ▶MoMA libr.
    cat.; Washington, DC (USA),
    Smithsonian Institution, National
    Museum of American Art,
    SHARING TRADITIONS...(1985) 40-
    43,49; ▶Witt checklist
    Johnston, Joshua   BA
Johnson, Karen (American architect,
    Chicago, Ill)   **AV**
    Bibl: Architecture: the AIA
    journal, 1989 May, v.78, no.5,
    p.144
Johnson, Kathryn (American artist,
    20th c.)   **BA**
    Bibl: Norton (MA, USA), Wheaton
    Coll., Collage (1980)
Johnson, Laura, Miss → see Knight,
    Laura

Johnson, Laurence   WC WI
  (British artist, op.1603)   WC
  (British artist, op.1603-)   WI
Johnson, Leon *(South African
  painter, b.ca.1960)*   BA
    Bibl: Rose, M., in ARTS MAG
    LX/8 (Apr 1986) 116
Johnson, Lester → see Johnson, Lester
  F.
Johnson, Lester F.   BA WI
  (American artist, 1919-)   WC
  (American artist, b.1919)   WI
  (American painter, b.1919)   BA
    Bibl: ART NEWS, 62 (Feb 1964),
    p.46-47; ▶Locus; ▶MoMA libr.
    cat.; ▶WW Amer. Art, 1976
Johnson, Lester   WC
Johnson, Lois Marlene *(American
  printmaker, b.1942)*   BA
    Bibl: ▶WW Amer. Art, 1976
Johnson, Marie E. *(American artist,
  b.1920)*   BA
    Bibl: ▶Cederholm, Afro-Amer.
    artists
Johnson, Marshall   BA WC WI
  (American artist, 1850-1921)   WI
  (American artist, 19th cent.)   WC
  *(American sailor, painter, ca.
  1850-1921)*   BA
    Bibl: ANTIQUES CXX (Nov 1981),
    p. 1218-1221; ▶Fielding's Amer.
    ptrs.; ▶Young, Amer. artists
Johnson, Martin   AV BA
  (British architect)   AV
  (British architect, 20th c.)   BA
    Bibl: ▶Avery period. idx.
Johnson, Martin Brian *(American
  painter, sculptor, b.1951.)*   BA
    Bibl: ARTS MAGAZINE LIV/5 (Jan
    1980), p.6; ▶WW Amer. Art,
    1986
Johnson, Mary *(British artist, op.
  1814-1829)*   WC WI
Johnson, Mel *(American artist,
  b.1925)*   WI
Johnson, Michael   BA WC
  *(American painter in AUS,
  b.1938)*   BA
  (Australian artist, 1938-)   WC
    Bibl: ▶ARTbibl. mod., 14/1, 17/1;
    Artscribe, 23 (June 1980) 22-29;
    ▶Babington Smith, Contemp.
    artists; ▶Gorenflo, Bild. Künstler;
    Paris (FRA), Gal. Baudoin Lebon,
    MICHAEL JOHNSON...(1989)
    BHA/FRA
Johnson, Nancy *(Canadian painter,
  20th c.)*   BA
    Bibl: ▶Intl. dir. exh. artists, 1983,
    1984, v.1
Johnson, Nerys *(British artist,
  b.1942)*   WI
Johnson, Nevill   WC WI
  (British artist, 20th cent.)   WC
  (British artist, op.1972-)   WI

Johnson, Nick *(Canadian artist, 20th
  c.)*   BA
    Bibl: Brodsky, M., ARTSCANADA,
    XXXIX/1 (Nov 1984), p.41; ▶Intl.
    dir. exh. artists, 1982, 1983
Johnson, P. *(American artist, op.
  19th c.)*   WI
Johnson, Paul *(American artist, 20th
  c.)*   BA
    Bibl: Huntington (NY, USA),
    Heckscher Mus., Kindred spirits
    (1981)
Johnson, Peter *(Australian
  architect)*   AV
    Bibl: Architecture Australia, 1986
    Mar., v.75, no.2, p.27
  Johnson, R. N.   AV
Johnson, Peter *(British artist,
  b.1948)*   WI
Johnson, Philip → see Johnson, Philip
  Cortelyou
Johnson, Philip Cortelyou   AV BA
  *(American architect and author,
  1906-)*   AV
  *(American architect, collector,
  b.1906)*   BA
    Bibl: ▶AIA Pro File; ▶Contemp.
    archts.; ▶Libr. of Congr. Name
    Auth. File; ▶WW Arch.
Johnson, Philip   AV
Johnson, Quincy *(American
  architect, Boca Raton, FL)*   AV
    Bibl: Builder, 1986 May., v.9,
    no.5, p.153
Johnson, R. A. *(Australian architect)*   AV
    Bibl: Architecture Australia, 1986
    July, v.75, no.5, p.55
Johnson, R. N. → see Johnson, Peter
Johnson, Ralph *(American architect,
  1948-)*   AV
    Bibl: Inland architect, 1985 Nov.-
    Dec., v.29, no.6, p.46
Johnson, Ray   BA WC WI
  (American artist, 1927-)   WC
  (American artist, b.1927)   BA WI
    Bibl: ▶Bénézit; ▶MoMA libr. cat.;
    ▶NY art yrbk.; ▶WW Amer. Art,
    1976
Johnson, Regitze *(Danish architect,
  1946-)*   AV
    Bibl: ▶Danske Arkitekters
    Landsforbund, 1988-89
Johnson, Richard Norman
  (Australian architect, 1923-)   AV
Johnson, Robert   BA WC
  (British artist, 1770-1796)   WC WI
  *(British printmaker, painter,
  1770-1796)*   BA
    Bibl: ▶Redgrave, Engl. school;
    ▶Thieme-Becker
Johnson, Robert I   WI
Johnson, Robert Ernest *(1946-)*   AV
    Bibl: ▶Libr. of Congr. Name Auth.
    File
Johnson, Robert I → see Johnson,
  Robert

Johnson, Robert II *(British artist,
  op.1927-)*   WI
Johnson, Ron *(American landscape
  painter, Conn)*   AV
    Bibl: House & Garden, 1986 Oct.,
    v.158, no.10, p.189
Johnson, S.Y. → see Johnson, Sidney
  Yates
Johnson, Sargent Claude
  *(American sculptor, printmaker,
  1888-1967)*   BA
    Bibl: ▶Cederholm, Afro-Amer.
    artists; ▶Havlice, Idx. art. bio.; Los
    Angeles (CA, USA), LACMA, Black
    Amer. art (1986); ▶Vollmer,
    Künst.-Lex. 20. Jhr.; ▶WW Amer.
    Art, 1940-1941
Johnson, Shawn Michael
  *(Architectural student, Oklahoma
  State Univ., 1984)*   AV
    Bibl: Architectural record, 1984
    Aug., v.172, no.9, p.65
Johnson, Sidney Yates   WI
  (British artist, 19th cent.)   WC
  (British artist, op.1901-1910)   WI
Johnson, S.Y.   WC
Johnson, Stephen *(British sculptor,
  b.1953)*   BA
    Bibl: ▶Art Index, Jan. 1984, Nov.
    1982-Oct. 1983; London (GBR),
    Camden Arts Ctr., Sculp. in
    garden (1982)
Johnson, Thomas *(British artist,
  furniture designer, act.1755-1778)*   BA
    Bibl: ▶Edwards, Engl. furniture,
    p.665; ▶Thieme-Becker
Johnson, Thomas *(Engraver, New
  York, NY., op.1893-1901)*   WI
Johnson, Thomas   BA GC WC
  (British architect, fl. 18th cent)   AV
  (British artist, op.1634-1685)   WI
  (British artist, op.1651-1685)   WC
  (British, act.1651-1685)   GC
  (English painter, act.1634-1676)   BA
    Bibl: ▶Bénézit; Country life, 1987
    Dec.31, v.181, no.53, p.48;
    Harris, THE ARTIST AND THE
    COUNTRY HOUSE;
    ▶Thieme-Becker; Whinney, Engl.
    art 1625-1714
Johnes, Thomas   AV
Johnson, Thomas I   WI
Johnson, Thomas → see Johnson,
  Thomas II
Johnson, Thomas → see Johnston,
  Thomas
Johnson, Thomas I → see Johnson,
  Thomas
Johnson, Thomas II   WI
  (British artist, 1709-1767)   WC WI
    Bibl: Mackenzie
Johnson, Thomas   WC
Johnson, Todd *(American architect,
  planner, Denver)*   AV
    Bibl: Progressive architecture,
    1985 Jan., v.66, no.1, p.132

Johnson, W.G.   **WC WI**
  (British artist, 19th cent.)   WC
  (British artist, op.19th c.)   WI
Johnson, W.Noel *(British artist, op.*
1887-1914)   **WI**
Johnson, William   **WC WI**
  (British artist, 18th cent.)   WC
  (British artist, op.18th c.)   WI
Johnson, William Carl *(American*
architect)   **AV**
  Bibl: Architectural digest, v.41,
  n.8, 1984, p.84
Johnson, William H. → see Johnson,
William Henry
Johnson, William Henry   **BA WI**
  (American artist, 1901-1970)   WC WI
  (American painter, printmaker,
  1901-1970)   BA
  Bibl: ▶Cederholm, Afro-Amer.
  artists; Los Angeles (CA, USA),
  LACMA, Black Amer. art (1986);
  Smithsonian Institution. National
  Collection of Fine Arts. WILLIAM
  H. JOHNSON 1901-1970 (1971)
  Johnson, William H.   **WC**
Johnson, William Templeton
  (American architect, 1877-1957)   **AV BA**
  Bibl: Apollo, v.115, n.244, 1982,
  p.432; ▶Avery obit. idx.; ▶Avery
  period. idx.; ▶WWW Amer., v.3
Johnson-Marshall, Stirrat, Sir   **AV**
Jöhnssen, Peter *(German architect,*
1930-)   **AV**
  Bibl: Deutsche Bauzeitung, 1985
  Feb., v.119, no.2, p.96
Johnston Forbes-Robertson → see
Forbes-Robertson, Johnstone
Johnston, Adam *(British in FRA,*
1784-1860)   **BA**
  Bibl: ▶Natl. union cat., pre-1956;
  Peltre, Pays Lorrain LXI/2 (1980),
  p.53-58; ▶Thieme-Becker
Johnston, Alan *(British artist,*
b.1945)   **WI**
Johnston, Alexander *(British artist,*
1815-1891)   **WC WI**
Johnston, Clarence H. *(American*
architect, St. Paul, Minn, 1859-
1936)   **AV**
  Bibl: ▶Withey, Amer. archts.
Johnston, David
  Claypoole   **BA GC WC WI**
  (American artist, 1797-1865)   WC WI
  (American painter, 1799-1865)   GC
  (American printmaker, 1799-
  1865)   BA
  Bibl: ▶Bénézit; ▶Dict. Amer. biog.;
  ▶Fielding's Amer. ptrs.; ▶Groce,
  Artists Amer.; ▶Natl. union cat.,
  pre-1956; ▶RILA/BHA; ▶WWW
  Amer., 1607; ▶Young, Amer.
  artists

Johnston, Frances Benjamin   **BA JG**
  (American photographer, 1864-
  1952)   BA
  (American, 1864-1952)   JG
  Bibl: ▶Auer, Encyc. photographes;
  ▶ICP encyc. photog.; ▶Macmillan
  photog. encyc.; ▶Rosenblum,
  World hist. photog.; ▶WWW
  Amer., v.3
Johnston, Francis   **AV BA**
  (1760-1829)   AV
  (Irish architect, 1761-1829)   BA
  Bibl: ▶Thieme-Becker
Johnston, Francis Hans   **BA**
  (Canadian artist, 1888-)   WC
  (Canadian painter, 1888-1949)   BA
  Bibl: ▶MacDonald, Can. artists;
  ▶Vollmer, Künst.-Lex. 20. Jhr.
  Johnston, Frank   BA
Johnston, Franz H.   **WC**
Johnston, Frank → see Johnston,
Francis Hans
Johnston, Franz H. → see Johnston,
Francis Hans
Johnston, Frederick *(British artist,*
op.1855-1868)   **WI**
Johnston, Harry Hamilton *(British*
artist, 1858-1927)   **WI**
Johnston, Henrietta   **BA WC WI**
  (American artist, op.1670-,
  d.1729)   WI
  (American artist,
  op.1703-m.1728/9)   WC
  (American painter, ca.1670-
  1728)   BA
  Bibl: ▶Collins, Women artists
  Amer.; ▶Dict. Amer. biog.;
  ▶Fielding's Amer. ptrs.; ▶Groce,
  Artists Amer.; Tufts, Amer.
  · Women artists; ▶WWW Amer.
  Branlieu, Henrietta de, Miss   WI
  Dering, Robert, Mrs., (Henrietta)   WI
  Johnstone, Henrietta   BA
Johnston, Henry *(English draftsman,*
act.1669)   **BA**
  Bibl: Routh, P.E.S., YORK
  ARCHAEOLOGICAL JOURNAL, LIV
  (1982) p.99
Johnston, Henry W. *(American*
architect, Wilmington, N.C)   **AV**
  Bibl: ▶AIA Pro File, 1985, p.569
Johnston, J. H. Eccleston *(American*
architect, Austin, TX)   **AV**
  Bibl: Texas architect, 1985 May-
  June, v.35, no.3, p.64
Johnston, John *(English architect,*
worked in Brazil, 19th cent.)   **AV**
  Bibl: ▶Avery period. idx., 1934-
  1978
Johnston, John   **BA WC WI**
  (American artist, 1752-1812)   WC
  (American artist, 1752-1818)   WI
  (American painter, 1753-1818)   BA
  Bibl: ▶Fielding's Amer. ptrs.;
  ▶Groce, Artists Amer.; ▶Young,
  Amer. artists

Johnston, John Humphreys   **WC WI**
  (American artist, 1857-)   WC
  (American artist, 1857-1941)   WI
Johnston, John R. *(American artist,*
op.1820-1872)   **WI**
Johnston, Joshua   **WC WI**
  (American artist, op.1793-1824)   WI
  (American artist, op.1796-1824)   WC
Johnston, Joshua → see Johnson,
Joshua
Johnston, Lawrence Waterbury   **AV BA**
  (British garden designer, 1871-
  1958)   AV
  (British landscape gardener,
  1871-1958)   BA
  Bibl: Boursier-Mougenot,
  MONUMENTS HISTORIQUES DE LA
  FRANCE 125 (1983), p.74;
  Country life, 1986 July 10, v.180,
  no.4638, p.81; Country life, 1989
  July 13, v.183, no.28, p.125;
  Lees-Milne, NATIONAL TRUST
  YEARBOOK, 1977-78, p.18-29;
  Sackville-West, HIDCOTE MANOR
  GARDEN
Johnston, Peter *(Canadian sculptor,*
b.1949)   **BA**
  Bibl: Kingston(Ont,CND), Queen's
  Univ., Etherington, PETER
  JOHNSTON..,1980
Johnston, Robert B. *(British artist,*
op.1880-1903)   **WI**
Johnston, Roy *(Irish painter,*
b.1936)   **BA**
  Bibl: Belfast (GBR), Ulster Mus.,
  Irish directions (1975), p.25
Johnston, Sarah J.F. *(American*
painter, 1850-1925)   **BA**
  Bibl: Amer. Art Jrnl. XIII/I (Winter
  1981) pp.17-46; ▶Petteys,
  Women artists; ▶WWW Amer. art
Johnston, Steve *(British*
photographer, b.1956)   **BA**
  Bibl: Arts Council GBR, Lives
  (1979)
Johnston, Thomas   **BA WI**
  (American artist, 1708-1767)   WC WI
  (American painter, japanner,
  printmaker, ca.1708-1767)   BA
  Bibl: ▶Dict. Amer. biog.; ▶Groce,
  Artists Amer.
  Johnson, Thomas   WI
Johnstone, Thomas   **WC**
Johnston, William   **BA GC WC WI**
  (American artist, 1732-1772)   WC WI
  (American painter, 1732-1772)   BA
  (American, 1732-1772)   GC
  Bibl: ▶Groce, Artists Amer.; ▶Witt
  checklist

Johnston, Ynez   **BA WC WI**
  (American artist, 20th cent.)   WC
  (American artist, b.1920)   WI
  (American painter, printmaker,
    b.1920)   BA
    Bibl: ▶Cummings, Contemp.
    Amer. artists; ▶MoMA libr. cat.;
    ▶Whitney Mus. cat.; WW Amer.,
    1976; ▶WW Amer. Art, 1976
Johnstone, Dorothy   **BA WC WI**
  (British artist, 1892-op.1949)   WI
  (British artist, 20th cent.)   WC
  (British painter, 1892-1980)   BA
    Bibl: Aberdeen (GBR), Art Gallery,
    DOROTHY JOHNSTONE (1982);
    ▶Johnson, Brit. artists; ▶Vollmer,
    Künst.-Lex. 20. Jhr.; ▶Who was
    who [GBR], v.7
  Sutherland, David M., Mrs.,
    (Dorothy)   WI
  Sutherland, Dorothy   BA
Johnstone, George Whitton
  (British artist, 1849-1901)   WI
Johnstone, Henrietta→see Johnston,
  Henrietta
Johnstone, Henry J.→see Johnstone,
  Henry James
Johnstone, Henry James   **WI**
  (British artist, 1835-1907)   WC WI
    Bibl: ▶Mallalieu, Brit. watercolour
    artists
  Johnstone, Henry J.   **WC**
Johnstone, John   **WC WI**
  (British artist, 20th cent.)   WC
  (British artist, op.1959-1966)   WI
Johnstone, M. (Engraver)   **WI**
Johnstone, Thomas→see Johnston,
  Thomas
Johnstone, William   **BA WC WI**
  (British artist, 1897-)   WC
  (British artist, 1897-1981)   WI
  (British painter, 1897-1981)   BA
    Bibl: ▶Fogg Mus. Libr. cat.;
    Thames & Hudson Brit. art;
    ▶Vollmer, Künst.-Lex. 20. Jhr.;
    ▶Waters, Brit. artists; ▶WW Art,
    1972
Johnstone, William Borthwick
  (British artist, 1804-1868)   WC WI
Joinet, M. (French artist, op.1804-
  1807)   WC
Joinville, Antoine Victor   **GC**
  (French artist, 1801-1849)   WC
  (French, 1801-1849)   GC
    Bibl: Getty Photo Study Coll.
    (Ptgs.); ▶Witt checklist
  Joinville, Antoine-Victor   **WC**
  Joinville, Edouard   GC
Joinville, Antoine-Victor→see
  Joinville, Antoine Victor
Joinville, Edouard→see Joinville,
  Antoine Victor
**Joinville, Francois Ferdinand
  Phillippe Louis Marie d'Orleans,
  Prince de** (French artist, 1818-
  1900)   WC

Jokela, Olli Pekka (Finnish architect) **AV**
  Bibl: Byggekunst, 1986, v.68,
    no.7, p.F2
Jokkinen, Leo (Finnish painter,
  b.1947)   **BA**
    Bibl: London (GBR), ICA,
    Workaday Finland (1974)
Jole→see Joli, Antonio
Jole, Joseph Gerardus van (Dutch
  draughtsman, 1877-1919)   **GC**
    Bibl: ▶Bénézit
Joli→see Joli, Antonio
Joli de Dipi, Antonio→see Joli,
  Antonio
Joli, Antonio   **AV BA GC PR**
  (Italian artist, c.1700-1777)   WC
  (Italian painter, ca. 1700-1777)   AV
  (Italian painter, ca.1700-
    1777)   BA GC PR
    Bibl: ▶Bolaffi; Getty Photo Study
    Coll. (Douwes coll.); ▶RILA/BHA,
    1986; RLIN BKS file, NYCG85-
    B46850; ▶Thieme-Becker
  A. Jolli   PR
  Antonio Joli   PR
  Eolli   PR
  Gioli, Antonio   BA GC
  Jole   PR
  Joli   PR
  Joli de Dipi, Antonio   GC
  Joli, Gioli, Jolli or Yoli, Antonio **WC**
  Jolli   PR
  Yoli, Antonio   BA GC
Joli, Gabriel→see Yoli, Gabriel
Joli, Gioli, Jolli or Yoli, Antonio→see
  Joli, Antonio
Jolin, Einar→see Jolin, Johan Einar
Jolin, François Gérard→see Jollain,
  François Gérard
Jolin, Johan Einar   **BA**
  (Swedish artist, 1890-)   WC
  (Swedish painter, b.1890)   BA
    Bibl: ▶Svenskt konst.-lex.;
    ▶Vollmer, Künst.-Lex. 20. Jhr.
  Jolin, Einar   BA **WC**
Jolivant, André→see Jolivard, André
Jolivard, André   **GC WC**
  (French artist, 1787-1851)   WC
  (French painter, 1787-1851)   GC
    Bibl: Getty Photo Study Coll.;
    ▶Thieme-Becker
  Jolivant, André   GC
Jolivet, Henri (French artist, op.
  1814-m.c.1825)   WC
Jolivet, L. (French artist, 18th cent.) WC
Jollain or Joullain, Nicolas Rene→see
  Jollain, Nicolas René
Jollain or Joullain, Pierre→see Jollain,
  Pierre
Jollain, Francois→see Jollain, François
  Gérard

Jollain, François Gérard   **BA**
  (French artist, c.1641-1704)   WC
  (French printmaker, act.1684-
    1719)   BA
    Bibl: ▶Bénézit; Cennerne
    Wilhelmb, Muvészettörténeti
    Értesíto, XXVI/I (1975) pp.62-66;
    ▶Thieme-Becker
  Jolin, François Gérard   BA
  Jollain, Francois   **WC**
Jollain, Gerard, I (French artist,
  -1683)   **WC**
Jollain, Nicolas René   **BA**
  (French artist, 1732-1804)   WC
  (French painter, 1732-1804)   BA
    Bibl: ▶Bénézit; ▶Thieme-Becker
  Jollain or Joullain, Nicolas Rene **WC**
  Joullain, Nicolas René   BA
Jollain, Pierre   **GC**
  (French artist, 1720-p.1762)   WC
  (French painter, b.1720)   GC
    Bibl: ▶Bénézit
  Jollain or Joullain, Pierre   **WC**
Jolli→see Joli, Antonio
Jolliffe, Michael (Canadian painter,
  printmaker, b.1945)   **BA**
    Bibl: ▶Intl. dir. exh. artists, 1983
Jollivet→see Jollivet, Pierre Jules
Jollivet, Pierre Jules   **BA PR WC**
  (French artist, 1794-1871)   WC
  (French painter, 1794-1871)   BA GC PR
    Bibl: ▶Bellier, Artistes fran.;
    ▶Bénézit; ▶RILA/BHA;
    ▶Thieme-Becker
  Jollivet   PR
  Jollivet, Pierre-Jules   **GC**
  Pierre Jules Jollivet   PR
Jollivet, Pierre-Jules→see Jollivet,
  Pierre Jules
Jolly, Ferdinand Louis (French
  painter, 1801-1861)   **GC**
    Bibl: ▶Bénézit
Jolly, Henri Jean Baptiste (Belgian
  artist, 1812-1853)   **WC**
Jolly, John (American lighting
  designer)   **AV**
    Bibl: Architectural lighting, 1988
    July, v.2, no.7, p.50
Jolly, Nicholas (British artist,
  b.1963)   **WI**
Joly, Alexis Victor (French artist,
  1798-1874)   **WC**
Joly, Andre (French artist, 1706-p.
  1781)   **WC**
Joly, Gabriel→see Yoli, Gabriel
Joly, Robert (1928-)   **AV**
Joly, Viktorine (de cadet) (French
  artist, op.1800-1830)   **WC**
Jolyet, Philippe   **GC WC**
  (French artist, 1832-1908)   WC
  (French painter, 1832-1908)   GC
    Bibl: ▶Bénézit

Jomantas, Vincas *(Australian draughtsman, b.1922)*   GC
    Bibl: ▶Encyc. Australian art; Gernsheim, Corpus Photog. of Drawings
Jomantas, Vincent   GC
Jomantas, Vincent → see Jomantas, Vincas

Jombert, Charles-Antoine *(French print publisher, 1712-1784)*   BA
    Bibl: ▶Natl. union cat., pre-1956; ▶Nouv. biog. gén.; ▶Thieme-Becker

Jombert, Pierre Charles *(French artist, c.1748/9-p.1777)*   WC

Jonas *(Active Dresden, late 19th century)*   JG
Jonas Lie → see Lie, Jonas

Jonas, Harry Maude *(British artist, 1893-1990)*   WI
Jonas, Henri → see Jonas, Henri Charles

Jonas, Henri Charles   GC
    (Dutch painter, 1878-1944)   GC
    (French artist, 1878-1944)   WC
    Bibl: ▶Vollmer, Künst.-Lex. 20. Jhr.
Jonas, Henri   WC

Jonas, Joan *(American artist, b.1936)*   BA
    Bibl: ▶Contemp. artists; ▶WW Amer. Art, 1978

Jonas, Joseph *(Czech artist, op. 1840-1850)*   WC

Jonas, Karl R. *(German artist, 1822-1888)*   WC

Jonas, Lucien Hector   GC WC
    (French artist, 1880-1947)   WC
    (French painter, b.1880)   GC
    Bibl: ▶Bénézit
Jonathan Fisher → see Fisher, Jonathon
Jonathan Richardson → see Richardson, Jonathan
Joncheer, Jacob de → see Jonckheer, Jacob de

Joncieres, Leonce J.V. de *(French artist, 1871-)*   WC
Joncker → see Juncker, Justus

Jonckheer, Jacob de   BA
    (Dutch artist, op.1668-1684)   WC
    (Dutch painter, printmaker, act. 1662-1672)   BA
    Bibl: ARTE VENETA, XXXII (1978), p.326-332; ▶Thieme-Becker; ▶Wurzbach, NLD Künst.-Lex.
Joncheer, Jacob de   BA
Jonckheer, Jonc-heer or Joncheer, Jacob de   WC
Jonckheer, Jonc-heer or Joncheer, Jacob de → see Jonckheer, Jacob de

Jonczyk, Leon *(Polish painter, printmaker in DEU, 20th c.)*   BA
    Bibl: ▶Intl. dir. arts; LEONARDO XVII/3 (1984), p.176-179
Jones → see Jones, Charles
Jones → see Jones, Thomas

Jones of Bath → see Jones, William IV
Jones, A. Quincy *(American architect, 1913-1979)*   AV
    Bibl: ▶Contemp. archts.; Process: architecture, n.41, Oct. 1983, p.162

Jones, Adrian *(British artist, 1845-1938)*   WC WI

Jones, Alexander Montgomery   WC WI
    (British artist, op.c.1820)   WC
    (British artist, op.circa 1820-)   WI

Jones, Alfred   WC WI
    (British artist, 1819-1900)   WC WI
    (Engraver, Yonkers, NY., 1819-1900)   WI

Jones, Alfred Garth   WI
    (British artist, 1872-circa 1932)   WI
    (British artist, 20th cent.)   WC
    Bibl: ▶Johnson, Brit. artists
Jones, Garth   WC

Jones, Allan L. *(American artist, b.1940)*   BA
    Bibl: New York (NY, USA), New Mus., Outside NY: Ohio (1980)

Jones, Allen   BA WC WI
    (British artist, 1937-)   WC
    (British artist, b.1937)   WI
    (British painter, printmaker, b.1937)   BA
    Bibl: ▶Bénézit; ▶Phaidon 20c. art; Russell, J., POP ART REDEFINED

Jones, Arthur E. *(American architect)*   AV

Jones, Asa *(American chairmaker, b.1790, act.1820)*   BA
    Bibl: Keno, Antiques CXVII (May 1980) 1100-1107

Jones, Ashley *(Australian painter, b.1951)*   BA
    Bibl: Melbourne (AUS), Natl. Gall. Victoria, New realism (1981)

Jones, Barbara   WC WI
    (British artist, 20th cent.)   WC
    (British artist, op.1940-, d.1978)   WI
Barry, Barbara, Mrs.   WI

Jones, Barry Owen *(British artist, op.20th c.)*   WI

Jones, Bayard   WC WI
    (American artist, 20th cent.)   WC
    (American artist, b.1869)   WI

Jones, Ben   BA WI
    (British artist, b.1947)   WI
    (British painter, b.1947)   BA
    Bibl: Bristol (GBR), Arnolfini Gallery, Style in the 70s (1979)

Jones, Bill *(American painter, photographer, b.1946)*   BA
    Bibl: ▶Artists Canada; Santa Barbara (CA, USA), UCSB Art Mus., Invented images (1980)
Jones, Bolton → see Jones, Hugh Bolton
Jones, Bolton (Hugh Bolton) → see Jones, Hugh Bolton
Jones, Bolton Hugh → see Jones, Hugh Bolton

Jones, C.M.   WC WI
    (British artist, 1836-)   WC
    (British artist, b.1836)   WI

Jones, Calvert Richard   WI
    (British artist, 1804-1877)   WI
    (British, 1804-1877, active Italy and Malta (also Rev. George Bridges and Rev. Calvert Richard Jones, active mid 19th century))   JG
Jones, Calvert Richard (Reverend)   JG
Jones, Calvert Richard (Reverend) → see Jones, Calvert Richard

Jones, Champion *(British artist, op. 1878-1901)*   WI

Jones, Charles   BA PR WC WI
    (British artist, 1836-1892)   WC WI
    (British painter, 1836-1892)   BA PR
    Bibl: ▶Bénézit; ▶RILA/BHA; ▶Thieme-Becker; ▶Wood, Victorian ptrs.
Charles Jones   PR
Jones   PR

Jones, Charlotte   WC WI
    (British artist, 1768-1847)   WI
    (British artist, op.1801-m.1847)   WC

Jones, Chester *(British interior designer)*   AV
    Bibl: Maison française, 1989 Oct., no.430, p.124

Jones, Chilion   BA FA
    (1835-1912; Architectural draftsman, Civil engineer, Contractor, Toronto)   FA
    (Canadian architect, 19th c.)   BA
    Bibl: Arthur, Toronto; Jrnl. Canadian art hist., III/1-2 (1976) pp.83-94

Jones, Chris *(British painter, b.1943)*   BA
    Bibl: Kingston-upon-Hull (GBR), Ferens Art Gallery, Drawing in action (1978)

Jones, Christopher   BA WI
    (British artist, b.1958)   WI
    (British painter, b.1958)   BA
    Bibl: ▶Intl. dir. exh. artists, 1982; Nottingham (GBR), Univ.Art Gallery, CHRISTOPHER JONES... (1985)

Jones, Christopher *(American painter, 20th c.)*   BA
    Bibl: Arts Mag. LV (Apr 1981), p.14

Jones, David *(American church architect, 19th cent)*   AV
    Bibl: Journal of the Society of Architectural Historians, 1987 Sept., v.46, no.3, p.215

Jones, David *(Australian sculptor, 20th c.)*   BA
    Bibl: Morse, Studio intl., CXCVI/1002 (Oct. 1983) p.48

Jones, David   **BA**
    (British artist, 1895-1974)   WC WI
    (British painter, printmaker,
      author, 1895-1974)   **BA**
      Bibl: London(GBR), Tate Gallery,
      DAVID JONES, 1981; STUDIO
      INTERNATIONAL, (Dec.1974),
      p.R3; ▶Who was who [GBR], v.7

Jones, David Michael   **WC WI**
Jones, David Michael→see Jones,
    David

Jones, David T. (American architect,
    Washington, D.C)   **AV**
      Bibl: ▶AIA Pro File, 1983

Jones, Derek John (British architect,
    London, son of Leslie Jones, 1933-
    1988)   **AV**
      Bibl: Architects' journal, 1988
      Mar.9, v.187, no.10, p.13; RIBA
      journal, 1988 July, v.95, no.7,
      p.92 [birth date]; ▶RIBA members,
      1987

Jones, Douglas, Mrs., (Vivien)→see
    Gribble, Vivien

Jones, E. Fay (American architect,
    professor at Univ. Of Ark. School
    of Architecture, Fayetteville, Ark,
    1921-)   **AV**
      Bibl: ▶AIA Pro File, 1987-88

Jones, E.H.   **WC WI**
    (British artist, op.1846-)   WI
    (British artist, op.c.1887-1891)   WC
Jones, E.M.   **WC WI**
    (British artist, op.1810)   WC
    (British artist, op.1810-)   WI
Jones, E.T.→see Jones, Edward T.
Jones, Earl (American artist, b.1937)   **WI**
Jones, Edward (British architect,
    practices in Toronto, Ont)   **AV**
      Bibl: Progressive architecture,
      1982 Nov., v.63, no.11, p.36

Jones, Edward   **BA**
    (American architect, d.1980)   BA
    (American restoration architect,
      1909-1980)   **AV**
      Bibl: Antiques magazine, v.123,
      n.5, May 1983, p.1014; NY Times
      obit., 6 Oct 1980

Jones, Edward Vason   **AV**
Jones, Edward T.   **WI**
    (British artist, 19th cent.)   WC
    (British artist, op.1901-1912)   WI
Jones, E.T.   **WC**
Jones, Edward Vason→see Jones,
    Edward

Jones, Elizabeth Burdick (American
    interior designer)   **AV**
      Bibl: House & garden, 1984 Aug.,
      v.156, no.8, p.117

Jones, Elizabeth Emma, Miss
    (Emma)→see Soyer, Elizabeth
    Emma
Jones, Emma→see Soyer, Elizabeth
    Emma

Jones, Fay (American painter,
    b.1936)   **BA**
      Bibl: ▶Intl. dir. exh. artists
Jones, Francis (British landscape
    architect)   **AV**
      Bibl: Building, 1984 Aug.24,
      v.247, no.34, p.34
Jones, Francis C.→see Jones, Francis
    Coates
Jones, Francis Coates   **WI**
    (American artist, 1857-1932)   WC WI
Jones, Francis C.   **WC**
Jones, Fred Cecil→see Jones,
    Frederick Cecil
Jones, Frederick (British artist, op.
    1867-1885)   **WC WI**
Jones, Frederick Cecil   **WI**
    (British artist, 1891-1956)   WC WI
Jones, Fred Cecil   **WC**
Jones, Frederick G.   **WC WI**
    (American artist, 20th cent.)   WC
    (American artist, op.20th c.)   WI
Jones, G. Smetham→see Smetham-
    Jones, G.W.
Jones, G.R. (British artist, 19th
    cent.)   **WC**
Jones, Gareth John (British
    sculptor, 20th c.)   **BA**
      Bibl: Cardiff (GBR), Oriel, The final
      proof (1981); RIBA Jrnl.,
      LXXXVII/3 (Mar. 1980) p.50
Jones, Garry A. (British artist, 20th
    c.)   **BA**
      Bibl: Cardiff (GBR), Oriel, The final
      proof (1981)
Jones, Garth→see Jones, Alfred
    Garth
Jones, Gavin (British artist, op.20th
    c.)   **WI**
Jones, George   **BA PR WC WI**
    (British artist, 1786-1869)   WC WI
    (British painter, 1786-1869)   BA PR
      Bibl: ▶Bénézit; ▶Dict. natl. biog.;
      ▶RILA/BHA
    George Jones   PR
Jones, George (American
    clockmaker, 1784-1867)   **BA**
      Bibl: ▶Britten, Old clocks
Jones, George Kingston (British
    artist, 1865-1948)   **WI**
      Bibl: ▶Houfe, Brit. book illus.
Jones, George Noble (American,
    1811-1876)   **BA**
      Bibl: ANTIQUES, CXVIII, (Sept
      1980), p.476-485
Jones, George Sydney (Australian
    architect, 1865-1927)   **AV**
      Bibl: Architecture Australia, Nov.
      1979, v.68, n.5, p.39-45
Jones, Glyn (British artist, op.1930-
    1934)   **WI**
Jones, Glyn (British painter, b.1936)   **BA**
      Bibl: ARTS MAGAZINE, LIV/2 (Oct
      1979), p.18; Cardiff (GBR), Oriel,
      GLYN JONES...(1981)

Jones, Grahame (British painter,
    b.1950)   **BA**
      Bibl: Bradford (GBR), City Art
      Gallery, Aislabie's gardens (1981)
Jones, H. Mansell   **WC WI**
    (British artist, 19th cent.)   WC
    (British artist, op.19th c.)   WI
Jones, H.F.→see Jones, H.F. & H.J.
Jones, H.F. & H.J.   **WI**
    (British artist, 19th cent.)   WC
    (British artist, op.1867-)   WI
      Bibl: Mitchell
Jones, H.F.   **WC**
Jones, H.J.   **WC**
Jones, H.J.→see Jones, H.F. & H.J.
Jones, Harold (British artist, b.1904)   **WI**
Jones, Harold Henry (American art
    administrator, photographer,
    b.1940)   **BA**
      Bibl: ▶WW Amer. Art, 1978
Jones, Harry Wild (American
    architect or designer)   **AV**
      Bibl: Architecture Minnesota,
      1984 Nov.-Dec., v.10, no.6, p.46
Jones, Helen (Wiz) (American artist,
    b.1926)   **BA**
      Bibl: Saint Louis (MO, USA), Art
      Mus., Wiz Jones (1980)
Jones, Horace   **BA WI**
    (British architect, 1819-1887)   AV BA
    (British artist, 1819-1887)   WC WI
      Bibl: ▶Dict. natl. biog.;
      ▶Thieme-Becker
Jones, Horace, Sir   **AV**
Jones, Sir Horace   **WC**
Jones, Horace, Sir→see Jones, Horace
Jones, Howard E. (American artist,
    op.1879-1886)   **WI**
Jones, Hugh Bolton   **BA PR WI**
    (American artist, 1848-)   WC
    (American artist, 1848-1927)   WI
    (American painter, 1848-1927)   BA PR
      Bibl: ▶Bénézit; ▶Fielding's Amer.
      ptrs.; ▶RILA/BHA; ▶Vollmer,
      Künst.-Lex. 20. Jhr.
    Hugh Bolton Jones   PR
    Jones, Bolton   BA
Jones, Bolton (Hugh Bolton)   **WC**
    Jones, Bolton Hugh   WI
Jones, Hugh G. (Canadian architect)   **AV**
      Bibl: ▶Avery period. idx.
Jones, Hugo   **WC WI**
    (British artist, op.1848)   WC
    (British artist, op.1848-)   WI
Jones, Inigo   **AV BA FA GC WC WI**
    (1573-1652)   AV
    (1573-21.VI.1652; Architect,
      England)   FA
    (British artist, 1573-1652)   WC WI
    (British, 1572-1652)   GC
    (English architect, 1573-1652)   BA
      Bibl: ▶Brit. Mus. cat.; ▶Dict. natl.
      biog.; Harris, J. and G. Higgott,
      Inigo Jones: Complete
      Architectural Drawings, 1989;
      ▶Macmillan encyc. archts., v.2,
      pp.504-513; ▶Thieme-Becker

Jones, Reginald T.   WI
    (British artist, 1857-1904)   WC WI
    Jones, Reginald   WC
Jones, Richard (British artist, 1767-
    1840)   WC WI
Jones, Robert (British artist, b.1953) WI
Jones, Robert Edmond   BA WC WI
    (American artist, 1887-1954) WC WI
    (American scenographer, 1887-
    1954)   BA
    Bibl: ▶WWW Amer.
Jones, Robert Trent (American golf
    course designer, Palo Alto, Calif) AV
    Bibl: Architecture Minnesota,
    1988 July-Aug., v.14, no.4, p.31
Jones, Roderick M.   AV
Jones, Ronald Warren (American
    artist, critic, b.1952)   BA
    Bibl: ▶WW Amer. Art, 1989
Jones, Royston   AV BA
    (British designer)   AV
    (British model maker, b.1948)   BA
    Bibl: Country life, 1988 Mar.24,
    v.182, no.12, p.128; Jill Heberden
    phone call to artist (RILA, GBR)
Jones, Russell (British architect)   AV
    Bibl: Building design, 1987
    Nov.20, no.862, p.16
Jones, Russell O. (American
    landscape architect)   AV
    Bibl: Southern accents, 1986 Jan.-
    Feb., v.9, no.1, p.74
Jones, S.I. (British artist, op.19th c.) WI
Jones, Samuel John Egbert   WC WI
    (British artist, op.1820-1845)   WC
    (British artist, op.1820-1855)   WI
    Bibl: Paviere, Brit. sporting ptrs
Jones, Sir Horace → see Jones, Horace
Jones, Sir Thomas Alfred → see Jones,
    Thomas Alfred
Jones, Stanley (British printmaker,
    20th c.)   BA
    Bibl: ▶Johnson, Brit. artists;
    ▶MoMA libr. cat.
Jones, Sydney Robert Fleming
    (British artist, 1881-1966)   WI
Jones, T.M. (British artist, b.1950)   WI
Jones, T.W. (British artist, op.1832-
    1871)   WC WI
Jones, Theophilus (British architect,
    b.1805, act.1840)   BA
    Bibl: Brayshay, DEVONSHIRE
    ASSOCIATION FOR THE
    ADVANCEMENT OF SCIENCE,
    LITERATURE AND ART. REPORT
    AND TRANSACTIONS, CXIV
    (1982), p.115-131

Jones, Thomas   AV BA PR WC
    (British artist, 1730/1743-1803)   WI
    (British artist, 1730/43-1803)   WC
    (British painter, 1742-1803)   BA PR
    (British painter, b. in Wales, act.
    in Italy, 1776-1783, 1742-
    1803)   AV
    Bibl: Apollo, (Oct 1974) 282-291;
    ▶Bénézit; ▶Dict. natl. biog.; FMR,
    1988 July-Aug., v.7, no.33, p.75;
    ▶RILA/BHA; ▶Thieme-Becker;
    Walpole Society, XXXII, MEMOIRS
    OF THOMAS JONES
    Jones   PR
Jones, Thomas I   WI
    T. Jones   PR
    Thomas Jones   PR
Jones, Thomas → see Jones, Thomas
    Howell
Jones, Thomas Alfred   WI
    (British artist, 1823-1893)   WC WI
    Jones, Sir Thomas Alfred   WC
Jones, Thomas Dow (American
    sculptor, 1811-1881)   BA
    Bibl: ▶WWW Amer.
Jones, Thomas Howell   WI
    (British artist, op.1836-1848)   WC WI
    Jones, Thomas   WC
Jones, Thomas I → see Jones, Thomas
Jones, Thomas II (British artist,
    1774-op.1846)   WI
Jones, Tim (British artist, op.20th c.) WI
Jones, Trevor   WC WI
    (British artist, 20th cent.)   WC
    (British artist, b.1945)   WI
Jones, V.M. → see Jones, Violet
    Madeline
Jones, Violet Madeline   WI
    (British artist, 19th cent.)   WC
    (British artist, op.1916-1929)   WI
    Jones, V.M.   WC
Jones, W.   WC WI
    (British artist, c.1798-1860)   WC
    (British artist, circa 1798-1860)   WI
Jones, W.F.   WC WI
    (British artist, op.1853)   WC
    (British artist, op.1853-)   WI
Jones, Walk (American architect,
    1904-)   AV
    Bibl: ▶Amer. archts. dir., 1970
Jones, Wendell   BA PR
    (American painter, 1899-aft.
    1939)   PR
    (American painter, 20th c.)   BA
    Bibl: ARCHIVES OF AA JOURNAL,
    XXIII/3 (1983), p.36-57; ▶WWW
    Amer. art
Jones, Wendell Cooley   PR
    Wendell Cooley Jones   PR
Jones, Wendell Cooley → see Jones,
    Wendell
Jones, Wesley C. (American
    architect)   AV
    Bibl: Architecture & urbanism,
    1987 Feb., no.197, p.75

Jones, William   AV BA
    (British architect, d.1757)   AV
    (English architect, d.1757)   BA
    Bibl: ▶Colvin, Brit. archts.;
    ▶Thieme-Becker
Jones, William (British artist, op.
    1779-1780)   WC
Jones, William → see Jones, William I
Jones, William → see Jones, William II
Jones, William → see Jones, William IV
Jones, William → see Jones, William V
Jones, William → see Jones, William VI
Jones, William E. (British artist, op.
    1849-1871)   WC WI
Jones, William I   WI
    (British artist, op.1632)   WC
    (British artist, op.1632-)   WI
    Jones, William   WC
Jones, William II   WI
    (British artist, op.1726-)   WI
    (British artist, op.1726-m.1747)   WC
    Jones, William   WC
Jones, William III (British artist, op.
    1744-1747)   WI
    Bibl: ▶Strickland, Irish artists
Jones, William IV   WI
    (British artist, op.1764-1775)   WC WI
    (British artist, op.1764-1777)   WI
    (British painter, act. 1764-1775)   PR
    Bibl: ▶Bénézit; ▶Thieme-Becker
    Jones of Bath   PR
Jones, William   PR WC
Jones, William, (of Bath)   WI
    William Jones   PR
Jones, William V   WI
    (British artist, op.1777)   WC
    (British artist, op.1777-)   WI
    Jones, William   WC
Jones, William VI   WI
    (British artist, op.1832-1836)   WC WI
    Jones, William   WC
Jones, William, (of Bath) → see Jones,
    William IV
Jones, Wynn (British artist, b.1941)   WI
Joney, E. (French artist, 19th cent.)   WC
Jong, Dirk de (Dutch artist, op.1779-
    1785)   WC
Jong, F. M. de (Architect,
    Netherlands (?))   AV
    Bibl: Detail, 1980 Sept.-Oct., no.5,
    p.657
Jong, Frans de   GC WC
    (Dutch artist, op.c.1666-m.1705) WC
    (Dutch painter, b. bef.1666-
    1705)   GC
    Bibl: ▶Thieme-Becker
Jong, Germ de (Dutch painter,
    1886-1967)   GC
    Bibl: ▶Thieme-Becker
Jong, Gerrit Pietersz. de (Dutch
    artist, op.1630-m.1642)   WC

Jong, Hans de *(Dutch ceramist, sculptor, b.1932)*   **BA**
   Bibl: Rotterdam, Museum Boymans, OVERZICHSTENTOONSTELLING CERAMIEK VAN HANS DE JONG, 1976

Jong, Harmen de *(Dutch architect, Leiden)*   **AV**
   Bibl: Abitare, 1985 July-Aug., no. 236, p.72

Jong, Pieter de Josselin de→see Josselin de Jong, Pieter de

jonge Moreels tot Utrecht→see Moreelse, Paulus

Jonge Pier→see Aertsen, Pieter

Jonge van Huysen→see Huysum, Jan van

Jonge Vermander→see Mander, Karel I van

Jonge, Eva Maria Alida de *(Dutch draughtsman, 1872-1951)*   **GC**
   Bibl: ▶Thieme-Becker

Jonge, Jacob de *(Netherlands artist, 17th cent.)*   **WC**

Jonge, Johan Antonie de *(Dutch draughtsman, 1864-1927)*   **GC**
   Bibl: ▶Thieme-Becker

Jonge, Nico de *(Dutch landscape architect)*   **AV**
   Bibl: ▶Libr. of Congr. Name Auth. File

Jonge, R.A. de *(Dutch draughtsman, act.1830-1832)*   **GC**
   Bibl: ▶Scheen, Ned. beeldende kunst.

Jonge, R.H. de *(Netherlands artist, 18th cent.)*   **WC**

Jongelincx, Jacques→see Jonghelinck, Jacques

jongen Mieris→see Mieris, Willem van

jonger Hals→see Hals, Harmen

Jongers, Alphonse   **WC WI**
   (American artist, 1872-)   **WC**
   (American artist, 1872-1945)   **WI**

Jongeward, Jean *(American interior designer, Seattle)*   **AV**
   Bibl: Architectural digest, 1984 Oct., v.41, no.10, p.140

Jongh→see Jongh, Ludolf de

Jongh, Claude de   **BA GC WC**
   (Dutch artist, op.1626-m.1663)   **WC**
   (Dutch painter, act.1628, d.1663)   **BA**
   (Dutch, act.1626-d.1663)   **GC**
   Bibl: Bok, M.J., Hoogsteder-Naumann Mercury; 10(1989) 41-56; Lyon (FRA), Université, Le Rôle de Lyon, p.52; ▶Thieme-Becker; ▶Witt checklist; ▶Wurzbach, NLD Künst.-Lex.

Jongh, Joannes de   **GC WC**
   (Dutch artist, op.1684)   **WC**
   (Dutch draughtsman, act.1684)   **GC**
   Bibl: Getty Photo Study Coll.; ▶Witt checklist

Jongh, Lendertsz. de→see Jongh, Ludolf de

Jongh, Leuff de→see Jongh, Ludolf de

Jongh, Leuven de→see Jongh, Ludolf de

Jongh, Lieve de→see Jongh, Ludolf de

Jongh, Ludolf de   **BA JG PR**
   (Dutch artist, 1616-1679)   **WC**
   (Dutch painter, 1616-1679)   **BA PR**
   (Dutch, 1616-1679)   **GC JG**
   Bibl: ▶Bénézit; ▶RILA/BHA; ▶Thieme-Becker; ▶Witt checklist
   De Jongh   **PR**
   Dejongh, Ludolf   **PR**
   Jongh   **PR**
   Jongh, Lendertsz. de   **BA**
   Jongh, Leuff de   **BA**
   Jongh, Leuven de   **BA**
   Jongh, Lieve de   **BA**

Jongh, Ludolph de   **GC PR**
Jongh, Ludolph or Leuven de   **WC**
   Jonghe   **PR**
   L. De Young   **PR**
   Ludolf de Jongh   **PR**
   Ludolph   **PR**

Jongh, Ludolph de→see Jongh, Ludolf de

Jongh, Ludolph or Leuven de→see Jongh, Ludolf de

Jongh, Martinus Johannes (Tinus) de *(Dutch artist, 1885-1942)*   **WC**

Jongh, Oene Romkes de   **GC WC**
   (Dutch artist, 1812-1896)   **WC**
   (Dutch painter, 1812-1896)   **GC**
   Bibl: ▶Wright, Ptgs. Dutch museums

Jonghe→see Jongh, Ludolf de

Jonghe→see Jonghe, Gustave Léonard de

Jonghe Vroom→see Vroom, Frederik

Jonghe, Clement de *(Dutch publisher, printmaker, act.1640, d.1679)*   **BA**
   Bibl: Francis, MARSYAS XXI (1981-1982), p.13-16; ▶Thieme-Becker; ▶Wurzbach, NLD Künst.-Lex.

Jonghe, Gustave de→see Jonghe, Gustave Léonard de

Jonghe, Gustave Léonard de   **GC PR WC**
   (Belgian artist, 1829-1893)   **WC**
   (Belgian painter, 1829-1893)   **PR**
   (Belgian, 1829-1893)   **GC**
   Bibl: Getty Photo Study Coll. (Ptgs.); ▶Thieme-Becker; ▶Witt checklist
   Gustave Leonard de Jonghe   **PR**
   Jonghe   **PR**
   Jonghe, Gustave de   **PR**
   Jonghes, Gustave de   **GC**

Jonghe, Jan Baptiste de *(Belgian artist, 1785-1844)*   **WC**

Jonghelinck, Jacques *(early Netherlandish sculptor, medalist, 1530-1606)*   **BA**
   Bibl: ▶Forrer, Medallists; ▶Thieme-Becker
   Jongelincx, Jacques   **BA**

Jonghes, Gustave de→see Jonghe, Gustave Léonard de

Jongkind→see Jongkind, Johan Barthold

Jongkind, Jean Berthold→see Jongkind, Johan Barthold

Jongkind, Johan→see Jongkind, Johan Barthold

Jongkind, Johan Barthold   **BA GC PR WC**
   (Dutch artist, 1819-1891)   **WC**
   (Dutch painter, 1819-1891)   **PR**
   (Dutch painter, printmaker, 1819-1891)   **BA**
   (Dutch, 1819-1891)   **GC**
   Bibl: ▶Encyc. world art; ▶RILA/BHA; ▶Thieme-Becker; ▶Witt checklist
   Johan Barthold Jongkind   **PR**
   Jongkind   **PR**
   Jongkind, Jean Berthold   **PR**
   Jongkind, Johan   **PR**
   Jongkind, Johan-Barthold   **PR**
   Jongkind, Johann Barthold   **PR**

Jongkind, Johan-Barthold→see Jongkind, Johan Barthold

Jongkind, Johann Barthold→see Jongkind, Johan Barthold

Joni→see Joni, Icilio Federico

Joni, Federico→see Joni, Icilio Federico

Joni, Icilio Federico   **BA PR**
   (Italian artist, 1866-)   **WC**
   (Italian painter, b. 1866)   **PR**
   (Italian painter, restorer, 1866-1946)   **BA**
   Bibl: ▶Comanducci, Diz.; Frinta, PANTHEON, XL/3 (July-Sept 1981), p.217-224; ▶Thieme-Becker; ▶Witt checklist
   Federico Joni   **PR**
   Joni   **PR**

Joni, Federico   **PR WC**

Jonker, Cornelis de *(Dutch artist, 1761-1830)*   **WC**

Jonnard *(Engraver)*   **WI**

Jonnarel *(Engraver)*   **WI**

Jonnevold→see Jonnevold, Carl Henrik

Jonnevold, Carl→see Jonnevold, Carl Henrik

Jonnevold, Carl Henrik *(American painter, 1856-ca.1930)*   **PR**
   Bibl: ▶Dawdy, Artists Amer. West
   Carl Henrik Jonnevold   **PR**
   Jonnevold   **PR**
   Jonnevold, Carl   **PR**

Jonniaux, Alfred *(Belgian artist, 1882-)*   **WC**

Jonson→see Johnson, Cornelius I

Jonson→see Jonson, Raymond

Jonson or Janssens van Ceulen (Koln), Cornelis, II → see Jonson, Cornelius II

Jonson van Ceulen, Cornelis → see Johnson, Cornelius I

Jonson van Ceulen, Cornelis (II) → see Jonson, Cornelius II

Jonson van Ceulen, Cornelis I → see Johnson, Cornelius I

Jonson van Ceulen, Cornelis II → see Jonson, Cornelius II

Jonson van Ceulen, Cornelis, the elder → see Johnson, Cornelius I

Jonson van Ceulen, Cornelis, the Younger → see Jonson, Cornelius II

Jonson van Ceulen, Cornelius → see Johnson, Cornelius I

Jonson van Ceulen, Cornelius → see Jonson, Cornelius II

Jonson, Cornelis (I) → see Johnson, Cornelius I

Jonson, Cornelis I → see Johnson, Cornelius I

Jonson, Cornelis II → see Jonson, Cornelius II

Jonson, Cornelius → see Johnson, Cornelius I

Jonson, Cornelius I → see Johnson, Cornelius I

Jonson, Cornelius II   **WI**
   (British artist, op.1622-1700)   WI
   (British artist, p.1622-p.1698)   WC
   (British, aft.1622-aft.1698)   GC
   (Dutch painter, aft.1622-aft. 1698)   PR
   Bibl: George Goldner; ▶Thieme-Becker; ▶Waterhouse, Brit. ptrs. 16-17cs.
   Cornelis Johnson (II)   PR
Johnson, Cornelis (II)   **PR**
Jonson or Janssens van Ceulen (Koln), Cornelis, II   **WC**
   Jonson van Ceulen, Cornelis (II)   PR
   Jonson van Ceulen, Cornelis II   GC
   Jonson van Ceulen, Cornelis, the Younger   PR
   Jonson van Ceulen, Cornelius   PR
Jonson, Cornelis II   **GC**

Jonson, Johnson, Jansen or Janssens van Ceulen, (Koln) Cornelis, I → see Johnson, Cornelius I

Jonson, Raymond *(American painter, 1891-1982)*   **BA PR**
   Bibl: Albuquerque (NM, USA), Museum, Transcendental ptg group (1982); ▶Fielding's Amer. ptrs.; ▶RILA/BHA; ▶WW Amer. Art, 1982; ▶Young, Amer. artists
   Jonson   PR
   Raymond Jonson   PR
Jonssens, Cornelius → see Johnson, Cornelius I

Jonsson, Agneta *(Scandinavian artist, 20th cent.)*   **WC**

Jónsson, Ásgrímur → see Ásgrímur Jónsson

Jonsson, Finnur *(Icelandic painter, act. ca.1925)*   **PR**
   Bibl: Yale UAG catalogue
   Finnur Jonsson   PR
Jonsson, Gudmundur → see Gudmundur Jónsson

Jonxis, Jan Lodewijk *(Dutch painter, 1789-1867)*   **GC**
   Bibl: ▶Thieme-Becker

Jonxis, Pieter Hendrik *(Dutch artist, c.1757-1843)*   **WC**

Jonxis, Pieter Hendrik Lodewijk   **GC WC**
   (Dutch artist, 1815-1852)   WC
   (Dutch painter, 1815-1852)   GC
   Bibl: ▶Thieme-Becker

Jonzen, Basil *(British artist, b.1916)*   **WI**

Joors, Eugene *(Belgian artist, 1850-1910)*   **WC**

Joos de Momper → see Momper, Joos de, the younger

Joos de Momper (I) → see Momper, Joos de, the elder

Joos van Cleve → see Cleve, Joos van

Joos van Craesbeeck → see Craesbeeck, Joos van

Joos van Gent → see Joos van Gent (Joos van Wassenhove)

Joos van Gent (Joos van Wassenhove)   **BA GC PR**
   (early Netherlandish painter, act.1460-1475)   BA
   (Netherlandish painter and draughtsman, act. ca.1460-1475)   GC
   (Netherlandish painter, act. 1460-1475)   PR
   (Netherlands artist, op.c.1460-1480)   WC
   Bibl: ▶Encyc. world art; ▶Friedländer, Early Neth. ptg., v.3, pp.43-58; ▶Panofsky, Early Neth. ptg.; ▶RILA/BHA, (var.); ▶Thieme-Becker; ▶Witt checklist; ▶Wurzbach, NLD Künst.-Lex.
   Gand, Juste de   BA
   Gent, Joos van   BA
   Ghent, Justus of   BA
   Giusto da Guanto   BA
   Giusto Guanto   GC
   Jodocus van Gent   BA
Joos van Gent   **GC PR**
   Joos van Wassenhove   BA GC PR
   Josse van Wassenhoven   BA
   Juste de Gand   BA
   Justus of Ghent   BA GC
Justus of Ghent (Joos van Wassenhove or Giusto da Guanto)   **WC**
   marked J. V. Ghert   PR
   Wassenhove   PR
   Wassenhove, Joos van   BA GC
Joos van Wassenhove → see Joos van Gent (Joos van Wassenhove)

Joos, Helmut *(West German architect, Frankfurt a. M)*   **AV**
   Bibl: Architectural record, 1986 Apr., v.174, no.4, p.49

Joosken van Utrecht *(early Netherlandish architect, sculptor, d.1481)*   **BA**
   Bibl: GOYA, 152 (Sept-Oct 1979), p.83-89; ▶Thieme-Becker
   Gusquin   BA
   Jusquin   BA

Joost Cornelisz. Droochsloot → see Droochsloot, Joost Cornelisz.

Joost van Geel → see Geel, Joost van

Joosten, Dirk Jan Hendrik   **GC WC**
   (Dutch artist, 1818-1882)   WC
   (Dutch painter, 1818-1882)   GC
   Bibl: ▶Thieme-Becker

Joostens, Antoon or Antoine L. *(Belgian artist, 1820-1886)*   **WC**

Joostens, Paul *(Belgian painter, 1889-1960)*   **BA**
   Bibl: ▶Bénézit; ▶Vollmer, Künst.-Lex. 20. Jhr.

Joosting, Pieter *(Dutch engineer, 1867-1942)*   **BA**
   Bibl: Boode, A. & P. van Oudheusden, De Hef: Biografie van een Spoorbrug, 34-36

Jope, Anne *(British artist, op.20th c.)*   **WI**

Jopling, Joseph Middleton *(British artist, 1831-1884)*   **WC WI**

Jopling, Louise   **WI**
   (British artist, 1843-1933)   WC WI
   (British artist, 19th cent.)   WC
   Goode, Louise, Miss   WI
Jobling, Louise   **WC**
Jopling, Louise, nee Goode (Mrs. Frank Romer)   **WC**
   Romer, Frank, Mrs., (Louise)   WI
   Rowe, George, Mrs., (Louise)   WI
Jopling, Louise, nee Goode (Mrs. Frank Romer) → see Jopling, Louise

Jorand, Jean Baptiste Joseph   **BA WC**
   (French artist, 1788-1850)   WC
   (French painter, printmaker, 1788-1850)   BA
   Bibl: ▶Bénézit; ▶Thieme-Becker

Jordaan → see Jordaens, Jacob

Jordaan, Denis *(British architect)*   **AV**
   Bibl: Architects' journal, 1984 Nov.7, v.180, no.45, p.64

Jordaan, Leendert Jurriaan *(Dutch caricaturist, illustrator, 1885-1980)*   **BA**
   Bibl: ▶Grote Winkler Prins; Mulder, Met eigen ogen, pp.173-183; ▶Scheen, Ned. beeldende kunst.

Jordaans → see Jordaens, Jacob

Jordaen → see Jordaens, Jacob

Jordaens → see Jordaens, Hans (I)

Jordaens → see Jordaens, Hans (IV)

Jordaens → see Jordaens, Jacob

Jordaens of Antwerp → see Jordaens, Jacob

Jordaens or Joerdaens, Hans, I→see
Jordaens, Hans (I)
Jordaens, A. *(Netherlands artist, op.*
1714)   **WC**
Jordaens, G.→see Jordaens, Jacob
Jordaens, Hans (I)   **PR**
   (Dutch painter, ca.1572-1630)   **PR**
   (Flemish artist, op.1572-m.1630) **WC**
   (Flemish, d.1630)   **GC**
     Bibl: ▶Thieme-Becker
   Hans Jordaens (I)   **PR**
   Jordaens   **PR**
   Jordaens or Joerdaens, Hans, I **WC**
   Jordaens, Hans I   **GC**
Jordaens, Hans (IV)   **PR**
   (Dutch artist, 1616-1680)   **WC**
   (Dutch painter, 1616-1680)   **PR**
   (Dutch, 1616-1680)   **GC**
     Bibl: ▶Thieme-Becker;
     Truchesessian Gallery, May 14,
     1804, lot 382
   Hans Jordaens (IV)   **PR**
   Jan Jordaens   **PR**
   Jan. Jordaens   **PR**
   Jordaens   **PR**
   Jordaens, Hans IV   **GC**
   Jordaens, Hans, IV (Polepel or
   Brypotlepel)   **WC**
Jordaens, Hans I→see Jordaens, Hans
(I)
Jordaens, Hans III   **GC**
   (Flemish artist, op.1619-m.1643) **WC**
   (Flemish, d.1643)   **GC**
     Bibl: ▶Thieme-Becker
   Jordaens, Hans, III   **WC**
Jordaens, Hans IV→see Jordaens,
Hans (IV)
Jordaens, Hans, III→see Jordaens,
Hans III
Jordaens, Hans, IV (Polepel or
Brypotlepel)→see Jordaens, Hans
(IV)
Jordaens, J.→see Jordaens, Jacob

Jordaens, Jacob   **BA GC JG PR**
   (Flemish artist, 1593-1678)   **WC WI**
   (Flemish painter, 1593-1678)   **BA PR**
   (Flemish, 1593-1678)   **GC JG**
     Bibl: George Goldner; ▶RILA/BHA;
     ▶Thieme-Becker; ▶Weilbach,
     Kunst.leks.
   after Jordaens   **PR**
   G. Jordaens   **PR**
   Giordano d'Olanda   **PR**
   J. Jordaen   **PR**
   J. Jordaens   **PR**
   J. Jordeans   **PR**
   Jac Jordaens   **PR**
   Jac. Jordaens   **PR**
   Jac. Jordeans   **PR**
   Jacob Jordaens   **PR**
   Jacques Jordaens   **PR**
   Jacques Jordans   **PR**
   Jaques Jordans   **PR**
   Joerdaens   **PR**
   Jordaan   **PR**
   Jordaans   **PR**
   Jordaen   **PR**
   Jordaens   **PR**
   Jordaens of Antwerp   **PR**
   Jordaens, G.   **PR**
   Jordaens, J.   **PR**
   Jordaens, Jacob I   **WI**
   Jordaens, Jacob, I   **WC**
   Jordaens, Jakob   **PR**
   Jordains   **PR**
   Jordanes   **PR**
   Jordans   **PR**
   Jordeanes   **PR**
   Jordeans   **PR**
   Jourdaens   **PR**
   Jourdains   **PR**
   Jourdano   **PR**
   P. Jordaens   **PR**
Jordaens, Jacob I→see Jordaens,
Jacob
Jordaens, Jacob, I→see Jordaens,
Jacob
Jordaens, Jakob→see Jordaens, Jacob
Jordaens, L. *(Netherlands artist, op.*
c.1660)   **WC**
Jordaens, Simon I   **GC**
   (Dutch artist, c.1590-c.1640)   **WC**
   (Flemish painter, ca.1590-1640)   **GC**
     Bibl: ▶Thieme-Becker
   Jordaens, Simon, I   **WC**
Jordaens, Simon, I→see Jordaens,
Simon I
Jordains→see Jordaens, Jacob
Jordan→see Giordano, Luca
Jordan Maalare *(Swedish altarpiece*
sculptor)   **AV**
     Bibl: Antikvariskt arkiv, 1985,
     v.72, p.1
   Jordan Painter   **AV**
Jordan Painter→see Jordan Maalare
Jordan, Carl *(German artist, 1826-*
1907)   **WC**
Jordan, Carl *(German artist, 1863-)* **WC**

Jordan, Charles *(American artist,*
op.19th c.)   **WI**
Jordan, Esteban *(Spanish artist,*
c.1543-1600)   **WC**
Jordan, Greg *(American interior*
designer, New York City)   **AV**
     Bibl: NYC phone bk., 1988
Jordan, Johanna *(American*
sculptor, 20th c.)   **BA**
     Bibl: Jordan, J., LEONARDO, 16/1
     (Winter 1983), p.43-45
Jordan, L. *(Spanish artist, 18th*
cent.)   **WC**
Jordan, Robert *(American painter,*
educator, b.1925)   **BA**
     Bibl: ▶WW Amer. Art
Jordan, Rudolf   **BA WC**
   (German artist, 1810-1887)   **WC**
   (German painter, 1810-1887)   **BA**
     Bibl: ▶Bénézit; ▶Thieme-Becker
Jordan, Samuel   **WC WI**
   (American artist, b.1803)   **WI**
   (American artist, op.1831)   **WC**
Jordanes→see Jordaens, Jacob
Jordanić, Petar *(Dalmatian painter,*
act.1469-1504)   **BA**
     Bibl: Branca, Umanesimo Istria,
     pp.225-229
Jordano→see Giordano, Luca
Jordans→see Jordaens, Jacob
Jordanus Hoorn→see Hoorn,
Jordanus
Jorde, Lars *(Norwegian artist,*
1865-)   **WC**
Jordeanes→see Jordaens, Jacob
Jordeans→see Jordaens, Jacob
Jorden, Noel *(British architect,*
Emsworth)   **AV**
     Bibl: ▶RIBA members, 1983
Jordens, Antoni *(Dutch artist, 1664-*
1715)   **WC**
Jordens, Daniël J. R. *(Dutch painter,*
1855-1939)   **BA**
     Bibl: ▶Busse, Maler u. Bildhauer
     19. Jahr.; ▶Scheen, Ned.
     beeldende kunst.
Jordi, Ernst *(Swiss sculptor, b.1945)* **BA**
     Bibl: ▶Lex. zeitgen. Schweiz.
     Künstler
Jordi, Eugen *(Swiss painter,*
printmaker, sculptor, 1894-1983)   **BA**
     Bibl: ▶Künst.-Lex. Schweiz 20.
     Jahrh.; ▶Lex. zeitgen. Schweiz.
     Künstler
Jorel, Colin *(French artist, op.1855)* **WC**
Joret, Guillaume *(French scribe,*
d.1518)   **BA**
     Bibl: Spencer, E., "Dom Louis de
     Busco's psalter",in GATHERINGS
     IN HONOR OF D.E. MINER (1974),
     p.231
Jörg Breu (the elder)→see Breu, Jörg,
the elder
Jorg Breu (the younger)→see Breu,
Jörg, the younger
Jorg P. Anders (Berlin)→see Anders,
Jörg P.

Jorg, Charles *(Swiss artist, 1933-)*   **WC**
Jörg, Hans *(German painter, act. 1760)*   **BA**
  Bibl: Reclams Bayern; Vollmer, Ars bavarica, 15-16 (1980) pp.97-104
Jorge Afonso→see Afonso, Jorge
Jorge del Castel Franco→see Giorgione (Giorgio da Castelfranco)
Jorge Ingles→see Inglés, Jorge
Jorge Manuel Theotocopuli→see Theotocopuli, Jorge Manuel
Jorgensen→see Jorgensen, Christian
Jørgensen, Børge *(Danish sculptor, b.1926)*   **BA**
  Bibl: København (DNK), Kastrupgårdsamlingen, Børge Jørgensen... (1981); ▸MoMA libr. cat.
Jorgensen, Chris→see Jorgensen, Christian
Jorgensen, Christian *(American painter, 1860-1935)*   **PR**
  Bibl: ▸WWW Amer. art
  Christian Jorgensen   PR
  Jorgensen   PR
  Jorgensen, Chris   PR
Jørgensen, Erling *(Danish painter, printmaker, 1905-1977)*   **BA**
  Bibl: ▸Nørregård-Nielsen, Dansk kunst; Schade, V., COLLAGE OM EN KUNSTNER..., 1985
Jørgensen, Frode *(Danish architect)*   **AV**
  Bibl: ▸Danske Arkitekters Landsforbund, 1984-85
Jorgensen, Johan *(Danish artist, op. 1640)*   **WC**
Jørgensen, Karl Aksel *(Danish painter, 1883-1957)*   **BA**
  Bibl: Fuente Pedersen, Cras, 49 (1987) pp.12-27; ▸Nørregård-Nielsen, Dansk kunst; ▸Thieme-Becker; ▸Vollmer, Künst.-Lex. 20. Jhr.; ▸Weilbach, Kunst.leks.
Jørgensen, Preben *(Danish painter, printmaker, b.1933)*   **BA**
  Bibl: ▸Nørregård-Nielsen, Dansk kunst; Steen, A., TRIUMPH OF LIFE: THE PAINTER AND THE MAN. ..,1983
Jorgensen, Robert R. *(American craftsman, b.1944)*   **BA**
  Bibl: Colorado Springs (CO, USA), Fine Arts Ctr., Woodworking in the Rockies (1982)
Jorgensen, Sven *(Norwegian artist, 1861-)*   **WC**
Jørgensen, Vetle *(Danish architect in Nairobi, Kenya, 1933-)*   **AV**
  Bibl: ▸Danske Arkitekters Landsforbund, 1984-85
Jorgenson, N.   **WC WI**
  (American artist, op.1894)   WC
  (American artist, op.1894-)   WI
Jorger, Johann Septimius Graf von *(German artist, 1594-1662)*   **WC**

Jorhan, Christian I *(German sculptor, 1727-1804)*   **BA**
  Bibl: ▸Brockhaus Enzyk.; ▸Thieme-Becker
Joris tot Franckfort [Unidentified] *(Unknown painter)*   **PR**
  Bibl: 1608 Morin inventory
Joris van der Hagen→see Hagen, Joris van der
Joris van Schooten→see Schooten, Joris van
Joris van Son→see Son, Joris van
Joris, David   **BA GC**
  (early Netherlandish glass painter, printmaker, author, ca.1501-1556)   BA
  (Flanders draughtsman, 1501-1556)   GC
  (Netherlands artist, 1501-1556)   WC
  Bibl: ▸Bénézit; ▸Natl. union cat., pre-1956; ▸RILA/BHA; ▸Thieme-Becker; Valentiner, BULLETIN OF THE DETROIT INSTITUTE OF ART, XIV (1934), p.3-5; Wayment, ARCHAEOLOGIA, CVII (1982), p. 141-152; ▸Wurzbach, NLD Künst.-Lex.
  Bruck, Johan von   BA
  Jorisz, Jan (called David)   GC
Jorisz, Jan or David (Jan van Brugge or Jan van Broek)   **WC**
Jorisz., Jan   **GC**
Joris, Pietro→see Joris, Pio
Joris, Pio   **GC PR WC**
  (Italian artist, 1843-1921)   WC
  (Italian painter, 1843-1921)   PR
  (Italian, 1843-1921)   GC
  Bibl: ▸Thieme-Becker; ▸Witt checklist
  Joris, Pietro   PR
  Pio Joris   PR
Jorisz, Jan (called David)→see Joris, David
Jorisz, Jan or David (Jan van Brugge or Jan van Broek)→see Joris, David
Jorisz., Jan→see Joris, David
Jorjion de Castelfranco→see Giorgione (Giorgio da Castelfranco)
Jorn, Asger→see Jorn, Asger Oluf
Jorn, Asger Oluf   **BA**
  (Danish painter, printmaker, ceramist, 1914-1973)   BA
  (Scandinavian artist, 1914-)   WC
  Bibl: ▸MoMA libr. cat.; ▸Nørregård-Nielsen, Dansk kunst; ▸Vollmer, Künst.-Lex. 20. Jhr.; ▸Weilbach, Kunst.leks.
Jorn, Asger   **WC**
Joron, Maurice *(French artist, 1883-)*   **WC**
Jorres, Carl *(German artist, 1870-1947)*   **WC**
Jörres, Rolf *(German sculptor, b.1933)*   **BA**
  Bibl: Krefeld (DEU), Museum Haus Lange, ROLF JÖRRES, 1976; ▸WW Arts DEU

Jos Boydell→see Boydell, Josiah
Jos. van Winghen→see Winghe, Jodocus van
Joscelyn, Nathaniel→see Jocelyn, Nathaniel
Jose Antolinez→see Antolínez, José
José Aparicio→see Aparicio, José
Jose Benlliure y Gil→see Benlliure y Gil, José
Jose Clemente Orozco→see Orozco, José Clemente
Josè De Rivera→see De Rivera, José
Jose del Castillo→see Castillo, José del
Jose Garcia y Ramos→see García y Ramos, José
Jose Gutierrez Solana→see Gutiérrez Solana, José
Jose Jimenes Aranda→see Jiménez Aranda, José
Jose Maria Jardines→see Jardines, José Maria
Jose Maria Sert Y Badia→see Sert y Badiá, José Mariá
Jose Maria Velasco→see Velasco, José Maria
Jose Moya Del Pino→see Moya del Pino, Jose
Jose Paez→see Paez, José
Jose Villegas y Cordero→see Villegas y Cordero, Jose
Jose Weiss→see Weiss, José
Josef Albers→see Albers, Josef
Josef Chelmonski→see Chelmonski, Josef
Josef Eberz→see Eberz, Josef
Josef Franz Adolph→see Adolph, Josef Franz
Josef Georg Edlinger→see Edlinger, Josef Georg von
Josef Heintz (the elder)→see Heintz, Joseph, the elder
Josef Kreutzinger→see Kreutzinger, Josef
Josef Munsch→see Munsch, Josef
Josef van Aken→see Aken, Joseph van
Josef Wenglein→see Wenglein, Josef
Joseph→see Baumhauer, Joseph
Joseph→see Joseph, George Francis
Joseph (Joseph Baumhauer)→see Baumhauer, Joseph
Joseph (Joseph Ettedgui)→see Ettedgui, Joseph
Joseph Albrier→see Albrier, Joseph
Joseph Alexander Ames→see Ames, Joseph Alexander
Joseph Amadeus Fleck→see Fleck, Joseph A.
Joseph Antolinez→see Antolínez, José
Joseph Badger→see Badger, Joseph
Joseph Bail→see Bail, Claude Joseph
Joseph Barber→see Barber, Joseph
Joseph Barney→see Barney, Joseph I

Joseph Bartholomew Kidd→see Kidd, Joseph Bartholomew

Joseph Beaume→see Beaume, Joseph

Joseph Blackburn→see Blackburn, Joseph

Joseph Bonomi (I)→see Bonomi, Joseph, the elder

Joseph Boze→see Boze, Joseph

Joseph Cesari→see Cesari, Giuseppe (Cavalier d'Arpino)

Joseph Charles Barrow→see Barrow, Joseph Charles

Joseph Christiaan Nicolie→see Nicolie, Joseph Christiaan

Joseph Christophe→see Christophe, Joseph

Joseph Clarendon Smith→see Smith, Joseph Clarendon

Joseph Cooper→see Cooper, Joseph

Joseph D. Strong→see Strong, Joseph D.

Joseph De Martini→see Martini, Joseph de

Joseph de Rivera→see Ribera, Jusepe de (lo Spagnoletto)

Joseph Decker→see Decker, Joseph

Joseph Ducreux→see Ducreux, Joseph

Joseph Farington→see Farington, Joseph

Joseph fils→see Baumhauer, Gaspard-Joseph

Joseph Fisher→see Fisher, Joseph

Joseph Floch→see Floch, Joseph

Joseph Florentin Leon Bonnat→see Bonnat, Léon

Joseph Florentin Lïon Bonnat→see Bonnat, Léon

Joseph Foxcroft Cole→see Cole, Joseph Foxcroft

Joseph Francois Millet→see Millet, Joseph François

Joseph Francois Parrocel→see Parrocel, Joseph

Joseph Frans Nollekens→see Nollekens, Joseph Frans

Joseph Fratel (I)→see Fratrel, Joseph (I)

Joseph Gall→see Gall, Joseph

Joseph Goodhue Chandler→see Chandler, Joseph Goodhue

Joseph Goupy→see Goupy, Joseph

Joseph Greenbaum→see Greenbaum, Joseph

Joseph Greenleaf Cole→see Cole, Joseph Greenleaf

Joseph H. Greenwood→see Greenwood, Joseph H.

Joseph H. Vignoles Fisher→see Fisher, Vignoles

Joseph Harrington→see Harrington, Joseph

Joseph Heintz (the elder)→see Heintz, Joseph, the elder

Joseph Heintz (the younger)→see Heintz, Joseph, the younger

Joseph Henry Sharp→see Sharp, Joseph Henry

Joseph Highmore→see Highmore, Joseph

Joseph Ibn Hayyim→see Ibn Hayyim, Joseph

Joseph Jefferson→see Jefferson, Joseph

Joseph Lacasse→see Lacasse, Joseph

Joseph Lane Hancock→see Hancock, Joseph Lane

Joseph Lee→see Lee, Joseph II

Joseph Leonardy→see Leonardy, Joseph [Unidentified]

Joseph Lindon Smith→see Smith, Joseph Lindon

Joseph Mallord William Turner→see Turner, Joseph Mallord William

Joseph Marie Vien→see Vien, Joseph Marie

Joseph Marsh Sheridan→see Sheridan, Joseph Marsh

Joseph napolitan→see Piscopo, Giuseppe

Joseph Nicolas Robert-Fleury→see Robert-Fleury, Joseph Nicolas

Joseph Peacock→see Peacock, Joseph

Joseph Pollet→see Pollet, Joseph

Joseph Porta→see Porta, Giuseppe (Giuseppe Salviati)

Joseph Powell→see Powell, Joseph

Joseph Raphael→see Raphael, Joseph

Joseph Ribera→see Ribera, Jusepe de (lo Spagnoletto)

Joseph Ribera, lo Spagnoletto→see Ribera, Jusepe de (lo Spagnoletto)

Joseph Riuera→see Ribera, Jusepe de (lo Spagnoletto)

Joseph Rodefer De Camp→see De Camp, Joseph Rodefer

Joseph Roos (I)→see Roos, Joseph (I)

Joseph Ropes→see Ropes, Joseph

Joseph Rusling Meeker→see Meeker, Joseph Rusling

Joseph Scheubel (II)→see Scheubel, Joseph (II)

Joseph Schex→see Schex, Joseph

Joseph Severn→see Severn, Joseph

Joseph Siffred Duplessis→see Duplessis, Joseph Siffred

Joseph Stella→see Stella, Joseph

Joseph Stewart→see Stewart, Joseph

Joseph Thors→see Thors, Joseph

Joseph Urbain Melin→see Melin, Joseph Urbain

Joseph van Aken→see Aken, Joseph van

Joseph van Bree→see Bree, Joseph van

Joseph Vavak→see Vavak, Joseph

Joseph Vernet→see Vernet, Joseph

Joseph Vivien→see Vivien, Joseph

Joseph W. Gies→see Gies, Joseph W.

Joseph Wright→see Wright, Joseph

Joseph Wright→see Wright, Joseph (Wright of Derby)

Joseph Wright of Derby→see Wright, Joseph (Wright of Derby)

Joseph Wright, of Derby→see Wright, Joseph (Wright of Derby)

Joseph Zahradniczek→see Zahradniczek, Joseph

Joseph Zaritzky→see Zaritzky, Joseph

Joseph, Amy (British artist, 1876-1961)   WI

Joseph, Douglas (British artist, op. circa 1921-)   WI

Joseph, George→see Joseph, George Francis

Joseph, George Francis   PR WC WI
    (British artist, 1764-1846)   WC WI
    (British painter, 1764-1846)   PR
    Bibl: Mackenzie; ▶Thieme-Becker
    George Francis Joseph   PR
    Joseph   PR
    Joseph, George   PR

Joseph, Hope (British artist, op. 1905-1936)   WI

Joseph, Jane   BA WI
    (British artist, b.1942)   WI
    (British painter, b.1942)   BA
    Bibl: Colchester (GBR), Minories, JANE JOSEPH:DRAWINGS, 1982; ▶Intl. dir. exh. artists

Joseph, Jasmin (Haitian artist, 1923-)   WC

Joseph, Lily Delissa   BA WI
    (British artist, 1864-1940)   WI
    (British painter, 1864-1940)   BA
    Bibl: ▶Johnson, Brit. artists; ▶Vollmer, Künst.-Lex. 20. Jhr.; WW Amer., 1934
    Solomon, Lily, Miss   WI

Joseph, Mary, Miss→see Cohen, Mary

Joseph, Peter   BA WC WI
    (British artist, 1929-)   WC
    (British artist, b.1929)   WI
    (British painter, b.1929)   BA
    Bibl: Chicago (IL,USA),Mus. of Contemporary Art, PETER JOSEPH (1983); ▶Dolman, Contemp. Brit. artists; Lucie Smith

Joseph, Richard   WC WI
    (American artist, 20th cent.)   WC
    (American artist, op.1968-)   WI

Joseph, Samuel (British sculptor, 1791-1850)   BA
    Bibl: COUNTRY LIFE, CLVII 4069 (June 26 1975), p.1692; ▶Dict. natl. biog.; ▶Thieme-Becker

Joseph, Sylvan (American architect, New York)   AV
    Bibl: Builder, 1984 Nov., v.7, no.11, p.89

Josephine Klippart→see Klippart, Josephine

Josephson, Ellen *(Swedish, 20th c.)* **BA**
  Bibl: KONSTHISTORISK TIDSKRIFT, LII/2 (1983), p.75-82

Josephson, Ernst **BA GC WC**
  (Swedish artist, 1851-1906) WC
  (Swedish painter, 1851-1906) BA
  (Swedish, 1851-1906) GC
  Bibl: ▶Bénézit; ▶Thieme-Becker; ▶Witt checklist

Josephson, Kenneth **BA JG**
  (American photographer, b.1932) BA
  (American, 1932-) JG
  Bibl: Providence (RI, USA), RISD, Spaces (1978)

Josephson, Ludvig *(Swedish, act. 1893)* **BA**
  Bibl: Abel, Sandblom coll.; Stockholm (SWE), National Museum, ERNST JOSEPHSON (1972)

Josephus Laurentius Dyckmans → see Dyckmans, Josephus Laurentius

Josey, Richard *(Engraver, 1841-1906)* **WI**

Joshua Bryant → see Bryant, Joshua
Joshua Reynolds → see Reynolds, Joshua
Joshua Shaw → see Shaw, Joshua, (of Bath)
Joshua Wallis → see Wallis, Joshua

Josi, Charles **WC WI**
  (British artist, op.1827-1851) WC
  (British artist, op.1827-1852) WI

Josiah Boydell → see Boydell, Josiah
Josias Boydell → see Boydell, Josiah

Josic, Alexis *(French architect, 1921-)* **AV**
  Bibl: ▶Contemp. archts.

Josic, Douchanka *(French architect, Paris)* **AV**
  Bibl: Architecture intérieure cree, 1986 Feb.-Mar., no.210, p.62

Jospey, Maxwell *(American, 20th c.)* **BA**
  Bibl: Mattison, R.S., ART INTERNATIONAL, XXV/9-10 (Nov-Dec 1982), p.8

Joss, Heinz *(Swiss architect, Zurich)* **AV**
  Bibl: ▶Schweiz. Ingen. u. Archit., 1984-1985

Josse Lieferinxe → see Lieferinxe, Josse
Josse van Wassenhoven → see Joos van Gent (Joos van Wassenhove)

Josse, C. *(German artist, 19th cent.)* **WC**

Josseau, Didier *(French architect)* **AV**
  Bibl: Architecture d'aujourd'hui, 1983 Sept., no.228, p.xv

Josselin de Jong, Pieter de **BA GC WC**
  (Dutch artist, 1861-1906) WC
  (Dutch painter and draughtsman, 1861-1906) GC
  (Dutch painter, printmaker, 1861-1906) BA
  Bibl: ▶Scheen, Ned. beeldende kunst.; ▶Thieme-Becker; ▶Witt checklist

  Jong, Pieter de Josselin de BA

Josseph de Rivera → see Ribera, Jusepe de (lo Spagnoletto)

Jossot, Henri-Gustave *(French artist, 1866-)* **WC**

[Jost] Cossiau → see Cossiau, Jan Joost van

Jost, Joseph *(German artist, 1875-)* **WC**

Jost, Wilhelm *(West German architect, fl. 1908)* **AV**
  Bibl: Architektur, Innenarchitektur, Technischer Ausbau, 1987 Sept., v.95, no.9, p.28

Jouanin, Auguste Adrien *(French artist, 1806-1887)* **WC**

Jouanon, Mlle. *(French artist, op. 1777)* **WC**

Jouas, Charles *(French artist, 20th cent.)* **WC**

Joubert l'aîné → see Joubert, Gilles

Joubert, Bernard *(French painter, b.1946)* **BA**
  Bibl: ▶ARTbibl. mod., 1975; ▶Bénézit; Sainte- Etienne (FRA), Musée d'art et d'industrie, BERNARD JOUBERT

Joubert, Daniel-Jean *(French silversmith, master 1745)* **GC**
  Bibl: ▶Nocq, Poinçon de Paris

Joubert, François *(French silversmith, master 1749)* **GC**
  Bibl: ▶Mabille, Orfèv. fran.

Joubert, Gilles **BA GC JG**
  (French cabinetmaker, 1689-1775) BA
  (French ébéniste, 1689-1775,) GC
  (French, 1689-1775, royal cabinetmaker 1763-1775) JG
  Bibl: ▶Boger, World pott. & porc.; ▶Penguin dec. arts; ▶Salverte, Ébénistes 18e s.; ▶Vial, Artistes décorateurs; Watson, Wallace Coll.

  Joubert l'aîné GC

Joubert, Leon *(French artist, op. 1883)* **WC**

Joubert, Mme. → see Drölling, Louise Adéone

Joubin, Georges *(French artist, 20th cent.)* **WC**

Jouderville → see Joudreville, Isaac de
Jouderville, Isaac de → see Joudreville, Isaac de

Joudreville, Isaac de **BA**
  (Dutch artist, c.1613-c.1645/8) WC
  (Dutch painter, 1613-1648) BA
  (Dutch painter, ca.1612-ca. 1645) PR
  (Dutch, 1613-1645/48) GC
  Bibl: ▶Bernt, Neth. ptrs. 17c.; ▶RILA/BHA; Sumowski, Gemälde Rembrandt-Schüler, II, 1434-1435; ▶Thieme-Becker; ▶Witt checklist; ▶Wurzbach, NLD Künst.-Lex.

  Isaac de Jouderville PR
  Jouderville PR

Jouderville, Isaac de **BA GC PR WC**
  Souderville PR

Jouett, Matthew Harris **BA WC WI**
  (American artist, 1787-1827) WI
  (American artist, 1788-1827) WC
  (American painter, 1787/88-1827) BA
  Bibl: ▶Dict. Amer. biog.; ▶Encyc. Britannica; ▶Fielding's Amer. ptrs.; ▶Groce, Artists Amer.; ▶Havlice, Idx. art. bio.; ▶Young, Amer. artists

Jouffroy, François *(French sculptor, 1806-1882)* **BA GC**
  Bibl: ▶Bénézit; ▶Encyc. world art; ▶Lami, Sculp. fran. 19e s.; ▶Mackay, Western sculp. bronze; ▶RILA/BHA

Jouffroy, Pierre **GC WC**
  (French artist, op.1743-1769) WC
  (French, act.1743-1769) GC
  Bibl: ▶Witt checklist

Jouillin, Amedee → see Joullin, Amédée

Joukovski, Stanislav Joulianovitch → see Žukovskij, Stanislav Julianovič

Joukovsky, Stanislav Joulianovitch → see Žukovskij, Stanislav Julianovič

Joullain, Francois *(French artist, 1697-1778)* **WC**

Joullain, Nicolas René → see Jollain, Nicolas René

Joullin → see Joullin, Amédée

Joullin, Amédée *(American painter, 1862-1917)* **PR**
  Bibl: ▶WWW Amer. art
  Amedee Joullin PR
  Jouillin, Amedee PR
  Joullin PR

Joumard *(Engraver)* **WI**

Jouravleff or Jouravlioff, Firs Sergeievitch *(Russian artist, 1836-1901)* **WC**
  Shurawljow, Firs Sergejevich WC

Jourd'Heuil, Jourdeville or Jourdheull *(French artist, 1759-1781)* **WC**

Jourda, Françoise-Hélène *(French architect)* **AV**
  Bibl: Architecture d'aujourd'hui, 1985 Feb., no.237, p.XX

Juan Hispalense→see Hispalense, Juan

Juan Hispalense or Hispalensis→see Hispalense, Juan

Juan II de Flandes *(Spanish artist, 16th cent.)* **WC**

Juan Labrador→see Labrador, Juan

Juan Laurent (Madrid)→see Laurent, Juan

Juan Miranda Carreno→see Carreño de Miranda, Juan

Juan Nunez→see Nunez, Juan

Juan Pantoja de la Cruz→see Pantoja de la Cruz, Juan

Juan Reco→see Reco, Juan [Unidentified]

Juan Rexach→see Rexach, Juan

Juan Rodriguez de Solis→see Solis, Juan Rodriguez de

Juan Rodriguez Juares→see Juares, Juan Rodriguez

Juan Sanchez Cotan→see Sánchez Cotán, Juan

Juan Simon Gutierrez→see Gutierrez, Juan Simón

Juan van der Hamen y León→see Hamen y León, Juan van der

Juan Zurbaran→see Zurbarán, Juan de

Juanes, Juan de→see Juanes, Juan de (Vicente Juan Macip)

Juanes, Juan de (Vicente Juan Macip) **BA**
  (Spanish artist, 1523(?)-1579) WC
  (Spanish painter, ca.1523-1579) **BA PR**
  (Spanish, ca.1500-1579) GC
  Bibl: ▶Aldana Fernández, Artistas valencianos; Angulo, Spanish drawings; ▶Ceán Bermúdez, Bellas artes ESP; ▶Encic. univ. ilus.; ▶Encyc. world art; George Goldner; ▶Kubler, Art & arch. ESP & PRT; ▶RILA/BHA; ▶Thieme-Becker; ▶Witt checklist
  Jean Joannès PR
  Joanes, Joan de BA
  Joannes PR
  Juan de Juanes BA GC PR
  Juanes, Juan de PR

Juanes, Juan de (Vincente Juan Macip) **PR**
  Maçip, Vicente Juan BA
  Masip, Vicent Juan BA

Masip, Vicente Juan (Juan de Juanes) **GC**

Masip, Vicente Juan, I (Juan de Juanes) **WC**
  Vincente Juan Macip PR
  Vincente Juan Masip Navarro PR

Juanes, Juan de (Vicente Juan Macip) →see Juanes, Juan de (Vicente Juan Macip)

Juanes, Juan Vicente→see Macip, Vicente II

Juanpere Miret, José *(Spanish architect, Barcelona)* **AV**
  Bibl: ▶Guia secreta Hermandad, 1984

Juara, Filippo→see Juvara, Filippo

Juares, Juan Rodriguez **BA PR**
  (Mexican painter, 18th c.) BA
  (Mexican painter, act. 18th century) PR
  (Spanish artist, 1676-1728) WC
  Bibl: ▶Bénézit; España entre el Mediterraneo y el Atlántico (1973); ▶RILA/BHA; ▶Thieme-Becker
  Juan Rodriguez Juares PR

Juarez or Xuarez, Juan Rodriguez **WC**
  Juarez, Juan Rodriguez PR
  Xuares, Juan Rodriguez BA

Juarez or Xuarez, Jose *(Spanish artist, op.1642-1698)* **WC**

Juarez or Xuarez, Juan Rodriguez→see Juares, Juan Rodriguez

Juarez, Agustin *(Spanish architect)* **AV**
  Bibl: El croquis, 1986 Jan., v.5, no.23, p.40

Juarez, Guadalupe *(Spanish artist, 19th cent.)* **WC**

Juarez, Juan Rodriquez→see Juares, Juan Rodriguez

Juarez, Luis *(Spanish artist, op.1610-1630)* **WC**

Juárez, Nicolás Rodríguez **BA WC**
  (Mexican artist, 1667-1734) WC
  (Mexican painter, 1667-1734) BA
  Bibl: Corpus Christi (TX, USA), Art Mus. So.Texas, Spain & new Spain (1979); ▶Thieme-Becker

Juarez, Roberto **BA WI**
  (American artist, b.1952) WI
  (American painter, b.1952.) BA
  Bibl: New York (NY, USA), Whitney Mus., Biennial (1987); ▶WW Amer. Art, 1986

Juchem Wtdewael→see Wtewael, Joachim Antonisz.

Jüchser, Hans *(German painter, printmaker, 1894-1977)* **BA**
  Bibl: DRESDENER KUNSTBLATTER, XXII/3 (1978); ▶Vollmer, Künst.-Lex. 20. Jhr.

Judd, David *(American cabinetmaker, act.1799-1827)* **BA**
  Bibl: Keno, Antiques CXVII (May 1980) 1100-1107

Judd, Don→see Judd, Donald

Judd, Donald **AV BA GC WI**
  (American artist, 1928-) WC
  (American artist, b.1928) WI
  (American sculptor, author, b.1928) BA
  (American sculptor, b.1928) GC
  (Sculptor, 1928-) AV
  Bibl: ▶Libr. of Congr. Name Auth. File; ▶NY art yrbk.; ▶RILA/BHA; WW Amer., 1987; ▶WW Amer. Art, 1976

Judd, Don **WC**

Judd, John *(British artist, op.1774-1793)* **WC WI**

Judenburg, Hans von→see Hans von Judenburg

Judet-Sloan, Anne *(French architect, Paris)* **AV**
  Bibl: ▶Annuaire archts. fran., 1978

Judge, Bernard **AV**

Judge, Mary Frances *(American painter, b.1935.)* **BA**
  Bibl: Art in Amer. 65 (Mar 1977), p.158; ARTS MAGAZINE, v.51 (Mar 1977), p.20; ▶WW Amer. Art, 1989

Judgement Painter *(Apulian vase-painter)* **GC**
  Bibl: Trendall, Attic red-fig. vases Apulia

Judith Leijster→see Leyster, Judith

Judith Leyster→see Leyster, Judith

Judith Molenaer→see Leyster, Judith

Judkin, Rev. Thomas James→see Judkin, Thomas James

Judkin, Thomas James **WI**
  (British artist, 1788-1871) WC WI

Judkin, Rev. Thomas James **WC**

Judlin, Alexis *(German artist, op. 1791-1793)* **WC**

Judovin, Solomon Borisovič *(Russian printmaker, b.1894)* **BA**
  Bibl: ▶Met. Mus. Art libr. cat.; Smatau, V.F.,BELARUSKAJA GRAFIKA 1917-1941 (1975)
  Yudovin, Solomon Borisovich BA

Judson→see Judson, C. Chapel

Judson, C. Chapel *(American painter, 1864-1946)* **PR**
  Bibl: ▶Dawdy, Artists Amer. West
  C. Chapel Judson PR
  Judson PR

Juechser, Hans *(German artist, 20th cent.)* **WC**

Juel, Cristence *(Swedish artist, 17th cent.(?))* **WC**

Juel, Jens **BA WC**
  (Danish artist, 1745-1802) WC
  (Danish painter, 1745-1802) BA
  Bibl: ▶Encyc. world art; ▶Thieme-Becker; ▶Weilbach, Kunst.leks.

Juel-Christiansen, Carsten *(Danish architect)* **AV**
  Bibl: Arkitekten, 1988 Sept.27, v.90, no.17, p.411

Juengling, Frederick (*Engraver, 1846-1889*)   **WI**

Juergens, Alfred   **WC WI**
  (*American artist, 1866-*)   WC
  (*American artist, 1866-circa 1934*)   WI

Juettner, Franz Albert (*German artist, 19th cent.*)   **WC**

juffr. Anna Maria van Honsem→see Honsem, Anna Maria van [Unidentified]

juffr. Hartop→see Hartop, Leonora [Unidentified]

juffr. Leonora Hartman→see Hartop, Leonora [Unidentified]

Juffr. van Peene→see Wolters, Henriette (née van Pee)

Juffre, Antonio→see Giuffre, Antonino

juffrouw Globers→see Glauber, Diana

juffrouw Oosterwijk→see Oosterwyck, Maria van

Juffrouw Rachel Ruys Pool→see Ruysch, Rachel

Juffrouw Rachel Ruysch Pool→see Ruysch, Rachel

Juffrouw Ruysch→see Ruysch, Rachel

Juffrouwen Rijgersbergen→see Rijgersbergen [Unidentified]

Jugel, Friedrich (Johann Friedrich) (*German artist, op.1787-m.1833*)   **WC**

Jügel, Henriette (*German painter, act.1794-1815*)   **GC**
  Bibl: ▶Thieme-Becker

Jugelet, Jean Marie Auguste   **GC WC**
  (*French artist, 1805-1875*)   WC
  (*French painter, 1805-1875*)   GC
  Bibl: ▶Bénézit

Juhl, Finn (*Danish designer, 1912-1989*)   **AV**
  Bibl: Arkitekten, 1989 Aug.15, v.91, no.14, p.356 (death date); ▶Libr. of Congr. Name Auth. File

Juillerat, J.V.C. (*Swiss artist, op. 1797*)   **WC**

Juillerat, Jacques Henri   **GC WC**
  (*Swiss artist, 1777-1860*)   WC
  (*Swiss painter, 1777-1860*)   GC
  Bibl: ▶Bénézit

Juilo Romano→see Giulio Romano (Giulio Pippi)

Jujol i Gibert, José Maria   **BA**
  (*Spanish architect, 1879-1949*)   AV BA
  Bibl: ▶Ars Hispaniae, v.22; ▶Contemp. archts.; Flores, Gaudí; ▶Hitchcock, Arch. 19 & 20cs, p.305; ▶Macmillan encyc. archts.; Pabon-Charneco, Arch. collaborators Gaudí

Jujol, Josep Maria   **AV**

Jujol, Josep Maria→see Jujol i Gibert, José Maria

Jukes, F. (*Engraver*)   **WI**

Jukes, Francis   **WC WI**
  (*British artist, 1745-1747-1812*)   WI
  (*British artist, 1747-1812*)   WC
  Bibl: ▶Mallalieu, Brit. watercolour artists

Jukes, J.→see Jukes, John

Jukes, John   **WI**
  (*British artist, 1772-1851*)   WI
  (*British artist, op.1791-1802*)   WC

Jukes, J.   **WC**

Jul. Romano→see Giulio Romano (Giulio Pippi)

Jule, Walter (*American artist, b.1940*)   **WI**

Jules Achille Noel→see Noël, Jules Achille

Jules Adolphe Aimé Louis Breton→see Breton, Jules Adolphe Aimé Louis

Jules Adolphe Goupil→see Goupil, Jules Adolphe

Jules Bastien-Lepage→see Bastien-Lepage, Jules

Jules Breton→see Breton, Jules Adolphe Aimé Louis

Jules Carpini→see Carpioni, Giulio I

Jules Charles Rozier→see Rozier, Jules Charles

Jules David (Paris)→see David, Jules

Jules Dupre→see Dupré, Jules

Jules Elie Delaunay→see Delaunay, Jules Elie

Jules Emile Santin→see Santin, Jules Emile

Jules Guerin→see Guerin, Jules

Jules Jacques Veyrassat→see Veyrassat, Jules Jacques

Jules James Rougeron→see Rougeron, Jules James

Jules Joseph Lefebvre→see Lefebvre, Jules Joseph

Jules Pages→see Pages, Jules

Jules Pascin→see Pascin, Jules

Jules R. Mersfelder→see Mersfelder, Jules R.

Jules Romain→see Giulio Romano (Giulio Pippi)

Jules Romain Joyant→see Joyant, Jules Romain

Jules Tavernier→see Tavernier, Jules

Jules Victor Genisson→see Génisson, Jules Victor

Jules Worms→see Worms, Jules

Jules, Mervin   **WC WI**
  (*American artist, 1912-*)   WC
  (*American artist, b.1912*)   WI

Juley, Paul→see Juley, Paul P.

Juley, Paul P. (*American photographer, 1890-1975*)   **GC**
  Bibl: Getty Photo Study Coll.; ▶Idx. Amer. photog. colls.

Juley, Paul   GC

Juley, Peter→see Juley, Peter A.

Juley, Peter A.   **GC JG**
  (*American (b. Germany), 1862-1937*)   JG
  (*American photographer, 1862-1937*)   GC
  Bibl: Getty Photo Study Coll.; ▶Idx. Amer. photog. colls.

Juley, Peter   GC

Julia Beatrice How→see How, Julia Beatrice

Julia E. Dunn→see Dunn, Julia E.

Julia Romana→see Giulio Romano (Giulio Pippi)

Julia Romano→see Giulio Romano (Giulio Pippi)

Julia, Ascencio ('El Pescadoret')→see Juliá, Ascensio

Julia, Ascencio (El Pescadoret)→see Juliá, Ascensio

Juliá, Ascensio   **BA**
  (*Spanish artist, a.1771-1816*)   WC
  (*Spanish painter, 1748-1832*)   BA
  (*Spanish, b. bef.1771-1816*)   GC
  Bibl: ARTS MAG., LVII, 4 (Dec 1982) 106-110; ▶Bénézit; Chabain, GOYA (1965); Gassier, Goya, 1971; Gil Salinas, GOYA, 192 (MAy-June 1986) p.348; ▶Lafuente Ferrari, Pint. española; ▶Thieme-Becker; ▶Witt checklist

Julia, Ascencio ('El Pescadoret')   **WC**
Julia, Ascencio (El Pescadoret)   **GC**

Julian Alden Weir→see Weir, Julian Alden

Julian de la Fuente, Carlos (*Architect*)   **AV**
  Bibl: Parametro, 1989 Jan.-Feb., no.170, p.80

Julian Walbridge Rix→see Rix, Julian Waldridge

Julian, Joanne (*American artist, 20th c.*)   **BA**
  Bibl: Arts Mag., "Arts Reviews: So. Calif." 3 Nov 1982

Julian, Rodolphe (*French painter, printmaker, art administrator, 1839-1907*)   **BA**
  Bibl: ▶Bénézit; Fehrer, Drawing, IV/2 (Jul.-Aug. 1982) pp.25-28; ▶Thieme-Becker

Julianis, Caterina de (*Italian sculptor, act.1695-1742*)   **BA**
  Bibl: ▶Bénézit; ▶Thieme-Becker

Juliard, Nicolas Jacques→see Juliard, Nicolas-Jacques

Juliard, Nicolas-Jacques   **GC**
  (*French artist, 1715/19-1790*)   WC
  (*French painter and draughtsman, 1715-1790*)   GC
  Bibl: ▶Bénézit; ▶Thieme-Becker; ▶Witt checklist

Juliard, Nicolas Jacques   GC
Juliart, Nicolas-Jacques   GC
Julliar, Nicolas-Jacques   GC

Julliard or Juliard, Jacques Nicolas   **WC**

Julliard, Jacques Nicolas   GC
Julliard, Nicolas-Jacques   GC

Juliart, Nicolas-Jacques→see Juliard, Nicolas-Jacques

Julien de Parme, Jean Antoine→see Julien, Jean-Antoine (Julien de Parme)

Julien Dupre→see Dupré, Julien

Julien Michel Gue→see Gué, Julien Michel

Julien or Jullien, Simon→see Julien, Simon

Julien, Anthelme Joseph Claude Julien (French artist, 1840-1867) **WC**

Julien, Henri (American artist, op. 20th c.) **WI**

Julien, Jean Antoine→see Julien, Jean-Antoine (Julien de Parme)

Julien, Jean-Antoine (Julien de Parme) BA

(French artist, 1736-1799) **WC**

(French painter, 1736-1799) **BA**

(French, 1736-1799) **GC**

Bibl: ▶Bellier, Artistes fran.; ▶Thieme-Becker; ▶Witt checklist

Julien de Parme, Jean Antoine WC

Julien, Jean Antoine GC

Julien, Marc (Canadian architect, Montreal) **AV**

Bibl: ▶Canad. arch. dir., 1985

Julien, Peter (Architect) **AV**

Bibl: ▶Arch. period. idx./RIBA, 1981

Julien, Pierre AV BA GC WC

(French artist, op.1731-1804) **WC**

(French sculptor, 1731-1804) **AV BA GC**

Bibl: ▶Bénézit; ▶RILA/BHA; ▶Thieme-Becker

Julien, Remy Eugene (Emile Julien)

(French artist, 1797-1868) **WC**

Julien, Simon BA GC

(French artist, 1735-1800) **WC**

(French painter, printmaker, 1735-1800) **BA**

(French, 1735-1800) **GC**

Bibl: ▶Bellier, Artistes fran.; ▶Bénézit; ▶Thieme-Becker; ▶Witt checklist

Julien or Jullien, Simon WC

Júlio (Júlio Maria dos Reis Pereira)

(Portuguese painter, printmaker, ceramist, 1902-1982) **BA**

Bibl: Colóquio: Artes 56 (Mar 1983) 67; ▶Tannock, Port. 20c. artists; ▶Tavares Chicó, Pint. portuguesa

Julio Carpioni→see Carpioni, Giulio I

Julio Romano→see Giulio Romano (Giulio Pippi)

Julius Bissier→see Bissier, Julius

Julius Bloch→see Bloch, Julius T.

Julius Caesar Ibbetson→see Ibbetson, Julius Caesar

Julius D. Katzieff→see Katzieff, Julius D.

Julius Friedrich Anton Schrader→see Schrader, Julius Friedrich Anton

Julius Gari Melchers→see Melchers, Gari

Julius Ibbetson→see Ibbetson, Julius Caesar

Julius Jacobus van de Sande Bakhuyzen→see Bakhuyzen, Julius Jacobus van de Sande

Julius Kockert→see Köckert, Julius

Julius Muhr→see Muhr, Julius

Julius Porcellis→see Porcellis, Julius

Julius Rolshoven→see Rolshoven, Julius C.

Julius Schnorr von Carolsfeld→see Schnorr von Carolsfeld, Julius

Julius Zimmermann→see Zimmermann, Julius

Julius, Leslie (British architect) **AV**

Bibl: RIBA journal, 1983 Apr., v.90, no.4, p.46

Julles Romain→see Giulio Romano (Giulio Pippi)

Jullian de la Fuente, Guillermo (Chilean architect, 1931-) **AV**

Bibl: Architecture SA, 1988 Mar.-Apr., p.27

Jullian, Phillippe (French artist, 19th cent.) **WC**

Julliar, Nicolas-Jacques→see Juliard, Nicolas-Jacques

Julliard or Juliard, Jacques Nicolas→see Juliard, Nicolas-Jacques

Julliard, Jacques Nicolas→see Juliard, Nicolas-Jacques

Julliard, Nicolas-Jacques→see Juliard, Nicolas-Jacques

Jullien, Benoît (French architect) **AV**

Bibl: ▶Annuaire archts. fran., 1978

Jullien, François (French architect, Paris) **AV**

Bibl: ▶Annuaire archts. fran., 1978

Jullio Romano→see Giulio Romano (Giulio Pippi)

Julliott, Mme. Made (French artist, 1887-1948) **WC**

Jumsai, Sumet (Thai architect, 1939-) **AV**

Bibl: ▶Contemp. archts.

Juncker→see Juncker, Justus

Juncker von Prag, Johann (German artist, op.1400) **WC**

Juncker von Prag, Wenzel (German artist, op.1400) **WC**

Juncker, Christian JG

Juncker, Hermann (German artist, 18th cent.) **WC**

Juncker, Justus BA GC PR WC

(German artist, 1703-1767) **WC**

(German painter, 1703-1767) **PR**

(German painter, printmaker, 1703-1767) **BA**

(German, 1703-1767) **GC**

Bibl: ▶Allgem. Deut. Biog.; ▶Bénézit; ▶Thieme-Becker; ▶Witt checklist

Joncker **PR**

Juncker **PR**

Juneker **PR**

Justus Juncker **PR**

Juncker, Wilhelm Karl (German painter, 1820-1901) **PR**

Bibl: ▶Thieme-Becker

Junker, Wilhelm **PR**

Wilhelm Karl Juncker **PR**

Jundt, Gusatave Adolphe (French artist, 1830-1884) **WC**

June, John (British artist, op.1740-1770) **WC WI**

Juneau, Denis→see Juneau, Dennis

Juneau, Dennis BA

(Canadian artist, 1925-) **WC**

(Canadian painter, b.1925) **BA**

Bibl: ▶Artists Canada; ▶Bénézit; ▶MacDonald, Can. artists; ▶Vollmer, Künst.-Lex. 20. Jhr.

Juneau, Denis WC

Juneau, Reynald (Canadian architect, Trois-Rivières, Quebec) **AV**

Bibl: ▶Canad. arch. dir., 1985

Junek, Lorris or Leo (Yugoslav artist, 1899-) **WC**

Juneker→see Juncker, Justus

Jünemann, Alfredo (Chilean architect) **AV**

Bibl: ARQ, 1986 May, no.11, p.12

Jung, Charles Frédéric (French painter, 1865-1936) **BA**

Bibl: ▶Bénézit; ▶Busse, Maler u. Bildhauer 19. Jahr.; Lyon (FRA), Mus. des B.-A., Fleurs de Lyon 1807-1917 (1982); ▶Vollmer, Künst.-Lex. 20. Jhr.

Jung, Gustaf (Finnish glassmaker, act.1681) **BA**

Bibl: Davis, Contl. glass; JOURNAL OF GLASS STUDIES XVI (1974) 57-86; Polak, Glass

Jung, Jakob (Johann Jakob) (German artist, 1819-1844) **WC**

Jung, Klaus (West German artist, 20th c.) **BA**

Bibl: Schmidt-Wulffen, Flash Art 121 (Mar. 1985), p. 70-73

Jung, Roland (West German artist in CHE, b.1941) **BA**

Bibl: ▶Lex. zeitgen. Schweiz. Künstler

Jung, Theodor (American photographer, b.1906) **BA**

Bibl: Akron (OH, USA), Art Institute, Ohio... (1980); ▶MoMA libr. cat.

Jung, Theodore   GC WC
  (French artist, 1803-1865)   WC
  (French, 1803-1865)   GC
    Bibl: ▶Thieme-Becker; ▶Witt
    checklist
Jung, W. *(Italian architect)*   AV
    Bibl: Lotus international, 1983,
    no.38, p.90
Jung, Walter *(German painter,*
    printmaker, b.1955)   BA
    Bibl: exh. cat., Karlsruhe (DEU),
    Staatliche Akademie der
    Bildenden Künste, 11 May-11
    June 1983
Jungblut, Johann → see Jungblut,
    Johann II
Jungblut, Johann II   GC
  (German artist, 1860-1912)   WC
  (German painter, 1860-1912)   GC
    Bibl: ▶Thieme-Becker
Jungblut, Johann   WC
Junge or Jung, Friedrich August
  (German artist, 1781-1841)   WC
Junge, Peter-Heinz *(East German*
    photographer, b.1928)   BA
    Bibl: BILDENDE KUNST 4 (1984)
    154
Jünger, Hermann *(German*
    goldsmith, b.1928)   BA
    Bibl: Darmstadt (DEU), Hess.
    Landesmus., 3 Goldschmeide
    (1978); ▶WW Arts DEU
Junger, Johann Christoph *(German*
    artist, op.1767)   WC
Junghanns, Julius Paul *(German*
    artist, 1876-)   WC
Jungheim, Carl *(German artist,*
    1830-1886)   WC
Jungling, J.F. *(Engraver, op.1850-)*   WI
Jungman, Maarten Johannes
    Balthasar → see Jungmann, Maarten
    Johannes Balthasar
Jungmann, Jean Paul *(French*
    architect, editor of the journal
    L'ivre des pierres)   AV
    Bibl: Daidalos, no.4, p.114
Jungmann, Maarten Johannes
    Balthasar   GC
  (Dutch artist, 1877-1964)   WC
  (Dutch painter, b.1877)   GC
    Bibl: ▶Thieme-Becker
Jungman, Maarten Johannes
    Balthasar   WC
Jungmann, Nico   GC WC
  (Dutch artist, 1872-)   WC
  (Dutch painter, b.1872)   GC
    Bibl: ▶Bénézit
Jungnick, Helene *(German designer,*
    20th c.)   BA
    Bibl: Wewerka, 1972-1982:
    BERICHT EINER DEUTSCHEN
    UNTERNEHMUNG

Jungnickel, Ludwig Heinrich BA GC WC
  (German artist, 1881-)   WC
  (German draughtsman, 1881-
    1965)   GC
  (German painter, printmaker,
    1881-1965)   BA
    Bibl: ▶Bénézit; ▶Neue deutsche
    Biog.; ▶Thieme-Becker; ▶Vollmer,
    Künst.-Lex. 20. Jhr.
Jungstedt, Axel Adolf Harald
  (Swedish artist, 1859-)   WC
Jungstedt, Kurt *(Swedish artist,*
    1894-)   WC
Jungwirth, Heinrich *(Austrian*
    architect, Vienna)   AV
    Bibl: Bauforum, 1988, v.21, no.
    125, p.54
Jungwirth, Joseph *(German artist,*
    1869-1950)   WC
Juni, Juan de *(Spanish sculptor,*
    painter, architect, ca.1507-1577)   BA
    Bibl: ▶Bénézit; ▶Encyc. world art;
    Griseri; Martin Cemzalez. Juan de
    Juni; ▶Thieme-Becker
Junient, Manuel de Amat y → see
    Amat y Junient, Manuel de
Junier van Lent → see Lent, Junier van
    [Unidentified]
Juniór, Affonso Risi *(Brazilian*
    architect)   AV
    Bibl: Projeto, 1988 Apr., no.109,
    p.72
Júnior, J. Barbosa *(Brazilian*
    architect)   AV
    Bibl: Projeto, 1988 Mar., no.108,
    p.108
Juniper, Robert *(Australian artist,*
    1929-)   WC
Junius Brutus Stearns → see Stearns,
    Junius Brutus
Junius, Isaak *(Dutch artist, op.1640-*
    1657)   WC
Junius, Marcel *(Canadian architect)*   AV
    Bibl: Section a, v.2, no.1, p.29
Junival, J. → see Junival, John
Junival, John   WI
  (American artist, 20th cent.)   WC
  (American artist, op.20th c.)   WI
Junival, J.   WC
Junker, Carl   AV BA
  (Austrian architect, 1827-1882)   BA
  (German architect, act. in
    Trieste, 19th cent)   AV
    Bibl: Arte in Friuli VII (1984) 135-
    143; TCI Friuli-Venezia-Giulia;
    ▶Thieme-Becker
    Iunker, Carl   BA
Junker, Wilhelm → see Juncker,
    Wilhelm Karl
Junker, Wolfgang *(East German*
    architect(?), 1929-)   AV
    Bibl: Architektur der DDR, 1989
    Feb., v.38, no.2, p.6
Junkers, Adja → see Yunkers, Adja

Junkin, Marion Montague
  (American painter, 1905-1977)   BA
    Bibl: ▶MoMA libr. cat.; ▶WW
    Amer. Art, 1978
Junno, Tapio *(Finnish sculptor,*
    b.1940)   BA
Junod, Pierre *(Swiss interior*
    designer, Basel)   AV
    Bibl: Abitare, 1983 Oct., no.218,
    p.20
Junor, D.   WC WI
  (British artist, op.1808)   WC
  (British artist, op.1808-)   WI
Junovič, Sofia *(Russian stage*
    designer, b.1910)   BA
Junquera, Jerónimo *(Spanish*
    architect)   AV
    Bibl: Arquitectura, 1984 May-
    June, v.65, no.248
Junyer, Joan *(Spanish artist, 20th*
    cent.)   WC
Juola, Heli *(Finnish architect)*   AV
    Bibl: Architektur + Wettbewerbe,
    1987 Sept., no.131, p.33
Juola, Tuomo *(Finnish architect)*   AV
    Bibl: Architektur + Wettbewerbe,
    1987 Sept., no.131, p.33
Juon, Andreas   BA WC
  (Swiss artist, 1895-)   WC
  (Swiss painter, b.1895)   BA
    Bibl: ▶Künst.-Lex. Schweiz 20.
    Jahrh.; ▶Lex. zeitgen. Schweiz.
    Künstler
Juon, Konstantin Fedorovič   BA
  (Russian artist, 1875-1958)   WC
  (Russian painter, printmaker,
    scenographer, 1875-1958)   BA
    Bibl: ▶Bowlt, Russian avant-garde;
    ▶WWW USSR
Juon, Konstantin Fjodorovitch   WC
Juon, Konstantin Fjodorovitch → see
    Juon, Konstantin Fedorovič
Jupp, Richard   AV BA
  (British architect, 1728-1799)   AV
  (British architect, surveyor,
    1728-1799)   BA
    Bibl: ▶Colvin, Brit. archts.; ▶Dict.
    natl. biog.; ▶Thieme-Becker
Juppe, Ludwig   BA GC
  (German sculptor, ca.1465-
    1538)   BA
  (German, ca.1465-aft.1538)   GC
    Bibl: ▶Bénézit; ▶Thieme-Becker
    Master Loedewich of Kalkar   BA
Jura, Thomasz *(Polish artist, 20th*
    cent.)   WC
Jurado, Carlos *(Mexican artist,*
    1926-)   WC
Jurgan Frederick Huge → see Huge,
    Jurgan Frederick
Jürgen Liepe (Berlin) → see Liepe,
    Jürgen
Jürgen Ovens → see Ovens, Jürgen
Jurgen, Lejda *(Russian designer,*
    20th c.)   BA

Jürgen-Fischer, Klaus *(German painter, printmaker, critic, b.1930)* **BA**
Bibl: ▶Bénézit; ▶Vollmer, Künst.-Lex. 20. Jhr.; ▶WW Arts DEU

Jürgens, Margarete *(German painter, 1899-1981)* **BA**
Bibl: Bonn (BRD), Kunstverein, GRETLE JÜRGENS... 1982; ▶Vollmer, Künst.-Lex. 20. Jhr.

Jürgensen, Axel *(Danish architect, Lyngby, 1923-)* **AV**
Bibl: ▶Danske Arkitekters Landsforbund, 1984-85

Jürgensen, Carla *(Danish architect, Lyngby)* **AV**
Bibl: Arkitektur DK, 1989, v.33, no.1, p.36

Jurgensen, Fritz (Georg Urban Frederik) *(Danish artist, 1818-1863)* **WC**

Jürgenssen, Birgit *(Austrian draftsman, b.1949)* **BA**
Bibl: ▶Babington Smith, Contemp. artists; ▶Intl. dir. exh. artists, 1983; Linz (AUT), Neue Galerie, Künstlerinnen (1983)

Juriaen van Streeck → see Streeck, Juriaen van
Juriana Ovens → see Ovens, Jürgen
Jurien Ovens → see Ovens, Jürgen
Jurjewitsch, Serge → see Youriévič, Serge

Jurkiewicz, Andrzej *(Polish painter, printmaker, 1907-1967)* **BA**
Bibl: ▶Vollmer, Künst.-Lex. 20. Jhr.; Warsaw, Muz. Narodowe, Andrzej Jurkiewicz 1907-1967, 1980

Jurkiewicz, Zdzisław *(Polish painter, printmaker, b.1931)* **BA**
Bibl: ▶Bénézit; Buffalo (NY, USA), Albright-Knox, 17 contemp. artists Poland (1976)

Jurkovič, Dušan → see Jurkovič, Dušan Samo

Jurkovič, Dušan Samo **BA**
(Czech architect, 1868-1947) **BA**
(Czechoslovakian architect, 1868-1947) **AV**
Bibl: "Architectural Association quarterly" Oct. 1981, p.45-50; ▶Macmillan encyc. archts.; ▶Portoghesi, Diz. arch. e urbanistica; ▶Thieme-Becker

Jurkovič, Dušan **AV**

Jurres → see Jurres, Johannes Hendricus

Jurres, Johannes Hendricus **GC PR WC**
(Dutch artist, 1875-1946) **WC**
(Dutch painter and draughtsman, b.1875) **GC**
(Dutch painter, 1875-1946) **PR**
Bibl: ▶Thieme-Becker
Johannes Hendricus Jurres **PR**
Jurres **PR**

Jurriaan Buttner → see Buttner, Jurriaan
Jurriaen Ovens → see Ovens, Jürgen
Jurriaen van Streek → see Streeck, Juriaen van

Jurt, Marc *(Swiss printmaker, b.1955)* **BA**
Bibl: ▶Lex. zeitgen. Schweiz. Künstler

Jury, Wilhelm (Johann Friedrich Wilhelm) *(German artist, 1763-1829)* **WC**

Jurysta, Gary *(American artist, 20th c.)* **BA**
Bibl: Arts Mag. LIV/7 (Mar 1980), p.18

Jusepe de Ribera → see Ribera, Jusepe de (lo Spagnoletto)
Jusepe de Riuera → see Ribera, Jusepe de (lo Spagnoletto)
Jusepe Leonardo → see Leonardo, Jusepe
Jusepe Rivera → see Ribera, Jusepe de (lo Spagnoletto)
Joseph de Riuexa → see Ribera, Jusepe de (lo Spagnoletto)
Joseph de Riuiera → see Ribera, Jusepe de (lo Spagnoletto)
Jusquin → see Joosken van Utrecht

Jussiant *(Belgian, 19th c.)* **BA**

Jussim, Boris Ossipovich *(American photographer, b.1890)* **BA**
Bibl: Hist of Photog I/3 (July 1971) 183-199

Jussow, Heinrich Christoph *(German architect, 1754-1825)* **BA**
Bibl: ▶Neue deutsche Biog.; ▶Thieme-Becker

Jussupoff, Aleksander *(Polish artist, 19th cent.)* **WC**

Just Another Asshole *(artist, 20th c.)* **BA**
Bibl: Artforum XVIII/6 (Feb. 1980), pp. 55-91

Just, Gunter *(East German architect, Dresden)* **AV**
Bibl: Deutsche Bauzeitschrift, 1987 Nov., v.35, no.11, p.137

Juste de Gand → see Joos van Gent (Joos van Wassenhove)

Juste family *(Italian sculptors in FRA, 16th c.)* **BA**
Bibl: ▶Diz. biog. ital.; ▶Encyc. world art; ▶Thieme-Becker
Giusto family **BA**

Juste, André *(Italian sculptor in FRA, b.1482-1487, act.1536)* **BA**
Bibl: ▶Bénézit; ▶Thieme-Becker

Juste, Antoine **BA GC**
(French sculptor, 1474-1519) **GC**
(Italian sculptor in FRA, 1479-1519) **BA**
Bibl: M. de VASSELOR, HISTOIRE DES SCULPTEURS FRANÇAIS, Paris 1888, pp.283-84; ▶Thieme-Becker
Antonio di Giusto Betti **GC**
Betti, Antonio di Giusto **GC**

Juste, Jean I *(Italian sculptor in FRA, 1485-1549)* **BA**
Bibl: ▶Bellier, Artistes fran.; ▶Bénézit; ▶Thieme-Becker
Betti, Giovanni di Giusto **BA**
Giusto, Giovanni di **BA**

Juste, Jérôme *(French stonecutter, b.ca.1456, act.1506)* **BA**
Bibl: ▶Bauchal, Archtes. fran.; ▶Lami, Sculp. fran. 19e s.; Quintero, in RENAISSANCE STUDIES IN HONOR OF CRAIG HUGH SMYTH (1985) II, 641; ▶Thieme-Becker

Juste, Just de (Giusto Betti) *(French artist, op.c.1537-m.c.1559)* **WC**

Juster, Norton *(American architect)* **AV**

Justerman → see Suttermans, Justus

Justesen, Kirsten *(Danish artist, b.1943)* **BA**
Bibl: Arnborg et al., Bidgrag 18 (1984) p.22; ▶Intl. dir. arts; ▶Køie, Kunst.leks.

Justi, Steven *(Interior designer)* **AV**
Bibl: Southern accents, 1985 Sept.-Oct., v.8, no.5, p.115

Justice, Martin *(American artist, op. 1911-)* **WI**

Justin Pope → see Pope-Stevens, Justin
Justin Pope-Stevens → see Pope-Stevens, Justin

Justinat, Justina or Justinar, Augustin Oudert *(French artist, -1743)* **WC**

Justinian → see Justinian, I, Emperor of the East

Justinian, I, Emperor of the East **AV**
(483?-565) **AV**
(Greek (Byzantine), b. Nissa, Yugoslavia, ca. 482; emperor 527 -) **JG**
Bibl: ▶Libr. of Congr. Name Auth. File
Giustiniano **AV**
Justinian **JG**

Justis, Gary Allen *(American sculptor, b.1953)* **BA**
Bibl: New York (NY, USA), New Mus., Dimensions Variable (1979)

Justitz, Alfréd *(Czech painter, 1879-1934)* **BA**
Bibl: ▶Encyk. českého výtv. umění; ▶Vollmer, Künst.-Lex. 20. Jhr.

Justus d'Allamagna   GC
    (German artist, op.1451)   WC
    (German painter, act.1451)   GC
    Bibl: ▶Thieme-Becker
    Justus d'Allemagna   GC
**Justus de Alemannia or
    Allamagna**   WC
Justus d'Allemagna →see Justus
    d'Allamagna
*Justus de Alemannia or
    Allamagna →see* Justus
    d'Allamagna
Justus de Allemagna →see Ammann,
    Jos
Justus Juncker →see Juncker, Justus
Justus of Ghent →see Joos van Gent
    (Joos van Wassenhove)
*Justus of Ghent (Joos van
    Wassenhove or Giusto da
    Guanto) →see* Joos van Gent (Joos
    van Wassenhove)
Justus Suttermans →see Suttermans,
    Justus
Justus van Egmont →see Egmont,
    Justus van
Justus van Huijsum →see Huysum,
    Justus van (I)
Justus van Huysum (I) →see Huysum,
    Justus van (I)
Justus Veerus ab Egmont →see
    Egmont, Justus van
Justyne, Percy William *(British
    artist, 1812-1883)*   WI
Juszczyk, James Joseph *(American
    painter, b.1943)*   BA
    Bibl: ▶NY art yrbk.; Rosa Esman
    Gallery, NY; ▶WW Amer. Art,
    1976
Jutsum, Henry *(British artist, 1816-
    1869)*   WC WI
Juttner, Bruno *(German artist,
    1880-)*   WC
Jutz, Carl →see Jutz, Carl I
Jutz, Carl I   GC
    (German artist, 1838-1916)   WC
    (German painter, 1838-1916)   GC
    Bibl: ▶Thieme-Becker
Jutz, Carl   WC
Juuel, Andreas *(Danish artist, 1817-
    1868)*   WC
Juul, Helle *(Danish architect,
    Copenhagen)*   AV
    Bibl: ▶Danske Arkitekters
    Landsforbund, 1984-85
Juul, Søren *(Danish architect)*   AV
    Bibl: Arkitektur DK, 1988 v.32,
    no.4, p.149
Juvara, Aloisio (Tommaso, Aloisio)
    (Italian artist, 1809-1875)   WC

Juvara, Filippo   AV BA FA GC
    *(1678-31.I.1736; Late Baroque
    Classical Architect,
    Scenography Designer,
    Madrid, Roma, Torino)*   FA
    *(Italian architect and
    printmaker, 1676-1736)*   GC
    (Italian architect, 1678-1736)   AV
    *(Italian architect, printmaker,
    1678-1736)*   BA
    (Italian artist, 1674/6-1736)   WC
    Bibl: ▶Bénézit; ▶Bessone-Aurelj,
    Scult. & arch. ital.; ▶Bolaffi;
    ▶Encic. italiana; ▶Libr. of Congr.
    Name Auth. File; ▶Macmillan
    encyc. archts., v.2, pp.519-533;
    Millon, H., Filippo Juvarra:
    Drawings from the Roman Period
    1704-1714--Part 1, 1984;
    ▶RILA/BHA, 1986;
    ▶Thieme-Becker, v.19, p.358 ff.
    Hovara, Filippo   AV
    Ivara, Filippo   FA
    Ivvara, Filippo   AV
    Juara, Filippo   FA
**Juvara, Ivara, Juarra or Juvarra,
    Filippo**   WC
Juvarra, Filippo   AV FA JG
Juvara, Francesco Natale *(Italian,
    1673-1759)*   JG
*Juvara, Ivara, Juarra or Juvarra,
    Filippo →see* Juvara, Filippo
Juvara, Romano *(Italian architect)*   AV
    Bibl: Abacus, 1989 June-July, v.5,
    no.19, p.75
Juvarra, Filippo →see Juvara, Filippo
Juvee, J.B. *(French artist, 19th
    cent.(?))*   WC
Juvenel or Juvenell, Nicolas, I →see
    Juvenel, Nicolas, the elder
Juvenel or Juvenell, Paul, I →see
    Juvenel, Paul I
Juvenel, Nicolas, the elder   BA
    *(German architect, painter, ca.
    1540-1597)*   BA
    *(Netherlands artist, op.1550-m.
    1597)*   WC
    Bibl: ▶Bénézit; ▶Thieme-Becker
Juvenel or Juvenell, Nicolas, I   WC
Juvenel, Paul I   BA GC
    (German artist, 1579-1643)   WC
    *(German painter and
    draughtsman, 1579-1643)*   GC
    (German painter, 1579-1643)   BA
    Bibl: ▶Bénézit; ▶Thieme-Becker
Juvenel or Juvenell, Paul, I   WC

Juvenet →see Jouvenet, Jean Baptiste
Juvenis [Unidentified] *(Unknown
    painter)*   PR
    Bibl: ([Nov. 16], 1801 lots 877-
    888, European Museum)
Juzefovič, I. *(Russian architect, 20th
    c.)*   BA
    Bibl: Barhin, AR HITEKTURA I
    GOVOD, (1979)
K-S Painter *(Apulian vase-painter)*   GC
    Bibl: Trendall, Attic red-fig. vases
    Apulia
K. Bed →see Bed, K. [Unidentified]
K. de Jardin →see Dujardin, Karel
K. de Moor →see Moor, Carel de
K. de Moore →see Moor, Carel de
K. Du Jardin →see Dujardin, Karel
K. du Jardine →see Dujardin, Karel
K. du Jardyn →see Dujardin, Karel
K. Dujardin →see Dujardin, Karel
K. Molenaer →see Molenaer, Klaes
K. Porter →see Porter, Robert Kerr, Sir
K...., Charlotte de *(French artist,
    op.1794)*   WC
K.D. Jardin →see Dujardin, Karel
Kaag, Werner *(West German
    architect, Stuttgart)*   AV
    Bibl: Deutsche Bauzeitung, 1989
    July, v.123, no.7, p.52
Kaalf →see Kalf, Willem
Kaalund, Bodil *(Danish painter,
    b.1930)*   BA
    Bibl: the artist: OEJE OG HAAND,
    1981
Kaas, Jacobus *(Dutch sculptor,
    painter, printmaker, 1898-1972)*   BA
    Bibl: Exh.cat. Amsterdams
    Historisch Museum, LEVEN EN
    WERK VAN BEELDHOUWER-
    TEKENAAR JAAP KAAS, Utrecht
    1987; ▶Scheen, Ned. beeldende
    kunst.
Kaasik, Veljo *(Estonian architect,
    20th century)*   AV
    Bibl: Casabella, 1986 Nov., v.50,
    no.529, p.4
Kaaz or Katz, Carl Ludwig →see Kaaz,
    Carl Ludwig
Kaaz, Carl Ludwig   BA GC
    (German artist, 1773-1810)   WC
    (German painter, 1773-1810)   BA
    (German, 1773-1810)   GC
    Bibl: ▶Bénézit; Getty Photo Study
    Coll. (Ptgs.); ▶Thieme-Becker;
    ▶Witt checklist
Kaaz or Katz, Carl Ludwig   WC
    Katz, Carl Ludwig   GC
Kabakov, Ilya *(Soviet artist, b.1933)*   BA
    Bibl: ▶Art Index, v.34, p.555; RLIN
    BKS file; Tupitsyn, Flash art 126
    (Feb-Mar 1986) 67-69
Kaballo, Klaus *(West German
    interior designer)*   AV
Kabel →see Cabel, Adrian van der

Kabel or Cabel, Adrian or Ary van der, or Adrian Vandercable, Vandrecable etc. →*see* Cabel, Adrian van der

Kabel or Cabel, Engel, Ange or Angelo van der *(Dutch artist, op. 1665-1695)* **WC**

Kabel, Adrian van der →*see* Cabel, Adrian van der

Kabele, Johann *(Austrian interior architect)* **AV**
Bibl: Bauforum, 1987, v.20, no. 124, p.42

Kabell, Ludvig Christian Brinck Seidelin *(Danish artist, 1853-1902)* **WC**

Kabotie, Fred *(American painter, designer, b.1900)* **BA**
Bibl: ▶WW Amer. Art, 1978

Kabraat, van [Unidentified]
(Unknown painter) **PR**
Bibl: (July 17, 1811, lot 40, Robins; February 1, 1812, lot 40, Robins)
Van Kabraat **PR**

Kacere, John →*see* Kacere, John C.

Kacere, John C. **BA WI**
(American artist, 20th cent.) **WC**
(American artist, b.1920) **WI**
(American painter, b.1920) **BA**
Bibl: Currier's guide 1645-1945; ▶Fielding's Amer. ptrs., 1983; Guide exh. artists: N. Amer. ptrs.; ▶Intl. dir. exh. artists, 1983; ▶WW Amer. Art, 1989-1990

Kacere, John **WC**

Kachadoorian, Zubel **WC WI**
(American artist, 1924/6-) **WC**
(American artist, b.1924) **WI**

Kachel, Johann Wilhelm Friedrich
(Dutch printmaker, 1826-1873) **GC**
Bibl: ▶Bénézit

Kachel, Ludwig *(German artist, 1830-1858)* **WC**

Kachlik, Jaroslav *(Polish or Yugoslavian architect)* **AV**
Bibl: Architektura ČSR, 1988, v.47, no.1, p.64

Kachrylion **GC**
Bibl: ▶Beazley, Attic red-fig. vase-ptrs.

Kachurin, I.V. *(Russian, 20th c.)* **BA**

Kacz, Endre Komaromi **WC**
(Hungarian artist, 1880) **WC**
(Hungarian artist, 1880-) **WC**

Komaromi-Kacz, Endre **WC**

Kaczorek, Janusz *(Polish architect, Warsaw)* **AV**
Bibl: Architektur + Wettbewerbe, 1988 Dec., no.136, p.59

Kada, Klaus *(Austrian architect, Leibnitz, 1940-)* **AV**
Bibl: Kenchiku bunka, 1984 Dec., v.39, p.458, p.100

Kadar →*see* Kádár, Béla

Kádár, Béla **BA GC PR WC**
(Hungarian artist, 1877-1955) **WC**
(Hungarian painter, 1877-1955) **BA PR**
(Hungarian, 1877-1955) **GC**
Bibl: ▶RILA/BHA; ▶Thieme-Becker; ▶Vollmer, Künst.-Lex. 20. Jhr., suppl.; ▶Witt checklist
Bela Kadar **PR**
Kadar **PR**

Kadar, Livia *(Hungarian artist, 1894-)* **WC**

Kaden, Siegfried *(German artist, b.1945)* **BA**
Bibl: Munich (BRD), Städt. Gal., Kunstf. Max., SIEGFRIED KADEN..., 1981

Kadish, Katherine *(American painter, printmaker, b.1939)* **BA**
Bibl: Binghamton (NY, USA), SUNY, Univ. Art Gallery, KATHERINE KADISH..., 1981

Kadish, Reuben *(American painter, sculptor, printmaker, b.1913)* **BA**
Bibl: Arts Mag. Lt/4 (dec 1976) 17; ▶Havlice, Idx. art. bio.

Kadishman, Menashe **BA WI**
(American artist, b.1932) **WI**
(Israeli sculptor, b.1932) **BA**
Bibl: ▶NY art yrbk.

Kadlik or Thadlik, Franz *(Czech artist, 1786-1840)* **WC**

Kadmos Painter *(vase-painter, ca. 420-390 BC)* **GC**
Bibl: ▶Beazley, Attic red-fig. vase-ptrs.; Richter, Attic red-fig. vases

Kadorizi, Catoriza or Kadoriza, Wolfgang Joseph *(German artist, op.1697-1730)* **WC**

Kadounis *(Greek artist, 17th cent.)* **WC**

Kadow, Jürgen *(West German artist, b.1954)* **BA**
Bibl: ▶Intl. dir. exh. artists, 1983; Nuremberg (DEU), Akademie der bildenden Künste, JURGEN KADOW, 1983

Kadz, Marco *(Architect)* **AV**
Bibl: Nieuw-neuf, 1987 Apr., no. 126, p.60

Kaelin →*see* Kaelin, Charles Salis

Kaelin, Charles →*see* Kaelin, Charles Salis

Kaelin, Charles S. →*see* Kaelin, Charles Salis

Kaelin, Charles Salis *(American painter, 1858-1929)* **PR**
Bibl: ▶WWW Amer. art
Charles Salis Kaelin **PR**
Kaelin **PR**
Kaelin, Charles **PR**
Kaelin, Charles S. **PR**

Kaemmerer →*see* Kaemmerer, Frederik Hendrik

Kaemmerer, Frederik Hendrik **GC PR WC**
(Dutch artist, 1839-1902) **WC**
(Dutch painter, 1839-1902) **PR**
(Dutch, 1839-1902) **GC**
Bibl: ▶Thieme-Becker; ▶Witt checklist
Frederik Hendrik Kaemmerer **PR**
Kaemmerer **PR**
Kaemmerer, Frederik Henri **PR**
Kaemmerer, Frederik Henri →*see* Kaemmerer, Frederik Hendrik

Kaemmerer, Johan Hendr *(Dutch artist, 1894-)* **WC**

Kaempffer, Eduard *(German artist, 1859-)* **WC**

Kaeser, Fritz *(American photographer, 20th c.)* **BA**
Bibl: Notre Dame, Univ. of N.D., Snite Mus., PHOTOGRAPHS BY FRITZ KAESER (1983)

Kaesermann, Kaisermann or Keiserman, Francois →*see* Kaisermaan, Franz

Kaesz, Gyula **AV BA**
(Hungarian architect, designer, 1897-1967) **BA**
(Hungarian designer, 1897-1967) **AV**
Bibl: Alte und moderne Kunst, 1985, v.30, no.201-202, pp. 30-33; ▶Vollmer, Künst.-Lex. 20. Jhr.

Kaesz-Lukáts, Kató *(Hungarian graphic artist, illustrator, b.1900)* **BA**
Bibl: Alte und moderne Kunst, 1985, v.30, no.201-202, pp.30-33

Kaex, L. de *(Dutch(?) artist, op. 1651)* **WC**

Kafka, Cestmir *(Czech painter, printmaker, b.1922)* **BA**
Bibl: Cincinnati (OH, USA), Art Mus., Eastern Euro. printmkrs. (1975); ▶Havlice, Idx. art. bio., Kafka Čestmír, 1922-; Czech painter

Kafka, Klaus *(German architect)* **AV**
Bibl: Detail, 1985 May, v.25, no.3, p.259

Kafrawi, Kamal el *(Egyptian architect)* **AV**
Bibl: Middle East construction, 1985 July, v.10, no.7, p.24
el Kafrawi, Kamal **AV**

Kagan, Michel *(French architect)* **AV**
Bibl: Architecture d'aujourd'hui, 1985 Apr., no.238, p.104

Kagan, Sasha *(British textile artist, b.1945)* **BA**
Bibl: Cardiff (GBR), Oriel, Sasha Kagan (1984)

Kåge, Wilhelm *(Swedish ceramist, 1889-1960)* **BA**
Bibl: ▶Danckert, Euro. Porzellans; ▶Encyc. world art; ▶Natl. union cat., 1976

Kager, F. *(Austrian goldsmith, 19th c.)*   **BA**
Bibl: Simoniti, Zbornik za umetnostno zgodovino XIV-XV (1978-1979) 199-209
Kager, Johann Mathias → see Kager, Johann Matthias
Kager, Johann Matthias   **BA**
(German artist, 1575-1634)   WC
(German painter, architect, 1575-1634)   BA
(German, 1575-1634)   GC
Bibl: ▶Allgem. Deut. Biog.; ▶Bénézit; ▶Brockhaus Enzyk.; ▶Thieme-Becker; ▶Witt checklist
Kager, Johann Mathias   **GC WC**
Kagie, Johannes Leonardus *(Dutch painter, b.1907)*   **BA**
Bibl: Amsterdam (NLD), Mus. Fodor, Uitlopers (1978); ▶Scheen, Ned. beeldende kunst.
Kagoshima, E'wao *(painter, 20th c.)* **BA**
Bibl: Arts Mag., LVII/1-4 (Sep.-Dec. 1983) pp.57-61, 85-89, 120-128
Kahan, Roger *(French, active Saint Ouen, France 1930s)*   **JG**
Kahane, Daniel *(French architect, Paris)*   **AV**
Bibl: ▶Annuaire archts. fran.
Kahane, Melanie *(American interior designer, New York, d. 1988)*   **AV**
Bibl: Connoisseur, 1984 Dec., v.214, no.874, p.75
Kähkönen, Seppo *(Finnish architect, Haukipudas)*   **AV**
Bibl: Architektur + Wettbewerbe, 1988 Mar., no.133, p.60
Kahl, Karl N. *(German artist, 1873-)*   **WC**
Kahl, Philipp *(West German architect, Hannover)*   **AV**
Bibl: Baumeister, 1987 Nov., v.84, no.11, p.28
Kahlen, Hans *(German architects, Aachen)*   **AV**
Bibl: Bauwelt, 1986 Mar.7, v.77, no.10, p.320
Kahlen, Wolf *(German artist, b.1940)*   **BA**
Bibl: ▶Intl. dir. arts, 1983-1984; ▶Intl. dir. exh. artists, 1983; ▶WW Arts DEU
Kahler, Eugen von *(Czech artist, 1882-1911)*   **WC**
Kahlfeldt, Ulrich Paul *(German architect, Berlin)*   **AV**
Bibl: Abitare, 1985 June, no.235, p.60
Kahlo, Frida   **BA**
(Mexican artist, 1910-)   WC
(Mexican painter, 1907-1954)   BA
Bibl: ▶Art Index, v.38; ▶ARTbibl. mod., 22/1; Chicago, Mus. of Contemp Art, fRIDA KAHLO...; ▶Libr. of Congr. Name Auth. File; ▶MoMA libr. cat.; NY Times obit.; ▶Vollmer, Künst.-Lex. 20. Jhr.
Kahlo, Frida (de Rivera)   **WC**

Kahlo, Frida (de Rivera) → see Kahlo, Frida
Kahn, Albert   **AV BA**
(American architect, 1869-1942)   BA
(American architect, New York, N.Y, 1869-1942)   AV
Bibl: ▶Withey, Amer. archts.; ▶WWW Amer., 1897-1942, 1943-1950
Kahn, Barry *(American artist, b.1938)*   **BA**
Bibl: Portland (OR, USA), Art Mus., West Coast now (1968)
Kahn, Eli Jacques → see Kahn, Ely Jacques
Kahn, Ely Jacques   **BA**
(American architect)   AV
(American architect, painter, 1884-1972)   BA
Bibl: ▶Avery obit. idx.; ▶Portoghesi, Diz. arch. e urbanistica; ▶Vollmer, Künst.-Lex. 20. Jhr.; ▶Withey, Amer. archts.; ▶WWW Amer., v.5
Kahn, Eli Jacques   **AV**
Kahn, Eric *(British artist, 1904-1979)*   **WI**
Kahn, Louis I. → see Kahn, Louis Isidore
Kahn, Louis Isidore   **BA**
(American architect, 1901-1974)   AV BA
Bibl: ▶Contemp. archts.; ▶Libr. of Congr. Name Auth. File; ▶Macmillan encyc. archts.; ▶WWW Amer., v.6
Kahn, Louis I.   **AV**
Kahn, Steve   **BA JG**
(American photographer, b.1943)   BA
(American, 1943-)   JG
Bibl: Los Angeles (CA, USA), UCLA Wight Gallery, Amer. photos (1976); ▶MoMA libr. cat.
Kahn, Tobi *(American painter, sculptor, b.1952)*   **BA**
Bibl: Dreishpoon, D., in ARTS MAGAZINE LVII/5 (Jan 1984) 7; New York (NY, USA), Guggenheim Mus., New horizons (1985)
Kahn, Wolf *(American painter, b.1927)*   **BA**
Bibl: Davenport (IA, USA), Munic. Art Gall., Family album (1975); ▶WW Amer. Art
Kahri, Esko *(Finnish architect)*   **AV**
Bibl: Arkkitehti, 1984, no.4, p.40
Kainen, Jacob   **BA WI**
(American artist, b.1909)   WI
(American painter, printmaker, b.1909)   BA
Bibl: WW Amer., 1984; ▶WW Amer. Art, 1984
Kainer, Ludwig *(German artist, 1885-)*   **WC**

Kainrath, Wilhelm *(Austrian architect, Vienna, 1939-1986)*   **AV**
Bibl: Der Aufbau, 1986 May, v.41, no.5, p.231
Kainz, Hanns *(American architect)*   **AV**
Kainzmaier, Stefan *(German painter, b.1926)*   **BA**
Bibl: Oldenburg (BRD), Stadtmuseum, STEFAN KAINZMAIER (29 Aug-26 Sept 1976)
Kaipa, Jouni *(Finnish architect or artist)*   **AV**
Bibl: Arkkitehti, 1988, v.85, no.1, p.74
Kairamo, Erkki *(Finnish architect, 1936-)*   **AV**
Bibl: Process: architecture, n.37, 1983, p.101
Kaiser, Charles James *(American painter, b.1939)*   **BA**
Bibl: ▶WW Amer. Art
Kaiser, Eduard *(German artist, 1820-1895)*   **WC**
Kaiser, Friedrich *(German artist, 1815-1890)*   **WC**
Kaiser, Gisela *(West German architect, Stuttgart, 1943-)*   **AV**
Bibl: ▶Bund Deut. Arch. Hdbch.
Kaiser, Hans *(German artist, 1914-)*   **WC**
Kaiser, Hans-Dieter *(West German architect, Stuttgart, 1940-)*   **AV**
Bibl: ▶Bund Deut. Arch. Hdbch.
Kaiser, Johan Wilhelm → see Kaiser, Johann Wilhelm
Kaiser, Johann Wilhelm   **BA**
(Dutch painter, printmaker, 1813-1900)   BA
(Dutch printmaker, 1813-1900)   GC
Bibl: ▶Bénézit; ▶Scheen, Ned. beeldende kunst.; ▶Thieme-Becker
Kaiser, Johan Wilhelm   **GC**
Kaiser, Josef *(East German architect)*   **AV**
Bibl: Deutsche Architektur, 1973, v.22, p.432
Kaiser, Ludwig Friedrich *(German artist, 1779-1819)*   **WC**
Kaiser, Raffi *(Israeli artist, b.1931)*   **BA**
Bibl: Heidelberg (DEU), Kunstverein, Raffi Kaiser: Grenzzonen (1985)
Kaiser, Richard   **GC WC**
(German artist, 1868-1941)   WC
(German painter, 1868-1941)   GC
Bibl: ▶Bénézit; ▶Schweers, Gemälde deut. Museen
Kaiser, Rudolf *(Swiss(?) architect)*   **AV**
Bibl: Japan architect, 1984 Jan., v.59, no.321, p.44
Kaiser-Herbst, Carl *(German artist, 1858-)*   **WC**

Kaisermaan, Franz GC
(Swiss artist, 1765-1833) WC
(Swiss painter, 1765-1833) GC
Bibl: ▶Bénézit
**Kaesermann, Kaisermann or
Keiserman, Francois** WC
Kaisermann, Franz WC
Kaisermann, Franz→see Kaisermaan,
Franz
Kaish, Luise BA GC
(American painter, sculptor,
20th c.) BA
(American sculptor, b.1925) GC
Bibl: Getty Photo Study Coll.;
▶Opitz, Amer. sculptors; ▶WW
Amer. Art
Kaish, Luise Meyers GC
Kaish, Luise Meyers→see Kaish, Luise
Kaish, Morton (American painter,
b.1927) BA
Bibl: ▶WW Amer. Art
Kaivanto, Kimmo (Finnish painter,
b.1932) BA
Kaja, Zbigniew (Polish artist, 20th
cent.) WC
Kajari, Gyula (Hungarian artist, 20th
cent.) WC
Kakabadze, David (Russian painter,
1889-1952) BA
Bibl: ▶Encyc. world art
Kåks, Olle (Swedish painter,
sculptor, b.1941) BA
Bibl: New York (NY, USA),
Guggenheim Mus., Sleeping
beauty (1982); ▶Svenska
konstnärer
Kalach, Alberto (Mexican architect) AV
Bibl: Interiors, 1989 Sept., v.149,
no.2, p.169
Kalamis (Greek sculptor, act. ca.470-
430 BC) GC
Bibl: ▶Bowder, WWW Greek,
p.70; Getty Photo Study Coll.
Kalaš, Bogoslav (Yugoslav painter,
b.1942) BA
Bibl: Ljubljana (YUG), Mala
Galerija, BUGOSLAV KALAŠ, 1983
Kalas, Ernest (French architect,
artist and city planner, 1861-) AV
Bibl: Cahiers de la recherche
architecturale, 1989, no.24-25,
p.88
Kalathiskos Painter (Lucanian vase-
painter) GC
Bibl: ▶Trendall, Red-fig. vases
Lucania
Kalayciyan, Kirkor (French(?)
architect, Paris) AV
Bibl: Mimar: architecture in
development, 1988 Mar., no.25,
p.12
Kalb, Marty Joel (American painter,
b.1941) BA
Bibl: ▶MoMA libr. cat.; ▶WW
Amer. Art
Kalberer, Alfred F. (American,
b.1907) BA

Kälberer, Dieter (West German
architect) AV
Kälberer, Ulrike (West German
architect) AV
Kalčevski, Risto (Yugoslav painter,
b.1933) BA
Bibl: ▶Bénézit
Kalckreuth, Leopold Carl Walther
Graf von→see Kalckreuth, Leopold
von
Kalckreuth, Leopold von BA GC
(German artist, 1855-1928) WC
(German painter, printmaker,
1855-1928) BA
(German, 1855-1928) GC
Bibl: ▶Busse, Maler u. Bildhauer
19. Jahr.; George Goldner; ▶Neue
deutsche Biog.; ▶Thieme-Becker;
▶Witt checklist
**Kalckreuth, Leopold Carl
Walther Graf von** WC
**Kalckreuth, Stanislaus (Eduard
Stanislaus) Graf von** (German
artist, 1820-1894) WC
Kalczyńska, Alina (Polish
printmaker, b.1936) BA
Bibl: WW Poland
Kaldemarckt, Gabriel (German
draftsman, act.1587) BA
Bibl: Scheicher, DIE KUNST- UND
WUNDERKAMMERN..., 1979
Kaldenbach or Caldenbac, Martin
(Hesse or Hess) (Master of the
Frankfurt Altar)→see Kaldenbach,
Martin (Hesse)
Kaldenbach, Jan Antonie (Dutch
artist, 1760-1818) WC
Kaldenbach, Martin (Hesse) GC
(German artist, p.1470-1518) WC
(German draughtsman, b. aft.
1470-1518) GC
Bibl: ▶Thieme-Becker
Caldenbach, Martin GC
**Kaldenbach or Caldenbac,
Martin (Hesse or Hess)
(Master of the Frankfurt
Altar)** WC
Kalding, Hans (German artist, 1514-) WC
Kaldis, Aristodemos (American
painter, 1899-1979) BA
Bibl: ▶Havlice, Idx. art. bio.; ▶NY
art yrbk.; NYT, 3 May 1979
Kaldis, Stephanie (American artist,
b.1952) BA
Bibl: Newport Beach (CA, USA),
Newport Harbor Art Mus.,
Houston (1978)
Kalec, Donald G. (American
architect) AV
Bibl: Architecture: the AIA
journal, 1987 May, v.76, no.5,
p.184
Kalendarev, Yuri (Israeli sculptor,
b.1947) BA
Kales, Arthur (American, 1882-1936) JG

Kaletsch, Clemens (West German
sculptor, b.1952) BA
Bibl: Karlsruhe (DEU), Badischer
Kunstverein, Ars Viva 84/85
(1984)
Kalf→see Kalf, Willem
Kalf, Willem BA GC JG PR WC
(Dutch artist, 1619-1693) WC
(Dutch painter, 1619-1693) BA GC
(Dutch painter, 1622-1693) PR
(Dutch, 1622-1693) JG
Bibl: ▶Bénézit; ▶Encyc. world art;
▶Fogg Mus. Libr. cat.; ▶Grote
Winkler Prins; ▶Mallett's idx.
artists; Pelican Hist. of Art;
▶RILA/BHA; ▶Thieme-Becker
Calf PR
G. Kalf PR
Kaalf PR
Kalf PR
Kalfe PR
Kalff PR
Kalff, Willem PR
W. Calf PR
Willem Kalf PR
Willem Kalff PR
Kalfe→see Kalf, Willem
Kalff→see Kalf, Willem
Kalff, Willem→see Kalf, Willem
Kalichew, G.L. (Russian artist, op.
1799) WC
Kalide, Theodor (German sculptor,
1801-1863) BA
Bibl: ▶Mackay, Western sculp.
bronze; ▶Neue deutsche Biog.;
▶Thieme-Becker
Kälin, Lina (Swiss architect) AV
Bibl: Abitare, 1982 July-Aug., no.
206, p.38
Kalin, Nancy (American designer and
decorator, Middlebranch, OH) AV
Bibl: Colonial homes, 1985 May-
June, v.11, no.3, p.67
Kälin, Otto (Swiss painter, b.1913) BA
Bibl: ▶Künst.-Lex. Schweiz 20.
Jahrh.; ▶Lex. zeitgen. Schweiz.
Künstler
Kalin, Zdenko (Yugoslav sculptor,
b.1911) BA
Bibl: THE STUDIO, 149, 1955
p.114; ▶Vollmer, Künst.-Lex. 20.
Jhr.
Kalina, Richard (American painter,
b.1946) BA
Bibl: ▶WW Amer. Art, 1980
Kalinderu Group (vase-painters, ca.
500-480 BC) GC
Bibl: ▶Beazley, Attic bl.-fig. vase-
ptrs.; Boardman, Attic Bl.-fig.
Vases
Kalinin, Vjačeslav (Russian painter,
20th c.) BA
Bibl: Artnews LXXV DEc 1976,
p.102; ▶Fogg Mus. Libr. cat.
Kalinowski, Horst Egon (German
painter, b.1924) BA
Bibl: ▶WW Arts DEU

Kalinyčeva, Klara *(Russian artist, b.1933)* **BA**
  Bibl: ▶Bénézit

Kalish, Lionel *(American painter, b.1931)* **BA**
  Bibl: ▶Babington Smith, Contemp. artists; ▶Intl. dir. exh. artists, 1983

Kalisz, Jacques **AV**

Kaljund, Tiit *(Estonian architect, 20th century)* **AV**
  Bibl: Casabella, 1986 Nov., v.50, no.529, p.4

Kalkar, Jan Joest von → see Joest, Jan
Kalkar, Jan Stephan van → see Calcar, Jan Stephan van

Kalke, Edwin *(American printmaker, b.1944)* **BA**
  Bibl: Milwaukee (WI, USA), Art Mus., Wisconsin printmkrs. (1982)

Kalkhof, Peter **WC WI**
  (British artist, 1933-) **WC**
  (British artist, b.1933) **WI**

Kalksma, Gea *(Dutch artist, b.1953)* **BA**
  Bibl: Exhibition Catalogue, Rotterdam, Museum Boymans-van Beuningen, KUNST UIT ROTTERDAM, 1984; ▶Intl. dir. exh. artists, 1982

Kallenbach, Gregor Maria *(German painter, b.1901)* **BA**
  Bibl: Bildende Kunst 7 1980 324-327; ▶Vollmer, Künst.-Lex. 20. Jhr.

Kallenbach, Otto *(German sculptor, b.1911)* **BA**
  Bibl: ▶Vollmer, Künst.-Lex. 20. Jhr.; ▶Who's Who [GBR]; ▶WW Arts DEU

Kallenberg, Anders Hansson *(Swedish artist, 1834-1902)* **WC**

Kallenberg, Jakob *(Swiss artist, op. 1535-1565)* **WC**

Kallenberger, Kreg *(American glass artist, 20th c.)* **BA**
  Bibl: Guide exh. artists: N. Amer. ptrs.; Tulsa (OK, USA), Philbrook Art Center, KALLENBERGER..., 1986

Kalliandrès, Syméon *(Greek ecclesiastic, scribe, 13th c.)* **BA**
  Bibl: Gehin, P., SCRIPTORIUM, XL/2 (1986), p.172-183

Kallierges, Zacharias → see Calliergi, Zaccaria

Kalliga, Charis *(Greek architect, 1941-)* **AV**
  Bibl: Architektonika Themata = Architecture in Greece, 1989, no.23, p.108

Kalligas, A. *(Architect, Greece)* **AV**
  Bibl: Architektonika themata, 1985, v.19, p.154

Kallikrates *(Greek architect, 5th c BC)* **GC**
  Bibl: ▶Brilliant, Anc. Greeks, p.192

Kallimachos **AV BA CE GC JG**
  (Greek sculptor, 5th c BC (late)) **GC**
  (Greek sculptor, metalworker, 5th c. B.C.) **BA**
  (Greek sculptor, painter, metalworker, 5th c. B.C) **AV**
  (Sculptor, post 500/ante 400 BC-post 410/ante 380/BC) **CE**
  Bibl: Becatti, AAGR, p.184; ▶Encyc. world art

Kallio, Heikki *(Finnish craftsman, b.1948)* **BA**
  Bibl: Sunderland (GBR), Arts Ctr., Suomen Lasi--Finnish glass (1979)

Kallis Painter **GC**
  Bibl: ▶Beazley, Attic bl.-fig. vase-ptrs.

Kallis, Sten *(Finnish architect)* **AV**
  Bibl: Arkkitehti, 1989, v.86, no.3, p.52

Kallistonikos of Thebes *(Greek sculptor, 4th c BC (1st half))* **GC**
  Bibl: ▶Robertson, Greek art, p.383

Kallmann, Gerhard M. *(American architect, Boston, Mass, 1915-)* **AV**
  Bibl: ▶Contemp. archts.

Kallmeyer, Hans Julius Bernhard *(German artist, 1882-)* **WC**

Kallmorgen, Friedrich **BA WC**
  (German artist, 1856-1924) **WC**
  (German painter, printmaker, 1856-1924) **BA**
  Bibl: ▶Met. Mus. Art libr. cat.; ▶Thieme-Becker

Kallmorgen, Georg *(West German architect)* **AV**
  Bibl: Bauwelt, 1988 Jan.29, v.79, no.5, p.214

Kallmorgen, Werner *(West German architect, 1902-1979)* **AV**
  Bibl: Bauwelt, 1988 Apr.8, v.79, no.14, p.594

Kallmus, Dora (Madame D'Ora) *(German photographer, 1881-1963)* **BA**
  Bibl: Hamburg (DEU), Mus. Kunst u. Gewerbe, Nicola Perscheid (1980)

Kallon of Aegina *(Greek sculptor, 5th c BC (early))* **GC**
  Bibl: ▶Robertson, Greek art, p.184

Kallos, Paul *(Hungarian artist, 1928-)* **WC**

Kallstenius, Gottfried Samuel Nikolaus *(Swedish artist, 1861-1943)* **WC**

Kalmakoff, Nicola *(Russian artist, op.1927)* **WC**

Kalman, Andras *(British, 20th c.)* **BA**

Kalman, Max M. *(American architect, Boston, Mass, early 20th cent)* **AV**
  Bibl: Boston Preservation Alliance letter, 1989 May, v.10, no.4, p.6

Kalmikov, Yu. *(Russian architect)* **AV**
  Bibl: Process: architecture, 1985 Jan., no.54, p.152

Kalnynsh or Kalnins, Edvards F. *(Russian artist, 1904-)* **WC**

Kalorkoti, Panayiotis *(Greek painter, printmaker in GBR, b.1957)* **BA**
  Bibl: ▶Intl. dir. exh. artists; Sunderland (GB), Arts Centre, Tricia Gillman (1982)

Kalouguine, Vladimir *(1931-)* **AV**

Kalraet → see Kalraet, Barend van

Kalraet, Abraham Pietersz. van **BA**
  (Dutch artist, 1642-1722) **WC**
  (Dutch painter, 1642-1722) **BA PR**
  (Dutch, 1642-1722) **GC**
  Bibl: ▶Bernt, Neth. ptrs. 17c.; George Goldner; Getty Photo Study Coll. (Ptgs.); Parière; ▶Thieme-Becker; ▶Witt checklist; ▶Wurzbach, NLD Künst.-Lex.

Abraham Calraet **PR**
Calraet **PR**
Calraet, Abraham **GC PR**
Calraet, Abraham van **PR**
Calraet, Calraat or Kalraet, Abraham Pietersz. **WC**
Kalraet, Abraham van **GC**
Kalraet, Abraham van → see Kalraet, Abraham Pietersz. van

Kalraet, Barend van **GC PR**
  (Dutch artist, 1649-1737) **WC**
  (Dutch painter, 1649-1737) **GC PR**
  Bibl: Getty Photo Study Coll.; Getty Photo Study Coll. (Ptgs.); ▶Thieme-Becker; ▶Witt checklist

Barend van Calraet **PR**
Barend van Kalraet **PR**
Calraet **PR**
Calraet, Barend van **PR**
Calraet, Barent Pietersz. **GC**
Calraet, Calraat or Kalraet, Barent Pietersz. **WC**
Kalraet **PR**

Kalsi, Amarjit *(British(?) architect)* **AV**
  Bibl: RIBA journal, 1983 June, v.90, no.6, p.16

Kalt, Michel *(French architect, Paris)* **AV**
  Bibl: ▶Annuaire archts. fran., 1978

Kaltenbach, Steven J. *(American artist, 20th c.)* **BA**
  Bibl: ▶Artweek idx.

Kaltenbacher, Franz *(Austrian architect)* **AV**
  Bibl: Planen Bauen Wohnen, 1989, no.127, p.26

Kaltenmoser, Karl *(German artist, 1853-1923)* **WC**

Kaltenmoser, Kaspar **GC WC**
  (German artist, 1806-1867) **WC**
  (German, 1806-1867) **GC**
  Bibl: ▶Thieme-Becker; ▶Witt checklist

Kaltenmoser, Max *(German artist, 1842-1887)* **WC**

Kaltenofer, Kalthoff or Koltenoffen, Peter *(German artist, op.1457-m.c.1490)* **WC**

Kaltner or Kalter, Joseph *(German artist, c.1758-p.1824)* **WC**

Kalvach, Rudolf *(German artist, 1883-)* **WC**

Kalvoda, Alois *(Czech artist, 1875-1934)* **WC**

Kalymnos Painter **GC**
Bibl: ▶Beazley, Attic red-fig. vase-ptrs.

Kalypso *(Greek painter, unknown)* **GC**
Bibl: ▶Robertson, Greek art, p.712

Kamal, Fawizah bte Haji→see Fawizah bte Haji Kamal

Kamal, Saman *(Iraqui architect)* **AV**
Bibl: RIBA journal, 1983 July, v.90, no.7, p.26

Kamali, Norma *(American fashion and furniture designer, New York City)* **AV**
Bibl: House & garden, 1988 Dec., p.142

Kamath, Revathi *(Indian architect, New Delhi, married to Vasant Kamath)* **AV**
Bibl: Architects' journal, 1987 July 22, v.186, no.29, p.69

Kamath, Vasant *(Indian architect, New Delhi, married to Revathi Kamath)* **AV**
Bibl: Indian Inst. Archts., Members Directory 1984

Kamenev, Lev Lvovich *(Russian artist, 1833-1886)* **WC**

Kamenow, Saszo *(Bulgarian artist, 20th cent.)* **WC**

Kamensetzer, Hans *(German woodcarver, act.1467)* **BA**
Bibl: Ramisch, Jahrb. der Staatl. Kunstsamml. Baden-Württemberg VII (1971), 19-34

Kamerlingh Onnes, Harm Hendrick **GC**
(Dutch artist, 1893-) **WC**
(Dutch painter, b.1893) **GC**
Bibl: Rijksmuseum

Onnes, Harm Henrick Kamerlingh **WC**

Kamerlingh Onnes, Jenny *(Dutch, act.1889-1894)* **BA**
Bibl: Jong Holland, II/4 (Dec 1986) 42

Kamieński, Antoni *(Polish painter, printmaker, 1860/61-1933)* **BA**
Bibl: ▶Bénézit; Biuletyn Historii Sztuki, XL/2 (1978) 165-192; ▶Wielka ilustr. encyk.

Kamihira, Ben **BA WC**
(American painter, b.1925) **BA**
(French artist, 20th cent.) **WC**
Bibl: ▶WW Amer. Art, 1978

Kamil Khan Mumtaz→see Mumtaz, Kamil Khan

Kamimura, Massayoshi *(Architect, works in Brazil)* **AV**
Bibl: Projeto, 1985 June, no.76, p.66

Kaminski, Aleksander *(Polish artist, 1823-1886)* **WC**

Kaminski, Max G. *(German painter, b.1938)* **BA**
Bibl: Berlin (BRD), Neuer Berliner Kunstrerein, MAX G. .KAMINSKI: BILDER UND ZEICHNUNGEN 1973-1977, 1977; LC slip

Kaminsky, Thomas *(German painter, b.1945)* **BA**
Bibl: ▶WW Arts DEU

Kaminsky, Walter *(German, active 1920s, Bauhaus)* **JG**

Kamiya, Ituo *(Japanese architect)* **AV**

Kamke, Georges *(French artist, 1889-)* **WC**

Kamke, Ivar *(Scandinavian artist, 1882-1936)* **WC**

Kamler, Richard *(American artist, 20th c.)* **BA**
Bibl: ▶Artweek idx.; San Francisco (CA, USA), SFMoMA, Desert project (1979)

Kamm *(German artist, 18th cent.)* **WC**

Kammann, Klaus *(West German architect)* **AV**
Bibl: Architectural review, 1987 Apr., v.181, no.1082, p.70

Kammer, Charles *(French interior designer, shoe designer)* **AV**
Bibl: Maison française, 1984 Sept., no.380, p.116

Kammerer, Hans **AV BA**
(1922-) **AV**
(German architect, b.1922) **BA**
Bibl: ▶WW Arts DEU; ▶WW Germany

Kamocki, Stanislas *(Polish artist, 1875-1944)* **WC**

Kamp, Anton *(American painter, 20th c.)* **BA**
Bibl: Archives Amer. Art Jrnl., XXIII/3 (1983) pp.34-37

Kamp, Karl *(German architect)* **AV**
Bibl: Deutsche Bauzeitung, 1986 Aug., v.120, no.8, p.34

Kampe, Gerhard *(West German architect, Arolsen)* **AV**
Bibl: Architektur, Innenarchitektur, Technischer Ausbau, 1987 Nov., v.95, no.11, p.44

Kampen, Jacob van→see Campen, Jacob van

Kampen, Joos van *(Dutch painter, act. 17th century)* **PR**
Bibl: ▶Thieme-Becker

Stoffade **PR**
Stokade **PR**

Kamper→see Kamper, Godaert

Kamper, Godaert **GC PR WC**
(Dutch artist, c.1613/14-1679) **WC**
(Dutch painter, 1613/14-1679) **PR**
(Dutch, ca.1613-1679) **GC**
Bibl: ▶Thieme-Becker; ▶Witt checklist

Godaert Kamper **PR**
Kamper **PR**

Kampf, Arthur **GC WC**
(German artist, 1864-1950) **WC**
(German painter and draughtsman, 1864-1950) **GC**
Bibl: ▶Thieme-Becker

Kampf, Eugen *(German artist, 1861-1902)* **WC**

Kämpf, Max **BA WC**
(Swiss artist, 1912-) **WC**
(Swiss painter, 1912-1982) **BA**
Bibl: Basel (CHE), Kunsthalle Basel, MAX KÄMPF, 1984; ▶Künst.-Lex. Schweiz 20. Jahrh.; ▶Lex. zeitgen. Schweiz. Künstler

Kamphuijsen→see Camphuysen, Dirck Raphaelsz.

Kamphuijsen→see Camphuysen, Govert Dircksz.

Kamphuijsen, Jan *(Dutch painter and draughtsman, 1760-1841)* **GC**
Bibl: ▶Bénézit; ▶Thieme-Becker

Camphuysen, Jan **GC**

Kamphuijssen→see Camphuysen, Dirck Raphaelsz.

Kamphuijssen→see Camphuysen, Govert Dircksz.

Kamphuyzen→see Camphuysen, Dirck Raphaelsz.

Kampik, Andreas *(West German architect, Munich)* **AV**
Bibl: Deutsches Architektenblatt, 1989 Oct.1, v.21, no.10, p.1447

Kampmann, Gustav *(German painter, printmaker, 1859-1917)* **BA**
Bibl: ▶Bénézit; ▶Thieme-Becker

Kampmann, Hack *(Danish architect, 1856-1920)* **AV BA**
Bibl: ▶Macmillan encyc. archts.; ▶Portoghesi, Diz. arch. e urbanistica; ▶Thieme-Becker

Kampmann, Walter *(German painter, sculptor, printmaker, 1887-1945)* **BA**
Bibl: ▶Vollmer, Künst.-Lex. 20. Jhr.

Kamrath, Karl *(American architect, Hoston, Tex, 1911-1988)* **AV**
Bibl: Texas architect, 1988 May-June, v.38, no.3, p.23; American architects directory 1970

Kamrowski, Gerome **BA WC WI**
(American artist, 1914-) **WC**
(American artist, b.1914) **WI**
(American painter, b.1914) **BA**
Bibl: ▶WW Amer. Art, 1976

Kamsetzer, Jan Baptist→see Kamsetzer, Jan Chrystian

Kamsetzer, Jan Chrystian **BA**
(German architect, printmaker in POL, 1753-1795) BA
(German artist, 1753-1795) WC
(Polish architect, 1753-1795) AV
Bibl: Bildhdbch. Kunst. Pol.;
▶Encyc. world art; ▶Hempel,
Baroque central Euro., p.309;
▶Łozínski, Arch. Poland, pp.249,
257; ▶Portoghesi, Diz. arch. e
urbanistica; ▶Slownik artystów
polskich; ▶Thieme-Becker

Kamsetzer, Jan Baptist **AV WC**

Kan, De-e *(Japanese architect)* **AV**
Bibl: Architettura; cronache e
storia, 1979 Apr., v.25, no.
4(282), p.234

Kan, Shiu-Kay *(Architect and lighting designer, London)* **AV**
Bibl: ▶RIBA members, 1987

Kanachos of Sikyon *(Greek sculptor, act. late 6th c BC)* **GC**
Bibl: Getty Photo Study Coll.;
▶Robertson, Greek art, p.182

Kanaga, Consuelo *(American photographer, 1894-1978)* **BA**
Bibl: NYT 2 Mar 1978 p.32

Kanda, Hiroshi *(Japanese architect, 1944-)* **AV**
Bibl: Process: architecture, 1986
May special issue, no.3, p.116

Kanda, Shun *(American architect)* **AV**
Bibl: Architectural record, 1985
May, v.173, no.6, p.110

Kandel, David **BA GC**
(German artist, c.1527-a.1596) WC
(German draughtsman, ca.1527-bef.1596) GC
(German painter, ca.1520/25-1592/96) BA
Bibl: ▶Hollstein, German, v.15b,
p.217; ▶Thieme-Becker

Kandel, Kandell, Kandler or Kannel, David **WC**
Kandler, David GC
Kannel, David GC
Kandel, Kandell, Kandler or Kannel, David → see Kandel, David

Kandel, Lutz *(West German architect, Stuttgart)* **AV**
Bibl: Garten + Landschaft, 1986
Aug., v.96, no.8, p.15

Kandell, Axel *(Swedish architect, Stockholm)* **AV**
Bibl: ▶Svenska Ark. Riks., 1984,
p.146

Kandinskij, Vasilij **BA**
(Russian artist, 1866-1944) WC WI
(Russian painter, 1866-1944) BA PR
(Russian, 1866-1944) GC
Bibl: ▶Encyc. world art; ▶Oxford
comp. 20c. art; ▶Phaidon 20c.
art; ▶RILA/BHA; ▶Seuphor,
Abstract ptg.; ▶Witt checklist
Kandinsky PR
Kandinsky, Vasily PR
Kandinsky, Wassily **GC PR**
Kandinsky, Wassily Wassiljewitsch **WC WI**
Wassily Kandinsky PR
Kandinsky → see Kandinskij, Vasilij
Kandinsky, Vasily → see Kandinskij, Vasilij
Kandinsky, Wassily → see Kandinskij, Vasilij
Kandinsky, Wassily Wassiljewitsch → see Kandinskij, Vasilij

Kandler, Charles Frederick I → see Kandler, Charles I

Kandler, Charles I **BA**
(British silversmith, act. from 1727) GC
(English goldsmith, silversmith, act.1727-1773) BA
Bibl: ▶Grimwade, London
goldsmiths, 1982, p.567;
▶Honour, Gold- & silversmiths,
p.171; Lever, Goldsmiths, p.53;
▶Thieme-Becker

Kandler, Charles Frederick I **GC**
Kandler, David → see Kandel, David

Kändler, Johann Joachim **BA GC JG**
(German porcelain modeller, 1706-1775) GC
(German sculptor, porcelain painter, 1706-1775) BA
(German, 1705-1775, active 1731) JG
Bibl: ▶Allgem. Deut. Biog.; ▶Art
Index, vs.24, 26; ▶Artist biog.
master idx.; Kunstland DDR;
▶Neue deutsche Biog.; ▶Penguin
dec. arts; ▶Thieme-Becker

Kandler, Wilhelm *(German artist, 1816-1896)* **WC**

Kandt-Horn, Susanne *(German painter, 20th c.)* **BA**
Bibl: Meuche, RAUM UND BILD.
1980

Kandzia, Christian *(West German architect, Stuttgart)* **AV**
Bibl: Architektur,
Innenarchitektur, Technischer
Ausbau 1985 Jan.-Feb., v.93,
no.1, p.24

Kane, John **BA PR WC WI**
(American artist, 1860-1934) WC WI
(American painter, 1860-1934) BA PR
Bibl: ▶Bénézit; ▶Jakovsky, Peintres
naïfs; ▶RILA/BHA
John Kane PR

Kane, Mitchell *(American artist, op. 1987-)* **WI**

Kane, Paul *(American painter, b.1939)* **BA**
Bibl: ▶Artweek idx.; Springfield
(MA, USA), MFA, Abstract
illusionism (1978)

Kane, Paul **BA WC**
(Canadian artist, 1810-1871) WC
(Canadian painter, 1810-1871) BA
Bibl: ▶Artist biog. master idx.;
Canad. encyc.; ▶Havlice, Idx. art.
bio.; ▶New Columbia encyc.

Kane, William *(American photographer, b.1951)* **BA**
Bibl: Afterimage, VIII/5 (Dec.
1980); ARTS MAG, LV (Jan 1981)
22

Kanelba, Rajmund → see Kanelba, Raymond

Kanelba, Raymond **GC**
(Polish artist, 1897-) WC
(Polish painter, b.1897) GC
Bibl: ▶Bénézit; Getty Photo Study
Coll.

Kanelba, Rajmund **WC**
Kanella, Raymond GC
Kanella, Raymond → see Kanelba, Raymond

Kanellopoulos, P. *(Greek, 20th c.)* **BA**
Bibl: BYZANTION, LIII/1 (1983)
17-35; ▶Libr. of Congr. Name
Auth. File

Kanemitsu, Matsumi *(American painter, b.1922)* **BA**
Bibl: ▶Bénézit; ▶Cummings,
Contemp. Amer. artists, 1971;
▶MoMA libr. cat.; ▶WW Amer.
Art, 1976

Kaneria, Raghav *(Indian sculptor, b.1936)* **BA**
Bibl: Cambridge (GBR), Camb.
Univ., Fitzwilliam Mus., Bernard
Meadows (1980)

Kanerva, Raimo Antti Olavi *(Finnish printmaker, painter, b.1941)* **BA**
Bibl: ▶Dict. Scand. biog.; Ljubljana
(YU), Mala Galerija, RAIMO
KANERVA (30 J-1 Aug 1976)

Kanfer, Robert *(Austrian architect, Vienna)* **AV**
Bibl: ▶Verzeich. Öst. Ziviltech.

Kaniewski, Xaver Jan *(Polish painter, printmaker, 1809-1870)* **BA**
Bibl: ▶Bénézit; ▶Thieme-Becker

Kánka, František Maximilian *(architect, 1674-1766)* **BA**

Kann, Adolphe *(French, 20th c.)* **BA**
Kannaletti → see Canaletto (Giovanni Antonio Canal)
Kannel, David → see Kandel, David

Kannemans, Christiaan Cornelis **GC WC**
(Dutch artist, 1812-1884) WC
(Dutch painter, 1812-1884) GC
Bibl: ▶Thieme-Becker

Kannwischer, Gustav (German
architect, Bad Kreuznach)　　**AV**
Bibl: Architektur,
Innenarchitektur, Technischer
Ausbau, 1986 Jan.-Feb., v.94, no.
1-2, p.24

Kano (American artist, 20th c.)　　**BA**
Bibl: ▶Art Index, Kano, n.d.; Arts
Mag., Lightning strikes, (3 Nov.
1982)

Kanoldt, Alexander　　**BA GC WC**
(German artist, 1881-1839)　　**WC**
(German painter, printmaker,
1881-1939)　　**BA**
(German, 1881-1939)　　**GC**
Bibl: ▶Bénézit; ▶Vollmer,
Künst.-Lex. 20. Jhr.; ▶Witt
checklist

Kanoldt, Edmund Friedrich　　**BA WC**
(German artist, 1845-1904)　　**WC**
(German painter, 1845-1904)　　**BA**
Bibl: ▶Bénézit; Boetticher,
Malerwerke 19. Jahrh.; ▶Busse,
Maler u. Bildhauer 19. Jahr.;
▶Darmstädter, Künstlerlex.;
▶Thieme-Becker

Kanovitz, Howard　　**BA WC WI**
(American artist, 1929-)　　**WC**
(American artist, b.1929)　　**WI**
(American painter, b.1929)　　**BA**
Bibl: ▶Brockhaus Enzyk.; ▶WW
Amer. Art

Kanstein, Cynthia (American
photographer, 20th c.)　　**BA**
Bibl: ▶Intl. dir. exh. artists, 1982,
1983

Kant, Immanuel (1724-1804)　　**AV**
Bibl: ▶Libr. of Congr. Name Auth.
File

Kantardziewa, Weni (Bulgarian
artist, 20th cent.)　　**WC**

Kanters, Hans (Dutch artist, 20th c.)　　**BA**
Bibl: Redeker, 8 Realisten

Kantharos Group　　**GC JG**
(Apulian vase-painters)　　**GC**
Bibl: Trendall, Attic red-fig. vases
Apulia

Kantor→see Kantor, Morris

Kantor, Martha Ryther (American
painter, ca.1896-1981)　　**BA**
Bibl: NY TIMES, 10 Jan 1981

Kantor, Morris　　**BA PR WC WI**
(American artist, 1896-)　　**WC**
(American artist, 1896-1974)　　**WI**
(American painter, 1896-1974)　　**BA PR**
Bibl: ▶RILA/BHA
Kantor　　**PR**
Morris Kantor　　**PR**

Kantor, Tadeusz　　**BA WC**
(Polish artist, 1915-)　　**WC**
(Polish painter, sculptor, theater
director, b.1915)　　**BA**
Bibl: ▶Artist biog. master idx.;
▶Contemp. artists; ▶Havlice, Idx.
art. bio.; Int. Herald Tribune
2/6/91, obit.; ▶Intl. dir. exh.
artists, 1983

Kantrowitz, Min (Project director)　　**AV**
Bibl: Progressive architecture,
1986 Jan., v.67, no.1, p.134

Kanz, Carl Christian (German artist,
1758-p.1818(?))　　**WC**

Kapadia, Sen (Indian architect)　　**AV**
Bibl: Architecture + design, 1988
Sept.-Oct., v.4, no.6, p.37

Kapanov, A. (Russian architect)　　**AV**
Bibl: Process: architecture, 1985
Jan., no.54, p.152

Kapell, P. (German artist, 19th cent.)　　**WC**

Kapeller (French artist, op.1771)　　**WC**

Kapeller, J. von (German artist, op.
1896)　　**WC**

**Kapeller, Kappeller or Kappler the
Younger, Joseph Anton** (German
artist, 1761-1806)　　**WC**

Kapéra, Jean (French painter,
sculptor, collagist, b.1924)　　**BA**
Bibl: ▶Bénézit; Morlaix (FRA), Mus.
de Jacobins, Kapera (1990)

Kapfenberger, Friedrich (Austrian
architect, Knittelfeld)　　**AV**
Bibl: ▶Verzeich. Öst. Ziviltech.
Kapfenberger, Fritz　　**AV**
Kapfenberger, Fritz→see
Kapfenberger, Friedrich

Kapfhammer, Wolfgang (West
German architect)　　**AV**

Kapfinger, Otto (Austrian architect,
1949-)　　**AV**
Bibl: Institute for Architecture and
Urban Studies. Catalogue, n.13,
1980, p.34

Kaphahn, Franz (German weapons
maker, 16th c.)　　**BA**
Bibl: Schaal, DRESDENER
KUNSTBLATTER XXX/41 (1986)
120-122

Kaplan, Anatoli→see Kaplan, Anatolij
L'vovič

Kaplan, Anatolij L'vovič　　**BA**
(Russian artist, 1902-)　　**WC**
(Russian artist, b.1902)　　**BA**
Bibl: Heider Gertrud '77
monograph, OCLC info

Kaplan, Anatoli　　**WC**

Kaplan, Enid (American jeweler,
sculptor, 20th c.)　　**BA**
Bibl: Women Artists News X/2
(Winter 1985) 8

Kaplan, Harvey (American designer,
Albany)　　**AV**
Bibl: Albany preservation report,
1983 Dec., p.5

Kaplan, Howard (American collector
and interior designer, New York
City)　　**AV**
Bibl: House beautiful, 1988 July,
v.130, no.7, p.9; NYC phone bk.,
1987

Kaplan, Joseph (American painter,
1900-1980)　　**BA**
Bibl: ▶MoMA libr. cat.; NY Times
12 Mar 1980; ▶WW Amer. Art

Kaplan, Kenneth (American
architect, New York City)　　**AV**
Bibl: A + U, 1989 Aug., no.
8(227), p.26

Kaplan, Louis S. (American
architect, New Jersey, 1896-1964)　　**AV**
Bibl: ▶Amer. archts. dir., 3rd ed.,
1970

Kaplan, Malvina (Israeli painter,
20th c.)　　**BA**
Bibl: Haifa. Mus. of Modern Art:
MALVINA KAPLAN..., 1977; ▶Intl.
dir. arts

Kaplan, Marion (American
photographer, 20th c.)　　**BA**
Bibl: Arts Mag., "Arts reviews", 3
Nov 1982

Kaplicky, Jan　　**AV BA**
(British architect, 1937-)　　**AV**
(Czech architect in GBR,
b.1937)　　**BA**
Bibl: Arch. & urbanism, 9(180)
(Sep. 1985) p.79; ▶Avery period.
idx., 4th suppl., 6th suppl.; Avery
Ref. File (RLIN); Davies, Arch.
review, CLXXVI/1049 (Jul. 1984)
p.76

Kaplin, Richard (Canadian architect,
Morin Heights, Quebec)　　**AV**
Bibl: ▶Canad. arch. dir., 1985

Kaplinski, Leon (Polish artist, 1826-
1873)　　**WC**

Kapljanskij, Boris (Russian sculptor,
20th c.)　　**BA**
Bibl: Soviet sculp. 1977

Kaplowitz, Jane (American artist,
op.1987-)　　**WI**

Kapnek, Theodore H. (American,
20th c.)　　**BA**

Kapociunas, Vytas Bronius
(Australian draughtsman, b.1943)　　**GC**
Bibl: ▶Encyc. Australian art

Kapoor, Anish　　**BA WI**
(British artist, op.20th c.)　　**WI**
(British sculptor, b.1954)　　**BA**
Bibl: Bristol (GBR), Arnolfini
Gallery, Objects (1981)

Kapp, David (American painter,
b.1953.)　　**BA**
Bibl: ARTS MAG, LVI (Oct 1981)
94-97; Jones, A., in ARTS MAG
LVIII/10 (summer 1984) 15

Kapp, Edmond Xavier　　**WC WI**
(British artist, 1890-)　　**WC**
(British artist, 1890-1978)　　**WI**

Kappe, Raymond (American
architect, Pacific Palisades, Calif)　　**AV**
Bibl: ▶AIA Pro File, 1987-88

Kappel, Philip (American printmaker,
author, b.1901)　　**BA**
Bibl: ▶WW Amer. Art, 1976

Kappel, Stephan (Danish architect,
Lyngby)　　**AV**
Bibl: ▶Danske Arkitekters
Landsforbund, 1984-85

Kappeler, Otto *(Swiss sculptor, 1884-1949)* **BA**
    Bibl: ▶Künst.-Lex. Schweiz 20. Jahrh.; ▶Thieme-Becker
Kappenberg, Meister von → *see* Baegert, Jan
Kappes, Alfred *(American artist, 1850-1894)* **WC WI**
Kappis → *see* Kappis, Albert
Kappis, A. → *see* Kappis, Albert
Kappis, Albert **PR WC**
    (German artist, 1836-1914) WC
    (German painter, 1836-1914) PR
    Bibl: ▶Thieme-Becker
    Albert Kappis PR
    Kappis PR
    Kappis, A. PR
Kappler, Hans Peter *(West German architect, 1935-)* **AV**
    Bibl: Deutsche Bauzeitung, 1988 Aug., v.122, no.8, p.47
Kaprasová, Ludmila *(Czech painter, sculptor, textile artist, b.1941)* **BA**
    Bibl: ▶Bénézit
Kaprov, Susan *(American painter, printmaker, 20th c.)* **BA**
    Bibl: ▶Art Index, Apr. 1978
Kaprow, Allan *(American artist, b.1927)* **BA WI**
    Bibl: ▶WW Amer. Art
Kaps, Andreas *(West German painter, b.1946)* **BA**
    Bibl: ▶Babington Smith, Contemp. artists; ▶Intl. dir. exh. artists, 1982
Kapterev, Valerij *(Russian printmaker, 20th c.)* **BA**
    Bibl: Bowlt, Abstract for Turova monograph, 1978
Kapus, Sergej *(Yugoslav painter, b.1950)* **BA**
    Bibl: ▶Intl. dir. exh. artists, 1981; Ljubljana (YUG), Emerik Bernard (1984)
Kapuscik, Andrzej *(Austrian architect)* **AV**
    Bibl: GA document, 1989 Apr., no.23, p.34
Kar, Ida *(British (b. Russia, now USSR), 1908)* **JG**
Karaffa, A.S. → *see* Caraff, A.S.
Karakaszew, Wilen *(Russian artist, 20th cent.)* **WC**
Karakosta, Seva *(Greek architect, 1938-)* **AV**
    Bibl: Architektonika Themata = Architecture in Greece, 1989, no.23, p.115
Karalis, Giovanni Jacopo → *see* Caraglio, Giovanni Jacopo
Karam, Nadim *(Lebanese architect, born in West Africa)* **AV**
    Bibl: (Mimar, 1989 June, no.32, p.16

Karamyšev, Lev Maksimovič *(Russian glassmaker, 1790-1836)* **BA**
    Bibl: Dek ISS SSR July 1976, p.38-39
Karas, Vekoslav *(Yugoslavian painter, 1821-1858)* **GC**
    Bibl: ▶Bénézit
Karavan, Dani **AV BA**
    (French artist) AV
    (Israeli sculptor, b.1930) BA
    Bibl: Architecture intérieure créé, 1985 Dec.-1986 Jan., no.209, p.52; Cape Town (ZAF), S. African Natl. Gallery, Israeli art (1980); KUNSTWERK XXXII 1 Feb 1979 12-17
Karazin, Nicholas Nicholaivich *(Russian artist, 1842-1908)* **WC**
Karban, Oldřich *(Czech sculptor, 20th c.)* **BA**
    Bibl: Vytvarná kultura V/5 (1981) 53-54
Karbowsky, Adrien *(French artist, 1855-p.1945)* **WC**
Kärcer, Amalie **GC**
    (German artist, c.1860-) WC
    (German painter, act. ca.1860) GC
    Bibl: DWA
Karcher, Amalie **WC**
Karcher, Amalie → *see* Kärcer, Amalie
Karcher, Giovanni *(early Netherlandish tapestry maker, act. 1517-1562)* **BA**
    Bibl: Fioravanti Baraldi, LA CATTEDRALE DI FERRARA, p.524; TCI Emilia-Romagna; ▶Thieme-Becker
Karcher, Nicolas *(early Netherlandish tapestry maker in ITA, act.1539-1556)* **BA**
    Bibl: ▶Thieme-Becker; ▶Thomson, Tapestry
Karcyganov, Evgenij Aleksandrovič *(Russian painter, printmaker, b.1932)* **BA**
    Bibl: Iskusstvo XXXVIII 7 1975, p.28; John Bowlt corresp., Nov. 1977
Karczewski, Eva *(French architect)* **AV**
    Bibl: Techniques et architecture, 1985 Dec.-1986 Jan., no.363, p.42
Karczewski, Jean *(French architect, Paris)* **AV**
    Bibl: ▶Annuaire archts. fran., 1978
Kardamitis, J. *(Greek artist, 1921-)* **WC**
Kardon, Dennis *(American painter, 20th c.)* **BA**
    Bibl: Meyer, J., in ARTS MAG LVII/9 (May 1983) 9
Kardorff, Konrad von *(German artist, 1877-1945)* **WC**
Kardovskij, Dmitrij Nikolaevič *(Russian painter, illustrator, 1866-1943)* **BA**
Karel Batist → *see* Batist, Karel

Karel Breydel → *see* Breydel, Karel
Karel du Jardin → *see* Dujardin, Karel
Karel du Jardyn → *see* Dujardin, Karel
Karel Dujardin → *see* Dujardin, Karel
Karel Ferdinand Venneman → *see* Venneman, Karel Ferdinand
Karel Krcal → *see* Krcal, Karel
Karel Philips Spierincks → *see* Spierincks, Karel Philips
Karel Roos → *see* Roos, Karel [Unidentified]
Karel Slabbaert → *see* Slabbaert, Karel
Karel van der Pluym → *see* Pluym, Karel van der
Karel Van Mander (I) → *see* Mander, Karel I van
Karel van Vogelaer → *see* Vogelaer, Karel van (Distelbloom)
Karel Vermander → *see* Mander, Karel I van
Karelin, Andrej Osipovič *(Russian photographer, 1837-1906)* **BA**
    Bibl: Hist. photography, I/4 (Oct. 1977) pp.327-347
Karelse, Thon *(Dutch architect, Groningen)* **AV**
    Bibl: De Architect, 1989 May, v.20, no.5 suppl., p.3
Kareoja, Pentti *(Finnish architect)* **AV**
    Bibl: Byggekunst, 1986, v.68, no.7, p.F2
Karev, Vasilij Vasil'evič *(Russian painter, b.1886)* **BA**
    Bibl: ▶Vollmer, Künst.-Lex. 20. Jhr.
Karfik, Vladimír *(Czech architect, 1901-)* **AV**
    Bibl: Czech functionalism 1918-1938 (1987)
Karfiol → *see* Karfiol, Bernard
Karfiol, Bernard **PR WC WI**
    (American artist, 1886-1952) WC
    (American artist, 1886-1955) WI
    (American painter, 1886-1952) PR
    Bibl: ▶Who was who [GBR]; ▶WWW Amer. art
    Bernard Karfiol PR
    Karfiol PR
Karg, Josef *(West German architect, Munich)* **AV**
    Bibl: Detail, 1986 May-June, v.26, no.3, p.237
Kargel, Reinhard **AV BA**
    (German architect) AV
    (West German architect, 20th c.) BA
    Bibl: ▶Avery period. idx., 6th suppl.; Kargel, Kunst in Hessen und am Mittelrhein 23-24 (1983-84) 23
Kärgel, Wolfgang *(East German architect, Potsdam)* **AV**
    Bibl: Architektur der DDR, 1986 Sept., v.35, no.9, p.514
Karger, Carl *(German artist, 1848-1913)* **WC**

Karhula, Matti *(Finnish architect, Oulu)*   **AV**
  Bibl: SAFA 87: Suomen Arkkit.
Karhunen, Anita *(Finnish architect)*   **AV**
  Bibl: Arkkitehti, 1985, no.5, p.62
Karhunen, Jukka *(Finnish architect)*   **AV**
  Bibl: ARkkitehti, 1989, v.86, no.1, p.37
Kari, Kaarina *(Finnish artist, 20th cent.)*   **WC**
Kari-Pasonen, Lotta *(Finnish architect)*   **AV**
  Bibl: Arkkitehti, 1985, no.1, p.44
Karil du Jardin→see Dujardin, Karel
Karina, Elena *(American ceramist, painter, printmaker, 20th c.)*   **BA**
  Bibl: Syracuse (NY, USA), Everson Museum of Art, ELENA KARINA (1979)
Karinger, Anton *(Yugoslav painter, 1829-1870)*   **BA**
  Bibl: ▶Bénézit; Ljubljana, Narodna Gal., ANTON KARINGER 1829-1870 (1984); ▶Thieme-Becker
Karkinos Painter   **GC**
  Bibl: ▶Beazley, Attic red-fig. vase-ptrs.
Kärkkäinen, Matti *(Finnish architect)*   **AV**
  Bibl: Arkkitehtuurikilpailuja, 1988, no.8, p.2
Karl Anderson→see Anderson, Karl
Karl August Aerttinger→see Aerttinger, Karl August
Karl Blechen→see Blechen, Karl
Karl Bodmer→see Bodmer, Karl
Karl Daubigny→see Daubigny, Karl
Karl Du Jardin→see Dujardin, Karel
Karl du Jardyn→see Dujardin, Karel
Karl Friedrich Lessing→see Lessing, Karl Friedrich
Karl Georg Naumann→see Naumann, Karl Georg
Karl Gottlob Schonherr→see Schönherr, Karl Gottlob
Karl Gussow→see Gussow, Karl
Karl Heinrich Beichling→see Beichling, Karl Heinrich
Karl Herbsthoffer→see Herbsthoffer, Karl
Karl Hetz→see Hetz, Karl
Karl Hoffmann→see Hoffmann, Karl
Karl Knaths→see Knaths, Karl
Karl Mattern→see Mattern, Karl
Karl More→see Moor, Carel de
Karl Muller→see Muller, Karl
Karl Roux→see Roux, Karl
Karl Schmidt-Rottluff→see Schmidt-Rottluff, Karl
Karl Sterrer→see Sterrer, Karl
Karl Theodor Fiodorovitch Goun→see Goun, Karl Theodor Fiodorovitch
Karl Theodor von Piloty→see Piloty, Karl Theodor von
Karl Wilhelm de Hamilton→see Hamilton, Karl Wilhelm de

Karl Wilhelm Hahn→see Hahn, Karl Wilhelm
Karlovsky, Bertelan (Bartolomaeus) *(Hungarian artist, 1858-1938)*   **WC**
Karlowska→see Karlowska, Stanislava de
Karlowska, Stanislava de   **WC WI**
  (British artist, 1880-1952)   **WC WI**
  (British painter, 1876-1952)   **PR**
  Bibl: ▶Johnson, Brit. artists; ▶Waters, Brit. artists
  De Karlowska   **PR**
  De Karlowska, Stanislawa   **PR**
  Karlowska   **PR**
  Karlowska, Stanislava de, Miss   **WI**
  Karlowska, Stanislawa de   **PR**
  Stanislawa de Karlowska   **PR**
Karlowska, Stanislava de, Miss→see Karlowska, Stanislava de
Karlowska, Stanislawa de→see Karlowska, Stanislava de
Karlsen, Anne Marie *(American painter, printmaker, b.1952)*   **BA**
  Bibl: ▶Art Index, v.32; ▶WW Amer. Art, 1984
Karlson, Axel Magnus Valfrid *(Swedish architect, Stockholm, b.1855)*   **AV**
  Bibl: ▶Thieme-Becker
Karlsruhe/Woodner Master *(Aegean sculptor, ca. 2700/2500 BC)*   **GC**
  Bibl: Getz-Preziosi, Early Cycladic sculp., p.70, pp.30, 70
Karlsson, Bror *(Swedish photographer)*   **AV**
  Bibl: Arkitektur: the Swedish review of architecture, 1988 Apr., v.88, no.3, p.34
Karlsteen, Arvid   **BA WC**
  (Swedish artist, 1647-1718)   **WC**
  (Swedish medalist, 1647-1718)   **BA**
  Bibl: ▶Bénézit; ▶Forrer, Medallists; ▶Svenskt konst.-lex.; ▶Thieme-Becker
Karlung, Åke *(Swedish sculptor, b.1930)*   **BA**
  Bibl: ▶Intl. dir. exh. artists, 1982
Karmann, Jacob *(German(?) artist, op.1824)*   **WC**
Karmi, Ada *(Israeli architect)*   **AV**
Karmi, Dov *(Israeli architect, 1905-1962)*   **AV**
  Bibl: ▶Contemp. archts.
Karmi, Ram *(Israeli architect, 1931-)*   **AV**
  Bibl: ▶Contemp. archts.
Karnec, J.E. *(German artist, 19th cent.)*   **WC**
Karneia Painter *(South Italian vase-painter, 4th century BC)*   **GC**
  Bibl: ▶Trendall, Red-fig. vases Lucania
Karnejeff, E. *(Russian artist, 18th cent.)*   **WC**

Karner, C. *(German painter, 18th century)*   **GC**
  Bibl: ▶Thieme-Becker
Karner, C. *(German artist, 18th cent.)*   **WC**
Karnow, Nadine *(American sculptor, 20th c.)*   **BA**
  Bibl: Philadelphia (PA, USA), Temple University, Samuel Paley Library, The Tyler show (1974)
Karol Hoppen→see Hoppen, Karol
Karolis, Adolfo de→see De Carolis, Adolfo
Karolus *(Flanders printmaker, 16th century)*   **GC**
  Bibl: ▶Bénézit
Karoly Lotz→see Lotz, Károly
Karp, Aaron S. *(American painter, b.1947)*   **BA**
  Bibl: ▶Intl. dir. exh. artists, 1983; ▶WW Amer. Art
Karp, Leon *(American artist, 1903-1951)*   **WC WI**
Karp, Raine *(Estonian architect, Tallinn, 1938-)*   **AV**
  Bibl: Architecture + design, 1988 Nov.-Dec., v.5, no.1, p.34
Karpathy, Jeno *(Hungarian artist, 1871-)*   **WC**
Karpff, Jean Jacques *(French, 1770-1829)*   **GC**
  Bibl: ▶Thieme-Becker
Karpinski, Alfons *(Polish artist, 1875-)*   **WC**
Karpion *(Greek architect(?), 5th c BC (2nd half))*   **GC**
  Bibl: ▶Robertson, Greek art, p.328
Karpoff, Giovanni *(Russian artist, 19th cent.)*   **WC**
Kars→see Kars, George
Kars or Karpeles, George→see Kars, George
Kars, George   **PR**
  (Czech artist, 1882-1945)   **WC**
  (Czechoslovakian painter, 1882-aft.1918)   **PR**
  (French painter, 1882-1945)   **GC**
  Bibl: ▶Bénézit; ▶Thieme-Becker
  George Kars   **PR**
  Kars   **PR**
  Kars or Karpeles, George   **WC**
  Kars, Georges   **GC**
Kars, Georges→see Kars, George
Karsch, Gerhard Joseph *(German artist, op.1700-1719)*   **WC**
Karsch, Joachim *(German sculptor, 1897-1945)*   **BA**
  Bibl: ▶Bénézit; ▶Brockhaus Enzyk.; ▶Thieme-Becker; ▶Vollmer, Künst.-Lex. 20. Jhr.
Karsen or Karssen, Kasparus→see Karsen, Kaspar

Karsen, Eduard   **GC**
   (Dutch artist, 1860-1941)   **WC**
   (Dutch painter, draughtsman,
     and printmaker, 1860-d. aft.
     1910)   **GC**
     Bibl: ▶Thieme-Becker
   Karsen, Jan Eduard   **GC**
Karsen, Johann Eduard (Eduard)   **WC**
Karsen, Jan Eduard→see Karsen,
   Eduard
Karsen, Johann Eduard (Eduard)→see
   Karsen, Eduard
Karsen, Kaspar   **BA GC**
   (Dutch artist, 1810-1896)   **WC**
   (Dutch painter and
     draughtsman, 1810-1896)   **GC**
   (Dutch painter, 1810-1896)   **BA**
     Bibl: ▶Bénézit; ▶RILA/BHA;
     ▶Thieme-Becker; ▶Wurzbach, NLD
     Künst.-Lex.
   Karsen or Karssen, Kasparus   **WC**
   Karssen   **GC**
Karsh, Yousuf   **BA WC**
   (American artist, 1908-)   **WC**
   (Canadian photographer,
     b.1908)   **BA**
     Bibl: UC Santa Barbara cat.
     sheets; World Exhib. of Photog.
Karskaya, Ida *(French painter,*
   printmaker, b.1905)   **BA**
     Bibl: ▶Bénézit; ▶Intl. dir. exh.
     artists, 1983; ▶Vollmer,
     Künst.-Lex. 20. Jhr.
Karssen→see Karsen, Kaspar
Karst, John *(Engraver, 1836-1922)*   **WI**
Karsten, Elisabet Charlotta
   (Kaschanoff) *(Swedish artist,*
   1789-p.1833)   **WC**
Karsten, Herman Thomas *(Dutch*
   architect, act. in Indonesia, 1885-)   **AV**
     Bibl: Muqarnas, 1985, v.3, p.138
Karsten, Ludvig   **BA WC**
   (Norwegian artist, 1876-1926)   **WC**
   (Norwegian painter, 1876-1926)   **BA**
     Bibl: ▶Bénézit; ▶MoMA libr. cat.;
     ▶Vollmer, Künst.-Lex. 20. Jhr.
Karsten, Magnus *(German bronze*
   founder, act.1573)   **BA**
     Bibl: Dehio: Niedersachsen;
     Pechstein, Anz. des Germ.
     Nationalmus. (1981) 80-83;
     ▶Thieme-Becker
Karsznicki, Józel *(Architect, Poland,*
   d.1809)   **AV**
     Bibl: Polska Akademia Nauk.
     Komisja Urbanistyki i
     Architektury. Teka, 1984, v.18,
     p.227; ▶Thieme-Becker
Kartarius, Marius→see Cartaro,
   Mario
Kartarus, Marius→see Cartaro, Mario
Karthaus, Frank *(West German*
   architect, Bielefeld)   **AV**
     Bibl: ▶Bund Deut. Arch. Hdbch.,
     1987; ▶Libr. of Congr. Name
     Auth. File

Kartvedt, Per *(Norwegian architect,*
   1940-)   **AV**
     Bibl: Das Kunstwerk, n.3-4, Sept.
     1983, p.109
Karuth, Ethel *(British artist, op.*
   1901-1910)   **WI**
Karyl du Jardin→see Dujardin, Karel
Kasai, Shuichiro *(Japanese architect,*
   1947-)   **AV**
     Bibl: Kenchiku bunka, 1987 Dec.,
     v.42, no.494, p.76
Kasak, Nikolai *(American painter,*
   sculptor, b.1917)   **BA**
     Bibl: Trenton (NJ, USA), NJ State
     Mus., Beyond the Plane (1983);
     ▶WW Amer. Art, 1984
Kasatkin, Nikolaj Alekseevič   **BA**
   (Russian artist, 1859-1930)   **WC**
   (Russian painter, sculptor, 1859-
     1930)   **BA**
     Bibl: ▶Bowlt, Russian avant-garde;
     ▶Valkenier, Russian realist art;
     ▶WWW USSR
   Kassatkin, Nikolaj Alexejewitsch   **WC**
Kaschauer, Jakob *(Austrian painter,*
   sculptor, act.1429, d. before 1463)   **BA**
     Bibl: ▶Bénézit; ▶Thieme-Becker
Kaschl, Reiner *(Austrian architect)*   **AV**
     Bibl: Bauforum, 1988, v.21, no.
     126, p.35
Kasdan, Paul   **WC WI**
   (British artist, 20th cent.)   **WC**
   (British artist, op.20th c.)   **WI**
Käsebier, Gertrude Stanton   **BA JG**
   (American photographer, 1852-
     1934)   **BA**
   (American, 1852-1934)   **JG**
     Bibl: ▶Art Index, 1932-1935;
     ▶Gernsheim, Hist. photog.;
     ▶Newhall, Photog.; PA;
     Szarkowski, Looking at Photos
Kaseweiss, Michael *(German artist,*
   op.1659-1671)   **WC**
Kasimir Dunin Markiewicz→see
   Markiewicz, Kasimir Dunin
Kasimir, Georg *(Austrian architect,*
   1927-)   **AV**
     Bibl: Deutsche Bauzeitung, 1985
     Apr., v.119, no.4, p.128
Kaskey, Raymond J. *(American*
   sculptor and architect)   **AV**
     Bibl: Architecture: the AIA
     journal, 1985 Dec., v.74, no.12,
     p.20
Kasnio, Kirsti *(Finnish architect)*   **AV**
     Bibl: Arkkitehti, 1986, no.4, p.32
Kaspar Waldmann→see Waldmann,
   Caspar
Kašpar, Adolf *(Czech printmaker,*
   illustrator, 1877-1934)   **BA**
     Bibl: ▶Encyk. českého výtv. umění;
     ▶Thieme-Becker; ▶Vollmer,
     Künst.-Lex. 20. Jhr.
Kasparides, Eduard *(German artist,*
   1858-1926)   **WC**
Kasper van Eyck→see Eyck, Kasper
   van

Kasper, Ernst   **AV BA**
   (German architect or planner,
     1935-)   **AV**
   (German architect, b.1935)   **BA**
     Bibl: Arch plus, 1981 July, no.
     57-58, p.40; ▶WW Arts DEU
Kasper, Ludwig *(Austrian sculptor,*
   1893-1945)   **BA**
Kasprick, Michael *(West German*
   architect, Bremen)   **AV**
     Bibl: Detail, 1982 July-Aug., no.4,
     p.442
Kass, Deborah *(American painter,*
   b.1952)   **BA**
     Bibl: ▶Intl. dir. exh. artists, 1983;
     Salz, Beyond boundaries
Kass, Jacob J. *(American painter,*
   b.1907)   **BA**
     Bibl: ART IN AMER, 69 (summer
     1981) 130-131; ARTS MAG., 55
     (Mar 1981), 71 (reprod.); Coral
     Gables, Univ. of Miami, Lowe
     A.M., JACOB J. KASS (1982)
Kassabaum, George E. *(American*
   architect, 1920-1982)   **AV**
     Bibl: AIA journal, Sept. 1982,
     p.17; ▶Contemp. archts.
Kassák, Lajos   **AV BA GC WC**
   (Hungarian artist)   **AV**
   (Hungarian artist, 1887-1967)   **WC**
   (Hungarian painter, 1887-1967)   **GC**
   (Hungarian painter, printmaker,
     author, 1887-1967)   **BA**
     Bibl: ▶Bénézit; ▶Libr. of Congr.
     Name Auth. File; ▶Thieme-Becker;
     ▶Vollmer, Künst.-Lex. 20. Jhr.
Kassatkin, Nikolaj Alexejewitsch→see
   Kasatkin, Nikolaj Alekseevič
Kasseböhmer, Axel *(West German*
   painter, b.1952)   **BA**
     Bibl: ▶Art Index, v.36; Guide exh.
     artists: Euro. ptrs.
Kassel, Ferdinand van→see Kessel,
   Ferdinand van
Kassiba, el Ghazzali *(Egyptian*
   architect)   **AV**
     Bibl: Middle East construction,
     1985 June, v.10, no.6, p.9
Kast, Lenna Tyler *(American artisan*
   who specializes in composition
     ornament, Los Angeles, Calif)   **AV**
     Bibl: Southern accents, 1989 Jan.-
     Feb., v.12, p.150
Kastan, Joseph *(Austrian architect,*
   act.1838-1851)   **BA**
     Bibl: Oesterreichisches
     Zeitschrift/XXVIII,1-2, 74, p.49-54
Kasteels, Frans van de→see Castello,
   Francesco da
Kasteev, Abylhan *(Russian*
   printmaker, b.1904)   **BA**
     Bibl: ▶Fogg Mus. Libr. cat.
Kastel, Peter *(American architect)*   **AV**
     Bibl: Metropolis, 1989 May, v.8,
     no.9, p.41
Kastemaa, Heikki *(Finnish artist,*
   20th cent.)   **WC**

Kasten, Barbara *(American
photographer, b.1936)* BA
    Bibl: Claremont (CA, USA),
    Galleries of the Claremont
    Colleges, Gallery as studio (1975)
Kasten, J.E.→see Kasten, Johann Elias
Kasten, Johann Elias GC
    (German artist, 18th cent.) WC
    (German painter, 18th/19th
    centuries) GC
    Bibl: ▶Bénézit
    Kasten, J.E. WC
Kasten, Karl *(New Zealand artist,
1916-)* WC
Kastenhetz *(German artist, 18th
cent.)* WC
Kastner, Johann Evangelist
(German artist, 1776-1827) WC
Kastner, Johannes *(Architect, New
York City)* AV
    Bibl: Architecture & urbanism,
    1989 Apr., no.4, p.123
Kastor, R. WC WI
    (British artist, 19th cent.) WC
    (British artist, op.1903-) WI
Kastrop, Bartold *(German sculptor,
1460/65-1531/32)* BA
    Bibl: Dehio, XI; Eckhardt, Jahrb.
    Hamburg. Kunstsamml. XXV
    (1980) 27-50; Reclams V
Kasturi, Hijjas bin→see Hijjas bin
Kasturi
Kasuba, Aleksandra *(American
sculptor, b.1923)* BA
    Bibl: Thompson, M.L., in
    WOMAN'S ART JOURNAL, IV/2
    (fall/winter 1983-1984) 35; ▶WW
    Amer. Art
Kasyn, John *(Canadian artist, 20th
cent.)* WC
Kat, Kees de *(Dutch architect)* AV
    Bibl: De Architect, 1988 July-Aug.,
    v.19, no.7-8. p.19
Kat, Otto Boudewijn de *(Dutch
painter, printmaker, b.1907)* BA
    Bibl: ▶Scheen, Ned. beeldende
    kunst.; ▶Vollmer, Künst.-Lex. 20.
    Jhr.
Katainen, Juhani *(Finnish architect)* AV
    Bibl: Arkkitehti, 1985, no.5, p.76
Katajamäki, Antti *(Finnish architect,
1938-)* AV
    Bibl: Process: architecture, n.37,
    1983, p.90
Katalan, Jak *(American painter,
sculptor, 20th c.)* BA
    Bibl: Pittsburgh (PA, USA),
    Carnegie-Mellon University,
    Hewlett Gallery, JAK KATALEN...,
    1985; UC Santa Barbara cat.
    sheets
Kataoka, Sankun *(Architect, Japan)* AV
    Bibl: Space design, 1984 Dec., no.
    243, p.21
Katay, Mihály *(Hungarian artist,
20th c.)* BA
    Bibl: Dekorativnoe iskusstvo SSSR,
    Sept 1975, p.47

Kate→see Kate, Jan Mari ten
Kate→see Kate, Johann Mari Henri
ten
Kate Freeman Clark→see Clark, Kate
Freeman
**Kate, Herman Frederik Carel
ten** GC WC
    (Dutch artist, 1822-1891) WC
    (Dutch, 1822-1891) GC
    Bibl: ▶Witt checklist
Kate, Jan Mari ten PR
    (Dutch artist, 1859-1896) WC
    (Dutch painter, 1859-1896) GC PR
    Bibl: ▶Thieme-Becker; ▶Wright,
    Ptgs. Dutch museums
    Jan Mari ten Kate PR
    Kate PR
**Kate, Johannes Marinus (Jan)
ten** WC
Kate, Johannes Marius ten GC
    Kate, ten PR
    Ten Kate, Johannes Marinus PR
*Kate, Johan Mari Henri (Mari)
ten→see* Kate, Johann Mari Henri
ten
Kate, Johan Mari Henri ten→see
Kate, Johann Mari Henri ten
Kate, Johann Mari Henri ten PR
    (Dutch artist, 1831-1910) WC
    (Dutch painter, 1831-1910) PR
    *(Dutch painter, draughtsman,
    and printmaker, 1831-1910)* GC
    Bibl: ▶Thieme-Becker
    Johann Mari Henri ten Kate PR
    Kate PR
**Kate, Johan Mari Henri (Mari)
ten** WC
Kate, Johan Mari Henri ten GC
    Kate, Mari ten PR
    Kate, ten PR
*Kate, Johannes Marinus (Jan)
ten→see* Kate, Jan Mari ten
Kate, Johannes Marius ten→see Kate,
Jan Mari ten
Kate, Lambert Hermansz. ten
    (Dutch draughtsman, 1674-1731) GC
    Bibl: ▶Thieme-Becker
Kate, Mari ten→see Kate, Johann
Mari Henri ten
Kate, ten→see Kate, Jan Mari ten
Kate, ten→see Kate, Johann Mari
Henri ten
Katharina van Hemessen→see
Hemessen, Katharina van
Katherine Dudley→see Dudley,
Katherine
Katherine Schmidt→see Schmidt,
Katherine
Katherine Sophie Dreier→see Dreier,
Katherine Sophie
Kathryn W. Leighton→see Leighton,
Kathryn W.
Kato, Akinori *(Japanese architect,
1946-)* AV

Kato, Hosei *(American artist, op.
1975-)* WI
Kato, Kiyashi *(American,
contemporary)* JG
Kato, Yoshio *(Japanese architect,
1941-)* AV
    Bibl: Kenchiku bunka, 1987 Dec.,
    v.42, no.494, p.78
Katodrytis, George *(Greek
architect, studied in London,
practices in London and Paris)* AV
    Bibl: Across architecture, [1987],
    no.4, p.22
Katschaloff, Grigorij *(Russian artist,
1711-p.1761)* WC
Katselas, Tasso *(American architect,
1927-)* AV
    Bibl: ▶Contemp. archts.; ▶Libr. of
    Congr. Name Auth. File
Katsiaficas, Diane *(American artist,
20th c.)* BA
    Bibl: ▶Art Index; Artweek Oct 18
    1980; Vanguard, X/8 (Oct. 1981)
    pp.10-15
Katsman, Evgenij Aleksandrovič
(Russian artist, b.1890) BA
    Bibl: ▶Bowlt, Russian avant-garde
Katterschafka, Rudolf *(Austrian
architect, Vienna)* AV
    Bibl: ▶Verzeich. Öst. Ziviltech.
Kattle *(Swiss artist, 18th cent.)* WC
Katz, Ada *(American, 20th c.)* BA
    Bibl: ART IN AMER, LXIX (Jan
    1981) 110-118
Katz, Alex BA WC WI
    (American artist, 1927-) WC
    (American artist, b.1927) WI
    *(American painter, printmaker,
    b.1927)* BA
    Bibl: ▶Contemp. artists; ▶Intl. dir.
    exh. artists, 1982-1983; ▶WW
    Amer. Art
Katz, Carl Ludwig→see Kaaz, Carl
Ludwig
Katz, Cima *(American printmaker,
b.1949)* BA
    Bibl: St. Louis (MO, USA), U.
    Missouri, Amer. women
    printmakers (1975)
Katz, Howard *(American builder,
Penn)* AV
    Bibl: Fine homebuilding, 1987
    Dec.-1988 Jan., no.43, p.72
Katz, Kalman *(Architect, Israel)* AV
    Bibl: AC: the fibrecement review
    XXX/1(iii) (Apr. 1985) p.73
Katz, Leo *(American artist, b.1887)* WI
Katz, Mel *(American sculptor,
b.1932)* BA
    Bibl: Pullman (Wash, USA), Wash
    State Univ., Mus. of Art, MEL
    KATZ..., 1979
Katz, Morton *(Canadian architect)* AV
    Bibl: Canadian architect, 1986
    Oct., v.31, no.10, p.28

Kaufman, Donald   AV BA WC WI
  *(American artist who produces
    custom-blended paints for
    interior use, New York City)*   AV
  (American artist, 1935-)   WC
  (American artist, b.1935)   WI
  (American painter, b.1935)   BA
  Bibl: House & garden, 1988 Dec.,
    p.68; ▶MoMA libr. cat.; NYC
    phone bk., 1988-89; ▶Parry,
    Contemp. art; Pasadena (CA,
    USA), Ca. Tech., Baxter Art
    Gallery, A PAINTING
    INSTALLATION (1979)
Kaufman, Elliot → see Kaufman, Elliott
Kaufman, Elliott   BA
  *(American photographer, 20th
    c.)*   BA
  (Photographer)   AV
  Bibl: ▶Libr. of Congr. Name Auth.
    File; Philadelphia. U. Penn. ICA
    ICA STREET SIGHTS 2, 1981
Kaufman, Elliot   AV
Kaufman, Jane A. *(American
  painter, b.1938)*   BA
  Bibl: ▶WW Amer. Art, 1976
Kaufman, Perla *(Israeli architect)*   AV
  Bibl: Architecture d'aujourd'hui,
    1987 Feb., no.249, p.xxii
Kaufman, W.   WC WI
  (British artist, 19th cent.)   WC
  (British artist, op.19th c.)   WI
**Kaufmann or Kauffmann, Johann
  Michael** *(German artist, 1713(?)-p.
  1786)*   WC
Kaufmann, Adolf *(German artist,
  1848/58-1916)*   WC
Kaufmann, Emil *(1891-1953)*   AV
Kaufmann, Gerd *(British architect,
  London)*   AV
  Bibl: ▶RIBA members, 1983
*Kaufmann, Gordon B. → see
  Kaufmann, Gordon Bernie*
Kaufmann, Gordon Bernie   BA
  (American architect, 1888-1949)   BA
  *(English architect, lived in
    southern Calif., fl. 1930's)*   AV
  Bibl: Architecture, the AIA
    journal, 1983 Dec., v.72, no.12,
    p.45; ▶Avery obit. idx.; ▶Withey,
    Amer. archts.; ▶WWW Amer., v.3
Kaufmann, Gordon B.   AV
Kaufmann, Hermann *(Austrian
  architect, 1955-)*   AV
  Bibl: Ottagono, 1988 Mar., p.20
Kaufmann, Ignaz   BA
  *(German painter, ca.1721-
    1781)*   BA GC
  Bibl: Getty Photo Study Coll.;
    Markmiller, Barockmaler;
    ▶RILA/BHA; ▶Thieme-Becker
Kauffmann, Ignatius   GC
Kaufmann, Isiidor *(Hungarian artist,
  1853-1921)*   WC
Kaufmann, Karl *(German artist,
  1843-)*   WC

Kaufmann, Oskar *(Hungarian
  architect, 1873-1956)*   BA
  Bibl: ▶Macmillan encyc. archts.;
    ▶Portoghesi, Diz. arch. e
    urbanistica; ▶Vollmer, Künst.-Lex.
    20. Jhr.
Kaufmann, Othon *(French, b.1905)*   BA
  Bibl: Paris, Musée natl. du Louvre,
    CATALOGUE DE LA DONATION
    OTHON KAUFMANN & FRANÇOIS
    SCHLAGETER..., 25
Kaufmann, Paul M. *(West German
  architect, Nürtingen)*   AV
  Bibl: ▶Bund Deut. Arch. Hdbch.,
    1987
Kaufmann, Rudolf *(West German
  landscape architect)*   AV
  Bibl: Garten und Landschaft,
    1987, v.97, no.12, p.27
Kaufmann, Theodor *(German artist,
  1814-p.1887)*   WC
Kaukas, Bernard *(British architect,
  20th c.)*   BA
  Bibl: RIBA JOURNAL, LXXXVI (Nov
    1979) 491-495
Kaul de Moor → see Moor, Carel de
Kaul du Jardin → see Dujardin, Karel
Kaula → see Kaula, William Jurian
Kaula, Lee Lufkin *(American artist,
  1865-1957)*   WI
*Kaula, William J. → see Kaula, William
  Jurian*
Kaula, William Jurian   PR WI
  (American artist, 1871-1953)   WI
  *(American painter, 1871-aft.
    1929)*   PR
  Bibl: ▶WWW Amer. art
  Kaula   PR
  Kaula, William J.   PR
  William Jurian Kaula   PR
*Kaulbach → see Kaulbach, Friedrich
  August von*
Kaulbach → see Kaulbach, Hermann
Kaulbach, Friedrich   BA GC WC
  (German artist, 1822-1903)   WC
  (German painter, 1822-1903)   BA GC
  Bibl: ▶Brockhaus Enzyk.;
    ▶Thieme-Becker
*Kaulbach, Friedrich August → see
  Kaulbach, Friedrich August von*
**Kaulbach, Friedrich August
  von**   BA GC PR WC
  (German artist, 1850-1920)   WC
  *(German painter, 1850-
    1920)*   BA GC PR
  Bibl: ▶Bénézit; ▶Brockhaus Enzyk.;
    ▶RILA/BHA; ▶Thieme-Becker
  Friedrich August von Kaulbach   PR
  Kaulbach   PR
  Kaulbach, Friedrich August   PR

Kaulbach, Hermann   BA GC PR WC
  (German artist, 1846-1909)   WC
  *(German painter, 1846-
    1909)*   BA GC PR
  Bibl: ▶Brockhaus Enzyk.;
    ▶RILA/BHA; ▶Thieme-Becker
  Hermann Kaulbach   PR
  Kaulbach   PR
*Kaulbach, Wilhelm → see Kaulbach,
  Wilhelm von*
*Kaulbach, Wilhelm (Bernhard Wilhelm
  Eliodorus) von → see Kaulbach,
  Wilhelm von*
Kaulbach, Wilhelm von   AV BA GC PR
  (German architect, 1805-1874)   AV
  (German artist, 1805-1874)   WC
  *(German draughtsman, 1805-
    1874)*   GC
  (German painter, 1805-1874)   PR
  *(German painter, illustrator,
    1805-1874)*   BA
  Bibl: ▶Bénézit; ▶Fogg Mus. Libr.
    cat.; ▶Libr. of Congr. Name Auth.
    File; ▶RILA/BHA; ▶Thieme-Becker
Kaulbach, Wilhelm   GC
**Kaulbach, Wilhelm (Bernhard
  Wilhelm Eliodorus) von**   WC
  Wilhelm von Kaulbach   PR
Kaulitz, Christian Ludwig *(German
  artist, -1744)*   WC
Kaulos   GC
  Bibl: ▶Beazley, Attic bl.-fig. vase-
    ptrs.
Kaupelis, Robert John *(American
  painter, author, b.1928)*   BA
  Bibl: ▶WW Amer. Art, 1978
Kauperz, Johann Veit *(German
  artist, 1741-1816)*   WC
Kauppinen, Timo *(Finnish architect)*   AV
  Bibl: Arkkitehti, 1985, no.3, p.66
Kaupunki-suunnittelu Ab, Oy
  (Finnish architect)   AV
  Bibl: Arkkitehti, 1984, no.4, p.43
Kaur, Updesh *(Indian architect)*   AV
  Bibl: Architecture + design, 1988
    July-Aug., v.4, no.5, p.75
Kaus → see Kaus, Max
Kaus, Max   BA PR WC
  (German artist, 1891-)   WC
  (German painter, b. 1891)   PR
  *(German painter, printmaker,
    b.1891)*   BA
  Bibl: ▶Bénézit; Berlin, Natl. Gall.
    cat.; ▶Brockhaus Enzyk.; ▶Kindlers
    Malerei Lex.; ▶Thieme-Becker;
    ▶Vollmer, Künst.-Lex. 20. Jhr.
  Kaus   PR
  Max Kaus   PR
Kausch, Werner *(German painter,
  printmaker, b.1924)*   BA
  Bibl: ▶Vollmer, Künst.-Lex. 20.
    Jhr.; ▶WW Arts DEU
Kausen, Manfred *(Dutch architect)*   AV
  Bibl: Forum voor architectuur en
    daarmee verbonden kunsten,
    1985-1986, v.30, no.3, p.131

Kausins, Vytautas *(Russian artist, 20th cent.)*   **WC**

Kaut, Franz *(West German architect)*   **AV**
Bibl: Arch Plus, 1987 Nov., no.92, p.32

Kaut, Gerd *(West German interior architect, Darmstadt)*   **AV**
Bibl: Architektur, Innenarchitektur, Technischer Ausbau, 1989 Apr., v.97, no.4, p.56

Kautreu → see Hautreu [Unidentified]

Kautzky, Johann *(Czech artist, 1827-1896)*   **WC**

Kauw, Albrecht I   **BA GC**
(Swiss artist, 1621-1681)   **WC**
(Swiss painter, 1621-1681)   **GC**
(Swiss painter, 1621-1681?)   **BA**
Bibl: ▶Bénézit; ▶Schweiz. Künst.-Lex.; ▶Thieme-Becker; ▶Witt checklist

Kauw, Albrecht, I   **WC**
Kauw, Albrecht, I → see Kauw, Albrecht I

Kavaleridze, Ivan Petrovič *(Russian sculptor, filmmaker, dramatist, b.1887)*   **BA**
Bibl: Iskusstvo XXXVIII #2, 1975, p.32

Kavalír, František   **AV BA**
(Czech architect, 20th c.)   **BA**
(Czechoslovak architect)   **AV**
Bibl: AMC, 1985 Mar., no.7, p.56; Svácha, Umění, XXVIII/4 (1980) pp.368-379

Kavan, Vladislav *(Russian artist, 20th cent.)*   **WC**

Kavanagh, John F. *(British sculptor, painter, b.1903)*   **BA**
Bibl: ▶Bénézit; ▶Waters, Brit. artists

Kavanagh, Joseph Malachy *(British artist, 1856-1918)*   **WC WI**

Kavanaugh, Gere *(American interior designer, Los Angeles, Calif)*   **AV**
Bibl: Interior design, 1989 Jan., p.226

Kavanaugh, Marion, Miss → see Wachtel, Marion Kavanaugh

Kavčič, Franc → see Caucig, Franz

Kavel, Martin *(French artist, 19th cent.)*   **WC**

Kavlashvili, Sh. *(Russian architect)*   **AV**
Bibl: Process: architecture, 1985 Jan., no.54, p.152

Kavli, Arne Texnes *(Norwegian artist, 1878-)*   **WC**

Kavurić-Kurtović, Nives *(Yugoslav painter, b.1938)*   **BA**
Bibl: Ljubljana (YUG), Mala Galerija, Nives Kavurić-Kurtović (1978); ▶MoMA libr. cat.

Kawa, Florence Kathryn *(American painter, b.1912)*   **BA**
Bibl: Des Moines, Art Center. FLORENCE KAWA (1976); ▶MoMA libr. cat.; ▶WW Amer. Art, 1976

Kawaguchi, Mamoru *(Architect ?, Japan)*   **AV**
Bibl: Kenchiku bunka, 1985 Jan., v.40, no.459, p.19

Kawai, Koji *(American artist, 20th c.)*   **BA**
Bibl: Arts Mag., "Arts reviews", 3 Nov 1982

Kawai, Tadashi *(Ceramic artist, born in Kyoto, Japan, 1926-)*   **AV**
Bibl: Japan architect, 1982 Oct., v.57, no.306, p.5

Kawakubo, Rei   **AV BA**
(Japanese designer, Tokyo; designs store interiors for her clothing line, Comme des Garçons, 1942-)   **AV**
(Japanese fashion designer, 20th c.)   **BA**
Bibl: Drier, ART IN AMER. LXXV (1987) 21; ▶Libr. of Congr. Name Auth. File; Steber, CONNOISSEUR CCXVI (1986) 117

Kawamata, Tadashi   **AV BA**
(Japanese architect or artist)   **AV**
(Japanese artist, b.1953)   **BA**
Bibl: Archis, 1989 Dec., no.12, p.2; Geneva (CHE), Musée Rath, Art japonais d'aujourd'hui (1983)

Kawara, On   **BA WC**
(Japanese artist, b.1933)   **BA**
(Oriental artist, 20th cent.)   **WC**
Bibl: ▶NY art yrbk.; ▶Parry, Contemp. art

Kawasaki, Kiyoshi *(Japanese architect)*   **AV**
Bibl: Japan architect, 1985 Apr., v.60, no.4 (336), p.61

Kawasaki, Takao *(Japanese architect or interior designer, 20th cent)*   **AV**
Bibl: Blueprint (London), 1989 May, no.57, p.30

Kawashima, Takeshi   **WC WI**
(American artist, 1930-)   **WC**
(American artist, b.1930)   **WI**

Kay Sage → see Sage, Kay

Kay, Andrew *(British woodworker, Kent, England; founder of Woodcraft workshop)*   **AV**
Bibl: Period homes, 1988 Apr., p.16

Kay, Archibald *(British artist, 1860-1935)*   **WC WI**

Kay, Arthur, Mrs., (Katherine) → see Cameron, Katherine

Kay, Bernard   **WC WI**
(British artist, 1927-)   **WC**
(British artist, b.1927)   **WI**

Kay, Dorothy *(South African painter, 1886-1977)*   **BA**
Bibl: CapeTown (SA), S. African Nat'l. Gall, DOROTHY KAY..., 1982

Kay, Gregory *(American lighting designer)*   **AV**
Bibl: Architectural lighting, 1989 Mar., v.3, no.3, p.22

Kay, Hanna *(American painter, 20th c.)*   **BA**
Bibl: Breslow, Arts mag., LVII/1 (Sep. 1982) p.13

Kay, James *(British artist, 1858-1942)*   **WC WI**

Kay, James *(Scottish painter and draughtsman, b.1838)*   **GC**
Bibl: ▶Bénézit

Kay, John *(British artist, op.1609)*   **WC**

Kay, John *(British artist, 1742-1826)*   **WC WI**

Kay, John *(English inventor, 1704-1764)*   **BA**
Bibl: ▶Dict. natl. biog.

Kay, John Illingworth *(British designer, 1870-1950)*   **BA**
Bibl: London (GBR), Mus. London, London design studio (1980)

Kay, Joseph *(British architect, 1775-1847)*   **AV BA**
Bibl: ▶Colvin, Brit. archts.; ▶Thieme-Becker

Kay, N.A.   **WC WI**
(British artist, 18th cent.)   **WC**
(British artist, op.18th c.)   **WI**

Kay, Pamela *(British artist, op.20th c.)*   **WI**

Kay, Thomas → see Kay, Tom

Kay, Tom   **BA**
(British architect, 20th c.)   **BA**
(English architect, London)   **AV**
Bibl: ▶Avery period. idx., 7th suppl.; London phone bk.; ▶RIBA members, 1986

Kay, Thomas   **AV**

Kay, William   **WC WI**
(British artist, op.1795)   **WC**
(British artist, op.1795-)   **WI**

Kay-Shuttleworth, Rachel Beatrice *(British textile designer, collector, 1886-1967)*   **BA**
Bibl: Museums Yearbook 1989/90; Parny, Country Life CLXXXII/23 (9 June 1988), 248-9

Kaye, Otis *(American artist, 1885-1974)*   **WI**

Kaye, Samuel H. *(American architect, Columbus, Miss)*   **AV**
Bibl: ▶AIA Pro File, 1987-88

Kayser, Alex *(Swiss photographer, b.1949)*   **BA**
Bibl: Amsterdam (NLD), Stedelijk Museum, Foto-sequenties (1977)

Kayser, Paul *(German artist, 1869-)*   **WC**

Kayser, Victor *(German sculptor, act.1516, d.ca.1552)*   **BA**
Bibl: ▶Encyc. world art; ▶Osten, Ptg. & sculp. DEU & NLD; ▶Thieme-Becker

---

Kazanjian, Milano (American
painter, performance artist,
b.1943) **BA**
    Bibl: Fullerton (CA, USA), CSU Art
    Gallery, Face to face (1984)

**Kazenberger or Katzenberger,
Balthasar** (German artist, op.1602-
1613) **WC**

Kazimir Severinovich Malevich → see
Malevič, Kazimir Severinovič

Kazimiria, Barthoso de (Polish
ceramist, 16th c.) **BA**
    Bibl: KERAMOS 76 Apr 1977,.
    15-26

Kazuko (American artist, 20th c.) **BA**
    Bibl: Arts Mag. LIII/9 (May 1979),
    p.16

Keable or Keeble, William → see
Keable, William

Keable, William **WI**
    (British artist, op.1714-, d.1774) **WI**
    (British artist, op.1753-1754) **WC**
  Keable or Keeble, William **WC**
  Keeble, William **WI**

Keaft → see Keaft, J.L. [Unidentified]

Keaft, J.L. [Unidentified] (Unknown
painter) **PR**
    Bibl: (April 23, 1802, lot 58, Evill)
  J.L. Keaft **PR**
  Keaft **PR**

Kealtes? **GC**
    Bibl: ▶Beazley, Attic bl.-fig. vase-
    ptrs.

Kean, Kirby (American, active
southern CA, U.S. 1930s-1940s) **JG**

Keane, John (British artist, b.1954) **WI**

Keane, Joseph B. (Irish architect,
d.1859) **BA**
    Bibl: Blue guide: Ireland; ▶Dict.
    natl. biog.; ▶Redgrave, Engl.
    school; ▶Thieme-Becker

Kearney, Francis **WI**
    (American artist, 1785-1837) **WC WI**
    (Engraver, 1785-1837) **WI**
  Kearny, Francis **WC**

Kearney, Nancy Jean (American
artist, b.1941) **WI**

Kearney, William Henry (British
artist, 1800-1858) **WC WI**

Kearns, Howard (American artist,
1907-1947) **WI**

Kearns, James **WC WI**
    (American artist, 1924-) **WC**
    (American artist, b.1924) **WI**

Kearns, Jerry Byron (American
artist, b.1943) **BA**
    Bibl: New York (NY, USA), New
    Mus. of Contemp. Art, Art &
    Videology (1984)

Kearny, Francis → see Kearney, Francis
Kearse, Mary, Mrs. → see Lawrence,
Mary
Kearsley → see Kearsley, Thomas

Kearsley, Harriet **WC WI**
    (British artist, op.1824-, d.1881) **WI**
    (British artist, op.1824-m.1881) **WC**

Kearsley, Thomas (British painter,
act. 1792-1802) **PR**
    Bibl: ▶Bénézit; ▶Graves Royal
    Acad. contribs.; ▶Thieme-Becker
  Kearsley **PR**
  Thomas Kearsley **PR**

Kearton, Cherry (British, 1871-1940
(also Cherry & Richard Kearton)) **JG**

Kearton, Richard (British, 1862-1928
(also Cherry & Richard Kearton)) **JG**

Keate, George (British artist, 1729-
1797) **WC WI**

Keating, Andrew (American painter,
20th c.) **BA**
    Bibl: ▶Babington Smith, Contemp.
    artists

Keating, Frank (British artist, op.
20th c.) **WI**

Keating, George (British artist,
1762-1842) **WC WI**

Keating, Richard **AV BA**
    (American architect) **AV**
    (American architect, 20th c.) **BA**
    Bibl: GA document, no.12, p.96;
    ▶Libr. of Congr. Name Auth. File;
    NEW ART EXAMINER, X/9 (June
    1983) 10

Keating, Sean (British artist, 1899-
1977) **WI**

Keating, Tom (British painter,
b.1917) **BA**
    Bibl: Art News LXXV/8 (Oct
    1976) 49-50; ▶Dict. natl. biog.,
    1981-85; His The Fake's progress,
    p.21; Keating, Tom, & Norman,
    G., THE FAKE'S PROGRESS, p.21

Keats, Don Juan Llanos y **WC WI**
    (British artist, 19th cent.) **WC**
    (British artist, op.19th c.) **WI**

Keats, John (British artist, 1795-
1821) **WC WI**

Keay, Lancelot, Sir (British
architect, Liverpool) **AV**
    Bibl: Architects' journal, 1988 July
    20, v.187, no.29, p.79

Kebar, Karel (Yugoslav painter,
1764-1810) **BA**
    Bibl: Gorskiletnik, 2 (1975) 129-
    130

Keck → see Kick, Cornelis

Keck, Anthony (British architect,
1726-1797) **AV BA**
    Bibl: ▶Colvin, Brit. archts.; Hussey,
    Engl. houses, v.2: Mid-Georgian

Keck, Charles (American sculptor,
1875-1951) **BA**
    Bibl: ▶Fielding's Amer. ptrs.;
    ▶Havlice, Idx. art. bio.; ▶Young,'
    Amer. artists

Keck, George Fred (American
architect, 1895-1980) **AV BA**
    Bibl: Boyce, George Fred Keck
    (1986); ▶Contemp. archts.; ▶Libr.
    of Congr. Name Auth. File; WW
    Amer.; ▶WWW Amer., v.7

Keck, Peter (Bohemian painter, act.
1679, d.1730) **BA**
    Bibl: ▶Bénézit; PANTHEON, XLII/4
    (Oct-Dec 1984) 335;
    ▶Thieme-Becker

Keck, William **AV BA**
    (American architect, b.1908) **BA**
    (American architect, Chicago,
    Ill, 1908-) **AV**
    Bibl: ▶Amer. archts. dir., 1970;
    WW Amer.

Keckhoven, Giacomo van der
(Dutch(?) painter, 17th century) **GC**
    Bibl: Sotheby's

Keddie, Ann **AV BA**
    (Australian architect) **AV**
    (Australian architect, 20th c.) **BA**
    Bibl: Architectural review, 1985
    Dec., v.178, no.1066, p.91;
    ▶Avery period. idx., 6th suppl.

Kederminster, John (English, act.
1613-1649) **BA**
    Bibl: Country Life CLXII/4195 (1
    Dec 1977) p.1576; Lewis, TOPO
    OF ENG. p.22; Murray's
    Buckinghamshire, p.5; Tipping,
    ENG. HOMES v.I

Kedzierski, Apolonusz (Polish artist,
1851/61-1939) **WC**

Keeble, William → see Keable, William

Keech, Pamela (American artist,
20th c.) **BA**
    Bibl: Arts Mag. LVII (2 Oct 1982),
    "Pamela Keechi, Neglect,
    Infidelity & Poisoning," pp.76-77

Keefe, Charles S. (American
architect, Kingston, NY, 1876-
1946) **AV**
    Bibl: ▶Withey, Amer. archts.

Keeler, Charlotte **WC WI**
    (American artist, 19th cent.) **WC**
    (American artist, op.19th c.) **WI**

Keeley Halswelle → see Halswelle,
Keeley

Keeley, Isaac H. **WI**
    (American artist, 1817-1891) **WI**
    (American painter, 1817-1891) **PR**
    Bibl: ▶Young, Amer. artists
  Isaac H. Keely **PR**
  Keeley, Josiah H. **WI**
  Keely **PR**
  Keely, Isaac H. **PR**

Keeley, Josiah H. → see Keeley, Isaac
H.

Keeley, Shelagh (American artist,
20th c.) **BA**
    Bibl: ▶Art Index, 1987; ▶ARTbibl.
    mod., 1988, pt.1; Mayer, ARTS,
    LXI (summer 1987), 96; NYC
    phone bk.

Keelhoff, Frans (Belgian artist,
1820-1891/3) **WC**

Keeling, E. Bassett   **BA**
  (British architect, 1837-1886)   AV BA
    Bibl: ▶Artist biog. master idx.;
    Curl, Country life, CLXXX/4650 (2
    Oct. 1986) pp.1030-1032;
    ▶Macmillan encyc. archts.; RIBA
    ldx. archts.
Keeling, Enoch Bassett   **AV**
Keeling, E.J.   **WC WI**
  (British artist, op.1856)   WC
  (British artist, op.1856-1873)   WI
*Keeling, Enoch Bassett→see Keeling,
  E. Bassett*
Keeling, Michael *(British artist,
  1750-1820)*   **WC WI**
Keeling, William Knight *(British
  artist, 1807-1886)*   **WC WI**
Keely →see Keeley, Isaac H.
Keely, Isaac H. → see Keeley, Isaac H.
Keely, Patrick Charles   **AV BA**
  *(Irish architect in USA, 1816-
  1896)*   BA
  *(Irish architect, practiced in
  Brooklyn, N.Y. from 1842,
  1816-1896)*   AV
    Bibl: ▶Macmillan encyc. archts.;
    ▶Withey, Amer. archts.; ▶WWW
    Amer. hist.
Keely, Robert Neff *(American,
  active Philadelphia, PA, U.S. 1846-
  1856,)*   **JG**
Keen, Charles Barton *(American
  architect, Philadelphia, 1868-1931)*   **AV**
    Bibl: Tatman, Philadelphia archts.,
    p.430
Keen, Henry *(British artist, op.20th
  c.)*   **WI**
Keen, Mary *(English garden
  designer)*   **AV**
    Bibl: House & garden, 1989 Sept.,
    v.161, no.9, p.174
Keen, Oskar M. *(Swedish artist,
  1867-1947)*   **WC**
Keen, Peter *(British photographer,
  20th c.)*   **BA**
    Bibl: Word & Image, II/1 (Jan-Mar
    1986) 33
Keenan, John *(American, active
  Philadelphia, PA, U.S. ca. 1854-
  1861)*   **JG**
Keenan, John   **WC WI**
  (British artist, op.1780-1819)   WI
  (British artist, op.1790-1819)   WC
Keene, Arthur *(British artist, op.
  20th c.)*   **WI**
Keene, Charles Samuel   **BA GC WC WI**
  (British artist, 1823-1891)   WC WI
  (British illustrator, 1823-1891)   BA
  (British, 1823-1891)   GC
    Bibl: ▶Dict. natl. biog.; ▶Houfe,
    Brit. book illus., p.357; Ray,
    Gordon. ILLUSTRATOR AND
    BOOK...; ▶Thieme-Becker

Keene, Henry *(British architect,
  1726-1776)*   **AV BA**
    Bibl: ▶Colvin, Brit. archts.; ▶Dict.
    natl. biog.; ▶Summerson, Arch.
    GBR; ▶Thieme-Becker
Keene, Henry Eddowes *(British
  artist, op.circa 1866-)*   **WI**
Keene, Norman *(British artist, op.
  20th c.)*   **WI**
Keene, Paul *(American painter,
  b.1920)*   **BA**
    Bibl: ▶WW Amer. Art
Keene, Thomas   **WC WI**
  (British artist, 20th cent.)   WC
  (British artist, op.20th c.)   WI
Keenen, John *(American architect,
  New York City, teaches at N.Y.
  Institute of Technology)*   **AV**
    Bibl: Assoc. of Collegiate Schools
    of Architecture. News, 1988 May,
    v.17, no.9, p.12
Keere, Pieter van den *(Dutch
  printmaker, dealer, publisher,
  1571-ca.1646)*   **BA**
    Bibl: Hollstein; Meurer, P.H.,
    BURGEN UND SCHLÖSSER, XXIV/2
    (Dec 1983), p. 106, 8; ▶Natl.
    union cat., pre-1956;
    ▶Thieme-Becker; ▶Wurzbach, NLD
    Künst.-Lex.
Keerend, Avo *(Russian printmaker,
  b.1920)*   **BA**
    Bibl: ▶Vollmer, Künst.-Lex. 20. Jhr.
Keerin →see Keirincx, Alexander
Keerincks →see Keirincx, Alexander
Keeringh →see Keirincx, Alexander
Keeringhs →see Keirincx, Alexander
Keerings →see Keirincx, Alexander
Keeringx →see Keirincx, Alexander
Keerinks →see Keirincx, Alexander
Keerinx →see Keirincx, Alexander
Keerl, Bayat *(American painter, 20th
  c.)*   **BA**
    Bibl: NYC phone bk.
*Kees van Dongen →see Dongen, Kees
  van*
Kees, Weldon *(American painter,
  poet, b.1914)*   **BA**
    Bibl: Arts Mag., LIII/1 (Sep. 1978)
    p.96; ▶MoMA libr. cat.; ▶Vollmer,
    Künst.-Lex. 20. Jhr.
Keesee, Tom *(American painter,
  b.1954)*   **BA**
    Bibl: Washington, DC (USA),
    Corcoran Gallery, 39th biennial
    (1985)
Keever, Kim *(American painter,
  printmaker, b.1950)*   **BA**
    Bibl: ARTS MAGAZINE, LIX/2 (Oct
    1984), p.5; ▶WW Amer. Art,
    1991
Keibel, Otto Samuel *(German
  goldsmith, jeweler in Russia, 1768-
  1809)*   **BA**
    Bibl: Solodkoff, Russian gold &
    silver; ▶Thieme-Becker

Keigerlin, Alois *(German artist, op.
  1830)*   **WC**
Keighley, Alexander *(British, 1861-
  1947)*   **JG**
Keijsers, W. H. A. M. *(Dutch city
  planner)*   **AV**
    Bibl: De Architect, 1989 June,
    v.20, no.6, p.95
Keikes, Tjeerd Annes *(Dutch
  silversmith, printmaker, 1804-
  1886)*   **BA**
    Bibl: ▶Forrer, Medallists; Keikes,
    ANTIEK, XV, 10 (May 1981) 575-
    584
*Keil, Bernard →see Keil, Bernhard
  (Monsù Bernardo)*
*Keil, Bernhard →see Keil, Bernhard
  (Monsù Bernardo)*
**Keil, Bernhard (Monsù
  Bernardo)**   **BA PR**
  (Danish artist, 1624-1687)   WC
  *(Danish painter,
  1624/26-1687)*   BA PR
  (Scandinavian, 1624-1687)   GC
    Bibl: ▶RILA/BHA; ▶Thieme-Becker
  Bernardi   PR
  Bernardo, Monsu   PR
  Bernhard Keil   PR
  Keil, Bernard   PR
  Keil, Bernhard   **GC** PR
  Keil, Bernhardt   PR
  Keil, Eberhard   PR
  **Keil, Kail, Kailo, Keilhau, Keillh,
  Keyl, or Keylhau, Bernhard
  (Eberhard?) (Monsu
  Bernardo)**   **WC**
  Monsieur Bernardo   PR
  Monsù Bernardo   PR
  Monsu' Bernardo   PR
  Monsu' Bernardo danese   PR
  Monsu' Bernardo danese di Roma   PR
*Keil, Bernhardt →see Keil, Bernhard
  (Monsù Bernardo)*
*Keil, Eberhard →see Keil, Bernhard
  (Monsù Bernardo)*
*Keil, Kail, Kailo, Keilhau, Keillh, Keyl,
  or Keylhau, Bernhard (Eberhard?)
  (Monsu Bernardo) →see Keil,
  Bernhard (Monsù Bernardo)*
Keil, Karl Philipp Franz *(German
  sculptor, 1838-1889)*   **BA**
    Bibl: Jahrb. Preussischer
    Kulturbesitz XX (1983) 95-117;
    ▶Mackay, Western sculp. bronze;
    ▶Thieme-Becker
Keil, Robert *(Austrian painter,
  b.1905)*   **BA**
    Bibl: Alte und moderne Kunst,
    XXX/202-202 (1985) 58;
    ▶Vollmer, Künst.-Lex. 20. Jhr.

Keiley, Joseph T. BA
(American photographer, critic, 1869-1914) BA
(American, 1869-1914) JG
Bibl: Homer.STIEGLITZ AND THE AMER AVANT-GARDE; Manchester (NH, USA), Currier Gallery, Stieglitz & photo-secession (1983); ▶Natl. union cat., pre-1956
Keiley, Joseph Turner JG
Keiley, Joseph Turner → see Keiley, Joseph T.
Keiller, Alexander *(British artist, b.1916)* WI
Keiller, Patrick *(British artist, b.1950)* BA
Bibl: London (GBR), Tate Gallery, Audio arts (1982)
Keim, Benno *(German draughtsman, 1798-1826)* GC
Bibl: ▶Bénézit
Keimal, Rudolf *(Austrian architect)* AV
Bibl: Bauforum, 1986, v.19, no. 117, p.66
Keimel, Rolf *(Austrian architect)* AV
Bibl: Bauforum, 1988, v.21, no. 127, p.57
Keir, Peter *(fl. 1852; Draftsman, England, Scotland)* FA
Bibl: Canad. Ctr. Arch. object file; Christie's East, NY, 19/10/83
Keira, Agnieshka *(Australian architect, city architect for Freemantle)* AV
Bibl: The Architect, W.A., 1987, v.27, no.2, p.13
Keirincx → see Keirincx, Alexander

Keirincx, Alexander BA GC PR
(Flemish artist, 1600-c.1652) WC
(Flemish painter in NLD, 1600-1652) BA
(Flemish painter, 1600-1652) GC
(Flemish painter, 1600-ca.1652) PR
Bibl: ▶Bénézit; ▶Nieuw NLD biog. woord.; ▶RILA/BHA; ▶Thieme-Becker; ▶Wurzbach, NLD Künst.-Lex.
Al. Kerincx PR
Alex. Keerings PR
Alexander Keirincx PR
Alexander Kerens PR
Alexander Kerings PR
Alexander Keyrinks PR
Keerin PR
Keerincks PR
Keeringh PR
Keeringhs PR
Keerings PR
Keeringx PR
Keerinks PR
Keerinx PR
Keirincx PR
Keirincx, Carings, Cierinx, Keerinckx, Keyrincx, Kierings etc., Alexander (also identified with Jacob or Johann-Carings or Cierings) WC
Kerincks PR
Keringhs PR
Kerings PR
Kerinks PR
Kierings PR
Kierinks PR
Kierinx PR
Kiernings PR
Kierynx PR
Keirincx, Carings, Cierinx, Keerinckx, Keyrincx, Kierings etc., Alexander (also identified with Jacob or Johann-Carings or Cierings) → see Keirincx, Alexander
Keiser, Carl *(Swiss(?) artist, op. 1762-1769)* WC
Keiser, Urs *(Swiss architect)* AV
Bibl: ▶Schweiz. Ingen. u. Archit., 1984-1985
Keisser, M. *(French architect)* AV
Bibl: Architecture d'aujourd'hui, 1987 Sept., no.252, p.13
Keister, Eugene *(American architect, 1850-1925)* BA
Bibl: Heal, Pendleton County Builder & His Houses, 1984; ▶Libr. of Congr. Name Auth. File
Keister, Steve *(American sculptor, b.1949)* BA
Bibl: Buffalo (NY, USA), Albright-Knox, 8 sculptors (1979)
Keith → see Keith, William
Keith Baynes → see Baynes, Keith Stuart
Keith, Boudinot, Mrs., (Dora) → see Keith, Dora Wheeler

Keith, Dora Wheeler BA
(American artist, 1857-1940) WI
(American painter, 1857-1940) BA
Bibl: ▶Fielding's Amer. ptrs.; ▶WWW Amer., 1897
Keith, Boudinot, Mrs., (Dora) WI
Wheeler, Dora WI
Keith, George *(American architect, Spokane, Wash., fl. ca. 1925)* AV
Bibl: Historic preservation, 1988 Jan.-Feb., p.72
Keith, John Frank *(American, active 1920s)* JG
Keith, Nancy, Lady *(American interior decorator, NYC)* AV
Bibl: House & Garden, 1987 Jan., v.159, no.1, p.66
Keith, Slim AV
Keith, Slim → see Keith, Nancy, Lady
Keith, Thomas BA
(British surgeon, photographer, 1827-1895) BA
(British, 1827-1885) JG
Bibl: ▶Gernsheim, Hist. photog.; ▶MoMA libr. cat.; ▶Newhall, Photog.; Szarkowski, Looking at Photos; ▶Szarkowski, Photog's eye
Keith, Thomas (Dr.) JG
Keith, Thomas (Dr.) → see Keith, Thomas
Keith, William BA GC PR WC WI
(American artist, 1839-1911) WC WI
(American painter, 1839-1911) PR
(American painter, printmaker, 1839-1911) BA
(American, 1839-1911) GC
Bibl: ▶Castagno, Amer. sigs.; ▶Dict. Amer. biog.; ▶Groce, Artists Amer.; ▶Havlice, Idx. art. bio.; ▶Hughes, Artists California; ▶Mallett's idx. artists; ▶RILA/BHA; ▶Samuels, Artists Amer. West; ▶Thieme-Becker; ▶Witt checklist; ▶WWW Amer. art; ▶Young, Amer. artists, p. 33
Keith PR
William Keith PR
Kejgelken [Unidentified] *(Unknown painter)* PR
Bibl: (June 8, 1815, lot 134, Stanley)
Kekrops Painter GC
Bibl: ▶Beazley, Attic red-fig. vase-ptrs.
Kelbaugh, Douglas S. *(American architect)* AV
Bibl: ▶AIA Pro File, 1985
Kelcey, Rose Finn → see Finn-Kelcey, Rose
Kelder → see Kelder, Toon (Antonius Bernardus)

Kelder, C.   **GC PR**
 (Dutch painter, act. 17th
  century)   PR
 (Dutch, act. ca.1684)   GC
  Bibl: ▶Bénézit; ▶Thieme-Becker
 C. Kelder   PR
Kelder, Toon → *see* Kelder, Toon
 (Antonius Bernardus)
Kelder, Toon (Antonius
 Bernardus)   **GC PR**
 (Dutch painter, b. 1894)   PR
 (Dutch painter, b.1894)   GC
  Bibl: ▶Thieme-Becker
 Kelder   PR
Kelder, Toon   **GC PR**
 Toon Kelder   PR
Kelderman, Jan   **GC WC**
 (Dutch artist, 1741-1820)   WC
 (Dutch painter, 1741-1820)   GC
  Bibl: ▶Thieme-Becker
Keldermans Family *(Seven*
 generation family of Flemish
 architects and sculptors, 14th-16th
 cent)   **AV**
  Bibl: ▶Thieme-Becker
Keldermans, Anthonis *(Flemish*
 architect and sculptor, ca.1450-
 1512)   **AV**
  Bibl: ▶Thieme-Becker
Keldermans, Rombout → *see*
 Keldermans, Rombout, the
 younger
Keldermans, Rombout, the
 younger   **BA**
 (Belgian architect, Mecheln, d.
  1531)   AV
 (early Netherlandish architect,
  ca.1460-1531)   BA
  Bibl: ▶Macmillan encyc. archts.;
  ▶Thieme-Becker
Keldermans, Rombout   **AV**
 Mansdale, Rombouts van, the
  younger   BA
Kelemen, Kristóf *(Hungarian*
 sculptor, b.1922)   **BA**
  Bibl: Szíj, R. JAKAB KÁROLY ES
  KELEMEN KRISTÓF, p.43
Keleti, Gusztáv Frigyes *(Hungarian*
 painter, critic, educator, 1834-
 1902)   **BA**
  Bibl: ▶Bénézit; ▶Thieme-Becker
Kelham, Augustus *(British, active*
 ca. 1865-1880)   **JG**
Kelhan, George W. *(American*
 architect, San Francisco, Calif)   **AV**
  Bibl: Assoc. for Preservation
  Technology. Bulletin, 1987, v.19,
  no.3, p.19; ▶Avery period. idx.
Keliutis, Raymond *(American*
 architect)   **AV**
Kell, Violet V. *(British artist, op.*
 1909-1912)   **WI**
Kellaway, Michael *(British artist,*
 b.1929)   **WI**

Kellen, David *(American architect,*
 Los Angeles)   **AV**
  Bibl: Architecture: the AIA
  journal, 1986 Apr., v.75, no.4,
  p.75
Kellen, David van der II   **GC**
 (Dutch artist, 1804-1879)   WC
 (Dutch, 1804-1879)   GC
  Bibl: ▶Witt checklist
 Kellen, David, II van der   **WC**
Kellen, David van der III *(Dutch*
 painter and draughtsman, 1827-
 1895)   **GC**
  Bibl: ▶Thieme-Becker
Kellen, David, II van der → *see* Kellen,
 David van der II
Kellen, Johan Philip van der *(Dutch*
 printmaker, art historian, 1831-
 1906)   **BA**
Kellenbach, Carel Frederick *(Dutch*
 artist, 1897-)   **WC**
Kellenberger, L'ubomír *(Czech*
 printmaker, 20th c.)   **BA**
Keller → *see* Keller, Johann Heinrich (II)
Keller → *see* Keller, Johann Sigmund
Keller, Albert von   **BA GC WC**
 (Swiss artist, 1844-1920)   WC
 (Swiss painter, 1844-1920)   BA
 (Swiss, 1844-1920)   GC
  Bibl: ▶Bénézit; ▶Schweiz.
  Künst.-Lex.; ▶Thieme-Becker;
  ▶Witt checklist
Keller, Arthur Ignatius   **WC WI**
 (American artist, 1866-)   WC
 (American artist, 1866-1924)   WI
Keller, Balthasar *(German artist,*
 1638-1702)   **WC**
Keller, Bruno *(Swiss architect)*   **AV**
  Bibl: ▶Schweiz. Ingen. u. Archit.,
  1984-1985
Keller, Charles   **BA WC WI**
 (American painter, b.1914)   BA
 (British artist, 20th cent.)   WC
 (British artist, op.20th c.)   WI
  Bibl: Apollo 94, Aug 1971, p.19
  front; Art news 44, Mar 15,
  1945, p.18; Ithaca (NY, USA),
  Cornell University, Herbert F.
  Johnson Museum of Art. Charles
  Keller: retrospective, 1976;
  ▶MoMA libr. cat.; ▶WW Amer.
  Art, 1940
Keller, Ernst *(Swiss printmaker,*
 1891-1968)   **BA**
  Bibl: ▶Art Index; ▶Künst.-Lex.
  Schweiz 20. Jahrh.; ▶Vollmer,
  Künst.-Lex. 20. Jhr.; ▶WW Graphic
  Art
Keller, Ferdinand   **BA GC**
 (German painter, illustrator,
  1842-1922)   BA
 (German, 1842-1922)   GC
  Bibl: ▶Bénézit; ▶Neue deutsche
  Biog.; ▶Thieme-Becker

Keller, Frank *(American painter,*
 20th c.)   **BA**
  Bibl: Arts Mag LVI 3 Nov 1981
  150-151
Keller, Franz   **AV BA**
 (d.1725)   AV
 (German architect, d.1725)   BA
  Bibl: ▶Thieme-Becker
Keller, Franz Xaver *(Austrian*
 sculptor, act.1780-after 1796)   **BA**
  Bibl: ▶Bénézit; Dehio:
  Oberösterreich; Kunstjarhb. Stadt
  Linz, (1973) pp.51-54;
  ▶Thieme-Becker
Keller, Friedrich von   **GC WC**
 (German artist, 1840-1914)   WC
 (German draughtsman, 1840-
  1914)   GC
  Bibl: ▶Bénézit
Keller, G. Edwin *(American*
 photographer, painter, 1877-1966)   **BA**
  Bibl: Buffalo (NY, USA), Albright-
  Knox, Photo-pictorialists (1981)
Keller, George W. *(American*
 architect, 1842-1935)   **BA**
  Bibl: LC slip; ▶Withey, Amer.
  archts., (Hartford, CT)
Keller, Germaine *(American*
 sculptor, 20th c.)   **BA**
  Bibl: ▶Art Index, v.48, no.3
Keller, Gottfried   **BA WC**
 (Swiss artist, 1819-1890)   WC
 (Swiss painter, author, 1819-
  1890)   BA
  Bibl: ▶Bénézit; ▶New Columbia
  encyc.; ▶Schweiz. Künst.-Lex.;
  ▶Thieme-Becker
Keller, Heinrich *(Swiss artist, 1778-*
 1862)   **WC**
Keller, Henry George *(American*
 artist, 1869-1949)   **WC WI**
Keller, Herbert *(Swiss architect,*
 1916-)   **AV**
  Bibl: Archithese, 1985 May, v.15,
  no.3, p.55
Keller, Johann Heinrich (II)   **PR**
 (Swiss artist, 1692-1765)   WC
 (Swiss painter, 1692-1765)   PR
 (Swiss, 1692-1765)   GC
  Bibl: ▶Thieme-Becker; ▶Witt
  checklist
 Johann Heinrich Keller (II)   PR
 Keller   PR
 Keller, Johann Heinrich II   **GC**
 Keller, Johann Heinrich, I   **WC**
Keller, Johann Heinrich II → *see* Keller,
 Johann Heinrich (II)
Keller, Johann Heinrich, I → *see* Keller,
 Johann Heinrich (II)
Keller, Johann Sigmund *(German*
 painter, act. 1785-1796)   **PR**
  Bibl: ▶Thieme-Becker
 J.S. Keller   PR
 Johann Sigmund Keller   PR
 Keller   PR

Keller, Josef GC
(German artist, 1740-1823) WC
(German, 1740-1823) GC
Bibl: ▶Thieme-Becker; ▶Witt
checklist

Keller, Joseph WC
Keller, Joseph → see Keller, Josef

Keller, Larry (American architect) AV
Bibl: ▶AIA Pro File, 1985

Keller, Mervyn (American architect,
Maine) AV
Bibl: Landmarks observer, 1989
spring, v.15, no.4, p.7

Keller, Paul Wilhelm → see Keller-
Reutlingen, Paul Wilhelm

Keller, Peter (German designer,
1898-1982) BA
Bibl: Wewerka, 1972-1982:
BERICHT EINER DEUTSCHEN
UNTERNEHMUNG

Keller, Peter A. (Swiss architect,
Zurich) AV
Bibl: ▶Schweiz. Ingen. u. Archit.,
1984-1985

Keller, Pierre BA WC
(Swiss artist, 20th cent.) WC
(Swiss painter, sculptor,
photographer, b.1945) BA
Bibl: ▶Intl. dir. arts, 1983-1984;
▶Lex. zeitgen. Schweiz. Künstler

Keller, Reinhardt (Swiss artist,
1759-1802) WC

Keller, Rolf AV BA
(Swiss architect, b.1931) BA
(Swiss architect, Zurich since
1960, 1930-) AV
Bibl: AC, 1984 Oct, v.29, no.
2(110), p.77; ▶Avery period. idx.;
Jones, Architectural review, 1985
June, v.177, no.1060

Keller, Werner (Swiss architect,
1948-) AV
Bibl: Deutsche Bauzeitung, 1986
June, v.120, no.6, p.164

Keller-Reutlingen → see Keller-
Reutlingen, Paul Wilhelm

Keller-Reutlingen, Paul Wilhelm PR WC
(German artist, 1854-1920) WC
(German painter, 1854-1920) PR
Bibl: ▶Thieme-Becker
Keller, Paul Wilhelm PR
Keller-Reutlingen PR
Paul Wilhelm Keller-Reutlingen PR

Kellerdaller, Daniel → see Kellerthaler,
Daniel

Kellerhoven, Moritz (German artist,
1758-1830) WC

Kellers, Michael WC WI
(American artist, 20th cent.) WC
(American artist, op.20th c.) WI

Kellerthaler or Kellerdaller,
Daniel → see Kellerthaler, Daniel

Kellerthaler, Daniel GC
(German artist, op.1598-
1665(?)) WC
(German draughtsman, bef.
1612-1665(?)) GC
Bibl: ▶Thieme-Becker
Kellerdaller, Daniel GC

**Kellerthaler or Kellerdaller,
Daniel** WC

Kellerthaler, Joannes or Hans, II
(German artist, c.1560-1637) WC

Kellerthaler, Johann (the Elder) GC
(German artist, 1530-p.1589) WC
(German painter and
draughtsman, ca.1530-aft.
1575) GC
Bibl: ▶Thieme-Becker

Kellerthaler, Johann, I WC
Kellerthaler, Johann, I → see
Kellerthaler, Johann (the Elder)

Kelley, Mike (American artist, b.ca.
1954) BA
Bibl: Directions, MIKE KELLEY:
"HALF A MAN" (1991); Eisenman,
S.F., in ARTS MAG LVII/3 (Nov
1982) 57; Gordon, Artforum,
XXIII/8 (Apr. 1985) pp.73-77;
▶Intl. dir. exh. artists; JOURNAL
OF SO. CALIF. ART MAG XXII
(Mar-Apr 1979) 51

Kelley, Richard (American painter,
b.1944) BA
Bibl: Des Moines (IA, USA), Art
Center.RICHARD KELLEY, 1976

Kelley, Ron (American
photographer, 20th c.) BA
Bibl: Afterimage IX 9 Apr 1981
p.12-15

Kellner, Gerhard (German artist,
20th c.) BA
Bibl: Künstler DDR

Kellner, Hermann I (German glass
painter, 1814-1877) BA
Bibl: ▶Bénézit; ▶Busse, Maler u.
Bildhauer 19. Jahr.;
▶Thieme-Becker

Kellner, Hermann, II (German artist,
1849-1926) WC

Kellner, Jakob (German painter, d.
ca.1775) GC
Bibl: ▶Thieme-Becker

Kello, Esther, Mrs. → see Inglis, Esther

Kellogg family (American
printmakers, 19th c.) BA
Bibl: Steinway, Imprint 13/1
(spring 1988) p.2-12 (docs)

Kellogg, Alice D. (American artist,
op.19th c.) WI

Kellogg, Kendrick Bangs (American
architect, San Diego, CA, 1934-) AV
Bibl: A & U, no.174, p.64

Kellogg, Milner Kilbourne → see
Kellogg, Miner Kilbourne

Kellogg, Miner Kilbourne BA WC
(American artist, 1814-1889) WC WI
(American painter, 1814-1889) BA
Bibl: ▶Bénézit; ▶Fielding's Amer.
ptrs.; ▶Thieme-Becker

Kellogg, Milner Kilbourne WI

Kellum, John (American architect,
New York City, 1809-1871) AV
Bibl: ▶Avery obit. idx.; ▶Macmillan
encyc. archts.

Kelly, Ben (Designer, Great Britain) AV
Bibl: World of interiors, 1984
Nov., p.198

Kelly, Bruce (American landscape
architect) AV

Kelly, Ellsworth BA GC WC WI
(American artist, 1923-) WC
(American artist, b.1923) WI
(American painter, b.1923) GC
(American painter, sculptor,
b.1923) BA
Bibl: ▶Cummings, Contemp.
Amer. artists; ▶RILA/BHA; ▶WW
Amer. Art, 1982

Kelly, Felix Runcie WC WI
(British artist, 1917-) WC
(British artist, b.1917) WI
Bibl: ▶Peppin, Bk. illus. 20c.

Kelly, Francis Robert WC WI
(British artist, 1927-) WC
(British artist, b.1927) WI

Kelly, Gerald → see Kelly, Gerald
Festus

Kelly, Gerald Festus BA PR WI
(British artist, 1879-1972) WC WI
(British painter, 1879-1972) BA PR
Bibl: ▶Bénézit; ▶Johnson, Brit.
artists; ▶Natl. union cat.;
▶RILA/BHA; ▶Witt checklist
Gerald Festus Kelly PR
Kelly, Gerald PR

Kelly, Sir Gerald Festus WC

Kelly, Harold Osman (American
painter, 1884-1955) PR
Bibl: ▶Artist biog. master idx.
Harold Osman Kelly PR

Kelly, Jack (American architect,
Chicago, Ill) AV
Bibl: Interior design, 1987 Dec.,
v.58, no.15, p.180

Kelly, James → see Kelly, James
Edward

Kelly, James Edward (American
sculptor, 1855-1933) GC
Bibl: Getty Photo Study Coll.;
▶Opitz, Amer. sculptors
Kelly, James GC

Kelly, Kathleen (American interior
designer) AV
Bibl: Interiors, 1988 May, v.147,
no.10, p.112

Kelly, Kathleen Irene
Ashburnham → see Newton,
Kathleen Irene Ashburnham

Kelly, Lee *(American architect, Portland, Oreg)*   **AV**
Bibl: Urban design international, 1985 Winter, v.5,no.2, p.34

Kelly, Leon *(American artist, b.1901)*   **WI**

Kelly, Mary *(American artist, b.1954)*   **BA**
Bibl: Paoletti, J.T., in ARTS MAGAZINE LX/2 (Oct 1985) 88

Kelly, Mary   **BA WI**
(American artist, b.1941)   WI
(American artist, educator in GBR, b.1941)   BA
Bibl: ▶Dolman, Contemp. Brit. artists; ▶Intl. dir. exh. artists, 1983; ▶WW Amer. Art

Kelly, Nicholas *(British artist, op. 1810-1831)*   **WC WI**

Kelly, Patrick *(American painter, b.1939)*   **BA**
Bibl: ▶NY art yrbk.

Kelly, Richard Barrett Talbot *(British artist, 1896-1971)*   **WC WI**

Kelly, Robert *(1944-)*   **AV**

Kelly, Robert George Talbot *(British artist, 1861-1934)*   **WC WI**
Bibl: Paviere, Landscape

Kelly, Roy *(Architect, California?, 1920s)*   **AV**
Bibl: World of interiors, 1984 Sept., p.100

Kelly, Sir Gerald Festus → see Kelly, Gerald Festus

Kelly, Thomas *(Engraver, circa 1795-circa 1841)*   **WI**

Kelly, William Joseph *(American painter, printmaker, b.1943)*   **BA**
Bibl: ▶MoMA libr. cat.; New Wilmington (PA, USA), Westminister College, Art Gallery, WILLIAM KELLY, 1980; ▶WW Amer. Art, 1978

Kelman   **WC WI**
(American artist, 20th cent.)   WC
(American artist, op.20th c.)   WI

Kelpe, Paul   **BA WC WI**
(American artist, 1902-)   WC
(American artist, b.1902)   WI
(American painter, b.1902)   BA
Bibl: ▶WW Amer. Art, 1973

Kels → see Kels, Franz

Kels, Franz   **PR WC**
(German artist, 1828-1893)   WC
(German painter, 1828-1893)   PR
Bibl: ▶Thieme-Becker
Franz Kels   PR
Kels   PR

Kels, Hans, the younger *(German medalist, sculptor, 1510-1565/66)*   **BA**
Bibl: ▶Forrer, Medallists; ▶Thieme-Becker

Kelsey, Albert *(American architect, d.1950)*   **AV**
Bibl: ▶Avery obit. idx.

Kelsey, Frank *(British artist, op. 1887-1926)*   **WI**

Kelsey, Mary *(American painter, b.1949)*   **BA**
Bibl: Syracuse (NY, USA), Everson Mus., New works in clay (1981)

Keltenhofer or Keltenofer, Christoph *(German artist, op. 1480-1524)*   **WC**

Kelterborn, Ludwig Adam *(German artist, 1811-1878)*   **WC**

Keltridge, William   **WC WI**
(British artist, op.1684)   WC
(British artist, op.1684-)   WI

Kelz, Adolph H. *(Austrian architect, Graz, 1957-)*   **AV**
Bibl: Transparent, 1988, v.19, no.6, p.37

Kemai Group *(South Italian vase-painters, 4th century BC)*   **GC**
Bibl: ▶Trendall, Red-fig. vases Lucania

Keman, Georges Antoine *(French artist, 1765-1830)*   **WC**

Kemble, Edward Windsor   **BA WI**
(American artist, 1861-1933)   WI
(American illustrator, author, 1861-1933)   BA
Bibl: ▶Fielding's Amer. ptrs.; ▶Smith, Idx. Amer. artists; ▶Vollmer, Künst.-Lex. 20. Jhr.; ▶WWW Amer., 1897; ▶Young, Amer. artists

Kemble, Mimi Maddock *(American interior designer, Palm Beach, Fla)*   **AV**
Bibl: House beautiful, 1989 Dec., p.68

Kemble, Richard *(American sculptor, printmaker, b.1932)*   **BA**
Bibl: ▶WW Amer. Art

Kemble, Roger *(Canadian architect)*   **AV**

Kemendy, Eugen (Jeno) *(Hungarian artist, 1860-1925)*   **WC**

Kemeny, Gyorgy *(Hungarian artist, 20th cent.)*   **WC**

Kemény, Zoltán   **BA WC**
(Hungarian artist, 1907-)   WC
(Hungarian artist, 1907-1965)   BA
Bibl: ▶Fogg Mus. Libr. cat.; ▶Vollmer, Künst.-Lex. 20. Jhr., suppl.

Kemkens, Alex *(West German photographer, b.1942)*   **BA**
Bibl: Munich (DEU), Galerie der Künstler, Fotografie: Porträt (1985)

Kemm, Robert *(British artist, op. 1874-1885)*   **WC WI**

Kemmelmeyer, Frederick   **BA WC WI**
(American artist, op.1788-1803)   WC
(American artist, op.1788-1810)   WI
(American painter, act.1788-1816)   BA
Bibl: ▶Fielding's Amer. ptrs.; ▶Groce, Artists Amer.; Washington, DC (USA), Corcoran Gallery, Charles Peale Polk (1981)

Kemmer, Johann   **GC WC**
(German artist, c.1495-p.1554)   WC
(German painter, ca.1495-1561)   GC
Bibl: ▶Thieme-Becker

Kemmeter, Johann Gottfried *(German architect, act.1734, d.1748)*   **BA**
Bibl: Deutsche Kunstdenk, Bd 14; ▶Macmillan encyc. archts.; ▶Portoghesi, Diz. arch. e urbanistica

Kemmler, Florence *(American, 1900-1972)*   **JG**

Kemna, Herman *(American architect)*   **AV**

Kemnat, Matthias von *(German, ca. 1430-1476)*   **JG**

Kemp or Camp, Nicolaes (Claes) de → see Kemp, Nicolaes de

Kemp, Anthony *(Canadian architect, Toronto)*   **AV**
Bibl: ▶Canad. arch. dir., 1985

Kemp, David Nathan *(British sculptor, painter, b.1945)*   **BA**
Bibl: ▶Contemp. artists, 1983; ▶Intl. dir. exh. artists, 1983, v.1

Kemp, George Meikle *(British architect, 1795-1844)*   **BA**
Bibl: ▶Portoghesi, Diz. arch. e urbanistica; ▶Thieme-Becker

Kemp, Guillaume *(French ébéniste, master 1764)*   **GC**
Bibl: ▶Salverte, Ébénistes 18e s.

Kemp, John   **WC WI**
(British artist, op.1861-1876)   WI
(British artist, op.1868-1876)   WC

Kemp, Kevin *(American architect)*   **AV**
Bibl: Architecture: the AIA journal, 1985 Oct., v.74, no.10, p.18

Kemp, Nicolaes de   **GC**
(Dutch artist, c.1574-1646)   WC
(Dutch painter, c.1574-1646)   GC
Bibl: ▶Thieme-Becker
Camp, Nicolaes de   GC

Kemp or Camp, Nicolaes (Claes) de   **WC**

Kemp, Oliver *(American artist, 1887-1934)*   **WC WI**

Kemp, Roger   **BA WC**
(Australian artist, 1908-)   WC
(Australian painter, b.1908)   BA
Bibl: ▶Encyc. Australian art; ▶Intl. dir. exh. artists, 1983; Kolenberg, H., in STUDIO INTERNATIONAL, CXCVI/1002 (Oct 1983) 51

Kemp, vander [Unidentified]
(Unknown painter)   **PR**
Bibl: (May 23, 1810, lot 54, Jarvis)
Vander Kemp   PR

Kemp-Welch, Lucy Elizabeth → see Kemp-Welch, Lucy Elizabeth

Kennedy, Cedric J.   WC WI
  (British artist, 1898-)   WC
  (British artist, 1898-1968)   WI
Kennedy, Charles→ see Kennedy,
  Charles Napier
Kennedy, Charles Napier   PR WC WI
  (British artist, 1852-1898)   WC WI
  (British painter, 1852-1898)   PR
    Bibl: ▶Thieme-Becker
  Charles Napier Kennedy   PR
  Kennedy, Charles   PR
Kennedy, Clarence   BA JG
  (American photographer, 1892-
    1972)   BA
  (American, 1892-1972)   JG
    Bibl: ▶Art Index, v.17; NY Times
    obit., index, 1969-1978;
    Williamstown (MA, USA), Sterling
    and Francine Clark Art Institute,
    CLARENCE KENNEDY, SCHOLAR-
    PHOTOGRAPHER (1980)
Kennedy, D.J.→ see Kennedy, David
  Johnston
Kennedy, David Johnston   WI
  (American artist, op.1841-1872)   WC
  (American artist, op.1870-)   WI
  Kennedy, D.J.   WC
Kennedy, Donald (American interior
  designer, d. 1987)   AV
    Bibl: Interior design, 1987 Dec.,
    v.58, no.15, p.43
Kennedy, Edward Sherrard (British
  artist, op.1863-1890)   WC WI
Kennedy, Florence (British artist,
  op.1880-1893)   WI
  Laing, Florence, Miss   WI
Kennedy, G.L. (British artist, op.
  20th c.)   WI
Kennedy, Garry Neill (Canadian
  painter, b.1935)   BA
    Bibl: ▶Artists Canada
Kennedy, Gibson B. (American
  photographer, 20th c.)   BA
    Bibl: Springfield (MA, USA), MFA,
    Platinum (1980)
Kennedy, Henry (British architect,
  act.1873-ca.1881)   BA
    Bibl: Haslam: Powys, pp.64, 156
Kennedy, Hugh Arthur (British
  glass painter, 19th c.)   BA
    Bibl: Harrison, Victorian stained
    glass
Kennedy, J.J. (fl. 1925; Architectural
  draftsman, United States of
  America)   FA
    Bibl: Natl. Archives object; Natl.
    Archives object file
Kennedy, John   WC WI
  (British artist, 19th cent.)   WC
  (British artist, op.19th c.)   WI
    Bibl: ▶Mallalieu, Brit. watercolour
    artists
Kennedy, Lewis   AV
Kennedy, Michael (American
  architect, St. Louis, MO, 1946-)   AV
    Bibl: Inland architect, 1985 Nov.-
    Dec., v.29, no.6, p.45

Kennedy, Peter (Australian artist,
  b.1945)   BA
    Bibl: ▶Intl. dir. exh. artists, 1983
Kennedy, Reinier Willem (Dutch
  artist, 1881-1960)   WC
Kennedy, Richard→ see Kennedy,
  Richard I
Kennedy, Richard→ see Kennedy,
  Richard II
Kennedy, Richard I   WI
  (British artist, op.1846-)   WI
  (British artist, op.c.1846)   WC
  Kennedy, Richard   WC
Kennedy, Richard II   WI
  (British artist, 1910-1989)   WI
  (British artist, 20th cent.)   WC
  Kennedy, Richard   WC
Kennedy, Tess (British interior
  designer, London)   AV
    Bibl: Architectural digest, 1987
    Jan., v.44, no.1, p.96
Kennedy, Thomas   WC WI
  (American artist, 19th cent.)   WC
  (American artist, op.19th c.)   WI
Kennedy, William   BA GC WC WI
  (British artist, 1859-1918)   WC WI
  (British painter, 1859-1918)   BA
  (Scottish painter, 1859-1918)   GC
    Bibl: ▶Bénézit; Billcliffe; ▶Harris,
    Scottish ptrs.; ▶Thieme-Becker;
    ▶Witt checklist
Kennedy, William→ see Kennedy,
  William Denholm
Kennedy, William Denholm   PR WC WI
  (British artist, 1813-1865)   WC WI
  (British painter, 1813-1865)   PR
    Bibl: ▶Thieme-Becker
  Kennedy, William   PR
  William Denholm Kennedy   PR
Kenneil, E., Mrs.→ see Nelson, E.,
  Miss
Kennely   WC WI
  (British artist, op.1800-)   WI
  (British(?) artist, op.c.1800)   WC
Kennerell (British, active Wisbech,
  England, U.K. 19th century)   JG
Kennerly, David Hume (American
  photographer, 20th c.)   BA
    Bibl: IMAGE, XXVII/3 (Sept 1984)
    1-36
Kennerly, J. (Engraver, op.18th c.)   WI
Kennet, Kathleen (British sculptor,
  1878-1947)   BA
    Bibl: ▶Johnson, Brit. artists;
    ▶Waters, Brit. artists; ▶Who was
    who [GBR]
Kenneth Hayes Miller→ see Miller,
  Kenneth Hayes
Kenneth K. Forbes→ see Forbes,
  Kenneth K.
Kennethson, George (British
  sculptor, b.1910)   BA
    Bibl: ▶Art Index, v.37; Kitchen,
    COUNTRY LIFE, CLXXXII/44 (3
    Nov 88), p.236

Kenney, Annson (American artist,
  musician, author, 1944-1981)   BA
    Bibl: ▶Intl. dir. exh. artists, 1982,
    1983; Philadelphia (PA, USA),
    Moore College of Art, Gallery,
    ANNSON KENNEY..., 1983
Kenney, John Theodore Eardley
  (British artist, 1911-1972)   WI
Kenney, Leo (American artist,
  b.1925)   BA
    Bibl: ▶MoMA libr. cat.; Portland
    (OR, USA), Art Mus., West Coast
    now (1968)
Kenning, David (British painter,
  b.1933)   BA
    Bibl: ▶Intl. dir. exh. artists
Kenning, J.B.   WC WI
  (British artist, 19th cent.)   WC
  (British artist, op.19th c.)   WI
Kennington, Eric Henri   BA WC WI
  (British artist, 1888-1960)   WC WI
  (British painter, sculptor, 1888-
    1960)   BA
    Bibl: ▶Johnson, Brit. artists;
    ▶Vollmer, Künst.-Lex. 20. Jhr.;
    ▶Who was who [GBR], v.5
Kennington, Thomas Benjamin
  (British artist, 1856-1916)   WC WI
Kennion, Edward   WC WI
  (British artist, 1743-1809)   WI
  (British artist, 1743/4-1809)   WC
    Bibl: ▶Mallalieu, Brit. watercolour
    artists
Kennon, Paul (American architect)   AV
Kenny, Michael   BA WI
  (British artist, b.1941)   WI
  (British sculptor, b.1941)   BA
    Bibl: ▶Art Index, 1969; ▶MoMA
    libr. cat.
Kenny, Nicholas   WC WI
  (British artist, 1807-op.1856)   WI
  (British artist, c.1807-p.1856)   WC
Kenny, Robert (American interior
  designer, New York City)   AV
    Bibl: Interior design, 1988 Feb.,
    v.59, no.3, p.292
Kennyman   WC WI
  (British artist, 17th cent.)   WC
  (British artist, op.17th c.)   WI
Kenoy, Franz van→ see Duquesnoy,
  François (il Fiammingo)
Kensett→ see Kensett, John Frederick
Kensett, John→ see Kensett, John
  Frederick

Kensett, John
    Frederick   **BA GC PR WC WI**
    (American artist, 1816-1872)   WI
    (American artist, 1818-1872)   WC
    (American painter, 1816-1872)   PR
    (American painter, printmaker,
    1816-1872)   BA
    (American, 1818-1972)   GC
    Bibl: Coral Gables (FL, USA), Lowe
    Art Mus., 19c. Amer. topographic
    ptrs. (1975); ▶Dict. Amer. biog.;
    ▶Fielding's Amer. ptrs.; ▶Groce,
    Artists Amer.; ▶RILA/BHA; ▶Witt
    checklist; ▶WWW Amer. art;
    ▶WWW Amer. hist.
  John Frederick Kensett   PR
  Kensett   PR
  Kensett, John   PR
Kensett, Thomas (American
    printmaker, 1786-1829)   **BA**
    Bibl: ▶Groce, Artists Amer.
Kensetu, Shin (Japanese architect)   **AV**
    Bibl: Kenchiku bunka, 1988 Sept.,
    v.43, no.503, p.115
Kensington Class   **GC**
    Bibl: ▶Beazley, Attic red-fig. vase-
    ptrs.
Kensington Painter   **GC**
    Bibl: ▶Beazley, Attic red-fig. vase-
    ptrs.
Kent→see Kent, Rockwell
Kent→see Kent, William
Kent, Caroline Cochrane (American
    artist, 20th c.)   **BA**
    Bibl: Visual Resources II, 1-3, fall-
    spr, 81/82, p.92-100
Kent, E.   **WC WI**
    (British artist, 17th cent.)   WC
    (British artist, op.17th c.)   WI
Kent, John (British artist, op.1770-
    1773)   **WC WI**
Kent, John Howe (American
    photographer, painter, 1827-1910)   **BA**
    Bibl: ▶Parry, Photo idx.; Pedzich,
    Image XXVII/1 (Mar 1984) 1
Kent, Rock→see Kent, Rockwell
Kent, Rockwell   **AV BA FA GC PR WC WI**
    (21.VI.1882-13.III.1971;
    Architectural draftsman,
    United States of America)   FA
    (American artist and author,
    trained in architecture at
    Columbia Univ, 1882-1971)   AV
    (American artist, 1882-)   WC
    (American artist, 1882-1971)   WI
    (American artist, author, 1882-
    1971)   BA
    (American painter, 1882-1971)   GC PR
    Bibl: ▶Fielding's Amer. ptrs.; Getty
    Photo Study Coll.; ▶Lowry,
    Building natl. image; ▶RILA/BHA;
    ▶Witt checklist; ▶WWW Amer.
  Kent   PR
  Kent, Rock   GC
  Rockwell Kent   PR

Kent, Sarah   **WC WI**
    (British artist, 1941-)   WC
    (British artist, b.1941)   WI
Kent, W.→see Kent, William
Kent, William   **AV BA PR WC WI**
    (British architect, designer,
    1685-1748)   AV
    (British artist, 1684-1748)   WC
    (British artist, 1685-1748)   WI
    (British painter, 1684-1748)   PR
    (English painter, architect,
    landscape gardener, 1684-
    1748)   BA
    Bibl: ▶Colvin, Brit. archts.; ▶Dict.
    natl. biog.; ▶Encyc. Britannica;
    ▶Libr. of Congr. Name Auth. File;
    ▶Macmillan encyc. archts.; ▶New
    Columbia encyc.; ▶RILA/BHA;
    ▶Thieme-Becker
  Kent   PR
  Kent, W.   PR
  William Kent   PR
Kent, William H. (Active London,
    England, U.K., daguerreotypist,
    active 1850-1856)   **JG**
Kenton, Elizabeth Macdowell
    (American painter, 19th-20th cs.)   **BA**
    Bibl: Hendricks, Life & Works of
    Thos. Eakins; Schendler, Thos.
    Eakins
Kenworthy, Jonathan (British
    sculptor, b.1943)   **BA**
    Bibl: ▶Babington Smith, Contemp.
    artists; Hemminway, J.
    Connoisseur CCXV/883 (Aug
    1985) 88
Kenyon Cox→see Cox, Kenyon
Kenyon, Arthur William (d.1969)   **AV**
Kenyon, F.P. (American, active New
    London, CT, U.S. 1855-1913)   **JG**
Kenyon, Lowell Anson (American
    architectural photographer)   **AV**
    Bibl: Architecture: the AIA
    journal, 1986 Apr., v.75, no.4,
    p.37
Keogh, Paul (Irish architect, Dublin)   **AV**
    Bibl: Architects' journal, 1984
    Oct.31, v.180, no.44, p.31
Keogh, Tom (American artist, op.
    1955-)   **WI**
Kepes, Gyorgy   **BA JG WC WI**
    (American artist, 1906-)   WC
    (American artist, b.1906)   WI
    (American painter, b.1906)   BA
    (American, born Hungary, 1906
    -)   JG
    Bibl: ▶WW Amer. Art, 1976
Kepets, Hugh→see Kepets, Hugh
  Michael
Kepets, Hugh Michael   **BA WI**
    (American artist, 1946-)   WC
    (American artist, b.1946)   WI
    (American painter, printmaker,
    b.1946)   BA
    Bibl: ▶WW Amer. Art
  Kepets, Hugh   **WC**

Kepfer, Maximilien Pierre (French
    artist, 1798-)   **WC**
Kephisodotos the Elder (Greek
    sculptor, act. 1st half 4th c BC)   **GC**
    Bibl: Getty Photo Study Coll.;
    ▶Robertson, Greek art, p.383
Kephisodotos the Younger (Greek
    sculptor, act. early 3rd c BC)   **GC**
    Bibl: Getty Photo Study Coll.;
    ▶Robertson, Greek art, p.383
Kephisophon Painter   **GC**
    Bibl: ▶Beazley, Attic bl.-fig. vase-
    ptrs.
Keppell, Niclauss (German
    printmaker, act.1588-1608)   **BA**
    Bibl: WALTERS ART GALL. BULL.,
    XXXIII (Jan 1981) 1-4
Keppelmann, H.W.   **WC WI**
    (American artist, 19th cent.)   WC
    (American artist, op.20th c.)   WI
Keppler, Joseph (American
    cartoonist, publisher, 1838-1894)   **BA**
    Bibl: Berkeley (CA, USA), UCB Art
    Mus., Amer. presidency political
    cartoons (1976); ▶Dict. Amer.
    biog.; Fielding's Amer. ptrs.;
    ▶Mallett's idx. artists
Ker Porter→see Porter, Robert Kerr,
  Sir
Ker Xavier Roussel→see Roussel, Ker
  Xavier
Ker, Dorian (British artist, 1948-op.
    1977)   **WI**
Ker, Wilhelmina Young (British
    artist, op.circa 1806-)   **WI**
Keranval, L.   **WC WI**
    (British artist, 19th cent.)   WC
    (British artist, op.19th c.)   WI
Kerbach, Ralf (West German
    painter, printmaker, b.1956)   **BA**
    Bibl: Ohff, Kunstwerk, XLII/1 (Mar
    1989) p.68
Kerbel', Lev Efimovič (Russian
    sculptor, b.1917)   **BA**
    Bibl: ▶Vollmer, Künst.-Lex. 20. Jhr.
Kerchlango, Jörg Wolfgang (Danish
    architect, Risskov, 1944-)   **AV**
    Bibl: ▶Danske Arkitekters
    Landsforbund, 1984-85
**Kerckhove or Kerchove, Joseph
    van den** (Flemish artist, 1667-
    1724)   **WC**
Kerckhove, Ernest van den
    (Belgian artist, 1840-1879)   **WC**
Kerckhove, F. van den (Dutch(?)
    artist, 17th cent.)   **WC**
Kerckhoven, Jacob van der   **GC**
    (Flemish painter, act.1649)   GC
    (Italian artist, c.1550-p.1600)   WC
    Bibl: Safarik; StaatsgalStuttgart;
    StaatsgalStuttgart (1962), p.101
  Castello, Giacomo da   **WC**
  Giacomo da Castello   GC
Kerdeoret, Gustav de (French
    artist, 19th cent.)   **WC**

Kerdijk, Herman *(Dutch architect)*   **AV**
    Bibl: Forum, 1988 Oct., v.32,
    no.4, p.16

Kerényi, Jenő *(Hungarian sculptor,*
    1908-1975)   **BA**
    Bibl: ▶Encyc. world art; ▶Fogg
    Mus. Libr. cat.; ▶Vollmer,
    Künst.-Lex. 20. Jhr.

Kerényi, József *(Hungarian*
    architect)   **AV**
    Bibl: Architecture: the AIA
    journal, 1984 Sept., v.73, no.9,
    p.108

Kerfers, Rita→see Lex-Kerfers, Rita

Kerfers, Robert *(West German*
    architect, Bockhorn)   **AV**
    Bibl: Deutsches Architektenblatt,
    1989 Oct.1, v.21, no.10, p.1447

Kerfoot, John B. *(American, active*
    ca. 1900)   **JG**

Kerg, Theo *(Dutch artist, b.1909)*   **BA**
    Bibl: Kunstler-Lex

Kergel→see Kergel, Ludwig
Kergel, Carl Franz Ludwig→see
    Kergel, Ludwig

Kergel, Ludwig   **PR**
    (German painter, 1814-1874)   **GC PR**
    Bibl: ▶Bénézit; ▶Thieme-Becker
    Kergel   PR

Kergel, Carl Franz Ludwig   **GC**
    Ludwig Kergel   PR

Kerhart, František   **AV BA**
    (Czech architect, 20th c.)   **BA**
    (Czechoslovak architect, 20th
    c.)   **AV**
    Bibl: AMC, 1985 Mar., no.7, p.56;
    Svácha, Umění, XXVIII/4 (1980)
    pp.368-379

Kerhart, Vojtěch *(Czechoslovak*
    architect, 20th c.)   **AV**
    Bibl: AMC, 1985 Mar., no.7, p.56

Kerincks→see Keirincx, Alexander
Keringhs→see Keirincx, Alexander
Kerings→see Keirincx, Alexander
Kerinks→see Keirincx, Alexander
Kerkam→see Kerkam, Earl Cavis
Kerkam, Earl→see Kerkam, Earl Cavis

Kerkam, Earl Cavis *(American*
    painter, 1890-1965)   **BA PR**
    Bibl: ▶Bénézit; ▶Fogg Mus. Libr.
    cat.; ▶RILA/BHA; ▶Vollmer,
    Künst.-Lex. 20. Jhr.; ▶WW Amer.
    Art, 1940-1941, 1966
    Earl Covis Kerkam   PR
    Kerkam   PR
    Kerkam, Earl   PR
    Kerkam, Earl Covis   PR

Kerkam, Earl Covis→see Kerkam, Earl
    Cavis

Kerkar, Elizabetha *(English(?)*
    interior designer)   **AV**
    Bibl: Restaurant/hotel design,
    1988 Nov., v.10, no.11, p.56

Kerken, A. van den *(Dutch artist,*
    op.1647)   **WC**

Kerkhoff, Daniel   **GC**
    (Dutch artist, 1766-1821)   **WC**
    (Dutch draughtsman, 1766-
    1821)   **GC**
    Bibl: ▶Thieme-Becker

Kerkhoff, Daniel Johannes
    Torman   **WC**
    Kerkhoff, Daniel Johannes
    Torman→see Kerkhoff, Daniel

Kerkhove→see Kerkhove, Jean van de

Kerkhove, Jean van de *(Belgian*
    painter, 1822-1881)   **PR**
    Bibl: ▶Thieme-Becker
    Jean van de Kerkhove   PR
    Kerkhove   PR

Kerkhoven, Leonard van den
    (Belgian painter, printmaker, ca.
    1828-1898)   **BA**
    Bibl: ▶Bénézit; ▶Thieme-Becker

Kerkovius, Ida   **BA WC**
    (German artist, 1879-1970)   **WC**
    (German painter, 1879-1970)   **BA**
    Bibl: ▶Bénézit; ▶Brockhaus Enzyk.;
    Hamburg (DEU), Kunsthalle,
    Meister des 19 Jahrh. (1969);
    ▶Kindlers Malerei Lex.;
    ▶Thieme-Becker; ▶Vollmer,
    Künst.-Lex. 20. Jhr.

Kerling, Anna E. *(Dutch*
    draughtsman, 1862-1955)   **GC**
    Bibl: ▶Thieme-Becker

Kerling, William *(British artist, op.*
    1895-)   **WI**

Kerlow, Isaac Victor *(American*
    artist, b.1958)   **BA**
    Bibl: Kerlow, I.V., LEONARDO,
    XIX/2 (1986) p. 131-134

Kerma, Ingrid   **BA WI**
    (British artist, b.1942)   **WI**
    (British painter, b.1942)   **BA**
    Bibl: Arts Council GBR, A free
    hand (1978)

Kermadec, Eugene Nestor de (Le)
    (French artist, 1899-)   **WC**

Kermarrec *(French artist, 20th cent.)*   **WC**

Kermode, William A. *(British artist,*
    op.1920-1930)   **WI**

Kern Group   **GC**
    Bibl: ▶Beazley, Attic bl.-fig. vase-
    ptrs.

Kern or Korne, Anton (Franz
    Anton)→see Kern, Anton

Kern, Anton   **BA GC**
    (Bohemian painter, 1710-1747)   **BA**
    (German artist, 1710-1747)   **WC**
    (German, 1710-1747)   **GC**
    Bibl: ▶Bénézit; ▶Nagler, Neues
    Künst.-Lex.; ▶Thieme-Becker;
    ▶Witt checklist

Kern or Korne, Anton (Franz
    Anton)   **WC**
    Körne, Anton   BA

Kern, Doreen *(British sculptor, 20th*
    c.)   **BA**
    Bibl: Cookham (GBR), Vicarage,
    Impact (1979)

Kern, Hermann *(Hungarian artist,*
    1839-1912)   **WC**

Kern, Hermann *(Austrian landscape*
    architect, Graz)   **AV**
    Bibl: Anthos, 1988 v.27, no.1,
    p.20

Kern, James (Jaya) *(American*
    painter, 20th c.)   **BA**
    Bibl: Kern, J., LEONARDO, XIII 3
    summer 1980 216-218

Kern, Johann Adam *(German artist,*
    1750-1800)   **WC**

Kern, Josef *(Austrian painter,*
    b.1953)   **BA**
    Bibl: Graz (AUT), Steiermarkisches
    Landesmus. Joanneum, Neue
    Galerie, JOSEF KERN, 1984

Kern, Leonhard *(German sculptor,*
    1585/88-1662)   **BA GC**
    Bibl: ▶Bénézit; ▶Encyc. world art;
    Gradmann. Die Monumental
    werke der Bildhaer familie Kern;
    ▶Nagler, Neues Künst.-Lex.;
    ▶RILA/BHA; ▶Thieme-Becker

Kern, Matthaus *(German artist,*
    1801-1852)   **WC**

Kern, Pascal *(French photographer,*
    b.1952)   **BA**
    Bibl: ▶Art Index, v.36; ▶ARTbibl.
    mod., v.17/1, p.232

Kern, Richard Hovenden *(American*
    painter, 1821-1853)   **BA**
    Bibl: ▶Dawdy, Artists Amer. West;
    ▶Groce, Artists Amer.; ▶WWW
    Amer. hist.; ▶Young, Amer. artists

Kern, Stephan *(German artist,*
    b.1955)   **BA**
    Bibl: Munich (BRD), Städt. Gal.,
    Kunstf. Max., STEPHEN KERN,
    1981

Kernan, J.   **WC WI**
    (British artist, 18th cent.)   **WC**
    (British artist, op.18th c.)   **WI**

Kerner, Nancy *(American*
    printmaker, 20th c.)   **BA**

Kernoff, Harry Aaron   **BA WI**
    (British artist, 1900-1974)   **WI**
    (British painter, 1900-1974)   **BA**
    Bibl: ▶Dolman, Contemp. Brit.
    artists; ▶Vollmer, Künst.-Lex. 20.
    Jhr.; ▶Waters, Brit. artists; ▶Who
    was who [GBR], index

Kerns, Ed *(American painter,*
    b.1945)   **BA**
    Bibl: ▶NY art yrbk.; ▶WW Amer.
    Art, 1976

Kerns, Thomas *(American architect)*   **AV**

Kernstok, Károly   **BA WC**
    (Hungarian artist, 1873-1940)   **WC**
    (Hungarian painter, printmaker,
    1873-1940)   **BA**
    Bibl: ▶Bénézit; Revai Nagy Lex.;
    ▶Thieme-Becker; ▶Uj magyar
    lexikon; ▶Vollmer, Künst.-Lex. 20.
    Jhr.

Kerpel, Lipót (Leopold) *(Hungarian*
    painter, 1818-1880)   **BA**

Kerpenter, or Kerpentier, P. →see
  Kerpenter, P.

Kerpenter, P.   **GC**
  (Flemish (?), act. ca.1650)   GC
  (Flemish(?) artist, op.c.1650)   WC
    Bibl: ▶Witt checklist

Kerpenter, or Kerpentier, P.   **WC**

Kerr, Bernadette *(British artist,*
  b.1958)   **WI**

Kerr, Charles Henry Malcolm
  (British artist, 1858-1907)   **WC WI**
    Bibl: ▶Waters, Brit. artists

Kerr, George Alexander *(Scottish*
  architect, Alloa, 1856-1927)   **AV**
    Bibl: Newsletter of the Charles
    Rennie Mackintosh Society, 1988
    summer, no.49, p.5

Kerr, George Cochrane *(British*
  artist, circa 1825-circa 1907)   **WI**

Kerr, Henry W. →see Kerr, Henry
  Wright

Kerr, Henry Wright   **WI**
  (British artist, 1857-1936)   WI
  (British artist, 19th cent.)   WC

Kerr, Henry W.   **WC**

Kerr, Illingworth Holey *(Canadian*
  painter, b.1905)   **BA**
    Bibl: ▶Artists Canada; Callahan,
    Winnipeg Art Gall. Magazine
    (Oct-Nov 1985), p. 10-11;
    ▶MacDonald, Can. artists

Kerr, J. Patrick *(American architect,*
  Paducah, Ky)   **AV**
    Bibl: ▶AIA Pro File, 1987-1988

Kerr, Robert *(British architect,*
  author, 1823-1904)   **BA**
    Bibl: ▶Portoghesi, Diz. arch. e
    urbanistica; ▶Thieme-Becker

Kerr, William *(Scottish architect,*
  Alloa, 1867-1940)   **AV**
    Bibl: Newsletter of the Charles
    Rennie Mackintosh Society, 1988
    summer, no.49, p.5

Kerr-Lawson, James   **BA WC WI**
  (British artist, 1865-1939)   WC WI
  (Canadian painter, printmaker,
  author, 1864-1939)   BA
    Bibl: ▶Bénézit; Guelph, Univ., Mac
    Stewart, JAMES KERR-LAWSON
    (1983); ▶Harper, Ptg. Canada;
    ▶Havlice, Idx. art. bio.; ▶Johnson,
    Brit. artists; ▶Thieme-Becker;
    ▶Waters, Brit. artists; ▶Witt
    checklist

Kerres, Bernhard *(German architect,*
  Stuttgart/Pforzheim)   **AV**
    Bibl: Deutsche Bauzeitung, 1985
    Oct., v.119, no.10, p.34

Kerrich, Thomas   **BA WC WI**
  (British artist, 1748-1828)   WC WI
  (British librarian, painter, author,
  1748-1828)   BA
    Bibl: ▶Dict. natl. biog.;
    ▶Thieme-Becker; ▶Witt checklist

Kerricx, Guillielmus *(Flemish*
  sculptor, 1652-1719)   **BA**
    Bibl: Brussels, Musée Royaux des
    Beaux-Arts, Sculpture...Rubens,
    1977; ▶Thieme-Becker;
    ▶Wurzbach, NLD Künst.-Lex.

Kerrigan, Maurie *(American*
  sculptor, b.1951)   **BA**
    Bibl: ARTS MAGAZINE
    LIV/4/Dec/1979 p.12; ▶WW
    Amer. Art, 1984

Kerrina [Unidentified] *(Unknown*
  painter)   **PR**
    Bibl: (May 22, 1813, lot 3, White)

Kerschbaumer, Anton *(German*
  painter, printmaker, 1885-1931)   **BA**
    Bibl: ▶Bénézit; ▶Kindlers Malerei
    Lex.; ▶Thieme-Becker; ▶Vollmer,
    Künst.-Lex. 20. Jhr.

Kerseboom →see Kerseboom,
  Frederic

Kerseboom, Casauban, Causabon or
  Kersseboom, Friedrich (A.R. de
  Charos) →see Kerseboom, Frederic

Kerseboom, Frederic   **PR**
  (German artist, 1632-1690)   WC
  (German painter, 1632-1690)   PR
    Bibl: ▶Thieme-Becker

Frederic Kerseboom   PR
Kerseboom   PR

Kerseboom, Casauban,
  Causabon or Kersseboom,
  Friedrich (A.R. de Charos)   **WC**

Kerseboom, J. (Johann?) *(German*
  artist, op.1680-m.1708)   **WC**

Kershaw, Dan   **WC WI**
  (American artist, op.1846)   WC
  (American artist, op.1846-)   WI

Kershaw, J. Franklin *(British artist,*
  d.1917)   **WI**

Kershaw, Thomas   **AV BA**
  (British decorator, 1819-1898)   BA
  (British gardener and marbler,
  1819-1898)   AV
    Bibl: ▶Bénézit; Jervis, Country life,
    CLXXIX/4625 (10 Apr. 1986)
    p.939; ▶Thieme-Becker

Kerssemakers, Antonius Cornelis
  Augustinus (Anton) *(Dutch*
  artist, 1846-1924)   **WC**

Kerstantsz., Jan *(Dutch*
  cabinetmaker, act.1539-1553)   **BA**

Kerstein, Vivian *(American artist,*
  b.1956)   **BA**
    Bibl: Claremont (CA, USA),
    Galleries of the Claremont
    Colleges, Contemp. triptychs
    (1982)

Kersten, Wilhelm *(German artist,*
  op.1830-1842)   **WC**

Kerstiaen de Coninck →see Keuninck,
  Kerstiaen de

Kersting, Carl Friedrich →see
  Kersting, Georg Friedrich

Kersting, Georg Friedrich   **BA GC WC**
  (German artist, 1785-1847)   WC
  (German painter, 1785-1847)   BA
  (German, 1785-1847)   GC
    Bibl: ▶Encyc. world art; ▶Fogg
    Mus. Libr. cat.; Getty Photo Study
    Coll. (Ptgs.); Novotny, Ptg. &
    sculp. Europe 1780-1880, p.59;
    Teske. Studien zur Genremalerei
    in Vormärz; ▶Thieme-Becker;
    ▶Witt checklist

Kersting, Carl Friedrich   GC

Kersting, Hermann Karl *(German*
  artist, 1825-1850)   **WC**

Kertész, András →see Kertész, André

Kertész, André   **BA JG**
  (American (b. Hungary), 1894-
  1985)   JG
  (American photographer, 1894-
  1985)   BA
  (Hungarian architect)   AV
    Bibl: ▶Contemp. photogs.; Magyar
    építömüvészet, 1987, v.78, no.3,
    p.36; National Public Radio (30
    Sept 1985); NT TIMES (30 Sept
    1985)

Kertész, András   **AV**

Kertészfi, Ágnes *(Hungarian stained*
  glass artist, Pécs)   **AV**
    Bibl: Müvészet, 1988 July, v.29,
    no.7, p.36

Kertson, M. *(Active New York, NY,*
  U.S. 1853-1855, daguerreotypist)   **JG**

Kerver, Jacob or Jacques
  (Monogrammist IK) *(French*
  artist, op.1535-m.1583)   **WC**

Kesegdans [Unidentified]
  (Unknown painter)   **PR**
    Bibl: January 24, 1807, lot 29,
    Christie's; July 30, 1807, lot 195,
    Dodd; June 5, 1806, lot 37,
    Cassano (Alexander)

Keserü, Ilona *(Hungarian painter,*
  b.1933)   **BA**
    Bibl: ARS HUNGARICA.
    VI/1/1978, pgs.65-79

Keskikastari, Paula *(Finnish*
  architect)   **AV**
    Bibl: Arkkitehtuurikilpailuja, 1989,
    no.9, p.2

Kesmarky, Arpad *(Hungarian*
  painter, printmaker, act.ca.1906-
  1914)   **BA**
    Bibl: Sheon, A., in ARTS
    MAGAZINE LVII/7 (Mar 1983) 103

Kessanlis, Nikos *(Greek artist,*
  1930-)   **WC**

Kessel →see Kessel, Hieronymus van
Kessel →see Kessel, Jan van
Kessel →see Kessel, Jan van I

Kessel, Bertel van *(early Netherlandish painter, sculptor, act.1460-1538)* **BA**
  Bibl: ▶Bénézit; Louvain (BEL), Sted. Mus., Laatgotische beeldsnijcentrum (1979); ▶Thieme-Becker; ▶Wurzbach, NLD Künst.-Lex.

Kessel, Ferdinand van **GC WC**
  (Flemish artist, 1648-p.1696) **WC**
  (Flemish, 1648-aft.1696) **GC**
  Bibl: Getty Photo Study Coll. (Ptgs.); ▶Witt checklist
  Kassel, Ferdinand van   GC

Kessel, Hieronymus van **PR WC**
  (Flemish artist, 1578-p.1636) **WC**
  (Flemish painter, 1576-aft.1636) **PR**
  Bibl: ▶Thieme-Becker
  Hieronymus van Kessel   PR
  Kessel   PR
  van Kessel   PR
Kessel, J.T. van→see Kessel, Jan Thomas van
Kessel, Jan III van→see Kessel, Jan van

Kessel, Jan Thomas van **PR WC**
  (Flemish artist, 1677-1741(?)) **WC**
  (Flemish painter, 1677-1741) **PR**
  Bibl: ▶Thieme-Becker
  Cavalier Van Cassel   PR
  Jan Thomas van Kessel   PR
  Kessel, J.T. van   PR
  van Kessel   PR

Kessel, Jan van **BA GC**
  (Dutch artist, 1641-1680) **WC**
  (Dutch painter and draughtsman, 1641-1680) **GC**
  (Dutch painter, 1641/42-1680) **BA PR**
  Bibl: ▶Artist biog. master idx.; ▶Bénézit; ▶Bernt, Neth. ptrs. 17c.; Getty Photo Study Coll. (Duits coll.); Getty Photo Study Coll. (Ptgs.); ▶RILA/BHA; ▶Thieme-Becker; ▶Wurzbach, NLD Künst.-Lex.
  J. van Kessel   PR
  Jan Kessel   PR
  Jan van Kessel   PR
  Kessel   PR
  Kessel, Jan III van   PR
  Kessel, Jan van (III)   **PR**
  Kessel, Jan van III   GC
  Kessel, Johan or Jan Thomasz. van   **WC**
  Kessel, Johan van   PR
  Kessel, Johannes van   GC
  Van Cassel   PR
  van Kessel   PR
Kessel, Jan van→see Kessel, Jan van I
Kessel, Jan van (I)→see Kessel, Jan van I
Kessel, Jan van (II)→see Kessel, Jan van II
Kessel, Jan van (III)→see Kessel, Jan van

Kessel, Jan van I **BA GC PR**
  (Flemish artist, 1626-1679) **WC**
  (Flemish painter, 1626-1679) **BA PR**
  (Flemish, 1626-1679) **GC**
  Bibl: ▶Bernt, Neth. ptrs. 17c.; ▶Grote Winkler Prins; ▶RILA/BHA; ▶Thieme-Becker; ▶Wurzbach, NLD Künst.-Lex.
  Jan van Kessel (I)   PR
  Jean Van Kessel père   PR
  Kessel   PR
  Kessel, Jan van   PR
  Kessel, Jan van (I)   **PR**
  Kessel, Jan, I van   **WC**
  V. Kessel   PR
  Van Cassel   PR
  Van Kessel   PR
  Van Kessell   PR
  Van Kessels   PR

Kessel, Jan van II **BA**
  (Flemish artist, 1654-1708) **WC**
  (Flemish painter, 1654-1708) **BA PR**
  Bibl: ▶Bénézit; ▶Kraam, Holl. en Vlaamsche kunst.; ▶RILA/BHA; ▶Thieme-Becker; ▶Winkler Prins van de kunst; ▶Wurzbach, NLD Künst.-Lex.
  Jan van Kessel (II)   PR
  John Van Kessel   PR
  John Van Kessel, 1682   PR
  Kessel, Jan van (II)   **PR**
  Kessel, Jan, II van   **WC**
  van Kessel   PR
Kessel, Jan van III→see Kessel, Jan van
Kessel, Jan, I van→see Kessel, Jan van I
Kessel, Jan, II van→see Kessel, Jan van II
Kessel, Johan or Jan Thomasz. van→see Kessel, Jan van
Kessel, Johan van→see Kessel, Jan van
Kessel, Johannes van→see Kessel, Jan van

Kessel, Peter van *(Flemish painter, d. 1668)* **PR**
  Bibl: Lewis, Dutch & Flem. still life ptrs., I
  Kessel, Pieter van   PR
  Peter van Kessel   PR
  T.V. Kessell   PR
Kessel, Pieter van→see Kessel, Peter van

Kessel, Theodor van **GC WC**
  (Dutch artist, c.1620-p.1660) **WC**
  (Dutch, ca.1620-aft.1660) **GC**
  Bibl: ▶Witt checklist

Kessel, W. van *(Netherlands artist, op.1721)* **WC**

Kesseler, Robert *(British artist, b.1951)* **WI**

Kessell, Mary **WC WI**
  (British artist, 20th cent.) **WC**
  (British artist, b.1914) **WI**

Kessels, Mathieu *(Belgian sculptor, 1784-1836)* **BA**
  Bibl: ▶Bénézit; BN; ▶Thieme-Becker

Kesselstadt, Franz Ludwig, Count von *(German artist, 1753-1841)* **WC**
Kessler or Kesseler, Franz→see Kessler, Franz

Kessler, Alan *(American painter, sculptor, b.1945)* **BA**
  Bibl: ▶WW Amer. Art, 1976

Kessler, C.A. *(German artist, op. 1814)* **WC**

Kessler, Christian Friedrich **GC WC**
  (German artist, 1790-1854) **WC**
  (German painter, 1799-1854) **GC**
  Bibl: ▶Bénézit

Kessler, David *(American architect)* **AV**
  Bibl: Architecture and urbanism, 1986 Aug., no.81(191), p.68

Kessler, Franz **GC**
  (German artist, c.1580-p.1650) **WC**
  (German, ca.1580-aft.1650) **GC**
  Bibl: ▶Witt checklist
  Kessler or Kesseler, Franz   **WC**

Kessler, George Edward *(American city planner and landscape architect, 1862-1923)* **AV**
  Bibl: AIA Journal, v.12, n.1, Jan. 1924, p.118-119

Kessler, Hans *(German painter, b.1906)* **BA**
  Bibl: Wangler, Schüler des Bauhauses, p.36

Kessler, Jon *(American artist, b.1957)* **BA**
  Bibl: ▶ARTbibl. mod., 21/1; Cooke, ARTSCRIBE, 69 (May 1988) p.50-54; Lyon (FRA), Espace lyonnais d'art cont., STATUS OF SCULPTURE (199); Santa Barbara (CA, USA), UCSB Art Mus., Scapes (1985)

Kessler, Joseph *(German artist, 1826-1887)* **WC**

Kessler, Michael *(American painter, b.1954)* **BA**
  Bibl: Carrier, Arts LXI (May 1987) 32-33; Narrett, NEW ART EXAMINER XIV (Apr 1987) 47; Stapen, ARTFORUM XXV (Apr 1987) 132
Kessler, Stephan→see Kessler, Stephan I

Kessler, Stephan I **BA**
  (Austrian painter, 1622-1700) **BA GC**
  (German artist, 1622-1700) **WC**
  Bibl: ▶Bénézit; ▶Neue deutsche Biog.; ▶Thieme-Becker; ▶Witt checklist
  Kessler, Stephan   **GC**
  Kessler, Stephan, I   **WC**
Kessler, Stephan, I→see Kessler, Stephan I

Kessler, Susanne *(German painter,*
  b.1955)   **BA**
    Bibl: London (GBR), Goethe Inst.,
    DAAD Scholarship-holders (1983)
Kessler, William H. *(American*
  architect, 1924-)   **AV**
    Bibl: ▶AIA Pro File, 1983; Process:
    architecture, n.7, 1978, p.210
Kestelman, Morris   **BA WC WI**
  (British artist, 20th cent.)   **WC**
  (British artist, b.1905)   **WI**
  (British painter, printmaker,
    b.1905)   **BA**
    Bibl: ▶Waters, Brit. artists; ▶WW
    Art
Kester, de   **WC WI**
  (British artist, op.18th c.)   **WI**
  (British(?) artist, 18th cent.)   **WC**
Kester, Leonard *(American stained*
  glass artist, Los Angeles, Calif)   **AV**
    Bibl: Stained glass, 1987 Fall,
    v.82, no.3, p.248
Kester, Wilmer *(American educator,*
  photographer, act.1897)   **BA**
    Bibl: Fritz, HISTORY OF
    PHOTOGRAPHY, 9/2 A-J '85
    p.148
Kesteren, Maria van *(Dutch*
  woodworker, b.1933)   **BA**
    Bibl: ex cat Stedelijk Mus.
    Amsterdam 1975-one man show;
    ▶Scheen, Ned. beeldende kunst.
Kesting, Edmund   **BA JG WC**
  (German artist, 1892-)   **WC**
  (German painter, printmaker,
    1892-1970)   **BA**
  (German, 1892-1970)   **JG**
    Bibl: ▶Bénézit; ▶MoMA libr. cat.;
    ▶Parry, Contemp. art; ▶Parry,
    Photo idx.; ▶Vollmer, Künst.-Lex.
    20. Jhr.
Kestner, August   **GC WC**
  (German artist, 1777-1853)   **WC**
  (German draughtsman, 1777-
    1853)   **GC**
    Bibl: ▶Bénézit
Kestoff *(Swiss artist, 20th cent.)* **WC**
Keston, Roger *(English, d.1409)*   **BA**
    Bibl: Transactions Mon. Brass
    Soc., XII/2 (1976) pp.185-189
Ket, Dick   **BA GC**
  (Dutch artist, 1902-1940)   **WC**
  (Dutch painter and
    draughtsman, 1902-1940)   **GC**
  (Dutch painter, 1902-1940)   **BA**
    Bibl: ▶Bénézit; ▶Vollmer,
    Künst.-Lex. 20. Jhr.
Ket, Dirk Hendrik (Dick)   **WC**
Ket, Dirk Hendrik (Dick)→see Ket,
  Dick
Ketchman, Nancy *(American*
  painter, 20th c.)   **BA**
    Bibl: ARTS MAG, LV (Jan 1981) 6

Ketchum, Morris *(American*
  architect, 1904-1984)   **AV**
    Bibl: Architecture: the AIA
    journal, 1985 Jan., v.74, no.1,
    p.92
Ketchum, Robert Glenn *(American*
  photographer, b.1947)   **BA**
    Bibl: Security Pacific Bank, Los
    Angeles. PHOTOGRAPHIC
    DIRECTIONS, 1979
Ketel→see Ketel, Cornelis
Ketel, Cornelis   **BA GC PR WC**
  (Dutch artist, 1548-1616)   **WC**
  (Dutch painter, 1548-1616)   **PR**
  (Dutch painter, architect, 1548-
    1616)   **BA**
  (North Netherlandish painter,
    1548-1616)   **GC**
    Bibl: European Authors, 1000-
    1900; Getty Photo Study Coll.;
    ▶RILA/BHA; ▶Thieme-Becker;
    ▶Witt checklist; ▶Wurzbach, NLD
    Künst.-Lex.
  Cornelis Ketel   **PR**
  Ketel   **PR**
Keteltrom→see Bunnik, Jan van
Ketle→see Kettle, Tilly
Kétoff, Maxime *(French architect,*
  1954-)   **AV**
    Bibl: Architecture d'aujourd'hui,
    1987 Oct., no.253, p.77; Das
    Kunstwerk, n.3-4, Sept. 1983,
    p.61
Ketoff, Sacha *(Architect, designer,*
  France, 1949-)   **AV**
    Bibl: Space design, 1985 Feb., no.
    245, p.58
Ketola, Irja *(Finnish artist in CAN,*
  b.1942)   **BA**
    Bibl: Oshawa (Ont, CAN),
    McLaughlin Gallery, 14 artists
    from Durham (1979)
Kett, Willem   **GC WC**
  (Dutch artist, op.c.1756-1795)   **WC**
  (Dutch draughtsman, act.
    c.1756-1795)   **GC**
    Bibl: ▶Bénézit
Kettel→see Kettle, Tilly
Kettell→see Kettle, Tilly
Kettemann, Erwin *(German artist,*
  1897-)   **WC**
Ketterlin, Andreas *(Swiss artist, op.*
  1732-m.1762)   **WC**
Kettle→see Kettle, Tilly
Kettle, Peter *(British artist, op.20th*
  c.)   **WI**
Kettle, Rupert Alfred   **WI**
  (British artist, 1817-1894)   **WC WI**
  Kettle, Sir Rupert A.   **WC**
Kettle, Sir Rupert A.→see Kettle,
  Rupert Alfred

Kettle, Tilly   **BA GC PR WC WI**
  (British artist, 1735-1786)   **WC WI**
  (British painter, 1735-1786)   **BA PR**
  (British, 1735-1786)   **GC**
    Bibl: ▶Bénézit; ▶Dict. natl. biog.;
    ▶Thieme-Becker; ▶Waterhouse,
    Brit. 18c. ptrs.; ▶Witt checklist
  Ketle   **PR**
  Kettel   **PR**
  Kettell   **PR**
  Kettle   **PR**
  Tilly Kettle   **PR**
Kettlewell [Unidentified] *(Unknown*
  painter)   **PR**
    Bibl: (May 29, 1807, lots 1[a] and
    1[b], Greenwood)
Kettner, David *(American artist,*
  20th c.)   **BA**
Kettner, Gerhard *(German*
  printmaker, b.1928)   **BA**
    Bibl: Berlin (DDR), Staatliche Mus.,
    Kupfer., GERHARD KETTNER...,
    1977; ▶Vollmer, Künst.-Lex. 20.
    Jhr.
Keulen, Floor van *(Dutch painter,*
  b.1951)   **BA**
    Bibl: Amsterdam (NLD), Stedelijk
    Museum, '60-'80: Attitudes,
    Concepts, Images (1982);
    Ottevanger, A., 'Floor van
    Keulen,' in Metropolis M III/2
    (Dec 1981) 41-50
Keull, Jacob→see Facht von
  Andernach, Jacob
Keun, Hendrik   **GC WC**
  (Dutch artist, 1738-1787)   **WC**
  (Dutch, 1738-1787)   **GC**
    Bibl: ▶Witt checklist
Keuninck, Kerstiaen de   **BA PR**
  (Flemish artist, op.1580-m.c.
    1632)   **WC**
  (Flemish painter, 1560-1635)   **PR**
  (Flemish painter,
    ca.1560-1632/35)   **BA**
  (Flemish, d.1635)   **GC**
    Bibl: Gerson, Art & arch. Belgium;
    Laes, MÉLANGES HULIN DE LOO,
    225-230; NY Met catalogue;
    ▶Thieme-Becker; ▶Witt checklist;
    ▶Wurzbach, NLD Künst.-Lex.
  Coninck   **PR**
  Coninck, Kauninck, Keuninc
    Keuning or Koninck,
    Kerstiaen de   **WC**
  Coninck, Kerstiaen de   **GC PR**
  Kerstiaen de Coninck   **PR**
Kever→see Kever, Jacobus Simon
  Hendrik
Kever, Gerard *(German painter,*
  b.1956)   **BA**
    Bibl: Artforum, XX/1 (Sep. 1981)
    pp.33-39; Kunstforum Int., issue
    47
Kever, Jacob Simon Hendrik→see
  Kever, Jacobus Simon Hendrik
Kever, Jacobus→see Kever, Jacobus
  Simon Hendrik

Kierkegaard, Svend *(Danish
landscape architect, 20th c.)*   **BA**
   Bibl: Arkitekten, LXXXV/3 (1983)
   pp.45-50
Kierner, Johann *(German sculptor in
Lithuania, b.1728)*   **BA**
Kiernings → see Keirincx, Alexander
Kiers, Catharina Isabella *(Dutch
painter, 1839-1930)*   **GC**
   Bibl: ▶Scheen, Ned. beeldende
   kunst.
Kiers, Elisabeth Alida → see Haanen,
   Elisabeth Alida
Kiers, George Laurens *(Dutch
painter and draughtsman, 1838-
1916)*   **GC**
   Bibl: ▶Thieme-Becker
Kiers, Petrus   **GC WC**
   (Dutch artist, 1807-1875)   **WC**
   (Dutch painter, 1807-1875)   **GC**
   Bibl: ▶Thieme-Becker
Kierschou, Frederik C. *(German
artist, 19th cent.)*   **WC**
Kierstede, Cornelius *(American
silversmith, 1674-1757)*   **BA**
   Bibl: Avery, Early Amer. silver;
   EARLY N.Y. SILVER; New Haven
   Silver
Kierynx → see Keirincx, Alexander
Kies, Helmut *(Austrian painter,
printmaker, b.1933)*   **BA**
   Bibl: ▶MoMA libr. cat.; ▶WW
   Austria
Kiesel, Conrad   **BA WC**
   (German artist, 1846-1921)   **WC**
   (German painter, 1846-1921)   **BA**
   Bibl: ▶Bénézit; ▶Thieme-Becker
Kiesel, Mathäus → see Küsel, Mathäus
Kieseling, Johannes Mattheus
   (Dutch glass engraver, 1691-1735)   **BA**
   Bibl: OUD HOLLAND, XCIX/3
   (1985) 190-200
Kieser, Eberhard *(German artist, op.
1609-1623)*   **WC**
Kieser, Jakob *(German
cabinetmaker, 1734-1786)*   **BA**
   Bibl: ▶Kreisel, Kunst deutschen
   Möbels, v.2; Stratmann, Jahrb.
   der Staatl. Kunstsamml.
   Baden-Württemberg XIX (1982)
   45-68
Kiesler, Frederick → see Kiesler,
   Frederick John

Kiesler, Frederick John   **BA**
   (American architect, 1890-1965)   **AV**
   *(Austrian architect, sculptor,
painter in USA, ca.1890-1965)*   **BA**
   Bibl: Art News 64 (Feb 1966) p.6;
   ▶Avery Libr. cat.; ▶Contemp.
   archts.; ▶Encyc. world art;
   ▶MoMA libr. cat.; New York (NY,
   USA), Whitney, FREDERICK
   KIESLER (1989) p.139; NY Times
   (28 Dec 1965) p.27; ▶Vollmer,
   Künst.-Lex. 20. Jhr.; ▶WWW
   Amer., 1961, v.4
   Kiesler, Frederick   **AV**
   Kiesler, Friedrich   **AV**
Kiesler, Friedrich → see Kiesler,
   Frederick John
Kiesler, Stefi *(Austrian artist,
d.1963)*   **BA**
   Bibl: Jong Holland, II/1 (Mar
   1986), 23-28
Kiessler, Uwe   **AV BA**
   (1937-)   **AV**
   (German architect, b.1937)   **BA**
   Bibl: KUNSTWERK XXXII 2-3 Apr-
   June 1979 78-79
Kiessling, Franz *(West German
architect, Munich)*   **AV**
   Bibl: Deutsche Bauzeitschrift,
   1986 Oct., v.34, no.10, p.1248
Kiessling, Johann Paul Adolf → see
   Kiessling, Paul
Kiessling, Paul   **GC**
   (German artist, 1836-1919)   **WC**
   (German, 1836-1919)   **GC**
   Bibl: Getty Photo Study Coll.
   (Ptgs.); ▶Witt checklist
   Kiessling, Johann Paul Adolf   **GC**
   **Kiessling, Paul (Johann Paul
   Adolf)**   **WC**
*Kiessling, Paul (Johann Paul
   Adolf) → see* Kiessling, Paul
Kietz, Ernst (Julius Ernst Benedikt)
   (German artist, 1815-1892)   **WC**
Kiev Painter   **GC**
   Bibl: ▶Beazley, Attic red-fig. vase-
   ptrs.
Kiewech, Steven *(American
sculptor, b.1955)*   **BA**
   Bibl: Purchase (NY, USA), SUNY,
   Area codes (1983)
Kiff, Ken   **BA WC WI**
   (British artist, 1935-)   **WC**
   (British artist, b.1935)   **WI**
   (British painter, b.1935)   **BA**
   Bibl: ▶Babington Smith, Contemp.
   artists; Guide exh. artists: N.
   Amer. ptrs.; ▶Intl. dir. exh. artists;
   New York, MOMA, New Work on
   Paper, 1981
Kiffer, Charles *(French artist, 1902-)*   **WC**
Kihara, Chitoshi *(Japanese architect,
1940-)*   **AV**
   Bibl: Kenchiku bunka, 1987 Dec.,
   v.42, no.494, p.92
Kihle, Harald *(Norwegian artist,
20th cent.)*   **WC**

Kihn → see Kihn, Wilfred Langdon
Kihn, W. Langdon → see Kihn, Wilfred
   Langdon
Kihn, Wilfred Langdon   **WC WI**
   (American artist, 1898-1957)   **WC WI**
   (American painter, 1898-1957)   **PR**
   Bibl: ▶WWW Amer. art
   Kihn   **PR**
   Kihn, W. Langdon   **PR**
   Kihn, William Langdon   **PR**
   William Langdon Kihn   **PR**
Kihn, William Langdon → see Kihn,
   Wilfred Langdon
Kiilsgaard, Christen *(Danish master
builder, 19th c.)*   **BA**
   Bibl: Licht, Frijsenborgkirker
   (1979) 199-211
Kiiskilä, Hannu *(Finnish architect)*   **AV**
   Bibl: Arkkitehti, 1986, no.2-3,
   p.48
Kijima, Yasufumi *(Japanese
architect, 1937-)*   **AV**
   Bibl: ▶Libr. of Congr. Name Auth.
   File
Kijno, Ladislas *(Polish artist, 20th
cent.)*   **WC**
Kikauka, Laura *(Canadian artist,
20th c.)*   **BA**
   Bibl: Kikauka, LEONARDO, XX/3
   (1987), p. 247-250
Kiki, John   **WC WI**
   (British artist, 1943-)   **WC**
   (British artist, b.1943)   **WI**
Kikkert, Adriaan (Ad) *(Dutch artist,
1914-)*   **WC**
*Kikkert, Conrad (Conrad Kikkert tot
den Egmond) → see* Kikkert, Conrad
   (J.C.)
Kikkert, Conrad (J.C.)   **GC**
   (Dutch artist, 1882-)   **WC**
   (Dutch painter, 1882-1970)   **GC**
   Bibl: ▶Thieme-Becker
   Kickert, Conrad   **GC**
   **Kikkert, Conrad (Conrad Kikkert
   tot den Egmond)**   **WC**
Kikoine, Michel *(French artist,
1892-)*   **WC**
Kikuchi, Makoto *(Japanese
architect, 1953-)*   **AV**
   Bibl: Japan architect, 1988 Nov.-
   Dec., v.63, no.11-12, p.44
Kikuchi-Yngojo, Alan *(American
photographer, b.1949)*   **BA**
   Bibl: Afterimage, VIII/5 (Dec.
   1980)
Kikutake, Kiyonori *(Japanese
architect, 1928-)*   **AV**
   Bibl: ▶Contemp. archts.
Kiland, Lance *(American painter,
b.1947)*   **BA**
   Bibl: Minneapolis (MN, USA), Inst.
   Arts, Bewildered image (1982);
   Washington, DC (USA), Corcoran
   Gallery, 39th biennial (1985)
Kilbourn, Oliver *(British artist, op.
1936-)*   **WI**

King, Charles B. →see King, Charles
    Bird
King, Charles Bird   **BA PR WI**
    (American artist, 1785-1862)   WI
    (American artist, 1785/6-1862)   WC
    (American painter, 1785-1862) BA PR
        Bibl: ▶Encyc. world art;
        ▶RILA/BHA; WW Amer.
    Charles Bird King   PR
    King, Charles B.   **WC**
King, Charles E. (American
    architect, Jacksonville, Fla)   **AV**
        Bibl: ▶AIA Pro File, 1987-88
King, Daniel   **BA GC WI**
    (British artist, circa 1622-circa
        1664)   WI
    (British, act.1630-ca.1661)   GC
    (English printmaker, d.ca.1664)   BA
        Bibl: ▶Bénézit; ▶Brit. Mus. cat.;
        ▶Dict. natl. biog.; ▶Thieme-Becker
King, Dave (British sculptor, b.1946) **BA**
        Bibl: Bristol (GBR), Arnolfini
        Gallery, Style in the 70s (1979)
King, Dennis (British glazier,
    conservator, 20th c.)   **BA**
        Bibl: Marks, Crown in glory, pp.
        7-11
King, Donald (Architect, Seattle,
    WA)   **AV**
        Bibl: ▶AIA Pro File, 1983
King, Edward R.   **WC WI**
    (British artist, 19th cent.)   WC
    (British artist, op.1883-1924)   WI
        Bibl: ▶Houfe, Brit. book illus.
King, Elizabeth (American sculptor,
    b.1950)   **BA**
        Bibl: Richmond (VA, USA), Virginia
        MFA, Process, image, portrait
        (1986), pp.17-19
King, Elizabeth Thomson (British
    artist, 1848-1914)   **WC WI**
King, Emma B., Mrs. →see Brownlow,
    Emma B.
King, Eric Mead (British artist, op.
    20th c.)   **WI**
        Bibl: ▶Johnson, Brit. artists
King, Ethel Slade (British artist, op.
    circa 1885-)   **WI**
    Gascoyne, George, Mrs., (Ethel
        Slade)   WI
King, F.C. (British artist, op.20th c.) **WI**
King, Francis Scott (Engraver,
    Newark, NJ., b.1850)   **WI**
King, Frederic Leonard   **WC WI**
    (American artist, 1879-)   WC
    (American artist, 1879-1947)   WI
King, Gilbert, Mrs., (Fannie) →see
    Moody, Fannie
King, Gunning (British artist, 1859-
    1940)   **WC WI**
King, Haynes   **BA WC WI**
    (British artist, 1831-1904)   WC WI
    (British painter, 1831-1904)   BA
        Bibl: ▶Johnson, Brit. artists;
        ▶Thieme-Becker

King, Henry John Yeend   **WI**
    (British artist, 1855-1924)   WC WI
King, Yeend (Henry John
    Yeend)   **WC**
King, Horatio B. (American, active
    Taunton, MA, U.S. 1850-1855,
    daguerreotypist)   **JG**
King, Ian C. (British architect,
    London)   **AV**
        Bibl: ▶RIBA members, 1987
King, Ingrid (American architect)   **AV**
        Bibl: ▶Architecture & urbanism,
        1989 Sept., no.9(228), p.21
King, J.W.   **WI**
    (American artist, op.1855-1864)   WC
    (American artist, op.19th c.)   WI
        Bibl: ▶Witt checklist
    King, John William   **WC**
King, Jeremy (British artist, op.20th
    c.)   **WI**
King, Jessie Marion   **BA WC WI**
    (British artist, 1875-1949)   WC WI
    (British painter, illustrator, 1875-
        1949)   BA
        Bibl: Edinburgh (GBR), Natl.
        Library of Scotland, Book
        illustrations of Jessie M. King
        (1976); ▶Vollmer, Künst.-Lex. 20.
        Jhr.; ▶Waters, Brit. artists
    Taylor, Ernest Archibald, Mrs.,
        (Jessie Marion)   WI
King, John (British artist, 1788-
    1847)   **WC WI**
King, John Crookshanks (American
    artist, 1806-1882)   **WC WI**
King, John Duncan   **WI**
    (British artist, 1789-1863)   WC WI
    King, Captain John Duncan   **WC**
King, John M. (American painter,
    1897-1977)   **BA**
        Bibl: ▶Bénézit; Dayton (O, USA),
        Art Institute, paintings by John
        King, 1977
King, John William →see King, J.W.
King, Jonathan   **AV**
        Bibl: ▶Libr. of Congr. Name Auth.
        File
King, Joseph Wallace   **WI**
    (American artist, op.20th c.)   WI
    (Italian artist, 20th cent.)   WC
    Vinciata   **WC WI**
King, Kenneth John (British
    architect, Norwich, d. 1988)   **AV**
        Bibl: Building design, 1988 Dec.2,
        no.913, p.4 [d. date]; ▶RIBA
        members, 1987
King, Louisa Yeomans (American
    gardener, 1863-1948)   **BA**
        Bibl: COUNTRY LIFE CLXIV/4240
        (12 Oct 1978) p.1141; ▶Natl.
        union cat., pre-1956; ▶WWW
        Amer., 1969
King, Louise Howland, Miss →see
    Cox, Louise Howland King
King, Margaret (British artist, op.
    1779-1787)   **WC WI**

King, Melvyn (British artist, op.20th
    c.)   **WI**
King, Mrs. W.A. →see King, S. Cecilia
    Cotter
King, Paul →see King, Paul Bernard
King, Paul Bernard   **WI**
    (American artist, 1867-1947)   WC WI
    King, Paul   **WC**
King, Perry A.   **AV BA**
    (Architect, based in Milan)   AV
    (British designer, b.1938)   BA
        Bibl: ▶Avery period. idx., 6th
        suppl.; Domus, 1984 Dec., no.
        656, p.46; Glancey, Arch. review,
        CLXXVI/1054 (Dec. 1984) pp.
        66-72; Philadelphia (PA, USA),
        Mus. of Art, Design Since 1945
        (1983), p.217
King, Phillip (American artist, 20th
    cent.)   **WC**
King, Phillip (British sculptor,
    b.1934)   **BA**
        Bibl: ▶Bénézit; Greater London
        Council, SILVER JUBILEE
        EXHIBITION (1977); ▶MoMA libr.
        cat.
King, Phyllis Gorlick   **WI**
    (American artist, b.1939)   WI
    (Engraver, b.1939)   WI
King, Ray (American artist)   **AV**
        Bibl: Stained glass, 1985 Summer,
        v.80, no.2, p.115
King, S. Cecilia →see King, S. Cecilia
    Cotter
King, S. Cecilia Cotter (American
    sculptor (b. Ireland), b.1874)   **GC**
        Bibl: Getty Photo Study Coll.;
        ▶Opitz, Amer. sculptors
    King, Cecilia   GC
    King, Mrs. W.A.   GC
    King, S. Cecilia   GC
King, Samuel   **BA WC**
    (American artist, 1749-1819)   WC WI
    (American painter, instrument
        maker, 1748-1819)   BA
        Bibl: ▶Dict. Amer. biog.; ▶Groce,
        Artists Amer.; ▶Thieme-Becker
King, Samuel, (USA)   **WI**
King, Samuel, (GBR) (British artist,
    op.20th c.)   **WI**
King, Samuel, (USA) →see King,
    Samuel
King, Stanley (Canadian architect,
    originator of a participatory
    design process called Co-Design)   **AV**
        Bibl: Canadian heritage, 1988
        Spring, v.14, no.1, p.20
King, Thomas →see King, Thomas I
King, Thomas →see King, Thomas II
King, Thomas Francis (painter, act.
    1885)   **GC**
        Bibl: Cleveland (OH, USA), Mus.
        Art, Euro. ptgs. bef. 1500 (1974)

King, Thomas Harper **AV BA**
  (British architect, b.1822, act.
  1868) **BA**
  (English architect, 1822-) **AV**
    Bibl: ▶Avery Libr. cat.; Cleven,
    Gentse Bijdragen XXVI (1981-84)
    45-58; ▶Natl. union cat., pre-1956

King, Thomas I **WI**
  (British artist, -c.1769) **WC**
  (British artist, op.1756-, d.1769) **WI**
King, Thomas **WC**
King, Thomas II **WI**
  (British artist, op.1826-1846) **WC WI**
    Bibl: Chichester Artists
King, Thomas **WC**
King, Tony *(American painter,*
  b.1944) **BA**
King, W. *(Irish landscape gardener,*
  act.ca.1780) **BA**
King, W.B. → see King, William B.
King, W.H. *(British artist, op.1808-*
  1836) **WC WI**
King, William *(American*
  cabinetmaker, 1771-1854) **BA**
    Bibl: Antiques CXI 2 MAy 1977,
    1032-1036; Complete encyc.
    antiques; ▶Groce, Artists Amer.;
    ▶Thieme-Becker; ▶Young, Amer.
    artists
King, William B. **WI**
  (American artist, 1880-1927) **WI**
  (American artist, 19th/20th
  cent.) **WC**
King, W.B. **WC**
King, William Dickey *(American*
  sculptor, b.1925) **BA**
    Bibl: ▶WW Amer. Art, 1976
King, Yeend *(Henry John*
  Yeend) → see King, Henry John
  Yeend
King-Farlow, Hazel *(British artist,*
  op.1936-1949) **WI**
Kingbourne, G.R. *(British designer,*
  20th c.) **BA**
    Bibl: London (GBR), Mus. London,
    London design studio (1980)
Kinger, Erwin *(Austrian architect)* **AV**
    Bibl: Bauforum, 1988, v.21, no.
    127, p.55
Kingerlee, John **WC WI**
  (American artist, 20th cent.) **WC**
  (American artist, op.20th c.) **WI**
Kinglake, Alexander William
  (British lawyer, historian,
  photographer, 1809-1891) **BA**
    Bibl: ▶Natl. union cat., pre-1956
Kingma, K. *(Dutch architect,*
  Rotterdam) **AV**
    Bibl: De Architect, 1988 Oct.,
    v.19, no.10, p.73
Kingman, Dong → see Kingman, Doug
Kingman, Doug **WI**
  (American artist, 1911-) **WC**
  (American artist, b.1911) **WI**
Kingman, Dong **WC**

Kingsbury, Alan *(British artist, op.*
  20th c.) **WI**
Kingsbury, Henry **WC WI**
  (British artist, op.1750-1798) **WI**
  (British artist, op.1775-1798) **WC**
  (Engraver, op.1750-1798) **WI**
Kingsland, James A. **AV**
Kingsley, Elbridge **WC WI**
  (American artist, 1841-1915) **WC WI**
  (Engraver, 1841-1915) **WI**
Kingsley, Harry *(British artist,*
  b.1914) **WI**
Kingston, Emily Fuller → see Fuller,
  Emily
Kingston, George Strickland, Sir
  (Australian architect, 1807-1880) **AV**
    Bibl: ▶Tanner, Archts. Australia
Kington, Louis Brent *(American*
  sculptor, educator, b.1934) **BA**
    Bibl: ▶WW Amer. Art
Kinigstein, Jonah **WC WI**
  (American artist, 1923-) **WC**
  (American artist, b.1923) **WI**
Kininger, Kieninger or Kinninger,
  Vincenz Georg → see Kininger,
  Vincenz Georg
Kininger, Vincenz Georg **GC**
  (Austrian miniaturist,
  draughtsman, engraver, and
  lithographer, 1767-1851) **GC**
  (German artist, 1767-1851) **WC**
    Bibl: ▶Thieme-Becker
Kininger, Kieninger or
  Kinninger, Vincenz Georg **WC**
Kinjo, Nobuyoshi **AV**
Kink, Martin von *(Austrian engineer,*
  industrialist, 1800-1877) **BA**
    Bibl: ▶Österr. biog. Lex. 1815-
    1950
Kinley, Peter **WC WI**
  (British artist, 1926-) **WC**
  (British artist, b.1926) **WI**
Kinloch, Ian *(British, 20th c.)* **BA**
    Bibl: Fox, PANTHEON, XL, 3(July-
    Sept 1982)
Kinmont, Robert *(American artist,*
  b.1937) **BA**
    Bibl: ▶Art Index, v.21; New
    Brunswick (NJ, USA), Rutgers U.,
    Response to the environment
    (1975)
Kinnaird, F.G. *(British artist, op.*
  1864-1881) **WC WI**
Kinnaird, Henry John **WC WI**
  (British artist, op.1880-1908) **WC**
  (British artist, op.1880-circa
  1920) **WI**
Kinnaird, John *(British painter,*
  b.1939) **BA**
    Bibl: Leeds (GBR), City Art Gall.,
    Atkinson, Chaplin, Kinnaird,
    Mitchell (1979)
Kinnard, W. *(British artist, op.circa*
  1807-) **WI**
Kinnear, James Balfour *(British*
  artist, op.circa 1880-) **WI**

Kinnebrew, Joseph Edwin
  (American sculptor, b.1942) **BA**
    Bibl: Grand Rapids (MI, USA), Art
    Mus., Artists of Grand Rapids
    (1981)
Kinnee, Sandy *(American painter,*
  printmaker, b.1947.) **BA**
    Bibl: ▶WW Amer. Art, 1989
Kinnermä, Marjaana *(Finnish*
  architect or artist) **AV**
    Bibl: Arkkitehti, 1988, v.85, no.1,
    p.74
Kinney, Troy *(American artist, 1871-*
  1938) **WI**
Kinoshita, Isami *(Japanese architect,*
  1954-) **AV**
    Bibl: Process: architecture, n.30,
    1982, p.163
Kinoshita, Michio *(Japanese*
  architect) **AV**
    Bibl: Space design, 1986 Dec., no.
    267, p.32
Kinoshita, Yoko *(Japanese architect)* **AV**
    Bibl: Japan architect, 1989 May,
    v.64, no.5(385), p.5
Kinross, John **AV BA**
  (British architect, ca.1855-1931) **BA**
  (British archtect, 1855-1931) **AV**
    Bibl: Clark Art Inst. Libr.; ▶Natl.
    union cat., pre-1956; ▶Who was
    who [GBR]
Kinsey, Chris *(British artist, op.20th*
  c.) **WI**
Kinsey, Darius Reynold → see Kinsey,
  Darius Reynolds
Kinsey, Darius Reynolds **BA**
  (American photographer, 1871-
  1945) **BA**
  (American, 1869-1945) **JG**
    Bibl: ▶Dict. Amer. biog.; ▶MoMA
    libr. cat.; ▶Natl. union cat., Jan-
    Mar 1976
Kinsey, Darius Reynold **JG**
Kinsey, Tabitha May *(American*
  photographer, 1875-1963) **BA**
    Bibl: ▶Natl. union cat., Jan-Mar
    1976
Kinsley, Albert *(British artist, 1852-*
  1945) **WI**
Kinsoen or Kinson, Francois
  Josephe → see Kinsoen, Francois
  Josephe
Kinsoen, Francois Josephe **GC**
  (Belgian artist, 1771-1839) **WC**
  (Belgian, 1771-1839) **GC**
    Bibl: ▶Witt checklist
Kinsoen or Kinson, Francois
  Josephe **WC**
Kinstler → see Kinstler, Everett
  Raymond

Kinstler, Everett Raymond   **PR WC WI**
    (American artist, 19th cent.)   WC
    (American artist, op.20th c.)   WI
    (American painter, act. 19th
      century)   PR
      Bibl: ▶Witt checklist
    Everett Raymond Kinstler   PR
    Kinstler   PR
Kintz, Georges *(French ébéniste,*
    master 1776, act. to 1805)   GC
      Bibl: ▶Salverte, Ébénistes 18e s.
Kinzel, Josef *(German artist, 1852-*
    1925)   WC
Kinzel, Peter *(West German*
    architect)   AV
      Bibl: Deutsche Bauzeitschrift,
      1989 July, v.37, no.7, p.879
Kinzing, Peter *(German, 1745-1816)*   JG
Kioerboe→see Kioerboe, Carl Fredrik
Kioerboe, Carl Fredrik   **PR**
    (Swedish artist, 1799-1876)   WC
    (Swedish painter, 1799-1876)   PR
    Carl Fredrik Kioerboe   PR
    Kioerboe   PR
    Kiorboé   PR
Kiorboe, Carl Frederik   **WC**
Kiolstrom, Isak *(Scandinavian artist,*
    op.1778-1792)   WC
Kiopini, Christian *(Canadian painter,*
    b.1949)   BA
      Bibl: ▶Intl. dir. exh. artists, 1983;
      Montreal (Que, CAN), MFA, 6
      propositions (1979)
Kiorboé→see Kioerboe, Carl Fredrik
Kiorboe, Carl Frederik→see Kioerboe,
    Carl Fredrik
Kiosa, Kawanabé *(Japanese artist,*
    19th c.)   BA
      Bibl: JAARBOEK VAN HET
      KONINKLIJK MUSEUM VOOR
      SCHONE
      KUNSTENANTWERP(1978), 205-
      221
Kip, Henry de Valcourt *(American*
    artist, 1830-circa 1900)   WI
Kip, Johannes   **BA WC**
    (Dutch artist, 1652/3-1722)   WC
    (Dutch printmaker in GBR,
      1652/53-1722)   BA
      Bibl: ▶Dict. natl. biog.; ▶Met.
      Mus. Art libr. cat.; ▶Strutt, Dict.
      engravers; ▶Thieme-Becker
Kip, Willem or William *(Dutch*
    artist, op.c.1598-1635)   WC
Kipling, Ann *(Canadian printmaker,*
    b.1934)   BA
      Bibl: ▶Artists Canada;
      ▶MacDonald, Can. artists
Kipling, John Lockwood   **AV BA**
    (British architect)   AV
    (British artist in IND, 1837-1911)   BA
      Bibl: ▶Dict. natl. biog.; Journal of
      the Tiles & Architectural Ceramics
      Society, 1987, v.2, p.21; ▶Who
      was who [GBR], v.1

Kipniss, Robert *(American painter,*
    printmaker, b.1931)   BA
      Bibl: ▶MoMA libr. cat.; ▶WW
      Amer. Art, 1976
Kipp, Karl *(American businessman,*
    designer, 20th c.)   BA
      Bibl: Clark, ARTS AND CRAFTS
      MOVEMENT; ▶Penguin dec. arts
Kipp, Lyman *(American sculptor,*
    b.1929)   BA
      Bibl: ▶Cummings, Contemp.
      Amer. artists, 1971; ▶WW Amer.
      Art, 1976
Kippenberger, Martin *(West*
    German artist, b.1953)   BA
      Bibl: Essen (DEU), Mus. Folkwang,
      Wahrheit ist Arbeit (1984)
Kippnick, Heinz *(German artist, 20th*
    cent.)   WC
Kiprenskij or Schwalbe, Orest
    Adamowitsch→see Kiprenskij,
    Orest Adamovič
Kiprenskij, Orest Adamovič   **BA**
    (Russian artist, 1773-1836)   WC
    (Russian painter, 1782-1836)   BA GC
      Bibl: ▶Encyc. world art; ▶Havlice,
      Idx. art. bio.; Sarabjanov, Orest
      Adamovic Kiprenskij: 1782-1836
      (1982); ▶Thieme-Becker; ▶Witt
      checklist
Kiprenskij or Schwalbe, Orest
    Adamowitsch   **WC**
Kiprenskij, Orest Adamowitsch   **GC**
Kiprenskij, Orest Adamowitsch→see
    Kiprenskij, Orest Adamovič
Kips, Erich *(German painter, b.1869)*   GC
      Bibl: ▶Thieme-Becker
Kipshaven, Isaack van   **GC WC**
    (Dutch artist, 1635/6(?)-p.1670)   WC
    (Dutch, 1636/36(?)-aft.1670)   GC
      Bibl: ▶Witt checklist
Kira, Hiromu *(1898-, active Seattle,*
    WA and Los Angeles, CA, U.S.
    1920s-1930s)   JG
Kiraly, John *(American artist and*
    garden designer, Key West, Fla)   AV
      Bibl: Garden design, 1987-1988
      Winter, v.6, no.4, p.54
Kiran, Ketil *(Norwegian architect)*   AV
      Bibl: Byggekunst, 1986, v.68,
      no.6, p.358
Kirberg, Otto Karl *(German artist,*
    1850-1926)   WC
Kirberger, Nikolaus   **GC WC**
    (German artist, op.1519-1521)   WC
    (German painter and
      draughtsman, act.1519-1521)   GC
      Bibl: ▶Thieme-Becker
Kirby, Charles F. *(American*
    architect, active in Boston)   AV
      Bibl: SAH journal, v.42, n.2, 1983,
      p.160
Kirby, Jack *(American cartoonist,*
    20th c.)   BA
      Bibl: Arts Mag., LVII/1-4 (Sep.-
      Dec. 1983) pp.57-61, 85-89, 120-
      128

Kirby, John Joshua   **BA WC WI**
    (British artist, 1716-1744)   WI
    (British artist, 1716-1774)   WC
    (British printmaker, author,
      1716-1774)   BA
      Bibl: ▶Dict. natl. biog.;
      ▶Thieme-Becker
Kirby, John Kynnersley *(British*
    artist, op.1914-1939)   **WC WI**
Kirby, Ron *(Architect, Zambia)*   AV
      Bibl: In situ, 1984 Nov., p.4
Kirby, Stephen *(British, act.ca.1730)*   GC
      Bibl: ▶Thieme-Becker
Kirch, Peter *(West German*
    architect, Freiburg, 1949-)   AV
      Bibl: Deutsche Bauzeitung, 1988
      Oct., v.122, no.10, p.208
Kirchbach, Franck *(German artist,*
    1859-)   WC
Kirchberger, Hermann *(German*
    artist, 1905-)   WC
Kirchdorffer, Lina *(German, act.*
    1867)   BA
      Bibl: Havlice, World ptg. idx.
Kirchebner, Josef *(German artist,*
    1756-1814)   WC
Kirchebner, Peter Paul *(German*
    artist, op.1827-m.1842)   WC
Kirchheim, Balthasar *(Swiss bell-*
    founder, act.1479-1499)   BA
      Bibl: ▶Schweiz. Künst.-Lex.;
      ▶Thieme-Becker
Kirchhoff, Hans Kurt *(West German*
    architect)   AV
Kirchhoffer, Henry   **WC WI**
    (British artist, 1781-1860)   WI
    (British artist, c.1781-1860)   WC
Kirchmaier or Kiermaier, Franz→see
    Kirchmaier, Franz
Kirchmaier or Kirchmair, Sebastian
    (German artist, op.1590-1610)   WC
Kirchmaier, Franz   **BA**
    (German artist, op.1560-m.
      1589)   WC
    (German painter, d.1589)   BA
      Bibl: ▶Hollstein, German, v.19,
      p.15; ▶Thieme-Becker
Kirchmaier or Kiermaier, Franz   **WC**
Kirchmaier, Michael→see Kirmer,
    Michel
Kirchmayer, Wolfgang *(Austrian*
    sculptor, act.1612)   BA
      Bibl: Dehio; ▶Thieme-Becker
Kirchner→see Kirchner, Ernst Ludwig
Kirchner, Albert Emil   **GC WC**
    (German artist, 1813-1885)   WC
    (German draughtsman, 1813-
      1885)   GC
      Bibl: ▶Bénézit
Kirchner, Erna→see Schilling, Erna
Kirchner, Ernest Ludwig→see
    Kirchner, Ernst Ludwig

Kirchner, Ernst Ludwig   **BA GC PR**
   (*German artist, 1880-1938*)   WC
   (*German painter, 1880-1938*)   PR
   (*German painter, printmaker,*
    1880-1938)   BA
   (*German, 1880-1938*)   GC
    Bibl: ▶RILA/BHA; ▶Vollmer,
    Künst.-Lex. 20. Jhr.; ▶Witt
    checklist
   Ernst Ludwig Kirchner   PR
   Kirchner   PR
   Kirchner, Ernest Ludwig   PR
Kirchner, Ernst-Ludwig   **WC**
   Marsalle, Louis de   BA
Kirchner, Ernst-Ludwig → see Kirchner,
   Ernst Ludwig
Kirchner, Hans (*Danish landscape*
   architect)   **AV**
    Bibl: Landskab, 1988 Nov., v.69,
    no.7, p.152
Kirchner, Heinrich (*West German*
   sculptor, Erlangen, 1902-)   **AV**
    Bibl: Garten und Landschaft,
    1989, v.99, no.9, p.44
Kirchner, Ingo (*German artist, 1930-*
   1983)   **BA**
    Bibl: Muschter, G., in BILDENDE
    KUNST, 1 (1984) 24
Kirchner, Johann Gottlieb (*German*
   ceramist, sculptor, 1706-after
   1737)   **BA**
    Bibl: ▶Boger, World pott. & porc.;
    ▶Neue deutsche Biog.; ▶Penguin
    dec. arts; ▶Thieme-Becker
Kirchner, Johann Jakob   **BA GC WC**
   (*German artist, 1796-1837*)   WC
   (*German painter, 1796-1837*)   GC
   (*German painter, printmaker,*
    1796-1837)   BA
    Bibl: ▶Bénézit; ▶Thieme-Becker
Kirchner, Matthias (*German artist,*
   1735-1805)   **WC**
Kirchner, Otto (*German artist,*
   1887-)   **WC**
Kirchoff, William (*American*
   photographer, N. J)   **AV**
    Bibl: Architecture New Jersey,
    1988, v.24, no.3, p.23
Kiriaki, Sapho (*Greek artist, 20th*
   cent.)   **WC**
Kirili, Alain (*French sculptor, b.1946*)   **BA**
    Bibl: ▶Bénézit; ▶DuMonts
    Künst.-Lex.; ▶MoMA libr. cat.
Kirillova, L.N. (*Russian artist, 20th*
   c.)   **BA**
    Bibl: Kuzmina, Molodye Sovetskie
    Hudozniki
Kirin, Vladimir (*Russian artist,*
   1894-)   **WC**
Kirk → see Kirk, Thomas
Kirk, Alexander H.   **WC WI**
   (*British artist, 19th cent.*)   WC
   (*British artist, op.19th c.*)   WI
Kirk, Barry (*British artist, op.20th c.*)   **WI**
Kirk, Eve (*British artist, 1900-*
   1969)   **WC WI**

Kirk, James (*British artist, op.1847-*
   1854)   **WC WI**
Kirk, Janet (*British artist, op.1910-*
   1938)   **WI**
Kirk, Michael (*American printmaker,*
   b.1947.)   **BA**
    Bibl: ▶WW Amer. Art, 1989
Kirk, Neil (*British architect*)   **AV**
    Bibl: RIBA journal, 1981 Apr.,
    v.88, no.4, p.59
Kirk, Thomas   **BA PR WC WI**
   (*British artist, 1765(?)-m.1797*)   WC
   (*British artist, 1765-1797*)   WI
   (*British painter, 1765-1797*)   PR
   (*English painter, printmaker, ca.*
    1765-1797)   BA
    Bibl: ▶Dict. natl. biog.;
    ▶RILA/BHA; ▶Thieme-Becker
   Kirk   PR
   Thomas Kirk   PR
Kirkall, Elisha   **BA WI**
   (*British artist, c.1682-1742*)   WC
   (*British artist, circa 1682-1742*)   WI
   (*English printmaker, ca.1682-*
    1742)   BA
   (*Engraver, circa 1682-1742*)   WI
    Bibl: ▶Dict. natl. biog.;
    ▶Thieme-Becker
Kirkall, Elisha (not Edward)   **WC**
Kirkall, Elisha (not Edward) → see
   Kirkall, Elisha
Kirkby, Thomas   **PR WC WI**
   (*British artist, 1775-circa 1847*)   WI
   (*British artist, op.1796-1847*)   WC
   (*British painter, act. 1796-1847*)   PR
    Bibl: ▶Thieme-Becker
   Thomas Kirkby   PR
Kirkeby, Per (*Danish painter,*
   printmaker, sculptor, b.1938)   **BA**
    Bibl: ▶Bénézit; Copenhagen(DNK),
    Ordrupgaard. PER KIRKEBY(1981);
    ▶Gorenflo, Bild. Künstler; Guide
    exh. artists: Sculp.; ▶Køie, Kunst.
    leks.; ▶Nørregård-Nielsen, Dansk
    kunst
Kirkerup, Andreas Johannes   **AV BA**
   (*Danish architect, 1749-1810*)   AV
   (*Danish builder, 1749-1810*)   BA
    Bibl: ▶Encyc. world art;
    ▶Thieme-Becker
Kirkland, Alexander (*British*
   architect in USA, 1824-1892)   **BA**
    Bibl: COMMITTEE FOR THE
    PRESERV. OF ARCH. RECORDS, 8
    (JAN1977) newsletter
Kirkland, George C. (*American,*
   active ca. 1900, Denver)   **JG**
Kirkland, J. Michael (*Canadian*
   architect)   **AV**
    Bibl: Progressive architecture,
    1982 Nov., v.63, no.11, p.36
Kirkland, Vance Hall (*American*
   painter, collector, b.1904)   **BA**
    Bibl: ▶WW Amer. Art, 1976
Kirkley, Caroline   **WC WI**
   (*British artist, op.1796-*)   WI
   (*British artist, op.1796-1797*)   WC

Kirkley, Miss S. → see Kirkley, S., Miss
Kirkley, S., Miss   **WI**
   (*British artist, op.1793-1797*)   WC WI
Kirkley, Miss S.   **WC**
Kirkman, Jacob (*German*
   harpsichord-maker in GBR, 1710-
   1792)   **BA**
    Bibl: Die Musik
Kirkman, Robert (*British model*
   maker)   **AV**
    Bibl: Building design, 1989 June
    9, no.940, p.12
Kirkpatrick → see Kirkpatrick, Harriet
Kirkpatrick, Betty Anne Stewart
   (Bask) (*American painter, 20th c.*)   **BA**
    Bibl: Long Beach (CA, USA), Mus.
    of Art, Bask: Tomorrow's Dragon
    (1979)
Kirkpatrick, Frank Le Brun
   (*American artist, 1853-1917*)   **WI**
Kirkpatrick, Harriet (*American*
   painter, 1877-1962)   **PR**
    Bibl: ▶WWW Amer. art
   Harriet Kirkpatrick   PR
   Kirkpatrick   PR
   Kirkpatrick, Harriet R.   PR
Kirkpatrick, Harriet R. → see
   Kirkpatrick, Harriet
Kirkpatrick, J. → see Kirkpatrick,
   Joseph
Kirkpatrick, Joey (*American glass*
   artist, b.1952)   **BA**
    Bibl: Guide exh. artists: N. Amer.
    ptrs.; ▶Intl. dir. exh. artists, 1983
Kirkpatrick, Joseph   **WI**
   (*British artist, 1872-circa 1930*)   WI
   (*British artist, 19th cent.*)   WC
Kirkpatrick, J.   **WC**
Kirkpatrick, W.A.B., Mrs. → see
   Powers, Marion
Kirkpatrick, William Arper-Brown
   (*American artist, b.1880*)   **WI**
Kirkup, Seymour Stocker   **WI**
   (*British artist, 1788-1880*)   WC WI
Kirkup, Seymour Stokes   **WC**
Kirkup, Seymour Stokes → see Kirkup,
   Seymour Stocker
Kirkwood, Ian (*British artist, op.*
   1980-)   **WI**
Kirkwood, John (*British artist,*
   b.1947)   **BA**
    Bibl: Edinburgh (GBR), Fruit
    Market Gallery, Scottish art now
    (1982)
Kirkwood, Peter (*American*
   silversmith, act.1790-1810)   **BA**
    Bibl: ANTIQUES, CXI/2(FEB 1977),
    note 13; Pleasants, Silversmiths
    1715-1830
Kirkwood, Robert (*British, 20th c.*)   **BA**
    Bibl: Allen, Burlington Mag.
    CXXV/961 (Apr. 1983) pp.195-
    196

Kirmer, Michel　　　　　　　GC
　(German artist, op.1552-1570)　WC
　(German draughtsman, act.
　　1550-d.1589)　　　　　　　GC
　　Bibl: ▶Bénézit; ▶Thieme-Becker
　Kirchmaier, Michael　　　　　GC
Kirmer, Michel or Michael　WC
Kirmer, Michel or Michael→see
　Kirmer, Michel
Kirn, Fritz (West German interior
　designer, Altensteig)　　　　AV
　　Bibl: Architektur,
　　Innenarchitektur, Technischer
　　Ausbau, 1988 Dec., v.96, no.12,
　　p.34
Kirnarsky (Russian artist, 19th cent.)　WC
Kirner, Bert (German painter,
　b.1951)　　　　　　　　　BA
　　Bibl: ▶Intl. dir. exh. artists, 1983
Kirner, Johann Baptist (German
　artist, 1806-1866)　　　　　WC
Kirner, Lukas (German artist, 1794-
　1851)　　　　　　　　　　WC
Kirov, Dimitar (Bulgarian artist, 20th
　cent.)　　　　　　　　　　WC
Kirsch　　　　　　　　WC WI
　(British artist, op.1843)　　　WC
　(British artist, op.1843-)　　WI
Kirsch, Emanuel (German artist,
　18th cent.)　　　　　　　　WC
Kirsch, Marilyn (American
　draftsman, b.1950)　　　　BA
　　Bibl: Santa Barbara (CA, USA),
　　UCSB Art Mus., Contemp.
　　drawings (1981)
Kirschen-Cole, Stephanie
　(American artist, 20th c.)　　BA
　　Bibl: ART IN AMERICA (Nov 1980)
　　140; ▶Intl. dir. exh. artists, 1983;
　　Withers, J., in ARTS MAGAZINE
　　LVIII/6 (Feb 1984) 2
Kirschenbaum, Bernard Edwin
　(American sculptor, b.1924)　BA
　　Bibl: ▶Art Index, Oct. 1976; ▶WW
　　Amer. Art, 1976
Kirschenbaum, Jules　　WC WI
　(American artist, 1930-)　　　WC
　(American artist, b.1930)　　WI
Kirschmann, J. (German artist, 18th
　cent.)　　　　　　　　　　WC
Kirschner, Friedrich (German
　painter, printmaker, 1748-1789)　BA
　　Bibl: ▶Bénézit; ▶Thieme-Becker
Kirsta, Georg (Russian artist, 20th
　cent.)　　　　　　　　　　WC
Kirstein, Joachim-Friedrich (French
　silversmith, d.1770, master 1729)　GC
　　Bibl: ▶Mabille, Orfèv. fran.
Kirwin, Steven (Norwegian(?)
　architect)　　　　　　　　AV
　　Bibl: Byggekunst: the Norwegian
　　review of architecture, 1988,
　　v.70, no.4, p.264
Kiryu, Mitsuru (Japanese architect,
　1944-)　　　　　　　　　　AV
　　Bibl: Kenchiku bunka, 1987 Dec.,
　　v.42, no.494, p.99

Kirzenbaum Painter (Apulian vase-
　painter)　　　　　　　　　GC
　　Bibl: Trendall, Attic red-fig. vases
　　Apulia
Kiščenko, A. (Russian artist, 20th c.)　BA
　　Bibl: Pugacova, DEKORATIVNOE
　　ISKUSSTVO SSSR 5(222), (MAY
　　1976), 23-25
Kisch, Gloria (American painter,
　sculptor, b.1941)　　　　　BA
　　Bibl: ▶WW Amer. Art, 1978
Kise, James N. (fl. 1956;
　Architectural draftsman, United
　States of America)　　　　　FA
　　Bibl: drawing inscription; Natl.
　　Archives object
Kiseleff, Constantin (Finnish
　architect, 1834-)　　　　　AV
　　Bibl: ▶Thieme-Becker
Kiselev, Aleksandr Aleksandrovič　BA
　(Russian artist, 1838-1911)　WC
　(Russian painter, 1838-1911)　BA
　　Bibl: ▶Bénézit; ▶Great Soviet
　　encyc.
**Kisseljoff, Alexander
　Alexejevitch**　　　　　　WC
Kisfaludi-Stróbl, Zsigmond
　(Hungarian sculptor, b.1884)　BA
　　Bibl: ▶Bénézit; ▶Encyc. world art;
　　▶Fogg Mus. Libr. cat.; ▶Vollmer,
　　Künst.-Lex. 20. Jhr.
　Stróbl, Zsigmond Kisfaludi　BA
Kish→see Kish, Maurice
Kish, Maurice (American painter, b.
　1898)　　　　　　　　　　PR
　　Bibl: ▶WWW Amer. art
　Kish　　　　　　　　　　PR
　Maurice Kish　　　　　　PR
Kishi, Masaki (Japanese architect,
　1949-)　　　　　　　　　　AV
　　Bibl: Kenchiku bunka, 1987 Dec.,
　　v.42, no.494, p.82
Kishi, Waro (Japanese architect)　AV
　　Bibl: Toshi jutaku, 1986 Nov., no.
　　229, p.9
Kishimoto, Tsutomu Ben
　(Architect, b. Japan, lives in
　Reston, Va., practices in
　Washington, D.C)　　　　　AV
　　Bibl: ▶AIA Pro File, 1987-88
Kisielev, Alexandr Alexeevich
　(Russian artist, 1855-)　　　WC
Kisil, Gerry (Canadian video artist,
　20th c.)　　　　　　　　　BA
　　Bibl: Madill, S., in WAG (Feb
　　1985) 12
Kiskunhalas Sub-Group (Apulian
　vase-painters)　　　　　　GC
　　Bibl: Trendall, Attic red-fig. vases
　　Apulia
Kisléghi Nagy, István (Hungarian
　artist or architect, 1906-)　　AV
　　Bibl: Magyar építőművészet,
　　1987, v.78, no.4-5, p.62
Kisling→see Kisling, Moïse
Kisling, Franz Joseph (German
　artist, op.1754-1770)　　　　WC

Kisling, Moïse　　　BA GC PR WC
　(French artist, 1891-1953)　　WC
　(French painter, 1891-1953)　PR
　(French painter, printmaker,
　　1891-1953)　　　　　　　BA
　(French, 1891-1953)　　　　GC
　　Bibl: ▶Bénézit; Clark Art Inst.
　　Libr.; ▶RILA/BHA; ▶Vollmer,
　　Künst.-Lex. 20. Jhr.; ▶Witt
　　checklist
　Kisling　　　　　　　　　PR
　Moise Kisling　　　　　　PR
Kiss Nagy, András→see Nagy, András
　Kiss
Kiss Painter (vase-painter, ca. 530-
　500 BC)　　　　　　　　　GC
　　Bibl: ▶Beazley, Attic red-fig. vase-
　　ptrs.; Richter, Attic red-fig. vases
Kiss, August Karl Eduard (German
　sculptor, 1802-1865)　　　　BA
　　Bibl: ▶Busse, Maler u. Bildhauer
　　19. Jahr.; ▶Thieme-Becker
Kiss, Bálint (Hungarian painter,
　printmaker, 1802-1868)　　　BA
　　Bibl: ▶Bénézit; ▶Thieme-Becker
Kiss, Gregory (American architect,
　New York City)　　　　　　AV
　　Bibl: Metropolis, 1987 Apr., v.6,
　　no.8, p.47
Kiss, J.G. (Hungarian(?) artist, op.c.
　1640)　　　　　　　　　　WC
Kiss, Laszlo　　　　　AV BA
　(American architect, b.1956)　BA
　(American architect, born in
　　Rumania, 1956-)　　　　AV
　　Bibl: ▶Avery period. idx., 4th
　　suppl.; Das Kunstwerk, n.3-4,
　　Sept. 1983, p.132
Kiss, Pál (Hungarian artist, 20th c.)　BA
　　Bibl: ARS HUNGARICA,
　　VII/2(1979), 237-242
Kisseljoff, Alexander
　Alexejevitch→see Kiselev,
　Aleksandr Aleksandrovič
Kissling, Richard (Swiss sculptor,
　1848-1919)　　　　　　　　BA
　　Bibl: ▶Bénézit; ▶Schweiz.
　　Künst.-Lex.; ▶Thieme-Becker
Kist, Bernd (German architect,
　Fellbach, 1939-)　　　　　　AV
　　Bibl: Deutsche Bauzeitung, 1985
　　Nov., v.119, no.11, p.126
Kiste, Adolf (German artist, 1812-
　1846)　　　　　　　　　　WC
Kistelegdi, István (Hungarian
　architect, 1944-)　　　　　AV
Kistler, Lynton R. (American printer,
　b.1897)　　　　　　　　　BA
　　Bibl: ▶Natl. union cat., pre-1956;
　　PRINT REVIEW, 7(1977), 28-43
Kita, Toshiyuki (Japanese furniture
　and product designer, Osaka,
　1941?-)　　　　　　　　　AV
　　Bibl: ID; Magazine of international
　　design, 1988 May-June, v.35,
　　no.3, p.47

Kitagawara, Atsushi *(Japanese architect, Tokyo, 1951-)*   **AV**
    Bibl: GA houses, n.14, 1983, p.288

Kitaj, R.B. → see Kitaj, Ronald B.

Kitaj, Ronald B.   **BA**
    (American artist, 1933-)   **WC**
    (American artist, b.1932)   **WI**
    (American painter, printmaker, b.1932)   **BA**
    Bibl: Clark Art Inst. Libr.; Guide exh. artists: N. Amer. ptrs.; ▶WW Amer. Art, 1989

    Kitaj, R.B.   **WC**
    Kitaj, Ronald Brooks   **WI**

Kitaj, Ronald Brooks → see Kitaj, Ronald B.

Kitamura, Rikuo *(Japanese architect, 1944-)*   **AV**
    Bibl: Space design, 1986 Dec., no. 267, p.30

Kitamura, Shuichi *(Japanese architect, 1949-)*   **AV**
    Bibl: Kenchiku bunka, 1987 Dec., v.42, no.494, p.88

Kitao Masayoshi → see Masayoshi (Keisai Kuwagata)

Kitao Shigemasa → see Shigemasa (Kitao Shigemasa)

Kitaoka, Setsuo *(Japanese designer, Tokyo, 1946-)*   **AV**
    Bibl: Ottagono, 1987 June, v.22, no.85, p.37

Kitayama, Koh *(Japanese architect)*   **AV**
    Bibl: Space design, 1986 Dec., no. 267, p.32

Kitayama, Kojiro *(Japanese architect)*   **AV**
    Bibl: Kenchiku bunka, 1985 Apr., v.40, no.462, p.23

Kitayama, Vin *(Japanese scientist, printmaker, 20th c.)*   **BA**
    Bibl: Kitayama, V., in LEONARDO, XVII/2 (1984) 91

Kitchel, Nancy *(American photographer, b.1941)*   **BA**
    Bibl: Sondheim, INDIVIDUALS:POST MOVEMENT ART IN AMERICA(1977)

Kitchell, H.M.   **WC WI**
    (American artist, 1862-1944)   **WI**
    (American artist, 19th cent.)   **WC**

Kitchen, Bert   **AV BA**
    (Architectural draughtsman)   **AV**
    (British painter, 20th c.)   **BA**
    Bibl: ▶Babington Smith, Contemp. artists; Jones, Architectural review, 1985 June, v.177, no. 1060; Jones, P.B., in ARCHITECTURAL REVIEW, CLXXVII/1060 (June 1985) 82

Kitchen, Robert *(American painter, 20th c.)*   **BA**
    Bibl: ▶Art Index, v.29; Arts Mag. LV (Feb 1981), 6; ▶Intl. dir. exh. artists, 1982

Kitchin, George Herbert *(British artist, op.circa 1883-)*   **WI**

Kitchin, L. Roy *(British sculptor, b.1926)*   **BA**
    Bibl: ▶Babington Smith, Contemp. artists; LEONARDO, XII(SUMMER 1979), 187

Kitchin, T.S. *(British artist, op.1833-1852)*   **WI**

Kitchin, Thomas   **WC WI**
    (British artist, op.1750-)   **WI**
    (British artist, op.c.1750)   **WC**

Kitchingman or Kitchinman, John → see Kitchingman, John

Kitchingman, John   **WI**
    (British artist, c.1740-1781)   **WC**
    (British artist, circa 1740-1781)   **WI**

    Kitchingman or Kitchinman, John   **WC**
    Kitchinman, John   **WI**

Kitchinman, John → see Kitchingman, John

Kite, Joseph Milner *(British artist, 1862-1946)*   **WC WI**

Kite, Victor *(British architect, London)*   **AV**
    Bibl: ▶RIBA members, 1983

Kithara Painter *(Etruscan vase-painter)*   **GC**
    Bibl: ▶Szilagyi, Etruszko-korinthosi

Kito, Azusa *(Japanese architect)*   **AV**
    Bibl: Kenchiku bunka, 1985 June, v.40, no.464, p.70

Kitsimagi *(Oriental artist, op.1969)*   **WC**

Kitson, Henry Hudson *(American sculptor, 1863/65-1947)*   **BA**
    Bibl: Boston (MA, USA), MFA, Sublime and beautiful (1979); ▶Fielding's Amer. ptrs.; NY Times obit.; ▶WWW Amer.; ▶Young, Amer. artists

Kitson, Linda → see Kitson, Linda F.

Kitson, Linda F.   **BA**
    (British artist, op.1989-)   **WI**
    (British painter, 20th c.)   **BA**
    Bibl: ▶Intl. dir. exh. artists, 1983

    Kitson, Linda   **WI**

Kitson, Robert Hawthorn   **WC WI**
    (British artist, 1873-1947)   **WI**
    (British artist, 19th cent.)   **WC**

Kitson, Sidney Decimus *(British architect, author, 1871-1937)*   **BA**
    Bibl: ▶Avery obit. idx.; ▶Who was who [GBR]

Kitt, Ferdinand *(Austrian painter, designer, 1887-1960)*   **BA**
    Bibl: ▶Vollmer, Künst.-Lex. 20. Jhr.

Kittel, Hermann *(Austrian architect, Vienna)*   **AV**
    Bibl: Der Aufbau, 1986, v.41, no.8, p.423

Kittel, Nicholas Biddle   **WI**
    (American artist, 1822-1894)   **WC WI**
    Kittell, Nicholas Biddle   **WC**

Kittell, Nicholas Biddle → see Kittel, Nicholas Biddle

Kittelsen, Theodor *(Norwegian artist, 1857-1914)*   **WC**

Kittensteyn, Cornelis van   **BA GC WC**
    (Dutch artist, c.1600-p.1638)   **WC**
    (Dutch printmaker, 1598-after 1652)   **BA**
    (Dutch, ca.1600-aft.1638)   **GC**
    Bibl: ▶Thieme-Becker; ▶Waller, Noord NLD Graveurs; ▶Witt checklist

Kittinger, Merrill *(American architect, Eugene, OR)*   **AV**
    Bibl: Builder, 1985 June, v.8, no.6, p.82

Kittner, Patrizius *(German artist, 1809-1900)*   **WC**

Kittos *(potter, ca. 400-350 BC)*   **GC**
    Bibl: ▶Beazley, Attic bl.-fig. vase-ptrs.; Boardman, Attic Bl.-fig. Vases

Kittos Group *(vase-painters, ca. 400-350 BC)*   **GC**
    Bibl: ▶Beazley, Attic bl.-fig. vase-ptrs.; Boardman, Attic Bl.-fig. Vases

Kitz, Peter *(German potter, act.ca. 1616-1627)*   **BA**
    Bibl: KERAMOS, 102 (Oct 1983) 45-54

Kitzel, Herbert *(German painter, 1928-1978)*   **BA**
    Bibl: ▶Wer ist wer

Kivchenko, Alexei Danilovitch → see Kivšenko, Aleksej Daniilovič

Kivett, B.Cory *(American artist, op. 1925-)*   **WI**

Kivland, Sharon *(German photographer in GBR, b.1955)*   **BA**
    Bibl: ▶Intl. dir. exh. artists

Kivšenko, Aleksej Daniilovič   **BA**
    (Russian artist, 1851-1895)   **WC**
    (Russian painter, 1851-1895)   **BA**
    Bibl: ▶Met. Mus. Art libr. cat.; ▶Thieme-Becker

    Kivchenko, Alexei Danilovitch   **WC**

Kiyooka, Roy Kenzie   **BA WC**
    (Canadian artist, 1926-)   **WC**
    (Canadian painter, sculptor, b.1926)   **BA**
    Bibl: ▶Artists Canada; ▶MacDonald, Can. artists

Kizberger, Joseph *(Austrian ceramist, act.1766, d.1780)*   **BA**
    Bibl: Langer, WELTKUNST, LV/2 (15Jan 1985), p. 116-121; ▶Thieme-Becker

Kizik, Roger *(American painter, b.1945)*   **BA**
    Bibl: Waltham(MA, USA), Brandeis Univ.,Rose Art Museum. ASPECTS OF THE '70'SMAVERICKS(1980)

Kjaergaard, Claus *(Danish architect)*   **AV**
    Bibl: Arkitekten, 1988 Dec.6, v.90, no.22, p.553

Kjaergaard, Poul Ernst *(Danish architect, b.1912)*   **BA**
    Bibl: TIL POUL KJAERGAARD (1982); ▶Weilbach, Kunst.leks.

Kjaerholm, Hanne   **AV BA**
    (Danish architect, 20th c.)   **BA**
    (Danish architect, Copenhagen, 1930-)   **AV**
    Bibl: ▶Danske Arkitekters Landsforbund, 1984-85; Hermansen, LIVING ARCHITECTURE 2 1984 p.46-51

Kjaerholm, Poul *(Danish designer, 1929-1980)*   **AV**
    Bibl: ▶Avery period. idx.; Contemp. designers

Kjarval, Jóhannes Sveinsson *(Icelandic painter, 1885-1972)*   **BA**
    Bibl: Reykjavik (ISL), Natl. Gall., Fjórirfrumberjar (1985); ▶Vollmer, Künst.-Lex. 20. Jhr.; ▶Weilbach, Kunst.leks.

Kjeldgard, Marinus J. *(Danish, active 1940s)*   **JG**

Kjerner, Esther *(Swedish artist, 1873-1952)*   **WC**

Kjerulf, Hjalmar *(Norwegian(?) artist, 19th cent.)*   **WC**

Kjoistrom, Isak *(Swedish artist, 1769-p.1799)*   **WC**

Klaarhamer *(Dutch architect, 20th c.)*   **BA**

Klaentschi, Hans *(English architect, Portsmouth)*   **AV**
    Bibl: Architects' journal, 1984 Aug.1, v.180,no.31

Klaes Molenaer→see Molenaer, Klaes
Klagstad→see Klagstad, Arnold Ness
Klagstad, Arnold→see Klagstad, Arnold Ness

Klagstad, Arnold Ness *(American painter, b. 1898)*   **PR**
    Bibl: ▶WWW Amer. art
Arnold Ness Klagstad   PR
Klagstad   PR
Klagstad, Arnold   PR

Klähn, Wolfgang *(German painter, b.1929)*   **BA**
    Bibl: ▶Havlice, Idx. art. bio.; ▶Kindlers Malerei Lex.; ▶WW Arts DEU

Klanzinget *(German(?) artist, 18th cent.)*   **WC**

Klaphauer, Johann Georg *(German artist, op.1634-1663)*   **WC**

Klapheck, Konrad   **BA WC**
    (German artist, 1935-)   **WC**
    (German painter, b.1935)   **BA**
    Bibl: ▶Babington Smith, Contemp. artists; ▶DuMonts Künst.-Lex.; ▶Gorenflo, Bild. Künstler; Guide exh. artists: Sculp.; ▶Intl. dir. exh. artists; ▶Vollmer, Künst.-Lex. 20. Jhr.

Klarin, Karla *(American painter, 20th c.)*   **BA**
    Bibl: ▶Intl. dir. exh. artists

Klarwein, Abdul Mati *(American painter, 20th c.)*   **BA**
    Bibl: Breslow, Arts mag., LVII/1 (Sep. 1982) p.13; White, ART MAGAZINE, LVII/10(JUNE 1983), 2

Klas, Aleksander *(Yugoslav artist, 20th cent.)*   **WC**

Klasen, Peter   **BA WC**
    (American artist, 20th cent.)   **WC**
    (West German painter, b.1935)   **BA**
    Bibl: ▶Babington Smith, Contemp. artists; Guide exh. artists: N. Amer. ptrs.

Klasen, Uwe *(East German architect, Berlin)*   **AV**
    Bibl: Architektur der DDR, 1987 Oct., v.36, no.10, p.15

Klass, Friedrich Christian *(German artist, 1752-1827)*   **WC**

Klassnik, Robin *(British artist, b.1947)*   **WI**

Klatt, Hans *(German artist, 1876-)*   **WC**

Klauber family *(German printmakers, publishers, 18th c.)*   **BA**
    Bibl: ▶Thieme-Becker

Klauber, Ignaz Sebastian   **GC WC**
    (German artist, 1753-1817)   **WC**
    (German draughtsman, 1753-1817)   **GC**
    Bibl: ▶Thieme-Becker

Klauber, Johann Baptist   **BA WC**
    (German artist, 1712-p.1787)   **WC**
    (German printmaker, publisher, 1712-1787)   **BA**
    Bibl: ▶Neue deutsche Biog.; ▶Thieme-Becker; ▶Witt checklist

Klauber, Joseph Sebastian   **BA WC**
    (German artist, c.1700-1768)   **WC**
    (German printmaker, publisher, 1710-1768)   **BA**
    Bibl: ▶Neue deutsche Biog.; ▶Thieme-Becker; ▶Witt checklist

Klauber, Kluber or Gluber, Hans Hug→see Kluber, Hans Hug

Klauke, Jürgen *(German artist, photographer, b.1943)*   **BA**
    Bibl: ▶DuMonts Künst.-Lex.; ▶WW Arts DEU

Klaus, Rudolf *(West German architect, Schloss Holte-Stukenbrock)*   **AV**
    Bibl: Architektur, Innenarchitektur, Technischer Ausbau, 1986 Oct., v.94, no.10, p.50

Klausener, Friedrich Wilhelm *(German architect, act.1846)*   **BA**
    Bibl: AACHENER KUNSTBLATTER, LII (1984) 255

Klauser, Johannes *(German architect, Karlsruhe)*   **AV**
    Bibl: Bauwelt, 1985 Dec.13, v.76, no.47, p.1844

Klauss, Ulrich *(Architect)*   **AV**
    Bibl: Deutsche Bauzeitung, 1986 Jan., v.120, no.1, p.31

Klaven, Marvin   **WC WI**
    (American artist, 1931-)   **WC**
    (American artist, b.1931)   **WI**

Kleanthes, Stamatios *(Greek architect, 19th c.)*   **BA**
    Bibl: Fountoulakis, ARCHITECTURA VII/1(1977), 46-51

Klearchos of Rhegium *(Greek sculptor, unknown)*   **GC**
    Bibl: ▶Robertson, Greek art, p.591

Kleczynski, Bohdan *(Polish artist, 1851-1916)*   **WC**

Klee→see Klee, Paul

Klee, Felix *(Swiss, b.1907)*   **BA**
    Bibl: BHA Paris; ▶Natl. union cat., 1968-1972

Klee, G.R.T. *(Swiss artist, 20th cent.)*   **WC**

Klee, Paul   **AV BA GC PR WC WI**
    (1879-1940)   **AV**
    (Swiss artist, 1879-1940)   **WC WI**
    (Swiss painter, 1879-1940)   **PR**
    (Swiss painter, printmaker, 1879-1940)   **BA**
    (Swiss, 1879-1940)   **GC**
    Bibl: ▶Brockhaus Enzyk.; ▶Encyc. Britannica; ▶Encyc. world art; Klee, F., THE DIARIES OF PAUL KLEE; ▶Künst.-Lex. Schweiz 20. Jahrh.; ▶Neue deutsche Biog.; ▶New Columbia encyc.; ▶RILA/BHA; ▶Vollmer, Künst.-Lex. 20. Jhr.; ▶Witt checklist
Klee   PR
Paul Klee   PR

Kleef, Hendrick III van→see Cleve, Hendrick III van
Kleef, Joos van→see Cleve, Joos van
Kleef, Marten I van→see Cleve, Marten I van

Kleehaas, Theodor *(German artist, 1854-)*   **WC**

Kleeman, Johann Jacob *(German artist, 1739-1790)*   **WC**

Kleeman, Ron   **BA WC WI**
    (American artist, 1937-)   **WC**
    (American artist, b.1937)   **WI**
    (American painter, b.1937)   **BA**
    Bibl: ▶WW Amer. Art, 1989

Kleemann, Nikolaus Moritz *(German artist, op.1726-m.1756)*   **WC**

Kleen, Lars *(Swedish painter, b.1941)*   **BA**
    Bibl: Bonn(DEU), Rheinisches Landesmuseum. NEUER REALISM AUS SCHWEDEN(1975)

Kleen, Thyra af *(Swedish artist, 1874-)*   **WC**

Kleene, David→see Kleijne, David

Kleeneknecht, Barent Cornelisz.   **GC**
    (Dutch artist, c.1608/10-1674)   **WC**
    (Dutch painter, c.1608-1674)   **GC**
    Bibl: ▶Thieme-Becker

Kleeneknecht, Cleeneknecht or Cleyneknecht, Barent Cornelisz.   **WC**

Kleeneknecht, Cleeneknecht or
  Cleyneknecht, Barent
  Cornelisz. → see Kleeneknecht,
  Barent Cornelisz.
Kleffel, Konstantin (West German
  architect, Hamburg)   **AV**
    Bibl: ▶Bund Deut. Arch. Hdbch.,
    1987
Kleihues, Josef Paul   **AV BA**
    (West German architect, 1933-) AV
    (West German architect,
    b.1933)   BA
    Bibl: ▶Contemp. archts.; ▶Wer ist
    wer, 1989-90
Kleijn, Johan Pieter Vaupel (Dutch
  artist, 1813-1870)   **WC**
Kleijn, Laurens Lodewijk (Dutch
  artist, 1826-1909)   **WC**
Kleijn, Lodewijk Johannes   **GC WC**
    (Dutch artist, 1817-1897)   WC
    (Dutch painter, 1817-1897)   GC
    Bibl: ▶Bénézit; ▶Thieme-Becker
    Kleyn, Lodewijk Johannes   GC
Kleijne, David   **BA**
    (Dutch painter and
    draughtsman, 1754-1805)   GC
    (Dutch painter, printmaker,
    1754-1805)   BA
    Bibl: ▶Bénézit; ▶Scheen, Ned.
    beeldende kunst.; ▶Thieme-Becker
    Kleene, David   GC
Kleyne, David   **GC**
Kleijnhens → see Kleynhens, Isaak
Kleimachos (potter, ca. 565-550 BC) **GC**
    Bibl: ▶Beazley, Attic bl.-fig. vase-
    ptrs.; Boardman, Attic Bl.-fig.
    Vases
Klein, Alexander   **AV BA**
    (German architect, b.1879)   BA
    (Israeli architect, 1879-1961) AV
    Bibl: Bauwelt, 1989 June 9, v.80,
    no.23, p.1042; ▶Portoghesi, Diz.
    arch. e urbanistica; ▶Vollmer,
    Künst.-Lex. 20. Jhr.
Klein, Anita (British artist, b.1960) **WI**
Klein, Astrid (West German
  photographer, b.1951)   **BA**
    Bibl: Lucerne(CHE), Kunstmuseum
    Luzern. ASTRID KLEIN(1984)
    RILA/CHE
Klein, Bernat (Yugoslav artist,
  1922-)   **WC**
Klein, Bernhard   **GC WC**
    (German artist, 1888-1967)   WC
    (German painter, 1888-1967)   GC
    Bibl: ▶Witt checklist
Klein, Carl August von (German
  artist, 1794-1870)   **WC**
Klein, Caspar (German artist, 18th
  cent.)   **WC**

Klein, Cesar   **BA**
    (German artist, 1876-1954)   WC
    (German painter, printmaker,
    scenographer, 1876-1954)   BA
    Bibl: ▶Bénézit; ▶Neue deutsche
    Biog.; ▶Vollmer, Künst.-Lex. 20.
    Jhr.
**Klein, Cesar Carl Robert
  Andreas**   **WC**
Klein, Cesar Carl Robert
  Andreas → see Klein, Cesar
Klein, Daniel, II (German artist, op.
  1745-1747)   **WC**
Klein, Ernst (West German
  landscape architect, Essen) **AV**
    Bibl: Deutsches Architektenblatt,
    1988 May, v.20, no.5, p.681
Klein, Franz → see Cleyn, Francis
Klein, Friedrich Franz Albert (Fred)
    (Dutch draughtsman, b.1898) **GC**
    Bibl: ▶Scheen, Ned. beeldende
    kunst.
Klein, Gerhardus (Dutch silversmith,
  act.1726, d.1730)   **BA**
    Bibl: Groningen (NLD), Groninger
    Museum voor Stad en Lande,
    Groninger Zilver (1975), 71-72;
    W.A. Hofman, in ANTIEK XVIII/1
    (June-July 1983), 19-24
Klein, Hanspeter (West German
  architect, Stuttgart)   **AV**
    Bibl: ▶Bund Deut. Arch. Hdbch.,
    1987
Klein, Henry (American architect) **AV**
    Bibl: ▶Amer. archts. dir., 1970
Klein, Johann Adam   **AV BA GC WC**
    (German artist, 1792-1875)   WC
    (German painter, printmaker,
    1792-1875)   BA
    (German, 1792-1875)   GC
    (Swedish artist, resided in
    Copenhagen after 1758,
    1792-1875)   AV
    Bibl: ▶Thieme-Becker; ▶Witt
    checklist
Klein, Johann L. (German artist,
  19th cent.)   **WC**
Klein, John (American architect) **AV**
Klein, Leslie (American artist, 20th
  c.)   **BA**
    Bibl: Ross, Southeast College Art
    Conf. Review X (Spr 1981) 24-27
Klein, Oscar   **BA WC**
    (American dealer, draftsman,
    20th c.)   BA
    (Czech artist, 20th cent.)   WC
    Bibl: Fine Arts Marketplace, 1975-
    1976, p.66; OSCAR
    KLEIN:DRAWINGS(1976)
Klein, Philipp   **GC WC**
    (German artist, 1871-1907)   WC
    (German painter, 1871-1907)   GC
    Bibl: ▶Thieme-Becker
Klein, Reiner (West German
  architect, Munich)   **AV**
    Bibl: Deutsches Architektenblatt,
    1987 Oct., v.18, no.10, p.1195

Klein, Sheila (American artist) **AV**
    Bibl: Arts + architecture, 1985,
    new ser., v.3, no.4, p.69
Klein, Stanley   **AV**
Klein, William   **BA JG**
    (American photographer,
    b.1928.)   BA
    (American, 1928 -)   JG
    Bibl: ▶Contemp. photogs., 1988;
    Minneapolis(MN, USA), Walker
    Art Gallery. VANISHING
    PRESENCE(1989); ▶MoMA libr.
    cat.
Klein, Yves   **BA WC**
    (French artist, 1928-)   WC
    (French painter, 1928-1962)   BA
    Bibl: ▶Bénézit; ▶Witt checklist
Klein-Berning, Jörn D. (West
  German architect, Augsburg) **AV**
    Bibl: Deutsches Architektenblatt,
    1988 Mar., v.20, no.3, p.517
Klein-Chevalier, Friedrich (German
  artist, 1862-)   **WC**
Klein-Hall (German artist, op.1846) **WC**
Klein-Moquay, Rotraut (German
  painter, sculptor, b.1938)   **BA**
    Bibl: Krefeld(DEU), Kaiser Wilhelm
    Museum.ROTRAUT KLEIN-
    MOQUAY(1975)
Kleinbard, Alexa (American artist,
  b.1952)   **BA**
    Bibl: New York (NY, USA), New
    Mus., Outside NY (1978)
Kleinberg, David (American interior
  decorator, New York City)   **AV**
    Bibl: House & garden, 1989 Oct.,
    v.161, no.10, p.238
Kleindienst, Gerhard (Austrian
  architect, Vienna)   **AV**
    Bibl: Der Aufbau, 1986, v.41,
    no.8, p.423
Kleine, Franz → see Cleyn, Francis
Kleine-Klopries, Heinz (German
  sculptor, b.1949)   **BA**
    Bibl: Duisburg (DEU), Wilhelm-
    Lehmbruck-Mus., Bella figura
    (1984)
Kleineh, Oscar Conrad (Finnish
  artist, 1846-1919)   **WC**
Kleinehanding, Heinz (West
  German architect)   **AV**
    Bibl: Arch Plus, 1987 Nov., no.92,
    p.60
Kleinenbroich, Wilhelm (German
  artist, 1814-1895)   **WC**
Kleiner, Salomon   **AV BA WC**
    (Austrian draftsman, engraver,
    1703-1761)   AV
    (German artist, 1700/3-1761) WC
    (German printmaker, publisher,
    1703-1761)   BA
    Bibl: Ars Bavarica, 1984, v.33-34,
    p.125; ▶Bénézit; ▶Thieme-Becker;
    ▶Witt checklist

Kleinert, Markus Friedrich   GC WC
  (German artist, 1694-1742)   WC
  (German painter, 1694-1742)   GC
    Bibl: ▶Bénézit

Kleinhammes, Hans Jürgen
  (German painter, printmaker,
  b.1937)   BA
    Bibl: ▶Intl. dir. exh. artists; ▶WW
    Arts DEU

Kleinhans, Franz (German architect,
  1699-1776)   BA
    Bibl: ▶Thieme-Becker

Kleinjohann, Günter (German
  architect, Trier)   AV
    Bibl: Deutsche Bauzeitschrift,
    1985 Dec., v.33, no.12, p.1587

Kleinknecht, Hermann (West
  German sculptor, b.1943)   BA
    Bibl: ▶Babington Smith, Contemp.
    artists; Guide exh. artists: Sculp.

**Kleinmichel, Julius (Ferdinand
  Julius Theodor)** (German artist,
  1846-1892)   WC

Kleinod, Karl (Austrian goldsmith,
  act.1852-1867)   BA
    Bibl: Simoniti, Zbornik za
    umetnostno zgodovino XVII
    (1981) 75-87

Kleinschmidt→see Kleinschmidt, Paul

Kleinschmidt, J.   WC
  (German artist, 1859-1905)   WC
  (German artist, 19th cent.)   WC

Kleinschmidt, Paul   BA PR WC
  (German artist, 1883-1949)   WC
  (German painter, 1883-1949)   PR
  (German painter, printmaker,
  1883-1949)   BA
    Bibl: ▶Bénézit; ▶RILA/BHA;
    ▶Thieme-Becker; ▶Vollmer,
    Künst.-Lex. 20. Jhr.
  Kleinschmidt   PR
  Paul Kleinschmidt   PR

Kleinschmidt, Robert   AV

Kleint, Boris Herbert   BA WC
  (German artist, 1903-)   WC
  (German painter, b.1903)   BA
    Bibl: ▶Bénézit; ▶Vollmer,
    Künst.-Lex. 20. Jhr.; ▶Witt
    checklist; ▶WW Arts DEU

Kleintje, Dieter (German artist,
  b.1944)   BA
    Bibl: ▶WW Arts DEU

Kleiser, Lorentz (American
  manufacturer, act.1913)   BA
    Bibl: ▶Who was who [GBR], index;
    Zrebibc, AMERICAN TAPESTRY
    MANUFACTURERS(1980)

Kleist, Heinrich von (German artist,
  op.c.1805)   WC

Kleist, Louis de (French artist, 19th
  cent.)   WC

Kleitias (vase-painter, ca. 575-560
  BC)   GC
    Bibl: ▶Beazley, Attic bl.-fig. vase-
    ptrs.; Boardman, Attic Bl.-fig.
    Vases

Klejman Painter (Apulian vase-
  painter)   GC
    Bibl: Trendall, Attic red-fig. vases
    Apulia

Klemens, Jozef Božetech   BA WC
  (Czech artist, 1817-1883)   WC
  (Czech painter, 1817-1883)   BA

Klement, Vera (American painter,
  printmaker, b.1929)   BA
    Bibl: ▶WW Amer. Art, 1984

Klemke, Werner (German
  printmaker, scenographer,
  illustrator, b.1917)   BA
    Bibl: ▶Vollmer, Künst.-Lex. 20. Jhr.

Klemm, Fritz (German painter,
  b.1902)   BA
    Bibl: ▶Vollmer, Künst.-Lex. 20.
    Jhr.; ▶WW Arts DEU

*Klemm, Ursula→see Fischer-Klemm,
  Ursula*

Klemm, Walther (German painter,
  illustrator, 1883-1957)   BA
    Bibl: ▶Thieme-Becker; ▶Vollmer,
    Künst.-Lex. 20. Jhr.

Klemm, Zsolt George (Australian
  architect, 1932-)   AV

Klemming, Frans G. (Swedish
  photographer, 1859-1922)   BA
    Bibl: Minneapolis (MN, USA),
    Walker Art Ctr., Frozen image
    (1982)

Klempner, Ernest S. (American
  artist, b.1867)   WI

Klenck, Paul (Swiss artist, 1844-)   WC

*Klengel→see Klengel, Johann
  Christian*

*Klengel or Klingel, Johann
  Christian→see Klengel, Johann
  Christian*

Klengel, Johann Christian   BA GC PR
  (German artist, 1751-1824)   WC
  (German painter, 1751-1824)   PR
  (German painter, printmaker,
  1751-1824)   BA
  (German, 1751-1824)   GC
    Bibl: ▶Brockhaus Enzyk.;
    ▶RILA/BHA; ▶Thieme-Becker
  Johann Christian Klengel   PR
  Klengel   PR

**Klengel or Klingel, Johann
  Christian**   WC

Klenk, Ulrich (West German
  architect, Backnang, 1951-)   AV
    Bibl: Deutsche Bauzeitung, 1989
    Jan., v.123, no.1, p.130

Klenze→see Klenze, Leo von

Klenze, Leo van→see Klenze, Leo von

Klenze, Leo von   AV BA GC JG PR WC
  (1784-1864)   AV
  (German architect, painter,
  1784-1864)   BA
  (German artist, 1784-1864)   WC
  (German draughtsman, 1784-
  1864)   GC
  (German painter, 1784-1864)   PR
  (German, 1784-1864)   JG
    Bibl: ▶Bénézit; ▶Encyc. world art;
    ▶RILA/BHA; ▶Thieme-Becker
  Klenze   PR
  Klenze, Leo van   PR
  Leo von Klenze   PR

Kleomelos Painter   GC JG
  (vase-painter, ca. 530-500 BC)   GC
    Bibl: ▶Beazley, Attic red-fig. vase-
    ptrs.; Richter, Attic red-fig. vases

Kleomenes (Roman copyist,
  unknown)   GC
    Bibl: ▶Robertson, Greek art, p.413

Kleophon Painter (vase-painter, ca.
  420-390 BC)   GC
    Bibl: ▶Beazley, Attic red-fig. vase-
    ptrs.; Richter, Attic red-fig. vases

Kleophrades   JG

Kleophrades Painter   JG

Kleophrades Painter (Epiktetos II)
  (vase-painter, ca. 500-475 BC)   GC
    Bibl: ▶Beazley, Attic bl.-fig. vase-
    ptrs.; ▶Beazley, Attic red-fig. vase-
    ptrs.; Richter, Attic red-fig. vases

Kleppan, Morten (Norwegian
  designer, 1958-)   AV
    Bibl: Byggekunst: the Norwegian
    review of architecture, 1988,
    v.70, no.5, p.338

Kleppen, Bettino [Unidentified]
  (Unknown painter, act. 18th
  century)   PR
    Bibl: Riccardi inventory dated
    1776
  Bettino Kleppen   PR

Klepper, Max Francis (German
  artist, 1861-1907)   WC

*Klerck, Hendrik de→see Clerck,
  Hendrik de*

Klerk, Michel de (Dutch architect,
  1884-1923)   AV BA
    Bibl: ▶Contemp. archts.;
    ▶Macmillan encyc. archts.;
    ▶Portoghesi, Diz. arch. e
    urbanistica
  De Klerk, Michel   AV

Klerk, Willem de   GC WC
  (Dutch artist, 1800-1876)   WC
  (Dutch painter, 1800-1876)   GC
    Bibl: ▶Bénézit

...kles (potter, ca. 550-520? BC)   GC
    Bibl: ▶Beazley, Attic bl.-fig. vase-
    ptrs.; Boardman, Attic Bl.-fig.
    Vases

Klett family (German weapons
  makers, 16th-17th cs.)   BA
    Bibl: Gumppenberg, ALTE U.
    MODERNE KUNST, XXX/198-199
    (1985) 42-45; ▶Thieme-Becker

Klett, Mark *(American photographer, b.1952)* **BA**
Bibl: ▶Alinder, Discovery & recognition; Los Angeles (CA, USA), LACMA, New Amer. photography (1985)

Kleudgen, Fritz *(German artist, 1846-)* **WC**

Kleukens, Friedrich Wilhelm *(German painter, printmaker, 1878-1956)* **BA**
Bibl: ▶Bénézit; ▶Vollmer, Künst.-Lex. 20. Jhr.

Klever, Julius Sergius (Julij Juljewitsch) von → see Klever, Juljus Sergjus

Klever, Juljus Sergjus **BA**
(Russian artist, 1850-1924) WC
(Russian painter, 1850-1924) BA
Bibl: ▶Thieme-Becker

Klever, Julius Sergius (Julij Juljewitsch) von **WC**

Kley, Hans *(West German architect, Biberach, 1933-)* **AV**
Bibl: Deutsche Bauzeitung, 1987 Oct., v.121, no.10, p.172

Kley, Heinrich *(German artist, 1863-1945)* **WC**

Kleyn → see Kleyn, Pieter Rudolph

Kleyn, A. *(Dutch painter, act. 17th century)* **GC**
Bibl: Getty Photo Study Coll. (Duits coll.)

Kleyn, Lodewijk Johannes → see Kleijn, Lodewijk Johannes

Kleyn, Pieter → see Kleyn, Pieter Rudolph

Kleyn, Pieter Rudolph **GC PR WC**
(Dutch artist, 1785-1816) WC
(Dutch painter and draughtsman, 1785-1816) GC
(Dutch painter, 1785-1816) PR
Bibl: ▶Bénézit; ▶Thieme-Becker
Kleyn PR
Kleyn, Pieter PR
Pieter Rudolph Kleyn PR

Kleyne, David → see Kleijne, David

Kleynhens, Isaak *(Dutch painter, 1634-1701)* **PR**
Bibl: ▶Thieme-Becker
Isaak Kleynhens PR
Kleijnhens PR

Klezmer, Michael *(American draftsman, b.1940.)* **BA**
Bibl: ▶Babington Smith, Contemp. artists

Kliczkowski, Hugo *(Argentine architect)* **AV**
Bibl: Architecture & urbanism, 1986 Dec., no.12 (195), p.43

Klieber, Edouard *(German artist, 1803-1879)* **WC**

Klieber, Josef *(German artist, 1773-1850)* **WC**

Klieber, Reichert *(German, d.1491)* **BA**
Bibl: Münchner Jahrb. Bild. Kunst, XXVI (1975) pp.65-88

Kliemann, Carl Heinz *(German artist, 1924-)* **WC**

Klien, Erika Giovanna *(Austrian painter in USA, 1900-1957)* **BA**
Bibl: Clark Art Inst. Libr.; Linz (AUT), Neue Galerie, Künstlerinnen (1983)

Klier, Hans von *(Designer)* **AV**
Bibl: L'Arca, 1989 Mar., no.25, p.92

Klíma, Milan *(Czech architect)* **AV**
Bibl: Architektura ČSR, 1988, v.47, no.1, p.42

Klimenko, Serge *(French? architect)* **AV**
Bibl: Maison Française, 1985 June, no.388, p.108

Kliment, Robert M. *(American architect, 1933-)* **AV**
Bibl: ▶AIA Pro File, 1985

Klimentov, Feoktist *(Russian painter, act.1708)* **BA**
Bibl: Soobscenija Hermitage XLIV (1979), 29-32

Klimes, Thomas *(German artist, op. 1780-1788)* **WC**

Klimesch, Winfried *(W. German architect, Tübingen)* **AV**
Bibl: Detail, 1986 Nov.-Dec., v.26, no.6

Klimkovic, Ignac *(Hungarian artist, 1800-)* **WC**

Klimowski, Andrezj → see Klimowski, Andrzej

Klimowski, Andrzej **BA**
(Polish artist, 20th cent.) WC
(Polish printmaker, b.1949) BA
Bibl: Arts & Artists XIV/5 (Sep 1979) 28-31

Klimowski, Andrezj **WC**

Klimsch, Eugen **GC WC**
(German artist, 1839-1896) WC
(German painter, 1839-1896) GC
Bibl: ▶Witt checklist

Klimsch, Fritz *(German sculptor, 1870-1960)* **BA GC**
Bibl: ▶Bénézit; ▶Neue deutsche Biog.; ▶Thieme-Becker

Klimt → see Klimt, Gustav

Klimt, Ernst **BA WC**
(Austrian painter, 1864-1892) BA
(German artist, 1864-1892) WC
Bibl: ▶Österr. biog. Lex. 1815-1950; ▶Thieme-Becker

Klimt, Gustav **AV BA GC PR WC**
(Austrian painter and designer, 1862-1918) AV
(Austrian painter and draughtsman, 1862-1918) GC
(Austrian painter, 1862-1918) BA PR
(German artist, 1862-1918) WC
Bibl: Getty Photo Study Coll.; ▶RILA/BHA; ▶Thieme-Becker; ▶Witt checklist
Gustave Klimt PR
Klimt PR

Klimt, Gustave **PR**
Klimt, Gustave → see Klimt, Gustav

Klinck, Germanns *(German artist, op.1609)* **WC**

Klinckenberg, Eugene *(Dutch artist, 1858-)* **WC**

Klinckowstrom, Axel Leonard **WI**
(American artist, 1775-1837) WC WI

Klinckowstrom, Axel Leonhard **WC**
Klinckowstrom, Axel Leonhard → see Klinckowstrom, Axel Leonard

Klinckowstrom, Harald *(Scandinavian artist, 1897-)* **WC**

Kline, Franz **BA WC WI**
(American artist, 1910-1962) WC WI
(American painter, 1910-1962) BA
Bibl: ▶Cummings, Contemp. Amer. artists; ▶Encyc. world art

Kline, Richard R. *(American painter, sculptor, 20th c.)* **BA**
Bibl: ▶WW Amer. Art, 1989

Kling, Anton *(Austrian painter, designer, 1881-1963)* **BA**
Bibl: ▶Bénézit; ▶Thieme-Becker; Vienna(AUT), Ost Museum fur ang.Kunst. ANTON KING...(1979)

Kling, Kathy *(American architect)* **AV**

Kling, Vincent G. **AV**

Klingel, J.C. *(German artist, 19th cent.)* **WC**

Klingelhöfer, Petra *(German architect, Stuttgart)* **AV**
Bibl: Architektur, Innenarchitektur, Technischer Ausbau, 1985 Mar., v.93, no.2, p.54

Klingelhöller, Harald *(West German artist, b.1954)* **BA**
Bibl: Bern (CHE), Kunsthalle Bern, Konstruierte Orte (1983)

Klinger, Albert *(German artist, 1869-1912)* **WC**

Klinger, Jörg *(Architect, Brunn)* **AV**
Bibl: ▶Verzeich. Öst. Ziviltech.

Klinger, Max **BA GC WC**
(German artist, 1857-1920) WC
(German painter, sculptor, and printmaker, 1857-1920) GC
(German painter, sculptor, printmaker, 1857-1920) BA
Bibl: ▶Encyc. Britannica; ▶Neue deutsche Biog.; ▶RILA/BHA; ▶Thieme-Becker

---

Klingeren, Frank van   AV BA
  (Dutch architect, Amsterdam)   AV
  (Dutch architect, b.1919.)   BA
  Bibl: ▶Avery period. idx.; Daidalos
  21 (15 Sep. 1986); ▶Federatie O
  jrbk., 1984

Klingerer, Jörg (Austrian architect)   AV
  Bibl: Architektur + Wettbewerbe,
  1986 Dec., no.128, p.18

Klingh, Franz Joseph (Unknown
  artist)   GC
  Bibl: Gernsheim, Corpus Photog.
  of Drawings, 1367

Klinghoffer, Clara (German artist,
  1900)   WC

Klingsor, Tristan   BA
  (French artist, 1874-1966)   WC
  (French poet, painter, critic,
  1874-1966)   BA
  Bibl: ▶Bénézit; ▶Larousse grande
  encyc.; ▶MoMA libr. cat.; Oxford
  comp. Fr. lit.; ▶Vollmer,
  Künst.-Lex. 20. Jhr.

Klingsor, Tristan (Leon Leclere)   WC
  Léon Leclère   BA

Klingsor, Tristan (Leon Leclere) → see
  Klingsor, Tristan

Klingstainer, Paul (German artist,
  op.1452-1461)   WC

Klingstedt or Klingstet, Carl
  Gustav → see Klingstedt, Karl
  Gustave

Klingstedt, Karl Gustave   GC
  (Swedish artist, 1657-1734)   WC
  (Swedish painter, 1657-1734)   GC
  Bibl: ▶Bénézit

**Klingstedt or Klingstet, Carl
  Gustav**   WC

Klinkan, Alfred (Austrian painter,
  b.1950)   BA
  Bibl: ▶Intl. dir. exh. artists, 1983

**Klinkenberg, Johannes Christiaan
  Karel**   BA GC WC
  (Dutch artist, 1852-1924)   WC
  (Dutch painter and
  draughtsman, 1852-1924)   GC
  (Dutch painter, 1852-1924)   BA
  Bibl: ▶Bénézit; ▶RILA/BHA;
  ▶Scheen, Ned. beeldende kunst.;
  ▶Thieme-Becker

Klinkerfuss, Johannes (German
  cabinetmaker, 1770-1831)   BA
  Bibl: Greber, ABSALAM UND
  DAVID ROENTGEN; Huth,
  Roentgen Furniture, p.70;
  ▶Kreisel, Kunst deutschen Möbels,
  v.3, p.67; Wiese, WELTKUNST,
  LVII/10 (15 May 1987),p.1380-
  1385

Klinkhamer, Hendrik Abraham
  (Dutch draughtsman, 1810-1872)   GC
  Bibl: ▶Thieme-Becker

Klinkowstein, Tom (American artist,
  20th c.)   BA
  Bibl: Klinkowstein, T., LEONARDO,
  XIX/2 (1986) p.107-112

**Klinkowstrom, Friedrich August
  von** (German artist, 1778-1835)   WC

Klint, Kaare   AV BA
  (Danish architect & painter, son
  of Peder V. Jensen-Klint,
  1888-1954)   AV
  (Danish architect, painter,
  furniture designer, 1888-
  1954)   BA
  Bibl: Anderson, KAARE KLINT'S
  MOBLER(1979); ▶Bénézit;
  ▶Macmillan encyc. archts.;
  ▶Thieme-Becker; ▶Weilbach,
  Kunst.leks.

Klint, Pedar Vilhelm Jensen → see
  Jensen-Klint, Peder Vilhelm

Klint, Peter Vilhelm Jensen → see
  Jensen-Klint, Peder Vilhelm

Klippart → see Klippart, Josephine

Klippart, Josephine (American
  painter, 1848-1936)   PR
  Bibl: ▶WWW Amer. art
  Josephine Klippart   PR
  Klippart   PR

Klippel, Robert (Australian
  sculptor, 1920-)   GC VO
  Bibl: Craftsman House Art
  Publishers, 1991 Complete List;
  Gernsheim, Corpus Photog. of
  Drawings, 1423; Gleeson, J.,
  Robert Klippel (1983); ▶Libr. of
  Congr. Name Auth. File,
  NAFL85233081; VCG

Klipper, Stuart David (American
  photographer, b.1941)   BA
  Bibl: ▶ARTbibl. mod.; ▶Macmillan
  photog. encyc.; ▶WW Amer. Art,
  1989-1990

Klitgaard, Christiana Brix, Miss → see
  May, Christiane Brix Klitgaard

Klitomenes   GC
  Bibl: ▶Beazley, Attic bl.-fig. vase-
  ptrs.

Klitsch, Peter (Austrian artist, 1934-)   WC
Kliun, Ivan → see Kljun, Ivan Vasil'evič

Kljun, Ivan Vasil'evič   BA
  (Russian artist, 20th cent.)   WC
  (Russian sculptor, painter, 1870-
  1942)   BA
  Bibl: ▶Bowlt, Russian avant-garde;
  WELTKUNST, LI/8(APR 1981),
  1154

Kliun, Ivan   WC
Kloack, A. → see Noack, Alfredo
Klocker or Kloker, David
  (Ehrenstrahl) → see Ehrenstrahl,
  David Klöcker
Klöcker, Anna Maria → see
  Ehrenstrahl, Anna Maria
Klocker, Anna Maria
  (Ehrenstrahl) → see Ehrenstrahl,
  Anna Maria
Klöcker, David → see Ehrenstrahl,
  David Klöcker
Klöcker, David (Ehrenstrahl) → see
  Ehrenstrahl, David Klöcker

Klode, Karl (German painter,
  b.1904)   BA
  Bibl: Wangler, Schüler des
  Bauhauses, p.42

**Klodt v. Jurgensburg, Michael (I)
  Konstantinowitsch** (Russian
  artist, 1832-1902)   WC

**Kloeber, August (Carl Friedrich)
  von** (German artist, 1793-1864)   WC
Klöker, David → see Ehrenstrahl, David
  Klöcker

Klokov, Vjačeslav Myhajlovyč
  (Russian sculptor, b.1928)   BA
  Bibl: Kal'nytska, VJACHESLAV
  KLOKOV AL'BOM

Klombeck, Johann Bernard   GC PR WC
  (Belgian painter, 1815-1893)   PR
  (Dutch artist, 1815-1893)   WC
  (Dutch painter, 1815-1893)   GC
  Bibl: ▶Busse, Maler u. Bildhauer
  19. Jahr.; LACMA catalogue;
  ▶Thieme-Becker

  Johann Bernard Klombeck   PR

Klomp → see Klomp, Albert Jansz.
Klomp or Clomp, Albert Jansz. → see
  Klomp, Albert Jansz.

Klomp, A.C. (Dutch contractor,
  architect, 20th c.)   BA
  Bibl: Brederoo, NEDERLANDS
  KUNSTHIST.JAARBK, XXXI(1980),
  555-562; Klomp, DE BERGENSCHE
  SCHOOL

Klomp, Aelbert → see Klomp, Albert
  Jansz.
Klomp, Albert → see Klomp, Albert
  Jansz.

Klomp, Albert Jansz.   BA PR
  (Dutch artist, c.1618-1688(?))   WC
  (Dutch painter,
  ca.1618-1688/89)   BA PR
  (Dutch, ca.1618-ca.1688)   GC
  Bibl: ▶Bénézit; George Goldner;
  ▶RILA/BHA; ▶Thieme-Becker;
  ▶Witt checklist; ▶Wurzbach, NLD
  Künst.-Lex.

  A. Klomp   PR
  Albert Jansz. Klomp   PR
  Albert Klomp   PR
  Clomp   PR
  Cloomp   PR
  Clump   PR
  Klomp   PR

Klomp or Clomp, Albert Jansz.   WC
Klomp, Aelbert   GC
  Klomp, Albert   PR
  Komp   PR
  Van Clomp   PR

Klomp, Folly (Dutch painter, b.1944)   BA
  Bibl: Amsterdam (NLD), Stedelijk
  Museum, 11 Schilders (1976)

Kloos, Jan (Dutch architect, b.1905)   BA
  Bibl: Bock, Somer, ARCHITECT J.P.
  KLOOS... (1986)

Klop, Jantje (Dutch draughtsman,
  b.1946)   GC
  Bibl: ▶Scheen, Ned. beeldende
  kunst.

Klophaus, Annalies *(German painter, poet, b.1940)*   BA
Bibl: ▸WW Arts DEU

Klophaus, Ute *(German photographer, 20th c.)*   BA
Bibl: Munich (DEU), Stadt. Gall. im Lenbachhaus. JOSEPH BEUYS: ZEIGE DEIRE WUNDE (1980)

Klopper, Brian *(Australian architect, North Fremantle)*   AV
Bibl: The Architect, W.A., 1987, v.27, no.2, p.21

Klopper, Jan *(Scandinavian artist, op.1702-m.1734)*   WC

Klos, Joachim *(German painter, printmaker, b.1931)*   BA
Bibl: ▸WW Arts DEU

Klose, Carl Friedrich Wilhelm
(German painter, architect, 1804-after 1863)   BA
Bibl: ▸Bénézit; ▸Thieme-Becker

Klose, Wilhelm   GC WC
(German artist, 1830-1914)   WC
(German, 1830-1914)   GC
Bibl: ▸Witt checklist

Klosowski, Alfred *(German artist, 20th cent.)*   WC

Kloss, Friedrich *(German artist, op. 1783-c.1790)*   WC

Kloss, Friedrich Theodor   BA
(German artist, 1802-1876)   WC
(German painter, printmaker, 1802-1876)   BA
Bibl: ▸Bénézit; ▸Busse, Maler u. Bildhauer 19. Jahr.; ▸Thieme-Becker; ▸Weilbach, Kunst.leks.

Kloss, Friedrich Theodore   WC
Kloss, Friedrich Theodore→see Kloss, Friedrich Theodor

Kloss, Gene (Alice Geneva Glasier)
(American printmaker, painter, b.1903)   BA
Bibl: ▸Havlice, Idx. art. bio.; ▸WW Amer. Art, 1976; ▸WWW Amer. art

Kloss, Hans *(German artist, 20th cent.)*   WC

Klossowski de Rola, Balthasar→see Balthus

Klossowski, Erich *(German artist, 1875-1949)*   WC

Klossowski, Pierre *(French painter, author, b.1905)*   BA
Bibl: ▸Bénézit; ▸Intl. dir. exh. artists, 1983; ▸MoMA libr. cat.

Kloster, Louis *(Norwegian architect, Stavenger, 1932-)*   AV
Bibl: Byggekunst: the Norwegian review of architecture, 1985, v.67, no.8, p.432

Kloth, Mark *(American artist, b.1954)*   BA
Bibl: New York (NY, USA), Guggenheim Mus., New horizons (1985)

Klotz, Bernard   GC WC
(Dutch artist, op.1672)   WC
(Dutch draughtsman, act.1672)   GC
Bibl: ▸Witt checklist

Klotz, Caspar Gerhard *(German artist, 1774-1847)*   WC

Klotz, Clemes *(German architect, 1886-)*   AV
Bibl: ▸Thieme-Becker

Klotz, Clots or Clotz, Valentin→see Klotz, Valentin

Klotz, Gustav-François *(French architect, 1810-1880)*   BA
Bibl: ▸Avery obit. idx., 1980; ▸Portoghesi, Diz. arch. e urbanistica; Prunet, Pierre, MONUMENTS HISTORIQUES DE LA FRANCE/153 (Oct, 1987) 45-49; Reclams, FRANKREICH II (1980)

Klotz, Heinrich *(West German architect and historian, Frankfurt, 1935-)*   AV
Bibl: ▸Libr. of Congr. Name Auth. File, date from 678 field

Klotz, Lenz   BA WC
(Swiss artist, 1925-)   WC
(Swiss painter, sculptor, b.1925)   BA
Bibl: ▸Lex. zeitgen. Schweiz. Künstler; LZK

Klotz, Lorenz→see Lorentz, Klotz

Klotz, Matthias   BA GC WC
(German artist, 1748-1821)   WC
(German painter, printmaker, 1748-1821)   BA
(German, 1748-1821)   GC
Bibl: ▸Bénézit; ▸Thieme-Becker; ▸Witt checklist

Klotz, Simon Petrus   GC WC
(German artist, 1776-1824)   WC
(German draughtsman, 1776-1824)   GC
Bibl: Getty Photo Study Coll.; ▸Thieme-Becker

Klotz, Trafford *(British artist, op. circa 1951-)*   WI

Klotz, Valentin   BA GC
(Dutch artist, op.1669-1697)   WC
(Dutch draftsman, engineer, act. 1669-1697)   BA
(Dutch, act.1669-1697)   GC
Bibl: ▸Thieme-Becker; ▸Witt checklist; ▸Wurzbach, NLD Künst.-Lex.

Klotz, Clots or Clotz, Valentin   WC

Klotz-Reilly, Suzanne Ruth
(American painter, sculptor, b.1944)   BA
Bibl: ▸WW Amer. Art, 1978

Klotza, Giorgio   BA
(Cretan painter, illuminator, 1540-1609)   BA
(Greek painter, 16th c.)   BA
Bibl: ARTE VENETA, XXXII(1978), 238-252; Bandera Viani, ARTE DOCUMENTO, 3 (1989), 72-87 BHA/ITA; Constantudaki-Kitromilides, THESAURISMATU, XVIII(1981), 145; Rice, Icons, p.61; Rothemund, B., ... IKONENKUNST (1966), p.79

Klotzas, George   BA
Klotzas, George→see Klotza, Giorgio

Klötzer, Bernd *(German artist, educator, b.1941)*   BA
Bibl: Munich(DEU), Stad.Gal.im Lenbachhaus. BERND KLOTZER... (1981); ▸WW Arts DEU

Klovic, Julije→see Clovio, Giorgio Giulio (Julije Klovic)

Kluber, Hans Hug   BA
(Swiss artist, 1535/6-1578)   WC
(Swiss painter, 1535/36-1578)   BA
Bibl: Clark Art Inst. Libr.; ▸Schweiz. Künst.-Lex.; ▸Thieme-Becker

Klauber, Kluber or Gluber, Hans Hug   WC

Klucis, Gustav Gustavovich→see Klutsis, Gustav Gustavovič

Klug, Ingo *(Austrian architect, Graz)*   AV
Bibl: ▸Verzeich. Öst. Ziviltech.

Kluge, Gustav *(West German painter, printmaker, b.1947)*   BA
Bibl: Bardon, A., PRINT COLLECTOR'S NEWSLETTER, XVII/5 (Nov-Dec 1986) p.163

Kluge, Janice *(American sculptor, 20th c.)*   BA
Bibl: Fariello, SOUTHEASTERN COLLEGE ART CONFERENCE REVIEW, XI/3 (1988), p. 233-235

Klügmann Painter *(vase-painter, ca. 450-420 BC)*   GC
Bibl: ▸Beazley, Attic red-fig. vase-ptrs.; Richter, Attic red-fig. vases

Klumb, Henry *(American architect, active in Puerto Rico, 1904-1984)*   AV
Bibl: Architecture: the AIA journal, 1985 Jan., v.74, no.1, p.94

Klumbke→see Klumpke, Anna Elizabeth

Klumbke, Anna Elisabeth→see Klumpke, Anna Elizabeth

Klumpke, Anna Elizabeth   PR WI
(American artist, 1856-1942)   WI
(American painter, 1856-1942)   PR
Bibl: ▸Fielding's Amer. ptrs.; ▸WWW Amer. art

Anna Elisabeth Klumbke   PR
Klumbke   PR

Klumbke, Anna Elisabeth   PR

Klumpp, Hans *(German architect, Stuttgart)*   AV
Bibl: Baumeister, 1985 Jan., v.82, no.1, p.62

Klumpp, Hermann (German artist, b.1902) **BA**
Bibl: Gardner, CONNOISSEUR CCXV/886 (Nov 1985) 1320135; Richard, Encyc. du Bauhaus, p.197; Wingler, Bauhaus, p.554

Klumpp, Thomas **AV BA**
(German architect, b.1943) **BA**
(West German architect, 1943-) **AV**
Bibl: Kunstwerk, XXXII/2-3 (Apr.-Jun. 1979) p.59

Klumpp, Walter (German architect) **AV**
Bibl: Bauwelt, 1986 May 23, v.77, no.19-20, p.693

Klunder, Harold (Dutch painter in CAN, b.1943) **BA**
Bibl: Montreal(ONT, CAN), Concord Univ.,Art Gallery. HAROLD KLUNDER(1985); Winnipeg(MAN, CAN), Art Gallery. DAVID CRAVEN...(1980)

Klur, Hans (German, b.1499) **BA**
Bibl: Jahrb. der Berliner Museen XXI (1979), 119-135

Klusemann, Georg (German painter, sculptor, printmaker, b.1942) **BA**
Bibl: Xanten(DEU), Regional Museum. GEORGE KLUSEMANN... (1980)

Kluska, Stanislaw (Polish artist, 20th cent.) **WC**

Kluth, Ewald (German artist, -1923) **WC**

Klutho, Henry John (American architect, 1873-1964) **BA**
Bibl: HISTORIC PRESERVATION, XXX/1(JAN-MAR 1978), 16-19

Klutsis, Gustav Gustavovič **BA**
(Russian artist, 1895-1944) **BA**
(Russian, active 20th century) **JG**
Bibl: ▶Bowlt, Russian avant-garde

Klucis, Gustav Gustavovich **JG**

Kluyver, Pieter Lodewijk Francisco **GC WC**
(Dutch artist, 1816-1900) **WC**
(Dutch painter, 1816-1900) **GC**
Bibl: ▶Thieme-Becker

Klyberg, Carl (Scandinavian artist, 1878-1952) **WC**

Klyčev, Izzat Nazarovič (Russian painter, b.1923) **BA**
Bibl: ▶Encyc. world art; ▶Fogg Mus. Libr. cat.; Prom. persons USSR

Klyher, Anton von (German, act.1729/31) **GC**
Bibl: ▶Thieme-Becker

Kmetty, János **BA WC**
(Hungarian artist, 1889-) **WC**
(Hungarian painter, printmaker, 1889-1976) **BA**
Bibl: Arts Council GBR, Hungarian avant-garde (1980); ▶Bénézit; ▶Vollmer, Künst.-Lex. 20. Jhr.

Kmit, Michael (Australian artist, 1910-) **WC**

Knaack, Donald (American artist, 20th c.) **BA**
Bibl: ▶Art Index; ARTS MAGAZINE, LVII(4 DEC 1982)

Knab, Ferdinand (German artist, 1834-1902) **WC**

Knabe, Hanns (German artist, op. 1481) **WC**

Knabl, Josef (German sculptor, 1819-1881) **BA**
Bibl: ▶Bénézit; ▶Thieme-Becker

Knackfuss Painter (Etruscan vase-painter) **GC**
Bibl: ▶Szilagyi, Etruszko-korinthosi

Knackfuss, Hermann Joseph Wilhelm (German artist, 1848-1915) **WC**

Knaefler, James A. (American architect, fl. 1920's) **AV**
Bibl: Architectural digest, 1987 Dec., v.44, no.12, p.112

Knap, G. (German artist, op.1770) **WC**

Knap, Jan (German painter, b.1949) **BA**
Bibl: Aachen (DEU), Neue Gallerie, Normal (1981)

Knapkiewicz, Katharina (Swiss architect, Zurich) **AV**
Bibl: Werk, Bauen + Wohnen. 1989 June, no.6, p.71

Knapp, Beate (German painter, b.1952) **BA**
Bibl: Stuttgart (DEU), Württemb. Kunstverein, 16 Künstler (1978)

Knapp, Charles W. (American artist, 1823-1900) **WC WI**

Knapp, Gerhard (West German architect) **AV**
Bibl: Deutsche Bauzeitung, 1989 Sept., v 123, no.9, p.44

Knapp, Heinz Josef (German architect, Baden-Baden) **AV**
Bibl: ▶Bund Deut. Arch. Hdbch., 1987

Knapp, Johann **GC WC**
(Austrian painter, 1778-1833) **GC**
(German artist, 1778-1833) **WC**
Bibl: Getty Photo Study Coll.; ▶Witt checklist

Knapp, Joseph (German artist, -1867) **WC**

Knapp, O. (German artist, 19th cent.) **WC**

Knapp, Peter (Swiss photographer, painter in FRA, b.1931) **BA**
Bibl: ▶Bénézit; ▶Vollmer, Künst.-Lex. 20. Jhr., suppl.

Knapp, Stefan **WC WI**
(British artist, 1921-) **WC**
(British artist, b.1921) **WI**

Knappe or Knapp, Carl Friedrich Ivanovitch (Russian artist, 1745-1808) **WC**

Knäpper, Gerd (German ceramist, 20th c.) **BA**
Bibl: CERAMICS M.,XXXIX(MAY 1981), 35-38

Knapton → see Knapton, George

Knapton, Charles (British artist, 1700-1760) **WC WI**

Knapton, George **GC PR WC WI**
(British artist, 1698-1778) **WC WI**
(British painter, 1698-1778) **PR**
(British, 1698-1778) **GC**
Bibl: ▶Thieme-Becker; ▶Witt checklist

George Knapton **PR**
Knapton **PR**

Knarren, Petrus Renier Hubertus (Belgian artist, 1826-1869) **WC**

Knaths → see Knaths, Karl

Knaths, Karl **BA PR WC WI**
(American artist, 1891-) **WC**
(American artist, 1891-1971) **WI**
(American painter, 1891-1971) **BA PR**
Bibl: ▶RILA/BHA; ▶WW Amer. Art

Karl Knaths **PR**
Knaths **PR**
Knaths, Otto Karl **PR**

Knaths, Otto Karl → see Knaths, Karl

Knauf, Werner (German ceramist, b.1895) **BA**
Bibl: Jahrb. der Staatl. Kunstsamml. Baden-Württemberg XII (1975), 205-212

Knaupp, Werner (West German painter, printmaker, b.1936) **BA**
Bibl: ▶Intl. dir. exh. artists, 1983; ▶WW Arts DEU

Knaus → see Knaus, Ludwig

Knaus, Ludwig **BA GC PR WC**
(German artist, 1829-1910) **WC**
(German painter, 1829-1910) **BA PR**
(German, 1829-1910) **GC**
Bibl: ▶Bénézit; ▶RILA/BHA; ▶Thieme-Becker; ▶Witt checklist; Zils, Ludwig Knaus

Knaus **PR**
Ludwig Knaus **PR**

Kneale, Bryan **BA WC WI**
(British artist, 1930-) **WC**
(British artist, b.1930) **WI**
(British sculptor, painter, printmaker, b.1930) **BA**
Bibl: ▶MoMA libr. cat.; ▶Vollmer, Künst.-Lex. 20. Jhr.; ▶Who's Who [GBR], 1977

Kneale, Deborah (American craftsman, b.1952) **BA**
Bibl: Colorado Springs (CO, USA), Fine Arts Ctr., Woodworking in the Rockies (1982)

Knebel, Franz (Swiss artist, 1809-1877) **WC**

Knecht, Hermann (Swiss painter, 1893-1978) **BA**
Bibl: ▶Künst.-Lex. Schweiz 20. Jahrh.; ▶Lex. zeitgen. Schweiz. Künstler

Knecht, Kurt (West German engineer, Ludwigsburg) **AV**
Bibl: Deutsches Architektenblatt, 1989 Mar.1, v.21, no.3, p.282

Knechtel, Tom *(American painter,
  20th c.)*   **BA**
  Bibl: Arts Mag. LIII/8 (Apr 1979),
  p.12; ▶Artweek idx.

Knechtl, Christian *(Austrian
  architect, 1954-)*   **AV**
  Bibl: Ottagono, 1988 Mar., p.20

Kneebone, Eugene *(Australian
  architect)*   **AV**
  Bibl: Architecture Australia, 1985
  Dec., v.74, no.8, p.31

Kneeland *(Active Northampton, MA,
  U.S. ca. 1850 (also J.D. Wells &
  Kneeland))*   **JG**

Kneeland, Gary Scott   **AV**

Kneeling Eros Group *(Campanian
  vase-painters)*   **GC**
  Bibl: ▶Trendall, Red-fig. vases
  Lucania

Kneeling Eros Painter *(South Italian
  vase-painter, 4th century BC)*   **GC**
  Bibl: ▶Trendall, Red-fig. vases
  Lucania

Kneen, William *(British artist, 1862-
  1921)*   **WC WI**

Kneib, Antoine *(French
  cabinetmaker, act.1855-1867)*   **BA**
  Bibl: Jedding, Jahrb. des Museums
  für Kunst und Gewerbe Hamburg
  II (1983), p.73-86

Kneipp, Georg *(German painter,
  1793-1862)*   **BA**
  Bibl: ▶Bénézit; ▶Thieme-Becker

Kneissl, Eberhard *(Austrian
  architect, Vienna)*   **AV**
  Bibl: Bauwelt, 1985 Feb.15, v.76,
  no.6-7, p.236

Knell, Adolphus *(British artist, op.
  1860-1880)*   **WI**
  Bibl: ▶Mallalieu, Brit. watercolour
  artists

Knell, William Adolphus   **GC WC WI**
  (British artist, circa 1808-1875)   **WI**
  (British artist, op.1825-m.1875)   **WC**
  (British, act.1825-d.1875)   **GC**
  Bibl: ▶Witt checklist

Knell, William Calcott   **WC WI**
  (British artist, 1830-op.1876)   **WI**
  (British artist, op.1848-1865)   **WC**
  Bibl: ▶Mallalieu, Brit. watercolour
  artists

*Kneller → see Kneller, Godfrey,
  baronet*
*Kneller or Kniller, Sir Gottfried or
  Godfrey → see Kneller, Godfrey,
  baronet*
*Kneller, Godfrey → see Kneller,
  Godfrey, baronet*

Kneller, Godfrey, baronet   **BA**
  (British artist, 1646-1723)   **WC WI**
  (British painter, 1646-1723)   **PR**
  (British, 1646-1723)   **GC**
  (English painter, 1646-1723)   **BA**
  Bibl: ▶Dict. natl. biog.; ▶Encyc.
  world art; ▶RILA/BHA;
  ▶Thieme-Becker; ▶Witt checklist

  G. Kneller   **PR**
  Godfrey Kneller   **PR**
  Kneller   **PR**

**Kneller or Kniller, Sir Gottfried
  or Godfrey**   **WC**
Kneller, Godfrey   **GC PR WI**
Kneller, Godfrey, Bart.   **PR**
  Kneller, Godfrey, Sir   **PR**
  Sir G Kneller   **PR**
  Sir G. Kneller   **PR**
  Sir Godfrey Kneller   **PR**
  Sir J. Kneller   **PR**
  Sir. G. Kneller   **PR**
  Sr Godfery Kneller   **PR**
  Sr Godfrey Kneler   **PR**
  Sr Godfrey Kneller   **PR**
  Sr Godfrey Neler   **PR**
*Kneller, Godfrey, Bart. → see Kneller,
  Godfrey, baronet*
*Kneller, Godfrey, Sir → see Kneller,
  Godfrey, baronet*

Kneller, John Zachary   **VO**
  (British painter, 1644-1702)   **VO**
  (German artist, 1644-1702)   **WC**
  Bibl: Croft-Murray, Dec. ptg.
  England, v. 1, p. 249; ▶Libr. of
  Congr. Name Auth. File,
  NAFR9233628

**Kniller or Kneller, Johann
  Zacharias**   **WC**

Knesl, Hans *(Austrian sculptor,
  1905-1971)*   **BA**
  Bibl: ▶Bénézit; Ingenl, BILDENDE
  KUNST, 2 (1984) 56-59

Knewstub, Walter Holmes *(British
  artist, op.circa 1882-)*   **WI**

Knewstub, Walter John *(British
  artist, 1831-1906)*   **WI**

Knez, Janez *(Yugoslav painter,
  printmaker, b.1931)*   **BA**
  Bibl: ▶Intl. dir. exh. artists, 1983;
  Ljubljana(YUG), Mala Galerija.
  JANEZ KNEZ(1982)

*Knibbergen → see Knibbergen,
  Francois*
*Knibbergen or Knipbergen, Francois
  van → see Knibbergen, Francois*

Knibbergen, Catharina van   **GC**
  (Dutch artist, op.1634-1672)   **WC**
  (Dutch painter, act.1634-1672)   **GC**
  Bibl: ▶Thieme-Becker
  Hen, Catharina de   **GC**

**Knibbergen, Catherina van
  (Catherina de Hen or de
  Witte)**   **WC**
  Witte, Catharina de   **GC**

*Knibbergen, Catherina van (Catherina
  de Hen or de Witte) → see
  Knibbergen, Catharina van*

Knibbergen, Francois   **GC PR**
  (Dutch artist, 1597(?)-p.1665)   **WC**
  *(Dutch painter, act. 17th
  century)*   **PR**
  (Dutch, b. ca.1597)   **GC**
  Bibl: George Goldner;
  Schoonsteen inventory 1647;
  ▶Thieme-Becker; ▶Witt checklist

  Cnibbergen   **PR**
  Francois Knibbergen   **PR**
  Francois Knipbergen   **PR**
  Knibbergen   **PR**

**Knibbergen or Knipbergen,
  Francois van**   **WC**
  Knipbergen   **PR**

Knibbs, Gary *(British interior
  designer)*   **AV**
  Bibl: Designers' journal, 1989 July-
  Aug., no.49, p.11

Knickerbocker *(Active New York,
  NY, U.S. 1844-1845,
  daguerreotypist)*   **JG**

Kniep, Christoph Heinrich   **BA GC WC**
  (German artist, 1755-1825)   **WC**
  (German painter, 1755-1825)   **BA**
  (German, 1755-1825)   **GC**
  Bibl: ▶Neue deutsche Biog.;
  ▶Thieme-Becker; ▶Witt checklist

*Knieper or Knipper, Hans (Johan von
  Antwerpen or Hans Maler) → see
  Knieper, Hans*

Knieper, Hans   **BA**
  *(Flemish painter in DNK, act.
  1577, d.1587)*   **BA**
  *(Netherlands artist, op.1577-m.
  1587)*   **WC**
  Bibl: ▶Nørregård-Nielsen, Dansk
  kunst; ▶Thieme-Becker

**Knieper or Knipper, Hans (Johan
  von Antwerpen or Hans
  Maler)**   **WC**

Knifton, Thomas *(English
  clockmaker, 1614-1666)*   **BA**
  Bibl: ▶Baillie, Watch- &
  clockmkrs.; Dawson et al, EARLY
  ENGLISH CLOCKS, p. 62; White,
  ANTIQUARIES JOURNAL, LXVII
  (1987), p. 324-337

Knight → see Knight, Frederic Charles
Knight → see Knight, Louis Aston

Knight family *(American painters,
  19th-20th cs.)*   **BA**
  Bibl: Ithaca (NY, USA), Cornell
  Univ., Johnson Mus. of Art,
  Pastoral legacy (1989);
  ▶Thieme-Becker

Knight, A. Roland   **WC WI**
  (British artist, 19th cent.)   **WC**
  (British artist, op.1810-1840)   **WI**

*Knight, Aston → see Knight, Louis
  Aston*
Knight, Avel de → see de Knight, Avel
Knight, Charles → see Knight, Charles I

Knight, Charles →see Knight, Charles III

Knight, Charles I   **WI**
   (British artist, 1743-c.1826)   WC
   (British artist, 1743-circa 1826)   WI
  Knight, Charles   **WC**
Knight, Charles II (British artist, 1791-1873)   **WI**
Knight, Charles III   **WI**
   (British artist, 1901-)   WC
   (British artist, b.1901)   WI
  Knight, Charles   **WC**
Knight, Charles Neil (British artist, 1865-op.1942)   **WI**
Knight, Charles Parsons (British artist, 1829-1897)   **WC WI**
Knight, Charles Robert (American artist, 1874-1953)   **WI**
Knight, Dame Laura, (nee Johnson) →see Knight, Laura
Knight, Daniel Ridgway   **PR WI**
   (American artist, 1839-1924)   WC WI
   (American painter, 1839-1824)   PR
   Bibl: ▶Thieme-Becker
  Knight, Ridgway   **PR**
  Knight, Ridgway (Daniel Ridgway)   **WC**
  Ridgway Knight   PR
Knight, Frederic C. →see Knight, Frederic Charles
Knight, Frederic Charles   **BA PR**
   (American painter, 1898-1979)   BA
   (American painter, b. 1898)   PR
   Bibl: ▶Artist biog. master idx.;
    ▶WWW Amer. art
  Frederic Charles Knight   PR
  Knight   PR
  Knight, Frederic C.   PR
Knight, George (British artist, op. circa 1875-)   **WI**
Knight, Harold (British artist, 1874-1961)   **WC WI**
Knight, Henry (English, 1737-1771)   **BA**
   Bibl: COUNTRY LIFE, CLXII(OCT 1977), 1006-9
Knight, Horace (British artist, op. 1917-1920)   **WI**
   Bibl: ▶Johnson, Brit. artists
Knight, John (American conceptual artist, b.1945.)   **BA**
   Bibl: ▶Intl. dir. exh. artists, 1983;
    ▶WW Amer. Art, 1989
Knight, John →see Knight, John William Buxton
Knight, John Baverstock (British artist, 1785-1859)   **WC WI**
Knight, John Prescott (British artist, 1803-1881)   **WC WI**

Knight, John William Buxton   **BA PR WC WI**
   (British artist, 1843-1908)   WC WI
   (British painter, 1842-1908)   PR
   (British painter, 1842/43-1908)   BA
   Bibl: ▶Fisher, Watercolour ptrs.;
    ▶RILA/BHA; ▶Wood, Victorian ptrs.
  John William Buxton Knight   PR
  Knight, John   PR
Knight, Joseph →see Knight, Joseph I
Knight, Joseph I   **WI**
   (British artist, 1837-1909)   WC WI
  Knight, Joseph   **WC**
Knight, Joseph II (British artist, 1870-1952)   **WI**
Knight, Laura   **BA PR WI**
   (British artist, 1877-1970)   WC WI
   (British painter, 1877-1970)   PR
   (British painter, printmaker, 1877-1970)   BA
   Bibl: ▶Johnson, Brit. artists;
    ▶RILA/BHA
  Johnson, Laura, Miss   WI
  Knight, Dame Laura, (nee Johnson)   **WC**
  Knight, Laura, Dame   PR
  Laura Knight   PR
Knight, Laura, Dame →see Knight, Laura
Knight, Lester B. (American architect)   **AV**
   Bibl: ▶AIA Pro File, 1985
Knight, Louis Aston   **BA PR WC WI**
   (American artist, 1873-1948)   WC WI
   (American painter, 1873-1948)   BA
   (French painter, 1873-1948)   PR
   Bibl: ▶Bénézit; ▶Fielding's Amer.
   ptrs.; Ithaca (NY, USA), Cornell
   Univ., Johnson Mus. of Art,
   Pastoral legacy (1989);
   ▶Thieme-Becker; ▶Witt checklist;
   ▶WWW Amer. art
  Knight   PR
  Knight, Aston   PR
  Louis Aston Knight   PR
Knight, Loxton   **WC WI**
   (British artist, 1905-)   WC
   (British artist, b.1905)   WI
Knight, Mary Ann (British artist, 1776-1851)   **WC WI**
Knight, Richard Payne (British classicist, connoisseur and aesthetician, noteworthy architecturally for Downton Castle, Hertfordshire, which he designed for himself, 1750-1824)   **AV**
   Bibl: ▶Macmillan encyc. archts.
Knight, Ridgway →see Knight, Daniel Ridgway
Knight, Ridgway (Daniel Ridgway) →see Knight, Daniel Ridgway
Knight, Robbert (Dutch painter, 17th century)   **GC**
   Bibl: ▶Bénézit

Knight, Robert (British artist, op. 20th c.)   **WI**
Knight, Russell W. (American, 20th c.)   **BA**
Knight, W.G.   **WC WI**
   (British artist, 19th cent.)   WC
   (British artist, op.19th c.)   WI
Knight, William (British artist, op. 1807-1845)   **WC WI**
Knight, William Henry (British artist, 1823-1863)   **WC WI**
Knightley, Thomas Edward (British architect, 1823-1905)   **BA**
   Bibl: ▶Arch. period. idx./RIBA;
   ▶Avery obit. idx.; ▶Wodehouse, Brit. archts.
Knights, Winifred, Miss →see Monington, Winifred
Knijff →see Knijff, Wouter
Knijff or Knijf, Wouter →see Knijff, Wouter
Knijff, Jacob →see Knyff, Jacob
Knijff, Leendert →see Knyff, Leonard
Knijff, Leendert or Leonard →see Knyff, Leonard
Knijff, Wouter   **GC PR**
   (Dutch artist, c.1607-p.1693)   WC
   (Dutch painter, ca.1607-aft. 1693)   PR
   (Dutch, ca.1607-aft.1693)   GC
   Bibl: ▶Thieme-Becker; ▶Witt checklist
  Knijff   PR
  Knijff or Knijf, Wouter   **WC**
  Knyff, Wouter   PR
  Wouter Knijff   PR
Knikker, Aris (Dutch painter, 1887-1962)   **GC**
   Bibl: ▶Scheen, Ned. beeldende kunst.
Knille, Otto (German artist, 1832-1898)   **WC**
Kniller or Kneller, Johann Zacharias →see Kneller, John Zachary
Kniller, Kneller or Knoller, Zacharias (German artist, 1611-1675)   **WC**
Knina, Gustav (Austrian scenographer, 20th c.)   **BA**
   Bibl: Golsmith-Reber, Turn of the Century, 291-310; Huesmann, Welt Theater Reinhardt
Knip, Antoinette Pauline Jacqueline, (nee Rifer de Courcelles) →see Knip, Pauline de
Knip, August (Dutch painter and printmaker, 1819-ca.1852)   **GC**
   Bibl: ▶Thieme-Becker
Knip, Hendrik Johannes   **GC WC**
   (Dutch artist, 1819-)   WC
   (Dutch painter, 1819-1897/1911)   GC
   Bibl: ▶Thieme-Becker

AV Avery Index   **BA** Bibl Hist of Art   **CE** Census Antique Works   **FA** Fndn Docs of Arch   **GC** Getty Ctr Photo Study Coll

Knip, Henriette Gertruide   GC WC
   (Dutch artist, 1783-1842)   WC
   (Dutch painter, 1783-1842)   GC
   Bibl: ▶Thieme-Becker
Knip, Joseph August   BA
   (Dutch artist, 1777-1847)   WC
   (Dutch painter, printmaker, 1777-1847)   BA
   (Dutch, 1777-1847)   GC
   Bibl: ▶Bénézit; George Goldner; ▶Nieuw NLD biog. woord.; ▶Thieme-Becker; ▶Witt checklist; ▶Wurzbach, NLD Künst.-Lex.
Knip, Josephus Augustus   GC WC
Knip, Josephus Augustus → see Knip, Joseph August
Knip, Marten Derk   GC
   (Dutch artist, 1785-1845)   WC
   (Dutch draughtsman, 1785-1845)   GC
   Bibl: ▶Thieme-Becker
Knip, Matthijs Dirk   WC
Knip, Matthijs Dirk → see Knip, Marten Derk
Knip, Nicolaas Frederik I   GC
   (Dutch artist, 1742-c.1809)   WC
   (Dutch painter, 1742-1809)   GC
   Bibl: ▶Thieme-Becker
Knip, Nicolaas Frederik, I   WC
Knip, Nicolaas Frederik, I → see Knip, Nicolaas Frederik I
Knip, Pauline de   GC
   (French artist, 1781-1851)   WC
   (French painter, 1781-1851)   GC
   Bibl: ▶Thieme-Becker
Knip, Antoinette Pauline Jacqueline, (nee Rifer de Courcelles)   WC
Knip, Willem Alexander   GC WC
   (Dutch artist, 1883-1967)   WC
   (Dutch painter, 1883-1967)   GC
   Bibl: ▶Vollmer, Künst.-Lex. 20. Jhr.
Knipbergen → see Knibbergen, Francois
Knipe, Eliza *(British artist, op.1784-1787)*   WC WI
Knipp, Günther *(German painter, b.1935)*   BA
   Bibl: ▶Intl. dir. exh. artists; ▶MoMA libr. cat.
Knipper, Johann Adam   AV WC
   (German architect, fl. 1780-1818)   AV
   (German artist, op.1780-1818)   WC
   Bibl: ▶Thieme-Becker; ▶Witt checklist
Knippert → see Knupfer, Nikolaus
Knipschild, Robert *(American painter, b.1927)*   BA
   Bibl: ▶WW Amer. Art, 1989
Knirsch, Jürgen *(German architect, Heidelberg)*   AV
   Bibl: Architektur, Innenarchitektur, Technischer Ausbau, 1984 Nov.-Dec., v.92, no.8, p.36

Knirsch, Otto   WC WI
   (American artist, op.1855-1865)   WI
   (American artist, op.c.1860)   WC
   (Engraver, op.1855-1865)   WI
Knispel, Ulrich *(German artist, 1911-)*   WC
Knížák, Milan *(Czech artist, musician, b.1940)*   BA
   Bibl: ▶Contemp. artists
Knöbell, Johann Friedrich *(German, 1724-1792)*   GC
   Bibl: ▶Thieme-Becker
Knobelsdorff, Georg Wenceslaus von   BA GC WC
   (German architect and artist, 1699-1753)   AV
   (German architect, painter, 1699-1753)   BA
   (German artist, 1699-1753)   WC
   (German painter, 1699-1753)   GC
   Bibl: ▶Brockhaus Enzyk.; ▶Thieme-Becker
Knobelsdorff, Georg Wenceslaus, Freiherr von   AV
   Knobelsdorff, George Wenzeslaus von   AV
Knobelsdorff, Georg Wenceslaus, Freiherr von → see Knobelsdorff, Georg Wenceslaus von
Knobelsdorff, George Wenzeslaus von → see Knobelsdorff, Georg Wenceslaus von
Knoblauch, Carl Heinrich Eduard *(German architect, 1801-1865)*   BA
   Bibl: ▶Macmillan encyc. archts.; ▶Natl. union cat.; ▶Thieme-Becker
Knoblock, Laura *(British artist, b.1957)*   WI
Knoche, Michael *(West German architect, Münster)*   AV
   Bibl: ▶Bund Deut. Arch. Hdbch., 1987
Knodel, Gerhardt *(American artist, b.1940)*   BA
   Bibl: ▶Babington Smith, Contemp. artists; Flint (MI, USA), Inst. Arts, Fiberworks: Michigan (1980)
Knoder, Hans *(act. ca.1508)*   GC
   Bibl: ▶Thieme-Becker
Knoebel, David *(American sculptor, b.1949.)*   BA
   Bibl: ▶Babington Smith, Contemp. artists; ▶WW Amer. Art, 1989
Knoebel, Imi *(German artist, b.1940)*   BA
   Bibl: ▶Guide exh. artists: Sculp.; ▶Intl. dir. exh. artists, 1983
Knoebel, Wolf *(German artist, b.1940)*   BA
   Bibl: ▶Babington Smith, Contemp. artists; ▶DuMonts Künst.-Lex.
Knoeller, Julius F. *(Swiss architect, worked in Brazil)*   AV
   Bibl: Architectural digest, 1987 Spring, v.44, no.3(supp.), p.38

Knoff, Anne-Lise *(Norwegian printmaker, painter, b.1937)*   BA
   Bibl: ▶Norsk Kunstner Leks., p.553
Knöffel, Johann Christoph   AV BA
   (1686-1752)   AV
   (German architect, 1686-1752)   BA
   Bibl: ▶Macmillan encyc. archts.; ▶Portoghesi, Diz. arch. e urbanistica; ▶Thieme-Becker
Knofler, Heinrich H. *(German artist, 1824-1886)*   WC
Knoll, Florence Schust *(American designer, b.1917)*   BA
   Bibl: ▶Art Index, v.12; ▶Avery period. idx.; WW Amer.
Knoll, Wolfgang *(Austrian architect, practices in Stuttgart, West Germany, 1937-)*   AV
   Bibl: Deutsche Bauzeitung, 1989 Jan., v.123, no.1, p.130
Knoller → see Knoller, Martin
Knoller, Martin   BA GC PR WC
   (Austrian painter and draughtsman, 1725-1804)   GC
   (Austrian painter, 1725-1804)   BA
   (German artist, 1725-1804)   WC
   (German painter, 1725-1804)   PR
   Bibl: ▶Bénézit; ▶Fuchs, Öst. Maler 19. Jahrh.; Getty Photo Study Coll.; ▶RILA/BHA; ▶Thieme-Becker
   Knoller   PR
   Martin Knoller   PR
Knöller, Paco R. *(West German draftsman, b.1950)*   BA
   Bibl: Ulm(DEU), Ulmer Museum. PACO KNOLLER...(1984)
Knoop, August → see Knoop, August Hermann
Knoop, August Hermann   GC
   (German artist, op.1856-1900)   WC
   (German painter, b.1856)   GC
   Bibl: ▶Thieme-Becker
Knoop, August   WC
Knoop, Jan *(Norwegian architect, Oslo)*   AV
   Bibl: Norske Ark. Lands. Årbok 1987
Knoop, Johannes H.   GC
   (Dutch artist, 1769-1833)   WC
   (Dutch painter, 1769-1833)   GC
   Bibl: ▶Thieme-Becker
Knoop, Johannes Hend(e)rik   WC
Knoop, Johannes Hend(e)rik → see Knoop, Johannes H.
Knoop, Ludwig *(German textile manufacturer in Russia, 1821-1894)*   BA
   Bibl: Thompstone, Textile Hist. XV/1 (spring 1984) 45
Knopf, Herbert *(East German architect; moved to West Berlin in 1987, 1942-)*   AV
   Bibl: Architects' journal, 1989 Feb.15, v.189, no.7, p.46
Knopfle, Olga (Olga van Iterson) *(Dutch artist, 1879-1961)*   WC

Knopp, Imre *(Hungarian artist, 1867-)*   **WC**

Knorr, Georg David Salomon *(German artist, 1844-1916)*   **WC**

Knorr, Hugo *(German artist, 1834-1904)*   **WC**

Knorre, Julius *(German artist, 1807-1884)*   **WC**

Knost, Keith H. *(American interior designer, Shepherdstown, W. Va)*   **AV**
Bibl: Southern accents, 1985 July-Aug., v.8, no.4, p.110

Knötel, Richard *(German painter, 1857-1914)*   **GC**
Bibl: ▶Thieme-Becker

Knott, Ralph *(British architect, 1878-1929)*   **BA**
Bibl: ▶Avery obit. idx.; ▶Wodehouse, Brit. archts.

Knott, Taverner   **WC WI**
(British artist, op.1858)   **WC**
(British artist, op.1858-1889)   **WI**

Knottenbelt, Marianna *(Canadian photographer, b.1949)*   **BA**
Bibl: Sackville (NB, CAN), Mt. Allison Univ. Owens Gall., 5 photographers

Knowles, Adrian   **WC WI**
(British artist, 20th cent.)   **WC**
(British artist, op.20th c.)   **WI**

Knowles, Alison *(American artist, b.1933)*   **BA**
Bibl: WW Amer., 1976

Knowles, Bridgett *(Architect, Philadelphia)*   **AV**
Bibl: ▶AIA Pro File, 1983

Knowles, Christopher *(American printmaker, conceptual artist, b.1959)*   **BA**
Bibl: ▶Babington Smith, Contemp. artists; ▶Intl. dir. exh. artists, 1983

Knowles, Davidson   **WC WI**
(British artist, op.1879-1896)   **WC**
(British artist, op.1879-1902)   **WI**

Knowles, Dorothy Elsie *(Canadian painter, b.1927)*   **BA**
Bibl: ▶MacDonald, Can. artists; ▶WW Amer. Art, 1978

Knowles, Edward F. *(American architect, Boston, Mass, 1929-)*   **AV**
Bibl: ▶Contemp. archts.

Knowles, Frederick J. *(British artist, 1874-op.1933)*   **WI**
Bibl: ▶Johnson, Brit. artists

Knowles, George Sheri → see Knowles, George Sheridan

Knowles, George Sheridan   **WI**
(British artist, 1863-1931)   **WC WI**

Knowles, George Sheri   **WC**

Knowles, Harry P. *(American architect, New York City, specialized in design of Masonic buildings, 1871-1944)*   **AV**
Bibl: ▶Withey, Amer. archts.

Knowles, Horace J. *(British artist, op.1908-1948)*   **WI**

Knowles, James Thomas I *(British editor, architect, ca.1806-1884)*   **BA**
Bibl: ▶Avery obit. idx.; ▶Macmillan encyc. archts.

Knowles, James Thomas II *(British architect, 1831-1908)*   **BA**
Bibl: ▶Macmillan encyc. archts.; ▶Wodehouse, Brit. archts.

Knowles, John Christopher *(Architect, Philadelphia)*   **AV**
Bibl: ▶AIA Pro File, 1983

Knowles, Justin   **WC WI**
(British artist, 20th cent.)   **WC**
(British artist, op.20th c.)   **WI**

Knowles, Mike   **BA WI**
(British artist, b.1941)   **WI**
(British painter, b.1941)   **BA**
Bibl: Kingston-upon-Hull (GBR), Ferens Art Gallery, Drawing in action (1978)

Knowles, Stuart *(British artist, b.1948)*   **WI**

Knowles, Victoria *(British artist, op. 20th c.)*   **WI**

Knowlton *(American, active Kankakee, IL, U.S. 19th century (Knowlton & Co.))*   **JG**

Knowlton, Grace Farrar *(American sculptor, photographer, b.1932)*   **BA**
Bibl: ▶Intl. dir. exh. artists, 1983; ▶WW Amer. Art, 1989

Knowlton, Helen Mary *(American painter, journalist, critic, 1832-1918)*   **BA**
Bibl: ▶Collins, Women artists Amer.; ▶Fielding's Amer. ptrs.; ▶Thieme-Becker; ▶Young, Amer. artists

Knowlton, Thomas *(British gardener, botanist, 1692-1781)*   **AV**
Bibl: ▶Hadfield, Brit. gardeners

Knox → see Knox, John

Knox, Archibald   **AV BA WI**
(British artist, 1864-1933)   **WI**
(British landscape painter, Isle of Man)   **AV**
(British painter, designer, 1864-1933)   **BA**
Bibl: ▶Johnson, Brit. artists; ▶Libr. of Congr. Name Auth. File; ▶Mallalieu, Brit. watercolour artists; ▶Wood, Victorian ptrs., v.2

Knox, Bronlow D. *(British artist, op. circa 1873-)*   **WI**

Knox, David   **AV**

Knox, G.J. → see Knox, George James

Knox, George James   **WI**
(British artist, 1810-1897)   **WI**
(British artist, op.1839-1863)   **WC**
Bibl: ▶Mallalieu, Brit. watercolour artists

Knox, G.J.   **WC**

Knox, Jack → see Knox, John

Knox, John   **BA PR WC**
(British artist, 1778-1845)   **WC WI**
(British painter, 1778-1845)   **PR**
(Scottish painter, 1778-1845)   **BA**
Bibl: ▶Bénézit; ▶Thieme-Becker

John Knox   **PR**

Knox   **PR**

Knox, John I   **WI**

Knox, John   **BA WI**
(British artist, 20th cent.)   **WC**
(British artist, b.1936)   **WI**
(British painter, b.1936)   **BA**
Bibl: Edinburgh (GBR), Fruit Market Gallery, Scottish art now (1982); ▶Intl. dir. exh. artists; ▶MoMA libr. cat.

Knox, Jack   **WC**

Knox, John I → see Knox, John

Knox, Mary, Mrs. → see Milward, Mary

Knox, Richard   **WC WI**
(American artist, 20th cent.)   **WC**
(American artist, op.20th c.)   **WI**

Knox, Sonia *(British artist, 20th c.)*   **BA**
Bibl: ▶Intl. dir. exh. artists, 1982; London (GBR), Tate Gallery, Audio arts (1982)

Knubel, F. Rudolf *(German photographer, sculptor, b.1938)*   **BA**
Bibl: Hannover (DEU), Kestner-Gesellschaft, Ursula Schulz-Dornburg (1981); ▶WW Arts DEU

Knud Merrild → see Merrild, Knud

Knudsen, Bertine *(Danish artist, b.1951)*   **BA**
Bibl: Petersen, NORTH-INFORMATION , 155 (1988), P.1-10; ▶RILA/BHA

Knudsen, Christian *(Canadian painter, b.1945)*   **BA**
Bibl: ▶Artists Canada; Montreal (Que, CAN), MFA, 6 propositions (1979); NGG

Knudsen, Jørgen Steen *(Danish architect, Odense, 1948-)*   **AV**
Bibl: ▶Danske Arkitekters Landsforbund, 1984-85

Knudsen, Karl *(Norwegian photographer, 1832-1915)*   **BA**
Bibl: Minneapolis (MN, USA), Walker Art Ctr., Frozen image (1982)

Knudsen, Knud *(Norwegian, active Bergen, Norway 1860s-1870s)*   **JG**

Knudsen, Lars Juel Thiis *(Danish architect, Aarhus, 1955-)*   **AV**
Bibl: ▶Danske Arkitekters Landsforbund, 1984-85

Knudsen, Per *(Norwegian architect)*   **AV**
Bibl: Byggekunst, 1984, no.5, p.236

Knuffer → see Knupfer, Nikolaus

Knupfer → see Knupfer, Nikolaus

Knupfer, Benes or Benesch *(Czech artist, 1848-1910)*   **WC**

Knupfer, Knipper, Knufer or Knupfer, Nicolaus → see Knupfer, Nikolaus

Knüpfer, Nicolaus → see Knupfer,
Nikolaus

Knupfer, Nikolaus **BA JG PR**
    (Dutch artist, c.1603-1655) WC
    (Dutch painter, 1603-1655) BA PR
    (Dutch, 1603-1655) JG
    (Dutch, ca.1603-1655) GC
       Bibl: ▶Aa, Biog. woordenboek
       NLD; ▶Met. Mus. Art libr. cat.;
       ▶RILA/BHA; ▶Thieme-Becker;
       ▶Witt checklist; ▶Wurzbach, NLD
       Künst.-Lex.
    Knippert PR
    Knuffer PR
    Knupfer PR
Knupfer, Knipper, Knufer or
   Knupfer, Nicolaus **WC**
Knüpfer, Nicolaus **GC**
    Nikolaus Knupfer PR

Knutsen, Gunnar *(Norwegian
   architect, Kristiansand)* **AV**
       Bibl: Deutsche Bauzeitung, 1987
       Nov., v.121, no.11, p.49

Knutsen, Knut *(Norwegian
   architect, 1903-1969)* **AV**
       Bibl: ▶Contemp. archts.

Knutson, Ann *(American sculptor,
   b.1948)* **BA**
       Bibl: New York (NY, USA), New
       Mus., Dimensions Variable (1979)

Knutsson, Anders *(American
   painter, b.1937)* **BA**
       Bibl: Guide exh. artists: N. Amer.
       ptrs.; Williamstown (MA, USA),
       Williams College, Mus. of Art,
       ANDERS KNUTSSON...(1989);
       Williamstown (MA, USA),
       Williams College, Mus. of Art,
       Radical Painting (1984), p. 47

Knychalla, Wolfgang *(German
   architect, Pilsach, 1950-)* **AV**
       Bibl: Deutsche Bauzeitung, 1985
       Dec., v.119, no.12, p.112

Knyff, Alfred de *(Belgian artist,
   1819-1885)* **WC**

Knyff, Jacob **BA**
    (Dutch artist, 1639-1681) WC
    *(Dutch painter in FRA, 1639-
    1681)* BA
    (Dutch painter, 1639-1681) GC
       Bibl: ▶Thieme-Becker; ▶Wurzbach,
       NLD Künst.-Lex.

Knijff, Jacob **GC WC**
Knyff, Leonard **BA**
    (Dutch artist, 1650-1721) WC
    *(Dutch painter in England, 1650-
    1721)* BA
    (Dutch, 1650-1721) GC
       Bibl: Clark Art Inst. Photo & Slide
       Dept.; ▶Dict. natl. biog.;
       ▶Thieme-Becker; ▶Witt checklist

Knijff, Leendert **GC**
Knijff, Leendert or Leonard **WC**
Knyff, Wouter → see Knijff, Wouter

Ko, Shun-min *(Japanese architect,
   1946-)* **AV**
       Bibl: Kenchiku bunka, 1987 Dec.,
       v.42, no.494, p.112

Kobakhidzé, Pierre-Alexis *(French
   architect, Paris)* **AV**
       Bibl: ▶Annuaire archts. fran.,
       1978

Kobayashi, Eiji *(Japanese architect,
   1947-)* **AV**
       Bibl: Kenchiku bunka, 1987 Dec.,
       v.42, no.494, p.118

Kobayashi, Haruto *(Japanese
   landscape architect, 1937-)* **AV**
       Bibl: Process: architecture, 1985
       June, no.59, p.142

Kobayashi, Hisashi *(Japanese
   architect, 1944-)* **AV**
       Bibl: Kenchiku bunka, 1987 Dec.,
       v.42, no.494, p.120

Kobayashi, Katsuhiro *(Japanese
   architect, 1955-)* **AV**
       Bibl: Japan architect, 1988 Nov.-
       Dec., v.63, no.11-12, p.28
       [dates]; ▶Libr. of Congr. Name
       Auth. File

Kobayashi, Kayoko *(Japanese
   architect)* **AV**
       Bibl: Japan architect, 1988 Mar.,
       v.63, no.3(371), p.41

Kobayashi, Milt *(American artist,
   b.1949)* **WI**
Kobayashi, Robert *(American
   painter, 20th c.)* **BA**
       Bibl: ARTS MAGAZINE, LVI/3(NOV
       1981), 10
Kobbel → see Kobell, Ferdinand
Kobel → see Kobell, Ferdinand
Köbel, Jacob *(German draughtsman,
   ca.1460-1533)* **GC**
       Bibl: ▶Thieme-Becker
Kobell → see Kobell, Ferdinand
Kobell family *(German painters,
   18th-19th cs.)* **BA**
       Bibl: ▶Allgem. Deut. Biog.;
       ▶Bénézit; ▶Busse, Maler u.
       Bildhauer 19. Jahr.; Grosse Enzyk.
       Malerei; Propyläen
       Kunstgeschichte [vol. not
       specified]; Singer, Allgem.
       Bildniskat.; ▶Thieme-Becker

Kobell, Ferdinand **BA GC PR WC**
    (German artist, 1740-1799) WC
    (German painter, 1740-1799) BA PR
    (German, 1740-1799) GC
       Bibl: ▶RILA/BHA; ▶Thieme-Becker;
       ▶Witt checklist
    Ferdinand Kobell PR
    Kobbel PR
    Kobel PR
    Kobell PR
Kobell, Franz Innocenz Josef **GC WC**
    (German artist, 1749-1822) WC
    (German, 1749-1822) GC
       Bibl: ▶Thieme-Becker; ▶Witt
       checklist
Kobell, Georg *(German artist, 1807-
   1894)* **WC**

Kobell, Hendrik **GC WC**
    (Dutch artist, 1751-1779) WC
    *(Dutch draughtsman, 1751-
    1779)* GC
       Bibl: ▶Bénézit
Kobell, Jan (II) **PR**
    (Dutch artist, 1778-1814) WC
    (Dutch painter, 1778-1814) PR
    (Dutch, 1778-1814) GC
       Bibl: Getty Photo Study Coll.
       (Ptgs.); ▶Thieme-Becker; ▶Witt
       checklist
    Jan Kobell (II) PR
    KObell, Jan (the younger) PR
Kobell, Jan II **GC**
Kobell, Jan, II (Baptist) **WC**
    Kobell, Johannes GC
KObell, Jan (the younger) → see
   Kobell, Jan (II)
Kobell, Jan I **GC**
    (Dutch artist, 1756/7-1833) WC
    (Dutch, 1756-1833) GC
       Bibl: ▶Thieme-Becker; ▶Witt
       checklist
Kobell, Jan, I **WC**
Kobell, Jan II → see Kobell, Jan (II)
Kobell, Jan III **GC**
    (Dutch artist, 1800-1838) WC
    (Dutch painter, 1800-1838) GC
       Bibl: ▶Bénézit
Kobell, Jan, III **WC**
Kobell, Jan, I → see Kobell, Jan I
Kobell, Jan, II (Baptist) → see Kobell,
   Jan (II)
Kobell, Jan, III → see Kobell, Jan III
Kobell, Johannes → see Kobell, Jan (II)
Kobell, Wilhelm Alexander von → see
   Kobell, Wilhelm Alexander
   Wolfgang von
Kobell, Wilhelm Alexander
   Wolfgang von **BA WC**
    (German artist, 1766-1855) WC
    *(German painter, printmaker,
    1766-1855)* BA
    (German, 1766-1855) GC
       Bibl: George Goldner;
       ▶Thieme-Becker; ▶Witt checklist
Kobell, Wilhelm Alexander von **GC**
Kober, Charles *(American architect)* **AV**
       Bibl: ▶AIA Pro File, 1983
Kober, Cober, Koeber or Koebner,
   Martin → see Kober, Marcin
Kober, Marcin **BA GC**
    *(German artist, op.1580-m.a.
    1609)* WC
    (German painter, act.1579-1609) GC
    (Polish painter, act.1580-1609) BA
       Bibl: ▶Bénézit; Giraudon;
       ▶RILA/BHA; ▶Thieme-Becker
Kober, Cober, Koeber or
   Koebner, Martin **WC**
Kober, Martin **GC**
Kober, Martin → see Kober, Marcin
Koberger, Anton *(German printer,
   ca.1445-1513)* **BA**
       Bibl: ▶New Columbia encyc.

Koberling, Bernd (*German painter, b.1938*)   BA
  Bibl: Berlin (DEU), Neuer Berliner Kunstverein, 8 from Berlin (1975); ▶Intl. dir. exh. artists; STUDIO 19(NOV 1975), 250
Koberwein, Georg (*German artist, 1820-1876*)   WC
Koberwein, Georgina, Miss →see Terrell, Georgina Koberwein
Koberwein, Rosa (*British artist, op. circa 1876-*)   WI
Kobilca, Ivana (*Yugoslav painter, 1861-1926*)   BA
  Bibl: ▶Bénézit; ▶Thieme-Becker
Kobitz, F.G. (*German artist, 18th cent.*)   WC
Kobke →see Købke, Christen Schiellerup
Kobke, Christen →see Købke, Christen Schiellerup
Kobke, Christen Schellerup →see Købke, Christen Schiellerup
Kobke, Christen Schiellerup →see Købke, Christen Schiellerup
Købke, Christen Schiellerup   BA PR
  (*Danish artist, 1810-1848*)   WC
  (*Danish painter, 1810-1848*)   GC PR
  (*Danish painter, printmaker, 1810-1848*)   BA
  (*Danish, 1810-1848*)   JG
  Bibl: ▶Bénézit; Clark Art Inst. Libr.; ▶Encyc. world art; ▶RILA/BHA; ▶Thieme-Becker; ▶Weilbach, Kunst.leks.
  Christen Schiellerup Kobke   PR
  Kobke   PR
  Kobke, Christen   PR
Kobke, Christen Schellerup   WC
  Kobke, Christen Schiellerup   PR
Kobke, Christen Schjellerup   JG
Købke, Christen Schjellerup   GC PR
Kobke, Christen Schjellerup →see Købke, Christen Schiellerup
Koblanos of Aphrodisias (*Greek sculptor, 1st c BC*)   GC
  Bibl: Getty Photo Study Coll.
Koblasa, Jan (*Czech sculptor in DEU, b.1932*)   BA
  Bibl: ▶WW Arts DEU
Kobler, Fritz (*German artist, op. 1516*)   WC
Koblic, Premysel (*Czech, active 1930s*)   JG
Kobliha, Frantisek (*Czech artist, 1877-1962*)   WC
Kobold, Gottlieb (*German draughtsman, 1769-1809*)   GC
  Bibl: ▶Thieme-Becker
Kobold, Werner (Johann Werner) (*German artist, c.1740-1803*)   WC
Kobro, Katarzyna (*Polish sculptor, author, 1898-1951*)   BA
  Bibl: ▶Bénézit; ▶Vollmer, Künst.-Lex. 20. Jhr.

Kobzdej, Aleksander (*Polish artist, 1920-*)   WC
Koca Sinan →see Sinan, Mimar
Kočergin, Nikolaj Mihajlovič (*Russian illustrator, designer, 20th c.*)   BA
  Bibl: Matafanov, NIKOLAJ MIHAJLOVIC KOCERGIN(1978)
Kocevar, Frank (*Canadian painter, 1899-1982*)   BA
  Bibl: Kingston (Ont, CAN), Queen's U. Etherington Art Ctr., Contemp. primitives (1982)
Koch, Andreas (*German interior designer, Kassel*)   AV
  Bibl: Architektur, Innenarchitektur, Technischer Ausbau, 1985 Sept., v.93, no.6, p.68
Koch, Carl (*American architect, 1912-*)   AV
  Bibl: ▶Contemp. archts.
Koch, Carl (*German artist, 1827-1905*)   WC
Koch, Dietrich (*East German architect, Frankfurt an der Oder*)   AV
  Bibl: Architektur der DDR, 1987 July, v.36, no.7, p.22
Koch, Elisa (*French artist, 19th cent.*)   WC
Koch, Emil (*German painter, 1902-1975*)   BA
  Bibl: Leipzig(DDR), Museum der bilden kunste. EMIL KOCH... (1978); ▶Vollmer, Künst.-Lex. 20. Jhr.
Koch, Franz Anton (*German artist, 19th cent.*)   WC
Koch, Frederick (*German, active ca. 1900*)   JG
Koch, Georg (Carl Georg) (*German artist, 1857-*)   WC
Koch, Georg Anton (*German artist, 1685-1757*)   WC
Koch, Günther (*German artist, b.1951*)   BA
  Bibl: London (GBR), Goethe Inst., Young German artists (1982)
Koch, Hans Halvorson (*Norwegian artist, op.1752-1796*)   WC
Koch, Hermann (*German artist, 1856-*)   WC
Koch, John   BA WC WI
  (*American artist, 1909-*)   WC
  (*American artist, 1909-1978*)   WI
  (*American painter, collector, 1909-1978*)   BA
  Bibl: ▶Havlice, Idx. art. bio.; NORTH ADAMS(MA, USA), TRANSCRIPT NEWSPAPER(4/21/78); ▶WW Amer. Art, 1976

Koch, Joseph Anton   BA GC WC
  (*Austrian painter, draughtsman, and printmaker, 1768-1839*)   GC
  (*Austrian painter, printmaker, 1768-1839*)   BA
  (*German artist, 1768-1839*)   WC
  Bibl: ▶Brockhaus Enzyk.; ▶Encyc. world art; Getty Photo Study Coll.; ▶RILA/BHA; ▶Thieme-Becker
Koch, Kai-Michael (*West German architect, Hannover*)   AV
  Bibl: Baumeister, 1987 Nov., v.84, no.11, p.28
Koch, Kenneth (*American artist, op. 20th c.*)   WI
Koch, Laura Anne (*American artist, b.1949*)   BA
  Bibl: Sacramento (CA, USA), Crocker Art Museum, Paper/art (1981)
Koch, Louis (*Swiss artist, op.1799-1802*)   WC
Koch, Ludwig (*Swiss artist, 1577-*)   WC
Koch, Ludwig (*German artist, 1866-1934*)   WC
Koch, Markus (*Architect, Austria (?)*)   AV
  Bibl: Aktuelles Bauen, 1985 Spring, v.20, p.36
Koch, Martin (*South African artist, 19th cent.*)   WC
Koch, Matthias   GC WC
  (*German artist, op.1802-1804*)   WC
  (*German printmaker, act.1802-1804*)   GC
  Bibl: ▶Witt checklist
Koch, Max (*German, active ca. 1895*)   JG
Koch, N. (*German(?) artist, op.1749*)   WC
Koch, Pyke   BA GC WC
  (*Dutch artist, 1901-*)   WC
  (*Dutch painter, b.1901*)   BA GC
  Bibl: ▶Bénézit; ▶Contemp. artists, 1983; ▶Intl. dir. exh. artists, 1982; ▶Scheen, Ned. beeldende kunst.; ▶Witt checklist
Koch, Samuel (*American painter, 1887-aft.1946*)   PR
  Bibl: ▶WWW Amer. art
  Kochmeister, Samuel   PR
  Samuel Koch   PR
  Samuel Kochmeister   PR
Koch-Gotha, Fritz (*German artist, 1877-1956*)   WC
Kochanowski, Roman (*Polish artist, 1856/7-1945*)   WC
Kocher, A. Lawrence →see Kocher, Alfred Lawrence
Kocher, Alfred Lawrence (*American architect, 1885-1969*)   AV BA
  Bibl: ▶Avery obit. idx.; ▶Macmillan encyc. archts.; S.A.H. journal, v.41, Dec. 1982, p.328; ▶WWW Amer.
  Kocher, A. Lawrence   AV
Kochmeister, Samuel →see Koch, Samuel

Kochseder, Franz (*West German printmaker, b.1947*)   **BA**
  Bibl: COURTAULD ARTIST INDEX; London(GBR), Goethe Institute. MAN UNDER THREAT...(1984), p.21

Kochta, Herbert (*German architect, Munich*)   **AV**
  Bibl: Detail, 1981 July-Aug., no.4, p.492

Kočíb, Zdeněk (*American painter, 20th c.*)   **BA**
  Bibl: Kočíb, Z., LEONARDO, XIX/2 p.141-144

Kock van Aelst, Pauwels → see Coecke van Aelst, Pauwels

Kock van Aelst, Pieter I → see Coecke van Aelst, Pieter I

Kock Wellens, Hieronymus → see Cock, Hieronymus

Köck, Hanns Peter (*Austrian architect, Salzburg, 1941-*)   **AV**
  Bibl: Deutsche Bauzeitung, 1986 Sept., v.120, no.9, p.182; ▶Verzeich. Öst. Ziviltech.

Kock, Hans (*German sculptor, b.1920*)   **BA**
  Bibl: ▶MoMA libr. cat.; ▶Vollmer, Künst.-Lex. 20. Jhr.; ▶Wer ist wer

Kock, Hieronymus → see Cock, Hieronymus

Kock, Jan Claudius de → see Cock, Jan Claudius de

Kock, Theodor Friedrich (*German artist, 1875-*)   **WC**

Kock, Wellens de → see Cock, Mathys

Kockert → see Köckert, Julius

Köckert, Julius   **GC PR WC**
  (*German artist, 1827-1918*)   **WC**
  (*German painter, 1827-1918*)   GC PR
  Bibl: ▶Bénézit; ▶Thieme-Becker; ▶Witt checklist
  Julius Kockert   PR
  Kockert   PR

Kocks, Adriaen (*Dutch ceramist, act.1686, d.1701*)   **BA**

Kocks, Pieter Adriaensz. (*Dutch ceramist, act.1687-1703*)   **BA**

Kockx, Jacques de → see Cock, Jacques de

Kocsis, Imre (*Hungarian painter, b.1937*)   **BA**
  Bibl: ▶Art Index, 1970; Bonn (DEU), Stadt. Kunstmus., Neue ungarische Konstruktivisten (1975)

Koczor, György (*Hungarian architect*)   **AV**
  Bibl: Magyar építömüvészet, 1987, v.78, no.3, p.44

Kodama, Yuichiro (*Japanese architect, Tsukuba, 1946-*)   **AV**
  Bibl: Kenchiku bunka, 1987 Dec., v.42, no.494, p.114

Koe, Laurence E. Leonard   **WC WI**
  (*British artist, 1868-1913*)   WI
  (*British artist, op.1885-m.1913*)   WC

Koebergher, Wenceslas → see Coebergher, Wenceslas

Koeck, Michele (Keck) (*German artist, 1760-1825*)   **WC**

Koed, Jan (*Danish architect, Copenhagen, 1948-*)   **AV**
  Bibl: ▶Danske Arkitekters Landsforbund, 1984-85

Koedijck → see Koedijck, Isaac

Koedijck, Isaac   **GC PR WC**
  (*Dutch artist, c.1616/18-c.1668*)   WC
  (*Dutch painter, ca.1616/18-ca.1668*)   PR
  (*Dutch, ca.1616/18-ca.1668*)   GC
  Bibl: ▶Thieme-Becker; ▶Witt checklist
  Coedik   PR
  Coedyk   PR
  Isaac Koedijck   PR
  Koedijck   PR
  Kouydyck   PR

Koegler, Kurt (*American, 20th c.*)   **BA**

Koehler, Florence Cary (*American painter, designer, 1861-1944*)   **BA**
  Bibl: Arts Mag. LIII/4 (Dec 1978), 108-117

Koehler, George Frederic → see Koehler, George Frederick

Koehler, George Frederick   **WI**
  (*British artist, op.1780-, d.1800*)   WI
  (*British artist, op.1780-m.1800*)   WC

Koehler, George Frederic   **WC**

Koehler, Henry   **WC WI**
  (*American artist, 1927-*)   WC
  (*American artist, b.1927*)   WI

Koehler, Mela (*German artist, 19th cent.*)   **WC**

Koehler, Reinhold (*West German painter, sculptor, 1919-1970*)   **BA**
  Bibl: Hannover (DEU), Sprengel-Museum, REINHOLD KOEHLER, 1919-1970..., 1985 (RILA/DEU); ▶MoMA libr. cat.; ▶Vollmer, Künst.-Lex. 20. Jhr., v.6

Koehler, Robert   **BA WC**
  (*American painter, printmaker, 1850-1917*)   BA
  (*German artist, 1850-1917*)   WC
  Bibl: ▶Bénézit; ▶Dict. Amer. biog.; ▶Fielding's Amer. ptrs.; ▶Thieme-Becker

Koekkoek → see Koekkoek, Barend Cornelis

Koekkoek, Barend Cornelis   **BA GC PR WC**
  (*Dutch artist, 1803-1862*)   WC
  (*Dutch painter, 1803-1862*)   BA GC PR
  Bibl: ▶Nieuw NLD biog. woord.; ▶RILA/BHA; ▶Scheen, Ned. beeldende kunst.; ▶Thieme-Becker
  Barend Cornelis Koekkoek   PR
  Koekkoek   PR
  Koekkoek, Barend Cornelius   PR

Koekkoek, Barend Cornelius → see Koekkoek, Barend Cornelis

Koekkoek, Gerard   **GC**
  (*Dutch artist, 1871-1956*)   WC
  (*Dutch painter, 1871-1956*)   GC
  Bibl: ▶Thieme-Becker; ▶Witt checklist
  Koekkoek, Gerardus Johannes   GC

Koekkoek, Gerardus Johannes (Gerard)   **WC**

Koekkoek, Gerardus Johannes → see Koekkoek, Gerard

Koekkoek, Gerardus Johannes (Gerard) → see Koekkoek, Gerard

Koekkoek, H.B. → see Koekkoek, Hendrik Barend

Koekkoek, Hendrik Barend   **GC**
  (*Dutch artist, op.1874*)   WC
  (*Dutch painter, 1849-ca.1885*)   GC
  Bibl: ▶Witt checklist

Koekkoek, H.B.   **WC**

Koekkoek, Hendrik Pieter   **GC WC**
  (*Dutch artist, 1843-*)   WC
  (*Dutch painter, 1843-ca.1890*)   GC
  Bibl: ▶Witt checklist

Koekkoek, Herman Willem   **GC PR**
  (*Dutch artist, 1867-1929*)   WC
  (*Dutch painter, 1867-1929*)   GC PR
  Bibl: NY Met catalogue; ▶Thieme-Becker
  Herman Willem Koekkoek   PR

Koekkoek, Hermanus Willem   **WC**

Koekkoek, Hermanus   **BA PR**
  (*Dutch artist, 1815-1882*)   WC
  (*Dutch painter and draughtsman, 1815-1882*)   GC
  (*Dutch painter, 1815-1882*)   BA PR
  Bibl: ▶Bénézit; Getty Photo Study Coll.; ▶Nieuw NLD biog. woord.; ▶RILA/BHA; ▶Thieme-Becker
  Hermanus Koekkoek   PR
  Koekkoek, Hermanus (the Elder)   GC

Koekkoek, Hermanus I   **GC**
Koekkoek, Hermanus, I   **WC**

Koekkoek, Hermanus (the Elder) → see Koekkoek, Hermanus

Koekkoek, Hermanus (the Younger) → see Koekkoek, Hermanus II

Koekkoek, Hermanus I → see Koekkoek, Hermanus

Koekkoek, Hermanus II   **GC**
  (*Dutch artist, 1836-1909*)   WC
  (*Dutch painter, 1836-1909*)   GC
  Bibl: Getty Photo Study Coll.; ▶Witt checklist
  Couver, Jan van   GC
  Koekkoek, Hermanus (the Younger)   GC

Koekkoek, Hermanus, II (Jan van Couver)   **WC**

Koekkoek, Hermanus Willem → see Koekkoek, Herman Willem

Koekkoek, Hermanus, I → see Koekkoek, Hermanus

Koekkoek, Hermanus, II (Jan van Couver) → see Koekkoek, Hermanus II

Koekkoek, Joannes Hermanus
  Barend→see Koekkoek, Johannes
  Herman Barend
Koekkoek, Johannes (Dutch
  painter, 1811-1831)   GC
    Bibl: ▶Bénézit
Koekkoek, Johannes Herman
  Barend   GC
    (Dutch artist, 1840-1912)   WC
    (Dutch painter, 1840-1912)   GC
    Bibl: ▶Thieme-Becker; ▶Witt
      checklist
  Koekkoek, Joannes Hermanus
    Barend   WC
Koekkoek, Johannes Hermanus GC WC
    (Dutch artist, 1778-1851)   WC
    (Dutch painter, 1778-1851)   GC
    Bibl: ▶Thieme-Becker; ▶Witt
      checklist
Koekkoek, Marinus Adrianus I   GC
    (Dutch artist, 1807-1870)   WC
    (Dutch, 1807-1870)   GC
    Bibl: ▶Witt checklist
  Koekkoek, Marinus Adrianus, I   WC
Koekkoek, Marinus Adrianus, I→see
  Koekkoek, Marinus Adrianus I
Koekkoek, Willem   GC WC
    (Dutch artist, 1839-1895)   WC
    (Dutch, 1839-1895)   GC
    Bibl: ▶Witt checklist
Koelhoff, Johann (German printer,
  act.1499)   BA
    Bibl: GESTA, XVII/2(1978), 33-36
Koelink, J. (Dutch architect, Delft) AV
    Bibl: De Architect, 1988 Oct.,
      v.19, no.10, p.73
Koelle, Fritz (German sculptor, 1895-
  1953)   BA
    Bibl: ▶Bénézit; Schmoll gen.
      Eisenwerth, Festschr. Eduard Trier
      (1981); ▶Vollmer, Künst.-Lex. 20.
      Jhr.
Koelman, Jan Philip   BA
    (Dutch painter, sculptor, author,
      1818-1893)   BA
    (Dutch printmaker, 1818-1893)   GC
    Bibl: ▶Grote Winkler Prins;
      ▶Scheen, Ned. beeldende kunst.;
      ▶Thieme-Becker
  Koelman, Johan Philip   GC
Koelman, Johan Daniel   GC WC
    (Dutch artist, 1831-1857)   WC
    (Dutch painter, draughtsman,
      and printmaker, 1831-1857)   GC
    Bibl: ▶Thieme-Becker
Koelman, Johan Hendrik (Dutch
  printmaker, 1820-1887)   GC
    Bibl: ▶Thieme-Becker
Koelman, Johan Philip→see Koelman,
  Jan Philip
Koeman, Jacques J. (Dutch
  printmaker, 1797-1837)   GC
    Bibl: Getty Photo Study Coll.
      (Douwes coll.)

Koen, Gerrit (Dutch goldsmith, act.
  1741-1773)   BA
    Bibl: ANTIEK, XIV(JAN 1980), 409-
      411
Koene→see Koene, Isaac
Koene or Koenen, Isaac→see Koene,
  Isaac
Koene, Isaac   BA GC PR
    (Dutch artist, c.1637/40-1713)   WC
    (Dutch painter, 1637/40-1713)   BA PR
    (Dutch, ca.1637/40-1713)   GC
    Bibl: ▶RILA/BHA; ▶Thieme-Becker;
      ▶Witt checklist; ▶Wurzbach, NLD
      Künst.-Lex.
  Isaac Koene   PR
  Koene   PR
  Koene or Koenen, Isaac   WC
Koenemann, Etvin (German artist,
  1883-1960)   BA
Koenig, Elizabeth (American
  sculptor, 20th c.)   BA
    Bibl: ▶Collins, Women artists
      Amer.; New London(CT, USA),
      Lyman Allyn Museum.
      SCULPTURE; ELIZA.KOENIG(1978)
Koenig, Fritz   BA WC
    (German artist, 1924-)   WC
    (German sculptor, b.1924)   BA
    Bibl: ▶Vollmer, Künst.-Lex. 20.
      Jhr.; ▶Wer ist wer; ▶WW
      Germany, 1974
Koenig, Ghisa→see Koenig, Ghisha
Koenig, Ghisha   BA
    (British artist, b.1922)   WI
    (British sculptor, b.1921)   BA
    Bibl: ▶Intl. dir. exh. artists, 1983;
      London (GBR), Serpentine Gallery,
      GHISKA KOENIG (1986); ▶WW Art
  Koenig, Ghisa   WI
Koenig, Johann→see König, Johann
Koenig, Jules Raymond (French
  painter, b.1872)   GC
    Bibl: ▶Bénézit
Koenig, Pierre (American architect,
  active in Los Angeles, Calif, 1925-) AV
    Bibl: ▶Contemp. archts.
Koenig, Robert (British sculptor,
  20th c.)   BA
    Bibl: Davies, Studio intl.,
      CXCVI/999 (Apr.-May 1983) pp.
      10-13; LCn 8136592
Koeniger→see Koeniger, Walter
Koeniger, Walter   PR WI
    (American artist, b.1881)   WI
    (American painter, 1881-1943)   PR
    Bibl: Univ of Arizona MA
      catalogue; ▶WWW Amer. art
  Koeniger   PR
  Walter Koeniger   PR
Koenigsberg, D. Franklin
    (American, 20th c.)   BA
Köening→see Koninck, Philips de
Koepfli, Elatia (American artist,
  b.1950)   BA
    Bibl: Irvine (CA, USA), UCI Art
      Gallery, Female fantasies (1977)

Koepp, Christian→see Köpp,
  Christian
Koeppel, Matthias (German painter,
  b.1937)   BA
    Bibl: ▶WW Arts DEU
Koeppel, Reinhold   GC WC
    (German artist, 1887-1951)   WC
    (German painter, 1887-1951)   GC
    Bibl: ▶Thieme-Becker
Koerbecke→see Koerbecke, Johann
Koerbecke, Johann   GC PR WC
    (German artist, op.1457-1471)   WC
    (German painter and
      draughtsman, act.1432-d.
      1491)   GC
    (German painter, act. 1457-
      1471)   PR
    Bibl: Berlin; Getty Photo Study
      Coll.; ▶Thieme-Becker; ▶Witt
      checklist
  Johann Koerbecke   PR
  Koerbecke   PR
Koerle, Pancraz (German artist,
  1823-1875)   WC
Koerner, Ernest Carl Eugen
    (German artist, 1846-1927)   WC
  Korner, Ernst   WC
Koerner, Henry (American painter,
  b.1915)   BA
    Bibl: NY Times obit., 9 Jul 1991;
      WW Amer., 1976; ▶WW Amer.
      Art, 1976
Koerner, William Henry David→see
  Koerner, William Henry Dethlef
Koerner, William Henry Dethlef BA WC
    (American artist, 1878-1938)   WI
    (American artist, 20th cent.)   WC
    (American illustrator, 1878-
      1938)   BA
    Bibl: ▶Dawdy, Artists Amer. West;
      ▶MoMA libr. cat.
  Koerner, William Henry David   WI
Koerten, Johanna   BA WC
    (Dutch artist, 1650-1715)   WC
    (Dutch painter, 1650-1715)   BA
    Bibl: ▶Bénézit; ▶Thieme-Becker
Koeslig, Franciscus (Netherlands
  artist, op.1696)   WC
Koester, Alexander→see Koester,
  Alexander Max
Koester, Alexander Max   BA GC
    (German artist, 1864-1932)   WC
    (German painter, 1864-1932)   BA GC
    Bibl: ▶Busse, Maler u. Bildhauer
      19. Jahr.; ▶Thieme-Becker;
      ▶Vollmer, Künst.-Lex. 20. Jhr.
  Koester, Alexander   WC
Koester, Christian (German artist,
  1784-1851)   WC
Koethe, Fritz (West German painter,
  b.1916)   BA
    Bibl: ▶WW Arts DEU
Koets or Coets, Roelof, I (Roelof
  Claessen)→see Koets, Roelof (I)
Koets, Andries (Dutch artist,
  1621/2-p.1661)   WC

Koets, Roelof (I)   PR
    (Dutch artist, c.1592/3-1655)   WC
    (Dutch painter, 1592/3-1655)   GC
    (Dutch painter,
        ca.1592/93-ca.1655)   PR
    Bibl: ▶Thieme-Becker
    Claessen, Roelof   GC
    Coets   PR
    Koets or Coets, Roelof, I
      (Roelof Claessen)   WC
    Koets, Roelof I (Roelof
      Claessen)   GC
    Roelof Koets (I)   PR
   Koets, Roelof I (Roelof
    Claessen)→see Koets, Roelof (I)
Koets, Roelof II   GC
    (Dutch artist, a.1650-1725)   WC
    (Dutch, bef.1650-1725)   GC
    Bibl: ▶Witt checklist
    Koets, Roelof, II   WC
  Koets, Roelof, II→see Koets, Roelof II
Koetschet, Achille *(Swiss artist,*
    1862-1895)   WC
Koetsier, Johannes (Hans) *(Dutch*
    artist, 1930-)   WC
Koetter, Fred   AV BA
    (American architect, 1938-)   AV
    (American architect, b.1938)   BA
    Bibl: ▶Avery period. idx.;
      Modulus, 16 (1983) p.126
Köfer, Kurt *(Austrian architect,*
    Vienna)   AV
    Bibl: ▶Verzeich. Öst. Ziviltech.
Koffermaker, Marcellus→see
    Coffermans, Marcellus
Koffermans, Marcellius→see
    Coffermans, Marcellus
Koffermans, Marcellus→see
    Coffermans, Marcellus
Koftlin, A. *(German artist, 19th*
    cent.)   WC
Kogan, Moissej→see Kogan, Moissey
Kogan, Moissey   BA
    (Russian artist, 1879-1930)   WC
    (Russian draughtsman, 1879-
      1943)   GC
    (Russian sculptor, printmaker in
      FRA, 1879-1943)   BA
    Bibl: ▶Busse, Maler u. Bildhauer
      19. Jahr.; Getty Photo Study Coll.;
      ▶RILA/BHA; Sohn, MOISSEY
      KOGAN...(1980); ▶Thieme-Becker;
      ▶Vollmer, Künst.-Lex. 20. Jhr., v.1,
      v.2; ▶Witt checklist
    Kogan, Moissej   GC WC
Kogan, Nina Ossipowna *(Russian*
    painter, 1887-ca.1942)   BA
    Bibl: Zurich, Galerie Schlegl, NINA
      OSSIPOWNA KOGAN... (1985)
Köglsberger, Philipp Jakob *(18th*
    century German architect)   AV
    Bibl: ▶Thieme-Becker
    Köglsperger, Philipp Jakob   AV
Koglsperger, Adolf *(German artist,*
    1891-)   WC

Köglsperger, Philipp Jakob→see
    Köglsberger, Philipp Jakob
Kohán, György   BA WC
    (Hungarian artist, 1910-)   WC
    (Hungarian painter, 1910-1967)   BA
    Bibl: Clark Art Inst. Libr.;
      MUVESZETTORTENETI ERTESTITO,
      XXIX[i.e.XXVIII]/1(1979), 51-64;
      ▶Németh, Mod. ungarische Kunst
Koharsky, T. *(Russian artist, 19th*
    cent.)   WC
Kohl, Bernhard *(West German*
    architect, Hamburg)   AV
    Bibl: ▶Bund Deut. Arch. Hdbch.,
      1987
Kohl, Clemens *(Austrian printmaker,*
    1754-1807)   BA
    Bibl: ▶Bénézit; ▶Thieme-Becker
Kohl, Hans *(W. German architect,*
    Munich, 1952-)   AV
    Bibl: Deutsche Bauzeitung, 1985
      Mar., v.119, no.3, p.114
Kohl, Ludwig *(German artist, 1746-*
    1821)   WC
Kohl, Pierre Ernest *(French artist,*
    1897-)   WC
Kohlberg, Bety *(American painter,*
    b.1936)   BA
    Bibl: ARTS MAGAZINE, LV(MAR
      1981), 18; Framingham (MA,
      USA), Danforth Mus., Abstract art
      New Engl. (1983)
Köhlemann, Horst *(West German*
    architect)   AV
    Bibl: Garten und Landschaft,
      1989, v.99, no.8, p.38
Kohler or Kioler, Per *(Swedish*
    artist, 1784-1810)   WC
Kohler, Albert *(German artist,*
    -1849)   WC
Kohler, Christian *(German artist,*
    1809-1861)   WC
Köhler, Fritz *(German painter, 1887-*
    1972)   BA
    Bibl: ▶Bénézit; Geymüller, DIE
      GEMÄLDE DES 20TH JH...
      DUSSELDORF (1977), p. 80;
      Kocks, WELTKUNST, LV, 5 (Mar.
      1985), p. 532-34; ▶Vollmer,
      Künst.-Lex. 20. Jhr.
Köhler, Gerhard *(German painter,*
    sculptor, b.1928)   BA
    Bibl: Freiburg im Bresgau,
      Augustinermuseum; Stuttgart
      (DEU), Galerie Maercklin
Kohler, H. *(Engraver)*   WI
Köhler, Heinrich *(German architect,*
    1830-1903)   BA
    Bibl: ▶Portoghesi, Diz. arch. e
      urbanistica; ▶Thieme-Becker
Köhler, Heinrich Gottlieb *(German*
    glass engraver, act.1746-1752)   BA
    Bibl: ▶Encyc. glass, p. 222;
      ▶Newman, Glass; ▶Norsk Kunstner
      Leks., v.2, 680-681; Polak, Glass

Kohler, Max *(Swiss painter,*
    printmaker, b.1919)   BA
    Bibl: ▶Künst.-Lex. Schweiz 20.
      Jahrh., v.1, p.540; ▶Lex. zeitgen.
      Schweiz. Künstler, p.202
Köhler, Waldo *(German painter,*
    b.1909)   BA
    Bibl: ▶Vollmer, Künst.-Lex. 20. Jhr.
Köhler, Wolfgang *(German*
    architect, Stuttgart, 1935-)   AV
    Bibl: Deutsche Bauzeitung, 1985
      June, v.119, no.6, p.136
Kohlhof *(German artist, 20th cent.)* WC
Kohlleppel, Ulrich   AV
Kohlmaier, Georg *(West German*
    architect)   AV
    Bibl: Transparent, 1985, v.16, no.
      5-6, p.4
Kohlmeyer, Ida→see Kohlmeyer, Ida
    R.
Kohlmeyer, Ida R.   BA
    (American artist, b.1912)   WI
    (American painter, b.1912)   BA
    Bibl: ▶WW Amer. Art, 1976
    Kohlmeyer, Ida   WI
Kohls, Ulrich *(East German*
    photographer, b.1936)   BA
    Bibl: BILDENDE KUNST 4 (1984)
      154
Kohlschein, Josef II *(German*
    painter, printmaker, 1884-1958)   BA
    Bibl: ▶Thieme-Becker; ▶Vollmer,
      Künst.-Lex. 20. Jhr.; WELTKUNST,
      LIV/18 (15 Sept 1984) 2438-2441
Kohlseisen, Josef *(Austrian*
    architect, Wien)   AV
    Bibl: ▶Verzeich. Öst. Ziviltech.
Kohn, A. Eugene *(American*
    architect, 1930-)   AV
    Bibl: ▶Amer. archts. dir., 3rd ed.,
      1970
Kohn, Bernhard *(Architect, France?)* AV
    Bibl: Bauwelt, 1985 Feb.22, v.76,
      no.8, p.258
Kohn, Gabriel *(American sculptor,*
    1910-1975)   BA
    Bibl: Washington(DC, USA),
      Corcoran Gallery of Art. GABRIEL
      KOHN 1910-1975 (1977); ▶WW
      Amer. Art, 1975
Kohn, Misch *(American painter,*
    printmaker, b.1916)   BA
    Bibl: ▶Vollmer, Künst.-Lex. 20.
      Jhr.; ▶WW Amer. Art, 1976
Kohn, Robert *(American artist,*
    b.1935)   BA
    Bibl: New York (NY, USA), New
      Mus., Outside NY: Ohio (1980)
Kohn, Robert D. *(American*
    architect, NYC, 1870?-1953)   AV
    Bibl: ▶Francis, Archts. NYC 1840-
      1900
Kohn, William Roth *(American*
    painter, b.1931)   BA
    Bibl: ▶WW Amer. Art, 1980

Kohoutek, Rudolf *(Austrian architect, 1941-)*   **AV**
Bibl: Institute for Architecture and Urban Studies. Catalogue, n.13, 1980, p.24

Kohring, John *(American painter, b.1946)*   **BA**
Bibl: Cambridge (MA, USA), MIT, Hayden Gallery, 4 ptrs. (1981)

Kohtz, Otto *(German architect, author, 1880-1956)*   **BA**
Bibl: ▶Neue deutsche Biog.; ▶Vollmer, Künst.-Lex. 20. Jhr.

Koinberg, Sture *(Swedish architect, Stockholm)*   **AV**
Bibl: Domus, 1988 Mar., no.692, p.52

Koios *(Greek metalworker, 6th c BC)*   **GC**
Bibl: Getty Photo Study Coll.

Koistinen, Karl *(Swedish architect, Lund, 1929-)*   **AV**
Bibl: ▶Svenska Ark. Riks., 1984

Koivula, Jukka *(Finnish architect)*   **AV**
Bibl: Arkkitehtuurikilpailuja, 1989, no.9, p.2

Koizumi, Hideo *(Japanese architect)*   **AV**
Bibl: Kenchiku bunka, 1988 Apr., v.43, no.498, p.29

Kojima, Kazuhiro *(Japanese architect)*   **AV**
Bibl: Space design, 1985 Dec., no.255, p.5

Kok, Abel Antoon *(Dutch architect, architectural historian, 1881-1951)*   **BA**
Bibl: Amsterdam, Gemeentelijk Archiefdienst, DRIE EEUWEN AMSTERDAMSE BOUWKUNST, 1984; ▶Natl. union cat., pre-1956

Kok, Jurriaan Jurriaan *(Dutch porcelain manufacturer, 1861-1919)*   **BA**
Bibl: ▶Boger, World pott. & porc.; The Hague(NLD), Haags Gemeentemuseum. ROZENBURG 1883-1917:GESCHIEDENIS VAN EEN HAAGSE FABRIEK(1983), 27

Kokas, Ignác   **BA WC**
(Hungarian artist, 1926-)   WC
(Hungarian painter, b.1926)   BA
Bibl: ARS HUNGARICA, IV/2(1976), 273-289

Koken, Edmund *(German artist, 1814-1872)*   **WC**

Kokkoris, P. *(Greek architect)*   **AV**
Bibl: Architektonika Themata = Architecture in Greece, 1989, no.23, p.185

Kokolja, Tripo *(Yugoslav painter, 1661-1713)*   **BA**
Bibl: Bildhdbch. Kunst. Jugo.; Mrlosevic, BAROCCO IN ITALIA E NEI PAESI SLAVI DEL SUD, 141-1616; ▶Thieme-Becker

Kokorekin, Aleksej Alekseevič *(Russian artist, 1906-1959)*   **BA**
Bibl: ▶Bénézit; ▶Encyc. world art; ▶Vollmer, Künst.-Lex. 20. Jhr.

Kokorin *(Russian artist, 20th cent.)*   **WC**

Kokoschka→see Kokoschka, Oskar
Kokoschka, Bohuslav *(German artist, 1893-)*   **WC**
Kokoschka, Olda *(Czech, b.ca.1910)*   **BA**
Bibl: ▶WW Germany
Kokoschka, Oscar→see Kokoschka, Oskar
Kokoschka, Oskar   **BA GC PR WC WI**
(Austrian painter and printmaker, 1886-1980)   GC
(Austrian painter, 1886-1980)   PR
(Austrian painter, printmaker, 1886-1980)   BA
(German artist, 1886-)   WC
(German artist, 1886-1980)   WI
Bibl: ▶Artist biog. master idx.; ▶Bénézit; ▶RILA/BHA
Kokoschka   PR
Kokoschka, Oscar   PR
Oskar Kokoschka   PR

Kokular, Alexandre *(Polish artist, 1793-1846)*   **WC**

Kokurin, V.G. *(Russian artist, 20th cent.)*   **WC**

Kolacio, Zdenko *(Yugoslav architect, 20th c.)*   **BA**

Kolář, Jiří   **BA WC**
(Czech artist, 20th cent.)   WC
(Czech artist, author, b.1914)   BA
Bibl: ▶Contemp. artists; ▶DuMonts Künst.-Lex.

Kolar, Vlastimir *(Architect, Czechoslovakia, 1924-)*   **AV**
Bibl: Architektur, Innenarchitektur, Technischer Ausbau, 1985 Jan.-Feb., v.93, no.1, p.10

Kolari, Pekka *(Finnish architect)*   **AV**
Bibl: Arkkitehti, 1986, no.5, p.62

Kolatan, Sulan *(Turkish-born architect, New York City)*   **AV**
Bibl: Metropolis, 1987 Apr., v.6, no.8, p.47

Kolb, Anton *(German businessman, print publisher in ITA, act.1504-1536)*   **BA**
Bibl: ART BULLETIN, LX/3(SEPT 1978), 428

Kolb, Ellsworth L. *(American, active early 20th century (also Kolb Brothers))*   **JG**

Kolb, Emery C. *(American, active early 20th century (also Kolb Brothers))*   **JG**

Kolb, Franz X. *(German architect, Munich)*   **AV**
Bibl: Detail, 1982 Mar.-Apr., no.2, p.162

Kolb, Gideon   **WC WI**
(British artist, 1911-)   WC
(British artist, b.1911)   WI

Kolb, Michele *(American interior designer, New York City)*   **AV**
Bibl: NYC phone bk., 1987-88

Kolb, Otto *(Architect and designer, Brüttisellen)*   **AV**
Bibl: Deutsche Bauzeitschrift, v.32, 1984, p.1147

Kolb, Paulus I *(German painter, d.1650)*   **GC**
Bibl: ▶Thieme-Becker

Kolb, Peter *(German artist, 1675-1726)*   **WC**
Kolbe→see Kolbe, Ernst
Kolbe, Carl Wilhelm (the Elder)→see Kolbe, Carl Wilhelm, the elder
Kolbe, Carl Wilhelm I→see Kolbe, Carl Wilhelm, the elder
Kolbe, Carl Wilhelm, I→see Kolbe, Carl Wilhelm, the elder

Kolbe, Carl Wilhelm, II *(German artist, 1781-1853)*   **WC**

Kolbe, Carl Wilhelm, the elder   **BA**
(German artist, 1757-1835)   WC
(German draughtsman and printmaker, 1757-1835)   GC
(German printmaker, author, 1759-1835)   BA
Bibl: ▶Bénézit; ▶Brockhaus Enzyk.; Getty Photo Study Coll.; Martens, DER ZEICHNER U.RADIERER CW KOLBE, p.10; ▶Thieme-Becker; ▶Witt checklist
Kolbe, Carl Wilhelm (the Elder)   GC
Kolbe, Carl Wilhelm I   **GC**
Kolbe, Carl Wilhelm, I   **WC**
Kolbe, Ernest→see Kolbe, Ernst

Kolbe, Ernst *(German painter, 1876-aft.1913)*   **PR**
Bibl: ▶Thieme-Becker
Ernst Kolbe   PR
Kolbe   PR
Kolbe, Ernest   PR

Kolbe, Georg   **BA GC WC**
(German artist, 1877-1947)   WC
(German sculptor, 1877-1947)   BA GC
Bibl: ▶Encyc. world art; ▶McGraw-Hill dict. art; ▶RILA/BHA

Kolbe, Heinrich Christoph   **GC WC**
(German artist, 1771-1836)   WC
(German painter, 1771-1836)   GC
Bibl: ▶Thieme-Becker

Kolbe, J.P. *(German artist, op.c. 1776)*   **WC**

Kolbowski, Silvia *(American conceptual artist, 20th c.)*   **BA**
Bibl: Lichtenstein, ARTS MAGAZINE LIX/10 (summer 1985) p.12; Lichtenstein, T., in ARTS MAGAZINE LIX/10 (summer 1985) 12; RLIN BKS file; Staniszewski, FLASH ART, 143 (Nov-Dec 1988) p.103

Kolderer, Keldrer, Kellrer, Koldrar, Kollrer etc. Jorg *(German artist, op.1497-m.1540)*   **WC**
Koldeweij, Bernard Marie→see Koldewey, Bernard Marie

Koldewey, Bernard Marie *(Dutch painter, 1859-1898)*   **GC**
> Bibl: ▶Thieme-Becker
Koldeweij, Bernard Marie   **GC**

Kolding, Peder Jensen *(Danish woodcarver, act.1630, d.1675)*   **BA**
> Bibl: ▶Nørregård-Nielsen, Dansk kunst; Norn, Konsthist. Tidskrift 58/1/ (1989), p.34-37; ▶Thieme-Becker; Trap, Kongeriget DNK: personalregister, v.8, p.410; ▶Weilbach, Kunst.leks.

Kolejčuk, Vjačeslav *(Czech sculptor, 20th c.)*   **BA**
> Bibl: Sokolov, VYTVARNA KULTURA, V/5 (1981), 28-34

Kolenc, Angelo A. *(fl.1975; Architect, Toronto)*   **FA**
> Bibl: CAAD Finding Aid J. Austin Floyd, 82303/27 Proj. 73008; Natl. Arch. of Canada, CAAD Finding Aid; Toronto City Directories

Kolesnikoff, Sergei M. *(Russian artist, 1889-)*   **WC**

Kolíbal, Stanislav *(Czech sculptor, illustrator, b.1925)*   **BA**
> Bibl: ▶Babington Smith, Contemp. artists; ▶Bénézit

Kolig, Anton   **BA WC**
> *(Austrian painter, 1886-1950)*   **BA**
> *(German artist, 1886-1950)*   **WC**
> Bibl: ▶Bénézit; ▶Encyc. world art; ▶Vollmer, Künst.-Lex. 20. Jhr.

Kolioppoulos, Peter *(American architect, Chicago, Ill)*   **AV**
> Bibl: Inland architect, 1988 July-Aug., v.32, no.4, p.5

Kolisnyk, Peter *(Canadian painter, sculptor, b.1934)*   **BA**
> Bibl: ▶Artists Canada; ▶MacDonald, Can. artists

Kolitz → see Kolitz, Louis

Kolitz, Louis   **GC PR WC**
> *(German artist, 1845-1914)*   **WC**
> *(German painter, 1845-1914)*   **GC PR**
> Bibl: ▶Thieme-Becker
Kolitz   **PR**
Louis Kolitz   **PR**

Kolkowitz, Allen *(American architect, New York, NY)*   **AV**
> Bibl: Interior design, 1984 Feb., v.55, no.2, p.157

Koll, Dieter *(German artist, b.1940)*   **BA**
> Bibl: Stuttgart (DEU), Württemb. Kunstverein, 16 Künstler (1978)

Kollakowski, Stanislaus Korvinus *(painter, act.1811)*   **BA**
> Bibl: ▶Thieme-Becker

Kollandsrud, Gullik *(Norwegian architect)*   **AV**
> Bibl: Architectural digest, 1985 Jan., v.41, no.1

Kollandsrud, Mari *(Norwegian architect)*   **AV**
> Bibl: Architectural digest, 1985 Jan., v.41, no.1

Kollanek or Kollanetz, Josef K. *(German artist, op.c.1760-1775)*   **WC**

Kolle, Claus Anton *(Danish artist, 1827-1872)*   **WC**

Kolle, Helmut (Helmut von Hugel) *(German artist, 1899-1931)*   **WC**

Koller → see Koller, Wilhelm

Koller, Broncia   **BA**
> *(Austrian painter, 1867-1934)*   **BA**
> *(German artist, 1867-)*   **WC**
> Bibl: ▶Busse, Maler u. Bildhauer 19. Jahr.; ▶Fuchs, Öst. Maler 19. Jahrh.; ▶Thieme-Becker

Koller, Broucia   **WC**
Koller, Broucia → see Koller, Broncia
Koller, Guillaume → see Koller, Wilhelm

Koller, Gustav   **GC WC**
> *(German artist, 1870-)*   **WC**
> *(German painter, b.1870)*   **GC**
> Bibl: ▶Bénézit

Koller, J.A. *(Swiss artist, 19th cent.)*   **WC**

Köller, Johann Caspar *(Swiss painter, 1808-1887)*   **GC**
> Bibl: ▶Bénézit
Koller, Johann Jacob → see Koller, Johann Jakob

Koller, Johann Jakob   **GC**
> *(Swedish artist, 1746-1805/6)*   **WC**
> *(Swiss painter, 1746-1805)*   **GC**
> Bibl: ▶Bénézit

Koller, Johann Jacob   **WC**

Koller, Johann Rudolf   **BA WC**
> *(Swiss artist, 1828-1905)*   **WC**
> *(Swiss painter, printmaker, 1828-1905)*   **BA**
> Bibl: BRUB; ▶Schweiz. Künst.-Lex.; ▶Thieme-Becker

Koller, Rolf M. *(West German painter, 20th cent)*   **AV**
> Bibl: Das Münster, 1989, v.42, no.1, p.31

Koller, Wilhelm   **BA GC PR**
> *(Austrian painter, 1829-1884/85)*   **BA GC PR**
> *(German artist, 1829-1884)*   **WC**
> Bibl: ▶Bénézit; ▶Fuchs, Öst. Maler 19. Jahrh.; Nürnberg (DEU), Stadtgesch. Mus., Wirkung u. Nachleben Durers (1976); ▶RILA/BHA; ▶Thieme-Becker
Koller   **PR**
Koller, Guillaume   **PR**

Koller, Wilhelm (Guillaume)   **WC**
Wilhelm Koller   **PR**
Koller, Wilhelm (Guillaume) → see Koller, Wilhelm

Kollhoff, Hans F. *(West German architect, 1946-)*   **AV**
> Bibl: Das Kunstwerk, n.3-4, Sept. 1983, p.126

Kollier, Edwaert → see Colyer, Edwaert

Köllinger, Michael *(Austrian goldsmith, act.1549-1550)*   **BA**
> Bibl: Hayward, Goldsmiths & Mannerism; ▶Thieme-Becker

Kollman, Michael S. *(American architect, Highland Park, Ill)*   **AV**
> Bibl: ▶AIA Pro File, 1987-1988, firm only

Kollmann or Kolman, Hans Friedrich *(Swiss artist, op.1592-m. c.1615)*   **WC**

Kollmann, Carl Ivanovitch *(Russian painter, 1788-1846)*   **GC**
> Bibl: ▶Bénézit

Köllner, Augustus   **BA FA WC WI**
> *(1813-ca.1870; Lithographer, Philadelphia)*   **FA**
> *(American artist, 1813-1900)*   **WI**
> *(German artist, 1813-1900)*   **WC**
> *(German painter in USA, 1813-1906)*   **BA**
> Bibl: Binghamton (NY, USA), SUNY, 19c. ptrs. Delaware Valley (1983); ▶Groce, Artists Amer.; Natl. Archives object; ▶Thieme-Becker; ▶Witt checklist; ▶Young, Amer. artists

Kollonitsch or Kolonitsch, Christian (not Carl) *(German artist, 1730-1802)*   **WC**

Kollwitz, Käthe   **BA GC**
> *(German artist, 1867-1945)*   **WC**
> *(German draughtsman and sculptor, 1867-1945)*   **GC**
> *(German printmaker, sculptor, 1867-1945)*   **BA**
> Bibl: Getty Photo Study Coll.; ▶Neue deutsche Biog.; ▶New Columbia encyc.; ▶RILA/BHA; ▶Vollmer, Künst.-Lex. 20. Jhr.; ▶Witt checklist

Kollwitz, Kathe, (nee Schmidt)   **WC**
Schmidt, Käthe   **BA**
Kollwitz, Kathe, (nee Schmidt) → see Kollwitz, Käthe

Kolm, Jan Sieuwertsz *(Dutch (?) draughtsman, act.1622)*   **GC**
> Bibl: ▶Thieme-Becker

Kolm, Wilhelm *(German wax modeler, b.1665/75, act.1714)*   **BA**
> Bibl: Theuerkauff, ZEIT.DES.DE. VEREINS FUR KUNST, XXXIV/1-4(1980), 100-119

Kolma, Imre *(Hungarian artist, 20th cent.)*   **WC**

Kolman, Colman or Koloman → see Helmschmied, Kolman

Kolodotschko, Igor *(British architect, real estate developer, and automobile dealer)*   **AV**
> Bibl: RIBA journal, 1984 July, v.91, no.7, p.4

Kolokytha-Antonakakis, Susanna → see Antonakakis, Suzana Maria

Kolom → see Colom, Cornelius

Kolos-Vary, Sigismond *(Hungarian artist, 1899-)*   **WC**

Kolotes of Herakleia *(Greek sculptor, 5th c BC (end))*   GC
    Bibl: ▶Robertson, Greek art, p.312
Kolotes of Teos *(Greek painter, ca. 400 BC)*   GC
    Bibl: ▶Robertson, Greek art, p.414
Kolowrat, Johann Libsteinsky von *(Austrian, act.1580)*   BA
    Bibl: Scheicher, Jahrb. d. Kunsthist. Samml. Wien, XLI (1981) pp.119-153, 119-153
Kolowrat, Magdalena Ludmilla *(Austrian, act.1659)*   BA
    Bibl: Blažíček, ARS AURO PRIOR: STUDIA IOANNI BIAŁOSTOCKI.... (1981) 528-529
Kolozsvar, Thomas de (Coloswar) → see Kolozsvári, Tamás
Kolozsvári, György *(Transylvanian sculptor, act.1373)*   BA
    Bibl: ▶Thieme-Becker
    György of Kolozsvár   BA
Kolozsvári, Márton *(Transylvanian sculptor, act.1373)*   BA
    Bibl: Kampis, Art Hungary; ▶Thieme-Becker
    Márton of Kolozsvár   BA
Kolozsvári, Tamás   BA
    (Hungarian artist, op.1427)   WC
    (Hungarian painter, 15th c.)   BA
    Bibl: Pogany, MAGYAR NEMZETI GALERIA EVKONYVE, II(1974), 51-63; Torok, INTERNATIONAL CONGRESS OF THE HIST. OF ART (1986) p.133-138
Kolozsvar, Thomas de (Coloswar)   WC
Kolozsvary, Lajos *(Hungarian artist, 1871-)*   WC
Kolpan, Steve *(American artist, 20th c.)*   BA
    Bibl: AFTERIMAGE, VII/4(NOV 1979, 4-5
Kölsch, Hans Ulrich *(German architect, collector, 20th c.)*   BA
Kölschbach, Josef *(German painter, 1892-1947)*   BA
    Bibl: Hannover (DEU), Kestner-Gesellschaft, August Macke (1979); ▶Vollmer, Künst.-Lex. 20. Jhr.
Kolscher, Bernhard *(German architect, 1834-1868)*   BA
    Bibl: Berlin(DDR), Staatiche Museen, Kunstbibliothek. ZEICHNUNGEN DES BERLINER ARCH.BERNARD KOLSCHER
Koltai, Ralph *(British scenographer, b.1924)*   BA
    Bibl: Koltai, ROYAL SOCIETY OF ARTS JOURNAL, CXXXV(MAR 1987), 298-309; Oxford comp. theatre
Kolthoff, Mark *(Dutch painter, photographer, filmmaker, b.1901)*   BA
    Bibl: ▶Scheen, Ned. beeldende kunst.

Kolunič-Rota, Martin → see Rota, Martino
Koman, Ilhan *(Turkish sculptor, b.1921)*   BA
    Bibl: ▶Bénézit
Komarin, Gary *(American painter, b.1951)*   BA
    Bibl: ▶WW Amer. Art, 1989
Komaris Painter   GC
    Bibl: ▶Beazley, Attic red-fig. vase-ptrs.
Komaromi-Kacz, Endre → see Kacz, Endre Komaromi
Komast Group: VIII, Unallotted *(vase-painters, ca. 585-570 BC)*   GC
    Bibl: ▶Beazley, Attic bl.-fig. vase-ptrs.; Boardman, Attic Bl.-fig. Vases, (Komast Group)
Komatsuda, Hirokazu *(Japanese architect)*   AV
    Bibl: Japan architect, 1982 Nov., v.57, no.307-308, p.68
Komili-Manetas, E. *(Architect, Greece)*   AV
    Bibl: Design + art in Greece, 1982, v.13, p.74
Komisar, Milton *(American sculptor, 20th c.)*   BA
    Bibl: ▶Art Index, v.34; ARTS MAGAZINE, LV(JUNE 1981), 85-87
Komisarek, Denise *(Mosaic artist, New York City subway system)*   AV
    Bibl: Sites, 1986, no.18, p.66
Komiyama, Akira *(Japanese architect, 1945-)*   AV
    Bibl: Kenchiku bunka, 1987 Dec., v.42, no.494, p.12
Komjati, Gyula Wanyerka *(Hungarian artist, 1894-)*   WC
Komlosy or Komlossy, Ede (Eduard) *(Hungarian artist, 1862-)*   WC
Kommerarius → see Camerarius, Adam
Komonen, Markku *(Finnish architect, 1945-)*   AV
    Bibl: Process: architecture, n.37, 1983, p.14
Komor, Marcell *(1868-1944)*   AV
Komp → see Klomp, Albert Jansz.
Kompatscher, Klaus *(Architect, based in Italy(?))*   AV
    Bibl: Ottagono, 1987 Dec., v.22, no.87, p.50
Komter, Auke   AV BA
    (Dutch architect)   AV
    (Dutch architect, b.1904)   BA
    Bibl: ▶Avery period. idx.; ▶Libr. of Congr. Name Auth. File
Komuro, Masanobu *(Japanese architect, 1952-)*   AV
    Bibl: Kenchiku bunka, 1987 Dec., v.42, no.494, p.124
Komuten, Mizusawa *(Japanese architect)*   AV
    Bibl: Process: architecture, 1984 Dec., no.53, p.150
Komuten, Takenaka *(Japanese architect)*   AV

Konarski, Marian *(Polish artist, b.1909)*   BA
    Bibl: Biuletyn Historii Sztuki, 3 (1974) p.303ff.
Konaševič, Vladimir Mihajlovič   BA
    (Russian artist, 1888-1963)   WC
    (Russian painter, printmaker, 1888-1963)   BA
    Bibl: ▶Thieme-Becker; ▶Witt checklist
Konashchevitch, Vladimir Mikhailovitch   WC
Konashchevitch, Vladimir Mikhailovitch → see Konaševič, Vladimir Mihajlovič
Končalovskij, Pëtr Petrovič   BA
    (Russian artist, 1876-)   WC
    (Russian artist, 20th cent.)   WC
    (Russian painter, 1876-1955)   BA
    Bibl: ▶Great Soviet encyc.; ▶Vollmer, Künst.-Lex. 20. Jhr.
Konchalovsky, P.P.   WC
Kontchalvoski, Piotr Petrowitsch   WC
Konchalovsky, P.P. → see Končalovskij, Pëtr Petrovič
Kondo, Kimio *(Japanese landscape architect, 1929-)*   AV
    Bibl: Process: architecture, 1985 June, no.59, p.142
Kondo, Shunji *(Japanese architect, 1953-)*   AV
    Bibl: Kenchiku bunka, 1987 Dec., v.42, no.494, p.126
Kondo, Yasuo *(Japanese architect, 1950-)*   AV
    Bibl: Ottagono, 1987 June, v.22, no.85, p.38
Kondor, Béla   BA WC
    (Hungarian artist, 1931-)   WC
    (Hungarian painter, printmaker, 1931-1972)   BA
Kondor, Gyorgy *(Hungarian artist, 1921-1945)*   WC
Kondor, Lajos *(Hungarian artist, 1926-)*   WC
Koneberg, Johann Michael → see Koneberg, Michael
Koneberg, Michael   GC
    (German artist, op.1765-1787)   WC
    (German draughtsman, act. 1765)   GC
    Bibl: ▶Thieme-Becker
Koneberg, Johann Michael   GC WC
Konecny, Joseph *(Czech artist, 1907-)*   WC
Konecsni, György *(Hungarian printmaker, illustrator, painter, 1908-1970)*   BA
    Bibl: Budapest(HUN), Magyar Nemzeti Galeria. GYORGY KONECSHI(1976); ▶Havlice, Idx. art. bio.; ▶WW Graphic Art
Konek, Ida *(Hungarian artist, 1856-p.1890)*   WC

Konekamp, Frederick *(German artist, 1897-)*   **WC**

Konenkov, Sergej Timofeevič *(Russian sculptor, 1874-1971)*   **BA**
    Bibl: ▶Bénézit; ▶Great Soviet encyc.; Kamenskij, KONENKOV(1975)

Koner, Max *(German artist, 1854-1900)*   **WC**

Konfar, Gyula *(Hungarian artist, 20th cent.)*   **WC**

Könholdt, Uwe *(West German architect, Hamburg)*   **AV**
    Bibl: Bauwelt, 1989 July 14, v.80, no.27, p.1302

Konig → see König, Johann

Konig, Anton Friedrich, I *(German artist, 1722-1787)*   **WC**

König, Franz Niklaus   **BA GC**
    (Swiss artist, 1765-1832)   WC
    (Swiss draughtsman, 1765-1832)   GC
    (Swiss painter, printmaker, 1765-1832)   BA
    Bibl: ▶Bénézit; ▶Schweiz. Künst.-Lex.; ▶Thieme-Becker

    Konig, Niklaus (Franz Niklaus)   **WC**

Konig, Franz Xaver *(German artist, c.1711-1782)*   **WC**

König, Gustav Ferdinand Leopold   **BA WC**
    (German artist, 1808-1869)   WC
    (German painter, illustrator, printmaker, 1808-1869)   BA
    Bibl: ▶Thieme-Becker

Konig, Hugo *(German artist, 1856-1899)*   **WC**

König, Ignaz Pallme → see Pallme-König, Ignaz

König, Johann   **BA GC PR**
    (German artist, 1586-1642)   WI
    (German artist, c.1586-1632/5)   WC
    (German painter, 1586-1623/25)   PR
    (German painter, ca.1586-1632/35)   GC
    (German painter, ca.1586-ca.1632)   BA
    Bibl: ▶Bénézit; ▶RILA/BHA; ▶Thieme-Becker; ▶Witt checklist

    J. Koenig   PR
    Johann König   PR
    John Konig   PR
    Koenig, Johann   **PR WI**
    Konig   PR

Konig, Johann or Hans (not Jakob)   **WC**

Konig, Johann or Hans (not Jakob) → see König, Johann

König, Jürgen *(W. German architect)*   **AV**
    Bibl: Architektur, Innenarchitektur, Technischer Ausbau, 1986 Nov., v.94, no.11, p.48

König, Leo Freiherr von → see König, Leo, Freiherr von

König, Leo, Freiherr von   **BA**
    (German artist, 1871-1944)   WC
    (German painter, 1871-1944)   BA
    (German, 1871-1944)   GC
    Bibl: ▶Thieme-Becker; ▶Vollmer, Künst.-Lex. 20. Jhr.; ▶Witt checklist

König, Leo Freiherr von   **GC WC**

Konig, Michael *(German artist, op. 1606)*   **WC**

Konig, Niklaus (Franz Niklaus) → see König, Franz Niklaus

König, Otto Freiherr von *(German, 1871-1944)*   **GC**
    Bibl: ▶Witt checklist

Konig, Rudolph (Georg Rudolph) *(Swiss artist, 1790-1815)*   **WC**

Königs, Tom *(West German member of the "Green" party, self-styled city planner)*   **AV**
    Bibl: Arch plus, 1988 Apr., no.94, p.70

Konigsberg, Johannes Muller von *(Austrian, 1436-1476)*   **JG**

Konigsberger, Jorge André *(Brazilian architect)*   **AV**
    Bibl: Projeto, 1987 Dec.-1988 Jan., no.106, p.108

Konigsbruggen, Rob van *(Dutch painter, b.1948)*   **BA**

Königswieser, Heinrich   **GC WC**
    (German artist, op.1552-m. 1583)   WC
    (German painter, act.1552-d. ca. 1583)   GC
    Bibl: ▶Thieme-Becker

Konijnenburg → see Konijnenburg, Willem Adriaan van

Konijnenburg, Willem A. van → see Konijnenburg, Willem Adriaan van

Konijnenburg, Willem Adriaan van   **GC PR WC**
    (Dutch artist, 1868-1943)   WC
    (Dutch painter, 1868-1943)   PR
    (Dutch painter, draughtsman, and printmaker, 1868-1943)   GC
    Bibl: ▶Bénézit; ▶Thieme-Becker; ▶Witt checklist

    Konijnenburg   PR
    Konijnenburg, Willem A. van   PR
    Willem Adriaan van Konijnenburg   PR

Koninck → see Koninck, Andries de
Koninck → see Koninck, Jacob (II)
Koninck → see Koninck, Jacob I
Koninck → see Koninck, Philips de
Koninck → see Koninck, Salomon

Koninck or Coning, Andries de → see Koninck, Andries de

Koninck, Andries de   **GC PR**
    (Dutch artist, op.c.1620)   WC
    (Dutch painter, act. 1620's-1630's, d. 1659)   PR
    (Dutch painter, act. c.1620)   GC
    Bibl: ▶Bénézit; Getty Museum; ▶Thieme-Becker; ▶Witt checklist

    Andries de Koninck   PR
    Coninck, A. de   PR
    Coning, Andries de   GC
    Koninck   PR

Koninck or Coning, Andries de   **WC**

Koninck, Coninck, Coning, Coningh, Konig, Konig etc., Jacob, II → see Koninck, Jacob (II)

Koninck, Coninckx or Koning, Philips Aertsz. (de) → see Koninck, Philips de

Koninck, Coning, Conningh or Koning, Jacob, I → see Koninck, Jacob I

Koninck, Gregorius de → see Coninck, Gregorius de

Koninck, Jacob (I) → see Koninck, Jacob I

Koninck, Jacob (II)   **PR**
    (Dutch artist, c.1648-1724)   WC
    (Dutch painter, ca.1648-1724)   PR
    (Dutch, ca.1648-1724)   GC
    Bibl: Getty Photo Study Coll. (Ptgs.); ▶Thieme-Becker

    Coning, Jacob   GC
    J. De Koeninck   PR
    Jacob Koninck (II)   PR
    Koninck   PR

Koninck, Coninck, Coning, Coningh, Konig, Konig etc., Jacob, II   **WC**

Koninck, Jacob II   **GC**

Koninck, Jacob I   **BA GC**
    (Dutch artist, c.1610/15-p.1690)   WC
    (Dutch painter, ca.1610/15-aft.1690)   GC
    (Dutch painter, ca.1616-1708)   PR
    (Dutch painter, printmaker, ca. 1616-1708)   BA
    Bibl: ▶Bénézit; ▶Bernt, Neth. ptrs. 17c.; ▶RILA/BHA; ▶Thieme-Becker; ▶Witt checklist; ▶Wurzbach, NLD Künst.-Lex.

    J. De Koeninck   PR
    Jacob Coninx   PR
    Jacob Koninck   PR
    Jacob Koninck (I)   PR
    Jan Coningh   PR
    Jan de Coninck   PR
    Koninck   PR

Koninck, Coning, Conningh or Koning, Jacob, I   **WC**

Koninck, Jacob (I)   **PR**

Koninck, Jacob II → see Koninck, Jacob (II)

Koninck, Jacob III *(Dutch painter, act.1695-d.1734)*   **GC**
    Bibl: ▶Thieme-Becker

Koninck, Louis Herman de *(Belgian architect, 1896-1984)* **AV**
Bibl: death date - Archives d'architecture moderne, 1985, no.28, p.95; ▶Macmillan encyc. archts.

De Koninck, Louis Herman **AV**
Koninck, Philips → see Koninck, Philips de

Koninck, Philips de **BA GC PR**
(Dutch artist, 1619-1688) **WC**
(Dutch painter, 1619-1688) **BA**
(Dutch painter, 1620-1688) **PR**
(Dutch, 1619-1688) **JG**
(Dutch, 1620-1688) **GC**
Bibl: ▶Encyc. world art; George Goldner; ▶RILA/BHA; ▶Wurzbach, NLD Künst.-Lex.

Colin **PR**
Coninck **PR**
D. Koninck **PR**
D. Koningh **PR**
D. Koningk **PR**
De Conigne **PR**
De Coningue **PR**
De Conink **PR**
De Kening **PR**
De Koening **PR**
De Koninch **PR**
De Koning **PR**
De Koningh **PR**
De Koningk **PR**
De Konink **PR**
De Konning **PR**
De Konyngh **PR**
De Krowning **PR**
De. Koningh **PR**
DeKoningh **PR**
Köening **PR**
Koninck **PR**

Koninck, Coninckx or Koning, Philips Aertsz. (de) **WC**
Koninck, Philips **JG PR**
Koningk **PR**
P. de Kningh **PR**
P. de Koningh **PR**
Philip Coninck **PR**
Philip Coningh **PR**
Philip de Coninck **PR**
Philip Konink **PR**
Philippus Coningh **PR**
Philips Coninck **PR**
Philips Coninx **PR**
Philips de Koninck **PR**
Philips Koning **PR**

Koninck, Salomon **BA GC PR WC**
(Dutch artist, 1609-1656) **WC**
(Dutch painter, 1609-1656) **PR**
(Dutch painter, printmaker, 1609-1656) **BA**
(Dutch, 1609-1656) **GC**
Bibl: HOLLSTEIN; ▶RILA/BHA; ▶Seyn, Écoles flam. et holl.; ▶Thieme-Becker; ▶Witt checklist; ▶Wurzbach, NLD Künst.-Lex.

Coninck **PR**
De Koninck **PR**
De Koningh **PR**
Deconing **PR**
DeKoningk **PR**
Koninck **PR**
S. Coninck **PR**
S. Coningh **PR**
Salomon d'Coning **PR**
Salomon Koninck **PR**
Koninckloo → see Coninxloo, Gilles van

Koninet, de [Unidentified]
(Unknown painter) **PR**
Bibl: (April 8, 1805, lot 108, King (Thomas))
De Koninet **PR**

Koning, Cornelis *(Dutch painter, printmaker, sculptor, 1893-1951)* **BA**
Bibl: ▶Scheen, Ned. beeldende kunst.; ▶Vollmer, Künst.-Lex. 20. Jhr.

Koning, Cornelis **GC WC**
(Dutch artist, op.1608(?)-m. 1671(?)) **WC**
(Dutch printmaker, ca.1610-1671) **GC**
Bibl: ▶Bénézit

Koning, Elisabeth Johanna (Elisabeth Johanna Stapert) → see Koning, Elizabeth Johanna

Koning, Elizabeth Johanna **GC**
(Dutch artist, 1816-1887) **WC**
(Dutch painter and draughtsman, 1816-1888) **GC**
Bibl: ▶Thieme-Becker

Koning, Elisabeth Johanna (Elisabeth Johanna Stapert) **WC**
Stapert, Elizabeth Johanna **GC**

Koning, Hank *(American architect)* **AV**
Bibl: GA houses, 1988 Oct., no.24, p.146

Koning, Hans Ebeling *(Dutch painter, b.1931)* **BA**
Bibl: Amsterdam (NLD), Stedelijk Museum, 11 Schilders (1976)

Koning, Jan *(Dutch architect)* **AV**
Bibl: Forum voor architectuur en daarmee verbonden kunsten, 1987, v.31, no.3, p.47

Koning, Roeland *(Dutch painter and draughtsman, b.1898)* **GC**
Bibl: ▶Scheen, Ned. beeldende kunst.

Koningh, Arie Kelting de **GC**
(Dutch artist, 1815-1867) **WC**
(Dutch painter and draughtsman, 1815-1867) **GC**
Bibl: ▶Bénézit

Koningh, Arie Ketting de **WC**
Koningh, Arie Ketting de → see Koningh, Arie Kelting de

Koningh, Leendert de **GC PR WC**
(Dutch artist, 1777-1849) **WC**
(Dutch painter, 1777-1849) **PR**
(Dutch, 1777-1849) **GC**
Bibl: Getty Photo Study Coll. (Ptgs.); ▶Thieme-Becker; ▶Witt checklist

De Konin **PR**
De Koning **PR**
Dekoning **PR**
Koningh, Leonard de **GC**
Leendert de Koningh **PR**
Koningh, Leonard de → see Koningh, Leendert de
Koningk → see Koninck, Philips de

Koningsbruggen, Rob van *(Dutch painter, b.1948)* **BA**
Bibl: Amsterdam (NLD), Stedelijk Museum, Fundamentele Schilderkunst (1975); ▶ARTbibl. mod., 13, 16

Konink or Coning, Daniel de *(Dutch artist, 1668-p.1720)* **WC**
Koninxlo → see Coninxloo, Gilles van

Konishi, Keisuke *(Westernized Oriental artist, 20th cent.)* **WC**

Könitz, Peter *(German sculptor, b.1942)* **BA**
Bibl: ▶Babington Smith, Contemp. artists; ▶Intl. dir. exh. artists, 1982; Munich(DEU), Stad Galim Lenbachhaus, Kunstf.Maxim. PETER KONITZ(1980)

Konnakis Painter **JG**

Kono, Yoshimi *(Architect)* **AV**
Bibl: Abitare, 1987 Nov., no.259, p.222

Konody, Paul G., Mrs.(Isabel) → see Codrington, Isabel

Konopka, Ladislav *(Czech architect, 1933-)* **AV**
Bibl: Architektura ČSR, 1988, v.47, no.4, p.20

Konrad Laib → see Laib, Konrad

Konrad von Friesach **BA GC WC**
(Austrian painter, act.1458) **BA**
(German artist, op.1458) **WC**
(German painter, act.1458) **GC**
Bibl: Öster. Zeit. für Kunst u. Denk. 32 (1978) 63-71; ▶Thieme-Becker

Friesach, Konrad von **GC**
Konrad von Soest → see Conrad von Soest

Konrad von Straubing *(German artist, op.c.1380)* **WC**
Konrad Weigand → see Weigand, Konrad

Konrad, Adolf Ferdinand *(American painter, b.1915)*   **BA**
 Bibl: ▶MoMA libr. cat.; ▶WW Amer. Art, 1989

Konrad, Anton *(German metalsmith, 1880-1938)*   **BA**
 Bibl: Dresdener kunstblatter, XXVI, 2-3 (1982) 56-64, 75-80

Konrad, James *(American printmaker, b.1943)*   **BA**
 Bibl: Davenport (IA, USA), Munic. Art Gall., Family album (1975)

Konrád, Miroslav *(Czech painter, 20th c.)*   **BA**
 Bibl: Vytvarna Kultura, V/5 (1981) pp.50-52

Konstant, Paul *(American architect)*   **AV**

Konstantin Andreevic Somov → *see* Somov, Konstantin Andreevič

Konstantin Egorovic Makovskij → *see* Makovskij, Konstantin Egorovič

Konstantine, Dimitrios → *see* Constantine, Dimitrios

Konstantinidis, Aris *(Greek architect, 1913-)*   **AV**
 Bibl: ▶Contemp. archts.

Kontchalvoski, Piotr Petrowitsch → *see* Končalovskij, Pëtr Petrovič

Konti, Isidore   **BA GC**
 (American sculptor (b. Hungary), 1862-1938)   **GC**
 (Hungarian sculptor in USA, 1862-1938)   **BA**
 Bibl: NY Times obit.; ▶RILA/BHA; ▶Thieme-Becker

Kontio, Jaakko *(Finnish architect)*   **AV**
 Bibl: Architektur + Wettbewerbe, 1985 Mar., no.121, p.68

Kontoglou, F. *(Greek artist, 20th cent.)*   **WC**

Kontozoglov, Kalliope K. *(British architect, London)*   **AV**
 Bibl: ▶RIBA members, 1987

Konupek, Jan *(Czech artist, 1883-1950)*   **WC**

Konzal, Joseph *(American sculptor, b.1905)*   **BA**
 Bibl: ARTS MAGAZINE, LIV/9(MAY 1980), 19; ▶MoMA libr. cat.

Koo, Rosalynn C.   **AV**

Koogen, Leendert van der → *see* Cooghen, Leendert van der

Koogh, Adrianus van der   **GC WC**
 (Dutch artist, 1796-1831)   **WC**
 (Dutch painter, 1796-1831)   **GC**
 Bibl: ▶Bénézit

Kooghe, Abraham de   **GC**
 (Dutch artist, op.1620-1680)   **WC**
 (Dutch painter, act.1632-d. aft. 1678)   **GC**
 Bibl: ▶Bénézit
 Coog, Abraham de   **GC**
 Cooge or Kooge, Abraham de   **WC**

Kooi, Willem Bartel van den → *see* Kooi, Willem Bartel van der

Kooi, Willem Bartel van der   **BA GC**
 (Dutch artist, 1768-1836)   **WC**
 (Dutch painter, 1768-1836)   **BA GC**
 Bibl: ▶Bénézit; ▶Scheen, Ned. beeldende kunst.; ▶Thieme-Becker

Kooi, Willem Bartel van den   **WC**

Kool → *see* Kool, Willem Gillisz.

Kool or Koolen, Jacobus *(Dutch artist, -1666/7)*   **WC**

Kool, Cool, Coolen or Koolen, Willem Gillisz. → *see* Kool, Willem Gillisz.

Kool, Sipke   **GC**
 (Dutch artist, 1836-1902)   **WC**
 (Dutch painter, 1836-1902)   **GC**
 Bibl: ▶Bénézit

Kool, Sipke (Cornelis)   **WC**
 Kool, Sipke (Cornelis) → *see* Kool, Sipke

Kool, Willem Gillisz.   **GC PR**
 (Dutch artist, 1608/9-1666)   **WC**
 (Dutch painter, 1608-1666)   **PR**
 (Dutch, 1608/9-1666)   **GC**
 Bibl: Getty Photo Study Coll. (Ptgs.); ▶Thieme-Becker; ▶Witt checklist
 Cool, Willem Gillisz.   **GC**
 Kool   **PR**

Kool, Cool, Coolen or Koolen, Willem Gillisz.   **WC**
 Koul   **PR**
 Willem Gillisz. Kool   **PR**

Koolhaas, Rem   **AV BA**
 (Dutch architect, b.1944)   **BA**
 (Dutch architect, Rotterdam and London, 1944-)   **AV**
 Bibl: Artforum (Sep 81) 41; Baumeister, 1988 May, v.85, no.5, p.41; Dyk, DUTCH ART&ARCH.TODAY(12 DEC 1982), 20; ▶Libr. of Congr. Name Auth. File

Koonce, Norman L. *(American architect, Bogalusa, La.; since 1989, president of the American Architectural Foundation)*   **AV**
 Bibl: ▶AIA Pro File, 1987-88

Kooning, Elaine de → *see* de Kooning, Elaine

Kooning, Elaine Marie Catherine de → *see* de Kooning, Elaine

Kooning, Willem de → *see* de Kooning, Willem

Kooninghsloo → *see* Coninxloo, Gilles van

Koons, Jeff *(American sculptor, b.1955)*   **BA**
 Bibl: ▶Art Index, v.37, Jan.1990; Tampa (FL, USA), Univ. So. Fla. Art Galleries, Objects, structures (1983)

Koop, Heinz *(German architect, Fellbach, 1942-)*   **AV**
 Bibl: Deutsche Bauzeitung, 1985 Nov., v.119, no.11, p.126

Koop, Wanda *(Canadian painter, b.1951)*   **BA**
 Bibl: Winnipeg (Man, CAN), Winnipeg Art Gallery, AIRPLANES AND THE WALL..., 1985

Koopman, Augustus → *see* Koopman, Augustus B.

Koopman, Augustus B.   **WI**
 (American artist, 1869-1914)   **WC WI**
 Koopman, Augustus   **WC**

Koornstra, Metten Teunis *(Dutch painter, printmaker, 1912-1978)*   **BA**
 Bibl: ▶Scheen, Ned. beeldende kunst.; Schiedem(NLD), STEDELIJK MUS., GRAFIELMANIFESTATIE(1978); Wessem, NEDERLANDS GRAFIEK NA 1945(1964), 77-78

Koorts, Hans *(South African architect)*   **AV**
 Bibl: Architecture SA = Argitektuur SA, 1989 Jan-Feb., no.1-2, p.33

Kop, David van de *(Dutch sculptor, b.1937)*   **BA**
 Bibl: ▶Scheen, Ned. beeldende kunst.

Kopac, Slavko *(Yugoslav artist, 20th cent.)*   **WC**

Kopallik, Franz *(German artist, 1860-)*   **WC**

Køpcke, Arthur Addi *(Danish painter, sculptor, 1928-1977)*   **BA**
 Bibl: ▶ARTbibl. mod., 20/1, #03064; KUNST OG MUSEUM, XIX(1984), 99-120; ▶Libr. of Congr. Name Auth. File, 1987-89; ▶Nørregård-Nielsen, Dansk kunst

Kopec, Luis *(Colombian architect)*   **AV**
 Bibl: Escala, 1988, no.138, p.5

Kopelijanski, Daniel G. *(Soviet architect, Moscow)*   **AV**
 Bibl: Architektur der DDR, 1986 Nov., v.35, no.11, p.686

Kopelson, Allen R. *(American architect, Morristown, N.J)*   **AV**
 Bibl: ▶AIA Pro File, 1987-88

Koper, Geoffrey L. *(American architect)*   **AV**

Kopetzki, Johan → *see* Kupezky, Johann

Kopf → *see* Kopf, Maxim

Kopf, Maxim   **PR WC**
 (German artist, 1892-)   **WC**
 (German painter, b. 1892)   **PR**
 Bibl: ▶Bénézit; ▶Witt checklist
 Kopf   **PR**
 Maxim Kopf   **PR**

Kopff, A. *(German(?) painter, 17th century)*   **GC**
 Bibl: Getty Photo Study Coll. (Duits coll.)

Kopff, J. ter *(Dutch painter, 17th century)*   **GC**
 Bibl: Getty Photo Study Coll. (Douwes coll.)

Kornhas, Carl (*German ceramist, sculptor, 1857-1931*)   **BA**
Bibl: ▶Thieme-Becker; ▶Vollmer, Künst.-Lex. 20. Jhr.

Kornhäusel, Josef → see Kornhäusel, Josef Georg

Kornhäusel, Josef Georg   **BA**
(*Austrian architect, 1782-1860*)   **BA**
(*Austrian architect, Vienna, 1782-1860*)   **AV**
(*German artist, 1782(?)-1860*)   **WC**
Bibl: ▶Macmillan encyc. archts.; ▶Österr. biog. Lex. 1815-1950; ▶Portoghesi, Diz. arch. e urbanistica; ▶Thieme-Becker

Kornhäusel, Josef   **AV WC**

Körnig, Hans (*German painter, printmaker, b.1905*)   **BA**
Bibl: ▶Intl. dir. exh. artists, 1982; ▶Vollmer, Künst.-Lex. 20. Jhr.

Korniloff, A. (*French architect*)   **AV**
Bibl: Techniques et architecture, 1986 Oct.-Nov., v.368, p.17

Kornis, Dezső (*Hungarian painter, b.1908*)   **BA**
Bibl: Lancz, ACTA HISTORIAE ARTIUM, XXI/1-2(1975), 167-194; NY MAGAZINE INDEX; ▶Vollmer, Künst.-Lex. 20. Jhr.

Korobkin, Barry (*American architect*)   **AV**
Bibl: Progressive architecture, 1985 Aug., v.66, no.8, p.103

Korobov, V.M. (*Russian artist, 20th cent.*)   **WC**

Korochansky, Michel (*French artist, 20th cent.*)   **WC**

Korolev, Boris Danilovič (*Russian sculptor, 1884-1963*)   **BA**
Bibl: ▶Bénézit; ▶Bowlt, Russian avant-garde; ▶Vollmer, Künst.-Lex. 20. Jhr.

Korolev, Jurij Konstantinovič (*Russian painter, printmaker, b.1929*)   **BA**
Bibl: John Bowlt corresp., Nov. 1977; Voronov, JURI KOROLEV(1976)

Korompay, Giovanni   **BA WC**
(*Italian artist, 1904-*)   **WC**
(*Italian painter, printmaker, b.1904*)   **BA**
Bibl: ▶Comanducci, Diz.; ▶Parry, Contemp. art

Koronaiou, S. (*Architect, Greece*)   **AV**
Bibl: Themata chorov + technon, 1984, v.15, p.155

Körösfői-Kriesch, Aladár (*Hungarian painter, printmaker, 1863-1920*)   **BA**
Bibl: ▶Bénézit; ▶Encyc. world art; Kampis, Art Hungary; ▶Thieme-Becker

Korot, Beryl (*American artist, b.1945*)   **BA**
Bibl: ▶WW Amer. Art, 1976

Korovin, Konstantin Alekseevič   **BA**
(*Russian artist, 1861-1939*)   **WC**
(*Russian painter, sculptor, printmaker, 1861-1939*)   **BA**
Bibl: ▶Bowlt, Russian avant-garde; ▶Encyc. world art; ▶Vollmer, Künst.-Lex. 20. Jhr.

Korowin, Konstantin Alexejewitsch   **WC**

Korovine, Alexei Konstantinovitch (*Russian artist, 1897-1950*)   **WC**

Korowin, Konstantin Alexejewitsch → see Korovin, Konstantin Alekseevič

Korrel du Jardin → see Dujardin, Karel

Korrodi, Ernesto (*Swiss decorator, architect in PRT, 1870-1944*)   **BA**
Bibl: GUIA...ARQUITECTONICO DE LISBOA (1987); ▶Natl. union cat., 1956; ▶NYPL Art & Arch. Div., Dict. catalog; ▶Portoghesi, Diz. arch. e urbanistica; ▶Thieme-Becker

Korsmo, Arne (*Norwegian architect, 1900-1968*)   **AV**
Bibl: ▶Contemp. archts.

Korsoukhine, Alexis (*Russian artist, 1835-1894*)   **WC**

Korte, Bernard (*Danish landscape architect*)   **AV**
Bibl: Landskab, 1989 May, v.70, no.3, p.62

Korteling, Bartus (*Dutch draughtsman, 1853-1930*)   **GC**
Bibl: ▶Scheen, Ned. beeldende kunst.

Korteweg, Neeltje (*Dutch sculptor, b.1944*)   **BA**
Bibl: Paris (FRA), Inst. néerlandais, 9 femmes constructivistes (1976)

Korth, Fred G. (*American (b. Germany), 1902-1983, active Chicago, IL, U.S. 1930s*)   **JG**

Korth, Karl T. (*American architect, San Francisco, CA*)   **AV**
Bibl: Progressive architecture, 1984 Jan., v.65, no.1, p.106

Kortright, Guy (*British artist, b.1877*)   **WI**

Kortright, Henry Somers (*British artist, 1870-1942*)   **WI**

Kortzau, Ole (*Danish architect, Copenhagen, 1939-*)   **AV**
Bibl: ▶Danske Arkitekters Landsforbund, 1984-85

Korumpany, Frantisek Vavrinec (*Russian artist, 19th cent.*)   **WC**

Korus, Gunter H. (*American artist, op.20th c.*)   **WI**

Korwan, Franz   **GC WC**
(*German artist, 1865-*)   **WC**
(*German painter, b.1865*)   **GC**
Bibl: ▶Thieme-Becker

Korybut, Kasimir (*American architect, Fla*)   **AV**
Bibl: Garden design, 1987 Spring, v.6, no.1, p.76

Korzeniewski, Swetik (*Australian architect, 1946-*)   **AV**
Bibl: Architecture & urbanism, 1987 Oct., no.10(205), p.56

Kós, Károly   **AV BA**
(*Hungarian architect and poet, 1883-1977*)   **AV**
(*Hungarian architect, 1883-1977*)   **BA**
Bibl: Öster. Zeit. für Kunst u. Denk. 33 (1979); ▶Portoghesi, Diz. arch. e urbanistica; ▶Thieme-Becker

Kos, Paul Joseph (*American sculptor, b.1942*)   **BA**
Bibl: ▶WW Amer. Art, 1976

Kosa, Emil Jean, Jr. (*American artist, 1903-1968*)   **WI**

Kosárek, Adolf   **BA WC**
(*Czech artist, 1830-1859*)   **WC**
(*Czech painter, 1830-1859*)   **BA**
Bibl: ▶Encyk. českého výtv. umění; ▶Thieme-Becker

Kosarek, N. Thomas → see Kosarek, Norman Thomas

Kosarek, Norman Thomas
(*American architect, Austin, Tex*)   **AV**
Bibl: ▶AIA Pro File, 1987-88
Kosarek, N. Thomas   **AV**

Koscianski, Leonard J. (*American painter, b.1952*)   **BA**
Bibl: ▶WW Amer. Art

Kosciuszko, Tadeusz (*Polish artist, 1746-1817*)   **WC**

Kosel, Gerhard (*East German architect, 1909-*)   **AV**
Bibl: Architektur der DDR, 1989 Jan., v.38, no.1, p.51

Kosel, Hermann (*German artist, 1896-*)   **WC**

Kosh, Feather (*American artist, 20th c.*)   **BA**
Bibl: Philadelphia (PA, USA), Temple University, Samuel Paley Library, The Tyler show (1974)

Koshiba, Junji (*Japanese architect*)   **AV**
Bibl: Interiors, 1989 Sept., v.149, no.2, p.181

Kosiński, Błażej (*Polish architect, stucco artist, act.1738-1752*)   **BA**
Bibl: ▶Thieme-Becker; ▶Wielka ilustr. encyk.

Kosinski, Jozef (*Polish artist, 1753-1821*)   **WC**

Koskinen, Harro Juhami (*Finnish painter, b.1945*)   **BA**
Bibl: Guide exh. artists: Sculp.

Koskova, Eva (*Czech architect*)   **AV**
Bibl: Architektura ČSR, 1988, v.47, no.1, p.42

Koskull, Anders Gustaf (*Scandinavian artist, 1831-1904*)   **WC**

Kösler, Michał (*Polish sculptor, act. 1699-1728*)   **BA**
Bibl: ▶Bénézit; ▶Thieme-Becker

Koslinsky, Vladimir → see Kozlinskij, Vladimir Ivanovič

Koslowskij, Michail Iwanowitsch
(Russian artist, 1753-1802) **WC**

Kosmalski, Chris *(American
designer, Los Angeles)* **AV**
Bibl: Builder, 1988 Apr., v.11,
no.4, p.6258

Kosmi, Brigit de *(French architect)* **AV**
Bibl: Architecture d'aujourd'hui,
1985 Apr., no.238, p.104

*Kosmowski, Magdalena
Abakanowicz→see Abakanowicz,
Magdalena*

Kosmulski, Leon *(Polish painter,
printmaker, 20th c.)* **BA**
Bibl: Rocznik Muz. Narodowega w
Warszawie, XXI (1977) pp.251-
292

Kosnick-Kloss, Hannah (Jeanne)
(German artist, 1892-) **WC**

Kosolapov, Alexander *(Russian
painter in USA, 20th c.)* **BA**
Bibl: Lerman, O., in ARTS
MAGAZINE LVIII/6 (Feb 1984) 115

Koss, Gene H. *(American sculptor,
b.1947)* **BA**
Bibl: Guide exh. artists: N. Amer.
ptrs.; ▶WW Amer. Art

Koss-Den'šina, Ėkaterina *(Russian
toymaker, 1901-1976)* **BA**
Bibl: DEKORATIVNOE ISKUSSTVO
SSSR, 12/229(DEC.1976), 37

Kossak, Jerzy *(Polish artist, 1890-
1963)* **WC**

Kossak, Juliusz Fortunat **BA WC**
(Polish artist, 1824-1899) **WC**
(Polish painter, 1824-1899) **BA**
Bibl: ▶Bénézit; ▶Thieme-Becker

Kossak, Wojciech **BA**
(French artist, 1857-1942) **WC**
(Polish painter, 1857-1942) **BA**

**Kossak, Wojciech (Adalbert),
Ritter von** **WC**

*Kossak, Wojciech (Adalbert), Ritter
von→see Kossak, Wojciech*

Kossatz, Les *(Australian painter,
sculptor, designer, b.1943)* **BA**

Kossdorff, Gert *(Austrian architect)* **AV**
Bibl: Bauforum, 1988, v.21, no.
127, p.39

Kossinsky, A. *(Russian architect)* **AV**
Bibl: Process: architecture, 1985
Jan., no.54, p.153

Kosso→see Eloul, Kosso

Kossoff, Leon **BA WC WI**
(British artist, 1926-) **WC**
(British artist, b.1926) **WI**
(British painter, b.1926) **BA**
Bibl: ▶Bénézit; ▶Contemp. artists;
▶Intl. dir. exh. artists; ▶MoMA
libr. cat.

Kossowska, Felicja *(Polish artist,
18th cent.)* **WC**

Kost **WC WI**
(American artist, op.1855-1865) **WI**
(American artist, op.c.1860) **WC**
*Kost, Frederick W.→see Kost,
Frederick Weller*

Kost, Frederick Weller **WI**
(American artist, 1865-1923) **WC WI**

Kost, Frederick W. **WC**

Kosta, Alex→see Alex, Kosta

Kostabi, Mark **BA WI**
(American artist, op.1983-) **WI**
*(American painter, sculptor,
b.1960)* **BA**
Bibl: ▶WW Amer. Art, 1986

Kostandi, Kiviak Konstantinovič
(Russian painter, 1852-1921) **BA**
Bibl: ▶Bénézit; ▶Encyc. world art;
▶Fogg Mus. Libr. cat.; ▶Larousse
grande encyc.; ▶Thieme-Becker

Kosteckij, Vladimir Nikolaevič
(Russian painter, b.1905) **BA**
Bibl: ▶Encyc. world art; ▶Vollmer,
Künst.-Lex. 20. Jhr.

Kostelac, Ante Josip von **AV BA**
*(West German architect, born in
Yugoslavia, 1937-)* **AV**
*(Yugoslav architect in DEU,
b.1937)* **BA**
Bibl: Das Kunstwerk, n.3-4, Sept.
1983, p.128; ▶WW Germany,
1974

Kostelanetz, Richard *(American
artist, author, b.1940)* **BA**
Bibl: ▶MoMA libr. cat.; NYMMA;
WW Amer., 1976

Koster→see Koster, Everhardus

Köster family *(German
cabinetmakers, 18th c.)* **BA**
Bibl: ▶Thieme-Becker

Koster or Coster, Simon de *(Dutch
artist, 1767-1831)* **WC**

*Koster, Antonie Lodewijk
(Anton)→see Koster, Antonie
Louis*

Koster, Antonie Louis **GC**
(Dutch artist, 1859-1937) **WC**
(Dutch painter, 1859-1937) **GC**
Bibl: ▶Thieme-Becker

**Koster, Antonie Lodewijk
(Anton)** **WC**

*Köster, Carl Georg→see Köster,
Georg*

Koster, Christian Philipp *(German
artist, 1784-1851)* **WC**

Koster, David *(British artist, b.1926)* **WI**

Koster, Everhardus **BA GC PR WC**
(1817-1892) **BA**
(Dutch artist, 1817-1892) **WC**
*(Dutch painter and printmaker,
1817-1892)* **GC**
(Dutch painter, 1817-1892) **PR**
Bibl: Portland (ME, USA), Mus of
Art, Sea & Sail; ▶Thieme-Becker

Everhardus Koster **PR**
Koster **PR**

Köster, Georg **GC**
(German artist, 1812-1893) **WC**
(German painter, 1812-1893) **GC**
Bibl: ▶Thieme-Becker

Köster, Carl Georg **GC WC**

Koster, J. M. De *(Dutch architect)* **AV**
Bibl: Gemeentewerken, 1986
Feb., v.15, no.2, p.34

Koster, Jo *(Dutch painter, 1869-
1944)* **GC**
Bibl: ▶Scheen, Ned. beeldende
kunst.; ▶Thieme-Becker

**Koster, Jojanna Petronella
Catharina Antoinetta** **GC**

Koster, Johannes *(Dutch painter,
b.1941)* **BA**
Bibl: Amsterdam (NLD), Museum
Fodor, JOHANNES KOSTER (1976)

*Koster, Jojanna Petronella Catharina
Antoinetta→see Koster, Jo*

Koster, Karl *(German artist, 1842-
1904)* **WC**

Köster, Peter *(German sculptor, ca.
1621-1669)* **BA**
Bibl: Krüger, DAS LEIBNIZHAUS IN
HANNOVER (1985) PhD diss.;
▶Thieme-Becker

Kösters, Bernd *(German architect,
Munster)* **AV**
Bibl: Deutsche Bauzeitschrift,
1986 Mar., v.34, no.3, p.303

Kostin, Konstantin K. *(Russian
artist, 20th c.)* **BA**
Bibl: DEKORATIVNOE ISKUSSTVO
(JUNE 1974), 38-40

Kostiuk, Michael Marion *(American
photographer, b.1944)* **BA**
Bibl: ▶WW Amer. Art, 1989

Kostka, Robert **WC WI**
(American artist, 20th cent.) **WC**
(American artist, b.1928) **WI**

Kostopoulos, K. *(Greek architect)* **AV**
Bibl: Architektonika Themata =
Architecture in Greece, 1989,
no.23, p.185

Kostritsky, George **AV**

Kostrzewa, Antoni *(Polish artist,
20th c.)* **BA**
Bibl: Berlin (DEU), Munzkabinett,
Polnischer Medaillen (1978)

Kostrzewski, Franciszek *(Polish
artist, 1826-1911)* **WC**

Kostulski, Thomas *(W. German
architect)* **AV**
Bibl: Arch Plus, 1986 Nov., no.87,
p.47

Kostyniuk, Ronald P. *(Canadian
sculptor, b.1941)* **BA**
Bibl: ▶Artists Canada; ▶WW
Amer. Art

Kosuth, Joseph **BA WC**
*(American conceptual artist,
b.1945)* **BA**
(Hungarian artist, 1945-) **WC**
Bibl: ▶Contemp. artists; ▶WW
Amer. Art, 1984

Koszatz, August *(German
cabinetmaker, act.1841)* **BA**
Bibl: Böhme, Dresd. Kstbl.
XXX/41 (1986) pp.115-119

Koszta, Josef→see Koszta, József

Koszta, József   **BA**
  (Hungarian painter, 1864-
  1949)   **BA GC**
  Bibl: ▶Bénézit; ▶Fogg Mus. Libr.
  cat.; Kampis, Art Hungary, p.389;
  ▶Thieme-Becker; ▶Uj magyar
  lexikon; ▶Vollmer, Künst.-Lex. 20.
  Jhr.

Koszta, Josef   **GC**

Kotas, Jeremy *(American architect)*   **AV**

Kotasz, Karoly (Karl) *(Hungarian
artist, 1872-1941)*   **WC**

Kotaya, Vojhef *(Hungarian medalist,
20th c.)*   **BA**
  Bibl: PUSHKIN

Kotchar, Ervand *(Russian artist,
1899-)*   **WC**

Kothgasser, Anton   **BA**
  *(Austrian glass painter,
porcelain painter, 1769-1851)*   **BA**
  (German artist, 1769-1851)   **WC**
  Bibl: ▶Honey, Euro. ceramic;
  ▶Thieme-Becker

**Kothgasser, Kothgassner or
Kottgassner, Anton**   **WC**
*Kothgasser, Kothgassner or
Kottgassner, Anton → see
Kothgasser, Anton*

Kotik, Jan *(Czech painter, author in
DEU, b.1916)*   **BA**

Kotík, Pravoslav *(Czech painter,
printmaker, b.1889)*   **BA**
  Bibl: ▶Bénézit; ▶Vollmer,
  Künst.-Lex. 20. Jhr.

Kotler, Martin *(American painter,
20th c.)*   **BA**
  Bibl: Rand, H., in ARTS MAGAZINE
  LIX/6 (Feb 1985) 20

Kotov, Petr Ivanovič   **BA**
  (Russian artist, 1889-1953)   **WC**
  (Russian painter, 1889-1953)   **BA**
  Bibl: ▶Fogg Mus. Libr. cat.;
  ▶Valkenier, Russian realist art;
  ▶Vollmer, Künst.-Lex. 20. Jhr.;
  ▶WWW USSR

Kotow, Piotr Ivanovitsh   **WC**
*Kotow, Piotr Ivanovitsh → see Kotov,
Petr Ivanovič*

Kotsch, Theodor   **BA WC**
  (German artist, 1818-1884)   **WC**
  (German painter, 1818-1884)   **BA**
  Bibl: ▶Thieme-Becker;
  Weschenfelder, K., NIEDERDTSCH.
  BEITRÄGE XXII (1983) 186-208

Kotschenreiter, Hugo   **GC WC**
  (German artist, 1854-1908)   **WC**
  (German painter, 1854-1908)   **GC**
  Bibl: ▶Thieme-Becker

Kotsis, Aleksander   **BA**
  (Polish artist, 1836-1877)   **WC**
  (Polish painter, 1836-1877)   **BA**
  Bibl: ▶Thieme-Becker; ▶Wielka
  ilustr. encyk.

Kotsis, Alexandre   **WC**
*Kotsis, Alexandre → see Kotsis,
Aleksander*

Koudelka, Josef *(Czech
photographer, b.1938)*   **BA**
  Bibl: Amsterdam (NLD), Stedelijk
  Museum, JOSEF KONDELKA
  (1978); ▶MoMA libr. cat.

Koudelka, Pauline Freiin von
(German artist, 1806-1840)   **WC**

Kouderov, Leonid *(Soviet architect)*   **AV**
  Bibl: Building, 1989 May 26,
  v.254, no.21, p.24

Koudra, Mike *(British architect,
head of Research and Statistics,
RIBA)*   **AV**
  Bibl: RIBA journal, 1984 Aug.,
  v.91, no.8, p.34

*Koudriachov, Ivan → see Kudrjashev,
Ivan*

Koukis, Yannis *(Greek architect)*   **AV**
  Bibl: Architecture: the AIA
  journal, 1985 Sept., v.74, no.9,
  p.140

Koul → see Kool, Willem Gillisz.

Koula, Jan *(Czechoslovak architect,
1855-1919)*   **AV**
  Bibl: Architectural Association
  quarterly, 1981, Oct., p.47

Koulermos, Panos *(Architect, "born
in Famagusta, Cyprus, in practice
in London, Milan, Athens and Los
Angeles", 1933-)*   **AV**
  Bibl: Architecture and urbanism,
  1979 May, no.104, p.67

Koulouridis, D. *(Architect, Greece)*   **AV**
  Bibl: Design + art in Greece,
  1982, v.13, p.130

Kounavine, A. *(Russian artist, 18th
cent.)*   **WC**

Kounelakis *(Greek artist, op.1864)*   **WC**

Kounellis, Jannis *(Italian artist,
b.1936)*   **BA**
  Bibl: ▶Bénézit; ▶Bolaffi;
  ▶Contemp. artists

Kourist, Werner *(German, 20th c.)*   **BA**

Koursaros, Harry *(American painter,
20th c.)*   **BA**
  Bibl: ▶Intl. dir. exh. artists

*Koustodieff → see Kustodiev, Boris
Mihajlovič*

*Koustodieff, Boris M. → see
Kustodiev, Boris Mihajlovič*

*Koustodieff, Boris Mikhailovitch → see
Kustodiev, Boris Mihajlovič*

Kouvela, Agne *(Architect, Greece)*   **AV**
  Bibl: Design + art in Greece,
  1982, v.13, p.85

Kouwen, Philip *(Dutch
draughtsman, b.1922)*   **GC**
  Bibl: ▶Scheen, Ned. beeldende
  kunst.

Kouwenbergh, Philip van *(Dutch
painter, 1671-1729)*   **BA**
  Bibl: ▶Bénézit; Meijer, F.G., OUD
  HOLLAND, CII/ 4 (1988), p. 313-
  321; ▶Thieme-Becker

*Kouwenbergh, Philip van → see
Couwenberg, Philips van*

*Kouwenhorn, Pieter → see
Couwenhorn, Pieter*

Kouwenhoven Jacob van *(Dutch
draughtsman, 1777-1825)*   **GC**
  Bibl: ▶Thieme-Becker

*Kouwerhoven, Pieter → see
Couwenhorn, Pieter*

Kouydyck → see Koedijck, Isaac

Kouzin, Yuri V. *(Russian architect)*   **AV**
  Bibl: Japan architect, 1988 Mar.,
  v.63, no.3(371), p.41

Kouzmanoff, Alexander   **AV BA**
  (American architect, b.1915)   **BA**
  *(American architect, New York,
N.Y, 1915-)*   **AV**
  Bibl: ▶AIA Pro File; ▶Macmillan
  encyc. archts.; NYC phone bk.

Kovac, Milan   **AV**

Kovacic, Josip *(Yugoslav artist,
1946-)*   **WC**

Kovačić, Viktor *(Croatian architect,
1874-1924)*   **AV**
  Bibl: ▶Thieme-Becker

Kovacs, Andrea *(American
photographer, b.1953)*   **BA**
  Bibl: ▶Babington Smith, Contemp.
  artists; New York (NY, USA), New
  Mus.,
  Deconstruction/reconstruction
  (1980)

Kovács, Attila *(Hungarian architect)*   **AV**

Kovacs, Margit *(Hungarian ceramist,
b.1902)*   **BA**
  Bibl: ▶Vollmer, Künst.-Lex. 20. Jhr.

Kovács, Mihály   **BA WC**
  (Hungarian artist, 1818-1892)   **WC**
  (Hungarian painter, 1818-1892)   **BA**
  Bibl: ▶Thieme-Becker

Kovács, Miklós *(Hungarian
architect, Budapest, 1938-)*   **AV**
  Bibl: Magyar építőművészet,
  1987, v.78, no.4-5

*Kovács, Petra de Castro y
Blanco → see Castro y Blanco, Petra
de*

Kovács, Sándor *(Hungarian
architect, Budapest, 1935-)*   **AV**
  Bibl: Magyar építőművészet,
  1987, v.78, no.6, p.23

Kovacs, Vilmas *(Hungarian artist,
20th cent.)*   **WC**

Kovalevsky, Pavel Osipovitch
(Russian artist, 1843-1903)   **WC**

Kovář, Jan *(Czech architect)*   **AV**
  Bibl: Architektura ČSR, 1988,
  v.47, no.4, p.62

Kovar, Stanislav *(Czech artist, 20th
cent.)*   **WC**

Kovatsch, Manfred *(Austrian
architect, 1940-)*   **AV**
  Bibl: Das Kunstwerk, no.3-4, Sept.
  1983, p.53

Kovrovskij, S. *(Russian painter, 20th
c.)*   **BA**
  Bibl: Drobov, Zivopis Sovetskoj
  Belorussij

Kowalewsky, Jobst *(West German architect, Mainz)*   **AV**
Bibl: Architektur, Innenarchitektur, Technischer Ausbau, 1989 Apr., v.97, no.4, p.46

Kowalke, Ron   **WC WI**
(American artist, 1936-)   WC
(American artist, b.1936)   WI

Kowalski, Alfred von Wierusz→see Kowalski-Wierusz, Alfred von

Kowalski, Dennis Allen *(American artist, b.1938)*   **BA**
Bibl: ▶WW Amer. Art, 1979

Kowalski, Ivan Ivanovitch *(Russian artist, 20th cent.)*   **WC**

Kowalski, Karla *(Austrian architect, 1941-)*   **AV**
Bibl: Kenchiku bunka, 1984 Dec., v.39, no.458, p.98

Szyszkowitz-Kowalski, Karla   AV

Kowalski, Piotr   **AV BA**
(French artist)   AV
(French sculptor, b.1927)   BA
Bibl: Architecture intérieure créé, 1985 Dec.-1986 Jan., no.209, p.52; ▶Bénézit; ▶Contemp. artists; ▶Intl. dir. arts; ▶Intl. dir. exh. artists, 1983; ▶MoMA libr. cat.; ▶Parry, Contemp. art

Kowalski, Stanisław *(Polish textile designer, 20th c.)*   **BA**
Bibl: Dek. Iskusstvo SSSR, 216 (Nov 1975) 4F

Kowalski-Wierusz→see Kowalski-Wierusz, Alfred von
Kowalski-Wierusz or Wierusz-Kowalski, Alfred von→see Kowalski-Wierusz, Alfred von
Kowalski-Wierusz, Alfred→see Kowalski-Wierusz, Alfred von

Kowalski-Wierusz, Alfred von   **PR**
(Polish artist, 1849-1915)   WC
(Polish painter, 1849-1915)   PR
(Polish, 1849-1915)   GC
Bibl: Getty Photo Study Coll. (Ptgs.); ▶Thieme-Becker; ▶Witt checklist

Alfred von Kowalski-Wierusz   PR
Kowalski, Alfred von Wierusz   PR
Kowalski-Wierusz   PR

Kowalski-Wierusz or Wierusz-Kowalski, Alfred von   **WC**
Kowalski-Wierusz, Alfred   **GC**
Wierusz-Kowalski, Alfred   GC
Wierusz-Kowalski, Alfred von   PR

Kowalsky, Anton Hermann *(German artist, 1813-)*   **WC**

Kowalsky, Elaine *(Canadian printmaker, painter, b.1948)*   **BA**
Bibl: Birmingham (GBR), Ikon Gallery, ELAINE KOWALSKY... (1986); ▶Intl. dir. exh. artists, 1982, 1983; ▶WW Art

Kowalyk, Ronald *(American ceramist, b.1946)*   **BA**
Bibl: Akron (OH, USA), Art Inst., Rips in reality (1978)

Kowarski, Felicjam Szczesny *(Polish artist, 1890-1948)*   **WC**

Kowner, Josef *(Russian artist, 1895-)*   **WC**

Koyabe, Ikuko *(Japanese architect)*   **AV**
Bibl: Japan architect, 1988 Aug., v.63, no.8(376), p.59

Koyama, Akira *(Japanese architect, 1951-)*   **AV**
Bibl: Japan architect, 1988 Nov.-Dec., v.63, no.11-12, p.68

Koyama, Hisao *(Japanese architect)*   **AV**
Bibl: Space design, 1984 Sep., no. 240, p.3

Koyanagui, Sei *(Westernized Oriental artist, 1896-)*   **WC**

Kozakiewicz, Anton *(Polish artist, 1841-)*   **WC**

Kozarewska, Magda *(British artist, b.1952)*   **WI**

Kožel, Janez *(Yugoslav architect, Llubljana)*   **AV**
Bibl: Bauwelt, 1989 Jan.27, v.80, no.5, p.156

Koželj, Matija *(Yugoslav painter, 1842-1917)*   **BA**
Bibl: ▶Busse, Maler u. Bildhauer 19. Jahr.; Kamnik, Kulturni center, MATIJA KOŽELJ (1986); ▶Thieme-Becker

Koželka, Karel   **AV**

Koźik, Gregor Thorsten *(German printmaker, b.1948)*   **BA**
Bibl: Hamburg (DEU), Kunstverein, Zeitvergleich (1982)

Kozina, Sándor *(Hungarian painter, 1808-1873)*   **BA**
Bibl: ▶Thieme-Becker

Kozjak, Ivan *(German architect, Hannover)*   **AV**
Bibl: Detail, 1981 Jan.-Feb., no.1, p.29

Kozlik, Lee *(Canadian painter, b.1953)*   **BA**
Bibl: Kingston(ONT, CAN), Etherington Centre. LEE KOZLIK... (1980)

Kozlinskij, Vladimir Ivanovič   **BA**
(Russian artist, 1891-1967)   WC
(Russian stage designer, printmaker, 1891-1967)   BA
Bibl: ▶Bowlt, Russian avant-garde

Koslinsky, Vladimir   **WC**

Kozloff, Joyce   **BA WI**
(American artist, b.1942)   WI
(American painter, printmaker, b.1942)   BA
Bibl: ▶WW Amer. Art, 1976

Blumberg, Joyce   WI

Kozloff, Max *(American photographer, critic, b.1933)*   **BA**
Bibl: ▶Intl. dir. exh. artists, 1983, v.2; ▶Macmillan photog. encyc.; ▶WW Amer. Art, 1989

Kozlovskij, Mihajl Ivanovič *(Russian sculptor, 1753-1802)*   **BA**
Bibl: ▶Thieme-Becker

Kozlow, Richard *(American painter, b.1926)*   **BA**
Bibl: ▶WW Amer. Art

Kozma, Lajos *(Hungarian illustrator, architect, designer, 1884-1948)*   **BA**
Bibl: ▶Libr. of Congr. Name Auth. File; ▶Vollmer, Künst.-Lex. 20. Jhr.

Kozniewska, Anna *(Polish artist, 20th cent.)*   **WC**

Kozzi, Kim *(Canadian artist, 20th c.)*   **BA**
Bibl: Oille, Vanguard, XI/8-9 (Oct.-Nov. 1982) p.18

Kraanen, Jacobus (Jaap) *(Dutch printmaker, painter, 1903-1973)*   **BA**
Bibl: Rotterdam(NLD), Museum Boymans-van Beuningen. GRAPHICS BY JAAP KRAANEN(1975); ▶Scheen, Ned. beeldende kunst.

Kraay, Dirck→see Craey, Dirck
Krab→see Asselyn, Jan

Krabbe, Elfriede Maria *(German, 1807-1843)*   **BA**
Bibl: ▶Allgem. Deut. Biog.; Vogel-Kohn, NIEDERDEUT.BEITRAGE Z.KUNST, XXI(1982), 129-136

Krabbé, Hendrik Maarten *(Dutch painter and draughtsman, 1868-1931)*   **GC**
Bibl: ▶Thieme-Becker

Krabbetie→see Asselyn, Jan
Krabbetje→see Asselyn, Jan

Kracht, Fritz André *(German photographer, b.1926)*   **BA**
Bibl: ▶Intl. dir. arts, 1983-84; ▶Intl. dir. exh. artists, 1983

Kracht, Yvonne Clothilde Julia *(Dutch printmaker, sculptor, b.1931)*   **BA**

Kracker, Johann Lucas   **BA WC**
(Czech artist, 1717-1779)   WC
(Czech painter, 1717-1779)   BA
Bibl: ▶Encyc. world art; ▶Encyk. českého výtv. umění; ▶Thieme-Becker

Kračun, Theodor *(Yugoslav painter, act.1762, d.1781)*   **BA**
Bibl: ▶Thieme-Becker

Kraeck, or Carrach, Jan, or Giovanni, Carracha, Carracka or Carragua, (Isidoro Carracca) *(Netherlands artist, op.1568-m. 1607)*   **WC**

Krael [Unidentified] *(Unknown painter)*   **PR**
Bibl: (February 11, 1804, lot 42, Christie's)

Kraemer, Friedrich Wilhelm *(West German architect, 1907-)* AV
  Bibl: ▶Contemp. archts.
Kraemer, Nathalie *(French artist, 1891-1943)* WC
Kraemer, Peter, I *(German artist, 1823-1907)* WC
Kraemer, Peter, II *(German artist, 1857-)* WC
Kraemer, Peter, III *(German artist, 1896-)* WC
Kraen, Adriaen → see Craen, Adriaen
Kraer, Johann Georg *(German artist, -c.1772)* WC
Kraetsch, George *(American architect, Des Moines, Iowa, fl. 1920's)* AV
  Bibl: Iowa architect, 1988 Mar.-Apr., v.36, no.2, p.38
Krafft → see Krafft, Carl R.
Krafft → see Krafft, Per (the elder)
Krafft, Barbara BA
  (Austrian painter, 1764-1825) BA
  (German artist, 1764-1825) WC
  Bibl: ▶Bénézit; ▶Fuchs, Öst. Maler 19. Jahrh.; ▶Thieme-Becker
Krafft, Barbara (Maria Barbara), (nee Steiner) WC
Krafft, Barbara (Maria Barbara), (nee Steiner) → see Krafft, Barbara
Krafft, Carl → see Krafft, Carl R.
Krafft, Carl R. PR WI
  (American artist, 1884-) WC
  (American artist, 1884-1938) WI
  (American painter, 1884-aft. 1930) PR
  Bibl: ▶Thieme-Becker
  Carl R. Krafft PR
  Krafft PR
Krafft, Carl WC
Krafft, David von GC WC
  (German artist, 1655-1724) WC
  (Swedish painter, 1655-1724) GC
  Bibl: ▶Bénézit
Krafft, Ingeborg *(Norwegian architect, 1902-1963)* AV
Krafft, Jan Lauwryn BA WC
  (Flemish artist, 1694-1765) WC
  (Flemish printmaker, 1694-after 1765) BA
  Bibl: ▶Bénézit; ▶Thieme-Becker; ▶Wurzbach, NLD Künst.-Lex.
Krafft, Johann August *(German artist, 1798-1829)* WC
Krafft, Johann Peter BA GC
  (Austrian painter, 1780-1856) BA GC
  (German artist, 1780-1856) WC
  Bibl: ▶Bénézit; ▶Busse, Maler u. Bildhauer 19. Jahr.; ▶Encyc. world art; ▶Neue deutsche Biog.; ▶Österr. biog. Lex. 1815-1950; ▶RILA/BHA; ▶Thieme-Becker; ▶Witt checklist
Krafft, Peter (Johann Peter) WC
Krafft, Josef *(German artist, 1787-1828)* WC

Krafft, Per (the elder) GC PR
  (Swedish artist, 1724-1793) WC
  (Swedish painter, 1724-1793) GC PR
  Bibl: ▶Bénézit; ▶Thieme-Becker
  Krafft PR
Krafft, Per I GC
Krafft, Per, I WC
  Kraft, Per, the Elder PR
  Per Krafft (the elder) PR
Krafft, Per I → see Krafft, Per (the elder)
Krafft, Per, I → see Krafft, Per (the elder)
Krafft, Per, II *(Swedish artist, 1777-1863)* WC
Krafft, Peter (Johann Peter) → see Krafft, Johann Peter
Krafft, Wilhelm (Johann Wilhelm) *(German artist, op.c.1828-1850/6)* WC
Krafft, Wilhelmina (Maria Wilhelmina) *(Swedish artist, 1778-1828)* WC
Kraft, Adam *(German sculptor, ca.1460-1508/09)* BA
  Bibl: ▶Brockhaus Enzyk.; ▶Encyc. world art; ▶Müller, Sculpture NLD DEU FRA ESP; ▶Thieme-Becker
Kraft, Johann → see Crato von Crafftheim, Johannes
Kraft, Per, the Elder → see Krafft, Per (the elder)
Kraft, Polly *(American painter, 20th c.)* BA
  Bibl: ▶Intl. dir. exh. artists
Kraft, Verena *(German artist, b.1942)* BA
  Bibl: Munich (DEU), Stadt. Gal. im Lenbachhaus, Verna Kraft/Kurt Petz (1982)
Krag, Eiler *(Danish painter, b.1908)* BA
  Bibl: Copenhagen(DNK), Statens Museum. EILER KRAG...(1981); ▶Weilbach, Kunst.leks.
Krag, Josef *(Architect, Munich, BRD)* AV
  Bibl: Detail, 1984 Sept.-Oct., v.24, no.5, p.481
Krag, Lilke *(Danish architect)* AV
  Bibl: Arkitekten, 1989 Feb.22, v.91, no.4, p.84
Kragulj, Radovan *(Yugoslav printmaker, b.1935)* BA
  Bibl: Ljubljana(YUG), Mala Galerija. RADOVAN KRAGULI.
Krahe → see Krahe, Wilhelm Lambert
Krahe, Peter Joseph BA WC
  (German architect, painter, 1758-1840) BA
  (German artist, 1758-1840) WC
  Bibl: ▶Avery Libr. cat.; ▶Bénézit; ▶Fogg Mus. Libr. cat.; ▶Lex. Kunst; ▶Thieme-Becker

Krahe, Wilhelm Lambert BA PR WC
  (German artist, 1712-1790) WC
  (German painter, 1712-1790) PR
  (German painter, printmaker, art administrator, 1712-1790) BA
  Bibl: ▶Allgem. Deut. Biog.; ▶Bénézit; ▶RILA/BHA; ▶Thieme-Becker
  Krahe PR
  L. Krahe PR
  Wilhelm Lambert Krahe PR
Krahn, Johannes *(German architect, b.1908)* BA
  Bibl: ▶Avery period. idx.; ▶Vollmer, Künst.-Lex. 20. Jhr.
Kraipale Painter *(vase-painter, ca. 450-420 BC)* GC
  Bibl: ▶Beazley, Attic red-fig. vase-ptrs.; Richter, Attic red-fig. vases
Kraisler, David *(American painter, sculptor, 20th c.)* BA
  Bibl: ▶Intl. dir. exh. artists, 1982-1983; Rigberg, L.R., in ARTS MAGAZINE, LX/5 (Jan 1986) 106
Krajewska, Helena *(Polish artist, 1910-)* WC
Krajewski, Andrzej *(Polish artist, 20th cent.)* WC
Krajewski, Juliusz *(Polish artist, 1905-)* WC
Krajewski, Marceli *(Polish painter, 1840-1920)* BA
  Bibl: Polanowska, BIULETYN HISTORII SZTUKI, XLVII/3-4 (1985), p. 275-288; ▶Wielka ilustr. encyk.
Krakora, Werner *(Austrian? architect)* AV
  Bibl: Planen, bauen, wohnen, v.105, p.17
Krakow Painter → see Cracow Painter
Kråkström, Erik *(Finnish architect, Espoo)* AV
  Bibl: Medlemmar av Finlands Arkitektförbund 1987
Král, Jaroslav *(Czech painter, 1883-1942)* BA
  Bibl: ▶Encyk. českého výtv. umění
Králíček, Emil *(Czech architect)* AV
  Bibl: Lukeš, Umění, XXXII/5 (1984) p.441
Kralicek, Vaclav *(Architect, Czechoslovakia, 1947-)* AV
  Bibl: Architektur, Innenarchitektur, Technischer Ausbau, 1985 Jan.-Feb., v.93, no.1, p.10
Kralinge, Jan *(German(?) artist, 17th cent.)* WC
Kramarsky, Siegfried, Mrs. *(American, 20th c.)* BA
  Bibl: ▶Intl. dir. arts, 1985-1986; Price, Burlington Mag. CXVII/872 (Nov 1975), 714-718
Kramer or Krammer, Gabriel *(Swiss artist, op.1598-m.c.1611)* WC

Kramer, Arnold *(American photographer, b.1944)*   **BA**
Bibl: ▶Art Index, vs.28, 30; ▶Macmillan photog. encyc.; Washington, DC (USA), Corcoran Gallery, Washington photography (1982)

Kramer, Dik G. *(Architect, New York City)*   **AV**
Bibl: Architecture & urbanism, 1989 Apr., no.4, p.121

Kramer, Ernst *(West German architect, author, b.1909)*   **BA**
Bibl: ▶Avery period. idx., 2nd suppl.; Clark Art Inst. Libr.; Krolopp, K. ERNST KRAMER, Fulda 1984; ▶Natl. union cat., pre-1956; ▶NYPL Art & Arch. Div., Dict. catalog

Kramer, Ferdinand   **AV BA**
(American architect, designer, 1898-1985)   **BA**
(German architect, active in Frankfurt, 1898-1985)   **AV**
Bibl: ▶Art Index, v.35; ▶Avery period. idx., suppl. 7,6; Bauwelt, 1985 Nov.22, v.76, no.44, p.1727; Berlin, Bauhaus. Archiv., FERDINAND KRAMER (1982)

Kramer, Friso   **AV BA**
(Dutch designer, b.1922)   **BA**
(Dutch industrial designer, 1922-)   **AV**
Bibl: Amsterdam, Stedelijk Museum, FRISO KRAMER (1977); ▶Avery period. idx., 4th suppl.; Dutch art + architecture today, n.10, Dec. 1981, p.[37]

Kramer, Gernot   **BA**
(Architect)   **AV**
(German architect, b.1928)   **BA**
Bibl: AC: fibrecement review, 1985 Apr, v.30, no.1(iii), p.70; ▶Art Index, v.16; ▶Avery period. idx., 3rd suppl., suppl.; KUNSTWERK, XXXII/2-3 (APR-JUN 1979), 96

Kramer, Gernoth   **AV**
Kramer, Gernoth → see Kramer, Gernot

Kramer, Harry *(American painter, b.1939)*   **BA**
Bibl: Pardee, ARTS MAGAZINE, 58 (SEP 1983), 69-71; Yonkers (NY, USA), Hudson River Mus., 6 ptrs. (1983)

Kramer, Harry *(German sculptor, b.1925)*   **BA**
Bibl: ▶Bénézit; Clark Art Inst. Libr.; ▶DuMonts Künst.-Lex.; ▶MoMA libr. cat.; ▶Oxford comp. 20c. art; ▶Parry, Contemp. art; ▶Phaidon 20c. art; ▶WW Arts DEU

Kramer, Heinrich *(German wax modeler, d.1632)*   **BA**
Bibl: Diemer, Anz. des Germ. Nationalmus. (1979) 121-140

Kramer, Helen Kroll *(American artist, collector, 1907-1977)*   **BA**
Bibl: Cornell University, Johnson Museum of Art, DR. AND MRS. M.L. KRAMER COLLECTION (1981); ▶Met. Mus. Art libr. cat.

Kramer, Hieronymus *(German goldsmith, act.1575-1595)*   **BA**
Bibl: Scheffler, Goldschmiede Niedersachsens, p.1137; Sponsel, FUHRER DURCH DIE GRUNE GEWOLBE 273,287; ▶Thieme-Becker

Kramer, Jacob   **BA WC**
(British artist, 20th cent.)   **WC**
(British painter, 1892-1962)   **BA**
Bibl: ▶Johnson, Brit. artists; ▶Waters, Brit. artists

Kramer, Johann Viktor *(German artist, 1861-1949)*   **WC**

Kramer, Konrad Joseph *(German sculptor, restorer, collector, 1835-1917)*   **BA**
Bibl: Trier & Weyres

Kramer, Linda Lewis *(American artist, b.1937)*   **BA**
Bibl: ▶Intl. dir. exh. artists, 1982, v.2; ▶WW Amer. Art, 1989-1990

Kramer, Loretta *(American printmaker, b.1938)*   **BA**
Bibl: Long Beach (CA, USA), Mus. Art, 2: New & unique (1982)

Kramer, Louise *(American sculptor, 20th c.)*   **BA**
Bibl: ▶Art Index, vs.21, 36; Arts Magazine, LI/9 (May 1977), 14; ▶Dunford, Women artists; Guide exh. artists: Sculp.; ▶Locus; ▶WW Amer. Art, 1989-1990

Krämer, Ludwig von   **GC WC**
(German artist, 1840-1908)   **WC**
(German painter, 1840-1908)   **GC**
Bibl: ▶Thieme-Becker

Kramer, Margia *(American artist, 20th c.)*   **BA**
Bibl: ▶Art Index, vs.33-35; ▶Intl. dir. arts, 1989-1990; Poughkeepsie (NY, USA), Vassar College, Art Gallery, THE ARTIST's PERCEPTION..., 1984; ▶WW Amer. Art, 1989-1990

Kramer, Michael *(German sculptor, builder, act.1569-1592)*   **BA**
Bibl: Krčálová, Umění, XXIII/2 (1975) pp.127-141

Kramer, Nikolaus *(German artist, 1521-1553)*   **WC**

Kramer, Oscar *(Austrian, active Vienna, Austria 1867-1869)*   **JG**

Kramer, Peter *(American artist, 1823-1907)*   **WI**

Kramer, Peter *(American architect, Minneapolis, Minn)*   **AV**
Bibl: Architecture Minnesota, 1988 Mar.-Apr., v.14, no.2, p.48
Kramer, Piet → see Kramer, Pieter Lodewijk

Kramer, Pieter Lodewijk *(1881-1961)*   **BA AV**
(Dutch architect, designer, 1881-1961)   **BA**
Bibl: ▶Macmillan encyc. archts.; ▶Portoghesi, Diz. arch. e urbanistica; ▶Vollmer, Künst.-Lex. 20. Jhr.

Kramer, Piet   **AV**

Kramer, Reuben Robert *(American sculptor, b.1909)*   **BA**
Bibl: ▶Artist biog. master idx.; ▶MoMA libr. cat.; ▶Vollmer, Künst.-Lex. 20. Jhr.; ▶WW Amer. Art, 1976, 1989-1990

Kramm, Christiaen *(Dutch painter, 1797-1875)*   **GC**
Bibl: ▶Thieme-Becker

Kramm, Rüdiger *(German architect, 1945-)*   **AV**
Bibl: Deutsche Bauzeitung, 1986 Apr., v.120, no.4, p.26

Krampe, Fritz *(German artist, 1913-1966)*   **WC**

Krampf, Gunther *(German, active London, England, U.K. 1907-1920s)*   **JG**

Kramskoj, Ivan Nikolaevič   **BA**
(Russian artist, 1837-1887)   **WC**
(Russian painter, printmaker, 1837-1887)   **BA**
(Russian, 1837-1887)   **GC**
Bibl: ▶Bénézit; ▶Busse, Maler u. Bildhauer 19. Jahr.; Getty Photo Study Coll. (Ptgs.); Pushkarev, Gosudarstvennyi Russkie Muzei; ▶Thieme-Becker; ▶Witt checklist

Kramskoj, Iwan Nikolajewitsch   **GC WC**
Kramskoy, Ivan Nikolaevich → GC
Kramskoj, Iwan Nikolajewitsch → see Kramskoj, Ivan Nikolaevič
Kramskoy, Ivan Nikolaevich → see Kramskoj, Ivan Nikolaevič

Kramsky, S. *(Russian artist, 1837-1887)*   **WC**

Kranner, Josef Andreas *(Bohemian architect, mason, 1801-1871)*   **BA**
Bibl: ▶Busse, Maler u. Bildhauer 19. Jahr.; Sturgis, Arch. & bldg.; ▶Thieme-Becker
Krans, Olaf → see Krans, Olof

Krans, Olof   **BA WC**
(American artist, 1836-1916)   **WI**
(American artist, 1838-1916)   **WC**
(American painter, 1838-1916)   **BA**
Bibl: ▶Art Index, vs.19-30; ▶ARTbibl. mod., 17/2 (1986); ▶Groce, Artists Amer.; Meyer, Folk artists biog. idx.; New York (NY, USA), Whitney Mus., Amer. folk ptrs. (1980); ▶Samuels, Artists Amer. West; ▶Young, Amer. artists

Krans, Olaf   **WI**

Krantz, Amelie *(German artist, op. 1820)*   **WC**

Kranz, Josef   **AV**

Kranz, Kurt *(German painter,*
printmaker, b.1910)   **BA**
   Bibl: ▶ARTbibl. mod., 12/2
   (1981); ▶Met. Mus. Art libr. cat.;
   ▶MoMA libr. cat.; ▶Vollmer,
   Künst.-Lex. 20. Jhr.; ▶WW Arts
   DEU
Kranz, M.   **WC WI**
   (American artist, op.1839)   WC
   (American artist, op.1839-)   WI
Kranzinger, Joseph   **GC WC**
   (Austrian painter, ca.1740-aft.
   1772)   GC
   (German artist, c.1740-1772)   WC
   Bibl: ▶Thieme-Becker
Kränzle, Nikolaus *(West German*
   architect)   **AV**
   Bibl: Kunst und das schöne Heim,
   v.95, n.12, p.859-866
Krapf, Kaspar *(Austrian*
   cabinetmaker, act.1591)   **BA**
   Bibl: KUNSTDENKMALER...
   KREMSMUNSTER, v.43 (1977), pp.
   375, 489
Krapfenbauer, Robert *(Austrian*
   architect, Vienna)   **AV**
   Bibl: Planen Bauen Wohnen,
   1986, no.115, p.5
Krapp, Herbert J. *(American*
   architect)   **AV**
   Bibl: Marquee, v.19, no.1, p.28
Krasickij, Fotij Stepanovič
   (Ukrainian painter, printmaker,
   1873-1944)   **BA**
   Bibl: ▶Thieme-Becker; ▶WWW
   USSR
Krasilnikov, V. *(Russian architect)*   **AV**
   Bibl: Process: architecture, 1985
   Jan., no.54, p.153
Krasiński, Edward *(Polish artist,*
   b.1925)   **BA**
   Bibl: ▶ARTbibl. mod., 7/2 (1975),
   16/2 (1985); ▶Bénézit; Buffalo
   (NY, USA), Albright-Knox, 17
   contemp. artists Poland (1976)
Kraskin, Sandra *(American painter,*
   20th c.)   **BA**
   Bibl: Minneapolis (MN, USA), Inst.
   Arts, Bewildered image (1982)
Krasner, Lee   **BA WI**
   (American artist, 1908-1984)   WI
   (American artist, 1909-)   WC
   (American painter, 1908-1984)   BA
   Bibl: ▶Bénézit; ▶Collins, Women
   artists Amer.; ▶Contemp. artists;
   ▶Fogg Mus. Libr. cat.; ▶Marks,
   Dict. world artists; Marlborough
   Graphics; ▶MoMA libr. cat.; ▶Natl.
   union cat.; NPR; Pace Gallery;
   Whitney Museum exh., p.37; WW
   Amer.; ▶WW Amer. Art, VIII
Krasner, Lee (Lee Pollock)   **WC**
   Pollock, Jackson, Mrs., (Lee
   Krasner)   WI
   Krasner, Lee (Lee Pollock)→see
   Krasner, Lee
   Krasnow→see Krasnow, Peter

Krasnow, Peter   **BA PR**
   (American artist, 1890-1979)   BA
   (American painter, 1890-1979)   PR
   Bibl: ▶Fielding's Amer. ptrs.;
   ▶Hughes, Artists California;
   ▶MoMA libr. cat.; ▶Moure, Art
   So. Calif.; ▶RILA/BHA; ▶WWW
   Amer. art
   Krasnow   PR
   Peter Krasnow   PR
Krašovec, Metka *(Yugoslav painter,*
   printmaker, b.1941)   **BA**
   Bibl: ▶Intl. dir. exh. artists, 1982;
   Ljubljana (YUG), Mala galerija,
   METKA KROŠOVEC (1975)
Krasovschi, Nicolae *(Romanian*
   painter, 1947-1977)   **BA**
   Bibl: ARTA, XXVI (1979), 31-33;
   ▶Barbosa, Art. romani contemp.
Kratinos *(Greek painter)*   **GC**
   Bibl: ▶Robertson, Greek art, p.712
Kratke→see Kratké, Charles Louis
Kratké, Charles Louis   **GC PR WC**
   (French artist, 1848-1921)   WC
   (French painter, 1848-1921/22)   PR
   (French, 1848-1921)   GC
   Bibl: ▶Bénézit; ▶Thieme-Becker;
   ▶Witt checklist
   Charles Louis Kratke   PR
   Kratke   PR
   Kratke, Charles-Louis   PR
   Kratke, Charles-Louis→see Kratké,
   Charles Louis
Kratochwil, Marian *(Polish artist,*
   20th cent.)   **WC**
Kratschkowskij, Iossif (Josef,
   Jewstafjewitsch) *(Russian artist,*
   1854-1914)   **WC**
Kratt, Wilhelm *(German actor,*
   photographer, 1869-1949)   **BA**
   Bibl: Karlsruhe, Staatliche
   Kunsthalle, STILLE ZERSTORUNG,
   1975-76, p.38
Kratzenstein Stub, Christian
   Gottlieb   **BA**
   (Danish artist, 1783-1816)   WC
   (Danish painter, 1783-1816)   BA
   Bibl: ▶Bénézit; ▶Thieme-Becker;
   ▶Weilbach, Kunst.leks.
Kratzenstein-Stub, Christian
   Gottlieb   **WC**
   Kratzenstein-Stub, Christian
   Gottlieb→see Kratzenstein Stub,
   Christian Gottlieb
Kratzer, Carl Edler von *(German*
   artist, 1827-1903)   **WC**
Kratzer, Nicolaus *(German artist,*
   16th cent.)   **WC**
Kraul, Karl Franz *(German artist,*
   1754-1796)   **WC**
   Kraus→see Kraus, Friedrich
Kraus, Anton *(German artist, 1838-*
   1872)   **WC**

Kraus, August *(German painter,*
   1852-1917)   **PR**
   Bibl: ▶Thieme-Becker
   August Kraus   PR
Kraus, August *(German sculptor,*
   1868-1934)   **BA**
   Bibl: ▶Bénézit; ▶Thieme-Becker;
   ▶Vollmer, Künst.-Lex. 20. Jhr.
Kraus, Erich Müller→see
   Müller-Kraus, Erich
Kraus, Franz Anton   **BA GC**
   (German artist, 1705-1752)   WC
   (German painter, 1705-1752)   BA
   (German, 1705-1752)   GC
   Bibl: ▶Allgem. Deut. Biog.;
   ▶Hempel, Baroque central Euro.;
   ▶Macmillan encyc. archts.;
   ▶Thieme-Becker; ▶Witt checklist
Kraus, Krause or Krauss, Franz
   Anton   **WC**
Kraus, Friedrich   **PR WC**
   (German artist, 1826-1894)   WC
   (German painter, 1826-1894)   PR
   Bibl: ▶Thieme-Becker
   Friedrich Kraus   PR
   Kraus   PR
   Kraus, Friedrick   PR
   Kraus, Friedrick→see Kraus, Friedrich
Kraus, Georg Melchior   **GC**
   (German artist, 1737-1806)   WC
   (German, 1737-1806)   GC
   Bibl: ▶Thieme-Becker; ▶Witt
   checklist
Kraus, Krause or Krauss, Georg
   Melchior   **WC**
Kraus, Gustav   **BA**
   (German artist, 1804-1852)   WC
   (German painter, printmaker,
   1804-1852)   BA
   Bibl: Pressler, C., GUSTAV KRAUS;
   ▶Thieme-Becker
Kraus, Gustav Wilhelm   **WC**
   Kraus, Gustav Wilhelm→see Kraus,
   Gustav
Kraus, Johann Ulrich   **BA GC WC**
   (German artist, 1655-1719)   WC
   (German printmaker, 1655-
   1719)   BA
   (German, 1655-1719)   GC
   Bibl: ▶Allgem. Deut. Biog., 1969;
   ▶Hollstein, German; ▶Natl. union
   cat.; ▶Thieme-Becker; ▶Witt
   checklist
   Krauss, Johann Ulrich   BA
   Kraus, Krause or Krauss, Franz
   Anton→see Kraus, Franz Anton
   Kraus, Krause or Krauss, Georg
   Melchior→see Kraus, Georg
   Melchior
Kraus, Romuald *(American sculptor,*
   1891-1954)   **BA**
   Bibl: ▶Havlice, Idx. art. bio.;
   ▶WWW Amer. art
Kraus, Victor *(West German painter,*
   b.1954)   **BA**
   Bibl: Münchn (DEU), Museum Villa
   Stuck, Victor Kraus: Bildov, 1984

Kraus, Wenzel (German artist, 1791-1849)   WC

Krause, Dorothea (East German architect)   AV
Bibl: Architektur der DDR, 1986 Oct., v.35, no.10, p.604

Krause, Franz   AV BA
(German artist, b.1897)   BA
(West German architect, 1897-1979)   AV
Bibl: ▶Art Index, v.28; ▶ARTbibl. mod., index 3 (1980); ▶Gorenflo, Bild. Künstler; Wuppertal (BRD), Von der Heydt-Mus., SCHLEMMER, BAUMEISTER, KRAUSE...(1979)

Krause, Franz Emil (German artist, 1836-1900)   WC

Krause, Hans (German artist, 1864-)   WC

Krause, Jerome C. (American painter, printmaker, photographer, b.1943)   BA
Bibl: ▶Art Index, v.29; ▶Intl. dir. exh. artists, 1983; Milwaukee (WI, USA), Art Ctr., Jerome Krause (1977)

Krause, LaVerne Erickson (American painter, printmaker, b.1924)   BA
Bibl: ▶Havlice, Idx. art. bio.; ▶WW Amer. Art, 1976, 1989-90

Krause, Paul (American architect, New York City)   AV
Bibl: Architectural digest, 1987 Sept., v.44, no.9, p.108

Krause, Rolf (German painter, printmaker, b.1908)   BA
Bibl: Dresdener Kunstblätter, XXII (1978) pp.54-61; ▶Gorenflo, Bild. Künstler; ▶Vollmer, Künst.-Lex. 20. Jhr.

Krause, Wilhelm August Leopold Christian   GC WC
(German artist, 1803-1864)   WC
(German painter, 1803-1864)   GC
Bibl: ▶Thieme-Becker

Krause, William (German artist, 1875-1925)   WC

Krause, Winfried (German architect)   AV
Bibl: Architektur der DDR, 1985 Sept., v.34, no.9, p.523

Krause, Wolfgang (East German landscape architect)   AV
Bibl: Architektur der DDR, 1986 Oct., v.35, no.10, p.604

Krauskopf, Bruno (German artist, 1892-)   WC

Krauss, Johann Ulrich → see Kraus, Johann Ulrich

Krauss, Rolf H. (German artist, collector, b.1930)   BA
Bibl: ▶Intl. dir. exh. artists, 1983; ▶WW Arts DEU

Krauss-Vonow, Katharina (Swiss photographer, b.1951)   BA
Bibl: Chur (CHE), Bundner Kunstmuseum, ERWEITERTE SAMMLUNGS...(1982); RLIN BKS file

Krausz, Michael (American painter, 20th c.)   BA
Bibl: ▶Art Index, v.28; ▶ARTbibl. mod., 12/1, 13/2; ▶Natl. Faculty Dir.; WW Amer., 1988-89

Krausz, Simon Andreas   GC WC
(Dutch artist, 1760-1825)   WC
(Dutch draughtsman, 1760-1825)   GC
Bibl: ▶Thieme-Becker

Krausz, Tiberiu (Rumanian artist, 1919-)   WC

Krausz, Wilhelm Victor (German artist, 1878-)   WC

Kraut, Susan (American painter, 20th c.)   BA
Bibl: ▶ARTbibl. mod., 13/1, 16/1; Bonesteel, Art in Amer., LXXIV/12 (Dec. 1986) p.49; ▶Intl. dir. exh. artists, 1982

Kravčenko, Aleksej (Russian printmaker, 1889-1940)   BA
Bibl: ▶Bénézit; ▶Encyc. world art

Kravietz, Juan (Argentinian architect)   AV
Bibl: Open house international, 1984, v.9, no.4, p.51

Krawczyk, Sabine (French printmaker, b.1953)   BA
Bibl: Rouen (FRA), Musée des B.-A., Rouen-Madrid (1981)

Kray, Wilhelm (German artist, 1828-89)   WC

Krayenbühl, Frank (Swiss architect, 1935-)   AV
Bibl: Architecture & urbanism, 1987 Oct., no.10(205), p.22

Krayl, Carl (German architect, 1890-)   AV

Krayn, Hugo (German artist, 1885-1919)   WC

Krbec, Rosemonde (Swiss artist, 20th cent.)   WC

Krcal → see Krcal, Karel

Krcal, Karel (Austrian painter, b.1888)   PR
Bibl: Boston MFA registrar files
Karel Krcal   PR
Krcal   PR

Krebs, Anne (Danish designer)   AV
Bibl: Arkitekten, 1988 Jan.20, v.90, no.1-2, p.27

Krebs, Eckart (German architect, Hildesheim)   AV
Bibl: Detail, 5 (Sep.-Oct. 1980) p.683

Krebs, Frederick (American artist, op.19th c.)   WI

Krebs, G. (West German architect, Berlin)   AV
Bibl: Abitare, 1984 July-Aug., no. 226

Krebs, Johanne Catherine (Danish painter, 1848-1924)   BA
Bibl: ▶Nørregård-Nielsen, Dansk kunst; ▶Petteys, Women artists

Krebs, Karsten   AV
(West German architect, 1945-)   AV
(West German architect, Hannover/Hamburg, 1945-)   AV
Bibl: Daidalos, 1989 Mar.15, no.31, p.135; Deutsche Bauzeitung, 1988 Oct., v.122, no.10, p.208

Krebs, Karsten K.   AV
Krebs, Karsten K. → see Krebs, Karsten

Krebs, Klaus D. (West German architect)   AV

Krebs, Konrad (German architect, mason, 1492-1540)   BA
Bibl: ▶Neue deutsche Biog.; ▶Thieme-Becker

Krebs, Monika (West German architect)   AV

Krebs, Patsy (American painter, b.1940)   BA
Bibl: Art News, 76 (Nov 1977), 206; ▶Babington Smith, Contemp. artists; ▶Intl. dir. exh. artists, 1982-1983; La Jolla (CA, USA), Mus. of Contemp. Art, Four Californians (1977)

Krebs, Rainer (West German architect, Hanau)   AV
Bibl: Deutsches Architektenblatt, 1989 Sept.1, v.21, no.9, p.1253

Krebs, Rockne (American sculptor, b.1938)   BA
Bibl: Art News, LXXX/8 (Oct 1981); ▶WW Amer. Art, 1976

Krebs, Thomas (German master builder, 16th c.)   BA
Bibl: Tietz-Strodel, DIE FUGGEREI IN AUGSBURG... (1981) docs

Krefft, Gerard (Australian artist, 19th cent.)   WC

Kreft, Jürgen (German architect)   AV
Bibl: Die Kunst, 1986 June, v.96, no.6, p.469

Kreft, Wilhelm (West German interior designer)   AV
Bibl: Architektur, Innenarchitektur, Technischer Ausbau, 1988 May, v.96, no.5, p.10

Kregar, Stane   WC
(Yugoslav artist, 1909-)   WC
(Yugoslav artist, op.1960)   WC
Stane, Kregar   WC

Kregten, Johannes Aurelius Richard Fedor (Fedor) van → see Kregten, Johannes Aurelius Richard Fedor van (Fedor)

Kregten, Johannes Aurelius
Richard Fedor van (Fedor) GC
  (Dutch artist, 1871-1937) WC
  (Dutch painter, 1871-1937) GC
    Bibl: ▸Witt checklist
Kregten, Johannes Aurelius
Richard Fedor (Fedor) van WC
Krehl, Hans → see Krell, Hans
Kreidolf, Ernst Konrad Theophil
  (Swiss artist, 1863-1956) WC
Kreienbühl, Jürg BA WC
  (Swiss artist, 1932-) WC
  (Swiss painter, b.1932) BA
    Bibl: ▸ARTbibl. mod., 15/1;
    ▸Gorenflo, Bild. Künstler; ▸Lex.
    zeitgen. Schweiz. Künstler
Kreienbül, Hans *(Swiss architect)* AV
    Bibl: Space design, 1986 Oct., no.
    265, p.5
Kreifelds, T.H. → see Creifelds, T.H.
Kreikenbaum, Hartmut *(West*
German architect) AV
    Bibl: Deutsches Architektenblatt,
    1987 Sept., v.19, no.9, p.993
Kreilick, Marjorie E. *(American*
mosaic artist, b.1925) BA
    Bibl: Columbia (SC, USA), Museum
    of Art, Mosaics by Marjorie
    Kreilick (1977); ▸Natl. Faculty Dir.,
    1989; ▸WW Amer. Art, 1976,
    1989-90
Kreilig von *(German artist, 20th*
cent.) WC
Kreimer *(German artist, 20th cent.)* WC
Kreiner, Günter *(Austrian interior*
architect) AV
    Bibl: Bauforum, XXII/134 (1989)
    p.59
Kreis, Henry *(American sculptor (b.*
Germany), 1899-1963) GC
    Bibl: ▸Opitz, Amer. sculptors
Kreis, Werner *(Swiss architect,*
1943-) AV
    Bibl: Das Kunstwerk, n.3-4, Sept.
    1983, p.45
Kreis, Wilhelm Heinrich AV BA WC
  (German architect, 1873-
1955) AV BA
  (German artist, 1873-1955) WC
    Bibl: ▸Avery obit. idx.; ▸Avery
    period. idx., 3rd suppl.;
    ▸Macmillan encyc. archts.; ▸Neue
    deutsche Biog.; ▸Portoghesi, Diz.
    arch. e urbanistica;
    ▸Thieme-Becker
Kreitter, Elias → see Greuter, Elias I
Kreitter, Elias II → see Greuter, Elias II
Krejcar, Jarómir AV BA
  (Czech architect, educator,
1895-1949) BA
  (Czechoslovakian architect,
1895-1949) AV
    Bibl: ▸Avery period. idx.; Czech
    functionalism 1918-1938 (1987);
    ▸Macmillan encyc. archts.;
    ▸Vollmer, Künst.-Lex. 20. Jhr.

Krejčí, Jan BA WC
  (Czech artist, 1942-) WC
  (Czech printmaker, b.1942) BA
    Bibl: ▸ARTbibl. mod., 19/2, 9/1;
    Cincinnati (OH, USA), Art Mus.,
    Eastern Euro. printmkrs. (1975)
Krejci, Johannes *(Austrian painter,*
b.1912) BA
    Bibl: Wacha.KUNSTJAHRBUCH DER
    STADT LINZ(1987),112-113
Kreler, Elisabeth *(German, ca.1488-*
after 1535) BA
    Bibl: Kobler, Jahrb. Zentralinst.
    Kunstgeschichte, I (1985) p.411
Kreler, Laux *(German goldsmith,*
1484-after 1535) BA
    Bibl: Kobler, Jahrb. Zentralinst.
    Kunstgeschichte, I (1985) p.409;
    ▸Seling, Augsburger
    Goldschmiede, v.3, p.34, no.525;
    ▸Thieme-Becker
Kreling, August von BA WC
  (German artist, 1819-1876) WC
  (German sculptor, painter,
printmaker, 1819-1876) BA
    Bibl: ▸Bénézit; ▸Thieme-Becker
Kreling, Wilhelm *(German artist,*
1855-) WC
Krell → see Krell, Hans
Krell, Hans GC PR
  (German artist, op.1522-m.c.
1586) WC
  (German painter, d. 1586) PR
  (German, act.1522-d.ca.1586) GC
    Bibl: Getty Photo Study Coll.
    (Ptgs.); ▸Thieme-Becker; ▸Witt
    checklist
  Hans Krell PR
  Krehl, Hans GC
  Krell PR
Krell, Krehl or Krel, Hans WC
Krell, Jan Krzysztof *(Polish*
goldsmith, act.1638) BA
    Bibl: Chrzanowski, Folia historiae
    artium, XVII (1981) p.145
Krell, Krehl or Krel, Hans → see Krell,
Hans
Kremberg, Jakob *(Swedish sculptor,*
act.1598, d.1641?) BA
Kremegne, Pinchus *(French artist,*
1890-) WC
Kremen, Irwin *(American*
psychiatrist, artist, b.1925) BA
    Bibl: East Lansing(MI, USA),
    WORD&COLLAGE(1979); ▸Natl.
    Faculty Dir., 1989
Kremer → see Kremer, Nicolaus
Kremer or Kraemer, Nicolaus → see
Kremer, Nicolaus
Kremer, E. *(Russian ceramist, act.*
1903) BA
Kremer, Eugène Jacques *(French*
glass manufacturer, 1867-1941) BA

Kremer, Nicolaus GC PR
  (German artist, op.1521-m.
1553) WC
  (German painter and
draughtsman, act.1521-d.
1553) GC
  (German painter, ca.1500-1553) PR
    Bibl: Getty Photo Study Coll.;
    ▸Thieme-Becker; Washington NG
    cat.; ▸Witt checklist
  Kremer PR
Kremer or Kraemer, Nicolaus WC
  Nicolaus Kremer PR
Kremer, Petrus GC WC
  (Belgian artist, 1801-1888) WC
  (Belgian painter and
draughtsman, 1801-1888) GC
    Bibl: ▸Bénézit
Kremlička, Rudolf BA WC
  (Czech artist, 1886-1932) WC
  (Czech painter, 1886-1932) BA
    Bibl: ▸Encyk. českého výtv. uměni;
    ▸Gorenflo, Bild. Künstler
Kremnitzer, August *(Austrian*
architect, Hartberg) AV
    Bibl: ▸Verzeich. Öst. Ziviltech.
Kremser, Engelbert AV BA
  (West German architect,
b.1938) BA
  (West German architect, Berlin) AV
    Bibl: Architectural review, 1985
    June, v.177, no.1060, p.86
Kremser-Schmidt, Martin Johann → see
Schmidt, Martin Johann
Krendovskij, Evgraf Fedorovič BA
  (Russian artist, 1810-) WC
  (Russian painter, b.1810) BA
Krendowskij, Jewgraf
Fjodorovitsch WC
Krendowskij, Jewgraf
Fjodorovitsch → see Krendovskij,
Evgraf Fedorovič
Krenn, Edmund *(German artist,*
1845/6-1902) WC
Krenn, Hans *(German artist, 1932-)* WC
Krenn, Walter *(Austrian architect)* AV
    Bibl: Bauforum, 1985, v.18, no.
    112, p.28
Kresilas *(Greek sculptor, act. ca.450-*
420 BC) GC
    Bibl: Getty Photo Study Coll.;
    ▸Robertson, Greek art, p.176
Kress, Hubert *(West German*
architect, Erlangen) AV
    Bibl: Baumeister, 1989 Aug., v.86,
    no.8, p.32
Kress, Siegfried *(East German*
architect, professor at
Bauakademie der DDR) AV
    Bibl: Architektur der DDR, 1987
    Sept., v.36, no.9, p.40
Kress, Tom *(American painter,*
b.1943) BA
Krestin, Lazar *(German artist, 1868-)* WC

Krethlow or Kretlow, Johann Ferdinand (German artist, 1767-1842)   WC

Kretschmar, Carl (Johann Carl Heinrich) (German artist, 1769-1847)   WC

Kretschmer, Albert (German artist, 1825-1891)   WC

Kretschmer, Robert   GC
(German artist, 1818-1872)   WC
(German, 1818-1872)   GC
    Bibl: ▶Thieme-Becker; ▶Witt checklist

Kretzchmer, Robert   WC
Kretzchmer, Robert → see Kretschmer, Robert

Kretzschmar, Bernhard (German artist, 1889-)   WC

Kretzschmer, Hermann (Johann Hermann) (German artist, 1811-1890)   WC

Kreuer, Willy   BA
(German architect and professor, 1910-1984)   AV
(German architect, b.1910)   BA
    Bibl: Bauwelt, 1984, v.75, no.35, p.213

Krever, Willy   AV

Kreuger, Nils   GC
(Swedish artist, 1858-1930)   WC
(Swedish painter, 1858-1930)   GC
    Bibl: ▶Bénézit

Kreuger, Nils Edvard   WC
Kreuger, Nils Edvard → see Kreuger, Nils
Kreuger, Ted → see Kreuger, Theodore

Kreuger, Theodore (American architect, New York City)   AV
    Bibl: A + U, 1989 Aug., no. 8(227), p.26
Kreuger, Ted   AV

Kreugher, J. [Unidentified]
(Unknown painter)   PR
    Bibl: (April 6, 1815, lot 52, Hoggart and Phillips)
J. Kreugher   PR

Kreul, Carl   GC
(German artist, 1804-1867)   WC
(German painter, 1804-1867)   GC
    Bibl: ▶Thieme-Becker

Kreul, Carl (Johann Friedrich Carl)   WC
Kreul, Johann Friedrich Carl   GC
Kreul, Carl (Johann Friedrich Carl) → see Kreul, Carl
Kreul, Johann Friedrich Carl → see Kreul, Carl

Kreul, Johann Lorenz   GC WC
(German artist, 1765-1840)   WC
(German painter, 1765-1840)   GC
    Bibl: ▶Thieme-Becker

Kreuser [Unidentified] (Unknown painter)   PR
    Bibl: (Friday, May 29th, 1801, lot 26, Christie's)
Kreuter, Elias → see Greuter, Elias I

Kreuter, Elias II → see Greuter, Elias II

Kreuter, Franz Jakob (German architect, 1813-1889)   BA

Kreutz, Heinz (West German painter, b.1923)   BA

Kreutzberg, Peter (Pit) (Russian artist, 19th cent.)   WC

Kreutzberger or Creutzberger, Paul (German artist, -c.1660)   WC

Kreutzberger, Charles (Engraver)   WI

Kreutzfelder, Johann → see Kreuzfelder, Johann

Kreutzinger → see Kreutzinger, Josef

Kreutzinger, Josef   PR
(Austrian painter, 1757-1829)   GC
(German artist, 1751/7-1829)   WC
(German painter, 1757-1829)   PR
    Bibl: ▶Bénézit; ▶Thieme-Becker
Josef Kreutzinger   PR
Kreutzinger   PR

Kreutzinger, Joseph   GC

Kreutzinger, Kreuzinger, Kreizinger, Kreiczinger, Josef   WC
Kreuzinger   PR
Krutzinger   PR
Kreutzinger, Joseph → see Kreutzinger, Josef
Kreutzinger, Kreuzinger, Kreizinger, Kreiczinger, Josef → see Kreutzinger, Josef

Kreuzfelder, Johann   GC WC
(German artist, 1577-1636)   WC
(German draughtsman, 1577-1636)   GC
    Bibl: ▶Thieme-Becker
Creuzfelder, Johann   GC
Kreutzfelder, Johann   GC

Kreuzhage, Werner (German painter, printmaker, b.1904)   BA
Kreuzinger → see Kreutzinger, Josef

Krevel, Ludwig (German painter, 1801-1876)   GC
    Bibl: ▶Thieme-Becker
Krever, Willy → see Kreuer, Willy

Krevit, Sheldon Howard (American painter, 20th c.)   BA

Kreybich, Georg Franz (Bohemian glass painter, glass engraver, dealer, 1662-1736?)   BA

Kreyder, Alexis (Joseph Alexis) (German artist, 1839-1912)   WC

Kreyssig, Hugo (German artist, 1873-p.1909)   WC

Krichbaum, Jörg (German photographer, b.1945)   BA
    Bibl: Ausstellung Fotomuseum im Münchner Stadtmuseum 1983; Ausstellung Karl Ernst Osthaus Museum, Hagen, 1984

Kricheldorf, Carl (German artist, 1863-)   WC

Kricheldorf, Hermann Gottlieb (German artist, 1867-1949)   WC

Kricke, Norbert (West German sculptor, 1922-1984)   BA

Krieble, John (American architect)   AV

Kriechbaum, Martin (German painter, sculptor, act.1473-ca. 1518)   BA
    Bibl: ARS BAVARICA, 31-32 (1983) 24; Dehio: Oberösterreich, p.126; Müller, Sculpture NLD DEU FRA ESP, p.176; Reclams Österreich, p.162; ▶Thieme-Becker

Kriechpaum, Ulrich → see Neunhauser, Ulrich

Krieg, Dieter (West German painter, printmaker, b.1937)   BA
    Bibl: ▶Babington Smith, Contemp. artists; ▶DuMonts Künst.-Lex.; Guide exh. artists: N. Amer. ptrs.; ▶Intl. dir. exh. artists, 1983

Krieg, Hans   GC
(German artist, c.1590-1643/7)   WC
(German draughtsman, ca.1590-1643/47)   GC
    Bibl: ▶Thieme-Becker
Krieg, Joannes   GC

Krieg, Krig, Kriegck, Krick, Kriag or Krieger(?), Hans (Joannes)   WC
Krieg, Joannes → see Krieg, Hans
Krieg, Krig, Kriegck, Krick, Kriag or Krieger(?), Hans (Joannes) → see Krieg, Hans

Kriegel, Willy (German artist, 1901-)   WC

Krieger, Alex (American architect)   AV
    Bibl: Architecture & urbanism, 1989 Mar., no.3(222), p.102

Krieger, Ernst-Friedrich (German architect, Darmstadt, 1938-)   AV
    Bibl: Deutsche Bauzeitung, 1985 Sept., v.119, no.9, p.25

Krieger, Johan Cornelius (Danish architect, 1683-1755)   AV BA
    Bibl: ▶Thieme-Becker

Krieger, Lisa (American garden and interior designer, Conn)   AV
    Bibl: House & garden, 1989 Sept., v.161, no.9, p.216

Krieger, Wilhelm (German sculptor, 1877-1945)   BA GC
    Bibl: ▶RILA/BHA

Krieghoff, Cornelius   BA WC
(Canadian artist, 1812-1872)   WC
(Canadian painter, 1815-1872)   BA

Kriehuber, Fritz (Austrian printmaker, painter, 1836-1871)   BA

Kriehuber, Joseph (German artist, 1800-1876)   WC

Krieken, Jan van (Dutch painter, printmaker, b.1942)   BA

Krier, Alexis (French architect)   AV
    Bibl: AMC, 1987 Oct., no.17, p.43

Krier, Leo → see Krier, Leon

Krier, Leon   **AV BA**
   (Architect, born in Luxembourg,
   private practice in London
   since 1974, 1946-)   AV
   (Luxembourger architect,
   theorist in GBR, b.1946)   BA
   Bibl: ▶Libr. of Congr. Name Auth.
   File
   Krier, Leo   AV
Krier, Rob → see Krier, Robert
Krier, Robert   **BA**
   (Austrian architect and author,
   brother of Leon Krier, 1938-)   AV
   (Austrian architect, b.1938)   BA
   Bibl: ▶Contemp. archts.
   Krier, Rob   **AV**
Krier, Walter *(Belgian architect,*
   brother of Leon Krier, 1950-)   **AV**
   Bibl: Building design, 1988 Apr.1,
   no.879, p.12
Kriesberg, Irving *(American painter,*
   b.1919)   **BA**
   Bibl: ▶Cummings, Contemp.
   Amer. artists, 1971, 1971, 1988;
   ▶MoMA libr. cat.; ▶NY Art Review
   1988, 1988; ▶WW Amer. Art
Kriester, Rainer *(German sculptor,*
   20th c.)   **BA**
Krik, Gerard van *(Dutch painter,*
   17th c.)   **BA**
Krikorian, Tamara *(British artist,*
   b.1944)   **BA**
Krílík, Emil *(Czech architect, 1880-*
   1946)   **BA**
   Bibl: ▶Encyk. českého výtv. umění;
   Lukeš, Umění, XXXII/5 (1984)
   p.441; ▶Vollmer, Künst.-Lex. 20.
   Jhr.
Krimmel, Johann Ludwig (John
   Lewis) → see Krimmel, John Lewis
Krimmel, John Lewis   **BA**
   (American painter, 1789-1821)   BA
   (German artist, 1787-1821)   WC
   Bibl: ▶Dict. Amer. biog.; ▶Groce,
   Artists Amer.
   Krimmel, Johann Ludwig (John
   Lewis)   **WC**
Krimmer, Eduard Mihajlovič
   (Russian artist, 1901-1974)   **BA**
Krimov, Nicolas P. *(Russian artist,*
   1884-)   **WC**
Krimper, Schulim   **AV BA**
   (Austrian cabinetmaker in AUS,
   1893-1971)   BA
   (Austrian(?) furniture designer
   and craftsman, immigrated to
   Australia)   AV
   Bibl: Transition, 1988 Autumn,
   no.24, p.85
Krims, Leslie Robert *(American*
   painter, photographer, b.1943)   **BA**
Krings, Herbert *(German painter,*
   b.1947)   **BA**
Krinskij, Vladimir Fedorovič
   (Russian architect, 1890-1971)   **BA**

Kripacz, Francisco *(Venezuelan born*
   designer of Yugoslavian ancestry,
   practicing in Los Angeles as a
   partner of the Canadian firm,
   Arthur Erickson Architects, 1944-)   **AV**
   Bibl: ▶AIA Pro File, 1983;
   Interiors, 1985 Jan., v.144, no.6,
   p.128
Krips, Maximilian *(German painter,*
   printmaker, b.1936)   **BA**
Kříš, Josef   **AV**
Krisan *(German artist, 19th cent.)*   **WC**
Krischanitz, Adolf *(Austrian*
   architect, 1946-)   **AV**
   Bibl: Institute for Architecture and
   Urban Studies. Catalogue, n.13,
   1980, p.34
Kristensen, Johan von
   (Scandinavian artist, 20th cent.)   **WC**
Kristensen, Poul *(Danish printer,*
   b.1922)   **BA**
   Bibl: ▶Dansk kunst. leks.; Kraks
   blå bog 1986; RLIN BKS file
Kristensen, Torkild *(Danish*
   architect, Odense)   **AV**
   Bibl: ▶Danske Arkitekters
   Landsforbund, 1984-85
Kristina von Post → see Post, Kristina
   von
Kristján Gudmundsson *(Icelandic*
   artist, b. 1941)   **BA**
   Bibl: ▶Art Index, v.39; ▶Intl. dir.
   exh. artists, 1983; Kvaren,
   TERSKEL, 2(1990) 30-37;
   Lucerne(CHE), Kunstmuseum.
   KRISTJAN GUDMUNDSSON...
   (1975)
Kristler, Hans Jakob *(German*
   architect, engineer, 1592-1645)   **BA**
Kristoffersen, John *(Norwegian*
   architect)   **AV**
   Bibl: Byggekunst, 1985, v.67,
   no.3, p.141
Kritikos, E. *(Architect, Greece)*   **AV**
   Bibl: Architektonika themata,
   1985, v.19, p.160
Kritios *(Greek sculptor, act. 1st half*
   5th c BC)   **GC**
   Bibl: Getty Photo Study Coll.;
   ▶Robertson, Greek art, p.176
Kritter, Ulrich von *(German, 20th*
   c.)   **BA**
Krivonogov, Petr Aleksandrovič
   (Russian painter, b.1911)   **BA**
Krivoutz, Vladimir *(Russian artist,*
   1901-)   **WC**
Kriwet, Ferdinand   **BA WC**
   (German artist, 20th cent.)   WC
   (German painter, poet, sculptor,
   b.1942)   BA
Kriz, Vilem *(American photographer,*
   b.1921)   **BA**
Krizan, Samuel Jan *(Canadian artist,*
   filmmaker, b.1939)   **BA**

Krizek, Katherine *(American*
   architect)   **AV**
   Bibl: Architecture & urbanism,
   1987 Feb., no.197, p.75
Krizia (Mariuccia Mandelli)   **BA**
   (Italian fashion designer, 20th
   c.)   BA
   (Italian interior designer)   AV
   Bibl: Artforum, XXI/3 (Nov 1982)
   78-80; Cambridge (MA, USA),
   MIT, Hayden Gallery, Intimate
   Architecture (1982); Contemp.
   designers, 1984; Maison
   française, 1985 Dec.-1986 Jan.,
   no.393, p.86
   Mandelli, Mariucca   **AV**
Krjukova, Irina Aleksandrovna
   (Russian art historian, artist,
   d.1974)   **BA**
Krock or Krogh, Hendrik → see Krock,
   Hendrick
Krock, Hendrick   **BA**
   (Danish painter, 1671-1738)   BA
   (German artist, 1671-1738)   WC
   (German, 1671-1738)   GC
   Bibl: ▶Thieme-Becker; ▶Witt
   checklist
   Krock or Krogh, Hendrik   **WC**
   Krock, Hendrik   **GC**
Krock, Hendrik → see Krock, Hendrick
Krodel, Crodel or Krotel, Martin
   (German artist, op.1539-1547)   **WC**
Krodel, Crodel or Krotel, Matthias,
   I → see Krodel, Matthias
Krodel, Crodel or Krotel, Matthias,
   II *(German artist, op.1593-m.1618)* **WC**
Krodel, Crodel or Krotel,
   Wolfgang *(German artist, a.1500-*
   1561)   **WC**
Krodel, Matthias   **GC**
   (German artist, op.1550-1605)   WC
   (German painter, act.1500-d.
   1605)   GC
   Bibl: Getty Photo Study Coll.
   Crodel, Matthias (the Elder)   GC
   Krodel, Crodel or Krotel,
   Matthias, I   **WC**
   Krötel, Matthias (the Elder)   GC
Kroese, Johannes Pieter *(Dutch*
   colckmaker, jeweler, act.1729,
   d.1788)   **BA**
   Bibl: ▶Baillie, Watch- &
   clockmkrs.; ▶Britten, Old clocks;
   J.H. Leopold, in ANTIEK, XX/8
   (Mar 2, 1986), p. 529
Kroesh, Jan van *(Dutch artist, 17th*
   cent.)   **WC**
Krog, Arnold *(Danish architect,*
   ceramist, 1856-1937)   **BA**
Kröger, Jürgen *(German architect,*
   b.1856)   **BA**
Kröger, Klaus *(German painter,*
   b.1920)   **BA**
   Bibl: Jahrb. Hamburger
   Kunstsamm., XIX (1974) pp.117-
   122; ▶Vollmer, Künst.-Lex. 20.
   Jhr., suppl.; ▶WW Arts DEU

Krogius, Björn (Finnish architect) **AV**
   Bibl: Arkkitehti, 1985, v.82, no. 6-7, p.40

Kroha, Jiří **AV BA**
   (Czech architect, painter, b.1893) **BA**
   (Czechoslovak architect, 1893-1974) **AV**
   Bibl: Czech functionalism 1918-1938 (1987)

Krohg → see Krohg, Per

Krohg, Christian **BA WC**
   (Norwegian artist, 1852-1925) **WC**
   (Norwegian painter, author, 1852-1925) **BA**
   Bibl: ▶Bénézit; Bonniers Folklex.; ▶Norsk Kunstner Leks.; ▶Thieme-Becker

Krohg, Oda, (nee Lasson)
   (Norwegian artist, 1860-1935) **WC**

Krohg, Per **BA**
   (Norwegian artist, 1889-) **WC**
   (Norwegian painter, 1889-aft. 1926) **PR**
   (Norwegian painter, costume designer, scenographer, 1889-1965) **BA**
   Bibl: ▶Artist biog. master idx.; Bugge, Festsch. Til Jens Thiis; ▶Havlice, Idx. art. bio.; ▶McGraw-Hill dict. art; ▶Norsk Kunstner Leks.; ▶Thieme-Becker; ▶Vollmer, Künst.-Lex. 20. Jhr.
   Krohg **PR**
   Krohg, Per Larson **PR**

Krohg, Per Lasson **PR WC**
   Per Lasson Krohg **PR**
Krohg, Per Larson → see Krohg, Per
Krohg, Per Lasson → see Krohg, Per

Krohl, Heinz (German artist, 20th cent.) **WC**

Krohn, B. (Dr.) (Czech, active ca. 1937) **JG**

Krohn, Inari (Finnish painter, b.1945) **BA**

Krøjer, Tom (Danish artist, b.1942) **BA**

Krokos, Kyriakos (Greek architect, 1941-) **AV**
   Bibl: Architektonika Themata = Architecture in Greece, 1989, no.23, p.120

Krokotos Group (vase-painters, ca. 520-500 BC) **GC**
   Bibl: ▶Beazley, Attic bl.-fig. vase-ptrs.; Boardman, Attic Bl.-fig. Vases

Krokotos Painter **GC**
   Bibl: Paralipomena

Krokstad, Harald (Norwegian painter, b.1946) **BA**
   Bibl: Lohne, HRYMFAXE, XIX (1989), 3-7; ▶Norsk Kunstner Leks.

Krol, Abraham (French artist, 1919-) **WC**

Krol, Stan **WC WI**
   (British artist, 1910-) **WC**
   (British artist, b.1910) **WI**

Kroll → see Kroll, Leon

Kroll, Leon **BA GC PR WC WI**
   (American artist, 1884-) **WC**
   (American artist, 1884-1974) **WI**
   (American painter, 1884-1974) **GC PR**
   (American painter, printmaker, 1884-1974) **BA**
   Bibl: ▶RILA/BHA
   Kroll **PR**
   Leon Kroll **PR**

Kroll, Lucien **AV BA**
   (Belgian architect, 1927-) **AV**
   (Belgian architect, b.1927) **BA**
   Bibl: ▶Contemp. archts.

Krolow, Wolfgang (West German photographer, b.1950) **BA**

Krombach, Max (Peter Paul)
   (German artist, 1867-) **WC**

Kromberger family → see Cromberger family

Kronberg → see Kronberg, Louis

Kronberg, Julius (Swedish artist, 1850-1921) **WC**

Kronberg, Louis **GC PR WC WI**
   (American artist, 1872-) **WC**
   (American artist, 1872-1965) **WI**
   (American painter, 1872-1965) **PR**
   (American, b.1872) **GC**
   Bibl: ▶Thieme-Becker; ▶Witt checklist; ▶WWW Amer. art
   Kronberg **PR**
   Louis Kronberg **PR**
Kronberger → see Kronberger, Carl

Kronberger, Carl **BA PR WC**
   (Austrian painter, 1841-1921) **BA PR**
   (German artist, 1841-1921) **WC**
   Bibl: ▶Bénézit; ▶RILA/BHA; ▶Thieme-Becker
   Carl Kronberger **PR**
   Kronberger **PR**
   Kronberger, Karl **PR**
Kronberger, Karl → see Kronberger, Carl

Krone, Hermann (German photographer, 1827-1916) **BA**
   Bibl: ▶ICP encyc. photog.; ▶Neue deutsche Biog.

Kronenburg, Robert Hermanus
   (British architect, Much Woolton, Liverpool) **AV**
   Bibl: ▶RIBA members, 1987

Kronenburgh, Tobias [Unidentified] (Unknown painter) **PR**
   Bibl: 1709 Rode inventory
   Tobias Kronenburgh **PR**

Kroner, Christian (Johann Christian) (German artist, 1838-1911) **WC**

Kronfuss, Juan (Argentine architect, 1872-1944) **AV**
   Bibl: Encic. arte en America

Kronlöf, Juha (Finnish architect) **AV**
   Bibl: Arkkitehtuurikilpailuja, 1989, no.3, p.2

Kronover, Irene **WC WI**
   (British artist, 20th cent.) **WC**
   (British artist, op.20th c.) **WI**

Kronsoble, Jeffrey Michael
   (American painter, b.1939) **BA**

Kronstrand, Bror. (Scandinavian artist, 1875-1950) **WC**

Kroon, Johannes Jacobus (Dutch painter, b.1903) **GC**
   Bibl: ▶Vollmer, Künst.-Lex. 20. Jhr.
Kroos, A. → see Croos, A.
Kroost → see Croos, Pieter van der
Krop, Hildebrand Lucien → see Krop, Hildo

Krop, Hildo (Dutch sculptor, 1884-1970) **BA**
   Bibl: ▶Bénézit; ▶Grote Winkler Prins
   Krop, Hildebrand Lucien **BA**

Kropf, J.A. (Swiss artist, op.1777) **WC**

Kropholler, Margaret (Dutch architect, 1891-1966) **BA**

Krotala Group **GC**
   Bibl: ▶Beazley, Attic bl.-fig. vase-ptrs.

Krötel, Matthias (the Elder) → see Krodel, Matthias

Krouchdaler, Hans (Swiss musical instrument maker, act.1685-1699) **BA**

Krouner, Robert D. (American architect) **AV**
   Bibl: ▶AIA Pro File, 1983

Krouthen, Johan Frederik (Swedish artist, 1858-1932) **WC**

Krouwel, Peter (Dutch designer, Leiden) **AV**
   Bibl: Abitare, 1985 July-Aug., no. 236, p.70

Kroyanker, David (Israeli architect, Jerusalem) **AV**
   Bibl: Preservation news, 1989 Jan., v.29, no.1, p.5

Kroyer → see Krøyer, Peder Severin

Krøyer, Marie Triepcke (Danish painter, 1867-1940) **BA**

Kroyer, Peder Severin → see Krøyer, Peder Severin

Krøyer, Peder Severin **BA PR**
   (Danish artist, 1851-1909) **WC**
   (Danish painter, 1851-1909) **GC PR**
   (Danish painter, sculptor, printmaker, 1851-1909) **BA**
   Bibl: Kent, Triumph of Light & Nature (1987); ▶RILA/BHA; ▶Thieme-Becker; ▶Weilbach, Kunst.leks.; ▶Witt checklist

Krøyer, Peter Severin **GC**
   Kroyer **PR**
   Kroyer, Peder Severin **PR**

Kroyer, Peter Severin **PR WC**
   Peder Severin Kroyer **PR**
Kroyer, Peter Severin → see Krøyer, Peder Severin
Krøyer, Peter Severin → see Krøyer, Peder Severin

Krumper, Hans   **BA**
   (*German architect and sculptor,*
    Weilheim, c.1570-1634)   **AV**
   (*German artist, c.1570-1634*)   **WC**
   (*German sculptor, architect, ca.*
    1570-1634)   **BA**
   (*German, ca.1570-1634*)   **GC**
    Bibl: ▶Encyc. world art;
    ▶Thieme-Becker; ▶Witt checklist
Krumpper, Hans   **AV GC**
Krumpper, Khrumpper,
   Krumper or Krumpter, Hans
   (Hans von Weilheim)   **WC**
Krumpper, Hans→see Krumper, Hans
Krumpper, Khrumpper, Krumper or
   Krumpter, Hans (Hans von
   Weilheim)→see Krumper, Hans
Krupa, Karen Jack (*American*
   designer, glass painter, b.1952)   **BA**
Krupka, Francis O. (*American*
   architect)   **AV**
    Bibl: Inland architect, 1988 Jan.-
    Feb., v.32, no.1, p.94
Krupka, Jaroslav (*Czech, active*
   Prague, Czechoslovakia 1920s)   **JG**
Krupy, Alex J. (*American (b. Russia,*
   now USSR), active Chicago, IL,
   U.S., 1930's-1920)   **JG**
Kruse→see Kruse, Alexander Zerdin
Kruse, Alexander→see Kruse,
   Alexander Zerdin
Kruse, Alexander Zerdin (*American*
   painter, 1890-1972)   **PR**
    Bibl: Univ of Arizona MA
    catalogue; ▶WWW Amer. art
   Alexander Zerdin Kruse   PR
   Kruse   PR
   Kruse, Alexander   PR
Kruse, Christian (*Scandinavian*
   artist, 1876-1953)   **WC**
Kruse, Max (*German sculptor, 1854-*
   1942)   **BA**
Kruse, Rasmus Henrik (*Danish*
   painter, 1796-1877)   **BA**
Kruse, Rod (*American architect, Des*
   Moines, IA)   **AV**
    Bibl: ▶AIA Pro File, 1985
Kruseman van Elten→see Kruseman
   van Elten, Hendrik Dirk
Kruseman van Elten, Hendrik
   Dirk   **GC PR WC**
   (*Dutch artist, 1829-1904*)   **WC**
   (*Dutch painter, 1829-1904*)   **GC PR**
    Bibl: ▶Thieme-Becker
   Elten, Kruseman, van   PR
   Hendrik Dirk Kruseman van Elten   PR
   Kruseman van Elten   PR
Kruseman, Cornelis   **GC WC**
   (*Dutch artist, 1797-1857*)   **WC**
   (*Dutch painter, draughtsman,*
    and printmaker, 1797-1857)   **GC**
    Bibl: ▶Thieme-Becker
Kruseman, F.W., Sr.→see Kruseman,
   Frederik Marianus

Kruseman, Frederik Marianus   **PR**
   (*Dutch artist, 1816-1882*)   **WC**
   (*Dutch painter, 1817-1860*)   **PR**
   (*Dutch, 1816-1882*)   **GC**
    Bibl: ▶Thieme-Becker; ▶Witt
    checklist
   Frederik Marianus Kruseman   PR
   Kruseman, F.W., Sr.   PR
Kruseman, Frederik Marinus   **GC WC**
Kruseman, Frederik Marinus→see
   Kruseman, Frederik Marianus
Kruseman, Jan Adam Jansz.   **BA**
   (*Dutch artist, 1804-1862*)   **WC**
   (*Dutch painter and printmaker,*
    1804-1862)   **GC**
   (*Dutch painter, 1804-1862*)   **BA**
    Bibl: ▶Thieme-Becker
Kruseman, Jan Adam
   Janszoon   **GC WC**
Kruseman, Jan Adam Janszoon→see
   Kruseman, Jan Adam Jansz.
Kruseman, Jan Theodoor   **GC**
   (*Dutch artist, 1835-1895*)   **WC**
   (*Dutch painter, 1835-1895*)   **GC**
    Bibl: ▶Thieme-Becker
Kruseman, Jan Theodor   **WC**
Kruseman, Jan Theodor→see
   Kruseman, Jan Theodoor
Krushenick, Nicholas   **BA WI**
   (*American artist, 1929-*)   **WC**
   (*American artist, b.1929*)   **WI**
   (*American painter, b.1929*)   **BA**
Krushenick, Nicolas   **WC**
Krushenick, Nicolas→see Krushenick,
   Nicholas
Kruszewski, Jozef (*Polish artist,*
   1856-1900)   **WC**
Krutikov, Georgij   **AV BA**
   (*Russian architect and urbanist,*
    1899-1958)   **AV**
   (*Russian architect, 1899-1958*)   **BA**
    Bibl: Cahiers du Musée National
    d'art Moderne, 1979, p.241
Krutzinger→see Kreutzinger, Josef
Kruyder, Herman Justus   **BA GC WC**
   (*Dutch artist, 1881-1935*)   **WC**
   (*Dutch painter and*
    draughtsman, 1881-1935)   **GC**
   (*Dutch painter, 1881-1935*)   **BA**
    Bibl: ▶RILA/BHA
Kruyder, Johanna Laura (Jo), (nee
   Bouman) (*Dutch artist, 1886-*)   **WC**
Kruyff, Cornelis de   **GC**
   (*Dutch artist, 1771-1854*)   **WC**
   (*Dutch painter and*
    draughtsman, 1771-1851)   **GC**
    Bibl: ▶Bénézit
Kruijff, Cornelis de   **WC**
Kruyl, Levyn→see Cruyl, Liévin
Kruys, Cornelius→see Cruys, Cornelis
Krylov, Porfirij Nikitič (*Russian*
   painter, printmaker, cartoonist,
   b.1902)   **BA**
Krymov, Nikolaj Petrovič (*Russian*
   painter, 1884-1958)   **BA**

Krynski, Sheila (*American painter,*
   20th c.)   **BA**
Kryzanovsky→see Kryzanovsky,
   Roman
Kryzanovsky, Roman (*American*
   painter, 1885-1929)   **PR**
    Bibl: ▶WWW Amer. art
   Kryzanovsky   PR
   Kryzanowsky, Roman   PR
   Roman Kryzanovsky   PR
Kryzanowsky, Roman→see
   Kryzanovsky, Roman
Kryževskij, J.J. (*Russian artist, 20th*
   c.)   **BA**
Krzczonowicz, Laurenty (*Lithuanian*
   printmaker, ca.1650-1704)   **BA**
Kržišnik, Tomaž (*Yugoslav artist,*
   b.1943)   **BA**
Krzywoblocki, Aleksander (*Polish*
   photographer, b.1901)   **BA**
Krzyzanowski, Conrad→see
   Krzyżanowski, Konrad
Krzyżanowski, Konrad   **BA**
   (*Polish artist, 1872-1922*)   **WC**
   (*Polish painter, 1872-1922*)   **BA**
Krzyzanowski, Conrad   **WC**
Krzyzanowski, Michel Szulc (*Dutch*
   photographer, b.1949)   **BA**
Ktesilaos (*Greek sculptor, 5th c BC*)   **GC**
    Bibl: ▶Robertson, Greek art, p.333
Kuba, Ludvík (*Czech painter,*
   musician, author, 1863-1956)   **BA**
Kuban Group   **GC JG**
   (*vase-painters, ca. 450-400 BC*)   **GC**
    Bibl: ▶Beazley, Attic bl.-fig. vase-
    ptrs.; Boardman, Attic Bl.-fig.
    Vases
Kubanek, Kurt (*Architect,*
   Nuremberg)   **AV**
    Bibl: Baumeister, 1985 Feb., v.82,
    no.2, p. 37
Kubanyi, Lajos (*Hungarian artist,*
   1855-1912)   **WC**
Kubarev, V. (*Russian artist, 20th c.*)   **BA**
Kübel, Mattheus (*Unknown artist*)   **GC**
    Bibl: Gernsheim, Corpus Photog.
    of Drawings, 1395
Kubicek, Jan (*Czech artist, 20th*
   cent.)   **WC**
Kubíček, Leoš (*Czech sculptor,*
   1887-1974)   **BA**
Kubicka, Margareta (*German artist,*
   b.1891)   **BA**
Kubicki, Benedykt (*Polish painter,*
   1874-1951)   **BA**
Kubicki, Jakob→see Kubicki, Jakub
Kubicki, Jakub   **BA GC**
   (*Polish architect and*
    draughtsman, 1758-1833)   **GC**
   (*Polish architect, 1758-1833*)   **AV BA**
    Bibl: ▶Portoghesi, Diz. arch. e
    urbanistica; ▶RILA/BHA;
    ▶Thieme-Becker; ▶Wielka ilustr.
    encyk.
Kubicki, Jakob   **AV**

Kubin, Alfred   **BA GC WC**
(Austrian painter and illustrator,
1877-1959)   GC
(Austrian painter, illustrator,
author, 1877-1959)   BA
(German artist, 1877-)   WC
Bibl: ▶Brockhaus Enzyk.; ▶Encyc.
world art; ▶McGraw-Hill dict. art;
▶Phaidon 20c. art; ▶RILA/BHA;
▶Thieme-Becker; ▶Witt checklist

Kubina, Horst-Dieter (German
architect, Munich)   AV
Bibl: Detail, 1981 Sept.-Oct., no.5,
p.642

Kubinzky, Karl (Czech artist, 1837-
1889)   WC

Kubišta, Bohumil   **BA WC**
(Czech artist, 1884-1918)   WC
(Czech painter, printmaker,
critic, 1884-1918)   BA
Bibl: ▶Bénézit; ▶Encyk. českého
výtv. uměni; ▶Gorenflo, Bild.
Künstler; ▶Thieme-Becker;
Tolman, Prokof, NORJ'LEONIK
CESKO.... (1936); ▶Vollmer,
Künst.-Lex. 20. Jhr.

Kübler, Arnold (Swiss draftsman,
author, b.1890)   BA

Kubler, Ludwig (German artist, op.
c.1850-1868)   WC

Kubler, Werli, II → see Kübler, Werner
(the Younger)

Kübler, Werner (the Younger)   GC
(German artist, 1582-1621)   WC
(Swiss, 1582-1621)   GC
Bibl: ▶Thieme-Becker

Kubler, Werli, II   WC

Kubler, Werner, (Werli), I (Swiss
artist, 1555-1586)   WC

Kubly, Felix Wilhelm (Swiss
architect, 1802-1872)   BA

Kubo, Paul (German surveyor,
architect, 20th c.)   BA

Kubo, Seichi (Japanese architect,
1953-)   AV
Bibl: Space design, 1986 Dec., no.
267, p.34

Kubota, Nobuo (Canadian sculptor,
architect, b.1932)   BA

Kubota, Shigeko (Japanese artist in
USA, b.1937)   BA

Kubovsky, Peter   **BA WC**
(Austrian printmaker, b.1930)   BA
(German artist, 1930-)   WC

Kubrick, Christiane (French artist,
20th cent.)   WC

Kuby, Hellmut (German architect)   AV
Bibl: Detail, 1981 May-June, no.3,
p.336

Kućanski, Boško (Yugoslav sculptor,
b.1931)   BA

Kučerová, Alena (Czech printmaker,
b.1935)   BA

Kučerová-Záveská, Hana   **AV BA**
(Czech architect, 20th c.)   BA
(Czechoslovak architect, 1902-
1944)   AV
Bibl: Czech functionalism 1918-
1938 (1987)

Kucharski → see Kucharski, Alexander
Kucharski, Aleksander → see
Kucharski, Alexander

Kucharski, Alexander   **GC PR**
(Polish artist, 1741-1819)   WC
(Polish painter, 1741-1819)   PR
(Polish, 1741-1819)   GC
Bibl: Getty Photo Study Coll.
(Ptgs.); ▶Thieme-Becker; ▶Witt
checklist

Alexander Kucharski   PR
Couasky, Alexander   GC
Kucharski   PR
Kucharski, Aleksander   PR

**Kucharski, Couasky, Kocharsky,
Kokarski, Kouarski etc.,
Alexander**   **WC**
Kucharski, Couasky, Kocharsky,
Kokarski, Kouarski etc.,
Alexander → see Kucharski,
Alexander

Küchel, Johann Jakob Michael   **BA**
(German architect, 1703-1769)   BA
(German artist, 1703-1769)   WC
Bibl: ▶Avery Libr. cat.; ▶Encyc.
world art; Knaurs: Deutschland, p.
825; ▶Thieme-Becker

**Kuchel, Michael (Johann Jakob
Michael)**   **WC**
Kuchel, Michael (Johann Jakob
Michael) → see Küchel, Johann
Jakob Michael

Kuchenmeister, Rainer (German
artist, 20th cent.)   WC

Kucher, Klaus (German architect,
b.1937)   BA

Kucher, Walter (West German
architect, Berlin)   AV
Bibl: Architecture and urbanism,
1987 May extra ed., no.5, p.158

Küchler, Albert   **BA WC**
(Danish painter, 1803-1886)   BA
(Scandinavian artist, 1803-1886)   WC

Küchler, Balthasar (German painter,
printmaker, ca.1571-1641)   BA
Bibl: ▶Natl. union cat.;
▶Thieme-Becker

Kuckei, Peter (German painter,
b.1938)   BA
Bibl: ▶Art Index, v.33; Ohff,
Kunstwerk, XXXVIII (Sep 1985)
pp.56-69

Kücker, Wilhelm   **AV BA**
(German architect, Munich)   AV
(West German architect, 20th
c.)   BA
Bibl: ▶Avery period. idx., 7th
suppl.; Deutsche Bauzeitung,
1984 Sept., v.118, no.9, p.23;
Jahrb. für Architektur (1983) 66

Kucsma, Kurt (American architect)   AV
Kucz, Jan (Polish sculptor, b.1936)   BA
Kucznierz, Guido (German artist,
b.1944)   BA
Kuczynska, Maria Theresa (Polish
sculptor, ceramist, 20th c.)   BA
Kudrin, Victor Petrovich (Russian
artist, 20th cent.)   WC
Kudrjashev, Ivan   BA
(Russian artist, 1896-)   WC
(Russian painter, 1896-1974)   BA
Koudriachov, Ivan   WC
Kudryashov, Oleg (Russian
printmaker, collagist in GBR,
b.1932)   BA
Bibl: ▶Art Index, vs.37-38; ▶Intl.
dir. exh. artists, 1982; ▶MoMA
libr. cat.

Kuehl → see Kuehl, Gotthardt Johann
Kuehl, Gotthardt → see Kuehl,
Gotthardt Johann

Kuehl, Gotthardt Johann   BA
(German artist, 1850-1915)   WC
(German painter, 1850-
1915)   BA GC PR
Bibl: ▶Bénézit; ▶Busse, Maler u.
Bildhauer 19. Jahr.;
▶Thieme-Becker

Gotthardt Kuehl   PR
Kuehl   PR

Kuehl, Gotthardt   **GC PR WC**
Kühl, Gotthardt Johann   GC

Kuehn, Frances   BA
(American artist, 20th cent.)   WC
(American artist, b.1943)   WI
(American painter, b.1943)   BA

Kuehn, Frances Tannebaum   **WC WI**
Kuehn, Frances Tannebaum → see
Kuehn, Frances

Kuehn, Frank Charles William
(American architect, 1884-1970)   BA
Bibl: Kinyon, PRAIRIE ARCHITECT
(1984)

Kuehn, Gary (American artist,
b.1939)   BA

Kuehn, Gernot (German
photographer, 20th c.)   BA
Kuehne → see Kuehne, Max

Kuehne, Max   **GC PR WI**
(American artist, 1880-1986)   WI
(American painter, b. 1880)   PR
(American sculptor, 20th
century)   GC
Bibl: Juley coll., NMAA;
▶Thieme-Becker

Kuehne   PR
Max Kuehne   PR

Kuen, Francoise (French artist, 20th
cent.)   WC

Kuen, Franz Martin (German artist,
1719-1771)   WC

Kuen, Johann Georg (Austrian
architect, 1642-1691)   BA

**Kuen, Khuen, Kuhen, Kuhn etc.,
Leonhard (J. Leonhard)** (German
artist, 1765-p.1797)   WC

Kuene, Konrad   **BA**
   (15th century German architect)   AV
   (German master builder,
   d.1469)   BA
   Kuhn, Konrad   **AV**
Küenzlen, Martin *(West German*
   architect, Berlin)   **AV**
   Bibl: Architektur + Wettbewerbe,
   1984 June, p.70
Kuess, Helmuth *(Austrian architect,*
   1952-)   **AV**
   Bibl: Ottagono, 1988 Mar., p.20
Küfer, Kuno → see Scheerbart, Paul
Kuffner, David *(American architect,*
   Northbrook, IL, 1947-)   **AV**
   Bibl: ▶AIA Pro File, 1985
Kugač, Jurij Petrovič *(Russian*
   painter, b.1917)   **BA**
Kugelgen, Carl (Ferdinand Carl)
   von *(German artist, 1772-1832)*   **WC**
Kugelgen, Gerhard (Franz Gerhard)
   von → see Kügelgen, Gerhard von
Kügelgen, Gerhard von   **BA GC**
   (German artist, 1772-1820)   WC
   (German painter, 1772-1820)   BA
   (German, 1772-1820)   GC
   Bibl: ▶Neue deutsche Biog.;
   ▶Thieme-Becker; ▶Witt checklist
   Kugelgen, Gerhard (Franz
   Gerhard) von   **WC**
Kügelgen, Wilhelm von   **BA GC WC**
   (German painter, author, 1802-
   1867)   BA
   (Russian artist, 1802-1867)   WC
   (Russian, 1802-1867)   GC
   Bibl: ▶Thieme-Becker; ▶Witt
   checklist
Kugler, Franz *(German artist, 1808-*
   1858)   **WC**
Kugler, Hermann *(West German*
   architect, Stuttgart)   **AV**
   Bibl: Deutsches Architektenblatt,
   1988 Nov.1, v.20, no.11, p.1563
Kugler, Luise *(German artist, 1811-*
   1884)   **WC**
Kügler, Martina *(German*
   printmaker, b.1945)   **BA**
Kuhalampi, Markku *(Finnish*
   architect, Haukipudas)   **AV**
   Bibl: Architektur + Wettbewerbe,
   1988 Mar., no.133, p.60
Kuhfuss, Paul *(German painter,*
   printmaker, 1883-1960)   **BA**
Kühl, Gotthardt Johann → see Kuehl,
   Gotthardt Johann
Kuhlen, Franz *(German artist, op.*
   1821-1854)   **WC**
Kuhler, Ingeborg *(West German*
   architect, 1943-)   **AV**
   Bibl: Das Kunstwerk, n.3-4, Sept.
   1983, p.130
Kuhlmann, Gerhard *(West German*
   architect, Stuttgart)   **AV**
   Bibl: Deutsches Architektenblatt,
   1987 Oct., v.19, no.10, p.1161
Kuhn → see Kuhn, Walt

Kühn, Achim *(German metalworker,*
   20th c.)   **BA**
Kuhn, B. *(French photographer, act.*
   1858-1875)   **GC**
   Bibl: ▶Idx. Amer. photog. colls.
   J. Kuhn (Paris)   GC
Kuhn, Beate *(German ceramist,*
   sculptor, painter, b.1927)   **BA**
   Bibl: ▶Gorenflo, Bild. Künstler;
   ▶Penguin dec. arts, 1987;
   ▶Vollmer, Künst.-Lex. 20. Jhr.
Kuhn, Franz J. *(German architect,*
   Trier, fl. 1911)   **AV**
   Bibl: Deutsche Bauzeitschrift,
   1988 July, v.36, no.7, p.362
Kuhn, Friedrich *(Swiss artist, 20th*
   cent.)   **WC**
Kuhn, Hans *(German painter,*
   b.1905)   **BA**
   Bibl: ▶Bénézit; Guide exh. artists:
   Euro. ptrs.; ▶WW Arts DEU
Kühn, Heinrich   **BA**
   (Austrian (b. Germany), 1866-
   1944)   JG
   (Austrian photographer, 1866-
   1944)   BA
Kuhn, Heinrich Carl Christian   **JG**
Kuhn, Heinrich Carl Christian → see
   Kühn, Heinrich
Kühn, Jan Hendrik *(Dutch jeweler,*
   ca.1751-1810)   **BA**
   Bibl: Amsterdam (NLD),
   Rijksmuseum. Catalogus van
   Meubelen (1952), p.259 #333;
   Baarsen, Bull. van het
   Rijksmuseum XXXI/2 1983,
   p.105-115
Kuhn, Jochen *(West German*
   painter, filmmaker, 20th c.)   **BA**
   Bibl: KUNSTFORUM INT'L 65, 9
   (Sept 1983), p.155-157
Kühn, Josef II *(German*
   draughtsman, b.1872)   **GC**
   Bibl: ▶Bénézit
Kühn, Justus Englehardt   **BA WC WI**
   (American artist, op.1708-1726)   WI
   (American artist, op.1708-m.
   1717)   WC
   (American painter, act.1708,
   d.1717)   BA
Kuhn, Konrad → see Kuene, Konrad
Kuhn, Max *(German artist, 1838-*
   1888)   **WC**
Kuhn, Thomas *(German sculptor,*
   b.1948)   **BA**
Kuhn, Walt   **BA GC PR WC WI**
   (American artist, 1877-1949)   WC WI
   (American painter, 1880-1949)   BA PR
   (American, 1877-1949)   GC
   Bibl: ▶Encyc. world art; ▶Fielding's
   Amer. ptrs.; ▶RILA/BHA;
   ▶Thieme-Becker; ▶Witt checklist;
   ▶WW Amer. Art, 1984 necrol.;
   ▶WWW Amer., v.2
   Kuhn   PR
   Walt Kuhn   PR

Kuhn, Walter   **AV BA**
   (Artist-turned-architect,
   Germany, 1913-1984)   AV
   (German architect, sculptor,
   b.1913)   BA
   Bibl: Bauwelt, 1984, v.75, no.39,
   p. 1661
Kühne, Claude *(Austrian architect)*   **AV**
   Bibl: Transparent, 1985, v.16, no.
   10-12, p.41
Kuhnel, Christian Friedrich
   (German artist, op.1719-1792)   **WC**
Kuhnert *(German artist, 19th cent.)*   **WC**
Kuhnert, Friedrich Wilhelm Karl → see
   Kuhnert, Wilhelm
Kuhnert, Horst *(German sculptor,*
   painter, b.1939)   **BA**
Kuhnert, Wilhelm   **GC**
   (German artist, 1865-1926)   WC
   (German painter, 1865-1926)   GC
   Bibl: ▶Thieme-Becker
   Kuhnert, Friedrich Wilhelm Karl   GC
   Kuhnert, Wilhelm (Friedrich
   Wilhelm Carl)   **WC**
Kuhnert, Wilhelm (Friedrich Wilhelm
   Carl) → see Kuhnert, Wilhelm
Kühnis, Felix *(Architect,*
   Switzerland?)   **AV**
   Bibl: DBZ, 1985 Jan., v.33, no.1,
   p.47
Kuhnle, Harry *(West German*
   architect)   **AV**
   Bibl: Deutsche Bauzeitschrift,
   1989 Jan., no.1, p.14
Kuhr, Fritz *(German, active 1920s-*
   1930s, Bauhaus)   **JG**
Kuhrt, Rolf   **BA WC**
   (German artist, 20th c.)   BA
   (German artist, 20th cent.)   WC
   Bibl: Lucke, BILDENDE KUNST, I
   (Jan 1988) 2-28
Kuhstoss, Paul *(Belgian artist, 1870-*
   1898)   **WC**
Kuijl → see Kuijl, Gerard van
Kuijl, Gerard van *(Dutch painter,*
   1604-1673)   **BA PR**
   Bibl: ▶RILA/BHA
   Gerard van Kuijl   PR
   Kuijl   PR
Kuijper → see Cuyper, Hendrick
Kuijpers, Toon *(Dutch painter, 20th*
   c.)   **BA**
   Bibl: ▶Art Index, v.36; Potter,
   ARTS
   MAGAZINE/LXII/5(JAN.'88)p.95
Kuijten, Henricus Johannes
   (Harrie) → see Kuyten, Harrie
Kuik, William Diederich *(Dutch*
   printmaker, b.1929)   **BA**
Kuil, Gysbert → see Kuyl, Gysbert van
   der
Kuindji, Arkhip Ivanovich → see
   Kuindži, Arksip Ivanovič
Kuindji, Arkhip Ivanovitch → see
   Kuindži, Arksip Ivanovič
Kuindzi → see Kuindži, Arksip Ivanovič

Kuindži, Arksip Ivanovič **BA PR**
  (Russian artist, 1842-1910) WC
  (Russian painter, 1842-1910) BA PR
  (Russian, 1842-1910) GC
  Bibl: ▶RILA/BHA; ▶Witt checklist
  Arksip Ivanovic Kuindzi PR
  Kuindji, Arkhip Ivanovich PR
Kuindji, Arkhip Ivanovitch **GC WC**
  Kuindzi PR
Kuipel(?), J.E.P. *(Dutch artist, op.*
  1694) WC
Kuiper → *see* Cuyper, Hendrick
Kuiper, Gijs *(Dutch architect, Zeist)* **AV**
  Bibl: ▶Federatie O jrbk.
Kuipers or Cuypers, C. → *see* Kuipers,
  C.
Kuipers, C. **GC**
  (Dutch artist, op.1756-1784) WC
  (Dutch painter, act.1756-1784) GC
  Bibl: ▶Bénézit
  Kuipers or Cuypers, C. **WC**
Kuipers, Hermann *(Architect,*
  Emlichheim) **AV**
  Bibl: Deutsche Bauzeitschrift,
  1984, v.32, p.1036
Kuipers, Michel *(Dutch artist,*
  b.1949) **BA**
Kujasalo, Matti *(Finnish painter,*
  b.1946) **BA**
  Bibl: Guide exh. artists: Euro.
  ptrs.; Philadelphia (PA, USA), Port
  of History Mus., Contemporaries
  (1982)
Kujawski, Jerzy *(Polish artist,*
  1921/2) **WC**
Kuka *(British artist, b.1948)* **WI**
Kükelhaus, Hugo *(Craftsman,*
  designer and interior architect in
  Werkstätte Dickerhoff, BRD, 1900-
  1984) **AV**
  Bibl: Arch+, 1984 Dec., no.78,
  p.36
Kukfeld, Peter *(British artist, op.*
  20th c.) **WI**
Kukkapuro, Yrjö *(Finnish designer,*
  1933-) **AV**
  Bibl: Living architecture, 1984,
  no.2, p.88
Kukkonen, Martti *(Finnish architect)* **AV**
Kukla, Reinhold *(German artist, op.*
  c.1920) **WC**
Kukryniksy (Three artists-P.N.
  Krylov, M.V. Kupriyanov and
  N.A. Sokolov) *(Russian artist,*
  20th cent.) **WC**
Kulbin, Nicolai → *see* Kulbin, Nikolaj
  Ivanovič
Kulbin, Nikolaj Ivanovič **BA**
  (Russian artist, 19th cent.) WC
  (Russian painter, 1868-1917) BA
  Kulbin, Nicolai **WC**
Kuldschun, Ingrid *(German*
  architect, Berlin, 1952-) **AV**
  Bibl: Bauwelt, 1985 Mar.15, v.76,
  no.11, p.372

Kuldschun, Peter *(German architect,*
  Berlin, 1947-) **AV**
  Bibl: Bauwelt, 1985 Mar.15, v.76,
  no.11, p.372
Kulhánek, Oldřich **BA WC**
  (Czech artist, 1940-) WC
  (Czech printmaker, b.1940) BA
Kulicke, Robert M. *(American*
  painter, b.1924) **BA**
Kulih, Jan *(Czech sculptor, 20th c.)* **BA**
Kulik, Bruce *(American landscape*
  architect, b.1939) **BA**
Kulikov, Afanacij Efremovič
  (Russian painter, caricaturist, 1884-
  1949) **BA**
Kulinyi, Istvan *(Hungarian artist,*
  20th cent.) **WC**
Kulisiewicz, Tadeusz **BA WC**
  (Polish artist, 1899-) WC
  (Polish printmaker, b.1899) BA
Kulka, Johann-Peter → *see* Kulka, Peter
Kulka, Peter **AV BA**
  (German architect, b.1937) BA
  (West German architect,
  Cologne, 1937-) AV
  Bibl: ▶Bund Deut. Arch. Hdbch.,
  1987
  Kulka, Johann-Peter AV
Kull, Hans Rudolf *(Swiss artist,*
  1802-1824) **WC**
Kull, Johann Baptist *(German artist,*
  18th cent.(?)) **WC**
Kulle, Axel Henrik *(Swedish artist,*
  1846-1908) **WC**
Kulle, Nils Jakob *(Swedish artist,*
  1838-1898) **WC**
Kulling, Ruedi *(Swiss artist, 20th*
  cent.) **WC**
Külling, V. *(Swiss(?) architect)* **AV**
  Bibl: Lotus international, 1988,
  no.57, p.59
Kullrich, Wilhelm Friedrich *(German*
  medalist, 1821-1887) **BA**
  Bibl: ▶Forrer, Medallists; MEDAL,
  10 (winter 1986), p. 21-25;
  ▶Thieme-Becker
Kulmala, Matti *(Finnish printmaker,*
  b.1946) **BA**
Kulmbach → *see* Kulmbach, Hans
  Suess von

Kulmbach, Hans Suess
von **BA GC PR WC**
  (German artist, c.1480-1522) WC
  (German painter, ca.1480-1522) PR
  (German painter, draughtsman,
  and printmaker, ca.1480-
  1522) GC
  (German painter, woodcutter,
  ca.1480-1522) BA
  (German, ca. 1480-1522) JG
  Bibl: George Goldner; Getty Photo
  Study Coll.; ▶RILA/BHA
  Han Suess von Kulmbach PR
  Kulmbach PR
  Kulmbach, Hans Suss von PR
  Kulmbach, Hans von **GC JG PR**
  Suess von Kulmbach, Hans PR
  Suess, Hans PR
Kulmbach, Hans Suss von → *see*
  Kulmbach, Hans Suess von
Kulmbach, Hans von → *see* Kulmbach,
  Hans Suess von
Kulmer, Ferdinand *(Yugoslav artist,*
  1925-) **WC**
Kulon, Stanislaw *(Polish sculptor,*
  b.1930) **BA**
Kulterer, Gernot *(Austrian architect,*
  professor, Villach, 1940-) **AV**
  Bibl: Bauforum, 1987, v.20, no.
  122, p.13
Kulusjärvi, Veli *(Finnish architect,*
  Oulu) **AV**
  Bibl: Baumeister, 1989 Oct., v.86,
  no.10, p.29
Kulvianski, Issai *(German painter,*
  sculptor, 1894-1940) **BA**
Külz, Walburga *(German ceramist,*
  b.1921) **BA**
Kuma, Helene *(Russian ceramist,*
  educator, collector, 20th c.) **BA**
Kuma, Kengo *(Japanese architect,*
  1954-) **AV**
  Bibl: Japan architect, 1988 Nov.-
  Dec., v.63, no.11-12, p.51
Kumagai, Yoshinobu *(Japanese*
  architect) **AV**
  Bibl: Japan architect, 1982 Feb.,
  v.57, no.298, p.69
Kumai, Michio *(Japanese architect)* **AV**
  Bibl: Toshi jutaku, 1983 May, no.
  187, p.14
Kümel, Lydia *(Belgian interior*
  designer) **AV**
  Bibl: Maison française, 1987 Oct.,
  no.410, p.104
Kumlien, Akke *(Swedish artist,*
  1884-) **WC**
Kumlien, Hjalmar *(Swedish artist,*
  1837-1897) **WC**
Kümmel, Heinrich August Georg
  (German sculptor in ITA, 1810-
  1855) **BA**
  Bibl: ▶Mackay, Western sculp.
  bronze; ▶Thieme-Becker

Kummer, Carl Robert   GC
(*German artist, 1810-1889*)   WC
(*German painter, 1810-1889*)   GC
   Bibl: ▶Bénézit
Kummer, Robert (Carl Robert)   WC
Kummer, Ernst (*German architect*)   AV
   Bibl: Bauwelt, 1986 May 23, v.77,
   no.19-20, p.696
Kummer, Peter, the elder (*German
architect, act.1572-1592*)   BA
Kummer, Raimund (*German
photographer, 20th c.*)   BA
   Bibl: ▶Art Index, v. 34 (July 1990);
   Deecke, KUNSTWERK,
   XXXVIII(SEPT 1988), 70-1
Kummer, Robert (Carl Robert) → *see*
   Kummer, Carl Robert
Kummert, Otto (*German artist, 20th
cent.*)   WC
Kump, Ernest J. (*American
architect, 1911-*)   AV
   Bibl: ▶Contemp. archts.
Kumrow, Klaus (*West German
artist, b.1959*)   BA
   Bibl: ▶Art Index, v.36; Purogel,
   Kunstwerk XL (Sep 1987), 49
Kunath → *see* Kunath, Oscar A.
Kunath, Oscar → *see* Kunath, Oscar A.
Kunath, Oscar A. (*German painter,
1830-1904*)   PR
   Bibl: ▶Dawdy, Artists Amer. West
Kunath   PR
Kunath, Oscar   PR
Oscar A. Kunath   PR
Kunau, Walther (*German artist,
b.1933*)   BA
Kunc, Milan (*West German painter,
b.1944*)   BA
Kunce, Ken (*American architect,
Chicago, Ill*)   AV
   Bibl: Inland architect, 1987 May-
   June, v.31, no.3, p.50
Kunckel, Georg Ernst (*German glass
engraver, 1692-1750*)   BA
Kündig, Reinhold (*Swiss painter,
b.1888*)   BA
Kundmann, Karl (*Austrian sculptor,
1838-1919*)   BA
Kúnffy, Lajos (*Hungarian painter,
1869-1962*)   BA
Küng, Beda (*Swiss architect*)   AV
   Bibl: ▶Schweiz. Ingen. u. Archit.,
   1984-1985
Kung, Edgar (*Swiss artist, 20th
cent.*)   WC
Küng, Erhard (*Swiss architect,
sculptor, act.1458, d.1506*)   BA
   Bibl: ▶Schweiz. Künst.-Lex.; Slade
   Czels, ZEITSCHR. FÜR SCHW.
   ARCH. U. KUNSTGESCH. XLIV/1
   (1987) 55-59; ▶Thieme-Becker
Kunikata, Hideo (*Japanese
architect*)   AV
   Bibl: Space design, 1988 July, no.
   286, p.49

Kunitsyna, L. (*Russian architect*)   AV
   Bibl: Process: architecture, 1985
   Jan., no.54, p.153
Kuniyoshi → *see* Kuniyoshi, Yasuo
Kuniyoshi (Utagawa Kuniyoshi)
(*Japanese printmaker, 1798-1861*)   BA
Kuniyoshi, Yasuo   BA GC JG PR WC WI
(*American (b. Japan), 1889-
1953*)   JG
(*American artist, 1889/94-1953*)   WC
(*American artist, 1893-1953*)   WI
(*American painter, 1889-
1953*)   BA GC PR
   Bibl: ▶RILA/BHA
Kuniyoshi   PR
Yasuo Kuniyoshi   PR
Kunkel, Jerry (*American artist, 20th
c.*)   BA
Kunkler, Jean Jules Adrien (*Swiss
artist, 1829-1866*)   WC
Kunkler, Johann Heinrich (*German
artist, 1756-1836*)   WC
Künnapu, Vilen (*Estonian architect,
20th century*)   AV
   Bibl: Casabella, 1986 Nov., v.50,
   no.529, p.4
Kunnas, Väinö (*Finnish painter,
1896-1929*)   BA
Kunst, Berend (*Dutch painter, 1794-
1881*)   BA
Kunst, Nicolas (*Netherlands artist,
op.1543*)   WC
Kunst, Pieter → *see* Cornelisz., Pieter
   (Pieter Kunst)
Kunstler, Morton (*American artist,
b.1931*)   WI
Kuntz, Carl → *see* Kuntz, Karl
Kuntz, Federico de Madrazo y → *see*
   Madrazo y Kuntz, Federico de
Kuntz, Karl   BA GC
(*German artist, 1770-1830*)   WC
(*German painter, 1770-1830*)   GC
(*German painter, printmaker,
1770-1830*)   BA
   Bibl: ▶Thieme-Becker
Kuntz, Carl   WC
*Kuntz, Kuntze, Cunz, Gunz or Konicz,
Thaddaus or Tadeusz* → *see* Kuntze,
   Tadeusz
Kuntz, Pietro (Pedro) (*Spanish
painter, 1795-1863*)   PR
   Bibl: ▶Thieme-Becker
Pedro Kuntz   PR
Kuntz, Rudolf (*German artist, 1797-
1848*)   WC
Kuntz, Taddeo → *see* Kuntze, Tadeusz
Kuntz, Thaddäus → *see* Kuntze,
   Tadeusz

Kuntze, Tadeusz   BA GC
(*German artist, 1731-1793*)   WC
(*Polish painter active in Italy,
18th cent*)   AV
(*Polish painter in ITA, ca.1731-
1793*)   BA
(*Polish painter, ca.1731-1793*)   GC
   Bibl: ANTICHITA VIVA, XX, 5 (Sep-
   Oct 1981), 23-29; Arte cristiana,
   1988 July-Aug., v.76, no.727,
   p.303; ▶Bénézit; ▶Encyc. world
   art; Getty Photo Study Coll.;
   Getty Photo Study Coll. (Ptgs.);
   ▶Havlice, Idx. art. bio.; ▶Kindlers
   Malerei Lex.; ▶RILA/BHA;
   ▶Slownik artystów polskich;
   ▶Thieme-Becker; ▶Wielka ilustr.
   encyk.
Cunze, Thaddaus   GC
Guntz, Thaddaeus   GC
**Kuntz, Kuntze, Cunz, Gunz or
Konicz, Thaddaus or Tadeusz**   WC
Kuntz, Taddeo   AV
Kuntz, Thaddäus   GC
Kunz, Adam (Ludwig Adam)
(*German artist, 1857-1929*)   WC
Kunz, Heinrich (*Architect,
Switzerland*)   AV
Kunz, Jurgen (*West German
architect*)   AV
   Bibl: Architecture d'aujourd'hui,
   1985 Feb., no.237, p.49
Kunz, Karl (*German painter,
printmaker, 1905-1971*)   BA
Kunze, Alfred (*German artist, 1866-
1943*)   WC
Künzel, Auguste (*Swiss architect,
Basel, fl. 1920's*)   AV
   Bibl: Archithese, 1988 Mar.-Apr.,
   v.19, no.2, p.61
Kupecky, Johann → *see* Kupezky,
   Johann
Kupelwieser, Leopold   BA WC
(*Austrian painter, 1796-1862*)   BA
(*German artist, 1796-1862*)   WC
Kuper (*German artist, 20th cent.*)   WC
Kupetski → *see* Kupezky, Johann
Kupetski, Johann → *see* Kupezky,
   Johann
Kupetsky, Jan → *see* Kupezky, Johann
Kupetsky, Johann → *see* Kupezky,
   Johann
Kupetzky → *see* Kupezky, Johann
Kupetzski, Jan → *see* Kupezky, Johann
Kupezcky, Johann → *see* Kupezky,
   Johann
Kupezky → *see* Kupezky, Johann

Kupezky, Johann   **BA PR**
  (Czech painter in Germany,
   1667-1740)   BA
  (Czechoslovakian painter, 1667-
   1740)   PR
  (German painter, 1666/67-1740)   GC
  (Hungarian artist, 1667-1740)   WC
  (Hungarian, 1667-1740)   GC
  Bibl: ▶Bénézit; Getty Photo Study
   Coll. (Ptgs.); ▶RILA/BHA; ▶Witt
   checklist
  Johann Kupezky   PR
  Kopetzki, Johan   GC
  Kupecky, Johann   GC
  Kupetski   PR
  Kupetski, Johann   GC
  Kupetsky, Jan   GC
  Kupetsky, Johann   **GC**
  Kupetzky   PR
  Kupetzski, Jan   GC
  Kupezcky, Johann   GC
  Kupezky   PR
  Kupezky, Johann (the Elder)   **GC**
  Kupezky, Kupetzki, Kupecky,
   Kupeczky etc. the Elder,
   Johann   **WC**
  Kupitski   PR
Kupezky, Johann (the Elder)→see
  Kupezky, Johann
Kupezky, Kupetzki, Kupecky,
  Kupeczky etc. the Elder,
  Johann→see Kupezky, Johann
Kupfer, Johann Michael *(German*
  artist, 1859-1917)   **WC**
Kupferman, Moshe *(Polish painter*
  in ISR, b.1926)   **BA**
  Bibl: ▶Art Index, 1974, v.37;
   ▶ARTbibl. mod., 19/1, #0379;
   ▶Intl. dir. exh. artists, 1983;
   Worcester Art Museum, 3 ISRAELI
   ARTISTS
Kupffer, Elisar von (Elisarion)
  (Swiss author, painter, 1872-1942)   **BA**
Kupiec, Robert E. *(American*
  architect)   **AV**
  Bibl: ▶AIA Pro File, 1983
Kupitski→see Kupezky, Johann
Kupka→see Kupka, František
Kupka, Frank→see Kupka, František
Kupka, Frans→see Kupka, František

Kupka, František   **BA PR**
  (Czech artist, 1871-1957)   WC
  (Czech painter in FRA, 1871-
   1957)   BA
  (Czech, 1871-1957)   GC
  (Czechoslovakian painter, 1871-
   1957)   PR
  Bibl: ▶Encyc. world art; ▶Havlice,
   Idx. art. bio.; ▶Libr. of Congr.
   Name Auth. File; McG; ▶Phaidon
   20c. art; ▶RILA/BHA;
   ▶Thieme-Becker; ▶Witt checklist
  Frantisek Kupka   PR
  Kupka   PR
  Kupka, Frank   **GC PR**
  Kupka, Frans   PR
  Kupka, Frantz   **WC**
  Kupka, Franz   PR
Kupka, Frantz→see Kupka, František
Kupka, Franz→see Kupka, František
Kupka, Pavel *(Czech architect,*
  Prague)   **AV**
  Bibl: Architecture: the AIA
   journal, 1988 Sept., v.77, no.9,
   p.96
Kupke, Joachim *(German painter,*
  draftsman, b.1947)   **BA**
Küpper, Christian Emil Marie→see
  Doesburg, Theo van (Christian Emil
  Marie Küpper)
Kupper, Eugene *(American*
  architect, 1939-)   **AV**
Küppers, Bernhard *(West German*
  architect, 20th c.)   **BA**
  Bibl: Müller, C., PANTHEON,
   XLII/3 (July-Sept 1984) 296-297
Kuppers, Leo *(German artist, 1884-)*   **WC**
Kuprejanov, Nikolaj Nikolaevič
  (Russian printmaker, 1894-1933)   **BA**
Kuprin, Aleksandr Vasil'evič
  (Russian painter, 1880-1960)   **BA**
Kuprjanov, Mihajl Vasil'evič
  (Russian painter, printmaker,
  cartoonist, b.1903)   **BA**
Kurahara, Ted *(American painter,*
  b.1925)   **BA**
Kuramata, Shiro *(Japanese interior,*
  furniture designer, 1934-)   **AV**
  Bibl: AMC, 1988 June, no.21,
   p.68
Kuramoto, Tatsuhiko G. *(Japanese*
  architect, 1946-)   **AV**
  Bibl: Kenchiku bunka, 1987 Dec.,
   v.42, no.494, p.102
Kurchan, Juan *(Argentine architect,*
  1913-)   **AV**
  Bibl: Summa, 1985 Oct., no.218,
   p.18
Kurelek, William   **BA WC**
  (Canadian artist, 20th cent.)   WC
  (Canadian painter, 1927-1977)   BA
Kurer, Thomas V. *(Swiss architect,*
  Zurich)   **AV**
  Bibl: ▶Schweiz. Ingen. u. Archit.,
   1984-1985, p.190

Kuretanoff, J. *(German artist, op.c.*
  1850)   **WC**
Kurfiss, Gottlieb *(Swiss painter,*
  b.1925)   **BA**
Kurhajec, Joseph A. *(American*
  sculptor, b.1938)   **BA**
Kuria, Francesco→see Curia,
  Francesco
Kurlander, Ira *(American architect,*
  San Francisco, CA)   **AV**
  Bibl: Architectural digest, 1985
   Oct., v.42, no.10, p.138
Kürmayr, August   **AV**
Kurnitzky, Günter *(German*
  architect, Berlin, 1909-1985)   **AV**
  Bibl: Bauwelt, 1985 May 31, v.76,
   no.20-21, p.755
Kurokawa, Kisho   **AV BA**
  (Japanese architect, b.1934)   BA
  (Japanese architect. Principal of
   Kisho Kurokawa, Architect
   and Associates, 1934-)   AV
  Bibl: ▶Avery period. idx., 1989
   suppl.; ▶Contemp. archts.;
   ▶Contemp. artists; Intl. who's
   who; ▶Macmillan encyc. archts.;
   ▶Natl. union cat., 1975
  Kurokawa, Noriaki Kisho   BA
Kurokawa, Masayuki   **AV BA**
  (Japanese architect, 1937-)   AV
  (Japanese architect, b.1937)   BA
  Bibl: ▶Avery period. idx., 7th
   suppl.; Kenchiku bunka, 1987
   Dec., v.42, no.494, p.108;
   Vorreiter-Wajed, ARCHITECTURAL
   REVIEW, CLXXX/1075 (Sept.
   1986), p. 91-94
Kurokawa, Noriaki Kisho→see
  Kurokawa, Kisho
Kurokawa, Tetsuro *(Japanese*
  architect, 1943-)   **AV**
  Bibl: Kenchiku bunka, 1987 Dec.,
   v.42, no.494, p.106
Kuronen, Pekka *(Finnish artist, 20th*
  cent.)   **WC**
Kurosaki, Akira *(Japanese*
  printmaker, b.1937)   **BA**
Kurosawa, Takashi *(Japanese*
  architect, 1941-)   **AV**
  Bibl: ▶Libr. of Congr. Name Auth.
   File
Kurrent, Friedrich *(Austrian*
  architect)   **AV**
  Bibl: Bauforum, 1988, v.21, no.
   126, p.20
Kürschner, Henning *(German*
  painter, printmaker, b.1941)   **BA**
Kurt Schwitters→see Schwitters, Kurt
Kurt, Kay   **BA WI**
  (American artist, 1944-)   WC
  (American artist, b.1944)   WI
  (American painter, b.1944)   BA
Kurt, Klay   **WC**
Kurt, Klay→see Kurt, Kay
Kurte, Joannes→see Cordua, Joannes
Kurte, Johannes→see Cordua,
  Joannes

Kurth, C.P. (German artist, 19th cent.) **WC**

Kurtycz, Jan Marek (Polish artist, 20th cent.) **WC**

Kurtz, Elaine (American painter, 20th c.) **BA**

Kurtz, Ellery (American painter, 20th c.) **BA**

Kurtz, Louis (Engraver, Chicago, IL., b.1834) **WI**

Kurtz, Wolf (German architect) **AV**
Bibl: Deutsche Bauzeitschrift, 1986 Apr., v.34, no.4, p.431

Kuryu, Akira (Japanese architect, 1947-) **AV**
Bibl: Kenchiku bunka, 1987 Dec., v.42, no.494, p.104

Kurz, Alois (German artist, op.c. 1825) **WC**

Kurz, Diana (American painter, 20th c.) **BA**

Kurz, Konrad (German sculptor, b.1934) **BA**

Kurz, Otho Orlando (German architect, Munich, fl. 1912) **AV**
Bibl: Der Architekt, 1987 July-Aug., no.7-8, p.358

Kurz, Rudolph Friedrich (Swiss painter, 1818-1871) **BA**

Kurz, Ursula (French architect) **AV**
Bibl: AMC, 1987 Oct., no.17, p.[30]

Kurzbauer, Eduard (German artist, 1840-1879) **WC**

Kurzen, Aaron (American sculptor, 20th c.) **BA**
Bibl: LEONARDO, XVI, 1 (winter 1983) 10-14

Kurzinger or Kirzinger, Franz (German artist, 1730-1795) **WC**

Kurzinger or Kirzinger, Marianna (German artist, 1770-1809) **WC**

Kurzweil, Max (German artist, 1867-1916) **WC**

Kusche, Alfred (German ceramist, 1884-1984) **BA**
Bibl: Budde, KERAMOS (1985) 63-68; ▶Thieme-Becker

Kuschnerus, Sigurd (German painter, b.1933) **BA**

Küsel family (German printmakers, goldsmiths, 17th-18th cs.) **BA**

Kusel, Ernst (Swedish artist, 1873-1942) **WC**

Küsel, Johanna Sibylla (German printmaker, act.1650-1717) **BA**

Kusel, Kusell, Kussell or Kiesel, Matthaus→see Küsel, Mathäus

Kusel, Kusell, Kussell, Kiesel or Kuuslin, Johanna Christina (Christiana) (German artist, 1665-) **WC**

Küsel, Mathäus **GC**
(German artist, 1629-1681) **WC**
(German draughtsman and printmaker, 1629-1681) **GC**
Bibl: Getty Photo Study Coll.; ▶Thieme-Becker; ▶Witt checklist
Kiesel, Mathäus **GC**
Kusel, Kusell, Kussell or Kiesel, Matthaus **WC**
Küsell, Mathäus **GC**
Küssell, Mathäus **GC**

Küsel, Melchior I (German designer, 1626-1683) **GC**
Bibl: ▶Thieme-Becker

Küsell, Mathäus→see Küsel, Mathäus

Kushner, Robert (American artist, b.1949) **BA WI**

Kusnezoff, Pawel Warfolomejewitsch→see Kuznecov, Pavel Varfolomeevič

Kuspezian, Aram Avakimovich (Russian artist, c.1928-) **WC**

Kuss (Austrian, active Vienna, Austria ca. 1880) **JG**

Kuss, Ferdinand (German artist, 1800-1886) **WC**

Kussaeus, Cornelis Ysbrantsz.→see Kussens, Cornelis Ysbrantsz.

Küssell, Mathäus→see Küsel, Mathäus

Kussens, Cornelis Ysbrantsz. **GC**
(Dutch draughtsman, act.1604-d.1618) **GC**
(Netherlands artist, op.1597-m.1618) **WC**
Bibl: ▶Thieme-Becker
Kussaeus, Cornelis Ysbrantsz. **GC**

Kussens, Cusseus or Kussaeus (also, erroneously, Kuffaeus, Kuffens or Kuffeus), Cornelis Ysbrantsz. **WC**

Kussens, Cusseus or Kussaeus (also, erroneously, Kuffaeus, Kuffens or Kuffeus), Cornelis Ysbrantsz.→see Kussens, Cornelis Ysbrantsz.

Kuster, Conrad (Swiss artist, c.1730-c.1802) **WC**

Kuster, Johann Kaspar (Swiss artist, 1747-1818) **WC**

Küsters, Hans Martin (German photographer, b.1946) **BA**

Küsthardt, Friedrich Heinrich Nicolaus, the elder (German sculptor, author, 1830-1900) **BA**

Küstner, Karl (German painter, 1861-1934) **BA**

Kustodiev, Boris Mihajlovič **BA**
(Russian artist, 1878-1927) **WC**
(Russian painter, 1878-1927) **PR**
(Russian painter, printmaker, scenographer, sculptor, 1878-1927) **BA**
Bibl: ▶Witt checklist
Boris M. Koustodieff **PR**
Koustodieff **PR**
Koustodieff, Boris M. **PR WC**
Koustodieff, Boris Mikhailovitch **PR**
Kustodjeff, Boris Michajlowitsch **WC**

Kustodieva, Irina (Russian, act. 1926) **BA**

Kustodjeff, Boris Michajlowitsch→see Kustodiev, Boris Mihajlovič

Kusztos, Endre (Hungarian artist, 1925-) **WC**

Kutcher, Arthur (American architect, b.1939) **BA**

Kütemeier, Klaus (German sculptor, b.1939) **BA**

Kuter, Leslie (American artist, 20th c.) **BA**

Kutter, Joseph (Dutch artist, 1894-1941) **WC**

Küttinger, Georg (West German architect) **AV**
Bibl: Kunst und Kirche, 1985, no.1, p.48

Küttinger, Ingrid (West German architect) **AV**
Bibl: Kunst und Kirche, 1985, no.1, p.48

Kuven, Johannes I→see Cuvenes, Johannes I

Kuvenet, J. (Dutch(?) artist, 18th cent.) **WC**

Kuwada, Wayne (American artist, b.1955) **BA**

Kuwagata, Keisai→see Masayoshi (Keisai Kuwagata)

Kuwasseg, Charles Euphrasie (French artist, 1833-1904) **WC**

Kuwasseg, Josef (German artist, 1799-1859) **WC**

Kuwasseg, Karl Joseph (German artist, 1802-1877) **WC**

Kuwayama, Tadaaki (American painter, b.1932) **BA**
Bibl: ▶Bénézit; ▶Contemp. artists, 1989; ▶WW Amer. Art, 1976, 1991-92

Kuyck, Frans Pieter Lodewijk van **GC WC**
(Belgian artist, 1852-1915) **WC**
(Belgian painter, 1852-1915) **GC**
Bibl: ▶Bénézit

Kuyck, Jean Louis (Louis) (Belgian artist, 1821-1871) **WC**

Kuyl or Kuil, Gysbert or Gysbrecht van der→see Kuyl, Gysbert van der